CODE OF FEDERAL REGULATIONS

Title 8
Aliens and Nationality

Revised as of January 1, 2019

Containing a codification of documents
of general applicability and future effect

As of January 1, 2019

Published by the Office of the Federal Register
National Archives and Records Administration
as a Special Edition of the Federal Register

Table of Contents

Cite this Code: CFR

To cite the regulations in this volume use title, part and section number. Thus, 8 CFR 1.1 *refers to title 8, part 1, section 1.*

Explanation

The Code of Federal Regulations is a codification of the general and permanent rules published in the Federal Register by the Executive departments and agencies of the Federal Government. The Code is divided into 50 titles which represent broad areas subject to Federal regulation. Each title is divided into chapters which usually bear the name of the issuing agency. Each chapter is further subdivided into parts covering specific regulatory areas.

Each volume of the Code is revised at least once each calendar year and issued on a quarterly basis approximately as follows:

Title 1 through Title 16	as of January 1
Title 17 through Title 27	as of April 1
Title 28 through Title 41	as of July 1
Title 42 through Title 50	as of October 1

The appropriate revision date is printed on the cover of each volume.

LEGAL STATUS

The contents of the Federal Register are required to be judicially noticed (44 U.S.C. 1507). The Code of Federal Regulations is prima facie evidence of the text of the original documents (44 U.S.C. 1510).

HOW TO USE THE CODE OF FEDERAL REGULATIONS

The Code of Federal Regulations is kept up to date by the individual issues of the Federal Register. These two publications must be used together to determine the latest version of any given rule.

To determine whether a Code volume has been amended since its revision date (in this case, January 1, 2019), consult the "List of CFR Sections Affected (LSA)," which is issued monthly, and the "Cumulative List of Parts Affected," which appears in the Reader Aids section of the daily Federal Register. These two lists will identify the Federal Register page number of the latest amendment of any given rule.

EFFECTIVE AND EXPIRATION DATES

Each volume of the Code contains amendments published in the Federal Register since the last revision of that volume of the Code. Source citations for the regulations are referred to by volume number and page number of the Federal Register and date of publication. Publication dates and effective dates are usually not the same and care must be exercised by the user in determining the actual effective date. In instances where the effective date is beyond the cut-off date for the Code a note has been inserted to reflect the future effective date. In those instances where a regulation published in the Federal Register states a date certain for expiration, an appropriate note will be inserted following the text.

OMB CONTROL NUMBERS

The Paperwork Reduction Act of 1980 (Pub. L. 96–511) requires Federal agencies to display an OMB control number with their information collection request.

Many agencies have begun publishing numerous OMB control numbers as amendments to existing regulations in the CFR. These OMB numbers are placed as close as possible to the applicable recordkeeping or reporting requirements.

PAST PROVISIONS OF THE CODE

Provisions of the Code that are no longer in force and effect as of the revision date stated on the cover of each volume are not carried. Code users may find the text of provisions in effect on any given date in the past by using the appropriate List of CFR Sections Affected (LSA). For the convenience of the reader, a "List of CFR Sections Affected" is published at the end of each CFR volume. For changes to the Code prior to the LSA listings at the end of the volume, consult previous annual editions of the LSA. For changes to the Code prior to 2001, consult the List of CFR Sections Affected compilations, published for 1949-1963, 1964-1972, 1973-1985, and 1986-2000.

"[RESERVED]" TERMINOLOGY

The term "[Reserved]" is used as a place holder within the Code of Federal Regulations. An agency may add regulatory information at a "[Reserved]" location at any time. Occasionally "[Reserved]" is used editorially to indicate that a portion of the CFR was left vacant and not accidentally dropped due to a printing or computer error.

INCORPORATION BY REFERENCE

What is incorporation by reference? Incorporation by reference was established by statute and allows Federal agencies to meet the requirement to publish regulations in the Federal Register by referring to materials already published elsewhere. For an incorporation to be valid, the Director of the Federal Register must approve it. The legal effect of incorporation by reference is that the material is treated as if it were published in full in the Federal Register (5 U.S.C. 552(a)). This material, like any other properly issued regulation, has the force of law.

What is a proper incorporation by reference? The Director of the Federal Register will approve an incorporation by reference only when the requirements of 1 CFR part 51 are met. Some of the elements on which approval is based are:

(a) The incorporation will substantially reduce the volume of material published in the Federal Register.

(b) The matter incorporated is in fact available to the extent necessary to afford fairness and uniformity in the administrative process.

(c) The incorporating document is drafted and submitted for publication in accordance with 1 CFR part 51.

What if the material incorporated by reference cannot be found? If you have any problem locating or obtaining a copy of material listed as an approved incorporation by reference, please contact the agency that issued the regulation containing that incorporation. If, after contacting the agency, you find the material is not available, please notify the Director of the Federal Register, National Archives and Records Administration, 8601 Adelphi Road, College Park, MD 20740-6001, or call 202-741-6010.

CFR INDEXES AND TABULAR GUIDES

A subject index to the Code of Federal Regulations is contained in a separate volume, revised annually as of January 1, entitled CFR INDEX AND FINDING AIDS. This volume contains the Parallel Table of Authorities and Rules. A list of CFR titles, chapters, subchapters, and parts and an alphabetical list of agencies publishing in the CFR are also included in this volume.

An index to the text of "Title 3—The President" is carried within that volume.

The Federal Register Index is issued monthly in cumulative form. This index is based on a consolidation of the "Contents" entries in the daily Federal Register.

A List of CFR Sections Affected (LSA) is published monthly, keyed to the revision dates of the 50 CFR titles.

REPUBLICATION OF MATERIAL

There are no restrictions on the republication of material appearing in the Code of Federal Regulations.

INQUIRIES

For a legal interpretation or explanation of any regulation in this volume, contact the issuing agency. The issuing agency's name appears at the top of odd-numbered pages.

For inquiries concerning CFR reference assistance, call 202–741–6000 or write to the Director, Office of the Federal Register, National Archives and Records Administration, 8601 Adelphi Road, College Park, MD 20740-6001 or e-mail *fedreg.info@nara.gov.*

SALES

The Government Publishing Office (GPO) processes all sales and distribution of the CFR. For payment by credit card, call toll-free, 866-512-1800, or DC area, 202-512-1800, M-F 8 a.m. to 4 p.m. e.s.t. or fax your order to 202-512-2104, 24 hours a day. For payment by check, write to: US Government Publishing Office – New Orders, P.O. Box 979050, St. Louis, MO 63197-9000.

ELECTRONIC SERVICES

The full text of the Code of Federal Regulations, the LSA (List of CFR Sections Affected), The United States Government Manual, the Federal Register, Public Laws, Public Papers of the Presidents of the United States, Compilation of Presidential Documents and the Privacy Act Compilation are available in electronic format via *www.govinfo.gov.* For more information, contact the GPO Customer Contact Center, U.S. Government Publishing Office. Phone 202-512-1800, or 866-512-1800 (toll-free). E-mail, *ContactCenter@gpo.gov.*

The Office of the Federal Register also offers a free service on the National Archives and Records Administration's (NARA) World Wide Web site for public law numbers, Federal Register finding aids, and related information. Connect to NARA's web site at *www.archives.gov/federal-register.*

The e-CFR is a regularly updated, unofficial editorial compilation of CFR material and Federal Register amendments, produced by the Office of the Federal Register and the Government Publishing Office. It is available at *www.ecfr.gov.*

OLIVER A. POTTS,
Director,
Office of the Federal Register
January 1, 2019

THIS TITLE

Title 8—ALIENS AND NATIONALITY is composed of one volume. This volume contains chapter I—Department of Homeland Security and chapter V—Executive Office for Immigration Review, Department of Justice. The contents of this volume represent all current regulations codified under this title of the CFR as of January 1, 2019.

For this volume, Gabrielle E. Burns was Chief Editor. The Code of Federal Regulations publication program is under the direction of the John Hyrum Martinez, assisted by Stephen J. Frattini.

Title 8—Aliens and Nationality

CHAPTER I—DEPARTMENT OF HOMELAND SECURITY

NOTE: This table shows sections of title 8 of the United States Code and corresponding sections of the Immigration and Nationality Act and of parts in subchapters A, B, and C of chapter I of title 8 of the Code of Federal Regulations. Those sections of title 8 of the United States Code bearing an asterisk do not have a corresponding part in chapter I of title 8 of the Code of Federal Regulations.

Sections 8 USC	Sections I. & N. Act and 8 CFR	Sections 8 USC	Sections I. & N. Act and 8 CFR	Sections 8 USC	Sections I. & N. Act and 8 CFR	Sections 8 USC	Sections I. & N. Act and 8 CFR
1101*	101	1254	244	1355*	285	1438	327
1102*	102	1255	245	1356*	286	1439	328
1103*	103	1256	246	1357	287	1440	329
1104*	104	1257	247	1358*	288	1441	330
1105*	105	1258	248	1359	289	1442*	331
1105a*	106	1259	249	1360*	290	1443	332
1151*	201	1260	250	1361*	291	1444	333
1152*	202	1281	251	1362	292	1445	334
1153*	203	1282	252	1401*	301	1446	335
1154	204	1283	253	1402*	302	1447	336
1155	205	1284*	254	1403*	303	1448	337
1156*	206	1285*	255	1404*	304	1449	338
1181	211	1286*	256	1405*	305	1450	339
1182	212	1287*	257	1406	306	1451	340
1183	213	1301*	261	1407*	307	1452	341
1184	214	1302*	262	1408*	308	1453	342
1185	215	1303*	263	1409*	309	1454	343
1201	221	1304	264	1421*	310	1455	344
1202*	222	1305	265	1422*	311	1457*	346
1203	223	1306*	266	1423	312	1458*	347
1204*	224	1321*	271	1424*	313	1459*	348
1221	231	1322*	272	1425*	314	1481	349
1222	232	1323*	273	1426*	315	1482*	350
1223	233	1324	274	1427	316	1483*	351
1224	234	1325*	275	1428*	317	1484*	352
1225	235	1326*	276	1429	318	1485*	353
1226	236	1327*	277	1430	319	1486*	354
1227	237	1328*	278	1431*	320	1487*	355
1228	238	1329*	279	1432*	321	1488*	356
1229	239	1330	280	1433	322	1489*	357
1230*	240	1351*	281	1434	323	1501*	358
1251	241	1352	282	1435	324	1502*	359
1252	242	1353*	283	1436*	325	1503*	360
1253	243	1354*	284	1437	326		

SUBCHAPTER A—GENERAL PROVISIONS

SUBCHAPTER C—NATIONALITY REGULATIONS

SUBCHAPTER A—GENERAL PROVISIONS

PART 1—DEFINITIONS

AUTHORITY: 8 U.S.C. 1101; 8 U.S.C. 1103; 5 U.S.C. 301; Pub. L. 107–296, 116 Stat. 2135; 6 U.S.C. 1 *et seq.*

SOURCE: 76 FR 53778, Aug. 29, 2011, unless otherwise noted.

§ 1.1 Applicability.

This part further defines some of the terms already described in section 101 and other sections of the Immigration and Nationality Act (66 Stat. 163), as amended, and such other enactments as pertain to immigration and nationality. These terms are used consistently by components within the Department of Homeland Security including U.S. Customs and Border Protection, U.S. Immigration and Customs Enforcement, and U.S. Citizenship and Immigration Services.

§ 1.2 Definitions.

As used in this chapter I, the term:

Act or *INA* means the Immigration and Nationality Act, as amended.

Aggravated felony means a crime (or a conspiracy or attempt to commit a crime) described in section 101(a)(43) of the Act. This definition applies to any proceeding, application, custody determination, or adjudication pending on or after September 30, 1996, but shall apply under section 276(b) of the Act only to violations of section 276(a) of the Act occurring on or after that date.

Application means benefit request.

Arriving alien means an applicant for admission coming or attempting to come into the United States at a port-of-entry, or an alien seeking transit through the United States at a port-of-entry, or an alien interdicted in international or United States waters and brought into the United States by any means, whether or not to a designated port-of-entry, and regardless of the means of transport. An arriving alien remains an arriving alien even if paroled pursuant to section 212(d)(5) of the Act, and even after any such parole is terminated or revoked. However, an arriving alien who was paroled into the United States before April 1, 1997, or who was paroled into the United States on or after April 1, 1997, pursuant to a grant of advance parole which the alien applied for and obtained in the United States prior to the alien's departure from and return to the United States, will not be treated, solely by reason of that grant of parole, as an arriving alien under section 235(b)(1)(A)(i) of the Act.

Attorney means any person who is eligible to practice law in, and is a member in good standing of the bar of, the highest court of any State, possession, territory, or Commonwealth of the United States, or of the District of Columbia, and is not under any order suspending, enjoining, restraining, disbarring, or otherwise restricting him or her in the practice of law.

Benefit request means any application, petition, motion, appeal, or other request relating to an immigration or naturalization benefit, whether such request is filed on a paper form or submitted in an electronic format, provided such request is submitted in a manner prescribed by DHS for such purpose.

Board means the Board of Immigration Appeals within the Executive Office for Immigration Review, Department of Justice, as defined in 8 CFR 1001.1(e).

Case, unless the context otherwise requires, means any proceeding arising under any immigration or naturalization law, Executive Order, or Presidential proclamation, or preparation for or incident to such proceeding, including preliminary steps by any private person or corporation preliminary to the filing of the application or petition by which any proceeding under the jurisdiction of the Service or the Board is initiated.

CBP means U.S. Customs and Border Protection.

Commissioner means the Commissioner of the Immigration and Naturalization Service prior to March 1,

2003. Unless otherwise specified, references after that date mean the Director of U.S. Citizenship and Immigration Services, the Commissioner of U.S. Customs and Border Protection, and the Director of U.S. Immigration and Customs Enforcement, as appropriate in the context in which the term appears.

Day, when computing the period of time for taking any action provided in this chapter I including the taking of an appeal, shall include Saturdays, Sundays, and legal holidays, except that when the last day of the period computed falls on a Saturday, Sunday, or a legal holiday, the period shall run until the end of the next day which is not a Saturday, Sunday, or a legal holiday.

Department or DHS, unless otherwise noted, means the Department of Homeland Security.

Director or district director prior to March 1, 2003, means the district director or regional service center director, unless otherwise specified. On or after March 1, 2003, pursuant to delegation from the Secretary of Homeland Security or any successive re-delegation, the terms mean, to the extent that authority has been delegated to such official: asylum office director; director, field operations; district director for interior enforcement; district director for services; field office director; service center director; or special agent in charge. The terms also mean such other official, including an official in an acting capacity, within U.S. Citizenship and Immigration Services, U.S. Customs and Border Protection, U.S. Immigration and Customs Enforcement, or other component of the Department of Homeland Security who is delegated the function or authority above for a particular geographic district, region, or area.

EOIR means the Executive Office for Immigration Review within the Department of Justice.

Executed or *execute* means fully completed.

Form when used in connection with a benefit or other request to be filed with DHS to request an immigration benefit, means a device for the collection of information in a standard format that may be submitted in paper format or in an electronic format as prescribed by USCIS on its official Internet Web site. The term Form followed by an immigration form number includes an approved electronic equivalent of such form as may be prescribed by the appropriate component on its official Internet Web site.

Form instructions means instructions on how to complete and where to file a benefit request, supporting evidence or fees, or any other required or preferred document or instrument with a DHS immigration component. Form instructions prescribed by USCIS or other DHS immigration components on their official Internet Web sites will be considered the currently applicable version, notwithstanding paper or other versions that may be in circulation, and may be issued through non-form guidance such as appendices, exhibits, guidebooks, or manuals.

ICE means U.S. Immigration and Customs Enforcement.

Immigration judge means an immigration judge as defined in 8 CFR 1001.1(l).

Immigration officer means the following employees of the Department of Homeland Security, including senior or supervisory officers of such employees, designated as immigration officers authorized to exercise the powers and duties of such officer as specified by the Act and this chapter I: aircraft pilot, airplane pilot, asylum officer, refugee corps officer, Border Patrol agent, contact representative, deportation officer, detention enforcement officer, detention officer, fingerprint specialist, forensic document analyst, general attorney (except with respect to CBP, only to the extent that the attorney is performing any immigration function), helicopter pilot, immigration agent (investigations), immigration enforcement agent, immigration information officer, immigration inspector, immigration officer, immigration services officer, investigator, intelligence agent, intelligence officer, investigative assistant, special agent, other officer or employee of the Department of Homeland Security or of the United States as designated by the Secretary of Homeland Security as provided in 8 CFR 2.1.

Lawfully admitted for permanent residence means the status of having been lawfully accorded the privilege of residing permanently in the United States as an immigrant in accordance with the immigration laws, such status not having changed. Such status terminates upon entry of a final administrative order of exclusion, deportation, or removal.

Petition. See Benefit request.

Practice means the act or acts of any person appearing in any case, either in person or through the preparation or filing of any brief or other document, paper, application, or petition on behalf of another person or client before or with DHS.

Preparation, constituting practice, means the study of the facts of a case and the applicable laws, coupled with the giving of advice and auxiliary activities, including the incidental preparation of papers, but does not include the lawful functions of a notary public or service consisting solely of assistance in the completion of blank spaces on printed DHS forms, by one whose remuneration, if any, is nominal and who does not hold himself or herself out as qualified in legal matters or in immigration and naturalization procedure.

Representation before DHS includes practice and preparation as defined in this section.

Representative refers to a person who is entitled to represent others as provided in 8 CFR 292.1(a)(2) through (6) and 8 CFR 292.1(b).

Respondent means an alien named in a Notice to Appear issued in accordance with section 239(a) of the Act, or in an Order to Show Cause issued in accordance with 8 CFR 242.1 (1997) as it existed prior to April 1, 1997.

Secretary, unless otherwise noted, means the Secretary of Homeland Security.

Service means U.S. Citizenship and Immigration Services, U.S. Customs and Border Protection, and/or U.S. Immigration and Customs Enforcement, as appropriate in the context in which the term appears.

Service counsel means any immigration officer assigned to represent the Service in any proceeding before an immigration judge or the Board of Immigration Appeals.

Transition program effective date as used with respect to extending the immigration laws to the Commonwealth of the Northern Mariana Islands means November 28, 2009.

USCIS means U.S. Citizenship and Immigration Services.

§ 1.3 Lawfully present aliens for purposes of applying for Social Security benefits.

(a) *Definition of the term an "alien who is lawfully present in the United States."* For the purposes of 8 U.S.C. 1611(b)(2) only, an "alien who is lawfully present in the United States" means:

(1) A qualified alien as defined in 8 U.S.C. 1641(b);

(2) An alien who has been inspected and admitted to the United States and who has not violated the terms of the status under which he or she was admitted or to which he or she has changed after admission;

(3) An alien who has been paroled into the United States pursuant to section 212(d)(5) of the Act for less than 1 year, except:

(i) Aliens paroled for deferred inspection or pending removal proceedings under section 240 of the Act; and

(ii) Aliens paroled into the United States for prosecution pursuant to 8 CFR 212.5(b)(3);

(4) An alien who belongs to one of the following classes of aliens permitted to remain in the United States because DHS has decided for humanitarian or other public policy reasons not to initiate removal proceedings or enforce departure:

(i) Aliens currently in temporary resident status pursuant to section 210 or 245A of the Act;

(ii) Aliens currently under Temporary Protected Status (TPS) pursuant to section 244 of the Act;

(iii) Cuban-Haitian entrants, as defined in section 202(b) of Pub. L. 99–603, as amended;

(iv) Family Unity beneficiaries pursuant to section 301 of Pub. L. 101–649, as amended;

(v) Aliens currently under Deferred Enforced Departure (DED) pursuant to a decision made by the President;

(vi) Aliens currently in deferred action status;

(vii) Aliens who are the spouse or child of a United States citizen whose visa petition has been approved and who have a pending application for adjustment of status;

(5) Applicants for asylum under section 208(a) of the Act and applicants for withholding of removal under section 241(b)(3) of the Act or under the Convention Against Torture who have been granted employment authorization, and such applicants under the age of 14 who have had an application pending for at least 180 days.

(b) *Non-issuance of a Notice to Appear and non-enforcement of deportation, exclusion, or removal orders.* An alien may not be deemed to be lawfully present solely on the basis of DHS's decision not to, or failure to:

(1) Issue a Notice to Appear; or

(2) Enforce an outstanding order of deportation, exclusion or removal.

§ 1.4 Definition of Form I–94

The term *Form I–94*, as used in this chapter I, includes the collection of arrival/departure and admission or parole information by DHS, whether in paper or electronic format, which is made available to the person about whom the information has been collected, as may be prescribed by DHS. The following terms, when used in the context of the *Form I–94*, are clarified as to their meaning to accommodate the collection of such information in an electronic format.

(a) The terms "annotate," "note," "indicate on," "stamp," and "endorse," unless used in part 231 of this chapter, include, but are not limited, to DHS amending, including or completing information in its electronic record of admission, or arrival/departure. For purposes of part 231, the term "endorse" includes but is not limited to the submission of electronic departure data to CBP.

(b) The terms "completed," "completely executed" and "completed and signed" include, but are not limited to, DHS completing its collection of information into its electronic record of admission, or arrival/departure.

(c) The terms "issuance" and "given" include, but are not limited to, the creation of an electronic record of admission, or arrival/departure by DHS following an inspection performed by an immigration officer.

(d) The term "original I–94" includes, but is not limited to, any printout or electronic transmission of information from DHS systems containing the electronic record of admission or arrival/departure.

(e) The terms "present," "presentation," or "submission" of a Form I–94, unless they are used in § 231.1 or § 231.2 of this chapter, include, but are not limited to, providing a printout of information from DHS systems containing an electronic record of admission or arrival/departure. For purposes of § 231.1 of this chapter, the terms "present" or "submission" of the Form I–94 includes ensuring that each passenger presents him/herself to a CBP Officer for inspection at a U.S. port-of-entry. For the purposes of § 231.2 of this chapter, the terms "present," "submit," or "submission" of the Form I–94 includes ensuring that each passenger is available for inspection by a CBP Officer upon request.

(f) The term "possession" with respect to a Form I–94 includes, but is not limited to, obtaining a copy or printout of the record of an electronic evidence of admission or arrival/departure from the appropriate CBP systems.

(g) The terms "surrendering," "turning in a Form I–94," and "departure I–94" includes, but is not limited to, complying with any departure controls under 8 CFR part 215 that may be prescribed by CBP in addition to the submission of electronic departure data to CBP by a carrier.

[78 FR 18472, Mar. 27, 2013]

PART 2—AUTHORITY OF THE SECRETARY OF HOMELAND SECURITY

AUTHORITY: 8 U.S.C. 1103; 5 U.S.C. 301; Public Law 107–296, 116 Stat. 2135 (6 U.S.C. 1 *et seq.*).

§ 2.1 Authority of the Secretary of Homeland Security.

All authorities and functions of the Department of Homeland Security to administer and enforce the immigration laws are vested in the Secretary of Homeland Security. The Secretary of

Homeland Security may, in the Secretary's discretion, delegate any such authority or function to any official, officer, or employee of the Department of Homeland Security, including delegation through successive redelegation, or to any employee of the United States to the extent authorized by law. Such delegation may be made by regulation, directive, memorandum, or other means as deemed appropriate by the Secretary in the exercise of the Secretary's discretion. A delegation of authority or function may in the Secretary's discretion be published in the FEDERAL REGISTER, but such publication is not required.

[68 FR 10923, Mar. 6, 2003]

PART 3—EXECUTIVE OFFICE FOR IMMIGRATION REVIEW

AUTHORITY: 5 U.S.C. 301; 8 U.S.C. 1101 note, 1103, 1252 note, 1252b, 1324b, 1362; 28 U.S.C. 509, 510, 1746; sec. 2, Reorg. Plan No. 2 of 1950, 3 CFR, 1949–1953 Comp., p. 1002; section 203 of Pub. L. 105–100, 111 Stat. 2196–200; sections 1506 and 1510 of Pub. L. 106–386; 114 Stat. 1527–29, 1531–32; section 1505 of Pub. L. 106–554, 114 Stat. 2763A–326 to –328.

§ 3.0 Executive Office for Immigration Review.

Regulations of the Executive Office for Immigration Review relating to the adjudication of immigration matters before immigration judges (referred to in some regulations as special inquiry officers) and the Board of Immigration Appeals are located in 8 CFR chapter V, part 1003.

[68 FR 9831, Feb. 28, 2003]

SUBCHAPTER B—IMMIGRATION REGULATIONS

PART 100—STATEMENT OF ORGANIZATION

AUTHORITY: 8 U.S.C. 1103; 8 U.S.C. 1185 note (section 7209 of Pub. L. 108–458); 8 CFR part 2.

SOURCE: 32 FR 9616, July 4, 1967, unless otherwise noted.

§ 100.1 Introduction.

The following components have been delegated authority under the Immigration and Nationality Act to administer and enforce certain provisions of the Immigration and Nationality Act and all other laws relating to immigration: U.S. Customs and Border Protection (CBP), U.S. Immigration and Customs Enforcement (ICE), and U.S. Citizenship and Immigration Services (USCIS).

[74 FR 26936, June 5, 2009]

§ 100.2 [Reserved]

§ 100.3 Places where, and methods whereby, information may be secured or submittals or requests made.

Any person desiring information relative to a matter handled by CBP, ICE or USCIS or any person desiring to make a submittal or request in connection with such a matter, should communicate either orally or in writing, with either CBP, ICE or USCIS as appropriate. When the submittal or request consists of a formal application for one of the documents, privileges, or other benefits provided for in the laws administered by CBP, ICE or USCIS or the regulations implementing those laws, follow the instructions on the form as to preparation and place of submission. Individuals can seek service or assistance from CBP, ICE or USCIS by visiting the CBP, ICE or USCIS Web site or calling CBP, ICE or USCIS.

[74 FR 26936, June 5, 2009]

§ 100.4 Field offices.

(a) *Ports-of-Entry for aliens arriving by vessel or by land transportation.* Subject to the limitations prescribed in this paragraph, the following places are hereby designated as Ports-of-Entry for aliens arriving by any means of travel other than aircraft. The designation of such a Port-of-Entry may be withdrawn whenever, in the judgment of the Commissioner, such action is warranted. The ports are listed according to location by districts and are designated either Class A, B, or C. Class A means that the port is a designated Port-of-Entry for all aliens. Class B means that the port is a designated Port-of-Entry for aliens who at the time of applying for admission are exempt from document requirements by § 212.1(c)(5) of this chapter or who are lawfully in possession of valid Permanent Resident Cards, and nonimmigrant aliens who are citizens of Canada or Bermuda or nationals of Mexico and who at the time of applying for admission are lawfully in possession of all valid documents required for admission as set forth in §§ 212.1(a) and (c) and 235.1(d) and (e) of this chapter and are admissible without further arrival documentation or immigration processing. Class C means that the port is a designated Port-of-Entry only for aliens who are arriving in the United States as crewmen as that term is defined in section 101(a)(10) of the Act with respect to vessels.

DISTRICT NO. 1 [RESERVED]

DISTRICT NO. 2—BOSTON, MASSACHUSETTS

Class A

Boston, MA (the port of Boston includes, among others, the port facilities at Beverly, Braintree, Chelsea, Everett, Hingham, Lynn, Manchester, Marblehead, Milton, Quincy, Revere, Salem, Saugus, and Weymouth, MA)
Gloucester, MA

Hartford, CT (the port at Hartford includes, among others, the port facilities at Bridgeport, Groton, New Haven, and New London, CT)
Providence, RI (the port of Providence includes, among others, the port facilities at Davisville, Melville, Newport, Portsmouth, Quonset Point, Saunderstown, Tiverton, and Warwick, RI; and at Fall River, New Bedford, and Somerset, MA)

Class C

Newburyport, MA
Plymouth, MA
Portsmouth, NH
Provincetown, MA
Sandwich, MA
Woods Hole, MA

DISTRICT NO. 3—NEW YORK, NEW YORK

Class A

New York, NY (the port of New York includes, among others, the port facilities at Bronx, Brooklyn, Buchanan, Manhattan, Montauk, Northport, Port Jefferson, Queens, Riverhead, Poughkeepsie, the Stapleton Anchorage-Staten Island, Staten Island, Stoney Point, and Yonkers, NY, as well as the East Side Passenger Terminal in Manhattan)

DISTRICT NO. 4—PHILADELPHIA, PENNSYLVANIA

Class A

Erie Seaport, PA
Philadelphia, PA (the port of Philadelphia includes, among others, the port facilities at Delaware City, Lewes, New Castle, and Wilmington, DE; and at Chester, Essington, Fort Mifflin, Marcus Hook, and Morrisville, PA)
Pittsburgh, PA

DISTRICT NO. 5—BALTIMORE, MARYLAND

Class A

Baltimore, MD
Patuxent River, MD

Class C

Piney Point, MD
Salisbury, MD

DISTRICT NO. 6—MIAMI, FLORIDA

Class A

Boca Grande, FL
Fernandina, FL
Fort Lauderdale/Port Everglades, FL, Seaport
Fort Pierce, FL
*Jacksonville, FL
Key West, FL
Miami Marine Unit, FL
Panama City, FL
Pensacola, FL
Port Canaveral, FL
St. Augustine, FL
St. Petersburg, FL
*Tampa, FL (includes Fort Myers)
West Palm Beach, FL

Class C

Manatee, FL
Port Dania, FL
Port St. Joe, FL

DISTRICT NO. 7—BUFFALO, NEW YORK

Class A

Albany, NY
Alexandria Bay, NY
Buffalo, NY
Cape Vincent, NY
Champlain, NY
Chateaugay, NY
Ft. Covington, NY
Massena, NY
Mooers, NY
Niagara Falls, NY (the port of Niagara Falls includes, among others, the port facilities at Lewiston Bridge, Rainbow Bridge, and Whirlpool Bridge, NY)
Ogdensburg, NY
Peace Bridge, NY
Rochester, NY
Rouses Point, NY
Thousand Islands Bridge, NY
Trout River, NY

Class B

Cannons Corner, NY
Churubusco, NY

Class C

Oswego, NY

DISTRICT NO. 8—DETROIT, MICHIGAN

Class A

Algonac, MI
Detroit, MI, Detroit and Canada Tunnel
Detroit, MI, Detroit International Bridge (Ambassador Bridge)
Grosse Isle, MI
Isle Royale, MI
Marine City, MI
Port Huron, MI
Sault Ste. Marie, MI

Class B

Alpena, MI
Detour, MI
Grand Rapids, MI
Mackinac Island, MI
Rogers City, MI

Class C

Alpena, MI
Baraga, MI

Bay City, MI
Cheboygan, MI
Detour, MI
Escanaba, MI
Grand Haven, MI
Holland, MI
Houghton, MI
Ludington, MI
Mackinac Island, MI
Manistee, MI
Marquette, MI
Menominee, MI
Monroe, MI
Munising, MI
Muskegon, MI
Pontiac, MI
Port Dolomite, MI
Port Inland, MI
Rogers City (Calcite), MI
Saginaw, MI
South Haven, MI

DISTRICT NO. 9—CHICAGO, ILLINOIS

Class A

Algoma, WI
Bayfield, WI
Chicago, IL
Green Bay, WI
*Milwaukee, WI

Class C

Ashland, WI
East Chicago, IL
Gary, IN
Kenosha, WI
Manitowoc, WI
Marinette, WI
Michigan City, IN
Racine, WI
Sheboygan, WI
Sturgeon Bay, WI

DISTRICT NO. 10—ST. PAUL, MINNESOTA

Class A

Ambrose, ND
Antler, ND
Baudette, MN
Carbury, ND
Duluth, MN (the port of Duluth includes, among others, the port facilities at Superior, WI)
Dunseith, ND
Ely, MN
Fortuna, ND
Grand Portage, MN
Hannah, ND
Hansboro, ND
International Falls, MN
Lancaster, MN
Maida, ND
Neche, ND
Noonan, ND
Northgate, ND
Noyes, MN
Pembina, ND
Pine Creek, MN
Portal, ND
Ranier, MN
Roseau, MN
Sarles, ND
Sherwood, ND
St. John, ND
Walhalla, ND
Warroad, MN
Westhope, ND

Class B

Crane Lake, MN
Oak Island, MN

Class C

Grand Marais, MN
Silver Bay, MN
Taconite Harbor, MN
Two Harbors, MN

DISTRICT NO. 11—KANSAS CITY, MISSOURI

Class A

Kansas City, MO

Class B

Wichita, KS

DISTRICT NO. 12—SEATTLE, WASHINGTON

Class A

Aberdeen, WA (the port of Aberdeen includes, among others, the port facilities at Raymond and South Bend, WA)
Anacortes, WA
Bellingham, WA
Blaine-Pacific Highway, WA
Blaine-Peach Arch, WA
Boundary, WA
Colville, WA
Danville, WA
Eastport, ID
Ferry, WA
Friday Harbor, WA (the port of Friday Harbor includes, among others, the port facilities at Roche Harbor, WA)
Frontier, WA
Kalama, WA
Laurier, WA
Longview, WA
Lynden, WA
Metaline Falls, WA
Neah Bay, WA
Olympia, WA
Oroville, WA
Point Roberts, WA
Port Angeles, WA
Port Townsend, WA
Porthill, WA
Seattle, WA (the port of Seattle includes, among others, the port facilities at Bangor, Blake Island, Bremerton, Eagle Harbor, Edmonds, Everett, Holmes Harbor, Houghton, Kennydale, Keyport, Kingston, Manchester, Mukilteo, Orchard Point,

Point Wells, Port Gamble, Port Ludlow, Port Orchard, Poulsbo, Shuffleton, and Winslow, WA)
Sumas, WA
Tacoma, WA (the port of Tacoma includes, among others, the port facilities at Dupont, WA)
Vancouver, WA
Yakima, WA

Class B

Nighthawk, WA

DISTRICT NO. 13—SAN FRANCISCO, CALIFORNIA

Class A

San Francisco, CA (the port of San Francisco includes, among others, the port facilities at Antioch, Benicia, Martinez, Oakland, Pittsburgh, Port Chicago Concord Naval Weapon Station, Redwood City, Richmond, Sacramento, San Pablo Bay, and Stockton, CA)

Class C

Eureka, CA

DISTRICT NO. 14—SAN ANTONIO, TEXAS

Class A

Amistad Dam, TX
Corpus Christi, TX (the port of Corpus Christi includes, among others, the port facilities at Harbor Island, Ingleside, and Port Lavaca-Point Comfort, TX)
Del Rio, TX
Laredo, TX (the port of Laredo includes, among others, the port facilities at Colombia Bridge, Convent Bridge, and Lincoln-Juarez Bridge, TX)
Maverick, TX

DISTRICT NO. 15—EL PASO, TEXAS

Class A

Columbus, NM
El Paso, TX (the port of El Paso includes, among others, the port facilities at Bridge of the Americas, Paso Del Norte Bridge, and Ysleta Bridge, TX)
Fabens, TX
Fort Hancock, TX
Presidio, TX
Santa Teresa, NM

Class B

Boquillas, TX

DISTRICT NO. 16—LOS ANGELES, CALIFORNIA

Class A

Los Angeles, CA (the port of Los Angeles includes, among others, the port facilities at Long Beach, Ontario, Port Hueneme, San Pedro, and Ventura, CA)
San Luis Obispo, CA (the port of San Luis Obispo includes, among others, the port facilities at Avila, Estero Bay, El Capitan, Elwood, Gaviota, Morro Bay, and Santa Barbara, CA)

DISTRICT NO. 17—HONOLULU, HAWAII

Class A

Agana, Guam, M.I (including the port facilities of Apra Harbor, Guam).
Honolulu, HI, Seaport (including all port facilities on the island of Oahu).
Rota, the Commonwealth of the Northern Mariana Islands.
Saipan, the Commonwealth of the Northern Mariana Islands.
Tinian, the Commonwealth of the Northern Mariana Islands.

Class C

Hilo, HI
Kahului, HI, Kahului Harbor
Nawiliwilli, HI, Nawiliwilli Harbor
Port Allen, HI, Port Allen Harbor

DISTRICT NO. 18—PHOENIX, ARIZONA

Class A

Douglas, AZ
Lukeville, AZ
Mariposa, AZ
Morley Gate, AZ
Naco, AZ
Nogales, AZ
Sasabe, AZ
San Luis, AZ

DISTRICT NO. 19—DENVER, COLORADO

Class A

Denver, CO
Grand Junction, CO
Pueblo, CO
Salt Lake City, UT

DISTRICT NO. 20 [RESERVED]

DISTRICT NO. 21—NEWARK, NEW JERSEY

Class A

Camden, NJ (the port of Camden includes, among others, the port facilities at Artificial Island, Billingsport, Burlington, Cape May, Deepwater Point, Fisher's Point, Gibbstown, Gloucester City, Paulsboro, Salem, and Trenton, NJ)
Newark, NJ (the port of Newark includes, among others, the port facilities at Bayonne, Carteret, Edgewater, Elizabeth, Jersey City, Leonardo, Linden, Perth Amboy, Port Newark, and Sewaren, NJ)

DISTRICT NO. 22—PORTLAND, MAINE

Class A

Alburg, VT

Alburg Springs, VT
Bangor, ME (the port of Bangor includes, among others, the port facilities at Bar Harbor, Belfast, Brewer, Bucksport Harbor, Prospect Harbor, Sandypoint, Seal Harbor, Searsport, and South West Harbor, ME)
Beebe Plain, VT
Beecher Falls, VT
Bridgewater, ME
Calais, ME (includes Ferry Point and Milltown Bridges)
Canaan, VT
Coburn Gore, ME
Derby Line, VT
Eastport, ME
East Richford, VT
Fort Fairfield, ME
Fort Kent, ME
Hamlin, ME
Highgate Springs, VT
Houlton, ME
Jackman, ME
Limestone, ME
Lubec, ME
Madawaska, ME
Morses Line, VT
North Troy, VT
Norton, VT
Pittsburgh, NH
Portland, ME
Richford, VT (includes the Pinnacle Port-of-Entry)
*St. Albans, VT
Van Buren, ME
Vanceboro, ME
West Berkshire, VT

Class B

Daaquam, ME
Easton, ME
Eastcourt, ME
Forest City, ME
Monticello, ME
Orient, ME
Robinston, ME
St. Aurelie, ME
St. Pamphile, ME

Class C

Bath, ME
Boothbay Harbor, ME
Kittery, ME
Rockland, ME
Wiscasset, ME

DISTRICT NO. 23 [RESERVED]

DISTRICT NO. 24—CLEVELAND, OHIO

Class A

Cincinnati, OH
Cleveland, OH
Columbus, OH
Put-In-Bay, OH
Sandusky, OH
Toledo, OH

Class C

Ashtabula, OH
Conneaut, OH
Fairport, OH
Huron, OH
Lorain, OH
Marblehead, OH

DISTRICT NO. 25—WASHINGTON, DC

Class A

Hopewell, VA
*Norfolk, VA—(the port of Norfolk includes, among others, the port facilities at Fort Monroe and Newport News, VA)
Richmond, VA
Washington, DC (includes the port facilities at Alexandria, VA)
Yorktown, VA

DISTRICT NO. 26—ATLANTA, GEORGIA

Class A

Charleston, SC (the port of Charleston includes, among others, the port facilities at Georgetown and Port Royal, SC)
Mobile, AL
Savannah, GA (the port of Savannah includes, among others, the port facilities at Brunswick and St. Mary's Seaport, GA)
Wilmington, NC (the port of Wilmington includes the port facilities at Morehead City, NC)

DISTRICT NO. 27—SAN JUAN, PUERTO RICO

Class A

Aguadilla, PR
*Charlotte Amalie, St. Thomas, VI
Christiansted, St. Croix, VI
Cruz Bay, St. John, VI
Ensenada, PR
Federiksted, St. Croix, VI
Fajardo, PR
Humacao, PR
Jobos, PR
Mayaguez, PR
Ponce, PR
Red Hook, St. Thomas, VI

Class B

Coral Bay, St. John, VI

DISTRICT NO. 28—NEW ORLEANS, LOUISIANA

Class A

Baton Rouge, LA
Gulfport, MS
Lake Charles, LA
Memphis, TN
Nashville, TN
New Orleans, LA (the port of New Orleans includes, among others, the port facilities at Avondale, Bell Chasse, Braithwaite, Burnside, Chalmette, Destrahan, Geismar, Gramercy, Gretna, Harvey, Marrero,

Norco, Port Sulphur, St. Rose, and Westwego, LA)

Class C

Morgan City, LA
Pascagoula, MS

DISTRICT NO. 29—OMAHA, NEBRASKA

Class A

Omaha, NE
Des Moines, IA

DISTRICT NO. 30—HELENA, MONTANA

Class A

Chief Mountain, MT (May-October)
Del Bonita, MT
Morgan, MT
Opheim, MT
Peigan, MT
Raymond, MT
Roosville, MT
Scobey, MT
Sweetgrass, MT
Turner, MT
Wildhorse, MT
Willow Creek, MT

Class B

Goat Haunt, MT
Trail Creek, MT
Whitlash, MT

DISTRICT NO. 31—PORTLAND, OREGON

Class A

Astoria, OR (the port of Astoria includes, among others, the port facilities at Bradwood, Pacific City, Taft, Tilliamook, (including Bay City and Garibaldi), Warrenton, Wauna, and Westport, OR)
Coos Bay, OR (the port of Coos Bay includes, among others, the port facilities at Bandon, Brookings, Depoe Bay, Florence, Frankfort, Gold Beach, Newport (including Toledo), Port Orford, Reedsport, Waldport, and Yachats, OR)
Portland, OR (the port of Portland includes, among others, the port facilities at Beaver, Columbia City, Prescott, Rainier, and St. Helens, OR)

DISTRICT NO. 32—ANCHORAGE, ALASKA

Class A

Alcan, AK
Anchorage, AK (the port of Anchorage includes, among others (for out of port inspections only), Afognak, Barrow, Cold Bay, Cordova, Homer, Kodiak, Kotzebue, Nikiski, Seward, Valdez, and Yakutat, AK)
Dalton's Cache, AK
Dutch Harbor, AK
Fairbanks, AK
Gambell, AK
Juneau, AK
Ketchikan, AK
Nome, AK
Poker Creek, AK
Skagway, AK

Class B

Eagle, AK
Hyder, AK

Class C

Valdez, AK

DISTRICT NO. 38—HOUSTON, TEXAS

Class A

Galveston, TX (the port of Galveston includes, among others, the port facilities at Freeport, Port Bolivar, and Texas City, TX)
Houston, TX (the port of Houston includes, among others, the port facilities at Baytown, TX)
Port Arthur, TX (the port of Port Arthur includes, among others, the port facilities at Beaumont, Orange, and Sabine, TX)

DISTRICT NO. 39—SAN DIEGO, CALIFORNIA

Class A

Andrade, CA
Calexico, CA
Otay Mesa, CA
San Ysidro, CA (including the Cross Border Xpress (CBX) facility)
Tecate, CA

DISTRICT NO. 40—HARLINGEN, TEXAS

Class A

Brownsville, TX (the port of Brownsville includes, among others, the port facilities at Brownsville Seaport, Port Isabel, Padre Island and Harlingen, TX, Ship Channel)
Brownsville, TX, Gateway Bridge and Brownsville/Matamoros Bridge
Falcon Heights, TX
Hidalgo, TX
Los Ebanos, TX
Los Indios, TX
Pharr, TX
Progreso, TX
Rio Grande City, TX
Roma, TX

(b) *Ports-of-Entry for aliens arriving by aircraft.* In addition to the following international airports which are hereby designated as Ports-of-Entry for aliens arriving by aircraft, other places where permission for certain aircraft to land officially has been given and places where emergency or forced landings are made under part 239 of this chapter shall be regarded as designated for the entry of aliens arriving by such aircraft:

DISTRICT NO. 1 [RESERVED]

DISTRICT NO. 2—BOSTON, MASSACHUSETTS

Boston, MA, Logan International Airport
Manchester, NH, Grenier Airport
Portsmouth, NH, Pease Air Force Base
Warwick, RI, T. F. Greene Airport
Windsor Locks, CT, Bradley International Airport

DISTRICT NO. 3—NEW YORK CITY, NEW YORK

Newburgh, NY, Stewart International Airport
Queens, NY, LaGuardia Airport
Westchester, NY, Westchester County Airport

DISTRICT NO. 4—PHILADELPHIA, PENNSYLVANIA

Charlestown, WV, Kanahwa Airport
Dover, DE, Dover Air Force Base
Erie, PA, Erie International Airport (USCS)
Harrisburg, PA, Harrisburg International Airport
Philadelphia, PA, Philadelphia International Airport
Pittsburgh, PA, Pittsburgh International Airport

DISTRICT NO. 5—BALTIMORE, MARYLAND

Baltimore, MD, Baltimore-Washington International Airport

DISTRICT NO. 6—MIAMI, FLORIDA

Daytona, FL, Daytona International Airport, FL
Fort Lauderdale, FL, Executive Airport
Fort Lauderdale, FL, Fort Lauderdale-Hollywood Airport
Fort Myers, FL, Southwest Regional International Airport
Freeport, Bahamas, Freeport International Airport
Jacksonville, FL, Jacksonville International Airport
Key West, FL, Key West International Airport
Melbourne, FL, Melbourne International Airport
Miami, FL, Chalks Flying Service Seaplane Base
Miami, FL, Miami International Airport
Nassau, Bahamas, Nassau International Airport
Orlando, FL, Orlando International Airport
Palm Beach, FL, Palm Beach International Airport
Paradise Island, Bahamas, Paradise Island Airport
Sanford, FL, Sanford International Airport
Sarasota, FL, Sarasota Airport
St. Petersburg, FL, St. Petersburg/Clearwater International Airport
Tampa, FL, Tampa International Airport

DISTRICT NO. 7—BUFFALO, NEW YORK

Albany, NY, Albany County Airport
Buffalo, NY, Buffalo Airport
Massena, NY, Massena Airport
Niagara Falls, NY, Niagara Falls International Airport
Ogdensburg, NY, Ogdensburg Municipal Airport
Rochester, NY, Rochester Airport
Syracuse, NY, Hancock International Airport
Watertown, NY, Watertown Municipal Airport

DISTRICT NO. 8—DETROIT, MICHIGAN

Battle Creek, MI, Battle Creek Airport
Chippewa, MI, Chippewa County International Airport
Detroit, MI, Detroit City Airport
Detroit, MI, Detroit Metropolitan Wayne County Airport
Port Huron, MI, St. Clair County International Airport
Sault Ste. Marie, MI, Sault Ste. Marie Airport

DISTRICT NO. 9—CHICAGO, ILLINOIS

Chicago, IL, Chicago Midway Airport
Chicago, IL, Chicago O'Hare International Airport
Indianapolis, IN, Indianapolis International Airport
Mitchell, WI, Mitchell International Airport

DISTRICT NO. 10—ST. PAUL, MINNESOTA

Baudette, MN, Baudette International Airport
Duluth, MN, Duluth International Airport
Duluth, MN, Sky Harbor Airport
Grand Forks, ND, Grand Forks International Airport
International Falls, MN, Falls International Airport
Minneapolis/St. Paul, MN, Minneapolis/St. Paul International Airport
Minot, ND, Minot International Airport
Pembina, ND, Port Pembina Airport
Portal, ND, Portal Airport
Ranier, MN, International Seaplane Base
Warroad, MN, Warroad International Airport
Williston, ND, Sioulin Field (Municipal)

DISTRICT NO. 11—KANSAS CITY, MISSOURI

Kansas City, MO, Kansas City International Airport
Springfield, MO, Springfield Regional Airport
St. Louis, MO, St. Louis Lambert International Airport
St. Louis, MO, Spirit of St. Louis Airport

DISTRICT NO. 12—SEATTLE, WASHINGTON

Bellingham, WA, Bellingham Airport

Friday Harbor, WA, Friday Harbor
McChord, WA, McChord Air Force Base
Oroville, WA, Dorothy Scott Municipal Airport
Oroville, WA, Dorothy Scott Seaplane Base
Point Roberts, WA, Point Roberts Airport
Port Townsend, WA, Jefferson County International Airport
SEA-TAC, WA, SEA-TAC International Airport
Seattle, WA, Boeing Municipal Air Field
Seattle, WA, Lake Union
Spokane, WA, Felts Field
Spokane, WA, Spokane International Airport

DISTRICT NO. 13—SAN FRANCISCO, CALIFORNIA

Alameda, CA, Alemeda Naval Air Station
Oakland, CA, Oakland International Airport
Sacramento, CA, Beale Air Force Base
San Francisco, CA, San Francisco International Airport
San Jose, CA, San Jose International Airport
Travis, CA, Travis Air Force Base

DISTRICT NO. 14—SAN ANTONIO, TEXAS

Austin, TX, Austin International Airport
Corpus Christi, TX, Corpus Christi Airport
Del Rio, TX, Del Rio International Airport
Laredo, TX, Laredo International Airport
Maverick, TX, Maverick County Airport
San Antonio, TX, San Antonio International Airport

DISTRICT NO. 15—EL PASO, TEXAS

Albuquerque, NM, Albuquerque International Airport
El Paso, TX, International Airport
Presidio, TX, Presidio Airport
Santa Teresa, NM, Santa Teresa Airport

DISTRICT NO. 16—LOS ANGELES, CALIFORNIA

Los Angeles, CA, Los Angeles International Airport
Ontario, CA, Ontario International Airport

DISTRICT NO. 17—HONOLULU, HAWAII

Agana, Guam, Guam International Airport Terminal.
Honolulu, HI, Honolulu International Airport.
Honolulu, HI, Hickam Air Force Base.
Rota, the Commonwealth of the Northern Mariana Islands.
Saipan, the Commonwealth of the Northern Mariana Islands.
Tinian, the Commonwealth of the Northern Mariana Islands.

DISTRICT NO. 18—PHOENIX, ARIZONA

Douglas, AZ, Bisbee-Douglas Airport
Las Vegas, NV, McCarren International Airport
Nogales, AZ, Nogales International Airport
Phoenix, AZ, Phoenix Sky Harbor International Airport
Reno, NV, Reno Carron International Airport
Tucson, AZ, Tucson International Airport
Yuma, AZ, Yuma International Airport

DISTRICT NO. 19—DENVER, COLORADO

Colorado Springs, CO, Colorado Springs Airport
Denver, CO, Denver International Airport
Salt Lake City, UT, Salt Lake City Airport

DISTRICT NO. 20—DALLAS, TEXAS

Dallas, TX, Dallas-Fort Worth International Airport
Oklahoma City, OK, Oklahoma City Airport (includes Altus and Tinker AFBs)

DISTRICT NO. 21—NEWARK, NEW JERSEY

Atlantic City, NJ, Atlantic City International Airport
Lakehurst, NJ, Lakehurst Naval Air Station
Morristown, NJ, Morristown Airport
Newark, NJ, Newark International Airport
Newark, NJ, Signature Airport
Teterboro, NJ, Teterboro Airport
Wrightstown, NJ, McGuire Air Force Base

DISTRICT NO. 22—PORTLAND, MAINE

Bangor, ME, Bangor International Airport
Burlington, VT, Burlington International Airport
Caribou, ME, Caribou Municipal Airport
Highgate Springs, VT, Franklin County Regional Airport
Newport, VT, Newport State Airport

DISTRICT NO. 23 [RESERVED]

DISTRICT NO. 24—CLEVELAND, OHIO

Akron, OH, Municipal Airport
Cincinnati, OH, Cincinnati International Airport
Cleveland, OH, Cleveland Hopkins Airport
Columbus, OH, Port Columbus International Airport
Sandusky, OH, Griffing/Sandusky Airport

DISTRICT NO. 25—WASHINGTON, D.C.

Camp Springs, MD, Andrews Air Force Base
Chantilly, VA, Washington Dulles International Airport
Winchester, VA, Winchester Airport

DISTRICT NO. 26—ATLANTA, GEORGIA

Atlanta, GA, Atlanta Hartsfield International Airport
Charleston, SC, Charleston International Airport
Charleston, SC, Charleston Air Force Base
Charlotte, NC, Charlotte International Airport
Raleigh, NC, Raleigh-Durham International Airport
Savannah, GA, Savannah International Airport

DISTRICT NO. 27—SAN JUAN, PUERTO RICO

San Juan, PR, San Juan International Airport

DISTRICT NO. 28—NEW ORLEANS, LOUISIANA

Louisville, KY, Louisville International Airport
New Orleans, LA, New Orleans International Airport
Memphis, TN, Memphis International Airport
Nashville, TN, Nashville International Airport

DISTRICT NO. 29—OMAHA, NEBRASKA

Des Moines, IA, Des Moines International Airport
Omaha, NE, Eppley International Airport
Omaha, NE, Offutt Air Force Base

DISTRICT NO. 30—HELENA, MONTANA

Billings, MT, Billings Airport
Boise, ID, Boise Airport
Cut Bank, MT, Cut Bank Airport
Glasgow, MT, Glasgow International Airport
Great Falls, MT, Great Falls International Airport
Havre, MT, Havre-Hill County Airport
Helena, MT, Helena Airport
Kalispel, MT, Kalispel Airport
Missoula, MT, Missoula Airport

DISTRICT NO. 31—PORTLAND, OREGON

Medford, OR, Jackson County Airport
Portland, OR, Portland International Airport

DISTRICT NO. 32—ANCHORAGE, ALASKA

Anchorage, AK, Anchorage International Airport
Juneau, AK, Juneau Airport (Seaplane Base Only)
Juneau, AK, Juneau Municipal Airport
Ketchikan, AK, Ketchikan Airport
Wrangell, AK, Wrangell Seaplane Base

DISTRICT NO. 38—HOUSTON, TEXAS

Galveston, TX, Galveston Airport
Houston, TX, Ellington Field
Houston, TX, Hobby Airport
Houston, TX, Houston Intercontinental Airport

DISTRICT NO. 39—SAN DIEGO, CALIFORNIA

Calexico, CA, Calexico International Airport
San Diego, CA, San Diego International Airport
San Diego, CA, San Diego Municipal Airport (Lindbergh Field)

DISTRICT NO. 40—HARLINGEN, TEXAS

Brownsville, TX, Brownsville/South Padre Island International Airport
Harlingen, TX, Valley International Airport
McAllen, TX, McAllen Miller International Airport

(c) *Border patrol sectors.* Border Patrol Sector Headquarters and Stations are situated at the following locations:

SECTOR NO. 1—HOULTON, MAINE

Calais, ME
Fort Fairfield, ME
Houlton, ME
Jackman, ME
Rangeley, ME
Van Buren, ME

SECTOR NO. 2—SWANTON, VERMONT

Beecher Falls, VT
Burke, NY
Champlain, NY
Massena, NY
Newport, VT
Ogdensburg, NY
Richford, VT
Swanton, VT

SECTOR NO. 3—RAMEY, PUERTO RICO

Ramey, Puerto Rico

SECTOR NO. 4—BUFFALO, NEW YORK

Buffalo, NY
Fulton, NY
Niagara Falls, NY
Watertown, NY

SECTOR NO. 5—DETROIT, MICHIGAN

Detroit, MI
Grand Rapids, MI
Port Huron, MI
Sault Ste. Marie, MI
Trenton, MI

SECTOR NO. 6—GRAND FORKS, NORTH DAKOTA

Bottineau, ND
Duluth, MN
Grand Forks, ND
Grand Marais, MN
International Falls, MN
Pembina, ND
Portal, ND
Warroad, MN

SECTOR NO. 7—HAVRE, MONTANA

Billings, MT
Havre, MT
Malta, MT
Plentywood, MT
Scobey, MT
Shelby, MT
St. Mary, MT
Sweetgrass, MT
Twin Falls, ID

SECTOR NO. 8—SPOKANE, WASHINGTON

Bonners Ferry, ID
Colville, WA

Eureka, MT
Oroville, WA
Pasco, WA
Spokane, WA
Wenatchee, WA
Whitefish, MT

SECTOR NO. 9—BLAINE, WASHINGTON

Bellingham, WA
Blaine, WA
Lynden, WA
Port Angeles, WA
Roseburg, OR

SECTOR NO. 10—LIVERMORE, CALIFORNIA

Bakersfield, CA
Fresno, CA
Livermore, CA
Oxnard, CA
Sacramento, CA
Salinas, CA
San Luis Obispo, CA
Stockton, CA

SECTOR NO. 11—SAN DIEGO, CALIFORNIA

Brown Field, CA
Campo, CA (Boulevard, CA)
Chula Vista, CA
El Cajon, CA (San Marcos and Julian, CA)
Imperial Beach, CA
San Clemente, CA
Temecula, CA

SECTOR NO. 12—EL CENTRO, CALIFORNIA

Calexico, CA
El Centro, CA
Indio, CA
Riverside, CA

SECTOR NO. 13—YUMA, ARIZONA

Blythe, CA
Boulder City, NV
Wellton, AZ
Yuma, AZ

SECTOR NO. 14—TUCSON, ARIZONA

Ajo, AZ
Casa Grande, AZ
Douglas, AZ
Naco, AZ
Nogales, AZ
Phoenix, AZ
Sonita, AZ
Tucson, AZ
Willcox, AZ

SECTOR NO. 15—EL PASO, TEXAS

Alamogordo, NM
Albuquerque, NM
Carlsbad, NM
Deming, NM
El Paso, TX
Fabens, TX
Fort Hancock, TX
Las Cruces, NM,
Lordsburg, NM
Truth or Consequences, NM
Ysleta, TX

SECTOR NO. 16—MARFA, TEXAS

Alpine, TX
Amarillo, TX
Fort Stockton, TX
Lubbock, TX
Marfa, TX
Midland, TX
Pecos, TX
Presidio, TX
Sanderson, TX
Sierra Blanca, TX
Van Horn, TX

SECTOR NO. 17—DEL RIO, TEXAS

Abilene, TX
Brackettville, TX
Carrizo Springs, TX
Comstock, TX
Del Rio, TX
Eagle Pass, TX
Llano, TX
Rocksprings, TX
San Angelo, TX
Uvalde, TX

SECTOR NO. 18—LAREDO, TEXAS

Cotulla, TX
Dallas, TX
Freer, TX
Hebbronville, TX
Laredo North, TX
Laredo South, TX
San Antonio, TX
Zapata, TX

SECTOR NO. 19—MCALLEN, TEXAS

Brownsville, TX
Corpus Christi, TX
Falfurrias, TX
Harlingen, TX
Kingsville, TX
McAllen, TX
Mercedes, TX
Port Isabel, TX
Rio Grande City, TX

SECTOR NO. 20—NEW ORLEANS, LOUISIANA

Baton Rouge, LA
Gulfport, MS
Lake Charles, LA
Little Rock, AR
Miami, OK
Mobile, AL
New Orleans, LA

SECTOR NO. 21—MIAMI, FLORIDA

Jacksonville, FL
Orlando, FL
Pembroke Pines, FL
Tampa, FL

West Palm Beach, FL

[60 FR 57166, Nov. 14, 1995, as amended at 61 FR 25778, May 23, 1996; 63 FR 70315, Dec. 21, 1998; 65 FR 39072, June 23, 2000; 66 FR 29672, June 1, 2001; 74 FR 2833, Jan. 16, 2009; 74 FR 26936, June 5, 2009; 77 FR 75824, Dec. 26, 2012; 77 FR 76352, Dec. 28, 2012; 79 FR 42451, July 22, 2014; 80 FR 75632, Dec. 3, 2015]

§ 100.5 Regulations.

The regulations of the Department of Homeland Security, published as chapter I of title 8 of the Code of Federal Regulations, contain information which under the provisions of section 552 of title 5 of the United States Code, is required to be published and is subdivided into subchapter A (General Provisions, parts 1 through 3, inclusive), subchapter B (Immigration Regulations, parts 100 through 299, inclusive), and subchapter C (Nationality Regulations, parts 306 through 499, inclusive). Any person desiring information with respect to a particular procedure (other than rule making) under the Immigration and Nationality Act should examine the part or section in chapter I of title 8 of the Code of Federal Regulations dealing with such procedures as well as the section of the Act implemented by such part or section.

[32 FR 9616, July 4, 1967, as amended at 74 FR 26936, June 5, 2009]

§ 100.6 [Reserved]

PART 101—PRESUMPTION OF LAWFUL ADMISSION

AUTHORITY: 8 U.S.C. 1103, 8 CFR part 2.

§ 101.1 Presumption of lawful admission.

A member of the following classes shall be presumed to have been lawfully admitted for permanent residence even though a record of his admission cannot be found, except as otherwise provided in this section, unless he abandoned his lawful permanent resident status or subsequently lost that status by operation of law:

(a) *Prior to June 30, 1906.* An alien who establishes that he entered the United States prior to June 30, 1906.

(b) *United States land borders.* An alien who establishes that, while a citizen of Canada or Newfoundland, he entered the United States across the Canadian border prior to October 1, 1906; an alien who establishes that while a citizen of Mexico he entered the United States across the Mexican border prior to July 1, 1908; an alien who establishes that, while a citizen of Mexico, he entered the United States at the port of Presidio, Texas, prior to October 21, 1918, and an alien for whom a record of his actual admission to the United States does not exist but who establishes that he gained admission to the United States prior to July 1, 1924, pursuant to preexamination at a United States immigration station in Canada and that a record of such preexamination exists.

(c) *Virgin Islands.* An alien who establishes that he entered the Virgin Islands of the United States prior to July 1, 1938, even though a record of his admission prior to that date exists as a non-immigrant under the Immigration Act of 1924.

(d) *Asiatic barred zone.* An alien who establishes that he is of a race indigenous to, and a native of a country within, the Asiatic zone defined in section 3 of the Act of February 5, 1917, as amended, that he was a member of a class of aliens exempted from exclusion by the provisions of that section, and that he entered the United States prior to July 1, 1924, provided that a record of his admission exists.

(e) *Chinese and Japanese aliens*—(1) *Prior to July 1, 1924.* A Chinese alien for whom there exists a record of his admission to the United States prior to July 1, 1924, under the laws and regulations formerly applicable to Chinese and who establishes that at the time of his admission he was a merchant, teacher, or student, and his son or daughter under 21 or wife accompanying or following to join him; a traveler for curiosity or pleasure and his accompanying son or daughter under 21 or accompanying wife; a wife of a United States citizen; a returning laborer; and a person erroneously admitted as a United States citizen under section 1993 of the Revised Statutes of the United States, as amended, his father not having resided in the United States prior to his birth.

(2) *On or after July 1, 1924.* A Chinese alien for whom there exists a record of his admission to the United States as a member of one of the following classes; an alien who establishes that he was readmitted between July 1, 1924, and December 16, 1943, inclusive, as a returning Chinese laborer who acquired lawful permanent residence prior to July 1, 1924; a person erroneously admitted between July 1, 1924, and June 6, 1927, inclusive, as a United States citizen under section 1993 of the Revised Statutes of the United States, as amended, his father not having resided in the United States prior to his birth; an alien admitted at any time after June 30, 1924, under section 4 (b) or (d) of the Immigration Act of 1924; an alien wife of a United States citizen admitted between June 13, 1930, and December 16, 1943, inclusive, under section 4(a) of the Immigration Act of 1924; an alien admitted on or after December 17, 1943, under section 4(f) of the Immigration Act of 1924; an alien admitted on or after December 17, 1943, under section 317(c) of the Nationality Act of 1940, as amended; an alien admitted on or after December 17, 1943, as a preference or nonpreference quota immigrant pursuant to section 2 of that act; and a Chinese or Japanese alien admitted to the United States between July 1, 1924, and December 23, 1952, both dates inclusive, as the wife or minor son or daughter of a treaty merchant admitted before July 1, 1924, if the husband-father was lawfully admitted to the United States as a treaty merchant before July 1, 1924, or, while maintaining another status under which he was admitted before that date, and his status changed to that of a treaty merchant or treaty trader after that date, and was maintaining the changed status at the time his wife or minor son or daughter entered the United States.

(f) *Citizens of the Philippine Islands*—(1) *Entry prior to May 1, 1934.* An alien who establishes that he entered the United States prior to May 1, 1934, and that he was on the date of his entry a citizen of the Philippine Islands, provided that for the purpose of petitioning for naturalization he shall not be regarded as having been lawfully admitted for permanent residence unless he was a citizen of the Commonwealth of the Philippines on July 2, 1946.

(2) *Entry between May 1, 1934, and July 3, 1946.* An alien who establishes that he entered Hawaii between May 1, 1934, and July 3, 1946, inclusive, under the provisions of the last sentence of section 8(a)(1) of the Act of March 24, 1934, as amended, that he was a citizen of the Philippine Islands when he entered, and that a record of such entry exists.

(g) *Temporarily admitted aliens.* The following aliens who when admitted expressed an intention to remain in the United States temporarily or to pass in transit through the United States, for whom records of admission exist, but who remained in the United States: An alien admitted prior to June 3, 1921, except if admitted temporarily under the 9th proviso to section 3 of the Immigration Act of 1917, or as an accredited official of a foreign government, his suite, family, or guest, or as a seaman in pursuit of his calling; an alien admitted under the Act of May 19, 1921, as amended, who was admissible for permanent residence under that Act notwithstanding the quota limitation's thereof and his accompanying wife or unmarried son or daughter under 21 who was admissible for permanent residence under that Act notwithstanding the quota limitations thereof; and an alien admitted under the Act of May 19, 1921, as amended, who was charged under that Act to the proper quota at the time of his admission or subsequently and who remained so charged.

(h) *Citizens of the Trust Territory of the Pacific Islands who entered Guam prior to December 24, 1952.* An alien who establishes that while a citizen of the Trust Territory of the Pacific Islands he entered Guam prior to December 24, 1952, by records, such as Service records subsequent to June 15, 1952, records of the Guamanian Immigration Service, records of the Navy or Air Force, or records of contractors of those agencies, and was residing in Guam on December 24, 1952.

(i) *Aliens admitted to Guam.* An alien who establishes that he was admitted to Guam prior to December 24, 1952, by records such as Service records subsequent to June 15, 1952, records of the Guamanian Immigration Service, records of the Navy or Air Force, or records of contractors of those agencies; that he was not excludable under the Act of February 5, 1917, as amended; and that he continued to reside in Guam until December 24, 1952, and thereafter was not admitted or readmitted into Guam as a nonimmigrant, provided that the provisions of this paragraph shall not apply to an alien who was exempted from the contract laborer provisions of section 3 of the Immigration Act of February 5, 1917, as amended, through the exercise, expressly or impliedly, of the 4th or 9th provisos to section 3 of that act.

(j) *Erroneous admission as United States citizens or as children of citizens.* (1)(i) An alien for whom there exists a record of admission prior to September 11, 1957, as a United States citizen who establishes that at the time of such admission he was the child of a United States citizen parent; he was erroneously issued a United States passport or included in the United States passport of his citizen parent accompanying him or to whom he was destined; no fraud or misrepresentation was practiced by him in the issuance of the passport or in gaining admission; he was otherwise admissible at the time of entry except for failure to meet visa or passport requirements; and he has maintained a residence in the United States since the date of admission, or (ii) an alien who meets all of the foregoing requirements except that if he were, in fact, a citizen of the United States a passport would not have been required, or it had been individually waived, and was erroneously admitted as a United States citizen by a Service officer. For the purposes of all of the foregoing, the terms *child* and *parent* shall be defined as in section 101(b) of the Immigration and Nationality Act, as amended.

(2) An alien admitted to the United States before July 1, 1948, in possession of a section 4(a) 1924 Act nonquota immigration visa issued in accordance with State Department regulations, including a child of a United States citizen after he reached the age of 21, in the absence of fraud or misrepresentation; a member of a naturalized person's family who was admitted to the United States as a United States citizen or as a section 4(a) 1924 Act nonquota immigrant on the basis of that naturalization, unless he knowingly participated in the unlawful naturalization of the parent or spouse rendered void by cancellation, or knew at any time prior to his admission to the United States of the cancellation; and a member of a naturalized person's family who knew at any time prior to his admission to the United States of the cancellation of the naturalization of his parent or spouse but was admitted to the United States as a United States citizen pursuant to a State Department or Service determination based upon a then prevailing administrative view, provided the State Department or Service knew of the cancellation.

[23 FR 9119, Nov. 26, 1958, as amended at 24 FR 2583, Apr. 3, 1959; 24 FR 6476, Aug. 12, 1959; 25 FR 581, Jan. 23, 1960; 31 FR 535, Jan. 15, 1966]

§ 101.2 Presumption of lawful admission; entry under erroneous name or other errors.

An alien who entered the United States as either an immigrant or nonimmigrant under any of the following circumstances shall be regarded as having been lawfully admitted in such status, except as otherwise provided in this part: An alien otherwise admissible whose entry was made and recorded under other than his full true and correct name or whose entry record contains errors in recording sex, names of relatives, or names of foreign places of birth or residence, provided that he establishes by clear, unequivocal, and convincing evidence that the record of the claimed admission relates to him, and, if entry occurred on or after May 22, 1918, if under other than his full, true and correct name that he also establishes that the name was not adopted for the purpose of concealing his identity when obtaining a passport or visa, or for the purpose of using the passport or visa of another person or otherwise evading any provision of the immigration laws, and that the name used at the time of entry was one by which he had been known for a sufficient length of time prior to making application for a passport or visa to have permitted the issuing authority or authorities to have made any necessary investigation concerning him or that his true identity was known to such officials.

[32 FR 9622, July 4, 1967]

§101.3 Creation of record of lawful permanent resident status for person born under diplomatic status in the United States.

(a) *Person born to foreign diplomat*—(1) *Status of person.* A person born in the United States to a foreign diplomatic officer accredited to the United States, as a matter of international law, is not subject to the jurisdiction of the United States. That person is not a United States citizen under the Fourteenth Amendment to the Constitution. Such a person may be considered a lawful permanent resident at birth.

(2) *Definition of foreign diplomatic officer. Foreign diplomatic officer* means a person listed in the State Department Diplomatic List, also known as the Blue List. It includes ambassadors, ministers, chargés d'affaires, counselors, secretaries and attachés of embassies and legations as well as members of the Delegation of the Commission of the European Communities. The term also includes individuals with comparable diplomatic status and immunities who are accredited to the United Nations or to the Organization of American States, and other individuals who are also accorded comparable diplomatic status.

(b) *Child born subject to the jurisdiction of the United States.* A child born in the United States is born subject to the jurisdiction of the United States and is a United States citizen if the parent is not a "foreign diplomatic officer" as defined in paragraph (a)(2) of this section. This includes, for example, a child born in the United States to one of the following foreign government officials or employees:

(1) Employees of foreign diplomatic missions whose names appear in the State Department list entitled "Employees of Diplomatic Missions Not Printed in the Diplomatic List," also known as the White List; employees of foreign diplomatic missions accredited to the United Nations or the Organization of American States; or foreign diplomats accredited to other foreign states. The majority of these individuals enjoy certain diplomatic immunities, but they are not "foreign diplomatic officers" as defined in paragraph (a)(2) of this section. The immunities, if any, of their family members are derived from the status of the employees or diplomats.

(2) Foreign government employees with limited or no diplomatic immunity such as consular officials named on the State Department list entitled "Foreign Consular Officers in the United States" and their staffs.

(c) *Voluntary registration as lawful permanent resident of person born to foreign diplomat.* Since a person born in the United States to a foreign diplomatic officer is not subject to the jurisdiction of the United States, his/her registration as a lawful permanent resident of the United States is voluntary. The provisions of section 262 of the Act do not apply to such a person unless and until that person ceases to have the rights, privileges, exemptions, or immunities which may be claimed by a foreign diplomatic officer.

(d) *Retention of lawful permanent residence.* To be eligible for lawful permanent resident status under paragraph (a) of this section, an alien must establish that he/she has not abandoned his/her residence in the United States. One of the tests for retention of lawful permanent resident status is continuous residence, not continuous physical presence, in the United States. Such a person will not be considered to have abandoned his/her residence in the United States solely by having been admitted to the United States in a nonimmigrant classification under paragraph (15)(A) or (15)(G) of section 101(a) of the Act after a temporary stay in a foreign country or countries on one or several occasions.

(Secs. 101(a)(20), 103, 262, 264 of the Immigration and Nationality Act, as amended; 8 U.S.C. 1101(a)(20), 1103, 1302, 1304)

[47 FR 940, Jan. 8, 1982]

§ 101.4 Registration procedure.

The procedure for an application for creation of a record of lawful permanent residence and a Permanent Resident Card, Form I–551, for a person eligible for presumption of lawful admission for permanent residence under § 101.1 or § 101.2 or for lawful permanent residence as a person born in the United States to a foreign diplomatic officer under § 101.3 is described in § 264.2 of this chapter.

(Secs. 101(a)(20), 103, 262, 264 of the Immigration and Nationality Act, as amended; 8 U.S.C. 1101(a)(20), 1103, 1302, 1304)

[47 FR 941, Jan. 8, 1982, as amended at 63 FR 70315, Dec. 21, 1998]

§ 101.5 Special immigrant status for certain G–4 nonimmigrants.

(a) *Application.* An application for adjustment to special immigrant status under section 101(a)(27)(I) of the INA shall be made on Form I–485. The application date of the I–485 shall be the date of acceptance by the Service as properly filed. If the application date is other than the fee receipt date it must be noted and initialed by a Service officer. The date of application for adjustment of status is the closing date for computing the residence and physical presence requirement. The applicant must have complied with all requirements as of the date of application.

(b) *Documentation.* All documents must be submitted in accordance with § 103.2(b) of this chapter. The application shall be accompanied by documentary evidence establishing the aggregate residence and physical presence required. Documentary evidence may include official employment verification, records of official or personnel transactions or recordings of events occurring during the period of claimed residence and physical presence. Affidavits of credible witnesses may also be accepted. Persons unable to furnish evidence in their own names may furnish evidence in the names of parents or other persons with whom they have been living, if affidavits of the parents or other persons are submitted attesting to the claimed residence and physical presence. The claimed family relationship to the principle G–4 international organization officer or employee must be substantiated by the submission of verifiable civil documents.

(c) *Residence and physical presence requirements.* All applicants applying under sections 101(a)(27)(I) (i), (ii), and (iii) of the INA must have resided and been physically present in the United States for a designated period of time.

For purposes of this section only, an absence from the United States to conduct official business on behalf of the employing organization, or approved customary leave shall not be subtracted from the aggregated period of required residence or physical presence for the current or former G–4 officer or employee or the accompanying spouse and unmarried sons or daughters of such officer or employee, provided residence in the United States is maintained during such absences, and the duty station of the principle G–4 nonimmigrant continues to be in the United States. Absence from the United States by the G–4 spouse or unmarried son or daughter without the principle G–4 shall not be subtracted from the aggregate period of residence and physical presence if on customary leave as recognized by the international organization employer. Absence by the unmarried son or daughter while enrolled in a school outside the United States will not be counted toward the physical presence requirement.

(d) *Maintenance of nonimmigrant status.* Section 101(a)(27)(I) (i), and (ii) requires the applicant to accrue the required period of residence and physical presence in the United States while maintaining status as a G–4 or N nonimmigrant. Section 101(a)(27)(I)(iii) requires such time accrued only in G–4 nonimmigrant status.

Maintaining G–4 status for this purpose is defined as maintaining qualified employment with a "G" international organization or maintaining the qualifying family relationship with the G–4 international organization officer or employee. Maintaining status as an N nonimmigrant for this purpose requires the qualifying family relationship to remain in effect. Unauthorized employment will not remove an otherwise eligible alien from G–4 status for residence and physical presence requirements, provided the qualifying G–4 status is maintained.

[54 FR 5927, Feb. 7, 1989]

PART 103—IMMIGRATION BENEFITS; BIOMETRIC REQUIREMENTS; AVAILABILITY OF RECORDS

Subpart A—Applying for Benefits, Surety Bonds, Fees

AUTHORITY: 5 U.S.C. 301, 552, 552a; 8 U.S.C. 1101, 1103, 1304, 1356; 31 U.S.C. 9701; 48 U.S.C. 1806; Pub. L. 107–296, 116 Stat. 2135 (6 U.S.C. 1 *et seq.*); E.O. 12356, 47 FR 14874, 15557; 3 CFR, 1982 Comp., p. 166; 8 CFR part 2; Pub. L. 112–54, 125 Stat 550.

SOURCE: 40 FR 44481, Sept. 26, 1975, unless otherwise noted.

Subpart A—Applying for Benefits, Surety Bonds, Fees

§ 103.1 [Reserved]

§ 103.2 Submission and adjudication of benefit requests.

(a) *Filing.* (1) *Preparation and submission.* Every form, benefit request, or other document must be submitted to DHS and executed in accordance with the form instructions regardless of a provision of 8 CFR chapter I to the contrary. The form's instructions are hereby incorporated into the regulations requiring its submission. Each form, benefit request, or other document must be filed with the fee(s) required by regulation. Filing fees generally are non-refundable and, except as otherwise provided in this chapter I, must be paid when the benefit request is filed.

(2) *Signature.* An applicant or petitioner must sign his or her benefit request. However, a parent or legal guardian may sign for a person who is less than 14 years old. A legal guardian may sign for a mentally incompetent person. By signing the benefit request, the applicant or petitioner, or parent or guardian certifies under penalty of perjury that the benefit request, and all evidence submitted with it, either at the time of filing or thereafter, is true and correct. Unless otherwise specified in this chapter, an acceptable signature on a benefit request that is being filed with the USCIS is one that is either handwritten or, for benefit requests filed electronically as permitted by the instructions to the form, in electronic format.

(3) *Representation.* An applicant or petitioner may be represented by an attorney in the United States, as defined in § 1.2 of this chapter, by an attorney outside the United States as defined in § 292.1(a)(6) of this chapter, or by an accredited representative as defined in § 292.1(a)(4) of this chapter. A beneficiary of a petition is not a recognized party in such a proceeding. A benefit request presented in person by someone who is not the applicant or petitioner, or his or her representative as defined in this paragraph, shall be treated as if received through the mail, and the person advised that the applicant or petitioner, and his or her representative,

will be notified of the decision. Where a notice of representation is submitted that is not properly signed, the benefit request will be processed as if the notice had not been submitted.

(4) *Oath.* Any required oath may be administered by an immigration officer or person generally authorized to administer oaths, including persons so authorized by Article 136 of the Uniform Code of Military Justice.

(5) *Translation of name.* If a document has been executed in an anglicized version of a name, the native form of the name may also be required.

(6) *Where to file.* All benefit requests must be filed in accordance with the form instructions.

(7) *Benefit requests submitted.* (i) USCIS will consider a benefit request received and will record the receipt date as of the actual date of receipt at the location designated for filing such benefit request whether electronically or in paper format.

(ii) A benefit request which is rejected will not retain a filing date. A benefit request will be rejected if it is not:

(A) Signed with valid signature;

(B) Executed;

(C) Filed in compliance with the regulations governing the filing of the specific application, petition, form, or request; and

(D) *Submitted with the correct fee(s).* If a check or other financial instrument used to pay a fee is returned as unpayable, USCIS will re-submit the payment to the remitter institution one time. If the instrument used to pay a fee is returned as unpayable a second time, the filing will be rejected and a charge will be imposed in accordance with 8 CFR 103.7(a)(2).

(iii) A rejection of a filing with USCIS may not be appealed.

(b) *Evidence and processing.* (1) *Demonstrating eligibility.* An applicant or petitioner must establish that he or she is eligible for the requested benefit at the time of filing the benefit request and must continue to be eligible through adjudication. Each benefit request must be properly completed and filed with all initial evidence required by applicable regulations and other USCIS instructions. Any evidence submitted in connection with a benefit request is incorporated into and considered part of the request.

(2) *Submitting secondary evidence and affidavits*—(i) *General.* The non-existence or other unavailability of required evidence creates a presumption of ineligibility. If a required document, such as a birth or marriage certificate, does not exist or cannot be obtained, an applicant or petitioner must demonstrate this and submit secondary evidence, such as church or school records, pertinent to the facts at issue. If secondary evidence also does not exist or cannot be obtained, the applicant or petitioner must demonstrate the unavailability of both the required document and relevant secondary evidence, and submit two or more affidavits, sworn to or affirmed by persons who are not parties to the petition who have direct personal knowledge of the event and circumstances. Secondary evidence must overcome the unavailability of primary evidence, and affidavits must overcome the unavailability of both primary and secondary evidence.

(ii) *Demonstrating that a record is not available.* Where a record does not exist, the applicant or petitioner must submit an original written statement on government letterhead establishing this from the relevant government or other authority. The statement must indicate the reason the record does not exist, and indicate whether similar records for the time and place are available. However, a certification from an appropriate foreign government that a document does not exist is not required where the Department of State's Foreign Affairs Manual indicates this type of document generally does not exist. An applicant or petitioner who has not been able to acquire the necessary document or statement from the relevant foreign authority may submit evidence that repeated good faith attempts were made to obtain the required document or statement. However, where USCIS finds that such documents or statements are generally available, it may require that the applicant or petitioner submit the required document or statement.

(iii) *Evidence provided with a self-petition filed by a spouse or child of abusive citizen or resident*. The USCIS will consider any credible evidence relevant to a self-petition filed by a qualified spouse or child of an abusive citizen or lawful permanent resident under section 204(a)(1)(A)(iii), 204(a)(1)(A)(iv), 204(a)(1)(B)(ii), or 204(a)(1)(B)(iii) of the Act. The self-petitioner may, but is not required to, demonstrate that preferred primary or secondary evidence is unavailable. The determination of what evidence is credible and the weight to be given that evidence shall be within the sole discretion of USCIS.

(3) *Translations*. Any document containing foreign language submitted to USCIS shall be accompanied by a full English language translation which the translator has certified as complete and accurate, and by the translator's certification that he or she is competent to translate from the foreign language into English.

(4) *Supporting documents*. Original or photocopied documents which are required to support any benefit request must be submitted in accordance with the form instructions.

(5) *Request for an original document*. USCIS may, at any time, request submission of an original document for review. The request will set a deadline for submission of the original document. Failure to submit the requested original document by the deadline may result in denial or revocation of the underlying benefit request. An original document submitted in response to such a request, when no longer required by USCIS, will be returned to the petitioner or applicant upon completion of the adjudication. If USCIS does not return an original document within a reasonable time after completion of the adjudication, the petitioner or applicant may request return of the original document in accordance with instructions provided by USCIS.

(6) *Withdrawal*. An applicant or petitioner may withdraw a benefit request at any time until a decision is issued by USCIS or, in the case of an approved petition, until the person is admitted or granted adjustment or change of status, based on the petition. However, a withdrawal may not be retracted.

(7) *Testimony*. The USCIS may require the taking of testimony, and may direct any necessary investigation. When a statement is taken from and signed by a person, he or she shall, upon request, be given a copy without fee. Any allegations made subsequent to filing a benefit request which are in addition to, or in substitution for, those originally made, shall be filed in the same manner as the original benefit request, or document, and acknowledged under oath thereon.

(8) *Request for Evidence; Notice of Intent to Deny*—(i) *Evidence of eligibility or ineligibility*. If the evidence submitted with the benefit request establishes eligibility, USCIS will approve the benefit request, except that in any case in which the applicable statute or regulation makes the approval of a benefit request a matter entrusted to USCIS discretion, USCIS will approve the benefit request only if the evidence of record establishes both eligibility and that the petitioner or applicant warrants a favorable exercise of discretion. If the record evidence establishes ineligibility, the benefit request will be denied on that basis.

(ii) *Initial evidence*. If all required initial evidence is not submitted with the benefit request or does not demonstrate eligibility, USCIS in its discretion may deny the benefit request for lack of initial evidence or for ineligibility or request that the missing initial evidence be submitted within a specified period of time as determined by USCIS.

(iii) *Other evidence*. If all required initial evidence has been submitted but the evidence submitted does not establish eligibility, USCIS may: deny the benefit request for ineligibility; request more information or evidence from the applicant or petitioner, to be submitted within a specified period of time as determined by USCIS; or notify the applicant or petitioner of its intent to deny the benefit request and the basis for the proposed denial, and require that the applicant or petitioner submit a response within a specified period of time as determined by USCIS.

(iv) *Process*. A request for evidence or notice of intent to deny will be communicated by regular or electronic mail and will specify the type of evidence required, and whether initial evidence or additional evidence is required, or the bases for the proposed denial sufficient to give the applicant or petitioner adequate notice and sufficient information to respond. The request for evidence or notice of intent to deny will indicate the deadline for response, but in no case shall the maximum response period provided in a request for evidence exceed twelve weeks, nor shall the maximum response time provided in a notice of intent to deny exceed thirty days. Additional time to respond to a request for evidence or notice of intent to deny may not be granted.

(9) *Appearance for interview or biometrics.* USCIS may require any applicant, petitioner, sponsor, beneficiary, or individual filing a benefit request, or any group or class of such persons submitting requests, to appear for an interview and/or biometric collection. USCIS may require the payment of the biometric services fee in 8 CFR 103.7(b)(1)(i)(C) or that the individual obtain a fee waiver. Such appearance and fee may also be required by law, regulation, form instructions, or FEDERAL REGISTER notice applicable to the request type. USCIS will notify the affected person of the date, time and location of any required appearance under this paragraph. Any person required to appear under this paragraph may, before the scheduled date and time of the appearance, either:

(i) Appear before the scheduled date and time;

(ii) For good cause, request that the biometric services appointment be rescheduled; or

(iii) Withdraw the benefit request.

(10) *Effect of a request for initial or additional evidence for fingerprinting or interview rescheduling*—(i) *Effect on processing.* The priority date of a properly filed petition shall not be affected by a request for missing initial evidence or request for other evidence. If a benefit request is missing required initial evidence, or an applicant, petitioner, sponsor, beneficiary, or other individual who requires fingerprinting requests that the fingerprinting appointment or interview be rescheduled, any time period imposed on USCIS processing will start over from the date of receipt of the required initial evidence or request for fingerprint or interview rescheduling. If USCIS requests that the applicant or petitioner submit additional evidence or respond to other than a request for initial evidence, any time limitation imposed on USCIS for processing will be suspended as of the date of request. It will resume at the same point where it stopped when USCIS receives the requested evidence or response, or a request for a decision based on the evidence.

(ii) *Effect on interim benefits.* Interim benefits will not be granted based on a benefit request held in suspense for the submission of requested initial evidence, except that the applicant or beneficiary will normally be allowed to remain while a benefit request to extend or obtain status while in the United States is pending. The USCIS may choose to pursue other actions to seek removal of a person notwithstanding the pending application. Employment authorization previously accorded based on the same status and employment as that requested in the current benefit request may continue uninterrupted as provided in 8 CFR 274a.12(b)(20) during the suspense period.

(11) *Responding to a request for evidence or notice of intent to deny.* In response to a request for evidence or a notice of intent to deny, and within the period afforded for a response, the applicant or petitioner may: submit a complete response containing all requested information at any time within the period afforded; submit a partial response and ask for a decision based on the record; or withdraw the benefit request. All requested materials must be submitted together at one time, along with the original USCIS request for evidence or notice of intent to deny. Submission of only some of the requested evidence will be considered a request for a decision on the record.

(12) *Effect where evidence submitted in response to a request does not establish eligibility at the time of filing.* A benefit request shall be denied where evidence submitted in response to a request for evidence does not establish filing eligibility at the time the benefit request was filed. A benefit request shall be denied where any benefit request upon which it was based was filed subsequently.

(13) *Effect of failure to respond to a request for evidence or a notice of intent to deny or to appear for interview or biometrics capture*—(i) *Failure to submit evidence or respond to a notice of intent to deny.* If the petitioner or applicant fails to respond to a request for evidence or to a notice of intent to deny by the required date, the benefit request may be summarily denied as abandoned, denied based on the record, or denied for both reasons. If other requested material necessary to the processing and approval of a case, such as photographs, are not submitted by the required date, the application may be summarily denied as abandoned.

(ii) *Failure to appear for biometrics capture, interview or other required in-person process.* Except as provided in 8 CFR 335.6, if USCIS requires an individual to appear for biometrics capture, an interview, or other required in-person process but the person does not appear, the benefit request shall be considered abandoned and denied unless by the appointment time USCIS has received a change of address or rescheduling request that the agency concludes warrants excusing the failure to appear.

(14) *Effect of request for decision.* Where an applicant or petitioner does not submit all requested additional evidence and requests a decision based on the evidence already submitted, a decision shall be issued based on the record. Failure to submit requested evidence which precludes a material line of inquiry shall be grounds for denying the benefit request. Failure to appear for required fingerprinting or for a required interview, or to give required testimony, shall result in the denial of the related benefit request.

(15) *Effect of withdrawal or denial due to abandonment.* The USCIS acknowledgement of a withdrawal may not be appealed. A denial due to abandonment may not be appealed, but an applicant or petitioner may file a motion to reopen under § 103.5. Withdrawal or denial due to abandonment does not preclude the filing of a new benefit request with a new fee. However, the priority or processing date of a withdrawn or abandoned benefit request may not be applied to a later application petition. Withdrawal or denial due to abandonment shall not itself affect the new proceeding; but the facts and circumstances surrounding the prior benefit request shall otherwise be material to the new benefit request.

(16) *Inspection of evidence.* An applicant or petitioner shall be permitted to inspect the record of proceeding which constitutes the basis for the decision, except as provided in the following paragraphs.

(i) *Derogatory information unknown to petitioner or applicant.* If the decision will be adverse to the applicant or petitioner and is based on derogatory information considered by the Service and of which the applicant or petitioner is unaware, he/she shall be advised of this fact and offered an opportunity to rebut the information and present information in his/her own behalf before the decision is rendered, except as provided in paragraphs (b)(16)(ii), (iii), and (iv) of this section. Any explanation, rebuttal, or information presented by or in behalf of the applicant or petitioner shall be included in the record of proceeding.

(ii) *Determination of statutory eligibility.* A determination of statutory eligibility shall be based only on information contained in the record of proceeding which is disclosed to the applicant or petitioner, except as provided in paragraph (b)(16)(iv) of this section.

(iii) *Discretionary determination.* Where an application may be granted or denied in the exercise of discretion, the decision to exercise discretion favorably or unfavorably may be based in whole or in part on classified information not contained in the record and not made available to the applicant, provided the USCIS Director or his or her designee has determined that such information is relevant and is classified under Executive Order No. 12356 (47 FR 14874; April 6, 1982) as requiring protection from unauthorized disclosure in the interest of national security.

(iv) *Classified information.* An applicant or petitioner shall not be provided any information contained in the record or outside the record which is classified under Executive Order No. 12356 (47 FR 14874; April 6, 1982) as requiring protection from unauthorized disclosure in the interest of national security, unless the classifying authority has agreed in writing to such disclosure. Whenever he/she believes he/she can do so consistently with safeguarding both the information and its source, the USCIS Director or his or her designee should direct that the applicant or petitioner be given notice of the general nature of the information and an opportunity to offer opposing evidence. The USCIS Director's or his or her designee's authorization to use such classified information shall be made a part of the record. A decision based in whole or in part on such classified information shall state that the information is material to the decision.

(17) *Verifying claimed permanent resident status*—(i) *Department records.* The status of an applicant or petitioner who claims that he or she is a permanent resident of the United States or was formerly a permanent resident of the United States will be verified from official Department records. These records include alien and other files, arrival manifests, arrival records, Department index cards, Immigrant Identification Cards, Certificates of Registry, Declarations of Intention issued after July 1, 1929, Permanent Resident Cards, or other registration receipt forms (provided that such forms were issued or endorsed to show admission for permanent residence), passports, and reentry permits. An official record of a Department index card must bear a designated immigrant visa symbol and must have been prepared by an authorized official of the Department in the course of processing immigrant admissions or adjustments to permanent resident status. Other cards, certificates, declarations, permits, and passports must have been issued or endorsed to show admission for permanent residence. Except as otherwise provided in 8 CFR part 101, and in the absence of countervailing evidence, such official records will be regarded as establishing lawful admission for permanent residence.

(ii) *Assisting self-petitioners who are spousal-abuse victims.* If a self-petitioner filing a petition under section 204(a)(1)(A)(iii), 204(a)(1)(A)(iv), 204(a)(1)(B)(ii), or 204(a)(1)(B)(iii) of the Act is unable to present primary or secondary evidence of the abuser's status, USCIS will attempt to electronically verify the abuser's citizenship or immigration status from information contained in the Department's automated or computerized records. Other Department records may also be reviewed at the discretion of the adjudicating officer. If USCIS is unable to identify a record as relating to the abuser, or the record does not establish the abuser's immigration or citizenship status, the self-petition will be adjudicated based on the information submitted by the self-petitioner.

(18) *Withholding adjudication.* USCIS may authorize withholding adjudication of a visa petition or other application if USCIS determines that an investigation has been undertaken involving a matter relating to eligibility or the exercise of discretion, where applicable, in connection with the benefit request, and that the disclosure of information to the applicant or petitioner in connection with the adjudication of the benefit request would prejudice the ongoing investigation. If an investigation has been undertaken and has not been completed within one year of its inception, USCIS will review the matter and determine whether adjudication of the benefit request should be held in abeyance for six months or until the investigation is completed, whichever comes sooner. If, after six months of USCIS's determination, the investigation has not been completed, the matter will be reviewed again by USCIS and, if it concludes that more time is needed to complete the investigation, adjudication may be held in abeyance for up to another six months. If the investigation is not completed at the end of that time, USCIS may authorize that adjudication be held in abeyance for another six months. Thereafter, if USCIS determines it is necessary to continue to withhold adjudication pending completion of the investigation, it will review that determination every six months.

(19) *Notification.* (i) *Unrepresented applicants or petitioners.* USCIS will only send original notices and documents evidencing lawful status based on the approval of a benefit request directly to the applicant or petitioner if the applicant or petitioner is not represented.

(ii) *Represented applicants or petitioners.* (A) *Notices.* When an applicant or petitioner is represented, USCIS will send original notices both to the applicant or petitioner and his or her authorized attorney or accredited representative. If provided in this title, on the applicable form, or on form instructions, an applicant or petitioner filing a paper application or petition may request that all original notices, such as requests for evidence and notices of decision, only be sent to the official business address of the applicant's or petitioner's authorized attorney or accredited representative, as reflected on a properly executed Notice of Entry of Appearance as Attorney or Accredited Representative. In such instances, a courtesy copy of the original notice will be sent to the applicant or petitioner.

(B) *Electronic notices.* For applications or petitions filed electronically, USCIS will notify both the applicant or petitioner and the authorized attorney or accredited representative electronically of any notices or decisions. Except as provided in paragraph (b)(19)(ii)(C) of this section, USCIS will not issue paper notices or decisions for electronically-filed applications or petitions, unless:

(*1*) The option exists for the applicant or petitioner to request to receive paper notices or decisions by mail through the U.S. Postal Service, by indicating this preference in his or her electronic online account profile in USCIS's electronic immigration system; or

(*2*) USCIS, in its discretion, determines that issuing a paper notice or decision for an electronically-filed application or petition is warranted.

(C) *Approval notices with attached Arrival-Departure Records.* USCIS will send an original paper approval notice with an attached Arrival-Departure Record, reflecting USCIS's approval of an applicant's request for an extension of stay or change of status, to the official business address of the applicant's or petitioner's attorney or accredited representative, as reflected on a properly executed Notice of Entry of Appearance as Attorney or Accredited Representative or in the address section of the online representative account profile in USCIS's electronic immigration system, unless the applicant specifically requests that the original approval notice with an attached Arrival-Departure Record be sent directly to his or her mailing address.

(iii) *Secure identity documents.* USCIS will send secure identification documents, such as a Permanent Resident Card or Employment Authorization Document, only to the applicant or self-petitioner unless the applicant or self-petitioner specifically consents to having his or her secure identification document sent to the official business address of the applicant's or self-petitioner's attorney of record or accredited representative, as reflected on a properly executed Notice of Entry of Appearance as Attorney or Accredited Representative or in the address section of the online representative account profile in USCIS's electronic immigration system.

(c)–(d) [Reserved]

[29 FR 11956, Aug. 21, 1964]

EDITORIAL NOTE: For FEDERAL REGISTER citations affecting § 103.2, see the List of CFR Sections Affected, which appears in the Finding Aids section of the printed volume and at *www.govinfo.gov*.

§ 103.3 Denials, appeals, and precedent decisions.

(a) *Denials and appeals*—(1) *General*—(i) *Denial of application or petition.* When a Service officer denies an application or petition filed under § 103.2 of this part, the officer shall explain in writing the specific reasons for denial. If Form I–292 (a denial form including notification of the right of appeal) is used to notify the applicant or petitioner, the duplicate of Form I–292 constitutes the denial order.

(ii) *Appealable decisions.* Certain unfavorable decisions on applications, petitions, and other types of cases may be appealed. Decisions under the appellate jurisdiction of the Board of Immigration Appeals (Board) are listed in § 3.1(b) of this chapter. Decisions under the appellate jurisdiction of the Associate Commissioner, Examinations, are listed in § 103.1(f)(2) of this part.

(iii) *Appeal*—(A) *Jurisdiction.* When an unfavorable decision may be appealed, the official making the decision shall state the appellate jurisdiction and shall furnish the appropriate appeal form.

(B) *Meaning of affected party.* For purposes of this section and §§ 103.4 and 103.5 of this part, *affected party* (in addition to the Service) means the person or entity with legal standing in a proceeding. It does not include the beneficiary of a visa petition. An affected party may be represented by an attorney or representative in accordance with part 292 of this chapter.

(C) *Record of proceeding.* An appeal and any cross-appeal or briefs become part of the record of proceeding.

(D) *Appeal filed by Service officer in case within jurisdiction of Board.* If an appeal is filed by a Service officer, a copy must be served on the affected party.

(iv) *Function of Administrative Appeals Unit (AAU).* The AAU is the appellate body which considers cases under the appellate jurisdiction of the Associate Commissioner, Examinations.

(v) *Summary dismissal.* An officer to whom an appeal is taken shall summarily dismiss any appeal when the party concerned fails to identify specifically any erroneous conclusion of law or statement of fact for the appeal. The filing by an attorney or representative accredited under 8 CFR 292.2(d) of an appeal which is summarily dismissed under this section may constitute frivolous behavior as defined in 8 CFR 292.3(a)(15). Summary dismissal of an appeal under § 103.3(a)(1)(v) in no way limits the other grounds and procedures for disciplinary action against attorneys or representatives provided in 8 CFR 292.2 or in any other statute or regulation.

(2) *AAU appeals in other than special agricultural worker and legalization cases*—(i) *Filing appeal.* The affected party must submit an appeal on Form I–290B. Except as otherwise provided in this chapter, the affected party must pay the fee required by § 103.7 of this part. The affected party must submit the complete appeal including any supporting brief as indicated in the applicable form instructions within 30 days after service of the decision.

(ii) *Reviewing official.* The official who made the unfavorable decision being appealed shall review the appeal unless the affected party moves to a new jurisdiction. In that instance, the official who has jurisdiction over such a proceeding in that geographic location shall review it.

(iii) *Favorable action instead of forwarding appeal to AAU.* The reviewing official shall decide whether or not favorable action is warranted. Within 45 days of receipt of the appeal, the reviewing official may treat the appeal as a motion to reopen or reconsider and take favorable action. However, that official is not precluded from reopening a proceeding or reconsidering a decision on his or her own motion under § 103.5(a)(5)(i) of this part in order to make a new decision favorable to the affected party after 45 days of receipt of the appeal.

(iv) *Forwarding appeal to AAU.* If the reviewing official will not be taking favorable action or decides favorable action is not warranted, that official shall promptly forward the appeal and the related record of proceeding to the AAU in Washington, DC.

(v) *Improperly filed appeal*—(A) *Appeal filed by person or entity not entitled to file it*—*(1) Rejection without refund of filing fee.* An appeal filed by a person or entity not entitled to file it must be rejected as improperly filed. In such a case, any filing fee the Service has accepted will not be refunded.

(2) Appeal by attorney or representative without proper Form G–28—*(i) General.* If an appeal is filed by an attorney or representative without a properly executed Notice of Entry of Appearance as Attorney or Representative (Form G–28) entitling that person to file the appeal, the appeal is considered improperly filed. In such a case, any filing fee the Service has accepted will not be refunded regardless of the action taken.

(ii) When favorable action warranted. If the reviewing official decides favorable action is warranted with respect to an otherwise properly filed appeal, that official shall ask the attorney or representative to submit Form G–28 to the official's office within 15 days of the request. If Form G–28 is not submitted within the time allowed, the official may, on his or her own motion, under § 103.5(a)(5)(i) of this part, make a new decision favorable to the affected party without notifying the attorney or representative.

(*iii*) *When favorable action not warranted.* If the reviewing official decides favorable action is not warranted with respect to an otherwise properly filed appeal, that official shall ask the attorney or representative to submit Form G–28 directly to the AAU. The official shall also forward the appeal and the relating record of proceeding to the AAU. The appeal may be considered properly filed as of its original filing date if the attorney or representative submits a properly executed Form G–28 entitling that person to file the appeal.

(B) *Untimely appeal—(1) Rejection without refund of filing fee.* An appeal which is not filed within the time allowed must be rejected as improperly filed. In such a case, any filing fee the Service has accepted will not be refunded.

(*2*) *Untimely appeal treated as motion.* If an untimely appeal meets the requirements of a motion to reopen as described in § 103.5(a)(2) of this part or a motion to reconsider as described in § 103.5(a)(3) of this part, the appeal must be treated as a motion, and a decision must be made on the merits of the case.

(vi) *Brief.* The affected party may submit a brief with Form I–290B.

(vii) *Additional time to submit a brief.* The affected party may make a written request to the AAU for additional time to submit a brief. The AAU may, for good cause shown, allow the affected party additional time to submit one.

(viii) *Where to submit supporting brief if additional time is granted.* If the AAU grants additional time, the affected party shall submit the brief directly to the AAU.

(ix) *Withdrawal of appeal.* The affected party may withdraw the appeal, in writing, before a decision is made.

(x) *Decision on appeal.* The decision must be in writing. A copy of the decision must be served on the affected party and the attorney or representative of record, if any.

(3) *Denials and appeals of special agricultural worker and legalization applications and termination of lawful temporary resident status under sections 210 and 245A.* (i) Whenever an application for legalization or special agricultural worker status is denied or the status of a lawful temporary resident is terminated, the alien shall be given written notice setting forth the specific reasons for the denial on Form I–692, Notice of Denial. Form I–692 shall also contain advice to the applicant that he or she may appeal the decision and that such appeal must be taken within 30 days after service of the notification of decision accompanied by any additional new evidence, and a supporting brief if desired. The Form I–692 shall additionally provide a notice to the alien that if he or she fails to file an appeal from the decision, the Form I–692 will serve as a final notice of ineligibility.

(ii) Form I–694, Notice of Appeal, in triplicate, shall be used to file the appeal, and must be accompanied by the appropriate fee. Form I–694 shall be furnished with the notice of denial at the time of service on the alien.

(iii) Upon receipt of an appeal, the administrative record will be forwarded to the Administrative Appeals Unit as provided by § 103.1(f)(2) of this part for review and decision. The decision on the appeal shall be in writing, and if the appeal is dismissed, shall include a final notice of ineligibility. A copy of the decision shall be served upon the applicant and his or her attorney or representative of record. No further administrative appeal shall lie from this decision, nor may the application be filed or reopened before an immigration judge or the Board of Immigration Appeals during exclusion or deportation proceedings.

(iv) Any appeal which is filed that:

(A) Fails to state the reason for appeal;

(B) Is filed solely on the basis of a denial for failure to file the application for adjustment of status under section 210 or 245A in a timely manner; or

(C) Is patently frivolous; will be summarily dismissed. An appeal received after the thirty (30) day period has tolled will not be accepted for processing.

(4) *Denials and appeal of Replenishment Agricultural Worker petitions and waivers and termination of lawful temporary resident status under section 210A.* (i) Whenever a petition for Replenishment Agricultural Worker status, or a request for a waiver incident to such filing, is denied in accordance with the

provisions of part 210a of this title, the alien shall be given written notice setting forth the specific reasons for the denial on Form I–692, Notice of Denial. Form I–692 shall also contain advice to the alien that he or she may appeal the decision and that such appeal must be taken within thirty (30) days after service of the notification of decision accompanied by any additional new evidence, and a supporting brief if desired. The Form I–692 shall additionally provide a notice to the alien that if he or she fails to file an appeal from the decision, the Form I–692 shall serve as a final notice of ineligibility.

(ii) Form I–694, Notice of Appeal, in triplicate, shall be used to file the appeal, and must be accompanied by the appropriate fee. Form I–694 shall be furnished with the notice of denial at the time of service on the alien.

(iii) Upon receipt of an appeal, the administrative record will be forwarded to the Administrative Appeals Unit as provided by § 103.1(f)(2) of this part for review and decision. The decision on the appeal shall be in writing, and if the appeal is dismissed, shall include a final notice of ineligibility. A copy of the decision shall be served upon the petitioner and his or her attorney or representative of record. No further administrative appeal shall lie from this decision, nor may the petition be filed or reopened before an immigration judge or the Board of Immigration Appeals during exclusion or deportation proceedings.

(iv) Any appeal which is filed that: Fails to state the reason for the appeal; is filed solely on the basis of a denial for failure to file the petition for adjustment of status under part 210a of this title in a timely manner; or is patently frivolous, will be summarily dismissed. An appeal received after the thirty (30) day period has tolled will not be accepted for processing.

(b) *Oral argument regarding appeal before AAU*—(1) *Request.* If the affected party desires oral argument, the affected party must explain in writing specifically why oral argument is necessary. For such a request to be considered, it must be submitted within the time allowed for meeting other requirements.

(2) *Decision about oral argument.* The Service has sole authority to grant or deny a request for oral argument. Upon approval of a request for oral argument, the AAU shall set the time, date, place, and conditions of oral argument.

(c) *Service precedent decisions.* The Secretary of Homeland Security, or specific officials of the Department of Homeland Security designated by the Secretary with the concurrence of the Attorney General, may file with the Attorney General decisions relating to the administration of the immigration laws of the United States for publication as precedent in future proceedings, and upon approval of the Attorney General as to the lawfulness of such decision, the Director of the Executive Office for Immigration Review shall cause such decisions to be published in the same manner as decisions of the Board and the Attorney General. In addition to Attorney General and Board decisions referred to in § 1003.1(g) of chapter V, designated Service decisions are to serve as precedents in all proceedings involving the same issue(s). Except as these decisions may be modified or overruled by later precedent decisions, they are binding on all Service employees in the administration of the Act. Precedent decisions must be published and made available to the public as described in 8 CFR 103.10(e).

[31 FR 3062, Feb. 24, 1966, as amended at 37 FR 927, Jan. 21, 1972; 48 FR 36441, Aug. 11, 1983; 49 FR 7355, Feb. 29, 1984; 52 FR 16192, May 1, 1987; 54 FR 29881, July 17, 1989; 55 FR 20769, 20775, May 21, 1990; 55 FR 23345, June 7, 1990; 57 FR 11573, Apr. 6, 1992; 68 FR 9832, Feb. 28, 2003; 76 FR 53781, Aug. 29, 2011]

§ 103.4 Certifications.

(a) *Certification of other than special agricultural worker and legalization cases*—(1) *General.* The Commissioner or the Commissioner's delegate may direct that any case or class of cases be certified to another Service official for decision. In addition, regional commissioners, regional service center directors, district directors, officers in charge in districts 33 (Bangkok, Thailand), 35 (Mexico City, Mexico), and 37 (Rome, Italy), and the Director, National Fines Office, may certify their decisions to the appropriate appellate authority (as designated in this chapter) when the case involves an unusually complex or novel issue of law or fact.

(2) *Notice to affected party.* When a case is certified to a Service officer, the official certifying the case shall notify the affected party using a Notice of Certification (Form I–290C). The affected party may submit a brief to the officer to whom the case is certified within 30 days after service of the notice. If the affected party does not wish to submit a brief, the affected party may waive the 30-day period.

(3) *Favorable action.* The Service officer to whom a case is certified may suspend the 30-day period for submission of a brief if that officer takes action favorable to the affected party.

(4) *Initial decision.* A case within the appellate jurisdiction of the Associate Commissioner, Examinations, or for which there is no appeal procedure may be certified only after an initial decision is made.

(5) *Certification to AAU.* A case described in paragraph (a)(4) of this section may be certified to the AAU.

(6) *Appeal to Board.* In a case within the Board's appellate jurisdiction, an unfavorable decision of the Service official to whom the case is certified (whether made initially or upon review) is the decision which may be appealed to the Board under §3.1(b) of this chapter.

(7) *Other applicable provisions.* The provisions of §103.3(a)(2)(x) of this part also apply to decisions on certified cases. The provisions of §103.3(b) of this part also apply to requests for oral argument regarding certified cases considered by the AAU.

(b) *Certification of denials of special agricultural worker and legalization applications.* The Regional Processing Facility director or the district director may, in accordance with paragraph (a) of this section, certify a decision to the Associate Commissioner, Examinations (Administrative Appeals Unit) (the appellate authority designated in §103.1(f)(2)) of this part, when the case involves an unusually complex or novel question of law or fact.

[52 FR 661, Jan. 8, 1987, as amended at 53 FR 43985, Oct. 31, 1988; 55 FR 20770, May 21, 1990]

§ 103.5 Reopening or reconsideration.

(a) *Motions to reopen or reconsider in other than special agricultural worker and legalization cases*—(1) *When filed by affected party*—(i) *General.* Except where the Board has jurisdiction and as otherwise provided in 8 CFR parts 3, 210, 242 and 245a, when the affected party files a motion, the official having jurisdiction may, for proper cause shown, reopen the proceeding or reconsider the prior decision. Motions to reopen or reconsider are not applicable to proceedings described in §274a.9 of this chapter. Any motion to reconsider an action by the Service filed by an applicant or petitioner must be filed within 30 days of the decision that the motion seeks to reconsider. Any motion to reopen a proceeding before the Service filed by an applicant or petitioner, must be filed within 30 days of the decision that the motion seeks to reopen, except that failure to file before this period expires, may be excused in the discretion of the Service where it is demonstrated that the delay was reasonable and was beyond the control of the applicant or petitioner.

(ii) *Jurisdiction.* The official having jurisdiction is the official who made the latest decision in the proceeding unless the affected party moves to a new jurisdiction. In that instance, the new official having jurisdiction is the official over such a proceeding in the new geographical locations.

(iii) *Filing Requirements*—A motion shall be submitted on Form I–290B and may be accompanied by a brief. It must be:

(A) In writing and signed by the affected party or the attorney or representative of record, if any;

(B) Accompanied by a nonrefundable fee as set forth in §103.7;

(C) Accompanied by a statement about whether or not the validity of the unfavorable decision has been or is the subject of any judicial proceeding and, if so, the court, nature, date, and status or result of the proceeding;

(D) Addressed to the official having jurisdiction; and

(E) Submitted to the office maintaining the record upon which the unfavorable decision was made for forwarding to the official having jurisdiction.

(iv) *Effect of motion or subsequent application or petition.* Unless the Service directs otherwise, the filing of a motion to reopen or reconsider or of a subsequent application or petition does not stay the execution of any decision in a case or extend a previously set departure date.

(2) *Requirements for motion to reopen.* A motion to reopen must state the new facts to be provided in the reopened proceeding and be supported by affidavits or other documentary evidence. A motion to reopen an application or petition denied due to abandonment must be filed with evidence that the decision was in error because:

(i) The requested evidence was not material to the issue of eligibility;

(ii) The required initial evidence was submitted with the application or petition, or the request for initial evidence or additional information or appearance was complied with during the allotted period; or

(iii) The request for additional information or appearance was sent to an address other than that on the application, petition, or notice of representation, or that the applicant or petitioner advised the Service, in writing, of a change of address or change of representation subsequent to filing and before the Service's request was sent, and the request did not go to the new address.

(3) *Requirements for motion to reconsider.* A motion to reconsider must state the reasons for reconsideration and be supported by any pertinent precedent decisions to establish that the decision was based on an incorrect application of law or Service policy. A motion to reconsider a decision on an application or petition must, when filed, also establish that the decision was incorrect based on the evidence of record at the time of the initial decision.

(4) *Processing motions in proceedings before the Service.* A motion that does not meet applicable requirements shall be dismissed. Where a motion to reopen is granted, the proceeding shall be reopened. The notice and any favorable decision may be combined.

(5) *Motion by Service officer*—(i) *Service motion with decision favorable to affected party.* When a Service officer, on his or her own motion, reopens a Service proceeding or reconsiders a Service decision in order to make a new decision favorable to the affected party, the Service officer shall combine the motion and the favorable decision in one action.

(ii) *Service motion with decision that may be unfavorable to affected party.* When a Service officer, on his or her own motion, reopens a Service proceeding or reconsiders a Service decision, and the new decision may be unfavorable to the affected party, the officer shall give the affected party 30 days after service of the motion to submit a brief. The officer may extend the time period for good cause shown. If the affected party does not wish to submit a brief, the affected party may waive the 30-day period.

(6) *Appeal to AAU from Service decision made as a result of a motion.* A field office decision made as a result of a motion may be applied to the AAU only if the original decision was appealable to the AAU.

(7) *Other applicable provisions.* The provisions of § 103.3(a)(2)(x) of this part also apply to decisions on motions. The provisions of § 103.3(b) of this part also apply to requests for oral argument regarding motions considered by the AAU.

(8) *Treating an appeal as a motion.* The official who denied an application or petition may treat the appeal from that decision as a motion for the purpose of granting the motion.

(b) *Motions to reopen or reconsider denials of special agricultural worker and legalization applications.* Upon the filing of an appeal to the Associate Commissioner, Examinations (Administrative Appeals Unit), the Director of a Regional Processing Facility or the consular officer at an Overseas Processing Office may *sua sponte* reopen any proceeding under his or her jurisdiction opened under part 210 or 245a of this chapter and may reconsider any decision rendered in such proceeding. The new decision must be served on the appellant within 45 days of receipt of any brief and/or new evidence, or upon expiration of the time allowed for the submission of a brief. The Associate Commissioner, Examinations, or the Chief of the Administrative Appeals Unit may *sua sponte* reopen any proceeding conducted by that Unit under part 210 or 245a of this chapter and reconsider any decision rendered in such proceeding. Motions to reopen a proceeding or reconsider a decision under part 210 or 245a of this chapter shall not be considered.

(c) *Motions to reopen or reconsider decisions on replenishment agricultural worker petitions.* (1) The director of a regional processing facility may *sua sponte* reopen any proceeding under part 210a of this title which is within his or her jurisdiction and may render a new decision. This decision may reverse a prior favorable decision when it is determined that there was fraud during the registration or petition processes and the petitioner was not entitled to the status granted. The petitioner must be given an opportunity to offer evidence in support of the petition and in opposition to the grounds for reopening the petition before a new decision is rendered.

(2) The Associate Commissioner, Examinations or the Chief of the Administrative Appeals Unit may *sua sponte* reopen any proceeding conducted by that unit under part 210a of this title and reconsider any decision rendered in such proceeding.

(3) Motions to reopen a proceeding or reconsider a decision under part 210a of this title shall not be considered.

[27 FR 7562, Aug. 1, 1962, as amended at 30 FR 12772, Oct. 7, 1965; 32 FR 271, Jan. 11, 1967; 52 FR 16193, May 1, 1987; 54 FR 29881, July 17, 1989; 55 FR 20770, 20775, May 21, 1990; 55 FR 25931, June 25, 1990; 56 FR 41782, Aug. 23, 1991; 59 FR 1463, Jan. 11, 1994; 61 FR 18909, Apr. 29, 1996; 62 FR 10336, Mar. 6, 1997; 70 FR 50957, Aug. 29, 2005]

§ 103.6 Surety bonds.

(a) *Posting of surety bonds*—(1) *Extension agreements; consent of surety; collateral security.* All surety bonds posted in immigration cases shall be executed on Form I–352, Immigration Bond, a copy of which, and any rider attached thereto, shall be furnished the obligor. A district director is authorized to approve a bond, a formal agreement to extension of liability of surety, a request for delivery of collateral security to a duly appointed and undischarged administrator or executor of the estate of a deceased depositor, and a power of attorney executed on Form I–312, Designation of Attorney in Fact. All other matters relating to bonds, including a power of attorney not executed on Form I–312 and a request for delivery of collateral security to other than the depositor or his or her approved attorney in fact, shall be forwarded to the regional director for approval.

(2) *Bond riders*—(i) *General.* Bond riders shall be prepared on Form I–351, Bond Riders, and attached to Form I–352. If a condition to be included in a bond is not on Form I–351, a rider containing the condition shall be executed.

(ii) [Reserved]

(b) *Acceptable sureties.* Either a company holding a certificate from the Secretary of the Treasury under 6 U.S.C. 6–13 as an acceptable surety on Federal bonds, or a surety who deposits cash or U.S. bonds or notes of the class described in 6 U.S.C. 15 and Treasury Department regulations issued pursuant thereto and which are not redeemable within 1 year from the date they are offered for deposit is an acceptable surety.

(c) *Cancellation*—(1) *Public charge bonds.* A public charge bond posted for an immigrant shall be cancelled when the alien dies, departs permanently from the United States or is naturalized, provided the immigrant did not become a public charge prior to death, departure, or naturalization. The district director may cancel a public charge bond at any time if he/she finds that the immigrant is not likely to become a public charge. A bond may also be cancelled in order to allow substitution of another bond. A public charge bond shall be cancelled by the district director upon review following the fifth anniversary of the admission of the immigrant, provided that the alien has filed Form I–356, Request for Cancellation of Public Charge Bond, and the district director finds that the immigrant did not become a public charge prior to the fifth anniversary. If Form I–356 is not filed, the bond shall remain in effect until the form is filed and the district director reviews the evidence supporting the form and renders a decision to breach or cancel the bond.

(2) *Maintenance of status and departure bonds.* When the status of a nonimmigrant who has violated the conditions of his admission has been adjusted as a result of administrative or legislative action to that of a permanent resident retroactively to a date prior to the violation, any outstanding maintenance of status and departure bond shall be canceled. If an application for adjustment of status is made by a nonimmigrant while he is in lawful temporary status, the bond shall be canceled if his status is adjusted to that of a lawful permanent resident or if he voluntarily departs within any period granted to him. As used in this paragraph, the term *lawful temporary status* means that there must not have been a violation of any of the conditions of the alien's nonimmigrant classification by acceptance of unauthorized employment or otherwise during the time he has been accorded such classification, and that from the date of admission to the date of departure or adjustment of status he must have had uninterrupted Service approval of his presence in the United States in the form of regular extensions of stay or dates set by which departure is to occur, or a combination of both. An alien admitted as a nonimmigrant shall not be regarded as having violated his nonimmigrant status by engaging in employment subsequent to his proper filing of an application for adjustment of status under section 245 of the Act and part 245 of this chapter. A maintenance of status and departure bond posted at the request of an American consular officer abroad in behalf of an alien who did not travel to the United States shall be canceled upon receipt of notice from an American consular officer that the alien is outside the United States and the nonimmigrant visa issued pursuant to the posting of the bond has been canceled or has expired.

(3) *Substantial performance.* Substantial performance of all conditions imposed by the terms of a bond shall release the obligor from liability.

(d) *Bond schedules*—(1) *Blanketbonds for departure of visitors and transits.* The amount of bond required for various numbers of nonimmigrant visitors or transits admitted under bond on Forms I–352 shall be in accordance with the following schedule:

Aliens

1 to 4—$500 each.
5 to 9—$2,500 total bond.
10 to 24—$3,500 total bond.
25 to 49—$5,000 total bond.
50 to 74—$6,000 total bond.
75 to 99—$7,000 total bond.
100 to 124—$8,000 total bond.
125 to 149—$9,000 total bond.
150 to 199—$10,000 total bond.
200 or more—$10,000 plus $50 for each alien over 200.

(2) *Blanket bonds for importation of workers classified as nonimmigrants under section 101(a)(15)(H).* The following schedule shall be employed by district directors when requiring employers or their agents or representatives to post bond as a condition to importing alien laborers into the United States from the West Indies, the British Virgin Islands, or from Canada:

Less than 500 workers—$15 *each*
500 to 1,000 workers—$10 *each*
1,000 or more workers—$5 *each*

A bond shall not be posted for less than $1,000 or for more than $12,000 irrespective of the number of workers involved. Failure to comply with conditions of the bond will result in the employer's liability in the amount of $200 as liquidated damages for each alien involved.

(e) *Breach of bond.* A bond is breached when there has been a substantial violation of the stipulated conditions. A final determination that a bond has been breached creates a claim in favor of the United States which may not be released or discharged by a Service officer. The district director having custody of the file containing the immigration bond executed on Form I–352 shall determine whether the bond shall be declared breached or cancelled, and shall notify the obligor on Form I–323 or Form I–391 of the decision, and, if declared breached, of the reasons therefor, and of the right to appeal in accordance with the provisions of this part.

[31 FR 11713, Sept. 7, 1966, as amended at 32 FR 9622, July 4, 1967; 33 FR 5255, Apr. 2, 1968; 33 FR 10504, July 24, 1968; 34 FR 1008, Jan. 23, 1969; 34 FR 14760, Sept. 25, 1969; 39 FR 12334, Apr. 5, 1974; 40 FR 42852, Sept. 17, 1975; 48 FR 51144, Nov. 7, 1983; 49 FR 24011, June 11, 1984; 60 FR 21974, May 4, 1995; 62 FR 10336, Mar. 6, 1997; 76 FR 53781, Aug. 29, 2011]

§ 103.7 Fees.

(a) *Remittances.* (1) Fees shall be submitted with any formal application or petition prescribed in this chapter in the amount prescribed by law or regulation. Except for fees remitted directly to the Board of Immigration Appeals pursuant to the provisions of 8 CFR 1003.8, or as the Attorney General otherwise may provide by regulation, any fee relating to any Department of Justice Executive Office for Immigration Review proceeding shall be paid to, and accepted by, any USCIS office authorized to accept fees. The immigration court does not collect fees. Payment of any fee under this section does not constitute filing of the document with the Board of Immigration Appeals or with the Immigration Court. The Department of Homeland Security shall return to the payer, at the time of payment, a receipt for any fee paid. The USCIS shall also return to the payer any documents, submitted with the fee, relating to any Immigration Court proceeding.

(2) Remittances must be drawn on a bank or other institution located in the United States and be payable in United States currency. Remittances must be made payable in accordance with the guidance specific to the applicable U.S. Government office when submitting to a Department of Homeland Security office located outside of the United States. Remittances to the Board of Immigration Appeals must be made payable to the "United States Department of Justice," in accordance with 8 CFR 1003.8. If a remittance in payment of a fee or any other matter is not honored by the bank or financial institution on which it is drawn:

(i) A charge of $30.00 will be imposed;

(ii) The provisions of 8 CFR 103.2(a)(7)(ii) apply, no receipt will be issued, and if a receipt was issued, it is void and the benefit request loses its receipt date; and

(iii) If the benefit request was approved, the approval may be revoked upon notice. If the approved benefit request requires multiple fees, this provision will apply if any fee submitted is not honored. Other fees that were paid for a benefit request that is revoked under this provision will be retained and not refunded. A revocation of an approval because the fee submitted is not honored may be appealed to the USCIS Administrative Appeals Office, in accordance with 8 CFR 103.3 and the applicable form instructions.

(b) *Amounts of fees*—(1) *Established fees and charges*—(i) *USCIS fees.* A request for immigration benefits submitted to USCIS must include the required fee as established under this section. The fees established in this section are associated with the benefit, the adjudication, or the type of request and not solely determined by the form number listed below. The term "form" as defined in 8 CFR part 1, may include a USCIS-approved electronic equivalent of such form as USCIS may provide on its official Web site at *http://www.uscis.gov.*

(A) *Certification of true copies:* $2.00 per copy.

(B) *Attestation under seal:* $2.00 each.

(C) *Biometric services fee.* For capturing, storing, and using biometric information (Biometric Fee). A service fee of $85 will be charged to pay for background checks and have their biometric information captured, stored, and used for any individual who is required to submit biometric information for an application, petition, or other request for certain immigration and naturalization benefits (other than asylum or refugee status) or actions. USCIS will not charge a biometric services fee when:

(*1*) An applicant under 8 CFR 204.3 submits to USCIS a written request for an extension of the approval period of an Application for Advance Processing of an Orphan Petition (Application), if the request is submitted before the approval period expires and the applicant has not yet filed a Petition to Classify

Orphan as an Immediate Relative (Petition) in connection with the approved Application. The applicant may submit only one extension request without having to pay an additional biometric services fee. If the extension of the approval expires before the applicant files an associated Petition, then the applicant must file either a new Application or a Petition, and pay a new filing fee and a new biometric services fee.

(*2*) The application or petition fee for the associated request has been waived under paragraph (c) of this section; or

(*3*) The associated benefit request is one of the following:

(*i*) Application for Posthumous Citizenship, Form N–644;

(*ii*) Refugee/Asylee Relative Petition, Form I–730;

(*iii*) Application for T Nonimmigrant Status, Form I–914;

(*iv*) Petition for U Nonimmigrant Status, Form I–918;

(*v*) Application for Naturalization, Form N–400, by an applicant who meets the requirements of sections 328 or 329 of the Act with respect to military service under paragraph (b)(1)(i)(WW) of this section;

(*vi*) Application to Register Permanent Residence or Adjust Status, Form I–485, from an asylee under paragraph (b)(1)(i)(U) of this section;

(*vii*) Application To Adjust Status under Section 245(i) of the Act, Supplement A to Form I–485, from an unmarried child less than 17 years of age, or when the applicant is the spouse, or the unmarried child less than 21 years of age of a legalized foreign national and who is qualified for and has applied for voluntary departure under the family unity program from an asylee under paragraph (b)(1)(i)(V) of this section; or

(*viii*) Petition for Amerasian, Widow(er), or Special Immigrant, Form I–360, meeting the requirements of paragraphs (b)(1)(i)(T)(*1*), (*2*), (*3*) or (*4*) of this section.

(D) *USCIS Immigrant Fee.* For DHS domestic processing and issuance of required documents after an immigrant visa is issued by the U.S. Department of State: $220.

(E) *Request for a search of indices to historical records to be used in genealogical research,* Form G–1041: $65. The search request fee is not refundable.

(F) *Request for a copy of historical records to be used in genealogical research,* Form G–1041A: $65. USCIS will refund the records request fee only when it is unable to locate the file previously identified in response to the index search request.

(G) *Application to Replace Permanent Resident Card,* Form I–90. For filing an application for a Permanent Resident Card, Form I–551, to replace an obsolete card or to replace one lost, mutilated, or destroyed, or for a change in name: $455.

(H) *Application for Replacement/Initial Nonimmigrant Arrival-Departure Document,* Form I–102. For filing a petition for an application for Arrival/Departure Record Form I–94, or Crewman's Landing Permit Form I–95, to replace one lost, mutilated, or destroyed: $445.

(I) *Petition for a Nonimmigrant Worker,* Form I–129. For filing a petition for a nonimmigrant worker: $460.

(J) *Petition for Nonimmigrant Worker in CNMI,* Form I–129CW. For an employer to petition on behalf of one or more beneficiaries: $460 plus a supplemental CNMI education funding fee of $150 per beneficiary per year. The CNMI education funding fee cannot be waived.

(K) *Petition for Alien Fiancé(e),* Form I–129F. For filing a petition to classify a nonimmigrant as a fiancée or fiancé under section 214(d) of the Act: $535; there is no fee for a K–3 spouse as designated in 8 CFR 214.1(a)(2) who is the beneficiary of an immigrant petition filed by a United States citizen on a Petition for Alien Relative, Form I–130.

(L) *Petition for Alien Relative,* Form I–130. For filing a petition to classify status of a foreign national relative for issuance of an immigrant visa under section 204(a) of the Act: $535.

(M) *Application for Travel Document,* Form I–131. For filing an application for travel document:

(*1*) $135 for a Refugee Travel Document for an individual age 16 or older.

(*2*) $105 for a Refugee Travel Document for a child under the age of 16.

(*3*) $575 for advance parole and any other travel document.

(*4*) No fee if filed in conjunction with a pending or concurrently filed Form I–485 with fee that was filed on or after July 30, 2007.

(N) *Immigrant Petition for Alien Worker*, Form I–140. For filing a petition to classify preference status of an alien on the basis of profession or occupation under section 204(a) of the Act: $700.

(O) *Application for Advance Permission to Return to Unrelinquished Domicile*, Form I–191. For filing an application for discretionary relief under section 212(c) of the Act: $930.

(P) *Application for Advance Permission to Enter as a Nonimmigrant*, Form I–192. For filing an application for discretionary relief under section 212(d)(3) of the Act, except in an emergency case or where the approval of the application is in the interest of the United States Government: $930. If filed with and processed by CBP: $585.

(Q) *Application for Waiver for Passport and/or Visa*, Form I–193. For filing an application for waiver of passport and/or visa: $585.

(R) *Application for Permission to Reapply for Admission into the United States After Deportation or Removal*, Form I–212. For filing an application for permission to reapply for an excluded, deported or removed alien, an alien who has fallen into distress, an alien who has been removed as an alien enemy, or an alien who has been removed at government expense instead of deportation: $930.

(S) *Notice of Appeal or Motion*, Form I–290B. For appealing a decision under the immigration laws in any type of proceeding over which the Board of Immigration Appeals does not have appellate jurisdiction: $675. The fee will be the same for appeal of a denial of a benefit request with one or multiple beneficiaries. There is no fee for an appeal or motion associated with a denial of a petition for a special immigrant visa filed by or on behalf of an individual seeking special immigrant visa or status as an Iraqi or Afghan national who was employed by or on behalf of the U.S. Government in Iraq or Afghanistan.

(T) *Petition for Amerasian, Widow(er), or Special Immigrant*, Form I–360. For filing a petition for an Amerasian, Widow(er), or Special Immigrant: $435. The following requests are exempt from this fee:

(*1*) A petition seeking classification as an Amerasian;

(*2*) A self-petition for immigrant status as a battered or abused spouse, parent, or child of a U.S. citizen or lawful permanent resident; or

(*3*) A petition for special immigrant juvenile status; or

(*4*) A petition seeking special immigrant visa or status an Iraqi or Afghan national who was employed by or on behalf of the U.S. Government in Iraq or Afghanistan.

(U) Application to Register Permanent Residence or Adjust Status, Form I–485. For filing an application for permanent resident status or creation of a record of lawful permanent residence:

(*1*) $1,140 for an applicant 14 years of age or older; or

(*2*) $750 for an applicant under the age of 14 years who submits the application concurrently with the Form I–485 of a parent.

(*3*) There is no fee if an applicant is filing as a refugee under section 209(a) of the Act.

(V) *Application to Adjust Status under Section 245(i) of the Act*, Supplement A to Form I–485. Supplement to Form I–485 for persons seeking to adjust status under the provisions of section 245(i) of the Act: $1,000. There is no fee when the applicant is an unmarried child less than 17 years of age, when the applicant is the spouse, or the unmarried child less than 21 years of age of an individual with lawful immigration status and who is qualified for and has applied for voluntary departure under the family unity program.

(W) *Immigrant Petition by Alien Entrepreneur*, Form I–526. For filing a petition for an alien entrepreneur: $3,675.

(X) *Application To Extend/Change Nonimmigrant Status*, Form I–539. For filing an application to extend or change nonimmigrant status: $370.

(Y) *Petition to Classify Orphan as an Immediate Relative*, Form I–600. For filing a petition to classify an orphan as an immediate relative for issuance of an immigrant visa under section 204(a) of the Act. Only one fee is required when more than one petition is submitted by the same petitioner on behalf of orphans who are brothers or sisters: $775.

(Z) *Application for Advance Processing of Orphan Petition*, Form I–600A. For filing an application for advance processing of orphan petition. (When more than one petition is submitted by the same petitioner on behalf of orphans who are brothers or sisters, only one fee will be required.): $775. No fee is charged if Form I–600 has not yet been submitted in connection with an approved Form I–600A subject to the following conditions:

(*1*) The applicant requests an extension of the approval in writing and the request is received by USCIS before the expiration date of approval; and

(*2*) The applicant's home study is updated and USCIS determines that proper care will be provided to an adopted orphan.

(*3*) A no fee extension is limited to one occasion. If the Form I–600A approval extension expires before submission of an associated Form I–600, then a complete application and fee must be submitted for any subsequent application.

(AA) *Application for Waiver of Ground of Inadmissibility*, Form I–601. For filing an application for waiver of grounds of inadmissibility: $930.

(BB) *Application for Provisional Unlawful Presence Waiver*, Form I–601A. For filing an application for provisional unlawful presence waiver: $630.

(CC) *Application for Waiver of the Foreign Residence Requirement (under Section 212(e) of the Immigration and Nationality Act, as Amended)*, Form I–612. For filing an application for waiver of the foreign-residence requirement under section 212(e) of the Act: $930.

(DD) *Application for Status as a Temporary Resident under Section 245A of the Immigration and Nationality Act*, Form I–687. For filing an application for status as a temporary resident under section 245A(a) of the Act: $1,130.

(EE) *Application for Waiver of Grounds of Inadmissibility under Sections 245A or 210 of the Immigration and Nationality Act*, Form I–690. For filing an application for waiver of a ground of inadmissibility under section 212(a) of the Act as amended, in conjunction with the application under sections 210 or 245A of the Act, or a petition under section 210A of the Act: $715.

(FF) *Notice of Appeal of Decision under Sections 245A or 210 of the Immigration and Nationality Act* (or a petition under section 210A of the Act), Form I–694. For appealing the denial of an application under sections 210 or 245A of the Act, or a petition under section 210A of the Act: $890.

(GG) *Application to Adjust Status from Temporary to Permanent Resident* (Under Section 245A of Pub. L. 99–603), Form I–698. For filing an application to adjust status from temporary to permanent resident (under section 245A of Pub. L. 99–603): $1,670. The adjustment date is the date of filing of the application for permanent residence or the applicant's eligibility date, whichever is later.

(HH) *Petition to Remove Conditions on Residence*, Form I–751. For filing a petition to remove the conditions on residence based on marriage: $595.

(II) *Application for Employment Authorization*, Form I–765. $410. No fee if filed in conjunction with a pending or concurrently filed Form I–485 with fee that was filed on or after July 30, 2007.

(JJ) *Petition to Classify Convention Adoptee as an Immediate Relative*, Form I–800.

(*1*) There is no fee for the first Form I–800 filed for a child on the basis of an approved Application for Determination of Suitability to Adopt a Child from a Convention Country, Form I–800A, during the approval period.

(*2*) If more than one Form I–800 is filed during the approval period for different children, the fee is $775 for the second and each subsequent petition submitted.

(*3*) If the children are already siblings before the proposed adoption, however, only one filing fee of $775 is required, regardless of the sequence of submission of the immigration benefit.

(KK) *Application for Determination of Suitability to Adopt a Child from a Convention Country*, Form I–800A. For filing an application for determination of suitability to adopt a child from a convention country: $775.

(LL) *Request for Action on Approved Application for Determination of Suitability to Adopt a Child from a Convention Country*, Form I–800A, Supplement 3. This filing fee is not charged if Form I–800 has not been filed based on the approval of the Form I– 800A, and Form I–800A Supplement 3 is filed in order to obtain a first extension of the approval of the Form I–800A: $385.

(MM) *Application for Family Unity Benefits*, Form I–817. For filing an application for voluntary departure under the Family Unity Program: $600.

(NN) *Application for Temporary Protected Status*, Form I–821. For first time applicants: $50. There is no fee for re-registration.

(OO) *Application for Action on an Approved Application or Petition*, Form I–824. For filing for action on an approved application or petition: $465.

(PP) *Petition by Entrepreneur to Remove Conditions*, Form I–829. For filing a petition by entrepreneur to remove conditions: $3,750.

(QQ) *Application for Suspension of Deportation or Special Rule Cancellation of Removal* (Pursuant to Section 203 of Pub. L. 105–100), Form I–881:

(*1*) $285 for adjudication by DHS, except that the maximum amount payable by family members (related as husband, wife, unmarried child under 21, unmarried son, or unmarried daughter) who submit applications at the same time will be $570.

(*2*) $165 for adjudication by the Immigration Court (a single fee of $165 will be charged whenever applications are filed by two or more foreign nationals in the same proceedings).

(*3*) The $165 fee is not required if the Form I–881 is referred to the Immigration Court by DHS.

(RR) *Application for Authorization to Issue Certification for Health Care Workers*, Form I–905: $230.

(SS) *Request for Premium Processing Service*, Form I–907. $1,410. The Request for Premium Processing Service fee:

(*1*) Must be paid in addition to, and in a separate remittance from, other filing fees.

(*2*) May be adjusted annually by notice in the FEDERAL REGISTER based on inflation according to the Consumer Price Index (CPI).

(*3*) May not be waived.

(TT) *Application for Civil Surgeon Designation*, Form I–910. For filing an application for civil surgeon designation: $785. There is no fee for an application from a medical officer in the U.S. Armed Forces or civilian physician employed by the U.S. Government who examines members and veterans of the Armed Forces and their dependents at a military, Department of Veterans Affairs, or U.S. Government facility in the United States.

(UU) *Application for T Nonimmigrant Status*, Form I–914. No fee.

(VV) *Application for U Nonimmigrant Status*, Form I–918. No fee.

(WW) *Application for Regional Center Designation under the Immigrant Investor Program*, Form I–924. For filing an application for regional center designation under the Immigrant Investor Program: $17,795.

(XX) *Annual Certification of Regional Center*, Form I–924A. To provide updated information and certify that an Immigrant Investor Regional Center has maintained their eligibility: $3,035.

(YY) *Petition for Qualifying Family Member of a U–1 Nonimmigrant*, Form I–929. For U–1 principal applicant to submit for each qualifying family member who plans to seek an immigrant visa or adjustment of U status: $230.

(ZZ) *Application to File Declaration of Intention*, Form N–300. For filing an application for declaration of intention to become a U.S. citizen: $270.

(AAA) *Request for a Hearing on a Decision in Naturalization Proceedings (Under section 336 of the Act)*, Form N–336. For filing a request for hearing on a decision in naturalization proceedings under section 336 of the Act: $700. There is no fee if filed on or after October 1, 2004, by an applicant who has filed an Application for Naturalization under sections 328 or 329 of the Act with respect to military service and whose application has been denied.

(BBB) *Application for Naturalization*, Form N–400. For filing an application for naturalization: $640. Except:

(*1*) The fee for an applicant whose documented income is greater than 150 percent and not more than 200 percent of the Federal poverty level is $320.

(*2*) No fee is charged an applicant who meets the requirements of sections 328 or 329 of the Act with respect to military service.

(CCC) *Application to Preserve Residence for Naturalization Purposes*, Form N–470. For filing an application for benefits under section 316(b) or 317 of the Act: $355.

(DDD) *Application for Replacement Naturalization/Citizenship Document*, Form N–565. For filing an application for a certificate of naturalization or declaration of intention in place of a certificate or declaration alleged to have been lost, mutilated, or destroyed; for a certificate of citizenship in a changed name under section 343(c) of the Act; or for a special certificate of naturalization to obtain recognition as a citizen of the United States by a foreign state under section 343(b) of the Act: $555. There is no fee when this application is submitted under 8 CFR 338.5(a) or 343a.1 to request correction of a certificate that contains an error.

(EEE) *Application for Certificate of Citizenship*, Form N–600. For filing an application for a certificate of citizenship under section 309(c) or section 341 of the Act: $1,170. There is no fee for any application filed by a member or veteran of any branch of the United States Armed Forces.

(FFF) *Application for Citizenship and Issuance of Certificate under section 322 of the Act*, Form N–600K. For filing an application for citizenship and issuance of certificate under section 322 of the Act: $1,170.

(GGG) *American Competitiveness and Workforce Improvement Act (ACWIA) fee.* For filing certain H–1B petitions as described in 8 CFR 214.2(h)(19) and USCIS form instructions: $1,500 or $750.

(HHH) *Fraud detection and prevention fee.* For filing certain H–1B and L petitions, and $150 for H–2B petitions as described in 8 CFR 214.2(h)(19): $500.

(III) *9–11 Response and Biometric Entry-Exit Fee for H–1B Visa.* For certain petitioners who employ 50 or more employees in the United States if more than 50 percent of the petitioner's employees are in H–1B, L–1A or L–1B nonimmigrant status: $4,000. Collection of this fee is scheduled to end on September 30, 2025.

(JJJ) *9–11 Response and Biometric Entry-Exit Fee for L–1 Visa.* For certain petitioners who employ 50 or more employees in the United States, if more than 50 percent of the petitioner's employees are in H–1B, L–1A or L–1B nonimmigrant status: $4,500. Collection of this fee is scheduled to end on September 30, 2025.

(KKK) *Application for Entrepreneur Parole (Form I–941).* For filing an application for parole for entrepreneurs: $1200.

(ii) *Other DHS immigration fees.* The following fees are applicable to one or more of the immigration components of DHS:

(A) DCL System Costs Fee. For use of a Dedicated Commuter Lane (DCL) located at specific ports-of-entry of the United States by an approved participant in a designated vehicle: $80.00, with the maximum amount of $160.00 payable by a family (husband, wife, and minor children under 18 years of age). Payable following approval of the application but before use of the DCL by each participant. This fee is non-refundable, but may be waived by DHS. If a participant wishes to enroll more than one vehicle for use in the PORTPASS system, he or she will be assessed with an additional fee of: $42 for each additional vehicle enrolled.

(B) *Form I–17.* For filing a petition for school certification: $1,700, plus a site visit fee of $655 for each location listed on the form.

(C) *Form I–68.* For application for issuance of the Canadian Border Boat Landing Permit under section 235 of the Act: $16.00. The maximum amount payable by a family (husband, wife, unmarried children under 21 years of age, and parents of either husband or wife) shall be $32.00.

(D) *Form I–94.* For issuance of Arrival/Departure Record at a land border port-of-entry: $6.00.

(E) *Form I–94W.* For issuance of Nonimmigrant Visa Waiver Arrival/Departure Form at a land border port-of-entry under section 217 of the Act: $6.00.

(F) *Form I–246.* For filing application for stay of deportation under 8 CFR part 243: $155.00.

(G) *Form I–823.* For application to a PORTPASS program under section 286 of the Act—$25.00, with the maximum amount of $50.00 payable by a family (husband, wife, and minor children under 18 years of age). The application fee may be waived by the district director. If fingerprints are required, the inspector will inform the applicant of the current Federal Bureau of Investigation fee for conducting fingerprint checks prior to accepting the application fee. Both the application fee (if not waived) and the fingerprint fee must be paid to CBP before the application will be processed. The fingerprint fee may not be waived. For replacement of PORTPASS documentation during the participation period: $25.00.

(H) *Form I–901.* For remittance of the I–901 SEVIS fee for F and M students: $200. For remittance of the I–901 SEVIS fee for certain J exchange visitors: $180. For remittance of the I–901 SEVIS fee for J–1 au pairs, camp counselors, and participants in a summer work/travel program: $35. There is no I–901 SEVIS fee remittance obligation for J exchange visitors in federally-funded programs with a program identifier designation prefix that begins with G–1, G–2, G–3 or G–7.

(I) *Special statistical tabulations*—a charge will be made to cover the cost of the work involved: DHS Cost.

(J) *Set of monthly, semiannual, or annual tables entitled "Passenger Travel Reports via Sea and Air":* $7.00. Available from DHS, then the Immigration & Naturalization Service, for years 1975 and before. Later editions are available from the United States Department of Transportation, contact: United States Department of Transportation, Transportation Systems Center, Kendall Square, Cambridge, MA 02142.

(K) *Classification of a citizen of Canada to be engaged in business activities at a professional level pursuant to section 214(e) of the Act (Chapter 16 of the North American Free Trade Agreement):* $50.00.

(L) *Request for authorization for parole of an alien into the United States:* $65.00.

(M) *Global Entry.* For filing an application for Global Entry—$100.

(N) *U.S. Asia-Pacific Economic Cooperation (APEC) Business Travel Card.* For filing an application for the card—$70.

(2) *Fees for copies of records.* Fees for production or disclosure of records under 5 U.S.C. 552 shall be charged in accordance with the regulations of the Department of Homeland Security at 6 CFR 5.11.

(3) *Adjustment to fees.* The fees prescribed in paragraph (b)(1)(i) of this section may be adjusted annually by publication of an inflation adjustment. The inflation adjustment will be announced by a publication of a notice in the FEDERAL REGISTER. The adjustment shall be a composite of the Federal civilian pay raise assumption and non-pay inflation factor for that fiscal year issued by the Office of Management and Budget for agency use in implementing OMB Circular A–76, weighted by pay and non-pay proportions of total funding for that fiscal year. If Congress enacts a different Federal civilian pay raise percentage than the percentage issued by OMB for Circular A–76, the Department of Homeland Security may adjust the fees, during the current year or a following year to reflect the enacted level. The prescribed fee or charge shall be the amount prescribed in paragraph (b)(1)(i) of this section, plus the latest inflation adjustment, rounded to the nearest $5 increment.

(4) *Fees for immigration court and Board of Immigration Appeals.* Fees for proceedings before immigration judges and the Board of Immigration Appeals are provided in 8 CFR 1103.7.

(c) *Waiver of fees.* (1) *Eligibility for a fee waiver.* Discretionary waiver of the fees provided in paragraph (b)(1)(i) of this section are limited as follows:

(i) The party requesting the benefit is unable to pay the prescribed fee.

(ii) A waiver based on inability to pay is consistent with the status or benefit sought including requests that require demonstration of the applicant's ability to support himself or herself, or individuals who seek immigration status based on a substantial financial investment.

(2) *Requesting a fee waiver.* To request a fee waiver, a person requesting an immigration benefit must submit a written request for permission to have their request processed without payment of a fee with their benefit request. The request must state the person's belief that he or she is entitled to or deserving of the benefit requested, the reasons for his or her inability to pay, and evidence to support the reasons indicated. There is no appeal of the denial of a fee waiver request.

(3) *USCIS fees that may be waived.* No fee relating to any application, petition, appeal, motion, or request made to U.S. Citizenship and Immigration Services may be waived except for the following:

(i) Biometric Fee, except for the biometric fee required for provisional unlawful presence waivers filed under 8 CFR 212.7(e).

(ii) Application to Replace Permanent Resident Card,

(iii) A Petition for a CNMI-Only Nonimmigrant Transitional Worker, or an Application to Extend/Change Nonimmigrant Status only in the case of an alien applying for CW–2 nonimmigrant status,

(iv) Application for Travel Document when filed to request humanitarian parole,

(v) Application for Advance Permission to Return to Unrelinquished Domicile,

(vi) Notice of Appeal or Motion, when there is no fee for the underlying application or petition or that fee may be waived,

(vii) Petition to Remove the Conditions of Residence based on marriage (Form I–751),

(viii) Application for Employment Authorization,

(ix) Application for Family Unity Benefits,

(x) Application for Temporary Protected Status,

(xi) Application for Suspension of Deportation or Special Rule Cancellation of Removal (pursuant to section 203 of Pub. L. 105–110),

(xii) Application to File Declaration of Intention, Request for a Hearing on a Decision in Naturalization Proceedings (under section 336 of the INA),

(xiii) Application for Naturalization,

(xiv) Application to Preserve Residence for Naturalization Purposes,

(xv) Application for Replacement Naturalization/Citizenship Document,

(xvi) Application for Certificate of Citizenship,

(xvii) Application for Citizenship and Issuance of Certificate under section 322 of this Act,

(xviii) Any fees associated with the filing of any benefit request by a VAWA self-petitioner or under sections 101(a)(15)(T) (T visas), 101(a)(15)(U) (U visas), 106 (battered spouses of A, G, E–3, or H nonimmigrants), 240A(b)(2) (battered spouse or child of a lawful permanent resident or U.S. citizen), and 244(a)(3) (Temporary Protected Status), of the Act (as in effect on March 31, 1997); and

(xix) Petition for Nonimmigrant Worker (Form I–129) or Application to Extend/Change Nonimmigrant Status (Form I–539), only in the case of an alien applying for E–2 CNMI Investor nonimmigrant status under 8 CFR 214.2(e)(23).

(4) The following fees may be waived only for an alien for which a determination of their likelihood of becoming a public charge under section 212(a)(4) of the Act is not required at the time of an application for admission or adjustment of status.:

(i) Application for Advance Permission to Enter as Nonimmigrant;

(ii) Application for Waiver for Passport and/or Visa;

(iii) Application to Register Permanent Residence or Adjust Status;

(iv) Application for Waiver of Grounds of Inadmissibility.

(5) *Immigration Court fees.* The provisions relating to the authority of the immigration judges or the Board to waive fees prescribed in paragraph (b) of this section in cases under their jurisdiction can be found at 8 CFR 1003.8 and 1003.24.

(6) *Fees under the Freedom of Information Act (FOIA).* FOIA fees may be waived or reduced if DHS determines that such action would be in the public interest because furnishing the information can be considered as primarily benefiting the general public.

(d) *Exceptions and exemptions.* The Director of USCIS may approve and suspend exemptions from any fee required by paragraph (b)(1)(i) of this section or provide that the fee may be waived for a case or specific class of cases that is not otherwise provided in this section, if the Director determines that such action would be in the public interest and the action is consistent with other applicable law. This discretionary authority will not be delegated to any official other than the USCIS Deputy Director.

(e) *Premium processing service.* A person submitting a request to USCIS may request 15 calendar day processing of certain employment-based immigration benefit requests.

(1) *Submitting a request for premium processing.* A request for premium processing must be submitted on the form prescribed by USCIS, including the required fee, and submitted to the address specified on the form instructions.

(2) *15-day limitation.* The 15 calendar day processing period begins when USCIS receives the request for premium processing accompanied by an eligible employment-based immigration benefit request.

(i) If USCIS cannot reach a final decision on a request for which premium processing was requested, as evidenced by an approval notice, denial notice, a notice of intent to deny, or a request for evidence, USCIS will refund the premium processing service fee, but continue to process the case.

(ii) USCIS may retain the premium processing fee and not reach a conclusion on the request within 15 days, and not notify the person who filed the request, if USCIS opens an investigation for fraud or misrepresentation relating to the benefit request.

(3) *Requests eligible for premium processing.*

(i) USCIS will designate the categories of employment-related benefit requests that are eligible for premium processing.

(ii) USCIS will announce by its official Internet Web site, currently *http://www.uscis.gov*, those requests for which premium processing may be requested, the dates upon which such availability commences and ends, and any conditions that may apply.

(f) *Authority to certify records.* The Director of USCIS, or such officials as he or she may designate, may certify records when authorized under 5 U.S.C. 552 or any other law to provide such records.

[38 FR 35296, Dec. 27, 1973]

EDITORIAL NOTE: For FEDERAL REGISTER citations affecting §103.7, see the List of CFR Sections Affected, which appears in the Finding Aids section of the printed volume and at *www.govinfo.gov*.

§103.8 Service of decisions and other notices.

This section states authorized means of service by the Service on parties and on attorneys and other interested persons of notices, decisions, and other papers (except warrants and subpoenas) in administrative proceedings before Service officers as provided in this chapter.

(a) *Types of service*—(1) *Routine service.* (i) Routine service consists of mailing the notice by ordinary mail addressed to the affected party and his or her attorney or representative of record at his or her last known address, or

(ii) If so requested by a party, advising the party of such notice by electronic mail and posting the decision to the party's USCIS account.

(2) *Personal service.* Personal service, which shall be performed by a Government employee, consists of any of the following, without priority or preference:

(i) Delivery of a copy personally;

(ii) Delivery of a copy at a person's dwelling house or usual place of abode by leaving it with some person of suitable age and discretion;

(iii) Delivery of a copy at the office of an attorney or other person, including a corporation, by leaving it with a person in charge;

(iv) Mailing a copy by certified or registered mail, return receipt requested, addressed to a person at his last known address; or

(v) If so requested by a party, advising the party by electronic mail and posting the decision to the party's USCIS account.

(3) *Personal service involving notices of intention to fine.* In addition to any of the methods of personal service listed in paragraph (a)(2) of this section, personal service of Form I–79, Notice of Intention to Fine, may also consist of delivery of the Form I–79 by a commercial delivery service at the carrier's address on file with the National Fines Office, the address listed on the Form I–849, Record for Notice of Intent to Fine, or to the office of the attorney or agent representing the carrier, provided that such a commercial delivery service requires the addressee or other responsible party accepting the package to sign for the package upon receipt.

(b) *Effect of service by mail.* Whenever a person has the right or is required to do some act within a prescribed period after the service of a notice upon him and the notice is served by mail, 3 days shall be added to the prescribed period. Service by mail is complete upon mailing.

(c) *When personal service required*—(1) *Generally*. In any proceeding which is initiated by the Service, with proposed adverse effect, service of the initiating notice and of notice of any decision by a Service officer shall be accomplished by personal service, except as provided in section 239 of the Act.

(2) *Persons confined, minors, and incompetents*—(i) *Persons confined*. If a person is confined in a penal or mental institution or hospital and is competent to understand the nature of the proceedings initiated against him, service shall be made both upon him and upon the person in charge of the institution or the hospital. If the confined person is not competent to understand, service shall be made only on the person in charge of the institution or hospital in which he is confined, such service being deemed service on the confined person.

(ii) *Incompetents and minors*. In case of mental incompetency, whether or not confined in an institution, and in the case of a minor under 14 years of age, service shall be made upon the person with whom the incompetent or the minor resides; whenever possible, service shall also be made on the near relative, guardian, committee, or friend.

(d) *When personal service not required*. Service of other types of papers in proceedings described in paragraph (c) of this section, and service of any type of papers in any other proceedings, may be accomplished either by routine service or by personal service.

[37 FR 11470, June 8, 1972, as amended at 39 FR 23247, June 27, 1974; 62 FR 10336, Mar. 6, 1997; 64 FR 17944, Apr. 13, 1999. Redesignated and amended at 76 FR 53781, Aug. 29, 2011]

§ 103.9 Request for further action on an approved benefit request.

(a) *Filing a request*. A person may request further action on an approved benefit request as prescribed by the form instructions. Requests for further action may be submitted with the original benefit request or following the approval of such benefit.

(b) *Processing*. The request will be approved if the requester has demonstrated eligibility for the requested action. There is no appeal from the denial of such request.

[Redesignated and amended at 76 FR 53781, Aug. 29, 2011]

§ 103.10 Precedent decisions.

(a) Proceedings before the immigration judges, the Board of Immigration Appeals and the Attorney General are governed by part 1003 of 8 CFR chapter V.

(b) *Decisions as precedents*. Except as Board decisions may be modified or overruled by the Board or the Attorney General, decisions of the Board, and decisions of the Attorney General, shall be binding on all officers and employees of the Department of Homeland Security or immigration judges in the administration of the immigration laws of the United States. By majority vote of the permanent Board members, selected decisions of the Board rendered by a three-member panel or by the Board en banc may be designated to serve as precedents in all proceedings involving the same issue or issues. Selected decisions designated by the Board, decisions of the Attorney General, and decisions of the Secretary of Homeland Security to the extent authorized in paragraph (i) of this section, shall serve as precedents in all proceedings involving the same issue or issues.

(c) *Referral of cases to the Attorney General*. (1) The Board shall refer to the Attorney General for review of its decision all cases which:

(i) The Attorney General directs the Board to refer to him.

(ii) The Chairman or a majority of the Board believes should be referred to the Attorney General for review.

(iii) The Secretary of Homeland Security, or specific officials of the Department of Homeland Security designated by the Secretary with the concurrence of the Attorney General, refers to the Attorney General for review.

(2) In any case the Attorney General decides, the Attorney General's decision shall be stated in writing and shall be transmitted to the Board or Secretary, as appropriate, for transmittal

and service as provided in paragraph (c) of this section or 8 CFR 1003.1(h)(2).

(d) *Publication of Secretary's precedent decisions.* The Secretary of Homeland Security, or specific officials of the Department of Homeland Security designated by the Secretary with the concurrence of the Attorney General, may file with the Attorney General Service precedent decisions as set forth in § 103.3(c).

(e) *Precedent decisions.* Bound volumes of designated precedent decisions, entitled "Administrative Decisions under Immigration and Nationality Laws of the United States," may be purchased from the Superintendent of Documents, U.S. Government Printing Office. Prior to publication in volume form, current precedent decisions are available from the Department of Justice, Executive Office for Immigration Review's Virtual Law Library at: *http://www.justice.gov/eoir/vll/libindex.html.*

(f) [Reserved]

[68 FR 9832, Feb. 28, 2003. Redesignated and amended at 76 FR 53781, Aug. 29, 2011]

Subpart B—Biometric Requirements

§ 103.16 Collection, use and storage of biometric information.

(a) *Use of biometric information.* An individual may be required to submit biometric information by law, regulation, FEDERAL REGISTER notice or the form instructions applicable to the request type or if required in accordance with 8 CFR 103.2(b)(9). DHS may collect and store for present or future use, by electronic or other means, the biometric information submitted by an individual. DHS may use this biometric information to conduct background and security checks, adjudicate immigration and naturalization benefits, and perform other functions related to administering and enforcing the immigration and naturalization laws.

(b) *Individuals residing abroad.* An individual who is required to provide biometric information and who is residing outside of the United States must report to a DHS-designated location to have his or her biometric information collected, whether by electronic or non-electronic means.

[76 FR 53782, Aug. 29, 2011, as amended at 81 FR 73331, Oct. 24, 2016]

§ 103.17 Biometric service fee.

(a) *Required fees.* DHS will charge a fee, as prescribed in 8 CFR 103.7(b)(1), for collecting biometric information at a DHS office, other designated collection site overseas, or a registered State or local law enforcement agency designated by a cooperative agreement with DHS to provide biometric collection services, to conduct required law enforcement checks, and to maintain this biometric information for reuse to support other benefit requests. Requests for benefits must be submitted with the biometric service fee for all individuals who are required to submit biometric information and a biometric services fee and who reside in the United States at the time of filing for the benefit.

(b) *Non-payment.* If a benefit request is received by DHS without the correct biometric services fee as provided in the form instructions, DHS will reject the benefit request.

[76 FR 53782, Aug. 29, 2011, as amended at 81 FR 73332, Oct. 24, 2016]

§§ 103.20–103.36 [Reserved]

Subpart C [Reserved]

Subpart D—Availability of Records

§ 103.38 Genealogy Program.

(a) *Purpose.* The Department of Homeland Security, U.S. Citizenship and Immigration Services Genealogy Program is a fee-for-service program designed to provide genealogical and historical records and reference services to genealogists, historians, and others seeking documents maintained within the historical record systems.

(b) *Scope and limitations.* Sections 103.38 through 103.41 comprise the regulations of the Genealogy Program. These regulations apply only to searches for and retrieval of records from the file series described as historical records in 8 CFR 103.39. These regulations set forth the procedures by which individuals may request searches for historical records and, if responsive records are located, obtain copies of those records.

[73 FR 28030, May 15, 2008]

§ 103.39 Historical Records.

Historical Records are files, forms, and documents now located within the following records series:

(a) *Naturalization Certificate Files (C–Files), from September 27, 1906 to April 1, 1956.* Copies of records relating to all U.S. naturalizations in Federal, State, county, or municipal courts, overseas military naturalizations, replacement of old law naturalization certificates, and the issuance of Certificates of Citizenship in derivative, repatriation, and resumption cases. The majority of C–Files exist only on microfilm. Standard C–Files generally contain at least one application form (Declaration of Intention and/or Petition for Naturalization, or other application) and a duplicate certificate of naturalization or certificate of citizenship. Many files contain additional documents, including correspondence, affidavits, or other records. Only C–Files dating from 1929 onward include photographs.

(b) *Microfilmed Alien Registration Forms, from August 1, 1940 to March 31, 1944.* Microfilmed copies of 5.5 million Alien Registration Forms (Form AR–2) completed by all aliens age 14 and older, residing in or entering the United States between August 1, 1940 and March 31, 1944. The two-page form called for the following information: Name; name at arrival; other names used; street address; post-office address; date of birth; place of birth; citizenship; sex; marital status; race; height; weight; hair and eye color; date, place, vessel, and class of admission of last arrival in United States; date of first arrival in United States; number of years in United States; usual occupation; present occupation; name, address, and business of present employer; membership in clubs, organizations, or societies; dates and nature of military or naval service; whether citizenship papers filed, and if so date, place, and court for declaration or petition; number of relatives living in the United States; arrest record, including date, place, and disposition of each arrest; whether or not affiliated with a foreign government; signature; and fingerprint.

(c) *Visa Files, from July 1, 1924 to March 31, 1944.* Original arrival records of immigrants admitted for permanent residence under provisions of the Immigration Act of 1924. Visa forms contain all information normally found on a ship passenger list of the period, as well as the immigrant's places of residence for 5 years prior to emigration, names of both the immigrant's parents, and other data. In most cases, birth records or affidavits are attached to the visa, and in some cases, marriage, military, or police records may also be attached to the visa.

(d) *Registry Files, from March 2, 1929 to March 31, 1944.* Original records documenting the creation of immigrant arrival records for persons who entered the United States prior to July 1, 1924, and for whom no arrival record could later be found. Most files also include documents supporting the immigrant's claims regarding arrival and residence (e.g., proofs of residence, receipts, and employment records).

(e) *Alien-Files numbered below 8 million (A8000000), and documents therein dated prior to May 1, 1951.* Individual alien case files (A–files) became the official file for all immigration records created or consolidated after April 1, 1944. The United States issued A–numbers ranging up to approximately 6 million to aliens and immigrants who were within or entered the United States between 1940 and 1945. The United States entered the 6 million and 7 million series of A–numbers between circa 1944 and May 1, 1951. Any documents dated after May 1, 1951, though found in an A–File numbered below 8 million, will remain subject to FOIA/PA restrictions.

[73 FR 28030, May 15, 2008]

§ 103.40 Genealogical Research Requests.

(a) *Nature of requests.* Genealogy requests are requests for searches and/or copies of historical records relating to a deceased person, usually for genealogy and family history research purposes.

(b) *Manner of requesting genealogical searches and records.* Requests must be submitted on Form G–1041, Genealogy Index Search Request, or Form G–

1041A, Genealogy Records Request, and mailed to the address listed on the form. Beginning on August 13, 2008, USCIS will accept requests electronically through its Web site at *http:// www.USCIS.gov*. A separate request on Form G–1041 must be submitted for each individual searched, and that form will call for the name, aliases, and all alternate spellings relating to the one individual immigrant. Form G–1041A may be submitted to request one or more separate records relating to separate individuals.

(c) *Information required to perform index search.* As required on Form G–1041, all requests for index searches to identify records of individual immigrants must include the immigrant's full name (including variant spellings of the name and/or aliases, if any), date of birth, and place of birth. The date of birth must be at least as specific as a year, and the place of birth must be at least as specific as a country (preferably the country name as it existed at the time of the immigrant's immigration or naturalization). Additional information about the immigrant's date of arrival in the United States, residence at time of naturalization, name of spouse, and names of children may be required to ensure a successful search.

(d) *Information required to retrieve records.* As required on Form G–1041A, requests for copies of historical records or files must identify the record by number or other specific data used by the Genealogy Program Office to retrieve the record. C–Files must be identified by a naturalization certificate number. Forms AR–2 and A–Files numbered below 8 million must be identified by Alien Registration Number. Visa Files must be identified by the Visa File Number. Registry Files must be identified by the Registry File Number (for example, R–12345).

(e) *Information required for release of records.* Subjects will be presumed deceased if their birth dates are more than 100 years prior to the date of the request. In other cases, the subject is presumed to be living until the requestor establishes to the satisfaction of the Genealogy Program Office that the subject is deceased. As required on Form G–1041A, primary or secondary documentary evidence of the subject's death will be required (including but not limited to death records, published obituaries or eulogies, published death notices, church or bible records, photographs of gravestones, and/or copies of official documents relating to payment of death benefits). All documentary evidence must be attached to Form G–1041A or submitted in accordance with instructions provided on Form G–1041A.

(f) *Processing of index search requests.* This service is designed for customers who are unsure whether USCIS has any record of their ancestor, or who suspect a record exists but cannot identify that record by number. Each request for index search services will generate a search of the indices to determine the existence of responsive historical records. If no record is found, USCIS will notify the customer accordingly. If records are found, USCIS will provide the customer with the search results, including the type of record found and the file number or other information identifying the record. The customer can use this information to request a copy of the record(s).

(g) *Processing of record copy requests.* This service is designed for customers who can identify a specific record or file to be retrieved, copied, reviewed, and released. Customers may identify one or more files in a single request. However, separate fees will apply to each file requested. Upon receipt of requests identifying specific records by number or other identifying information, USCIS will retrieve, review, duplicate, and then mail the record(s) to the requester. It is possible that USCIS will find a record that contains data that is not releasable to the customer. An example would be names and birth dates of persons who might be living. The FOIA/PA only permits release of this type of information when the affected individual submits a release authorization to USCIS. Therefore, the Genealogy Program Office will contact and inform the customer of this requirement. The customer will have the opportunity to submit the release authorization. The customer can also agree to the transfer of the document request to the FOIA/PA program for treatment as a FOIA/PA request as described in 6 CFR Part 5. Document retrieval charges will apply in all cases where documents are retrieved.

[73 FR 28031, May 15, 2008]

§ 103.41 Genealogy request fees.

(a) *Genealogy search fee.* See 8 CFR 103.7(b)(1).

(b) *Genealogy records fees.* See 8 CFR 103.7(b)(1).

(c) *Manner of submission.* The application and fee must be submitted in accordance with form instructions.

[73 FR 28031, May 15, 2008, as amended at 76 FR 53782, Aug. 29, 2011]

§ 103.42 Rules relating to the Freedom of Information Act (FOIA) and the Privacy Act.

Immigration-related regulations relating to FOIA and the Privacy Act are located in 6 CFR part 5.

[76 FR 53782, Aug. 29, 2011]

PART 109 [RESERVED]

PART 204—IMMIGRANT PETITIONS

Subpart A—Immigrant Visa Petitions

Subpart B [Reserved]

Subpart C—Intercountry Adoption of a Convention Adoptee

AUTHORITY: 8 U.S.C. 1101, 1103, 1151, 1153, 1154, 1182, 1184, 1186a, 1255, 1324a, 1641; 8 CFR part 2.

Subpart A—Immigrant Visa Petitions

§ 204.1 General information about immediate relative and family-sponsored petitions.

(a) *Types of petitions.* Petitions may be filed for an alien's classification as an immediate relative under section 201(b) of the Act or as a preference immigrant under section 203(a) of the Act based on a qualifying relationship to a citizen or lawful permanent resident of the United States, as follows:

(1) A citizen or lawful permanent resident of the United States petitioning under section 204(a)(1)(A)(i) or 204(a)(1)(B)(i) of the Act for a qualifying relative's classification as an immediate relative under section 201(b) of the Act or as a preference immigrant under section 203(a) of the Act must file a Form I–130, Petition for Alien Relative. These petitions are described in § 204.2;

(2) A widow or widower of a United States citizen self-petitioning under

section 204(a)(1)(A)(ii) of the Act as an immediate relative under section 201(b) of the Act must file a Form I–360, Petition for Amerasian, Widow, or Special Immigrant. These petitions are described in § 204.2;

(3) A spouse or child of an abusive citizen or lawful permanent resident of the United States self-petitioning under section 204(a)(1)(A)(iii), 204(a)(1)(A)(iv), 204(a)(1)(B)(ii), or 204(a)(1)(B)(iii) of the Act for classification as an immediate relative under section 201(b) of the Act or as a preference immigrant under section 203(a) of the Act must file a Form I–360, Petition for Amerasian, Widow, or Special Immigrant. These petitions are described in § 204.2;

(4) A U.S. citizen seeking to have USCIS accord immediate relative status to a child based on the citizen's adoption of the child as an orphan, as defined in section 101(b)(1)(F) of the Act, must follow the procedures in § 204.3.

(5) A U.S. citizen seeking to have USCIS accord immediate relative status to a child under section 101(b)(1)(G) of the Act on the basis of a Convention adoption must:

(i) File a Form I–800A, Application to Determine Suitability as Adoptive Parents for a Convention adoptee; and

(ii) After USCIS approves the Form I–800A, file a Form I–800, Petition to Classify Convention adoptee as Immediate Relative, as provided in 8 CFR part 204, subpart C.

(6) Any person filing a petition under section 204(f) of the Act as, or on behalf of, an Amerasian for classification as an immediate relative under section 201(b) of the Act or as a preference immigrant under section 203(a)(1) or 203(a)(3) of the Act must file a Form I–360, Petition for Amerasian, Widow, or Special Immigrant. These petitions are described in § 204.4.

(b) *Proper filing.* A petition for alien relative and a petition for Amerasian, widow(er), or special immigrant must be filed on the form prescribed by USCIS in accordance with the form instructions, and will be considered properly filed when the petition is filed in accordance with 8 CFR 103.2. The filing date of a petition is the date it is properly filed and received by USCIS. That date will constitute the priority date.

(c)–(e) [Reserved].

(f) *Supporting documentation.* (1) Documentary evidence consists of those documents which establish the United States citizenship or lawful permanent resident status of the petitioner and the claimed relationship of the petitioner to the beneficiary. They must be in the form of primary evidence, if available. When it is established that primary evidence is not available, secondary evidence may be accepted. To determine the availability of primary documents, the Service will refer to the Department of State's Foreign Affairs Manual (FAM). When the FAM shows that primary documents are generally available in the country of issue but the petitioner claims that his or her document is unavailable, a letter from the appropriate registrar stating that the document is not available will not be required before the Service will accept secondary evidence. The Service will consider any credible evidence relevant to a self-petition filed by a qualified spouse or child of an abusive citizen or lawful permanent resident under section 204(a)(1)(A)(iii), 204(a)(1)(A)(iv), 204(a)(1)(B)(ii), or 204(a)(1)(B)(iii) of the Act. The self-petitioner may, but is not required to, demonstrate that preferred primary or secondary evidence is unavailable. The determination of what evidence is credible and the weight to be given that evidence shall be within the sole discretion of the Service.

(2) Original documents or legible, true copies of original documents are acceptable. The Service reserves the right to require submission of original documents when deemed necessary. Documents submitted with the petition will not be returned to the petitioner, except when originals are requested by the Service. If original documents are requested by the Service, they will be returned to the petitioner after a decision on the petition has been rendered, unless their validity or authenticity is in question. When an interview is required, all original documents must be presented for examination at the interview.

(3) Foreign language documents must be accompanied by an English translation which has been certified by a competent translator.

(g) *Evidence of petitioner's United States citizenship or lawful permanent residence*—(1) *Primary evidence.* A petition must be accompanied by one of the following:

(i) A birth certificate that was issued by a civil authority and that establishes the petitioner's birth in the United States;

(ii) An unexpired United States passport issued initially for a full ten-year period to a petitioner over the age of eighteen years as a citizen of the United States (and not merely as a noncitizen national);

(iii) An unexpired United States passport issued initially for a full five-year period to the petitioner under the age of eighteen years as a citizen of the United States (and not merely as a noncitizen national);

(iv) A statement executed by a United States consular officer certifying the petitioner to be a United States citizen and the bearer of a currently valid United States passport;

(v) The petitioner's Certificate of Naturalization or Certificate of Citizenship;

(vi) Department of State Form FS–240, Report of Birth Abroad of a Citizen of the United States, relating to the petitioner;

(vii) The petitioner's Form I–551, Permanent Resident Card, or other proof given by the Service as evidence of lawful permanent residence. Photocopies of Form I–551 or of a Certificate of Naturalization or Certificate of Citizenship may be submitted as evidence of status as a lawfully permanent resident or United States citizen, respectively.

(2) *Secondary evidence.* If primary evidence is unavailable, the petitioner must present secondary evidence. Any evidence submitted as secondary evidence will be evaluated for authenticity and credibility. Secondary evidence may include, but is not limited to, one or more of the following documents:

(i) A baptismal certificate with the seal of the church, showing the date and place of birth in the United States and the date of baptism;

(ii) Affidavits sworn to by persons who were living at the time and who have personal knowledge of the event to which they attest. The affidavits must contain the affiant's full name and address, date and place of birth, relationship to the parties, if any, and complete details concerning how the affiant acquired knowledge of the event;

(iii) Early school records (preferably from the first school) showing the date of admission to the school, the child's date and place of birth, and the name(s) and place(s) of birth of the parent(s);

(iv) Census records showing the name, place of birth, and date of birth or age of the petitioner; or

(v) If it is determined that it would cause unusual delay or hardship to obtain documentary proof of birth in the United States, a United States citizen petitioner who is a member of the Armed Forces of the United States and who is serving outside the United States may submit a statement from the appropriate authority of the Armed Forces. The statement should attest to the fact that the personnel records of the Armed Forces show that the petitioner was born in the United States on a certain date.

(3) *Evidence submitted with a self-petition.* If a self-petitioner filing under section 204(a)(1)(A)(iii), 204(a)(1)(A)(iv), 204(a)(1)(B)(ii), or 204(a)(1)(B)(iii) of the Act is unable to present primary or secondary evidence of the abuser's status, the Service will attempt to electronically verify the abuser's citizenship or immigration status from information contained in Service computerized records. Other Service records may also be reviewed at the discretion of the adjudicating officer. If the Service is unable to identify a record as relating to the abuser or the record does not establish the abuser's immigration or citizenship status, the self-petition will

be adjudicated based on the information submitted by the self-petitioner.

[57 FR 41056, Sept. 9, 1992, as amended at 58 FR 48778, Sept. 20, 1993; 61 FR 13072, 13073, Mar. 26, 1996; 63 FR 70315, Dec. 21, 1998; 72 FR 19106, Apr. 17, 2007; 72 FR 56853, Oct. 4, 2007; 74 FR 26936, June 5, 2009; 76 FR 28305, May 17, 2011]

§ 204.2 Petitions for relatives, widows and widowers, and abused spouses and children.

(a) *Petition for a spouse*—(1) *Eligibility*. A United States citizen or alien admitted for lawful permanent residence may file a petition on behalf of a spouse.

(i) *Marriage within five years of petitioner's obtaining lawful permanent resident status*. (A) A visa petition filed on behalf of an alien by a lawful permanent resident spouse may not be approved if the marriage occurred within five years of the petitioner being accorded the status of lawful permanent resident based upon a prior marriage to a United States citizen or alien lawfully admitted for permanent residence, unless:

(*1*) The petitioner establishes by clear and convincing evidence that the marriage through which the petitioner gained permanent residence was not entered into for the purposes of evading the immigration laws; or

(*2*) The marriage through which the petitioner obtained permanent residence was terminated through death.

(B) *Documentation*. The petitioner should submit documents which cover the period of the prior marriage. The types of documents which may establish that the prior marriage was not entered into for the purpose of evading the immigration laws include, but are not limited to:

(*1*) Documentation showing joint ownership of property;

(*2*) A lease showing joint tenancy of a common residence;

(*3*) Documentation showing commingling of financial resources;

(*4*) Birth certificate(s) of child(ren) born to the petitioner and prior spouse;

(*5*) Affidavits sworn to or affirmed by third parties having personal knowledge of the bona fides of the prior marital relationship. (Each affidavit must contain the full name and address, date and place of birth of the person making the affidavit; his or her relationship, if any, to the petitioner, beneficiary or prior spouse; and complete information and details explaining how the person acquired his or her knowledge of the prior marriage. The affiant may be required to testify before an immigration officer about the information contained in the affidavit. Affidavits should be supported, if possible, by one or more types of documentary evidence listed in this paragraph.); or

(*6*) Any other documentation which is relevant to establish that the prior marriage was not entered into in order to evade the immigration laws of the United States.

(C) The petitioner must establish by clear and convincing evidence that the prior marriage was not entered into for the purpose of evading the immigration laws. Failure to meet the "clear and convincing evidence" standard will result in the denial of the petition. Such a denial shall be without prejudice to the filing of a new petition once the petitioner has acquired five years of lawful permanent residence. The director may choose to initiate deportation proceedings based upon information gained through the adjudication of the petition; however, failure to initiate such proceedings shall not establish that the petitioner's prior marriage was not entered into for the purpose of evading the immigration laws. Unless the petition is approved, the beneficiary shall not be accorded a filing date within the meaning of section 203(c) of the Act based upon any spousal second preference petition.

(ii) *Fraudulent marriage prohibition*. Section 204(c) of the Act prohibits the approval of a visa petition filed on behalf of an alien who has attempted or conspired to enter into a marriage for the purpose of evading the immigration laws. The director will deny a petition for immigrant visa classification filed on behalf of any alien for whom there is substantial and probative evidence of such an attempt or conspiracy, regardless of whether that alien received a benefit through the attempt or conspiracy. Although it is not necessary that the alien have been convicted of, or even prosecuted for, the attempt or conspiracy, the evidence of the attempt or conspiracy must be contained in the alien's file.

(iii) *Marriage during proceedings—general prohibition against approval of visa petition.* A visa petition filed on behalf of an alien by a United States citizen or a lawful permanent resident spouse shall not be approved if the marriage creating the relationship occurred on or after November 10, 1986, and while the alien was in exclusion, deportation, or removal proceedings, or judicial proceedings relating thereto. Determination of commencement and termination of proceedings and exemptions shall be in accordance with § 245.1(c)(9) of this chapter, except that the burden in visa petition proceedings to establish eligibility for the exemption in § 245.1(c)(9)(iii)(F) of this chapter shall rest with the petitioner.

(A) *Request for exemption.* No application or fee is required to request an exemption. The request must be made in writing and submitted with the Form I–130. The request must state the reason for seeking the exemption and must be supported by documentary evidence establishing eligibility for the exemption.

(B) *Evidence to establish eligibility for the bona fide marriage exemption.* The petitioner should submit documents which establish that the marriage was entered into in good faith and not entered into for the purpose of procuring the alien's entry as an immigrant. The types of documents the petitioner may submit include, but are not limited to:

(*1*) Documentation showing joint ownership of property;

(*2*) Lease showing joint tenancy of a common residence;

(*3*) Documentation showing commingling of financial resources;

(*4*) Birth certificate(s) of child(ren) born to the petitioner and beneficiary;

(*5*) Affidavits of third parties having knowledge of the bona fides of the marital relationship (Such persons may be required to testify before an immigration officer as to the information contained in the affidavit. Affidavits must be sworn to or affirmed by people who have personal knowledge of the marital relationship. Each affidavit must contain the full name and address, date and place of birth of the person making the affidavit and his or her relationship to the spouses, if any. The affidavit must contain complete information and details explaining how the person acquired his or her knowledge of the marriage. Affidavits should be supported, if possible, by one or more types of documentary evidence listed in this paragraph); or

(*6*) Any other documentation which is relevant to establish that the marriage was not entered into in order to evade the immigration laws of the United States.

(C) *Decision.* Any petition filed during the prohibited period shall be denied, unless the petitioner establishes eligibility for an exemption from the general prohibition. The petitioner shall be notified in writing of the decision of the director.

(D) *Denials.* The denial of a petition because the marriage took place during the prohibited period shall be without prejudice to the filing of a new petition after the beneficiary has resided outside the United States for the required period of two years following the marriage. The denial shall also be without prejudice to the consideration of a new petition or a motion to reopen the visa petition proceedings if deportation or exclusion proceedings are terminated after the denial other than by the beneficiary's departure from the United States. Furthermore, the denial shall be without prejudice to the consideration of a new petition or motion to reopen the visa petition proceedings, if the petitioner establishes eligibility for the bona fide marriage exemption contained in this part: *Provided,* That no motion to reopen visa petition proceedings may be accepted if the approval of the motion would result in the beneficiary being accorded a priority date within the meaning of section 203(c) of the Act earlier than November 29, 1990.

(E) *Appeals.* The decision of the Board of Immigration Appeals concerning the denial of a relative visa petition because the petitioner failed to establish eligibility for the bona fide marriage exemption contained in this part will constitute the single level of appellate review established by statute.

(F) *Priority date.* A preference beneficiary shall not be accorded a priority date within the meaning of section

203(c) of the Act based upon any relative petition filed during the prohibited period, unless an exemption contained in this part has been granted. Furthermore, a preference beneficiary shall not be accorded a priority date prior to November 29, 1990, based upon the approval of a request for consideration for the bona fide marriage exemption contained in this part.

(2) *Evidence for petition for a spouse.* In addition to evidence of United States citizenship or lawful permanent residence, the petitioner must also provide evidence of the claimed relationship. A petition submitted on behalf of a spouse must be accompanied by a recent ADIT-style photograph of the petitioner, a recent ADIT-style photograph of the beneficiary, a certificate of marriage issued by civil authorities, and proof of the legal termination of all previous marriages of both the petitioner and the beneficiary. However, non-ADIT-style photographs may be accepted by the district director when the petitioner or beneficiary reside(s) in a country where such photographs are unavailable or cost prohibitive.

(3) *Decision on and disposition of petition.* The approved petition will be forwarded to the Department of State's Processing Center. If the beneficiary is in the United States and is eligible for adjustment of status under section 245 of the Act, the approved petition will be retained by the Service. If the petition is denied, the petitioner will be notified of the reasons for the denial and of the right to appeal in accordance with the provisions of 8 CFR 3.3.

(4) *Derivative beneficiaries.* No alien may be classified as an immediate relative as defined in section 201(b) of the Act unless he or she is the direct beneficiary of an approved petition for that classification. Therefore, a child of an alien approved for classification as an immediate relative spouse is not eligible for derivative classification and must have a separate petition filed on his or her behalf. A child accompanying or following to join a principal alien under section 203(a)(2) of the Act may be included in the principal alien's second preference visa petition. The child will be accorded second preference classification and the same priority date as the principal alien. However, if the child reaches the age of twenty-one prior to the issuance of a visa to the principal alien parent, a separate petition will be required. In such a case, the original priority date will be retained if the subsequent petition is filed by the same petitioner. Such retention of priority date will be accorded only to a son or daughter previously eligible as a derivative beneficiary under a second preference spousal petition.

(b) *Petition by widow or widower of a United States citizen*—(1) *Eligibility.* A widow or widower of a United States citizen may file a petition and be classified as an immediate relative under section 201(b) of the Act if:

(i) He or she had been married for at least two years to a United States citizen.

(NOTE: The United States citizen is not required to have had the status of United States citizen for the entire two year period, but must have been a United States citizen at the time of death.)

(ii) The petition is filed within two years of the death of the citizen spouse or before November 29, 1992, if the citizen spouse died before November 29, 1990;

(iii) The alien petitioner and the citizen spouse were not legally separated at the time of the citizen's death; and

(iv) The alien spouse has not remarried.

(2) *Evidence for petition of widow or widower.* If a petition is submitted by the widow or widower of a deceased United States citizen, it must be accompanied by evidence of citizenship of the United States citizen and primary evidence, if available, of the relationship in the form of a marriage certificate issued by civil authorities, proof of the termination of all prior marriages of both husband and wife, and the United States citizen's death certificate issued by civil authorities. To determine the availability of primary documents, the Service will refer to the Department of State's Foreign Affairs Manual (FAM). When the FAM shows that primary documents are generally available in the country at issue but the petitioner claims that his or her document is unavailable, a letter from the appropriate registrar stating that the document is not available will

be required before the Service will accept secondary evidence. Secondary evidence will be evaluated for its authenticity and credibility. Secondary evidence may include:

(i) Such evidence of the marriage and termination of prior marriages as religious documents, tribal records, census records, or affidavits; and

(ii) Such evidence of the United States citizen's death as religious documents, funeral service records, obituaries, or affidavits. Affidavits submitted as secondary evidence pursuant to paragraphs (b)(2)(i) and (b)(2)(ii) of this section must be sworn to or affirmed by people who have personal knowledge of the event to which they attest. Each affidavit should contain the full name and address, date and place of birth of the person making the affidavit and his or her relationship, if any, to the widow or widower. Any such affidavit must contain complete information and details explaining how knowledge of the event was acquired.

(3) *Decision on and disposition of petition.* The approved petition will be forwarded to the Department of State's Processing Center. If the widow or widower is in the United States and is eligible for adjustment of status under section 245 of the Act, the approved petition will be retained by the Service. If the petition is denied, the widow or widower will be notified of the reasons for the denial and of the right to appeal in accordance with the provisions of 8 CFR 3.3.

(4) *Derivative beneficiaries.* A child of an alien widow or widower classified as an immediate relative is eligible for derivative classification as an immediate relative. Such a child may be included in the principal alien's immediate relative visa petition, and may accompany or follow to join the principal alien to the United States. Derivative benefits do not extend to an unmarried or married son or daughter of an alien widow or widower.

(c) *Self-petition by spouse of abusive citizen or lawful permanent resident*—(1) *Eligibility*—(i) *Basic eligibility requirements.* A spouse may file a self-petition under section 204(a)(1)(A)(iii) or 204(a)(1)(B)(ii) of the Act for his or her classification as an immediate relative or as a preference immigrant if he or she:

(A) Is the spouse of a citizen or lawful permanent resident of the United States;

(B) Is eligible for immigrant classification under section 201(b)(2)(A)(i) or 203(a)(2)(A) of the Act based on that relationship;

(C) Is residing in the United States;

(D) Has resided in the United States with the citizen or lawful permanent resident spouse;

(E) Has been battered by, or has been the subject of extreme cruelty perpetrated by, the citizen or lawful permanent resident during the marriage; or is that parent of a child who has been battered by, or has been the subject of extreme cruelty perpetrated by, the citizen or lawful permanent resident during the marriage;

(F) Is a person of good moral character;

(G) Is a person whose deportation would result in extreme hardship to himself, herself, or his or her child; and

(H) Entered into the marriage to the citizen or lawful permanent resident in good faith.

(ii) *Legal status of the marriage.* The self-petitioning spouse must be legally married to the abuser when the petition is properly filed with the Service. A spousal self-petition must be denied if the marriage to the abuser legally ended through annulment, death, or divorce before that time. After the self-petition has been properly filed, the legal termination of the marriage will have no effect on the decision made on the self-petition. The self-petitioner's remarriage, however, will be a basis for the denial of a pending self-petition.

(iii) *Citizenship or immigration status of the abuser.* The abusive spouse must be a citizen of the United States or a lawful permanent resident of the United States when the petition is filed and when it is approved. Changes in the abuser's citizenship or lawful permanent resident status after the approval will have no effect on the self-petition. A self-petition approved on the basis of a relationship to an abusive lawful permanent resident spouse will not be automatically upgraded to immediate relative status. The self-petitioner would not be precluded, however, from filing a new self-petition for immediate relative classification after the abuser's naturalization, provided the self-petitioner continues to meet the self-petitioning requirements.

(iv) *Eligibility for immigrant classification.* A self-petitioner is required to comply with the provisions of section 204(c) of the Act, section 204(g) of the Act, and section 204(a)(2) of the Act.

(v) *Residence.* A self-petition will not be approved if the self-petitioner is not residing in the United States when the self-petition is filed. The self-petitioner is not required to be living with the abuser when the petition is filed, but he or she must have resided with the abuser in the United States in the past.

(vi) *Battery or extreme cruelty.* For the purpose of this chapter, the phrase "was battered by or was the subject of extreme cruelty" includes, but is not limited to, being the victim of any act or threatened act of violence, including any forceful detention, which results or threatens to result in physical or mental injury. Psychological or sexual abuse or exploitation, including rape, molestation, incest (if the victim is a minor), or forced prostitution shall be considered acts of violence. Other abusive actions may also be acts of violence under certain circumstances, including acts that, in and of themselves, may not initially appear violent but that are a part of an overall pattern of violence. The qualifying abuse must have been committed by the citizen or lawful permanent resident spouse, must have been perpetrated against the self-petitioner or the self-petitioner's child, and must have taken place during the self-petitioner's marriage to the abuser.

(vii) *Good moral character.* A self-petitioner will be found to lack good moral character if he or she is a person described in section 101(f) of the Act. Extenuating circumstances may be taken into account if the person has not been convicted of an offense or offenses but admits to the commission of an act or acts that could show a lack of good moral character under section 101(f) of the Act. A person who was subjected to abuse in the form of forced prostitution or who can establish that he or she was forced to engage in other behavior that could render the person excludable under section 212(a) of the Act would not be precluded from being found to be a person of good moral character, provided the person has not been convicted for the commission of the offense or offenses in a court of law. A self-petitioner will also be found to lack good moral character, unless he or she establishes extenuating circumstances, if he or she willfully failed or refused to support dependents; or committed unlawful acts that adversely reflect upon his or her moral character, or was convicted or imprisoned for such acts, although the acts do not require an automatic finding of lack of good moral character. A self-petitioner's claim of good moral character will be evaluated on a case-by-case basis, taking into account the provisions of section 101(f) of the Act and the standards of the average citizen in the community. If the results of record checks conducted prior to the issuance of an immigrant visa or approval of an application for adjustment of status disclose that the self-petitioner is no longer a person of good moral character or that he or she has not been a person of good moral character in the past, a pending self-petition will be denied or the approval of a self-petition will be revoked.

(viii) *Extreme hardship.* The Service will consider all credible evidence of extreme hardship submitted with a self-petition, including evidence of hardship arising from circumstances surrounding the abuse. The extreme hardship claim will be evaluated on a case-by-case basis after a review of the evidence in the case. Self-petitioners are encouraged to cite and document all applicable factors, since there is no guarantee that a particular reason or reasons will result in a finding that deportation would cause extreme hardship. Hardship to persons other than the self-petitioner or the self-petitioner's child cannot be considered in determining whether a self-petitioning spouse's deportation would cause extreme hardship.

(ix) *Good faith marriage.* A spousal self-petition cannot be approved if the self-petitioner entered into the marriage to the abuser for the primary purpose of circumventing the immigration laws. A self-petition will not be denied, however, solely because the spouses are not living together and the marriage is no longer viable.

(2) *Evidence for a spousal self-petition*—(i) *General.* Self-petitioners are encouraged to submit primary evidence whenever possible. The Service will consider, however, any credible evidence relevant to the petition. The determination of what evidence is credible and the weight to be given that evidence shall be within the sole discretion of the Service.

(ii) *Relationship.* A self-petition filed by a spouse must be accompanied by evidence of citizenship of the United States citizen or proof of the immigration status of the lawful permanent resident abuser. It must also be accompanied by evidence of the relationship. Primary evidence of a marital relationship is a marriage certificate issued by civil authorities, and proof of the termination of all prior marriages, if any, of both the self-petitioner and the abuser. If the self-petition is based on a claim that the self-petitioner's child was battered or subjected to extreme cruelty committed by the citizen or lawful permanent resident spouse, the self-petition should also be accompanied by the child's birth certificate or other evidence showing the relationship between the self-petitioner and the abused child.

(iii) *Residence.* One or more documents may be submitted showing that the self-petitioner and the abuser have resided together in the United States. One or more documents may also be submitted showing that the self-petitioner is residing in the United States when the self-petition is filed. Employment records, utility receipts, school records, hospital or medical records, birth certificates of children born in the United States, deeds, mortgages, rental records, insurance policies, affidavits or any other type of relevant credible evidence of residency may be submitted.

(iv) *Abuse.* Evidence of abuse may include, but is not limited to, reports and affidavits from police, judges and other court officials, medical personnel, school officials, clergy, social workers, and other social service agency personnel. Persons who have obtained an order of protection against the abuser or have taken other legal steps to end the abuse are strongly encouraged to submit copies of the relating legal documents. Evidence that the abuse victim sought safe-haven in a battered women's shelter or similar refuge may be relevant, as may a combination of documents such as a photograph of the visibly injured self-petitioner supported by affidavits. Other forms of credible relevant evidence will also be considered. Documentary proof of non-qualifying abuses may only be used to establish a pattern of abuse and violence and to support a claim that qualifying abuse also occurred.

(v) *Good moral character.* Primary evidence of the self-petitioner's good moral character is the self-petitioner's affidavit. The affidavit should be accompanied by a local police clearance or a state-issued criminal background check from each locality or state in the United States in which the self-petitioner has resided for six or more months during the 3-year period immediately preceding the filing of the self-petition. Self-petitioners who lived outside the United States during this time should submit a police clearance, criminal background check, or similar report issued by the appropriate authority in each foreign country in which he or she resided for six or more months during the 3-year period immediately preceding the filing of the self-petition. If police clearances, criminal background checks, or similar reports are not available for some or all locations, the self-petitioner may include an explanation and submit other evidence with his or her affidavit. The Service will consider other credible evidence of good moral character, such as affidavits from responsible persons who can knowledgeably attest to the self-petitioner's good moral character.

(vi) *Extreme hardship.* Evidence of extreme hardship may include affidavits, birth certificates of children, medical reports, protection orders and other court documents, police reports, and other relevant credible evidence.

(vii) *Good faith marriage.* Evidence of good faith at the time of marriage may include, but is not limited to, proof that one spouse has been listed as the other's spouse on insurance policies, property leases, income tax forms, or bank accounts; and testimony or other evidence regarding courtship, wedding ceremony, shared residence and experiences. Other types of readily available evidence might include the birth certificates of children born to the abuser and the spouse; police, medical, or court documents providing information about the relationship; and affidavits of persons with personal knowledge of the relationship. All credible relevant evidence will be considered.

(3) *Decision on and disposition of the petition*—(i) *Petition approved.* If the self-petitioning spouse will apply for adjustment of status under section 245 of the Act, the approved petition will be retained by the Service. If the self-petitioner will apply for an immigrant visa abroad, the approved self-petition will be forwarded to the Department of State's National Visa Center.

(ii) *Petition denied.* If the self-petition is denied, the self-petitioner will be notified in writing of the reasons for the denial and of the right to appeal the decision.

(4) *Derivative beneficiaries.* A child accompanying or following-to-join the self-petitioning spouse may be accorded the same preference and priority date as the self-petitioner without the necessity of a separate petition, if the child has not been classified as an immigrant based on his or her own self-petition. A derivative child who had been included in a parent's self-petition may later file a self-petition, provided the child meets the self-petitioning requirements. A child who has been classified as an immigrant based on a petition filed by the abuser or another relative may also be derivatively included in a parent's self-petition. The derivative child must be unmarried, less than 21 years old, and otherwise qualify as the self-petitioner's child under section 101(b)(1)(F) of the Act until he or she becomes a lawful permanent resident based on the derivative classification.

(5) *Name change.* If the self-petitioner's current name is different than the name shown on the documents, evidence of the name change (such as the petitioner's marriage certificate, legal document showing name change, or other similar evidence) must accompany the self-petition.

(6) *Prima facie determination.* (i) Upon receipt of a self-petition under paragraph (c)(1) of this section, the Service shall make a determination as to whether the petition and the supporting documentation establish a "prima facie case" for purposes of 8 U.S.C. 1641, as amended by section 501 of Public Law 104–208.

(ii) For purposes of paragraph (c)(6)(i) of this section, a prima facie case is established only if the petitioner submits a completed Form I–360 and other evidence supporting all of the elements required of a self-petitioner in paragraph (c)(1) of this section. A finding of prima facie eligibility does not relieve the petitioner of the burden of providing additional evidence in support of the petition and does not establish eligibility for the underlying petition.

(iii) If the Service determines that a petitioner has made a "prima facie case," the Service shall issue a Notice of Prima Facie Case to the petitioner. Such Notice shall be valid until the Service either grants or denies the petition.

(iv) For purposes of adjudicating the petition submitted under paragraph (c)(1) of this section, a prima facie determination—

(A) Shall not be considered evidence in support of the petition;

(B) Shall not be construed to make a determination of the credibility or probative value of any evidence submitted along with that petition; and,

(C) Shall not relieve the self-petitioner of his or her burden of complying with all of the evidentiary requirements of paragraph (c)(2) of this section.

(d) *Petition for a child or son or daughter*—(1) *Eligibility.* A United States citizen may file a petition on behalf of an unmarried child under twenty-one years of age for immediate relative classification under section 201(b) of the Act. A United States citizen may file a petition on behalf of an unmarried son or daughter over twenty-one years of age under section 203(a)(1) or for a married son or daughter for preference classification under section 203(a)(3) of the Act. An alien lawfully admitted for permanent residence may file a petition on behalf of a child or an unmarried son or daughter for preference classification under section 203(a)(2) of the Act.

(2) *Evidence to support petition for child or son or daughter.* In addition to evidence of United States citizenship or lawful permanent resident, the petitioner must also provide evidence of the claimed relationship.

(i) *Primary evidence for a legitimate child or son or daughter.* If a petition is submitted by the mother, the birth certificate of the child showing the mother's name must accompany the petition. If the mother's name on the birth certificate is different from her name on the petition, evidence of the name change must also be submitted. If a petition is submitted by the father, the birth certificate of the child, a marriage certificate of the parents, and proof of legal termination of the parents' prior marriages, if any, issued by civil authorities must accompany the petition. If the father's name has been legally changed, evidence of the name change must also accompany the petition.

(ii) *Primary evidence for a legitimated child or son or daughter.* A child can be legitimated through the marriage of his or her natural parents, by the laws of the country or state of the child's residence or domicile, or by the laws of the country or state of the father's residence or domicile. If the legitimation is based on the natural parents' marriage, such marriage must have taken place while the child was under the age of eighteen. If the legitimation is based on the laws of the country or state of the child's residence or domicile, the law must have taken effect before the child's eighteenth birthday. If the legitimation is based on the laws of the country or state of the father's residence or domicile, the father must have resided—while the child was under eighteen years of age—in the country or state under whose laws the child has been legitimated. Primary evidence of the relationship should consist of the beneficiary's birth certificate and the parents' marriage certificate or other evidence of legitimation issued by civil authorities.

(iii) *Primary evidence for an illegitimate child or son or daughter.* If a petition is submitted by the mother, the child's birth certificate, issued by civil authorities and showing the mother's name, must accompany the petition. If the mother's name on the birth certificate is different from her name as reflected in the petition, evidence of the name change must also be submitted. If the petition is submitted by the purported father of a child or son or daughter born out of wedlock, the father must show that he is the natural father and that a bona fide parent-child relationship was established when the child or son or daughter was unmarried and under twenty-one years of age. Such a relationship will be deemed to exist or to have existed where the father demonstrates or has demonstrated an active concern for the child's support, instruction, and general welfare. Primary evidence to establish that the petitioner is the child's natural father is the beneficiary's birth certificate, issued by civil authorities and showing the father's name. If the father's name has been legally changed, evidence of the name change must accompany the petition. Evidence of a parent/child relationship should establish more than merely a biological relationship. Emotional and/or financial ties or a genuine concern and interest by the father for the child's support, instruction, and general welfare must be shown. There should be evidence that the father and child actually lived together or that the father held the child out as being his own, that he provided for some or all of the child's needs, or that in general the father's behavior evidenced a genuine concern for the child. The most persuasive evidence for establishing a bona fide parent/child relationship and financial responsibility by the father is documentary evidence which was contemporaneous with the events in question. Such evidence may include, but is not limited to: money order receipts or cancelled checks showing the father's financial support of the beneficiary; the father's income tax returns; the father's medical or insurance records which include the beneficiary as a dependent; school records for the beneficiary; correspondence between the parties; or notarized affidavits of friends, neighbors, school officials, or other associates knowledgeable about the relationship.

(iv) *Primary evidence for a stepchild.* If a petition is submitted by a stepparent on behalf of a stepchild or stepson or stepdaughter, the petition must be supported by the stepchild's or stepson's or stepdaughter's birth certificate, issued by civil authorities and showing the name of the beneficiary's parent to whom the petitioner is married, a marriage certificate issued by civil authorities which shows that the petitioner and the child's natural parent were married before the stepchild or stepson or stepdaughter reached the age of eighteen; and evidence of the termination of any prior marriages of the petitioner and the natural parent of the stepchild or stepson or stepdaughter.

(v) *Secondary evidence.* When it is established that primary evidence is not available, secondary evidence may be accepted. To determine the availability of primary documents, the Service will refer to the Department of State's Foreign Affairs Manual (FAM). When the FAM shows that primary documents are generally available in the country at issue but the petitioner claims that his or her document is unavailable, a letter from the appropriate registrar stating that the document is not available will be required before the Service will accept secondary evidence. Secondary evidence will be evaluated for its authenticity and credibility. Secondary evidence may take the form of historical evidence; such evidence must have been issued contemporaneously with the event which it documents any may include, but is not limited to, medical records, school records, and religious documents. Affidavits may also by accepted. When affidavits are submitted, they must be sworn to by persons who were born at the time of and who have personal knowledge of the event to which they attest. Any affidavit must contain the affiant's full name and address, date and place of birth, relationship to the party, if any, and complete details concerning how the affiant acquired knowledge of the event.

(vi) *Blood tests.* The director may require that a specific Blood Group Antigen Test be conducted of the beneficiary and the beneficiary's father and mother. In general, blood tests will be required only after other forms of evidence have proven inconclusive. If the specific Blood Group Antigen Test is also found not to be conclusive and the director determines that additional evidence is needed, a Human Leucocyte Antigen (HLA) test may be requested. Tests will be conducted, at the expense of the petitioner or beneficiary, by the United States Public Health Service physician who is authorized overseas or by a qualified medical specialist designated by the district director. The results of the test should be reported on Form G-620. Refusal to submit to a Specific Blood Group Antigen or HLA test when requested may constitute a basis for denial of the petition, unless a legitimate religious objection has been established. When a legitimate religious objection is established, alternate forms of evidence may be considered based upon documentation already submitted.

(vii) *Primary evidence for an adopted child or son or daughter.* A petition may be submitted on behalf of an adopted child or son or daughter by a United States citizen or lawful permanent resident if the adoption took place before the beneficiary's sixteenth birthday, and if the child has been in the legal custody of the adopting parent or parents and has resided with the adopting parent or parents for at least two years. A copy of the adoption decree, issued by the civil authorities, must accompany the petition.

(A) *Legal custody* means the assumption of responsibility for a minor by an adult under the laws of the state and under the order or approval of a court of law or other appropriate government entity. This provision requires that a legal process involving the courts or other recognized government entity take place. If the adopting parent was granted legal custody by the court or recognized governmental entity prior to the adoption, that period may be counted toward fulfillment of the two-year legal custody requirement. However, if custody was not granted prior to the adoption, the adoption decree shall be deemed to mark the commencement of legal custody. An informal custodial or guardianship document, such as a sworn affidavit signed before a notary public, is insufficient for this purpose.

(B) Evidence must also be submitted to show that the beneficiary resided with the petitioner for at least two years. Generally, such documentation must establish that the petitioner and the beneficiary resided together in a familial relationship. Evidence of parental control may include, but is not limited to, evidence that the adoptive parent owns or maintains the property where the child resides and provides financial support and day-to-day supervision. The evidence must clearly indicate the physical living arrangements of the adopted child, the adoptive parent(s), and the natural parent(s) for the period of time during which the adoptive parent claims to have met the residence requirement. When the adopted child continued to reside in the same household as a natural parent(s) during the period in which the adoptive parent petitioner seeks to establish his or her compliance with this requirement, the petitioner has the burden of establishing that he or she exercised primary parental control during that period of residence.

(C) Legal custody and residence occurring prior to or after the adoption will satisfy both requirements. Legal custody, like residence, is accounted for in the aggregate. Therefore, a break in legal custody or residence will not affect the time already fulfilled. To meet the definition of child contained in sections 101(b)(1)(E) and 101(b)(2) of the Act, the child must have been under 16 years of age when the adoption is finalized.

(D) On or after the Convention effective date, as defined in 8 CFR part 204.301, a United States citizen who is habitually resident in the United States, as determined under 8 CFR 204.303, may not file a Form I–130 under this section on behalf of child who was habitually resident in a Convention country, as determined under 8 CFR 204.303, unless the adoption was completed before the Convention effective date. In the case of any adoption occurring on or after the Convention effective date, a Form I–130 may be filed and approved only if the United States citizen petitioner was not habitually resident in the United States at the time of the adoption.

(E) For purposes of paragraph (d)(2)(vii)(D) of this section, USCIS will deem a United States citizen, 8 CFR 204.303 notwithstanding, to have been habitually resident outside the United States, if the citizen satisfies the 2-year joint residence and custody requirements by residing with the child outside the United States.

(F) For purposes of paragraph (d)(2)(vii)(D) of this section, USCIS will not approve a Form I–130 under section 101(b)(1)(E) of the Act on behalf of an alien child who is present in the United States based on an adoption that is entered on or after the Convention effective date, but whose habitual residence immediately before the child's arrival in the United States was in a Convention country. However, the U.S. citizen seeking the child's adoption may file a Form I–800A and Form I–800 under 8 CFR part 204, subpart C.

(3) *Decision on and disposition of petition.* The approved petition will be forwarded to the Department of State's Processing Center. If the beneficiary is in the United States and is eligible for adjustment of status under section 245 of the Act, the approved petition will be retained by the Service. If the petition is denied, the petitioner will be notified of the reasons for the denial and of the right to appeal in accordance with the provisions of 8 CFR 3.3.

(4) *Derivative beneficiaries.* A spouse or child accompanying or following to join a principal alien as used in this section may be accorded the same preference and priority date as the principal alien without the necessity of a separate petition. However, a child of an alien who is approved for classification as an immediate relative is not eligible for derivative classification and must have a separate petition approved on his or her behalf.

(5) *Name change.* When the petitioner's name does not appear on the child's birth certificate, evidence of the name change (such as the petitioner's marriage certificate, legal document showing name change, or other similar

evidence) must accompany the petition. If the beneficiary's name has been legally changed, evidence of the name change must also accompany the petition.

(e) *Self-petition by child of abusive citizen or lawful permanent resident*—(1) *Eligibility.* (i) A child may file a self-petition under section 204(a)(1)(A)(iv) or 204(a)(1)(B)(iii) of the Act if he or she:

(A) Is the child of a citizen or lawful permanent resident of the United States;

(B) Is eligible for immigrant classification under section 201(b)(2)(A)(i) or 203(a)(2)(A) of the Act based on that relationship;

(C) Is residing in the United States;

(D) Has resided in the United States with the citizen or lawful permanent resident parent;

(E) Has been battered by, or has been the subject of extreme cruelty perpetrated by, the citizen or lawful permanent resident parent while residing with that parent;

(F) Is a person of good moral character; and

(G) Is a person whose deportation would result in extreme hardship to himself or herself.

(ii) *Parent-child relationship to the abuser.* The self-petitioning child must be unmarried, less than 21 years of age, and otherwise qualify as the abuser's child under the definition of child contained in section 101(b)(1) of the Act when the petition is filed and when it is approved. Termination of the abuser's parental rights or a change in legal custody does not alter the self-petitioning relationship provided the child meets the requirements of section 101(b)(1) of the Act.

(iii) *Citizenship or immigration status of the abuser.* The abusive parent must be a citizen of the United States or a lawful permanent resident of the United States when the petition is filed and when it is approved. Changes in the abuser's citizenship or lawful permanent resident status after the approval will have no effect on the self-petition. A self-petition approved on the basis of a relationship to an abusive lawful permanent resident will not be automatically upgraded to immediate relative status. The self-petitioning child would not be precluded, however, from filing a new self-petition for immediate relative classification after the abuser's naturalization, provided the self-petitioning child continues to meet the self-petitioning requirements.

(iv) *Eligibility for immigrant classification.* A self-petitioner is required to comply with the provisions of section 204(c) of the Act, section 204(g) of the Act, and section 204(a)(2) of the Act.

(v) *Residence.* A self-petition will not be approved if the self-petitioner is not residing in the United States when the self-petition is filed. The self-petitioner is not required to be living with the abuser when the petition is filed, but he or she must have resided with the abuser in the United States in the past.

(vi) *Battery or extreme cruelty.* For the purpose of this chapter, the phrase "was battered by or was the subject of extreme cruelty" includes, but is not limited to, being the victim of any act or threatened act of violence, including any forceful detention, which results or threatens to result in physical or mental injury. Psychological or sexual abuse or exploitation, including rape, molestation, incest (if the victim is a minor), or forced prostitution shall be considered acts of violence. Other abusive actions may also be acts of violence under certain circumstances, including acts that, in and of themselves, may not initially appear violent but are a part of an overall pattern of violence. The qualifying abuse must have been committed by the citizen or lawful permanent resident parent, must have been perpetrated against the self-petitioner, and must have taken place while the self-petitioner was residing with the abuser.

(vii) *Good moral character.* A self-petitioner will be found to lack good moral character if he or she is a person described in section 101(f) of the Act. Extenuating circumstances may be taken into account if the person has not been convicted of an offense or offenses but admits to the commission of an act or acts that could show a lack of good moral character under section 101(f) of the Act. A person who was subjected to abuse in the form of forced prostitution or who can establish that he or she was forced to engage in other behavior that could render the person excludable under section 212(a) of the Act would not be precluded from being found to be a person of good moral character, provided the person has not been convicted for the commission of the offense or offenses in a court of law. A self-petitioner will also be found to lack good moral character, unless he or she establishes extenuating circumstances, if he or she willfully failed or refused to support dependents; or committed unlawful acts that adversely reflect upon his or her moral character, or was convicted or imprisoned for such acts, although the acts do not require an automatic finding of lack of good moral character. A self-petitioner's claim of good moral character will be evaluated on a case-by-case basis, taking into account the provisions of section 101(f) of the Act and the standards of the average citizen in the community. If the results of record checks conducted prior to the issuance of an immigrant visa or approval of an application for adjustment of status disclose that the self-petitioner is no longer a person of good moral character or that he or she has not been a person of good moral character in the past, a pending self-petition will be denied or the approval of a self-petition will be revoked.

(viii) *Extreme hardship.* The Service will consider all credible evidence of extreme hardship submitted with a self-petition, including evidence of hardship arising from circumstances surrounding the abuse. The extreme hardship claim will be evaluated on a case-by-case basis after a review of the evidence in the case. Self-petitioners are encouraged to cite and document all applicable factors, since there is no guarantee that a particular reason or reasons will result in a finding that deportation would cause extreme hardship. Hardship to persons other than the self-petitioner cannot be considered in determining whether a self-petitioning child's deportation would cause extreme hardship.

(2) *Evidence for a child's self-petition*—(i) *General.* Self-petitioners are encouraged to submit primary evidence whenever possible. The Service will consider, however, any credible evidence relevant to the petition. The determination of what evidence is credible and the weight to be given that evidence shall be within the sole discretion of the Service.

(ii) *Relationship.* A self-petition filed by a child must be accompanied by evidence of citizenship of the United States citizen or proof of the immigration status of the lawful permanent resident abuser. It must also be accompanied by evidence of the relationship. Primary evidence of the relationship between:

(A) The self-petitioning child and an abusive biological mother is the self-petitioner's birth certificate issued by civil authorities;

(B) A self-petitioning child who was born in wedlock and an abusive biological father is the child's birth certificate issued by civil authorities, the marriage certificate of the child's parents, and evidence of legal termination of all prior marriages, if any;

(C) A legitimated self-petitioning child and an abusive biological father is the child's birth certificate issued by civil authorities, and evidence of the child's legitimation;

(D) A self-petitioning child who was born out of wedlock and an abusive biological father is the child's birth certificate issued by civil authorities showing the father's name, and evidence that a bona fide parent-child relationship has been established between the child and the parent;

(E) A self-petitioning stepchild and an abusive stepparent is the child's birth certificate issued by civil authorities, the marriage certificate of the child's parent and the stepparent showing marriage before the stepchild reached 18 years of age, and evidence of legal termination of all prior marriages of either parent, if any; and

(F) An adopted self-petitioning child and an abusive adoptive parent is an adoption decree showing that the adoption took place before the child reached 16 years of age, and evidence that the child has been residing with and in the legal custody of the abusive adoptive parent for at least 2 years.

(iii) *Residence.* One or more documents may be submitted showing that the self-petitioner and the abuser have resided together in the United States. One or more documents may also be submitted showing that the self-petitioner is residing in the United States when the self-petition is filed. Employment records, school records, hospital or medical records, rental records, insurance policies, affidavits or any other type of relevant credible evidence of residency may be submitted.

(iv) *Abuse.* Evidence of abuse may include, but is not limited to, reports and affidavits from police, judges and other court officials, medical personnel, school officials, clergy, social workers, and other social service agency personnel. Persons who have obtained an order of protection against the abuser or taken other legal steps to end the abuse are strongly encouraged to submit copies of the relating legal documents. Evidence that the abuse victim sought safe-haven in a battered women's shelter or similar refuge may be relevant, as may a combination of documents such as a photograph of the visibly injured self-petitioner supported by affidavits. Other types of credible relevant evidence will also be considered. Documentary proof of non-qualifying abuse may only be used to establish a pattern of abuse and violence and to support a claim that qualifying abuse also occurred.

(v) *Good moral character.* Primary evidence of the self-petitioner's good moral character is the self-petitioner's affidavit. The affidavit should be accompanied by a local police clearance or a state-issued criminal background check from each locality or state in the United States in which the self-petitioner has resided for six or more months during the 3-year period immediately preceding the filing of the self-petition. Self-petitioners who lived outside the United States during this time should submit a police clearance, criminal background check, or similar report issued by the appropriate authority in the foreign country in which he or she resided for six or more months during the 3-year period immediately preceding the filing of the self-petition. If police clearances, criminal background checks, or similar reports are not available for some or all locations, the self-petitioner may include an explanation and submit other evidence with his or her affidavit. The Service will consider other credible evidence of good moral character, such as affidavits from responsible persons who can knowledgeably attest to the self-petitioner's good moral character. A child who is less than 14 years of age is presumed to be a person of good moral character and is not required to submit affidavits of good moral character, police clearances, criminal background checks, or other evidence of good moral character.

(vi) *Extreme hardship.* Evidence of extreme hardship may include affidavits, medical reports, protection orders and other court documents, police reports, and other relevant credible evidence.

(3) *Decision on and disposition of the petition*—(i) *Petition approved.* If the self-petitioning child will apply for adjustment of status under section 245 of the Act, the approved petition will be retained by the Service. If the self-petitioner will apply for an immigrant visa abroad, the approved self-petition will be forwarded to the Department of State's National Visa Center.

(ii) *Petition denied.* If the self-petition is denied, the self-petitioner will be notified in writing of the reasons for the denial and of the right to appeal the decision.

(4) *Derivative beneficiaries.* A child of a self-petitioning child is not eligible for derivative classification and must have a petition filed on his or her behalf if seeking immigrant classification.

(5) *Name change.* If the self-petitioner's current name is different than the name shown on the documents, evidence of the name change (such as the petitioner's marriage certificate, legal document showing the name change, or other similar evidence) must accompany the self-petition.

(6) *Prima facie determination.* (i) Upon receipt of a self-petition under paragraph (e)(1) of this section, the Service shall make a determination as to whether the petition and the supporting documentation establish a "prima facie case" for purposes of 8 U.S.C. 1641, as amended by section 501 of Public Law 104–208.

(ii) For purposes of paragraph (e)(6)(i) of this section, a prima facie case is established only if the petitioner submits a completed Form I–360 and other evidence supporting all of the elements required of a self-petitioner in paragraph (e)(1) of this section. A finding of prima facie eligibility does not relieve the petitioner of the burden of providing additional evidence in support of the petition and does not establish eligibility for the underlying petition.

(iii) If the Service determines that a petitioner has made a "prima facie case" the Service shall issue a Notice of Prima Facie Case to the petitioner. Such Notice shall be valid until the Service either grants or denies the petition.

(iv) For purposes of adjudicating the petition submitted under paragraph (e)(1) of this section, a prima facie determination:

(A) Shall not be considered evidence in support of the petition;

(B) Shall not be construed to make a determination of the credibility or probative value of any evidence submitted along with that petition; and,

(C) Shall not relieve the self-petitioner of his or her burden of complying with all of the evidentiary requirements of paragraph (e)(2) of this section.

(f) *Petition for a parent*—(1) *Eligibility.* Only a United States citizen who is twenty-one years of age or older may file a petition on behalf of a parent for classification under section 201(b) of the Act.

(2) *Evidence to support a petition for a parent.* In addition to evidence of United States citizenship as listed in § 204.1(g) of this part, the petitioner must also provide evidence of the claimed relationship.

(i) *Primary evidence if petitioner is a legitimate son or daughter.* If a petition is submitted on behalf of the mother, the birth certificate of the petitioner showing the mother's name must accompany the petition. If the mother's name on the birth certificate is different from her name as reflected in the petition, evidence of the name change must also be submitted. If a petition is submitted on behalf of the father, the birth certificate of the petitioner, a marriage certificate of the parents, and proof of legal termination of the parents' prior marriages, if any, issued by civil authorities must accompany the petition. If the father's name on the birth certificate has been legally changed, evidence of the name change must also accompany the petition.

(ii) *Primary evidence if petitioner is a legitimated son or daughter.* A child can be legitimated through the marriage of his or her natural parents, by the laws of the country or state of the child's residence or domicile, or by the laws of the country or state of the father's residence or domicile. If the legitimation is based on the natural parent's marriage, such marriage must have taken place while the child was under the age of eighteen. If the legitimation is based on the laws of the country or state of the child's residence or domicile, the law must have taken effect before the child's eighteenth birthday. If the legitimation is based on the laws of the country or state of the father's residence or domicile, the father must have resided—while the child was under eighteen years of age—in the country or state under whose laws the child has been legitimated. Primary evidence of the relationship should consist of petitioner's birth certificate and the parents' marriage certificate or other evidence of legitimation issued by civil authorities.

(iii) *Primary evidence if the petitioner is an illegitimate son or daughter.* If a petition is submitted on behalf of the mother, the petitioner's birth certificate, issued by civil authorities and showing the mother's name, must accompany the petition. If the mother's name on the birth certificate is different from her name as reflected in the petition, evidence of the name change must also be submitted. If the petition is submitted on behalf of the purported father of the petitioner, the petitioner must show that the beneficiary is his or her natural father and that a bona fide parent-child relationship was established when the petitioner was unmarried and under twenty-one years of age. Such a relationship will be deemed to exist or to have existed where the father demonstrates or has demonstrated an active concern for the child's support, instruction, and general welfare. Primary evidence to establish that the beneficiary is the petitioner's natural father is the petitioner's birth certificate, issued by civil authorities and showing the father's name. If the father's name has been legally changed, evidence of the name change must accompany the petition. Evidence of a parent/child relationship should establish more than merely a biological relationship. Emotional and/or financial ties or a genuine concern and interest by the father for the child's support, instruction, and general welfare must be shown. There should be evidence that the father and child actually lived together or that the father held the child out as being his own, that he provided for some or all of the child's needs, or that in general the father's behavior evidenced a genuine concern for the child. The most persuasive evidence for establishing a bona fide parent/child relationship is documentary evidence which was contemporaneous with the events in question. Such evidence may include, but is not limited to: money order receipts or cancelled checks showing the father's financial support of the beneficiary; the father's income tax returns; the father's medical or insurance records which include the petitioner as a dependent; school records for the petitioner; correspondence between the parties; or notarized affidavits of friends, neighbors, school officials, or other associates knowledgeable as to the relationship.

(iv) *Primary evidence if petitioner is an adopted son or daughter.* A petition may be submitted for an adoptive parent by a United States citizen who is twenty-one years of age or older if the adoption took place before the petitioner's sixteenth birthday and if the two year legal custody and residence requirements have been met. A copy of the adoption decree, issued by the civil authorities, must accompany the petition.

(A) *Legal custody* means the assumption of responsibility for a minor by an adult under the laws of the state and under the order or approval of a court of law or other appropriate government entity. This provision requires that a legal process involving the courts or other recognized government entity take place. If the adopting parent was granted legal custody by the court or recognized governmental entity prior to the adoption, that period may be counted toward fulfillment of the two-year legal custody requirement. However, if custody was not granted prior to the adoption, the adoption decree shall be deemed to mark the commencement of legal custody. An informal custodial or guardianship document, such as a sworn affidavit signed before a notary public, is insufficient for this purpose.

(B) Evidence must also be submitted to show that the beneficiary resided with the petitioner for at least two years. Generally, such documentation must establish that the petitioner and the beneficiary resided together in a parental relationship. The evidence must clearly indicate the physical living arrangements of the adopted child, the adoptive parent(s), and the natural parent(s) for the period of time during which the adoptive parent claims to have met the residence requirement.

(C) Legal custody and residence occurring prior to or after the adoption will satisfy both requirements. Legal custody, like residence, is accounted for in the aggregate. Therefore, a break in legal custody or residence will not affect the time already fulfilled. To meet the definition of child contained in sections 101(b)(1)(E) and 101(b)(2) of the Act, the child must have been under 16 years of age when the adoption is finalized.

(v) *Name change.* When the petition is filed by a child for the child's parent, and the parent's name is not on the child's birth certificate, evidence of the name change (such as the parent's marriage certificate, a legal document showing the parent's name change, or other similar evidence) must accompany the petition. If the petitioner's name has been legally changed, evidence of the name change must also accompany the petition.

(3) *Decision on and disposition of petition.* The approved petition will be forwarded to the Department of State's Processing Center. If the beneficiary is in the United States and is eligible for adjustment of status under section 245 of the Act, the approved petition will be retained by the Service. If the petition is denied, the petitioner will be notified of the reasons for the denial and of the right to appeal in accordance with the provisions of 8 CFR 3.3.

(4) *Derivative beneficiaries.* A child or a spouse of a principal alien who is approved for classification as an immediate relative is not eligible for derivative classification and must have a separate petition approved on his or her behalf.

(g) *Petition for a brother or sister*—(1) *Eligibility.* Only a United States citizen who is twenty-one years of age or older may file a petition of a brother or sister for classification under section 203(a)(4) of the Act.

(2) *Evidence to support a petition for brother or sister.* In addition to evidence of United States citizenship, the petitioner must also provide evidence of the claimed relationship.

(i) *Primary evidence if the siblings share a common mother or are both legitimate children of a common father.* If a sibling relationship is claimed through a common mother, the petition must be supported by a birth certificate of the petitioner and a birth certificate of the beneficiary showing a common mother. If the mother's name on one birth certificate is different from her name as reflected on the other birth certificate or in the petition, evidence of the name change must also be submitted. If a sibling relationship is claimed through a common father, the birth certificates of the beneficiary and petitioner, a marriage certificate of the parents' and proof of legal termination of the parents, prior marriage(s), if any, issued by civil authorities must accompany the petition. If the father's name has been legally changed, evidence of the name change must also accompany the petition.

(ii) *Primary evidence if either or both siblings are legitimated.* A child can be legitimated through the marriage of his or her natural parents, by the laws of the country or state of the child's residence or domicile, or by the laws of the country or state of the father's residence or domicile. If the legitimation is based on the natural parents' marriage, such marriage must have taken place while the child was under the age of eighteen. If the legitimation is based on the laws of the country or state of the child's residence or domicile, the law must have taken effect before the child's eighteenth birthday. If based on the laws of the country or state of the father's residence or domicile, the father must have resided—while the child was under eighteen years of age—in the country or state under whose laws the child has been legitimated. Primary evidence of the relationship should consist of the petitioner's birth certificate, the beneficiary's birth certificate, and the parents' marriage certificate or other evidence of legitimation issued by civil authorities.

(iii) *Primary evidence if either sibling is illegitimate.* If one or both of the siblings is (are) the illegitimate child(ren) of a common father, the petitioner must show that they are the natural children of the father and that a bona fide parent-child relationship was established when the illegitimate child(ren) was (were) unmarried and under twenty-one years of age. Such a relationship will be deemed to exist or to have existed where the father demonstrates or has demonstrated an active concern for the child's support, instruction, and general welfare. Primary evidence is the petitioner's and beneficiary's birth certificates, issued by civil authorities and showing the father's name, and evidence that the siblings have or had a bona fide parent/child relationship with the natural father. If the father's name has been legally changed, evidence of the name change must accompany the petition. Evidence of a parent/child relationship should establish more than merely a biological relationship. Emotional and/or financial ties or a genuine concern and interest by the father for the child's support, instruction, and general welfare must be shown. There should be evidence that the father and child actually lived together or that the father held the child out as being his own, that he provided for some or all of the child's needs, or that in general the father's behavior evidenced a genuine concern for the child. The most persuasive evidence for establishing a bona fide parent/child relationship is documentary evidence which was contemporaneous with the events in question. Such evidence may include, but is not limited to: money order receipts or canceled checks showing the father's financial support of the beneficiary; the father's income tax returns; the father's medical or insurance records which include the beneficiary as a dependent; school records for the beneficiary; correspondence between the parties; or notarized affidavits of friends, neighbors, school officials, or other associates knowledgeable about the relationship.

(iv) *Primary evidence for stepsiblings.* If the petition is submitted on behalf of a brother or sister having a common father, the relationship of both the petitioner and the beneficiary to the father must be established as required in paragraphs (g)(2)(ii) and (g)(2)(iii) of this section. If the petitioner and beneficiary are stepsiblings through the marriages of their common father to different mothers, the marriage certificates of the parents and evidence of the termination of any prior marriages of the parents must be submitted.

(3) *Decision on and disposition of petition.* The approved petition will be forwarded to the Department of State's Processing Center. If the beneficiary is in the United States and is eligible for adjustment of status under section 245 of the Act, the approved petition will be retained by the Service. If the petition is denied, the petitioner will be notified of the reasons for the denial and of the right to appeal in accordance with the provisions of 8 CFR 3.3.

(4) *Derivative beneficiaries.* A spouse or a child accompanying or following to join a principal alien beneficiary under this section may be accorded the same preference and priority date as the principal alien without the necessity of a separate petition.

(5) *Name change.* If the name of the petitioner, the beneficiary, or both has been legally changed, evidence showing the name change (such as a marriage certificate, a legal document showing the name change, or other similar evidence) must accompany the petition.

(h) *Validity of approved petitions*—(1) *General.* Unless terminated pursuant to section 203(g) of the Act or revoked pursuant to part 205 of this chapter, the approval of a petition to classify an alien as a preference immigrant under paragraphs (a)(1), (a)(2), (a)(3), or (a)(4) of section 203 of the Act, or as an immediate relative under section 201(b) of the Act, shall remain valid for the duration of the relationship to the petitioner and of the petitioner's status as established in the petition.

(2) *Subsequent petition by same petitioner for same beneficiary.* When a visa petition has been approved, and subsequently a new petition by the same petitioner is approved for the same preference classification on behalf of the same beneficiary, the latter approval shall be regarded as a reaffirmation or reinstatement of the validity of the original petition, except when the original petition has been terminated pursuant to section 203(g) of the Act or revoked pursuant to part 205 of this chapter, or when an immigrant visa has been issued to the beneficiary as a result of the petition approval. A self-petition filed under section 204(a)(1)(A)(iii), 204(a)(1)(A)(iv), 204(a)(1)(B)(ii), 204(a)(1)(B)(iii) of the Act based on the relationship to an abusive citizen or lawful permanent resident of the United States will not be regarded as a reaffirmation or reinstatement of a petition previously filed by the abuser. A self-petitioner who has been the beneficiary of a visa petition filed by the abuser to accord the self-petitioner immigrant classification as his or her spouse or child, however, will be allowed to transfer the visa petition's priority date to the self-petition. The visa petition's priority date may be assigned to the self-petition without regard to the current validity of the visa petition. The burden of proof to establish the existence of and the filing date of the visa petition lies with the self-petitioner, although the Service will attempt to verify a claimed filing through a search of the Service's computerized records or other records deemed appropriate by the adjudicating officer. A new self-petition filed under section 204(a)(1)(A)(iii), 204(a)(1)(A)(iv), 204(a)(1)(B)(ii), or 204(a)(1)(B)(iii) of the Act will not be regarded as a reaffirmation or reinstatement of the original self-petition unless the prior and the subsequent self-petitions are based on the relationship to the same abusive citizen or lawful permanent resident of the United States.

(i) *Automatic conversion of preference classification*—(1) *By change in beneficiary's marital status.* (i) A currently valid petition previously approved to classify the beneficiary as the unmarried son or daughter of a United States citizen under section 203(a)(1) of the Act shall be regarded as having been approved for preference status under section 203(a)(3) of the Act as of the date the beneficiary marries. The beneficiary's priority date is the same as the date the petition for classification under section 203(a)(1) of the Act was properly filed.

(ii) A currently valid petition previously approved to classify a child of a United States citizen as an immediate relative under section 201(b) of the Act shall be regarded as having been approved for preference status under section 203(a)(3) of the Act as of the date the beneficiary marries. The beneficiary's priority date is the same as the date the petition for 201(b) classification was properly filed.

(iii) A currently valid petition classifying the married son or married daughter of a United States citizen for preference status under section 203(a)(3) of the Act shall, upon legal termination of the beneficiary's marriage, be regarded as having been approved under section 203(a)(1) of the Act if the beneficiary is over twenty-one years of age. The beneficiary's priority date is the same as the date the petition for classification under section 203(a)(3) of the Act was properly filed. If the beneficiary is under twenty-one years of age, the petition shall be regarded as having been approved for classification as an immediate relative under section 201(b) of the Act as of the date the petition for classification under section 203(a)(3) of the Act was properly filed.

(iv) A currently valid visa petition previously approved to classify the beneficiary as an immediate relative as the spouse of a United States citizen must be regarded, upon the death of the petitioner, as having been approved as a Form I–360, Petition for Amerasian, Widow(er) or Special Immigrant for classification under paragraph (b) of this section, if, on the date of the petitioner's death, the beneficiary satisfies the requirements of paragraph (b)(1) of this section. If the petitioner dies before the petition is approved, but, on the date of the petitioner's death, the beneficiary satisfies the requirements of paragraph (b)(1) of this section, then the petition shall be adjudicated as if it had been filed as a Form I–360, Petition for Amerasian, Widow(er) or Special Immigrant under paragraph (b) of this section.

(2) *By the beneficiary's attainment of the age of twenty-one years.* A currently valid petition classifying the child of a United States citizen as an immediate relative under section 201(b) of the Act shall be regarded as having been approved for preference status under section 203(a)(1) of the Act as of the beneficiary's twenty-first birthday. The beneficiary's priority date is the same as the date the petition for section 201(b) classification was filed.

(3) *By the petitioner's naturalization.* Effective upon the date of naturalization of a petitioner who had been lawfully admitted for permanent residence, a currently valid petition according preference status under section 203(a)(2) of the Act to the petitioner's spouse and unmarried children under twenty-one years of age shall be regarded as having been approved for immediate relative status under section 201(b) of the Act. Similarly, a currently valid petition according preference status under section 203(a)(2) of the Act for the unmarried son or daughter over twenty-one years of age shall be regarded as having been approved under section 203(a)(1) of the Act. In any case of conversion to classification under section 203(a)(1) of the Act, the beneficiary's priority date is the same as the date the petition for classification under section 203(a)(2) of the Act was properly filed. A self-petition filed under section 204(a)(1)(B)(ii) or 204(a)(1)(B)(iii) of the Act based on the relationship to an abusive lawful permanent resident of the United States for classification under section 203(a)(2) of the Act will not be affected by the abuser's naturalization and will not be automatically converted to a petition for immediate relative classification.

[57 FR 41057, Sept. 9, 1992, as amended at 60 FR 34090, June 30, 1995; 60 FR 38948, July 31, 1995; 61 FR 13073, 13075, 13077, Mar. 26, 1996; 62 FR 10336, Mar. 6, 1997; 62 FR 60771, Nov. 13, 1997; 71 FR 35749, June 21, 2006; 72 FR 19107, Apr. 17, 2007; 72 FR 56853, Oct. 4, 2007]

§ 204.3 Orphan cases under section 101(b)(1)(F) of the Act (non-Convention cases).

(a) This section addresses the immigration classification of alien orphans as provided for in section 101(b)(1)(F) of the Act.

(1) Except as provided in paragraph (a)(2) of this section, a child who meets the definition of orphan contained in section 101(b)(1)(F) of the Act is eligible for classification as the immediate relative of a U.S. citizen if:

(i) The U.S. citizen seeking the child's immigration can document that the citizen (and his or her spouse, if any) are capable of providing, and will provide, proper care for an alien orphan; and

(ii) The child is an orphan under section 101(b)(1)(F) of the Act.

A U.S. citizen may submit the documentation necessary for each of these determinations separately or at one time, depending on when the orphan is identified.

(2) Form I–600A or Form I–600 may not be filed under this section on or after the Convention effective date, as defined in 8 CFR 204.301, on behalf of a child who is habitually resident in a Convention country, as defined in 8 CFR 204.301. On or after the Convention effective date, USCIS may approve a Form I–600 on behalf of a child who is habitually resident in a Convention country only if the Form I–600A or Form I–600 was filed before the Convention effective date.

(b) *Definitions.* As used in this section, the term:

Abandonment by both parents means that the parents have willfully forsaken all parental rights, obligations, and claims to the child, as well as all control over and possession of the child, without intending to transfer, or without transferring, these rights to any specific person(s). Abandonment must include not only the intention to surrender all parental rights, obligations, and claims to the child, and control over and possession of the child, but also the actual act of surrending such rights, obligations, claims, control, and possession. A relinquishment or release by the parents to the prospective adoptive parents or for a specific adoption does not constitute abandonment. Similarly, the relinquishment or release of the child by the parents to a third party for custodial care in anticipation of, or preparation for, adoption does not constitute abandonment unless the third party (such as a governmental agency, a court of competent jurisdiction, an adoption agency, or an orphanage) is authorized under the child welfare laws of the foreign-sending country to act in such a capacity. A child who is placed temporarily in an orphanage shall not be considered to be abandoned if the parents express an intention to retrieve the child, are contributing or attempting to contribute to the support of the child, or otherwise exhibit ongoing parental interest in the child. A child who has been given unconditionally to an orphanage shall be considered to be abandoned.

Adult member of the prospective adoptive parents' household means an individual, other than a prospective adoptive parent, over the age of 18 whose principal or only residence is the home of the prospective adoptive parents. This definition excludes any child of the prospective adoptive parents, whose principal or only residence is the home of the prospective adoptive parents, who reaches his or her eighteenth birthday after the prospective adoptive parents have filed the advanced processing application (or the advanced processing application concurrently with the orphan petition) unless the director has an articulable and substantive reason for requiring an evaluation by a home study preparer and/or fingerprint check.

Advanced processing application means Form I–600A (Application for Advanced Processing of Orphan Petition) completed in accordance with the form's instructions and submitted with the required supporting documentation and the fee as required in 8 CFR 103.7(b)(1). The application must be signed in accordance with the form's instructions by the married petitioner and spouse, or by the unmarried petitioner.

Application is synonymous with *advanced processing application.*

Competent authority means a court or governmental agency of a foreign-sending country having jurisdiction and authority to make decisions in matters of child welfare, including adoption.

Desertion by both parents means that the parents have willfully forsaken their child and have refused to carry out their parental rights and obligations and that, as a result, the child has become a ward of a competent authority in accordance with the laws of the foreign-sending country.

Disappearance of both parents means that both parents have unaccountably or inexplicably passed out of the child's life, their whereabouts are unknown, there is no reasonable hope of their reappearance, and there has been a reasonable effort to locate them as determined by a competent authority in accordance with the laws of the foreign-sending country.

Foreign-sending country means the country of the orphan's citizenship, or if he or she is not permanently residing in the country of citizenship, the country of the orphan's habitual residence. This excludes a country to which the orphan travels temporarily, or to which he or she travels either as a prelude to, or in conjunction with, his or her adoption and/or immigration to the United States.

Home study preparer means any party licensed or otherwise authorized under the law of the State of the orphan's proposed residence to conduct the research and preparation for a home study, including the required personal interview(s). This term includes a public agency with authority under that State's law in adoption matters, public or private adoption agencies licensed or otherwise authorized by the laws of that State to place children for adoption, and organizations or individuals licensed or otherwise authorized to conduct the research and preparation for a home study, including the required personal interview(s), under the laws of the State of the orphan's proposed residence. In the case of an orphan whose adoption has been finalized abroad and whose adoptive parents reside abroad, the home study preparer includes any party licensed or otherwise authorized to conduct home studies under the law of any State of the United States, or any party licensed or otherwise authorized by the foreign country's adoption authorities to conduct home studies under the laws of the foreign country.

Incapable of providing proper care means that a sole or surviving parent is unable to provide for the child's basic needs, consistent with the local standards of the *foreign sending country*.

Loss from both parents means the involuntary severance or detachment of the child from the parents in a permanent manner such as that caused by a natural disaster, civil unrest, or other calamitous event beyond the control of the parents, as verified by a competent authority in accordance with the laws of the foreign sending country.

Orphan petition means Form I–600 (Petition to Classify Orphan as an Immediate Relative). The petition must be completed in accordance with the form's instructions and submitted with the required supporting documentation and, if there is not an advanced processing application approved within the previous 18 months or pending, the fee as required in 8 CFR 103.7(b)(1). The petition must be signed in accordance with the form's instructions by the married petitioner and spouse, or the unmarried petitioner.

Overseas site means the Department of State immigrant visa-issuing post having jurisdiction over the orphan's residence, or in foreign countries in which the Services has an office or offices, the Service office having jurisdiction over the orphan's residence.

Petition is synonymous with *orphan petition*.

Petitioner means a married United States citizen of any age, or an unmarried United States citizen who is at least 24 years old at the time he or she files the advanced processing application and at least 25 years old at the time he or she files the orphan petition. In the case of a married couple, both of whom are United States citizens, either party may be the petitioner.

Prospective adoptive parents means a married United States citizen of any age and his or her spouse of any age, or an unmarried United States citizen who is at least 24 years old at the time he or she files the advanced processing application and at least 25 years old at the time he or she files the orphan petition. The spouse of the United States citizen may be a citizen or an alien. An alien spouse must be in lawful immigration status if residing in the United States.

Separation from both parents means the involuntary severance of the child from his or her parents by action of a competent authority for good cause and in accordance with the laws of the foreign-sending country. The parents must have been properly notified and granted the opportunity to contest such action. The termination of all parental rights and obligations must be permanent and unconditional.

Sole parent means the mother when it is established that the child is illegitimate and has not acquired a parent within the meaning of section 101(b)(2) of the Act. An illegitimate child shall be considered to have a sole parent if his or her father has severed all parental ties, rights, duties, and obligations to the child, or if his or her father has, in writing, irrevocably released the child for emigration and adoption. This definition is not applicable to children born in countries which make no distinction between a child born in or out of wedlock, since all such children are considered to be legitimate. In all cases, a sole parent must be *incapable of providing proper care* as that term is defined in this section.

Surviving parent means the child's living parent when the child's other parent is dead, and the child has not acquired another parent within the meaning of section 101(b)(2) of the Act. In all cases, a surviving parent must be *incapable of providing proper care* as that term is defined in this section.

(c) *Supporting documentation for an advanced processing application.* The prospective adoptive parents may file an advanced processing application before an orphan is identified in order to secure the necessary clearance to file the orphan petition. Any document not in the English language must be accompanied by a certified English translation.

(1) *Required supporting documentation that must accompany the advanced processing application.* The following supporting documentation must accompany an advanced processing application at the time of filing:

(i) Evidence of the petitioner's United States citizenship as set forth in § 204.1(g) and, if the petitioner is married and the married couple is residing in the United States, evidence of the spouse's United States citizenship or lawful immigration status;

(ii) A copy of the petitioner's marriage certificate to his or her spouse, if the petitioner is currently married;

(iii) Evidence of legal termination of all previous marriages for the petitioner and/or spouse, if previously married; and

(iv) Evidence of compliance with preadoption requirements, if any, of the State of the orphan's proposed residence in cases where it is known that there will be no adoption abroad, or that both members of the married prospective adoptive couple or the unmarried prospective adoptive parent will not personally see the child prior to, or during, the adoption abroad, and/or that the adoption abroad will not be full and final. Any preadoption requirements which cannot be met at the time the advanced processing application is filed because of operation of State law must be noted and explained when the application is filed. Preadoption requirements must be met at the time the petition is filed, except for those which cannot be met until the orphan arrives in the United States.

(2) *Home study.* The home study must comply with the requirements contained in paragraph (e) of this section. If the home study is not submitted when the advanced processing application is filed, it must be submitted within one year of the filing date of the advanced processing application, or the application will be denied pursuant to paragraph (h)(5) of this section.

(3) After receipt of a properly filed advanced processing application, USCIS will fingerprint each member of the married prospective adoptive couple or the unmarried prospective adoptive parent, as prescribed in 8 CFR 103.16. USCIS will also fingerprint each additional adult member of the prospective adoptive parents' household, as prescribed in 8 CFR 103.16. USCIS may waive the requirement that each

additional adult member of the prospective adoptive parents' household be fingerprinted when it determines that such adult is physically unable to be fingerprinted because of age or medical condition.

(d) *Supporting documentation for a petition for an identified orphan.* Any document not in the English language must be accompanied by a certified English translation. If an orphan has been identified for adoption and the advanced processing application is pending, the prospective adoptive parents may file the orphan petition at the Service office where the application is pending. The prospective adoptive parents who have an approved advanced processing application must file an orphan petition and all supporting documents within eighteen months of the date of the approval of the advanced processing application. If the prospective adoptive parents fail to file the orphan petition within the eighteen-month period, the advanced processing application shall be deemed abandoned pursuant to paragraph (h)(7) of this section. If the prospective adoptive parents file the orphan petition after the eighteen-month period, the petition shall be denied pursuant to paragraph (h)(13) of this section. Prospective adoptive parents who do not have an advanced processing application approved or pending may file the application and petition concurrently on one Form I–600 if they have identified an orphan for adoption. An orphan petition must be accompanied by full documentation as follows:

(1) *Filing an orphan petition after the advanced processing application has been approved.* The following supporting documentation must accompany an orphan petition filed after approval of the advanced processing application:

(i) Evidence of approval of the advanced processing application;

(ii) The orphan's birth certificate, or if such a certificate is not available, an explanation together with other proof of identity and age;

(iii) Evidence that the child is an orphan as appropriate to the case:

(A) Evidence that the orphan has been abandoned or deserted by, separated or lost from both parents, or that both parents have disappeared as those terms are defined in paragraph (b) of this section; or

(B) The death certificate(s) of the orphan's parent(s), if applicable;

(C) If the orphan has only a sole or surviving parent, as defined in paragraph (b) of this section, evidence of this fact and evidence that the sole or surviving parent is incapable of providing for the orphan's care and has irrevocably released the orphan for emigration and adoption; and

(iv) Evidence of adoption abroad or that the prospective adoptive parents have, or a person or entity working on their behalf has, custody of the orphan for emigration and adoption in accordance with the laws of the foreign-sending country:

(A) A legible, certified copy of the adoption decree, if the orphan has been the subject of a full and final adoption abroad, and evidence that the unmarried petitioner, or married petitioner and spouse, saw the orphan prior to or during the adoption proceeding abroad; or

(B) If the orphan is to be adopted in the United States because there was no adoption abroad, or the unmarried petitioner, or married petitioner and spouse, did not personally see the orphan prior to or during the adoption proceeding abroad, and/or the adoption abroad was not full and final:

(*1*) Evidence that the prospective adoptive parents have, or a person or entity working on their behalf has, secured custody of the orphan in accordance with the laws of the foreign-sending country;

(*2*) An irrevocable release of the orphan for emigration and adoption from the person, organization, or competent authority which had the immediately previous legal custody or control over the orphan if the adoption was not full and final under the laws of the foreign-sending country;

(*3*) Evidence of compliance with all preadoption requirements, if any, of the State of the orphan's proposed residence. (Any such requirements that cannot be complied with prior to the orphan's arrival in the United States because of State law must be noted and explained); and

(*4*) Evidence that the State of the orphan's proposed residence allows readoption or provides for judicial recognition of the adoption abroad if there was an adoption abroad which does not meet statutory requirements pursuant to section 101(b)(1)(F) of the Act, because the unmarried petitioner, or married petitioner *and* spouse, did not personally see the orphan prior to or during the adoption proceeding abroad, and/or the adoption abroad was not full and final.

(2) *Filing an orphan petition while the advanced processing application is pending.* An orphan petition filed while an advanced processing application is pending must be filed at the Service office where the application is pending. The following supporting documentation must accompany an orphan petition filed while the advanced processing application is pending:

(i) A photocopy of the fee receipt relating to the advanced processing application, or if not available, other evidence that the advanced processing application has been filed, such as a statement including the date when the application was filed;

(ii) The home study, if not already submitted; and

(iii) The supporting documentation for an orphan petition required in paragraph (d)(1) of this section, except for paragraph (d)(1)(i) of this section.

(3) *Filing an orphan petition concurrently with the advanced processing application.* A petition filed concurrently with the advanced processing application must be submitted on Form I–600, completed and signed in accordance with the form's instructions. (Under this concurrent procedure, Form I–600 serves as both the Forms I–600A and I–600, and the prospective adoptive parents should not file a separate Form I–600A). The following supporting documentation must accompany a petition filed concurrently with the application under this provision:

(i) The supporting documentation for an advanced processing application required in paragraph (c) of this section; and

(ii) The supporting documentation for an orphan petition required in paragraph (d)(1) of this section, except for paragraph (d)(1)(i) of this section.

(e) *Home study requirements.* For immigration purposes, a home study is a process for screening and preparing prospective adoptive parents who are interested in adopting an orphan from another country. The home study should be tailored to the particular situation of the prospective adoptive parents: for example, a family which previously has adopted children will require different preparation than a family that has no adopted children. If there are any additional adult members of the prospective adoptive parents' household, the home study must address this fact. The home study preparer must interview any additional adult member of the prospective adoptive parents' household and assess him or her in light of the requirements of paragraphs (e)(1), (e)(2)(i), (iii), (iv), and (v) of this section. A home study must be conducted by a home study preparer, as defined in paragraph (b) of this section. The home study, or the most recent update to the home study, must not be more than six months old at the time the home study is submitted to the Service. Only one copy of the home study must be submitted to the Service. Ordinarily, a home study (or a home study and update as discussed above) will not have to be updated after it has been submitted to the Service unless there is a significant change in the household of the prospective adoptive parents such as a change in residence, marital status, criminal history, financial resources, and/or the addition of one or more children or other dependents to the family prior to the orphan's immigration into the United States. In addition to meeting any State, professional, or agency requirements, a home study must include the following:

(1) *Personal interview(s) and home visit(s).* The home study preparer must conduct at least one interview in person, and at least one home visit, with the prospective adoptive couple or the unmarried prospective adoptive parent. Each additional adult member of the prospective adoptive parents' household must also be interviewed in person at least once. The home study report must state the number of such interviews and visits, and must specify any other contacts with the prospective

adoptive parents and any adult member of the prospective adoptive parents' household.

(2) *Assessment of the capabilities of the prospective adoptive parents to properly parent the orphan.* The home study must include a discussion of the following areas:

(i) *Assessment of the physical, mental, and emotional capabilities of the prospective adoptive parents to properly parent the orphan.* The home study preparer must make an initial assessment of how the physical, mental, and emotional health of the prospective adoptive parents would affect their ability to properly care for the prospective orphan. If the home study preparer determines that there are areas beyond his or her expertise which need to be addressed, he or she shall refer the prospective adoptive parents to an appropriate licensed professional, such as a physician, psychiatrist, clinical psychologist, or clinical social worker for an evaluation. Some problems may not necessarily disqualify applicants. For example, certain physical limitations may indicate which categories of children may be most appropriately placed with certain prospective adoptive parents. Certain mental and emotional health problems may be successfully treated. The home study must include the home study preparer's assessment of any such potential problem areas, a copy of any outside evaluation(s), and the home study preparer's recommended restrictions, if any, on the characteristics of the child to be placed in the home. Additionally, the home study preparer must apply the requirements of this paragraph to each adult member of the prospective adoptive parents' household.

(ii) *Assessment of the finances of the prospective adoptive parents.* The financial assessment must include a description of the income, financial resources, debts, and expenses of the prospective adoptive parents. A statement concerning the evidence that was considered to verify the source and amount of income and financial resources must be included. Any income designated for the support of one or more children in the care and custody of the prospective adoptive parents, such as funds for foster care, or any income designated for the support of another member of the household must not be counted towards the financial resources available for the support of a prospective orphan. The Service will not routinely require a detailed financial statement or supporting financial documents. However, should the need arise, the Service reserves the right to ask for such detailed documentation.

(iii) *History of abuse and/or violence*—(A) *Screening for abuse and violence*—(*1*) *Checking available child abuse registries.* The home study preparer must ensure that a check of each prospective adoptive parent and each adult member of the prospective adoptive parents' household has been made with available child abuse registries and must include in the home study the results of the checks including, if applicable, a report that no record was found to exist. Depending on the access allowed by the state of proposed residence of the orphan, the home study preparer must take one of the following courses of action:

(*i*) If the home study preparer is allowed access to information from the child abuse registries, he or she shall make the appropriate checks for each of the prospective adoptive parents and for each adult member of the prospective adoptive parents' household;

(*ii*) If the State requires the home study preparer to secure permission from each of the prospective adoptive parents and for each adult member of the prospective adoptive parents' household before gaining access to information in such registries, the home study preparer must secure such permission from those individuals, and make the appropriate checks;

(*iii*) If the State will only release information directly to each of the prospective adoptive parents and directly to the adult member of the prospective adoptive parents' household, those individuals must secure such information and provide it to the home study preparer. The home study preparer must include the results of these checks in the home study;

(*iv*) If the State will not release information to either the home study preparer or the prospective adoptive parents and the adult members of the prospective adoptive parents' household, this must be noted in the home study; or

(*v*) If the State does not have a child abuse registry, this must be noted in the home study.

(*2*) *Inquiring about abuse and violence.* The home study preparer must ask each prospective adoptive parent whether he or she has a history of substance abuse, sexual or child abuse, or domestic violence, even if it did not result in an arrest or conviction. The home study preparer must include each prospective adoptive parent's response to the questions regarding abuse and violence. Additionally, the home study preparer must apply the requirements of this paragraph to each adult member of the prospective adoptive parents' household.

(B) *Information concerning history of abuse and/or violence.* If the petitioner and/or spouse, if married, disclose(s) any history of abuse and/or violence as set forth in paragraph (e)(2)(iii)(A) of this section, or if, in the absence of such disclosure, the home study preparer becomes aware of any of the foregoing, the home study report must contain an evaluation of the suitability of the home for adoptive placement of an orphan in light of this history. This evaluation must include information concerning all arrests or convictions or history of substance abuse, sexual or child abuse, and/or domestic violence and the date of each occurrence. A certified copy of the documentation showing the final disposition of each incident, which resulted in arrest, indictment, conviction, and/or any other judicial or administrative action, must accompany the home study. Additionally, the prospective adoptive parent must submit a signed statement giving details including mitigating circumstances, if any, about each incident. The home study preparer must apply the requirements of this paragraph to each adult member of the prospective adoptive parents' household.

(C) *Evidence of rehabilitation.* If a prospective adoptive parent has a history of substance abuse, sexual or child abuse, and/or domestic violence, the home study preparer may, nevertheless, make a favorable finding if the prospective adoptive parent has demonstrated appropriate rehabilitation. In such a case, a discussion of such rehabilitation which demonstrates that the prospective adoptive parent is and will be able to provide proper care for the orphan must be included in the home study. Evidence of rehabilitation may include an evaluation of the seriousness of the arrest(s), conviction(s), or history of abuse, the number of such incidents, the length of time since the last incident, and any type of counseling or rehabilitation programs which have been successfully completed. Evidence of rehabilitation may also be provided by an appropriate licensed professional, such as a psychiatrist, clinical psychologist, or clinical social worker. The home study report must include all facts and circumstances which the home study preparer has considered, as well as the preparer's reasons for a favorable decision regarding the prospective adoptive parent. Additionally, if any adult member of the prospective adoptive parents' household has a history of substance abuse, sexual or child abuse, and/or domestic violence, the home study preparer must apply the requirements of this paragraph to that adult member of the prospective adoptive parents' household.

(D) *Failure to disclose or cooperate.* Failure to disclose an arrest, conviction, or history of substance abuse, sexual or child abuse, and/or domestic violence by the prospective adoptive parents or an adult member of the prospective adoptive parents' household to the home study preparer and to the Service, may result in the denial of the advanced processing application or, if applicable, the application and orphan petition, pursuant to paragraph (h)(4) of this section. Failure by the prospective adoptive parents or an adult member of the prospective adoptive parents' household to cooperate in having available child abuse registries in accordance with paragraphs (e)(2)(iii)(A)(*1*) and (e)(2)(iii)(A)(*1*)(*i*) through (e)(2)(iii)(A)(*1*)(*iii*) of this section will result in the denial of the advanced processing application or, if applicable, the application and orphan petition, pursuant to paragraph (h)(4) of this section.

(iv) *Previous rejection for adoption or prior unfavorable home study.* The home study preparer must ask each prospective adoptive parent whether he or she previously has been rejected as a prospective adoptive parent or has been the subject of an unfavorable home study, and must include each prospective adoptive parent's response to this question in the home study report. If a prospective adoptive parent previously has been rejected or found to be unsuitable, the reasons for such a finding must be set forth as well as the reason(s) why he or she is not being favorably considered as a prospective adoptive parent. A copy of each previous rejection and/or unfavorable home study must be attached to the favorable home study. Additionally, the home study preparer must apply the requirements of this paragraph to each adult member of the prospective adoptive parents' household.

(v) *Criminal history.* The prospective adoptive parents and the adult members of the prospective adoptive parents' household are expected to disclose to the home study preparer and the Service any history of arrest and/or conviction early in the advanced processing procedure. Failure to do so may result in denial pursuant to paragraph (h)(4) of this section or in delays. Early disclosure provides the prospective adoptive parents with the best opportunity to gather and present evidence, and it gives the home study preparer and the Service the opportunity to properly evaluate the criminal record in light of such evidence. When such information is not presented early in the process, it comes to light when the fingerprint checks are received by the Service. By that time, the prospective adoptive parents are usually well into preadoption proceedings of identifying a child and may even have firm travel plans. At times, the travel plans have to be rescheduled while the issues raised by the criminal record are addressed. It is in the best interests of all parties to have any criminal records disclosed and resolved early in the process.

(3) *Living accommodations.* The home study must include a detailed description of the living accommodations where the prospective adoptive parents currently reside. If the prospective adoptive parents are planning to move, the home study must include a description of the living accommodations where the child will reside with the prospective adoptive parents, if known. If the prospective adoptive parents are residing abroad at the time of the home study, the home study must include a description of the living accommodations where the child will reside in the United States with the prospective adoptive parents, if known. Each description must include an assessment of the suitability of accommodations for a child and a determination whether such space meets applicable State requirements, if any.

(4) *Handicapped or special needs orphan.* A home study conducted in conjunction with the proposed adoption of a special needs or handicapped orphan must contain a discussion of the prospective adoptive parents' preparation, willingness, and ability to provide proper care for such an orphan.

(5) *Summary of the counseling given and plans for post-placement counseling.* The home study must include a summary of the counseling given to prepare the prospective adoptive parents for an international adoption and any plans for post-placement counseling. Such preadoption counseling must include a discussion of the processing, expenses, difficulties, and delays associated with international adoptions.

(6) *Specific approval of the prospective adoptive parents for adoption.* If the home study preparer's findings are favorable, the home study must contain his or her specific approval of the prospective adoptive parents for adoption and a discussion of the reasons for such approval. The home study must include the number of orphans which the prospective adoptive parents may adopt. The home study must state whether there are any specific restrictions to the adoption such as nationality, age, or gender of the orphan. If the home study preparer has approved the prospective parents for a handicapped or special needs adoption, this fact must be clearly stated.

(7) *Home study preparer's certification and statement of authority to conduct home studies.* The home study must include a statement in which the home study preparer certifies that he or she is licensed or otherwise authorized by

the State of the orphan's proposed residence to research and prepare home studies. In the case of an orphan whose adoption was finalized abroad and whose adoptive parents reside abroad, the home study preparer must certify that he or she is licensed or otherwise authorized to conduct home studies under the law of any State of the United States, or authorized by the adoption authorities of the foreign country to conduct home studies under the laws of the foreign country. In every case, this statement must cite the State or country under whose authority the home study preparer is licensed or authorized, the specific law or regulation authorizing the preparer to conduct home studies, the license number, if any, and the expiration date, if any, of this authorization or license.

(8) *Review of home study.* If the prospective adoptive parents reside in a State which requires the State to review the home study, such a review must occur and be documented before the home study is submitted to the Service. If the prospective adoptive parents reside abroad, an appropriate public or private adoption agency licensed, or otherwise authorized, by any State of the United States to place children for adoption, must review and favorably recommend the home study before it is submitted to the Service.

(9) *Home study updates and amendments*—(i) *Updates.* If the home study is more than six months old at the time it would be submitted to the Service, the prospective adoptive parents must ensure that it is updated by a home study preparer before it is submitted to the Service. Each update must include screening in accordance with paragraphs (e)(2)(iii) (A) and (B) of this section.

(ii) *Amendments.* If there have been any significant changes, such as a change in the residence of the prospective adoptive parents, marital status, criminal history, financial resources, and/or the addition of one or more children or other dependents to the family, the prospective adoptive parents must ensure that the home study is amended by a home study preparer to reflect any such changes. If the orphan's proposed State of residence has changed, the home study amendment must contain a recommendation in accordance with paragraph (e)(8) of this section, if required by State law. Any preadoption requirements of the new State must be complied with in the case of an orphan coming to the United States to be adopted.

(10) *"Grandfather" provision for home study.* A home study properly completed in conformance with the regulations in force prior to September 30, 1994, shall be considered acceptable if submitted to the Service within 90 days of September 30, 1994. Any such home study accepted under this "grandfather" provision must include screening in accordance with paragraphs (e)(2)(iii) (A) and (B) of this section. Additionally, any such home study submitted under this "grandfather" provision which is more than six months old at the time of its submission must be amended or updated pursuant to the requirements of paragraph (e)(9) of this section.

(f) *State preadoption requirements*—(1) *General.* Many States have preadoption requirements which, under the Act, must be complied with in every case in which a child is coming to such a State as an orphan to be adopted in the United States.

(2) *Child coming to be adopted in the United States.* An orphan is coming to be adopted in the United States if he or she will not be or has not been adopted abroad, or if the unmarried petitioner or both the married petitioner and spouse did not or will not personally see the orphan prior to or during the adoption proceeding abroad, and/or if the adoption abroad will not be, or was not, full and final. If the prospective adoptive parents reside in a State with preadoption requirements and they plan to have the child come to the United States for adoption, they must submit evidence of compliance with the State's preadoption requirements to the Service. Any preadoption requirements which by operation of State law cannot be met before filing the advanced processing application must be noted. Such requirements must be met prior to filing the petition, except for those which cannot be met by operation of State law until the orphan is physically in the United

States. Those requirements which cannot be met until the orphan is physically present in the United States must be noted.

(3) *Special circumstances.* If both members of the prospective adoptive couple or the unmarried prospective adoptive parent intend to travel abroad to see the child prior to or during the adoption, the Act permits the application and/or petition, if otherwise approvable, to be approved without preadoption requirements having been met. However, if plans change and both members of the prospective adoptive couple or the unmarried prospective adoptive parent fail to see the child prior to or during the adoption, then preadoption requirements must be met before the immigrant visa can be issued, except for those preadoption requirements that cannot be met until the child is physically in the United States because of operation of State law.

(4) *Evidence of compliance.* In every case where compliance with preadoption requirements is required, the evidence of compliance must be in accordance with applicable State law, regulation, and procedure.

(g) *Where to file.* Form I–600, Petition to Classify Orphan as an Immediate Relative, and Form I–600A, Application for Advanced Processing of Orphan Petition, must be filed in accordance with the instructions on the form.

(h) *Adjudication and decision*—(1) *"Grandfather" provision for advanced processing application and/or orphan petition.* All applications and petitions filed under prior regulations which are filed before and are still pending on September 30, 1994, shall be processed and adjudicated under the prior regulations.

(2) *Director's responsibility to make an independent decision in an advanced processing application.* No advanced processing application shall be approved unless the director is satisfied that proper care will be provided for the orphan. If the director has reason to believe that a favorable home study, or update, or both are based on an inadequate or erroneous evaluation of all the facts, he or she shall attempt to resolve the issue with the home study preparer, the agency making the recommendation pursuant to paragraph (e)(8) of this section, if any, and the prospective adoptive parents. If such consultations are unsatisfactory, the director may request a review and opinion from the appropriate State Government authorities.

(3) *Advanced processing application approved.* (i) If the advanced processing application is approved, the prospective adoptive parents shall be advised in writing. The application and supporting documents shall be forwarded to the overseas site where the orphan resides. Additionally, if the petitioner advises the director that he or she intends to travel abroad to file the petition, telegraphic notification shall be sent overseas as detailed in paragraph (j)(1) of this section. The approved application shall be valid for 18 months from its approval date, unless the approval period is extended as provided in paragraph (h)(3)(ii) of this section. During this time, the prospective adoptive parents may file an orphan petition for one orphan without fee. If approved in the home study for more than one orphan, the prospective adoptive parents may file a petition for each of the additional children, to the maximum number approved. If the orphans are siblings, no additional fee is required. If the orphans are not siblings, an additional fee is required for each orphan beyond the first orphan. Approval of an advanced processing application does not guarantee that the orphan petition will be approved.

(ii) If the USCIS Director, or an officer designated by the USCIS Director, determines that the ability of a prospective adoptive parent to timely file a petition has been adversely affected by the outbreak of Severe Acute Respiratory Syndrome (SARS) in a foreign country, such Director or designated officer may extend the validity period of the approval of the advance processing request, either in an individual case or for a class of cases. An extension of the validity of the advance processing request may be subject to such conditions as the USCIS Director, or officer designated by the USCIS Director may establish.

(4) *Advanced processing application denied for failure to disclose history of abuse and/or violence, or for failure to*

disclose a criminal history, or for failure to cooperate in checking child abuse registries. Failure to disclose an arrest, conviction, or history of substance abuse, sexual or child abuse, and/or domestic violence, or a criminal history to the home study preparer and to the Service in accordance with paragraphs (e)(2)(iii) (A) and (B) and (e)(2)(v) of this section may result in the denial of the advanced processing application, or if applicable, the application and orphan petition filed concurrently. Failure by the prospective adoptive parents or an adult member of the prospective adoptive parents' household to cooperate in having available child abuse registries checked in accordance with paragraphs (e)(2)(iii)(A)(*1*) and (e)(2)(iii)(A)(*1*)(*i*) through (e)(2)(iii)(A)(*1*)(*iii*) of this section will result in the denial of the advanced processing application or, if applicable, the application and orphan petition filed concurrently. Any new application and/or petition filed within a year of such denial will also be denied.

(5) *Advanced processing denied for failure to submit home study.* If the home study is not submitted within one year of the filing date of the advanced processing application, the application shall be denied. This action shall be without prejudice to a new filing at any time with fee.

(6) *Advanced processing application otherwise denied.* If the director finds that the prospective adoptive parents have otherwise failed to establish eligibility, the applicable provisions of 8 CFR part 103 regarding a letter of intent to deny, if appropriate, and denial and notification of appeal rights shall govern.

(7) *Advanced processing application deemed abandoned for failure to file orphan petition within eighteen months of application's approval date.* If an orphan petition is not properly filed within eighteen months of the approval date of the advanced processing application, the application shall be deemed abandoned. Supporting documentation shall be returned to the prospective adoptive parents, except for documentation submitted by a third party which shall be returned to the third party, and documentation relating to the fingerprint checks. The director shall dispose of documentation relating to fingerprint checks in accordance with current policy. Such abandonment shall be without prejudice to a new filing at any time with fee.

(8) *Orphan petition approved by a stateside Service office.* If the orphan petition is approved by a stateside Service office, the prospective adoptive parents shall be advised in writing, telegraphic notification shall be sent to the immigrant visa-issuing post pursuant to paragraph (j)(3) of this section, and the petition and supporting documents shall be forwarded to the Department of State.

(9) *Orphan petition approved by an overseas Service office.* If the orphan petition is approved by an overseas Service office located in the country of the orphan's residence, the prospective adoptive parents shall be advised in writing, and the petition and supporting documents shall be forwarded to the immigrant visa-issuing post having jurisdiction for immigrant visa processing.

(10) *Orphan petition approved at an immigrant visa-issuing post.* If the orphan petition is approved at an immigrant visa-issuing post, the post shall initiate immigrant visa processing.

(11) *Orphan petition found to be "not readily approvable" by a consular officer.* If the consular officer adjudicating the orphan petition finds that it is "not readily approvable," he or she shall notify the prospective adoptive parents in his or her consular district and forward the petition, the supporting documents, the findings of the I–604 investigation conducted pursuant to paragraph (k)(1) of this section, and any other relating documentation to the overseas Service office having jurisdiction pursuant to § 100.4(b) of this chapter.

(12) *Orphan petition denied: petitioner fails to establish that the child is an orphan.* If the director finds that the petitioner has failed to establish that the child is an orphan who is eligible for the benefits sought, the applicable provisions of 8 CFR part 103 regarding a letter of intent to deny and notification of appeal rights shall govern.

(13) *Orphan petition denied: petitioner files orphan petition more than eighteen*

months after the approval of the advanced processing application. If the petitioner files the orphan petition more than eighteen months after the approval date of the advanced processing application, the petition shall be denied. This action shall be without prejudice to a new filing at any time with fee.

(14) *Revocation.* The approval of an advanced processing application or an orphan petition shall be automatically revoked in accordance with § 205.1 of this chapter, if an applicable reason exists. The approval of an advanced processing application or an orphan petition shall be revoked if the director becomes aware of information that would have resulted in denial had it been known at the time of adjudication. Such a revocation or any other revocation on notice shall be made in accordance with § 205.2 of this chapter.

(i) *Child-buying as a ground for denial.* An orphan petition must be denied under this section if the prospective adoptive parents or adoptive parent(s), or a person or entity working on their behalf, have given or will given money or other consideration either directly or indirectly to the child's parent(s), agent(s), other individual(s), or entity as payment for the child or as an inducement to release the child. Nothing in this paragraph shall be regarded as precluding reasonable payment for necessary activities such as administrative, court, legal, translation, and/or medical services related to the adoption proceedings.

(j) *Telegraphic notifications*—(1) *Telegraphic notification of approval of advanced processing application.* Unless conditions preclude normal telegraphic transmissions, whenever an advanced processing application is approved in the United States, the director shall send telegraphic notification of the approval to the overseas site if a prospective adoptive parent advises the director that the petitioner intends to travel abroad and file the orphan petition abroad.

(2) *Requesting a change in visa-issuing posts.* If a prospective adoptive parent is in the United States, he or she may request the director to transfer notification of the approved advanced processing application to another visa-issuing post. Such a request shall be made on Form I–824 (Application for Action on an Approved Application or Petition) with the appropriate fee. The director shall send a Visas 37 telegram to both the previously and the newly designated posts. The following shall be inserted after the last numbered standard entry. "To: [insert name of previously designated visa-issuing post or overseas Service office]. Pursuant to the petitioner's request, the Visas 37 cable previously sent to your post/office in this matter is hereby invalidated. The approval is being transferred to the other post/office addressed in this telegram. Please forward the approved advanced processing application to that destination." Prior to sending such a telegram, the director must ensure that the change in posts does not alter any conditions of the approval.

(3) *Telegraphic notification of approval of an orphan petition.* Unless conditions preclude normal telegraphic transmissions, whenever a petition is approved by a stateside Service office, the director shall send telegraphic notification of the approval to the immigrant visa-issuing post.

(k) *Other considerations*—(1) *I–604 investigations.* An I–604 investigation must be completed in every orphan case. The investigation must be completed by a consular officer except when the petition is properly filed at a Service office overseas, in which case it must be completed by a Service officer. An I–604 investigation shall be completed before a petition is adjudicated abroad. When a petition is adjudicated by a stateside Service office, the I–604 investigation is normally completed after the case has been forwarded to visa-issuing post abroad. However, in a case where the director of a stateside Service office adjudicating the petition has articulable concerns that can only be resolved through the I–604 investigation, he or she shall request the investigation prior to adjudication. In any case in which there are significant differences between the facts presented in the approved advanced processing application and/or orphan petition and the facts uncovered by the I–604 investigation, the overseas site may consult directly with the appropriate Service office. In any instance where an I–604 investigation reveals negative information sufficient to sustain a denial or revocation, the investigation report, supporting documentation, and petition shall be forwarded to the appropriate Service office for action. Depending on the circumstances surrounding the case, the I–604 investigation shall include, but shall not necessarily be limited to, document checks, telephonic checks, interview(s) with the natural parent(s), and/or a field investigation.

(2) *Authority of consular officers.* An American consular officer is authorized to approve an orphan petition if the Service has made a favorable determination on the related advanced processing application, and the petitioner, who has traveled abroad to a country with no Service office in order to locate or adopt an orphan, has properly filed the petition, and the petition is approvable. A consular officer, however, shall refer any petition which is "not clearly approvable" for a decision by the Service office having jurisdiction pursuant to §100.4(b) of this chapter. The consular officer's adjudication includes all aspects of eligibility for classification as an orphan under section 101(b)(1)(F) of the Act other than the issue of the ability of the prospective adoptive parents to furnish proper care to the orphan. However, if the consular officer has a well-founded and substantive reason to believe that the advanced processing approval was obtained on the basis of fraud or misrepresentation, or has knowledge of a change in material fact subsequent to the approval of the advanced processing application, he or she shall consult with the Service office having jurisdiction pursuant to §100.4(b) of this chapter.

(3) *Child in the United States.* A child who is in parole status and who has not been adopted in the United States is eligible for the benefits of an orphan petition when all the requirements of sections 101(b)(1)(F) and 204 (d) and (e) of the Act have been met. A child in the United States either illegally or as a nonimmigrant, however, is ineligible for the benefits of an orphan petition.

(4) *Liaison.* Each director shall develop and maintain liaison with State Government adoption authorities having jurisdiction within his or her jurisdiction, including the administrator(s) of the Interstate Compact on the Placement of Children, and with other parties with interest in international adoptions. Such parties include, but are not necessarily limited to, adoption agencies, organizations representing adoption agencies, organizations representing adoptive parents, and adoption attorneys.

[59 FR 38881, Aug. 1, 1994; 59 FR 42878, Aug. 19, 1994, as amended at 63 FR 12986, Mar. 17, 1998; 68 FR 46926, Aug. 7, 2003; 72 FR 56853, Oct. 4, 2007; 74 FR 26936, June 5, 2009; 76 FR 53782, Aug. 29, 2011]

§204.4 Amerasian child of a United States citizen.

(a) *Eligibility.* An alien is eligible for benefits under Public Law 97–359 as the Amerasian child or son or daughter of a United States citizen if there is reason to believe that the alien was born in Korea, Vietnam, Laos, Kampuchea, or Thailand after December 31, 1950, and before October 22, 1982, and was fathered by a United States citizen. Such an alien is eligible for classification under sections 201(b), 203(a)(1), or 203(a)(3) of the Act as the Amerasian child or son or daughter of a United States citizen, pursuant to section 204(f) of the Act.

(b) *Filing petition.* Any alien claiming to be eligible for benefits as an Amerasian under Public Law 97–359, or any person on the alien's behalf, may file a petition, Form I–360, Petition for Amerasian, Widow, or Special Immigrant. Any person filing the petition must either be eighteen years of age or older or be an emancipated minor. In addition, a corporation incorporated in the United States may file the petition on the alien's behalf.

(c) *Jurisdiction.* The petition must be filed in accordance with the instructions on the form.

(d) *Two-stage processing*—(1) *Preliminary processing.* Upon initial submission of a petition with the documentary evidence required in paragraph (f)(1) of this section, the director shall adjudicate the petition to determine whether there is reason to believe the beneficiary was fathered by a United

States citizen. If the preliminary processing is completed in a satisfactory manner, the director shall advise the petitioner to submit the documentary evidence required in paragraph (f)(1) of this section and shall fingerprint the sponsor in accordance with 8 CFR 103.16. The petitioner must submit all required documents within one year of the date of the request or the petition will be considered to have been abandoned. To reactivate an abandoned petition, the petitioner must submit a new petition, without the previously submitted documentation, to the Service office having jurisdiction over the prior petition.

(2) *Final processing.* Upon submission of the documentary evidence required in paragraph (f)(1) of this section, the director shall complete the adjudication of the petition.

(e) *One-stage processing.* If all documentary evidence required in paragraph (f)(1) of this section is available when the petition is initially filed, the petitioner may submit it at that time. In that case, the director shall consider all evidence without using the two-stage processing procedure set out in paragraph (d) of this section.

(f) *Evidence to support a petition for an Amerasian child of a United States citizen*—(1) *Two-stage processing of petition*—(i) *Preliminary processing.* (A) A petition filed by or on behalf of an Amerasian under this section must be accompanied by evidence that the beneficiary was born in Korea, Vietnam, Laos, Kampuchea, or Thailand after December 31, 1950, and before October 22, 1982. If the beneficiary was born in Vietnam, the beneficiary's ID card must be submitted, if available. If it is not available, the petitioner must submit an affidavit explaining why the beneficiary's ID card is not available. Evidence that the beneficiary was fathered by a United States citizen must also be presented. The putative father must have been a United States citizen at the time of the beneficiary's birth or at the time of the father's death, if his death occurred prior to the beneficiary's birth. It is not required that the name of the father be given. Such evidence may include, but need not be limited to:

(*1*) The beneficiary's birth and baptismal certificates or other religious documents;

(*2*) Local civil records;

(*3*) Affidavits from knowledgeable witnesses;

(*4*) Letters or evidence of financial support from the beneficiary's putative father;

(*5*) Photographs of the beneficiary's putative father, especially with the beneficiary; and

(*6*) Evidence of the putative father's United States citizenship.

(B) The beneficiary's photograph must be submitted.

(C) The beneficiary's marriage certificate, if married, and evidence of the termination of any previous marriages, if applicable, is required.

(D) If the beneficiary is under eighteen years of age, a written irrevocable release for emigration must be received from the beneficiary's mother or legal guardian. The mother or legal guardian must authorize the placing agency or agencies to make decisions necessary for the child's immediate care until the sponsor receives custody. Interim costs are the responsibility of the sponsor. The mother or legal guardian must show an understanding of the effects of the release and state before signing the release whether any money was paid or any coercion was used. The signature of the mother or legal guardian must be authenticated by the local registrar, the court of minors, or a United States immigration or consular officer. The release must include the mother's or legal guardian's full name, date and place of birth, and current or permanent address.

(ii) *Final processing.* (A) If the director notifies the petitioner that all preliminary processing has been completed in a satisfactory manner, the petitioner must then submit Form I–361, Affidavit of Financial Support and Intent to Petition for Legal Custody for Public Law 97–359 Amerasian, executed by the beneficiary's sponsor, along with the documentary evidence of the sponsor's financial ability required by that form. If the beneficiary is under eighteen years of age, the sponsor must agree to petition the court having jurisdiction, within thirty days of the beneficiary's arrival in the United

States, for legal custody under the laws of the state where the beneficiary will reside until the beneficiary is eighteen years of age. The term "legal custody" as used in this section means the assumption of responsibility for a minor by an adult under the laws of the state in a court of law. The sponsor must be a United States citizen or lawful permanent resident who is twenty-one years of age or older and who is of good moral character.

(B) Other documents necessary to support the petition are:

(*1*) Evidence of the age of the beneficiary's sponsor;

(*2*) Evidence of United States citizenship or lawful permanent residence of the sponsor as provided in §204.1(f); and

(C) If the beneficiary is under eighteen years of age, evidence that a public, private, or state agency licensed in the United States to place children and actively involved, with recent experience, in the intercountry placement of children has arranged the beneficiary's placement in the United States. Evidence must also be provided that the sponsor with whom the beneficiary is being placed is able to accept the beneficiary for care in the sponsor's home under the laws of the state of the beneficiary's intended residence. The evidence must demonstrate the agency's capability, including financial capability, to arrange the placement as described in paragraph (f)(1) of this section, either directly or through cooperative agreement with other suitable provider(s) of service.

(iii) *Arrangements for placement of beneficiary under eighteen years of age.* (A) If the beneficiary is under eighteen years of age, the petitioner must submit evidence of the placement arrangement required under paragraph (f)(1) of this section. A favorable home study of the sponsor is necessary and must be conducted by an agency in the United States legally authorized to conduct that study. If the sponsor resides outside the United States, a home study of the sponsor must be conducted by an agency legally authorized to conduct home studies in the state of the sponsor's and beneficiary's intended residence in the United States and must be submitted with a favorable recommendation by the agency.

(B) A plan from the agency to provide follow-up services, including mediation and counselling, is required to ensure that the sponsor and the beneficiary have satisfactorily adjusted to the placement and to determine whether the terms of the sponsorship are being observed. A report from the agency concerning the placement, including information regarding any family separation or dislocation abroad that results from the placement, must also be submitted. In addition, the agency must submit to the Director, Outreach Program, Immigration and Naturalization Service, Washington, DC, within 90 days of each occurrence, reports of any breakdowns in sponsorship that occur, and reports of the steps taken to remedy these breakdowns. The petitioner must also submit a statement from the agency:

(*1*) Indicating that, before signing the sponsorship agreement, the sponsor has been provided a report covering pre-placement screening and evaluation, including a health evaluation, of the beneficiary;

(*2*) Describing the agency's orientation of both the sponsor and the beneficiary on the legal and cultural aspects of the placement;

(*3*) Describing the initial facilitation of the placement through introduction, translation, and similar services; and

(*4*) Describing the contingency plans to place the beneficiary in another suitable home if the initial placement fails. The new sponsor must execute and submit a Form I–361 to the Service office having jurisdiction over the beneficiary's residence in the United States. The original sponsor nonetheless retains financial responsibility for the beneficiary under the terms of the guarantee of financial support and intent to petition for legal custody which that sponsor executed, unless that responsibility is assumed by a new sponsor. In the event that the new sponsor does not comply with the terms of the new guarantee of financial support and intent to petition for legal custody and if, for any reason, that guarantee is not enforced, the original sponsor again becomes financially responsible for the beneficiary.

(2) *One-stage processing of petition.* If the petitioner chooses to have the petition processed under the one-stage processing procedure described in paragraph (e) of this section, the petitioner must submit all evidence required by paragraph (f)(1) of this section.

(g) *Decision*—(1) *General.* The director shall notify the petitioner of the decision and, if the petition is denied, of the reasons for the denial. If the petition is denied, the petitioner may appeal the decision under part 103 of this chapter.

(2) *Denial upon completion of preliminary processing.* The director may deny the petition upon completion of the preliminary processing under paragraph (d) of this section for:

(i) Failure to establish that there is reason to believe the alien was fathered by a United States citizen; or

(ii) Failure to meet the sponsorship requirements if the fingerprints of the sponsor, required in paragraph (f)(1) of this section, were submitted during the preliminary processing and the completed background check of the sponsor discloses adverse information resulting in a finding that the sponsor is not of good moral character.

(3) *Denial upon completion of final processing.* The director may deny the petition upon completion of final processing if it is determined that the sponsorship requirements, or one or more of the other applicable requirements, have not been met.

(4) *Denial upon completion of one-stage processing.* The director may deny the petition upon completion of all processing if any of the applicable requirements in a case being processed under the one-stage processing described in paragraph (e) of this section are not met.

(h) *Classification of Public Law 97–359 Amerasian.* If the petition is approved the beneficiary is classified as follows:

(1) An unmarried beneficiary under the age of twenty-one is classified as the child of a United States citizen under section 201(b) of the Act;

(2) An unmarried beneficiary twenty-one years of age or older is classified as the unmarried son or daughter of a United States citizen under section 203(a)(1) of the Act; and

(3) A married beneficiary is classified as the married son or daughter of a United States citizen under section 203(a)(3) of the Act.

(i) *Enforcement of affidavit of financial support and intent to petition for legal custody.* A guarantee of financial support and intent to petition for legal custody on Form I–361 may be enforced against the alien's sponsor in a civil suit brought by the Attorney General in the United States District Court for the district in which the sponsor resides, except that the sponsor's estate is not liable under the guarantee if the sponsor dies or is adjudicated as bankrupt under title 11, United States Code. After admission to the United States, if the beneficiary of a petition requires enforcement of the guarantee of financial support and intent to petition for legal custody executed by the beneficiary's sponsor, the beneficiary may file Form I–363 with USCIS. If the beneficiary is under eighteen years of age, any agency or individual (other than the sponsor) having legal custody of the beneficiary, or a legal guardian acting on the alien's behalf, may file Form I–363.

[57 FR 41066, Sept. 9, 1992, as amended at 63 FR 12986, Mar. 17, 1998; 74 FR 26936, June 5, 2009; 76 FR 53782, Aug. 29, 2011]

§ 204.5 Petitions for employment-based immigrants.

(a) *General.* A petition to classify an alien under section 203(b)(1), 203(b)(2), or 203(b)(3) of the Act must be filed on Form I–140, Petition for Immigrant Worker. A petition to classify an alien under section 203(b)(4) (as it relates to special immigrants under section 101(a)(27)(C)) must be filed on kForm I–360, Petition for Amerasian, Widow, or Special Immigrant. A separate Form I–140 or I–360 must be filed for each beneficiary, accompanied by the applicable fee. A petition is considered properly filed if it is:

(1) Accepted for processing under the provisions of part 103;

(2) Accompanied by any required individual labor certification, application for Schedule A designation, or evidence that the alien's occupation qualifies as a shortage occupation within the Department of Labor's Labor Market Information Pilot Program; and

(3) Accompanied by any other required supporting documentation.

(b) *Jurisdiction.* Form I-140 or I-360 must be filed in accordance with the instructions on the form.

(c) *Filing petition.* Any United States employer desiring and intending to employ an alien may file a petition for classification of the alien under section 203(b)(1)(B), 203(b)(1)(C), 203(b)(2), or 203(b)(3) of the Act. An alien, or any person in the alien's behalf, may file a petition for classification under section 203(b)(1)(A) or 203(b)(4) of the Act (as it relates to special immigrants under section 101(a)(27)(C) of the Act).

(d) *Priority date.* The priority date of any petition filed for classification under section 203(b) of the Act which is accompanied by an individual labor certification from the Department of Labor shall be the date the labor certification application was accepted for processing by any office of the Department of Labor. The priority date of any petition filed for a classification under section 203(b) of the Act which does not require a labor certification from the Department of Labor shall be the date the completed, signed petition (including all initial evidence and the correct fee) is properly filed with USCIS. The priority date of any petition filed for classification under section 203(b) of the Act which is accompanied by an application for Schedule A designation shall be the date the completed, signed petition (including all initial evidence and the correct fee) is properly filed with USCIS. The priority date of an alien who filed for classification as a special immigrant under section 203(b)(4) of the Act prior to October 1, 1991, and who is the beneficiary of an approved petition for special immigrant status after October 1, 1991, shall be the date the alien applied for an immigrant visa or adjustment of status.

(e) *Retention of section 203(b)(1), (2), or (3) priority date.* (1) A petition approved on behalf of an alien under sections 203(b)(1), (2), or (3) of the Act accords the alien the priority date of the approved petition for any subsequently filed petition for any classification under section 203(b)(1), (2), or (3) of the Act for which the alien may qualify. In the event that the alien is the beneficiary of multiple approved petitions under section 203(b)(1), (2), or (3) of the Act, the alien shall be entitled to the earliest priority date.

(2) The priority date of a petition may not be retained under paragraph (e)(1) of this section if at any time USCIS revokes the approval of the petition because of:

(i) Fraud, or a willful misrepresentation of a material fact;

(ii) Revocation by the Department of Labor of the approved permanent labor certification that accompanied the petition;

(iii) Invalidation by USCIS or the Department of State of the permanent labor certification that accompanied the petition; or

(iv) A determination by USCIS that petition approval was based on a material error.

(3) A denied petition will not establish a priority date.

(4) A priority date is not transferable to another alien.

(5) A petition filed under section 204(a)(1)(F) of the Act for an alien shall remain valid with respect to a new employment offer as determined by USCIS under section 204(j) of the Act and 8 CFR 245.25. An alien will continue to be afforded the priority date of such petition, if the requirements of paragraph (e) of this section are met.

(f) *Maintaining the priority date of a third or sixth preference petition filed prior to October 1, 1991.* Any petition filed before October 1, 1991, and approved on any date, to accord status under section 203(a)(3) or 203(a)(6) of the Act, as in effect before October 1, 1991, shall be deemed a petition approved to accord status under section 203(b)(2) or within the appropriate classification under section 203(b)(3), respectively, of the Act as in effect on or after October 1, 1991, provided that the alien applies for an immigrant visa or adjustment of status within the two years following notification that an immigrant visa is immediately available for his or her use.

(g) *Initial evidence*—(1) *General.* Specific requirements for initial supporting documents for the various employment-based immigrant classifications are set forth in this section. In general, ordinary legible photocopies of such documents (except for labor certifications from the Department of Labor) will be acceptable for initial filing and approval. However, at the discretion of the director, original documents may be required in individual cases. Evidence relating to qualifying experience or training shall be in the form of letter(s) from current or former employer(s) or trainer(s) and shall include the name, address, and title of the writer, and a specific description of the duties performed by the alien or of the training received. If such evidence is unavailable, other documentation relating to the alien's experience or training will be considered.

(2) *Ability of prospective employer to pay wage.* Any petition filed by or for an employment-based immigrant which requires an offer of employment must be accompanied by evidence that the prospective United States employer has the ability to pay the proffered wage. The petitioner must demonstrate this ability at the time the priority date is established and continuing until the beneficiary obtains lawful permanent residence. Evidence of this ability shall be either in the form of copies of annual reports, federal tax returns, or audited financial statements. In a case where the prospective United States employer employs 100 or more workers, the director may accept a statement from a financial officer of the organization which establishes the prospective employer's ability to pay the proffered wage. In appropriate cases, additional evidence, such as profit/loss statements, bank account records, or personnel records, may be submitted by the petitioner or requested by the Service.

(h) *Aliens with extraordinary ability.* (1) An alien, or any person on behalf of the alien, may file an I–140 visa petition for classification under section 203(b)(1)(A) of the Act as an alien of extraordinary ability in the sciences, arts, education, business, or athletics.

(2) *Definition.* As used in this section:

Extraordinary ability means a level of expertise indicating that the individual is one of that small percentage who have risen to the very top of the field of endeavor.

(3) *Initial evidence.* A petition for an alien of extraordinary ability must be accompanied by evidence that the alien has sustained national or international acclaim and that his or her achievements have been recognized in the field of expertise. Such evidence shall include evidence of a one-time achievement (that is, a major, international recognized award), or at least three of the following:

(i) Documentation of the alien's receipt of lesser nationally or internationally recognized prizes or awards for excellence in the field of endeavor;

(ii) Documentation of the alien's membership in associations in the field for which classification is sought, which require outstanding achievements of their members, as judged by recognized national or international experts in their disciplines or fields;

(iii) Published material about the alien in professional or major trade publications or other major media, relating to the alien's work in the field for which classification is sought. Such evidence shall include the title, date, and author of the material, and any necessary translation;

(iv) Evidence of the alien's participation, either individually or on a panel, as a judge of the work of others in the same or an allied field of specification for which classification is sought;

(v) Evidence of the alien's original scientific, scholarly, artistic, athletic, or business-related contributions of major significance in the field;

(vi) Evidence of the alien's authorship of scholarly articles in the field, in professional or major trade publications or other major media;

(vii) Evidence of the display of the alien's work in the field at artistic exhibitions or showcases;

(viii) Evidence that the alien has performed in a leading or critical role for organizations or establishments that have a distinguished reputation;

(ix) Evidence that the alien has commanded a high salary or other significantly high remuneration for services, in relation to others in the field; or

(x) Evidence of commercial successes in the performing arts, as shown by box office receipts or record, cassette, compact disk, or video sales.

(4) If the above standards do not readily apply to the beneficiary's occupation, the petitioner may submit comparable evidence to establish the beneficiary's eligibility.

(5) *No offer of employment required.* Neither an offer for employment in the United States nor a labor certification is required for this classification; however, the petition must be accompanied by clear evidence that the alien is coming to the United States to continue work in the area of expertise. Such evidence may include letter(s) from prospective employer(s), evidence of prearranged commitments such as contracts, or a statement from the beneficiary detailing plans on how he or she intends to continue his or her work in the United States.

(i) *Outstanding professors and researchers.* (1) Any United States employer desiring and intending to employ a professor or researcher who is outstanding in an academic field under section 203(b)(1)(B) of the Act may file an I–140 visa petition for such classification.

(2) *Definitions.* As used in this section:

Academic field means a body of specialized knowledge offered for study at an accredited United States university or institution of higher education.

Permanent, in reference to a research position, means either tenured, tenure-track, or for a term of indefinite or unlimited duration, and in which the employee will ordinarily have an expectation of continued employment unless there is good cause for termination.

(3) *Initial evidence.* A petition for an outstanding professor or researcher must be accompanied by:

(i) Evidence that the professor or researcher is recognized internationally as outstanding in the academic field specified in the petition. Such evidence shall consist of at least two of the following:

(A) Documentation of the alien's receipt of major prizes or awards for outstanding achievement in the academic field;

(B) Documentation of the alien's membership in associations in the academic field which require outstanding achievements of their members;

(C) Published material in professional publications written by others about the alien's work in the academic field. Such material shall include the title, date, and author of the material, and any necessary translation;

(D) Evidence of the alien's participation, either individually or on a panel, as the judge of the work of others in the same or an allied academic field;

(E) Evidence of the alien's original scientific or scholarly research contributions to the academic field; or

(F) Evidence of the alien's authorship of scholarly books or articles (in scholarly journals with international circulation) in the academic field;

(ii) If the standards in paragraph (i)(3)(i) of this section do not readily apply, the petitioner may submit comparable evidence to establish the beneficiary's eligibility.

(iii) Evidence that the alien has at least three years of experience in teaching and/or research in the academic field. Experience in teaching or research while working on an advanced degree will only be acceptable if the alien has acquired the degree, and if the teaching duties were such that he or she had full responsibility for the class taught or if the research conducted toward the degree has been recognized within the academic field as outstanding. Evidence of teaching and/or research experience shall be in the form of letter(s) from current or former employer(s) and shall include the name, address, and title of the writer, and a specific description of the duties performed by the alien; and

(iv) An offer of employment from a prospective United States employer. A labor certification is not required for this classification. The offer of employment shall be in the form of a letter from:

(A) A United States university or institution of higher learning offering the alien a tenured or tenure-track teaching position in the alien's academic field;

(B) A United States university or institution of higher learning offering the alien a permanent research position in the alien's academic field; or

(C) A department, division, or institute of a private employer offering the alien a permanent research position in the alien's academic field. The department, division, or institute must demonstrate that it employs at least three persons full-time in research positions, and that it has achieved documented accomplishments in an academic field.

(j) *Certain multinational executives and managers.* (1) A United States employer may file a petition on Form I–140 for classification of an alien under section 203(b)(1)(C) of the Act as a multinational executive or manager.

(2) *Definitions.* As used in this section:

Affiliate means:

(A) One of two subsidiaries both of which are owned and controlled by the same parent or individual;

(B) One of two legal entities owned and controlled by the same group of individuals, each individual owning and controlling approximately the same share or proportion of each entity; or

(C) In the case of a partnership that is organized in the United States to provide accounting services, along with managerial and/or consulting services, and markets its accounting services under an internationally recognized name under an agreement with a worldwide coordinating organization that is owned and controlled by the member accounting firms, a partnership (or similar organization) that is organized outside the United States to provide accounting' services shall be considered to be an affiliate of the United States partnership if it markets its accounting services under the same internationally recognized name under the agreement with the worldwide coordinating organization of which the United States partnership is also a member.

Doing business means the regular, systematic, and continuous provision of goods and/or services by a firm, corporation, or other entity and does not include the mere presence of an agent or office.

Executive capacity means an assignment within an organization in which the employee primarily:

(A) Directs the management of the organization or a major component or function of the organization;

(B) Establishes the goals and policies of the organization, component, or function;

(C) Exercises wide latitude in discretionary decisionmaking; and

(D) Receives only general supervision or direction from higher level executives, the board of directors, or stockholders of the organization.

Managerial capacity means an assignment within an organization in which the employee primarily:

(A) Manages the organization, or a department, subdivision, function, or component of the organization;

(B) Supervises and controls the work of other supervisory, professional, or managerial employees, or manages an essential function within the organization, or a department or subdivision of the organization;

(C) If another employee or other employees are directly supervised, has the authority to hire and fire or recommend those as well as other personnel actions (such as promotion and leave authorization), or, if no other employee is directly supervised, functions at a senior level within the organizational hierarchy or with respect to the function managed; and

(D) Exercises direction over the day-to-day operations of the activity or function for which the employee has authority.

Multinational means that the qualifying entity, or its affiliate, or subsidiary, conducts business in two or more countries, one of which is the United States.

Subsidiary means a firm, corporation, or other legal entity of which a parent owns, directly or indirectly, more than half of the entity and controls the entity; or owns, directly or indirectly, half of the entity and controls the entity; or owns, directly or indirectly, 50 percent of a 50–50 joint venture and has equal control and veto power over the entity; or owns, directly or indirectly, less than half of the entity, but in fact controls the entity.

(3) *Initial evidence*—(i) *Required evidence.* A petition for a multinational executive or manager must be accompanied by a statement from an authorized official of the petitioning United States employer which demonstrates that:

(A) If the alien is outside the United States, in the three years immediately preceding the filing of the petition the alien has been employed outside the United States for at least one year in a managerial or executive capacity by a firm or corporation, or other legal entity, or by an affiliate or subsidiary of such a firm or corporation or other legal entity; or

(B) If the alien is already in the United States working for the same employer or a subsidiary or affiliate of the firm or corporation, or other legal entity by which the alien was employed overseas, in the three years preceding entry as a nonimmigrant, the alien was employed by the entity abroad for at least one year in a managerial or executive capacity;

(C) The prospective employer in the United States is the same employer or a subsidiary or affiliate of the firm or corporation or other legal entity by which the alien was employed overseas; and

(D) The prospective United States employer has been doing business for at least one year.

(ii) *Appropriate additional evidence.* In appropriate cases, the director may request additional evidence.

(4) *Determining managerial or exectuve capacities*—(i) *Supervisors as managers.* A first-line supervisor is not considered to be acting in a managerial capacity merely by virtue of his or her supervisory duties unless the employees supervised are professional.

(ii) *Staffing levels.* If staffing levels are used as a factor in determining whether an individual is acting in a managerial or executive capacity, the reasonable needs of the organization, component, or function, in light of the overall purpose and stage of development of the organization, component, or function, shall be taken into account. An individual shall not be considered to be acting in a managerial or executive capacity merely on the basis of the number of employees that the individual supervises or has supervised or directs or has directed.

(5) *Offer of employment.* No labor certification is required for this classification; however, the prospective employer in the United States must furnish a job offer in the form of a statement which indicates that the alien is to be employed in the United States in a managerial or executive capacity. Such letter must clearly describe the duties to be performed by the alien.

(k) *Aliens who are members of the professions holding advanced degrees or aliens of exceptional ability.* (1) Any United States employer may file a petition on Form I–140 for classification of an alien under section 203(b)(2) of the Act as an alien who is a member of the professions holding an advanced degree or an alien of exceptional ability in the sciences, arts, or business. If an alien is claiming exceptional ability in the sciences, arts, or business and is seeking an exemption from the requirement of a job offer in the United States pursuant to section 203(b)(2)(B) of the Act, then the alien, or anyone in the alien's behalf, may be the petitioner.

(2) *Definitions.* As used in this section: *Advanced degree* means any United States academic or professional degree or a foreign equivalent degree above that of baccalaureate. A United States baccalaureate degree or a foreign equivalent degree followed by at least five years of progressive experience in the specialty shall be considered the equivalent of a master's degree. If a doctoral degree is customarily required by the specialty, the alien must have a United States doctorate or a foreign equivalent degree.

Exceptional ability in the sciences, arts, or business means a degree of expertise significantly above that ordinarily encountered in the sciences, arts, or business.

Profession means one of the occupations listed in section 101(a)(32) of the Act, as well as any occupation for which a United States baccalaureate degree or its foreign equivalent is the minimum requirement for entry into the occupation.

(3) *Initial evidence.* The petition must be accompanied by documentation showing that the alien is a professional holding an advanced degree or an alien of exceptional ability in the sciences, the arts, or business.

(i) To show that the alien is a professional holding an advanced degree, the petition must be accompanied by:

(A) An official academic record showing that the alien has a United States advanced degree or a foreign equivalent degree; or

(B) An official academic record showing that the alien has a United States baccalaureate degree or a foreign equivalent degree, and evidence in the form of letters from current or former employer(s) showing that the alien has at least five years of progressive post-baccalaureate experience in the specialty.

(ii) To show that the alien is an alien of exceptional ability in the sciences, arts, or business, the petition must be accompanied by at least three of the following:

(A) An official academic record showing that the alien has a degree, diploma, certificate, or similar award from a college, university, school, or other institution of learning relating to the area of exceptional ability;

(B) Evidence in the form of letter(s) from current or former employer(s) showing that the alien has at least ten years of full-time experience in the occupation for which he or she is being sought;

(C) A license to practice the profession or certification for a particular profession or occupation;

(D) Evidence that the alien has commanded a salary, or other renumeration for services, which demonstrates exceptional ability;

(E) Evidence of membership in professional associations; or

(F) Evidence of recognition for achievements and significant contributions to the industry or field by peers, governmental entities, or professional or business organizations.

(iii) If the above standards do not readily apply to the beneficiary's occupation, the petitioner may submit comparable evidence to establish the beneficiary's eligibility.

(4) *Labor certification or evidence that alien qualifies for Labor Market Information Pilot Program*—(i) *General.* Every petition under this classification must be accompanied by an individual labor certification from the Department of Labor, by an application for Schedule A designation (if applicable), or by documentation to establish that the alien qualifies for one of the shortage occupations in the Department of Labor's Labor Market Information Pilot Program. To apply for Schedule A designation or to establish that the alien's occupation is within the Labor Market Information Program, a fully executed uncertified Form ETA–750 in duplicate must accompany the petition. The job offer portion of the individual labor certification, Schedule A application, or Pilot Program application must demonstrate that the job requires a professional holding an advanced degree or the equivalent or an alien of exceptional ability.

(ii) *Exemption from job offer.* The director may exempt the requirement of a job offer, and thus of a labor certification, for aliens of exceptional ability in the sciences, arts, or business if exemption would be in the national interest. To apply for the exemption, the petitioner must submit Form ETA–750B, Statement of Qualifications of Alien, in duplicate, as well as evidence to support the claim that such exemption would be in the national interest.

(l) *Skilled workers, professionals, and other workers.* (1) Any United States employer may file a petition on Form I–140 for classification of an alien under section 203(b)(3) as a skilled worker, professional, or other (unskilled) worker.

(2) *Definitions.* As used in this part:

Other worker means a qualified alien who is capable, at the time of petitioning for this classification, of performing unskilled labor (requiring less than two years training or experience), not of a temporary or seasonal nature, for which qualified workers are not available in the United States.

Professional means a qualified alien who holds at least a United States baccalaureate degree or a foreign equivalent degree and who is a member of the professions.

Skilled worker means an alien who is capable, at the time of petitioning for this classification, of performing skilled labor (requiring at least two years training or experience), not of a temporary or seasonal nature, for which qualified workers are not available in the United States. Relevant post-secondary education may be considered as training for the purposes of this provision.

(3) *Initial evidence*—(i) *Labor certification or evidence that alien qualifies for Labor Market Information Pilot Program.* Every petition under this classification

must be accompanied by an individual labor certification from the Department of Labor, by an application for Schedule A designation, or by documentation to establish that the alien qualifies for one of the shortage occupations in the Department of Labor's Labor Market Information Pilot Program. To apply for Schedule A designation or to establish that the alien's occupation is a shortage occupation with the Labor Market Pilot Program, a fully executed uncertified Form ETA-750 in duplicate must accompany the petition. The job offer portion of an individual labor certification, Schedule A application, or Pilot Program application for a professional must demonstrate that the job requires the minimum of a baccalaureate degree.

(ii) *Other documentation*—(A) *General.* Any requirements of training or experience for skilled workers, professionals, or other workers must be supported by letters from trainers or employers giving the name, address, and title of the trainer or employer, and a description of the training received or the experience of the alien.

(B) *Skilled workers.* If the petition is for a skilled worker, the petition must be accompanied by evidence that the alien meets the educational, training or experience, and any other requirements of the individual labor certification, meets the requirements for Schedule A designation, or meets the requirements for the Labor Market Information Pilot Program occupation designation. The minimum requirements for this classification are at least two years of training or experience.

(C) *Professionals.* If the petition is for a professional, the petition must be accompanied by evidence that the alien holds a United States baccalaureate degree or a foreign equivalent degree and by evidence that the alien is a member of the professions. Evidence of a baccalaureate degree shall be in the form of an official college or university record showing the date the baccalaureate degree was awarded and the area of concentration of study. To show that the alien is a member of the professions, the petitioner must submit evidence showing that the minimum of a baccalaureate degree is required for entry into the occupation.

(D) *Other workers.* If the petition is for an unskilled (other) worker, it must be accompanied by evidence that the alien meets any educational, training and experience, and other requirements of the labor certification.

(4) *Differentiating between skilled and other workers.* The determination of whether a worker is a skilled or other worker will be based on the requirements of training and/or experience placed on the job by the prospective employer, as certified by the Department of Labor. In the case of a Schedule A occupation or a shortage occupation within the Labor Market Pilot Program, the petitioner will be required to establish to the director that the job is a skilled job, *i.e.*, one which requires at least two years of training and/or experience.

(m) *Religious workers.* This paragraph governs classification of an alien as a special immigrant religious worker as defined in section 101(a)(27)(C) of the Act and under section 203(b)(4) of the Act. To be eligible for classification as a special immigrant religious worker, the alien (either abroad or in the United States) must:

(1) For at least the two years immediately preceding the filing of the petition have been a member of a religious denomination that has a bona fide non-profit religious organization in the United States.

(2) Be coming to the United States to work in a full time (average of at least 35 hours per week) compensated position in one of the following occupations as they are defined in paragraph (m)(5) of this section:

(i) Solely in the vocation of a minister of that religious denomination;

(ii) A religious vocation either in a professional or nonprofessional capacity; or

(iii) A religious occupation either in a professional or nonprofessional capacity.

(3) Be coming to work for a bona fide non-profit religious organization in the United States, or a bona fide organization which is affiliated with the religious denomination in the United States.

(4) Have been working in one of the positions described in paragraph (m)(2) of this section, either abroad or in lawful immigration status in the United States, and after the age of 14 years continuously for at least the two-year period immediately preceding the filing of the petition. The prior religious work need not correspond precisely to the type of work to be performed. A break in the continuity of the work during the preceding two years will not affect eligibility so long as:

(i) The alien was still employed as a religious worker;

(ii) The break did not exceed two years; and

(iii) The nature of the break was for further religious training or for sabbatical that did not involve unauthorized work in the United States. However, the alien must have been a member of the petitioner's denomination throughout the two years of qualifying employment.

(5) *Definitions.* As used in paragraph (m) of this section, the term:

Bona fide non-profit religious organization in the United States means a religious organization exempt from taxation as described in section 501(c)(3) of the Internal Revenue Code of 1986, subsequent amendment or equivalent sections of prior enactments of the Internal Revenue Code, and possessing a currently valid determination letter from the IRS confirming such exemption.

Bona fide organization which is affiliated with the religious denomination means an organization which is closely associated with the religious denomination and which is exempt from taxation as described in section 501(c)(3) of the Internal Revenue Code of 1986, subsequent amendment or equivalent sections of prior enactments of the Internal Revenue Code and possessing a currently valid determination letter from the IRS confirming such exemption.

Denominational membership means membership during at least the two-year period immediately preceding the filing date of the petition, in the same type of religious denomination as the United States religious organization where the alien will work.

Minister means an individual who:

(A) Is fully authorized by a religious denomination, and fully trained according to the denomination's standards, to conduct such religious worship and perform other duties usually performed by authorized members of the clergy of that denomination;

(B) Is not a lay preacher or a person not authorized to perform duties usually performed by clergy;

(C) Performs activities with a rational relationship to the religious calling of the minister; and

(D) Works solely as a minister in the United States, which may include administrative duties incidental to the duties of a minister.

Petition means USCIS Form I–360, Petition for Amerasian, Widow(er), or Special Immigrant, a successor form, or other form as may be prescribed by USCIS, along with a supplement containing attestations required by this section, the fee specified in 8 CFR 103.7(b)(1), and supporting evidence filed as provided by this part.

Religious denomination means a religious group or community of believers that is governed or administered under a common type of ecclesiastical government and includes one or more of the following:

(A) A recognized common creed or statement of faith shared among the denomination's members;

(B) A common form of worship;

(C) A common formal code of doctrine and discipline;

(D) Common religious services and ceremonies;

(E) Common established places of religious worship or religious congregations; or

(F) Comparable indicia of a bona fide religious denomination.

Religious occupation means an occupation that meets all of the following requirements:

(A) The duties must primarily relate to a traditional religious function and be recognized as a religious occupation within the denomination.

(B) The duties must be primarily related to, and must clearly involve, inculcating or carrying out the religious creed and beliefs of the denomination.

(C) The duties do not include positions that are primarily administrative or support such as janitors, maintenance workers, clerical employees, fund raisers, persons solely involved in the solicitation of donations, or similar positions, although limited administrative duties that are only incidental to religious functions are permissible.

(D) Religious study or training for religious work does not constitute a religious occupation, but a religious worker may pursue study or training incident to status.

Religious vocation means a formal lifetime commitment, through vows, investitures, ceremonies, or similar indicia, to a religious way of life. The religious denomination must have a class of individuals whose lives are dedicated to religious practices and functions, as distinguished from the secular members of the religion. Examples of individuals practicing religious vocations include nuns, monks, and religious brothers and sisters.

Religious worker means an individual engaged in and, according to the denomination's standards, qualified for a religious occupation or vocation, whether or not in a professional capacity, or as a minister.

Tax-exempt organization means an organization that has received a determination letter from the IRS establishing that it, or a group that it belongs to, is exempt from taxation in accordance with sections 501(c)(3) of the Internal Revenue Code of 1986 or subsequent amendments or equivalent sections of prior enactments of the Internal Revenue Code.

(6) *Filing requirements.* A petition must be filed as provided in the petition form instructions either by the alien or by his or her prospective United States employer. After the date stated in section 101(a)(27)(C) of the Act, immigration or adjustment of status on the basis of this section is limited solely to ministers.

(7) *Attestation.* An authorized official of the prospective employer of an alien seeking religious worker status must complete, sign and date an attestation prescribed by USCIS and submit it along with the petition. If the alien is a self-petitioner and is also an authorized official of the prospective employer, the self-petitioner may sign the attestation. The prospective employer must specifically attest to all of the following:

(i) That the prospective employer is a bona fide non-profit religious organization or a bona fide organization which is affiliated with the religious denomination and is exempt from taxation;

(ii) The number of members of the prospective employer's organization;

(iii) The number of employees who work at the same location where the beneficiary will be employed and a summary of the type of responsibilities of those employees. USCIS may request a list of all employees, their titles, and a brief description of their duties at its discretion;

(iv) The number of aliens holding special immigrant or nonimmigrant religious worker status currently employed or employed within the past five years by the prospective employer's organization;

(v) The number of special immigrant religious worker and nonimmigrant religious worker petitions and applications filed by or on behalf of any aliens for employment by the prospective employer in the past five years;

(vi) The title of the position offered to the alien, the complete package of salaried or non-salaried compensation being offered, and a detailed description of the alien's proposed daily duties;

(vii) That the alien will be employed at least 35 hours per week;

(viii) The specific location(s) of the proposed employment;

(ix) That the alien has worked as a religious worker for the two years immediately preceding the filing of the application and is otherwise qualified for the position offered;

(x) That the alien has been a member of the denomination for at least two years immediately preceding the filing of the application;

(xi) That the alien will not be engaged in secular employment, and any salaried or non-salaried compensation for the work will be paid to the alien by the attesting employer; and

(xii) That the prospective employer has the ability and intention to compensate the alien at a level at which the alien and accompanying family members will not become public charges, and that funds to pay the alien's compensation do not include any monies obtained from the alien, excluding reasonable donations or tithing to the religious organization.

(8) *Evidence relating to the petitioning organization.* A petition shall include the following initial evidence relating to the petitioning organization:

(i) A currently valid determination letter from the Internal Revenue Service (IRS) establishing that the organization is a tax-exempt organization; or

(ii) For a religious organization that is recognized as tax-exempt under a group tax-exemption, a currently valid determination letter from the IRS establishing that the group is tax-exempt; or

(iii) For a bona fide organization that is affiliated with the religious denomination, if the organization was granted tax-exempt status under section 501(c)(3) of the Internal Revenue Code of 1986, or subsequent amendment or equivalent sections of prior enactments of the Internal Revenue Code, as something other than a religious organization:

(A) A currently valid determination letter from the IRS establishing that the organization is a tax-exempt organization;

(B) Documentation that establishes the religious nature and purpose of the organization, such as a copy of the organizing instrument of the organization that specifies the purposes of the organization;

(C) Organizational literature, such as books, articles, brochures, calendars, flyers and other literature describing the religious purpose and nature of the activities of the organization; and

(D) A religious denomination certification. The religious organization must complete, sign and date a religious denomination certification certifying that the petitioning organization is affiliated with the religious denomination. The certification is to be submitted by the petitioner along with the petition.

(9) *Evidence relating to the qualifications of a minister.* If the alien is a minister, the petitioner must submit the following:

(i) A copy of the alien's certificate of ordination or similar documents reflecting acceptance of the alien's qualifications as a minister in the religious denomination; and

(ii) Documents reflecting acceptance of the alien's qualifications as a minister in the religious denomination, as well as evidence that the alien has completed any course of prescribed theological education at an accredited theological institution normally required or recognized by that religious denomination, including transcripts, curriculum, and documentation that establishes that the theological institution is accredited by the denomination, or

(iii) For denominations that do not require a prescribed theological education, evidence of:

(A) The denomination's requirements for ordination to minister;

(B) The duties allowed to be performed by virtue of ordination;

(C) The denomination's levels of ordination, if any; and

(D) The alien's completion of the denomination's requirements for ordination.

(10) *Evidence relating to compensation.* Initial evidence must include verifiable evidence of how the petitioner intends to compensate the alien. Such compensation may include salaried or non-salaried compensation. This evidence may include past evidence of compensation for similar positions; budgets showing monies set aside for salaries, leases, etc.; verifiable documentation that room and board will be provided; or other evidence acceptable to USCIS. If IRS documentation, such as IRS Form W–2 or certified tax returns, is available, it must be provided. If IRS documentation is not available, an explanation for its absence must be provided, along with comparable, verifiable documentation.

(11) *Evidence relating to the alien's prior employment.* Qualifying prior experience during the two years immediately preceding the petition or preceding any acceptable break in the continuity of the religious work, must have occurred after the age of 14, and if acquired in the United States, must have been authorized under United States immigration law. If the alien was employed in the United States during the two years immediately preceding the filing of the application and:

(i) Received salaried compensation, the petitioner must submit IRS documentation that the alien received a salary, such as an IRS Form W-2 or certified copies of income tax returns.

(ii) Received non-salaried compensation, the petitioner must submit IRS documentation of the non-salaried compensation if available.

(iii) Received no salary but provided for his or her own support, and provided support for any dependents, the petitioner must show how support was maintained by submitting with the petition additional documents such as audited financial statements, financial institution records, brokerage account statements, trust documents signed by an attorney, or other verifiable evidence acceptable to USCIS.

If the alien was employed outside the United States during such two years, the petitioner must submit comparable evidence of the religious work.

(12) *Inspections, evaluations, verifications, and compliance reviews.* The supporting evidence submitted may be verified by USCIS through any means determined appropriate by USCIS, up to and including an on-site inspection of the petitioning organization. The inspection may include a tour of the organization's facilities, an interview with the organization's officials, a review of selected organization records relating to compliance with immigration laws and regulations, and an interview with any other individuals or review of any other records that the USCIS considers pertinent to the integrity of the organization. An inspection may include the organization headquarters, satellite locations, or the work locations planned for the applicable employee. If USCIS decides to conduct a pre-approval inspection, satisfactory completion of such inspection will be a condition for approval of any petition.

(n) *Closing action*—(1) *Approval.* An approved employment-based petition will be forwarded to the National Visa Center of the Department of State if the beneficiary resides outside of the United States. If the Form I–140 petition indicates that the alien has filed or will file an application for adjustment to permanent residence in the United States (Form I–485) the approved visa petition (Form I–140), will be retained by the Service for consideration with the application for permanent residence (Form I–485). If a visa is available, and Form I–485 has not been filed, the alien will be instructed on the Form I–797, Notice of Action, (mailed out upon approval of the Form I–140 petition) to file the Form I–485.

(2) *Denial.* The denial of a petition for classification under section 203(b)(1), 203(b)(2), 203(b)(3), or 203(b)(4) of the Act (as it relates to special immigrants under section 101(a)(27)(C) of the Act) shall be appealable to the Associate Commissioner for Examinations. The petitioner shall be informed in plain language of the reasons for denial and of his or her right to appeal.

(3) *Validity of approved petitions.* Unless approval is revoked under section 203(g) or 205 of the Act, an employment-based petition is valid indefinitely.

(o) *Denial of petitions under section 204 of the Act based on a finding by the Department of Labor.* Upon debarment by the Department of Labor pursuant to 20 CFR 655.31, USCIS may deny any employment-based immigrant petition filed by that petitioner for a period of at least 1 year but not more than 5 years. The time period of such bar to petition approval shall be based on the severity of the violation or violations. The decision to deny petitions, the time period for the bar to petitions, and the reasons for the time period will be explained in a written notice to the petitioner.

(p) *Eligibility for employment authorization in compelling circumstances*—(1) *Eligibility of principal alien.* An individual who is the principal beneficiary of an approved immigrant petition for classification under sections 203(b)(1), 203(b)(2) or 203(b)(3) of the Act may be eligible to receive employment authorization, upon application, if:

(i) In the case of an initial request for employment authorization, the individual is in E–3, H–1B, H–1B1, O–1, or L–1 nonimmigrant status, including the periods authorized by § 214.1(l)(1) and (2), as well as any other periods of admission authorized by this chapter before a validity period begins or after the expiration of a validity period, on the date the application for employment authorization (Form I–765) is filed;

(ii) An immigrant visa is not authorized for issuance to the principal beneficiary based on his or her priority date on the date the application for employment authorization is filed; and

(iii) USCIS determines, as a matter of discretion, that the principal beneficiary demonstrates compelling circumstances that justify the issuance of employment authorization.

(2) *Eligibility of spouses and children.* The family members, as described in section 203(d) of the Act, of a principal beneficiary, who are in nonimmigrant status at the time the principal beneficiary applies for employment authorization under paragraph (p)(1) of this section, are eligible to apply for employment authorization provided that the principal beneficiary has been granted employment authorization under paragraph (p) of this section and such employment authorization has not been terminated or revoked. Such family members may apply for employment authorization concurrently with the principal beneficiary, but cannot be granted employment authorization until the principal beneficiary is so authorized. The validity period of employment authorization granted to family members may not extend beyond the validity period of employment authorization granted to the principal beneficiary.

(3) *Eligibility for renewal of employment authorization.* An alien may be eligible to renew employment authorization granted under paragraph (p) of this section, upon submission of a new application before the expiration of such employment authorization, if:

(i) He or she is the principal beneficiary of an approved immigrant petition for classification under section 203(b)(1), 203(b)(2) or 203(b)(3) of the Act and either:

(A) An immigrant visa is not authorized for issuance to the principal beneficiary based on his or her priority date on the date the application for employment authorization, (Form I–765) is filed; and USCIS determines, as a matter of discretion that the principal beneficiary demonstrates compelling circumstances that justify the issuance of employment authorization; or

(B) The difference between the principal beneficiary's priority date and the date upon which immigrant visas are authorized for issuance for the principal beneficiary's preference category and country of chargeability is 1 year or less according to the Department of State Visa Bulletin in effect on the date the application for employment authorization (Form I–765), is filed. For example, if the Department of State Visa Bulletin in effect on the date the renewal application is filed indicates immigrant visas are authorized for issuance for the applicable preference category and country of chargeability to individuals with priority dates earlier than November 1, 2000, USCIS may grant a renewal to a principal beneficiary whose priority date is on or between October 31, 1999 and October 31, 2001; or

(ii) He or she is a family member, as described under paragraph (p)(2) of this section, of a principal beneficiary granted a renewal of employment authorization under paragraph (p)(3)(i) that remains valid, except that the family member need not be maintaining nonimmigrant status at the time the principal beneficiary applies for renewal of employment authorization under paragraph (p) of this section. A family member may file an application to renew employment authorization concurrently with an application to renew employment authorization filed by the principal beneficiary or while such application by the principal beneficiary is pending, but the family member's renewal application cannot be approved unless the principal beneficiary's application is granted. The validity period of a renewal of employment authorization granted to family members may not extend beyond the validity period of the renewal of employment authorization granted to the principal beneficiary.

(4) *Application for employment authorization.* To request employment authorization, an eligible applicant described in paragraph (p)(1), (2), or (3) of this section must file an application for employment authorization (Form I–765), with USCIS, in accordance with 8 CFR 274a.13(a) and the form instructions.

Such applicant is subject to the collection of his or her biometric information and the payment of any biometric services fee as provided in the form instructions. Employment authorization under this paragraph may be granted solely in 1-year increments.

(5) *Ineligibility for employment authorization.* An alien is not eligible for employment authorization, including renewal of employment authorization, under this paragraph if the alien has been convicted of any felony or two or more misdemeanors.

[56 FR 60905, Nov. 29, 1991, as amended at 59 FR 502, Jan. 5, 1994; 59 FR 27229, May 26, 1994; 60 FR 29753, June 6, 1995; 61 FR 33305, June 27, 1996; 67 FR 49563, July 31, 2002; 73 FR 72291, Nov. 26, 2008; 73 FR 78127, Dec. 19, 2008; 74 FR 26936, June 5, 2009; 81 FR 2083, Jan. 15, 2016; 81 FR 82484, Nov. 18, 2016]

§ 204.6 Petitions for employment creation aliens.

(a) *General.* A petition to classify an alien under section 203(b)(5) of the Act must be filed on Form I–526, Immigrant Petition by Alien Entrepreneur. The petition must be accompanied by the appropriate fee. Before a petition is considered properly filed, the petition must be signed by the petitioner, and the initial supporting documentation required by this section must be attached. Legible photocopies of supporting documents will ordinarily be acceptable for initial filing and approval. However, at the discretion of the director, original documents may be required.

(b) [Reserved]

(c) *Eligibility to file.* A petition for classification as an alien entrepreneur may only be filed by any alien on his or her own behalf.

(d) *Priority date.* The priority date of a petition for classification as an alien entrepreneur is the date the petition is properly filed with the Service or, if filed prior to the effective date of these regulations, the date the Form I–526 was received at the appropriate Service Center.

(e) *Definitions.* As used in this section:

Capital means cash, equipment, inventory, other tangible property, cash equivalents, and indebtedness secured by assets owned by the alien entrepreneur, provided that the alien entrepreneur is personally and primarily liable and that the assets of the new commercial enterprise upon which the petition is based are not used to secure any of the indebtedness. All capital shall be valued at fair market value in United States dollars. Assets acquired, directly or indirectly, by unlawful means (such as criminal activities) shall not be considered capital for the purposes of section 203(b)(5) of the Act.

Commercial enterprise means any for-profit activity formed for the ongoing conduct of lawful business including, but not limited to, a sole proprietorship, partnership (whether limited or general), holding company, joint venture, corporation, business trust, or other entity which may be publicly or privately owned. This definition includes a commercial enterprise consisting of a holding company and its wholly-owned subsidiaries, provided that each such subsidiary is engaged in a for-profit activity formed for the ongoing conduct of a lawful business. This definition shall not include a noncommercial activity such as owning and operating a personal residence.

Employee means an individual who provides services or labor for the new commercial enterprise and who receives wages or other remuneration directly from the new commercial enterprise. In the case of the Immigrant Investor Pilot Program, "employee" also means an individual who provides services or labor in a job which has been created indirectly through investment in the new commercial enterprise. This definition shall not include independent contractors.

Full-time employment means employment of a qualifying employee by the new commercial enterprise in a position that requires a minimum of 35 working hours per week. In the case of the Immigrant Investor Pilot Program, "full-time employment" also means employment of a qualifying employee in a position that has been created indirectly through revenues generated from increased exports resulting from the Pilot Program that requires a minimum of 35 working hours per week. A job-sharing arrangement whereby two or more qualifying employees share a full-time position shall count as full-time employment provided the hourly requirement per week is met. This definition shall not include combinations of part-time positions even if, when combined, such positions meet the hourly requirement per week.

High employment area means a part of a metropolitan statistical area that at the time of investment:

(i) Is not a targeted employment area; and

(ii) Is an area with an unemployment rate significantly below the national average unemployment rates.

Invest means to contribute capital. A contribution of capital in exchange for a note, bond, convertible debt, obligation, or any other debt arrangement between the alien entrepreneur and the new commercial enterprise does not constitute a contribution of capital for the purposes of this part.

New means established after November 29, 1990.

Qualifying employee means a United States citizen, a lawfully admitted permanent resident, or other immigrant lawfully authorized to be employed in the United States including, but not limited to, a conditional resident, a temporary resident, an asylee, a refugee, or an alien remaining in the United States under suspension of deportation. This definition does not include the alien entrepreneur, the alien entrepreneur's spouse, sons, or daughters, or any nonimmigrant alien.

Regional center means any economic unit, public or private, which is involved with the promotion of economic growth, including increased export sales, improved regional productivity, job creation, and increased domestic capital investment.

Rural area means any area not within either a metropolitan statistical area (as designated by the Office of Management and Budget) or the outer boundary of any city or town having a population of 20,000 or more.

Targeted employment area means an area which, at the time of investment, is a rural area or an area which has experienced unemployment of at least 150 percent of the national average rate.

Troubled business means a business that has been in existence for at least two years, has incurred a net loss for accounting purposes (determined on the basis of generally accepted accounting principles) during the twelve- or twenty-four month period prior to the priority date on the alien entrepreneur's Form I–526, and the loss for such period is at least equal to twenty percent of the troubled business's net worth prior to such loss. For purposes of determining whether or not the troubled business has been in existence for two years, successors in interest to the troubled business will be deemed to have been in existence for the same period of time as the business they succeeded.

(f) *Required amounts of capital*—(1) *General.* Unless otherwise specified, the amount of capital necessary to make a qualifying investment in the United States is one million United States dollars ($1,000,000).

(2) *Targeted employment area.* The amount of capital necessary to make a qualifying investment in a targeted employment area within the United States is five hundred thousand United States dollars ($500,000).

(3) *High employment area.* The amount of capital necessary to make a qualifying investment in a high employment area within the United States, as defined in section 203(b)(5)(C)(iii) of the Act, is one million United States dollars ($1,000,000).

(g) *Multiple investors*—(1) *General.* The establishment of a new commercial enterprise may be used as the basis of a petition for classification as an alien entrepreneur by more than one investor, provided each petitioning investor has invested or is actively in the process of investing the required amount for the area in which the new commercial enterprise is principally doing business, and provided each individual investment results in the creation of at least ten full-time positions for qualifying employees. The establishment of a new commercial enterprise may be used as the basis of a petition for classification as an alien entrepreneur even though there are several owners of the enterprise, including persons who are not seeking classification under section 203(b)(5) of the Act and non-natural persons, both foreign and domestic, provided that the source(s) of all capital invested is identified and all invested capital has been derived by lawful means.

(2) *Employment creation allocation.* The total number of full-time positions created for qualifying employees shall be allocated solely to those alien entrepreneurs who have used the establishment of the new commercial enterprise as the basis of a petition on Form I–526. No allocation need be made among persons not seeking classification under section 203(b)(5) of the Act or among non-natural persons, either foreign or domestic. The Service shall recognize any reasonable agreement made among the alien entrepreneurs in regard to the identification and allocation of such qualifying positions.

(h) *Establishment of a new commercial enterprise.* The establishment of a new commercial enterprise may consist of:

(1) The creation of an original business;

(2) The purchase of an existing business and simultaneous or subsequent restructuring or reorganization such that a new commercial enterprise results; or

(3) The expansion of an existing business through the investment of the required amount, so that a substantial change in the net worth or number of employees results from the investment of capital. Substantial change means a 40 percent increase either in the net worth, or in the number of employees, so that the new net worth, or number of employees amounts to at least 140 percent of the pre-expansion net worth or number of employees. Establishment of a new commercial enterprise in this manner does not exempt the petitioner from the requirements of 8 CFR 204.6(j)(2) and (3) relating to the required amount of capital investment and the creation of full-time employment for ten qualifying employees. In the case of a capital investment in a troubled business, employment creation may meet the criteria set forth in 8 CFR 204.6(j)(4)(ii).

(i) *State designation of a high unemployment area.* The state government of any state of the United States may designate a particular geographic or political subdivision located within a metropolitan statistical area or within a city or town having a population of 20,000 or more within such state as an area of high unemployment (at least 150 percent of the national average rate). Evidence of such designation, including a description of the boundaries of the geographic or political subdivision and the method or methods by which the unemployment statistics were obtained, may be provided to a prospective alien entrepreneur for submission with Form I–526. Before any such designation is made, an official of the state must notify the Associate Commissioner for Examinations of the agency, board, or other appropriate governmental body of the state which shall be delegated the authority to certify that the geographic or political subdivision is a high unemployment area.

(j) *Initial evidence to accompany petition.* A petition submitted for classification as an alien entrepreneur must be accompanied by evidence that the alien has invested or is actively in the process of investing lawfully obtained capital in a new commercial enterprise in the United States which will create full-time positions for not fewer than 10 qualifying employees. In the case of petitions submitted under the Immigrant Investor Pilot Program, a petition must be accompanied by evidence that the alien has invested, or is actively in the process of investing, capital obtained through lawful means within a regional center designated by the Service in accordance with paragraph (m)(4) of this section. The petitioner may be required to submit information or documentation that the Service deems appropriate in addition to that listed below.

(1) To show that a new commercial enterprise has been established by the petitioner in the United States, the petition must be accompanied by:

(i) As applicable, articles of incorporation, certificate of merger or consolidation, partnership agreement, certificate of limited partnership, joint venture agreement, business trust agreement, or other similar organizational document for the new commercial enterprise;

(ii) A certificate evidencing authority to do business in a state or municipality or, if the form of the business does not require any such certificate or the State or municipality does not issue such a certificate, a statement to that effect; or

(iii) Evidence that, as of a date certain after November 29, 1990, the required amount of capital for the area in which an enterprise is located has been transferred to an existing business, and that the investment has resulted in a substantial increase in the net worth or number of employees of the business to which the capital was transferred. This evidence must be in the form of stock purchase agreements, investment agreements, certified financial reports, payroll records, or any similar instruments, agreements, or documents evidencing the investment in the commercial enterprise and the resulting substantial change in the net worth, number of employees.

(2) To show that the petitioner has invested or is actively in the process of investing the required amount of capital, the petition must be accompanied by evidence that the petitioner has placed the required amount of capital at risk for the purpose of generating a return on the capital placed at risk. Evidence of mere intent to invest, or of prospective investment arrangements entailing no present commitment, will not suffice to show that the petitioner is actively in the process of investing. The alien must show actual commitment of the required amount of capital. Such evidence may include, but need not be limited to:

(i) Bank statement(s) showing amount(s) deposited in United States business account(s) for the enterprise;

(ii) Evidence of assets which have been purchased for use in the United States enterprise, including invoices, sales receipts, and purchase contracts containing sufficient information to identify such assets, their purchase costs, date of purchase, and purchasing entity;

(iii) Evidence of property transferred from abroad for use in the United States enterprise, including United States Customs Service commercial entry documents, bills of lading, and transit insurance policies containing ownership information and sufficient information to identify the property and to indicate the fair market value of such property;

(iv) Evidence of monies transferred or committed to be transferred to the new commercial enterprise in exchange for shares of stock (voting or nonvoting, common or preferred). Such stock may not include terms requiring the new commercial enterprise to redeem it at the holder's request; or

(v) Evidence of any loan or mortgage agreement, promissory note, security agreement, or other evidence of borrowing which is secured by assets of the petitioner, other than those of the new commercial enterprise, and for which the petitioner is personally and primarily liable.

(3) To show that the petitioner has invested, or is actively in the process of investing, capital obtained through lawful means, the petition must be accompanied, as applicable, by:

(i) Foreign business registration records;

(ii) Corporate, partnership (or any other entity in any form which has filed in any country or subdivision thereof any return described in this subpart), and personal tax returns including income, franchise, property (whether real, personal, or intangible), or any other tax returns of any kind filed within five years, with any taxing jurisdiction in or outside the United States by or on behalf of the petitioner;

(iii) Evidence identifying any other source(s) of capital; or

(iv) Certified copies of any judgments or evidence of all pending governmental civil or criminal actions, governmental administrative proceedings, and any private civil actions (pending or otherwise) involving monetary judgments against the petitioner from any court in or outside the United States within the past fifteen years.

(4) *Job creation*—(i) *General.* To show that a new commercial enterprise will create not fewer than ten (10) full-time positions for qualifying employees, the petition must be accompanied by:

(A) Documentation consisting of photocopies of relevant tax records, Form I–9, or other similar documents for ten (10) qualifying employees, if such employees have already been hired following the establishment of the new commercial enterprise; or

(B) A copy of a comprehensive business plan showing that, due to the nature and projected size of the new commercial enterprise, the need for not fewer than ten (10) qualifying employees will result, including approximate dates, within the next two years, and when such employees will be hired.

(ii) *Troubled business.* To show that a new commercial enterprise which has been established through a capital investment in a troubled business meets the statutory employment creation requirement, the petition must be accompanied by evidence that the number of existing employees is being or will be maintained at no less than the pre-investment level for a period of at least two years. Photocopies of tax records, Forms I–9, or other relevant documents for the qualifying employees and a comprehensive business plan shall be submitted in support of the petition.

(iii) *Immigrant Investor Pilot Program.* To show that the new commercial enterprise located within a regional center approved for participation in the Immigrant Investor Pilot Program meets the statutory employment creation requirement, the petition must be accompanied by evidence that the investment will create full-time positions for not fewer than 10 persons either directly or indirectly through revenues generated from increased exports resulting from the Pilot Program. Such evidence may be demonstrated by reasonable methodologies including those set forth in paragraph (m)(3) of this section.

(5) To show that the petitioner is or will be engaged in the management of the new commercial enterprise, either through the exercise of day-to-day managerial control or through policy formulation, as opposed to maintaining a purely passive role in regard to the investment, the petition must be accompanied by:

(i) A statement of the position title that the petitioner has or will have in the new enterprise and a complete description of the position's duties;

(ii) Evidence that the petitioner is a corporate officer or a member of the corporate board of directors; or

(iii) If the new enterprise is a partnership, either limited or general, evidence that the petitioner is engaged in either direct management or policy making activities. For purposes of this section, if the petitioner is a limited partner and the limited partnership agreement provides the petitioner with certain rights, powers, and duties normally granted to limited partners under the Uniform Limited Partnership Act, the petitioner will be considered sufficiently engaged in the management of the new commercial enterprise.

(6) If applicable, to show that the new commercial enterprise has created or will create employment in a targeted employment area, the petition must be accompanied by:

(i) In the case of a rural area, evidence that the new commercial enterprise is principally doing business within a civil jurisdiction not located within any standard metropolitan statistical area as designated by the Office of Management and Budget, or within any city or town having a population of 20,000 or more as based on the most recent decennial census of the United States; or

(ii) In the case of a high unemployment area:

(A) Evidence that the metropolitan statistical area, the specific county within a metropolitan statistical area, or the county in which a city or town with a population of 20,000 or more is located, in which the new commercial enterprise is principally doing business has experienced an average unemployment rate of 150 percent of the national average rate; or

(B) A letter from an authorized body of the government of the state in which the new commercial enterprise is located which certifies that the geographic or political subdivision of the metropolitan statistical area or of the city or town with a population of 20,000 or more in which the enterprise is principally doing business has been designated a high unemployment area. The letter must meet the requirements of 8 CFR 204.6(i).

(k) *Decision.* The petitioner will be notified of the decision, and, if the petition is denied, of the reasons for the denial and of the petitioner's right of appeal to the Associate Commissioner for Examinations in accordance with the provisions of part 103 of this chapter. The decision must specify whether or not the new commercial enterprise is principally doing business within a targeted employment area.

(l) [Reserved]

(m) *Immigrant Investor Pilot Program*—(1) *Scope*. The Immigrant Investor Pilot Program is established solely pursuant to the provisions of section 610 of the Departments of Commerce, Justice, and State, the Judiciary, and Related Agencies Appropriation Act, and subject to all conditions and restrictions stipulated in that section. Except as provided herein, aliens seeking to obtain immigration benefits under this paragraph continue to be subject to all conditions and restrictions set forth in section 203(b)(5) of the Act and this section.

(2) *Number of immigrant visas allocated*. The annual allocation of the visas available under the Immigrant Investor Pilot Program is set at 300 for each of the five fiscal years commencing on October 1, 1993.

(3) *Requirements for regional centers*. Each regional center wishing to participate in the Immigrant Investor Pilot Program shall submit a proposal to the Assistant Commissioner for Adjudications, which:

(i) Clearly describes how the regional center focuses on a geographical region of the United States, and how it will promote economic growth through increased export sales, improved regional productivity, job creation, and increased domestic capital investment;

(ii) Provides in verifiable detail how jobs will be created indirectly through increased exports;

(iii) Provides a detailed statement regarding the amount and source of capital which has been committed to the regional center, as well as a description of the promotional efforts taken and planned by the sponsors of the regional center;

(iv) Contains a detailed prediction regarding the manner in which the regional center will have a positive impact on the regional or national economy in general as reflected by such factors as increased household earnings, greater demand for business services, utilities, maintenance and repair, and construction both within and without the regional center; and

(v) Is supported by economically or statistically valid forecasting tools, including, but not limited to, feasibility studies, analyses of foreign and domestic markets for the goods or services to be exported, and/or multiplier tables.

(4) *Submission of proposals to participate in the Immigrant Investor Pilot Program*. On August 24, 1993, the Service will accept proposals from regional centers seeking approval to participate in the Immigrant Investor Pilot Program. Regional centers that have been approved by the Assistant Commissioner for Adjudications will be eligible to participate in the Immigrant Investor Pilot Program.

(5) *Decision to participate in the Immigrant Investor Pilot Program*. The Assistant Commissioner for Adjudications shall notify the regional center of his or her decision on the request for approval to participate in the Immigrant Investor Pilot Program, and, if the petition is denied, of the reasons for the denial and of the regional center's right of appeal to the Associate Commissioner for Examinations. Notification of denial and appeal rights, and the procedure for appeal shall be the same as those contained in 8 CFR 103.3.

(6) *Continued participation requirements for regional centers*. (i) Regional centers approved for participation in the program must:

(A) Continue to meet the requirements of section 610(a) of the Appropriations Act.

(B) Provide USCIS with updated information annually, and/or as otherwise requested by USCIS, to demonstrate that the regional center is continuing to promote economic growth, including increased export sales, improved regional productivity, job creation, and increased domestic capital investment in the approved geographic area, using a form designated for this purpose; and

(C) Pay the fee provided by 8 CFR 103.7(b)(1)(i)(XX).

(ii) USCIS will issue a notice of intent to terminate the designation of a regional center in the program if:

(A) A regional center fails to submit the information required in paragraph (m)(6)(i)(B) of this section, or pay the associated fee; or

(B) USCIS determines that the regional center no longer serves the purpose of promoting economic growth, including increased export sales, improved regional productivity, job creation, and increased domestic capital investment.

(iii) A notice of intent to terminate the designation of a regional center will be sent to the regional center and set forth the reasons for termination.

(iv) The regional center will be provided 30 days from receipt of the notice of intent to terminate to rebut the ground or grounds stated in the notice of intent to terminate.

(v) USCIS will notify the regional center of the final decision. If USCIS determines that the regional center's participation in the program should be terminated, USCIS will state the reasons for termination. The regional center may appeal the final termination decision in accordance with 8 CFR 103.3.

(vi) A regional center may elect to withdraw from the program and request a termination of the regional center designation. The regional center must notify USCIS of such election in the form of a letter or as otherwise requested by USCIS. USCIS will notify the regional center of its decision regarding the withdrawal request in writing.

(7) *Requirements for alien entrepreneurs.* An alien seeking an immigrant visa as an alien entrepreneur under the Immigrant Investor Pilot Program must demonstrate that his or her qualifying investment is within a regional center approved pursuant to paragraph (m)(4) of this section and that such investment will create jobs indirectly through revenues generated from increased exports resulting from the new commercial enterprise.

(i) *Exports.* For purposes of paragraph (m) of this section, the term "exports" means services or goods which are produced directly or indirectly through revenues generated from a new commercial enterprise and which are transported out of the United States;

(ii) *Indirect job creation.* To show that 10 or more jobs are actually created indirectly by the business, reasonable methodologies may be used. Such methodologies may include multiplier tables, feasibility studies, analyses of foreign and domestic markets for the goods or services to be exported, and other economically or statistically valid forecasting devices which indicate the likelihood that the business will result in increased employment.

(8) *Time for submission of petitions for classification as an alien entrepreneur under the Immigrant Investor Pilot Program.* Commencing on October 1, 1993, petitions will be accepted for filing and adjudicated in accordance with the provisions of this section if the alien entrepreneur has invested or is actively in the process of investing within a regional center which has been approved by the Service for participation in the Pilot Program.

(9) *Effect of termination of approval of regional center to participate in the Immigrant Investor Pilot Program.* Upon termination of approval of a regional center to participate in the Immigrant Investor Pilot Program, the director shall send a formal written notice to any alien within the regional center who has been granted lawful permanent residence on a conditional basis under the Pilot Program, and who has not yet removed the conditional basis of such lawful permanent residence, of the termination of the alien's permanent resident status, unless the alien can establish continued eligibility for alien entrepreneur classification under section 203(b)(5) of the Act.

[56 FR 60910, Nov. 29, 1991, as amended at 57 FR 1860, Jan. 16, 1992; 58 FR 44608, 44609, Aug. 24, 1993; 74 FR 26937, June 5, 2009; 75 FR 58990, Sept. 24, 2010; 76 FR 53782, Aug. 29, 2011; 81 FR 73332, Oct. 24, 2016]

§204.7 Preservation of benefits contained in savings clause of Immigration and Nationality Act Amendments of 1976.

In order to be considered eligible for the benefits of the savings clause contained in section 9 of the Immigration and Nationality Act Amendments of 1976, an alien must show that the facts established prior to January 1, 1977 upon which the entitlement to such benefits was based continue to exist.

[41 FR 55849, Dec. 23, 1976]

§ 204.8 [Reserved]

§ 204.9 Special immigrant status for certain aliens who have served honorably (or are enlisted to serve) in the Armed Forces of the United States for at least 12 years.

(a) *Petition for Armed Forces special immigrant.* An alien may not be classified as an Armed Forces special immigrant unless the alien is the beneficiary of an approved petition to classify such an alien as a special immigrant under section 101(a)(27)(K) of the Act. The petition must be filed on Form I–360, Petition for Amerasian, Widow or Special Immigrant.

(1) *Who may file.* An alien Armed Forces enlistee or veteran may file the petition for Armed Forces special immigrant status in his or her own behalf. The person filing the petition is not required to be a citizen or lawful permanent resident of the United States.

(2) *Where to file.* The petition must be filed in accordance with the instructions on the form.

(b) *Eligibility.* An alien is eligible for classification as a special immigrant under section 101(a)(27)(K) of the Act if:

(1) The alien has served honorably on active duty in the Armed Forces of the United States after October 15, 1978;

(2) The alien's original lawful enlistment was outside the United States (under a treaty or agreement in effect October 1, 1991) for a period or periods aggregating—

(i) Twelve years, and who, if separated from such service, was never separated except under honorable conditions; or

(ii) Six years, in the case of an immigrant who is on active duty at the time of seeking special immigrant status under this rule and who has reenlisted to incur a total active duty service obligation of at least 12 years;

(3) The alien is a national of an independent state which maintains a treaty or agreement allowing nationals of that state to enlist in the United States Armed Forces each year; and

(4) The executive department under which the alien has served or is serving has recommended the granting of special immigrant status to the immigrant.

(c) *Derivative beneficiaries.* A spouse or child accompanying or following to join a principal immigrant who has requested benefits under this section may be accorded the same special immigrant classification as the principal alien. This may occur whether or not the spouse or child is named in the petition and without the approval of a separate petition, but only if the executive department under which the immigrant serves or served recommends the granting of special immigrant status to the principal immigrant.

(1) The relationship of spouse and child as defined in section 101(b)(1) of the Act must have existed at the time the principal alien's special immigrant application under section 101(a)(27)(K) of the Act was approved. The spouse or child of an immigrant classified as a section 103(a)(27)(K) special immigrant is entitled to a derivative status corresponding to the classification and priority date of the beneficiary of the petition.

(2) When a spouse or child of an alien granted special immigrant status under section 101(a)(27)(K) of the Act is in the United States but was not included in the principal alien's application, the spouse or child shall file Form I–485, Application to Register Permanent Residence or Adjust Status, in accordance with the instructions on the form, regardless of the status of that spouse or child in the United States. The application must be supported by evidence that the principal alien has been granted special immigrant status under section 101(a)(27)(K) of the Act.

(3) *Revocation of derivative status.* The termination of special immigrant status for a person who was the principal applicant shall result in termination of the special immigrant status of a spouse or child whose status was based on the special immigrant application of the principal.

(d) *Documents which must be submitted in support of the petition.* (1) A petition to classify an immigrant as a special immigrant under section 101(a)(27)(K) of the Act must be accompanied by the following:

(i) Certified proof of reenlistment (after 6 years of active duty service), or certification of past active duty status of 12 years, issued by the authorizing official of the executive department in which the applicant serves or has served, which certifies that the applicant has the required honorable active duty service and commitment. The authorizing official need not be at a level above the "local command". The certification must be submitted with Form I-360, Petition for Amerasian, Widow(er), or Special Immigrant; and

(ii) Birth certificate of the applicant establishing that the applicant is a national of an independent state which maintains a treaty or agreement allowing nationals of that state to enlist in the United States Armed Forces each year.

(2) Any documents submitted in support of the petition must meet the evidentiary requirements as set forth in 8 CFR part 103.

(3) Submission of an original Form DD–214, Certificate of Release or Discharge from Active Duty; Form G–325b, Biographic Information; and Form N–426, Request for Certification of Military or Naval Service, is not required for approval of a petition for special immigrant status.

(e) *Decision.* The petitioner will be notified of the director's decision and, if the petition is denied, of the reasons for the denial. If the petition is denied, the petitioner will also be notified of the petitioner's right to appeal the decision to the Associate Commissioner for Examinations in accordance with 8 CFR part 103.

(f) *Revocation under section 205 of the Act.* An alien who has been granted special immigrant classification under section 101(a)(27)(K) of the Act must meet the qualifications set forth in the Act at the time he or she is admitted to the United States for lawful permanent residence. If an Armed Forces special immigrant ceases to be a qualified enlistee by failing to complete the required active duty service obligation for reasons other than an honorable discharge prior to entering the United States with an immigrant visa or approval of an application for adjustment of status to that of an alien lawfully admitted for permanent residence, the petition designating his or her classification as a special immigrant is revoked automatically under the general provisions of section 205 of the Act. The Service shall obtain a current Form DD–214, Certificate of Release or Discharge from Active Duty, from the appropriate executive department for verification of the alien's failure to maintain eligibility for the classification under section 101(a)(27)(K) of the Act.

[57 FR 33861, July 31, 1992, as amended at 58 FR 50836, Sept. 29, 1993; 74 FR 26937, June 5, 2009]

§204.10 [Reserved]

§204.11 Special immigrant status for certain aliens declared dependent on a juvenile court (special immigrant juvenile).

(a) *Definitions.*

Eligible for long-term foster care means that a determination has been made by the juvenile court that family reunification is no longer a viable option. A child who is eligible for long-term foster care will normally be expected to remain in foster care until reaching the age of majority, unless the child is adopted or placed in a guardianship situation. For the purposes of establishing and maintaining eligibility for classification as a special immigrant juvenile, a child who has been adopted or placed in guardianship situation after having been found dependent upon a juvenile court in the United States will continue to be considered to be eligible for long-term foster care.

Juvenile court means a court located in the United States having jurisdiction under State law to make judicial determinations about the custody and care of juveniles.

(b) *Petition for special immigrant juvenile.* An alien may not be classified as a special immigrant juvenile unless the alien is the beneficiary of an approved petition to classify an alien as a special immigrant under section 101(a)(27) of the Act. The petition must be filed on Form I–360, Petition for Amerasian, Widow(er) or Special Immigrant. The alien, or any person acting on the alien's behalf, may file the petition for special immigrant juvenile status. The person filing the petition is not required to be a citizen or lawful permanent resident of the United States.

(c) *Eligibility.* An alien is eligible for classification as a special immigrant under section 101(a)(27)(J) of the Act if the alien:

(1) Is under twenty-one years of age;

(2) Is unmarried;

(3) Has been declared dependent upon a juvenile court located in the United States in accordance with state law governing such declarations of dependency, while the alien was in the United States and under the jurisdiction of the court;

(4) Has been deemed eligible by the juvenile court for long-term foster care;

(5) Continues to be dependent upon the juvenile court and eligible for long-term foster care, such declaration, dependency or eligibility not having been vacated, terminated, or otherwise ended; and

(6) Has been the subject of judicial proceedings or administrative proceedings authorized or recognized by the juvenile court in which it has been determined that it would not be in the alien's best interest to be returned to the country of nationality or last habitual residence of the beneficiary or his or her parent or parents; or

(7) On November 29, 1990, met all the eligibility requirements for special immigrant juvenile status in paragraphs (c)(1) through (c)(6) of this section, and for whom a petition for classification as a special immigrant juvenile is filed on Form I–360 before June 1, 1994.

(d) *Initial documents which must be submitted in support of the petition.* (1) Documentary evidence of the alien's age, in the form of a birth certificate, passport, official foreign identity document issued by a foreign government, such as a Cartilla or a Cedula, or other document which in the discretion of the director establishes the beneficiary's age; and

(2) One or more documents which include:

(i) A juvenile court order, issued by a court of competent jurisdiction located in the United States, showing that the court has found the beneficiary to be dependent upon that court;

(ii) A juvenile court order, issued by a court of competent jurisdiction located in the United States, showing that the court has found the beneficiary eligible for long-term foster care; and

(iii) Evidence of a determination made in judicial or administrative proceedings by a court or agency recognized by the juvenile court and authorized by law to make such decisions, that it would not be in the beneficiary's best interest to be returned to the country of nationality or last habitual residence of the beneficiary or of his or her parent or parents.

(e) *Decision.* The petitioner will be notified of the director's decision, and, if the petition is denied, of the reasons for the denial. If the petition is denied, the petitioner will also be notified of the petitioner's right to appeal the decision to the Associate Commissioner, Examinations, in accordance with part 103 of this chapter.

[58 FR 42850, Aug. 12, 1993, as amended at 74 FR 26937, June 5, 2009]

§ 204.12 How can second-preference immigrant physicians be granted a national interest waiver based on service in a medically underserved area or VA facility?

(a) *Which physicians qualify?* Any alien physician (namely doctors of medicine and doctors of osteopathy) for whom an immigrant visa petition has been filed pursuant to section 203(b)(2) of the Act shall be granted a national interest waiver under section 203(b)(2)(B)(ii) of the Act if the physician requests the waiver in accordance with this section and establishes that:

(1) The physician agrees to work full-time (40 hours per week) in a clinical practice for an aggregate of 5 years (not including time served in J–1 nonimmigrant status); and

(2) The service is;

(i) In a geographical area or areas designated by the Secretary of Health and Human Services (HHS) as a Medically Underserved Area, a Primary Medical Health Professional Shortage Area, or a Mental Health Professional Shortage Area, and in a medical speciality that is within the scope of the Secretary's designation for the geographical area or areas; or

(ii) At a health care facility under the jurisdiction of the Secretary of Veterans Affairs (VA); and

(3) A Federal agency or the department of public health of a State, territory of the United States, or the District of Columbia, has previously determined that the physician's work in that area or facility is in the public interest.

(b) *Is there a time limit on how long the physician has to complete the required medical service?* (1) If the physician already has authorization to accept employment (other than as a J–1 exchange alien), the beneficiary physician must complete the aggregate 5 years of qualifying full-time clinical practice during the 6-year period beginning on the date of approval of the Form I–140.

(2) If the physician must obtain authorization to accept employment before the physician may lawfully begin working, the physician must complete the aggregate 5 years of qualifying full-time clinical practice during the 6-year period beginning on the date of the Service issues the necessary employment authorization document.

(c) *Are there special requirements for these physicians?* Petitioners requesting the national interest waiver as described in this section on behalf of a qualified alien physician, or alien physicians self-petitioning for second preference classification, must meet all eligibility requirements found in paragraphs (k)(1) through (k)(3) of § 204.5. In addition, the petitioner or self-petitioner must submit the following evidence with Form I–140 to support the request for a national interest waiver. Physicians planning to divide the practice of full-time clinical medicine between more than one underserved area must submit the following evidence for each area of intended practice.

(1)(i) If the physician will be an employee, a full-time employment contract for the required period of clinical medical practice, or an employment commitment letter from a VA facility. The contract or letter must have been issued and dated within 6 months prior to the date the petition is filed.

(ii) If the physician will establish his or her own practice, the physician's sworn statement committing to the full-time practice of clinical medicine for the required period, and describing the steps the physician has taken or intends to actually take to establish the practice.

(2) Evidence that the physician will provide full-time clinical medical service:

(i) In a geographical area or areas designated by the Secretary of HHS as having a shortage of health care professionals and in a medical speciality that is within the scope of the Secretary's designation for the geographical area or areas; or

(ii) In a facility under the jurisdiction of the Secretary of VA.

(3) A letter (issued and dated within 6 months prior to the date on which the petition is filed) from a Federal agency or from the department of public health (or equivalent) of a State or territory of the United States or the District of Columbia, attesting that the alien physician's work is or will be in the public interest.

(i) An attestation from a Federal agency must reflect the agency's knowledge of the alien's qualifications and the agency's background in making determinations on matters involving medical affairs so as to substantiate the finding that the alien's work is or will be in the public interest.

(ii) An attestation from the public health department of a State, territory, or the District of Columbia must reflect that the agency has jurisdiction over the place where the alien physician intends to practice clinical medicine. If the alien physician intends to practice clinical medicine in more than one underserved area, attestations from each intended area of practice must be included.

(4) Evidence that the alien physician meets the admissibility requirements established by section 212(a)(5)(B) of the Act.

(5) Evidence of the Service-issued waivers, if applicable, of the requirements of sections 212(e) of the Act, if the alien physician has been a J–1 nonimmigrant receiving medical training within the United States.

(d) *How will the Service process petitions filed on different dates?*—(1) *Petitions filed on or after November 12, 1999.* For petitions filed on or after November 12, 1999, the Service will approve a national interest waiver provided the petitioner or beneficiary (if self-petitioning) submits the necessary documentation to satisfy the requirements of section 203(b)(2)(B)(ii) of the Act and this section, and the physician is otherwise eligible for classification as a second preference employment-based immigrant. Nothing in this section relieves the alien physician from any other requirement other than that of fulfilling the labor certification process as provided in § 204.5(k)(4).

(2) *Petitions pending on November 12, 1999.* Section 203(b)(2)(B)(ii) of the Act applies to all petitions that were pending adjudication as of November 12, 1999 before a Service Center, before the associate Commissioner for Examinations, or before a Federal court. Petitioners whose petitions were pending on November 12, 1999, will not be required to submit a new petition, but may be required to submit supplemental evidence noted in paragraph (c) of this section. The requirement that supplemental evidence be issued and dated within 6 months prior to the date on which the petition is filed is not applicable to petitions that were pending as of November 12, 1999. If the case was pending before the Associate Commissioner for Examinations or a Federal court on November 12, 1999, the petitioner should ask for a remand to the proper Service Center for consideration of this new evidence.

(3) *Petitions denied on or after November 12, 1999.* The Service Center or the Associate Commissioner for Examinations shall reopen any petition affected by the provision of section 203(b)(2)(B)(ii) of the Act that the Service denied on or after November 12, 1999, but prior to the effective date of this rule.

(4) *Petitions filed prior to November 1, 1998.* For petitions filed prior to November 1, 1998, and still pending as of November 12, 1999, the Service will approve a national interest waiver provided the beneficiary fulfills the evidence requirements of paragraph (c) of this section. Alien physicians that are beneficiaries of pre-November 1, 1998, petitions are only required to work full-time as a physician practicing clinical medicine for an aggregate of 3 years, rather than 5 years, not including time served in J–1 nonimmigrant status, prior to the physician either adjusting status under section 245 of the Act or receiving a visa issued under section 204(b) of the Act. The physician must complete the aggregate of 3 years of medical service within the 4-year period beginning on the date of the approval of the petition, if the physician already has authorization to accept employment (other than as a J–1 exchange alien). If the physician does not already have authorization to accept employment, the physician must perform the service within the 4-year period beginning the date the Service issues the necessary employment authorization document.

(5) *Petitions filed and approved before November 12, 1999.* An alien physician who obtained approval of a second preference employment-based visa petition and a national interest waiver before November 12, 1999, is not subject to the service requirements imposed in section 203(b)(2)(B)(ii) of the Act. If the physician obtained under section 214(l) of the Act a waiver of the foreign residence requirement imposed under section 212(e) of the Act, he or she must comply with the requirements of section 214(l) of the Act in order to continue to have the benefit of that waiver.

(6) *Petitions denied prior to November 12, 1999.* If a prior Service decision denying a national interest waiver under section 203(b)(2)(B) of the Act became administratively final before November 12, 1999, an alien physician who believes that he or she is eligible for the waiver under the provisions of section 203(b)(2)(B)(ii) of the Act may file a new Form I–140 petition accompanied by the evidence required in paragraph (c) of this section. The Service must deny any motion to reopen or reconsider a decision denying an immigrant visa petition if the decision became final before November 12, 1999, without prejudice to the filing of a new visa petition with a national interest waiver request that comports with section 203(b)(2)(B)(ii) of the Act.

(e) *May physicians file adjustment of status applications?* Upon approval of a second preference employment-based immigrant petition, Form I–140, and national interest waiver based on a full-time clinical practice in a shortage area or areas of the United States, an alien physician may submit Form I–485, Application to Register Permanent Residence or Adjust Status, to the appropriate Service Center. The Service will not approve the alien physician's application for adjustment of status until the alien physician submits evidence documenting that the alien physician has completed the period of required service. Specific instructions for alien physicians filing adjustment applications are found in §245.18 of this chapter.

(f) *May a physician practice clinical medicine in a different underserved area?* Physicians in receipt of an approved Form I–140 with a national interest waiver based on full-time clinical practice in a designated shortage area and a pending adjustment of status application may apply to the Service if the physician is offered new employment to practice full-time in another underserved area of the United States.

(1) If the physician beneficiary has found a new employer desiring to petition the Service on the physician's behalf, the new petitioner must submit a new Form I–140 (with fee) with all the evidence required in paragraph (c) of this section, including a copy of the approval notice from the initial Form I–140. If approved, the new petition will be matched with the pending adjustment of status application. The beneficiary will retain the priority date from the initial Form I–140. The Service will calculate the amount of time the physician was between employers so as to adjust the count of the aggregate time served in an underserved area. This calculation will be based on the evidence the physician submits pursuant to the requirements of §245.18(d) of this chapter. An approved change of practice to another underserved area does not constitute a new 6-year period in which the physician must complete the aggregate 5 years of service.

(2) If the physician intends to establish his or her own practice, the physician must submit a new Form I–140 (with fee) will all the evidence required in paragraph (c) of this section, including the special requirement of paragraph (c)(1)(ii) of this section and a copy of the approval notice from the initial Form I–140. If approved, the new petition will be matched with the pending adjustment of status application. The beneficiary will retain the priority date from the initial Form I–140. The Service will calculate the amount of time the physician was between practices so as to adjust the count of the aggregate time served in an underserved area. This calculation will be based on the evidence the physician submits pursuant to the requirements of §245.18(d) of this chapter. An approved change of practice to another underserved area does not constitute a new 6-year period in which the physician must complete the aggregate 5 years of service.

(g) *Do these provisions have any effect on physicians with foreign residence requirements?* Because the requirements of section 203(b)(2)(B)(ii) of the Act are not exactly the same as the requirements of section 212(e) or 214(l) of the Act, approval of a national interest waiver under section 203(b)(2)(B)(ii) of the Act and this paragraph does not relieve the alien physician of any foreign residence requirement that the alien physician may have under section 212(e) of the Act.

[65 FR 53893, Sept. 6, 2000; 65 FR 57861, Sept. 26, 2000]

§204.13 How can the International Broadcasting Bureau of the United States Broadcasting Board of Governors petition for a fourth preference special immigrant broadcaster?

(a) *Which broadcasters qualify?* Under section 203(b)(4) of the Act, the International Broadcasting Bureau of the United States Broadcasting Board of Governors (BBG), or a grantee of the BBG, may petition for an alien (and the alien's accompanying spouse and children) to work as a broadcaster for the BBG or a grantee of the BBG in the United States. For the purposes of this section, the terms:

BBG grantee means Radio Free Asia, Inc (RFA) or Radio Free Europe/Radio Liberty, Inc. (RFE/RL); and

Broadcaster means a reporter, writer, translator, editor, producer or announcer for news broadcasts; hosts for news broadcasts, news analysis, editorial and other broadcast features; or a news analysis specialist. The term broadcaster does not include individuals performing purely technical or support services for the BBG or a BBG grantee.

(b) *Is there a yearly limit on the number of visas available for alien broadcasters petitioned by the BBG or a BBG grantee?* (1) Under the provisions of section 203(b)(4) of the Act, a yearly limit of 100 fourth preference special immigrant visas are available to aliens intending to work as broadcasters in the United States for the BBG or a BBG grantee. These 100 visas are available in any fiscal year beginning on or after October 1, 2000.

(2) The alien broadcaster's accompanying spouse and children are not counted towards the 100 special broadcaster visa limit.

(c) *What form should the BBG use to petition for these special alien broadcasters?* The BBG or a BBG grantee shall use Form I–360, Petition for Amerasian, Widow(er), or Special Immigrant, to petition for an alien broadcaster. The petition must be submitted with the correct fee noted on the form.

(d) *Will the BBG need to submit supplemental evidence with Form I–360 for alien broadcasters?* (1) All Form I–360 petitions submitted by the BBG or a BBG grantee on behalf of an alien for a broadcaster position with the BBG or BBG grantee must be accompanied by a signed and dated supplemental attestation that contains the following information about the prospective alien broadcaster:

(i) The job title and a full description of the job to be performed; and

(ii) The broadcasting expertise held by the alien, including how long the alien has been performing duties that relate to the prospective position or a statement as to how the alien possesses the necessary skills that make him or her qualified for the broadcasting-related position within the BBG or BBG grantee.

(2) [Reserved]

[66 FR 51821, Oct. 11, 2001, as amended at 74 FR 26937, June 5, 2009]

Subpart B [Reserved]

Subpart C—Intercountry Adoption of a Convention Adoptee

SOURCE: 72 FR 56854, Oct. 4, 2007, unless otherwise noted.

§ 204.300 Scope of this subpart.

(a) *Convention adoptees.* This subpart governs the adjudication of a Form I–800A or Form I–800 for a Convention adoptee under section 101(b)(1)(G) of the Act. The provisions of this subpart enter into force on the Convention effective date, as defined in 8 CFR 204.301.

(b) *Orphan cases.* On or after the Convention effective date, no Form I–600A or I–600 may be filed under section 101(b)(1)(F) of the Act and 8 CFR 204.3 in relation to the adoption of a child who is habitually resident in a Convention country. If a Form I–600A or Form I–600 was filed before the Convention effective date, the case will continue to be governed by 8 CFR 204.3, as in effect before the Convention effective date.

(c) *Adopted children.* This subpart does not apply to the immigrant visa classification of adopted children, as defined in section 101(b)(1)(E) of the Act. For the procedures that govern classification of adopted children as defined in section 101(b)(1)(E) of the Act, see 8 CFR 204.2.

§ 204.301 Definitions.

The definitions in 22 CFR 96.2 apply to this subpart C. In addition, as used in this subpart C, the term:

Abandonment means:

(1) That a child's parent has willfully forsaken all parental rights, obligations, and claims to the child, as well as all custody of the child without intending to transfer, or without transferring, these rights to any specific individual(s) or entity.

(2) The child's parent must have actually surrendered such rights, obligations, claims, control, and possession.

(3) That a parent's knowledge that a specific person or persons may adopt a child does not void an abandonment; however, a purported act of abandonment cannot be conditioned on the child's adoption by that specific person or persons.

(4) That if the parent(s) entrusted the child to a third party for custodial care

in anticipation of, or preparation for, adoption, the third party (such as a governmental agency, a court of competent jurisdiction, an adoption agency, or an orphanage) must have been authorized under the Convention country's child welfare laws to act in such a capacity.

(5) That, if the parent(s) entrusted the child to an orphanage, the parent(s) did not intend the placement to be merely temporary, with the intention of retaining the parent-child relationship, but that the child is abandoned if the parent(s) entrusted the child permanently and unconditionally to an orphanage.

(6) That, although a written document from the parent(s) is not necessary to prove abandonment, if any written document signed by the parent(s) is presented to prove abandonment, the document must specify whether the parent(s) who signed the document was (were) able to read and understand the language in which the document is written. If the parent is not able to read or understand the language in which the document is written, then the document is not valid unless the document is accompanied by a declaration, signed by an identified individual, establishing that that identified individual is competent to translate the language in the document into a language that the parent understands and that the individual, on the date and at the place specified in the declaration, did in fact read and explain the document to the parent in a language that the parent understands. The declaration must also indicate the language used to provide this explanation. If the person who signed the declaration is an officer or employee of the Central Authority (but not of an agency or entity authorized to perform a Central Authority function by delegation) or any other governmental agency, the person must certify the truth of the facts stated in the declaration. Any other individual who signs a declaration must sign the declaration under penalty of perjury under United States law.

Adoption means the judicial or administrative act that establishes a permanent legal parent-child relationship between a minor and an adult who is not already the minor's legal parent and terminates the legal parent-child relationship between the adoptive child and any former parent(s).

Adult member of the household means:

(1) Any individual other than the applicant, who has the same principal residence as the applicant and who had reached his or her 18th birthday on or before the date a Form I–800A is filed; or

(2) Any person who has not yet reached his or her 18th birthday before the date a Form I–800A is filed, or who does not actually live at the same residence, but whose presence in the residence is relevant to the issue of suitability to adopt, if the officer adjudicating the Form I–800A concludes, based on the facts of the case, that it is necessary to obtain an evaluation of how that person's presence in the home affects the determination whether the applicant is suitable as the adoptive parent(s) of a Convention adoptee.

Applicant means the U.S. citizen (and his or her spouse, if any) who has filed a Form I–800A under this subpart C. The applicant may be an unmarried U.S. citizen who is at least 24 years old when the Form I–800A is filed, or a married U.S. citizen of any age and his or her spouse of any age. Although the singular term "applicant" is used in this subpart, the term includes both a married U.S. citizen and his or her spouse.

Birth parent means a "natural parent" as used in section 101(b)(1)(G) of the Act.

Central Authority means the entity designated as such under Article 6(1) of the Convention by any Convention country or, in the case of the United States, the United States Department of State. Except as specified in this Part, "Central Authority" also means, solely for purposes of this Part, an individual who or entity that is performing a Central Authority function, having been authorized to do so by the designated Central Authority, in accordance with the Convention and the law of the Central Authority's country.

Competent authority means a court or governmental agency of a foreign country that has jurisdiction and authority to make decisions in matters of child welfare, including adoption.

Convention means the Convention on Protection of Children and Co-operation in Respect of Intercountry Adoption, opened for signature at The Hague on May 29, 1993.

Convention adoptee means a child habitually resident in a Convention country who is eligible to immigrate to the United States on the basis of a Convention adoption.

Convention adoption, except as specified in 8 CFR 204.300(b), means the adoption, on or after the Convention effective date, of an alien child habitually resident in a Convention country by a U.S. citizen habitually resident in the United States, when in connection with the adoption the child has moved, or will move, from the Convention country to the United States.

Convention country means a country that is a party to the Convention and with which the Convention is in force for the United States.

Convention effective date means the date on which the Convention enters into force for the United States as announced by the Secretary of State under 22 CFR 96.17.

Custody for purposes of emigration and adoption exists when:

(1) The competent authority of the country of a child's habitual residence has, by a judicial or administrative act (which may be either the act granting custody of the child or a separate judicial or administrative act), expressly authorized the petitioner, or an individual or entity acting on the petitioner's behalf, to take the child out of the country of the child's habitual residence and to bring the child to the United States for adoption in the United States.

(2) If the custody order shows that custody was given to an individual or entity acting on the petitioner's behalf, the custody order must indicate that the child is to be adopted in the United States by the petitioner.

(3) A foreign judicial or administrative act that is called an adoption but that does not terminate the legal parent-child relationship between the former parent(s) and the adopted child and does not create the permanent legal parent-child relationship between the petitioner and the adopted child will be deemed a grant of custody of the child for purposes of this part, but only if the judicial or administrative act expressly authorizes the custodian to take the child out of the country of the child's habitual residence and to bring the child to the United States for adoption in the United States by the petitioner.

Deserted or desertion means that a child's parent has willfully forsaken the child and has refused to carry out parental rights and obligations and that, as a result, the child has become a ward of a competent authority in accordance with the laws of the Convention country.

Disappeared or Disappearance means that a child's parent has unaccountably or inexplicably passed out of the child's life so that the parent's whereabouts are unknown, there is no reasonable expectation of the parent's reappearance, and there has been a reasonable effort to locate the parent as determined by a competent authority in accordance with the laws of the Convention country. A stepparent who under the definition of "Parent" in this section is deemed to be a child's legal parent, may be found to have disappeared if it is established that the stepparent either never knew of the child's existence, or never knew of their legal relationship to the child.

Home study preparer means a person (whether an individual or an agency) authorized under 22 CFR part 96 to conduct home studies for Convention adoption cases, either as a public domestic authority, an accredited agency, a temporarily accredited agency, approved person, supervised provider, or exempted provider and who (if not a public domestic authority) holds any license or other authorization that may be required to conduct adoption home studies under the law of the jurisdiction in which the home study is conducted.

Incapable of providing proper care means that, in light of all the relevant circumstances including but not limited to economic or financial concerns, extreme poverty, medical, mental, or emotional difficulties, or long term-incarceration, the child's two living birth parents are not able to provide for the child's basic needs, consistent with the local standards of the Convention country.

Irrevocable consent means a document which indicates the place and date the document was signed by a child's legal custodian, and which meets the other requirements specified in this definition, in which the legal custodian freely consents to the termination of the legal custodian's legal relationship with the child. If the irrevocable consent is signed by the child's birth mother or any legal custodian other than the birth father, the irrevocable consent must have been signed after the child's birth; the birth father may sign an irrevocable consent before the child's birth if permitted by the law of the child's habitual residence. This provision does not preclude a birth father from giving consent to the termination of his legal relationship to the child before the child's birth, if the birth father is permitted to do so under the law of the country of the child's habitual residence.

(1) To qualify as an irrevocable consent under this definition, the document must specify whether the legal custodian is able to read and understand the language in which the consent is written. If the legal custodian is not able to read or understand the language in which the document is written, then the document does not qualify as an irrevocable consent unless the document is accompanied by a declaration, signed, by an identified individual, establishing that that identified individual is competent to translate the language in the irrevocable consent into a language that the parent understands, and that the individual, on the date and at the place specified in the declaration, did in fact read and explain the consent to the legal custodian in a language that the legal custodian understands. The declaration must also indicate the language used to provide this explanation. If the person who signed the declaration is an officer or employee of the Central Authority (but not of an agency or entity authorized to perform a Central Authority function by delegation) or any other governmental agency, the person must certify the truth of the facts stated in the declaration. Any other individual who signs a declaration must sign the declaration under penalty of perjury under United States law.

(2) If more than one individual or entity is the child's legal custodian, the consent of each legal custodian may be recorded in one document, or in an additional document, but all documents, taken together, must show that each legal custodian has given the necessary irrevocable consent.

Legal custodian means the individual who, or entity that, has legal custody of a child, as defined in 22 CFR 96.2.

Officer means a USCIS officer with jurisdiction to adjudicate Form I–800A or Form I–800 or a Department of State officer with jurisdiction, by delegation from USCIS, to grant either provisional or final approval of a Form I–800.

Parent means any person who is related to a child as described in section 101(b)(1)(A), (B), (C), (D), (E), (F), or (G) and section 101(b)(2) of the Act, except that a stepparent described in section 101(b)(1)(B) of the Act is not considered a child's parent, solely for purposes of classification of the child as a Convention adoptee, if the petitioner establishes that, under the law of the Convention country, there is no legal parent-child relationship between a stepparent and stepchild. This definition includes a stepparent if the stepparent adopted the child, or if the stepparent, under the law of the Convention country, became the child's legal parent by marrying the other legal parent. A stepparent who is a legal parent may consent to the child's adoption, or may be found to have abandoned or deserted the child, or to have disappeared from the child's life, in the same manner as would apply to any other legal parent.

Petitioner means the U.S. citizen (and his or her spouse, if any) who has filed a Form I–800 under this subpart C. The petitioner may be an unmarried U.S. citizen who is at least 25 years old when the Form I–800 is filed, or a married U.S. citizen of any age and his or her spouse of any age. Although the singular term "petitioner" is used in this subpart, the term includes both a married U.S. citizen and his or her spouse.

Sole parent means:

(1) The child's mother, when the competent authority has determined that

the child's father has abandoned or deserted the child, or has disappeared from the child's life; or

(2) The child's father, when the competent authority has determined that the child's mother has abandoned or deserted the child, or has disappeared from the child's life; except that

(3) A child's parent is not a sole parent if the child has acquired another parent within the meaning of section 101(b)(2) of the Act and this section.

Suitability as adoptive parent(s) means that USCIS is satisfied, based on the evidence of record, that it is reasonable to conclude that the applicant is capable of providing, and will provide, proper parental care to an adopted child.

Surviving parent means the child's living parent when the child's other parent is dead, and the child has not acquired another parent within the meaning of section 101(b)(2) of the Act and this section.

§ 204.302 Role of service providers.

(a) *Who may provide services in Convention adoption cases.* Subject to the limitations in paragraph (b) or (c) of this section, a U.S. citizen seeking to file a Form I–800A or I–800 may use the services of any individual or entity authorized to provide services in connection with adoption, except that the U.S. citizen must use the services of an accredited agency, temporarily accredited agency, approved person, supervised provider public domestic authority or exempted provider when required to do so under 22 CFR part 96.

(b) *Unauthorized practice of law prohibited.* An adoption agency or facilitator, including an individual or entity authorized under 22 CFR part 96 to provide the six specific adoption services identified in 22 CFR 96.2, may not engage in any act that constitutes the legal representation, as defined in 8 CFR 1.2, of the applicant (for a Form I–800A case) or petitioner (for a Form I–800 case) unless authorized to do so as provided in 8 CFR part 292. An individual authorized under 8 CFR part 292 to practice before USCIS may provide legal services in connection with a Form I–800A or I–800 case, but may not provide any of the six specific adoption services identified in 22 CFR 96.2, unless the individual is authorized to do so under 22 CFR part 96 (for services provided in the United States) or under the laws of the country of the child's habitual residence (for services performed outside the United States). The provisions of 8 CFR 292.5 concerning sending notices about a case do not apply to an adoption agency or facilitator that is not authorized under 8 CFR part 292 to engage in representation before USCIS.

(c) *Application of the Privacy Act.* Except as permitted by the Privacy Act, 5 U.S.C. 552a and the relevant Privacy Act notice concerning the routine use of information, USCIS may not disclose or give access to any information or record relating to any applicant or petitioner who has filed a Form I–800A or Form I–800 to any individual or entity other than that person, including but not limited to an accredited agency, temporarily accredited agency, approved person, public domestic authority, exempted provider, or supervised provider, unless the applicant who filed the Form I–800A or the petitioner who filed Form I–800 has filed a written consent to disclosure, as provided by the Privacy Act, 5 U.S.C. 552a.

[72 FR 56854, Oct. 4, 2007, as amended at 76 FR 53782, Aug. 29, 2011]

§ 204.303 Determination of habitual residence.

(a) *U.S. Citizens.* For purposes of this subpart, a U.S. citizen who is seeking to have an alien classified as the U.S. citizen's child under section 101(b)(1)(G) of the Act is deemed to be habitually resident in the United States if the individual:

(1) Has his or her domicile in the United States, even if he or she is living temporarily abroad; or

(2) Is not domiciled in the United States but establishes by a preponderance of the evidence that:

(i) The citizen will have established a domicile in the United States on or before the date of the child's admission to the United States for permanent residence as a Convention adoptee; or

(ii) The citizen indicates on the Form I–800 that the citizen intends to bring the child to the United States after adopting the child abroad, and before the child's 18th birthday, at which time the child will be eligible for, and will apply for, naturalization under section 322 of the Act and 8 CFR part 322. This option is not available if the child will be adopted in the United States.

(b) *Convention adoptees.* A child whose classification is sought as a Convention adoptee is, generally, deemed for purposes of this subpart C to be habitually resident in the country of the child's citizenship. If the child's actual residence is outside the country of the child's citizenship, the child will be deemed habitually resident in that other country, rather than in the country of citizenship, if the Central Authority (or another competent authority of the country in which the child has his or her actual residence) has determined that the child's status in that country is sufficiently stable for that country properly to exercise jurisdiction over the child's adoption or custody. This determination must be made by the Central Authority itself, or by another competent authority of the country of the child's habitual residence, but may not be made by a nongovernmental individual or entity authorized by delegation to perform Central Authority functions. The child will not be considered to be habitually resident in any country to which the child travels temporarily, or to which he or she travels either as a prelude to, or in conjunction with, his or her adoption and/or immigration to the United States.

§ 204.304 Improper inducement prohibited.

(a) *Prohibited payments.* Neither the applicant/petitioner, nor any individual or entity acting on behalf of the applicant/petitioner may, directly or indirectly, pay, give, offer to pay, or offer to give to any individual or entity or request, receive, or accept from any individual or entity, any money (in any amount) or anything of value (whether the value is great or small), directly or indirectly, to induce or influence any decision concerning:

(1) The placement of a child for adoption;

(2) The consent of a parent, a legal custodian, individual, or agency to the adoption of a child;

(3) The relinquishment of a child to a competent authority, or to an agency or person as defined in 22 CFR 96.2, for the purpose of adoption; or

(4) The performance by the child's parent or parents of any act that makes the child a Convention adoptee.

(b) *Permissible payments.* Paragraph (a) of this section does not prohibit an applicant/petitioner, or an individual or entity acting on behalf of an applicant/petitioner, from paying the reasonable costs incurred for the services designated in this paragraph. A payment is not reasonable if it is prohibited under the law of the country in which the payment is made or if the amount of the payment is not commensurate with the costs for professional and other services in the country in which any particular service is provided. The permissible services are:

(1) The services of an adoption service provider in connection with an adoption;

(2) Expenses incurred in locating a child for adoption;

(3) Medical, hospital, nursing, pharmaceutical, travel, or other similar expenses incurred by a mother or her child in connection with the birth or any illness of the child;

(4) Counseling services for a parent or a child for a reasonable time before and after the child's placement for adoption;

(5) Expenses, in an amount commensurate with the living standards in the country of the child's habitual residence, for the care of the birth mother while pregnant and immediately following the birth of the child;

(6) Expenses incurred in obtaining the home study;

(7) Expenses incurred in obtaining the reports on the child as described in 8 CFR 204.313(d)(3) and (4);

(8) Legal services, court costs, and travel or other administrative expenses connected with an adoption, including any legal services performed for a parent who consents to the adoption of a child or relinquishes the child to an agency; and

(9) Any other service the payment for which the officer finds, on the basis of the facts of the case, was reasonably necessary.

(c) *Department of State requirements.* See 22 CFR 96.34, 96.36 and 96.40 for additional regulatory information concerning fees in relation to Convention adoptions.

§ 204.305 State preadoption requirements.

State preadoption requirements must be complied with when a child is coming into the State as a Convention adoptee to be adopted in the United States. A qualified Convention adoptee is deemed to be coming to be adopted in the United States if either of the following factors exists:

(a) The applicant/petitioner will not complete the child's adoption abroad; or

(b) In the case of a married applicant/petitioner, the child was adopted abroad only by one of the spouses, rather than by the spouses jointly, so that it will be necessary for the other spouse to adopt the child after the child's admission.

§ 204.306 Classification as an immediate relative based on a Convention adoption.

(a) Unless 8 CFR 204.309 requires the denial of a Form I–800A or Form I–800, a child is eligible for classification as an immediate relative, as defined in section 201(b)(2)(A)(i) of the Act, on the basis of a Convention adoption, if the U.S. citizen who seeks to adopt the child establishes that:

(1) The United States citizen is (or, if married, the United States citizen and the United States citizen's spouse are) eligible and suitable to adopt; and

(2) The child is a Convention adoptee.

(b) A U.S. citizen seeking to have USCIS classify an alien child as the U.S. citizen's child under section 101(b)(1)(G) of the Act must complete a two-step process:

(1) First, the U.S. citizen must file a Form I–800A under 8 CFR 204.310;

(2) Then, once USCIS has approved the Form I–800A and a child has been identified as an alien who may qualify as a Convention adoptee, the U.S. citizen must file a Form I–800 under 8 CFR 204.313.

§ 204.307 Who may file a Form I–800A or Form I–800.

(a) *Eligibility to file Form I–800A.* Except as provided in paragraph (c) of this section, the following persons may file a Form I–800A:

(1) An unmarried United States citizen who is at least 24 years old and who is habitually resident in the United States, as determined under 8 CFR 204.303(a); or

(2) A married United States citizen, who is habitually resident in the United States, as determined under 8 CFR 204.303(a), and whose spouse will also adopt any child adopted by the citizen based on the approval of a Form I–800A; and

(3) The citizen's spouse must also be either a U.S. citizen, a non-citizen U.S. national, or an alien who, if living in the United States, holds a lawful status under U.S. immigration law. If an alien spouse is present in a lawful status other than the status of an alien lawfully admitted for permanent residence, such status will be a factor evaluated in determining whether the family's situation is sufficiently stable to support a finding that the applicant is suitable as the adoptive parents of a Convention adoptee.

(b) *Eligibility to file a Form I–800.* Except as provided in paragraph (c) of this section, the following persons may file a Form I–800:

(1) An unmarried United States citizen who is at least 25 years old and who is habitually resident in the United States, as determined under 8 CFR 204.303(a); or

(2) A married United States citizen, who is habitually resident in the United States as determined under 8 CFR 204.303(a), and whose spouse will also adopt the child the citizen seeks to adopt. The spouse must be either a United States citizen or a non-citizen U.S. national or an alien who, if living in the United States, holds a lawful status under U.S. immigration law; and

(3) The person has an approved and unexpired Form I–800A.

(c) *Exceptions.* (1) No applicant may file a Form I–800A, and no petitioner may file a Form I–800, if:

(i) The applicant filed a prior Form I–800A that USCIS denied under 8 CFR 204.309(a); or

(ii) The applicant filed a prior Form I-600A under 8 CFR 204.3 that USCIS denied under 8 CFR 204.3(h)(4); or

(iii) The petitioner filed a prior Form I-800 that USCIS denied under 8 CFR 204.309(b)(3); or

(iv) The petitioner filed a prior Form I-600 under 8 CFR 204.3 that USCIS denied under 8 CFR 204.3(i).

(2) This bar against filing a subsequent Form I-800A or Form I-800 expires one year after the date on which the decision denying the prior Form I-800A, I-600A, I-800 or I-600 became administratively final. If the applicant (for a Form I-800A or I-600A case) or the petitioner (for a Form I-800 or I-600 case) does not appeal the prior decision, the one-year period ends one year after the date of the original decision denying the prior Form I-800A, I-600A, I-800 or I-600. Any Form I-800A, or Form I-800 filed during this one-year period will be denied. If the applicant (for a Form I-800A or Form I-600A case) or petitioner (for a Form I-800 or I-600 case) appeals the prior decision, the bar to filing a new Form I-800A or I-800 applies while the appeal is pending and ends one year after the date of an Administrative Appeals Office decision affirming the denial.

(3) Any facts underlying a prior denial of a Form I-800A, I-800, I-600A, or I-600 are relevant to the adjudication of any subsequently filed Form I-800A or Form I-800 that is filed after the expiration of this one year bar.

§204.308 Where to file Form I-800A or Form I-800.

(a) *Form I-800A.* An applicant must file a Form I-800A with the USCIS office identified in the instructions that accompany Form I-800A.

(b) *Form I-800.* After a Form I-800A has been approved, a petitioner may file a Form I-800 on behalf of a Convention adoptee with the stateside or overseas USCIS office identified in the instructions that accompany Form I-800. The petitioner may also file the Form I-800 with a visa-issuing post that would have jurisdiction to adjudicate a visa application filed by or on behalf of the Convention adoptee, when filing with the visa-issuing post is permitted by the instructions that accompany Form I-800.

(c) *Final approval of Form I-800.* Once a Form I-800 has been provisionally approved under 8 CFR 204.313(g) and the petitioner has either adopted or obtained custody of the child for purposes of emigration and adoption, the Department of State officer with jurisdiction to adjudicate the child's application for an immigrant or nonimmigrant visa has jurisdiction to grant final approval of the Form I-800. The Department of State officer may approve the Form I-800, but may not deny it; the Department of State officer must refer any Form I-800 that is "not clearly approvable" for a decision by a USCIS office having jurisdiction over Form I-800 cases. If the Department of State officer refers the Form I-800 to USCIS because it is "not clearly approvable," then USCIS has jurisdiction to approve or deny the Form I-800. In the case of an alien child who is in the United States and who is eligible both under 8 CFR 204.309(b)(4) for approval of a Form I-800 and under 8 CFR part 245 for adjustment of status, the USCIS office with jurisdiction to adjudicate the child's adjustment of status application also has jurisdiction to grant final approval of the Form I-800.

(d) *Use of electronic filing.* When, and if, USCIS adopts electronic, internet-based or other digital means for filing Convention cases, the terms "filing a Form I-800A" and "filing a Form I-800" will include an additional option. Rather than filing the Form I-800A or Form I-800 and accompanying evidence in a paper format, the submission of the same required information and accompanying evidence may be filed according to the digital filing protocol that USCIS adopts.

§204.309 Factors requiring denial of a Form I-800A or Form I-800.

(a) *Form I-800A.* A USCIS officer must deny a Form I-800A if:

(1) The applicant or any additional adult member of the household failed to disclose to the home study preparer or to USCIS, or concealed or misrepresented, any fact(s) about the applicant or any additional member of the household concerning the arrest, conviction, or history of substance abuse, sexual abuse, child abuse, and/or family violence, or any other criminal history as

an offender; the fact that an arrest or conviction or other criminal history has been expunged, sealed, pardoned, or the subject of any other amelioration does not relieve the applicant or additional adult member of the household of the obligation to disclose the arrest, conviction or other criminal history;

(2) The applicant, or any additional adult member of the household, failed to cooperate in having available child abuse registries checked in accordance with 8 CFR 204.311;

(3) The applicant, or any additional adult member of the household, failed to disclose, as required by 8 CFR 204.311, each and every prior adoption home study, whether completed or not, including those that did not favorably recommend for adoption or custodial care, the person(s) to whom the prior home study related; or

(4) The applicant is barred by 8 CFR 204.307(c) from filing the Form I–800A.

(b) *Form I–800.* A USCIS officer must deny a Form I–800 if:

(1) Except as specified in 8 CFR 204.312(e)(2)(ii) with respect to a new Form I–800 filed with a new Form I–800A to reflect a change in marital status, the petitioner completed the adoption of the child, or acquired legal custody of the child for purposes of emigration and adoption, before the provisional approval of the Form I–800 under 8 CFR 204.313(g). This restriction will not apply if a competent authority in the country of the child's habitual residence voids, vacates, annuls, or terminates the adoption or grant of custody and then, after the provisional approval of the Form I–800, and after receipt of notice under article 5(c) of the Convention that the child is, or will be, authorized to enter and reside permanently in the United States, permits a new grant of adoption or custody. The prior adoption must be voided, vacated, annulled or otherwise terminated before the petitioner files a Form I–800.

(2) Except as specified in 8 CFR 204.312(e)(2)(ii) with respect to a new Form I–800 filed with a new Form I–800A to reflect a change in marital status, the petitioner, or any additional adult member of the household had met with, or had any other form of contact with, the child's parents, legal custodian, or other individual or entity who was responsible for the child's care when the contact occurred, unless the contact was permitted under this paragraph. An authorized adoption service provider's sharing of general information about a possible adoption placement is not "contact" for purposes of this section. Contact is permitted under this paragraph if:

(i) The first such contact occurred only after USCIS had approved the Form I–800A filed by the petitioner, and after the competent authority of the Convention country had determined that the child is eligible for intercountry adoption and that the required consents to the adoption have been given; or

(ii) The competent authority of the Convention country had permitted earlier contact, either in the particular instance or through laws or rules of general application, and the contact occurred only in compliance with the particular authorization or generally applicable laws or rules. If the petitioner first adopted the child without complying with the Convention, the competent authority's decision to permit the adoption to be vacated, and to allow the petitioner to adopt the child again after complying with the Convention, will also constitute approval of any prior contact; or

(iii) The petitioner was already, before the adoption, the father, mother, son, daughter, brother, sister, uncle, aunt, first cousin (that is, the petitioner, or either spouse, in the case of a married petitioner had at least one grandparent in common with the child's parent), second cousin (that is, the petitioner, or either spouse, in the case of a married petitioner, had at least one great-grandparent in common with the child's parent) nephew, niece, husband, former husband, wife, former wife, father-in-law, mother-in-law, son-in-law, daughter-in-law, brother-in-law, sister-in-law, stepfather, stepmother, stepson, stepdaughter, stepbrother, stepsister, half brother, or half sister of the child's parent(s).

(3) The USCIS officer finds that the petitioner, or any individual or entity acting on behalf of the petitioner has engaged in any conduct related to the adoption or immigration of the child that is prohibited by 8 CFR 204.304, or

that the petitioner has concealed or misrepresented any material facts concerning payments made in relation to the adoption;

(4) The child is present in the United States, unless the petitioner, after compliance with the requirements of this subpart, either adopt(s) the child in the Convention country, or else, after having obtained custody of the child under the law of the Convention country for purposes of emigration and adoption, adopt(s) the child in the United States. This subpart does not require the child's actual return to the Convention country; whether to permit the child's adoption without the child's return is a matter to be determined by the Central Authority of the country of the child's habitual residence, but approval of a Form I–800 does not relieve an alien child of his or her ineligibility for adjustment of status under section 245 of the Act, if the child is present in the United States without inspection or is otherwise ineligible for adjustment of status. If the child is in the United States but is not eligible for adjustment of status, the Form I–800 may be provisionally approved only if the child will leave the United States after the provisional approval and apply for a visa abroad before the final approval of the Form I–800.

(5) Except as specified in 8 CFR 204.312(e)(2)(ii) with respect to a new Form I–800 filed with a new Form I–800A to reflect a change in marital status, the petitioner files the Form I–800:

(i) Before the approval of a Form I–800A, or

(ii) After the denial of a Form I–800A; or

(iii) After the expiration of the approval of a Form I–800A;

(6) The petitioner is barred by 8 CFR 204.307(c) from filing the Form I–800.

(c) *Notice of intent to deny.* Before denying a Form I–800A under paragraph (a) or a Form I–800 under paragraph (b) of this section, the USCIS officer will notify the applicant (for a Form I–800A case) or petitioner (for a Form I–800 case) in writing of the intent to deny the Form I–800A or Form I–800 and provide 30 days in which to submit evidence and argument to rebut the claim that this section requires denial of the Form I–800A or Form I–800.

(d) *Rebuttal of intent to deny.* If USCIS notifies the applicant that USCIS intends to deny a Form I–800A under paragraph (a) of this section, because the applicant or any additional adult member(s) of the household failed to disclose to the home study preparer or to USCIS, or concealed or misrepresented, any fact(s) concerning the arrest, conviction, or history of substance abuse, sexual abuse or child abuse, and/or family violence, or other criminal history, or failed to cooperate in search of child abuse registries, or failed to disclose a prior home study, the applicant may rebut the intent to deny only by establishing, by clear and convincing evidence that:

(1) The applicant or additional adult member of the household did, in fact, disclose the information; or

(2) If it was an additional adult member of the household who failed to cooperate in the search of child abuse registries, or who failed to disclose to the home study preparer or to USCIS, or concealed or misrepresented, any fact(s) concerning the arrest, conviction, or history of substance abuse, sexual abuse or child abuse, and/or family violence, or other criminal history, or failed to disclose a prior home study, that that person is no longer a member of the household and that that person's conduct is no longer relevant to the suitability of the applicant as the adoptive parent of a Convention adoptee.

§ 204.310 Filing requirements for Form I–800A.

(a) *Completing and filing the Form.* A United States citizen seeking to be determined eligible and suitable as the adoptive parent of a Convention adoptee must:

(1) Complete Form I–800A, including a Form I–800A Supplement 1 for each additional adult member of the household, in accordance with the instructions that accompany the Form I–800A.

(2) Sign the Form I–800A personally. One spouse cannot sign for the other, even under a power of attorney or similar agency arrangement.

(3) File the Form I–800A with the USCIS office that has jurisdiction under 8 CFR 204.308(a) to adjudicate the Form I–800A, together with:

(i) The fee specified in 8 CFR 103.7(b)(1) for the filing of Form I–800A;

(ii) The additional biometrics information collection fee required under 8 CFR 103.7(b)(1) for the applicant and each additional adult member of the household;

(iii) Evidence that the applicant is a United States citizen, as set forth in 8 CFR 204.1(g), or, in the case of a married applicant, evidence either that both spouses are citizens or, if only one spouse is a United States citizen, evidence of that person's citizenship and evidence that the other spouse, if he or she lives in the United States, is either a non-citizen United States national or an alien who holds a lawful status under U.S. immigration law.

(iv) A copy of the current marriage certificate, unless the applicant is not married;

(v) If the applicant has been married previously, a death certificate or divorce or dissolution decree to establish the legal termination of all previous marriages, regardless of current marital status;

(vi) If the applicant is not married, his or her birth certificate, U.S. passport biographical information page, naturalization or citizenship certificate, or other evidence, to establish that he or she is at least 24 years old;

(vii) A written description of the preadoption requirements, if any, of the State of the child's proposed residence in cases where it is known that any child the applicant may adopt will be adopted in the United States, and of the steps that have already been taken or that are planned to comply with these requirements. The written description must include a citation to the State statutes and regulations establishing the requirements. Any preadoption requirements which cannot be met at the time the Form I–800A is filed because of the operation of State law must be noted and explained when the Form I–800A is filed.

(viii) A home study that meets the requirements of 8 CFR 204.311 and that bears the home study preparer's original signature. If the home study is not included with the Form I–800A, the director of the office that has jurisdiction to adjudicate the Form I–800A will make a written request for evidence, directing the applicant to submit the home study. If the applicant fails to submit the home study within the period specified in the request for evidence, the director of the office that has jurisdiction to adjudicate the Form I–800A will deny the Form I–800A. Denial of a Form I–800A under this paragraph for failure to submit a home study is not subject to appeal, but the applicant may file a new Form I–800A, accompanied by a new filing fee.

(b) *Biometrics.* Upon the proper filing of a Form I–800A, USCIS will arrange for the collection of biometrics from the applicant and each additional adult member of the household, as prescribed in 8 CFR 103.16, but with no upper age limit. It will be necessary to collect the biometrics of each of these persons again, if the initial collection expires before approval of the Form I–800A. USCIS may waive this requirement for any particular individual if USCIS determines that that person is physically unable to comply. However, USCIS will require the submission of affidavits, police clearances, or other evidence relating to whether that person has a criminal history in lieu of collecting the person's biometrics.

(c) *Change in marital status.* If, while a Form I–800A is pending, an unmarried applicant marries, or the marriage of a married applicant ends, an amended Form I–800A and amended home study must be filed to reflect the change in marital status. No additional filing fee is required to file an amended Form I–800A while the original Form I–800A is still pending. See 8 CFR 204.312(e)(2) concerning the need to file a new Form I–800A if the marital status changes after approval of a Form I–800A.

[72 FR 56854, Oct. 4, 2007, as amended at 76 FR 53782, Aug. 29, 2011]

§ 204.311 Convention adoption home study requirements.

(a) *Purpose.* For immigration purposes, a home study is a process for screening and preparing an applicant who is interested in adopting a child from a Convention country.

(b) *Preparer.* Only an individual or entity defined under 8 CFR 204.301 as a home study preparer for Convention cases may complete a home study for a Convention adoption. In addition, the individual or entity must be authorized to complete adoption home studies under the law of the jurisdiction in which the home study is conducted.

(c) *Study requirements.* The home study must:

(1) Be tailored to the particular situation of the applicant and to the specific Convention country in which the applicant intends to seek a child for adoption. For example, an applicant who has previously adopted children will require different preparation than an applicant who has no adopted children. A home study may address the applicant's suitability to adopt in more than one Convention country, but if the home study does so, the home study must separately assess the applicant's suitability as to each specific Convention country.

(2) If there are any additional adult members of the household, identify each of them by name, alien registration number (if the individual has one), and date of birth.

(3) Include an interview by the preparer of any additional adult member of the household and an assessment of him or her in light of the requirements of this section.

(4) Be no more than 6 months old at the time the home study is submitted to USCIS.

(5) Include the home study preparer's assessment of any potential problem areas, a copy of any outside evaluation(s), and the home study preparer's recommended restrictions, if any, on the characteristics of the child to be placed in the home. See 8 CFR 204.309(a) for the consequences of failure to disclose information or cooperate in completion of a home study.

(6) Include the home study preparer's signature, in accordance with paragraph (f) of this section.

(7) State the number of interviews and visits, the participants, date and location of each interview and visit, and the date and location of any other contacts with the applicant and any additional adult member of the household.

(8) Summarize the pre-placement preparation and training already provided to the applicant concerning the issues specified in 22 CFR 96.48(a) and (b), the plans for future preparation and training with respect to those issues, or with respect to a particular child, as specified in 22 CFR 96.48(c), and the plans for post-placement monitoring specified in 22 CFR 96.50, in the event that the child will be adopted in the United States rather than abroad.

(9) Specify whether the home study preparer made any referrals as described in paragraph (g)(4) of this section, and include a copy of the report resulting from each referral, the home study preparer's assessment of the impact of the report on the suitability of the applicant to adopt, and the home study preparer's recommended restrictions, if any, on the characteristics of the child to be placed in the home.

(10) Include results of the checks conducted in accordance with paragraph (i) of this section including that no record was found to exist, that the State or foreign country will not release information to the home study preparer or anyone in the household, or that the State or foreign country does not have a child abuse registry.

(11) Include each person's response to the questions regarding abuse and violence in accordance with paragraph (j) of this section.

(12) Include a certified copy of the documentation showing the final disposition of each incident which resulted in arrest, indictment, conviction, and/or any other judicial or administrative action for anyone subject to the home study and a written statement submitted with the home study giving details, including any mitigating circumstances about each arrest, signed, under penalty of perjury, by the person to whom the arrest relates.

(13) Contain an evaluation of the suitability of the home for adoptive placement of a child in light of any applicant's or additional adult member of the household's history of abuse and/or violence as an offender, whether this history is disclosed by an applicant or any additional adult member of the household or is discovered by home study preparer, regardless of the source of the home study preparer's discovery. A single incident of sexual abuse, child abuse, or family violence is sufficient to constitute a "history" of abuse and/or violence.

(14) Contain an evaluation of the suitability of the home for adoptive placement of a child in light of disclosure by an applicant, or any additional adult member of the household, of a history of substance abuse. A person has a history of substance abuse if his or her current or past use of alcohol, controlled substances, or other substances impaired or impairs his or her ability to fulfill obligations at work, school, or home, or creates other social or interpersonal problems that may adversely affect the applicant's suitability as an adoptive parent.

(15) Include a general description of the information disclosed in accordance with paragraph (m) of this section concerning the physical, mental, and emotional health of the applicant and of any additional adult member of the household.

(16) Identify the agency involved in each prior or terminated home study in accordance with paragraph (o) of this section, when the prior home study process began, the date the prior home study was completed, and whether the prior home study recommended for or against finding the applicant or additional adult member of the household suitable for adoption, foster care, or other custodial care of a child. If a prior home study was terminated without completion, the current home study must indicate when the prior home study began, the date of termination, and the reason for the termination.

(d) *Duty to disclose.* (1) The applicant, and any additional adult members of the household, each has a duty of candor and must:

(i) Give true and complete information to the home study preparer.

(ii) Disclose any arrest, conviction, or other adverse criminal history, whether in the United States or abroad, even if the record of the arrest, conviction or other adverse criminal history has been expunged, sealed, pardoned, or the subject of any other amelioration. A person with a criminal history may be able to establish sufficient rehabilitation.

(iii) Disclose other relevant information, such as physical, mental or emotional health issues, or behavioral issues, as specified in paragraph (m) of this section. Such problems may not necessarily preclude approval of a Form I–800A, if, for example, they have been or are being successfully treated.

(2) This duty of candor is an ongoing duty, and continues while the Form I–800A is pending, after the Form I–800A is approved, and while any subsequent Form I–800 is pending, and until there is a final decision admitting the Convention adoptee to the United States with a visa. The applicant and any additional adult member of the household must notify the home study preparer and USCIS of any new event or information that might warrant submission of an amended or updated home study.

(e) *State standards.* In addition to the requirements of this section, the home study preparer must prepare the home study according to the requirements that apply to a domestic adoption in the State of the applicant's actual or proposed residence in the United States.

(f) *Home study preparer's signature.* The home study preparer (or, if the home study is prepared by an entity, the officer or employee who has authority to sign the home study for the entity) must personally sign the home study, and any updated or amended home study. The home study preparer's signature must include a declaration, under penalty of perjury under United States law, that:

(1) The signer personally, and with the professional diligence reasonably necessary to protect the best interests of any child whom the applicant might adopt, either actually conducted or supervised the home study, including personal interview(s), the home visits, and all other aspects of the investigation needed to prepare the home study; if the signer did not personally conduct the home study, the person who actually did so must be identified;

(2) The factual statements in the home study are true and correct, to the best of the signer's knowledge, information and belief; and

(3) The home study preparer has advised the applicant of the duty of candor under paragraph (d) of this section, specifically including the on-going duty under paragraph (d)(2) of this section concerning disclosure of new

events or information warranting submission of an updated or amended home study.

(g) *Personal interview(s) and home visit(s).* The home study preparer must:

(1) Conduct at least one interview in person, and at least one home visit, with the applicant.

(2) Interview, at least once, each additional adult member of the household, as defined in 8 CFR 204.301. The interview with an additional adult member of the household should also be in person, unless the home study preparer determines that interviewing that individual in person is not reasonably feasible and explains in the home study the reason for this conclusion.

(3) Provide information on and assess the suitability of the applicant as the adoptive parent of a Convention adoptee based on the applicant's background, family and medical history (including physical, mental and emotional health), social environment, reasons for adoption, ability to undertake an intercountry adoption, and the characteristics of the child(ren) for whom they would be qualified to care.

(4) Refer the applicant to an appropriate licensed professional, such as a physician, psychiatrist, clinical psychologist, clinical social worker, or professional substance abuse counselor, for an evaluation and written report, if the home study preparer determines that there are areas beyond his or her expertise that need to be addressed. The home study preparer must also make such a referral if such a referral would be required for a domestic adoption under the law of the State of the applicant's actual or proposed place of residence in the United States.

(5) Apply the requirements of this paragraph to each additional adult member of the household.

(h) *Financial considerations.* (1) Assessment of the finances of the applicant must include:

(i) A description of the applicant's income, financial resources, debts, and expenses.

(ii) A statement concerning the evidence that was considered to verify the source and amount of income and financial resources.

(2) Any income designated for the support of one or more children in the applicant's care and custody, such as funds for foster care, or any income designated for the support of another member of the household, must not be counted towards the financial resources available for the support of a prospective adoptive child.

(3) USCIS will not routinely require a detailed financial statement or supporting financial documents. However, should the need arise, USCIS reserves the right to ask for such detailed documentation.

(i) *Checking available child abuse registries.* The home study preparer must ensure that a check of the applicant, and of each additional adult member of the household, has been made with available child abuse registries in any State or foreign country that the applicant, or any additional adult member of the household, has resided in since that person's 18th birthday. USCIS may also conduct its own check of any child abuse registries to which USCIS has access. Depending on the extent of access to a relevant registry allowed by the State or foreign law, the home study preparer must take one of the following courses of action:

(1) If the home study preparer is allowed access to information from the child abuse registries, he or she must make the appropriate checks for the applicant and each additional adult member of the household;

(2) If the State or foreign country requires the home study preparer to secure permission from the applicant and each additional adult member of the household before gaining access to information in such registries, the home study preparer must secure such permission from those individuals and make the appropriate checks;

(3) If the State or foreign country will only release information directly to an individual to whom the information relates, then the applicant and the additional adult member of the household must secure such information and provide it to the home study preparer.

(4) If the State or foreign country will release information neither to the home study preparer nor to the person to whom the information relates, or has not done so within 6 months of a written request for the information,

this unavailability of information must be noted in the home study.

(j) *Inquiring about history of abuse or violence as an offender.* The home study preparer must ask each applicant and each additional adult member of the household whether he or she has a history as an offender, whether in the United States or abroad, of substance abuse, sexual abuse, or child abuse, or family violence, even if such history did not result in an arrest or conviction. This evaluation must include:

(1) The dates of each arrest or conviction or history of substance abuse, sexual abuse or child abuse, and/or family violence; or,

(2) If not resulting in an arrest, the date or time period (if occurring over an extended period of time) of each occurrence and

(3) Details including any mitigating circumstances about each incident.

Each statement must be signed, under penalty of perjury, by the person to whom the incident relates.

(k) *Criminal history.* The applicant, and any additional adult members of the household, must also disclose to the home study preparer and USCIS any history, whether in the United States or abroad, of any arrest and/or conviction (other than for minor traffic offenses) in addition to the information that the person must disclose under paragraph (j) of this section. If an applicant or an additional adult member of the household has a criminal record, the officer may still find that the applicant will be suitable as the adoptive parent of a Convention adoptee, if there is sufficient evidence of rehabilitation as described in paragraph (l) of this section.

(l) *Evidence of rehabilitation.* If an applicant, or any additional adult member of the household, has a history of substance abuse, sexual abuse or child abuse, and/or family violence as an offender, or any other criminal history, the home study preparer may, nevertheless, make a favorable finding if the applicant has demonstrated that the person with this adverse history has achieved appropriate rehabilitation. A favorable recommendation cannot be made based on a claim of rehabilitation while an applicant or any additional adult member of the household is on probation, parole, supervised release, or other similar arrangement for any conviction. The home study must include a discussion of the claimed rehabilitation, which demonstrates that the applicant is suitable as the adoptive parent(s) of a Convention adoptee. Evidence of rehabilitation may include:

(1) An evaluation of the seriousness of the arrest(s), conviction(s), or history of abuse, the number of such incidents, the length of time since the last incident, the offender's acceptance of responsibility for his or her conduct, and any type of counseling or rehabilitation programs which have been successfully completed, or

(2) A written opinion from an appropriate licensed professional, such as a psychiatrist, clinical psychologist, or clinical social worker.

(m) *Assessment with respect to physical, mental and emotional health or behavioral issues.* The home study must address the current physical, mental and emotional health of the applicant, or any additional adult member of the household, as well as any history of illness or of any mental, emotional, psychological, or behavioral instability if the home study preparer determines, in the exercise of reasonable professional judgment, that the suitability of the applicant as an adoptive parent may be affected adversely by such history. Paragraph (g)(4) of this section, regarding referral to professionals, applies to any home study involving prior psychiatric care, or issues arising from sexual abuse, child abuse, or family violence issues if, in the home study preparer's reasonable professional judgment, such referral(s) may be necessary or helpful to the proper completion of the home study.

(n) *Prior home study.* The home study preparer must ask each applicant, and any additional adult member of the household, whether he or she previously has had a prior home study completed, or began a home study process in relation to an adoption or to any form of foster or other custodial care of a child that was not completed, whether or not the prior home study related to an intercountry adoption, and must include each individual's response to this question in the home study report. A copy of any previous home study that did not favorably recommend the applicant or additional adult member of the household must be attached to any home study submitted with a Form I–800A. If a copy of any prior home study that did not favorably recommend the applicant or additional adult member of the household is no longer available, the current home study must explain why the prior home study is no longer available. The home study preparer must evaluate the relevance of any prior unfavorable or uncompleted home study to the suitability of the applicant as the adoptive parent of a Convention adoptee.

(o) *Living accommodations.* The home study must include a detailed description of the living accommodations where the applicant currently resides. If the applicant is planning to move, the home study must include a description of the living accommodations where the child will reside with the applicant, if known. If the applicant is residing abroad at the time of the home study, the home study must include a description of the living accommodations where the child will reside in the United States with the applicant, if known. Each description must include an assessment of the suitability of accommodations for a child and a determination whether such space meets applicable State requirements, if any.

(p) *Handicapped or special needs child.* A home study conducted in conjunction with the proposed adoption of a special needs or handicapped child must contain a discussion of the preparation, willingness, and ability of the applicant to provide proper care for a child with the handicap or special needs. This information will be used to evaluate the suitability of the applicant as the adoptive parent of a special needs or handicapped child. If this information is not included in the home study, an updated or amended home study will be necessary if the applicant seeks to adopt a handicapped or special needs child.

(q) *Addressing a Convention country's specific requirements.* If the Central Authority of the Convention country has notified the Secretary of State of any specific requirements that must be met in order to adopt in the Convention country, the home study must include a full and complete statement of all facts relevant to the applicant's eligibility for adoption in the Convention country, in light of those specific requirements.

(r) *Specific approval for adoption.* If the home study preparer's findings are favorable, the home study must contain his or her specific approval of the applicant for adoption of a child from the specific Convention country or countries, and a discussion of the reasons for such approval. The home study must include the number of children the applicant may adopt at the same time. The home study must state whether there are any specific restrictions to the adoption based on the age or gender, or other characteristics of the child. If the home study preparer has approved the applicant for a handicapped or special needs adoption, this fact must be clearly stated.

(s) *Home study preparer's authority to conduct home studies.* The home study must include a statement in which the home study preparer certifies that he or she is authorized under 22 CFR part 96 to complete home studies for Convention adoption cases. The certification must specify the State or country under whose authority the home study preparer is licensed or authorized, cite the specific law or regulation authorizing the preparer to conduct home studies, and indicate the license number, if any, and the expiration date, if any, of this authorization or license. The certification must also specify the basis under 22 CFR part 96 (public domestic authority, accredited agency, temporarily accredited agency, approved person, exempted provider, or supervised provider) for his or her authorization to conduct Convention adoption home studies.

(t) *Review of home study.* (1) If the law of the State in which the applicant resides requires the competent authority in the State to review the home study, such a review must occur and be documented before the home study is submitted to USCIS.

(2) When the home study is not performed in the first instance by an accredited agency or temporarily accredited agency, as defined in 22 CFR part

96, then an accredited agency or temporarily accredited agency, as defined in 22 CFR part 96, must review and approve the home study as specified in 22 CFR 96.47(c) before the home study is submitted to USCIS. This requirement for review and approval by an accredited agency or temporarily accredited agency does not apply to a home study that was actually prepared by a public domestic authority, as defined in 22 CFR 96.2.

(u) *Home study updates and amendments.* (1) A new home study amendment or update will be required if there is:

(i) A significant change in the applicant's household, such as a change in residence, marital status, criminal history, financial resources; or

(ii) The addition of one or more children in the applicant's home, whether through adoption or foster care, birth, or any other means. Even if the original home study provided for the adoption of more than one adopted child, the applicant must submit an amended home study recommending adoption of an additional child, because the addition of the already adopted child(ren) to the applicant's household is a significant change in the household that should be assessed before the adoption of any additional child(ren);

(iii) The addition of other dependents or additional adult member(s) of the household to the family prior to the prospective child's immigration into the United States;

(iv) A change resulting because the applicant is seeking to adopt a handicapped or special needs child, if the home study did not already address the applicant's suitability as the adoptive parent of a child with the particular handicap or special need;

(v) A change to a different Convention country. This change requires the updated home study to address suitability under the requirements of the new Convention country;

(vi) A lapse of more than 6 months between the date the home study is completed and the date it is submitted to USCIS; or

(vii) A change to the child's proposed State of residence. The preadoption requirements of the new State must be complied with in the case of a child coming to the United States to be adopted.

(2) Any updated or amended home study must:

(i) Meet the requirements of this section;

(ii) Be accompanied by a copy of the home study that is being updated or amended, including all prior updates and amendments;

(iii) Include a statement from the preparer that he or she has reviewed the home study that is being updated or amended and is personally and fully aware of its contents; and

(iv) Address whether the home study preparer recommends approval of the proposed adoption and the reasons for the recommendation.

(3) If submission of an updated or amended home study becomes necessary before USCIS adjudicates the Form I–800A, the applicant may simply submit the updated or amended home study to the office that has jurisdiction over the Form I–800A.

(4) If it becomes necessary to file an updated or amended home study after USCIS has approved the Form I–800A, the applicant must file a Form I–800A Supplement 3 with the filing fee specified in 8 CFR 103.7(b)(1) and the amended or updated home study. If USCIS determines that the amended or updated home study shows that the applicant remains suitable as the adoptive parent(s) of a Convention adoptee, USCIS will issue a new approval notice that will expire on the same date as the original approval. If the applicant also wants to have USCIS extend the approval period for the Form I–800A, the applicant must submit the updated or amended home study with an extension request under 8 CFR 204.312(e)(3), rather than under this paragraph (u) of this section.

(5) Each update must indicate that the home study preparer has updated the screening of the applicant and any additional adult member of the household under paragraphs (i) through (l) of this section, and must indicate the results of this updated screening.

§ 204.312 Adjudication of the Form I-800A.

(a) *USCIS action.* The USCIS officer must approve a Form I–800A if the officer finds, based on the evidence of record, that the applicant is eligible under 8 CFR 204.307(a) to file a Form I-800A and the USCIS officer is satisfied that the applicant is suitable as the adoptive parent of a child from the specified Convention country. If the applicant sought approval for more than one Convention country, the decision will specify each country for which the Form I–800A is approved, and will also specify whether the Form I–800A is denied with respect to any particular Convention country.

(b) *Evaluation of the home study.* In determining suitability to adopt, the USCIS officer will give considerable weight to the home study, but is not bound by it. Even if the home study is favorable, the USCIS officer must deny the Form I–800A if, on the basis of the evidence of record, the officer finds, for a specific and articulable reason, that the applicant has failed to establish that he or she is suitable as the adoptive parent of a child from the Convention country. The USCIS officer may consult the accredited agency or temporarily accredited agency that approved the home study, the home study preparer, the applicant, the relevant State or local child welfare agency, or any appropriate licensed professional, as needed to clarify issues concerning whether the applicant is suitable as the adoptive parent of a Convention adoptee. If this consultation yields evidence that is adverse to the applicant, the USCIS officer may rely on the evidence only after complying with the provisions of 8 CFR 103.2(b)(16) relating to the applicant's right to review and rebut adverse information.

(c) *Denial of application.* (1) The USCIS officer will deny the Form I-800A if the officer finds that the applicant has failed to establish that the applicant is:

(i) Eligible under 8 CFR 204.307(a) to file Form I–800A; or

(ii) Suitable as the adoptive parent of a child from the Convention country.

(2) Before denying a Form I–800A, the USCIS officer will comply with 8 CFR 103.2(b)(16), if required to do so under that provision, and may issue a request for evidence or a notice of intent to deny under 8 CFR 103.2(b)(8).

(3) A denial will be in writing, giving the reason for the denial and notifying the applicant of the right to appeal, if any, as provided in 8 CFR 204.314.

(4) It is for the Central Authority of the other Convention country to determine how its own adoption requirements, as disclosed in the home study under 8 CFR 204.311(q), should be applied in a given case. For this reason, the fact that the applicant may be ineligible to adopt in the other Convention country under those requirements, will not warrant the denial of a Form I–800A, if USCIS finds that the applicant has otherwise established eligibility and suitability as the adoptive parent of a Convention adoptee.

(d) *Approval notice.* (1) If USCIS approves the Form I–800A, USCIS will notify the applicant in writing as well as the Department of State. The notice of approval will specify:

(i) The expiration date for the notice of approval, as determined under paragraph (e) of this section, and

(ii) The name(s) and marital status of the applicant; and

(iii) If the applicant is not married and not yet 25 years old, the applicant's date of birth.

(2) Once USCIS approves the Form I-800A, or extends the validity period for a prior approval under paragraph (e) of this section, any submission of the home study to the Central Authority of the country of the child's habitual residence must consist of the entire and complete text of the same home study and of any updates or amendments submitted to USCIS.

(e) *Duration or revocation of approval.* (1) A notice of approval expires 15 months after the date on which USCIS received the FBI response on the applicant's, and any additional adult member of the household's, biometrics, unless approval is revoked. If USCIS received the responses on different days, the 15-month period begins on the earliest response date. The notice of approval will specify the expiration date. USCIS may extend the validity period for the approval of a Form I–800A only as provided in paragraph (e)(3) of this section.

(2) (i) The approval of a Form I–800A is automatically revoked if before the final decision on a Convention adoptee's application for admission with an immigrant visa or for adjustment of status:

(A) The marriage of the applicant terminates; or

(B) An unmarried applicant marries; or

(C) In the case of a married applicant, either spouse files with a USCIS or Department of State officer a written document withdrawing his or her signature on the Form I–800A.

(ii) This revocation is without prejudice to the filing of a new Form I–800A, with fee, accompanied by a new or amended home study, reflecting the change in marital status. If a Form I–800 had already been filed based on the approval of the prior Form I–800A, a new Form I–800 must also be filed with the new Form I–800A under this paragraph. The new Form I–800 will be adjudicated only if the new Form I–800A is approved. The new Form I–800 will not be subject to denial under 8 CFR 204.309(b)(1) or (2), unless the original Form I–800 would have been subject to denial under either of those provisions.

(3)(i) If the 15-month validity period for a Form I–800A approval is about to expire, and the applicant has not filed a Form I–800, the applicant may file Form I–800A Supplement 3, with the filing fee under 8 CFR 103.7(b)(1), if required. The applicant may not file a Form I–800A Supplement 3 seeking extension of an approval notice more than 90 days before the expiration of the validity period for the Form I–800A approval, but must do so on or before the date on which the validity period expires. The applicant is not required to pay the Form I–800A Supplement 3 filing fee for the first request to extend the approval of a Form I–800A. If the applicant files a second or subsequent Form I–800A Supplement 3 to obtain a second or subsequent extension, however, the applicant must pay the Form I–800A Supplement 3 filing fee, as specified in 8 CFR 103.7(b), for the second, or any subsequent, Form I–800A Supplement 3 that is filed to obtain a second or subsequent extension. Any Form I–800A Supplement 3 that is filed to obtain an extension of the approval of a Form I–800A must be accompanied by:

(A) A statement, signed by the applicant under penalty of perjury, detailing any changes to the answers given to the questions on the original Form I–800A;

(B) An updated or amended home study as required under 8 CFR 204.311(u); and

(C) A photocopy of the Form I–800A approval notice.

(ii) Upon receipt of the Form I–800A Supplement 3, USCIS will arrange for the collection of the biometrics of the applicant and of each additional adult member of the applicant's household.

(iii) If USCIS continues to be satisfied that the applicant remains suitable as the adoptive parent of a Convention adoptee, USCIS will extend the approval of the Form I–800A to a date not more than 15 months after the date on which USCIS received the new biometric responses. If new responses are received on different dates, the new 15-month period begins on the earliest response date. The new notice of approval will specify the new expiration date.

(iv) There is no limit to the number of extensions that may be requested and granted under this section, so long as each request is supported by an updated or amended home study that continues to recommend approval of the applicant for intercountry adoption and USCIS continues to find that the applicant remain suitable as the adoptive parent(s) of a Convention adoptee.

(4) In addition to the automatic revocation provided for in paragraph (e)(2) of this section, the approval of a Form I–800A may be revoked pursuant to 8 CFR 205.1 or 205.2.

§ 204.313 Filing and adjudication of a Form I–800.

(a) *When to file.* Once a Form I–800A has been approved and the Central Authority has proposed placing a child for adoption by the petitioner, the petitioner may file the Form I–800. The petitioner must complete the Form I–800 in accordance with the instructions that accompany the Form I–800, and must sign the Form I–800 personally. In the case of a married petitioner, one spouse cannot sign for the other, even under a power of attorney or similar agency arrangement. The petitioner may then file the Form I–800 with the stateside or overseas USCIS office or the visa issuing post that has jurisdiction under 8 CFR 204.308(b) to adjudicate the Form I–800, together with the evidence specified in this section and the filing fee specified in 8 CFR 103.7(b)(1), if more than one Form I–800 is filed for children who are not siblings.

(b) *What to include on the Form.* (1) The petitioner must specify on the Form I–800 either that:

(i) The child will seek an immigrant visa, if the Form I–800 is approved, because the child will reside in the United States with the petitioner (in the case of a married petitioner, if only one spouse is a United States citizen, with that spouse) after the child's admission to the United States on the basis of the proposed adoption; or

(ii) The child will seek a nonimmigrant visa, in order to travel to the United States to obtain naturalization under section 322 of the Act, because the petitioner intends to complete the adoption abroad and the petitioner and the child will continue to reside abroad immediately following the adoption, rather than residing in the United States with the petitioner. This option is not available if the child will be adopted in the United States.

(2) In applying this paragraph (b), if a petitioner is a United States citizen who is domiciled in the United States, but who is posted abroad temporarily under official orders as a member of the Uniformed Services as defined in 5 U.S.C. 2101, or as a civilian officer or employee of the United States Government, the child will be deemed to be coming to the United States to reside in the United States with that petitioner.

(c) *Filing deadline.* (1) The petitioner must file the Form I–800 before the expiration of the notice of the approval of the Form I–800A and before the child's 16th birthday. Paragraphs (c)(2) and (3) of this section provide special rules for determining that this requirement has been met.

(2) If the appropriate Central Authority places the child with the petitioner for intercountry adoption more than 6 months after the child's 15th birthday but before the child's 16th birthday, the petitioner must still file the Form I–800 before the child's 16th birthday. If the evidence required by paragraph (d)(3) or (4) of this section is not yet available, instead of that evidence, the petitioner may submit a statement from the primary provider, signed under penalty of perjury under United States law, confirming that the Central Authority has, in fact, made the adoption placement on the date specified in the statement. Submission of a Form I–800 with this statement will satisfy the statutory requirement that the petition must be submitted before the child's 16th birthday, but no provisional or final approval of the Form I–800 will be granted until the evidence required by paragraph (d)(3) or (4) of this section has been submitted. When submitted, the evidence required by paragraph (d)(3) and (4) must affirmatively show that the Central Authority did, in fact, make the adoption placement decision before the child's 16th birthday.

(3) If the Form I–800A was filed after the child's 15th birthday but before the child's 16th birthday, the filing date of the Form I–800A will be deemed to be the filing date of the Form I–800, provided the Form I–800 is filed not more than 180 days after the initial approval of the Form I–800A.

(d) *Required evidence.* Except as specified in paragraph (c)(2) of this section, the petitioner must submit the following evidence with the properly completed Form I–800:

(1) The Form I–800A approval notice and, if applicable, proof that the approval period has been extended under 8 CFR 204.312(e);

(2) A statement from the primary provider, as defined in 22 CFR 96.2, signed under penalty of perjury under United States law, indicating that all of the pre-placement preparation and training provided for in 22 CFR 96.48 has been completed;

(3) The report required under article 16 of the Convention, specifying the child's name and date of birth, the reasons for making the adoption placement, and establishing that the competent authority has, as required under article 4 of the Convention:

(i) Established that the child is eligible for adoption;

(ii) Determined, after having given due consideration to the possibility of placing the child for adoption within the Convention country, that intercountry adoption is in the child's best interests;

(iii) Ensured that the legal custodian, after having been counseled as required, concerning the effect of the child's adoption on the legal custodian's relationship to the child and on the child's legal relationship to his or her family of origin, has freely consented in writing to the child's adoption, in the required legal form;

(iv) Ensured that if any individual or entity other than the legal custodian must consent to the child's adoption, this individual or entity, after having been counseled as required concerning the effect of the child's adoption, has freely consented in writing, in the required legal form, to the child's adoption;

(v) Ensured that the child, after having been counseled as appropriate concerning the effects of the adoption; has freely consented in writing, in the required legal form, to the adoption, if the child is of an age that, under the law of the country of the child's habitual residence, makes the child's consent necessary, and that consideration was given to the child's wishes and opinions; and

(vi) Ensured that no payment or inducement of any kind has been given to obtain the consents necessary for the adoption to be completed.

(4) The report under paragraph (d)(3) of this section must be accompanied by:

(i) A copy of the child's birth certificate, or secondary evidence of the child's age; and

(ii) A copy of the irrevocable consent(s) signed by the legal custodian(s) and any other individual or entity who must consent to the child's adoption unless, as permitted under article 16 of the Convention, the law of the country of the child's habitual residence provides that their identities may not be disclosed, so long as the Central Authority of the country of the child's habitual residence certifies in its report that the required documents exist and that they establish the child's age and availability for adoption;

(iii) A statement, signed under penalty of perjury by the primary provider (or an authorized representative if the primary provider is an agency or other juridical person), certifying that the report is a true, correct, and complete copy of the report obtained from the Central Authority of the Convention country;

(iv) A summary of the information provided to the petitioner under 22 CFR 96.49(d) and (f) concerning the child's medical and social history. This summary, or a separate document, must include:

(A) A statement concerning whether, from any examination as described in 22 CFR 96.49(e) or for any other reason, there is reason to believe that the child has any medical condition that makes the child inadmissible under section 212(a)(1) of the Act; if the medical information that is available at the provisional approval stage is not sufficient to assess whether the child may be inadmissible under section 212(a)(1), the submission of this information may be deferred until the petitioner seeks final approval of the Form I–800;

(B) If both of the child's birth parents were the child's legal custodians and signed the irrevocable consent, the factual basis for determining that they are incapable of providing proper care for the child, as defined in 8 CFR 204.301;

(C) Information about the circumstances of the other birth parent's death, if applicable, supported by a copy of the death certificate, unless paragraph (d)(4)(ii) of this section makes it unnecessary to provide a copy of the death certificate;

(D) If a sole birth parent was the legal custodian, the circumstances leading to the determination that the other parent abandoned or deserted the child, or disappeared from the child's life; and

(E) If the legal custodian was the child's prior adoptive parent(s) or any individual or entity other than the child's birth parent(s), the circumstances leading to the custodian's acquisition of custody of the child and the legal basis of that custody.

(v) If the child will be adopted in the United States, the primary provider's written report, signed under penalty of perjury by the primary provider (or an authorized representative if the primary provider is an agency or other juridical person) detailing the primary adoption service provider's plan for post-placement duties, as specified in 22 CFR 96.50; and

(5) If the child may be inadmissible under any provision of section 212(a) for which a waiver is available, a properly completed waiver application for each such ground; and

(6) Either a Form I–864W, Intending Immigrant's I–864 Exemption, or a Form I–864, Affidavit of Support, as specified in 8 CFR 213a.2.

(e) *Obtaining the home study and supporting evidence.* The materials from the Form I–800A proceeding will be included in the record of the Form I–800 proceeding.

(f) *Investigation.* An investigation concerning the alien child's status as a Convention adoptee will be completed before the Form I–800 is adjudicated in any case in which the officer with jurisdiction to grant provisional or final approval of the Form I–800 determines, on the basis of specific facts, that completing the investigation will aid in the provisional or final adjudication of the Form I–800. Depending on the circumstances surrounding the case, the investigation may include, but is not limited to, document checks, telephone checks, interview(s) with the birth or prior adoptive parent(s), a field investigation, and any other appropriate investigatory actions. In any case in which there are significant differences between the facts presented in the approved Form I–800A or Form I–800 and the facts uncovered by the investigation, the office conducting the investigation may consult directly with the appropriate USCIS office. In any instance where the investigation reveals negative information sufficient to sustain a denial of the Form I–800 (including a denial of a Form I–800 that had been provisionally approved) or the revocation of the final approval of the Form I–800, the results of the investigation, including any supporting documentation, and the Form I–800 and its supporting documentation will be forwarded to the appropriate USCIS office for action. Although USCIS is not precluded from denying final approval of a Form I–800 based on the results of an investigation under this paragraph, the grant of provisional approval under paragraph (g), and the fact that the Department of State has given the notice contemplated by article 5(c) of the Convention, shall constitute prima facie evidence that the grant of adoption or custody for purposes of adoption will, ordinarily, warrant final approval of the Form I–800. The Form I–800 may still be denied, however, if the Secretary of State declines to issue the certificate provided for under section 204(d)(2) of the Act or if the investigation under this paragraph establishes the existence of facts that clearly warrant denial of the petition.

(g) *Provisional approval.* (1) The officer will consider the evidence described in paragraph (d) of this section and any additional evidence acquired as a result of any investigation completed under paragraph (f) of this section, to determine whether the preponderance of the evidence shows that the child qualifies as a Convention adoptee. Unless 8 CFR 204.309(b) prohibits approval of the Form I–800, the officer will serve the petitioner with a written order provisionally approving the Form I–800 if the officer determines that the child does qualify for classification as a "child" under section 101(b)(1)(G), and that the proposed adoption or grant of custody will meet the Convention requirements.

(i) The provisional approval will expressly state that the child will, upon adoption or acquisition of custody, be eligible for classification as a Convention adoptee, adjudicate any waiver application and (if any necessary waiver of inadmissibility is granted) direct the petitioner to obtain and present the evidence required under paragraph (h) of this section in order to obtain final approval of the Form I–800.

(ii) The grant of a waiver of inadmissibility in conjunction with the provisional approval of a Form I–800 is conditioned upon the issuance of an immigrant or nonimmigrant visa for the child's admission to the United States based on the final approval of the same Form I–800. If the Form I–800 is finally denied or the immigrant or nonimmigrant visa application is denied, the waiver is void.

(2) If the petitioner filed the Form I-800 with USCIS and the child will apply for an immigrant or nonimmigrant visa, then, upon provisional approval of the Form I-800, the officer will forward the notice of provisional approval, Form I-800, and all supporting evidence to the Department of State. If the child will apply for adjustment of status, USCIS will retain the record of proceeding.

(h) *Final approval.* (1) To obtain final approval of a provisionally approved Form I-800, the petitioner must submit to the Department of State officer who has jurisdiction of the child's application for an immigrant or nonimmigrant visa, or to the USCIS officer who has jurisdiction of the child's adjustment of status application, a copy of the following document(s):

(i) If the child is adopted in the Convention country, the adoption decree or administrative order from the competent authority in the Convention country showing that the petitioner has adopted the child; in the case of a married petitioner, the decree or order must show that both spouses adopted the child; or

(ii) If the child will be adopted in the United States:

(A) The decree or administrative order from the competent authority in the Convention country giving custody of the child for purposes of emigration and adoption to the petitioner or to an individual or entity acting on behalf of the petitioner. In the case of a married petitioner, an adoption decree that shows that the child was adopted only by one spouse, but not by both, will be deemed to show that the petitioner has acquired sufficient custody to bring the child to the United States for adoption by the other spouse;

(B) If not already provided before the provisional approval (because, for example, the petitioner thought the child would be adopted abroad, but that plan has changed so that the child will now be adopted in the United States), a statement from the primary provider, signed under penalty of perjury under United States law, summarizing the plan under 22 CFR 96.50 for monitoring of the placement until the adoption is finalized in the United States;

(C) If not already provided before the provisional approval (because, for example, the petitioner thought the child would be adopted abroad, but that plan has changed so that the child will now be adopted in the United States), a written description of the preadoption requirements that apply to adoptions in the State of the child's proposed residence and a description of when and how, after the child's immigration, the petitioner intends to complete the child's adoption. The written description must include a citation to the relevant State statutes or regulations and specify how the petitioner intends to comply with any requirements that can be satisfied only after the child arrives in the United States.

(2) If the Secretary of State, after reviewing the evidence that the petitioner provides under paragraph (h)(1)(i) or (ii) of this section, issues the certificate required under section 204(d)(2) of the Act, the Department of State officer who has jurisdiction over the child's visa application has authority, on behalf of USCIS, to grant final approval of a Form I-800. In the case of an alien who will apply for adjustment of status, the USCIS officer with jurisdiction of the adjustment application has authority to grant this final approval upon receiving the Secretary of State's certificate under section 204(d)(2) of the Act.

(i) *Denial of Form I-800.* (1) A USCIS officer with authority to grant provisional or final approval will deny the Form I-800 if the officer finds that the child does not qualify as a Convention adoptee, or that 8 CFR 204.309(b) of this section requires denial of the Form I-800. Before denying a Form I-800, the officer will comply with the requirements of 8 CFR 103.2(b)(16)), if required to do so under that provision, and may issue a request for evidence or a notice of intent to deny under 8 CFR 103.2(b)(8).

(2) The decision will be in writing, specifying the reason(s) for the denial and notifying the petitioner of the right to appeal, if any, as specified in 8 CFR 204.314.

(3) If a Department of State officer finds, either at the provisional approval stage or the final approval stage, that the Form I–800 is "not clearly approvable," or that 8 CFR 204.309(b) warrants denial of the Form I–800, the Department of State officer will forward the Form I–800 and accompanying evidence to the USCIS office with jurisdiction over the place of the child's habitual residence for review and decision.

§204.314 Appeal.

(a) *Decisions that may be appealed.* (1) Except as provided in paragraph (b) of this section:

(i) An applicant may appeal the denial of a Form I–800A (including the denial of a request to extend the prior approval of a Form I–800A) and

(ii) A petitioner may appeal the denial of a Form I–800.

(2) The provisions of 8 CFR 103.3, concerning how to file an appeal, and how USCIS adjudicates an appeal, apply to the appeal of a decision under this subpart C.

(b) *Decisions that may not be appealed.* There is no appeal from the denial of:

(1) Form I–800A because the Form I–800A was filed during any period during which 8 CFR 204.307(c) bars the filing of a Form I–800A; or

(2) Form I–800A for failure to timely file a home study as required by 8 CFR 204.310(a)(3)(viii); or

(3) Form I–800 that is denied because the Form I–800 was filed during any period during which 8 CFR 204.307(c) bars the filing of a Form I–800;

(4) Form I–800 filed either before USCIS approved a Form I–800A or after the expiration of the approval of a Form I–800A.

PART 205—REVOCATION OF APPROVAL OF PETITIONS

AUTHORITY: 8 U.S.C. 1101, 1103, 1151, 1153, 1154, 1155, 1182, 1324a, and 1186a.

§205.1 Automatic revocation.

(a) *Reasons for automatic revocation.* The approval of a petition or self-petition made under section 204 of the Act and in accordance with part 204 of this chapter is revoked as of the date of approval:

(1) If the Secretary of State shall terminate the registration of the beneficiary pursuant to the provisions of section 203(e) of the Act before October 1, 1991, or section 203(g) of the Act on or after October 1, 1994;

(2) [Reserved]

(3) If any of the following circumstances occur before the beneficiary's or self-petitioner's journey to the United States commences or, if the beneficiary or self-petitioner is an applicant for adjustment of status to that of a permanent resident, before the decision on his or her adjustment application becomes final:

(i) *Immediate relative and family-sponsored petitions, other than Amerasian petitions.* (A) Upon written notice of withdrawal filed by the petitioner or self-petitioner with any officer of the Service who is authorized to grant or deny petitions.

(B) Upon the death of the beneficiary or the self-petitioner.

(C) Upon the death of the petitioner, unless:

(*1*) The petition is deemed under 8 CFR 204.2(i)(1)(iv) to have been approved as a Form I–360, Petition for Amerasian, Widow(er) or Special Immigrant under 8 CFR 204.2(b); or

(*2*) U.S. Citizenship and Immigration Services (USCIS) determines, as a matter of discretion exercised for humanitarian reasons in light of the facts of a particular case, that it is inappropriate to revoke the approval of the petition. USCIS may make this determination only if the principal beneficiary of the visa petition asks for reinstatement of the approval of the petition and establishes that a person related to the principal beneficiary in one of the ways described in section 213A(f)(5)(B) of the Act is willing and able to file an affidavit of support under 8 CFR part 213a as a substitute sponsor.

(D) Upon the legal termination of the marriage when a citizen or lawful permanent resident of the United States has petitioned to accord his or her spouse immediate relative or family-sponsored preference immigrant classification under section 201(b) or section 203(a)(2) of the Act. The approval of a spousal self-petition based on the relationship to an abusive citizen or lawful permanent resident of the United States filed under section 204(a)(1)(A)(iii) or 204(a)(1)(B)(ii) of the Act, however, will not be revoked solely because of the termination of the marriage to the abuser.

(E) Upon the remarriage of the spouse of an abusive citizen or lawful permanent resident of the United States when the spouse has self-petitioned under section 204(a)(1)(A)(iii) or 204(a)(1)(B)(ii) of the Act for immediate relative classification under section 201(b) of the Act or for preference classification under section 203(a)(2) of the Act.

(F) Upon a child reaching the age of 21, when he or she has been accorded immediate relative status under section 201(b) of the Act. A petition filed on behalf of a child under section 204(a)(1)(A)(i) of the Act or a self-petition filed by a child of an abusive United States citizen under section 204(a)(1)(A)(iv) of the Act, however, will remain valid for the duration of the relationship to accord preference status under section 203(a)(1) of the Act if the beneficiary remains unmarried, or to accord preference status under section 203(a)(3) of the Act if he or she marries.

(G) Upon the marriage of a child, when he or she has been accorded immediate relative status under section 201(b) of the Act. A petition filed on behalf of the child under section 204(a)(1)(A)(i) of the Act or a self-petition filed by a child of an abusive United States citizen under section 204(a)(1)(A)(iv) of the Act, however, will remain valid for the duration of the relationship to accord preference status under section 203(a)(3) of the Act if he or she marries.

(H) Upon the marriage of a person accorded preference status as a son or daughter of a United States citizen under section 203(a)(1) of the Act. A petition filed on behalf of the son or daughter, however, will remain valid for the duration of the relationship to accord preference status under section 203(a)(3) of the Act.

(I) Upon the marriage of a person accorded status as a son or daughter of a lawful permanent resident alien under section 203(a)(2) of the Act.

(J) Upon legal termination of the petitioner's status as an alien admitted for lawful permanent residence in the United States unless the petitioner became a United States citizen. The provisions of 8 CFR 204.2(i)(3) shall apply if the petitioner became a United States citizen.

(ii) *Petition for Pub. L. 97–359 Amerasian.* (A) Upon formal notice of withdrawal filed by the petitioner with the officer who approved the petition.

(B) Upon the death of the beneficiary.

(C) Upon the death or bankruptcy of the sponsor who executed Form I–361, Affidavit of Financial Support and Intent to Petition for Legal Custody for Pub. L. 97–359 Amerasian. In that event, a new petition may be filed in the beneficiary's behalf with the documentary evidence relating to sponsorship and, in the case of a beneficiary under 18 years of age, placement. If the new petition is approved, it will be given the priority date of the previously approved petition.

(D) Upon the death or substitution of the petitioner if other than the beneficiary or sponsor. However, if the petitioner dies or no longer desires or is able to proceed with the petition, and another person 18 years of age or older, an emancipated minor, or a corporation incorporated in the United States desires to be substituted for the deceased or original petitioner, a written request may be submitted to the Service or American consular office where the petition is located to reinstate the petition and restore the original priority date.

(E) Upon the beneficiary's reaching the age of 21 when the beneficiary has been accorded classification under section 201(b) of the Act. Provided that all requirements of section 204(f) of the Act continue to be met, however, the petition is to be considered valid for purposes of according the beneficiary preference classification under section 203(a)(1) of the Act if the beneficiary remains unmarried or under section 203(a)(3) if the beneficiary marries.

(F) Upon the beneficiary's marriage when the beneficiary has been accorded classification under section 201(b) or section 203(a)(1) of the Act. Provided that all requirements of section 204(f) of the Act continue to be met, however, the petition is to be considered valid for purposes of according the beneficiary preference classification under section 203(a)(3) of the Act.

(iii) *Petitions under section 203(b), other than special immigrant juvenile petitions.* (A) Upon invalidation pursuant to 20 CFR Part 656 of the labor certification in support of the petition.

(B) Upon the death of the petitioner or beneficiary.

(C) In employment-based preference cases, upon written notice of withdrawal filed by the petitioner to any officer of USCIS who is authorized to grant or deny petitions, where the withdrawal is filed less than 180 days after approval of the employment-based preference petition, unless an associated adjustment of status application has been pending for 180 days or more. A petition that is withdrawn 180 days or more after its approval, or 180 days or more after the associated adjustment of status application has been filed, remains approved unless its approval is revoked on other grounds. If an employment-based petition on behalf of an alien is withdrawn, the job offer of the petitioning employer is rescinded and the alien must obtain a new employment-based preference petition in order to seek adjustment of status or issuance of an immigrant visa as an employment-based immigrant, unless eligible for adjustment of status under section 204(j) of the Act and in accordance with 8 CFR 245.25.

(D) Upon termination of the petitioning employer's business less than 180 days after petition approval under section 203(b)(1)(B), 203(b)(1)(C), 203(b)(2), or 203(b)(3) of the Act, unless an associated adjustment of status application has been pending for 180 days or more. If a petitioning employer's business terminates 180 days or more after petition approval, or 180 days or more after an associated adjustment of status application has been filed, the petition remains approved unless its approval is revoked on other grounds. If a petitioning employer's business terminates the job offer of the petitioning employer is rescinded and the beneficiary must obtain a new employment-based preference petition on his or her behalf in order to seek adjustment of status or issuance of an immigrant visa as an employment-based immigrant, unless eligible for adjustment of status under section 204(j) of the Act and in accordance with 8 CFR 245.25.

(iv) *Special immigrant juvenile petitions.* Unless the beneficiary met all of the eligibility requirements as of November 29, 1990, and the petition requirements as of November 29, 1990, and the petition for classification as a special immigrant juvenile was filed before June 1, 1994, or unless the change in circumstances resulted from the beneficiary's adoption or placement in a guardianship situation:

(A) Upon the beneficiary reaching the age of 21;

(B) Upon the marriage of the beneficiary;

(C) Upon the termination of the beneficiary's dependency upon the juvenile court;

(D) Upon the termination of the beneficiary's eligibility for long-term foster care; or

(E) Upon the determination in administrative or judicial proceedings that it is in the beneficiary's best interest to be returned to the country of nationality or last habitual residence of the beneficiary or of his or her parent or parents.

(b) *Notice.* When it shall appear to the director that the approval of a petition has been automatically revoked, he or she shall cause a notice of such revocation to be sent promptly to the consular office having jurisdiction over the visa application and a copy of such notice to be mailed to the petitioner's last known address.

[61 FR 13077, Mar. 26, 1996, as amended at 71 FR 35749, June 21, 2006; 81 FR 73332, Oct. 24, 2016; 81 FR 82486, Nov. 18, 2016]

§ 205.2 Revocation on notice.

(a) *General.* Any Service officer authorized to approve a petition under section 204 of the Act may revoke the approval of that petition upon notice to the petitioner on any ground other than those specified in § 205.1 when the necessity for the revocation comes to the attention of this Service.

(b) *Notice of intent.* Revocation of the approval of a petition of self-petition under paragraph (a) of this section will be made only on notice to the petitioner or self-petitioner. The petitioner or self-petitioner must be given the opportunity to offer evidence in support of the petition or self-petition and in opposition to the grounds alleged for revocation of the approval.

(c) *Notification of revocation.* If, upon reconsideration, the approval previously granted is revoked, the director shall provide the petitioner or the self-petitioner with a written notification of the decision that explains the specific reasons for the revocation. The director shall notify the consular officer having jurisdiction over the visa application, if applicable, of the revocation of an approval.

(d) *Appeals.* The petitioner or self-petitioner may appeal the decision to revoke the approval within 15 days after the service of notice of the revocation. The appeal must be filed as provided in part 3 of this chapter, unless the Associate Commissioner for Examinations exercises appellate jurisdiction over the revocation under part 103 of this chapter. Appeals filed with the Associate Commissioner for Examinations must meet the requirements of part 103 of this chapter.

[48 FR 19156, Apr. 28, 1983, as amended at 58 FR 42851, Aug. 12, 1993; 61 FR 13078, Mar. 26, 1996]

PART 207—ADMISSION OF REFUGEES

Sec.

AUTHORITY: 8 U.S.C. 1101, 1103, 1151, 1157, 1159, 1182; 8 CFR part 2.

SOURCE: 46 FR 45118, Sept. 10, 1981, unless otherwise noted.

§ 207.1 Eligibility.

(a) *Filing.* Any alien who believes he or she is a refugee as defined in section 101(a)(42) of the Act, and is included in a refugee group identified in section 207(a) of the Act, may apply for admission to the United States by submitting an application, including biometric information, in accordance with the form instructions, as defined in 8 CFR 1.2.

(b) *Firmly resettled.* Any applicant (other than an applicant for derivative refugee status under 8 CFR 207.7) who has become firmly resettled in a foreign country is not eligible for refugee status under this chapter I. A refugee is considered to be "firmly resettled" if he or she has been offered resident status, citizenship, or some other type of permanent resettlement by a country other than the United States and has traveled to and entered that country as a consequence of his or her flight from persecution. Any applicant who claims not to be firmly resettled in a foreign country must establish that the conditions of his or her residence in that country are so restrictive as to deny resettlement. In determining whether or not an applicant is firmly resettled in a foreign country, the officer reviewing the matter shall consider the conditions under which other residents of the country live:

(1) Whether permanent or temporary housing is available to the refugee in the foreign country;

(2) Nature of employment available to the refugee in the foreign country; and

(3) Other benefits offered or denied to the refugee by the foreign country which are available to other residents, such as right to property ownership, travel documentation, education, public welfare, and citizenship.

(c) *Immediate relatives and special immigrants.* Any applicant for refugee status who qualifies as an immediate relative or as a special immigrant shall not be processed as a refugee unless it is in the public interest. The alien shall be advised to obtain an immediate relative or special immigrant visa and shall be provided with the proper petition forms to send to any prospective petitioners. An applicant who may be eligible for classification under sections 203(a) or 203(b) of the Act, and for whom a visa number is now available, shall be advised of such eligibility but is not required to apply.

[76 FR 53782, Aug. 29, 2011]

§ 207.2 Applicant processing.

(a) *Interview.* Each applicant 14 years old or older shall appear in person before an immigration officer for inquiry under oath to determine his or her eligibility for admission as a refugee.

(b) *Medical examination.* Each applicant shall submit to a medical examination as required by sections 221(d) and 232(b) of the Act.

(c) *Sponsorship.* Each applicant must be sponsored by a responsible person or organization. Transportation for the applicant from his or her present abode to the place of resettlement in the United States must be guaranteed by the sponsor.

[76 FR 53783, Aug. 29, 2011]

§ 207.3 Waivers of inadmissibility.

(a) *Authority.* Section 207(c)(3) of the Act sets forth grounds of inadmissibility under section 212(a) of the Act which are not applicable and those which may be waived in the case of an otherwise qualified refugee and the conditions under which such waivers may be approved.

(b) *Filing requirements.* An applicant may request a waiver by submitting an application for a waiver in accordance with the form instructions. The burden is on the applicant to show that the waiver should be granted based upon humanitarian grounds, family unity, or the public interest. The applicant shall be notified in writing of the decision, including the reasons for denial if the application is denied. There is no appeal from such decision.

[76 FR 53783, Aug. 29, 2011]

§ 207.4 Approved application.

Approval of a refugee application by USCIS outside the United States authorizes CBP to admit the applicant conditionally as a refugee upon arrival at the port within four months of the date the refugee application was approved. There is no appeal from a denial of refugee status under this chapter.

[76 FR 53783, Aug. 29, 2011]

§ 207.5 Waiting lists and priority handling.

Waiting lists are maintained for each designated refugee group of special humanitarian concern. Each applicant whose application is accepted for filing by USCIS shall be registered as of the date of filing. The date of filing is the priority date for purposes of case control. Refugees or groups of refugees may be selected from these lists in a manner that will best support the policies and interests of the United States. The Secretary may adopt appropriate criteria for selecting the refugees and assignment of processing priorities for each designated group based upon such considerations as reuniting families, close association with the United States, compelling humanitarian concerns, and public interest factors.

[76 FR 53783, Aug. 29, 2011]

§ 207.6 Control over approved refugee numbers.

Current numerical accounting of approved refugees is maintained for each special group designated by the President. As refugee status is authorized for each applicant, the total count is reduced correspondingly from the appropriate group so that information is readily available to indicate how many refugee numbers remain available for issuance.

§ 207.7 Derivatives of refugees.

(a) *Eligibility.* A spouse, as defined in section 101(a)(35) of the Act, and/or child(ren), as defined in section 101(b)(1)(A), (B), (C), (D), or (E) of the Act, shall be granted refugee status if accompanying or following-to-join the principal alien. An accompanying derivative is a spouse or child of a refugee who is in the physical company of the principal refugee when he or she is admitted to the United States, or a spouse or child of a refugee who is admitted within 4 months following the principal refugee's admission. A following-to-join derivative, on the other hand, is a spouse or child of a refugee who seeks admission more than 4 months after the principal refugee's admission to the United States.

(b) *Ineligibility*. The following relatives of refugees are ineligible for accompanying or following-to-join benefits:

(1) A spouse or child who has previously been granted asylee or refugee status;

(2) An adopted child, if the adoption took place after the child became 16 years old, or if the child has not been in the legal custody and living with the parent(s) for at least 2 years;

(3) A stepchild, if the marriage that created this relationship took place after the child became 18 years old;

(4) A husband or wife if each/both were not physically present at the marriage ceremony, and the marriage was not consummated (section 101(a)(35) of the Act);

(5) A husband or wife if the Secretary has determined that such alien has attempted or conspired to enter into a marriage for the purpose of evading immigration laws; and

(6) A parent, sister, brother, grandparent, grandchild, nephew, niece, uncle, aunt, cousin or in-law.

(c) *Relationship*. The relationship of a spouse and child as defined in sections 101(a)(35) and 101(b) (1)(A), (B), (C), (D), or (E), respectively, of the Act, must have existed prior to the refugee's admission to the United States and must continue to exist at the time of filing for accompanying or following-to-join benefits and at the time of the spouse or child's subsequent admission to the United States. If the refugee proves that the refugee is the parent of a child who was born after the refugee's admission as a refugee, but who was *in utero* on the date of the refugee's admission as a refugee, the child shall be eligible to accompany or follow-to-join the refugee. The child's mother, if not the principal refugee, shall not be eligible to accompany or follow-to-join the principal refugee unless the child's mother was the principal refugee's spouse on the date of the principal refugee's admission as a refugee.

(d) *Filing*. A refugee may request accompanying or following-to-join benefits for his or her spouse and unmarried, minor child(ren) (whether the spouse and children are inside or outside the United States) by filing a separate Request for Refugee/Asylee Relative in accordance with the form instructions for each qualifying family member. The request may only be filed by the principal refugee. Family members who derived their refugee status are not eligible to request derivative benefits on behalf of their spouse and child(ren). A separate Request for Refugee/Asylee Relative must be filed for each qualifying family member within two years of the refugee's admission to the United States unless USCIS determines that the filing period should be extended for humanitarian reasons. There is no time limit imposed on a family member's travel to the United States once the Request for Refugee/Asylee Relative has been approved, provided that the relationship of spouse or child continues to exist and approval of the Request for Refugee/Asylee Relative has not been subsequently revoked. There is no fee for this benefit request.

(e) *Evidence*. Documentary evidence consists of those documents which establish that the petitioner is a refugee, and evidence of the claimed relationship of the petitioner to the beneficiary. The burden of proof is on the petitioner to establish by a preponderance of the evidence that any person on whose behalf he/she is making a request under this section is an eligible spouse or unmarried, minor child. Evidence to establish the claimed relationship for a spouse or unmarried, minor child as set forth in 8 CFR part 204 must be submitted with the request for accompanying or following-to-join benefits. Where possible this will consist of the documents specified in § 204.2(a)(1)(i)(B), (a)(1)(iii)(B), (a)(2), (d)(2), and (d)(5) of this chapter.

(f) *Approvals*. (1) *Spouse or child in the United States*. When a spouse or child of a refugee is in the United States and the Request for Refugee/Asylee Relative is approved, USCIS will notify the refugee of such approval. Employment will be authorized incident to status.

(2) *Spouse or child outside the United States*. When a spouse or child of a refugee is outside the United States and the Request for Refugee/Asylee Relative is approved, USCIS will notify the refugee of such approval. USCIS will send the approved request to the

Department of State for transmission to the U.S. Embassy or Consulate having jurisdiction over the area in which the refugee's spouse or child is located.

(3) *Benefits.* The approval of the Request for Refugee/Asylee Relative will remain valid for the duration of the relationship to the refugee and, in the case of a child, while the child is under 21 years of age and unmarried, provided also that the principal's status has not been revoked. However, the approved Request for Refugee/Asylee Relative will cease to confer immigration benefits after it has been used by the beneficiary for admission to the United States as a derivative of a refugee. For a derivative inside or arriving in the United States, USCIS will issue a document reflecting the derivative's current status as a refugee to demonstrate employment authorization, or the derivative may apply, under 8 CFR 274a.12(a), for evidence of employment authorization.

(g) *Denials.* If the spouse or child of a refugee is found to be ineligible for derivative status, a written notice explaining the basis for denial shall be forwarded to the principal refugee. There shall be no appeal from this decision. However, the denial shall be without prejudice to the consideration of a new petition or motion to reopen the refugee or asylee relative petition proceeding, if the refugee establishes eligibility for the accompanying or following-to-join benefits contained in this part.

[63 FR 3795, Jan. 27, 1998, as amended at 76 FR 53783, Aug. 29, 2011; 76 FR 73476, Nov. 29, 2011]

§ 207.8 Physical presence in the United States.

For the purpose of adjustment of status under section 209(a)(1) of the Act, the required one year physical presence of the applicant in the United States is computed from the date the applicant entered the United States as a refugee.

[46 FR 45118, Sept. 10, 1981. Redesignated at 63 FR 3795, Jan. 27, 1998]

§ 207.9 Termination of refugee status.

The refugee status of any alien (and of the spouse or child of the alien) admitted to the United States under section 207 of the Act will be terminated by USCIS if the alien was not a refugee within the meaning of section 101(a)(42) of the Act at the time of admission. USCIS will notify the alien in writing of its intent to terminate the alien's refugee status. The alien will have 30 days from the date notice is served upon him or her in accordance with 8 CFR 103.8, to present written or oral evidence to show why the alien's refugee status should not be terminated. There is no appeal under this chapter I from the termination of refugee status by USCIS. Upon termination of refugee status, USCIS will process the alien under sections 235, 240, and 241 of the Act.

[76 FR 53784, Aug. 29, 2011]

PART 208—PROCEDURES FOR ASYLUM AND WITHHOLDING OF REMOVAL

Subpart A—Asylum and Withholding of Removal

Sec.

Subpart B—Credible Fear of Persecution

AUTHORITY: 8 U.S.C. 1101, 1103, 1158, 1226, 1252, 1282; Title VII of Public Law 110–229; 8 CFR part 2.

SOURCE: 62 FR 10337, Mar. 6, 1997, unless otherwise noted.

Subpart A—Asylum and Withholding of Removal

§ 208.1 General.

(a) *Applicability.* (1) *General.* Unless otherwise provided in this chapter I, this subpart A shall apply to all applications for asylum under section 208 of the Act or for withholding of deportation or withholding of removal under section 241(b)(3) of the Act, or under the Convention Against Torture, whether before an asylum officer or an immigration judge, regardless of the date of filing. For purposes of this chapter I, withholding of removal shall also mean withholding of deportation under section 243(h) of the Act, as it appeared prior to April 1, 1997, except as provided in § 208.16(d). Such applications are referred to as "asylum applications." The provisions of this part 208 shall not affect the finality or validity of any decision made by a district director, an immigration judge, or the Board of Immigration Appeals in any such case prior to April 1, 1997. No asylum application that was filed with a district director, asylum officer, or immigration judge prior to April 1, 1997, may be reopened or otherwise reconsidered under the provisions of this part 208 except by motion granted in the exercise of discretion by the Board of Immigration Appeals, an immigration judge, or an asylum officer for proper cause shown. Motions to reopen or reconsider must meet the requirements of sections 240(c)(6) and (c)(7) of the Act, and 8 CFR parts 103 and 1003, as applicable.

(2) *Commonwealth of the Northern Mariana Islands.* The provisions of this subpart A shall not apply prior to January 1, 2015, to an alien physically present in or arriving in the Commonwealth of the Northern Mariana Islands seeking to apply for asylum. No application for asylum may be filed prior to January 1, 2015, pursuant to section 208 of the Act by an alien physically present in or arriving in the Commonwealth of the Northern Mariana Islands. Effective on the transition program effective date, the provisions of this subpart A shall apply to aliens physically present in or arriving in the CNMI with respect to withholding of removal under section 241(b)(3) of the Act and withholding and deferral of removal under the Convention Against Torture.

(b) *Training of asylum officers.* The Associate Director of USCIS Refugee, Asylum, and International Operations (RAIO) shall ensure that asylum officers receive special training in international human rights law, nonadversarial interview techniques, and other relevant national and international refugee laws and principles. The Associate Director of USCIS Refugee, Asylum, and International Operations (RAIO) shall also, in cooperation with the Department of State and other appropriate sources, compile and disseminate to asylum officers information concerning the persecution of persons in other countries on account of race, religion, nationality, membership in a particular social group, or political opinion, torture of persons in other countries, and other information relevant to asylum determinations, and shall maintain a documentation center with information on human rights conditions.

[64 FR 8487, Feb. 19, 1999, as amended at 74 FR 55736, Oct. 28, 2009; 76 FR 53784, Aug. 29, 2011]

§ 208.2 Jurisdiction.

(a) *Refugee, Asylum, and International Operations (RAIO)* Except as provided in paragraph (b) or (c) of this section, RAIO shall have initial jurisdiction over an asylum application filed by an alien physically present in the United States or seeking admission at a port-of-entry. RAIO shall also have initial jurisdiction over credible fear determinations under §208.30 and reasonable fear determinations under §208.31.

(b) *Jurisdiction of Immigration Court in general.* Immigration judges shall have exclusive jurisdiction over asylum applications filed by an alien who has been served a Form I–221, Order to Show Cause; Form I–122, Notice to Applicant for Admission Detained for a Hearing before an Immigration Judge; or Form I–862, Notice to Appear, after the charging document has been filed with the Immigration Court. Immigration judges shall also have jurisdiction over any asylum applications filed prior to April 1, 1997, by alien crewmembers who have remained in the United States longer than authorized, by applicants for admission under the Visa Waiver Pilot Program, and by aliens who have been admitted to the United States under the Visa Waiver Pilot Program. Immigration judges shall also have the authority to review reasonable fear determinations referred to the Immigration Court under §208.31, and credible fear determinations referred to the Immigration Court under §208.30.

(c) *Certain aliens not entitled to proceedings under section 240 of the Act*—(1)*Asylum applications and withholding of removal applications only.* After Form I–863, Notice of Referral to Immigration Judge, has been filed with the Immigration Court, an immigration judge shall have exclusive jurisdiction over any asylum application filed on or after April 1, 1997, by:

(i) An alien crewmember who:

(A) Is an applicant for a landing permit;

(B) Has been refused permission to land under section 252 of the Act; or

(C) On or after April 1, 1997, was granted permission to land under section 252 of the Act, regardless of whether the alien has remained in the United States longer than authorized;

(ii) An alien stowaway who has been found to have a credible fear of persecution or torture pursuant to the procedures set forth in subpart B of this part;

(iii) An alien who is an applicant for admission pursuant to the Visa Waiver Program under section 217 of the Act, except that if such an alien is an applicant for admission to the Commonwealth of the Northern Mariana Islands, then he or she shall not be eligible for asylum prior to January 1, 2015;

(iv) An alien who was admitted to the United States pursuant to the Visa Waiver Program under section 217 of the Act and has remained longer than authorized or has otherwise violated his or her immigration status, except that if such an alien was admitted to the Commonwealth of the Northern Mariana Islands, then he or she shall not be eligible for asylum in the Commonwealth of the Northern Mariana Islands prior to January 1, 2015;

(v) An alien who has been ordered removed under §235(c) of the Act, as described in §235.8(a) of this chapter (applicable only in the event that the alien is referred for proceedings under this paragraph by the Regional Director pursuant to section 235.8(b)(2)(ii) of this chapter);

(vi) An alien who is an applicant for admission, or has been admitted, as an alien classified under section 101(a)(15)(S) of the Act (applicable only in the event that the alien is referred for proceedings under this paragraph by the district director);

(vii) An alien who is an applicant for admission to Guam or the Commonwealth of the Northern Mariana Islands pursuant to the Guam-CNMI Visa Waiver Program under section 212(l) of the Act, except that if such an alien is an applicant for admission to the Commonwealth of the Northern Mariana Islands, then he or she shall not be eligible for asylum prior to January 1, 2015; or

(viii) An alien who was admitted to Guam or the Commonwealth of the Northern Mariana Islands pursuant to the Guam-CNMI Visa Waiver Program under section 212(l) of the Act and has remained longer than authorized or has otherwise violated his or her immigration status, except that if such an alien was admitted to the Commonwealth of the Northern Mariana Islands, then he or she shall not be eligible for asylum in the Commonwealth of the Northern Mariana Islands prior to January 1, 2015.

(2) *Withholding of removal applications only.* After Form I–863, Notice of Referral to Immigration Judge, has been filed with the Immigration Court, an immigration judge shall have exclusive jurisdiction over any application for withholding of removal filed by:

(i) An alien who is the subject of a reinstated removal order pursuant to section 241(a)(5) of the Act; or

(ii) An alien who has been issued an administrative removal order pursuant to section 238 of the Act as an alien convicted of committing an aggravated felony.

(3) *Rules of procedure*—(i)*General.* Except as provided in this section, proceedings falling under the jurisdiction of the immigration judge pursuant to paragraph (c)(1) or (c)(2) of this section shall be conducted in accordance with the same rules of procedure as proceedings conducted under 8 CFR part 240, subpart A. The scope of review in proceedings conducted pursuant to paragraph (c)(1) of this section shall be limited to a determination of whether the alien is eligible for asylum or withholding or deferral of removal, and whether asylum shall be granted in the exercise of discretion. The scope of review in proceedings conducted pursuant to paragraph (c)(2) of this section shall be limited to a determination of whether the alien is eligible for withholding or deferral of removal. During such proceedings, all parties are prohibited from raising or considering any other issues, including but not limited to issues of admissibility, deportability, eligibility for waivers, and eligibility for any other form of relief.

(ii) *Notice of hearing procedures and in-absentia decisions.* The alien will be provided with notice of the time and place of the proceeding. The request for asylum and withholding of removal submitted by an alien who fails to appear for the hearing shall be denied. The denial of asylum and withholding of removal for failure to appear may be reopened only upon a motion filed with the immigration judge with jurisdiction over the case. Only one motion to reopen may be filed, and it must be filed within 90 days, unless the alien establishes that he or she did not receive notice of the hearing date or was in Federal or State custody on the date directed to appear. The motion must include documentary evidence, which demonstrates that:

(A) The alien did not receive the notice;

(B) The alien was in Federal or State custody and the failure to appear was through no fault of the alien; or

(C) "Exceptional circumstances," as defined in section 240(e)(1) of the Act, caused the failure to appear.

(iii) *Relief.* The filing of a motion to reopen shall not stay removal of the alien unless the immigration judge issues an order granting a stay pending disposition of the motion. An alien who fails to appear for a proceeding under this section shall not be eligible for relief under section 240A, 240B, 245, 248, or 249 of the Act for a period of 10 years after the date of the denial, unless the applicant can show exceptional circumstances resulted in his or her failure to appear.

[65 FR 76130, Dec. 6, 2000, as amended at 74 FR 55736, Oct. 28, 2009; 76 FR 53784, Aug. 29, 2011]

§ 208.3 Form of application.

(a) An asylum applicant must file Form I–589, Application for Asylum and for Withholding of Removal, together with any additional supporting evidence in accordance with the instructions on the form. The applicant's spouse and children shall be listed on the application and may be included in the request for asylum if they are in the United States. One additional copy of the principal applicant's Form I–589 must be submitted for each dependent included in the principal's application.

(b) An asylum application shall be deemed to constitute at the same time an application for withholding of removal, unless adjudicated in deportation or exclusion proceedings commenced prior to April 1, 1997. In such instances, the asylum application shall be deemed to constitute an application for withholding of deportation under section 243(h) of the Act, as that section existed prior to April 1, 1997. Where a determination is made that an applicant is ineligible to apply for asylum under section 208(a)(2) of the Act, an asylum application shall be construed as an application for withholding of removal.

(c) Form I–589 shall be filed under the following conditions and shall have the following consequences:

(1) If the application was filed on or after January 4, 1995, information provided in the application may be used as a basis for the initiation of removal proceedings, or to satisfy any burden of proof in exclusion, deportation, or removal proceedings;

(2) The applicant and anyone other than a spouse, parent, son, or daughter of the applicant who assists the applicant in preparing the application must sign the application under penalty of perjury. The applicant's signature establishes a presumption that the applicant is aware of the contents of the application. A person other than a relative specified in this paragraph who assists the applicant in preparing the application also must provide his or her full mailing address;

(3) An asylum application that does not include a response to each of the questions contained in the Form I–589, is unsigned, or is unaccompanied by the required materials specified in paragraph (a) of this section is incomplete. The filing of an incomplete application shall not commence the 150-day period after which the applicant may file an application for employment authorization in accordance with §208.7. An application that is incomplete shall be returned by mail to the applicant within 30 days of the receipt of the application by the Service. If the Service has not mailed the incomplete application back to the applicant within 30 days, it shall be deemed complete. An application returned to the applicant as incomplete shall be resubmitted by the applicant with the additional information if he or she wishes to have the application considered;

(4) Knowing placement of false information on the application may subject the person placing that information on the application to criminal penalties under title 18 of the United States Code and to civil or criminal penalties under section 274C of the Act; and

(5) Knowingly filing a frivolous application on or after April 1, 1997, so long as the applicant has received the notice required by section 208(d)(4) of the Act, shall render the applicant permanently ineligible for any benefits under the Act pursuant to §208.20.

[62 FR 10337, Mar. 6, 1997, as amended at 65 FR 76131, Dec. 6, 2000]

§ 208.4 Filing the application.

Except as prohibited in paragraph (a) of this section, asylum applications shall be filed in accordance with paragraph (b) of this section.

(a) *Prohibitions on filing.* Section 208(a)(2) of the Act prohibits certain aliens from filing for asylum on or after April 1, 1997, unless the alien can demonstrate to the satisfaction of the Attorney General that one of the exceptions in section 208(a)(2)(D) of the Act applies. Such prohibition applies only to asylum applications under section 208 of the Act and not to applications for withholding of removal under §208.16. If an applicant files an asylum application and it appears that one or more of the prohibitions contained in section 208(a)(2) of the Act apply, an asylum officer, in an interview, or an immigration judge, in a hearing, shall review the application and give the applicant the opportunity to present any relevant and useful information bearing on any prohibitions on filing to determine if the application should be rejected. For the purpose of making determinations under section 208(a)(2) of the Act, the following rules shall apply:

(1) *Authority.* Only an asylum officer, an immigration judge, or the Board of Immigration Appeals is authorized to make determinations regarding the prohibitions contained in section 208(a)(2)(B) or (C) of the Act.

(2) *One-year filing deadline.* (i) For purposes of section 208(a)(2)(B) of the Act, an applicant has the burden of proving:

(A) By clear and convincing evidence that the application has been filed within 1 year of the date of the alien's arrival in the United States, or

(B) To the satisfaction of the asylum officer, the immigration judge, or the Board that he or she qualifies for an exception to the 1-year deadline.

(ii) The 1-year period shall be calculated from the date of the alien's last arrival in the United States or April 1,

1997, whichever is later. When the last day of the period so computed falls on a Saturday, Sunday, or legal holiday, the period shall run until the end of the next day that is not a Saturday, Sunday, or legal holiday. For the purpose of making determinations under section 208(a)(2)(B) of the Act only, an application is considered to have been filed on the date it is received by the Service, pursuant to § 103.2(a)(7) of this chapter. In a case in which the application has not been received by the Service within 1 year from the applicant's date of entry into the United States, but the applicant provides clear and convincing documentary evidence of mailing the application within the 1-year period, the mailing date shall be considered the filing date. For cases before the Immigration Court in accordance with § 3.13 of this chapter, the application is considered to have been filed on the date it is received by the Immigration Court. For cases before the Board of Immigration Appeals, the application is considered to have been filed on the date it is received by the Board. In the case of an application that appears to have been filed more than a year after the applicant arrived in the United States, the asylum officer, the immigration judge, or the Board will determine whether the applicant qualifies for an exception to the deadline. For aliens present in or arriving in the Commonwealth of the Northern Mariana Islands, the 1-year period shall be calculated from either January 1, 2015, or from the date of the alien's last arrival in the United States (including the Commonwealth of the Northern Mariana Islands), whichever is later. No period of physical presence in the Commonwealth of the Northern Mariana Islands prior to January 1, 2015, shall count toward the 1-year period. After November 28, 2009, any travel to the Commonwealth of the Northern Mariana Islands from any other State shall not re-start the calculation of the 1-year period.

(3) *Prior denial of application.* For purposes of section 208(a)(2)(C) of the Act, an asylum application has not been denied unless denied by an immigration judge or the Board of Immigration Appeals.

(4) *Changed circumstances.* (i) The term "changed circumstances" in section 208(a)(2)(D) of the Act shall refer to circumstances materially affecting the applicant's eligibility for asylum. They may include, but are not limited to:

(A) Changes in conditions in the applicant's country of nationality or, if the applicant is stateless, country of last habitual residence;

(B) Changes in the applicant's circumstances that materially affect the applicant's eligibility for asylum, including changes in applicable U.S. law and activities the applicant becomes involved in outside the country of feared persecution that place the applicant at risk; or

(C) In the case of an alien who had previously been included as a dependent in another alien's pending asylum application, the loss of the spousal or parent-child relationship to the principal applicant through marriage, divorce, death, or attainment of age 21.

(ii) The applicant shall file an asylum application within a reasonable period given those "changed circumstances." If the applicant can establish that he or she did not become aware of the changed circumstances until after they occurred, such delayed awareness shall be taken into account in determining what constitutes a "reasonable period."

(5) The term "extraordinary circumstances" in section 208(a)(2)(D) of the Act shall refer to events or factors directly related to the failure to meet the 1-year deadline. Such circumstances may excuse the failure to file within the 1-year period as long as the alien filed the application within a reasonable period given those circumstances. The burden of proof is on the applicant to establish to the satisfaction of the asylum officer, the immigration judge, or the Board of Immigration Appeals that the circumstances were not intentionally created by the alien through his or her own action or inaction, that those circumstances were directly related to the alien's failure to file the application within the 1-year period, and that the delay was reasonable under the circumstances. Those circumstances may include but are not limited to:

(i) Serious illness or mental or physical disability, including any effects of persecution or violent harm suffered in the past, during the 1-year period after arrival;

(ii) Legal disability (e.g., the applicant was an unaccompanied minor or suffered from a mental impairment) during the 1-year period after arrival;

(iii) Ineffective assistance of counsel, provided that:

(A) The alien files an affidavit setting forth in detail the agreement that was entered into with counsel with respect to the actions to be taken and what representations counsel did or did not make to the respondent in this regard;

(B) The counsel whose integrity or competence is being impugned has been informed of the allegations leveled against him or her and given an opportunity to respond; and

(C) The alien indicates whether a complaint has been filed with appropriate disciplinary authorities with respect to any violation of counsel's ethical or legal responsibilities, and if not, why not;

(iv) The applicant maintained Temporary Protected Status, lawful immigrant or nonimmigrant status, or was given parole, until a reasonable period before the filing of the asylum application;

(v) The applicant filed an asylum application prior to the expiration of the 1-year deadline, but that application was rejected by the Service as not properly filed, was returned to the applicant for corrections, and was refiled within a reasonable period thereafter; and

(vi) The death or serious illness or incapacity of the applicant's legal representative or a member of the applicant's immediate family.

(6) *Safe Third Country Agreement.* Asylum officers have authority to apply section 208(a)(2)(A) of the Act, relating to the determination that the alien may be removed to a safe country pursuant to a bilateral or multilateral agreement, only as provided in 8 CFR 208.30(e). For provisions relating to the authority of immigration judges with respect to section 208(a)(2)(A), *see* 8 CFR 1240.11(g).

(b) *Filing location.* Form I–589, Application for Asylum and Withholding of Removal, must be filed in accordance with the instructions on the form.

(c) *Amending an application after filing.* Upon request of the alien and as a matter of discretion, the asylum officer or immigration judge having jurisdiction may permit an asylum applicant to amend or supplement the application, but any delay caused by such request shall extend the period within which the applicant may not apply for employment authorization in accordance with §208.7(a).

[62 FR 10337, Mar. 6, 1997, as amended at 64 FR 8488, Feb. 19, 1999; 64 FR 13881, Mar. 23, 1999; 65 FR 76131, Dec. 6, 2000; 69 FR 69488, Nov. 29, 2004; 74 FR 26937, June 5, 2009; 74 FR 55737, Oct. 28, 2009]

§208.5 Special duties toward aliens in custody of DHS.

(a) *General.* When an alien in the custody of DHS requests asylum or withholding of removal, or expresses a fear of persecution or harm upon return to his or her country of origin or to agents thereof, DHS shall make available the appropriate application forms and shall provide the applicant with the information required by section 208(d)(4) of the Act, except in the case of an alien who is in custody pending a credible fear determination under 8 CFR 208.30 or a reasonable fear determination pursuant to 8 CFR 208.31. Although DHS does not have a duty in the case of an alien who is in custody pending a credible fear or reasonable fear determination under either 8 CFR 208.30 or 8 CFR 208.31, DHS may provide the appropriate forms, upon request. Where possible, expedited consideration shall be given to applications of detained aliens. Except as provided in paragraph (c) of this section, such alien shall not be excluded, deported, or removed before a decision is rendered on his or her asylum application. Furthermore, except as provided in paragraph (c) of this section, an alien physically present in or arriving in the Commonwealth of the Northern Mariana Islands shall not be excluded, deported, or removed before a decision is rendered on his or her application for withholding of removal pursuant to section 241(b)(3) of the Act and withholding of removal under the Convention Against Torture. No application for asylum may be filed prior to January 1, 2015, under section 208 of the Act by an alien physically present in or arriving in the Commonwealth of the Northern Mariana Islands.

(b) *Certain aliens aboard vessels.* (1) If an alien crewmember or alien stowaway on board a vessel or other conveyance alleges, claims, or otherwise makes known to an immigration inspector or other official making an examination on the conveyance that he or she is unable or unwilling to return to his or her country of nationality or last habitual residence (if not a national of any country) because of persecution or a fear of persecution in that country on account of race, religion, nationality, membership in a particular social group, or political opinion, or if the alien expresses a fear of torture upon return to that country, the alien shall be promptly removed from the conveyance. If the alien makes such fear known to an official while off such conveyance, the alien shall not be returned to the conveyance but shall be retained in or transferred to the custody of the Service.

(i) An alien stowaway will be referred to an asylum officer for a credible fear determination under § 208.30.

(ii) An alien crewmember shall be provided the appropriate application forms and information required by section 208(d)(4) of the Act and may then have 10 days within which to submit an asylum application in accordance with the instructions on the form. The DHS may extend the 10-day filing period for good cause. Once the application has been filed, the DHS shall serve Form I–863 on the alien and immediately forward any such application to the appropriate Immigration Court with a copy of the Form I–863 being filed with that court.

(iii) An alien crewmember physically present in or arriving in the Commonwealth of the Northern Mariana Islands can request withholding of removal pursuant to section 241(b)(3) of the Act and withholding of removal under the Convention Against Torture. However, such an alien crewmember is not eligible to request asylum pursuant to section 208 of the Act prior to January 1, 2015.

(2) Pending adjudication of the application, and, in the case of a stowaway the credible fear determination and any review thereof, the alien may be detained by the Service or otherwise paroled in accordance with § 212.5 of this chapter. However, pending the credible fear determination, parole of an alien stowaway may be permitted only when the Secretary determines, in the exercise of discretion, that parole is required to meet a medical emergency or is necessary for a legitimate law enforcement objective.

(c) *Exception to prohibition on removal.* A motion to reopen or an order to remand accompanied by an asylum application pursuant to § 208.4(b)(3)(iii) shall not stay execution of a final exclusion, deportation, or removal order unless such stay is specifically granted by the Board of Immigration Appeals or the immigration judge having jurisdiction over the motion.

[62 FR 10337, Mar. 6, 1997, as amended at 64 FR 8488, Feb. 19, 1999; 65 FR 76132, Dec. 6, 2000; 74 FR 26937, June 5, 2009; 74 FR 55737, Oct. 28, 2009; 76 FR 53784, Aug. 29, 2011]

§ 208.6 Disclosure to third parties.

(a) Information contained in or pertaining to any asylum application, records pertaining to any credible fear determination conducted pursuant to § 208.30, and records pertaining to any reasonable fear determination conducted pursuant to § 208.31, shall not be disclosed without the written consent of the applicant, except as permitted by this section or at the discretion of the Attorney General.

(b) The confidentiality of other records kept by the Service and the Executive Office for Immigration Review that indicate that a specific alien has applied for asylum, received a credible fear or reasonable fear interview, or received a credible fear or reasonable fear review shall also be protected from disclosure. The Service will coordinate with the Department of State to ensure that the confidentiality of those records is maintained if they are transmitted to Department of State offices in other countries.

(c) This section shall not apply to any disclosure to:

(1) Any United States Government official or contractor having a need to examine information in connection with:

(i) The adjudication of asylum applications;

(ii) The consideration of a request for a credible fear or reasonable fear interview, or a credible fear or reasonable fear review;

(iii) The defense of any legal action arising from the adjudication of, or failure to adjudicate, the asylum application, or from a credible fear determination or reasonable fear determination under §208.30 or §208.31;

(iv) The defense of any legal action of which the asylum application, credible fear determination, or reasonable fear determination is a part; or

(v) Any United States Government investigation concerning any criminal or civil matter; or

(2) Any Federal, State, or local court in the United States considering any legal action:

(i) Arising from the adjudication of, or failure to adjudicate, the asylum application, or from a credible fear or reasonable fear determination under §208.30 or §208.31; or

(ii) Arising from the proceedings of which the asylum application, credible fear determination, or reasonable fear determination is a part.

[65 FR 76133, Dec. 6, 2000]

§208.7 Employment authorization.

(a) *Application and approval.* (1) Subject to the restrictions contained in sections 208(d) and 236(a) of the Act, an applicant for asylum who is not an aggravated felon shall be eligible pursuant to §§274a.12(c)(8) and 274a.13(a) of this chapter to request employment authorization. Except in the case of an alien whose asylum application has been recommended for approval, or in the case of an alien who filed an asylum application prior to January 4, 1995, the application shall be submitted no earlier than 150 days after the date on which a complete asylum application submitted in accordance with §§208.3 and 208.4 has been received. In the case of an applicant whose asylum application has been recommended for approval, the applicant may apply for employment authorization when he or she receives notice of the recommended approval. If an asylum application has been returned as incomplete in accordance with §208.3(c)(3), the 150-day period will commence upon receipt by the Service of a complete asylum application. An applicant whose asylum application has been denied by an asylum officer or by an immigration judge within the 150-day period shall not be eligible to apply for employment authorization. If an asylum application is denied prior to a decision on the application for employment authorization, the application for employment authorization shall be denied. If the asylum application is not so denied, the Service shall have 30 days from the date of filing of the request employment authorization to grant or deny that application, except that no employment authorization shall be issued to an asylum applicant prior to the expiration of the 180-day period following the filing of the asylum application filed on or after April 1, 1997.

(2) The time periods within which the alien may not apply for employment authorization and within which USCIS must respond to any such application and within which the asylum application must be adjudicated pursuant to section 208(d)(5)(A)(iii) of the Act shall begin when the alien has filed a complete asylum application in accordance with §§208.3 and 208.4. Any delay requested or caused by the applicant shall not be counted as part of these time periods, including delays caused by failure without good cause to follow the requirements for fingerprint processing. Such time periods shall also be extended by the equivalent of the time between issuance of a request for evidence pursuant to §103.2(b)(8) of this chapter and the receipt of the applicant's response to such request.

(3) The provisions of paragraphs (a)(1) and (a)(2) of this section apply to applications for asylum filed on or after January 4, 1995.

(4) Employment authorization pursuant to §274a.12(c)(8) of this chapter may not be granted to an alien who fails to appear for a scheduled interview before an asylum officer or a hearing before an immigration judge, unless the applicant demonstrates that the failure to

appear was the result of exceptional circumstances.

(b) *Renewal and termination.* Employment authorization shall be renewable, in increments to be determined by USCIS, for the continuous period of time necessary for the asylum officer or immigration judge to decide the asylum application and, if necessary, for completion of any administrative or judicial review.

(1) If the asylum application is denied by the asylum officer, the employment authorization shall terminate at the expiration of the employment authorization document or 60 days after the denial of asylum, whichever is longer.

(2) If the application is denied by the immigration judge, the Board of Immigration Appeals, or a Federal court, the employment authorization terminates upon the expiration of the employment authorization document, unless the applicant has filed an appropriate request for administrative or judicial review.

(c) *Supporting evidence for renewal of employment authorization.* In order for employment authorization to be renewed under this section, the alien must request employment authorization in accordance with the form instructions. USCIS may require that an alien establish that he or she has continued to pursue an asylum application before an immigration judge or sought administrative or judicial review. For purposes of employment authorization, pursuit of an asylum application is established by presenting one of the following, depending on the stage of the alien's immigration proceedings:

(1) If the alien's case is pending in proceedings before the immigration judge, and the alien wishes to continue to pursue his or her asylum application, a copy of any asylum denial, referral notice, or charging document placing the alien in such proceedings;

(2) If the immigration judge has denied asylum, a copy of the document issued by the Board of Immigration Appeals to show that a timely appeal has been filed from a denial of the asylum application by the immigration judge; or

(3) If the Board of Immigration Appeals has dismissed the alien's appeal of a denial of asylum, or sustained an appeal by the Service of a grant of asylum, a copy of the petition for judicial review or for habeas corpus pursuant to section 242 of the Act, date stamped by the appropriate court.

(d) In order for employment authorization to be renewed before its expiration, the application for renewal must be received by the Service 90 days prior to expiration of the employment authorization.

[62 FR 10337, Mar. 6, 1997, as amended at 63 FR 12986, Mar. 17, 1998; 76 FR 53784, Aug. 29, 2011]

§ 208.8 Limitations on travel outside the United States.

(a) An applicant who leaves the United States without first obtaining advance parole under § 212.5(f) of this chapter shall be presumed to have abandoned his or her application under this section.

(b) An applicant who leaves the United States pursuant to advance parole under § 212.5(f) of this chapter and returns to the country of claimed persecution shall be presumed to have abandoned his or her application, unless the applicant is able to establish compelling reasons for such return.

[62 FR 10337, Mar. 6, 1997, as amended at 65 FR 82255, Dec. 28, 2000]

§ 208.9 Procedure for interview before an asylum officer.

(a) The Service shall adjudicate the claim of each asylum applicant whose application is complete within the meaning of § 208.3(c)(3) and is within the jurisdiction of the Service.

(b) The asylum officer shall conduct the interview in a nonadversarial manner and, except at the request of the applicant, separate and apart from the general public. The purpose of the interview shall be to elicit all relevant and useful information bearing on the applicant's eligibility for asylum. At the time of the interview, the applicant must provide complete information regarding his or her identity, including name, date and place of birth, and nationality, and may be required to register this identity. The applicant may have counsel or a representative present, may present witnesses, and may submit affidavits of witnesses and other evidence.

(c) The asylum officer shall have authority to administer oaths, verify the identity of the applicant (including through the use of electronic means), verify the identity of any interpreter, present and receive evidence, and question the applicant and any witnesses.

(d) Upon completion of the interview, the applicant or the applicant's representative shall have an opportunity to make a statement or comment on the evidence presented. The asylum officer may, in his or her discretion, limit the length of such statement or comment and may require its submission in writing. Upon completion of the interview, the applicant shall be informed that he or she must appear in person to receive and to acknowledge receipt of the decision of the asylum officer and any other accompanying material at a time and place designated by the asylum officer, except as otherwise provided by the asylum officer. An applicant's failure to appear to receive and acknowledge receipt of the decision shall be treated as delay caused by the applicant for purposes of § 208.7(a)(3) and shall extend the period within which the applicant may not apply for employment authorization by the number of days until the applicant does appear to receive and acknowledge receipt of the decision or until the applicant appears before an immigration judge in response to the issuance of a charging document under § 208.14(c).

(e) The asylum officer shall consider evidence submitted by the applicant together with his or her asylum application, as well as any evidence submitted by the applicant before or at the interview. As a matter of discretion, the asylum officer may grant the applicant a brief extension of time following an interview during which the applicant may submit additional evidence. Any such extension shall extend by an equivalent time the periods specified by § 208.7 for the filing and adjudication of any employment authorization application.

(f) The asylum application, all supporting information provided by the applicant, any comments submitted by the Department of State or by the Service, and any other information specific to the applicant's case and considered by the asylum officer shall comprise the record.

(g) An applicant unable to proceed with the interview in English must provide, at no expense to the Service, a competent interpreter fluent in both English and the applicant's native language or any other language in which the applicant is fluent. The interpreter must be at least 18 years of age. Neither the applicant's attorney or representative of record, a witness testifying on the applicant's behalf, nor a representative or employee of the applicant's country of nationality, or if stateless, country of last habitual residence, may serve as the applicant's interpreter. Failure without good cause to comply with this paragraph may be considered a failure to appear for the interview for purposes of § 208.10.

[62 FR 10337, Mar. 6, 1997, as amended at 65 FR 76133, Dec. 6, 2000; 76 FR 53784, Aug. 29, 2011]

§ 208.10 Failure to appear at an interview before an asylum officer or failure to follow requirements for fingerprint processing.

Failure to appear for a scheduled interview without prior authorization may result in dismissal of the application or waiver of the right to an interview. Failure to comply with fingerprint processing requirements without good cause may result in dismissal of the application or waiver of the right to an adjudication by an asylum officer. Failure to appear shall be excused if the notice of the interview or fingerprint appointment was not mailed to the applicant's current address and such address had been provided to the USCIS by the applicant prior to the date of mailing in accordance with section 265 of the Act and regulations promulgated thereunder, unless the asylum officer determines that the applicant received reasonable notice of the interview or fingerprinting appointment. Failure to appear at the interview or fingerprint appointment will be excused if the applicant demonstrates that such failure was the result of exceptional circumstances.

[63 FR 12986, Mar. 17, 1998, as amended at 76 FR 53784, Aug. 29, 2011]

§ 208.11 Comments from the Department of State.

(a) U.S. Citizenship and Immigration Services (USCIS) may request, at its discretion, specific comments from the Department of State regarding individual cases or types of claims under consideration, or such other information as USCIS deems appropriate.

(b) With respect to any asylum application, the Department of State may provide, at its discretion, to USCIS:

(1) Detailed country conditions information relevant to eligibility for asylum or withholding of removal;

(2) An assessment of the accuracy of the applicant's assertions about conditions in his or her country of nationality or habitual residence and his or her particular situation;

(3) Information about whether persons who are similarly situated to the applicant are persecuted or tortured in the applicant's country of nationality or habitual residence and the frequency of such persecution or torture; or

(4) Such other information as it deems relevant.

(c) Any comments received pursuant to paragraph (b) of this section shall be made part of the record. Unless the comments are classified under the applicable Executive Order, the applicant shall be provided an opportunity to review and respond to such comments prior to the issuance of any decision to deny the application.

[74 FR 15369, Apr. 6, 2009]

§ 208.12 Reliance on information compiled by other sources.

(a) In deciding an asylum application, or in deciding whether the alien has a credible fear of persecution or torture pursuant to § 208.30 of this part, or a reasonable fear of persecution or torture pursuant to § 208.31, the asylum officer may rely on material provided by the Department of State, other USCIS offices, or other credible sources, such as international organizations, private voluntary agencies, news organizations, or academic institutions.

(b) Nothing in this part shall be construed to entitle the applicant to conduct discovery directed toward the records, officers, agents, or employees of the Service, the Department of Justice, or the Department of State. Persons may continue to seek documents available through a Freedom of Information Act (FOIA) request pursuant to 8 CFR part 103.

[62 FR 10337, Mar. 6, 1997, as amended at 64 FR 8488, Feb. 19, 1999; 65 FR 76133, Dec. 6, 2000; 76 FR 53784, Aug. 29, 2011]

§ 208.13 Establishing asylum eligibility.

(a) *Burden of proof.* The burden of proof is on the applicant for asylum to establish that he or she is a refugee as defined in section 101(a)(42) of the Act. The testimony of the applicant, if credible, may be sufficient to sustain the burden of proof without corroboration. The fact that the applicant previously established a credible fear of persecution for purposes of section 235(b)(1)(B) of the Act does not relieve the alien of the additional burden of establishing eligibility for asylum.

(b) *Eligibility.* The applicant may qualify as a refugee either because he or she has suffered past persecution or because he or she has a well-founded fear of future persecution.

(1) *Past persecution.* An applicant shall be found to be a refugee on the basis of past persecution if the applicant can establish that he or she has suffered persecution in the past in the applicant's country of nationality or, if stateless, in his or her country of last habitual residence, on account of race, religion, nationality, membership in a particular social group, or political opinion, and is unable or unwilling to return to, or avail himself or herself of the protection of, that country owing to such persecution. An applicant who has been found to have established such past persecution shall also be presumed to have a well-founded fear of persecution on the basis of the original claim. That presumption may be rebutted if an asylum officer or immigration judge makes one of the findings described in paragraph (b)(1)(i) of this section. If the applicant's fear of future persecution is unrelated to the past persecution, the applicant bears the burden of establishing that the fear is well-founded.

(i) *Discretionary referral or denial.* Except as provided in paragraph (b)(1)(iii) of this section, an asylum officer shall, in the exercise of his or her discretion, refer or deny, or an immigration judge, in the exercise of his or her discretion, shall deny the asylum application of an alien found to be a refugee on the basis of past persecution if any of the following is found by a preponderance of the evidence:

(A) There has been a fundamental change in circumstances such that the applicant no longer has a well-founded fear of persecution in the applicant's country of nationality or, if stateless, in the applicant's country of last habitual residence, on account of race, religion, nationality, membership in a particular social group, or political opinion; or

(B) The applicant could avoid future persecution by relocating to another part of the applicant's country of nationality or, if stateless, another part of the applicant's country of last habitual residence, and under all the circumstances, it would be reasonable to expect the applicant to do so.

(ii) *Burden of proof.* In cases in which an applicant has demonstrated past persecution under paragraph (b)(1) of this section, the Service shall bear the burden of establishing by a preponderance of the evidence the requirements of paragraphs (b)(1)(i)(A) or (B) of this section.

(iii) *Grant in the absence of well-founded fear of persecution.* An applicant described in paragraph (b)(1)(i) of this section who is not barred from a grant of asylum under paragraph (c) of this section, may be granted asylum, in the exercise of the decision-maker's discretion, if:

(A) The applicant has demonstrated compelling reasons for being unwilling or unable to return to the country arising out of the severity of the past persecution; or

(B) The applicant has established that there is a reasonable possibility that he or she may suffer other serious harm upon removal to that country.

(2) *Well-founded fear of persecution.* (i) An applicant has a well-founded fear of persecution if:

(A) The applicant has a fear of persecution in his or her country of nationality or, if stateless, in his or her country of last habitual residence, on account of race, religion, nationality, membership in a particular social group, or political opinion;

(B) There is a reasonable possibility of suffering such persecution if he or she were to return to that country; and

(C) He or she is unable or unwilling to return to, or avail himself or herself of the protection of, that country because of such fear.

(ii) An applicant does not have a well-founded fear of persecution if the applicant could avoid persecution by relocating to another part of the applicant's country of nationality or, if stateless, another part of the applicant's country of last habitual residence, if under all the circumstances it would be reasonable to expect the applicant to do so.

(iii) In evaluating whether the applicant has sustained the burden of proving that he or she has a well-founded fear of persecution, the asylum officer or immigration judge shall not require the applicant to provide evidence that there is a reasonable possibility he or she would be singled out individually for persecution if:

(A) The applicant establishes that there is a pattern or practice in his or her country of nationality or, if stateless, in his or her country of last habitual residence, of persecution of a group of persons similarly situated to the applicant on account of race, religion, nationality, membership in a particular social group, or political opinion; and

(B) The applicant establishes his or her own inclusion in, and identification with, such group of persons such that his or her fear of persecution upon return is reasonable.

(3) *Reasonableness of internal relocation.* For purposes of determinations under paragraphs (b)(1)(i), (b)(1)(ii), and (b)(2) of this section, adjudicators should consider, but are not limited to considering, whether the applicant would face other serious harm in the place of suggested relocation; any ongoing civil strife within the country; administrative, economic, or judicial infrastructure; geographical limitations; and social and cultural constraints, such as age, gender, health, and social and familial ties. Those factors may, or may not, be relevant, depending on all the circumstances of the

case, and are not necessarily determinative of whether it would be reasonable for the applicant to relocate.

(i) In cases in which the applicant has not established past persecution, the applicant shall bear the burden of establishing that it would not be reasonable for him or her to relocate, unless the persecution is by a government or is government-sponsored.

(ii) In cases in which the persecutor is a government or is government-sponsored, or the applicant has established persecution in the past, it shall be presumed that internal relocation would not be reasonable, unless the Service establishes by a preponderance of the evidence that, under all the circumstances, it would be reasonable for the applicant to relocate.

(c) *Mandatory denials*—(1) *Applications filed on or after April 1, 1997.* For applications filed on or after April 1, 1997, an applicant shall not qualify for asylum if section 208(a)(2) or 208(b)(2) of the Act applies to the applicant. If the applicant is found to be ineligible for asylum under either section 208(a)(2) or 208(b)(2) of the Act, the applicant shall be considered for eligibility for withholding of removal under section 241(b)(3) of the Act. The applicant shall also be considered for eligibility for withholding of removal under the Convention Against Torture if the applicant requests such consideration or if the evidence presented by the alien indicates that the alien may be tortured in the country of removal.

(2) *Applications filed before April 1, 1997.* (i) An immigration judge or asylum officer shall not grant asylum to any applicant who filed his or her application before April 1, 1997, if the alien:

(A) Having been convicted by a final judgment of a particularly serious crime in the United States, constitutes a danger to the community;

(B) Has been firmly resettled within the meaning of § 208.15;

(C) Can reasonably be regarded as a danger to the security of the United States;

(D) Has been convicted of an aggravated felony, as defined in section 101(a)(43) of the Act; or

(E) Ordered, incited, assisted, or otherwise participated in the persecution of any person on account of race, religion, nationality, membership in a particular social group, or political opinion.

(F) Is described within section 212(a)(3)(B)(i)(I),(II), and (III) of the Act as it existed prior to April 1, 1997, and as amended by the Anti-terrorist and Effective Death Penalty Act of 1996 (AEDPA), unless it is determined that there are no reasonable grounds to believe that the individual is a danger to the security of the United States.

(ii) If the evidence indicates that one of the above grounds apply to the applicant, he or she shall have the burden of proving by a preponderance of the evidence that he or she did not so act.

(3) *Additional limitation on eligibility for asylum.* For applications filed after November 9, 2018, an alien shall be ineligible for asylum if the alien is subject to a presidential proclamation or other presidential order suspending or limiting the entry of aliens along the southern border with Mexico that is issued pursuant to subsection 212(f) or 215(a)(1) of the Act on or after November 9, 2018 and the alien enters the United States after the effective date of the proclamation or order contrary to the terms of the proclamation or order. This limitation on eligibility does not apply if the proclamation or order expressly provides that it does not affect eligibility for asylum, or expressly provides for a waiver or exception that makes the suspension or limitation inapplicable to the alien.

[62 FR 10337, Mar. 6, 1997, as amended at 64 FR 8488, Feb. 19, 1999; 65 FR 76133, Dec. 6, 2000; 83 FR 55952, Nov. 9, 2018]

§ 208.14 Approval, denial, referral, or dismissal of application.

(a) *By an immigration judge.* Unless otherwise prohibited in § 208.13(c), an immigration judge may grant or deny asylum in the exercise of discretion to an applicant who qualifies as a refugee under section 101(a)(42) of the Act.

(b) *Approval by an asylum officer.* In any case within the jurisdiction of the RAIO, unless otherwise prohibited in § 208.13(c), an asylum officer may grant, in the exercise of his or her discretion, asylum to an applicant who qualifies as a refugee under section 101(a)(42) of the Act, and whose identity has been checked pursuant to section 208(d)(5)(A)(i) of the Act.

(c) *Denial, referral, or dismissal by an asylum officer.* If the asylum officer does not grant asylum to an applicant after an interview conducted in accordance with § 208.9, or if, as provided in § 208.10, the applicant is deemed to have waived his or her right to an interview or an adjudication by an asylum officer, the asylum officer shall deny, refer, or dismiss the application, as follows:

(1) *Inadmissible or deportable aliens.* Except as provided in paragraph (c)(4) of this section, in the case of an applicant who appears to be inadmissible or deportable under section 212(a) or 237(a) of the Act, the asylum officer shall refer the application to an immigration judge, together with the appropriate charging document, for adjudication in removal proceedings (or, where charging documents may not be issued, shall dismiss the application).

(2) *Alien in valid status.* In the case of an applicant who is maintaining valid immigrant, nonimmigrant, or Temporary Protected Status at the time the application is decided, the asylum officer shall deny the application for asylum.

(3) *Alien with valid parole.* If an applicant has been paroled into the United States and the parole has not expired or been terminated by the Service, the asylum officer shall deny the application for asylum.

(4) *Alien paroled into the United States whose parole has expired or is terminated*—(i) *Alien paroled prior to April 1, 1997, or with advance authorization for parole.* In the case of an applicant who was paroled into the United States prior to April 1, 1997, or who, prior to departure from the United States, had received an advance authorization for parole, the asylum officer shall refer the application, together with the appropriate charging documents, to an immigration judge for adjudication in removal proceedings if the parole has expired, the Service has terminated parole, or the Service is terminating parole through issuance of the charging documents, pursuant to § 212.5(d)(2)(i) of this chapter.

(ii) *Alien paroled on or after April 1, 1997, without advance authorization for parole.* In the case of an applicant who is an arriving alien or is otherwise subject to removal under § 235.3(b) of this chapter, and was paroled into the United States on or after April 1, 1997, without advance authorization for parole prior to departure from the United States, the asylum officer will take the following actions, if the parole has expired or been terminated:

(A) *Inadmissible under section 212(a)(6)(C) or 212(a)(7) of the Act.* If the applicant appears inadmissible to the United States under section 212(a)(6)(C) or 212(a)(7) of the Act and the asylum officer does not intend to lodge any additional charges of inadmissibility, the asylum officer shall proceed in accordance with § 235.3(b) of this chapter. If such applicant is found to have a credible fear of persecution or torture based on information elicited from the asylum interview, an asylum officer may refer the applicant directly to an immigration judge in removal proceedings under section 240 of the Act, without conducting a separate credible fear interview pursuant to § 208.30. If such applicant is not found to have a credible fear based on information elicited at the asylum interview, an asylum officer will conduct a credible fear interview and the applicant will be subject to the credible fear process specified at § 208.30(b).

(B) *Inadmissible on other grounds.* In the case of an applicant who was paroled into the United States on or after April 1, 1997, and will be charged as inadmissible to the United States under provisions of the Act other than, or in addition to, sections 212(a)(6)(C) or 212(a)(7), the asylum officer shall refer the application to an immigration judge for adjudication in removal proceedings.

(d) *Applicability of § 103.2(b) of this chapter.* No application for asylum or withholding of deportation shall be subject to denial pursuant to § 103.2(b) of this chapter.

(e) *Duration.* If the applicant is granted asylum, the grant will be effective for an indefinite period, subject to termination as provided in § 208.24.

(f) *Effect of denial of principal's application on separate applications by dependents.* The denial of an asylum application filed by a principal applicant for asylum shall also result in the denial of asylum status to any dependents of that principal applicant who are included in that same application. Such denial shall not preclude a grant of asylum for an otherwise eligible dependent who has filed a separate asylum application, nor shall such denial result in an otherwise eligible dependent becoming ineligible to apply for asylum due to the provisions of section 208(a)(2)(C) of the Act.

(g) *Applicants granted lawful permanent residence status.* If an asylum applicant is granted adjustment of status to lawful permanent resident, the Service may provide written notice to the applicant that his or her asylum application will be presumed abandoned and dismissed without prejudice, unless the applicant submits a written request within 30 days of the notice, that the asylum application be adjudicated. If an applicant does not respond within 30 days of the date the written notice was sent or served, the Service may presume the asylum application abandoned and dismiss it without prejudice.

[62 FR 10337, Mar. 6, 1997, as amended at 63 FR 12986, Mar. 17, 1998; 64 FR 27875, May 21, 1999; 65 FR 76134, Dec. 6, 2000; 76 FR 53784, Aug. 29, 2011]

§ 208.15 Definition of "firm resettlement."

An alien is considered to be firmly resettled if, prior to arrival in the United States, he or she entered into another country with, or while in that country received, an offer of permanent resident status, citizenship, or some other type of permanent resettlement unless he or she establishes:

(a) That his or her entry into that country was a necessary consequence of his or her flight from persecution, that he or she remained in that country only as long as was necessary to arrange onward travel, and that he or she did not establish significant ties in that country; or

(b) That the conditions of his or her residence in that country were so substantially and consciously restricted by the authority of the country of refuge that he or she was not in fact resettled. In making his or her determination, the asylum officer or immigration judge shall consider the conditions under which other residents of the country live; the type of housing, whether permanent or temporary, made available to the refugee; the types and extent of employment available to the refugee; and the extent to which the refugee received permission to hold property and to enjoy other rights and privileges, such as travel documentation that includes a right of entry or reentry, education, public relief, or naturalization, ordinarily available to others resident in the country.

[65 FR 76135, Dec. 6, 2000]

§ 208.16 Withholding of removal under section 241(b)(3)(B) of the Act and withholding of removal under the Convention Against Torture.

(a) *Consideration of application for withholding of removal.* An asylum officer shall not decide whether the exclusion, deportation, or removal of an alien to a country where the alien's life or freedom would be threatened must be withheld, except in the case of an alien who is otherwise eligible for asylum but is precluded from being granted such status due solely to section 207(a)(5) of the Act. In exclusion, deportation, or removal proceedings, an immigration judge may adjudicate both an asylum claim and a request for withholding of removal whether or not asylum is granted.

(b) *Eligibility for withholding of removal under section 241(b)(3) of the Act; burden of proof.* The burden of proof is on the applicant for withholding of removal under section 241(b)(3) of the Act to establish that his or her life or freedom would be threatened in the proposed country of removal on account of race, religion, nationality, membership in a particular social group, or political opinion. The testimony of the applicant, if credible, may be sufficient to sustain the burden of proof without corroboration. The evidence shall be evaluated as follows:

(1) *Past threat to life or freedom.* (i) If the applicant is determined to have suffered past persecution in the proposed country of removal on account of race, religion, nationality, membership in a particular social group, or political opinion, it shall be presumed that the applicant's life or freedom would be threatened in the future in the country

of removal on the basis of the original claim. This presumption may be rebutted if an asylum officer or immigration judge finds by a preponderance of the evidence:

(A) There has been a fundamental change in circumstances such that the applicant's life or freedom would not be threatened on account of any of the five grounds mentioned in this paragraph upon the applicant's removal to that country; or

(B) The applicant could avoid a future threat to his or her life or freedom by relocating to another part of the proposed country of removal and, under all the circumstances, it would be reasonable to expect the applicant to do so.

(ii) In cases in which the applicant has established past persecution, the Service shall bear the burden of establishing by a preponderance of the evidence the requirements of paragraphs (b)(1)(i)(A) or (b)(1)(i)(B) of this section.

(iii) If the applicant's fear of future threat to life or freedom is unrelated to the past persecution, the applicant bears the burden of establishing that it is more likely than not that he or she would suffer such harm.

(2) *Future threat to life or freedom.* An applicant who has not suffered past persecution may demonstrate that his or her life or freedom would be threatened in the future in a country if he or she can establish that it is more likely than not that he or she would be persecuted on account of race, religion, nationality, membership in a particular social group, or political opinion upon removal to that country. Such an applicant cannot demonstrate that his or her life or freedom would be threatened if the asylum officer or immigration judge finds that the applicant could avoid a future threat to his or her life or freedom by relocating to another part of the proposed country of removal and, under all the circumstances, it would be reasonable to expect the applicant to do so. In evaluating whether it is more likely than not that the applicant's life or freedom would be threatened in a particular country on account of race, religion, nationality, membership in a particular social group, or political opinion, the asylum officer or immigration judge shall not require the applicant to provide evidence that he or she would be singled out individually for such persecution if:

(i) The applicant establishes that in that country there is a pattern or practice of persecution of a group of persons similarly situated to the applicant on account of race, religion, nationality, membership in a particular social group, or political opinion; and

(ii) The applicant establishes his or her own inclusion in and identification with such group of persons such that it is more likely than not that his or her life or freedom would be threatened upon return to that country.

(3) *Reasonableness of internal relocation.* For purposes of determinations under paragraphs (b)(1) and (b)(2) of this section, adjudicators should consider, among other things, whether the applicant would face other serious harm in the place of suggested relocation; any ongoing civil strife within the country; administrative, economic, or judicial infrastructure; geographical limitations; and social and cultural constraints, such as age, gender, health, and social and familial ties. These factors may or may not be relevant, depending on all the circumstances of the case, and are not necessarily determinative of whether it would be reasonable for the applicant to relocate.

(i) In cases in which the applicant has not established past persecution, the applicant shall bear the burden of establishing that it would not be reasonable for him or her to relocate, unless the persecutor is a government or is government-sponsored.

(ii) In cases in which the persecutor is a government or is government-sponsored, or the applicant has established persecution in the past, it shall be presumed that internal relocation would not be reasonable, unless the Service establishes by a preponderance of the evidence that under all the circumstances it would be reasonable for the applicant to relocate.

(c) *Eligibility for withholding of removal under the Convention Against Torture.* (1) For purposes of regulations under Title II of the Act, "Convention Against Torture" shall refer to the United Nations Convention Against

Torture and Other Cruel, Inhuman or Degrading Treatment or Punishment, subject to any reservations, understandings, declarations, and provisos contained in the United States Senate resolution of ratification of the Convention, as implemented by section 2242 of the Foreign Affairs Reform and Restructuring Act of 1998 (Pub. L. 105–277, 112 Stat. 2681, 2681–821). The definition of torture contained in § 208.18(a) of this part shall govern all decisions made under regulations under Title II of the Act about the applicability of Article 3 of the Convention Against Torture.

(2) The burden of proof is on the applicant for withholding of removal under this paragraph to establish that it is more likely than not that he or she would be tortured if removed to the proposed country of removal. The testimony of the applicant, if credible, may be sufficient to sustain the burden of proof without corroboration.

(3) In assessing whether it is more likely than not that an applicant would be tortured in the proposed country of removal, all evidence relevant to the possibility of future torture shall be considered, including, but not limited to:

(i) Evidence of past torture inflicted upon the applicant;

(ii) Evidence that the applicant could relocate to a part of the country of removal where he or she is not likely to be tortured;

(iii) Evidence of gross, flagrant or mass violations of human rights within the country of removal, where applicable; and

(iv) Other relevant information regarding conditions in the country of removal.

(4) In considering an application for withholding of removal under the Convention Against Torture, the immigration judge shall first determine whether the alien is more likely than not to be tortured in the country of removal. If the immigration judge determines that the alien is more likely than not to be tortured in the country of removal, the alien is entitled to protection under the Convention Against Torture. Protection under the Convention Against Torture will be granted either in the form of withholding of removal or in the form of deferral of removal. An alien entitled to such protection shall be granted withholding of removal unless the alien is subject to mandatory denial of withholding of removal under paragraphs (d)(2) or (d)(3) of this section. If an alien entitled to such protection is subject to mandatory denial of withholding of removal under paragraphs (d)(2) or (d)(3) of this section, the alien's removal shall be deferred under § 208.17(a).

(d) *Approval or denial of application*—(1) *General.* Subject to paragraphs (d)(2) and (d)(3) of this section, an application for withholding of deportation or removal to a country of proposed removal shall be granted if the applicant's eligibility for withholding is established pursuant to paragraphs (b) or (c) of this section.

(2) *Mandatory denials.* Except as provided in paragraph (d)(3) of this section, an application for withholding of removal under section 241(b)(3) of the Act or under the Convention Against Torture shall be denied if the applicant falls within section 241(b)(3)(B) of the Act or, for applications for withholding of deportation adjudicated in proceedings commenced prior to April 1, 1997, within section 243(h)(2) of the Act as it appeared prior to that date. For purposes of section 241(b)(3)(B)(ii) of the Act, or section 243(h)(2)(B) of the Act as it appeared prior to April 1, 1997, an alien who has been convicted of a particularly serious crime shall be considered to constitute a danger to the community. If the evidence indicates the applicability of one or more of the grounds for denial of withholding enumerated in the Act, the applicant shall have the burden of proving by a preponderance of the evidence that such grounds do not apply.

(3) *Exception to the prohibition on withholding of deportation in certain cases.* Section 243(h)(3) of the Act, as added by section 413 of Pub. L. 104–132 (110 Stat. 1214), shall apply only to applications adjudicated in proceedings commenced before April 1, 1997, and in which final action had not been taken before April 24, 1996. The discretion permitted by that section to override section 243(h)(2) of the Act shall be exercised

only in the case of an applicant convicted of an aggravated felony (or felonies) where he or she was sentenced to an aggregate term of imprisonment of less than 5 years and the immigration judge determines on an individual basis that the crime (or crimes) of which the applicant was convicted does not constitute a particularly serious crime. Nevertheless, it shall be presumed that an alien convicted of an aggravated felony has been convicted of a particularly serious crime. Except in the cases specified in this paragraph, the grounds for denial of withholding of deportation in section 243(h)(2) of the Act as it appeared prior to April 1, 1997, shall be deemed to comply with the Protocol Relating to the Status of Refugees, Jan. 31, 1967, T.I.A.S. No. 6577.

(e) *Reconsideration of discretionary denial of asylum.* In the event that an applicant is denied asylum solely in the exercise of discretion, and the applicant is subsequently granted withholding of deportation or removal under this section, thereby effectively precluding admission of the applicant's spouse or minor children following to join him or her, the denial of asylum shall be reconsidered. Factors to be considered will include the reasons for the denial and reasonable alternatives available to the applicant such as reunification with his or her spouse or minor children in a third country.

(f) *Removal to third country.* Nothing in this section or § 208.17 shall prevent the Service from removing an alien to a third country other than the country to which removal has been withheld or deferred.

[62 FR 10337, Mar. 6, 1997, as amended at 64 FR 8488, Feb. 19, 1999; 65 FR 76135, Dec. 6, 2000]

§ 208.17 Deferral of removal under the Convention Against Torture.

(a) *Grant of deferral of removal.* An alien who: has been ordered removed; has been found under § 208.16(c)(3) to be entitled to protection under the Convention Against Torture; and is subject to the provisions for mandatory denial of withholding of removal under § 208.16(d)(2) or (d)(3), shall be granted deferral of removal to the country where he or she is more likely than not to be tortured.

(b) *Notice to alien.* (1) After an immigration judge orders an alien described in paragraph (a) of this section removed, the immigration judge shall inform the alien that his or her removal to the country where he or she is more likely than not to be tortured shall be deferred until such time as the deferral is terminated under this section. The immigration judge shall inform the alien that deferral of removal:

(i) Does not confer upon the alien any lawful or permanent immigration status in the United States;

(ii) Will not necessarily result in the alien being released from the custody of the Service if the alien is subject to such custody;

(iii) Is effective only until terminated; and

(iv) Is subject to review and termination if the immigration judge determines that it is not likely that the alien would be tortured in the country to which removal has been deferred, or if the alien requests that deferral be terminated.

(2) The immigration judge shall also inform the alien that removal has been deferred only to the country in which it has been determined that the alien is likely to be tortured, and that the alien may be removed at any time to another country where he or she is not likely to be tortured.

(c) *Detention of an alien granted deferral of removal under this section.* Nothing in this section shall alter the authority of the Service to detain an alien whose removal has been deferred under this section and who is otherwise subject to detention. In the case of such an alien, decisions about the alien's release shall be made according to part 241 of this chapter.

(d) *Termination of deferral of removal.* (1) At any time while deferral of removal is in effect, the INS District Counsel for the District with jurisdiction over an alien whose removal has been deferred under paragraph (a) of this section may file a motion with the Immigration Court having administrative control pursuant to § 3.11 of this chapter to schedule a hearing to consider whether deferral of removal should be terminated. The Service motion shall be granted if it is accompanied by evidence that is relevant to the possibility that the alien would be tortured in the country to which removal has been deferred and that was not presented at the previous hearing. The Service motion shall not be subject to the requirements for reopening in §§ 3.2 and 3.23 of this chapter.

(2) The Immigration Court shall provide notice to the alien and the Service of the time, place, and date of the termination hearing. Such notice shall inform the alien that the alien may supplement the information in his or her initial application for withholding of removal under the Convention Against Torture and shall provide that the alien must submit any such supplemental information within 10 calendar days of service of such notice (or 13 calendar days if service of such notice was by mail). At the expiration of this 10 or 13 day period, the Immigration Court shall forward a copy of the original application, and any supplemental information the alien or the Service has submitted, to the Department of State, together with notice to the Department of State of the time, place and date of the termination hearing. At its option, the Department of State may provide comments on the case, according to the provisions of § 208.11 of this part.

(3) The immigration judge shall conduct a hearing and make a *de novo* determination, based on the record of proceeding and initial application in addition to any new evidence submitted by the Service or the alien, as to whether the alien is more likely than not to be tortured in the country to which removal has been deferred. This determination shall be made under the standards for eligibility set out in § 208.16(c). The burden is on the alien to establish that it is more likely than not that he or she would be tortured in the country to which removal has been deferred.

(4) If the immigration judge determines that the alien is more likely than not to be tortured in the country to which removal has been deferred, the order of deferral shall remain in place. If the immigration judge determines that the alien has not established that he or she is more likely than not to be tortured in the country to which removal has been deferred, the deferral of removal shall be terminated and the alien may be removed to that country. Appeal of the immigration judge's decision shall lie to the Board.

(e) *Termination at the request of the alien.* (1) At any time while deferral of removal is in effect, the alien may make a written request to the Immigration Court having administrative control pursuant to § 3.11 of this chapter to terminate the deferral order. If satisfied on the basis of the written submission that the alien's request is knowing and voluntary, the immigration judge shall terminate the order of deferral and the alien may be removed.

(2) If necessary the immigration judge may calendar a hearing for the sole purpose of determining whether the alien's request is knowing and voluntary. If the immigration judge determines that the alien's request is knowing and voluntary, the order of deferral shall be terminated. If the immigration judge determines that the alien's request is not knowing and voluntary, the alien's request shall not serve as the basis for terminating the order of deferral.

(f) *Termination pursuant to § 208.18(c).* At any time while deferral of removal is in effect, the Attorney General may determine whether deferral should be terminated based on diplomatic assurances forwarded by the Secretary of State pursuant to the procedures in § 208.18(c).

[64 FR 8489, Feb. 19, 1999]

§ 208.18 Implementation of the Convention Against Torture.

(a) *Definitions.* The definitions in this subsection incorporate the definition of torture contained in Article 1 of the Convention Against Torture, subject to the reservations, understandings, declarations, and provisos contained in the United States Senate resolution of ratification of the Convention.

(1) Torture is defined as any act by which severe pain or suffering, whether physical or mental, is intentionally inflicted on a person for such purposes as obtaining from him or her or a third person information or a confession, punishing him or her for an act he or she or a third person has committed or is suspected of having committed, or

intimidating or coercing him or her or a third person, or for any reason based on discrimination of any kind, when such pain or suffering is inflicted by or at the instigation of or with the consent or acquiescence of a public official or other person acting in an official capacity.

(2) Torture is an extreme form of cruel and inhuman treatment and does not include lesser forms of cruel, inhuman or degrading treatment or punishment that do not amount to torture.

(3) Torture does not include pain or suffering arising only from, inherent in or incidental to lawful sanctions. Lawful sanctions include judicially imposed sanctions and other enforcement actions authorized by law, including the death penalty, but do not include sanctions that defeat the object and purpose of the Convention Against Torture to prohibit torture.

(4) In order to constitute torture, mental pain or suffering must be prolonged mental harm caused by or resulting from:

(i) The intentional infliction or threatened infliction of severe physical pain or suffering;

(ii) The administration or application, or threatened administration or application, of mind altering substances or other procedures calculated to disrupt profoundly the senses or the personality;

(iii) The threat of imminent death; or

(iv) The threat that another person will imminently be subjected to death, severe physical pain or suffering, or the administration or application of mind altering substances or other procedures calculated to disrupt profoundly the sense or personality.

(5) In order to constitute torture, an act must be specifically intended to inflict severe physical or mental pain or suffering. An act that results in unanticipated or unintended severity of pain and suffering is not torture.

(6) In order to constitute torture an act must be directed against a person in the offender's custody or physical control.

(7) Acquiescence of a public official requires that the public official, prior to the activity constituting torture, have awareness of such activity and thereafter breach his or her legal responsibility to intervene to prevent such activity.

(8) Noncompliance with applicable legal procedural standards does not *per se* constitute torture.

(b) *Applicability of §§ 208.16(c) and 208.17(a)*—(1) *Aliens in proceedings on or after March 22, 1999.* An alien who is in exclusion, deportation, or removal proceedings on or after March 22, 1999 may apply for withholding of removal under § 208.16(c), and, if applicable, may be considered for deferral of removal under § 208.17(a).

(2) *Aliens who were ordered removed, or whose removal orders became final, before March 22, 1999.* An alien under a final order of deportation, exclusion, or removal that became final prior to March 22, 1999 may move to reopen proceedings for the sole purpose of seeking protection under § 208.16(c). Such motions shall be governed by §§ 3.23 and 3.2 of this chapter, except that the time and numerical limitations on motions to reopen shall not apply and the alien shall not be required to demonstrate that the evidence sought to be offered was unavailable and could not have been discovered or presented at the former hearing. The motion to reopen shall not be granted unless:

(i) The motion is filed within June 21, 1999; and

(ii) The evidence sought to be offered establishes a prima facie case that the applicant's removal must be withheld or deferred under §§ 208.16(c) or 208.17(a).

(3) *Aliens who, on March 22, 1999, have requests pending with the Service for protection under Article 3 of the Convention Against Torture.* (i) Except as otherwise provided, after March 22, 1999, the Service will not:

(A) Consider, under its pre-regulatory administrative policy to ensure compliance with the Convention Against Torture, whether Article 3 of that Convention prohibits the removal of an alien to a particular country, or

(B) Stay the removal of an alien based on a request filed with the Service for protection under Article 3 of that Convention.

(ii) For each alien who, on or before March 22, 1999, filed a request with the Service for protection under Article 3 of the Convention Against Torture, and whose request has not been finally decided by the Service, the Service shall provide written notice that, after March 22, 1999, consideration for protection under Article 3 can be obtained only through the provisions of this rule.

(A) The notice shall inform an alien who is under an order of removal issued by EOIR that, in order to seek consideration of a claim under §§ 208.16(c) or 208.17(a), such an alien must file a motion to reopen with the immigration court or the Board of Immigration Appeals. This notice shall be accompanied by a stay of removal, effective until 30 days after service of the notice on the alien. A motion to reopen filed under this paragraph for the limited purpose of asserting a claim under §§ 208.16(c) or 208.17(a) shall not be subject to the requirements for reopening in §§ 3.2 and 3.23 of this chapter. Such a motion shall be granted if it is accompanied by a copy of the notice described in paragraph (b)(3)(ii) or by other convincing evidence that the alien had a request pending with the Service for protection under Article 3 of the Convention Against Torture on March 22, 1999. The filing of such a motion shall extend the stay of removal during the pendency of the adjudication of this motion.

(B) The notice shall inform an alien who is under an administrative order of removal issued by the Service under section 238(b) of the Act or an exclusion, deportation, or removal order reinstated by the Service under section 241(a)(5) of the Act that the alien's claim to withholding of removal under § 208.16(c) or deferral of removal under § 208.17(a) will be considered under § 208.31.

(C) The notice shall inform an alien who is under an administrative order of removal issued by the Service under section 235(c) of the Act that the alien's claim to protection under the Convention Against Torture will be decided by the Service as provided in § 208.18(d) and 235.8(b)(4) and will not be considered under the provisions of this part relating to consideration or review by an immigration judge, the Board of Immigration Appeals, or an asylum officer.

(4) *Aliens whose claims to protection under the Convention Against Torture were finally decided by the Service prior to March 22, 1999.* Sections 208.16(c) and 208.17 (a) and paragraphs (b)(1) through (b)(3) of this section do not apply to cases in which, prior to March 22, 1999, the Service has made a final administrative determination about the applicability of Article 3 of the Convention Against Torture to the case of an alien who filed a request with the Service for protection under Article 3. If, prior to March 22, 1999, the Service determined that an applicant cannot be removed consistent with the Convention Against Torture, the alien shall be considered to have been granted withholding of removal under § 208.16(c), unless the alien is subject to mandatory denial of withholding of removal under § 208.16(d)(2) or (d)(3), in which case the alien will be considered to have been granted deferral of removal under 208.17(a). If, prior to March 22, 1999, the Service determined that an alien can be removed consistent with the Convention Against Torture, the alien will be considered to have been finally denied withholding of removal under § 208.16(c) and deferral of removal under § 208.17(a).

(c) *Diplomatic assurances against torture obtained by the Secretary of State.* (1) The Secretary of State may forward to the Attorney General assurances that the Secretary has obtained from the government of a specific country that an alien would not be tortured there if the alien were removed to that country.

(2) If the Secretary of State forwards assurances described in paragraph (c)(1) of this section to the Attorney General for consideration by the Attorney General or her delegates under this paragraph, the Attorney General shall determine, in consultation with the Secretary of State, whether the assurances are sufficiently reliable to allow the alien's removal to that country consistent with Article 3 of the Convention Against Torture. The Attorney General's authority under this paragraph may be exercised by the Deputy Attorney General or by the Commissioner, Immigration and Naturalization Service, but may not be further delegated.

(3) Once assurances are provided under paragraph (c)(2) of this section,

the alien's claim for protection under the Convention Against Torture shall not be considered further by an immigration judge, the Board of Immigration Appeals, or an asylum officer.

(d) *Cases involving aliens ordered removed under section 235(c) of the Act.* With respect to an alien terrorist or other alien subject to administrative removal under section 235(c) of the Act who requests protection under Article 3 of the Convention Against Torture, the Service will assess the applicability of Article 3 through the removal process to ensure that a removal order will not be executed under circumstances that would violate the obligations of the United States under Article 3. In such cases, the provisions of Part 208 relating to consideration or review by an immigration judge, the Board of Immigration Appeals, or an asylum officer shall not apply.

(e) *Judicial review of claims for protection from removal under Article 3 of the Convention Against Torture.* (1) Pursuant to the provisions of section 2242(d) of the Foreign Affairs Reform and Restructuring Act of 1998, there shall be no judicial appeal or review of any action, decision, or claim raised under the Convention or that section, except as part of the review of a final order of removal pursuant to section 242 of the Act; provided however, that any appeal or petition regarding an action, decision, or claim under the Convention or under section 2242 of the Foreign Affairs Reform and Restructuring Act of 1998 shall not be deemed to include or authorize the consideration of any administrative order or decision, or portion thereof, the appeal or review of which is restricted or prohibited by the Act.

(2) Except as otherwise expressly provided, nothing in this paragraph shall be construed to create a private right of action or to authorize the consideration or issuance of administrative or judicial relief.

[64 FR 8490, Feb. 19, 1999; 64 FR 13881, Mar. 23, 1999]

§208.19 Decisions.

The decision of an asylum officer to grant or to deny asylum or to refer an asylum application, in accordance with §208.14(b) or (c), shall be communicated in writing to the applicant. Pursuant to §208.9(d), an applicant must appear in person to receive and to acknowledge receipt of the decision to grant or deny asylum, or to refer an asylum application unless, in the discretion of the asylum office director, service by mail is appropriate. A letter communicating denial of asylum or referral of the application shall state the basis for denial or referral and include an assessment of the applicant's credibility.

[65 FR 76136, Dec. 6, 2000]

§208.20 Determining if an asylum application is frivolous.

For applications filed on or after April 1, 1997, an applicant is subject to the provisions of section 208(d)(6) of the Act only if a final order by an immigration judge or the Board of Immigration Appeals specifically finds that the alien knowingly filed a frivolous asylum application. For purposes of this section, an asylum application is frivolous if any of its material elements is deliberately fabricated. Such finding shall only be made if the immigration judge or the Board is satisfied that the applicant, during the course of the proceedings, has had sufficient opportunity to account for any discrepancies or implausible aspects of the claim. For purposes of this section, a finding that an alien filed a frivolous asylum application shall not preclude the alien from seeking withholding of removal.

[64 FR 8492, Feb. 19, 1999. Redesignated at 65 FR 76136, Dec. 6, 2000]

§208.21 Admission of the asylee's spouse and children.

(a) *Eligibility.* In accordance with section 208(b)(3) of the Act, a spouse, as defined in section 101(a)(35) of the Act, 8 U.S.C. 1101(a)(35), or child, as defined in section 101(b)(1) of the Act, also may be granted asylum if accompanying, or following to join, the principal alien who was granted asylum, unless it is determined that the spouse or child is ineligible for asylum under section 208(b)(2)(A)(i), (ii), (iii), (iv) or (v) of the Act for applications filed on or after April 1, 1997, or under §208.13(c)(2)(i)(A), (C), (D), (E), or (F) for applications filed before April 1, 1997.

(b) *Relationship.* The relationship of spouse and child as defined in sections 101(a)(35) and 101(b)(1) of the Act must have existed at the time the principal alien's asylum application was approved and must continue to exist at the time of filing for accompanying or following-to-join benefits and at the time of the spouse or child's subsequent admission to the United States. If the asylee proves that the asylee is the parent of a child who was born after asylum was granted, but who was *in utero* on the date of the asylum grant, the child shall be eligible to accompany or follow-to-join the asylee. The child's mother, if not the principal asylee, shall not be eligible to accompany or follow-to-join the principal asylee unless the child's mother was the principal asylee's spouse on the date the principal asylee was granted asylum.

(c) *Spouse or child in the United States.* When a spouse or child of an alien granted asylum is in the United States, but was not included in the asylee's benefit request, the asylee may request accompanying or following-to-join benefits for his or her spouse or child, by filing for each qualifying family member a Request for Refugee/Asylee Relative, with supporting evidence, and in accordance with the form instructions, regardless of the status of that spouse or child in the United States. A separate Request for Refugee/Asylee Relative must be filed by the asylee for each qualifying family member within two years of the date in which he or she was granted asylum status, unless it is determined by USCIS that this period should be extended for humanitarian reasons. Upon approval of the Request for Refugee/Asylee Relative, USCIS will notify the asylee of such approval. Employment will be authorized incident to status. To demonstrate employment authorization, USCIS will issue a document reflecting the derivative's current status as an asylee, or the derivative may apply, under 8 CFR 274a.12(a), for employment authorization. The approval of the Request for Refugee/Asylee Relative will remain valid for the duration of the relationship to the asylee and, in the case of a child, while the child is under 21 years of age and unmarried, provided also that the principal's status has not been revoked. However, the approved Request for Refugee/Asylee Relative will cease to confer immigration benefits after it has been used by the beneficiary for admission to the United States as a derivative of an asylee.

(d) *Spouse or child outside the United States.* When a spouse or child of an alien granted asylum is outside the United States, the asylee may request accompanying or following-to-join benefits for his or her spouse or child(ren) by filing a separate Request for Refugee/Asylee Relative for each qualifying family member in accordance with the form instructions. A separate Request for Refugee/Asylee Relative for each qualifying family member must be filed within two years of the date in which the asylee was granted asylum, unless USCIS determines that the filing period should be extended for humanitarian reasons. When the Request for Refugee/Asylee Relative is approved, USCIS will notify the asylee of such approval. USCIS also will send the approved request to the Department of State for transmission to the U.S. Embassy or Consulate having jurisdiction over the area in which the asylee's spouse or child is located. The approval of the Request for Refugee/Asylee Relative will remain valid for the duration of the relationship to the asylee and, in the case of a child, while the child is under 21 years of age and unmarried, provided also that the principal's status has not been revoked. However, the approved Request for Refugee/Asylee Relative will cease to confer immigration benefits after it has been used by the beneficiary for admission to the United States as a derivative of an asylee.

(e) *Denial.* If the spouse or child is found to be ineligible for the status accorded under section 208(c) of the Act, a written notice stating the basis for denial shall be forwarded to the principal alien. No appeal shall lie from this decision.

(f) *Burden of proof.* To establish the claimed relationship of spouse or child as defined in sections 101(a)(35) and 101(b)(1) of the Act, evidence must be submitted with the request as set forth in part 204 of this chapter. Where possible this will consist of the documents specified in § 204.2 (a)(1)(i)(B), (a)(1)(iii)(B), (a)(2), (d)(2), and (d)(5) of this chapter. The burden of proof is on the principal alien to establish by a preponderance of the evidence that any person on whose behalf he or she is making a request under this section is an eligible spouse or child.

(g) *Duration.* The spouse or child qualifying under section 208(c) of the Act shall be granted asylum for an indefinite period unless the principal's status is revoked.

[62 FR 10337, Mar. 6, 1997, as amended at 63 FR 3796, Jan. 27, 1998. Redesignated at 64 FR 8490, Feb. 19, 1999 and further redesignated and amended at 65 FR 76136, Dec. 6, 2000; 76 FR 53784, Aug. 29, 2011; 76 FR 73476, Nov. 29, 2011]

§ 208.22 Effect on exclusion, deportation, and removal proceedings.

An alien who has been granted asylum may not be deported or removed unless his or her asylum status is terminated pursuant to § 208.24. An alien in exclusion, deportation, or removal proceedings who is granted withholding of removal or deportation, or deferral of removal, may not be deported or removed to the country to which his or her deportation or removal is ordered withheld or deferred unless the withholding order is terminated pursuant to § 208.24 or deferral is terminated pursuant to § 208.17(d) or (e).

[64 FR 8492, Feb. 19, 1999. Revised at 65 FR 76136, Dec. 6, 2000]

§ 208.23 Restoration of status.

An alien who was maintaining his or her nonimmigrant status at the time of filing an asylum application and has such application denied may continue in or be restored to that status, if it has not expired.

[62 FR 10337, Mar. 6, 1997. Redesignated at 64 FR 8490, Feb. 19, 1999 and further redesignated at 65 FR 76136, Dec. 6, 2000]

§ 208.24 Termination of asylum or withholding of removal or deportation.

(a) *Termination of asylum by USCIS.* Except as provided in paragraph (e) of this section, an asylum officer may terminate a grant of asylum made under the jurisdiction of USCIS if, following an interview, the asylum officer determines that:

(1) There is a showing of fraud in the alien's application such that he or she was not eligible for asylum at the time it was granted;

(2) As to applications filed on or after April 1, 1997, one or more of the conditions described in section 208(c)(2) of the Act exist; or

(3) As to applications filed before April 1, 1997, the alien no longer has a well-founded fear of persecution upon return due to a change of country conditions in the alien's country of nationality or habitual residence or the alien has committed any act that would have been grounds for denial of asylum under § 208.13(c)(2).

(b) *Termination of withholding of deportation or removal by USCIS.* Except as provided in paragraph (e) of this section, an asylum officer may terminate a grant of withholding of deportation or removal made under the jurisdiction of USCIS if the asylum officer determines, following an interview, that:

(1) The alien is no longer entitled to withholding of deportation or removal because, owing to a fundamental change in circumstances relating to the original claim, the alien's life or freedom no longer would be threatened on account of race, religion, nationality, membership in a particular social group, or political opinion in the country from which deportation or removal was withheld.

(2) There is a showing of fraud in the alien's application such that the alien was not eligible for withholding of removal at the time it was granted;

(3) The alien has committed any other act that would have been grounds for denial of withholding of removal under section 241(b)(3)(B) of the Act had it occurred prior to the grant of withholding of removal; or

(4) For applications filed in proceedings commenced before April 1, 1997, the alien has committed any act that would have been grounds for denial of withholding of deportation under section 243(h)(2) of the Act.

(c) *Procedure.* Prior to the termination of a grant of asylum or withholding of deportation or removal, the alien shall be given notice of intent to terminate, with the reasons therefor, at least 30 days prior to the interview specified in paragraph (a) of this section before an asylum officer. The alien shall be provided the opportunity to present evidence showing that he or she is still eligible for asylum or withholding of deportation or removal. If the asylum officer determines that the alien is no longer eligible for asylum or withholding of deportation or removal, the alien shall be given written notice that asylum status or withholding of deportation or removal and any employment authorization issued pursuant thereto, are terminated.

(d) *Termination of derivative status.* The termination of asylum status for a person who was the principal applicant shall result in termination of the asylum status of a spouse or child whose status was based on the asylum application of the principal. Such termination shall not preclude the spouse or child of such alien from separately asserting an asylum or withholding of deportation or removal claim.

(e) *Removal proceedings.* When an alien's asylum status or withholding of removal or deportation is terminated under this section, the Service shall initiate removal proceedings, as appropriate, if the alien is not already in exclusion, deportation, or removal proceedings. Removal proceedings may take place in conjunction with a termination hearing scheduled under § 208.24(f).

(f) *Termination of asylum, or withholding of deportation or removal, by an immigration judge or the Board of Immigration Appeals.* An immigration judge or the Board of Immigration Appeals may reopen a case pursuant to 8 CFR 1003.2 and 8 CFR 1003.23 for the purpose of terminating a grant of asylum, or a withholding of deportation or removal. In such a reopened proceeding, the Service must establish, by a preponderance of evidence, one or more of the grounds set forth in paragraphs (a) or (b) of this section. In addition, an immigration judge may terminate a grant of asylum, or a withholding of deportation or removal, made under the jurisdiction of USCIS at any time after the alien has been provided a notice of intent to terminate by USCIS. Any termination under this paragraph may occur in conjunction with an exclusion, deportation, or removal proceeding.

(g) *Termination of asylum for arriving aliens.* If the Service determines that an applicant for admission who had previously been granted asylum in the United States falls within conditions set forth in § 208.24 and is inadmissible, the Service shall issue a notice of intent to terminate asylum and initiate removal proceedings under section 240 of the Act. The alien shall present his or her response to the intent to terminate during proceedings before the immigration judge.

[62 FR 10337, Mar. 6, 1997. Redesignated at 64 FR 8490, Feb. 19, 1999, and further redesignated and amended at 65 FR 76136, Dec. 6, 2000; 76 FR 53785, Aug. 29, 2011; 78 FR 22771, Apr. 17, 2013]

§§ 208.25–208.29 [Reserved]

Subpart B—Credible Fear of Persecution

§ 208.30 Credible fear determinations involving stowaways and applicants for admission who are found inadmissible pursuant to section 212(a)(6)(C) or 212(a)(7) of the Act or whose entry is limited or suspended under section 212(f) or 215(a)(1) of the Act.

(a) *Jurisdiction.* The provisions of this subpart B apply to aliens subject to sections 235(a)(2) and 235(b)(1) of the Act. Pursuant to section 235(b)(1)(B) of the Act, DHS has exclusive jurisdiction to make credible fear determinations, and the Executive Office for Immigration Review has exclusive jurisdiction to review such determinations. Except as otherwise provided in this subpart B, paragraphs (b) through (g) of this section are the exclusive procedures applicable to credible fear interviews, determinations, and reviews under section 235(b)(1)(B) of the Act. Prior to January 1, 2015, an alien present in or arriving in the Commonwealth of the Northern Mariana Islands is ineligible to apply for asylum and may only establish eligibility for withholding of removal pursuant to section 241(b)(3) of the Act or withholding or deferral of removal under the Convention Against Torture.

(b) *Treatment of dependents.* A spouse or child of an alien may be included in that alien's credible fear evaluation and determination, if such spouse or child:

(1) Arrived in the United States concurrently with the principal alien; and

(2) Desires to be included in the principal alien's determination. However, any alien may have his or her credible fear evaluation and determination made separately, if he or she expresses such a desire.

(c) *Authority.* Asylum officers conducting credible fear interviews shall have the authorities described in §208.9(c).

(d) *Interview.* The asylum officer, as defined in section 235(b)(1)(E) of the Act, will conduct the interview in a nonadversarial manner, separate and apart from the general public. The purpose of the interview shall be to elicit all relevant and useful information bearing on whether the applicant has a credible fear of persecution or torture, and shall conduct the interview as follows:

(1) If the officer conducting the credible fear interview determines that the alien is unable to participate effectively in the interview because of illness, fatigue, or other impediments, the officer may reschedule the interview.

(2) At the time of the interview, the asylum officer shall verify that the alien has received Form M-444, Information about Credible Fear Interview in Expedited Removal Cases. The officer shall also determine that the alien has an understanding of the credible fear determination process.

(3) The alien may be required to register his or her identity.

(4) The alien may consult with a person or persons of the alien's choosing prior to the interview or any review thereof, and may present other evidence, if available. Such consultation shall be at no expense to the Government and shall not unreasonably delay the process. Any person or persons with whom the alien chooses to consult may be present at the interview and may be permitted, in the discretion of the asylum officer, to present a statement at the end of the interview. The asylum officer, in his or her discretion, may place reasonable limits on the number of persons who may be present at the interview and on the length of the statement.

(5) If the alien is unable to proceed effectively in English, and if the asylum officer is unable to proceed competently in a language chosen by the alien, the asylum officer shall arrange for the assistance of an interpreter in conducting the interview. The interpreter must be at least 18 years of age and may not be the applicant's attorney or representative of record, a witness testifying on the applicant's behalf, a representative or employee of the applicant's country of nationality, or, if the applicant is stateless, the applicant's country of last habitual residence.

(6) The asylum officer shall create a summary of the material facts as stated by the applicant. At the conclusion of the interview, the officer shall review the summary with the alien and provide the alien with an opportunity to correct any errors therein.

(e) *Determination.* (1) The asylum officer shall create a written record of his or her determination, including a summary of the material facts as stated by the applicant, any additional facts relied on by the officer, and the officer's determination of whether, in light of such facts, the alien has established a credible fear of persecution or torture.

(2) An alien will be found to have a credible fear of persecution if there is a significant possibility, taking into account the credibility of the statements made by the alien in support of the alien's claim and such other facts as are known to the officer, the alien can establish eligibility for asylum under section 208 of the Act or for withholding of removal under section 241(b)(3) of the Act. However, prior to January 1, 2015, in the case of an alien physically present in or arriving in the Commonwealth of the Northern Mariana Islands, the officer may only find a credible fear of persecution if there is a significant possibility that the alien can establish eligibility for withholding of removal pursuant to section 241(b)(3) of the Act.

(3) An alien will be found to have a credible fear of torture if the alien shows that there is a significant possibility that he or she is eligible for withholding of removal or deferral of

removal under the Convention Against Torture, pursuant to 8 CFR 208.16 or 208.17.

(4) In determining whether the alien has a credible fear of persecution, as defined in section 235(b)(1)(B)(v) of the Act, or a credible fear of torture, the asylum officer shall consider whether the alien's case presents novel or unique issues that merit consideration in a full hearing before an immigration judge.

(5) Except as provided in paragraph (e)(6) of this section, if an alien is able to establish a credible fear of persecution or torture but appears to be subject to one or more of the mandatory bars to applying for, or being granted, asylum contained in section 208(a)(2) and 208(b)(2) of the Act, or to withholding of removal contained in section 241(b)(3)(B) of the Act, the Department of Homeland Security shall nonetheless place the alien in proceedings under section 240 of the Act for full consideration of the alien's claim, if the alien is not a stowaway. If the alien is a stowaway, the Department shall place the alien in proceedings for consideration of the alien's claim pursuant to 8 CFR 208.2(c)(3). If the alien is found to be an alien described in 8 CFR 208.13(c)(3), then the asylum officer shall enter a negative credible fear determination with respect to the alien's application for asylum. The Department shall nonetheless place the alien in proceedings under section 240 of the Act for full consideration of the alien's claim for withholding of removal under section 241(b)(3) of the Act, or for withholding or deferral of removal under the Convention Against Torture if the alien establishes a reasonable fear of persecution or torture. However, if an alien fails to establish, during the interview with the asylum officer, a reasonable fear of either persecution or torture, the asylum officer will provide the alien with a written notice of decision, which will be subject to immigration judge review consistent with paragraph (g) of this section, except that the immigration judge will review the reasonable fear findings under the reasonable fear standard instead of the credible fear standard described in paragraph (g) and in 8 CFR 1208.30(g).

(6) Prior to any determination concerning whether an alien arriving in the United States at a U.S.-Canada land border port-of-entry or in transit through the U.S. during removal by Canada has a credible fear of persecution or torture, the asylum officer shall conduct a threshold screening interview to determine whether such an alien is ineligible to apply for asylum pursuant to section 208(a)(2)(A) of the Act and subject to removal to Canada by operation of the Agreement Between the Government of the United States and the Government of Canada For Cooperation in the Examination of Refugee Status Claims from Nationals of Third Countries ("Agreement"). In conducting this threshold screening interview, the asylum officer shall apply all relevant interview procedures outlined in paragraph (d) of this section, provided, however, that paragraph (d)(2) of this section shall not apply to aliens described in this paragraph. The asylum officer shall advise the alien of the Agreement's exceptions and question the alien as to applicability of any of these exceptions to the alien's case.

(i) If the asylum officer, with concurrence from a supervisory asylum officer, determines that an alien does not qualify for an exception under the Agreement during this threshold screening interview, the alien is ineligible to apply for asylum in the United States. After the asylum officer's documented finding is reviewed by a supervisory asylum officer, the alien shall be advised that he or she will be removed to Canada in order to pursue his or her claims relating to a fear of persecution or torture under Canadian law. Aliens found ineligible to apply for asylum under this paragraph shall be removed to Canada.

(ii) If the alien establishes by a preponderance of the evidence that he or she qualifies for an exception under the terms of the Agreement, the asylum officer shall make a written notation of the basis of the exception, and then proceed immediately to a determination concerning whether the alien has a credible fear of persecution or torture under paragraph (d) of this section.

(iii) An alien qualifies for an exception to the Agreement if the alien is not being removed from Canada in transit through the United States and

(A) Is a citizen of Canada or, not having a country of nationality, is a habitual resident of Canada;

(B) Has in the United States a spouse, son, daughter, parent, legal guardian, sibling, grandparent, grandchild, aunt, uncle, niece, or nephew who has been granted asylum, refugee, or other lawful status in the United States, provided, however, that this exception shall not apply to an alien whose relative maintains only nonimmigrant visitor status, as defined in section 101(a)(15)(B) of the Act, or whose relative maintains only visitor status based on admission to the United States pursuant to the Visa Waiver Program;

(C) Has in the United States a spouse, son, daughter, parent, legal guardian, sibling, grandparent, grandchild, aunt, uncle, niece, or nephew who is at least 18 years of age and has an asylum application pending before U.S. Citizenship and Immigration Services, the Executive Office for Immigration Review, or on appeal in federal court in the United States;

(D) Is unmarried, under 18 years of age, and does not have a parent or legal guardian in either Canada or the United States;

(E) Arrived in the United States with a validly issued visa or other valid admission document, other than for transit, issued by the United States to the alien, or, being required to hold a visa to enter Canada, was not required to obtain a visa to enter the United States; or

(F) The Director of USCIS, or the Director's designee, determines, in the exercise of unreviewable discretion, that it is in the public interest to allow the alien to pursue a claim for asylum, withholding of removal, or protection under the Convention Against Torture, in the United States.

(iv) As used in 8 CFR 208.30(e)(6)(iii)(B), (C) and (D) only, "legal guardian" means a person currently vested with legal custody of such an alien or vested with legal authority to act on the alien's behalf, provided that such an alien is both unmarried and less than 18 years of age, and provided further that any dispute with respect to whether an individual is a legal guardian will be resolved on the basis of U.S. law.

(7) An asylum officer's determination shall not become final until reviewed by a supervisory asylum officer.

(f) *Procedures for a positive credible fear finding.* If an alien, other than an alien stowaway, is found to have a credible fear of persecution or torture, the asylum officer will so inform the alien and issue a Form I–862, Notice to Appear, for full consideration of the asylum and withholding of removal claim in proceedings under section 240 of the Act. If an alien stowaway is found to have a credible fear of persecution or torture, the asylum officer will so inform the alien and issue a Form I–863, Notice of Referral to Immigration Judge, for full consideration of the asylum claim, or the withholding of removal claim, in proceedings under § 208.2(c). Parole of the alien may be considered only in accordance with section 212(d)(5) of the Act and § 212.5 of this chapter.

(g) *Procedures for a negative credible fear finding.* (1) If an alien is found not to have a credible fear of persecution or torture, the asylum officer shall provide the alien with a written notice of decision and inquire whether the alien wishes to have an immigration judge review the negative decision, using Form I–869, Record of Negative Credible Fear Finding and Request for Review by Immigration Judge. The alien shall indicate whether he or she desires such review on Form I–869. A refusal by the alien to make such indication shall be considered a request for review.

(i) If the alien requests such review, or refuses to either request or decline such review, the asylum officer shall arrange for detention of the alien and serve him or her with a Form I–863, Notice of Referral to Immigration Judge, for review of the credible fear determination in accordance with paragraph (f)(2) of this section.

(ii) If the alien is not a stowaway and does not request a review by an immigration judge, the officer shall order the alien removed and issue a Form I–860, Notice and Order of Expedited Removal, after review by a supervisory asylum officer.

(iii) If the alien is a stowaway and the alien does not request a review by an immigration judge, the asylum officer shall refer the alien to the district director for completion of removal proceedings in accordance with section 235(a)(2) of the Act.

(2) Review by immigration judge of a negative credible fear finding.

(i) Immigration judges will review negative credible fear findings as provided in 8 CFR 1208.30(g)(2).

(ii) The record of the negative credible fear determination, including copies of the Form I–863, the asylum officer's notes, the summary of the material facts, and other materials upon which the determination was based shall be provided to the immigration judge with the negative determination.

[65 FR 76136, Dec. 6, 2000, as amended at 69 FR 69488, Nov. 29, 2004; 74 FR 55737, Oct. 28, 2009; 76 FR 53785, Aug. 29, 2011; 83 FR 55952, Nov. 9, 2018]

§ 208.31 Reasonable fear of persecution or torture determinations involving aliens ordered removed under section 238(b) of the Act and aliens whose removal is reinstated under section 241(a)(5) of the Act.

(a) *Jurisdiction.* This section shall apply to any alien ordered removed under section 238(b) of the Act or whose deportation, exclusion, or removal order is reinstated under section 241(a)(5) of the Act who, in the course of the administrative removal or reinstatement process, expresses a fear of returning to the country of removal. USCIS has exclusive jurisdiction to make reasonable fear determinations, and EOIR has exclusive jurisdiction to review such determinations.

(b) *Initiation of reasonable fear determination process.* Upon issuance of a Final Administrative Removal Order under § 238.1 of this chapter, or notice under § 241.8(b) of this chapter that an alien is subject to removal, an alien described in paragraph (a) of this section shall be referred to an asylum officer for a reasonable fear determination. In the absence of exceptional circumstances, this determination will be conducted within 10 days of the referral.

(c) *Interview and procedure.* The asylum officer shall conduct the interview in a non-adversarial manner, separate and apart from the general public. At the time of the interview, the asylum officer shall determine that the alien has an understanding of the reasonable fear determination process. The alien may be represented by counsel or an accredited representative at the interview, at no expense to the Government, and may present evidence, if available, relevant to the possibility of persecution or torture. The alien's representative may present a statement at the end of the interview. The asylum officer, in his or her discretion, may place reasonable limits on the number of persons who may be present at the interview and the length of the statement. If the alien is unable to proceed effectively in English, and if the asylum officer is unable to proceed competently in a language chosen by the alien, the asylum officer shall arrange for the assistance of an interpreter in conducting the interview. The interpreter may not be a representative or employee of the applicant's country or nationality, or if the applicant is stateless, the applicant's country of last habitual residence. The asylum officer shall create a summary of the material facts as stated by the applicant. At the conclusion of the interview, the officer shall review the summary with the alien and provide the alien with an opportunity to correct errors therein. The asylum officer shall create a written record of his or her determination, including a summary of the material facts as stated by the applicant, any additional facts relied on by the officers, and the officer's determination of whether, in light of such facts, the alien has established a reasonable fear of persecution or torture. The alien shall be determined to have a reasonable fear of persecution or torture if the alien establishes a reasonable possibility that he or she would be persecuted on account of his or her race, religion, nationality, membership in a particular social group or political opinion, or a reasonable possibility that he or she would be tortured in the country of removal. For purposes of the screening determination, the bars to eligibility for withholding of removal under section 241(b)(3)(B) of the Act shall not be considered.

(d) *Authority*. Asylum officers conducting screening determinations under this section shall have the authority described in §208.9(c).

(e) *Referral to Immigration Judge*. If an asylum officer determines that an alien described in this section has a reasonable fear of persecution or torture, the officer shall so inform the alien and issue a Form I–863, Notice of Referral to the Immigration Judge, for full consideration of the request for withholding of removal only. Such cases shall be adjudicated by the immigration judge in accordance with the provisions of §208.16. Appeal of the immigration judge's decision shall lie to the Board of Immigration Appeals.

(f) *Removal of aliens with no reasonable fear of persecution or torture*. If the asylum officer determines that the alien has not established a reasonable fear of persecution or torture, the asylum officer shall inform the alien in writing of the decision and shall inquire whether the alien wishes to have an immigration judge review the negative decision, using Form I–898, Record of Negative Reasonable Fear Finding and Request for Review by Immigration Judge, on which the alien shall indicate whether he or she desires such review.

(g) *Review by immigration judge*. The asylum officer's negative decision regarding reasonable fear shall be subject to review by an immigration judge upon the alien's request. If the alien requests such review, the asylum officer shall serve him or her with a Form I–863. The record of determination, including copies of the Form I–863, the asylum officer's notes, the summary of the material facts, and other materials upon which the determination was based shall be provided to the immigration judge with the negative determination. In the absence of exceptional circumstances, such review shall be conducted by the immigration judge within 10 days of the filing of the Form I–863 with the immigration court. Upon review of the asylum officer's negative reasonable fear determination:

(1) If the immigration judge concurs with the asylum officer's determination that the alien does not have a reasonable fear of persecution or torture, the case shall be returned to the Service for removal of the alien. No appeal shall lie from the immigration judge's decision.

(2) If the immigration judge finds that the alien has a reasonable fear of persecution or torture, the alien may submit Form I–589, Application for Asylum and Withholding of Removal.

(i) The immigration judge shall consider only the alien's application for withholding of removal under §208.16 and shall determine whether the alien's removal to the country of removal must be withheld or deferred.

(ii) Appeal of the immigration judge's decision whether removal must be withheld or deferred lies to the Board of Immigration Appeals. If the alien or the Service appeals the immigration judge's decision, the Board shall review only the immigration judge's decision regarding the alien's eligibility for withholding or deferral of removal under §208.16.

[64 FR 8493, Feb. 19, 1999; 64 FR 13881, Mar. 23, 1999; 76 FR 53785, Aug. 29, 2011]

PART 209—ADJUSTMENT OF STATUS OF REFUGEES AND ALIENS GRANTED ASYLUM

Sec.

AUTHORITY: 8 U.S.C. 1101, 1103, 1157, 1158, 1159, 1228, 1252, 1282; Title VII of Public Law 110–229; 8 CFR part 2.

§209.1 Adjustment of status of refugees.

The provisions of this section shall provide the sole and exclusive procedure for adjustment of status by a refugee admitted under section 207 of the Act whose application is based on his or her refugee status.

(a) *Eligibility*. (1) Every alien in the United States who is classified as a refugee under 8 CFR part 207, whose status has not been terminated, is required to apply to USCIS one year after entry in order for USCIS to determine his or her admissibility under section 212 of the Act, without regard to paragraphs (4), (5), and (7)(A) of section 212(a) of the Act.

(2) Every alien processed by the Immigration and Naturalization Service

abroad and paroled into the United States as a refugee after April 1, 1980, and before May 18, 1980, shall be considered as having entered the United States as a refugee under section 207(a) of the Act.

(b) *Application.* Upon admission to the United States, every refugee entrant will be notified of the requirement to submit an application for permanent residence one year after entry. An application for the benefits of section 209(a) of the Act must be submitted along with the biometrics required by 8 CFR 103.16 and in accordance with the applicable form instructions.

(c) *Medical examination.* A refugee seeking adjustment of status under section 209(a) of the Act is not required to repeat the medical examination performed under § 207.2(c), unless there were medical grounds of inadmissibility applicable at the time of admission. The refugee is, however, required to establish compliance with the vaccination requirements described under section 212(a)(1)(A)(ii) of the Act.

(d) *Interview.* USCIS will determine, on a case-by-case basis, whether an interview by an immigration officer is necessary to determine the applicant's admissibility for permanent resident status under this part.

(e) *Decision.* USCIS will notify the applicant in writing of the decision on his or her application. There is no appeal of a denial, but USCIS will notify an applicant of the right to renew the request for permanent residence in removal proceedings under section 240 of the Act. If the applicant is found to be admissible for permanent residence under section 209(a) of the Act, USCIS will approve the application, admit the applicant for lawful permanent residence as of the date of the alien's arrival in the United States, and issue proof of such status.

(f) *Inadmissible Alien.* An applicant who is inadmissible to the United States as described in 8 CFR 209.1(a)(1), may, under section 209(c) of the Act, have the grounds of inadmissibility waived by USCIS except for those grounds under sections 212(a)(2)(C) and 212(a)(3)(A), (B), (C), or (E) of the Act for humanitarian purposes, to ensure family unity, or when it is otherwise in the public interest. An application for the waiver may be requested with the application for adjustment, in accordance with the form instructions.

[63 FR 30109, June 3, 1998, as amended at 76 FR 53785, Aug. 29, 2011]

§ 209.2 Adjustment of status of alien granted asylum.

The provisions of this section shall be the sole and exclusive procedure for adjustment of status by an asylee admitted under section 208 of the Act whose application is based on his or her asylee status.

(a) *Eligibility.* (1) Except as provided in paragraph (a)(2) or (a)(3) of this section, the status of any alien who has been granted asylum in the United States may be adjusted by USCIS to that of an alien lawfully admitted for permanent residence, provided the alien:

(i) Applies for such adjustment;

(ii) Has been physically present in the United States for at least one year after having been granted asylum;

(iii) Continues to be a refugee within the meaning of section 101(a)(42) of the Act, or is the spouse or child of a refugee;

(iv) Has not been firmly resettled in any foreign country; and

(v) Is admissible to the United States as an immigrant under the Act at the time of examination for adjustment without regard to paragraphs (4), (5)(A), (5)(B), and (7)(A)(i) of section 212(a) of the Act, and (vi) has a refugee number available under section 207(a) of the Act.

(2) An alien, who was granted asylum in the United States prior to November 29, 1990 (regardless of whether or not such asylum has been terminated under section 208(b) of the Act), and is no longer a refugee due to a change in circumstances in the foreign state where he or she feared persecution, may also have his or her status adjusted by USCIS to that of an alien lawfully admitted for permanent residence even if he or she is no longer able to demonstrate that he or she continues to be a refugee within the meaning of section 101(a)(42) of the Act, or to be a spouse or child of such a refugee or to have been physically present in the United States for at least one year

after being granted asylum, so long as he or she is able to meet the requirements noted in paragraphs (a)(1)(i), (iv), and (v) of this section.

(3) No alien arriving in or physically present in the Commonwealth of the Northern Mariana Islands may apply to adjust status under section 209(b) of the Act in the Commonwealth of the Northern Mariana Islands prior to January 1, 2015.

(b) *Inadmissible alien*. An applicant who is not admissible to the United States as described in 8 CFR 209.2(a)(1)(v), may, under section 209(c) of the Act, have the grounds of inadmissibility waived by USCIS except for those grounds under sections 212(a)(2)(C) and 212(a)(3)(A), (B), (C), or (E) of the Act for humanitarian purposes, to ensure family unity, or when it is otherwise in the public interest. An application for the waiver may be requested with the application for adjustment, in accordance with the form instructions. An applicant for adjustment under this part who has had the status of an exchange alien nonimmigrant under section 101(a)(15)(J) of the Act, and who is subject to the foreign resident requirement of section 212(e) of the Act, shall be eligible for adjustment without regard to the foreign residence requirement if otherwise eligible for adjustment.

(c) *Application*. An application for the benefits of section 209(b) of the Act may be filed in accordance with the form instructions. If an alien has been placed in removal, deportation, or exclusion proceedings, the application can be filed and considered only in proceedings under section 240 of the Act.

(d) *Medical examination*. For an alien seeking adjustment of status under section 209(b) of the Act, the alien shall submit a medical examination to determine whether any grounds of inadmissibility described under section 212(a)(1)(A) of the Act apply. The asylee is also required to establish compliance with the vaccination requirements described under section 212(a)(1)(A)(ii) of the Act.

(e) *Interview*. USCIS will determine, on a case-by-case basis, whether an interview by an immigration officer is necessary to determine the applicant's admissibility for permanent resident status under this part.

(f) *Decision*. USCIS will notify the applicant in writing of the decision on his or her application. There is no appeal of a denial, but USCIS will notify an applicant of the right to renew the request in removal proceedings under section 240 of the Act. If the application is approved, USCIS will record the alien's admission for lawful permanent residence as of the date one year before the date of the approval of the application, but not earlier than the date of the approval for asylum in the case of an applicant approved under paragraph (a)(2) of this section.

[46 FR 45119, Sept. 10, 1981, as amended at 56 FR 26898, June 12, 1991; 57 FR 42883, Sept. 17, 1992; 63 FR 30109, June 3, 1998; 74 FR 55737, Oct. 28, 2009; 76 FR 53785, Aug. 29, 2011]

PART 210—SPECIAL AGRICULTURAL WORKERS

Sec.

AUTHORITY: 8 U.S.C. 1103, 1160, 8 CFR part 2.

SOURCE: 53 FR 10064, Mar. 29, 1988, unless otherwise noted.

§210.1 Definition of terms used in this part.

(a) *Act*. The Immigration and Nationality Act, as amended by the Immigration Reform and Control Act of 1986.

(b) *ADIT. Alien Documentation, Identification and Telecommunications card, Form I–89*. Used to collect key data concerning an alien. When processed together with an alien's photographs, fingerprints and signature, this form becomes the source document for generation of Form I–551, Permanent Resident Card.

(c) *Application period*. The 18-month period during which an application for adjustment of status to that of a temporary resident may be accepted, begins on June 1, 1987, and ends on November 30, 1988.

(d) *Complete application.* A complete application consists of an executed Form I–700, Application for Temporary Resident Status as a Special Agricultural Worker, evidence of qualifying agricultural employment and residence, a report of medical examination, and the prescribed number of photographs. An application is not complete until the required fee has been paid and recorded.

(e) *Determination process.* Determination process as used in this part means reviewing and evaluating all information provided pursuant to an application for the benefit sought and making a determination thereon. If fraud, willful misrepresentation of a material fact, a false writing or document, or any other activity prohibited by section 210(b)(7) of the Act is discovered during the determination process the Service shall refer the case to a U.S. Attorney for possible prosecution.

(f) *Family unity.* The term *family unity* as used in section 210(c)(2)(B)(i) of the Act means maintaining the family group without deviation or change. The family group shall include the spouse, unmarried minor children who are not members of some other household, and parents who reside regularly in the household of the family group.

(g) *Group 1.* Special agricultural workers who have performed qualifying agricultural employment in the United States for at least 90 man-days in the aggregate in each of the twelve-month periods ending on May 1, 1984, 1985, and 1986, and who have resided in the United States for six months in the aggregate in each of those twelve-month periods.

(h) *Group 2.* Special agricultural workers who during the twelve-month period ending on May 1, 1986 have performed at least 90 man-days in the aggregate of qualifying agricultural employment in the United States.

(i) *Legalization Office.* Legalization offices are local offices of the Immigration and Naturalization Service which accept and process applications for legalization or special agricultural worker status, under the authority of the district directors in whose districts such offices are located.

(j) *Man-day.* The term *man-day* means the performance during any day of not less than one hour of qualifying agricultural employment for wages paid. If employment records relating to an alien applicant show only piece rate units completed, then any day in which piece rate work was performed shall be counted as a man-day. Work for more than one employer in a single day shall be counted as no more than one man-day for the purposes of this part.

(k) *Nonfrivolous application.* A complete application will be determined to be nonfrivolous at the time the applicant appears for an interview at a legalization or overseas processing office if it contains:

(1) Evidence or information which shows on its face that the applicant is admissible to the United States or, if inadmissible, that the applicable grounds of excludability may be waived under the provisions of section 210(c)(2)(i) of the Act,

(2) Evidence or information which shows on its face that the applicant performed at least 90 man-days of qualifying employment in seasonal agricultural services during the twelve-month period from May 1, 1985 through May 1, 1986, and

(3) Documentation which establishes a reasonable inference of the performance of the seasonal agricultural services claimed by the applicant.

(l) *Overseas processing office.* Overseas processing offices are offices outside the United States at which applications for adjustment to temporary resident status as a special agricultural worker are received, processed, referred to the Service for adjudication or denied. The Secretary of State has designated for this purpose the United States Embassy at Mexico City, and in all other countries the immigrant visa issuing of office at which the alien, if an applicant for an immigrant visa, would make such application. Consular officers assigned to such offices are authorized to recommend approval of an application for special agricultural worker status to the Service if the alien establishes eligibility for approval and to deny such an application if the alien fails to establish eligibility for approval or is found to have committed fraud or misrepresented facts in the application process.

(m) *Preliminary application.* A preliminary application is defined as a fully completed and signed application with fee and photographs which contains specific information concerning the performance of qualifying employment in the United States, and identifies documentary evidence which the applicant intends to submit as proof of such employment. The applicant must be otherwise admissible to the United States and must establish to the satisfaction of the examining officer during an interview that his or her claim to eligibility for special agriculture worker status is credible.

(n) *Public cash assistance.* Public cash assistance means income or needs-based monetary assistance. This includes but is not limited to supplemental security income received by the alien or his immediate family members through federal, state, or local programs designed to meet subsistence levels. It does not include assistance in kind, such as food stamps, public housing, or other non-cash benefits, nor does it include work-related compensation or certain types of medical assistance (Medicare, Medicaid, emergency treatment, services to pregnant women or children under 18 years of age, or treatment in the interest of public health).

(o) *Qualified designated entity.* A qualified designated entity is any state, local, church, community, or voluntary agency, farm labor organization, association of agricultural employers or individual designated by the Service to assist aliens in the preparation of applications for Legalization and/or Special Agricultural Worker status.

(p) *Qualifying agricultural employment.* Qualifying agricultural employment means the performance of "seasonal agricultural services" described at section 210(h) of the Act as that term is defined in regulations by the Secretary of Agriculture at 7 CFR part 1d.

(q) *Regional processing facility.* Regional Processing Facilities are Service offices established in each of the four Service regions to adjudicate, under the authority of the Directors of the Regional Processing Facilities, applications for adjustment of status under sections 210 and 245a of the Act.

(r) *Service.* The Immigration and Naturalization Service (INS).

(s) *Special agricultural worker.* Any individual granted temporary resident status in the Group 1 or Group 2 classification or permanent resident status under section 210(a) of the Act.

[53 FR 10064, Mar. 29, 1988, as amended at 54 FR 50339, Dec. 6, 1989; 63 FR 70315, Dec. 21, 1998]

§ 210.2 Application for temporary resident status.

(a)(1) *Application for temporary resident status.* An alien agricultural worker who believes that he or she is eligible for adjustment of status under the provisions of § 210.3 of this part may file an application for such adjustment at a qualified designated entity, at a legalization office, or at an overseas processing office outside the United States. Such application must be filed within the application period.

(2) *Application for Group 1 status.* An alien who believes that he or she qualifies for Group 1 status as defined in § 210.1(f) of this part and who desires to apply for that classification must so endorse his or her application at the time of filing. Applications not so endorsed will be regarded as applications for Group 2 status as defined in § 210.1(g) of this part.

(3) *Numerical limitations.* The numerical limitations of sections 201 and 202 of the Act do not apply to the adjustment of aliens to lawful temporary or permanent resident status under section 210 of the Act. No more than 350,000 aliens may be granted temporary resident status in the Group 1 classification. If more than 350,000 aliens are determined to be eligible for Group 1 classification, the first 350,000 applicants (in chronological order by date the application is filed at a legalization or overseas processing office) whose applications are approved for Group 1 status shall be accorded that classification. Aliens admitted to the United States under the transitional admission standard placed in effect between July 1, 1987, and November 1, 1987, and under the preliminary application standard at § 210.2(c)(4) who claim eligibility for Group 1 classification shall be registered as applicants for that classification on the date of

submission to a legalization office of a complete application as defined in § 210.1(c) of this part. Other applicants who may be eligible for Group 1 classification shall be classified as Group 2 aliens. There is no limitation on the number of aliens whose resident status may be adjusted from temporary to permanent in Group 2 classification.

(b) *Filing date of application*—(1) *General.* The date the alien submits an application to a qualified designated entity, legalization office or overseas processing office shall be considered the filing date of the application, provided that in the case of an application filed at a qualified designated entity the alien has consented to have the entity forward the application to a legalization office. Qualified designated entities are required to forward completed applications to the appropriate legalization office within 60 days after the applicant gives consent for such forwarding.

(2) [Reserved]

(c) *Filing of application*—(1) *General.* The application must be filed on Form I–700 at a qualified designated entity, at a legalization office, at a designated port of entry, or at an overseas processing office within the eighteen-month period beginning on June 1, 1987 and ending on November 30, 1988.

(2) *Applications in the United States.* (i) The application must be filed on Form I–700 with the required fee and, if the applicant is 14 years or older, the application must be accompanied by a completed Form FD–258 (Fingerprint Card).

(ii) All fees for applications filed in the United States, other than those within the provisions of § 210.2(c)(4), must be submitted in the exact amount in the form of a money order, cashier's check, or bank check made payable to the Immigration and Naturalization Service. No personal checks or currency will be accepted. Fees will not be waived or refunded under any circumstances.

(iii) In the case of an application filed at a legalization office, including an application received from a qualified designated entity, the district director may, at his or her discretion, require filing either by mail or in person, or may permit filing in either manner.

(iv) Each applicant, regardless of age, must appear at the appropriate Service legalization office and must be fingerprinted for the purpose of issuance of Form I–688A. Each applicant shall be interviewed by an immigration officer, except that the interview may be waived when it is impractical because of the health of the applicant.

(3) *Filing at overseas processing offices.* (i) The application must be filed on Form I–700 and must include a completed State Department Form OF–179 (Biographic Data for Visa Purposes).

(ii) Every applicant must appear at the appropriate overseas processing office to be interviewed by a consular officer. The overseas processing office will inform each applicant of the date and time of the interview. At the time of the interview every applicant shall submit the required fee.

(iii) All fees for applications submitted to an overseas processing office shall be submitted in United States currency, or in the currency of the country in which the overseas processing office is located. Fees will not be waived or refunded under any circumstances.

(iv) An applicant at an overseas processing office whose application is recommended for approval shall be provided with an entry document attached to the applicant's file. Upon admission to the United States, the applicant shall proceed to a legalization office for presentation or completion of Form FD–258 (Fingerprint Card), presentation of the applicant's file and issuance of the employment authorization Form I–688A.

(4) *Border processing.* The Commissioner will designate specific ports of entry located on the southern land border to accept and process applications under this part. Ports of entry so designated will process preliminary applications as defined at § 210.1(l) under the authority of the district directors in whose districts they are located. The ports of entry at Calexico, California, Otay Mesa, California, and Laredo, Texas have been designated to conduct preliminary application processing. Designated ports of entry may be closed or added at the discretion of the Commissioner.

(i) *Admission standard.* The applicant must present a fully completed and signed Form I–700, Application for Temporary Resident Status with the required fee and photographs at a designated port of entry. The application must contain specific information concerning the performance of qualifying employment in the United States and identify documentary evidence which the applicant intends to submit as proof of such employment. The applicant must establish to the satisfaction of the examining officer during an interview that his or her claim to eligibility for special agricultural worker classification is credible, and that he or she is otherwise admissible to the United States under the provisions of § 210.3(e) of this part including, if required, approval of an application for waiver of grounds of excludability.

(ii) *Procedures.* The fee for any application under this paragraph including applications for waivers of grounds of excludability, must be submitted in United States currency. Application fees shall not be collected until the examining immigration officer has determined that the applicant has presented a preliminary application and is admissible to the United States including, if required, approval of an application for waiver of grounds of excludability as provided in this paragraph. Applicants at designated ports of entry must present proof of identity in the form of a valid passport, a "cartilla" (Mexican military service registration booklet), a Form 13 ("Forma trece"—Mexican lieu passport identity document), or a certified copy of a birth certificate accompanied by additional evidence of identity bearing a photograph and/or fingerprint of the applicant. Upon a determination by an immigration officer at a designated port of entry that an applicant has presented a preliminary application, the applicant shall be admitted to the United States as an applicant for special agricultural worker status. All preliminary applicants shall be considered as prospective applicants for the Group 2 classification. However, such applicants may later submit a complete application for either the Group 1 or Group 2 classification to a legalization office. Preliminary applicants are not required to pay the application fee a second time when submitting the complete application to a legalization office.

(iii) *Conditions of admission.* Aliens who present a preliminary application shall be admitted to the United States for a period of ninety (90) days with authorization to accept employment, if they are determined by an immigration officer to be admissible to the United States. Such aliens are required, within that ninety-day period, to submit evidence of eligibility which meets the provisions of § 210.3 of this part; to complete Form FD–258 (Fingerprint Card); to obtain a report of medical examination in accordance with § 210.2(d) of this part; and to submit to a legalization office a complete application as defined at § 210.1(c) of this part. The INS may, for good cause, extend the ninety-day period and grant further authorization to accept employment in the United States if an alien demonstrates he or she was unable to perfect an application within the initial period. If an alien described in this paragraph fails to submit a complete application to a legalization office within ninety days or within such additional period as may have been authorized, his or her application may be denied for lack of prosecution, without prejudice.

(iv) Deportation is not stayed for an alien subject to deportation and removal under the INA, notwithstanding a claim to eligibility for SAW status, unless that alien has filed a nonfrivolous application.

(d) *Medical examination.* An applicant under this part must be examined at no expense to the government by a designated civil surgeon or, in the case of an applicant abroad, by a physician or clinic designated to perform medical examinations of immigrant visa applicants. The medical report setting forth the findings concerning the mental and physical condition of the applicant shall be incorporated into the record. Any applicant certified under paragraph (1), (2), (3), (4), or (5) of section 212(a) of the Act may appeal to a Board of Medical Officers of the U.S. Public Health Service as provided in section 234 of the Act and part 235 of this chapter.

(e) *Limitation on access to information and confidentiality.* (1) Except for consular officials engaged in the processing of applications overseas and employees of a qualified designated entity where an application is filed with that entity, no person other than a sworn officer or employee of the Department of Justice or bureau or agency thereof, or contract personnel employed by the Service to work in connection with the legalization program, will be permitted to examine individual applications.

(2) Files and records prepared by qualified designated entities under this section are confidential. The Attorney General and the Service shall not have access to these files and records without the consent of the alien.

(3) All information furnished pursuant to an application for temporary resident status under this part including documentary evidence filed with the application shall be used only in the determination process, including a determination under § 210.4(d) of this part, or to enforce the provisions of section 210(b)(7) of the Act, relating to prosecutions for fraud and false statements made in connection with applications, as provided in paragraph (e)(4) of this section.

(4) If a determination is made by the Service that the alien has, in connection with his or her application, engaged in fraud or willful misrepresentation or concealment of a material fact, knowingly provided a false writing or document in making his or her application, knowingly made a false statement or representation, or engaged in any other activity prohibited by section 210(b)(7) of the Act, the Service shall refer the matter to the U.S. Attorney for prosecution of the alien or any person who created or supplied a false writing or document for use in an application for adjustment of status under this part.

(f) *Decision.* The applicant shall be notified in writing of the decision and, if the application is denied, of the reason(s) therefor. An adverse decision under this part including an overseas application may be appealed to the Associate Commissioner, Examinations (Administrative Appeals Unit) on Form I–694. The appeal with the required fee shall be filed with the Regional Processing Facility in accordance with the provisions of § 103.3(a)(2) of this chapter. An applicant for Group 1 status as defined in § 210.1(f) of this part who is determined to be ineligible for that status may be classified as a temporary resident under Group 2 as defined in § 210.1(g) of this part if otherwise eligible for Group 2 status. In such a case the applicant shall be notified of the decision to accord him or her Group 2 status and to deny Group 1 status. He or she is entitled to file an appeal in accordance with the provisions of § 103.3(a)(2) of this chapter from that portion of the decision denying Group 1 status. In the case of an applicant who is represented in the application process in accordance with 8 CFR part 292, the applicant's representative shall also receive notification of decision specified in this section.

(g) *Motions.* In accordance with the provisions of § 103.5(b) of this chapter, the director of a regional processing facility or a consular officer at an overseas processing office may *sua sponte* reopen any proceeding under this part under his or her jurisdiction and reverse any adverse decision in such proceeding when appeal is taken under § 103.3(a)(2) of this part from such adverse decision; the Associate Commissioner, Examinations, and the Chief of the Administrative Appeals Unit may *sua sponte* reopen any proceeding conducted by that unit under this part and reconsider any decision rendered in such proceeding. The decision must be served on the appealing party within forty-five (45) days of receipt of any briefs and/or new evidence, or upon expiration of the time allowed for the submission of any briefs. Motions to reopen a proceeding or reconsider a decision shall not be considered under this part.

(h) *Certifications.* The regional processing facility director may, in accordance with § 103.4 of this chapter, certify a decision to the Associate Commissioner, Examinations when the case involves an unusually complex or novel question of law or fact. A consular officer assigned to an overseas processing office is authorized to certify a decision in the same manner and upon the same basis.

[53 FR 10064, Mar. 29, 1988, as amended at 55 FR 12629, Apr. 5, 1990; 60 FR 21975, May 4, 1995]

§210.3 Eligibility.

(a) *General.* An alien who, during the twelve-month period ending on May 1, 1986, has engaged in qualifying agricultural employment in the United States for at least 90 man-days is eligible for status as an alien lawfully admitted for temporary residence if otherwise admissible under the provisions of section 210(c) of the Act and if he or she is not ineligible under the provisions of paragraph (d) of this section.

(b) *Proof of eligibility*—(1) *Burden of proof.* An alien applying for adjustment of status under this part has the burden of proving by a preponderance of the evidence that he or she has worked the requisite number of man-days, is admissible to the United States under the provisions of section 210(c) of the Act, is otherwise eligible for adjustment of status under this section and in the case of a Group 1 applicant, has resided in the United States for the requisite periods. If the applicant cannot provide documentation which shows qualifying employment for each of the requisite man-days, or in the case of a Group 1 applicant, which meets the residence requirement, the applicant may meet his or her burden of proof by providing documentation sufficient to establish the requisite employment or residence as a matter of just and reasonable inference. The inference to be drawn from the documentation provided shall depend on the extent of the documentation, its credibility and amenability to verification as set forth in paragraphs (b)(2) and (3) of this section. If an applicant establishes that he or she has in fact performed the requisite qualifying agricultural employment by producing sufficient evidence to show the extent of that employment as a matter of just and reasonable inference, the burden then shifts to the Service to disprove the applicant's evidence by showing that the inference drawn from the evidence is not reasonable.

(2) *Evidence.* The sufficiency of all evidence produced by the applicant will be judged according to its probative value and credibility. Original documents will be given greater weight than copies. To meet his or her burden of proof, an applicant must provide evidence of eligibility apart from his or her own testimony. Analysis of evidence submitted will include consideration of the fact that work performed by minors and spouses is sometimes credited to a principal member of a family.

(3) *Verification.* Personal testimony by an applicant which is not corroborated, in whole or in part, by other credible evidence (including testimony of persons other than the applicant) will not serve to meet an applicant's burden of proof. All evidence of identity, qualifying employment, admissibility, and eligibility submitted by an applicant for adjustment of status under this part will be subject to verification by the Service. Failure by an applicant to release information protected by the Privacy Act or related laws when such information is essential to the proper adjudication of an application may result in denial of the benefit sought. The Service may solicit from agricultural producers, farm labor contractors, collective bargaining organizations and other groups or organizations which maintain records of employment, lists of workers against which evidence of qualifying employment can be checked. If such corroborating evidence is not available and the evidence provided is deemed insufficient, the application may be denied.

(4) *Securing SAW employment records.* When a SAW applicant alleges that an employer or farm labor contractor refuses to provide him or her with records relating to his or her employment and the applicant has reason to believe such records exist, the Service shall attempt to secure such records. However, prior to any attempt by the Service to secure the employment records, the following conditions must be met: a SAW application (Form I–700) must have been filed; an interview must have been conducted; the applicant's testimony must support credibly his or her claim; and, the Service must determine that the application cannot

be approved in the absence of the employer or farm labor contractor records. Provided each of these conditions has been met, and after unsuccessful attempts by the Service for voluntary compliance, the District Directors shall utilize section 235 of the Immigration and Nationality Act and issue a subpoena in accordance with 8 CFR 287.4, in such cases where the employer or farm labor contractor refuses to release the needed employment records.

(c) *Documents.* A complete application for adjustment of status must be accompanied by proof of identity, evidence of qualifying employment, evidence of residence and such evidence of admissibility or eligibility as may be requested by the examining immigration officer in accordance with requirements specified in this part. At the time of filing, certified copies of documents may be submitted in lieu of originals. However, at the time of the interview, wherever possible, the original documents must be presented except for the following: Official government records; employment or employment related records maintained by employers, unions, or collective bargaining organizations; medical records; school records maintained by a school or school board; or other records maintained by a party other than the applicant. Copies of records maintained by parties other than the applicant which are submitted in evidence must be certified as true and correct by such parties and must bear their seal or signature or the signature and title of persons authorized to act in their behalf. If at the time of the interview the return of original documents is desired by the applicant, they must be accompanied by notarized copies or copies certified true and correct by a qualified designated entity or by the alien's representative in the format prescribed in § 204.2(j)(1) or (2) of this chapter. At the discretion of the district director or consular officer, original documents, even if accompanied by certified copies, may be temporarily retained for further examination.

(1) *Proof of identity.* Evidence to establish identity is listed below in descending order of preference:

(i) Passport;

(ii) Birth certificate;

(iii) Any national identity document from a foreign country bearing a photo and/or fingerprint (e.g., "cedula", "cartilla", "carte d'identite," etc.);

(iv) Driver's license or similar document issued by a state if it contains a photo;

(v) Baptismal record or marriage certificate;

(vi) Affidavits, or

(vii) Such other documentation which may establish the identity of the applicant.

(2) *Assumed names*—(i) *General.* In cases where an applicant claims to have met any of the eligibility criteria under an assumed name, the applicant has the burden of proving that the applicant was in fact the person who used that name.

(ii) *Proof of common identity.* The most persuasive evidence is a document issued in the assumed name which identifies the applicant by photograph, fingerprint or detailed physical description. Other evidence which will be considered are affidavit(s) by a person or persons other than the applicant, made under oath, which identify the affiant by name and address and state the affiant's relationship to the applicant and the basis of the affiant's knowledge of the applicant's use of the assumed name. Affidavits accompanied by a photograph which has been identified by the affiant as the individual known to the affiant under the assumed name in question will carry greater weight. Other documents showing the assumed name may serve to establish the common identity when substantiated by corroborating detail.

(3) *Proof of employment.* The applicant may establish qualifying employment through government employment records, or records maintained by agricultural producers, farm labor contractors, collective bargaining organizations and other groups or organizations which maintain records of employment, or such other evidence as worker identification issued by employers or collective bargaining organizations, union membership cards or other union records such as dues receipts or records of the applicant's involvement or that

of his or her immediate family with organizations providing services to farmworkers, or work records such as pay stubs, piece work receipts, W-2 Forms or certification of the filing of Federal income tax returns on IRS Form 6166, or state verification of the filing of state income tax returns. Affidavits may be submitted under oath, by agricultural producers, foremen, farm labor contractors, union officials, fellow employees, or other persons with specific knowledge of the applicant's employment. The affiant must be identified by name and address; the name of the applicant and the relationship of the affiant to the applicant must be stated; and the source of the information in the affidavit (e.g. personal knowledge, reliance on information provided by others, etc.) must be indicated. The affidavit must also provide information regarding the crop and the type of work performed by the applicant and the period during which such work was performed. The affiant must provide a certified copy of corroborating records or state the affiant's willingness to personally verify the information provided. The weight and probative value of any affidavit accepted will be determined on the basis of the substance of the affidavit and any documents which may be affixed thereto which may corroborate the information provided.

(4) *Proof of residence.* Evidence to establish residence in the United States during the requisite period(s) includes: Employment records as described in paragraph (c)(3) of this section; utility bills (gas, electric, phone, etc.), receipts, or letters from companies showing the dates during which the applicant received service; school records (letters, report cards, etc.) from the schools that the applicant or his or her children have attended in the United States showing the name of school, name and, if available, address of student, and periods of attendance, and hospital or medical records showing similar information; attestations by churches, unions, or other organizations to the applicant's residence by letter which: Identify applicant by name, are signed by an official (whose title is shown), show inclusive dates of membership, state the address where applicant resided during the membership period, include the seal of the organization impressed on the letter, establish how the author knows the applicant, and the origin of the information; and additional documents that could show that the applicant was in the United States at a specific time, such as: Money order receipts for money sent out of the country; passport entries; birth certificates of children born in the United States; bank books with dated transactions; letters of correspondence between the applicant and another person or organization; Social Security card; Selective Service card; automobile license receipts, title, vehicle registration, etc.; deeds, mortgages, contracts to which applicant has been a party; tax receipts; insurance policies, receipts, or letters; and any other document that will show that applicant was in the United States at a specific time. For Group 2 eligibility, evidence of performance of the required 90 man-days of seasonal agricultural services shall constitute evidence of qualifying residence.

(5) *Proof of financial responsibility.* Generally, the evidence of employment submitted under paragraph (c)(3) of this section will serve to demonstrate the alien's financial responsibility. If it appears that the applicant may be inadmissible under section 212(a)(15) of the Act, he or she may be required to submit documentation showing a history of employment without reliance on public cash assistance for all periods of residence in the United States.

(d) *Ineligible classes.* The following classes of aliens are ineligible for temporary residence under this part:

(1) An alien who at any time was a nonimmigrant exchange visitor under section 101(a)(15)(J) of the Act who is subject to the two-year foreign residence requirement unless the alien has complied with that requirement or the requirement has been waived pursuant to the provisions of section 212(e) of the Act;

(2) An alien excludable under the provisions of section 212(a) of the Act whose grounds of excludability may not be waived, pursuant to section 210(c)(2)(B)(ii) of the Act;

(3) An alien who has been convicted of a felony, or three or more misdemeanors.

(e) *Exclusion grounds*—(1) *Grounds of exclusion not to be applied.* Sections (14), (20), (21), (25), and (32) of section 212(a) of the Act shall not apply to applicants applying for temporary resident status.

(2) *Waiver of grounds for exclusion.* Except as provided in paragraph (e)(3) of this section, the Service may waive any other provision of section 212(a) of the Act only in the case of individual aliens for humanitarian purposes, to assure family unity, or when the granting of such a waiver is in the public interest. If an alien is excludable on grounds which may be waived as set forth in this paragraph, he or she shall be advised of the procedures for applying for a waiver of grounds of excludability on Form I–690. When an application for waiver of grounds of excludability is submitted in conjunction with an application for temporary residence under this section, it shall be accepted for processing at the legalization office, overseas processing office, or designated port of entry. If an application for waiver of grounds of excludability is submitted after the alien's preliminary interview at the legalization office it shall be forwarded to the appropriate regional processing facility. All applications for waivers of grounds of excludability must be accompanied by the correct fee in the exact amount. All fees for applications filed in the United States other than those within the provisions of § 210.2(c)(4) must be in the form of a money order, cashier's check, or bank check. No personal checks or currency will be accepted. Fees for waiver applications filed at the designated port of entry under the preliminary application standard must be submitted in United States currency. Fees will not be waived or refunded under any circumstances. Generally, an application for waiver of grounds of excludability under this part submitted at a legalization office or overseas processing office will be approved or denied by the director of the regional processing facility in whose jurisdiction the applicant's application for adjustment of status was filed. However, in cases involving clear statutory ineligibility or admitted fraud, such application for a waiver may be denied by the district director in whose jurisdiction the application is filed; in cases filed at overseas processing offices, such application for a waiver may be denied by a consular officer; or, in cases returned to a legalization office for reinterview, such application may be approved at the discretion of the district director. Waiver applications filed at the port of entry under the preliminary application standard will be approved or denied by the district director having jurisdiction over the port of entry. The applicant shall be notified of the decision and, if the application is denied, of the reason(s) therefor. The applicant may appeal the decision within 30 days after the service of the notice pursuant to the provisions of § 103.3(a)(2) of this chapter.

(3) *Grounds of exclusion that may not be waived.* The following provisions of section 212(a) of the Act may not be waived:

(i) Paragraphs (9) and (10) (criminals);

(ii) Paragraph (15) (public charge) except as provided in paragraph (c)(4) of this section.

(iii) Paragraph (23) (narcotics) except for a single offense of simple possession of thirty grams or less of marijuana.

(iv) Paragraphs (27), (prejudicial to the public interest), (28), (communists), and (29) (subversive);

(v) Paragraph (33) (Nazi persecution).

(4) *Special Rule for determination of public charge.* An applicant who has a consistent employment history which shows the ability to support himself and his or her family, even though his income may be below the poverty level, is not excludable under paragraph (e)(3)(ii) of this section. The applicant's employment history need not be continuous in that it is uninterrupted. It should be continuous in the sense that the applicant shall be regularly attached to the workforce, has an income over a substantial period of the applicable time, and has demonstrated the capacity to exist on his or her income and maintain his or her family without reliance on public cash assistance. This regulation is prospective in that the Service shall determine, based on the applicant's history, whether he or she

is likely to become a public charge. Past acceptance of public cash assistance within a history of consistent employment will enter into this decision. The weight given in considering applicability of the public charge provisions will depend on many factors, but the length of time an applicant has received public cash assistance will constitute a significant factor.

[53 FR 10064, Mar. 29, 1988, as amended at 53 FR 27335, July 20, 1988; 54 FR 4757, Jan. 31, 1989; 55 FR 12629, Apr. 5, 1990]

§210.4 Status and benefits.

(a) *Date of adjustment.* The status of an alien whose application for temporary resident status is approved shall be adjusted to that of a lawful temporary resident as of the date on which the fee was paid at a legalization office, except that the status of an alien who applied for such status at an overseas processing office whose application has been recommended for approval by that office shall be adjusted as of the date of his or her admission into the United States.

(b) *Employment and travel authorization*—(1) *General.* Authorization for employment and travel abroad for temporary resident status applicants under section 210 of the Act be granted by the INS. In the case of an application which has been filed with a qualified designated entity, employment authorization may only be granted after a nonfrivolous application has been received at a legalization office, and receipt of the fee has been recorded.

(2) *Employment and travel authorization prior to the granting of temporary resident status.* Permission to travel abroad and to accept employment will be granted to the applicant after an interview has been conducted in connection with a nonfrivolous application at a Service office. If an interview appointment cannot be scheduled within 30 days from the date an application is filed at a Service office, authorization to accept employment will be granted, valid until the scheduled appointment date. Employment authorization, both prior and subsequent to an interview, will be restricted to increments not exceeding 1 year, pending final determination on the application for temporary resident status. If a final determination has not been made prior to the expiration date on the Employment Authorization Document (Form I–766, Form I–688A or Form I–688B) that date may be extended upon return of the employment authorization document by the applicant to the appropriate Service office. Persons submitting applications who currently have work authorization incident to status as defined in §274a.12(b) of this chapter shall be granted work authorization by the Service effective on the date the alien's prior work authorization expires. Permission to travel abroad shall be granted in accordance with the Service's advance parole provisions contained in §212.5(f) of this chapter.

(3) *Employment and travel authorization upon grant of temporary resident status.* Upon the granting of an application for adjustment to temporary resident status, the service center will forward a notice of approval to the applicant at his or her last known address and to his or her qualified designated entity or representative. The applicant may appear at any Service office, and upon surrender of the previously issued Employment Authorization Document, will be issued Form I–688, Temporary Resident Card. An alien whose status is adjusted to that of a lawful temporary resident under section 210 of the Act has the right to reside in the United States, to travel abroad (including commuting from a residence abroad), and to accept employment in the United States in the same manner as aliens lawfully admitted to permanent residence.

(c) *Ineligibility for immigration benefits.* An alien whose status is adjusted to that of a lawful temporary resident under section 210 of the Act is not entitled to submit a petition pursuant to section 203(a)(2) of the Act or to any other benefit or consideration accorded under the Act to aliens lawfully admitted for permanent residence, except as provided in paragraph (b)(3) of this section.

(d) *Termination of temporary resident status*—(1) *General.* The temporary resident status of a special agricultural worker is terminated automatically and without notice under section 210(a)(3) of the Act upon entry of a final order of deportation by an immigration judge based on a determination that the alien is deportable under section 241 of the Act.

(2) The status of an alien lawfully admitted for temporary residence under section 210(a)(2) of the Act, may be terminated before the alien becomes eligible for adjustment of status under §210.5 of this part, upon the occurrence of any of the following:

(i) It is determined by a preponderance of the evidence that the adjustment to temporary resident status was the result of fraud or willful misrepresentation as provided in section 212(a)(19) of the Act;

(ii) The alien commits an act which renders him or her inadmissible as an immigrant, unless a waiver is secured pursuant to §210.3(e)(2) of this part;

(iii) The alien is convicted of any felony, or three or more misdemeanors in the United States.

(3) *Procedure.* (i) Termination of an alien's status under paragraph (d)(2) of this section will be made only on notice to the alien sent by certified mail directed to his or her last known address, and to his or her representative. The alien must be given an opportunity to offer evidence in opposition to the grounds alleged for termination of his or her status. Evidence in opposition must be submitted within thirty (30) days after the service of the Notice of Intent to Terminate. If the alien's status is terminated, the director of the regional processing facility shall notify the alien of the decision and the reasons for the termination, and further notify the alien that any Service Form I–94 (see §1.4), Arrival-Departure Record or other official Service document issued to the alien authorizing employment and/or travel abroad, or any Form I–688, Temporary Resident Card previously issued to the alien will be declared void by the director of the regional processing facility within thirty (30) days if no appeal of the termination decision is filed within that period. The alien may appeal the decision to the Associate Commissioner, Examinations (Administrative Appeals Unit) using Form I–694. Any appeal with the required fee shall be filed with the regional processing facility within thirty (30) days after the service of the notice of termination. If no appeal is filed within that period, the Forms I–94, I–688 or other official Service document shall be deemed void, and must be surrendered without delay to an immigration officer or to the issuing office of the Service.

(ii) Termination proceedings must be commenced before the alien becomes eligible for adjustment of status under §210.5 of this part. The timely commencement of termination proceedings will preclude the alien from becoming a lawful permanent resident until a final determination is made in the proceedings, including any appeal.

[53 FR 10064, Mar. 29, 1988, as amended at 55 FR 12629, Apr. 5, 1990; 60 FR 21975, May 4, 1995; 61 FR 46536, Sept. 4, 1996; 65 FR 82255, Dec. 28, 2000; 78 FR 18472, Mar. 27, 2013]

§210.5 Adjustment to permanent resident status.

(a) *Eligibility and date of adjustment to permanent resident status.* The status of an alien lawfully admitted to the United States for temporary residence under section 210(a)(1) of the Act, if the alien has otherwise maintained such status as required by the Act, shall be adjusted to that of an alien lawfully admitted to the United States for permanent residence as of the following dates:

(1) *Group 1.* Aliens determined to be eligible for Group 1 classification, whose adjustment to temporary residence occurred prior to November 30, 1988, shall be adjusted to lawful permanent residence as of December 1, 1989. Those aliens whose adjustment to temporary residence occurred after November 30, 1988 shall be adjusted to lawful permanent residence one year from the date of the adjustment to temporary residence.

(2) *Group 2.* Aliens determined to be eligible for Group 2 classification whose adjustment to temporary residence occurred prior to November 30, 1988, shall be adjusted to lawful permanent residence as of December 1, 1990. Those aliens whose adjustment to temporary residence occurred after November 30, 1988 shall be adjusted to lawful permanent residence two years from the date of the adjustment to temporary residence.

(b) *ADIT processing*—(1) *General.* To obtain proof of permanent resident status an alien described in paragraph (a) of this section must appear at a legalization or Service office designated for this purpose for preparation of Form I–551, Permanent Resident Card. Such appearance may be prior to the date of adjustment, but only upon invitation by the Service. Form I–551 shall be issued subsequent to the date of adjustment.

(2) Upon appearance at a Service office for preparation of Form I–551, an alien must present proof of identity, suitable ADIT photographs, and a fingerprint and signature must be obtained from the alien on Form I–89.

[53 FR 10064, Mar. 29, 1988, as amended at 54 FR 50339, Dec. 6, 1989; 63 FR 70315, Dec. 21, 1998]

PART 211—DOCUMENTARY REQUIREMENTS: IMMIGRANTS; WAIVERS

AUTHORITY: 8 U.S.C. 1101, 1103, 1181, 1182, 1203, 1225, 1257; 8 CFR part 2.

SOURCE: 62 FR 10346, Mar. 6, 1997, unless otherwise noted.

§211.1 Visas.

(a) *General.* Except as provided in paragraph (b)(1) of this section, each arriving alien applying for admission (or boarding the vessel or aircraft on which he or she arrives) into the United States for lawful permanent residence, or as a lawful permanent resident returning to an unrelinquished lawful permanent residence in the United States, shall present one of the following:

(1) A valid, unexpired immigrant visa;

(2) A valid, unexpired Form I–551, Permanent Resident Card, if seeking readmission after a temporary absence of less than 1 year, or in the case of a crewmember regularly serving on board a vessel or aircraft of United States registry seeking readmission after any temporary absence connected with his or her duties as a crewman;

(3) A valid, unexpired Form I–327, Permit to Reenter the United States;

(4) A valid, unexpired Form I–571, Refugee Travel Document, properly endorsed to reflect admission as a lawful permanent resident;

(5) An expired Form I–551, Permanent Resident Card, accompanied by a filing receipt issued within the previous 6 months for either a Form I–751, Petition to Remove the Conditions on Residence, or Form I–829, Petition by Entrepreneur to Remove Conditions, if seeking admission or readmission after a temporary absence of less than 1 year;

(6) A Form I–551, whether or not expired, presented by a civilian or military employee of the United States Government who was outside the United States pursuant to official orders, or by the spouse or child of such employee who resided abroad while the employee or serviceperson was on overseas duty and who is preceding, accompanying or following to join within 4 months the employee, returning to the United States; or

(7) Form I–551, whether or not expired, or a transportation letter issued by an American consular officer, presented by an employee of the American University of Beirut, who was so employed immediately preceding travel to the United States, returning temporarily to the United States before resuming employment with the American University of Beirut, or resuming permanent residence in the United States.

(b) *Waivers.* (1) A waiver of the visa required in paragraph (a) of this section shall be granted without fee or application by the district director, upon presentation of the child's birth certificate, to a child born subsequent to the issuance of an immigrant visa to his or her accompanying parent who applies for admission during the validity of such a visa; or a child born during the temporary visit abroad of a mother who is a lawful permanent resident alien, or a national, of the United States, provided that the child's application for admission to the United States is made within 2 years of birth, the child is accompanied by the parent who is applying for readmission as a permanent resident upon the first return of the parent to the United States after the birth of the child, and the accompanying parent is found to be admissible to the United States.

(2) For an alien described in paragraph (b)(1) of this section, recordation of the child's entry shall be on Form I–181, Memorandum of Creation of Record of Admission for Lawful Permanent Residence. The carrier of such alien shall not be liable for a fine pursuant to section 273 of the Act.

(3) If an immigrant alien returning to an unrelinquished lawful permanent residence in the United States after a temporary absence abroad believes that good cause exists for his or her failure to present an unexpired immigrant visa, permanent resident card, or reentry permit, the alien may file an application for a waiver of this requirement with the DHS officer with jurisdiction over the port of entry where the alien arrives. To apply for this waiver, the alien must file the designated form with the fee prescribed in 8 CFR 103.7(b)(1). If the alien's permanent resident card was lost or stolen and the alien has been absent for less than one year, rather than the waiver application the alien must apply for a replacement card as described in 8 CFR 264.5. In the exercise of discretion, the DHS officer who has jurisdiction over the port of entry where the alien arrives may waive the alien's lack of an immigrant visa, permanent resident card, or reentry permit and admit the alien as a returning resident if DHS is satisfied that the alien has established good cause for the alien's failure to present an immigrant visa, permanent resident card, or reentry permit. Filing a request to replace a lost or stolen card will serve as both application for replacement and as application for waiver of passport and visa, without the obligation to file a separate waiver application.

(c) *Immigrants having occupational status defined in section 101(a)(15) (A), (E), or (G) of the Act.* An immigrant visa, reentry permit, or Form I–551 shall be invalid when presented by an alien who has an occupational status under section 101(a)(15) (A), (E), or (G) of the Act, unless he or she has previously submitted, or submits at the time he or she applies for admission to the United States, the written waiver required by section 247(b) of the Act and 8 CFR part 247.

[62 FR 10346, Mar. 6, 1997, as amended at 63 FR 39218, July 22, 1998; 63 FR 70315, Dec. 21, 1998; 74 FR 26937, June 5, 2009; 76 FR 53786, Aug. 29, 2011]

§211.2 Passports.

(a) A passport valid for the bearer's entry into a foreign country at least 60 days beyond the expiration date of his or her immigrant visa shall be presented by each immigrant except an immigrant who:

(1) Is the parent, spouse, or unmarried son or daughter of a United States citizen or of an alien lawful permanent resident of the United States;

(2) Is entering under the provisions of §211.1(a)(2) through (a)(7);

(3) Is a child born during the temporary visit abroad of a mother who is a lawful permanent resident alien, or a national, of the United States, provided that the child's application for admission to the United States is made within 2 years of birth, the child is accompanied by the parent who is applying for readmission as a permanent resident upon the first return of the parent to the United States after the birth of the child, and the accompanying parent is found to be admissible to the United States;

(4) Is a stateless person or a person who because of his or her opposition to Communism is unwilling or unable to obtain a passport from the country of his or her nationality, or is the accompanying spouse or unmarried son or daughter of such immigrant; or

(5) Is a member of the Armed Forces of the United States.

(b) Except as provided in paragraph (a) of this section, if an alien seeking admission as an immigrant with an immigrant visa believes that good cause exists for his or her failure to present a passport, the alien may file an application for a waiver of this requirement with the *DHS officer who has jurisdiction over the port of entry where the alien arrives*. To apply for this waiver, the alien must apply on the form specified by USCIS, with the fee prescribed in 8

CFR 103.7(b)(1). In the exercise of discretion, the *DHS officer with jurisdiction over the port of entry*, may waive the alien's lack of passport and admit the alien as an immigrant, if DHS is satisfied that the alien has established good cause for his or her failure to present a passport.

[62 FR 10346, Mar. 6, 1997, as amended at 74 FR 26937, June 5, 2009; 76 FR 53786, Aug. 29, 2011]

§211.3 Expiration of immigrant visa or other travel document.

An immigrant visa, reentry permit, refugee travel document, or a permanent resident card shall be regarded as unexpired if the rightful holder embarked or enplaned before the expiration of his or her immigrant visa, reentry permit, or refugee travel document, or with respect to a permanent resident card, before the first anniversary of the date on which he or she departed from the United States, provided that the vessel or aircraft on which he or she so embarked or enplaned arrives in the United States or foreign contiguous territory on a continuous voyage. The continuity of the voyage shall not be deemed to have been interrupted by scheduled or emergency stops of the vessel or aircraft en route to the United States or foreign contiguous territory, or by a layover in foreign contiguous territory necessitated solely for the purpose of effecting a transportation connection to the United States.

[62 FR 10346, Mar. 6, 1997, as amended at 76 FR 53786, Aug. 29, 2011]

§211.4 Waiver of documents for returning residents.

(a) Pursuant to the authority contained in section 211(b) of the Act, an alien previously lawfully admitted to the United States for permanent residence who, upon return from a temporary absence was inadmissible because of failure to have or to present a valid passport, immigrant visa, reentry permit, border crossing card, or other document required at the time of entry, may be granted a waiver of such requirement in the discretion of the district director if the district director determines that such alien:

(1) Was not otherwise inadmissible at the time of entry, or having been otherwise inadmissible at the time of entry is with respect thereto qualified for an exemption from deportability under section 237(a)(1)(H) of the Act; and

(2) Is not otherwise subject to removal.

(b) Denial of a waiver by the district director is not appealable but shall be without prejudice to renewal of an application and reconsideration in proceedings before the immigration judge.

§211.5 Alien commuters.

(a) *General.* An alien lawfully admitted for permanent residence or a special agricultural worker lawfully admitted for temporary residence under section 210 of the Act may commence or continue to reside in foreign contiguous territory and commute as a special immigrant defined in section 101(a)(27)(A) of the Act to his or her place of employment in the United States. An alien commuter engaged in seasonal work will be presumed to have taken up residence in the United States if he or she is present in this country for more than 6 months, in the aggregate, during any continuous 12-month period. An alien commuter's address report under section 265 of the Act must show his or her actual residence address even though it is not in the United States.

(b) *Loss of residence status.* An alien commuter who has been out of regular employment in the United States for a continuous period of 6 months shall be deemed to have lost residence status, notwithstanding temporary entries in the interim for other than employment purposes. An exception applies when employment in the United States was interrupted for reasons beyond the individual's control other than lack of a job opportunity or the commuter can demonstrate that he or she has worked 90 days in the United States in the aggregate during the 12-month period preceding the application for admission into the United States. Upon loss of status, the alien's permanent resident card becomes invalid and must be surrendered to an immigration officer.

(c) *Eligibility for benefits under the immigration and nationality laws.* Until he or she has taken up residence in the United States, an alien commuter cannot satisfy the residence requirements of the naturalization laws and cannot qualify for any benefits under the immigration laws on his or her own behalf or on behalf of his or her relatives other than as specified in paragraph (a) of this section. When an alien commuter takes up residence in the United States, he or she shall no longer be regarded as a commuter. He or she may facilitate proof of having taken up such residence by notifying the Service as soon as possible, preferably at the time of his or her first reentry for that purpose. Application for issuance of a new Permanent Resident Card to show that he or she has taken up residence in the United States shall be made in accordance with 8 CFR 264.5.

[62 FR 10346, Mar. 6, 1997, as amended at 63 FR 70315, Dec. 21, 1998; 76 FR 53786, Aug. 29, 2011]

PART 212—DOCUMENTARY REQUIREMENTS: NONIMMIGRANTS; WAIVERS; ADMISSION OF CERTAIN INADMISSIBLE ALIENS; PAROLE

Sec.

AUTHORITY: 6 U.S.C. 111, 202(4) and 271; 8 U.S.C. 1101 and note, 1102, 1103, 1182 and note, 1184, 1185 note (section 7209 of Pub. L. 108–458), 1187, 1223, 1225, 1226, 1227, 1255, 1359; 8 CFR part 2.

Section 212.1(q) also issued under section 702, Pub. L. 110–229, 122 Stat. 754, 854.

SOURCE: 17 FR 11484, Dec. 19, 1952, unless otherwise noted.

§ 212.0 Definitions.

For purposes of § 212.1 and § 235.1 of this chapter:

Adjacent islands means Bermuda and the islands located in the Caribbean Sea, except Cuba.

Cruise ship means a passenger vessel over 100 gross tons, carrying more than 12 passengers for hire, making a voyage lasting more than 24 hours any part of which is on the high seas, and for which passengers are embarked or disembarked in the United States or its territories.

Ferry means any vessel operating on a pre-determined fixed schedule and route, which is being used solely to provide transportation between places that are no more than 300 miles apart and which is being used to transport passengers, vehicles, and/or railroad cars.

Pleasure vessel means a vessel that is used exclusively for recreational or personal purposes and not to transport passengers or property for hire.

United States means "United States" as defined in section 215(c) of the Immigration and Nationality Act of 1952, as amended (8 U.S.C. 1185(c)).

U.S. citizen means a United States citizen or a U.S. non-citizen national.

United States qualifying tribal entity means a tribe, band, or other group of Native Americans formally recognized by the United States Government which agrees to meet WHTI document standards.

[73 FR 18415, Apr. 3, 2008]

§212.1 Documentary requirements for nonimmigrants.

A valid unexpired visa that meets the requirements of part 215, subpart B, of this chapter, if applicable, and an unexpired passport, shall be presented by each arriving nonimmigrant alien except that the passport validity period for an applicant for admission who is a member of a class described in section 102 of the Act is not required to extend beyond the date of his application for admission if so admitted, and except as otherwise provided in the Act, this chapter, and for the following classes:

(a) *Citizens of Canada or Bermuda, Bahamian nationals or British subjects resident in certain islands.* (1) *Canadian citizens.* A visa is generally not required for Canadian citizens, except those Canadians that fall under nonimmigrant visa categories E, K, S, or V as provided in paragraphs (h), (l), and (m) of this section and 22 CFR 41.2. A valid unexpired passport is required for Canadian citizens arriving in the United States, except when meeting one of the following requirements:

(i) *NEXUS Program.* A Canadian citizen who is traveling as a participant in the NEXUS program, and who is not otherwise required to present a passport and visa as provided in paragraphs (h), (l), and (m) of this section and 22 CFR 41.2, may present a valid unexpired NEXUS program card when using a NEXUS Air kiosk or when entering the United States from contiguous territory or adjacent islands at a land or sea port-of-entry. A Canadian citizen who enters the United States by pleasure vessel from Canada under the remote inspection system may present a valid unexpired NEXUS program card.

(ii) *FAST Program.* A Canadian citizen who is traveling as a participant in the FAST program, and who is not otherwise required to present a passport and visa as provided in paragraphs (h), (l), and (m) of this section and 22 CFR 41.2, may present a valid unexpired FAST card at a land or sea port-of-entry prior to entering the United States from contiguous territory or adjacent islands.

(iii) *SENTRI Program.* A Canadian citizen who is traveling as a participant in the SENTRI program, and who is not otherwise required to present a passport and visa as provided in paragraphs (h), (l), and (m) of this section and 22 CFR 41.2, may present a valid unexpired SENTRI card at a land or sea port-of-entry prior to entering the United States from contiguous territory or adjacent islands.

(iv) *Canadian Indians.* If designated by the Secretary of Homeland Security, a Canadian citizen holder of a Indian and Northern Affairs Canada ("INAC") card issued by the Canadian Department of Indian Affairs and North Development, Director of Land and Trust Services ("LTS") in conformance with security standards agreed upon by the Governments of Canada and the United States, and containing a machine readable zone and who is arriving from Canada may present the card prior to entering the United States at a land port-of-entry.

(v) *Children.* A child who is a Canadian citizen arriving from contiguous territory may present for admission to the United States at sea or land ports-of-entry certain other documents if the arrival meets the requirements described below.

(A) *Children Under Age 16.* A Canadian citizen who is under the age of 16 is permitted to present an original or a copy of his or her birth certificate, a Canadian Citizenship Card, or a Canadian Naturalization Certificate when arriving in the United States from contiguous territory at land or sea ports-of-entry.

(B) *Groups of Children Under Age 19.* A Canadian citizen, under age 19 who is traveling with a public or private school group, religious group, social or cultural organization, or team associated with a youth sport organization is permitted to present an original or a copy of his or her birth certificate, a Canadian Citizenship Card, or a Canadian Naturalization Certificate when arriving in the United States from contiguous territory at land or sea ports-of-entry, when the group, organization or team is under the supervision of an adult affiliated with the organization and when the child has parental or legal guardian consent to travel. For purposes of this paragraph, an adult is considered to be a person who is age 19 or older. The following requirements will apply:

(*1*) The group, organization, or team must provide to CBP upon crossing the border, on organizational letterhead:

(*i*) The name of the group, organization or team, and the name of the supervising adult;

(*ii*) A trip itinerary, including the stated purpose of the trip, the location of the destination, and the length of stay;

(*iii*) A list of the children on the trip;

(*iv*) For each child, the primary address, primary phone number, date of birth, place of birth, and name of a parent or legal guardian.

(*2*) The adult leading the group, organization, or team must demonstrate parental or legal guardian consent by certifying in the writing submitted in paragraph (a)(1)(v)(B)(1) of this section that he or she has obtained for each child the consent of at least one parent or legal guardian.

(*3*) The inspection procedure described in this paragraph is limited to members of the group, organization, or team who are under age 19. Other members of the group, organization, or team must comply with other applicable document and/or inspection requirements found in this part or parts 211 or 235 of this subchapter.

(2) *Citizens of the British Overseas Territory of Bermuda.* A visa is generally not required for Citizens of the British Overseas Territory of Bermuda, except those Bermudians that fall under nonimmigrant visa categories E, K, S, or V as provided in paragraphs (h), (l), and (m) of this section and 22 CFR 41.2. A passport is required for Citizens of the British Overseas Territory of Bermuda arriving in the United States.

(3) *Bahamian nationals or British subjects resident in the Bahamas.* A passport is required. A visa required of such an alien unless, prior to or at the time of embarkation for the United States on a vessel or aircraft, the alien satisfied the examining U.S. immigration officer at the Bahamas, that he or she is clearly and beyond a doubt entitled to admission, under section 212(a) of the Immigration and Nationality Act, in all other respects.

(4) *British subjects resident in the Cayman Islands or in the Turks and Caicos Islands.* A passport is required. A visa is required of such an alien unless he or she arrives directly from the Cayman Islands or the Turks and Caicos Islands and presents a current certificate from the Clerk of Court of the Cayman Islands or the Turks and Caicos Islands indicating no criminal record.

(b) *Nationals of the British Virgin Islands.* A visa is not required of a national of the British Virgin Islands who has his or her residence in the British Virgin Islands, if:

(1) The alien is seeking admission solely to visit the Virgin Islands of the United States; or

(2) At the time of embarking on an aircraft at St. Thomas, U.S. Virgin Islands, the alien meets each of the following requirements:

(i) The alien is traveling to any other part of the United States by aircraft as a nonimmigrant visitor for business or pleasure (as described in section 101(a)(15)(B) of the Act);

(ii) The alien satisfies the examining U.S. immigration officer at the port-of-entry that he or she is clearly and beyond doubt entitled to admission in all other respects; and

(iii) The alien presents a current certificate issued by the Royal Virgin Islands Police Force indicating that he or she has no criminal record.

(c) *Mexican nationals.* (1) A visa and a passport are not required of a Mexican national who:

(i) Is applying for admission as a temporary visitor for business or pleasure from Mexico at a land port-of-entry, or arriving by pleasure vessel or ferry, if the national is in possession of a Form DSP–150, B–1/B–2 Visa and Border Crossing Card issued by the Department of State, containing a machine-readable biometric identifier; or.

(ii) Is applying for admission from contiguous territory or adjacent islands at a land or sea port-of-entry, if the national is a member of the Texas Band of Kickapoo Indians or Kickapoo Tribe of Oklahoma who is in possession of a Form I–872 American Indian Card.

(2) A visa shall not be required of a Mexican national who:

(i) Is in possession of a Form DSP–150, with a biometric identifier, issued by the DOS, and a passport, and is applying for admission as a temporary visitor for business or pleasure from other than contiguous territory;

(ii) Is a crew member employed on an aircraft belonging to a Mexican company owned carrier authorized to engage in commercial transportation into the United States; or

(iii) Bears a Mexican diplomatic or official passport and who is a military or civilian official of the Federal Government of Mexico entering the United States for 6 months or less for a purpose other than on assignment as a permanent employee to an office of the Mexican Federal Government in the United States, and the official's spouse or any of the official's dependent family members under 19 years of age, bearing diplomatic or official passports, who are in the actual company of such official at the time of admission into the United States. This provision does not apply to the spouse or any of the official's family members classifiable under section 101(a)(15)(F) or (M) of the Act.

(3) A Mexican national who presents a BCC at a POE must present the DOS-issued DSP–150 containing a machine-readable biometric identifier. The alien will not be permitted to cross the border into the United States unless the biometric identifier contained on the card matches the appropriate biometric characteristic of the alien.

(4) Mexican nationals presenting a combination B–1/B–2 nonimmigrant visa and border crossing card (or similar stamp in a passport), issued by DOS prior to April 1, 1998, that does not contain a machine-readable biometric identifier, may be admitted on the basis of the nonimmigrant visa only, provided it has not expired and the alien remains admissible. A passport is also required.

(5) *Aliens entering pursuant to International Boundary and Water Commission Treaty.* A visa and a passport are not required of an alien employed either directly or indirectly on the construction, operation, or maintenance of works in the United States undertaken in accordance with the treaty concluded on February 3, 1944, between the United States and Mexico regarding the functions of the International Boundary and Water Commission, and entering the United States temporarily in connection with such employment.

(d) *Citizens of the Freely Associated States, formerly Trust Territory of the Pacific Islands.* Citizens of the Republic of the Marshall Islands and the Federated States of Micronesia may enter into, lawfully engage in employment, and establish residence in the United States and its territories and possessions without regard to paragraphs (14), (20) and (26) of section 212(a) of the Act pursuant to the terms of Pub. L. 99–239. Pending issuance by the aforementioned governments of travel documents to eligible citizens, travel documents previously issued by the Trust Territory of the Pacific Islands will continue to be accepted for purposes of identification and to establish eligibility for admission into the United States, its territories and possessions.

(e) *Aliens entering Guam pursuant to section 14 of Pub. L. 99–396, "Omnibus Territories Act."* (1) Until November 28, 2009, a visa is not required of an alien who is a citizen of a country enumerated in paragraph (e)(3) of this section who:

(i) Is classifiable as a vistor for business or pleasure;

(ii) Is solely entering and staying on Guam for a period not to exceed fifteen days;

(iii) Is in possession of a round-trip nonrefundable and nontransferable transportation ticket bearing a confirmed departure date not exceeding fifteen days from the date of admission to Guam;

(iv) Is in possession of a completed and signed Visa Waiver Information Form (Form I–736);

(v) Waives any right to review or appeal the immigration officer's determination of admissibility at the port of entry at Guam; and

(vi) Waives any right to contest any action for deportation, other than on the basis of a request for asylum.

(2) An alien is eligible for the waiver provision if all of the eligibility criteria in paragraph (e)(1) of this section have been met prior to embarkation and the alien is a citizen of a country that:

(i) Has a visa refusal rate of 16.9% or less, or a country whose visa refusal rate exceeds 16.9% and has an established preinspection or preclearance program, pursuant to a bilateral agreement with the United States under which its citizens traveling to Guam without a valid United States visa are inspected by the Immigration and Naturalization Service prior to departure from that country;

(ii) Is within geographical proximity to Guam, unless the country has a substantial volume of nonimmigrant admissions to Guam as determined by the Commissioner and extends reciprocal privileges to citizens of the United States;

(iii) Is not designated by the Department of State as being of special humanitarian concern; and

(iv) Poses no threat to the welfare, safety or security of the United States, its territories, or commonwealths.

Any potential threats to the welfare, safety, or security of the United States, its territories, or commonwealths will be dealt with on a country by country basis, and a determination by the Commissioner of the Immigration and Naturalization Service that a threat exists will result in the immediate deletion of that country from the listing in paragraph (e)(3) of this section.

(3)(i) The following geographic areas meet the eligibility criteria as stated in paragraph (e)(2) of this section: Australia, Brunei, Indonesia, Japan, Malaysia, Nauru, New Zealand, Papua New Guinea, Republic of Korea, Singapore, Solomon Islands, Taiwan (residents thereof who begin their travel in Taiwan and who travel on direct flights from Taiwan to Guam without an intermediate layover or stop except that the flights may stop in a territory of the United States enroute), the United Kingdom (including the citizens of the colony of Hong Kong), Vanuatu, and Western Samoa. The provision that flights transporting residents of Taiwan to Guam may stop at a territory of the United States enroute may be rescinded whenever the number of inadmissible passengers arriving in Guam who have transited a territory of the United States enroute to Guam exceeds 20 percent of all the inadmissible passengers arriving in Guam within any consecutive two-month period. Such rescission will be published in the FEDERAL REGISTER.

(ii) For the purposes of this section, the term *citizen of a country* as used in 8 CFR 212.1(e)(1) when applied to Taiwan refers only to residents of Taiwan who are in possession of Taiwan National Identity Cards and a valid Taiwan passport with a valid re-entry permit issued by the Taiwan Ministry of Foreign Affairs. It does not refer to any other holder of a Taiwan passport or a passport issued by the People's Republic of China.

(4) Admission under this section renders an alien ineligible for:

(i) Adjustment of status to that of a temporary resident or, except as provided by section 245(i) of the Act or as an immediate relative as defined in section 201(b) of the Act, to that of a lawful permanent resident.

(ii) Change of nonimmigrant status; or

(iii) Extension of stay.

(5) A transportation line bringing any alien to Guam pursuant to this section shall:

(i) Enter into a contract on Form I–760, made by the Commissioner of the Immigration and Naturalization Service in behalf of the government;

(ii) Transport only an alien who is a citizen and in possession of a valid passport of a country enumerated in paragraph (e)(3) of this section;

(iii) Transport only an alien in possession of a round-trip, nontransferable transportation ticket:

(A) Bearing a confirmed departure date not exceeding fifteen days from the date of admission to Guam,

(B) Valid for a period of not less than one year,

(C) Nonrefundable except in the country in which issued or in the country of the alien's nationality or residence,

(D) Issued by a carrier which has entered into an agreement described in part (5)(i) of this section, and

(E) Which the carrier will unconditionally honor when presented for return passage; and

(iv) Transport only an alien in possession of a completed and signed Visa Waiver Information Form I–736.

(f) *Direct transits.* (1)–(2) [Reserved]

(3) *Foreign government officials in transit.* If an alien is of the class described in section 212(d)(8) of the Act, only a

valid unexpired visa and a travel document valid for entry into a foreign country for at least 30 days from the date of admission to the United States are required.

(g) *Unforeseen emergency.* A nonimmigrant seeking admission to the United States must present an unexpired visa and passport valid for the amount of time set forth in section 212(a)(7)(B)(i) of the Act, 8 U.S.C. 1182(a)(7)(B)(i), or a valid biometric border crossing card issued by the DOS on Form DSP–150, at the time of application for admission, unless the nonimmigrant satisfies the requirements described in one or more of paragraphs (a) through (f) or (i), (o), or (p) of this section. Upon a nonimmigrant's application on Form I–193, or successor form, "Application for Waiver of Passport and/or Visa," a district director may, in the exercise of its discretion, on a case-by-case basis, waive either or both of the documentary requirements of section 212(a)(7)(B)(i) if satisfied that the nonimmigrant cannot present the required documents because of an unforeseen emergency. The district director may at any time revoke a waiver previously authorized pursuant to this paragraph and notify the nonimmigrant in writing to that effect.

(h) *Nonimmigrant spouses, fiancées, fiancés, and children of U.S. citizens.* Notwithstanding any of the provisions of this part, an alien seeking admission as a spouse, fiancée, fiancé, or child of a U.S. citizen, or as a child of the spouse, fiané, or finacée of a U.S. citizen, pursuant to section 101(a)(15)(K) of the Act shall be in possession of an unexpired nonimmigrant visa issued by an American consular officer classifying the alien under that section, or be inadmissible under section 212(a)(7)(B) of the Act.

(i) *Visa Waiver Pilot Program.* A visa is not required of any alien who is eligible to apply for admission to the United States as a Visa Waiver Pilot Program applicant pursuant to the provisions of section 217 of the Act and part 217 of this chapter if such alien is a national of a country designated under the Visa Waiver Pilot Program, who seeks admission to the United States for a period of 90 days or less as a visitor for business or pleasure.

(j) *Officers authorized to act upon recommendations of United States consular officers for waiver of visa and passport requirements.* All district directors, the officers in charge are authorized to act upon recommendations made by United States consular officers or by officers of the Visa Office, Department of State, pursuant to the provisions of 22 CFR 41.7 for waiver of visa and passport requirements under the provisions of section 212(d)(4)(A) of the Act. The District Director at Washington, DC, has jurisdiction in such cases recommended to the Service at the seat of Government level by the Department of State. Neither an application nor fee are required if the concurrence in a passport or visa waiver is requested by a U.S. consular officer or by an officer of the Visa Office. The district director or the Deputy Commissioner, may at any time revoke a waiver previously authorized pursuant to this paragraph and notify the nonimmigrant alien in writing to that effect.

(k) *Cancellation of nonimmigrant visas by immigration officers.* Upon receipt of advice from the Department of State that a nonimmigrant visa has been revoked or invalidated, and request by that Department for such action, immigration officers shall place an appropriate endorsement thereon.

(l) *Treaty traders and investors.* Notwithstanding any of the provisions of this part, an alien seeking admission as a treaty trader or investor under the provisions of Chapter 16 of the North American Free Trade Agreement (NAFTA) pursuant to section 101(a)(15)(E) of the Act, shall be in possession of a nonimmigrant visa issued by an American consular officer classifying the alien under that section.

(m) *Aliens in S classification.* Notwithstanding any of the provisions of this part, an alien seeking admission pursuant to section 101(a)(15)(S) of the Act must be in possession of appropriate documents issued by a United States consular officer classifying the alien under that section.

(n) [Reserved]

(o) *Alien in T–2 through T–6 classification.* USCIS may apply paragraph (g) of this section to individuals seeking T–2,

T–3, T–4, T–5, or T–6 nonimmigrant status upon request by the applicant.

(Secs. 103, 104, 212 of the Immigration and Nationality Act, as amended (8 U.S.C. 1103, 1104, 1132))

(p) *Alien in U–1 through U–5 classification.* Individuals seeking U–1 through U–5 nonimmigrant status may avail themselves of the provisions of paragraph (g) of this section, except that the authority to waive documentary requirements resides with the director of the USCIS office having jurisdiction over the adjudication of Form I–918, "Petition for U Nonimmigrant Status."

(q) *Aliens admissible under the Guam-CNMI Visa Waiver Program*—(1) *Eligibility for Program.* In accordance with Public Law 110–229, beginning November 28, 2009, the Secretary, in consultation with the Secretaries of the Departments of Interior and State, may waive the visa requirement in the case of a nonimmigrant alien who seeks admission to Guam or to the Commonwealth of the Northern Mariana Islands (CNMI) under the Guam-CNMI Visa Waiver Program. To be admissible under the Guam-CNMI Visa Waiver Program, prior to embarking on a carrier for travel to Guam or the CNMI, each nonimmigrant alien must:

(i) Be a national of a country or geographic area listed in paragraph (q)(2) of this section;

(ii) Be classifiable as a visitor for business or pleasure;

(iii) Be solely entering and staying on Guam or the CNMI for a period not to exceed forty-five days;

(iv) Be in possession of a round trip ticket that is nonrefundable and nontransferable and bears a confirmed departure date not exceeding forty-five days from the date of admission to Guam or the CNMI. "Round trip ticket" includes any return trip transportation ticket issued by a participating carrier, electronic ticket record, airline employee passes indicating return passage, individual vouchers for return passage, group vouchers for return passage for charter flights, or military travel orders which include military dependents for return to duty stations outside the United States on U.S. military flights;

(v) Be in possession of a completed and signed Guam-CNMI Visa Waiver Information Form (CBP Form I–736);

(vi) Be in possession of a completed and signed I–94 (see §1.4), Arrival-Departure Record (CBP Form I–94);

(vii) Be in possession of a valid unexpired ICAO compliant, machine readable passport issued by a country that meets the eligibility requirements of paragraph (q)(2) of this section;

(viii) Have not previously violated the terms of any prior admissions. Prior admissions include those under the Guam-CNMI Visa Waiver Program, the prior Guam Visa Waiver Program, the Visa Waiver Program as described in section 217(a) of the Act and admissions pursuant to any immigrant or nonimmigrant visa;

(ix) Waive any right to review or appeal an immigration officer's determination of admissibility at the port of entry into Guam or the CNMI;

(x) Waive any right to contest any action for deportation or removal, other than on the basis of: An application for withholding of removal under section 241(b)(3) of the INA; withholding or deferral of removal under the regulations implementing Article 3 of the United Nations Convention Against Torture and Other Cruel, Inhuman or Degrading Treatment or Punishment; or, an application for asylum if permitted under section 208 of the Act; and

(xi) If a resident of Taiwan, possess a Taiwan National Identity Card and a valid Taiwan passport with a valid reentry permit issued by the Taiwan Ministry of Foreign Affairs.

(2) *Program Countries and Geographic Areas*—(i) *General Eligibility Criteria.* (A) A country or geographic area may not participate in the Guam-CNMI Visa Waiver Program if the country or geographic area poses a threat to the welfare, safety or security of the United States, its territories, or commonwealths;

(B) A country or geographic area may not participate in the Guam-CNMI Visa Waiver Program if it has been designated a Country of Particular Concern under the International Religious Freedom Act of 1998 by the Department of State, or identified by the Department of State as a source country of refugees designated of special humanitarian concern to the United States;

(C) A country or geographic area may not participate in the Guam-CNMI Visa Waiver Program if that country, not later than three weeks after the issuance of a final order of removal, does not accept for repatriation any citizen, former citizen, or national of the country against whom a final executable order of removal is issued. Nothing in this subparagraph creates any duty for the United States or any right for any alien with respect to removal or release. Nothing in this subparagraph gives rise to any cause of action or claim under this paragraph or any other law against any official of the United States or of any State to compel the release, removal or reconsideration for release or removal of any alien.

(D) DHS may make a determination regarding a country's eligibility based on other factors including, but not limited to, rate of refusal for nonimmigrant visas, rate of overstays, cooperation in information exchange with the United States, electronic travel authorizations, and any other factors deemed relevant by DHS.

(ii) *Eligible Countries and Geographic Areas.* Nationals of the following countries are eligible to participate in the Guam-CNMI Visa Waiver Program for purposes of admission to both Guam and the CNMI: Australia, Brunei, Japan, Malaysia, Nauru, New Zealand, Papua New Guinea, Republic of Korea, Singapore, and the United Kingdom. Travelers with a connection to one of the following geographic areas—the Hong Kong Special Administrative Region (Hong Kong) or Taiwan—may also be eligible to participate in the Guam-CNMI Visa Waiver Program for purposes of admission to both Guam and the CNMI, *see* paragraphs (q)(2)(ii)(A) and (q)(2)(ii)(B) respectively.

(A) *Hong Kong Special Administrative Region (Hong Kong).* To be eligible to participate in the program as a result of a connection to Hong Kong, the following documentation is required: A Hong Kong Special Administrative Region (SAR) passport with a Hong Kong identification card; or a British National (Overseas) (BN(O)) passport with a Hong Kong identification card.

(B) *Taiwan.* To be eligible to participate in the program as a result of a connection to Taiwan, one must be a resident of Taiwan who begins his or her travel in Taiwan and who travels on direct flights from Taiwan to Guam or the CNMI without an intermediate layover or stop, except that the flights may stop in a territory of the United States en route.

(iii) *Significant Economic Benefit Criteria.* If, in addition to the considerations enumerated under paragraph (q)(2)(i) of this section, DHS determines that the CNMI has received a significant economic benefit from the number of visitors for pleasure from particular countries during the period of May 8, 2007 through May 8, 2008, those countries are eligible to participate in the Guam-CNMI Visa Waiver Program unless the Secretary of Homeland Security determines that such country's inclusion in the Guam-CNMI Visa Waiver Program would represent a threat to the welfare, safety, or security of the United States and its territories.

(iv) *Additional Eligible Countries or Geographic Areas Based on Significant Economic Benefit.* [Reserved]

(3) *Suspension of Program Countries or Geographic Areas.* (i) Suspension of a country or geographic area from the Guam-CNMI Visa Waiver Program may be made on a country-by-country basis for good cause including, but not limited to if: The admissions of visitors from a country have resulted in an unacceptable number of visitors from a country remaining unlawfully in Guam or the CNMI, unlawfully obtaining entry to other parts of the United States, or seeking withholding of removal or seeking asylum; or that visitors from a country pose a risk to law enforcement or security interests, including the enforcement of immigration laws of Guam, the CNMI, or the United States.

(ii) A country or geographic area may be suspended from the Guam-CNMI Visa Waiver Program if that country or geographic area is designated as a Country of Particular Concern under the International Religious Freedom Act of 1998 by the Department of State, or identified by the Department of State as a source country of refugees designated of special humanitarian concern to the United States, pending an evaluation and determination by the Secretary.

(iii) A country or geographic area may be suspended from the Guam-CNMI Visa Waiver Program by the Secretary of Homeland Security, in consultation with the Secretary of the Interior and the Secretary of State, based on the evaluation of all factors the Secretary deems relevant including, but not limited to, electronic travel authorization, procedures for reporting lost and stolen passports, repatriation of aliens, rates of refusal for nonimmigrant visitor visas, overstays, exit systems and information exchange.

(4) Admission under this section renders an alien ineligible for:

(i) Adjustment of status to that of a temporary resident or, except as provided by section 245(i) of the Act or as an immediate relative as defined in section 201(b) of the Act, to that of a lawful permanent resident.

(ii) Change of nonimmigrant status; or

(iii) Extension of stay.

(5) *Requirements for transportation lines.* A transportation line bringing any alien to Guam or the CNMI pursuant to this section must:

(i) Enter into a contract on CBP Form I–760, made by the Commissioner of Customs and Border Protection on behalf of the government;

(ii) Transport an alien who is a citizen or national and in possession of a valid unexpired ICAO compliant, machine readable passport of a country enumerated in paragraph (q)(2) of this section;

(iii) Transport an alien only if the alien is in possession of a round trip ticket as defined in paragraph (q)(1)(iv) of this section bearing a confirmed departure date not exceeding forty-five days from the date of admission to Guam or the CNMI which the carrier will unconditionally honor when presented for return passage. This ticket must be:

(A) Valid for a period of not less than one year,

(B) Nonrefundable except in the country in which issued or in the country of the alien's nationality or residence, and

(C) Issued by a carrier which has entered into an agreement described in paragraph (q)(5) of this section.

(iv) Transport an alien in possession of a completed and signed Guam-CNMI Visa Waiver Information Form (CBP Form I–736), and

(v) Transport an alien in possession of completed I–94, Arrival-Departure Record (CBP Form I–94).

(6) *Bonding.* The Secretary may require a bond on behalf of an alien seeking admission under the Guam-CNMI Visa Waiver Program, in addition to the requirements enumerated in this section, when the Secretary deems it appropriate. Such bonds may be required of an individual alien or of an identified subset of participants.

(7) *Maintenance of status*—(i) *Satisfactory departure.* If an emergency prevents an alien admitted under the Guam-CNMI Visa Waiver Program, as set forth in this paragraph (q), from departing from Guam or the CNMI within his or her period of authorized stay, an immigration officer having jurisdiction over the place of the alien's temporary stay may, in his or her discretion, grant a period of satisfactory departure not to exceed 15 days. If departure is accomplished during that period, the alien is to be regarded as having satisfactorily accomplished the visit without overstaying the allotted time.

(8) *Inadmissibility and Deportability*—(i) *Determinations of inadmissibility.* (A) An alien who applies for admission under the provisions of the Guam-CNMI Visa Waiver Program, who is determined by an immigration officer to be inadmissible to Guam or the CNMI under one or more of the grounds of inadmissibility listed in section 212 of the Act (other than for lack of a visa), or who is in possession of and presents fraudulent or counterfeit travel documents, will be refused admission into Guam or the CNMI and removed. Such refusal and removal shall be effected without referral of the alien to an immigration judge for further inquiry, examination, or hearing, except that an alien who presents himself or herself as an applicant for admission to Guam under the Guam-CNMI Visa Waiver Program, who applies for asylum, withholding of removal under section 241(b)(3) of the INA or withholding or

deferral of removal under the regulations implementing Article 3 of the United Nations Convention Against Torture and Other Cruel, Inhuman or Degrading Treatment or Punishment must be issued a Form I–863, Notice of Referral to Immigration Judge, for a proceeding in accordance with 8 CFR 208.2(c)(1) and (2). The provisions of 8 CFR subpart 208 subpart A shall not apply to an alien present or arriving in the CNMI seeking to apply for asylum prior to January 1, 2015. No application for asylum may be filed pursuant to section 208 of the Act by an alien present or arriving in the CNMI prior to January 1, 2015; however, aliens physically present in the CNMI during the transition period who express a fear of persecution or torture only may establish eligibility for withholding of removal pursuant to INA 241(b)(3) or pursuant to the regulations implementing Article 3 of the United Nations Convention Against Torture and Other Cruel, Inhuman or Degrading Treatment or Punishment.

(B) The removal of an alien under this section may be deferred if the alien is paroled into the custody of a Federal, State, or local law enforcement agency for criminal prosecution or punishment. This section in no way diminishes the discretionary authority of the Secretary enumerated in section 212(d) of the Act.

(C) Refusal of admission under this paragraph shall not constitute removal for purposes of the Act.

(ii) *Determination of deportability.* (A) An alien who has been admitted to either Guam or the CNMI under the provisions of this section who is determined by an immigration officer to be deportable from either Guam or the CNMI under one or more of the grounds of deportability listed in section 237 of the Act, shall be removed from either Guam or the CNMI to his or her country of nationality or last residence. Such removal will be determined by DHS authority that has jurisdiction over the place where the alien is found, and will be effected without referral of the alien to an immigration judge for a determination of deportability, except that an alien admitted to Guam under the Guam-CNMI Visa Waiver Program who applies for asylum or other form of protection from persecution or torture must be issued a Form I–863 for a proceeding in accordance with 8 CFR 208.2(c)(1) and (2). The provisions of 8 CFR part 208 subpart A shall not apply to an alien present or arriving in the CNMI seeking to apply for asylum prior to January 1, 2015. No application for asylum may be filed pursuant to section 208 of the INA by an alien present or arriving in the CNMI prior to January 1, 2015; however, aliens physically present or arriving in the CNMI prior to January 1, 2015, may apply for withholding of removal under section 241(b)(3) of the Act and withholding and deferral of removal under the regulations implementing Article 3 of the United Nations Convention Against Torture, Inhuman or Degrading Treatment or Punishment.

(B) Removal by DHS under paragraph (b)(1) of this section is equivalent in all respects and has the same consequences as removal after proceedings conducted under section 240 of the Act.

(iii) *Removal of inadmissible aliens who arrived by air or sea.* Removal of an alien from Guam or the CNMI under this section may be effected using the return portion of the round trip passage presented by the alien at the time of entry to Guam and the CNMI. Such removal shall be on the first available means of transportation to the alien's point of embarkation to Guam or the CNMI. Nothing in this part absolves the carrier of the responsibility to remove any inadmissible or deportable alien at carrier expense, as provided in the carrier agreement.

[26 FR 12066, Dec. 16, 1961]

EDITORIAL NOTE: For FEDERAL REGISTER citations affecting §212.1, see the List of CFR Sections Affected, which appears in the Finding Aids section of the printed volume and at *www.govinfo.gov*.

§212.2 Consent to reapply for admission after deportation, removal or departure at Government expense.

(a) *Evidence.* Any alien who has been deported or removed from the United States is inadmissible to the United States unless the alien has remained outside of the United States for five consecutive years since the date of deportation or removal. If the alien has been convicted of an aggravated felony, he or she must remain outside of the United States for twenty consecutive years from the deportation date before he or she is eligible to re-enter the United States. Any alien who has been deported or removed from the United States and is applying for a visa, admission to the United States, or adjustment of status, must present proof that he or she has remained outside of the United States for the time period required for re-entry after deportation or removal. The examining consular or immigration officer must be satisfied that since the alien's deportation or removal, the alien has remained outside the United States for more than five consecutive years, or twenty consecutive years in the case of an alien convicted of an aggravated felony as defined in section 101(a)(43) of the Act. Any alien who does not satisfactorily present proof of absence from the United States for more than five consecutive years, or twenty consecutive years in the case of an alien convicted of an aggravated felony, to the consular or immigration officer, and any alien who is seeking to enter the United States prior to the completion of the requisite five- or twenty-year absence, must apply for permission to reapply for admission to the United States as provided under this part. A temporary stay in the United States under section 212(d)(3) of the Act does not interrupt the five or twenty consecutive year absence requirement.

(b) *Alien applying to consular officer for nonimmigrant visa or nonresident alien border crossing card.* (1) An alien who is applying to a consular officer for a nonimmigrant visa or a nonresident alien border crossing card, must request permission to reapply for admission to the United States if five years, or twenty years if the alien's deportation was based upon a conviction for an aggravated felony, have not elapsed since the date of deportation or removal. This permission shall be requested in the manner prescribed through the consular officer, and may be granted only in accordance with sections 212(a)(9)(A) and 212(d)(3)(A) of the Act and 8 CFR 212.4. However, the alien may apply for such permission by submitting an application on the form designated by USCIS with the fee prescribed in 8 CFR 103.7(b)(1), in accordance with the form instructions, to the consular officer if that officer is willing to accept the application, and recommends to the district director that the alien be permitted to apply.

(2) The consular officer shall forward the application to the district director with jurisdiction over the place where the deportation or removal proceedings were held.

(c) *Special provisions for an applicant for nonimmigrant visa under section 101(a)(15)(K) of the Act.* (1) An applicant for a nonimmigrant visa under section 101(a)(15)(K) must:

(i) Be the beneficiary of a valid visa petition approved by the Service; and

(ii) File the application on the form designated by USCIS with the fee prescribed in 8 CFR 103.7(b)(1), in accordance with the form instructions with the consular officer for permission to reapply for admission to the United States after deportation or removal.

(2) The consular officer must forward the application to the designated USCIS office. If the alien is ineligible on grounds which, upon the applicant's marriage to the United States citizen petitioner, may be waived under section 212 (g), (h), or (i) of the Act, the consular officer must also forward a recommendation as to whether the waiver should be granted.

(d) *Applicant for immigrant visa.* Except as provided in paragraph (g)(2) of this section, an applicant for an immigrant visa who is not physically present in the United States and who requires permission to reapply must file the waiver request on the form designated by USCIS. Except as provided in paragraph (g)(2) of this section, if the applicant also requires a waiver under section 212(g), (h), or (i) of the Act, he or she must file both waiver requests simultaneously on the forms designated by USCIS with the fees prescribed in 8 CFR 103.7(b)(1) and in accordance with the form instructions.

(e) *Applicant for adjustment of status.* An applicant for adjustment of status under section 245 of the Act and part 245 of this chapter must request permission to reapply for entry in conjunction with his or her application for adjustment of status. This request is made by filing the application on the form designated by USCIS. If the application under section 245 of the Act has been initiated, renewed, or is pending in a proceeding before an immigration judge, the district director must refer the application to the immigration judge for adjudication.

(f) *Applicant for admission at port of entry.* An alien may request permission at a port of entry to reapply for admission to the United States within 5 years of the deportation or removal, or 20 years in the case of an alien deported, or removed 2 or more times, or at any time after deportation or removal in the case of an alien convicted of an aggravated felony. The alien must file the , where required, with the DHS officer having jurisdiction over the port of entry.

(g) *Other applicants.* (1) Any applicant for permission to reapply for admission under circumstances other than those described in paragraphs (b) through (f) of this section must apply on the form designated by USCIS with the fee prescribed in 8 CFR 103.7(b)(1) and in accordance with the form instructions.

(2) An alien who is an applicant for parole authorization under 8 CFR 245.15(t)(2) or 8 CFR 245.13(k)(2) and requires consent to reapply for admission after deportation, removal, or departure at Government expense, or a waiver under section 212(g), 212(h), or 212(i) of the Act, must file the requisite waiver form concurrently with the parole request.

(h) *Decision.* An applicant who has submitted a request for consent to reapply for admission after deportation or removal must be notified of the decision. If the application is denied, the applicant must be notified of the reasons for the denial and of his or her right to appeal as provided in part 103 of this chapter. Except in the case of an applicant seeking to be granted advance permission to reapply for admission prior to his or her departure from the United States, the denial of the application shall be without prejudice to the renewal of the application in the course of proceedings before an immigration judge under section 242 of the Act and this chapter.

(i) *Retroactive approval.* (1) If the alien filed the application when seeking admission at a port of entry, the approval of the application shall be retroactive to either:

(i) The date on which the alien embarked or reembarked at a place outside the United States; or

(ii) The date on which the alien attempted to be admitted from foreign contiguous territory.

(2) If the alien filed Form I–212 in conjunction with an application for adjustment of status under section 245 of the Act, the approval of the application shall be retroactive to the date on which the alien embarked or reembarked at a place outside the United States.

(j) *Advance approval.* An alien whose departure will execute an order of deportation shall receive a conditional approval depending upon his or her satisfactory departure. However, the grant of permission to reapply does not waive inadmissibility under section 212(a)(9)(A) of the Act resulting from exclusion, deportation, or removal proceedings which are instituted subsequent to the date permission to reapply is granted.

[56 FR 23212, May 21, 1991, as amended at 64 FR 25766, May 12, 1999; 65 FR 15854, Mar. 24, 2000; 74 FR 26937, June 5, 2009; 76 FR 53787, Aug. 29, 2011]

§212.3 Application for the exercise of discretion under section 212(c).

(a) *Jurisdiction.* An application for the exercise of discretion under section 212(c) of the Act must be submitted on the form designated by USCIS with the fee prescribed in 8 CFR 103.7(b)(1) and in accordance with the form instructions. If the application is made in the course of proceedings under sections 235, 236, or 242 of the Act, the application shall be made to the Immigration Court.

(b) *Filing of application.* The application may be filed prior to, at the time of, or at any time after the applicant's departure from or arrival into the United States. All material facts and/or circumstances which the applicant knows or believes apply to the grounds of excludability or deportability must be described. The applicant must also submit all available documentation relating to such grounds.

(c) *Decision of the District Director.* A district director may grant or deny an application for advance permission to return to an unrelinquished domicile under section 212(c) of the Act, in the exercise of discretion, unless otherwise prohibited by paragraph (f) of this section. The applicant shall be notified of the decision and, if the application is denied, of the reason(s) for denial. No appeal shall lie from denial of the application, but the application may be renewed before an Immigration Judge as provided in paragraph (e) of this section.

(d) *Validity.* Once an application is approved, that approval is valid indefinitely. However, the approval covers only those specific grounds of excludability or deportability that were described in the application. An application who failed to describe any other grounds of excludability or deportability, or failed to disclose material facts existing at the time of the approval of the application, remains excludable or deportable under the previously unidentified grounds. If at a later date, the applicant becomes subject to exclusion or deportation based upon these previously unidentified grounds or upon new ground(s), a new application must be filed.

(e) *Filing or renewal of applications before an Immigration Judge.* (1) An application for the exercise of discretion under section 212(c) of the Act may be renewed or submitted in proceedings before an Immigration Judge under sections 235, 236, or 242 of the Act, and under this chapter. Such application shall be adjudicated by the Immigration Judge, without regard to whether the applicant previously has made application to the district director.

(2) The Immigration Judge may grant or deny an application for advance permission to return to an unrelinquished domicile under section 212(c) of the Act, in the exercise of discretion, unless otherwise prohibited by paragraph (f) of this section.

(3) An alien otherwise entitled to appeal to the Board of Immigration Appeals may appeal the denial by the Immigration Judge of this application in accordance with the provisions of § 3.36 of this chapter.

(f) Limitations on discretion to grant an application under section 212(c) of the Act. An application for advance permission to enter under section 212 of the Act shall be denied if:

(1) The alien has not been lawfully admitted for permanent residence;

(2) The alien has not maintained lawful domicile in the United States, as either a lawful permanent resident or a lawful temporary resident pursuant to section 245A or section 210 of the Act, for at least seven consecutive years immediately preceding the filing of the application;

(3) The alien is subject to exclusion from the United States under paragraphs (3)(A), (3)(B), (3)(C), or (3)(E) of section 212(a) of the Act;

(4) The alien has been convicted of an aggravated felony, as defined by section 101(a)(43) of the Act, and has served a term of imprisonment of at least five years for such conviction; or

(5) The alien applies for relief under section 212(c) within five years of the barring act as enumerated in one or more sections of section 242B(e) (1) through (4) of the Act.

(g) *Relief for certain aliens who were in deportation proceedings before April 24, 1996.* Section 440(d) of Antiterrorism and Effective Death Penalty Act of 1996 (AEDPA) shall not apply to any applicant for relief under this section whose deportation proceedings were commenced before the Immigration Court before April 24, 1996.

[56 FR 50034, Oct. 3, 1991, as amended at 60 FR 34090, June 30, 1995; 61 FR 59825, Nov. 25, 1996; 66 FR 6446, Jan. 22, 2001; 74 FR 26938, June 5, 2009; 76 FR 53787, Aug. 29, 2011]

§ 212.4 Applications for the exercise of discretion under section 212(d)(1) and 212(d)(3).

(a) *Applications under section 212(d)(3)(A)*—(1) *General.* District directors and officers in charge outside the United States in the districts of Bangkok, Thailand; Mexico City, Mexico; and Rome, Italy are authorized to act upon recommendations made by consular officers for the exercise of discretion under section 212(d)(3)(A) of the Act. The District Director, Washington, DC, has jurisdiction in such cases recommended to the Service at the seat-of-government level by the Department of State. When a consular officer or other State Department official recommends that the benefits of section 212(d)(3)(A) of the Act be accorded an alien, neither an application nor fee shall be required. The recommendation shall specify:

(i) The reasons for inadmissibility and each section of law under which the alien is inadmissible;

(ii) Each intended date of arrival;

(iii) The length of each proposed stay in the United States;

(iv) The purpose of each stay;

(v) The number of entries which the alien intends to make; and

(vi) The justification for exercising the authority contained in section 212(d)(3) of the Act.

If the alien desires to make multiple entries and the consular officer or other State Department official believes that the circumstances justify the issuance of a visa valid for multiple entries rather than for a specified number of entries, and recommends that the alien be accorded an authorization valid for multiple entries, the information required by items (ii) and (iii) shall be furnished only with respect to the initial entry. Item (ii) does not apply to a bona fide crewman. The consular officer or other State Department official shall be notified of the decision on his recommendation. No appeal by the alien shall lie from an adverse decision made by a Service officer on the recommendation of a consular officer or other State Department official.

(2) *Authority of consular officers to approve section 212(d)(3)(A) recommendations pertaining to aliens inadmissible under section 212(a)(28)(C).* In certain categories of visa cases defined by the Secretary of State, United States consular officers assigned to visa-issuing posts abroad may, on behalf of the Attorney General pursuant to section 212(d)(3)(A) of the Act, approve a recommendation by another consular officer that an alien be admitted temporarily despite visa ineligibility solely because the alien is of the class of aliens defined at section 212(a)(28)(C) of the Act, as a result of presumed or actual membership in, or affiliation with, an organization described in that section. Authorizations for temporary admission granted by consular officers shall be subject to the terms specified in §212.4(c) of this chapter. Any recommendation which is not clearly approvable shall, and any recommendation may, be presented to the appropriate official of the Immigration and Naturalization Service for a determination.

(b) *Applications under section 212(d)(3)(B).* An application for the exercise of discretion under section 212(d)(3)(B) of the Act shall be submitted on the form designated by USCIS with the fee prescribed in 8 CFR 103.7(b)(1), and in accordance with the form instructions. (For Department of State procedure when a visa is required, see 22 CFR 41.95 and paragraph (a) of this section.) If the application is made because the applicant may be inadmissible due to present or past membership in or affiliation with any Communist or other totalitarian party or organization, there shall be attached to the application a written statement of the history of the applicant's membership or affiliation, including the period of such membership or affiliation, whether the applicant held any office in the organization, and whether his membership or affiliation was voluntary or involuntary. If the applicant alleges that his membership or affiliation was involuntary, the statement shall include the basis for that allegation. When the application is made because the applicant may be inadmissible due to disease, mental or physical defect, or disability of any kind, the application shall describe the disease, defect, or disability. If the purpose of seeking admission to the United States is for treatment, there shall be attached to the application statements in writing to establish that satisfactory treatment cannot be obtained outside the United States; that arrangements have been completed for treatment, and where and from whom treatment will be received; what financial arrangements for payment of expenses incurred in connection with the treatment have been made, and that a bond will be available if required. When the application is made because the applicant may be inadmissible due to the conviction of one or more crimes, the designation of each crime, the date and place of its commission and of the conviction thereof, and the sentence or other judgment of the court shall be stated in the application; in such a case the application shall be supplemented by the official record of each conviction, and any other documents relating to commutation of sentence, parole, probation, or pardon. If the application is made at the time of the applicant's arrival to the district director at a port of entry, the applicant shall establish that he was not aware of the ground of inadmissibility and that it could not have been ascertained by the exercise of reasonable diligence, and he shall be in possession of a passport and visa, if required, or have been granted a waiver thereof. The applicant shall be notified of the decision and if the application is denied of the reasons therefor and of his right to appeal to the Board within 15 days after the mailing of the notification of decision in accordance with the Provisions of part 3 of this chapter. If denied, the denial shall be without prejudice to renewal of the application in the course of proceedings before a special inquiry officer under sections 235 and 236 of the Act and this chapter. When an appeal may not be taken from a decision of a special inquiry officer excluding an alien but the alien has applied for the exercise of discretion under section 212(d)(3)(B) of the Act, the alien may appeal to the Board from a denial of such application in accordance with the provisions of § 236.5(b) of this chapter.

(c) *Terms of authorization*—(1) *General.* Except as provided in paragraph (c)(2) of this section, each authorization under section 212(d)(3)(A) or (B) of the Act shall specify:

(i) Each section of law under which the alien is inadmissible;

(ii) The intended date of each arrival, unless the applicant is a bona fide crewman. However, if the authorization is valid for multiple entries rather than for a specified number of entries, this information shall be specified only with respect to the initial entry;

(iii) The length of each stay authorized in the United States, which shall not exceed the period justified and shall be subject to limitations specified in 8 CFR part 214. However, if the authorization is valid for multiple entries rather than for a specified number of entries, this information shall be specified only with respect to the initial entry;

(iv) The purpose of each stay;

(v) The number of entries for which the authorization is valid;

(vi) Subject to the conditions set forth in paragraph (c)(2) of this section, the dates on or between which each application for admission at POEs in the United States is valid;

(vii) The justification for exercising the authority contained in section 212(d)(3) of the Act; and

(viii) That the authorization is subject to revocation at any time.

(2) *Conditions of admission.* (i) For aliens issued an authorization for temporary admission in accordance with this section, admissions pursuant to section 212(d)(3) of the Act shall be subject to the terms and conditions set forth in the authorization.

(ii) The period for which the alien's admission is authorized pursuant to this section shall not exceed the period justified, or the limitations specified, in 8 CFR part 214 for each class of nonimmigrant, whichever is less.

(3) *Validity.* (i) Authorizations granted to crew members may be valid for a maximum period of 2 years for application for admission at U.S. POEs and may be valid for multiple entries.

(ii) An authorization issued in conjunction with an application for a Form DSP–150, B–1/B–2 Visa and Border Crossing Card, issued by the DOS shall be valid for a period not to exceed the validity of the biometric BCC for applications for admission at U.S. POEs and shall be valid for multiple entries.

(iii) A multiple entry authorization for a person other than a crew member or applicant for a Form DSP–150 may be made valid for a maximum period of 5 years for applications for admission at U.S. POEs.

(iv) An authorization that was previously issued in conjunction with Form I–185, Nonresident Alien Canadian Border Crossing Card, and that is noted on the card may remain valid. Although the waiver may remain valid, the non-biometric border crossing card portion of this document is not valid after that date. This waiver authorization shall cease if otherwise revoked or voided.

(v) A single-entry authorization to apply for admission at a U.S. POE shall not be valid for more than 6 months from the date the authorization is issued.

(vi) An authorization may not be revalidated. Upon expiration of the authorization, a new application and authorization are required.

(d) *Admission of groups inadmissible under section 212(a)(28) for attendance at international conferences.* When the Secretary of State recommends that a group of nonimmigrant aliens and their accompanying family members be admitted to attend international conferences notwithstanding their inadmissibility under section 212(a)(28) of the Act, the Deputy Commissioner, may enter an order pursuant to the authority contained in section 212(d)(3)(A) of the Act specifying the terms and conditions of their admission and stay.

(e) *Inadmissibility under section 212(a)(1)(A)(iii).* Pursuant to the authority contained in section 212(d)(3) of the Act, the temporary admission of a nonimmigrant visitor is authorized notwithstanding inadmissibility under section 212(a)(1)(A)(iii)(I) or (II) of the Act due to a mental disorder and associated threatening or harmful behavior, if such alien is accompanied by a member of his/her family, or a guardian who will be responsible for him/her during the period of admission authorized.

(f) *Inadmissibility under section 212(a)(1) for aliens inadmissible due to HIV*—(1) *General.* Pursuant to the authority in section 212(d)(3)(A)(i) of the Act, any alien who is inadmissible under section 212(a)(1)(A)(i) of the Act due to infection with the etiologic agent for acquired immune deficiency syndrome (HIV infection) may be issued a B–1 (business visitor) or B–2 (visitor for pleasure) nonimmigrant visa by a consular officer or the Secretary of State, and be authorized for temporary admission into the United States for a period not to exceed 30 days, subject to authorization of an additional period or periods under paragraph (f)(5) of this section, provided that the authorization is granted in accordance with paragraphs (f)(2) through (f)(7) of this section. Application under this paragraph (f) may not be combined with any other waiver of inadmissibility.

(2) *Conditions.* An alien who is HIV-positive who applies for a nonimmigrant visa before a consular officer may be issued a B–1 (business visitor) or B–2 (visitor for pleasure) nonimmigrant visa and admitted to the United States for a period not to exceed 30 days, provided that the applicant establishes that:

(i) The applicant has tested positive for HIV;

(ii) The applicant is not currently exhibiting symptoms indicative of an active, contagious infection associated with acquired immune deficiency syndrome;

(iii) The applicant is aware of, has been counseled on, and understands the nature, severity, and the communicability of his or her medical condition;

(iv) The applicant's admission poses a minimal risk of danger to the public health in the United States and poses a minimal risk of danger of transmission of the infection to any other person in the United States;

(v) The applicant will have in his or her possession, or will have access to, as medically appropriate, an adequate supply of antiretroviral drugs for the anticipated stay in the United States and possesses sufficient assets, such as insurance that is accepted in the United States, to cover any medical care that the applicant may require in the event of illness at any time while in the United States;

(vi) The applicant's admission will not create any cost to the United States, or a state or local government, or any agency thereof, without the prior written consent of the agency;

(vii) The applicant is seeking admission solely for activities that are consistent with the B–1 (business visitor) or B–2 (visitor for pleasure) nonimmigrant classification;

(viii) The applicant is aware that no single admission to the United States will be for a period that exceeds 30 days (subject to paragraph (f)(5) of this section);

(ix) The applicant is otherwise admissible to the United States and no other ground of inadmissibility applies;

(x) The applicant is aware that he or she cannot be admitted under section 217 of the Act (Visa Waiver Program);

(xi) The applicant is aware that any failure to comply with any condition of admission set forth under this paragraph (f) will thereafter make him or her ineligible for authorization under this paragraph; and

(xii) The applicant, for the purpose of admission pursuant to authorization under this paragraph (f), waives any opportunity to apply for an extension of nonimmigrant stay (except as provided in paragraph (f)(5) of this section), a change of nonimmigrant status, or adjustment of status to that of permanent resident.

(A) Nothing in this paragraph (f) precludes an alien admitted under this paragraph (f) from applying for asylum pursuant to section 208 of the Act.

(B) Any alien admitted under this paragraph (f) who applies for adjustment of status under section 209 of the Act after being granted asylum must establish his or her eligibility to adjust status under all applicable provisions of the Act and 8 CFR part 209. Any applicable ground of inadmissibility must be waived by approval of an appropriate waiver(s) under section 209(c) of the Act and 8 CFR 209.2(b).

(C) Nothing within this paragraph (f) constitutes a waiver of inadmissibility under section 209 of the Act or 8 CFR part 209.

(3) *Nonimmigrant visa.* A nonimmigrant visa issued to the applicant for purposes of temporary admission under section 212(d)(3)(A)(i) of the Act and this paragraph (f) may not be valid for more than 12 months or for more than two applications for admission during the 12-month period. The authorized period of stay will be for 30 calendar days calculated from the initial admission under this visa.

(4) *Application at U.S. port.* If otherwise admissible, a holder of the nonimmigrant visa issued under section 212(d)(3)(A)(i) of the Act and this paragraph (f) is authorized to apply for admission at a United States port of entry at any time during the period of validity of the visa in only the B–1 (business visitor) or B–2 (visitor for pleasure) nonimmigrant categories.

(5) *Admission limited; satisfactory departure.* Notwithstanding any other provision of this chapter, no single period of admission under section 212(d)(3)(A)(i) of the Act and this paragraph (f) may be authorized for more than 30 days; if an emergency prevents a nonimmigrant alien admitted under this paragraph (f) from departing from the United States within his or her period of authorized stay, the director (or other appropriate official) having jurisdiction over the place of the alien's temporary stay may, in his or her discretion, grant an additional period (or periods) of satisfactory departure, each such period not to exceed 30 days. If departure is accomplished during that period, the alien is to be regarded as having satisfactorily accomplished the visit without overstaying the allotted time.

(6) *Failure to comply.* No authorization under section 212(d)(3)(A)(i) of the Act and this paragraph (f) may be provided to any alien who has previously failed to comply with any condition of an admission authorized under this paragraph.

(7) *Additional limitations.* The Secretary of Homeland Security or the Secretary of State may require additional evidence or impose additional conditions on granting authorization for temporary admissions under this paragraph (f) as international (or other relevant) conditions may indicate.

(8) *Option for case-by-case determination.* If the applicant does not meet the criteria under this paragraph (f), or does not wish to agree to the conditions for the streamlined 30-day visa under this paragraph (f), the applicant may elect to utilize the process described in either paragraph (a) or (b) of this section, as applicable.

(g) *Action upon alien's arrival.* Upon admitting an alien who has been granted the benefits of section 212(d)(3)(A) of the Act, the immigration officer shall be guided by the conditions and limitations imposed in the authorization and noted by the consular officer in the alien's passport. When admitting any alien who has been granted the benefits of section 212(d)(3)(B) of the Act, the Immigration officer shall note on the arrival-departure record, Form I–94 (see § 1.4), or crewman's landing permit, Form I–95, issued to the alien, the conditions and limitations imposed in the authorization.

(h) *Authorizations issued to crewmen without limitation as to period of validity.* When a crewman who has a valid section 212(d)(3) authorization without any time limitation comes to the attention of the Service, his travel document shall be endorsed to show that the validity of his section 212(d)(3) authorization expires as of a date six months thereafter, and any previously-issued Form I–184 shall be lifted and Form I–95 shall be issued in its place and similarly endorsed.

(i) *Revocation.* The Deputy Commissioner or the district director may at any time revoke a waiver previously authorized under section 212(d)(3) of the Act and shall notify the nonimmigrant in writing to that effect.

(j) *Alien witnesses and informants*—(1) *Waivers under section 212(d)(1) of the Act.* Upon the application of a federal or state law enforcement authority ("LEA"), which shall include a state or federal court or United States Attorney's Office, pursuant to the filing for nonimmigrant classification described in section 101(a)(15)(S) of the Act, USCIS will determine whether a ground of exclusion exists with respect to the alien for whom classification is sought and, if so, whether it is in the national interest to exercise the discretion to waive the ground of excludability, other than section 212(a)(3)(E) of the Act. USCIS may at any time revoke a waiver previously authorized under section 212(d)(1) of the Act. In the event USCIS decides to revoke a previously authorized waiver for an S nonimmigrant, the Assistant Attorney General, Criminal Division, and the relevant LEA shall be notified in writing to that effect. The Assistant Attorney General, Criminal Division, shall concur in or object to the decision. Unless the Assistant Attorney General, Criminal Division, objects within 7 days, he or she shall be deemed to have concurred in the decision. In the event of an objection by the Assistant Attorney General, Criminal Division, the matter will be expeditiously referred to the Deputy Attorney General for a final resolution. In no circumstances shall the alien or the relevant LEA have a right of appeal from any decision to revoke.

(2) *Grounds of removal.* Nothing shall prohibit the Service from removing from the United States an alien classified pursuant to section 101(a)(15)(S) of the Act for conduct committed after the alien has been admitted to the United States as an S nonimmigrant, or after the alien's change to S classification, or for conduct or a condition undisclosed to the Attorney General prior to the alien's admission in, or change to, S classification, unless such conduct or condition is waived prior to admission and classification. In the event USCIS decides to remove an S nonimmigrant from the United States, the Assistant Attorney General, Criminal Division, and the relevant LEA shall be notified in writing to that effect. The Assistant Attorney General, Criminal Division, shall concur in or object to that decision. Unless the Assistant Attorney General, Criminal Division, objects within 7 days, he or she shall be deemed to have concurred in the decision. In the event of an objection by the Assistant Attorney General, Criminal Division, the matter will be expeditiously referred to the Deputy Attorney General for a final resolution. In no circumstances shall the alien or the relevant LEA have a right of appeal from any decision to remove.

[29 FR 15252, Nov. 13, 1964, as amended at 30 FR 12330, Sept. 28, 1965; 31 FR 10413, Aug. 3, 1966; 32 FR 15469, Nov. 7, 1967; 35 FR 3065, Feb. 17, 1970; 35 FR 7637, May 16, 1970; 40 FR 30470, July 21, 1975; 51 FR 32295, Sept. 10, 1986; 53 FR 40867, Oct. 19, 1988; 60 FR 44264, Aug. 25, 1995; 60 FR 52248, Oct. 5, 1995; 67 FR 71448, Dec. 2, 2002; 73 FR 58030, Oct. 6, 2008; 76 FR 53787, Aug. 29, 2011; 78 FR 18472, Mar. 27, 2013]

§212.5 Parole of aliens into the United States.

(a) The authority of the Secretary to continue an alien in custody or grant parole under section 212(d)(5)(A) of the Act shall be exercised by the Assistant Commissioner, Office of Field Operations; Director, Detention and Removal; directors of field operations; port directors; special agents in charge; deputy special agents in charge; associate special agents in charge; assistant special agents in charge; resident agents in charge; field office directors; deputy field office directors; chief patrol agents; district directors for services; and those other officials as may be designated in writing, subject to the parole and detention authority of the Secretary or his designees. The Secretary or his designees may invoke, in the exercise of discretion, the authority under section 212(d)(5)(A) of the Act.

(b) The parole of aliens within the following groups who have been or are detained in accordance with § 235.3(b) or (c) of this chapter would generally be justified only on a case-by-case basis for "urgent humanitarian reasons" or "significant public benefit," provided the aliens present neither a security risk nor a risk of absconding:

(1) Aliens who have serious medical conditions in which continued detention would not be appropriate;

(2) Women who have been medically certified as pregnant;

(3) Aliens who are defined as juveniles in § 236.3(a) of this chapter. The Director, Detention and Removal; directors of field operations; field office directors; deputy field office directors; or chief patrol agents shall follow the guidelines set forth in § 236.3(a) of this chapter and paragraphs (b)(3)(i) through (iii) of this section in determining under what conditions a juvenile should be paroled from detention:

(i) Juveniles may be released to a relative (brother, sister, aunt, uncle, or grandparent) not in Service detention who is willing to sponsor a minor and the minor may be released to that relative notwithstanding that the juvenile has a relative who is in detention.

(ii) If a relative who is not in detention cannot be located to sponsor the minor, the minor may be released with an accompanying relative who is in detention.

(iii) If the Service cannot locate a relative in or out of detention to sponsor the minor, but the minor has identified a non-relative in detention who accompanied him or her on arrival, the question of releasing the minor and the accompanying non-relative adult shall be addressed on a case-by-case basis;

(4) Aliens who will be witnesses in proceedings being, or to be, conducted by judicial, administrative, or legislative bodies in the United States; or

(5) Aliens whose continued detention is not in the public interest as determined by those officials identified in paragraph (a) of this section.

(c) In the case of all other arriving aliens, except those detained under § 235.3(b) or (c) of this chapter and paragraph (b) of this section, those officials listed in paragraph (a) of this section may, after review of the individual case, parole into the United States temporarily in accordance with section 212(d)(5)(A) of the Act, any alien applicant for admission, under such terms and conditions, including those set forth in paragraph (d) of this section, as he or she may deem appropriate. An alien who arrives at a port-of-entry and applies for parole into the United States for the sole purpose of seeking adjustment of status under section 245A of the Act, without benefit of advance authorization as described in paragraph (f) of this section shall be denied parole and detained for removal in accordance with the provisions of § 235.3(b) or (c) of this chapter. An alien seeking to enter the United States for the sole purpose of applying for adjustment of status under section 210 of the Act shall be denied parole and detained for removal under § 235.3(b) or (c) of this chapter, unless the alien has been recommended for approval of such application for adjustment by a consular officer at an Overseas Processing Office.

(d) *Conditions*. In any case where an alien is paroled under paragraph (b) or (c) of this section, those officials listed in paragraph (a) of this section may require reasonable assurances that the alien will appear at all hearings and/or depart the United States when required to do so. Not all factors listed need be present for parole to be exercised. Those officials should apply reasonable discretion. The consideration of all relevant factors includes:

(1) The giving of an undertaking by the applicant, counsel, or a sponsor to ensure appearances or departure, and a bond may be required on Form I–352 in such amount as may be deemed appropriate;

(2) Community ties such as close relatives with known addresses; and

(3) Agreement to reasonable conditions (such as periodic reporting of whereabouts).

(e) *Termination of parole*—(1) *Automatic*. Parole shall be automatically terminated without written notice (i) upon the departure from the United States of the alien, or, (ii) if not departed, at the expiration of the time for which parole was authorized, and in the latter case the alien shall be processed in accordance with paragraph (e)(2) of this section except that no written notice shall be required.

(2)(i) *On notice*. In cases not covered by paragraph (e)(1) of this section, upon accomplishment of the purpose for which parole was authorized or when in the opinion of one of the officials listed in paragraph (a) of this section, neither humanitarian reasons nor public benefit warrants the continued presence of the alien in the United States, parole shall be terminated upon written notice to the alien and he or she shall be restored to the status that he or she had at the time of parole. When a charging document is served on the alien, the charging document will constitute written notice of termination of parole, unless otherwise specified. Any further inspection or hearing shall be conducted under section 235 or 240 of the Act and this chapter, or any order of exclusion, deportation, or removal previously entered shall be executed. If the exclusion, deportation, or removal order cannot be executed within a reasonable time, the alien shall again be released on parole unless in the opinion of the official listed in paragraph (a) of this section the public interest requires that the alien be continued in custody.

(ii) An alien who is granted parole into the United States after enactment of the Immigration Reform and Control Act of 1986 for other than the specific purpose of applying for adjustment of status under section 245A of the Act shall not be permitted to avail him or herself of the privilege of adjustment thereunder. Failure to abide by this provision through making such an application will subject the alien to termination of parole status and institution of proceedings under sections 235 and 236 of the Act without the written notice of termination required by §212.5(e)(2)(i) of this chapter.

(iii) Any alien granted parole into the United States so that he or she may transit through the United States in the course of removal from Canada shall have his or her parole status terminated upon notice, as specified in 8 CFR 212.5(e)(2)(i), if he or she makes known to an immigration officer of the United States a fear of persecution or an intention to apply for asylum. Upon termination of parole, any such alien shall be regarded as an arriving alien, and processed accordingly by the Department of Homeland Security.

(f) *Advance authorization*. When parole is authorized for an alien who will travel to the United States without a visa, the alien shall be issued an appropriate document authorizing travel.

(g) *Parole for certain Cuban nationals*. Notwithstanding any other provision respecting parole, the determination whether to release on parole, or to revoke the parole of, a native of Cuba who last came to the United States between April 15, 1980, and October 20, 1980, shall be governed by the terms of §212.12.

(h) *Effect of parole of Cuban and Haitian nationals*. (1) Except as provided in paragraph (h)(2) of this section, any national of Cuba or Haiti who was paroled into the United States on or after October 10, 1980, shall be considered to have been paroled in the special status for nationals of Cuba or Haiti, referred to in section 501(e)(1) of the Refugee Education Assistance Act of 1980, Public Law 96–422, as amended (8 U.S.C. 1522 note).

(2) A national of Cuba or Haiti shall not be considered to have been paroled in the special status for nationals of Cuba or Haiti, referred to in section 501(e)(1) of the Refugee Education Assistance Act of 1980, Public Law 96–422, as amended, if the individual was paroled into the United States:

(i) In the custody of a Federal, State or local law enforcement or prosecutorial authority, for purposes of criminal prosecution in the United States; or

(ii) Solely to testify as a witness in proceedings before a judicial, administrative, or legislative body in the United States.

[47 FR 30045, July 9, 1982, as amended at 47 FR 46494, Oct. 19, 1982; 52 FR 16194, May 1, 1987; 52 FR 48802, Dec. 28, 1987; 53 FR 17450, May 17, 1988; 61 FR 36611, July 12, 1996; 62 FR 10348, Mar. 6, 1997; 65 FR 80294, Dec. 21, 2000; 65 FR 82255, Dec. 28, 2000; 67 FR 39257, June 7, 2002; 68 FR 35152, June 12, 2003; 69 FR 69489, Nov. 29, 2004; 76 FR 53787, Aug. 29, 2011]

§212.6 Border crossing identification cards.

(a) *Application for Form DSP–150, B–1/B–2 Visa and Border Crossing Card, issued by the Department of State.* A citizen of Mexico, who seeks to travel temporarily to the United States for business or pleasure without a visa and passport, must apply to the DOS on Form DS–156, Visitor Visa Application, to obtain a Form DSP–150 in accordance with the applicable DOS regulations at 22 CFR 41.32 and/or instructions.

(b) *Use*—(1) *Application for admission with Non-resident Canadian Border Crossing Card, Form I–185, containing separate waiver authorization; Canadian residents bearing DOS-issued combination B–1/B–2 visa and border crossing card (or similar stamp in a passport).* (i) A Canadian citizen or other person sharing common nationality with Canada and residing in Canada who presents a Form I–185 that contains a separate notation of a waiver authorization issued pursuant to §212.4 may be admitted on the basis of the waiver, provided the waiver has not expired or otherwise been revoked or voided. Although the waiver may remain valid on or after October 1, 2002, the non-biometric border crossing card portion of the document is not valid after that date.

(ii) A Canadian resident who presents a combination B–1/B–2 visa and border crossing card (or similar stamp in a passport) issued by the DOS prior to April 1, 1998, that does not contain a machine-readable biometric identifier, may be admitted on the basis of the nonimmigrant visa only, provided it has not expired and the alien remains otherwise admissible.

(2) *Application for admission by a national of Mexico—Form DSP–150 issued by the DOS; DOS-issued combination B–1/B–2 visa and border crossing card (or similar stamp in a passport).* (i) The rightful holder of a Form DSP–150 issued by the DOS may be admitted under §235.1(f) of this chapter if found otherwise admissible and if the biometric identifier contained on the card matches the appropriate biometric characteristic of the alien.

(ii) The bearer of a combination B–1/B–2 nonimmigrant visa and border crossing card (or similar stamp in a passport) issued by DOS prior to April 1, 1998, that does not contain a machine-readable biometric identifier, may be admitted on the basis of the nonimmigrant visa only, provided it has not expired and the alien remains otherwise admissible. A passport is also required.

(iii) Any alien seeking admission as a visitor for business or pleasure, must also present a valid passport with his or her border crossing card, and shall be issued a Form I–94 (see §1.4) if the alien is applying for admission from:

(A) A country other than Mexico or Canada, or

(B) Canada if the alien has been in a country other than the United States or Canada since leaving Mexico.

(c) *Validity.* Forms I–185, I–186, and I–586 are invalid on or after October 1, 2002. If presented on or after that date, these documents will be voided at the POE.

(d) *Voidance for reasons other than expiration of the validity of the form*—(1) *At a POE.* (i) In accordance with 22 CFR 41.122, a Form DSP–150 or combined B–1/B–2 visitor visa and non-biometric border crossing identification card or (a similar stamp in a passport), issued by the DOS, may be physically cancelled and voided by a supervisory immigration officer at a POE if it is considered void pursuant to section 222(g) of the Act when presented at the time of application for admission, or as the alien departs the United States. If the card is considered void and if the applicant for admission is not otherwise subject to expedited removal in accordance with 8 CFR part 235, the applicant shall be advised in writing that he or she may request a hearing before an immigration judge. The purpose of the hearing shall be to determine his/her admissibility in accordance with §235.6

of this chapter. The applicant may be represented at this hearing by an attorney of his/her own choice at no expense to the Government. He or she shall also be advised of the availability of free legal services provided by organizations and attorneys qualified under 8 CFR part 3, and organizations recognized under §292.2 of this chapter located in the district where the removal hearing is to be held. If the applicant requests a hearing, the Form DSP–150 or combined B–1/B–2 visitor visa and non-biometric border crossing identification card (or similar stamp in a passport), issued by the DOS, shall be held by the Service for presentation to the immigration judge.

(ii) If the applicant chooses not to have a hearing, the Form DSP–150 or combined B–1/B–2 visitor visa and non-biometric BCC (or similar stamp in a passport) issued by the DOS, shall be voided and physically cancelled. The alien to whom the card or stamp was issued by the DOS shall be notified of the action taken and the reasons for such action by means of Form I–275, Withdrawal of Application for Admission/Consular Notification, delivered in person or by mailing the Form I–275 to the last known address. The DOS shall be notified of the cancellation of the biometric Form DSP–150 or combined B–1/B–2 visitor visa and non-biometric BCC (or similar stamp in a passport) issued by DOS, by means of a copy of the original Form I–275. Nothing in this paragraph limits the Service's ability to remove an alien pursuant to 8 CFR part 235 where applicable.

(2) *Within the United States.* In accordance with former section 242 of the Act (before amended by section 306 of the IIRIRA of 1996, Div. C, Public Law 104–208, 110 Stat. 3009 (Sept. 30, 1996,) or current sections 235(b), 238, and 240 of the Act, if the holder of a Form DSP–150, or other combined B–1/B–2 visa and BCC, or (similar stamp in a passport) issued by the DOS, is placed under removal proceedings, no action to cancel the card or stamp shall be taken pending the outcome of the hearing. If the alien is ordered removed or granted voluntary departure, the card or stamp shall be physically cancelled and voided by an immigration officer. In the case of an alien holder of a BCC who is granted voluntary departure without a hearing, the card shall be declared void and physically cancelled by an immigration officer who is authorized to issue a Notice to Appear or to grant voluntary departure.

(3) *In Mexico or Canada.* Forms I–185, I–186 or I–586 issued by the Service and which are now invalid, or a Form DSP–150 or combined B–1/B–2 visitor visa and non-biometric BCC, or (similar stamp in a passport) issued by the DOS may be declared void by United States consular officers or United States immigration officers in Mexico or Canada.

(4) *Grounds.* Grounds for voidance of a Form I–185, I–186, I–586, a DOS-issued non-biometric BCC, or the biometric Form DSP–150 shall be that the holder has violated the immigration laws; that he/she is inadmissible to the United States; that he/she has abandoned his/her residence in the country upon which the card was granted; or if the BCC is presented for admission on or after October 1, 2002, it does not contain a machine-readable biometric identifier corresponding to the bearer and is invalid on or after October 1, 2002.

(e) *Replacement.* If a valid Border Crossing Card (Forms I–185, I–186, or I–586) previously issued by the Service, a non-biometric border crossing card issued by the DOS before April 1998, or a Form DSP–150 issued by the DOS has been lost, stolen, mutilated, or destroyed, the person to whom the card was issued may apply for a new card as provided for in the DOS regulations found at 22 CFR 41.32 and 22 CFR 41.103.

[67 FR 71448, Dec. 2, 2002, as amended at 78 FR 18472, Mar. 27, 2013]

§212.7 Waiver of certain grounds of inadmissibility.

(a) (1) *Application.* Except as provided by 8 CFR 212.7(e), an applicant for an immigrant visa, adjustment of status, or a K or V nonimmigrant visa who is inadmissible under any provision of section 212(a) of the Act for which a waiver is available under section 212 of the Act may apply for the related waiver by filing the form designated by USCIS, with the fee prescribed in 8 CFR 103.7(b)(1), and in accordance with the form instructions. Certain immigrants may apply for a provisional unlawful presence waiver of inadmissibility as specified in 8 CFR 212.7(e).

(2) *Termination of application for lack of prosecution.* An applicant may withdraw the application at any time prior to the final decision, whereupon the case will be closed and the consulate notified. If the applicant fails to prosecute the application within a reasonable time either before or after interview the applicant shall be notified that if he or she fails to prosecute the application within 30 days the case will be closed subject to being reopened at the applicant's request. If no action has been taken within the 30-day period immediately thereafter, the case will be closed and the appropriate consul notified.

(3) *Decision.* If the waiver application is denied, USCIS will provide a written decision and notify the applicant and his or her attorney or accredited representative and will advise the applicant of appeal procedures, if any, in accordance with 8 CFR 103.3. The denial of a provisional unlawful presence waiver is governed by 8 CFR 212.7(e).

(4) *Validity.* (i) A provisional unlawful presence waiver granted according to paragraph (e) of this section is valid subject to the terms and conditions as specified in paragraph (e) of this section. In any other case, approval of an immigrant waiver of inadmissibility under this section applies only to the grounds of inadmissibility, and the related crimes, events, or incidents that are specified in the application for waiver.

(ii) Except for K–1 and K–2 nonimmigrants and aliens lawfully admitted for permanent residence on a conditional basis, an immigrant waiver of inadmissibility is valid indefinitely, even if the applicant later abandons or otherwise loses lawful permanent resident status.

(iii) For a K–1 or K–2 nonimmigrant, approval of the waiver is conditioned on the K–1 nonimmigrant marrying the petitioner; if the K–1 nonimmigrant marries the K nonimmigrant petitioner, the waiver becomes valid indefinitely, subject to paragraph (a)(4)(iv) of this section, even if the applicant later abandons or otherwise loses lawful permanent resident status. If the K–1 does not marry the K nonimmigrant petitioner, the K–1 and K–2 nonimmigrants remain inadmissible for purposes of any application for a benefit on any basis other than the proposed marriage between the K–1 and the K nonimmigrant petitioner.

(iv) For an alien lawfully admitted for permanent residence on a conditional basis under section 216 of the Act, removal of the conditions on the alien's status renders the waiver valid indefinitely, even if the applicant later abandons or otherwise loses lawful permanent resident status. Termination of the alien's status as an alien lawfully admitted for permanent residence on a conditional basis also terminates the validity of a waiver of inadmissibility based on sections 212(h) or 212(i) of the Act that was granted to the alien. Separate notification of the termination of the waiver is not required when an alien is notified of the termination of residence under section 216 of the Act, and no appeal will lie from the decision to terminate the waiver on this basis. If the alien challenges the termination in removal proceedings, and the removal proceedings end in the restoration of the alien's status, the waiver will become effective again.

(v) Nothing in this subsection precludes USCIS from reopening and reconsidering a decision if the decision is determined to have been made in error.

(b) *Section 212(g) waivers for certain medical conditions.* (1) *Application.* Any alien who is inadmissible under section 212(a)(1)(A)(i), (ii), or (iii) of the Act and who is eligible for a waiver under section 212(g) of the Act may file an application as described in paragraph (a)(1) of this section. The family member specified in section 212(g) of the Act may file the waiver application for the applicant if the applicant is incompetent to file the waiver personally.

(2) *Section 212(a) (1) or (3) (certain mental conditions)*—(i) *Arrangements for submission of medical report.* If the alien is excludable under section 212(a)(1)(A)(iii) of the Act he or his sponsoring family member shall submit a waiver request with a statement that arrangements have been made for the submission to that office of a medical report. The medical report shall

contain a complete medical history of the alien, including details of any hospitalization or institutional care or treatment for any physical or mental condition; findings as to the current physical condition of the alien, including reports of chest X-ray examination and of serologic test for syphilis if the alien is 15 years of age or over, and other pertinent diagnostic tests; and findings as to the current mental condition of the alien, with information as to prognosis and life expectancy and with a report of a psychiatric examination conducted by a psychiatrist who shall, in case of mental retardation, also provide an evaluation of the alien's intelligence. For an alien with a past history of mental illness, the medical report shall also contain available information on which the U.S. Public Health Service can base a finding as to whether the alien has been free of such mental illness for a period of time sufficient in the light of such history to demonstrate recovery.

(ii) *Submission of statement.* Upon being notified that the medical report has been reviewed by the U.S. Public Health Service and determined to be acceptable, the alien or the alien's sponsoring family member shall submit a statement to the consular or Service office. The statement must be from a clinic, hospital, institution, specialized facility, or specialist in the United States approved by the U.S. Public Health Service. The alien or alien's sponsor may be referred to the mental retardation or mental health agency of the state of proposed residence for guidance in selecting a post-arrival medical examining authority who will complete the evaluation and provide an evaluation report to the Centers for Disease Control. The statement must specify the name and address of the specialized facility, or specialist, and must affirm that:

(A) The specified facility or specialist agrees to evaluate the alien's mental status and prepare a complete report of the findings of such evaluation.

(B) The alien, the alien's sponsoring family member, or another responsible person has made complete financial arrangements for payment of any charges that may be incurred after arrival for studies, care, training and service;

(C) The Director, Division of Quarantine, Center for Prevention Services, Centers for Disease Control, Atlanta, GA. 30333 shall be furnished:

(*1*) The report evaluating the alien's mental status within 30 days after the alien's arrival; and

(*2*) Prompt notification of the alien's failure to report to the facility or specialist within 30 days after being notified by the U.S. Public Health Service that the alien has arrived in the United States.

(D) The alien shall be in an outpatient, inpatient, study, or other specified status as determined by the responsible local physcian or specialist during the initial evaluation.

(3) *Assurances: Bonds.* In all cases under paragraph (b) of this section the alien or his or her sponsoring family member shall also submit an assurance that the alien will comply with any special travel requirements as may be specified by the U.S. Public Health Service and that, upon the admission of the alien into the United States, he or she will proceed directly to the facility or specialist specified for the initial evaluation, and will submit to such further examinations or treatment as may be required, whether in an outpatient, inpatient, or other status. The alien, his or her sponsoring family member, or other responsible person shall provide such assurances or bond as may be required to assure that the necessary expenses of the alien will be met and that he or she will not become a public charge. For procedures relating to cancellation or breaching of bonds, see part 103 of this chapter.

(c) *Section 212(e).* (1) An alien who was admitted to the United States as an exchange visitor, or who acquired that status after admission, is subject to the foreign residence requirement of section 212(e) of the Act if his or her participation in an exchange program was financed in whole or in part, directly or indirectly, by a United States government agency or by the government of the country of his or her nationality or last foreign residence.

(2) An alien is also subject to the foreign residence requirement of section

212(e) of the Act if at the time of admission to the United States as an exchange visitor or at the time of acquisition of exchange visitor status after admission to the United States, the alien was a national or lawful permanent resident of a country which the Director of the United States Information Agency had designated, through public notice in the FEDERAL REGISTER, as clearly requiring the services of persons engaged in the field of specialized knowledge or skill in which the alien was to engage in his or her exchange visitor program.

(3) An alien is also subject to the foreign residence requirement of section 212(e) of the Act if he or she was admitted to the United States as an exchange visitor on or after January 10, 1977 to receive graduate medical education or training, or following admission, acquired such status on or after that date for that purpose. However, an exchange visitor already participating in an exchange program of graduate medical education or training as of January 9, 1977 who was not then subject to the foreign residence requirement of section 212(e) and who proceeds or has proceeded abroad temporarily and is returning to the United States to participate in the same program, continues to be exempt from the foreign residence requirement.

(4) A spouse or child admitted to the United States or accorded status under section 101(a)(15)(J) of the Act to accompany or follow to join an exchange visitor who is subject to the foreign residence requirement of section 212(e) of the Act is also subject to that requirement.

(5) An alien who is subject to the foreign residence requirement and who believes that compliance therewith would impose exceptional hardship upon his/her spouse or child who is a citizen of the United States or a lawful permanent resident alien, or that he or she cannot return to the country of his or her nationality or last residence because he or she will be subject to persecution on account of race, religion, or political opinion, may apply for a waiver on the form designated by USCIS. The alien's spouse and minor children, if also subject to the foreign residence requirement, may be included in the application, provided the spouse has not been a participant in an exchange program.

(6) Each application based upon a claim to exceptional hardship must be accompanied by the certificate of marriage between the applicant and his or her spouse and proof of legal termination of all previous marriages of the applicant and spouse; the birth certificate of any child who is a United States citizen or lawful permanent resident alien, if the application is based upon a claim of exceptional hardship to a child, and evidence of the United States citizenship of the applicant's spouse or child, when the application is based upon a claim of exceptional hardship to a spouse or child who is a citizen of the United States.

(7) Evidence of United States citizenship and of status as a lawful permanent resident shall be in the form provided in part 204 of this chapter. An application based upon exceptional hardship shall be supported by a statement, dated and signed by the applicant, giving a detailed explanation of the basis for his or her belief that his or her compliance with the foreign residence requirement of section 212(e) of the Act, as amended, would impose exceptional hardship upon his or her spouse or child who is a citizen of the United States or a lawful permanent resident thereof. The statement shall include all pertinent information concerning the incomes and savings of the applicant and spouse. If exceptional hardship is claimed upon medical grounds, the applicant shall submit a medical certificate from a qualified physician setting forth in terms understandable to a layman the nature and effect of the illness and prognosis as to the period of time the spouse or child will require care or treatment.

(8) An application based upon the applicant's belief that he or she cannot return to the country of his or her nationality or last residence because the applicant would be subject to persecution on account of race, religion, or political opinion, must be supported by a statement, dated and signed by the applicant, setting forth in detail why the applicant believes he or she would be subject to persecution.

(9) *Waivers under Pub. L. 103–416 based on a request by a State Department of Public Health (or equivalent).* In accordance with section 220 of Pub. L. 103–416, an alien admitted to the United States as a nonimmigrant under section 101(a)(15)(J) of the Act, or who acquired status under section 101(a)(15)(J) of the Act after admission to the United States, to participate in an exchange program of graduate medical education or training (as of January 9, 1977), may apply for a waiver of the 2-year home country residence and physical presence requirement (the "2-year requirement") under section 212(e)(iii) of the Act based on a request by a State Department of Public Health, or its equivalent. To initiate the application for a waiver under Pub. L. 103–416, the Department of Public Health, or its equivalent, or the State in which the foreign medical graduate seeks to practice medicine, must request the Director of USIA to recommend a waiver to the Service. The waiver may be granted only if the Director of USIA provides the Service with a favorable waiver recommendation. Only the Service, however, may grant or deny the waiver application. If granted, such a waiver shall be subject to the terms and conditions imposed under section 214(l) of the Act (as redesignated by section 671(a)(3)(A) of Pub. L. 104–208). Although the alien is not required to submit a separate waiver application to the Service, the burden rests on the alien to establish eligibility for the waiver. If the Service approves a waiver request made under Pub. L. 103–416, the foreign medical graduate (and accompanying dependents) may apply for change of nonimmigrant status, from J–1 to H–1B and, in the case of dependents of such a foreign medical graduate, from J–2 to H–4. Aliens receiving waivers under section 220 of Pub. L. 103–416 are subject, in all cases, to the provisions of section 214(g)(1)(A) of the Act.

(i) *Eligiblity criteria.* J–1 foreign medical graduates (with accompanying J–2 dependents) are eligible to apply for a waiver of the 2-year requirement under Pub. L. 103–416 based on a request by a State Department of Public Health (or its equivalent) if:

(A) They were admitted to the United States under section 101(a)(15)(J) of the Act, or acquired J nonimmigrant status before June 1, 2002, to pursue graduate medical education or training in the United States.

(B) They have entered into a bona fide, full-time employment contract for 3 years to practice medicine at a health care facility located in an area or areas designated by the Secretary of Health and Human Services as having a shortage of health care professionals ("HHS-designated shortage area");

(C) They agree to commence employment within 90 days of receipt of the waiver under this section and agree to practice medicine for 3 years at the facility named in the waiver application and only in HHS-designated shortage areas. The health care facility named in the waiver application may be operated by:

(*1*) An agency of the Government of the United States or of the State in which it is located; or

(*2*) A charitable, educational, or other not-for-profit organization; or

(*3*) Private medical practitioners.

(D) The Department of Public Health, or its equivalent, in the State where the health care facility is located has requested the Director, USIA, to recommend the waiver, and the Director, USIA, submits a favorable waiver recommendation to the Service; and

(E) Approval of the waiver will not cause the number of waivers granted pursuant to Pub. L. 103–416 and this section to foreign medical graduates who will practice medicine in the same state to exceed 20 during the current fiscal year.

(ii) *Decision on waivers under Pub. L. 103–416 and notification to the alien*—(A) *Approval.* If the Director of USIA submits a favorable waiver recommendation on behalf of a foreign medical graduate pursuant to Pub. L. 103–416, and the Service grants the waiver, the alien shall be notified of the approval on Form I–797 (or I–797A or I–797B, as appropriate). The approval notice shall clearly state the terms and conditions imposed on the waiver, and the Service's records shall be noted accordingly.

(B) *Denial.* If the Director of USIA issues a favorable waiver recommendation under Pub. L. 103–416 and the Service denies the waiver, the alien shall be notified of the decision and of the right to appeal under 8 CFR part 103. However, no appeal shall lie where the basis for denial is that the number of waivers granted to the State in which the foreign medical graduate will be employed would exceed 20 for that fiscal year.

(iii) *Conditions.* The foreign medical graduate must agree to commence employment for the health care facility specified in the waiver application within 90 days of receipt of the waiver under Pub. L. 103–416. The foreign medical graduate may only fulfill the requisite 3-year employment contract as an H–1B nonimmigrant. A foreign medical graduate who receives a waiver under Pub. L. 103–416 based on a request by a State Department of Public Health (or equivalent), and changes his or her nonimmigrant classification from J–1 to H–1B, may not apply for permanent residence or for any other change of nonimmigrant classification unless he or she has fulfilled the 3-year employment contract with the health care facility and in the specified HHS-designated shortage area named in the waiver application.

(iv) *Failure to fulfill the three-year employment contract due to extenuating circumstances.* A foreign medical graduate who fails to meet the terms and conditions imposed on the waiver under section 214(l) of the Act and this paragraph will once again become subject to the 2-year requirement under section 212(e) of the Act.

Under section 214(l)(1)(B) of the Act, however, the Service, in the exercise of discretion, may excuse early termination of the foreign medical graduate's 3-year period of employment with the health care facility named in the waiver application due to extenuating circumstances. Extenuating circumstances may include, but are not limited to, closure of the health care facility or hardship to the alien. In determining whether to excuse such early termination of employment, the Service shall base its decision on the specific facts of each case. In all cases, the burden of establishing eligibility for a favorable exercise of discretion rests with the foreign medical graduate. Depending on the circumstances, closure of the health care facility named in the waiver application may, but need not, be considered an extenuating circumstance excusing early termination of employment. Under no circumstances will a foreign medical graduate be eligible to apply for change of status to another nonimmigrant category, for an immigrant visa or for status as a lawful permanent resident prior to completing the requisite 3-year period of employment for a health care facility located in an HHS-designated shortage area.

(v) *Required evidence.* A foreign medical graduate who seeks to have early termination of employment excused due to extenuating circumstances shall submit documentary evidence establishing such a claim. In all cases, the foreign medical graduate shall submit an employment contract with another health care facility located in an HHS-designated shortage area for the balance of the required 3-year period of employment. A foreign medical graduate claiming extenuating circumstances based on hardship shall also submit evidence establishing that such hardship was caused by unforeseen circumstances beyond his or her control. A foreign medical graduate claiming extenuating circumstances based on closure of the health care facility named in the waiver application shall also submit evidence that the facility has closed or is about to be closed.

(vi) *Notification requirements.* A J–1 foreign medical graduate who has been granted a waiver of the 2-year requirement pursuant to Pub. L. 103–416, is required to comply with the terms and conditions specified in section 214(l) of the Act and the implementing regulations in this section. If the foreign medical graduate subsequently applies for and receives H–1B status, he or she must also comply with the terms and conditions of that nonimmigrant status. Such compliance shall also include notifying USCIS of any material change in the terms and conditions of the H–1B employment, by filing either an amended or a new H–1B petition, as required, under §§214.2(h)(2)(i)(D),

214.2(h)(2)(i)(E), and 214.2(h)(11) of this chapter.

(A) *Amended H–1B petitions.* The health care facility named in the waiver application and H–1B petition shall file an amended H–1B petition, as required under §214.2(h)(2)(i)(E) of this chapter, if there are any material changes in the terms and conditions of the beneficiary's employment or eligibility as specified in the waiver application filed under Pub. L. 103–416 and in the subsequent H–1B petition. In such a case, an amended H–1B petition shall be accompanied by evidence that the alien will continue practicing medicine with the original employer in an HHS-designated shortage area.

(B) *New H–1B petitions.* A health care facility seeking to employ a foreign medical graduate who has been granted a waiver under Pub. L. 103–416 (prior to the time the alien has completed his or her 3-year contract with the facility named in the waiver application and original H–1B petition), shall file a new H–1B petition, as required under §§214.2(h)(2)(i) (D) and (E) of this chapter. Although a new waiver application need not be filed, the new H–1B petition shall be accompanied by the documentary evidence generally required under §214.2(h) of this chapter, and the following additional documents:

(*1*) A copy of the USCIS approval notice relating to the waiver and nonimmigrant H status granted under Pub. L. 103–416;

(*2*) An explanation from the foreign medical graduate, with supporting evidence, establishing that extenuating circumstances necessitate a change in employment;

(*3*) An employment contract establishing that the foreign medical graduate will practice medicine at the health care facility named in the new H–1B petition for the balance of the required 3-year period; and

(*4*) Evidence that the geographic area or areas of intended employment indicated in the new H–1B petition are in HHS-designated shortage areas.

(C) *Review of amended and new H–1B petitions for foreign medical graduates granted waivers under Pub. L. 103–416 and who seek to have early termination of employment excused due to extenuating circumstances*—(*1*) *Amended H–1B petitions.* The waiver granted under Pub. L. 103–416 may be affirmed, and the amended H–1B petition may be approved, if the petitioning health care facility establishes that the foreign medical graduate otherwise remains eligible for H–1B classification and that he or she will continue practicing medicine in an HHS-designated shortage area.

(*2*) *New H–1B petitions.* The Service shall review a new H–1B petition filed on behalf of a foreign medical graduate who has not yet fulfilled the required 3-year period of employment with the health care facility named in the waiver application and in the original H–1B petition to determine whether extenuating circumstances exist which warrant a change in employment, and whether the waiver granted under Pub. L. 103–416 should be affirmed. In conducting such a review, the Service shall determine whether the foreign medical graduate will continue practicing medicine in an HHS-designated shortage area, and whether the new H–1B petitioner and the foreign medical graduate have satisfied the remaining H–1B eligibility criteria described under section 101(a)(15)(H) of the Act and §214.2(h) of this chapter. If these criteria have been satisfied, the waiver granted to the foreign medical graduate under Pub. L. 103–416 may be affirmed, and the new H1–B petition may be approved in the exercise of discretion, thereby permitting the foreign medical graduate to serve the balance of the requisite 3-year employment period at the health care facility named in the new H–1B petition.

(D) *Failure to notify the Service of any material changes in employment.* Foreign medical graduates who have been granted a waiver of the 2-year requirement and who have obtained H–1B status under Pub. L. 103–416 but fail to: Properly notify the Service of any material change in the terms and conditions of their H–1B employment, by having their employer file an amended or a new H–1B petition in accordance with this section and §214.2(h) of this chapter; or establish continued eligibility for the waiver and H–1B status, shall (together with their dependents) again become subject to the 2-year requirement. Such foreign medical graduates and their accompanying H–4 dependents also become subject to deportation under section 241(a)(1)(C)(i) of the Act.

(10) The applicant and his or her spouse may be interviewed by an immigration officer in connection with the application and consultation may be had with the Director, United States Information Agency and the sponsor of any exchange program in which the applicant has been a participant.

(11) The applicant shall be notified of the decision, and if the application is denied, of the reasons therefor and of the right of appeal in accordance with the provisions of part 103 of this chapter. However, no appeal shall lie from the denial of an application for lack of a favorable recommendation from the Secretary of State. When an interested United States Government agency requests a waiver of the two-year foreign-residence requirement and the Director, United States Information Agency had made a favorable recommendation, the interested agency shall be notified of the decision on its request and, if the request is denied, of the reasons thereof, and of the right of appeal. If the foreign country of the alien's nationality or last residence has furnished statement in writing that it has no objection to his/her being granted a waiver of the foreign residence requirement and the Director, United States Information Agency has made a favorable recommendation, the Director shall be notified of the decision and, if the foreign residence requirement is not waived, of the reasons therefor and of the foregoing right of appeal. However, this "no objection" provision is not applicable to the exchange visitor admitted to the United States on or after January 10, 1977 to receive graduate medical education or training, or who acquired such status on or after that date for such purpose; except that the alien who commenced a program before January 10, 1977 and who was readmitted to the United States on or after that date to continue participation in the same program, is eligible for the "no objection" waiver.

(d) *Criminal grounds of inadmissibility involving violent or dangerous crimes.* The Attorney General, in general, will not favorably exercise discretion under section 212(h)(2) of the Act (8 U.S.C. 1182(h)(2)) to consent to an application or reapplication for a visa, or admission to the United States, or adjustment of status, with respect to immigrant aliens who are inadmissible under section 212(a)(2) of the Act in cases involving violent or dangerous crimes, except in extraordinary circumstances, such as those involving national security or foreign policy considerations, or cases in which an alien clearly demonstrates that the denial of the application for adjustment of status or an immigrant visa or admission as an immigrant would result in exceptional and extremely unusual hardship. Moreover, depending on the gravity of the alien's underlying criminal offense, a showing of extraordinary circumstances might still be insufficient to warrant a favorable exercise of discretion under section 212(h)(2) of the Act.

(e) *Provisional unlawful presence waivers of inadmissibility.* The provisions of this paragraph (e) apply to certain aliens who are pursuing consular immigrant visa processing.

(1) *Jurisdiction.* USCIS has exclusive jurisdiction to grant a provisional unlawful presence waiver under this paragraph (e). An alien applying for a provisional unlawful presence waiver must file with USCIS the form designated by USCIS, with the fees prescribed in 8 CFR 103.7(b), and in accordance with the form instructions.

(2) *Provisional unlawful presence waiver; in general.* (i) USCIS may adjudicate applications for a provisional unlawful presence waiver of inadmissibility based on section 212(a)(9)(B)(v) of the Act filed by eligible aliens described in paragraph (e)(3) of this section. USCIS will only approve such provisional unlawful presence waiver applications in accordance with the conditions outlined in paragraph (e) of this section. Consistent with section 212(a)(9)(B)(v) of the Act, the decision whether to approve a provisional unlawful presence waiver application is discretionary. A pending or approved provisional unlawful presence waiver does not constitute

a grant of a lawful immigration status or a period of stay authorized by the Secretary.

(ii) A pending or an approved provisional unlawful presence waiver does not support the filing of any application for interim immigration benefits, such as employment authorization or an advance parole document. Any application for an advance parole document or employment authorization that is submitted in connection with a provisional unlawful presence waiver application will be rejected.

(3) *Eligible aliens.* Except as provided in paragraph (e)(4) of this section, an alien may be eligible to apply for and receive a provisional unlawful presence waiver for the grounds of inadmissibility under section 212(a)(9)(B)(i)(I) or (II) of the Act if he or she meets the requirements in this paragraph. An alien may be eligible to apply for and receive a waiver if he or she:

(i) Is present in the United States at the time of filing the application for a provisional unlawful presence waiver;

(ii) Provides biometrics to USCIS at a location in the United States designated by USCIS;

(iii) Upon departure, would be inadmissible only under section 212(a)(9)(B)(i) of the Act at the time of the immigrant visa interview;

(iv) Has a case pending with the Department of State, based on:

(A) An approved immigrant visa petition, for which the Department of State immigrant visa processing fee has been paid; or

(B) Selection by the Department of State to participate in the Diversity Visa Program under section 203(c) of the Act for the fiscal year for which the alien registered;

(v) Will depart from the United States to obtain the immigrant visa; and

(vi) Meets the requirements for a waiver provided in section 212(a)(9)(B)(v) of the Act.

(4) *Ineligible aliens.* Notwithstanding paragraph (e)(3) of this section, an alien is ineligible for a provisional unlawful presence waiver under paragraph (e) of this section if:

(i) The alien is under the age of 17;

(ii) The alien does not have a case pending with the Department of State, based on:

(A) An approved immigrant visa petition, for which the Department of State immigrant visa processing fee has been paid; or

(B) Selection by the Department of State to participate in the Diversity Visa program under section 203(c) of the Act for the fiscal year for which the alien registered;

(iii) The alien is in removal proceedings, in which no final order has been entered, unless the removal proceedings are administratively closed and have not been recalendared at the time of filing the application for a provisional unlawful presence waiver;

(iv) The alien is subject to an administratively final order of removal, deportation, or exclusion under any provision of law (including an *in absentia* order under section 240(b)(5) of the Act), unless the alien has already filed and USCIS has already granted, before the alien applies for a provisional unlawful presence waiver under 8 CFR 212.7(e), an application for consent to reapply for admission under section 212(a)(9)(A)(iii) of the Act and 8 CFR 212.2(j);

(v) CBP or ICE, after service of notice under 8 CFR 241.8, has reinstated a prior order of removal under section 241(a)(5) of the Act, either before the filing of the provisional unlawful presence waiver application or while the provisional unlawful presence waiver application is pending; or

(vi) The alien has a pending application with USCIS for lawful permanent resident status.

(5) *Filing.* (i) An alien must file an application for a provisional unlawful presence waiver of the unlawful presence inadmissibility bars under section 212(a)(9)(B)(i)(I) or (II) of the Act on the form designated by USCIS, in accordance with the form instructions, with the fee prescribed in 8 CFR 103.7(b), and with the evidence required by the form instructions.

(ii) An application for a provisional unlawful presence waiver will be rejected and the fee and package returned to the alien if the alien:

(A) Fails to pay the required filing fee or correct filing fee for the provisional unlawful presence waiver application;

(B) Fails to sign the provisional unlawful presence waiver application;

(C) Fails to provide his or her family name, domestic home address, and date of birth;

(D) Is under the age of 17;

(E) Does not include evidence of:

(1) An approved immigrant visa petition;

(2) Selection by the Department of State to participate in the Diversity Visa Program under section 203(c) of the Act for the fiscal year for which the alien registered; or

(3) Eligibility as a derivative beneficiary of an approved immigrant visa petition or of an alien selected for participation in the Diversity Visa Program as provided in this section and outlined in section 203(d) of the Act.

(F) Fails to include documentation evidencing:

(1) That the alien has paid the immigrant visa processing fee to the Department of State for the immigrant visa application upon which the alien's approved immigrant visa petition is based; or

(2) In the case of a diversity immigrant, that the Department of State selected the alien to participate in the Diversity Visa Program for the fiscal year for which the alien registered.

(6) *Biometrics.* (i) All aliens who apply for a provisional unlawful presence waiver under this section will be required to provide biometrics in accordance with 8 CFR 103.16 and 103.17, as specified on the form instructions.

(ii) *Failure to appear for biometric services.* If an alien fails to appear for a biometric services appointment or fails to provide biometrics in the United States as directed by USCIS, a provisional unlawful presence waiver application will be considered abandoned and denied under 8 CFR 103.2(b)(13). The alien may not appeal or file a motion to reopen or reconsider an abandonment denial under 8 CFR 103.5.

(7) *Burden and standard of proof.* The alien has the burden to establish, by a preponderance of the evidence, eligibility for a provisional unlawful presence waiver as described in this paragraph, and under section 212(a)(9)(B)(v) of the Act, including that the alien merits a favorable exercise of discretion.

(8) *Adjudication.* USCIS will adjudicate a provisional unlawful presence waiver application in accordance with this paragraph and section 212(a)(9)(B)(v) of the Act. If USCIS finds that the alien is not eligible for a provisional unlawful presence waiver, or if USCIS determines in its discretion that a waiver is not warranted, USCIS will deny the waiver application. Notwithstanding 8 CFR 103.2(b)(16), USCIS may deny an application for a provisional unlawful presence waiver without prior issuance of a request for evidence or notice of intent to deny.

(9) *Notice of decision.* (i) USCIS will notify the alien and the alien's attorney of record or accredited representative of the decision in accordance with 8 CFR 103.2(b)(19). USCIS may notify the Department of State of the denial of an application for a provisional unlawful presence waiver. A denial is without prejudice to the alien's filing another provisional unlawful presence waiver application under this paragraph (e), provided the alien meets all of the requirements in this part, including that the alien's case must be pending with the Department of State. An alien also may elect to file a waiver application under paragraph (a)(1) of this section after departing the United States, appearing for his or her immigrant visa interview at the U.S. Embassy or consulate abroad, and after the Department of State determines the alien's admissibility and eligibility for an immigrant visa.

(ii) Denial of an application for a provisional unlawful presence waiver is not a final agency action for purposes of section 10(c) of the Administrative Procedure Act, 5 U.S.C. 704.

(10) *Withdrawal of waiver applications.* An alien may withdraw his or her application for a provisional unlawful presence waiver at any time before USCIS makes a final decision. Once the case is withdrawn, USCIS will close the case and notify the alien and his or her attorney or accredited representative. The alien may file a new application for a provisional unlawful presence

waiver, in accordance with the form instructions and required fees, provided that the alien meets all of the requirements included in this paragraph (e).

(11) *Appeals and motions to reopen.* There is no administrative appeal from a denial of a request for a provisional unlawful presence waiver under this section. The alien may not file, pursuant to 8 CFR 103.5, a motion to reopen or reconsider a denial of a provisional unlawful presence waiver application under this section.

(12) *Approval and conditions.* A provisional unlawful presence waiver granted under this section:

(i) Does not take effect unless, and until, the alien who applied for and obtained the provisional unlawful presence waiver:

(A) Departs from the United States;

(B) Appears for an immigrant visa interview at a U.S. Embassy or consulate; and

(C) Is determined to be otherwise eligible for an immigrant visa by the Department of State in light of the approved provisional unlawful presence waiver.

(ii) Waives, upon satisfaction of the conditions described in paragraph (e)(12)(i), the alien's inadmissibility under section 212(a)(9)(B) of the Act only for purposes of the application for an immigrant visa and admission to the United States as an immigrant based on the approved immigrant visa petition upon which a provisional unlawful presence waiver application is based or selection by the Department of State to participate in the Diversity Visa Program under section 203(c) of the Act for the fiscal year for which the alien registered, with such selection being the basis for the alien's provisional unlawful presence waiver application;

(iii) Does not waive any ground of inadmissibility other than, upon satisfaction of the conditions described in paragraph (e)(12)(i), the grounds of inadmissibility under section 212(a)(9)(B)(i)(I) or (II) of the Act.

(13) *Validity.* Until the provisional unlawful presence waiver takes full effect as provided in paragraph (e)(12) of this section, USCIS may reopen and reconsider its decision at any time. Once a provisional unlawful presence waiver takes full effect as defined in paragraph (e)(12) of this section, the period of unlawful presence for which the provisional unlawful presence waiver is granted is waived indefinitely, in accordance with and subject to paragraph (a)(4) of this section.

(14) *Automatic revocation.* The approval of a provisional unlawful presence waiver is revoked automatically if:

(i) The Department of State denies the immigrant visa application after completion of the immigrant visa interview based on a finding that the alien is ineligible to receive an immigrant visa for any reason other than inadmissibility under section 212(a)(9)(B)(i)(I) or (II) of the Act. This automatic revocation does not prevent the alien from applying for a waiver of inadmissibility for unlawful presence under section 212(a)(9)(B)(v) of the Act and 8 CFR 212.7(a) or for any other relief from inadmissibility on any other ground for which a waiver is available and for which the alien may be eligible;

(ii) The immigrant visa petition approval associated with the provisional unlawful presence waiver is at any time revoked, withdrawn, or rendered invalid but not otherwise reinstated for humanitarian reasons or converted to a widow or widower petition;

(iii) The immigrant visa registration is terminated in accordance with section 203(g) of the Act, and has not been reinstated in accordance with section 203(g) of the Act; or

(iv) The alien enters or attempts to reenter the United States without inspection and admission or parole at any time after the alien files the provisional unlawful presence waiver application and before the approval of the provisional unlawful presence waiver takes effect in accordance with paragraph (e)(12) of this section.

(Secs. 103, 203, 212 of the Immigration and Nationality Act, as amended by secs. 4, 5, 18 of Pub. L. 97–116, 95 Stat. 1611, 1620, (8 U.S.C. 1103, 1153, 1182)

[29 FR 12584, Sept. 4, 1964]

EDITORIAL NOTE: For FEDERAL REGISTER citations affecting §212.7, see the List of CFR Sections Affected, which appears in the Finding Aids section of the printed volume and at *www.govinfo.gov*.

§§ 212.8–212.9 [Reserved]

§ 212.10 Section 212(k) waiver.

Any applicant for admission who is in possession of an immigrant visa, and who is inadmissible under section 212(a)(5)(A) or 212(a)(7)(A)(i) of the Act, may apply at the port of entry for a waiver under section 212(k) of the Act. If the application for waiver is denied, the application may be renewed in removal proceedings before an immigration judge as provided in 8 CFR part 1240.

[76 FR 53787, Aug. 29, 2011]

§ 212.11 [Reserved]

§ 212.12 Parole determinations and revocations respecting Mariel Cubans.

(a) *Scope.* This section applies to any native of Cuba who last came to the United States between April 15, 1980, and October 20, 1980 (hereinafter referred to as *Mariel Cuban*) and who is being detained by the Immigration and Naturalization Service (hereinafter referred to as the *Service*) pending his or her exclusion hearing, or pending his or her return to Cuba or to another country. It covers Mariel Cubans who have never been paroled as well as those Mariel Cubans whose previous parole has been revoked by the Service. It also applies to any Mariel Cuban, detained under the authority of the Immigration and Nationality Act in any facility, who has not been approved for release or who is currently awaiting movement to a Service or Bureau Of Prisons (BOP) facility. In addition, it covers the revocation of parole for those Mariel Cubans who have been released on parole at any time.

(b) *Parole authority and decision.* The authority to grant parole under section 212(d)(5) of the Act to a detained Mariel Cuban shall be exercised by the Commissioner, acting through the Associate Commissioner for Enforcement, as follows:

(1) *Parole decisions.* The Associate Commissioner for Enforcement may, in the exercise of discretion, grant parole to a detained Mariel Cuban for emergent reasons or for reasons deemed strictly in the public interest. A decision to retain in custody shall briefly set forth the reasons for the continued detention. A decision to release on parole may contain such special conditions as are considered appropriate. A copy of any decision to parole or to detain, with an attached copy translated into Spanish, shall be provided to the detainee. Parole documentation for Mariel Cubans shall be issued by the district director having jurisdiction over the alien, in accordance with the parole determination made by the Associate Commissioner for Enforcement.

(2) *Additional delegation of authority.* All references to the Commissioner and Associate Commissioner for Enforcement in this section shall be deemed to include any person or persons (including a committee) designated in writing by the Commissioner or Associate Commissioner for Enforcement to exercise powers under this section.

(c) *Review Plan Director.* The Associate Commissioner for Enforcement shall appoint a Director of the Cuban Review Plan. The Director shall have authority to establish and maintain appropriate files respecting each Mariel Cuban to be reviewed for possible parole, to determine the order in which the cases shall be reviewed, and to coordinate activities associated with these reviews.

(d) *Recommendations to the Associate Commissioner for Enforcement.* Parole recommendations for detained Mariel Cubans shall be developed in accordance with the following procedures.

(1) *Review Panels.* The Director shall designate a panel or panels to make parole recommendations to the Associate Commissioner for Enforcement. A Cuban Review Panel shall, except as otherwise provided, consist of two persons. Members of a Review Panel shall be selected from the professional staff of the Service. All recommendations by a two-member Panel shall be unanimous. If the vote of a two-member Panel is split, it shall adjourn its deliberations concerning that particular detainee until a third Panel member is added. A recommendation by a three-member Panel shall be by majority vote. The third member of any Panel shall be the Director of the Cuban Review Plan or his designee.

(2) *Criteria for Review.* Before making any recommendation that a detainee

be granted parole, a majority of the Cuban Review Panel members, or the Director in case of a record review, must conclude that:

(i) The detainee is presently a nonviolent person;

(ii) The detainee is likely to remain nonviolent;

(iii) The detainee is not likely to pose a threat to the community following his release; and

(iv) The detainee is not likely to violate the conditions of his parole.

(3) *Factors for consideration.* The following factors should be weighed in considering whether to recommend further detention or release on parole of a detainee:

(i) The nature and number of disciplinary infractions or incident reports received while in custody;

(ii) The detainee's past history of criminal behavior;

(iii) Any psychiatric and psychological reports pertaining to the detainee's mental health;

(iv) Institutional progress relating to participation in work, educational and vocational programs;

(v) His ties to the United States, such as the number of close relatives residing lawfully here;

(vi) The likelihood that he may abscond, such as from any sponsorship program; and

(vii) Any other information which is probative of whether the detainee is likely to adjust to life in a community, is likely to engage in future acts of violence, is likely to engage in future criminal activity, or is likely to violate the conditions of his parole.

(4) *Procedure for review.* The following procedures will govern the review process:

(i) *Record review.* Initially, the Director or a Panel shall review the detainee's file. Upon completion of this record review, the Director or the Panel shall issue a written recommendation that the detainee be released on parole or scheduled for a personal interview.

(ii) *Personal interview.* If a recommendation to grant parole after only a record review is not accepted or if the detainee is not recommended for release, a Panel shall personally interview the detainee. The scheduling of such interviews shall be at the discretion of the Director. The detainee may be accompanied during the interview by a person of his choice, who is able to attend at the time of the scheduled interview, to assist in answering any questions. The detainee may submit to the Panel any information, either orally or in writing, which he believes presents a basis for release on parole.

(iii) *Panel recommendation.* Following completion of the interview and its deliberations, the Panel shall issue a written recommendation that the detainee be released on parole or remain in custody pending deportation or pending further observation and subsequent review. This written recommendation shall include a brief statement of the factors which the Panel deems material to its recommendation. The recommendation and appropriate file material shall be forwarded to the Associate Commissioner for Enforcement, to be considered in the exercise of discretion pursuant to §212.12(b).

(e) *Withdrawal of parole approval.* The Associate Commissioner for Enforcement may, in his or her discretion, withdraw approval for parole of any detainee prior to release when, in his or her opinion, the conduct of the detainee, or any other circumstance, indicates that parole would no longer be appropriate.

(f) *Sponsorship.* No detainee may be released on parole until suitable sponsorship or placement has been found for the detainee. The paroled detainee must abide by the parole conditions specified by the Service in relation to his sponsorship or placement. The following sponsorships and placements are suitable:

(1) Placement by the Public Health Service in an approved halfway house or mental health project;

(2) Placement by the Community Relations Service in an approved halfway house or community project; and

(3) Placement with a close relative such as a parent, spouse, child, or sibling who is a lawful permanent resident or a citizen of the United States.

(g) *Timing of reviews.* The timing of review shall be in accordance with the following guidelines.

(1) *Parole revocation cases.* The Director shall schedule the review process in the case of a new or returning detainee whose previous immigration parole has been revoked. The review process will commence with a scheduling of a file review, which will ordinarily be expected to occur within approximately three months after parole is revoked. In the case of a Mariel Cuban who is in the custody of the Service, the Cuban Review Plan Director may, in his or her discretion, suspend or postpone the parole review process if such detainee's prompt deportation is practicable and proper.

(2) *Continued detention cases.* A subsequent review shall be commenced for any detainee within one year of a refusal to grant parole under § 212.12(b), unless a shorter interval is specified by the Director.

(3) *Discretionary reviews.* The Cuban Review Plan Director, in his discretion, may schedule a review of a detainee at any time when the Director deems such a review to be warranted.

(h) *Revocation of parole.* The Associate Commissioner for Enforcement shall have authority, in the exercise of discretion, to revoke parole in respect to Mariel Cubans. A district director may also revoke parole when, in the district director's opinion, revocation is in the public interest and circumstances do not reasonably permit referral of the case to the Associate Commissioner. Parole may be revoked in the exercise of discretion when, in the opinion of the revoking official:

(1) The purposes of parole have been served;

(2) The Mariel Cuban violates any condition of parole;

(3) It is appropriate to enforce an order of exclusion or to commence proceedings against a Mariel Cuban; or

(4) The period of parole has expired without being renewed.

[52 FR 48802, Dec. 28, 1987, as amended at 59 FR 13870, Mar. 24, 1994; 65 FR 80294, Dec. 21, 2000]

§ 212.13 [Reserved]

§ 212.14 Parole determinations for alien witnesses and informants for whom a law enforcement authority ("LEA") will request S classification.

(a) *Parole authority.* Parole authorization under section 212(d)(5) of the Act for aliens whom LEAs seek to bring to the United States as witnesses or informants in criminal/counter terrorism matters and to apply for S classification shall be exercised as follows:

(1) *Grounds of eligibility.* The Commissioner may, in the exercise of discretion, grant parole to an alien (and the alien's family members) needed for law enforcement purposes provided that a state or federal LEA:

(i) Establishes its intention to file, within 30 days after the alien's arrival in the United States, an application for S nonimmigrant status on the form designated for such purposes, with the Assistant Attorney General, Criminal Division, Department of Justice, in accordance with the instructions on or attached to the form, which will include the names of qualified family members for whom parole is sought;

(ii) Specifies the particular operational reasons and basis for the request, and agrees to assume responsibility for the alien during the period of the alien's temporary stay in the United States, including maintaining control and supervision of the alien and the alien's whereabouts and activities, and further specifies any other terms and conditions specified by the Service during the period for which the parole is authorized;

(iii) Agrees to advise the Service of the alien's failure to report quarterly any criminal conduct by the alien, or any other activity or behavior on the alien's part that may constitute a ground of excludability or deportability;

(iv) Assumes responsibility for ensuring the alien's departure on the date of termination of the authorized parole (unless the alien has been admitted in S nonimmigrant classification pursuant to the terms of paragraph (a)(2) of this section), provides any and all assistance needed by the Service, if necessary, to ensure departure, and verifies departure in a manner acceptable to the Service;

(v) Provide LEA seat-of-government certification that parole of the alien is essential to an investigation or prosecution, is in the national interest, and is requested pursuant to the terms and authority of section 212(d)(5) of the Act;

(vi) Agrees that no promises may be, have been, or will be made by the LEA to the alien that the alien will or may:

(A) Remain in the United States in parole status or any other nonimmigrant classification;

(B) Adjust status to that of lawful permanent resident; or

(C) Otherwise attempt to remain beyond the authorized parole. The alien (and any family member of the alien who is 18 years of age or older) shall sign a statement acknowledging an awareness that parole only authorizes a temporary stay in the United States and does not convey the benefits of S nonimmigrant classification, any other nonimmigrant classification, or any entitlement to further benefits under the Act; and

(vii) Provides, in the case of a request for the release of an alien from Service custody, certification that the alien is eligible for parole pursuant to § 235.3 of this chapter.

(2) *Authorization.* (i) Upon approval of the request for parole, the Commissioner shall notify the Assistant Attorney General, Criminal Division, of the approval.

(ii) Upon notification of approval of a request for parole, the LEA will advise the Commissioner of the date, time, and place of the arrival of the alien. The Commissioner will coordinate the arrival of the alien in parole status with the port director prior to the time of arrival.

(iii) Parole will be authorized for a period of thirty (30) days to commence upon the alien's arrival in the United States in order for the LEA to submit the completed application to the Assistant Attorney General, Criminal Division. Upon the submission to the Assistant Attorney General of the completed application for S classification, the period of parole will be automatically extended while the request is being reviewed. The Assistant Attorney General, Criminal Division, will notify the Commissioner of the submission of the application.

(b) *Termination of parole*—(1) *General.* The Commissioner may terminate parole for any alien (including a member of the alien's family) in parole status under this section where termination is in the public interest. A district director may also terminate parole when, in the district director's opinion, termination is in the public interest and circumstances do not reasonably permit referral of the case to the Commissioner. In such a case, the Commissioner shall be notified immediately. In the event the Commissioner, or in the appropriate case, a district director, decides to terminate the parole of an alien witness or informant authorized under the terms of this paragraph, the Assistant Attorney General, Criminal Division, and the relevant LEA shall be notified in writing to that effect. The Assistant Attorney General, Criminal Division, shall concur in or object to that decision. Unless the Assistant Attorney General, Criminal Division, objects within 7 days, he or she shall be deemed to have concurred in the decision. In the event of an objection by the Assistant Attorney General, Criminal Division, the matter will be expeditiously referred to the Deputy Attorney General for a final resolution. In no circumstances shall the alien or the relevant LEA have a right of appeal from any decision to terminate parole.

(2) *Termination of parole and admission in S classification.* When an LEA has filed a request for an alien in authorized parole status to be admitted in S nonimmigrant classification and that request has been approved by the Commissioner pursuant to the procedures outlines in 8 CFR 214.2(t), the Commissioner may, in the exercise of discretion:

(i) Terminate the alien's parole status;

(ii) Determine eligibility for waivers; and

(iii) Admit the alien in S nonimmigrant classification pursuant to the terms and conditions of section 101(a)(15(S) of the Act and 8 CFR 214.2(t).

(c) *Departure.* If the alien's parole has been terminated and the alien has been ordered excluded from the United States, the LEA shall ensure departure from the United States and so inform the district director in whose jurisdiction the alien has last resided. The district director, if necessary, shall oversee the alien's departure from the United States and, in any event, shall notify the Commissioner of the alien's departure. The Commissioner shall be notified in writing of the failure of any alien authorized parole under this paragraph to depart in accordance with an order of exclusion and deportation entered after parole authorized under this paragraph has been terminated.

(d) *Failure to comply with procedures.* Any failure to adhere to the parole procedures contained in this section shall immediately be brought to the attention of the Commissioner, who will notify the Attorney General.

[60 FR 44265, Aug. 25, 1995, as amended at 76 FR 53787, Aug. 29, 2011]

§212.15 Certificates for foreign health care workers.

(a) *General certification requirements.* (1) Except as provided in paragraph (b) or paragraph (d)(1) of this section, any alien who seeks admission to the United States as an immigrant or as a nonimmigrant for the primary purpose of performing labor in a health care occupation listed in paragraph (c) of this section is inadmissible unless the alien presents a certificate from a credentialing organization, listed in paragraph (e) of this section.

(2) In the alternative, an eligible alien who seeks to enter the United States for the primary purpose of performing labor as a nurse may present a certified statement as provided in paragraph (h) of this section.

(3) A certificate or certified statement described in this section does not constitute professional authorization to practice in that health care occupation.

(b) *Inapplicability of the ground of inadmissibility.* This section does not apply to:

(1) Physicians;

(2) Aliens seeking admission to the United States to perform services in a non-clinical health care occupation. A non-clinical care occupation is one in which the alien is not required to perform direct or indirect patient care. Occupations which are considered to be non-clinical include, but are not limited to, medical teachers, medical researchers, and managers of health care facilities;

(3) Aliens coming to the United States to receive training as an H–3 nonimmigrant, or receiving training as part of an F or J nonimmigrant program.

(4) The spouse and dependent children of any immigrant or nonimmigrant alien;

(5) Any alien applying for adjustment of status to that of a permanent resident under any provision of law other than under section 245 of the Act, or any alien who is seeking adjustment of status under section 245 of the Act on the basis of a relative visa petition approved under section 203(a) of the Act, or any alien seeking adjustment of status under section 245 of the Act on the basis of an employment-based petition approved pursuant to section 203(b) of the Act for employment that does not fall under one of the covered health care occupations listed in paragraph (c) of this section.

(c) *Covered health care occupations.* With the exception of the aliens described in paragraph (b) of this section, this paragraph (c) applies to any alien seeking admission to the United States to perform labor in one of the following health care occupations, regardless of where he or she received his or her education or training:

(1) Licensed Practical Nurses, Licensed Vocational Nurses, and Registered Nurses.

(2) Occupational Therapists.

(3) Physical Therapists.

(4) Speech Language Pathologists and Audiologists.

(5) Medical Technologists (Clinical Laboratory Scientists).

(6) Physician Assistants.

(7) Medical Technicians (Clinical Laboratory Technicians)

(d) *Presentation of certificate or certified statements*—(1) *Aliens required to obtain visas.* Except as provided in paragraph (n) of this section, if 8 CFR 212.1 requires an alien who is described in paragraph (a) of this section and who is applying for admission as a nonimmigrant seeking to perform labor in a health care occupation as described in this section to obtain a nonimmigrant visa, the alien must present a certificate or certified statement to a consular officer at the time of visa issuance and to the Department of Homeland Security (DHS) at the time of admission. The certificate or certified statement must be valid at the time of visa issuance and admission at a port-of-entry. An alien who has previously presented a foreign health care worker certification or certified statement for a particular health care occupation will be required to present it again at the time of visa issuance or each admission to the United States.

(2) *Aliens not requiring a nonimmigrant visa.* Except as provided in paragraph (n) of this section, an alien described in paragraph (a) of this section who, pursuant to 8 CFR 212.1, is not required to obtain a nonimmigrant visa to apply for admission to the United States must present a certificate or certified statement as provided in this section to an immigration officer at the time of initial application for admission to the United States to perform labor in a particular health care occupation. An alien who has previously presented a foreign health care worker certification or certified statement for a particular health care occupation will be required to present it again at the time of each application for admission.

(e) *Approved credentialing organizations for health care workers.* An alien may present a certificate from any credentialing organization listed in this paragraph (e) with respect to a particular health care field. In addition to paragraphs (e)(1) through (e)(3) of this section, the DHS will notify the public of additional credentialing organizations through the publication of notices in the FEDERAL REGISTER.

(1) The Commission on Graduates of Foreign Nursing Schools (CGFNS) is authorized to issue certificates under section 212(a)(5)(C) of the Act for nurses, physical therapists, occupational therapists, speech-language pathologists and audiologists, medical technologists (also known as clinical laboratory scientists), medical technicians (also known as clinical laboratory technicians), and physician assistants.

(2) The National Board for Certification in Occupational Therapy (NBCOT) is authorized to issue certificates in the field of occupational therapy pending final adjudication of its credentialing status under this part.

(3) The Foreign Credentialing Commission on Physical Therapy (FCCPT) is authorized to issue certificates in the field of physical therapy pending final adjudication of its credentialing status under this part.

(f) *Requirements for issuance of health care certification.* (1) Prior to issuing a certification to an alien, the organization must verify the following:

(i) That the alien's education, training, license, and experience are comparable with that required for an American health care worker of the same type;

(ii) That the alien's education, training, license, and experience are authentic and, in the case of a license, unencumbered;

(iii) That the alien's education, training, license, and experience meet all applicable statutory and regulatory requirements for admission into the United States. This verification is not binding on the DHS; and

(iv) Either that the alien has passed a test predicting success on the occupation's licensing or certification examination, provided such a test is recognized by a majority of states licensing the occupation for which the certification is issued, or that the alien has passed the occupation's licensing or certification examination.

(2) A certificate issued under section 212(a)(5)(C) of the Act must contain the following:

(i) The name, address, and telephone number of the credentialing organization, and a point of contact to verify the validity of the certificate;

(ii) The date the certificate was issued;

(iii) The health care occupation for which the certificate was issued; and

(iv) The alien's name, and date and place of birth.

(g) *English language requirements.* (1) With the exception of those aliens described in paragraph (g)(2) of this section, every alien must meet certain English language requirements in order to obtain a certificate. The Secretary of HHS has sole authority to set standards for these English language requirements, and has determined that an alien must have a passing score on one of the three tests listed in paragraph (g)(3) of this section before he or she can be granted a certificate. HHS will notify The Department of Homeland Security of additions or deletions to this list, and The Department of Homeland Security will publish such changes in the FEDERAL REGISTER.

(2) The following aliens are exempt from the English language requirements:

(i) Alien nurses who are presenting a certified statement under section 212(r) of the Act; and

(ii) Aliens who have graduated from a college, university, or professional training school located in Australia, Canada (except Quebec), Ireland, New Zealand, the United Kingdom, or the United States.

(3) The following English testing services have been approved by the Secretary of HHS:

(i) Educational Testing Service (ETS).

(ii) Test of English in International Communication (TOEIC) Service International.

(iii) International English Language Testing System (IELTS).

(4) Passing English test scores for various occupations.

(i) *Occupational and physical therapists.* An alien seeking to perform labor in the United States as an occupational or physical therapist must obtain the following scores on the English tests administered by ETS: Test Of English as a Foreign Language (TOEFL): Paper-Based 560, Computer-Based 220; Test of Written English (TWE): 4.5; Test of Spoken English (TSE): 50. The certifying organizations shall not accept the results of the TOEIC, or the IELTS for the occupation of occupational therapy or physical therapy.

(ii) *Registered nurses and other health care workers requiring the attainment of a baccalaureate degree.* An alien coming to the United States to perform labor as a registered nurse (other than a nurse presenting a certified statement under section 212(r) of the Act) or to perform labor in another health care occupation requiring a baccalaureate degree (other than occupational or physical therapy) must obtain one of the following combinations of scores to obtain a certificate:

(A) ETS: TOEFL: Paper-Based 540, Computer-Based 207; TWE: 4.0; TSE: 50;

(B) TOEIC Service International: TOEIC: 725; plus TWE: 4.0 and TSE: 50; or

(C) IELTS: 6.5 overall with a spoken band score of 7.0. This would require the Academic module.

(iii) *Occupations requiring less than a baccalaureate degree.* An alien coming to the United States to perform labor in a health care occupation that does not require a baccalaureate degree must obtain one of the following combinations of scores to obtain a certificate:

(A) ETS: TOEFL: Paper-Based 530, Computer-Based 197; TWE: 4.0; TSE: 50;

(B) TOEIC Service International: TOEIC: 700; plus TWE 4.0 and TSE: 50; or

(C) IELTS: 6.0 overall with a spoken band score of 7.0. This would allow either the Academic or the General module.

(h) *Alternative certified statement for certain nurses.* (1) CGFNS is authorized to issue certified statements under section 212(r) of the Act for aliens seeking to enter the United States to perform labor as nurses. The DHS will notify the public of new organizations that are approved to issue certified statements through notices published in the FEDERAL REGISTER.

(2) An approved credentialing organization may issue a certified statement to an alien if each of the following requirements is satisfied:

(i) The alien has a valid and unrestricted license as a nurse in a state where the alien intends to be employed and such state verifies that the foreign licenses of alien nurses are authentic and unencumbered;

(ii) The alien has passed the National Council Licensure Examination for registered nurses (NCLEX-RN);

(iii) The alien is a graduate of a nursing program in which the language of instruction was English;

(iv) The nursing program was located in Australia, Canada (except Quebec), Ireland, New Zealand, South Africa, the United Kingdom, or the United

States; or in any other country designated by unanimous agreement of CGFNS and any equivalent credentialing organizations which have been approved for the certification of nurses and which are listed at paragraph (e) of this section; and

(v) The nursing program was in operation on or before November 12, 1999, or has been approved by unanimous agreement of CGFNS and any equivalent credentialing organizations that have been approved for the certification of nurses.

(3) An individual who obtains a certified statement need not comply with the certificate requirements of paragraph (f) or the English language requirements of paragraph (g) of this section.

(4) A certified statement issued to a nurse under section 212(r) of the Act must contain the following information:

(i) The name, address, and telephone number of the credentialing organization, and a point of contact to verify the validity of the certified statement;

(ii) The date the certified statement was issued; and

(iii) The alien's name, and date and place of birth.

(i) *Streamlined certification process*—(1) *Nurses.* An alien nurse who has graduated from an entry level program accredited by the National League for Nursing Accreditation Commission (NLNAC) or the Commission on Collegiate Nursing Education (CCNE) is exempt from the educational comparability review and English language proficiency testing.

(2) *Occupational Therapists.* An alien occupational therapist who has graduated from a program accredited by the Accreditation Council for Occupational Therapy Education (ACOTE) of the American Occupational Therapy Association (AOTA) is exempt from the educational comparability review and English language proficiency testing.

(3) *Physical therapists.* An alien physical therapist who has graduated from a program accredited by the Commission on Accreditation in Physical Therapy Education (CAPTE) of the American Physical Therapy Association (APTA) is exempt from the educational comparability review and English language proficiency testing.

(4) *Speech language pathologists and audiologists.* An alien speech language pathologists and/or audiologist who has graduated from a program accredited by the Council on Academic Accreditation in Audiology and Speech Language Pathology (CAA) of the American Speech-Language-Hearing Association (ASHA) is exempt from the educational comparability review and English language proficiency testing.

(j) *Application process for credentialing organizations*—(1) *Organizations other than CGFNS.* An organization, other than CGFNS, seeking to obtain approval to issue certificates to health care workers, or certified statements to nurses must apply on the form designated by USCIS in accordance with the form instructions. An organization seeking authorization to issue certificates or certified statements must agree to submit all evidence required by the DHS and, upon request, allow the DHS to review the organization's records related to the certification process. The application must:

(i) Clearly describe and identify the organization seeking authorization to issue certificates;

(ii) List the occupations for which the organization desires to provide certificates;

(iii) Describe how the organization substantially meets the standards described at paragraph (k) of this section;

(iv) Describe the organization's expertise, knowledge, and experience in the health care occupation(s) for which it desires to issue certificates;

(v) Provide a point of contact;

(vi) Describe the verification procedure the organization has designed in order for the DHS to verify the validity of a certificate; and

(vii) Describe how the organization will process and issue in a timely manner the certificates.

(2) *Applications filed by CGFNS.* (i) CGFNS must apply to ensure that it will be in compliance with the regulations governing the issuance and content of certificates to nurses, physical therapists, occupational therapists, speech-language pathologists and audiologists, medical technologists (also

known as clinical laboratory scientists), medical technicians (also known as clinical laboratory technicians), and physician assistants under section 212(a)(5)(C) of the Act, or issuing certified statements to nurses under section 212(r) of the Act.

(ii) Prior to issuing certificates for any other health care occupations, CGFNS must apply on the form designated by USCIS with the fee prescribed in 8 CFR 103.7(b)(1) and in accordance with the form instructions for authorization to issue such certificates. The DHS will evaluate CGFNS' expertise with respect to the particular health care occupation for which authorization to issue certificates is sought, in light of CGFNS' statutory designation as a credentialing organization.

(3) *Procedure for review of applications by credentialing organizations.* (i) USCIS will, forward a copy of the application and supporting documents to the Secretary of HHS in order to obtain an opinion on the merits of the application. The DHS will not render a decision on the request until the Secretary of HHS provides an opinion. The DHS shall accord the Secretary of HHS' opinion great weight in reaching its decision. The DHS may deny the organization's request notwithstanding the favorable recommendation from the Secretary of HHS, on grounds unrelated to the credentialing of health care occupations or health care services.

(ii) The DHS will notify the organization of the decision on its application in writing and, if the request is denied, of the reasons for the denial. Approval of authorization to issue certificates to foreign health care workers or certified statements to nurses will be made in 5-year increments, subject to the review process described at paragraph (l) of this section.

(iii) If the application is denied, the decision may be appealed pursuant to 8 CFR 103.3.

(k) *Standards for credentialing organizations.* The DHS will evaluate organizations, including CGFNS, seeking to obtain approval from the DHS to issue certificates for health care workers, or certified statements for nurses. Any organization meeting the standards set forth in paragraph (k)(1) of this section can be eligible for authorization to issue certificates. While CGFNS has been specifically listed in the statute as an entity authorized to issue certificates, it is not exempt from governmental oversight. All organizations will be reviewed, including CGFNS, to guarantee that they continue to meet the standards required of all certifying organizations, under the following:

(1) *Structure of the organization.* (i) The organization shall be incorporated as a legal entity.

(ii)(A) The organization shall be independent of any organization that functions as a representative of the occupation or profession in question or serves as or is related to a recruitment/placement organization.

(B) The DHS shall not approve an organization that is unable to render impartial advice regarding an individual's qualifications regarding training, experience, and licensure.

(C) The organization must also be independent in all decision making matters pertaining to evaluations and/or examinations that it develops including, but not limited to: policies and procedures; eligibility requirements and application processing; standards for granting certificates and their renewal; examination content, development, and administration; examination cut-off scores, excluding those pertaining to English language requirements; grievance and disciplinary processes; governing body and committee meeting rules; publications about qualifying for a certificate and its renewal; setting fees for application and all other services provided as part of the screening process; funding, spending, and budget authority related to the operation of the certification organization; ability to enter into contracts and grant arrangements; ability to demonstrate adequate staffing and management resources to conduct the program(s) including the authority to approve selection of, evaluate, and initiate dismissal of the chief staff member.

(D) An organization whose fees are based on whether an applicant receives a visa may not be approved.

(iii) The organization shall include the following representation in the portion of its organization responsible for overseeing certification and, where applicable, examinations:

(A) Individuals from the same health care discipline as the alien health care worker being evaluated who are eligible to practice in the United States; and

(B) At least one voting public member to represent the interests of consumers and protect the interests of the public at large. The public member shall not be a member of the discipline or derive significant income from the discipline, its related organizations, or the organization issuing the certificate.

(iv) The organization must have a balanced representation such that the individuals from the same health care discipline, the voting public members, and any other appointed individuals have an equal say in matters relating to credentialing and/or examinations.

(v) The organization must select representatives of the discipline using one of the following recommended methods, or demonstrate that it has a selection process that meets the intent of these methods:

(A) Be selected directly by members of the discipline eligible to practice in the United States;

(B) Be selected by members of a membership organization representing the discipline or by duly elected representatives of a membership organization; or

(C) Be selected by a membership organization representing the discipline from a list of acceptable candidates supplied by the credentialing body.

(vi) The organization shall use formal procedures for the selection of members of the governing body that prohibit the governing body from selecting a majority of its successors. Not-for-profit corporations which have difficulty meeting this requirement may provide in their applications evidence that the organization is independent, and free of material conflicts of interest regarding whether an alien receives a visa.

(vii) The organization shall be separate from the accreditation and educational functions of the discipline, except for those entities recognized by the Department of Education as having satisfied the requirement of independence.

(viii) The organization shall publish and make available a document which clearly defines the responsibilities of the organization and outlines any other activities, arrangements, or agreements of the organization that are not directly related to the certification of health care workers.

(2) *Resources of the organization.* (i) The organization shall demonstrate that its staff possess the knowledge and skills necessary to accurately assess the education, work experience, licensure of health care workers, and the equivalence of foreign educational institutions, comparable to those of United States-trained health care workers and institutions.

(ii) The organization shall demonstrate the availability of financial and material resources to effectively and thoroughly conduct regular and ongoing evaluations on an international basis.

(iii) If the health care field is one for which a majority of the states require a predictor test, the organization shall demonstrate the ability to conduct examinations in those countries with educational and evaluation systems comparable to the majority of states.

(iv) The organization shall have the resources to publish and make available general descriptive materials on the procedures used to evaluate and validate credentials, including eligibility requirements, determination procedures, examination schedules, locations, fees, reporting of results, and disciplinary and grievance procedures.

(3) *Candidate evaluation and testing mechanisms.* (i) The organization shall publish and make available a comprehensive outline of the information, knowledge, or functions covered by the evaluation/examination process, including information regarding testing for English language competency.

(ii) The organization shall use reliable evaluation/examination mechanisms to evaluate individual credentials and competence that is objective, fair to all candidates, job related, and based on knowledge and skills needed in the discipline.

(iii) The organization shall conduct ongoing studies to substantiate the reliability and validity of the evaluation/examination mechanisms.

(iv) The organization shall implement a formal policy of periodic review of the evaluation/examination mechanism to ensure ongoing relevance of the mechanism with respect to knowledge and skills needed in the discipline.

(v) The organization shall use policies and procedures to ensure that all aspects of the evaluation/examination procedures, as well as the development and administration of any tests, are secure.

(vi) The organization shall institute procedures to protect against falsification of documents and misrepresentation, including a policy to request each applicant's transcript(s) and degree(s) directly from the educational licensing authorities.

(vii) The organization shall establish policies and procedures that govern the length of time the applicant's records must be kept in their original format.

(viii) The organization shall publish and make available, at least annually, a summary of all screening activities for each discipline including, at least, the number of applications received, the number of applicants evaluated, the number receiving certificates, the number who failed, and the number receiving renewals.

(4) *Responsibilities to applicants applying for an initial certificate or renewal.* (i) The organization shall not discriminate among applicants as to age, sex, race, religion, national origin, disability, or marital status and shall include a statement of nondiscrimination in announcements of the evaluation/examination procedures and renewal certification process.

(ii) The organization shall provide all applicants with copies of formalized application procedures for evaluation/examination and shall uniformly follow and enforce such procedures for all applicants. Instructions shall include standards regarding English language requirements.

(iii) The organization shall implement a formal policy for the periodic review of eligibility criteria and application procedures to ensure that they are fair and equitable.

(iv) Where examinations are used, the organization shall provide competently proctored examination sites at least once annually.

(v) The organization shall report examination results to applicants in a uniform and timely fashion.

(vi) The organization shall provide applicants who failed either the evaluation or examination with information on general areas of deficiency.

(vii) The organization shall implement policies and procedures to ensure that each applicant's examination results are held confidential and delineate the circumstances under which the applicant's certification status may be made public.

(viii) The organization shall have a formal policy for renewing the certification if an individual's original certification has expired before the individual first seeks admission to the United States or applies for adjustment of status. Such procedures shall be restricted to updating information on licensure to determine the existence of any adverse actions and the need to reestablish English competency.

(ix) The organization shall publish due process policies and procedures for applicants to question eligibility determinations, examination or evaluation results, and eligibility status.

(x) The organization shall provide all qualified applicants with a certificate in a timely manner.

(5) *Maintenance of comprehensive and current information.* (i) The organization shall maintain comprehensive and current information of the type necessary to evaluate foreign educational institutions and accrediting bodies for purposes of ensuring that the quality of foreign educational programs is equivalent to those training the same occupation in the United States. The organization shall examine, evaluate, and validate the academic and clinical requirements applied to each country's accrediting body or bodies, or in countries not having such bodies, of the educational institution itself.

(ii) The organization shall also evaluate the licensing and credentialing system(s) of each country or licensing jurisdiction to determine which systems are equivalent to that of the majority of the licensing jurisdictions in the United States.

(6) *Ability to conduct examinations fairly and impartially.* An organization undertaking the administration of a predictor examination, or a licensing or certification examination shall demonstrate the ability to conduct such examination fairly and impartially.

(7) *Criteria for awarding and governing certificate holders.* (i) The organization shall issue a certificate after the education, experience, license, and English language competency have been evaluated and determined to be equivalent to their United States counterparts. In situations where a United States nationally recognized licensure or certification examination, or a test predicting the success on the licensure or certification examination, is offered overseas, the applicant must pass the examination or the predictor test prior to receiving certification. Passage of a test predicting the success on the licensure or certification examination may be accepted only if a majority of states (and Washington, DC) licensing the profession in which the alien intends to work recognize such a test.

(ii) The organization shall have policies and procedures for the revocation of certificates at any time if it is determined that the certificate holder was not eligible to receive the certificate at the time that it was issued. If the organization revokes an individual's certificate, it must notify the DHS, via the Nebraska Service Center, and the appropriate state regulatory authority with jurisdiction over the individual's health care profession. The organization may not reissue a certificate to an individual whose certificate has been revoked.

(8) *Criteria for maintaining accreditation.* (i) The organization shall advise the DHS of any changes in purpose, structure, or activities of the organization or its program(s).

(ii) The organization shall advise the DHS of any major changes in the evaluation of credentials and examination techniques, if any, or in the scope or objectives of such examinations.

(iii) The organization shall, upon the request of the DHS, submit to the DHS, or any organization designated by the DHS, information requested of the organization and its programs for use in investigating allegations of non-compliance with standards and for general purposes of determining continued approval as an independent credentialing organization.

(iv) The organization shall establish performance outcome measures that track the ability of the certificate holders to pass United States licensure or certification examinations. The purpose of the process is to ensure that certificate holders pass United States licensure or certification examinations at the same pass rate as graduates of United States programs. Failure to establish such measures, or having a record showing an inability of persons granted certificates to pass United States licensure examinations at the same rate as graduates of United States programs, may result in a ground for termination of approval. Information regarding the passage rates of certificate holders shall be maintained by the organization and provided to HHS on an annual basis, to the DHS as part of the 5-year reauthorization application, and at any other time upon request by HHS or the DHS.

(v) The organization shall be in ongoing compliance with other policies specified by the DHS.

(l) *DHS review of the performance of certifying organizations.* The DHS will review credentialing organizations every 5 years to ensure continued compliance with the standards described in this section. Such review will occur concurrent with the adjudication of a request for reauthorization to issue health care worker certificates. The DHS will notify the credentialing organization in writing of the results of the review and request for reauthorization. The DHS may conduct a review of the approval of any request for authorization to issue certificates at any time within the 5-year period of authorization for any reason. If at any time the DHS determines that an organization is not complying with the terms of its authorization or if other adverse information relating to eligibility to issue certificates is developed, the DHS may initiate termination proceedings.

(m) *Termination of certifying organizations.* (1) If the DHS determines that an organization has been convicted, or the directors or officers of an authorized credentialing organization have individually been convicted of the violation of state or federal laws, or other information is developed such that the fitness of the organization to continue to issue certificates or certified statements is called into question, the DHS shall automatically terminate authorization for that organization to issue certificates or certified statements by issuing to the organization a notice of termination of authorization to issue certificates to foreign health care workers. The notice shall reference the specific conviction that is the basis of the automatic termination.

(2) If the DHS determines that an organization is not complying with the terms of its authorization or other adverse information relating to eligibility to issue certificates is uncovered during the course of a review or otherwise brought to the DHS' attention, or if the DHS determines that an organization currently authorized to issue certificates or certified statements has not submitted an application or provided all information required on the request within 6 months of July 25, 2003, the DHS will issue a Notice of Intent to Terminate authorization to issue certificates to the credentialing organization. The Notice shall set forth reasons for the proposed termination.

(i) The credentialing organization shall have 30 days from the date of the Notice of Intent to Terminate authorization to rebut the allegations, or to cure the noncompliance identified in the DHS's notice of intent to terminate.

(ii) DHS will forward to HHS upon receipt any information received in response to a Notice of Intent to Terminate an entity's authorization to issue certificates. Thirty days after the date of the Notice of Intent to Terminate, the DHS shall forward any additional evidence and shall request an opinion from HHS regarding whether the organization's authorization should be terminated. The DHS shall accord HHS' opinion great weight in determining whether the authorization should be terminated. After consideration of the rebuttal evidence, if any, and consideration of HHS' opinion, the DHS will promptly provide the organization with a written decision. If termination of credentialing status is made, the written decision shall set forth the reasons for the termination.

(3) An adverse decision may be appealed pursuant to 8 CFR 103.3 to the Associate Commissioner for Examinations. Termination of credentialing status shall remain in effect until and unless the terminated organization reapplies for credentialing status and is approved, or its appeal of the termination decision is sustained by the Administrative Appeals Office. There is no waiting period for an organization to re-apply for credentialing status.

(n) *Transition*—(1) *One year waiver.* (i) Pursuant to section 212(d)(3) of the Act (and, for cases described in paragraph (d)(1) of this section, upon the recommendation of the Secretary of State), the Secretary has determined that until July 26, 2004 (or until July 26, 2005, in the case of a citizen of Canada or Mexico who, before September 23, 2003, was employed as a TN or TC nonimmigrant health care worker and held a valid license from a U.S. jurisdiction), DHS, subject to the conditions in paragraph (n)(2) of this section, may in its discretion admit, extend the period of authorized stay, or change the nonimmigrant status of an alien described in paragraph (d)(1) or paragraph (d)(2) of this section, despite the alien's inadmissibility under section 212(a)(5)(C) of the Act, provided the alien is not otherwise inadmissible.

(ii) After July 26, 2004 (or, after July 26, 2005, in the case of a citizen of Canada or Mexico, who, before September 23, 2003, was employed as a TN or TC nonimmigrant health care worker and held a valid license from a U.S. jurisdiction), such discretion shall be applied on a case-by-case basis.

(2) *Conditions.* Until July 26, 2004 (or until July 26, 2005, in the case of a citizen of Canada or Mexico, who, before September 23, 2003, was employed as a TN or TC nonimmigrant health care worker and held a valid license from a U.S. jurisdiction), the temporary admission, extension of stay, or change of status of an alien described in 8 CFR part 212(d)(1) or (d)(2) of this section that is provided for under this paragraph (n) is subject to the following conditions:

(i) The admission, extension of stay, or change of status may not be for a period longer than 1 year from the date of the decision, even if the relevant provision of 8 CFR 214.2 would ordinarily permit the alien's admission for a longer period;

(ii) The alien must obtain the certification required by paragraph (a) of this section within 1 year of the date of decision to admit the alien or to extend the alien's stay or change the alien's status; and,

(iii) Any subsequent petition or application to extend the period of the alien's authorized stay or change the alien's nonimmigrant status must include proof that the alien has obtained the certification required by paragraph (a) of this section, if the extension or stay or change of status is sought for the primary purpose of the alien's performing labor in a health care occupation listed in paragraph (c) of this section.

(3) *Immigrant aliens.* An alien described in paragraph (a) of this section, who is coming to the United States as an immigrant or is applying for adjustment of status pursuant to section 245 of the Act (8 U.S.C. 1255), to perform labor in a health care occupation described in paragraph (c) of this section, must submit the certificate or certified statement as provided in this section at the time of visa issuance or adjustment of status.

(4) *Expiration of certificate or certified statement.* The individual's certification or certified statement must be used for any admission into the United States, change of status within the United States, or adjustment of status within 5 years of the date that it is issued.

(5) *Revocation of certificate or certified statement.* When a credentialing organization notifies the DHS, via the Nebraska Service Center, that an individual's certification or certified statement has been revoked, the DHS will take appropriate action, including, but not limited to, revocation of approval of any related petitions, consistent with the Act and DHS regulations at 8 CFR 205.2, 8 CFR 214.2(h)(11)(iii), and 8 CFR 214.6(d)(5)(iii).

[68 FR 43915, July 25, 2003, as amended at 69 FR 43731, July 22, 2004; 74 FR 26938, June 5, 2009; 76 FR 53788, Aug. 29, 2011; 76 FR 73477, Nov. 29, 2011]

§ 212.16 Applications for exercise of discretion relating to T nonimmigrant status.

(a) *Requesting the waiver.* An alien requesting a waiver of inadmissibility under section 212(d)(3)(B) or (d)(13) of the Act must submit a waiver form as designated by USCIS in accordance with 8 CFR 103.2.

(b) *Treatment of waiver request.* USCIS, in its discretion, may grant a waiver request based on section 212(d)(13) of the Act of the applicable ground(s) of inadmissibility, except USCIS may not waive a ground of inadmissibility based on sections 212(a)(3), (a)(10)(C), or (a)(10)(E) of the Act. An applicant for T nonimmigrant status is not subject to the ground of inadmissibility based on section 212(a)(4) of the Act (public charge) and is not required to file a waiver form for the public charge ground. Waiver requests are subject to a determination of national interest and connection to victimization as follows.

(1) *National interest.* USCIS, in its discretion, may grant a waiver of inadmissibility request if it determines that it is in the national interest to exercise discretion to waive the applicable ground(s) of inadmissibility.

(2) *Connection to victimization.* An applicant requesting a waiver under section 212(d)(13) of the Act on grounds other than the health-related grounds described in section 212(a)(1) of the Act must establish that the activities rendering him or her inadmissible were caused by, or were incident to, the victimization described in section 101(a)(15)(T)(i)(I) of the Act.

(3) *Criminal grounds.* In exercising its discretion, USCIS will consider the number and seriousness of the criminal offenses and convictions that render an applicant inadmissible under the criminal and related grounds in section 212(a)(2) of the Act. In cases involving violent or dangerous crimes, USCIS will only exercise favorable discretion in extraordinary circumstances, unless

the criminal activities were caused by, or were incident to, the victimization described under section 101(a)(15)(T)(i)(I) of the Act.

(c) *No appeal.* There is no appeal of a decision to deny a waiver request. Nothing in this section is intended to prevent an applicant from re-filing a request for a waiver of a ground of inadmissibility in appropriate cases.

(d) *Revocation.* USCIS, at any time, may revoke a waiver previously authorized under section 212(d) of the Act. There is no appeal of a decision to revoke a waiver.

[81 FR 92304, Dec. 19, 2016]

§ 212.17 Applications for the exercise of discretion relating to U nonimmigrant status.

(a) *Filing the waiver application.* An alien applying for a waiver of inadmissibility under section 212(d)(3)(B) or (d)(14) of the Act (waivers of inadmissibility), 8 U.S.C. 1182(d)(3)(B) or (d)(14), in connection with a petition for U nonimmigrant status being filed pursuant to 8 CFR 214.14, must submit the waiver request and the petition for U nonimmigrant status on the forms designated by USCIS in accordance with the form instructions. An alien in U nonimmigrant status who is seeking a waiver of section 212(a)(9)(B) of the Act, 8 U.S.C. 1182(a)(9)(B) (unlawful presence ground of inadmissibility triggered by departure from the United States), must file the waiver request prior to his or her application for reentry to the United States in accordance with the form instructions.

(b) *Treatment of waiver application.* (1) USCIS, in its discretion, may grant the waiver based on section 212(d)(14) of the Act, 8 U.S.C. 1182(d)(14), if it determines that it is in the public or national interest to exercise discretion to waive the applicable ground(s) of inadmissibility. USCIS may not waive a ground of inadmissibility based upon section 212(a)(3)(E) of the Act, 8 U.S.C. 1182(a)(3)(E). USCIS, in its discretion, may grant the waiver based on section 212(d)(3) of the Act, 8 U.S.C. 1182(d)(3), except where the ground of inadmissibility arises under sections 212(a)(3)(A)(i)(I), (3)(A)(ii), (3)(A)(iii), (3)(C), or (3)(E) of the Act, 8 U.S.C. 1182(a)(3)(A)(i)(I), (3)(A)(ii), (3)(A)(iii), (3)(C), or (3)(E).

(2) In the case of applicants inadmissible on criminal or related grounds, in exercising its discretion USCIS will consider the number and severity of the offenses of which the applicant has been convicted. In cases involving violent or dangerous crimes or inadmissibility based on the security and related grounds in section 212(a)(3) of the Act, USCIS will only exercise favorable discretion in extraordinary circumstances.

(3) There is no appeal of a decision to deny a waiver. However, nothing in this paragraph is intended to prevent an applicant from re-filing a request for a waiver of ground of inadmissibility in appropriate cases.

(c) *Revocation.* The Secretary of Homeland Security, at any time, may revoke a waiver previously authorized under section 212(d) of the Act, 8 U.S.C. 118(d). Under no circumstances will the alien or any party acting on his or her behalf have a right to appeal from a decision to revoke a waiver.

[72 FR 53035, Sept. 17, 2007, as amended at 76 FR 53788, Aug. 29, 2011]

§ 212.18 Applications for waivers of inadmissibility in connection with an application for adjustment of status by T nonimmigrant status holders.

(a) *Filing the waiver application.* An alien applying for a waiver of inadmissibility under section 245(*l*)(2) of the Act in connection with an application for adjustment of status under 8 CFR 245.23(a) or (b) must submit:

(1) A completed Form I–485 application package;

(2) The appropriate fee in accordance with 8 CFR 103.7(b)(1) or an application for a fee waiver; and, as applicable,

(3) Form I–601, Application for Waiver of Grounds of Excludability.

(b) *Treatment of waiver application.* (1) USCIS may not waive an applicant's inadmissibility under sections 212(a)(3), 212(a)(10)(C), or 212(a)(10)(E) of the Act.

(2) If an applicant is inadmissible under sections 212(a)(1) or (4) of the Act, USCIS may waive such inadmissibility if it determines that granting a waiver is in the national interest.

(3) If any other provision of section 212(a) renders the applicant inadmissible, USCIS may grant a waiver of inadmissibility if the activities rendering the alien inadmissible were caused by or were incident to the victimization and USCIS determines that it is in the national interest to waive the applicable ground or grounds of inadmissibility.

(c) *Other waivers.* Nothing in this section shall be construed as limiting an alien's ability to apply for any other waivers of inadmissibility for which he or she may be eligible.

(d) *Revocation.* The Secretary of Homeland Security may, at any time, revoke a waiver previously granted through the procedures described in 8 CFR 103.5.

[73 FR 75557, Dec. 12, 2008]

§212.19 Parole for entrepreneurs.

(a) *Definitions.* For purposes of this section, the following definitions apply:

(1) *Entrepreneur* means an alien who possesses a substantial ownership interest in a start-up entity and has a central and active role in the operations of that entity, such that the alien is well-positioned, due to his or her knowledge, skills, or experience, to substantially assist the entity with the growth and success of its business. For purposes of this section, an alien may be considered to possess a substantial ownership interest if he or she possesses at least a 10 percent ownership interest in the start-up entity at the time of adjudication of the initial grant of parole and possesses at least a 5 percent ownership interest in the start-up entity at the time of adjudication of a subsequent period of re-parole. During the period of initial parole, the entrepreneur may continue to reduce his or her ownership interest in the start-up entity, but must, at all times during the period of initial parole, maintain at least a 5 percent ownership interest in the entity. During the period of re-parole, the entrepreneur may continue to reduce his or her ownership interest in the start-up entity, but must, at all times during the period of parole, maintain an ownership interest in the entity.

(2) *Start-up entity* means a U.S. business entity that was recently formed, has lawfully done business during any period of operation since its date of formation, and has substantial potential for rapid growth and job creation. An entity that is the basis for a request for parole under this section may be considered recently formed if it was created within the 5 years immediately preceding the filing date of the alien's initial parole request. For purposes of paragraphs (a)(3) and (5) of this section, an entity may be considered recently formed if it was created within the 5 years immediately preceding the receipt of the relevant grant(s), award(s), or investment(s).

(3) *Qualified government award or grant* means an award or grant for economic development, research and development, or job creation (or other similar monetary award typically given to start-up entities) made by a federal, state, or local government entity (not including foreign government entities) that regularly provides such awards or grants to start-up entities. This definition excludes any contractual commitment for goods or services.

(4) *Qualified investment* means an investment made in good faith, and that is not an attempt to circumvent any limitations imposed on investments under this section, of lawfully derived capital in a start-up entity that is a purchase from such entity of its equity, convertible debt, or other security convertible into its equity commonly used in financing transactions within such entity's industry. Such an investment shall not include an investment, directly or indirectly, from the entrepreneur; the parents, spouse, brother, sister, son, or daughter of such entrepreneur; or any corporation, limited liability company, partnership, or other entity in which such entrepreneur or the parents, spouse, brother, sister, son, or daughter of such entrepreneur directly or indirectly has any ownership interest.

(5) *Qualified investor* means an individual who is a U.S. citizen or lawful permanent resident of the United States, or an organization that is located in the United States and operates through a legal entity organized under the laws of the United States or any

state, that is majority owned and controlled, directly and indirectly, by U.S. citizens or lawful permanent residents of the United States, provided such individual or organization regularly makes substantial investments in start-up entities that subsequently exhibit substantial growth in terms of revenue generation or job creation. The term "qualified investor" shall not include an individual or organization that has been permanently or temporarily enjoined from participating in the offer or sale of a security or in the provision of services as an investment adviser, broker, dealer, municipal securities dealer, government securities broker, government securities dealer, bank, transfer agent or credit rating agency, barred from association with any entity involved in the offer or sale of securities or provision of such services, or otherwise found to have participated in the offer or sale of securities or provision of such services in violation of law. For purposes of this section, such an individual or organization may be considered a qualified investor if, during the preceding 5 years:

(i) The individual or organization made investments in start-up entities in exchange for equity, convertible debt or other security convertible into equity commonly used in financing transactions within their respective industries comprising a total in such 5-year period of no less than $600,000; and

(ii) Subsequent to such investment by such individual or organization, at least 2 such entities each created at least 5 qualified jobs or generated at least $500,000 in revenue with average annualized revenue growth of at least 20 percent.

(6) *Qualified job* means full-time employment located in the United States that has been filled for at least 1 year by one or more qualifying employees.

(7) *Qualifying employee* means a U.S. citizen, a lawful permanent resident, or other immigrant lawfully authorized to be employed in the United States, who is not an entrepreneur of the relevant start-up entity or the parent, spouse, brother, sister, son, or daughter of such an entrepreneur. This definition shall not include independent contractors.

(8) *Full-time employment* means paid employment in a position that requires a minimum of 35 working hours per week. This definition does not include combinations of part-time positions even if, when combined, such positions meet the hourly requirement per week.

(9) *U.S. business entity* means any corporation, limited liability company, partnership, or other entity that is organized under federal law or the laws of any state, and that conducts business in the United States, that is not an investment vehicle primarily engaged in the offer, purchase, sale or trading of securities, futures contracts, derivatives or similar instruments.

(10) *Material change* means any change in facts that could reasonably affect the outcome of the determination whether the entrepreneur provides, or continues to provide, a significant public benefit to the United States. Such changes include, but are not limited to, the following: Any criminal charge, conviction, plea of no contest, or other judicial determination in a criminal case concerning the entrepreneur or start-up entity; any complaint, settlement, judgment, or other judicial or administrative determination concerning the entrepreneur or start-up entity in a legal or administrative proceeding brought by a government entity; any settlement, judgment, or other legal determination concerning the entrepreneur or start-up entity in a legal proceeding brought by a private individual or organization other than proceedings primarily involving claims for damages not exceeding 10 percent of the current assets of the entrepreneur or start-up entity; a sale or other disposition of all or substantially all of the start-up entity's assets; the liquidation, dissolution or cessation of operations of the start-up entity; the voluntary or involuntary filing of a bankruptcy petition by or against the start-up entity; a significant change with respect to ownership and control of the start-up entity; and a cessation of the entrepreneur's qualifying ownership interest in the start-up entity or the entrepreneur's central and active role in the operations of that entity.

(b) *Initial parole*—(1) *Filing of initial parole request form*. An alien seeking an initial grant of parole as an entrepreneur of a start-up entity must file an Application for Entrepreneur Parole (Form I-941) with USCIS, with the required fees (including biometric services fees), and supporting documentary evidence in accordance with this section and the form instructions, demonstrating eligibility as provided in paragraph (b)(2) of this section.

(2) *Criteria for consideration*—(i) *In general.* An alien may be considered for parole under this section if the alien demonstrates that a grant of parole will provide a significant public benefit to the United States based on his or her role as an entrepreneur of a start-up entity.

(ii) *General criteria.* An alien may meet the standard described in paragraph (b)(2)(i) of this section by providing a detailed description, along with supporting evidence:

(A) Demonstrating that the alien is an entrepreneur as defined in paragraph (a)(1) of this section and that his or her entity is a start-up entity as defined in paragraph (a)(2) of this section; and

(B) Establishing that the alien's entity has:

(*1*) Received, within 18 months immediately preceding the filing of an application for initial parole, a qualified investment amount of at least $250,000 from one or more qualified investors; or

(*2*) Received, within 18 months immediately preceding the filing of an application for initial parole, an amount of at least $100,000 through one or more qualified government awards or grants.

(iii) *Alternative criteria.* An alien who satisfies the criteria in paragraph (b)(2)(ii)(A) of this section and partially meets one or both of the criteria in paragraph (b)(2)(ii)(B) of this section may alternatively meet the standard described in paragraph (b)(2)(i) of this section by providing other reliable and compelling evidence of the start-up entity's substantial potential for rapid growth and job creation.

(c) *Additional periods of parole*—(1) *Filing of re-parole request form.* Prior to the expiration of the initial period of parole, an entrepreneur parolee may request an additional period of parole based on the same start-up entity that formed the basis for his or her initial period of parole granted under this section. To request such parole, an entrepreneur parolee must timely file the Application for Entrepreneur Parole (Form I-941) with USCIS, with the required fees (including biometric services fees), and supporting documentation in accordance with the form instructions, demonstrating eligibility as provided in paragraph (c)(2) of this section.

(2) *Criteria for consideration*—(i) *In general.* An alien may be considered for re-parole under this section if the alien demonstrates that a grant of parole will continue to provide a significant public benefit to the United States based on his or her role as an entrepreneur of a start-up entity.

(ii) *General criteria.* An alien may meet the standard described in paragraph (c)(2)(i) of this section by providing a detailed description, along with supporting evidence:

(A) Demonstrating that the alien continues to be an entrepreneur as defined in paragraph (a)(1) of this section and that his or her entity continues to be a start-up entity as defined in paragraph (a)(2) of this section; and

(B) Establishing that the alien's entity has:

(*1*) Received at least $500,000 in qualifying investments, qualified government grants or awards, or a combination of such funding, during the initial parole period;

(*2*) Created at least 5 qualified jobs with the start-up entity during the initial parole period; or

(*3*) Reached at least $500,000 in annual revenue in the United States and averaged 20 percent in annual revenue growth during the initial parole period.

(iii) *Alternative criteria.* An alien who satisfies the criteria in paragraph (c)(2)(ii)(A) of this section and partially meets one or more of the criteria in paragraph (c)(2)(ii)(B) of this section may alternatively meet the standard described in paragraph (c)(2)(i) of this section by providing other reliable and compelling evidence of the start-up entity's substantial potential for rapid growth and job creation.

(d) *Discretionary authority; decision; appeals and motions to reopen*—(1) *Discretionary authority.* DHS may grant parole under this section in its sole discretion on a case-by-case basis if the

Department determines, based on the totality of the evidence, that an applicant's presence in the United States will provide a significant public benefit and that he or she otherwise merits a favorable exercise of discretion. In determining whether an alien's presence in the United States will provide a significant public benefit and whether the alien warrants a favorable exercise of discretion, USCIS will consider and weigh all evidence, including any derogatory evidence or information, such as but not limited to, evidence of criminal activity or national security concerns.

(2) *Initial parole.* DHS may grant an initial period of parole based on the start-up entity listed in the request for parole for a period of up to 30 months from the date the individual is initially paroled into the United States. Approval by USCIS of such a request must be obtained before the alien may appear at a port of entry to be granted parole, in lieu of admission.

(3) *Re-parole.* DHS may re-parole an entrepreneur for one additional period of up to 30 months from the date of the expiration of the initial parole period. If the entrepreneur is in the United States at the time that USCIS approves the request for re-parole, such approval shall be considered a grant of re-parole. If the alien is outside the United States at the time that USCIS approves the request for re-parole, the alien must appear at a port of entry to be granted parole, in lieu of admission.

(4) *Appeals and motions to reopen.* There is no appeal from a denial of parole under this section. USCIS will not consider a motion to reopen or reconsider a denial of parole under this section. On its own motion, USCIS may reopen or reconsider a decision to deny the Application for Entrepreneur Parole (Form I–941), in accordance with 8 CFR 103.5(a)(5).

(e) *Payment of biometric services fee and collection of biometric information.* An alien seeking parole or re-parole under this section will be required to pay the biometric services fee as prescribed by 8 CFR 103.7(b)(1)(i)(C). An alien seeking an initial grant of parole will be required to submit biometric information. An alien seeking re-parole may be required to submit biometric information.

(f) *Limitations.* No more than three entrepreneurs may be granted parole under this section based on the same start-up entity. An alien shall not receive more than one initial grant of entrepreneur parole or more than one additional grant of entrepreneur re-parole based on the same start-up entity, for a maximum period of parole of five years.

(g) *Employment authorization.* An entrepreneur who is paroled into the United States pursuant to this section is authorized for employment with the start-up entity incident to the conditions of his or her parole.

(h) *Spouse and children.* (1) The entrepreneur's spouse and children who are seeking parole as derivatives of such entrepreneur must individually file an Application for Travel Document (Form I–131). Such application must also include evidence that the derivative has a qualifying relationship to the entrepreneur and otherwise merits a grant of parole in the exercise of discretion. A biometric services fee is required to be filed with the application. Such spouse or child will be required to appear for collection of biometrics in accordance with the form instructions or upon request.

(2) The spouse and children of an entrepreneur granted parole under this section may be granted parole under this section for no longer than the period of parole granted to such entrepreneur.

(3) The spouse of the entrepreneur parolee, after being paroled into the United States, may be eligible for employment authorization on the basis of parole under this section. To request employment authorization, an eligible spouse paroled into the United States must file an Application for Employment Authorization (Form I–765), in accordance with 8 CFR 274a.13 and form instructions. An Application for Employment Authorization must be accompanied by documentary evidence establishing eligibility, including evidence of the spousal relationship.

(4) Notwithstanding 8 CFR 274a.12(c)(11), a child of the entrepreneur parolee may not be authorized

for and may not accept employment on the basis of parole under this section.

(i) *Conditions on parole.* As a condition of parole under this section, a parolee must maintain household income that is greater than 400 percent of the federal poverty line for his or her household size as defined by the Department of Health and Human Services. USCIS may impose other such reasonable conditions in its sole discretion with respect to any alien approved for parole under this section, and it may request verification of the parolee's compliance with any such condition at any time. Violation of any condition of parole may lead to termination of the parole in accordance with paragraph (k) of this section or denial of re-parole.

(j) *Reporting of material changes.* An alien granted parole under this section must immediately report any material change(s) to USCIS. If the entrepreneur will continue to be employed by the start-up entity and maintain a qualifying ownership interest in the start-up entity, the entrepreneur must submit a form prescribed by USCIS, with any applicable fee (not including any biometric fees), in accordance with the form instructions to notify USCIS of the material change(s). The entrepreneur parolee must immediately notify USCIS in writing if he or she will no longer be employed by the start-up entity or ceases to possess a qualifying ownership stake in the start-up entity.

(k) *Termination of parole*—(1) *In general.* DHS, in its discretion, may terminate parole granted under this section at any time and without prior notice or opportunity to respond if it determines that the alien's continued parole in the United States no longer provides a significant public benefit. Alternatively, DHS, in its discretion, may provide the alien notice and an opportunity to respond prior to terminating the alien's parole under this section.

(2) *Automatic termination.* Parole granted under this section will be automatically terminated without notice upon the expiration of the time for which parole was authorized, unless the alien timely files a non-frivolous application for re-parole. Parole granted under this section may be automatically terminated when USCIS receives written notice from the entrepreneur parolee that he or she will no longer be employed by the start-up entity or ceases to possess a qualifying ownership stake in the start-up entity in accordance with paragraph (j) of this section. Additionally, parole of the spouse or child of the entrepreneur will be automatically terminated without notice if the parole of the entrepreneur has been terminated. If parole is terminated, any employment authorization based on that parole is automatically revoked.

(3) *Termination on notice.* USCIS may terminate on notice or provide the entrepreneur or his or her spouse or children, as applicable, written notice of its intent to terminate parole if USCIS believes that:

(i) The facts or information contained in the request for parole were not true and accurate;

(ii) The alien failed to timely file or otherwise comply with the material change reporting requirements in this section;

(iii) The entrepreneur parolee is no longer employed in a central and active role by the start-up entity or ceases to possess a qualifying ownership stake in the start-up entity;

(iv) The alien otherwise violated the terms and conditions of parole; or

(v) Parole was erroneously granted.

(4) *Notice and decision.* A notice of intent to terminate issued under this paragraph should generally identify the grounds for termination of the parole and provide a period of up to 30 days for the alien's written rebuttal. The alien may submit additional evidence in support of his or her rebuttal, when applicable, and USCIS will consider all relevant evidence presented in deciding whether to terminate the alien's parole. Failure to timely respond to a notice of intent to terminate will result in termination of the parole. When a charging document is served on the alien, the charging document will constitute written notice of termination of parole (if parole has not already been terminated), unless otherwise specified. Any further immigration and removal actions will be conducted in accordance with the Act and this chapter. The decision to terminate parole may not be appealed. USCIS will

not consider a motion to reopen or reconsider a decision to terminate parole under this section. On its own motion, USCIS may reopen or reconsider a decision to terminate.

(l) *Increase of investment and revenue amount requirements.* The investment and revenue amounts in this section will be automatically adjusted every 3 years by the Consumer Price Index and posted on the USCIS Web site at *www.uscis.gov.* Investment and revenue amounts adjusted under this paragraph will apply to all applications filed on or after the beginning of the fiscal year for which the adjustment is made.

[82 FR 5286, Jan. 17, 2017]

PART 213—ADMISSION OF ALIENS ON GIVING BOND OR CASH DEPOSIT

AUTHORITY: 8 U.S.C. 1103; 8 CFR part 2.

§ 213.1 Admission under bond or cash deposit.

The district director having jurisdiction over the intended place of residence of an alien may accept a public charge bond prior to the issuance of an immigrant visa to the alien upon receipt of a request directly from a United States consular officer or upon presentation by an interested person of a notification from the consular officer requiring such a bond. Upon acceptance of such a bond, the district director shall notify the U.S. consular officer who requested the bond, giving the date and place of acceptance and the amount of the bond. The district director having jurisdiction over the place where the examination for admission is being conducted or the special inquiry officer to whom the case is referred may exercise the authority contained in section 213 of the Act. All bonds and agreements covering cash deposits given as a condition of admission of an alien under section 213 of the Act shall be executed on Form I–352 and shall be in the sum of not less than $1,000. The officer accepting such deposit shall give his receipt therefor on Form I–305. For procedures relating to bond riders, acceptable sureties, cancellation or breaching of bonds, see § 103.6 of this chapter.

[29 FR 10579, July 30, 1964, as amended at 32 FR 9626, July 4, 1967; 62 FR 10349, Mar. 6, 1997]

PART 213a—AFFIDAVITS OF SUPPORT ON BEHALF OF IMMIGRANTS

Sec.

AUTHORITY: 8 U.S.C. 1183a; 8 CFR part 2.

SOURCE: 62 FR 54352, Oct. 20, 1997, unless otherwise noted.

§ 213a.1 Definitions.

As used in this part, the term:

Domicile means the place where a sponsor has his or her principal residence, as defined in section 101(a)(33) of the Act, with the intention to maintain that residence for the foreseeable future.

Federal poverty line means the level of income equal to the poverty guidelines as issued by the Secretary of Health and Human Services in accordance with 42 U.S.C. 9902 that is applicable to a household of the size involved. For purposes of considering the Form I–864, Affidavit of Support Under Section 213A of the Act, the Service and Consular Posts will use the most recent income-poverty guidelines published in the FEDERAL REGISTER by the Department of Health and Human Services. These guidelines are updated annually, and the Service and Consular Posts will begin to use updated guidelines on the first day of the second month after the date the guidelines are published in the FEDERAL REGISTER.

Household income means the income used to determine whether the sponsor meets the minimum income requirements under sections 213A(f)(1)(E), 213A(f)(3), or 213A(f)(5) of the Act. It includes the income of the sponsor, and of the sponsor's spouse and any other person included in determining the sponsor's household size, if the spouse or other person is at least 18 years old and has signed the form designated by

USCIS for this purpose, on behalf of the sponsor and intending immigrants. The "household income" may not, however, include the income of an intending immigrant, unless the intending immigrant is either the sponsor's spouse or has the same principal residence as the sponsor and the preponderance of the evidence shows that the intending immigrant's income results from the intending immigrant's lawful employment in the United States or from some other lawful source that will continue to be available to the intending immigrant after he or she acquires permanent resident status. The prospect of employment in the United States that has not yet actually begun will not be sufficient to meet this requirement.

Household size means the number obtained by adding the number of persons specified in this definition. In calculating household size, no individual shall be counted more than once. If the intending immigrant's spouse or child is a citizen or already holds the status of an alien lawfully admitted for permanent residence, then the sponsor should not include that spouse or child in determining the total household size, unless the intending immigrant's spouse or child is a dependent of the sponsor.

(1) In all cases, the household size includes the sponsor, the sponsor's spouse and all of the sponsor's children, as defined in section 101(b)(1) of the Act (other than a stepchild who meets the requirements of section 101(b)(1)(B) of the Act, if the stepchild does not reside with the sponsor, is not claimed by the sponsor as a dependent for tax purposes, and is not seeking to immigrate based on the stepparent/stepchild relationship), unless these children have reached the age of majority under the law of the place of domicile and the sponsor did not claim them as dependents on the sponsor's Federal income tax return for the most recent tax year. The following persons must also be included in calculating the sponsor's household size: Any other persons (whether related to the sponsor or not) whom the sponsor has claimed as dependents on the sponsor's Federal income tax return for the most recent tax year, even if such persons do not have the same principal residence as the sponsor, plus the number of aliens the sponsor has sponsored under any other affidavit of support for whom the sponsor's support obligation has not terminated, plus the number of aliens to be sponsored under the current affidavit of support, even if such aliens do not or will not have the same principal residence as the sponsor. If a child, as defined in section 101(b)(1) of the Act, or spouse of the principal intending immigrant is an alien who does not currently reside in the United States and who either is not seeking to immigrate at the same time as, or will not seek to immigrate within six months of the principal intending immigrant's immigration, the sponsor may exclude that child or spouse in calculating the sponsor's household size.

(2) If the sponsor chooses to do so, the sponsor may add to the number of persons specified in the first part of this definition the number of relatives (as defined in this section) of the sponsor who have the same principal residence as the sponsor and whose income will be relied on to meet the requirements of section 213A of the Act and this part.

Immigration Officer, solely for purposes of this part, includes a Consular Officer, as defined by section 101(a)(9) of the Act, as well as an Immigration Officer, as defined by §103.1(j) of this chapter.

Income means an individual's total income (adjusted gross income for those who file IRS Form 1040EZ) for purposes of the individual's U.S. Federal income tax liability, including a joint income tax return (e.g., line 22 on the 2004 IRS Form 1040, line 15 on the 2004 IRS Form 1040A, or line 4 on the 2004 IRS Form 1040EZ or the corresponding line on any future revision of these IRS Forms). Only an individual's Federal income tax return—that is, neither a state or territorial income tax return nor an income tax return filed with a foreign government—shall be filed with an affidavit of support, unless the individual had no duty to file a Federal income tax return, and claims that his or her state, territorial or foreign taxable income is sufficient to establish the sufficiency of the affidavit of support.

Intending immigrant means any beneficiary of an immigrant visa petition filed under section 204 of the Act, including any alien who will accompany or follow-to-join the principal beneficiary.

Joint sponsor means any individual who meets the requirements of section 213A(f)(1)(A), (B), (C), and (E) of the Act and 8 CFR 213a.2(c)(1)(i), and who, as permitted by section 213A(f)(5)(A) of the Act, is willing to submit a an affidavit of support and accept joint and several liability with the sponsor or substitute sponsor, in any case in which the sponsor's or substitute sponsor's household income is not sufficient to satisfy the requirements of section 213A of the Act.

Means-tested public benefit means either a Federal means-tested public benefit, which is any public benefit funded in whole or in part by funds provided by the Federal Government that the Federal agency administering the Federal funds has determined to be a Federal means-tested public benefit under the Personal Responsibility and Work Opportunity Reconciliation Act of 1996, Public Law 104–193, or a State means-tested public benefit, which is any public benefit for which no Federal funds are provided that a State, State agency, or political subdivision of a State has determined to be a means-tested public benefit. No benefit shall be considered to be a means-tested public benefit if it is a benefit described in sections 401(b), 411(b), 422(b) or 423(d) of Public Law 104–193.

Program official means the officer or employee of any Federal, State, or local government agency or of any private agency that administers any means-tested public benefit program who has authority to act on the agency's behalf in seeking reimbursement of means-tested public benefits.

Relative means a husband, wife, father, mother, child, adult son, adult daughter, brother, or sister.

Significant ownership interest means an ownership interest of 5 percent or more in a for-profit entity that filed an immigrant visa petition to accord a prospective employee an immigrant status under section 203(b) of the Act.

Sponsor means an individual who is either required to execute or has executed an affidavit of support under this part.

Sponsored immigrant means any alien who was an intending immigrant, once that person has been lawfully admitted for permanent residence, so that the affidavit of support filed for that person under this part has entered into force.

Substitute sponsor means an individual who meets the requirements of section 213A(f)(1)(A), (B), (C), and (E) of the Act and 8 CFR 213a.2(c)(1)(i), who is related to the principal intending immigrant in one of the ways described in section 213A(f)(5)(B) of the Act, and who is willing to sign the affidavit of support in place of the now-deceased person who filed ta relative or fiancé(e) petition that provides the basis for the intending immigrant's ability to seek permanent residence.

[62 FR 54352, Oct. 20, 1997, as amended at 71 FR 35749, June 21, 2006; 76 FR 53788, Aug. 29, 2011]

§ 213a.2 Use of affidavit of support.

(a) *Applicability of section 213a affidavit of support.* (1)(i)(A) In any case specified in paragraph (a)(2) of this section, an intending immigrant is inadmissible as an alien likely to become a public charge, unless the qualified sponsor specified in paragraph (b) of this section or a substitute sponsor and, if necessary, a joint sponsor, has executed on behalf of the intending immigrant an affidavit of support on the applicable form designated by USCIS in accordance with the requirements of section 213A of the Act and the form instructions. Each reference in this section to the affidavit of support or the form is deemed to be a reference to all such forms designated by USCIS for use by a sponsor for compliance with section 213A of the Act.

(B) If the intending immigrant claims that, under paragraph (a)(2)(ii)(A), (C), or (E) of this section, the intending immigrant is exempt from the requirement to file an affidavit of support, the intending immigrant must include with his or her application for an immigrant visa or adjustment of status an exemption request on the form designated by USCIS for this purpose.

(ii) An affidavit of support is executed when a sponsor signs and submits the appropriate forms in accordance with the form instructions to USCIS or the Department of State, as appropriate.

(iii) A separate affidavit of support is required for each principal beneficiary.

(iv) Each immigrant who will accompany the principal intending immigrant must be included on the affidavit. See paragraph (f) of this section for further information concerning immigrants who intend to accompany or follow the principal intending immigrant to the United States.

(v)(A) Except as provided for under paragraph (a)(1)(v)(B) of this section, the Department of State consular officer, immigration officer, or immigration judge will determine the sufficiency of the affidavit of support based on the sponsor's, substitute sponsor's, or joint sponsor's reasonably expected household income in the year in which the intending immigrant filed the application for an immigrant visa or for adjustment of status, and based on the evidence submitted with the affidavit of support and the Poverty Guidelines in effect when the intending immigrant filed the application for an immigrant visa or adjustment of status.

(B) If more than one year passes between the filing of the affidavit of support or required affidavit of support attachment form and the hearing, interview, or examination of the intending immigrant concerning the intending immigrant's application for an immigrant visa or adjustment of status, and the Department of State officer, immigration officer or immigration judge determines, in the exercise of discretion, that the particular facts of the case make the submission of additional evidence necessary to the proper adjudication of the case, then the Department of State officer, immigration officer or immigration judge may direct the intending immigrant to submit additional evidence. A Department of State officer or immigration officer shall make the request in writing, and provide the intending immigrant not less than 30 days to submit the additional evidence. An immigration judge may direct the intending immigrant to submit additional evidence and also set the deadline for submission of the initial evidence in any manner permitted under subpart C of 8 CFR part 1003 and any local rules of the Immigration Court. If additional evidence is required under this paragraph, an intending immigrant must submit additional evidence (including copies or transcripts of any income tax returns for the most recent tax year) concerning the income or employment of the sponsor, substitute sponsor, joint sponsor, or household member in the year in which the Department of State officer, immigration officer, or immigration judge makes the request for additional evidence. In this case, the sufficiency of the affidavit of support and any required affidavit of support attachment will be determined based on the sponsor's, substitute sponsor's, or joint sponsor's reasonably expected household income in the year the Department of State officer, immigration officer or immigration judge makes the request for additional evidence, and based on the evidence submitted in response to the request for additional evidence and on the Poverty Guidelines in effect when the request for evidence was issued.

(2)(i) Except for cases specified in paragraph (a)(2)(ii) of this section, paragraph (a)(1) of this section applies to any application for an immigrant visa or for adjustment of status filed on or after December 19, 1997, in which an intending immigrant seeks an immigrant visa, admission as an immigrant, or adjustment of status as:

(A) An immediate relative under section 201(b)(2)(A)(i) of the Act, including orphans and any alien admitted as a K nonimmigrant when the alien seeks adjustment of status;

(B) A family-based immigrant under section 203(a) of the Act; or

(C) An employment-based immigrant under section 203(b) of the Act, if a relative (as defined in 8 CFR 213a.1) of the intending immigrant is a citizen or an alien lawfully admitted for permanent residence who either filed the employment-based immigrant petition or has a significant ownership interest in the entity that filed the immigrant visa petition on behalf of the intending immigrant. An affidavit of support under this section is not required, however, if the relative is a brother or sister of the intending immigrant, unless the brother or sister is a citizen.

(ii) Paragraph (a)(1) of this section shall not apply if the intending immigrant:

(A) Filed a visa petition on his or her own behalf pursuant to section 204(a)(1)(A)(ii), (iii), or (iv) or section 204(a)(1)(B)(ii) or (iii) of the Act, or who seeks to accompany or follow-to-join an immigrant who filed a visa petition on his or his own behalf pursuant to section 204(a)(1)(A)(ii), (iii), or (iv) or section 204(a)(1)(B)(ii) or (iii) of the Act;

(B) Seeks admission as an immigrant on or after December 19, 1997, in a category specified in paragraph (a)(2)(i) of this section with an immigrant visa issued on the basis of an immigrant visa application filed with the Department of State officer before December 19, 1997;

(C) Establishes, on the basis of the alien's own Social Security Administration record or those of his or her spouse or parent(s), that he or she has already worked, or under section 213A(a)(3)(B) of the Act, can already be credited with, 40 qualifying quarters of coverage as defined under title II of the Social Security Act, 42 U.S.C. 401, *et seq;*

(D) Is a child admitted under section 211(a) of the Act and 8 CFR 211.1(b)(1); or

(E) Is the child of a citizen, if the child is not likely to become a public charge (other than because of the provision of section 212(a)(4)(C) of the Act), and the child's lawful admission for permanent residence will result automatically in the child's acquisition of citizenship under section 320 of the Act, as amended. This exception applies to an alien orphan if the citizen parent(s) has (or have) legally adopted the alien orphan before the alien orphan's acquisition of permanent residence, and if both adoptive parents personally saw and observed the alien orphan before or during the foreign adoption proceeding. An affidavit of support under this part is still required if the citizen parent(s) will adopt the alien orphan in the United States only after the alien orphan's acquisition of permanent residence. If the citizen parent(s) adopted the alien orphan abroad, but at least one of the adoptive parents did not see and observe the alien orphan before or during the foreign adoption proceeding, then an affidavit of support under this part is still required, unless the citizen parent establishes that, under the law of the State of the alien orphan's intended residence in the United States, the foreign adoption decree is entitled to recognition without the need for a formal administrative or judicial proceeding in the State of proposed residence. In the case of a child who immigrates as a Convention adoptee, as defined in 8 CFR 204.301, this exception applies if the child was adopted by the petitioner in the Convention country. An affidavit of support under this part is still required in the case of a child who immigrates as a Convention adoptee if the petitioner will adopt the child in the United States only after the child's acquisition of permanent residence.

(b) *Affidavit of support sponsors.* The following individuals must execute an affidavit of support on behalf of the intending immigrant in order for the intending immigrant to be found admissible on public charge grounds:

(1) *For immediate relatives and family-based immigrants.* The person who filed a relative, orphan or fiancé(e) petition, the approval of which forms the basis of the intending immigrant's eligibility to apply for an immigrant visa or adjustment of status as an immediate relative or a family-based immigrant, must execute a an affidavit of support on behalf of the intending immigrant. If the intending immigrant is the beneficiary of more than one approved immigrant visa petition, it is the person who filed the petition that is actually the basis for the intending immigrant's eligibility to apply for an immigrant visa or adjustment of status who must file the an affidavit of support.

(2) *For employment-based immigrants.* A relative of an intending immigrant seeking an immigrant visa under section 203(b) of the Act must file a if the relative either filed the immigrant visa petition on behalf of the intending immigrant or owns a significant ownership interest in an entity that filed an immigrant visa petition on behalf of

the intending immigrant, but only if the relative is a citizen or an alien lawfully admitted for permanent residence. If the intending immigrant is the beneficiary of more than one relative's employment-based immigrant visa petition, it is the relative who filed the petition that is actually the basis for the intending immigrant's eligibility to apply for an immigrant visa or adjustment of status who must file the an affidavit of support.

(c) *Sponsorship requirements*—(1)(i) *General*. A sponsor must be:

(A) At least 18 years of age;

(B) Domiciled in the United States or any territory or possession of the United States; and

(C)(*1*) A citizen or an alien lawfully admitted for permanent residence in the case described in paragraph (a)(2)(i) of this section; or

(*2*) A citizen or national or an alien lawfully admitted for permanent residence if the individual is a substitute sponsor or joint sponsor.

(ii) *Determination of domicile*. (A) If the sponsor is residing abroad, but only temporarily, the sponsor bears the burden of proving, by a preponderance of the evidence, that the sponsor's domicile (as that term is defined in 8 CFR 213a.1) remains in the United States, *provided*, that a permanent resident who is living abroad temporarily is considered to be domiciled in the United States if the permanent resident has applied for and obtained the preservation of residence benefit under section 316(b) or section 317 of the Act, *and provided further*, that a citizen who is living abroad temporarily is considered to be domiciled in the United States if the citizen's employment abroad meets the requirements of section 319(b)(1) of the Act.

(B) If the sponsor is not domiciled in the United States, the sponsor can still sign and submit an affidavit of support so long as the sponsor satisfies the Department of State officer, immigration officer, or immigration judge, by a preponderance of the evidence, that the sponsor will establish a domicile in the United States on or before the date of the principal intending immigrant's admission or adjustment of status. The intending immigrant will be inadmissible under section 212(a)(4) of the Act, and the immigration officer or immigration judge must deny the intending immigrant's application for admission or adjustment of status, if the sponsor has not, in fact, established a domicile in the United States on or before the date of the decision on the principal intending immigrant's application for admission or adjustment of status. In the case of a sponsor who comes to the United States intending to establish his or her principal residence in the United States at the same time as the principal intending immigrant's arrival and application for admission at a port-of-entry, the sponsor shall be deemed to have established a domicile in the United States for purposes of this paragraph, unless the sponsor is also a permanent resident alien and the sponsor's own application for admission is denied and the sponsor leaves the United States under a removal order or as a result of the sponsor's withdrawal of the application for admission.

(2) *Demonstration of ability to support intending immigrants*. In order for the intending immigrant to overcome the public charge ground of inadmissibility, the sponsor must demonstrate the means to maintain the intending immigrant at an annual income of at least 125 percent of the Federal poverty line. If the sponsor is on active duty in the Armed Forces of the United States (other than active duty for training) and the intending immigrant is the sponsor's spouse or child, the sponsor's ability to maintain income must equal at least 100 percent of the Federal poverty line.

(i) *Proof of income*. (A) The sponsor must include with the an affidavit of support either a photocopy or an Internal Revenue Service-issued transcript of his or her complete Federal income tax return for the most recent taxable year (counting from the date of the signing, rather than the filing, of the an affidavit of support. However, the sponsor may, at his or her option, submit tax returns for the three most recent years if the sponsor believes that these additional tax returns may help in establishing the sponsor's ability to maintain his or her income at the applicable threshold set forth in the Poverty Guidelines. Along with each transcript or photocopy, the sponsor must also submit as initial evidence copies of all schedules filed with each return and (if the sponsor submits a photocopy, rather than an IRS transcript of the tax return(s)) all Forms W–2 (if the sponsor relies on income from employment) and Forms 1099 (if the sponsor relies on income from sources documented on Forms 1099) in meeting the income threshold. The sponsor may also include as initial evidence: Letter(s) evidencing his or her current employment and income, paycheck stub(s) (showing earnings for the most recent six months, financial statements, or other evidence of the sponsor's anticipated household income for the year in which the intending immigrant files the application for an immigrant visa or adjustment of status. By executing an affidavit of support, the sponsor certifies under penalty of perjury under United States law that the evidence of his or her current household income is true and correct and that each transcript or photocopy of each income tax return is a true and correct transcript or photocopy of the return that the sponsor filed with the Internal Revenue Service for that taxable year.

(B) If the sponsor had no legal duty to file a Federal income tax return for the most recent tax year, the sponsor must explain why he or she had no legal duty to a file a Federal income tax return for that year. If the sponsor claims he or she had no legal duty to file for any reason other than the level of the sponsor's income for that year, the initial evidence submitted with the an affidavit of support must also include any evidence of the amount and source of the income that the sponsor claims was exempt from taxation and a copy of the provisions of any statute, treaty, or regulation that supports the claim that he or she had no duty to file an income tax return with respect to that income. If the sponsor had no legal obligation to file a Federal income tax return, he or she may submit other evidence of annual income. The fact that a sponsor had no duty to file a Federal income tax return does not relieve the sponsor of the duty to file an affidavit of support.

(C)(*1*) The sponsor's ability to meet the income requirement will be determined based on the sponsor's household income. In establishing the household income, the sponsor may rely entirely on his or her personal income, if it is sufficient to meet the income requirement. The sponsor may also rely on the income of the sponsor's spouse and of any other person included in determining the sponsor's household size, if the spouse or other person is at least 18 years old and has completed and signed an affidavit of support attachment. A person does not need to be a U.S. citizen, national, or alien lawfully admitted for permanent residence in order to sign an affidavit of support attachment.

(*2*) Each individual who signs an affidavit of support attachment agrees, in consideration of the sponsor's signing of the an affidavit of support, to provide to the sponsor as much financial assistance as may be necessary to enable the sponsor to maintain the intending immigrants at the annual income level required by section 213A(a)(1)(A) of the Act, to be jointly and severally liable for any reimbursement obligation that the sponsor may incur, and to submit to the personal jurisdiction of any court that has subject matter jurisdiction over a civil suit to enforce the contract or the affidavit of support. The sponsor, as a party to the contract, may bring suit to enforce the contract. The intending immigrants and any Federal, state, or local agency or private entity that provides a means-tested public benefit to an intending immigrant are third party beneficiaries of the contract between the sponsor and the other individual or individuals on whose income the sponsor relies and may bring an action to enforce the contract in the same manner as third party beneficiaries of other contracts.

(*3*) If there is no spouse or child immigrating with the intending immigrant, then there will be no need for the intending immigrant to sign a Form I–864A, even if the sponsor will rely on the continuing income of the intending immigrant to meet the income requirement. If, however, the sponsor seeks to rely on an intending immigrant's continuing income to establish the sponsor's ability to support the intending immigrant's spouse or children, then the intending immigrant whose income is to be relied on must sign the .

(*4*) If the sponsor relies on the income of any individual who has signed an affidavit of support attachment, the sponsor must also include with thean affidavit of support and an affidavit of support attachment, with respect to the person who signed the an affidavit of support attachment, the initial evidence required under paragraph (c)(2)(i)(A) of this section. The household member's tax return(s) must be for the same tax year as the sponsor's tax return(s). An individual who signs an affidavit of support attachment certifies, under penalty of perjury, that the submitted transcript or photocopy of the tax return is a true and correct transcript or photocopy of the Federal income tax return filed with the Internal Revenue Service, and that the information concerning that person's employment and income is true and correct.

(*5*) If the person who signs the affidavit of support attachment is not an intending immigrant, and is any person other than the sponsor's spouse or a claimed dependent of the sponsor, the sponsor must also attach proof that the person is a relative (as defined in 8 CFR 213a.1) of the sponsor and that the affidavit of support attachment signer has the same principal residence as the sponsor. If an intending immigrant signs an affidavit of support attachment, the sponsor must also provide proof that the sponsored immigrant has the same principal residence as the sponsor, unless the sponsored immigrant is the sponsor's spouse.

(D) *Effect of failure to file income tax returns.* If a sponsor, substitute sponsor, joint sponsor, or household member did not file a Federal income tax return for the year for which a transcript or photocopy must be provided, the affidavit of support or an affidavit of support attachment will not be considered sufficient to satisfy the requirements of section 213A of the Act, even if the household income meets the requirements of section 213A of the Act, unless the sponsor, substitute sponsor, joint sponsor, or household member proves, by a preponderance of the evidence, that he or she had no duty to file. If the sponsor, substitute sponsor, joint sponsor or household member cannot prove that he or she had no duty to file, then the affidavit of support or an affidavit of support attachment will not be considered sufficient to satisfy the requirements of section 213A of the Act until the sponsor, substitute sponsor, joint sponsor, or household member proves that he or she has satisfied the obligation to file the tax return and provides a transcript or copy of the return.

(ii) *Determining the sufficiency of an affidavit of support.* The sufficiency of an affidavit of support shall be determined in accordance with this paragraph.

(A) *Income.* The sponsor must first calculate the total income attributable to the sponsor under paragraph (c)(2)(i)(C) of this section for the year in which the intending immigrant filed the application for an immigrant visa or adjustment of status.

(B) *Number of persons to be supported.* The sponsor must then determine his or her household size as defined in 8 CFR 213a.1.

(C) *Sufficiency of income.* Except as provided in this paragraph, or in paragraph (a)(1)(v)(B) of this section, the sponsor's affidavit of support shall be considered sufficient to satisfy the requirements of section 213A of the Act and this section if the reasonably expected household income for the year in which the intending immigrant filed the application for an immigrant visa or adjustment of status, calculated under paragraph (c)(2)(iii)(A) of this section, would equal at least 125 percent of the Federal poverty line for the sponsor's household size as defined in 8 CFR 213a.1, under the Poverty Guidelines in effect when the intending immigrant filed the application for an immigrant visa or for adjustment of status, except that the sponsor's income need only equal at least 100 percent of the Federal poverty line for the sponsor's household size, if the sponsor is on active duty (other than for training) in the Armed Forces of the United States and the intending immigrant is the sponsor's spouse or child. The sponsor's household income for the year in which the intending immigrant filed the application for an immigrant visa or adjustment of status shall be given the greatest evidentiary weight; any tax return and other information relating to the sponsor's financial history will serve as evidence tending to show whether the sponsor is likely to be able to maintain his or her income in the future. If the projected household income for the year in which the intending immigrant filed the application for an immigrant visa or adjustment of status meets the applicable income threshold, the affidavit of support may be held to be insufficient on the basis of the household income but only if, on the basis of specific facts, including a material change in employment or income history of the sponsor, substitute sponsor, joint sponsor or household member, the number of aliens included in affidavit of support that the sponsor has signed but that have not yet entered into force in accordance with paragraph (e) of this section, or other relevant facts, it is reasonable to infer that the sponsor will not be able to maintain his or her household income at a level sufficient to meet his or her support obligations.

(iii) *Inability to meet income requirement.* (A) If the sponsor is unable to meet the minimum income requirement in paragraph (c)(2)(iii) of this section, the intending immigrant is inadmissible under section 212(a)(4) of the Act unless:

(*1*) The sponsor, the intending immigrant or both, can meet the significant assets provision of paragraph (c)(2)(iv)(B) of this section; or

(*2*) A joint sponsor executes a separate affidavit of support.

(B) *Significant assets.* The sponsor may submit evidence of the sponsor's ownership of significant assets, such as savings accounts, stocks, bonds, certificates of deposit, real estate, or other assets. An intending immigrant may submit evidence of the intending immigrant's assets as a part of the affidavit of support, even if the intending immigrant is not required to sign an affidavit of support attachment. The assets of any person who has signed an affidavit of support attachment may also be considered in determining whether the assets are sufficient to meet this requirement. To qualify as "significant assets" the combined cash value of all the assets (the total value of the assets less any offsetting liabilities) must exceed:

(*1*) If the intending immigrant is the spouse or child of a United States citizen (and the child has reached his or her 18th birthday), three times the difference between the sponsor's household income and the Federal poverty line for the sponsor's household size (including all immigrants sponsored in any affidavit of support in force or submitted under this section);

(*2*) If the intending immigrant is an alien orphan who will be adopted in the United States after the alien orphan acquires permanent residence (or in whose case the parents will need to seek a formal recognition of a foreign adoption under the law of the State of the intending immigrant's proposed residence because at least one of the parents did not see the child before or during the adoption), and who will, as a result of the adoption or formal recognition of the foreign adoption, acquire citizenship under section 320 of the Act, the difference between the sponsor's household income and the Federal poverty line for the sponsor's household size (including all immigrants sponsored in any affidavit of support in force or submitted under this section);

(*3*) In all other cases, five times the difference between the sponsor's household income and the Federal poverty line for the sponsor's household size (including all immigrants sponsored in any affidavit of support in force or submitted under this section).

(C) *Joint sponsor.* A joint sponsor must execute a separate affidavit of support on behalf of the intending immigrant(s) and be willing to accept joint and several liabilities with the sponsor or substitute sponsor. A joint sponsor must meet all the eligibility requirements under paragraph (c)(1) of this section, except that the joint sponsor is not required to file a visa petition on behalf of the intending immigrant. The joint sponsor must demonstrate his or her ability to support the intending immigrant in the manner specified in paragraph (c)(2) of this section. A joint sponsor's household income must meet or exceed the income requirement in paragraph (c)(2)(iii) of this section unless the joint sponsor can demonstrate significant assets as provided in paragraph (c)(2)(iv)(A) of this section. The joint sponsor's household income must equal at least 125 percent of the Poverty Guidelines for the joint sponsor's household size, unless the joint sponsor is on active duty in the Armed Forces and the intending immigrant is the joint sponsor's spouse or child, in which case the joint sponsor's household income is sufficient if it equals at least 100 percent of the Poverty Guidelines for the joint sponsor's household size. An intending immigrant may not have more than one joint sponsor, but, if the joint sponsor's household income is not sufficient to meet the income requirement with respect to the principal intending immigrant, any spouse and all the children who, under section 203(d) of the Act, seek to accompany the principal intending immigrant, then the joint sponsor may specify on the affidavit that it is submitted only on behalf of the principal intending immigrant and those accompanying family members specifically listed on the affidavit. The remaining accompanying family members will then be inadmissible under section 212(a)(4) of the Act unless a second joint sponsor submits an affidavit(s) on behalf of all the remaining family members who seek to accompany the principal intending immigrant and who are not included in the first joint sponsor's affidavit. There may not be more than two joint sponsors for the family group consisting of the principal intending immigrant and the accompanying spouse and children.

(D) *Substitute sponsor.* In a family-sponsored case, if the visa petitioner dies after approval of the visa petition, but the U.S. Citizenship and Immigration Services determines, under 8 CFR 205.1(a)(3)(i)(C), that for humanitarian reasons it would not be appropriate to revoke approval of the visa petition, then a substitute sponsor, as defined in 8 CFR 213a.1, may sign the an affidavit of support. The substitute sponsor must meet all the requirements of this section that would have applied to the visa petitioner, had the visa petitioner survived and been the sponsor. The substitute sponsor's household income must equal at least 125% of the Poverty Guidelines for the substitute sponsor's household size, unless the intending immigrant is the substitute sponsor's spouse or child and the substitute sponsor is on active duty in the Armed Forces (other than active duty for training), in which case the substitute sponsor's household income is sufficient if it equals at least 100% of the Poverty Guidelines for the substitute sponsor's household size. If the substitute sponsor's household income is not sufficient to meet the requirements of section 213A(a)(f)(1)(E) of the Act and paragraph (c)(2) of this section, the alien will be inadmissible unless a joint sponsor signs an affidavit of support.

(iv) *Remaining inadmissibility on public charge grounds.* Notwithstanding the filing of a sufficient affidavit of support under section 213A of the Act and this section, an alien may be found to be inadmissible under section 212(a)(4) of the Act if the alien's case includes evidence of specific facts that, when considered in light of section 212(a)(4)(B) of the Act, support a reasonable inference that the alien is likely at any time to become a public charge.

(v) *Verification of employment, income, and assets.* The Federal Government may pursue verification of any information provided on or with an affidavit of support, including information on employment, income, or assets, with the employer, financial or other institutions, the Internal Revenue Service, or the Social Security Administration. To facilitate this verification process, the sponsor, joint sponsor, substitute sponsor, or household member must sign and submit any necessary waiver form when directed to do so by the immigration officer, immigration judge, or Department of State officer who has jurisdiction to adjudicate the case to which the affidavit of support or an affidavit of support attachment relates. A sponsor's, substitute sponsor's, joint sponsor's, or household member's failure or refusal to sign any waiver needed to verify the information when directed to do so constitutes a withdrawal of the affidavit of support or an affidavit of support attachment, so that, in adjudicating the intending immigrant's application for an immigrant visa or adjustment of status, the affidavit of support or an affidavit of support attachment will be deemed not to have been filed.

(vi) *Effect of fraud or material concealment or misrepresentation.* An affidavit of support or an affidavit of support attachment is insufficient to satisfy the requirements of section 213A of the Act and this part, and the affidavit of support shall be found insufficient to establish that the intending immigrant is not likely to become a public charge, if the Department of State officer, immigration officer or immigration judge finds that an affidavit of support or an affidavit of support attachment is forged, counterfeited, or otherwise falsely executed, or if the affidavit of support or an affidavit of support attachment conceals or misrepresents facts concerning household size, household income, employment history, or any other material fact. Any person who knowingly participated in the forgery, counterfeiting, or false production of an affidavit of support or an affidavit of support attachment, or in any concealment or misrepresentation of any material fact, may be subject to a civil penalty under section 274C of the Act, to criminal prosecution, or to both, to the extent permitted by law. If the person is an alien, the person may also be subject to removal from the United States.

(d) *Legal effect of affidavit of support.* Execution of an affidavit of support under this section creates a contract between the sponsor and the U.S. Government for the benefit of the sponsored immigrant, and of any Federal, State, or local governmental agency or private entity that administers any means-tested public benefits program. The sponsored immigrant, or any Federal, State, or local governmental agency or private entity that provides any means-tested public benefit to the sponsored immigrant after the sponsored immigrant acquires permanent resident status, may seek enforcement of the sponsor's obligations through an appropriate civil action.

(e) *Commencement and termination of support obligation.* (1) With respect to any intending immigrant, the support obligation and change of address obligation imposed on a sponsor, substitute sponsor, or joint sponsor under an affidavit of support, and any household member's support obligation under an affidavit of support attachment, all begin when the immigration officer or the immigration judge grants the intending immigrant's application for admission as an immigrant or for adjustment of status on the basis of an application for admission or adjustment that included the affidavit of support or an affidavit of support attachment. Any person completing and submitting an affidavit of support as a joint sponsor or an affidavit of support attachment as a household member is not bound to any obligations under section 213A of the Act if, notwithstanding his or her signing of an affidavit of support or an affidavit of support attachment, the Department of State officer (in deciding an application for an immigrant visa) or the immigration officer or immigration judge (in deciding an application for admission or adjustment of status) includes in the decision a specific finding that the sponsor or substitute sponsor's own household income is sufficient to meet the income requirements under section 213A of the Act.

(2)(i) The support obligation and the change of address reporting requirement imposed on a sponsor, substitute sponsor and joint sponsor under an affidavit of support, and any household member's support obligation under an affidavit of support attachment, all terminate by operation of law when the sponsored immigrant:

(A) Becomes a citizen of the United States;

(B) Has worked, or can be credited with, 40 qualifying quarters of coverage under title II of the Social Security Act, 42 U.S.C. 401, *et seq., provided* that the sponsored immigrant is not credited with any quarter beginning after December 31, 1996, during which the sponsored immigrant receives or received any Federal means-tested public benefit;

(C) Ceases to hold the status of an alien lawfully admitted for permanent residence and departs the United States (if the sponsored immigrant has not abandoned permanent resident status, executing the form designated by USCIS for recording such action this provision will apply only if the sponsored immigrant is found in a removal proceeding to have abandoned that status while abroad);

(D) Obtains in a removal proceeding a new grant of adjustment of status as relief from removal (in this case, if the sponsored immigrant is still subject to the affidavit of support requirement under this part, then any individual(s) who signed an affidavit of support or an affidavit of support attachment in relation to the new adjustment application will be subject to the obligations of this part, rather than those who signed an affidavit of support or an affidavit of support attachment in relation to an earlier grant of admission as an immigrant or of adjustment of status); or

(E) Dies.

(ii) The support obligation under an affidavit of support also terminates if the sponsor, substitute sponsor or joint sponsor dies. A household member's obligation under an affidavit of support attachment terminates when the household member dies. The death of one person who had a support obligation under an affidavit of support or an affidavit of support attachment does not terminate the support obligation of any other sponsor, substitute sponsor, joint sponsor, or household member with respect to the same sponsored immigrant.

(3) The termination of the sponsor's, substitute sponsor's, or joint sponsor's obligations under an affidavit of support or of a household member's obligations under an affidavit of support attachment does not relieve the sponsor, substitute sponsor, joint sponsor, or household member (or their respective estates) of any reimbursement obligation under section 213A(b) of the Act and this section that accrued before the support obligation terminated.

(f) *Withdrawal of affidavit of support and any required attachments.* (1) In an immigrant visa case, once the sponsor, substitute sponsor, joint sponsor, household member, or intending immigrant has presented a signed affidavit of support and any required attachments to a Department of State officer, the sponsor, substitute sponsor, joint sponsor, or household member may disavow his or her agreement to act as sponsor, substitute sponsor, joint sponsor, or household member if he or she does so in writing and submits the document to the Department of State officer before the actual issuance of an immigrant visa to the intending immigrant. Once the intending immigrant has obtained an immigrant visa, a sponsor, substitute sponsor, joint sponsor, or household member cannot disavow his or her agreement to act as a sponsor, joint sponsor, or household member unless the person or entity who filed the visa petition withdraws the visa petition in writing, as specified in 8 CFR 205.1(a)(3)(i)(A) or 8 CFR 205.1(a)(3)(iii)(C), and also notifies the Department of State officer who issued the visa of the withdrawal of the petition.

(2) In an adjustment of status case, once the sponsor, substitute sponsor, joint sponsor, household member, or intending immigrant has presented a signed affidavit of support and any required attachments to an immigration officer or immigration judge, the sponsor, substitute sponsor, joint sponsor, or household member may disavow his or her agreement to act as sponsor, substitute sponsor, joint sponsor, or household member only if he or she does so in writing and submits the document to the immigration officer or immigration judge before the decision on the adjustment application.

(g) *Aliens who accompany or follow-to-join a principal intending immigrant.* (1) To avoid inadmissibility under section 212(a)(4) of the Act, an alien who applies for an immigrant visa, admission, or adjustment of status as an alien who is accompanying, as defined in 22 CFR 40.1, a principal intending immigrant must submit clear and true photocopies of any relevant affidavit(s) and attachments filed on behalf of the principal intending immigrant.

(2)(i) To avoid inadmissibility under section 212(a)(4) of the Act, an alien who applies for an immigrant visa, admission, or adjustment of status as an alien who is following-to-join a principal intending immigrant must submit a new affidavit(s) of support, together with all documents or other evidence necessary to prove that the new affidavits comply with the requirements of section 213A of the Act and 8 CFR part 213a.

(ii) When paragraph (g)(2)(i) of this section requires the filing of a new affidavit for an alien who seeks to follow-to-join a principal sponsored immigrant, the same sponsor who filed the visa petition and affidavit of support for the principal sponsored immigrant must file the new affidavit on behalf of the alien seeking to follow-to-join. If that person has died, then the alien seeking to follow-to-join is inadmissible unless a substitute sponsor, as defined by 8 CFR 213a.1, signs a new affidavit that meets the requirements of this section. Persons other than the person or persons who signed the original joint affidavits on behalf of the principal sponsored immigrant may sign a new joint affidavit on behalf of an alien who seeks to follow-to-join a principal sponsored immigrant.

(iii) If a joint sponsor is needed in the case of an alien who seeks to follow-to-join a principal sponsored immigrant, and the principal sponsored immigrant also required a joint sponsor when the principal sponsored immigrant immigrated, that same person may, but is not required to be, the joint sponsor for the alien who seeks to follow-to-join the principal sponsored immigrant.

[62 FR 54352, Oct. 20, 1997; 62 FR 60122, Nov. 6, 1997; 62 FR 64048, Dec. 3, 1997; 71 FR 35750, June 21, 2006; 72 FR 56867, Oct. 4, 2007; 76 FR 53788, Aug. 29, 2011; 76 FR 73477, Nov. 29, 2011]

§ 213a.3 Change of address.

(a) *Submission of address change*—(1) *Filing requirements.* If the address of a sponsor (including a substitute sponsor or joint sponsor) changes while the sponsor's support obligation is in effect, the sponsor shall file a change of address notice within 30 days, in a manner as prescribed by USCIS on its address change form instructions.

(2) *Proof of mailing.* USCIS will accept a photocopy of the change of address form together with proof of the form's delivery to USCIS as evidence that the sponsor has complied with this requirement.

(3) *Electronic notices.* USCIS will provide the sponsor with a receipt notice for an address change.

(4) *Alien sponsors.* If the sponsor is an alien, the sponsor must still comply with the requirements of 8 CFR 265.1 to notify USCIS of his or her change of address.

(b) *Civil penalty.* If the sponsor fails to give notice in accordance with paragraph (a) of this section, DHS may impose on the sponsor a civil penalty in an amount within the penalty range established in section 213A(d)(2)(A) of the Act. Except, if the sponsor, knowing that the sponsored immigrant has received any means-tested public benefit, fails to give notice in accordance with paragraph (a) of this section, DHS may impose on the sponsor a civil penalty in an amount within the penalty range established in section 213A(d)(2)(B) of the Act. The procedure for imposing a civil penalty is established at 8 CFR part 280.

[76 FR 53789, Aug. 29, 2011]

§ 213a.4 Actions for reimbursement, public notice, and congressional reports.

(a) *Requests for reimbursement; commencement of civil action*—(1) *By agencies.* (i) If an agency that provides a means-tested public benefit to a sponsored immigrant wants to seek reimbursement from a sponsor, household member, or joint sponsor, the program official must arrange for service of a written request for reimbursement upon the sponsor, household member, or joint sponsor, by personal service, as defined by 8 CFR 103.8(a)(2), except that the person making personal service need not be a Federal Government officer or employee.

(ii) The request for reimbursement must specify the date the sponsor, household member, or joint sponsor's support obligation commenced (this is the date the sponsored immigrant became a permanent resident), the sponsored immigrant's name, alien registration number, address, and date of birth, as well as the types of means-tested public benefit(s) that the sponsored immigrant received, the dates the sponsored immigrant received the means-tested public benefit(s), and the total amount of the means-tested public benefit(s) received.

(iii) It is not necessary to make a separate request for each type of means-tested public benefit, nor for each separate payment. The agency may instead aggregate in a single request all benefit payments the agency has made as of the date of the request. A state or local government may make a single reimbursement request on behalf of all of the state or local government agencies that have provided means-tested public benefits.

(iv) So that the sponsor, household member, or joint sponsor may verify the accuracy of the request, the request for reimbursement must include an itemized statement supporting the claim for reimbursement. The request for reimbursement must also include a notification to the sponsor, household member, or joint sponsor that the sponsor, household member, or joint sponsor must, within 45 days of the date of service, respond to the request for reimbursement either by paying the reimbursement or by arranging to commence payments pursuant to a payment schedule that is agreeable to the program official.

(v) Prior to filing a lawsuit against a sponsor, household member, or joint sponsor to enforce the sponsor, household member, or joint sponsor's support obligation under section 213A(b)(2) of the Act, a Federal, state, or local governmental agency or a private entity must wait 45 days from the date it serves a written request for reimbursement in accordance with this section.

(2) *By the sponsored immigrant.* Section 213A(b) of the Act does not require a sponsored immigrant to request the sponsor or joint sponsor to comply with the support obligation, before bringing an action to compel compliance.

(3) *Role of USCIS and DHS.* Upon the receipt of a duly issued subpoena, USCIS may provide a certified copy of an affidavit of support that has been filed on behalf of a specific alien for use as evidence in a civil action to enforce an affidavit of support, and may also disclose the last known address and social security number of the sponsor, substitute sponsor, or joint sponsor. Requesting information through the Systematic Alien Verification for Entitlement (SAVE) Programis sufficient, and a subpoena is not required, to obtain the sponsored immigrant's current immigration or citizenship status or the name, social security number and last known address of a sponsor, substitute sponsor, or joint sponsor.

(b) *Designation of means-tested public benefits.* Federal, State, and local government agencies should issue public notice of determinations regarding which benefits are considered "means-tested public benefits" prior to December 19, 1997, the date the new affidavit of support goes into effect, or as soon as possible thereafter. Additional notices should be issued whenever an agency revises its determination of which benefits are considered "means-tested public benefits." A sponsor, joint sponsor, or household member is not liable to reimburse any agency for any benefit with respect to which a public notice of the determination that the benefit is a means-tested public benefit was not published until after the date the benefit was first provided to the immigrant.

(c) *Congressional reports.* (1) For purposes of section 213A(i)(3) of the Act, USCIS will consider a sponsor or joint sponsor to be in compliance with the financial obligations of section 213A of the Act unless a party that has obtained a final judgment enforcing the sponsor or joint sponsor's obligations under section 213A(a)(1)(A) or 213A(b) of the Act has provided a copy of the final judgment to the USCIS by mailing a certified copy to the address listed in paragraph (c)(3) of this section. The copy should be accompanied by a cover letter that includes the reference "Civil Judgments for Congressional Reports under section 213A(i)(3) of the Act." Failure to file a certified copy of the final civil judgment in accordance with this section has no effect on the plaintiff's ability to collect on the judgment pursuant to law.

(2) If a Federal, state, or local agency or private entity that administers any means-tested public benefit makes a determination under section 421(e) of the Personal Responsibility and Work Opportunity Reconciliation Act of 1996

in the case of any sponsored immigrant, the program official shall send written notice of the determination, including the name of the sponsored immigrant and of the sponsor, to the address listed in paragraph (c)(3) of this section. The written notice should include the reference "Determinations under 421(e) of the Personal Responsibility and Work Opportunity Reconciliation Act of 1996."

(3) The address referred to in paragraphs (c)(1) and (c)(2) of this section is: Office of Program and Regulation Development, U.S. Citizenship and Immigration Services, 20 Massachusetts Avenue, NW., Washington, DC, 20529.

[62 FR 54352, Oct. 20, 1997, as amended at 71 FR 35755, June 21, 2006; 76 FR 53790, Aug. 29, 2011]

§ 213a.5 Relationship of this part to other affidavits of support.

Nothing in this part precludes the continued use of other affidavits of support provided by USCIS in a case other than a case described in § 213a.2(a)(2). The obligations of section 213A of the Act do not bind a person who executes such other USCIS affidavits of support. Persons sponsoring an Amerasian alien described in section 204(f)(2) of the Act remain subject to the provisions of section 204(f)(4)(B) of the Act and 8 CFR 204.4(i), as appropriate.

[76 FR 53790, Aug. 29, 2011]

PART 214—NONIMMIGRANT CLASSES

Sec.

AUTHORITY: 6 U.S.C. 202, 236; 8 U.S.C. 1101, 1102, 1103, 1182, 1184, 1186a, 1187, 1221, 1281, 1282, 1301–1305 and 1372; sec. 643, Pub. L. 104–208, 110 Stat. 3009–708; Public Law 106–386, 114 Stat. 1477–1480; section 141 of the Compacts of Free Association with the Federated States of Micronesia and the Republic of the Marshall Islands, and with the Government of Palau, 48 U.S.C. 1901 note, and 1931 note, respectively; 48 U.S.C. 1806; 8 CFR part 2.

§ 214.1 Requirements for admission, extension, and maintenance of status.

(a) *General*—(1) *Nonimmigrant classes.* For the purpose of administering the nonimmigrant provisions of the Act, the following administrative subclassifications of nonimmigrant classifications as defined in section 101(a)(15) of the Act are established:

(i) Section 101(a)(15)(B) is divided into (B)(i) for visitors for business and (B)(ii) for visitors for pleasure;

(ii) Section 101(a)(15)(C) is divided into (C)(i) for aliens who are not diplomats and are in transit through the United States; (C)(ii) for aliens in transit to and from the United Nations Headquarters District; and (C)(iii) for alien diplomats in transit through the United States;

(iii) Section 101(a)(15)(H) is divided to create an (H)(iv) subclassification for the spouse and children of a nonimmigrant classified under section 101(a)(15) (H) (i), (ii), or (iii);

(iv) Section 101(a)(15)(J) is divided into (J)(i) for principal aliens and (J)(ii) for such alien's spouse and children;

(v) Section 101(a)(15)(K) is divided into (K)(i) for the fianceé(e), (K)(ii) for the spouse, and (K)(iii) for the children of either;

(vi) Section 101(a)(15)(L) is divided into (L)(i) for principal aliens and

(L)(ii) for such alien's spouse and children;

(vii) Section 101(a)(15)(Q)(ii) is divided to create a (Q)(iii) for subclassification for the spouse and children of a nonimmigrant classified under section 101(a)(15)(Q)(ii) of the Act;

(viii) Section 101(a)(15)(T)(ii) is divided into (T)(ii), (T)(iii), (T)(iv), and (T)(v) for the spouse, child, parent, and unmarried sibling under 18 years of age, respectively, of a principal nonimmigrant classified under section 101(a)(15)(T)(i); and T(vi) for the adult or minor child of a derivative nonimmigrant classified under section 101(a)(15)(T)(ii); and

(ix) Section 101(a)(15)(U)(ii) is divided into (U)(ii), (U)(iii), (U)(iv), and (U)(v) for the spouse, child, parent, and siblings, respectively, of a nonimmigrant classified under section 101(a)(15)(U)(i); and

(2) *Classification designations.* For the purpose of this chapter the following nonimmigrant designations are established. The designation in the second column may be used to refer to the appropriate nonimmigrant classification.

Section	Designation
101(a)(15)(A)(i)	A–1.
101(a)(15)(A)(ii)	A–2.
101(a)(15)(A)(iii)	A–3.
101(a)(15)(B)(i)	B–1.
101(a)(15)(B)(ii)	B–2.
101(a)(15)(C)(i)	C–1.
101(a)(15)(C)(ii)	C–2.
101(a)(15)(C)(iii)	C–3.
101(a)(15)(D)(i)	D–1.
101(a)(15)(D)(ii)	D–2.
101(a)(15)(E)(i)	E–1.
101(a)(15)(E)(ii)	E–2.
101(a)(15)(F)(i)	F–1.
101(a)(15)(F)(ii)	F–2.
101(a)(15)(G)(i)	G–1.
101(a)(15)(G)(ii)	G–2.
101(a)(15)(G)(iii)	G–3.
101(a)(15)(G)(iv)	G–4.
101(a)(15)(g)(v)	G–5.
101(a)(15)(H)(i)(B)	H–1B.
101(a)(15)(H)(i)(C)	H–1C.
101(a)(15)(H)(ii)(A)	H–2A.
101(a)(15)(H)(ii)(B)	H–2B.
101(a)(15)(H)(iii)	H–3.
101(a)(15)(H)(iv)	H–4.
101(a)(15)(I)	I.
101(a)(15)(J)(i)	J–1.
101(a)(15)(J)(ii)	J–2.
101(a)(15)(K)(i)	K–1.
101(a)(15)(K)(ii)	K–3.
101(a)(15)(K)(iii)	K–2; K–4.
101(a)(15)(L)(i)	L–1.
101(a)(15)(L)(ii)	L–2.
101(a)(15)(M)(i)	M–1.
101(a)(15)(M)(ii)	M–2.
101(a)(15)(N)(i)	N–8.
101(a)(15)(N)(ii)	N–9.
101(a)(15)(O)(i)	O–1.
101(a)(15)(O)(ii)	O–2.
101(a)(15)(O)(iii)	O–3.
101(a)(15)(P)(i)	P–1.
101(a)(15)(P)(ii)	P–2.
101(a)(15)(P)(iii)	P–3.
101(a)(15)(P)(iv)	P–4.
101(a)(15)(Q)(i)	Q–1.
101(a)(15)(Q)(ii)	Q–2.
101(a)(15)(Q)(iii)	Q–3.
101(a)(15)(R)(i)	R–1.
101(a)(15)(R)(ii)	R–2.
101(a)(15)(S)(i)	S–5.
101(a)(15)(S)(ii)	S–6.
101(a)(15)(S) qualified family members	S–7.
101(a)(15)(T)(i)	T–1
101(a)(15)(T)(ii)	T–2
101(a)(15)(T)(iii)	T–3
101(a)(15)(T)(iv)	T–4
101(a)(15)(T)(v)	T–5
101(a)(15)(T)(vi)	T–6
101(a)(15)(U)(i)	U–1
101(a)(15)(U)(ii)	U–2, U–3, U–4, U–5
101(a)(15)(V)	V–1, V–2, or V–3
NAFTA, Principal	TN.
NAFTA, Dependent	TD.
Visa Waiver, Business	WB.
Visa Waiver, Tourist	WT.

NOTE 1: The classification designation K–2 is for the child of a K–1. The classification designation K–4 is for the child of a K–3.

NOTE 2: The classification designation V–1 is for the spouse of a lawful permanent resident; the classification designation V–2 is for the principal beneficiary of an I–130 who is the child of an LPR; the classification V–3 is for the derivative child of a V–1 or V–2 alien.

(3) *General requirements.* (i) Every nonimmigrant alien who applies for admission to, or an extension of stay in, the United States, must establish that he or she is admissible to the United States, or that any ground of inadmissibility has been waived under section 212(d)(3) of the Act. Upon application for admission, the alien must present a valid passport and valid visa unless either or both documents have been waived. A nonimmigrant alien's admission to the United States is conditioned on compliance with any inspection requirement in §235.1(d) or of this chapter, as well as compliance with part 215, subpart B, of this chapter, if applicable. The passport of an alien applying for admission must be valid for a minimum of six months from the expiration date of the contemplated period of stay, unless otherwise provided in this chapter, and the alien must agree to abide by the terms and conditions of his or her admission. An alien

applying for extension of stay must present a passport only if requested to do so by the Department of Homeland Security. The passport of an alien applying for extension of stay must be valid at the time of application for extension, unless otherwise provided in this chapter, and the alien must agree to maintain the validity of his or her passport and to abide by all the terms and conditions of his extension.

(ii) At the time of admission or extension of stay, every nonimmigrant alien must also agree to depart the United States at the expiration of his or her authorized period of admission or extension of stay, or upon abandonment of his or her authorized nonimmigrant status, and to comply with the departure procedures at section 215.8 of this chapter if such procedures apply to the particular alien. The nonimmigrant alien's failure to comply with those departure requirements, including any requirement that the alien provide biometric identifiers, may constitute a failure of the alien to maintain the terms of his or her nonimmigrant status.

(iii) At the time a nonimmigrant alien applies for admission or extension of stay, he or she must post a bond on Form I–352 in the sum of not less than $500, to ensure the maintenance of his or her nonimmigrant status and departure from the United States, if required to do so by the Commissioner of CBP, the Director of U.S. Citizenship and Immigration Services, an immigration judge, or the Board of Immigration Appeals.

(b) *Readmission of nonimmigrants under section 101(a)(15) (F), (J), (M), or (Q)(ii) to complete unexpired periods of previous admission or extension of stay*—(1) *Section 101(a)(15)(F).* The inspecting immigration officer shall readmit for duration of status as defined in § 214.2(f)(5)(iii), any nonimmigrant alien whose nonimmigrant visa is considered automatically revalidated pursuant to 22 CFR 41.125(f) and who is applying for readmission under section 101(a)(15)(F) of the Act, if the alien:

(i) Is admissible;

(ii) Is applying for readmission after an absence from the United States not exceeding thirty days solely in contiguous territory or adjacent islands;

(iii) Is in possession of a valid passport unless exempt from the requirement for presentation of a passport; and

(iv) Presents, or is the accompanying spouse or child of an alien who presents, an Arrival-Departure Record, Form I–94 (see § 1.4), issued to the alien in connection with the previous admission or stay, the alien's Form I–20 ID copy, and either:

(A) A properly endorsed page 4 of Form I-20A-B if there has been no substantive change in the information on the student's most recent Form I-20A since the form was initially issued; or

(B) A new Form I-20A-B if there has been any substantive change in the information on the student's most recent Form I-20A since the form was initially issued.

(2) *Section 101(a)(15)(J).* The inspecting immigration officer shall readmit for the unexpired period of stay authorized prior to the alien's departure, any nonimmigrant alien whose nonimmigrant visa is considered automatically revalidated pursuant to 22 CFR 41.125(f) and who is applying for readmission under section 101(a)(15)(J) of the Act, if the alien:

(i) Is admissible;

(ii) Is applying for readmission after an absence from the United States not exceeding thirty days solely in contiguous territory or adjacent islands;

(iii) Is in possession of a valid passport unless exempt from the requirement for the presentation of a passport; and

(iv) Presents, or is the accompanying spouse or child of an alien who presents, Form I–94 issued to the alien in connection with the previous admission or stay or copy three of the last Form IAP–66 issued to the alien. Form I–94 or Form IAP–66 must show the unexpired period of the alien's stay endorsed by the Service.

(3) *Section 101(a)(15)(M).* The inspecting immigration officer shall readmit for the unexpired period of stay authorized prior to the alien's departure, any nonimmigrant alien whose nonimmigrant visa is considered automatically revalidated pursuant to 22 CFR 41.125(f) and who is applying for readmission under section 101(a)(15)(M) of the Act, if the alien:

(i) Is admissible;

(ii) Is applying for readmission after an absence not exceeding thirty days solely in contiguous territory;

(iii) Is in possession of a valid passport unless exempt from the requirement for presentation of a passport; and

(iv) Presents, or is the accompanying spouse or child of an alien who presents, Form I–94 issued to the alien in connection with the previous admission or stay, the alien's Form I–20 ID copy, and a properly endorsed page 4 of Form I–20M–N.

(4) *Section 101(a)(15)(Q)(ii).* The inspecting immigration officer shall readmit for the unexpired period of stay authorized prior to the alien's departure, if the alien:

(i) Is admissible;

(ii) Is applying for readmission after an absence from the United States not exceeding 30 days solely in contiguous territory or adjacent islands;

(iii) Is in possession of a valid passport;

(iv) Presents, or is the accompanying spouse or child of an alien who presents, an Arrival-Departure Record, Form I–94, issued to the alien in connection with the previous admission or stay. The principal alien must also present a Certification Letter issued by the Department of State's Program Administrator.

(c) *Extensions of stay*—(1) *Extension of stay for certain employment-based nonimmigrant workers.* A petitioner seeking the services of an E–1, E–2, E–3, H–1B, H–1B1, H–2A, H–2B, H–3, L–1, O–1, O–2, P–1, P–2, P–3, Q–1, R–1, or TN nonimmigrant beyond the period previously granted, must apply for an extension of stay on the form designated by USCIS, with the fee prescribed in 8 CFR 103.7(b)(1), with the initial evidence specified in §214.2, and in accordance with the form instructions. Dependents holding derivative status may be included in the petition if it is for only one worker and the form version specifically provides for their inclusion. In all other cases dependents of the worker should file on Form I–539.

(2) *Filing on Form I–539.* Any other nonimmigrant alien, except an alien in F or J status who has been granted duration of status, who seeks to extend his or her stay beyond the currently authorized period of admission, must apply for an extension of stay on Form I–539 with the fee required in §103.7 of this chapter together with any initial evidence specified in the applicable provisions of §214.2, and on the application form. More than one person may be included in an application where the co-applicants are all members of a single family group and either all hold the same nonimmigrant status or one holds a nonimmigrant status and the other co-applicants are his or her spouse and/or children who hold derivative nonimmigrant status based on his or her status. Extensions granted to members of a family group must be for the same period of time. The shortest period granted to any member of the family shall be granted to all members of the family. In order to be eligible for an extension of stay, nonimmigrant aliens in K–3/K–4 status must do so in accordance with §214.2(k)(10).

(3) *Ineligible for extension of stay.* A nonimmigrant in any of the following classes is ineligible for an extension of stay:

(i) B–1 or B–2 where admission was pursuant to the Visa Waiver Pilot Program;

(ii) C–1, C–2, C–3;

(iii) D–1, D–2;

(iv) K–1, K–2;

(v) Any nonimmigrant admitted for duration of status, other than as provided in §214.2(f)(7);

(vi) Any nonimmigrant who is classified pursuant to section 101(a)(15)(S) of the Act beyond a total of 3 years; or

(vii) Any nonimmigrant who is classified according to section 101(a)(15)(Q)(ii) of the Act beyond a total of 3 years.

(viii) Any nonimmigrant admitted pursuant to the Guam-CNMI Visa Waiver Program, as provided in section 212(l) of the Act.

(4) *Timely filing and maintenance of status.* An extension of stay may not be approved for an applicant who failed to maintain the previously accorded status or where such status expired before the application or petition was filed, except that failure to file before the period of previously authorized status expired may be excused in the discretion

of the Service and without separate application, with any extension granted from the date the previously authorized stay expired, where it is demonstrated at the time of filing that:

(i) The delay was due to extraordinary circumstances beyond the control of the applicant or petitioner, and the Service finds the delay commensurate with the circumstances;

(ii) The alien has not otherwise violated his or her nonimmigrant status;

(iii) The alien remains a bona fide nonimmigrant; and

(iv) The alien is not the subject of deportation proceedings under section 242 of the Act (prior to April 1, 1997) or removal proceedings under section 240 of the Act.

(5) *Decision in Form I–129 or I–539 extension proceedings.* Where an applicant or petitioner demonstrates eligibility for a requested extension, it may be granted at the discretion of the Service. There is no appeal from the denial of an application for extension of stay filed on Form I–129 or I–539.

(d) *Termination of status.* Within the period of initial admission or extension of stay, the nonimmigrant status of an alien shall be terminated by the revocation of a waiver authorized on his or her behalf under section 212(d) (3) or (4) of the Act; by the introduction of a private bill to confer permanent resident status on such alien; or, pursuant to notification in the FEDERAL REGISTER, on the basis of national security, diplomatic, or public safety reasons.

(e) *Employment.* A nonimmigrant in the United States in a class defined in section 101(a)(15)(B) of the Act as a temporary visitor for pleasure, or section 101(a)(15)(C) of the Act as an alien in transit through this country, may not engage in any employment. Any other nonimmigrant in the United States may not engage in any employment unless he has been accorded a nonimmigrant classification which authorizes employment or he has been granted permission to engage in employment in accordance with the provisions of this chapter. A nonimmigrant who is permitted to engage in employment may engage only in such employment as has been authorized. Any unauthorized employment by a nonimmigrant constitutes a failure to maintain status within the meaning of section 241(a)(1)(C)(i) of the Act.

(f) *False information.* A condition of a nonimmigrant's admission and continued stay in the United States is the full and truthful disclosure of all information requested by DHS. A nonimmigrant's willful failure to provide full and truthful information requested by DHS (regardless of whether or not the information requested was material) constitutes a failure to maintain nonimmigrant status under section 237(a)(1)(C)(i) of the Act.

(g) *Criminal activity.* A condition of a nonimmigrant's admission and continued stay in the United States is obedience to all laws of United States jurisdictions which prohibit the commission of crimes of violence and for which a sentence of more than one year imprisonment may be imposed. A nonimmigrant's conviction in a jurisdiction in the United States for a crime of violence for which a sentence of more than one year imprisonment may be imposed (regardless of whether such sentence is in fact imposed) constitutes a failure to maintain status under section 241(a)(1)(C)(i) of the Act.

(h) *Education privacy and F, J, and M nonimmigrants.* As authorized by section 641(c)(2) of Division C of Pub. L. 104–208, 8 U.S.C. 1372, and § 2.1(a) of this chapter, the Service has determined that, with respect to F and M nonimmigrant students and J nonimmigrant exchange visitors, waiving the provisions of the Family Educational Rights and Privacy Act (FERPA), 20 U.S.C. 1232g, is necessary for the proper implementation of 8 U.S.C. 1372. An educational agency or institution may not refuse to report information concerning an F or M nonimmigrant student or a J nonimmigrant exchange visitor that the educational agency or institution is required to report under 8 U.S.C. 1372 and § 214.3(g) (or any corresponding Department of State regulation concerning J nonimmigrants) on the basis of FERPA and any regulation implementing FERPA. The waiver of FERPA under this paragraph authorizes and requires an educational agency or institution to report information concerning an F, J or M nonimmigrant that would ordinarily be protected by FERPA, but only to the extent that 8 U.S.C. 1372 and §214.3(g) (or any corresponding Department of State regulation concerning J nonimmigrants) requires the educational agency or institution to report information.

(i) *Employment in a health care occupation.* (1) Except as provided in 8 CFR 212.15(n), any alien described in 8 CFR 212.15(a) who is coming to the United States to perform labor in a health care occupation described in 8 CFR 212.15(c) must obtain a certificate from a credentialing organization described in 8 CFR 212.15(e). The certificate or certified statement must be presented to the Department of Homeland Security in accordance with 8 CFR 212.15(d). In the alternative, an eligible alien seeking admission as a nurse may obtain a certified statement as provided in 8 CFR 212.15(h).

(2) A TN nonimmigrant may establish that he or she is eligible for a waiver described at 8 CFR 212.15(n) by providing evidence that his or her initial admission as a TN (or TC) nonimmigrant health care worker occurred before September 23, 2003, and he or she was licensed and employed in the United States as a health care worker before September 23, 2003. Evidence may include, but is not limited to, copies of TN or TC approval notices, copies of Form I–94 Arrival/Departure Records, employment verification letters and/or pay-stubs or other employment records, and state health care worker licenses.

(j) *Extension of stay or change of status for health care worker.* In the case of any alien admitted temporarily as a nonimmigrant under section 212(d)(3) of the Act and 8 CFR 212.15(n) for the primary purpose of the providing labor in a health care occupation described in 8 CFR 212.15(c), the petitioning employer may file a Form I–129 to extend the approval period for the alien's classification for the nonimmigrant status. If the alien is in the United States and is eligible for an extension of stay or change of status, the Form I–129 also serves as an application to extend the period of the alien's authorized stay or to change the alien's status. Although the Form I–129 petition may be approved, as it relates to the employer's request to classify the alien, the application for an extension of stay or change of status shall be denied if:

(1) The petitioner or applicant fails to submit the certification required by 8 CFR 212.15(a) with the petition or application to extend the alien's stay or change the alien's status; or

(2) The petition or application to extend the alien's stay or change the alien's status does include the certification required by 8 CFR 212.15(a), but the alien obtained the certification more than 1 year after the date of the alien's admission under section 212(d)(3) of the Act and 8 CFR 212.15(n). While DHS may admit, extend the period of authorized stay, or change the status of a nonimmigrant health care worker for a period of 1 year if the alien does not have certification on or before July 26, 2004 (or on or before July 26, 2005, in the case of a citizen of Canada or Mexico, who, before September 23, 2003, was employed as a TN or TC nonimmigrant health care worker and held a valid license from a U.S. jurisdiction), the alien will not be eligible for a subsequent admission, change of status, or extension of stay as a health care worker if the alien has not obtained the requisite certification 1 year after the initial date of admission, change of status, or extension of stay as a health care worker.

(k) *Denial of petitions under section 214(c) of the Act based on a finding by the Department of Labor.* Upon debarment by the Department of Labor pursuant to 20 CFR part 655, USCIS may deny any petition filed by that petitioner for nonimmigrant status under section 101(a)(15)(H) (except for status under sections 101(a)(15)(H)(i)(b1)), (L), (O), and (P)(i) of the Act) for a period of at least 1 year but not more than 5 years. The length of the period shall be based on the severity of the violation or violations. The decision to deny petitions, the time period for the bar to petitions, and the reasons for the time period will be explained in a written notice to the petitioner.

(l) *Period of stay.* (1) An alien admissible in E–1, E–2, E–3, H–1B, L–1, or TN classification and his or her dependents may be admitted to the United States or otherwise provided such status for the validity period of the petition, or for a validity period otherwise authorized for the E–1, E–2, E–3, and TN classifications, plus an additional period of up to 10 days before the validity period begins and 10 days after the validity period ends. Unless authorized under 8 CFR 274a.12, the alien may not work except during the validity period.

(2) An alien admitted or otherwise provided status in E–1, E–2, E–3, H–1B, H–1B1, L–1, O–1 or TN classification and his or her dependents shall not be considered to have failed to maintain nonimmigrant status solely on the basis of a cessation of the employment on which the alien's classification was based, for up to 60 consecutive days or until the end of the authorized validity period, whichever is shorter, once during each authorized validity period. DHS may eliminate or shorten this 60-day period as a matter of discretion. Unless otherwise authorized under 8 CFR 274a.12, the alien may not work during such a period.

(3) An alien in any authorized period described in paragraph (l) of this section may apply for and be granted an extension of stay under paragraph (c)(4) of this section or change of status under 8 CFR 248.1, if otherwise eligible.

[26 FR 12067, Dec. 16, 1961]

EDITORIAL NOTE: For FEDERAL REGISTER citations affecting § 214.1, see the List of CFR Sections Affected, which appears in the Finding Aids section of the printed volume and at *www.govinfo.gov*.

§ 214.2 Special requirements for admission, extension, and maintenance of status.

The general requirements in § 214.1 are modified for the following nonimmigrant classes:

(a) *Foreign government officials*—(1) *General.* The determination by a consular officer prior to admission and the recognition by the Secretary of State subsequent to admission is evidence of the proper classification of a nonimmigrant under section 101(a)(15)(A) of the Act. An alien who has a nonimmigrant status under section 101(a)(15)(A)(i) or (ii) of the Act is to be admitted for the duration of the period for which the alien continues to be recognized by the Secretary of State as being entitled to that status. An alien defined in section (101)(a)(15)(A)(iii) of the Act is to be admitted for an initial period of not more than three years, and may be granted extensions of temporary stay in increments of not more than two years. In addition, the application for extension of temporary stay must be accompanied by a statement signed by the employing official stating that he/she intends to continue to employ the applicant and describing the type of work the applicant will perform.

(2) *Definition of A–1 or A–2 dependent.* For purposes of employment in the United States, the term *dependent* of an A–1 or A–2 principal alien, as used in § 214.2(a), means any of the following immediate members of the family habitually residing in the same household as the principal alien who is an officer or employee assigned to a diplomatic or consular office in the United States:

(i) Spouse;

(ii) Unmarried children under the age of 21;

(iii) Unmarried sons or daughters under the age of 23 who are in full-time attendance as students at post-secondary educational institutions;

(iv) Unmarried sons or daughters under the age of 25 who are in full-time attendance as students at post-secondary educational institutions if a formal bilateral employment agreement permitting their employment in the United States was signed prior to November 21, 1988, and such bilateral employment agreement does not specify 23 as the maximum age for employment of such sons and daughters. The Office of Protocol of the Department of State shall maintain a listing of foreign states with which the United States has such bilateral employment agreements;

(v) Unmarried sons or daughters who are physically or mentally disabled to the extent that they cannot adequately care for themselves or cannot establish, maintain or re-establish their own households. The Department of State or the Service may require certification(s) as it deems sufficient to document such mental or physical disability; or

(vi) An immediate family member of an A–1 or A–2 principal alien described in 22 CFR 41.21(a)(3)(i) to (iv) with A–1 or A–2 nonimmigrant status, who falls within a category of aliens recognized by the Department of State as qualifying dependents.

(3) *Applicability of a formal bilateral agreement or an informal de facto arrangement for A–1 or A–2 dependents.* The applicability of a formal bilateral agreement shall be based on the foreign state which employs the principal alien and not on the nationality of the principal alien or dependent. The applicability of an informal de facto arrangement shall be based on the foreign state which employs the principal alien, but under a de facto arrangement the principal alien also must be a national of the foreign state which employs him/her in the United States.

(4) *Income tax, Social Security liability; non-applicability of certain immunities.* Dependents who are granted employment authorization under this section are responsible for payment of all federal, state and local income, employment and related taxes and Social Security contributions on any remuneration received. In addition, immunity from civil or administrative jurisdiction in accordance with Article 37 of the Vienna Convention on Diplomatic Relations or other international agreements does not apply to these dependents with respect to matters arising out of their employment.

(5) *Dependent employment pursuant to formal bilateral employment agreements and informal de facto reciprocal arrangements.* (i) The Office of Protocol shall maintain a listing of foreign states which have entered into formal bilateral employment agreements. Dependents of an A–1 or A–2 principal alien assigned to official duty in the United States may accept or continue in unrestricted employment based on such formal bilateral agreements upon favorable recommendation by the Department of State and issuance of employment authorization documentation by the Service in accordance with 8 CFR part 274a. The application procedures are set forth in paragraph (a)(6) of this section.

(ii) For purposes of this section, an informal de facto reciprocal arrangement exists when the Department of State determines that a foreign state allows appropriate employment on the local economy for dependents of certain United States officials assigned to duty in that foreign state. The Office of Protocol shall maintain a listing of countries with which such reciprocity exists. Dependents of an A–1 or A–2 principal alien assigned to official duty in the United States may be authorized to accept or continue in employment based upon informal de facto arrangements upon favorable recommendation by the Department of State and issuance of employment authorization by the Service in accordance with 8 CFR part 274a. Additionally, the procedures set forth in paragraph (a)(6) of this section must be complied with, and the following conditions must be met:

(A) Both the principal alien and the dependent desiring employment are maintaining A–1 or A–2 status as appropriate;

(B) The principal's assignment in the United States is expected to last more than six months;

(C) Employment of a similar nature for dependents of United States Government officials assigned to official duty in the foreign state employing the principal alien is not prohibited by that foreign state's government;

(D) The proposed employment is not in an occupation listed in the Department of Labor Schedule B (20 CFR part 656), or otherwise determined by the Department of Labor to be one for which there is an oversupply of qualified U.S. workers in the area of proposed employment. This Schedule B restriction does not apply to a dependent son or daughter who is a full-time student if the employment is part-time, consisting of not more than 20 hours per week, and/or if it is temporary employment of not more than 12 weeks during school holiday periods; and

(E) The proposed employment is not contrary to the interest of the United States. Employment contrary to the interest of the United States includes, but is not limited to, the employment of A–1 or A–2 dependents: who have criminal records; who have violated United States immigration laws or regulations, or visa laws or regulations; who have worked illegally in the United States; and/or who cannot establish that they have paid taxes and social security on income from current or previous United States employment.

(6) *Application procedures.* The following procedures are applicable to dependent employment applications under bilateral agreements and de facto arrangements:

(i) The dependent must submit a completed Form I–566 to the Department of State through the office, mission, or organization which employs his/her principal alien. A dependent applying under paragraph (a)(2)(iii) or (iv) of this section must submit a certified statement from the post-secondary educational institution confirming that he/she is pursuing studies on a full-time basis. A dependent applying under paragraph (a)(2)(v) of this section must submit medical certification regarding his/her condition. The certification should identify the dependent and the certifying physician and give the physician's phone number; identify the condition, describe the symptoms and provide a prognosis; and certify that the dependent is unable to maintain a home of his or her own. Additionally, a dependent applying under the terms of a de facto arrangement must attach a statement from the prospective employer which includes the dependent's name; a description of the position offered and the duties to be performed; the salary offered; and verification that the dependent possesses the qualifications for the position.

(ii) The Department of State reviews and verifies the information provided, makes its determination, and endorses the Form I–566.

(iii) If the Department of State's endorsement is favorable, the dependent may apply to USCIS for employment authorization. When applying to USCIS for employment authorization, the dependent must present his or her Form I–566 with a favorable endorsement from the Department of State and any additional documentation as may be required by the Secretary.

(7) *Period of time for which employment may be authorized.* If approved, an application to accept or continue employment under this section shall be granted in increments of not more than three years each.

(8) *No appeal.* There shall be no appeal from a denial of permission to accept or continue employment under this section.

(9) *Dependents or family members of principal aliens classified A–3.* A dependent or family member of a principal alien classified A–3 may not be employed in the United States under this section.

(10) *Unauthorized employment.* An alien classified under section 101(a)(15)(A) of the Act who is not a principal alien and who engages in employment outside the scope of, or in a manner contrary to this section, may be considered in violation of section 241(a)(1)(C)(i) of the Act. An alien who is classified under section 101(a)(15)(A) of the Act who is a principal alien and who engages in employment outside the scope of his/her official position may be considered in violation of section 241(a)(1)(C)(i) of the Act.

(b) *Visitors*—(1) *General.* Any B–1 visitor for business or B–2 visitor for pleasure may be admitted for not more than one year and may be granted extensions of temporary stay in increments of not more than six months each, except that alien members of a religious denomination coming temporarily and solely to do missionary work in behalf of a religious denomination may be granted extensions of not more than one year each, provided that such work does not involve the selling of articles or the solicitation or acceptance of donations. Those B–1 and B–2 visitors admitted pursuant to the waiver provided at § 212.1(e) of this chapter may be admitted to and stay on Guam for period not to exceed fifteen days and are not eligible for extensions of stay.

(2) *Minimum six month admissions.* Any B–2 visitor who is found otherwise admissible and is issued a Form I–94 (see § 1.4), will be admitted for a minimum period of six months, regardless of whether less time is requested, provided, that any required passport is valid as specified in section 212(a)(26) of the Act. Exceptions to the minimum six month admission may be made only in individual cases upon the specific approval of the district director for good cause.

(3) *Visa Waiver Pilot Program.* Special requirements for admission and maintenance of status for visitors admitted to the United States under the Visa Waiver Pilot Program are set forth in section 217 of the Act and part 217 of this chapter.

(4) *Admission of aliens pursuant to the North American Free Trade Agreement (NAFTA).* A citizen of Canada or Mexico seeking temporary entry for purposes set forth in paragraph (b)(4)(i) of this section, who otherwise meets existing requirements under section 101(a)(15)(B) of the Act, including but not limited to requirements regarding the source of remuneration, shall be admitted upon presentation of proof of such citizenship in the case of Canadian applicants, and valid, unexpired entry documents such as a passport and visa, or a passport and BCC in the case of Mexican applicants, a description of the purpose for which the alien is seeking admission, and evidence demonstrating that he or she is engaged in one of the occupations or professions set forth in paragraph (b)(4)(i) of this section. Existing requirements, with respect to Canada, are those requirements which were in effect at the time of entry into force of the Canada/U.S. Free Trade Agreement and, with respect to Mexico, are those requirements which were in effect at the time of entry into force of the NAFTA. Additionally, nothing shall preclude the admission of a citizen of Mexico or Canada who meets the requirements of paragraph (b)(4)(ii) of this section.

(i) *Occupations and professions set forth in Appendix 1603.A.1 to Annex 1603 of the NAFTA*—(A) *Research and design.* Technical scientific and statistical researchers conducting independent research or research for an enterprise located in the territory of another Party.

(B) *Growth, manufacture and production* (*1*) Harvester owner supervising a harvesting crew admitted under applicable law. (Applies only to harvesting of agricultural crops: Grain, fiber, fruit and vegetables.)

(*2*) Purchasing and production management personnel conducting commercial transactions for an enterprise located in the territory of another Party.

(C) *Marketing.* (*1*) Market researchers and analyst conducting independent research or analysis, or research or analysis for an enterprise located in the territory of another Party.

(*2*) Trade fair and promotional personnel attending a trade convention.

(D) *Sales.* (*1*) Sales representatives and agents taking orders or negotiating contracts for goods or services for an enterprise located in the territory of another Party but not delivering goods or providing services.

(*2*) Buyers purchasing for an enterprise located in the territory of another Party.

(E) *Distribution.* (*1*) Transportation operators transporting goods or passengers to the United States from the territory of another Party or loading and transporting goods or passengers from the United States to the territory of another Party, with no unloading in the United States, to the territory of another Party. (These operators may make deliveries in the United States if all goods or passengers to be delivered were loaded in the territory of another Party. Furthermore, they may load from locations in the United States if all goods or passengers to be loaded will be delivered in the territory of another Party. Purely domestic service or solicitation, in competition with the United States operators, is not permitted.)

(*2*) Customs brokers performing brokerage duties associated with the export of goods from the United States to or through Canada.

(F) *After-sales service.* Installers, repair and maintenance personnel, and supervisors, possessing specialized knowledge essential to the seller's contractual obligation, performing services or training workers to perform services, pursuant to a warranty or other service contract incidental to the sale of commercial or industrial equipment or machinery, including computer software, purchased from an enterprise located outside the United States, during the life of the warranty or service agreement. (For the purposes of this provision, the commercial or industrial equipment or machinery, including computer software, must have been manufactured outside the United States.)

(G) *General service.* (*1*) Professionals engaging in a business activity at a professional level in a profession set out in Appendix 1603.D.1 to Annex 1603 of the NAFTA, but receiving no salary or other remuneration from a United States source (other than an expense allowance or other reimbursement for expenses incidental to the temporary stay) and otherwise satisfying the requirements of Section A to Annex 1063 of the NAFTA.

(*2*) Management and supervisory personnel engaging in commercial transactions for an enterprise located in the territory of another Party.

(*3*) Financial services personnel (insurers, bankers or investment brokers) engaging in commercial transactions for an enterprise located in the territory of another Party.

(*4*) Public relations and advertising personnel consulting with business associates, or attending or participating in conventions.

(*5*) Tourism personnel (tour and travel agents, tour guides or tour operators) attending or participating in conventions or conducting a tour that has begun in the territory of another Party. (The tour may begin in the United States; but must terminate in foreign territory, and a significant portion of the tour must be conducted in foreign territory. In such a case, an operator may enter the United States with an empty conveyance and a tour guide may enter on his or her own and join the conveyance.)

(*6*) Tour bus operators entering the United States:

(*i*) With a group of passengers on a bus tour that has begun in, and will return to, the territory of another Party.

(*ii*) To meet a group of passengers on a bus tour that will end, and the predominant portion of which will take place, in the territory of another Party.

(*iii*) With a group of passengers on a bus tour to be unloaded in the United States and returning with no passengers or reloading with the group for transportation to the territory of another Party.

(*7*) Translators or interpreters performing services as employees of an enterprise located in the territory of another Party.

(ii) Occupations and professions not listed in Appendix 1603.A.1 to Annex 1603 of the NAFTA. Nothing in this paragraph shall preclude a business person engaged in an occupation or profession other than those listed in Appendix 1603.A.1 to Annex 1603 of the NAFTA from temporary entry under section 101(a)(15)(B) of the Act, if such person otherwise meets the existing requirements for admission as prescribed by the Attorney General.

(5) *Construction workers not admissible.* Aliens seeking to enter the country to perform building or construction work, whether on-site or in-plant, are not eligible for classification or admission as B–1 nonimmigrants under section 101(a)(15)(B) of the Act. However, alien nonimmigrants otherwise qualified as B–1 nonimmigrants may be issued visas and may enter for the purpose of supervision or training of others engaged in building or construction work, but not for the purpose of actually performing any such building or construction work themselves.

(6) [Reserved]

(7) *Enrollment in a course of study prohibited.* An alien who is admitted as, or changes status to, a B–1 or B–2 nonimmigrant on or after April 12, 2002, or who files a request to extend the period of authorized stay in B–1 or B–2 nonimmigrant status on or after such date, violates the conditions of his or her B–1 or B–2 status if the alien enrolls in a course of study. Such an alien who desires to enroll in a course of study must either obtain an F–1 or M–1 nonimmigrant visa from a consular officer abroad and seek readmission to the United States, or apply for and obtain a change of status under section 248 of the Act and 8 CFR part 248. The alien may not enroll in the course of study until the Service has admitted the alien as an F–1 or M–1 nonimmigrant or has approved the alien's application under part 248 of this chapter and changed the alien's status to that of an F–1 or M–1 nonimmigrant.

(c) *Transits.* (1) [Reserved]

(2) *United Nations Headquarters District.* An alien of the class defined in section 101(a)(15)(C) of the Act, whose visa is limited to transit to and from the United Nations Headquarters District, if otherwise admissible, shall be

admitted on the additional conditions that he proceed directly to the immediate vicinity of the United Nations Headquarters District, and remain there continuously, departing therefrom only if required in connection with his departure from the United States, and that he have a document establishing his ability to enter some country other than the United States following his sojourn in the United Nations Headquarters District. The immediate vicinity of the United Nations Headquarters District is that area lying within a twenty-five mile radius of Columbus Circle, New York, NY.

(3) *Others.* The period of admission of an alien admitted under section 101(a)(15)(C) of the Act shall not exceed 29 days.

(d) *Crewmen.* (1) The provisions of parts 251, 252, 253, and 258 of this chapter shall govern the landing of crewmen as nonimmigrants of the class defined in section 101(a)(15)(D) of the Act. An alien in this status may be employed only in a crewman capacity on the vessel or aircraft of arrival, or on a vessel or aircraft of the same transportation company, and may not be employed in connection with domestic flights or movements of a vessel or aircraft. However, nonimmigrant crewmen may perform crewmember duties through stopovers on an international flight for any United States carrier where such flight uses a single aircraft and has an origination or destination point outside the United States.

(2) *Denial of crewman status in the case of certain labor disputes (D nonimmigrants).* (i) An alien shall be denied D crewman status as described in section 101(a)(15)(D) of the Act if:

(A) The alien intends to land for the purpose of performing service on a vessel of the United States (as defined in 46 U.S.C. 2101(46)) or an aircraft of an air carrier (as defined in section 101(3) of the Federal Aviation Act of 1958); and

(B) A labor dispute consisting of a strike or lockout exists in the bargaining unit of the employer in which the alien intends to perform such service; and

(C) The alien is not already an employee of the company (as described in paragraph (d)(2)(iv) of this section).

(ii) *Refusal to land.* Any alien (except a qualified current employee as described in paragraph (d)(2)(iv) of this section) who the examining immigration officer determines has arrived in the United States for the purpose of performing service on board a vessel or an aircraft of the United States when a strike or lockout is under way in the bargaining unit of the employer, shall be refused a conditional landing permit under section 252 of the Act.

(iii) *Ineligibility for parole.* An alien described in paragraph (d)(2)(i) of this section may not be paroled into the United States under section 212(d)(5) of the Act for the purpose of performing crewmember duties unless the Attorney General determines that the parole of such alien is necessary to protect the national security of the United States. This paragraph does not prohibit the granting of parole for other purposes, such as medical emergencies.

(iv) *Qualified current employees.* (A) Paragraphs (d)(2)(i), (d)(2)(ii), and (d)(2)(iii) of this section do not apply to an alien who is already an employee of the owner or operator of the vessel or air carrier and who at the time of inspection presents true copies of employer work records which satisfy the examining immigration officer that the alien:

(*1*) Has been an employee of such employer for a period of not less than one year preceding the date that a strike or lawful lockout commenced;

(*2*) Has served as a qualified crewman for such employer at least once in three different months during the 12-month period preceding the date that the strike or lockout commenced; and

(*3*) Shall continue to provide the same crewman services that he or she previously provided to the employer.

(B) An alien crewman who qualifies as a current employee under this paragraph remains subject to the restrictions on his or her employment in the United States contained in paragraph (d)(1) of this section.

(v) *Strike or lockout determination.* These provisions will take effect if the Attorney General, through the Commissioner of the Immigration and Naturalization Service or his or her designee, after consultation with the National Mediation Board, determines that a strike, lockout, or labor dispute involving a work stoppage is in progress in the bargaining unit of the employer for whom the alien intends to perform such service.

(e) *Treaty traders and investors*—(1) *Treaty trader.* An alien, if otherwise admissible, may be classified as a nonimmigrant treaty trader (E–1) under the provisions of section 101(a)(15)(E)(i) of the Act if the alien:

(i) Will be in the United States solely to carry on trade of a substantial nature, which is international in scope, either on the alien's behalf or as an employee of a foreign person or organization engaged in trade principally between the United States and the treaty country of which the alien is a national, taking into consideration any conditions in the country of which the alien is a national which may affect the alien's ability to carry on such substantial trade; and

(ii) Intends to depart the United States upon the expiration or termination of treaty trader (E–1) status.

(2) *Treaty investor.* An alien, if otherwise admissible, may be classified as a nonimmigrant treaty investor (E–2) under the provision of section 101(a)(15)(E)(ii) of the Act if the alien:

(i) Has invested or is actively in the process of investing a substantial amount of capital in a bona fide enterprise in the United States, as distinct from a relatively small amount of capital in a marginal enterprise solely for the purpose of earning a living;

(ii) Is seeking entry solely to develop and direct the enterprise; and

(iii) Intends to depart the United States upon the expiration or termination of treaty investor (E–2) status.

(3) *Employee of treaty trader or treaty investor.* An alien employee of a treaty trader, if otherwise admissible, may be classified as E–1, and an alien employee of a treaty investor, if otherwise admissible, may be classified as E–2 if the employee is in or is coming to the United States to engage in duties of an executive or supervisory character, or, if employed in a lesser capacity, the employee has special qualifications that make the alien's services essential to the efficient operation of the enterprise. The employee must have the same nationality as the principal alien employer. In addition, the employee must intend to depart the United States upon the expiration or termination of E–1 or E–2 status. The principal alien employer must be:

(i) A person in the United States having the nationality of the treaty country and maintaining nonimmigrant treaty trader or treaty investor status or, if not in the United States, would be classifiable as a treaty trader or treaty investor; or

(ii) An enterprise or organization at least 50 percent owned by persons in the United States having the nationality of the treaty country and maintaining nonimmigrant treaty trader or treaty investor status or who, if not in the United States, would be classifiable as treaty traders or treaty investors.

(4) *Spouse and children of treaty trader or treaty investor.* The spouse and child of a treaty trader or treaty investor accompanying or following to join the principal alien, if otherwise admissible, may receive the same classification as the principal alien. The nationality of a spouse or child of a treaty trader or treaty investor is not material to the classification of the spouse or child under the provisions of section 101(a)(15)(E) of the Act.

(5) *Nonimmigrant intent.* An alien classified under section 101(a)(15)(E) of the Act shall maintain an intention to depart the United States upon the expiration or termination of E–1 or E–2 status. However, an application for initial admission, change of status, or extension of stay in E classification may not be denied solely on the basis of an approved request for permanent labor certification or a filed or approved immigrant visa preference petition.

(6) *Treaty country.* A treaty country is, for purposes of this section, a foreign state with which a qualifying Treaty of Friendship, Commerce, or Navigation or its equivalent exists with the United States. A treaty country includes a foreign state that is accorded treaty visa privileges under section 101(a)(15)(E) of the Act by specific legislation.

(7) *Treaty country nationality.* The nationality of an individual treaty trader or treaty investor is determined by the authorities of the foreign state of which the alien is a national. In the

case of an enterprise or organization, ownership must be traced as best as is practicable to the individuals who are ultimately its owners.

(8) *Terms and conditions of E treaty status*—(i) *Limitations on employment.* The Service determines the terms and conditions of E treaty status at the time of admission or approval of a request to change nonimmigrant status to E classification. A treaty trader, treaty investor, or treaty employee may engage only in employment which is consistent with the terms and conditions of his or her status and the activity forming the basis for the E treaty status.

(ii) *Subsidiary employment.* Treaty employees may perform work for the parent treaty organization or enterprise, or any subsidiary of the parent organization or enterprise. Performing work for subsidiaries of a common parent enterprise or organization will not be deemed to constitute a substantive change in the terms and conditions of the underlying E treaty employment if, at the time the E treaty status was determined, the applicant presented evidence establishing:

(A) The enterprise or organization, and any subsidiaries thereof, where the work will be performed; the requisite parent-subsidiary relationship; and that the subsidiary independently qualifies as a treaty organization or enterprise under this paragraph;

(B) In the case of an employee of a treaty trader or treaty investor, the work to be performed requires executive, supervisory, or essential skills; and

(C) The work is consistent with the terms and conditions of the activity forming the basis of the classification.

(iii) *Substantive changes.* Prior Service approval must be obtained where there will be a substantive change in the terms or conditions of E status. In such cases, a treaty alien must file a new application on Form I–129 and E supplement, in accordance with the instructions on that form, requesting extension of stay in the United States. In support of an alien's Form I–129 application, the treaty alien must submit evidence of continued eligibility for E classification in the new capacity. Alternatively, the alien must obtain from a consular officer a visa reflecting the new terms and conditions and subsequently apply for admission at a port-of-entry. The Service will deem there to have been a substantive change necessitating the filing of a new Form I–129 application in cases where there has been a fundamental change in the employing entity's basic characteristics, such as a merger, acquisition, or sale of the division where the alien is employed.

(iv) *Non-substantive changes.* Prior approval is not required, and there is no need to file a new Form I–129, if there is no substantive, or fundamental, change in the terms or conditions of the alien's employment which would affect the alien's eligibility for E classification. Further, prior approval is not required if corporate changes occur which do not affect the previously approved employment relationship, or are otherwise non-substantive. To facilitate admission, the alien may:

(A) Present a letter from the treaty-qualifying company through which the alien attained E classification explaining the nature of the change;

(B) Request a new Form I–797, Approval Notice, reflecting the non-substantive change by filing Form I–129, with fee, and a complete description of the change, or;

(C) Apply directly to Department of State for a new E visa reflecting the change. An alien who does not elect one of the three options contained in paragraph (e)(8)(iv) (A) through (C) of this section, is not precluded from demonstrating to the satisfaction of the immigration officer at the port-of-entry in some other manner, his or her admissibility under section 101(a)(15)(E) of the Act.

(v) *Advice.* To ascertain whether a change is substantive, an alien may file Form I–129, with fee, and a complete description of the change, to request appropriate advice. In cases involving multiple employees, an alien may request that USCIS determine if a merger or other corporate restructuring requires the filing of separate applications by filing a single Form I–129, with fee, and attaching a list of the related receipt numbers for the employees involved and an explanation of the change or changes.

(vi) *Approval.* If an application to change the terms and conditions of E status or employment is approved, the Service shall notify the applicant on Form I–797. An extension of stay in nonimmigrant E classification may be granted for the validity of the approved application. The alien is not authorized to begin the new employment until the application is approved. Employment is authorized only for the period of time the alien remains in the United States. If the alien subsequently departs from the United States, readmission in E classification may be authorized where the alien presents his or her unexpired E visa together with the Form I–797, Approval Notice, indicating Service approval of a change of employer or of a change in the substantive terms or conditions of treaty status or employment in E classification, or, in accordance with 22 CFR 41.112(d), where the alien is applying for readmission after an absence not exceeding 30 days solely in contiguous territory.

(vii) An unauthorized change of employment to a new employer will constitute a failure to maintain status within the meaning of section 237(a)(1)(C)(i) of the Act. In all cases where the treaty employee will be providing services to a subsidiary under this paragraph, the subsidiary is required to comply with the terms of 8 CFR part 274a.

(9) *Trade—definitions.* For purposes of this paragraph: *Items of trade* include but are not limited to goods, services, international banking, insurance, monies, transportation, communications, data processing, advertising, accounting, design and engineering, management consulting, tourism, technology and its transfer, and some news-gathering activities. For purposes of this paragraph, goods are tangible commodities or merchandise having extrinsic value. Further, as used in this paragraph, services are legitimate economic activities which provide other than tangible goods.

Trade is the existing international exchange of items of trade for consideration between the United States and the treaty country. Existing trade includes successfully negotiated contracts binding upon the parties which call for the immediate exchange of items of trade. Domestic trade or the development of domestic markets without international exchange does not constitute trade for purposes of section 101(a)(15)(E) of the Act. This exchange must be traceable and identifiable. Title to the trade item must pass from one treaty party to the other.

(10) *Substantial trade.* Substantial trade is an amount of trade sufficient to ensure a continuous flow of international trade items between the United States and the treaty country. This continuous flow contemplates numerous transactions over time. Treaty trader status may not be established or maintained on the basis of a single transaction, regardless of how protracted or monetarily valuable the transaction. Although the monetary value of the trade item being exchanged is a relevant consideration, greater weight will be given to more numerous exchanges of larger value. There is no minimum requirement with respect to the monetary value or volume of each individual transaction. In the case of smaller businesses, an income derived from the value of numerous transactions which is sufficient to support the treaty trader and his or her family constitutes a favorable factor in assessing the existence of substantial trade.

(11) *Principal trade.* Principal trade between the United States and the treaty country exists when over 50 percent of the volume of international trade of the treaty trader is conducted between the United States and the treaty country of the treaty trader's nationality.

(12) *Investment.* An investment is the treaty investor's placing of capital, including funds and other assets (which have not been obtained, directly or indirectly, through criminal activity), at risk in the commercial sense with the objective of generating a profit. The treaty investor must be in possession of and have control over the capital invested or being invested. The capital must be subject to partial or total loss if investment fortunes reverse. Such

investment capital must be the investor's unsecured personal business capital or capital secured by personal assets. Capital in the process of being invested or that has been invested must be irrevocably committed to the enterprise. The alien has the burden of establishing such irrevocable commitment. The alien may use any legal mechanism available, such as the placement of invested funds in escrow pending admission in, or approval of, E classification, that would not only irrevocably commit funds to the enterprise, but might also extend personal liability protection to the treaty investor in the event the application for E classification is denied.

(13) *Bona fide enterprise.* The enterprise must be a real, active, and operating commercial or entrepreneurial undertaking which produces services or goods for profit. The enterprise must meet applicable legal requirements for doing business in the particular jurisdiction in the United States.

(14) *Substantial amount of capital.* A substantial amount of capital constitutes an amount which is:

(i) Substantial in relationship to the total cost of either purchasing an established enterprise or creating the type of enterprise under consideration;

(ii) Sufficient to ensure the treaty investor's financial commitment to the successful operation of the enterprise; and

(iii) Of a magnitude to support the likelihood that the treaty investor will successfully develop and direct the enterprise. Generally, the lower the cost of the enterprise, the higher, proportionately, the investment must be to be considered a substantial amount of capital.

(15) *Marginal enterprise.* For purposes of this section, an enterprise may not be marginal. A marginal enterprise is an enterprise that does not have the present or future capacity to generate more than enough income to provide a minimal living for the treaty investor and his or her family. An enterprise that does not have the capacity to generate such income, but that has a present or future capacity to make a significant economic contribution is not a marginal enterprise. The projected future income-generating capacity should generally be realizable within 5 years from the date the alien commences the normal business activity of the enterprise.

(16) *Solely to develop and direct.* An alien seeking classification as a treaty investor (or, in the case of an employee of a treaty investor, the owner of the treaty enterprise) must demonstrate that he or she does or will develop and direct the investment enterprise. Such an applicant must establish that he or she controls the enterprise by demonstrating ownership of at least 50 percent of the enterprise, by possessing operational control through a managerial position or other corporate device, or by other means.

(17) *Executive and supervisory character.* The applicant's position must be principally and primarily, as opposed to incidentally or collaterally, executive or supervisory in nature. Executive and supervisory duties are those which provide the employee ultimate control and responsibility for the enterprise's overall operation or a major component thereof. In determining whether the applicant has established possession of the requisite control and responsibility, a Service officer shall consider, where applicable:

(i) That an executive position is one which provides the employee with great authority to determine the policy of, and the direction for, the enterprise;

(ii) That a position primarily of supervisory character provides the employee supervisory responsibility for a significant proportion of an enterprise's operations and does not generally involve the direct supervision of low-level employees, and;

(iii) Whether the applicant possesses executive and supervisory skills and experience; a salary and position title commensurate with executive or supervisory employment; recognition or indicia of the position as one of authority and responsibility in the overall organizational structure; responsibility for making discretionary decisions, setting policies, directing and managing business operations, supervising other professional and supervisory personnel; and that, if the position requires some routine work usually performed by a staff employee, such functions may only be of an incidental nature.

(18) *Special qualifications.* Special qualifications are those skills and/or aptitudes that an employee in a lesser capacity brings to a position or role that are essential to the successful or efficient operation of the treaty enterprise. In determining whether the skills possessed by the alien are essential to the operation of the employing treaty enterprise, a Service officer must consider, where applicable:

(i) The degree of proven expertise of the alien in the area of operations involved; whether others possess the applicant's specific skill or aptitude; the length of the applicant's experience and/or training with the treaty enterprise; the period of training or other experience necessary to perform effectively the projected duties; the relationship of the skill or knowledge to the enterprise's specific processes or applications, and the salary the special qualifications can command; that knowledge of a foreign language and culture does not, by itself, meet the special qualifications requirement, and;

(ii) Whether the skills and qualifications are readily available in the United States. In all cases, in determining whether the applicant possesses special qualifications which are essential to the treaty enterprise, a Service officer must take into account all the particular facts presented. A skill that is essential at one point in time may become commonplace at a later date. Skills that are needed to start up an enterprise may no longer be essential after initial operations are complete and running smoothly. Some skills are essential only in the short-term for the training of locally hired employees. Under certain circumstances, an applicant may be able to establish his or her essentiality to the treaty enterprise for a longer period of time, such as, in connection with activities in the areas of product improvement, quality control, or the provision of a service not yet generally available in the United States. Where the treaty enterprise's need for the applicant's special qualifications, and therefore, the applicant's essentiality, is time-limited, Service officers may request that the applicant provide evidence of the period for which skills will be needed and a reasonable projected date for completion of start-up or replacement of the essential skilled workers.

(19) *Period of admission.* Periods of admission are as follows:

(i) A treaty trader or treaty investor may be admitted for an initial period of not more than 2 years.

(ii) The spouse and minor children accompanying or following to join a treaty trader or treaty investor shall be admitted for the period during which the principal alien is in valid treaty trader or investor status. The temporary departure from the United States of the principal trader or investor shall not affect the derivative status of the dependent spouse and minor unmarried children, provided the familial relationship continues to exist and the principal remains eligible for admission as an E nonimmigrant to perform the activity.

(iii) Unless otherwise provided for in this chapter, an alien shall not be admitted in E classification for a period of time extending more than 6 months beyond the expiration date of the alien's passport.

(20) *Extensions of stay.* Requests for extensions of stay may be granted in increments of not more than 2 years. A treaty trader or treaty investor in valid E status may apply for an extension of stay by filing an application for extension of stay on Form I–129 and E Supplement, with required accompanying documents, in accordance with §214.1 and the instructions on that form.

(i) For purposes of eligibility for an extension of stay, the alien must prove that he or she:

(A) Has at all times maintained the terms and conditions of his or her E nonimmigrant classification;

(B) Was physically present in the United States at the time of filing the application for extension of stay; and

(C) Has not abandoned his or her extension request.

(ii) With limited exceptions, it is presumed that employees of treaty enterprises with special qualifications who are responsible for start-up operations should be able to complete their objectives within 2 years. Absent special circumstances, therefore, such employees will not be eligible to obtain an extension of stay.

(iii) Subject to paragraph (e)(5) of this section and the presumption noted in paragraph (e)(22)(ii) of this section, there is no specified number of extensions of stay that a treaty trader or treaty investor may be granted.

(21) *Change of nonimigrant status.* (i) An alien in another valid nonimmigrant status may apply for change of status to E classification by filing an application for change of status on Form I–129 and E Supplement, with required accompanying documents establishing eligibility for a change of status and E classification, in accordance with 8 CFR part 248 and the instructions on Form I–129 and E Supplement.

(ii) The spouse or minor children of an applicant seeking a change of status to that of treaty trader or treaty investor alien shall file concurrent applications for change of status to derivative treaty classification on the appropriate Service form. Applications for derivative treaty status shall:

(A) Be approved only if the principal treaty alien is granted treaty alien status and continues to maintain that status;

(B) Be approved for the period of admission authorized in paragraph (e)(20) of this section.

(22) *Denial of treaty trader or treaty investor status to citizens of Canada or Mexico in the case of certain labor disputes.* (i) A citizen of Canada or Mexico may be denied E treaty trader or treaty investor status as described in section 101(a)(15)(E) of the Act and section B of Annex 1603 of the NAFTA if:

(A) The Secretary of Labor certifies to or otherwise informs the Commissioner that a strike or other labor dispute involving a work stoppage of workers in the alien's occupational classification is in progress at the place where the alien is or intends to be employed; and

(B) Temporary entry of that alien may affect adversely either:

(*1*) The settlement of any labor dispute that is in progress at the place or intended place of employment, or

(*2*) The employment of any person who is involved in such dispute.

(ii) If the alien has already commenced employment in the United States and is participating in a strike or other labor dispute involving a work stoppage of workers, whether or not such strike or other labor dispute has been certified by the Secretary of Labor, or whether the Service has been otherwise informed that such a strike or labor dispute is in progress, the alien shall not be deemed to be failing to maintain his or her status solely on account of past, present, or future participation in a strike or other labor dispute involving a work stoppage of workers, but is subject to the following terms and conditions:

(A) The alien shall remain subject to all applicable provisions of the Immigration and Nationality Act, and regulations promulgated in the same manner as all other E nonimmigrants; and

(B) The status and authorized period of stay of such an alien is not modified or extended in any way by virtue of his or her participation in a strike or other labor dispute involving a work stoppage of workers.

(iii) Although participation by an E nonimmigrant alien in a strike or other labor dispute involving a work stoppage of workers will not constitute a ground for deportation, any alien who violates his or her status or who remains in the United States after his or her authorized period of stay has expired will be subject to deportation.

(iv) If there is a strike or other labor dispute involving a work stoppage of workers in progress, but such strike or other labor dispute is not certified under paragraph (e)(22)(i) of this section, or the Service has not otherwise been informed by the Secretary that such a strike or labor dispute is in progress, the Commissioner shall not deny entry to an applicant for E status.

(23) *Special procedures for classifying foreign investors in the Commonwealth of the Northern Mariana Islands (CNMI) as E–2 nonimmigrant treaty investors under*

title VII of the Consolidated Natural Resources Act of 2008 (Pub. L. 110–229), 48 U.S.C. 1806.

(i) *E–2 CNMI Investor eligibility.* During the period ending on January 18, 2013, an alien may, upon application to the Secretary of Homeland Security, be classified as a CNMI-only nonimmigrant treaty investor (E–2 CNMI Investor) under section 101(a)(15)(E)(ii) of the Act if the alien:

(A) Was lawfully admitted to the CNMI in long-term investor status under the immigration laws of the CNMI before the transition program effective date and had that status on the transition program effective date;

(B) Has continuously maintained residence in the CNMI;

(C) Is otherwise admissible to the United States; and

(D) Maintains the investment or investments that formed the basis for such long-term investment status.

(ii) *Definitions.* For purposes of paragraph (e)(23) of this section, the following definitions apply:

(A) *Approved investment or residence* means an investment or residence approved by the CNMI government.

(B) *Approval letter* means a letter issued by the CNMI government certifying the acceptance of an approved investment subject to the minimum investment criteria and standards provided in 4 N. Mar. I. Code section 5941 *et seq.* (long-term business certificate), 4 N. Mar. I. Code section 5951 *et seq.* (foreign investor certificate), and 4 N. Mar. I. Code section 50101 *et seq.* (foreign retiree investment certificate).

(C) *Certificate* means a certificate or certification issued by the CNMI government to an applicant whose application has been approved by the CNMI government.

(D) *Continuously maintained residence in the CNMI* means that the alien has maintained his or her residence within the CNMI since being lawfully admitted as a long-term investor and has been physically present therein for periods totaling at least half of that time. Absence from the CNMI for any continuous period of more than six months but less than one year after such lawful admission shall break the continuity of such residence, unless the subject alien establishes to the satisfaction of DHS that he or she did not in fact abandon residence in the CNMI during such period. Absence from the CNMI for any period of one year or more during the period for which continuous residence is required shall break the continuity of such residence.

(E) *Public organization* means a CNMI public corporation or an agency of the CNMI government.

(F) *Transition period* means the period beginning on the transition program effective date and ending on December 31, 2014.

(iii) *Long-term investor status.* Long-term investor status under the immigration laws of the CNMI includes only the following investor classifications under CNMI immigration laws as in effect on or before November 27, 2009:

(A) *Long-term business investor.* An alien who has an approved investment of at least $50,000 in the CNMI, as evidenced by a Long-Term Business Certificate.

(B) *Foreign investor.* An alien in the CNMI who has invested either a minimum of $100,000 in an aggregate approved investment in excess of $2,000,000, or a minimum of $250,000 in a single approved investment, as evidenced by a Foreign Investment Certificate.

(C) *Retiree investor.* An alien in the CNMI who:

(*1*) Is over the age of 55 years and has invested a minimum of $100,000 in an approved residence on Saipan or $75,000 in an approved residence on Tinian or Rota, as evidenced by a Foreign Retiree Investment Certification; or

(*2*) Is over the age of 55 years and has invested a minimum of $150,000 in an approved residence to live in the CNMI, as evidenced by a Foreign Retiree Investment Certificate.

(iv) *Maintaining investments.* An alien in long-term investor status under the immigration laws of the CNMI is maintaining his or her investments if that alien investor is in compliance with the terms upon which the investor certificate was issued.

(v) *Filing procedures.* An alien seeking classification under E–2 CNMI Investor nonimmigrant status must file an application for E–2 CNMI investor nonimmigrant status, along with accompanying evidence, with USCIS in accordance with the form instructions before January 18, 2013. An application filed after the filing date deadline will be rejected.

(vi) *Appropriate documents.* Documentary evidence establishing eligibility for E–2 CNMI nonimmigrant investor status is required.

(A) Required evidence of admission includes a valid unexpired foreign passport and a properly endorsed CNMI admission document (*e.g.*, entry permit or certificate) reflecting lawful admission to the CNMI in long-term business investor, foreign investor, or retiree foreign investor status.

(B) Required evidence of long-term investor status includes:

(*1*) An unexpired Long-Term Business Certificate, in the case of an alien in long-term business investor status.

(*2*) An unexpired Foreign Investment Certificate, in the case of an alien in foreign investor status.

(*3*) A Foreign Retiree Investment Certification or a Foreign Retiree Investment Certificate, in the case of an alien in retiree investor status.

(C) Required evidence that the long-term investor is maintaining his or her investment includes all of the following, as applicable:

(*1*) An approval letter issued by the CNMI government.

(*2*) Evidence that capital has been invested, including bank statements showing amounts deposited in CNMI business accounts, invoices, receipts or contracts for assets purchased, stock purchase transaction records, loan or other borrowing agreements, land leases, financial statements, business gross tax receipts, or any other agreements supporting the application.

(*3*) Evidence that the applicant has invested at least the minimum amount required, including evidence of assets which have been purchased for use in the enterprise, evidence of property transferred from abroad for use in the enterprise, evidence of monies transferred or committed to be transferred to the new or existing enterprise in exchange for shares of stock, any loan or mortgage, promissory note, security agreement, or other evidence of borrowing which is secured by assets of the applicant.

(*4*) A comprehensive business plan for new enterprises.

(*5*) Articles of incorporation, by-laws, partnership agreements, joint venture agreements, corporate minutes and annual reports, affidavits, declarations, or certifications of paid-in capital.

(*6*) Current business licenses.

(*7*) Foreign business registration records, recent tax returns of any kind, evidence of other sources of capital.

(*8*) A listing of all resident and nonresident employees.

(*9*) A listing of all holders of business certificates for the business establishment.

(*10*) A listing of all corporations in which the applicant has a controlling interest.

(*11*) In the case of a holder of a certificate of foreign investment, copies of annual reports of investment activities in the CNMI containing sufficient information to determine whether the certificate holder is under continuing compliance with the standards of issuance, accompanied by annual financial audit reports performed by an independent certified public accountant.

(*12*) In the case of an applicant who is a retiree investor, evidence that he or she has an interest in property in the CNMI (*e.g.*, lease agreement), evidence of the value of the property interest (*e.g.*, an appraisal regarding the value of the property), and, as applicable, evidence of the value of the improvements on the property (*e.g.*, receipts or invoices of the costs of construction, the amount paid for a preexisting structure, or an appraisal of improvements).

(vii) *Physical presence in the CNMI.* Physical presence in the CNMI at the time of filing or during the pendency of the application is not required, but an application may not be filed by, or E–2 CNMI Investor status granted to, any alien present in U.S. territory other than in the CNMI. If an alien with CNMI long-term investor status departs the CNMI on or after the transition program effective date but before being granted E–2 CNMI Investor status, he or she may not be re-admitted to the CNMI without a visa or appropriate inadmissibility waiver under the U.S. immigration laws. If USCIS grants E–2 CNMI Investor nonimmigrant classification to an alien who is not physically present in the CNMI at the time of the grant, such alien must obtain an E–2 CNMI Investor nonimmigrant visa at a consular office abroad in order to seek admission to the CNMI in E–2 CNMI Investor status.

(viii) *Information for background checks.* USCIS may require an applicant for E–2 CNMI Investor status, including but not limited to any applicant for derivative status as a spouse or child, to submit biometric information. An applicant present in the CNMI must pay or obtain a waiver of the biometric services fee described in 8 CFR 103.7(b) for any biometric services provided, including but not limited to reuse of previously provided biometric information for background checks.

(ix) *Denial.* A grant of E–2 CNMI Investor status is a discretionary determination, and the application may be denied for failure of the applicant to demonstrate eligibility or for other good cause. Denial of the application may be appealed to the USCIS Administrative Appeals Office or any successor body.

(x) *Spouse and children of an E–2 CNMI Investor*—(A) *Classification.* The spouse and children of an E–2 CNMI Investor accompanying or following-to-join the principal alien, if otherwise admissible, may receive the same classification as the principal alien. The nationality of a spouse or child of an E–2 CNMI investor is not material to the classification of the spouse or child.

(B) *Employment authorization.* The spouse of an E–2 CNMI Investor lawfully admitted in the CNMI in E–2 CNMI Investor nonimmigrant status, other than the spouse of an E–2 CNMI investor who obtained such status based upon a Foreign Retiree Investment Certificate, is eligible to apply for employment authorization under 8 CFR 274a.12(c)(12) while in E–2 CNMI Investor nonimmigrant status. Employment authorization acquired under this paragraph is limited to employment in the CNMI only.

(xi) *Terms and conditions of E–2 CNMI Investor nonimmigrant status*—(A) *Nonimmigrant status.* E–2 CNMI Investor nonimmigrant status and any derivative status are only applicable in the CNMI. Entry, employment, and residence in the rest of the United States (including Guam) require the appropriate visa or visa waiver eligibility. An E–2 CNMI Investor who enters, attempts to enter or attempts to travel to any other part of the United States without the appropriate visa or visa waiver eligibility, or who violates conditions of nonimmigrant stay applicable to any such authorized status in any other part of the United States, will be deemed to have violated the terms and conditions of his or her E–2 CNMI Investor status. An E–2 CNMI Investor who departs the CNMI will require an E–2 CNMI investor visa for readmission to the CNMI as an E–2 CNMI Investor.

(B) *Employment authorization.* An alien with E–2 CNMI Investor nonimmigrant status is only employment authorized in the CNMI for the enterprise that is the basis for his or her CNMI Foreign Investment Certificate or Long-Term Business Certificate, to the extent that such Certificate authorized such activity. An alien with E–2 CNMI Investor nonimmigrant status based upon a Foreign Retiree Investor Certificate is not employment authorized.

(C) *Changes in E–2 CNMI investor nonimmigrant status.* If there are any substantive changes to an alien's compliance with the terms and conditions of qualification for E–2 CNMI Investor nonimmigrant status, the alien must file a new application for E–2 CNMI Investor nonimmigrant status, in accordance with the appropriate form instructions to request an extension of stay in the United States. Prior approval is not required if corporate changes occur that do not affect a previously approved employment relationship, or are otherwise non-substantive.

(D) *Unauthorized change of employment.* An unauthorized change of employment to a new employer will constitute a failure to maintain status within the meaning of section 237(a)(1)(C)(i) of the Act.

(E) *Periods of admission.* (*1*) An E–2 CNMI Investor may be admitted for an initial period of not more than two years.

(*2*) The spouse and children accompanying or following-to-join an E–2 CNMI Investor may be admitted for the period during which the principal alien is in valid E–2 CNMI Investor nonimmigrant status. The temporary departure from the United States of the principal E–2 CNMI Investor shall not affect the derivative status of the dependent spouse and children, provided the familial relationship continues to exist and the principal alien remains eligible for admission as an E–2 CNMI Investor.

(xii) *Extensions of stay.* Requests for extensions of E–2 CNMI Investor nonimmigrant status may be granted in increments of not more than two years, until the end of the transition period. To request an extension of stay, an E–2 CNMI Investor must file with USCIS an application for extension of stay, with required accompanying documents, in accordance with the appropriate form instructions. To qualify for an extension of E–2 CNMI Investor nonimmigrant status, each alien must demonstrate:

(A) Continuous maintenance of the terms and conditions of E–2 CNMI Investor nonimmigrant status;

(B) Physical presence in the CNMI at the time of filing the application for extension of stay; and

(C) That he or she did not leave during the pendency of the application.

(xiii) *Change of status.* An alien lawfully admitted to the United States in another valid nonimmigrant status who is continuing to maintain that status may apply to change nonimmigrant status to E–2 CNMI Investor in accordance with paragraph (e)(21) of this section, if otherwise eligible, including but not limited to having been in CNMI long-term investor status on the transition date and within the period provided by paragraph (e)(23)(v) of this section.

(xiv) *Expiration of initial transition period.* Upon expiration of the initial transition period, the E–2 CNMI Investor nonimmigrant status will automatically terminate.

(xv) *Fee waiver.* An alien applying for E–2 CNMI Investor nonimmigrant status is eligible for a waiver of the required fee for an application based upon inability to pay as provided by 8 CFR 103.7(c)(1).

(xvi) *Waiver of inadmissibility for applicants present in the CNMI.* An applicant for E–2 CNMI Investor nonimmigrant status, who is otherwise eligible for such status and otherwise admissible to the United States, and who has provided all appropriate documents as described in paragraph (e)(23)(vi) of this section, may be granted a waiver of inadmissibility under section 212(d)(3)(A)(ii) of the Act, including the grounds of inadmissibility described in sections 212(a)(6)(A)(i) (to the extent such grounds arise solely because of the alien's presence in the CNMI on November 28, 2009) and 212(a)(7)(B)(i)(II) of the Act, for the purpose of granting the E–2 CNMI Investor nonimmigrant status. Such waiver may be granted without additional form or fee required. In the case of an application by a spouse or child as described in paragraph (e)(23)(x) of this section who is present in the CNMI, the appropriate documents required for such waiver are a valid unexpired passport and evidence that the spouse or child is lawfully present in the CNMI under section 1806(e) of title 48, U.S. Code (which may include evidence of a grant of parole by USCIS or by the Department of Homeland Security pursuant to a grant of advance parole by USCIS in furtherance of section 1806(e) of title 48, U.S. Code).

(f) *Students in colleges, universities, seminaries, conservatories, academic high schools, elementary schools, other academic institutions, and in language training programs*—(1) *Admission of student*—(i) *Eligibility for admission.* A nonimmigrant student may be admitted into the United States in nonimmigrant status under section 101(a)(15)(F) of the Act, if:

(A) The student presents a SEVIS Form I–20 issued in his or her own name by a school approved by the Service for attendance by F–1 foreign students. (In the alternative, for a student seeking admission prior to August 1, 2003, the student may present a currently-valid Form I–20A–B/I–20ID, if that form was issued by the school prior to January 30, 2003);

(B) The student has documentary evidence of financial support in the amount indicated on the SEVIS Form I–20 (or the Form I–20A–B/I–20ID);

(C) For students seeking initial admission only, the student intends to attend the school specified in the student's visa (or, where the student is exempt from the requirement for a visa, the school indicated on the SEVIS Form I–20 (or the Form I–20A–B/I–20ID)); and

(D) In the case of a student who intends to study at a public secondary school, the student has demonstrated that he or she has reimbursed the local educational agency that administers the school for the full, unsubsidized per capita cost of providing education at the school for the period of the student's attendance.

(ii) *Disposition of Form I–20 A–B/I–20 ID.* Form I–20 A–B/I–20 ID contains two copies, the I–20 School Copy and the I–20 ID (Student) Copy. For purposes of clarity, the entire Form I–20 A–B/I–20 ID shall be referred to as Form I–20 A–B and the I–20 ID (Student) Copy shall be referred to as the I–20 ID. When an F–1 student applies for admission with a complete Form I–20 A–B, the inspecting officer shall:

(A) Transcribe the student's admission number from Form I–94 onto his or her Form I–20 A–B (for students seeking initial admission only);

(B) Endorse all copies of the Form I–20 A–B;

(C) Return the I–20 ID to the student; and

(D) Forward the I–20 School Copy to the Service's processing center for data entry. (The school copy of Form I–20 A–B will be sent back to the school as a notice of the student's admission after data entry.)

(iii) *Use of SEVIS.* On January 30, 2003, the use of the Student and Exchange Visitor Information System (SEVIS) will become mandatory for the issuance of any new Form I–20. A student or dependent who presents a non-SEVIS Form I–20 issued on or after January 30, 2003, will not be accepted for admission to the United States. Non-SEVIS Forms I–20 issued prior to January 30, 2003, will continue to be acceptable until August 1, 2003. However, schools must issue a SEVIS Form I–20 to any current student requiring a reportable action (e.g., extension of status, practical training, and requests for employment authorization) or a new Form I–20, or for any aliens who must obtain a new nonimmigrant student visa. As of August 1, 2003, the records of all current or continuing students must be entered in SEVIS.

(2) *I–20 ID.* An F–1 student is expected to safekeep the initial I–20 ID bearing the admission number and any subsequent copies which have been issued to him or her. Should the student lose his or her current I–20 ID, a replacement copy bearing the same information as the lost copy, including any endorsement for employment and notations, may be issued by the designated school official (DSO) as defined in 8 CFR 214.3(*l*)(1)(i).

(3) *Admission of the spouse and minor children of an F–1 student.* The spouse and minor children accompanying an F–1 student are eligible for admission in F–2 status if the student is admitted in F–1 status. The spouse and minor children following-to-join an F–1 student are eligible for admission to the United States in F–2 status if they are able to demonstrate that the F–1 student has been admitted and is, or will be within 30 days, enrolled in a full course of study, or engaged in approved practical training following completion of studies. In either case, at the time they seek admission, the eligible spouse and minor children of an F–1 student with a SEVIS Form I–20 must individually present an original SEVIS Form I–20 issued in the name of each F–2 dependent issued by a school authorized by the Service for attendance by F–1 foreign students. Prior to August 1, 2003, if exigent circumstances are demonstrated, the Service will allow the dependent of an F–1 student in possession of a SEVIS Form I–20 to enter the United States using a copy of the F–1 student's SEVIS Form I–20. (In the alternative, for dependents seeking admission to the United States prior to August 1, 2003, a copy of the F–1 student's current Form I–20ID issued prior to January 30, 2003, with proper endorsement by the DSO will satisfy this requirement.) A new SEVIS Form I–20

(or Form I–20A–B) is required for a dependent where there has been any substantive change in the F–1 student's current information.

(4) *Temporary absence.* An F–1 student returning to the United States from a temporary absence of five months or less may be readmitted for attendance at a Service-approved educational institution, if the student presents:

(i) A current SEVIS Form I–20 (or, for readmission prior to August 1, 2003, a current Form I–20ID which was issued prior to January 30, 2003), properly endorsed by the DSO for reentry if there has been no substantive change to the most recent Form I–20 information; or

(ii) A new SEVIS Form I–20 (or, for readmission prior to August 1, 2003, a new Form I–20ID which was issued prior to January 30, 2003), if there has been a substantive change in the information on the student's most recent Form I–20 information, such as in the case of a student who has changed the major area of study, who intends to transfer to another Service approved institution or who has advanced to a higher level of study.

(5) *Duration of status*—(i) *General.* Except for border commuter students covered by the provisions of paragraph (f)(18) of this section, an F–1 student is admitted for duration of status. Duration of status is defined as the time during which an F–1 student is pursuing a full course of study at an educational institution approved by the Service for attendance by foreign students, or engaging in authorized practical training following completion of studies, except that an F–1 student who is admitted to attend a public high school is restricted to an aggregate of 12 months of study at any public high school(s). An F–1 student may be admitted for a period up to 30 days before the indicated report date or program start date listed on Form I–20. The student is considered to be maintaining status if he or she is making normal progress toward completing a course of study.

(ii) *Change in educational levels.* An F–1 student who continues from one educational level to another is considered to be maintaining status, provided that the transition to the new educational level is accomplished according to transfer procedures outlined in paragraph (f)(8) of this section.

(iii) *Annual vacation.* An F–1 student at an academic institution is considered to be in status during the annual (or summer) vacation if the student is eligible and intends to register for the next term. A student attending a school on a quarter or trimester calendar who takes only one vacation a year during any one of the quarters or trimesters instead of during the summer is considered to be in status during that vacation, if the student has completed the equivalent of an academic year prior to taking the vacation.

(iv) *Preparation for departure.* An F–1 student who has completed a course of study and any authorized practical training following completion of studies will be allowed an additional 60-day period to prepare for departure from the United States or to transfer in accordance with paragraph (f)(8) of this section. An F–1 student authorized by the DSO to withdraw from classes will be allowed a 15-day period for departure from the United States. However, an F–1 student who fails to maintain a full course of study without the approval of the DSO or otherwise fails to maintain status is not eligible for an additional period for departure.

(v) *Emergent circumstances as determined by the Commissioner.* Where the Commissioner has suspended the applicability of any or all of the requirements for on-campus or off-campus employment authorization for specified students pursuant to paragraphs (f)(9)(i) or (f)(9)(ii) of this section by notice in the FEDERAL REGISTER, an affected student who needs to reduce his or her full course of study as a result of accepting employment authorized by such notice in the FEDERAL REGISTER will be considered to be in status during the authorized employment, subject to any other conditions specified in the notice, provided that, for the duration of the authorized employment, the student is registered for the number of semester or quarter hours of instruction per academic term specified in the notice, which in no event shall be less than 6 semester or quarter hours of instruction per academic term if the student is at the undergraduate level or less than 3 semester or quarter hours of instruction per academic term if the student is at the graduate level, and is continuing to make progress toward completing the course of study.

(vi) *Extension of duration of status and grant of employment authorization.* (A) The duration of status, and any employment authorization granted under 8 CFR 274a.12(c)(3)(i)(B) or (C), of an F–1 student who is the beneficiary of an H–1B petition subject to section 214(g)(1)(A) of the Act (8 U.S.C. 1184(g)(1)(A)) and request for change of status shall be automatically extended until October 1 of the fiscal year for which such H–1B status is being requested where such petition:

(*1*) Has been timely filed; and

(*2*) Requests an H–1B employment start date of October 1 of the following fiscal year.

(B) The automatic extension of an F–1 student's duration of status and employment authorization under paragraph (f)(5)(vi)(A) of this section shall automatically terminate upon the rejection, denial, revocation, or withdrawal of the H–1B petition filed on such F–1 student's behalf or upon the denial or withdrawal of the request for change of nonimmigrant status, even if the H–1B petition filed on the F–1 student's behalf is approved for consular processing.

(C) In order to obtain the automatic extension of stay and employment authorization under paragraph (f)(5)(vi)(A) of this section, the F–1 student, consistent with 8 CFR part 248, must not have violated the terms or conditions of his or her nonimmigrant status.

(D) An automatic extension of an F–1 student's duration of status under paragraph (f)(5)(vi)(A) of this section also applies to the duration of status of any F–2 dependent aliens.

(6) *Full course of study*—(i) *General.* Successful completion of the full course of study must lead to the attainment of a specific educational or professional objective. A course of study at an institution not approved for attendance by foreign students as provided in § 214.3(a)(3) does not satisfy this requirement. A "full course of study" as required by section 101(a)(15)(F)(i) of the Act means:

(A) Postgraduate study or postdoctoral study at a college or university, or undergraduate or postgraduate study at a conservatory or religious seminary, certified by a DSO as a full course of study;

(B) Undergraduate study at a college or university, certified by a school official to consist of at least twelve semester or quarter hours of instruction per academic term in those institutions using standard semester, trimester, or quarter hour systems, where all undergraduate students who are enrolled for a minimum of twelve semester or quarter hours are charged full-time tuition or are considered full-time for other administrative purposes, or its equivalent (as determined by the district director in the school approval process), except when the student needs a lesser course load to complete the course of study during the current term;

(C) Study in a postsecondary language, liberal arts, fine arts, or other non-vocational program at a school which confers upon its graduates recognized associate or other degrees or has established that its credits have been and are accepted unconditionally by at least three institutions of higher learning which are either: (1) A school (or school system) owned and operated as a public educational institution by the United States or a State or political subdivision thereof; or (2) a school accredited by a nationally recognized accrediting body; and which has been certified by a designated school official to consist of at least twelve clock hours of instruction a week, or its equivalent as determined by the district director in the school approval process;

(D) Study in any other language, liberal arts, fine arts, or other nonvocational training program, certified by a designated school official to consist of at least eighteen clock hours of attendance a week if the dominant part of the course of study consists of classroom instruction, or to consist of at least twenty-two clock hours a week if the dominant part of the course of study consists of laboratory work; or

(E) Study in a curriculum at an approved private elementary or middle school or public or private academic high school which is certified by a designated school official to consist of class attendance for not less than the minimum number of hours a week prescribed by the school for normal progress toward graduation.

(F) Notwithstanding paragraphs (f)(6)(i)(A) and (f)(6)(i)(B) of this section, an alien who has been granted employment authorization pursuant to the terms of a document issued by the Commissioner under paragraphs (f)(9)(i) or (f)(9)(ii) of this section and published in the FEDERAL REGISTER shall be deemed to be engaged in a "full course of study" if he or she remains registered for no less than the number of semester or quarter hours of instruction per academic term specified by the Commissioner in the notice for the validity period of such employment authorization.

(G) For F–1 students enrolled in classes for credit or classroom hours, no more than the equivalent of one class or three credits per session, term, semester, trimester, or quarter may be counted toward the full course of study requirement if the class is taken on-line or through distance education and does not require the student's physical attendance for classes, examination or other purposes integral to completion of the class. An on-line or distance education course is a course that is offered principally through the use of television, audio, or computer transmission including open broadcast, closed circuit, cable, microwave, or satellite, audio conferencing, or computer conferencing. If the F–1 student's course of study is in a language study program, no on-line or distance education classes may be considered to count toward a student's full course of study requirement.

(H) On-campus employment pursuant to the terms of a scholarship, fellowship, or assistantship is deemed to be part of the academic program of a student otherwise taking a full course of study.

(ii) *Institution of higher learning.* For purposes of this paragraph, a college or university is an institution of higher learning which awards recognized associate, bachelor's, master's, doctorate, or professional degrees. Schools which devote themselves exclusively or primarily to vocational, business, or language instruction are not included in the category of colleges or universities. Vocational or business schools which are classifiable as M–1 schools are provided for by regulations under 8 CFR 214.2(m).

(iii) *Reduced course load.* The designated school official may allow an F–1 student to engage in less than a full course of study as provided in this paragraph (f)(6)(iii). Except as otherwise noted, a reduced course load must consist of at least six semester or quarter hours, or half the clock hours required for a full course of study. A student who drops below a full course of study without the prior approval of the DSO will be considered out of status. On-campus employment pursuant to the terms of a scholarship, fellowship, or assistantship is deemed to be part of the academic program of a student otherwise taking a full course of study.

(A) *Academic difficulties.* The DSO may authorize a reduced course load on account of a student's initial difficulty with the English language or reading requirements, unfamiliarity with U.S. teaching methods, or improper course level placement. The student must resume a full course of study at the next available term, session, or semester, excluding a summer session, in order to maintain student status. A student previously authorized to drop below a full course of study due to academic difficulties is not eligible for a second authorization by the DSO due to academic difficulties while pursuing a course of study at that program level. A student authorized to drop below a full course of study for academic difficulties while pursuing a course of study at a particular program level may still be authorized for a reduced course load due to an illness medical condition as provided for in paragraph (B) of this section.

(B) *Medical conditions.* The DSO may authorize a reduced course load (or, if necessary, no course load) due to a student's temporary illness or medical condition for a period of time not to exceed an aggregate of 12 months while the student is pursuing a course of study at a particular program level. In order to authorize a reduced course load based upon a medical condition, the student must provide medical documentation from a licensed medical doctor, doctor of osteopathy, or licensed clinical psychologist, to the DSO to substantiate the illness or medical condition. The student must provide current medical documentation and the DSO must reauthorize the drop below full course of study each new term, session, or semester. A student previously authorized to drop below a full course of study due to illness or medical condition for an aggregate of 12 months may not be authorized by a DSO to reduce his or her course load on subsequent occasions while pursuing a course of study at the same program level. A student may be authorized to reduce course load for a reason of illness or medical condition on more than one occasion while pursuing a course of study, so long as the aggregate period of that authorization does not exceed 12 months.

(C) *Completion of course of study.* The DSO may authorize a reduced course load in the student's final term, semester, or session if fewer courses are needed to complete the course of study. If the student is not required to take any additional courses to satisfy the requirements for completion, but continues to be enrolled for administrative purposes, the student is considered to have completed the course of study and must take action to maintain status. Such action may include application for change of status or departure from the U.S.

(D) *Reporting requirements for non-SEVIS schools.* A DSO must report to the Service any student who is authorized to reduce his or her course load. Within 21 days of the authorization, the DSO must send a photocopy of the student's current Form I–20ID along with Form I–538 to Service's data processing center indicating the date and reason that the student was authorized to drop below full time status. Similarly, the DSO will report to the Service no more than 21 days after the student has resumed a full course of study by submitting a current copy of the students' Form I–20ID to the Service's data processing center indicating the date a full course of study was resumed and the new program end date with Form I–538, if applicable.

(E) *SEVIS reporting requirements.* In order for a student to be authorized to drop below a full course of study, the DSO must update SEVIS prior to the student reducing his or her course load. The DSO must update SEVIS with the date, reason for authorization, and the start date of the next term or session. The DSO must also notify SEVIS within 21 days of the student's commencement of a full course of study. If an extension of the program end date is required due to the drop below a full course of study, the DSO must update SEVIS by completing a new SEVIS Form I–20 with the new program end date in accordance with paragraph (f)(7) of this section.

(iv) *Concurrent enrollment.* An F–1 student may be enrolled in two different Service-approved schools at one time as long as the combined enrollment amounts to a full time course of study. In cases where a student is concurrently enrolled, the school from which the student will earn his or her degree or certification should issue the Form I–20, and conduct subsequent certifications and updates to the Form I–20. The DSO from this school is also responsible for all of the reporting requirements to the Service. In instances where a student is enrolled in programs with different full course of study requirements (e.g., clock hours vs. credit hours), the DSO is permitted to determine what constitutes a full time course of study.

(7) *Extension of stay*—(i) *General.* An F–1 student who is admitted for duration of status is not required to apply for extension of stay as long as the student is maintaining status and making normal progress toward completion of his or her educational objective. An F–1 student who is currently maintaining status and making normal progress toward completing his or her educational objective, but who is unable to complete his or her course of study by the program end date on the Form I–20, must apply prior to the program end date for a program extension pursuant to paragraph (f)(7)(iii) of this section.

(ii) *Report date and program completion date on Form I–20.* When determining the report date on the Form I–20, the DSO may choose a reasonable date to accommodate a student's need to be in attendance for required activities at the school prior to the actual start of classes. Such required activities may include, but are not limited to, research projects and orientation sessions. However, for purposes of employment, the DSO may not indicate a report date more than 30 days prior to the start of classes. When determining the program completion date on Form I–20, the DSO should make a reasonable estimate based upon the time an average student would need to complete a similar program in the same discipline.

(iii) *Program extension for students in lawful status.* An F–1 student who is unable to meet the program completion date on the Form I–20 may be granted an extension by the DSO if the DSO certifies that the student has continually maintained status and that the delays are caused by compelling academic or medical reasons, such as changes of major or research topics, unexpected research problems, or documented illnesses. Delays caused by academic probation or suspension are not acceptable reasons for program extensions. A DSO may not grant an extension if the student did not apply for an extension until after the program end date noted on the Form I–20. An F–1 student who is unable to complete the educational program within the time listed on Form I–20 and who is ineligible for program extension pursuant to this paragraph (f)(7) is considered out of status. If eligible, the student may apply for reinstatement under the provisions of paragraph (f)(16) of this section.

(iv) *Notification.* Upon granting a program extension, a DSO at a non-SEVIS school must immediately submit notification to the Service's data processing center using Form I–538 and the top page of Form I–20A–B showing the new program completion date. For a school enrolled in SEVIS, a DSO may grant a program extension only by updating SEVIS and issuing a new Form I–20 reflecting the current program end date. A DSO may grant an extension any time prior to the program end date listed on the student's original Form I–20.

(8) *School transfer.* (i) A student who is maintaining status may transfer to another Service approved school by following the notification procedure prescribed in paragraph (f)(8)(ii) of this section. However, an F–1 student is not permitted to remain in the United States when transferring between schools or programs unless the student will begin classes at the transfer school or program within 5 months of transferring out of the current school or within 5 months of the program completion date on his or her current Form I–20, whichever is earlier. In the case of an F–1 student authorized to engage in post-completion optional practical training (OPT), the student must be able resume classes within 5 months of transferring out of the school that recommended OPT or the date the OPT authorization ends, whichever is earlier. An F–1 student who was not pursuing a full course of study at the school he or she was last authorized to attend is ineligible for school transfer and must apply for reinstatement under the provisions of paragraph (f)(16) of this section, or, in the alternative, may depart the country and return as an initial entry in a new F–1 nonimmigrant status.

(ii) *Transfer procedure.* To transfer schools, an F–1 student must first notify the school he or she is attending of the intent to transfer, then obtain a Form I–20 A–B, issued in accordance with the provisions of 8 CFR 214.3(k), from the school to which he or she intends to transfer. The transfer will be effected only if the F–1 student completes the Student Certification portion of the Form I–20 A–B and returns the form to a designated school official on campus within 15 days of beginning attendance at the new school.

(A) *Non-SEVIS School to Non-SEVIS school.* To transfer from one non-SEVIS school to a different non-SEVIS school, the student must first notify the school he or she is attending of the intent to transfer, then obtain a Form I–20 issued in accordance with the provisions of 8 CFR 214.3(k) from the school to which he or she intends to transfer. Prior to issuance of any Form I–20, the DSO at the transfer school is responsible for determining that the student has been maintaining status at his or her current school and is eligible for transfer to the new school. The transfer will be effected only if the student completes the Student Certification portion of the Form I–20 and returns the form to a DSO of the transfer school within 15 days of the program start date listed on Form I–20. Upon receipt of the student's Form I–20 the DSO must note "transfer completed on (date)" in the space provided for the DSO's remarks, thereby acknowledging the student's attendance at the transfer school; return the Form I–20 to the student; submit the School copy of the Form I–20 to Service's Data Processing Center within 30 days of receipt from the student; and forward a photocopy of the school copy to the school from which the student transferred.

(B) *Non-SEVIS school to SEVIS school.* To transfer from a non-SEVIS school to a SEVIS school, the student must first notify the school he or she is attending of the intent to transfer, then obtain a SEVIS Form I–20 issued in accordance with the provisions of 8 CFR 214.3(k) from the school to which he or she intends to transfer. Prior to issuance of any Form I–20, the DSO at the transfer school is responsible for determining that the student has been maintaining status at his or her current school and is eligible for transfer to the new school. Once the transfer school has issued the SEVIS Form I–20 to the student indicating a transfer, the transfer school becomes responsible for updating and maintaining the student's record in SEVIS. The student is then required to notify the DSO at the transfer school within 15 days of the program start date listed on SEVIS Form I–20. Upon notification that the student is enrolled in classes, the DSO of the transfer school must update SEVIS to reflect the student's registration and current address, thereby acknowledging that the student has completed the transfer process. In the remarks section of the student's SEVIS Form I–20, the DSO must note that the transfer has been completed, including the date, and return the form to the student. The transfer is effected when the transfer school updates SEVIS indicating that the student has registered in classes within the 30 days required by § 214.3(g)(3)(iii).

(C) *SEVIS school to SEVIS school.* To transfer from a SEVIS school to a SEVIS school the student must first notify his or her current school of the intent to transfer and must indicate the school to which he or she intends to transfer. Upon notification by the student, the current school will update the student's record in SEVIS as a "transfer out" and indicate the school to which the student intends to transfer, and a release date. The release date will be the current semester or session completion date, or the date of expected transfer if earlier than the established academic cycle. The current school will retain control over the student's record in SEVIS until the student completes the current term or reaches the release date. At the request of the student, the DSO of the current school may cancel the transfer request at any time prior to the release date. As of the release date specified by the current DSO, the transfer school will be granted full access to the student's SEVIS record and then becomes responsible for that student. The current school conveys authority and responsibility over that student to the transfer school, and will no longer have full SEVIS access to that student's record. As such, a transfer request may not be cancelled by the current DSO after the release date has been reached. After the release date, the transfer DSO must complete the transfer of the student's record in SEVIS and may issue a SEVIS Form I–20. The student is then required to contact the DSO at the transfer school within 15 days of the program start date listed on the SEVIS Form I–20. Upon notification that the student is enrolled in classes, the DSO of the transfer school must update SEVIS to reflect the student's registration and current address, thereby acknowledging that the student has completed the transfer process. In the remarks section of the student's SEVIS Form I–20, the DSO must note that the transfer has been completed, including the date, and return the form to the student. The transfer is effected when the transfer school notifies SEVIS that the student has enrolled in classes in accordance with the 30 days required by § 214.3(g)(3)(iii).

(D) *SEVIS school to non-SEVIS school.* To transfer from a SEVIS school to a non-SEVIS school, the student must first notify his or her current school of the intent to transfer and must indicate the school to which he or she intends to transfer. Upon notification by the student, the current school will update the student's status in SEVIS as "a transfer out", enter a "release" or expected transfer date, and update the transfer school as "non-SEVIS." The student must then notify the school to which the he or she intends to transfer of his or her intent to enroll. After the student has completed his or her current term or session, or has reached the expected transfer date, the DSO at the current school will no longer have full access to the student's SEVIS record. At this point, if the student has notified the transfer school of his or her intent to transfer, and the transfer school has determined that the student has been maintaining status at his or her current school, the transfer school may issue the student a Form I-20. The transfer will be effected only if the student completes the Student Certification portion of the Form I–20 and returns the form to a designated school official of the transfer school within 15 days of the program start date listed on Form I-20. Upon receipt of the student's Form I–20 the DSO must do as follows: note "transfer completed on (date)" in the space provided for the DSO's remarks, thereby acknowledging the student's attendance; return the Form I–20 to the student; submit the school copy of the Form I–20 to the Service's data processing center within 30 days of receipt from the student; and forward a photocopy of the school copy to the school from which the student transferred.

(iii) *Notification.* Upon receipt of the student's Form I–20 A–B, the DSO must:

(A) Note "transfer completed on (date)" on the student's I–20 ID in the space provided for the DSO's remarks, thereby acknowledging the student's attendance;

(B) Return the I–20 ID to the student;

(C) Submit the I–20 School copy to the Service's Data Processing Center within 30 days of receipt from the student; and

(D) Forward a photocopy of the Form I–20 A-B School Copy to the school from which the student transferred.

(9) *Employment*—(i) *On-campus employment.* On-campus employment must either be performed on the school's premises, (including on-location commercial firms which provide services for students on campus, such as the school bookstore or cafeteria), or at an off-campus location which is educationally affiliated with the school. Employment with on-site commercial firms, such as a construction company building a school building, which do not provide direct student services is not deemed on-campus employment for the purposes of this paragraph. In the case of off-campus locations, the educational affiliation must be associated with the school's established curriculum or related to contractually funded research projects at the postgraduate level. In any event, the employment must be an integral part of the student's educational program. Employment authorized under this paragraph must not exceed 20 hours a week while school is in session, unless the Commissioner suspends the applicability of this limitation due to emergent circumstances, as determined by the Commissioner, by means of notice in the FEDERAL REGISTER, the student demonstrates to the DSO that the employment is necessary to avoid severe economic hardship resulting from the emergent circumstances, and the DSO notates the Form I–20 in accordance with the FEDERAL REGISTER document. An F–1 student may, however, work on campus full-time when school is not in session or during the annual vacation. A student who has been issued a Form I–20 A-B to begin a new program in accordance with the provision of 8 CFR 214.3(k) and who intends to enroll for the next regular academic year, term, or session at the institution which issued the Form I–20 A-B may continue on-campus employment incident to status. Otherwise, an F-1 student may not engage in on-campus employment after completing a course of study, except employment for practical training as authorized under paragraph (f)(10) of this section. An F-I student may engage in any on-campus employment authorized under this paragraph which will not displace United States residents. In the case of a transfer in SEVIS, the student may only engage in

on-campus employment at the school having jurisdiction over the student's SEVIS record. Upon initial entry to begin a new course of study, an F–1 student may not begin on-campus employment more than 30 days prior to the actual start of classes.

(ii) *Off-campus work authorization*—(A) *General.* An F–1 student may be authorized to work off-campus on a part-time basis in accordance with paragraph (f)(9)(ii) (B) or (C) of this section after having been in F–1 status for one full academic year provided that the student is in good academic standing as determined by the DSO. Part-time off-campus employment authorized under this section is limited to no more than twenty hours a week when school is in session. A student who is granted off-campus employment authorization may work full-time during holidays or school vacation. The employment authorization is automatically terminated whenever the student fails to maintain status. In emergent circumstances as determined by the Commissioner, the Commissioner may suspend the applicability of any or all of the requirements of paragraph (f)(9)(ii) of this section by notice in the FEDERAL REGISTER.

(B) [Reserved]

(C) *Severe economic hardship.* If other employment opportunities are not available or are otherwise insufficient, an eligible F–1 student may request off-campus employment work authorization based upon severe economic hardship caused by unforeseen circumstances beyond the student's control. These circumstances may include loss of financial aid or on-campus employment without fault on the part of the student, substantial fluctuations in the value of currency or exchange rate, inordinate increases in tuition and/or living costs, unexpected changes in the financial condition of the student's source of support, medical bills, or other substantial and unexpected expenses.

(D) *Procedure for off-campus employment authorization due to severe economic hardship.* The student must request a recommendation from the DSO for off-campus employment. The DSO at a non-SEVIS school must make such a certification on Form I–538, Certification by Designated School Official. The DSO of a SEVIS school must complete such certification in SEVIS. The DSO may recommend the student for work off-campus for one year intervals by certifying that:

(*1*) The student has been in F–1 status for one full academic year;

(*2*) The student is in good standing as a student and is carrying a full course of study as defined in paragraph (f)(6) of this section;

(*3*) The student has demonstrated that acceptance of employment will not interfere with the student's carrying a full course of study; and

(*4*) The student has demonstrated that the employment is necessary to avoid severe economic hardship due to unforeseen circumstances beyond the student's control pursuant to paragraph (f)(9)(ii)(C) of this section and has demonstrated that employment under paragraph (f)(9)(i) of this section is unavailable or otherwise insufficient to meet the needs that have arisen as a result of the unforeseen circumstances.

(E) [Reserved]

(F) *Severe economic hardship application.* (*1*) The applicant should submit the economic hardship application for employment authorization on Form I–765, with the fee required by 8 CFR 103.7(b)(1), to the service center having jurisdiction over his or her place of residence. Applicants at a non-SEVIS school should submit Form I–20, Form I–538, and any other supporting materials such as affidavits which further detail the unforeseen circumstances that require the student to seek employment authorization and the unavailability or insufficiency of employment under paragraph (f)(9)(i) of this section. Students enrolled in a SEVIS school should submit the SEVIS Form I–20 with the employment page demonstrating the DSO's comments and certification.

(*2*) The Service shall adjudicate the application for work authorization based upon severe economic hardship on the basis of Form I–20 ID, Form I–538, and Form I–765, and any additional supporting materials. If employment is authorized, the adjudicating officer shall issue an EAD. The Service director shall notify the student of the decision, and, if the application is denied, of the reason or reasons for the denial. No appeal shall lie from a decision to deny a request for employment authorization under this section. The employment authorization may be granted in one year intervals up to the expected date of completion of the student's current course of study. A student has permission to engage in off-campus employment only if the student receives the EAD endorsed to that effect. Off-campus employment authorization may be renewed by the Service only if the student is maintaining status and good academic standing. The employment authorization is automatically terminated whenever the student fails to maintain status.

(iii) *Internship with an international organization.* A bona fide F–1 student who has been offered employment by a recognized international organization within the meaning of the International Organization Immunities Act (59 Stat. 669) must apply for employment authorization to the service center having jurisdiction over his or her place of residence. A student seeking employment authorization under this provision is required to present a written certification from the international organization that the proposed employment is within the scope of the organization's sponsorship, Form I–20 ID or SEVIS Form I–20 with employment page completed by DSO certifying eligibility for employment, and a completed Form I–765, with required fee as contained in §103.7(b)(1) of this chapter.

(10) *Practical training.* Practical training may be authorized to an F–1 student who has been lawfully enrolled on a full time basis, in a Service-approved college, university, conservatory, or seminary for one full academic year. This provision also includes students who, during their course of study, were enrolled in a study abroad program, if the student had spent at least one full academic term enrolled in a full course of study in the United States prior to studying abroad. A student may be authorized 12 months of practical training, and becomes eligible for another 12 months of practical training when he or she changes to a higher educational level. Students in English language training programs are ineligible for practical training. An eligible student may request employment authorization for practical training in a position that is directly related to his or her major area of study. There are two types of practical training available:

(i) *Curricular practical training.* An F–1 student may be authorized by the DSO to participate in a curricular practical training program that is an integral part of an established curriculum. Curricular practical training is defined to be alternative work/study, internship, cooperative education, or any other type of required internship or practicum that is offered by sponsoring employers through cooperative agreements with the school. Students who have received one year or more of full time curricular practical training are ineligible for post-completion academic training. Exceptions to the one academic year requirement are provided for students enrolled in graduate studies that require immediate participation in curricular practical training. A request for authorization for curricular practical training must be made to the DSO. A student may begin curricular practical training only after receiving his or her Form I–20 with the DSO endorsement.

(A) *Non-SEVIS process.* A student must request authorization for curricular practical training using Form I–538. Upon approving the request for authorization, the DSO shall: certify Form I–538 and send the form to the Service's data processing center; endorse the student's Form I–20 ID with "full-time (or part-time) curricular practical training authorized for (employer) at (location) from (date) to (date)"; and sign and date the Form I–20ID before returning it to the student.

(B) *SEVIS process.* To grant authorization for a student to engage in curricular practical training, a DSO at a SEVIS school will update the student's record in SEVIS as being authorized for curricular practical training that is directly related to the student's major area of study. The DSO will indicate whether the training is full-time or part-time, the employer and location, and the employment start and end date. The DSO will then print a copy of the employment page of the SEVIS Form I–20 indicating that curricular practical training has been approved. The DSO must sign, date, and return the SEVIS Form I–20 to the student prior to the student's commencement of employment.

(ii) *Optional practical training*— (A) *General.* Consistent with the application and approval process in paragraph (f)(11) of this section, a student may apply to USCIS for authorization for temporary employment for optional practical training directly related to the student's major area of study. The student may not begin optional practical training until the date indicated on his or her employment authorization document, Form I–766. A student may be granted authorization to engage in temporary employment for optional practical training:

(*1*) During the student's annual vacation and at other times when school is not in session, if the student is currently enrolled, and is eligible for registration and intends to register for the next term or session;

(*2*) While school is in session, provided that practical training does not exceed 20 hours a week while school is in session; or

(*3*) After completion of the course of study, or, for a student in a bachelor's, master's, or doctoral degree program, after completion of all course requirements for the degree (excluding thesis or equivalent). Continued enrollment, for the school's administrative purposes, after all requirements for the degree have been met does not preclude eligibility for optional practical training. A student must complete all practical training within a 14-month period following the completion of study, except that a 24-month extension pursuant to paragraph (f)(10)(ii)(C) of this section does not need to be completed within such 14-month period.

(B) *Termination of practical training.* Authorization to engage in optional practical training employment is automatically terminated when the student transfers to another school or begins study at another educational level.

(C) *24-month extension of post-completion OPT for a science, technology, engineering, or mathematics (STEM) degree.* Consistent with paragraph (f)(11)(i)(C) of this section, a qualified student may apply for an extension of OPT while in a valid period of post-completion OPT authorized under 8 CFR 274a.12(c)(3)(i)(B). An extension will be for 24 months for the first qualifying degree for which the student has completed all course requirements (excluding thesis or equivalent), including any qualifying degree as part of a dual degree program, subject to the requirement in paragraph (f)(10)(ii)(C)(*3*) of this section that previously obtained degrees must have been conferred. If a student completes all such course requirements for another qualifying degree at a higher degree level than the first, the student may apply for a second 24-month extension of OPT while in a valid period of post-completion OPT authorized under 8 CFR 274a.12(c)(3)(i)(B). In no event may a student be authorized for more than two lifetime STEM OPT extensions. A student who was granted a 17-month OPT extension under the rule issued at 73 FR 18944, whether or not such student requests an additional 7-month period of STEM OPT under 8 CFR 214.16, is considered to have been authorized for one STEM OPT extension, and may be eligible for only one more STEM OPT extension. Any subsequent application for an additional 24-month OPT extension under this paragraph (f)(10)(ii)(C) must be based on a degree at a higher degree level than the degree that was the basis for the student's first OPT extension. In order to qualify for an extension of post-completion OPT based upon a STEM degree, all of the following requirements must be met.

(*1*) *Accreditation.* The degree that is the basis for the 24-month OPT extension is from a U.S. educational institution accredited by an accrediting agency recognized by the Department of Education at the time of application.

(*2*) *DHS-approved degree.* The degree that is the basis for the 24-month OPT extension is a bachelor's, master's, or doctoral degree in a field determined by the Secretary, or his or her designee, to qualify within a science, technology, engineering, or mathematics field.

(*i*) The term "science, technology, engineering or mathematics field" means a field included in the Department of

Education's Classification of Instructional Programs taxonomy within the two-digit series or successor series containing engineering, biological sciences, mathematics, and physical sciences, or a related field. In general, related fields will include fields involving research, innovation, or development of new technologies using engineering, mathematics, computer science, or natural sciences (including physical, biological, and agricultural sciences).

(*ii*) The Secretary, or his or her designee, will maintain the STEM Designated Degree Program List, which will be a complete list of qualifying degree program categories, published on the Student and Exchange Visitor Program Web site at *http://www.ice.gov/sevis*. Changes that are made to the Designated Degree Program List may also be published in a notice in the FEDERAL REGISTER. All program categories included on the list must be consistent with the definition set forth in paragraph (f)(10)(ii)(C)(*2*)(*i*) of this section.

(*iii*) At the time the DSO recommends a 24-month OPT extension under this paragraph (f)(10)(ii)(C) in SEVIS, the degree that is the basis for the application for the OPT extension must be contained within a category on the STEM Designated Degree Program List.

(*3*) *Previously obtained STEM degree(s)*. The degree that is the basis for the 24-month OPT extension under this paragraph (f)(10)(ii)(C) may be, but is not required to be, the degree that is the basis for the post-completion OPT period authorized under 8 CFR 274a.12(c)(3)(i)(B). If an application for a 24-month OPT extension under this paragraph (f)(10)(ii)(C) is based upon a degree obtained previous to the degree that provided the basis for the period of post-completion OPT authorized under 8 CFR 274a.12(c)(3)(i)(B), that previously obtained degree must have been conferred from a U.S. educational institution that is accredited and SEVP-certified at the time the student's DSO recommends the student for the 24-month OPT extension and must be in a degree program category included on the current STEM Designated Degree Program List at the time of the DSO recommendation. That previously obtained degree must have been conferred within the 10 years preceding the date the DSO recommends the student for the 24-month OPT extension.

(*4*) *Eligible practical training opportunity*. The STEM practical training opportunity that is the basis for the 24-month OPT extension under this paragraph (f)(10)(ii)(C) must be directly related to the degree that qualifies the student for such extension, which may be the previously obtained degree described in paragraph (f)(10)(ii)(C)(*3*) of this section.

(*5*) *Employer qualification*. The student's employer is enrolled in E-Verify, as evidenced by either a valid E-Verify Company Identification number or, if the employer is using an employer agent to create its E-Verify cases, a valid E-Verify Client Company Identification number, and the employer remains a participant in good standing with E-Verify, as determined by USCIS. An employer must also have an employer identification number (EIN) used for tax purposes.

(*6*) *Employer reporting*. A student may not be authorized for employment with an employer pursuant to paragraph (f)(10)(ii)(C)(*2*) of this section unless the employer agrees, by signing the Training Plan for STEM OPT Students, Form I–983 or successor form, to report the termination or departure of an OPT student to the DSO at the student's school, if the termination or departure is prior to the end of the authorized period of OPT. Such reporting must be made within five business days of the termination or departure. An employer shall consider a student to have departed when the employer knows the student has left the practical training opportunity, or if the student has not reported for his or her practical training for a period of five consecutive business days without the consent of the employer, whichever occurs earlier.

(*7*) *Training Plan for STEM OPT Students, Form I–983 or successor form*. (*i*) A student must fully complete an individualized Form I–983 or successor form and obtain requisite signatures from an appropriate individual in the employer's organization on the form, consistent with form instructions, before the DSO may recommend a 24-month OPT extension under paragraph (f)(10)(ii)(C)(*2*) of this section in SEVIS. A student must submit the Form I–983 or successor form, which includes a certification of adherence to the training plan completed by an appropriate individual in the employer's organization who has signatory authority for the employer, to the student's DSO, prior to the new DSO recommendation. A student must present his or her signed and completed Form I–983 or successor form to a DSO at the educational institution of his or her most recent enrollment. A student, while in F–1 student status, may also be required to submit the Form I–983 or successor form to ICE and/or USCIS upon request or in accordance with form instructions.

(*ii*) The training plan described in the Form I–983 or successor form must identify goals for the STEM practical training opportunity, including specific knowledge, skills, or techniques that will be imparted to the student, and explain how those goals will be achieved through the work-based learning opportunity with the employer; describe a performance evaluation process; and describe methods of oversight and supervision. Employers may rely on their otherwise existing training programs or policies to satisfy the requirements relating to performance evaluation and oversight and supervision, as applicable.

(*iii*) The training plan described in the Form I–983 or successor form must explain how the training is directly related to the student's qualifying STEM degree.

(*iv*) If a student initiates a new practical training opportunity with a new employer during his or her 24-month OPT extension, the student must submit, within 10 days of beginning the new practical training opportunity, a new Form I–983 or successor form to the student's DSO, and subsequently obtain a new DSO recommendation.

(*8*) *Duties, hours, and compensation for training.* The terms and conditions of a STEM practical training opportunity during the period of the 24-month OPT extension, including duties, hours, and compensation, must be commensurate with terms and conditions applicable to the employer's similarly situated U.S. workers in the area of employment. A student may not engage in practical training for less than 20 hours per week, excluding time off taken consistent with leave-related policies applicable to the employer's similarly situated U.S. workers in the area of employment. If the employer does not employ and has not recently employed more than two similarly situated U.S. workers in the area of employment, the employer nevertheless remains obligated to attest that the terms and conditions of a STEM practical training opportunity are commensurate with the terms and conditions of employment for other similarly situated U.S. workers in the area of employment. "Similarly situated U.S. workers" includes U.S. workers performing similar duties subject to similar supervision and with similar educational backgrounds, industry expertise, employment experience, levels of responsibility, and skill sets as the student. The duties, hours, and compensation of such students are "commensurate" with those offered to U.S. workers employed by the employer in the same area of employment when the employer can show that the duties, hours, and compensation are consistent with the range of such terms and conditions the employer has offered or would offer to similarly situated U.S. employees. The student must disclose his or her compensation, including any adjustments, as agreed to with the employer, on the Form I–983 or successor form.

(*9*) *Evaluation requirements and Training Plan modifications.* (*i*) A student may not be authorized for employment with an employer pursuant to paragraph (f)(10)(ii)(C)(*2*) of this section unless the student submits a self-evaluation of the student's progress toward the training goals described in the Form I–983 or successor form. All required evaluations must be completed prior to the conclusion of a STEM practical training opportunity, and the student and an appropriate individual in the employer's organization must sign each evaluation to attest to its accuracy. All STEM practical training opportunities require an initial evaluation within 12 months of the approved starting date on the employment authorization document granted pursuant to the student's 24-month OPT extension application, and a concluding evaluation. The student is responsible for ensuring the DSO receives his or her 12-month evaluation and final evaluation no later than 10 days following the conclusion of the reporting period or conclusion of his or her practical training opportunity, respectively.

(*ii*) If any material change to or deviation from the training plan described in the Form I–983 or successor form occurs, the student and employer must sign a modified Form I–983 or successor form reflecting the material change(s) or deviation(s). Material changes and deviations relating to training may include, but are not limited to, any change of Employer Identification Number resulting from a corporate restructuring, any reduction in compensation from the amount previously submitted on the Form I–983 or successor form that is not tied to a reduction in hours worked, any significant decrease in hours per week that a student engages in a STEM training opportunity, and any decrease in hours worked below the minimum hours for the 24-month extension as described in paragraph (f)(10)(ii)(C)(*8*) of this section. Material changes and deviations also include any change or deviation that renders an employer attestation inaccurate, or renders inaccurate the information in the Form I–983 or successor form on the nature, purpose, oversight, or assessment of the student's practical training opportunity. The student and employer must ensure that the modified Form I–983 or successor form is submitted to the student's DSO at the earliest available opportunity.

(*iii*) The educational institution whose DSO is responsible for duties associated with the student's latest OPT extension under paragraph (f)(10)(ii)(C)(*2*) of this section is responsible for ensuring the Student and Exchange Visitor Program has access to each individualized Form I–983 or successor form and associated student evaluations (electronic or hard copy), including through SEVIS if technologically available, beginning within 30 days after the document is submitted to the DSO and continuing for a period of three years following the completion of each STEM practical training opportunity.

(*10*) *Additional STEM opportunity obligations*. A student may only participate in a STEM practical training opportunity in which the employer attests, including by signing the Form I–983 or successor form, that:

(*i*) The employer has sufficient resources and personnel available and is prepared to provide appropriate training in connection with the specified opportunity at the location(s) specified in the Form I–983 or successor form;

(*ii*) The student on a STEM OPT extension will not replace a full- or part-time, temporary or permanent U.S. worker; and

(*iii*) The student's opportunity assists the student in reaching his or her training goals.

(*11*) *Site visits*. DHS, at its discretion, may conduct a site visit of any employer. The purpose of the site visit is for DHS to ensure that each employer possesses and maintains the ability and resources to provide structured and guided work-based learning experiences consistent with any Form I–983 or successor form completed and signed by the employer. DHS will provide notice to the employer 48 hours in advance of any site visit, except notice may not be provided if the visit is triggered by a complaint or other evidence of noncompliance with the regulations in this paragraph (f)(10)(ii)(C).

(D) *Duration of status while on post-completion OPT*. For a student with approved post-completion OPT, the duration of status is defined as the period beginning on the date that the student's application for OPT was properly filed and pending approval, including the authorized period of post-completion OPT, and ending 60 days after the OPT employment authorization expires.

(E) *Periods of unemployment during post-completion OPT*. During post-completion OPT, F–1 status is dependent upon employment. Students may not accrue an aggregate of more than 90 days of unemployment during any post-completion OPT period described in 8 CFR 274a.12(c)(3)(i)(B). Students granted a 24-month OPT extension under paragraph (f)(10)(ii)(C)(*2*) of this section may not accrue an aggregate of more than 150 days of unemployment during a total OPT period, including any post-completion OPT period described in 8 CFR 274a.12(c)(3)(i)(B) and any subsequent 24-month extension period.

(11) *OPT application and approval process*—(i) *Student responsibilities.* A student must initiate the OPT application process by requesting a recommendation for OPT from his or her DSO. Upon making the recommendation, the DSO will provide the student a signed Form I–20 indicating that recommendation.

(A) *Applications for employment authorization.* The student must properly file an Application for Employment Authorization, Form I–765 or successor form, with USCIS, accompanied by the required fee, and the supporting documents, as described in the form's instructions.

(B) *Applications and filing deadlines for pre-completion OPT and post-completion OPT*—(*1*) *Pre-completion OPT.* For pre-completion OPT, the student may properly file his or her Form I–765 or successor form up to 90 days before being enrolled for one full academic year, provided that the period of employment will not start prior to the completion of the full academic year.

(*2*) *Post-completion OPT.* For post-completion OPT, not including a 24-month OPT extension under paragraph (f)(10)(ii)(C)(*2*) of this section, the student may properly file his or her Form I–765 or successor form up to 90 days prior to his or her program end date and no later than 60 days after his or her program end date. The student must also file his or her Form I–765 or successor form with USCIS within 30 days of the date the DSO enters the recommendation for OPT into his or her SEVIS record.

(C) *Applications and filing deadlines for 24-month OPT extension.* A student meeting the eligibility requirements for a 24-month OPT extension under paragraph (f)(10)(ii)(C) of this section may request an extension of employment authorization by filing Form I–765 or successor form, with the required fee and supporting documents, up to 90 days prior to the expiration date of the student's current OPT employment authorization. The student seeking such 24-month OPT extension must properly file his or her Form I–765 or successor form with USCIS within 60 days of the date the DSO enters the recommendation for the OPT extension into his or her SEVIS record. If a student timely and properly files an application for such 24-month OPT extension and timely and properly requests a DSO recommendation, including by submitting the fully executed Form I–983 or successor form to his or her DSO, but the Employment Authorization Document, Form I–766 or successor form, currently in the student's possession expires prior to the decision on the student's application for the OPT extension, the student's Form I–766 or successor form is extended automatically pursuant to the terms and conditions specified in 8 CFR 274a.12(b)(6)(iv).

(D) *Start of OPT employment.* A student may not begin OPT employment prior to the approved start date on his or her Employment Authorization Document, Form I–766 or successor form, except as described in paragraph (f)(11)(i)(C) of this section. A student may not request a start date that is more than 60 days after the student's program end date. Employment authorization will begin on the date requested or the date the employment authorization is adjudicated, whichever is later.

(ii) *Additional DSO responsibilities.* A student must have a recommendation from his or her DSO in order to apply for OPT. When a DSO recommends a student for OPT, the school assumes the added responsibility for maintaining the SEVIS record of that student for the entire period of authorized OPT, consistent with paragraph (f)(12) of this section.

(A) Prior to making a recommendation, the DSO at the educational institution of the student's most recent enrollment must ensure that the student is eligible for the given type and period of OPT and that the student is aware of the student's responsibilities for maintaining status while on OPT. Prior to recommending a 24-month OPT extension under paragraph (f)(10)(ii)(C) of this section, the DSO at the educational institution of the student's most recent enrollment must certify that the student's degree being used to qualify that student for the 24-month OPT extension, as shown in SEVIS or official transcripts, is a bachelor's, master's, or doctorate degree with a degree code that is contained within a category on the current STEM Designated Degree Program List at the time the recommendation is made. A DSO may recommend a student for a 24-month OPT extension under paragraph (f)(10)(ii)(C) of this section only if the Form I–983 or successor form described in paragraph (f)(10)(ii)(C)(*7*) of this section has been properly completed and executed by the student and prospective employer. A DSO may not recommend a student for an OPT extension under paragraph (f)(10)(ii)(C) of this section if the practical training would be conducted by an employer who has failed to meet the requirements under paragraphs (f)(10)(ii)(C)(*5*) through (*9*) of this section or has failed to provide the required assurances of paragraph (f)(10)(ii)(C)(*10*) of this section.

(B) The DSO must update the student's SEVIS record with the DSO's recommendation for OPT before the student can apply to USCIS for employment authorization. The DSO will indicate in SEVIS whether the OPT employment is to be full-time or part-time, or for a student seeking a recommendation for a 24-month OPT extension under paragraph (f)(10)(ii)(C) of this section whether the OPT employment meets the minimum hours requirements described in paragraph (f)(10)(ii)(C)(*8*) of this section, and note in SEVIS the OPT start and end dates.

(C) The DSO must provide the student with a signed, dated Form I–20 or successor form indicating that OPT has been recommended.

(iii) *Decision on application for OPT employment authorization.* USCIS will adjudicate a student's Form I–765 or successor form on the basis of the DSO's recommendation and other eligibility considerations.

(A) If granted, the employment authorization period for post-completion OPT begins on the requested date of commencement or the date the Form I–765 or successor form is approved, whichever is later, and ends at the conclusion of the remaining time period of post-completion OPT eligibility. The employment authorization period for a 24-month OPT extension under paragraph (f)(10)(ii)(C) of this section begins on the day after the expiration of the initial post-completion OPT employment authorization and ends 24 months thereafter, regardless of the date the actual extension is approved.

(B) USCIS will notify the applicant of the decision on the Form I–765 or successor form in writing, and, if the application is denied, of the reason or reasons for the denial.

(C) The applicant may not appeal the decision.

(12) *Reporting while on optional practical training*—(i) *General.* An F–1 student who is granted employment authorization by USCIS to engage in optional practical training is required to report any change of name or address, or interruption of such employment to the DSO for the duration of the optional practical training. A DSO who recommends a student for OPT is responsible for updating the student's record to reflect these reported changes for the duration of the time that training is authorized.

(ii) *Additional reporting obligations for students with an approved 24-month OPT extension.* Students with an approved 24-month OPT extension under paragraph (f)(10)(ii)(C) of this section have additional reporting obligations. Compliance with these reporting requirements is required to maintain F–1 status. The reporting obligations are:

(A) Within 10 days of the change, the student must report to the student's DSO a change of legal name, residential or mailing address, employer name, employer address, and/or loss of employment.

(B) The student must complete a validation report, confirming that the information required by paragraph (f)(12)(ii)(A) of this section has not changed, every six months. The requirement for validation reporting starts on the date the 24-month OPT extension begins and ends when the student's F–1 status expires or the 24-month OPT extension concludes, whichever is first. The validation report is due to the student's DSO within 10 business days of each reporting date.

(13) *Temporary absence from the United States of F–1 student granted employment authorization.* (i) A student returning from a temporary trip abroad with an unexpired off-campus employment authorization on his or her I–20 ID may resume employment only if the student is readmitted to attend the same school which granted the employment authorization.

(ii) An F–1 student who has an unexpired EAD issued for post-completion practical training and who is otherwise admissible may return to the United States to resume employment after a period of temporary absence. The EAD must be used in combination with an I–20 ID endorsed for reentry by the DSO within the last six months.

(14) *Effect of strike or other labor dispute.* Any employment authorization, whether or not part of an academic program, is automatically suspended upon certification by the Secretary of Labor or the Secretary's designee to the Commissioner of the Immigration and Naturalization Service or the Commissioner's designee, that a strike or other labor dispute involving a work stoppage of workers is in progress in the occupation at the place of employment. As used in this paragraph, "place of employment" means the facility or facilities where a labor dispute exists. The employer is prohibited from transferring F–1 students working at other facilities to the facility where the work stoppage is occurring.

(15) *Spouse and children of F–1 student.* The F–2 spouse and minor children of an F–1 student shall each be issued an individual SEVIS Form I–20 in accordance with the provisions of § 214.3(k).

(i) *Employment.* The F–2 spouse and children of an F–1 student may not accept employment.

(ii) *Study*—(A) *F–2 post-secondary/vocational study*—(*1*) *Authorized study at SEVP-certified schools.* An F–2 spouse or F–2 child may enroll in less than a full course of study, as defined in paragraphs (f)(6)(i)(A) through (D) and (m)(9)(i) through (iv), in any course of study described in paragraphs (f)(6)(i)(A) through (D) or (m)(9)(i) through (iv) of this section at an SEVP-certified school. Notwithstanding paragraphs (f)(6)(i)(B) and (m)(9)(i) of this section, study at an undergraduate college or university or at a community college or junior college is not a full course of study solely because the F–2 nonimmigrant is engaging in a lesser course load to complete a course of study during the current term. An F–2 spouse or F–2 child enrolled in less than a full course of study is not eligible to engage in employment pursuant to paragraphs (f)(9) and (10) of this section or pursuant to paragraph (m)(14) of this section.

(*2*) *Full course of study.* Subject to paragraphs (f)(15)(ii)(B) and (f)(18) of this section, an F–2 spouse and child may engage in a full course of study only by applying for and obtaining a change of status to F–1, M–1 or J–1 nonimmigrant status, as appropriate, before beginning a full course of study. An F–2 spouse and child may engage in study that is avocational or recreational in nature, up to and including on a full-time basis.

(B) *F–2 elementary or secondary study.* An F–2 child may engage in full-time study, including any full course of study, in any elementary or secondary school (kindergarten through twelfth grade).

(C) An F–2 spouse and child violates his or her nonimmigrant status by enrolling in any study except as provided in paragraph (f)(15)(ii)(A) or (B) of this section.

(16) *Reinstatement to student status*—(i) *General.* The district director may consider reinstating a student who makes a request for reinstatement on Form I–539, Application to Extend/Change Nonimmigrant Status, accompanied by a properly completed SEVIS Form I–20 indicating the DSO's recommendation for reinstatement (or a properly completed Form I–20A-B issued prior to January 30, 2003, from the school the student is attending or intends to attend prior to August 1, 2003). The district director may consider granting the request if the student:

(A) Has not been out of status for more than 5 months at the time of filing the request for reinstatement (or demonstrates that the failure to file within the 5 month period was the result of exceptional circumstances and that the student filed the request for reinstatement as promptly as possible under these exceptional circumstances);

(B) Does not have a record of repeated or willful violations of Service regulations;

(C) Is currently pursuing, or intending to pursue, a full course of study in the immediate future at the school which issued the Form I–20;

(D) Has not engaged in unauthorized employment;

(E) Is not deportable on any ground other than section 237(a)(1)(B) or (C)(i) of the Act; and

(F) Establishes to the satisfaction of the Service, by a detailed showing, either that:

(*1*) The violation of status resulted from circumstances beyond the student's control. Such circumstances might include serious injury or illness, closure of the institution, a natural disaster, or inadvertence, oversight, or neglect on the part of the DSO, but do not include instances where a pattern of repeated violations or where a willful failure on the part of the student resulted in the need for reinstatement; or

(*2*) The violation relates to a reduction in the student's course load that would have been within a DSO's power to authorize, and that failure to approve reinstatement would result in extreme hardship to the student.

(ii) *Decision.* If the Service reinstates the student, the Service shall endorse the student's copy of Form I–20 to indicate the student has been reinstated and return the form to the student. If the Form I–20 is from a non-SEVIS school, the school copy will be forwarded to the school. If the Form I–20 is from a SEVIS school, the adjudicating officer will update SEVIS to reflect the Service's decision. In either case, if the Service does not reinstate the student, the student may not appeal that decision.

(17) *Current name and address.* A student must inform the DSO and the Service of any legal changes to his or her name or of any change of address, within 10 days of the change, in a manner prescribed by the school. A student enrolled at a SEVIS school can satisfy the requirement in 8 CFR 265.1 of notifying the Service by providing a notice of a change of address within 10 days to the DSO, who in turn shall enter the information in SEVIS within 21 days of notification by the student. A student enrolled at a non-SEVIS school must submit a notice of change of address to the Service, as provided in 8 CFR 265.1, within 10 days of the change. Except in the case of a student who cannot receive mail where he or she resides, the address provided by the student must be the actual physical location where the student resides rather than a mailing address. In cases where a student provides a mailing address, the school must maintain a record of, and must provide upon request from the Service, the actual physical location where the student resides.

(18) *Special rules for certain border commuter students*—(i) *Applicability.* For purposes of the special rules in this paragraph (f)(18), the term "border commuter student" means a national of Canada or Mexico who is admitted to the United States as an F–1 nonimmigrant student to enroll in a full course of study, albeit on a part-time basis, in an approved school located within 75 miles of a United States land border. A border commuter student must maintain actual residence and place of abode in the student's country of nationality, and seek admission to the United States at a land border port-of-entry. These special rules do not apply to a national of Canada or Mexico who is:

(A) Residing in the United States while attending an approved school as an F–1 student, or

(B) Enrolled in a full course of study as defined in paragraph (f)(6) of this section.

(ii) *Full course of study.* The border commuter student must be enrolled in a full course of study at the school that leads to the attainment of a specific educational or professional objective, albeit on a part-time basis. A designated school official at the school may authorize an eligible border commuter student to enroll in a course load below that otherwise required for a full course of study under paragraph (f)(6) of this section, provided that the reduced course load is consistent with the border commuter student's approved course of study.

(iii) *Period of admission.* An F–1 nonimmigrant student who is admitted as a border commuter student under this paragraph (f)(18) will be admitted until a date certain. The DSO is required to specify a completion date on the Form I–20 that reflects the actual semester or term dates for the commuter student's current term of study. A new Form I–20 will be required for each new semester or term that the border commuter student attends at the school. The provisions of paragraphs (f)(5) and (f)(7) of this section, relating to duration of status and extension of stay, are not applicable to a border commuter student.

(iv) *Employment.* A border commuter student may not be authorized to accept any employment in connection with his or her F–1 student status, except for curricular practical training as provided in paragraph (f)(10)(i) of this section or post-completion optional practical training as provided in paragraph (f)(10)(ii)(A)(*3*) of this section.

(19) *Remittance of the fee.* An alien who applies for F–1 or F–3 nonimmigrant status in order to enroll in a program of study at a Department of Homeland Security (DHS)-approved educational institution is required to pay the Student and Exchange Visitor Information System (SEVIS) fee to DHS, pursuant to 8 CFR 214.13, except as otherwise provided in that section.

(g) *Representatives to international organizations*—(1) *General.* The determination by a consular officer prior to admission and the recognition by the Secretary of State subsequent to admission is evidence of the proper classification of a nonimmigrant under section 101(a)(15)(G) of the Act. An alien who has a nonimmigrant status under section 101(a)(15)(G) (i), (ii), (iii) or (iv) of the Act is to be admitted for the duration of the period for which the alien continues to be recognized by the Secretary of State as being entitled to that status. An alien defined in section (101)(a)(15)(G)(v) of the Act is to be admitted for an initial period of not more than three years, and may be granted extensions of temporary stay in increments of not more than two years. In addition, the application for extension of temporary stay must be accompanied by a statement signed by the employing official stating that he or she intends to continue to employ the applicant and describing the type of work the applicant will perform.

(2) *Definition of G–1, G–3, or G–4 dependent.* For purposes of employment in the United States, the term *dependent* of a G–1, G–3, or G–4 principal alien, as used in § 214.2(g), means any of the following immediate members of the family habitually residing in the same household as the principal alien who is an officer or employee assigned to a mission, to an international organization, or is employed by an international organization in the United States:

(i) Spouse;

(ii) Unmarried children under the age of 21;

(iii) Unmarried sons or daughters under the age of 23 who are in full-time attendance as students at post-secondary educational institutions;

(iv) Unmarried sons or daughters under the age of 25 who are in full-time attendance as students at post-secondary educational institutions if a formal bilateral employment agreement permitting their employment in the United States was signed prior to November 21, 1988, and such bilateral employment agreement does not specify 23 as the maximum age for employment of such sons and daughters. The Office of Protocol of the Department of State shall maintain a listing of foreign states which the United States has such bilateral employment agreements. The provisions of this paragraph apply only to G–1 and G–3 dependents under certain bilateral agreements and are not applicable to G–4 dependents;

(v) Unmarried sons or daughters who are physically or mentally disabled to the extent that they cannot adequately care for themselves or cannot establish, maintain, or re-establish their own households. The Department of State or the Service may require certification(s) as it deems sufficient to document such mental or physical disability; or

(vi) An immediate family member of a G–1, G–3, or G–4 principal alien described in 22 CFR 41.21(a)(3)(i) to (iv) with G–1, G–3, or G–4 nonimmigrant status who falls within a category of aliens designated by the Department of State as qualifying dependents.

(3) *Applicability of a formal bilateral agreement or an informal de facto arrangement for G–1 and G–3 dependents.* The applicability of a formal bilateral agreement shall be based on the foreign state which employs the principal alien and not on the nationality of the principal alien or dependent. The applicability of an informal de facto arrangement shall be based on the foreign state which employs the principal alien, but under a de facto arrangement the principal alien also must be a national of the foreign state which employs him or her in the United States.

(4) *Income tax, Social Security liability; non-applicability of certain immunities.* Dependents who are granted employment authorization under this section are responsible for payment of all federal, state and local income, employment and related taxes and Social Security contributions on any remuneration received. In addition, immunity from civil or administrative jurisdiction in accordance with Article 37 of the Vienna Convention on Diplomatic Relations or other international agreements does not apply to these dependents with respect to matters arising out of their employment.

(5) *G–1 and G–3 dependent employment pursuant to formal bilateral employment agreements and informal de facto reciprocal arrangements, and G–4 dependent employment.* (i) The Office of Protocol shall maintain a listing of foreign states which have entered into formal bilateral employment agreements. Dependents of a G–1 or G–3 principal alien assigned to official duty in the United States may accept or continue in unrestricted employment based on such formal bilateral agreements, if the applicable agreement includes persons in G–1 or G–3 visa status, upon favorable recommendation by the Department of State and issuance of employment authorization documentation by the Service in accordance with 8 CFR part 274a. The application procedures are set forth in paragrpah (g)(6) of this section.

(ii) For purposes of this section, an informal de facto reciprocal arrangement exists when the Department of State determines that a foreign state allows appropriate employment on the local economy for dependents of certain United States officials assigned to duty in that foreign state. The Office of Protocol shall maintain a listing of countries with which such reciprocity exists. Dependents of a G–1 or G–3 principal alien assigned to official duty in the United States may be authorized to accept or continue in employment based upon informal de facto arrangements, and dependents of a G–4 principal alien assigned to official duty in the United States may be authorized to accept or continue in employment upon favorable recommendation by the Department of State and issuance of employment authorization by the Service in accordance with 8 CFR part 274a. Additionally, the procedures set forth in paragraph (g)(6) of this section must be complied with, and the following conditions must be met:

(A) Both the principal alien and the dependent desiring employment are maintaining G–1, G–3, or G–4 status as appropriate;

(B) The principal's assignment in the United States is expected to last more than six months;

(C) Employment of a similar nature for dependents of United States Government officials assigned to official duty in the foreign state employing the principal alien is not prohibited by that foreign government. The provisions of this paragraph apply only to G–1 and G–3 dependents;

(D) The proposed employment is not in an occupation listed in the Department of Labor Schedule B (20 CFR part 656), or otherwise determined by the Department of Labor to be one for which there is an oversupply of qualified U.S. workers in the area of proposed employment. This Schedule B restriction does not apply to a dependent son or daughter who is a full-time student if the employment is part-time, consisting of not more than 20 hours per week, and/or if it is temporary employment of not more than 12 weeks during school holiday periods; and

(E) The proposed employment is not contrary to the interest of the United States. Employment contrary to the interest of the United States includes, but is not limited to, the employment of G–1, G–3, or G–4 dependents: who have criminal records; who have violated United States immigration laws or regulations, or visa laws or regulations; who have worked illegally in the United States; and/or who cannot establish that they have paid taxes and social security on income from current or previous United States employment. Additionally, the Department of State may determine a G–4 dependent's employment is contrary to the interest of the United States when the principal alien's country of nationality has one or more components of an international organization or international organizations within its borders and does not allow the employment of dependents of United States citizens employed by such component(s) or organization(s).

(6) *Application procedures.* The following procedures are applicable to G–1 and G–3 dependent employment applications under bilateral agreements and de facto arrangements, as well as to G–4 dependent employment applications:

(i) The dependent must submit a completed Form I–566 to the Department of State through the office, mission, or organization which employs his or her principal alien. If the principal is assigned to or employed by the United Nations, the Form I–566 must be submitted to the U.S. Mission to the United Nations. All other applications must be submitted to the Office of Protocol of the Department of State. A dependent applying under paragraph (g)(2) (iii) or (iv) of this section must submit a certified statement from the post-secondary educational institution confirming that he or she is pursuing studies on a full-time basis. A dependent applying under paragraph (g)(2)(v) of this section must submit medical certification regarding his or her condition. The certification should identify the dependent and the certifying physician and give the physician's phone number; identify the condition, describe the symptoms and provide a prognosis; certify that the dependent is unable to establish, re-establish, and maintain a home or his or her own. Additionally, a G–1 or G–3 dependent applying under the terms of a de facto arrangement or a G–4 dependent must attach a statement from the prospective employer which includes the dependent's name; a description of the position offered and the duties to be performed; the salary offered; and verification that the dependent possesses the qualifications for the position.

(ii) The Department of State reviews and verifies the information provided, makes its determination, and endorses the Form I–566.

(iii) If the Department of State's endorsement is favorable, the dependent may apply to USCIS for employment authorization. When applying to USCIS for employment authorization, the dependent must present his or her Form I–566 with a favorable endorsement from the Department of State and any additional documentation as may be required by the Secretary.

(7) *Period of time for which employment may be authorized.* If approved, an application to accept or continue employment under this section shall be granted in increments of not more than three years each.

(8) *No appeal.* There shall be no appeal from a denial of permission to accept or continue employment under this section.

(9) *Dependents or family members of principal aliens classified G–2 or G–5.* A dependent or family member of a principal alien classified G–2 or G–5 may not be employed in the United States under this section.

(10) *Unauthorized employment.* An alien classified under section 101(a)(15)(G) of the Act who is not a principal alien and who engages in employment outside the scope of, or in a manner contrary to this section, may be considered in violation of section 241(a)(1)(C)(i) of the Act. An alien who is classified under section 101(a)(15)(G) of the Act who is a principal alien and who engages in employment outside the scope of his/her official position may be considered in violation of section 241(a)(1)(C)(i) of the Act.

(11) *Special provision.* As of February 16, 1990 no new employment authorization will be granted and no pre-existing employment authorization will be extended for a G–1 dependent absent an appropriate bilateral agreement or de

facto arrangement. However, a G–1 dependent who has been granted employment authorization by the Department of State prior to the effective date of this section and who meets the definition of dependent under §214.2(g)(2) (i), (ii), (iii) or (v) of this part but is not covered by the terms of a bilateral agreement or de facto arrangement may be allowed to continue in employment until whichever of the following occurs first:

(i) The employment authorization by the Department of State expires; or

(ii) He or she no longer qualifies as a dependent as that term is defined in this section; or

(iii) March 19, 1990.

(h) *Temporary employees*—(1) *Admission of temporary employees*—(i) *General.* Under section 101(a)(15)(H) of the Act, an alien may be authorized to come to the United States temporarily to perform services or labor for, or to receive training from, an employer, if petitioned for by that employer. Under this nonimmigrant category, the alien may be classified as follows: under section 101(a)(15)(H)(i)(c) of the Act as a registered nurse; under section 101(a)(15)(H)(i)(b) of the Act as an alien who is coming to perform services in a specialty occupation, services relating to a Department of Defense (DOD) cooperative research and development project or coproduction project, or services as a fashion model who is of distinguished merit and ability; under section 101(a)(15)(H)(ii)(a) of the Act as an alien who is coming to perform agricultural labor or services of a temporary or seasonal nature; under section 101(a)(15)(H)(ii)(b) of the Act as an alien coming to perform other temporary services or labor; or under section 101(a)(15)(H)(iii) of the Act as an alien who is coming as a trainee or as a participant in a special education exchange visitor program. These classifications are called H–1C, H–1B, H–2A, H–2B, and H–3, respectively. The employer must file a petition with the Service for review of the services or training and for determination of the alien's eligibility for classification as a temporary employee or trainee, before the alien may apply for a visa or seek admission to the United States. This paragraph sets forth the standards and procedures applicable to these classifications.

(ii) *Description of classifications.* (A) An H–1C classification applies to an alien who is coming temporarily to the United States to perform services as a registered nurse, meets the requirements of section 212(m)(1) of the Act, and will perform services at a facility (as defined at section 212(m)(6) of the Act) for which the Secretary of Labor has determined and certified to the Attorney General that an unexpired attestation is on file and in effect under section 212(m)(2) of the Act. This classification will expire 4 years from June 11, 2001.

(B) An H–1B classification applies to an alien who is coming temporarily to the United States:

(*1*) To perform services in a specialty occupation (except agricultural workers, and aliens described in section 101(a)(15) (O) and (P) of the Act) described in section 214(i)(1) of the Act, that meets the requirements of section 214(i)(2) of the Act, and for whom the Secretary of Labor has determined and certified to the Attorney General that the prospective employer has filed a labor condition application under section 212(n)(1) of the Act;

(*2*) To perform services of an exceptional nature requiring exceptional merit and ability relating to a cooperative research and development project or a coproduction project provided for under a Government-to-Government agreement administered by the Secretary of Defense;

(*3*) To perform services as a fashion model of distinguished merit and ability and for whom the Secretary of Labor has determined and certified to the Attorney General that the prospective employer has filed a labor condition application under section 212(n)(1) of the Act.

(C) An H–2A classification applies to an alien who is coming temporarily to the United States to perform agricultural work of a temporary or seasonal nature.

(D) An H–2B classification applies to an alien who is coming temporarily to the United States to perform nonagricultural work of a temporary or seasonal nature, if there are not sufficient workers who are able, willing, qualified, and available at the time of application for a visa and admission to the United States and at the place where the alien is to perform such services or labor. This classification does not apply to graduates of medical schools coming to the United States to perform services as members of the medical profession. The temporary or permanent nature of the services or labor described on the approved temporary labor certification are subject to review by USCIS. This classification requires a temporary labor certification issued by the Secretary of Labor or the Governor of Guam prior to the filing of a petition with USCIS.

(E) An H–3 classification applies to an alien who is coming temporarily to the United States:

(*1*) As a trainee, other than to receive graduate medical education or training, or training provided primarily at or by an academic or vocational institution, or

(*2*) As a participant in a special education exchange visitor program which provides for practical training and experience in the education of children with physical, mental, or emotional disabilities.

(2) *Petitions*—(i) *Filing of petitions*—(A) *General.* A United States employer seeking to classify an alien as an H–1B, H–2A, H–2B, or H–3 temporary employee must file a petition on Form I–129, Petition for Nonimmigrant Worker, as provided in the form instructions.

(B) *Service or training in more than one location.* A petition that requires services to be performed or training to be received in more than one location must include an itinerary with the dates and locations of the services or training and must be filed with USCIS as provided in the form instructions. The address that the petitioner specifies as its location on the Form I–129 shall be where the petitioner is located for purposes of this paragraph.

(C) *Services or training for more than one employer.* If the beneficiary will perform nonagricultural services for, or receive training from, more than one employer, each employer must file a separate petition with USCIS as provided in the form instructions.

(D) *Change of employers.* If the alien is in the United States and seeks to change employers, the prospective new employer must file a petition on Form I–129 requesting classification and an extension of the alien's stay in the United States. If the new petition is approved, the extension of stay may be granted for the validity of the approved petition. The validity of the petition and the alien's extension of stay must conform to the limits on the alien's temporary stay that are prescribed in paragraph (h)(13) of this section. Except as provided by 8 CFR 274a.12(b)(21) or section 214(n) of the Act, 8 U.S.C. 1184(n), the alien is not authorized to begin the employment with the new petitioner until the petition is approved. An H–1C nonimmigrant alien may not change employers.

(E) *Amended or new petition.* The petitioner shall file an amended or new petition, with fee, with the Service Center where the original petition was filed to reflect any material changes in the terms and conditions of employment or training or the alien's eligibility as specified in the original approved petition. An amended or new H–1C, H–1B, H–2A, or H–2B petition must be accompanied by a current or new Department of Labor determination. In the case of an H–1B petition, this requirement includes a new labor condition application.

(F) *Agents as petitioners.* A United States agent may file a petition in cases involving workers who are traditionally self-employed or workers who use agents to arrange short-term employment on their behalf with numerous employers, and in cases where a foreign employer authorizes the agent to act on its behalf. A United States agent may be: the actual employer of the beneficiary, the representative of both the employer and the beneficiary, or, a person or entity authorized by the employer to act for, or in place of, the employer as it agent. A petition filed by a United States agent is subject to the following conditions;

(*1*) An agent performing the function of an employer must guarantee the wages and other terms and conditions of employment by contractual agreement with the beneficiary or beneficiaries of the petition. The agent/employer must also provide an itinerary of definite employment and information on any other services planned for the period of time requested.

(*2*) A person or company in business as an agent may file the H petition involving multiple employers as the representative of both the employers and the beneficiary or beneficiaries if the supporting documentation includes a complete itinerary of services or engagements. The itinerary shall specify the dates of each service or engagement, the names and addresses of the actual employers, and the names and addresses of the establishment, venues, or locations where the services will be performed. In questionable cases, a contract between the employers and the beneficiary or beneficiaries may be required. The burden is on the agent to explain the terms and conditions of the employment and to provide any required documentation.

(*3*) A foreign employer who, through a United States agent, files a petition for an H nonimmigrant alien is responsible for complying with all of the employer sanctions provisions of section 274A of the Act and 8 CFR part 274a.

(G) *Multiple H–1B petitions.* An employer may not file, in the same fiscal year, more than one H–1B petition on behalf of the same alien if the alien is subject to the numerical limitations of section 214(g)(1)(A) of the Act or is exempt from those limitations under section 214(g)(5)(C) of the Act. If an H–1B petition is denied, on a basis other than fraud or misrepresentation, the employer may file a subsequent H–1B petition on behalf of the same alien in the same fiscal year, provided that the numerical limitation has not been reached or if the filing qualifies as exempt from the numerical limitation. Otherwise, filing more than one H–1B petition by an employer on behalf of the same alien in the same fiscal year will result in the denial or revocation of all such petitions. If USCIS believes that related entities (such as a parent company, subsidiary, or affiliate) may not have a legitimate business need to file more than one H–1B petition on behalf of the same alien subject to the numerical limitations of section 214(g)(1)(A) of the Act or otherwise eligible for an exemption under section 214(g)(5)(C) of the Act, USCIS may issue a request for additional evidence or notice of intent to deny, or notice of intent to revoke each petition. If any of the related entities fail to demonstrate a legitimate business need to file an H–1B petition on behalf of the same alien, all petitions filed on that alien's behalf by the related entities will be denied or revoked.

(H) *H–1B portability.* An eligible H–1B nonimmigrant is authorized to start concurrent or new employment under section 214(n) of the Act upon the filing, in accordance with 8 CFR 103.2(a), of a nonfrivolous H–1B petition on behalf of such alien, or as of the requested start date, whichever is later.

(*1*) *Eligible H–1B nonimmigrant.* For H–1B portability purposes, an eligible H–1B nonimmigrant is defined as an alien:

(*i*) Who has been lawfully admitted into the United States in, or otherwise provided, H–1B nonimmigrant status;

(*ii*) On whose behalf a nonfrivolous H–1B petition for new employment has been filed, including a petition for new employment with the same employer, with a request to amend or extend the H–1B nonimmigrant's stay, before the H–1B nonimmigrant's period of stay authorized by the Secretary of Homeland Security expires; and

(*iii*) Who has not been employed without authorization in the United States from the time of last admission through the filing of the petition for new employment.

(*2*) *Length of employment.* Employment authorized under paragraph (h)(2)(i)(H) of this section automatically ceases upon the adjudication of the H–1B petition described in paragraph (h)(2)(i)(H)(*1*)(*ii*) of this section.

(*3*) *Successive H–1B portability petitions.* (*i*) An alien maintaining authorization for employment under paragraph (h)(2)(i)(H) of this section, whose status, as indicated on the Arrival-Departure Record (Form I-94), has expired, shall be considered to be in a period of stay authorized by the Secretary of Homeland Security for purposes of paragraph (h)(2)(i)(H)(*1*)(*ii*) of this section. If otherwise eligible under paragraph (h)(2)(i)(H) of this section, such alien may begin working in a subsequent position upon the filing of another H–1B petition or from the requested start date, whichever is later, notwithstanding that the previous H-1B petition upon which employment is authorized under paragraph (h)(2)(i)(H) of this section remains pending and regardless of whether the validity period of an approved H–1B petition filed on the alien's behalf expired during such pendency.

(*ii*) A request to amend the petition or for an extension of stay in any successive H–1B portability petition cannot be approved if a request to amend the petition or for an extension of stay in any preceding H–1B portability petition in the succession is denied, unless the beneficiary's previously approved period of H–1B status remains valid.

(*iii*) Denial of a successive portability petition does not affect the ability of the H–1B beneficiary to continue or resume working in accordance with the terms of an H–1B petition previously approved on behalf of the beneficiary if that petition approval remains valid and the beneficiary has maintained H-1B status or been in a period of authorized stay and has not been employed in the United States without authorization.

(ii) *Multiple beneficiaries.* More than one beneficiary may be included in an H–1C, H–2A, H–2B, or H–3 petition if the beneficiaries will be performing the same service, or receiving the same training, for the same period of time, and in the same location H–2A and H-2B petitions for workers from countries not designated in accordance with paragraph (h)(6)(i)(E) of this section should be filed separately.

(iii) *Naming beneficiaries.* H–1B, H–1C, and H–3 petitions must include the name of each beneficiary. Except as provided in this paragraph (h), all H–2A and H–2B petitions must include the name of each beneficiary who is currently in the United States, but need not name any beneficiary who is not currently in the United States. Unnamed beneficiaries must be shown on the petition by total number. USCIS may require the petitioner to name H-2B beneficiaries where the name is needed to establish eligibility for H–2B nonimmigrant status. If all of the beneficiaries covered by an H–2A or H-2B temporary labor certification have not been identified at the time a petition is filed, multiple petitions for subsequent beneficiaries may be filed at different times but must include a copy of the same temporary labor certification. Each petition must reference all previously filed petitions associated with that temporary labor certification. All H–2A and H–2B petitions on behalf of workers who are not from a country that has been designated as a participating country in accordance with paragraphs (h)(5)(i)(F)(*1*) or (h)(6)(i)(E)(*1*) of this section must name all the workers in the petition who fall within these categories. All H–2A and H–2B petitions must state the nationality of all beneficiaries, whether or not named, even if there are beneficiaries from more than one country.

(iv) [Reserved]

(v) *H–2A Petitions.* Special criteria for admission, extension, and maintenance of status apply to H–2A petitions and are specified in paragraph (h)(5) of this section. The other provisions of § 214.2(h) apply to H–2A only to the extent that they do not conflict with the special agricultural provisions in paragraph (h)(5) of this section.

(3) *Petition for registered nurse (H-1C)*—(i) *General.* (A) For purposes of H-1C classification, the term "registered nurse" means a person who is or will be authorized by a State Board of Nursing to engage in registered nurse practice in a state or U.S. territory or possession, and who is or will be practicing at a facility which provides health care services.

(B) A United States employer which provides health care services is referred to as a *facility*. A *facility* may file an H–1C petition for an alien nurse to perform the services of a registered nurse, if the *facility* meets the eligibility standards of 20 CFR 655.1111 and the other requirements of the Department of Labor's regulations in 20 CFR part 655, subpart L.

(C) The position must involve nursing practice and require licensure or other authorization to practice as a registered nurse from the State Board of Nursing in the state of intended employment.

(ii) [Reserved]

(iii) *Beneficiary requirements.* An H–1C petition for a nurse shall be accompanied by evidence that the nurse:

(A) Has obtained a full and unrestricted license to practice nursing in the country where the alien obtained nursing education, or has received nursing education in the United States;

(B) Has passed the examination given by the Commission on Graduates of Foreign Nursing Schools (CGFNS), or has obtained a full and unrestricted (permanent) license to practice as a registered nurse in the state of intended employment, or has obtained a full and unrestricted (permanent) license in any state or territory of the United States and received temporary authorization to practice as a registered nurse in the state of intended employment; and

(C) Is fully qualified and eligible under the laws (including such temporary or interim licensing requirements which authorize the nurse to be employed) governing the place of intended employment to practice as a registered nurse immediately upon admission to the United States, and is authorized under such laws to be employed by the employer. For purposes of this paragraph, the temporary or interim licensing may be obtained immediately after the alien enters the United States.

(iv) *Petitioner requirements.* The petitioning facility shall submit the following with an H–1C petition:

(A) A current copy of the DOL's notice of acceptance of the filing of its attestation on Form ETA 9081;

(B) A statement describing any limitations which the laws of the state or jurisdiction of intended employment place on the alien's services; and

(C) Evidence that the alien(s) named on the petition meets the definition of a registered nurse as defined at 8 CFR 214.2(h)(3)(i)(A), and satisfies the requirements contained in section 212(m)(1) of the Act.

(v) *Licensure requirements.* (A) A nurse who is granted H–1C classification based on passage of the CGFNS examination must, upon admission to the United States, be able to obtain temporary licensure or other temporary authorization to practice as a registered nurse from the State Board of Nursing in the state of intended employment.

(B) An alien who was admitted as an H–1C nonimmigrant on the basis of a temporary license or authorization to practice as a registered nurse must comply with the licensing requirements for registered nurses in the state of intended employment. An alien admitted as an H–1C nonimmigrant is required to obtain a full and unrestricted license if required by the state of intended employment. The Service must be notified pursuant to § 214.2(h)(11) when an H–1C nurse is no longer licensed as a registered nurse in the state of intended employment.

(C) A nurse shall automatically lose his or her eligibility for H–1C classification if he or she is no longer performing the duties of a registered professional nurse. Such a nurse is not authorized to remain in employment unless he or she otherwise receives authorization from the Service.

(vi) *Other requirements.* (A) If the Secretary of Labor notifies the Service that a facility which employs H–1C nonimmigrant nurses has failed to meet a condition in its attestation, or that there was a misrepresentation of a material fact in the attestation, the Service shall not approve petitions for H–1C nonimmigrant nurses to be employed by the facility for a period of at least 1 year from the date of receipt of such notice. The Secretary of Labor shall make a recommendation with respect to the length of debarment. If the Secretary of Labor recommends a longer period of debarment, the Service will give considerable weight to that recommendation.

(B) If the facility's attestation expires, or is suspended or invalidated by DOL, the Service will not suspend or revoke the facility's approved petitions for nurses, if the facility has agreed to comply with the terms of the attestation under which the nurses were admitted or subsequent attestations accepted by DOL for the duration of the nurses' authorized stay.

(4) *Petition for alien to perform services in a specialty occupation, services relating to a DOD cooperative research and development project or coproduction project, or services of distinguished merit and ability in the ield of fashion modeling (H–1B)—*

(i)(A) *Types of H–1B classification.* An H–1B classification may be granted to an alien who:

(*1*) Will perform services in a specialty occupation which requires theoretical and practical application of a body of highly specialized knowledge and attainment of a baccalaureate or higher degree or its equivalent as a minimum requirement for entry into the occupation in the United States, and who is qualified to perform services in the specialty occupation because he or she has attained a baccalaureate or higher degree or its equivalent in the specialty occupation;

(*2*) Based on reciprocity, will perform services of an exceptional nature requiring exceptional merit and ability relating to a DOD cooperative research and development project or a coproduction project provided for under a Government-to-Government agreement administered by the Secretary of Defense;

(*3*) Will perform services in the field of fashion modeling and who is of distinguished merit and ability.

(B) *General requirements for petitions involving a specialty occupation.* (*1*) Before filing a petition for H–1B classification in a specialty occupation, the petitioner shall obtain a certification from the Department of Labor that it has filed a labor condition application in the occupational specialty in which the alien(s) will be employed.

(*2*) Certification by the Department of Labor of a labor condition application in an occupational classification does not constitute a determination by that agency that the occupation in question is a specialty occupation. The director shall determine if the application involves a specialty occupation as defined in section 214(i)(1) of the Act. The director shall also determine whether the particular alien for whom H–1B classification is sought qualifies to perform services in the specialty occupation as prescribed in section 214(i)(2) of the Act.

(*3*) If all of the beneficiaries covered by an H–1B labor condition application have not been identified at the time a petition is filed, petitions for newly identified beneficiaries may be filed at any time during the validity of the labor condition application using photocopies of the same application. Each petition must refer by file number to all previously approved petitions for that labor condition application.

(*4*) When petitions have been approved for the total number of workers specified in the labor condition application, substitution of aliens against previously approved openings shall not be made. A new labor condition application shall be required.

(*5*) If the Secretary of Labor notifies the Service that the petitioning employer has failed to meet a condition of paragraph (B) of section 212(n)(1) of the Act, has substantially failed to meet a condition of paragraphs (C) or (D) of section 212(n)(1) of the Act, has willfully failed to meet a condition of paragraph (A) of section 212(n)(1) of the Act, or has misrepresented any material fact in the application, the Service shall not approve petitions filed with respect to that employer under section 204 or 214(c) of the Act for a period of at least one year from the date of receipt of such notice.

(*6*) If the employer's labor condition application is suspended or invalidated by the Department of Labor, the Service will not suspend or revoke the employer's approved petitions for aliens already employed in specialty occupations if the employer has certified to the Department of Labor that it will comply with the terms of the labor condition application for the duration of the authorized stay of aliens it employs.

(C) *General requirements for petitions involving an alien of distinguished merit and ability in the field of fashion modeling.* H–1B classification may be granted to an alien who is of distinguished merit and ability in the field of fashion modeling. An alien of distinguished merit and ability in the field of fashion modeling is one who is prominent in the field of fashion modeling. The alien must also be coming to the United States to perform services which require a fashion model of prominence.

(ii) *Definitions.*

Prominence means a high level of achievement in the field of fashion modeling evidenced by a degree of skill and recognition substantially above that ordinarily encountered to the extent that a person described as prominent is renowned, leading, or well-known in the field of fashion modeling.

Regonized authority means a person or an organization with expertise in a particular field, special skills or knowledge in that field, and the expertise to render the type of opinion requested. Such an opinion must state:

(*1*) The writer's qualifications as an expert;

(*2*) The writer's experience giving such opinions, citing specific instances where past opinions have been accepted as authoritative and by whom;

(*3*) How the conclusions were reached; and

(*4*) The basis for the conclusions supported by copies or citations of any research material used.

Specialty occupation means an occupation which requires theoretical and practical application of a body of highly specialized knowledge in fields of human endeavor including, but not limited to, architecture, engineering, mathematics, physical sciences, social sciences, medicine and health, education, business specialties, accounting, law, theology, and the arts, and which requires the attainment of a bachelor's degree or higher in a specific specialty, or its equivalent, as a minimum for entry into the occupation in the United States.

United States employer means a person, firm, corporation, contractor, or other association, or organization in the United States which:

(*1*) Engages a person to work within the United States;

(*2*) Has an employer-employee relationship with respect to employees under this part, as indicated by the fact that it may hire, pay, fire, supervise, or otherwise control the work of any such employee; and

(*3*) Has an Internal Revenue Service Tax identification number.

(iii) *Criteria for H–1B petitions involving a specialty occupation*—(A) *Standards for specialty occupation position.* To qualify as a specialty occupation, the position must meet one of the following criteria:

(*1*) A baccalaureate or higher degree or its equivalent is normally the minimum requirement for entry into the particular position;

(*2*) The degree requirement is common to the industry in parallel positions among similar organizations or, in the alternative, an employer may show that its particular position is so complex or unique that it can be performed only by an individual with a degree;

(*3*) The employer normally requires a degree or its equivalent for the position; or

(*4*) The nature of the specific duties are so specialized and complex that knowledge required to perform the duties is usually associated with the attainment of a baccalaureate or higher degree.

(B) *Petitioner requirements.* The petitioner shall submit the following with an H–1B petition involving a specialty occupation:

(*1*) A certification from the Secretary of Labor that the petitioner has filed a labor condition application with the Secretary,

(*2*) A statement that it will comply with the terms of the labor condition application for the duration of the alien's authorized period of stay,

(*3*) Evidence that the alien qualifies to perform services in the specialty occupation as described in paragraph (h)(4)(iii)(A) of this section, and

(C) *Beneficiary qualifications.* To qualify to perform services in a specialty occupation, the alien must meet one of the following criteria:

(*1*) Hold a United States baccalaureate or higher degree required by the specialty occupation from an accredited college or university;

(*2*) Hold a foreign degree determined to be equivalent to a United States baccalaureate or higher degree required by the specialty occupation from an accredited college or university;

(*3*) Hold an unrestricted State license, registration or certification which authorizes him or her to fully practice the specialty occupation and be immediately engaged in that specialty in the state of intended employment; or

(*4*) Have education, specialized training, and/or progressively responsible experience that is equivalent to completion of a United States baccalaureate or higher degree in the specialty occupation, and have recognition of expertise in the specialty through progressively responsible positions directly related to the specialty.

(D) *Equivalence to completion of a college degree.* For purposes of paragraph (h)(4)(iii)(C)(*4*) of this section, equivalence to completion of a United States baccalaureate or higher degree shall mean achievement of a level of knowledge, competence, and practice in the specialty occupation that has been determined to be equal to that of an individual who has a baccalaureate or higher degree in the specialty and shall be determined by one or more of the following:

(*1*) An evaluation from an official who has authority to grant college-level credit for training and/or experience in the specialty at an accredited college or university which has a program for granting such credit based on an individual's training and/or work experience;

(*2*) The results of recognized college-level equivalency examinations or special credit programs, such as the College Level Examination Program (CLEP), or Program on Noncollegiate Sponsored Instruction (PONSI);

(*3*) An evaluation of education by a reliable credentials evaluation service which specializes in evaluating foreign educational credentials;

(*4*) Evidence of certification or registration from a nationally-recognized professional association or society for the specialty that is known to grant certification or registration to persons in the occupational specialty who have achieved a certain level of competence in the specialty;

(*5*) A determination by the Service that the equivalent of the degree required by the specialty occupation has been acquired through a combination of education, specialized training, and/or work experience in areas related to the specialty and that the alien has achieved recognition of expertise in the specialty occupation as a result of such training and experience. For purposes of determining equivalency to a baccalaureate degree in the specialty, three years of specialized training and/or work experience must be demonstrated for each year of college-level training the alien lacks. For equivalence to an advanced (or Masters) degree, the alien must have a baccalaureate degree followed by at least five years of experience in the specialty. If required by a specialty, the alien must hold a Doctorate degree or its foreign equivalent. It must be clearly demonstrated that the alien's training and/or work experience included the theoretical and practical application of specialized knowledge required by the specialty occupation; that the alien's experience was gained while working with peers, supervisors, or subordinates who have a degree or its equivalent in the specialty occupation; and that the alien has recognition of expertise in the specialty evidenced by at least one type of documentation such as:

(*i*) Recognition of expertise in the specialty occupation by at least two recognized authorities in the same specialty occupation;

(*ii*) Membership in a recognized foreign or United States association or society in the specialty occupation;

(*iii*) Published material by or about the alien in professional publications, trade journals, books, or major newspapers;

(*iv*) Licensure or registration to practice the specialty occupation in a foreign country; or

(*v*) Achievements which a recognized authority has determined to be significant contributions to the field of the specialty occupation.

(E) *Liability for transportation costs.* The employer will be liable for the reasonable costs of return transportation of the alien abroad if the alien is dismissed from employment by the employer before the end of the period of authorized admission pursuant to section 214(c)(5) of the Act. If the beneficiary voluntarily terminates his or her employment prior to the expiration of the validity of the petition, the alien has not been dismissed. If the beneficiary believes that the employer has not complied with this provision, the beneficiary shall advise the Service Center which adjudicated the petition in writing. The complaint will be retained in the file relating to the petition. Within the context of this paragraph, the term "abroad" refers to the alien's last place of foreign residence. This provision applies to any employer whose offer of employment became the basis for an alien obtaining or continuing H–1B status.

(iv) *General documentary requirements for H–1B classification in a specialty occupation.* An H–1B petition involving a specialty occupation shall be accompanied by:

(A) Documentation, certifications, affidavits, declarations, degrees, diplomas, writings, reviews, or any other required evidence sufficient to establish that the beneficiary is qualified to perform services in a specialty occupation as described in paragraph (h)(4)(i) of this section and that the services the beneficiary is to perform are in a specialty occupation. The evidence shall conform to the following:

(*1*) School records, diplomas, degrees, affidavits, declarations, contracts, and similar documentation submitted must reflect periods of attendance, courses of study, and similar pertinent data, be executed by the person in charge of the records of the educational or other institution, firm, or establishment where education or training was acquired.

(*2*) Affidavits or declarations made under penalty of perjury submitted by present or former employers or recognized authorities certifying as to the recognition and expertise of the beneficiary shall specifically describe the beneficiary's recognition and ability in factual terms and must set forth the expertise of the affiant and the manner in which the affiant acquired such information.

(B) Copies of any written contracts between the petitioner and beneficiary, or a summary of the terms of the oral agreement under which the beneficiary will be employed, if there is no written contract.

(v) *Licensure for H classification*—(A) *General.* If an occupation requires a state or local license for an individual to fully perform the duties of the occupation, an alien (except an H–1C nurse) seeking H classification in that occupation must have that license prior to approval of the petition to be found qualified to enter the United States and immediately engage in employment in the occupation.

(B) *Temporary licensure.* If a temporary license is available and the alien is allowed to perform the duties of the occupation without a permanent license, the director shall examine the nature of the duties, the level at which the duties are performed, the degree of supervision received, and any limitations placed on the alien. If an analysis of the facts demonstrates that the alien under supervision is authorized to fully perform the duties of the occupation, H classification may be granted.

(C) *Duties without licensure.* (*1*) In certain occupations which generally require licensure, a state may allow an individual without licensure to fully practice the occupation under the supervision of licensed senior or supervisory personnel in that occupation. In such cases, USCIS shall examine the nature of the duties and the level at which they are performed, as well as evidence provided by the petitioner as to the identity, physical location, and credentials of the individual(s) who will supervise the alien, and evidence that the petitioner is complying with state requirements. If the facts demonstrate that the alien under supervision will fully perform the duties of the occupation, H classification may be granted.

(*2*) An H–1B petition filed on behalf of an alien who does not have a valid state or local license, where a license is otherwise required to fully perform the duties in that occupation, may be approved for a period of up to 1 year if:

(*i*) The license would otherwise be issued provided the alien was in possession of a valid Social Security number, was authorized for employment in the United States, or met a similar technical requirement; and

(*ii*) The petitioner demonstrates, through evidence from the state or local licensing authority, that the only obstacle to the issuance of a license to the beneficiary is the lack of a Social Security number, a lack of employment authorization in the United States, or a failure to meet a similar technical requirement that precludes the issuance of the license to an individual who is not yet in H–1B status.

The petitioner must demonstrate that the alien is fully qualified to receive the state or local license in all other respects, meaning that all educational, training, experience, and other substantive requirements have been met. The alien must have filed an application for the license in accordance with applicable state and local rules and procedures, provided that state or local rules or procedures do not prohibit the alien from filing the license application without provision of a Social Security number or proof of employment authorization or without meeting a similar technical requirement.

(*3*) An H–1B petition filed on behalf of an alien who has been previously accorded H–1B classification under paragraph (h)(4)(v)(C)(*2*) of this section may not be approved unless the petitioner demonstrates that the alien has obtained the required license, is seeking to employ the alien in a position requiring a different license, or the alien will be employed in that occupation in a different location which does not require a state or local license to fully perform the duties of the occupation.

(D) *H–1C nurses.* For purposes of licensure, H–1C nurses must provide the evidence required in paragraph (h)(3)(iii) of this section.

(E) *Limitation on approval of petition.* Where licensure is required in any occupation, including registered nursing, the H petition may only be approved for a period of one year or for the period that the temporary license is valid, whichever is longer, unless the alien already has a permanent license to practice the occupation. An alien who is accorded H classification in an occupation which requires licensure may not be granted an extension of stay or accorded a new H classification after the one year unless he or she has obtained a permanent license in the state of intended employment or continues to hold a temporary license valid in the same state for the period of the requested extension.

(vi) *Criteria and documentary requirements for H–1B petitions involving DOD cooperative research and development projects or coproduction projects*—(A) *General.* (*1*) For purposes of H–1B classification, services of an exceptional nature relating to DOD cooperative research and development projects or coproduction projects shall be those services which require a baccalaureate or higher degree, or its equivalent, to perform the duties. The existence of this special program does not preclude the DOD from utilizing the regular H–1B provisions provided the required guidelines are met.

(*2*) The requirements relating to a labor condition application from the Department of Labor shall not apply to petitions involving DOD cooperative research and development projects or coproduction projects.

(B) *Petitioner requirements.* (*1*) The petition must be accompanied by a verification letter from the DOD project manager for the particular project stating that the alien will be working on a cooperative research and development project or a coproduction project under a reciprocal Government-to-Government agreement administered by DOD. Details about the specific project are not required.

(*2*) The petitioner shall provide a general description of the alien's duties on the particular project and indicate the actual dates of the alien's employment on the project.

(*3*) The petitioner shall submit a statement indicating the names of aliens currently employed on the project in the United States and their dates of employment. The petitioner shall also indicate the names of aliens whose employment on the project ended within the past year.

(C) *Beneficiary requirement.* The petition shall be accompanied by evidence that the beneficiary has a baccalaureate or higher degree or its equivalent in the occupational field in which he or she will be performing services in accordance with paragraph (h)(4)(iii)(C) and/or (h)(4)(iii)(D) of this section.

(vii) *Criteria and documentary requirements for H–1B petitions for aliens of distinguished merit and ability in the field of fashion modeling*—(A) *General.* Prominence in the field of fashion modeling may be established in the case of an individual fashion model. The work which a prominent alien is coming to perform in the United States must require the services of a prominent alien. A petition for an H–1B alien of distinguished merit and ability in the field of fashion modeling shall be accompanied by:

(*1*) Documentation, certifications, affidavits, writings, reviews, or any other required evidence sufficient to establish that the beneficiary is a fashion model of distinguished merit and ability. Affidavits submitted by present or former employers or recognized experts certifying to the recognition and distinguished ability of the beneficiary shall specifically describe the beneficiary's recognition and ability in factual terms and must set forth the expertise of the affiant and the manner in which the affiant acquired such information.

(*2*) Copies of any written contracts between the petitioner and beneficiary, or a summary of the terms of the oral agreement under which the beneficiary will be employed, if there is no written contract.

(B) *Petitioner's requirements.* To establish that a position requires prominence, the petitioner must establish that the position meets one of the following criteria:

(*1*) The services to be performed involve events or productions which have a distinguished reputation;

(*2*) The services are to be performed for an organization or establishment that has a distinguished reputation for, or record of, employing prominent persons.

(C) *Beneficiary's requirements.* A petitioner may establish that a beneficiary is a fashion model of distinguished merit and ability by the submission of two of the following forms of documentation showing that the alien:

(*1*) Has achieved national or international recognition and acclaim for outstanding achievement in his or her field as evidenced by reviews in major newspapers, trade journals, magazines, or other published material;

(*2*) Has performed and will perform services as a fashion model for employers with a distinguished reputation;

(*3*) Has received recognition for significant achievements from organizations, critics, fashion houses, modeling agencies, or other recognized experts in the field; or

(*4*) Commands a high salary or other substantial remuneration for services evidenced by contracts or other reliable evidence.

(viii) *Criteria and documentary requirements for H–1B petitions for physicians*—(A) *Beneficiary's requirements.* An H–1B petition for a physician shall be accompanied by evidence that the physician:

(*1*) Has a license or other authorization required by the state of intended employment to practice medicine, or is exempt by law therefrom, if the physician will perform direct patient care and the state requires the license or authorization, and

(*2*) Has a full and unrestricted license to practice medicine in a foreign state or has graduated from a medical school in the United States or in a foreign state.

(B) *Petitioner's requirements.* The petitioner must establish that the alien physician:

(*1*) Is coming to the United States primarily to teach or conduct research, or both, at or for a public or nonprofit private educational or research institution or agency, and that no patient care will be performed, except that which is incidental to the physician's teaching or research; or

(*2*) The alien has passed the Federation Licensing Examination (or an equivalent examination as determined by the Secretary of Health and Human Services) or is a graduate of a United States medical school; and

(*i*) Has competency in oral and written English which shall be demonstrated by the passage of the English language proficiency test given by the Educational Commission for Foreign Medical Graduates; or

(*ii*) Is a graduate of a school of medicine accredited by a body or bodies approved for that purpose by the Secretary of Education.

(C) *Exception for physicians of national or international renown.* A physician who is a graduate of a medical school in a foreign state and who is of national or international renown in the field of medicine is exempt from the requirements of paragraph (h)(4)(viii)(B) of this section.

(5) *Petition for alien to perform agricultural labor or services of a temporary or seasonal nature (H–2A)*—(i) *Filing a petition*—(A) *General.* An H–2A petition

must be filed on Form I–129 with a single valid temporary agricultural labor certification. The petition may be filed by either the employer listed on the temporary labor certification, the employer's agent, or the association of United States agricultural producers named as a joint employer on the temporary labor certification.

(B) *Multiple beneficiaries*. The total number of beneficiaries of a petition or series of petitions based on the same temporary labor certification may not exceed the number of workers indicated on that document. A single petition can include more than one beneficiary if the total number does not exceed the number of positions indicated on the relating temporary labor certification.

(C) [Reserved]

(D) *Evidence*. An H–2A petitioner must show that the proposed employment qualifies as a basis for H–2A status, and that any named beneficiary qualifies for that employment. A petition will be automatically denied if filed without the certification evidence required in paragraph (h)(5)(i)(A) of this section and, for each named beneficiary, the initial evidence required in paragraph (h)(5)(v) of this section.

(E) *Special filing requirements*. Where a certification shows joint employers, a petition must be filed with an attachment showing that each employer has agreed to the conditions of H–2A eligibility. A petition filed by an agent must be filed with an attachment in which the employer has authorized the agent to act on its behalf, has assumed full responsibility for all representations made by the agent on its behalf, and has agreed to the conditions of H–2A eligibility.

(F) *Eligible Countries*. (*1*)(*i*) H–2A petitions may only be approved for nationals of countries that the Secretary of Homeland Security has designated as participating countries, with the concurrence of the Secretary of State, in a notice published in the FEDERAL REGISTER, taking into account factors, including but not limited to:

(*A*) The country's cooperation with respect to issuance of travel documents for citizens, subjects, nationals and residents of that country who are subject to a final order of removal;

(*B*) The number of final and unexecuted orders of removal against citizens, subjects, nationals and residents of that country;

(*C*) The number of orders of removal executed against citizens, subjects, nationals and residents of that country; and

(*D*) Such other factors as may serve the U.S. interest.

(*ii*) A national from a country not on the list described in paragraph (h)(5)(i)(F)(*1*)(*i*) of this section may be a beneficiary of an approved H–2A petition upon the request of a petitioner or potential H–2A petitioner, if the Secretary of Homeland Security, in his sole and unreviewable discretion, determines that it is in the U.S. interest for that alien to be a beneficiary of such petition. Determination of such a U.S. interest will take into account factors, including but not limited to:

(*A*) Evidence from the petitioner demonstrating that a worker with the required skills is not available either from among U.S. workers or from among foreign workers from a country currently on the list described in paragraph (h)(5)(i)(F)(*1*)(*i*) of this section;

(*B*) Evidence that the beneficiary has been admitted to the United States previously in H–2A status;

(*C*) The potential for abuse, fraud, or other harm to the integrity of the H–2A visa program through the potential admission of a beneficiary from a country not currently on the list; and

(*D*) Such other factors as may serve the U.S. interest.

(*2*) Once published, any designation of participating countries pursuant to paragraph (h)(5)(i)(F)(*1*)(*i*) of this section shall be effective for one year after the date of publication in the FEDERAL REGISTER and shall be without effect at the end of that one-year period.

(ii) *Effect of the labor certification process*. The temporary agricultural labor certification process determines whether employment is as an agricultural worker, whether it is open to U.S. workers, if qualified U.S. workers are available, the adverse impact of employment of a qualified alien, and whether employment conditions, including housing, meet applicable requirements. In petition proceedings a petitioner must establish that the employment and beneficiary meet the requirements of paragraph (h)(5) of this section.

(iii) *Ability and intent to meet a job offer*—(A) *Eligibility requirements.* An H–2A petitioner must establish that each beneficiary will be employed in accordance with the terms and conditions of the certification, which includes that the principal duties to be performed are those on the certification, with other duties minor and incidental.

(B) *Intent and prior compliance.* Requisite intent cannot be established for two years after an employer or joint employer, or a parent, subsidiary or affiliate thereof, is found to have violated section 274(a) of the Act or to have employed an H–2A worker in a position other than that described in the relating petition.

(C) *Initial evidence.* Representations required for the purpose of labor certification are initial evidence of intent.

(iv) *Temporary and seasonal employment*—(A) *Eligibility requirements.* An H–2A petitioner must establish that the employment proposed in the certification is of a temporary or seasonal nature. Employment is of a seasonal nature where it is tied to a certain time of year by an event or pattern, such as a short annual growing cycle or a specific aspect of a longer cycle, and requires labor levels far above those necessary for ongoing operations. Employment is of a temporary nature where the employer's need to fill the position with a temporary worker will, except in extraordinary circumstances, last no longer than one year.

(B) *Effect of Department of Labor findings.* In temporary agricultural labor certification proceedings the Department of Labor separately tests whether employment qualifies as temporary or seasonal. Its finding that employment qualifies is normally sufficient for the purpose of an H–2A petition, However, notwithstanding that finding, employment will be found not to be temporary or seasonal where an application for permanent labor certification has been filed for the same alien, or for another alien to be employed in the same position, by the same employer or by its parent, subsidiary or affiliate. This can only be overcome by the petitioner's demonstration that there will be at least a six month interruption of employment in the United States after H–2A status ends. Also, eligibility will not be found, notwithstanding the issuance of a temporary agricultural labor certification, where there is substantial evidence that the employment is not temporary or seasonal.

(v) *The beneficiary's qualifications*—(A) *Eligibility requirements.* An H–2A petitioner must establish that any named beneficiary met the stated minimum requirements and was fully able to perform the stated duties when the application for certification was filed. It must be established at time of application for an H–2A visa, or for admission if a visa is not required, that any unnamed beneficiary either met these requirements when the certification was applied for or passed any certified aptitude test at any time prior to visa issuance, or prior to admission if a visa is not required.

(B) *Evidence of employment/job training.* For petitions with named beneficiaries, a petition must be filed with evidence that the beneficiary met the certification's minimum employment and job training requirements, if any are prescribed, as of the date of the filing of the labor certification application. For petitions with unnamed beneficiaries, such evidence must be submitted at the time of a visa application or, if a visa is not required, at the time the applicant seeks admission to the United States. Evidence must be in the form of the past employer or employers' detailed statement(s) or actual employment documents, such as company payroll or tax records. Alternately, a petitioner must show that such evidence cannot be obtained, and submit affidavits from persons who worked with the beneficiary that demonstrate the claimed employment or job training.

(C) *Evidence of education and other training.* For petitions with named beneficiaries, a petition must be filed with evidence that the beneficiary met all of the certification's post-secondary education and other formal training requirements, if any are prescribed in the labor certification application as of date of the filing of the labor certification application. For petitions with unnamed beneficiaries, such evidence must be submitted at the time of a visa application or, if a visa is not required, at the time the applicant seeks admission to the United States. Evidence must be in the form of documents, issued by the relevant institution(s) or organization(s), that show periods of attendance, majors and degrees or certificates accorded.

(vi) *Petitioner consent and notification requirements*—(A) *Consent.* In filing an H–2A petition, a petitioner and each employer consents to allow access to the site by DHS officers where the labor is being performed for the purpose of determining compliance with H–2A requirements.

(B) *Agreements.* The petitioner agrees to the following requirements:

(*1*) To notify DHS, within 2 workdays, and beginning on a date and in a manner specified in a notice published in the FEDERAL REGISTER if:

(*i*) An H–2A worker fails to report to work within 5 workdays of the employment start date on the H–2A petition or within 5 workdays of the start date established by his or her employer, whichever is later;

(*ii*) The agricultural labor or services for which H–2A workers were hired is completed more than 30 days earlier than the employment end date stated on the H–2A petition; or

(*iii*) The H–2A worker absconds from the worksite or is terminated prior to the completion of agricultural labor or services for which he or she was hired.

(*2*) To retain evidence of such notification and make it available for inspection by DHS officers for a 1-year period beginning on the date of the notification. To retain evidence of a different employment start date if it is changed from that on the petition by the employer and make it available for inspection by DHS officers for the 1-year period beginning on the newly-established employment start date.

(*3*) To pay $10 in liquidated damages for each instance where the employer cannot demonstrate that it has complied with the notification requirements, unless, in the case of an untimely notification, the employer demonstrates with such notification that good cause existed for the untimely notification, and DHS, in its discretion, waives the liquidated damages amount.

(C) *Process.* If DHS has determined that the petitioner has violated the notification requirements in paragraph (h)(5)(vi)(B)(1) of this section and has not received the required notification, the petitioner will be given written notice and 30 days to reply before being given written notice of the assessment of liquidated damages.

(D) *Failure to pay liquidated damages.* If liquidated damages are not paid within 10 days of assessment, an H–2A petition may not be processed for that petitioner or any joint employer shown on the petition until such damages are paid.

(E) *Abscondment.* An H–2A worker has absconded if he or she has not reported for work for a period of 5 consecutive workdays without the consent of the employer.

(vii) *Validity.* An approved H–2A petition is valid through the expiration of the relating certification for the purpose of allowing a beneficiary to seek issuance of an H–2A nonimmigrant visa, admission or an extension of stay for the purpose of engaging in the specific certified employment.

(viii) *Admission*—(A) *Effect of violations of status.* An alien may not be accorded H–2A status who, at any time during the past 5 years, USCIS finds to have violated, other than through no fault of his or her own (e.g., due to an employer's illegal or inappropriate conduct), any of the terms or conditions of admission into the United States as an H–2A nonimmigrant, including remaining beyond the specific period of authorized stay or engaging in unauthorized employment.

(B) *Period of admission.* An alien admissible as an H–2A nonimmigrant shall be admitted for the period of the approved petition. Such alien will be admitted for an additional period of up to one week before the beginning of the approved period for the purpose of travel to the worksite, and a 30-day period following the expiration of the H–2A petition for the purpose of departure or to seek an extension based on a subsequent offer of employment. Unless authorized under 8 CFR 274a.12 or section 214(n) of the Act, the beneficiary may not work except during the validity period of the petition.

(C) *Limits on an individual's stay.* Except as provided in paragraph (h)(5)(viii)(B) of this section, an alien's stay as an H–2A nonimmigrant is limited by the term of an approved petition. An alien may remain longer to engage in other qualifying temporary agricultural employment by obtaining an extension of stay. However, an individual who has held H–2A status for a total of 3 years may not again be granted H–2A status until such time as he or she remains outside the United States for an uninterrupted period of 3 months. An absence from the United States can interrupt the accrual of time spent as an H–2A nonimmigrant against the 3-year limit. If the accumulated stay is 18 months or less, an absence is interruptive if it lasts for at least 45 days. If the accumulated stay is greater than 18 months, an absence is interruptive if it lasts for at least 2 months. Eligibility under paragraph (h)(5)(viii)(C) of this section will be determined in admission, change of status or extension proceedings. An alien found eligible for a shorter period of H–2A status than that indicated by the petition due to the application of this paragraph (h)(5)(viii)(C) of this section shall only be admitted for that abbreviated period.

(ix) *Substitution of beneficiaries after admission.* An H–2A petition may be filed to replace H–2A workers whose employment was terminated earlier than the end date stated on the H–2A petition and before the completion of work; who fail to report to work within five days of the employment start date on the H–2A petition or within five days of the start date established by his or her employer, whichever is later; or who abscond from the worksite. The petition must be filed with a copy of the certification document, a copy of the approval notice covering the workers for which replacements are sought, and other evidence required by paragraph (h)(5)(i)(D) of this section. It must also be filed with a statement giving each terminated or absconded worker's name, date and country of birth, termination date, and the reason for termination, and the date that USCIS was notified that the alien was terminated or absconded, if applicable. A petition for a replacement will not be approved where the requirements of paragraph (h)(5)(vi) of this section have not been met. A petition for replacements does not constitute the notification required by paragraph (h)(5)(vi)(B)(*1*) of this section.

(x) *Extensions in emergent circumstances.* In emergent circumstances, as determined by USCIS, a single H–2A petition may be extended for a period not to exceed 2 weeks without an additional approved labor certification if filed on behalf of one or more beneficiaries who will continue to be employed by the same employer that previously obtained an approved petition on the beneficiary's behalf, so long as the employee continues to perform the same duties and will be employed for no longer than 2 weeks after the expiration of previously-approved H–2A petition. The previously approved H–2A petition must have been based on an approved temporary labor certification, which shall be considered to be extended upon the approval of the extension of H–2A status.

(xi) *Treatment of petitions and alien beneficiaries upon a determination that fees were collected from alien beneficiaries*—(A) *Denial or revocation of petition.* As a condition to approval of an H–2A petition, no job placement fee or other compensation (either direct or indirect) may be collected at any time, including before or after the filing or approval of the petition, from a beneficiary of an H–2A petition by a petitioner, agent, facilitator, recruiter, or similar employment service as a condition of H–2A employment (other than the lesser of the fair market value or actual costs of transportation and any government-mandated passport, visa, or inspection fees, to the extent that the payment of such costs and fees by the beneficiary is not prohibited by statute or Department of Labor regulations, unless the employer agent, facilitator, recruiter, or employment service has agreed with the alien to pay such costs and fees).

(*1*) If USCIS determines that the petitioner has collected, or entered into an agreement to collect, such prohibited fee or compensation, the H–2A petition will be denied or revoked on notice unless the petitioner demonstrates that, prior to the filing of the petition, the petitioner has reimbursed the alien in full for such fees or compensation, or, where such fee or compensation has not yet been paid by the alien worker, that the agreement has been terminated.

(*2*) If USCIS determines that the petitioner knew or should have known at the time of filing the petition that the beneficiary has paid or agreed to pay any facilitator, recruiter, or similar employment service such fees or compensation as a condition of obtaining the H–2A employment, the H–2A petition will be denied or revoked on notice unless the petitioner demonstrates that, prior to the filing of the petition, the petitioner or the facilitator, recruiter, or similar employment service has reimbursed the alien in full for such fees or compensation or, where such fee or compensation has not yet been paid by the alien worker, that the agreement has been terminated.

(*3*) If USCIS determines that the beneficiary paid the petitioner such fees or compensation as a condition of obtaining the H–2A employment after the filing of the H–2A petition, the petition will be denied or revoked on notice.

(*4*) If USCIS determines that the beneficiary paid or agreed to pay the agent, facilitator, recruiter, or similar employment service such fees or compensation as a condition of obtaining the H–2A employment after the filing of the H–2A petition and with the knowledge of the petitioner, the petition will be denied or revoked unless the petitioner demonstrates that the petitioner or facilitator, recruiter, or similar employment service has reimbursed the beneficiary in full or where such fee or compensation has not yet been paid by the alien worker, that the agreement has been terminated, or notifies DHS within 2 workdays of obtaining knowledge in a manner specified in a notice published in the FEDERAL REGISTER.

(B) *Effect of petition revocation.* Upon revocation of an employer's H–2A petition based upon paragraph (h)(5)(xi)(A) of this section, the alien beneficiary's stay will be authorized and the alien will not accrue any period of unlawful presence under section 212(a)(9) of the Act (8 U.S.C. 1182(a)(9)) for a 30-day period following the date of the revocation for the purpose of departure or extension of stay based upon a subsequent offer of employment.

(C) *Reimbursement as condition to approval of future H–2A petitions*—(*1*) *Filing subsequent H–2A petitions within 1 year of denial or revocation of previous H–2A petition.* A petitioner filing an H–2A petition within 1 year after the decision denying or revoking on notice an H–2A petition filed by the same petitioner on the basis of paragraph (h)(5)(xi)(A) of this section must demonstrate to the satisfaction of USCIS, as a condition of approval of such petition, that the petitioner or agent, facilitator, recruiter, or similar employment service has reimbursed the beneficiary in full or that the petitioner has failed to locate the beneficiary. If the petitioner demonstrates to the satisfaction of USCIS that the beneficiary was reimbursed in full, such condition of approval shall be satisfied with respect to any subsequently filed H–2A petitions, except as provided in paragraph (h)(5)(xi)(C)(*2*). If the petitioner demonstrates to the satisfaction of USCIS that it has made reasonable efforts to locate the beneficiary with respect to each H–2A petition filed within 1 year after the decision denying or revoking the previous H–2A petition on the basis of paragraph (h)(5)(xi)(A) of this section but has failed to do so, such condition of approval shall be deemed satisfied with respect to any H–2A petition filed 1 year or more after the denial or revocation. Such reasonable efforts shall include contacting any of the beneficiary's known addresses.

(*2*) *Effect of subsequent denied or revoked petitions.* An H–2A petition filed by the same petitioner subsequent to a denial under paragraph (h)(5)(xi)(A) of this section shall be subject to the condition of approval described in paragraph (h)(5)(xi)(C)(*1*) of this section, regardless of prior satisfaction of such condition of approval with respect to a previously denied or revoked petition.

(xii) *Treatment of alien beneficiaries upon revocation of labor certification.* The approval of an employer's H–2A petition is immediately and automatically revoked if the Department of

Labor revokes the labor certification upon which the petition is based. Upon revocation of an H–2A petition based upon revocation of labor certification, the alien beneficiary's stay will be authorized and the alien will not accrue any period of unlawful presence under section 212(a)(9) of the Act for a 30-day period following the date of the revocation for the purpose of departure or extension of stay based upon a subsequent offer of employment.

(6) *Petition for alien to perform temporary nonagricultural services or labor (H–2B)*—(i) *Petition*—(A) *H–2B nonagricultural temporary worker.* An H–2B nonagricultural temporary worker is an alien who is coming temporarily to the United States to perform temporary services or labor without displacing qualified United States workers available to perform such services or labor and whose employment is not adversely affecting the wages and working conditions of United States workers.

(B) *Denial or revocation of petition upon a determination that fees were collected from alien beneficiaries.* As a condition of approval of an H–2B petition, no job placement fee or other compensation (either direct or indirect) may be collected at any time, including before or after the filing or approval of the petition, from a beneficiary of an H–2B petition by a petitioner, agent, facilitator, recruiter, or similar employment service as a condition of an offer or condition of H–2B employment (other than the lower of the actual cost or fair market value of transportation to such employment and any government-mandated passport, visa, or inspection fees, to the extent that the passing of such costs to the beneficiary is not prohibited by statute, unless the employer, agent, facilitator, recruiter, or similar employment service has agreed with the beneficiary that it will pay such costs and fees).

(*1*) If USCIS determines that the petitioner has collected or entered into an agreement to collect such fee or compensation, the H–2B petition will be denied or revoked on notice, unless the petitioner demonstrates that, prior to the filing of the petition, either the petitioner reimbursed the beneficiary in full for such fees or compensation or the agreement to collect such fee or compensation was terminated before the fee or compensation was paid by the beneficiary.

(*2*) If USCIS determines that the petitioner knew or should have known at the time of filing the petition that the beneficiary has paid or agreed to pay any agent, facilitator, recruiter, or similar employment service as a condition of an offer of the H–2B employment, the H–2B petition will be denied or revoked on notice unless the petitioner demonstrates that, prior to filing the petition, either the petitioner or the agent, facilitator, recruiter, or similar employment service reimbursed the beneficiary in full for such fees or compensation or the agreement to collect such fee or compensation was terminated before the fee or compensation was paid by the beneficiary.

(*3*) If USCIS determines that the beneficiary paid the petitioner such fees or compensation as a condition of an offer of H–2B employment after the filing of the H–2B petition, the petition will be denied or revoked on notice.

(*4*) If USCIS determines that the beneficiary paid or agreed to pay the agent, facilitator, recruiter, or similar employment service such fees or compensation after the filing of the H–2B petition and that the petitioner knew or had reason to know of the payment or agreement to pay, the petition will be denied or revoked unless the petitioner demonstrates that the petitioner or agent, facilitator, recruiter, or similar employment service reimbursed the beneficiary in full, that the parties terminated any agreement to pay before the beneficiary paid the fees or compensation, or that the petitioner has notified DHS within 2 work days of obtaining knowledge, in a manner specified in a notice published in the FEDERAL REGISTER.

(C) *Effect of petition revocation.* Upon revocation of an employer's H–2B petition based upon paragraph (h)(6)(i)(B) of this section, the alien beneficiary's stay will be authorized and the beneficiary will not accrue any period of unlawful presence under section 212(a)(9) of the Act (8 U.S.C. 1182(a)(9)) for a 30-day period following the date of the revocation for the purpose of departure or extension of stay based upon a subsequent offer of employment. The employer shall be liable for the alien beneficiary's reasonable costs of return transportation to his or her last place of foreign residence abroad, unless such alien obtains an extension of stay based on an approved H–2B petition filed by a different employer.

(D) *Reimbursement as condition to approval of future H–2B petitions*—(1) *Filing subsequent H–2B petitions within 1 year of denial or revocation of previous H–2B petition.* A petitioner filing an H–2B petition within 1 year after a decision denying or revoking on notice an H–2B petition filed by the same petitioner on the basis of paragraph (h)(6)(i)(B) of this section must demonstrate to the satisfaction of USCIS, as a condition of the approval of the later petition, that the petitioner or agent, facilitator, recruiter, or similar employment service reimbursed in full each beneficiary of the denied or revoked petition from whom a prohibited fee was collected or that the petitioner has failed to locate each such beneficiary despite the petitioner's reasonable efforts to locate them. If the petitioner demonstrates to the satisfaction of USCIS that each such beneficiary was reimbursed in full, such condition of approval shall be satisfied with respect to any subsequently filed H–2B petitions, except as provided in paragraph (h)(6)(i)(D)(*2*) of this section. If the petitioner demonstrates to the satisfaction of USCIS that it has made reasonable efforts to locate but has failed to locate each such beneficiary within 1 year after the decision denying or revoking the previous H–2B petition on the basis of paragraph (h)(6)(i)(B) of this section, such condition of approval shall be deemed satisfied with respect to any H–2B petition filed 1 year or more after the denial or revocation. Such reasonable efforts shall include contacting all of each such beneficiary's known addresses.

(*2*) *Effect of subsequent denied or revoked petitions.* An H–2B petition filed by the same petitioner subsequent to a denial under paragraph (h)(6)(i)(B) of this section shall be subject to the condition of approval described in paragraph (h)(6)(i)(D)(*1*) of this section, regardless of prior satisfaction of such condition of approval with respect to a previously denied or revoked petition.

(E) *Eligible countries.* (*1*) H–2B petitions may be approved for nationals of countries that the Secretary of Homeland Security has designated as participating countries, with the concurrence of the Secretary of State, in a notice published in the FEDERAL REGISTER, taking into account factors, including but not limited to:

(*i*) The country's cooperation with respect to issuance of travel documents for citizens, subjects, nationals and residents of that country who are subject to a final order of removal;

(*ii*) The number of final and unexecuted orders of removal against citizens, subjects, nationals, and residents of that country;

(*iii*) The number of orders of removal executed against citizens, subjects, nationals and residents of that country; and

(*iv*) Such other factors as may serve the U.S. interest.

(*2*) A national from a country not on the list described in paragraph (h)(6)(i)(E)(*1*) of this section may be a beneficiary of an approved H–2B petition upon the request of a petitioner or potential H–2B petitioner, if the Secretary of Homeland Security, in his sole and unreviewable discretion, determines that it is in the U.S. interest for that alien to be a beneficiary of such petition. Determination of such a U.S. interest will take into account factors, including but not limited to:

(*i*) Evidence from the petitioner demonstrating that a worker with the required skills is not available from among foreign workers from a country currently on the list described in paragraph (h)(6)(i)(E)(*1*) of this section;

(*ii*) Evidence that the beneficiary has been admitted to the United States previously in H–2B status;

(*iii*) The potential for abuse, fraud, or other harm to the integrity of the H–2B visa program through the potential admission of a beneficiary from a country not currently on the list; and

(*iv*) Such other factors as may serve the U.S. interest.

(*3*) Once published, any designation of participating countries pursuant to paragraph (h)(6)(i)(E)(*1*) of this section shall be effective for one year after the date of publication in the FEDERAL REGISTER and shall be without effect at the end of that one-year period.

(F) *Petitioner agreements and notification requirements—(1) Agreements.* The petitioner agrees to notify DHS, within 2 work days, and beginning on a date and in a manner specified in a notice published in the FEDERAL REGISTER if: An H–2B worker fails to report for work within 5 work days after the employment start date stated on the petition; the nonagricultural labor or services for which H–2B workers were hired were completed more than 30 days early; or an H–2B worker absconds from the worksite or is terminated prior to the completion of the nonagricultural labor or services for which he or she was hired. The petitioner also agrees to retain evidence of such notification and make it available for inspection by DHS officers for a one-year period beginning on the date of the notification.

(2) Abscondment. An H–2B worker has absconded if he or she has not reported for work for a period of 5 consecutive work days without the consent of the employer.

(ii) *Temporary services or labor*—(A) *Definition.* Temporary services or labor under the H–2B classification refers to any job in which the petitioner's need for the duties to be performed by the employee(s) is temporary, whether or not the underlying job can be described as permanent or temporary.

(B) *Nature of petitioner's need.* Employment is of a temporary nature when the employer needs a worker for a limited period of time. The employer must establish that the need for the employee will end in the near, definable future. Generally, that period of time will be limited to one year or less, but in the case of a one-time event could last up to 3 years. The petitioner's need for the services or labor shall be a one-time occurrence, a seasonal need, a peak load need, or an intermittent need.

(1) One-time occurance. The petitioner must establish that it has not employed workers to perform the services or labor in the past and that it will not need workers to perform the services or labor in the future, or that it has an employment situation that is otherwise permanent, but a temporary event of short duration has created the need for a temporary worker.

(2) Seasonal need. The petitioner must establish that the services or labor is traditionally tied to a season of the year by an event or pattern and is of a recurring nature. The petitioner shall specify the period(s) of time during each year in which it does not need the services or labor. The employment is not seasonal if the period during which the services or labor is not needed is unpredictable or subject to change or is considered a vacation period for the petitioner's permanent employees.

(3) Peakload need. The petitoner must establish that it regularly employs permanent workers to perform the services or labor at the place of employment and that it needs to supplement its permanent staff at the place of employment on a temporary basis due to a seasonal or short-term demand and that the temporary additions to staff will not become a part of the petitioner's regular operation.

(4) Intermittent need. The petitioner must establish that it has not employed permanent or full-time workers to perform the services or labor, but occasionally or intermittently needs temporary workers to perform services or labor for short periods.

(iii) *Procedures.* (A) Prior to filing a petition with the director to classify an alien as an H–2B worker, the petitioner shall apply for a temporary labor certification with the Secretary of Labor for all areas of the United States, except the Territory of Guam. In the Territory of Guam, the petitioning employer shall apply for a temporary labor certification with the Governor of Guam. The labor certification shall be advice to the director on whether or not United States workers capable of performing the temporary services or labor are available and whether or not the alien's employment will adversely affect the wages and working conditions of similarly employed United States workers.

(B) An H–2B petitioner shall be a United States employer, a United States agent, or a foreign employer filing through a United States agent. For purposes of paragraph (h) of this section, a foreign employer is any employer who is not amenable to service of process in the United States. A foreign employer may not directly petition for an H–2B nonimmigrant but must use the services of a United States agent to file a petition for an H–2B nonimmigrant. A United States agent petitioning on behalf of a foreign employer must be authorized to file the petition, and to accept service of process in the United States in proceedings under section 274A of the Act, on behalf of the employer. The petitioning employer shall consider available United States workers for the temporary services or labor, and shall offer terms and conditions of employment which are consistent with the nature of the occupation, activity, and industry in the United States.

(C) The petitioner may not file an H–2B petition unless the United States petitioner has applied for a labor certification with the Secretary of Labor or the Governor of Guam within the time limits prescribed or accepted by each, and has obtained a favorable labor certification determination as required by paragraph (h)(6)(iv) or (h)(6)(v) of this section.

(D) The Governor of Guam shall separately establish procedures for administering the temporary labor program under his or her jurisdiction. The Secretary of Labor shall separately establish for the temporary labor program under his or her jurisdiction, by regulation at 20 CFR 655, procedures for administering that temporary labor program under his or her jurisdiction, and shall determine the prevailing wage applicable to an application for temporary labor certification for that temporary labor program in accordance with the Secretary of Labor's regulation at 20 CFR 655.10.

(E) After obtaining a favorable determination from the Secretary of Labor or the Governor of Guam, as appropriate, the petitioner shall file a petition on I–129, accompanied by the labor certification determination and supporting documents, with the director having jurisdiction in the area of intended employment.

(iv) *Labor certifications, except Guam*—(A) *Secretary of Labor's determination.* An H–2B petition for temporary employment in the United States, except for temporary employment on Guam, shall be accompanied by an approved temporary labor certification from the Secretary of Labor stating that qualified workers in the United States are not available and that the alien's employment will not adversely affect wages and working conditions of similarly employed United States workers.

(B) *Validity of the labor certification.* The Secretary of Labor may issue a temporary labor certification for a period of up to one year.

(C) *U.S. Virgin Islands.* Temporary labor certifications filed under section 101(a)(15)(H)(ii)(b) of the Act for employment in the United States Virgin Islands may be approved only for entertainers and athletes and only for periods not to exceed 45 days.

(D) *Employment start date.* Beginning with petitions filed for workers for fiscal year 2010, an H–2B petition must state an employment start date that is the same as the date of need stated on the approved temporary labor certification. A petitioner filing an amended H–2B petition due to the unavailability of originally requested workers may state an employment start date later than the date of need stated on the previously approved temporary labor certification accompanying the amended H–2B petition.

(v) *Labor certification for Guam*—(A) *Governor of Guam's determination.* An H–2B petition for temporary employment on Guam shall be accompanied by an approved temporary labor certification issued by the Governor of Guam stating that qualified workers in the United States are not available to perform the required services, and that the alien's employment will not adversely affect the wages and working conditions of United States resident workers who are similarly employed on Guam.

(B) *Validity of labor certification.* The Governor of Guam may issue a temporary labor certification for a period up to one year.

(C)–(D) [Reserved]

(E) *Criteria for Guam labor certifications.* The Governor of Guam shall, in consultation with the Service, establish systematic methods for determining the prevailing wage rates and working conditions for individual occupations on Guam and for making determinations as to availability of qualified United States residents.

(*1*) *Prevailing wage and working conditions.* The system to determine wages and working conditions must provide for consideration of wage rates and employment conditions for occupations in both the private and public sectors, in Guam and/or in the United States (as defined in section 101(a)(38) of the Act), and may not consider wages and working conditions outside of the United States. If the system includes utilitzation of advisory opinions and consultations, the opinions must be provided by officially sanctioned groups which reflect a balance of the interests of the private and public sectors, government, unions and management.

(*2*) *Availability of United States workers.* The system for determining availability of qualified United States workers must require the prospective employer to:

(*i*) Advertise the availability of the position for a minimum of three consecutive days in the newspaper with the largest daily circulation on Guam;

(*ii*) Place a job offer with an appropriate agency of the Territorial Government which operates as a job referral service at least 30 days in advance of the need for the services to commence, except that for applications from the armed forces of the United States and those in the entertainment industry, the 30-day period may be reduced by the Governor to 10 days;

(*iii*) Conduct appropriate recruitment in other areas of the United States and its territories if sufficient qualified United States construction workers are not available on Guam to fill a job. The Governor of Guam may require a job order to be placed more than 30 days in advance of need to accommodate such recruitment;

(*iv*) Report to the appropriate agency the names of all United States resident workers who applied for the position, indicating those hired and the job-related reasons for not hiring;

(*v*) Offer all special considerations, such as housing and transportation expenses, to all United States resident workers who applied for the position, indicating those hired and the job-related reasons for not hiring;

(*vi*) Meet the prevailing wage rates and working conditions determined under the wages and working conditions system by the Governor; and

(*vii*) Agree to meet all Federal and Territorial requirements relating to employment, such as nondiscrimination, occupational safety, and minimum wage requirements.

(F) *Approval and publication of employment systems on Guam—(1) Systems.* The Commissioner of Immigration and Naturalization must approve the system to determine prevailing wages and working conditions and the system to determine availability of United States resident workers and any future modifications of the systems prior to implementation. If the Commissioner, in consultation with the Secretary of Labor, finds that the systems or modified systems meet the requirements of this section, the Commissioner shall publish them as a notice in the FEDERAL REGISTER and the Governor shall publish them as a public record in Guam.

(*2*) *Approval of construction wage rates.* The Commissioner must approve specific wage data and rates used for construction occupations on Guam prior to implementation of new rates. The Governor shall submit new wage survey data and proposed rates to the Commissioner for approval at least eight weeks before authority to use existing rates expires. Surveys shall be conducted at least every two years, unless the Commissioner prescribes a lesser period.

(G) *Reporting.* The Governor shall provide the Commissioner statistical data on temporary labor certification workload and determinations. This information shall be submitted quarterly no later than 30 days after the quarter ends.

(H) *Invalidation of temporary labor certification issued by the Governor of Guam—(1) General.* A temporary labor certification issued by the Governor of Guam may be invalidated by a director if it is determined by the director or a court of law that the certification request involved fraud or willful misrepresentation. A temporary labor certification may also be invalidated if the director determines that the certification involved gross error.

(*2*) *Notice of intent to invalidate.* If the director intends to invalidate a temporary labor certification, a notice of intent shall be served upon the employer, detailing the reasons for the intended invalidation. The employer shall have 30 days in which to file a written response in rebuttal to the notice of intent. The director shall consider all evidence submitted upon rebuttal in reaching a decision.

(*3*) *Appeal of invalidation.* An employer may appeal the invalidation of a temporary labor certification in accordance with part 103 of this chapter.

(vi) *Evidence for H–2B petitions.* An H–2B petition shall be accompanied by:

(A) *Labor certification.* An approved temporary labor certification issued by the Secretary of Labor or the Governor of Guam, as appropriate;

(B) [Reserved]

(C) *Alien's qualifications.* In petitions where the temporary labor certification application requires certain education, training, experience, or special requirements of the beneficiary who is present in the United States, documentation that the alien qualifies for the job offer as specified in the application for such temporary labor certification. This requirement also applies to the named beneficiary who is abroad on the basis of special provisions stated in paragraph (h)(2)(iii) of this section;

(D) *Statement of need.* A statement describing in detail the temporary situation or conditions which make it necessary to bring the alien to the United States and whether the need is a one-time occurrence, seasonal, peakload, or intermittent. If the need is seasonal, peakload, or intermittent, the statement shall indicate whether the situation or conditions are expected to be recurrent; or

(E) *Liability for transportation costs.* The employer will be liable for the reasonable costs of return transportation of the alien abroad, if the alien is dismissed from employment for any reason by the employer before the end of the period of authorized admission pursuant to section 214(c)(5) of the Act. If the beneficiary voluntarily terminates his or her employment prior to the expiration of the validity of the petition, the alien has not been dismissed. If the beneficiary believes that the employer has not complied with this provision, the beneficiary shall advise the Service Center which adjudicated the petition in writing. The complaint will be retained in the file relating to the petition. Within the context of this paragraph, the term "abroad" means the alien's last place of foreign residence. This provision applies to any employer whose offer of employment became the basis for the alien obtaining or continuing H–2B status.

(vii) *Traded professional H–2B athletes.* In the case of a professional H–2B athlete who is traded from one organization to another organization, employment authorization for the player will automatically continue for a period of 30 days after the player's acquisition by the new organization, within which time the new organization is expected to file a new Form I–129 for H–2B nonimmigrant classification. If a new Form I–129 is not filed within 30 days, employment authorization will cease. If a new Form I–129 is filed within 30 days, the professional athlete shall be deemed to be in valid H–2B status, and employment shall continue to be authorized, until the petition is adjudicated. If the new petition is denied, employment authorization will cease.

(viii) *Substitution of beneficiaries.* Beneficiaries of H–2B petitions that are approved for named or unnamed beneficiaries who have not been admitted may be substituted only if the employer can demonstrate that the total number of beneficiaries will not exceed the number of beneficiaries certified in the original temporary labor certification. Beneficiaries who were admitted to the United States may not be substituted without a new petition accompanied by a newly approved temporary labor certification.

(A) To substitute beneficiaries who were previously approved for consular processing but have not been admitted with aliens who are outside of the United States, the petitioner shall, by letter and a copy of the petition approval notice, notify the consular office at which the alien will apply for a visa or the port of entry where the alien will apply for admission. The petitioner shall also submit evidence of the qualifications of beneficiaries to the consular office or port of entry prior to issuance of a visa or admission, if applicable.

(B) To substitute beneficiaries who were previously approved for consular processing but have not been admitted with aliens who are currently in the United States, the petitioner shall file an amended petition with fees at the USCIS Service Center where the original petition was filed, with a copy of the original petition approval notice, a statement explaining why the substitution is necessary, evidence of the qualifications of beneficiaries, if applicable, evidence of the beneficiaries' current status in the United States, and evidence that the number of beneficiaries will not exceed the number allocated on the approved temporary labor certification, such as employment records or other documentary evidence to establish that the number of visas sought in the amended petition were not already issued. The amended petition must retain a period of employment within the same half of the same fiscal year as the original petition. Otherwise, a new temporary labor certification issued by DOL or the Governor of Guam and subsequent H–2B petition are required.

(ix) *Enforcement.* The Secretary of Labor may investigate employers to enforce compliance with the conditions of a petition and Department of Labor-approved temporary labor certification to admit or otherwise provide status to an H–2B worker.

(7) *Petition for alien trainee or participant in a special education exchange visitor program (H–3)*—(i) *Alien trainee.* The H–3 trainee is a nonimmigrant who seeks to enter the United States at the invitation of an organization or individual for the purpose of receiving training in any field of endeavor, such as agriculture, commerce, communications, finance, government, transportation, or the professions, as well as training in a purely industrial establishment. This category shall not apply to physicians, who are statutorily ineligible to use H–3 classification in order to receive any type of graduate medical education or training.

(A) *Externs.* A hospital approved by the American Medical Association or the American Osteopathic Association for either an internship or residency program may petition to classify as an H–3 trainee a medical student attending a medical school abroad, if the alien will engage in employment as an extern during his/her medical school vacation.

(B) *Nurses.* A petitioner may seek H–3 classification for a nurse who is not H–1 if it can be established that there is a genuine need for the nurse to receive a brief period of training that is unavailable in the alien's native country and such training is designed to benefit the nurse and the overseas employer upon the nurse's return to the country of origin, if:

(*1*) The beneficiary has obtained a full and unrestricted license to practice professional nursing in the country where the beneficiary obtained a nursing education, or such education was obtained in the United States or Canada; and

(*2*) The petitioner provides a statement certifying that the beneficiary is fully qualified under the laws governing the place where the training will be received to engage in such training, and that under those laws the petitioner is authorized to give the beneficiary the desired training.

(ii) *Evidence required for petition involving alien trainee*—(A) *Conditions.* The petitioner is required to demonstrate that:

(*1*) The proposed training is not available in the alien's own country;

(*2*) The beneficiary will not be placed in a position which is in the normal operation of the business and in which citizens and resident workers are regularly employed;

(*3*) The beneficiary will not engage in productive employment unless such employment is incidental and necessary to the training; and

(*4*) The training will benefit the beneficiary in pursuing a career outside the United States.

(B) *Description of training program.* Each petition for a trainee must include a statement which:

(*1*) Describes the type of training and supervision to be given, and the structure of the training program;

(*2*) Sets forth the proportion of time that will be devoted to productive employment;

(*3*) Shows the number of hours that will be spent, respectively, in classroom instruction and in on-the-job training;

(*4*) Describes the career abroad for which the training will prepare the alien;

(*5*) Indicates the reasons why such training cannot be obtained in the alien's country and why it is necessary for the alien to be trained in the United States; and

(*6*) Indicates the source of any remuneration received by the trainee and any benefit which will accrue to the petitioner for providing the training.

(iii) *Restrictions on training program for alien trainee.* A training program may not be approved which:

(A) Deals in generalities with no fixed schedule, objectives, or means of evaluation;

(B) Is incompatible with the nature of the petitioner's business or enterprise;

(C) Is on behalf of a beneficiary who already possesses substantial training and expertise in the proposed field of training;

(D) Is in a field in which it is unlikely that the knowledge or skill will be used outside the United States;

(E) Will result in productive employment beyond that which is incidental and necessary to the training;

(F) Is designed to recruit and train aliens for the ultimate staffing of domestic operations in the United States;

(G) Does not establish that the petitioner has the physical plant and sufficiently trained manpower to provide the training specified; or

(H) Is designed to extend the total allowable period of practical training previously authorized a nonimmigrant student.

(iv) *Petition for participant in a special education exchange visitor program*—(A) *General Requirements.* (*1*) The H–3 participant in a special education training program must be coming to the United States to participate in a structured program which provides for practical training and experience in the education of children with physical, mental, or emotional disabilities.

(*2*) The petition must be filed by a facility which has professionally trained staff and a structured program for providing education to children with disabilities, and for providing training and hands-on experience to participants in the special education exchange visitor program.

(*3*) The requirements in this section for alien trainees shall not apply to petitions for participants in a special education exchange visitor program.

(B) *Evidence.* An H–3 petition for a participant in a special education exchange visitor program shall be accompanied by:

(*1*) A description of the training program and the facility's professional staff and details of the alien's participation in the training program (any custodial care of children must be incidental to the training), and

(*2*) Evidence that the alien participant is nearing completion of a baccalaureate or higher degree in special education, or already holds such a degree, or has extensive prior training and experience in teaching children with physical, mental, or emotional disabilities.

(8) *Numerical limits*—(i) *Limits on affected categories.* During each fiscal year, the total number of aliens who can be provided nonimmigrant classification is limited as follows:

(A) Aliens classified as H–1B nonimmigrants, excluding those involved in Department of Defense research and development projects or coproduction projects, may not exceed the limits identified in section 214(g)(1)(A) of the Act.

(B) Aliens classified as H–1B nonimmigrants to work for DOD research and development projects or coproduction projects may not exceed 100 at any time.

(C) Aliens classified as H–2B nonimmigrants may not exceed 66,000.

(D) Aliens classified as H–3 nonimmigrant participants in a special education exchange visitor program may not exceed 50.

(E) Aliens classified as H–1C nonimmigrants may not exceed 500 in a fiscal year.

(ii) *Procedures.* (A) Each alien issued a visa or otherwise provided nonimmigrant status under sections 101(a)(15)(H)(i)(b), 101(a)(15)(H)(i)(c), or 101(a)(15)(H)(ii) of the Act shall be counted for purposes of any applicable numerical limit, unless otherwise exempt from such numerical limit. Requests for petition extension or extension of an alien's stay shall not be counted for the purpose of the numerical limit. The spouse and children of principal H aliens are classified as H–4 nonimmigrants and shall not be counted against numerical limits applicable to principals.

(B) When calculating the numerical limitations or the number of exemptions under section 214(g)(5)(C) of the Act for a given fiscal year, USCIS will make numbers available to petitions in the order in which the petitions are filed. USCIS will make projections of the number of petitions necessary to achieve the numerical limit of approvals, taking into account historical data related to approvals, denials, revocations, and other relevant factors. USCIS will monitor the number of petitions (including the number of beneficiaries requested when necessary) received and will notify the public of the date that USCIS has received the necessary number of petitions (the "final receipt date"). The day the news is published will not control the final receipt date. When necessary to ensure the fair and orderly allocation of numbers in a particular classification subject to a numerical limitation or the exemption under section 214(g)(5)(C) of the Act, USCIS may randomly select from among the petitions received on the final receipt date the remaining number of petitions deemed necessary to generate the numerical limit of approvals. This random selection will be made via computer-generated selection as validated by the Office of Immigration Statistics. Petitions subject to a numerical limitation not randomly selected or that were received after the final receipt date will be rejected. Petitions filed on behalf of aliens otherwise eligible for the exemption under section 214(g)(5)(C) of the Act not randomly selected or that were received after the final receipt date will be rejected if the numerical limitation under 214(g)(1) of the Act has been reached for that fiscal year. Petitions indicating that they are exempt from the numerical limitation but that are determined by USCIS after the final receipt date to be subject to the numerical limit will be denied and filing fees will not be returned or refunded. If the final receipt date is any of the first five business days on which petitions subject to the applicable numerical limit may be received (*i.e.*, if the numerical limit is reached on any one of the first five business days that filings can be made), USCIS will randomly apply all of the numbers among the petitions received on any of those five business days, conducting the random selection among the petitions subject to the exemption under section 214(g)(5)(C) of the Act first.

(C) When an approved petition is not used because the beneficiary(ies) does not apply for admission to the United States, the petitioner shall notify the Service Center Director who approved the petition that the number(s) has not been used. The petition shall be revoked pursuant to paragraph (h)(11)(ii) of this section and USCIS will take into account the unused number during the appropriate fiscal year.

(D) If the total numbers available in a fiscal year are used, new petitions and the accompanying fee shall be rejected and returned with a notice that numbers are unavailable for the particular nonimmigrant classification until the beginning of the next fiscal year. Petitions received after the total numbers available in a fiscal year are used stating that the alien beneficiaries are exempt from the numerical limitation will be denied and filing fees will not be returned or refunded if USCIS later determines that such beneficiaries are subject to the numerical limitation.

(E) The 500 H–1C nonimmigrant visas issued each fiscal year shall be allocated in the following manner:

(*1*) For each fiscal year, the number of visas issued to the states of California, Florida, Illinois, Michigan, New York, Ohio, Pennsylvania, and Texas shall not exceed 50 each (except as provided for in paragraph (h)(8)(ii)(F)(*3*) of this section).

(*2*) For each fiscal year, the number of visas issued to the states not listed in paragraph (h)(8)(ii)(F)(*1*) of this section shall not exceed 25 each (except as provided for in paragraph (h)(8)(ii)(F)(*3*) of this section).

(*3*) If the total number of visas available during the first three quarters of a fiscal year exceeds the number of approvable H–1C petitions during those quarters, visas may be issued during the last quarter of the fiscal year to nurses who will be working in a state whose cap has already been reached for that fiscal year.

(*4*) When an approved H–1C petition is not used because the alien(s) does not obtain H–1C classification, e.g., the alien is never admitted to the United States, or the alien never worked for the facility, the facility must notify the Service according to the instructions contained in paragraph (h)(11)(ii) of this section. The Service will subtract H–1C petitions approved in the current fiscal year that are later revoked from the total count of approved H–1C petitions, provided that the alien never commenced employment with the facility.

(*5*) If the number of alien nurses included in an H–1C petition exceeds the number available for the remainder of a fiscal year, the Service shall approve the petition for the beneficiaries to the allowable amount in the order that they are listed on the petition. The remaining beneficiaries will be considered for approval in the subsequent fiscal year.

(*6*) Once the 500 cap has been reached, the Service will reject any new petitions subsequently filed requesting a work start date prior to the first day of the next fiscal year.

(F) *Cap exemptions under sections 214(g)(5)(A) and (B) of the Act.* An alien is not subject to the numerical limitations identified in section 214(g)(1)(A) of the Act if the alien qualifies for an exemption under section 214(g)(5) of the Act. For purposes of section 214(g)(5)(A) and (B) of the Act:

(*1*) "Institution of higher education" has the same definition as described at section 101(a) of the Higher Education Act of 1965 (20 U.S.C. 1001(a)).

(*2*) A nonprofit entity shall be considered to be related to or affiliated with an institution of higher education if it satisfies any one of the following conditions:

(*i*) The nonprofit entity is connected to or associated with an institution of higher education through shared ownership or control by the same board or federation;

(*ii*) The nonprofit entity is operated by an institution of higher education;

(*iii*) The nonprofit entity is attached to an institution of higher education as a member, branch, cooperative, or subsidiary; or

(*iv*) The nonprofit entity has entered into a formal written affiliation agreement with an institution of higher education that establishes an active working relationship between the nonprofit entity and the institution of higher education for the purposes of research or education, and a fundamental activity of the nonprofit entity is to directly contribute to the research or education mission of the institution of higher education.

(*3*) An entity is considered a "nonprofit entity" if it meets the definition described at paragraph (h)(19)(iv) of this section. "Nonprofit research organization" and "governmental research organization" have the same definitions as described at paragraph (h)(19)(iii)(C) of this section.

(*4*) An H–1B beneficiary who is not directly employed by a qualifying institution, organization or entity identified in section 214(g)(5)(A) or (B) of the Act shall qualify for an exemption under such section if the H–1B beneficiary will spend the majority of his or her work time performing job duties at a qualifying institution, organization or entity and those job duties directly and predominately further the essential purpose, mission, objectives or functions of the qualifying institution, organization or entity, namely, either higher education, nonprofit research or government research. The burden is on the H–1B petitioner to establish that there is a nexus between the duties to be performed by the H–1B beneficiary and the essential purpose, mission, objectives or functions of the qualifying institution, organization or entity.

(*5*) If cap-exempt employment ceases, and if the alien is not the beneficiary of a new cap-exempt petition, then the alien will be subject to the cap if not previously counted within the 6-year period of authorized admission to which the cap-exempt employment applied. If cap-exempt employment converts to cap-subject employment subject to the numerical limitations in section 214(g)(1)(A) of the Act, USCIS may revoke the petition authorizing such employment consistent with paragraph (h)(11)(iii) of this section.

(*6*) Concurrent H–1B employment in a cap-subject position of an alien that qualifies for an exemption under section 214(g)(5)(A) or (B) of the Act shall not subject the alien to the numerical limitations in section 214(g)(1)(A) of the Act. When petitioning for concurrent cap-subject H–1B employment, the petitioner must demonstrate that the H–1B beneficiary is employed in valid H–1B status under a cap exemption under section 214(g)(5)(A) or (B) of the Act, the beneficiary's employment with the cap-exempt employer is expected to continue after the new cap-subject petition is approved, and the beneficiary can reasonably and concurrently perform the work described in each employer's respective positions.

(*i*) Validity of a petition for concurrent cap-subject H–1B employment approved under paragraph (h)(8)(ii)(F)(*6*) of this section cannot extend beyond the period of validity specified for the cap-exempt H–1B employment.

(*ii*) If H–1B employment subject to a cap exemption under section 214(g)(5)(A) or (B) of the Act is terminated by a petitioner, or otherwise ends before the end of the validity period listed on the approved petition filed on the alien's behalf, the alien who is concurrently employed in a cap-subject position becomes subject to the numerical limitations in section 214(g)(1)(A) of the Act, unless the alien was previously counted with respect to the 6-year period of authorized H–1B admission to which the petition applies or another exemption applies. If such an alien becomes subject to the numerical limitations in section 214(g)(1)(A) of the Act, USCIS may revoke the cap-subject petition described in paragraph (h)(8)(ii)(F)(*6*) of this section consistent with paragraph (h)(11)(iii) of this section.

(9) *Approval and validity of petition*—(i) *Approval*. The director shall consider all the evidence submitted and such other evidence as he or she may independently require to assist his or her adjudication. The director shall notify the petitioner of the approval of the petition on Form I–797, Notice of Action. The approval shall be as follows:

(A) The approval notice shall include the beneficiary's(ies') name(s) and classification and the petition's period of validity. A petition for more than one beneficiary and/or multiple services may be approved in whole or in part. The approval notice shall cover only those beneficiaries approved for classification under section 101(a)(15)(H) of the Act.

(B) The petition may not be filed or approved earlier than 6 months before the date of actual need for the beneficiary's services or training, except that an H–2B petition for a temporary nonagricultural worker may not be filed or approved more than 120 days before the date of the actual need for the beneficiary's temporary nonagricultural services that is identified on the temporary labor certification.

(ii) *Recording the validity of petitions*. Procedures for recording the validity period of petitions are:

(A) If a new H petition is approved before the date the petitioner indicates that the services or training will begin, the approved petition and approval notice shall show the actual dates requested by the petitoner as the validity period, not to exceed the limits specified by paragraph (h)(9)(iii) of this section or other Service policy.

(B) If a new H petition is approved after the date the petitioner indicates that the services or training will begin, the aproved petition and approval notice shall show a validity period commencing with the date of approval and ending with the date requested by the petitioner, as long as that date does not exceed either the limits specified by paragraph (h)(9)(iii) of this section or other Service policy.

(C) If the period of services or training requested by the petitioner exceeds the limit specified in paragraph (h)(9)(iii) of this section, the petition shall be approved only up to the limit specified in that paragraph.

(iii) *Validity*. The initial approval period of an H petition shall conform to the limits prescribed as follows:

(A)(*1*) *H–1B petition in a specialty occupation*. An approved petition classified under section 101(a)(15)(H)(i)(b) of the Act for an alien in a specialty occupation shall be valid for a period of up to three years but may not exceed the validity period of the labor condition application.

(*2*) *H–1B petition involving a DOD research and development or coproduction project*. An approved petition classified under section 101(a)(15)(H)(i)(b) of the Act for an alien involved in a DOD research and development project or a coproduction project shall be valid for a period of up to five years.

(*3*) *H–1B petition involving an alien of distinguished merit and ability in the field of fashion modeling*. An approved petition classified under section 101(a)(15)(H)(i)(b) of the Act for an alien of distinguished merit and ability in the field of fashion modeling shall be valid for a period of up to three years.

(B) *H–2B petition*. The approval of the petition to accord an alien a classification under section 101(a)(15)(H)(ii)(b) of the Act shall be valid for the period of the approved temporary labor certification.

(C)(*1*) *H–3 petition for alien trainee*. An approved petition for an alien trainee classified under section 101(a)(15)(H)(iii) of the Act shall be valid for a period of up to two years.

(*2*) *H–3 petition for alien participant in a special education training program*. An approved petition for an alien classified under section 101(a)(15)(H)(iii) of the Act as a participant in a special education exchange visitor program shall be valid for a period of up to 18 months.

(D) *H–1C petition for a registered nurse*. An approved petition for an alien classified under section 101(a)(15)(H)(i)(c) of the Act shall be valid for a period of 3 years.

(iv) *H–4 dependents*. The spouse and children of an H nonimmigrant, if they are accompanying or following to join such H nonimmigrant in the United States, may be admitted, if otherwise admissible, as H–4 nonimmigrants for the same period of admission or extension as the principal spouse or parent. H–4 nonimmigrant status does not confer eligibility for employment authorization incident to status. An H–4 nonimmigrant spouse of an H–1B nonimmigrant may be eligible for employment authorization only if the H–1B nonimmigrant is the beneficiary of an approved Immigrant Petition for Alien Worker, or successor form, or the H–1B nonimmigrant's period of stay in H–1B status is authorized in the United States under sections 106(a) and (b) of the American Competitiveness in the Twenty-first Century Act of 2000 (AC21), Public Law 106–313, as amended by the 21st Century Department of Justice Appropriations Authorization Act, Public Law 107–273 (2002). To request employment authorization, an eligible H–4 nonimmigrant spouse must file an Application for Employment Authorization, or a successor form, in accordance with 8 CFR 274a.13 and the form instructions. An Application for Employment Authorization must be accompanied by documentary evidence establishing eligibility, including evidence of the spousal relationship and that the principal H–1B is the beneficiary of an approved Immigrant Petition for Alien Worker or has been provided H–1B status under sections 106(a) and (b) of AC21, as amended by the 21st Century Department of Justice Appropriations Authorization Act, the H–1B beneficiary is currently in H–1B status, and the H–4 nonimmigrant spouse is currently in H–4 status.

(10) *Denial of petition*—(i) *Multiple beneficiaries*. A petition for multiple beneficiaries may be denied in whole or in part.

(ii) *Notice of denial*. The petitioner shall be notified of the reasons for the denial and of the right to appeal the denial of the petition under 8 CFR part 103. The petition will be denied if it is determined that the statements on the petition were inaccurate, fraudulent, or misrepresented a material fact. There is no appeal from a decision to deny an extension of stay to the alien.

(11) *Revocation of approval of petition*—(i) *General*. (A) The petitioner shall immediately notify the Service of any changes in the terms and conditions of employment of a beneficiary which may affect eligibility under section 101(a)(15)(H) of the Act and paragraph (h) of this section. An amended petition on Form I-129 should be filed when the petitioner continues to employ the beneficiary. If the petitioner no longer employs the beneficiary, the petitioner shall send a letter explaining the change(s) to the director who approved the petition. However, H-2A and H-2B petitioners must send notification to DHS pursuant to paragraphs (h)(5)(vi) and (h)(6)(i)(F) of this section respectively.

(B) The director may revoke a petition at any time, even after the expiration of the petition.

(ii) *Immediate and automatic revocation*. The approval of any petition is immediately and automatically revoked if the petitioner goes out of business, files a written withdrawal of the petition, or the Department of Labor revokes the labor certification upon which the petition is based.

(iii) *Revocation on notice*—(A) *Grounds for revocation*. The director shall send to the petitioner a notice of intent to revoke the petition in relevant part if he or she finds that:

(*1*) The beneficiary is no longer employed by the petitioner in the capacity specified in the petition, or if the beneficiary is no longer receiving training as specified in the petition; or

(*2*) The statement of facts contained in the petition or on the application for a temporary labor certification was not true and correct, inaccurate, fraudulent, or misrepresented a material fact; or

(*3*) The petitioner violated terms and conditions of the approved petition; or

(*4*) The petitioner violated requirements of section 101(a)(15)(H) of the Act or paragraph (h) of this section; or

(*5*) The approval of the petition violated pargraph (h) of this section or involved gross error.

(B) *Notice and decision*. The notice of intent to revoke shall contain a detailed statement of the grounds for the revocation and the time period allowed for the petitioner's rebuttal. The petitioner may submit evidence in rebuttal within 30 days of receipt of the notice. The director shall consider all relevant evidence presented in deciding whether to revoke the petition in whole or in part. If the petition is revoked in part, the remainder of the petition shall remain approved and a revised approval notice shall be sent to the petitioner with the revocation notice.

(12) *Appeal of a denial or a revocation of a petition*—(i) *Denial*. A petition denied in whole or in part may be appealed under part 103 of this chapter.

(ii) *Revocation*. A petition that has been revoked on notice in whole or in part may be appealed under part 103 of this chapter. Automatic revocations may not be appealed.

(13) *Admission*—(i) *General*. (A) Except as set forth in 8 CFR 214.1(l) with respect to H-1B beneficiaries and their dependents and paragraph (h)(5)(viii)(B) of this section with respect to H-2A beneficiaries, a beneficiary shall be admitted to the United States for the validity period of the petition, plus a period of up to 10 days before the validity period begins and 10 days after the validity period ends. The beneficiary may not work except during the validity period of the petition.

(B) When an alien in an H classification has spent the maximum allowable period of stay in the United States, a new petition under sections 101(a)(15)(H) or (L) of the Act may not be approved unless that alien has resided and been physically present outside the United States, except for brief trips for business or pleasure, for the time limit imposed on the particular H classification. Brief trips to the United States for business or pleasure during the required time abroad are not interruptive, but do not count towards fulfillment of the required time abroad. A certain period of absence from the United States of H-2A and H-2B aliens can interrupt the accrual of time spent in such status against the 3-year limit set forth in 8 CFR 214.2(h)(13)(iv). The petitioner shall provide information about the alien's employment, place of residence, and the dates and purposes of any trips to the United States during the period that the alien was required to reside abroad.

(ii) *H–1C limitation on admission.* The maximum period of admission for an H–1C nonimmigrant alien is 3 years. The maximum period of admission for an H–1C alien begins on the date the H–1C alien is admitted to the United and ends on the third anniversary of the alien's admission date. Periods of time spent out of the United States for business or personal reasons during the validity period of the H–1C petition count towards the alien's maximum period of admission. When an H–1C alien has reached the 3-year maximum period of admission, the H–1C alien is no longer eligible for admission to the United States as an H–1C nonimmigrant alien.

(iii) *H–1B limitation on admission*—(A) *Alien in a specialty occupation or an alien of distinguished merit and ability in the field of fashion modeling.* An H–1B alien in a specialty occupation or an alien of distinguished merit and ability who has spent six years in the United States under section 101(a)(15)(H) and/or (L) of the Act may not seek extension, change status, or be readmitted to the United States under section 101(a)(15) (H) or (L) of the Act unless the alien has resided and been physically present outside the United States, except for brief trips for business or pleasure, for the immediate prior year.

(B) *Alien involved in a DOD research and development or coproduction project.* An H–1B alien involved in a DOD research and development or coproduction project who has spent 10 years in the United States under section 101(a)(15) (H) and/or (L) of the Act may not seek extension, change status, or be readmitted to the United States under section 101(a)(15) (H) or (L) of the Act to perform services involving a DOD research and development project or coproduction project. A new petition or change of status under section 101(a)(15) (H) or (L) of the Act may not be approved for such an alien unless the alien has resided and been physically present outside the United States, except for brief trips for business or pleasure, for the immediate prior year.

(C) *Calculating the maximum H–1B admission period.* Time spent physically outside the United States exceeding 24 hours by an alien during the validity of an H–1B petition that was approved on the alien's behalf shall not be considered for purposes of calculating the alien's total period of authorized admission under section 214(g)(4) of the Act, regardless of whether such time meaningfully interrupts the alien's stay in H–1B status and the reason for the alien's absence. Accordingly, such remaining time may be recaptured in a subsequent H–1B petition on behalf of the alien, at any time before the alien uses the full period of H–1B admission described in section 214(g)(4) of the Act.

(*1*) It is the H–1B petitioner's burden to request and demonstrate the specific amount of time for recapture on behalf of the beneficiary. The beneficiary may provide appropriate evidence, such as copies of passport stamps, Arrival-Departure Records (Form I–94), or airline tickets, together with a chart, indicating the dates spent outside of the United States, and referencing the relevant independent documentary evidence, when seeking to recapture the alien's time spent outside the United States. Based on the evidence provided, USCIS may grant all, part, or none of the recapture period requested.

(*2*) If the beneficiary was previously counted toward the H–1B numerical cap under section 214(g)(1) of the Act with respect to the 6-year maximum period of H–1B admission from which recapture is sought, the H–1B petition seeking to recapture a period of stay as an H–1B nonimmigrant will not subject the beneficiary to the H–1B numerical cap, whether or not the alien has been physically outside the United States for 1 year or more and would be otherwise eligible for a new period of admission under such section of the Act. An H–1B petitioner may either seek such recapture on behalf of the alien or, consistent with paragraph (h)(13)(iii) of this section, seek a new period of admission on behalf of the alien under section 214(g)(1) of the Act.

(D) *Lengthy adjudication delay exemption from 214(g)(4) of the Act.* (*1*) An alien who is in H–1B status or has previously held H–1B status is eligible for H–1B status beyond the 6-year limitation under section 214(g)(4) of the Act, if at least 365 days have elapsed since:

(*i*) The filing of a labor certification with the Department of Labor on the alien's behalf, if such certification is required for the alien to obtain status under section 203(b) of the Act; or

(*ii*) The filing of an immigrant visa petition with USCIS on the alien's behalf to accord classification under section 203(b) of the Act.

(*2*) H–1B approvals under paragraph (h)(13)(iii)(D) of this section may be granted in up to 1-year increments until either the approved permanent labor certification expires or a final decision has been made to:

(*i*) Deny the application for permanent labor certification, or, if approved, to revoke or invalidate such approval;

(*ii*) Deny the immigrant visa petition, or, if approved, revoke such approval;

(*iii*) Deny or approve the alien's application for an immigrant visa or application to adjust status to lawful permanent residence; or

(*iv*) Administratively or otherwise close the application for permanent labor certification, immigrant visa petition, or application to adjust status.

(*3*) *No final decision while appeal available or pending.* A decision to deny or revoke an application for labor certification, or to deny or revoke the approval of an immigrant visa petition, will not be considered final under paragraph (h)(13)(iii)(D)(*2*)(*i*) or (*ii*) of this section during the period authorized for filing an appeal of the decision, or while an appeal is pending.

(*4*) *Substitution of beneficiaries.* An alien who has been replaced by another alien, on or before July 16, 2007, as the beneficiary of an approved permanent labor certification may not rely on that permanent labor certification to establish eligibility for H–1B status based on this lengthy adjudication delay exemption. Except for a substitution of a beneficiary that occurred on or before July 16, 2007, an alien establishing eligibility for this lengthy adjudication delay exemption based on a pending or approved labor certification must be the named beneficiary listed on the permanent labor certification.

(*5*) *Advance filing.* A petitioner may file an H–1B petition seeking a lengthy adjudication delay exemption under paragraph (h)(13)(iii)(D) of this section within 6 months of the requested H–1B start date. The petition may be filed before 365 days have elapsed since the labor certification application or immigrant visa petition was filed with the Department of Labor or USCIS, respectively, provided that the application for labor certification or immigrant visa petition must have been filed at least 365 days prior to the date the period of admission authorized under this exemption will take effect. The petitioner may request any time remaining to the beneficiary under the maximum period of admission described at section 214(g)(4) of the Act along with the exemption request, but in no case may the approved H–1B period of validity exceed the limits specified by paragraph (h)(9)(iii) of this section. Time remaining to the beneficiary under the maximum period of admission described at section 214(g)(4) of the Act may include any request to recapture unused H–1B, L–1A, or L–1B time spent outside of the United States.

(*6*) *Petitioners seeking exemption.* The H–1B petitioner need not be the employer that filed the application for labor certification or immigrant visa petition that is used to qualify for this exemption.

(*7*) *Subsequent exemption approvals after the 7th year.* The qualifying labor certification or immigrant visa petition need not be the same as that used to qualify for the initial exemption under paragraph (h)(13)(iii)(D) of this section.

(*8*) *Aggregation of time not permitted.* A petitioner may not aggregate the number of days that have elapsed since the filing of one labor certification or immigrant visa petition with the number of days that have elapsed since the filing of another such application or petition to meet the 365-day requirement.

(*9*) *Exemption eligibility.* Only a principal beneficiary of a nonfrivolous labor certification application or immigrant visa petition filed on his or her behalf may be eligible under paragraph (h)(13)(iii)(D) of this section for an exemption to the maximum period of admission under section 214(g)(4) of the Act.

(*10*) *Limits on future exemptions from the lengthy adjudication delay.* An alien is ineligible for the lengthy adjudication delay exemption under paragraph (h)(13)(iii)(D) of this section if the alien is the beneficiary of an approved petition under section 203(b) of the Act and fails to file an adjustment of status application or apply for an immigrant visa within 1 year of an immigrant visa being authorized for issuance based on his or her preference category and country of chargeability. If the accrual of such 1-year period is interrupted by the unavailability of an immigrant visa, a new 1-year period shall be afforded when an immigrant visa again becomes immediately available. USCIS may excuse a failure to file in its discretion if the alien establishes that the failure to apply was due to circumstances beyond his or her control. The limitations described in this paragraph apply to any approved immigrant visa petition under section 203(b) of the Act, including petitions withdrawn by the petitioner or those filed by a petitioner whose business terminates 180 days or more after approval.

(E) *Per-country limitation exemption from section 214(g)(4) of the Act.* An alien who currently maintains or previously held H–1B status, who is the beneficiary of an approved immigrant visa petition for classification under section 203(b)(1), (2), or (3) of the Act, and who is eligible to be granted that immigrant status but for application of the per country limitation, is eligible for H–1B status beyond the 6-year limitation under section 214(g)(4) of the Act. The petitioner must demonstrate such visa unavailability as of the date the H–1B petition is filed with USCIS.

(*1*) *Validity periods.* USCIS may grant validity periods for petitions approved under this paragraph in increments of up to 3 years for as long as the alien remains eligible for this exemption.

(*2*) H–1B approvals under paragraph (h)(13)(iii)(E) of this section may be granted until a final decision has been made to:

(*i*) Revoke the approval of the immigrant visa petition; or

(*ii*) Approve or deny the alien's application for an immigrant visa or application to adjust status to lawful permanent residence.

(*3*) *Current H–1B status not required.* An alien who is not in H–1B status at the time the H–1B petition on his or her behalf is filed, including an alien who is not in the United States, may seek an exemption of the 6-year limitation under 214(g)(4) of the Act under this clause, if otherwise eligible.

(*4*) *Subsequent petitioners may seek exemptions.* The H–1B petitioner need not be the employer that filed the immigrant visa petition that is used to qualify for this exemption. An H–1B petition may be approved under paragraph (h)(13)(iii)(E) of this section with respect to any approved immigrant visa petition, and a subsequent H–1B petition may be approved with respect to a different approved immigrant visa petition on behalf of the same alien.

(*5*) *Advance filing.* A petitioner may file an H–1B petition seeking a per-country limitation exemption under paragraph (h)(13)(iii)(E) of this section within 6 months of the requested H–1B start date. The petitioner may request any time remaining to the beneficiary under the maximum period of admission described in section 214(g)(4) of the Act along with the exemption request, but in no case may the H–1B approval period exceed the limits specified by paragraph (h)(9)(iii) of this section.

(*6*) *Exemption eligibility.* Only the principal beneficiary of an approved immigrant visa petition for classification under section 203(b)(1), (2), or (3) of the Act may be eligible under paragraph (h)(13)(iii)(E) of this section for an exemption to the maximum period of admission under section 214(g)(4) of the Act.

(iv) *H–2B and H–3 limitation on admission.* An H–2B alien who has spent 3 years in the United States under section 101(a)(15)(H) and/or (L) of the Act may not seek extension, change status, or be readmitted to the United States under sections 101(a)(15)(H) and/or (L) of the Act unless the alien has resided and been physically present outside the United States for the immediately preceding 3 months. An H–3 alien participant in a special education program who has spent 18 months in the United States under sections 101(a)(15)(H) and/or (L) of the Act; and an H–3 alien trainee who has spent 24 months in the United States under sections 101(a)(15)(H) and/or (L) of the Act may not seek extension, change status, or be readmitted to the United States under sections 101(a)(15)(H) and/or (L) of the Act unless the alien has resided and been physically present outside the United States for the immediate prior 6 months.

(v) *Exceptions.* The limitations in paragraphs (h)(13)(iii) through (h)(13)(iv) of this section shall not apply to H–1B, H–2B, and H–3 aliens who did not reside continually in the United States and whose employment in the United States was seasonal or intermittent or was for an aggregate of 6 months or less per year. In addition, the limitations shall not apply to aliens who reside abroad and regularly commute to the United States to engage in part-time employment. An absence from the United States can interrupt the accrual of time spent as an H–2B nonimmigrant against the 3-year limit. If the accumulated stay is 18 months or less, an absence is interruptive if it lasts for at least 45 days. If the accumulated stay is greater than 18 months, an absence is interruptive if it lasts for at least two months. To qualify for this exception, the petitioner and the alien must provide clear and convincing proof that the alien qualifies for such an exception. Such proof shall consist of evidence such as arrival and departure records, copies of tax returns, and records of employment abroad.

(14) *Extension of visa petition validity.* The petitioner shall file a request for a petition extension on Form I–129 to extend the validity of the original petition under section 101(a)(15)(H) of the Act. Supporting evidence is not required unless requested by the director. A request for a petition extension may be filed only if the validity of the original petition has not expired.

(15) *Extension of stay*—(i) *General.* The petitioner shall apply for extension of an alien's stay in the United States by filing a petition extension on Form I–129 accompanied by the documents described for the particular classification in paragraph (h)(15)(ii) of this section. The petitioner must also request a petition extension. The dates of extension shall be the same for the petition and the beneficiary's extension of stay. The beneficiary must be physically present in the United States at the time of the filing of the extension of stay. Even though the requests to extend the petition and the alien's stay are combined on the petition, the director shall make a separate determination on each. If the alien is required to leave the United States for business or personal reasons while the extension requests are pending, the petitioner may request the director to cable notification of approval of the petition extension to the consular office abroad where the alien will apply for a visa. When the total period of stay in an H classification has been reached, no further extensions may be granted.

(ii) *Extension periods*—(A) *H–1C extension of stay.* The maximum period of admission for an H–1C alien is 3 years. An H–1C alien who was initially admitted to the United States for less than 3 years may receive an extension of stay up to the third anniversary date of his or her initial admission. An H–1C nonimmigrant may not receive an extension of stay beyond the third anniversary date of his or her initial admission to the United States.

(B) *H–1B extension of stay*—*(1) Alien in a specialty occupation or an alien of distinguished merit and ability in the field of fashion modeling.* An extension of stay may be authorized for a period of up to three years for a beneficiary of an H–1B petition in a specialty occupation or an alien of distinguished merit and ability. The alien's total period of stay may not exceed six years. The request for extension must be accompanied by either a new or a photocopy of the prior certification from the Department of Labor that the petitioner continues to have on file a labor condition application valid for the period of time requested for the occupation.

(2) Alien in a DOD research and development or coproduction project. An extension of stay may be authorized for a period up to five years for the beneficiary of an H–1B petition involving a DOD research and development project or coproduction project. The total period of stay may not exceed 10 years.

(C) *H–2A or H–2B extension of stay.* An extension of stay for the beneficiary of an H–2A or H–2B petition may be authorized for the validity of the labor certification or for a period of up to one year, except as provided for in paragraph (h)(5)(x) of this section. The alien's total period of stay as an H–2A or H–2B worker may not exceed three years, except that in the Virgin Islands, the alien's total period of stay may not exceed 45 days.

(D) *H–3 extension of stay*. An extension of stay may be authorized for the length of the training program for a total period of stay as an H–3 trainee not to exceed two years, or for a total period of stay as a participant in a special education training program not to exceed 18 months.

(16) *Effect of approval of a permanent labor certification or filing of a preference petition on H classification*—(i) *H–1B or H–1C classification*. The approval of a permanent labor certification or the filing of a preference petition for an alien shall not be a basis for denying an H–1C or H–1B petition or a request to extend such a petition, or the alien's admission, change of status, or extension of stay. The alien may legitimately come to the United States for a temporary period as an H–1C or H–1B nonimmigrant and depart voluntarily at the end of his or her authorized stay and, at the same time, lawfully seek to become a permanent resident of the United States.

(ii) *H–2A, H–2B, and H–3 classification*. The approval of a permanent labor certification, or the filing of a preference petition for an alien currently employed by or in a training position with the same petitioner, shall be a reason, by itself, to deny the alien's extension of stay.

(17) *Effect of a strike*. (i) If the Secretary of Labor certifies to the Commissioner that a strike or other labor dispute involving a work stoppage of workers is in progress in the occupation and at the place where the beneficiary is to be employed or trained, and that the employment of training of the beneficiary would adversely affect the wages and working conditions of U.S. citizens and lawful resident workers:

(A) A petition to classify an alien as a nonimmigrant as defined in section 101(a)(15)(H) of the Act shall be denied.

(B) If a petition has already been approved, but the alien has not yet entered the United States, or has entered the United States but has not commenced the employment, the approval of the petition is automatically suspended, and the application for admission on the basis of the petition shall be denied.

(ii) If there is a strike or other labor dispute involving a work stoppage of workers in progress, but such strike or other labor dispute is not certified under paragraph (h)(17)(i), the Commissioner shall not deny a petition or suspend an approved petition.

(iii) If the alien has already commenced employment in the United States under an approved petition and is participating in a strike or other labor dispute involving a work stoppage of workers, whether or not such strike or other labor dispute has been certified by the Department of Labor, the alien shall not be deemed to be failing to maintain his or her status solely on account of past, present, or future participation in a strike or other labor dispute involving a work stoppage of workers, but is subject to the following terms and conditions:

(A) The alien shall remain subject to all applicable provisions of the Immigration and Nationality Act, and regulations promulgated in the same manner as all other H nonimmigrants;

(B) The status and authorized period of stay of such an alien is not modified or extended in any way by virtue of his or her participation in a strike or other labor dispute involving a work stoppage of workers; and

(C) Although participation by an H nonimmigrant alien in a strike or other labor dispute involving a work stoppage of workers will not constitute a ground for deportation, any alien who violates his or her status or who remains in the United States after his or her authorized period of stay has expired will be subject to deportation.

(18) *Use of approval notice, Form I–797*. The Service shall notify the petitioner on Form I–797 whenever a visa petition, an extension of a visa petition, or an alien's extension of stay is approved under the H classification. The beneficiary of an H petition who does not require a nonimmigrant visa may present a copy of the approval notice at a port of entry to facilitate entry into the United States. A beneficiary

who is required to present a visa for admission and whose visa will have expired before the date of his or her intended return may use a copy of Form I–797 to apply for a new or revalidated visa during the validity period of the petition. The copy of Form I–797 shall be retained by the beneficiary and presented during the validity of the petition when reentering the United States to resume the same employment with the same petitioner.

(19) *Additional fee for filing certain H–1B petitions.* (i) A United States employer (other than an exempt employer defined in paragraph (h)(19)(iii) of this section, or an employer filing a petition described in paragraph (h)(19)(v) of this section) who files a Petition for Nonimmigrant Worker (Form I–129) must include the additional American Competitiveness and Workforce Improvement Act (ACWIA) fee referenced in §103.7(b)(1) of this chapter, if the petition is filed for any of the following purposes:

(A) An initial grant of H–1B status under section 101(a)(15)(H)(i)(b) of the Act;

(B) An initial extension of stay, as provided in paragraph (h)(15)(i) of this section; or

(C) Authorization for a change in employers, as provided in paragraph (h)(2)(i)(D) of this section.

(ii) A petitioner must submit with the petition the ACWIA fee, and any other applicable fees, in accordance with §103.7 of this chapter, and form instructions. Payment of all applicable fees must be made at the same time, but the petitioner may submit separate checks. USCIS will accept payment of the ACWIA fee only from the United States employer or its representative of record, as defined in 8 CFR 103.2(a) and 8 CFR part 292.

(iii) The following exempt organizations are not required to pay the additional fee:

(A) *An institution of higher education,* as defined in section 101(a) of the Higher Education Act of 1965;

(B) *An affiliated or related nonprofit entity.* A nonprofit entity shall be considered to be related to or affiliated with an institution of higher education if it satisfies any one of the following conditions:

(*1*) The nonprofit entity is connected to or associated with an institution of higher education through shared ownership or control by the same board or federation;

(*2*) The nonprofit entity is operated by an institution of higher education;

(*3*) The nonprofit entity is attached to an institution of higher education as a member, branch, cooperative, or subsidiary; or

(*4*) The nonprofit entity has entered into a formal written affiliation agreement with an institution of higher education that establishes an active working relationship between the nonprofit entity and the institution of higher education for the purposes of research or education, and a fundamental activity of the nonprofit entity is to directly contribute to the research or education mission of the institution of higher education;

(C) *A nonprofit research organization or governmental research organization.* A nonprofit research organization is an organization that is primarily engaged in basic research and/or applied research. A governmental research organization is a federal, state, or local entity whose primary mission is the performance or promotion of basic research and/or applied research. Basic research is general research to gain more comprehensive knowledge or understanding of the subject under study, without specific applications in mind. Basic research is also research that advances scientific knowledge, but does not have specific immediate commercial objectives although it may be in fields of present or potential commercial interest. It may include research and investigation in the sciences, social sciences, or humanities. Applied research is research to gain knowledge or understanding to determine the means by which a specific, recognized need may be met. Applied research includes investigations oriented to discovering new scientific knowledge that has specific commercial objectives with respect to products, processes, or services. It may include research and investigation in the sciences, social sciencies, or humanities;

(D) A primary or secondary education institution; or

(E) A nonprofit entity which engages in an established curriculum-related clinical training of students registered at an institution of higher education.

(iv) *Non-profit or tax exempt organizations.* For purposes of paragraphs (h)(19)(iii) (B) and (C) of this section, a nonprofit organization or entity is:

(A) Defined as a tax exempt organization under the Internal Revenue Code of 1986, section 501(c)(3), (c)(4) or (c)(6), 26 U.S.C. 501(c)(3), (c)(4) or (c)(6), and

(B) Has been approved as a tax exempt organization for research or educational purposes by the Internal Revenue Service.

(v) *Filing situations where the* American Competitiveness and Workforce Improvement Act of 1998 *(ACWIA) fee is not required.* The ACWIA fee is not required if:

(A) The petition is an amended H–1B petition that does not contain any requests for an extension of stay;

(B) The petition is an H–1B petition filed for the sole purpose of correcting a Service error; or

(C) The petition is the second or subsequent request for an extension of stay filed by the employer regardless of when the first extension of stay was filed or whether the ACWIA fee was paid on the initial petition or the first extension of stay.

(vi) *ACWIA fee exemption evidence.* (A) Employer claiming to be exempt. An employer claiming to be exempt from the ACWIA fee must file a Petition for Nonimmigrant Worker (Form I–129), in accordance with the form instructions, including supporting evidence establishing that it meets one of the exemptions described at paragraph (h)(19)(iii) of this section. A United States employer claiming an exemption from the ACWIA fee on the basis that it is a non-profit research organization must submit evidence that it has tax exempt status under the Internal Revenue Code of 1986, section 501(c)(3), (c)(4) or (c)(6), 26 U.S.C. 501(c)(3), (c)(4) or (c)(6). All other employers claiming an exemption must submit a statement describing why the organization or entity is exempt.

(B) Exempt filing situations. Any non-exempt employer who claims that the ACWIA fee does not apply with respect to a particular filing for one of the reasons described in paragraph (h)(19)(v) of this section must indicate why the ACWIA fee is not required.

(20) *Retaliatory action claims.* If credible documentary evidence is provided in support of a petition seeking an extension of H–1B stay in or change of status to another classification indicating that the beneficiary faced retaliatory action from his or her employer based on a report regarding a violation of that employer's labor condition application obligations under section 212(n)(2)(C)(iv) of the Act, USCIS may consider a loss or failure to maintain H–1B status by the beneficiary related to such violation as due to, and commensurate with, "extraordinary circumstances" as defined by §214.1(c)(4) and 8 CFR 248.1(b).

(i) *Representatives of information media.* The admission of an alien of the class defined in section 101(a)(15)(I) of the Act constitutes an agreement by the alien not to change the information medium or his or her employer until he or she obtains permission to do so from the district director having jurisdiction over his or her residence. An alien classified as an information media nonimmigrant (I) may be authorized admission for the duration of employment.

(j) *Exchange aliens*—(1) *General*—(i) *Eligibility for admission.* A nonimmigrant exchange visitor and his or her accompanying spouse and minor children may be admitted into the United States in J–1 and J–2 classifications under section 101(a)(15)(J) of the Act, if the exchange visitor and his or her accompanying spouse and children each presents a SEVIS Form DS–2019 issued in his or her own name by a program approved by the Department of State for participation by J–1 exchange visitors. Prior to August 1, 2003, if exigent circumstances are demonstrated, the Service will allow the dependent of an exchange visitor possessing a SEVIS Form DS–2019 to enter the United States using a copy of the exchange visitor's SEVIS Form DS–2019. However, where the exchange visitor presents a properly completed Form DS–2019, Certificate of Eligibility for Exchange Visitor (J–1) Status, which was issued to the J–1 exchange visitor by a program approved by the Department of State for participation by exchange visitors and which remains valid for the admission of the exchange visitor, the accompanying spouse and children may be admitted on the basis of the J–1's non-SEVIS Form DS–2019.

(ii) *Admission period.* An exchange alien, and J–2 spouse and children, may be admitted for a period up to 30 days before the report date or start of the approved program listed on Form DS–2019. The initial admission of an exchange visitor, spouse and children may not exceed the period specified on Form DS–2019, plus a period of 30 days for the purposes of travel or for the period designated by the Commissioner as provided in paragraph (j)(1)(vi) of this section. Regulations of the Department of State published at 22 CFR part 62 give general limitations on the stay of the various classes of exchange visitors. A spouse or child may not be admitted for longer than the principal exchange visitor.

(iii) *Readmission.* An exchange alien may be readmitted to the United States for the remainder of the time authorized on Form I–94, without presenting Form IAP–66, if the alien is returning from a visit solely to foreign contiguous territory or adjacent islands after an absence of less than 30 days and if the original Form I–94 is presented. All other exchange aliens must present a valid Form IAP–66. An original Form IAP–66 or copy three (the pink copy) of a previously issued form presented by an exchange alien returning from a temporary absence shall be retained by the exchange alien for re-entries during the balance of the alien's stay.

(iv) *Extensions of Stay.* If an exchange alien requires an extension beyond the initial admission period, the alien shall apply by submitting a new Form DS–2019 which indicates the date to which the alien's program is extended. The extension may not exceed the period specified on Form DS–2019, plus a period of 30 days for the purpose of travel. Extensions of stay for the alien's spouse and children require, as an attachment to Form DS–2019, Form I–94 for each dependent, and a list containing the names of the applicants, dates and places of birth, passport numbers, issuing countries, and expiration dates. An accompanying spouse or child may not be granted an extension of stay for longer than the principal exchange alien.

(v) *Employment.* (A) The accompanying spouse and minor children of a J–1 exchange visitor may accept employment only with authorization by the Immigration and Naturalization Service. A request for employment authorization must be made on Form I–765, Application for Employment Authorization, with fee, as required by the Service, to the district director having jurisdiction over the J–1 exchange visitor's temporary residence in the United States. Income from the spouse's or dependent's employment may be used to support the family's customary recreational and cultural activities and related travel, among other things. Employment will not be authorized if this income is needed to support the J–1 principal alien.

(B) J–2 employment may be authorized for the duration of the J–1 principal alien's authorized stay as indicated on Form I–94 or a period of four years, whichever is shorter. The employment authorization is valid only if the J–1 is maintaining status. Where a J–2 spouse or dependent child has filed a timely application for extension of stay, only upon approval of the request for extension of stay may he or she apply for a renewal of the employment authorization on a Form I–765 with the required fee.

(vi) *Extension of duration of status.* The Commissioner may, by notice in the FEDERAL REGISTER, at any time she determines that the H–1B numerical limitation as described in section 214(g)(1)(A) of the Act will likely be reached prior to the end of a current fiscal year, extend for such a period of time as the Commissioner deems necessary to complete the adjudication of the H–1B application, the duration of status of any J–1 alien on behalf of whom an employer has timely filed an application for change of status to H–1B. The alien, in accordance with 8 CFR part 248, must not have violated the terms of his or her nonimmigrant stay and is not subject to the 2-year foreign residence requirement at 212(e) of the Act. Any J–1 student whose duration of status has been extended shall be considered to be maintaining lawful nonimmigrant status for all purposes under the Act, provided that the alien does not violate the terms and conditions of his or her J nonimmigrant stay. An extension made under this paragraph also applies to the J–2 dependent aliens.

(vii) *Use of SEVIS.* At a date to be established by the Department of State, the use of the Student and Exchange Visitor Information System (SEVIS) will become mandatory for designated program sponsors. After that date, which will be announced by publication in the FEDERAL REGISTER, all designated program sponsors must begin issuance of the SEVIS Form DS–2019.

(viii) *Current name and address.* A J–1 exchange visitor must inform the Service and the responsible officer of the exchange visitor program of any legal changes to his or her name or of any change of address, within 10 days of the change, in a manner prescribed by the program sponsor. A J–1 exchange visitor enrolled in a SEVIS program can satisfy the requirement in 8 CFR 265.1 of notifying the Service by providing a notice of a change of address within 10 days to the responsible officer, who in turn shall enter the information in SEVIS within 21 days of notification by the exchange visitor. A J–1 exchange visitor enrolled at a non-SEVIS program must submit a change of address to the Service, as provided in 8 CFR 265.1, within 10 days of the change. Except in the case of an exchange visitor who cannot receive mail where he or she resides, the address provided by the exchange visitor must be the actual physical location where the exchange visitor resides rather than a mailing address. In cases where an exchange visitor provides a mailing address, the exchange visitor program must maintain a record of, and must provide upon request from the Service, the actual physical location where the exchange visitor resides.

(2) *Special reporting requirement.* Each exchange alien participating in a program of graduate medical education or training shall file Form I–644 (Supplementary Statement for Graduate Medical Trainees) annually with the Service attesting to the conditions as specified on the form. The exchange alien shall also submit Form I–644 as an attachment to a completed Form DS–2019 when applying for an extension of stay.

(3) *Alien in cancelled programs.* When the approval of an exchange visitor program is withdrawn by the Director of the United States Information Agency, the district director shall send a notice of the withdrawal to each participant in the program and a copy of each such notice shall be sent to the program sponsor. If the exchange visitor is currently engaged in activities authorized by the cancelled program, the participant is authorized to remain in the United States to engage in those activities until expiration of the period of stay previously authorized. The district director shall notify participants in cancelled programs that permission to remain in the United States as an exchange visitor, or extension of stay may be obtained if the participant is accepted in another approved program and a Form DS–2019, executed by the new program sponsor, is submitted. In this case, a release from the sponsor of the cancelled program will not be required.

(4) *Eligibility requirements for section 101(a)(15)(J) classification for aliens desiring to participate in programs under which they will receive graduate medical education or training*—(i) *Requirements.* Any alien coming to the United States as an exchange visitor to participate in a program under which the alien will receive graduate medical education or training, or any alien seeking to change nonimmigrant status to that of an exchange visitor on Form I–506 for that purpose, must have passed parts of I and II of the National Board of Medical Examiners Examination (or an equivalent examination as determined by the Secretary of Health and Human Services), and must be competent in oral and written English, and shall submit a completely executed and valid Form DS–2019.

(ii) *Exemptions.* From January 10, 1978 until December 31, 1983, any alien who has come to or seeks to come to the United States as an exchange visitor to participate in an accredited program of graduate medical education or training, or any alien who seeks to change nonimmigrant status for that purpose, may be admitted to participate in such program without regard to the requirements stated in subparagraphs (A) and (B)(ii)(I) of section 212(j)(1) of the Act if a substantial disruption in the health services provided by such program would result from not permitting the alien to participate in the program: *Provided* that the exemption will not increase the total number of aliens then participating in such programs to a level greater than that participating on January 10, 1978.

(5) *Remittance of the fee.* An alien who applies for J–1 nonimmigrant status in order to commence participation in a Department of State-designated exchange visitor program is required to pay the SEVIS fee to DHS, pursuant to 8 CFR 214.13, except as otherwise provided in that section.

(k) *Spouses, Fiancées, and Fiancés of United States Citizens*—(1) *Petition and supporting documents.* To be classified as a fiance or fiancee as defined in section 101(a)(15)(K)(i) of the Act, an alien must be the beneficiary of an approved visa petition filed on Form I–129F. A copy of a document submitted in support of a visa petition filed pursuant to section 214(d) of the Act and this paragraph may be accepted, though unaccompanied by the original, if the copy bears a certification by an attorney, typed or rubber-stamped, in the language set forth in §204.2(j) of this chapter. However, the original document shall be submitted if requested by the Service.

(2) *Requirement that petitioner and K–1 beneficiary have met.* The petitioner shall establish to the satisfaction of the director that the petitioner and K–1 beneficiary have met in person within the two years immediately preceding the filing of the petition. As a matter of discretion, the director may exempt the petitioner from this requirement only if it is established that compliance would result in extreme hardship to the petitioner or that compliance would violate strict and long-established customs of the K–1 beneficiary's foreign culture or social practice, as where marriages are traditionally arranged by the parents of the contracting parties and the prospective bride and groom are prohibited from meeting subsequent to the arrangement and prior to the wedding day. In addition to establishing that the required meeting would be a violation of custom or practice, the petitioner must also establish that any and all other aspects of the traditional arrangements have been or will be met in accordance with the custom or practice. Failure to establish that the petitioner and K–1 beneficiary have met within the required period or that compliance with the requirement should be waived shall result in the denial of the petition. Such denial shall be without prejudice to the filing of a new petition once the petitioner and K–1 beneficiary have met in person.

(3) *Children of beneficiary.* Without the approval of a separate petition on his or her behalf, a child of the beneficiary (as defined in section 101(b)(1)(A), (B), (C), (D), or (E) of the Act) may be accorded the same nonimmigrant classification as the beneficiary if accompanying or following to join him or her.

(4) *Notification.* The petitioner shall be notified of the decision and, if the petition is denied, of the reasons therefor and of the right to appeal in accordance with the provisions of part 103 of this chapter.

(5) *Validity.* The approval of a petition under this paragraph shall be valid for a period of four months. A petition which has expired due to the passage of time may be revalidated by a director or a consular officer for a period of four months from the date of revalidation upon a finding that the petitioner and K–1 beneficiary are free to marry and intend to marry each other within 90 days of the beneficiary's entry into the United States. The approval of any petition is automatically terminated when the petitioner dies or files a written withdrawal of the petition before the beneficiary arrives in the United States.

(6) *Adjustment of status from nonimmigrant to immigrant.*

(i) [Reserved]

(ii) *Nonimmigrant visa issued on or after November 10, 1986.* Upon contracting a valid marriage to the petitioner within 90 days of his or her admission as a nonimmigrant pursuant to a valid K–1 visa issued on or after November 10, 1986, the K–1 beneficiary and his or her minor children may apply for adjustment of status to lawful permanent resident under section 245 of the Act. Upon approval of the application the director shall record their lawful admission for permanent residence in accordance with that section and subject to the conditions prescribed in section 216 of the Act.

(7) *Eligibility, petition and supporting documents for K–3/K–4 classification.* To be classified as a K–3 spouse as defined in section 101(a)(15)(k)(ii) of the Act, or the K–4 child of such alien defined in section 101(a)(15)(K)(iii) of the Act, the alien spouse must be the beneficiary of an immigrant visa petition filed by a U.S. citizen on Form I–130, Petition for Alien Relative, and the beneficiary of an approved petition for a K–3 nonimmigrant visa filed on Form I–129F.

(8) *Period of admission for K3/K–4 status.* Aliens entering the United States as a K–3 shall be admitted for a period of 2 years. Aliens entering the United States as a K–4 shall be admitted for a period of 2 years or until that alien's 21st birthday, whichever is shorter.

(9) *Employment authorization.* An alien admitted to the United States as a nonimmigrant under section 101(a)(15)(K) of the Act shall be authorized to work incident to status for the period of authorized stay. K–1/K–2 aliens seeking work authorization must apply, with fee, to the Service for work authorization pursuant to § 274a.12(a)(6) of this chapter. K–3/K–4 aliens must apply to the Service for a document evidencing employment authorization pursuant to § 274a.12(a)(9) of this chapter. Employment authorization documents issued to K–3/K–4 aliens may be renewed only upon a showing that the applicant has an application or petition awaiting approval, equivalent to the showing required for an extension of stay pursuant to § 214.2(k)(10).

(10) *Extension of stay for K–3/K–4 status*—(i) *General.* A K–3/K–4 alien may apply for extension of stay, on Form I–539, Application to Extend/Change Nonimmigrant Status, 120 days prior to the expiration of his or her authorized stay. Extensions for K–4 status must be filed concurrently with the alien's parent's K–3 status extension application. In addition, the citizen parent of a K–4 alien filing for extension of K status should file Form I–130 on their behalf. Extension will be granted in 2-year intervals upon a showing of eligibility pursuant to section 101(a)(15)(K)(ii) or (iii) of the Act. Aliens wishing to extend their period of stay as a K–3 or K–4 alien pursuant to § 214.1(c)(2) must show that one of the following has been filed with the Service or the Department of State, as applicable, and is awaiting approval:

(A) The Form I–130, Petition for Alien Relative, filed by the K–3's U.S. citizen spouse who filed the Form I–129F;

(B) An application for an immigrant visa based on a Form I–130 described in § 214.2(K)(10)(i);

(C) A Form I–485, Application for Adjustment to that of Permanent Residence, based on a Form I–130 described in § 214.2(k)(10)(i);

(ii) *"Good Cause" showing.* Aliens may file for an extension of stay as a K–3/K–4 nonimmigrant after a Form I–130 filed on their behalf has been approved, without filing either an application for adjustment of status or an immigrant visa upon a showing of "good cause." A showing of "good cause" may include an illness, a job loss, or some other catastrophic event that has prevented the filing of an adjustment of status application by the K–3/K–4 alien. The event or events must have taken place since the alien entered the United States as a K–3/K–4 nonimmigrant. The burden of establishing "good cause" rests solely with the applicant. Whether the applicant has shown "good cause" is a purely discretionary decision by the Service from which there is no appeal.

(11) *Termination of K–3/K–4 status.* The status of an alien admitted to the United States as a K–3/K–4 under section 101(a)(15)(K)(ii) or (iii) of the Act, shall be automatically terminated 30 days following the occurrence of any of the following:

(i) The denial or revocation of the Form I–130 filed on behalf of that alien;

(ii) The denial or revocation of the immigrant visa application filed by that alien;

(iii) The denial or revocation of the alien's application for adjustment of status to that of lawful permanent residence;

(iv) The K–3 spouse's divorce from the U.S. citizen becomes final;

(v) The marriage of an alien in K–4 status.

(vi) The denial of any of these petitions or applications to a K–3 also results in termination of a dependent K–4's status. For purposes of this section, there is no denial or revocation of a petition or application until the administrative appeal applicable to that application or petition has been exhausted.

(l) *Intracompany transferees*—(1) *Admission of intracompany transferees*—(i) *General.* Under section 101(a)(15)(L) of the Act, an alien who within the preceding three years has been employed abroad for one continuous year by a qualifying organization may be admitted temporarily to the United States to be employed by a parent, branch, affiliate, or subsidiary of that employer in a managerial or executive capacity, or in a position requiring specialized knowledge. An alien transferred to the United States under this nonimmigrant classification is referred to as an intracompany transferee and the organization which seeks the classification of an alien as an intracompany transferee is referred to as the petitioner. The Service has responsibility for determining whether the alien is eligible for admission and whether the petitioner is a qualifying organization. These regulations set forth the standards applicable to these classifications. They also set forth procedures for admission of intracompany transferees and appeal of adverse decisions. Certain petitioners seeking the classification of aliens as intracompany transferees may file blanket petitions with the Service. Under the blanket petition process, the Service is responsible for determining whether the petitioner and its parent, branches, affiliates, or subsidiaries specified are qualifying organizations. The Department of State or, in certain cases, the Service is responsible for determining the classification of the alien.

(ii) *Definitions*—(A) *Intracompany transferee* means an alien who, within three years preceding the time of his or her application for admission into the United States, has been employed abroad continuously for one year by a firm or corporation or other legal entity or parent, branch, affiliate, or subsidiary thereof, and who seeks to enter the United States temporarily in order to render his or her services to a branch of the same employer or a parent, affiliate, or subsidiary thereof in a capacity that is managerial, executive, or involves specialized knowledge. Periods spent in the United States in lawful status for a branch of the same employer or a parent, affiliate, or subsidiary thereof and brief trips to the United States for business or pleasure shall not be interruptive of the one year of continuous employment abroad but such periods shall not be counted toward fulfillment of that requirement.

(B) *Managerial capacity* means an assignment within an organization in which the employee primarily:

(*1*) Manages the organization, or a department, subdivision, function, or component of the organization;

(*2*) Supervises and controls the work of other supervisory, professional, or managerial employees, or manages an essential function within the organization, or a department or subdivision of the organization;

(*3*) Has the authority to hire and fire or recommend those as well as other personnel actions (such as promotion and leave authorization) if another employee or other employees are directly supervised; if no other employee is directly supervised, functions at a senior level within the organizational hierarchy or with respect to the function managed; and

(*4*) Exercises discretion over the day-to-day operations of the activity or function for which the employee has authority. A first-line supervisor is not considered to be acting in a managerial capacity merely by virtue of the supervisor's supervisory duties unless the employees supervised are professional.

(C) *Executive capacity* means an assignment within an organization in which the employee primarily:

(*1*) Directs the management of the organization or a major component or function of the organization;

(*2*) Establishes the goals and policies of the organization, component, or function;

(*3*) Exercises wide latitude in discretionary decision-making; and

(*4*) Receives only general supervision or direction from higher level executives, the board of directors, or stockholders of the organization.

(D) *Specialized knowledge* means special knowledge possessed by an individual of the petitioning organization's product, service, research, equipment, techniques, management, or other interests and its application in international markets, or an advanced level of knowledge or expertise in the organization's processes and procedures.

(E) *Specialized knowledge professional* means an individual who has specialized knowledge as defined in paragraph (l)(1)(ii)(D) of this section and is a member of the professions as defined in section 101(a)(32) of the Immigration and Nationality Act.

(F) *New office* means an organization which has been doing business in the United States through a parent, branch, affiliate, or subsidiary for less than one year.

(G) *Qualifying organization* means a United States or foreign firm, corporation, or other legal entity which:

(*1*) Meets exactly one of the qualifying relationships specified in the definitions of a parent, branch, affiliate or subsidiary specified in paragraph (l)(1)(ii) of this section;

(*2*) Is or will be doing business (engaging in international trade is not required) as an employer in the United States and in at least one other country directly or through a parent, branch, affiliate, or subsidiary for the duration of the alien's stay in the United States as an intracompany transferee; and

(*3*) Otherwise meets the requirements of section 101(a)(15)(L) of the Act.

(H) *Doing business* means the regular, systematic, and continuous provision of goods and/or services by a qualifying organization and does not include the mere presence of an agent or office of the qualifying organization in the United States and abroad.

(I) *Parent* means a firm, corporation, or other legal entity which has subsidiaries.

(J) *Branch* means an operating division or office of the same organization housed in a different location.

(K) *Subsidiary* means a firm, corporation, or other legal entity of which a parent owns, directly or indirectly, more than half of the entity and controls the entity; or owns, directly or indirectly, half of the entity and controls the entity; or owns, directly or indirectly, 50 percent of a 50–50 joint venture and has equal control and veto power over the entity; or owns, directly or indirectly, less than half of the entity, but in fact controls the entity.

(L) *Affiliate* means (*1*) One of two subsidiaries both of which are owned and controlled by the same parent or individual, or

(*2*) One of two legal entities owned and controlled by the same group of individuals, each individual owning and controlling approximately the same share or proportion of each entity, or

(*3*) In the case of a partnership that is organized in the United States to provide accounting services along with managerial and/or consulting services and that markets its accounting services under an internationally recognized name under an agreement with a worldwide coordinating organization that is owned and controlled by the member accounting firms, a partnership (or similar organization) that is organized outside the United States to provide accounting services shall be considered to be an affiliate of the United States partnership if it markets its accounting services under the same internationally recognized name under the agreement with the worldwide coordinating organization of which the United States partnership is also a member.

(M) *Director* means a Service Center director with delegated authority at 8 CFR 103.1.

(2) *Filing of petitions.* (i) Except as provided in paragraph (l)(2)(ii) and (l)(17) of this section, a petitioner seeking to classify an alien as an intracompany transferee must file a petition on Form I–129, Petition for Nonimmigrant Worker. The petitioner shall advise USCIS whether a previous petition for the same beneficiary has been filed, and certify that another petition for the same beneficiary will not be filed unless the circumstances and conditions in the initial petition have

changed. Failure to make a full disclosure of previous petitions filed may result in a denial of the petition.

(ii) A United States petitioner which meets the requirements of paragraph (l)(4) of this section and seeks continuing approval of itself and its parent, branches, specified subsidiaries and affiliates as qualifying organizations and, later, classification under section 101(a)(15)(L) of the Act multiple numbers of aliens employed by itself, its parent, or those branches, subsidiaries, or affiliates may file a blanket petition on Form I–129. The blanket petition shall be maintained at the adjudicating office. The petitioner shall be the single representative for the qualifying organizations with which USCIS will deal regarding the blanket petition.

(3) *Evidence for individual petitions.* An individual petition filed on Form I–129 shall be accompanied by:

(i) Evidence that the petitioner and the organization which employed or will employ the alien are qualifying organizations as defined in paragraph (l)(1)(ii)(G) of this section.

(ii) Evidence that the alien will be employed in an executive, managerial, or specialized knowledge capacity, including a detailed description of the services to be performed.

(iii) Evidence that the alien has at least one continuous year of full-time employment abroad with a qualifying organization within the three years preceding the filing of the petition.

(iv) Evidence that the alien's prior year of employment abroad was in a position that was managerial, executive, or involved specialized knowledge and that the alien's prior education, training, and employment qualifies him/her to perform the intended services in the United States; however, the work in the United States need not be the same work which the alien performed abroad.

(v) If the petition indicates that the beneficiary is coming to the United States as a manager or executive to open or to be employed in a new office in the United States, the petitioner shall submit evidence that:

(A) Sufficient physical premises to house the new office have been secured;

(B) The beneficiary has been employed for one continuous year in the three year period preceding the filing of the petition in an executive or managerial capacity and that the proposed employment involved executive or managerial authority over the new operation; and

(C) The intended United States operation, within one year of the approval of the petition, will support an executive or managerial position as defined in paragraphs (l)(1)(ii) (B) or (C) of this section, supported by information regarding:

(*1*) The proposed nature of the office describing the scope of the entity, its organizational structure, and its financial goals;

(*2*) The size of the United States investment and the financial ability of the foreign entity to remunerate the beneficiary and to commence doing business in the United States; and

(*3*) The organizational structure of the foreign entity.

(vi) If the petition indicates that the beneficiary is coming to the United States in a specialized knowledge capacity to open or to be employed in a new office, the petitioner shall submit evidence that:

(A) Sufficient physical premises to house the new office have been secured;

(B) The business entity in the United States is or will be a qualifying organization as defined in paragraph (l)(1)(ii)(G) of this section; and

(C) The petitioner has the financial ability to remunerate the beneficiary and to commence doing business in the United States.

(vii) If the beneficiary is an owner or major stockholder of the company, the petition must be accompanied by evidence that the beneficiary's services are to be used for a temporary period and evidence that the beneficiary will be transferred to an assignment abroad upon the completion of the temporary services in the United States.

(viii) Such other evidence as the director, in his or her discretion, may deem necessary.

(4) *Blanket petitions.* (i) A petitioner which meets the following requirements may file a blanket petition seeking continuing approval of itself and

some or all of its parent, branches, subsidiaries, and affiliates as qualifying organizations if:

(A) The petitioner and each of those entities are engaged in commercial trade or services;

(B) The petitioner has an office in the United States that has been doing business for one year or more;

(C) The petitioner has three or more domestic and foreign branches, subsidiaries, or affiliates; and

(D) The petitioner and the other qualifying organizations have obtained approval of petitions for at least ten "L" managers, executives, or specialized knowledge professionals during the previous 12 months; or have U.S. subsidiaries or affiliates with combined annual sales of at least $25 million; or have a United States work force of at least 1,000 employees.

(ii) Managers, executives, and specialized knowledge professionals employed by firms, corporations, or other entities which have been found to be qualifying organizations pursuant to an approved blanket petition may be classified as intracompany transferees and admitted to the United States as provided in paragraphs (l) (5) and (11) of this section.

(iii) When applying for a blanket petition, the petitioner shall include in the blanket petition all of its branches, subsidiaries, and affiliates which plan to seek to transfer aliens to the United States under the blanket petition. An individual petition may be filed by the petitioner or organizations in lieu of using the blanket petition procedure. However, the petitioner and other qualifying organizations may not seek L classification for the same alien under both procedures, unless a consular officer first denies eligibility. Whenever a petitioner which has blanket L approval files an individual petition to seek L classification for a manager, executive, or specialized knowledge professional, the petitioner shall advise the Service that it has blanket L approval and certify that the beneficiary has not and will not apply to a consular officer for L classification under the approved blanket petition.

(iv) *Evidence.* A blanket petition filed on Form I–129 shall be accompanied by:

(A) Evidence that the petitioner meets the requirements of paragraph (l)(4)(i) of this section.

(B) Evidence that all entities for which approval is sought are qualifying organizations as defined in subparagraph (l)(1)(ii)(G) of this section.

(C) Such other evidence as the director, in his or her discretion, deems necessary in a particular case.

(5) *Certification and admission procedures for beneficiaries under blanket petition*—(i) *Jurisdiction.* United States consular officers shall have authority to determine eligibility of individual beneficiaries outside the United States seeking L classification under blanket petitions, except for visa-exempt nonimmigrants. An application for a visa-exempt nonimmigrant seeking L classification under a blanket petition or by an alien in the United States applying for change of status to L classification under a blanket petition shall be filed with the Service office at which the blanket petition was filed.

(ii) *Procedures.* (A) When one qualifying organization listed in an approved blanket petition wishes to transfer an alien outside the United States to a qualifying organization in the United States and the alien requires a visa to enter the United States, that organization shall complete Form I–129S, Certificate of Eligibility for Intracompany Transferee under a Blanket Petition, in an original and three copies. The qualifying organization shall retain one copy for its records and send the original and two copies to the alien. A copy of the approved Form I–797 must be attached to the original and each copy of Form I–129S.

(B) After receipt of Form I–797 and Form I–129S, a qualified employee who is being transferred to the United States may use these documents to apply for visa issuance with the consular officer within six months of the date on Form I–129S.

(C) When the alien is a visa-exempt nonimmigrant seeking L classification under a blanket petition, or when the alien is in the United States and is seeking a change of status from another nonimmigrant classification to L classification under a blanket petition, the petitioner shall submit Form I–

129S, Certificate of Eligibility, and a copy of the approval notice, Form I-797, to the USCIS office with which the blanket petition was filed.

(D) The consular or Service officer shall determine whether the position in which the alien will be employed in the United States is with an organization named in the approved petition and whether the specific job is for a manager, executive, or specialized knowledge professional. The consular or Service officer shall determine further whether the alien's immediate prior year of continuous employment abroad was with an organization named in the petition and was in a position as manager, executive, or specialized knowledge professional.

(E) Consular officers may grant "L" classification only in clearly approvable applications. If the consular officer determines that the alien is eligible for L classification, the consular officer may issue a nonimmigrant visa, noting the visa classification "Blanket L-1" for the principal alien and "Blanket L-2" for any accompanying or following to join spouse and children. The consular officer shall also endorse all copies of the alien's Form I-129S with the blanket L-1 visa classification and return the original and one copy to the alien. When the alien is inspected for entry into the United States, both copies of the Form I-129S shall be stamped to show a validity period not to exceed three years and the second copy collected and sent to the appropriate Regional Service Center for control purposes. Service officers who determine eligibility of aliens for L-1 classification under blanket petitions shall endorse both copies of Form I-129S with the blanket L-1 classification and the validity period not to exceed three years and retain the second copy for Service records.

(F) If the consular officer determines that the alien is ineligible for L classification under a blanket petition, the consular officer's decision shall be final. The consular officer shall record the reasons for the denial on Form I-129S, retain one copy, return the original of I-129S to the USCIS office which approved the blanket petition, and provide a copy to the alien. In such a case, an individual petition may be filed for the alien on Form I-129, Petition for Nonimmigrant Worker. The petition shall state the reason the alien was denied L classification and specify the consular office which made the determination and the date of the determination.

(G) An alien admitted under an approved blanket petition may be reassigned to any organization listed in the approved petition without referral to the Service during his/her authorized stay if the alien will be performing virtually the same job duties. If the alien will be performing different job duties, the petitioner shall complete a new Certificate of Eligibility and send it for approval to the director who approved the blanket petition.

(6) *Copies of supporting documents.* The petitioner may submit a legible photocopy of a document in support of the visa petition, in lieu of the original document. However, the original document shall be submitted if requested by the Service.

(7) *Approval of petition*—(i) *General.* The director shall notify the petitioner of the approval of an individual or a blanket petition within 30 days after the date a completed petition has been filed. If additional information is required from the petitioner, the 30 day processing period shall begin again upon receipt of the information. The original Form I-797 received from the USCIS with respect to an approved individual or blanket petition may be duplicated by the petitioner for the beneficiary's use as described in paragraph (l)(13) of this section.

(A) *Individual petition*—(*1*) Form I-797 shall include the beneficiary's name and classification and the petition's period of validity.

(*2*) An individual petition approved under this paragraph shall be valid for the period of established need for the beneficiary's services, not to exceed three years, except where the beneficiary is coming to the United States to open or to be employed in a new office.

(*3*) If the beneficiary is coming to the United States to open or be employed in a new office, the petition may be approved for a period not to exceed one year, after which the petitioner shall demonstrate as required by paragraph (l)(14)(ii) of this section that it is doing business as defined in paragraph (l)(1)(ii)(H) of this section to extend the validity of the petition.

(B) *Blanket petition.* (*1*) Form I–797 shall identify the approved organizations included in the petition and the petition's period of validity.

(*2*) A blanket petition approved under this paragraph shall be valid initially for a period of three years and may be extended indefinitely thereafter if the qualifying organizations have complied with these regulations.

(*3*) A blanket petition may be approved in whole or in part and shall cover only qualifying organizations.

(C) *Amendments.* The petitioner must file an amended petition, with fee, at the USCIS office where the original petition was filed to reflect changes in approved relationships, additional qualifying organizations under a blanket petition, change in capacity of employment (*i.e.*, from a specialized knowledge position to a managerial position), or any information which would affect the beneficiary's eligibility under section 101(a)(15)(L) of the Act.

(ii) *Spouse and dependents.* The spouse and unmarried minor children of the beneficiary are entitled to L nonimmigrant classification, subject to the same period of admission and limits as the beneficiary, if the spouse and unmarried minor children are accompanying or following to join the beneficiary in the United States. Neither the spouse nor any child may accept employment unless he or she has been granted employment authorization.

(8) *Denial of petition*—(i) *Individual petition.* If an individual is denied, the petitioner shall be notified within 30 days after the date a completed petition has been filed of the denial, the reasons for the denial, and the right to appeal the denial.

(ii) *Blanket petition.* If a blanket petition is denied in whole or in part, the petitioner shall be notified within 30 days after the date a completed petition has been filed of the denial, the reasons for the denial, and the right to appeal the denial. If the petition is denied in part, the USCIS office issuing the denial shall forward to the petitioner, along with the denial, a Form I–797 listing those organizations which were found to quality. If the decision to deny is reversed on appeal, a new Form I–797 shall be sent to the petitioner to reflect the changes made as a result of the appeal.

(9) *Revocation of approval of individual and blanket petitions*—(i) *General.* The director may revoke a petition at any time, even after the expiration of the petition.

(ii) *Automatic revocation.* The approval of any individual or blanket petition is automatically revoked if the petitioner withdraws the petition or the petitioner fails to request indefinite validity of a blanket petition.

(iii) *Revocation on notice.* (A) The director shall send to the petitioner a notice of intent to revoke the petition in relevant part if he/she finds that:

(*1*) One or more entities are no longer qualifying organizations;

(*2*) The alien is no longer eligible under section 101(a)(15)(L) of the Act;

(*3*) A qualifying organization(s) violated requirements of section 101(a)(15)(L) and these regulations;

(*4*) The statement of facts contained in the petition was not true and correct; or

(*5*) Approval of the petition involved gross error; or

(*6*) None of the qualifying organizations in a blanket petition have used the blanket petition procedure for three consecutive years.

(B) The notice of intent to revoke shall contain a detailed statement of the grounds for the revocation and the time period allowed for the petitioner's rebuttal. Upon receipt of this notice, the petitioner may submit evidence in rebuttal within 30 days of the notice. The director shall consider all relevant evidence presented in deciding whether to revoke the petition in whole or in part. If a blanket petition is revoked in part, the remainder of the petition shall remain approved, and a revised Form I–797 shall be sent to the petitioner with the revocation notice.

(iv) *Status of beneficiaries.* If an individual petition is revoked, the beneficiary shall be required to leave the United States, unless the beneficiary has obtained other work authorization from the Service. If a blanket petition is revoked and the petitioner and beneficiaries already in the United States are otherwise eligible for L classification, the director shall extend the blanket petition for a period necessary to support the stay of those blanket L beneficiaries. The approval notice, Form I–171C, shall include only the names of qualifying organizations and covered beneficiaries. No new beneficiaries may be classified or admitted under this limited extension.

(10) *Appeal of denial or revocation of individual or blanket petition.* (i) A petition denied in whole or in part may be appealed under 8 CFR part 103. Since the determination on the Certificate of Eligibility, Form I–129S, is part of the petition process, a denial or revocation of approval of an I–129S is appealable in the same manner as the petition.

(ii) A petition that has been revoked on notice in whole or in part may be appealed under part 103 of this chapter. Automatic revocations may not be appealed.

(11) *Admission.* A beneficiary may apply for admission to the United States only while the individual or blanket petition is valid. The beneficiary of an individual petition shall not be admitted for a date past the validity period of the petition. The beneficiary of a blanket petition may be admitted for three years even though the initial validity period of the blanket petition may expire before the end of the three-year period. If the blanket petition will expire while the alien is in the United States, the burden is on the petitioner to file for indefinite validity of the blanket petition or to file an individual petition in the alien's behalf to support the alien's status in the United States. The admission period for any alien under section 101(a)(15)(L) shall not exceed three years unless an extension of stay is granted pursuant to paragraph (l)(15) of this section.

(12) *L–1 limitation on period of stay*—(i) *Limits.* An alien who has spent five years in the United States in a specialized knowledge capacity or seven years in the United States in a managerial or executive capacity under section 101(a)(15) (L) and/or (H) of the Act may not be readmitted to the United States under section 101(a)(15) (L) or (H) of the Act unless the alien has resided and been physically present outside the United States, except for brief visits for business or pleasure, for the immediate prior year. Such visits do not interrupt the one year abroad, but do not count towards fulfillment of that requirement. In view of this restriction, a new individual petition may not be approved for an alien who has spent the maximum time period in the United States under section 101(a)(15) (L) and/or (H) of the Act, unless the alien has resided and been physically present outside the United States, except for brief visits for business or pleasure, for the immediate prior year. The petitioner shall provide information about the alien's employment, place of residence, and the dates and purpose of any trips to the United States for the previous year. A consular or Service officer may not grant L classification under a blanket petition to an alien who has spent five years in the United States as a professional with specialized knowledge or seven years in the United States as a manager or executive, unless the alien has met the requirements contained in this paragraph.

(ii) *Exceptions.* The limitations of paragraph (l)(12)(i) of this section shall not apply to aliens who do not reside continually in the United States and whose employment in the United States is seasonal, intermittent, or consists of an aggregate of six months or less per year. In addition, the limitations will not apply to aliens who reside abroad and regularly commute to the United States to engage in part-time employment. The petitioner and the alien must provide clear and convincing proof that the alien qualifies for an exception. Clear and convincing proof shall consist of evidence such as arrival and departure records, copies of tax returns, and records of employment abroad.

(13) *Beneficiary's use of Form I–797 and Form I–129S*—(i) *Beneficiary of an individual petition.* The beneficiary of an individual petition who does not require a nonimmigrant visa may present a copy of Form I–797 at a port of entry to facilitate entry into the United States. The copy of Form I–797 shall be retained by the beneficiary and presented

during the validity of the petition (provided that the beneficiary is entering or reentering the United States) for entry and reentry to resume the same employment with the same petitioner (within the validity period of the petition) and to apply for an extension of stay. A beneficiary who is required to present a visa for admission and whose visa will have expired before the date of his or her intended return may use an original Form I–797 to apply for a new or revalidated visa during the validity period of the petition and to apply for an extension of stay.

(ii) *Beneficiary of a blanket petition.* Each alien seeking L classification and admission under a blanket petition shall present a copy of Form I–797 and a Form I–129S from the petitioner which identifies the position and organization from which the employee is transferring, the new organization and position to which the employee is destined, a description of the employee's actual duties for both the new and former positions, and the positions, dates, and locations of previous L stays in the United States. A current copy of Form I–797 and Form I–129S should be retained by the beneficiary and used for leaving and reentering the United States to resume employment with a qualifying organization during his/her authorized period of stay, for applying for a new or revalidated visa, and for applying for readmission at a port of entry. The alien may be readmitted even though reassigned to a different organization named on the Form I–797 than the one shown on Form I–129S if the job duties are virtually the same.

(14) *Extension of visa petition validity*—(i) *Individual petition.* The petitioner shall file a petition extension on Form I–129 to extend an individual petition under section 101(a)(15)(L) of the Act. Except in those petitions involving new offices, supporting documentation is not required, unless requested by the director. A petition extension may be filed only if the validity of the original petition has not expired.

(ii) *New offices.* A visa petition under section 101(a)(15)(L) which involved the opening of a new office may be extended by filing a new Form I–129, accompanied by the following:

(A) Evidence that the United States and foreign entities are still qualifying organizations as defined in paragraph (l)(1)(ii)(G) of this section;

(B) Evidence that the United States entity has been doing business as defined in paragraph (l)(1)(ii)(H) of this section for the previous year;

(C) A statement of the duties performed by the beneficiary for the previous year and the duties the beneficiary will perform under the extended petition;

(D) A statement describing the staffing of the new operation, including the number of employees and types of positions held accompanied by evidence of wages paid to employees when the beneficiary will be employed in a managerial or executive capacity; and

(E) Evidence of the financial status of the United States operation.

(iii) *Blanket petitions*—(A) *Extension procedure.* A blanket petition may only be extended indefinitely by filing a new Form I–129 with a copy of the previous approval notice and a report of admissions during the preceding three years. The report of admissions shall include a list of the aliens admitted under the blanket petition during the preceding three years, including positions held during that period, the employing entity, and the dates of initial admission and final departure of each alien. The petitioner shall state whether it still meets the criteria for filing a blanket petition and shall document any changes in approved relationships and additional qualifying organizations.

(B) *Other conditions.* If the petitioner in an approved blanket petition fails to request indefinite validity or if indefinite validity is denied, the petitioner and its other qualifying organizations shall seek L classification by filing individual petitions until another three years have expired; after which the petitioner may seek approval of a new blanket petition.

(15) *Extension of stay.* (i) In individual petitions, the petitioner must apply for the petition extension and the alien's extension of stay concurrently on Form I–129. When the alien is a beneficiary under a blanket petition, a new certificate of eligibility, accompanied by a copy of the previous approved certificate of eligibility, shall be filed by

the petitioner to request an extension of the alien's stay. The petitioner must also request a petition extension. The dates of extension shall be the same for the petition and the beneficiary's extension of stay. The beneficiary must be physically present in the United States at the time the extension of stay is filed. Even though the requests to extend the visa petition and the alien's stay are combined on the petition, the director shall make a separate determination on each. If the alien is required to leave the United States for business or personal reasons while the extension requests are pending, the petitioner may request the director to cable notification of approval of the petition extension to the consular office abroad where the alien will apply for a visa.

(ii) An extension of stay may be authorized in increments of up to two years for beneficiaries of individual and blanket petitions. The total period of stay may not exceed five years for aliens employed in a specialized knowledge capacity. The total period of stay for an alien employed in a managerial or executive capacity may not exceed seven years. No further extensions may be granted. When an alien was initially admitted to the United States in a specialized knowledge capacity and is later promoted to a managerial or executive position, he or she must have been employed in the managerial or executive position for at least six months to be eligible for the total period of stay of seven years. The change to managerial or executive capacity must have been approved by the Service in an amended, new, or extended petition at the time that the change occurred.

(16) *Effect of filing an application for or approval of a permanent labor certification, preference petition, or filing of an application for adjustment of status on L-1 classification.* An alien may legitimately come to the United States for a temporary period as an L-1 nonimmigrant and, at the same time, lawfully seek to become a permanent resident of the United States provided he or she intends to depart voluntarily at the end of his or her authorized stay. The filing of an application for or approval of a permanent labor certification, an immigrant visa preference petition, or the filing of an application of readjustment of status for an L-1 nonimmigrant shall not be the basis for denying:

(i) An L-1 petition filed on behalf of the alien,

(ii) A request to extend an L-1 petition which had previously been filed on behalf of the alien;

(iii) An application for admission as an L-1 nonimmigrant by the alien, or as an L-2 nonimmigrant by the spouse or child of such alien;

(iv) An application for change of status to H-1 or L-2 nonimmigrant filed by the alien, or to H-1, H-4, or L-1 status filed by the L-2 spouse or child of such alien;

(v) An application for change of status to H-4 nonimmigrant filed by the L-1 nonimmigrant, if his or her spouse has been approved for classification as an H-1; or

(vi) An application for extension of stay filed by the alien, or by the L-2 spouse or child of such alien.

(17) *Filing of individual petitions and certifications under blanket petitions for citizens of Canada under the North American Free Trade Agreement (NAFTA)*—(i) *Individual petitions.* Except as provided in paragraph (1)(2)(ii) of this section (filing of blanket petitions), a United States or foreign employer seeking to classify a citizen of Canada as an intracompany transferee may file an individual petition in duplicate on Form I-129 in conjunction with an application for admission of the citizen of Canada. Such filing may be made with an immigration officer at a Class A port of entry located on the United States-Canada land border or at a United States pre-clearance/pre-flight station in Canada. The petitioning employer need not appear, but Form I-129 must bear the authorized signature of the petitioner.

(ii) *Certification of eligibility for intracompany transferree under the blanket petition.* An immigration officer at a location identified in paragraph (1)(17)(i) of this section may determine eligibility of individual citizens of Canada seeking L classification under approved blanket petitions. At these locations, such citizens of Canada shall present the original and two copies of Form I-129S, Intracompany Transferee

Certificate of Eligibility, prepared by the approved organization, as well as three copies of Form I–797, Notice of Approval of Nonimmigrant Visa Petition.

(iii) Nothing in this section shall preclude or discourage the advance filing of petitions and certificates of eligibility in accordance with paragraph (l)(2) of this section.

(iv) *Deficient or deniable petitions or certificates of eligibility.* If a petition or certificate of eligibility submitted concurrently with an application for admission is lacking necessary supporting documentation or is otherwise deficient, the inspecting immigration officer shall return it to the applicant for admission in order to obtain the necessary documentation from the petitioner or for the deficiency to be overcome. The fee to file the petition will be remitted at such time as the documentary or other deficiency is overcome. If the petition or certificate of eligibility is clearly deniable, the immigration officer will accept the petition (with fee) and the petitioner shall be notified of the denial, the reasons for denial, and the right of appeal. If a formal denial order cannot be issued by the port of entry, the petition with a recommendation for denial shall be forwarded to the appropriate Service Center for final action. For the purposes of this provision, the appropriate Service Center will be the one within the same Service region as the location where the application for admission is made.

(v) *Spouse and dependent minor children accompanying or following to join.* (A) The Canadian citizen spouse and Canadian citizen unmarried minor children of a Canadian citizen admitted under this paragraph shall be entitled to the same nonimmigrant classification and same length of stay subject to the same limits as the principal alien. They shall not be required to present visas, and they shall be admitted under the classification symbol L–2.

(B) A non-Canadian citizen spouse or non-Canadian citizen unmarried minor child shall be entitled to the same nonimmigrant classification and the same length of stay subject to the same limits as the principal, but shall be required to present a visa upon application for admission as an L–2 unless otherwise exempt under § 212.1 of this chapter.

(C) The spouse and dependent minor children shall not accept employment in the United States unless otherwise authorized under the Act.

(18) *Denial of intracompany transferee status to citizens of Canada or Mexico in the case of certain labor disputes.* (i) If the Secretary of Labor certifies to or otherwise informs the Commissioner that a strike or other labor dispute involving a work stoppage of workers is in progress where the beneficiary is to be employed, and the temporary entry of the beneficiary may affect adversely the settlement of such labor dispute or the employment of any person who is involved in such dispute, a petition to classify a citizen of Mexico or Canada as an L–1 intracompany transferee may be denied. If a petition has already been approved, but the alien has not yet entered the United States, or has entered the United States but not yet commenced employment, the approval of the petition may be suspended, and an application for admission on the basis of the petition may be denied.

(ii) If there is a strike or other labor dispute involving a work stoppage of workers in progress, but such strike or other labor dispute is not certified under paragraph (l)(18)(i) of this section, or the Service has not otherwise been informed by the Secretary that such a strike or labor dispute is in progress, the Commissioner shall not deny a petition or suspend an approved petition.

(iii) If the alien has already commended employment in the United States under an approved petition and is participating in a strike or other labor dispute involving a work stoppage of workers, whether or not such strike or other labor dispute has been certified by the Department of Labor, the alien shall not be deemed to be failing to maintain his or her status solely on account of past, present, or future participation in a strike or other labor dispute involving a work stoppage of workers, but is subject to the following terms and conditions.

(A) The alien shall remain subject to all applicable provisions of the Immigration and Nationality Act, and regulations promulgated in the same manner as all other L nonimmigrants;

(B) The status and authorized period of stay of such an alien is not modified or extended in any way by virtue of his or her participation in a strike or other labor dispute involving work stoppage of workers; and

(C) Although participation by an L nonimmigrant alien in a strike or other labor dispute involving a work stoppage of workers will not constitute a ground for deportation, any alien who violates his or her status or who remains in the United States after his or her authorized period of stay has expired will be subject to deportation.

(m) *Students in established vocational or other recognized nonacademic institutions, other than in language training programs*—(1) *Admission of student*—(i) *Eligibility for admission.* A nonimmigrant student may be admitted into the United States in nonimmigrant status under section 101(a)(15)(M) of the Act, if:

(A) The student presents a SEVIS Form I–20 issued in his or her own name by a school approved by the Service for attendance by M–1 foreign students. (In the alternative, for a student seeking admission prior to August 1, 2003, the student may present a currently-valid Form I–20M–N/I–20ID, if that form was issued by the school prior to January 30, 2003);

(B) The student has documentary evidence of financial support in the amount indicated on the SEVIS Form I–20 (or the Form I–20M–N/I–20ID); and

(C) For students seeking initial admission only, the student intends to attend the school specified in the student's visa (or, where the student is exempt from the requirement for a visa, the school indicated on the SEVIS Form I–20 (or the Form I–20M–N/I–20ID)).

(ii) *Disposition of Form I–20M–N.* When a student is admitted to the United States, the inspecting officer shall forward Form I–20M–N to the Service's processing center. The processing center shall forward Form I–20N to the school which issued the form to notify the school of the student's admission.

(iii) *Use of SEVIS.* On January 30, 2003, the use of the Student and Exchange Visitor Information System (SEVIS) will become mandatory for the issuance of any new Form I–20. A student or dependent who presents a non-SEVIS Form I–20 issued on or after January 30, 2003, will not be accepted for admission to the United States. Non-SEVIS Forms I–20 issued prior to January 30, 2003, will continue to be accepted for admission to the United States until August 1, 2003. However, schools must issue a SEVIS Form I–20 to any current student requiring a reportable action (e.g., extension of status, practical training, and requests for employment authorization) or a new Form I–20, or for any aliens who must obtain a new nonimmigrant student visa. As of August 1, 2003, the records of all current or continuing students must be entered in SEVIS.

(2) *Form I–20 ID copy.* The first time an M–1 student comes into contact with the Service for any reason, the student must present to the Service a Form I–20M–N properly and completely filled out by the student and by the designated official of the school the student is attending or intends to attend. The student will be issued a Form I–20 ID copy with his or her admission number. The student must have the Form I–20 ID copy with him or her at all times. If the student loses the Form I–20 ID copy, the student must request a new Form I–20 ID copy on Form I–102 from the Service office having jurisdiction over the school the student was last authorized to attend.

(3) *Admission of the spouse and minor children of an M–1 student.* The spouse and minor children accompanying an M–1 student are eligible for admission in M–2 status if the student is admitted in M–1 status. The spouse and minor children following-to-join an M–1 student are eligible for admission to the United States in M–2 status if they are able to demonstrate that the M–1 student has been admitted and is, or will be within 30 days, enrolled in a full course of study, or engaged in approved practical training following completion of studies. In either case, at the time they seek admission, the eligible spouse and minor children of an M–1 student with a SEVIS Form I–20 must

individually present an original SEVIS Form I–20 issued in the name of each M–2 dependent issued by a school authorized by the Service for attendance by M–1 foreign students. Prior to August 1, 2003, if exigent circumstances are demonstrated, the Service will allow the dependent of an M–1 student in possession of a SEVIS Form I–20 to enter the United States using a copy of the M–1 student's SEVIS Form I–20. (In the alternative, for dependents seeking admission to the United States prior to August 1, 2003, a copy of the M–1 student's current Form I–20ID issued prior to January 30, 2003, with proper endorsement by the DSO will satisfy this requirement.) A new SEVIS Form I–20 (or Form I–20M–N) is required for a dependent where there has been any substantive change in the M–1 student's current information.

(i) A properly endorsed page 4 of Form I–20M–N if there has been no substantive change in the information on the student's most recent Form I–20M since the form was initially issued; or

(ii) A new Form I–20M–N if there has been any substantive change in the information on the student's most recent Form I–20M since the form was initially issued.

(4) *Temporary absence*—(i) *General.* An M–1 student returning to the United States from a temporary absence to attend the school which the student was previously authorized to attend must present either—

(A) A properly endorsed page 4 of Form I–20M–N if there has been no substantive change in the information on the student's most recent Form I–20M since the form was initially issued; or

(B) A new Form I–20M–N if there has been any substantive change in the information on the student's most recent Form I–20M since the form was initially issued.

(ii) *Student who transferred between schools.* If an M–1 student has been authorized to transfer between schools and is returning to the United States from a temporary absence in order to attend the school to which transfer was authorized as indicated on the student's Form I–20 ID copy, the name of the school to which the student is destined does not need to be specified in the student's visa.

(5) *Period of stay.* A student in M nonimmigrant status is admitted for a fixed time period, which is the period necessary to complete the course of study indicated on the Form I–20, plus practical training following completion of the course of study, plus an additional 30 days to depart the United States, but not to exceed a total period of one year. An M–1 student may be admitted for a period up to 30 days before the report date or start date of the course of study listed on the Form I–20. An M–1 student who fails to maintain a full course of study or otherwise fails to maintain status is not eligible for the additional 30-day period of stay.

(6)–(8) [Reserved]

(9) *Full course of study.* Successful completion of the course of study must lead to the attainment of a specific educational or vocational objective. A "full course of study" as required by section 101(a)(15)(M)(i) of the Act means—

(i) Study at a community college or junior college, certified by a school official to consist of at least twelve semester or quarter hours of instruction per academic term in those institutions using standard semester, trimester, or quarter-hour systems, where all students enrolled for a minimum of twelve semester or quarter hours are charged full-time tuition or considered full-time for other administrative purposes, or its equivalent (as determined by the district director), except when the student needs a lesser course load to complete the course of study during the current term;

(ii) Study at a postsecondary vocational or business school, other than in a language training program except as provided in § 214.3(a)(2)(iv), which confers upon its graduates recognized associate or other degrees or has established that its credits have been and are accepted unconditionally by at least three institutions of higher learning which are either: (1) A school (or school system) owned and operated as a public educational institution by the United States or a State or political subdivision thereof; or (2) a school accredited by a nationally recognized accrediting body; and which has been certified by a designated school official to consist of at least twelve hours of instruction a week, or its equivalent as determined by the district director;

(iii) Study in a vocational or other nonacademic curriculum, other than in a language training program except as provided in § 214.3(a)(2)(iv), certified by a designated school official to consist of at least eighteen clock hours of attendance a week if the dominant part of the course of study consists of classroom instruction, or at least twenty-two clock hours a week if the dominant part of the course of study consists of shop or laboratory work; or

(iv) Study in a vocational or other nonacademic high school curriculum, certified by a designated school official to consist of class attendance for not less than the minimum number of hours a week prescribed by the school for normal progress towards graduation.

(v) *On-line courses/distance education programs.* No on-line or distance education classes may be considered to count toward an M–1 student's full course of study requirement if such classes do not require the student's physical attendance for classes, examination or other purposes integral to completion of the class. An on-line or distance education course is a course that is offered principally through the use of television, audio, or computer transmission including open broadcast, closed circuit, cable, microwave, or satellite, audio conferencing, or computer conferencing.

(vi) *Reduced course load.* The designated school official may authorize an M–1 student to engage in less than a full course of study only where the student has been compelled by illness or a medical condition that has been documented by a licensed medical doctor, doctor of osteopathy, or licensed clinical psychologist, to interrupt or reduce his or her course of study. A DSO may not authorize a reduced course load for more than an aggregate of 5 months per course of study. An M–1 student previously authorized to drop below a full course of study due to illness or medical condition for an aggregate of 5 months, may not be authorized by the DSO to reduce his or her course load on subsequent occasions during his or her particular course of study.

(A) *Non-SEVIS schools.* A DSO must report any student who has been authorized by the DSO to carry a reduced course load. Within 21 days of the authorization, the DSO must send a photocopy of the student's Form I–20 to the Service's data processing center indicating the date that authorization was granted. The DSO must also report to the Service's data processing center when the student has resumed a full course of study, no more than 21 days from the date the student resumed a full course of study. In this case, the DSO must submit a photocopy of the student's Form I–20 indicating the date that a full course of study was resumed, with a new program end date.

(B) *SEVIS reporting.* In order for a student to be authorized to drop below a full course of study, the DSO must update SEVIS prior to the student reducing his or her course load. The DSO must update SEVIS with the date, reason for authorization, and the start date of the next term or session. The DSO must also notify SEVIS within 21 days of the student's commencement of a full course of study.

(10) *Extension of stay*—(i) *Eligibility.* The cumulative time of extensions that can be granted to an M–1 student is limited to a period of 3 years from the M–1 student's original start date, plus 30 days. No extension can be granted to an M–1 student if the M–1 student is unable to complete the course of study within 3 years of the original program start date. This limit includes extensions that have been granted due to a drop below full course of study, a transfer of schools, or reinstatement. An M–1 student may be granted an extension of stay if it is established that:

(A) He or she is a bona fide nonimmigrant currently maintaining student status;

(B) Compelling educational or medical reasons have resulted in a delay to his or her course of study. Delays caused by academic probation or suspension are not acceptable reasons for program extension; and

(C) He or she is able to, and in good faith intends to, continue to maintain that status for the period for which the extension is granted.

(ii) *Application.* A student must apply to the Service for an extension on Form I–539, Application to Extend/ Change Nonimmigrant Status. A student's M–2 spouse and children seeking an extension of stay must be included in the application. The student must submit the application to the service center having jurisdiction over the school the student is currently authorized to attend, at least 15 days but not more than 60 days before the program end date on the student's Form I–20. The application must also be accompanied by the student's Form I–20 and the Forms I–94 of the student's spouse and children, if applicable.

(iii) *Period of stay.* If an application for extension is granted, the student and the student's spouse and children, if applicable, are to be given an extension of stay for the period of time necessary to complete the course of study, plus 30 days within which to depart from the United States, or for a total period of one year, whichever is less. A student's M–2 spouse and children are not eligible for an extension unless the M–1 student is granted an extension of stay, or for a longer period than is granted to the M–1 student.

(iv) *SEVIS update.* A DSO must update SEVIS to recommend that a student be approved for an extension of stay. The SEVIS Form I–20 must be printed with the recommendation and new program end date for submission by mail to the service center, with Form I–539, and Forms I–94 if applicable.

(11) *School transfer*—(i) *Eligibility.* An M–1 student may not transfer to another school after six months from the date the student is first admitted as, or changes nonimmigrant classification to that of, an M–1 student unless the student is unable to remain at the school to which the student was initially admitted due to circumstances beyond the student's control. An M–1 student may be otherwise eligible to transfer to another school if the student—

(A) Is a bona fide nonimmigrant;

(B) Has been pursuing a full course of study at the school the student was last authorized to attend;

(C) Intends to pursue a full course of study at the school to which the student intends to transfer; and

(D) Is financially able to attend the school to which the student intends to transfer.

(ii) *Procedure.* A student must apply to the Service on Form I–539 for permission to transfer between schools. Upon application for school transfer, a student may effect the transfer subject to approval of the application. A student who transfers without complying with this requirement or whose application is denied after transfer pursuant to this regulation is considered to be out of status. If the application is approved, the approval of the transfer will be determined to be the program start date listed on the Form I–20, and the student will be granted an extension of stay for the period of time necessary to complete the new course of study plus 30 days, or for a total period of one year, whichever is less.

(A) *Non-SEVIS school.* The application must be accompanied by the Form I–20ID copy and the Form I–94 of the student's spouse and children, if applicable. The Form I–539 must also be accompanied by Form I–20M–N properly and completely filled out by the student and by the designated official of the school which the student wishes to attend. Upon approval, the adjudicating officer will endorse the name of the school to which the transfer is authorized on the student's Form I–20ID copy and return it to the student. The officer will also endorse Form I–20M–N to indicate that a school transfer has been authorized and forward it to the Service's processing center for updating. The processing center will forward Form I–20M–N to the school to which the transfer has been authorized to notify the school of the action taken.

(B) *SEVIS school.* The student must first notify his or her current school of the intent to transfer and indicate the school to which the student intends to transfer. Upon notification by the student, the current school must update SEVIS to show the student as a "transfer out" and input the "release date" for transfer. Once updated as a "transfer out" the transfer school is permitted to generate a SEVIS Form I–20 for transfer but will not gain access to the student's SEVIS record until the release date is reached. Upon receipt of the SEVIS Form I–20 from the transfer school, the student must submit Form I–539 in accordance with § 214.2(m)(11). The student may enroll in the transfer school at the next available term or session and is required to notify the DSO of the transfer school immediately upon beginning attendance. The transfer school must update the student's registration record in SEVIS in accordance with § 214.3(g)(3). Upon approval of the transfer application, the Service officer will endorse the name of the school to which the transfer is authorized on the student's SEVIS Form I–20 and return it to the student.

(C) *Transition process.* Once SEVIS is fully operational and interfaced with the service center benefit processing system, the Service officer will transmit the approval of the transfer to SEVIS and endorse the name of the school to which transfer is authorized on the student's SEVIS Form I–20 and return it to the student. As part of a transitional process until that time, the student is required to notify the DSO at the transfer school of the decision of the Service within 15 days of the receipt of the adjudication by the Service. Upon notification by the student of the approval of the Service, the DSO must immediately update SEVIS to show that approval of the transfer has been granted. The DSO must then print an updated SEVIS Form I–20 for the student indicating that the transfer has been completed. If the application for transfer is denied, the student is out of status and the DSO must terminate the student's record in SEVIS.

(iii) *Student who has not been pursuing a full course of study.* If an M–1 student who has not been pursuing a full course of study at the school the student was last authorized to attend desires to attend a different school, the student must apply for reinstatement to student status under paragraph (m)(16) of this section.

(12) *Change in educational objective.* An M–1 student may not change educational objective.

(13) *Employment.* Except as provided in paragraph (m)(14) of this section, a student may not accept employment.

(14) *Practical training*—(i) *When practical training may be authorized.* Temporary employment for practical training may be authorized only after completion of the student's course of study.

(A) The proposed employment is recommended for the purpose of practical training;

(B) The proposed employment is related to the student's course of study; and

(C) Upon the designated school official's information and belief, employment comparable to the proposed employment is not available to the student in the country of the student's foreign residence.

(ii) *Application.* A M–1 student must apply for permission to accept employment for practical training on Form I–765, with fee as contained in 8 CFR 103.7(b)(1), accompanied by a Form I–20 that has been endorsed for practical training by the designated school official. The application must be submitted prior to the program end date listed on the student's Form I–20 but not more than 90 days before the program end date. The designated school official must certify on Form I–538 that—

(A) The proposed employment is recommended for the purpose of practical training;

(B) The proposed employment is related to the student's course of study; and

(C) Upon the designated school official's information and belief, employment comparable to the proposed employment is not available to the student in the country of the student's foreign residence.

(iii) *Duration of practical training.* When the student is authorized to engage in employment for practical training, he or she will be issued an employment authorization document. The M–1 student may not begin employment until he or she has been issued an employment authorization document by the Service. One month of employment authorization will be granted for each four months of full-time study that the M–1 student has completed. However, an M–1 student may not engage in more than six months of practical training in the aggregate. The student will not be granted employment authorization if he or she cannot complete the requested practical training within six months.

(iv) *Temporary absence of M–1 student granted practical training.* An M–1 student who has been granted permission to accept employment for practical training and who temporarily departs from the United States, may be readmitted for the remainder of the authorized period indicated on the student's Form I–20 ID copy. The student must be returning to the United States to perform the authorized practical training. A student may not be readmitted to begin practical training which was not authorized prior to the student's departure from the United States.

(v) *Effect of strike or other labor dispute.* Authorization for all employment for practical training is automatically suspended upon certification by the Secretary of Labor or the Secretary's designee to the Commissioner of Immigration and Naturalization or the Commissioner's designee that a strike or other labor dispute involving a work stoppage of workers is in progress in the occupation at the place of employment. As used in this paragraph, "place of employment" means wherever the employer or joint employer does business.

(vi) *SEVIS process.* The DSO must update the student's record in SEVIS to recommend that the Service approve the student for practical training, and print SEVIS Form I–20 with the recommendation, for the student to submit to the Service with Form I–765 as provided in this paragraph (m)(14).

(15) *Decision on application for extension, permission to transfer to another school, or permission to accept employment for practical training.* The Service shall notify the applicant of the decision and, if the application is denied, of the reason(s) for the denial. The applicant may not appeal the decision.

(16) *Reinstatement to student status*—(i) *General.* A district director may consider reinstating a student who makes a request for reinstatement on Form I–539, Application to Extend/Change Nonimmigrant Status, accompanied by a properly completed SEVIS Form I–20 indicating the DSO's recommendation for reinstatement (or a properly completed Form I–20M–N issued prior to January 30, 2003, from the school the student is attending or intends to attend prior to August 1, 2003). The district director may consider granting the request only if the student:

(A) Has not been out of status for more than 5 months at the time of filing the request for reinstatement (or demonstrates that the failure to file within the 5 month period was the result of exceptional circumstances and that the student filed the request for reinstatement as promptly as possible under these exceptional circumstances);

(B) Does not have a record of repeated or willful violations of the Service regulations;

(C) Is currently pursuing, or intends to pursue, a full course of study at the school which issued the Form I–20M–N or SEVIS Form I–20;

(D) Has not engaged in unlawful employment;

(E) Is not deportable on any ground other than section 237(a)(1)(B) or (C)(i) of the Act; and

(F) Establishes to the satisfaction of the Service, by a detailed showing, either that:

(*1*) The violation of status resulted from circumstances beyond the student's control. Such circumstances might include serious injury or illness, closure of the institution, a natural disaster, or inadvertence, oversight or neglect on the part of the DSO, but do not include instances where a pattern of repeated violations or where a willful failure on the part of the student resulted in the need for reinstatement; or

(*2*) The violation relates to a reduction in the student's course load that would have been within a DSO's power to authorize, and that failure to approve reinstatement would result in extreme hardship to the student.

(ii) *Decision.* If the Service reinstates the student, the Service shall endorse the student's copy of Form I–20 to indicate that the student has been reinstated and return the form to the student. If the Form I–20 is from a non-SEVIS school, the school copy will be forwarded to the school. If the Form I–

20 is from a SEVIS school, the adjudicating officer will update SEVIS to reflect the Service's decision. In either case, if the Service does not reinstate the student, the student may not appeal the decision. The district director will send notification to the school of the decision.

(17) *Spouse and children of M–1 student.* The M–2 spouse and minor children of an M–1 student shall each be issued an individual SEVIS Form I–20 in accordance with the provisions of § 214.3(k).

(i) *Employment.* The M–2 spouse and children may not accept employment.

(ii) *Study*—(A) *M–2 post-secondary/vocational study*—(*1*) *Authorized study at SEVP-certified schools.* An M–2 spouse or M–2 child may enroll in less than a full course of study, as defined in paragraphs (f)(6)(i)(A) through (D) or (m)(9)(i) through (v), in any course of study described in paragraphs (f)(6)(i)(A) through (D) or (m)(9)(i) through (v) of this section at an SEVP-certified school. Notwithstanding paragraphs (f)(6)(i)(B) and (m)(9)(i) of this section, study at an undergraduate college or university or at a community college or junior college is not a full course of study solely because the M–2 nonimmigrant is engaging in a lesser course load to complete a course of study during the current term. An M–2 spouse or M–2 child enrolled in less than a full course of study is not eligible to engage in employment pursuant to paragraph (m)(14) of this section or pursuant to paragraphs (f)(9) through (10) of this section.

(*2*) *Full course of study.* Subject to paragraph (m)(17)(ii)(B) of this section, an M–2 spouse and child may engage in a full course of study only by applying for and obtaining a change of status to F–1, M–1, or J–1 status, as appropriate, before beginning a full course of study. An M–2 spouse and M–2 child may engage in study that is avocational or recreational in nature, up to and including on a full-time basis.

(B) *M–2 elementary or secondary study.* An M–2 child may engage in full-time study, including any full course of study, in any elementary or secondary school (kindergarten through twelfth grade).

(C) An M–2 spouse or child violates his or her nonimmigrant status by enrolling in any study except as provided in paragraph (m)(17)(ii)(A) or (B) of this section.

(18) *Current name and address.* A student must inform the Service and the DSO of any legal changes to his or her name or of any change of address, within 10 days of the change, in a manner prescribed by the school. A student enrolled at a SEVIS school can satisfy the requirement in 8 CFR 265.1 of notifying the Service by providing a notice of a change of address within 10 days to the DSO, and the DSO in turn shall enter the information in SEVIS within 21 days of notification by the student. A nonimmigrant student enrolled at a non-SEVIS institution must submit a notice of change of address to the Service, as provided in 8 CFR 265.1, within 10 days of the change. Except in the case of a student who cannot receive mail where he or she resides, the address provided by the student must be the actual physical location where the student resides rather than a mailing address. In cases where a student provides a mailing address, the school must maintain a record of, and must provide upon request from the Service, the actual physical location where the student resides.

(19) *Special rules for certain border commuter students*—(i) *Applicability.* For purposes of the special rules in this paragraph (m)(19), the term "border commuter student" means a national of Canada or Mexico who is admitted to the United States as an M–1 student to enroll in a full course of study, albeit on a part-time basis, in an approved school located within 75 miles of a United States land border. The border commuter student must maintain actual residence and place of abode in the student's country of nationality, and seek admission to the United States at a land border port-of-entry. These special rules do not apply to a national of Canada or Mexico who is:

(A) Residing in the United States while attending an approved school as an M–1 student, or

(B) Enrolled in a full course of study as defined in paragraph (m)(9) of this section.

(ii) *Full course of study.* The border commuter student must be enrolled in a full course of study at the school that leads to the attainment of a specific educational or vocational objective, albeit on a part-time basis. A designated school official at the school may authorize an eligible border commuter student to enroll in a course load below that otherwise required for a full course of study under paragraph (m)(9) of this section, provided that the reduced course load is consistent with the border commuter student's approved course of study.

(iii) *Period of stay.* An M–1 border commuter student is not entitled to an additional 30-day period of stay otherwise available under paragraph (m)(5) of this section.

(iv) *Employment.* A border commuter student may not be authorized to accept any employment in connection with his or her M–1 student status, except for practical training as provided in paragraph (m)(14) of this section.

(20) *Remittance of the fee.* An alien who applies for M–1 or M–3 nonimmigrant status in order to enroll in a program of study at a DHS-approved vocational educational institution is required to pay the SEVIS fee to DHS, pursuant to 8 CFR 214.13, except as otherwise provided in that section.

(n) *Certain parents and children of section 101(a)(27)(I) special immigrants*—(1) *Parent of special immigrant.* Upon application, a parent of a child accorded special immigrant status under section 101(a)(27)(I)(i) of the Act may be granted status under section 101(a)(15)(N)(i) of the Act as long as the permanent resident child through whom eligibility is derived remains a child as defined in section 101(b)(1) of the Act.

(2) *Child of section 101(a)(27)(I) special immigrants and section 101(a)(15)(N)(i) nonimmigrants.* Children of parents granted nonimmigrant status under section 101(a)(15)(N)(i) of the Act, or of parents who have been granted special immigrant status under section 101(a)(27)(I) (ii), (iii) or (iv) of the Act may be granted status under section 101(a)(15)(N)(ii) of the Act for such time as each remains a child as defined in section 101(b)(1) of the Act.

(3) *Admission and extension of stay.* A nonimmigrant granted (N) status shall be admitted for not to exceed three years with extensions in increments up to but not to exceed three years. Status as an (N) nonimmigrant shall terminate on the date the child described in paragraph (n)(1) or (n)(2) of this section no longer qualifies as a child as defined in section 101(b)(1) of the Act.

(4) *Employment.* A nonimmigrant admitted in or granted (N) status is authorized employment incident to (N) status without restrictions as to location or type of employment.

(o) *Aliens of extraordinary ability or achievement*—(1) *Classifications*—(i) *General.* Under section 101(a)(15)(O) of the Act, a qualified alien may be authorized to come to the United States to perform services relating to an event or events if petitioned for by an employer. Under this nonimmigrant category, the alien may be classified under section 101(a)(15)(O)(i) of the Act as an alien who has extraordinary ability in the sciences, arts, education, business, or athletics, or who has a demonstrated record of extraordinary achievement in the motion picture or television industry. Under section 101(a)(15)(O)(ii) of the Act, an alien having a residence in a foreign country which he or she has no intention of abandoning may be classified as an accompanying alien who is coming to assist in the artistic or athletic performance of an alien admitted under section 101(a)(15)(O)(i) of the Act. The spouse or child of an alien described in section 101(a)(15)(O)(i) or (ii) of the Act who is accompanying or following to join the alien is entitled to classification pursuant to section 101(a)(15)(O)(iii) of the Act. These classifications are called the O–1, O–2, and O–3 categories, respectively. The petitioner must file a petition with the Service for a determination of the alien's eligibility for O–1 or O–2 classification before the alien may apply for a visa or seek admission to the United States. This paragraph sets forth the standards and procedures applicable to these classifications.

(ii) *Description of classifications.* (A) An O–1 classification applies to:

(*1*) An individual alien who has extraordinary ability in the sciences, arts, education, business, or athletics which has been demonstrated by sustained national or international acclaim and who is coming temporarily to the United States to continue work in the area of extraordinary ability; or

(*2*) An alien who has a demonstrated record of extraordinary achievement in motion picture and/or television productions and who is coming temporarily to the United States to continue work in the area of extraordinary achievement.

(B) An O–2 classification applies to an accompanying alien who is coming temporarily to the United States solely to assist in the artistic or athletic performance by an O–1. The O–2 alien must:

(*1*) Be an integral part of the actual performances or events and posses critical skills and experience with the O–1 alien that are not of a general nature and which are not possessed by others; or

(*2*) In the case of a motion picture or television production, have skills and experience with the O–1 alien which are not of a general nature and which are critical, either based on a pre-existing and longstanding working relationship or, if in connection with a specific production only, because significant production (including pre- and post-production) will take place both inside and outside the United States and the continuing participation of the alien is essential to the successful completion of the production.

(2) *Filing of petitions*—(i) *General.* Except as provided for in paragraph (o)(2)(iv)(A) of this section, a petitioner seeking to classify an alien as an O–1 or O–2 nonimmigrant shall file a petition on Form I–129, Petition for a Nonimmigrant Worker. The petition may not be filed more than one year before the actual need for the alien's services. An O–1 or O–2 petition shall be adjudicated at the appropriate Service Center, even in emergency situations. Only one beneficiary may be included on an O–1 petition. O–2 aliens must be filed for on a separate petition from the O–1 alien. An O–1 or O–2 petition may only be filed by a United States employer, a United States agent, or a foreign employer through a United States agent. For purposes of paragraph (o) of this section, a foreign employer is any employer who is not amenable to service of process in the United States. A foreign employer may not directly petition for an O nonimmigrant alien but instead must use the services of a United States agent to file a petition for an O nonimmigrant alien. A United States agent petitioning on behalf of a foreign employer must be authorized to file the petition, and to accept services of process in the United States in proceedings under section 274A of the Act, on behalf of the foreign employer. An O alien may not petition for himself or herself.

(ii) *Evidence required to accompany a petition.* Petitions for O aliens shall be accompanied by the following:

(A) The evidence specified in the particular section for the classification;

(B) Copies of any written contracts between the petitioner and the alien beneficiary or, if there is no written contract, a summary of the terms of the oral agreement under which the alien will be employed;

(C) An explanation of the nature of the events or activities, the beginning and ending dates for the events or activities, and a copy of any itinerary for the events or activities; and

(D) A written advisory opinion(s) from the appropriate consulting entity or entities.

(iii) *Form of documentation.* The evidence submitted with an O petition shall conform to the following:

(A) Affidavits, contracts, awards, and similar documentation must reflect the nature of the alien's achievement and be executed by an officer or responsible person employed by the institution, firm, establishment, or organization where the work was performed.

(B) Affidavits written by present or former employers or recognized experts certifying to the recognition and extraordinary ability, or in the case of a motion picture or television production, the extraordinary achievement of the alien, shall specifically describe the alien's recognition and ability or achievement in factual terms and set forth the expertise of the affiant and the manner in which the affiant acquired such information.

(C) A legible photocopy of a document in support of the petition may be submitted in lieu of the original. However, the original document shall be submitted if requested by the Director.

(iv) *Other filing situations*—(A) *Services in more than one location.* A petition which requires the alien to work in more than one location must include an itinerary with the dates and locations of work.

(B) *Services for more than one employer.* If the beneficiary will work concurrently for more than one employer within the same time period, each employer must file a separate petition unless an established agent files the petition.

(C) *Change of employer.* If an O–1 or O–2 alien in the United States seeks to change employers, the new employer must file a petition and a request to extend the alien's stay. An O–2 alien may change employers only in conjunction with a change of employers by the principal O–1 alien. If the O–1 or O–2 petition was filed by an agent, an amended petition must be filed with evidence relating to the new employer and a request for an extension of stay.

(D) *Amended petition.* The petitioner shall file an amended petition on Form I–129, with fee, to reflect any material changes in the terms and conditions of employment or the beneficiary's eligibility as specified in the original approved petition. In the case of a petition filed for an artist or entertainer, a petitioner may add additional performances or engagements during the validity period of the petition without filing an amended petition, provided the additional performances or engagements require an alien of O–1 caliber.

(E) *Agents as petitioners.* A United States agent may file a petition in cases involving workers who are traditionally self-employed or workers who use agents to arrange short-term employment on their behalf with numerous employers, and in cases where a foreign employer authorizes the agent to act in its behalf. A United States agent may be: The actual employer of the beneficiary, the representative of both the employer and the beneficiary; or, a person or entity authorized by the employer to act for, or in place of, the employer as its agent. A petition filed by an agent is subject to the following conditions:

(*1*) An agent performing the function of an employer must provide the contractual agreement between the agent and the beneficiary which specifies the wage offered and the other terms and conditions of employment of the beneficiary.

(*2*) A person or company in business as an agent may file the petition involving multiple employers as the representative of both the employers and the beneficiary, if the supporting documentation includes a complete itinerary of the event or events. The itinerary must specify the dates of each service or engagement, the names and addresses of the actual employers, and the names and addresses of the establishments, venues, or locations where the services will be performed. A contract between the employers and the beneficiary is required. The burden is on the agent to explain the terms and conditions of the employment and to provide any required documentation.

(*3*) A foreign employer who, through a United States agent, files a petition for an O nonimmigrant alien is responsible for complying with all of the employer sanctions provisions of section 274A of the Act and 8 CFR part 274a.

(F) *Multiple beneficiaries.* More than one O–2 accompanying alien may be included on a petition if they are assisting the same O–1 alien for the same events or performances, during the same period of time, and in the same location.

(G) *Traded professional O–1 athletes.* In the case of a professional O–1 athlete who is traded from one organization to another organization, employment authorization for the player will automatically continue for a period of 30 days after acquisition by the new organization, within which time the new organization is expected to file a new Form I–129. If a new Form I–129 is not filed within 30 days, employment authorization will cease. If a new Form I–129 is filed within 30 days, the professional athlete shall be deemed to be in valid O–1 status, and employment shall continue to be authorized, until the petition is adjudicated. If the new petition is denied, employment authorization will cease.

(3) *Petition for alien of extraordinary ability or achievement (O–1)*—(i) *General.* Extraordinary ability in the sciences, arts, education, business, or athletics, or extraordinary achievement in the case of an alien in the motion picture or television industry, must be established for an individual alien. An O–1 petition must be accompanied by evidence that the work which the alien is coming to the United States to continue is in the area of extraordinary ability, and that the alien meets the criteria in paragraph (o)(3)(iii) or (iv) of this section.

(ii) *Definitions.* As used in this paragraph, the term:

Arts includes any field of creative activity or endeavor such as, but not limited to, fine arts, visual arts, culinary arts, and performing arts. Aliens engaged in the field of arts include not only the principal creators and performers but other essential persons such as, but not limited to, directors, set designers, lighting designers, sound designers, choreographers, choreologists, conductors, orchestrators, coaches, arrangers, musical supervisors, costume designers, makeup artists, flight masters, stage technicians, and animal trainers.

Event means an activity such as, but not limited to, a scientific project, conference, convention, lecture series, tour, exhibit, business project, academic year, or engagement. Such activity may include short vacations, promotional appearances, and stopovers which are incidental and/or related to the event. A group of related activities may also be considered to be an event. In the case of an O–1 athlete, the event could be the alien's contract.

Extraordinary ability in the field of arts means distinction. Distinction means a high level of achievement in the field of arts evidenced by a degree of skill and recognition substantially above that ordinarily encountered to the extent that a person described as prominent is renowned, leading, or well-known in the field of arts.

Extraordinary ability in the field of science, education, business, or athletics means a level of expertise indicating that the person is one of the small percentage who have arisen to the very top of the field of endeavor.

Extraordinary achievement with respect to motion picture and television productions, as commonly defined in the industry, means a very high level of accomplishment in the motion picture or television industry evidenced by a degree of skill and recognition significantly above that ordinarily encountered to the extent that the person is recognized as outstanding, notable, or leading in the motion picture or television field.

Peer group means a group or organization which is comprised of practitioners of the alien's occupation. If there is a collective bargaining representative of an employer's employees in the occupational classification for which the alien is being sought, such a representative may be considered the appropriate peer group for purposes of consultation.

(iii) *Evidentiary criteria for an O–1 alien of extraordinary ability in the fields of science, education, business, or athletics.* An alien of extraordinary ability in the fields of science, education, business, or athletics must demonstrate sustained national or international acclaim and recognition for achievements in the field of expertise by providing evidence of:

(A) Receipt of a major, internationally recognized award, such as the Nobel Prize; or

(B) At least three of the following forms of documentation:

(*1*) Documentation of the alien's receipt of nationally or internationally recognized prizes or awards for excellence in the field of endeavor;

(*2*) Documentation of the alien's membership in associations in the field for which classification is sought, which require outstanding achievements of their members, as judged by recognized national or international experts in their disciplines or fields;

(*3*) Published material in professional or major trade publications or major media about the alien, relating to the alien's work in the field for which classification is sought, which shall include the title, date, and author of such published material, and any necessary translation;

(*4*) Evidence of the alien's participation on a panel, or individually, as a judge of the work of others in the same or in an allied field of specialization to that for which classification is sought;

(*5*) Evidence of the alien's original scientific, scholarly, or business-related contributions of major significance in the field;

(*6*) Evidence of the alien's authorship of scholarly articles in the field, in professional journals, or other major media;

(*7*) Evidence that the alien has been employed in a critical or essential capacity for organizations and establishments that have a distinguished reputation;

(*8*) Evidence that the alien has either commanded a high salary or will command a high salary or other remuneration for services, evidenced by contracts or other reliable evidence.

(C) If the criteria in paragraph (o)(3)(iii) of this section do not readily apply to the beneficiary's occupation, the petitioner may submit comparable evidence in order to establish the beneficiary's eligibility.

(iv) *Evidentiary criteria for an O–1 alien of extraordinary ability in the arts.* To qualify as an alien of extraordinary ability in the field of arts, the alien must be recognized as being prominent in his or her field of endeavor as demonstrated by the following:

(A) Evidence that the alien has been nominated for, or has been the recipient of, significant national or international awards or prizes in the particular field such as an Academy Award, an Emmy, a Grammy, or a Director's Guild Award; or

(B) At least three of the following forms of documentation:

(*1*) Evidence that the alien has performed, and will perform, services as a lead or starring participant in productions or events which have a distinguished reputation as evidenced by critical reviews, advertisements, publicity releases, publications contracts, or endorsements;

(*2*) Evidence that the alien has achieved national or international recognition for achievements evidenced by critical reviews or other published materials by or about the individual in major newspapers, trade journals, magazines, or other publications;

(*3*) Evidence that the alien has performed, and will perform, in a lead, starring, or critical role for organizations and establishments that have a distinguished reputation evidenced by articles in newspapers, trade journals, publications, or testimonials;

(*4*) Evidence that the alien has a record of major commercial or critically acclaimed successes as evidenced by such indicators as title, rating, standing in the field, box office receipts, motion pictures or television ratings, and other occupational achievements reported in trade journals, major newspapers, or other publications;

(*5*) Evidence that the alien has received significant recognition for achievements from organizations, critics, government agencies, or other recognized experts in the field in which the alien is engaged. Such testimonials must be in a form which clearly indicates the author's authority, expertise, and knowledge of the alien's achievements; or

(*6*) Evidence that the alien has either commanded a high salary or will command a high salary or other substantial remuneration for services in relation to others in the field, as evidenced by contracts or other reliable evidence; or

(C) If the criteria in paragraph (o)(3)(iv) of this section do not readily apply to the beneficiary's occupation, the petitioner may submit comparable evidence in order to establish the beneficiary's eligibility.

(v) *Evidentiary criteria for an alien of extraordinary achievement in the motion picture or television industry.* To qualify as an alien of extraordinary achievement in the motion picture or television industry, the alien must be recognized as having a demonstrated record of extraordinary achievement as evidenced by the following:

(A) Evidence that the alien has been nominated for, or has been the recipient of, significant national or international awards or prizes in the particular field such as an Academy Award, an Emmy, a Grammy, or a Director's Guild Award; or

(B) At least three of the following forms of documentation:

(*1*) Evidence that the alien has performed, and will perform, services as a lead or starring participant in productions or events which have a distinguished reputation as evidenced by critical reviews, advertisements, publicity releases, publications contracts, or endorsements;

(*2*) Evidence that the alien has achieved national or international recognition for achievements evidenced by critical reviews or other published materials by or about the individual in major newspapers, trade journals, magazines, or other publications;

(*3*) Evidence that the alien has performed, and will perform, in a lead, starring, or critical role for organizations and establishments that have a distinguished reputation evidenced by articles in newspapers, trade journals, publications, or testimonials;

(*4*) Evidence that the alien has a record of major commercial or critically acclaimed successes as evidenced by such indicators as title, rating, standing in the field, box office receipts, motion picture or television ratings, and other occupational achievements reported in trade journals, major newspapers, or other publications;

(*5*) Evidence that the alien has received significant recognition for achievements from organizations, critics, government agencies, or other recognized experts in the field in which the alien is engaged. Such testimonials must be in a form which clearly indicates the author's authority, expertise, and knowledge of the alien's achievements; or

(*6*) Evidence that the alien has either commanded a high salary or will command a high salary or other substantial remuneration for services in relation to other in the field, as evidenced by contracts or other reliable evidence.

(4) *Petition for an O–2 accompanying alien*—(i) *General.* An O–2 accompanying alien provides essential support to an O–1 artist or athlete. Such aliens may not accompany O–1 aliens in the fields of science, business, or education. Although the O–2 alien must obtain his or her own classification, this classification does not entitle him or her to work separate and apart from the O–1 alien to whom he or she provides support. An O–2 alien must be petitioned for in conjunction with the services of the O–1 alien.

(ii) *Evidentiary criteria for qualifying as an O–2 accompanying alien*—(A) *Alien accompanying an O–1 artist or athlete of extraordinary ability.* To qualify as an O–2 accompanying alien, the alien must be coming to the United States to assist in the performance of the O–1 alien, be an integral part of the actual performance, and have critical skills and experience with the O–1 alien which are not of a general nature and which are not possessed by a U.S. worker.

(B) *Alien accompanying an O–1 alien of extraordinary achievement.* To qualify as an O–2 alien accompanying and O–1 alien involved in a motion picture or television production, the alien must have skills and experience with the O–1 alien which are not of a general nature and which are critical based on a pre-existing longstanding working relationship or, with respect to the specific production, because significant production (including pre- and post-production work) will take place both inside and outside the United States and the continuing participation of the alien is essential to the successful completion of the production.

(C) The evidence shall establish the current essentiality, critical skills, and experience of the O–2 alien with the O–1 alien and that the alien has substantial experience performing the critical skills and essential support services for the O–1 alien. In the case of a specific motion picture or television production, the evidence shall establish that significant production has taken place outside the United States, and will take place inside the United States, and that the continuing participation of the alien is essential to the successful completion of the production.

(5) *Consultation*—(i) *General.* (A) Consultation with an appropriate U.S. peer group (which could include a person or persons with expertise in the field), labor and/or management organization regarding the nature of the work to be done and the alien's qualifications is mandatory before a petition for an O–1 or O–2 classification can be approved.

(B) Except as provided in paragraph (o)(5)(i)(E) of this section, evidence of consultation shall be in the form of a written advisory opinion from a peer group (which could include a person or persons with expertise in the field), labor and/or management organization with expertise in the specific field involved.

(C) Except as provided in paragraph (o)(5)(i)(E) of this section, the petitioner shall obtain a written advisory opinion from a peer group (which could include a person or persons with expertise in the field), labor, and/or management organization with expertise in the specific field involved. The advisory opinion shall be submitted along with the petition when the petition is filed. If the advisory opinion is not favorable to the petitioner, the advisory opinion must set forth a specific statement of facts which supports the conclusion reached in the opinion. Advisory opinions must be submitted in writing and must be signed by an authorized official of the group or organization.

(D) Except as provided in paragraph (o)(5)(i)(E) and (G) of this section, written evidence of consultation shall be included in the record in every approved O petition. Consultations are advisory and are not binding on the Service.

(E) In a case where the alien will be employed in the field of arts, entertainment, or athletics, and the Service has determined that a petition merits expeditious handling, the Service shall contact the appropriate labor and/or management organization and request an advisory opinion if one is not submitted by the petitioner. The labor and/or management organization shall have 24 hours to respond to the Service's request. The Service shall adjudicate the petition after receipt of the response from the consulting organization. The labor and/or management organization shall then furnish the Service with a written advisory opinion within 5 days of the initiating request. If the labor and/or management organization fails to respond within 24 hours, the Service shall render a decision on the petition without the advisory opinion.

(F) In a routine processing case where the petition is accompanied by a written opinion from a peer group, but the peer group is not a labor organization, the Director will forward a copy of the petition and all supporting documentation to the national office of the appropriate labor organization within 5 days of receipt of the petition. If there is a collective bargaining representative of an employer's employees in the occupational classification for which the alien is being sought, that representative shall be the appropriate labor organization for purposes of this section. The labor organization will then have 15 days from receipt of the petition and supporting documents to submit to the Service a written advisory opinion, comment, or letter of no objection. Once the 15-day period has expired, the Director shall adjudicate the petition in no more than 14 days. The Director may shorten this time in his or her discretion for emergency reasons, if no unreasonable burden would be imposed on any participant in the process. If the labor organization does not respond within 15 days, the Director will render a decision on the record without the advisory opinion.

(G) In those cases where it is established by the petitioner that an appropriate peer group, including a labor organization, does not exist, the Service shall render a decision on the evidence of record.

(ii) *Consultation requirements for an O–1 alien for extraordinary ability*—(A) *Content.* Consultation with a peer group in the area of the alien's ability (which may include a labor organization), or a person or persons with expertise in the area of the alien's ability, is required in an O–1 petition for an alien of extraordinary ability. If the advisory opinion is not favorable to the petitioner, the advisory opinion must set forth a specific statement of facts which supports the conclusion reached in the opinion. If the advisory opinion is favorable to the petitioner, it should describe the alien's ability and achievements in the field of endeavor, describe the nature of the duties to be performed, and state whether the position requires the services of an alien of extraordinary ability. A consulting organization may also submit a letter of no objection in lieu of the above if it has no objection to the approval of the petition.

(B) *Waiver of consultation of certain aliens of extraordinary ability in the field of arts.* Consultation for an alien of extraordinary ability in the field of arts shall be waived by the Director in those instances where the alien seeks readmission to the United States to perform similar services within 2 years of the date of a previous consultation. The director shall, within 5 days of granting the waiver, forward a copy of the petition and supporting documentation to the national office of an appropriate labor organization. Petitioners desiring to avail themselves of the waiver should submit a copy of the prior consultation with the petition and advise the Director of the waiver request.

(iii) *Consultation requirements for an O–1 alien of extraordinary achievement.* In the case of an alien of extraordinary achievement who will be working on a motion picture or television production, consultation shall be made with the appropriate union representing the alien's occupational peers and a management organization in the area of the alien's ability. If an advisory opinion is not favorable to the petitioner, the advisory opinion must set forth a specific statement of facts which supports the conclusion reached in the opinion. If the advisory opinion is favorable to the petitioner, the written advisory opinion from the labor and management organizations should describe the alien's achievements in the motion picture or television field and state whether the position requires the services of an alien of extraordinary achievement. If a consulting organization has no objection to the approval of the petition, the organization may submit a letter of no objection in lieu of the above.

(iv) *Consultation requirements for an O–2 accompanying alien.* Consultation with a labor organization with expertise in the skill area involved is required for an O–2 alien accompanying an O–1 alien of extraordinary ability. In the case of an O–2 alien seeking entry for a motion picture or television production, consultation with a labor organization and a management organization in the area of the alien's ability is required. If an advisory opinion is not favorable to the petitioner, the advisory opinion must set forth a specific statement of facts which supports the conclusion reached in the opinion. If the advisory opinion is favorable to the petitioner, the opinion provided by the labor and/or management organization should describe the alien's essentiality to, and working relationship with, the O–1 artist or athlete and state whether there are available U.S. workers who can perform the support services. If the alien will accompany an O–1 alien involved in a motion picture or television production, the advisory opinion should address the alien's skills and experience wit the O–1 alien and whether the alien has a pre-existing longstanding working relationship with the O–1 alien, or whether significant production will take place in the United States and abroad and if the continuing participation of the alien is essential to the successful completion of the production. A consulting organization may also submit a letter of no objection in lieu of the above if it has no objection to the approval of the petition.

(v) *Organizations agreeing to provide advisory opinions.* The Service will list in its Operations Instructions for O classification those peer groups, labor organizations, and/or management organizations which have agreed to provide advisory opinions to the Service and/or petitioners. The list will not be an exclusive or exhaustive list. The Service and petitioners may use other sources, such as publications, to identify appropriate peer groups, labor organizations, and management organizations. Additionally, the Service will list in its Operations Instructions those occupations or fields of endeavor where the nonexistence of an appropriate consulting entity has been verified.

(6) *Approval and validity of petition*—(1) *Approval.* The Director shall consider all of the evidence submitted and such other evidence as may be independently required to assist in the adjudication. The Director shall notify the petitioner of the approval of the petition on Form I–797, Notice of Action. The approval notice shall include the alien beneficiary name, the classification, and the petition's period of validity.

(ii) *Recording the validity of petitions.* Procedures for recording the validity period of petitions are as follows;

(A) If a new O petition is approved before the date the petitioner indicates the services will begin, the approved petition and approval notice shall show the actual dates requested by the petitioner, not to exceed the limit specified by paragraph (o)(6)(iii) of this section or other Service policy.

(B) If a new 0 petition is approved after the date the petitioner indicates the services will begin, the approved petition and approval notice shall generally show a validity period commencing with the date of approval and ending with the date requested by the petitioner, not to exceed the limit specified by paragraph (o)(6)(iii) of this section or other Service policy.

(C) If the period of services requested by the petitioner exceeds the limit specified in paragraph (o)(6)(iii) of this section, the petition shall be approved only up to the limit specified in that paragraph.

(iii) *Validity*—(A) *O–1 petition.* An approved petition for an alien classified under section 101(a)(15)(O)(i) of the Act shall be valid for a period of time determined by the Director to be necessary to accomplish the event or activity, not to exceed 3 years.

(B) *O–2 petition.* An approved petition for an alien classified under section 101(a)(15)(O)(ii) of the Act shall be valid for a period of time determined to be necessary to assist the O–1 alien to accomplish the event or activity, not to exceed 3 years.

(iv) *Spouse and dependents.* The spouse and unmarried minor children of the O–1 or O–2 alien beneficiary are entitled to O–3 nonimmigrant classification, subject to the same period of admission and limitations as the alien beneficiary, if they are accompanying or following to join the alien beneficiary in the United States. Neither the spouse nor a child of the alien beneficiary may accept employment unless he or she has been granted employment authorization.

(7) The petitioner shall be notified of the decision, the reasons for the denial, and the right to appeal the denial under 8 CFR part 103.

(8) *Revocation of approval of petition*—(i) *General.* (A) The petitioner shall immediately notify the Service of any changes in the terms and conditions of employment of a beneficiary which may affect eligibility under section 101(a)(15)(O) of the Act and paragraph (o) of this section. An amended petition should be filed when the petitioner continues to employ the beneficiary. If the petitioner no longer employs the beneficiary, the petitioner shall send a letter explaining the change(s) to the Director who approved the petition.

(B) The Director may revoke a petition at any time, even after the validity of the petition has expired.

(ii) *Automatic revocation.* The approval of an unexpired petition is automatically revoked if the petitioner, or the named employer in a petition filed by an agent, goes out of business, files a written withdrawal of the petition, or notifies the Service that the beneficiary is no longer employed by the petitioner.

(iii) *Revocation on notice*—(A) *Grounds for revocation.* The Director shall send to the petitioner a notice of intent to revoke the petition in relevant part if is determined that:

(*1*) The beneficiary is no longer employed by the petitioner in the capacity specified in the petition;

(*2*) The statement of facts contained in the petition was not true and correct;

(*3*) The petitioner violated the terms or conditions of the approved petition;

(*4*) The petitioner violated the requirements of section 101(a)(15)(O) of the Act or paragraph (o) of this section; or

(*5*) The approval of the petition violated paragraph (o) of this section or involved gross error.

(B) *Notice and decision.* The notice of intent to revoke shall contain a detailed statement of the grounds for the revocation and the time period allowed for the petitioner's rebuttal. The petitioner may submit evidence in rebuttal within 30 days of the date of the notice. The Director shall consider all relevant evidence presented in deciding whether to revoke the petition.

(9) *Appeal of a denial or a revocation of a petition*—(i) *Denial.* A denied petition may be appealed under 8 CFR part 103.

(ii) *Revocation.* A petition that has been revoked on notice may be appealed under 8 CFR part 103. Automatic revocations may not be appealed.

(10) *Admission.* A beneficiary may be admitted to the United States for the validity period of the petition, plus a period of up to 10 days before the validity period begins and 10 days after the validity period ends. The beneficiary may only engage in employment during the validity period of the petition.

(11) *Extention of visa petition validity.* The petitioner shall file a request to extend the validity of the original petition under section 101(a)(15)(O) of the Act on Form I–129, Petition for a Nonimmigrant Worker, in order to continue or complete the same activities or events specified in the original petition. Supporting documents are not required unless requested by the Director. A petition extension may be filed only if the validity of the original petition has not expired.

(12) *Extension of stay*—(i) *Extension procedure.* The petitioner shall request extension of the alien's stay to continue or complete the same event or activity by filing Form I–129, accompanied by a statement explaining the reasons for the extension. The petitioner must also request a petition extension. The dates of extension shall be the same for the petition and the beneficiary's extension of stay. The alien beneficiary must be physically present in the United States at the time of filing of the extension of stay. Even though the request to extend the petition and the alien's stay are combined on the petition, the Director shall make a separate determination on each. If the alien leaves the United States for business or personal reasons while the extension requests are pending, the petitioner may request the Director to cable notification of approval of the petition extension to the consular office abroad where the alien will apply for a visa.

(ii) *Extension period.* An extension of stay may be authorized in increments of up to 1 year for an O–1 or O–2 beneficiary to continue or complete the same event or activity for which he or she was admitted plus an additional 10 days to allow the beneficiary to get his or her personal affairs in order.

(iii) *Denial of an extension of stay.* The denial of the request for the alien's extension of temporary stay may not be appealed.

(13) *Effect of approval of a permanent labor certification or filing of a preference petition on O classification.* The approval of a permanent labor certification or the filing of a preference petition for an alien shall not be a basis for denying an O–1 petition, a request to extend such a petition, or the alien's application for admission, change of status, or extension of stay. The alien may legitimately come to the United States for a temporary period as an O–1 nonimmigrant and depart voluntarily at the end of his or her authorized stay and, at the same time, lawfully seek to become a permanent resident of the United States.

(14) *Effect of a strike.* (i) If the Secretary of Labor certifies to the Commissioner that a strike or other labor dispute involving a work stoppage of workers is in progress in the occupation at the place where the beneficiary is to be employed, and that the employment of the beneficiary would adversely affect the wages and working conditions of U.S. citizens and lawful resident workers:

(A) A petition to classify an alien as a nonimmigrant as defined in section 101(a)(15)(O) of the Act shall be denied; or

(B) If a petition has been approved, but the alien has not yet entered the United States, or has entered the United States but has not commenced employment, the approval of the petition is automatically suspended, and the application for admission on the basis of the petition shall be denied.

(ii) If there is a strike or other labor dispute involving a work stoppage of workers in progress, but such strike or other labor dispute is not certified under paragraph (o)(14)(i) of this section, the Commissioner shall not deny a petition or suspend an approved petition.

(iii) If the alien has already commenced employment in the United States under an approved petition and is participating in a strike or labor dispute involving a work stoppage of workers, whether or not such strike or other labor dispute has been certified by the Secretary of Labor, the alien shall not be deemed to be failing to maintain his or her status solely on account of past, present, or future participation in a strike or other labor dispute involving a work stoppage of workers but is subject to the following terms and conditions:

(A) The alien shall remain subject to all applicable provisions of the Immigration and Nationality Act and regulations promulgated thereunder in the same manner as are all other O nonimmigrants;

(B) The status and authorized period of stay of such an alien is not modified or extended in any way by virtue of his or her participation in a strike or other labor dispute involving a work stoppage of workers; and

(C) Although participation by an O nonimmigrant alien in a strike or other labor dispute involving a work stoppage of workers will not constitute a ground for deportation, and alien who violates his or her status or who remains in the United States after his or her authorized period of stay has expired will be subject to deportation.

(15) *Use of approval notice, Form I–797.* The Service shall notify the petitioner of Form I–797 whenever a visa petition or an extension of a visa petition is approved under the O classification. The beneficiary of an O petition who does not require a nonimmigrant visa may present a copy of the approval notice at a Port-of-Entry to facilitate entry into the United States. A beneficiary who is required to present a visa for admission, and who visa will have expired before the date of his or her intended return, may use Form I–797 to apply for a new or revalidated visa during the validity period of the petition. A copy of Form I–797 shall be retained by the beneficiary and presented during the validity of the petition when reentering the United States to resume the same employment with the same petitioner.

(16) *Return transportation requirement.* In the case of an alien who enters the United States under section 101(a)(15(O) of the Act and whose employment terminates for reasons other than voluntary resignation, the employer whose offer of employment formed the basis of such nonimmigrant status and the petitioner are jointly and severally liable for the reasonable cost of return transportation of the alien abroad. For the purposes of this paragraph, the term "abroad" means the alien's last place of residence prior to his or her entry into the United States.

(p) *Artists, athletes, and entertainers*—(1) *Classifications*—(i) *General.* Under section 101(a)(15)(P) of the Act, an alien having a residence in a foreign country which he or she has not intention or abandoning may be authorized to come to the United States temporarily to perform services for an employer or a sponsor. Under the nonimmigrant category, the alien may be classified under section 101(a)(15)(P)(i) of the Act as an alien who is coming to the United States to perform services as an internationally recognized athlete, individually or as part of a group or team, or member of an internationally recognized entertainment group; under section 101(a)(15)(P)(ii) of the Act, who is coming to perform as an artist or entertainer under a reciprocal exchange program; under section 101(a)(15)(P)(iii) of the Act, as an alien who is coming solely to perform, teach, or coach under a program that is culturally unique; or under section 101(a)(15)(P)(iv) of the Act, as the spouse or child of an alien described in section 101(a)(15)(P) (i), (ii), or (iii) of the Act who is accompanying or following to join the alien. These classifications are called P–1, P–2, P–3, and P–4 respectively. The employer or sponsor must file a petition with the Service for review of the services to be performed and for determination of the alien's eligibility for P–1, P–2, or P–3 classification before the alien may apply for a visa or seek admission to the United States. This paragraph sets forth the standards and procedures applicable to these classifications.

(ii) *Description of classification.* (A) A P–1 classification applies to an alien who is coming temporarily to the United States:

(*1*) To perform at specific athletic competition as an athlete, individually or as part of a group or team, at an internationally recognized level or performance, or

(*2*) To perform with, or as an integral and essential part of the performance of, and entertainment group that has been recognized internationally as being outstanding in the discipline for a sustained and substantial period of time, and who has had a sustained and substantial relationship with the group (ordinarily for at least 1 year) and provides functions integral to the performance of the group.

(B) A P–2 classification applies to an alien who is coming temporarily to the United States to perform as an artist or entertainer, individually or as part of a group, or to perform as an integral part of the performance of such a group, and who seeks to perform under a reciprocal exchange program which is between an organization or organizations in the United States and an organization or organizations in one or more foreign states, and which provides for the temporary exchange of artists and entertainers, or groups of artists and entertainers.

(C) A P–3 classification applies to an alien artist or entertainer who is coming temporarily to the United States, either individually or as part of a group, or as an integral part of the performance of the group, to perform, teach, or coach under a commercial or noncommercial program that is culturally unique.

(2) *Filing of petitions*—(i) *General.* A P–1 petition for an athlete or entertainment group shall be filed by a United States employer, a United States sponsoring organization, a United States agent, or a foreign employer through a United States agent. For purposes of paragraph (p) of this section, a foreign employer is any employer who is not amenable to service of process in the United States. Foreign employers seeking to employ a P–1 alien may not directly petition for the alien but must use a United States agent. A United States agent petitioning on behalf of a foreign employer must be authorized to file the petition, and to accept service of process in the United States in proceedings under section 274A of the Act, on behalf of the foreign employer. A P–2 petition for an artist or entertainer in a reciprocal exchange program shall be filed by the United States labor organization which negotiated the reciprocal exchange agreement, the sponsoring organization, or a United States employer. A P–3 petition for an artist or entertainer in a culturally unique program shall be filed by the sponsoring organization or a United States employer. Essential support personnel may not be included on the petition filed for the principal alien(s). These aliens require a separate petition. The petitioner must file a P petition on Form I–129, Petition for Nonimmigrant Worker. The petition may not be filed more than one year before the actual need for the alien's services. A P–1, P–2, or P–3 petition shall be adjudicated at the appropriate Service Center, even in emergency situations.

(ii) *Evidence required to accompany a petition for a P nonimmigrant.* Petitions for P nonimmigrant aliens shall be accompanied by the following:

(A) The evidence specified in the specific section of this part for the classification;

(B) Copies of any written contracts between the petitioner and the alien beneficiary or, if there is no written contract, a summary of the terms of the oral agreement under which the alien(s) will be employed;

(C) An explanation of the nature of the events or activities, the beginning and ending dates for the events or activities, and a copy of any itinerary for the events or activities; and

(D) A written consultation from a labor organization.

(iii) *Form of documentation.* The evidence submitted with an P petition should conform to the following:

(A) Affidavits, contracts, awards, and similar documentation must reflect the nature of the alien's achievement and be executed by an officer or responsible person employed by the institution, establishment, or organization where the work has performed.

(B) Affidavits written by present or former employers or recognized experts certifying to the recognition and extraordinary ability, or, in the case of a motion picture or television production, the extraordinary achievement of the alien, which shall specifically describe the alien's recognition and ability or achievement in factual terms. The affidavit must also set forth the expertise of the affiant and the manner in which the affiant acquired such information.

(C) A legible copy of a document in support of the petition may be submitted in lieu of the original. However, the original document shall be submitted if requested by the Director.

(iv) *Other filing situations*—(A) *Services in more than one location.* A petition which requires the alien to work in more than one location (e.g., a tour) must include an itinerary with the dates and locations of the performances.

(B) *Services for more than one employer.* If the beneficiary or beneficiaries will work for more than one employer within the same time period, each employer must file a separate petition unless an agent files the petition pursuant to paragraph (p)(2)(iv)(E) of this section.

(C) *Change of employer*—(*1*) *General.* If a P–1, P–2, or P–3 alien in the United States seeks to change employers or sponsors, the new employer or sponsor must file both a petition and a request to extend the alien's stay in the United States. The alien may not commence employment with the new employer or sponsor until the petition and request for extension have been approved.

(*2*) *Traded professional P–1 athletes.* In the case of a professional P–1 athlete who is traded from one organization to another organization, employment authorization for the player will automatically continue for a period of 30 days after acquisition by the new organization, within which time the new organization is expected to file a new Form I–129 for P–1 nonimmigrant classification. If a new Form I–129 is not filed within 30 days, employment authorization will cease. If a new Form I–129 is filed within 30 days, the professional athlete shall be deemed to be in valid P–1 status, and employment shall continue to be authorized, until the petition is adjudicated. If the new petition is denied, employment authorization will cease.

(D) *Amended petition.* The petitioner shall file an amended petition, with fee, with the Service Center where the original petition was filed to reflect any material changes in the terms and conditions of employment or the beneficiary's eligibility as specified in the original approved petition. A petitioner may add additional, similar or comparable performance, engagements, or competitions during the validity period of the petition without filing an amended petition.

(E) *Agents as petitioners.* A United States agent may file a petition in cases involving workers who are traditionally self-employed or workers who use agents to arrange short-term employment on their behalf with numerous employers, and in cases where a foreign employer authorizes the agent to act on its behalf. A United States agent may be: the actual employer of the beneficiary; the representative of both the employer and the beneficiary; or, a person or entity authorized by the employer to act for, or in place of, the employer as its agent. A petition filed by an United States agent is subject to the following conditions:

(*1*) An agent performing the function of an employer must specify the wage offered and the other terms and conditions of employment by contractual agreement with the beneficiary or beneficiaries. The agent/employer must also provide an itinerary of definite employment and information on any other services planned for the period of time requested.

(*2*) A person or company in business as an agent may file the P petition involving multiple employers as the representative of both the employers and the beneficiary or beneficiaries if the supporting documentation includes a complete itinerary of services or engagements. The itinerary shall specify the dates of each service or engagement, the names and addresses of the actual employers, the names and addresses of the establishment, venues, or locations where the services will be performed. In questionable cases, a contract between the employer(s) and the beneficiary or beneficiaries may be required. The burden is on the agent to explain the terms and conditions of the employment and to provide any required documentation.

(*3*) A foreign employer who, through a United States agent, files a petition for a P nonimmigrant alien is responsible for complying with all of the employer sanctions provisions of section 274A of the Act and 8 CFR part 274a.

(F) *Multiple beneficiaries.* More than one beneficiary may be included in a P petition if they are members of a group seeking classification based on the reputation of the group as an entity, or if they will provide essential support to P–1, P–2, or P–3 beneficiaries performing in the same location and in the same occupation.

(G) *Named beneficiaries.* Petitions for P classification must include the names of beneficiaries and other required information at the time of filing.

(H) *Substitution of beneficiaries.* A petitioner may request substitution of beneficiaries in approved P–1, P–2, and P–3 petitions for groups. To request substitution, the petitioner shall submit a letter requesting such substitution, along with a copy of the petitioner's approval notice, to the consular office at which the alien will apply for a visa or the Port-of-Entry where the alien will apply for admission. Essential support personnel may not be substituted at consular offices or at Ports-of-entry. In order to add additional new essential support personnel, a new I–129 petition must be filed.

(3) *Definitions.* As used in this paragraph, the term:

Arts includes fields of creative activity or endeavor such as, but not limited to, fine arts, visual arts, and performing arts.

Competition, event, or performance means an activity such as an athletic competition, athletic season, tournament, tour, exhibit, project, entertainment event, or engagement. Such activity could include short vacations, promotional appearances for the petitioning employer relating to the competition, event, or performance, and stopovers which are incidental and/or related to the activity. An athletic competition or entertainment event could include an entire season of performances A group of related activities will also be considered an event. In the case of a P–2 petition, the event may be the duration of the reciprocal exchange agreement. In the case of a P–1 athlete, the event may be the duration of the alien's contract.

Contract means the written agreement between the petitioner and the beneficiary(ies) that explains the terms and conditions of employment. The contract shall describe the services to be performed, and specify the wages, hours of work, working conditions, and any fringe benefits.

Culturally unique means a style of artistic expression, methodology, or medium which is unique to a particular country, nation, society, class, ethnicity, religion, tribe, or other group of persons.

Essential support alien means a highly skilled, essential person determined by the Director to be an integral part of the performance of a P–1, P–2, or P–3 alien because he or she performs support services which cannot be readily performed by a United States worker and which are essential to the successful performance of services by the P–1, P–2, alien. Such alien must have appropriate qualifications to perform the services, critical knowledge of the specific services to be performed, and experience in providing such support to the P–1, P–2, or P–3 alien.

Group means two or more persons established as one entity or unit to perform or to provide a service.

Internationally recognized means having a high level of achievement in a field evidenced by a degree of skill and recognition substantially above that ordinarily encountered, to the extent that such achievement is renowned, leading, or well-known in more than one country.

Member of a group means a person who is actually performing the entertainment services.

Sponsor means an established organization in the United States which will not directly employ a P–1, P–2, or P–3 alien but will assume responsibility for the accuracy of the terms and conditions specified in the petition.

Team means two or more persons organized to perform together as a competitive unit in a competitive event.

(4) *Petition for an internationally recognized athlete or member of an internationally recognized entertainment group (P–1)*—(i) *Types of classification*—(A) *P–1 classification as an athlete in an individual capacity.* A P–1 classification may be granted to an alien who is an internationally recognized athlete based on his or her own reputation and achievements as an individual. The alien must be coming to the United

States to perform services which require an internationally recognized athlete.

(B) *P–1 classification as a member of an entertainment group or an athletic team.* An entertainment group or athletic team consists of two or more persons who function as a unit. The entertainment group or athletic team as a unit must be internationally recognized as outstanding in the discipline and must be coming to perform services which require an internationally recognized entertainment group or athletic team. A person who is a member of an internationally recognized entertainment group or athletic team may be granted P–1 classification based on that relationship, but may not perform services separate and apart from the entertainment group or athletic team. An entertainment group must have been established for a minimum of 1 year, and 75 percent of the members of the group must have been performing entertainment services for the group for a minimum of 1 year.

(ii) *Criteria and documentary requirements for P–1 athletes*—(A) *General.* A P–1 athlete must have an internationally recognized reputation as an international athlete or he or she must be a member of a foreign team that is internationally recognized. The athlete or team must be coming to the United States to participate in an athletic competition which has a distinguished reputation and which requires participation of an athlete or athletic team that has an international reputation.

(B) *Evidentiary requirements for an internationally recognized athlete or athletic team.* A petition for an athletic team must be accompanied by evidence that the team as a unit has achieved international recognition in the sport. Each member of the team is accorded P–1 classification based on the international reputation of the team. A petition for an athlete who will compete individually or as a member of a U.S. team must be accompanied by evidence that the athlete has achieved international recognition in the sport based on his or her reputation. A petition for a P–1 athlete or athletic team shall include:

(*1*) A tendered contract with a major United States sports league or team, or a tendered contract in an individual sport commensurate with international recognition in that sport, if such contracts are normally executed in the sport, and

(*2*) Documentation of at least two of the following:

(*i*) Evidence of having participated to a significant extent in a prior season with a major United States sports league;

(*ii*) Evidence of having participated in international competition with a national team;

(*iii*) Evidence of having participated to a significant extent in a prior season for a U.S. college or university in intercollegiate competition;

(*iv*) A written statement from an official of the governing body of the sport which details how the alien or team is internationally recognized;

(*v*) A written statement from a member of the sports media or a recognized expert in the sport which details how the alien or team is internationally recognized;

(*vi*) Evidence that the individual or team is ranked if the sport has international rankings; or

(*vii*) Evidence that the alien or team has received a significant honor or award in the sport.

(iii) *Criteria and documentary requirements for members of an internationally recognized entertainment group*—(A) *General.* A P–1 classification shall be accorded to an entertainment group to perform as a unit based on the international reputation of the group. Individual entertainers shall not be accorded P–1 classification to perform separate and apart from a group. Except as provided in paragraph (p)(4)(iii)(C)(*2*) of this section, it must be established that the group has been internationally recognized as outstanding in the discipline for a sustained and substantial period of time. Seventy-five percent of the members of the group must have had a sustained and substantial relationship with the group for at least 1 year and must provide functions integral to the group's performance.

(B) *Evidentiary criteria for members of internationally recognized entertainment groups.* A petition for P–1 classification for the members of an entertainment group shall be accompanied by:

(*1*) Evidence that the group has been established and performing regularly for a period of at least 1 year;

(*2*) A statement from the petitioner listing each member of the group and the exact dates for which each member has been employed on a regular basis by the group; and

(*3*) Evidence that the group has been internationally recognized in the discipline for a sustained and substantial period of time. This may be demonstrated by the submission of evidence of the group's nomination or receipt of significant international awards or prices for outstanding achievement in its field or by three of the following different types of documentation:

(*i*) Evidence that the group has performed, and will perform, as a starring or leading entertainment group in productions or events which have a distinguished reputation as evidenced by critical reviews, advertisements, publicity releases, publications, contracts, or endorsements;

(*ii*) Evidence that the group has achieved international recognition and acclaim for outstanding achievement in its field as evidenced by reviews in major newspapers, trade journals, magazines, or other published material;

(*iii*) Evidence that the group has performed, and will perform, services as a leading or starring group for organizations and establishments that have a distinguished reputation evidenced by articles in newspapers, trade journals, publications, or testimonials;

(*iv*) Evidence that the group has a record of major commercial or critically acclaimed successes, as evidenced by such indicators as ratings; standing in the field; box office receipts; record, cassette, or video sales; and other achievements in the field as reported in trade journals, major newspapers, or other publications;

(*v*) Evidence that the group has achieved significant recognition for achievements from organizations, critics, government agencies, or other recognized experts in the field. Such testimonials must be in a form that clearly indicates the author's authority, expertise, and knowledge of the alien's achievements; or

(*vi*) Evidence that the group has either commanded a high salary or will command a high salary or other substantial remuneration for services comparable to other similarly situated in the field as evidenced by contracts or other reliable evidence.

(C) *Special provisions for certain entertainment groups*—(*1*) *Alien circus personnel.* The 1-year group membership requirement and the international recognition requirement are not applicable to alien circus personnel who perform as part of a circus or circus group, or who constitute an integral and essential part of the performance of such circus or circus group, provided that the alien or aliens are coming to join a circus that has been recognized nationally as outstanding for a sustained and substantial period of time or as part of such a circus.

(*2*) *Certain nationally known entertainment groups.* The Director may waive the international recognition requirement in the case of an entertainment group which has been recognized nationally as being outstanding in its discipline for a sustained and substantial period of time in consideration of special circumstances. An example of a special circumstances would be when an entertainment group may find it difficult to demonstrate recognition in more than one country due to such factors as limited access to news media or consequences of geography.

(*3*) *Waiver of 1-year relationship in exigent circumstances.* The Director may waive the 1-year relationship requirement for an alien who, because of illness or unanticipated and exigent circumstances, replaces an essential member of a P–1 entertainment group or an alien who augments the group by performing a critical role. The Department of State is hereby delegated the authority to waive the 1-year relationship requirement in the case of consular substitutions involving P–1 entertainment groups.

(iv) *P–1 classification as an essential support alien*—(A) *General.* An essential support alien as defined in paragraph (p)(3) of this section may be granted P–1 classification based on a support relationship with an individual P–1 athlete,

P–1 athletic team, or a P–1 entertainment group.

(B) *Evidentiary criteria for a P–1 essential support petition.* A petition for P–1 essential support personnel must be accompanied by:

(*1*) A consultation from a labor organization with expertise in the area of the alien's skill;

(*2*) A statement describing the alien(s) prior essentiality, critical skills, and experience with the principal alien(s); and

(*3*) A copy of the written contract or a summary of the terms of the oral agreement between the alien(s) and the employer.

(5) *Petition for an artist or entertainer under a reciprocal exchange program (P–2)*—(i) *General.* (A) A P–2 classification shall be accorded to artists or entertainers, individually or as a group, who will be performing under a reciprocal exchange program which is between an organization or organizations in the United States, which may include a management organization, and an organization or organizations in one or more foreign states and which provides for the temporary exchange of artists and entertainers, or groups of artists and entertainers.

(B) The exchange of artists or entertainers shall be similar in terms of caliber of artists or entertainers, terms and conditions of employment, such as length of employment, and numbers of artists or entertainers involved in the exchange. However, this requirement does not preclude an individual for group exchange.

(C) An alien who is an essential support person as defined in paragraph (p)(3) of this section may be accorded P–2 classification based on a support relationship to a P–2 artist or entertainer under a reciprocal exchange program.

(ii) *Evidentiary requirements for petition involving a reciprocal exchange program.* A petition for P–2 classification shall be accompanied by:

(A) A copy of the formal reciprocal exchange agreement between the U.S. organization or organizations which sponsor the aliens and an organization or organizations in a foreign country which will receive the U.S. artist or entertainers;

(B) A statement from the sponsoring organization describing the reciprocal exchange of U.S. artists or entertainers as it relates to the specific petition for which P–2 classification is being sought;

(C) Evidence that an appropriate labor organization in the United States was involved in negotiating, or has concurred with, the reciprocal exchange of U.S. and foreign artists or entertainers; and

(D) Evidence that the aliens for whom P–2 classification is being sought and the U.S. artists or entertainers subject to the reciprocal exchange agreement are artists or entertainers with comparable skills, and that the terms and conditions of employment are similar.

(iii) *P–2 classification as an essential support alien*—(A) *General.* An essential support alien as defined in paragraph (p)(3) of this section may be granted P–2 classification based on a support relationship with a P–2 entertainer or P–2 entertainment group.

(B) *Evidentiary criteria for a P–2 essential support petition.* A petition for P–2 essential support personnel must be accompanied by:

(*1*) A consultation from a labor organization with expertise in the area of the alien's skill;

(*2*) A statement describing the alien(s) prior essentiality, critical skills, and experience with the principal alien(s); and

(*3*) A copy of the written contract or a summary of the terms of the oral agreement between the alien(s) and the employer.

(6) *Petition for an artist or entertainer under a culturally unique program*—(i) *General.* (A) A P–3 classification may be accorded to artists or entertainers, individually or as a group, coming to the United States for the purpose of developing, interpreting, representing, coaching, or teaching a unique or traditional ethnic, folk, cultural, musical, theatrical, or artistic performance or presentation.

(B) The artist or entertainer must be coming to the United States to participate in a cultural event or events which will further the understanding or development of his or her art form.

The program may be of a commercial or noncommercial nature.

(ii) *Evidentiary criteria for a petition involving a culturally unique program.* A petition for P–3 classification shall be accompanied by:

(A) Affidavits, testimonials, or letters from recognized experts attesting to the authenticity of the alien's or the group's skills in performing, presenting, coaching, or teaching the unique or traditional art form and giving the credentials of the expert, including the basis of his or her knowledge of the alien's or group's skill, or

(B) Documentation that the performance of the alien or group is culturally unique, as evidence by reviews in newspapers, journals, or other published materials; and

(C) Evidence that all of the performances or presentations will be culturally unique events.

(iii) *P–3 classification as an essential support alien*—(A) *General.* An essential support alien as defined in paragraph (p)(3) of this section may be granted P–3 classification based on a support relationship with a P–3 entertainer or P–3 entertainment group.

(B) *Evidentiary criteria for a P–3 essential support petition.* A petition for P–3 essential support personnel must be accompanied by:

(*1*) A consultation from a labor organization with expertise in the area of the alien's skill;

(*2*) A statement describing the alien(s) prior essentiality, critical skills and experience with the principal alien(s); and

(*3*) A copy of the written contract or a summary of the terms of the oral agreement between the alien(s) and the employer.

(7) *Consultation*—(i) *General.* (A) Consultation with an appropriate labor organization regarding the nature of the work to be done and the alien's qualifications is mandatory before a petition for P–1, P–2, or P–3 classification can be approved.

(B) Except as provided in paragraph (p)(7)(i)(E) of this section, evidence of consultation shall be a written advisory opinion from an appropriate labor organization.

(C) Except as provided in paragraph (p)(7)(i)(E) of this section, the petitioner shall obtain a written advisory opinion from an appropriate labor organization. The advisory opinion shall be submitted along with the petition when the petition is filed. If the advisory opinion is not favorable to the petitioner, the advisory opinion must set forth a specific statement of facts which support the conclusion reached in the opinion. Advisory opinions must be submitted in writing and signed by an authorized official of the organization.

(D) Except as provided in paragraph (p)(7)(i) (E) and (F) of this section, written evidence of consultation shall be included in the record of every approved petition. Consultations are advisory and are not binding on the Service.

(E) In a case where the Service has determined that a petition merits expeditious handling, the Service shall contact the labor organization and request an advisory opinion if one is not submitted by the petitioner. The labor organization shall have 24 hours to respond to the Service's request. The Service shall adjudicate the petition after receipt of the response from the labor organization. The labor organization shall then furnish the Service with a written advisory opinion within 5 working days of the request. If the labor organization fails to respond within 24 hours, the Service shall render a decision on the petition without the advisory opinion.

(F) In those cases where it is established by the petitioner that an appropriate labor organization does not exist, the Service shall render a decision on the evidence of record.

(ii) *Consultation requirements for P–1 athletes and entertainment groups.* Consultation with a labor organization that has expertise in the area of the alien's sport or entertainment field is required in the case of a P–1 petition. If the advisory opinion is not favorable to the petitioner, the advisory opinion must set forth a specific statement of facts which support the conclusion reached in the opinion. If the advisory opinion provided by the labor organization is favorable to the petitioner it should evaluate and/or describe the alien's or group's ability and achievements in the field of endeavor, comment on whether the alien or group is internationally recognized for achievements, and state whether the services the alien or group is coming to perform are appropriate for an internationally recognized athlete or entertainment group. In lieu of the above, a labor organization may submit a letter of no objection if it has no objection to the approval of the petition.

(iii) *Consultation requirements for P–1 circus personnel.* The advisory opinion provided by the labor organization should comment on whether the circus which will employ the alien has national recognition as well as any other aspect of the beneficiary's or beneficiaries' qualifications which the labor organization deems appropriate. If the advisory opinion is not favorable to the petitioner, it must set forth a specific statement of facts which support the conclusion reached in the opinion. In lieu of the above, a labor organization may submit a letter of no objection if it has no objection to the approval of the petition.

(iv) *Consultation requirements for P–2 alien in a reciprocal exchange program.* In P–2 petitions where an artist or entertainer is coming to the United States under a reciprocal exchange program, consultation with the appropriate labor organization is required to verify the existence of a viable exchange program. The advisory opinion from the labor organization shall comment on the bona fides of the reciprocal exchange program and specify whether the exchange meets the requirements of paragraph (p)(5) of this section. If the advisory opinion is not favorable to the petitioner, it must also set forth a specific statement of facts which support the conclusion reached in the opinion.

(v) *Consultation requirements for P–3 in a culturally unique program.* Consultation with an appropriate labor organization is required for P–3 petitions involving aliens in culturally unique programs. If the advisory opinion is favorable to the petitioner, it should evaluate the cultural uniqueness of the alien's skills, state whether the events are cultural in nature, and state whether the event or activity is appropriate for P–3 classification. If the advisory opinion is not favorable to the petitioner, it must also set forth a specific statement of facts which support the conclusion reached in the opinion. In lieu of the above, a labor organization may submit a letter of no objection if it has no objection to the approval of the petition.

(vi) *Consultation requirements for essential support aliens.* Written consultation on petitions for P–1, P–2, or P–3 essential support aliens must be made with a labor organization with expertise in the skill area involved. If the advisory opinion provided by the labor organization is favorable to the petitioner, it must evaluate the alien's essentiality to and working relationship with the artist or entertainer, and state whether United States workers are available who can perform the support services. If the advisory opinion is not favorable to the petitioner, it must also set forth a specific statement of facts which support the conclusion reached in the opinion. A labor organization may submit a letter of no objection if it has no objection to the approval of the petition.

(vii) *Labor organizations agreeing to provide consultations.* The Service shall list in its Operations Instructions for P classification those organizations which have agreed to provide advisory opinions to the Service and/or petitioners. The list will not be an exclusive or exhaustive list. The Service and petitioners may use other sources, such as publications, to identify appropriate labor organizations. The Service will also list in its Operations Instructions those occupations or fields of endeavor where it has been determined by the Service that no appropriate labor organization exists.

(8) *Approval and validity of petition*—(i) *Approval.* The Director shall consider all the evidence submitted and such other evidence as he or she may independently require to assist in his or her adjudication. The Director shall notify the petitioner of the approval of the petition on Form I–797, Notice of Action. The approval notice shall include the alien beneficiary's name and classification and the petition's period of validity.

(ii) *Recording the validity of petitions.* Procedures for recording the validity period of petitions are:

(A) If a new P petition is approved before the date the petitioner indicates the services will begin, the approved petition and approval notice shall show the actual dates requested by the petitioner as the validity period, not to exceed the limit specified in paragraph (p)(8)(iii) of this section or other Service policy.

(B) If a new P petition is approved after the date the petitioner indicates the services will begin, the approved petition and approval notice shall generally show a validity period commencing with the date of approval and ending with the date requested by the petitioner, not to exceed the limit specified in paragraph (p)(8)(iii) of this section or other Service policy.

(C) If the period of services requested by the petitioner exceeds the limit specified in paragraph (p)(8)(iii) of this section, the petition shall be approved only up to the limit specified in that paragraph.

(iii) *Validity.* The approval period of a P petition shall conform to the limits prescribed as follows:

(A) *P-1 petition for athletes.* An approved petition for an individual athlete classified under section 101(a)(15)(P)(i) of the Act shall be valid for a period up to 5 years. An approved petition for an athletic team classified under section 101(a)(15)(P)(i) of the Act shall be valid for a period of time determined by the Director to complete the competition or event for which the alien team is being admitted, not to exceed 1 year.

(B) *P-1 petition for an entertainment group.* An approved petition for an entertainment group classified under section 101(a)(15)(P)(i) of the Act shall be valid for a period of time determined by the Director to be necessary to complete the performance or event for which the group is being admitted, not to exceed 1 year.

(C) *P-2 and P-3 petitions for artists or entertainers.* An approved petition for an artist or entertainer under section 101(a)(15)(P)(ii) or (iii) of the Act shall be valid for a period of time determined by the Director to be necessary to complete the event, activity, or performance for which the P-2 or P-3 alien is admitted, not to exceed 1 year.

(D) *Spouse and dependents.* The spouse and unmarried minor children of a P-1, P-2, or P-3 alien beneficiary are entitled to P-4 nonimmigrant classification, subject to the same period of admission and limitations as the alien beneficiary, if they are accompanying or following to join the alien beneficiary in the United States. Neither the spouse nor a child of the alien beneficiary may accept employment unless he or she has been granted employment authorization.

(E) *Essential support aliens.* Petitions for essential support personnel to P-1, P-2, and P-3 aliens shall be valid for a period of time determined by the Director to be necessary to complete the event, activity, or performance for which the P-1, P-2, or P-3 alien is admitted, not to exceed 1 year.

(9) The petitioner shall be notified of the decision, the reasons for the denial, and the right to appeal the denial under 8 CFR part 103. There is no appeal from a decision to deny an extension of stay to the alien or a change of nonimmigrant status.

(10) *Revocation of approval of petition*—(i) *General.* (A) The petitioner shall immediately notify the Service of any changes in the terms and conditions of employment of a beneficiary which may affect eligibility under section 101(a)(15)(P) of the Act and paragraph (p) of this section. An amended petition should be filed when the petitioner continues to employ the beneficiary. If the petitioner no longer employs the beneficiary, the petitioner shall send a letter explaining the change(s) to the Director who approved the petition.

(B) The Director may revoke a petition at any time, even after the validity of the petition has expired.

(ii) *Automatic revocation.* The approval of an unexpired petition is automatically revoked if the petitioner, or the employer in a petition filed by an agent, goes out of business, files a written withdrawal of the petition, or notifies the Service that the beneficiary is no longer employed by the petitioner.

(iii) *Revocation on notice*—(A) *Grounds for revocation.* The Director shall send to the petitioner a notice of intent to revoke the petition in relevant part if he or she finds that:

(*1*) The beneficiary is no longer employed by the petitioner in the capacity specified in the petition;

(*2*) The statement of facts contained in the petition were not true and correct;

(*3*) The petitioner violated the terms or conditions of the approved petition;

(*4*) The petitioner violated requirements of section 101(a)(15)(P) of the Act or paragraph (p) of this section; or

(*5*) The approval of the petition violated paragraph (p) of this section or involved gross error.

(B) *Notice and decision.* The notice of intent to revoke shall contain a detailed statement of the grounds for the revocation and the time period allowed for the petitioner's rebuttal. The petitioner may submit evidence in rebuttal within 30 days of the date of the notice. The Director shall consider all relevant evidence presented in deciding whether to revoke the petition.

(11) *Appeal of a denial or a revocation of a petition*—(i) *Denial.* A denied petition may be appealed under 8 CFR part 103.

(ii) *Revocation.* A petition that has been revoked on notice may be appealed under 8 CFR part 103. Automatic revocations may not be appealed.

(12) *Admission.* A beneficiary may be admitted to the United States for the validity period of the petition, plus a period of up to 10 days before the validity period begins and 10 days after the validity period ends. The beneficiary may not work except during the validity period of the petition.

(13) *Extension of visa petition validity.* The petitioner shall file a request to extend the validity of the original petition under section 101(a)(15)(P) of the Act on Form I–129 in order to continue or complete the same activity or event specified in the original petition. Supporting documents are not required unless requested by the Director. A petition extension may be filed only if the validity of the original petition has not expired.

(14) *Extension of stay*—(i) *Extension procedure.* The petitioner shall request extension of the alien's stay to continue or complete the same event or activity by filing Form I–129, accompanied by a statement explaining the reasons for the extension. The petitioner must also request a petition extension. The extension dates shall be the same for the petition and the beneficiary's stay. The beneficiary must be physically present in the United States at the time the extension of stay is filed. Even though the requests to extend the petition and the alien's stay are combined on the petition, the Director shall make a separate determination on each. If the alien leaves the United States for business or personal reasons while the extension requests are pending, the petitioner may request the Director to cable notification of approval of the petition extension to the consular office abroad where the alien will apply for a visa.

(ii) *Extension periods*—(A) *P–1 individual athlete.* An extension of stay for a P–1 individual athlete and his or her essential support personnel may be authorized for a period up to 5 years for a total period of stay not to exceed 10 years.

(B) *Other P–1, P–2, and P–3 aliens.* An extension of stay may be authorized in increments of 1 year for P–1 athletic teams, entertainment groups, aliens in reciprocal exchange programs, aliens in culturally unique programs, and their essential support personnel to continue or complete the same event or activity for which they were admitted.

(15) *Effect of approval of a permanent labor certification or filing of a preference petition on P classification.* The approval of a permanent labor certification or the filing of a preference petition for an alien shall not be a basis for denying a P petition, a request to extend such a petition, or the alien's admission, change of status, or extension of stay. The alien may legitimately come to the United States for a temporary period as a P nonimmigrant and depart voluntarily at the end of his or her authorized stay and, at the same time, lawfully seek to become a permanent resident of the United States. This provision does not include essential support personnel.

(16) *Effect of a strike.* (i) If the Secretary of Labor certifies to the Commissioner that a strike or other labor dispute involving a work stoppage of

workers is in progress in the occupation at the place where the beneficiary is to be employed, and that the employment of the beneficiary would adversely affect the wages and working conditions of U.S. citizens and lawful resident workers:

(A) A petition to classify an alien as a nonimmigrant as defined in section 101(a)(15)(P) of the Act shall be denied; or

(B) If a petition has been approved, but the alien has not yet entered the United States, or has entered the United States but has not commenced employment, the approval of the petition is automatically suspended, and the application for admission of the basis of the petition shall be denied.

(ii) If there is a strike or other labor dispute involving a work stoppage of workers in progress, but such strike or other labor dispute is not certified under paragraph (p)(16)(i) of this section, the Commissioner shall not deny a petition or suspend an approved petition.

(iii) If the alien has already commenced employment in the United States under an approved petition and is participating in a strike or labor dispute involving a work stoppage of workers, whether or not such strike or other labor dispute has been certified by the Secretary of Labor, the alien shall not be deemed to be failing to maintain his or her status solely on account of past, present, or future participation in a strike or other labor dispute involving a work stoppage of workers but is subject to the following terms and conditions:

(A) The alien shall remain subject to all applicable provisions of the Immigration and Nationality Act and regulations promulgated thereunder in the same manner as all other P nonimmigrant aliens;

(B) The status and authorized period of stay of such an alien is not modified or extended in any way by virtue of his or her participation in a strike or other labor dispute involving a work stoppage of workers; and

(C) Although participation by a P nonimmigrant alien in a strike or other labor dispute involving a work stoppages of workers will not constitute a ground for deportation, an alien who violates his or her status or who remains in the United States after his or her authorized period of stay has expired, will be subject to deportation.

(17) *Use of approval of notice, Form I–797.* The Service has notify the petitioner on Form I–797 whenever a visa petition or an extension of a visa petition is approved under the P classification. The beneficiary of a P petition who does not require a nonimmigrant visa may present a copy of the approved notice at a Port-of-Entry to facilitate entry into the United States. A beneficiary who is required to present a visa for admission, and whose visa expired before the date of his or her intended return, may use Form I–797 to apply for a new or revalidated visa during the validity period of the petition. The copy of Form I–797 shall be retained by the beneficiary and present during the validity of the petition when reentering the United States to resume the same employment with the same petitioner.

(18) *Return transportation requirement.* In the case of an alien who enters the United States under section 101(a)(15)(P) of the Act and whose employment terminates for reasons other than voluntary resignation, the employer whose offer of employment formed the basis of suh nonimmigrant status and the petitioner are jointly and severally liable for the reasonable cost of return transporation of the alien abroad. For the purposes of this paragraph, the term "abroad" means the alien's last place of residence prior to his or her entry into the United States.

(q) *Cultural visitors*—(1)(i) *International cultural exchange visitors program.* Paragraphs (q)(2) through (q)(11) of this section provide the rules governing nonimmigrant aliens who are visiting the United States temporarily in an international cultural exchange visitors program (Q–1).

(ii) *Irish peace process cultural and training program.* Paragraph (q)(15) of this section provides the rules governing nonimmigrant aliens who are visiting the United States temporarily under the Irish peace process cultural and training program (Q–2) and their dependents (Q–3).

(iii) *Definitions.* As used in this section:

Country of nationality means the country of which the participant was a national at the time of the petition seeking international cultural exchange visitor status for him or her.

Doing business means the regular, systematic, and continuous provision of goods and/or services (including lectures, seminars and other types of cultural programs) by a qualified employer which has employees, and does not include the mere presence of an agent or office of the qualifying employer.

Duration of program means the time in which a qualified employer is conducting an approved international cultural exchange program in the manner as established by the employer's petition for program approval, provided that the period of time does not exceed 15 months.

International cultural exchange visitor means an alien who has a residence in a foreign country which he or she has no intention of abandoning, and who is coming temporarily to the United States to take part in an international cultural exchange program approved by the Attorney General.

Petitioner means the employer or its designated agent who has been employed by the qualified employer on a permanent basis in an executive or managerial capacity. The designated agent must be a United States citizen, an alien lawfully admitted for permanent residence, or an alien provided temporary residence status under sections 210 or 245A of the Act.

Qualified employer means a United States or foreign firm, corporation, non-profit organization, or other legal entity (including its U.S. branches, subsidiaries, affiliates, and franchises) which administers an international cultural exchange program designated by the Attorney General in accordance with the provisions of section 101(a)(15)(Q)(i) of the Act.

(2) *Admission of international cultural exchange visitor*—(i) *General.* A nonimmigrant alien may be authorized to enter the United States as a participant in an international cultural exchange program approved by the Attorney General for the purpose of providing practical training, employment, and the sharing of the history, culture, and traditions of the country of the alien's nationality. The period of admission is the duration of the approved international cultural exchange program or fifteen (15) months, whichever is shorter. A nonimmigrant alien admitted under this provision is classifiable as an international cultural exchange visitor in Q–1 status.

(ii) *Limitation on admission.* Any alien who has been admitted into the United States as an international cultural exchange visitor under section 101(a)(15)(Q)(i) of the Act shall not be readmitted in Q–1 status unless the alien has resided and been physically present outside the United States for the immediate prior year. Brief trips to the United States for pleasure or business during the immediate prior year do not break the continuity of the one-year foreign residency.

(3) *International cultural exchange program*—(i) *General.* A United States employer shall petition the Attorney General on Form I–129, Petition for a Nonimmigrant Worker, for approval of an international cultural exchange program which is designed to provide an opportunity for the American public to learn about foreign cultures. The United States employer must simultaneously petition on the same Form I–129 for the authorization for one or more individually identified nonimmigrant aliens to be admitted in Q–1 status. These aliens are to be admitted to engage in employment or training of which the essential element is the sharing with the American public, or a segment of the public sharing a common cultural interest, of the culture of the alien's country of nationality. The international cultural exchange visitor's eligibility for admission will be considered only if the international cultural exchange program is approved.

(ii) *Program validity.* Each petition for an international cultural exchange program will be approved for the duration of the program, which may not exceed 15 months, plus 30 days to allow time for the participants to make travel arrangements. Subsequent to the approval of the initial petition, a new petition must be filed each time the qualified employer wishes to bring in additional cultural visitors. A qualified employer may replace or substitute a participant named on a previously approved petition for the remainder of the program in accordance with paragraph (q)(6) of this section. The replacement or substituting alien may be admitted in Q–1 status until the expiration date of the approved petition.

(iii) *Requirements for program approval.* An international cultural exchange program must meet all of the following requirements:

(A) *Accessibility to the public.* The international cultural exchange program must take place in a school, museum, business or other establishment where the American public, or a segment of the public sharing a common cultural interest, is exposed to aspects of a foreign culture as part of a structured program. Activities that take place in a private home or an isolated business setting to which the American public, or a segment of the public sharing a common cultural interest, does not have direct access do not qualify.

(B) *Cultural component.* The international cultural exchange program must have a cultural component which is an essential and integral part of the international cultural exchange visitor's employment or training. The cultural component must be designed, on the whole, to exhibit or explain the attitude, customs, history, heritage, philosophy, or traditions of the international cultural exchange visitor's country of nationality. A cultural component may include structured instructional activities such as seminars, courses, lecture series, or language camps.

(C) *Work component.* The international cultural exchange visitor's employment or training in the United States may not be independent of the cultural component of the international cultural exchange program. The work component must serve as the vehicle to achieve the objectives of the cultural component. The sharing of the culture of the international cultural exchange visitor's country of nationality must result from his or her employment or training with the qualified employer in the United States.

(iv) *Requirements for international cultural exchange visitors.* To be eligible for international cultural exchange visitor status, an alien must be a bona fide nonimmigrant who:

(A) Is at least 18 years of age at the time the petition is filed;

(B) Is qualified to perform the service or labor or receive the type of training stated in the petition;

(C) Has the ability to communicate effectively about the cultural attributes of his or her country of nationality to the American public; and

(D) Has resided and been physically present outside of the United States for the immediate prior year, if he or she was previously admitted as an international cultural exchange visitor.

(4) *Supporting documentation*—(i) *Documentation by the employer.* To establish eligibility as a qualified employer, the petitioner must submit with the completed Form I–129 appropriate evidence that the employer:

(A) Maintains an established international cultural exchange program in accordance with the requirements set forth in paragraph (q)(3) of this section;

(B) Has designated a qualified employee as a representative who will be responsible for administering the international cultural exchange program and who will serve as liaison with the Immigration and Naturalization Service;

(C) Is actively doing business in the United States;

(D) Will offer the alien(s) wages and working conditions comparable to those accorded local domestic workers similarly employed; and

(E) Has the financial ability to remunerate the participant(s).

(ii) *Certification by petitioner.* (A) The petitioner must give the date of birth, country of nationality, level of education, position title, and a brief job description for each international cultural exchange visitor included in the petition. The petitioner must verify and certify that the prospective participants are qualified to perform the service or labor, or receive the type of training, described in the petition.

(B) The petitioner must report the international cultural exchange visitors' wages and certify that such cultural exchange visitors are offered wages and working conditions comparable to those accorded to local domestic workers similarly employed.

(iii) Supporting documentation as prescribed in paragraphs (q)(4)(i) and (q)(4)(ii) of this section must accompany a petition filed on Form I–129 in all cases except where the employer files multiple petitions in the same calendar year. When petitioning to repeat a previously approved international cultural exchange program, a copy of the initial program approval notice may be submitted in lieu of the documentation required under paragraph (q)(4)(i) of this section. The Service will request additional documentation only when clarification is needed.

(5) *Filing of petitions for international cultural exchange visitor program*—(i) *General.* A United States employer seeking to bring in international cultural exchange visitors must file a petition on Form I-129, Petition for a Nonimmigrant Worker, with the applicable fee, along with appropriate documentation. A new petition on Form I–129, with the applicable fee, must be filed with the appropriate service center each time a qualified employer wants to bring in additional international cultural exchange visitors. Each person named on an approved petition will be admitted only for the duration of the approved program. Replacement or substitution may be made for any person named on an approved petition as provided in paragraph (q)(6) of this section, but only for the remainder of the approved program.

(ii) *Petition for multiple participants.* The petitioner may include more than one participant on the petition. The petitioner shall include the name, date of birth, nationality, and other identifying information required on the petition for each participant. The petitioner must also indicate the United States consulate at which each participant will apply for a Q–1 visa. For participants who are visa-exempt under 8 CFR 212.1(a), the petitioner must indicate the port of entry at which each participant will apply for admission to the United States.

(iii) *Service, labor, or training in more than one location.* A petition which requires the international cultural exchange visitor to engage in employment or training (with the same employer) in more than one location must include an itinerary with the dates and locations of the services, labor, or training.

(iv) *Services, labor, or training for more than one employer.* If the international cultural exchange visitor will perform services or labor for, or receive training from, more than one employer, each employer must file a separate petition. The international cultural exchange visitor may work part-time for multiple employers provided that each employer has an approved petition for the alien.

(v) *Change of employers.* If an international cultural exchange visitor is in the United States under section 101(a)(15)(Q)(i) of the Act and decides to change employers, the new employer must file a petition. However, the total period of time the international cultural exchange visitor may stay in the United States remains limited to fifteen (15) months.

(6) *Substitution or replacements of participants in an international cultural exchange visitor program.* The petitioner may substitute for or replace a person named on a previously approved petition for the remainder of the program without filing a new Form I–129. The substituting international cultural exchange visitor must meet the qualification requirements prescribed in paragraph (q)(3)(iv) of this section. To request substitution or replacement, the petitioner shall, by letter, notify the consular office at which the alien will apply for a visa or, in the case of visa-exempt aliens, the Service office at the port of entry where the alien will apply for admission. A copy of the petition's approval notice must be included with the letter. The petitioner must state the date of birth, country of nationality, level of education, and position title of each prospective international cultural exchange visitor and must certify that each is qualified to perform the service or labor or receive the type of training described in the approved petition. The petitioner must also indicate each international cultural exchange visitor's wages and certify that the international cultural exchange visitor is offered wages and working

conditions comparable to those accorded to local domestic workers in accordance with paragraph (q)(11)(ii) of this section.

(7) *Approval of petition for international cultural exchange visitor program.* (i) The director shall consider all the evidence submitted and request other evidence as he or she may deem necessary.

(ii) The director shall notify the petitioner and the appropriate United States consulate(s) of the approval of a petition. For participants who are visa-exempt under 8 CFR 212.1(a), the director shall give notice of the approval to the director of the port of entry at which each such participant will apply for admission to the United States. The notice of approval shall include the name of the international cultural exchange visitors, their classification, and the petition's period of validity.

(iii) An approved petition for an alien classified under section 101(a)(15)(Q)(i) of the Act is valid for the length of the approved program or fifteen (15) months, whichever is shorter.

(iv) A petition shall not be approved for an alien who has an aggregate of fifteen (15) months in the United States under section 101(a)(15)(Q)(i) of the Act, unless the alien has resided and been physically present outside the United States for the immediate prior year.

(8) *Denial of the petition*—(i) *Notice of denial.* The petitioner shall be notified of the denial of a petition, the reasons for the denial, and the right to appeal the denial under part 103 of this chapter.

(ii) *Multiple participants.* A petition for multiple international cultural exchange visitors may be denied in whole or in part.

(9) *Revocation of approval of petition*—(i) *General.* The petitioner shall immediately notify the appropriate Service center of any changes in the employment of a participant which would affect eligibility under section 101(a)(15)(Q)(i) of the Act.

(ii) *Automatic revocation.* The approval of any petition is automatically revoked if the qualifying employer goes out of business, files a written withdrawal of the petition, or terminates the approved international cultural exchange program prior to its expiration date. No further action or notice by the Service is necessary in the case of automatic revocation. In any other case, the Service shall follow the revocation procedures in paragraphs (q)(9) (iii) through (v) of this section.

(iii) *Revocation on notice.* The director shall send the petitioner a notice of intent to revoke the petition in whole or in part if he or she finds that:

(A) The international cultural exchange visitor is no longer employed by the petitioner in the capacity specified in the petition, or if the international cultural exchange visitor is no longer receiving training as specified in the petition;

(B) The statement of facts contained in the petition was not true and correct;

(C) The petitioner violated the terms and conditions of the approved petition; or

(D) The Service approved the petition in error.

(iv) *Notice and decision.* The notice of intent to revoke shall contain a detailed statement of the grounds for the revocation and the period of time allowed for the petitioner's rebuttal. The petitioner may submit evidence in rebuttal within 30 days of receipt of the notice. The director shall consider all relevant evidence presented in deciding whether to revoke the petition in whole or in part. If the petition is revoked in part, the remainder of the petition shall remain approved and a revised approval notice shall be sent to the petitioner with the revocation notice.

(v) *Appeal of a revocation of a petition.* Revocation with notice of a petition in whole or in part may be appealed to the Associate Commissioner for Examinations under part 103 of this chapter. Automatic revocation may not be appealed.

(10) *Extension of stay.* An alien's total period of stay in the United States under section 101(a)(15)(Q)(i) of the Act cannot exceed fifteen (15) months. The authorized stay of an international cultural exchange visitor may be extended within the 15-month limit if he or she is the beneficiary of a new petition filed in accordance with paragraph (q)(3) of this section. The new petition, if filed by the same employer, should

include a copy of the previous petition's approval notice and a letter from the petitioner indicating any terms and conditions of the previous petition that have changed.

(11) *Employment provisions*—(i) *General.* An alien classified under section 101(a)(15)(Q)(i) of the Act may be employed only by the qualified employer through which the alien attained Q–1 nonimmigrant status. An alien in this class is not required to apply for an employment authorization document. Employment outside the specific program violates the terms of the alien's Q–1 nonimmigrant status within the meaning of section 237(a)(1)(C)(i) of the Act.

(ii) *Wages and working conditions.* The wages and working conditions of an international cultural exchange visitor must be comparable to those accorded to domestic workers similarly employed in the geographical area of the alien's employment. The employer must certify on the petition that such conditions are met as in accordance with paragraph (q)(4)(iii)(B) of this section.

(12)–(14) [Reserved]

(15) *Irish peace process cultural and training program visitors (Q–2) and their dependents (Q–3)*—(i) *General.* An Irish Peace Process Cultural and Training Program (IPPCTP) visitor is a nonimmigrant alien coming to the United States temporarily to gain or upgrade work skills through training and temporary employment and to experience living in a diverse and peaceful environment.

(ii) *What are the requirements for participation?* (A) The principal alien must have been physically resident in either Northern Ireland or the counties of Louth, Monaghan, Cavan, Leitrim, Sligo, and Donegal in the Republic of Ireland, for at least 3 months immediately preceding application to the program and must show that he or she has no intention of abandoning this residence.

(B) The principal alien must be between the ages of 18 and 35.

(C) The principal alien must:

(*1*) Be unemployed for at least 3 months, or have completed or currently be enrolled in a training/employment program sponsored by the Training and Employment Agency of Northern Ireland (T&EA) or by the Training and Employment Authority of Ireland (FAS), or by other such publicly funded programs, or have been made redundant from employment (*i.e.*, lost their job), or have received a notice of redundancy (termination of employment); or

(*2*) Be a currently employed person whose employer has nominated him/her to participate in this program for additional training or job experience that is to benefit both the participant and his/her employer upon returning home.

(D) The principal alien must intend to come to the United States temporarily, for a period not to exceed 36 months, in order to obtain training, employment, and the experience of coexistence and conflict resolution in a diverse society.

(iii) *Are there any limitations on admissions?* (A) No more than 4,000 participants, including spouses and any minor children of principal aliens, may be admitted annually for 3 consecutive program years, beginning with FY 2000 (October 1, 1999, through September 30, 2000).

(B) For each alien admitted under section 101(a)(15)(Q)(ii) of the Act, the number of aliens admitted under section 101(a)(15)(H)(ii)(b) of the Act is reduced by one for that fiscal year or the subsequent fiscal year.

(C) This program expires on October 1, 2005.

(iv) *What are the requirements for initial admission to the United States?* (A) Principal aliens, their spouses, and minor children of principal aliens must present valid passports and either a Q–2 or Q–3 visa at the time of inspection.

(B) Initial admission for those principal and dependent aliens in this program who received their visas at either the U.S. Embassy in Dublin or the U.S. Consulate in Belfast must take place at the Service's Pre-Flight Inspection facilities at either the Shannon or Dublin airports in the Republic of Ireland.

(C) The principal alien will be required to present a Certification Letter issued by the Department of State's (DOS') Program Administrator documenting him or her as an individual selected for participation in the IPPCTP. Eligible dependents may be requested to present written documentation certifying their relationship to the principal.

(v) *May the principal alien and dependents make brief visits outside the United States?* (A) The principal alien, spouse, and any minor children of the principal alien may make brief departures, for periods not to exceed 3 consecutive months, and may be readmitted without having to obtain a new visa. However, such periods of time spent outside the United States will not be added to the end of stay, which is not to exceed a total of 3 years from the initial date of entry of the principal alien.

(B) Those participants or dependents who remain outside the United States in excess of 3 consecutive months will not be readmitted by the Service on their initial Q–2 or Q–3 visa. Instead, any such individual and eligible dependents wishing to rejoin the program will be required to reapply to the program and be in receipt of a new Q–2 or Q–3 visa and a Certification Letter issued by the DOS' Program Administrator, prior to any subsequent admission to the United States.

(vi) *How long may a Q–2 or Q–3 visa holder remain in the United States under this program?* (A) The principal alien and any accompanying, or following-to-join, spouse or minor children of the principal alien are admitted for the duration of the principal alien's planned cultural and training program or 36 months, whichever is shorter.

(B) Those participants and eligible dependents admitted for specific periods less than 36 months may extend their period of stay through the Service so that their total period of stay is 36 months, provided the extension of stay is related to employment or training certified by the DOS' Program Administrator.

(vii) *How is employment authorized under this program?* (A) Following endorsement of his/her Form I–94, Arrival-Departure Record, by a Service officer, any principal alien admitted under section 101(a)(15)(Q)(ii) of the Act is permitted to work for an employer or employers listed on the Certification Letter issued by the DOS' Program Administrator.

(B) The accompanying spouse and minor children of the principal alien may not accept employment, unless the spouse has also been designated as a principal alien (Q–2) in this program and has been issued a Certification Letter by the DOS' Program Administrator.

(viii) *May the principal alien change employers?* Principal aliens wishing to change employers must request such a change through the DOS' Program Administrator to the Service. Following review and consideration of the request by the Service, the Service will inform the participant of the decision. The Service will grant such approval of employers only if the new employer has been approved by DOS in accordance with its regulations and such approval is communicated to the Service through the DOS' Program Administrator. If approved, the participant's Form I–94 will be annotated to show the new employer. If denied, there is no appeal under this section.

(ix) *May the principal alien hold other jobs during his/her U.S. visit?* No; any principal alien classified as an Irish peace process cultural and training program visitor may only engage in employment that has been certified by the DOS' Program Administrator and approved by the DOS or the Service as endorsed on the Form I–94. An alien who engages in unauthorized employment violates the terms of the Q-2 visa and will be considered to have violated section 237(a)(1)(C)(i) of the Act.

(x) *What happens if a principal alien loses his/her job?* A principal alien, who loses his or her job, will have 30 days from his/her last date of employment to locate appropriate employment or training, to have the job offer certified by the DOS' Program Administrator in accordance with the DOS' regulations and to have it approved by the Service. If appropriate employment or training cannot be found within this 30-day-period, the principal alien and any accompany family members will be required to depart the United States.

(r) *Religious workers.* This paragraph governs classification of an alien as a nonimmigrant religious worker (R–1).

(1) To be approved for temporary admission to the United States, or extension and maintenance of status, for the purpose of conducting the activities of

a religious worker for a period not to exceed five years, an alien must:

(i) Be a member of a religious denomination having a bona fide non-profit religious organization in the United States for at least two years immediately preceding the time of application for admission;

(ii) Be coming to the United States to work at least in a part time position (average of at least 20 hours per week);

(iii) Be coming solely as a minister or to perform a religious vocation or occupation as defined in paragraph (r)(3) of this section (in either a professional or nonprofessional capacity);

(iv) Be coming to or remaining in the United States at the request of the petitioner to work for the petitioner; and

(v) Not work in the United States in any other capacity, except as provided in paragraph (r)(2) of this section.

(2) An alien may work for more than one qualifying employer as long as each qualifying employer submits a petition plus all additional required documentation as prescribed by USCIS regulations.

(3) *Definitions.* As used in this section, the term:

Bona fide non-profit religious organization in the United States means a religious organization exempt from taxation as described in section 501(c)(3) of the Internal Revenue Code of 1986, subsequent amendment or equivalent sections of prior enactments of the Internal Revenue Code, and possessing a currently valid determination letter from the Internal Revenue Service (IRS) confirming such exemption.

Bona fide organization which is affiliated with the religious denomination means an organization which is closely associated with the religious denomination and which is exempt from taxation as described in section 501(c)(3) of the Internal Revenue Code of 1986, or subsequent amendment or equivalent sections of prior enactments of the Internal Revenue Code, and possessing a currently valid determination letter from the IRS confirming such exemption.

Denominational membership means membership during at least the two-year period immediately preceding the filing date of the petition, in the same type of religious denomination as the United States religious organization where the alien will work.

Minister means an individual who:

(A) Is fully authorized by a religious denomination, and fully trained according to the denomination's standards, to conduct religious worship and perform other duties usually performed by authorized members of the clergy of that denomination;

(B) Is not a lay preacher or a person not authorized to perform duties usually performed by clergy;

(C) Performs activities with a rational relationship to the religious calling of the minister; and

(D) Works solely as a minister in the United States which may include administrative duties incidental to the duties of a minister.

Petition means USCIS Form I–129, Petition for a Nonimmigrant Worker, a successor form, or any other form as may be prescribed by USCIS, along with a supplement containing attestations required by this section, the fee specified in 8 CFR 103.7(b)(1), and supporting evidence required by this part.

Religious denomination means a religious group or community of believers that is governed or administered under a common type of ecclesiastical government and includes one or more of the following:

(A) A recognized common creed or statement of faith shared among the denomination's members;

(B) A common form of worship;

(C) A common formal code of doctrine and discipline;

(D) Common religious services and ceremonies;

(E) Common established places of religious worship or religious congregations; or

(F) Comparable indicia of a bona fide religious denomination.

Religious occupation means an occupation that meets all of the following requirements:

(A) The duties must primarily relate to a traditional religious function and be recognized as a religious occupation within the denomination;

(B) The duties must be primarily related to, and must clearly involve, inculcating or carrying out the religious creed and beliefs of the denomination;

(C) The duties do not include positions which are primarily administrative or support such as janitors, maintenance workers, clerical employees, fund raisers, persons solely involved in the solicitation of donations, or similar positions, although limited administrative duties that are only incidental to religious functions are permissible; and

(D) Religious study or training for religious work does not constitute a religious occupation, but a religious worker may pursue study or training incident to status.

Religious vocation means a formal lifetime commitment, through vows, investitures, ceremonies, or similar indicia, to a religious way of life. The religious denomination must have a class of individuals whose lives are dedicated to religious practices and functions, as distinguished from the secular members of the religion. Examples of vocations include nuns, monks, and religious brothers and sisters.

Religious worker means an individual engaged in and, according to the denomination's standards, qualified for a religious occupation or vocation, whether or not in a professional capacity, or as a minister.

Tax-exempt organization means an organization that has received a determination letter from the IRS establishing that it, or a group it belongs to, is exempt from taxation in accordance with sections 501(c)(3) of the Internal Revenue Code of 1986, or subsequent amendments or equivalent sections of prior enactments of the Internal Revenue Code.

(4) *Requirements for admission/change of status; time limits*—(i) *Principal applicant (R–1 nonimmigrant).* If otherwise admissible, an alien who meets the requirements of section 101(a)(15)(R) of the Act may be admitted as an R–1 alien or changed to R–1 status for an initial period of up to 30 months from date of initial admission. If visa-exempt, the alien must present original documentation of the petition approval.

(ii) *Spouse and children (R–2 status).* The spouse and unmarried children under the age of 21 of an R–1 alien may be accompanying or following to join the R–1 alien, subject to the following conditions:

(A) R–2 status is granted for the same period of time and subject to the same limits as the principal, regardless of the time such spouse and children may have spent in the United States in R–2 status;

(B) Neither the spouse nor children may accept employment while in the United States in R–2 status; and

(C) The primary purpose of the spouse or children coming to the United States must be to join or accompany the principal R–1 alien.

(5) *Extension of stay or readmission.* An R–1 alien who is maintaining status or is seeking readmission and who satisfies the eligibility requirements of this section may be granted an extension of R–1 stay or readmission in R–1 status for the validity period of the petition, up to 30 months, provided the total period of time spent in R–1 status does not exceed a maximum of five years. A Petition for a Nonimmigrant Worker to request an extension of R–1 status must be filed by the employer with a supplement prescribed by USCIS containing attestations required by this section, the fee specified in 8 CFR 103.7(b)(1), and the supporting evidence, in accordance with the applicable form instructions.

(6) *Limitation on total stay.* An alien who has spent five years in the United States in R–1 status may not be readmitted to or receive an extension of stay in the United States under the R visa classification unless the alien has resided abroad and has been physically present outside the United States for the immediate prior year. The limitations in this paragraph shall not apply to R–1 aliens who did not reside continually in the United States and whose employment in the United States was seasonal or intermittent or was for an aggregate of six months or less per year. In addition, the limitations shall not apply to aliens who reside abroad and regularly commute to the United States to engage in part-time employment. To qualify for this exception, the petitioner and the alien must provide clear and convincing proof that the alien qualifies for such an exception. Such proof shall consist of evidence such as arrival and departure records,

transcripts of processed income tax returns, and records of employment abroad.

(7) *Jurisdiction and procedures for obtaining R–1 status.* An employer in the United States seeking to employ a religious worker, by initial petition or by change of status, shall file a petition in accordance with the applicable form instructions.

(8) *Attestation.* An authorized official of the prospective employer of an R–1 alien must complete, sign and date an attestation prescribed by USCIS and submit it along with the petition. The prospective employer must specifically attest to all of the following:

(i) That the prospective employer is a bona fide non-profit religious organization or a bona fide organization which is affiliated with the religious denomination and is exempt from taxation;

(ii) That the alien has been a member of the denomination for at least two years and that the alien is otherwise qualified for the position offered;

(iii) The number of members of the prospective employer's organization;

(iv) The number of employees who work at the same location where the beneficiary will be employed and a summary of the type of responsibilities of those employees. USCIS may request a list of all employees, their titles, and a brief description of their duties at its discretion;

(v) The number of aliens holding special immigrant or nonimmigrant religious worker status currently employed or employed within the past five years by the prospective employer's organization;

(vi) The number of special immigrant religious worker and nonimmigrant religious worker petitions and applications filed by or on behalf of any aliens for employment by the prospective employer in the past five years;

(vii) The title of the position offered to the alien and a detailed description of the alien's proposed daily duties;

(viii) Whether the alien will receive salaried or non-salaried compensation and the details of such compensation;

(ix) That the alien will be employed at least 20 hours per week;

(x) The specific location(s) of the proposed employment; and

(xi) That the alien will not be engaged in secular employment.

(9) *Evidence relating to the petitioning organization.* A petition shall include the following initial evidence relating to the petitioning organization:

(i) A currently valid determination letter from the IRS showing that the organization is a tax-exempt organization; or

(ii) For a religious organization that is recognized as tax-exempt under a group tax-exemption, a currently valid determination letter from the IRS establishing that the group is tax-exempt; or

(iii) For a bona fide organization that is affiliated with the religious denomination, if the organization was granted tax-exempt status under section 501(c)(3), or subsequent amendment or equivalent sections of prior enactments, of the Internal Revenue Code, as something other than a religious organization:

(A) A currently valid determination letter from the IRS establishing that the organization is a tax-exempt organization;

(B) Documentation that establishes the religious nature and purpose of the organization, such as a copy of the organizing instrument of the organization that specifies the purposes of the organization;

(C) Organizational literature, such as books, articles, brochures, calendars, flyers, and other literature describing the religious purpose and nature of the activities of the organization; and

(D) A religious denomination certification. The religious organization must complete, sign and date a statement certifying that the petitioning organization is affiliated with the religious denomination. The statement must be submitted by the petitioner along with the petition.

(10) *Evidence relating to the qualifications of a minister.* If the alien is a minister, the petitioner must submit the following:

(i) A copy of the alien's certificate of ordination or similar documents reflecting acceptance of the alien's qualifications as a minister in the religious denomination; and

(ii) Documents reflecting acceptance of the alien's qualifications as a minister in the religious denomination, as well as evidence that the alien has completed any course of prescribed theological education at an accredited theological institution normally required or recognized by that religious denomination, including transcripts, curriculum, and documentation that establishes that the theological education is accredited by the denomination, or

(iii) For denominations that do not require a prescribed theological education, evidence of:

(A) The denomination's requirements for ordination to minister;

(B) The duties allowed to be performed by virtue of ordination;

(C) The denomination's levels of ordination, if any; and

(D) The alien's completion of the denomination's requirements for ordination.

(11) *Evidence relating to compensation.* Initial evidence must state how the petitioner intends to compensate the alien, including specific monetary or in-kind compensation, or whether the alien intends to be self-supporting. In either case, the petitioner must submit verifiable evidence explaining how the petitioner will compensate the alien or how the alien will be self-supporting. Compensation may include:

(i) *Salaried or non-salaried compensation.* Evidence of compensation may include past evidence of compensation for similar positions; budgets showing monies set aside for salaries, leases, etc.; verifiable documentation that room and board will be provided; or other evidence acceptable to USCIS. IRS documentation, such as IRS Form W-2 or certified tax returns, must be submitted, if available. If IRS documentation is unavailable, the petitioner must submit an explanation for the absence of IRS documentation, along with comparable, verifiable documentation.

(ii) *Self support.* (A) If the alien will be self-supporting, the petitioner must submit documentation establishing that the position the alien will hold is part of an established program for temporary, uncompensated missionary work, which is part of a broader international program of missionary work sponsored by the denomination.

(B) An established program for temporary, uncompensated work is defined to be a missionary program in which:

(*1*) Foreign workers, whether compensated or uncompensated, have previously participated in R-1 status;

(*2*) Missionary workers are traditionally uncompensated;

(*3*) The organization provides formal training for missionaries; and

(*4*) Participation in such missionary work is an established element of religious development in that denomination.

(C) The petitioner must submit evidence demonstrating:

(*1*) That the organization has an established program for temporary, uncompensated missionary work;

(*2*) That the denomination maintains missionary programs both in the United states and abroad;

(*3*) The religious worker's acceptance into the missionary program;

(*4*) The religious duties and responsibilities associated with the traditionally uncompensated missionary work; and

(*5*) Copies of the alien's bank records, budgets documenting the sources of self-support (including personal or family savings, room and board with host families in the United States, donations from the denomination's churches), or other verifiable evidence acceptable to USCIS.

(12) *Evidence of previous R-1 employment.* Any request for an extension of stay as an R-1 must include initial evidence of the previous R-1 employment. If the beneficiary:

(i) Received salaried compensation, the petitioner must submit IRS documentation that the alien received a salary, such as an IRS Form W-2 or certified copies of filed income tax returns, reflecting such work and compensation for the preceding two years.

(ii) Received non-salaried compensation, the petitioner must submit IRS documentation of the non-salaried compensation if available. If IRS documentation is unavailable, an explanation for the absence of IRS documentation must be provided, and the petitioner must provide verifiable evidence of all financial support, including stipends, room and board, or other support for the beneficiary by submitting a description of the location where the beneficiary lived, a lease to establish where the beneficiary lived, or other evidence acceptable to USCIS.

(iii) Received no salary but provided for his or her own support, and that of any dependents, the petitioner must show how support was maintained by submitting with the petition verifiable documents such as audited financial statements, financial institution records, brokerage account statements, trust documents signed by an attorney, or other evidence acceptable to USCIS.

(13) *Change or addition of employers.* An R–1 alien may not be compensated for work for any religious organization other than the one for which a petition has been approved or the alien will be out of status. A different or additional employer seeking to employ the alien may obtain prior approval of such employment through the filing of a separate petition and appropriate supplement, supporting documents, and fee prescribed in 8 CFR 103.7(b)(1).

(14) *Employer obligations.* When an R–1 alien is working less than the required number of hours or has been released from or has otherwise terminated employment before the expiration of a period of authorized R–1 stay, the R–1 alien's approved employer must notify DHS within 14 days using procedures set forth in the instructions to the petition or otherwise prescribed by USCIS on the USCIS Internet Web site at *www.uscis.gov.*

(15) *Nonimmigrant intent.* An alien classified under section 101(a)(15)(R) of the Act shall maintain an intention to depart the United States upon the expiration or termination of R–1 or R–2 status. However, a nonimmigrant petition, application for initial admission, change of status, or extension of stay in R classification may not be denied solely on the basis of a filed or an approved request for permanent labor certification or a filed or approved immigrant visa preference petition.

(16) *Inspections, evaluations, verifications, and compliance reviews.* The supporting evidence submitted may be verified by USCIS through any means determined appropriate by USCIS, up to and including an on-site inspection of the petitioning organization. The inspection may include a tour of the organization's facilities, an interview with the organization's officials, a review of selected organization records relating to compliance with immigration laws and regulations, and an interview with any other individuals or review of any other records that the USCIS considers pertinent to the integrity of the organization. An inspection may include the organization headquarters, or satellite locations, or the work locations planned for the applicable employee. If USCIS decides to conduct a pre-approval inspection, satisfactory completion of such inspection will be a condition for approval of any petition.

(17) *Denial and appeal of petition.* USCIS will provide written notification of the reasons for the denial under 8 CFR 103.3(a)(1). The petitioner may appeal the denial under 8 CFR 103.3.

(18) *Revocation of approved petitions*—(i) *Director discretion.* The director may revoke a petition at any time, even after the expiration of the petition.

(ii) *Automatic revocation.* The approval of any petition is automatically revoked if the petitioner ceases to exist or files a written withdrawal of the petition.

(iii) *Revocation on notice*—(A) *Grounds for revocation.* The director shall send to the petitioner a notice of intent to revoke the petition in relevant part if he or she finds that:

(*1*) The beneficiary is no longer employed by the petitioner in the capacity specified in the petition;

(*2*) The statement of facts contained in the petition was not true and correct;

(*3*) The petitioner violated terms and conditions of the approved petition;

(*4*) The petitioner violated requirements of section 101(a)(15)(R) of the Act or paragraph (r) of this section; or

(*5*) The approval of the petition violated paragraph (r) of this section or involved gross error.

(B) *Notice and decision.* The notice of intent to revoke shall contain a detailed statement of the grounds for the revocation and the time period allowed for the petitioner's rebuttal. The petitioner may submit evidence in rebuttal within 30 days of receipt of the notice. The director shall consider all relevant evidence presented in deciding whether to revoke the petition.

(19) *Appeal of a revocation of a petition.* A petition that has been revoked on notice in whole or in part may be appealed under 8 CFR 103.3. Automatic revocations may not be appealed.

(s) *NATO nonimmigrant aliens*—(1) *General*—(i) *Background.* The North Atlantic Treaty Organization (NATO) is constituted of nations signatory to the North Atlantic Treaty. The Agreement Between the Parties to the North Atlantic Treaty Regarding the Status of Their Forces, signed in London, June 1951 (NATO Status of Forces Agreement), is the agreement between those nations that defines the terms of the status of their armed forces while serving abroad.

(A) Nonimmigrant aliens classified as NATO-1 through NATO-5 are officials, employees, or persons associated with NATO, and members of their immediate families, who may enter the United States in accordance with the NATO Status of Forces Agreement or the Protocol on the Status of International Military Headquarters set up pursuant to the North Atlantic Treaty (Paris Protocol). The following specific classifications shall be assigned to such NATO nonimmigrants:

(*1*) NATO-1—A principal permanent representative of a Member State to NATO (including any of its subsidiary bodies) resident in the United States and resident members of permanent representative's official staff; Secretary General, Deputy Secretary General, Assistant Secretaries General and Executive Secretary of NATO; other permanent NATO officials of similar rank; and the members of the immediate family of such persons.

(*2*) NATO-2—Other representatives of Member States to NATO (including any of its subsidiary bodies) including representatives, advisers and technical experts of delegations, and the members of the immediate family of such persons; dependents of members of a force entering in accordance with the provisions of the NATO Status of Forces Agreement or in accordance with the provisions of the Paris Protocol; members of such a force, if issued visas.

(*3*) NATO-3—Official clerical staff accompanying a representative of a Member State to NATO (including any of its subsidiary bodies) and the members of the immediate family of such persons.

(*4*) NATO-4—Officials of NATO (other than those classifiable under NATO-1) and the members of their immediate family

(*5*) NATO-5—Experts, other than NATO officials classifiable under NATO-4, employed on missions on behalf of NATO and their dependents.

(B) Nonimmigrant aliens classified as NATO-6 are civilians, and members of their immediate families, who may enter the United States as employees of a force entering in accordance with the NATO Status of Forces Agreement, or as members of a civilian component attached to or employed by NATO Headquarters, Supreme Allied Commander, Atlantic (SACLANT), set up pursuant to the Paris Protocol.

(C) Nonimmigrant aliens classified as NATO-7 are attendants, servants, or personal employees of nonimmigrant aliens classified as NATO-1, NATO-2, NATO-3, NATO-4, NATO-5, and NATO-6, who are authorized to work only for the NATO-1 through NATO-6 nonimmigrant from whom they derive status, and members of their immediate families.

(ii) *Admission and extension of stay.* NATO-1, NATO-2, NATO-3, NATO-4, and NATO-5 aliens are normally exempt from inspection under 8 CFR 235.1(c). NATO-6 aliens may be authorized admission for duration of status. NATO-7 aliens may be admitted for not more than 3 years and may be granted extensions of temporary stay in increments of not more than 2 years. In addition, an application for extension of temporary stay for a NATO-7 alien must be accompanied by a statement signed by the employing official stating that he or she intends to continue to employ the NATO-7 applicant, describing the work the applicant will perform, and acknowledging that this is, and will be, the sole employment of the NATO-7 applicant.

(2) *Definition of a dependent of a NATO-1, NATO-2, NATO-3, NATO-4, NATO-5, or NATO-6.* For purposes of

employment in the United States, the term *dependent* of a NATO–1, NATO–2, NATO–3, NATO–4, NATO–5, or NATO–6 principal alien, as used in this section, means any of the following immediate members of the family habitually residing in the same household as the NATO–1, NATO–2, NATO–3, NATO–4, NATO–5, or NATO–6 principal alien assigned to official duty in the United States:

(i) Spouse;

(ii) Unmarried children under the age of 21;

(iii) Unmarried sons or daughters under the age of 23 who are in full-time attendance as students at post-secondary educational institutions;

(iv) Unmarried sons or daughters under the age of 25 who are in full-time attendance as students at post-secondary educational institutions if a formal bilateral employment agreement permitting their employment in the United States was signed prior to November 21, 1988, and such bilateral employment agreements do not specify under the age of 23 as the maximum age for employment of such sons and daughters;

(v) Unmarried sons or daughters who are physically or mentally disabled to the extent that they cannot adequately care for themselves or cannot establish, maintain, or re-establish their own households. The Service may require medical certification(s) as it deems necessary to document such mental or physical disability.

(3) *Dependent employment requirements based on formal bilateral employment agreements and informal de facto reciprocal arrangements*—(i) *Formal bilateral employment agreements*. The Department of State's Family Liaison office (FLO) shall maintain all listing of NATO Member States which have entered into formal bilateral employment agreements that include NATO personnel. A dependent of a NATO–1, NATO–2, NATO–3, NATO–4, NATO–5, or NATO–6 principal alien assigned to official duty in the United States may accept, or continue in, unrestricted employment based on such formal bilateral agreement upon favorable recommendation by SACLANT, pursuant to paragraph (s)(5) of this section, and issuance of employment authorization documentation by the Service in accordance with 8 CFR part 274a. The application procedures are set forth in paragraph (s)(5) of this section.

(ii) *Informal de facto reciprocal arrangements*. For purposes of this section, an informal de facto reciprocal arrangement exists when the Office of the Secretary of Defense, Foreign Military Rights Affairs (OSD/FMRA), certifies, with State Department concurrence, that a NATO Member State allows appropriate employment in the local economy for dependents of members of the force and members of the civilian component of the United States assigned to duty in the NATO Member State. OSD/FMRA and State's FLO shall maintain a listing of countries with which such reciprocity exists. Dependents of a NATO–1, NATO–2, NATO–3, NATO–4, NATO–5, or NATO–6 principal alien assigned to official duty in the United States may be authorized to accept, or continue in, employment based upon informal de facto arrangements upon favorable recommendation by SACLANT, pursuant to paragraph (s)(5) of this section, and issuance of employment authorization by the Service in accordance with 8 CFR part 274a. Additionally, the application procedures set forth in paragraph (s)(5) of this section must be complied with, and the following conditions must be met:

(A) Both the principal alien and the dependent requesting employment are maintaining NATO–1, NATO–2, NATO–3, NATO–4, NATO–5, or NATO–6 status, as appropriate;

(B) The principal alien's total length of assignment in the United States is expected to last more than 6 months;

(C) Employment of a similar nature for dependents of members of the force and members of the civilian component of the United States assigned to official duty in the NATO Member State employing the principal alien is not prohibited by the NATO Member State;

(D) The proposed employment is not in an occupation listed in the Department of Labor's Schedule B (20 CFR part 656), or otherwise determined by the Department of Labor to be one for which there is an oversupply of qualified United States workers in the area of proposed employment. This Schedule B restriction does not apply to a dependent son or daughter who is a full-time student if the employment is part-time, consisting of not more than 20 hours per week, of if it is temporary employment of not more than 12 weeks during school holiday periods; and

(E) The proposed employment is not contrary to the interest of the United States. Employment contrary to the interest of the United States includes, but is not limited to, the employment of NATO–1, NATO–2, NATO–3, NATO–4, NATO–5, or NATO–6 dependents who have criminal records; who have violated United States immigration laws or regulations, or visa laws or regulations; who have worked illegally in the United States; or who cannot establish that they have paid taxes and social security on income from current or previous United States employment.

(iii) State's FLO shall inform the Service, by contacting Headquarters, Adjudications, Attention: Chief, Business and Trade Services Branch, 425 I Street, NW., Washington, DC 20536, of any additions or changes to the formal bilateral employment agreements and informal de facto reciprocal arrangements.

(4) *Applicability of a formal bilateral agreement or an informal de facto arrangement for NATO–1, NATO–2, NATO–3, NATO–4, NATO–5, or NATO–6 dependents.* The applicability of a formal bilateral agreement shall be based on the NATO Member State which employs the principal alien and not on the nationality of the principal alien or dependent. The applicability of an informal de facto arrangement shall be based on the NATO Member State which employs the principal alien, and the principal alien also must be a national of the NATO Member State which employs him or her in the United States. Dependents of SACLANT employees receive bilateral agreement or de facto arrangement employment privileges as appropriate based upon the nationality of the SACLANT employee (principal alien).

(5) *Application procedures.* The following procedures are required for dependent employment applications under bilateral agreements and de facto arrangements:

(i) The dependent of a NATO alien shall submit a complete application for employment authorization, including Form I–765 and Form I–566, completed in accordance with the instructions on, or attached to, those forms. The complete application shall be submitted to SACLANT for certification of the Form I–566 and forwarding to the Service.

(ii) In a case where a bilateral dependent employment agreement containing a numerical limitation on the number of dependents authorized to work is applicable, the certifying officer of SACLANT shall not forward the application for employment authorization to the Service unless, following consultation with State's Office of Protocol, the certifying officer has confirmed that this numerical limitation has not been reached. The countries with such limitations are indicated on the bilateral/de facto dependent employment listing issued by State's FLO.

(iii) SACLANT shall keep copies of each application and certified Form I–566 for 3 years from the date of the certification.

(iv) A dependent applying under the terms of a de facto arrangement must also attach a statement from the prospective employer which includes the dependent's name, a description of the position offered, the duties to be performed, the hours to be worked, the salary offered, and verification that the dependent possesses the qualifications for the position.

(v) A dependent applying under paragraph (s)(2) (iii) or (iv) of this section must also submit a certified statement from the post-secondary educational institution confirming that he or she is pursuing studies on a full-time basis.

(vi) A dependent applying under paragraph (s)(2)(v) of this section must also submit medical certification regarding his or her condition. The certification should identify both the dependent and the certifying physician, give the physician's phone number, identify the condition, describe the symptoms, provide a clear prognosis, and certify that the dependent is unable to maintain a home of his or her own.

(vii) The Service may require additional supporting documentation, but only after consultation with SACLANT.

(6) *Period of time for which employment may be authorized.* If approved, an application to accept or continue employment under this paragraph shall be granted in increments of not more than 3 years.

(7) *Income tax and Social Security liability.* Dependents who are granted employment authorization under this paragraph are responsible for payment of all Federal, state, and local income taxes, employment and related taxes and Social Security contributions on any remuneration received.

(8) *No appeal.* There shall be no appeal from a denial of permission to accept or continue employment under this paragraph.

(9) *Unauthorized employment.* An alien classified as a NATO–1, NATO–2, NATO–3, NATO–4, NATO–5, NATO–6, or NATO–7 who is not a NATO principal alien and who engages in employment outside the scope of, or in a manner contrary to, this paragraph may be considered in violation of status pursuant to section 237(a)(1)(C)(i) of the Act. A NATO principal alien in those classifications who engages in employment outside the scope of his or her official position may be considered in violation of status pursuant to section 237(a)(1)(C)(i) of the Act.

(t) *Alien witnesses and informants*—(1) *Alien witness or informant in criminal matter.* An alien may be classified as an S–5 alien witness or informant under the provisions of section 101(a)(15)(S)(i) of the Act if, in the exercise of discretion pursuant to an application on Form I–854 by an interested federal or state law enforcement authority ("LEA"), it is determined by the Commissioner that the alien:

(i) Possesses critical reliable information concerning a criminal organization or enterprise;

(ii) Is willing to supply, or has supplied, such information to federal or state LEA; and

(iii) Is essential to the success of an authorized criminal investigation or the successful prosecution of an individual involved in the criminal organization or enterprise.

(2) *Alien witness or informant in counterterrorism matter.* An alien may be classified as an S–6 alien counterterrorism witness or informant under the provisions of section 101(a)(15)(S)(ii) of the Act if it is determined by the Secretary of State and the Commissioner acting jointly, in the exercise of their discretion, pursuant to an application on Form I–854 by an interested federal LEA, that the alien:

(i) Possesses critical reliable information concerning a terrorist organization, enterprise, or operation;

(ii) Is willing to supply or has supplied such information to a federal LEA;

(iii) Is in danger or has been placed in danger as a result of providing such information; and

(iv) Is eligible to receive a reward under section 36(a) of the State Department Basic Authorities Act of 1956, 22 U.S.C. 2708(a).

(3) *Spouse, married and unmarried sons and daughters, and parents of alien witness or informant in criminal or counterterrorism matter.* An alien spouse, married or unmarried son or daughter, or parent of an alien witness or informant may be granted derivative S classification (S–7) when accompanying, or following to join, the alien witness or informant if, in the exercise of discretion by, with respect to paragraph (t)(1) of this section, the Commissioner, or, with respect to paragraph (t)(2) of this section, the Secretary of State and the Commissioner acting jointly, consider it to be appropriate. A nonimmigrant in such derivative S–7 classification shall be subject to the same period of admission, limitations, and restrictions as the alien witness or informant and must be identified by the requesting LEA on the application Form I–854 in order to qualify for S nonimmigrant classification. Family members not identified on the Form I–854 application will not be eligible for S nonimmigrant classification.

(4) *Request for S nonimmigrant classification.* An application on Form I–854, requesting S nonimmigrant classification for a witness or informant, may only be filed by a federal or state LEA (which shall include a federal or state court or a United States Attorney's Office) directly in need of the information to be provided by the alien witness

or informant. The completed application is filed with the Assistant Attorney General, Criminal Division, Department of Justice, who will forward only properly certified applications that fall within the numerical limitation to the Commissioner, Immigration and Naturalization Service, for approval, pursuant to the following process.

(i) *Filing request.* For an alien to qualify for status as an S nonimmigrant, S nonimmigrant classification must be requested by an LEA. The LEA shall recommend an alien for S nonimmigrant classification by: Completing Form I–854, with all necessary endorsements and attachments, in accordance with the instructions on, or attached to, that form, and agreeing, as a condition of status, that no promises may be, have been, or will be made by the LEA that the alien will or may remain in the United States in S or any other nonimmigrant classification or parole, adjust status to that of lawful permanent resident, or otherwise attempt to remain beyond a 3-year period other than by the means authorized by section 101(a)(15)(S) of the Act. The alien, including any derivative beneficiary who is 18 years or older, shall sign a statement, that is part of or affixed to Form I–854, acknowledging awareness that he or she is restricted by the terms of S nonimmigrant classification to the specific terms of section 101(a)(15)(S) of the Act as the exclusive means by which he or she may remain permanently in the United States.

(A) *District director referral.* Any district director or Service officer who receives a request by an alien, an eligible LEA, or other entity seeking S nonimmigrant classification shall advise the requestor of the process and the requirements for applying for S nonimmigrant classification. Eligible LEAs seeking S nonimmigrant classification shall be referred to the Commissioner.

(B) *United States Attorney certification.* The United States Attorney with jurisdiction over a prosecution or investigation that forms the basis for a request for S nonimmigrant classification must certify and endorse the application on Form I–854 and agree that no promises may be, have been, or will be made that the alien will or may remain in the United States in S or any other nonimmigrant classification or parole, adjust status to lawful permanent resident, or attempt to remain beyond the authorized period of admission.

(C) *LEA certification.* LEA certifications on Form I–854 must be made at the seat-of-government level, if federal, or the highest level of the state LEA involved in the matter. With respect to the alien for whom S nonimmigrant classification is sought, the LEA shall provide evidence in the form of attachments establishing the nature of the alien's cooperation with the government, the need for the alien's presence in the United States, all conduct or conditions which may constitute a ground or grounds of excludability, and all factors and considerations warranting a favorable exercise of discretionary waiver authority by the Attorney General on the alien's behalf. The attachments submitted with a request for S nonimmigrant classification may be in the form of affidavits, statements, memoranda, or similar documentation. The LEA shall review Form I–854 for accuracy and ensure the alien understands the certifications made on Form I–854.

(D) *Filing procedure.* Upon completion of Form I–854, the LEA shall forward the form and all required attachments to the Assistant Attorney General, Criminal Division, United States Department of Justice, at the address listed on the form.

(ii) *Assistant Attorney General, Criminal Division review*—(A) *Review of information.* Upon receipt of a complete application for S nonimmigrant classification on Form I–854, with all required attachments, the Assistant Attorney General, Criminal Division, shall ensure that all information relating to the basis of the application, the need for the witness or informant, and grounds of excludability under section 212 of the Act has been provided to the Service on Form I–854, and shall consider the negative and favorable factors warranting an exercise of discretion on the alien's behalf. No application may be acted on by the Assistant Attorney

General unless the eligible LEA making the request has proceeded in accordance with the instructions on, or attached to, Form I–854 and agreed to all provisions therein.

(B) *Advisory panel.* Where necessary according to procedures established by the Assistant Attorney General, Criminal Division, an advisory panel, composed of representatives of the Service, Marshals Service, Federal Bureau of Investigation, Drug Enforcement Administration, Criminal Division, and the Department of State, and those representatives of other LEAs, including state and federal courts designated by the Attorney General, will review the completed application and submit a recommendation to the Assistant Attorney General, Criminal Division, regarding requests for S nonimmigrant classification. The function of this advisory panel is to prioritize cases in light of the numerical limitation in order to determine which cases will be forwarded to the Commissioner.

(C) *Assistant Attorney General certification.* The certification of the Assistant Attorney General, Criminal Division, to the Commissioner recommending approval of the application for S nonimmigrant classification shall contain the following:

(*1*) All information and attachments that may constitute, or relate to, a ground or grounds of excludability under section 212(a) of the Act;

(*2*) Each section of law under which the alien appears to be inadmissible;

(*3*) The reasons that waiver(s) of inadmissibility are considered to be justifiable and in the national interest;

(*4*) A detailed statement that the alien is eligible for S nonimmigrant classification, explaining the nature of the alien's cooperation with the government and the government's need for the alien's presence in the United States;

(*5*) The intended date of arrival;

(*6*) The length of the proposed stay in the United States;

(*7*) The purpose of the proposed stay; and

(*8*) A statement that the application falls within the statutorily specified numerical limitation.

(D) *Submission of certified requests for S nonimmigrant classification to Service.* (*1*) The Assistant Attorney General, Criminal Division, shall forward to the Commissioner only qualified applications for S–5 nonimmigrant classification that have been certified in accordance with the provisions of this paragraph and that fall within the annual numerical limitation.

(*2*) The Assistant Attorney General Criminal Division, shall forward to the Commissioner applications for S–6 nonimmigrant classification that have been certified in accordance with the provisions of this paragraph, certified by the Secretary of State or eligibility for S–6 classification, and that fall within the annual numerical limitation.

(5) *Decision on application.* (i) The Attorney General's authority to waive grounds of excludability pursuant to section 212 of the Act is delegated to the Commissioner and shall be exercised with regard to S nonimmigrant classification only upon the certification of the Assistant Attorney General, Criminal Division. Such certification is nonreviewable as to the matter's significance, importance, and/or worthwhileness to law enforcement. The Commissioner shall make the final decision to approve or deny a request for S nonimmigrant classification certified by the Assistant Attorney General, Criminal Division.

(ii) *Decision to approve application.* Upon approval of the application on Form I–854, the Commissioner shall notify the Assistant Attorney General, Criminal Division, the Secretary of State, and Service officers as appropriate. Admission shall be authorized for a period not to exceed 3 years.

(iii) *Decision to deny application.* In the event the Commissioner decides to deny an application for S nonimmigrant classification on Form I–854, the Assistant Attorney General, Criminal Division, and the relevant LEA shall be notified in writing to that effect. The Assistant Attorney General, Criminal Division, shall concur in or object to that decision. Unless the Assistant Attorney General, Criminal Division, objects within 7 days, he or she shall be deemed to have concurred in the decision. In the event of an objection by the Assistant Attorney General, Criminal Division, the matter will be expeditiously referred to the Deputy Attorney General for a final resolution. In no circumstances shall the alien or the relevant LEA have a right of appeal from any decision to deny.

(6) *Submission of requests for S nonimmigrant visa classification to Secretary of State.* No request for S nonimmigrant visa classification may be presented to the Secretary of State unless it is approved and forwarded by the Commissioner.

(7) *Conditions of status.* An alien witness or informant is responsible for certifying and fulfilling the terms and conditions specified on Form I–854 as a condition of status. The LEA that assumes responsibility for the S nonimmigrant must:

(i) Ensure that the alien:

(A) Reports quarterly to the LEA on his or her whereabouts and activities, and as otherwise specified on Form I–854 or pursuant to the terms of his or her S nonimmigrant classification;

(B) Notifies the LEA of any change of home or work address and phone numbers or any travel plans;

(C) Abides by the law and all specified terms, limitations, or restrictions on the visa, Form I–854, or any waivers pursuant to classification; and

(D) Cooperates with the responsible LEA in accordance with the terms of his or her classification and any restrictions on Form I–854;

(ii) Provide the Assistant Attorney General, Criminal Division, with the name of the control agent on an ongoing basis and provide a quarterly report indicating the whereabouts, activities, and any other control information required on Form I–854 or by the Assistant Attorney General;

(iii) Report immediately to the Service any failure on the alien's part to:

(A) Report quarterly;

(B) Cooperate with the LEA;

(C) Comply with the terms and conditions of the specific S nonimmigrant classification; or

(D) Refrain from criminal activity that may render the alien deportable, which information shall also be forwarded to the Assistant Attorney General, Criminal Division; and

(iv) Report annually to the Assistant Attorney General, Criminal Division, on whether the alien's S nonimmigrant classification and cooperation resulted in either:

(A) A successful criminal prosecution or investigation or the failure to produce a successful resolution of the matter; or

(B) The prevention or frustration of terrorist acts or the failure to prevent such acts.

(v) Assist the alien in his or her application to the Service for employment authorization.

(8) *Annual report.* The Assistant Attorney General, Criminal Division, in consultation with the Commissioner, shall compile the statutorily mandated annual report to the Committee on the Judiciary of the House of Representatives and the Committee on the Judiciary of the Senate.

(9) *Admission.* The responsible LEA will coordinate the admission of an alien in S nonimmigrant classification with the Commissioner as to the date, time, place, and manner of the alien's arrival.

(10) *Employment.* An alien classified under section 101(a)(15)(S) of the Act may apply for employment authorization by filing Form I–765, Application for Employment Authorization, with fee, in accordance with the instructions on, or attached to, that form pursuant to §274a.12(c)(21) of this chapter.

(11) *Failure to maintain status.* An alien classified under section 101(a)(15)(S) of the Act shall abide by all the terms and conditions of his or her S nonimmigrant classification imposed by the Attorney General. If the terms and conditions of S nonimmigrant classification will not be or have not been met, or have been violated, the alien is convicted of any criminal offense punishable by a term of imprisonment of 1 year or more, is otherwise rendered deportable, or it is otherwise appropriate or in the public interest to do so, the Commissioner shall proceed to deport an alien pursuant to the terms of 8 CFR 242.26. In the event the Commissioner decides to deport an alien witness or informant in S nonimmigrant classification, the Assistant Attorney General, Criminal Division, and the relevant LEA shall be notified in writing to that effect. The Assistant Attorney General, Criminal Division, shall concur in or object to

that decision. Unless the Assistant Attorney General, Criminal Division, objects within 7 days, he or she shall be deemed to have concurred in the decision. In the event of an objection by the Assistant Attorney General, Criminal Division, the matter will be expeditiously referred to the Deputy Attorney General for a final resolution. In no circumstances shall the alien or the relevant LEA have a right of appeal from any decision to deport.

(12) *Change of classification.* (i) An alien in S nonimmigrant classification is prohibited from changing to any other nonimmigrant classification.

(ii) An LEA may request that any alien lawfully admitted to the United States and maintaining status in accordance with the provisions of § 248.1 of this chapter, except for those aliens enumerated in 8 CFR 248.2, have his or her nonimmigrant classification changed to that of an alien classified pursuant to section 101(a)(15)(S) of the Act as set forth in 8 CFR 248.3(h).

(u) [Reserved]

(v) *Certain spouses and children of LPRs.* Section 214.15 of this chapter provides the procedures and requirements pertaining to V nonimmigrant status.

(w) *CNMI-Only Transitional Worker (CW–1)*—(1) *Definitions.* The following definitions apply to petitions for and maintenance of CW status in the Commonwealth of the Northern Mariana Islands (the CNMI or the Commonwealth):

(i) *Direct Guam transit* means travel from the CNMI to the Philippines by an alien in CW status, or from the Philippines to the CNMI by an alien with a valid CW visa, on a direct itinerary involving a flight stopover or connection in Guam (and no other place) within 8 hours of arrival in Guam, without the alien leaving the Guam airport.

(ii) *Doing business* means the regular, systematic, and continuous provision of goods or services by an employer as defined in this paragraph and does not include the mere presence of an agent or office of the employer in the CNMI.

(iii) *Employer* means a person, firm, corporation, contractor, or other association, or organization which:

(A) Engages a person to work within the CNMI; and

(B) Has or will have an employer-employee relationship with the CW–1 nonimmigrant being petitioned for.

(iv) *Employer-employee relationship* means that the employer will hire, pay, fire, supervise, and control the work of the employee.

(v) *Lawfully present in the CNMI* means that the alien:

(A) At the time the application for CW status is filed, is an alien lawfully present in the CNMI under 48 U.S.C. 1806(e); or

(B) Was lawfully admitted or paroled into the CNMI under the immigration laws on or after the transition program effective date, other than an alien admitted or paroled as a visitor for business or pleasure (B–1 or B–2, under any visa-free travel provision or parole of certain visitors from Russia and the People's Republic of China), and remains in a lawful immigration status.

(vi) *Legitimate business* means a real, active, and operating commercial or entrepreneurial undertaking which produces services or goods for profit, or is a governmental, charitable or other validly recognized nonprofit entity. The business must meet applicable legal requirements for doing business in the CNMI. A business will not be considered legitimate if it engages directly or indirectly in prostitution, trafficking in minors, or any other activity that is illegal under Federal or CNMI law. DHS will determine whether a business is legitimate.

(vii) *Minor child* means a child as defined in section 101(b)(1) of the Act who is under 18 years of age.

(viii) *Numerical limitation* means the maximum number of persons who may be granted CW–1 status in a given fiscal year or other period as determined by DHS, as follows:

(A) For fiscal year 2011, the numerical limitation is 22,417 per fiscal year.

(B) For fiscal year 2012, the numerical limitation is 22,416 per fiscal year.

(C) For each fiscal year beginning on October 1, 2012 until the end of the transition period, the numerical limitation will be a number less than 22,416 that is determined by DHS and published via Notice in the FEDERAL REGISTER. The numerical limitation for any fiscal year will be less than the number for the previous fiscal year, and will be a number reasonably calculated in DHS's discretion to reduce the number of CW–1 nonimmigrants to zero by the end of the transition period.

(D) DHS may adjust the numerical limitation for a fiscal year or other period in its discretion at any time via Notice in the FEDERAL REGISTER, as long as such adjustment is consistent with paragraph (w)(1)(viii)(C) of this section.

(E) If the numerical limitation is not reached for a specified fiscal year, unused numbers do not carry over to the next fiscal year.

(ix) *Occupational category* means those employment activities that DHS has determined require alien workers to supplement the resident workforce and includes:

(A) Professional, technical, or management occupations;

(B) Clerical and sales occupations;

(C) Service occupations;

(D) Agricultural, fisheries, forestry, and related occupations;

(E) Processing occupations;

(F) Machine trade occupations;

(G) Benchwork occupations;

(H) Structural work occupations; and

(I) Miscellaneous occupations.

(x) *Petition* means USCIS Form I–129CW, Petition for a CNMI-Only Nonimmigrant Transitional Worker, a successor form, other form, or electronic equivalent, any supplemental information requested by USCIS, and additional evidence as may be prescribed or requested by USCIS.

(xi) *Transition period* means the period beginning on the transition program effective date and ending on December 31, 2014, unless the CNMI-only transitional worker program is extended by the Secretary of Labor, in which case the transition period will end for purposes of the CW transitional worker program on the date designated by the Secretary of Labor.

(xii) *United States worker* means a national of the United States, an alien lawfully admitted for permanent residence, or a national of the Federated States of Micronesia, the Republic of the Marshall Islands, or the Republic of Palau who is eligible for nonimmigrant admission and is employment-authorized under the Compacts of Free Association between the United States and those nations.

(2) *Eligible aliens*. Subject to the numerical limitation, an alien may be classified as a CW–1 nonimmigrant if, during the transition period, the alien:

(i) Will enter or remain in the CNMI for the purpose of employment in the transition period in an occupational category that DHS has designated as requiring alien workers to supplement the resident workforce;

(ii) Is petitioned for by an employer;

(iii) Is not present in the United States, other than the CNMI;

(iv) If present in the CNMI, is lawfully present in the CNMI;

(v) Is not inadmissible to the United States as a nonimmigrant or has been granted a waiver of each applicable ground of inadmissibility; and

(vi) Is ineligible for status in a nonimmigrant worker classification under section 101(a)(15) of the Act.

(3) *Derivative beneficiaries—CW–2 nonimmigrant classification*. The spouse or minor child of a CW–1 nonimmigrant may accompany or follow the alien as a CW–2 nonimmigrant if the alien:

(i) Is not present in the United States, other than the CNMI;

(ii) If present in the CNMI, is lawfully present in the CNMI; and

(iii) Is not inadmissible to the United States as a nonimmigrant or has been granted a waiver of each applicable ground of inadmissibility.

(4) *Eligible employers*. To be eligible to petition for a CW–1 nonimmigrant worker, an employer must:

(i) Be engaged in legitimate business;

(ii) Consider all available United States workers for the position being filled by the CW–1 worker;

(iii) Offer terms and conditions of employment which are consistent with the nature of the petitioner's business and the nature of the occupation, activity, and industry in the CNMI; and

(iv) Comply with all Federal and Commonwealth requirements relating to employment, including but not limited to nondiscrimination, occupational safety, and minimum wage requirements.

(5) *Petition requirements*. An employer who seeks to classify an alien as a CW–1 worker must file a petition with USCIS and pay the requisite petition

fee plus the CNMI education fee of $150 per beneficiary per year. An employer filing a petition is eligible to apply for a waiver of the fee based upon inability to pay as provided by 8 CFR 103.7(c). If the beneficiary will perform services for more than one employer, each employer must file a separate petition with fees with USCIS.

(6) *Appropriate documents.* Documentary evidence establishing eligibility for CW status is required. A petition must be accompanied by:

(i) Evidence demonstrating the petitioner meets the definition of eligible employer in this section;

(ii) An attestation by the petitioner certified as true and accurate by an appropriate official of the petitioner, of the following:

(A) No qualified United States worker is available to fill the position;

(B) The employer is doing business as defined in paragraph (w)(1)(ii) of this section;

(C) The employer is a legitimate business as defined in paragraph (w)(1)(vi) of this section;

(D) The employer is an eligible employer as described in paragraph (w)(4) of this section and will continue to comply with the requirements for an eligible employer until such time as the employer no longer employs the CW–1 nonimmigrant worker;

(E) The beneficiary meets the qualifications for the position;

(F) The beneficiary, if present in the CNMI, is lawfully present in the CNMI;

(G) The position is not temporary or seasonal employment, and the petitioner does not reasonably believe it to qualify for any other nonimmigrant worker classification; and

(H) The position falls within the list of occupational categories designated by DHS.

(iii) Evidence of licensure if an occupation requires a Commonwealth or local license for an individual to fully perform the duties of the occupation. Categories of valid licensure for CW–1 classification are:

(A) *Licensure.* An alien seeking CW–1 classification in that occupation must have that license prior to approval of the petition to be found qualified to enter the CNMI and immediately engage in employment in the occupation.

(B) *Temporary licensure.* If a temporary license is available and allowed for the occupation with a temporary license, USCIS may grant the petition at its discretion after considering the duties performed, the degree of supervision received, and any limitations placed on the alien by the employer and/or pursuant to the temporary license.

(C) *Duties without licensure.* If the CNMI allows an individual to fully practice the occupation that usually requires a license without a license under the supervision of licensed senior or supervisory personnel in that occupation, USCIS may grant CW–1 status at its discretion after considering the duties performed, the degree of supervision received, and any limitations placed on the alien if the facts demonstrate that the alien under supervision could fully perform the duties of the occupation.

(7) *Change of employers.* A change of employment to a new employer inconsistent with paragraphs (w)(7)(i) and (ii) of this section will constitute a failure to maintain status within the meaning of section 237(a)(1)(C)(i) of the Act. A CW–1 nonimmigrant may change employers if:

(i) The prospective new employer files a petition to classify the alien as a CW–1 worker in accordance with paragraph (w)(5) of this section, and

(ii) An extension of the alien's stay is requested if necessary for the validity period of the petition.

(iii) A CW–1 may work for a prospective new employer after the prospective new employer files a Form I–129CW petition on the employee's behalf if:

(A) The prospective employer has filed a nonfrivolous petition for new employment before the date of expiration of the CW–1's authorized period of stay; and

(B) Subsequent to his or her lawful admission, the CW–1 has not been employed without authorization in the United States.

(iv) Employment authorization shall continue for such alien until the new petition is adjudicated. If the new petition is denied, such authorization shall cease.

(v) If a CW–1's employment has been terminated prior to the filing of a petition by a prospective new employer consistent with paragraphs (w)(7)(i) and (ii), the CW–1 will not be considered to be in violation of his or her CW–1 status during the 30-day period immediately following the date on which the CW–1's employment terminated if a nonfrivolous petition for new employment is filed consistent with this paragraph within that 30-day period and the CW–1 does not otherwise violate the terms and conditions of his or her status during that 30-day period.

(8) *Amended or new petition.* If there are any material changes in the terms and conditions of employment, the petitioner must file an amended or new petition to reflect the changes.

(9) *Multiple beneficiaries.* A petitioning employer may include more than one beneficiary in a CW–1 petition if the beneficiaries will be working in the same occupational category, for the same period of time, and in the same location.

(10) *Named beneficiaries.* The petition must include the name of the beneficiary and other required information, as indicated in the form instructions, at the time of filing. Unnamed beneficiaries will not be permitted.

(11) *Early termination.* The petitioning employer must pay the reasonable cost of return transportation of the alien to the alien's last place of foreign residence if the alien is dismissed from employment for any reason by the employer before the end of the period of authorized admission.

(12) *Approval.* USCIS will consider all the evidence submitted and such other evidence required in the form instructions to adjudicate the petition. USCIS will notify the petitioner of the approval of the petition on Form I–797, Notice of Action, or in another form as USCIS may prescribe:

(i) The approval notice will include the classification and name of the beneficiary or beneficiaries and the petition's period of validity. A petition for more than one beneficiary may be approved in whole or in part.

(ii) The petition may not be filed or approved earlier than six months before the date of actual need for the beneficiary's services.

(13) *Petition validity.* An approved petition will be valid for a period of up to one year.

(14) *How to apply for CW–1 or CW–2 status.* (i) Upon approval of the petition, a beneficiary, his or her eligible spouse, and or his or her minor child(ren) outside the CNMI will be informed in the approval notice of where they may apply for a visa authorizing admission in CW–1 or CW–2 status.

(ii) If the beneficiary is present in the CNMI, the petition also serves as the application for a grant of status as a CW–1.

(iii) If the eligible spouse and/or minor child(ren) are present in the CNMI, the spouse or child(ren) may apply for CW–2 dependent status on Form I–539 (or such alternative form as USCIS may designate) in accordance with the form instructions. The CW–2 status may not be approved until approval of the CW–1 petition. A spouse or child applying for CW–2 status on Form I–539 is eligible to apply for a waiver of the fee based upon inability to pay as provided by 8 CFR 103.7(c).

(15) *Biometrics and other information.* The beneficiary of a CW–1 petition or the spouse or child applying for a grant or, extension of CW–2 status, or a change of status to CW–2 status, must submit biometric information as requested by USCIS. For a Form I–129CW petition where the beneficiary is present in the CNMI, the employer must submit the biometric service fee described in 8 CFR 103.7(b)(1) with the petition for each beneficiary for which CW–1 status is being requested or request a fee waiver for any biometric services provided, including but not limited to reuse of previously provided biometric information for background checks. For a Form I–539 application where the applicant is present in the CNMI, the applicant must submit a biometric service fee for each CW–2 nonimmigrant on the application with the application or obtain a waiver of the biometric service fee described in 8 CFR 103.7(b)(1) for any biometric services provided, including but not limited to reuse of previously provided biometric information for background checks. A biometric service fee is not required for beneficiaries under the age of 14, or who are at least 79 years of age.

(16) *Period of admission.* (i) A CW–1 nonimmigrant will be admitted for the period of petition validity, plus up to 10 days before the validity period begins and 10 days after the validity period ends. The CW–1 nonimmigrant may not work except during the validity period of the petition. A CW–2 spouse will be admitted for the same period as the principal alien. A CW–2 minor child will be admitted for the same period as the principal alien, but such admission will not extend beyond the child's 18th birthday.

(ii) The temporary departure from the CNMI of the CW–1 nonimmigrant will not affect the derivative status of the CW–2 spouse and minor children, provided the familial relationship continues to exist and the principal remains eligible for admission as a CW–1 nonimmigrant.

(17) *Extension of petition validity and extension of stay.* (i) The petitioner may request an extension of an employee's CW–1 nonimmigrant status by filing a new petition.

(ii) A request for a petition extension may be filed only if the validity of the original petition has not expired.

(iii) Extensions of CW–1 status may be granted for a period of up to 1 year until the end of the transition period, subject to the numerical limitation.

(iv) To qualify for an extension of stay, the petitioner must demonstrate that the beneficiary or beneficiaries:

(A) Continuously maintained the terms and conditions of CW–1 status;

(B) Remains admissible to the United States; and

(C) Remains eligible for CW–1 classification.

(v) The derivative CW–2 nonimmigrant may file an application for extension of nonimmigrant stay on Form I–539 (or such alternative form as USCIS may designate) in accordance with the form instructions. The CW–2 status extension may not be approved until approval of the CW–1 extension petition.

(18) *Change or adjustment of status.* A CW–1 or CW–2 nonimmigrant can apply to change nonimmigrant status under section 248 of the Act or apply for adjustment of status under section 245 of the Act, if otherwise eligible. During the transition period, CW–1 or CW–2 nonimmigrants may be the beneficiary of a petition for or may apply for any nonimmigrant or immigrant visa classification for which they may qualify.

(19) *Effect of filing an application for or approval of a permanent labor certification, preference petition, or filing of an application for adjustment of status on CW–1 or CW–2 classification.* An alien may be granted, be admitted in and maintain lawful CW–1 or CW–2 nonimmigrant status while, at the same time, lawfully seeking to become a lawful permanent resident of the United States, provided he or she intends to depart the CNMI voluntarily at the end of the period of authorized stay. The filing of an application for or approval of a permanent labor certification or an immigrant visa preference petition, the filing of an application for adjustment of status, or the lack of residence abroad will not be the basis for denying:

(i) A CW–1 petition filed on behalf of the alien;

(ii) A request to extend a CW–1 status pursuant to a petition previously filed on behalf of the alien;

(iii) An application for CW–2 classification filed by an alien;

(iv) A request to extend CW–2 status pursuant to the extension of a related CW–1 alien's extension; or

(v) An application for admission as a CW–1 or CW–2 nonimmigrant.

(20) *Rejection.* USCIS may reject an employer's petition for new or extended CW–1 status if the numerical limitation has been met. In that case, the petition and accompanying fee will be rejected and returned with the notice that numbers are unavailable for the CW nonimmigrant classification. The beneficiary's application for admission based upon an approved petition will not be rejected based upon the numerical limitation.

(21) *Denial.* The ultimate decision to grant or deny CW–1 or CW–2 classification or status is a discretionary determination, and the petition or the application may be denied for failure of the petitioner or the applicant to demonstrate eligibility or for other good cause. The denial of a petition to classify an alien as a CW–1 may be appealed to the USCIS Administrative Appeals Office or any successor body.

The denial of a grant of CW–1 or CW–2 status within the CNMI, or of an application for change or extension of status filed under this section, may not be appealed.

(22) *Terms and conditions of CW Nonimmigrant status*—(i) *Geographical limitations.* CW–1 and CW–2 statuses are only applicable in the CNMI. Entry, employment and residence in the rest of the United States (including Guam) require the appropriate visa or visa waiver. Except as provided in paragraph (w)(22)(iii) of this section, an alien with CW–1 or CW–2 status who enters or attempts to enter, or travels or attempts to travel to any other part of the United States without an appropriate visa or visa waiver, or who violates conditions of nonimmigrant stay applicable to any such authorized status in any other part of the United States, will be deemed to have violated CW–1 or CW–2 status.

(ii) *Re-entry.* An alien with CW–1 or CW–2 status who travels abroad from the CNMI will require a CW–1 or CW–2 or other appropriate visa to be re-admitted to the CNMI.

(iii) *Direct Guam transit*—(A) *Travel from the CNMI to the Philippines.* An alien with CW–1 or CW–2 status who is a national of the Philippines may travel to the Philippines via a direct Guam transit without being deemed to violate that status.

(B) *Travel from the Philippines to the CNMI.* An alien who is a national of the Philippines may travel to the CNMI via a direct Guam transit under the following conditions: If an immigration officer determines that the alien warrants a discretionary exercise of parole authority, the alien may be paroled into Guam via direct Guam transit to undergo preinspection outbound from Guam for admission to the CNMI pursuant to 8 CFR 235.5(a) or to proceed for inspection upon arrival in the CNMI. During any such preinspection, the alien will be admitted in CW–1 or CW–2 status if the immigration officer in Guam determines that the alien is admissible to the CNMI. A condition of the admission is that the alien must complete the direct Guam transit. DHS, in its discretion, may exempt such alien from the provisions of 8 CFR 235.5(a) relating to separation and boarding of passengers after inspection.

(iv) *Employment authorization.* An alien with CW–1 nonimmigrant status is only authorized employment in the CNMI for the petitioning employer. An alien with CW–2 status is not authorized to be employed.

(23) *Expiration of status.* CW–1 status expires when the alien violates his or her CW–1 status (or in the case of a CW–1 status violation caused solely by termination of the alien's employment, at the end of the 30 day period described in section 214.2(w)(7)(v)), 10 days after the end of the petition's validity period, or at the end of the transitional worker program, whichever is earlier. CW–2 nonimmigrant status expires when the status of the related CW–1 alien expires, on a CW–2 minor child's 18th birthday, when the alien violates his or her status, or at the end of the transitional worker program, whichever is earlier. No alien will be eligible for admission to the CNMI in CW–1 or CW–2 status, and no CW–1 or CW–2 visa will be valid for travel to the CNMI, after the transitional worker program ends.

(24) *Waivers of inadmissibility for applicants lawfully present in the CNMI.* An applicant for CW–1 or CW–2 nonimmigrant status, who is otherwise eligible for such status and otherwise admissible to the United States, and who possesses appropriate documents demonstrating that the applicant is lawfully present in the CNMI, may be granted a waiver of inadmissibility under section 212(d)(3)(A)(ii) of the Act, including the grounds of inadmissibility described in sections 212(a)(6)(A)(i) and 212(a)(7)(B)(i)(II) of the Act, as a matter of discretion for the purpose of granting the CW–1 or CW–2 nonimmigrant status. Such waiver may be granted without additional form or fee. Appropriate documents required for such a waiver include a valid unexpired passport and other documentary evidence demonstrating that the applicant is lawfully present in the CNMI, such as an "umbrella permit" or a DHS-issued Form I–94. Evidence that the applicant possesses appropriate documents may be provided by an employer to accompany a petition, by an

eligible spouse or minor child to accompany the Form I–539 (or such alternative form as USCIS may designate), or in such other manner as USCIS may designate.

(Title VI of the Health Professions Educational Assistance Act of 1976 (Pub. L. 94–484; 90 Stat. 2303); secs. 103 and 214, Immigration and Nationality Act (8 U.S.C. 1103 and 1184))

[38 FR 35425, Dec. 28, 1973]

EDITORIAL NOTE: For FEDERAL REGISTER citations affecting §214.2, see the List of CFR Sections Affected, which appears in the Finding Aids section of the printed volume and at *www.govinfo.gov.*

§214.3 Approval of schools for enrollment of F and M nonimmigrants.

(a) *Filing petition*—(1) *General.* A school or school system seeking initial or continued authorization for attendance by nonimmigrant students under sections 101(a)(15)(F)(i) or 101(a)(15)(M)(i) of the Act, or both, must file a petition for certification or recertification with SEVP, using the Student and Exchange Visitor Information System (SEVIS), in accordance with the procedures at paragraph (h) of this section. The petition must state whether the school or school system is seeking certification or recertification for attendance of nonimmigrant students under section 101(a)(15)(F)(i) or 101(a)(15)(M)(i) of the Act or both. The petition must identify by name and address each location of the school that is included in the petition for certification or recertification, specifically including any physical location in which a nonimmigrant can attend classes through the school (*i.e.*, campus, extension campuses, satellite campuses, etc.).

(i) *School systems.* A school system, as used in this section, means public school (grades 9–12) or private school (grades kindergarten–12). A petition by a school system must include a list of the names and addresses of those schools included in the petition with the supporting documents.

(ii) *Submission requirements.* Certification and recertification petitions require that a complete Form I–17, Petition for Approval of School for Attendance by Nonimmigrant Student, including supplements A and B and bearing original signatures, be included with the school's submission of supporting documentation. In submitting the Form I–17, a school certifies that the designated school officials (DSOs) signing the form have read and understand DHS regulations relating to: Nonimmigrant students at 8 CFR 214.1, 214.2(f), and/or 214.2(m); change of nonimmigrant classification for students at 8 CFR 248; school certification and recertification under this section; withdrawal of school certification under this section and 8 CFR 214.4; that both the school and its DSOs intend to comply with these regulations at all times; and that, to the best of its knowledge, the school is eligible for SEVP certification. Willful misstatements may constitute perjury (18 U.S.C. 1621).

(2) *Approval for F–1 or M–1 classification, or both*—(i) *F–1 classification.* The following schools may be approved for attendance by nonimmigrant students under section 101(a)(15)(F)(i) of the Act:

(A) A college or university, *i.e.*, an institution of higher learning which awards recognized bachelor's, master's doctor's or professional degrees.

(B) A community college or junior college which provides instruction in the liberal arts or in the professions and which awards recognized associate degrees.

(C) A seminary.

(D) A conservatory.

(E) An academic high school.

(F) A private elementary school.

(G) An institution which provides language training, instruction in the liberal arts or fine arts, instruction in the professions, or instruction or training in more than one of these disciplines.

(ii) *M–1 classification.* The following schools are considered to be vocational or nonacademic institutions and may be approved for attendance by nonimmigrant students under section 101(a)(15)(M)(i) of the Act:

(A) A community college or junior college which provides vocational or technical training and which awards recognized associate degrees.

(B) A vocational high school.

(C) A school which provides vocational or nonacademic training other than language training.

(iii) *Both F–1 and M–1 classification.* A school may be approved for attendance by nonimmigrant students under both sections 101(a)(15)(F)(i) and 101(a)(15)(M)(i) of the Act if it has both instruction in the liberal arts, fine arts, language, religion, or the professions and vocational or technical training. In that case, a student whose primary intent is to pursue studies in liberal arts, fine arts, language, religion, or the professions at the school is classified as a nonimmigrant under section 101(a)(15)(F)(i) of the Act. A student whose primary intent is to pursue vocational or technical training at the school is classified as a nonimmigrant under section 101(a)(15)(M)(i) of the Act.

(iv) *English language training for a vocational student.* A student whose primary intent is to pursue vocational or technical training who takes English language training at the same school solely for the purpose of being able to understand the vocational or technical course of study is classified as a nonimmigrant under section 101(a)(15)(M)(i) of the Act.

(v) The following may not be approved for attendance by foreign students:

(A) A home school,

(B) A public elementary school, or

(C) An adult education program, as defined by section 203(l) of the Adult Education and Family Literacy Act, Public Law 105–220, as amended, 20 U.S.C. 9202(l), if the adult education program is funded in whole or in part by a grant under the Adult Education and Family Literacy Act, or by any other Federal, State, county or municipal funding.

(3) *Eligibility.* (i) The petitioner, to be eligible for certification, must establish at the time of filing that it:

(A) Is a bona fide school;

(B) Is an established institution of learning or other recognized place of study;

(C) Possesses the necessary facilities, personnel, and finances to conduct instruction in recognized courses; and

(D) Is, in fact, engaged in instruction in those courses.

(ii) The petitioner, to be eligible for recertification, must establish at the time of filing that it:

(A) Remains eligible for certification in accordance with paragraph (a)(3)(i) of this section;

(B) Has complied during its previous period of certification or recertification with recordkeeping, retention, and reporting requirements and all other requirements of paragraphs (g), (j), (k), and (l) of this section.

(b) *Supporting documents.* Institutions petitioning for certification or recertification must submit certain supporting documents as follows, pursuant to sections 101(a)(15)(F) and (M) of the Act. A petitioning school or school system owned and operated as a public educational institution or system by the United States or a State or a political subdivision thereof shall submit a certification to that effect signed by the appropriate public official who shall certify that he or she is authorized to do so. A petitioning private or parochial elementary or secondary school system shall submit a certification signed by the appropriate public official who shall certify that he or she is authorized to do so to the effect that it meets the requirements of the State or local public educational system. Any other petitioning school shall submit a certification by the appropriate licensing, approving, or accrediting official who shall certify that he or she is authorized to do so to the effect that it is licensed, approved, or accredited. In lieu of such certification a school which offers courses recognized by a State-approving agency as appropriate for study for veterans under the provisions of 38 U.S.C. 3675 and 3676 may submit a statement of recognition signed by the appropriate official of the State approving agency who shall certify that he or she is authorized to do so. A charter shall not be considered a license, approval, or accreditation. A school catalogue, if one is issued, shall also be submitted with each petition. If not included in the catalogue, or if a catalogue is not issued, the school shall furnish a written statement containing information concerning the size of its physical plant, nature of its facilities for study and training, educational, vocational or professional qualifications of the teaching staff, salaries of the teachers, attendance and scholastic grading policy, amount and character of supervisory and consultative services available to students and trainees, and finances (including a certified copy of the accountant's last statement of school's net worth, income, and expenses). Neither a catalogue nor such a written statement need be included with a petition submitted by:

(1) A school or school system owned and operated as a public educational institution or system by the United States or a State or a political subdivision thereof;

(2) A school accredited by a nationally recognized accrediting body; or

(3) A secondary school operated by or as part of a school so accredited.

(c) *Other evidence.* If the petitioner is a vocational, business, or language school, or American institution of research recognized as such by the Secretary of Homeland Security, it must submit evidence that its courses of study are accepted as fulfilling the requirements for the attainment of an educational, professional, or vocational objective, and are not avocational or recreational in character. If the petitioner is a vocational, business, or language school, or American institution of research recognized as such by the Attorney General, it must submit evidence that its courses of study are accepted as fulfilling the requirements for the attainment of an educational, professional, or vocational objective, and are not avocational or recreational in character. If the petitioner is an institution of higher education and is not within the category described in paragraph (b) (1) or (2) of this section, it must submit evidence that it confers upon its graduates recognized bachelor, master, doctor, professional, or divinity degrees, or if it does not confer such degrees that its credits have been and are accepted unconditionally by at least three such institutions of higher learning. If the petitioner is an elementary or secondary school and is not within the category described in paragraph (b) (1) or (3) of this section, it must submit evidence that attendance at the petitioning institution satisfies the compulsory attendance requirements of the State in which it is located and that the petitioning school qualifies graduates for acceptance by schools of a higher educational level within the category described in paragraph (b) (1), (2), or (3) of this section.

(d) *Interview of petitioner.* The petitioner or an authorized representative of the petitioner may be required to appear in person before or be interviewed by telephone by a DHS representative prior to the adjudication of a petition for certification or recertification. The interview will be conducted under oath.

(e) *Notices to schools related to certification or recertification petitions or to out-of-cycle review*—(1) *General.* All notices from SEVP to schools or school systems related to school certification, recertification, or out-of-cycle review (including, but not limited to, notices related to the collection of evidence, testimony, and appearance pertaining to petitions for recertification encompassing compliance with the recordkeeping, retention and reporting, and other requirements of paragraphs (f), (g), (j), (k), and (l) of this section, as well as to eligibility) will be served in accordance with the procedures at 8 CFR 103.2(b)(1), (4)–(16), (18) and (19), with the exception that all procedures will be conducted by SEVP, the SEVP Director, and the Assistant Secretary, ICE, as appropriate, and except as provided in this section. All such notices will be served (*i.e.*, generated and transmitted) through SEVIS and/or by e-mail. The date of service is the date of transmission of the e-mail notice. DSOs must maintain current contact information, including current e-mail addresses, at all times. Failure of a school to receive SEVP notices due to inaccurate DSO e-mail addresses in SEVIS or blockages of the school's e-mail system caused by spam filters is not grounds for appeal of a denial or withdrawal. The term "in writing" means either a paper copy bearing original signatures or an electronic copy bearing electronic signatures.

(2) *SEVP approval notification and SEVIS updating by certified schools.* SEVP will notify the petitioner by updating SEVIS to reflect approval of the petition and by e-mail upon approval of a certification or recertification petition. The certification or recertification is valid only for the type of program and nonimmigrant classification

specified in the certification or recertification approval notice. The certification must be recertified every two years and may be subject to out-of-cycle review at any time. Approval may be withdrawn in accordance with 8 CFR 214.4.

(3) *Modifications to Form I–17 while a school is SEVP-certified.* Any modification made by an SEVP-certified school on the Form I–17 at any time after certification and for the duration of a school's authorization to enroll F and/or M students must be reported to SEVP and will be processed by SEVP in accordance with the provisions of paragraphs (f)(1), (g)(2) and (h)(3)(i) of this section.

(4) *Notice of Intent to Withdraw (NOIW) SEVP certification*—(i) *Automatic withdrawal.* SEVP will serve the school with an NOIW 30 days prior to a school's SEVP certification expiration date if the school has not submitted to SEVP a completed recertification petition, in accordance with paragraph (h)(2) of this section. The school will be automatically withdrawn immediately, in accordance with 8 CFR 214.4(a)(3), if it has not submitted a completed recertification petition by the school's certification expiration date.

(ii) *Withdrawal on notice.* SEVP will serve a Withdrawal on Notice, in accordance with 8 CFR 214.4(b), if SEVP determines that a school reviewed out-of-cycle has failed to sustain eligibility or has failed to comply with the recordkeeping, retention, reporting and other requirements of paragraphs (f), (g), (j), (k), and (l) of this section. When a school fails to file an answer to an NOIW within the 30-day period, SEVP will withdraw the school's certification and notify the DSOs of the decision, in accordance with 8 CFR 214.4(d). Such withdrawal of certification may not be appealed.

(5) *Notice of Denial.* A Notice of Denial will be served to a school when SEVP denies a petition for initial certification or recertification. The notice will address appeals options. Schools denied recertification must comply with 8 CFR 214.4(i).

(6) *Notice of Automatic Withdrawal.* Schools that relinquish SEVP certification for any of the reasons cited in 8 CFR 214.4(a)(3) will be served a Notice of Automatic Withdrawal.

(7) *Notice of Withdrawal.* A school found to be ineligible for continued SEVP certification as a result of an out-of-cycle review will receive a Notice of Withdrawal. Schools withdrawn must comply with 8 CFR 214.4(i).

(8) *Notice of SEVIS Access Termination Date.* The Notice of SEVIS Access Termination Date gives the official date for the school's denial or withdrawal to be final and SEVIS access to be terminated. In most situations, SEVP will not determine a SEVIS access termination date for that school until the appeals process has concluded and the initial denial or withdrawal has been upheld, in accordance with 8 CFR 214.4(i)(3). The school will no longer be able to access SEVIS and SEVP will automatically terminate any remaining Active SEVIS records for that school on that date.

(f) *Adjudication of a petition for SEVP certification or recertification*—(1) *Approval.* The school is required to immediately report through SEVIS any change to its school information upon approval of a petition for SEVP certification or recertification. Modification to school information listed in paragraph (h)(3) of this section will require a determination of continued eligibility for certification. The certification or recertification is valid only for the type of program and student specified in the approval notice. The certification may be withdrawn in accordance with the provisions of 8 CFR 214.4, is subject to review at any time, and will be reviewed every two years.

(2) *Denial.* The petitioner will be notified of the reasons for the denial and appeal rights, in accordance with the provisions of 8 CFR part 103 and 8 CFR 214.4, if SEVP denies a petition for certification or recertification.

(g) *Recordkeeping and reporting requirements*—(1) *Student records.* An SEVP-certified school must keep records containing certain specific information and documents relating to each F–1 or M–1 student to whom it has issued a Form I–20, while the student is attending the school and until the school notifies SEVP, in accordance with the requirements of paragraphs (g)(1) and (2) of this section, that the student is not pursuing a full course of study. Student information not required for entry in SEVIS may be kept in the school's student system of records, but must be accessible to DSOs. The school must keep a record of having complied with the reporting requirements for at least three years after the student is no longer pursuing a full course of study. The school must maintain records on the student in accordance with paragraphs (g)(1) and (2) of this section if a school recommends reinstatement for a student who is out of status. The school must maintain records on the student for three years from the date of the denial if the reinstatement is denied. The DSO must make the information and documents required by this paragraph available, including academic transcripts, and must furnish them to DHS representatives upon request. Schools must maintain and be able to provide an academic transcript or other routinely maintained student records that reflect the total, unabridged academic history of the student at the institution, in accordance with paragraph (g)(1)(iv) of this section. All courses must be recorded in the academic period in which the course was taken and graded. The information and documents that the school must keep on each student are as follows:

(i) Identification of the school, to include name and full address.

(ii) Identification of the student, to include name while in attendance (record any legal name change), date and place of birth, country of citizenship, and school's student identification number.

(iii) Current address where the student and his or her dependents physically reside. In the event the student or his or her dependents cannot receive mail at such physical residence, the school must provide a mailing address in SEVIS. If the mailing address and the physical address are not the same, the school must maintain a record of both mailing and physical addresses and provide the physical location of residence of the student and his or her dependents to DHS upon request.

(iv) Record of coursework. Identify the student's degree program and field of study. For each course, give the periods of enrollment, course identification code and course title; the number of credits or contact hours, and the grade; the number of credits or clock hours, and for credit hour courses the credit unit; the term unit (semester hour, quarter hour, etc.). Include the date of withdrawal if the student withdrew from a course. Show the grade point average for each session or term. Show the cumulative credits or clock hours and cumulative grade point average. Narrative evaluation will be accepted in lieu of grades when the school uses no other type of grading.

(v) Record of transfer credit or clock hours accepted. Type of hours, course identification, grades.

(vi) Academic status. Include the effective date or period if suspended, dismissed, placed on probation, or withdrawn.

(vii) Whether the student has been certified for practical training, and the beginning and end dates of certification.

(viii) Statement of graduation (if applicable). Title of degree or credential received, date conferred, program of study or major.

(ix) Termination date and reason.

(x) The documents referred to in paragraph (k) of this section.

NOTE TO PARAGRAPH (g)(1): A DHS officer may request any or all of the data in paragraphs (g)(1)(i) through (x) of this section on any individual student or class of students upon notice. This notice will be in writing if requested by the school. The school will have three work days to respond to any request for information concerning an individual student, and ten work days to respond to any request for information concerning a class of students. The school will respond orally on the same day the request for information is made if DHS requests information on a student who is being held in custody, and DHS will provide a written notification that the request was made after the fact, if the school so desires. DHS will first attempt to gain information concerning a class of students from DHS record systems.

(2) *Reporting changes in student and school information.* (i) Schools must update SEVIS with the current information within 21 days of a change in any of the information contained in paragraphs (f)(1) and (h)(3) of this section.

(ii) Schools are also required to report within 21 days any change of the information contained in paragraph (g)(1) or the occurrence of the following events:

(A) Any student who has failed to maintain status or complete his or her program;

(B) A change of the student's or dependent's legal name or U.S. address;

(C) Any student who has graduated early or prior to the program end date listed on SEVIS Form I–20;

(D) Any disciplinary action taken by the school against the student as a result of the student being convicted of a crime; and

(E) Any other notification request not covered by paragraph (g)(1) of this section made by DHS with respect to the current status of the student.

(F) For F–1 students authorized by USCIS to engage in a 24-month extension of OPT under 8 CFR 214.2(f)(10)(ii)(C):

(*1*) Any change that the student reports to the school concerning legal name, residential or mailing address, employer name, or employer address; and

(*2*) The end date of the student's employment reported by a former employer in accordance with 8 CFR 214.2(f)(10)(ii)(C)(6).

(iii) Each term or session and no later than 30 days after the deadline for registering for classes, schools are required to report the following registration information:

(A) Whether the student has enrolled at the school, dropped below a full course of study without prior authorization by the DSO, or failed to enroll;

(B) The current address of each enrolled student; and

(C) *The start date of the student's next session, term, semester, trimester, or quarter.* For initial students, the start date is the "program start date" or "report date." (These terms are used interchangeably.) The DSO may choose a reasonable date to accommodate a student's need to be in attendance for required activities at the school prior to the actual start of classes when determining the report date on the Form I–20. Such required activities may include, but are not limited to, research projects and orientation sessions. The DSO may not, however, indicate a report date more than 30 days prior to the start of classes. The next session start date is the start of classes for continuing students.

(D) *Adjustment to the program completion date.* Any factors that influence the student's progress toward program completion (e.g., deferred attendance, authorized drop below, program extension) must be reflected by making an adjustment updating the program completion date.

(3) *Administrative correction of a student's record.* In instances where technological or computer problems on the part of SEVIS cause an error in the student's record, the DSO may request the SEVIS system administrator, without fee, to administratively correct the student's record.

(h) *SEVP certification, recertification, out-of-cycle review, and oversight of schools*—(1) *Certification.* A school seeking SEVP certification for attendance by nonimmigrants under section 101(a)(15)(F)(i) or 101(a)(15)(m)(i) of the Act must use SEVIS to file an electronic petition (which compiles the data for the Form I–17) and must submit the nonrefundable certification petition fee on-line.

(i) *Filing a petition.* The school must access the SEVP Web site at *http://www.ice.gov/sevis* to file a certification petition in SEVIS. The school will be issued a temporary ID and password in order to access SEVIS to complete and submit an electronic Form I–17. The school must submit the proper nonrefundable certification petition fee as provided in 8 CFR 103.7(b)(1).

(ii) *Site visit, petition adjudication and school notification.* SEVP will conduct a site visit for each petitioning school and its additional schools or campuses. SEVP will contact the school to arrange the site visit. The school must comply with and complete the visit within 30 days after the date SEVP contacts the school to arrange the visit, or the petition for certification will be denied as abandoned. DSOs and school officials that have signed the school's Form I–17 petition must be able to demonstrate to DHS representatives how they obtain access to the regulations cited in the certification as part of the site visit. Paper or electronic access is acceptable. DSOs must be able to extract pertinent citations within the regulations related to their requirements and responsibilities. SEVP will serve a notice of approval and SEVIS will be updated to reflect the school's certification if SEVP approves the school's certification petition.

(iii) *Certification denial.* SEVP will serve a notice of denial in accordance with paragraph (f)(2) of this section if a school's petition for certification is denied.

(2) *Recertification.* Schools are required to file a completed petition for SEVP recertification before the school's certification expiration date, which is two years from the date of their previous SEVP certification or recertification expiration date, except for the first recertification cycle after publication of the recertification rule. There is no recertification petition fee. SEVP will review a petitioning school's compliance with the recordkeeping, retention and reporting, and other requirements of paragraphs (f), (g), (j), (k), and (l) of this section, as well as continued eligibility for certification, pursuant to paragraph (a)(3) of this section.

(i) *Filing of petition for recertification.* Schools must submit a completed Form I–17 (including supplements A and B) using SEVIS, and submit a paper copy of the Form I–17 bearing original signatures of all officials. SEVP will notify all DSOs of a previously certified school 180 days prior to the school's certification expiration date that the school may submit a petition for recertification. A school may file its recertification petition at any time after receipt of this notification. A school must submit a complete recertification petition package, as outlined in the submission guidelines, by its certification expiration date. SEVP will send a notice of confirmation of complete filing or rejection to the school upon receipt of any filing of a petition for recertification.

(A) Notice of confirmation assures a school of uninterrupted access to SEVIS while SEVP adjudicates the school's petition for recertification. A school that has complied with the petition submission requirements will continue to have SEVIS access after its certification expiration date while the adjudication for recertification is pending. The school is required to comply with all regulatory recordkeeping, retention and reporting, and other requirements of paragraphs (f), (g), (j), (k), and (l) of this section during the period the petition is pending.

(B) Notice of rejection informs a school that it must take prompt corrective action in regard to its recertification petition prior to its certification expiration date to ensure that its SEVIS access will not be terminated and its petition for recertification will be accepted for adjudication.

(ii) *Consequence of failure to petition.* SEVP will serve an NOIW to the school 30 days prior to a school's certification expiration date. SEVP will no longer accept a petition for recertification from the school and will immediately withdraw the school's certification if the school does not petition for recertification, abandons its petition, or does not submit a complete recertification petition package by the certification expiration date, in accordance with the automatic withdrawal criteria in 8 CFR 214.4(a)(3). The school must comply with 8 CFR 214.4(i) upon withdrawal.

(iii) *School recertification process*—(A) *General.* School recertification reaffirms the petitioning school's eligibility for SEVP certification and the school's compliance with recordkeeping, retention, reporting and other requirements of paragraphs (f), (g), (j), (k), and (l) of this section since its previous certification.

(B) *Compliance.* Assessment by SEVP of a school petitioning for recertification will focus primarily on overall school compliance, but may also include examination of individual DSO compliance as data and circumstances warrant. Past performance of these individuals, whether or not they continue to serve as principal designated school officials (PDSOs) or DSOs, will be considered in any petition for recertification of the school.

(C) *On-site review for recertification.* All schools are subject to on-site review, at the discretion of SEVP, in conjunction with recertification. The school must comply with and complete an on-site review within 30 days of the notification by a DHS representative of a school that it has been selected for an on-site review for recertification, or the petition for recertification will be denied as abandoned, resulting in the school's withdrawal from SEVIS.

(iv) *Recertification approval.* SEVP will serve a notice of approval if a school's petition for recertification is approved. The date of the subsequent recertification review will be two years after the school's certification expiration date from this petition cycle.

(v) *Recertification denial.* SEVP will serve a notice of denial if a school's petition for recertification is denied, in accordance with 8 CFR 103.3(a)(1)(i).

(vi) *Adjustment of certification expiration date.* Schools eligible for recertification before March 25, 2009 will, at a minimum, have their certification expiration date extended to March 25, 2009. SEVP may extend the certification expiration date beyond this date during the first cycle of recertification.

(3) *Out-of-cycle review and oversight of SEVP-certified schools.* (i) SEVP will determine if out-of-cycle review is required upon receipt in SEVIS of any changes from an SEVP-certified school to its Form I–17 information. The Form I–17 information that requires out-of-cycle review when changed includes:

(A) Approval for attendance of students (F/M/both);

(B) Name of school system; name of main campus;

(C) Mailing address of the school;

(D) Location of the school;

(E) School type;

(F) Public/private school indicator;

(G) Private school owner name;

(H) The school is engaged in;

(I) The school operates under the following Federal, State, Local or other authorization;

(J) The school has been approved by the following national, regional, or state accrediting association or agency;

(K) Areas of study;

(L) Degrees available from the school;

(M) If the school is engaged in elementary or secondary education;

(N) If the school is engaged in higher education;

(O) If the school is engaged in vocational or technical education;

(P) If the school is engaged in English language training;

(Q) Adding or deleting campuses;

(R) Campus name;

(S) Campus mailing address; and

(T) Campus location address.

(ii) SEVP may request a school to electronically update all Form I–17 fields in SEVIS and provide SEVP with documentation supporting the update. The school must complete such updates in SEVIS and submit the supporting documentation to SEVP within 10 business days of the request from SEVP.

(iii) SEVP may review a school's certification at any time to verify the school's compliance with the recordkeeping, retention, reporting and other requirements of paragraphs (f), (g), (j), (k), and (l) of this section to verify the school's continued eligibility for SEVP certification pursuant to paragraph (a)(3) of this section. SEVP may initiate remedial action with the school, as appropriate, and may initiate withdrawal proceedings against the school pursuant to 8 CFR 214.4(b) if noncompliance or ineligibility of a school is identified.

(iv) *On-site review.* SEVP-certified schools are subject to on-site review at any time. SEVP will initiate withdrawal proceedings against a certified school, pursuant to 8 CFR 214.4(b), if the certified school selected for on-site review prior to its certification expiration date fails to comply with and complete the review within 30 days of the date SEVP contacted the school to arrange the review.

(v) *Notice of Continued Eligibility.* SEVP will serve the school a notice of continued eligibility if, upon completion of an out-of-cycle review, SEVP determines that the school remains eligible for certification. Such notice will not change the school's previously-determined certification expiration date unless specifically notified by SEVP.

(vi) *Withdrawal of certification.* SEVP will institute withdrawal proceedings in accordance with 8 CFR 214.4(b) if, upon completion of an out-of-cycle review, SEVP determines that a school or its programs are no longer eligible for certification.

(vii) *Voluntary withdrawal.* A school can voluntarily withdraw from SEVP certification at any time or in lieu of complying with an out-of-cycle review or request. Failure of a school to comply with an out-of-cycle review or request by SEVP will be treated as a voluntary withdrawal. A school must initiate voluntary withdrawal by sending a request for withdrawal on official school letterhead to SEVP.

(i) *Administration of student regulations.* DHS officials may conduct out-of-cycle, on-site reviews on the campuses of SEVP-certified schools to determine whether nonimmigrant students on those campuses are complying with DHS regulations pertaining to them, including the requirement that each maintains a valid passport. DHS officers will take appropriate action regarding violations of the regulations by nonimmigrant students.

(j) *Advertising.* In any advertisement, catalogue, brochure, pamphlet, literature, or other material hereafter printed or reprinted by or for an approved school, any statement which may appear in such material concerning approval for attendance by nonimmigrant students shall be limited solely to the following: This school is authorized under Federal law to enroll nonimmigrant alien students.

(k) *Issuance of Certificate of Eligibility.* A DSO of an SEVP-certified school must sign any completed Form I–20 issued for either a prospective or continuing student or a dependent. A Form I–20 issued by a certified school system must state which school within the system the student will attend. Only a DSO of an SEVP-certified school may issue a Form I–20 to a prospective student and his or her dependents, and only after the following conditions are met:

(1) The prospective student has made a written application to the school.

(2) The written application, the student's transcripts or other records of courses taken, proof of financial responsibility for the student, and other supporting documents have been received, reviewed, and evaluated at the school's location in the United States.

(3) The appropriate school authority has determined that the prospective student's qualifications meet all standards for admission.

(4) The official responsible for admission at the school has accepted the prospective student for enrollment in a full course of study.

(l) *Designated Official.* (1) Meaning of term *Designated Official.* As used in §§ 214.1(b), 214.2(b), 214.2(f), 214.2(m), and 214.4, a *Designated Official, Designated School Official (DSO),* or *Principal Designated School Official (PDSO),* means a regularly employed member of the school administration whose office is located at the school and whose compensation does not come from commissions for recruitment of foreign students. An individual whose principal obligation to the school is to recruit foreign students for compensation does not qualify as a designated official. The PDSO and any other DSO must be named by the president, owner, or head of a school or school system. The PDSO and DSO may not delegate this designation to any other person.

(i) A PDSO and DSO must be either a citizen or lawful permanent resident of the United States.

(ii) Each campus must have one PDSO. The PDSO is responsible for updating SEVIS to reflect the addition or deletion of any DSO on his or her associated campus. SEVP will use the PDSO as the point of contact on any issues that relate to the school's compliance with the regulations, as well as any system alerts generated by SEVIS. SEVP may also designate certain functions in SEVIS for use by the PDSO only. The PDSO of the main campus is the only DSO authorized to submit a Form I–17 for recertification. The PDSO and DSO will share the same responsibilities in all other respects.

(iii) School officials may nominate as many DSOs in addition to PDSOs as they determine necessary to adequately provide recommendations to F and/or M students enrolled at the school regarding maintenance of nonimmigrant status and to support timely and complete recordkeeping and reporting to DHS, as required by this section. School officials must not permit a DSO or PDSO nominee access to SEVIS until DHS approves the nomination.

(2) *Name, title, and sample signature.* Petitions for SEVP certification, review and recertification must include the names, titles, and sample signatures of designated officials. An SEVP-certified school must update SEVIS

upon any changes to the persons who are principal or designated officials, and furnish the name, title and e-mail address of any new official within 21 days of the change. Any changes to the PDSO or DSO must be made by the PDSO within 21 days of the change. DHS may, at its discretion, reject the submission of any individual as a DSO or withdraw a previous submission by a school of an individual.

(3) *Statement of designated officials.* A petition for school approval must include a statement by each designated official certifying that the official is familiar with the Service regulations relating to the requirements for admission and maintenance of status of nonimmigrant students, change of nonimmigrant status under part 248 of this chapter, and school approval under §§ 214.3 and 214.4, and affirming the official's intent to comply with these regulations. At the time a new designated official is added, the designated official must make the same certification.

[30 FR 919, Jan. 29, 1965]

EDITORIAL NOTE: For FEDERAL REGISTER citations affecting § 214.3, see the List of CFR Sections Affected, which appears in the Finding Aids section of the printed volume and at *www.govinfo.gov*.

§ 214.4 Denial of certification, denial of recertification or withdrawal of SEVP certification.

(a) *General*—(1) *Denial of certification.* The petitioning school will be notified of the reasons and appeal rights if a petition for certification is denied, in accordance with the provisions of 8 CFR 103.3(a)(1)(iii). No fee is required with appeals related to SEVP certification. A petitioning school denied certification may file a new petition for certification at any time.

(2) *Denial of recertification or withdrawal on notice.* The school must wait at least one calendar year from the date of denial of recertification or withdrawal on notice before being eligible to petition again for SEVP certification if a school's petition for recertification is denied by SEVP pursuant to 8 CFR 214.3(h)(3)(v), or its certification is withdrawn on notice pursuant to paragraph (b) of this section. Eligibility to re-petition will be at the discretion of the Director of SEVP. SEVP certification of a school or school system for the attendance of nonimmigrant students, pursuant to sections 101(a)(15)(F)(i) and/or 101(a)(15)(M)(i) of the Immigration and Nationality Act, will be withdrawn on notice subsequent to out-of-cycle review, or recertification denied, if the school or school system is determined to no longer be entitled to certification for any valid and substantive reason including, but not limited to, the following:

(i) Failure to comply with 8 CFR 214.3(g)(1) without a subpoena.

(ii) Failure to comply with 8 CFR 214.3(g)(2).

(iii) Failure of a DSO to notify SEVP of the attendance of an F–1 transfer student as required by 8 CFR 214.2(f)(8)(ii).

(iv) Failure of a DSO to identify on the Form I–20 which school within the system the student must attend, in compliance with 8 CFR 214.3(k).

(v) Willful issuance by a DSO of a false statement, including wrongful certification of a statement by signature, in connection with a student's school transfer or application for employment or practical training.

(vi) Conduct on the part of a DSO that does not comply with the regulations.

(vii) The designation as a DSO of an individual who does not meet the requirements of 8 CFR 214.3(l)(1).

(viii) Failure to provide SEVP paper copies of the school's Form I–17 bearing the names, titles, and signatures of DSOs as required by 8 CFR 214.3(l)(2).

(ix) Failure to submit statements of DSOs as required by 8 CFR 214.3(l)(3).

(x) Issuance of Forms I–20 to students without receipt of proof that the students have met scholastic, language, or financial requirements as required by 8 CFR 214.3(k)(2).

(xi) Issuance of Forms I–20 to aliens who will not be enrolled in or carry full courses of study, as defined in 8 CFR 214.2(f)(6) or 214.2(m)(9).

(xii) Failure to operate as a bona fide institution of learning.

(xiii) Failure to employ adequate qualified professional personnel.

(xiv) Failure to limit advertising in the manner prescribed in 8 CFR 214.3(j).

(xv) Failure to maintain proper facilities for instruction.

(xvi) Failure to maintain accreditation or licensing necessary to qualify graduates as represented in the school's Form I–17.

(xvii) Failure to maintain the physical plant, curriculum, and teaching staff in the manner represented in the Form I–17.

(xviii) Failure to comply with the procedures for issuance of Forms I–20 as set forth in 8 CFR 214.3(k).

(xix) Failure of a DSO to notify SEVP of material changes, such as changes to the school's name, address, or curricular changes that represent material change to the scope of institution offerings (e.g., addition of a program, class or course for which the school is issuing Forms I–20, but which does not have Form I–17 approval), as required by 8 CFR 214.3(f)(1).

(3) *Automatic withdrawal*. A school that is automatically withdrawn and subsequently wishes to enroll nonimmigrant students in the future may file a new petition for SEVP certification at any time. The school must use the certification petition procedures described in 8 CFR 214.3(h)(1) to gain access to SEVIS for submitting its petition. Past compliance with the recordkeeping, retention, reporting and other requirements of 8 CFR 214.3(f), (g), (j), (k), and (l), and with the requirements for transition of students under paragraph (i) of this section will be considered in the evaluation of a school's subsequent petition for certification. SEVP certification will be automatically withdrawn:

(i) As of the date of termination of operations, if an SEVP-certified school terminates its operations.

(ii) As of a school's certification expiration date, if an SEVP-certified school does not submit a completed recertification petition in the manner required by 8 CFR 214.3(h)(2).

(iii) Sixty days after the change of ownership if an SEVP-certified school changes ownership, unless the school files a new petition for SEVP certification, in accordance with the procedures at 8 CFR 214.3(h)(1), within 60 days of the change of ownership. SEVP will review the petition if the school properly files such petition to determine whether the school still meets the eligibility requirements of 8 CFR 214.3(a)(3) and is still in compliance with the recordkeeping, retention, reporting and other requirements of 8 CFR 214.3(f), (g), (j), (k), and (l). SEVP will institute withdrawal proceedings in accordance with paragraph (b) of this section if, upon completion of the review, SEVP finds that the school is no longer eligible for certification, or is not in compliance with the recordkeeping, retention, reporting and other requirements of 8 CFR 214.3(f), (g), (j), (k), and (l).

(iv) If an SEVP-certified school voluntarily withdraws from its certification.

(4) *Automatic withdrawal as of SEVIS mandatory compliance date*. The present approval of any school that has not filed for enrollment in SEVIS by the mandatory compliance date for attendance of nonimmigrant students under section 101(a)(15)(F)(i) or 101(a)(15)(M)(i) of the Act is automatically withdrawn as of the day following the mandatory compliance date for SEVIS. Given the time necessary to conduct a review of each school, the Service will review and adjudicate Form I–17 petitions for approval in SEVIS prior to the SEVIS mandatory compliance date only for Form I–17 petitions filed at least 75 days prior to this mandatory date. If a Form I–17 petition is filed less than 75 days prior to the mandatory compliance date and is not adjudicated prior to the mandatory compliance date, the school will not be authorized to access SEVIS and will be unable to issue any SEVIS Forms I–20 until the adjudication is complete.

(b) *Withdrawal on notice*. SEVP will initiate an out-of-cycle review and serve the school with an NOIW if SEVP has information that a school or school system may no longer be entitled to SEVP certification prior to the school being due for its two-year recertification. The NOIW will inform the school of:

(1) The grounds for withdrawing SEVP certification.

(2) The 30-day deadline from the date of the service of the NOIW for the school to submit sworn statements, and documentary or other evidence, to rebut the grounds for withdrawal of

certification in the NOIW. An NOIW is not a means for the school to submit evidence that it should have previously submitted as a part of its established reporting requirements.

(3) The school's right to submit a written request (including e-mail) within 30 days of the date of service of the NOIW for a telephonic interview in support of its response to the NOIW.

(c) *Assistance of counsel.* The school or school system shall also be informed in the notice of intent to withdraw approval that it may be assisted or represented by counsel of its choice qualified under part 292 of this chapter, at no expense to the Government, in preparation of its answer or in connection with the interview.

(d) *Allegations admitted or no answer filed.* If the school or school system admits all of the allegations in the notice of intent to withdraw approval, or if the school or school system fails to file an answer within the 30-day period, the district director shall withdraw the approval previously granted and he/she shall notify the designated school official of the decision. No appeal shall lie from the district director's decision if all allegations are admitted or no answer is filed within the 30-day period.

(e) *Allegations denied.* If the school or school system denies the allegations in the notice of intent to withdraw approval, then the school or school system shall, in its answer, provide all information or evidence on which the answer is based.

(f) *Interview requested.* (1) If in its answer to the notice of intent to withdraw approval the school or school system requests an interview, the school or school system shall be given notice of the date set for the interview.

(2) A summary of the information provided by the school or school system at the interview shall be prepared and included in the record. In the discretion of the district director, the interview may be recorded.

(g) *Decision.* The decision of SEVP will be in accordance with 8 CFR 103.3(a)(1).

(h) *Appeals.* Notices of denial or withdrawal of SEVP certification will include appeal alternatives and filing instructions. Any appeal must be taken within 15 days after the service of the decision by stating the reasons for the appeal in the notice of appeal provided with the instructions, and supported by a statement or brief specifically setting forth the grounds for contesting the withdrawal of the approval. No fee is required with appeals related to denial of SEVP recertification or withdrawal of SEVP certification.

(i) *Operations at a school when SEVP certification is relinquished or withdrawn, or whose recertification is denied and on the SEVIS access termination date*—(1) *General.* A school whose certification is relinquished or withdrawn, or whose recertification is denied may, at SEVP discretion, no longer be able to create Initial student records or issue new Forms I–20, Certificate of Eligibility for Nonimmigrant Student, for initial attendance. Schools must comply with the instructions given in the notice of withdrawal or denial with regard to management of status for their Initial and continuing F and/or M students. All other SEVIS functionality, including event reporting for students, will remain unchanged until the school's SEVIS access termination date. The school must continue to comply with the recordkeeping, retention, reporting and other requirements of 8 CFR 214.3(f), (g), (j), (k), and (l) until its SEVIS access termination date.

(2) *SEVIS access termination.* In determining the SEVIS access termination date, SEVP will consider the impact that such date will have upon SEVP, the school, and the school's nonimmigrant students in determining the SEVIS access termination date. In most situations, SEVP will not determine a SEVIS access termination date for that school until the appeals process has concluded and the initial denial or withdrawal has been upheld unless a school whose certification is withdrawn or whose recertification is denied is suspected of criminal activity or poses a potential national security threat. The school will no longer be able to access SEVIS, and SEVP will automatically terminate any remaining Active SEVIS records for that school on the SEVIS access termination date.

(3) *Legal obligations and ramifications for a school and its DSOs when a school is having SEVP certification denied or*

withdrawn. Schools are obligated to their students to provide the programs of study to which they have committed themselves in the students' application for enrollment and acceptance process. Schools are obligated to the U.S. government to comply with the recordkeeping, retention, reporting and other requirements contained in 8 CFR 214.3. With any new petition for SEVP certification, SEVP will consider the extent to which a school has fulfilled these obligations to students and the U.S. government during any previous period of SEVP certification.

[37 FR 17463, Aug. 29, 1972, as amended at 48 FR 14592, Apr. 5, 1983; 48 FR 19867, May 3, 1983; 48 FR 22131, May 17, 1983; 49 FR 41015, Oct. 19, 1984; 50 FR 9991, Mar. 13, 1985; 54 FR 19544, May 8, 1989; 55 FR 41988, Oct. 17, 1990; 67 FR 60112, Sept. 25, 2002; 73 FR 55702, Sept. 26, 2008]

§ 214.5 Libyan and third country nationals acting on behalf of Libyan entities.

(a) Notwithstanding any other provision of this title, the nonimmigrant status of any Libyan national, or of any other foreign national acting on behalf of a Libyan entity, who is engaging in aviation maintenance, flight operations, or nuclear-related studies or training is terminated.

(b) Notwithstanding any other provision of this chapter, the following benefits will not be available to any Libyan national or any other foreign national acting on behalf of a Libyan entity where the purpose is to engage in, or seek to obtain aviation maintenance, flight operations or nuclear-related studies or training:

(1) Application for school transfer.

(2) Application for extension of stay.

(3) Employment authorization or practical training.

(4) Request for reinstatement of student status.

(5) Application for change of nonimmigrant status.

(Secs. 103, 212, 214, 248; 8 U.S.C. 1103, 1182, 1184, 1258)

[48 FR 10297, Mar. 3, 1983]

§ 214.6 Citizens of Canada or Mexico seeking temporary entry under NAFTA to engage in business activities at a professional level.

(a) *General.* Under section 214(e) of the Act, a citizen of Canada or Mexico who seeks temporary entry as a business person to engage in business activities at a professional level may be admitted to the United States in accordance with the North American Free Trade Agreement (NAFTA).

(b) *Definitions.* As used in this section, the terms:

Business activities at a professional level means those undertakings which require that, for successful completion, the individual has a least a baccalaureate degree or appropriate credentials demonstrating status as a professional in a profession set forth in Appendix 1603.D.1 of the NAFTA.

Business person, as defined in the NAFTA, means a citizen of Canada or Mexico who is engaged in the trade of goods, the provision of services, or the conduct of investment activities.

Engage in business activities at a professional level means the performance of prearranged business activities for a United States entity, including an individual. It does not authorize the establishment of a business or practice in the United States in which the professional will be, in substance, self-employed. A professional will be deemed to be self-employed if he or she will be rendering services to a corporation or entity of which the professional is the sole or controlling shareholder or owner.

Temporary entry, as defined in the NAFTA, means entry without the intent to establish permanent residence. The alien must satisfy the inspecting immigration officer that the proposed stay is temporary. A temporary period has a reasonable, finite end that does not equate to permanent residence. In order to establish that the alien's entry will be temporary, the alien must demonstrate to the satisfaction of the inspecting immigration officer that his or her work assignment in the United States will end at a predictable time and that he or she will depart upon completion of the assignment.

(c) *Appendix 1603.D.1 to Annex 1603 of the NAFTA.* Pursuant to the NAFTA, an applicant seeking admission under this section shall demonstrate business activity at a professional level in one of the professions set forth in Appendix 1603.D.1 to Annex 1603. The professions in Appendix 1603.D.1 and the minimum requirements for qualification for each are as follows:[1]

APPENDIX 1603.D.1 (ANNOTATED)

—Accountant—Baccalaureate or Licenciatura Degree; or C.P.A., C.A., C.G.A., or C.M.A.
—Architect—Baccalaureate or Licenciatura Degree; or state/provincial license.[2]
—Computer Systems Analyst—Baccalaureate or Licenciatura Degree; or Post-Secondary Diploma[3] or Post Secondary Certificate[4] and three years' experience.
—Disaster relief insurance claims adjuster (claims adjuster employed by an insurance company located in the territory of a Party, or an independent claims adjuster)—Baccalaureate or Licenciatura Degree and successful completion of training in the appropriate areas of insurance adjustment pertaining to disaster relief claims; or three years experience in claims adjustment and successful completion of training in the appropriate areas of insurance adjustment pertaining to disaster relief claims.
—Economist—Baccalaureate or Licenciatura Degree.
—Engineer—Baccalaureate or Licenciatura Degree; or state/provincial license.
—Forester—Baccalaureate or Licenciatura Degree; or state/provincial license.
—Graphic Designer—Baccalaureate or Licenciatura Degree; or Post-Secondary Diploma or Post-Secondary Certificate and three years experience.
—Hotel Manager—Baccalaureate or Licenciatura Degree in hotel/restaurant management; or Post-Secondary Diploma or Post Secondary Certificate in hotel/restaurant management and three years experience in hotel/restaurant management.
—Industrial Designer—Baccalaureate or Licenciatura Degree; or Post-Secondary Diploma or Post Secondary Certificate, and three years experience.
—Interior Designer—Baccalaureate or Licenciatura Degree or Post-Secondary Diploma or Post-Secondary Certificate, and three years experience.
—Land Surveyor—Baccalaureate or Licenciatura Degree or state/provincial/federal license.
—Landscape Architect—Baccalaureate or Licenciatura Degree.
—Lawyer (including Notary in the province of Quebec)—L.L.B., J.D., L.L.L., B.C.L., or Licenciatura degree (five years); or membership in a state/provincial bar.
—Librarian—M.L.S., or B.L.S. (for which another Baccalaureate or Licenciatura Degree was a prerequisite).
—Management Consultant—Baccalaureate or Licenciatura Degree; or equivalent professional experience as established by statement or professional credential attesting to five years experience as a management consultant, or five years experience in a field of specialty related to the consulting agreement.
—Mathematician (including Statistician)—Baccalaureate or Licenciatura Degree.[5]
—Range Manager/Range Conservationist—Baccalaureate or Licenciatura Degree.
—Research Assistant (working in a post-secondary educational institution)—Baccalaureate or Licenciatura Degree.
—Scientific Technician/Technologist[6]—Possession of (a) theoretical knowledge of any of the following disciplines: agricultural sciences, astronomy, biology,

[1] A business person seeking temporary employment under this Appendix may also perform training functions relating to the profession, including conducting seminars.

[2] The terms "state/provincial license" and "state/provincial/federal license" mean any document issued by a state, provincial, or federal government, as the case may be, or under its authority, but not by a local government, that permits a person to engage in a regulated activity or profession.

[3] "Post Secondary Diploma" means a credential issued, on completion of two or more years of post secondary education, by an accredited academic institution in Canada or the United States.

[4] "Post Secondary Certificate" means a certificate issued, on completion of two or more years of post secondary education at an academic institution, by the federal government of Mexico or a state government in Mexico, an academic institution recognized by the federal government or a state government, or an academic institution created by federal or state law.

[5] The term "Mathematician" includes the profession of Actuary. An Actuary must satisfy the necessary requirements to be recognized as an actuary by a professional actuarial association or society. A professional actuarial association or society means a professional actuarial association or society operating in the territory of at least one of the Parties.

[6] A business person in this category must be seeking temporary entry for work in direct support of professionals in agricultural sciences, astronomy, biology, chemistry, engineering, forestry, geology, geophysics, meteorology or physics.

chemistry, engineering, forestry, geology, geophysics, meteorology, or physics; and (b) the ability to solve practical problems in any of those disciplines, or the ability to apply principles of any of those disciplines to basic or applied research.

—Social Worker—Baccalaureate or Licenciatura Degree.

—Sylviculturist (including Forestry Specialist)—Baccalaureate or Licenciatura Degree.

—Technical Publications Writer—Baccalaureate or Licenciatura Degree, or Post-Secondary Diploma or Post-Secondary Certificate, and three years experience.

—Urban Planner (including Geographer)—Baccalaureate or Licenciatura Degree.

—Vocational Counselor—Baccalaureate or Licenciatura Degree.

Medical/Allied Professionals

—Dentist—D.D.S., D.M.D., Doctor en Odontologia or Doctor en Cirugia Dental or state/provincial license.

—Dietitian—Baccalaureate or Licenciatura Degree; or state/provincial license.

—Medical Laboratory Technologist (Canada)/Medical Technologist (Mexico and the United States)[7]—Baccalaureate or Licenciatura Degree; or Post-Secondary Diploma or Post-Secondary Certificate, and three years experience.

—Nutritionist—Baccalaureate or Licenciatura Degree.

—Occupational Therapist—Baccalaureate or Licenciatura Degree; or state/provincial license.

—Pharmacist—Baccalaureate or Licenciatura Degree; or state/provincial license.

—Physician (teaching or research only)—M.D. Doctor en Medicina; or state/provincial license.

—Physiotherapist/Physical Therapist—Baccalaureate or Licenciatura Degree; or state/provincial license.

—Psychologist—state/provincial license; or Licenciatura Degree.

—Recreational Therapist-Baccalaureate or Licenciatura Degree.

—Registered nurse—state/provincial license or Licenciatura Degree.

—Veterinarian—D.V.M., D.M.V., or Doctor en Veterinaria; or state/provincial license.

—SCIENTIST

—Agriculturist (including Agronomist)—Baccalaureate or Licenciatura Degree.

—Animal Breeder—Baccalaureate or Licenciatura Degree.

—Animal Scientist—Baccalaureate or Licenciatura Degree.

—Apiculturist—Baccalaureate or Licenciatura Degree.

—Astronomer—Baccalaureate or Licenciatura Degree.

—Biochemist—Baccalaureate or Licenciatura Degree.

—Biologist—Baccalaureate or Licenciatura Degree.[8]

—Chemist—Baccalaureate or Licenciatura Degree.

—Dairy Scientist—Baccalaureate or Licenciatura Degree.

—Entomologist—Baccalaureate or Licenciatura Degree.

—Epidemiologist—Baccalaureate or Licenciatura Degree.

—Geneticist—Baccalaureate or Licenciatura Degree.

—Geochemist—Baccalaureate or Licenciatura Degree.

—Geologist—Baccalaureate or Licenciatura Degree.

—Geophysicist (including Oceanographer in Mexico and the United States)—Baccalaureate or Licenciatura Degree.

—Horticulturist—Baccalaureate or Licenciatura Degree.

—Meteorologist—Baccalaureate or Licenciatura Degree.

—Pharmacologist—Baccalaureate or Licenciatura Degree.

—Physicist (including Oceanographer in Canada—Baccalaureate or Licenciatura Degree.

—Plant Breeder—Baccalaureate or Licenciatura Degree.

—Poultry Scientist—Baccalaureate or Licenciatura Degree.

—Soil Scientist—Baccalaureate or Licenciatura Degree.

—Zoologist—Baccalaureate or Licenciatura Degree.

—TEACHER

—College—Baccalaureate or Licenciatura Degree.

—Seminary—Baccalaureate or Licenciatura Degree.

—University—Baccalaureate or Licenciatura Degree.

(d) *Classification of citizens of Canada or Mexico as TN professionals under the NAFTA*—(1) *Citizens of Mexico.* A citizen of Mexico who seeks temporary entry as a business person to engage in business activities at a professional level may be admitted to the United States in accordance with NAFTA upon presentation of a valid passport and valid

[7] A business person in this category must be seeking temporary entry to perform in a laboratory chemical, biological, hematological, immunologic, microscopic or bacteriological tests and analyses for diagnosis, treatment, or prevention of diseases.

[8] The term "Biologist" includes the profession of Plant Pathologist.

TN nonimmigrant visa at a United States Class A port-of-entry, at a United States airport handling international traffic, or at a United States pre-clearance/pre-flight station.

(2) *Citizens of Canada*. A citizen of Canada seeking temporary entry as a business person to engage in business activities at a professional level shall make application for admission with a Department officer at the United States Class A port-of-entry, at a United States airport handling international traffic, or at a United States pre-clearance/pre-flight station.

(3) *Documentation*. Upon application for a visa at a United States consular office, or, in the case of a citizen of Canada making application for admission at a port-of-entry, an applicant under this section shall present the following:

(i) *Proof of citizenship*. A Mexican citizen applying for admission as a TN nonimmigrant must establish such citizenship by presenting a valid passport. Canadian citizens, while not required to present a valid passport for admission unless traveling from outside the Western hemisphere, must establish Canadian citizenship.

(ii) *Documentation demonstrating engagement in business activities at a professional level and demonstrating professional qualifications*. The applicant must present documentation sufficient to satisfy the consular officer (in the case of a Mexican citizen) or the Department officer (in the case of a Canadian citizen) that the applicant is seeking entry to the United States to engage in business activities for a United States employer(s) or entity(ies) at a professional level, and that the applicant meets the criteria to perform at such a professional level. This documentation may be in the form of a letter from the prospective employer(s) in the United States or from the foreign employer, and must be supported by diplomas, degrees or membership in a professional organization. Degrees received by the applicant from an educational institution not located within Canada, Mexico, or the United States must be accompanied by an evaluation by a reliable credentials evaluation service which specializes in evaluating foreign educational credentials. The documentation shall fully affirm:

(A) The Appendix 1603.D.1 profession of the applicant;

(B) A description of the professional activities, including a brief summary of daily job duties, if appropriate, in which the applicant will engage in for the United States employer/entity;

(C) The anticipated length of stay;

(D The educational qualifications or appropriate credentials which demonstrate that the Canadian or Mexican citizen has professional level status; and

(E) The arrangements for remuneration for services to be rendered.

(e) *Procedures for admission*. A citizen of Canada or Mexico who qualifies for admission under this section shall be provided confirming documentation and shall be admitted under the classification symbol TN for a period not to exceed three years. The conforming document provided shall bear the legend "multiple entry." The fee prescribed under 8 CFR 103.7(b)(1) shall be remitted by Canadian Citizens upon admission to the United States pursuant to the terms and conditions of the NAFTA. Upon remittance of the prescribed fee, the TN applicant for admission shall be provided a DHS-issued receipt on the appropriate form.

(f) [Reserved]

(g) *Readmission*—(1) *With a Form I-94*. An alien may be readmitted to the United States in TN classification for the remainder of the authorized period of TN admission on Form I-94 (see §1.4), without presentation of the letter or supporting documentation described in paragraph (d)(3) of this section, and without the prescribed fee set forth in 8 CFR 103.7(b)(1), provided that the original intended professional activities and employer(s) have not changed, and the Form I-94 has not expired.

(2) *Without a valid I-94*. If the alien seeking readmission to the United States in TN classification is no longer in possession of a valid, unexpired Form I-94, and the period of initial admission in TN classification has not lapsed, then a new Form I-94 may be issued for the period of validity that remains on the TN nonimmigrant's original Form I-94 with the legend "multiple entry" and the alien can

then be readmitted in TN status if the alien presents alternate evidence as follows:

(i) For Canadian citizens, alternate evidence may include, but is not limited to, a fee receipt for admission as a TN or a previously issued admission stamp as TN in a passport, and a confirming letter from the United States employer(s).

(ii) For Mexican citizens seeking re-admission as TN nonimmigrants, alternate evidence shall consist of presentation of a valid unexpired TN visa and evidence of a previous admission.

(h) *Extension of stay.* (1) *Filing.* A United States employer of a citizen of Canada or Mexico who is currently maintaining valid TN nonimmigrant status, or a United States entity (in the case of a citizen of Canada or Mexico who is currently maintaining valid TN nonimmigrant status and is employed by a foreign employer), may request an extension of stay, subject to the following conditions:

(i) An extension of stay must be requested by filing the appropriate form with the fee provided at 8 CFR 103.7(b)(1), in accordance with the form instructions with USCIS.

(ii) The beneficiary must be physically present in the United States at the time of the filing of the appropriate form requesting an extension of stay as a TN nonimmigrant. If the alien is required to leave the United States for any reason while the petition is pending, the petitioner may request that USCIS notify the consular office where the beneficiary is required to apply for a visa or, if visa exempt, a DHS-designated port-of-entry where the beneficiary will apply for admission to the United States, of the approval.

(iii) An extension of stay in TN status may be approved by USCIS for a maximum period of three years.

(iv) There is no specific limit on the total period of time an alien may be in TN status provided the alien continues to be engaged in TN business activities for a U.S. employer or entity at a professional level, and otherwise continues to properly maintain TN nonimmigrant status.

(2) *Readmission at the border.* Nothing in paragraph (h)(1) of this section shall preclude a citizen of Canada or Mexico who has previously been admitted to the United States in TN status, and who has not violated such status while in the United States, from applying at a DHS-designated port-of-entry, prior to the expiration date of the previous period of admission, for a new three-year period of admission. The application for a new period of admission must be supported by a new letter from the United States employer or the foreign employer, in the case of a citizen of Canada who is providing prearranged services to a United States entity, which meets the requirements of paragraph (d) of this section, together with the appropriate filing fee as noted in 8 CFR 103.7(b)(1). Citizens of Mexico must present a valid passport and a valid, unexpired TN nonimmigrant visa when applying for readmission, as outlined in paragraph (d)(1) of this section.

(i) *Request for change or addition of United States employers*—(1) *Filing at the service center.* A citizen of Canada or Mexico admitted into the United States as a TN nonimmigrant who seeks to change or add a United States employer during the period of admission must have the new employer file a Form I–129 with appropriate supporting documentation, including a letter from the new employer describing the services to be performed, the time needed to render such services, and the terms of remuneration for services. Employment with a different or with an additional employer is not authorized prior to Department approval of the request.

(2) *Readmission at the border.* Nothing in paragraph (i)(1) of those section precludes a citizen of Canada or Mexico from applying for readmission to the United States for the purpose of presenting documentation from a different or additional United States or foreign employer. Such documentation shall meet the requirements prescribed in paragraph (d) of this section. The fee prescribed under 8 CFR 103.7(b)(1) shall be remitted by Canadian citizens upon admission to the United States pursuant to the terms and conditions of the NAFTA. Citizens of Mexico may present documentation from a different or additional United States or foreign employer to a consular officer as evidence in support of a new nonimmigrant TN visa application.

(3) No action shall be required on the part of a citizen of Canada or Mexico in TN status who is transferred to another location by the same United States employer to perform the same services. Such an acceptable transfer would be to a branch or office of the employer. In a case of a transfer to a separately incorporated subsidiary or affiliate, the requirements of paragraphs (i)(1) and (i)(2) of this section will apply.

(j) *Spouse and unmarried minor children accompanying or following to join.* (1) The spouse or unmarried minor children of a citizen of Canada or Mexico admitted in TN nonimmigrant status, if otherwise admissible, may be admitted initially, readmitted, or granted a change of nonimmigrant status or an extension of his or her period of stay for the same period of time granted to the TN nonimmigrant. Such spouse or unmarried minor children shall, upon approval of an application for admission, readmission, change of status or extension of stay be classified as TD nonimmigrants. A request for a change of status to TD or an extension of stay of a TD nonimmigrant may be made on the appropriate form together with appropriate filing fees and evidence of the principal alien's current TN status.

(2) The spouse or unmarried minor children of a citizen of Canada or Mexico admitted in TN nonimmigrant status shall be required to present a valid, unexpired TD nonimmigrant visa unless otherwise exempt under 8 CFR 212.1.

(3) The spouse and unmarried minor children of a citizen of Canada or Mexico admitted in TN nonimmigrant status shall be issued confirming documentation bearing the legend "multiple entry." There shall be no fee required for admission of the spouse and unmarried minor children.

(4) The spouse and unmarried minor children of a citizen of Canada or Mexico admitted in TN nonimmigrant status shall not accept employment in the United States unless otherwise authorized under the Act.

(k) *Effect of a strike.* (1) If the Secretary of Labor certifies or otherwise informs the Director of USCIS that a strike or other labor dispute involving a work stoppage of workers is in progress, and the temporary entry of a citizen of Mexico or Canada in TN nonimmigrant status may adversely affect the settlement of any labor dispute or the employment of any person who is involved in such dispute, the United States may refuse to issue an immigration document authorizing the entry or employment of such an alien.

(2) If the alien has already commenced employment in the United States and is participating in a strike or other labor dispute involving a work stoppage of workers, whether or not such strike or other labor dispute has been certified by the Department of Labor, or whether USCIS has been otherwise informed that such a strike or labor dispute is in progress, the alien shall not be deemed to be failing to maintain his or her status solely on account of past, present, or future participation in a strike or other labor dispute involving a work stoppage of workers, but is subject to the following terms and conditions:

(i) The alien shall remain subject to all applicable provisions of the Immigration and Nationality Act and regulations promulgated in the same manner as all other TN nonimmigrants;

(ii) The status and authorized period of stay of such an alien is not modified or extended in any way by virtue of his or her participation in a strike or other labor dispute involving a work stoppage of workers; and

(iii) Although participation by a TN nonimmigrant alien in a strike or other labor dispute involving a work stoppage of workers will not constitute a ground for removal, any alien who violates his or her status or who remains in the United States after his or her authorized period of stay has expired will be subject to removal.

(3) If there is a strike or other labor dispute involving a work stoppage of workers in progress but such strike or other labor dispute is not certified under paragraph (k)(1) of this section, or USCIS has not otherwise been informed by the Secretary that such a strike or labor dispute is in progress, Director of USCIS shall not deny a petition or deny entry to an applicant for

TN status based upon such strike or other labor dispute.

[58 FR 69212, Dec. 30, 1993, as amended at 63 FR 1335, Jan. 9, 1998; 69 FR 11289, Mar. 10, 2004; 69 FR 60941, Oct. 13, 2004; 73 FR 61334, Oct. 16, 2008; 78 FR 18472, Mar. 27, 2013]

§ 214.7 Habitual residence in the territories and possessions of the United States and consequences thereof.

(a) *Definitions.* As used in this section, the term:

(1) *Compacts* means the agreements of free association between the United States and the governments of the Republic of the Marshall Islands, the Federated States of Micronesia, and Palau, approved by Public Law 99–239 with respect to the governments of the Republic of the Marshall Islands and the Federated States of Micronesia, and by Public Law 99–658, with respect to Palau.

(2) *Freely associated states (FAS)* means the following parts of the former Trust Territories of the Pacific Islands, namely, the Republic of the Marshall Islands, the Federated States of Micronesia, and Palau.

(3) *Territories and possessions of the United States* means all territories and possessions of the United States to which the Act applies, including those commonwealths of the United States that are not States. It does not include American Samoa, as long as the Act does not apply to it.

(4)(i) *Habitual resident* means a citizen of the FAS who has been admitted to a territory or possession of the United States (other than American Samoa, as long as the Act is not applicable to it) pursuant to section 141(a) of the Compacts and who occupies in such territory or possession a habitual residence as that term is defined in section 461 of the Compacts, namely a place of general abode or a principal, actual dwelling place of a continuing or lasting nature. The term "habitual resident" does not apply to:

(A) A person who has established a continuing residence in a territory or possession of the United States, but whose cumulative physical presence in the United States amounts to less than 365 days; or

(B) A dependent of a resident representative described in section 152 of the Compacts; or

(C) A person who entered the United States for the purpose of full-time studies as long as such person maintains that status.

(ii) Since the term "habitual" resident requires that the person have entered the United States pursuant to section 141(a) of the Compacts, the term does not apply to FAS citizens whose presence in the territories or possessions is based on an authority other than section 141(a), such as:

(A) Members of the Armed Forces of the United States described in 8 CFR § 235.1(c);

(B) Persons lawfully admitted for permanent residence in the United States; or

(C) Persons having nonimmigrant status whose entry into the United States is based on provisions of the Compacts or the Act other than section 141(a) of the Compacts.

(5) *Dependent* means a citizen of the FAS, as defined in section 141(a) of the Compacts, who:

(i) Is a habitual resident;

(ii) Resides with a principal habitual resident;

(iii) Relies for financial support on that principal habitual resident; and

(iv) Is either the parent, spouse, or unmarried child under the age of 21 of the principal habitual resident or the parent or child of the spouse of the principal habitual resident.

(6) *Principal habitual resident* means a habitual resident with whom one or more dependents reside and on whom dependent(s) rely for financial support.

(7) *Self-supporting* means:

(i) Having a lawful occupation of a current and continuing nature that provides 40 hours of gainful employment each week. A part-time student attending an accredited college or institution of higher learning in a territory or possession of the United States receives for each college or graduate credit-hour of study a three-hour credit toward the 40-hour requirement; or

(ii) If the person cannot meet the 40-hour employment requirement, having lawfully derived funds that meet or exceed 100 percent of the official poverty guidelines for Hawaii for a family unit of the appropriate size as published annually by the Department of Health and Human Services.

(8) *Receipt of unauthorized public benefits* means the acceptance of public benefits by fraud or willful misrepresentation in violation of section 401 or 411 of the Personal Responsibility and Work Opportunity Reconciliation Act of 1996, Public Law 104–193, 110 Stat. 2261, 2268, as amended by sections 5561 and 5565 of the Balanced Budget Act of 1997, Public Law 105–33, 111 Stat. 638. 639.

(b) *Where do these rules regarding habitual residence apply?* The rules in this section apply to habitual residents living in a territory or possession of the United States to which the Act applies. Those territories and possessions are at present Guam, the Commonwealth of Puerto Rico, the American Virgin Islands, and the Commonwealth of the Northern Mariana Islands. These rules do not apply to habitual residents living in American Samoa as long as the Act does not extend to it. These rules are not applicable to habitual residents living in the fifty States or the District of Columbia.

(c) *When is an arriving FAS citizen presumed to be a habitual resident?* (1) An arriving FAS citizen will be subject to the rebuttable presumption that he or she is a habitual resident if the Service has reason to believe that the arriving FAS citizen was previously admitted to the territory or possession more than one year ago; and

(2) That the arriving FAS citizen either;

(i) Failed to turn in his or her Form I–94 (see §1.4) when he or she previously departed from the United States; or

(ii) Failed to apply for a replacement Form I–94.

(d) *What rights do habitual residents have?* Habitual residents have the right to enter, reside, study, and work in the United States, its territories or possessions, in nonimmigrant status without regard to the requirements of sections 212(a)(5)(A) and 212(a)(7)(A) and (B) of the Act.

(e) *What are the limitations on the rights of habitual residents?* (1) A habitual resident who is not a dependent is subject to removal if he or she:

(i) Is not and has not been self-supporting for a period exceeding 60 consecutive days for reasons other than a lawful strike or other labor dispute involving work stoppage; or

(ii) Has received unauthorized public benefits by fraud or willful misrepresentation; or

(iii) Is subject to removal pursuant to section 237 of the Act, or any other provision of the Act.

(2) Any dependent is removable from a territory or possession of the United States if:

(i) The principal habitual resident who financially supports him or her and with whom he or she resides, becomes subject to removal unless the dependent establishes that he or she has become a dependent of another habitual resident or becomes self-supporting; or

(ii) The dependent, as an individual, receives unauthorized public benefits by fraud or willful misrepresentation; or

(iii) The dependent, as an individual, is subject to removal pursuant to section 237 of the Act, or any other provision of the Act.

[65 FR 56465, Sept. 19, 2000, as amended at 74 FR 55738, Oct. 28, 2009; 78 FR 18472, Mar. 27, 2013]

§§214.8–214.10 [Reserved]

§214.11 Alien victims of severe forms of trafficking in persons.

(a) *Definitions.* Where applicable, USCIS will apply the definitions provided in section 103 and 107(e) of the Trafficking Victims Protection Act (TVPA) with due regard for the definitions and application of these terms in 28 CFR part 1100 and the provisions of 18 U.S.C. 77. As used in this section the term:

Application for derivative T nonimmigrant status means a request by a principal alien on behalf of an eligible family member for derivative T–2, T–3, T–4, T–5, or T–6 nonimmigrant status on the form designated by USCIS for that purpose.

Application for T nonimmigrant status means a request by a principal alien for T–1 nonimmigrant status on the form designated by USCIS for that purpose.

Bona fide determination means a USCIS determination that an application for T–1 nonimmigrant status has been initially reviewed and determined that the application does not appear to be fraudulent, is complete and properly filed, includes completed fingerprint and background checks, and presents prima facie evidence of eligibility for T–1 nonimmigrant status including admissibility.

Child means a person described in section 101(b)(1) of the Act.

Coercion means threats of serious harm to or physical restraint against any person; any scheme, plan, or pattern intended to cause a person to believe that failure to perform an act would result in serious harm to or physical restraint against any person; or the abuse or threatened abuse of the legal process.

Commercial sex act means any sex act on account of which anything of value is given to or received by any person.

Debt bondage means the status or condition of a debtor arising from a pledge by the debtor of his or her personal services or of those of a person under his or her control as a security for debt, if the value of those services as reasonably assessed is not applied toward the liquidation of the debt or the length and nature of those services are not respectively limited and defined.

Derivative T nonimmigrant means an eligible family member who has been granted T–2, T–3, T–4, T–5, or T–6 derivative status. A family member outside of the United States is not a derivative T nonimmigrant until he or she is granted a T–2, T–3, T–4, T–5, or T–6 visa by the Department of State and is admitted to the United States in derivative T nonimmigrant status.

Eligible family member means a family member who may be eligible for derivative T nonimmigrant status based on his or her relationship to an alien victim and, if required, upon a showing of a present danger or retaliation; and:

(1) In the case of an alien victim who is 21 years of age or older, means the spouse and children of such alien;

(2) In the case of an alien victim under 21 years of age, means the spouse, children, unmarried siblings under 18 years of age, and parents of such alien; and

(3) Regardless of the age of an alien victim, means any parent or unmarried sibling under 18 years of age, or adult or minor child of a derivative of such alien where the family member faces a present danger of retaliation as a result of the alien victim's escape from a severe form of trafficking or cooperation with law enforcement.

Involuntary servitude means a condition of servitude induced by means of any scheme, plan, or pattern intended to cause a person to believe that, if the person did not enter into or continue in such condition, that person or another person would suffer serious harm or physical restraint; or a condition of servitude induced by the abuse or threatened abuse of legal process. Involuntary servitude includes a condition of servitude in which the victim is forced to work for the defendant by the use or threat of physical restraint or physical injury, or by the use or threat of coercion through the law or the legal process. This definition encompasses those cases in which the defendant holds the victim in servitude by placing the victim in fear of such physical restraint or injury or legal coercion.

Law Enforcement Agency (LEA) means a Federal, State, or local law enforcement agency, prosecutor, judge, labor agency, children's protective services agency, or other authority that has the responsibility and authority for the detection, investigation, and/or prosecution of severe forms of trafficking in persons. Federal LEAs include but are not limited to the following: U.S. Attorneys' Offices, Civil Rights Division, Criminal Division, U.S. Marshals Service, Federal Bureau of Investigation (Department of Justice); U.S. Immigration and Customs Enforcement (ICE), U.S. Customs and Border Protection (CBP); Diplomatic Security Service (Department of State); and Department of Labor.

Law Enforcement Agency (LEA) endorsement means an official LEA endorsement on the form designated by USCIS for such purpose.

Peonage means a status or condition of involuntary servitude based upon real or alleged indebtedness.

Principal T nonimmigrant means the victim of a severe form of trafficking in persons who has been granted T–1 nonimmigrant status.

Reasonable request for assistance means a request made by an LEA to a victim to assist in the investigation or prosecution of the acts of trafficking in persons or the investigation of crime where acts of trafficking are at least one central reason for the commission of that crime. The "reasonableness" of the request depends on the totality of the circumstances. Factors to consider include, but are not limited to: General law enforcement and prosecutorial practices; the nature of the victimization; the specific circumstances of the victim; severe trauma (both mental and physical); access to support services; whether the request would cause further trauma: The safety of the victim or the victim's family; compliance with other requests and the extent of such compliance; whether the request would yield essential information; whether the information could be obtained without the victim's compliance; whether an interpreter or attorney was present to help the victim understand the request; cultural, religious, or moral objections to the request; the time the victim had to comply with the request; and the age and maturity of the victim.

Severe form of trafficking in persons means sex trafficking in which a commercial sex act is induced by force, fraud, or coercion, or in which the person induced to perform such act is under the age of 18 years; or the recruitment, harboring, transportation, provision, or obtaining of a person for labor or services through the use of force, fraud, or coercion for the purpose of subjection to involuntary servitude, peonage, debt bondage, or slavery.

Sex trafficking means the recruitment, harboring, transportation, provision, obtaining, patronizing, or soliciting of a person for the purpose of a commercial sex act.

United States means the fifty States of the United States, the District of Columbia, the Commonwealth of Puerto Rico, the U.S. Virgin Islands, Guam, and the Commonwealth of the Northern Mariana Islands.

Victim of a severe form of trafficking in persons (victim) means an alien who is or has been subject to a severe form of trafficking in persons.

(b) *Eligibility for T–1 status.* An alien is eligible for T–1 nonimmigrant status under section 101(a)(15)(T)(i) of the Act if he or she demonstrates all of the following, subject to section 214(o) of the Act:

(1) *Victim.* The alien is or has been a victim of a severe form of trafficking in persons.

(2) *Physical presence.* The alien is physically present in the United States or at a port-of-entry thereto, according to paragraph (g) of this section.

(3) *Compliance with any reasonable request for assistance.* The alien has complied with any reasonable request for assistance in a Federal, State, or local investigation or prosecution of acts of trafficking in persons, or the investigation of a crime where acts of trafficking in persons are at least one central reason for the commission of that crime, or meets one of the conditions described below.

(i) *Exemption for minor victims.* An alien under 18 years of age is not required to comply with any reasonable request.

(ii) *Exception for trauma.* An alien who, due to physical or psychological trauma, is unable to cooperate with a reasonable request for assistance in the Federal, State, or local investigation or prosecution of acts of trafficking in persons, or the investigation of a crime where acts of trafficking in persons are at least one central reason for the commission of that crime, is not required to comply with such reasonable request.

(4) *Hardship.* The alien would suffer extreme hardship involving unusual and severe harm upon removal.

(5) *Prohibition against traffickers in persons.* No alien will be eligible to receive T nonimmigrant status under section 101(a)(15)(T) of the Act if there is substantial reason to believe that the alien has committed an act of a severe form of trafficking in persons.

(c) *Period of admission.* (1) *T–1 Principal.* T–1 nonimmigrant status may be approved for a period not to exceed 4 years, except as provided in section 214(o)(7) of the Act.

(2) *Derivative family members.* A derivative family member who is otherwise eligible for admission may be granted T–2, T–3, T–4, T–5, or T–6 nonimmigrant

status for an initial period that does not exceed the expiration date of the initial period approved for the T–1 principal alien, except as provided in section 214(o)(7) of the Act.

(3) *Notice.* At the time an alien is approved for T nonimmigrant status or receives an extension of T nonimmigrant status, USCIS will notify the alien when his or her T nonimmigrant status will expire. USCIS also will notify the alien that the failure to apply for adjustment of status to lawful permanent resident, as set forth in 8 CFR 245.23, will result in termination of the alien's T nonimmigrant status in the United States at the end of the 4-year period or any extension.

(d) *Application.* USCIS has sole jurisdiction over all applications for T nonimmigrant status.

(1) *Filing an application.* An alien seeking T–1 nonimmigrant status must submit an application for T nonimmigrant status on the form designated by USCIS in accordance with 8 CFR 103.2 and with the evidence described in paragraph (d) of this section.

(i) *Applicants in pending immigration proceedings.* An alien in removal proceedings under section 240 of the Act, or in exclusion or deportation proceedings under former sections 236 or 242 of the Act (as in effect prior to April 1, 1997), and who wishes to apply for T–1 nonimmigrant status must file an application for T nonimmigrant status directly with USCIS. In its discretion, DHS may agree to the alien's request to file with the immigration judge or the Board a joint motion to administratively close or terminate proceedings without prejudice, whichever is appropriate, while an application for T nonimmigrant status is adjudicated by USCIS.

(ii) *Applicants with final orders of removal, deportation, or exclusion.* An alien subject to a final order of removal, deportation, or exclusion may file an application for T–1 nonimmigrant status directly with USCIS. The filing of an application for T nonimmigrant status has no effect on DHS authority or discretion to execute a final order of removal, although the alien may request an administrative stay of removal pursuant to 8 CFR 241.6(a). If the alien is in detention pending execution of the final order, the period of detention (under the standards of 8 CFR 241.4) reasonably necessary to bring about the applicant's removal will be extended during the period the stay is in effect. If USCIS subsequently determines under the procedures in paragraph (e) of this section that the application is bona fide, DHS will automatically grant an administrative stay of the final order of removal, deportation, or exclusion, and the stay will remain in effect until a final decision is made on the application for T nonimmigrant status.

(iii) *Minor applicants.* When USCIS receives an application from a minor principal alien under the age of 18, USCIS will notify the Department of Health and Human Services to facilitate the provision of interim assistance.

(2) *Initial evidence.* An application for T nonimmigrant status must include:

(i) The applicant's signed statement describing the facts of the victimization and compliance with any reasonable law enforcement request (or a basis for why he or she has not complied) and any other eligibility requirements in his or her own words;

(ii) Any credible evidence that the applicant would like USCIS to consider supporting any of the eligibility requirements set out in paragraphs (f), (g), (h) and (i) of this section; and

(iii) *Inadmissible applicants.* If an applicant is inadmissible based on a ground that may be waived, he or she must also submit a request for a waiver of inadmissibility on the form designated by USCIS with the fee prescribed by 8 CFR 103.7(b)(1), in accordance with form instructions and 8 CFR 212.16, and accompanied by supporting evidence.

(3) *Evidence from law enforcement.* An applicant may wish to submit evidence from an LEA to help establish certain eligibility requirements for T nonimmigrant status. Evidence from an LEA is optional and is not given any special evidentiary weight.

(i) *Law Enforcement Agency (LEA) endorsement.* An LEA endorsement is optional evidence that can be submitted to help demonstrate victimization and/

or compliance with reasonable requests. An LEA endorsement is not mandatory and is not given any special evidentiary weight. An LEA endorsement itself does not grant a benefit and is one form of possible evidence but it does not lead to automatic approval of the application for T nonimmigrant status by USCIS. If provided, the LEA endorsement must be submitted on the form designated by USCIS in accordance with the form instructions and must be signed by a supervising official responsible for the detection, investigation or prosecution of severe forms of trafficking in persons. The LEA endorsement must attach the results of any name or database inquiries performed and describe the victimization (including dates where known) and the cooperation of the victim. USCIS, not the LEA, will determine if the applicant was or is a victim of a severe form of trafficking in persons, and otherwise meets the eligibility requirements for T nonimmigrant status. The decision whether to complete an LEA endorsement is at the discretion of the LEA. A formal investigation or prosecution is not required to complete an LEA endorsement.

(ii) *Disavowed or revoked LEA endorsement.* An LEA may revoke or disavow the contents of a previously submitted endorsement in writing. After revocation or disavowal, the LEA endorsement will no longer be considered as evidence.

(iii) *Continued Presence.* An applicant granted Continued Presence under 28 CFR 110.35 should submit documentation of the grant of Continued Presence. If Continued Presence has been revoked, it will no longer be considered as evidence.

(iv) *Other evidence.* An applicant may also submit any evidence regarding entry or admission into the United States or permission to remain in the United States or note that such evidence is contained in an applicant's immigration file.

(4) *Biometric services.* All applicants for T–1 nonimmigrant status must submit biometrics in accordance with 8 CFR 103.16.

(5) *Evidentiary standards and burden of proof.* The burden is on the applicant to demonstrate eligibility for T–1 nonimmigrant status. The applicant may submit any credible evidence relating to a T nonimmigrant application for consideration by USCIS. USCIS will conduct a de novo review of all evidence and may investigate any aspect of the application. Evidence previously submitted by the applicant for any immigration benefit or relief may be used by USCIS in evaluating the eligibility of an applicant for T–1 nonimmigrant status. USCIS will not be bound by previous factual determinations made in connection with a prior application or petition for any immigration benefit or relief. USCIS will determine, in its sole discretion, the evidentiary value of previously or concurrently submitted evidence.

(6) *Interview.* USCIS may require an applicant for T nonimmigrant status to participate in a personal interview. The necessity and location of the interview is determined solely by USCIS in accordance with 8 CFR part 103. Every effort will be made to schedule the interview in a location convenient to the applicant.

(7) *Bona fide determination.* Once an alien submits an application for T–1 nonimmigrant status, USCIS will conduct an initial review to determine if the application is a bona fide application for T–1 nonimmigrant status under the provisions of paragraph (e) of this section.

(8) *Decision.* After completing its de novo review of the application and evidence, USCIS will issue a decision approving or denying the application in accordance with 8 CFR 103.3.

(9) *Approval.* If USCIS determines that the applicant is eligible for T–1 nonimmigrant status, USCIS will approve the application and grant T–1 nonimmigrant status, subject to the annual limitation as provided in paragraph (j) of this section. USCIS will provide the applicant with evidence of T–1 nonimmigrant status. USCIS may also notify other parties and entities of the approval as it determines appropriate, including any LEA providing an LEA endorsement and the Department of Health and Human Service's Office of Refugee Resettlement, consistent with 8 U.S.C. 1367.

(i) *Applicants with an outstanding order of removal, deportation or exclusion issued by DHS.* For an applicant who is the subject of an order of removal, deportation or exclusion issued by DHS, the order will be deemed cancelled by operation of law as of the date of the USCIS approval of the application.

(ii) *Applicants with an outstanding order of removal, deportation or exclusion issued by the Department of Justice.* An applicant who is the subject of an order of removal, deportation or exclusion issued by an immigration judge or the Board may seek cancellation of such order by filing a motion to reopen and terminate removal proceedings with the immigration judge or the Board. ICE may agree, as a matter of discretion, to join such motion to overcome any applicable time and numerical limitations of 8 CFR 1003.2 and 1003.23.

(10) *Denial.* Upon denial of an application, USCIS will notify the applicant in accordance with 8 CFR 103.3. USCIS may also notify any LEA providing an LEA endorsement and the Department of Health and Human Service's Office of Refugee Resettlement. If an applicant appeals a denial in accordance with 8 CFR 103.3, the denial will not become final until the administrative appeal is decided.

(i) *Effect on bona fide determination.* Upon denial of an application, any benefits derived from a bona fide determination will automatically be revoked when the denial becomes final.

(ii) *Applicants previously in removal proceedings.* In the case of an applicant who was previously in removal proceedings that were terminated on the basis of a pending application for T nonimmigrant status, once a denial becomes final, DHS may file a new Notice to Appear to place the individual in removal proceedings again.

(iii) *Applicants subject to an order of removal, deportation or exclusion.* In the case of an applicant who is subject to an order of removal, deportation or exclusion that had been stayed due to the pending application for T nonimmigrant status, the stay will be automatically lifted as of the date the denial becomes final.

(11) *Employment authorization.* An alien granted T–1 nonimmigrant status is authorized to work incident to status. There is no need for an alien to file a separate form to be granted employment authorization. USCIS will issue an initial Employment Authorization Document (EAD) to such aliens, which will be valid for the duration of the alien's T–1 nonimmigrant status. An alien granted T–1 nonimmigrant status seeking to replace an EAD that was lost, stolen, or destroyed must file an application on the form designated by USCIS in accordance with form instructions.

(e) *Bona fide determination.* Once an alien submits an application for T–1 nonimmigrant status, USCIS will conduct an initial review to determine if the application is a bona fide application for T–1 nonimmigrant status.

(1) *Criteria.* After initial review, an application will be determined to be bona fide if:

(i) The application is properly filed and is complete;

(ii) The application does not appear to be fraudulent;

(iii) The application presents prima facie evidence of each eligibility requirement for T–1 nonimmigrant status;

(iv) Biometrics and background checks are complete; and

(v) The applicant is:

(A) Admissible to the United States; or

(B) Inadmissible to the United States based on a ground that may be waived (other than section 212(a)(4) of the Act); and either the applicant has filed a waiver of a ground of inadmissibility described in section 212(d)(13) of the Act concurrently with the application for T nonimmigrant status, or USCIS has already granted a waiver with respect to any ground of inadmissibility that applies to the applicant. USCIS may request further evidence from the applicant. All waivers are discretionary and require a request for waiver, on the form designated by USCIS.

(2) *USCIS determination.* An application will not be treated as bona fide until USCIS provides notice to the applicant.

(i) *Incomplete or insufficient application.* If an application is incomplete or if an application is complete but does not present sufficient evidence to establish prima facie eligibility for each eligibility requirement for T–1 nonimmigrant status, USCIS may request additional information, issue a notice of intent to deny as provided in 8 CFR 103.2(b)(8), or may adjudicate the application on the basis of the evidence presented under the procedures of this section.

(ii) *Notice*. Once USCIS determines an application is bona fide, USCIS will notify the applicant. An application will be treated as a bona fide application as of the date of the notice.

(3) *Stay of final order of removal, deportation, or exclusion*. If USCIS determines that an application is bona fide it automatically stays the execution of any final order of removal, deportation, or exclusion. This administrative stay will remain in effect until any adverse decision becomes final. The filing of an application for T nonimmigrant status does not automatically stay the execution of a final order unless USCIS has determined that the application is bona fide. Neither an immigration judge nor the Board has jurisdiction to adjudicate an application for a stay of removal, deportation, or exclusion on the basis of the filing of an application for T nonimmigrant status.

(f) *Victim of a severe form of trafficking in persons*. To be eligible for T–1 nonimmigrant status an applicant must meet the definition of a victim of a severe form of trafficking in persons described in paragraph (a) of this section.

(1) *Evidence*. The applicant must submit evidence that demonstrates that he or she is or has been a victim of a severe form of trafficking in persons. Except in instances of sex trafficking involving victims under 18 years of age, severe forms of trafficking in persons must involve both a particular means (force, fraud, or coercion) and a particular end or a particular intended end (sex trafficking, involuntary servitude, peonage, debt bondage, or slavery). If a victim has not performed labor or services, or a commercial sex act, the victim must establish that he or she was recruited, transported, harbored, provided, or obtained for the purposes of subjection to sex trafficking, involuntary servitude, peonage, debt bondage, or slavery, or patronized or solicited for the purposes of subjection to sex trafficking. The applicant may satisfy this requirement by submitting:

(i) An LEA endorsement as described in paragraph (d)(3) of this section;

(ii) Documentation of a grant of Continued Presence under 28 CFR 1100.35; or

(iii) Any other evidence, including but not limited to, trial transcripts, court documents, police reports, news articles, copies of reimbursement forms for travel to and from court, and/or affidavits. In the victim's statement prescribed by paragraph (d)(2) of this section, the applicant should describe what the alien has done to report the crime to an LEA and indicate whether criminal records relating to the trafficking crime are available.

(2) If the Continued Presence has been revoked or the contents of the LEA endorsement have been disavowed based on a determination that the applicant is not or was not a victim of a severe form of trafficking in persons, it will no longer be considered as evidence.

(g) *Physical presence*. To be eligible for T–1 nonimmigrant status an applicant must be physically present in the United States, American Samoa, or at a port-of-entry thereto on account of such trafficking.

(1) *Applicability*. The physical presence requirement requires USCIS to consider the alien's presence in the United States at the time of application. The requirement reaches an alien who:

(i) Is present because he or she is currently being subjected to a severe form of trafficking in persons;

(ii) Was liberated from a severe form of trafficking in persons by an LEA;

(iii) Escaped a severe form of trafficking in persons before an LEA was involved, subject to paragraph (g)(2) of this section;

(iv) Was subject to a severe form of trafficking in persons at some point in the past and whose continuing presence in the United States is directly related to the original trafficking in persons; or

(v) Is present on account of the alien having been allowed entry into the United States for participation in investigative or judicial processes associated with an act or perpetrator of trafficking.

(2) *Departure from the United States.* An alien who has voluntarily departed from (or has been removed from) the United States at any time after the act of a severe form of trafficking in persons is deemed not to be present in the United States as a result of such trafficking in persons unless:

(i) The alien's reentry into the United States was the result of the continued victimization of the alien;

(ii) The alien is a victim of a new incident of a severe form of trafficking in persons; or

(iii) The alien has been allowed reentry into the United States for participation in investigative or judicial processes associated with an act or perpetrator of trafficking, described in paragraph (g)(4) of this section.

(3) *Presence for participation in investigative or judicial processes.* An alien who was allowed initial entry or reentry into the United States for participation in investigative or judicial processes associated with an act or perpetrator of trafficking will be deemed to be physically present in the United States on account of trafficking in persons, regardless of where such trafficking occurred. To satisfy this section, an alien must submit documentation to show valid entry into the United States and evidence that this valid entry is for participation in investigative or judicial processes associated with an act or perpetrator of trafficking.

(4) *Evidence.* The applicant must submit evidence that demonstrates that his or her physical presence in the United States or at a port-of-entry thereto, is on account of trafficking in persons, including physical presence on account of the alien having been allowed entry into the United States for participation in investigative or judicial processes associated with an act or a perpetrator of trafficking. USCIS will consider all evidence presented to determine the physical presence requirement, including the alien's responses to questions on the application for T nonimmigrant status about when he or she escaped from the trafficker, what activities he or she has undertaken since that time including the steps he or she may have taken to deal with the consequences of having been trafficked, and the applicant's ability to leave the United States. The applicant may satisfy this requirement by submitting:

(i) An LEA endorsement, described in paragraph (d)(3) of this section;

(ii) Documentation of a grant of Continued Presence under 28 CFR 1100.35;

(iii) Any other documentation of entry into the United States or permission to remain in the United States, such as parole under section 212(d)(5) of the Act, or a notation that such evidence is contained in the applicant's immigration file; or

(iv) Any other credible evidence, including a personal statement from the applicant, stating the date and place (if known) and the manner and purpose (if known) for which the applicant entered the United States and demonstrating that the applicant is now present on account of the trafficking.

(h) *Compliance with any reasonable request for assistance in an investigation or prosecution.* To be eligible for T–1 nonimmigrant status, an applicant must have complied with any reasonable request for assistance from an LEA in an investigation or prosecution of acts of trafficking or the investigation of a crime where acts of trafficking are at least one central reason for the commission of that crime, unless the applicant meets an exemption described in paragraph (h)(4) of this section.

(1) *Applicability.* An applicant must have had, at a minimum, contact with an LEA regarding the acts of a severe form of trafficking in persons. An applicant who has never had contact with an LEA regarding the acts of a severe form of trafficking in persons will not be eligible for T–1 nonimmigrant status, unless he or she meets an exemption described in paragraph (h)(4) of this section.

(2) *Unreasonable requests.* An applicant need only show compliance with reasonable requests made by an LEA for assistance in the investigation or prosecution of the acts of trafficking in persons. The reasonableness of the request depends on the totality of the circumstances. Factors to consider include, but are not limited to:

(i) General law enforcement and prosecutorial practices;

(ii) The nature of the victimization;

(iii) The specific circumstances of the victim;

(iv) Severity of trauma suffered (both mental and physical) or whether the request would cause further trauma;

(v) Access to support services;

(vi) The safety of the victim or the victim's family;

(vii) Compliance with previous requests and the extent of such compliance;

(viii) Whether the request would yield essential information;

(ix) Whether the information could be obtained without the victim's compliance;

(x) Whether an interpreter or attorney was present to help the victim understand the request;

(xi) Cultural, religious, or moral objections to the request;

(xii) The time the victim had to comply with the request; and

(xiii) The age and maturity of the victim.

(3) *Evidence.* An applicant must submit evidence that demonstrates that he or she has complied with any reasonable request for assistance in a Federal, State, or local investigation or prosecution of trafficking in persons, or a crime where trafficking in persons is at least one central reason for the commission of that crime. In the alternative, an applicant can submit evidence to demonstrate that he or she should be exempt under paragraph (h)(4) of this section. If USCIS has any question about whether the applicant has complied with a reasonable request for assistance, USCIS may contact the LEA. The applicant may satisfy this requirement by submitting any of the following:

(i) An LEA endorsement as described in paragraph (d)(3) of this section;

(ii) Documentation of a grant of Continued Presence under 28 CFR 1100.35; or

(iii) Any other evidence, including affidavits of witnesses. In the victim's statement prescribed by paragraph (d)(2) of this section, the applicant should show that an LEA that has responsibility and authority for the detection, investigation, or prosecution of severe forms of trafficking in persons has information about such trafficking in persons, that the victim has complied with any reasonable request for assistance in the investigation or prosecution of such acts of trafficking, and, if the victim did not report the crime, why the crime was not previously reported.

(4) An applicant who has not had contact with an LEA or who has not complied with any reasonable request may be exempt from the requirement to comply with any reasonable request for assistance in an investigation or prosecution if either of the following two circumstances applies:

(i) *Trauma.* The applicant is unable to cooperate with a reasonable request for assistance in the Federal, State, or local investigation or prosecution of acts of trafficking in persons due to physical or psychological trauma. An applicant must submit evidence of the trauma. An applicant may satisfy this by submitting an affirmative statement describing the trauma and any other credible evidence. "Any other credible evidence" includes, for instance, a signed statement from a qualified professional, such as a medical professional, social worker, or victim advocate, who attests to the victim's mental state, and medical, psychological, or other records which are relevant to the trauma. USCIS reserves the authority and discretion to contact the LEA involved in the case, if appropriate; or

(ii) *Age.* The applicant is under 18 years of age. An applicant under 18 years of age is exempt from the requirement to comply with any reasonable request for assistance in an investigation or prosecution, but he or she must submit evidence of age. Applicants should include, where available, an official copy of the alien's birth certificate, a passport, or a certified medical opinion. Other evidence regarding the age of the applicant may be submitted in accordance with 8 CFR 103.2(b)(2)(i).

(i) *Extreme hardship involving unusual and severe harm.* To be eligible for T–1 nonimmigrant status, an applicant must demonstrate that removal from the United States would subject the applicant to extreme hardship involving unusual and severe harm.

(1) *Standard.* Extreme hardship involving unusual and severe harm is a

higher standard than extreme hardship as described in 8 CFR 240.58. A finding of extreme hardship involving unusual and severe harm may not be based solely upon current or future economic detriment, or the lack of, or disruption to, social or economic opportunities. The determination of extreme hardship is made solely by USCIS.

(2) *Factors*. Factors that may be considered in evaluating whether removal would result in extreme hardship involving unusual and severe harm should include both traditional extreme hardship factors and factors associated with having been a victim of a severe form of trafficking in persons. These factors include, but are not limited to:

(i) The age, maturity, and personal circumstances of the applicant;

(ii) Any physical or psychological issues the applicant has which necessitates medical or psychological care not reasonably available in the foreign country;

(iii) The nature and extent of the physical and psychological consequences of having been a victim of a severe form of trafficking in persons;

(iv) The impact of the loss of access to the United States courts and the criminal justice system for purposes relating to the incident of a severe form of trafficking in persons or other crimes perpetrated against the applicant, including criminal and civil redress for acts of trafficking in persons, criminal prosecution, restitution, and protection;

(v) The reasonable expectation that the existence of laws, social practices, or customs in the foreign country to which the applicant would be returned would penalize the applicant severely for having been the victim of a severe form of trafficking in persons;

(vi) The likelihood of re-victimization and the need, ability, and willingness of foreign authorities to protect the applicant;

(vii) The likelihood of harm that the trafficker in persons or others acting on behalf of the trafficker in the foreign country would cause the applicant; or

(viii) The likelihood that the applicant's individual safety would be threatened by the existence of civil unrest or armed conflict.

(3) *Evidence*. An applicant must submit evidence that demonstrates he or she would suffer extreme hardship involving unusual and severe harm if removed from the United States. An applicant is encouraged to describe and document all factors that may be relevant to the case, as there is no guarantee that a particular reason(s) will satisfy the requirement. Hardship to persons other than the alien victim cannot be considered in determining whether an applicant would suffer the requisite hardship. The applicant may satisfy this requirement by submitting any credible evidence regarding the nature and scope of the hardship if the applicant was removed from the United States, including evidence of hardship arising from circumstances surrounding the victimization and any other circumstances. An applicant may submit a personal statement or other evidence, including evidence from relevant country condition reports and any other public or private sources of information.

(j) *Annual cap*. In accordance with section 214(o)(2) of the Act, DHS may not grant T–1 nonimmigrant status to more than 5,000 aliens in any fiscal year.

(1) *Waiting list*. All eligible applicants who, due solely to the cap, are not granted T–1 nonimmigrant status will be placed on a waiting list and will receive written notice of such placement. Priority on the waiting list will be determined by the date the application was properly filed, with the oldest applications receiving the highest priority. In the next fiscal year, USCIS will issue a number to each application on the waiting list, in the order of the highest priority, providing the applicant remains admissible and eligible for T nonimmigrant status. After T–1 nonimmigrant status has been issued to qualifying applicants on the waiting list, any remaining T–1 nonimmigrant numbers for that fiscal year will be issued to new qualifying applicants in the order that the applications were properly filed.

(2) *Unlawful presence*. While an applicant for T nonimmigrant status who was granted deferred action or parole is

on the waiting list, the applicant will not accrue unlawful presence under section 212(a)(9)(B) of the Act while maintaining parole or deferred action.

(3) *Removal from the waiting list.* An applicant may be removed from the waiting list and the deferred action or parole may be terminated consistent with law and policy. Applicants on the waiting list must remain admissible to the United States and otherwise eligible for T nonimmigrant status. If at any time prior to final adjudication USCIS receives information that an applicant is no longer eligible for nonimmigrant status, the applicant may be removed from the waiting list and the deferred action or parole may be terminated. USCIS will provide notice to the applicant of that decision.

(k) *Application for eligible family members.* (1) *Eligibility.* Subject to section 214(o) of the Act, an alien who has applied for or has been granted T–1 nonimmigrant status (principal alien) may apply for the admission of an eligible family member, who is otherwise admissible to the United States, in derivative T nonimmigrant status if accompanying or following to join the principal alien.

(i) *Principal alien 21 years of age or older.* For a principal alien who is 21 years of age or over, eligible family member means a T–2 (spouse) or T–3 (child).

(ii) *Principal alien under 21 years of age.* For a principal alien who is under 21 years of age, eligible family member means a T–2 (spouse), T–3 (child), T–4 (parent), or T–5 (unmarried sibling under the age of 18).

(iii) *Family member facing danger of retaliation.* Regardless of the age of the principal alien, if the eligible family member faces a present danger of retaliation as a result of the principal alien's escape from the severe form of trafficking or cooperation with law enforcement, in consultation with the law enforcement officer investigating a severe form of trafficking, eligible family member means a T–4 (parent), T–5 (unmarried sibling under the age of 18), or T–6 (adult or minor child of a derivative of the principal alien).

(iv) *Admission requirements.* The principal applicant must demonstrate that the alien for whom derivative T nonimmigrant status is being sought is an eligible family member of the T–1 principal alien, as defined in paragraph (a) of this section, and is otherwise eligible for that status.

(2) *Application.* A T–1 principal alien may submit an application for derivative T nonimmigrant status on the form designated by USCIS in accordance with the form instructions. The application for derivative T nonimmigrant status for an eligible family member may be filed with the T–1 application, or separately. Derivative T nonimmigrant status is dependent on the principal alien having been granted T–1 nonimmigrant status and the principal alien maintaining T–1 nonimmigrant status. If a principal alien granted T–1 nonimmigrant status cannot maintain status due to his or her death, the provisions of section 204(l) of the Act may apply.

(i) *Eligible family members in pending immigration proceedings.* If an eligible family member is in removal proceedings under section 240 of the Act, or in exclusion or deportation proceedings under former sections 236 or 242 of the Act (as in effect prior to April 1, 1997), the principal alien must file an application for derivative T nonimmigrant status directly with USCIS. In its discretion and at the request of the eligible family member, ICE may agree to file a joint motion to administratively close or terminate proceedings without prejudice with the immigration judge or the Board, whichever is appropriate, while USCIS adjudicates an application for derivative T nonimmigrant status.

(ii) *Eligible family members with final orders of removal, deportation, or exclusion.* If an eligible family member is the subject of a final order of removal, deportation, or exclusion, the principal alien may file an application for derivative T nonimmigrant status directly with USCIS. The filing of an application for derivative T nonimmigrant status has no effect on ICE's authority or discretion to execute a final order, although the alien may file a request for an administrative stay of removal pursuant to 8 CFR 241.6(a). If the eligible family member is in detention pending execution of the final order, the period of detention (under the standards of 8 CFR 241.4) will be extended while a stay is in effect for the period reasonably necessary to bring about the applicant's removal.

(3) *Required supporting evidence.* In addition to the form, an application for derivative T nonimmigrant status must include the following:

(i) Biometrics submitted in accordance with 8 CFR 103.16;

(ii) Evidence demonstrating the relationship of an eligible family member, as provided in paragraph (k)(4) of this section;

(iii) In the case of an alien seeking derivative T nonimmigrant status on the basis of danger of retaliation, evidence demonstrating this danger as provided in paragraph (k)(6) of this section.

(iv) *Inadmissible applicants.* If an eligible family member is inadmissible based on a ground that may be waived, a request for a waiver of inadmissibility under section 212(d)(13) or section 212(d)(3) of the Act must be filed in accordance with 8 CFR 212.16 and submitted with the completed application package.

(4) *Relationship.* Except as described in paragraphs (k)(5) of this section, the family relationship must exist at the time:

(i) The application for the T–1 nonimmigrant status is filed;

(ii) The application for the T–1 nonimmigrant status is adjudicated;

(iii) The application for derivative T nonimmigrant status is filed;

(iv) The application for derivative T nonimmigrant status is adjudicated; and

(v) The eligible family member is admitted to the United States if residing abroad.

(5) *Relationship and age-out protections.* (i) *Protection for new child of a principal alien.* If the T–1 principal alien proves that he or she had a child after filing the application for T–1 nonimmigrant status, the child will be deemed to be an eligible family member eligible to accompany or follow to join the T–1 principal alien.

(ii) *Age-out protection for eligible family members of a principal alien under 21 years of age.* If the T–1 principal alien was under 21 years of age when he or she filed for T–1 nonimmigrant status, USCIS will continue to consider a parent or unmarried sibling as an eligible family member. A parent or unmarried sibling will remain eligible even if the principal alien turns 21 years of age before adjudication of the T–1 application. An unmarried sibling will remain eligible even if the unmarried sibling is over 18 years of age at the time of adjudication of the T–1 application, so long as the unmarried sibling was under 18 years of age at the time of the T–1 application. The age of an unmarried sibling when USCIS adjudicates the T–1 application, when the unmarried sibling files the derivative application, when USCIS adjudicates the derivative application, or when the unmarried sibling is admitted to the United States does not affect eligibility.

(iii) *Age-out protection for child of a principal alien 21 years of age or older.* If a T–1 principal alien was 21 years of age or older when he or she filed for T–1 nonimmigrant status, USCIS will continue to consider a child as an eligible family member if the child was under 21 years of age at the time the principal filed for T–1 nonimmigrant status. The child will remain eligible even if the child is over 21 years of age at the time of adjudication of the T–1 application. The age of the child when USCIS adjudicates the T–1 application, when the child files the derivative application, when USCIS adjudicates the derivative application, or when the child is admitted to the United States does not affect eligibility.

(iv) *Marriage of an eligible family member.* An eligible family member seeking T–3 or T–5 status must be unmarried when the principal files an application for T–1 status, when USCIS adjudicates the T–1 application, when the eligible family member files for T–3 or T–5 status, when USCIS adjudicates the T–3 or T–5 application, and when the family member is admitted to the United States. If a T–1 marries subsequent to filing the application for T–1 status, USCIS will not consider the spouse eligible as a T–2 eligible family member.

(6) *Evidence demonstrating a present danger of retaliation.* An alien seeking derivative T nonimmigrant status on the basis of facing a present danger of

retaliation as a result of the T–1 victim's escape from a severe form of trafficking or cooperation with law enforcement, must demonstrate the basis of this danger. USCIS may contact the LEA involved, if appropriate. An applicant may satisfy this requirement by submitting:

(i) Documentation of a previous grant of advance parole to an eligible family member;

(ii) A signed statement from a law enforcement official describing the danger of retaliation;

(iii) An affirmative statement from the applicant describing the danger the family member faces and how the danger is linked to the victim's escape or cooperation with law enforcement (ordinarily an applicant's statement alone is not sufficient to prove present danger); and/or

(iv) Any other credible evidence, including trial transcripts, court documents, police reports, news articles, copies of reimbursement forms for travel to and from court, and affidavits from other witnesses.

(7) *Biometric collection; evidentiary standards.* The provisions for biometric capture and evidentiary standards described in paragraph (d)(2) and (d)(4) of this section apply to an eligible family member's application for derivative T nonimmigrant status.

(8) *Review and decision.* USCIS will review the application and issue a decision in accordance with paragraph (d) of this section.

(9) *Derivative approvals.* Aliens whose applications for derivative T nonimmigrant status are approved are not subject to the annual cap described in paragraph (j) of this section. USCIS will not approve applications for derivative T nonimmigrant status until USCIS has approved T–1 nonimmigrant status to the related principal alien.

(i) *Approvals for eligible family members in the United States.* When USCIS approves an application for derivative T nonimmigrant status for an eligible family member in the United States, USCIS will concurrently approve derivative T nonimmigrant status. USCIS will notify the T–1 principal alien of such approval and provide evidence of derivative T nonimmigrant status to the derivative.

(ii) *Approvals for eligible family members outside the United States.* When USCIS approves an application for an eligible family member outside the United States, USCIS will notify the T–1 principal alien of such approval and provide the necessary documentation to the Department of State for consideration of visa issuance.

(10) *Employment authorization.* An alien granted derivative T nonimmigrant status may apply for employment authorization by filing an application on the form designated by USCIS with the fee prescribed in 8 CFR 103.7(b)(1) in accordance with form instructions. For derivatives in the United States, the application may be filed concurrently with the application for derivative T nonimmigrant status or at any later time. For derivatives outside the United States, an application for employment authorization may only be filed after admission to the United States in T nonimmigrant status. If the application for employment authorization is approved, the derivative alien will be granted employment authorization pursuant to 8 CFR 274a.12(c)(25) for the period remaining in derivative T nonimmigrant status.

(l) *Extension of T nonimmigrant status*—(1) *Eligibility.* USCIS may grant extensions of T–1 nonimmigrant status beyond 4 years from the date of approval in 1-year periods from the date the T–1 nonimmigrant status ends if:

(i) An LEA investigating or prosecuting activity related to human trafficking certifies that the presence of the alien in the United States is necessary to assist in the investigation or prosecution of such activity;

(ii) The Secretary of Homeland Security determines that an extension is warranted due to exceptional circumstances; or

(iii) The alien has a pending application for adjustment of status to that of a lawful permanent resident.

(2) *Application for a discretionary extension of status.* Upon application, USCIS may extend T–1 nonimmigrant status based on law enforcement need or exceptional circumstances. A T–1 nonimmigrant may apply for an extension by submitting the form designated by USCIS with the prescribed fee and in accordance with form instructions.

A T–1 nonimmigrant should indicate on the application whether USCIS should apply the extension to any family member holding derivative T nonimmigrant status.

(3) *Timely filing.* An alien should file the application to extend nonimmigrant status before the expiration of T–1 nonimmigrant status. If T–1 nonimmigrant status has expired, the applicant must explain in writing the reason for the untimely filing. USCIS may exercise its discretion to approve an untimely filed application for extension of T nonimmigrant status.

(4) *Evidence.* In addition to the application, a T–1 nonimmigrant must include evidence to support why USCIS should grant an extension of T nonimmigrant status. The nonimmigrant bears the burden of establishing eligibility for an extension of status.

(5) *Evidence of law enforcement need.* An applicant may demonstrate law enforcement need by submitting evidence that comes directly from an LEA, including:

(i) A new LEA endorsement;

(ii) Evidence from a law enforcement official, prosecutor, judge, or other authority who can investigate or prosecute human trafficking activity, such as a letter on the agency's letterhead, email, or fax; or

(iii) Any other credible evidence.

(6) *Evidence of exceptional circumstances.* An applicant may demonstrate exceptional circumstances by submitting:

(i) The applicant's affirmative statement; or

(ii) Any other credible evidence, including medical records, police or court records, news articles, correspondence with an embassy or consulate, and affidavits of witnesses.

(7) *Mandatory extensions of status for adjustment of status applicants.* USCIS will automatically extend T–1 nonimmigrant status when a T nonimmigrant properly files an application for adjustment of status in accordance with 8 CFR 245.23. No separate application for extension of T nonimmigrant status, or supporting evidence, is required.

(m) *Revocation of approved T nonimmigrant status*—(1) *Automatic revocation of derivative status.* An approved application for derivative T nonimmigrant status will be revoked automatically if the beneficiary of the approved derivative application notifies USCIS that he or she will not apply for admission to the United States.

(2) *Revocation on notice/grounds for revocation.* USCIS may revoke an approved application for T nonimmigrant status following issuance of a notice of intent to revoke. USCIS may revoke an approved application for T nonimmigrant status based on one or more of the following reasons:

(i) The approval of the application violated the requirements of section 101(a)(15)(T) of the Act or 8 CFR 214.11 or involved error in preparation, procedure, or adjudication that affects the outcome;

(ii) In the case of a T–2 spouse, the alien's divorce from the T–1 principal alien has become final;

(iii) In the case of a T–1 principal alien, an LEA with jurisdiction to detect or investigate the acts of severe forms of trafficking in persons notifies USCIS that the alien has refused to comply with reasonable requests to assist with the investigation or prosecution of the trafficking in persons and provides USCIS with a detailed explanation in writing; or

(iv) The LEA that signed the LEA endorsement withdraws it or disavows its contents and notifies USCIS and provides a detailed explanation of its reasoning in writing.

(3) *Procedures.* Procedures for revocation and appeal follow 8 CFR 103.3. If USCIS revokes approval of the previously granted T nonimmigrant status application, USCIS may notify the LEA who signed the LEA endorsement, any consular officer having jurisdiction over the applicant, or the Office of Refugee Resettlement of the Department of Health and Human Services.

(4) *Effect of revocation.* Revocation of a principal alien's application for T–1 nonimmigrant status will result in termination of T–1 status for the principal alien and, consequently, the automatic termination of the derivative T nonimmigrant status for all derivatives. If a derivative application is pending at the time of revocation, it will be denied. Revocation of an approved application for T–1 nonimmigrant status or

an application for derivative T nonimmigrant status also revokes any waiver of inadmissibility granted in conjunction with such application. The revocation of an alien's T-1 status will have no effect on the annual cap described in paragraph (j) of this section.

(n) *Removal proceedings.* Nothing in this section prohibits DHS from instituting removal proceedings for conduct committed after admission, or for conduct or a condition that was not disclosed prior to the granting of T nonimmigrant status, including misrepresentations of material facts in the application for T-1 nonimmigrant status or in an application for derivative T nonimmigrant status, or after revocation of T nonimmigrant status.

(o) *USCIS employee referral.* Any USCIS employee who, while carrying out his or her official duties, comes into contact with an alien believed to be a victim of a severe form of trafficking in persons and is not already working with an LEA should consult, as necessary, with the ICE officials responsible for victim protection, trafficking investigations and prevention, and deterrence. The ICE office may, in turn, refer the victim to another LEA with responsibility for investigating or prosecuting severe forms of trafficking in persons. If the alien has a credible claim to victimization, USCIS may advise the alien that he or she can submit an application for T nonimmigrant status and seek any other benefit or protection for which he or she may be eligible, provided doing so would not compromise the alien's safety.

(p) *Restrictions on use and disclosure of information relating to applicants for T nonimmigrant classification.* (1) The use or disclosure (other than to a sworn officer or employee of DHS, the Department of Justice, the Department of State, or a bureau or agency of any of those departments, for legitimate department, bureau, or agency purposes) of any information relating to the beneficiary of a pending or approved application for T nonimmigrant status is prohibited unless the disclosure is made in accordance with an exception described in 8 U.S.C. 1367(b).

(2) Information protected under 8 U.S.C. 1367(a)(2) may be disclosed to federal prosecutors to comply with constitutional obligations to provide statements by witnesses and certain other documents to defendants in pending federal criminal proceedings.

(3) Agencies receiving information under this section, whether governmental or non-governmental, are bound by the confidentiality provisions and other restrictions set out in 8 U.S.C. 1367.

(4) DHS officials are prohibited from making adverse determinations of admissibility or deportability based on information obtained solely from the trafficker, unless the alien has been convicted of a crime or crimes listed in section 237(a)(2) of the Act.

[81 FR 92304, Dec. 19, 2016]

§214.12 Preliminary enrollment of schools in the Student and Exchange Visitor Information System (SEVIS).

(a) Private elementary and private secondary schools, public high schools, post-secondary schools, language schools, and vocational schools are eligible for preliminary enrollment in Student and Exchange Visitor Information System (SEVIS), beginning on or after July 1, 2002, but only if the school is accredited by an accrediting agency recognized by the United States Department of Education, CAPE, or AACS, or in the case of a public high school, the school provides certification from the appropriate public official that the school meets the requirements of the state or local public educational system and has been continuously approved by the Service for a minimum of three years, as of July 1, 2002, for the admission of F or M nonimmigrant students. A school may establish that it is accredited by showing that it has been designated as an eligible school under Title IV of the Higher Education Act of 1965.

(b) Preliminary enrollment in SEVIS is optional for eligible schools. The preliminary enrollment period will be open from July 1, 2002, through August 16, 2002, or, if later, until the Service begins the SEVIS full scale certification process. The process for eligible schools to apply for preliminary enrollment through the Internet is as follows:

(1) Eligible institutions must access the Internet site, *http://www.ins.usdoj.gov/sevis.* Upon accessing the site, the president, owner, head of the school or designated school official will be asked to enter the following information: the school's name; the first, middle, and last name of the contact person for the school; and the e-mail address and phone number of the contact person.

(2) Once this information has been submitted, the Service will issue the school a temporary ID and password, which will be forwarded to the e-mail address listed. When the contact person receives this temporary ID and password, the school will again access the Internet site and will electronically enter the school's information for its Form I–17.

(c) The Service will review the information by a school submitted as provided in paragraph (b) of this section, and will preliminarily enroll a school in SEVIS, if it is determined to be eligible under the standards of paragraph (a) of this section. If the officer determines that the school is eligible for preliminary enrollment, the officer will update SEVIS and enroll the school and permanent user IDs and passwords will be automatically generated via e-mail to the DSOs listed on the Form I–17. Schools that are not approved by the Service for preliminary enrollment will be notified that they must apply for certification in accordance with the Interim Certification Rule. A school that is granted preliminary enrollment will have to use SEVIS for the issuance of any new Form I–20 to a new or continuing student.

(d) Schools granted preliminary enrollment in SEVIS will not have to apply for certification at this time. However, all such schools will be required to apply for certification, and pay the certification fee, prior to May 14, 2004.

(e) Eligible schools that meet the standards of paragraph (a) of this section, but do not apply for preliminary enrollment in SEVIS prior to the close of the preliminary enrollment period will have to apply for certification review under the Interim Certification Rule and pay the certification fee before enrolling in SEVIS. However, once a school meeting the standards of paragraph (a) of this section applies for certification review, the Service will have the discretion, after a review of the school's application, to allow the school to enroll in SEVIS without requiring an on-site visit prior to enrollment. If the Service permits such a school to enroll in SEVIS prior to completion of the on-site visit, the on-site visit must be completed prior to May 14, 2004.

(f) Schools that are not eligible to apply for preliminary enrollment in SEVIS under this section—including flight schools—will have to apply for certification under the Interim Certification Rule, pay the certification fee, and undergo a full certification review including an on-site visit, prior to being allowed to enroll in SEVIS.

[67 FR 44346, July 1, 2002]

§ 214.13 SEVIS fee for certain F, J, and M nonimmigrants.

(a) *Applicability.* The following aliens are required to submit a payment in the amount indicated for their status to the Student and Exchange Visitor Program (SEVP) in advance of obtaining nonimmigrant status as an F or M student or J exchange visitor, in addition to any other applicable fees, except as otherwise provided for in this section:

(1) An alien who applies for F–1 or F–3 status in order to enroll in a program of study at an SEVP-certified institution of higher education, as defined in section 101(a) of the Higher Education Act of 1965, as amended, or in a program of study at any other SEVP-certified academic or language-training institution including private elementary and secondary schools and public secondary schools, the amount of $200;

(2) An alien who applies for J–1 status in order to commence participation in an exchange visitor program designated by the Department of State (DoS), the amount of $180, with a reduced fee for certain exchange visitor categories as provided in paragraphs (b)(1) and (c) of this section; and

(3) An alien who applies for M–1 or M–3 status in order to enroll in a program of study at an SEVP-certified vocational educational institution, including a flight school, in the amount of $200.

(b) *Aliens not subject to a fee.* No SEVIS fee is required with respect to:

(1) A J–1 exchange visitor who is coming to the United States as a participant in an exchange visitor program sponsored by the Federal government, identified by a program identifier designation prefix of G–1, G–2, G–3, or G–7;

(2) Dependents of F, M, or J nonimmigrants. The principal alien must pay the fee, when required under this section, in order for his/her qualifying dependents to obtain F–2, J–2, or M–2 status. However, an F–2, J–2, or M–2 dependent is not required to pay a separate fee under this section in order to obtain that status or during the time he/she remains in that status.

(3) A nonimmigrant described in paragraph (a) of this section whose Form I–20 or Form DS–2019 for initial attendance was issued on or before August 31, 2004.

(c) *Special Fee for Certain J–1 Nonimmigrants.* A J–1 exchange visitor coming to the United States as an au pair, camp counselor, or participant in a summer work/travel program is subject to a fee of $35.

(d) *Time for payment of SEVIS fee.* An alien who is subject to payment of the SEVIS fee must remit the fee directly to DHS as follows:

(1) An alien seeking an F–1, F–3, J–1, M–1, or M–3 visa from a consular officer abroad for initial attendance at a DHS-approved school or to commence participation in a Department of State-designated exchange visitor program, must pay the fee to DHS before issuance of the visa.

(2) An alien who is exempt from the visa requirement described in section 212(d)(4) of the Act must pay the fee to DHS before the alien applies for admission at a U.S. port-of-entry to begin initial attendance at a DHS-approved school or initial participation in a Department of State-designated exchange visitor program.

(3) A nonimmigrant alien in the United States seeking a change of status to F–1, F–3, J–1, M–1, or M–3 must pay the fee to DHS before the alien is granted the change of nonimmigrant status, except as provided in paragraph (e)(4) of this section.

(4) A J–1 nonimmigrant who is applying for a change of program category within the United Status, in accordance with 22 CFR 62.42, must pay the fee associated with that new category, if any, prior to being granted such a change.

(5) A J–1 nonimmigrant initially granted J–1 status to participate in a program sponsored by the Federal government, as defined in paragraph (b)(1) of this section, and transferring in accordance with 22 CFR 62.42 to a program that is not similarly sponsored, must pay the fee associated with the new program prior to completing the transfer.

(6) A J–1 nonimmigrant who is applying for reinstatement after a substantive violation of status, or who has been out of program status for longer than 120 days but less than 270 days during the course of his/her program must pay a new fee to DHS, if applicable, prior to being granted a reinstatement to valid J–1 status.

(7) An F or M student who is applying for reinstatement of student status because of a violation of status, and who has been out of status for a period of time that exceeds the presumptive ineligibility deadline set forth in 8 CFR 214.2(f)(16)(i)(A) or (m)(16)(i)(A), must pay a new fee to DHS prior to being granted a return to valid status.

(8) An F–1, F–3, M–1, or M–3 nonimmigrant who has been absent from the United States for a period that exceeds 5 months in duration, and wishes to reenter the United States to engage in further study in the same course of study, with the exception of students who have been working toward completion of a U.S. course of study in authorized overseas study, must pay a new fee to DHS prior to being granted student status.

(e) *Circumstances where no new fee is required.* (1) Extension of stay, transfer, or optional practical training for students. An F–1, F–3, M–1, or M–3 nonimmigrant is not required to pay a new fee in connection with:

(i) An application for an extension of stay, as provided in 8 CFR 214.2(f)(7) or (m)(10);

(ii) An application for transfer, as provided in 8 CFR 214.2(f)(8) or (m)(11);

(iii) A change in educational level, as provided in 8 CFR 214.2(f)(5)(ii); or

(iv) An application for post-completion practical training, as provided in 8 CFR 214.2(f)(10)(ii) or (m)(14).

(2) Extension of program or transfer for exchange visitors. A J–1 nonimmigrant is not required to pay a new fee in connection with:

(i) An application for an extension of program, as provided in 22 CFR 62.43; or

(ii) An application for transfer of program, as provided in 22 CFR 62.42.

(3) Visa issuance for a continuation of study. An F–1, F–3, J–1, M–1, or M–3 nonimmigrant who has previously paid the fee is not required to pay a new fee in order to be granted a visa to return to the United States as a continuing student or exchange visitor in a single course of study, so long as the nonimmigrant is not otherwise required to pay a new fee in accordance with the other provisions in this section.

(4) Certain changes in student classification.

(i) No fee is required for changes between the F–1 and F–3 classifications, and no fee is required for changes between the M–1 and M–3 classifications.

(ii) Institutional reclassification. DHS retains the discretionary authority to waive the additional fee requirement when a nonimmigrant changes classification between F and M, if the change of status is due solely to institutional reclassification by the Student and Exchange Visitor Program during that nonimmigrant's course of study.

(5) Re-application following denial of application by consular officer. An alien who fully paid a SEVIS fee in connection with an initial application for an F–1, F–3, M–1, or M–3 visa, or a J–1 visa in a particular program category, whose initial application was denied, and who is reapplying for the same status, or the same J–1 exchange visitor category, within 12 months following the initial notice of denial is not required to repay the SEVIS fee.

(6) Re-application following denial of an application for a change of status. A nonimmigrant who fully paid a SEVIS fee in connection with an initial application for a change of status within in the United States to F–1, F–3, M–1, or M–3 classification, or for a change of status to a particular J–1 exchange visitor category, whose initial application was denied, and who is granted a motion to reopen the denied case is not required to repay the SEVIS fee if the motion to reopen is granted within 12 months of receipt of initial notice of denial.

(f) [Reserved]

(g) *Procedures for payment of the SEVIS fee*—(1) *Options for payment.* An alien subject to payment of a fee under this section may pay the fee by any procedure approved by DHS, including:

(i) Submission of Form I–901, to DHS by mail, along with the proper fee paid by check, money order, or foreign draft drawn on a financial institution in the United States and payable in United States currency, as provided by 8 CFR 103.7(a)(1);

(ii) Electronic submission of Form I–901 to DHS using a credit card or other electronic means of payment accepted by DHS; or,

(iii) A designated payment service and receipt mechanism approved and set forth in future guidance by DHS.

(2) *Receipts.* DHS will provide a receipt for each fee payment under paragraph (g)(1) of this section until such time as DHS issues a notice in the FEDERAL REGISTER that paper receipts will no longer be necessary. Further receipt provisions include:

(i) DHS will provide for an expedited delivery of the receipt, upon request and receipt of an additional fee;

(ii) If payment was made electronically, both DHS and the Department of State will accept a properly completed receipt that is printed-out electronically, in lieu of the receipt generated by DHS;

(iii) If payment was made through an approved payment service, DHS and the Department of State will accept a properly completed receipt issued by the payment service, in lieu of the receipt generated by DHS.

(3) *Electronic record of fee payment.* DHS will maintain an electronic record of payment for the alien as verification of receipt of the required fee under this

section. If DHS records indicate that the fee has been paid, an alien who has lost or did not receive a receipt for a fee payment under this section will not be denied an immigration benefit, including visa issuance or admission to the United States, solely because of a failure to present a paper receipt of fee payment.

(4) *Third-party payments.* DHS will accept payment of the required fee for an alien from an approved school or a designated exchange visitor program sponsor, or from another source, in accordance with procedures approved by DHS.

(h) *Failure to pay the fee.* The failure to pay the required fee is grounds for denial of F, M, or J nonimmigrant status or status-related benefits. Payment of the fee does not preserve the lawful status of any F, J, or M nonimmigrant that has violated his or her status in some other manner.

(1) For purposes of reinstatement to F or M status, failure to pay the required fee will be considered a "willful violation" under 8 CFR 214.2(f)(16) or (m)(16), unless DHS determines that there are sufficient extenuating circumstances (as determined at the discretion of the Student and Exchange Visitor Program).

(2) For purposes of reinstatement to valid J program status, failure to pay the required fee will not be considered a "minor or technical infraction" under 22 CFR 62.45.

[69 FR 39825, July 1, 2004; 69 FR 41388, July 9, 2004, as amended at 73 FR 55704, Sept. 26, 2008]

§214.14 Alien victims of certain qualifying criminal activity.

(a) *Definitions.* As used in this section, the term:

(1) *BIWPA* means Battered Immigrant Women Protection Act of 2000 of the Victims of Trafficking and Violence Protection Act of 2000, div. B, Violence Against Women Act of 2000, tit. V, Pub. L. 106–386, 114 Stat. 1464, (2000), *amended by* Violence Against Women and Department of Justice Reauthorization Act of 2005, tit. VIII, Pub. L. 109–162, 119 Stat. 2960 (2006), *amended by* Violence Against Women and Department of Justice Reauthorization Act—Technical Corrections, Pub. L. 109–271, 120 Stat. 750 (2006).

(2) *Certifying agency* means a Federal, State, or local law enforcement agency, prosecutor, judge, or other authority, that has responsibility for the investigation or prosecution of a qualifying crime or criminal activity. This definition includes agencies that have criminal investigative jurisdiction in their respective areas of expertise, including, but not limited to, child protective services, the Equal Employment Opportunity Commission, and the Department of Labor.

(3) *Certifying official* means:

(i) The head of the certifying agency, or any person(s) in a supervisory role who has been specifically designated by the head of the certifying agency to issue U nonimmigrant status certifications on behalf of that agency; or

(ii) A Federal, State, or local judge.

(4) *Indian Country* is defined as:

(i) All land within the limits of any Indian reservation under the jurisdiction of the United States Government, notwithstanding the issuance of any patent, and including rights-of-way running through the reservation;

(ii) All dependent Indian communities within the borders of the United States whether within the original or subsequently acquired territory thereof, and whether within or without the limits of a state; and

(iii) All Indian allotments, the Indian titles to which have not been extinguished, including rights-of-way running through such allotments.

(5) *Investigation or prosecution* refers to the detection or investigation of a qualifying crime or criminal activity, as well as to the prosecution, conviction, or sentencing of the perpetrator of the qualifying crime or criminal activity.

(6) *Military Installation* means any facility, base, camp, post, encampment, station, yard, center, port, aircraft, vehicle, or vessel under the jurisdiction of the Department of Defense, including any leased facility, or any other location under military control.

(7) *Next friend* means a person who appears in a lawsuit to act for the benefit of an alien under the age of 16 or incapacitated or incompetent, who has suffered substantial physical or mental abuse as a result of being a victim of qualifying criminal activity. The next

friend is not a party to the legal proceeding and is not appointed as a guardian.

(8) *Physical or mental abuse* means injury or harm to the victim's physical person, or harm to or impairment of the emotional or psychological soundness of the victim.

(9) *Qualifying crime or qualifying criminal activity* includes one or more of the following or any similar activities in violation of Federal, State or local criminal law of the United States: Rape; torture; trafficking; incest; domestic violence; sexual assault; abusive sexual contact; prostitution; sexual exploitation; female genital mutilation; being held hostage; peonage; involuntary servitude; slave trade; kidnapping; abduction; unlawful criminal restraint; false imprisonment; blackmail; extortion; manslaughter; murder; felonious assault; witness tampering; obstruction of justice; perjury; or attempt, conspiracy, or solicitation to commit any of the above mentioned crimes. The term "any similar activity" refers to criminal offenses in which the nature and elements of the offenses are substantially similar to the statutorily enumerated list of criminal activities.

(10) *Qualifying family member* means, in the case of an alien victim 21 years of age or older who is eligible for U nonimmigrant status as described in section 101(a)(15)(U) of the Act, 8 U.S.C. 1101(a)(15)(U), the spouse or child(ren) of such alien; and, in the case of an alien victim under the age of 21 who is eligible for U nonimmigrant status as described in section 101(a)(15)(U) of the Act, *qualifying family member* means the spouse, child(ren), parents, or unmarried siblings under the age of 18 of such an alien.

(11) *Territories and Possessions of the United States* means American Samoa, Swains Island, Bajo Nuevo (the Petrel Islands), Baker Island, Howland Island, Jarvis Island, Johnston Atoll, Kingman Reef, Midway Atoll, Navassa Island, Palmyra Atoll, Serranilla Bank, and Wake Atoll.

(12) *U nonimmigrant status certification* means Form I–918, Supplement B, "U Nonimmigrant Status Certification," which confirms that the petitioner has been helpful, is being helpful, or is likely to be helpful in the investigation or prosecution of the qualifying criminal activity of which he or she is a victim.

(13) *U interim relief* refers to the interim benefits that were provided by USCIS to petitioners for U nonimmigrant status, who requested such benefits and who were deemed prima facie eligible for U nonimmigrant status prior to the publication of the implementing regulations.

(14) *Victim of qualifying criminal activity* generally means an alien who has suffered direct and proximate harm as a result of the commission of qualifying criminal activity.

(i) The alien spouse, children under 21 years of age and, if the direct victim is under 21 years of age, parents and unmarried siblings under 18 years of age, will be considered victims of qualifying criminal activity where the direct victim is deceased due to murder or manslaughter, or is incompetent or incapacitated, and therefore unable to provide information concerning the criminal activity or be helpful in the investigation or prosecution of the criminal activity. For purposes of determining eligibility under this definition, USCIS will consider the age of the victim at the time the qualifying criminal activity occurred.

(ii) A petitioner may be considered a victim of witness tampering, obstruction of justice, or perjury, including any attempt, solicitation, or conspiracy to commit one or more of those offenses, if:

(A) The petitioner has been directly and proximately harmed by the perpetrator of the witness tampering, obstruction of justice, or perjury; and

(B) There are reasonable grounds to conclude that the perpetrator committed the witness tampering, obstruction of justice, or perjury offense, at least in principal part, as a means:

(*1*) To avoid or frustrate efforts to investigate, arrest, prosecute, or otherwise bring to justice the perpetrator for other criminal activity; or

(*2*) To further the perpetrator's abuse or exploitation of or undue control over the petitioner through manipulation of the legal system.

(iii) A person who is culpable for the qualifying criminal activity being investigated or prosecuted is excluded from being recognized as a victim of qualifying criminal activity.

(b) *Eligibility*. An alien is eligible for U–1 nonimmigrant status if he or she demonstrates all of the following in accordance with paragraph (c) of this section:

(1) The alien has suffered substantial physical or mental abuse as a result of having been a victim of qualifying criminal activity. Whether abuse is substantial is based on a number of factors, including but not limited to: The nature of the injury inflicted or suffered; the severity of the perpetrator's conduct; the severity of the harm suffered; the duration of the infliction of the harm; and the extent to which there is permanent or serious harm to the appearance, health, or physical or mental soundness of the victim, including aggravation of pre-existing conditions. No single factor is a prerequisite to establish that the abuse suffered was substantial. Also, the existence of one or more of the factors automatically does not create a presumption that the abuse suffered was substantial. A series of acts taken together may be considered to constitute substantial physical or mental abuse even where no single act alone rises to that level;

(2) The alien possesses credible and reliable information establishing that he or she has knowledge of the details concerning the qualifying criminal activity upon which his or her petition is based. The alien must possess specific facts regarding the criminal activity leading a certifying official to determine that the petitioner has, is, or is likely to provide assistance to the investigation or prosecution of the qualifying criminal activity. In the event that the alien has not yet reached 16 years of age on the date on which an act constituting an element of the qualifying criminal activity first occurred, a parent, guardian or next friend of the alien may possess the information regarding a qualifying crime. In addition, if the alien is incapacitated or incompetent, a parent, guardian, or next friend may possess the information regarding the qualifying crime;

(3) The alien has been helpful, is being helpful, or is likely to be helpful to a certifying agency in the investigation or prosecution of the qualifying criminal activity upon which his or her petition is based, and since the initiation of cooperation, has not refused or failed to provide information and assistance reasonably requested. In the event that the alien has not yet reached 16 years of age on the date on which an act constituting an element of the qualifying criminal activity first occurred, a parent, guardian or next friend of the alien may provide the required assistance. In addition, if the petitioner is incapacitated or incompetent and, therefore, unable to be helpful in the investigation or prosecution of the qualifying criminal activity, a parent, guardian, or next friend may provide the required assistance; and

(4) The qualifying criminal activity occurred in the United States (including Indian country and U.S. military installations) or in the territories or possessions of the United States, or violated a U.S. federal law that provides for extraterritorial jurisdiction to prosecute the offense in a U.S. federal court.

(c) *Application procedures for U nonimmigrant status*—(1) *Filing a petition*. USCIS has sole jurisdiction over all petitions for U nonimmigrant status. An alien seeking U–1 nonimmigrant status must submit, by mail, Form I–918, "Petition for U Nonimmigrant Status," applicable biometric fee (or request for a fee waiver as provided in 8 CFR 103.7(c)), and initial evidence to USCIS in accordance with this paragraph and the instructions to Form I–918. A petitioner who received interim relief is not required to submit initial evidence with Form I–918 if he or she wishes to rely on the law enforcement certification and other evidence that was submitted with the request for interim relief.

(i) *Petitioners in pending immigration proceedings*. An alien who is in removal proceedings under section 240 of the Act, 8 U.S.C. 1229a, or in exclusion or deportation proceedings initiated under former sections 236 or 242 of the Act, 8 U.S.C. 1226 and 1252 (as in effect prior to April 1, 1997), and who would like to apply for U nonimmigrant status must file a Form I–918 directly with USCIS. U.S. Immigration and Customs Enforcement (ICE) counsel may agree, as a matter of discretion, to file, at the request of the alien petitioner, a joint motion to terminate proceedings without prejudice with the immigration judge or Board of Immigration Appeals, whichever is appropriate, while a petition for U nonimmigrant status is being adjudicated by USCIS.

(ii) *Petitioners with final orders of removal, deportation, or exclusion.* An alien who is the subject of a final order of removal, deportation, or exclusion is not precluded from filing a petition for U–1 nonimmigrant status directly with USCIS. The filing of a petition for U–1 nonimmigrant status has no effect on ICE's authority to execute a final order, although the alien may file a request for a stay of removal pursuant to 8 CFR 241.6(a) and 8 CFR 1241.6(a). If the alien is in detention pending execution of the final order, the time during which a stay is in effect will extend the period of detention (under the standards of 8 CFR 241.4) reasonably necessary to bring about the petitioner's removal.

(2) *Initial evidence.* Form I–918 must include the following initial evidence:

(i) Form I–918, Supplement B, "U Nonimmigrant Status Certification," signed by a certifying official within the six months immediately preceding the filing of Form I–918. The certification must state that: the person signing the certificate is the head of the certifying agency, or any person(s) in a supervisory role who has been specifically designated by the head of the certifying agency to issue U nonimmigrant status certifications on behalf of that agency, or is a Federal, State, or local judge; the agency is a Federal, State, or local law enforcement agency, or prosecutor, judge or other authority, that has responsibility for the detection, investigation, prosecution, conviction, or sentencing of qualifying criminal activity; the applicant has been a victim of qualifying criminal activity that the certifying official's agency is investigating or prosecuting; the petitioner possesses information concerning the qualifying criminal activity of which he or she has been a victim; the petitioner has been, is being, or is likely to be helpful to an investigation or prosecution of that qualifying criminal activity; and the qualifying criminal activity violated U.S. law, or occurred in the United States, its territories, its possessions, Indian country, or at military installations abroad.

(ii) Any additional evidence that the petitioner wants USCIS to consider to establish that: the petitioner is a victim of qualifying criminal activity; the petitioner has suffered substantial physical or mental abuse as a result of being a victim of qualifying criminal activity; the petitioner (or, in the case of a child under the age of 16 or petitioner who is incompetent or incapacitated, a parent, guardian or next friend of the petitioner) possesses information establishing that he or she has knowledge of the details concerning the qualifying criminal activity of which he or she was a victim and upon which his or her application is based; the petitioner (or, in the case of a child under the age of 16 or petitioner who is incompetent or incapacitated, a parent, guardian or next friend of the petitioner) has been helpful, is being helpful, or is likely to be helpful to a Federal, State, or local law enforcement agency, prosecutor, or authority, or Federal or State judge, investigating or prosecuting the criminal activity of which the petitioner is a victim; or the criminal activity is qualifying and occurred in the United States (including Indian country and U.S. military installations) or in the territories or possessions of the United States, or violates a U.S. federal law that provides for extraterritorial jurisdiction to prosecute the offense in a U.S. federal court;

(iii) A signed statement by the petitioner describing the facts of the victimization. The statement also may include information supporting any of the eligibility requirements set out in paragraph (b) of this section. When the petitioner is under the age of 16, incapacitated, or incompetent, a parent, guardian, or next friend may submit a statement on behalf of the petitioner; and

(iv) If the petitioner is inadmissible, Form I–192, "Application for Advance

Permission to Enter as Non-Immigrant," in accordance with 8 CFR 212.17.

(3) *Biometric capture.* All petitioners for U–1 nonimmigrant status must submit to biometric capture and pay a biometric capture fee. USCIS will notify the petitioner of the proper time and location to appear for biometric capture after the petitioner files Form I–918.

(4) *Evidentiary standards and burden of proof.* The burden shall be on the petitioner to demonstrate eligibility for U–1 nonimmigrant status. The petitioner may submit any credible evidence relating to his or her Form I–918 for consideration by USCIS. USCIS shall conduct a de novo review of all evidence submitted in connection with Form I–918 and may investigate any aspect of the petition. Evidence previously submitted for this or other immigration benefit or relief may be used by USCIS in evaluating the eligibility of a petitioner for U–1 nonimmigrant status. However, USCIS will not be bound by its previous factual determinations. USCIS will determine, in its sole discretion, the evidentiary value of previously or concurrently submitted evidence, including Form I–918, Supplement B, "U Nonimmigrant Status Certification."

(5) *Decision.* After completing its de novo review of the petition and evidence, USCIS will issue a written decision approving or denying Form I–918 and notify the petitioner of this decision. USCIS will include in a decision approving Form I–918 a list of nongovernmental organizations to which the petitioner can refer regarding his or her options while in the United States and available resources.

(i) *Approval of Form I–918, generally.* If USCIS determines that the petitioner has met the requirements for U–1 nonimmigrant status, USCIS will approve Form I–918. For a petitioner who is within the United States, USCIS also will concurrently grant U–1 nonimmigrant status, subject to the annual limitation as provided in paragraph (d) of this section. For a petitioner who is subject to an order of exclusion, deportation, or removal issued by the Secretary, the order will be deemed canceled by operation of law as of the date of USCIS' approval of Form I–918. A petitioner who is subject to an order of exclusion, deportation, or removal issued by an immigration judge or the Board may seek cancellation of such order by filing, with the immigration judge or the Board, a motion to reopen and terminate removal proceedings. ICE counsel may agree, as a matter of discretion, to join such a motion to overcome any applicable time and numerical limitations of 8 CFR 1003.2 and 1003.23.

(A) *Notice of Approval of Form I–918 for U–1 petitioners within the United States.* After USCIS approves Form I–918 for an alien who filed his or her petition from within the United States, USCIS will notify the alien of such approval on Form I–797, "Notice of Action," and include Form I–94 (see § 1.4), "Arrival-Departure Record," indicating U–1 nonimmigrant status.

(B) *Notice of Approval of Form I–918 for U–1 petitioners outside the United States.* After USCIS approves Form I–918 for an alien who filed his or her petition from outside the United States, USCIS will notify the alien of such approval on Form I–797, "Notice of Action," and will forward notice to the Department of State for delivery to the U.S. Embassy or Consulate having jurisdiction over the area in which the alien is located, or, for a visa exempt alien, to the appropriate port of entry.

(ii) *Denial of Form I–918.* USCIS will provide written notification to the petitioner of the reasons for the denial. The petitioner may appeal a denial of Form I–918 to the Administrative Appeals Office (AAO) in accordance with the provisions of 8 CFR 103.3. For petitioners who appeal a denial of their Form I–918 to the AAO, the denial will not be deemed administratively final until the AAO issues a decision affirming the denial. Upon USCIS' final denial of a petition for a petitioner who was in removal proceedings that were terminated pursuant to 8 CFR 214.14(c)(1)(i), DHS may file a new Notice to Appear (see section 239 of the Act, 8 U.S.C. 1229) to place the individual in proceedings again. For petitioners who are subject to an order of removal, deportation, or exclusion and whose order has been stayed, USCIS' denial of the petition will result in the stay being lifted automatically as of the date the denial becomes administratively final.

(6) *Petitioners granted U interim relief.* Petitioners who were granted U interim relief as defined in paragraph (a)(13) of this section and whose Form I–918 is approved will be accorded U–1 nonimmigrant status as of the date that a request for U interim relief was initially approved.

(7) *Employment authorization.* An alien granted U–1 nonimmigrant status is employment authorized incident to status. USCIS automatically will issue an initial Employment Authorization Document (EAD) to such aliens who are in the United States. For principal aliens who applied from outside the United States, the initial EAD will not be issued until the petitioner has been admitted to the United States in U nonimmigrant status. After admission, the alien may receive an initial EAD, upon request and submission of a copy of his or her Form I–94, "Arrival-Departure Record," to the USCIS office having jurisdiction over the adjudication of petitions for U nonimmigrant status. No additional fee is required. An alien granted U–1 nonimmigrant status seeking to renew his or her expiring EAD or replace an EAD that was lost, stolen, or destroyed, must file Form I–765 in accordance with the instructions to the form.

(d) *Annual cap on U–1 nonimmigrant status*—(1) *General.* In accordance with section 214(p)(2) of the Act, 8 U.S.C. 1184(p)(2), the total number of aliens who may be issued a U–1 nonimmigrant visa or granted U–1 nonimmigrant status may not exceed 10,000 in any fiscal year.

(2) *Waiting list.* All eligible petitioners who, due solely to the cap, are not granted U–1 nonimmigrant status must be placed on a waiting list and receive written notice of such placement. Priority on the waiting list will be determined by the date the petition was filed with the oldest petitions receiving the highest priority. In the next fiscal year, USCIS will issue a number to each petition on the waiting list, in the order of highest priority, providing the petitioner remains admissible and eligible for U nonimmigrant status. After U–1 nonimmigrant status has been issued to qualifying petitioners on the waiting list, any remaining U–1 nonimmigrant numbers for that fiscal year will be issued to new qualifying petitioners in the order that the petitions were properly filed. USCIS will grant deferred action or parole to U–1 petitioners and qualifying family members while the U–1 petitioners are on the waiting list. USCIS, in its discretion, may authorize employment for such petitioners and qualifying family members.

(3) *Unlawful presence.* During the time a petitioner for U nonimmigrant status who was granted deferred action or parole is on the waiting list, no accrual of unlawful presence under section 212(a)(9)(B) of the INA, 8 U.S.C. 1182(a)(9)(B), will result. However, a petitioner may be removed from the waiting list, and the deferred action or parole may be terminated at the discretion of USCIS.

(e) *Restrictions on use and disclosure of information relating to petitioners for U nonimmigrant classification*—(1) *General.* The use or disclosure (other than to a sworn officer or employee of DHS, the Department of Justice, the Department of State, or a bureau or agency of any of those departments, for legitimate department, bureau, or agency purposes) of any information relating to the beneficiary of a pending or approved petition for U nonimmigrant status is prohibited unless the disclosure is made:

(i) By the Secretary of Homeland Security, at his discretion, in the same manner and circumstances as census information may be disclosed by the Secretary of Commerce under 13 U.S.C. 8;

(ii) By the Secretary of Homeland Security, at his discretion, to law enforcement officials to be used solely for a legitimate law enforcement purpose;

(iii) In conjunction with judicial review of a determination in a manner that protects the confidentiality of such information;

(iv) After adult petitioners for U nonimmigrant status or U nonimmigrant status holders have provided written consent to waive the restrictions prohibiting the release of information;

(v) To Federal, State, and local public and private agencies providing benefits, to be used solely in making determinations of eligibility for benefits pursuant to 8 U.S.C. 1641(c);

(vi) After a petition for U nonimmigrant status has been denied in a final decision;

(vii) To the chairmen and ranking members of the Committee on the Judiciary of the Senate or the Committee on the Judiciary of the House of Representatives, for the exercise of congressional oversight authority, provided the disclosure relates to information about a closed case and is made in a manner that protects the confidentiality of the information and omits personally identifying information (including locational information about individuals);

(viii) With prior written consent from the petitioner or derivative family members, to nonprofit, nongovernmental victims' service providers for the sole purpose of assisting the victim in obtaining victim services from programs with expertise working with immigrant victims; or

(ix) To federal prosecutors to comply with constitutional obligations to provide statements by witnesses and certain other documents to defendants in pending federal criminal proceedings.

(2) Agencies receiving information under this section, whether governmental or non-governmental, are bound by the confidentiality provisions and other restrictions set out in 8 U.S.C. 1367.

(3) Officials of the Department of Homeland Security are prohibited from making adverse determinations of admissibility or deportability based on information obtained solely from the perpetrator of substantial physical or mental abuse and the criminal activity.

(f) *Admission of qualifying family members*—(1) *Eligibility*. An alien who has petitioned for or has been granted U–1 nonimmigrant status (*i.e.*, principal alien) may petition for the admission of a qualifying family member in a U–2 (spouse), U–3 (child), U–4 (parent of a U–1 alien who is a child under 21 years of age), or U–5 (unmarried sibling under the age of 18) derivative status, if accompanying or following to join such principal alien. A qualifying family member who committed the qualifying criminal activity in a family violence or trafficking context which established the principal alien's eligibility for U nonimmigrant status shall not be granted U–2, U–3, U–4, or U–5 nonimmigrant status. To be eligible for U–2, U–3, U–4, or U–5 nonimmigrant status, it must be demonstrated that:

(i) The alien for whom U–2, U–3, U–4, or U–5 status is being sought is a qualifying family member, as defined in paragraph (a)(10) of this section; and

(ii) The qualifying family member is admissible to the United States.

(2) *Filing procedures*. A petitioner for U–1 nonimmigrant status may apply for derivative U nonimmigrant status on behalf of qualifying family members by submitting a Form I–918, Supplement A, "Petition for Qualifying Family Member of U–1 Recipient," for each family member either at the same time the petition for U–1 nonimmigrant status is filed, or at a later date. An alien who has been granted U–1 nonimmigrant status may apply for derivative U nonimmigrant status on behalf of qualifying family members by submitting Form I–918, Supplement A for each family member. All Forms I–918, Supplement A must be accompanied by initial evidence and the required fees specified in the instructions to the form. Forms I–918, Supplement A that are not filed at the same time as Form I–918 but are filed at a later date must be accompanied by a copy of the Form I–918 that was filed by the principal petitioner or a copy of his or her Form I–94 demonstrating proof of U–1 nonimmigrant status, as applicable.

(i) Qualifying family members in pending immigration proceedings. The principal alien of a qualifying family member who is in removal proceedings under section 240 of the Act, 8 U.S.C. 1229a, or in exclusion or deportation proceedings initiated under former sections 236 or 242 of the Act, 8 U.S.C. 1226 and 1252 (as in effect prior to April 1, 1997), and who is seeking U nonimmigrant status, must file a Form I–918, Supplement A directly with USCIS. ICE counsel may agree to file, at the request of the qualifying family member, a joint motion to terminate proceedings without prejudice with the immigration judge or Board of Immigration Appeals, whichever is appropriate, while the petition for U nonimmigrant status is being adjudicated by USCIS.

(ii) Qualifying family members with final orders of removal, deportation, or exclusion. An alien who is the subject of a final order of removal, deportation, or exclusion is not precluded from filing a petition for U–2, U–3, U–4, or U–5 nonimmigrant status directly with USCIS. The filing of a petition for U–2, U–3, U–4, or U–5 nonimmigrant status has no effect on ICE's authority to execute a final order, although the alien may file a request for a stay of removal pursuant to 8 CFR 241.6(a) and 8 CFR 1241.6(a). If the alien is in detention pending execution of the final order, the time during which a stay is in effect will extend the period of detention (under the standards of 8 CFR 241.4) reasonably necessary to bring about the alien's removal.

(3) *Initial evidence.* Form I–918, Supplement A, must include the following initial evidence:

(i) Evidence demonstrating the relationship of a qualifying family member, as provided in paragraph (f)(4) of this section;

(ii) If the qualifying family member is inadmissible, Form I–192, "Application for Advance Permission to Enter as a Non-Immigrant," in accordance with 8 CFR 212.17.

(4) *Relationship.* Except as set forth in paragraphs (f)(4)(i) and (ii) of this section, the relationship between the U–1 principal alien and the qualifying family member must exist at the time Form I–918 was filed, and the relationship must continue to exist at the time Form I–918, Supplement A is adjudicated, and at the time of the qualifying family member's subsequent admission to the United States.

(i) If the U–1 principal alien proves that he or she has become the parent of a child after Form I–918 was filed, the child shall be eligible to accompany or follow to join the U–1 principal alien.

(ii) If the principal alien was under 21 years of age at the time he or she filed Form I–918, and filed Form I–918, Supplement A for an unmarried sibling under the age of 18, USCIS will continue to consider such sibling as a qualifying family member for purposes of U nonimmigrant status even if the principal alien is no longer under 21 years of age at the time of adjudication, and even if the sibling is no longer under 18 years of age at the time of adjudication.

(5) *Biometric capture and evidentiary standards.* The provisions for biometric capture and evidentiary standards in paragraphs (c)(3) and (c)(4) of this section also are applicable to petitions for qualifying family members.

(6) *Decision.* USCIS will issue a written decision approving or denying Form I–918, Supplement A and send notice of this decision to the U–1 principal petitioner. USCIS will include in a decision approving Form I–918 a list of nongovernmental organizations to which the qualifying family member can refer regarding his or her options while in the United States and available resources. For a qualifying family member who is subject to an order of exclusion, deportation, or removal issued by the Secretary, the order will be deemed canceled by operation of law as of the date of USCIS' approval of Form I–918, Supplement A. A qualifying family member who is subject to an order of exclusion, deportation, or removal issued by an immigration judge or the Board may seek cancellation of such order by filing, with the immigration judge or the Board, a motion to reopen and terminate removal proceedings. ICE counsel may agree, as a matter of discretion, to join such a motion to overcome any applicable time and numerical limitations of 8 CFR 1003.2 and 1003.23.

(i) *Approvals for qualifying family members within the United States.* When USCIS approves a Form I–918, Supplement A for a qualifying family member who is within the United States, it will concurrently grant that alien U–2, U–3, U–4, or U–5 nonimmigrant status. USCIS will notify the principal of such approval on Form I–797, "Notice of Action," with Form I–94, "Arrival-Departure Record," indicating U–2, U–3, U–4, or U–5 nonimmigrant status. Aliens who were previously granted U interim relief as defined in paragraph (a)(13) of this section will be accorded U nonimmigrant status as of the date that the request for U interim relief was approved. Aliens who are granted U–2, U–3, U–4, or U–5 nonimmigrant status are not subject to an annual numerical limit. USCIS may not approve Form I–918, Supplement A unless it has approved the principal alien's Form I–918.

(ii) *Approvals for qualifying family members outside the United States.* When USCIS approves Form I–918, Supplement A for a qualifying family member who is outside the United States, USCIS will notify the principal alien of such approval on Form I–797. USCIS will forward the approved Form I–918, Supplement A to the Department of State for delivery to the U.S. Embassy or Consulate having jurisdiction over the area in which the qualifying family member is located, or, for a visa exempt alien, to the appropriate port of entry.

(iii) *Denial of the Form I–918, Supplement A.* In accordance with 8 CFR 103.3(a)(1), USCIS will provide written notification of the reasons for the denial. The principal alien may appeal the denial of Form I–918, Supplement A to the Administrative Appeals Office in accordance with the provisions of 8 CFR 103.3. Upon USCIS' final denial of Form I–918, Supplement A for a qualifying family member who was in removal proceedings that were terminated pursuant to 8 CFR 214.14(f)(2)(i), DHS may file a new Notice to Appear (see section 239 of the INA, 8 U.S.C. 1229) to place the individual in proceedings again. For qualifying family members who are subject to an order of removal, deportation, or exclusion and whose order has been stayed, USCIS' denial of the petition will result in the stay being lifted automatically as of the date the denial becomes administratively final.

(7) *Employment authorization.* An alien granted U–2, U–3, U–4, or U–5 nonimmigrant status is employment authorized incident to status. To obtain an Employment Authorization Document (EAD), such alien must file Form I–765, "Application for Employment Authorization," with the appropriate fee or a request for a fee waiver, in accordance with the instructions to the form. For qualifying family members within the United States, the Form I–765 may be filed concurrently with Form I–918, Supplement A, or at any time thereafter. For qualifying family members who are outside the United States, Form I–765 only may be filed after admission to the United States in U nonimmigrant status.

(g) *Duration of U nonimmigrant status*—(1) *In general.* U nonimmigrant status may be approved for a period not to exceed 4 years in the aggregate. A qualifying family member granted U–2, U–3, U–4, and U–5 nonimmigrant status will be approved for an initial period that does not exceed the expiration date of the initial period approved for the principal alien.

(2) *Extension of status.* (i) Where a U nonimmigrant's approved period of stay on Form I–94 is less than 4 years, he or she may file Form I–539, "Application to Extend/Change Nonimmigrant Status," to request an extension of U nonimmigrant status for an aggregate period not to exceed 4 years. USCIS may approve an extension of status for a qualifying family member beyond the date when the U–1 nonimmigrant's status expires when the qualifying family member is unable to enter the United States timely due to delays in consular processing, and an extension of status is necessary to ensure that the qualifying family member is able to attain at least 3 years in nonimmigrant status for purposes of adjusting status under section 245(m) of the Act, 8 U.S.C. 1255.

(ii) Extensions of U nonimmigrant status beyond the 4-year period are available upon attestation by the certifying official that the alien's presence in the United States continues to be necessary to assist in the investigation or prosecution of qualifying criminal activity. In order to obtain an extension of U nonimmigrant status based upon such an attestation, the alien must file Form I–539 and a newly executed Form I–918, Supplement B in accordance with the instructions to Form I–539.

(h) *Revocation of approved petitions for U nonimmigrant status*—(1) *Automatic revocation.* An approved petition for U–1 nonimmigrant status will be revoked automatically if, pursuant to 8 CFR 214.14(d)(1), the beneficiary of the approved petition notifies the USCIS office that approved the petition that he or she will not apply for admission to the United States and, therefore, the petition will not be used.

(2) *Revocation on notice.* (i) USCIS may revoke an approved petition for U nonimmigrant status following a notice of intent to revoke. USCIS may revoke an approved petition for U nonimmigrant status based on one or more of the following reasons:

(A) The certifying official withdraws the U nonimmigrant status certification referred to in 8 CFR 214.14(c)(2)(i) or disavows the contents in writing;

(B) Approval of the petition was in error;

(C) Where there was fraud in the petition;

(D) In the case of a U–2, U–3, U–4, or U–5 nonimmigrant, the relationship to the principal petitioner has terminated; or

(E) In the case of a U–2, U–3, U–4, or U–5 nonimmigrant, the principal U–1's nonimmigrant status is revoked.

(ii) The notice of intent to revoke must be in writing and contain a statement of the grounds for the revocation and the time period allowed for the U nonimmigrant's rebuttal. The alien may submit evidence in rebuttal within 30 days of the date of the notice. USCIS shall consider all relevant evidence presented in deciding whether to revoke the approved petition for U nonimmigrant status. The determination of what is relevant evidence and the weight to be given to that evidence will be within the sole discretion of USCIS. If USCIS revokes approval of a petition and thereby terminates U nonimmigrant status, USCIS will provide the alien with a written notice of revocation that explains the specific reasons for the revocation.

(3) *Appeal of a revocation of approval.* A revocation on notice may be appealed to the Administrative Appeals Office in accordance with 8 CFR 103.3 within 30 days after the date of the notice of revocation. Automatic revocations may not be appealed.

(4) *Effects of revocation of approval.* Revocation of a principal alien's approved Form I–918 will result in termination of status for the principal alien, as well as in the denial of any pending Form I–918, Supplement A filed for qualifying family members seeking U–2, U–3, U–4, or U–5 nonimmigrant status. Revocation of a qualifying family member's approved Form I–918, Supplement A will result in termination of status for the qualifying family member. Revocation of an approved Form I–918 or Form I–918, Supplement A also revokes any waiver of inadmissibility granted in conjunction with such petition.

(i) *Removal proceedings.* Nothing in this section prohibits USCIS from instituting removal proceedings under section 240 of the Act, 8 U.S.C. 1229(a), for conduct committed after admission, for conduct or a condition that was not disclosed to USCIS prior to the granting of U nonimmigrant status, for misrepresentations of material facts in Form I–918 or Form I–918, Supplement A and supporting documentation, or after revocation of U nonimmigrant status.

[72 FR 53036, Sept. 17, 2007, as amended at 72 FR 54813, Sept. 27, 2007; 74 FR 55738, Oct. 28, 2009; 78 FR 18472, Mar. 27, 2013]

§ 214.15 Certain spouses and children of lawful permanent residents.

(a) *Aliens abroad.* Under section 101(a)(15)(v) of the Act, certain eligible spouses and children of lawful permanent residents may apply for a V nonimmigrant visa at a consular office abroad and be admitted to the United States in V–1 (spouse), V–2 (child), or V–3 (dependent child of the spouse or child who is accompanying or following to join the principal beneficiary) nonimmigrant status to await the approval of:

(1) A relative visa petition;

(2) The availability of an immigrant visa number; or

(3) Lawful permanent resident (LPR) status through adjustment of status or an immigrant visa.

(b) *Aliens already in the United States.* Eligible aliens already in the United States may apply to the Service to obtain V nonimmigrant status for the same purpose. Aliens in the United States in V nonimmigrant status are entitled to reside in the United States as V nonimmigrants and obtain employment authorization.

(c) *Eligibility.* Subject to section 214(o) of the Act, an alien who is the beneficiary (including a child of the principal alien, if eligible to receive a visa under section 203(d) of the Act) of an immigrant visa petition to accord a status under section 203(a)(2)(A) of the Act that was filed with the Service under section 204 of the Act on or before December 21, 2000, may apply for V nonimmigrant status if:

(1) Such immigrant visa petition has been pending for 3 years or more; or

(2) Such petition has been approved, and 3 or more years have passed since such filing date, in either of the following circumstances:

(i) An immigrant visa is not immediately available to the alien because of a waiting list of applicants for visas under section 203(a)(2)(A) of the Act; or

(ii) The alien's application for an immigrant visa, or the alien's application for adjustment of status under section 245 of the Act, pursuant to the approval of such petition, remains pending.

(d) *The definition of "pending petition."* For purposes of this section, a pending petition is defined as a petition to accord a status under section 203(a)(2)(A) of the Act that was filed with USCIS under section 204 of the Act on or before December 21, 2000, and has not been adjudicated. In addition, the petition must have been properly filed according to 8 CFR 103.2(a), and if, subsequent to filing, USCIS returns the petition to the applicant for any reason or makes a request for evidence or issues a notice of intent to deny under 8 CFR 103.2(b), the petitioner must comply with the request within the time period set by USCIS. If USCIS denies a petition but the petitioner appeals that decision, the petition will be considered pending until the administrative appeal is decided by USCIS. A petition rejected by USCIS as not properly filed is not considered to be pending.

(e) *Classification process for aliens outside the United States*—(1) *V nonimmigrant visa.* An eligible alien may obtain a V nonimmigrant visa from the Department of State at a consular office abroad pursuant to the procedures set forth in 22 CFR 41.86.

(2) *Aliens applying for admission to the United States as a V nonimmigrant at a port-of-entry.* Aliens applying under section 235 of the Act for admission to the United States at a port-of-entry as a V nonimmigrant must have a visa in the appropriate category. Such aliens are exempt from the ground of inadmissibility under section 212(a)(9)(B) of the Act.

(f) *Application by aliens in the United States.* An alien described in paragraph (c) of this section who is in the United States may apply to the Service to obtain V nonimmigrant status pursuant to the procedures set forth in this section and 8 CFR part 248. The alien must be admissible to the United States, except that, in determining the alien's admissibility in V nonimmigrant status, sections 212(a)(6)(A), (a)(7), and (a)(9)(B) of the Act do not apply.

(1) *Contents of application.* To apply for V nonimmigrant status, an eligible alien must submit:

(i) Form I–539, Application to Extend/Change Nonimmigrant Status, with the fee required by § 103.7(b)(1) of this chapter;

(ii) The fingerprint fee as required by § 103.2(e)(4) of this chapter;

(iii) Form I–693, Medical Examination of Aliens Seeking Adjustment of Status, without the vaccination supplement; and

(iv) Evidence of eligibility as described by Supplement A to Form I–539 and in paragraph (f)(2) of this section.

(2) *Evidence.* Supplement A to Form I–539 provides instructions regarding the submission of evidence. An alien applying for V nonimmigrant status with the Service should submit proof of filing of the immigrant petition that qualifies the alien for V status. Proof of filing may include Form I–797, Notice of Action, which serves as a receipt of the petition or as a notice of approval, or a receipt for a filed petition or notice of approval issued by a local district office. If the alien does not have such proof, the Service will review other forms of evidence, such as correspondence to or from the Service regarding a pending petition. If the alien does not have any of the items previously mentioned in this paragraph, but believes he or she is eligible for V nonimmigrant status, he or she should state where and when the petition was filed, the name and alien number of the petitioner, and the names of all beneficiaries (if known).

(g) *Period of admission*—(1) *Spouse of an LPR.* An alien admitted to the United States in V–1 nonimmigrant status (or whose status in the United States is changed to V–1) will be granted a period of admission not to exceed 2 years.

(2) *Child of an LPR or derivative child.* An alien admitted to the United States in V–2 or V–3 nonimmigrant status (or whose status in the United States is changed to V–2 or V–3) will be granted a period of admission not to exceed 2 years or the day before the alien's 21st birthday, whichever comes first.

(3) *Extension of status.* An alien may apply to the Service for an extension of V nonimmigrant status pursuant to this part and 8 CFR part 248. Aliens may apply for the extension of V nonimmigrant status, submitting Form I–539, and the associated filing fee, on or before 120 days before the expiration of their status. If approved, the Service will grant an extension of status to aliens in V nonimmigrant status who remain eligible for V nonimmigrant status for a period not to exceed 2 years, or in the case of a child in V–2 or V–3 status, the day before the alien's 21st birthday, whichever comes first.

(4) *Special rules.* The following special rules apply with respect to aliens who have a current priority date in the United States, but do not have a pending application for an immigrant visa abroad or an application to adjust status.

(i) For an otherwise eligible alien who applies for admission to the United States in a V nonimmigrant category at a designated Port-of-Entry and has a current priority date but does not have a pending immigrant visa abroad or application for adjustment of status in the United States, the Service will admit the alien for a 6-month period (or to the date of the day before the alien's 21st birthday, as appropriate).

(ii) For such an alien in the United States who applies for extension of V nonimmigrant status, the Service will grant a one-time extension not to exceed 6 months.

(iii) If the alien has not filed an application, either for adjustment of status or for an immigrant visa within that 6-month period, the alien cannot extend or be admitted or readmitted to V nonimmigrant status. If the alien does file an application, either for adjustment of status or for an immigrant visa within the time allowed, the alien will continue to be eligible for further extensions of V nonimmigrant status as provided in this section while that application remains pending.

(h) *Employment authorization.* An alien in V nonimmigrant status may apply to the Service for employment authorization pursuant to this section and §274a.12(a)(15) of this chapter. An alien must file Form I–765, Application for Employment Authorization, with the fee required by 8 CFR 103.7. The Service will grant employment authorization to aliens in V nonimmigrant status who remain eligible for V nonimmigrant status valid for a period equal to the alien's authorized admission as a V nonimmigrant.

(i) *Travel abroad; unlawful presence*—(1) *V nonimmigrant status in the United States.* An alien who applies for and obtains V nonimmigrant status in the United States will be issued Form I–797, Notice of Action, indicating the alien's V status in the United States. Form I–797 does not serve as a travel document. If such an alien departs the United States, he or she must obtain a V visa from a consular office abroad in order to be readmitted to the United States as a V nonimmigrant. This visa requirement, however, does not apply if the alien traveled to contiguous territory or adjacent islands, possesses another valid visa, and is eligible for automatic revalidation.

(2) *V nonimmigrants with a pending Form I–485.* An alien in V nonimmigrant status with a pending Form I–485 (Application to Register Permanent Residence or Adjust Status) that was properly filed with the Service does not have to obtain advance parole in order to prevent the abandonment of that application when the alien departs the United States.

(3) *Unlawful presence*—(i) *Nonimmigrant admission.* An alien otherwise eligible for admission as a V nonimmigrant is not subject to the ground of inadmissibility under section 212(a)(9)(B) of the Act. This is true even if the alien had accrued more than 180 days of unlawful presence in the United

States and is applying for admission as a nonimmigrant after travel abroad.

(ii) *Permanent resident status.* A V nonimmigrant alien is subject to the ground of inadmissibility under section 212(a)(9)(B) of the Act when applying for an immigrant visa or for adjustment of status to that of a lawful permanent resident. Therefore, a departure from the United States at any time after having accrued more than 180 days of unlawful presence will render the alien inadmissible under that section for the purpose of adjustment of status or admission as an immigrant, unless he or she has obtained a waiver under section 212(a)(9)(B)(v) of the Act or falls within one of the exceptions in section 212(a)(9)(B)(iii) of the Act.

(j) *Termination of status*—(1) *General.* The status of an alien admitted to the United States as a V nonimmigrant under section 101(a)(15)(V) of the Act shall be automatically terminated 30 days following the occurrence of any of the following:

(i) The denial, withdrawal, or revocation of the Form I–130, Petition for Immediate Relative, filed on behalf of that alien;

(ii) The denial or withdrawal of the immigrant visa application filed by that alien;

(iii) The denial or withdrawal of the alien's application for adjustment of status to that of lawful permanent residence;

(iv) The V–1 spouse's divorce from the LPR becomes final; or

(v) The marriage of an alien in V–2 or V–3 status.

(2) *Dependents.* When a principal alien's V nonimmigrant status is terminated, the V nonimmigrant status of any alien listed as a V–3 dependent or who is seeking derivative benefits is also terminated.

(3) *Appeals.* If the denial of the immigrant visa petition is appealed, the alien's V nonimmigrant status does not terminate until 30 days after the administrative appeal is dismissed.

(4) *Violations of status.* Nothing in this section precludes the Service from immediately initiating removal proceedings for other violations of an alien's V nonimmigrant status.

(k) *Naturalization of the petitioner.* If the lawful permanent resident who filed the qualifying Form I–130 immigrant visa petition subsequently naturalizes, the V nonimmigrant status of the spouse and any children will terminate after his or her current period of admission ends. However, in such a case, the alien spouse or child will be considered an immediate relative of a U.S. citizen as defined in section 201(b) of the Act and will immediately be eligible to apply for adjustment of status and related employment authorization. If the V–1 spouse or V–2 child had already filed an application for adjustment of status by the time the LPR naturalized, a new application for adjustment will not be required.

(l) *Aliens in proceedings.* An alien who is already in immigration proceedings and believes that he or she may have become eligible to apply for V nonimmigrant status should request before the immigration judge or the Board, as appropriate, that the proceedings be administratively closed (or before the Board that a previously-filed motion for reopening or reconsideration be indefinitely continued) in order to allow the alien to pursue an application for V nonimmigrant status with the Service. If the alien appears eligible for V nonimmigrant status, the immigration judge or the Board, whichever has jurisdiction, shall administratively close the proceeding or continue the motion indefinitely. In the event that the Service finds an alien eligible for V nonimmigrant status, the Service can adjudicate the change of status under this section. In the event that the Service finds an alien ineligible for V nonimmigrant status, the Service shall recommence proceedings by filing a motion to re-calendar.

[66 FR 46702, Sept. 7, 2001, as amended at 72 FR 19107, Apr. 17, 2007]

§214.16 Transition Procedures for OPT Applications for Employment Authorization

(a) *STEM OPT Applications for Employment Authorization that are filed prior to, and remain pending on May 10, 2016.* (1) On or after May 10, 2016, USCIS will issue Requests for Evidence (RFEs) to students whose applications for a 17-month OPT extension under the rule issued at 73 FR 18944 are still pending. The RFEs will request documentation that will establish that the student is eligible for a 24-month OPT extension under 8 CFR 214.2(f)(10)(ii)(C), including a Form I–20 endorsed on or after May 10, 2016, indicating that the Designated School Official (DSO) recommends the student for a 24-month OPT extension and that the requirements for such an extension have been met. Submission of the Form I–20 in response to an RFE issued under 8 CFR 214.16(a) will be regarded as fulfilling the requirement in 8 CFR 214.2(f)(11)(i) that a student must initiate the OPT application process by requesting a recommendation for OPT by his or her DSO.

(2) Forms I–765 that are filed prior to, and remain pending on, May 10, 2016, will be regarded as being covered by 8 CFR 214.2(f)(11)(i)(C) and 8 CFR 274a.12(b)(6)(iv).

(b) *STEM OPT Applications for Employment Authorization that are filed and approved before May 10, 2016.* A student whose Form I–765 is filed and approved prior to May 10, 2016 will be issued an Employment Authorization Document, Form I–766, that is valid for 17 months even if the student requested a 24-month OPT extension.

(c) *Students with 17-Month STEM OPT employment authorization.* (1) Subject to paragraph (c)(3) of this section, any Employment Authorization Document, Form I–766, indicating a 17-month OPT extension under the rule issued at 73 FR 18944 that has been issued and is valid prior to May 10, 2016 remains valid until such Form I–766 expires or is terminated or revoked under 8 CFR 274a.14, and the student, the student's employer, and the student's DSO must continue to abide by all the terms and conditions that were in effect when the Form I–766 was issued.

(2) Subject to the requirements in paragraphs (c)(2)(i) through (iii) of this section, F–1 students with a 17-month OPT extension under the rule issued at 73 FR 18944 are eligible to apply for an additional 7-month period of OPT. The F–1 student applying for the additional 7-month period of OPT must:

(i) Properly file a Form I–765, with USCIS on or after May 10, 2016 and on or before August 8, 2016, and within 60 days of the date the DSO enters the recommendation for the 24-month OPT extension into the student's SEVIS record, with applicable fees and supporting documentation, as described in the form instructions;

(ii) Have at least 150 calendar days remaining prior to the end of his or her 17-month OPT extension at the time the Form I–765, is properly filed; and

(iii) Meet all the requirements for the 24-month OPT extension as described in 8 CFR 214.2(f)(10)(ii)(C), except the requirement that the student must be in a valid period of post-completion OPT authorized under 8 CFR 274a.12(c)(3)(i)(B).

(3) Students on a 17-month OPT extension who apply for and are granted an additional 7-month period of OPT shall be considered to be in a period of 24-month OPT extension, as authorized under 8 CFR 214.2(f)(10)(ii)(C). Upon proper filing of the application for the additional 7-month OPT extension, the student, the student's employer as identified in the student's completed Form I–983 and the student's DSO are subject to all requirements of the 24-month OPT extension period, except for the 150-day unemployment limit described in 8 CFR 214.2(f)(10)(ii)(E), which applies to students only upon approval of the additional 7-month OPT extension. Subsequent to any denial of the application for the additional 7-month extension, the student, the student's employer, and the student's DSO must abide by all the terms and conditions that were in effect when the 17-month OPT extension was issued throughout the remaining validity period of the 17-month OPT extension.

[81 FR 13121, Mar. 11, 2016]

EFFECTIVE DATE NOTE: At 81 FR 13121, Mar. 11, 2016, § 214.16 was added, effective May 10, 2016, through May 10, 2019.

PART 215—CONTROLS OF ALIENS DEPARTING FROM THE UNITED STATES; ELECTRONIC VISA UPDATE SYSTEM

Subpart A—Controls of Aliens Departing from the United States

Sec.

Subpart B—Electronic Visa Update System

AUTHORITY: 6 U.S.C. 202(4), 236; 8 U.S.C. 1101, 1103, 1104, 1184, 1185 (pursuant to Executive Order 13323 (Dec. 30, 2003)), 1365a note, 1379, 1731–32; and 8 CFR part 2.

SOURCE: 45 FR 65516, Oct. 3, 1980, unless otherwise noted.

Subpart A—Controls of Aliens Departing from the United States

§215.1 Definitions.

For the purpose of this subpart:

(a) The term *alien* means any person who is not a citizen or national of the United States.

(b) The term *Commissioner* means the Commissioner of Immigration and Naturalization.

(c) The term *regional commissioner* means an officer of the Immigration and Naturalization Service duly appointed or designated as a regional commissioner, or an officer who has been designated to act as a regional commissioner.

(d) The term *district director* means an officer of the Immigration and Naturalization Service duly appointed or designated as a district director, or an officer who has been designated to act as a district director.

(e) The term *United States* means the several States, the District of Columbia, Puerto Rico, the Virgin Islands, Guam, American Samoa, Swains Island, the Commonwealth of the Northern Mariana Islands (beginning November 28, 2009), and all other territory and waters, continental and insular, subject to the jurisdiction of the United States.

(f) The term *continental United States* means the District of Columbia and the several States, except Alaska and Hawaii.

(g) The term *geographical part of the United States* means:

(1) The continental United States,

(2) Alaska,

(3) Hawaii,

(4) Puerto Rico,

(5) The Virgin Islands,

(6) Guam,

(7) American Samoa,

(8) Swains Island, or

(9) The Commonwealth of the Northern Mariana Islands (beginning November 28, 2009).

(h) The term *depart from the United States* means depart by land, water, or air: (1) From the United States for any foreign place, or (2) from one geographical part of the United States for a separate geographical part of the United States: *Provided*, That a trip or journey upon a public ferry, passenger vessel sailing coastwise on a fixed schedule, excursion vessel, or aircraft, having both termini in the continental United States or in any one of the other geographical parts of the United States and not touching any territory or waters under the jurisdiction or control of a foreign power, shall not be deemed a departure from the United States.

(i) The term *departure-control officer* means any immigration officer as defined in the regulations of the Immigration and Naturalization Service who is designated to supervise the departure of aliens, or any officer or employee of the United States designated by the Governor of the Canal Zone, the High Commissioner of the Trust Territory of the Pacific Islands, or the governor of an outlying possession of the United States, to supervise the departure of aliens.

(j) The term *port of departure* means a port in the continental United States, Alaska, Guam, Hawaii, Puerto Rico, the Commonwealth of the Northern Mariana Islands (beginning November 28, 2009), or the Virgin Islands, designated as a port of entry by the Secretary, or in exceptional circumstances such other place as the departure-control officer may, in his discretion, designate in an individual case, or a port in American Samoa, or Swains Island, designated as a port of entry by the chief executive officer thereof.

(k) The term *special inquiry officer* shall have the meaning ascribed thereto in section 101(b)(4) of the Immigration and Nationality Act.

[45 FR 65516, Oct. 3, 1980, as amended at 74 FR 2836, Jan. 16, 2009; 74 FR 25388, May 28, 2009; 81 FR 72491, Oct. 20, 2016]

§ 215.2 Authority of departure-control officer to prevent alien's departure from the United States.

(a) No alien shall depart, or attempt to depart, from the United States if his departure would be prejudicial to the interests of the United States under the provisions of § 215.3. Any departure-control officer who knows or has reason to believe that the case of an alien in the United States comes within the provisions of § 215.3 shall temporarily prevent the departure of such alien from the United States and shall serve him with a written temporary order directing him not to depart, or attempt to depart, from the United States until notified of the revocation of the order.

(b) The written order temporarily preventing an alien, other than an enemy alien, from departing from the United States shall become final 15 days after the date of service thereof upon the alien, unless prior thereto the alien requests a hearing as hereinafter provided. At such time as the alien is served with an order temporarily preventing his departure from the United States, he shall be notified in writing concerning the provisions of this paragraph, and shall be advised of his right to request a hearing if entitled thereto under § 215.4. In the case of an enemy alien, the written order preventing departure shall become final on the date of its service upon the alien.

(c) Any alien who seeks to depart from the United States may be required, in the discretion of the departure-control officer, to be examined under oath and to submit for official inspection all documents, articles, and other property in his possession which are being removed from the United States upon, or in connection with, the alien's departure. The departure-control officer may permit certain other persons, including officials of the Department of State and interpreters, to participate in such examination or inspection and may exclude from presence at such examination or inspection any person whose presence would not further the objectives of such examination or inspection. The departure-control officer shall temporarily prevent the departure of any alien who refuses to submit to such examination or inspection, and may, if necessary to the enforcement of this requirement, take possession of the alien's passport or other travel document.

§ 215.3 Alien whose departure is deemed prejudicial to the interests of the United States.

The departure from the United States of any alien within one or more of the following categories shall be deemed prejudicial to the interests of the United States.

(a) Any alien who is in possession of, and who is believed likely to disclose to unauthorized persons, information concerning the plans, preparation, equipment, or establishments for the national defense and security of the United States.

(b) Any alien who seeks to depart from the United States to engage in, or who is likely to engage in, activities of any kind designed to obstruct, impede, retard, delay or counteract the effectiveness of the national defense of the United States or the measures adopted by the United States or the United Nations for the defense of any other country.

(c) Any alien who seeks to depart from the United States to engage in, or who is likely to engage in, activities which would obstruct, impede, retard, delay, or counteract the effectiveness of any plans made or action taken by any country cooperating with the United States in measures adopted to promote the peace, defense, or safety of the United States or such other country.

(d) Any alien who seeks to depart from the United States for the purpose of organizing, directing, or participating in any rebellion, insurrection, or violent uprising in or against the United States or a country allied with the United States, or of waging war against the United States or its allies, or of destroying, or depriving the United States of sources of supplies or materials vital to the national defense of the United States, or to the effectiveness of the measures adopted by the United States for its defense, or for the defense of any other country allied with the United States.

(e) Any alien who is subject to registration for training and service in the Armed Forces of the United States and who fails to present a Registration Certificate (SSS Form No. 2) showing that he has complied with his obligation to register under the Universal Military Training and Service Act, as amended.

(f) Any alien who is a fugitive from justice on account of an offense punishable in the United States.

(g) Any alien who is needed in the United States as a witness in, or as a party to, any criminal case under investigation or pending in a court in the United States: *Provided*, That any alien who is a witness in, or a party to, any criminal case pending in any criminal court proceeding may be permitted to depart from the United States with the consent of the appropriate prosecuting authority, unless such alien is otherwise prohibited from departing under the provisions of this part.

(h) Any alien who is needed in the United States in connection with any investigation or proceeding being, or soon to be, conducted by any official executive, legislative, or judicial agency in the United States or by any governmental committee, board, bureau, commission, or body in the United States, whether national, state, or local.

(i) Any alien whose technical or scientific training and knowledge might be utilized by an enemy or a potential enemy of the United States to undermine and defeat the military and defensive operations of the United States or of any nation cooperating with the United States in the interests of collective security.

(j) Any alien, where doubt exists whether such alien is departing or seeking to depart from the United States voluntarily except an alien who is departing or seeking to depart subject to an order issued in extradition, exclusion, or deportation proceedings.

(k) Any alien whose case does not fall within any of the categories described in paragraphs (a) to (j), inclusive, of this section, but which involves circumstances of a similar character rendering the alien's departure prejudicial to the interests of the United States.

§ 215.4 Procedure in case of alien prevented from departing from the United States.

(a) Any alien, other than an enemy alien, whose departure has been temporarily prevented under the provisions of § 215.2, may, within 15 days of the service upon him of the written order temporarily preventing his departure, request a hearing before a special inquiry officer. The alien's request for a hearing shall be made in writing and shall be addressed to the district director having administrative jurisdiction over the alien's place of residence. If the alien's request for a hearing is timely made, the district director shall schedule a hearing before a special inquiry officer, and notice of such hearing shall be given to the alien. The notice of hearing shall, as specifically as security considerations permit, inform the alien of the nature of the case against him, shall fix the time and place of the hearing, and shall inform the alien of his right to be represented, at no expense to the Government, by counsel of his own choosing.

(b) Every alien for whom a hearing has been scheduled under paragraph (a) of this section shall be entitled: (1) To appear in person before the special inquiry officer, (2) to be represented by counsel of his own choice, (3) to have the opportunity to be heard and to present evidence, (4) to cross-examine the witnesses who appear at the hearing, except that if, in the course of the examination, it appears that further examination may divulge information of a confidential or security nature, the special inquiry officer may, in his discretion, preclude further examination of the witness with respect to such matters, (5) to examine any evidence in possession of the Government which is to be considered in the disposition of the case, provided that such evidence is not of a confidential or security nature the disclosure of which would be prejudicial to the interests of the United States, (6) to have the time and opportunity to produce evidence and witnesses on his own behalf, and (7) to reasonable continuances, upon request, for good cause shown.

(c) Any special inquiry officer who is assigned to conduct the hearing provided for in this section shall have the authority to: (1) Administer oaths and affirmations, (2) present and receive evidence, (3) interrogate, examine, and cross examine under oath or affirmation both the alien and witnesses, (4) rule upon all objections to the introduction of evidence or motions made during the course of the hearing, (5) take or cause depositions to be taken, (6) issue subpoenas, and (7) take any further action consistent with applicable provisions of law, Executive orders, proclamations, and regulations.

§ 215.5 Hearing procedure before special inquiry officer.

(a) The hearing before the special inquiry officer shall be conducted in accordance with the following procedure:

(1) The special inquiry officer shall advise the alien of the rights and privileges accorded him under the provisions of § 215.4.

(2) The special inquiry officer shall enter of record: (i) A copy of the order served upon the alien temporarily preventing his departure from the United States, and (ii) a copy of the notice of hearing furnished the alien.

(3) The alien shall be interrogated by the special inquiry officer as to the matters considered pertinent to the proceeding, with opportunity reserved to the alien to testify thereafter in his own behalf, if he so chooses.

(4) The special inquiry officer shall present on behalf of the Government such evidence, including the testimony of witnesses and the certificates or written statements of Government officials or other persons, as may be necessary and available. In the event such certificates or statements are received in evidence, the alien may request and, in the discretion of the special inquiry officer, be given an opportunity to interrogate such officials or persons, by deposition or otherwise, at a time and place and in a manner fixed by the special inquiry officer: *Provided*, That when in the judgment of the special inquiry officer any evidence relative to the disposition of the case is of a confidential or security nature the disclosure of which would be prejudicial to the interests of the United States, such evidence shall not be presented at the hearing but shall be taken into consideration in arriving at a decision in the case.

(5) The alien may present such additional evidence, including the testimony of witnesses, as is pertinent and available.

(b) A complete verbatim transcript of the hearing, except statements made off the record shall be recorded. The alien shall be entitled, upon request, to the loan of a copy of the transcript, without cost, subject to reasonable conditions governing its use.

(c) Following the completion of the hearing, the special inquiry officer shall make and render a recommended decision in the case, which shall be governed by and based upon the evidence presented at the hearing and any evidence of a confidential or security nature which the Government may have in its possession. The decision of the special inquiry officer shall recommend: (1) That the temporary order preventing the departure of the alien from the United States be made final, or (2) that the temporary order preventing the departure of the alien from the United States be revoked. This recommended decision of the special inquiry officer shall be made in writing and shall set forth the officer's reasons for such decision. The alien concerned shall at his request be furnished a copy of the recommended decision of the special inquiry officer, and shall be allowed a reasonable time, not to exceed 10 days, in which to submit representations with respect thereto in writing.

(d) As soon as practicable after the completion of the hearing and the rendering of a decision by the special inquiry officer, the district director shall forward the entire record of the case, including the recommended decision of the special inquiry officer and any written representations submitted by the alien, to the regional commissioner having jurisdiction over his district. After reviewing the record, the regional commissioner shall render a decision in the case, which shall be based upon the evidence in the record and on any evidence or information of a confidential or security nature which he deems pertinent. Whenever any decision is based in whole or in part on confidential or security information not included in the record, the decision shall state that such information was considered. A copy of the regional commissioner's decision shall be furnished the alien, or his attorney or representative. No administrative appeal shall lie from the regional commissioner's decision.

(e) Notwithstanding any other provision of this part, the Administrator of the Bureau of Security and Consular Affairs referred to in section 104(b) of the Immigration and Nationality Act, or such other officers of the Department of State as he may designate, after consultation with the Commissioner, or such other officers of the Immigration and Naturalization Service as he may designate, may at any time permit the departure of an individual alien or of a group of aliens from the United States if he determines that such action would be in the national interest. If the Administrator specifically requests the Commissioner to prevent the departure of a particular alien or of a group of aliens, the Commissioner shall not permit the departure of such alien or aliens until he has consulted with the Administrator.

(f) In any case arising under §§215.1 to 215.7, the Administrator shall, at his request, be kept advised, in as much detail as he may indicate is necessary, of the facts and of any action taken or proposed.

§215.6 Departure from the Canal Zone, the Trust Territory of the Pacific Islands, or outlying possessions of the United States.

(a) In addition to the restrictions and prohibitions imposed by the provisions of this part upon the departure of aliens from the United States, any alien who seeks to depart from the Canal Zone, the Trust Territory of the Pacific Islands, or an outlying possession of the United States shall comply with such other restrictions and prohibitions as may be imposed by regulations prescribed, with the concurrence of the Administrator of the Bureau of Security and Consular Affairs and the Commissioner, by the Governor of the Canal Zone, the High Commissioner of the Trust Territory of the Pacific Islands, or by the governor of an outlying possession of the United States, respectively. No alien shall be prevented from departing from such zone, territory, or possession without first being accorded a hearing as provided in §§215.4 and 215.5.

(b) The Governor of the Canal Zone, the High Commissioner of the Trust Territory of the Pacific Islands, or the governor of any outlying possession of the United States shall have the authority to designate any employee or class of employees of the United States as hearing officers for the purpose of conducting the hearing referred to in paragraph (a) of this section. The hearing officer so designated shall exercise the same powers, duties, and functions as are conferred upon special inquiry officers under the provisions of this part. The chief executive officer of such zone, territory, or possession shall, in lieu of the regional commissioner, review the recommended decision of the hearing officer, and shall render a decision in any case referred to him, basing it on evidence in the record and on any evidence or information of a confidential or a security nature which he deems pertinent.

§215.7 Instructions from the Administrator required in certain cases.

In the absence of appropriate instructions from the Administrator of the Bureau of Security and Consular Affairs, departure-control officers shall not exercise the authority conferred by §215.2 in the case of any alien who seeks to depart from the United States in the status of a nonimmigrant under section 101(a)(15) (A) or (G) of the Immigration and Nationality Act, or in the status of a nonimmigrant under section 11(3), 11(4), or 11(5) of the Agreement between the United Nations and the United States of America regarding the Headquarters of the United Nations (61 Stat. 756): *Provided*, That in cases of extreme urgency, where the national security so requires, a departure-control officer may preliminarily exercise the authority conferred by § 215.2 pending the outcome of consultation with the Administrator, which shall be undertaken immediately. In all cases arising under this section, the decision of the Administrator shall be controlling: *Provided*, That any decision to prevent the departure of an alien shall be based upon a hearing and record as prescribed in this part.

§ 215.8 Requirements for biometric identifiers from aliens on departure from the United States.

(a)(1) The Secretary of Homeland Security, or his designee, may establish pilot programs at land border ports of entry, and at up to fifteen air or sea ports of entry, designated through notice in the FEDERAL REGISTER, through which the Secretary or his delegate may require an alien admitted to or paroled into the United States, other than aliens exempted under paragraph (a)(2) of this section or Canadian citizens under section 101(a)(15)(B) of the Act who were not otherwise required to present a visa or have been issued Form I–94 (see § 1.4) or Form I–95 upon arrival at the United States, who departs the United States from a designated port of entry, to provide fingerprints, photograph(s) or other specified biometric identifiers, documentation of his or her immigration status in the United States, and such other evidence as may be requested to determine the alien's identity and whether he or she has properly maintained his or her status while in the United States.

(2) The requirements of paragraph (a)(1) shall not apply to:

(i) Aliens younger than 14 or older than 79 on date of departure;

(ii) Aliens admitted on A–1, A–2, C–3 (except for attendants, servants, or personal employees of accredited officials), G–1, G–2, G–3, G–4, NATO–1, NATO–2, NATO–3, NATO–4, NATO–5, or NATO–6 visas, and certain Taiwan officials who hold E–1 visas and members of their immediate families who hold E–1 visas who are maintaining such status at time of departure, unless the Secretary of State and the Secretary of Homeland Security jointly determine that a class of such aliens should be subject to the requirements of paragraph (a)(1);

(iii) Classes of aliens to whom the Secretary of Homeland Security and the Secretary of State jointly determine it shall not apply; or

(iv) An individual alien to whom the Secretary of Homeland Security, the Secretary of State, or the Director of Central Intelligence determines it shall not apply.

(b) An alien who is required to provide biometric identifiers at departure pursuant to paragraph (a)(1) and who fails to comply with the departure requirements may be found in violation of the terms of his or her admission, parole, or other immigration status. In addition, failure of a covered alien to comply with the departure requirements could be a factor in support of a determination that the alien is ineligible to receive a future visa or other immigration status documentation, or to be admitted to the United States. In making this determination, the officer will consider the totality of the circumstances, including, but not limited to, all positive and negative factors related to the alien's ability to comply with the departure procedures.

(c) A covered alien who leaves the United States without complying with the departure requirements in this section may be found to have overstayed the period of his or her last admission where the available evidence clearly indicates that the alien did not depart the United States within the time period authorized at his or her last admission or extension of stay. A determination that the alien previously overstayed the terms of his admission may result in a finding of inadmissibility for accruing prior unlawful presence in the United States under section 212(a)(9) of the Immigration and Nationality Act or that the alien is otherwise ineligible for a visa or other authorization to reenter the United States, provided that all other requirements of section 212(a)(9) have been met. A determination that an alien who was admitted on the basis of a nonimmigrant visa has remained in the

United States beyond his or her authorized period of stay may result in such visa being deemed void pursuant to section 222(g) of the Act (8 U.S.C. 1202(g)) where all other requirements of that section are also met.

[69 FR 480, Jan. 5, 2004, as amended at 69 FR 53333, Aug. 31, 2004; 69 FR 58037, Sept. 29, 2004; 73 FR 77491, Dec. 19, 2008; 78 FR 18472, Mar. 27, 2013]

§215.9 Temporary Worker Visa Exit Program.

An alien admitted on certain temporary worker visas at a port of entry participating in the Temporary Worker Visa Exit Program must also depart at the end of his or her authorized period of stay through a port of entry participating in the program and must present designated biographic and/or biometric information upon departure. U.S. Customs and Border Protection will publish a Notice in the FEDERAL REGISTER designating which temporary workers must participate in the Temporary Worker Visa Exit Program, which ports of entry are participating in the program, which biographical and/or biometric information would be required, and the format for submission of that information by the departing designated temporary workers.

[73 FR 78130, Dec. 19, 2008]

Subpart B—Electronic Visa Update System

SOURCE: 81 FR 72491, Oct. 20, 2016, unless otherwise noted.

§215.21 Purpose.

The purpose of this subpart is to establish an electronic visa update system for nonimmigrant aliens who hold a passport issued by an identified country containing a U.S. nonimmigrant visa of a designated category.

§215.22 Applicability.

This subpart is applicable to nonimmigrant aliens who hold a passport issued by an identified country containing a U.S. nonimmigrant visa of a designated category. The Secretary, in the Secretary's discretion and in consultation with the Secretary of State, may identify countries and designate nonimmigrant visa categories for purposes of this subpart. Notice of the identified countries and designated nonimmigrant visa categories will be published in the FEDERAL REGISTER.

§215.23 Definitions.

The following definitions apply for purposes of this subpart.

(a) *Covered alien.* A covered alien is a nonimmigrant alien who holds a passport issued by an EVUS country (as defined in paragraph (c) of this section) containing a U.S. nonimmigrant visa of a designated category.

(b) *Electronic Visa Update System (EVUS).* The Electronic Visa Update System (EVUS) is the electronic system used by a covered alien to provide required information to DHS after the receipt of his or her visa of a designated category.

(c) *EVUS country.* An EVUS country is a country that has been identified for inclusion in EVUS, through publication of a notice in the FEDERAL REGISTER, by the Secretary after consultation with the Secretary of State.

(d) *Notification of compliance.* A notification of compliance is a verification from CBP that a covered alien has successfully enrolled in EVUS. A notification of compliance is a positive determination that an alien's visa is:

(1) Not automatically provisionally revoked pursuant to 22 CFR 41.122(b)(3); and

(2) Is considered valid for travel to the United States as of the time of notification.

§215.24 Electronic Visa Update System (EVUS) requirements.

(a) *Enrollment required.* Each covered alien must initially enroll in EVUS, in accordance with paragraph (c)(1) of this section, by providing the information set forth in paragraph (d) of this section electronically through EVUS. Each covered alien who intends to travel to the United States must have a valid notification of compliance as set forth in paragraph (c)(2) of this section. Upon each successful enrollment or re-enrollment, CBP will issue a notification of compliance.

(b) *Validity period of notification of compliance*—(1) *General validity period.* A notification of compliance will generally be valid for a period of two years from the date the notification of compliance is issued, except as provided in paragraph (b)(2) or (3) of this section.

(2) *Exception.* If the nonimmigrant alien's passport or nonimmigrant visa will expire in less than two years from the date the notification of compliance is issued, the notification will be valid until the date of expiration of the passport or nonimmigrant visa, whichever is sooner.

(3) *Change in validity period of notification of compliance.* The Secretary, in consultation with the Secretary of State, may increase or decrease the notification of compliance validity period otherwise authorized by paragraph (b)(1) of this section for an EVUS country. Any such increase or decrease would apply to subsequently issued notifications of compliance. Any changes to the validity period will be done through rulemaking. The EVUS Web site will be updated to reflect the specific duration of notification of compliance validity periods for each EVUS country.

(4) *Relation to nonimmigrant visa validity.* A notification of compliance is not valid unless the alien's nonimmigrant visa also is valid.

(c) *Schedule for EVUS enrollment*—(1) *Initial EVUS enrollment*—(i) *Visas received prior to November 29, 2016.* Each covered alien who received his or her nonimmigrant visa of a designated category prior to November 29, 2016 must initially enroll in EVUS by December 14, 2016, unless the covered alien intends to travel to the United States before that date, in which case the requirements for EVUS enrollment outlined in paragraph (c)(2) of this section apply.

(ii) *Visas received on or after November 29, 2016.* Each covered alien who received his or her nonimmigrant visa of a designated category on or after November 29, 2016 must initially enroll in EVUS upon receipt of such visa.

(2) *EVUS re-enrollment requirements prior to travel to the United States*—(i) *Individuals arriving at air or sea ports of entry.* Each covered alien who intends to travel by air or sea to the United States on a nonimmigrant visa of a designated category must have a notification of compliance that is valid, as described in paragraph (b) of this section, prior to boarding a carrier destined for travel to the United States through the date when the covered alien will arrive at a U.S. port of entry.

(ii) *Individuals arriving at land ports of entry.* Each covered alien who intends to travel by land to the United States on a nonimmigrant visa of a designated category must have a notification of compliance that is valid, as described in paragraph (b) of this section, through the date of application for admission to the United States.

(d) *Required EVUS enrollment elements.* DHS will collect such information from covered aliens as DHS deems necessary in its discretion, after consultation with the Department of State. The required information will be reflected in the EVUS enrollment questions.

(e) *EVUS re-enrollment required.* Each covered alien must re-enroll in EVUS and obtain a new notification of compliance from CBP if any of the following occurs:

(1) The alien is issued a new passport or new nonimmigrant visa of a designated category;

(2) The alien changes his or her name;

(3) The alien changes his or her gender;

(4) There is any change to the alien's country of citizenship or nationality, including becoming a dual national; or

(5) The circumstances underlying the alien's previous responses to any of the EVUS enrollment questions requiring a "yes" or "no" response (eligibility questions) have changed.

(f) *Limitation.* A notification of compliance is not a determination that the covered alien is admissible to the United States. A determination of admissibility is made after an applicant for admission is inspected by a CBP officer at a U.S. port of entry.

(g) *Noncompliance, expiration of notification of compliance, and change in EVUS status resulting in rescission of notification of compliance*—(1) *Initial EVUS enrollment.* Failure to initially enroll in EVUS in accordance with paragraph (c)(1) of this section will result in the automatic provisional revocation of the covered alien's nonimmigrant visa pursuant to 22 CFR 41.122(b)(3), pending enrollment.

(2) *Expiration of notification of compliance.* Upon expiration of a notification of compliance, as described in paragraph (b) of this section, the covered alien's nonimmigrant visa will be automatically provisionally revoked pursuant to 22 CFR 41.122(b)(3), pending re-enrollment. To prevent the automatic provisional revocation of his or her nonimmigrant visa due to the expiration of the notification of compliance, each covered alien must re-enroll in EVUS prior to such expiration.

(3) *Unsuccessful EVUS enrollment.* If a covered alien's EVUS enrollment or re-enrollment is unsuccessful, his or her nonimmigrant visa will be automatically provisionally revoked pursuant to 22 CFR 41.122(b)(3), pending successful enrollment or re-enrollment.

(4) *Change in EVUS status after receipt of a notification of compliance.* In the event that irreconcilable errors are discovered after the issuance of a notification of compliance, or other circumstances occur including but not limited to a change in the validity period of the notification of compliance as provided in paragraph (b) of this section, CBP may rescind the notification of compliance. If a covered alien's notification of compliance is rescinded, his or her nonimmigrant visa will be automatically provisionally revoked pursuant to 22 CFR 41.122(b)(3), pending successful enrollment. CBP will attempt to provide notification of a change in EVUS status to the covered alien through the provided email address.

(h) *Reversal of an automatically provisionally revoked visa and steps to address an unsuccessful EVUS enrollment or rescission of a notification of compliance*—(1) *Reversal of an automatically provisionally revoked visa.* If a covered alien's nonimmigrant visa has been automatically provisionally revoked as described in paragraph (g)(1) or (2) of this section, the revocation of the alien's visa will be automatically reversed, following compliance with EVUS, if the visa remains valid and was not also revoked on other grounds. After a reversal of the revocation the visa will immediately resume the validity provided for on its face, pursuant to 22 CFR 41.122(b)(3), after the alien enrolls in EVUS and receives a notification of compliance.

(2) *Unsuccessful EVUS enrollment.* If a covered alien's EVUS enrollment is unsuccessful per paragraph (g)(3) of this section, the covered alien may re-attempt enrollment or contact CBP.

(3) *Rescission of notification of compliance.* If a covered alien's nonimmigrant visa has been automatically provisionally revoked as described in paragraph (g)(4) of this section, the covered alien may re-attempt enrollment or contact CBP.

PART 216—CONDITIONAL BASIS OF LAWFUL PERMANENT RESIDENCE STATUS

Sec.

AUTHORITY: 8 U.S.C. 1101, 1103, 1154, 1184, 1186a, 1186b, and 8 CFR part 2.

SOURCE: 53 FR 30018, Aug. 10, 1988, unless otherwise noted.

§216.1 Definition of conditional permanent resident.

A *conditional permanent resident* is an alien who has been lawfully admitted for permanent residence within the meaning of section 101(a)(20) of the Act, except that a conditional permanent resident is also subject to the conditions and responsibilities set forth in section 216 or 216A of the Act, whichever is applicable, and part 216 of this chapter. Unless otherwise specified, the rights, privileges, responsibilities and duties which apply to all other lawful permanent residents apply equally to conditional permanent residents, including but not limited to the right to apply for naturalization (if otherwise eligible), the right to file petitions on behalf of qualifying relatives, the privilege of residing permanently in the

United States as an immigrant in accordance with the immigration laws, such status not having changed; the duty to register with the Selective Service System, when required; and the responsibility for complying with all laws and regulations of the United States. All references within this chapter to lawful permanent residents apply equally to conditional permanent residents, unless otherwise specified. The conditions of section 216 of the Act shall not apply to lawful permanent resident status based on a self-petitioning relationship under section 204(a)(1)(A)(iii), 204(a)(1)(A)(iv), 204(a)(1)(b)(ii), or 204(a)(1)(B)(iii) of the Act or based on eligibility as the derivative child of a self-petitioning spouse under section 204(a)(1)(A)(iii) or 204(a)(1)(B)(ii) of the Act, regardless of the date on which the marriage to the abusive citizen or lawful permanent resident occurred.

[53 FR 30018, Aug. 10, 1988, as amended at 59 FR 26590, May 23, 1994; 61 FR 13079, Mar. 26, 1996]

§216.2 Notification requirements.

(a) *When alien acquires status of conditional permanent resident.* At the time an alien acquires conditional permanent residence through admission to the United States with an immigrant visa or adjustment of status under section 245 of the Act, the Service shall notify the alien of the conditional basis of the alien's status, of the requirement that the alien apply for removal of the conditions within the ninety days immediately preceding the second anniversary of the alien's having been granted such status, and that failure to apply for removal of the conditions will result in automatic termination of the alien's lawful status in the United States.

(b) *When alien is required to apply for removal of the conditional basis of lawful permanent resident status.* Approximately 90 days before the second anniversary of the date on which the alien obtained conditional permanent residence, the Service should notify the alien a second time of the requirement that the alien and the petitioning spouse or alien entrepreneur must file a petition to remove the conditional basis of the alien's lawful permanent residence. Such notification shall be mailed to the alien's last known address.

(c) *Effect of failure to provide notification.* Failure of the Service to provide notification as required by either paragraph (a) or (b) of this section does not relieve the alien and the petitioning spouse, or alien entrepreneur of the requirement to file a petition to remove conditions within the 90 days immediately preceding the second anniversary of the date on which the alien obtained permanent residence.

[53 FR 30018, Aug. 10, 1988, as amended at 59 FR 26590, May 23, 1994]

§216.3 Termination of conditional resident status.

(a) *During the two-year conditional period.* The director shall send a formal written notice to the conditional permanent resident of the termination of the alien's conditional permanent resident status if the director determines that any of the conditions set forth in section 216(b)(1) or 216A(b)(1) of the Act, whichever is applicable, are true, or it becomes known to the government that an alien entrepreneur who was admitted pursuant to section 203(b)(5) of the Act obtained his or her investment capital through other than legal means (such as through the sale of illegal drugs). If the Service issues a notice of intent to terminate an alien's conditional resident status, the director shall not adjudicate Form I–751 or Form I–829 until it has been determined that the alien's status will not be terminated. During this time, the alien shall continue to be a lawful conditional permanent resident with all the rights, privileges, and responsibilities provided to persons possessing such status. Prior to issuing the notice of termination, the director shall provide the alien with an opportunity to review and rebut the evidence upon which the decision is to be based, in accordance with §103.2(b)(2) of this chapter. The termination of status, and all of the rights and privileges concomitant thereto (including authorization to accept or continue in employment in this country), shall take effect as of the date of such determination by the director, although the alien may request a review of such determination in removal proceedings. In addition to the notice of termination, the director shall issue a notice to appear in accordance with 8 CFR part 239. During the ensuing removal proceedings, the alien may submit evidence to rebut the determination of the director. The burden of proof shall be on the Service to establish, by a preponderance of the evidence, that one or more of the conditions in section 216(b)(1) or 216A(b)(1) of the Act, whichever is applicable, are true, or that an alien entrepreneur who was admitted pursuant to section 203(b)(5) of the Act obtained his or her investment capital through other than legal means (such as through the sale of illegal drugs).

(b) *Determination of fraud after two years.* If, subsequent to the removal of the conditional basis of an alien's permanent resident status, the director determines that an alien spouse obtained permanent resident status through a marriage which was entered into for the purpose of evading the immigration laws or an alien entrepreneur obtained permanent resident status through a commercial enterprise which was improper under section 216A(b)(1) of the Act, the director may institute rescission proceedings pursuant to section 246 of the Act (if otherwise appropriate) or removal proceedings under section 240 of the Act.

[62 FR 10349, Mar. 6, 1997]

§216.4 Joint petition to remove conditional basis of lawful permanent resident status for alien spouse.

(a) *Filing the petition*—(1) *General procedures.* Within the 90-day period immediately preceding the second anniversary of the date on which the alien obtained permanent residence, the alien and the alien's spouse who filed the original immigrant visa petition or fiance/fiancee petition through which the alien obtained permanent residence must file a Petition to Remove the Conditions on Residence (Form I–751) with the Service. The petition shall be filed within this time period regardless of the amount of physical presence which the alien has accumulated in the United States. Before Form I–751 may be considered as properly filed, it must be accompanied by the fee required under §103.7(b) of this chapter and by documentation as described in paragraph (a)(5) of this section, and it must be properly signed by the alien and the alien's spouse. If the joint petition cannot be filed due to the termination of the marriage through annulment, divorce, or the death of the petitioning spouse, or if the petitioning spouse refuses to join in the filing of the petition, the conditional permanent resident may apply for a waiver of the requirement to file the joint petition in accordance with the provisions of §216.5 of this part. Upon receipt of a properly filed Form I–751, the alien's conditional permanent resident status shall be extended automatically, if necessary, until such time as the director has adjudicated the petition.

(2) *Dependent children.* Dependent children of a conditional permanent resident who acquired conditional permanent resident status concurrently with the parent may be included in the joint petition filed by the parent and the parent's petitioning spouse. A child shall be deemed to have acquired conditional residence status concurrently with the parent if the child's residence was acquired on the same date or within 90 days thereafter. Children who cannot be included in a joint petition filed by the parent and parent's petitioning spouse due to the child's not having acquired conditional resident status concurrently with the parent, the death of the parent, or other reasons may file a separate Petition to Remove the Conditions on Residence (Form I–751).

(3) [Reserved]

(4) *Physical presence at time of filing.* A petition may be filed regardless of whether the alien is physically present in the United States. However, if the alien is outside the United States at the time of filing, he or she must return to the United States, with his or her spouse and dependent children, to comply with the interview requirements contained in the Act. Furthermore, if the documentation submitted in support of the petition includes affidavits of third parties having knowledge of the bona fides of the marital relationship, the petitioner must arrange for the affiants to be present at the

interview, at no expense to the government. Once the petition has been properly filed, the alien may travel outside the United States and return if in possession of documentation as set forth in §211.1(b)(1) of this chapter, provided the alien and the petitioning spouse comply with the interview requirements described in §216.4(b). An alien who is not physically present in the United States during the filing period but subsequently applies for admission to the United States shall be processed in accordance with §235.11 of this chapter.

(5) *Documentation.* Form I–751 shall be accompanied by evidence that the marriage was not entered into for the purpose of evading the immigration laws of the United States. Such evidence may include:

(i) Documentation showing joint ownership of property;

(ii) Lease showing joint tenancy of a common residence;

(iii) Documentation showing commingling of financial resources;

(iv) Birth certificates of children born to the marriage;

(v) Affidavits of third parties having knowledge of the bona fides of the marital relationship, or

(vi) Other documentation establishing that the marriage was not entered into in order to evade the immigration laws of the United States.

(6) *Termination of status for failure to file petition.* Failure to properly file Form I–751 within the 90-day period immediately preceding the second anniversary of the date on which the alien obtained lawful permanent residence on a conditional basis shall result in the automatic termination of the alien's permanent residence status and the initiation of proceedings to remove the alien from the United States. In such proceedings the burden shall be on the alien to establish that he or she complied with the requirement to file the joint petition within the designated period. Form I–751 may be filed after the expiration of the 90-day period only if the alien establishes to the satisfaction of the director, in writing, that there was good cause for the failure to file Form I–751 within the required time period. If the joint petition is filed prior to the jurisdiction vesting with the immigration judge in removal proceedings and the director excuses the late filing and approves the petition, he or she shall restore the alien's permanent residence status, remove the conditional basis of such status and cancel any outstanding notice to appear in accordance with §239.2 of this chapter. If the joint petition is not filed until after jurisdiction vests with the immigration judge, the immigration judge may terminate the matter upon joint motion by the alien and the Service.

(b) *Interview*—(1) *Authority to waive interview.* The director of the regional service center shall review the Form I–751 filed by the alien and the alien's spouse to determine whether to waive the interview required by the Act. If satisfied that the marriage was not for the purpose of evading the immigration laws, the regional service center director may waive the interview and approve the petition. If not so satisfied, then the regional service center director shall forward the petition to the district director having jurisdiction over the place of the alien's residence so that an interview of both the alien and the alien's spouse may be conducted. The director must either waive the requirement for an interview and adjudicate the petition or arrange for an interview within 90 days of the date on which the petition was properly filed.

(2) *Location of interview.* Unless waived, an interview on the Form I–751 shall be conducted by an immigration examiner or other officer so designated by the district director at the district office, files control office or suboffice having jurisdiction over the residence of the joint petitioners.

(3) *Termination of status for failure to appear for interview.* If the conditional resident alien and/or the petitioning spouse fail to appear for an interview in connection with the joint petition required by section 216(c) of the Act, the alien's permanent residence status will be automatically terminated as of the second anniversary of the date on which the alien obtained permanent residence. The alien shall be provided with written notification of the termination and the reasons therefor, and a notice to appear shall be issued placing

the alien under removal proceedings. The alien may seek review of the decision to terminate his or her status in such proceedings, but the burden shall be on the alien to establish compliance with the interview requirements. If the alien submits a written request that the interview be rescheduled or that the interview be waived, and the director determines that there is good cause for granting the request, the interview may be rescheduled or waived, as appropriate. If the interview is rescheduled at the request of the petitioners, the Service shall not be required to conduct the interview within the 90-day period following the filing of the petition.

(c) *Adjudication of petition.* The director shall adjudicate the petition within 90 days of the date of the interview, unless the interview is waived in accordance with paragraph (b)(1) of this section. In adjudicating the petition the director shall determine whether—

(1) The qualifying marriage was entered into in accordance with the laws of the place where the marriage took place;

(2) The qualifying marriage has been judicially annulled or terminated, other than through the death of a spouse;

(3) The qualifying marriage was entered into for the purpose of procuring permanent residence status for the alien; or

(4) A fee or other consideration was given (other than a fee or other consideration to an attorney for assistance in preparation of a lawful petition) in connection with the filing of the petition through which the alien obtained conditional permanent residence. If derogatory information is determined regarding any of these issues, the director shall offer the petitioners the opportunity to rebut such information. If the petitioners fail to overcome such derogatory information the director may deny the joint petition, terminate the alien's permanent residence, and issue a notice to appear to initiate removal proceedings. If derogatory information not relating to any of these issues is determined during the course of the interview, such information shall be forwarded to the investigations unit for appropriate action. If no unresolved derogatory information is determined relating to these issues, the petition shall be approved and the conditional basis of the alien's permanent residence status removed, regardless of any action taken or contemplated regarding other possible grounds for removal.

(d) *Decision*—(1) *Approval.* If the director approves the joint petition he or she shall provide written notice of the decision to the alien and shall require the alien to report to the appropriate office of the Service for processing for a new Permanent Resident Card (if necessary), at which time the alien shall surrender any Permanent Resident Card previously issued.

(2) *Denial.* If the director denies the joint petition, he or she shall provide written notice to the alien of the decision and the reason(s) therefor and shall issue a notice to appear under section 239 of the Act and 8 CFR part 239. The alien's lawful permanent resident status shall be terminated as of the date of the director's written decision. The alien shall also be instructed to surrender any Permanent Resident Card previously issued by the Service. No appeal shall lie from the decision of the director; however, the alien may seek review of the decision in removal proceedings. In such proceedings the burden of proof shall be on the Service to establish, by a preponderance of the evidence, that the facts and information set forth by the petitioners are not true or that the petition was properly denied.

[53 FR 30018, Aug. 10, 1988, as amended at 54 FR 30369, July 20, 1989; 59 FR 26590, May 23, 1994; 62 FR 10349, Mar. 6, 1997; 63 FR 70315, Dec. 21, 1998; 74 FR 26939, June 5, 2009]

§216.5 Waiver of requirement to file joint petition to remove conditions by alien spouse.

(a) *General.* (1) A conditional resident alien who is unable to meet the requirements under section 216 of the Act for a joint petition for removal of the conditional basis of his or her permanent resident status may file Form I–751, Petition to Remove the Conditions on Residence, if the alien requests a waiver, was not at fault in failing to meet the filing requirement, and the conditional resident alien is able to establish that:

(i) Deportation or removal from the United States would result in extreme hardship;

(ii) The marriage upon which his or her status was based was entered into in good faith by the conditional resident alien, but the marriage was terminated other than by death, and the conditional resident was not at fault in failing to file a timely petition; or

(iii) The qualifying marriage was entered into in good faith by the conditional resident but during the marriage the alien spouse or child was battered by or subjected to extreme cruelty committed by the citizen or permanent resident spouse or parent.

(2) A conditional resident who is in exclusion, deportation, or removal proceedings may apply for the waiver only until such time as there is a final order of exclusion, deportation or removal.

(b) *Fee.* Form I–751 shall be accompanied by the appropriate fee required under §103.7(b) of this Chapter.

(c) [Reserved]

(d) *Interview.* The service center director may refer the application to the appropriate local office and require that the alien appear for an interview in connection with the application for a waiver. The director shall deny the application and initiate removal proceedings if the alien fails to appear for the interview as required, unless the alien establishes good cause for such failure and the interview is rescheduled.

(e) *Adjudication of waiver application*—(1) *Application based on claim of hardship.* In considering an application for a waiver based upon an alien's claim that extreme hardship would result from the alien's removal from the United States, the director shall take into account only those factors that arose subsequent to the alien's entry as a conditional permanent resident. The director shall bear in mind that any removal from the United States is likely to result in a certain degree of hardship, and that only in those cases where the hardship is extreme should the application for a waiver be granted. The burden of establishing that extreme hardship exists rests solely with the applicant.

(2) *Application for waiver based upon the alien's claim that the marriage was entered into in good faith.* In considering whether an alien entered into a qualifying marriage in good faith, the director shall consider evidence relating to the amount of commitment by both parties to the marital relationship. Such evidence may include—

(i) Documentation relating to the degree to which the financial assets and liabilities of the parties were combined;

(ii) Documentation concerning the length of time during which the parties cohabited after the marriage and after the alien obtained permanent residence;

(iii) Birth certificates of children born to the marriage; and

(iv) Other evidence deemed pertinent by the director.

(3) *Application for waiver based on alien's claim of having been battered or subjected to extreme mental cruelty.* A conditional resident who entered into the qualifying marriage in good faith, and who was battered or was the subject of extreme cruelty or whose child was battered by or was the subject of extreme cruelty perpetrated by the United States citizen or permanent resident spouse during the marriage, may request a waiver of the joint filing requirement. The conditional resident parent of a battered or abused child may apply for the waiver regardless of the child's citizenship or immigration status.

(i) For the purpose of this chapter the phrase "was battered by or was the subject of extreme cruelty" includes, but is not limited to, being the victim of any act or threatened act of violence, including any forceful detention, which results or threatens to result in physical or mental injury. Psychological or sexual abuse or exploitation, including rape, molestation, incest (if the victim is a minor) or forced prostitution shall be considered acts of violence.

(ii) A conditional resident or former conditional resident who has not departed the United States after termination of resident status may apply for the waiver. The conditional resident may apply for the waiver regardless of his or her present marital status. The conditional resident may still be residing with the citizen or permanent resident spouse, or may be divorced or separated.

(iii) Evidence of physical abuse may include, but is not limited to, expert testimony in the form of reports and affidavits from police, judges, medical personnel, school officials and social service agency personnel. The Service must be satisfied with the credibility of the sources of documentation submitted in support of the application.

(iv) The Service is not in a position to evaluate testimony regarding a claim of extreme mental cruelty provided by unlicensed or untrained individuals. Therefore, all waiver applications based upon claims of extreme mental cruelty must be supported by the evaluation of a professional recognized by the Service as an expert in the field. An evaluation which was obtained in the course of the divorce proceedings may be submitted if it was provided by a professional recognized by the Service as an expert in the field.

(v) The evaluation must contain the professional's full name, professional address and license number. It must also identify the licensing, certifying, or registering authority. The Service retains the right to verify the professional's license.

(vi) The Service's decision on extreme mental cruelty waivers will be based upon the evaluation of the recognized professional. The Service reserves the right to request additional evaluations from expert witnesses chosen by the Service. Requests for additional evaluations must be authorized by the Assistant Regional Commissioner for Adjudications.

(vii) Licensed clinical social workers, psychologists, and psychiatrists are professionals recognized by the Service for the purpose of this section. A clinical social worker who is not licensed only because the state in which he or she practices does not provide for licensing will be considered a licensed professional recognized by the Service if he or she is included in the Register of Clinical Social Workers published by the National Association of Social Workers or is certified by the American Board of Examiners in Clinical Social Work.

(viii) As directed by the statute, the information contained in the application and supporting documents shall not be released without a court order or the written consent of the applicant; or, in the case of a child, the written consent of the parent or legal guardian who filed the waiver application on the child's behalf. Information may be released only to the applicant, his or her authorized representative, an officer of the Department of Justice, or any federal or State law enforcement agency. Any information provided under this part may be used for the purposes of enforcement of the Act or in any criminal proceeding.

(f) *Decision.* The director shall provide the alien with written notice of the decision on the application for waiver. If the decision is adverse, the director shall advise the alien of the reasons therefor, notify the alien of the termination of his or her permanent residence status, instruct the alien to surrender any Permanent Resident Card issued by the Service and issue a notice to appear placing the alien in removal proceedings. No appeal shall lie from the decision of the director; however, the alien may seek review of such decision in removal proceedings.

[53 FR 30018, Aug. 10, 1988, as amended at 56 FR 22637, May 16, 1991; 59 FR 26591, May 23, 1994; 62 FR 10350, Mar. 6, 1997; 63 FR 70315, Dec. 21, 1998; 74 FR 26939, June 5, 2009]

§216.6 Petition by entrepreneur to remove conditional basis of lawful permanent resident status.

(a) *Filing the petition*—(1) *General procedures.* A petition to remove the conditional basis of the permanent resident status of an alien accorded conditional permanent residence pursuant to section 203(b)(5) of the Act must be filed by the alien entrepreneur on Form I–829, Petition by Entrepreneur to Remove Conditions. The alien entrepreneur must file Form I–829 within the 90-day period preceding the second anniversary of his or her admission to the United States as a conditional permanent resident. Before Form I–829 may be considered as properly filed, it must be accompanied by the fee required under §103.7(b)(1) of this chapter, and by documentation as described in paragraph (a)(4) of this section, and it must be properly signed by the alien. Upon receipt of a properly filed Form I–829, the alien's conditional permanent resident status shall be extended automatically, if necessary, until such time as the director has adjudicated the petition. The entrepreneur's spouse and children should be included in the petition to remove conditions. Children who have reached the age of twenty-one or who have married during the period of conditional permanent residence and the former spouse of an entrepreneur, who was divorced from the entrepreneur during the period of conditional permanent residence, may be included in the alien entrepreneur's petition or may file a separate petition.

(2) [Reserved]

(3) *Physical presence at time of filing.* A petition may be filed regardless of whether the alien is physically present in the United States. However, if the alien is outside the United States at the time of filing, he or she must return to the United States, with his or her spouse and children, if necessary, to comply with the interview requirements contained in the Act. Once the petition has been properly filed, the alien may travel outside the United States and return if in possession of documentation as set forth in §211.1(b)(1) of this chapter, provided the alien complies with the interview requirements described in paragraph (b) of this section. An alien who is not physically present in the United States during the filing period but subsequently applies for admission to the United States shall be processed in accordance with §235.11 of this chapter.

(4) *Documentation.* The petition for removal of conditions must be accompanied by the following evidence:

(i) Evidence that a commercial enterprise was established by the alien. Such evidence may include, but is not limited to, Federal income tax returns;

(ii) Evidence that the alien invested or was actively in the process of investing the requisite capital. Such evidence may include, but is not limited to, an audited financial statement or other probative evidence; and

(iii) Evidence that the alien sustained the actions described in paragraph (a)(4)(i) and (a)(4)(ii) of this section throughout the period of the alien's residence in the United States. The alien will be considered to have sustained the actions required for removal of conditions if he or she has, in good faith, substantially met the capital investment requirement of the statute and continuously maintained his or her capital investment over the two years of conditional residence. Such evidence may include, but is not limited to, bank statements, invoices, receipts, contracts, business licenses, Federal or State income tax returns, and Federal or State quarterly tax statements.

(iv) Evidence that the alien created or can be expected to create within a reasonable time ten full-time jobs for qualifying employees. In the case of a "troubled business" as defined in 8 CFR 204.6(j)(4)(ii), the alien entrepreneur must submit evidence that the commercial enterprise maintained the number of existing employees at no less than the pre-investment level for the period following his or her admission as a conditional permanent resident. Such evidence may include payroll records, relevant tax documents, and Forms I–9.

(5) *Termination of status for failure to file petition.* Failure to properly file Form I–829 within the 90-day period immediately preceding the second anniversary of the date on which the alien obtained lawful permanent residence on a conditional basis shall result in the automatic termination of the alien's permanent resident status and the initiation of deportation proceedings. The director shall send a written notice of termination and an order to show cause to an alien entrepreneur who fails to timely file a petition for removal of conditions. No appeal shall lie from this decision; however, the alien may request a review of the determination during deportation proceedings. In deportation proceedings, the burden of proof shall rest with the alien to show by a preponderance of the evidence that he or she complied with the requirement to file the petition within the designated period. The director may deem the petition to have been filed prior to the second anniversary of the alien's obtaining conditional permanent resident status and accept and consider a late

petition if the alien demonstrates to the director's satisfaction that failure to file a timely petition was for good cause and due to extenuating circumstances. If the late petition is filed prior to jurisdiction vesting with the immigration judge in deportation proceedings and the director excuses the late filing and approves the petition, he or she shall restore the alien's permanent resident status, remove the conditional basis of such status, and cancel any outstanding order to show cause in accordance with §242.7 of this chapter. If the petition is not filed until after jurisdiction vests with the immigration judge, the immigration judge may terminate the matter upon joint motion by the alien and the Service.

(6) *Death of entrepreneur and effect on spouse and children.* If an entrepreneur dies during the prescribed two-year period of conditional permanent residence, the spouse and children of the entrepreneur will be eligible for removal of conditions if it can be demonstrated that the conditions set forth in paragraph (a)(4) of this section have been met.

(b) *Petition review*—(1) *Authority to waive interview.* The director of the service center shall review the Form I–829 and the supporting documents to determine whether to waive the interview required by the Act. If satisfied that the requirements set forth in paragraph (c)(1) of this section have been met, the service center director may waive the interview and approve the petition. If not so satisfied, then the service center director shall forward the petition to the district director having jurisdiction over the location of the alien entrepreneur's commercial enterprise in the United States so that an interview of the alien entrepreneur may be conducted. The director must either waive the requirement for an interview and adjudicate the petition or arrange for an interview within 90 days of the date on which the petition was properly filed.

(2) *Location of interview.* Unless waived, an interview relating to the Form I–829 shall be conducted by an immigration examiner or other officer so designated by the district director at the district office that has jurisdiction over the location of the alien entrepreneur's commercial enterprise in the United States.

(3) *Termination of status for failure to appear for interview.* If the alien fails to appear for an interview in connection with the petition when requested by the Service, the alien's permanent resident status will be automatically terminated as of the second anniversary of the date on which the alien obtained permanent residence. The alien will be provided with written notification of the termination and the reasons therefore, and an order to show cause shall be issued placing the alien under deportation proceedings. The alien may seek review of the decision to terminate his or her status in such proceedings, but the burden shall be on the alien to establish by a preponderance of the evidence that he or she complied with the interview requirements. If the alien has failed to appear for a scheduled interview, he or she may submit a written request to the district director asking that the interview be rescheduled or that the interview be waived. That request should explain his or her failure to appear for the scheduled interview, and if a request for waiver of the interview, the reasons such waiver should be granted. If the district director determines that there is good cause for granting the request, the interview may be rescheduled or waived, as appropriate. If the district director waives the interview, he or she shall restore the alien's conditional permanent resident status, cancel any outstanding order to show cause in accordance with §242.7 of this chapter, and proceed to adjudicate the alien's petition. If the district director reschedules that alien's interview, he or she shall restore the alien's conditional permanent resident status, and cancel any outstanding order to show cause in accordance with §242.7 of this chapter. If the interview is rescheduled at the request of the alien, the Service shall not be required to conduct the interview within the 90-day period following the filing of the petition.

(c) *Adjudication of petition.* (1) The decision on the petition shall be made within 90 days of the date of filing or within 90 days of the interview, whichever is later. In adjudicating the petition, the director shall determine whether:

(i) A commercial enterprise was established by the alien;

(ii) The alien invested or was actively in the process of investing the requisite capital; and

(iii) The alien sustained the actions described in paragraphs (c)(1)(i) and (c)(1)(ii) of this section throughout the period of the alien's residence in the United States. The alien will be considered to have sustained the actions required for removal of conditions if he or she has, in good faith, substantially met the capital investment requirement of the statute and continuously maintained his or her capital investment over the two years of conditional residence.

(iv) The alien created or can be expected to create within a reasonable period of time ten full-time jobs to qualifying employees. In the case of a "troubled business" as defined in 8 CFR 204.6(j)(4)(ii), the alien maintained the number of existing employees at no less than the pre-investment level for the previous two years.

(2) If derogatory information is determined regarding any of these issues or it becomes known to the government that the entrepreneur obtained his or her investment funds through other than legal means (such as through the sale of illegal drugs), the director shall offer the alien entrepreneur the opportunity to rebut such information. If the alien entrepreneur fails to overcome such derogatory information or evidence the investment funds were obtained through other than legal means, the director may deny the petition, terminate the alien's permanent resident status, and issue an order to show cause. If derogatory information not relating to any of these issues is determined during the course of the interview, such information shall be forwarded to the investigations unit for appropriate action. If no unresolved derogatory information is determined relating to these issues, the petition shall be approved and the conditional basis of the alien's permanent resident status removed, regardless of any action taken or contemplated regarding other possible grounds for deportation.

(d) *Decision*—(1) *Approval.* If, after initial review or after the interview, the director approves the petition, he or she will remove the conditional basis of the alien's permanent resident status as of the second anniversary of the alien's entry as a conditional permanent resident. He or she shall provide written notice of the decision to the alien and shall require the alien to report to the appropriate district office for processing for a new Permanent Resident Card, Form I–551, at which time the alien shall surrender any Permanent Resident Card previously issued.

(2) *Denial.* If, after initial review or after the interview, the director denies the petition, he or she shall provide written notice to the alien of the decision and the reason(s) therefor, and shall issue an order to show cause why the alien should not be deported from the United States. The alien's lawful permanent resident status and that of his or her spouse and any children shall be terminated as of the date of the director's written decision. The alien shall also be instructed to surrender any Permanent Resident Card previously issued by the Service. No appeal shall lie from this decision; however, the alien may seek review of the decision in deportation proceedings. In deportation proceedings, the burden shall rest with the Service to establish by a preponderance of the evidence that the facts and information in the alien's petition for removal of conditions are not true and that the petition was properly denied.

[59 FR 26591, May 23, 1994, as amended at 63 FR 70315, Dec. 21, 1998; 74 FR 26939, June 5, 2009]

PART 217—VISA WAIVER PROGRAM

Sec.

AUTHORITY: 8 U.S.C. 1103, 1187; 8 CFR part 2.

SOURCE: 53 FR 24901, June 30, 1988, unless otherwise noted.

§217.1 Scope.

The Visa Waiver Pilot Program (VWPP) described in this section is established pursuant to the provisions of section 217 of the Act.

[62 FR 10351, Mar. 6, 1997]

§217.2 Eligibility.

(a) *Definitions.* As used in this part, the term:

Carrier refers to the owner, charterer, lessee, or authorized agent of any commercial vessel or commercial aircraft engaged in transporting passengers to the United States from a foreign place.

Designated country refers to Andorra, Australia, Austria, Belgium, Brunei, Chile, Czech Republic, Denmark, Estonia, Finland, France, Germany, Greece, Hungary, Iceland, Ireland, Italy, Japan, Latvia, Liechtenstein, Lithuania, Luxembourg, Malta, Monaco, the Netherlands, New Zealand, Norway, Portugal, Republic of Korea, San Marino, Singapore, Slovak Republic, Slovenia, Spain, Sweden, Switzerland, Taiwan, and the United Kingdom. The United Kingdom refers only to British citizens who have the unrestricted right of permanent abode in the United Kingdom (England, Scotland, Wales, Northern Ireland, the Channel Islands and the Isle of Man); it does not refer to British overseas citizens, British dependent territories' citizens, or citizens of British Commonwealth countries. Taiwan refers only to individuals who have unrestricted right of permanent abode on Taiwan and are in possession of an electronic passport bearing a personal identification (household registration) number.

Round trip ticket means any return trip transportation ticket in the name of an arriving Visa Waiver Pilot Program applicant on a participating carrier valid for at least 1 year, electronic ticket record, airline employee passes indicating return passage, individual vouchers for return passage, group vouchers for return passage for charter flights, and military travel orders which include military dependents for return to duty stations outside the United States on U.S. military flights. A period of validity of 1 year need not be reflected on the ticket itself, provided that the carrier agrees that it will honor the return portion of the ticket at any time, as provided in Form I-775, Visa Waiver Pilot Program Agreement.

(b) *Special program requirements*—(1) *General.* In addition to meeting all of the requirements for the Visa Waiver Pilot Program specified in section 217 of the Act, each applicant must possess a valid, unexpired passport issued by a designated country and present a completed, signed Form I-94W, Nonimmigrant Visa Waiver Arrival/Departure Form.

(2) *Persons previously removed as deportable aliens.* Aliens who have been deported or removed from the United States, after having been determined deportable, require the consent of the Attorney General to apply for admission to the United States pursuant to section 212(a)(9)(A)(iii) of the Act. Such persons may not be admitted to the United States under the provisions of this part notwithstanding the fact that the required consent of the Attorney General may have been secured. Such aliens must secure a visa in order to be admitted to the United States as nonimmigrants, unless otherwise exempt.

(c) *Restrictions on manner of arrival*—(1) *Applicants arriving by air and sea.* Applicants must arrive on a carrier that is signatory to a Visa Waiver Pilot Program Agreement and at the time of arrival must have a round trip ticket that will transport the traveler out of the United States to any other foreign port or place as long as the trip does not terminate in contiguous territory or an adjacent island; except that the round trip ticket may transport the traveler to contiguous territory or an adjacent island, if the traveler is a resident of the country of destination.

(2) *Applicants arriving at land border ports-of-entry.* Any Visa Waiver Pilot Program applicant arriving at a land border port-of-entry must provide evidence to the immigration officer of financial solvency and a domicile abroad to which the applicant intends to return. An applicant arriving at a land-border port-of-entry will be charged a fee as prescribed in §103.7(b)(1) of this

chapter for issuance of Form I–94W, Nonimmigrant Visa Waiver Arrival/Departure Form. A round-trip transportation ticket is not required of applicants at land border ports-of-entry.

(d) *Aliens in transit.* An alien who is in transit through the United States is eligible to apply for admission under the Visa Waiver Pilot Program, provided the applicant meets all other program requirements.

[62 FR 10351, Mar. 6, 1997, as amended at 62 FR 50999, Sept. 30, 1997; 64 FR 42007, Aug. 3, 1999; 67 FR 7945, Feb. 21, 2002; 68 FR 10957, Mar. 7, 2003; 73 FR 67712, Nov. 17, 2008; 73 FR 79597, Dec. 30, 2008; 75 FR 15992, Mar. 31, 2010; 77 FR 64411, Oct. 22, 2012; 79 FR 17854, Mar. 31, 2014]

§ 217.3 Maintenance of status.

(a) *Satisfactory departure.* If an emergency prevents an alien admitted under this part from departing from the United States within his or her period of authorized stay, the district director having jurisdiction over the place of the alien's temporary stay may, in his or her discretion, grant a period of satisfactory departure not to exceed 30 days. If departure is accomplished during that period, the alien is to be regarded as having satisfactorily accomplished the visit without overstaying the allotted time.

(b) *Readmission after departure to contiguous territory or adjacent island.* An alien admitted to the United States under this part may be readmitted to the United States after a departure to foreign contiguous territory or adjacent island for the balance of his or her original Visa Waiver Pilot Program admission period if he or she is otherwise admissible and meets all the conditions of this part with the exception of arrival on a signatory carrier.

[62 FR 10351, Mar. 6, 1997]

§ 217.4 Inadmissibility and deportability.

(a) *Determinations of inadmissibility.* (1) An alien who applies for admission under the provisions of section 217 of the Act, who is determined by an immigration officer not to be eligible for admission under that section or to be inadmissible to the United States under one or more of the grounds of inadmissibility listed in section 212 of the Act (other than for lack of a visa), or who is in possession of and presents fraudulent or counterfeit travel documents, will be refused admission into the United States and removed. Such refusal and removal shall be made at the level of the port director or officer-in-charge, or an officer acting in that capacity, and shall be effected without referral of the alien to an immigration judge for further inquiry, examination, or hearing, except that an alien who presents himself or herself as an applicant for admission under section 217 of the Act and applies for asylum in the United States must be issued a Form I–863, Notice of Referral to Immigration Judge, for a proceeding in accordance with 8 CFR 208.2(c)(1) and (c)(2).

(2) The removal of an alien under this section may be deferred if the alien is paroled into the custody of a Federal, State, or local law enforcement agency for criminal prosecution or punishment. This section in no way diminishes the discretionary authority of the Attorney General enumerated in section 212(d) of the Act.

(3) Refusal of admission under paragraph (a)(1) of this section shall not constitute removal for purposes of the Act.

(b) *Determination of deportability.* (1) An alien who has been admitted to the United States under the provisions of section 217 of the Act and of this part who is determined by an immigration officer to be deportable from the United States under one or more of the grounds of deportability listed in section 237 of the Act shall be removed from the United States to his or her country of nationality or last residence. Such removal shall be determined by the district director who has jurisdiction over the place where the alien is found, and shall be effected without referral of the alien to an immigration judge for a determination of deportability, except that an alien who was admitted as a Visa Waiver Program visitor who applies for asylum in the United States must be issued a Form I–863 for a proceeding in accordance with 8 CFR 208.2(c)(1) and (c)(2).

(2) Removal by the district director under paragraph (b)(1) of this section is equivalent in all respects and has the same consequences as removal after

proceedings conducted under section 240 of the Act.

(c)(1) *Removal of inadmissible aliens who arrived by air or sea.* Removal of an alien from the United States under this section may be effected using the return portion of the round trip passage presented by the alien at the time of entry to the United States as required by section 217(a)(7) of the Act. Such removal shall be on the first available means of transportation to the alien's point of embarkation to the United States. Nothing in this part absolves the carrier of the responsibility to remove any inadmissible or deportable alien at carrier expense, as provided in the carrier agreement.

(2) *Removal of inadmissible and deportable aliens who arrived at land border ports-of-entry.* Removal under this section will be by the first available means of transportation deemed appropriate by the district director.

[53 FR 24901, June 30, 1988, as amended at 56 FR 32953, July 18, 1991; 62 FR 10351, Mar. 6, 1997; 74 FR 55738, Oct. 28, 2009]

§217.5 Electronic System for Travel Authorization.

(a) *Travel authorization required.* Each nonimmigrant alien intending to travel by air or sea to the United States under the Visa Waiver Program (VWP) must, within the time specified in paragraph (b) of this section, receive a travel authorization, which is a positive determination of eligibility to travel to the United States under the VWP via the Electronic System for Travel Authorization (ESTA), from CBP. In order to receive a travel authorization, each nonimmigrant alien intending to travel to the United States by air or sea under the VWP must provide the data elements set forth in paragraph (c) of this section to CBP, in English, in the manner specified herein, and must pay a fee as described in paragraph (h) of this section.

(b) *Time.* Each alien falling within the provisions of paragraph (a) of this section must receive a travel authorization prior to embarking on a carrier for travel to the United States.

(c) *Required elements.* ESTA will collect such information as the Secretary deems necessary to issue a travel authorization, as reflected by the I–94W Nonimmigrant Alien Arrival/Departure Form (I–94W).

(d) *Duration.* (1) *General Rule.* A travel authorization issued under ESTA will be valid for a period of two years from the date of issuance, unless the passport of the authorized alien will expire in less than two years, in which case the authorization will be valid until the date of expiration of the passport.

(2) *Exception.* For travelers from countries which have not entered into agreements with the United States whereby their passports are recognized as valid for the return of the bearer to the country of the foreign-issuing authority for a period of six months beyond the expiration date specified in the passport, a travel authorization issued under ESTA is not valid beyond the six months prior to the expiration date of the passport. Travelers from these countries whose passports will expire in six months or less will not receive a travel authorization.

(3) The Secretary, in consultation with the Secretary of State, may increase or decrease ESTA travel authorization validity period otherwise authorized by subparagraph (1) for a designated VWP country. Notice of any change to ESTA travel authorization validity periods will be published in the FEDERAL REGISTER. The ESTA Web site will be updated to reflect the specific ESTA travel authorization validity period for each VWP country.

(e) *New travel authorization required.* A new travel authorization is required if any of the following occur:

(1) The alien is issued a new passport;

(2) The alien changes his or her name;

(3) The alien changes his or her gender;

(4) The alien's country of citizenship changes; or

(5) The circumstances underlying the alien's previous responses to any of the ESTA application questions requiring a "yes" or "no" response (eligibility questions) have changed.

(f) *Limitations.* (1) *Current authorization period.* An authorization under ESTA is a positive determination that an alien is eligible, and grants the alien permission, to travel to the United States under the VWP and to apply for admission under the VWP during the period of time the travel authorization is valid. An authorization under ESTA is not a determination that the alien is admissible to the United States. A determination of admissibility is made only after an applicant for admission is inspected by a CBP Officer at a U.S. port of entry.

(2) *Not a determination of visa eligibility.* A determination under ESTA that an alien is not eligible to travel to the United States under the VWP is not a determination that the alien is ineligible for a visa to travel to the United States and does not preclude the alien from applying for a visa before a United States consular officer.

(3) *Judicial review.* Notwithstanding any other provision of law, a determination under ESTA is not subject to judicial review pursuant to 8 U.S.C. 217(h)(3)(C)(iv).

(4) *Revocation.* A determination under ESTA that an alien is eligible to travel to the United States to apply for admission under the VWP may be revoked at the discretion of the Secretary.

(g) *Compliance date.* Once ESTA is implemented as a mandatory program, 60 days following publication by the Secretary of a notice in the FEDERAL REGISTER, citizens and eligible nationals of countries that participate in the VWP planning to travel to the United States under the VWP must comply with the requirements of this section. As new countries are added to the VWP, citizens and eligible nationals of those countries will be required to obtain a travel authorization via ESTA prior to traveling to the United States under the VWP.

(h) *Fee.* (1) Until September 30, 2015, the fee for an approved ESTA is $14.00, which is the sum of two amounts: a $10 travel promotion fee to fund the Corporation for Travel Promotion and a $4.00 operational fee to at least ensure recovery of the full costs of providing and administering the system. In the event the ESTA application is denied, the fee is $4.00 to cover the operational costs.

(2) Beginning October 1, 2020, the fee for using ESTA is an operational fee of $4.00 to at least ensure recovery of the full costs of providing and administering the system.

[73 FR 32452, June 9, 2008, as amended at 75 FR 47708, Aug. 9, 2010; 80 FR 32294, June 8, 2015]

§217.6 Carrier agreements.

(a) *General.* The carrier agreements referred to in section 217(e) of the Act shall be made by the Commissioner on behalf of the Attorney General and shall be on Form I–775, Visa Waiver Pilot Program Agreement.

(b) *Termination of agreements.* The Commissioner, on behalf of the Attorney General, may terminate any carrier agreement under this part, with 5 days notice to a carrier, for the carrier's failure to meet the terms of such agreement. As a matter of discretion, the Commissioner may notify a carrier of the existence of a basis for termination of a carrier agreement under this part and allow the carrier a period not to exceed 15 days within which the carrier may bring itself into compliance with the terms of the carrier agreement. The agreement shall be subject to cancellation by either party for any reason upon 15 days' written notice to the other party.

[62 FR 10352, Mar. 6, 1997]

§217.7 Electronic data transmission requirement.

(a) An alien who applies for admission under the provisions of section 217 of the Act after arriving via sea or air at a port of entry will not be admitted under the Visa Waiver Program unless an appropriate official of the carrier transporting the alien electronically transmitted to Customs and Border Protection (CBP) passenger arrival manifest data relative to that alien passenger in accordance with 19 CFR 4.7b or 19 CFR 122.49a. Upon departure from the United States by sea or air of an alien admitted under the Visa Waiver Program, an appropriate official of the transporting carrier must electronically transmit to CBP departure manifest data relative to that alien passenger in accordance with 19 CFR 4.64 and 19 CFR 122.75a.

(b) If a carrier fails to submit the required electronic arrival or departure manifests specified in paragraph (a) of this section, CBP will evaluate the carrier's compliance with immigration requirements as a whole. CBP will inform the carrier of any noncompliance and then may revoke any contract agreements between CBP and the carrier. The carrier may also be subject to fines for failure to comply with manifest requirements or other statutory provisions. CBP will also review each Visa Waiver Program applicant who applies for admission and, on a case-by-case basis, may authorize a waiver under current CBP policy and guidelines or deny the applicant admission into the United States.

[70 FR 17848, Apr. 7, 2005]

PART 221—ADMISSION OF VISITORS OR STUDENTS

AUTHORITY: 8 U.S.C. 1101, 1103, 1201; 8 CFR part 2.

§ 221.1 Admission under bond.

The district director having jurisdiction over the intended place of residence of an alien may accept a bond on behalf of an alien defined in section 101(a)(15)(B) or (F) of the Act prior to the issuance of a visa to the alien or upon receipt of a request directly from a U.S. consular officer or upon presentation by an interested person of a notification from the consular officer requiring such a bond; such a bond also may be accepted by the district director with jurisdiction over the port of entry or preinspection station where inspection of the alien takes place. Upon acceptance of such a bond, the district director shall notify the United States consular officer who requested the bond, giving the date and place of acceptance and amount of the bond. All bonds given as a condition of admission of an alien under section 221(g) of the Act shall be executed on Form I–352. For procedures relating to bond riders, acceptable sureties, cancellation, or breaching of bonds, see § 103.6 of this chapter.

[32 FR 9626, July 4, 1967, as amended at 34 FR 1008, Jan. 23, 1969; 62 FR 10352, Mar. 6, 1997]

PART 223—REENTRY PERMITS, REFUGEE TRAVEL DOCUMENTS, AND ADVANCE PAROLE DOCUMENTS

AUTHORITY: 8 U.S.C. 1103, 1181, 1182, 1186a, 1203, 1225, 1226, 1227, 1251; Protocol Relating to the Status of Refugees, November 1, 1968, 19 U.S.T. 6223 (TIAS) 6577; 8 CFR part 2.

SOURCE: 59 FR 1464, Jan. 11, 1994, unless otherwise noted.

§ 223.1 Purpose of documents.

(a) *Reentry permit.* A reentry permit allows a permanent resident to apply for admission to the United States upon return from abroad during the period of the permit's validity without the necessity of obtaining a returning resident visa.

(b) *Refugee travel document.* A refugee travel document is issued pursuant to this part and article 28 of the United Nations Convention of July 29, 1951, for the purpose of travel. Except as provided in § 223.3(d)(2)(i), a person who holds refugee status pursuant to section 207 of the Act, or asylum status pursuant to section 208 of the Act, must have a refugee travel document to return to the United States after temporary travel abroad unless he or she is in possession of a valid advance parole document.

[59 FR 1464, Jan. 11, 1994, as amended at 62 FR 10352, Mar. 6, 1997]

§ 223.2 Application and processing.

(a) *Application.* An applicant must submit an application for a reentry permit, refugee travel document, or advance parole on the form designated by USCIS with the fee prescribed in 8 CFR 103.7(b)(1) and in accordance with the form instructions.

(b) *Filing eligibility*—(1) *Reentry permit.* An applicant for a reentry permit must file such application while in the United States and in status as a lawful permanent resident or conditional permanent resident.

(2) *Refugee travel document.* (i) Except as provided in paragraph (b)(2)(ii) of this section, an applicant for a refugee

travel document must submit the application while in the United States and in valid refugee status under section 207 of the Act, valid asylum status under section 208 of the Act or is a permanent resident who received such status as a direct result of his or her asylum or refugee status.

(ii) *Discretionary authority to accept a refugee travel document application from an alien not within the United States.* As a matter of discretion, the Service office with jurisdiction over a port-of-entry or pre-flight inspection location where the alien is seeking admission, or the overseas Service office where the alien is physically present, may accept and adjudicate an application for a refugee travel document from an alien who previously had been admitted to the United States as a refugee, or who previously had been granted asylum status in the United States, and who departed from the United States without having applied for such refugee travel document, provided the officer:

(A) Is satisfied that the alien did not intend to abandon his or her refugee or asylum status at the time of departure from the United States;

(B) The alien did not engage in any activities while outside the United States that would be inconsistent with continued refugee or asylum status; and

(C) The alien has been outside the United States for less than 1 year since his or her last departure.

(c) *Ineligibility*—(1) *Prior document still valid.* An application for a reentry permit or refugee travel document will be denied if the applicant was previously issued a reentry permit or refugee travel document which is still valid, unless it was returned to USCIS or it is demonstrated that it was lost.

(2) *Extended absences.* A reentry permit issued to a person who, since becoming a permanent resident or during the last five years, whichever is less, has been outside the United States for more than four years in the aggregate, shall be limited to a validity of one year, except that a permit with a validity of two years may be issued to:

(i) A permanent resident described in 8 CFR 211.1(a)(6) or (a)(7);

(ii) A permanent resident employed by a public international organization of which the United States is a member by treaty or statute, and his or her permanent resident spouse and children; or

(iii) A permanent resident who is a professional athlete who regularly competes in the United States and worldwide.

(3) *Permanent resident entitled to nonimmigrant diplomatic or treaty status.* A permanent resident entitled to nonimmigrant status under section 101(a)(15)(A), (E), or (G) of the Act because of occupational status may only be issued a reentry permit if the applicant executes and submits with the application, or has previously executed and submitted, a written waiver as required by 8 CFR part 247.

(d) *Effect of travel before a decision is made.* Departure from the United States before a decision is made on an application for a reentry permit or refugee travel document will not affect the application.

(e) *Processing.* USCIS may approve or deny a request for a reentry permit or refugee travel document as an exercise of discretion. If it approves the application, USCIS will issue an appropriate document.

(f) *Effect on proceedings.* Issuance of a reentry permit or refugee travel document to a person in exclusion, deportation, or removal proceedings shall not affect those proceedings.

(g) *Appeal.* Denial of an application for a reentry permit or refugee travel document may be appealed in accordance with 8 CFR 103.3.

[76 FR 53790, Aug. 29, 2011]

§ 223.3 Validity and effect on admissibility.

(a) *Validity*—(1) *Reentry permit.* Except as provided in § 223.2(c)(2), a reentry permit issued to a permanent resident shall be valid for 2 years from the date of issuance. A reentry permit issued to a conditional permanent resident shall be valid for 2 years from the date of issuance, or to the date the conditional permanent resident must apply for removal of the conditions on his or her status, whichever comes first.

(2) *Refugee travel document.* A refugee travel document shall be valid for 1 year, or to the date the refugee or asylee status expires, whichever comes first.

(b) *Invalidation.* A document issued under this part is invalid if obtained through material false representation or concealment, or if the person is ordered excluded or deported. A refugee travel document is also invalid if the United Nations Convention of July 28, 1951, ceases to apply or does not apply to the person as provided in Article 1C, D, E, or F of the convention.

(c) *Extension.* A reentry permit or refugee travel document may not be extended.

(d) *Effect on admissibility*—(1) *Reentry permit.* A permanent resident or conditional permanent resident in possession of a valid reentry permit who is otherwise admissible shall not be deemed to have abandoned status based solely on the duration of an absence or absences while the permit is valid.

(2) *Refugee travel document*—(i) *Inspection and immigration status.* Upon arrival in the United States, an alien who presents a valid unexpired refugee travel document, or who has been allowed to file an application for a refugee travel document and this application has been approved under the procedure set forth in § 223.2(b)(2)(ii), shall be examined as to his or her admissibility under the Act. An alien shall be accorded the immigration status endorsed in his or her refugee travel document, or (in the case of an alien discussed in § 223.2(b)(2)(ii)) which will be endorsed in such document, unless he or she is no longer eligible for that status, or he or she applies for and is found eligible for some other immigration status.

(ii) *Inadmissibility.* If an alien who presents a valid unexpired refugee travel document appears to the examining immigration officer to be inadmissible, he or she shall be referred for proceedings under section 240 of the Act. Section 235(c) of the Act shall not be applicable.

[59 FR 1464, Jan. 11, 1994, as amended at 62 FR 10353, Mar. 6, 1997]

PART 231—ARRIVAL AND DEPARTURE MANIFESTS

Sec.

AUTHORITY: 8 U.S.C. 1101, 1103, 1182, 1221, 1228, 1229; 8 CFR part 2.

§ 231.1 Electronic manifest and I–94 requirement for passengers and crew onboard arriving vessels and aircraft.

(a) *Electronic submission of manifests.* Provisions setting forth requirements applicable to commercial carriers regarding the electronic transmission of arrival manifests covering passengers and crew members under section 231 of the Act are set forth in 19 CFR 4.7b (passengers and crew members onboard vessels) and in 19 CFR 122.49a (passengers onboard aircraft) and 122.49b (crew members onboard aircraft).

(b) *Submission of Form I–94*—(1) *General requirement.* In addition to the electronic manifest transmission requirement specified in paragraph (a) of this section, and subject to the exception of paragraph (2) of this paragraph (b), the master or commanding officer, or authorized agent, owner or consignee, of each commercial vessel or aircraft arriving in the United States from any place outside the United States must present to a Customs and Border Protection (CBP) officer at the port of entry a properly completed Arrival/Departure Record, Form I–94 (see § 1.4), for each arriving passenger.

(2) *Exceptions.* The Form I–94 requirement of paragraph (1) of this paragraph (b) does not apply to United States citizens, lawful permanent residents of the United States, immigrants to the United States, or passengers in transit through the United States; nor does it apply to vessels or aircraft arriving directly from Canada on a trip originating in that country or arriving in the Virgin Islands of the United States directly from a trip originating in the British Virgin Islands.

(c) *Progressive clearance.* Inspection of arriving passengers may be deferred at the request of the carrier to an onward port of debarkation. However, verification of transmission of the electronic manifest referred to in paragraph (a) of this section must occur at the first port of arrival. Authorization for this progressive clearance may be granted by the Director, Field Operations, at the first port of arrival. When progressive clearance is requested, the carrier must present the Form I–92 referred to in paragraph (d) of this section in duplicate at the initial port of entry. The original Form I–92 will be processed at the initial port of entry, and the duplicate will be noted and returned to the carrier for presentation at the onward port of debarkation.

(d) *Aircraft/Vessel Report.* A properly completed Aircraft/Vessel Report, Form I–92, must be completed for each arriving aircraft and vessel that is transporting passengers. Submission of the Form I–92 to the CBP officer must be accomplished on the day of arrival.

[70 FR 17849, Apr. 7, 2005, as amended at 78 FR 18472, Mar. 27, 2013]

§ 231.2 Electronic manifest and I–94 requirement for passengers and crew onboard departing vessels and aircraft.

(a) *Electronic submission of manifests.* Provisions setting forth requirements applicable to commercial carriers regarding the electronic transmission of departure manifests covering passengers and crew members under section 231 of the Act are set forth in 19 CFR 4.64 (passengers and crew members onboard vessels) and in 19 CFR 122.75a (passengers onboard aircraft) and 122.75b (crew members onboard aircraft).

(b) *Submission of Form I–94*—(1) *General requirement.* In addition to the electronic manifest transmission requirement specified in paragraph (a) of this section, and subject to the exception of paragraph (2) of this paragraph (b), the master or commanding officer, or authorized agent, owner, or consignee, of each commercial vessel or aircraft departing from the United States to any place outside the United States must present a properly completed departure portion of an Arrival/Departure Record, Form I–94 (see § 1.4), to the Customs and Border Protection (CBP) officer at the port of departure for each person on board. Whenever possible, the departure Form I–94 presented must be the same form given to the alien at the time of arrival in the United States. The carrier must endorse the I–94 with the departure information on the reverse of the form. Submission of the I–94 to the CBP officer must be accomplished within 48 hours of the departure, exclusive of Saturdays, Sundays, and legal holidays. Failure to submit the departure I–94 within this period may be regarded as a failure to comply with section 231(g) of the Act, unless prior authorization for delayed delivery is obtained from CBP. A non-immigrant alien departing on an aircraft proceeding directly to Canada on a flight terminating in that country must surrender any Form I–94 in his/her possession to the airline agent at the port of departure.

(2) *Exceptions.* The form I–94 requirement of paragraph (1) of this paragraph (b) does not apply to United States citizens, lawful permanent residents of the United States, or passengers in transit through the United States; nor does it apply to a vessel or aircraft departing on a trip directly for and terminating in Canada or departing from the United States Virgin Islands directly to the British Virgin Islands on a trip terminating there.

(c) *Aircraft/Vessel Report.* A properly completed Aircraft/Vessel Report, Form I–92, must be completed for each departing aircraft and vessel that is transporting passengers. Submission of the Form I–92 to the CBP officer must be accomplished on the day of departure.

[70 FR 17849, Apr. 7, 2005, as amended at 78 FR 18472, Mar. 27, 2013]

§ 231.3 Exemptions for private vessels and aircraft.

The provision of this part relating to the presentation of arrival and departure manifests shall not apply to a private vessel or private aircraft. Private aircraft as defined in 19 CFR 122.1(h) are subject to the arrival and departure manifest presentation requirements set forth in 19 CFR 122.22.

[73 FR 68309, Nov. 18, 2008]

PART 232—DETENTION OF ALIENS FOR PHYSICAL AND MENTAL EXAMINATION

Sec.

AUTHORITY: 8 U.S.C. 1103, 1222, 1224, 1252; 8 CFR part 2.

§ 232.1 General.

The manner in which the physical and mental examination of aliens shall be conducted is set forth in 42 CFR part 34.

[38 FR 33061, Nov. 30, 1973, as amended at 38 FR 34315, Dec. 13, 1973. Redesignated at 62 FR 10353, Mar. 6, 1997]

§ 232.2 Examination in the United States of alien applicants for benefits under the immigration laws and other aliens.

(a) *General.* When a medical examination is required of an alien who files an application for status as a permanent resident under section 245 of the Act or part 245 of this chapter, it shall be made by a selected civil surgeon. Such examination shall be performed in accordance with 42 CFR part 34 and any additional instructions and guidelines as may be considered necessary by the U.S. Public Health Service. In any other case in which the Service requests a medical examination of an alien, the examination shall be made by a medical officer of the U.S. Public Health Service, or by a civil surgeon if a medical officer of the U.S. Public Health Service is not located within a reasonable distance or is otherwise not available.

(b) *Selection of civil surgeons.* When a civil surgeon is to perform the examination, he shall be selected by the district director having jurisdiction over the area of the alien's residence. The district director shall select as many civil surgeons, including clinics and local, county and state health departments employing qualified civil surgeons, as he determines to be necessary to serve the needs of the Service in a locality under his jurisdiction. Each civil surgeon selected shall be a licensed physician with no less than 4 years' professional experience. Under usual circumstances physicians will be required to meet the 4 year professional experience criteria. However, at the district director's discretion other physicians with less experience can be designated to address unusual or unforeseen situations as the need arises. Officers of local health departments and medical societies may be consulted to obtain the names of competent surgeons and clinics willing to make the examinations. An understanding shall be reached with respect to the fee which the surgeon or clinic will charge for the examination. The alien shall pay the fee agreed upon directly to the surgeon making the examination.

(c) *Civil surgeon reports*—(1) *Applicants for status of permanent resident.* (i) When an applicant for status as a permanent resident is found upon examination to be free of any defect, disease, or disability listed in section 212(a) of the Act, the civil surgeon shall endorse Form I–486A, Medical Examination and Immigration Interview, and forward it with the X-ray and other pertinent laboratory reports to the immigration office from which the alien was referred, The immigration office may return the X-ray and laboratory reports to the alien. If the applicant is found to be afflicted with a defect, disease or disability listed under section 212(a) of the Act, the civil surgeon shall complete Form OF–157 in duplicate, and forward it with Form I–486A, X-ray, and other pertinent laboratory reports to the immigration office from which the alien was referred.

(ii) If the applicant is found to be afflicted with active tuberculosis and a waiver is granted under section 212(g) of the Act, the immigration office will forward a copy of the completed Form I–601 (Application for Waiver of Grounds of Excludability) and a copy of the Form OF–157 to the Director, Division of Quarantine, Center for Prevention Sevices, Centers for Disease Control, Atlanta, GA 30333.

(iii) If an alien who if found to be mentally retarded or to have had one or more previous attacks of insanity, applies for a waiver of excludability under section 212(g) of the Act, the immigration office will submit to the Director, Division of Quarantine, Center for Prevention Services, Centers for Disease Control, Atlanta, GA 30333, the completed Form I–601, including a copy of the medical report specified in the instructions attached to that form, and a copy of Form OF–157. This official shall review the medical report and advise the Service whether it is acceptable, in accordance with § 212.7(b)(4)(ii) of this chapter.

(iv) In any other case where the applicant has been found to be afflicted with active or inactive tuberculosis or an infectious or noninfectious leprosy condition, the immigration office will forward a copy of Form OF–157 with the applicant's address endorsed on the reverse to the Director, Division of Quarantine, Center for Prevention Services, Centers for Disease Control, Atlanta, GA 30333.

(2) *Other aliens.* The results of the examination of an alien who is not an applicant for status as a permanent resident shall be entered on Form I–141, Medical Certificate, in duplicate. This form shall be returned to the Service office by which the alien was referred.

(d) *U.S. Public Health Service hospital and outpatient clinic reports.* When an applicant for a benefit under the immigration laws, other than an applicant for status as a permanent resident, is examined by a medical officer of the U.S. Public Health Service, the results of the examination shall be entered on Form I–141, Medical Certificate, in duplicate. The form shall be returned to the Service office by which the alien was referred.

[38 FR 33061, Nov. 30, 1973, as amended at 48 FR 30610, July 5, 1983; 52 FR 16194, May 1, 1987. Redesignated at 62 FR 10353, Mar. 6, 1997]

§ 232.3 Arriving aliens.

When a district director has reasonable grounds for believing that persons arriving in the United States should be detained for reasons specified in section 232 of the Act, he or she shall, after consultation with the United States Public Health Service at the port-of-entry, notify the master or agent of the arriving vessel or aircraft of his or her intention to effect such detention by serving on the master or agent Form I–259 in accordance with § 235.3(a) of this chapter.

[62 FR 10353, Mar. 6, 1997]

PART 233—CONTRACTS WITH TRANSPORTATION LINES

Sec.

AUTHORITY: 8 U.S.C. 1101, 1103, 1182, 1221, 1228, 1229, 8 CFR part 2.

SOURCE: Redesignated at 62 FR 10353, Mar. 6, 1997.

§ 233.1 Contracts.

The contracts with transportation lines referred to in section 233(c) of the Act may be entered into by the Executive Associate Commissioner for Programs, or by an immigration officer designated by the Executive Associate Commissioner for Programs on behalf of the government and shall be documented on Form I–420. The contracts with transportation lines referred to in section 233(a) of the Act shall be made by the Commissioner on behalf of the government and shall be documented on Form I–426. The contracts with transportation lines desiring their passengers to be preinspected at places outside the United States shall be made by the Commissioner on behalf of the government and shall be documented on Form I–425; except that contracts for irregularly operated charter flights may be entered into by the Associate Commissioner for Examinations or an immigration officer designated by the Executive Associate Commissioner for Programs and having jurisdiction over the location where the inspection will take place.

[62 FR 10353, Mar. 6, 1997]

§233.2 Transportation lines bringing aliens to the United States from or through foreign contiguous territory or adjacent islands.

Form I–420 shall be signed in duplicate and forwarded to the Headquarters Office of Inspections. After acceptance, each Regional Office of Inspections, the district office and the carrier will be furnished with one copy of the agreement. The transmittal letter to the Headquarters Office of Inspections shall indicate whether the signatory to the agreement is a subsidiary or affiliate of a line which has already signed a similar agreement. Correspondence regarding ancillary contracts for office space and other facilities to be furnished by transportation lines at Service stations in Canada shall be similarly handled.

[57 FR 59907, Dec. 17, 1992]

§233.3 [Reserved]

§233.4 Preinspection outside the United States.

(a) *Form I–425 agreements.* A transportation line bringing applicants for admission to the United States through preinspection sites outside the United States shall enter into an agreement on Form I–425. Such an agreement shall be negotiated directly by the Service's Headquarters Office of Inspections and the head office of the transportation line.

(b) *Signatory lines.* A list of transportation lines with currently valid transportation agreements on Form I–425 is maintained by the Service's Headquarters Office of Inspections and is available upon written request.

[62 FR 10353, Mar. 6, 1997]

§233.5 Aliens entering Guam pursuant to section 14 of Public Law 99–396, "Omnibus Territories Act."

A transportation line bringing aliens to Guam under the visa waiver provisions of §212.1(e) of this chapter shall enter into an agreement on Form I–760. Such agreements shall be negotiated directly by the Service's Headquarters and head offices of the transportation lines.

[62 FR 10353, Mar. 6, 1997]

§233.6 Aliens entering Guam or the Commonwealth of the Northern Mariana Islands pursuant to Title VII of Public Law 110–229, "Consolidated Natural Resources Act of 2008."

A transportation line bringing aliens to Guam or the Commonwealth of the Northern Mariana Islands under the visa waiver provisions of §212.1(q) of this chapter must enter into an agreement on CBP Form I–760. Such agreements must be negotiated directly by Customs and Border Protection and head offices of the transportation lines.

[74 FR 2836, Jan. 16, 2009]

PART 234—DESIGNATION OF PORTS OF ENTRY FOR ALIENS ARRIVING BY CIVIL AIRCRAFT

Sec.

AUTHORITY: 8 U.S.C. 1103, 1221, 1229; 8 CFR part 2.

SOURCE: Redesignated at 62 FR 10353, Mar. 6, 1997.

§234.1 Definitions.

(a) *Scheduled Airline.* This term means any individual, partnership, corporation, or association engaged in air transportation upon regular schedules to, over, or away from the United States, or from one place to another in the United States, and holding a Foreign Air Carrier permit or a Certificate of Public Convenience and Necessity issued pursuant to the Federal Aviation Act of 1958 (72 Stat. 731).

(b) *International Airport.* An international airport is one designated by the Commissioner for the entry of aliens with the prior approval of the Secretary of Commerce, Secretary of the Treasury and the Secretary of Health and Human Services.

(c) *Landing Rights Airport.* An airport, although not designated as international, at which permission to land has been granted to aircraft operated by scheduled airlines by the Commissioner of Customs.

[49 FR 50018, Dec. 26, 1984]

§ 234.2 Landing requirements.

(a) *Place of landing.* Aircraft carrying passengers or crew required to be inspected under the Act must land at the international air ports of entry enumerated in part 100 of this chapter unless permission to land elsewhere is first obtained from the Commissioner of U.S. Customs and Border Protection (CBP) in the case of aircraft operated by scheduled airlines, and in all other cases from the port director of CBP or other CBP officer having jurisdiction over the CBP port of entry nearest the intended place of landing.

(b) *Advance notice of arrival.* Aircraft carrying passengers or crew required to be inspected under the Immigration and Nationality Act, except aircraft of a scheduled airline arriving in accordance with the regular schedule filed with the Service at the place of landing, shall furnish notice of the intended flight to the immigration officer at or nearest the intended place of landing, or shall furnish similar notice to the district director of Customs or other Customs officer in charge at such place. Such notice shall specify the type of aircraft, the registration marks thereon, the name of the aircraft commander, the place of last departure, the airport of entry, or other place at which landing has been authorized, number of alien passengers, number of citizen passengers, and the estimated time of arrival. The notice shall be sent in sufficient time to enable the officers designated to inspect the aircraft to reach the airport of entry or such other place of landing prior to the arrival of the aircraft.

(c) *Permission to discharge or depart.* Aircraft carrying passengers or crew required to be inspected under the Immigration and Nationality Act shall not discharge or permit to depart any passenger or crewman without permission from an immigration officer.

(d) *Emergency or forced landing.* Should any aircraft carrying passengers or crew required to be inspected under the Immigration and Nationality Act make a forced landing in the United States, the commanding officer or person in command shall not allow any passenger or crewman thereon to depart from the landing place without permission of an immigration officer, unless such departure is necessary for purposes of safety or the preservation of life or property. As soon as practicable, the commanding officer or person in command, or the owner of the aircraft, shall communicate with the nearest immigration officer and make a full report of the circumstances of the flight and of the emergency or forced landing.

[22 FR 9795, Dec. 6, 1957, as amended at 32 FR 9631, July 4, 1967; 45 FR 29243, May 1, 1980; 49 FR 50019, Dec. 26, 1984; 54 FR 102, Jan. 4, 1989; 54 FR 1050, Jan. 11, 1989; 65 FR 58903, Oct. 3, 2000; 76 FR 5060, Jan. 28, 2011; 81 FR 14953, Mar. 21, 2016]

§ 234.3 Aircraft; how considered.

Except as otherwise specifically provided in the Immigration and Nationality Act and this chapter, aircraft arriving in or departing from the continental United States or Alaska directly from or to foreign contiguous territory or the French island of St. Pierre or Miquelon shall be regarded for the purposes of the Immigration and Nationality Act and this chapter as other transportation lines or companies arriving or departing over the land borders of the United States.

[22 FR 9795, Dec. 6, 1957. Redesignated and amended at 62 FR 10353, Mar. 6, 1997]

§ 234.4 International airports for entry of aliens.

International airports for the entry of aliens shall be those airports designated as such by the Commissioner. An application for designation of an airport as an international airport for the entry of aliens shall be made to the Commissioner and shall state whether the airport: (a) Has been approved by the Secretary of Commerce as a properly equipped airport, (b) has been designated by the Secretary of the Treasury as a port of entry for aircraft arriving in the United States from any place outside thereof and for the merchandise carried thereon, and (c) has been designated by the Secretary of Health, Education, and Welfare as a place for quarantine inspection. An airport shall not be so designated by the Commissioner without such prior approval and designation, and unless it appears to the satisfaction of the Commissioner that conditions render such designation necessary or advisable, and unless adequate facilities have been or will be provided at such airport without cost to the Federal Government for the proper inspection and disposition of aliens, including office space and such temporary detention quarters as may be found necessary. The designation of an airport as an international airport for the entry of aliens may be withdrawn whenever, in the judgment of the Commissioner, there appears just cause for such action.

[22 FR 9795, Dec. 6, 1957]

PART 235—INSPECTION OF PERSONS APPLYING FOR ADMISSION

Sec.

AUTHORITY: 8 U.S.C. 1101 and note, 1103, 1183, 1185 (pursuant to E.O. 13323, 69 FR 241, 3 CFR, 2004 Comp., p.278), 1201, 1224, 1225, 1226, 1228, 1365a note, 1365b, 1379, 1731–32; Title VII of Public Law 110–229; 8 U.S.C. 1185 note (section 7209 of Pub. L. 108–458); Pub. L. 112–54.

§ 235.1 Scope of examination.

(a) *General.* Application to lawfully enter the United States shall be made in person to an immigration officer at a U.S. port-of-entry when the port is open for inspection, or as otherwise designated in this section.

(b) *U.S. Citizens.* A person claiming U.S. citizenship must establish that fact to the examining officer's satisfaction and must present a U.S. passport or alternative documentation as required by 22 CFR part 53. If such applicant for admission fails to satisfy the examining immigration officer that he or she is a U.S. citizen, he or she shall thereafter be inspected as an alien. A U.S. citizen must present a valid unexpired U.S. passport book upon entering the United States, unless he or she presents one of the following documents:

(1) *Passport card.* A U.S. citizen who possesses a valid unexpired United States passport card, as defined in 22 CFR 53.1, may present the passport card when entering the United States from contiguous territory or adjacent islands at land or sea ports-of-entry.

(2) *Merchant Mariner Document.* A U.S. citizen who holds a valid Merchant Mariner Document (MMD) issued by the U.S. Coast Guard may present an unexpired MMD used in conjunction with official maritime business when entering the United States.

(3) *Military identification.* Any U.S. citizen member of the U.S. Armed Forces who is in the uniform of, or bears documents identifying him or her as a member of, such Armed Forces, and who is coming to or departing from the United States under official orders or permit of such Armed Forces, may present a military identification card and the official orders when entering the United States.

(4) *Trusted traveler programs.* A U.S. citizen who travels as a participant in the NEXUS, FAST, or SENTRI programs may present a valid NEXUS program card when using a NEXUS Air kiosk or a valid NEXUS, FAST, or SENTRI card at a land or sea port-of-entry prior to entering the United States from contiguous territory or adjacent islands. A U.S. citizen who enters the United States by pleasure vessel from Canada using the remote inspection system may present a NEXUS program card.

(5) *Certain cruise ship passengers.* A U.S. citizen traveling entirely within the Western Hemisphere is permitted to present a government-issued photo identification document in combination with either an original or a copy of his or her birth certificate, a Consular Report of Birth Abroad issued by the Department of State, or a Certificate of Naturalization issued by U.S.

Citizenship and Immigration Services for entering the United States when the United States citizen:

(i) Boards a cruise ship at a port or place within the United States; and,

(ii) Returns on the return voyage of the same cruise ship to the same United States port or place from where he or she originally departed.

On such cruises, U.S. Citizens under the age of 16 may present an original or a copy of a birth certificate, a Consular Report of Birth Abroad, or a Certificate of Naturalization issued by U.S. Citizenship and Immigration Services.

(6) *Native American holders of an American Indian card.* A Native American holder of a Form I–872 American Indian Card arriving from contiguous territory or adjacent islands may present the Form I–872 card prior to entering the United States at a land or sea port-of-entry.

(7) *Native American holders of tribal documents.* A U.S. citizen holder of a tribal document issued by a United States qualifying tribal entity or group of United States qualifying tribal entities, as provided in paragraph (e) of this section, who is arriving from contiguous territory or adjacent islands may present the tribal document prior to entering the United States at a land or sea port-of-entry.

(8) *Children.* A child who is a United States citizen entering the United States from contiguous territory at a sea or land ports-of-entry may present certain other documents, if the arrival falls under subsection (i) or (ii).

(i) *Children under Age 16.* A U.S. citizen who is under the age of 16 is permitted to present either an original or a copy of his or her birth certificate, a Consular Report of Birth Abroad issued by the Department of State, or a Certificate of Naturalization issued by U.S. Citizenship and Immigration Services when entering the United States from contiguous territory at land or sea ports-of-entry.

(ii) *Groups of Children under Age 19.* A U.S. citizen, who is under age 19 and is traveling with a public or private school group, religious group, social or cultural organization, or team associated with a youth sport organization is permitted to present either an original or a copy of his or her birth certificate, a Consular Report of Birth Abroad issued by the Department of State, or a Certificate of Naturalization issued by U.S. Citizenship and Immigration Services when arriving from contiguous territory at land or sea ports-of-entry, when the group, organization, or team is under the supervision of an adult affiliated with the group, organization, or team and when the child has parental or legal guardian consent to travel. For purposes of this paragraph, an adult is considered to be a person age 19 or older. The following requirements will apply:

(A) The group or organization must provide to CBP upon crossing the border, on organizational letterhead:

(*1*) The name of the group, organization or team, and the name of the supervising adult;

(*2*) A list of the children on the trip;

(*3*) For each child, the primary address, primary phone number, date of birth, place of birth, and name of a parent or legal guardian.

(B) The adult leading the group, organization, or team must demonstrate parental or legal guardian consent by certifying in the writing submitted in paragraph (b)(8)(ii)(A) of this section that he or she has obtained for each child the consent of at least one parent or legal guardian.

(C) The inspection procedure described in this paragraph is limited to members of the group, organization, or team who are under age 19. Other members of the group, organization, or team must comply with other applicable document and/or inspection requirements found in this part.

(c) *Alien members of United States Armed Forces and members of a force of a NATO country.* Any alien member of the United States Armed Forces who is in the uniform of, or bears documents identifying him or her as a member of, such Armed Forces, and who is coming to or departing from the United States under official orders or permit of such Armed Forces is not subject to the removal provisions of the Act. A member of the force of a NATO country signatory to Article III of the Status of Forces Agreement seeking to enter the United States under official orders is exempt from the control provision of the Act. Any alien who is a member of either of the foregoing classes may, upon request, be inspected and his or her entry as an alien may be recorded. If the alien does not appear to the examining immigration officer to be clearly and beyond a doubt entitled to enter the United States under the provisions of the Act, the alien shall be so informed and his or her entry shall not be recorded.

(d) *Enhanced Driver's License Projects; alternative requirements.* Upon the designation by the Secretary of Homeland Security of an enhanced driver's license as an acceptable document to denote identity and citizenship for purposes of entering the United States, U.S. and Canadian citizens may be permitted to present these documents in lieu of a passport upon entering or seeking admission to the United States according to the terms of the agreements entered between the Secretary of Homeland Security and the entity. The Secretary of Homeland Security will announce, by publication of a notice in the FEDERAL REGISTER, documents designated under this paragraph. A list of the documents designated under this paragraph will also be made available to the public.

(e) *Native American Tribal Cards; alternative requirements.* Upon the designation by the Secretary of Homeland Security of a United States qualifying tribal entity document as an acceptable document to denote identity and citizenship for purposes of entering the United States, Native Americans may be permitted to present tribal cards upon entering or seeking admission to the United States according to the terms of the voluntary agreement entered between the Secretary of Homeland Security and the tribe. The Secretary of Homeland Security will announce, by publication of a notice in the FEDERAL REGISTER, documents designated under this paragraph. A list of the documents designated under this paragraph will also be made available to the public.

(f) *Alien applicants for admission.* (1) Each alien seeking admission at a United States port-of-entry must present whatever documents are required and must establish to the satisfaction of the inspecting officer that the alien is not subject to removal under the immigration laws, Executive Orders, or Presidential Proclamations, and is entitled, under all of the applicable provisions of the immigration laws and this chapter, to enter the United States.

(i) A person claiming to have been lawfully admitted for permanent residence must establish that fact to the satisfaction of the inspecting officer and must present proper documents in accordance with §211.1 of this chapter.

(ii) The Secretary of Homeland Security or his designee may require any alien, other than aliens exempted under paragraph (iv) of this section or Canadian citizens under section 101(a)(15)(B) of the Act who are not otherwise required to present a visa or be issued Form I–94 (see §1.4) or Form I–95 for admission or parole into the United States, to provide fingerprints, photograph(s) or other specified biometric identifiers, documentation of his or her immigration status in the United States, and such other evidence as may be requested to determine the alien's identity and whether he or she has properly maintained his or her status while in the United States and/or whether he or she is admissible. The failure of an alien at the time of inspection to comply with any requirement to provide biometric identifiers may result in a determination that the alien is inadmissible under section 212(a) of the Immigration and Nationality Act or any other law.

(iii) Aliens who are required under paragraph (d)(1)(ii) to provide biometric identifier(s) at inspection may also be subject to the departure requirements for biometrics contained in §215.8 of this chapter, unless otherwise exempted.

(iv) The requirements of paragraph (d)(1)(ii) shall not apply to:

(A) Aliens younger than 14 or older than 79 on date of admission;

(B) Aliens admitted on A–1, A–2, C–3 (except for attendants, servants, or personal employees of accredited officials), G–1, G–2, G–3, G–4, NATO–1, NATO–2, NATO–3, NATO–4, NATO–5, or NATO–6 visas, and certain Taiwan officials who hold E–1 visas and members of their immediate families who hold E–1 visas unless the Secretary of State and the Secretary of Homeland Security jointly determine that a class of such aliens should be subject to the requirements of paragraph (d)(1)(ii);

(C) Classes of aliens to whom the Secretary of Homeland Security and the Secretary of State jointly determine it shall not apply; or

(D) An individual alien to whom the Secretary of Homeland Security, the Secretary of State, or the Director of Central Intelligence determines it shall not apply.

(2) An alien present in the United States who has not been admitted or paroled or an alien who seeks entry at other than an open, designated port-of-entry, except as otherwise permitted in this section, is subject to the provisions of section 212(a) of the Act and to removal under section 235(b) or 240 of the Act.

(3) An alien who is brought to the United States, whether or not to a designated port-of-entry and regardless of the means of transportation, after having been interdicted in international or United States waters, is considered an applicant for admission and shall be examined under section 235(b) of the Act.

(4) An alien stowaway is not an applicant for admission and may not be admitted to the United States. A stowaway shall be removed from the United States under section 235(a)(2) of the Act. The provisions of section 240 of the Act are not applicable to stowaways, nor is the stowaway entitled to further hearing or review of the removal, except that an alien stowaway who indicates an intention to apply for asylum, or expresses a fear of persecution, a fear of torture, or a fear of return to the country of proposed removal shall be referred to an asylum officer for a determination of credible fear of persecution or torture in accordance with section 235(b)(1)(B) of the Act and § 208.30 of this chapter. An alien stowaway who is determined to have a credible fear of persecution or torture shall have his or her asylum application adjudicated in accordance with § 208.2(b)(2) of this chapter.

(g) *U.S. citizens, lawful permanent residents of the United States, and other aliens, entering the United States along the northern border, other than at a port-of-entry.* A citizen of Canada or a permanent resident of Canada who is a national of a country listed in § 217.2(a) of this chapter may, if in possession of a valid, unexpired, Canadian Border Boat Landing Permit(Form I–68) or evidence of enrollment in any other Service Alternative Inspections program (e.g., the Immigration and Naturalization Service Passenger Accelerated Service System (INSPASS) or the Port Passenger Accelerated Service System (PORTPASS)), enter the United States by means of a pleasure craft along the northern border of the United States from time-to-time without further inspection. No persons other than those described in this paragraph may participate in this program. Permanent residents of Canada who are nationals of a designated Visa Waiver Program country listed in § 217.2(a) of this chapter must be in possession of a valid, unexpired passport issued by his or her country of nationality, and an unexpired multiple entry Form I–94W, Nonimmigrant Visa Waiver Arrival/Departure Form, or an unexpired passport, valid unexpired United States visa and I–94 Arrival/Departure Form. When an entry to the United States is made by a person who is a Canadian citizen or a permanent resident of Canada who is a national of a designated Visa Waiver Program country listed in § 217.2(a) of this chapter, entry may be made under this program only for a purpose as described in section 101(a)(15)(B)(ii) of the Act as a visitor for pleasure. Persons seeking to enter the United States for any other purpose must do so at a port-of-entry staffed by immigration inspectors. Persons aboard a vessel which has crossed the international boundary between the United States and Canada and who do not intend to land in the United States, other than at a staffed port-of-entry, are not required to be in possession of Form I–68, Canadian Border Boat Landing Permit, or evidence of enrollment in an Alternative Inspections program merely because they have crossed the international boundary. However, the Service retains the right to conduct inspections or examinations of all persons applying for admission or readmission to or seeking transit through the United States in accordance with the Act.

(1) *Application.* An eligible applicant may apply for a Canadian Border Boat Landing Permit by completing the Form I–68 in triplicate. Application forms will be made readily available through the Internet, from a Service office, or by mail. A family may apply on a single application. For the purposes of this paragraph, a family is defined as a husband, wife, unmarried children under the age of 21, and the parents of either husband or wife, who reside at the same address. In order for the I–68 application to be considered complete, it must be accompanied by the following:

(i) For each person included on the application, evidence of citizenship, and, if not a citizen of the Untied States or Canada, evidence of legal permanent resident status in either the United States or Canada. Evidence of residency must be submitted by all applicants. It is not required that all persons on the application be of the same nationality; however, they must all be individually eligible to participate in this program.

(ii) If multiple members of a family, as defined in paragraph (e)(1) of this section, are included on a single application, evidence of the familial relationship.

(iii) A fee as prescribed in § 103.7(b)(1) of this chapter.

(iv) A copy of any previously approved Form I–68.

(v) A permanent resident of Canada who is a national of a Visa Waiver Program may apply for admission simultaneously with the Form I–68 application and thereby obtain a Form I–94 or I–94W.

(2) *Submission of Form I–68.* Except as indicated in this paragraph, Form I–68 shall be properly completed and submitted in person, along with the documentary evidence and the required fee as specified in § 103.7(b)(1) of this chapter, to a United States immigration officer at a Canadian border Port-of-Entry located within the district having jurisdiction over the applicant's residence or intended place of landing. Persons previously granted Form I–68 approval may apply by mail to the issuing Service office for renewal if a copy of the previous Form I–68 is included in the application. At the discretion of the district director concerned, any applicant for renewal of Form I–68 may be required to appear for an interview in person if the applicant does not appear to be clearly eligible for renewal.

(3) *Denial of Form I–68.* If the applicant has committed a violation of any immigration or customs regulation or, in the case of an alien, is inadmissible to the United States, approval of the Form I–68 shall be denied. However, if, in the exercise of discretion, the district director waives under section 212(d)(3) of the Act all applicable grounds of inadmissibility, the I–68 application may be approved for such non-citizens. If the Form I–68 application is denied, the applicant shall be given written notice of and the reasons for the denial by letter from the district director. There is no appeal from the denial of the Form I–68 application, but the denial is without prejudice to a subsequent application for this program or any other Service benefit, except that the applicant may not submit a subsequent Form I–68 application for 90 days after the date of the last denial.

(4) *Validity.* Form I–68 shall be valid for 1 year from the date of issuance, or until revoked or violated by the Service.

(5) *Conditions for participation in the I–68 program.* Upon being inspected and positively identified by an immigration officer and found admissible and eligible for participation in the I–68 program, a participant must agree to abide by the following conditions:

(i) Form I–68 may be used only when entering the United States by means of a vessel exclusively used for pleasure, including chartered vessels when such vessel has been chartered by an approved Form I–68 holder. When used by a person who is a not a citizen or a lawful permanent resident of the United States, admission shall be for a period not to exceed 72 hours to visit within 25 miles of the shore line along the northern border of the United States, including the shore line of Lake Michigan and Puget Sound.

(ii) Participants must be in possession of any authorization documents issued for participation in this program or another Service Alternative Inspections program (INSPASS or

PORTPASS). Participants over the age of 15 years and who are not in possession of an INSPASS or PORTPASS enrollment card must also be in possession of a photographic identification document issued by a governmental agency. Participants who are permanent residents of Canada who are nationals of a Visa Waiver Program country listed in § 217.2(a) of this chapter must also be in possession of proper documentation as described in paragraph (e) of this section.

(iii) Participants may not import merchandise or transport controlled or restricted items while entering the United States under this program. The entry of any merchandise or goods must be in accordance with the laws and regulations of all Federal Inspection Services.

(iv) Participants must agree to random checks or inspections that may be conducted by the Service, at any time and at any location, to ensure compliance.

(v) Participants must abide by all Federal, state, and local laws regarding the importation of alcohol or agricultural products or the importation or possession of controlled substances as defined in section 101 of the Controlled Substance Act (21 U.S.C. 802).

(vi) Participants acknowledge that all devices, decals, cards, or other Federal Government supplied identification or technology used to identify or inspect persons or vessels seeking entry via this program remain the property of the United States Government at all times, and must be surrendered upon request by a Border Patrol Agent or any other officer of a Federal Inspection Service.

(vii) The captain, charterer, master, or owner (if aboard) of each vessel bringing persons into the United States is responsible for determining that all persons aboard the vessel are in possession of a valid, unexpired Form I–68 or other evidence of participation in a Service Alternative Inspections program (INSPASS or PORTPASS) prior to entry into the territorial waters of the United States. If any person on board is not in possession of such evidence, the captain, charterer, master, or owner must transport such person to a staffed United States Port-of-Entry for an in-person immigration inspection.

(6) *Revocation.* The district director, the chief patrol agent, or their designated representatives may revoke the designation of any participant who violates any condition of this program, as contained in paragraph (e)(5) of this section, or who has violated any immigration law or regulation, or a law or regulation of the United States Customs Service or other Federal Inspection Service, has abandoned his or her residence in the United States or Canada, is inadmissible to the United States, or who is otherwise determined by an immigration officer to be ineligible for continued participation in this program. Such persons may be subject to other applicable sanctions, such as criminal and/or administrative prosecution or deportation, as well as possible seizure of goods and/or vessels. If permission to participate is revoked, a written request to the district director for restoration of permission to participate may be made. The district director will notify the person of his or her decision and the reasons therefore in writing.

(7) *Compliance checking.* Participation in this program does not relieve the holder from responsibility to comply with all other aspects of United States Immigration, Customs, or other Federal inspection service laws or regulations. To prevent abuse, the United States Immigration and Naturalization Service retains the right to conduct inspections or examinations of all persons applying for admission or readmission to or seeking transit through the United States in accordance with the Immigration and Nationality Act.

(h) *Form I–94, Arrival-Departure Record.* (1) Unless otherwise exempted, each arriving nonimmigrant who is admitted to the United States will be issued a Form I–94 as evidence of the terms of admission. For land border admission, a Form I–94 will be issued only upon payment of a fee, and will be considered issued for multiple entries unless specifically annotated for a limited number of entries. A Form I–94 issued at other than a land border port-of-entry, unless issued for multiple entries, must be surrendered upon departure from the United States in accordance with the instructions on the form. Form I-94 is not required by:

(i) Any nonimmigrant alien described in §212.1(a) of this chapter and 22 CFR 41.33 who is admitted as a visitor for business or pleasure or admitted to proceed in direct transit through the United States;

(ii) Any nonimmigrant alien residing in the British Virgin Islands who was admitted only to the U.S. Virgin Islands as a visitor for business or pleasure under §212.1(b) of this chapter;

(iii) Except as provided in paragraph (h)(1)(v) of this section, any Mexican national admitted as a nonimmigrant visitor who is:

(A) Exempt from a visa and passport pursuant to §212.1(c)(1) of this chapter and is admitted for a period not to exceed 30 days to visit within 25 miles of the border; or

(B) In possession of a valid visa and passport and is admitted for a period not to exceed 72 hours to visit within 25 miles of the border;

(iv) Bearers of Mexican diplomatic or official passports described in §212.1(c) of this chapter; or

(v) Any Mexican national admitted as a nonimmigrant visitor who is:

(A) Exempt from a visa and passport pursuant to §212.1(c)(1) of this chapter and is admitted at the Mexican border POEs in the State of Arizona at Sasabe, Nogales, Mariposa, Naco or Douglas to visit within the State of Arizona within 75 miles of the border for a period not to exceed 30 days; or

(B) In possession of a valid visa and passport and is admitted at the Mexican border POEs in the State of Arizona at Sasabe, Nogales, Mariposa, Naco or Douglas to visit within the State of Arizona within 75 miles of the border for a period not to exceed 72 hours; or

(C) Exempt from visa and passport pursuant to §212.1(c)(1) of this chapter and is admitted for a period not to exceed 30 days to visit within the State of New Mexico within 55 miles of the border or the area south of and including Interstate Highway I-10, whichever is further north; or

(D) In possession of a valid visa and passport and is admitted for a period not to exceed 72 hours to visit within the State of New Mexico within 55 miles of the border or the area south of and including Interstate Highway I-10, whichever is further north.

(2) *Paroled aliens.* Any alien paroled into the United States under section 212(d)(5) of the Act, including any alien crewmember, shall be issued a completely executed Form I-94, endorsed with the parole stamp.

[62 FR 10353, Mar. 6, 1997, as amended at 62 FR 47751, Sept. 11, 1997; 64 FR 8494, Feb. 19, 1999; 64 FR 36561, July 7, 1999; 64 FR 68617, Dec. 8, 1999; 67 FR 71449, Dec. 2, 2002; 68 FR 5193, Jan. 31, 2003; 69 FR 480, Jan. 5, 2004; 69 FR 50053, Aug. 13, 2004; 69 FR 53333, Aug. 31, 2004; 69 FR 58037, Sept. 29, 2004; 71 FR 68429, Nov. 24, 2006; 73 FR 18416, Apr. 3, 2008; 73 FR 77491, Dec. 19, 2008; 74 FR 2837, Jan. 16, 2009; 78 FR 18472, Mar. 27, 2013; 78 FR 35107, June 12, 2013]

§235.2 Parole for deferred inspection.

(a) A district director may, in his or her discretion, defer the inspection of any vessel or aircraft, or of any alien, to another Service office or port-of-entry. Any alien coming to a United States port from a foreign port, from an outlying possession of the United States, from Guam, Puerto Rico, or the Virgin Islands of the United States, or from another port of the United States at which examination under this part was deferred, shall be regarded as an applicant for admission at that onward port.

(b) An examining immigration officer may defer further examination and refer the alien's case to the district director having jurisdiction over the place where the alien is seeking admission, or over the place of the alien's residence or destination in the United States, if the examining immigration officer has reason to believe that the alien can overcome a finding of inadmissibility by:

(1) Posting a bond under section 213 of the Act;

(2) Seeking and obtaining a waiver under section 211 or 212(d)(3) or (4) of the Act; or

(3) Presenting additional evidence of admissibility not available at the time and place of the initial examination.

(c) Such deferral shall be accomplished pursuant to the provisions of section 212(d)(5) of the Act for the period of time necessary to complete the deferred inspection.

(d) Refusal of a district director to authorize admission under section 213 of the Act, or to grant an application for the benefits of section 211 or section 212(d) (3) or (4) of the Act, shall be without prejudice to the renewal of such application or the authorizing of such admission by the immigration judge without additional fee.

(e) Whenever an alien on arrival is found or believed to be suffering from a disability that renders it impractical to proceed with the examination under the Act, the examination of such alien, members of his or her family concerning whose admissibility it is necessary to have such alien testify, and any accompanying aliens whose protection or guardianship will be required should such alien be found inadmissible shall be deferred for such time and under such conditions as the district director in whose district the port is located imposes.

[62 FR 10355, Mar. 6, 1997]

§ 235.3 Inadmissible aliens and expedited removal.

(a) *Detention prior to inspection.* All persons arriving at a port-of-entry in the United States by vessel or aircraft shall be detained aboard the vessel or at the airport of arrival by the owner, agent, master, commanding officer, person in charge, purser, or consignee of such vessel or aircraft until admitted or otherwise permitted to land by an officer of the Service. Notice or order to detain shall not be required. The owner, agent, master, commanding officer, person in charge, purser, or consignee of such vessel or aircraft shall deliver every alien requiring examination to an immigration officer for inspection or to a medical officer for examination. The Service will not be liable for any expenses related to such detention or presentation or for any expenses of a passenger who has not been presented for inspection and for whom a determination has not been made concerning admissibility by a Service officer.

(b) *Expedited removal*—(1) *Applicability.* The expedited removal provisions shall apply to the following classes of aliens who are determined to be inadmissible under section 212(a)(6)(C) or (7) of the Act:

(i) Arriving aliens, as defined in 8 CFR 1.2;

(ii) As specifically designated by the Commissioner, aliens who arrive in, attempt to enter, or have entered the United States without having been admitted or paroled following inspection by an immigration officer at a designated port-of-entry, and who have not established to the satisfaction of the immigration officer that they have been physically present in the United States continuously for the 2-year period immediately prior to the date of determination of inadmissibility. The Commissioner shall have the sole discretion to apply the provisions of section 235(b)(1) of the Act, at any time, to any class of aliens described in this section. The Commissioner's designation shall become effective upon publication of a notice in the FEDERAL REGISTER. However, if the Commissioner determines, in the exercise of discretion, that the delay caused by publication would adversely affect the interests of the United States or the effective enforcement of the immigration laws, the Commissioner's designation shall become effective immediately upon issuance, and shall be published in the FEDERAL REGISTER as soon as practicable thereafter. When these provisions are in effect for aliens who enter without inspection, the burden of proof rests with the alien to affirmatively show that he or she has the required continuous physical presence in the United States. Any absence from the United States shall serve to break the period of continuous physical presence. An alien who was not inspected and admitted or paroled into the United States but who establishes that he or she has been continuously physically present in the United States for the 2-year period immediately prior to the date of determination of inadmissibility shall be detained in accordance with section 235(b)(2) of the Act for a proceeding under section 240 of the Act.

(2) *Determination of inadmissibility*—(i) *Record of proceeding*. An alien who is arriving in the United States, or other alien as designated pursuant to paragraph (b)(1)(ii) of this section, who is determined to be inadmissible under section 212(a)(6)(C) or 212(a)(7) of the Act (except an alien for whom documentary requirements are waived under § 211.1(b)(3) or § 212.1 of this chapter), shall be ordered removed from the United States in accordance with section 235(b)(1) of the Act. In every case in which the expedited removal provisions will be applied and before removing an alien from the United States pursuant to this section, the examining immigration officer shall create a record of the facts of the case and statements made by the alien. This shall be accomplished by means of a sworn statement using Form I–867AB, Record of Sworn Statement in Proceedings under Section 235(b)(1) of the Act. The examining immigration officer shall read (or have read) to the alien all information contained on Form I–867A. Following questioning and recording of the alien's statement regarding identity, alienage, and inadmissibility, the examining immigration officer shall record the alien's response to the questions contained on Form I–867B, and have the alien read (or have read to him or her) the statement, and the alien shall sign and initial each page of the statement and each correction. The examining immigration officer shall advise the alien of the charges against him or her on Form I–860, Notice and Order of Expedited Removal, and the alien shall be given an opportunity to respond to those charges in the sworn statement. After obtaining supervisory concurrence in accordance with paragraph (b)(7) of this section, the examining immigration official shall serve the alien with Form I–860 and the alien shall sign the reverse of the form acknowledging receipt. Interpretative assistance shall be used if necessary to communicate with the alien.

(ii) *No entitlement to hearings and appeals*. Except as otherwise provided in this section, such alien is not entitled to a hearing before an immigration judge in proceedings conducted pursuant to section 240 of the Act, or to an appeal of the expedited removal order to the Board of Immigration Appeals.

(iii) *Detention and parole of alien in expedited removal*. An alien whose inadmissibility is being considered under this section or who has been ordered removed pursuant to this section shall be detained pending determination and removal, except that parole of such alien, in accordance with section 212(d)(5) of the Act, may be permitted only when the Attorney General determines, in the exercise of discretion, that parole is required to meet a medical emergency or is necessary for a legitimate law enforcement objective.

(3) *Additional charges of inadmissibility*. In the expedited removal process, the Service may not charge an alien with any additional grounds of inadmissibility other than section 212(a)(6)(C) or 212(a)(7) of the Act. If an alien appears to be inadmissible under other grounds contained in section 212(a) of the Act, and if the Service wishes to pursue such additional grounds of inadmissibility, the alien shall be detained and referred for a removal hearing before an immigration judge pursuant to sections 235(b)(2) and 240 of the Act for inquiry into all charges. Once the alien is in removal proceedings under section 240 of the Act, the Service is not precluded from lodging additional charges against the alien. Nothing in this paragraph shall preclude the Service from pursuing such additional grounds of inadmissibility against the alien in any subsequent attempt to reenter the United States, provided the additional grounds of inadmissibility still exist.

(4) *Claim of asylum or fear of persecution or torture*. If an alien subject to the expedited removal provisions indicates an intention to apply for asylum, or expresses a fear of persecution or torture, or a fear of return to his or her country, the inspecting officer shall not proceed further with removal of the alien until the alien has been referred for an interview by an asylum officer in accordance with 8 CFR 208.30. The examining immigration officer shall record sufficient information in the sworn statement to establish and record that the alien has indicated such intention, fear, or concern, and to establish the alien's inadmissibility.

(i) *Referral.* The referring officer shall provide the alien with a written disclosure on Form M–444, Information About Credible Fear Interview, describing:

(A) The purpose of the referral and description of the credible fear interview process;

(B) The right to consult with other persons prior to the interview and any review thereof at no expense to the United States Government;

(C) The right to request a review by an immigration judge of the asylum officer's credible fear determination; and

(D) The consequences of failure to establish a credible fear of persecution or torture.

(ii) *Detention pending credible fear interview.* Pending the credible fear determination by an asylum officer and any review of that determination by an immigration judge, the alien shall be detained. Parole of such alien in accordance with section 212(d)(5) of the Act may be permitted only when the Attorney General determines, in the exercise of discretion, that parole is required to meet a medical emergency or is necessary for a legitimate law enforcement objective. Prior to the interview, the alien shall be given time to contact and consult with any person or persons of his or her choosing. Such consultation shall be made available in accordance with the policies and procedures of the detention facility where the alien is detained, shall be at no expense to the government, and shall not unreasonably delay the process.

(5) *Claim to lawful permanent resident, refugee, or asylee status or U.S. citizenship*—(i) *Verification of status.* If an applicant for admission who is subject to expedited removal pursuant to section 235(b)(1) of the Act claims to have been lawfully admitted for permanent residence, admitted as a refugee under section 207 of the Act, granted asylum under section 208 of the Act, or claims to be a U.S. citizen, the immigration officer shall attempt to verify the alien's claim. Such verification shall include a check of all available Service data systems and any other means available to the officer. An alien whose claim to lawful permanent resident, refugee, asylee status, or U.S. citizen status cannot be verified will be advised of the penalties for perjury, and will be placed under oath or allowed to make a declaration as permitted under 28 U.S.C. 1746, concerning his or her lawful admission for permanent residence, admission as a refugee under section 207 of the Act, grant of asylum status under section 208 of the Act, or claim to U.S. citizenship. A written statement shall be taken from the alien in the alien's own language and handwriting, stating that he or she declares, certifies, verifies, or states that the claim is true and correct. The immigration officer shall issue an expedited order of removal under section 235(b)(1)(A)(i) of the Act and refer the alien to the immigration judge for review of the order in accordance with paragraph (b)(5)(iv) of this section and § 235.6(a)(2)(ii). The person shall be detained pending review of the expedited removal order under this section. Parole of such person, in accordance with section 212(d)(5) of the Act, may be permitted only when the Attorney General determines, in the exercise of discretion, that parole is required to meet a medical emergency or is necessary for a legitimate law enforcement objective.

(ii) *Verified lawful permanent residents.* If the claim to lawful permanent resident status is verified, and such status has not been terminated in exclusion, deportation, or removal proceedings, the examining immigration officer shall not order the alien removed pursuant to section 235(b)(1) of the Act. The examining immigration officer will determine in accordance with section 101(a)(13)(C) of the Act whether the alien is considered to be making an application for admission. If the alien is determined to be seeking admission and the alien is otherwise admissible, except that he or she is not in possession of the required documentation, a discretionary waiver of documentary requirements may be considered in accordance with section 211(b) of the Act and § 211.1(b)(3) of this chapter or the alien's inspection may be deferred to an onward office for presentation of the required documents. If the alien appears to be inadmissible, the immigration officer may initiate removal proceedings against the alien under section 240 of the Act.

(iii) *Verified refugees and asylees.* If a check of Service records or other means indicates that the alien has been granted refugee status or asylee status, and such status has not been terminated in deportation, exclusion, or removal proceedings, the immigration officer shall not order the alien removed pursuant to section 235(b)(1) of the Act. If the alien is not in possession of a valid, unexpired refugee travel document, the examining immigration officer may accept an application for a refugee travel document in accordance with §223.2(b)(2)(ii) of this chapter. If accepted, the immigration officer shall readmit the refugee or asylee in accordance with §223.3(d)(2)(i) of this chapter. If the alien is determined not to be eligible to file an application for a refugee travel document the immigration officer may initiate removal proceedings against the alien under section 240 of the Act.

(iv) *Review of order for claimed lawful permanent residents, refugees, asylees, or U.S. citizens.* A person whose claim to U.S. citizenship has been verified may not be ordered removed. When an alien whose status has not been verified but who is claiming under oath or under penalty of perjury to be a lawful permanent resident, refugee, asylee, or U.S. citizen is ordered removed pursuant to section 235(b)(1) of the Act, the case will be referred to an immigration judge for review of the expedited removal order under section 235(b)(1)(C) of the Act and §235.6(a)(2)(ii). If the immigration judge determines that the alien has never been admitted as a lawful permanent resident or as a refugee, granted asylum status, or is not a U.S. citizen, the order issued by the immigration officer will be affirmed and the Service will remove the alien. There is no appeal from the decision of the immigration judge. If the immigration judge determines that the alien was once so admitted as a lawful permanent resident or as a refugee, or was granted asylum status, or is a U.S. citizen, and such status has not been terminated by final administrative action, the immigration judge will terminate proceedings and vacate the expedited removal order. The Service may initiate removal proceedings against such an alien, but not against a person determined to be a U.S. citizen, in proceedings under section 240 of the Act. During removal proceedings, the immigration judge may consider any waivers, exceptions, or requests for relief for which the alien is eligible.

(6) *Opportunity for alien to establish that he or she was admitted or paroled into the United States.* If the Commissioner determines that the expedited removal provisions of section 235(b)(1) of the Act shall apply to any or all aliens described in paragraph (b)(2)(ii) of this section, such alien will be given a reasonable opportunity to establish to the satisfaction of the examining immigration officer that he or she was admitted or paroled into the United States following inspection at a port-of-entry. The alien will be allowed to present evidence or provide sufficient information to support the claim. Such evidence may consist of documentation in the possession of the alien, the Service, or a third party. The examining immigration officer will consider all such evidence and information, make further inquiry if necessary, and will attempt to verify the alien's status through a check of all available Service data systems. The burden rests with the alien to satisfy the examining immigration officer of the claim of lawful admission or parole. If the alien establishes that he or she was lawfully admitted or paroled, the case will be examined to determine if grounds of deportability under section 237(a) of the Act are applicable, or if paroled, whether such parole has been, or should be, terminated, and whether the alien is inadmissible under section 212(a) of the Act. An alien who cannot satisfy the examining officer that he or she was lawfully admitted or paroled will be ordered removed pursuant to section 235(b)(1) of the Act.

(7) *Review of expedited removal orders.* Any removal order entered by an examining immigration officer pursuant to section 235(b)(1) of the Act must be reviewed and approved by the appropriate supervisor before the order is considered final. Such supervisory review shall not be delegated below the level of the second line supervisor, or a person acting in that capacity. The supervisory review shall include a review

of the sworn statement and any answers and statements made by the alien regarding a fear of removal or return. The supervisory review and approval of an expedited removal order for an alien described in section 235(b)(1)(A)(iii) of the Act must include a review of any claim of lawful admission or parole and any evidence or information presented to support such a claim, prior to approval of the order. In such cases, the supervisor may request additional information from any source and may require further interview of the alien.

(8) *Removal procedures relating to expedited removal.* An alien ordered removed pursuant to section 235(b)(1) of the Act shall be removed from the United States in accordance with section 241(c) of the Act and 8 CFR part 241.

(9) *Waivers of documentary requirements.* Nothing in this section limits the discretionary authority of the Attorney General, including authority under sections 211(b) or 212(d) of the Act, to waive the documentary requirements for arriving aliens.

(10) *Applicant for admission under section 217 of the Act.* The provisions of § 235.3(b) do not apply to an applicant for admission under section 217 of the Act.

(c) *Arriving aliens placed in proceedings under section 240 of the Act.* Except as otherwise provided in this chapter, any arriving alien who appears to the inspecting officer to be inadmissible, and who is placed in removal proceedings pursuant to section 240 of the Act shall be detained in accordance with section 235(b) of the Act. Parole of such alien shall only be considered in accordance with § 212.5(b) of this chapter. This paragraph shall also apply to any alien who arrived before April 1, 1997, and who was placed in exclusion proceedings.

(d) *Service custody.* The Service will assume custody of any alien subject to detention under paragraph (b) or (c) of this section. In its discretion, the Service may require any alien who appears inadmissible and who arrives at a land border port-of-entry from Canada or Mexico, to remain in that country while awaiting a removal hearing. Such alien shall be considered detained for a proceeding within the meaning of section 235(b) of the Act and may be ordered removed in absentia by an immigration judge if the alien fails to appear for the hearing.

(e) *Detention in non-Service facility.* Whenever an alien is taken into Service custody and detained at a facility other than at a Service Processing Center, the public or private entities contracted to perform such service shall have been approved for such use by the Service's Jail Inspection Program or shall be performing such service under contract in compliance with the Standard Statement of Work for Contract Detention Facilities. Both programs are administered by the Detention and Deportation section having jurisdiction over the alien's place of detention. Under no circumstances shall an alien be detained in facilities not meeting the four mandatory criteria for usage. These are:

(1) 24-Hour supervision,

(2) Conformance with safety and emergency codes,

(3) Food service, and

(4) Availability of emergency medical care.

(f) *Privilege of communication.* The mandatory notification requirements of consular and diplomatic officers pursuant to § 236.1(e) of this chapter apply when an inadmissible alien is detained for removal proceedings, including for purpose of conducting the credible fear determination.

[62 FR 10355, Mar. 6, 1997, as amended at 64 FR 8494, Feb. 19, 1999; 65 FR 82256, Dec. 28, 2000; 69 FR 69490, Nov. 29, 2004; 76 FR 53790, Aug. 29, 2011; 82 FR 4771, Jan. 17, 2017]

§ 235.4 Withdrawal of application for admission.

The Attorney General may, in his or her discretion, permit any alien applicant for admission to withdraw his or her application for admission in lieu of removal proceedings under section 240 of the Act or expedited removal under section 235(b)(1) of the Act. The alien's decision to withdraw his or her application for admission must be made voluntarily, but nothing in this section shall be construed as to give an alien the right to withdraw his or her application for admission. Permission to withdraw an application for admission should not normally be granted unless the alien intends and is able to depart the United States immediately. An alien permitted to withdraw his or her application for admission shall normally remain in carrier or Service custody pending departure, unless the district director determines that parole of the alien is warranted in accordance with § 212.5(b) of this chapter.

[62 FR 10358, Mar. 6, 1997; 62 FR 15363, Apr. 1, 1997; 65 FR 82256, Dec. 28, 2000]

§ 235.5 Preinspection.

(a) *In United States territories and possessions.* In the case of any aircraft proceeding from Guam, the Commonwealth of the Northern Mariana Islands (beginning November 28, 2009), Puerto Rico, or the United States Virgin Islands destined directly and without touching at a foreign port or place, to any other of such places, or to one of the States of the United States or the District of Columbia, the examination of the passengers and crew required by the Act may be made prior to the departure of the aircraft, and in such event, final determination of admissibility will be made immediately prior to such departure. The examination will be conducted in accordance with sections 232, 235, and 240 of the Act and 8 CFR parts 235 and 240. If it appears to the immigration officer that any person in the United States being examined under this section is prima facie removable from the United States, further action with respect to his or her examination will be deferred and further proceedings regarding removability conducted as provided in section 240 of the Act and 8 CFR part 240. When the foregoing inspection procedure is applied to any aircraft, persons examined and found admissible will be placed aboard the aircraft, or kept at the airport separate and apart from the general public until they are permitted to board the aircraft. No other person will be permitted to depart on such aircraft until and unless he or she is found to be admissible as provided in this section.

(b) *In foreign territory.* In the case of any aircraft, vessel, or train proceeding directly, without stopping, from a port or place in foreign territory to a port-of-entry in the United States, the examination and inspection of passengers and crew required by the Act and final determination of admissibility may be made immediately prior to such departure at the port or place in the foreign territory and shall have the same effect under the Act as though made at the destined port-of-entry in the United States.

[62 FR 10358, Mar. 6, 1997, as amended at 74 FR 2836, Jan. 16, 2009; 74 FR 25388, May 28, 2009]

§ 235.6 Referral to immigration judge.

(a) *Notice*—(1) *Referral by Form I–862, Notice to Appear.* An immigration officer or asylum officer will sign and deliver a Form I–862 to an alien in the following cases:

(i) If, in accordance with the provisions of section 235(b)(2)(A) of the Act, the examining immigration officer detains an alien for a proceeding before an immigration judge under section 240 of the Act; or

(ii) If an asylum officer determines that an alien in expedited removal proceedings has a credible fear of persecution or torture and refers the case to the immigration judge for consideration of the application for asylum, except that, prior to January 1, 2015, an alien arriving in the Commonwealth of the Northern Mariana Islands is not eligible to apply for asylum but the immigration judge may consider eligibility for withholding of removal pursuant to section 241(b)(3) of the Act or withholding or deferral of removal under the Convention Against Torture.

(iii) If the immigration judge determines that an alien in expedited removal proceedings has a credible fear of persecution or torture and vacates the expedited removal order issued by the asylum officer, except that, prior to January 1, 2015, an alien physically present in or arriving in the Commonwealth of the Northern Mariana Islands is not eligible to apply for asylum but an immigration judge may consider eligibility for withholding of removal pursuant to section 241(b)(3) of the Act or withholding or deferral of removal under the Convention Against Torture.

(iv) If an immigration officer verifies that an alien subject to expedited removal under section 235(b)(1) of the Act has been admitted as a lawful permanent resident refugee, or asylee, or upon review pursuant to § 235.3(b)(5)(iv) an immigration judge determines that the alien was once so admitted, provided that such status has not been terminated by final administrative action, and the Service initiates removal proceedings against the alien under section 240 of the Act.

(2) *Referral by Form I–863, Notice of Referral to Immigration Judge.* An immigration officer will sign and deliver a Form I–863 to an alien in the following cases:

(i) If an asylum officer determines that an alien does not have a credible fear of persecution or torture, and the alien requests a review of that determination by an immigration judge; or

(ii) If, in accordance with section 235(b)(1)(C) of the Act, an immigration officer refers an expedited removal order entered on an alien claiming to be a lawful permanent resident, refugee, asylee, or U.S. citizen for whom the officer could not verify such status to an immigration judge for review of the order.

(iii) If an immigration officer refers an applicant described in § 208.2(b)(1) of this chapter to an immigration judge for an asylum hearing under § 208.2(b)(2) of this chapter.

(b) *Certification for mental condition; medical appeal.* An alien certified under sections 212(a)(1) and 232(b) of the Act shall be advised by the examining immigration officer that he or she may appeal to a board of medical examiners of the United States Public Health Service pursuant to section 232 of the Act. If such appeal is taken, the district director shall arrange for the convening of the medical board.

[62 FR 10358, Mar. 6, 1997, as amended at 64 FR 8494, Feb. 19, 1999; 74 FR 55739, Oct. 28, 2009]

§ 235.7 Automated inspection services.

(a) *PORTPASS Program*—(1) *Definitions*—(i) *Port Passenger Accelerated Service System (PORTPASS).* A system in which certain ports-of-entry (POEs) are identified and designated by the Service as providing access to the United States for a group of identified, low-risk, border crossers. Alien participants in the PORTPASS program are personally inspected, identified, and screened in advance of approval for participation in the program by an immigration officer, and may apply to enter the United States through a dedicated commuter lane (DCL) or through an automated permit port (APP). Such advance inspection and identification, when the enrolled participant satisfies the conditions and requirements set fourth in this section, satisfies the reporting requirements of § 235.1(a). Each successful use of PORTPASS constitutes a separate and completed inspection and application for entry by the alien program participants on the date PORTPASS is used. United States citizens who meet the eligibility requirements for participation are subject to all rules, procedures, and conditions for use set forth in this section.

(ii) *Automated Permit Port (APP).* A POE designated by the Service to provide access to the United States by an identified, low-risk, border crosser through the use of automation when the POE is not staffed. An APP has limited hours of operation and is located at a remote location on a land border. This program is limited to the northern border of the United States.

(iii) *Dedicated Commuter Lane (DCL).* A special lane set apart from the normal flow of traffic at a land border POE which allows an accelerated inspection for identified, low-risk travelers. This program is limited to the northern border of the United States and the California-Mexico border.

(iv) *DCL system costs fee.* A fee charged to a participant to cover the cost of the implementation and operation of the PORTPASS system. If a participant wishes to enroll more than one vehicle for use in the PORTPASS system, he or she will be assessed an *additional vehicle fee* for each additional vehicle enrolled. Regardless of when the additional vehicle is enrolled, the expiration date for use of that vehicle in the DCL will be the same date that the respective participant's authorized use of the lane expires, or is otherwise revoked.

(2) *Designation of POEs for PORTPASS access.* The following criteria shall be used by the Service in the selection of a POE when classifying the POE as having PORTPASS access:

(i) The location has an identifiable group of low-risk border crossers;

(ii) The institution of PORTPASS access will not significantly inhibit normal traffic flow;

(iii) The POE selected for access via a DCL has a sufficient number of Service personnel to perform primary and secondary inspection functions.

(3) *General eligibility requirements for PORTPASS program applicants.* Applicants to PORTPASS must be citizens or lawful permanent residents of the United States, or nonimmigrants determined to be eligible by the Commissioner of the Service. Non-United States citizens must meet all applicable documentary and entry eligibility requirements of the Act. Applicants must agree to furnish all information requested on the application, and must agree to terms set forth for use of the PORTPASS program. Use of the PORTPASS program constitutes application for entry into the United States. Criminal justice information databases will be checked to assist in determining the applicant's eligibility for the PORTPASS program at the time the Form I–823, Application—Alternative Inspection Services, is submitted. Criminal justice information on PORTPASS participants will be updated regularly, and the results will be checked electronically at the time of each approved participant's use of PORTPASS. Notwithstanding the provisions of 8 CFR part 264, fingerprints on Form FD–258 or in the manner prescribed by the Service may be required.

(4) *Application.* (i) Application for PORTPASS access shall be made on Form I–823, Application—Alternative Inspection Services. Applications may be submitted during regular working hours at the principal Port-of-Entry having jurisdiction over the Port-of-Entry for which the applicant requests access. Applications may also be submitted by mail.

(ii) Each person seeking PORTPASS access must file a separate application.

(iii) The number of persons and vehicles which can use a DCL is limited numerically by the technology of the system. For this reason, distribution of applications at each POE may be limited.

(iv) Applications must be supported by evidence of citizenship, and, in the case of lawful permanent residents of the United States, evidence of lawful permanent resident status in the United States. Alien applicants required to possess a valid visa must present documentation establishing such possession and any other documentation as required by the Act at the time of the application, and must be in possession of such documentation at the time of each entry, and at all times while present in the United States. Evidence of residency must be submitted by all applicants. Evidence of employment may be required to be furnished by the applicant. A current valid driver's license, and evidence of vehicle registration and insurance for the vehicle which will be occupied by the applicant as a driver or passenger when he or she uses the DCL or APP must be presented to the Service prior to approval of the application.

(v) A completed Form I–823 must be accompanied by the fee as prescribed in §103.7(b)(1) of this chapter. Each PORTPASS applicant 14 years-of-age or older must complete the application and pay the application fee. Applicants under the age of 14 will be required to complete the application, but will not be required to pay the application fee. An application for a replacement PORTPASS card must be made on the Form I–823, and filed with the fee prescribed in §103.7(b)(1). The district director having jurisdiction over the POE where the applicant requests access may, in his or her discretion, waive the application or replacement fee.

(vi) If fingerprints are required to assist in a determination of eligibility at that POE, the applicant will be so advised by the Service prior to submitting his or her application. The applicant shall also be informed at that time of the current Federal Bureau of Investigation fee for conducting a fingerprint check. This fee must be paid by the applicant to the Service before any processing of the application shall occur. The fingerprint fee may be not be waived.

(vii) Each applicant must present himself or herself for an inspection and/or positive identification at a time designated by the Service prior to approval of the application.

(viii) Each vehicle that a PORTPASS participant desires to register in PORTPASS must be inspected and approved by the Service prior to use in the PORTPASS system. Evidence of valid, current registration and vehicle insurance must be presented to the Service at the time the vehicle is inspected. If the vehicle is not owned by the participant, the participant may be required to present written permission from the registered owner authorizing use of the vehicle in the PORTPASS program throughout the PORTPASS registration period.

(ix) An applicant, whether an occupant or driver, may apply to use more than one vehicle in the DCL. The first vehicle listed on the Form I–823 will be designated as the applicant's primary vehicle. The second vehicle, if not designated by another applicant as his or her primary vehicle, is subject to the additional vehicle charge as prescribed by the Service.

(x) An application may be denied in the discretion of the district director having jurisdiction over the POE where the applicant requests access. Notice of such denial shall be given to the applicant. There is no appeal from the denial, but denial is without prejudice to reapplying for this or any other Service benefit. Re-applications, or applications following revocation of permission to use the lane, will not be considered by the Service until 90 days have passed following the date of denial or revocation. Criteria which will be considered in the decision to approve or deny the application include the following: admissibility to the United States and documentation so evidencing, criminal history and/or evidence of criminality, purpose of travel, employment, residency, prior immigration history, possession of current driver's license, vehicle insurance and registration, and vehicle inspection.

(xi) Applications approved by the Service will entitle the applicant to seek entry via a designated PORTPASS Program POE for a period of 2 years from the date of approval of the application unless approval is otherwise withdrawn. An application for a replacement card will not extend the initial period of approval.

(5) By applying for and participating in the PORTPASS program, each approved participant acknowledges and agrees to all of the following:

(i) The installation and/or use of, in the vehicle approved for use in the PORTPASS program, any and all decals, devices, technology or other methodology deemed necessary by the Service to ensure inspection of the person(s) seeking entry through a DCL, in addition to any fee and/or monetary deposit assessed by the Service pending return of any and all such decals, devices, technology, and other methodology in undamaged condition.

(ii) That all devices, decals, or other equipment, methodology, or technology used to identify or inspect persons or vehicles seeking entry via any PORTPASS program remains the property of the United States Government at all times, and must be surrendered upon request by the Service. Each participant agrees to abide by the terms set forth by the Service for use of any device, decal, or other equipment, method or technology.

(iii) The payment of a system costs fee as determined by the Service to be necessary to cover the costs of implementing, maintaining, and operating the PORTPASS program.

(iv) That each occupant of a vehicle applying for entry through PORTPASS must have current approval from the Service to apply for entry through the PORTPASS program in that vehicle.

(v) That a participant must be in possession of any authorization document(s) issued for PORTPASS access and any other entry document(s) as required by the Act or by regulation at the time of each entry to the United States.

(vi) That a participant must positively identify himself or herself in the manner prescribed by the Service at the time of each application for entry via the PORTPASS.

(vii) That each use of PORTPASS constitutes a separate application for entry to the United States by the alien participant.

(viii) That each participant agrees to be responsible for all contents of the vehicle that he or she occupies when using PORTPASS.

(ix) That a participant may not import merchandise or transport controlled or restricted items using PORTPASS. The entry of any merchandise or goods must be in accordance with the laws and regulations of all other Federal inspection agencies.

(x) That a participant must abide by all Federal, state and local laws regarding the importation of alcohol or agricultural products or the importation or possession of controlled substances as defined in section 101 of the Controlled Substance Act (21 U.S.C. §802).

(xi) That a participant will be subject to random checks or inspections that may be conducted by the Service at any time and at any location, to ensure compliance.

(xii) That current vehicle registration and, if applicable, current permission to use the vehicle in PORTPASS, and evidence of current vehicle insurance, shall be in the vehicle at all times during use of PORTPASS.

(xiii) Participant agrees to notify the Service if a vehicle approved for use in a PORTPASS program is sold, stolen, damaged, or disposed of otherwise. If a vehicle is sold, it is the responsibility of the participant to remove or obliterate any identifying device or other authorization for participation in the program or at the time of sale unless otherwise notified by the Service. If any license plates are replaced on an enrolled vehicle, the participant must submit a properly executed Form I–823, without fee, prior to use of the vehicle in the PORTPASS program.

(xiv) That APP-approved participants who wish to enter the United States through a POE other than one designated as an APP through which they may pass must present themselves for inspection or examination by an immigration officer during normal business hours. Entry to the United States during hours when a Port of Entry is not staffed may be made only through a POE designated as an APP.

(b) *Violation of condition of the PORTPASS program.* A PORTPASS program participant who violates any condition of the PORTPASS program, or who has violated any immigration law or regulation, or a law or regulation of the United States Customs Service or other Federal Inspection Service, or who is otherwise determined by an immigration officer to be inadmissible to the United States or ineligible to participate in PORTPASS, may have the PORTPASS access revoked at the discretion of the district director or the chief patrol agent and may be subject to other applicable sanctions, such as criminal and/or administrative prosecution or deportation, as well as possible seizure of goods and/or vehicles.

(c) *Judicial review.* Nothing in this section is intended to create any right or benefit, substantive or procedural, enforceable in law or equity by a party against the Department of Justice, the Immigration and Naturalization Service, their officers or any employees of the Department of Justice.

[61 FR 53831, Oct. 16, 1996. Redesignated at 62 FR 10358, Mar. 6, 1997; 68 FR 10145, Mar. 4, 2003]

§235.8 Inadmissibility on security and related grounds.

(a) *Report.* When an immigration officer or an immigration judge suspects that an arriving alien appears to be inadmissible under section 212(a)(3)(A) (other than clause (ii)), (B), or (C) of the Act, the immigration officer or immigration judge shall order the alien removed and report the action promptly to the district director who has administrative jurisdiction over the place where the alien has arrived or where the hearing is being held. The immigration officer shall, if possible, take a brief sworn question-and-answer statement from the alien, and the alien shall be notified by personal service of Form I–147, Notice of Temporary Inadmissibility, of the action taken and the right to submit a written statement and additional information for consideration by the Attorney General. The district director shall forward the report to the regional director for further action as provided in paragraph (b) of this section.

(b) *Action by regional director.* (1) In accordance with section 235(c)(2)(B) of the Act, the regional director may deny any further inquiry or hearing by an immigration judge and order the alien removed by personal service of Form I–148, Notice of Permanent Inadmissibility, or issue any other order disposing of the case that the regional director considers appropriate.

(2) If the regional director concludes that the case does not meet the criteria contained in section 235(c)(2)(B) of the Act, the regional director may direct that:

(i) An immigration officer shall conduct a further examination of the alien, concerning the alien's admissibility; or,

(ii) The alien's case be referred to an immigration judge for a hearing, or for the continuation of any prior hearing.

(3) The regional director's decision shall be in writing and shall be signed by the regional director. Unless the written decision contains confidential information, the disclosure of which would be prejudicial to the public interest, safety, or security of the United States, the written decision shall be served on the alien. If the written decision contains such confidential information, the alien shall be served with a separate written order showing the disposition of the case, but with the confidential information deleted.

(4) The Service shall not execute a removal order under this section under circumstances that violate section 241(b)(3) of the Act or Article 3 of the Convention Against Torture. The provisions of part 208 of this chapter relating to consideration or review by an immigration judge, the Board of Immigration Appeals, or an asylum officer shall not apply.

(c) *Finality of decision.* The regional director's decision under this section is final when it is served upon the alien in accordance with paragraph (b)(3) of this section. There is no administrative appeal from the regional director's decision.

(d) *Hearing by immigration judge.* If the regional director directs that an alien subject to removal under this section be given a hearing or further hearing before an immigration judge, the hearing and all further proceedings in the matter shall be conducted in accordance with the provisions of section 240 of the Act and other applicable sections of the Act to the same extent as though the alien had been referred to an immigration judge by the examining immigration officer. In a case where the immigration judge ordered the alien removed pursuant to paragraph (a) of this section, the Service shall refer the case back to the immigration judge and proceedings shall be automatically reopened upon receipt of the notice of referral. If confidential information, not previously considered in the matter, is presented supporting the inadmissibility of the alien under section 212(a)(3)(A) (other than clause (ii)), (B) or (C) of the Act, the disclosure of which, in the discretion of the immigration judge, may be prejudicial to the public interest, safety, or security, the immigration judge may again order the alien removed under the authority of section 235(c) of the Act and further action shall be taken as provided in this section.

(e) *Nonapplicability.* The provisions of this section shall apply only to arriving aliens, as defined in 8 CFR 1.2. Aliens present in the United States who have not been admitted or paroled may be subject to proceedings under Title V of the Act.

[62 FR 10358, Mar. 6, 1997, as amended at 64 FR 8494, Feb. 19, 1999; 76 FR 53790, Aug. 29, 2011]

§ 235.9 Northern Marianas identification card.

During the two-year period that ended July 1, 1990, the Service issued Northern Marianas Identification Cards to aliens who acquired United States citizenship when the Covenant to Establish a Commonwealth of the Northern Mariana Islands in Political Union with the United States entered into force on November 3, 1986. These cards remain valid as evidence of United States citizenship. Although the Service no longer issues these cards, a United States citizen to whom a card was issued may file Form I–777, Application for Issuance or Replacement of Northern Marianas Card, to obtain replacement of a lost, stolen, or mutilated Northern Marianas Identification Card.

[62 FR 10359, Mar. 6, 1997]

§ 235.10 U.S. Citizen Identification Card.

(a) *General.* Form I–197, U.S. Citizen Identification Card, is no longer issued by the Service but valid existing cards will continue to be acceptable documentation of U.S. citizenship. Possession of the identification card is not mandatory for any purpose. A U.S. Citizen Identification Card remains the property of the United States. Because the identification card is no longer issued, there are no provisions for replacement cards.

(b) *Surrender and voidance*—(1) *Institution of proceeding under section 240 or 342 of the Act.* A U.S. Citizen Identification Card must be surrendered provisionally to a Service office upon notification by the district director that a proceeding under section 240 or 342 of the Act is being instituted against the person to whom the card was issued. The card shall be returned to the person if the final order in the proceeding does not result in voiding the card under this paragraph. A U.S. Citizen Identification Card is automatically void if the person to whom it was issued is determined to be an alien in a proceeding conducted under section 240 of the Act, or if a certificate, document, or record relating to that person is canceled under section 342 of the Act.

(2) *Investigation of validity of identification card.* A U.S. Citizen Identification Card must be surrendered provisionally upon notification by a district director that the validity of the card is being investigated. The card shall be returned to the person who surrendered it if the investigation does not result in a determination adverse to his or her claim to be a United States citizen. When an investigation results in a tentative determination adverse to the applicant's claim to be a United States citizen, the applicant shall be notified by certified mail directed to his or her last known address. The notification shall inform the applicant of the basis for the determination and of the intention of the district director to declare the card void unless within 30 days the applicant objects and demands an opportunity to see and rebut the adverse evidence. Any rebuttal, explanation, or evidence presented by the applicant must be included in the record of proceeding. The determination whether the applicant is a United States citizen must be based on the entire record and the applicant shall be notified of the determination. If it is determined that the applicant is not a United States citizen, the applicant shall be notified of the reasons, and the card deemed void. There is no appeal from the district director's decision.

(3) *Admission of alienage.* A U.S. Citizen Identification Card is void if the person to whom it was issued admits in a statement signed before an immigration officer that he or she is an alien and consents to the voidance of the card. Upon signing the statement the card must be surrendered to the immigration officer.

(4) *Surrender of void card.* A void U.S. Citizen Identification Card which has not been returned to the Service must be surrendered without delay to an immigration officer or to the issuing office of the Service.

(c) *U.S. Citizen Identification Card previously issued on Form I–179.* A valid Form I–179, U.S. Citizen Identification Card, continues to be valid subject to the provisions of this section.

[62 FR 10359, Mar. 6, 1997]

§235.11 Admission of conditional permanent residents.

(a) *General*—(1) *Conditional residence based on family relationship.* An alien seeking admission to the United States with an immigrant visa as the spouse or son or daughter of a United States citizen or lawful permanent resident shall be examined to determine whether the conditions of section 216 of the Act apply. If so, the alien shall be admitted conditionally for a period of 2 years. At the time of admission, the alien shall be notified that the alien and his or her petitioning spouse must file a Form I–751, Petition to Remove the Conditions on Residence, within the 90-day period immediately preceding the second anniversary of the alien's admission for permanent residence.

(2) *Conditional residence based on entrepreneurship.* An alien seeking admission to the United States with an immigrant visa as an alien entrepreneur (as defined in section 216A(f)(1) of the Act) or the spouse or unmarried minor child of an alien entrepreneur shall be admitted conditionally for a period of 2 years. At the time of admission, the alien shall be notified that the principal alien (entrepreneur) must file a

Form I–829, Petition by Entrepreneur to Remove Conditions, within the 90-day period immediately preceding the second anniversary of the alien's admission for permanent residence.

(b) *Correction of endorsement on immigrant visa.* If the alien is subject to the provisions of section 216 of the Act, but the classification endorsed on the immigrant visa does not so indicate, the endorsement shall be corrected and the alien shall be admitted as a lawful permanent resident on a conditional basis, if otherwise admissible. Conversely, if the alien is not subject to the provisions of section 216 of the Act, but the visa classification endorsed on the immigrant visa indicates that the alien is subject thereto (e.g., if the second anniversary of the marriage upon which the immigrant visa is based occurred after the issuance of the visa and prior to the alien's application for admission) the endorsement on the visa shall be corrected and the alien shall be admitted as a lawful permanent resident without conditions, if otherwise admissible.

(c) *Expired conditional permanent resident status.* The lawful permanent resident alien status of a conditional resident automatically terminates if the conditional basis of such status is not removed by the Service through approval of a Form I–751, Petition to Remove the Conditions on Residence or, in the case of an alien entrepreneur (as defined in section 216A(f)(1) of the Act), Form I–829, Petition by Entrepreneur to Remove Conditions. Therefore, an alien who is seeking admission as a returning resident subsequent to the second anniversary of the date on which conditional residence was obtained (except as provided in § 211.1(b)(1) of this chapter) and whose conditional basis of such residence has not been removed pursuant to section 216(c) or 216A(c) of the Act, whichever is applicable, shall be placed under removal proceedings. However, in a case where conditional residence was based on a marriage, removal proceedings may be terminated and the alien may be admitted as a returning resident if the required Form I–751 is filed jointly, or by the alien alone (if appropriate), and approved by the Service. In the case of an alien entrepreneur, removal proceedings may be terminated and the alien admitted as a returning resident if the required Form I–829 is filed by the alien entrepreneur and approved by the Service.

[62 FR 10360, Mar. 6, 1997]

§ 235.12 Global Entry program.

(a) *Program description.* The Global Entry program is a voluntary international trusted traveler program consisting of an integrated passenger processing system that expedites the movement of low-risk air travelers into the United States by providing an alternate inspection process for pre-approved, pre-screened travelers. In order to participate, a person must meet the eligibility requirements specified in this section, apply in advance, undergo pre-screening by CBP, and be accepted into the program. The Global Entry program allows participants expedited entry into the United States at selected airports identified by CBP at *www.globalentry.gov.* Participants will be processed through the use of CBP-approved technology that will include the use of biometrics to validate identity and to perform enforcement queries.

(b) *Program eligibility criteria*—(1) *Eligible individuals.* The following individuals, who hold a valid, machine-readable passport, a valid, machine-readable U.S. Lawful Permanent Resident Card (Form I–551), or other appropriate travel document as determined by CBP, may apply to participate in Global Entry:

(i) U.S. citizens, U.S. nationals, and U.S. lawful permanent residents absent any of the disqualifying factors described in paragraph (b)(2) of this section.

(ii) Certain nonimmigrant aliens from countries that have entered into arrangements with CBP concerning international trusted traveler programs absent any of the disqualifying factors described in paragraph (b)(2) of this section, and subject to the conditions set forth in the particular arrangement. Individuals from a country that has entered into such an arrangement with CBP may be eligible to apply for participation in Global Entry only after CBP announces the arrangement by publication of a notice in the

FEDERAL REGISTER. The notice will include the country, the scope of eligibility of nonimmigrant aliens from that country (*e.g.*, whether only citizens of the foreign country or citizens and non-citizens are eligible) and other conditions that may apply based on the terms of the arrangement. CBP may change or terminate these arrangements without prior notice to the public, but will announce such actions as soon as practicable on *www.globalentry.gov* and by publication of a notice in the FEDERAL REGISTER.

(iii) Persons under the age of 18 who meet the eligibility criteria of paragraph (b)(1)(i) or (ii) of this section must have the consent of a parent or legal guardian to participate in Global Entry and provide proof of such consent in accordance with CBP instructions.

(2) *Disqualifying factors.* An individual is ineligible to participate in Global Entry if CBP, at its sole discretion, determines that the individual presents a potential risk for terrorism, criminality (such as smuggling), or is otherwise not a low-risk traveler. This risk determination will be based in part upon an applicant's ability to demonstrate past compliance with laws, regulations, and policies. Reasons why an applicant may not qualify for participation include:

(i) The applicant provides false or incomplete information on the application;

(ii) The applicant has been arrested for, or convicted of, any criminal offense or has pending criminal charges or outstanding warrants in any country;

(iii) The applicant has been found in violation of any customs, immigration, or agriculture regulations, procedures, or laws in any country;

(iv) The applicant is the subject of an investigation by any federal, state, or local law enforcement agency in any country;

(v) The applicant is inadmissible to the United States under applicable immigration laws or has, at any time, been granted a waiver of inadmissibility or parole;

(vi) The applicant is known or suspected of being or having been engaged in conduct constituting, in preparation for, in aid of, or related to terrorism; or

(vii) The applicant cannot satisfy CBP of his or her low-risk status or meet other program requirements.

(c) *Participating airports.* The Global Entry program allows participants expedited entry into the United States at the locations identified at *www.globalentry.gov*. Expansions of the Global Entry program to new airports will be announced by publication in the FEDERAL REGISTER and at *www.globalentry.gov*.

(d) *Program application.* (1) Each applicant must complete and submit the program application electronically through an approved application process as determined by CBP. The application and application instructions for the Global Entry program are available at *www.globalentry.gov*.

(2) Each applicant must pay a non-refundable fee in the amount set forth at 8 CFR 103.7(b)(1)(ii)(M) for "Global Entry" at the time of application. The fee is to be paid to CBP at the time of application through the Federal Government's on-line payment system, Pay.gov or other CBP-approved process.

(3) Every applicant accepted into Global Entry is accepted for a period of 5 years provided participation is not suspended or terminated by CBP prior to the end of the 5-year period. Each applicant may apply to renew participation up to one year prior to the close of the participation period.

(4) Each applicant may check the status of his or her application through his or her account with the application system in use for Global Entry.

(e) *Interview and enrollment.* (1) After submitting the application, the applicant will be notified by CBP to schedule an in-person interview at a Global Entry enrollment center.

(2) Each applicant must bring to the interview with CBP the original of the identification document specified in his or her application. During the interview, CBP will collect biometric information from the applicant (*e.g.*, a set of ten fingerprints and/or digital photograph) to conduct background checks or as otherwise required for participation in the program.

(3) CBP may provide for alternative enrollment procedures, as necessary, to facilitate enrollment and ensure an applicant's eligibility for the program.

(f) *Valid machine-readable passport or valid lawful permanent resident card.* Each participant must possess a valid, machine-readable passport, a valid, machine-readable U.S. Lawful Permanent Resident Card (Form I–551), or other appropriate travel document as determined by CBP.

(g) *Arrival procedures.* In order to utilize the Global Entry program upon arrival in the United States, each participant must:

(1) Use the Global Entry kiosk and follow the on-screen instructions;

(2) Declare all articles being brought into the United States pursuant to 19 CFR 148.11. A Global Entry participant will be redirected to the nearest open passport control primary inspection station if the participant declares any of the following:

(i) Commercial merchandise or commercial samples, or items that exceed the applicable personal exemption amount;

(ii) More than $10,000 in currency or other monetary instruments (checks, money orders, *etc.*), or foreign equivalent in any form; or

(iii) Restricted/prohibited goods, such as agricultural products, firearms, mace, pepper spray, endangered animals, birds, controlled substances, fireworks, Cuban goods, and plants.

(h) *Application for entry, examination and inspection.* Each successful use of Global Entry constitutes a separate and completed inspection and application for entry by the participant on the date that Global Entry is used. Pursuant to the enforcement provisions of 19 CFR Part 162, Global Entry participants may be subject to further CBP examination and inspection at any time during the arrival process.

(i) *Pilot participant enrollment.* Upon implementation of the Global Entry Program, participants in the Global Entry pilot will be automatically enrolled in the Global Entry Program for 5 years from the date of enrollment in the pilot.

(j) *Denial, removal and suspension.* (1) If an applicant is denied participation in Global Entry, CBP will notify the applicant of the denial, and the reasons for the denial. CBP will also provide instructions regarding how to proceed if the applicant wishes to seek additional information as to the reason for the denial.

(2) A Global Entry participant may be suspended or removed from the program for any of the following reasons:

(i) CBP, at its sole discretion, determines that the participant has engaged in any disqualifying activities under the Global Entry program as outlined in § 235.12(b)(2);

(ii) CBP, at its sole discretion, determines that the participant provided false information in the application and/or during the application process;

(iii) CBP, at its sole discretion, determines that the participant failed to follow the terms, conditions and requirements of the program;

(iv) CBP, at its sole discretion, determines that the participant has been arrested or convicted of a crime or otherwise no longer meets the program eligibility criteria; or

(v) CBP, at its sole discretion, determines that such action is otherwise necessary.

(3) CBP will notify the participant of his or her suspension or removal in writing. Such suspension or removal is effective immediately.

(4) An applicant or participant denied, suspended, or removed does not receive a refund, in whole or in part, of his or her application processing fee.

(k) *Redress.* An individual whose application is denied or whose participation is suspended or terminated has three possible methods for redress. These processes do not create or confer any legal right, privilege or benefit on the applicant or participant, and are wholly discretionary on the part of CBP. The methods of redress are:

(1) *Enrollment center.* The applicant/participant may contest his or her denial, suspension or removal by writing to the enrollment center where that individual's interview was conducted. The enrollment center addresses are available at *www.globalentry.gov*. The letter must be received by CBP within 30 calendar days of the date provided as the date of suspension or removal. The individual should write on the envelope "Redress Request RE: Global Entry."

The letter should address any facts or conduct listed in the notification from CBP as contributing to the denial, suspension or removal and why the applicant/participant believes the reason for the action is invalid. If the applicant/participant believes that the denial, suspension or revocation was based upon inaccurate information, the individual should also include any reasonably available supporting documentation with the letter. After review, CBP will inform the individual of its redress decision. If the individual's request for redress is successful, the individual's eligibility to participate in Global Entry will resume immediately.

(2) *DHS Traveler Redress Inquiry Program (DHS TRIP).* The applicant/participant may choose to initiate the redress process through DHS TRIP. An applicant/participant seeking redress may obtain the necessary forms and information to initiate the process on the DHS TRIP Web site at *www.dhs.gov/trip*, or by contacting DHS TRIP by mail at the address on this Web site.

(3) *Ombudsman.* Applicants (including applicants who were not scheduled for an interview at an enrollment center) and participants may contest a denial, suspension or removal by writing to the CBP Trusted Traveler Ombudsman at the address listed on the Web site *www.globalentry.gov.*

[77 FR 5690, Feb. 6, 2012]

§235.13 U.S. Asia-Pacific Economic Cooperation Business Travel Card Program.

(a) *Description.* The U.S. Asia-Pacific Economic Cooperation (APEC) Business Travel Card Program is a voluntary program designed to facilitate travel for bona fide U.S. business persons engaged in business in the APEC region and U.S. government officials actively engaged in APEC business within the APEC region. Participants will receive a U.S. APEC Business Travel Card that will enable them access to fast-track immigration lanes at participating airports in foreign APEC member economies. In order to obtain a U.S. APEC Business Travel Card, an individual must meet the eligibility requirements specified in this section, apply in advance, pay any requisite fee and be approved as a card holder. The APEC member economies are identified at *http://www.apec.org.*

(b) *Program eligibility criteria*—(1) *Eligible individuals.* An individual is eligible for the U.S. APEC Business Travel Card if he or she is:

(i) A U.S. citizen;

(ii) An existing member in good standing of a CBP trusted traveler program or approved for membership in a CBP trusted traveler program during the application process described in paragraph (c) of this section; and

(iii) A bona fide U.S. business person engaged in business in the APEC region or U.S. Government official actively engaged in APEC business.

(A) "APEC business" means U.S. government activities that support the work of APEC.

(B) A "bona fide business person engaged in business in the APEC region" means a person engaged in the trade of goods, the provision of services, or the conduct of investment activities in the APEC region. Professional athletes, news correspondents, entertainers, musicians, artists or persons engaged in similar occupations are not considered to be bona fide business persons engaged in business in the APEC region.

(2) *Conditions regarding the use of the U.S. APEC Business Travel Card.* (i) The U.S. APEC Business Travel Card is not transferable and may be used only by the U.S. APEC Business Travel Card holder and not by anyone else including the card holder's spouse or child.

(ii) The U.S. APEC Business Travel Card can be used only if the card holder is traveling solely for business purposes to a foreign APEC member economy and is not engaging in paid employment in the foreign APEC member economy.

(c) *Application process.* (1) Each applicant must complete and submit an application electronically through the Global Entry Enrollment System (GOES) or other applicable process as determined by CBP. The application and application instructions for the card are available as an add-on to the CBP trusted traveler application at *www.globalentry.gov.*

(2) Each applicant must certify that he or she is an existing member in good

standing in a CBP trusted traveler program or that he or she has submitted an application to a CBP trusted traveler program; that he or she is a bona fide U.S. business person engaged in business in the APEC region or U.S. Government official actively engaged in APEC business; and, that he or she is not a professional athlete, news correspondent, entertainer, musician, artist or person engaged in a similar occupation.

(3) Each applicant must provide his or her signature so that the signature will appear on the face of the card.

(4) If the applicant is not a member of a CBP trusted traveler program, the applicant must concurrently apply for membership in a CBP trusted traveler program and be approved for such membership. Applicants for a CBP trusted traveler program must have an in-person interview, undergo a vetting process and pay the relevant CBP trusted traveler fee. Active membership in a CBP trusted traveler program is necessary for the entire duration of the U.S. APEC Business Travel Card. If membership in the CBP trusted traveler program is set to lapse before the U.S. APEC Business Travel Card expires, the individual must renew his or her CBP trusted traveler membership prior to its expiration date in order to retain membership in the U.S. APEC Business Travel Card Program.

(5) Each applicant must pay a non-refundable fee in the amount set forth at 8 CFR 103.7(b)(1)(ii)(N) for "U.S. Asia-Pacific Economic Cooperation (APEC) Business Travel Card" at the time of application. The fee is to be paid to CBP at the time of application through the Federal Government's on-line payment system, Pay.gov or other CBP-approved process.

(6) The U.S. APEC Business Travel Card is valid for a period of five years or until the expiration date of the card holder's passport if that is earlier, provided that membership is not terminated by CBP prior to the end of this period. CBP can terminate use of the U.S. APEC Business Travel Card if the card holder is no longer a member of a CBP trusted traveler program or if the individual is not compliant with the program requirements. Each applicant may apply to renew the card prior to its expiration.

(d) *Expedited entry privileges.* The U.S. APEC Business Travel Card will enable card holders access to a dedicated fast-track lane for expedited immigration processing at participating airports in foreign APEC member economies.

(e) *Entry requirements.* U.S. APEC Business Travel Card holders must present any travel or identity documentation, such as a passport and visa, required by the foreign APEC member economies.

(f) *Denial and removal.* (1) If an applicant is denied a U.S. APEC Business Travel Card, CBP will notify the applicant of the denial, and the reasons for the denial. CBP will also provide instructions regarding how to proceed if the applicant wishes to seek additional information as to the reason for the denial.

(2) A U.S. APEC Business Travel Card holder may be removed from the U.S. APEC Business Travel Card Program if CBP determines at its sole discretion that:

(i) The U.S. APEC Business Travel Card holder provided false information in the application and/or during the application process;

(ii) The U.S. APEC Business Travel Card holder failed to follow the terms, conditions and requirements of the program (including continued active membership in a CBP trusted traveler program);

(iii) The U.S. APEC Business Travel Card holder has been arrested or convicted of a crime or otherwise no longer meets the program eligibility criteria; or

(iv) Such action is otherwise necessary.

(3) CBP will notify the U.S. APEC Business Travel Card holder of his or her removal in writing. Such removal is effective immediately.

(4) A U.S. APEC Business Travel Card applicant or a U.S. APEC Business Travel Card holder who is denied or removed will not receive a refund, in whole or in part, of the application fee.

(g) *Redress.* An individual whose application is denied or whose participation is suspended or terminated has two possible methods of redress. These processes do not create or confer any legal right, privilege, or benefit on the applicant or participant, and are wholly discretionary on the part of CBP. The methods of redress are:

(1) *Enrollment center*. If the applicant or participant applied concurrently for the U.S. APEC Business Travel Card and a CBP trusted traveler program, the applicant or participant may contest his or her denial or removalby writing to the enrollment center where that individual's CBP trusted traveler program interview was conducted. If the applicant or participant was already a member of a CBP trusted traveler program, the applicant or participant may contest his or her denial or removal by writing to the enrollment center where that individual's signature was collected for the U.S. APEC Business Travel Card. The enrollment center addresses are available at *www.globalentry.gov*, *http://www.globalentry.gov/nexus.html* and *http://www.globalentry.gov/sentri.html*. The letter must be received by CBP within 30 calendar days of the date provided as the date of removal. The individual should write on the envelope "Redress Request RE: U.S. APEC Business Travel Card." The letter should address any facts or conduct listed in the notification from CBP as contributing to the denial or removal and why the applicant or participant believes the reason for the action is invalid. If the applicant or participant believes that the denial or removal was based upon inaccurate information, the individual should also include any reasonably available supporting documentation with the letter. After review, CBP will inform the individual of its redress decision. If the individual's request for redress is successful, the individual's eligibility to be a U.S. APEC Business Travel Card holder will continue immediately.

(2) *Ombudsman*. Applicants and participants may contest a denial or removal by writing to the CBP Trusted Traveler Ombudsman at the address listed on the Web site www.globalentry.gov.

(h) *Duration of U.S. APEC Business Travel Card Program*. DHS will issue U.S. APEC Business Travel Cards through September 30, 2018. Unless revoked, U.S. APEC Business Travel Cards issued on or before September 30, 2018 are valid until their expiration date, even if the expiration date is after September 30, 2018.

[79 FR 27174, May 13, 2014, as amended at 81 FR 84415, Nov. 23, 2016]

PART 236—APPREHENSION AND DETENTION OF INADMISSIBLE AND DEPORTABLE ALIENS; REMOVAL OF ALIENS ORDERED REMOVED

Subpart A—Detention of Aliens Prior to Order of Removal

Subpart B—Family Unity Program

AUTHORITY: 5 U.S.C. 301, 552, 552a; 8 U.S.C. 1103, 1182, 1224, 1225, 1226, 1227, 1231, 1362; 18 U.S.C. 4002, 4013(c)(4); 8 CFR part 2.

SOURCE: 62 FR 10360, Mar. 6, 1997, unless otherwise noted.

Subpart A—Detention of Aliens Prior to Order of Removal

§ 236.1 Apprehension, custody, and detention.

(a) *Detainers*. The issuance of a detainer under this section shall be governed by the provisions of § 287.7 of this chapter.

(b) *Warrant of arrest*—(1) *In general*. At the time of issuance of the notice to appear, or at any time thereafter and up to the time removal proceedings are completed, the respondent may be arrested and taken into custody under the authority of Form I–200, Warrant of Arrest. A warrant of arrest may be issued only by those immigration officers listed in § 287.5(e)(2) of this chapter and may be served only by those immigration officers listed in § 287.5(e)(3) of this chapter.

(2) If, after the issuance of a warrant of arrest, a determination is made not to serve it, any officer authorized to issue such warrant may authorize its cancellation.

(c) *Custody issues and release procedures*—(1) *In general.* (i) After the expiration of the Transition Period Custody Rules (TPCR) set forth in section 303(b)(3) of Div. C of Pub. L. 104–208, no alien described in section 236(c)(1) of the Act may be released from custody during removal proceedings except pursuant to section 236(c)(2) of the Act.

(ii) Paragraph (c)(2) through (c)(8) of this section shall govern custody determinations for aliens subject to the TPCR while they remain in effect. For purposes of this section, an alien "subject to the TPCR" is an alien described in section 303(b)(3)(A) of Div. C of Pub. L. 104–208 who is in deportation proceedings, subject to a final order of deportation, or in removal proceedings. The TPCR do not apply to aliens in exclusion proceedings under former section 236 of the Act, aliens in expedited removal proceedings under section 235(b)(1) of the Act, or aliens subject to a final order of removal.

(2) *Aliens not lawfully admitted.* Subject to paragraph (c)(6)(i) of this section, but notwithstanding any other provision within this section, an alien subject to the TPCR who is not lawfully admitted is not eligible to be considered for release from custody.

(i) An alien who remains in status as an alien lawfully admitted for permanent residence, conditionally admitted for permanent residence, or lawfully admitted for temporary residence is "lawfully admitted" for purposes of this section.

(ii) An alien in removal proceedings, in deportation proceedings, or subject to a final order of deportation, and not described in paragraph (c)(2)(i) of this section, is not "lawfully admitted" for purposes of this section unless the alien last entered the United States lawfully and is not presently an applicant for admission to the United States.

(3) *Criminal aliens eligible to be considered for release.* Except as provided in this section, or otherwise provided by law, an alien subject to the TPCR may be considered for release from custody if lawfully admitted. Such an alien must first demonstrate, by clear and convincing evidence, that release would not pose a danger to the safety of other persons or of property. If an alien meets this burden, the alien must further demonstrate, by clear and convincing evidence, that the alien is likely to appear for any scheduled proceeding (including any appearance required by the Service or EOIR) in order to be considered for release in the exercise of discretion.

(4) *Criminal aliens ineligible to be considered for release except in certain special circumstances.* An alien, other than an alien lawfully admitted for permanent residence, subject to section 303(b)(3)(A) (ii) or (iii) of Div. C. of Pub. L. 104–208 is ineligible to be considered for release if the alien:

(i) Is described in section 241(a)(2)(C) of the Act (as in effect prior to April 1, 1997), or has been convicted of a crime described in section 101(a)(43)(B), (E)(ii) or (F) of the Act (as in effect on April 1, 1997);

(ii) Has been convicted of a crime described in section 101(a)(43)(G) of the Act (as in effect on April 1, 1997) or a crime or crimes involving moral turpitude related to property, and sentenced therefor (including in the aggregate) to at least 3 years' imprisonment;

(iii) Has failed to appear for an immigration proceeding without reasonable cause or has been subject to a bench warrant or similar legal process (unless quashed, withdrawn, or cancelled as improvidently issued);

(iv) Has been convicted of a crime described in section 101(a)(43)(Q) or (T) of the Act (as in effect on April 1, 1997);

(v) Has been convicted in a criminal proceeding of a violation of section 273, 274, 274C, 276, or 277 of the Act, or has admitted the factual elements of such a violation;

(vi) Has overstayed a period granted for voluntary departure;

(vii) Has failed to surrender or report for removal pursuant to an order of exclusion, deportation, or removal;

(viii) Does not wish to pursue, or is statutorily ineligible for, any form of relief from exclusion, deportation, or removal under this chapter or the Act; or

(ix) Is described in paragraphs (c)(5)(i)(A), (B), or (C) of this section but has not been sentenced, including in the aggregate but not including any portions suspended, to at least 2 years' imprisonment, unless the alien was lawfully admitted and has not, since the commencement of proceedings and within the 10 years prior thereto, been convicted of a crime, failed to comply with an order to surrender or a period of voluntary departure, or been subject to a bench warrant or similar legal process (unless quashed, withdrawn, or cancelled as improvidently issued). An alien eligible to be considered for release under this paragraph must meet the burdens described in paragraph (c)(3) of this section in order to be released from custody in the exercise of discretion.

(5) *Criminal aliens ineligible to be considered for release.* (i) A criminal alien subject to section 303(b)(3)(A)(ii) or (iii) of Div. C of Pub. L. 104–208 is ineligible to be considered for release if the alien has been sentenced, including in the aggregate but not including any portions suspended, to at least 2 years' imprisonment, and the alien

(A) Is described in section 237(a)(2)(D)(i) or (ii) of the Act (as in effect on April 1, 1997), or has been convicted of a crime described in section 101(a)(43)(A), (C), (E)(i), (H), (I), (K)(iii), or (L) of the Act (as in effect on April 1, 1997);

(B) Is described in section 237(a)(2)(A)(iv) of the Act; or

(C) Has escaped or attempted to escape from the lawful custody of a local, State, or Federal prison, agency, or officer within the United States.

(ii) Notwithstanding paragraph (c)(5)(i) of this section, a permanent resident alien who has not, since the commencement of proceedings and within the 15 years prior thereto, been convicted of a crime, failed to comply with an order to surrender or a period of voluntary departure, or been subject to a bench warrant or similar legal process (unless quashed, withdrawn, or cancelled as improvidently issued), may be considered for release under paragraph (c)(3) of this section.

(6) *Unremovable aliens and certain long-term detainees.* (i) If the district director determines that an alien subject to section 303(b)(3)(A)(ii) or (iii) of Div. C of Pub. L. 104–208 cannot be removed from the United States because the designated country of removal or deportation will not accept the alien's return, the district director may, in the exercise of discretion, consider release of the alien from custody upon such terms and conditions as the district director may prescribe, without regard to paragraphs (c)(2), (c)(4), and (c)(5) of this section.

(ii) The district director may also, notwithstanding paragraph (c)(5) of this section, consider release from custody, upon such terms and conditions as the district director may prescribe, of any alien described in paragraph (c)(2)(ii) of this section who has been in the Service's custody for six months pursuant to a final order of deportation terminating the alien's status as a lawful permanent resident.

(iii) The district director may release an alien from custody under this paragraph only in accordance with the standards set forth in paragraph (c)(3) of this section and any other applicable provisions of law.

(iv) The district director's custody decision under this paragraph shall not be subject to redetermination by an immigration judge, but, in the case of a custody decision under paragraph (c)(6)(ii) of this section, may be appealed to the Board of Immigration Appeals pursuant to paragraph (d)(3)(iii) of this section.

(7) *Construction.* A reference in this section to a provision in section 241 of the Act as in effect prior to April 1, 1997, shall be deemed to include a reference to the corresponding provision in section 237 of the Act as in effect on April 1, 1997. A reference in this section to a "crime" shall be considered to include a reference to a conspiracy or attempt to commit such a crime. In calculating the 10-year period specified in paragraph (c)(4) of this section and the 15-year period specified in paragraph

(c)(5) of this section, no period during which the alien was detained or incarcerated shall count toward the total. References in paragraph (c)(6)(i) of this section to the "district director" shall be deemed to include a reference to any official designated by the Assistant Secretary/Director of ICE to exercise custody authority over aliens covered by that paragraph. Nothing in this part shall be construed as prohibiting an alien from seeking reconsideration of the Service's determination that the alien is within a category barred from release under this part.

(8) Any officer authorized to issue a warrant of arrest may, in the officer's discretion, release an alien not described in section 236(c)(1) of the Act, under the conditions at section 236(a)(2) and (3) of the Act; provided that the alien must demonstrate to the satisfaction of the officer that such release would not pose a danger to property or persons, and that the alien is likely to appear for any future proceeding. Such an officer may also, in the exercise of discretion, release an alien in deportation proceedings pursuant to the authority in section 242 of the Act (as designated prior to April 1, 1997), except as otherwise provided by law.

(9) When an alien who, having been arrested and taken into custody, has been released, such release may be revoked at any time in the discretion of the district director, acting district director, deputy district director, assistant district director for investigations, assistant district director for detention and deportation, or officer in charge (except foreign), in which event the alien may be taken into physical custody and detained. If detained, unless a breach has occurred, any outstanding bond shall be revoked and canceled.

(10) The provisions of § 103.6 of this chapter shall apply to any bonds authorized. Subject to the provisions of this section, the provisions of § 1003.19 of this chapter shall govern availability to the respondent of recourse to other administrative authority for release from custody.

(11) An immigration judge may not exercise the authority provided in this section, and the review process described in paragraph (d) of this section shall not apply, with respect to any alien beyond the custody jurisdiction of the immigration judge as provided in § 1003.19(h) of this chapter.

(d) *Appeals from custody decisions*—(1) *Application to immigration judge.* After an initial custody determination by the district director, including the setting of a bond, the respondent may, at any time before an order under 8 CFR part 240 becomes final, request amelioration of the conditions under which he or she may be released. Prior to such final order, and except as otherwise provided in this chapter, the immigration judge is authorized to exercise the authority in section 236 of the Act (or section 242(a)(1) of the Act as designated prior to April 1, 1997 in the case of an alien in deportation proceedings) to detain the alien in custody, release the alien, and determine the amount of bond, if any, under which the respondent may be released, as provided in § 1003.19 of this chapter. If the alien has been released from custody, an application for amelioration of the terms of release must be filed within 7 days of release.

(2) *Application to the district director.* After expiration of the 7-day period in paragraph (d)(1) of this section, the respondent may request review by the district director of the conditions of his or her release.

(3) *Appeal to the Board of Immigration Appeals.* An appeal relating to bond and custody determinations may be filed to the Board of Immigration Appeals in the following circumstances:

(i) In accordance with § 1003.38 of this chapter, the alien or the Service may appeal the decision of an immigration judge pursuant to paragraph (d)(1) of this section.

(ii) The alien, within 10 days, may appeal from the district director's decision under paragraph (d)(2)(i) of this section.

(4) *Effect of filing an appeal.* The filing of an appeal from a determination of an immigration judge or district director under this paragraph shall not operate to delay compliance with the order (except as provided in § 1003.19(i), nor stay the administrative proceedings or removal.

(e) *Privilege of communication.* Every detained alien shall be notified that he or she may communicate with the consular or diplomatic officers of the country of his or her nationality in the United States. Existing treaties with the following countries require immediate communication with appropriate consular or diplomatic officers whenever nationals of the following countries are detained in removal proceedings, whether or not requested by the alien and even if the alien requests that no communication be undertaken in his or her behalf. When notifying consular or diplomatic officials, Service officers shall not reveal the fact that any detained alien has applied for asylum or withholding of removal.

Algeria[1]
Antigua and Barbuda
Armenia
Azerbaijan
Bahamas, The
Barbados
Belarus
Belize
Brunei
Bulgaria
China (People's Republic of)[2]
Costa Rica
Cyprus
Czech Republic
Dominica
Fiji
Gambia, The
Georgia
Ghana
Grenada
Guyana
Hong Kong[3]
Hungary
Jamaica
Kazakhstan
Kiribati
Kuwait
Kyrgyzstan
Malaysia
Malta
Mauritius
Moldova
Mongolia
Nigeria
Philippines
Poland[4]
Romania
Russian Federation
St. Kitts and Nevis
St. Lucia
St. Vincent/Grenadines
Seychelles
Sierra Leone
Singapore
Slovak Republic
Tajikistan
Tanzania
Tonga
Trinidad and Tobago
Tunisia
Turkmenistan
Tuvalu
Ukraine
United Kingdom[5]
U.S.S.R.[6]
Uzbekistan
Zambia
Zimbabwe

---

[1] Arrangements with the countries listed in 8 CFR 236.1(e) provide that U.S. authorities shall notify responsible representatives within 72 hours of the arrest or detention of one of their nationals.

[2] Notification is not mandatory in the case of any person who carries a "Republic of China" passport issued by Taiwan. Such persons should be informed without delay that the nearest office of the Taipei Economic and Cultural Representative Office ("TECRO"), the unofficial entity representing Taiwan's interests in the United States, can be notified at their request.

[3] Hong Kong reverted to Chinese sovereignty on July 1, 1997, and is now officially referred to as the Hong Kong Special Administrative Region, or "S.A.R." Under paragraph 3(f)(2) of the March 25, 1997, U.S.-China Agreement on the Maintenance of the U.S. Consulate General in the Hong Kong Special Administrative Region, U.S. officials are required to notify Chinese officials of the arrest or detention of the bearers of Hong Kong passports in the same manner as is required for bearers of Chinese passports—i.e., immediately, and in any event, within four days of the arrest or detention.

[4] Consular communication is not mandatory for any Polish national who has been admitted for permanent residence in the United States. Such notification should only be provided upon request by a Polish national with permanent residency in the United States.

[5] United Kingdom includes England, Scotland, Wales, Northern Ireland and Islands and the British dependencies of Anguilla, British Virgin Islands, Bermuda, Montserrat, and the Turks and Caicos Islands. Their residents carry British passports.

[6] All U.S.S.R. successor states are covered by this agreement. They are: Armenia, Azerbaijan, Belarus, Georgia, Kazakhstan, Kyrgyzstan, Moldova, Russian Federation, Tajikistan, Turkmenistan, Ukraine, and Uzbekistan. Although the U.S.S.R. no longer exists, the U.S.S.R is listed here, because some nationals of its successor states may still be traveling on a U.S.S.R. passport. Mandatory consular notification applies to any national of such a state, including one traveling on a U.S.S.R. passport.

(f) *Notification to Executive Office for Immigration Review of change in custody status.* The Service shall notify the Immigration Court having administrative control over the Record of Proceeding of any change in custody location or of release from, or subsequent taking into, Service custody of a respondent/applicant pursuant to § 1003.19(g) of this chapter.

(g) *Notice of custody determination*—(1) *In general.* At the time of issuance of the notice to appear, or at any time thereafter and up to the time removal proceedings are completed, an immigration official may issue a Form I–286, Notice of Custody Determination. A notice of custody determination may be issued by those immigration officials listed in 8 CFR 287.5(e)(2) and may be served by those immigration officials listed in 8 CFR 287.5(e)(3), or other officers or employees of the Department or the United States who are delegated the authority to do so pursuant to 8 CFR 2.1.

(2) *Cancellation.* If after the issuance of a notice of custody determination, a determination is made not to serve it, any official authorized to issue such notice may authorize its cancellation.

[62 FR 10360, Mar. 6, 1997; 62 FR 15363, Apr. 1, 1997, as amended at 63 FR 27449, May 19, 1998; 65 FR 80294, Dec. 21, 2000; 70 FR 67088, Nov. 4, 2005; 72 FR 1924, Jan. 17, 2007; 81 FR 62355, Sept. 9, 2016]

§ 236.2 Confined aliens, incompetents, and minors.

(a) *Service.* If the respondent is confined, or if he or she is an incompetent, or a minor under the age of 14, the notice to appear, and the warrant of arrest, if issued, shall be served in the manner prescribed in § 239.1 of this chapter upon the person or persons specified by 8 CFR 103.8(c).

(b) *Service custody and cost of maintenance.* An alien confined because of physical or mental disability in an institution or hospital shall not be accepted into physical custody by the Service until an order of removal has been entered and the Service is ready to remove the alien. When such an alien is an inmate of a public or private institution at the time of the commencement of the removal proceedings, expenses for the maintenance of the alien shall not be incurred by the Government until he or she is taken into physical custody by the Service.

[62 FR 10360, Mar. 6, 1997, as amended at 76 FR 53790, Aug. 29, 2011]

§ 236.3 Detention and release of juveniles.

(a) *Juveniles.* A juvenile is defined as an alien under the age of 18 years.

(b) *Release.* Juveniles for whom bond has been posted, for whom parole has been authorized, or who have been ordered released on recognizance, shall be released pursuant to the following guidelines:

(1) Juveniles shall be released, in order of preference, to:

(i) A parent;

(ii) Legal guardian; or

(iii) An adult relative (brother, sister, aunt, uncle, grandparent) who is not presently in Service detention, unless a determination is made that the detention of such juvenile is required to secure his or her timely appearance before the Service or the Immigration Court or to ensure the juvenile's safety or that of others. In cases where the parent, legal guardian, or adult relative resides at a location distant from where the juvenile is detained, he or she may secure release at a Service office located near the parent, legal guardian, or adult relative.

(2) If an individual specified in paragraphs (b)(1)(i) through (iii) of this section cannot be located to accept custody of a juvenile, and the juvenile has identified a parent, legal guardian, or adult relative in Service detention, simultaneous release of the juvenile and the parent, legal guardian, or adult relative shall be evaluated on a discretionary case-by-case basis.

(3) In cases where the parent or legal guardian is in Service detention or outside the United States, the juvenile may be released to such person as is designated by the parent or legal guardian in a sworn affidavit, executed before an immigration officer or consular officer, as capable and willing to care for the juvenile's well-being. Such person must execute an agreement to care for the juvenile and to ensure the

juvenile's presence at all future proceedings before the Service or an immigration judge.

(4) In unusual and compelling circumstances and in the discretion of the Director of the Office of Juvenile Affairs, a juvenile may be released to an adult, other than those identified in paragraphs (b)(1)(i) through (b)(1)(iii) of this section, who executes an agreement to care for the juvenile's well-being and to ensure the juvenile's presence at all future proceedings before the Service or an immigration judge.

(c) *Juvenile coordinator.* The case of a juvenile for whom detention is determined to be necessary should be referred to the "Juvenile Coordinator," whose responsibilities should include, but not be limited to, finding suitable placement of the juvenile in a facility designated for the occupancy of juveniles. These may include juvenile facilities contracted by the Service, state or local juvenile facilities, or other appropriate agencies authorized to accommodate juveniles by the laws of the state or locality.

(d) *Detention.* In the case of a juvenile for whom detention is determined to be necessary, for such interim period of time as is required to locate suitable placement for the juvenile, whether such placement is under paragraph (b) or (c) of this section, the juvenile may be temporarily held by Service authorities or placed in any Service detention facility having separate accommodations for juveniles.

(e) *Refusal of release.* If a parent of a juvenile detained by the Service can be located, and is otherwise suitable to receive custody of the juvenile, and the juvenile indicates a refusal to be released to his or her parent, the parent(s) shall be notified of the juvenile's refusal to be released to the parent(s), and they shall be afforded the opportunity to present their views to the district director, chief patrol agent, Director of the Office of Juvenile Affairs or immigration judge before a custody determination is made.

(f) *Notice to parent of application for relief.* If a juvenile seeks release from detention, voluntary departure, parole, or any form of relief from removal, where it appears that the grant of such relief may effectively terminate some interest inherent in the parent-child relationship and/or the juvenile's rights and interests are adverse with those of the parent, and the parent is presently residing in the United States, the parent shall be given notice of the juvenile's application for relief, and shall be afforded an opportunity to present his or her views and assert his or her interest to the district director, Director of the Office of Juvenile Affairs or immigration judge before a determination is made as to the merits of the request for relief.

(g) *Voluntary departure.* Each juvenile, apprehended in the immediate vicinity of the border, who resides permanently in Mexico or Canada, shall be informed, prior to presentation of the voluntary departure form or being allowed to withdraw his or her application for admission, that he or she may make a telephone call to a parent, close relative, a friend, or to an organization found on the free legal services list. A juvenile who does not reside in Mexico or Canada who is apprehended shall be provided access to a telephone and must in fact communicate either with a parent, adult relative, friend, or with an organization found on the free legal services list prior to presentation of the voluntary departure form. If such juvenile, of his or her own volition, asks to contact a consular officer, and does in fact make such contact, the requirements of this section are satisfied.

(h) *Notice and request for disposition.* When a juvenile alien is apprehended, he or she must be given a Form I–770, Notice of Rights and Disposition. If the juvenile is less than 14 years of age or unable to understand the notice, the notice shall be read and explained to the juvenile in a language he or she understands. In the event a juvenile who has requested a hearing pursuant to the notice subsequently decides to accept voluntary departure or is allowed to withdraw his or her application for admission, a new Form I–770 shall be given to, and signed by the juvenile.

[62 FR 10360, Mar. 6, 1997, as amended at 67 FR 39258, June 7, 2002]

§ 236.4 Removal of S–5, S–6, and S–7 nonimmigrants.

(a) *Condition of classification.* As a condition of classification and continued stay in classification pursuant to section 101(a)(15)(S) of the Act, nonimmigrants in S classification must have executed Form I–854, Part B, Inter-agency Alien Witness and Informant Record, certifying that they have knowingly waived their right to a removal hearing and right to contest, other than on the basis of an application for withholding of deportation or removal, any removal action, including detention pending deportation or removal, instituted before lawful permanent resident status is obtained.

(b) *Determination of deportability.* (1) A determination to remove a deportable alien classified pursuant to section 101(a)(15)(S) of the Act shall be made by the district director having jurisdiction over the place where the alien is located.

(2) A determination to remove such a deportable alien shall be based on one or more of the grounds of deportability listed in section 237 of the Act based on conduct committed after, or conduct or a condition not disclosed to the Service prior to, the alien's classification as an S nonimmigrant under section 101(a)(15)(S) of the Act, or for a violation of, or failure to adhere to, the particular terms and conditions of status in S nonimmigrant classification.

(c) *Removal procedures.* (1) A district director who determines to remove an alien witness or informant in S nonimmigrant classification shall notify the Commissioner, the Assistant Attorney General, Criminal Division, and the relevant law enforcement agency in writing to that effect. The Assistant Attorney General, Criminal Division, shall concur in or object to that decision. Unless the Assistant Attorney General, Criminal Division, objects within 7 days, he or she shall be deemed to have concurred in the decision. In the event of an objection by the Assistant Attorney General, Criminal Division, the matter will be expeditiously referred to the Deputy Attorney General for a final resolution. In no circumstances shall the alien or the relevant law enforcement agency have a right of appeal from any decision to remove.

(2) A district director who has provided notice as set forth in paragraph (c)(1) of this section and who has been advised by the Commissioner that the Assistant Attorney General, Criminal Division, has not objected shall issue a Warrant of Removal. The alien shall immediately be arrested and taken into custody by the district director initiating the removal. An alien classified under the provisions of section 101(a)(15)(S) of the Act who is determined, pursuant to a warrant issued by a district director, to be deportable from the United States shall be removed from the United States to his or her country of nationality or last residence. The agency that requested the alien's presence in the United States shall ensure departure from the United States and so inform the district director in whose jurisdiction the alien has last resided. The district director, if necessary, shall oversee the alien's departure from the United States and, in any event, shall notify the Commissioner of the alien's departure.

(d) *Withholding of removal.* An alien classified pursuant to section 101(a)(15)(S) of the Act who applies for withholding of removal shall have 10 days from the date the Warrant of Removal is served upon the alien to file an application for such relief with the district director initiating the removal order. The procedures contained in §§ 208.2 and 208.16 of this chapter shall apply to such an alien who applies for withholding of removal.

(e) *Inadmissibility.* An alien who applies for admission under the provisions of section 101(a)(15)(S) of the Act who is determined by an immigration officer not to be eligible for admission under that section or to be inadmissible to the United States under one or more of the grounds of inadmissibility listed in section 212 of the Act and which have not been previously waived by the Commissioner will be taken into custody. The district director having jurisdiction over the port-of-entry shall follow the notification procedures specified in paragraph (c)(1) of this section. A district director who has provided such notice and who has been advised by the Commissioner that the Assistant Attorney General, Criminal Division, has not objected shall remove the alien without further hearing. An alien may not contest such removal, other than by applying for withholding of removal.

§236.5 Fingerprints and photographs.

Every alien 14 years of age or older against whom proceedings based on deportability under section 237 of the Act are commenced under this part by service of a notice to appear shall be fingerprinted and photographed. Such fingerprints and photographs shall be made available to Federal, State, and local law enforcement agencies upon request to the district director or chief patrol agent having jurisdiction over the alien's record. Any such alien, regardless of his or her age, shall be photographed and/or fingerprinted if required by any immigration officer authorized to issue a notice to appear. Every alien 14 years of age or older who is found to be inadmissible to the United States and ordered removed by an immigration judge shall be fingerprinted, unless during the preceding year he or she has been fingerprinted at an American consular office.

§236.6 Information regarding detainees.

No person, including any state or local government entity or any privately operated detention facility, that houses, maintains, provides services to, or otherwise holds any detainee on behalf of the Service (whether by contract or otherwise), and no other person who by virtue of any official or contractual relationship with such person obtains information relating to any detainee, shall disclose or otherwise permit to be made public the name of, or other information relating to, such detainee. Such information shall be under the control of the Service and shall be subject to public disclosure only pursuant to the provisions of applicable federal laws, regulations and executive orders. Insofar as any documents or other records contain such information, such documents shall not be public records. This section applies to all persons and information identified or described in it, regardless of when such persons obtained such information, and applies to all requests for public disclosure of such information, including requests that are the subject of proceedings pending as of April 17, 2002.

[67 FR 19511, Apr. 22, 2002]

§§236.7–236.9 [Reserved]

Subpart B—Family Unity Program

§236.10 Description of program.

The family unity program implements the provisions of section 301 of the Immigration Act of 1990, Public Law 101–649. This Act is referred to in this subpart as "IMMACT 90".

§236.11 Definitions.

In this subpart, the term:

Eligible immigrant means a qualified immigrant who is the spouse or unmarried child of a legalized alien.

For purposes of §§236.10 to 236.18 only, *Legalized alien* means an alien who:

(1) Is a temporary or permanent resident under section 210 or 245A of the Act;

(2) Is a permanent resident under section 202 of the Immigration Reform and Control Act of 1986 (Cuban/Haitian Adjustment); or

(3) Is a naturalized U.S. citizen who was a permanent resident under section 210 or 245A of the Act or section 202 of the Immigrant Reform and Control Act of 1986 (IRCA) (Cuban/Haitian Adjustment), and maintained such a status until his or her naturalization.

[62 FR 10360, Mar. 6, 1997, as amended at 65 FR 43679, July 14, 2000]

§236.12 Eligibility.

(a) *General.* An alien who is not a lawful permanent resident is eligible to apply for benefits under the Family Unity Program if he or she establishes:

(1) That he or she entered the United States before May 5, 1988 (in the case of a relationship to a legalized alien described in subsection (b)(2)(B) or (b)(2)(C) of section 301 of IMMACT 90), or as of December 1, 1988 (in the case of

a relationship to a legalized alien described in subsection (b)(2)(A) of section 301 of IMMACT 90), and has been continuously residing in the United States since that date; and

(2) That as of May 5, 1988, (in the case of a relationship to a legalized alien described in subsection (b)(2)(B) or (b)(2)(C) of section 301 of IMMACT 90) or as of December 1, 1988, (in the case of a relationship to a legalized alien described in subsection (b)(2) (A) of section 301 of IMMACT 90), he or she was the spouse or unmarried child of a legalized alien, and that he or she has been eligible continuously since that time for family-sponsored immigrant status under section 203(a) (1), (2), or (3) or as an immediate relative under section 201 (b)(2) of the Act based on the same relationship.

(b) *Legalization application pending as of May 5, 1988 or December 1, 1988.* An alien whose legalization application was filed on or before May 5, 1988 (in the case of a relationship to a legalized alien described in subsection (b)(2)(B) or (b)(2)(C) of section 301 of IMMACT 90), or as of December 1, 1988 (in the case of a relationship to a legalized alien described in subsection (b)(2)(A) of section 301 of IMMACT 90), but not approved until after that date will be treated as having been a legalized alien as of May 5, 1988 (in the case of a relationship to a legalized alien described in subsection (b)(2)(B) or (b)(2)(C) of section 301 of IMMACT 90), or as of December 1, 1988 (in the case of a relationship to a legalized alien described in subsection (b)(2)(A) of section 301 of IMMACT 90), for purposes of the Family Unity Program.

[62 FR 10360, Mar. 6, 1997, as amended at 65 FR 43679, July 14, 2000]

§ 236.13 Ineligible aliens.

The following categories of aliens are ineligible for benefits under the Family Unity Program:

(a) An alien who is deportable under any paragraph in section 237(a) of the Act, except paragraphs (1)(A), (1)(B), (1)(C), and (3)(A); provided that an alien who is deportable under section 237(a)(1)(A) of such Act is also ineligible for benefits under the Family Unity Program if deportability is based upon a ground of inadmissibility described in section 212(a)(2) or (3) of the Act;

(b) An alien who has been convicted of a felony or three or more misdemeanors in the United States;

(c) An alien described in section 241(b)(3)(B) of the Act; or

(d) An alien who has committed an act of juvenile delinquency (as defined in 18 U.S.C. 5031) which if committed by an adult would be classified as:

(1) A felony crime of violence that has an element the use or attempted use of physical force against another individual; or

(2) A felony offense that by its nature involves a substantial risk that physical force against another individual may be used in the course of committing the offense.

[62 FR 10360, Mar. 6, 1997, as amended at 65 FR 43680, July 14, 2000]

§ 236.14 Filing.

(a) *General.* A Form I–817, Application for Family Unity Benefits, must be filed with the correct fee required in § 103.7(b)(1) of this chapter and the required supporting documentation. A separate application with appropriate fee and documentation must be filed for each person claiming eligibility.

(b) *Decision.* The service center director has sole jurisdiction to adjudicate an application for benefits under the Family Unity Program. The director will provide the applicant with specific reasons for any decision to deny an application. Denial of an application may not be appealed. An applicant who believes that the grounds for denial have been overcome may submit another application with the appropriate fee and documentation.

(c) *Referral of denied cases for consideration of issuance of notice to appear.* If an application is denied, the case will be referred to the district director with jurisdiction over the alien's place of residence for consideration of whether to issue a notice to appear. After an initial denial, an applicant's case will not be referred for issuance of a notice to appear until 90 days from the date of the initial denial, to allow the alien the opportunity to file a new Form I–817 application in order to attempt to overcome the basis of the denial. However, if the applicant is found not to be eligible for benefits under §236.13(b), the Service reserves the right to issue a notice to appear at any time after the initial denial.

[62 FR 10360, Mar. 6, 1997, as amended at 65 FR 43680, July 14, 2000; 66 FR 29672, June 1, 2001; 74 FR 26939, June 5, 2009]

§236.15 Voluntary departure and eligibility for employment.

(a) *Authority.* Voluntary departure under this section implements the provisions of section 301 of IMMACT 90, and authority to grant voluntary departure under the family unity program derives solely from that section. Voluntary departure under the family unity program shall be governed solely by this section, notwithstanding the provisions of section 240B of the Act and 8 CFR part 240.

(b) *Children of legalized aliens.* Children of legalized aliens residing in the United States, who were born during an authorized absence from the United States of mothers who are currently residing in the United States under voluntary departure pursuant to the Family Unity Program, may be granted voluntary departure under section 301 of IMMACT 90 for a period of 2 years.

(c) *Duration of voluntary departure.* An alien whose application for benefits under the Family Unity Program is approved will receive voluntary departure for 2 years, commencing with the date of approval of the application. Voluntary departure under this section shall be considered effective from the date on which the application was properly filed.

(d) *Employment authorization.* An alien granted benefits under the Family Unity Program is authorized to be employed in the United States and will receive an employment authorization document. The validity period of the employment authorization document will coincide with the period of voluntary departure.

(e) *Extension of voluntary departure.* An application for an extension of voluntary departure under the Family Unity Program must be filed by the alien on Form I-817 along with the correct fee required in §103.7(b)(1) of this chapter and the required supporting documentation. The submission of a copy of the previous approval notice will assist in shortening the processing time. An extension may be granted if the alien continues to be eligible for benefits under the Family Unity Program. However, an extension may not be approved if the legalized alien is a lawful permanent resident, or a naturalized U.S. citizen who was a lawful permanent resident under section 210 or 245A of the Act or section 202 of the Immigration Reform and Control Act of 1986 (IRCA), Pub. L. 66–903, and maintained such status until his or her naturalization, and a petition for family-sponsored immigrant status has not been filed on behalf of the applicant. In such case, the Service will notify the alien of the reason for the denial and afford him or her the opportunity to file another Form I-817 once the petition, Form I-130, has been filed on his or her behalf. No charging document will be issued for a period of 90 days from the date of the denial.

(f) *Supporting documentation for extension application.* Supporting documentation need not include documentation provided with the previous application(s). The extension application shoud only include changes to previous applications and evidence of continuing eligibility since the date of prior approval.

[62 FR 10360, Mar. 6, 1997, as amended at 65 FR 43680, July 14, 2000]

§236.16 Travel outside the United States.

An alien granted Family Unity Program benefits who intends to travel outside the United States temporarily must apply for advance authorization in accordance with 8 CFR 223.2(a). The authority to grant an application for advance authorization for an alien granted Family Unity Program benefits rests solely with USCIS. An alien who is granted advance authorization and returns to the United States in accordance with such authorization, and who is found not to be inadmissible under section 212(a)(2) or (3) of the Act, shall be inspected and admitted in the same immigration status as the alien had at the time of departure, and shall be provided the remainder of the voluntary departure period previously granted under the Family Unity Program.

[62 FR 10360, Mar. 6, 1997, as amended at 76 FR 53790, Aug. 29, 2011]

§ 236.17 Eligibility for Federal financial assistance programs.

An alien granted Family Unity Program benefits based on a relationship to a legalized alien as defined in § 236.11 is ineligible for public welfare assistance in the same manner and for the same period as the legalized alien who is ineligible for such assistance under section 245A(h) or 210(f) of the Act, respectively.

§ 236.18 Termination of Family Unity Program benefits.

(a) *Grounds for termination.* The Service may terminate benefits under the Family Unity Program whenever the necessity for the termination comes to the attention of the Service. Such grounds will exist in situations including, but not limited to, those in which:

(1) A determination is made that Family Unity Program benefits were acquired as the result of fraud or willful misrepresentation of a material fact;

(2) The beneficiary commits an act or acts which render him or her inadmissible as an immigrant ineligible for benefits under the Family Unity Program;

(3) The legalized alien upon whose status benefits under the Family Unity Program were based loses his or her legalized status;

(4) The beneficiary is the subject of a final order of exclusion, deportation, or removal issued subsequent to the grant of Family Unity benefits unless such final order is based on entry without inspection; violation of status; or failure to comply with section 265 of the Act; or inadmissibility at the time of entry other than inadmissibility pursuant to section 212(a)(2) or 212(a)(3) of the Act, regardless of whether the facts giving rise to such ground occurred before or after the benefits were granted; or

(5) A qualifying relationship to a legalized alien no longer exists.

(b) *Notice procedure.* Notice of intent to terminate and of the grounds thereof shall be served pursuant to the provisions of 8 CFR 103.8(a)(2). The alien shall be given 30 days to respond to the notice and may submit to the Service additional evidence in rebuttal. Any final decision of termination shall also be served pursuant to the provisions of 8 CFR 103.8(a)(2). Nothing in this section shall preclude the Service from commencing exclusion or deportation proceedings prior to termination of Family Unity Program benefits.

(c) *Effect of termination.* Termination of benefits under the Family Unity Program, other than as a result of a final order of removal, shall render the alien amenable to removal proceedings under section 240 of the Act. If benefits are terminated, the period of voluntary departure under this section is also terminated.

[62 FR 10360, Mar. 6, 1997, as amended at 65 FR 43680, July 14, 2000; 76 FR 53791, Aug. 29, 2011]

PART 237 [RESERVED]

PART 238—EXPEDITED REMOVAL OF AGGRAVATED FELONS

AUTHORITY: 8 U.S.C. 1228; 8 CFR part 2.

§ 238.1 Proceedings under section 238(b) of the Act.

(a) *Definitions.* As used in this part the term:

Deciding Service officer means a district director, chief patrol agent, or another immigration officer designated by a district director, chief patrol agent, the Deputy Executive Associate Commissioner for Detention and Removal, or the Director of the Office of Juvenile Affairs, so long as that person is not the same person as the Issuing Service Officer.

Issuing Service officer means any Service officer listed in § 239.1 of this chapter as authorized to issue notices to appear.

(b) *Preliminary consideration and Notice of Intent to Issue a Final Administrative Deportation Order; commencement of proceedings*—(1) *Basis of Service charge.* An issuing Service officer shall cause to be served upon an alien a Form I–851, Notice of Intent to Issue a Final Administrative Deportation Order (Notice of Intent), if the officer is satisfied that there is sufficient evidence, based upon questioning of the alien by an immigration officer and upon any other evidence obtained, to support a finding that the individual:

(i) Is an alien;

(ii) Has not been lawfully admitted for permanent residence, or has conditional permanent resident status under section 216 of the Act;

(iii) Has been convicted (as defined in section 101(a)(48) of the Act and as demonstrated by any of the documents or records listed in § 1003.41 of this chapter) of an aggravated felony and such conviction has become final; and

(iv) Is deportable under section 237(a)(2)(A)(iii) of the Act, including an alien who has neither been admitted nor paroled, but who is conclusively presumed deportable under section 237(a)(2)(A)(iii) by operation of section 238(c) of the Act ("Presumption of Deportability").

(2) *Notice.* (i) Removal proceedings under section 238(b) of the Act shall commence upon personal service of the Notice of Intent upon the alien, as prescribed by8 CFR 103.8. The Notice of Intent shall set forth the preliminary determinations and inform the alien of the Service's intent to issue a Form I–851A, Final Administrative Removal Order, without a hearing before an immigration judge. The Notice of Intent shall constitute the charging document. The Notice of Intent shall include allegations of fact and conclusions of law. It shall advise that the alien: has the privilege of being represented, at no expense to the government, by counsel of the alien's choosing, as long as counsel is authorized to practice in removal proceedings; may request withholding of removal to a particular country if he or she fears persecution or torture in that country; may inspect the evidence supporting the Notice of Intent; may rebut the charges within 10 calendar days after service of such Notice (or 13 calendar days if service of the Notice was by mail).

(ii) The Notice of Intent also shall advise the alien that he or she may designate in writing, within the rebuttal period, the country to which he or she chooses to be deported in accordance with section 241 of the Act, in the event that a Final Administrative Removal Order is issued, and that the Service will honor such designation only to the extent permitted under the terms, limitations, and conditions of section 241 of the Act.

(iii) The Service must determine that the person served with the Notice of Intent is the person named on the notice.

(iv) The Service shall provide the alien with a list of available free legal services programs qualified under 8 CFR part 3 and organizations recognized pursuant to 8 CFR part 292, located within the district or sector where the Notice of Intent is issued.

(v) The Service must either provide the alien with a written translation of the Notice of Intent or explain the contents of the Notice of Intent to the alien in the alien's native language or in a language that the alien understands.

(c) *Alien's response*—(1) *Time for response.* The alien will have 10 calendar days from service of the Notice of Intent or 13 calendar days if service is by mail, to file a response to the Notice of Intent. In the response, the alien may: designate his or her choice of country for removal; submit a written response rebutting the allegations supporting the charge and/or requesting the opportunity to review the Government's evidence; and/or submit a statement indicating an intention to request withholding of removal under 8 CFR 208.16 of this chapter, and/or request in writing an extension of time for response, stating the specific reasons why such an extension is necessary.

(2) *Nature of rebuttal or request to review evidence.* (i) If an alien chooses to rebut the allegations contained in the Notice of Intent, the alien's written response must indicate which finding(s) are being challenged and should be accompanied by affidavit(s), documentary information, or other specific evidence supporting the challenge.

(ii) If an alien's written response requests the opportunity to review the Government's evidence, the Service shall serve the alien with a copy of the evidence in the record of proceeding upon which the Service is relying to support the charge. The alien may, within 10 calendar days following service of the Government's evidence (13 calendar days if service is by mail), furnish a final response in accordance with paragraph (c)(1) of this section. If the alien's final response is a rebuttal of the allegations, such a final response should be accompanied by affidavit(s), documentary information, or other specific evidence supporting the challenge.

(d) *Determination by deciding Service officer*—(1) *No response submitted or concession of deportability.* If the deciding Service officer does not receive a timely response and the evidence in the record of proceeding establishes deportability by clear, convincing, and unequivocal evidence, or if the alien concedes deportability, then the deciding Service officer shall issue and cause to be served upon the alien a Final Administrative Removal Order that states the reasons for the deportation decision. The alien may, in writing, waive the 14-day waiting period before execution of the final order of removal provided in a paragraph (f) of this section.

(2) *Response submitted*—(i) *Insufficient rebuttal; no genuine issue of material fact.* If the alien timely submits a rebuttal to the allegations, but the deciding Service officer finds that deportability is established by clear, convincing, and unequivocal evidence in the record of proceeding, the deciding Service officer shall issue and cause to be served upon the alien a Final Administrative Removal Order that states the reasons for the decision of deportability.

(ii) *Additional evidence required.* (A) If the deciding Service officer finds that the record of proceeding, including the alien's timely rebuttal, raises a genuine issue of material fact regarding the preliminary findings, the deciding Service officer may either obtain additional evidence from any source, including the alien, or cause to be issued a notice to appear to initiate removal proceedings under section 240 of the Act. The deciding Service officer may also obtain additional evidence from any source, including the alien, if the deciding Service officer deems that such additional evidence may aid the officer in the rendering of a decision.

(B) If the deciding Service officer considers additional evidence from a source other than the alien, that evidence shall be made a part of the record of proceeding, and shall be provided to the alien. If the alien elects to submit a response to such additional evidence, such response must be filed with the Service within 10 calendar days of service of the additional evidence (or 13 calendar days if service is by mail). If the deciding Service officer finds, after considering all additional evidence, that deportability is established by clear, convincing, and unequivocal evidence in the record of proceeding, the deciding Service officer shall issue and cause to be served upon the alien a Final Administrative Removal Order that states the reasons for the decision of deportability.

(iii) *Conversion to proceedings under section 240 of the Act.* If the deciding Service officer finds that the alien is not amenable to removal under section 238 of the Act, the deciding Service officer shall terminate the expedited proceedings under section 238 of the Act and shall, where appropriate, cause to be issued a notice to appear for the purpose of initiating removal proceedings before an immigration judge under section 240 of the Act.

(3) *Termination of proceedings by deciding Service officer.* Only the deciding Service officer may terminate proceedings under section 238 of the Act, in accordance with this section.

(e) *Proceedings commenced under section 240 of the Act.* In any proceeding commenced under section 240 of the Act which is based on deportability under section 237 of the Act, if it appears that the respondent alien is subject to removal pursuant to section 238 of the Act, the immigration judge may, upon the Service's request, terminate the case and, upon such termination, the Service may commence administrative proceedings under section 238 of the Act. However, in the absence of any such request, the immigration judge shall complete the proceeding commenced under section 240 of the Act.

(f) *Executing final removal order of deciding Service officer*—(1) *Time of execution.* Upon the issuance of a Final Administrative Removal Order, the Service shall issue a Warrant of Removal in accordance with § 241.2 of this chapter; such warrant shall be executed no sooner than 14 calendar days after the date the Final Administrative Removal Order is issued, unless the alien knowingly, voluntarily, and in writing waives the 14-day period.

(2) *Country to which alien is to be removed.* The deciding Service officer shall designate the country of removal in the manner prescribed by section 241 of the Act.

(3) *Withholding of removal.* If the alien has requested withholding of removal under §208.16 of this chapter, the deciding officer shall, upon issuance of a Final Administrative Removal Order, immediately refer the alien's case to an asylum officer to conduct a reasonable fear determination in accordance with §208.31 of this chapter.

(g) *Arrest and detention.* At the time of issuance of a Notice of Intent or at any time thereafter and up to the time the alien becomes the subject of a Warrant of Removal, the alien may be arrested and taken into custody under the authority of a Warrant of Arrest issued by an officer listed in §287.5(e)(2) of this chapter. The decision of the Service concerning custody or bond shall not be administratively appealable during proceedings initiated under section 238 of the Act and this part.

(h) *Record of proceeding.* The Service shall maintain a record of proceeding for judicial review of the Final Administrative Removal Order sought by any petition for review. The record of proceeding shall include, but not necessarily be limited to: the charging document (Notice of Intent); the Final Administrative Removal Order (including any supplemental memorandum of decision); the alien's response, if any; all evidence in support of the charge; and any admissible evidence, briefs, or documents submitted by either party respecting deportability. The executed duplicate of the Notice of Intent in the record of proceedings shall be retained as evidence that the individual upon whom the notice for the proceeding was served was, in fact, the alien named in the notice.

[62 FR 10365, Mar. 6, 1997, as amended at 64 FR 8494, Feb. 19, 1999; 67 FR 39258, June 7, 2002; 76 FR 53791, Aug. 29, 2011; 81 FR 62355, Sept. 9, 2016]

PART 239—INITIATION OF REMOVAL PROCEEDINGS

Sec.

AUTHORITY: 8 U.S.C. 1103, 1221, 1229; Homeland Security Act of 2002, Public Law 107–296; 8 CFR part 2.

SOURCE: 62 FR 10366, Mar. 6, 1997, unless otherwise noted.

§239.1 Notice to appear.

(a) *Issuance of notice to appear.* Any immigration officer, or supervisor thereof, performing an inspection of an arriving alien at a port-of-entry may issue a notice to appear to such alien. In addition, the following officers, or officers acting in such capacity, may issue a notice to appear:

(1) District directors (except foreign);

(2) Deputy district directors (except foreign);

(3) Chief patrol agents;

(4) Deputy chief patrol agents;

(5) Division chiefs;

(6) Assistant chief patrol agents;

(7) Patrol agents in charge;

(8) Deputy patrol agents in charge;

(9) Border patrol watch commanders;

(10) Special operations supervisors;

(11) Supervisory border patrol agents;

(12) Directors of air operations;

(13) Directors of marine operations;

(14) Supervisory air and marine interdiction agents;

(15) Service center directors;

(16) Deputy service center directors;

(17) Assistant service center directors for examinations;

(18) Supervisory immigration services officers;

(19) Supervisory immigration officers;

(20) Supervisory asylum officers;

(21) Officers in charge (except foreign);

(22) Assistant officers in charge (except foreign);

(23) Special agents in charge;

(24) Deputy special agents in charge;

(25) Associate special agents in charge;

(26) Assistant special agents in charge;

(27) Resident agents in charge;

(28) Supervisory special agents;

(29) Directors of investigations;

(30) District directors for interior enforcement;

(31) Deputy or assistant district directors for interior enforcement;

(32) Director of enforcement and removal operations;

(33) Field office directors;

(34) Deputy field office directors;

(35) Supervisory deportation officers;

(36) Supervisory detention and deportation officers;

(37) Directors or officers in charge of detention facilities;

(38) Directors of field operations;

(39) Assistant directors of field operations;

(40) Port directors;

(41) Assistant port directors;

(42) Field operations watch commanders;

(43) Field operations chiefs;

(44) Unit Chief, Law Enforcement Support Center;

(45) Section Chief, Law Enforcement Support Center; or

(46) Other duly authorized officers or employees of the Department of Homeland Security or of the United States who are delegated the authority as provided by 8 CFR 2.1 to issue notices to appear, and who have successfully completed any required immigration law enforcement training.

(b) *Service of notice to appear.* Service of the notice to appear shall be in accordance with section 239 of the Act.

[68 FR 35275, June 13, 2003, as amended at 70 FR 67089, Nov. 4, 2005; 81 FR 62355, Sept. 9, 2016]

§ 239.2 Cancellation of notice to appear.

(a) Any officer authorized by § 239.1(a) to issue a notice to appear may cancel such notice prior to jurisdiction vesting with the immigration judge pursuant to § 3.14 of this chapter provided the officer is satisfied that:

(1) The respondent is a national of the United States;

(2) The respondent is not deportable or inadmissible under immigration laws;

(3) The respondent is deceased;

(4) The respondent is not in the United States;

(5) The notice was issued for the respondent's failure to file a timely petition as required by section 216(c) of the Act, but his or her failure to file a timely petition was excused in accordance with section 216(d)(2)(B) of the Act;

(6) The notice to appear was improvidently issued, or

(7) Circumstances of the case have changed after the notice to appear was issued to such an extent that continuation is no longer in the best interest of the government.

(b) A notice to appear issued pursuant to section 235(b)(3) of the Act may be canceled under provisions in paragraphs (a)(2) and (a)(6) of this section only by the issuing officer, unless it is impracticable for the issuing officer to cancel the notice.

(c) *Motion to dismiss.* After commencement of proceedings pursuant to 8 CFR 1003.14, ICE counsel, or any officer enumerated in paragraph (a) of this section, may move for dismissal of the matter on the grounds set out under paragraph (a) of this section.

(d) *Motion for remand.* After commencement of the hearing, ICE counsel, or any officer enumerated in paragraph (a) of this section may move for remand of the matter to district jurisdiction on the ground that the foreign relations of the United States are involved and require further consideration.

(e) *Warrant of arrest.* When a notice to appear is canceled or proceedings are terminated under this section any outstanding warrant of arrest is canceled.

[62 FR 10366, Mar. 6, 1997, as amended at 68 FR 35276, June 13, 2003]

§ 239.3 Effect of filing notice to appear.

The filing of a notice to appear shall have no effect in determining periods of unlawful presence as defined in section 212(a)(9)(B) of the Act.

PART 240—VOLUNTARY DEPARTURE, SUSPENSION OF DEPORTATION AND SPECIAL RULE CANCELLATION OF REMOVAL

Subpart A—Removal Proceedings [Reserved]

Subpart B—Cancellation of Removal

Subpart C—Voluntary Departure

Subpart D—Exclusion of Aliens (for Proceedings Commenced Prior to April 1, 1997) [Reserved]

Subpart E—Proceedings To Determine Deportability of Aliens in the United States: Hearing and Appeal (for Proceedings Commenced Prior to April 1, 1997) [Reserved]

Subpart F—Suspension of Deportation and Voluntary Departure (for Proceedings Commenced Prior to April 1, 1997) [Reserved]

Subpart G—Civil Penalties for Failure To Depart [Reserved]

Subpart H—Applications for Suspension of Deportation or Special Rule Cancellation of Removal Under Section 203 of Pub. L. 105–100

AUTHORITY: 8 U.S.C. 1103; 1182, 1186a, 1224, 1225, 1226, 1227, 1251, 1252 note, 1252a, 1252b, 1362; secs. 202 and 203, Pub. L. 105-100 (111 Stat. 2160, 2193); sec. 902, Pub. L. 105-277 (112 Stat. 2681); 8 CFR part 2.

SOURCE: 62 FR 10367, Mar. 6, 1997, unless otherwise noted.

Subpart A—Removal Proceedings [Reserved]

Subpart B—Cancellation of Removal

§ 240.21 Suspension of deportation and adjustment of status under section 244(a) of the Act (as in effect before April 1, 1997) and cancellation of removal and adjustment of status under section 240A(b) of the Act for certain nonpermanent residents.

(a) *Applicability of annual cap on suspension of deportation or cancellation of removal.* (1) As used in this section, the term *cap* means the numerical limitation of 4,000 grants of suspension of deportation or cancellation of removal in any fiscal year (except fiscal year 1998, which has a limitation of 8,000 grants) pursuant to section 240A(e) of the Act.

(2) The provisions of this section apply to grants of suspension of deportation pursuant to section 244(a) of the Act (as in effect before April 1, 1997) or cancellation of removal pursuant to section 240A(b) of the Act that are subject to a numerical limitation in section 240A(e) of the Act for any fiscal year. This section does not apply to grants of suspension of deportation or cancellation of removal to aliens described in section 309(c)(5)(C)(i) of the Illegal Immigration Reform and Immigrant Responsibility Act (IIRIRA), as amended by section 203(a)(1) of the Nicaraguan Adjustment and Central American Relief Act (NACARA), or aliens in deportation proceedings prior to April 1, 1997, who apply for suspension of deportation pursuant to section 244(a)(3) of the Act (as in effect prior to April 1, 1997). The Immigration Court and the Board shall no longer issue conditional grants of suspension of deportation or cancellation of removal as provided in 8 CFR 240.21 (as in effect prior to September 30, 1998).

(b) *Conditional grants of suspension of deportation or cancellation of removal in fiscal year 1998 cases*—(1) *Conversion to grants.* Except with respect to cases described in paragraphs (b)(2) and (b)(3) of this section, EOIR shall grant suspension of deportation or cancellation of removal without condition prior to October 1, 1998, to the first 8,000 aliens given conditional grants of suspension of deportation or cancellation of removal (as determined by the date of the immigration judge's order or, if the order was appealed to the Board, the date such order was entered by the Board.)

(2) *Treatment of certain nationals of Nicaragua and Cuba who received conditional grants of suspension of deportation or cancellation of removal on or before September 30, 1998*—(i) *NACARA adjustment request.* An application for suspension of deportation or cancellation of removal filed by a national of Nicaragua or Cuba that was granted on a conditional basis on or before September 30, 1998, shall be deemed to be a request for adjustment of status pursuant to section 202 of NACARA ("NACARA adjustment") for the period starting September 30, 1998 and ending December 31, 1998. The Service shall provide the applicant with notice of the date, time, and place at which the applicant must appear before a Service officer to perfect the request for NACARA adjustment. Such notice shall include an attestation form, Attestation of Alien and Memorandum of Creation of Record of Lawful Permanent Residence, Form I–895, regarding the applicant's eligibility for NACARA adjustment.

(ii) *Submission of documentation.* To perfect the request for NACARA adjustment, the applicant must appear before a Service officer on the date scheduled with the following documentation:

(A) The order granting suspension of deportation or cancellation of removal on a conditional basis issued on or before September 30, 1998;

(B) A completed, but unsigned Form I–895, which the applicant shall be required to sign and to attest to the veracity of the information contained therein in the presence of a Service officer;

(C) Any applicable applications for waiver of inadmissibility; and

(D) Two "ADIT-style" photographs; meeting the specifications in the instructions attached to Form I–895.

(iii) *Waiver of documentation and fees.* The provisions of § 245.13(e) and (f) of this chapter relating to documentary requirements for NACARA adjustment are waived with respect to an alien seeking to perfect a request for adjustment of status pursuant to paragraph (b)(2) of this section. In addition, the fees for the NACARA adjustment and for any applications for waivers of inadmissibility submitted in conjunction with perfecting a request for NACARA adjustment shall be waived.

(iv) *NACARA adjustment determination.* In determining an applicant's eligibility for NACARA adjustment under the provisions of paragraph (b)(2) of this section, unless the Service officer before whom the applicant appears is not satisfied that the applicant is admissible to the United States in accordance with section 202(a)(1)(B) of NACARA, and has continuously resided in the United States from December 1, 1995, through the date of appearance before the Service officer (not counting an absence or absences from the United States totaling 180 days or less or any absences that occurred pursuant to advance authorization for parole (Form I–512 issued by the Service)), the Service officer shall accept an alien's attestation of admissibility and/or continuous physical presence as sufficient evidence that the applicant has met the admissibility and/or continuous physical presence requirement for NACARA adjustment. If the Service officer grants NACARA adjustment, then the Service officer shall create a record of lawful permanent residence and the prior order granting suspension of deportation or cancellation of removal on a conditional basis shall be automatically vacated and the deportation or removal proceedings shall be automatically terminated. The Service officer (whose decision in this regard is not subject to appeal) shall not adjust the applicant to lawful permanent resident status pursuant to section 202 of NACARA if:

(A) The Service officer is not satisfied that the applicant is eligible for NACARA adjustment and so indicates on the attestation form; or

(B) The applicant indicates on the attestation form that he or she does not wish to receive NACARA adjustment.

(v) *Automatic conversion.* If the Service officer does not adjust the applicant to lawful permanent resident status pursuant to section 202 of NACARA, the applicant's conditional grant of suspension of deportation or cancellation of removal shall be automatically converted to a grant of suspension of deportation or cancellation of removal. Upon such a conversion, the Service shall create a record of lawful permanent residence based upon the grant of suspension of deportation or cancellation of removal.

(vi) *Failure to appear.* An alien who fails to appear to perfect his or her request for NACARA adjustment shall have his or her conditional grant of suspension of deportation or cancellation of removal automatically converted by the Immigration Court or the Board to a grant of suspension of deportation or cancellation of removal effective December 31, 1998.

(3) *Conditional grants not converted in fiscal year 1998.* The provisions of paragraphs (b)(1) and (b)(2) of this section for granting relief shall not apply with respect to:

(i) Any case in which a conditional grant of suspension of deportation or cancellation of removal is pending on appeal before the Board as of September 30, 1998 or, if the right to appeal to the Board has not been waived, the time for an appeal has not expired. After the Board issues its decision or the time for appeal has expired, the conditional grant shall be converted to a grant when a grant is available.

(ii) Any other conditional grant not described in paragraphs (b)(1), (b)(2) or (b)(3)(i) of this section, which was not converted to a grant in fiscal year 1998. Such a conditional grant shall be converted to a grant when a grant is available.

(4) *Motion to reopen.* The Service may file a motion to reopen within 90 days after the alien is issued a grant of suspension of deportation or cancellation of removal pursuant to paragraphs (b)(1), (b)(2), or (b)(3) of this section, if after the issuance of a conditional grant by the Immigration Court or the Board the applicant committed an act that would have rendered him or her ineligible for suspension of deportation or cancellation or removal at the time of the conversion.

(5) *Travel for aliens conditionally granted suspension of deportation or cancellation of removal.* If the Immigration Court or the Board granted suspension of deportation or cancellation of removal on a conditional basis or, if the conditional grant by the Immigration Court was appealed to the Board and the Board issued such a conditional grant, the alien shall retain the conditional grant of suspension of deportation or cancellation of removal upon return to the United States following a temporary absence abroad and be permitted to resume completion of his or her case, provided that:

(i) The alien departed on or before September 30, 1998 with or without a grant of advance parole from the District Director; or

(ii) The alien, prior to his or her departure from the United States after September 30, 1998, obtained a grant of advance parole from the District Director in accordance with section 212(d)(5) of the Act and § 212.5 of this chapter and complied with the terms and conditions of the advance parole.

(c) *Grants of suspension of deportation or cancellation of removal in fiscal years subsequent to fiscal year 1998.* On and after October 1, 1998, the Immigration Court and the Board may grant applications for suspension of deportation and adjustment of status under section 244(a) of the Act (as in effect prior to April 1, 1997) or cancellation of removal and adjustment of status under section 240A(b) of the Act that meet the statutory requirements for such relief and warrant a favorable exercise of discretion until the annual numerical limitation has been reached in that fiscal year. The awarding of such relief shall be determined according to the date the order granting such relief becomes final as defined in §§ 3.1(d)(3) and 3.39 of this chapter.

(1) *Applicability of the annual cap.* When grants are no longer available in a fiscal year, further decisions to grant or deny such relief shall be reserved until such time as a grant becomes available under the annual limitation in a subsequent fiscal year. Immigration judges and the Board may deny without reserving decision or may pretermit those suspension of deportation or cancellation of removal applications in which the applicant has failed to establish statutory eligibility for relief. The basis of such denial or pretermission may not be based on an

unfavorable exercise of discretion, a finding of no good moral character on a ground not specifically noted in section 101(f) of the Act, a failure to establish exceptional or extremely unusual hardship to a qualifying relative in cancellation cases, or a failure to establish extreme hardship to the applicant and/or qualifying relative in suspension cases.

(2) *Aliens applying for additional forms of relief.* Whether or not the cap has been reached, the Immigration Court or the Board shall adjudicate concurrently all other forms of relief for which the alien has applied. Applications for suspension of deportation or cancellation of removal shall be denied in the exercise of discretion if the alien is granted asylum or adjustment of status, including pursuant to section 202 of NACARA, while the suspension of deportation or cancellation of removal application is pending. Where an appeal of a decision granting asylum or adjustment is sustained by the Board, a decision to deny as a matter of discretion an application for suspension of deportation or cancellation of removal on this basis shall be reconsidered.

[63 FR 52138, Sept. 30, 1998, as amended at 66 FR 6446, Jan. 22, 2001]

Subpart C—Voluntary Departure

§ 240.25 Voluntary departure—authority of the Service.

(a) *Authorized officers.* The authority contained in section 240B(a) of the Act to permit aliens to depart voluntarily from the United States may be exercised in lieu of being subject to proceedings under section 240 of the Act by district directors, assistant district directors for investigations, assistant district directors for examinations, officers in charge, chief patrol agents, the Deputy Executive Associate Director for Enforcement and Removal Operations, the Director of the Office of Juvenile Affairs, service center directors, and assistant service center directors for examinations.

(b) *Conditions.* The Service may attach to the granting of voluntary departure any conditions it deems necessary to ensure the alien's timely departure from the United States, including the posting of a bond, continued detention pending departure, and removal under safeguards. The alien shall be required to present to the Service, for inspection and photocopying, his or her passport or other travel documentation sufficient to assure lawful entry into the country to which the alien is departing. The Service may hold the passport or documentation for sufficient time to investigate its authenticity. A voluntary departure order permitting an alien to depart voluntarily shall inform the alien of the penalties under section 240B(d) of the Act.

(c) *Decision.* The authorized officer, in his or her discretion, shall specify the period of time permitted for voluntary departure, and may grant extensions thereof, except that the total period allowed, including any extensions, shall not exceed 120 days. Every decision regarding voluntary departure shall be communicated in writing on Form I–210, Notice of Action—Voluntary Departure. Voluntary departure may not be granted unless the alien requests such voluntary departure and agrees to its terms and conditions.

(d) *Application.* Any alien who believes himself or herself to be eligible for voluntary departure under this section may apply therefor at any office of the Service. After the commencement of removal proceedings, the application may be communicated through the Service counsel. If the Service agrees to voluntary departure after proceedings have commenced, it may either:

(1) Join in a motion to terminate the proceedings, and if the proceedings are terminated, grant voluntary departure; or

(2) Join in a motion asking the immigration judge to permit voluntary departure in accordance with § 240.26.

(e) *Appeals.* An appeal shall not lie from a denial of an application for voluntary departure under this section, but the denial shall be without prejudice to the alien's right to apply to the immigration judge for voluntary departure in accordance with § 240.26 or for relief from removal under any provision of law.

(f) *Revocation.* If, subsequent to the granting of an application for voluntary departure under this section, it is ascertained that the application should not have been granted, that grant may be revoked without advance notice by any officer authorized to grant voluntary departure under §240.25(a). Such revocation shall be communicated in writing, citing the statutory basis for revocation. No appeal shall lie from revocation.

[62 FR 10367, Mar. 6, 1997, as amended at 67 FR 39258, June 7, 2002; 81 FR 62355, Sept. 9, 2016]

Subpart D—Exclusion of Aliens (for Proceedings Commenced Prior to April 1, 1997) [Reserved]

Subpart E—Proceedings To Determine Deportability of Aliens in the United States: Hearing and Appeal (for Proceedings Commenced Prior to April 1, 1997) [Reserved]

Subpart F—Suspension of Deportation and Voluntary Departure (for Proceedings Commenced Prior to April 1, 1997) [Reserved]

Subpart G—Civil Penalties for Failure To Depart [Reserved]

Subpart H—Applications for Suspension of Deportation or Special Rule Cancellation of Removal Under Section 203 of Pub. L. 105–100

SOURCE: 64 FR 27876, May 21, 1999, unless otherwise noted.

§240.60 Definitions.

As used in this subpart the term:

ABC means *American Baptist Churches* v. *Thornburgh*, 760 F. Supp. 796 (N.D. Cal. 1991).

ABC class member refers to:

(1) Any Guatemalan national who first entered the United States on or before October 1, 1990; and

(2) Any Salvadoran national who first entered the United States on or before September 19, 1990.

Asylum application pending adjudication by the Service means any asylum application for which the Service has not served the applicant with a final decision or which has not been referred to the Immigration Court.

Filed an application for asylum means the proper filing of a principal asylum application or filing a derivative asylum application by being properly included as a dependent spouse or child in an asylum application pursuant to the regulations and procedures in effect at the time of filing the principal or derivative asylum application.

IIRIRA means the Illegal Immigration Reform and Immigrant Responsibility Act of 1996, enacted as Pub. L. 104–208 (110 Stat. 3009–625).

NACARA means the Nicaraguan Adjustment and Central American Relief Act (NACARA), enacted as title II of Pub. L. 105–100 (111 Stat. 2160, 2193), as amended by the Technical Corrections to the Nicaraguan Adjustment and Central American Relief Act, Pub. L. 105–139 (111 Stat. 2644).

Registered ABC class member means an ABC class member who:

(1) In the case of an *ABC* class member who is a national of El Salvador, properly submitted an ABC registration form to the Service on or before October 31, 1991, or applied for temporary protected status on or before October 31, 1991; or

(2) In the case of an *ABC* class member who is a national of Guatemala, properly submitted an *ABC* registration form to the Service on or before December 31, 1991.

§240.61 Applicability.

(a) Except as provided in paragraph (b) of this section, this subpart H applies to the following aliens:

(1) A registered *ABC* class member who has not been apprehended at the time of entry after December 19, 1990;

(2) A Guatemalan or Salvadoran national who filed an application for asylum with the Service on or before April 1, 1990, either by filing an application with the Service or filing the application with the Immigration Court and serving a copy of that application on the Service.

(3) An alien who entered the United States on or before December 31, 1990,

filed an application for asylum on or before December 31, 1991, and, at the time of filing the application, was a national of the Soviet Union, Russia, any republic of the former Soviet Union, Latvia, Estonia, Lithuania, Poland, Czechoslovakia, Romania, Hungary, Bulgaria, Albania, East Germany, Yugoslavia, or any state of the former Yugoslavia;

(4) An alien who is the spouse or child of an individual described in paragraph (a)(1), (a)(2), or (a)(3) of this section at the time a decision is made to suspend the deportation, or cancel the removal, of the individual described in paragraph (a)(1), (a)(2), or (a)(3) of this section;

(5) An alien who is:

(i) The unmarried son or unmarried daughter of an individual described in paragraph (a)(1), (a)(2), or (a)(3) of this section and is 21 years of age or older at the time a decision is made to suspend the deportation, or cancel the removal, of the parent described in paragraph (a)(1), (a)(2), or (a)(3) of this section; and

(ii) Entered the United States on or before October 1, 1990.

(b) This subpart H does not apply to any alien who has been convicted at any time of an aggravated felony, as defined in section 101(a)(43) of the Act.

§ 240.62 Jurisdiction.

(a) *Office of International Affairs.* Except as provided in paragraph (b) of this section, the Office of International Affairs shall have initial jurisdiction to grant or refer to the Immigration Court or Board an application for suspension of deportation or special rule cancellation of removal filed by an alien described in § 240.61, provided:

(1) In the case of a national of El Salvador described in § 240.61(a)(1), the alien filed a complete asylum application on or before January 31, 1996 (with an administrative grace period extending to February 16, 1996), or otherwise met the asylum application filing deadline pursuant to the *ABC* settlement agreement, and the application is still pending adjudication by the Service;

(2) In the case of a national of Guatemala described in § 240.61(a)(1), the alien filed a complete asylum application on or before January 3, 1995, or otherwise met the asylum application filing deadline pursuant to the *ABC* settlement agreement, and the application is still pending adjudication by the Service;

(3) In the case of an individual described in § 240.61(a)(2) or (3), the individual's asylum application is pending adjudication by the Service;

(4) In the case of an individual described in § 240.61(a)(4) or (5), the individual's parent or spouse has an application pending with the Service under this subpart H or has been granted relief by the Service under this subpart.

(b) *Immigration Court.* The Immigration Court shall have exclusive jurisdiction over an application for suspension of deportation or special rule cancellation of removal filed pursuant to section 309(f)(1)(A) or (B) of IIRIRA, as amended by NACARA, by an alien who has been served Form I–221, Order to Show Cause, or Form I–862, Notice to Appear, after a copy of the charging document has been filed with the Immigration Court, unless the alien is covered by one of the following exceptions:

(1) *Certain ABC class members.* (i) The alien is a registered *ABC* class member for whom proceedings before the Immigration Court or the Board have been administratively closed or continued (including those aliens who had final orders of deportation or removal who have filed and been granted a motion to reopen as required under 8 CFR 3.43);

(ii) The alien is eligible for benefits of the *ABC* settlement agreement and has not had a *de novo* asylum adjudication pursuant to the settlement agreement; and

(iii) The alien has not moved for and been granted a motion to recalendar proceedings before the Immigration Court or the Board to request suspension of deportation.

(2) *Spouses, children, unmarried sons, and unmarried daughters.* (i) The alien is described in § 240.61(a) (4) or (5);

(ii) The alien's spouse or parent is described in § 240.61(a)(1), (a)(2), or (a)(3) and has a Form I–881 pending with the Service; and

(iii) The alien's proceedings before the Immigration Court have been administratively closed, or the alien's proceedings before the Board have been continued, to permit the alien to file an application for suspension of deportation or special rule cancellation of removal with the Service.

§240.63 Application process.

(a) *Form and fees.* Except as provided in paragraph (b) of this section, the application must be made on a Form I–881, Application for Suspension of Deportation or Special Rule Cancellation of Removal (pursuant to section 203 of Public Law 105–100 (NACARA)), and filed in accordance with the instructions for that form. An applicant who submitted to EOIR a completed Form EOIR–40, Application for Suspension of Deportation, before the effective date of the Form I–881 may apply with the Service by submitting the completed Form EOIR–40 attached to a completed first page of the Form I–881. Each application must be filed with the filing and fingerprint fees as provided in §103.7(b)(1) of this chapter, or a request for fee waiver, as provided in §103.7(c) of this chapter. The fact that an applicant has also applied for asylum does not exempt the applicant from the fingerprinting fees associated with the Form I–881.

(b) *Applications filed with EOIR.* If jurisdiction rests with the Immigration Court under §260.62(b), the application must be made on the Form I–881, if filed subsequent to June 21, 1999. The application form, along with any supporting documents, must be filed with the Immigration Court and served on the Service's district counsel in accordance with the instructions on or accompanying the form. Applications for suspension of deportation or special rule cancellation of removal filed prior to June 21, 1999 shall be filed on Form EOIR–40.

(c) *Applications filed with the Service.* If jurisdiction rests with the Service under §240.62(a), the Form I–881 and supporting documents must be filed in accordance with the instructions on or accompanying the form.

(d) *Conditions and consequences of filing.* Applications filed under this section shall be filed under the following conditions and shall have the following consequences:

(1) The information provided in the application may be used as a basis for the initiation of removal proceedings, or to satisfy any burden of proof in exclusion, deportation, or removal proceedings;

(2) The applicant and anyone other than a spouse, parent, son, or daughter of the applicant who assists the applicant in preparing the application must sign the application under penalty of perjury. The applicant's signature establishes a presumption that the applicant is aware of the contents of the application. A person other than a relative specified in this paragraph who assists the applicant in preparing the application also must provide his or her full mailing address;

(3) An application that does not include a response to each of the questions contained in the application, is unsigned, or is unaccompanied by the required materials specified in the instructions to the application is incomplete and shall be returned by mail to the applicant within 30 days of receipt of the application by the Service; and

(4) Knowing placement of false information on the application may subject the person supplying that information to criminal penalties under title 18 of the United States Code and to civil penalties under section 274C of the Act.

[64 FR 27876, May 21, 1999, as amended at 74 FR 26939, June 5, 2009]

§240.64 Eligibility—general.

(a) *Burden and standard of proof.* The burden of proof is on the applicant to establish by a preponderance of the evidence that he or she is eligible for suspension of deportation or special rule cancellation of removal and that discretion should be exercised to grant relief.

(b) *Calculation of continuous physical presence and certain breaks in presence.* For purposes of calculating continuous physical presence under this section, section 309(c)(5)(A) of IIRIRA and section 240A(d)(1) of the Act shall not apply to persons described in §240.61. For purposes of this subpart H, a single absence of 90 days or less or absences which in the aggregate total no more than 180 days shall be considered brief.

(1) For applications for suspension of deportation made under former section 244 of the Act, as in effect prior to April 1, 1997, the burden of proof is on

the applicant to establish that any breaks in continuous physical presence were brief, casual, and innocent and did not meaningfully interrupt the period of continuous physical presence in the United States. For purposes of evaluating whether an absence is brief, single absences in excess of 90 days, or absences that total more than 180 days in the aggregate will be evaluated on a case-by-case basis. An applicant must establish that any absence from the United States was casual and innocent and did not meaningfully interrupt the period of continuous physical presence.

(2) For applications for special rule cancellation of removal made under section 309(f)(1) of IIRIRA, as amended by NACARA, the applicant shall be considered to have failed to maintain continuous physical presence in the United States if he or she has departed from the United States for any period in excess of 90 days or for any periods in the aggregate exceeding 180 days. The applicant must establish that any period of absence less than 90 days was casual and innocent and did not meaningfully interrupt the period of continuous physical presence in the United States.

(3) For all applications made under this subpart, a period of continuous physical presence is terminated whenever an alien is removed from the United States under an order issued pursuant to any provision of the Act or the alien has voluntarily departed under the threat of deportation or when the departure is made for purposes of committing an unlawful act.

(4) The requirements of continuous physical presence in the United States under this subpart shall not apply to an alien who:

(i) Has served for a minimum period of 24 months in an active-duty status in the Armed Forces of the United States and, if separated from such service, was separated under honorable conditions, and

(ii) At the time of the alien's enlistment or induction, was in the United States.

(c) *Factors relevant to extreme hardship.* Except as described in paragraph (d) of this section, extreme hardship shall be determined as set forth in § 240.58.

(d) *Rebuttable presumption of extreme hardship for certain classes of aliens*—(1) *Presumption of extreme hardship.* An applicant described in paragraphs (a)(1) or (a)(2) of § 240.61 who has submitted a completed Form I–881 or Form EOIR–40 to either the Service or the Immigration Court, in accordance with § 240.63, shall be presumed to have established that deportation or removal from the United States would result in extreme hardship to the applicant or to his or her spouse, parent, or child, who is a citizen of the United States or an alien lawfully admitted for permanent residence.

(2) *Rebuttal of presumption.* A presumption of extreme hardship as described in paragraph (d)(1) of this section shall be rebutted if the evidence in the record establishes that it is more likely than not that neither the applicant nor a qualified relative would suffer extreme hardship if the applicant were deported or removed from the United States. In making such a determination, the adjudicator shall consider relevant factors, including those listed in § 240.58.

(3) *Burden of proof.* In those cases where a presumption of extreme hardship applies, the burden of proof shall be on the Service to establish that it is more likely than not that neither the applicant nor a qualified relative would suffer extreme hardship if the applicant were deported or removed from the United States.

(4) *Effect of rebuttal.* (i) A determination that it is more likely than not that neither the applicant nor a qualified relative would suffer extreme hardship if the applicant were deported or removed from the United States shall be grounds for referral to the Immigration Court or dismissal of an application submitted initially to the Service. The applicant is entitled to a *de novo* adjudication and will again be considered to have a presumption of extreme hardship before the Immigration Court.

(ii) If the Immigration Court determines that extreme hardship will not result from deportation or removal from the United States, the application will be denied.

[64 FR 27876, May 21, 1999; 64 FR 33386, June 23, 1999]

§ 240.65 Eligibility for suspension of deportation.

(a) *Applicable statutory provisions.* To establish eligibility for suspension of deportation under this section, the applicant must be an individual described in § 240.61; must establish that he or she is eligible under former section 244 of the Act, as in effect prior to April 1, 1997; must not be subject to any bars to eligibility in former section 242B(e) of the Act, as in effect prior to April 1, 1997, or any other provisions of law; and must not have been convicted of an aggravated felony or be an alien described in former section 241(a)(4)(D) of the Act, as in effect prior to April 1, 1997 (relating to Nazi persecution and genocide).

(b) *General rule.* To establish eligibility for suspension of deportation under former section 244(a)(1) of the Act, as in effect prior to April 1, 1997, an alien must be deportable under any law of the United States, except the provisions specified in paragraph (c) of this section, and must establish:

(1) The alien has been physically present in the United States for a continuous period of not less than 7 years immediately preceding the date the application was filed;

(2) During all of such period the alien was and is a person of good moral character; and

(3) The alien's deportation would, in the opinion of the Attorney General, result in extreme hardship to the alien or to the alien's spouse, parent, or child, who is a citizen of the United States or an alien lawfully admitted for permanent residence.

(c) *Aliens deportable on criminal or certain other grounds.* To establish eligibility for suspension of deportation under former section 244(a)(2) of the Act, as in effect prior to April 1, 1997, an alien who is deportable under former section 241(a) (2), (3), or (4) of the Act, as in effect prior to April 1, 1997 (relating to criminal activity, document fraud, failure to register, and security threats), must establish that:

(1) The alien has been physically present in the United States for a continuous period of not less than 10 years immediately following the commission of an act, or the assumption of a status constituting a ground for deportation;

(2) The alien has been and is a person of good moral character during all of such period; and

(3) The alien's deportation would, in the opinion of the Attorney General, result in exceptional and extremely unusual hardship to the alien, or to the alien's spouse, parent, or child, who is a citizen of the United States or an alien lawfully admitted for permanent residence.

(d) *Battered spouses and children.* To establish eligibility for suspension of deportation under former section 244(a)(3) of the Act, as in effect prior to April 1, 1997, an alien must be deportable under any law of the United States, except under former section 241(a)(1)(G) of the Act, as in effect prior to April 1, 1997 (relating to marriage fraud), and except under the provisions specified in paragraph (c) of this section, and must establish that:

(1) The alien has been physically present in the United States for a continuous period of not less than 3 years immediately preceding the date the application was filed;

(2) The alien has been battered or subjected to extreme cruelty in the United States by a spouse or parent who is a United States citizen or lawful permanent resident (or is the parent of a child of a United States citizen or lawful permanent resident and the child has been battered or subjected to extreme cruelty in the United States by such citizen or permanent resident parent); and

(3) During all of such time in the United States the alien was and is a person of good moral character; and

(4) The alien's deportation would, in the opinion of the Attorney General, result in extreme hardship to the alien or the alien's parent or child.

§ 240.66 Eligibility for special rule cancellation of removal.

(a) *Applicable statutory provisions.* To establish eligibility for special rule cancellation of removal, the applicant must show he or she is eligible under section 309(f)(1) of IIRIRA, as amended by section 203 of NACARA. The applicant must be described in § 240.61, must be inadmissible or deportable, must not be subject to any bars to eligibility in sections 240(b)(7), 240A(c), or 240B(d) of the Act, or any other provisions of law, and must not have been convicted of an aggravated felony or be an alien described in section 241(b)(3)(B)(I) of the Act (relating to persecution of others).

(b) *General rule.* To establish eligibility for special rule cancellation of removal under section 309(f)(1)(A) of IIRIRA, as amended by section 203 of NACARA, the alien must establish that:

(1) The alien is not inadmissible under section 212(a)(2) or (3) or deportable under section 237(a)(2), (3) or (4) of the Act (relating to criminal activity, document fraud, failure to register, and security threats);

(2) The alien has been physically present in the United States for a continuous period of 7 years immediately preceding the date the application was filed;

(3) The alien has been a person of good moral character during the required period of continuous physical presence; and

(4) The alien's removal from the United States would result in extreme hardship to the alien, or to the alien's spouse, parent or child who is a United States citizen or an alien lawfully admitted for permanent residence.

(c) *Aliens inadmissible or deportable on criminal or certain other grounds.* To establish eligibility for special rule cancellation of removal under section 309(f)(1)(B) of IIRIRA, as amended by section 203 of NACARA, the alien must be described in § 240.61 and establish that:

(1) The alien is inadmissible under section 212(a)(2) of the Act (relating to criminal activity), or deportable under paragraphs (a)(2) (other than section 237(a)(2)(A)(iii), relating to aggravated felony convictions), or (a)(3) of section 237 of the Act (relating to criminal activity, document fraud, and failure to register);

(2) The alien has been physically present in the United States for a continuous period of not less than 10 years immediately following the commission of an act, or the assumption of a status constituting a ground for removal;

(3) The alien has been a person of good moral character during the required period of continuous physical presence; and

(4) The alien's removal from the United States would result in exceptional and extremely unusual hardship to the alien or to the alien's spouse, parent, or child, who is a United States citizen or an alien lawfully admitted for permanent residence.

§ 240.67 Procedure for interview before an asylum officer.

(a) *Fingerprinting requirements.* USCIS will notify each applicant 14 years of age or older to appear for an interview only after the applicant has complied with fingerprinting requirements pursuant to 8 CFR 103.16, and USCIS has received a definitive response from the FBI that a full criminal background check has been completed. A definitive response that a full criminal background check on an applicant has been completed includes:

(1) Confirmation from the FBI that an applicant does not have an administrative or criminal record;

(2) Confirmation from the FBI that an applicant has an administrative or a criminal record; or

(3) Confirmation from the FBI that two properly prepared fingerprint cards (Form FD–258) have been determined unclassifiable for the purpose of conducting a criminal background check and have been rejected.

(b) *Interview.* (1) The asylum officer shall conduct the interview in a non-adversarial manner and, except at the request of the applicant, separate and apart from the general public. The purpose of the interview shall be to elicit all relevant and useful information bearing on the applicant's eligibility for suspension of deportation or special rule cancellation of removal. If the applicant has an asylum application pending with the Service, the asylum officer may also elicit information relating to the application for asylum in accordance with § 208.9 of this chapter. At the time of the interview, the applicant must provide complete information regarding the applicant's identity, including name, date and place of birth, and nationality, and may be required to register this identity electronically or through any other means designated by the Attorney General.

(2) The applicant may have counsel or a representative present, may

present witnesses, and may submit affidavits of witnesses and other evidence.

(3) An applicant unable to proceed with the interview in English must provide, at no expense to the Service, a competent interpreter fluent in both English and a language in which the applicant is fluent. The interpreter must be at least 18 years of age. The following individuals may not serve as the applicant's interpreter: the applicant's attorney or representative of record; a witness testifying on the applicant's behalf; or, if the applicant also has an asylum application pending with the Service, a representative or employee of the applicant's country of nationality, or, if stateless, country of last habitual residence. Failure without good cause to comply with this paragraph may be considered a failure to appear for the interview for purposes of §240.68.

(4) The asylum officer shall have authority to administer oaths, verify the identity of the applicant (including through the use of electronic means), verify the identity of any interpreter, present and receive evidence, and question the applicant and any witnesses.

(5) Upon completion of the interview, the applicant or the applicant's representative shall have an opportunity to make a statement or comment on the evidence presented. The asylum officer may, in the officer's discretion, limit the length of such statement or comment and may require its submission in writing. Upon completion of the interview, and except as otherwise provided by the asylum officer, the applicant shall be informed of the requirement to appear in person to receive and to acknowledge receipt of the decision and any other accompanying material at a time and place designated by the asylum officer.

(6) The asylum officer shall consider evidence submitted by the applicant with the application, as well as any evidence submitted by the applicant before or at the interview. As a matter of discretion, the asylum officer may grant the applicant a brief extension of time following an interview, during which the applicant may submit additional evidence.

[64 FR 27876, May 21, 1999, as amended at 76 FR 53791, Aug. 29, 2011]

§240.68 Failure to appear at an interview before an asylum officer or failure to follow requirements for fingerprinting.

(a) Failure to appear for a scheduled interview without prior authorization may result in dismissal of the application or waiver of the right to an adjudication by an asylum officer. A written request to reschedule will be granted if it is an initial request and is received by the Asylum Office at least 2 days before the scheduled interview date. All other requests to reschedule the interview, including those submitted after the interview date, will be granted only if the applicant has a reasonable excuse for not appearing, and the excuse was received by the Asylum Office in writing within a reasonable time after the scheduled interview date.

(b) Failure to comply with fingerprint processing requirements without reasonable excuse may result in dismissal of the application or waiver of the right to an adjudication by an asylum officer.

(c) Failure to appear shall be excused if the notice of the interview or fingerprint appointment was not mailed to the applicant's current address and such address had been provided to the Office of International Affairs by the applicant prior to the date of mailing in accordance with section 265 of the Act and Service regulations, unless the asylum officer determines that the applicant received reasonable notice of the interview or fingerprinting appointment.

§240.69 Reliance on information compiled by other sources.

In determining whether an applicant is eligible for suspension of deportation or special rule cancellation of removal, the asylum officer may rely on material described in §208.12 of this chapter. Nothing in this subpart shall be construed to entitle the applicant to conduct discovery directed toward records, officers, agents, or employees of the Service, the Department of Justice, or the Department of State.

§240.70 Decision by the Service.

(a) *Service of decision.* Unless the asylum officer has granted the application for suspension of deportation or special rule cancellation of removal at the time of the interview or as otherwise provided by an Asylum Office, the applicant will be required to return to the Asylum Office to receive service of the decision on the applicant's application. If the applicant does not speak English fluently, the applicant shall bring an interpreter when returning to the office to receive service of the decision.

(b) *Grant of suspension of deportation.* An asylum officer may grant suspension of deportation to an applicant eligible to apply for this relief with the Service who qualifies for suspension of deportation under former section 244(a)(1) of the Act, as in effect prior to April 1, 1997, who is not an alien described in former section 241(a)(4)(D) of the Act, as in effect prior to April 1, 1997, and who admits deportability under any law of the United States, excluding former section 241(a)(2), (3), or (4) of the Act, as in effect prior to April 1, 1997. If the Service has made a preliminary decision to grant the applicant suspension of deportation under this subpart, the applicant shall be notified of that decision and will be asked to sign an admission of deportability or inadmissibility. The applicant must sign the admission before the Service may grant the relief sought. If suspension of deportation is granted, the Service shall adjust the status of the alien to lawful permanent resident, effective as of the date that suspension of deportation is granted.

(c) *Grant of cancellation of removal.* An asylum officer may grant cancellation of removal to an applicant who is eligible to apply for this relief with the Service, and who qualifies for cancellation of removal under section 309(f)(1)(A) of IIRIRA, as amended by section 203 of NACARA, and who admits deportability under section 237(a), excluding paragraphs (2), (3), and (4), of the Act, or inadmissibility under section 212(a), excluding paragraphs (2) or (3), of the Act. If the Service has made a preliminary decision to grant the applicant cancellation of removal under this subpart, the applicant shall be notified of that decision and asked to sign an admission of deportability or inadmissibility. The applicant must sign the concession before the Service may grant the relief sought. If the Service grants cancellation of removal, the Service shall adjust the status of the alien to lawful permanent resident, effective as of the date that cancellation of removal is granted.

(d) *Referral of the application.* Except as provided in paragraphs (e) and (f) of this section, and unless the applicant is granted asylum or is in lawful immigrant or non-immigrant status, an asylum officer shall refer the application for suspension of deportation or special rule cancellation of removal to the Immigration Court for adjudication in deportation or removal proceedings, and will provide the applicant with written notice of the statutory or regulatory basis for the referral, if:

(1) The applicant is not clearly eligible for suspension of deportation under former section 244(a)(1) of the Act as in effect prior to April 1, 1997, or for cancellation of removal under section 309(f)(1)(A) of IIRIRA, as amended by NACARA;

(2) The applicant does not appear to merit relief as a matter of discretion;

(3) The applicant appears to be eligible for suspension of deportation or special rule cancellation of removal under this subpart, but does not admit deportability or inadmissibility; or

(4) The applicant failed to appear for a scheduled interview with an asylum officer or failed to comply with fingerprinting processing requirements and such failure was not excused by the Service, unless the application is dismissed.

(e) *Dismissal of the application.* An asylum officer shall dismiss without prejudice an application for suspension of deportation or special rule cancellation of removal submitted by an applicant who has been granted asylum, or who is in lawful immigrant or non-immigrant status. An asylum officer may also dismiss an application for failure to appear, pursuant to § 240.68. The asylum officer will provide the applicant written notice of the statutory or regulatory basis for the dismissal.

(f) *Special provisions for certain ABC class members whose proceedings before EOIR were administratively closed or continued.* The following provisions shall apply with respect to an *ABC* class member who was in proceedings before the Immigration Court or the Board, and those proceedings were closed or continued pursuant to the *ABC* settlement agreement:

(1) *Suspension of deportation or asylum granted.* If an asylum officer grants asylum or suspension of deportation, the previous proceedings before the Immigration Court or Board shall be terminated as a matter of law on the date relief is granted.

(2) *Asylum denied and application for suspension of deportation not approved.* If an asylum officer denies asylum and does not grant the applicant suspension of deportation, the Service shall move to recalendar proceedings before the Immigration Court or resume proceedings before the Board, whichever is appropriate. The Service shall refer to the Immigration Court or the Board the application for suspension of deportation. In the case where jurisdiction rests with the Board, an application for suspension of deportation that is referred to the Board will be remanded to the Immigration Court for adjudication.

(g) *Special provisions for dependents whose proceedings before EOIR were administratively closed or continued.* If an asylum officer grants suspension of deportation or special rule cancellation of removal to an applicant described in §240.61(a)(4) or (a)(5), whose proceedings before EOIR were administratively closed or continued, those proceedings shall terminate as of the date the relief is granted. If suspension of deportation or special rule cancellation of removal is not granted, the Service shall move to recalendar proceedings before the Immigration Court or resume proceedings before the Board, whichever is appropriate. The Service shall refer to the Immigration Court or the Board the application for suspension of deportation or special rule cancellation of removal. In the case where jurisdiction rests with the Board, an application for suspension of deportation or special rule cancellation of removal that is referred to the Board will be remanded to the Immigration Court for adjudication.

(h) *Special provisions for applicants who depart the United States and return under a grant of advance parole while in deportation proceedings.* Notwithstanding paragraphs (f) and (g) of this section, for purposes of adjudicating an application for suspension of deportation or special rule cancellation of removal under this subpart, if an applicant departs and returns to the United States pursuant to a grant of advance parole while in deportation proceedings, including deportation proceedings administratively closed or continued pursuant to the *ABC* settlement agreement, the deportation proceedings will be considered terminated as of the date of applicant's departure from the United States. A decision on the NACARA application shall be issued in accordance with paragraph (a), and paragraphs (c) through (e) of this section.

PART 241—APPREHENSION AND DETENTION OF ALIENS ORDERED REMOVED

Subpart A—Post-hearing Detention and Removal

Sec.

Subpart B—Deportation of Excluded Aliens (for Hearings Commenced Prior to April 1, 1997)

Subpart C—Deportation of Aliens in the United States (for Hearings Commenced Prior to April 1, 1997)

AUTHORITY: 5 U.S.C. 301, 552, 552a; 8 U.S.C. 1103, 1182, 1223, 1224, 1225, 1226, 1227, 1228, 1231, 1251, 1253, 1255, 1330, 1362; 18 U.S.C. 4002, 4013(c)(4); Pub. L. 107–296, 116 Stat. 2135 (6 U.S.C. 101, *et seq.*); 8 CFR part 2.

SOURCE: 62 FR 10378, Mar. 6, 1997, unless otherwise noted.

Subpart A—Post-hearing Detention and Removal

§ 241.1 Final order of removal.

An order of removal becomes final in accordance with 8 CFR 1241.1.

[70 FR 673, Jan. 5, 2005]

§ 241.2 Warrant of removal.

(a) *Issuance of a warrant of removal*—(1) *In general.* A Form I–205, Warrant of Removal, based on the final administrative removal order in the alien's case will be issued by any of the following immigration officials:

(i) Director, Enforcement and Removal Operations;

(ii) Deputy Assistant Director, Field Operations;

(iii) Field Office Directors;

(iv) Deputy Field Office Directors;

(v) Assistant Field Office Directors;

(vi) Officers in Charge;

(vii) Special Agents in Charge;

(viii) Deputy Special Agents in Charge;

(ix) Associate Special Agents in Charge;

(x) Assistant Special Agents in Charge;

(xi) Group Supervisors;

(xii) Resident Agents in Charge;

(xiii) District Field Officers;

(xiv) Chief Patrol Agents;

(xv) Deputy Chief Patrol Agents;

(xvi) Division Chiefs;

(xvii) Assistant Chief Patrol Agents;

(xviii) Patrol Agents in Charge;

(xix) Deputy Patrol Agents in Charge;

(xx) Watch Commanders, Border Patrol;

(xxi) Director of Air Operations;

(xxii) Director of Marine Operations;

(xxiii) Supervisory Air and Marine Interdiction Agents;

(xxiv) Unit Chief, Law Enforcement Support Center;

(xxv) Section Chief, Law Enforcement Support Center;

(xxvi) Port Directors;

(xxvii) Assistant Port Directors;

(xxviii) Directors, Field Operations;

(xxix) Assistant Directors, Field Operations;

(xxx) Watch Commanders, Field Operations;

(xxxi) Chiefs, Field Operations; and

(xxxii) Other duly authorized officers or employees of the Department of Homeland Security or the United States who are delegated the authority as provided in 8 CFR 2.1 to issue Warrants of Removal, and who have successfully completed any required immigration law enforcement training.

(2) *Costs and care during removal.* The immigration officials listed in paragraphs (a)(1)(i) through (xxxi) of this section, and other officers or employees of the Department or the United States who are delegated the authority as provided in 8 CFR 2.1, shall exercise the authority contained in section 241 of the Act to determine at whose expense the alien shall be removed and whether his or her mental or physical condition requires personal care and attention en route to his or her destination.

(b) *Execution of the warrant of removal.* Any officer authorized by 8 CFR 287.5(e)(3) to execute administrative warrants of arrest may execute a warrant of removal.

[70 FR 67089, Nov. 4, 2005, as amended at 81 FR 62355, Sept. 9, 2016]

§241.3 Detention of aliens during removal period.

(a) *Assumption of custody.* Once the removal period defined in section 241(a)(1) of the Act begins, an alien in the United States will be taken into custody pursuant to the warrant of removal.

(b) *Cancellation of bond.* Any bond previously posted will be canceled unless it has been breached or is subject to being breached.

(c) *Judicial stays.* The filing of (or intention to file) a petition or action in a Federal court seeking review of the issuance or execution of an order of removal shall not delay execution of the Warrant of Removal except upon an affirmative order of the court.

(d) *Information regarding detainees.* Disclosure of information relating to detainees shall be governed by the provisions of 8 CFR 236.3.

[62 FR 10378, Mar. 6, 1997, as amended at 70 FR 673, Jan. 5, 2005]

§241.4 Continued detention of inadmissible, criminal, and other aliens beyond the removal period.

(a) *Scope.* The authority to continue an alien in custody or grant release or parole under sections 241(a)(6) and 212(d)(5)(A) of the Act shall be exercised by the Commissioner or Deputy Commissioner, as follows: Except as otherwise directed by the Commissioner or his or her designee, the Executive Associate Commissioner for Field Operations (Executive Associate Commissioner), the Deputy Executive Associate Commissioner for Detention and Removal, the Director of the Detention and Removal Field Office or the district director may continue an alien in custody beyond the removal period described in section 241(a)(1) of the Act pursuant to the procedures described in this section. Except as provided for in paragraph (b)(2) of this section, the provisions of this section apply to the custody determinations for the following group of aliens:

(1) An alien ordered removed who is inadmissible under section 212 of the Act, including an excludable alien convicted of one or more aggravated felony offenses and subject to the provisions of section 501(b) of the Immigration Act of 1990, Public Law 101–649, 104 Stat. 4978, 5048 (codified at 8 U.S.C. 1226(e)(1) through (e)(3)(1994));

(2) An alien ordered removed who is removable under section 237(a)(1)(C) of the Act;

(3) An alien ordered removed who is removable under sections 237(a)(2) or 237(a)(4) of the Act, including deportable criminal aliens whose cases are governed by former section 242 of the Act prior to amendment by the Illegal Immigration Reform and Immigrant Responsibility Act of 1996, Div. C of Public Law 104–208, 110 Stat. 3009–546; and

(4) An alien ordered removed who the decision-maker determines is unlikely to comply with the removal order or is a risk to the community.

(b) *Applicability to particular aliens*—(1) *Motions to reopen.* An alien who has filed a motion to reopen immigration proceedings for consideration of relief from removal, including withholding or deferral of removal pursuant to 8 CFR 208.16 or 208.17, shall remain subject to the provisions of this section unless the motion to reopen is granted. Section 236 of the Act and 8 CFR 236.1 govern custody determinations for aliens who are in pending immigration proceedings before the Executive Office for Immigration Review.

(2) *Parole for certain Cuban nationals.* The review procedures in this section do not apply to any inadmissible Mariel Cuban who is being detained by the Service pending an exclusion or removal proceeding, or following entry of a final exclusion or pending his or her return to Cuba or removal to another country. Instead, the determination whether to release on parole, or to revoke such parole, or to detain, shall in the case of a Mariel Cuban be governed by the procedures in 8 CFR 212.12.

(3) *Individuals granted withholding or deferral of removal.* Aliens granted withholding of removal under section 241(b)(3) of the Act or withholding or deferral of removal under the Convention Against Torture who are otherwise subject to detention are subject to the provisions of this part 241. Individuals subject to a termination of deferral hearing under 8 CFR 208.17(d) remain subject to the provisions of this part 241 throughout the termination process.

(4) *Service determination under 8 CFR 241.13.* The custody review procedures in this section do not apply after the Service has made a determination, pursuant to the procedures provided in 8 CFR 241.13, that there is no significant likelihood that an alien under a final order of removal can be removed in the reasonably foreseeable future. However, if the Service subsequently determines, because of a change of circumstances, that there is a significant likelihood that the alien may be removed in the reasonably foreseeable future to the country to which the alien was ordered removed or to a third country, the alien shall again be subject to the custody review procedures under this section.

(c) *Delegation of authority.* The Attorney General's statutory authority to make custody determinations under sections 241(a)(6) and 212(d)(5)(A) of the Act when there is a final order of removal is delegated as follows:

(1) *District Directors and Directors of Detention and Removal Field Offices.* The initial custody determination described in paragraph (h) of this section and any further custody determination concluded in the 3 month period immediately following the expiration of the 90-day removal period, subject to the provisions of paragraph (c)(2) of this section, will be made by the district director or the Director of the Detention and Removal Field Office having jurisdiction over the alien. The district director or the Director of the Detention and Removal Field Office shall maintain appropriate files respecting each detained alien reviewed for possible release, and shall have authority to determine the order in which the cases shall be reviewed, and to coordinate activities associated with these reviews in his or her respective jurisdictional area.

(2) *Headquarters Post-Order Detention Unit (HQPDU).* For any alien the district director refers for further review after the removal period, or any alien who has not been released or removed by the expiration of the three-month period after the review, all further custody determinations will be made by the Executive Associate Commissioner, acting through the HQPDU.

(3) *The HQPDU review plan.* The Executive Associate Commissioner shall appoint a Director of the HQPDU. The Director of the HQPDU shall have authority to establish and maintain appropriate files respecting each detained alien to be reviewed for possible release, to determine the order in which the cases shall be reviewed, and to coordinate activities associated with these reviews.

(4) *Additional delegation of authority.* All references to the Executive Associate Commissioner, the Director of the Detention and Removal Field Office, and the district director in this section shall be deemed to include any person or persons (including a committee) designated in writing by the Executive Associate Commissioner, the Director of the Detention and Removal Field Office, or the district director to exercise powers under this section.

(d) *Custody determinations.* A copy of any decision by the district director, Director of the Detention and Removal Field Office, or Executive Associate Commissioner to release or to detain an alien shall be provided to the detained alien. A decision to retain custody shall briefly set forth the reasons for the continued detention. A decision to release may contain such special conditions as are considered appropriate in the opinion of the Service. Notwithstanding any other provisions of this section, there is no appeal from the district director's or the Executive Associate Commissioner's decision.

(1) *Showing by the alien.* The district director, Director of the Detention and Removal Field Office, or Executive Associate Commissioner may release an alien if the alien demonstrates to the satisfaction of the Attorney General or her designee that his or her release will not pose a danger to the community or to the safety of other persons or to property or a significant risk of flight pending such alien's removal from the United States. The district director, Director of the Detention and Removal Field Office, or Executive Associate Commissioner may also, in accordance with the procedures and consideration of the factors set forth in this section, continue in custody any alien described in paragraphs (a) and (b)(1) of this section.

(2) *Service of decision and other documents.* All notices, decisions, or other documents in connection with the custody reviews conducted under this section by the district director, Director of the Detention and Removal Field Office, or Executive Associate Commissioner shall be served on the alien, in accordance with 8 CFR 103.8, by the Service district office having jurisdiction over the alien. Release documentation (including employment authorization if appropriate) shall be issued by the district office having jurisdiction over the alien in accordance with the custody determination made by the district director or by the Executive Associate Commissioner. Copies of all such documents will be retained in the alien's record and forwarded to the HQPDU.

(3) *Alien's representative.* The alien's representative is required to complete Form G–28, Notice of Entry of Appearance as Attorney or Representative, at the time of the interview or prior to reviewing the detainee's records. The Service will forward by regular mail a copy of any notice or decision that is being served on the alien only to the attorney or representative of record. The alien remains responsible for notification to any other individual providing assistance to him or her.

(e) *Criteria for release.* Before making any recommendation or decision to release a detainee, a majority of the Review Panel members, or the Director of the HQPDU in the case of a record review, must conclude that:

(1) Travel documents for the alien are not available or, in the opinion of the Service, immediate removal, while proper, is otherwise not practicable or not in the public interest;

(2) The detainee is presently a nonviolent person;

(3) The detainee is likely to remain nonviolent if released;

(4) The detainee is not likely to pose a threat to the community following release;

(5) The detainee is not likely to violate the conditions of release; and

(6) The detainee does not pose a significant flight risk if released.

(f) *Factors for consideration.* The following factors should be weighed in considering whether to recommend further detention or release of a detainee:

(1) The nature and number of disciplinary infractions or incident reports received when incarcerated or while in Service custody;

(2) The detainee's criminal conduct and criminal convictions, including consideration of the nature and severity of the alien's convictions, sentences imposed and time actually served, probation and criminal parole history, evidence of recidivism, and other criminal history;

(3) Any available psychiatric and psychological reports pertaining to the detainee's mental health;

(4) Evidence of rehabilitation including institutional progress relating to participation in work, educational, and vocational programs, where available;

(5) Favorable factors, including ties to the United States such as the number of close relatives residing here lawfully;

(6) Prior immigration violations and history;

(7) The likelihood that the alien is a significant flight risk or may abscond to avoid removal, including history of escapes, failures to appear for immigration or other proceedings, absence without leave from any halfway house or sponsorship program, and other defaults; and

(8) Any other information that is probative of whether the alien is likely to—

(i) Adjust to life in a community,

(ii) Engage in future acts of violence,

(iii) Engage in future criminal activity,

(iv) Pose a danger to the safety of himself or herself or to other persons or to property, or

(v) Violate the conditions of his or her release from immigration custody pending removal from the United States.

(g) *Travel documents and docket control for aliens continued in detention*—(1) *Removal period.* (i) The removal period for an alien subject to a final order of removal shall begin on the latest of the following dates:

(A) the date the order becomes administratively final;

(B) If the removal order is subject to judicial review (including review by habeas corpus) and if the court has ordered a stay of the alien's removal, the date on which, consistent with the court's order, the removal order can be executed and the alien removed; or

(C) If the alien was detained or confined, except in connection with a proceeding under this chapter relating to removability, the date the alien is released from the detention or confinement.

(ii) The removal period shall run for a period of 90 days. However, the removal period is extended under section 241(a)(1)(C) of the Act if the alien fails or refuses to make timely application in good faith for travel or other documents necessary to the alien's departure or conspires or acts to prevent the alien's removal subject to an order of removal. The Service will provide such an alien with a Notice of Failure to Comply, as provided in paragraph (g)(5) of this section, before the expiration of the removal period. The removal period shall be extended until the alien demonstrates to the Service that he or she has complied with the statutory obligations. Once the alien has complied with his or her obligations under the law, the Service shall have a reasonable period of time in order to effect the alien's removal.

(2) *In general.* The district director shall continue to undertake appropriate steps to secure travel documents for the alien both before and after the expiration of the removal period. If the district director is unable to secure travel documents within the removal period, he or she shall apply for assistance from Headquarters Detention and Deportation, Office of Field Operations. The district director shall promptly advise the HQPDU Director when travel documents are obtained for an alien whose custody is subject to review by the HQPDU. The Service's determination that receipt of a travel document is likely may by itself warrant continuation of detention pending the removal of the alien from the United States.

(3) *Availability of travel document.* In making a custody determination, the district director and the Director of the HQPDU shall consider the ability to obtain a travel document for the alien. If it is established at any stage of a custody review that, in the judgment of the Service, travel documents can be obtained, or such document is forthcoming, the alien will not be released unless immediate removal is not practicable or in the public interest.

(4) *Removal.* The Service will not conduct a custody review under these procedures when the Service notifies the alien that it is ready to execute an order of removal.

(5) *Alien's compliance and cooperation.* (i) Release will be denied and the alien may remain in detention if the alien fails or refuses to make timely application in good faith for travel documents necessary to the alien's departure or conspires or acts to prevent the alien's removal. The detention provisions of section 241(a)(2) of the Act will continue to apply, including provisions that mandate detention of certain criminal and terrorist aliens.

(ii) The Service shall serve the alien with a Notice of Failure to Comply, which shall advise the alien of the following: the provisions of sections 241(a)(1)(C) (extension of removal period) and 243(a) of the Act (criminal penalties related to removal); the circumstances demonstrating his or her failure to comply with the requirements of section 241(a)(1)(C) of the Act; and an explanation of the necessary steps that the alien must take in order to comply with the statutory requirements.

(iii) The Service shall advise the alien that the Notice of Failure to Comply shall have the effect of extending the removal period as provided by law, if the removal period has not yet expired, and that the Service is not obligated to complete its scheduled custody reviews under this section until the alien has demonstrated compliance with the statutory obligations.

(iv) The fact that the Service does not provide a Notice of Failure to Comply, within the 90-day removal period, to an alien who has failed to comply with the requirements of section 241(a)(1)(C) of the Act, shall not have the effect of excusing the alien's conduct.

(h) *District director's or Director of the Detention and Removal Field Office's custody review procedures.* The district director's or Director of the Detention and Removal Field Office's custody determination will be developed in accordance with the following procedures:

(1) *Records review.* The district director or Director of the Detention and Removal Field Office will conduct the initial custody review. For aliens described in paragraphs (a) and (b)(1) of this section, the district director or Director of the Detention and Removal Field Office will conduct a records review prior to the expiration of the removal period. This initial post-order custody review will consist of a review of the alien's records and any written information submitted in English to the district director by or on behalf of the alien. However, the district director or Director of the Detention and Removal Field Office may in his or her discretion schedule a personal or telephonic interview with the alien as part of this custody determination. The district director or Director of the Detention and Removal Field Office may also consider any other relevant information relating to the alien or his or her circumstances and custody status.

(2) *Notice to alien.* The district director or Director of the Detention and Removal Field Office will provide written notice to the detainee approximately 30 days in advance of the pending records review so that the alien may submit information in writing in support of his or her release. The alien may be assisted by a person of his or her choice, subject to reasonable security concerns at the institution and panel's discretion, in preparing or submitting information in response to the district director's notice. Such assistance shall be at no expense to the Government. If the alien or his or her representative requests additional time to prepare materials beyond the time when the district director or Director of the Detention and Removal Field Office expects to conduct the records review, such a request will constitute a waiver of the requirement that the review occur prior to the expiration of the removal period.

(3) *Factors for consideration.* The district director's or Director of the Detention and Removal Field Office's review will include but is not limited to consideration of the factors described in paragraph (f) of this section. Before making any decision to release a detainee, the district director must be able to reach the conclusions set forth in paragraph (e) of this section.

(4) *District director's or Director of the Detention and Removal Field Office's decision.* The district director or Director of the Detention and Removal Field Office will notify the alien in writing that he or she is to be released from custody, or that he or she will be continued in detention pending removal or further review of his or her custody status.

(5) *District office or Detention and Removal Field office staff.* The district director or the Director of the Detention and Removal Field Office may delegate the authority to conduct the custody review, develop recommendations, or render the custody or release decisions to those persons directly responsible for detention within his or her geographical areas of responsibility. This includes the deputy district director, the assistant director for detention and deportation, the officer-in-charge of a detention center, the assistant director of the detention and removal field office, the director of the detention and removal resident office, the assistant director of the detention and removal resident office, officers in charge of service processing centers, or such other persons as the district director or the Director of the Detention and Removal Field Office may designate from the professional staff of the Service.

(i) *Determinations by the Executive Associate Commissioner.* Determinations by the Executive Associate Commissioner to release or retain custody of aliens shall be developed in accordance with the following procedures.

(1) *Review panels.* The HQPDU Director shall designate a panel or panels to make recommendations to the Executive Associate Commissioner. A Review Panel shall, except as otherwise provided, consist of two persons. Members of a Review Panel shall be selected from the professional staff of the Service. All recommendations by the two-

member Review Panel shall be unanimous. If the vote of the two-member Review Panel is split, it shall adjourn its deliberations concerning that particular detainee until a third Review Panel member is added. The third member of any Review Panel shall be the Director of the HQPDU or his or her designee. A recommendation by a three-member Review Panel shall be by majority vote.

(2) *Records review.* Initially, and at the beginning of each subsequent review, the HQPDU Director or a Review Panel shall review the alien's records. Upon completion of this records review, the HQPDU Director or the Review Panel may issue a written recommendation that the alien be released and reasons therefore.

(3) *Personal interview.* (i) If the HQPDU Director does not accept a panel's recommendation to grant release after a records review, or if the alien is not recommended for release, a Review Panel shall personally interview the detainee. The scheduling of such interviews shall be at the discretion of the HQPDU Director. The HQPDU Director will provide a translator if he or she determines that such assistance is appropriate.

(ii) The alien may be accompanied during the interview by a person of his or her choice, subject to reasonable security concerns at the institution's and panel's discretion, who is able to attend at the time of the scheduled interview. Such assistance shall be at no expense to the Government. The alien may submit to the Review Panel any information, in English, that he or she believes presents a basis for his or her release.

(4) *Alien's participation.* Every alien shall respond to questions or provide other information when requested to do so by Service officials for the purpose of carrying out the provisions of this section.

(5) *Panel recommendation.* Following completion of the interview and its deliberations, the Review Panel shall issue a written recommendation that the alien be released or remain in custody pending removal or further review. This written recommendation shall include a brief statement of the factors that the Review Panel deems material to its recommendation.

(6) *Determination.* The Executive Associate Commissioner shall consider the recommendation and appropriate custody review materials and issue a custody determination, in the exercise of discretion under the standards of this section. The Executive Associate Commissioner's review will include but is not limited to consideration of the factors described in paragraph (f) of this section. Before making any decision to release a detainee, the Executive Associate Commissioner must be able to reach the conclusions set forth in paragraph (e) of this section. The Executive Associate Commissioner is not bound by the panel's recommendation.

(7) *No significant likelihood or removal.* During the custody review process as provided in this paragraph (i), or at the conclusion of that review, if the alien submits, or the record contains, information providing a substantial reason to believe that the removal of a detained alien is not significantly likely in the reasonably foreseeable future, the HQPDU shall treat that as a request for review and initiate the review procedures under § 241.13. To the extent relevant, the HQPDU may consider any information developed during the custody review process under this section in connection with the determinations to be made by the Service under § 241.13. The Service shall complete the custody review under this section unless the HQPDU is able to make a prompt determination to release the alien under an order of supervision under § 241.13 because there is no significant likelihood that the alien will be removed in the reasonably foreseeable future.

(j) *Conditions of release*—(1) *In general.* The district director, Director of the Detention and Removal Field Office, or Executive Associate Commissioner shall impose such conditions or special conditions on release as the Service considers appropriate in an individual case or cases, including but not limited to the conditions of release noted in 8 CFR 212.5(c) and § 241.5. An alien released under this section must abide by the release conditions specified by the

Service in relation to his or her release or sponsorship.

(2) *Sponsorship.* The district director, Director of the Detention and Removal Field Office, or Executive Associate Commissioner may, in the exercise of discretion, condition release on placement with a close relative who agrees to act as a sponsor, such as a parent, spouse, child, or sibling who is a lawful permanent resident or a citizen of the United States, or may condition release on the alien's placement or participation in an approved halfway house, mental health project, or community project when, in the opinion of the Service, such condition is warranted. No detainee may be released until sponsorship, housing, or other placement has been found for the detainee, if ordered, including but not limited to, evidence of financial support.

(3) *Employment authorization.* The district director, Director of the Detention and Removal Field Office, and the Executive Associate Commissioner, may, in the exercise of discretion, grant employment authorization under the same conditions set forth in § 241.5(c) for aliens released under an order of supervision.

(4) *Withdrawal of release approval.* The district director, Director of the Detention and Removal Field Office, or Executive Associate Commissioner may, in the exercise of discretion, withdraw approval for release of any detained alien prior to release when, in the decision-maker's opinion, the conduct of the detainee, or any other circumstance, indicates that release would no longer be appropriate.

(k) *Timing of reviews.* The timing of reviews shall be in accordance with the following guidelines:

(1) *District director or Director of the Detention and Removal Field Office.* (i) Prior to the expiration of the removal period, the district director or Director of the Detention and Removal Field Office shall conduct a custody review for an alien described in paragraphs (a) and (b)(1) of this section where the alien's removal, while proper, cannot be accomplished during the period, or is impracticable or contrary to the public interest. As provided in paragraph (h)(4) of this section, the district director or Director of the Detention and Removal Field Office will notify the alien in writing that he or she is to be released from custody, or that he or she will be continued in detention pending removal or further review of his or her custody status.

(ii) When release is denied pending the alien's removal, the district director or Director of the Detention and Removal Field Office in his or her discretion may retain responsibility for custody determinations for up to three months after expiration of the removal period, during which time the district director or Director of the Detention and Removal Field Office may conduct such additional review of the case as he or she deems appropriate. The district director may release the alien if he or she is not removed within the three-month period following the expiration of the removal period, in accordance with paragraphs (e), (f), and (j) of this section, or the district director or Director of the Detention and Removal Field Office may refer the alien to the HQPDU for further custody review.

(2) *HQPDU reviews*—(i) *District director or Director of the Detention and Removal Field Office referral for further review.* When the district director or Director of the Detention and Removal Field Office refers a case to the HQPDU for further review, as provided in paragraph (c)(2) of this section, authority over the custody determination transfers to the Executive Associate Commissioner, according to procedures established by the HQPDU. The Service will provide the alien with approximately 30 days notice of this further review, which will ordinarily be conducted by the expiration of the removal period or as soon thereafter as practicable.

(ii) *District director or Director of the Detention and Removal Field Office retains jurisdiction.* When the district director or Director of the Detention and Removal Field Office has advised the alien at the 90-day review as provided in paragraph (h)(4) of this section that he or she will remain in custody pending removal or further custody review, and the alien is not removed within three months of the district director's decision, authority over the custody determination transfers from the district director or Director of the Detention and Removal Field Office to the Executive Associate Commissioner. The initial HQPDU review will ordinarily be conducted at the expiration of the three-month period after the 90-day review or as soon thereafter as practicable. The Service will provide the alien with approximately 30 days notice of that review.

(iii) *Continued detention cases.* A subsequent review shall ordinarily be commenced for any detainee within approximately one year of a decision by the Executive Associate Commissioner declining to grant release. Not more than once every three months in the interim between annual reviews, the alien may submit a written request to the HQPDU for release consideration based on a proper showing of a material change in circumstances since the last annual review. The HQPDU shall respond to the alien's request in writing within approximately 90 days.

(iv) *Review scheduling.* Reviews will be conducted within the time periods specified in paragraphs (k)(1)(i), (k)(2)(i), (k)(2)(ii), and (k)(2)(iii) of this section or as soon as possible thereafter, allowing for any unforeseen circumstances or emergent situation.

(v) *Discretionary reviews.* The HQPDU Director, in his or her discretion, may schedule a review of a detainee at shorter intervals when he or she deems such review to be warranted.

(3) *Postponement of review.* In the case of an alien who is in the custody of the Service, the district director or the HQPDU Director may, in his or her discretion, suspend or postpone the custody review process if such detainee's prompt removal is practicable and proper, or for other good cause. The decision and reasons for the delay shall be documented in the alien's custody review file or A file, as appropriate. Reasonable care will be exercised to ensure that the alien's case is reviewed once the reason for delay is remedied or if the alien is not removed from the United States as anticipated at the time review was suspended or postponed.

(4) *Transition provisions.* (i) The provisions of this section apply to cases that have already received the 90-day review. If the alien's last review under the procedures set out in the Executive Associate Commissioner memoranda entitled *Detention Procedures for Aliens Whose Immediate Repatriation is Not Possible or Practicable,* February 3, 1999; *Supplemental Detention Procedures,* April 30, 1999; *Interim Changes and Instructions for Conduct of Post-order Custody Reviews,* August 6, 1999; *Review of Long-term Detainees,* October 22, 1999, was a records review and the alien remains in custody, the HQPDU will conduct a custody review within six months of that review (Memoranda available at *http://www.ins.usdoj.gov*). If the alien's last review included an interview, the HQPDU review will be scheduled one year from the last review. These reviews will be conducted pursuant to the procedures in paragraph (i) of this section, within the time periods specified in this paragraph or as soon as possible thereafter, allowing for resource limitations, unforeseen circumstances, or an emergent situation.

(ii) Any case pending before the Board on December 21, 2000 will be completed by the Board. If the Board affirms the district director's decision to continue the alien in detention, the next scheduled custody review will be conducted one year after the Board's decision in accordance with the procedures in paragraph (i) of this section.

(l) *Revocation of release*—(1) *Violation of conditions of release.* Any alien described in paragraph (a) or (b)(1) of this section who has been released under an order of supervision or other conditions of release who violates the conditions of release may be returned to custody. Any such alien who violates the conditions of an order of supervision is subject to the penalties described in section 243(b) of the Act. Upon revocation, the alien will be notified of the reasons for revocation of his or her release or parole. The alien will be afforded an initial informal interview promptly after his or her return to Service custody to afford the alien an opportunity to respond to the reasons for revocation stated in the notification.

(2) *Determination by the Service.* The Executive Associate Commissioner shall have authority, in the exercise of discretion, to revoke release and return

to Service custody an alien previously approved for release under the procedures in this section. A district director may also revoke release of an alien when, in the district director's opinion, revocation is in the public interest and circumstances do not reasonably permit referral of the case to the Executive Associate Commissioner. Release may be revoked in the exercise of discretion when, in the opinion of the revoking official:

(i) The purposes of release have been served;

(ii) The alien violates any condition of release;

(iii) It is appropriate to enforce a removal order or to commence removal proceedings against an alien; or

(iv) The conduct of the alien, or any other circumstance, indicates that release would no longer be appropriate.

(3) *Timing of review when release is revoked.* If the alien is not released from custody following the informal interview provided for in paragraph (l)(1) of this section, the HQPDU Director shall schedule the review process in the case of an alien whose previous release or parole from immigration custody pursuant to a decision of either the district director, Director of the Detention and Removal Field Office, or Executive Associate Commissioner under the procedures in this section has been or is subject to being revoked. The normal review process will commence with notification to the alien of a records review and scheduling of an interview, which will ordinarily be expected to occur within approximately three months after release is revoked. That custody review will include a final evaluation of any contested facts relevant to the revocation and a determination whether the facts as determined warrant revocation and further denial of release. Thereafter, custody reviews will be conducted annually under the provisions of paragraphs (i), (j), and (k) of this section.

[65 FR 80294, Dec. 21, 2000, as amended at 66 FR 56976, 56977, Nov. 14, 2001; 67 FR 39259, June 7, 2002; 70 FR 673, Jan. 5, 2005; 76 FR 53791, Aug. 29, 2011]

§241.5 Conditions of release after removal period.

(a) *Order of supervision.* An alien released pursuant to §241.4 shall be released pursuant to an order of supervision. The Commissioner, Deputy Commissioner, Executive Associate Commissioner Field Operations, regional director, district director, acting district director, deputy district director, assistant district director for investigations, assistant district director for detention and deportation, or officer-in-charge may issue Form I-220B, Order of Supervision. The order shall specify conditions of supervision including, but not limited to, the following:

(1) A requirement that the alien report to a specified officer periodically and provide relevant information under oath as directed;

(2) A requirement that the alien continue efforts to obtain a travel document and assist the Service in obtaining a travel document;

(3) A requirement that the alien report as directed for a mental or physical examination or examinations as directed by the Service;

(4) A requirement that the alien obtain advance approval of travel beyond previously specified times and distances; and

(5) A requirement that the alien provide DHS with written notice of any change of address in the prescribed manner.

(b) *Posting of bond.* An officer authorized to issue an order of supervision may require the posting of a bond in an amount determined by the officer to be sufficient to ensure compliance with the conditions of the order, including surrender for removal.

(c) *Employment authorization.* An officer authorized to issue an order of supervision may, in his or her discretion, grant employment authorization to an alien released under an order of supervision if the officer specifically finds that:

(1) The alien cannot be removed in a timely manner; or

(2) The removal of the alien is impracticable or contrary to public interest.

[62 FR 10378, Mar. 6, 1997, as amended at 65 FR 80298, Dec. 21, 2000; 70 FR 673, Jan. 5, 2005; 76 FR 53791, Aug. 29, 2011]

§ 241.6 Administrative stay of removal.

(a) Any request of an alien under a final order of deportation or removal for a stay of deportation or removal shall be filed on Form I–246, Stay of Removal, with the district director having jurisdiction over the place where the alien is at the time of filing. The Commissioner, Deputy Commissioner, Executive Associate Commissioner for Field Operations, Deputy Executive Associate Commissioner for Detention and Removal, the Director of the Office of Juvenile Affairs, regional directors, or district director, in his or her discretion and in consideration of factors listed in 8 CFR 212.5 and section 241(c) of the Act, may grant a stay of removal or deportation for such time and under such conditions as he or she may deem appropriate. Neither the request nor failure to receive notice of disposition of the request shall delay removal or relieve the alien from strict compliance with any outstanding notice to surrender for deportation or removal.

(b) Denial by the Commissioner, Deputy Commissioner, Executive Associate Commissioner for Field Operations, Deputy Executive Associate Commissioner for Detention and Removal, Director of the Office of Juvenile Affairs, regional director, or district director of a request for a stay is not appealable, but such denial shall not preclude an immigration judge or the Board from granting a stay in connection with a previously filed motion to reopen or a motion to reconsider as provided in 8 CFR part 3.

(c) The Service shall take all reasonable steps to comply with a stay granted by an immigration judge or the Board. However, such a stay shall cease to have effect if granted (or communicated) after the alien has been placed aboard an aircraft or other conveyance for removal and the normal boarding has been completed.

[65 FR 80298, Dec. 21, 2000, as amended at 67 FR 39259, June 7, 2002]

§ 241.7 Self-removal.

A district director, the Deputy Executive Associate Commissioner for Detention and Removal, or the Director of the Office of Juvenile Affairs may permit an alien ordered removed (including an alien ordered excluded or deported in proceedings prior to April 1, 1997) to depart at his or her own expense to a destination of his or her own choice. Any alien who has departed from the United States while an order of deportation or removal is outstanding shall be considered to have been deported, excluded and deported, or removed, except that an alien who departed before the expiration of the voluntary departure period granted in connection with an alternate order of deportation or removal shall not be considered to be so deported or removed.

[67 FR 39260, June 7, 2002]

§ 241.8 Reinstatement of removal orders.

(a) *Applicability.* An alien who illegally reenters the United States after having been removed, or having departed voluntarily, while under an order of exclusion, deportation, or removal shall be removed from the United States by reinstating the prior order. The alien has no right to a hearing before an immigration judge in such circumstances. In establishing whether an alien is subject to this section, the immigration officer shall determine the following:

(1) Whether the alien has been subject to a prior order of removal. The immigration officer must obtain the prior order of exclusion, deportation, or removal relating to the alien.

(2) The identity of the alien, *i.e.*, whether the alien is in fact an alien who was previously removed, or who departed voluntarily while under an order of exclusion, deportation, or removal. In disputed cases, verification of identity shall be accomplished by a comparison of fingerprints between those of the previously excluded, deported, or removed alien contained in Service records and those of the subject alien. In the absence of fingerprints in a disputed case the alien shall

not be removed pursuant to this paragraph.

(3) Whether the alien unlawfully reentered the United States. In making this determination, the officer shall consider all relevant evidence, including statements made by the alien and any evidence in the alien's possession. The immigration officer shall attempt to verify an alien's claim, if any, that he or she was lawfully admitted, which shall include a check of Service data systems available to the officer.

(b) *Notice.* If an officer determines that an alien is subject to removal under this section, he or she shall provide the alien with written notice of his or her determination. The officer shall advise the alien that he or she may make a written or oral statement contesting the determination. If the alien wishes to make such a statement, the officer shall allow the alien to do so and shall consider whether the alien's statement warrants reconsideration of the determination.

(c) *Order.* If the requirements of paragraph (a) of this section are met, the alien shall be removed under the previous order of exclusion, deportation, or removal in accordance with section 241(a)(5) of the Act.

(d) *Exception for applicants for benefits under section 902 of HRIFA or sections 202 or 203 of NACARA.* If an alien who is otherwise subject to this section has applied for adjustment of status under either section 902 of Division A of Public Law 105–277, the Haitian Refugee Immigrant Fairness Act of 1998 (HRIFA), or section 202 of Public Law 105–100, the Nicaraguan Adjustment and Central American Relief Act (NACARA), the provisions of section 241(a)(5) of the Immigration and Nationality Act shall not apply. The immigration officer may not reinstate the prior order in accordance with this section unless and until a final decision to deny the application for adjustment has been made. If the application for adjustment of status is granted, the prior order shall be rendered moot.

(e) *Exception for withholding of removal.* If an alien whose prior order of removal has been reinstated under this section expresses a fear of returning to the country designated in that order, the alien shall be immediately referred to an asylum officer for an interview to determine whether the alien has a reasonable fear of persecution or torture pursuant to §208.31 of this chapter.

(f) *Execution of reinstated order.* Execution of the reinstated order of removal and detention of the alien shall be administered in accordance with this part.

[62 FR 10378, Mar. 6, 1997, as amended at 64 FR 8495, Feb. 19, 1999; 66 FR 29451, May 31, 2001]

§241.9 Notice to transportation line of alien's removal.

(a) An alien who has been ordered removed shall, immediately or as promptly as the circumstances permit, be offered for removal to the owner, agent, master, commanding officer, person in charge, purser, or consignee of the vessel or aircraft on which the alien is to be removed, as determined by the district director, with a written notice specifying the cause of inadmissibility or deportability, the class of travel in which such alien arrived and is to be removed, and with the return of any documentation that will assist in effecting his or her removal. If special care and attention are required, the provisions of §241.10 shall apply.

(b) Failure of the carrier to accept for removal an alien who has been ordered removed shall result in the carrier being assessed any costs incurred by the Service for detention after the carrier's failure to accept the alien for removal, including the cost of any transportation as required under section 241(e) of the Act. The User Fee Account shall not be assessed for expenses incurred because of the carrier's violation of the provisions of section 241 of the Act and this paragraph. The Service will, at the carrier's option, retain custody of the alien for an additional 7 days beyond the date of the removal order. If, after the third day of this additional 7-day period, the carrier has not made all the necessary transportation arrangements for the alien to be returned to his or her point of embarkation by the end of the additional 7-day period, the Service will make the arrangements and bill the carrier for its costs.

§ 241.10 Special care and attention of removable aliens.

When, in accordance with section 241(c)(3) of the Act, a transportation line is responsible for the expenses of an inadmissible or deportable alien's removal, and the alien requires special care and attention, the alien shall be delivered to the owner, agent, master, commanding officer, person in charge, purser, or consignee of the vessel or aircraft on which the alien will be removed, who shall be given Forms I–287, I–287A, and I–287B. The reverse of Form I–287A shall be signed by the officer of the vessel or aircraft to whom the alien has been delivered and immediately returned to the immigration officer effecting delivery. Form I–287B shall be retained by the receiving officer and subsequently filled out by the agents or persons therein designated and returned by mail to the district director named on the form. The transportation line shall at its own expense forward the alien from the foreign port of disembarkation to the final destination specified on Form I–287. The special care and attention shall be continued to such final destination, except when the foreign public officers decline to allow such attendant to proceed and they take charge of the alien, in which case this fact shall be recorded by the transportation line on the reverse of Form I–287B. If the transportation line fails, refuses, or neglects to provide the necessary special care and attention or comply with the directions of Form I–287, the district director shall thereafter and without notice employ suitable persons, at the expense of the transportation line, and effect such removal.

§ 241.11 Detention and removal of stowaways.

(a) *Presentation of stowaways.* The owner, agent, master, commanding officer, charterer, or consignee of a vessel or aircraft (referred to in this section as the carrier) bringing any alien stowaway to the United States is required to detain the stowaway on board the vessel or aircraft, at the expense of the owner of the vessel or aircraft, until completion of the inspection of the alien by an immigration officer. If detention on board the vessel or aircraft pending inspection is not possible, the carrier shall advise the Service of this fact without delay, and the Service may authorize that the carrier detain the stowaway at another designated location, at the expense of the owner, until the immigration officer arrives. No notice to detain the alien shall be required. Failure to detain an alien stowaway pending inspection shall result in a civil penalty under section 243(c)(1)(A) of the Act. The owner, agent, master, commanding officer, charterer, or consignee of a vessel or aircraft must present the stowaway for inspection, along with any documents or evidence of identity or nationality in the possession of the alien or obtained by the carrier relating to the alien stowaway, and must provide any available information concerning the alien's boarding or apprehension.

(b) *Removal of stowaways from vessel or aircraft for medical treatment.* The district director may parole an alien stowaway into the United States for medical treatment, but the costs of detention and treatment of the alien stowaway shall be at the expense of the owner of the vessel or aircraft, and such removal of the stowaway from the vessel or aircraft does not relieve the carrier of the requirement to remove the stowaway from the United States once such medical treatment has been completed.

(c) *Repatriation of stowaways*—(1) *Requirements of carrier.* Following inspection, an immigration officer may order the owner, agent, master, commanding officer, charterer, or consignee of a vessel or aircraft bringing any alien stowaway to the United States to remove the stowaway on the vessel or aircraft of arrival, unless it is impracticable to do so or other factors exist which would preclude removal on the same vessel or aircraft. Such factors may include, but are not limited to, sanitation, health, and safety concerns for the crew and/or stowaway, whether the stowaway is a female or a juvenile, loss of insurance coverage on account of the stowaway remaining aboard, need for repairs to the vessel, and other similar circumstances. If the owner, agent, master, commanding officer, charterer, or consignee requests that he or she be allowed to remove the stowaway by other means, the Service shall favorably consider any such request, provided the carrier has obtained, or will obtain in a timely manner, any necessary travel documents and has made or will make all transportation arrangements. The owner, agent, master, commanding officer, charterer, or consignee shall transport the stowaway or arrange for secure escort of the stowaway to the vessel or aircraft of departure to ensure that the stowaway departs the United States. All expenses relating to removal shall be borne by the owner. Other than requiring compliance with the detention and removal requirements contained in section 241(d)(2) of the Act, the Service shall not impose additional conditions on the carrier regarding security arrangements. Failure to comply with an order to remove an alien stowaway shall result in a civil penalty under section 243(c)(1)(A) of the Act.

(2) *Detention of stowaways ordered removed.* If detention of the stowaway is required pending removal on other than the vessel or aircraft of arrival, or if the stowaway is to be removed on the vessel or aircraft of arrival but departure of the vessel or aircraft is not imminent and circumstances preclude keeping the stowaway on board the vessel or aircraft, the Service shall take the stowaway into Service custody. The owner is responsible for all costs of maintaining and detaining the stowaway pending removal, including costs for stowaways seeking asylum as described in paragraph (d) of this section. Such costs will be limited to those normally incurred in the detention of an alien by the Service, including, but not limited to, housing, food, transportation, medical expenses, and other reasonable costs incident to the detention of the stowaway. The Service may require the posting of a bond or other surety to ensure payment of costs of detention.

(d) *Stowaways claiming asylum*—(1) *Referral for credible fear determination.* A stowaway who indicates an intention to apply for asylum or a fear of persecution or torture upon return to his or her native country or country of last habitual residence (if not a national of any country) shall be removed from the vessel or aircraft of arrival in accordance with §208.5(b) of this chapter. The immigration officer shall refer the alien to an asylum officer for a determination of credible fear in accordance with section 235(b)(1)(B) of the Act and §208.30 of this chapter. The stowaway shall be detained in the custody of the Service pending the credible fear determination and any review thereof. Parole of such alien, in accordance with section 212(d)(5) of the Act, may be permitted only when the Attorney General determines, in the exercise of discretion, that parole is required to meet a medical emergency or is necessary for a legitimate law enforcement objective. A stowaway who has established a credible fear of persecution or torture in accordance with §208.30 of this chapter may be detained or paroled pursuant to §212.5 of this chapter during any consideration of the asylum application. In determining whether to detain or parole the alien, the Service shall consider the likelihood that the alien will abscond or pose a security risk.

(2) *Costs of detention of asylum-seeking stowaways.* The owner of the vessel or aircraft that brought the stowaway to the United States shall reimburse the Service for the costs of maintaining and detaining the stowaway pending a determination of credible fear under section 235(b)(1)(B) of the Act, up to a maximum period of 72 hours. The owner is also responsible for the costs of maintaining and detaining the stowaway during the period in which the stowaway is pursuing his or her asylum application, for a maximum period of 15 working days, excluding Saturdays, Sundays, and holidays. The 15-day period shall begin on the day following the day in which the alien is determined to have a credible fear of persecution by the asylum officer, or by the immigration judge if such review was requested by the alien pursuant to section 235(b)(1)(B)(iii)(III) of the Act, but not later than 72 hours after the stowaway was initially presented to the Service for inspection. Following the determination of credible fear, if the stowaway's application for asylum is not adjudicated within 15 working days, the Service shall pay the costs of detention beyond this time period. If the stowaway is determined not to

have a credible fear of persecution, or if the stowaway's application for asylum is denied, including any appeals, the carrier shall be notified and shall arrange for repatriation of the stowaway at the expense of the owner of the vessel or aircraft on which the stowaway arrived.

[62 FR 10378, Mar. 6, 1997, as amended at 64 FR 8495, Feb. 19, 1999]

§ 241.12 Nonapplication of costs of detention and maintenance.

The owner of a vessel or aircraft bringing an alien to the United States who claims to be exempt from payment of the costs of detention and maintenance of the alien pursuant to section 241(c)(3)(B) of the Act shall establish to the satisfaction of the district director in charge of the port of arrival that such costs should not be applied. The district director shall afford the owner a reasonable time within which to submit affidavits and briefs to support the claim. There is no appeal from the decision of the district director.

§ 241.13 Determination of whether there is a significant likelihood of removing a detained alien in the reasonably foreseeable future.

(a) *Scope.* This section establishes special review procedures for those aliens who are subject to a final order of removal and are detained under the custody review procedures provided at § 241.4 after the expiration of the removal period, where the alien has provided good reason to believe there is no significant likelihood of removal to the country to which he or she was ordered removed, or to a third country, in the reasonably foreseeable future.

(b) *Applicability to particular aliens*—(1) *Relationship to § 241.4.* Section 241.4 shall continue to govern the detention of aliens under a final order of removal, including aliens who have requested a review of the likelihood of their removal under this section, unless the Service makes a determination under this section that there is no significant likelihood of removal in the reasonably foreseeable future. The Service may release an alien under an order of supervision under § 241.4 if it determines that the alien would not pose a danger to the public or a risk of flight, without regard to the likelihood of the alien's removal in the reasonably foreseeable future.

(2) *Continued detention pending determinations.* (i) The Service's Headquarters Post-order Detention Unit (HQPDU) shall continue in custody any alien described in paragraph (a) of this section during the time the Service is pursuing the procedures of this section to determine whether there is no significant likelihood the alien can be removed in the reasonably foreseeable future. The HQPDU shall continue in custody any alien described in paragraph (a) of this section for whom it has determined that special circumstances exist and custody procedures under § 241.14 have been initiated.

(ii) The HQPDU has no obligation to release an alien under this section until the HQPDU has had the opportunity during a six-month period, dating from the beginning of the removal period (whenever that period begins and unless that period is extended as provided in section 241(a)(1) of the Act), to make its determination as to whether there is a significant likelihood of removal in the reasonably foreseeable future.

(3) *Limitations.* This section does not apply to:

(i) Arriving aliens, including those who have not entered the United States, those who have been granted immigration parole into the United States, and Mariel Cubans whose parole is governed by § 212.12 of this chapter;

(ii) Aliens subject to a final order of removal who are still within the removal period, including aliens whose removal period has been extended for failure to comply with the requirements of section 241(a)(1)(C) of the Act; or

(iii) Aliens who are ordered removed by the Alien Terrorist Removal Court pursuant to title 5 of the Act.

(c) *Delegation of authority.* The HQPDU shall conduct a review under this section, in response to a request from a detained alien, in order to determine whether there is no significant likelihood that the alien will be removed in the reasonably foreseeable future. If so, the HQPDU shall determine whether the alien should be released from custody under appropriate conditions of supervision or should be referred for a determination under §241.14 as to whether the alien's continued detention may be justified by special circumstances.

(d) *Showing by the alien*—(1) *Written request.* An eligible alien may submit a written request for release to the HQPDU asserting the basis for the alien's belief that there is no significant likelihood that the alien will be removed in the reasonably foreseeable future . The alien may submit whatever documentation to the HQPDU he or she wishes in support of the assertion that there is no significant likelihood of removal in the reasonably foreseeable future.

(2) *Compliance and cooperation with removal efforts.* The alien shall include with the written request information sufficient to establish his or her compliance with the obligation to effect his or her removal and to cooperate in the process of obtaining necessary travel documents.

(3) *Timing of request.* An eligible alien subject to a final order of removal may submit, at any time after the removal order becomes final, a written request under this section asserting that his or her removal is not significantly likely in the reasonably foreseeable future. However, the Service may, in the exercise of its discretion, postpone its consideration of such a request until after expiration of the removal period.

(e) *Review by HQPDU*—(1) *Initial response.* Within 10 business days after the HQPDU receives the request (or, if later, the expiration of the removal period), the HQPDU shall respond in writing to the alien, with a copy to counsel of record, by regular mail, acknowledging receipt of the request for a review under this section and explaining the procedures that will be used to evaluate the request. The notice shall advise the alien that the Service may continue to detain the alien until it has made a determination under this section whether there is a significant likelihood the alien can be removed in the reasonably foreseeable future.

(2) *Lack of compliance, failure to cooperate.* The HQPDU shall first determine if the alien has failed to make reasonable efforts to comply with the removal order, has failed to cooperate fully in effecting removal, or has obstructed or hampered the removal process. If so, the HQPDU shall so advise the alien in writing, with a copy to counsel of record by regular mail. The HQPDU shall advise the alien of the efforts he or she needs to make in order to assist in securing travel documents for return to his or her country of origin or a third country, as well as the consequences of failure to make such efforts or to cooperate, including the provisions of section 243(a) of the Act. The Service shall not be obligated to conduct a further consideration of the alien's request for release until the alien has responded to the HQPDU and has established his or her compliance with the statutory requirements.

(3) *Referral to the State Department.* If the HQPDU believes that the alien's request provides grounds for further review, the Service may, in the exercise of its discretion, forward a copy of the alien's release request to the Department of State for information and assistance. The Department of State may provide detailed country conditions information or any other information that may be relevant to whether a travel document is obtainable from the country at issue. The Department of State may also provide an assessment of the accuracy of the alien's assertion that he or she cannot be returned to the country at issue or to a third country. When the Service bases its decision, in whole or in part, on information provided by the Department of State, that information shall be made part of the record.

(4) *Response by alien.* The Service shall permit the alien an opportunity to respond to the evidence on which the Service intends to rely, including the Department of State's submission, if any, and other evidence of record presented by the Service prior to any HQPDU decision. The alien may provide any additional relevant information to the Service, including reasons why his or her removal would not be significantly likely in the reasonably foreseeable future even though the Service has generally been able to accomplish the removal of other aliens to the particular country.

(5) *Interview.* The HQPDU may grant the alien an interview, whether telephonically or in person, if the HQPDU determines that an interview would provide assistance in reaching a decision. If an interview is scheduled, the HQPDU will provide an interpreter upon its determination that such assistance is appropriate.

(6) *Special circumstances.* If the Service determines that there are special circumstances justifying the alien's continued detention nowithstanding the determination that removal is not significantly likely in the reasonably foreseeable future, the Service shall initiate the review procedures in § 241.14, and provide written notice to the alien. In appropriate cases, the Service may initiate review proceedings under § 241.14 before completing the HQPDU review under this section.

(f) *Factors for consideration.* The HQPDU shall consider all the facts of the case including, but not limited to, the history of the alien's efforts to comply with the order of removal, the history of the Service's efforts to remove aliens to the country in question or to third countries, including the ongoing nature of the Service's efforts to remove this alien and the alien's assistance with those efforts, the reasonably foreseeable results of those efforts, and the views of the Department of State regarding the prospects for removal of aliens to the country or countries in question. Where the Service is continuing its efforts to remove the alien, there is no presumptive period of time within which the alien's removal must be accomplished, but the prospects for the timeliness of removal must be reasonable under the circumstances.

(g) *Decision.* The HQPDU shall issue a written decision based on the administrative record, including any documentation provided by the alien, regarding the likelihood of removal and whether there is a significant likelihood that the alien will be removed in the reasonably foreseeable future under the circumstances. The HQPDU shall provide the decision to the alien, with a copy to counsel of record, by regular mail.

(1) *Finding of no significant likelihood of removal.* If the HQPDU determines at the conclusion of the review that there is no significant likelihood that the alien will be removed in the reasonably foreseeable future, despite the Service's and the alien's efforts to effect removal, then the HQPDU shall so advise the alien. Unless there are special circumstances justifying continued detention, the Service shall promptly make arrangements for the release of the alien subject to appropriate conditions, as provided in paragraph (h) of this section. The Service may require that the alien submit to a medical or psychiatric examination prior to establishing appropriate conditions for release or determining whether to refer the alien for further proceedings under § 214.14 because of special circumstances justifying continued detention. The Service is not required to release an alien if the alien refuses to submit to a medical or psychiatric examination as ordered.

(2) *Denial.* If the HQPDU determines at the conclusion of the review that there is a significant likelihood that the alien will be removed in the reasonably foreseeable future, the HQPDU shall deny the alien's request under this section. The denial shall advise the alien that his or her detention will continue to be governed under the established standards in § 214.4. There is no administrative appeal from the HQPDU decision denying a request from an alien under this section.

(h) *Conditions of release*—(1) *In general.* An alien's release pursuant to an HQPDU determination that the alien's removal is not significantly likely in the reasonably foreseeable future shall be upon appropriate conditions specified in this paragraph and in the order of supervision, in order to protect the public safety and to promote the ability of the Service to effect the alien's removal as ordered, or removal to a third country, should circumstances change in the future. The order of supervision shall include all of the conditions provided in section 241(a)(3) of the Act, and § 241.5, and shall also include the conditions that the alien obey all laws, including any applicable prohibitions on the possession or use of firearms (*see, e.g.,* 18 U.S.C. 922(g)); and that the alien continue to seek to obtain travel documents and provide the Service with all correspondence to Embassies/Consulates requesting the issuance of travel documents and any reply from the Embassy/Consulate. The order of supervision may also include any other conditions that the HQPDU considers necessary to ensure public safety and guarantee the alien's compliance with the order of removal, including, but not limited to, attendance at any rehabilitative/sponsorship program or submission for medical or psychiatric examination, as ordered.

(2) *Advice of consequences for violating conditions of release.* The order of supervision shall advise an alien released under this section that he or she must abide by the conditions of release specified by the Service. The order of supervision shall also advise the alien of the consequences of violation of the conditions of release, including the authority to return the alien to custody and the sanctions provided in section 243(b) of the Act.

(3) *Employment authorization.* The Service may, in the exercise of its discretion, grant employment authorization under the same conditions set forth in § 241.5(c) for aliens released under an order of supervision.

(4) *Withdrawal of release approval.* The Service may, in the exercise of its discretion, withdraw approval for release of any alien under this section prior to release in order to effect removal in the reasonably foreseeable future or where the alien refuses to comply with the conditions of release.

(i) *Revocation of release*—(1) *Violation of conditions of release.* Any alien who has been released under an order of supervision under this section who violates any of the conditions of release may be returned to custody and is subject to the penalties described in section 243(b) of the Act. In suitable cases, the HQPDU shall refer the case to the appropriate U.S. Attorney for criminal prosecution. The alien may be continued in detention for an additional six months in order to effect the alien's removal, if possible, and to effect the conditions under which the alien had been released.

(2) *Revocation for removal.* The Service may revoke an alien's release under this section and return the alien to custody if, on account of changed circumstances, the Service determines that there is a significant likelihood that the alien may be removed in the reasonably foreseeable future. Thereafter, if the alien is not released from custody following the informal interview provided for in paragraph (h)(3) of this section, the provisions of § 241.4 shall govern the alien's continued detention pending removal.

(3) *Revocation procedures.* Upon revocation, the alien will be notified of the reasons for revocation of his or her release. The Service will conduct an initial informal interview promptly after his or her return to Service custody to afford the alien an opportunity to respond to the reasons for revocation stated in the notification. The alien may submit any evidence or information that he or she believes shows there is no significant likelihood he or she be removed in the reasonably foreseeable future, or that he or she has not violated the order of supervision. The revocation custody review will include an evaluation of any contested facts relevant to the revocation and a determination whether the facts as determined warrant revocation and further denial of release.

(j) *Subsequent requests for review.* If the Service has denied an alien's request for release under this section, the alien may submit a request for review of his or her detention under this section, six months after the Service's last denial of release under this section. After applying the procedures in this section, the HQPDU shall consider any additional evidence provided by the alien or available to the Service as well as the evidence in the prior proceedings but the HQPDC shall render a *de novo* decision on the likelihood of removing the alien in the reasonably foreseeable future under the circumstances.

[66 FR 56977, Nov. 14, 2001, as amended at 70 FR 673, Jan. 5, 2005]

§ 241.14 Continued detention of removable aliens on account of special circumstances.

(a) *Scope.* The Service may invoke the procedures of this section in order to continue detention of particular removable aliens on account of special circumstances even though there is no significant likelihood that the alien will be removed in the reasonably foreseeable future.

(1) *Applicability*. This section applies to removable aliens as to whom the Service has made a determination under § 241.13 that there is no significant likelihood of removal in the reasonably foreseeable future. This section does not apply to aliens who are not subject to the special review provisions under § 241.13.

(2) *Jurisdiction*. The immigration judges and the Board have jurisdiction with respect to determinations as to whether release of an alien would pose a special danger to the public, as provided in paragraphs (f) through (k) of this section, but do not have jurisdiction with respect to aliens described in paragraphs (b), (c), or (d) of this section.

(b) *Aliens with a highly contagious disease that is a threat to public safety*. If, after a medical examination of the alien, the Service determines that a removable alien presents a threat to public safety initiate efforts with the Public Health Service or proper State and local government officials to secure appropriate arrangements for the alien's continued medical care or treatment.

(1) *Recommendation*. The Service shall not invoke authority to continue detention of an alien under this paragraph except upon the express recommendation of the Public Health Service. The Service will provide every reasonably available form of treatment while the alien remains in the custody of the Service.

(2) *Conditions of release*. If the Service, in consultation with the Public Health Service and the alien, identifies an appropriate medical facility that will treat the alien, then the alien may be released on condition that he or she continue with appropriate medical treatment until he or she no longer poses a threat to public safety because of a highly contagious disease.

(c) *Aliens detained on account of serious adverse foreign policy consequences of release*—(1) *Certification*. The Service shall continue to detain a removable alien where the Attorney General or Deputy Attorney General has certified in writing that:

(i) Without regard to the grounds upon which the alien has been found inadmissible or removable, the alien is a person described in section 212(a)(3)(C) or section 237(a)(4)(C) of the Act;

(ii) The alien's release is likely to have serious adverse foreign policy consequences for the United States; and

(iii) No conditions of release can reasonably be expected to avoid those serious adverse foreign policy consequences,

(2) *Foreign policy consequences*. A certification by the Attorney General or Deputy Attorney General that an alien should not be released from custody on account of serious adverse foreign policy consequences shall be made only after consultation with the Department of State and upon the recommendation of the Secretary of State.

(3) *Ongoing review*. The certification is subject to ongoing review on a semiannual basis but is not subject to further administrative review.

(d) *Aliens detained on account of security or terrorism concerns*—(1) *Standard for continued detention*. Subject to the review procedures under this paragraph (d), the Service shall continue to detain a removable alien based on a determination in writing that:

(i) The alien is a person described in section 212(a)(3)(A) or (B) or section 237(a)(4)(A) of (B) of the Act or the alien has engaged or will likely engage in any other activity that endangers the national security;

(ii) The alien's release presents a significant threat to the national security or a significant risk of terrorism; and

(iii) No conditions of release can reasonably be expected to avoid the threat to the national security or the risk of terrorism, as the case may be.

(2) *Procedure*. Prior to the Commissioner's recommendation to the Attorney General under paragraph (d)(5) of this section, the alien shall be notified of the Service's intention to continue the alien in detention and of the alien's right to submit a written statement and additional information for consideration by the Commissioner. The Service shall continue to detain the

alien pending the decision of the Attorney General under this paragraph. To the greatest extent consistent with protection of the national security and classified information:

(i) The Service shall provide a description of the factual basis for the alien's continued detention; and

(ii) The alien shall have a reasonable opportunity to examine evidence against him or her, and to present information on his or her own behalf.

(3) *Aliens ordered removed on grounds other than national security or terrorism.* If the alien's final order of removal was based on grounds of inadmissibility other than any of those stated in section 212(a)(3)(A)(i), (A)(iii), or (B) of the Act, or on grounds of deportability other than any of those stated in section 237(a)(4)(A) or (B) of the Act:

(i) An immigration officer shall, if possible, conduct an interview in person and take a sworn question-and-answer statement from the alien, and the Service shall provide an interpreter for such interview, if such assistance is determined to be appropriate; and

(ii) The alien may be accompanied at the interview by an attorney or other representative of his or her choice in accordance with 8 CFR part 292, at no expense to the government.

(4) *Factors for consideration.* In making a recommendation to the Attorney General that an alien should not be released from custody on account of security or terrorism concerns, the Commissioner shall take into account all relevant information, including but not limited to:

(i) The recommendations of appropriate enforcement officials of the Service, including the director of the Headquarters Post-order Detention Unit (HQPDU), and of the Federal Bureau of Investigation or other federal law enforcement or national security agencies;

(ii) The statements and information submitted by the alien, if any;

(iii) The extent to which the alien's previous conduct (including but not limited to the commission of national security or terrorism-related offenses, engaging in terrorist activity or other activity that poses a danger to the national security and any prior convictions in a federal, state or foreign court) indicates a likelihood that the alien's release would present a significant threat to the national security or a significant risk of terrorism; and

(iv) Other special circumstances of the alien's case indicating that release from detention would present a significant threat to the national security or a significant risk of terrorism.

(5) *Recommendation to the Attorney General.* The Commissioner shall submit a written recommendation and make the record available to the Attorney General. If the continued detention is based on a significant risk of terrorism, the recommendation shall state in as much detail as practicable the factual basis for this determination.

(6) *Attorney General certification.* Based on the record developed by the Service, and upon this recommendation of the Commissioner and the Director of the Federal Bureau of Investigation, the Attorney General may certify that an alien should continue to be detained on account of security or terrorism grounds as provided in this paragraph (d). Before making such a certification, the Attorney General shall order any further procedures or reviews as may be necessary under the circumstances to ensure the development of a complete record, consistent with the obligations to protect national security and classified information and to comply with the requirements of due process.

(7) *Ongoing review.* The detention decision under this paragraph (d) is subject to ongoing review on a semi-annual basis as provided in this paragraph (d), but is not subject to further administrative review. After the initial certification by the Attorney General, further certifications under paragraph (d)(6) of this section may be made by the Deputy Attorney General.

(e) [Reserved]

(f) *Detention of aliens determined to be specially dangerous*—(1) *Standard for continued detention.* Subject to the review procedures provided in this section, the Service shall continue to detain an alien if the release of the alien would pose a special danger to the public, because:

(i) The alien has previously committed one or more crimes of violence as defined in 18 U.S.C. 16;

(ii) Due to a mental condition or personality disorder and behavior associated with that condition or disorder, the alien is likely to engage in acts of violence in the future; and

(iii) No conditions of release can reasonably be expected to ensure the safety of the public.

(2) *Determination by the Commissioner.* The Service shall promptly initiate review proceedings under paragraph (g) of this section if the Commissioner has determined in writing that the alien's release would pose a special danger to the public, according to the standards of paragraph (f)(1) of this section.

(3) *Medical or mental health examination.* Before making such a determination, the Commissioner shall arrange for a report by a physician employed or designated by the Public Health Service based on a full medical and psychiatric examination of the alien. The report shall include recommendations pertaining to whether, due to a mental condition or personality disorder and behavior associated with that condition or disorder, the alien is likely to engage in acts of violence in the future.

(4) *Detention pending review.* After the Commissioner or Deputy Commissioner has made a determination under this paragraph, the Service shall continue to detain the alien, unless an immigration judge or the Board issues an administratively final decision dismissing the review proceedings under this section.

(g) *Referral to Immigration Judge.* Jurisdiction for an immigration judge to review a determination by the Service pursuant to paragraph (f) of this section that an alien is specially dangerous shall commence with the filing by the Service of a Notice of Referral to the Immigration Judge (Form I–863) with the Immigration Court having jurisdiction over the place of the alien's custody. The Service shall promptly provide to the alien by personal service a copy of the Notice of Referral to the Immigration Judge and all accompanying documents.

(1) *Factual basis.* The Service shall attach a written statement that contains a summary of the basis for the Commissioner's determination to continue to detain the alien, including a description of the evidence relied upon to reach the determination regarding the alien's special dangerousness. The Service shall attach copies of all relevant documents used to reach its decision to continue to detain the alien.

(2) *Notice of reasonable cause hearing.* The Service shall attach a written notice advising the alien that the Service is initiating proceedings for the continued detention of the alien and informing the alien of the procedures governing the reasonable cause hearing, as set forth at paragraph (h) of this section.

(3) *Notice of alien's rights.* The Service shall also provide written notice advising the alien of his or her rights during the reasonable cause hearing and the merits hearing before the Immigration Court, as follows:

(i) The alien shall be provided with a list of free legal services providers, and may be represented by an attorney or other representative of his or her choice in accordance with 8 CFR part 292, at no expense to the Government;

(ii) The Immigration Court shall provide an interpreter for the alien, if necessary, for the reasonable cause hearing and the merits hearing.

(iii) The alien shall have a reasonable opportunity to examine evidence against the alien, to present evidence in the alien's own behalf, and to cross-examine witnesses presented by the Service; and

(iv) The alien shall have the right, at the merits hearing, to cross-examine the author of any medical or mental health reports used as a basis for the determination under paragraph (f) of this section that the alien is specially dangerous.

(4) *Record.* All proceedings before the immigration judge under this section shall be recorded. The Immigration Court shall create a record of proceeding that shall include all testimony and documents related to the proceedings.

(h) *Reasonable cause hearing.* The immigration judge shall hold a preliminary hearing to determine whether the evidence supporting the Service's determination is sufficient to establish reasonable cause to go forward with a merits hearing under paragraph (i) of this section. A finding of reasonable cause under this section will be sufficient to warrant the alien's continued detention pending the completion of the review proceedings under this section.

(1) *Scheduling of hearing.* The reasonable cause hearing shall be commenced not later than 10 business days after the filing of the Form I-863. The Immigration Court shall provide prompt notice to the alien and to the Service of the time and place of the hearing. The hearing may be continued at the request of the alien or his or her representative.

(2) *Evidence.* The Service must show that there is reasonable cause to conduct a merits hearing under a merits hearing under paragraph (i) of this section. The Service may offer any evidence that is material and relevant to the proceeding. Testimony of witnesses, if any, shall be under oath or affirmation. The alien may, but is not required to, offer evidence on his or her own behalf.

(3) *Decision.* The immigration judge shall render a decision, which should be in summary form, within 5 business days after the close of the record, unless that time is extended by agreement of both parties, by a determination from the Chief Immigration Judge that exceptional circumstances make it impractical to render the decision on a highly expedited basis, or because of delay caused by the alien. If the immigration judge determines that the Service has met its burden of establishing reasonable cause, the immigration judge shall advise the alien and the Service, and shall schedule a merits hearing under paragraph (i) of this section to review the Service's determination that the alien is specially dangerous. If the immigration judge determines that the Service has not met its burden, the immigration judge shall order that the review proceedings under this section be dismissed. The order and any documents offered shall be included in the record of proceedings, and may be relied upon in a subsequent merits hearing.

(4) *Appeal.* If the immigration judge dismisses the review proceedings, the Service may appeal to the Board of Immigration Appeals in accordance with §3.38 of this chapter, except that the Service must file the Notice of Appeal (Form EOIR-26) with the Board within 2 business days after the immigration judge's order. The Notice of Appeal should state clearly and conspicuously that it is an appeal of a reasonable cause decision under this section.

(i) If the Service reserves appeal of a dismissal of the reasonable cause hearing, the immigration judge's order shall be stayed until the expiration of the time to appeal. Upon the Service's filing of a timely Notice of Appeal, the immigration judge's order shall remain in abeyance pending a final decision of the appeal. The stay shall expire if the Service fails to file a timely Notice of Appeal.

(ii) The Board will decide the Service's appeal, by single Board Member review, based on the record of proceedings before the immigration judge. The Board shall expedite its review as far as practicable, as the highest priority among the appeals filed by detained aliens, and shall determine the issue within 20 business days of the filing of the notice of appeal, unless that time is extended by agreement of both parties, by a determination from the Chairman of the Board that exceptional circumstances make it impractical to render the decision on a highly expedited basis, or because of delay caused by the alien.

(iii) If the Board determines that the Service has met its burden of showing reasonable cause under this paragraph (h), the Board shall remand the case to the immigration judge for the scheduling of a merits hearing under paragraph (i) of this section. If the Board determines that the Service has not met its burden, the Board shall dismiss the review proceedings under this section.

(i) *Merits hearing.* If there is reasonable cause to conduct a merits hearing under this section, the immigration judge shall promptly schedule the hearing and shall expedite the proceedings as far as practicable. The immigration judge shall allow adequate time for the parties to prepare for the merits hearing, but, if requested by the alien, the hearing shall commence within 30 days. The hearing may be continued at the request of the alien or his or her representative, or at the request of the Service upon a showing of exceptional circumstances by the Service.

(1) *Evidence.* The Service shall have the burden of proving, by clear and convincing evidence, that the alien should remain in custody because the alien's release would pose a special danger to the public, under the standards of paragraph (f)(1) of this section. The immigration judge may receive into evidence any oral or written statement that is material and relevant to this determination. Testimony of witnesses shall be under oath or affirmation. The alien may, but is not required to, offer evidence on his or her own behalf.

(2) *Factors for consideration.* In making any determination in a merits hearing under this section, the immigration judge shall consider the following non-exclusive list of factors:

(i) The alien's prior criminal history, particularly the nature and seriousness of any prior crimes involving violence or threats of violence;

(ii) The alien's previous history of recidivism, if any, upon release from either Service or criminal custody;

(iii) The substantiality of the Service's evidence regarding the alien's current mental condition or personality disorder;

(iv) The likelihood that the alien will engage in acts of violence in the future; and

(v) The nature and seriousness of the danger to the public posed by the alien's release.

(3) *Decision.* After the closing of the record, the immigration judge shall render a decision as soon as practicable. The decision may be oral or written. The decision shall state whether or not the Service has met its burden of establishing that the alien should remain in custody because the alien's release would pose a special danger to the public, under the standards of paragraph (f)(1) of this section. The decision shall also include the reasons for the decision under each of the standards of paragraph (f)(1) of this section, although a formal enumeration of findings is not required. Notice of the decision shall be served in accordance with § 240.13(a) or (b).

(i) If the immigration judge determines that the Service has met its burden, the immigration judge shall enter an order providing for the continued detention of the alien.

(ii) If the immigration judge determines that the Service has failed to meet its burden, the immigration judge shall order that the review proceedings under this section be dismissed.

(4) *Appeal.* Either party may appeal an adverse decision to the Board of Immigration Appeals in accordance with § 3.38 of this chapter, except that, if the immigration judge orders dismissal of the proceedings, the Service shall have only 5 business days to file a Notice of Appeal with the Board. The Notice of Appeal should state clearly and conspicuously that this is an appeal of a merits decision under this section.

(i) If the Service reserves appeal of a dismissal, the immigration judge's order shall be stayed until the expiration of the time to appeal. Upon the Service's filing of a timely Notice of Appeal, the immigration judge's order shall remain in abeyance pending a final decision of the appeal. The stay shall expire if the Service fails to file a timely Notice of Appeal.

(ii) The Board shall conduct its review of the appeal as provided in 8 CFR part 3, but shall expedite its review as far as practicable, as the highest priority among the appeals filed by detained aliens. The decision of the Board shall be final as provided in § 3.1(d)(3) of this chapter.

(j) *Release of alien upon dismissal of proceedings.* If there is an administratively final decision by the immigration judge or the Board dismissing the review proceedings under this section upon conclusion of the reasonable cause hearing or the merits hearing, the Service shall promptly release the alien on conditions of supervision, as determined by the Service, pursuant to § 241.13. The conditions of supervision shall not be subject to review by the immigration judge or the Board.

(k) *Subsequent review for aliens whose release would pose a special danger to the public*—(1) *Periodic review.* In any case where the immigration judge or the Board has entered an order providing for the alien to remain in custody after a merits hearing pursuant to paragraph

(i) of this section, the Service shall continue to provide an ongoing, periodic review of the alien's continued detention, according to §241.4 and paragraphs (f)(1)(ii) and (f)(1)(iii) of this section.

(2) *Alien's request for review.* The alien may also request a review of his or her custody status because of changed circumstances, as provided in this paragraph (k). The request shall be in writing and directed to the HQPDU.

(3) *Time for review.* An alien may only request a review of his or her custody status under this paragraph (k) no earlier than six months after the last decision of the immigration judge under this section or, if the decision was appealed, the decision of the Board.

(4) *Showing of changed circumstances.* The alien shall bear the initial burden to establish a material change in circumstances such that the release of the alien would no longer pose a special danger to the public under the standards of paragraph (f)(1) of this section.

(5) *Review by the Service.* If the Service determines, upon consideration of the evidence submitted by the alien and other relevant evidence, that the alien is not likely to commit future acts of violence or that the Service will be able to impose adequate conditions of release so that the alien will not pose a special danger to the public, the Service shall release the alien from custody pursuant to the procedures in §241.13. If the Service determines that continued detention is needed in order to protect the public, the Service shall provide a written notice to the alien stating the basis for the Service's determination, and provide a copy of the evidence relied upon by the Service. The notice shall also advise the alien of the right to move to set aside the prior review proceedings under this section.

(6) *Motion to set aside determination in prior review proceedings.* If the Service denies the alien's request for release from custody, the alien may file a motion with the Immigration Court that had jurisdiction over the merits hearing to set aside the determination in the prior review proceedings under this section. The immigration judge shall consider any evidence submitted by the alien or relied upon by the Service and shall provide an opportunity for the Service to respond to the motion.

(i) If the immigration judge determines that the alien has provided good reason to believe that, because of a material change in circumstances, releasing the alien would no longer pose a special danger to the public under the standards of paragraph (f)(1) of this section, the immigration judge shall set aside the determination in the prior review proceedings under this section and schedule a new merits hearing as provided in paragraph (i) of this section.

(ii) Unless the immigration judge determines that the alien has satisfied the requirements under paragraph (k)(6)(i) of this section, the immigration judge shall deny the motion. Neither the immigration judge nor the Board may *sua sponte* set aside a determination in prior review proceedings. Notwithstanding 8 CFR 3.23 or 3.2 (motions to reopen), the provisions set forth in this paragraph (k) shall be the only vehicle for seeking review based on material changed circumstances.

(iii) The alien may appeal an adverse decision to the Board in accordance with §3.38 of this chapter. The Notice of Appeal should state clearly and conspicuously that this is an appeal of a denial of a motion to set aside a prior determination in review proceedings under this section.

[66 FR 56979, Nov. 14, 2001]

§241.15 Countries to which aliens may be removed.

(a) *Country.* For the purposes of section 241(b) of the Act (8 U.S.C. 1231(b)), the Secretary retains discretion to remove an alien to any country described in section 241(b) of the Act (8 U.S.C. 1231(b)), without regard to the nature or existence of a government.

(b) *Acceptance.* For the purposes of section 241(b) of the Act (8 U.S.C. 1231(b)), the Secretary retains discretion to determine the effect, if any, of acceptance or lack thereof, when an acceptance by a country is required, and what constitutes sufficient acceptance.

(c) *Absence or lack of response.* The absence of or lack of response from a de jure or functioning government (whether recognized by the United States, or otherwise) or a body acting as a de jure or functioning government in the receiving country does not preclude the removal of an alien to a receiving country.

(d) *Prior commitment.* No commitment of acceptance by the receiving country is required prior to designation of the receiving country, before travel arrangements are made, or before the alien is transported to the receiving country.

(e) *Specific provisions regarding acceptance.* Where the Department cannot remove an alien under section 241(b)(2)(A)–(D) of the Act, acceptance is not required to remove an alien to a receiving country pursuant to section 241(b)(2)(E)(i)–(vi) of the Act. Where the Department cannot remove an arriving alien under section 241(b)(1)(A) or (B) of the Act, acceptance is not required to remove an alien to a receiving country pursuant to section 241(b)(1)(C)(i)–(iii) of the Act.

(f) *Interest of the United States controlling.* The Secretary or his designee may designate a country previously identified in section 241(b)(2)(A)–(D) of the Act when selecting a removal country under section 241(b)(2)(E) of the Act (and may designate a country previously identified in section 241(b)(1)(A) or (B) of the Act when selecting an alternative removal country under subsection 241(b)(1)(C) of the Act) if the Secretary or his designee determines that such designation is in the best interests of the United States.

(g) *Limitation on construction.* Nothing in this section shall be construed to create any substantive or procedural right or benefit that is legally enforceable by any party against the United States or its agencies or officers or any other person.

[70 FR 673, Jan. 5, 2005]

§§ 241.16–241.19 [Reserved]

Subpart B—Deportation of Excluded Aliens (for Hearings Commenced Prior to April 1, 1997)

§ 241.20 Proceedings commenced prior to April 1, 1997.

Subpart B of 8 CFR part 241 applies to exclusion proceedings commenced prior to April 1, 1997. All references to the Act contained in this subpart are references to the Act in effect prior to April 1, 1997.

§ 241.21 Stay of deportation of excluded alien.

The district director in charge of the port of arrival may stay the immediate deportation of an excluded alien pursuant to sections 237 (a) and (d) of the Act under such conditions as he or she may prescribe.

§ 241.22 Notice to surrender for deportation.

An alien who has been finally excluded pursuant to 8 CFR part 240, subpart D may at any time surrender himself or herself to the custody of the Service and shall surrender to such custody upon notice in writing of the time and place for his or her surrender. The Service may take the alien into custody at any time. An alien taken into custody either upon notice to surrender or by arrest shall not be deported less than 72 hours thereafter without his or her consent thereto filed in writing with the district director in charge of the place of his or her detention. An alien in foreign contiguous territory shall be informed that he or she may remain there in lieu of surrendering to the Service, but that he or she will be deemed to have acknowledged the execution of the order of exclusion and deportation in his or her case upon his or her failure to surrender at the time and place prescribed.

§ 241.23 Cost of maintenance not assessed.

A claim pursuant to section 237(a)(1) of the Act shall be established to the satisfaction of the district director in charge of the port of arrival, from whose adverse decision no appeal shall lie. The district director shall afford the line a reasonable time within which to submit affidavits and briefs to support its claim.

§241.24 Notice to transportation line of alien's exclusion.

(a) An excluded alien shall, immediately or as promptly as the circumstances permit, be offered for deportation to the master, commanding officer, purser, person in charge, agent, owner, or consignee of the vessel or aircraft on which the alien is to be deported, as determined by the district director, with a written notice specifying the cause of exclusion, the class of travel in which such alien arrived and is to be deported, and with the return of any documentation that will assist in effecting his or her deportation. If special care and attention are required, the provisions of §241.10 shall apply.

(b) Failure of the carrier to accept for removal an alien who has been ordered excluded and deported shall result in the carrier being assessed any costs incurred by the Service for detention after the carrier's failure to accept the alien for removal including the cost of any transportation. The User Fee Account shall not be assessed for expenses incurred because of the carrier's violation of the provisions of section 237 of the Act and this paragraph. The Service will, at the carrier's option, retain custody of the excluded alien for an additional 7 days beyond the date of the deportation/exclusion order. If, after the third day of this additional 7-day period, the carrier has not made all the necessary transportation arrangements for the excluded alien to be returned to his or her point of embarkation by the end of the additional 7-day period, the Service will make the arrangements and bill the carrier for its costs.

§241.25 Deportation.

(a) *Definitions of terms.* For the purposes of this section, the following terms mean:

(1) *Adjacent island*—as defined in section 101(b)(5) of the Act.

(2) *Foreign contiguous territory*—any country sharing a common boundary with the United States.

(3) *Residence in foreign contiguous territory or adjacent island*—any physical presence, regardless of intent, in a foreign contiguous territory or an adjacent island if the government of such territory or island agrees to accept the alien.

(4) *Aircraft or vessel*—any conveyance and other mode of travel by which arrival is effected.

(5) *Next available flight*—the carrier's next regularly scheduled departure to the excluded alien's point of embarkation regardless of seat availability. If the carrier's next regularly scheduled departure to the excluded aliens point of embarkation is full, the carrier has the option of arranging for return transportation on other carriers which service the excluded aliens point of embarkation.

(b) *Place to which deported.* Any alien (other than an alien crewmember or an alien who boarded an aircraft or vessel in foreign contiguous territory or an adjacent island) who is ordered excluded shall be deported to the country where the alien boarded the vessel or aircraft on which the alien arrived in the United States. Otherwise, the Secretary may, as a matter of discretion, deport the alien to the country of which the alien is a subject, citizen, or national; the country where the alien was born; the country where the alien has a residence; or any other country.

(c) *Contiguous territory and adjacent islands.* Any alien ordered excluded who boarded an aircraft or vessel in foreign contiguous territory or in any adjacent island shall be deported to such foreign contiguous territory or adjacent island if the alien is a native, citizen, subject, or national of such foreign contiguous territory or adjacent island, or if the alien has a residence in such foreign contiguous territory or adjacent island. Otherwise, the alien shall be deported, in the first instance, to the country in which is located the port at which the alien embarked for such foreign contiguous territory or adjacent island.

(d) *Land border pedestrian arrivals.* Any alien ordered excluded who arrived at a land border on foot shall be deported in the same manner as if the alien had boarded a vessel or aircraft in foreign contiguous territory.

[62 FR 10378, Mar. 6, 1997, as amended at 70 FR 673, Jan. 5, 2005]

§§ 241.26–241.29 [Reserved]

Subpart C—Deportation of Aliens in the United States (for Hearings Commenced Prior to April 1, 1997)

§ 241.30 Proceedings commenced prior to April 1, 1997.

Subpart C of 8 CFR part 241 applies to deportation proceedings commenced prior to April 1, 1997. All references to the Act contained in this subpart are references to the Act in effect prior to April 1, 1997.

§ 241.31 Final order of deportation.

An order of deportation becomes final in accordance with 8 CFR 1241.31.

[70 FR 673, Jan. 5, 2005]

§ 241.32 Warrant of deportation.

A Form I–205, Warrant of Deportation, based upon the final administrative order of deportation in the alien's case shall be issued by a district director. The district director shall exercise the authority contained in section 243 of the Act to determine at whose expense the alien shall be deported and whether his or her mental or physical condition requires personal care and attention en route to his or her destination.

§ 241.33 Expulsion.

(a) *Execution of order*. Except in the exercise of discretion by the district director, and for such reasons as are set forth in § 212.5(b) of this chapter, once an order of deportation becomes final, an alien shall be taken into custody and the order shall be executed. An order of deportation becomes final in accordance with 8 CFR 1241.31.

(b) *Service of decision*. In the case of an order entered by any of the authorities enumerated above, the order shall be executed no sooner than 72 hours after service of the decision, regardless of whether the alien is in Service custody, provided that such period may be waived on the knowing and voluntary request of the alien. Nothing in this paragraph shall be construed, however, to preclude assumption of custody by the Service at the time of issuance of the final order.

[62 FR 10378, Mar. 6, 1997, as amended at 65 FR 82256, Dec. 28, 2000; 70 FR 674, Jan. 5, 2005]

PARTS 242–243 [RESERVED]

PART 244—TEMPORARY PROTECTED STATUS FOR NATIONALS OF DESIGNATED STATES

Sec.

AUTHORITY: 8 U.S.C. 1103, 1254, 1254a note, 8 CFR part 2.

§ 244.1 Definitions.

As used in this part:

Brief, casual, and innocent absence means a departure from the United States that satisfies the following criteria:

(1) Each such absence was of short duration and reasonably calculated to accomplish the purpose(s) for the absence;

(2) The absence was not the result of an order of deportation, an order of voluntary departure, or an administrative grant of voluntary departure without the institution of deportation proceedings; and

(3) The purposes for the absence from the United States or actions while outside of the United States were not contrary to law.

Charging document means the written instrument which initiates a proceeding before an Immigration Judge. For proceedings initiated prior to April 1, 1997, these documents include an Order to Show Cause, a Notice to Applicant for Admission Detained for Hearing before Immigration Judge, and a Notice of Intention to Rescind and Request for Hearing by Alien. For proceedings initiated after April 1, 1997, these documents include a Notice to Appear, a Notice of Referral to Immigration Judge, and a Notice of Intention to Rescind and Request for Hearing by Alien.

Continuously physically present means actual physical presence in the United States for the entire period specified in the regulations. An alien shall not be considered to have failed to maintain continuous physical presence in the United States by virtue of brief, casual, and innocent absences as defined within this section.

Continuously resided means residing in the United States for the entire period specified in the regulations. An alien shall not be considered to have failed to maintain continuous residence in the United States by reason of a brief, casual and innocent absence as defined within this section or due merely to a brief temporary trip abroad required by emergency or extenuating circumstances outside the control of the alien.

Felony means a crime committed in the United States, punishable by imprisonment for a term of more than one year, regardless of the term such alien actually served, if any, except: When the offense is defined by the State as a misdemeanor and the sentence actually imposed is one year or less regardless of the term such alien actually served. Under this exception for purposes of section 244 of the Act, the crime shall be treated as a misdemeanor.

Foreign state means any foreign country or part thereof as designated by the Attorney General pursuant to section 244 of the Act.

Misdemeanor means a crime committed in the United States, either:

(1) Punishable by imprisonment for a term of one year or less, regardless of the term such alien actually served, if any, or

(2) A crime treated as a misdemeanor under the term "felony" of this section.

For purposes of this definition, any crime punishable by imprisonment for a maximum term of five days or less shall not be considered a felony or misdemeanor.

Prima facie means eligibility established with the filing of a completed application for Temporary Protected Status containing factual information that if unrebutted will establish a claim of eligibility under section 244 of the Act.

Register means to properly file, with the director, a completed application, with proper fee, for Temporary Protected Status during the registration period designated under section 244(b) of the Act.

[56 FR 619, Jan. 7, 1991, as amended at 56 FR 23497, May 22, 1991. Redesignated at 62 FR 10367, 10382, Mar. 6, 1997, as amended at 63 FR 63595, Nov. 16, 1998; 64 FR 4781, Feb. 1, 1999]

§244.2 Eligibility.

Except as provided in §§244.3 and 244.4, an alien may in the discretion of the director be granted Temporary Protected Status if the alien establishes that he or she:

(a) Is a national, as defined in section 101(a)(21) of the Act, of a foreign state designated under section 244(b) of the Act;

(b) Has been continuously physically present in the United States since the effective date of the most recent designation of that foreign state;

(c) Has continuously resided in the United States since such date as the Attorney General may designate;

(d) Is admissible as an immigrant except as provided under §244.3;

(e) Is not ineligible under §244.4; and

(f)(1) Registers for Temporary Protected Status during the initial registration period announced by public notice in the FEDERAL REGISTER, or

(2) During any subsequent extension of such designation if at the time of the initial registration period:

(i) The applicant is a nonimmigrant or has been granted voluntary departure status or any relief from removal;

(ii) The applicant has an application for change of status, adjustment of status, asylum, voluntary departure, or any relief from removal which is pending or subject to further review or appeal;

(iii) The applicant is a parolee or has a pending request for reparole; or

(iv) The applicant is a spouse or child of an alien currently eligible to be a TPS registrant.

(3) Eligibility for late initial registration in a currently designated foreign state shall also continue until January 15, 1999, for any applicant who would have been eligible to apply previously if paragraph (f)(2) of this section as revised had been in effect before November 16, 1998.

(g) Has filed an application for late registration with the appropriate Service director within a 60-day period immediately following the expiration or termination of conditions described in paragraph (f)(2) of this section.

[63 FR 63595, Nov. 16, 1998]

§ 244.3 Applicability of grounds of inadmissibility.

(a) *Grounds of inadmissibility not to be applied.* Paragraphs (4), (5) (A) and (B), and (7)(A)(i) of section 212(a) of the Act shall not render an alien ineligible for Temporary Protected Status.

(b) *Waiver of grounds of inadmissibility.* Except as provided in paragraph (c) of this section, USCIS may waive any other provision of section 212(a) of the Act in the case of individual aliens for humanitarian purposes, to assure family unity, or when the granting of such a waiver is in the public interest. If an alien is inadmissible on grounds which may be waived as set forth in this paragraph, he or she shall be advised of the procedures for applying for a waiver.

(c) *Grounds of inadmissibility that may not be waived.* USCIS may not waive the following provisions of section 212(a) of the Act:

(1) Paragraphs (2)(A)(i), (2)(B), and (2)(C) (relating to criminals and drug offenses);

(2) Paragraphs (3)(A), (3)(B), (3)(C), and (3)(D) (relating to national security); or

(3) Paragraph (3)(E) (relating to those who assisted in the Nazi persecution).

[56 FR 619, Jan. 7, 1991, as amended at 58 FR 58937, Nov. 5, 1993. Redesignated at 62 FR 10367, 10382, Mar. 6, 1997; 76 FR 53791, Aug. 29, 2011]

§ 244.4 Ineligible aliens.

An alien is ineligible for Temporary Protected Status if the alien:

(a) Has been convicted of any felony or two or more misdemeanors, as defined in § 244.1, committed in the United States, or

(b) Is an alien described in section 208(b)(2)(A) of the Act.

[56 FR 619, Jan. 7, 1991, as amended at 56 FR 23497, May 22, 1991. Redesignated at 62 FR 10367, 10382, Mar. 6, 1997, as amended at 63 FR 63596, Nov. 16, 1998; 76 FR 53791, Aug. 29, 2011]

§ 244.5 Temporary treatment benefits for eligible aliens.

(a) *Prior to the registration period.* Prior to the registration period established by DHS, a national of a foreign state designated by DHS shall be afforded temporary treatment benefits upon the filing, after the effective date of such designation, of a completed application for Temporary Protected Status which establishes the alien's *prima facie* eligibility for benefits under section 244 of the Act. This application may be filed without fee. Temporary treatment benefits, if granted, shall terminate unless the registration fee is paid or a waiver is sought within the first thirty days of the registration period designated by DHS. If the registration fee is paid or a waiver is sought within such thirty day period, temporary treatment benefits shall continue until terminated under § 244.13. The denial of temporary treatment benefits prior to the registration period designated by DHS shall be without prejudice to the filing of an application for Temporary Protected Status during such registration period.

(b) *During the registration period.* Upon the filing of an application for Temporary Protected Status, the alien shall be afforded temporary treatment benefits, if the application establishes the alien's *prima facie* eligibility for Temporary Protected Status. Such temporary treatment benefits shall continue until terminated under §244.13.

(c) *Denied benefits*. There shall be no appeal from the denial of temporary treatment benefits.

[56 FR 619, May 22, 1991, as amended at 56 FR 23497, May 22, 1991. Redesignated at 62 FR 10367, 10382, Mar. 6, 1997, as amended at 63 FR 63596, Nov. 16, 1998; 76 FR 53791, Aug. 29, 2011]

§244.6 Application.

(a) An application for Temporary Protected Status must be submitted in accordance with the form instructions, the applicable country-specific FEDERAL REGISTER notice that announces the procedures for TPS registration or re-registration, and 8 CFR 103.2, except as otherwise provided in this section, with the appropriate fees and biometric information as described in 8 CFR 103.7(b)(1), 103.16, and 103.17.

(b) An applicant for TPS may also request employment authorization pursuant to 8 CFR 274a. Those applicants between the ages of 14 and 65 who are not requesting authorization to work will not be charged a fee for an application for employment authorization.

[76 FR 53791, Aug. 29, 2011]

§244.7 Filing the application.

(a) An application for Temporary Protected Status must be filed on the form designated by USCIS with any prescribed fees and in accordance with the form instructions.

(b) An application for Temporary Protected Status must be filed during the registration period established by DHS, except in the case of an alien described in §244.2(f)(2).

(c) Each applicant must pay a fee, as determined at the time of the designation of the foreign state, except as provided in §244.5(a).

(d) If the alien has a pending deportation or exclusion proceeding before the immigration judge or Board of Immigration Appeals at the time a foreign state is designated under section 244(b) of the Act, the alien shall be given written notice concerning Temporary Protected Status. Such alien shall have the opportunity to submit an application for Temporary Protected Status to the director under paragraph (a) of this section during the published registration period unless the basis of the charging document, if established, would render the alien ineligible for Temporary Protected Status under §244.3(c) or §244.4. Eligibility for Temporary Protected Status in the latter instance shall be decided by the Executive Office for Immigration Review during such proceedings.

[63 FR 63596, Nov. 16, 1998, as amended at 74 FR 26940, June 5, 2009; 76 FR 53791, Aug. 29, 2011; 76 FR 73477, Nov. 29, 2011]

§244.8 Appearance.

The applicant may be required to appear in person before an immigration officer. The applicant may be required to present documentary evidence to establish his or her eligibility. The applicant may have a representative as defined in §292.1 of this chapter present during any examination. Such representative shall not directly participate in the examination; however, such representative may consult with and provide advice to the applicant. The record of examination shall consist of the application, documents relating to the application, and the decision of the director.

[56 FR 619, Jan. 7, 1991, as amended at 56 FR 23497, May 22, 1991. Redesignated at 62 FR 10367, 10382, Mar. 6, 1997, as amended at 63 FR 63596, Nov. 16, 1998]

§244.9 Evidence.

(a) *Documentation*. Applicants shall submit all documentation as required in the instructions or requested by the Service. The Service may require proof of unsuccessful efforts to obtain documents claimed to be unavailable. If any required document is unavailable, an affidavit or other credible evidence may be submitted.

(1) *Evidence of identity and nationality*. Each application must be accompanied by evidence of the applicant's identity and nationality, if available. If these documents are unavailable, the applicant shall file an affidavit showing proof of unsuccessful efforts to obtain such identity documents, explaining why the consular process is unavailable, and affirming that he or she is a national of the designated foreign state. A personal interview before an immigration officer shall be required for each applicant who fails to provide

documentary proof of identity or nationality. During this interview, the applicant may present any secondary evidence that he or she feels would be helpful in showing nationality. Acceptable evidence in descending order of preference may consist of:

(i) Passport;

(ii) Birth certificate accompanied by photo identification; and/or

(iii) Any national identity document from the alien's country of origin bearing photo and/or fingerprint.

(2) *Proof of residence*. Evidence to establish proof of continuous residence in the United States during the requisite period of time may consist of any of the following:

(i) Employment records, which may consist of pay stubs, W-2 Forms, certification of the filing of Federal, State, or local income tax returns; letters from employer(s) or, if the applicant has been self employed, letters from banks, and other firms with whom he or she has done business. In all of the above, the name of the alien and the name of the employer or other interested organization must appear on the form or letter, as well as relevant dates. Letters from employers must be in affidavit form, and shall be signed and attested to by the employer under penalty of perjury. Such letters from employers must include:

(A) Alien's address(es) at the time of employment;

(B) Exact period(s) of employment;

(C) Period(s) of layoff; and

(D) Duties with the company.

(ii) Rent receipts, utility bills (gas, electric, telephone, etc.), receipts, or letters from companies showing the dates during which the applicant received service;

(iii) School records (letters, report cards, etc.) from the schools that the applicant or his or her children have attended in the United States showing name of school and period(s) of school attendance;

(iv) Hospital or medical records showing medical treatment or hospitalization of the applicant or his or her children, showing the name of the medical facility or physician as well as the date(s) of the treatment or hospitalization;

(v) Attestations by churches, unions, or other organizations of the applicant's residence by letter which:

(A) Identifies applicant by name;

(B) Is signed by an official whose title is also shown;

(C) Shows inclusive dates of membership;

(D) States the address where applicant resided during the membership period;

(E) Includes the seal of the organization impressed on the letter or is on the letterhead of the organization, if the organization has letterhead stationery;

(F) Establishes how the attestor knows the applicant; and

(G) Establishes the origin of the information being attested to.

(vi) Additional documents to support the applicant's claim, which may include:

(A) Money order receipts for money sent in or out of the country;

(B) Passport entries;

(C) Birth certificates of children born in the United States;

(D) Bank books with dated transactions;

(E) Correspondence between the applicant and other persons or organizations;

(F) Social Security card;

(G) Selective Service card;

(H) Automobile license receipts, title, vehicle registration, etc;

(I) Deeds, mortgages, contracts to which applicant has been a party;

(J) Tax receipts;

(K) Insurance policies, receipts, or letters; and/or

(L) Any other relevant document.

(3) *Evidence of eligibility under section 244(c)(2) of the Act*. An applicant has the burden of showing that he or she is eligible for benefits under this part.

(4) *Evidence of valid immigrant or nonimmigrant status*. In the case of an alien described in § 244.2(f)(2), evidence of admission for lawful permanent residence or nonimmigrant status must be submitted by the applicant.

(b) *Sufficiency of evidence*. The sufficiency of all evidence will be judged according to its relevancy, consistency, credibility, and probative value. To meet his or her burden of proof the applicant must provide supporting documentary evidence of eligibility apart from his or her own statements.

(c) *Failure to timely respond.* Failure to timely respond to a request for information, or to appear for a scheduled interview, without good cause, will be deemed an abandonment of the application and will result in a denial of the application for lack of prosecution. Such failure shall be excused if the request for information, or the notice of the interview was not mailed to the applicant's most recent address provided to the Service.

[56 FR 619, Jan. 7, 1991, as amended at 56 FR 23497, May 22, 1991; 58 FR 58937, Nov. 5, 1993. Redesignated at 62 FR 10367, 10382, Mar. 6, 1997, as amended at 63 FR 63596, Nov. 16, 1998; 76 FR 53791, Aug. 29, 2011]

§ 244.10 Decision and appeal.

(a) *Temporary treatment benefits.* USCIS will grant temporary treatment benefits to the applicant if the applicant establishes prima facie eligibility for Temporary Protected Status in accordance with 8 CFR 244.5.

(b) *Temporary Protected Status.* Upon review of the evidence presented, USCIS may approve or deny the application for Temporary Protected Status in the exercise of discretion, consistent with the standards for eligibility in 8 CFR 244.2, 244.3, and 244.4.

(c) *Denial.* The initial decision to deny Temporary Protected Status, a waiver of inadmissibility, or temporary treatment benefits shall be in writing served in person or by mail to the alien's most recent address provided to the Service and shall state the reason(s) for the denial. Except as otherwise provided in this section, the alien will be given written notice of his or her right to appeal. If an appeal is filed, the administrative record shall be forwarded to the USCIS AAO for review and decision, except as otherwise provided in this section.

(1) If the basis for the denial of the Temporary Protected Status constitutes a ground for deportability or inadmissibility which renders the alien ineligible for Temporary Protected Status under § 244.4 or inadmissible under § 244.3(c), the decision shall include a charging document which sets forth such ground(s).

(2) If such a charging document is issued, the alien shall not have the right to appeal the USCIS decision denying Temporary Protected Status as provided in 8 CFR 103.3. However, the decision will also apprise the alien of his or her right to a *de novo* determination of his or her eligibility for Temporary Protected Status in removal proceedings pursuant to section 240 of the Act and 8 CFR 1244.18.

(d) *Administrative appeal.* The appellate decision will be served in accordance with 8 CFR 103.8. If the appeal is dismissed, the decision must state the reasons for dismissal.

(1) If the appeal is dismissed on appeal under 8 CFR 244.18(b), the decision shall also apprise the alien of his or her right to a *de novo* determination of eligibility for Temporary Protected Status in removal proceedings pursuant to section 240 of the Act and 8 CFR 1244.18.

(2) If the appeal is dismissed, USCIS may issue a charging document if no charging document is presently filed with the Immigration Court.

(3) If a charging document has previously been filed or is pending before the Immigration Court, either party may move to re-calendar the case after the administrative appeal is dismissed.

(e) *Grant of temporary treatment benefits.* (1) Temporary treatment benefits shall be evidenced by the issuance of an employment authorization document. The alien shall be given, in English and in the language of the designated foreign state or a language that the alien understands, a notice of the registration requirements for Temporary Protected Status and a notice of the following benefits:

(i) Temporary stay of deportation; and

(ii) Temporary employment authorization.

(2) Unless terminated under § 244.13, temporary treatment benefits shall remain in effect until a final decision has been made on the application for Temporary Protected Status.

(f) *Grant of temporary protected status.* (1) The decision to grant Temporary Protected Status shall be evidenced by the issuance of an alien registration document. For those aliens requesting employment authorization, the employment authorization document will act as alien registration.

(2) The alien shall be provided with a notice, in English and in the language of the designated foreign state or a language that the alien understands, of the following benefits:

(i) The alien shall not be deported while maintaining Temporary Protected Status;

(ii) Employment authorization;

(iii) The privilege to travel abroad with the prior consent of the director as provided in § 244.15;

(iv) For the purposes of adjustment of status under section 245 of the Act and change of status under section 248 of the Act, the alien is considered as being in, and maintaining, lawful status as a nonimmigrant while the alien maintains Temporary Protected Status.

(v) An alien eligible to apply for Temporary Protected Status under § 244.2(f)(2), who was prevented from filing a late application for registration because the regulations failed to provide him or her with this opportunity, will be considered to have been maintaining lawful status as a nonimmigrant until the benefit is granted.

(3) The benefits contained in the notice are the only benefits the alien is entitled to under Temporary Protected Status.

(4) Such notice shall also advise the alien of the following:

(i) The alien must remain eligible for Temporary Protected Status;

(ii) The alien must register annually with the district office or service center having jurisdiction over the alien's place of residence; and

(iii) The alien's failure to comply with paragraphs (f)(4) (i) or (ii) of this section will result in the withdrawal of Temporary Protected Status, including work authorization granted under this Program, and may result in the alien's deportation from the United States.

[56 FR 619, Jan. 7, 1991, as amended at 56 FR 23497, May 22, 1991; 58 FR 58937, Nov. 5, 1993; 60 FR 34090, June 30, 1995. Redesignated at 62 FR 10367, 10382, Mar. 6, 1997, as amended at 63 FR 63596, Nov. 16, 1998; 64 FR 4782, Feb. 1, 1999; 76 FR 53791, Aug. 29, 2011]

§ 244.11 Renewal of application; appeal to the Board of Immigration Appeals.

If a charging document is served on the alien with a notice of denial or withdrawal of Temporary Protected Status, an alien may renew the application for Temporary Protected Status in deportation or exclusion proceedings. The decision of the immigration judge as to eligibility for Temporary Protected Status may be appealed to the Board of Immigration Appeals pursuant to 8 CFR 1003. The provisions of this section do not extend the benefits of Temporary Protected Status beyond the termination of a foreign state's designation pursuant to § 244.19.

[56 FR 619, Jan. 7, 1991, as amended at 56 FR 23497, May 22, 1991. Redesignated at 62 FR 10367, 10382, Mar. 6, 1997, as amended at 63 FR 63596, Nov. 16, 1998; 76 FR 53792, Aug. 29, 2011]

§ 244.12 Employment authorization.

(a) Upon approval of an application for Temporary Protected Status, USCIS shall grant an employment authorization document valid during the initial period of the foreign state's designation (and any extensions of such period).

(b) If the alien's Temporary Protected Status is withdrawn under § 244.14, employment authorization expires upon notice of withdrawal or on the date stated on the employment authorization document, whichever occurs later.

(c) If Temporary Protected Status is denied by USCIS, employment authorization shall terminate upon notice of denial or at the expiration of the employment authorization document, whichever occurs later.

(d) If the application is renewed or appealed in deportation or exclusion proceedings, or pending administrative appeal pursuant to § 244.18(b), employment authorization will be extended during the pendency of the renewal and/or appeal.

[56 FR 619, Jan. 7, 1991, as amended at 56 FR 23498, May 22, 1991; 60 FR 21975, May 4, 1995. Redesignated at 62 FR 10367, 10382, Mar. 6, 1997, as amended at 63 FR 63596, Nov. 16, 1998; 64 FR 4782, Feb. 1, 1999; 76 FR 53792, Aug. 29, 2011]

§244.13 Termination of temporary treatment benefits.

(a) Temporary treatment benefits terminate upon a final determination with respect to the alien's eligibility for Temporary Protected Status.

(b) Temporary treatment benefits terminate, in any case, sixty (60) days after the date that notice is published of the termination of a foreign state's designation under section 244(b)(3) of the Act.

[56 FR 619, Jan. 7, 1991. Redesignated at 62 FR 10367, 10382, Mar. 6, 1997, as amended at 63 FR 63596, Nov. 16, 1998]

§244.14 Withdrawal of Temporary Protected Status.

(a) *Authority of USCIS.* USCIS may withdraw the status of an alien granted Temporary Protected Status under section 244 of the Act at any time upon the occurrence of any of the following:

(1) The alien was not in fact eligible at the time such status was granted, or at any time thereafter becomes ineligible for such status;

(2) The alien has not remained continuously physically present in the United States from the date the alien was first granted Temporary Protected Status under this part. For the purpose of this provision, an alien granted Temporary Protected Status under this part shall be deemed not to have failed to maintain continuous physical presence in the United States if the alien departs the United States after first obtaining permission from USCIS to travel pursuant to §244.15;

(3) The alien fails without good cause to register with DHS annually within thirty (30) days before the end of each 12-month period after the granting of Temporary Protected Status.

(b) *Decision by USCIS.* (1) Withdrawal of an alien's status under paragraph (a) of this section shall be in writing and served by personal service pursuant to 8 CFR 103.8(a)(2). If the ground for withdrawal is 8 CFR 244.14(a)(3), the notice shall provide that the alien has thirty (30) days within which to provide evidence of good cause for failure to register. If the alien fails to respond within thirty (30) days, Temporary Protected Status shall be withdrawn without further notice.

(2) Withdrawal of the alien's Temporary Protected Status under paragraph (b)(1) of this section may subject the applicant to exclusion or deportation proceedings under sections 235, 236, 237, 238, 240, or 241 of the Act as appropriate.

(3) If the basis for the withdrawal of Temporary Protected Status constitutes a ground of deportability or excludability which renders an alien ineligible for Temporary Protected Status under §244.4 or inadmissible under §244.3(c), the decision shall include a charging document which sets forth such ground(s) with notice of the right of a *de novo* determination of eligibility for Temporary Protected Status in deportation or exclusion proceedings. If the basis for withdrawal does not constitute such a ground, the alien shall be given written notice of his or her right to appeal to the AAU. Upon receipt of an appeal, the administrative record will be forwarded to the AAU for review and decision pursuant to the authority delegated under §103.1(f)(2). Temporary Protected Status benefits will be extended during the pendency of an appeal.

(c) *Decision by AAU.* If a decision to withdraw Temporary Protected Status is entered by the AAU, the AAU shall notify the alien of the decision and the right to a *de novo* determination of eligibility for Temporary Protected Status in deportation or exclusion proceedings, if the alien is then deportable or excludable, as provided by §244.10(d).

[56 FR 619, Jan. 7, 1991, as amended at 56 FR 23498, May 22, 1991. Redesignated at 62 FR 10367, 10382, Mar. 6, 1997, as amended at 63 FR 63596, 63597, Nov. 16, 1998; 76 FR 53792, Aug. 29, 2011; 76 FR 73477, Nov. 29, 2011]

§244.15 Travel abroad.

(a) After the grant of Temporary Protected Status, the alien must remain continuously physically present in the United States under the provisions of section 244(c)(3)(B) of the Act. The grant of Temporary Protected Status shall not constitute permission to travel abroad. Permission to travel may be granted by the director pursuant to the Service's advance parole provisions. There is no appeal from a denial of advance parole.

(b) Failure to obtain advance parole prior to the alien's departure from the United States may result in the withdrawal of Temporary Protected Status and/or the institution or recalendering of deportation or exclusion proceedings against the alien.

[56 FR 619, Jan. 7, 1991, as amended at 56 FR 23498, May 22, 1991. Redesignated at 62 FR 10367, 10382, Mar. 6, 1997, as amended at 63 FR 63597, Nov. 16, 1998; 64 FR 4782, Feb. 1, 1999]

§ 244.16 Confidentiality.

The information contained in the application and supporting documents submitted by an alien shall not be released in any form whatsoever to a third party requester without a court order, or the written consent of the alien. For the purpose of this provision, a third party requester means any requester other than the alien, his or her authorized representative, an officer of DHS, or any federal or State law enforcement agency. Any information provided under this part may be used for purposes of enforcement of the Act or in any criminal proceeding.

[56 FR 619, Jan. 7, 1991. Redesignated at 62 FR 10367, 10382, Mar. 6, 1997; 76 FR 53792, Aug. 29, 2011]

§ 244.17 Periodic registration.

(a) Aliens granted Temporary Protected Status must re-register periodically in accordance with USCIS instructions. Such registration applies to nationals of those foreign states designated or redesignated for more than one year by DHS. Applicants for periodic re-registration must apply during the registration period provided by USCIS. Re-registering applicants will not need to re-pay the TPS application fee that was required for initial registration except that aliens requesting employment authorization must submit the application fee for employment authorization. The biometric service fee described in 103.7(b), or an approved fee waiver, will be required of applicants age 14 and over. By completing the application, applicants attest to their continuing eligibility. Such applicants do not need to submit additional supporting documents unless USCIS requests them to do so.

(b) If an alien fails to register without good cause, USCIS will withdraw Temporary Protected Status. USCIS may, for good cause, accept and approve an untimely registration request.

[76 FR 53792, Aug. 29, 2011]

§ 244.18 Issuance of charging documents; detention.

(a) A charging document may be issued against an alien granted Temporary Protected Status on grounds of deportability or excludability which would have rendered the alien statutorily ineligible for such status pursuant to §§ 244.3(c) and 244.4. Aliens shall not be deported for a particular offense for which the Service has expressly granted a waiver. If the alien is deportable on a waivable ground, and no such waiver for the charged offense has been previously granted, then the alien may seek such a waiver in deportation or exclusion proceedings. The charging document shall constitute notice to the alien that his or her status in the United States is subject to withdrawal. A final order of deportation or exclusion against an alien granted Temporary Protected Status shall constitute a withdrawal of such status.

(b) The filing of the charging document by DHS with the Immigration Court renders inapplicable any other administrative, adjudication or review of eligibility for Temporary Protected Status. The alien shall have the right to a *de novo* determination of his or her eligibility for Temporary Protected Status in removal proceedings pursuant to section 240 of the Act and 8 CFR 1244.18. Review by the Board of Immigration Appeals shall be the exclusive administrative appellate review procedure. If an appeal is already pending before the Administrative Appeals Office (AAO), USCIS will notify the AAO of the filing of the charging document, in which case the pending appeal shall be dismissed and the record of proceeding returned to the jurisdiction where the charging document was filed.

(c) Upon denial of Temporary Protected Status by the Administrative Appeals Unit, the Administrative Appeals Unit shall immediately forward the record of proceeding to the director having jurisdiction over the alien's place of residence. The director shall, as soon as practicable, file a charging document with the Immigration Court if the alien is then deportable or excludable under section 241(a) or section 212(a) of the Act, respectively.

(d) An alien who is determined by USCIS deportable or inadmissible upon grounds which would have rendered the alien ineligible for such status as provided in 8 CFR 244.3(c) and 8 CFR 244.4 may be detained under the provisions of this chapter pending removal proceedings. Such alien may be removed from the United States upon entry of a final order of removal.

[56 FR 619, Jan. 7, 1991, as amended at 56 FR 23498, May 22, 1991; 60 FR 34090, June 30, 1995. Redesignated at 62 FR 10367, 10382, Mar. 6, 1997, as amended at 63 FR 63597, Nov. 16, 1998; 64 FR 4782, Feb. 1, 1999; 76 FR 53792, Aug. 29, 2011]

§244.19 Termination of designation.

Upon the termination of designation of a foreign state, those nationals afforded temporary Protected Status shall, upon the sixtieth (60th) day after the date notice of termination is published in the FEDERAL REGISTER, or on the last day of the most recent extension of designation by the Attorney General, automatically and without further notice or right of appeal, lose Temporary Protected Status in the United States. Such termination of a foreign state's designation is not subject to appeal.

[56 FR 619, Jan. 7, 1991. Redesignated at 62 FR 10367, 10382, Mar. 6, 1997, as amended at 63 FR 63597, Nov. 16, 1998]

PART 245—ADJUSTMENT OF STATUS TO THAT OF PERSON ADMITTED FOR PERMANENT RESIDENCE

Sec.

AUTHORITY: 8 U.S.C. 1101, 1103, 1182, 1255; Pub. L. 105–100, section 202, 111 Stat. 2160, 2193; Pub. L. 105–277, section 902, 112 Stat. 2681; Pub. L. 110–229, tit. VII, 122 Stat. 754; 8 CFR part 2.

§245.1 Eligibility.

(a) *General.* Any alien who is physically present in the United States, except for an alien who is ineligible to apply for adjustment of status under paragraph (b) or (c) of this section, may apply for adjustment of status to that of a lawful permanent resident of the United States if the applicant is eligible to receive an immigrant visa and an immigrant visa is immediately available at the time of filing of the application. A special immigrant described under section 101(a)(27)(J) of the Act shall be deemed, for the purpose of applying the adjustment to status provisions of section 245(a) of the Act, to have been paroled into the United States, regardless of the actual method of entry into the United States.

(b) *Restricted aliens.* The following categories of aliens are ineligible to apply for adjustment of status to that of a lawful permanent resident alien under section 245 of the Act, unless the alien establishes eligibility under the provisions of section 245(i) of the Act and § 245.10, is not included in the categories of aliens prohibited from applying for adjustment of status listed in § 245.1(c), is eligible to receive an immigrant visa, and has an immigrant visa immediately available at the time of filing the application for adjustment of status:

(1) Any alien who entered the United States in transit without a visa;

(2) Any alien who, on arrival in the United States, was serving in any capacity on board a vessel or aircraft or was destined to join a vessel or aircraft in the United States to serve in any capacity thereon;

(3) Any alien who was not admitted or paroled following inspection by an immigration officer;

(4) Any alien who, on or after January 1, 1977, was employed in the United States without authorization prior to filing an application for adjustment of status. This restriction shall not apply to an alien who is:

(i) An immediate relative as defined in section 201(b) of the Act;

(ii) A special immigrant as defined in section 101(a)(27)(H) or (J) of the Act;

(iii) Eligible for the benefits of Public Law 101–238 (the Immigration Nursing Relief Act of 1989) and files an application for adjustment of status on or before October 17, 1991; or

(iv) Eligible for the benefits of Public Law 101–238 (the Immigration Nursing Relief Act of 1989), and has not entered into or continued in unauthorized employment on or after November 29, 1990.

(5) Any alien who on or after November 6, 1986 is not in lawful immigration status on the date of filing his or her application for adjustment of status, except an applicant who is an immediate relative as defined in section 201(b) or a special immigrant as defined in section 101(a)(27) (H), (I), or (J).

(6) Any alien who files an application for adjustment of status on or after November 6, 1986, who has failed (other than through no fault of his or her own or for technical reasons) to maintain continuously a lawful status since entry into the United States, except an applicant who is an immediate relative as defined in section 201(b) of the Act or a special immigrant as defined in section 101(a)(27) (H), (I), or (J) of the Act;

(7) Any alien admitted as a visitor under the visa waiver provisions of 8 CFR 212.1(e) or (q), other than an immediate relative as defined in section 201(b) of the Act;

(8) Any alien admitted as a Visa Waiver Pilot Program visitor under the provisions of section 217 of the Act and part 217 of this chapter other than an immediate relative as defined in section 201(b) of the Act;

(9) Any alien who seeks adjustment of status pursuant to an employment-based immigrant visa petition under section 203(b) of the Act and who is not maintaining a lawful nonimmigrant status at the time he or she files an application for adjustment of status; and

(10) Any alien who was ever employed in the United States without the authorization of the Service or who has otherwise at any time violated the terms of his or her admission to the United States as a nonimmigrant, except an alien who is an immediate relative as defined in section 201(b) of the Act or a special immigrant as defined in section 101(a)(27)(H), (I), (J), or (K) of the Act. For purposes of this paragraph, an alien who meets the requirements of § 274a.12(c)(9) of this chapter shall not be deemed to have engaged in unauthorized employment during the pendency of his or her adjustment application.

(c) *Ineligible aliens.* The following categories of aliens are ineligible to apply for adjustment of status to that of a lawful permanent resident alien under section 245 of the Act:

(1) Any nonpreference alien who is seeking or engaging in gainful employment in the United States who is not the beneficiary of a valid individual or blanket labor certification issued by the Secretary of Labor or who is not exempt from certification requirements under § 212.8(b) of this chapter;

(2) Except for an alien who is applying for residence under the provisions of section 133 of the Immigration Act of 1990, any alien who has or had the status of an exchange visitor under section 101(a)(15)(J) of the Act and who is subject to the foreign residence requirement of section 212(e) of the Act, unless the alien has complied with the foreign residence requirement or has

been granted a waiver of that requirement, under that section. An alien who has been granted a waiver under section 212(e)(iii) of the Act based on a request by a State Department of Health (or its equivalent) under Pub. L. 103–416 shall be ineligible to apply for adjustment of status under section 245 of the Act if the terms and conditions specified in section 214(l) of the Act and §212.7(c)(9) of this chapter have not been met;

(3) Any alien who has nonimmigrant status under paragraph (15)(A), (15)(E), or (15)(G) of section 101(a) of the Act, or has an occupational status which would, if the alien were seeking admission to the United States, entitle the alien to nonimmigrant status under those paragraphs, unless the alien first executes and submits the written waiver required by section 247(b) of the Act and part 247 of this chapter;

(4) Any alien who claims immediate relative status under section 201(b) or preference status under sections 203(a) or 203(b) of the Act, unless the applicant is the beneficiary of a valid unexpired visa petition filed in accordance with part 204 of this chapter;

(5) Any alien who is already an alien lawfully admitted to the United States for permanent residence on a conditional basis pursuant to section 216 or 216A of the Act, regardless of any other quota or non-quota immigrant visa classification for which the alien may otherwise be eligible;

(6) Any alien admitted to the United States as a nonimmigrant defined in section 101(a)(15)(K) of the Act, unless:

(i) In the case of a K–1 fianceé(e) under section 101(a)(15)(K)(i) of the Act or the K–2 child of a fianceé(e) under section 101(a)(15)(K)(iii) of the Act, the alien is applying for adjustment of status based upon the marriage of the K–1 fianceé(e) which was contracted within 90 days of entry with the United States citizen who filed a petition on behalf of the K–1 fianceé(e) pursuant to §214.2(k) of this chapter;

(ii) In the case of a K–3 spouse under section 101(a)(15)(K)(ii) of the Act or the K–4 child of a spouse under section 101(a)(15)(K)(iii) of the Act, the alien is applying for adjustment of status based upon the marriage of the K–3 spouse to the United States citizen who filed a petition on behalf of the K–3 spouse pursuant to §214.2(k) of this chapter;

(7) A nonimmigrant classified pursuant to section 101(a)(15)(S) of the Act, unless the nonimmigrant is applying for adjustment of status pursuant to the request of a law enforcement authority, the provisions of section 101(a)(15)(S) of the Act, and 8 CFR 245.11;

(8) Any alien who seeks to adjust status based upon a marriage which occurred on or after November 10, 1986, and while the alien was in exclusion, deportation, or removal proceedings, or judicial proceedings relating thereto.

(i) *Commencement of proceedings.* The period during which the alien is in deportation, exclusion, or removal proceedings or judicial proceedings relating thereto, commences:

(A) With the issuance of the Form I–221, Order to Show Cause and Notice of Hearing prior to June 20, 1991;

(B) With the filing of a Form I–221, Order to Show Cause and Notice of Hearing, issued on or after June 20, 1991, with the Immigration Court;

(C) With the issuance of Form I–122, Notice to Applicant for Admission Detained for Hearing Before Immigration Judge, prior to April 1, 1997,

(D) With the filing of a Form I–862, Notice to Appear, with the Immigration Court, or

(E) With the issuance and service of Form I–860, Notice and Order of Expedited Removal.

(ii) *Termination of proceedings.* The period during which the alien is in exclusion, deportation, or removal proceedings, or judicial proceedings relating thereto, terminates:

(A) When the alien departs from the United States while an order of exclusion, deportation, or removal is outstanding or before the expiration of the voluntary departure time granted in connection with an alternate order of deportation or removal;

(B) When the alien is found not to be inadmissible or deportable from the United States;

(C) When the Form I–122, I–221, I–860, or I–862 is canceled;

(D) When proceedings are terminated by the immigration judge or the Board of Immigration Appeals; or

(E) When a petition for review or an action for habeas corpus is granted by a Federal court on judicial review.

(iii) *Exemptions.* This prohibition shall no longer apply if:

(A) The alien is found not to be inadmissible or deportable from the United States;

(B) Form I–122, I–221, I–860, or I–862, is canceled;

(C) Proceedings are terminated by the immigration judge or the Board of Immigration Appeals;

(D) A petition for review or an action for habeas corpus is granted by a Federal court on judicial review;

(E) The alien has resided outside the United States for 2 or more years following the marriage; or

(F) The alien establishes the marriage is bona fide by providing clear and convincing evidence that the marriage was entered into in good faith and in accordance with the laws of the place where the marriage took place, was not entered into for the purpose of procuring the alien's entry as an immigrant, and no fee or other consideration was given (other than to an attorney for assistance in preparation of a lawful petition) for the filing of a petition.

(iv) *Request for exemption.* No application or fee is required to request the exemption under section 245(e) of the Act. The request must be made in writing and submitted with the Form I–485. Application for Permanent Residence. The request must state the basis for requesting consideration for the exemption and must be supported by documentary evidence establishing eligibility for the exemption.

(v) *Evidence to establish eligibility for the bona fide marriage exemption.* Section 204(g) of the Act provides that certain visa petitions based upon marriages entered into during deportation, exclusion or related judicial proceedings may be approved only if the petitioner provides clear and convincing evidence that the marriage is bona fide. Evidence that a visa petition based upon the same marriage was approved under the bona fide marriage exemption to section 204(g) of the Act will be considered primary evidence of eligibility for the bona fide marriage exemption provided in this part. The applicant will not be required to submit additional evidence to qualify for the bona fide marriage exemption provided in this part, unless the district director determines that such additional evidence is needed. In cases where the district director notifies the applicant that additional evidence is required, the applicant must submit documentary evidence which clearly and convincingly establishes that the marriage was entered into in good faith and not entered into for the purpose of procuring the alien's entry as an immigrant. Such evidence may include:

(A) Documentation showing joint ownership of property;

(B) Lease showing joint tenancy of a common residence;

(C) Documentation showing commingling of financial resources;

(D) Birth certificates of children born to the applicant and his or her spouse;

(E) Affidavits of third parties having knowledge of the bona fides of the marital relationship, or

(F) Other documentation establishing that the marriage was not entered into in order to evade the immigration laws of the United States.

(vi) *Decision.* An application for adjustment of status filed during the prohibited period shall be denied, unless the applicant establishes eligibility for an exemption from the general prohibition.

(vii) *Denials.* The denial of an application for adjustment of status because the marriage took place during the prohibited period shall be without prejudice to the consideration of a new application or a motion to reopen a previously denied application, if deportation or exclusion proceedings are terminated while the alien is in the United States. The denial shall also be without prejudice to the consideration of a new application or motion to reopen the adjustment of status application, if the applicant presents clear and convincing evidence establishing eligibility for the bona fide marriage exemption contained in this part.

(viii) *Appeals.* An application for adjustment of status to lawful permanent resident which is denied by the district director solely because the applicant failed to establish eligibility for the bona fide marriage exemption contained in this part may be appealed to the Associate Commissioner, Examinations, in accordance with 8 CFR part 103. The appeal to the Associate Commissioner, Examinations, shall be the single level of appellate review established by statute.

(d) *Definitions*—(1) *Lawful immigration status.* For purposes of section 245(c)(2) of the Act, the term "lawful immigration status" will only describe the immigration status of an individual who is:

(i) In lawful permanent resident status;

(ii) An alien admitted to the United States in nonimmigrant status as defined in section 101(a)(15) of the Act, whose initial period of admission has not expired or whose nonimmigrant status has been extended in accordance with part 214 of this chapter;

(iii) In refugee status under section 207 of the Act, such status not having been revoked;

(iv) In asylee status under section 208 of the Act, such status not having been revoked;

(v) In parole status which has not expired, been revoked or terminated; or

(vi) Eligible for the benefits of Public Law 101–238 (the Immigration Nursing Relief Act of 1989) and files an application for adjustment of status on or before October 17, 1991.

(2) *No fault of the applicant or for technical reasons.* The parenthetical phrase *other than through no fault of his or her own or for technical reasons* shall be limited to:

(i) Inaction of another individual or organization designated by regulation to act on behalf of an individual and over whose actions the individual has no control, if the inaction is acknowledged by that individual or organization (as, for example, where a designated school official certified under §214.2(f) of this chapter or an exchange propram sponsor under §214.2(j) of this chapter did not provide required notification to the Service of continuation of status, or did not forward a request for continuation of status to the Service); or

(ii) A technical violation resulting from inaction of the Service (as for example, where an applicant establishes that he or she properly filed a timely request to maintain status and the Service has not yet acted on that request). An individual whose refugee or asylum status has expired through passage of time, but whose status has not been revoked, will be considered to have gone out of status for a technical reason.

(iii) A technical violation caused by the physical inability of the applicant to request an extension of nonimmigrant stay from the Service either in person or by mail (as, for example, an individual who is hospitalized with an illness at the time nonimmigrant stay expires). The explanation of such a technical violation shall be accompanied by a letter explaining the circumstances from the hospital or attending physician.

(iv) A technical violation resulting from the Service's application of the maximum five/six year period of stay for certain H–1 nurses only if the applicant was subsequently reinstated to H–1 status in accordance with the terms of Public Law 101–656 (Immigration Amendments of 1988).

(3) *Effect of departure.* The departure and subsequent reentry of an individual who was employed without authorization in the United States after January 1, 1977 does not erase the bar to adjustment of status in section 245(c)(2) of the Act. Similarly, the departure and subsequent reentry of an individual who has not maintained a lawful immigration status on any previous entry into the United States does not erase the bar to adjustment of status in section 245(c)(2) of the Act for any application filed on or after November 6, 1986.

(e) *Special categories*—(1) *Alien medical graduates.* Any alien who is a medical graduate qualified for special immigrant classification under section 101(a)(27)(H) of the Act and is the beneficiary of an approved petition as required under section 204(a)(1)(E)(i) of the Act is eligible for adjustment of status. An accompanying spouse and children also may apply for adjustment of status under this section. Temporary absences from the United States for 30 days or less, during which the applicant was practicing or studying medicine, do not interrupt the continuous presence requirement. Temporary absences authorized under the Service's advance parole procedures will not be considered interruptive of continuous presence when the alien applies for adjustment of status.

(2) [Reserved]

(3) *Special immigrant juveniles.* Any alien qualified for special immigrant classification under section 101(a)(27)(J) of the Act shall be deemed, for the purpose of section 245(a) of the Act, to have been paroled into the United States, regardless of the alien's actual method of entry into the United States. Neither the provisions of section 245(c)(2) nor the exclusion provisions of sections 212(a)(4), (5)(A), or (7)(A) of the Act shall apply to a qualified special immigrant under section 101(a)(27)(J) of the Act. The exclusion provisions of sections 212(a)(2)(A), (2)(B), (2)(C) (except for so much of such paragraph as related to a single offense of simple possession of 30 grams or less of marijuana), (3)(A), (3)(B), (3)(C), or (3)(E) of the Act may not be waived. Any other exclusion provision may be waived on an individual basis for humanitarian purposes, family unity, or when it is otherwise in the public interest; however, the relationship between the alien and the alien's natural parents or prior adoptive parents shall not be considered a factor in a discretionary waiver determination.

(f) *Concurrent applications to overcome grounds of inadmissibility.* Except as provided in 8 CFR parts 235 and 249, an application under this part shall be the sole method of requesting the exercise of discretion under sections 212(g), (h), (i), and (k) of the Act, as they relate to the inadmissibility of an alien in the United States. No fee is required for filing an application to overcome the grounds of inadmissibility of the Act if filed concurrently with an application for adjustment of status under the provisions of the Act of October 28, 1977, and of this part.

(g) *Availability of immigrant visas under section 245 and priority dates*—(1) *Availability of immigrant visas under section 245.* An alien is ineligible for the benefits of section 245 of the Act unless an immigrant visa is immediately available to him or her at the time the application is filed. If the applicant is a preference alien, the current Department of State Bureau of Consular Affairs Visa Bulletin will be consulted to determine whether an immigrant visa is immediately available. A preference immigrant visa is considered available for accepting and processing if the applicant has a priority date on the waiting list which is earlier than the date shown in the Bulletin (or the Bulletin shows that numbers for visa applicants in his or her category are current). Information concerning the immediate availability of an immigrant visa may be obtained at any Service office.

(2) *Priority dates.* The priority date of an applicant who is seeking the allotment of an immigrant visa number under one of the preference classes specified in section 203(a) or 203(b) of the Act by virtue of a valid visa petition approved in his or her behalf shall be fixed by the date on which such approved petition was filed.

(h) *Conditional basis of status.* Whenever an alien spouse (as defined in section 216(g)(1) of the Act), an alien son or daughter (as defined in section 216(g)(2) of the Act), an alien entrepreneur (as defined in section 216A(f)(1) of the Act), or an alien spouse or child (as defined in section 216A(f)(2) of the Act) is granted adjustment of status to that of lawful permanent residence, the alien shall be considered to have obtained such status on a conditional basis subject to the provisions of section 216 or 216A of the Act, as appropriate.

(i) *Adjustment of status from K–3/K–4 status.* An alien admitted to the United States as a K–3 under section 101(a)(15)(K)(ii) of the Act may apply for adjustment of status to that of a permanent resident pursuant to section 245 of the Act at any time following the approval of the Form I–130 petition filed on the alien's behalf, by the same citizen who petitioned for the alien's K–3 status. An alien admitted to the United States as a K–4 under section 101(a)(15)(K)(iii) of the Act may apply for adjustment of status to that of permanent residence pursuant to section 245 of the Act at any time following the approval of the Form I–130 petition filed on the alien's behalf, by the same citizen who petitioned for the alien's parent's K–3 status. Upon approval of the application, the director shall record his or her lawful admission for permanent residence in accordance with that section and subject to the conditions prescribed in section 216 of the Act. An alien admitted to the U.S. as a K–3/K–4 alien may not adjust to that of permanent resident status in any way other than as a spouse or child of the U.S. citizen who originally filed the petition for that alien's K–3/K–4 status.

(Title I of Pub. L. 95–145 enacted Oct. 28, 1977 (91 Stat. 1223), sec. 103 of the Immigration and Nationality Act (8 U.S.C. 1103). Interpret or apply secs. 101, 212, 242 and 245 (8 U.S.C. 1101, 1182, 1252 and 1255))

[30 FR 14778, Nov. 30, 1965]

EDITORIAL NOTE: For FEDERAL REGISTER citations affecting §245.1, see the List of CFR Sections Affected, which appears in the Finding Aids section of the printed volume and at *www.govinfo.gov*.

§245.2 Application.

(a) *General*—(1) *Jurisdiction.* USCIS has jurisdiction to adjudicate an application for adjustment of status filed by any alien, unless the immigration judge has jurisdiction to adjudicate the application under 8 CFR 1245.2(a)(1).

(2) *Proper filing of application*—(i) *Under section 245.* (A) An immigrant visa must be immediately available in order for an alien to properly file an adjustment application under section 245 of the Act See §245.1(g)(1) to determine whether an immigrant visa is immediately available.

(B) If, at the time of filing, approval of a visa petition filed for classification under section 201(b)(2)(A)(i), section 203(a) or section 203(b)(1), (2) or (3) of the Act would make a visa immediately available to the alien beneficiary, the alien beneficiary's adjustment application will be considered properly filed whether submitted concurrently with or subsequent to the visa petition, provided that it meets the filing requirements contained in parts 103 and 245. For any other classification, the alien beneficiary may file the adjustment application only after the Service has approved the visa petition.

(C) A visa petition and an adjustment application are concurrently filed only if:

(*1*) The visa petitioner and adjustment applicant each file their respective form at the same time, bundled together within a single mailer or delivery packet, with the proper filing fees on the same day and at the same Service office, or;

(*2*) the visa petitioner filed the visa petition, for which a visa number has become immediately available, on, before or after July 31, 2002, and the adjustment applicant files the adjustment application, together with the proper filing fee and a copy of the Form I–797, Notice of Action, establishing the receipt and acceptance by the Service of the underlying Form I–140 visa petition, at the same Service office at which the visa petitioner filed the visa petition, or;

(*3*) The visa petitioner filed the visa petition, for which a visa number has become immediately available, on, before, or after July 31, 2002, and the adjustment applicant files the adjustment application, together with proof of payment of the filing fee with the Service and a copy of the Form I–797 Notice of Action establishing the receipt and acceptance by the Service of the underlying Form I–140 visa petition, with the Immigration Court or the Board of Immigration Appeals when jurisdiction lies under paragraph (a)(1) of this section.

(ii) *Under the Act of November 2, 1966.* An application for the benefits of section 1 of the Act of November 2, 1966 is not properly filed unless the applicant was inspected and admitted or paroled into the United States subsequent to January 1, 1959. An applicant is ineligible for the benefits of the Act of November 2, 1966 unless he or she has been physically present in the United States for one year (amended from two years by the Refugee Act of 1980).

(3) *Submission of documents*—(i) *General.* A separate application shall be filed by each applicant for benefits under section 245, or the Act of November 2, 1966. Each application shall be accompanied by an executed Form G–325A, if the applicant has reached his or her 14th birthday. Form G–325A

shall be considered part of the application. An application under this part shall be accompanied by the document specified in the instructions which are attached to the application.

(ii) *Under section 245.* An application for adjustment of status is submitted on Form I–485, Application for Permanent Residence. The application must be accompanied by the appropriate fee as explained in the instructions to the application.

(iii) *Under section 245(i).* An alien who seeks adjustment of status under the provisions of section 245(i) of the Act must file Form I–485, with the required fee. The alien must also file Supplement A to Form I–485, with any required additional sum.

(iv) *Under the Act of November 2, 1966.* An application for adjustment of status is made on Form I–485A. The application must be accompanied by Form I–643, Health and Human Services Statistical Data Sheet. The application must include a clearance from the local police jurisdiction for any area in the United States when the applicant has lived for six months or more since his or her 14th birthday.

(4) *Effect of departure*—(i) *General.* The effect of a departure from the United States is dependent upon the law under which the applicant is applying for adjustment.

(ii) *Under section 245 of the Act.* (A) The departure from the United States of an applicant who is under exclusion, deportation, or removal proceedings shall be deemed an abandonment of the application constituting grounds for termination of the proceeding by reason of the departure. Except as provided in paragraph (a)(4)(ii)(B) and (C) of this section, the departure of an applicant who is not under exclusion, deportation, or removal proceedings shall be deemed an abandonment of the application constituting grounds for termination of any pending application for adjustment of status, unless the applicant was previously granted advance parole by the Service for such absences, and was inspected upon returning to the United States. If the adjustment application of an individual granted advance parole is subsequently denied the individual will be treated as an applicant for admission, and subject to the provisions of section 212 and 235 of the Act.

(B) The travel outside of the United States by an applicant for adjustment who is not under exclusion, deportation, or removal proceedings shall not be deemed an abandonment of the application if he or she was previously granted advance parole by the Service for such absences, and was inspected and paroled upon returning to the United States. If the adjustment of status application of such individual is subsequently denied, he or she will be treated as an applicant for admission, and subject to the provisions of section 212 and 235 of the Act.

(C) The travel outside of the United States by an applicant for adjustment of status who is not under exclusion, deportation, or removal proceeding and who is in lawful H–1 or L–1 status shall not be deemed an abandonment of the application if, upon returning to this country, the alien remains eligible for H or L status, is coming to resume employment with the same employer for whom he or she had previously been authorized to work as an H–1 or L–1 nonimmigrant, and, is in possession of a valid H or L visa (if required). The travel outside of the United States by an applicant for adjustment of status who is not under exclusion, deportation, or removal proceeding and who is in lawful H–4 or L–2 status shall not be deemed an abandonment of the application if the spouse or parent of such alien through whom the H–4 or L–2 status was obtained is maintaining H–1 or L–1 status and the alien remains otherwise eligible for H–4 or L–2 status, and, the alien is in possession of a valid H–4 or L–2 visa (if required). The travel outside of the United States by an applicant for adjustment of status, who is not under exclusion, deportation, or removal proceeding and who is in lawful K–3 or K–4 status shall not be deemed an abandonment of the application if, upon returning to this country, the alien is in possession of a valid K–3 or K–4 visa and remains eligible for K–3 or K–4 status.

(D) The travel outside of the United States by an applicant for adjustment of status who is not under exclusion, deportation, or removal proceeding and who is in lawful V status shall not be deemed an abandonment of the application if, upon returning to this country, the alien is admissible as a V nonimmigrant.

(iii) *Under the Act of November 2, 1966.* If an applicant who was admitted or paroled subsequent to January 1, 1959, later departs from the United States temporarily with no intention of abandoning his or her residence, and is readmitted or paroled upon return, the temporary absence shall be disregarded for purposes of the applicant's "last arrival" into the United States in regard to cases filed under section 1 of the Act of November 2, 1966.

(5) *Decision*—(i) *General.* The applicant shall be notified of the decision of the director and, if the application is denied, the reasons for the denial.

(ii) *Under section 245 of the Act.* If the application is approved, the applicant's permanent residence shall be recorded as of the date of the order approving the adjustment of status. An application for adjustment of status, as a preference alien, shall not be approved until an immigrant visa number has been allocated by the Department of State. No appeal lies from the denial of an application by the director, but the applicant, if not an arriving alien, retains the right to renew his or her application in proceedings under 8 CFR part 240. Also, an applicant who is a parolee and meets the two conditions described in §245.2(a)(1) may renew a denied application in proceedings under 8 CFR part 240 to determine admissibility. At the time of renewal of the application, an applicant does not need to meet the statutory requirement of section 245(c) of the Act, or §245.1(g), if, in fact, those requirements were met at the time the renewed application was initially filed with the director. Nothing in this section shall entitle an alien to proceedings under section 240 of the Act who is not otherwise so entitled.

(iii) *Under the Act of November 2, 1966.* If the application is approved, the applicant's permanent residence shall be recorded in accordance with the provisions of section 1. No appeal lies from the denial of an application by the director, but the applicant, if not an arriving alien, retains the right to renew his or her application in proceedings under 8 CFR part 240. Also, an applicant who is a parolee and meets the two conditions described in §245.2(a)(1) may renew a denied application in proceedings under 8 CFR part 240 to determine admissibility.

(b) *Application under section 2 of the Act of November 2, 1966.* An application by a native or citizen of Cuba or by his spouse or child residing in the United States with him, who was lawfully admitted to the United States for permanent residence prior to November 2, 1966, and who desires such admission to be recorded as of an earlier date pursuant to section 2 of the Act of November 2, 1966, shall be made on Form I–485A. The application shall be accompanied by the Permanent Resident Card, Form I–151 or I–551, issued to the applicant in connection with his lawful admission for permanent residence. No appeal shall lie from the decision. If the application is approved, the applicant will be furnished with a replacement of his Form I–151 or I–551 bearing the new date as of which the lawful admission for permanent residence has been recorded.

(c) *Application under section 214(d) of the Act.* An application for permanent resident status pursuant to section 214(d) of the Act shall be filed on Form I–485. A separate application shall be filed by each applicant. If the application is approved, USCIS shall record the lawful admission of the applicant as of the date of approval. The applicant shall be notified of the decision and, if the application is denied, of the reasons therefor. No appeal shall lie from the denial of an application but such denial shall be without prejudice to the alien's right to renew his or her application in proceedings under 8 CFR part 240.

[30 FR 14778, Nov. 30, 1965]

EDITORIAL NOTE: For FEDERAL REGISTER citations affecting §245.2, see the List of CFR Sections Affected, which appears in the Finding Aids section of the printed volume and at *www.govinfo.gov.*

§245.3 Adjustment of status under section 13 of the Act of September 11, 1957, as amended.

Any application for benefits under section 13 of the Act of September 11, 1957, as amended, must be filed on

Form I–485 with the director having jurisdiction over the applicant's place of residence. The benefits under section 13 are limited to aliens who were admitted into the United States under section 101, paragraphs (a)(15)(A)(i), (a)(15)(A)(ii), (a)(15)(G)(i), or (a)(15)(G)(ii) of the Immigration and Nationality Act who performed diplomatic or semi-diplomatic duties and to their immediate families, and who establish that there are compelling reasons why the applicant or the member of the applicant's immediate family is unable to return to the country represented by the government which accredited the applicant and that adjustment of the applicant's status to that of an alien lawfully admitted for permanent residence would be in the national interest. Aliens whose duties were of a custodial, clerical, or menial nature, and members of their immediate families, are not eligible for benefits under section 13. In view of the annual limitation of 50 on the number of aliens whose status may be adjusted under section 13, any alien who is prima facie eligible for adjustment of status to that of a lawful permanent resident under another provision of law shall be advised to apply for adjustment pursuant to such other provision of law. An applicant for the benefits of section 13 shall not be subject to the labor certification requirement of section 212(a)(14) of the Immigration and Nationality Act. The applicant shall be notified of the decision and, if the application is denied, of the reasons for the denial and of the right to appeal under the provisions of part 103 of this chapter. Any applications pending with the Service before December 29, 1981 must be resubmitted to comply with the requirements of this section.

(Secs. 103, 245, of the Immigration and Nationality Act, as amended; 71 Stat. 642, as amended, sec. 17, Pub. L. 97–116, 95 Stat. 1619 (8 U.S.C. 1103, 1255, 1255b))

[47 FR 44238, Oct. 7, 1982, as amended at 59 FR 33905, July 1, 1994]

§ 245.4 Documentary requirements.

The provisions of part 211 of this chapter relating to the documentary requirements for immigrants shall not apply to an applicant under this part.

(Secs. 103, 214, 245 Immigration and Nationality Act, as amended; (8 U.S.C. 1103, 1184, 8 U.S.C. 1255, Sec. 2, 96 Stat. 1157, 8 U.S.C. 1255 note))

[30 FR 14779, Nov. 30, 1965. Redesignated at 48 FR 4770, Feb. 3, 1983, and further redesignated at 52 FR 6322, Mar. 3, 1982, and further redesignated at 56 FR 49481, Oct. 2, 1991]

§ 245.5 Medical examination.

Pursuant to section 232(b) of the Act, an applicant for adjustment of status shall be required to have a medical examination by a designated civil surgeon, whose report setting forth the findings of the mental and physical condition of the applicant, including compliance with section 212(a)(1)(A)(ii) of the Act, shall be incorporated into the record. A medical examination shall not be required of an applicant for adjustment of status who entered the United States as a nonimmigrant spouse, fianceé, or fianceeé of a United States citizen or the child of such an alien as defined in section 101(a)(15)(K) of the Act and § 214.2(k) of this chapter if the applicant was medically examined prior to, and as a condition of, the issuance of the nonimmigrant visa; provided that the medical examination must have occurred not more than 1 year prior the date of application for adjustment of status. Any applicant certified under paragraphs (1)(A)(ii) or (1)(A)(iii) of section 212(a) of the Act may appeal to a Board of Medical Officers of the U.S. Public Health Service as provided in section 234 of the Act and part 235 of this chapter.

[56 FR 49841, Oct. 2, 1991, as amended at 62 FR 10384, Mar. 6, 1997; 66 FR 42595, Aug. 14, 2001]

§ 245.6 Interview.

Each applicant for adjustment of status under this part shall be interviewed by an immigration officer. This interview may be waived in the case of a child under the age of 14; when the applicant is clearly ineligible under section 245(c) of the Act or § 245.1 of this chapter; or when it is determined by the Service that an interview is unnecessary.

[57 FR 49375, Nov. 2, 1992]

§ 245.7 Adjustment of status of certain Soviet and Indochinese parolees under the Foreign Operations Appropriations Act for Fiscal Year 1990 (Pub. L. 101–167).

(a) *Application.* Each person applying for benefits under section 599E of Public Law 101–167, 103 Stat. 1195, 1263, must file an application on the form prescribed by USCIS with the fee prescribed in 8 CFR 103.7(b)(1) and in accordance with the form instructions.

(b) *Aliens eligible to apply for adjustment.* The benefits of this section shall only apply to an alien who:

(1) Was a national of the Soviet Union, Vietnam, Laos, or Cambodia, and

(2) Was inspected and granted parole into the United States during the period beginning on August 15, 1988, and ending on September 30, 1990, after being denied refugee status.

(c) *Eligibility.* Benefits under Section 599E of Public Law 101–167 are limited to any alien described in paragraph (b) of this section who:

(1) Applies for such adjustment,

(2) Has been physically present in the United States for at least one year and is physically present in the United States on the date the application for such adjustment is filed,

(3) Is admissible to the United States as an immigrant, except as provided in paragraph (d) of this section, and

(4) Pays a fee for the processing of such application.

(d) *Waiver of certain grounds for inadmissibility.* The provisions of paragraphs (14), (15), (20), (21), (25), (28) (other than subparagraph (F), and (32) of section 212(a) of the Act shall not apply to adjustment under this section. The Attorney General may waive any other provision of section 212(a) (other than paragraph (23)(B), (27), (29), or (33)) with respect to such an adjustment for humanitarian purposes, to assure family unity, or when it is otherwise in the public interest.

(e) *Date of approval.* Upon approval of such an application for adjustment of status, the Attorney General shall create a record of the alien's admission as a lawful permanent resident as of the date of the alien's inspection and parole described in paragraph (b)(2) of this section.

(f) *No offset in number of visas available.* When an alien is granted the status of having been lawfully admitted for permanent residence under this section, the Secretary of State shall not be required to reduce the number of immigrant visas authorized to be issued under the Immigration and Nationality Act.

[55 FR 24860, July 19, 1990. Redesignated at 56 FR 49841, Oct. 2, 1991, as amended at 59 FR 33905, July 1, 1994; 63 FR 12987, Mar. 17, 1998; 74 FR 26940, June 5, 2009; 76 FR 53792, Aug. 29, 2011]

§ 245.8 Adjustment of status as a special immigrant under section 101(a)(27)(K) of the Act.

(a) *Application.* Each person applying for adjustment of status as a special immigrant under section 101(a)(27)(K) of the Act must file a Form I–485, Application to Register Permanent Residence or Adjust Status. Benefits under this section are limited to aliens who have served honorably (or are enlisted to serve) in the Armed Forces of the United States for at least 12 years, and their spouses and children. For purposes of this section, special immigrants described in section 101(a)(27)(K) of the Act and his or her spouse and children shall be deemed to have been paroled into the United States pursuant to section 245(g) of the Act. Each applicant must file a separate application with the appropriate fee.

(b) *Eligibility.* The benefits of this section shall apply only to an alien described in section 101(a)(27)(K) of the Act who applies for such adjustment. The accompanying spouse or child of an applicant for adjustment of status who benefits from Public Law 102–110 may also apply for adjustment of status. The provisions of section 245(c) of the Act do not apply to the principal Armed Forces special immigrant or to his or her spouse or child.

(c) *Interview of the applicant.* Upon completion of the adjustment of status interview for a special immigrant under section 101(a)(27)(K) of the Act, the director shall make a *prima facie* determination regarding eligibility for naturalization benefits if the applicant is to be granted status as an alien lawfully admitted for permanent residence. If the director determines that the applicant is immediately eligible for naturalization under section 328 or 329 of the Act, the director shall advise the applicant that he or she is eligible to apply for naturalization on Form N–400, Application to File Petition for Naturalization. If the applicant wishes to apply for naturalization, the director shall instruct the applicant concerning the requirements for naturalization and provide him or her with the necessary forms.

(d) *Spouse or child outside the United States.* When a spouse or child of an alien granted special immigrant status under section 101(a)(27)(K) of the Act is outside the United States, the principal alien may file Form I–824, Application for Action on an Approved Application or Petition, with the office which approved the original application.

(e) *Removal provisions of section 237 of the Act.* If the Service is made aware by notification from the appropriate executive department or by any other means that a section 101(a)(27)(K) special immigrant who has already been granted permanent residence fails to complete his or her total active duty service obligation for reasons other than an honorable discharge, the alien may become subject to the removal provisions of section 237 of the Act, provided the alien is in one or more of the classes of deportable aliens specified in section 237 of the Act. The Service shall obtain a current Form DD–214, Certificate of Release or Discharge from Active Duty, from the appropriate executive department for verification of the alien's failure to maintain eligibility.

(f) *Rescission proceedings under section 246 of the Act.* If the Service determines that a military special immigrant under section 101(a)(27)(K) of the Act was not in fact eligible for adjustment of status, the Service may pursue rescission proceedings under section 246 of the Act.

[57 FR 33862, July 31, 1992, as amended at 58 FR 50836, Sept. 29, 1993; 62 FR 10384, Mar. 6, 1997; 74 FR 26940, June 5, 2009]

§ 245.9 [Reserved]

§ 245.10 Adjustment of status upon payment of additional sum under section 245(i).

(a) *Definitions.* As used in this section the term:

(1)(i) *Grandfathered alien* means an alien who is the beneficiary (including a spouse or child of the alien beneficiary if eligible to receive a visa under section 203(d) of the Act) of:

(A) A petition for classification under section 204 of the Act which was properly filed with the Attorney General on or before April 30, 2001, and which was approvable when filed; or

(B) An application for labor certification under section 212(a)(5)(A) of the Act that was properly filed pursuant to the regulations of the Secretary of Labor on or before April 30, 2001, and which was approvable when filed.

(ii) If the qualifying visa petition or application for labor certification was filed after January 14, 1998, the alien must have been physically present in the United States on December 21, 2000. This requirement does not apply with respect to a spouse or child accompanying or following to join a principal alien who is a grandfathered alien as described in this section.

(2) *Properly filed* means:

(i) With respect to a qualifying immigrant visa petition, that the application was physically received by the Service on or before April 30, 2001, or if mailed, was postmarked on or before April 30, 2001, and accepted for filing as provided in § 103.2(a)(1) and (a)(2) of this chapter; and

(ii) With respect to a qualifying application for labor certification, that the application was properly filed and accepted pursuant to the regulations of the Secretary of Labor, 20 CFR 656.21.

(3) *Approvable when filed* means that, as of the date of the filing of the qualifying immigrant visa petition under section 204 of the Act or qualifying application for labor certification, the qualifying petition or application was properly filed, meritorious in fact, and non-frivolous ("frivolous" being defined herein as patently without substance). This determination will be made based on the circumstances that

existed at the time the qualifying petition or application was filed. A visa petition that was properly filed on or before April 30, 2001, and was approvable when filed, but was later withdrawn, denied, or revoked due to circumstances that have arisen after the time of filing, will preserve the alien beneficiary's grandfathered status if the alien is otherwise eligible to file an application for adjustment of status under section 245(i) of the Act.

(4) *Circumstances that have arisen after the time of filing* means circumstances similar to those outlined in §205.1(a)(3)(i) or (a)(3)(ii) of this chapter.

(b) *Eligibility.* An alien who is included in the categories of restricted aliens under §245.1(b) and meets the definition of a "grandfathered alien" may apply for adjustment of status under section 245 of the Act if the alien meets the requirements of paragraphs (b)(1) through (b)(7) of this section:

(1) Is physically present in the United States;

(2) Is eligible for immigrant classification and has an immigrant visa number immediately available at the time of filing for adjustment of status;

(3) Is not inadmissible from the United States under any provision of section 212 of the Act, or all grounds for inadmissibility have been waived;

(4) Properly files Form I–485, Application to Register Permanent Residence or Adjust Status on or after October 1, 1994, with the required fee for that application;

(5) Properly files Supplement A to Form I–485 on or after October 1, 1994;

(6) Pays an additional sum of $1,000, unless payment of the additional sum is not required under section 245(i) of the Act; and

(7) Will adjust status under section 245 of the Act to that of lawful permanent resident of the United States on or after October 1, 1994.

(c) *Payment of additional sum.* An adjustment applicant filing under the provisions of section 245(i) of the Act must pay the standard adjustment application filing fee as specified in §103.7(b)(1) of this chapter. Each application submitted under the provisions of section 245(i) of the Act must be submitted with an additional sum of $1,000. An applicant must submit the additional sum of $1,000 only once per application for adjustment of status submitted under the provisions of section 245(i) of the Act. However, an applicant filing under the provisions of section 245(i) of the Act is not required to pay the additional sum if, at the time the application for adjustment of status is filed, the alien is:

(1) Unmarried and less than 17 years of age;

(2) The spouse of a legalized alien, qualifies for and has properly filed Form I–817, Application for Voluntary Departure under the Family Unity Program, and submits a copy of his or her receipt or approval notice for filing Form I–817; or

(3) The child of a legalized alien, is unmarried and less than 21 years of age, qualifies for and has filed Form I–817, and submits a copy of his or her receipt or approval notice for filing Form I–817. Such an alien must pay the additional sum if he or she has reached the age of 21 years at the time of filing for adjustment of status. Such an alien must meet all other conditions for adjustment of status contained in the Act and in this chapter.

(d) *Pending adjustment application with the Service or Executive Office for Immigration Review filed without Supplement A to Form I–485 and additional sum.* An alien who filed an adjustment of status application with the Service in accordance with §103.2 of this chapter will be allowed the opportunity to amend such an application to request consideration under the provisions of section 245(i) of the Act, if it appears that the alien is not otherwise ineligible for adjustment of status. The Service shall notify the applicant in writing of the Service's intent to deny the adjustment of status application, and any other requests for benefits that derive from the adjustment application, unless Supplement A to Form I–485 and any required additional sum is filed within 30 days of the date of the notice. If the application for adjustment of status is pending before the Executive Office for Immigration Review (EOIR), EOIR will allow the respondent an opportunity to amend an adjustment of status application filed in accordance with § 103.2 of this chapter (to include Supplement A to Form I–485 and proof of remittance to the INS of the required additional sum) in order to request consideration under the provisions of section 245(i) of the Act.

(e) *Applications for Adjustment of Status filed before October 1, 1994.* The provisions of section 245(i) of the Act shall not apply to an application for adjustment of status that was filed before October 1, 1994. The provisions of section 245(i) of the Act also shall not apply to a motion to reopen or reconsider an application for adjustment of status if the application for adjustment of status was filed before October 1, 1994. An applicant whose pre-October 1, 1994, application for adjustment of status has been denied may file a new application for adjustment of status pursuant to section 245(i) of the Act on or after October 1, 1994, provided that such new application is accompanied by: the required fee; Supplement A to Form I–485; the additional sum required by section 245(i) of the Act; and all other required initial and additional evidence.

(f) *Effect of section 245(i) on completed adjustment applications before the Service.* (1) Any motion to reopen or reconsider before the Service alleging availability of section 245(i) of the Act must be filed in accordance with § 103.5 of this chapter. If said motion to reopen with the Service is granted, the alien must remit to the Service Supplement A to Form I–485 and the additional sum required by section 245(i) of the Act. If the alien had previously remitted Supplement A to Form I–485 and the additional sum with the application which is the subject of the motion to reopen, then no additional sum need be remitted upon such reopening.

(2) An alien whose adjustment application was adjudicated and denied by the Service because of ineligibility under section 245(a) or (c) of the Act and now alleges eligibility due to the availability of section 245(i) of the Act may file a new application for adjustment of status pursuant to section 245(i) of the Act, provided that such new application is accompanied by the required fee for the application, Supplement A to Form I–485, additional sum required by section 245(i) of the Act and all other required and additional evidence.

(g) *Aliens deportable under section 237(a)(4)(B) of the Act are ineligible to adjust status.* Section 237(a)(4)(B) of the Act renders any alien who has engaged, is engaged, or at any time after admission engages in any terrorist activity, as defined in section 212(a)(3)(B)(iii) of the Act, deportable. Under section 245(c)(6) of the Act, persons who are deportable under section 237(a)(4)(B) of the Act are ineligible to adjust status under section 245(a) of the Act. Any person who is deportable under section 237(a)(4)(B) of the Act is also ineligible to adjust status under section 245(i) of the Act.

(h) *Asylum or diversity immigrant visa applications.* An asylum application, diversity visa lottery application, or diversity visa lottery-winning letter does not serve to grandfather the alien for purposes of section 245(i) of the Act. However, an otherwise grandfathered alien may use winning a diversity visa as a basis for adjustment.

(i) *Denial, withdrawal, or revocation of the approval of a visa petition or application for labor certification.* The denial, withdrawal, or revocation of the approval of a qualifying immigrant visa petition, or application for labor certification, that was properly filed on or before April 30, 2001, and that was approvable when filed, will not preclude its grandfathered alien (including the grandfathered alien's family members) from seeking adjustment of status under section 245(i) of the Act on the basis of another approved visa petition, a diversity visa, or any other ground for adjustment of status under the Act, as appropriate.

(j) *Substitution of a beneficiary on an application for a labor certification.* Only the alien who was the beneficiary of the application for the labor certification on or before April 30, 2001, will be considered to have been grandfathered for purposes of filing an application for adjustment of status under section 245(i) of the Act. An alien who was previously the beneficiary of the application for the labor certification but was subsequently replaced by another alien on or before April 30, 2001, will not be considered to be a grandfathered alien. An alien who was substituted for the previous beneficiary of the application for the labor certification after April 30, 2001, will not be considered to be a grandfathered alien.

(k) *Changes in employment.* An applicant for adjustment under section 245(i) of the Act who is adjusting status through an employment-based category is not required to work for the petitioner who filed the petition that grandfathered the alien, unless he or she is seeking adjustment based on employment for that same petitioner.

(l) *Effects of grandfathering on an alien's nonimmigrant status.* An alien's nonimmigrant status is not affected by the fact that he or she is a grandfathered alien. Lawful immigration status for a nonimmigrant is defined in § 245.1(d)(1)(ii).

(m) *Effect of grandfathering on unlawful presence under section 212(a)(9)(B) and (c) of the Act.* If the alien is not in a period of stay authorized by the Attorney General, the fact that he or she is a grandfathered alien does not prevent the alien from accruing unlawful presence under section 212(a)(9)(B) and (C) of the Act.

(n) *Evidentiary requirement to demonstrate physical presence on December 21, 2000.* (1) Unless the qualifying immigrant visa petition or application for labor certification was filed on or before January 14, 1998, a principal grandfathered alien must establish that he or she was physically present in the United States on December 21, 2000, to be eligible to apply to adjust status under section 245(i) of the Act. If no one document establishes the alien's physical presence on December 21, 2000, he or she may submit several documents establishing his or her physical presence in the United States prior to, and after December 21, 2000.

(2) To demonstrate physical presence on December 21, 2000, the alien may submit copies of documents issued by the former INS or EOIR such as arrival-departure forms or notices to appear in immigration court.

(3) To demonstrate physical presence on December 21, 2000, the alien may submit other government documentation. Other government documentation issued by a Federal, state, or local authority must bear the signature, seal, or other authenticating instrument of such authority (if the document normally bears such instrument), be dated at the time of issuance, and bear a date of issuance not later than December 21, 2000. For this purpose, the term Federal, state, or local authority includes any governmental, educational, or administrative function operated by Federal, state, county, or municipal officials. Examples of such other documentation include, but are not limited to:

(i) A state driver's license;

(ii) A state identification card;

(iii) A county or municipal hospital record;

(iv) A public college or public school transcript;

(v) Income tax records;

(vi) A certified copy of a Federal, state, or local governmental record which was created on or prior to December 21, 2000, shows that the applicant was present in the United States at the time, and establishes that the applicant sought on his or her own behalf, or some other party sought on the applicant's behalf, a benefit from the Federal, state, or local governmental agency keeping such record;

(vii) A certified copy of a Federal, state, or local governmental record which was created on or prior to December 21, 2000, that shows that the applicant was present in the United States at the time, and establishes that the applicant submitted an income tax return, property tax payment, or similar submission or payment to the Federal, state, or local governmental agency keeping such record;

(viii) A transcript from a private or religious school that is registered with, or approved or licensed by, appropriate State or local authorities, accredited by the State or regional accrediting body, or by the appropriate private school association, or maintains enrollment records in accordance with State or local requirements or standards.

(4) To demonstrate physical presence on December 21, 2000, the alien may

submit non-government documentation. Examples of documentation establishing physical presence on December 21, 2000, may include, but are not limited to:

(i) School records;

(ii) Rental receipts;

(iii) Utility bill receipts;

(iv) Any other dated receipts;

(v) Personal checks written by the applicant bearing a bank cancellation stamp;

(vi) Employment records, including pay stubs;

(vii) Credit card statements showing the dates of purchase, payment, or other transaction;

(viii) Certified copies of records maintained by organizations chartered by the Federal or State government, such as public utilities, accredited private and religious schools, and banks;

(ix) If the applicant established that a family unit was in existence and cohabiting in the United States, documents evidencing the presence of another member of the same family unit; and

(x) For applicants who have ongoing correspondence or other interaction with the Service, a list of the types and dates of such correspondence or other contact that the applicant knows to be contained or reflected in Service records.

(5)(i) The adjudicator will evaluate all evidence on a case-by-case basis and will not accept a personal affidavit attesting to physical presence on December 21, 2000, without requiring an interview or additional evidence to validate the affidavit.

(ii) In all cases, any doubts as to the existence, authenticity, veracity, or accuracy of the documentation shall be resolved by the official government record, with records of the Service and the Executive Office for Immigration Review (EOIR) having precedence over the records of other agencies. Furthermore, determinations as to the weight to be given any particular document or item of evidence shall be solely within the discretion of the adjudicating authority (*i.e.*, the Service or EOIR). It shall be the responsibility of the applicant to obtain and submit copies of the records of any other government agency that the applicant desires to be considered in support of his or her application.

[59 FR 51095, Oct. 7, 1994; 59 FR 53020, Oct. 20, 1994, as amended at 62 FR 10384, Mar. 6, 1997; 62 FR 39424, July 23, 1997; 62 FR 55153, Oct. 23, 1997; 66 FR 16388, Mar. 26, 2001; 76 FR 53793, Aug. 29, 2011]

§ 245.11 Adjustment of aliens in S nonimmigrant classification.

(a) *Eligibility*. An application on Form I–854, requesting that an alien witness or informant in S nonimmigrant classification be allowed to adjust status to that of lawful permanent resident, may only be filed by the federal or state law enforcement authority ("LEA") (which shall include a federal or state court or a United States Attorney's Office) that originally requested S classification for the alien. The completed application shall be filed with the Assistant Attorney General, Criminal Division, Department of Justice, who will forward only properly certified applications to the Commissioner, Immigration and Naturalization Service, for approval. Upon receipt of an approved Form I–854 allowing the S nonimmigrant to adjust status to that of lawful permanent resident, the alien may proceed to file with that Form, Form I–485, Application to Register Permanent Residence or Adjust Status, pursuant to the following process.

(1) *Request to allow S nonimmigrant to apply for adjustment of status to that of lawful permanent resident*. The LEA that requested S nonimmigrant classification for an S nonimmigrant witness or informant pursuant to section 101(a)(15)(S) of the Act may request that the principal S nonimmigrant be allowed to apply for adjustment of status by filing Form I–854 with the Assistant Attorney General, Criminal Division, in accordance with the instructions on, or attached to, that form and certifying that the alien has fulfilled the terms of his or her admission and classification. The same Form I–854 may be used by the LEA to request that the principals nonimmigrant's spouse, married and unmarried sons and daughters, regardless of age, and parents who are in derivative S nonimmigrant classification and who are qualified family members as described

in paragraph (b) of this section similarly be allowed to apply for adjustment of status pursuant to section 101(a)(15)(S) of the Act.

(2) *Certification.* Upon receipt of an LEA's request for the adjustment of an alien in S nonimmigrant classification on Form I–854, the Assistant Attorney General, Criminal Division, shall review the information and determine whether to certify the request to the Commissioner in accordance with the instructions on the form.

(3) *Submission of requests for adjustment of status to the Commissioner.* No application by an LEA on Form I–854 requesting the adjustment to lawful permanent resident status of an S nonimmigrant shall be forwarded to the Commissioner unless first certified by the Assistant Attorney General, Criminal Division.

(4) *Decision on request to allow adjustment of S nonimmigrant.* The Commissioner shall make the final decision on a request to allow an S nonimmigrant to apply for adjustment of status to lawful permanent resident.

(i) In the event the Commissioner decides to deny an application on Form I–854 to allow an S nonimmigrant to apply for adjustment of status, the Assistant Attorney General, Criminal Division, and the relevant LEA shall be notified in writing to that effect. The Assistant Attorney General, Criminal Division, shall concur in or object to that decision. Unless the Assistant Attorney General, Criminal Division, objects within 7 days, he or she shall be deemed to have concurred in the decision. In the event of an objection by the Assistant Attorney General, Criminal Division, the matter will be expeditiously referred to the Deputy Attorney General for a final resolution. In no circumstances shall the alien or the relevant LEA have a right of appeal from any decision to deny.

(ii) Upon approval of the request on Form I–854, the Commissioner shall forward a copy of the approved form to the Assistant Attorney General and the S nonimmigrant, notifying them that the S nonimmigrant may proceed to file Form I–485 and request adjustment of status to that of lawful permanent resident, and that, to be eligible for adjustment of status, the nonimmigrant must otherwise:

(A) Meet the requirements of paragraph (b) of this section, if requesting adjustment as a qualified family member of the certified principal S nonimmigrant witness or informant;

(B) Be admissible to the United States as an immigrant, unless the ground of inadmissibility has been waived;

(C) Establish eligibility for adjustment of status under all provisions of section 245 of the Act, unless the basis for ineligibility has been waived; and

(D) Properly file with his or her Form I–485, Application to Register Permanent Residence or Adjust Status, the approved Form I–854.

(b) *Family members*—(1) *Qualified family members.* A qualified family member of an S nonimmigrant includes the spouse, married or unmarried son or daughter, or parent of a principal S nonimmigrant who meets the requirements of paragraph (a) of this section, provided that:

(i) The family member qualified as the spouse, married or unmarried son or daughter, or parent (as defined in section 101(b) of the Act) of the principal S nonimmigrant when the family member was admitted as or granted a change of status to that of a nonimmigrant under section 101(a)(15)(S) of the Act;

(ii) The family member was admitted in S nonimmigrant classification to accompany, or follow to join, the principal S–5 or S–6 alien pursuant to the LEA's request;

(iii) The family member is not inadmissible from the United States as a participant in Nazi persecution or genocide as described in section 212(a)(3)(E) of the Act;

(iv) The qualifying relationship continues to exist; and

(v) The principal alien has adjusted status, has a pending application for adjustment of status or is concurrently filing an application for adjustment of status under section 101(a)(15)(S) of the Act.

(vi) Paragraphs (b)(1)(iv) and (v) of this section do not apply if the alien witness or informant has died and, in the opinion of the Attorney General, was in compliance with the terms of his or her S classification under section 245(i) (1) and (2) of the Act.

(2) *Other family member.* The adjustment provisions in this section do not apply to a family member who has not been classified as an S nonimmigrant pursuant to a request on Form I–854 or who does not otherwise meet the requirements of paragraph (b) of this section. However, a spouse or an unmarried child who is less than 21 years old, and whose relationship to the principal S nonimmigrant or qualified family member was established prior to the approval of the principal S nonimmigrant's adjustment of status application, may be accorded the priority date and preference category of the principal S nonimmigrant or qualified family member, in accordance with the provisions of section 203(d) of the Act. Such a spouse or child:

(i) May use the principal S nonimmigrant or qualified member's priority date and category when it becomes current, in accordance with the limitations set forth in sections 201 and 202 of the Act;

(ii) May seek immigrant visa issuance abroad or adjustment of status to that of a lawful permanent resident of the United States when the priority date becomes current for the spouse's or child's country of chargeability under the fourth employment-based preference classification;

(iii) Must meet all the requirements for immigrant visa issuance or adjustment of status, unless those requirements have been waived;

(iv) Is not applying for adjustment of status under 101(a)(15)(S) of the Act, is not required to file Form I–854, and is not required to obtain LEA certification; and

(v) Will lose eligibility for benefits if the child marries or has his or her twenty-first birthday before being admitted with an immigrant visa or granted adjustment of status.

(c) *Waivers of inadmissibility.* An alien seeking to adjust status pursuant to the provisions of section 101(a)(15)(S) of the Act may not be denied adjustment of status for conduct or a condition that:

(1) Was disclosed to the Attorney General prior to admission; and

(2) Was specifically waived pursuant to the waiver provisions set forth at section 212(d)(1) and 212(d)(3) of the Act.

(d) *Application.* Each S nonimmigrant requesting adjustment of status under section 101(a)(15)(S) of the Act must:

(1) File Form I–485, with the prescribed fee, accompanied by the approved Form I–854, and the supporting documents specified in the instructions to Form I–485 and described in 8 CFR 245.2. Secondary evidence may be submitted if the nonimmigrant is unable to obtain the required primary evidence as provided in 8 CFR 103.2(b)(2). The S nonimmigrant applying to adjust must complete Part 2 of Form I–485 by checking box "h-other" and writing "S" or "S-Qualified Family Member." Qualified family members must submit documentary evidence of the relationship to the principal S nonimmigrant witness or informant.

(2) Submit detailed and inclusive evidence of eligibility for the adjustment of status benefits of S classification, which shall include:

(i) A photocopy of all pages of the alien's most recent passport or an explanation of why the alien does not have a passport; or

(ii) An attachment on a plain piece of paper showing the dates of all arrivals and departures from the United States in S nonimmigrant classification and the reason for each departure; and

(iii) Primary evidence of a qualifying relationship to the principal S nonimmigrant, such as birth or marriage certificate. If any required primary evidence is unavailable, church or school records, or other secondary evidence may be submitted. If such documents are unavailable, affidavits may be submitted as provided in 8 CFR 103.2(b)(2).

(e) *Priority date.* The S nonimmigrant's priority date shall be the date his or her application for adjustment of status as an S nonimmigrant is properly filed with the Service.

(f) *Visa number limitation.* An adjustment of status application under section 101(a)(15)(S) of the Act may be filed regardless of the availability of immigrant visa numbers. The adjustment of status application may not, however, be approved and the alien's adjustment of status to that of lawful permanent resident of the United States may not be granted until a visa number becomes available for the alien under the worldwide allocation for employment-based immigrants under section 201(d) and section 203(b)(4) of the Act. The applicant may request employment authorization or permission to travel outside the United States while the application is pending by filing an application pursuant to 8 CFR 274a.13 or 8 CFR 223.2.

(g) *Filing and decision.* An application for adjustment of status filed by an S nonimmigrant under section 101(a)(15)(S) of the Act shall be filed with the district director having jurisdiction over the alien's place of residence. Upon approval of adjustment of status under this section, the district director shall record the alien's lawful admission for permanent residence as of the date of such approval. The district director shall notify the Commissioner and the Assistant Attorney General, Criminal Division, of the adjustment.

(h) *Removal under section 237 of the Act.* Nothing in this section shall prevent an alien adjusted pursuant to the terms of these provisions from being removed for conviction of a crime of moral turpitude committed within 10 years after being provided lawful permanent residence under this section or for any other ground under section 237 of the Act.

(i) *Denial of application.* In the event the district director decides to deny an application on Form I-485 and an approved Form I-854 to allow an S nonimmigrant to adjust status, the Assistant Attorney General, Criminal Division, and the relevant LEA shall be notified in writing to that effect. The Assistant Attorney General, Criminal Division, shall concur in or object to that decision. Unless the Assistant Attorney General, Criminal Division, objects within 7 days, he or she shall be deemed to have concurred in the decision. In the event of an objection by the Assistant Attorney General, Criminal Division, the matter will be expeditiously referred to the Deputy Attorney General for a final resolution. In no circumstances shall the alien or the relevant LEA have a right of appeal from any decision to deny. A denial of an adjustment application under this paragraph may not be renewed in subsequent removal proceedings.

[60 FR 44269, Aug. 25, 1995; 60 FR 52248, Oct. 5, 1995, as amended at 62 FR 10384, Mar. 6, 1997; 76 FR 53793, Aug. 29, 2011]

§§245.12–245.14 [Reserved]

§245.15 Adjustment of status of certain Haitian nationals under the Haitian Refugee Immigrant Fairness Act of 1998 (HRIFA).

(a) *Definitions.* As used in this section, the terms:

Abandoned and *abandonment* mean that both parents have, or the sole or surviving parent has, or in the case of a child who has been placed into a guardianship, the child's guardian or guardians have, willfully forsaken all parental or guardianship rights, obligations, and claims to the child, as well as all control over and possession of the child, without intending to transfer these rights to any specific person(s).

Guardian means a person lawfully invested (by order of a competent Federal, State, or local authority) with the power, and charged with the duty, of taking care of, including managing the property, rights, and affairs of, a child.

Orphan and *orphaned* refer to the involuntary detachment or severance of a child from his or her parents due to any of the following:

(1) The death or disappearance of, desertion by, or separation or loss from both parents, as those terms are defined in §204.3(b) of this chapter;

(2) The irrevocable and written release of all parental rights by the sole parent, as that term is defined in §204.3(b) of this chapter, based upon the inability of that parent to provide proper care (within the meaning of that phrase in §204.3(b) of this chapter) for the child, provided that at the time of such irrevocable release such parent is legally obligated to provide such care; or

(3) The death or disappearance, as that term is defined in §204.3(b) of this chapter, of one parent and the irrevocable and written release of all parental rights by the sole remaining parent based upon the inability of that parent to provide proper care (within the

meaning of that phrase in § 204.3(b) of this chapter) for the child, provided that at the time of such irrevocable release such parent is legally obligated to provide such care.

Parent, father, or *mother* means a parent, father, or mother only where the relationship exists by reason of any of the circumstances set forth in paragraphs (A) through (E) of section 101(b)(1) of the Act.

Sole remaining parent means a person who is the child's only parent because:

(1) The child's other parent has died; or

(2) The child's other parent has been certified by competent Haitian authorities to be presumed dead as a result of his or her disappearance, within the meaning of that term as set forth in § 204.3(b) of this chapter.

(b) *Applicability of provisions of section 902 of HRIFA in general.* Section 902 of Division A of Pub. L. 105–277, the Haitian Refugee Immigrant Fairness Act of 1998 (HRIFA), provides special rules for adjustment of status for certain nationals of Haiti, and without regard to section 241(a)(5) of the Act, if they meet the other requirements of HRIFA.

(1) *Principal applicants.* Section 902(b)(1) of HRIFA defines five categories of principal applicants who may apply for adjustment of status, if the alien was physically present in the United States on December 31, 1995:

(i) An alien who filed for asylum before December 31, 1995;

(ii) An alien who was paroled into the United States prior to December 31, 1995, after having been identified as having a credible fear of persecution, or paroled for emergent reasons or reasons deemed strictly in the public interest; or

(iii) An alien who at the time of arrival in the United States and on December 31, 1995, was unmarried and under 21 years of age and who:

(A) Arrived in the United States without parents in the United States and has remained, without parents, in the United States since his or her arrival;

(B) Became orphaned subsequent to arrival in the United States; or

(C) Was abandoned by parents or guardians prior to April 1, 1998, and has remained abandoned since such abandonment.

(2) *Dependents.* Section 902(d) of HRIFA provides for certain Haitian nationals to apply for adjustment of status as the spouse, child, or unmarried son or daughter of a principal HRIFA beneficiary, even if the individual would not otherwise be eligible for adjustment under section 902. The eligibility requirements for dependents are described further in paragraph (d) of this section.

(c) *Eligibility of principal HRIFA applicants.* A Haitian national who is described in paragraph (b)(1) of this section is eligible to apply for adjustment of status under the provisions of section 902 of HRIFA if the alien meets the following requirements:

(1) *Physical presence.* The alien is physically present in the United States at the time the application is filed;

(2) *Proper application.* The alien properly files an application for adjustment of status in accordance with this section, including the evidence described in paragraphs (h), (i), (j), and (k) of this section. For purposes of § 245.15 of this chapter only, an Application to Register Permanent Residence or Adjust Status (Form I–485) submitted by a principal applicant for benefits under HRIFA may be considered to have been properly filed if it:

(i) Is received not later than March 31, 2000, at the Nebraska Service Center, the Board, or the Immigration Court having jurisdiction;

(ii) Has been properly completed and signed by the applicant;

(iii) Identifies the provision of HRIFA under which the applicant is seeking adjustment of status; and

(iv) Is accompanied by either:

(A) The correct fee as specified in § 103.7(b)(1) of this chapter; or

(B) A request for a fee waiver in accordance with § 103.7(c) of this chapter, provided such fee waiver request is subsequently granted; however, if such a fee waiver request is subsequently denied and the applicant submits the require fee within 30 days of the date of any notice that the fee waiver request had been denied, the application shall be regarded as having been filed before the statutory deadline. In addition, in a case over which the Board has jurisdiction, an application received by the Board before April 1, 2000, that has been properly signed and executed shall be considered filed before the statutory deadline without payment of the fee or submission of a fee waiver request. Upon remand by the Board, the payment of the fee or a request for a fee waiver shall be made upon submission of the application to the Immigration Court in accordance with 8 CFR 240.11(f). If a request for a fee waiver is denied, the application shall be considered as having been properly filed with the Immigration Court before the statutory deadline provided that the applicant submits the required fee within 30 days of the date of any notice that the fee waiver request has been denied.

(3) *Admissibility*. The alien is not inadmissible to the United States for permanent residence under any provisions of section 212(a) of the Act, except as provided in paragraph (e) of this section; and

(4) *Continuous physical presence*. The alien has been physically present in the United States for a continuous period beginning on December 31, 1995, and ending on the date the application for adjustment is granted, except for the following periods of time:

(i) Any period or periods of absence from the United States not exceeding 180 days in the aggregate; and

(ii) Any periods of absence for which the applicant received an advance parole authorization prior to his or her departure from the United States, provided the applicant returned to the United States in accordance with the conditions of such authorization.

(iii) Any periods of absence from the United States occurring after October 21, 1998, and before July 12, 1999, provided the applicant departed the United States prior to December 31, 1998.

(d) *Eligibility of dependents of a principal HRIFA beneficiary*. A Haitian national who is the spouse, child, or unmarried son or daughter of a principal beneficiary eligible for adjustment of status under the provisions of HRIFA is eligible to apply for benefits as a dependent, if the dependent alien meets the following requirements:

(1) *Physical presence*. The alien is physically present in the United States at the time the application is filed;

(2) *Proper application*. The alien properly files an application for adjustment of status as a dependent in accordance with this section, including the evidence described in paragraphs (h) and (l) of this section;

(3) *Admissibility*. The alien is not inadmissible to the United States for permanent residence under any provisions of section 212(a) of the Act, except as provided in paragraph (e) of this section;

(4) *Relationship*. The qualifying relationship to the principal alien must have existed at the time the principal was granted adjustment of status and must continue to exist at the time the dependent alien is granted adjustment of status. To establish the qualifying relationship to the principal alien, evidence must be submitted in accordance with § 204.2 of this chapter. Such evidence should consist of the documents specified in § 204.2(a)(1)(i)(B), (a)(1)(iii)(B), (a)(2), (d)(2), and (d)(5) of this chapter;

(5) *Continuous physical presence*. If the alien is applying as the unmarried son or unmarried daughter of a principal HRIFA beneficiary, he or she must have been physically present in the United States for a continuous period beginning not later than December 31, 1995, and ending on the date the application for adjustment is granted, as provided in paragraphs (c)(4) and (j) of this section.

(e) *Applicability of grounds of inadmissibility contained in section 212(a)*—(1) *Certain grounds of inadmissibility inapplicable to HRIFA applicants*. Paragraphs (4), (5), (6)(A), (7)(A) and (9)(B) of section 212(a) of the Act are inapplicable to HRIFA principal applicants and their dependents. Accordingly, an applicant for adjustment of status under section 902 of HRIFA need not establish admissibility under those provisions in order to be able to adjust his or her status to that of permanent resident.

(2) *Availability of individual waivers*. If a HRIFA applicant is inadmissible under any of the other provisions of section 212(a) of the Act for which an

immigrant waiver is available, the applicant may apply for one or more of the immigrant waivers of inadmissibility under section 212 of the Act, in accordance with § 212.7 of this chapter. In considering an application for waiver under section 212(g) of the Act by an otherwise statutorily eligible applicant for adjustment of status under HRIFA who was paroled into the United States from the U.S. Naval Base at Guantanamo Bay, for the purpose of receiving treatment of an HIV or AIDS condition, the fact that his or her arrival in the United States was the direct result of a government decision to provide such treatment should be viewed as a significant positive factor when weighing discretionary factors. In considering an application for waiver under section 212(i) of the Act by an otherwise statutorily eligible applicant for adjustment of status under HRIFA who used counterfeit documents to travel from Haiti to the United States, the adjudicator shall, when weighing discretionary factors, take into consideration the general lawlessness and corruption which was widespread in Haiti at the time of the alien's departure, the difficulties in obtaining legitimate departure documents at that time, and other factors unique to Haiti at that time which may have induced the alien to commit fraud or make willful misrepresentations.

(3) *Special rule for waiver of inadmissibility grounds for HRIFA applicants under section 212(a)(9)(A) and 212(a)(9)(C) of the Act.* An applicant for adjustment of status under HRIFA who is inadmissible under section 212(a)(9)(A) or 212(a)(9)(C) of the Act, may apply for a waiver of these grounds of inadmissibility while present in the United States. Such an alien must file Form I–601, Application for Waiver of Grounds of Excludability. If the application for adjustment is pending at the Nebraska Service Center, Form I–601 must be filed with the director of that office. If the application for adjustment is pending at a district office, Form I–601 must be filed with the district director having jurisdiction over the application. If the application for adjustment is pending before the immigration court, Form I–601 must be filed with the immigration judge having jurisdiction, or with the Board of Immigration Appeals if the appeal is pending before the Board.

(f) *Time for filing of applications*—(1) *Applications for HRIFA benefits by a principal HRIFA applicant.* The application period begins on June 11, 1999. To benefit from the provisions of section 902 of HRIFA, an alien who is applying for adjustment as a principal applicant must properly file an application for adjustment of status before April 1, 2000.

(2) *Applications by dependent aliens.* The spouse, minor child, or unmarried son or daughter of an alien who is eligible for adjustment of status as a principal beneficiary under HRIFA may file an application for adjustment of status under this section concurrently with or subsequent to the filing of the application of the principal HRIFA beneficiary. An application filed by a dependent may not be approved prior to approval of the principal's application.

(g) *Jurisdiction for filing of applications*—(1) *Filing of applications with USCIS.* USCIS has jurisdiction over all applications for the benefits of section 902 of HRIFA as a principal applicant or as a dependent under this section, except for applications filed by aliens who are in pending immigration proceedings as provided in paragraph (g)(2) of this section. All applications filed with USCIS for the benefits of section 902 of HRIFA must be submitted on the form designated by USCIS with the fees prescribed in 8 CFR 103.7(b)(1) and in accordance with the form instructions. After proper filing of the application, USCIS will instruct the applicant to appear for biometrics collection as prescribed in 8 CFR 103.16.

(2) *Filing of applications by aliens in pending exclusion, deportation, or removal proceedings.* An alien who is in exclusion, deportation, or removal proceedings pending before the Immigration Court or the Board, or who has a pending motion to reopen or motion to reconsider filed with the Immigration Court or the Board on or before May 12, 1999, must apply for HRIFA benefits to the Immigration Court or the Board, as provided in paragraph (p)(1) of this section, rather than to the Service. However, an alien whose proceeding has

been administratively closed (see paragraph (p)(4) of this section) may only apply for HRIFA benefits with the Service as provided in paragraph (g)(1) of this section.

(3)(i) *Filing of applications with the Service by aliens who are subject to a final order of exclusion, deportation, or removal.* An alien who is subject to a final order of exclusion, deportation, or removal, and who has not been denied adjustment of status under section 902 of HRIFA by the Immigration Court or the Board, may only apply for HRIFA benefits with the Service as provided in paragraph (g)(1) of this section. This includes applications for HRIFA benefits filed by aliens who have filed a motion to reopen or motion to reconsider a final order after May 12, 1999.

(ii) An alien present in the United States who is subject to a final order of exclusion, deportation, or removal and has been denied adjustment of status under section 902 of HRIFA by the Immigration Court or the Board, or who never applied for adjustment of status with the Service, an Immigration Court, or the Board on or before March 31, 2000, and who was made eligible for HRIFA benefits under the Legal Immigration Family Equity Act of 2000 (LIFE Act) and LIFE amendments, Public Law 106–553 and Public Law 106–554, respectively, may file a motion to reopen with either the Immigration Court or the Board, whichever had jurisdiction last. As provided by the LIFE Act, motions to reopen must be filed on or before June 19, 2001.

(iii) *Stay of final order of exclusion, deportation, or removal.* The filing of an application for adjustment under section 902 of HRIFA with the Service shall not stay the execution of such final order unless the applicant has requested and been granted a stay in connection with the HRIFA application. An alien who has filed a HRIFA application with the Service may file an Application for Stay of Removal (Form I–246) in accordance with section 241(c)(2) of the Act and § 241.6 of this chapter.

(iv) *Grant of stay.* Absent evidence of the applicant's statutory ineligibility for adjustment of status under section 902 of HRIFA or significant negative discretionary factors, a Form I–246 filed by a bona fide applicant for adjustment under section 902 of HRIFA shall be approved and the removal of the applicant shall be stayed until such time as the Service has adjudicated the application for adjustment in accordance with this section.

(h) *Application and supporting documents.* Each applicant for adjustment of status must file an Application to Register Permanent Residence or Adjust Status (Form I–485). An applicant should complete Part 2 of Form I–485 by checking box "h—other" and writing "HRIFA—Principal" or "HRIFA—Dependent" next to that block. Each application must be accompanied by:

(1) *Application fee.* The fee for Form I–485 prescribed in § 103.7(b)(1) of this chapter;

(2) *Fingerprinting fee.* If the applicant is 14 years of age or older, the fee for fingerprinting prescribed in § 103.7(b)(1) of this chapter;

(3) *Identifying information.* (i) A copy of the applicant's birth certificate or other record of birth as provided in paragraph (m) of this section;

(ii) A completed Biographic Information Sheet (Form G–325A), if the applicant is between 14 and 79 years of age;

(iii) A report of medical examination, as specified in § 245.5 of this chapter; and

(iv) Two photographs, as described in the instructions to Form I–485;

(4) *Arrival-Departure Record.* A copy of the Form I–94 (see § 1.4), Arrival-Departure Record, issued at the time of the applicant's arrival in the United States, if the alien was inspected and admitted or paroled;

(5) *Police clearances.* If the applicant is 14 years old or older, a police clearance from each municipality where the alien has resided for 6 months or longer since arriving in the United States. If there are multiple local law enforcement agencies (e.g., city police and county sheriff) with jurisdiction over the alien's residence, the applicant may obtain a clearance from either agency. If the applicant resides or resided in a State where the State police maintain a compilation of all local arrests and convictions, a statewide clearance is sufficient. If the applicant presents a letter from the local police agencies involved, or other evidence, to the effect that the applicant attempted

to obtain such clearance but was unable to do so because of local or State policy, the director or immigration judge having jurisdiction over the application may waive the local police clearance. Furthermore, if such local police agency has provided the Service or the Immigration Court with a blanket statement that issuance of such police clearance is against local or State policy, the director or immigration judge having jurisdiction over the case may waive the local police clearance requirement regardless of whether the applicant individually submits a letter from that local police agency;

(6) *Proof of Haitian nationality.* If the applicant acquired Haitian nationality other than through birth in Haiti, a copy of the certificate of naturalization or certificate of citizenship issued by the Haitian government; and

(7) *Additional supporting evidence.* Additional supporting evidence pertaining to the applicant as provided in paragraphs (i) through (l) of this section.

(i) *Evidence of presence in the United States on December 31, 1995.* An alien seeking HRIFA benefits as a principal applicant must provide with the application evidence establishing the alien's presence in the United States on December 31, 1995. Such evidence may consist of the evidence listed in § 245.22.

(j) *Evidence of continuity of presence in the United States since December 31, 1995.* An alien seeking HRIFA benefits as a principal applicant, or as the unmarried son or daughter of a principal applicant, must provide with the application evidence establishing continuity of the alien's physical presence in the United States since December 31, 1995. (This requirement does not apply to a dependent seeking HRIFA benefits as the spouse or minor child of a principal applicant.)

(1) *Evidence establishing presence.* Evidence establishing the continuity of the alien's physical presence in the United States since December 31, 1995, may consist of any documentation issued by any governmental or nongovernmental authority, provided such evidence bears the name of the applicant, was dated at the time it was issued, and bears the signature, seal, or other authenticating instrument of the authorized representative of the issuing authority, if the document would normally contain such authenticating instrument.

(2) *Examples.* Documentation establishing continuity of physical presence may include, but is not limited to:

(i) School records;

(ii) Rental receipts;

(iii) Utility bill receipts;

(iv) Any other dated receipts;

(v) Personal checks written by the applicant bearing a dated bank cancellation stamp;

(vi) Employment records, including pay stubs;

(vii) Credit card statements showing the dates of purchase, payment, or other transaction;

(viii) Certified copies of records maintained by organizations chartered by the Federal or State government, such as public utilities, accredited private and religious schools, and banks;

(ix) If the applicant establishes that a family unit was in existence and cohabiting in the United States, documents evidencing presence of another member of that same family unit; and

(x) For applicants who have had ongoing correspondence or other interaction with the Service, a list of the types and dates of such correspondence or other contact that the applicant knows to be contained or reflected in Service records.

(3) *Evidence relating to absences from the United States since December 31, 1995.* If the alien is applying as a principal applicant, or as the unmarried son or daughter of a principal applicant, and has departed from and returned to the United States since December 31, 1995, the alien must provide with the application an attachment on a plain piece of paper showing:

(i) The date of the applicant's last arrival in the United States before December 31, 1995;

(ii) The date of each departure (if any) from the United States since that arrival;

(iii) The reason for each departure; and

(iv) The date, manner, and place of each return to the United States.

(k) *Evidence establishing the alien's eligibility under section 902(b) of HRIFA.* An alien seeking HRIFA benefits as a principal applicant must provide with the application evidence establishing that the alien satisfies one of the eligibility standards described in paragraph (b)(1) of this section.

(1) *Applicant for asylum.* If the alien is a principal applicant who filed for asylum before December 31, 1995, the applicant must provide with the application either:

(i) A photocopy of the first page of the Application for Asylum and Withholding of Removal (Form I–589); or

(ii) If the alien is not in possession of a photocopy of the first page of the Form I–589, a statement to that effect giving the date of filing and the location of the Service office or Immigration Court at which it was filed;

(2) *Parolee.* If the alien is a principal applicant who was paroled into the United States prior to December 31, 1995, after having been identified as having a credible fear of persecution, or paroled for emergent reasons or reasons deemed strictly in the public interest, the applicant must provide with the application either:

(i) A photocopy of the Arrival-Departure Record (Form I–94) issued when he or she was granted parole; or

(ii) If the alien is not in possession of the original Form I–94, a statement to that effect giving the date of parole and the location of the Service port-of-entry at which parole was authorized.

(3) *Child without parents.* If the alien is a principal applicant who arrived in the United States as a child without parents in the United States, the applicant must provide with the application:

(i) Evidence, showing the date, location, and manner of his or her arrival in the United States, such as:

(A) A photocopy of the Form I–94 issued at the time of the alien's arrival in the United States;

(B) A copy of the airline or vessel records showing transportation to the United States;

(C) Other similar documentation; or

(D) If none of the documents in paragraphs (k)(3)(i)(A)–(C) of this section are available, a statement from the applicant, accompanied by whatever evidence the applicant is able to submit in support of that statement; and

(ii) Evidence establishing the absence of the child's parents, which may include either:

(A) Evidence showing the deaths of, or disappearance or desertion by, the applicant's parents; or

(B) Evidence showing that the applicant's parents did not live in the United States with the applicant. Such evidence may include, but is not limited to, documentation or affidavits showing that the applicant's parents have been continuously employed outside the United States, are deceased, disappeared, or abandoned the applicant prior to the applicant's arrival, or were otherwise engaged in activities showing that they were not in the United States, or (if they have been in the United States) that the applicant and his or her parents did not reside together.

(4) *Orphaned child.* If the alien is a principal applicant who is or was a child who became orphaned subsequent to arrival in the United States, the applicant must provide with the application:

(i) Evidence, showing the date, location, and manner of his or her arrival in the United States, such as:

(A) A photocopy of the Form I–94 issued at the time of the alien's arrival in the United States;

(B) A copy of the airline or vessel records showing transportation to the United States;

(C) Other similar documentation; or

(D) If none of the documents in paragraphs (k)(4)(i)(A)–(C) of this section are available, a statement from the applicant, accompanied by whatever evidence the applicant is able to submit in support of that statement; and

(ii) Either:

(A) The death certificates of both parents (or in the case of a child having only one parent, the death certificate of the sole parent) showing that the death or deaths occurred after the date of the applicant's arrival in the United States;

(B) Evidence from a State, local, or other court or governmental authority having jurisdiction and authority to make decisions in matters of child welfare establishing the disappearance of, the separation or loss from, or desertion by, both parents (or, in the case of a child born out of wedlock who has not been legitimated, the sole parent); or

(C) Evidence of:

(*1*) Either:

(*i*) The child having only a sole parent, as that term is defined in § 204.3(b) of this chapter;

(*ii*) The death of one parent; or

(*iii*) Certification by competent Haitian authorities that one parent is presumed dead as a result of his or her disappearance, within the meaning of that term as set forth in § 204.3(b) of this chapter; and

(*2*) A copy of a written statement executed by the sole parent, or the sole remaining parent, irrevocably releasing all parental rights based upon the inability of that parent to provide proper care for the child.

(5) *Abandoned child.* If the alien is a principal applicant who was abandoned by parents or guardians prior to April 1, 1998, and has remained abandoned since such abandonment, the applicant must provide with the application:

(i) Evidence, showing the date, location, and manner of his or her arrival in the United States, such as:

(A) A photocopy of the Form I–94 issued at the time of the alien's arrival in the United States;

(B) A copy of the airline or vessel records showing transportation to the United States;

(C) Other similar documentation; or

(D) If none of the documents in paragraphs (k)(5)(i)(A)–(C) of this section are available, a statement from the applicant, accompanied by whatever evidence the applicant is able to submit in support of that statement; and

(ii) Either:

(A) Evidence from a State, local, or other court or governmental authority having jurisdiction and authority to make decisions in matters of child welfare establishing such abandonment; or

(B) Evidence to establish that the applicant would have been considered to be abandoned according to the laws of the State where he or she resides, or where he or she resided at the time of the abandonment, had the issue been presented to the proper authorities.

(l) *Evidence relating to applications by dependents under section 902(d) of HRIFA*—(1) *Evidence of spousal relationship.* If the alien is applying as the spouse of a principal HRIFA beneficiary, the applicant must provide with the application a copy of their certificate of marriage and copies of documents showing the legal termination of all other marriages by the applicant or the other beneficiary.

(2) *Evidence of parent-child relationship.* If the applicant is applying as the child, unmarried son, or unmarried daughter of a principal HRIFA beneficiary, and the principal beneficiary is not the applicant's biological mother, the applicant must provide with the application evidence to demonstrate the parent-child relationship between the principal beneficiary and the applicant. Such evidence may include copies of the applicant's parent's marriage certificate and documents showing the legal termination of all other marriages, an adoption decree, or other relevant evidence.

(m) *Secondary evidence.* Except as otherwise provided in this paragraph, if the primary evidence required in this section is unavailable, church or school records, or other secondary evidence pertinent to the facts in issue, may be submitted. If such documents are unavailable, affidavits may be submitted. The applicant may submit as many types of secondary evidence as necessary to establish birth, marriage, or other relevant events. Documentary evidence establishing that primary evidence is unavailable must accompany secondary evidence of birth or marriage in the home country. The unavailability of such documents may be shown by submission of a copy of the written request for a copy of such documents which was sent to the official keeper of the records. In adjudicating the application for adjustment of status under section 902 of HRIFA, the Service or immigration judge shall determine the weight to be given such secondary evidence. Secondary evidence may not be submitted in lieu of the documentation specified in paragraphs (i) or (j) of this section. However, subject to verification by the Service, if the documentation specified in this paragraph or in paragraphs (h)(3)(i), (i), (j), (l)(1), and (l)(2) of this section is already contained in the Service's file relating to the applicant, the applicant may submit an affidavit to that effect in lieu of the actual documentation.

(n) *Authorization to be employed in the United States while the application is pending*—(1) *Application for employment authorization.* An applicant for adjustment of status under section 902 of HRIFA who wishes to obtain initial or continued employment authorization during the pendency of the adjustment application must file an application on the form designated by USCIS with the fee prescribed in 8 CFR 103.7(b)(1) and in accordance with the form instructions. The applicant may submit the application either concurrently with or subsequent to the filing of the application for HRIFA benefits.

(2) *Adjudication and issuance.* Employment authorization may not be issued to an applicant for adjustment of status under section 902 of HRIFA until the adjustment application has been pending for 180 days, unless USCIS verifies that DHS records contain evidence that the applicant meets the criteria set forth in section 902(b) or 902(d) of HRIFA, and determines that there is no indication that the applicant is clearly ineligible for adjustment of status under section 902 of HRIFA, in which case USCIS may approve the application for employment authorization, and issue the resulting document, immediately upon such verification. If USCIS fails to adjudicate the application for employment authorization upon the expiration of the 180-day waiting period, or within 90 days of the filing of application for employment authorization, whichever comes later, the applicant shall be eligible for an employment authorization document. Nothing in this section shall preclude an applicant for adjustment of status under HRIFA from being granted an initial employment authorization or an extension of employment authorization under any other provision of law or regulation for which the applicant may be eligible.

(o) *Adjudication of HRIFA applications filed with the Service*—(1) *Referral for interview.* Except as provided in paragraphs (o)(2) and (o)(3) of this section, all aliens filing applications for adjustment of status with the Service under this section must be personally interviewed by an immigration officer at a local office of the Service. If the Director of the Nebraska Service Center determines that an interview of the applicant is necessary, the Director shall forward the case to the appropriate local Service office for interview and adjudication.

(2) *Approval without interview.* Upon examination of the application, including all other evidence submitted in support of the application, all relevant Service records and all other relevant law enforcement indices, the Director may approve the application without an interview if the Director determines that:

(i) The alien's claim to eligibility for adjustment of status under section 902 of HRIFA is verified through existing Service records; and

(ii) The alien is clearly eligible for adjustment of status.

(3) *Denial without interview.* If, upon examination of the application, all supporting documentation, all relevant Service records, and all other relevant law enforcement indices, the Director determines that the alien is clearly ineligible for adjustment of status under HRIFA and that an interview of the applicant is not necessary, the Director may deny the application.

(p) *Adjudication of HRIFA applications filed in pending exclusion, deportation, or removal proceedings*—(1) *Proceedings pending before an Immigration Court.* Except as provided in paragraph (p)(4) of this section, the Immigration Court shall have sole jurisdiction over an application for adjustment of status under this section filed by an alien who is in exclusion, deportation, or removal proceedings pending before an immigration judge or the Board, or who has a pending motion to reopen or motion to reconsider filed with an immigration judge or the Board on or before May 12, 1999. The immigration judge having jurisdiction over the exclusion, deportation, or removal proceedings shall have jurisdiction to accept and adjudicate any application for adjustment of status under section 902 of HRIFA during the course of such proceedings. All applications for adjustment of status under section 902 of HRIFA filed with an Immigration

Court shall be subject to the requirements of §§ 3.11 and 3.31 of this chapter.

(2) *Motion to reopen or motion to reconsider.* If an alien who has a pending motion to reopen or motion to reconsider timely filed with an immigration judge on or before May 12, 1999, files an application for adjustment of status under section 902 of HRIFA, the immigration judge shall reopen the alien's proceedings for consideration of the adjustment application, unless the alien is clearly ineligible for adjustment of status under section 902 of HRIFA.

(3) *Proceedings pending before the Board.* Except as provided in paragraph (d)(4) of this section, in the case of an alien who either has a pending appeal with the Board or has a pending motion to reopen or motion to reconsider timely filed with the Board on or before May 12, 1999, the Board shall remand, or reopen and remand, the proceedings to the Immigration Court for the sole purpose of adjudicating an application for adjustment of status under section 902 of HRIFA, unless the alien is clearly ineligible for adjustment of status under section 902 of HRIFA. If the immigration judge denies, or the alien fails to file, the application for adjustment of status under section 902 of HRIFA, the immigration judge shall certify the decision to the Board for consideration in conjunction with the applicant's previously pending appeal or motion.

(4) *Administrative closure of exclusion, deportation, or removal proceedings.* (i) An alien who is in exclusion, deportation, or removal proceedings, or who has a pending motion to reopen or a motion to reconsider such proceedings filed on or before May 12, 1999, may request that the proceedings be administratively closed, or that the motion be indefinitely continued, in order to allow the alien to file such application with the Service as prescribed in paragraph (g) of this section. If the alien appears to be eligible to file an application for adjustment of status under this section, the Immigration Court or the Board (whichever has jurisdiction) shall, with the concurrence of the Service, administratively close the proceedings or continue indefinitely the motion.

(ii) In the case of an otherwise-eligible alien whose exclusion, deportation, or removal proceedings have been administratively closed for reasons not specified in this section, the alien may only apply before the Service for adjustment of status under this section.

(q) *Approval of HRIFA applications*—(1) *Applications approved by the Service.* If the Service approves the application for adjustment of status under the provisions of section 902 of HRIFA, the director shall record the alien's lawful admission for permanent residence as of the date of such approval and notify the applicant accordingly. The director shall also advise the alien regarding the delivery of his or her Permanent Resident Card and of the process for obtaining temporary evidence of alien registration. If the alien had previously been issued a final order of exclusion, deportation, or removal, such order shall be deemed canceled as of the date of the director's approval of the application for adjustment of status. If the alien had been in exclusion, deportation, or removal proceedings that were administratively closed, such proceedings shall be deemed terminated as of the date of approval of the application for adjustment of status by the director.

(2) *Applications approved by an immigration judge or the Board.* If an immigration judge or (upon appeal) the Board grants an application for adjustment under the provisions of section 902 of HRIFA, the date of the alien's lawful admission for permanent residence shall be the date of such grant.

(r) *Review of decisions by the Service denying HRIFA applications*—(1)(i) *Denial notification.* If the Service denies the application for adjustment of status under the provisions of section 902 of HRIFA, the director shall notify the applicant of the decision and of any right to renew the application in proceedings before the Immigration Court.

(ii) An alien made eligible for adjustment of status under HRIFA by the LIFE Act amendments and whose case has not been referred to EOIR under paragraphs (r)(2) or (r)(3) of this section, may file a motion to reopen with the Service.

(2) *Renewal of application for HRIFA benefits in removal, deportation, or exclusion proceedings.* An alien who is not the subject of a final order of removal, deportation, or exclusion may renew his or her application for adjustment under section 902 of HRIFA during the course of such removal, deportation, or exclusion proceedings.

(i) *Initiation of removal proceedings.* In the case of an alien who is not maintaining valid nonimmigrant status and who had not previously been placed in exclusion, deportation, or removal proceedings, the director shall initiate removal proceedings in accordance with § 239.1 of this chapter.

(ii) *Recalendaring or reinstatement of prior proceedings.* In the case of an alien whose previously initiated exclusion, deportation, or removal proceeding had been administratively closed or continued indefinitely under paragraph (p)(4) of this section, the director shall make a request for recalendaring or reinstatement to the Immigration Court that had administratively closed the proceeding, or the Board, as appropriate, when the application has been denied. The Immigration Court or the Board will then recalendar or reinstate the prior exclusion, deportation, or removal proceeding.

(iii) *Filing of renewed application.* A principal alien may file a renewed application for HRIFA benefits with the Immigration Court either before or after March 31, 2000, if he or she had filed his or her initial application for such benefits with the Service on or before March 31, 2000. A dependent of a principal applicant may file such renewed application with the Immigration Court either before or after March 31, 2000, regardless of when he or she filed his or her initial application for HRIFA benefits with the Service.

(3) *Aliens with final orders.* In the case of an alien who is the subject of an outstanding final order of exclusion, deportation, or removal, the Service shall refer the decision to deny the application by filing a Notice of Certification (Form I–290C) with the Immigration Court that issued the final order for consideration in accordance with paragraph (s) of this section.

(4)(i) An alien whose case has been referred to the Immigration Court under paragraphs (r)(2) or (r)(3) of this section, or who filed an appeal with the Board after his or her application for adjustment of status under section 902 of HRIFA was denied, and whose proceedings are pending, and who is now eligible for adjustment of status under HRIFA as amended by section 1505(b) of the LIFE Act and its amendments, may renew the application for adjustment of status with either the Immigration Court or the Board, whichever has jurisdiction. The application will be adjudicated in accordance with section 1505(b) of the LIFE Act and its amendments.

(ii) An alien present in the United States who is subject to a final order of exclusion, deportation or removal after his or her HRIFA adjustment application was denied by an Immigration Court or the Board, but who was made eligible for HRIFA adjustment as a result of section 1505(b) of the LIFE Act and its amendments, may file a motion to reopen with either the Immigration Court or the Board, whichever had jurisdiction last. Such motion to reopen must be filed on or before June 19, 2001.

(s) *Action of immigration judge upon referral of decision by a notice of certification*—(1) *General.* Upon the referral by a notice of certification of a decision to deny the application, in accordance with paragraph (r)(3) of this section, the immigration judge will conduct a hearing to determine whether the alien is eligible for adjustment of status under section 902 of HRIFA in accordance with this paragraph (s)(1).

(2) *Stay pending review.* When the Service refers a decision to the Immigration Court on a Notice of Certification (Form I–290C) in accordance with paragraph (r)(3) of this section, the referral shall not stay the execution of the final order. Execution of such final order shall proceed unless a stay of execution is specifically granted by the immigration judge, the Board, or an authorized Service officer.

(3) *Appeal of Immigration Court decision.* Once the immigration judge issues his or her decision on the application, either the alien or the Service may appeal the decision to the Board. Such appeal must be filed pursuant to the requirements for appeals to the Board

from an Immigration Court decision set forth in §§ 3.3 and 3.8 of this chapter.

(4) *Rescission or reopening of the decision of an Immigration Court.* The decision of an Immigration Court under paragraph (s)(1) of this section denying an application for adjustment under section 902 of HRIFA for failure to appear may be rescinded or reopened only:

(i) Upon a motion to reopen filed within 180 days after the date of the denial if the alien demonstrates that the failure to appear was because of exceptional circumstances as defined in section 240(e)(1) of the Act;

(ii) Upon a motion to reopen filed at any time if the alien demonstrates that he or she did not receive notice of the hearing in person (or, if personal service was not practicable, through service by mail to the alien or to the alien's counsel of record, if any) or the alien demonstrates that he or she was in Federal or State custody and the failure to appear was through no fault of the alien; or

(iii) Upon a motion to reopen filed not later than June 19, 2001, by an alien present in the United States who became eligible for adjustment of status under HRIFA, as amended by section 1505, of Public Law 106–554.

(t) *Parole authorization for purposes of travel*—(1) *Travel from and return to the United States while the application for adjustment of status is pending.* If an applicant for benefits under section 902 of HRIFA desires to travel outside, and return to, the United States while the application for adjustment of status is pending, he or she must file a request for advance parole authorization on the form designated by USCIS with the fee prescribed in 8 CFR 103.7(b)(1) and in accordance with the form instructions. Unless the applicant files an advance parole request prior to departing from the United States and USCIS approves such request, his or her application for adjustment of status under section 902 of HRIFA is deemed to be abandoned as of the moment of departure. Parole may only be authorized pursuant to the authority contained in, and the standards prescribed in, section 212(d)(5) of the Act.

(2) *Parole authorization for the purpose of filing an application for adjustment of status under section 902 of HRIFA.* (i) An otherwise eligible applicant who is outside the United States and wishes to come to the United States in order to apply for benefits under section 902 of HRIFA may request parole authorization for such purpose by filing a request on the form designated by USCIS with the fee prescribed in 8 CFR 103.7(b)(1) and in accordance with the form instructions. Such application must be supported by a photocopy of the application for adjustment of status that the alien will file once he or she has been paroled into the United States. The applicant must include photocopies of all the supporting documentation listed in paragraph (h) of this section, except the filing fee, the medical report, the fingerprint card, and the local police clearances.

(ii) If the Director of the Nebraska Service Center is satisfied that the alien will be eligible for adjustment of status once the alien has been paroled into the United States and files the application, he or she may issue an Authorization for Parole of an Alien into the United States (Form I–512) to allow the alien to travel to, and be paroled into, the United States for a period of 60 days.

(iii) The applicant shall have 60 days from the date of parole to file the application for adjustment of status. If the alien files the application for adjustment of status within that 60-day period, the Service may re-parole the alien for such time as is necessary for adjudication of the application. Failure to file such application for adjustment of status within 60 days shall result in the alien being returned to the custody of the Service and being examined as an arriving alien applying for admission. Such examination will be conducted in accordance with the provisions of section 235(b)(1) of the Act if the alien is inadmissible under section 212(a)(6)(C) or 212(a)(7) of the Act, or section 240 of the Act if the alien is inadmissible under any other grounds.

(iv) Parole may only be authorized pursuant to the authority contained in, and the standards prescribed in, section 212(d)(5) of the Act. The authority of the Director of the Nebraska Service Center to authorize parole from outside the United States under this provision shall expire on March 31, 2000.

(3) *Effect of departure on an outstanding warrant of exclusion, deportation, or removal.* If an alien who is the subject of an outstanding final order of exclusion, deportation, or removal departs from the United States, with or without an advance parole authorization, such final order shall be executed by the alien's departure. The execution of such final order shall not preclude the applicant from filing an Application for Permission to Reapply for Admission Into the United States After Deportation or Removal (Form I–212) in accordance with §212.2 of this chapter.

(u) *Tolling the physical presence in the United States provision for certain individuals*—(1) *Departure with advance authorization for parole.* In the case of an alien who departed the United States after having been issued an Authorization for Parole of an Alien into the United States (Form I–512), and who returns to the United States in accordance with the conditions of that document, the physical presence in the United States requirement of section 902(b)(1) of HRIFA is tolled while the alien is outside the United States pursuant to the issuance of the Form I–512.

(2) *Request for parole authorization from outside the United States.* In the case of an alien who is outside the United States and submits an application for parole authorization in accordance with paragraph (t)(2) of this section, and such application for parole authorization is granted by the Service, the physical presence requirement contained in section 902(b)(1) of HRIFA is tolled from the date the application is received at the Nebraska Service Center until the alien is paroled into the United States pursuant to the issuance of the Form I–512.

(3) *Departure without advance authorization for parole.* In the case of an otherwise-eligible applicant who departed the United States on or before December 31, 1998, the physical presence in the United States provision of section 902(b)(1) of HRIFA is tolled as of October 21, 1998, and until July 12, 1999.

(v) *Judicial review of HRIFA adjustment of status determinations.* Pursuant to the provisions of section 902(f) of HRIFA, there shall be no judicial appeal or review of any administrative determination as to whether the status of an alien should be adjusted under the provisions of section 902 of HRIFA.

[64 FR 25767, May 12, 1999, as amended at 65 FR 15844, Mar. 24, 2000; 66 FR 29452, May 1, 2001; 67 FR 78673, Dec. 26, 2002; 76 FR 53793, Aug. 29, 2011; 78 FR 18472, Mar. 27, 2013]

§245.18 Physicians with approved employment-based petitions serving in a medically underserved area or a Veterans Affairs facility.

(a) *Which physicians are eligible for this benefit?* Any alien physician who has been granted a national interest waiver under §204.12 of this chapter may submit Form I–485 during the 6-year period following Service approval of a second preference employment-based immigrant visa petition.

(b) *Do alien physicians have special time-related requirements for adjustment?* (1) Alien physicians who have been granted a national interest waiver under §204.12 of this chapter must meet all the adjustment of status requirements of this part.

(2) The Service shall not approve an adjustment application filed by an alien physician who obtained a waiver under section 203(b)(2)(B)(ii) of the Act until the alien physician has completed the period of required service established in §204.12 of this chapter.

(c) *Are the filing procedures and documentary requirements different for these particular alien physicians?* Alien physicians submitting adjustment applications upon approval of an immigrant petition are required to follow the procedures outlined within this part with the following modifications.

(1) Delayed fingerprinting. Fingerprinting, as noted in the Form I–485 instructions, will not be scheduled at the time of filing. Fingerprinting will be scheduled upon the physician's completion of the required years of service.

(2) Delayed medical examination. The required medical examination, as specified in §245.5, shall not be submitted with Form I–485. The medical examination report shall be submitted with the documentary evidence noting the physician's completion of the required years of service.

(d) *Employment authorization.* (1) Once USCIS has approved a petition described in paragraph (a) of this section, the alien physician may apply for permanent residence and employment authorization on the forms designated by USCIS with the fee prescribed in 8 CFR 103.7(b)(1) and in accordance with the form instructions.

(2) Since section 203(b)(2)(B)(ii) of the Act requires the alien physician to complete the required employment before USCIS can approve the alien physician's adjustment application, an alien physician who was in lawful nonimmigrant status when he or she filed the adjustment application is not required to maintain a nonimmigrant status while the adjustment application remains pending. Even if the alien physician's nonimmigrant status expires, the alien physician shall not be considered to be unlawfully present, so long as the alien physician is practicing medicine in accordance with § 204.5(k)(4)(iii) of this chapter.

(e) *When does the Service begin counting the physician's 5-year or 3-year medical practice requirement?* Except as provided in this paragraph, the 6-year period during which a physician must provide the required 5 years of service begins on the date of the notice approving the Form I–140 and the national interest waiver. Alien physicians who have a 3-year medical practice requirement must complete their service within the 4-year period beginning on that date.

(1) If the physician does not already have employment authorization and so must obtain employment authorization before the physician can begin working, then the period begins on the date the Service issues the employment authorization document.

(2) If the physician formerly held status as a J–1 nonimmigrant, but obtained a waiver of the foreign residence requirement and a change of status to that of an H–1B nonimmigrant, pursuant to section 214(l) of the Act, as amended by section 220 of Public Law 103–416, and § 212.7(c)(9) of this chapter, the period begins on the date of the alien's change from J–1 to H–1B status. The Service will include the alien's compliance with the 3-year period of service required under section 214(l) in calculating the alien's compliance with the period of service required under section 203(b)(2)(B)(ii)(II) of the Act and this section.

(3) An alien may not include any time employed as a J–1 nonimmigrant physician in calculating the alien's compliance with the 5 or 3-year medical practice requirement. If an alien is still in J–1 nonimmigrant status when the Service approves a Form I–140 petition with a national interest job offer waiver, the aggregate period during which the medical practice requirement period must be completed will begin on the date the Service issues an employment authorization document.

(f) *Will the Service provide information to the physician about evidence and supplemental filings?* The Service shall provide the physician with the information and the projected timetables for completing the adjustment process, as described in this paragraph. If the physician either files the Form I–485 concurrently with or waits to subsequently file the Form I–485 while the previously filed Form I–140 is still pending, then the Service will given this information upon approval of the Form I–140. If the physician does not file the adjustment application until after approval of the Form I–140 visa petition, the Service shall provide this information upon receipt of the Form I–485 adjustment application.

(1) The Service shall note the date that the medical service begins (provided the physician already had work authorization at the time the Form I–140 was filed) or the date that an employment authorization document was issued.

(2) A list of the evidence necessary to satisfy the requirements of paragraphs (g) and (h) of this section.

(3) A projected timeline noting the dates that the physician will need to submit preliminary evidence two years and 120 days into his or her medical service in an underserved area or VA facility, and a projected date six years and 120 days in the future on which the physician's final evidence of completed medical service will be due.

(g) *Will physicians be required to file evidence prior to the end of the 5 or 3-year period?* (1) For physicians with a 5-year service requirement, no later than 120 days after the second anniversary of the approval of Petition for Immigrant Worker, Form I–140, the alien physician must submit to the Service Center having jurisdiction over his or her place of employment documentary evidence that proves the physician has in fact fulfilled at least 12 months of qualifying employment. This may be accomplished by submitting the following.

(i) Evidence noted in paragraph (h) of this section that is available at the second anniversary of the I–140 approval.

(ii) Documentation from the employer attesting to the fill-time medical practice and the date on which the physician began his or her medical service.

(2) Physicians with a 3-year service requirement are not required to make a supplemental filing, and must only comply with the requirements of paragraph (h) of this section.

(h) *What evidence is needed to prove final compliance with the service requirement?* No later than 120 days after completion of the service requirement established under § 204.12(a) of this section, an alien physician must submit to the Service Center having jurisdiction over his or her place of employment documentary evidence that proves the physician has in fact satisfied the service requirement. Such evidence must include, but is not limited to:

(1) Individual Federal income tax returns, including copies of the alien'sW-2 forms, for the entire 3-year period or the balance years of the 5-year period that follow the submission of the evidence required in paragraph (e) of this section;

(2) Documentation from the employer attesting to the full-time medical service rendered during the required aggregate period. The documentation shall address instances of breaks in employment, other than routine breaks such as paid vacations;

(3) If the physician established his or her own practice, documents noting the actual establishment of the practice, including incorporation of the medical practice (if incorporated), the business license, and the business tax returns and tax withholding documents submitted for the entire 3 year period, or the balance years of the 5-year period that follow the submission of the evidence required in paragraph (e) of this section.

(i) *What if the physician does not comply with the requirements of paragraphs (f) and (g) of this section?* If an alien physician does not submit (in accordance with paragraphs (f) and (g) of this section) proof that he or she has completed the service required under 8 CFR 204.12(a), USCIS shall serve the alien physician with a written notice of intent to deny the alien physician's application for adjustment of status and, after the denial is finalized, to revoke approval of the Form I–140 and national interest waiver. The written notice shall require the alien physician to provide the evidence required by paragraph (f) or (g) of this section. If the alien physician fails to submit the evidence within the allotted time, USCIS shall deny the alien physician's application for adjustment of status and shall revoke approval of the Form I–140 and of the national interest waiver.

(j) *Will a Service officer interview the physician?* (1) Upon submission of the evidence noted in paragraph (h) of this section, the Service shall match the documentary evidence with the pending form I–485 and schedule the alien physician for fingerprinting at an Application Support Center.

(2) The local Service office shall schedule the alien for an adjustment interview with a Service officer, unless the Service waives the interview as provided in § 245.6. The local Service office shall also notify the alien if supplemental documentation should either be mailed to the office, or brought to the adjustment interview.

(k) *Are alien physicians allowed to travel outside the United States during the mandatory 3 or 5-year service period?* An alien physician who has been granted a national interest waiver under § 204.12 of this chapter and has a pending application for adjustment of status may travel outside of the United States during the required 3 or 5-year service period by obtaining advanced parole prior to traveling. Such physicians may apply for advance parole on the form designated by USCIS with the fee prescribed in 8 CFR 103.7(b)(1) and in accordance with the form instructions.

(l) *What if the Service denies the adjustment application?* If the Service denies the adjustment application, the alien physician may renew the application in removal proceedings.

[65 FR 53895, Sept. 6, 2000; 65 FR 57861, Sept. 26, 2000; 65 FR 57944, Sept. 27, 2000; 67 FR 49563, July 31, 2002; 72 FR 19107, Apr. 17, 2007; 76 FR 53793, Aug. 29, 2011; 81 FR 82490, Nov. 18, 2016]

§ 245.20 [Reserved]

§ 245.21 Adjustment of status of certain nationals of Vietnam, Cambodia, and Laos (section 586 of Public Law 106–429).

(a) *Eligibility.* USCIS may adjust the status to that of a lawful permanent resident, a native or citizen of Vietnam, Cambodia, or Laos who:

(1) Was inspected and paroled into the United States before October 1, 1997;

(2) Was paroled into the United States from Vietnam under the auspices of the Orderly Departure Program (ODP), a refugee camp in East Asia, or a displaced person camp administered by the United Nations High Commissioner for Refugees (UNHCR) in Thailand;

(3) Was physically present in the United States prior to and on October 1, 1997; and

(4) Is otherwise eligible to receive an immigrant visa and is otherwise admissible as an immigrant to the United States except as provided in paragraphs (e) and (f) of this section.

(b) *Application.* An applicant must submit an application on the form designated by USCIS with the fee specified in 8 CFR 103.7(b)(1) and in accordance with the form instructions. Applicants who are 14 through 79 years of age must also submit the biometrics service fee described in 8 CFR 103.17.

(c) *Applications from aliens in immigration proceedings.* An alien in pending immigration proceedings who believes he or she is eligible for adjustment of status under section 586 of Public Law 106–429 must apply directly to USCIS in accordance with paragraph (b) of this section. An immigration judge or the Board of Immigration Appeals may not adjudicate applications for adjustment of status under this section. An alien who is currently in immigration proceedings who alleges eligibility for adjustment of status under section 586 of Public Law 106–429 may contact USCIS counsel after filing an application to request the consent of USCIS to the filing of a joint motion for administrative closure. Unless USCIS consents to such a motion, the immigration judge or the Board may not defer or dismiss the proceeding in connection with section 586 of Public Law 106–429.

(d) *Applications from aliens with final orders of removal, deportation, or exclusion.* An alien with a final order of removal, deportation, or exclusion who believes he or she is eligible for adjustment of status under section 586 of Public Law 106–429 must apply directly to USCIS in accordance with paragraph (b) of this section.

(1) An application under this section does not automatically stay the order of removal, deportation, or exclusion. An alien who is eligible for adjustment of status under section 586 of Public Law 106–429 may request a stay of removal during the pendency of the application. The regulations governing such a request are found at 8 CFR 241.6.

(2) DHS will exercise its discretion not to grant a stay of removal, deportation, or exclusion with respect to an alien who is inadmissible on any of the grounds specified in paragraph (m)(3) of this section, unless there is substantial reason to believe that USCIS will grant the necessary waivers of inadmissibility.

(3) An immigration judge or the Board may not grant a motion to reopen or stay in connection with an application under this section.

(4) If USCIS approves the application, the approval will constitute the automatic re-opening of the alien's immigration proceedings, vacating of the final order of removal, deportation, or exclusion, and termination of the reopened proceedings.

(e) *Grounds of inadmissibility that do not apply.* In making a determination of whether an applicant is otherwise eligible for admission to the United States for lawful permanent residence under the provisions of section 586 of Public Law 106–429, the grounds of inadmissibility under sections 212(a)(4), (a)(5), (a)(7)(A), and (a)(9) of the Act shall not apply.

(f) *Waiver of grounds of inadmissibility.* In connection with an application for adjustment of status under this section, the alien may apply for a waiver of the grounds of inadmissibility under sections 212(a)(1), (a)(6)(B), (a)(6)(C), (a)(6)(F), (a)(8)(A), (a)(10)(B), and (a)(10)(D) of the Act as provided in section 586(c) of Public Law 106–429, if the alien demonstrates that a waiver is necessary to prevent extreme hardship to the alien, or to the alien's spouse, parent, son or daughter who is a U.S. citizen or an alien lawfully admitted for permanent residence. In addition, the alien may apply for any other waiver of inadmissibility under section 212 of the Act, if eligible. In order to obtain a waiver for any of these grounds, the applicant must submit an application on the form designated by USCIS with the fee prescribed in 8 CFR 103.7(b)(1) and in accordance with the form instructions.

(g) *Evidence.* Applicants must submit evidence that demonstrates they are eligible for adjustment of status under section 586 of Public Law 106–429. Such evidence shall include the following:

(1) A birth certificate or other record of birth;

(2) Documentation to establish that the applicant was physically present in the United States on October 1, 1997, under the standards set forth in § 245.22 of this chapter.

(3) A copy of the applicant's Arrival-Departure Record (Form I–94) (see § 1.4) or other evidence that the alien was inspected or paroled into the United States prior to October 1, 1997, from one of the three programs listed in paragraph (a)(2) of this section. Subject to verification, documentation pertaining to paragraph (a)(2) of this section is already contained in USCIS files and the applicant may submit an affidavit to that effect in lieu of actual documentation.

(h) *Employment authorization.* Applicants who want to obtain employment authorization based on a pending application for adjustment of status under this section may apply on the form specified by USCIS with the fee prescribed in 8 CFR 103.7(b)(1) and in accordance with the form instructions.

(i) *Travel while an application to adjust status is pending.* An applicant who wishes to travel outside the United States while the application is pending must obtain advance permission by filing the application specified by USCIS with the fee prescribed in 8 CFR 103.7(b)(1) and in accordance with the form instructions.

(j) *Approval and date of admission as a lawful permanent resident.* When USCIS approves an application to adjust status to that of lawful permanent resident based on section 586 of Public Law 106–429, the applicant will be notified in writing of USCIS's decision. In addition, the record of the alien's admission as a lawful permanent resident will be recorded as of the date of the alien's inspection and parole into the United States, as described in paragraph (a)(1) of this section.

(k) *Notice of denial.* When USCIS denies an application to adjust status to that of lawful permanent resident based on section 586 of Public Law 106–429, the applicant will be notified of the decision in writing.

(l) *Administrative review.* An alien whose application for adjustment of status under section 586 of Public Law 106–429 is denied by USCIS may appeal the decision to the Administrative Appeals Office in accordance with 8 CFR 103.3(a)(2).

[67 FR 78673, Dec. 26, 2002, as amended at 76 FR 53793, Aug. 29, 2011; 76 FR 73477, Nov. 29, 2011; 78 FR 18472, Mar. 27, 2013]

§ 245.22 Evidence to demonstrate an alien's physical presence in the United States on a specific date.

(a) *Evidence.* Generally, an alien who is required to demonstrate his or her physical presence in the United States on a specific date in connection with an application to adjust status to that of an alien lawfully admitted for permanent residence should submit evidence according to this section. In cases where a more specific regulation relating to a particular adjustment of status provision has been issued in the 8 CFR, such regulation is controlling to the extent that it conflicts with this section.

(b) *The number of documents.* If no one document establishes the alien's physical presence on the required date, he or she may submit several documents establishing his or her physical presence in the United States prior to and after that date.

(c) *DHS-issued documentation.* An applicant for permanent residence may demonstrate physical presence by submitting DHS-issued (or predecessor agency-issued) documentation such as an arrival-departure form or notice to appear in immigration proceedings.

(d) *Government-issued documentation.* To demonstrate physical presence on the required date, the alien may submit other government documentation. Other government documentation issued by a Federal, State, or local authority must bear the signature, seal, or other authenticating instrument of such authority (if the document normally bears such instrument), be dated at the time of issuance, and bear a date of issuance not later than the required date. For this purpose, the term Federal, State, or local authority includes any governmental, educational, or administrative function operated by Federal, State, county, or municipal officials. Examples of such other documentation include, but are not limited to:

(1) A state driver's license;

(2) A state identification card;

(3) A county or municipal hospital record;

(4) A public college or public school transcript;

(5) Income tax records;

(6) A certified copy of a Federal, State, or local governmental record that was created on or prior to the required date, shows that the applicant was present in the United States at the time, and establishes that the applicant sought in his or her own behalf, or some other party sought in the applicant's behalf, a benefit from the Federal, State, or local governmental agency keeping such record;

(7) A certified copy of a Federal, State, or local governmental record that was created on or prior to the required date, that shows that the applicant was present in the United States at the time, and establishes that the applicant submitted an income tax return, property tax payment, or similar submission or payment to the Federal, State, or local governmental agency keeping such record; or

(8) A transcript from a private or religious school that is registered with, or approved or licensed by, appropriate State or local authorities, accredited by the State or regional accrediting body, or by the appropriate private school association, or maintains enrollment records in accordance with State or local requirements or standards. Such evidence will only be accepted to document the physical presence of an alien who was in attendance and under the age of 21 on the specific date that physical presence in the United States is required.

(e) *Copies of records.* It shall be the responsibility of the applicant to obtain and submit copies of the records of any other government agency that the applicant desires to be considered in support of his or her application. If the alien is not in possession of such a document or documents, but believes that a copy is already contained in the Service file relating to him or her, he or she may submit a statement as to the name and location of the issuing Federal, State, or local government agency, the type of document and the date on which it was issued.

(f) *Other relevant document(s) and evaluation of evidence.* The adjudicator will consider any other relevant document(s) as well as evaluate all evidence submitted, on a case-by-case basis. The Service may require an interview when necessary.

(g) *Accuracy of documentation.* In all cases, any doubts as to the existence, authenticity, veracity, or accuracy of the documentation shall be resolved by the official government record, with records of the Service having precedence over the records of other agencies. Furthermore, determinations as to the weight to be given any particular document or item of evidence shall be solely within the discretion of the adjudicating authority.

[67 FR 78674, Dec. 26, 2002, as amended at 76 FR 53794, Aug. 29, 2011]

§ 245.23 Adjustment of aliens in T nonimmigrant classification.

(a) *Eligibility of principal T–1 applicants.* Except as described in paragraph (c) of this section, an alien may be granted adjustment of status to that of an alien lawfully admitted for permanent residence, provided the alien:

(1) Applies for such adjustment;

(2)(i) Was lawfully admitted to the United States as a T–1 nonimmigrant, as defined in 8 CFR 214.11(a)(2); and

(ii) Continues to hold such status at the time of application, or accrued 4 years in T–1 nonimmigrant status and files a complete application before April 13, 2009;

(3) Has been physically present in the United States for a continuous period of at least 3 years since the first date of lawful admission as a T–1 nonimmigrant, or has been physically present in the United States for a continuous period during the investigation or prosecution of acts of trafficking and the Attorney General has determined that the investigation or prosecution is complete, whichever period is less; except

(i) If the applicant has departed from the United States for any single period in excess of 90 days or for any periods in the aggregate exceeding 180 days, the applicant shall be considered to have failed to maintain continuous physical presence in the United States for purposes of section 245(l)(1)(A) of the Act; and

(ii) If the alien was granted T nonimmigrant status under 8 CFR 214.11, such alien's physical presence in the CNMI before, on, or after November 28, 2009, and subsequent to the grant of T nonimmigrant status, is considered as equivalent to presence in the United States pursuant to an admission in T nonimmigrant status.

(4) Is admissible to the United States under the Act, or otherwise has been granted a waiver by USCIS of any applicable ground of inadmissibility, at the time of examination for adjustment;

(5) Has been a person of good moral character since first being lawfully admitted as a T–1 nonimmigrant and until USCIS completes the adjudication of the application for adjustment of status; and

(6)(i) Has, since first being lawfully admitted as a T–1 nonimmigrant and until the conclusion of adjudication of the application, complied with any reasonable request for assistance in the investigation or prosecution of acts of trafficking, as defined in 8 CFR 214.11(a), or

(ii) Would suffer extreme hardship involving unusual and severe harm upon removal from the United States, as provided in 8 CFR 214.11(i).

(b) *Eligibility of derivative family members.* A derivative family member of a T–1 nonimmigrant status holder may be granted adjustment of status to that of an alien lawfully admitted for permanent residence, provided:

(1) The T–1 principal nonimmigrant has applied for adjustment of status under this section and meets the eligibility requirements described under subsection (a);

(2) The derivative family member was lawfully admitted to the United States in derivative T nonimmigrant status under section 101(a)(15)(T)(ii) of the Act, and continues to hold such status at the time of application;

(3) The derivative family member has applied for such adjustment; and

(4) The derivative family member is admissible to the United States under the Act, or otherwise has been granted a waiver by USCIS of any applicable ground of inadmissibility, at the time of examination for adjustment.

(c) *Exceptions.* An alien is not eligible for adjustment of status under paragraphs (a) or (b) of this section if:

(1) The alien's T nonimmigrant status has been revoked pursuant to 8 CFR 214.11(s);

(2) The alien is described in sections 212(a)(3), 212(a)(10)(C), or 212(a)(10)(E) of the Act; or

(3) The alien is inadmissible under any other provisions of section 212(a) of the Act and has not obtained a waiver of inadmissibility in accordance with 8 CFR 212.18 or 214.11(j). Where the applicant establishes that the victimization was a central reason for the applicant's unlawful presence in the United States, section 212(a)(9)(B)(iii) of the Act is not applicable, and the applicant need not obtain a waiver of that ground of inadmissibility. The applicant, however, must submit with the Form I–485 evidence sufficient to demonstrate that the victimization suffered was a central reason for the unlawful presence in the United States. To qualify for this exception, the victimization need not

be the sole reason for the unlawful presence but the nexus between the victimization and the unlawful presence must be more than tangential, incidental, or superficial.

(d) *Jurisdiction.* USCIS shall determine whether a T–1 applicant for adjustment of status under this section was lawfully admitted as a T–1 nonimmigrant and continues to hold such status, has been physically present in the United States during the requisite period, is admissible to the United States or has otherwise been granted a waiver of any applicable ground of inadmissibility, and has been a person of good moral character during the requisite period. The Attorney General shall determine whether the applicant received a reasonable request for assistance in the investigation or prosecution of acts of trafficking as defined in 8 CFR 214.11(a), and, if so, whether the applicant complied in such request. If the Attorney General determines that the applicant failed to comply with any reasonable request for assistance, USCIS shall deny the application for adjustment of status unless USCIS finds that the applicant would suffer extreme hardship involving unusual and severe harm upon removal from the United States.

(e) *Application*—(1) *General.* Each T–1 principal applicant and each derivative family member who is applying for adjustment of status must file Form I–485, Application to Register Permanent Residence or Adjust Status, and

(i) Accompanying documents, in accordance with the form instructions;

(ii) The fee prescribed in 8 CFR 103.7(b)(1) or an application for a fee waiver;

(iii) The biometric services fee prescribed by 8 CFR 103.7(b)(1) or an application for a fee waiver;

(iv) A photocopy of the alien's Form I–797, Notice of Action, granting T nonimmigrant status;

(v) A photocopy of all pages of the alien's most recent passport or an explanation of why the alien does not have a passport;

(vi) A copy of the alien's Form I–94 (see §1.4), Arrival-Departure Record; and

(vii) Evidence that the applicant was lawfully admitted in T nonimmigrant status and continues to hold such status at the time of application. For T nonimmigrants who traveled outside the United States and re-entered using an advance parole document issued under 8 CFR 245.2(a)(4)(ii)(B), the date that the alien was first admitted in lawful T status will be the date of admission for purposes of this section, regardless of how the applicant's Form I–94 "Arrival-Departure Record" is annotated.

(2) *T–1 principal applicants.* In addition to the items in paragraph (e)(1) of this section, T–1 principal applicants must submit:

(i) Evidence, including an affidavit from the applicant and a photocopy of all pages of all of the applicant's passports valid during the required period (or equivalent travel document or a valid explanation of why the applicant does not have a passport), that he or she has been continuously physically present in the United States for the requisite period as described in paragraph (a)(2) of this section. Applicants should submit evidence described in 8 CFR 245.22. A signed statement from the applicant attesting to the applicant's continuous physical presence alone will not be sufficient to establish this eligibility requirement. If additional documentation is not available, the applicant must explain why in an affidavit and provide additional affidavits from others with first-hand knowledge who can attest to the applicant's continuous physical presence by specific facts.

(A) If the applicant has departed from and returned to the United States while in T–1 nonimmigrant status, the applicant must submit supporting evidence showing the dates of each departure from the United States and the date, manner and place of each return to the United States.

(B) Applicants applying for adjustment of status under this section who have less than 3 years of continuous physical presence while in T–1 nonimmigrant status must submit a document signed by the Attorney General or his designee, attesting that the investigation or prosecution is complete.

(ii) Evidence of good moral character in accordance with paragraph (g) of this section; and (iii)(A) Evidence that the alien has complied with any reasonable request for assistance in the investigation or prosecution of the trafficking as described in paragraph (f)(1) of this section since having first been lawfully admitted in T–1 nonimmigrant status and until the adjudication of the application; or

(B) Evidence that the alien would suffer extreme hardship involving unusual and severe harm if removed from the United States as described in paragraph (f)(2) of this section.

(3) *Evidence relating to discretion.* Each T applicant bears the burden of showing that discretion should be exercised in his or her favor. Where adverse factors are present, an applicant may offset these by submitting supporting documentation establishing mitigating equities that the applicant wants USCIS to consider. Depending on the nature of adverse factors, the applicant may be required to clearly demonstrate that the denial of adjustment of status would result in exceptional and extremely unusual hardship. Moreover, depending on the gravity of the adverse factors, such a showing might still be insufficient. For example, only the most compelling positive factors would justify a favorable exercise of discretion in cases where the applicant has committed or been convicted of a serious violent crime, a crime involving sexual abuse committed upon a child, or multiple drug-related crimes, or where there are security- or terrorism-related concerns.

(f) *Assistance in the investigation or prosecution or a showing of extreme hardship.* Each T–1 principal applicant must establish, to the satisfaction of the Attorney General, that since having been lawfully admitted as a T–1 nonimmigrant and up until the adjudication of the application, he or she complied with any reasonable request for assistance in the investigation or prosecution of the acts of trafficking, as defined in 8 CFR 214.11(a), or establish, to the satisfaction of USCIS, that he or she would suffer extreme hardship involving unusual and severe harm upon removal from the United States.

(1) Each T–1 applicant for adjustment of status under section 245(*l*) of the Act must submit a document issued by the Attorney General or his designee certifying that the applicant has complied with any reasonable requests for assistance in the investigation or prosecution of the human trafficking offenses during the requisite period; or

(2) In lieu of showing continued compliance with requests for assistance, an applicant may establish, to the satisfaction of USCIS, that he or she would suffer extreme hardship involving unusual and severe harm upon removal from the United States. The hardship determination will be evaluated on a case-by-case basis, in accordance with the factors described in 8 CFR 214.11(i). Where the basis for the hardship claim represents a continuation of the hardship claimed in the application for T nonimmigrant status, the applicant need not re-document the entire claim, but rather may submit evidence to establish that the previously established hardship is ongoing. However, in reaching its decision regarding hardship under this section, USCIS is not bound by its previous hardship determination made under 8 CFR 214.11(i).

(g) *Good moral character.* A T–1 nonimmigrant applicant for adjustment of status under this section must demonstrate that he or she has been a person of good moral character since first being lawfully admitted as a T–1 nonimmigrant and until USCIS completes the adjudication of their applications for adjustment of status. Claims of good moral character will be evaluated on a case-by-case basis, taking into account section 101(f) of the Act and the standards of the community. The applicant must submit evidence of good moral character as follows:

(1) An affidavit from the applicant attesting to his or her good moral character, accompanied by a local police clearance or a state-issued criminal background check from each locality or state in the United States in which the applicant has resided for 6 or more months during the requisite period in continued presence or T–1 nonimmigrant status.

(2) If police clearances, criminal background checks, or similar reports are not available for some or all locations, the applicant may include an explanation and submit other evidence with his or her affidavit.

(3) USCIS will consider other credible evidence of good moral character, such as affidavits from responsible persons who can knowledgeably attest to the applicant's good moral character.

(4) An applicant who is under 14 years of age is generally presumed to be a person of good moral character and is not required to submit evidence of good moral character. However, if there is reason to believe that an applicant who is under 14 years of age may lack good moral character, USCIS may require evidence of good moral character.

(h) *Filing and decision.* An application for adjustment of status from a T nonimmigrant under section 245(*l*) of the Act shall be filed with the USCIS office identified in the instructions to Form I–485. Upon approval of adjustment of status under this section, USCIS will record the alien's lawful admission for permanent residence as of the date of such approval and will notify the applicant in writing. Derivative family members' applications may not be approved before the principal applicant's application is approved.

(i) *Denial.* If the application for adjustment of status or the application for a waiver of inadmissibility is denied, USCIS will notify the applicant in writing of the reasons for the denial and of the right to appeal the decision to the Administrative Appeals Office (AAO) pursuant to the AAO appeal procedures found at 8 CFR 103.3. Denial of the T–1 principal applicant's application will result in the automatic denial of a derivative family member's application.

(j) *Effect of Departure.* If an applicant for adjustment of status under this section departs the United States, he or she shall be deemed to have abandoned the application, and it will be denied. If, however, the applicant is not under exclusion, deportation, or removal proceedings, and he or she filed a Form I–131, Application for Travel Document, in accordance with the instructions on the form, or any other appropriate form, and was granted advance parole by USCIS for such absences, and was inspected and paroled upon returning to the United States, he or she will not be deemed to have abandoned the application. If the adjustment of status application of such an individual is subsequently denied, he or she will be treated as an applicant for admission subject to sections 212 and 235 of the Act. If an applicant for adjustment of status under this section is under exclusion, deportation, or removal proceedings, USCIS will deem the application for adjustment of status abandoned as of the moment of the applicant's departure from the United States.

(k) *Inapplicability of 8 CFR 245.1 and 245.2.* Sections 245.1 and 245.2 of this chapter do not apply to aliens seeking adjustment of status under this section.

(l) *Annual cap of T–1 principal applicant adjustments.* (1) *General.* The total number of T–1 principal applicants whose status is adjusted to that of lawful permanent residents under this section may not exceed the statutory cap in any fiscal year.

(2) *Waiting list.* All eligible applicants who, due solely to the limit imposed in section 245(*l*)(4) of the Act and paragraph (m)(1) of this section, are not granted adjustment of status will be placed on a waiting list. USCIS will send the applicant written notice of such placement. Priority on the waiting list will be determined by the date the application was properly filed, with the oldest applications receiving the highest priority. In the following fiscal year, USCIS will proceed with granting adjustment of status to applicants on the waiting list who remain admissible and eligible for adjustment of status in order of highest priority until the available numbers are exhausted for the given fiscal year. After the status of qualifying applicants on the waiting list has been adjusted, any remaining numbers for that fiscal year will be issued to new qualifying applicants in the order that the applications were properly filed.

[73 FR 75558, Dec. 12, 2008, as amended at 78 FR 18472, Mar. 27, 2013; 81 FR 92312, Dec. 19, 2016]

§ 245.24 Adjustment of aliens in U nonimmigrant status.

(a) *Definitions.* As used in this section, the term:

(1) *Continuous Physical Presence* means the period of time that the alien has been physically present in the

United States and must be a continuous period of at least 3 years since the date of admission as a U nonimmigrant continuing through the date of the conclusion of adjudication of the application for adjustment of status. If the alien has departed from the United States for any single period in excess of 90 days or for any periods in the aggregate exceeding 180 days, the applicant must include a certification from the agency that signed the Form I-918, Supplement B, in support of the alien's U nonimmigrant status that the absences were necessary to assist in the criminal investigation or prosecution or were otherwise justified.

(2) *Qualifying Family Member* means a U-1 principal applicant's spouse, child, or, in the case of an alien child, a parent who has never been admitted to the United States as a nonimmigrant under sections 101(a)(15)(U) and 214(p) of the Act.

(3) *U Interim Relief* means deferred action and work authorization benefits provided by USCIS or the Immigration and Naturalization Service to applicants for U nonimmigrant status deemed *prima facie* eligible for U nonimmigrant status prior to publication of the U nonimmigrant status regulations.

(4) *U Nonimmigrant* means an alien who is in lawful U-1, U-2, U-3, U-4, or U-5 status.

(5) *Refusal to Provide Assistance in a Criminal Investigation or Prosecution* is the refusal by the alien to provide assistance to a law enforcement agency or official that had responsibility for the investigation or prosecution of persons in connection with the qualifying criminal activity after the alien was granted U nonimmigrant status. The Attorney General will determine whether the alien's refusal was unreasonable under the totality of the circumstances based on all available affirmative evidence. The Attorney General may take into account such factors as general law enforcement, prosecutorial, and judicial practices; the kinds of assistance asked of other victims of crimes involving an element of force, coercion, or fraud; the nature of the request to the alien for assistance; the nature of the victimization; the applicable guidelines for victim and witness assistance; and the specific circumstances of the applicant, including fear, severe traumatization (both mental and physical), and the age and maturity of the applicant.

(b) *Eligibility of U Nonimmigrants.* Except as described in paragraph (c) of this section, an alien may be granted adjustment of status to that of an alien lawfully admitted for permanent residence, provided the alien:

(1) Applies for such adjustment;

(2)(i) Was lawfully admitted to the United States as either a U-1, U-2, U-3, U-4 or U-5 nonimmigrant, as defined in 8 CFR 214.1(a)(2), and

(ii) Continues to hold such status at the time of application; or accrued at least 4 years in U interim relief status and files a complete adjustment application within 120 days of the date of approval of the Form I-918, Petition for U Nonimmigrant Status;

(3) Has continuous physical presence for 3 years as defined in paragraph (a)(1) of this section;

(4) Is not inadmissible under section 212(a)(3)(E) of the Act;

(5) Has not unreasonably refused to provide assistance to an official or law enforcement agency that had responsibility in an investigation or prosecution of persons in connection with the qualifying criminal activity after the alien was granted U nonimmigrant status, as determined by the Attorney General, based on affirmative evidence; and

(6) Establishes to the satisfaction of the Secretary that the alien's presence in the United States is justified on humanitarian grounds, to ensure family unity, or is in the public interest.

(c) *Exception.* An alien is not eligible for adjustment of status under paragraph (b) of this section if the alien's U nonimmigrant status has been revoked pursuant to 8 CFR 214.14(h).

(d) *Application Procedures for U nonimmigrants.* Each U nonimmigrant who is requesting adjustment of status must submit:

(1) Form I-485, Application to Register Permanent Residence or Adjust Status, in accordance with the form instructions;

(2) The fee prescribed in 8 CFR 103.7(b)(1) or an application for a fee waiver;

(3) The biometric services fee as prescribed in 8 CFR 103.7(b)(1) or an application for a fee waiver;

(4) A photocopy of the alien's Form I–797, Notice of Action, granting U nonimmigrant status;

(5) A photocopy of all pages of all of the applicant's passports valid during the required period (or equivalent travel document or a valid explanation of why the applicant does not have a passport) and documentation showing the following:

(i) The date of any departure from the United States during the period that the applicant was in U nonimmigrant status;

(ii) The date, manner, and place of each return to the United States during the period that the applicant was in U nonimmigrant status; and

(iii) If the applicant has been absent from the United States for any period in excess of 90 days or for any periods in the aggregate of 180 days or more, a certification from the investigating or prosecuting agency that the absences were necessary to assist in the investigation or prosecution of the criminal activity or were otherwise justified;

(6) A copy of the alien's Form I–94 (see § 1.4), Arrival-Departure Record;

(7) Evidence that the applicant was lawfully admitted in U nonimmigrant status and continues to hold such status at the time of application;

(8) Evidence pertaining to any request made to the alien by an official or law enforcement agency for assistance in an investigation or prosecution of persons in connection with the qualifying criminal activity, and the alien's response to such request;

(9) Evidence, including an affidavit from the applicant, that he or she has continuous physical presence for at least 3 years as defined in paragraph (a)(1) of this section. Applicants should submit evidence described in 8 CFR 245.22. A signed statement from the applicant attesting to continuous physical presence alone will not be sufficient to establish this eligibility requirement. If additional documentation is not available, the applicant must explain why in an affidavit and provide additional affidavits from others with first-hand knowledge who can attest to the applicant's continuous physical presence by specific facts;

(10) *Evidence establishing that approval is warranted.* Any other information required by the instructions to Form I–485, including whether adjustment of status is warranted as a matter of discretion on humanitarian grounds, to ensure family unity, or is otherwise in the public interest; and

(11) *Evidence relating to discretion.* An applicant has the burden of showing that discretion should be exercised in his or her favor. Although U adjustment applicants are not required to establish that they are admissible, USCIS may take into account all factors, including acts that would otherwise render the applicant inadmissible, in making its discretionary decision on the application. Where adverse factors are present, an applicant may offset these by submitting supporting documentation establishing mitigating equities that the applicant wants USCIS to consider when determining whether or not a favorable exercise of discretion is appropriate. Depending on the nature of the adverse factors, the applicant may be required to clearly demonstrate that the denial of adjustment of status would result in exceptional and extremely unusual hardship. Moreover, depending on the gravity of the adverse factors, such a showing might still be insufficient. For example, USCIS will generally not exercise its discretion favorably in cases where the applicant has committed or been convicted of a serious violent crime, a crime involving sexual abuse committed upon a child, or multiple drug-related crimes, or where there are security- or terrorism-related concerns.

(e) *Continued assistance in the investigation or prosecution.* Each applicant for adjustment of status under section 245(m) of the Act must provide evidence of whether or not any request was made to the alien to provide assistance, after having been lawfully admitted as a U nonimmigrant, in an investigation or prosecution of persons in connection with the qualifying criminal activity, and his or her response to any such requests.

(1) An applicant for adjustment of status under section 245(m) of the Act

may submit a document signed by an official or law enforcement agency that had responsibility for the investigation or prosecution of persons in connection with the qualifying criminal activity, affirming that the applicant complied with (or did not unreasonably refuse to comply with) reasonable requests for assistance in the investigation or prosecution during the requisite period. To meet this evidentiary requirement, applicants may submit a newly executed Form I–918, Supplement B, "U Nonimmigrant Status Certification."

(2) If the applicant does not submit a document described in paragraph (e)(1) of this section, the applicant may submit an affidavit describing the applicant's efforts, if any, to obtain a newly executed Form I–918, Supplement B, or other evidence describing whether or not the alien received any request to provide assistance in a criminal investigation or prosecution, and the alien's response to any such request.

(i) The applicant should also include, when possible, identifying information about the law enforcement personnel involved in the case and any information, of which the applicant is aware, about the status of the criminal investigation or prosecution, including any charges filed and the outcome of any criminal proceedings, or whether the investigation or prosecution was dropped and the reasons.

(ii) If applicable, an applicant may also provide a more detailed description of situations where the applicant refused to comply with requests for assistance because the applicant believed that the requests for assistance were unreasonable.

(3) In determining whether the applicant has satisfied the continued assistance requirement, USCIS or the Department of Justice may at its discretion contact the certifying agency that executed the applicant's original Form I–918, Supplement B, "U Nonimmigrant Status Certification" or any other law enforcement agency.

(4) In accordance with procedures determined by the Department of Justice and the Department of Homeland Security, USCIS will refer certain applications for adjustment of status to the Department of Justice for determination of whether the applicant unreasonably refused to provide assistance in a criminal investigation or prosecution. If the applicant submits a document described in paragraph (e)(1) of this section, USCIS will not refer the application for consideration by the Department of Justice absent extraordinary circumstances. In other cases, USCIS will only refer an application to the Department of Justice if an official or law enforcement agency has provided evidence that the alien has refused to comply with requests to provide assistance in an investigation or prosecution of persons in connection with the qualifying criminal activity or if there are other affirmative evidence in the record suggesting that the applicant may have unreasonably refused to provide such assistance. In these instances, USCIS will request that the Department of Justice determine, based on all available affirmative evidence, whether the applicant unreasonably refused to provide assistance in a criminal investigation or prosecution. The Department of Justice will have 90 days to provide a written determination to USCIS, or where appropriate, request an extension of time to provide such a determination. After such time, USCIS may adjudicate the application whether or not the Department of Justice has provided a response.

(f) *Decision.* The decision to approve or deny a Form I–485 filed under section 245(m) of the Act is a discretionary determination that lies solely within USCIS's jurisdiction. After completing its review of the application and evidence, USCIS will issue a written decision approving or denying Form I–485 and notify the applicant of this decision.

(1) *Approvals.* If USCIS determines that the applicant has met the requirements for adjustment of status and merits a favorable exercise of discretion, USCIS will approve the Form I–485. Upon approval of adjustment of status under this section, USCIS will record the alien's lawful admission for permanent residence as of the date of such approval.

(2) *Denials.* Upon the denial of an application for adjustment of status under section 245(m) of the Act, the applicant will be notified in writing of

the decision and the reason for the denial in accordance with 8 CFR part 103. If an applicant chooses to appeal the denial to the Administrative Appeals Office pursuant to the provisions of 8 CFR 103.3, the denial will not become final until the appeal is adjudicated.

(g) *Filing petitions for qualifying family members*. A principal U–1 applicant may file an immigrant petition under section 245(m)(3) of the Act on behalf of a qualifying family member as defined in paragraph (a)(2) of this section, provided that:

(1) The qualifying family member has never held U nonimmigrant status;

(2) The qualifying family relationship, as defined in paragraph (a)(2) of this section, exists at the time of the U–1 principal's adjustment and continues to exist through the adjudication of the adjustment or issuance of the immigrant visa for the qualifying family member;

(3) The qualifying family member or the principal U–1 alien, would suffer extreme hardship as described in 8 CFR 245.24(g) (to the extent the factors listed are applicable) if the qualifying family member is not allowed to remain in or enter the United States; and

(4) The principal U–1 alien has adjusted status to that of a lawful permanent resident, has a pending application for adjustment of status, or is concurrently filing an application for adjustment of status.

(h) *Procedures for filing petitions for qualifying family members*—(1) *Required documents*. For each qualifying family member who plans to seek an immigrant visa or adjustment of status under section 245(m)(3) of the Act, the U–1 principal applicant must submit, either concurrently with, or after he or she has filed, his or her Form I–485:

(i) Form I–929 in accordance with the form instructions;

(ii) The fee prescribed in 8 CFR 103.7(b)(1) or an application for a fee waiver;

(iii) Evidence of the relationship listed in paragraph (a)(2) of this section, such as a birth or marriage certificate. If primary evidence is unavailable, secondary evidence or affidavits may be submitted in accordance with 8 CFR 103.2(b)(2);

(iv) Evidence establishing that either the qualifying family member or the U–1 principal alien would suffer extreme hardship if the qualifying family member is not allowed to remain in or join the principal in the United States. Extreme hardship is evaluated on a case-by-case basis, taking into account the particular facts and circumstances of each case. Applicants are encouraged to document all applicable factors in their applications, as the presence or absence of any one factor may not be determinative in evaluating extreme hardship. To establish extreme hardship to a qualifying family member who is physically present in the United States, an applicant must demonstrate that removal of the qualifying family member would result in a degree of hardship beyond that typically associated with removal. Factors that may be considered in evaluating whether removal would result in extreme hardship to the alien or to the alien's qualifying family member include, but are not limited to:

(A) The nature and extent of the physical or mental abuse suffered as a result of having been a victim of criminal activity;

(B) The impact of loss of access to the United States courts and criminal justice system, including but not limited to, participation in the criminal investigation or prosecution of the criminal activity of which the alien was a victim, and any civil proceedings related to family law, child custody, or other court proceeding stemming from the criminal activity;

(C) The likelihood that the perpetrator's family, friends, or others acting on behalf of the perpetrator in the home country would harm the applicant or the applicant's children;

(D) The applicant's needs for social, medical, mental health, or other supportive services for victims of crime that are unavailable or not reasonably accessible in the home country;

(E) Where the criminal activity involved arose in a domestic violence context, the existence of laws and social practices in the home country that punish the applicant or the applicant's child(ren) because they have been victims of domestic violence or have taken steps to leave an abusive household;

(F) The perpetrator's ability to travel to the home country and the ability and willingness of authorities in the home country to protect the applicant or the applicant's children; and

(G) The age of the applicant, both at the time of entry to the United States and at the time of application for adjustment of status; and

(v) Evidence, including a signed statement from the qualifying family member and other supporting documentation, to establish that discretion should be exercised in his or her favor. Although qualifying family members are not required to establish that they are admissible on any of the grounds set forth in section 212(a) of the Act other than on section 212(a)(3)(E) of the Act, USCIS may take into account all factors, including acts that would otherwise render the applicant inadmissible, in making its discretionary decision on the application. Where adverse factors are present, an applicant may offset these by submitting supporting documentation establishing mitigating equities that the applicant wants USCIS to consider when determining whether or not a favorable exercise of discretion is appropriate. Depending on the nature of the adverse factors, the applicant may be required to clearly demonstrate that the denial of adjustment of status would result in exceptional and extremely unusual hardship. Moreover, depending on the gravity of the adverse factors, such a showing might still be insufficient. For example, USCIS will generally not exercise its discretion favorably in cases where the applicant has committed or been convicted of a serious violent crime, a crime involving sexual abuse committed upon a child, or multiple drug-related crimes, or where there are security- or terrorism-related concerns.

(2) *Decision*. The decision to approve or deny a Form I–929 is a discretionary determination that lies solely within USCIS's jurisdiction. The Form I–929 for a qualifying family member may not be approved, however, until such time as the principal U–1 applicant's application for adjustment of status has been approved. After completing its review of the application and evidence, USCIS will issue a written decision and notify the applicant of that decision in writing.

(i) *Approvals*. (A) For qualifying family members who are outside of the United States, if the Form I–929 is approved, USCIS will forward notice of the approval either to the Department of State's National Visa Center so the applicant can apply to the consular post for an immigrant visa, or to the appropriate port of entry for a visa exempt alien.

(B) For qualifying family members who are physically present in the United States, if the Form I–929 is approved, USCIS will forward notice of the approval to the U–1 principal applicant.

(ii) *Denials*. If the Form I–929 is denied, the applicant will be notified in writing of the reason(s) for the denial in accordance with 8 CFR part 103. If an applicant chooses to appeal the denial to the Administrative Appeals Office pursuant to 8 CFR 103.3, the denial will not become final until the appeal is adjudicated. Denial of the U–1 principal applicant's application will result in the automatic denial of a qualifying family member's Form I–929. There shall be no appeal of such an automatic denial.

(i) *Application procedures for qualifying family members who are physically present in the United States to request adjustment of status*. (1) *Required documents*. Qualifying family members in the United States may request adjustment of status by submitting:

(i) Form I–485, Application to Register Permanent Residence or Adjust Status, in accordance with the form instructions;

(ii) An approved Form I–929, Petition for Qualifying Family Member of a U–1 Nonimmigrant;

(iii) The fee prescribed in 8 CFR 103.7(b)(1) or an application for a fee waiver; and

(iv) The biometric services fee as prescribed in 8 CFR 103.7(b)(1) or an application for a fee waiver.

(2) *Decision*. The decision to approve or deny Form I–485 is a discretionary determination that lies solely within USCIS's jurisdiction. After completing

its review of the application and evidence, USCIS will issue a written decision approving or denying Form I–485 and notify the applicant of this decision in writing.

(i) *Approvals.* Upon approval of a Form I–485 under this section, USCIS shall record the alien's lawful admission for permanent residence as of the date of such approval.

(ii) *Denial.* Upon the denial of any application for adjustment of status, the applicant will be notified in writing of the decision and the reason for the denial in accordance with 8 CFR part 103. If an applicant chooses to appeal the denial to the Administrative Appeals Office pursuant to the provisions of 8 CFR 103.3, the denial will not become final until the appeal is adjudicated. During the appeal period, the applicant may not obtain or renew employment authorization under 8 CFR 274a.12(c)(9). Denial of the U–1 principal applicant's application will result in the automatic denial of a qualifying family member's Form I–485; such an automatic denial is not appealable.

(j) *Effect of departure.* If an applicant for adjustment of status under this section departs the United States, he or she shall be deemed to have abandoned the application, and it will be denied. If, however, the applicant is not under exclusion, deportation, or removal proceedings, and he or she filed a Form I–131, Application for Travel Document, in accordance with the instructions on the form, or any other appropriate form, and was granted advance parole by USCIS for such absences, and was inspected and paroled upon returning to the United States, he or she will not be deemed to have abandoned the application. If the adjustment of status application of such an individual is subsequently denied, he or she will be treated as an applicant for admission subject to sections 212 and 235 of the Act. If an applicant for adjustment of status under this section is under exclusion, deportation, or removal proceedings, USCIS will deem the application for adjustment of status abandoned as of the moment of the applicant's departure from the United States.

(k) *Exclusive jurisdiction.* USCIS shall have exclusive jurisdiction over adjustment applications filed under section 245(m) of the Act.

(l) *Inapplicability of 8 CFR 245.1 and 245.2.* The provisions of 8 CFR 245.1 and 245.2 do not apply to aliens seeking adjustment of status under section 245(m) of the Act.

[73 FR 75560, Dec. 12, 2008; 74 FR 395, Jan. 6, 2009; 78 FR 18472, Mar. 27, 2013]

§ 245.25 Adjustment of status of aliens with approved employment-based immigrant visa petitions; validity of petition and offer of employment.

(a) *Validity of petition for continued eligibility for adjustment of status.* An alien who has a pending application to adjust status to that of a lawful permanent resident based on an approved employment-based immigrant visa petition filed under section 204(a)(1)(F) of the Act on the applicant's behalf must have a valid offer of employment based on a valid petition at the time the application to adjust status is filed and at the time the alien's application to adjust status is adjudicated, and the applicant must intend to accept such offer of employment. Prior to a final administrative decision on an application to adjust status, USCIS may require that the applicant demonstrate, or the applicant may affirmatively demonstrate to USCIS, on Form I–485 Supplement J, with any supporting material and credible documentary evidence, in accordance with the form instructions that:

(1) The employment offer by the petitioning employer is continuing; or

(2) Under section 204(j) of the Act, the applicant has a new offer of employment from the petitioning employer or a different U.S. employer, or a new offer based on self-employment, in the same or a similar occupational classification as the employment offered under the qualifying petition, provided that:

(i) The alien's application to adjust status based on a qualifying petition has been pending for 180 days or more; and

(ii) The qualifying immigrant visa petition:

(A) Has already been approved; or

(B) Is pending when the beneficiary notifies USCIS of a new job offer 180 days or more after the date the alien's adjustment of status application was filed, and the petition is subsequently approved:

(*1*) Adjudication of the pending petition shall be without regard to the requirement in 8 CFR 204.5(g)(2) to continuously establish the ability to pay the proffered wage after filing and until the beneficiary obtains lawful permanent residence; and

(*2*) The pending petition will be approved if it was eligible for approval at the time of filing and until the alien's adjustment of status application has been pending for 180 days, unless approval of the qualifying immigrant visa petition at the time of adjudication is inconsistent with a requirement of the Act or another applicable statute; and

(iii) The approval of the qualifying petition has not been revoked.

(3) In all cases, the applicant and his or her intended employer must demonstrate the intention for the applicant to be employed under the continuing or new employment offer (including self-employment) described in paragraphs (a)(1) and (2) of this section, as applicable, within a reasonable period upon the applicant's grant of lawful permanent resident status.

(b) *Definition of same or similar occupational classification.* The term "same occupational classification" means an occupation that resembles in every relevant respect the occupation for which the underlying employment-based immigrant visa petition was approved. The term "similar occupational classification" means an occupation that shares essential qualities or has a marked resemblance or likeness with the occupation for which the underlying employment-based immigrant visa petition was approved.

[81 FR 82490, Nov. 18, 2016]

PART 245a—ADJUSTMENT OF STATUS TO THAT OF PERSONS ADMITTED FOR TEMPORARY OR PERMANENT RESIDENT STATUS UNDER SECTION 245A OF THE IMMIGRATION AND NATIONALITY ACT

Subpart A—Immigration Reform and Control Act of 1986 (RICA) Legalization Provisions

Sec.

Subpart B—Legal Immigration Family Equity (LIFE) Act Legalization Provisions

Subpart C—LIFE Act Amendments Family Unity Provisions

AUTHORITY: 8 U.S.C. 1101, 1103, 1255a and 1255a note.

SOURCE: 52 FR 16208, May 1, 1987, unless otherwise noted.

Subpart A—Immigration Reform and Control Act of 1986 (IRCA) Legalization Provisions

§ 245a.1 Definitions.

As used in this chapter:

(a) *Act* means the Immigration and Nationality Act, as amended by The Immigration Reform and Control Act of 1986.

(b) *Service* means the Immigration and Naturalization Service (INS).

(c)(1) *Resided continuously* as used in section 245A(a)(2) of the Act, means that the alien shall be regarded as having resided continuously in the United States if, at the time of filing of the application for temporary resident status:

An alien who after appearing for a scheduled interview to obtain an immigrant visa at a Consulate or Embassy in Canada or Mexico but who subsequently is not issued an immigrant visa and who is paroled back into the United States, pursuant to the stateside criteria program, shall be regarded as having been granted advance parole by the Service.

(i) No single absence from the United States has exceeded forty-five (45) days, and the aggregate of all absences has not exceeded one hundred and eighty (180) days between January 1, 1982 through the date the application for temporary resident status is filed, unless the alien can establish that due to emergent reasons, his or her return to the United States could not be accomplished within the time period allowed;

(ii) The alien was maintaining residence in the United States; and

(iii) The alien's departure from the United States was not based on an order of deportation.

An alien who has been absent from the United States in accordance with the Service's advance parole procedures shall not be considered as having interrupted his or her continuous residence as required at the time of filing an application.

(2) *Continuous residence,* as used in section 245A(b)(1)(B) of the Act, means that the alien shall be regarded as having resided continuously in the United States if, at the time of applying for adjustment from temporary residence to permanent resident status: No single absence from the United States has exceeded thirty (30) days, and the aggregate of all absences has not exceeded ninety (90) days between the date of granting of lawful temporary resident status and of applying for permanent resident status, unless the alien can establish that due to emergent reasons the return to the United States could not be accomplished within the time period(s) allowed.

(d) In the term *alien's unlawful status was known to the government,* the term *government* means the Immigration and Naturalization Service. An alien's unlawful status was *known to the government* only if:

(1) The Service received factual information constituting a violation of the alien's nonimmigrant status from any agency, bureau or department, or subdivision thereof, of the Federal government, and such information was stored or otherwise recorded in the official Service alien file, whether or not the Service took follow-up action on the information received. In order to meet the standard of *information constituting a violation of the alien's nonimmigrant status,* the alien must have made a clear statement or declaration to the other federal agency, bureau or department that he or she was in violation of nonimmigrant status; or

(2) An affirmative determination was made by the Service prior to January 1, 1982 that the alien was subject to deportation proceedings. Evidence that may be presented by an alien to support an assertion that such a determination was made may include, but is not limited to, official Service documents issued prior to January 1, 1982, *i.e.,* Forms I–94 (see § 1.4), Arrival-Departure Records granting a period of time in which to depart the United States without imposition of proceedings; Forms I–210, Voluntary Departure Notice letter; and Forms I–221, Order to Show Cause and Notice of Hearing. Evidence from Service records that may be used to support a finding

that such a determination was made may include, but is not limited to, record copies of the aforementioned forms and other documents contained in alien files, *i.e.*, Forms I–213, Record of Deportable Alien;

Unexecuted Forms I–205, Warrant of Deportation; Forms I–265, Application for Order to Show Cause and Processing Sheet; Forms I–541, Order of Denial of Application for Extension of Stay granting a period of time in which to depart the United States without imposition of proceedings, or any other Service record reflecting that the alien's nonimmigrant status was considered by the Service to have terminated or the alien was otherwise determined to be subject to deportation proceedings prior to January 1, 1982, whether or not deportation proceedings were instituted; or

(3) A copy of a response by the Service to any other agency which advised that agency that a particular alien had no legal status in the United States or for whom no record could be found.

(4) The applicant produces documentation from a school approved to enroll foreign students under § 214.3 which establishes that the said school forwarded to the Service a report that clearly indicated the applicant had violated his or her nonimmigrant student status prior to January 1, 1982. A school may submit an affirmation that the school did forward to the Service the aforementioned report and that the school no longer has available copies of the actual documentation sent. In order to be eligible under this part, the applicant must not have been reinstated to nonimmigrant student status.

(e) The term *to make a determination* as used in § 245a.2(t)(3) of this part means obtaining and reviewing all information required to adjudicate an application for the benefit sought and making a decision thereon. If fraud, willful misrepresentation or concealment of a material fact, knowingly providing a false writing or document, knowingly making a false statement or representation, or any other activity prohibited by section 245A(c)(6) of the Act is established during the process of making the determination on the application, the Service shall refer to the United States Attorney for prosecution of the alien or of any person who created or supplied a false writing or document for use in an application for adjustment of status under this part.

(f) The term *continuous physical presence* as used in section 245A(a)(3)(A) of the Act means actual continuous presence in the United States since November 6, 1986 until filing of any application for adjustment of status. Aliens who were outside of the United States on the date of enactment or departed the United States after enactment may apply for legalization if they reentered prior to May 1, 1987, provided they meet the continuous residence requirements, and are otherwise eligible for legalization.

(g) *Brief, casual, and innocent* means a departure authorized by the Service (advance parole) subsequent to May 1, 1987 of not more than thirty (30) days for legitimate emergency or humanitarian purposes unless a further period of authorized departure has been granted in the discretion of the district director or a departure was beyond the alien's control.

(h) The term *brief and casual absences* as used in section 245a(b)(3)(A) of the Act permits temporary trips abroad as long as the alien establishes a continuing intention to adjust to lawful permanent resident status. However, such absences must comply with § 245a.3(b)(2) of this chapter in order for the alien to maintain continuous residence as specified in the Act.

(i) *Public cash assistance* means income or needs-based monetary assistance to include, but not limited to, supplemental security income received by the alien through federal, state, or local programs designed to meet subsistence levels. It does not include assistance in kind, such as food stamps, public housing, or other non-cash benefits, nor does it include work-related compensation or certain types of medical assistance (Medicare, Medicaid, emergency treatment, services to pregnant women or children under 18 years of age, or treatment in the interest of public health).

(j) *Legalization Office* means local offices of the Immigration and Naturalization Service which accept and process applications for Legalization or

Special Agricultural Worker status, under the authority of the INS district directors in whose districts such offices are located.

(k) *Regional Processing Facility* means Service offices established in each of the four Service regions to adjudicate, under the authority of the INS Directors of the Regional Processing Facilities, applications for adjustment of status under section 210, 245A(a) or 245A(b)(1) of the Act.

(l) *Designated entity* means any state, local, church, community, farm labor organization, voluntary organization, association of agricultural employers or individual determined by the Service to be qualified to assist aliens in the preparation of applications for Legalization status.

(m) The term *family unity* as used in section 245(d)(2)(B)(i) of the Act means maintaining the family group without deviation or change. The family group shall include the spouse, unmarried minor children under 18 years of age who are not members of some other household, and parents who reside regularly in the household of the family group.

(n) The term *prima facie* as used in section 245(e)(1) and (2) of the Act means eligibility is established if the applicant presents a completed I–687 and specific factual information which in the absence of rebuttal will establish a claim of eligibility under this part.

(o) *Misdemeanor* means a crime committed in the United States, either (1) punishable by imprisonment for a term of one year or less, regardless of the term such alien actually served, if any, or (2) a crime treated as a misdemeanor under 8 CFR 245a.1(p). For purposes of this definition, any crime punishable by imprisonment for a maximum term of five days or less shall not be considered a misdemeanor.

(p) *Felony* means a crime committed in the United States, punishable by imprisonment for a term of more than one year, regardless of the term such alien actually served, if any, except: When the offense is defined by the State as a misdemeanor and the sentence actually imposed is one year or less regardless of the term such alien actually served. Under this exception, for purposes of 8 CFR part 245a, the crime shall be treated as a misdemeanor.

(q) *Subject of an Order to Show Cause* means actual service of the Order to Show Cause upon the alien through the mail or by personal service.

(r) *A qualified designated entity in good-standing with the Service* means those designated entities whose cooperative agreements were not suspended or terminated by the Service or those whose agreements were not allowed to lapse by the Service prior to January 30, 1989 (the expiration date of the INS cooperative agreements for all designated entities), or those whose agreements were not terminated for cause by the Service subsequent to January 30, 1989.

Subsequent to January 30, 1989, and throughout the period ending on November 6, 1990, a QDE in good-standing may: (1) Serve as an authorized course provider under § 245a.3(b)(5)(i)(C) of this chapter; (2) Administer the IRCA Test for Permanent Residency (proficiency test), provided an agreement has been entered into with and authorization has been given by INS under § 245a.1(s)(5) of this chapter; and, (3) Certify as true and complete copies of original documents submitted in support of Form I–698 in the format prescribed in § 245a.3(d)(2) of this chapter.

(s) *Satisfactorily pursuing,* as used in section 245A(b)(1)(D)(i)(II) of the Act, means:

(1) An applicant for permanent resident status has attended a recognized program for at least 40 hours of a minimum 60-hour course as appropriate for his or her ability level, and is demonstrating progress according to the performance standards of the English/citizenship course prescribed by the recognized program in which he or she is enrolled (as long as enrollment occurred on or after May 1, 1987, course standards include attainment of particular functional skills related to communicative ability, subject matter knowledge, and English language competency, and attainment of these skills is measured either by successful completion of learning objectives appropriate to the applicant's ability level, or attainment of a determined score on a test or tests, or both of these); or

(2) An applicant presents a high school diploma or general educational development diploma (GED) from a school in the United States. A GED gained in a language other than English is acceptable only if a GED English proficiency test has been passed. (The curriculum for both the high school diploma and the GED must have included at least 40 hours of instruction in English and U.S. history and government); or

(3) An applicant has attended for a period of one academic year (or the equivalent thereof according to the standards of the learning institution), a state recognized, accredited learning institution in the United States and that institution certifies such attendance (as long as the curriculum included at least 40 hours of instruction in English and U.S. history and government); or

(4) An applicant has attended courses conducted by employers, social, community, or private groups certified (retroactively, if necessary, as long as enrollment occurred on or after May 1, 1987, and the curriculum included at least 40 hours of instruction in English and U.S. history and government) by the district director or the Director of the Outreach Program under § 245a.3(b)(5)(i)(D) of this chapter; or

(5) An applicant attests to having completed at least 40 hours of individual study in English and U.S. history and government and passes the proficiency test for legalization, called the IRCA Test for Permanent Residency, indicating that the applicant is able to read and understand minimal functional English within the context of the history and government of the United States. Such test may be given by INS, as well as, State Departments of Education (SDEs) (and their accredited educational agencies) and Qualified Designated Entities in good-standing (QDEs) upon agreement with and authorization by INS. Those SDEs and QDEs wishing to participate in this effort should write to the Director of the INS Outreach Program at 425 "I" Street, NW., Washington, DC 20536, for further information.

(t) Minimal understanding of ordinary English as used in section 245A(b)(1)(D)(i) of the Act means an applicant can satisfy basic survival needs and routine social demands. The person can handle jobs that involve following simple oral and very basic written communication.

(u) *Curriculum* means a defined course for an instructional program. Minimally, the curriculum prescribes what is to be taught, how the course is to be taught, with what materials, and when and where. The curriculum must:

(1) Teach words and phrases in ordinary, everyday usage;

(2) Include the content of the Federal Citizenship Text series as the basis for curriculum development (other texts with similar content may be used in addition to, but not in lieu of, the Federal Citizenship Text series);

(3) Be designed to provide at least 60 hours of instruction per class level;

(4) Be relevant and educationally appropriate for the program focus and the intended audience; and

(5) Be available for examination and review by INS as requested.

(v) The term *developmentally disabled* means the same as the term *developmental disability* defined in section 102(5) of the Developmental Disabilities Assistance and Bill of Rights Act of 1987, Public Law 100–146. As a convenience to the public, that definition is printed here in its entirety:

The term *developmental disability* means a severe, chronic disability of a person which:

(1) Is attributable to a mental or physical impairment or combination of mental and physical impairments;

(2) Is manifested before the person attains age twenty-two;

(3) Is likely to continue indefinitely;

(4) Results in substantial functional limitations in three or more of the following areas of major life activity: (i) Self-care, (ii) receptive and expressive language, (iii) learning, (iv) mobility, (v) self direction, (vi) capacity for independent living, and (vii) economic self-sufficiency; and

(5) Reflects the person's need for a combination and sequence of special, interdisciplinary, or generic care, treatment, or other services which are of lifelong or extended duration and are individually planned and coordinated.

[52 FR 16208, May 1, 1987, as amended at 52 FR 43845, Nov. 17, 1987; 53 FR 9863, Mar. 28, 1988; 53 FR 23382, June 22, 1988; 53 FR 43992, Oct. 31, 1988; 54 FR 29448, July 12, 1989; 56 FR 31061, July 9, 1991; 78 FR 18472, Mar. 27, 2013]

§ 245a.2 Application for temporary residence.

(a) *Application period for temporary residence.* (1) An alien who has resided unlawfully in the United States since January 1, 1982, who believes that he or she meets the eligibility requirements of section 245A of the Act must make application within the twelve month period beginning on May 5, 1987 and ending on May 4, 1988, except as provided in the following paragraphs.

(2)(i) [Reserved]

(ii) An alien who is the subject of an Order to Show Cause issued under section 242 of the Act during the period beginning on May 5, 1987 and ending on April 4, 1988 must file an application for adjustment of status to that of a temporary resident prior to the thirty-first day after the issuance of the Order to Show Cause.

(iii) An alien who is the subject of an Order to Show Cause issued under section 242 of the Act during the period beginning on April 5, 1988 and ending on May 4, 1988 must file an application for adjustment of status to that of a temporary resident not later than May 4, 1988.

(iv) An alien, described in paragraphs (a)(2)(i) through (iii) of this section, who fails to file an application for adjustment of status to that of a temporary resident under section 245A(a) of the Act during the respective time period(s), will be statutorily ineligible for such adjustment of status.

(b) *Eligibility.* The following categories of aliens, who are otherwise eligible to apply for legalization, may file for adjustment to temporary residence status:

(1) An alien (other than an alien who entered as a nonimmigrant) who establishes that he or she entered the United States prior to January 1, 1982, and who has thereafter resided continuously in the United States in an unlawful status, and who has been physically present in the United States from November 6, 1986, until the date of filing the application.

(2) An alien who establishes that he or she entered the United States as a nonimmigrant prior to January 1, 1982, and whose period of authorized admission expired through the passage of time prior to January 1, 1982, and who has thereafter resided continuously in the United States in an unlawful status, and who has been physically present in the United States from November 6, 1986, until the date of filing the application.

(3) An alien who establishes that he or she entered the United States as a nonimmigrant prior to January 1, 1982, and whose unlawful status was known to the Government as of January 1, 1982, and who has thereafter resided continuously in the United States in an unlawful status, and who has been physically present in the United States from November 6, 1986, until the date of filing the application.

(4) An alien described in paragraphs (b) (1) through (3) of this section who was at any time a nonimmigrant exchange visitor (as defined in section 101(a)(15)(J) of the Act), must establish that he or she was not subject to the two-year foreign residence requirements of section 212(e) or has fulfilled that requirement or has received a waiver of such requirements and has resided continuously in the United States in unlawful status since January 1, 1982.

(5) An alien who establishes that he or she was granted voluntary departure, voluntary return, extended voluntary departure or placed in deferred action category by the Service prior to January 1, 1982 and who has thereafter resided continuously in such status in the United States and who has been physically present in the United States from November 6, 1986 until the date of filing the application.

(6) An alien who establishes that he or she was paroled into the United States prior to January 1, 1982, and whose parole status terminated prior to January 1, 1982, and who has thereafter resided continuously in such status in the United States, and who has been physically present in the United States from November 6, 1986, until the date of filing the application.

(7) An alien who establishes that he or she is a Cuban or Haitian Entrant who was physically present in the United States prior to January 1, 1982, and who has thereafter resided continuously in the United States, and who has been physically present in the United States from November 6, 1986,

until the date of filing the application, without regard to whether such alien has applied for adjustment of status pursuant to section 202 of the Act.

(8) An alien's eligibility under the categories described in section 245(a)(2)(b) (1) through (7) and (9) through (15) shall not be affected by entries to the United States subsequent to January 1, 1982 that were not documented on Service Form I-94 (see §1.4), Arrival-Departure Record.

(9) An alien who would be otherwise eligible for legalization and who was present in the United States in an unlawful status prior to January 1, 1982, and reentered the United States as a nonimmigrant, such entry being documented on Service Form I-94, Arrival-Departure Record, in order to return to an unrelinquished unlawful residence.

(10) An alien described in paragraph (b)(9) of this section must receive a waiver of the excludable charge 212(a)(19) as an alien who entered the United States by fraud.

(11) A nonimmigrant who entered the United States for duration of status ("D/S") is one of the following classes, A, A-1, A-2, G, G-1, G-2, G-3 or G-4, whose qualifying employment terminated or who ceased to be recognized by the Department of State as being entitled to such classification prior to January 1, 1982, and who has thereafter continued to reside in the United States in an unlawful status. An alien who was a dependent family member and who may be otherwise eligible for legalization may be considered a member of this class of eligible aliens if the dependent family member was also in A and G status when the principal A or G alien's status terminated or ceased to be recognized by the Department of State.

(12) A nomimmigrant who entered the United States for duration of status ("D/S") in one of the following classes, F, F-1, or F-2, who completed a full course of study, including practical training and whose time period if any to depart the United States after completion of study expired prior to January 1, 1982 and who has remained in the United States in an unlawful status since that time. A dependent F-2 alien otherwise eligible who was admitted into the United States with a specific time period, as opposed to duration of status, documented on Service Form I-94, Arrival-Departure Record that extended beyond January 1, 1982 is considered eligible if the principal F-1 alien is found eligible.

(13) An alien who establishes that he or she is a member of the class in the Silva-Levi lawsuit (No. 76-C-4268 (N.D. ILL. March 22, 1977)); that is, an alien from an independent country of the Western Hemisphere who was present in the United States prior to March 11, 1977, and was known by the Immigration and Naturalization Service (INS) to have a priority date for the issuance of an immigrant visa between July 1, 1968 and December 31, 1976, inclusive, and who was clearly eligible for an immigrant visa.

(14) An alien who filed an asylum application prior to January 1, 1982 and whose application was subsequently denied or whose application has not yet been decided is considered an alien in an unlawful status known to the government.

(15) An alien, otherwise eligible who departed the United States and was paroled into the United States on or before May 1, 1987 in order to return to an unrelinquished unlawful residence.

(c) *Ineligible aliens.* (1) An alien who has been convicted of a felony, or three or more misdemeanors.

(2) An alien who has assisted in the persecution of any person or persons on account of race, religion, nationality, membership in a particular social group or political opinion.

(3) An alien excludable under the provisions of section 212(a) of the Act whose grounds of excludability may not be waived, pursuant to section 245A(d)(2)(B)(ii) of this Act.

(4) An alien who at any time was a nonimmigrant exchange visitor who is subject to the two-year foreign residence requirement unless the requirement has been satisfied or waived pursuant to the provisions of section 212(e) of the Act who has resided continuously in the United States in an unlawful status since January 1, 1982.

(5) [Reserved]

(6) An alien who is the subject of an Order to Show Cause issued under section 242 of the Act during the period beginning on May 5, 1987 and ending on

April 4, 1988 who does not file an application for adjustment of status to that of temporary resident under section 245A(a) of the Act prior to the thirty-first day after issuance of the order.

(7) An alien who is the subject of an Order to Show Cause issued under section 242 of the Act during the period beginning on April 5, 1988 and ending on May 4, 1988 who does not file an application for adjustment of status to that of a temporary resident under section 245A(a) of the Act prior to May 5, 1988.

(8) An alien who was paroled into the United States prior to January 1, 1982 and whose parole status terminated or expired subsequent to January 1, 1982, except an alien who was granted advance parole.

(d) *Documentation.* Evidence to support an alien's eligibility for the legalization program shall include documents establishing proof of identity, proof of residence, and proof of financial responsibility, as well as photographs, a completed fingerprint card (Form FD–258), and a completed medical report of examination (Form I–693). All documentation submitted will be subject to Service verification. Applications submitted with unverifiable documentation may be denied. Failure by an applicant to authorize release to INS of information protected by the Privacy Act and/or related laws in order for INS to adjudicate a claim may result in denial of the benefit sought. Acceptable supporting documents for these three categories are discussed below.

(1) *Proof of identity.* Evidence to establish identity is listed below in descending order of preference:

(i) Passport;

(ii) Birth certificate;

(iii) Any national identity document from the alien's country of origin bearing photo and fingerprint (e.g., a "cedula" or "cartilla");

(iv) Driver's license or similar document issued by a state if it contains a photo;

(v) Baptismal Record/Marriage Certificate; or

(vi) Affidavits.

(2) *Assumed names*—(i) *General.* In cases where an applicant claims to have met any of the eligibility criteria under an assumed name, the applicant has the burden of proving that the applicant was in fact the person who used that name. The applicant's true identity is established pursuant to the requirements of paragraph (d)(1) of this section. The assumed name must appear in the documentation provided by the applicant to establish eligibility. To meet the requirements of this paragraph documentation must be submitted to prove the common identity, *i.e.*, that the assumed name was in fact used by the applicant.

(ii) *Proof of common identity.* The most persuasive evidence is a document issued in the assumed name which identifies the applicant by photograph, fingerprint or detailed physical description. Other evidence which will be considered are affidavit(s) by a person or persons other than the applicant, made under oath, which identify the affiant by name and address, state the affiant's relationship to the applicant and the basis of the affiant's knowledge of the applicant's use of the assumed name. Affidavits accompanied by a photograph which has been identified by the affiant as the individual known to affiant under the assumed name in question will carry greater weight.

(3) *Proof of residence.* Evidence to establish proof of continuous residence in the United States during the requisite period of time may consist of any combination of the following:

(i) Past employment records, which may consist of pay stubs, W-2 Forms, certification of the filing of Federal income tax returns on IRS Form 6166, state verification of the filing of state income tax returns, letters from employer(s) or, if the applicant has been in business for himself or herself, letters from banks and other firms with whom he or she has done business. In all of the above, the name of the alien and the name of the employer or other interested organization must appear on the form or letter, as well as relevant dates. Letters from employers should be on employer letterhead stationery, if the employer has such stationery, and must include:

(A) Alien's address at the time of employment;

(B) Exact period of employment;

(C) Periods of layoff;

(D) Duties with the company;

(E) Whether or not the information was taken from official company records; and

(F) Where records are located and whether the Service may have access to the records.

If the records are unavailable, an affidavit form-letter stating that the alien's employment records are unavailable and why such records are unavailable may be accepted in lieu of (3)(i)(E) and (3)(i)(F) of this paragraph. This affidavit form-letter shall be signed, attested to by the employer under penalty of perjury, and shall state the employer's willingness to come forward and give testimony if requested.

(ii) Utility bills (gas, electric, phone, etc.), receipts, or letters from companies showing the dates during which the applicant received service are acceptable documentation.

(iii) School records (letters, report cards, etc.) from the schools that the applicant or their children have attended in the United States must show name of school and periods of school attendance.

(iv) Hospital or medical records showing treatment or hospitalization of the applicant or his or her children must show the name of the medical facility or physician and the date(s) of the treatment or hospitalization.

(v) Attestations by churches, unions, or other organizations to the applicant's residence by letter which:

(A) Identifies applicant by name;

(B) Is signed by an official (whose title is shown);

(C) Shows inclusive dates of membership;

(D) States the address where applicant resided during membership period;

(E) Includes the seal of the organization impressed on the letter or the letterhead of the organization, if the organization has letterhead stationery;

(F) Establishes how the author knows the applicant; and

(G) Establishes the origin of the information being attested to.

(vi) Additional documents to support the applicant's claim may include:

(A) Money order receipts for money sent in or out of the country;

(B) Passport entries;

(C) Birth certificates of children born in the United States;

(D) Bank books with dated transactions;

(E) Letters or correspondence between applicant and another person or organization;

(F) Social Security card;

(G) Selective Service card;

(H) Automobile license receipts, title, vehicle registration, etc.;

(I) Deeds, mortgages, contracts to which applicant has been a party;

(J) Tax receipts;

(K) Insurance policies, receipts, or letters; and

(L) Any other relevant document.

(4) *Proof of financial responsibility.* An applicant for adjustment of status under this part is subject to the provisions of section 212(a)(15) of the Act relating to excludability of aliens likely to become public charges. Generally, the evidence of employment submitted under paragraph (d)(3)(i) of this section will serve to demonstrate the alien's financial responsibility during the documented period(s) of employment. If the alien's period(s) of residence in the United States include significant gaps in employment or if there is reason to believe that the alien may have received public assistance while employed, the alien may be required to provide proof that he or she has not received public cash assistance. An applicant for residence who is determined likely to become a public charge and is unable to overcome this determination after application of the special rule will be denied adjustment. The burden of proof to demonstrate the inapplicability of this provision of law lies with the applicant who may provide:

(i) Evidence of a history of employment (*i.e.*, employment letter, W-2 Forms, income tax returns, etc.);

(ii) Evidence that he/she is self-supporting (*i.e.*, bank statements, stocks, other assets, etc.); or

(iii) Form I–134, Affidavit of Support, completed by a spouse in behalf of the applicant and/or children of the applicant or a parent in behalf of children which guarantees complete or partial financial support. Acceptance of the affidavit of support shall be extended to other family members where family circumstances warrant.

(5) *Burden of proof.* An alien applying for adjustment of status under this part has the burden of proving by a preponderance of the evidence that he or she has resided in the United States for the requisite periods, is admissible to the United States under the provisions of section 245a of the Act, and is otherwise eligible for adjustment of status under this section. The inference to be drawn from the documentation provided shall depend on the extent of the documentation, its credibility and amenability to verification as set forth in paragraph (d) of this section.

(6) *Evidence.* The sufficiency of all evidence produced by the applicant will be judged according to its probative value and credibility. To meet his or her burden of proof, an applicant must provide evidence of eligibility apart from his or her own testimony. In judging the probative value and credibility of the evidence submitted, greater weight will be given to the submission of original documentation.

(e) *Filing of application.* (1) The application must be filed on Form I–687 at an office of a designated entity or at a Service Legalization Office within the jurisdiction of the District wherein the applicant resides. If the application is filed with a designated entity, the alien must have consented to having the designated entity forward the application to the legalization office. In the case of applications filed at a legalization office, the district director may, at his or her discretion:

(i) Require the applicant to file the application in person; or

(ii) Require the applicant to file the application by mail; or

(iii) Permit the filing of applications either by mail or in person.

The applicant must appear for a personal interview at the legalization office as scheduled. If the applicant is 14 years of age or older, the application must be accompanied by a completed Form FD–258 (Applicant Card).

(2) At the time of the interview, wherever possible, original documents must be submitted except the following: Official government records; employment or employment-related records maintained by employers, unions, or collective bargaining organizations; medical records; school records maintained by a school or school board; or other records maintained by a party other than the applicant. Copies of records maintained by parties other than the applicant which are submitted in evidence must be certified as true and correct by such parties and must bear their seal or signature or the signature and title of persons authorized to act in their behalf. If at the time of the interview the return of original documents is desired by the applicant, they must be accompanied by notarized copies or copies certified true and correct by a qualified designated entity or by the alien's representative in the format prescribed in §204.2(j)(1) or (2) of this chapter. At the discretion of the district director, original documents, even if accompanied by certified copies, may be temporarily retained for forensic examination by the Document Analysis Unit at the Regional Processing Facility having jurisdiction over the legalization office to which the documents were submitted.

(3) A separate application (I–687) must be filed by each eligible applicant. All fees required by §103.7(b)(1) of this chapter must be submitted in the exact amount in the form of a money order, cashier's check, or certified bank check, made payable to the Immigration and Naturalization Service. No personal checks or currency will be accepted. Fees will not be waived or refunded under any circumstances.

(f) *Filing date of application.* The date the alien submits a completed application to a Service Legalization Office or designated entity shall be considered the filing date of the application, provided that in the case of an application filed at a designated entity the alien has consented to having the designated entity forward the application to the Service Legalization Office having jurisdiction over the location of the alien's residence. The designated entities are required to forward completed applications to the appropriate Service Legalization Office within sixty days of receipt.

(g) *Selective Service registration.* At the time of filing an application under this section, male applicants over the age of 17 and under the age of 26 are required to be registered under the Military Selective Service Act. An applicant shall present evidence that he has previously registered under that Act in the form of a letter of acknowledgement from the Selective Service System, or such alien shall present a completed and signed Form SSS–1 at the time of filing Form I–687 with the Immigration and Naturalization Service or a designated entity. Form SSS–1 will be forwarded to the Selective Service System by the Service.

(h) *Continuous residence.* (1) For the purpose of this Act, an applicant for *temporary resident status* shall be regarded as having resided continuously in the United States if, at the time of filing of the application:

(i) No single absence from the United States has exceeded forty-five (45) days, and the aggregate of all absences has not exceeded one hundred and eighty (180) days between January 1, 1982 through the date the application for temporary resident status is filed, unless the alien can establish that due to emergent reasons, his or her return to the United States could not be accomplished within the time period allowed;

(ii) The alien was maintaining a residence in the United States; and

(iii) The alien's departure from the United States was not based on an order of deportation.

(2) An alien who has been absent from the United States in accordance with the Service's advance parole procedures shall not be considered as having interrupted his or her continuous residence as required at the time of filing an application under this section.

(i) *Medical examination.* An applicant under this part shall be required to submit to an examination by a designated civil surgeon at no expense to the government. The designated civil surgeon shall report on the findings of the mental and physical condition of the applicant and the determination of the alien's immunization status. Results of the medical examination must be presented to the Service at the time of interview and shall be incorporated into the record. Any applicant certified under paragraphs (1), (2), (3), (4), or (5) of section 212(a) of the Act may appeal to a Board of Medical Officers of the U.S. Public Health Service as provided in section 234 of the Act and part 235 of this chapter.

(j) *Interview.* Each applicant, regardless of age, must appear at the appropriate Service Office and must be fingerprinted for the purpose of issuance of an employment authorization document and Form I–688. Each applicant shall be interviewed by an immigration officer, except that the interview may be waived for a child under 14, or when it is impractical because of the health or advanced age of the applicant.

(k) *Applicability of exclusion grounds*—(1) *Grounds of exclusion not to be applied.* The following paragraphs of section 212(a) of the Act shall not apply to applicants for temporary resident status: (14) Workers entering without Labor Certification; (20) immigrants not in possession of a valid entry document; (21) visas issued without compliance with section 203; (25) illiterates; and (32) graduates of non-accredited medical schools.

(2) *Waiver of grounds of exclusion.* Except as provided in paragraph (k)(3) of this section, the Attorney General may waive any other provision of section 212(a) of the Act only in the case of individual aliens for humanitarian purposes, to assure family unity, or when the granting of such a waiver is in the public interest. If an alien is excludable on grounds which may be waived as set forth in this paragraph, he or she shall be advised of the procedures for applying for a waiver of grounds of excludability on Form I–690. When an application for waiver of grounds of excludability is filed jointly with an application for temporary residence under this section, it shall be accepted for processing at the legalization office. If an application for waiver of grounds of excludability is submitted after the alien's preliminary interview at the legalization office, it shall be forwarded to the appropriate Regional Processing Facility. All applications for waivers of grounds of excludability must be accompanied by the correct fee in the exact amount. All fees for applications filed in the United States must be in the form of a money order, cashier's check, or bank check. No personal

checks or currency will be accepted. Fees will not be waived or refunded under any circumstances. An application for waiver of grounds of excludability under this part shall be approved or denied by the director of the Regional Processing Facility in whose jurisdiction the applicant's application for adjustment of status was filed except that in cases involving clear statutory ineligibility or admitted fraud, such application may be denied by the district director in whose jurisdiction the application is filed, and in cases returned to a Service Legalization Office for re-interview, such application may be approved at the discretion of the district director. The applicant shall be notified of the decision and, if the application is denied, of the reason therefor. Appeal from an adverse decision under this part may be taken by the applicant on Form I–694 within 30 days after the service of the notice only to the Service's Administrative Appeals Unit pursuant to the provisions of § 103.3(a) of this chapter.

(3) *Grounds of exclusion that may not be waived.* Notwithstanding any other provision of the Act, the following provisions of section 212(a) may not be waived by the Attorney General under paragraph (k)(2) of this section:

(i) Paragraphs (9) and (10) (criminals);

(ii) Paragraph (23) (narcotics) except for a single offense of simple possession of thirty grams or less of marijuana;

(iii) Paragraphs (27) (prejudicial to the public interest), (28) (communist), and (29) (subversive);

(iv) Paragraph (33) (participated in Nazi persecution).

(4) *Special rule for determination of public charge.* An alien who has a consistent employment history which shows the ability to support himself or herself even though his or her income may be below the poverty level, may be admissible. The alien's employment history need not be continuous in that it is uninterrupted. It should be continuous in the sense that the alien shall be regularly attached to the workforce, has an income over a substantial period of the applicable time, and has demonstrated the capacity to exist on his or her income without recourse to public cash assistance. This regulation is prospective in that the Service shall determine, based on the alien's history, whether he or she is likely to become a public charge. Past acceptance of public cash assistance within a history of consistent employment will enter into this decision. The weight given in considering applicability of the public charge provisions will depend on many factors, but the length of time an applicant has received public cash assistance will constitute a significant factor.

(5) *Public assistance and criminal history verification.* Declarations by an applicant that he or she has not been the recipient of public cash assistance and/or has not had a criminal record are subject to a verification of facts by the Service. The applicant must agree to fully cooperate in the verification process. Failure to assist the Service in verifying information necessary for the adjudication of the application may result in a denial of the application.

(l) *Continous physical presence since November 6, 1986.* (1) An alien applying for adjustment to temporary resident status must establish that he or she has been continuously physically present in the United States since November 6, 1986. Aliens who were outside of the United States on the date of enactment or departed the United States after enactment may apply for legalization if they reentered prior to May 1, 1987, and meet the continuous residence requirements and are otherwise eligible for legalization.

(2) A brief, casual and innocent absence means a departure authorized by the Service (advance parole) subsequent to May 1, 1987 of not more than thirty (30) days for legitimate emergency or humanitarian purposes unless a further period of authorized departure has been granted in the discretion of the district director or a departure was beyond the alien's control.

(m) *Departure.* (1) During the time period from the date that an alien's application establishing prima facie eligibility for temporary resident status is reviewed at a Service Legalization Office and the date status as a temporary resident is granted, the alien applicant can only be readmitted to the United States provided his or her departure was authorized under the Service's advance parole provisions contained in §212.5(f) of this chapter.

(2) An alien whose application for temporary resident status has been approved may be admitted to the United States upon return as a returning temporary resident provided he or she:

(i) Is not under deportation proceedings, such proceedings having been instituted subsequent to the approval of temporary resident status. A temporary resident alien will not be considered deported if that alien departs the United States while under an outstanding order of deportation issued prior to the approval of temporary resident status;

(ii) Has not been absent from the United States more than thirty (30) days on the date application for admission is made;

(iii) Has not been absent from the United States for an aggregate period of more than 90 days since the date the alien was granted lawful temporary resident status;

(iv) Presents Form I–688;

(v) Presents himself or herself for inspection; and

(vi) Is otherwise admissible.

(3) The periods of time in paragraph (m)(2)(ii) and (m)(2)(iii) of this section may be waived at the discretion of the Attorney General in cases where the absence from the United States was due merely to a brief temporary trip abroad due to emergent or extenuating circumstances beyond the alien's control.

(n)(1) *Employment and travel authorization; general.* Authorization for employment and travel abroad for temporary resident status applicants under section 245A(a) of the Act may only be granted by a Service Office. INS district directors will determine the Service location for the completion of processing of travel documentation. In the case of an application which has been filed with a designated entity, employment authorization may only be granted by the Service after the application has been properly received at the Service Office.

(2) *Employment authorization prior to the granting of temporary resident status.* (i) Permission to travel abroad and accept employment may be granted to the applicant after an interview has been conducted in connection with an application establishing prima facie eligibility for temporary resident status. Permission to travel abroad may be granted in emergent circumstances in accordance with the Service's advance parole provisions contained in §212.5(f) of this chapter after an interview has been conducted in connection with an application establishing prima facie eligiblity for temporary resident status.

(ii) If an interview appointment cannot be scheduled within 30 days from the date an application is filed at a Service office, authorization to accept employment will be granted, valid until the scheduled appointment date. Employment authorization, both prior and subsequent to an interview, will be restricted to increments of 1 year, pending final determination on the application for temporary resident status. If a final determination has not been made prior to the expiration date on the Employment Authorization Document (Form I–766, Form I–688A or Form I–688B), that date may be extended upon return of the employment authorization document by the applicant to the appropriate Service office.

(3) *Employment and travel authorization upon grant of temporary resident status.* Upon the granting of an application for adjustment to temporary resident status, the service center will forward a notice of approval to the applicant at his or her last known address and to his or her qualified designated entity or representative. The applicant may appear at any Service office and, upon surrender of the previously issued Employment Authorization Document, will be issued Form I–688, Temporary Resident Card, authorizing employment and travel abroad.

(4) *Revocation of employment authorization upon denial of temporary resident status.* Upon denial of an application for adjustment to temporary resident status the alien will be notified that if a timely appeal is not submitted, employment authorization shall be automatically revoked on the final day of the appeal period.

(o) *Decision.* The applicant shall be notified in writing of the decision, and, if the application is denied, of the reason therefor. An appeal from an adverse decision under this part may be taken by the applicant on Form I–694.

(p) *Appeal process.* An adverse decision under this part may be appealed to the Associate Commissioner, Examinations (Administrative Appeals Unit). Any appeal with the required fee shall be filed with the Regional Processing Facility within thirty (30) days after service of the notice of denial in accordance with the procedures of § 103.3(a) of this chapter. An appeal received after the thirty (30) day period has tolled will not be accepted. The thirty (30) day period includes any time required for service or receipt by mail.

(q) *Motions.* The Regional Processing Facility director may *sua sponte* reopen and reconsider any adverse decision. When an appeal to the Associate Commissioner, Examinations (Administrative Appeals Unit) has been filed, the INS director of the Regional Processing Facility may issue a new decision that will grant the benefit which has been requested. The director's new decision must be served on the appealing party within 45 days of receipt of any briefs and/or new evidence, or upon expiration of the time allowed for the submission of any briefs. Motions to reopen a proceeding or reconsider a decision shall not be considered under this part.

(r) *Certifications.* The Regional Processing Facility director may, in accordance with § 103.4 of this chapter, certify a decision to the Associate Commissioner, Examinations (Administrative Appeals Unit) when the case involves an unusually complex or novel question of law or fact. The party affected shall be given notice of such certification and of the right to submit a brief within thirty (30) days from service of the notice.

(s) *Date of adjustment to temporary residence.* The status of an alien whose application for temporary resident status is approved shall be adjusted to that of a lawful temporary resident as of the date indicated on the application fee receipt issued at Service Legalization Office.

(t) *Limitation on access to information and confidentiality.* (1) No person other than a sworn officer or employee of the Justice Department or bureau of agency thereof, will be permitted to examine individual applications, except employees of designated entities where applications are filed with the same designated entity. For purposes of this part, any individual employed under contract by the Service to work in connection with the legalization program shall be considered an "employee of the Justice Department or bureau or agency thereof."

(2) Files and records prepared by designated entities under this section are confidential. The Attorney General and the Service shall not have access to these files and records without the consent of the alien.

(3) No information furnished pursuant to an application for legalization under this section shall be used for any purpose except: (i) To make a determination on the application; or, (ii) for the enforcement of the provisions encompassed in section 245A(c)(6) of the Act, except as provided in paragraph (t)(4) of this section.

(4) If a determination is made by the Service that the alien has, in connection with his or her application, engaged in fraud or willful misrepresentation or concealment of a material fact, knowingly provided a false writing or document in making his or her application, knowingly made a false statement or representation, or engaged in any other activity prohibited by section 245A(c)(6) of the Act, the Service shall refer the matter to the United States Attorney for prosecution of the alien or of any person who created or supplied a false writing or document for use in an application for adjustment of status under this part.

(5) Information obtained in a granted legalization application and contained in the applicant's file is subject to subsequent review in reference to future benefits applied for (including petitions for naturalization and permanent resident status for relatives).

(u) *Termination of temporary resident staus*—(1) *Termination of temporary resident status; General.* The status of an alien lawfully admitted for temporary residence under section 245A(a)(1) of the Act may be terminated at any time in accordance with section 245A(b)(2) of the Act. It is not necessary that a final order of deportation be entered in order to terminate temporary resident status. The temporary resident status may be terminated upon the occurance of any of the following:

(i) It is determined that the alien was ineligible for temporary residence under section 245A of this Act;

(ii) The alien commits an act which renders him or her inadmissible as an immigrant, unless a waiver is secured pursuant to § 245a.2(k)(2).

(iii) The alien is convicted of any felony, or three or more misdemeanors;

(iv) The alien fails to file for adjustment of status from temporary resident to permanent resident on Form I-698 within forty-three (43) months of the date he/she was granted status as a temporary resident under § 245a.1 of this part.

(2) *Procedure*—(i) *Termination by the Service.* Except as provided in paragraph (u)(2)(ii) of this section, termination of an alien's temporary resident status under paragraph (u)(1) of this section will be made before instituting deportation proceedings against a temporary resident alien and only on notice sent to the alien by certified mail directed to his or her last known address, and to his or her representative, if any. The alien must be given an opportunity to offer evidence in opposition to the grounds alleged for termination of his or her status. Evidence in opposition must be submitted within thirty (30) days after the service of the Notice of Intent to Terminate. If the alien's status is terminated, the director of the regional processing facility shall notify the alien of the decision and the reasons for the termination, and further notify the alien that any Service Form I-94, Arrival-Departure Record or other official Service document issued to the alien authorizing employment and/or travel abroad, or any Form I-688, Temporary Resident Card previously issued to the alien will be declared void by the director of the regional processing facility within thirty (30) days if no appeal of the termination decision is filed within that period. The alien may appeal the decision to the Associate Commissioner, Examinations (Administrative Appeals Unit). Any appeal with the required fee shall be filed with the regional processing facility within thirty (30) days after the service of the notice of termination. If no appeal is filed within that period, the I-94, I-688 or other official Service document shall be deemed void, and must be surrendered without delay to an immigration officer or to the issuing office of the Service.

(ii) *Termination upon entry of final order of deportation or exclusion.* (A) The Service may institute deportation or exclusion proceedings against a temporary resident alien without regard to the procedures set forth in paragraph (u)(2)(i) of this section:

(*1*) If the ground for deportation arises under section 241(a)(2)(A)(iii) of the Act (8 U.S.C. 1251(a)(2)(A)(iii));

(*2*) If the ground for deportation arises after the acquisition of temporary resident status, and the basis of such ground of deportation is not waivable pursuant to section 245A(d)(2)(B)(ii) of the Act (8 U.S.C. 1255a(d)(2)(B)(ii)); or

(*3*) If the ground for exclusion arises after the acquisition of temporary resident status and is not waivable pursuant to section 245A(d)(2)(B)(ii) of the Act (8 U.S.C. 1255a(d)(2)(B)(ii)).

(B) In such cases, the entry of a final order of deportation or exclusion will automatically terminate an alien's temporary resident status acquired under section 245A(a)(1) of the Act.

(3) *Termination not construed as rescission under section 246.* For the purposes of this part the phrase *termination of status* of an alien granted lawful temporary residence under section 245A(a) of the Act shall not be construed to necessitate a rescission of status as described in section 246 of the Act, and the proceedings required by the regulations issued thereunder shall not apply.

(4) *Return to unlawful status after termination.* Termination of the status of any alien previously adjusted to lawful temporary residence under section 245A(a) of the Act shall act to return such alien to the unlawful status held prior to the adjustment, and render him or her amenable to exclusion or deportation proceedings under section 236 or 242 of the Act, as appropriate.

(v) *Ineligibility for immigration benefits.* An alien whose status is adjusted to that of a lawful temporary resident under section 245A of the Act is not entitled to submit a petition pursuant to section 203(a)(2) or to any other benefit or consideration accorded under the Act to aliens lawfuly admitted for permanent residence.

(w) *Declaration of Intending Citizen.* An alien who has been granted the status of temporary resident under section 245A(a)(1) of this Act may assert a claim of discrimination on the basis of citizenship status under section 274B of the Act only if he or she has previously filed Form I–772 (Declaration of Intending Citizen) after being granted such status. The Declaration of Intending Citizen is not required as a basis for filing a petition for naturalization; nor shall it be regarded as a right to United States citizenship; nor shall it be regarded as evidence of a person's status as a resident.

[52 FR 16208, May 1, 1987, as amended at 52 FR 43845, 43846, Nov. 17, 1987; 53 FR 23382, June 22, 1988; 54 FR 29449, July 12, 1989; 56 FR 31061, July 9, 1991; 58 FR 45236, Aug. 27, 1993; 60 FR 21040, May 1, 1995; 60 FR 21975, May 4, 1995; 61 FR 46536, Sept. 4, 1996; 65 FR 82256, Dec. 28, 2000; 78 FR 18472, Mar. 27, 2013]

§ 245a.3 Application for adjustment from temporary to permanent resident status.

(a) *Application period for permanent residence.* (1) An alien may submit an application for lawful permanent resident status, with fee, immediately subsequent to the granting of lawful temporary resident status. Any application received prior to the alien's becoming eligible for adjustment to permanent resident status will be administratively processed and held by the INS, but will not be considered filed until the beginning of the nineteenth month after the date the alien was granted temporary resident status as defined in §245a.2(s) of this chapter.

(2) No application shall be denied for failure to timely apply before the end of 43 months from the date of actual approval of the temporary resident application.

(3) The Service Center Director shall sua sponte reopen and reconsider without fee any application which was previously denied for late filing. No additional fee will be required for those applications which are filed during the twelve month extension period but prior to July 9, 1991.

(b) *Eligibility.* Any alien who has been lawfully admitted for temporary resident status under section 245A(a) of the Act, such status not having been terminated, may apply for adjustment of status of that of an alien lawfully admitted for permanent residence if the alien:

(1) Applies for such adjustment anytime subsequent to the granting of temporary resident status but on or before the end of 43 months from the date of actual approval of the termporary resident application. The alien need not be physically present in the United States at the time of application; however, the alien must establish continuous residence in the United States in accordance with the provisions of paragraph (b)(2) of this section and must be physically present in the United States at the time of interview and/or processing for permanent resident status (ADIT processing);

(2) Establishes continuous residence in the United States since the date the alien was granted such temporary residence status. An alien shall be regarded as having resided continuously in the United States for the purpose of this part if, at the time of applying for adjustment from temporary to permanent resident status, or as of the date of eligibility for permanent residence, whichever is later, no single absence from the United States has exceeded thirty (30) days, and the aggregate of all absences has not exceeded ninety (90) days between the date of approval of the temporary resident application, Form I-687 (not the "roll-back" date) and the date the alien applied or became eligible for permanent resident status, whichever is later, unless the alien can establish that due to emergent reasons or circumstances beyond his or her control, the return to the United States could not be accomplished within the time period(s) allowed. A single absence from the United States of more than 30 days, and aggregate absences of more than 90 days during the period for which continuous residence is required for adjustment to permanent residence, shall break the continuity of such residence,

unless the temporary resident can establish to the satisfaction of the district director or the Director of the Regional Processing Facility that he or she did not, in fact, abandon his or her residence in the United States during such period;

(3) Is admissible to the United States as an immigrant, except as otherwise provided in paragraph (g) of this section; and has not been convicted of any felony, or three or more misdemeanors; and

(4)(i)(A) Can demonstrate that the alien meets the requirements of section 312 of the Immigration and Nationality Act, as amended (relating to minimal understanding of ordinary English and a knowledge and understanding of the history and government of the United States); or

(B) Is satisfactorily pursuing a course of study recognized by the Attorney General to achieve such an understanding of English and such a knowledge and understanding of the history and government of the United States.

(ii) The requirements of paragraph (b)(4)(i) of this section must be met by each applicant. However, these requirements shall be waived without formal application for persons who, as of the date of application or the date of eligibility for permanent residence under this part, whichever date is later, are:

(A) Under 16 years of age; or

(B) 65 years of age or older; or

(C) Over 50 years of age who have resided in the United States for at least 20 years and submit evidence establishing the 20-year qualification requirement. Such evidence must be submitted pursuant to the requirements contained in Section 245a.2(d)(3) of this chapter; or

(D) Developmentally disabled as defined at § 245a.1(v) of this chapter. Such persons must submit medical evidence concerning their developmental disability; or

(E) Physically unable to comply. The physical disability must be of a nature which renders the applicant unable to acquire the four language skills of speaking, understanding, reading, and writing English in accordance with the criteria and precedence established in OI 312.1(a)(2)(iii) (Interpretations). Such persons must submit medical evidence concerning their physical disability.

(iii)(A) Literacy and basic citizenship skills may be demonstrated for purposes of complying with paragraph (b)(4)(i)(A) of this section by:

(*1*) Speaking and understanding English during the course of the interview for permanent resident status. An applicant's ability to read and write English shall be tested by excerpts from one or more parts of the Federal Textbooks on Citizenship at the elementary literacy level. The test of an applicant's knowledge and understanding of the history and form of government of the United States shall be given in the English language. The scope of the testing shall be limited to subject matter covered in the revised (1987) Federal Textbooks on Citizenship or other approved training material. The test questions shall be selected from a list of 100 standardized questions developed by the Service. In choosing the subject matter and in phrasing questions, due consideration shall be given to the extent of the applicant's education, background, age, length of residence in the United States, opportunities available and efforts made to acquire the requisite knowledge, and any other elements or factors relevant to an appraisal of the adequacy of his or her knowledge and understanding; or

(*2*) By passing a standardized section 312 test (effective retroactively as of November 7, 1988) such test being given in the English language by the Legalization Assistance Board with the Educational Testing Service (ETS) or the California State Department of Education with the Comprehensive Adult Student Assessment System (CASAS). The scope of the test is based on the 1987 edition of the Federal Textbooks on Citizenship series written at the elementary literacy level. An applicant may evidence passing of the standardized section 312 test by submitting the approved testing organization's standard notice of passing test results at the time of filing Form I–698, subsequent to filing the application but prior to the interview, or at the time of the interview. The test results may be independently verified by INS, if necessary.

(B) An applicant who fails to pass the English literacy and/or the U.S. history and government tests at the time of the interview, shall be afforded a second opportunity after six (6) months (or earlier, at the request of the applicant) to pass the tests, submit evidence of passing an INS approved section 312 standardized examination or submit evidence of fulfillment of any one of the "satisfactorily pursuing" alternatives listed at § 245a.1(s) of this chapter. The second interview shall be conducted prior to the denial of the application for permanent residence and may be based solely on the failure to pass the basic citizenship skills requirements. An applicant whose period of eligibility expires prior to the end of the six-month re-test period, shall still be accorded the entire six months within which to be re-tested.

(iv) To satisfy the English language and basic citizenship skills requirements under the "satisfactorily pursuing" standard as defined at § 245a.1(s) of this chapter the applicant must submit evidence of such satisfactory pursuit in the form of a "Certificate of Satisfactory Pursuit" (Form I–699) issued by the designated school or program official attesting to the applicant's satisfactory pursuit of the course of study as defined at § 245a.1(s)(1) and (4) of this chapter; or a high school diploma or general educational development diploma (GED) under § 245a.1(s)(2) of this chapter; or certification on letterhead stationery from a state recognized, accredited learning institution under § 245a.1(s)(3) of this chapter; or evidence of having passed the IRCA Test for Permanent Residency under § 245a.1(s)(5) of this chapter. Such applicants shall not then be required to demonstrate that they meet the requirements of § 245a.3(b)(4)(i)(A) of this chapter in order to be granted lawful permanent residence provided they are otherwise eligible. Evidence of "Satisfactory Pursuit" may be submitted at the time of filing Form I–698, subsequent to filing the application but prior to the interview, or at the time of the interview (the applicant's name and A90M number must appear on any such evidence submitted). An applicant need not necessarily be enrolled in a recognized course of study at the time of application for permanent residency.

(v) Enrollment in a recognized course of study as defined in § 245a.3(b)(5) and issuance of a "Certificate of Satisfactory Pursuit" must occur subsequent to May 1, 1987.

(5) A course of study in the English language and in the history and government of the United States shall satisfy the requirement of paragraph (b)(4)(i) of this section if the course materials for such instruction include textbooks published under the authority of section 346 of the Act, and it is

(i) Sponsored or conducted by: (A) An established public or private institution of learning recognized as such by a qualified state certifying agency; (B) An institution of learning approved to issue Forms I–20 in accordance with § 214.3 of this chapter; (C) A qualified designated entity within the meaning of section 245A(c)(2) of the Act, in good-standing with the Service; or (D) Is certified by the district director in whose jurisdiction the program is conducted, or is certified by the Director of the Outreach Program nationally.

(ii) A program seeking certification as a course of study recognized by the Attorney General under paragraph (b)(5)(i)(D) of this section shall file Form I–803, Petition for Attorney General Recognition to Provide Course of Study for Legalization: Phase II, with the Director of Outreach for national level programs or with the district director having jurisdiction over the area in which the school or program is located. In the case of local programs, a separate petition must be filed with each district director when a parent organization has schools or programs in more than one INS district. A petition must identify by name and address those schools or programs included in the petition. No fee shall be required to file Form I–803;

(A) The Director of Outreach and the district directors may approve a petition where they have determined that (*1*) a need exists for a course of study in addition to those already certified under § 245a.3(b)(5)(i) (A), (B), or (C); and/or (*2*) of this chapter the petitioner has historically provided educational services in English and U.S. history and government but is not already certified under §245a.3(b)(5)(i)(A), (B), or (C); and (*3*) of this chapter the petitioner is otherwise qualified to provide such course of study;

(B) Upon approval of the petition the Director of Outreach and district directors shall issue a Certificate of Attorney General Recognition on Form I–804 to the petitioner. If the petition is denied, the petitioner shall be notified in writing of the decision therefor. No appeal shall lie from a denial of Form I–803, except that in such case where the petitions of a local, cross-district program are approved in one district and denied in another within the same State, the petitioner may request review of the denied petition by the appropriate Regional Commissioner. The Regional Commissioner shall then make a determination in this case;

(C) Each district director shall compile and maintain lists of programs approved under paragraph (b)(5)(i)(D) of this section within his or her jurisdiction. The Director of Outreach shall compile and maintain lists of approved national level programs.

(6) *Notice of participation.* All courses of study recognized under §245a.3(b)(5)(i)(A) through (C) of this chapter which are already conducting or will conduct English and U.S. history and government courses for temporary residents must submit a Notice of Participation to the district director in whose jurisdiction the program is conducted. Acceptance of "Certificates of Satisfactory Pursuit" (Form I–699) shall be delayed until such time as the course provider submits the Notice of Participation, which notice shall be in the form of a letter typed on the letterhead of the course provider (if available) and include the following:

(i) The name(s) of the school(s)/program(s).

(ii) The complete addresses and telephone numbers of sites where courses will be offered, and class schedules.

(iii) The complete names of persons who are in charge of conducting English and U.S. history and government courses of study.

(iv) A statement that the course of study will issue "Certificates of Satisfactory Pursuit" to temporary resident enrollees according to INS regulations.

(v) A list of designated officials of the recognized course of study authorized to sign "Certificates of Satisfactory Pursuit", and samples of their original signatures.

(vi) A statement that if a course provider charges a fee to temporary resident enrollees, the fee will not be excessive.

(vii) Evidence of recognition under 8 CFR 245a.3(b)(5)(i)(A), (B), or (C) (e.g., certification from a qualified state certifying agency; evidence of INS approval for attendance by nonimmigrant students, such as the school code number, or the INS identification number from the QDE cooperative agreement). The course provider shall notify the district director, in writing, of any changes to the information contained in the Notice of Participation subsequent to its submission within ten (10) days of such change.

A Certificate of Attorney General Recognition to Provide Course of Study for Legalization (Phase II), Form I–804, shall be issued to course providers who have submitted a Notice of Participation in accordance with the provisions of this section by the distict director. A Notice of Participation deficient in any way shall be returned to the course provider to correct the deficiency. Upon the satisfaction of the district director that the deficiency has been corrected, the course provider shall be issued Form I–804. Each district director shall compile and maintain lists of recognized courses within his or her district.

(7) *Fee structure.* No maximum fee standard will be imposed by the Attorney General. However, if it is believed that a fee charged is excessive, this factor alone will justify non-certification of the course provider by INS as provided in §245a.3(b)(10) and/or (12) of this section. Once fees are established, any change in fee without prior approval of the district director or the Director of Outreach may justify de-certification. In determining whether or not a fee is excessive, district directors and the Director of Outreach shall consider such factors as the means of instruction, class size, prevailing wages of instructors in the area of the program, and additional costs such as rent, materials, utilities, insurance, and taxes. District

directors and the Director of Outreach may also seek the assistance of various Federal, State and local entities as the need arises (e.g., State Departments of Education) to determine the appropriateness of course fees.

(8) The Citizenship textbooks to be used by applicants for lawful permanent residence under section 245A of the Act shall be distributed by the Service to appropriate representatives of public schools. These textbooks may otherwise be purchased from the Superintendent of Documents, Government Printing Office, Washington, DC 20402, and are also available at certain public institutions.

(9) *Maintenance of Student Records.* Course providers conducting courses of study recognized under § 245a.3(b)(5) of this chapter shall maintain for each student, for a period of three years from the student's enrollment, the following information and documents:

(i) Name (as copied exactly from the I–688A or I–688);

(ii) A-number (90 million series);

(iii) Date of enrollment;

(iv) Attendance records;

(v) Assessment records;

(vi) Photocopy of signed "Certificate of Satisfactory Pursuit" issued to the student.

(10) *Issuance of "Certificate of Satisfactory Pursuit" (I–699).* (i) Each recognized course of study shall prepare a standardized certificate that is signed by the designated official. The Certificate shall be issued to an applicant who has attended a recognized course of study for at least 40 hours of a minimum of 60-hour course as appropriate for his or her ability level, and is demonstrating progress according to the performance standards of the English and U.S. history and government course prescribed. Such standards shall conform with the provisions of § 245a.1(s) of this chapter.

(ii) The district director shall reject a certificate if it is determined that the certificate is fraudulent or was fraudulently issued.

(iii) The district director shall reject a Certificate if it is determined that the course provider is not complying with INS regulations. In the case of non-compliance, the district director will advise the course provider in writing of the specific deficiencies and give the provider thirty (30) days within which to correct such deficiencies.

(iv) District directors will accept Certificates from course providers once it is determined that the deficiencies have been satisfactorily corrected.

(v) Course providers which engage in fraudulent activities or fail to conform with INS regulations will be removed from the list of INS approved programs. INS will not accept Certificates from these providers.

(vi) Certificates may be accepted if a program is cited for deficiencies or decertified at a later date and no fraud was involved.

(vii) Certificates shall not be accepted from a course provider that has been decertified unless the alien enrolled in and had been issued a certificate prior to the decertification, provided that no fraud was involved.

(viii) The appropriate State agency responsible for SLIAG funding shall be notified of all decertifications by the district director.

(11) *Designated official.* (i) The designated official is the authorized person from each recognized course of study whose signature appears on all "Certificates of Satisfactory Pursuit" issued by that course;

(ii) The designated official must be a regularly employed member of the school administration whose office is located at the school and whose compensation does not come from commissions for recruitment of foreign students;

(iii)(A) The head of the school system or school, the director of the Qualified Designated Entity, the head of a program approved by the Attorney General, or the president or owner of other institutions recognized by the Attorney General must specify a *designated official.* Such designated official may not delegate this designation to any other person. Each school or institution may have up to three (3) designated officials at any one time. In a multi-campus institution, each campus may have up to three (3) designated officials at any one time;

(B) Each designated official shall have read and otherwise be familiar with the "Requirements and Guidelines for Courses of Study Recognized by the Attorney General". The signature of a designated official shall affirm the official's compliance with INS regulations;

(C) The name, title, and sample signature of each designated official for each recognized course of study shall be on file with the district director in whose jurisdiction the program is conducted.

(12) *Monitoring by INS.* (i) INS Outreach personnel in conjunction with the district director shall monitor the course providers in each district in order to:

(A) Assure that the program is a course of study recognized by the Attorney General under the provisions of § 245a.3(b)(5).

(B) Verify the existence of curriculm as defined in § 245a.1(u) on file for each level of instruction provided in English language and U.S. history and government classes.

(C) Assure that "Certificates of Satisfactory Pursuit" are being issued in accordance with § 245a.3(b)(10).

(D) Assure that records are maintained on each temporary resident enrollee in accordance with § 245a.3(b)(9).

(E) Assure that fees (if any) assessed by the course provider are in compliance in accordance with § 245a.3(b)(7).

(ii) If INS has reason to believe that the service is not being provided to the applicant, INS will issue a 24-hour minimum notice to the service provider before any site visit is conducted.

(iii) If it is determined that a course provider is not performing according to the standards established in either § 245a.3(b)(10) or (12) of this chapter, the district director shall institute decertification proceedings. Notice of Intent to Decertify shall be provided to the course provider. The course provider has 30 days within which to correct performance according to standards established. If after the 30 days, the district director is not satisfied that the basis for decertification has been overcome, the course provider will be decertified. The appropriate State agency shall be notified in accordance with § 245a.3(b)(10)(viii) of this chapter. A copy of the notice of decertification shall be sent to the State agency.

(13) Courses of study recognized by the Attorney General as defined at § 245a.3(b)(5) of this chapter shall provide certain standards for the selection of teachers. Since some programs may be in locations where selection of qualified staff is limited, or where budget constraints restrict options, the following list of qualities for teacher selection is provided as guidance. Teacher selections should include as many of the following qualities as possible:

(i) Specific training in Teaching English to Speakers of Other Languages (TESOL);

(ii) Experience as a classroom teacher with adults;

(iii) Cultural sensitivity and openness;

(iv) Familiarity with compentency-based education;

(v) Knowledge of curriculum and materials adaptation;

(vi) Knowledge of a second language.

(c) *Ineligible aliens.* (1) An alien who has been convicted of a felony, or three or more misdemeanors in the United States.

(2) An alien who is inadmissible to the United States as an immigrant, except as provided in § 245a.3(g)(1).

(3) An alien who was previously granted temporary resident status pursuant to section 245A(a) of the Act who has not filed an application for permanent resident status under section 245A(b)(1) of the Act by the end of 43 months from the date of actual approval of the temporary resident application.

(4) An alien who was not previously granted temporary resident status under section 245A(a) of the Act.

(5) An alien whose temporary resident status has been terminated under § 245a.2(u) of this chapter

(d) *Filing the application.* The provisions of part 211 of this chapter relating to the documentary requirements for immigrants shall not apply to an applicant under this part.

(1) The application must be filed on Form I–698. Form I–698 must be accompanied by the correct fee and documents specified in the instructions. The application will be mailed to the director having jurisdiction over the applicant's place of residence.

(2) *Certification of documents.* The submission of original documents is not required at the time of filing Form I–698. A copy of a document submitted in

support of Form I–698 filed pursuant to section 245A(b) of the Act and this part may be accepted, though unaccompanied by the original, if the copy is certified as true and complete by

(i) An attorney in the format prescribed in § 204.2(j)(1) of this chapter; or

(ii) An alien's representative in the format prescribed in § 204.2(j)(2) of this chapter; or

(iii) A qualified designated entity (QDE) in good standing as defined in § 245a.1(r) of this chapter, if the copy bears a certification by the QDE in good-standing, typed or rubber-stamped in the following language:

I certify that I have compared this copy with its original and it is a true and complete copy.

Signed: __________
Date: __________
Name: __________
QDE in good-standing representative
Name of QDE in good-standing: __________
Address of QDE in good-standing: __________
INS-QDE Cooperative Agreement Number: __

(iv) *Authentication.* Certification of documents must be authenticated by an original signature. A facsimile signature on a rubber stamp will not be acceptable.

(v) *Original documents.* Original documents must be presented when requested by the Service. Official government records, employment or employment-related records maintained by employers, unions, or collective bargaining organizations, medical records, school records maintained by a school or school board or other records maintained by a party other than the applicant which are submitted in evidence must be certified as true and complete by such parties and must bear their seal or signature or the signature and title of persons authorized to act in their behalf. At the discretion of the district director and/or the Regional Processing Facility director, original documents may be kept for forensic examination.

(3) A separate application (I–698) must be filed by each eligible applicant. All fees required by § 103.7(b)(1) of this chapter must be submitted in the exact amount in the form of a money order, cashier's check or certified bank check. No personal checks or currency will be accepted. Fees will not be waived or refunded under any circumstances.

(4) Applicants who filed for temporary resident status prior to December 1, 1987, are required to submit the results of a serologic test for HIV virus on Form I–693, "Medical Examination of Aliens Seeking Adjustment of Status", completed by a designated civil surgeon, unless the serologic test for HIV was performed and the results were submitted on Form I–693 when the applicant filed for temporary resident status. Applicants who did submit an I–693 reflecting a serologic test for HIV was performed prior to December 1, 1987, must submit evidence of this fact when filing the I–698 application in order to be relieved from the requirement of submitting another I–693. If such evidence is not available, applicants may note on their I–698 application their prior submission of the results of the serologic test for HIV. This information shall then be verified at the Regional Processing Facility. Applicants having to submit an I–693 pursuant to this section are not required to have a complete medical examination. All HIV-positive applicants shall be advised that a waiver of the ground of excludability under section 212(a)(6) of the Act is available and shall be provided the opportunity to apply for the waiver. To be eligible for the waiver, the applicant must establish that:

(i) The danger to the public health of the United States created by the alien's admission to the United States is minimal,

(ii) The possibility of the spread of the infection created by the alien's admission to the United States is minimal, and

(iii) There will be no cost incurred by any government agency without prior consent of that agency. Provided these criteria are met, the waiver may be granted only for humanitarian purposes, to assure family unity, or when the granting of such a waiver is in the public interest in accordance with § 245a.3(g)(2) of this chapter.

(5) If necessary, the validity of an alien's temporary resident card (I–688) will be extended in increments of one (1) year until such time as the decision on an alien's properly filed application for permanent residence becomes final.

(6) An application lacking the proper fee or incomplete in any way shall be returned to the applicant with request for the proper fee, correction, additional information, and/or documentation. Once an application has been accepted by the Service and additional information and/or documentation is required, the applicant shall be sent a notice to submit such information and/or documentation. In such case the application Form I–698 shall be retained at the RPF. If a response to this request is not received within 60 days, a second request for correction, additional information, and/or documentation shall be made. If the second request is not complied with by the end of 43 months from the date the application for temporary residence, Form I–687, was approved the application for permanent residence will be adjudicated on the basis of the existing record.

(e) *Interview.* Each applicant regardless of age, must appear at the appropriate Service office and must be fingerprinted for the purpose of issuance of Form I–551. Each applicant shall be interviewed by an immigration officer, except that the adjudicative interview may be waived for a child under 14, or when it is impractical because of the health or advanced age of the applicant. An applicant failing to appear for the scheduled interview may, for good cause, be afforded another interview. Where an applicant fails to appear for two scheduled interviews, his or her application shall be held in abeyance until the end of 43 months from the date the application for temporary residence was approved and adjudicated on the basis of the existing record.

(f) *Numerical limitations.* The numerical limitations of sections 201 and 202 of the Act do not apply to the adjustment of aliens to lawful permanent resident status under section 245A(b) of the Act.

(g) *Applicability of exclusion grounds*—(1) *Grounds of exclusion not to be applied.* The following paragraphs of section 212(a) of the Act shall not apply to applicants for adjustment of status from temporary resident to permanent resident status: (14) workers entering without labor certification; (20) immigrants not in possession of valid entry documents; (21) visas issued without compliance of section 203; (25) illiterates; and (32) graduates of non-accredited medical schools.

(2) *Waiver of grounds of excludability.* Except as provided in paragraph (g)(3) of this section, the Service may waive any provision of section 212(a) of the Act only in the case of individual aliens for humanitarian purposes, to assure family unity, or when the granting of such a waiver is otherwise in the public interest. In any case where a provision of section 212(a) of the Act has been waived in connection with an alien's application for lawful temporary resident status under section 245A(a) of the Act, no additional waiver of the same ground of excludability will be required when the alien applies for permanent resident status under section 245A(b)(1) of the Act. In the event that the alien was excludable under any provision of section 212(a) of the Act at the time of temporary residency and failed to apply for a waiver in connection with the application for temporary resident status, or becomes excludable subsequent to the date temporary residence was granted, a waiver of the ground of excludability, if available, will be required before permanent resident status may be granted.

(3) *Grounds of exclusion that may not be waived.* Notwithstanding any other provisions of the Act the following provisions of section 212(a) of the Act may not be waived by the Attorney General under paragraph (g)(2) of this section:

(i) Paragraphs (9) and (10) (criminals);

(ii) Paragraph (15) (public charge) except for an alien who is or was an aged, blind, or disabled individual (as defined in section 1614(a)(1) of the Social Security Act);

(iii) Paragraph (23) (narcotics), except for a single offense of simple possession of thirty grams or less of marijuana;

(iv) Paragraphs (27) (prejudicial to the public interest), (28) (communists), and (29) (subversives);

(v) Paragraph (33) (participated in Nazi persecution).

(4) *Determination of Likely to become a public charge* and Special Rule. Prior to

use of the special rule for determination of public charge, paragraph (g)(4)(iii) of this section, an alien must first be determined to be excludable under section 212(a)(15) of the Act. If the applicant is determined to be *likely to become a public charge*, he or she may still be admissible under the terms of the Special Rule.

(i) In determining whether an alien is *likely to become a public charge* financial responsibility of the alien is to be established by examining the totality of the alien's circumstances at the time of his or her application for legalization. The existence or absence of a particular factor should never be the sole criteria for determining if an alien is likely to become a public charge. The determination of financial responsibility should be a prospective evaluation based on the alien's age, health, income, and vocation.

(ii) The Special Rule for determination of public charge, paragraph (g)(4)(iii) of this section, is to be applied only after an initial determination that the alien is inadmissible under the provisions of section 212(a)(15) of the act.

(iii) *Special Rule*. An alien who has a consistent employment history which shows the ability to support himself or herself even though his or her income may be below the poverty level is not excludable under paragraph (g)(3)(ii) of this section. The alien's employment history need not be continuous in that it is uninterrupted. It should be continuous in the sense that the alien shall be regularly attached to the workforce, has an income over a substantial period of the applicable time, and has demonstrated the capacity to exist on his or her income without recourse to public cash assistance. The Special Rule is prospective in that the Service shall determine, based on the alien's history, whether he or she is likely to become a public charge. Past acceptance of public cash assistance within a history of consistent employment will enter into this decision. The weight given in considering applicability of the public charge provisions will depend on many factors, but the length of time an applicant has received public cash assistance will constitute a significant factor. It is not necessary to file a waiver in order to apply the Special Rule for Determination of Public Charge.

(5) *Public cash assistance and criminal history verification*. Declarations by an applicant that he or she has not been the recipient of public cash assistance and/or has not had a criminal record are subject to a verification of facts by the Service. The applicant must agree to fully cooperate in the verification process. Failure to assist the Service in verifying information necessary for proper adjudication may result in denial of the application.

(h) *Departure*. An applicant for adjustment to lawful permanent resident status under section 245A(b)(1) of the Act who was granted lawful temporary resident status under section 245A(a) of the Act, shall be permitted to return to the United States after such brief and casual trips abroad, as long as the alien reflects a continuing intention to adjust to lawful permanent resident status. However, such absences from the United States must not exceed the periods of time specified in § 245a.3(b)(2) of this chapter in order for the alien to maintain continuous residence as specified in the Act.

(i) *Decision*. The applicant shall be notified in writing of the decision, and, if the application is denied, of the reason therefor. Applications for permanent residence under this chapter will not be denied at local INS offices (districts, suboffices, and legalization offices) until the entire record of proceeding has been reviewed. An application will not be denied if the denial is based on adverse information not previously furnished to the Service by the alien without providing the alien an opportunity to rebut the adverse information and to present evidence in his or her behalf. If inconsistencies are found between information submitted with the adjustment application and information previously furnished to the Service, the applicant shall be afforded the opportunity to explain discrepancies or rebut any adverse information. A party affected under this part by an adverse decision is entitled to file an appeal on Form I–694. If an application is denied, work authorization will be granted until a final decision has been rendered on an appeal or until the end of the appeal period if no appeal is filed. An applicant whose appeal period has ended is no longer considered to be an Eligible Legalized Alien for the purposes of the administration of State Legalization Impact Assistance Grants (SLIAG) funding. An alien whose application is denied will not be required to surrender his or her temporary resident card (I–688) until such time as the appeal period has tolled, or until expiration date of the I-688, whichever date is later. After exhaustion of an appeal, an applicant who believes that the grounds for denial have been overcome may submit another application with fee, provided that the application is submitted within his or her eligibility period.

(j) *Appeal process.* An adverse decision under this part may be appealed to the Associate Commissioner, Examinations (Administrative Appeals Unit) the appellate authority designated in § 103.1(f)(2). Any appeal shall be submitted to the Regional Processing Facility with the required fee within thirty (30) days after service of the Notice of Denial in accordance with the procedures of § 103.3(a) of this chapter. An appeal received after the thirty (30) day period has tolled will not be accepted. The thirty (30) day period for submitting an appeal begins three days after the notice of denial is mailed. If a review of the Record of Proceeding (ROP) is requested by the alien or his or her legal representative and an appeal has been properly filed, an additional thirty (30) days will be allowed for this review from the time the Record of Proceeding is photocopied and mailed. A brief may be submitted with the appeal form or submitted up to thirty (30) calendar days from the date of receipt of the appeal form at the Regional Processing Facility. Briefs filed after submission of the appeal should be mailed directly to the Regional Processing Facility. For good cause shown, the time within which a brief supporting an appeal may be submitted may be extended by the Director of the Regional Processing Facility.

(k) *Motions.* The Regional Processing Facility director may reopen and reconsider any adverse decision *sua sponte.* When an appeal to the Associate Commissioner, Examinations (Administrative Appeals Unit) has been filed, the INS director of the Regional Processing Facility may issue a new decision that will grant the benefit which has been requested. The director's new decision must be served on the appealing party within forty-five (45) days of receipt of any briefs and/or new evidence, or upon expiration of the time allowed for the submission of any briefs.

(l) *Certifications.* The Regional Processing Facility director or district director may, in accordance with § 103.4 of this chapter, certify a decision to the Associate Commissioner, Examinations (Administrative Appeals Unit) when the case involves an unusually complex or novel question of law or fact. The decision on an appealed case subsequently remanded back to either the Regional Processing Facility director or the district director will be certified to the Administrative Appeals Unit.

(m) *Date of adjustment to permanent residence.* The status of an alien whose application for permanent resident status is approved shall be adjusted to that of a lawful permanent resident as of the date of filing of the application for permanent residence or the eligibility date, whichever is later. For purposes of making application to petition for naturalization, the continuous residence requirements for naturalization shall begin as of the date the alien's status is adjusted to that of a person lawfully admitted for permanent residence under this part.

(n) *Limitation on access to information and confidentiality.* (1) No person other than a sworn officer or employee of the Department of Justice or bureau of agency thereof, will be permitted to examine individual applications. For purposes of this part, any individual employed under contract by the Service to work in connection with the Legalization Program shall be considered an *employee of the Department of Justice or bureau or agency thereof.*

(2) No information furnished pursuant to an application for permanent resident status under this section shall be used for any purpose except: (i) To make a determination on the application; or (ii) for the enforcement of the provisions encompassed in section

245A(c)(6) of the Act, except as provided in paragraph (n)(3) of this section.

(3) If a determination is made by the Service that the alien has, in connection with his or her application, engaged in fraud or willful misrepresentation or concealment of a material fact, knowingly provided a false writing or document in making his or her application, knowingly made a false statement or representation, or engaged in any other activity prohibited by section 245A(c)(6) of the Act, the Service shall refer the matter to the United States Attorney for prosecution of the alien and/or of any person who created or supplied a false writing or document for use in an application for adjustment of status under this part.

(4) Information contained in granted legalization files may be used by the Service at a later date to make a decision (i) On an immigrant visa petition or other status filed by the applicant under section 204(a) of the Act; (ii) On a naturalization application submitted by the applicant; (iii) For the preparation of reports to Congress under section 404 of IRCA, or; (iv) For the furnishing of information, at the discretion of the Attorney General, in the same manner and circumstances as census information may be disclosed by the Secretary of Commerce under section 8 of title 13, Unites States Code.

(o) *Rescission.* Rescission of adjustment of status under 245a shall occur under the guidelines established in section 246 of the Act.

[54 FR 29449, July 12, 1989; 54 FR 43384, Oct. 24, 1989, as amended at 56 FR 31061, July 9, 1991; 57 FR 3926, Feb. 3, 1992; 59 FR 33905, July 1, 1994]

§ 245a.4 Adjustment to lawful resident status of certain nationals of countries for which extended voluntary departure has been made available.

(a) *Definitions.* As used in this section: (1) *Act* means the Immigration and Nationality Act, as amended by the Immigration Reform and Control Act of 1986.

(2) *Service* means the Immigration and Naturalization Service (INS).

(3) *Resided continuously* means that the alien shall be regarded as having resided continuously in the United States if, at the time of filing of the application for temporary resident status:

(i) No single absence from the United States has exceeded 45 days, and the aggregate of all absences has not exceeded 180 days between July 21, 1984, through the date the application for temporary resident status is filed, unless the alien can establish that due to emergent reasons, his or her return to the United States could not be accomplished within the time period allowed;

(ii) The alien was maintaining residence in the United States; and

(iii) The alien's departure from the United States was not based on an order of deportation.

An alien who has been absent from the United States in accordance with the Service's advance parole procedures shall not be considered as having interrupted his or her continuous residence as required at the time of filing an application. An alien who, after appearing for a scheduled interview to obtain an immigrant visa at a Consulate or Embassy in Canada or Mexico but who subsequently is not issued an immigrant visa and who is paroled back into the United States pursuant to the stateside criteria program, shall be considered as having *resided continuously*.

(4) *Continous residence* means that the alien shall be regarded as having resided continously in the United States if, at the time of applying for adjustment from temporary residence to permanent resident status: No single absence from the United States has exceeded 30 days, and the aggregate of all absences has not exceeded 90 days between the date on which lawful temporary resident status was granted and the date permanent resident status was applied for, unless the alien can establish that due to emergent reasons or extenuating circumstances beyond his or her control, the return to the United States could not be accomplished within the time period(s) allowed. A single absence from the United States of more than 30 days, and aggregate absences of more than 90 days during the period for which continuous residence is required for adjustment to permanent resident status, shall break the continuity of such residence unless the temporary

resident can establish to the satisfaction of the district director that he or she did not, in fact, abandon his or her residence in the United States during such period.

(5) *To make a determination* means obtaining and reviewing all information required to adjudicate an application for the benefit sought and making a decision thereon. If fraud, willful misrepresentation or concealment of a material fact, knowingly providing a false writing or document, knowingly making a false statement or representation, or any other activity prohibited by the Act is established during the process of making the determination on the application, the Service shall refer the matter to the United States Attorney for prosecution of the alien or of any person who created or supplied a false writing or document for use in an application for adjustment of status under this part.

(6) *Continuous physical presence* means actual continuous presence in the United States since December 22, 1987, until filing of any application for adjustment of status. Aliens who were outside of the United States after enactment may apply for temporary residence if they reentered prior to March 21, 1988, provided they meet the continuous residence requirements, and are otherwise eligible for legalization.

(7) *Brief, casual, and innocent* means a departure authorized by the Service (advance parole) subsequent to March 21, 1988, for not more than 30 days for legitimate emergency or humanitarian purposes unless a further period of authorized departure has been granted in the discretion of the district director or a departure was beyond the alien's control.

(8) *Brief and casual* means temporary trips abroad as long as the alien establishes a continuing intention to adjust to lawful permanent resident status. However, such absences must not exceed the specific periods of time required in order to maintain continuous residence.

(9) *Certain nationals of countries for which extended voluntary departure has been made available on the basis of a nationality group determination at any time during the 5-year period ending on November 1, 1987* is limited to nationals of Poland, Afghanistan, Ethiopia, and Uganda.

(10) *Public cash assistance* means income or need-based monetary assistance to include, but not limited to, supplemental security income received by the alien through federal, state, or local programs designed to meet subsistence levels. It does not include assistance in kind, such as food stamps, public housing, or other non-cash benefits, nor does it include work related compensation or certain types of medical assistance (Medicare, Medicaid, emergency treatment, services to pregnant women or children under 18 years of age, or treatment in the interest of public health).

(11) *Designated entity* means any state, local, church, community, farm labor organization, voluntary organization, association of agricultural employers or individual determined by the Service to be qualified to assist aliens in the preparation of applications for legalization status.

(12) *Through the passage of time* means through the expiration date of the nonimmigrant permission to remain in the United States, including any extensions and/or change of status.

(13) *Prima facie eligibility* means eligibility is established if the applicant presents a completed I–687 and specific factual information which in the absence of rebuttal will establish a claim of eligibility under this part.

(b) *Application for temporary residence*—(1) *Application for temporary residence.* (i) An alien who is a national of Poland, Uganda, Ethiopia, or Afghanistan who has resided continuously in the United States since prior to July 21, 1984, and who believes that he or she meets the eligibility requirements of section 245A of the Act must make application within the 21-month period beginning on March 21, 1988, and ending on December 22, 1989.

(ii) An alien who fails to file an application for adjustment of status to that of a temporary resident under § 245A.4 of this part during the time period, will be statutorily ineligible for such adjustment of status.

(2) *Eligibility* (i) The following categories of aliens who are not otherwise excludable under section 212(a) of the Act are eligible to apply for status to

that of a person admitted for temporary residence:

(A) An alien who is a national of Poland, Uganda, Ethiopia, or Afghanistan, (other than an alien who entered as a nonimmigrant) who establishes that he or she entered the United States prior to July 21, 1984, and who has thereafter resided continuously in the United States, and who has been physically present in the United States from December 22, 1987, until the date of filing the application.

(B) An alien who is a national of Poland, Uganda, Ethiopia, or Afghanistan, and establishes that he or she entered the United States as a nonimmigrant prior to July 21, 1984, and whose period of authorized admission expired through the passage of time prior to January 21, 1985, and who has thereafter resided continuously in the United States, and who has been physically present in the United States from December 22, 1987, until the date of filing the application.

(C) An alien who is a national of Poland, Uganda, Ethiopia, or Afghanistan, and establishes that he or she entered the United States as a nonimmigrant prior to July 21, 1984, and who applied for asylum prior to July 21, 1984, and who has thereafter resided continuously in the United States, and who has been physically present in the United States from December 22, 1987, until the date of filing the application.

(D) An alien who is a national of Poland, Uganda, Ethiopia, or Afghanistan, who would otherwise be eligible for temporary resident status and who establishes that he or she resided continuously in the United States prior to July 21, 1984, and who subsequently reentered the United States as a nonimmigrant in order to return to an unrelinquished residence. An alien described in this paragraph must have received a waiver of 212(a)(19) as an alien who entered the United States by fraud.

(E) An alien who is a national of Poland, Uganda, Ethiopia, or Afghanistan, and was a nonimmigrant who entered the United States in the classification A, A–1, A–2, G, G–1, G–2, G–3, or G–4, for Duration of Status (D/S), and whose qualifying employment terminated or who ceased to be recognized by the Department of State as being entitled to such classification prior to January 21, 1985, and who thereafter continued to reside in the United States.

(F) An alien who is a national of Poland, Uganda, Ethiopia, or Afghanistan, and who was a nonimmigrant who entered the United States as an F, F–1, or F–2 for Duration of Status (D/S), and who completed a full course of studies, including practical training (if any), and whose time period to depart the United States after completion of studies expired prior to January 21, 1985, and who has thereafter continued to reside in the United States. Those students placed in a *nunc pro tunc* retroactive student status which would otherwise preclude their eligibility for legalization under this section, must present evidence that they had otherwise terminated their status during the requisite time period. A dependent F–2 alien otherwise eligible who was admitted into the United States with a specific time period, as opposed to duration of status, documented on Service Form I–94 (see §1.4), Arrival-Departure Record that extended beyond July 21, 1984 is considered eligible if the principal F–1 alien is found eligible.

(3) *Ineligible aliens.* (i) An alien who has been convicted of a felony, or three or more misdemeanors.

(ii) An alien who has assisted in the persecution of any person or persons on account of race, religion, nationality, membership in a particular social group, or political opinion.

(iii) An alien excludable under the provisions of section 212(a) of the Act whose grounds of excludability may not be waived.

(4) *Documentation.* Evidence to support an alien's eligibility for temporary residence status shall include documents establishing proof of identity, proof of nationality, proof of residence, and proof of financial responsibility, as well as photographs, a completed fingerprint card (Form FD–258), and a completed medical report of examination (Form I–693). All documentation submitted will be subject to Service verification. Applications submitted with unverifiable documentation may be denied. Failure by an applicant to authorize release to INS of

information protected by the Privacy Act and/or related laws in order for INS to adjudicate a claim may result in denial of the benefit sought. Acceptable supporting documents for the four categories of documentation are discussed as follows:

(i) *Proof of identity.* Evidence to establish identity is listed below in descending order of preference:

(A) Passport;

(B) Birth certificate;

(C) Any national identity document from the alien's country of origin bearing photo and fingerprint;

(D) Driver's license or similar document issued by a state if it contains a photo;

(E) Baptismal Record/Marriage Certificate; or

(F) Affidavits.

(ii) *Proof of nationality.* Evidence to establish nationality is listed as follows:

(A) Passport;

(B) Birth certificate;

(C) Any national identity document from the alien's country of origin bearing photo and fingerprint;

(D) Other credible documents, including those created by, or in the possession of the INS, or any other documents (excluding affidavits) that, when taken singly, or together as a whole, establish the alien's nationality.

(iii) *Assumed names*—(A) *General.* In cases where an applicant claims to have met any of the eligibility criteria under an assumed name, the applicant has the burden of proving that the applicant was in fact the person who used that name. The applicant's true identity is established pursuant to the requirements of paragraph (b)(4)(i) and (ii) of this section. The assumed name must appear in the documentation provided by the applicant to establish eligibility. To meet the requirement of this paragraph, documentation must be submitted to prove the common identity, *i.e.*, that the assumed name was in fact used by the applicant.

(B) *Proof of common identity.* The most persuasive evidence is a document issued in the assumed name which identifies the applicant by photograph, fingerprint, or detailed physical description. Other evidence which will be considered are affidavit(s) by a person or persons other than the applicant, made under oath, which identify the affiant by name and address, state the affiant's relationship to the applicant and the basis of the affiant's knowledge of the applicant's use of the assumed name. Affidavits accompanied by a photograph which has been identified by the affiant as the individual known to the affiant under the assumed name in question will carry greater weight.

(iv) *Proof of residence.* Evidence to establish proof of continuous residence in the United States during the requisite period of time may consist of any combination of the following:

(A) Past employment records, which may consist of pay stubs, W-2 Forms, certification of the filing of Federal income tax returns on IRS Form 6166, a state verification of the filing of state income tax returns, letters from employer(s) or, if the applicant has been in business for himself or herself, letters from banks and other firms with whom he or she has done business. In all of the above, the name of the alien and the name of the employer or other interested organizations must appear on the form or letter, as well as relevant dates. Letters from employers should be on employer letterhead stationery, if the employer has such stationery, and must include:

(*1*) Alien's address at the time of employment;

(*2*) Exact period of employment;

(*3*) Periods of layoff;

(*4*) Duties with the company;

(*5*) Whether or not the information was taken from official company records; and

(*6*) Where records are located, whether the Service may have access to the records.

If the records are unavailable, an affidavit form letter stating that the alien's employment records are unavailable and why such records are unavailable may be accepted in lieu of paragraphs (b)(4)(iv)(A)(*5*) and (*6*) of this section. This affidavit form letter shall be signed, attested to by the employer under penalty of perjury, and shall state the employer's willingness to come forward and give testimony if requested.

(B) Utility bills (gas, electric, phone, etc.) receipts, or letters from companies showing the dates during which the applicant received service are acceptable documentation.

(C) School records (letters, report cards, etc.) from the schools that the applicant or his or her children have attended in the United States must show the name of school and periods of school attendance.

(D) Hospital or medical records showing treatment or hospitalization of the applicant or his or her children must show the name of the medical facility or physician and the date(s) of the treatment or hospitalization.

(E) Attestations by churches, unions, or other organizations as to the applicant's residence by letter which:

(*1*) Identify applicant by name;

(*2*) Are signed by an official (whose title is shown);

(*3*) Show inclusive dates of membership;

(*4*) State the address where applicant resided during membership period;

(*5*) Include the seal of the organization impressed on the letter or the letterhead of the organization, if the organization has letterhead stationery;

(*6*) Establish how the author knows the applicant; and

(*7*) Establish the origin of the information being attested to.

(F) Additional documents to support the applicant's claim may include:

(*1*) Money order receipts for money sent into or out of the country;

(*2*) Passport entries;

(*3*) Birth certificates of children born in the United States;

(*4*) Bank books with dated transactions;

(*5*) Letters or correspondence between applicant and other person or organization;

(*6*) Social Security card;

(*7*) Selective Service card;

(*8*) Automobile license receipts, title, vehicle registration, etc.;

(*9*) Deeds, mortgages, contracts to which applicant has been a party;

(*10*) Tax receipts;

(*11*) Insurance policies, receipts, or letters; and

(*12*) Any other relevant document.

(v) *Proof of financial responsibility.* An applicant for adjustment of status under this part is subject to the provisions of section 212(a)(15) of the Act relating to excludability of aliens likely to become public charges. Generally, the evidence of employment submitted under paragraph (b)(4)(iv)(A) of this section will serve to demonstrate the alien's financial responsibility during the documented period(s) of employment. If the alien's period(s) of residence in the United States include significant gaps in employment or if there is reason to believe that the alien may have received public assistance while employed, the alien may be required to provide proof that he or she has not received public cash assistance. An applicant for residence who is determined likely to become a public charge and is unable to overcome this determination after application of the Special Rule under paragraph (b)(11)(iv)(C) of this section will be denied adjustment. The burden of proof to demonstrate the inapplicability of this provision of law lies with the applicant who may provide:

(A) Evidence of a history of employment (*i.e.*, employment letter, W-2 forms, income tax returns, etc.);

(B) Evidence that he/she is self-supporting (*i.e.*, bank statements, stocks, other assets, etc.); or

(C) Form I–134. Affidavit of Support, completed by a spouse on behalf of the applicant and/or children of the applicant or a parent in behalf of children which guarantees complete or partial financial support. Acceptance of the Affidavit of Support shall be extended to other family members in unusual family circumstances.

Generally, the evidence of employment submitted under paragraph (b)(4)(iv)(A) of this section will serve to demonstrate the alien's financial responsibility during the documented period(s) of employment. If the alien's period(s) of residence in the United States include significant gaps in employment or if there is reason to believe that the alien may have received public assistance while employed, the alien may be required to provide proof that he or she has not received public cash assistance. An applicant for residence who is likely to become a public charge will be denied adjustment.

(vi) *Burden of proof.* An alien applying for adjustment of status under this part has the burden of proving by a preponderance of the evidence that he or she has resided in the United States for the requisite periods, is admissible to the United States under the provisions of section 245A of the Act, and is otherwise eligible for adjustment of status under this section. The inference to be drawn from the documentation provided shall depend on the extent of the documentation, its credibility and amenability to verification.

(vii) *Evidence.* The sufficiency of all evidence produced by the applicant will be judged according to its probative value and credibility. To meet his or her burden of proof, an applicant must provide evidence of eligibility apart from his or her own testimony. In judging the probative value and credibility of the evidence submitted, greater weight will be given to the submission of original documentation.

(5) *Filing of application.* (i) The application must be filed on Form I–687 at an office of a designated entity or at a Service office within the jurisdiction of the district where the applicant resides. If the application is filed with a designated entity, the alien must have consented to having the designated entity forward the application to the Service office. In the case of applications filed at a Service office, the district director may, at his or her discretion:

(A) Require the applicant to file the application in person; or

(B) Require the applicant to file the application by mail; or

(C) Permit the filing of applications whether by mail or in person.

The applicant must appear for a personal interview at the Service office as scheduled. If the applicant is 14 years of age or older, the application must be accompanied by a completed Form FD–258 (Applicant Card).

(ii) At the time of the interview, whenever possible, original documents must be submitted except the following: Official government records; employment or employment-related records maintained by employers, union, or collective bargaining organizations; medical records; school records maintained by a school or school board; or other records maintained by a party other than the applicant. Copies of records maintained by parties other than the applicant which are submitted in evidence must be certified as true and correct by such parties and must bear their seal or signature or the signature and title of persons authorized to act in their behalf. If at the time of the interview the return of the original document is desired by the applicant, the document must be accompanied by notarized copies or copies certified true and correct by a qualified designated entity or by the alien's representative in the format prescribed in § 204.2(j)(1) or (2) of this chapter. At the discretion of the district director, original documents, even if accompanied by certified copies, may be temporarily retained for forensic examination by the Document Analysis Unit at the Regional Processing Facility having jurisdiction over the Service office to which the documents were submitted.

(iii) A separate application (I–687) must be filed by each eligible applicant. All fees required by § 103.7(b)(1) of this chapter must be submitted in the exact amount in the form of a money order, cashier's check, or certified bank check, made payable to the Immigration and Naturalization Service. No personal checks or currency will be accepted. Fees will not be waived or refunded under any circumstances.

(6) *Filing date of application.* The date the alien submits a completed application to a Service office or designated entity shall be considered the filing date of the application, provided that in the case of an application filed at a designated entity the alien has consented to having the designated entity forward the application to the Service office having jurisdiction over the location of the alien's residence. Designated entities are required to forward completed applications to the appropriate Service office within 60 days of receipt.

(7) *Selective Service registration.* At the time of filing an application under this section, male applicants over the age of 17 and under the age of 26, are required to be registered under the Military Selective Service Act. An applicant shall present evidence that he has

previously registered under that Act in the form of a letter of acknowledgement from the Selective Service System, or such alien shall present a completed and signed Form SSS–1 at the time of filing Form I–687 with the Immigration and Naturalization Service or a designated entity. Form SSS–1 will be forwarded to the Selective Service System by the Service.

(8) *Continuous residence.* (i) For the purpose of this Act, an applicant for temporary residence status shall be regarded as having resided continuously in the United States if, at the time of filing of the application:

(A) No single absence from the United States has exceeded 45 days, and the aggregate of all absences has not exceeded 180 days between July 21, 1984, through the date the application for temporary resident status is filed, unless the alien can establish that due to emergent reasons, his or her return to the United States could not be accomplished within the time period allowed;

(B) The alien was maintaining a residence in the United States; and

(C) The alien's departure from the United States was not based on an order of deportation.

(ii) An alien who has been absent from the United States in accordance with the Service's advance parole procedures shall not be considered as having interrupted his or her continuous residence as required at the time of filing an application under this section.

(9) *Medical examination.* (i) An applicant under this part shall be required to submit to an examination by a designated civil surgeon at no expense to the government. The designated civil surgeon shall report on the findings of the mental and physical condition of the applicant and the determination of the alien's immunization status on Form I–693, "Medical Examination of Aliens Seeking Adjustment of Status, (Pub. L. 99–603)". Results of the medical examination must be presented to the Service at the time of interview and shall be incorporated into the record. Any applicant certified under paragraphs (1), (2), (3), (4) or (5) of section 212(a) of the Act may appeal to a Board of Medical Officers of the U.S. Public Health Service as provided in section 234 of the Act and part 235 of this chapter.

(ii) All applicants who file for temporary resident status are required to include the results of a serological test for the HIV virus on the I–693. All HIV-positive applicants shall be advised that a waiver is available and shall be provided with the opportunity to apply for a waiver.

(10) *Interview.* Each applicant, regardless of age, must appear at the appropriate Service office and must be fingerprinted for the purpose of issuance of an employment authorization document and Form I–688. Each applicant shall be interviewed by an immigration officer, except that the interview may be waived for a child under 14 years of age, or when it is impractical because of the health or advanced age of the applicant.

(11) *Applicability of exclusion grounds*—(i) *Grounds of exclusion not to be applied.* Paragraphs (14), (workers entering without labor certification); (20), (immigrants not in possession of a valid entry document); (21), (visas issued without compliance with section 203); (25), (illiterates); and (32) (graduates of non-accredited medical schools) of section 212(a) of the Act shall not apply to applicants for temporary resident status.

(ii) *Waiver of grounds of exclusion.* Except as provided in paragraph (b)(11)(iii) of this section, the Attorney General may waive any other provision of section 212(a) of the Act only in the case of individual aliens for humanitarian purposes, to assure family unity, or when the granting of such a waiver is in the public interest. If an alien is excludable on grounds which may be waived as set forth in this paragraph, he or she shall be advised of the procedures for applying for a waiver of grounds of excludability on Form I–690. When an application for waiver of grounds of excludability is filed jointly with an application for temporary residence under this section, it shall be accepted for processing at the Service office. If an application for waiver of grounds of excludability is submitted after the alien's preliminary interview at the Service office, it shall be forwarded to the appropriate Regional Processing Facility. All applications for waivers of grounds of excludability must be accompanied by the correct fee in the exact amount. All fees for applications filed in the United States must be in the form of a money order, cashier's check, or bank check. No personal checks or currency will be accepted. Fees will not be waived or refunded under any circumstances. An application for waiver of grounds of excludability under this part shall be approved or denied by the director of the Regional Processing Facility in whose jurisdiction the alien's application for adjustment of status was filed except that in cases involving clear statutory ineligibility or fraud, such application may be denied by the district director in whose jurisdiction the application is filed, and in cases returned to a Service office for re-interview, such application may be approved at the discretion of the district director. The applicant shall be notified of the decision and, if the application is denied, of the reason therefore. Appeal from an adverse decision under this part may be taken by the applicant on Form I–694 within 30 days after the service of the notice only to the Service's Administrative Appeals Unit pursuant to the provisions of section 103.3(a) of this chapter.

(iii) *Grounds of exclusion that may not be waived.* Notwithstanding any other provision of the Act, the following provisions of section 212(a) may not be waived by the Attorney General under paragraph (b)(11)(ii) of this section:

(A) Paragraphs (9) and (10) (criminals);

(B) Paragraph (23) (narcotics) except for a single offense of simple possession of thirty grams or less of marijuana;

(C) Paragraphs (27) (prejudicial to the public interest), (28) (communist), and (29) (subversive);

(D) Paragraph (33) (participated in Nazi persecution).

(iv) *Determination of Likely to become a public charge* and the special rule. (A) Prior to use of the special rule for determination of public charge, an alien must first be determined to be excludable under section 212(a)(15) of the Act. If the applicant is determined to be *likely to become a public charge,* he or she may still be admissible under the terms of the Special Rule.

(B) In determining whether an alien is *likely to become a public charge,* financial responsibility of the alien is to be established by examining the totality of the alien's circumstances at the time of his or her application for legalization. The existence or absence of a particular factor should never be the sole criterion for determining if an alien is likely to become a public charge. The determination of financial responsibility should be a prospective evaluation based on the alien's age, health, income and vocation.

(C) An alien who has a consistent employment history which shows the ability to support himself or herself even though his or her income may be below the poverty level may be admissible under this section. The alien's employment history need not be continuous in that it is uninterrupted. It should be continuous in the sense that the alien shall be regularly attached to the workforce, has an income over a substantial period of the applicable time, and has demonstrated the capacity to exist on his or her income without recourse to public cash assistance. The Special Rule is prospective in that the Service shall determine, based on the alien's history, whether he or she is likely to become a public charge. Past acceptance of public cash assistance within a history of consistent employment will enter into this decision. The weight given in considering applicability of the public charge provisions will depend on many factors, but the length of time an applicant has received public cash assistance will constitute a significant factor. It is not necessary to file a waiver in order to apply the Special Rule for Determination of Public Charge.

(v) *Public assistance and criminal history verification.* Declarations by an applicant that he or she has not been the recipient of public cash assistance and/or has not had a criminal record are subject to a verification of facts by the Service. The applicant must agree to fully cooperate in the verification process. Failure to assist the Service in verifying information necessary for the adjudication of the application may result in a denial of the application.

(12) *Continuous physical presence since December 22, 1987.* (i) An alien applying

for adjustment to temporary resident status must establish that he or she has been continuously physically present in the United States since December 22, 1987. Aliens who were outside of the United States on the date of enactment or departed the United States after enactment may apply for legalization if they reentered prior to March 21, 1988, and meet the continuous residence requirements and are otherwise eligible for legalization.

(ii) A brief, casual and innocent absence means a departure authorized by the Service (advance parole) subsequent to March 21, 1988, of not more than thirty (30) days for legitimate emergency or humanitarian purposes unless a further period of authorized departure has been granted in the discretion of the district director or a departure was beyond the alien's control.

(13) *Departure.* (i) During the time period from the date that an alien's application establishing prima facie eligibility for temporary resident status is reviewed at a Service office and the date status as a temporary resident is granted, the alien applicant can be readmitted to the United States provided his or her departure was authorized under the Service's advance parole provisions contained in §212.5(f) of this chapter.

(ii) An alien whose application for temporary resident status has been approved may be admitted to the United States upon return as a returning temporary resident provided he or she:

(A) Is not under deportation proceedings, such proceedings having been instituted subsequent to the approval of temporary resident status. A temporary resident alien will not be considered deported if that alien departs the United States while under an outstanding order of deportation issued prior to the approval of temporary resident status;

(B) Has not been absent from the United States for more than 30 days on the date application for admission is made;

(C) Has not been absent from the United States for an aggregate period of more than 90 days since the date the alien was granted lawful temporary resident status;

(D) Presents Form I–688;

(E) Presents himself or herself for inspection; and

(F) Is otherwise admissible.

(iii) The periods of time in paragraphs (b)(13)(ii)(B) and (C) of this section may be waived at the discretion of the Attorney General in cases where the absence from the United States was due merely to a brief and casual trip abroad due to emergent or extenuating circumstances beyond the alien's control.

(14) *Employment and travel authorization*—(i) *General.* Authorization for employment and travel abroad for temporary resident status applicants under this section may be granted only by a Service office. INS district directors will determine the Service location for the completion of processing travel documentation. In the case of an application which has been filed with a designated entity, employment authorization may be granted by the Service only after the application has been properly received at the Service office.

(ii) *Employment and travel authorization prior to the granting of temporary resident status.* (A) Permission to travel abroad and accept employment may be granted to the applicant after an interview has been conducted in connection with an application establishing prima facie eligibility for temporary resident status. Permission to travel abroad may be granted in emergent circumstances in accordance with the Service's advance parole provisions contained in §212.5(f) of this chapter after an interview has been conducted in connection with an application establishing prima facie eligibility for temporary resident status.

(B) If an appointment cannot be scheduled within 30 days, authorization to accept employment will be granted, valid until the scheduled appointment date. The appointment letter will be endorsed with the temporary employment authorization. An employment authorization document will be given to the applicant after an interview has been completed by an immigration officer unless a formal denial is issued by a Service office. This temporary employment authorization will be restricted to six-months duration, pending final determination on the application for temporary resident status.

(iii) *Employment and travel authorization upon grant of temporary resident status.* Upon grant of an application for adjustment to temporary resident status by a Regional Processing Facility, the processing facility will forward a notice of approval to the alien at his or her last known address, or to his or her legal representative. The alien will be required to return to the appropriate INS office, surrender the I–688A or employment authorization document previously issued, and obtain Form I–688, Temporary Resident Card, authorizing employment and travel abroad.

(iv) *Revocation of employment authorization upon denial of temporary resident status.* Upon denial of an application for adjustment to temporary resident status, the alien will be notified that if a timely appeal is not submitted, employment authorization shall be automatically revoked on the final day of the appeal period. An applicant whose appeal period has ended is no longer considered to be an Eligible Legalized Alien for the purposes of the administration of State Legalization Impact Assistance Grants (SLIAG) funding.

(15) *Decision.* The applicant shall be notified in writing of the decision. If the application is denied, the reason(s) for the decision shall be provided to the applicant. An appeal from an adverse decision under this part may be taken by the applicant on Form I–694.

(16) *Appeal process.* An adverse decision under this part may be appealed to the Associate Commissioner, Examinations (Administrative Appeals Unit), the appellate authority designated in § 103.1(f)(2). Any appeal shall be submitted to the Regional Processing Facility (RPF) with the required fee within 30 days after service of the Notice of Denial in accordance with the procedures of § 103.3(a) of this chapter. An appeal received after the 30-day period will not be accepted. The 30-day period for submission of an appeal begins three days after the Notice of Denial is mailed as provided in 8 CFR 103.8(b). If a review of the Record of Proceeding (ROP) is requested by the alien or his or her legal representative and an appeal has been properly filed, an additional 30 days will be allowed for this review beginning at the time the ROP is mailed. A brief may be submitted with the appeal form or submitted up to 30 calendar days from the date of receipt of the appeal form at the RPF. Briefs filed after submission of the appeal should be mailed directly to the RPF. For good cause shown, the time within which a brief supporting an appeal may be submitted may be extended by the Director of the Regional Processing Facility.

(17) *Motions.* The Regional Processing Facility director may *sua sponte* reopen and reconsider any adverse decision. When an appeal to the Associate Commissioner, Examinations (Administrative Appeals Unit) has been filed, the INS director of the Regional Processing Facility may issue a new decision granting the benefit which has been requested. The director's new decision must be served on the appealing party within 45 days of receipt of any briefs and/or new evidence, or upon expiration of the time allowed for the submission of any briefs. Motions to reopen a proceeding or reconsider a decision shall not be considered under this part.

(18) *Certifications.* The Regional Processing Facility director may, in accordance with § 103.4 of this chapter, certify a decision to the Associate Commissioner, Examinations (Administrative Appeals Unit) when the case involves an unusually complex or novel question of law or fact. The decision on an appealed case subsequently remanded to the Regional Processing Facility director will be certified to the Administrative Appeals Unit.

(19) *Date of adjustment to temporary residence.* The status of an alien whose application for temporary resident status is approved shall be adjusted to that of a lawful temporary resident as of the date indicated on the application fee receipt issued at the Service office.

(20) *Termination of temporary resident status*—(i) *Termination of temporary resident status (General).* The status of an alien lawfully admitted for temporary residence under § 245a.4 of this part may be terminated at any time. It is not necessary that a final order of deportation be entered in order to terminate temporary resident status. The temporary resident status may be terminated upon the occurrence of any of the following:

(A) It is determined that the alien was ineligible for temporary residence under § 245a.4 of this part;

(B) The alien commits an act which renders him or her inadmissible as an immigrant unless a waiver is obtained, as provided in this part;

(C) The alien is convicted of any felony, or three or more misdemeanors;

(D) The alien fails to file for adjustment of status from temporary resident to permanent resident within 31 months of the date he or she was granted status as a temporary resident.

(ii) *Procedure.* Termination of an alien's status will be made only on notice to the alien sent by certified mail directed to his or her last known address, and, if applicable, to his or her representative. The alien must be given an opportunity to offer evidence in opposition to the grounds alleged for termination of his or her status. Evidence in opposition must be submitted within 30 days after the service of the Notice of Intent to Terminate. If the alien's status is terminated, the director of the Regional Processing Facility shall notify the alien of the decision and the reason for the termination, and further notify the alien that any Service Form issued to the alien authorizing employment and/or travel abroad, or any Form I–688, Temporary Resident Card previously issued to the alien will be declared void by the director of the Regional Processing Facility within 30 days if no appeal of the termination decision is filed within that period. The alien may appeal the decision to the Associate Commissioner, Examinations (Administrative Appeals Unit). Any appeal along with the required fee, shall be filed with the Regional Processing Facility within 30 days after the service of the notice of termination. If no appeal is filed within that period, the official Service document shall be deemed void, and must be surrendered without delay to an immigration officer or to the issuing office of the Service.

(iii) *Termination not construed as rescission under section 246.* For the purposes of this part the phrase *termination of status* of an alien granted lawful temporary residence under this section shall not be construed to necessitate a rescission of status as described in section 246 of the Act, and the proceedings required by the regulations issued thereunder shall not apply.

(iv) *Return to unlawful status after termination.* Termination of the status of any alien previously adjusted to lawful temporary residence shall act to return such alien to the status held prior to the adjustment, and render him or her amenable to exclusion or deportation proceedings under sections 236 or 242 of the Act, as appropriate.

(21) *Ineligibility for immigration benefits.* An alien whose status is adjusted to that of a lawful temporary resident under § 245a.4 of this part is not entitled to submit a petition pursuant to section 203(a)(2), nor is such alien entitled to any other benefit or consideration accorded under the Act to aliens lawfully admitted for permanent residence.

(22) *Declaration of intending citizen.* An alien who has been granted the status of temporary resident under § 245a.4 of this part may assert a claim of discrimination on the basis of citizenship status under section 274B of the Act only if he or she has previously filed Form I–772 (Declaration of Intending Citizen) after being granted such status. The Declaration of Intending Citizen is not required as a basis for filing a petition for naturalization; nor shall it be regarded as a right to United States citizenship; nor shall it be regarded as evidence of a person's status as a resident.

(23) *Limitation on access to information and confidentiality.* (i) No person other than a sworn officer or employee of the Department of Justice or bureau or agency thereof, will be permitted to examine individual applications. For purposes of this part, any individual employed under contract by the Service to work in connection with the Legalization Program shall be considered an *employee of the Department of Justice or bureau or agency thereof.*

(ii) No information furnished pursuant to an application for temporary or permanent resident status under this section shall be used for any purpose except:

(A) To make a determination on the application; or,

(B) for the enforcement of the provisions encompassed in section 245A(c)(6) of the Act, except as provided in paragraph (b)(23)(iii) of this section.

(iii) If a determination is made by the Service that the alien has, in connection with his or her application, engaged in fraud or willful misrepresentation or concealment of a material fact, knowingly provided a false writing or document in making his or her application, knowingly made a false statement or representation, or engaged in any other activity prohibited by section 245A(c)(6) of the Act, the Service shall refer the matter to the United States Attorney for prosecution of the alien or of any person who created or supplied a false writing or document for use in an application for adjustment of status under this part.

(iv) Information contained in granted legalization files may be used by the Service at a later date to make a decision on an immigrant visa petition (or other status petition) filed by the applicant under section 204(a), or for naturalization applications submitted by the applicant.

(c) *Adjustment from temporary to permanent resident status.* The provisions of § 245a.3 of this part shall be applied to aliens adjusting to permanent residence under this part.

[54 FR 6505, Feb. 13, 1989, as amended at 54 FR 29455, July 12, 1989; 54 FR 47676, Nov. 16, 1989; 60 FR 21976, May 4, 1995; 65 FR 82256, Dec. 28, 2000; 76 FR 53794, Aug. 29, 2011; 78 FR 18472, Mar. 27, 2013]

§ 245a.5 Temporary disqualification of certain newly legalized aliens from receiving benefits from programs of financial assistance furnished under federal law.

(a) Except as provided in § 245a.5(b), any alien who has obtained the status of an alien lawfully admitted for temporary residence pursuant to section 245A of the Act (Adjustment of Status of Certain Entrants Before January 1, 1982, to that of Person Admitted for Lawful Residence) or 210A of the Act (Determinations of Agricultural Labor Shortages and Admission of Additional Special Agricultural Workers) is ineligible, for a period of five years from the date such status was obtained, for benefits financed directly or indirectly, in whole or in part, through the programs identified in § 245a.5(c) of this chapter.

(b)(1) Section 245a.5(a) shall not apply to a Cuban or Haitian entrant (as defined in paragraph (1) or (2)(A) of section 501(e) of Public Law 96–422, as in effect on April 1, 1983), or in the case of assistance (other than aid to families with dependent children) which is furnished to an alien who is an aged, blind, or disabled individual (as defined in section 1614(a)(1) of the Social Security Act).

(2) With respect to any alien who has obtained the status of an alien lawfully admitted for temporary residence pursuant to section 210A of the Act only, assistance furnished under the Legal Services Corporation Act (42 U.S.C. 2996, *et seq.*) or title V of the Housing Act of 1949 (42 U.S.C. 1471 *et seq.*) shall not be construed to be financial assistance referred to in § 245a.5(a).

(3) Section 245a.5(a) shall not apply to benefits financed through the programs identified in § 245a.5(c), which are marked with an asterisk (*), except to the extent that such benefits:

(i) Consist of, or are financed by, financial assistance in the form of grants, wages, loan, loan guarantees, or otherwise, which is furnished by the Federal Government directly, or indirectly through a State or local government or a private entity, to eligible individuals or to private suppliers of goods or services to such individuals, or is furnished to a State or local government that provides to such individuals goods or services of a kind that is offered by private suppliers, and

(ii) Are targeted to individuals in financial need; either (A) in order to be eligible, individuals must establish that their income or wealth is below some maximum level, or, with respect to certain loan or loan guarantee programs, that they are unable to obtain financing from alternative sources, or at prevailing interest rates, or at rates that would permit the achievement of program goals, or (B) distribution of assistance is directed, geographically or otherwise, in a way that is intended to primarily benefit persons in financial need, as evidenced by references to such intent in the authorizing legislation.

(c) The programs of Federal financial assistance referred to in § 245a.5(a) are those identified in the list set forth below. The General Services Administration (GSA) Program Numbers set forth in the right column of the program list refer to the program identification numbers used in the Catalog of Federal Domestic Assistance, published by the United States General Services Administration, as updated through December, 1986.

	GSA Program Numbers
Department of Agriculture:	
Farm Operating Loans	10.406
Farm Ownership Loans	10.407
Department of Health and Human Services:	
Assistance Payments—Maintenance Assistance (Maintenance Assistance; Emergency Assistance; State Aid; Aid to Families with Dependent Children)	13.780
Low-Income Home Energy Assistance	13.789
*Community Services Block Grant	13.792
*Community Services Block Grant—Discretionary Awards	13.793
Department of Housing and Urban Development:	
Mortgage Insurance—Housing in Older, Declining Areas (223(e))	14.123
Mortgage Insurance—Special Credit Risks (237)	14.140
*Community Development Block Grants/Entitlement Grants	14.218
*Community Development Block Grants/Small Cities Program (Small Cities)	14.219
Section 312 Rehabilitation Loans (312)	14.220
*Urban development action grants	14.221
*Community Development Block Grants/State's Program	14.228
Section 221(d)(3) Mortgage Insurance for Multifamily Rental Housing for Low and Moderate Income Families (Below Market Interest Rate)	14.136
Department of Labor:	
Senior Community Service Employment Program (SCSEP)	17.235
Office of Personnel Management:	
Federal Employment for Disadvantaged Youth—Part-Time (Stay-in-School Program)	27.003
Federal Employment for Disadvantaged Youth—Summer (Summer Aides)	27.004
Small Business Administration:	
Small Business Loans (7(a) Loans)	59.012
Department of Energy:	
Weatherization Assistance for Low-Income Persons	81.042
Department of Education:	
Patricia Roberts Harris Fellowships (Graduate and Professional Study; Graduate and Professional Study Opportunity Fellowships; Public Service Education Fellowships)	84.094
Legal Training for the Disadvantaged (The American Bar Association Fund for Public Education)	84.136
Allen J. Ellender Fellowship Program (Ellender Fellowship)	84.148
Legal Services Corporation:	
Payments to Legal Services Corporation	....

[54 FR 29437, July 12, 1989, as amended at 54 FR 49964, Dec. 4, 1989]

§ 245a.6 Treatment of denied application under part 245a, Subpart B.

If the district director finds that an eligible alien as defined at § 245a.10 has not established eligibility under section 1104 of the LIFE Act (part 245a, Subpart B), the district director shall consider whether the eligible alien has established eligibility for adjustment to temporary resident status under section 245A of the Act, as in effect before enactment of section 1104 of the LIFE Act (part 245a, Subpart A). In such an adjudication using this Subpart A, the district director will deem the "date of filing the application" to be the date the eligible alien establishes that he or she was "front-desked" or that, though he or she took concrete steps to apply, the front-desking policy was a substantial cause of his or her failure to apply. If the eligible alien has established eligibility for adjustment to temporary resident status, the LIFE Legalization application shall be deemed converted to an application for temporary residence under this Subpart A.

[67 FR 38350, June 4, 2002]

Subpart B—Legal Immigration Family Equity (LIFE) Act Legalization Provisions

SOURCE: 66 FR 29673, June 1, 2001, unless otherwise noted.

§ 245a.10 Definitions.

In this Subpart B, the terms:

Eligible alien means an alien (including a spouse or child as defined at section 101(b)(1) of the Act of the alien who was such as of the date the alien alleges that he or she attempted to file or was discouraged from filing an application for legalization during the original application period) who, before October 1, 2000, filed with the Attorney General a written claim for class membership, with or without filing fee, pursuant to a court order issued in the case of:

(1) *Catholic Social Services, Inc.* v. *Meese*, vacated sub nom. *Reno* v. *Catholic Social Services, Inc.*, 509 U.S. 43 (1993) (*CSS*);

(2) *League of United Latin American Citizens* v. *INS*, vacated sub nom. *Reno* v. *Catholic Social Services, Inc.*, 509 U.S. 43 (1993) (*LULAC*); or

(3) *Zambrano* v. *INS*, vacated, 509 U.S. 918 (1993) (*Zambrano*).

Lawful Permanent Resident (LPR) means the status of having been lawfully accorded the privilege of residing permanently in the United States as an immigrant in accordance with the immigration laws, such status not having changed.

LIFE Act means the Legal Immigration Family Equity Act and the LIFE Act Amendments of 2000.

LIFE Legalization means the provisions of section 1104 of the LIFE Act and section 1503 of the LIFE Act Amendments.

Prima facie means eligibility is established if an "eligible alien" presents a properly filed and completed Form I-485 and specific factual information which in the absence of rebuttal will establish a claim of eligibility under this Subpart B.

Written claim for class membership means a filing, in writing, in one of the forms listed in §245a.14 that provides the Attorney General with notice that the applicant meets the class definition in the cases of *CSS*, *LULAC* or *Zambrano*.

[66 FR 29673, June 1, 2001, as amended at 67 FR 38350, June 4, 2002; 67 FR 66532, Nov. 1, 2002]

§ 245a.11 Eligibility to adjust to LPR status.

An eligible alien, as defined in §245a.10, may adjust status to LPR status under LIFE Legalization if:

(a) He or she properly files, with fee, Form I-485, Application to Register Permanent Residence or Adjust Status, with the Service during the application period beginning June 1, 2001, and ending June 4, 2003.

(b) He or she entered the United States before January 1, 1982, and resided continuously in the United States in an unlawful status since that date through May 4, 1988;

(c) He or she was continuously physically present in the United States during the period beginning on November 6, 1986, and ending on May 4, 1988;

(d) He or she is not inadmissible to the United States for permanent residence under any provisions of section 212(a) of the Act, except as provided in §245a.18, and that he or she:

(1) Has not been convicted of any felony or of three or more misdemeanors committed in the United States;

(2) Has not assisted in the persecution of any person or persons on account of race, religion, nationality, membership in a particular social group, or political opinion; and

(3) Is registered or registering under the Military Selective Service Act, if the alien is required to be so registered; and

(e) He or she can demonstrate basic citizenship skills.

[66 FR 29673, June 1, 2001, as amended at 67 FR 38350, June 4, 2002]

§ 245a.12 Filing and applications.

(a) *When to file.* The application period began on June 1, 2001, and ends on June 4, 2003. To benefit from the provisions of LIFE Legalization, an alien must properly file an application for adjustment of status, Form I-485, with appropriate fee, to the Service during the application period as described in this section. All applications, whether filed in the United States or filed from abroad, must be postmarked on or before June 4, 2003, to be considered timely filed.

(1) If the postmark is illegible or missing, and the application was mailed from within the United States, the Service will consider the application to be timely filed if it is *received* on or before June 9, 2003.

(2) If the postmark is illegible or missing, and the application was mailed from outside the United States, the Service will consider the application to be timely filed if it is *received* on or before June 18, 2003.

(3) If the postmark is made by other than the United States Post Office, and is filed from within the United States, the application must bear a date on or before June 4, 2003, and must be received on or before June 9, 2003.

(4) If an application filed from within the United States bears a postmark that was made by other than the United States Post Office, bears a date

on or before June 4, 2003, and is received after June 9, 2003, the alien must establish:

(i) That the application was actually deposited in the mail before the last collection of the mail from the place of deposit that was postmarked by the United States Post Office June 4, 2003; and

(ii) That the delay in receiving the application was due to a delay in the transmission of the mail; and

(iii) The cause of such delay.

(5) If an application filed from within the United States bears both a postmark that was made by other than the United States Post Office and a postmark that was made by the United States Post Office, the Service shall disregard the postmark that was made by other than the United States Post Office.

(6) If an application filed from abroad bears both a foreign postmark and a postmark that was subsequently made by the United States Post Office, the Service shall disregard the postmark that was made by the United States Post Office.

(7) In all instances, the burden of proof is on the applicant to establish timely filing of an application for LIFE Legalization.

(b) *Filing of applications in the United States.* The Service has jurisdiction over all applications for the benefits of LIFE Legalization under this Subpart B. All applications filed with the Service for the benefits of LIFE Legalization must be submitted by *mail* to the Service. After proper filing of the application, the Service will instruct the applicant to appear for fingerprinting as prescribed in 8 CFR 103.16. The Director of the Missouri Service Center shall have jurisdiction over all applications filed with the Service for LIFE Legalization adjustment of status, unless the Director refers the applicant for a personal interview at a local Service office as provided in § 245a.19.

(1) *Aliens in exclusion, deportation, or removal proceedings, or who have a pending motion to reopen or motion to reconsider.* An alien who is prima facie eligible for adjustment of status under LIFE Legalization who is in exclusion, deportation, or removal proceedings before the Immigration Court or the Board of Immigration Appeals (Board), or who is awaiting adjudication of a motion to reopen or motion to reconsider filed with the Immigration Court of the Board, may request that the proceedings be administratively closed or that the motion filed be indefinitely continued, in order to allow the alien to pursue a LIFE Legalization application with the Service. In the request to administratively close the matter or indefinitely continue the motion, the alien must include documents demonstrating prima facie eligibility for the relief, and proof that the application for relief had been properly filed with the Service as prescribed in this section. With the concurrence of Service counsel, if the alien appears eligible to file for relief under LIFE Legalization, the Immigration Court or the Board, whichever has jurisdiction, shall administratively close the proceeding or continue the motion indefinitely.

(2) If an alien has a matter before the Immigration Court or the Board that has been administratively closed for reasons unrelated to this Subpart B, the alien may apply before the Service for LIFE Legalization adjustment of status.

(3) *Aliens with final orders of exclusion, deportation, or removal.* An alien, who is prima facie eligible for adjustment of status under LIFE Legalization, and who is subject to a final order of exclusion, deportation, or removal, may apply to the Service for LIFE Legalization adjustment.

(c) *Filing of applications from outside the United States.* An applicant for LIFE Legalization may file an application for LIFE Legalization from abroad. An application for LIFE Legalization filed from outside the United States shall be submitted by mail to the Service according to the instructions on the application. The Missouri Service Center Director shall have jurisdiction over all applications filed with the Service for LIFE Legalization adjustment of status. After reviewing the application and all evidence with the application, the Service shall notify the applicant of any further requests for evidence regarding the application and, if eligible, how an interview will be conducted.

(d) *Application and supporting documentation.* Each applicant for LIFE Legalization adjustment of status must file Form I–485. An applicant should complete Part 2 of Form I–485 by checking box "h—other" and writing "LIFE Legalization" next to that block. Each application must be accompanied by:

(1) The Form I–485 application fee as contained in 8 CFR 103.7(b)(1).

(2) The fee for fingerprinting as contained in 8 CFR 103.7(b)(1), if the applicant is between the ages of 14 and 79.

(3) Evidence to establish identity, such as a passport, birth certificate, any national identity document from the alien's country of origin bearing photo and fingerprint, driver's license or similar document issued by a state if it contains a photo, or baptismal record/marriage certificate.

(4) A completed Form G–325A, Biographic Information Sheet, if the applicant is between the ages of 14 and 79.

(5) A report of medical examination, as specified in § 245.5 of this chapter.

(6) Two photographs, as described in the instructions to Form I–485.

(7) Proof of application for class membership in *CSS*, *LULAC*, or *Zambrano* class action lawsuits as described in § 245a.14.

(8) Proof of continuous residence in an unlawful status since prior to January 1, 1982, through May 4, 1988, as described in § 245a.15.

(9) Proof of continuous physical presence from November 6, 1986, through May 4, 1988, as described in § 245a.16.

(10) Proof of citizenship skills as described in § 245a.17. This proof may be submitted either at the time of filing the application, subsequent to filing the application but prior to the interview, or at the time of the interview.

(e) *Burden of proof.* An alien applying for adjustment of status under this part has the burden of proving by a preponderance of the evidence that he or she has resided in the United States for the requisite periods, is admissible to the United States under the provisions of section 212(a) of the Act, and is otherwise eligible for adjustment of status under this Subpart B. The inference to be drawn from the documentation provided shall depend on the extent of the documentation, its credibility and amenability to verification as set forth in paragraph (f) of this section.

(f) *Evidence.* The sufficiency of all evidence produced by the applicant will be judged according to its probative value and credibility. To meet his or her burden of proof, an applicant must provide evidence of eligibility apart from his or her own testimony. In judging the probative value and credibility of the evidence submitted, greater weight will be given to the submission of original documentation. Subject to verification by the Service, if the evidence required to be submitted by the applicant is already contained in the Service's file or databases relating to the applicant, the applicant may submit a statement to that effect in lieu of the actual documentation.

[66 FR 29673, June 1, 2001, as amended at 67 FR 38350, June 4, 2002; 76 FR 53794, Aug. 29, 2011]

§ 245a.13 During pendency of application.

(a) *In general.* When an eligible alien in the United States submits a prima facie application for adjustment of status under LIFE Legalization during the application period, until a final determination on his or her application has been made, the applicant:

(1) May not be deported or removed from the United States;

(2) Is authorized to engage in employment in the United States and is provided with an "employment authorized" endorsement or other appropriate work permit; and

(3) Is allowed to travel and return to the United States as described at paragraph (e) of this section. Any domestic LIFE Legalization applicant who departs the United States while his or her application is pending without advance parole may be denied re-admission to the United States as described at paragraph (e) of this section.

(b) *Determination of filing of claim for class membership.* With respect to each LIFE Legalization application for adjustment of status that is properly filed under this Subpart B during the application period, the Service will first determine whether or not the applicant is an "eligible alien" as defined under §245a.10 of this Subpart B by virtue of having filed with the Service a claim of class membership in the *CSS*, *LULAC*, or *Zambrano* lawsuit before October 1, 2000. If the Service's records indicate, or if the evidence submitted by the applicant with the application establishes, that the alien had filed the requisite claim of class membership before October 1, 2000, then the Service will proceed to adjudicate the application under the remaining standards of eligibility.

(c) *Prima facie eligibility*. Unless the Service has evidence indicating ineligibility due to criminal grounds of inadmissibility, an application for adjustment of status shall be treated as a prima facie application during the pendency of application, until the Service has made a final determination on the application, if:

(1) The application was properly filed under this Subpart B during the application period; and

(2) The applicant establishes that he or she filed the requisite claim for class membership in the *CSS*, *LULAC*, or *Zambrano* lawsuit.

(d) *Authorization to be employed in the United States while the application is pending*—(1) *Application for employment authorization*. An applicant for adjustment of status under LIFE Legalization who wishes to obtain initial or continued employment authorization during the pendency of the adjustment application must file a Form I–765, Application for Employment Authorization, with the Service, including the fee as set forth in §103.7(b)(1) of this chapter. The applicant may submit Form I–765 either concurrently with or subsequent to the filing of the application for adjustment of status benefits on Form I–485.

(2) *Adjudication and issuance*. Until a final determination on the application has been made, an eligible alien who submits a prima facie application for adjustment of status under this Subpart B shall be authorized to engage in employment in the United States and be provided with an "employment authorized" endorsement or other appropriate work permit in accordance with §274a.12(c)(24) of this chapter. An alien shall not be granted employment authorization pursuant to LIFE Legalization until he or she has submitted a prima facie application for adjustment of status under this Subpart B. If the Service finds that additional evidence is required from the alien in order to establish prima facie eligibility for LIFE Legalization, the Service shall request such evidence from the alien in writing. Nothing in this section shall preclude an applicant for adjustment of status under LIFE Legalization from being granted an initial employment authorization or an extension of employment authorization under any other provision of law or regulation for which the alien may be eligible.

(e) *Travel while the application is pending*. This paragraph is authorized by section 1104(c)(3) of the LIFE Act relating to the ability of an alien to travel abroad and return to the United States while his or her LIFE Legalization adjustment application is pending. Parole authority is granted to the Missouri Service Center Director for the purposes described in this section. Nothing in this section shall preclude an applicant for adjustment of status under LIFE Legalization from being granted advance parole or admission into the United States under any other provision of law or regulation for which the alien may be eligible.

(1) An applicant for LIFE Legalization benefits who wishes to travel during the pendency of the application and who is applying from within the United States should file, with his or her application for adjustment, at the Missouri Service Center, a Form I–131, Application for Travel Document, with fee as set forth in §103.7(b)(1) of this chapter. The Service shall approve the Form I–131 and issue an advance parole document, unless the Service finds that the alien's application does not establish a prima facie claim to adjustment of status under LIFE Legalization.

(2) An eligible alien who has properly filed a Form I–485 pursuant to this Subpart B, and who needs to travel abroad pursuant to the standards prescribed in section 212(d)(5) of the Act, may file a Form I–131 with the district director having jurisdiction over his or her place of residence.

(3) If an alien travels abroad and returns to the United States with a grant of advance parole, the Service shall

presume that the alien is entitled to return under section 1104(c)(3)(B) of the LIFE Act, unless, in a removal or expedited removal proceeding, the Service shows by a preponderance of the evidence, that one or more of the provisions of §245a.11(d) makes the alien ineligible for adjustment of status under LIFE Legalization.

(4) If an alien travels abroad and returns without a grant of advance parole, he or she shall be denied admission and shall be subject to removal or expedited removal unless the alien establishes, clearly and beyond doubt, that:

(i) He or she filed an application for adjustment pursuant to LIFE Legalization during the application period that presented a prima facie claim to adjustment of status under LIFE Legalization; and,

(ii) His or her absence was either a brief and casual trip consistent with an intention on the alien's part to pursue his or her LIFE Legalization adjustment application, or was a brief temporary trip that occurred because of the alien's need to tend to family obligations relating to a close relative's death or illness or similar family need.

(5) An applicant for LIFE Legalization benefits who applies for admission into the United States shall not be subject to the provisions of section 212(a)(9)(B) of the Act.

(6) Denial of admission under this section is not a denial of the alien's application for adjustment. The alien may continue to pursue his or her application for adjustment from abroad, and may also appeal any denial of such application from abroad. Such application shall be adjudicated in the same manner as other applications filed from abroad.

(f) *Stay of final order of exclusion, deportation, or removal.* The filing of a LIFE Legalization adjustment application on or after June 1, 2001, and on or before June 4, 2003, stays the execution of any final order of exclusion, deportation, or removal. This stay shall remain in effect until there is a final decision on the LIFE Legalization application, unless the district director who intends to execute the order makes a formal determination that the applicant does not present a prima facie claim to LIFE Legalization eligibility pursuant to §§245a.18(a)(1) or (a)(2), or §§245a.18(c)(2)(i), (c)(2)(ii), (c)(2)(iii), (c)(2)(iv), (c)(2)(v), or (c)(2)(vi), and serves the applicant with a written decision explaining the reason for this determination. Any such stay determination by the district director is not appealable. Neither an Immigration Judge nor the Board has jurisdiction to adjudicate an application for stay of execution of an exclusion, deportation, or removal order, on the basis of the alien's having filed a LIFE Legalization adjustment application.

[66 FR 29673, June 1, 2001, as amended at 67 FR 38351, June 4, 2002]

§245a.14 Application for class membership in the *CSS, LULAC,* or *Zambrano* lawsuit.

The Service will first determine whether an alien filed a written claim for class membership in the *CSS, LULAC,* or *Zambrano* lawsuit as reflected in the Service's indices, a review of the alien's administrative file with the Service, and by all evidence provided by the alien. An alien must provide with the application for LIFE Legalization evidence establishing that, before October 1, 2000, he or she was a class member applicant in the *CSS, LULAC,* or *Zambrano* lawsuit. An alien should include as many forms of evidence as the alien has available to him or her. Such forms of evidence include, but are not limited to:

(a) An Employment Authorization Document (EAD) or other employment document issued by the Service pursuant to the alien's class membership in the *CSS, LULAC,* or *Zambrano* lawsuit (if a photocopy of the EAD is submitted, the alien's name, A-number, issuance date, and expiration date should be clearly visible);

(b) Service document(s) addressed to the alien, or his or her representative, granting or denying the class membership, which includes date, alien's name and A-number;

(c) The questionnaire for class member applicant under *CSS, LULAC,* or *Zambrano* submitted with the class membership application, which includes date, alien's full name and date of birth;

(d) Service document(s) addressed to the alien, or his or her representative, discussing matters pursuant to the class membership application, which includes date, alien's name and A-number. These include, but are not limited to the following:

(1) Form I–512, Parole authorization, or denial of such;

(2) Form I–221, Order to Show Cause;

(3) Form I–862, Notice to Appear;

(4) Final order of removal or deportation;

(5) Request for evidence letter (RFE); or

(6) Form I–687 submitted with the class membership application.

(e) Form I–765, Application for Employment Authorization, submitted pursuant to a court order granting interim relief.

(f) An application for a stay of deportation, exclusion, or removal pursuant to a court's order granting interim relief.

(g) Any other relevant document(s).

[66 FR 29673, June 1, 2001, as amended at 67 FR 38351, June 4, 2002]

§ 245a.15 Continuous residence in an unlawful status since prior to January 1, 1982, through May 4, 1988.

(a) *General.* The Service will determine whether an alien entered the United States before January 1, 1982, and resided in continuous unlawful status since such date through May 4, 1988, based on the evidence provided by the alien. An alien must provide with the application for LIFE Legalization evidence establishing that he or she entered the United States before January 1, 1982, and resided in continuous unlawful status since that date through May 4, 1988.

(b) *Evidence.* (1) A list of evidence that may establish an alien's continuous residence in the United States can be found at § 245a.2(d)(3).

(2) The following evidence may establish an alien's unlawful status in the United States:

(i) Form I–94 (see § 1.4), Arrival-Departure Record;

(ii) Form I–20A–B, Certificate of Eligibility for Nonimmigrant (F–1) Student Status—For Academic and Language Students;

(iii) Form IAP–66, Certificate of Eligibility for Exchange Visitor Status;

(iv) A passport; or

(v) Nonimmigrant visa(s) issued to the alien.

(c) *Continuous residence.* An alien shall be regarded as having resided continuously in the United States if:

(1) No single absence from the United States has exceeded forty-five (45) days, and the aggregate of all absences has not exceeded one hundred and eighty (180) days between January 1, 1982, and May 4, 1988, unless the alien can establish that due to emergent reasons, his or her return to the United States could not be accomplished within the time period allowed;

(2) The alien was maintaining residence in the United States; and

(3) The alien's departure from the United States was not based on an order of deportation.

(d) *Unlawful status.* The following categories of aliens, who are otherwise eligible to adjust to LPR status pursuant to LIFE Legalization, may file for adjustment of status provided they resided continuously in the United States in an unlawful status since prior to January 1, 1982, through May 4, 1988:

(1) An eligible alien who entered the United States without inspection prior to January 1, 1982.

(2) *Nonimmigrants.* An eligible alien who entered the United States as a nonimmigrant before January 1, 1982, whose authorized period of admission as a nonimmigrant expired before January 1, 1982, through the passage of time, or whose unlawful status was known to the Government before January 1, 1982. Known to the Government means documentation existing in one or more Federal Government agencies' files such that when such document is taken as a whole, it warrants a finding that the alien's status in the United States was unlawful. Any absence of mandatory annual and/or quarterly registration reports from Federal Government files does not warrant a finding that the alien's unlawful status was known to the Government.

(i) *A or G nonimmigrants.* An eligible alien who entered the United States for duration of status (D/S) in one of the following nonimmigrant classes, A–1,

A–2, G–1, G–2, G–3 or G–4, whose qualifying employment terminated or who ceased to be recognized by the Department of State as being entitled to such classification prior to January 1, 1982. A dependent family member may be considered a member of this class if the dependent family member was also in A or G status when the principal A or G alien's status terminated or ceased to be recognized by the Department of State.

(ii) *F nonimmigrants.* An eligible alien who entered the United States for D/S in one of the following nonimmigrant classes, F–1 or F–2, who completed a full course of study, including practical training, and whose time period, if any, to depart the United States after completion of study expired prior to January 1, 1982. A dependent F–2 alien otherwise eligible who was admitted into the United States with a specific time period, as opposed to duration of status, documented on Form I–94, Arrival-Departure Record, that extended beyond January 1, 1982, is considered eligible if the principal F–1 alien is found eligible.

(iii) *Nonimmigrant exchange visitors.* An eligible alien who was at any time a nonimmigrant exchange alien (as defined in section 101(a)(15)(J) of the Act), who entered the United States before January 1, 1982, and who:

(A) Was not subject to the 2-year foreign residence requirement of section 212(e) of the Act; or

(B) Has fulfilled the 2-year foreign residence requirement of section 212(e) of the Act; or

(C) Has received a waiver for the 2-year foreign residence requirement of section 212(e) of the Act.

(3) *Asylum applicants.* An eligible alien who filed an asylum application prior to January 1, 1982, and whose application was subsequently denied or whose application was not decided by May 4, 1988.

(4) *Aliens considered to be in unlawful status.* Aliens who were present in the United States in one of the following categories were considered to be in unlawful status:

(i) An eligible alien who was granted voluntary departure, voluntary return, extended voluntary departure, or placed in deferred action category by the Service prior to January 1, 1982.

(ii) An eligible alien who is a Cuban or Haitian entrant (as described in paragraph (1) or (2)(A) of section 501(e) of Public Law 96–422 and at §212.5(g) of this chapter), who entered the United States before January 1, 1982. Pursuant to section 1104(c)(2)(B)(iv) of the LIFE Act, such alien is considered to be in an unlawful status in the United States.

(iii) An eligible alien who was paroled into the United States prior to January 1, 1982, and whose parole status terminated prior to January 1, 1982.

(iv) An eligible alien who entered the United States before January 1, 1982, and whose entries to the United States subsequent to January 1, 1982, were not documented on Form I–94.

[66 FR 29673, June 1, 2001, as amended at 78 FR 18472, Mar. 27, 2013]

§245a.16 Continuous physical presence from November 6, 1986, through May 4, 1988.

(a) The Service will determine whether an alien was continuously physically present in the United States from November 6, 1986, through May 4, 1988, based on the evidence provided by the alien. An alien must provide with the application evidence establishing his or her continuous physical presence in the United States from November 6, 1986, through May 4, 1988. Evidence establishing the alien's continuous physical presence in the United States from November 6, 1986, to May 4, 1988, may consist of any documentation issued by any governmental or nongovernmental authority, provided such evidence bears the name of the applicant, was dated at the time it was issued, and bears the signature, seal, or other authenticating instrument of the authorized representative of the issuing authority, if the document would normally contain such authenticating instrument.

(b) For purposes of this section, an alien shall not be considered to have failed to maintain continuous physical presence in the United States by virtue of brief, casual, and innocent absences from the United States. Also, brief, casual, and innocent absences from the

United States are not limited to absences with advance parole. Brief, casual, and innocent absence(s) as used in this paragraph means temporary, occasional trips abroad as long as the purpose of the absence from the United States was consistent with the policies reflected in the immigration laws of the United States.

(c) An alien who has been absent from the United States in accordance with the Service's advance parole procedures shall not be considered as having interrupted his or her continuous physical presence as required at the time of filing an application under this section.

[66 FR 29673, June 1, 2001, as amended at 67 FR 38351, June 4, 2002]

§ 245a.17 Citizenship skills.

(a) *Requirements.* Applicants for adjustment under LIFE Legalization must meet the requirements of section 312(a) of the Act (8 U.S.C. 1423(a)) (relating to minimal understanding of ordinary English and a knowledge and understanding of the history and government of the United States). Unless an exception under paragraph (c) of this section applies to the applicant, LIFE Legalization applicants must establish that:

(1) He or she has complied with the same requirements as those listed for naturalization applicants under §§ 312.1 and 312.2 of this chapter; or

(2) He or she has a high school diploma or general educational development diploma (GED) from a school in the United States. A GED gained in a language other than English is acceptable only if a GED English proficiency test has been passed. (The curriculum for both the high school diploma and the GED must have included at least 40 hours of instruction in English and United States history and government). The applicant may submit a high school diploma or GED either at the time of filing Form I–485, subsequent to filing the application but prior to the interview, or at the time of the interview (the applicant's name and A-number must appear on any such evidence submitted); or

(3) He or she has attended, or is attending, a state recognized, accredited learning institution in the United States, and that institution certifies such attendance. The course of study at such learning institution must be for a period of one academic year (or the equivalent thereof according to the standards of the learning institution) and the curriculum must include at least 40 hours of instruction in English and United States history and government. The applicant may submit certification on letterhead stationery from a state recognized, accredited learning institution either at the time of filing Form I–485, subsequent to filing the application but prior to the interview, or at the time of the interview (the applicant's name and A-number must appear on any such evidence submitted).

(b) *Second interview.* An applicant who fails to pass the English literacy and/or the United States history and government tests at the time of the interview, shall be afforded a second opportunity after 6 months (or earlier, at the request of the applicant) to pass the tests or submit evidence as described in paragraphs (a)(2) or (a)(3) of this section. The second interview shall be conducted prior to the denial of the application for permanent residence and may be based solely on the failure to pass the basic citizenship skills requirements.

(c) *Exceptions.* LIFE Legalization applicants are exempt from the requirements listed under paragraph (a)(1) of this section if he or she has qualified for the same exceptions as those listed for naturalization applicants under §§ 312.1(b)(3) and 312.2(b) of this chapter. Further, at the discretion of the Attorney General, the requirements listed under paragraph (a) of this section may be waived if the LIFE Legalization applicant:

(1) Is 65 years of age or older on the date of filing; or

(2) Is developmentally disabled as defined under § 245a.1(v).

[66 FR 29673, June 1, 2001, as amended at 67 FR 38351, June 4, 2002]

§ 245a.18 Ineligibility and applicability of grounds of inadmissibility.

(a) *Ineligible aliens.* (1) An alien who has been convicted of a felony or of three or misdemeanors committed in the United States is ineligible for adjustment to LPR status under this Subpart B; or

(2) An alien who has assisted in the persecution of any person or persons on account of race, religion, nationality, membership in a particular social group, or political opinion is ineligible for adjustment of status under this Subpart B.

(b) *Grounds of inadmissibility not to be applied.* Section 212(a)(5) of the Act (labor certification requirements) and section 212(a)(7)(A) of the Act (immigrants not in possession of valid visa and/or travel documents) shall not apply to applicants for adjustment to LPR status under this Subpart B.

(c) *Waiver of grounds of inadmissibility.* Except as provided in paragraph (c)(2) of this section, the Service may waive any provision of section 212(a) of the Act only in the case of individual aliens for humanitarian purposes, to ensure family unity, or when the granting of such a waiver is otherwise in the public interest. If available, an applicant may apply for an individual waiver as provided in paragraph (c)(1) of this section without regard to section 241(a)(5) of the Act.

(1) *Special rule for waiver of inadmissibility grounds for LIFE Legalization applicants under sections 212(a)(9)(A) and 212(a)(9)(C) of the Act.* An applicant for adjustment of status under LIFE Legalization who is inadmissible under section 212(a)(9)(A) or 212(a)(9)(C) of the Act, may apply for a waiver of these grounds of inadmissibility while present in the United States, without regard to the normal requirement that a Form I–212, Application for Permission to Reapply for Admission into the United States After Deportation or Removal, be filed prior to embarking or re-embarking for travel to the United States, and without regard to the length of time since the alien's removal or deportation from the United States. Such an alien shall file Form I–690, Application for Waiver of Grounds of Excludability Under Sections 245A or 210 of the Immigration and Nationality Act, with the district director having jurisdiction over the applicant's case if the application for adjustment of status is pending at a local office, or with the Director of the Missouri Service Center. Approval of a waiver of inadmissibility under section 212(a)(9)(A) or section 212(a)(9)(C) of the Act does not cure a break in continuous residence resulting from a departure from the United States at any time during the period from January 1, 1982, and May 4, 1988, if the alien was subject to a final exclusion or deportation order at the time of the departure.

(2) *Grounds of inadmissibility that may not be waived.* Notwithstanding any other provisions of the Act, the following provisions of section 212(a) of the Act may not be waived by the Attorney General under paragraph (c) of this section:

(i) Section 212(a)(2)(A)(i)(I) (crimes involving moral turpitude);

(ii) Section 212(a)(2)(A)(i)(II) (controlled substance, except for so much of such paragraph as relates to a single offense of simple possession of 30 grams or less of marijuana);

(iii) Section 212(a)(2)(B) (multiple criminal convictions);

(iv) Section 212(a)(2)(C) (controlled substance traffickers);

(v) Section 212(a)(3) (security and related grounds); and

(vi) Section 212(a)(4) (public charge) except for an alien who is or was an aged, blind, or disabled individual (as defined in section 1614(a)(1) of the Social Security Act). If a LIFE Legalization applicant is determined to be inadmissible under section 212(a)(4) of the Act, he or she may still be admissible under the Special Rule described under paragraph (d)(3) of this section.

(d)(1) In determining whether an alien is "likely to become a public charge", financial responsibility of the alien is to be established by examining the totality of the alien's circumstance at the time of his or her application for adjustment. The existence or absence of a particular factor should never be the sole criteria for determining if an alien is likely to become a public charge. The determination of financial responsibility should be a prospective evaluation based on the alien's age, health, family status, assets, resources, education and skills.

(2) An alien who has a consistent employment history that shows the ability to support himself or herself even though his or her income may be below

the poverty level is not excludable under paragraph (c)(2)(vi) of this section. The alien's employment history need not be continuous in that it is uninterrupted. In applying the Special Rule, the Service will take into account an alien's employment history in the United States to include, but not be limited to, employment prior to and immediately following the enactment of IRCA on November 6, 1986. However, the Service will take into account that an alien may not have consistent employment history due to the fact that an eligible alien was in an unlawful status and was not authorized to work. Past acceptance of public cash assistance within a history of consistent employment will enter into this decision. The weight given in considering applicability of the public charge provisions will depend on many factors, but the length of time an applicant has received public cash assistance will constitute a significant factor. It is not necessary to file a waiver in order to apply the Special Rule for determination of public charge.

(3) In order to establish that an alien is not inadmissible under paragraph (c)(2)(vi) of this section, an alien may file as much evidence available to him or her establishing that the alien is not likely to become a public charge. An alien may have filed on his or her behalf a Form I–134, Affidavit of Support. The failure to submit Form I–134 shall not constitute an adverse factor.

(e) *Public cash assistance and criminal history verification.* Declarations by an alien that he or she has not been the recipient of public cash assistance and/or has not had a criminal record are subject to a verification by the Service. The alien must agree to fully cooperate in the verification process. Failure to assist the Service in verifying information necessary for proper adjudication may result in denial of the application.

[66 FR 29673, June 1, 2001, as amended at 67 FR 38351, June 4, 2002]

§ 245a.19 Interviews.

(a) All aliens filing applications for adjustment of status with the Service under this section must be personally interviewed, except that the adjudicative interview may be waived for a child under the age of 14, or when it is impractical because of the health or advanced age of the applicant. Applicants will be interviewed by an immigration officer as determined by the Director of the Missouri Service Center. An applicant failing to appear for the scheduled interview may, for good cause, be afforded another interview. Where an applicant fails to appear for two scheduled interviews, his or her application shall be denied for lack of prosecution. Applications for LIFE Legalization adjustment may be denied without interview if the applicant is determined to be statutorily ineligible.

(b) At the time of the interview, wherever possible, original documents must be submitted except the following: official government records; employment or employment-related records maintained by employers, unions, or collective bargaining organizations; medical records; school records maintained by a school or school board; or other records maintained by a party other than the applicant. Copies of records maintained by parties other than the applicant which are submitted in evidence must be certified as true and correct by such parties and must bear their seal or signature or the signature and title of persons authorized to act in their behalf.

(c) If at the time of the interview the return of original documents is desired by the applicant, they must be accompanied by notarized copies or copies certified true and correct by the alien's representative. At the discretion of the district director, original documents, even if accompanied by certified copies, may be temporarily retained for forensic examination by the Service.

§ 245a.20 Decisions, appeals, motions, and certifications.

(a) *Decisions*—(1) *Approval of applications.* If the Service approves the application for adjustment of status under LIFE Legalization, the district director shall record the alien's lawful admission for permanent residence as of the date of such approval and notify the alien accordingly. The district director shall also advise the alien regarding the delivery of his or her Form I–551, Permanent Resident Card, and of the process for obtaining temporary evidence of alien registration. If the alien has previously been issued a final order of exclusion, deportation, or removal, such order shall be deemed canceled as of the date of the district director's approval of the application for adjustment of status. If the alien had been in exclusion, deportation, or removal proceedings that were administratively closed, such proceedings shall be deemed terminated as of the date of approval of the application for adjustment of status by the district director.

(2) *Denials*. The alien shall be notified in writing of the decision of denial and of the reason(s) therefore. An applicant affected under this part by an adverse decision is entitled to file an appeal on Form I–290B Notice of Appeal to the Administrative Appeals Office (AAO), with the required fee specified in 8 CFR 103.7(b)(1). Renewal of employment authorization issued pursuant to 8 CFR 245a.13 will be granted until a final decision has been rendered on appeal or until the end of the appeal period if no appeal is filed. After exhaustion of an appeal, an alien who believes that the grounds for denial have been overcome may submit another application with fee, provided that the application is submitted on or before June 4, 2003.

(b) *Appeals process*. An adverse decision under this part may be appealed to the Associate Commissioner, Examinations, Administrative Appeals Office (AAO), who is the appellate authority designated in § 103.1(f)(3) of this chapter. Any appeal shall be submitted to the Service office that rendered the decision with the required fee.

(1) If an appeal is filed from within the United States, it must be received by the Service within 30 calendar days after service of the Notice of Denial (NOD) in accordance with the procedures of § 103.3(a) of this chapter. An appeal received after the 30 day period has tolled will not be accepted. The 30 day period for submitting an appeal begins 3 days after the NOD is mailed. If a review of the Record of Proceeding (ROP) is requested by the alien or his or her legal representative, and an appeal has been properly filed, an additional 30 days will be allowed for this review from the time the ROP is photocopied and mailed.

(2) If an applicant's last known address of record was outside the United States, and the NOD was mailed to that foreign address, the appeal must be received by the Service within 60 calendar days after service of the NOD in accordance with the procedures of § 103.3(a) of this chapter. An appeal received after the 60 day period has tolled will not be accepted. The 60-day period for submitting an appeal begins 3 days after the NOD is mailed.

(c) *Motions*. The Service director who denied the application may reopen and reconsider any adverse decision *sua sponte*. When an appeal to the AAO has been filed, the director may issue a new decision that will grant the benefit that has been requested. Motions to reopen a proceeding or reconsider a decision shall not be considered under this Subpart B.

(d) *Certifications*. The Service director who adjudicates the application may, in accordance with § 103.4 of this chapter, certify a decision to the AAO when the case involves an unusually complex or novel question of law or fact.

(e) *Effect of final adjudication of application on aliens previously in proceedings*—(1) *Upon the granting of an application*. If the application for LIFE Legalization is granted, proceedings shall be deemed terminated or a final order of exclusion, deportation, or removal shall be deemed canceled as of the date of the approval of the LIFE Legalization application for adjustment of status.

(2) *Upon the denial of an application*—(i) *Where proceedings were administratively closed*. In the case of an alien whose previously initiated exclusion, deportation or removal proceeding had been administratively closed or continued indefinitely under § 245a.12(b)(1), the director shall make a request for recalendaring to the Immigration Court that had administratively closed the proceeding, or the Board, as appropriate, when there is a final decision denying the LIFE Legalization application. The Immigration Court or the Board will then recalendar the prior proceeding.

(ii) *Where final order was stayed*. If the application for LIFE Legalization is denied, the stay of a final order of exclusion, deportation, or removal afforded in § 245a.13(f) shall be deemed lifted as of the date of such denial.

[66 FR 29673, June 1, 2001, as amended at 67 FR 38352, June 4, 2002; 72 FR 19107, Apr. 17, 2007]

§ 245a.21 Confidentiality.

(a) No person other than a sworn officer or employee of the Department of Justice or bureau or agency thereof, will be permitted to examine individual applications. For purposes of this part, any individual employed under contract by the Service to work in connection with the LIFE Legalization provisions shall be considered an employee of the Department of Justice or bureau or agency thereof.

(b) No information furnished pursuant to an application for permanent resident status under this Subpart B shall be used for any purpose except:

(1) To make a determination on the application;

(2) For the enforcement of the provisions encompassed in section 245A(c)(6) of the Act, except as provided in paragraphs (c) of this section; or

(3) For the purposes of rescinding, pursuant to section 246(a) of the Act (8 U.S.C. 1256(a)), any adjustment of status obtained by the alien.

(c) If a determination is made by the Service that the alien has, in connection with his or her application, engaged in fraud or willful misrepresentation or concealment of a material fact, knowingly provided a false statement or document in making his or her application, knowingly made a false statement or representation, or engaged in any other activity prohibited by section 245A(c)(6) of the Act, the Service shall refer the matter to the United States Attorney for prosecution of the alien and/or of any person who created or supplied a false statement or document for use in an application for adjustment of status under this Subpart B.

(d) Information contained in granted files may be used by the Service at a later date to make a decision:

(1) On an immigrant visa petition or other status filed by the applicant under section 204(a) of the Act;

(2) On a naturalization application submitted by the applicant;

(3) For the preparation of reports to Congress under section 404 of the Immigration Reform and Control Act of 1986; or

(4) For the furnishing of information, at the discretion of the Attorney General, in the same manner and circumstances as census information may be disclosed by the Secretary of Commerce under 13 U.S.C. 8.

(e) Information concerning whether the applicant has at any time been convicted of a crime may be used or released for immigration enforcement or law enforcement purposes.

§ 245a.22 Rescission.

(a) Rescission of adjustment of status under LIFE Legalization shall occur only under the procedures of 8 CFR part 246.

(b) Information furnished by an eligible alien pursuant to any application filed under LIFE Legalization may be used by the Attorney General, and other officials and employees of the Department of Justice and any bureau or agency thereof, for purposes of rescinding, pursuant to 8 CFR part 246, any adjustment of status obtained by the alien.

§§ 245a.23–245a.29 [Reserved]

Subpart C—LIFE Act Amendments Family Unity Provisions

SOURCE: 66 FR 29673, June 1, 2001, unless otherwise noted.

§ 245a.30 Description of program.

This Subpart C implements the Family Unity provisions of section 1504 of the LIFE Act Amendments, Public Law 106–554.

§ 245a.31 Eligibility.

An alien who is currently in the United States may obtain Family Unity benefits under section 1504 of the LIFE Act Amendments if he or she establishes that:

(a) He or she is the spouse or unmarried child under the age of 21 of an eligible alien (as defined under § 245a.10) at the time the alien's application for

Family Unity benefits is adjudicated and thereafter;

(b) He or she entered the United States before December 1, 1988, and resided in the United States on such date; and

(c) If applying for Family Unity benefits on or after June 5, 2003, he or she is the spouse or unmarried child under the age of 21 of an alien who has filed a Form I–485 pursuant to this Subpart B.

[66 FR 29673, June 1, 2001, as amended at 67 FR 38352, June 4, 2002]

§ 245a.32 Ineligible aliens.

The following categories of aliens are ineligible for Family Unity benefits under the LIFE Act Amendments:

(a) An alien who has been convicted of a felony or of three or more misdemeanors in the United States; or

(b) An alien who has ordered, incited, assisted, or otherwise participated in the persecution of an individual because of the individual's race, religion, nationality, membership in a particular social group, or political opinion; or

(c) An alien who has been convicted by a final judgment of a particularly serious crime and who is a danger to the community of the United States; or

(d) An alien who the Attorney General has serious reasons to believe has committed a serious nonpolitical crime outside the United States before the alien arrived in the United States; or

(e) An alien who the Attorney General has reasonable grounds to believe is a danger to the security of the United States.

§ 245a.33 Filing.

(a) *General.* An application for Family Unity benefits under section 1504 of the LIFE Act Amendments must be filed on a Form I–817, Application for Family Unity Benefits, with the Missouri Service Center. A Form I–817 must be filed with the correct fee required in § 103.7(b)(1) of this chapter and the required supporting documentation. A separate application with appropriate fee and documentation must be filed for each person claiming eligibility.

(b) *Decision.* The Missouri Service Center Director has sole jurisdiction to adjudicate an application for Family Unity benefits under the LIFE Act Amendments. The Director will provide the applicant with specific reasons for any decision to deny an application. Denial of an application may not be appealed. An applicant who believes that the grounds for denial have been overcome may submit another application with the appropriate fee and documentation.

(c) *Referral of denied cases for consideration of issuance of notice to appear.* If an application is denied, the case will be referred to the district director with jurisdiction over the alien's place of residence for consideration of whether to issue a notice to appear. After an initial denial, an applicant's case will not be referred for issuance of a notice to appear until 90 days from the date of the initial denial, to allow the alien the opportunity to file a new Form I–817 application in order to attempt to overcome the basis of the denial. However, if the applicant is found not to be eligible for benefits under § 245a.32(a), the Service reserves the right to issue a notice to appear at any time after the initial denial.

[66 FR 29673, June 1, 2001, as amended at 72 FR 19107, Apr. 17, 2007]

§ 245a.34 Protection from removal, eligibility for employment, and period of authorized stay.

(a) *Scope of protection.* Nothing in this Subpart C shall be construed to limit the authority of the Service to commence removal proceedings against an applicant for or beneficiary of Family Unity benefit under this Subpart C on any ground of removal. Also, nothing in this Subpart C shall be construed to limit the authority of the Service to take any other enforcement action against such an applicant or beneficiary with respect to any ground of removal not specified in paragraphs (a)(1) through (a)(4) of this section. Protection from removal under this Subpart C is limited to the grounds of removal specified in:

(1) Section 237(a)(1)(A) of the Act (aliens who were inadmissible at the time of entry or adjustment of status), except that the alien may be removed if he or she is inadmissible because of a ground listed in section 212(a)(2)

(criminal and related grounds) or in section 212(a)(3) (security and related grounds) of the Act; or

(2) Section 237(a)(1)(B) of the Act (aliens present in the United States in violation of the Act or any other law of the United States);

(3) Section 237(a)(1)(C) of the Act (aliens who violated their nonimmigrant status or violated the conditions of entry); or

(4) Section 237(a)(3)(A) of the Act (aliens who failed to comply with the change of address notification requirements).

(b) *Duration of protection from removal.* When an alien whose application for Family Unity benefits under the LIFE Act Amendments is approved, he or she will receive protection from removal, commencing with the date of approval of the application. A grant of protection from removal under this section shall be considered effective from the date on which the application was properly filed.

(1) In the case of an alien who has been granted Family Unity benefits under the LIFE Act Amendments based on the principal alien's application for LIFE Legalization, any evidence of protection from removal shall be dated to expire 1 year after the date of approval, or the day before the alien's 21st birthday, whichever comes first.

(2) In the case of an alien who has been granted Family Unity benefits under the LIFE Act Amendments based on the principal alien's adjustment to LPR status pursuant to his or her LIFE Legalization application, any evidence of protection from removal shall be dated to expire 2 years after the date of approval, or the day before the alien's 21st birthday, whichever comes first.

(c) *Employment authorization.* An alien granted Family Unity benefits under the LIFE Act Amendments is authorized to be employed in the United States.

(1) In the case of an alien who has been granted Family Unity benefits based on the principal alien's application for LIFE Legalization, the validity period of the employment authorization document shall be dated to expire 1 year after the date of approval of the Form I–817, or the day before the alien's 21st birthday, whichever comes first.

(2) In the case of an alien who has been granted Family Unity benefits based on the principal alien's adjustment to LPR status pursuant to his or her LIFE Legalization application, the validity period of the employment authorization document shall be dated to expire 2 years after the date of approval of the Form I–817, or the day before the alien's 21st birthday, whichever comes first.

(d) *Period of authorized stay.* An alien granted Family Unity benefits under the LIFE Act Amendments is deemed to have received an authorized period of stay approved by the Attorney General within the scope of section 212(a)(9)(B) of the Act.

[66 FR 29673, June 1, 2001, as amended at 67 FR 38352, June 4, 2002]

§ 245a.35 Travel outside the United States.

(a) An alien who departs the United States while his or her application for Family Unity benefits is pending will be deemed to have abandoned the application and the application will be denied.

(b) An alien granted Family Unity benefits under the LIFE Act Amendments who intends to travel outside the United States temporarily must apply for advance authorization using Form I–131. The authority to grant an application for advance authorization for an alien granted Family Unity benefits under the LIFE Act Amendments rests solely with the Service. An alien who is granted advance authorization and returns to the United States in accordance with such authorization, and who is found not to be inadmissible under section 212(a)(2) or (3) of the Act, shall be paroled into the United States. He or she shall be provided the remainder of the protection from removal period previously granted under the Family Unity provisions of the LIFE Act Amendments.

§ 245a.36 [Reserved]

§ 245a.37 Termination of Family Unity Program benefits.

(a) *Grounds for termination*. The Service may terminate Family Unity benefits under the LIFE Act Amendments whenever the necessity for the termination comes to the attention of the Service. Such grounds will exist in situations including, but not limited to, those in which:

(1) A determination is made that Family Unity benefits were acquired as the result of fraud or willful misrepresentation of a material fact;

(2) The beneficiary commits an act or acts which render him or her ineligible for Family Unity benefits under the LIFE Act Amendments;

(3) The alien, upon whose status Family Unity benefits under the LIFE Act were based, fails to apply for LIFE Legalization by June 4, 2003, has his or her LIFE Legalization application denied, or loses his or her LPR status; or

(4) A qualifying relationship to the alien, upon whose status Family Unity benefits under the LIFE Act Amendments were based, no longer exists.

(b) *Notice procedure*. Notice of intent to terminate and of the grounds thereof shall be served pursuant to the provisions of 8 CFR 103.8. The alien shall be given 30 days to respond to the notice and may submit to the Service additional evidence in rebuttal. Any final decision of termination shall also be served pursuant to the provisions of 8 CFR 103.8. Nothing in this section shall preclude the Service from commencing removal proceedings prior to termination of Family Unity benefits.

(c) *Effect of termination*. Termination of Family Unity benefits under the LIFE Act Amendments shall render the alien amenable to removal under any ground specified in section 237 of the Act (including those grounds described in § 245a.34(a)). In addition, the alien will no longer be considered to be in a period of stay authorized by the Attorney General as of the date of such termination.

[66 FR 29673, June 1, 2001, as amended at 67 FR 38352, June 4, 2002; 76 FR 53794, Aug. 29, 2011]

PART 246—RESCISSION OF ADJUSTMENT OF STATUS

Sec.

AUTHORITY: 8 U.S.C. 1103, 1254, 1255, 1256, 1259; 8 CFR part 2.

SOURCE: 62 FR 10385, Mar. 6, 1997, unless otherwise noted.

§ 246.1 Notice.

If it appears to a district director that a person residing in his or her district was not in fact eligible for the adjustment of status made in his or her case, or it appears to an asylum office director that a person granted adjustment of status by an asylum officer pursuant to 8 CFR 240.70 was not in fact eligible for adjustment of status, a proceeding shall be commenced by the personal service upon such person of a notice of intent to rescind, which shall inform him or her of the allegations upon which it is intended to rescind the adjustment of his or her status. In such a proceeding the person shall be known as the respondent. The notice shall also inform the respondent that he or she may submit, within thirty days from the date of service of the notice, an answer in writing under oath setting forth reasons why such rescission shall not be made, and that he or she may, within such period, request a hearing before an immigration judge in support of, or in lieu of, his or her written answer. The respondent shall further be informed that he or she may have the assistance of or be represented by counsel or representative of his or her choice qualified under part 292 of this chapter, at no expense to the Government, in the preparation of his or her answer or in connection with his or her hearing, and that he or she may present such evidence in his or her behalf as may be relevant to the rescission.

[62 FR 10385, Mar. 6, 1997, as amended at 64 FR 27881, May 21, 1999]

§ 246.2 Allegations admitted; no answer filed; no hearing requested.

If the answer admits the allegations in the notice, or if no answer is filed within the thirty-day period, or if no hearing is requested within such period, the district director or asylum office director shall rescind the adjustment of status previously granted, and no appeal shall lie from his decision.

[62 FR 10385, Mar. 6, 1997, as amended at 64 FR 27881, May 21, 1999]

§ 246.3 Allegations contested or denied; hearing requested.

If, within the prescribed time following service of the notice pursuant to § 246.1, the respondent has filed an answer which contests or denies any allegation in the notice, or a hearing is requested, a hearing pursuant to § 246.5 shall be conducted by an immigration judge, and the requirements contained in §§ 240.3, 240.4, 240.5, 240.6, 240.7, and 240.9 of this chapter shall be followed.

§ 246.4 Immigration judge's authority; withdrawal and substitution.

In any proceeding conducted under this part, the immigration judge shall have authority to interrogate, examine, and cross-examine the respondent and other witnesses, to present and receive evidence, to determine whether adjustment of status shall be rescinded, to make decisions thereon, including an appropriate order, and to take any other action consistent with applicable provisions of law and regulations as may be appropriate to the disposition of the case. Nothing contained in this part shall be construed to diminish the authority conferred on immigration judges by the Act. The immigration judge assigned to conduct a hearing shall, at any time, withdraw if he or she deems himself or herself disqualified. If a hearing has begun but no evidence has been adduced other than the notice and answer, if any, pursuant to §§ 246.1 and 246.2, or if an immigration judge becomes unavailable to complete his or her duties within a reasonable time, or if at any time the respondent consents to a substitution, another immigration judge may be assigned to complete the case. The new immigration judge shall familiarize himself or herself with the record in the case and shall state for the record that he or she is familiar with the record in the case.

§ 246.5 Hearing.

(a) *Service counsel.* The Government shall be represented at the hearing by a Service counsel who shall have authority to present evidence, and to interrogate, examine, and cross-examine the respondent and other witnesses. The Service counsel is authorized to appeal from a decision of the immigration judge pursuant to § 246.7 and to move for reopening or reconsideration pursuant to § 3.23 of this chapter.

(b) *Opening.* The immigration judge shall advise the respondent of the nature of the proceeding and the legal authority under which it is conducted; advise the respondent of his or her right to representation, at no expense to the Government, by counsel or representative of his or her own choice qualified under part 292 of this chapter and require him or her to state then and there whether he or she desires representation; advise the respondent that he or she will have a reasonable opportunity to examine and object to the evidence against him or her, to present evidence in his or her own behalf, and to cross-examine witnesses presented by the Government; place the respondent under oath; read the allegations in the notice to the respondent and explain them in nontechnical language, and enter the notice and respondent's answer, if any, as exhibits in the record.

(c) *Pleading by respondent.* The immigration judge shall require the respondent to state for the record whether he or she admits or denies the allegations contained in the notice, or any of them, and whether he or she concedes that his or her adjustment of status should be rescinded. If the respondent admits all of the allegations and concedes that the adjustment of status in his or her case should be rescinded under the allegations set forth in the notice, and the immigration judge is satisfied that no issues of law or fact remain, he or she may determine that rescission as alleged has been established by the respondent's admissions. The allegations contained in the notice shall be taken as admitted when the respondent, without reasonable cause, fails or refuses to attend or remain in attendance at the hearing.

§246.6 Decision and order.

The decision of the immigration judge may be oral or written. The formal enumeration of findings is not required. The order shall direct either that the proceeding be terminated or that the adjustment of status be rescinded. Service of the decision and finality of the order of the immigration judge shall be in accordance with, and as stated in §§240.13 (a) and (b) and 240.14 of this chapter.

§246.7 Appeals.

Pursuant to 8 CFR part 3, an appeal shall lie from a decision of an immigration judge under this part to the Board of Immigration Appeals. An appeal shall be taken within 30 days after the mailing of a written decision or the stating of an oral decision. The reasons for the appeal shall be specifically identified in the Notice of Appeal (Form EOIR 26); failure to do so may constitute a ground for dismissal of the appeal by the Board.

§246.8 [Reserved]

§246.9 Surrender of Form I–551.

A respondent whose status as a permanent resident has been rescinded in accordance with section 246 of the Act and this part, shall, upon demand, promptly surrender to the district director having administrative jurisdiction over the office in which the action under this part was taken, the Form I–551 issued to him or her at the time of the grant of permanent resident status.

PART 247—ADJUSTMENT OF STATUS OF CERTAIN RESIDENT ALIENS

Sec.

AUTHORITY: 8 U.S.C. 1101, 1103, and 1257.

§247.1 Scope of part.

The provisions of this part apply to an alien who is lawfully admitted for permanent residence and has an occupational status which, if he were seeking admission to the United States, would entitle him to a nonimmigrant status under paragraph (15)(A) or (15)(G) of section 101(a) of the Act, and to his immediate family; also, an alien who was lawfully admitted for permanent residence and has an occupational status which, if he were seeking admission to the United States, would entitle him to a nonimmigrant status under paragraph (15)(E) of section 101(a) of the Act, and to his spouse and children.

[22 FR 9801, Dec. 6, 1957]

§247.11 Notice.

If it appears to a district director that an alien residing in his district, who was lawfully admitted for permanent residence, has an occupational status described in section 247 of the Act, he shall cause a notice on Form I–509 to be served on such alien by personal service informing him that it is proposed to adjust his status, unless the alien requests that he be permitted to retain his status as a resident alien and executes and files with such district director a Form I–508 (Waiver of Rights, Privileges, Exemptions and Immunities) and, if a French national receiving salary from the French Republic, Form I–508F (election as to tax exemption under the Convention between the United States and the French Republic), within 10 days after service of the notice, or the alien, within such 10-day period, files with the district director a written answer under oath setting forth reasons why his status should not be adjusted. The notice shall also advise the person that he may, within such period and upon his request have an opportunity to appear in person, in support or in lieu of his written answer, before an immigration officer designated for that purpose. The person shall further be advised that he may have the assistance of counsel without expense to the Government of the

United States in the preparation of his answer or in connection with such personal appearance, and may examine the evidence upon which it is proposed to base such adjustment.

[22 FR 9801, Dec. 6, 1957, as amended at 37 FR 11471, June 8, 1972]

§ 247.12 Disposition of case.

(a) *Allegations admitted or no answer filed.* If the waiver Form I–508 and, if applicable, Form I–508F is not filed by the alien within the time prescribed, and the answer admits the allegations in the notice, or no answer is filed, the district director shall place a notation on the notice describing the alien's adjusted nonimmigrant status and shall cause a set of Forms I–94 (see § 1.4) to be prepared evidencing the nonimmigrant classification to which the alien has been adjusted and no appeal shall lie from such decision. Form I–94A shall be delivered to the alien and shall constitute notice to him of such adjustment. The alien's nonimmigrant status shall be for such time, under such conditions, and subject to such regulations as are applicable to the particular nonimmigrant status granted and shall be subject to such other terms and conditions, including the exaction of bond as the district director may deem appropriate.

(b) *Answer filed; personal appearance.* Upon receipt of an answer asserting a defense to the allegations made in the notice without requesting a personal appearance, or if a personal appearance is requested or directed, the case shall be assigned to an immigration officer. Pertinent evidence, including testimony of witnesses, shall be incorporated in the record. The immigration officer shall prepare a report summarizing the evidence and containing his findings and recommendation. The record, including the report and recommendation of the immigration officer, shall be forwarded to the district director who caused the notice to be served. The district director shall note on the report of the immigration officer whether he approves or disapproves the recommendation of the immigration officer. If the decision of the district director is that the matter be terminated, the alien shall be informed of such decision. If the decision of the district director is that the status of the alien should be adjusted to that of a nonimmigrant, his decision shall provide that unless the alien, within 10 days of receipt of notification of such decision, requests permission to retain his status as an immigrant and files with the district director Form I–508 and, if applicable, Form I–508F, the alien's immigrant status be adjusted to that of a nonimmigrant. The alien shall be informed of such decision and of the reasons therefor, and of his right to appeal in accordance with the provisions of part 103 of this chapter. If the alien does not request that he be permitted to retain status and file the Form I–508 and, if applicable, Form I–508F within the period provided therefor, the district director, without further notice to the alien, shall cause a set of Forms I–94 to be prepared evidencing the nonimmigrant classification to which the alien has been adjusted. Form I–94A shall be delivered to the alien. The alien's nonimmigrant status shall be for such time, under such conditions, and subject to such regulations as are applicable to the particular nonimmigrant status created and shall be subject to such other terms and conditions, including the exaction of bond, as the district director may deem appropriate.

[22 FR 9801, Dec. 6, 1957, as amended at 23 FR 9124, Nov. 26, 1958; 35 FR 13829, Sept. 1, 1970; 78 FR 18472, Mar. 27, 2013]

§ 247.13 Disposition of Form I–508.

If Form I–508 is executed and filed, the duplicate copy thereof (noted to show the election made on Form I–508F, if applicable) shall be filed in the office of the Assistant Commissioner, Administrative Division, and may be made available for inspection by any interested officer or agency of the United States.

[35 FR 13829, Sept. 1, 1970]

§ 247.14 Surrender of documents.

An alien whose status as a permanent resident has been adjusted to that of a nonimmigrant in accordance with section 247 of the Act and this part, shall, upon demand, promptly surrender to the district director having administrative jurisdiction over the office in which the action under this part was taken any documents (such as Form I–151 or I–551 or any other form of Permanent Resident Card, immigrant identification card, resident alien's border-crossing identification card (Form I–187), certificate of registry, or certificate of lawful entry) in his possession evidencing his former permanent resident status.

[22 FR 9802, Dec. 6, 1957, as amended at 45 FR 32657, May 19, 1980; 63 FR 70316, Dec. 21, 1998]

PART 248—CHANGE OF NONIMMIGRANT CLASSIFICATION

AUTHORITY: 8 U.S.C. 1101, 1103, 1184, 1258; 8 CFR part 2.

§248.1 Eligibility.

(a) *General.* Except for those classes enumerated in §248.2, any alien lawfully admitted to the United States as a nonimmigrant, including an alien who acquired such status pursuant to section 247 of the Act, 8 U.S.C. 1257, who is continuing to maintain his or her nonimmigrant status, may apply to have his or her nonimmigrant classification changed to any nonimmigrant classification other than that of a spouse or fianc(e), or the child of such alien, under section 101(a)(15)(K) of the Act, 8 U.S.C. 1101(a)(15)(K), or as an alien in transit under section 101(a)(15)(C) of the Act, 8 U.S.C. 1101(a)(15)(C). An alien defined by section 101(a)(15)(V), or 101(a)(15)(U) of the Act, 8 U.S.C. 1101(a)(15)(V) or 8 U.S.C. 1101(a)(15)(U), may be accorded nonimmigrant status in the United States by following the procedures set forth respectively in §214.15(f) or §214.14 of this chapter.

(b) Except in the case of an alien applying to obtain V nonimmigrant status in the United States under §214.15(f) of this chapter, a change of status may not be approved for an alien who failed to maintain the previously accorded status or whose status expired before the application or petition was filed, except that failure to file before the period of previously authorized status expired may be excused in the discretion of USCIS, and without separate application, where it is demonstrated at the time of filing that:

(1) The failure to file a timely application was due to extraordinary circumstances beyond the control of the applicant or petitioner, and USCIS finds the delay commensurate with the circumstances;

(2) The alien has not otherwise violated his or her nonimmigrant status;

(3) The alien remains a bona fide nonimmigrant; and

(4) The alien is not the subject of removal proceedings under 8 CFR part 240.

(c) *Change of nonimmigrant classification to that of a nonimmigrant student.* (1) Except as provided in paragraph (c)(3) of this section, a nonimmigrant applying for a change of classification as an F–1 or M–1 student is not considered ineligible for such a change solely because the applicant may have started attendance at school before the application was submitted. USCIS will deny an application for a change to classification as an M–1 student if the applicant intends to pursue the course of study solely in order to qualify for a subsequent change of nonimmigrant classification to that of an alien temporary worker under section 101(a)(15)(H) of the Act. Furthermore, an alien may not change from classification as an M–1 student to that of an F–1 student.

(2) [Reserved]

(3) A nonimmigrant who is admitted as, or changes status to, a B–1 or B–2 nonimmigrant on or after April 12, 2002, or who files a request to extend the period of authorized stay as a B–1 or B–2 nonimmigrant on or after such date, may not pursue a course of study at an approved school unless the Service has approved his or her application for change of status to a classification as an F–1 or M–1 student. USCIS will deny the change of status if the B–1 or B–2 nonimmigrant enrolled in a course of study before filing the application for change of status or while the application is pending.

(d) *Application for change of nonimmigrant classification from that of a student under section 101(a)(15)(M)(i) to that described in section 101(a)(15)(H).* A district director shall deny an application for change of nonimmigrant classification from that of an M–1 student to that of an alien temporary worker under section 101(a)(15)(H) of the Act if the education or training which the student received while an M–1 student enables the student to meet the qualifications for temporary worker classification under section 101(a)(15)(H) of the Act.

(e) *Change of nonimmigrant classification to that as described in section 101(a)(15)(N).* An application for change to N status shall not be denied on the grounds the applicant is an intending immigrant. Change of status shall be granted for three years not to exceed termination of eligibility under section 101(a)(15)(N) of the Act. Employment authorization pursuant to section 274(A) of the Act may be granted to an alien accorded nonimmigrant status under section 101(a)(15)(N) of the Act. Employment authorization is automatically terminated when the alien changes status or is no longer eligible for classification under section 101(a)(15)(N) of the Act.

[36 FR 9001, May 18, 1971, as amended at 48 FR 14592, Apr. 5, 1983; 52 FR 11621, Apr. 10, 1987; 59 FR 1465, Jan. 11, 1994; 62 FR 10386, Mar. 6, 1997; 66 FR 42595, Aug. 14, 2001; 66 FR 46704, Sept. 7, 2001; 67 FR 18064, Apr. 12, 2002; 72 FR 53041, Sept. 17, 2007; 76 FR 53794, Aug. 29, 2011]

§ 248.2 Ineligible classes.

(a) Except as described in paragraph (b) of this section, the following categories of aliens are not eligible to change their nonimmigrant status under section 248 of the Act, 8 U.S.C. 1258:

(1) Any alien in immediate and continuous transit through the United States without a visa;

(2) Any alien classified as a nonimmigrant under section 101(a)(15) (C), (D), (K), or (S) of the Act;

(3) Any alien admitted as a nonimmigrant under section 101(a)(15)(J) of the Act, or who acquired such status after admission in order to receive graduate medical education or training, whether or not the alien was subject to, received a waiver of, or fulfilled the two-year foreign residence requirement of section 212(e) of the Act. This restriction shall not apply when the alien is a foreign medical graduate who was granted a waiver under section 212(e)(iii) of the Act pursuant to a request made by a State Department of Public Health (or its equivalent) under Pub. L. 103–416, and the alien complies with the terms and conditions imposed on the waiver under section 214(k) of the Act and the implementing regulations at § 212.7(c)(9) of this chapter. A foreign medical graduate who was granted a waiver under Pub. L. 103–416 and who does not fulfill the requisite 3-year employment contract or otherwise comply with the terms and conditions imposed on the waiver is ineligible to apply for change of status to any other nonimmigrant classification; and

(4) Any alien classified as a nonimmigrant under section 101(a)(15)(J) of the Act (other than an alien described in paragraph (c) of this section) who is subject to the foreign residence requirement of section 212(e) of the Act and who has not received a waiver of the residence requirement, except when the alien applies to change to a classification under section 101(a)(15)(A) or (G) of the Act.

(5) Any alien admitted as a visitor under the visa waiver provisions of § 212.1(e) of this chapter.

(6) Any alien admitted as a Visa Waiver Pilot Program visitor under the provisions of section 217 of the Act and part 217 of this chapter.

(b) The prohibition against a change of nonimmigrant status for the categories of aliens described in paragraphs (a)(1) through (6) of this section is inapplicable to aliens applying for a change of nonimmigrant status to that of a nonimmigrant under section 101(a)(15)(U) of the Act, 8 U.S.C. 1101(a)(15)(U).

[47 FR 44238, Oct. 7, 1982, as amended at 48 FR 41017, Sept. 13, 1983; 52 FR 48084, Dec. 18, 1987; 53 FR 24903, June 30, 1988; 60 FR 26683, May 18, 1995; 60 FR 44271, Aug. 25, 1995; 72 FR 53041, Sept. 17, 2007]

§ 248.3 Petition and application.

Requests for a change of status must be filed on the form designated by USCIS with the fee prescribed in 8 CFR

103.7(b) and in accordance with the form instructions.

(a) *Requests by petitioners.* A petitioner must submit a request for a change of status to E-1, E-2, E-3, H-1C, H-1B, H-1B1, H-2A, H-2B, H-3, L-1, O-1, O-2, P-1, P-2, P-3, Q-1, R-1, or TN nonimmigrant.

(b) *Application by nonimmigrant.* (1) *Individual applicant.* Any nonimmigrant who seeks to change status to:

(i) A dependent nonimmigrant classification as the spouse or child of a principal whose nonimmigrant classification is listed in paragraph (a) of this section, or

(ii) Any other nonimmigrant classification not listed in paragraph (a) of this section must apply for a change of status on his or her own behalf.

(2) *Multiple applicants.* More than one person may be included in an application where the co-applicants are all members of a single family group and either all hold the same nonimmigrant status or one holds a nonimmigrant status and the co-applicants are his or her spouse and/or children who hold derivative nonimmigrant status based on the principal's nonimmigrant status.

(c) *Special provisions for change of nonimmigrant classification to, or from, a position classified under section 101(a)(15) (A) or (G) of the Act.* Each application for change of nonimmigrant classification to, or from, a position classified under section 101(a)(15)(A) or (G) must be filed on the prescribed application accompanied by the appropriate endorsement from the Department of State recommending the change of status. If the Department of State recommends against the change, the application shall be denied. An application for a change of classification by a principal alien in a position classified A-1, A-2, G-1, G-2, G-3, or G-4 shall be processed without fee. Members of the principal alien's immediate family who are included on the principal alien's application shall also be processed without fee.

(d) [Reserved]

(e) *Change of classification not required.* The following do not need to request a change of classification:

(1) An alien classified as a visitor for business under section 101(a)(15)(B) of the Act who intends to remain in the United States temporarily as a visitor for pleasure during the period of authorized admission; or

(2) An alien classified under sections 101(a)(15)(A) or 101(a)(15)(G) of the Act as a member of the immediate family of a principal alien classified under the same section, or an alien classified under sections 101(a)(15)(E), (H), (I), (J), or (L) of the Act as the spouse or child who accompanied or followed-to-join a principal alien who is classified under the same section, may attend school in the United States, provided that the principal alien or spouse or child maintain their nonimmigrant status.

(f) *Approval of application.* If the application is granted, the applicant shall be notified of the decision and granted a new period of time to remain in the United States without the requirement of filing a separate application and paying a separate fee for an extension of stay. The applicant's nonimmigrant status under his new classification shall be subject to the terms and conditions applicable generally to such classification and to such other additional terms and conditions, including exaction of bond, which USCIS deems appropriate to the case.

(g) *Denial of application.* When the application is denied, the applicant shall be notified of the decision and the reasons for the denial. There is no appeal from the denial of the application under this chapter.

(h) *Change to S nonimmigrant classification.* An eligible state or federal law enforcement agency ("LEA"), which shall include a state or federal court or a United States Attorney's Office, may seek to change the nonimmigrant classification of a nonimmigrant lawfully admitted to the United States, except those enumerated in § 248.2 of this chapter, to that of an alien witness or informant pursuant to section 101(a)(15)(S) of the Act by filing with the Assistant Attorney General, Criminal Division, the forms designated by USCIS with the fee prescribed in 8 CFR 103.7(b)(1) and in accordance with the form instructions establishing eligibility for the change of nonimmigrant classification.

(1) If the Assistant Attorney General, Criminal Division, certifies the request

for S nonimmigrant classification in accordance with the procedures set forth in 8 CFR 214.2(t), the Assistant Attorney General shall forward the LEA's request on Form I–854 with Form I–539 to the Commissioner. No request for change of nonimmigrant classification to S classification may proceed to the Commissioner unless it has first been certified by the Assistant Attorney General, Criminal Division.

(2) In the event the Commissioner decides to deny an application to change nonimmigrant classification to S nonimmigrant classification, the Assistant Attorney General, Criminal Division, and the relevant LEA shall be notified in writing to that effect. The Assistant Attorney General, Criminal Division, shall concur in or object to that decision. Unless the Assistant Attorney General, Criminal Division, objects within 7 days, he or she shall be deemed to have concurred in the decision. In the event of an objection by the Assistant Attorney General, Criminal Division, the matter will be expeditiously referred to the Deputy Attorney General for a final resolution. In no circumstances shall the alien or the relevant LEA have a right of appeal from any decision to deny.

(i) *Change of nonimmigrant status to perform labor in a health care occupation.* A request for a change of nonimmigrant status filed by, or on behalf of, an alien seeking to perform labor in a health care occupation as provided in 8 CFR 212.15(c), must be accompanied by a certificate as described in 8 CFR 212.15(f), or if the alien is eligible, a certified statement as described in 8 CFR 212.15(h). See 8 CFR 214.1(j) for a special rule concerning applications for change of status for aliens admitted temporarily under section 212(d)(3) of the Act and 8 CFR 212.15(n).

[36 FR 9001, May 18, 1971, as amended at 48 FR 14593, Apr. 5, 1983; 48 FR 41017, Sept. 13, 1983; 48 FR 44763, Sept. 30, 1983; 50 FR 25697, June 21, 1985; 59 FR 1466, Jan. 11, 1994; 60 FR 44271, Aug. 25, 1995; 65 FR 14779, 14780, Mar. 17, 2000; 65 FR 18432, Apr. 7, 2000; 67 FR 76280, Dec. 11, 2002; 68 FR 43921, July 25, 2003; 73 FR 61336, Oct. 16, 2008; 74 FR 26940, June 5, 2009; 76 FR 53794, Aug. 29, 2011; 81 FR 2084, Jan. 15, 2016]

PART 249—CREATION OF RECORDS OF LAWFUL ADMISSION FOR PERMANENT RESIDENCE

Sec.

AUTHORITY: 8 U.S.C. 1103, 1182, 1259; 8 CFR part 2.

§ 249.1 Waiver of inadmissibility.

In conjunction with an application under section 249 of the Act, an otherwise eligible alien who is inadmissible under paragraph (9), (10), or (12) of section 212(a) of the Act or so much of paragraph (23) of section 212(a) of the Act as relates to a single offense of simple possession of 30 grams or less of marihuana may request a waiver of such ground of inadmissibility under section 212(h) of the Act. Any alien within the classes described in subparagraphs (B) through (H) of section 212(a)(28) of the Act may apply for the benefits of section 212(a)(28)(I)(ii) in conjunction with an application under section 249 of the Act.

[47 FR 44238, Oct. 7, 1982]

§ 249.2 Application.

(a) *Jurisdiction.* An application by an alien, other than an arriving alien, who has been served with a notice to appear or warrant of arrest shall be considered only in proceedings under 8 CFR part 240. In any other case, an alien who believes he or she meets the eligibility requirements of section 249 of the Act shall apply to the district director having jurisdiction over his or her place of residence. The application shall be made on Form I–485 and shall be accompanied by Form G–325A, which shall be considered part of the application. The application shall also be accompanied by documentary evidence establishing continuous residence in the United States since prior to January 1, 1972, or since entry and prior to July 1, 1924. All documents must be submitted in accordance with § 103.2(b) of this chapter. Documentary evidence may include any records of official or personal transactions or recordings of events occurring during the period of claimed residence. Affidavits of credible witnesses may also be accepted. Persons unemployed and unable to furnish evidence in their own names may furnish evidence in the names of parents or other persons with whom they have been living, if affidavits of the parents or other persons are submitted attesting to the residence. The numerical limitations of sections 201 and 202 of the Act shall not apply.

(b) *Decision.* The applicant shall be notified of the decision and, if the application is denied, of the reasons therefor. If the application is granted, a Form I–551, showing that the applicant has acquired the status of an alien lawfully admitted for permanent residence, shall not be issued until the applicant surrenders any other document in his or her possession evidencing compliance with the alien registration requirements of former or existing law. No appeal shall lie from the denial of an application by the district director. However, an alien, other than an arriving alien, may renew the denied application in proceedings under 8 CFR part 240.

[52 FR 6322, Mar. 3, 1987, as amended at 62 FR 10386, Mar. 6, 1997]

§249.3 Reopening and reconsideration.

An applicant who alleged entry and residence since prior to July 1, 1924, but in whose case a record was created as of the date of approval of the application because evidence of continuous residence prior to July 1, 1924, was not submitted, may have his case reopened and reconsidered pursuant to §103.5 of this chapter. Upon the submission of satisfactory evidence, a record of admission as of the date of alleged entry may be created.

[29 FR 11494, Aug. 11, 1964]

PART 250—REMOVAL OF ALIENS WHO HAVE FALLEN INTO DISTRESS

Sec.

AUTHORITY: Secs. 103, 250, 66 Stat. 173, 219; 8 U.S.C. 1103, 1260.

§250.1 Application.

Application for removal shall be made on Form I–243. No appeal shall lie from the decision of the district director.

[22 FR 9802, Dec. 6, 1957]

§250.2 Removal authorization.

If the district director grants the application he shall issue an authorization for the alien's removal on Form I–202. Upon issuance of the authorization, or as soon thereafter as practicable, the alien may be removed from the United States at government expense.

[22 FR 9802, Dec. 6, 1957]

PART 251—ARRIVAL AND DEPARTURE MANIFESTS AND LISTS: SUPPORTING DOCUMENTS

Sec.

AUTHORITY: 8 U.S.C. 1103, 1182, 1221, 1281, 1282, 8 CFR part 2.

§251.1 Arrival manifests and lists.

(a) *Vessels*—(1) *General.* The master or agent of every vessel arriving in the United States from a foreign place or an outlying possession of the United States shall present to the immigration officer at the port where the immigration inspection is performed a manifest of all crewmen on board on Form I–418, Passenger List and Crew List, in accordance with the instructions contained thereon.

(2) *Longshore work notations.* The master or agent of the vessel shall indicate in writing immediately below the name of the last alien listed on the Form I–418 whether or not crewmen aboard the vessel will be used to perform longshore work at any United States port before the vessel departs the United States.

(i) If no longshore work will be performed, no further notation regarding longshore work is required.

(ii) If longshore work will be performed, the master or agent shall note which exception listed in section 258 of the Act permits the work. The exceptions are:

(A) The hazardous cargo exception;

(B) The prevailing practice exception in accordance with a port's collective bargaining agreements;

(C) The prevailing practice exception at a port where there is no collective bargaining agreement, but for which the vessel files an attestation;

(D) The prevailing practice exception for automated vessels; and

(E) The reciprocity exception.

(iii) If longshore work will be performed under the hazardous cargo exception, the vessel must either be a tanker or be transporting dry bulk cargo that qualifies as hazardous. All tankers qualify for the hazardous cargo exception, except for a tanker that has been gas-freed to load non-hazardous dry bulk commodities.

(A) To invoke the exception for tankers, the master or agent shall note on the manifest that the vessel is a qualifying tanker.

(B) If the vessel is transporting dry bulk hazardous cargo, the master or agent shall note on the manifest that the vessel's dry bulk cargo is hazardous and shall show the immigration officer the dangerous cargo manifest that is signed by the master or an authorized representative of the owner, and that under 46 CFR 148.02 must be kept in a conspicuous place near the bridge house.

(iv) If longshore work will be performed under the prevailing practice exception, the master or agent shall note on the manifest each port at which longshore work will be performed under this exception. Additionally, for each port the master or agent shall note either that:

(A) The practice of nonimmigrant crewmen doing longshore work is in accordance with all collective bargaining agreements covering 30 percent or more of the longshore workers in the port;

(B) The port has no collective bargaining agreement covering 30 percent or more of the longshore workers in the port and an attestation has been filed with the Secretary of Labor;

(C) An attestation that was previously filed is still valid and the vessel continues to comply with the conditions stated in that attestation; or

(D) The longshore work consists of operating an automated, self-unloading conveyor belt or a vacuum-actuated system.

(v) If longshore work will be performed under the reciprocity exception, the master or agent shall note on the manifest that the work will be done under the reciprocity exception, and will note the nationality of the vessel's registry and the nationality or nationalities of the holders of a majority of the ownership interest in the vessel.

(3) *Exception for certain Great Lakes vessels.* (i) A manifest shall not be required for a vessel of United States, Canadian, or British registry engaged solely in traffic on the Great Lakes or the St. Lawrence River and connecting waterways, herein designated as a Great Lakes vessel, unless:

(A) The vessel employs nonimmigrant crewmen who will do longshore work at a port in the United States; or

(B) The vessel employs crewmen of other than United States, Canadian, or British citizenship.

(ii) In either situation, the master shall note the manifest in the manner prescribed in paragraph (a)(2) of this section.

(iii) After submission of a manifest on the first voyage of a calendar year, a manifest shall not be required on subsequent arrivals unless a nonimmigrant crewman of other than Canadian or British citizenship is employed on the vessel who was not aboard and listed on the last prior manifest, or a change has occurred regarding the performance of longshore work in the United States by nonimmigrant crewmen, or a change has occurred in the exception that the master or agent of the vessel wishes to invoke which was not noted on the last prior manifest.

(4) The master or agent of a vessel that only bunkers at a United States port en route to another United States

port shall annotate Form I–418 presented at the onward port to indicate the time, date, and place of bunkering.

(5) If documentation is required to support an exception, as described in §258.2 of this chapter, it must accompany the manifest.

(b) *Aircraft.* The captain or agent of every aircraft arriving in the United States from a foreign place or from an outlying possession of the United States, except an aircraft arriving in the United States directly from Canada on a flight originating in that country, shall present to the immigration officer at the port where the inspection is performed a manifest on United States Customs Service Form 7507 or on the International Civil Aviation Organization's General Declaration of all the alien crewmembers on board, including alien crewmembers who are returning to the United States after taking an aircraft of the same line from the United States to a foreign place or alien crewmembers who are entering the United States as passengers solely for the purpose of taking an aircraft of the same line from the United States to a foreign port. The captain or agent of an aircraft that only refuels at the United States en route to another United States port must annotate the manifest presented at the onward port to indicate the time, date, and place of refueling. The surname, given name, and middle initial of each alien crewman listed also shall be shown on the manifest. In addition, the captain or agent of the aircraft shall indicate the total number of United States citizen crewmembers and total number of alien crewmembers.

(c) *Additional documents.* The master, captain, or agent shall prepare as a part of the manifest, when one is required for presentation to an immigration officer, a completely executed set of Forms I–95, Conditional Landing Permit, for each nonimmigrant alien crewman on board, except:

(1) A Canadian or British citizen crewman serving on a vessel plying solely between Canada and the United States; or

(2) A nonimmigrant crewman who is in possession of an unmutilated Form I–184, Alien Crewman Landing Permit and Identification Card, or an unmutilated Form I–95 with space for additional endorsements previously issued to him or her as a member of the crew of the same vessel or an aircraft of the same line on his or her last prior arrival in the United States, following which he or she departed from the United States as a member of the crew of the same vessel or an aircraft of the same line.

[62 FR 10386, Mar. 6, 1997]

§251.2 Notification of illegal landings.

As soon as discovered, the master or agent of any vessel from which an alien crewman has illegally landed or deserted in the United States shall inform the immigration officer in charge of the port where the illegal landing or desertion occurred, in writing, of the name, nationality, passport number and, if known, the personal description, circumstances and time of such illegal landing or desertion of such alien crewman, and furnish any other information and documents that might aid in his or her apprehension, including any passport surrendered pursuant to §252.1(d) of this chapter. Failure to file notice of illegal landing or desertion and to furnish any surrendered passport within 24 hours of the time of such landing or desertion becomes known shall be regarded as lack of compliance with section 251(d) of the Act.

[62 FR 10387, Mar. 6, 1997]

§251.3 Departure manifests and lists for vessels.

(a) *Form I–418, Passenger List-Crew List.* The master or agent of every vessel departing from the United States shall submit to the immigration officer at the port from which such vessel is to depart directly to some foreign place or outlying possession of the United States, except when a manifest is not required pursuant to §251.1(a), a single Form I–418 completed in accordance with the instructions on the form. Submission of a Form I–418 that lacks any required endorsement shall be regarded as lack of compliance with section 251(c) of the Act.

(b) *Exception for certain Great Lakes vessels.* The required list need not be submitted for Canadian or British crewmembers of Great Lakes vessels described in § 251.1(a)(3).

[62 FR 10387, Mar. 6, 1997]

§ 251.4 Departure manifests and lists for aircraft.

(a) *United States Customs Service Form 7507 or International Civil Aviation Organization's General Declaration.* The captain or agent of every aircraft departing from the United States for a foreign place or an outlying possession of the United States, except on a flight departing for and terminating in Canada, shall submit to the immigration officer at the port from which such aircraft is to depart a completed United States Customs Service Form 7507 or the International Civil Aviation Organization's General Declaration. The form shall contain a list of all alien crewmen on board, including alien crewmen who arrived in the United States as crewmen on an aircraft of the same line and who are departing as passengers. The surname, given name, and middle initial of each such alien crewman listed shall be shown. In addition, the captain or agent of the aircraft shall indicate the total number of alien crewmembers and the total number of United States citizen crewmembers.

(b) *Notification of changes in employment for aircraft.* The agent of the air transportation line shall immediately notify in writing the nearest immigration office of the termination of employment in the United States of each alien employee of the line furnishing the name, birth date, birthplace, nationality, passport number, and other available information concerning such alien. The procedure to follow in obtaining permission to pay off or discharge an alien crewman in the United States after initial immigration inspection, other than an alien lawfully admitted for permanent residence, is set forth in § 252.1(f) of this chapter.

[62 FR 10387, Mar. 6, 1997]

§ 251.5 Paper arrival and departure manifests for crew.

In addition to the electronic manifest transmission requirement applicable to crew members specified in §§ 231.1 and 231.2 of this chapter, the master or commanding officer, or authorized agent, owner, or consignee, of a commercial vessel or commercial aircraft arriving in or departing from the United States must submit arrival and departure manifests in a paper format in accordance with §§ 251.1, 251.3, and 251.4.

[70 FR 17849, Apr. 7, 2005]

§ 251.6 Exemptions for private vessels and aircraft.

The provisions of this part relating to the presentation of arrival and departure manifests do not apply to a private vessel or private aircraft not engaged directly or indirectly in the carrying of persons or cargo for hire.

[70 FR 17849, Apr. 7, 2005]

PART 252—LANDING OF ALIEN CREWMEN

AUTHORITY: 8 U.S.C. 1103, 1184, 1185 (pursuant to E.O. 13323 published on January 2, 2004) , 1258, 1281, 1282; 8 CFR part 2.

§ 252.1 Examination of crewmen.

(a) *Detention prior to examination.* All persons employed in any capacity on board any vessel or aircraft arriving in the United States shall be detained on board the vessel or at the airport of arrival by the master or agent of such vessel or aircraft until admitted or otherwise permitted to land by an officer of the Service.

(b) *Classes of aliens subject to examination under this part.* The examination of every nonimmigrant alien crewman arriving in the United States shall be in accordance with this part except that the following classes of persons employed on vessels or aircraft shall be examined in accordance with the provisions of 8 CFR parts 235 and 240:

(1) Canadian or British citizen crewmen serving on vessels plying solely

between Canada and the United States; or

(2) Canadian or British citizen crewmen of aircraft arriving in a State of the United States directly from Canada on flights originating in that country. The crew of a vessel arriving at a United States port that may not require inspection by or clearance from the United States Customs Service is, nevertheless, subject to examination under this part; however, the master of such a vessel is not required to present Form I–95 for any crewman who is not an applicant for a conditional landing permit.

(c) *Requirements for landing permits.* Every alien crewman applying for landing privileges in the United States is subject to the provisions of 8 CFR 235.1(d)(1)(ii) and (iii), and must make his or her application in person before a Customs and Border Protection (CBP) officer, present whatever documents are required, establish to the satisfaction of the inspecting officer that he or she is not inadmissible under any provision of the law, and is entitled clearly and beyond doubt to landing privileges in the United States.

(d) *Authorization to land.* The immigration officer in his discretion may grant an alien crewman authorization to land temporarily in the United States for: (1) Shore leave purposes during the period of time the vessel or aircraft is in the port of arrival or other ports in the United States to which it proceeds directly without touching at a foreign port or place, not exceeding 29 days in the aggregate, if the immigration officer is satisfied that the crewman intends to depart on the vessel on which he arrived or on another aircraft of the same transportation line, and the crewman's passport is surrendered for safe keeping to the master of the arriving vessel, or (2) the purpose of departing from the United States as a crewman on a vessel other than the one on which he arrived, or departing as a passenger by means of other transportation, within a period of 29 days, if the immigration officer is satisfied that the crewman intends to depart in that manner, that definite arrangements for such departure have been made, and the immigration officer has consented to the pay off or discharge of the crewman from the vessel on which he arrived. A crewman granted a conditional permit to land under section 252(a)(1) of the Act and paragraph (d)(1) of this section is required to depart with his vessel from its port of arrival and from each other port in the United States to which it thereafter proceeds coastwise without touching at a foreign port or place; however, he may rejoin his vessel at another port in the United States before it touches at a foreign port or place if he has advance written permission from the master or agent to do so.

(e) *Conditional permits to land.* Unless the crewman is in possession of Form I–184 and is landed under paragraph (d)(1) of this section, the immigration officer shall give to each alien nonimmigrant crewman permitted to land a copy of the Form I–95 presented by the crewman, endorsed to show the date and place of admission and the type of conditional landing permit.

(f) *Change of status.* An alien nonimmigrant crewman landed pursuant to the provisions of this part shall be ineligible for any extension of stay or for a change of nonimmigrant classification under part 248 of this chapter. A crewman admitted under paragraph (d)(1) of this section may, if still maintaining status, apply for a conditional landing permit under paragraph (d)(2) of this section. The application shall not be approved unless an application on Form I–408, filed pursuant to paragraph (h) of this section, has been approved authorizing the master or agent of the vessel on which the crewman arrived to pay off or discharge the crewman and unless evidence is presented by the master or agent of the vessel to which the crewman will be transferred that a specified position on that vessel has been authorized for him or that satisfactory arrangements have been completed for the repatriation of the alien crewman. If the application is approved, the crewman shall be given a new Form I–95 endorsed to show landing authorized under paragraph (d)(2) of this section for the period necessary to accomplish his scheduled reshipment, which shall not exceed 29 days from the date of his landing, upon surrendering any conditional landing permit previously issued to him on Form I–95.

(g) *Refusal of conditional landing permit.* When an alien crewman is refused a conditional landing permit for any reason, the Form I–95 presented by him at time of examination shall be endorsed "Permission to land temporarily at all U.S. ports is refused" and the Form I–95 shall be given to the master or agent of the vessel or aircraft and, in the case of vessels, the alien crewman's name shall be listed on the Form I–410 delivered to the master of the vessel upon completion of the examination of the crew. If an alien crewman who has been refused a conditional landing permit is in possession of Form I–184, the Form I–184 shall be lifted by the examining immigration officer and, except in the case of an alien crewman who is refused a conditional landing permit solely because he is not in possession of a valid passport or visa, the Form I–184 shall be voided. In the case of an alien crewman refused a conditional landing permit because he is not in possession of a valid passport or visa, the Form I–184 shall be delivered to the master or agent of the vessel with instructions to return it to the alien crewman after the vessel has departed from the United States.

(h) *Authorization to pay off or discharge an alien crewman.* Application to pay off or discharge an alien crewman, except an alien lawfully admitted for permanent residence, shall be made by the owner, agent, consignee, charterer, master, or commanding officer of the vessel or aircraft on which the alien crewman arrived on Form I–408 filed with the immigration officer having jurisdiction over the area in which the vessel or aircraft is located at the time of application. The applicant shall be notified of the decision, and, if the application is denied, of the reasons therefor. There shall be no appeal from the denial of an application on Form I–408.

[23 FR 2788, Apr. 26, 1958, as amended at 27 FR 11875, Dec. 1, 1962; 29 FR 13243, Sept. 24, 1964; 29 FR 14432, Oct. 21, 1964; 32 FR 9633, July 4, 1967; 33 FR 9332, June 26, 1968; 33 FR 17137, Nov. 19, 1968; 58 FR 48779, Sept. 20, 1993; 62 FR 10388, Mar. 6, 1997; 69 FR 53333, Aug. 31, 2004]

§ 252.2 Revocation of conditional landing permits; removal.

(a) *Revocation and removal while vessel is in the United States.* A crewman whose landing permit is subject to revocation pursuant to section 252(b) of the Act may be taken into custody by any immigration officer without a warrant of arrest and be transferred to the vessel of arrival, if the vessel is in any port in the United States and has not departed foreign since the crewman was issued his or her conditional landing permit. Detention and removal of the crewman shall be at the expense of the transportation line on which the crewman arrived. Removal may be effected on the vessel of arrival or, if the master of the vessel has requested in writing, by alternate means if removal on the vessel of arrival is impractical.

(b) *Revocation and removal after vessel has departed the United States.* A crewman who was granted landing privileges prior to April 1, 1997, and who has not departed foreign on the vessel of arrival, or on another vessel or aircraft if such permission was granted pursuant to § 252.1(f), is subject to removal proceedings under section 240 of the Act as an alien deportable pursuant to section 237(a)(1)(C)(i) of the Act. A crewman who was granted landing privileges on or after April 1, 1997, and who has not departed foreign on the vessel of arrival, or on another vessel or aircraft if such permission was granted pursuant to § 252.1(f), shall be removed from the United States without a hearing, except as provided in § 208.2(b)(1) of this chapter. In either case, if the alien is removed within 5 years of the date of landing, removal of the crewman shall be at the expense of the owner of the vessel. In the case of a crewman ordered removed more than

5 years after the date of landing, removal shall be at the expense of the appropriation for the enforcement of the Act.

[62 FR 10388, Mar. 6, 1997]

§252.3 Great Lakes vessels and tugboats arriving in the United States from Canada; special procedures.

(a) *United States vessels and tugboats.* An immigration examination shall not be required of any crewman aboard a Great Lakes vessel of United States registry or a tugboat of United States registry arriving from Canada at a port of the United States who has been examined and admitted by an immigration officer as a member of the crew of the same vessel or tugboat or of any other vessel or tugboat of the same company during the current calendar year.

(b) *Canadian or British vessels or tugboats.* An alien crewman need not be presented for inspection if the alien crewman:

(1) Serves aboard a Great Lakes vessel of Canadian or British registry or aboard a tugboat of Canadian or British registry arriving at a United States port-of-entry from Canada;

(2) Seeks admission for a period of less than 29 days;

(3) Has, during the current calendar year, been inspected and admitted by an immigration officer as a member of the crew of the same vessel or tugboat, or of any other vessel or tugboat of the same company;

(4) Is either a British or Canadian citizen or is in possession of a valid Form I–95 previously issued to him or her as a member of the crew of the same vessel or tugboat, or of any other vessel or tugboat of the same company;

(5) Does not request or require landing privileges in the United States beyond the time the vessel or tugboat will be in port; and,

(6) Will depart to Canada with the vessel or tugboat.

[62 FR 10388, Mar. 6, 1997]

§252.4 Permanent landing permit and identification card.

A Form I–184 is valid until revoked. It shall be revoked when an immigration officer finds that the crewman is in the United States in willful violation of the terms and conditions of his or her permission to land, or that he or she is inadmissible to the United States. On revocation, the Form I–184 shall be surrendered to an immigration officer. No appeal shall lie from the revocation of Form I–184.

[62 FR 10388, Mar. 6, 1997]

§252.5 Special procedures for deserters from Spanish or Greek ships of war.

(a) *General.* Under E.O. 11267 of January 19, 1966 (31 FR 807) and 28 CFR 0.109, and E.O. 11300 of August 17, 1966, (31 FR 11009), and 28 CFR 0.110, the Commissioner and immigration officers (as defined in §103.1(j) of this chapter) are designated as "competent national authorities" on the part of the United States within the meaning of Article XXIV of the 1903 Treaty of Friendship and General Relations between the United States and Spain (33 Stat. 2105, 2117), and "local authorities" and "competent officers" on the part of the United States within the meaning of Article XIII of the Convention between the United States and Greece (33 Stat. 2122, 2131).

(b) *Application for restoration.* On application of a Consul General, Consul, Vice-Consul, or Consular-Agent of the Spanish or Greek Government, made in writing pursuant to Article XXIV of the treaty, or Article XIII of the Convention, respectively, stipulating for the restoration of crewmen deserting, stating that the person named therein has deserted from a ship of war of that government, while in any port of the United States, and on proof by the exhibition of the register, crew list, or official documents of the vessel, or a copy or extract therefrom, duly certified, that the person named belonged, at the time of desertion, to the crew of such vessel, such person shall be taken into custody by any immigration officer without a warrant of arrest. Written notification of charges shall be served on the alien when he or she is taken into custody or as soon as practical thereafter.

(c) *Examination.* Within a reasonable period of time after the arrest, the alien shall be accorded an examination by the district director, acting district director, or the deputy district director having jurisdiction over the place of arrest. The alien shall be informed that he or she may have the assistance of or be represented by a counsel or representative of his or her choice qualified under 8 CFR part 292 without expense to the Government, and that he or she may present such evidence in his or her behalf as may be relevant to this proceeding. If, upon the completion of such examination, it is determined that:

(1) The individual sought by the Spanish or Greek authorities had deserted from a Spanish or Greek ship of war in a United States port;

(2) The individual actually arrested and detained is the person sought;

(3) The individual is not a citizen of the United States; and

(4) The individual had not previously been arrested for the same cause and set at liberty because he or she had been detained for more than 3 months, or more than 2 months in the case of a deserter from a Greek ship of war, from the day of his or her arrest without the Spanish or Greek authorities having found an opportunity to send him or her home, the individual shall be served with a copy of the findings, from which no appeal shall lie, and be surrendered forthwith to the Spanish or Greek authorities if they are prepared to remove him or her from the United States. On written request of the Spanish or Greek authorities, the individual shall be detained, at their expense, for a period not exceeding 3 months or 2 months, respectively, from the day of arrest to afford opportunity to arrange for his or her departure from the United States.

(d) *Timely departure not effected.* If the Spanish authorities delay in sending the individual home for more than 3 months, or if the Greek authorities delay in sending the individual home for more than 2 months, from the day of his or her arrest, the individual shall be dealt with as any other alien unlawfully in the United States under the removal provisions of the Act, as amended.

(e) *Commission of crime.* If the individual has committed any crime or offense in the United States, he or she shall not be placed at the disposal of the consul until after the proper tribunal having jurisdiction in his or her case shall have pronounced sentence, and such sentence shall have been executed.

[62 FR 10388, Mar. 6, 1997]

PART 253—PAROLE OF ALIEN CREWMEN

Sec.

AUTHORITY: 8 U.S.C. 1103, 1182, 1282, 1283, 1285; 8 CFR part 2.

§ 253.1 Parole.

(a) *General.* When a crewman is paroled into the United States pursuant to the provisions of this part under the provisions of section 212(d)(5) of the Act, he shall be given Form I–94 (see § 1.4), reflecting the terms of parole. A notice on Form I–259 shall be served upon the agent, and, if available, upon the owner and master or commanding officer of the vessel or aircraft, which shall specify the purpose of the parole and the conditions under which the alien crewman is paroled into the United States. The Form I–259 shall also specify the Service office to which the alien crewman is to be presented for inspection upon termination of the parole. The guarantee of payment for medical and other related expenses required by section 253 of the Act shall be executed by the owner, agent, consignee, commanding officer or master on Form I–510.

(b) *Afflicted crewman.* Any alien crewman afflicted with feeblemindedness, insanity, epilepsy, tuberculosis in any form, leprosy, or any dangerous contagious disease, or an alien crewman suspected of being so afflicted shall upon arrival at the first port of call in the United States, be paroled to the medical institution designated by the district director in whose district the port is located, in the custody (other than during the period of time he is in such medical institution) of the agent of the vessel or aircraft on which such alien arrived in the United States and at the expense of the transportation line for a period initially not to exceed thirty days, for treatment and observation, under the provisions of section 212(d)(5) of the Act. Unless the Public Health Surgeon at the first port certifies that such parole be effected immediately for emergent reasons, the district director may defer execution of parole to a subsequent port of the United States to which the vessel or aircraft will proceed, if facilities not readily available at the first port are readily available at such subsequent port of call. Notice to remove an afflicted alien crewman shall be served by the examining immigration officer upon the master or agent of the vessel or aircraft on Form I–259 and shall specify the date when and the place to which such alien crewman shall be removed and the reasons therefor.

(c) *Disabled crewman.* Any alien crewman who becomes disabled in any port of the United States, whom the master or agent of the vessel or aircraft is obliged under foreign law to return to another country, may be paroled into the United States under the provisions of section 212(d)(5) of the Act for the period of time and under the conditions set by the district director in whose district the port is located, in the custody of the agent of the vessel or aircraft for the purpose of passing through the United States and transferring to another vessel or aircraft for departure to such foreign country, by the most direct and expeditious route.

(d) *Shipwrecked or castaway seamen or airmen.* A shipwrecked or castaway alien seaman or airman who is rescued by or transferred at sea to a vessel or aircraft destined directly for the United States and who is brought to the United States on such vessel or aircraft other than as a member of its crew shall be paroled into the United States under the provisions of section 212(d)(5) of the Act for the period of time and under the conditions set by the district director in whose district the port is located, in the custody of the appropriate foreign consul or the agent of the aircraft or vessel which was wrecked or from which such seaman or airman was removed, for the purpose of treatment or observation in a hospital, if such is required, and for departure to the appropriate foreign country by the most direct and expeditious route.

(e) *Medical treatment or observation.* Any alien crewman denied a conditional landing permit or whose conditional landing permit issued under §252.1(d)(1) of this chapter is revoked may, upon the request of the master or agent, be paroled into the United States under the provisions of section 212(d)(5) of the Act in the custody of the agent of the vessel or aircraft and at the expense of the transportation line for medical treatment or observation.

(f) *Crewman, stowaway, or alien removable under section 235(c) alleging persecution or torture.* Any alien crewman, stowaway, or alien removable under section 235(c) of the Act who alleges that he or she cannot return to his or her country of nationality or last habitual residence (if not a national of any country) because of fear of persecution in that country on account of race, religion, nationality, membership in a particular social group, or political opinion, or because of fear of torture is eligible to apply for asylum or withholding of removal under 8 CFR part 208. Service officers shall take particular care to ensure that the provisions of §208.5(b) of this chapter regarding special duties toward aliens aboard certain vessels are closely followed.

(g) *Other crewmen.* In the discretion of the district director, any alien crewman not within the purview of paragraphs (b) through (f) of this section may for other emergent reasons or for reasons deemed strictly in the public interest be paroled into the United States under the provisions of section 212(d)(5) of the Act for the period of time and under the conditions set by the district director having jurisdiction over the area where the alien crewman is located.

[22 FR 9804, Dec. 6, 1957, as amended at 26 FR 11797, Dec. 8, 1961; 32 FR 4341, Mar. 22, 1967; 32 FR 9633, July 4, 1967; 55 FR 30687, July 27, 1990; 62 FR 10389, Mar. 6, 1997; 64 FR 8495, Feb. 19, 1999; 78 FR 18472, Mar. 27, 2013]

§253.2 Termination of parole.

(a) *General.* At the expiration of the period of parole authorized by the district director, or when the purpose of the parole has been served, whichever is earlier, the agent upon whom the relating Form I–259 was served as provided in § 253.1, shall present the alien crewman for inspection to an immigration officer at the Service office specified in the Form I–259. If the agent cannot present the alien crewman, the agent shall immediately submit a report of the reasons therefor to the district director. The district director shall take such further action as the circumstances may require. If the vessel or aircraft on which the alien crewman arrived in the United States is still in the United States when he is presented for inspection, he shall be treated as an applicant for a conditional landing permit and his case shall be dealt with in the same manner as any other applicant for a conditional landing permit. If the vessel or aircraft on which the alien crewman arrived in the United States departed before he was presented for inspection, the agent shall be directed by means of written notice on Form I–259 to arrange for the removal of the alien crewman from the United States, and if such alien crewman thereafter departs voluntarily from the United States within the time specified by the district director, such departure shall not be considered a deportation within the meaning of this section.

(b) *Revocation of parole.* When an immigration officer has reason to believe that an alien crewman paroled into the United States pursuant to the provisions of § 253.1 has violated the conditions of parole, the immigration officer may take such alien crewman into custody without a warrant of arrest. Following such action, the alien crewman shall be accorded, without undue delay, an examination by another immigration officer. If it is determined on the basis of such examination that the individual detained is an alien crewman who was paroled into the United States pursuant to the provisions of § 253.1 and that he has violated the conditions of the parole or has remained in the United States beyond the period authorized by the district director, the district director shall cause to be served upon the alien crewman a written notice that his parole has been revoked, setting forth the reasons for such action. If the vessel or aircraft upon which the alien crewman arrived in the United States is still in the United States, the alien crewman shall be delivered to that vessel or aircraft and Form I–259 shall be served upon the master or commanding officer of the vessel or aircraft directing that the alien crewman be detained on board the vessel or aircraft and deported from the United States. A copy of Form I–259 shall also be served on the agent for the vessel or aircraft. If the vessel or aircraft upon which the alien crewman arrived in the United States has departed from the United States, the agent or owner of the vessel or aircraft shall be directed by means of a notice on Form I–259 to effect the deportation of the alien crewman from the United States. Pending deportation, the alien crewman shall be continued in custody, unless the district director authorizes his release on parole under such conditions, including the posting of a suitable bond, as the district director may prescribe.

[32 FR 4342, Mar. 22, 1967]

PART 258—LIMITATIONS ON PERFORMANCE OF LONGSHORE WORK BY ALIEN CREWMEN

Sec.

AUTHORITY: 8 U.S.C. 1101, 1103, 1281; 8 CFR part 2.

SOURCE: 57 FR 40834, Sept. 8, 1992, unless otherwise noted.

§ 258.1 Limitations—General.

(a) *Longshore work defined.* Longshore work means any activity relating to the loading and unloading of cargo, the operation of cargo-related equipment [whether or not integral to the vessel], and the handling of mooring lines on the dock when the vessel is made fast or let go, in the United States or the coastal waters thereof.

(1) Longshore work is not included in the term "normal operation and service on board a vessel" for the purposes of section 101(a)(15)(D)(i) of the Act except as provided in sections 258 (c) or (d) of the Act.

(2) A vessel that uses nonimmigrant crewmen to perform longshore work, other than the activities allowed in particular circumstances under § 258.2 (a)(2), (b), or (c) of this part, shall be subject to a fine under section 251(d) of the Act.

(b) *Port defined.* For purposes of this section, the term *port* means a geographic area, either on a seacoast, lake, river, or other navigable body of water, which contains one or more publicly or privately owned terminals, piers, docks, or maritime facilities, which is commonly regarded as a port by other government maritime related agencies, such as the Maritime Administration.

§ 258.2 Exceptions.

Any master or agent who uses nonimmigrant crewmen to perform longshore work at any United States port under the exceptions provided for in paragraphs (a)(2), (b), or (c) of this section must so indicate on the crew manifest and shall note under which exception the work will be performed.

(a) *Hazardous cargo.* (1) The term *longshore work* does not include the loading and unloading of any cargo for which the Secretary of Transportation has prescribed regulations under authority contained in chapter 37 of title 46, United States Code, section 311 of the Federal Water Pollution Control Act, section 4106 of the Oil Pollution Act of 1990, or section 105 or 106 of the Hazardous Materials Transportation Act.

(2) In order to invoke the hazardous cargo exception for safety and environmental protection, the master or agent shall note on the manifest that the vessel is a qualifying tanker or carries hazardous dry bulk cargo.

(i) All tankers qualify for the hazardous cargo exception, including parcel tankers, except for a tanker that has been gas-freed to transport nonhazardous dry bulk commodities.

(ii) In order for a vessel to qualify for the hazardous cargo exception as a dry bulk hazardous cargo carrier, the master or agent must show the immigration officer the dangerous cargo manifest that is required by Coast Guard regulation 46 CFR 148.02–3(a) to be kept near the bridge house.

(b) *Prevailing practice exception.* (1) Nonimmigrant crewmen may perform longshore work under this exception if:

(i) There is in effect in the local port one or more collective bargaining agreements, each covering at least 30 percent of the persons performing longshore work at the port, and each of which permits the longshore activity to be performed by the nonimmigrant crewman, or

(ii) There is no collective bargaining agreement in effect in the local port covering at least 30 percent of the persons performing longshore work at the port, and the employer of the crewmen has filed an attestation with the Secretary of Labor that the Secretary of Labor has accepted.

(2) *Documentation to be presented under the prevailing practice exception.* (i) If the master or agent states on the manifest, Form I–418, that nonimmigrant crewmen will perform longshore work at a port under the prevailing practice exception as permitted by all collective bargaining agreements covering 30 percent or more of the persons performing longshore work at the port, then the master or agent must present to the examining immigration officer an affidavit from the local stevedore. The stevedore or a union representative of the employees' association must state on the affidavit that all bargaining agreements covering 30 percent or more of the longshore workers at the port allow nonimmigrant crewmen either to perform all longshore work or to perform those specified longshore activities that crewmen on the vessel intend to perform.

(ii) Where there is no collective bargaining agreement in effect at a port covering at least 30 percent of the persons who do longshore work, and the master or agent states on the manifest that nonimmigrant crewmen will perform such work under the prevailing practice exception, then the master or agent shall present a copy of the notification received from the Secretary of Labor that the attestation required for this exception has been accepted.

(iii) When an unanticipated emergency occurs, the master or agent of a vessel may file an attestation with the Secretary of Labor up to the date on which crewmen perform longshore work.

(A) If, because of an unanticipated emergency, crewmen on a vessel perform longshore work under the prevailing practice exception at a port, a revised manifest shall be submitted together with complete documentation, as specified in paragraph (b)(2)(ii) of this section, within 14 days of the longshore work having been done. Failure to present the required documentation may result in a fine under section 251 of the Act.

(B) All documents submitted after inspection shall be sent to the Immigration and Naturalization Service seaport office that inspected the vessel.

(iv) Attestations are valid for one year from the date of filing and cover nonimmigrant crewmen landing during that period if the master or agent states on the manifest that the vessel's crew continue to comply with the conditions in the attestation. When the vessel's master or agent intends to use a previously accepted attestation that is still valid, the master or agent shall submit a copy of the notification from the Secretary of Labor that the attestation was accepted and shall note on the manifest that the vessel continues to comply with the conditions of the attestation.

(3) *Use of automated self-unloading conveyor belt or vacuum-actuated system on a vessel.* An automated self-unloading conveyor belt or a vacuum-actuated system may be operated by a nonimmigrant crewman under the prevailing practice exception when no collective bargaining agreement at the local port prevents it. The master or agent is not required to file an attestation for nonimmigrant crewmen to perform such activity in such a circumstance unless the Secretary of Labor has determined that such activity is not the prevailing practice at that port, and has publicized this finding. When invoking this exception, the master or agent of the vessel shall annotate the manifest that the longshore work consists of operating a self-unloading conveyor belt or a vacuum-actuated system on the vessel under the prevailing practice exception.

(4) *Sanctions upon notification by the Secretary of Labor.* If the Immigration and Naturalization Service is notified by the Secretary of Labor that an entity has either misrepresented facts in its attestation or has failed to meet a condition attested to, then the Immigration and Naturalization Service will take the necessary steps to prevent the landing of vessels owned or chartered by the offending entity in accordance with section 258(c)(E)(i) of the Act. The Service may also impose a sanction as provided in that section, including the prohibition of any vessel owned or chartered by the violating entity from landing at any United States port for up to one year.

(5) The three variations of the prevailing practice exception—collective bargaining agreement, attestation process, and automated equipment—are port specific. If a vessel is to use nonimmigrant crewmen to perform longshore work under the prevailing practice exception, the appropriate documentation required under paragraph (b)(2) of this section must be presented for each port at which the longshore work will be performed.

(c) *Reciprocity exception.* Nonimmigrant crewmen may perform longshore work in a United States port under this exception if:

(1) The vessel on which the crewmen serve is registered in a country that does not prohibit crewmen aboard United States vessels from performing longshore work, or a specified longshore activity, when United States vessels land in that country, as determined by the Secretary of State; and

(2) The master or agent presents an affidavit from the crewmen's employer or the vessel's owner that a majority of the ownership interest in the vessel is held by nationals of a country or countries that do not prohibit such longshore activity by crewmen aboard United States vessels when they land in those countries.

(d) *Vessels that qualify for multiple exceptions.* A vessel that qualifies for more than one exception under this section may invoke the exception that the master or agent chooses.

(e) *Lack of documentation required by an exception.* If a vessel invokes an exception to the prohibition against nonimmigrant crewmen performing longshore work, but lacks any documentation required to accompany the manifest when invoking the exception, then the vessel's crewmen shall not perform longshore work. If the longshore work is performed despite the lack of documentation that the immigration officer has noted on the Form I–410, then the vessel is subject to fine under section 251(d) of the Act.

§ 258.3 Action upon arrival.

(a) The master or agent of the vessel shall state on the manifest at the first port of entry:

(1) Whether or not nonimmigrant crewmen aboard the vessel will perform longshore work at any port before departing the United States; and

(2) If nonimmigrant crewmen will perform longshore work, which exception in section 258 of the Act permits them to do so.

(b) If nonimmigrant crewmen will perform longshore work, the master or agent of the vessel shall present with the manifest any documentation required by 8 CFR 258.2 for the exception invoked.

(c) If, at the time of inspection, the master or agent fails to present the documentation required for the exception invoked, then the vessel is prohibited from using nonimmigrant crewmen to perform longshore work. If crewmen aboard the vessel perform longshore work despite the prohibition, the vessel is subject to fine under section 251(d) of the Act.

(d) The examining immigration officer shall give the master or agent a Receipt for Crew List, Form I–410, on which the officer shall note whether or not nonimmigrant crewmen will do longshore work at any port of call and, if so, under which exception. The officer shall also note which documentation supporting the exception accompanied the manifest, and any failure to present documentation which failure would prohibit crewmen from performing longshore work under the exception that the vessel invoked.

(e) If a vessel's crewmen perform longshore activity not sanctioned by an exception but performed to prevent the imminent destruction of goods or property; severe damage to vessels, docks, or real estate; possible environmental contamination; or possible injury or death to a person, a concise report of the incident shall be made within 14 days of the incident to the Immigration and Naturalization Service seaport office that performed the inspection. If the Service agrees that the situation was one of imminent danger requiring immediate action, no fine will be imposed for the performance of a longshore activity in this isolated instance.

(f) Failure to deliver true and complete information on the manifest or any documentation required to support an exception may result in a fine against the owner, agent, consignee, master, or commanding officer under section 251(d) of the Act.

PART 264—REGISTRATION AND FINGERPRINTING OF ALIENS IN THE UNITED STATES

Sec.

AUTHORITY: 8 U.S.C. 1103, 1201, 1303–1305; 8 CFR part 2.

§ 264.1 Registration and fingerprinting.

(a) *Prescribed registration forms.* The following forms are prescribed as registration forms:

FORM NO. AND CLASS

I–67, Inspection Record—Hungarian refugees (Act of July 25, 1958).

I–94, Arrival-Departure Record—Aliens admitted as nonimmigrants; aliens paroled into the United States under section 212(d)(5) of the Immigration and Nationality Act; aliens whose claimed entry prior to July 1, 1924, cannot be verified, they having satisfactorily established residence in the United States since prior to July 1, 1924; aliens lawfully admitted to the United States for permanent residence who have not been registered previously; aliens who are granted permission to depart without the institution of deportation proceedings or against whom deportation proceedings are being instituted.

I–95, Crewmen's Landing Permit—Crewmen arriving by vessel or aircraft.

I–181, Memorandum of Creation of Record of Lawful Permanent Residence—Aliens presumed to be lawfully admitted to the United States under 8 CFR 101.1.

I–485, Application for Status as Permanent Resident—Applicants under sections 245 and 249 of the Immigration and Nationality Act as amended, and section 13 of the Act of September 11, 1957.

I–590, Registration for Classification as Refugee—Escapee—Refugee-escapees paroled pursuant to section 1 of the Act of July 14, 1960.

I–687, Application for Status as a Temporary Resident—Applicants under section 245A of the Immigration and Nationality Act, as amended.

I–691, Notice of Approval for Status as a Temporary Resident—Aliens adjusted to lawful temporary residence under 8 CFR 210.2 and 245A.2.

I–698, Application to Adjust Status from Temporary to Permanent Resident—Applicants under section 245A of the Immigration and Nationality Act, as amended.

I–700, Application for Status as a Temporary Resident—Applicants under section 210 of the Immigration and Nationality Act, as amended.

I–817, Application for Voluntary Departure under the Family Unity Program.

(b) *Evidence of registration.* The following forms constitute evidence of registration:

FORM NO. AND CLASS

I–94, Arrival-Departure Record—Aliens admitted as nonimmigrants; aliens paroled into the United States under section 212(d)(5) of the Immigration and Nationality Act; aliens whose claimed entry prior to July 1, 1924, cannot be verified, they having satisfactorily established residence in the United States since prior to July 1, 1924; and aliens granted permission to depart without the institution of deportation proceedings.

I–95, Crewmen's Landing Permit—Crewmen arriving by vessel or aircraft.

I–184, Alien Crewman Landing Permit and Identification Card—Crewmen arriving by vessel.

I–185, Nonresident Alien Canadian Border Crossing Card—Citizens of Canada or British subjects residing in Canada.

I–186, Nonresident Alien Mexican Border Crossing Card—Citizens of Mexico residing in Mexico.

I–221, Order to Show Cause and Notice of Hearing—Aliens against whom deportation proceedings are being instituted.

I–221S, Order to Show Cause, Notice of Hearing, and Warrant for Arrest of Alien—Aliens against whom deportation proceedings are being instituted.

I–551, Permanent Resident Card—Lawful permanent resident of the United States.

I–766, Employment Authorization Document.

Form I–862, Notice to Appear—Aliens against whom removal proceedings are being instituted.

Form I–863, Notice of Referral to Immigration Judge—Aliens against whom removal proceedings are being instituted.

NOTE TO PARAGRAPH (b): In addition to the forms noted in this paragraph (b), a valid, unexpired nonimmigrant DHS admission or parole stamp in a foreign passport constitutes evidence of registration.

(c) *Replacement of alien registration.* Any alien whose registration document is not available for any reason must immediately apply for a replacement document in the manner prescribed by USCIS.

(d) *Surrender of registration.* If an alien is naturalized, dies, permanently departs, or is deported from the United States, or evidence of registration is found by a person other than the one to whom such evidence was issued, the person in possession of the document shall forward it to a USCIS office.

(e) *Fingerprinting waiver.* (1) Fingerprinting is waived for nonimmigrant aliens admitted as foreign government officials and employees; international organization representatives, officers and employees; NATO representatives, officers and employees, and holders of diplomatic visas while they maintain such nonimmigrant status. Fingerprinting is also waived for other nonimmigrant aliens, while they maintain nonimmigrant status, who are nationals of countries which do not require fingerprinting of United States citizens temporarily residing therein.

(2) Fingerprinting is waived for every nonimmigrant alien not included in paragraph (e)(1) of this section who departs from the United States within one year of his admission, provided he maintains his nonimmigrant status during that time; each such alien not previously fingerprinted shall apply therefor at once if he remains in the United States in excess of one year.

(3) Every nonimmigrant alien not previously fingerprinted shall apply therefor at once upon his failure to maintain his nonimmigrant status.

(f) [Reserved]

(g) *Registration and fingerprinting of children who reach age 14.* Within 30 days after reaching the age of 14, any alien in the United States not exempt from alien registration under the Act and this chapter must apply for registration and fingerprinting, unless fingerprinting is waived under paragraph (e) of this section, in accordance with applicable form instructions.

(1) *Permanent residents.* If such alien is a lawful permanent resident of the United States and is temporarily absent from the United States when he reaches the age of 14, he must apply for registration and provide a photograph within 30 days of his or her return to the United States in accordance with applicable form instructions. The alien, if a lawful permanent resident of the United States, must surrender any prior evidence of alien registration. USCIS will issue the alien new evidence of alien registration.

(2) *Others.* In the case of an alien who is not a lawful permanent resident, the alien's previously issued registration document will be noted to show that he or she has been registered and the date of registration.

[25 FR 10495, Nov. 2, 1960]

EDITORIAL NOTE: For FEDERAL REGISTER citations affecting § 264.1, see the List of CFR Sections Affected, which appears in the Finding Aids section of the printed volume and at *www.govinfo.gov.*

§ 264.2 Application for creation of record of permanent residence.

(a) *Jurisdiction.* An applicant who believes that he/she is eligible for presumption of lawful admission for permanent residence under § 101.1 or § 101.2 of this chapter or for lawful permanent residence as a person born in the United States to a foreign diplomatic officer under § 101.3 of this chapter shall submit his/her application for creation of a record of lawful permanent residence on Form I–485 in accordance with the instructions on the form and paragraph (c) of this section. The applicant must be physically present in the United States at the time of submission of his/her application.

(b) *Applicant under eighteen years old.* If the applicant is under eighteen years old, the applicant's parent or legal guardian shall prepare and sign the application in the applicant's behalf.

(c) *Filing application*—(1) *Presumption of lawful admission for permanent residence.* An applicant who believes that he/she is eligible for presumption of lawful admission for permanent residence under § 101.1 or § 101.2 of this chapter shall submit the following:

(i) A completed Form I–485, with the fee required in 8 CFR 103.7(b)(1) and any initial evidence required on the application form and in this section.

(ii) Form G–325A, Biographic Information.

(iii) [Reserved]

(iv) A list of all the applicant's arrivals in and departures from the United States.

(v) A statement signed by the applicant indicating the basis of the applicant's claim to presumption of lawful admission for permanent residence.

(vi) Documentary evidence substantiating the applicant's claim to presumption of lawful admission for permanent residence, including proof of continuous residence in the United States.

(vii) Two photographs prepared in accordance with the specifications outlined in the instructions on the application form. The immigration officer to whom the application is submitted, however, may waive the photographs for just cause.

(2) *Lawful permanent residence as a person born in the United States under diplomatic status.* An applicant who believes that he/she is eligible for lawful permanent residence as a person born in the United States to a foreign diplomatic officer under § 101.3 of this chapter shall submit the following:

(i) A completed Form I–485, with the fee required in 8 CFR 103.7(b)(1) and any initial evidence required in this application form and in this section.

(ii) Form G–325A, Biographic Information.

(iii) [Reserved]

(iv) The applicant's birth certificate.

(v) An executed Form I–508, Waiver of Rights, Privileges, Exemptions, and Immunities.

(vi) Official confirmation of the diplomatic classification and occupational title of the applicant's parent(s) at the time of the applicant's birth.

(vii) A list of all the applicant's arrivals in and departures from the United States.

(viii) Proof of continuous residence in the United States.

(ix) Two photographs prepared in accordance with the specifications outlined in the instructions on the application form. The immigration officer to whom the application is submitted, however, may waive the photographs for just cause.

(3) *Applicant under fourteen years old.* An applicant under fourteen years old shall not submit Form G–325A, Biographic Information.

(d) *Fingerprinting.* After filing an application, each applicant 14 years of age or older shall be fingerprinted as prescribed in 8 CFR 103.16.

(e) *Personal appearance.* Each applicant, including an applicant under eighteen years of age, must submit his/her application in person. This requirement may be waived at the discretion of the immigration officer to whom the application is submitted because of confinement of age, physical infirmity, illiteracy, or other compelling reason.

(f) *Interview.* The applicant may be required to appear in person before an immigration officer prior to adjudication of the application to be interviewed under oath concerning his/her eligibility for creation of a record of lawful permanent residence.

(g) *Decision.* The decision regarding creation of a record of lawful permanent residence for an alien eligible for presumption of lawful admission for permanent residence or for a person born in the United States to a foreign diplomatic officer will be made by the district director having jurisdiction over the applicant's place of residence.

(h) *Date of record of lawful permanent residence*—(1) *Presumption of lawful admission for permanent residence.* If the application is granted, the applicant's permanent residence will be recorded as of the date of the applicant's arrival in the United States under the conditions which caused him/her to be eligible for presumption of lawful admission for permanent residence.

(2) *Lawful permanent residence as a person born in the United States under diplomatic status.* If the application is granted, the applicant's permanent residence will be recorded as of his/her date of birth.

(i) *Denied application.* If the application is denied, the decision may not be appealed.

(Secs. 101(a)(20), 103, 262, 264 of the Immigration and Nationality Act, as amended; 8 U.S.C. 1101(a)(20), 1103, 1302, 1304)

[47 FR 941, Jan. 8, 1982, as amended at 58 FR 48779, Sept. 20, 1993; 63 FR 12987, Mar. 17, 1998; 74 FR 26940, June 5, 2009; 76 FR 53795, Aug. 29, 2011]

§ 264.4 [Reserved]

§ 264.5 Application for a replacement Permanent Resident Card.

(a) *Filing instructions.* A request to replace a Permanent Resident Card must be filed in accordance with the appropriate form instructions and with the fee specified in 8 CFR 103.7(b)(1); except that no fee is required for an application filed pursuant to paragraphs (b)(7) through (9) of this section, or paragraphs (d)(2) or (4) of this section.

(b) *Permanent residents required to file.* A permanent resident shall apply for a replacement Permanent Resident Card:

(1) When the previous card has been lost, stolen, or destroyed;

(2) When the existing card will be expiring within six months;

(3) When the existing card has been mutilated;

(4) When the bearer's name or other biographic information has been legally changed since issuance of the existing card;

(5) When the applicant is taking up actual residence in the United States after having been a commuter, or is a permanent resident taking up commuter status;

(6) When the applicant has been automatically converted to permanent resident status;

(7) When the previous card was issued but never received;

(8) When the bearer of the card reaches the age of 14 years, unless the existing card will expire prior to the bearer's 16th birthday; or

(9) If the existing card bears incorrect data on account of Service error.

(c) *Other filings by a permanent resident.* (1) A permanent resident shall apply on the designated form to replace a prior edition of the alien registration card issued on Form AR–3, AR–103, or I–151.

(2) A permanent resident may apply on the designated form to replace any edition of the Permanent Resident Card for any other reason not specified in paragraphs (b) and (c)(1) of this section.

(d) *Conditional permanent residents required to file.* A conditional permanent resident whose card is expiring may apply to have the conditions on residence removed in accordance with 8 CFR 216.4 or 8 CFR 216.6. A conditional resident who seeks to replace a permanent resident card that is not expiring within 90 days may apply for a replacement card on the form prescribed by USCIS:

(1) To replace a card that was lost, stolen, or destroyed;

(2) To replace a card that was issued but never received;

(3) Where the prior card has been mutilated;

(4) Where the prior card is incorrect on account of Service error; or

(5) Where his or her name or other biographic data has changed since the card was issued.

(e) *Supporting documentation.* (1) The prior Permanent Resident Card must be surrendered to USCIS if a new card is being requested in accordance with paragraphs (b)(2) through (5) and (b)(8) and (9) of this section.

(2) A request to replace a Permanent Resident Card filed pursuant to paragraph (b)(4) of this section must include evidence of the name change such as a court order or marriage certificate.

(3) A request to replace a Permanent Resident Card in order to change any other biographic data on the card must include documentary evidence verifying the new data.

(f) *Decision.* If an application is denied, the applicant shall be notified of the reasons for denial. No appeal shall lie from this decision.

(g) *Eligibility for evidence of permanent residence while in deportation, exclusion, or removal proceedings.* A person in deportation, exclusion, or removal proceedings is entitled to evidence of permanent resident status until ordered excluded, deported, or removed. USCIS will issue such evidence in the form of a temporary permanent resident document that will remain valid until the proceedings are concluded. Issuance of evidence of permanent residence to an alien who had permanent resident status when the proceedings commenced shall not affect those proceedings.

(h) *Temporary evidence of registration.* USCIS may issue temporary evidence of registration and lawful permanent resident status to a lawful permanent resident alien who is departing temporarily from the United States and has applied for issuance of a replacement permanent resident card if USCIS is unable to issue and deliver such card prior to the alien's contemplated return to the United States. The alien must surrender such temporary evidence upon receipt of his or her permanent resident card.

(i) *Waiver of requirements.* USCIS may waive the photograph, in person filing, and fingerprinting requirements of this section in cases of confinement due to advanced age or physical infirmity.

[58 FR 48779, Sept. 20, 1993, as amended at 59 FR 1466, Jan. 11, 1994; 59 FR 33905, July 1, 1994; 63 FR 12987, Mar. 17, 1998; 63 FR 70316, Dec. 21, 1998; 65 FR 57724, Sept. 26, 2000; 74 FR 26940, June 5, 2009; 76 FR 53795, Aug. 29, 2011]

§ 264.6 Application for a nonimmigrant arrival-departure record.

(a) *Eligibility.* USCIS may issue a new or replacement arrival-departure record to a nonimmigrant who seeks:

(1) To replace a lost or stolen record;

(2) To replace a mutilated record; or

(3) Was not issued an arrival-departure record pursuant to 8 CFR 235.1(h)(1)(i), (iii), (iv), (v), or (vi) when last admitted as a nonimmigrant, and has not since been issued such record but now requires one.

(b) *Application.* A nonimmigrant may request issuance or replacement of a nonimmigrant arrival-departure record by applying on the form designated by USCIS with the fee prescribed in 8 CFR 103.7(b)(1) and in accordance with the form instructions.

(c) *Processing.* A pending application filed under paragraph (a) of this section is temporary evidence of registration. If the application is approved, USCIS will issue an arrival-departure document. There is no appeal from the denial of this application.

[76 FR 53795, Aug. 29, 2011]

PART 265—NOTICES OF ADDRESS

AUTHORITY: 8 U.S.C. 1103 and 1305.

§ 265.1 Reporting change of address.

Except for those exempted by section 263(b) of the Act, all aliens in the United States required to register under section 262 of the Act must report each change of address and new address within 10 days of such change in accordance with instructions provided by USCIS.

[76 FR 53796, Aug. 29, 2011]

PART 270—PENALTIES FOR DOCUMENT FRAUD

AUTHORITY: 8 U.S.C. 1101, 1103, and 1324c; Pub. L. 101–410, 104 Stat. 890, as amended by Pub. L. 104–134, 110 Stat. 1321 and Pub. L. 114–74, 129 Stat. 599.

SOURCE: 57 FR 33866, July 31, 1992, unless otherwise noted.

§ 270.1 Definitions.

For the purpose of this part—

Document means an instrument on which is recorded, by means of letters, figures, or marks, matters which may be used to fulfill any requirement of the Act. The term "document" includes, but is not limited to, an application required to be filed under the Act and any other accompanying document or material;

Entity means any legal entity, including, but not limited to, a corporation, partnership, joint venture, governmental body, agency, proprietorship, or association, including an agent or anyone acting directly or indirectly in the interest thereof.

§ 270.2 Enforcement procedures.

(a) *Procedures for the filing of complaints.* Any person or entity having knowledge of a violation or potential violation of section 274C of the Act may submit a signed, written complaint to the Service office having jurisdiction over the business or residence of the potential violator or the location where the violation occurred. The signed, written complaint must contain sufficient information to identify both the complainant and the alleged violator, including their names and addresses. The complaint should also contain detailed factual allegations relating to the potential violation including the date, time and place of the alleged violation and the specific act or conduct alleged to constitute a violation of the Act. Written complaints may be delivered either by mail to the appropriate Service office or by personally appearing before any immigration officer at a Service office.

(b) *Investigation.* When the Service receives complaints from a third party in accordance with paragraph (a) of this section, it shall investigate only those complaints which, on their face, have a substantial probability of validity. The Service may also conduct investigations for violations on its own initiative, and without having received a written complaint. If it is determined after investigation that the person or entity has violated section 274C of the Act, the Service may issue and serve upon the alleged violator a Notice of Intent to Fine.

(c) *Issuance of a subpoena.* Service officers shall have reasonable access to examine any relevant evidence of any person or entity being investigated. The Service may issue subpoenas pursuant to its authority under sections 235(a) and 287 of the Act, in accordance with the procedures set forth in § 287.4 of this chapter.

(d) *Notice of Intent to Fine.* The proceeding to assess administrative penalties under section 274C of the Act is commenced when the Service issues a Notice of Intent to Fine. Service of this notice shall be accomplished by personal service pursuant to 8 CFR 103.8(a)(2). Service is effective upon receipt, as evidenced by the certificate of service or the certified mail return receipt. The person or entity identified in the Notice of Intent to Fine shall be known as the respondent. The Notice of

Intent to Fine may be issued by an officer defined in §242.1 of this chapter or by an INS port director designated by his or her district director.

(e) *Contents of the Notice of Intent to Fine.* (1) The Notice of Intent to Fine shall contain the basis for the charge(s) against the respondent, the statutory provisions alleged to have been violated, and the monetary amount of the penalty the Service intends to impose.

(2) The Notice of Intent to Fine shall provide the following advisals to the respondent:

(i) That the person or entity has the right to representation by counsel of his or her own choice at no expense to the government;

(ii) That any statement given may be used against the person or entity;

(iii) That the person or entity has the right to request a hearing before an administrative law judge pursuant to 5 U.S.C. 554–557, and that such request must be filed with INS within 60 days from the service of the Notice of Intent to Fine; and

(iv) That if a written request for a hearing is not timely filed, the Service will issue a final order from which there is no appeal.

(f) *Request for hearing before an administrative law judge.* If a respondent contests the issuance of a Notice of Intent to Fine, the respondent must file with the INS, within 60 days of the Notice of Intent to Fine, a written request for a hearing before an administrative law judge. Any written request for a hearing submitted in a foreign language must be accompanied by an English language translation. A request for hearing is deemed filed when it is either received by the Service office designated in the Notice of Intent to Fine, or addressed to such office, stamped with the proper postage, and postmarked within the 60-day period. In computing the 60-day period prescribed by this section, the day of service of the Notice of Intent to Fine shall not be included. In the request for a hearing, the respondent may, but is not required to, respond to each allegation listed in the Notice of Intent to Fine. A respondent may waive the 60-day period in which to request a hearing before an administrative law judge and ask that the INS issue a final order from which there is no appeal. Prior to execution of the waiver, a respondent who is not a United States citizen will be advised that a waiver of a section 274C hearing will result in the issuance of a final order and that the respondent will be excludable and/or deportable from the United States pursuant to the Act.

(g) *Failure to file a request for hearing.* If the respondent does not file a written request for a hearing within 60 days of service of the Notice of Intent to Fine, the INS shall issue a final order from which there shall be no appeal.

(h) *Issuance of the final order.* A final order may be issued by an officer defined in §242.1 of this chapter, by an INS port director designated by his or her district director, or by the Director of the INS National Fines Office.

(i) *Service of the final order*—(1) *Generally.* Service of the final order shall be accomplished by personal service pursuant to 8 CFR 103.8(a)(2). Service is effective upon receipt, as evidenced by the certificate of service or the certified mail return receipt.

(2) *Alternative provisions for service in a foreign country.* When service is to be effected upon a party in a foreign country, it is sufficient if service of the final order is made: (i) In the manner prescribed by the law of the foreign country for service in that country in an action in any of its courts of general jurisdiction; or

(ii) As directed by the foreign authority in response to a letter rogatory, when service in either case is reasonably calculated to give actual notice; or

(iii) When applicable, pursuant to §103.5a(a)(2) of this chapter.

Service is effective upon receipt of the final order. Proof of service may be made as prescribed by the law of the foreign country, or, when service is pursuant to §103.5a(a)(2) of this chapter, as evidenced by the certificate of service or the certified mail return receipt.

(j) *Declination to file charges for document fraud committed by refugees at the time of entry.* The Service shall not issue a Notice of Intent to Fine for acts of document fraud committed by an alien pursuant to direct departure from a country in which the alien has a well-founded fear of persecution or from which there is a significant danger that the alien would be returned to a country in which the alien would have a well-founded fear of persecution, provided that the alien has presented himself or herself without delay to an INS officer and shown good cause for his or her illegal entry or presence. Other acts of document fraud committed by such an alien may result in the issuance of a Notice of Intent to Fine and the imposition of civil money penalties.

[57 FR 33866, July 31, 1992, as amended at 76 FR 53796, Aug. 29, 2011]

§ 270.3 Penalties.

(a) *Criminal penalties.* Nothing in section 274C of the Act shall be construed to diminish or qualify any of the penalties available for activities prohibited by this section but proscribed as well in title 18, United States Code.

(b) *Civil penalties.* A person or entity may face civil penalties for a violation of section 274C of the Act. Civil penalties may be imposed by the Service or by an administrative law judge for violations under section 274C of the Act. The Service may charge multiple violations of section 274C of the Act in a single Notice of Intent to Fine, and may impose separate penalties for each such unlawful act in a single proceeding or determination. However, in determining whether an offense is a first offense or a subsequent offense, a finding of more than one violation in the course of a single proceeding or determination will be counted as a single offense.

(1) A respondent found by the Service or an administrative law judge to have violated section 274C of the Act shall be subject to an order:

(i) To cease and desist from such behavior; and

(ii) To pay a civil penalty as follows:

(A) *First offense under section 274C(a)(1) through (a)(4).* Not less than $275 and not exceeding $2,200 for each fraudulent document or each proscribed activity described in section 274C(a)(1) through (a)(4) of the Act before March 27, 2008; not less than $375 and not exceeding $3,200 for each fraudulent document or each proscribed activity described in section 274C(a)(1) through (a)(4) of the Act on or after March 27, 2008 and on or before November 2, 2015; and not less than $461 and not exceeding $3,695 for each fraudulent document or each proscribed activity described in section 274C(a)(1) through (a)(4) of the Act after November 2, 2015.

(B) *First offense under section 274C(a)(5) or (a)(6).* Not less than $250 and not exceeding $2,000 for each fraudulent document or each proscribed activity described in section 274C(a)(5) or (a)(6) of the Act before March 27, 2008; not less than $275 and not exceeding $2,200 for each fraudulent document or each proscribed activity described in section 274C(a)(5) or (a)(6) of the Act on or after March 27, 2008 and on or before November 2, 2015; and not less than $390 and not exceeding $3,116 for each fraudulent document or each proscribed activity described in section 274C(a)(5) or (a)(6) of the Act after November 2, 2015.

(C) *Subsequent offenses under section 274C(a)(1) through (a)(4).* Not less than $2,200 and not more than $5,500 for each fraudulent document or each proscribed activity described in section 274C(a)(1) through (a)(4) of the Act before March 27, 2008; not less than $3,200 and not exceeding $6,500 for each fraudulent document or each proscribed activity described in section 274C(a)(1) through (a)(4) of the Act occurring on or after March 27, 2008 and on or before November 2, 2015; and not less than $3,695 and not more than $9,239 for each fraudulent document or each proscribed activity described in section 274C(a)(1) through (a)(4) of the Act after November 2, 2015.

(D) *Subsequent offenses under section 274C(a)(5) or (a)(6).* Not less than $2,000 and not more than $5,000 for each fraudulent document or each proscribed activity described in section 274C(a)(5) or (a)(6) of the Act before March 27, 2008; not less than $2,200 and not exceeding $5,500 for each fraudulent document or each proscribed activity described in section 274C(a)(5) or (a)(6) of the Act occurring on or after March 27, 2008 and on or before November 2, 2015; and not less than $3,116 and not more than $7,791 for each fraudulent document or each proscribed activity described in section 274C(a)(5) or (a)(6) of the Act after November 2, 2015.

(2) Where an order is issued to a respondent composed of distinct, physically separate subdivisions each of which provides separately for the hiring, recruiting, or referring for a fee for employment (without reference to the practices of, and not under the common control of or common control with, another subdivision), each subdivision shall be considered a separate person or entity.

[57 FR 33866, July 31, 1992, as amended at 64 FR 47101, Aug. 30, 1999; 73 FR 10135, Feb. 26, 2008; 81 FR 43001, July 1, 2016; 82 FR 8579, Jan. 27, 2017; 83 FR 13834, Apr. 2, 2018]

PART 271—DILIGENT AND REASONABLE EFFORTS TO PREVENT THE UNAUTHORIZED ENTRY OF ALIENS BY THE OWNERS OF RAILROAD LINES, INTERNATIONAL BRIDGES OR TOLL ROADS

AUTHORITY: 8 U.S.C. 1103 and 1321.

§ 271.1 Procedures for inspections.

(a) *Applicability*. The following terms and conditions apply to those owners or operators of railroad lines, international bridges, or toll roads, which provide a means for an alien to come to the United States.

(b) *Inspection of facility*. Based upon a written request by the owners or operators, the INS district director or his designee shall inspect the facility or method utilized in order to ensure that owners and operators have acted diligently in taking adequate steps to prevent the unlawful entry of aliens into the United States. Such measures may include but are not necessarily limited to fencing, barricades, lighting, or security guards. If the district director determines that preventive measures are inadequate, he or she shall advise the owners or operators in writing, citing the reasons for such determination. If the owners or operators believe the requirements of the district director to be excessive or unnecessary, they may request that the Regional Commissioner having jurisdiction over the location where the facility is located, review the district director's requirements. The Regional Commissioner shall advise the owners or operators in writing of the results of his or her review.

(c) *Preventive measures and certification*. Upon a determination by the district director that reasonable and adequate preventive measures have been taken by the owners and operators, he or she shall certify that the owners and operators shall not be liable for the penalty described in section 271(a), so long as the facility or method utilized is maintained in the condition in which approved and certified.

(d) *Revocation of certification*. The District Director having jurisdiction over the location where the facility is located, in his or her discretion, may at any time, conduct an inspection of said facility to determine if any violation is occurring. If the facility is found to be not in compliance, said certification will be revoked.

[53 FR 26036, July 11, 1988]

PART 273—CARRIER RESPONSIBILITIES AT FOREIGN PORTS OF EMBARKATION; REDUCING, REFUNDING, OR WAIVING FINES UNDER SECTION 273 OF THE ACT

Sec.

AUTHORITY: 8 U.S.C. 1103, 1323; 8 CFR part 2.

SOURCE: 63 FR 23655, Apr. 30, 1998, unless otherwise noted.

§ 273.1 General.

In any fines case in which a fine is imposed under section 273 of the Act involving an alien brought to the United States after December 24, 1994, the carrier may seek a reduction, refund, or waiver of fine, as provided for by section 273(e) of the Act, in accordance with this part. The provisions of section 273(e) of the Act and of this part do not apply to any fine imposed under any provision other than section 273 (a)(1) and (b) of the Act.

§ 273.2 Definition.

As used in this part, the term *Carrier* means an individual or organization engaged in transporting passengers or goods for hire to the United States.

§ 273.3 Screening procedures.

(a) *Applicability.* The terms and conditions contained in paragraph (b) of this section apply to those owners, operators, or agents of carriers which transport passengers to the United States.

(b) *Procedures at ports of embarkation.* At each port of embarkation carriers shall take reasonable steps to prevent the boarding of improperly documented aliens destined to the United States by taking the following steps:

(1) Screening of passengers by carrier personnel prior to boarding and examination of their travel documents to ensure that:

(i) The passport or travel document presented is not expired and is valid for entry into the United States;

(ii) The passenger is the rightful holder;

(iii) If the passenger requires a visa, the visa is valid for the holder and any other accompanying passengers named in the passport; and

(iv) Passengers described in part 215, subpart B, of this chapter have complied with EVUS requirements as appropriate.

(2) Refusing to board any passenger determined to be improperly documented. Failure to refuse boarding when advised to do so by a Service or Consular Officer may be considered by the Service as a factor in its evaluation of applications under § 273.5.

(3) Implementing additional safeguards such as, but not necessarily limited to, the following:

(i) For instances in which the carrier suspects fraud, assessing the adequacy of the documents presented by asking additional, pertinent questions or by taking other appropriate steps to corroborate the identity of passengers, such as requesting secondary information.

(ii) Conducting a second check of passenger documents, when necessary at high-risk ports of embarkation, at the time of boarding to verify that all passengers are properly documented consistent with paragraph (b)(1) of this section. This includes a recheck of documents at the final foreign port of embarkation for all passengers, including those originally boarded at a prior stop or who are being transported to the United States under the Transit Without Visa (TWOV) or International-to-International (ITI) Programs.

(iii) Providing a reasonable level of security during the boarding process so that passengers are unable to circumvent any carrier document checks.

(4) *Transmitting visa numbers.* Carriers must transmit to U.S. Customs and Border Protection the visa number for any passenger who requires a visa. The visa number must be transmitted using the Advance Passenger Information System, consistent with the procedural requirements for transmission of electronic passenger manifests in 19 CFR parts 4 (vessel) and 122 (aircraft).

[63 FR 23655, Apr. 30, 1998, as amended at 81 FR 72493, Oct. 20, 2016]

§ 273.4 Demonstration by carrier that screening requirements were met.

(a) To be eligible to apply for reduction, refund, or waiver of a fine, the carrier shall provide evidence that it screened all passengers on the conveyance for the instant flight or voyage in accordance with the procedures listed in § 273.3.

(b) The Service may, at any time, conduct an inspection of a carrier's document screening procedures at ports of embarkation to determine compliance with the procedures listed in § 273.3, to the extent permitted by the local competent authority responsible for port access or security. If necessary, the carrier shall use its good offices to obtain this permission from the local authority. If the carrier's port of embarkation operation is found not to be in compliance, the carrier will be notified by the Service that it will not be eligible for refund, reduction, or waiver of fines under section 273(e) of the Act unless the carrier can establish that lack of compliance was beyond the carrier's control.

§ 273.5 General criteria used for reduction, refund, or waiver of fines.

(a) Upon application by the carrier, the Service shall determine whether circumstances exist which would justify a reduction, refund, or waiver of fines pursuant to section 273(e) of the Act.

(b) Applications for reduction, refund, or waiver of fine under section 273(e) of the Act shall be made in accordance with the procedures outlined in 8 CFR 280.12 and 8 CFR 280.51.

(c) In determining the amount of the fine reduction, refund, or waiver, the Service shall consider:

(1) The effectiveness of the carrier's screening procedures;

(2) The carrier's history of fines violations, including fines, liquidated damages, and user fee payment records; and,

(3) The existence of any extenuating circumstances.

§ 273.6 Memorandum of Understanding.

(a) Carriers may apply to enter into a Memorandum of Understanding (MOU) with the Service for an automatic reduction, refund, or waiver of fines imposed under section 273 of the Act.

(b) Carriers signatory to an MOU will not be required to apply for reduction, refund, or waiver of fines in accordance with the procedures outlined in 8 CFR 280.12 and 8 CFR 280.51, but will follow procedures as set forth in the MOU.

(c) Carriers signatory to an MOU will have fines reduced, refunded, or waived according to performance standards enumerated in the MOU or as determined by the Service.

(d) Carriers signatory to an MOU are not precluded from seeking additional reduction, refund, or waiver of fines in accordance with the procedures outlined in 8 CFR 280.12 and 8 CFR 280.51.

PART 274—SEIZURE AND FORFEITURE OF CONVEYANCES

Sec.

AUTHORITY: 8 U.S.C. 1103, 1324(b); 18 U.S.C. 983, 19 U.S.C. 66, 1600, 1618, 1619, 1624; 22 U.S.C. 401; 31 U.S.C. 5321; 49 U.S.C. 80304.

SOURCE: 53 FR 43187, Oct. 26, 1988, unless otherwise noted.

§ 274.1 Seizure and forfeiture authority.

Any officer of Customs and Border Protection or Immigration and Customs Enforcement may seize and forfeit any property that has been or is being used in the commission of a violation of any statutory authority involving the unlawful introduction of aliens, contraband or proceeds of such introduction, pursuant to, but not limited to, section 274(a) of the Act (8 U.S.C. 1324(a)). All seizures and forfeitures in such cases will be administered in accordance with 19 CFR parts 162 and 171.

[73 FR 9011, Feb. 19, 2008]

§ 274.2 Delegation of authority.

All powers provided to Fines, Penalties and Forfeitures Officers in 19 CFR parts 162 and 171 are provided to the Chief, Office of Border Patrol or his designees, for purposes of administering seizures and forfeitures made by Border Patrol Officers.

[73 FR 9011, Feb. 19, 2008]

PART 274a—CONTROL OF EMPLOYMENT OF ALIENS

Subpart A—Employer Requirements

Sec.

Subpart B—Employment Authorization

AUTHORITY: 8 U.S.C. 1101, 1103, 1324a; 48 U.S.C. 1806; 8 CFR part 2; Pub. L. 101–410, 104

Stat. 890, as amended by Pub. L. 114–74, 129 Stat. 599.

SOURCE: 52 FR 16221, May 1, 1987, unless otherwise noted.

Subpart A—Employer Requirements

§274a.1 Definitions.

For the purpose of this part—

(a) The term *unauthorized alien* means, with respect to employment of an alien at a particular time, that the alien is not at that time either: (1) Lawfully admitted for permanent residence, or (2) authorized to be so employed by this Act or by the Attorney General;

(b) The term *entity* means any legal entity, including but not limited to, a corporation, partnership, joint venture, governmental body, agency, proprietorship, or association;

(c) The term *hire* means the actual commencement of employment of an employee for wages or other remuneration. For purposes of section 274A(a)(4) of the Act and 8 CFR 274a.5, a hire occurs when a person or entity uses a contract, subcontract, or exchange entered into, renegotiated, or extended after November 6, 1986 (or, with respect to the Commonwealth of the Northern Mariana Islands, after the transition program effective date as defined in 8 CFR 1.1), to obtain the labor of an alien in the United States, knowing that the alien is an unauthorized alien;

(d) The term *refer for a fee* means the act of sending or directing a person or transmitting documentation or information to another, directly or indirectly, with the intent of obtaining employment in the United States for such person, for remuneration whether on a retainer or contingency basis; however, this term does not include union hiring halls that refer union members or non-union individuals who pay union membership dues;

(e) The term *recruit for a fee* means the act of soliciting a person, directly or indirectly, and referring that person to another with the intent of obtaining employment for that person, for remuneration whether on a retainer or contingency basis; however, this term does not include union hiring halls that refer union members or non-union individuals who pay union membership dues;

(f) The term *employee* means an individual who provides services or labor for an employer for wages or other remuneration but does not mean independent contractors as defined in paragraph (j) of this section or those engaged in casual domestic employment as stated in paragraph (h) of this section;

(g) The term *employer* means a person or entity, including an agent or anyone acting directly or indirectly in the interest thereof, who engages the services or labor of an employee to be performed in the United States for wages or other remuneration. In the case of an independent contractor or contract labor or services, the term *employer* shall mean the independent contractor or contractor and not the person or entity using the contract labor;

(h) The term *employment* means any service or labor performed by an employee for an employer within the United States, including service or labor performed on a vessel or aircraft that has arrived in the United States and has been inspected, or otherwise included within the provisions of the Anti-Reflagging Act codified at 46 U.S.C. 8704, but not including duties performed by nonimmigrant crewmen defined in sections 101 (a)(10) and (a)(15)(D) of the Act. However, employment does not include casual employment by individuals who provide domestic service in a private home that is sporadic, irregular or intermittent;

(i) The term *State employment agency* means any State government unit designated to cooperate with the United States Employment Service in the operation of the public employment service system;

(j) The term *independent contractor* includes individuals or entities who carry on independent business, contract to do a piece of work according to their own means and methods, and are subject to control only as to results. Whether an individual or entity is an independent contractor, regardless of what the individual or entity calls itself, will be determined on a case-by-case basis. Factors to be considered in that determination include, but are not limited to, whether the individual or entity: supplies the tools or materials; makes services available to the general public; works for a number of clients at the same time; has an opportunity for profit or loss as a result of labor or services provided; invests in the facilities for work; directs the order or sequence in which the work is to be done and determines the hours during which the work is to be done. The use of labor or services of an independent contractor are subject to the restrictions in section 274A(a)(4) of the Act and §274a.5 of this part;

(k) The term *pattern* or *practice* means regular, repeated, and intentional activities, but does not include isolated, sporadic, or accidental acts;

(l)(1) The term *knowing* includes not only actual knowledge but also knowledge which may fairly be inferred through notice of certain facts and circumstances which would lead a person, through the exercise of reasonable care, to know about a certain condition. Constructive knowledge may include, but is not limited to, situations where an employer:

(i) Fails to complete or improperly completes the Employment Eligibility Verification Form, I–9;

(ii) Has information available to it that would indicate that the alien is not authorized to work, such as Labor Certification and/or an Application for Prospective Employer; or

(iii) Acts with reckless and wanton disregard for the legal consequences of permitting another individual to introduce an unauthorized alien into its work force or to act on its behalf.

(2) Knowledge that an employee is unauthorized may not be inferred from an employee's foreign appearance or accent. Nothing in this definition should be interpreted as permitting an employer to request more or different documents than are required under section 274(b) of the Act or to refuse to honor documents tendered that on their face reasonably appear to be genuine and to relate to the individual.

[52 FR 16221, May 1, 1987, as amended at 53 FR 8612, Mar. 16, 1988; 55 FR 25931, June 25, 1990; 56 FR 41783, Aug. 23, 1991; 72 FR 45623, Aug. 15, 2007; 73 FR 63867, Oct. 28, 2008; 74 FR 51452, Oct. 7, 2009; 74 FR 55739, Oct. 28, 2009]

§274a.2 Verification of identity and employment authorization.

(a) *General.* This section establishes requirements and procedures for compliance by persons or entities when hiring, or when recruiting or referring for a fee, or when continuing to employ individuals in the United States.

(1) *Recruiters and referrers for a fee.* For purposes of complying with section 274A(b) of the Act and this section, all references to recruiters and referrers for a fee are limited to a person or entity who is either an agricultural association, agricultural employer, or farm labor contractor (as defined in section 3 of the Migrant and Seasonal Agricultural Worker Protection Act, Pub. L. 97–470 (29 U.S.C. 1802)).

(2) *Verification form.* Form I–9, Employment Eligibility Verification Form, is used in complying with the requirements of this 8 CFR 274a.1—274a.11. In the Commonwealth of the Northern Mariana Islands (CNMI) only, for a 2-year period starting from the transition program effective date (as defined in 8 CFR 1.1), the Form I–9 CNMI Employment Eligibility Verification Form must be used in lieu of Form I–9 in complying with the requirements of 8 CFR 274a.1 through 274a.11. Whenever "Form I–9" is mentioned in this title 8, "Form I–9" means Form I–9 or, when used in the CNMI for a 2-year period starting from the transition program effective date (as defined in 8 CFR 1.1), Form I–9 CNMI. Form I–9 can be in paper or electronic format. In paper format, the Form I–9 may be obtained in limited quantities at USCIS district offices, or ordered from the Superintendent of Documents, Washington, DC 20402. In electronic format, a fillable electronic Form I–9 may be downloaded from *http://www.uscis.gov.* Alternatively, Form I–9 can be electronically generated or retained, provided that the resulting form is legible; there is no change to the name, content, or sequence of the data elements and instructions; no additional data elements or language are inserted; and the standards specified under 8 CFR 274a.2(e), (f), (g), (h), and (i), as applicable, are met. When copying or printing the paper Form I–9, the text of the two-

sided form may be reproduced by making either double-sided or single-sided copies.

(3) *Attestation Under Penalty and Perjury*. In conjunction with completing the Form I–9, an employer or recruiter or referrer for a fee must examine documents that evidence the identity and employment authorization of the individual. The employer or recruiter or referrer for a fee and the individual must each complete an attestation on the Form I–9 under penalty of perjury.

(b) *Employment verification requirements*—(1) *Examination of documents and completion of Form I–9*. (i) A person or entity that hires or recruits or refers for a fee an individual for employment must ensure that the individual properly:

(A) Completes section 1—"Employee Information and Verification"—on the Form I–9 at the time of hire and signs the attestation with a handwritten or electronic signature in accordance with paragraph (h) of this section; or if an individual is unable to complete the Form I–9 or needs it translated, someone may assist him or her. The preparer or translator must read the Form I–9 to the individual, assist him or her in completing Section 1—"Employee Information and Verification," and have the individual sign or mark the Form I–9 by a handwritten signature, or an electronic signature in accordance with paragraph (h) of this section, in the appropriate place; and

(B) Present to the employer or the recruiter or referrer for a fee documentation as set forth in paragraph (b)(1)(v) of this section establishing his or her identity and employment authorization within the time limits set forth in paragraphs (b)(1)(ii) through (b)(1)(v) of this section.

(ii) Except as provided in paragraph (b)(1)(viii) of this section, an employer, his or her agent, or anyone acting directly or indirectly in the interest thereof, must within three business days of the hire:

(A) Physically examine the documentation presented by the individual establishing identity and employment authorization as set forth in paragraph (b)(1)(v) of this section and ensure that the documents presented appear to be genuine and to relate to the individual; and

(B) Complete section 2—"Employer Review and Verification"—on the Form I–9 within three business days of the hire and sign the attestation with a handwritten signature or electronic signature in accordance with paragraph (i) of this section.

(iii) An employer who hires an individual for employment for a duration of less than three business days must comply with paragraphs (b)(1)(ii)(A) and (b)(1)(ii)(B) of this section at the time of the hire. An employer may not accept a receipt, as described in paragraph (b)(1)(vi) of this section, in lieu of the required document if the employment is for less than three business days.

(iv) A recruiter or referrer for a fee for employment must comply with paragraphs (b)(1)(ii)(A) and (b)(1)(ii)(B) of this section within three business days of the date the referred individual is hired by the employer. Recruiters and referrers may designate agents to complete the employment verification procedures on their behalf including but not limited to notaries, national associations, or employers. If a recruiter or referrer designates an employer to complete the employment verification procedures, the employer need only provide the recruiter or referrer with a photocopy or printed electronic image of the Form I–9, electronic Form I–9, or a Form I–9 on microfilm or microfiche.

(v) The individual may present either an original document which establishes both employment authorization and identity, or an original document which establishes employment authorization and a separate original document which establishes identity. Only unexpired documents are acceptable. The identification number and expiration date (if any) of all documents must be noted in the appropriate space provided on the Form I–9.

(A) The following documents, so long as they appear to relate to the individual presenting the document, are acceptable to evidence both identity and employment authorization:

(*1*) A United States passport;

(*2*) An Alien Registration Receipt Card or Permanent Resident Card (Form I–551);

(*3*) A foreign passport that contains a temporary I–551 stamp, or temporary I–551 printed notation on a machine-readable immigrant visa;

(*4*) An Employment Authorization Document which contains a photograph (Form I–766);

(*5*) In the case of an individual who is employment-authorized incident to status or parole with a specific employer, a foreign passport with an Arrival/Departure Record, Form I–94 (as defined in 8 CFR 1.4) or Form I–94A, bearing the same name as the passport and containing an endorsement by DHS indicating such employment-authorized status or parole, as long as the period of endorsement has not yet expired and the employment is not in conflict with the individual's employment-authorized status or parole;

(*6*) A passport from the Federated States of Micronesia (FSM) or the Republic of the Marshall Islands (RMI) with Form I–94 or Form I–94A indicating nonimmigrant admission under the Compact of Free Association Between the United States and the FSM or RMI;

(*7*) In the case of an individual lawfully enlisted for military service in the Armed Forces under 10 U.S.C. 504, a military identification card issued to such individual may be accepted only by the Armed Forces.

(B) The following documents are acceptable to establish identity only:

(*1*) For individuals 16 years of age or older:

(*i*) A driver's license or identification card containing a photograph, issued by a state (as defined in section 101(a)(36) of the Act) or an outlying possession of the United States (as defined by section 101(a)(29) of the Act). If the driver's license or identification card does not contain a photograph, identifying information shall be included such as: name, date of birth, sex, height, color of eyes, and address;

(*ii*) School identification card with a photograph;

(*iii*) Voter's registration card;

(*vi*) U.S. military card or draft record;

(*v*) Identification card issued by federal, state, or local government agencies or entities. If the identification card does not contain a photograph, identifying information shall be included such as: name, date of birth, sex, height, color of eyes, and address;

(*vi*) Military dependent's identification card;

(*vii*) Native American tribal documents;

(*viii*) United States Coast Guard Merchant Mariner Card;

(*ix*) Driver's license issued by a Canadian government authority;

(*2*) For individuals under age 18 who are unable to produce a document listed in paragraph (b)(1)(v)(B)(*1*) of this section, the following documents are acceptable to establish identity only:

(*i*) School record or report card;

(*ii*) Clinic doctor or hospital record;

(*iii*) Daycare or nursery school record.

(*3*) Minors under the age of 18 who are unable to produce one of the identity documents listed in paragraph (b)(1)(v)(B) (*1*) or (*2*) of this section are exempt from producing one of the enumerated identity documents if:

(*i*) The minor's parent or legal guardian completes on the Form I–9 Section 1—"Employee Information and Verification" and in the space for the minor's signature, the parent or legal guardian writes the words, "minor under age 18."

(*ii*) The minor's parent or legal guardian completes on the Form I–9 the "Preparer/Translator certification."

(*iii*) The employer or the recruiter or referrer for a fee writes in Section 2—"Employer Review and Verification" under List B in the space after the words "Document Identification #" the words, "minor under age 18."

(*4*) Individuals with handicaps, who are unable to produce one of the identity documents listed in paragraph (b)(1)(v)(B) (*1*) or (*2*) of this section, who are being placed into employment by a nonprofit organization, association or as part of a rehabilitation program, may follow the procedures for establishing identity provided in this section for minors under the age of 18, substituting where appropriate, the term "special placement" for "minor under age 18'', and permitting, in addition to a parent or legal guardian, a representative from the nonprofit organization, association or rehabilitation program placing the individual into a position of employment, to fill out and sign in the appropriate section, the Form I–9. For purposes of this section the term *individual with handicaps* means any person who

(*i*) Has a physical or mental impairment which substantially limits one or more of such person's major life activities,

(*ii*) Has a record of such impairment, or

(*iii*) Is regarded as having such impairment.

(C) The following are acceptable documents to establish employment authorization only:

(*1*) A Social Security account number card other than one that specifies on the face that the issuance of the card does not authorize employment in the United States;

(*2*) Certification or report of birth issued by the Department of State, including Forms FS–545, DS–1350, FS–240;

(*3*) An original or certified copy of a birth certificate issued by a State, county, municipal authority or outlying possession of the United States bearing an official seal;

(*4*) Native American tribal document;

(*5*) United States Citizen Identification Card, Form I–197;

(*6*) Identification card for use of resident citizen in the United States, Form I–179;

(*7*) An employment authorization document issued by the Department of Homeland Security.

(D) The following are acceptable documents to establish both identity and employment authorization in the Commonwealth of the Northern Mariana Islands only, for a two-year period starting from the transition program effective date (as defined in 8 CFR 1.1), in addition to those documents listed in paragraph (b)(1)(v)(A) of this section:

(1) In the case of an alien with employment authorization in the Commonwealth of the Northern Mariana Islands incident to status for a period of up to two years following the transition program effective date that is unrestricted or otherwise authorizes a change of employer:

(i) The unexpired foreign passport and an Alien Entry Permit with red band issued to the alien by the Office of the Attorney General, Division of Immigration of the Commonwealth of the Northern Mariana Islands before the transition program effective date, as long as the period of employment authorization has not yet expired, or

(ii) An unexpired foreign passport and temporary work authorization letter issued by the Department of Labor of the Commonwealth of the Northern Mariana Islands before the transition program effective date, and containing the name and photograph of the individual, as long as the period of employment authorization has not yet expired and the proposed employment is not in conflict with any restrictions or limitations identified on the Temporary Work Authorization letter;

(iii) An unexpired foreign passport and a permanent resident card issued by the Commonwealth of the Northern Mariana Islands.

(*2*) [Reserved]

(vi) *Special rules for receipts.* Except as provided in paragraph (b)(1)(iii) of this section, unless the individual indicates or the employer or recruiter or referrer for a fee has actual or constructive knowledge that the individual is not authorized to work, an employer or recruiter or referrer for a fee must accept a receipt for the application for a replacement document or a document described in paragraphs (b)(1)(vi)(B)(*1*) and (b)(1)(vi)(C)(*1*) of this section in lieu of the required document in order to comply with any requirement to examine documentation imposed by this section, in the following circumstances:

(A) *Application for a replacement document.* The individual:

(*1*) Is unable to provide the required document within the time specified in this section because the document was lost, stolen, or damaged;

(*2*) Presents a receipt for the application for the replacement document within the time specified in this section; and

(*3*) Presents the replacement document within 90 days of the hire or, in the case of reverification, the date employment authorization expires; or

(B) *Form I–94 or I–94A indicating temporary evidence of permanent resident status.* The individual indicates in section 1 of the Form I–9 that he or she is a lawful permanent resident and the individual:

(*1*) Presents the arrival portion of Form I–94 or Form I–94A containing an unexpired "Temporary I–551" stamp and a photograph of the individual, which is designated for purposes of this section as a receipt for Form I–551; and

(*2*) Presents the Form I–551 by the expiration date of the "Temporary I–551" stamp or, if the stamp has no expiration date, within one year from the issuance date of the arrival portion of the Form I–94 or Form I–94A; or

(C) *Form I–94 or I–94A indicating refugee status.* The individual indicates in section 1 of the Form I–9 that he or she is an alien authorized to work and the individual:

(*1*) Presents the departure portion of Form I–94 or I–94A containing an unexpired refugee admission stamp, which is designated for purposes of this section as a receipt for the Form I–766, or a social security account number card that contains no employment restrictions; and

(*2*) Presents, within 90 days of the hire or, in the case of reverification, the date employment authorization expires, either an unexpired Form I–766, or a social security account number card that contains no employment restrictions and a document described under paragraph (b)(1)(v)(B) of this section.

(vii) If an individual's employment authorization expires, the employer, recruiter or referrer for a fee must reverify on the Form I–9 to reflect that the individual is still authorized to work in the United States; otherwise, the individual may no longer be employed, recruited, or referred. Reverification on the Form I–9 must occur not later than the date work authorization expires. If an Employment Authorization Document (Form I–766) as described in § 274a.13(d) was presented for completion of the Form I–9 in combination with a Notice of Action (Form I–797C), stating that the original Employment Authorization Document has been automatically extended for up to 180 days, reverification applies upon the expiration of the automatically extended validity period under § 274a.13(d) and not upon the expiration date indicated on the face of the individual's Employment Authorization Document. In order to reverify on the Form I–9, the employee or referred individual must present a document that either shows continuing employment eligibility or is a new grant of work authorization. The employer or the recruiter or referrer for a fee must review this document, and if it appears to be genuine and relate to the individual, reverify by noting the document's identification number and expiration date, if any, on the Form I–9 and signing the attestation by a handwritten signature or electronic signature in accordance with paragraph (i) of this section.

(viii) An employer will not be deemed to have hired an individual for employment if the individual is continuing in his or her employment and has a reasonable expectation of employment at all times.

(A) An individual is continuing in his or her employment in one of the following situations:

(*1*) An individual takes approved paid or unpaid leave on account of study, illness or disability of a family member, illness or pregnancy, maternity or paternity leave, vacation, union business, or other temporary leave approved by the employer;

(*2*) An individual is promoted, demoted, or gets a pay raise;

(*3*) An individual is temporarily laid off for lack of work;

(*4*) An individual is on strike or in a labor dispute;

(*5*) An individual is reinstated after disciplinary suspension for wrongful termination, found unjustified by any court, arbitrator, or administrative body, or otherwise resolved through reinstatement or settlement;

(*6*) An individual transfers from one distinct unit of an employer to another distinct unit of the same employer; the employer may transfer the individual's Form I–9 to the receiving unit;

(*7*) An individual continues his or her employment with a related, successor, or reorganized employer, provided that the employer obtains and maintains from the previous employer records and Forms I–9 where applicable. For this purpose, a related, successor, or reorganized employer includes:

(*i*) The same employer at another location;

(*ii*) An employer who continues to employ some or all of a previous employer's workforce in cases involving a corporate reorganization, merger, or sale of stock or assets;

(*iii*) An employer who continues to employ any employee of another employer's workforce where both employers belong to the same multi-employer association and the employee continues to work in the same bargaining unit under the same collective bargaining agreement. For purposes of this subsection, any agent designated to complete and maintain the Form I–9 must record the employee's date of hire and/or termination each time the employee is hired and/or terminated by an employer of the multi-employer association; or

(*8*) An individual is engaged in seasonal employment.

(B) The employer who is claiming that an individual is continuing in his or her employment must also establish that the individual expected to resume employment at all times and that the individual's expectation is reasonable. Whether an individual's expectation is reasonable will be determined on a case-by-case basis taking into consideration several factors. Factors which would indicate that an individual has a reasonable expectation of employment include, but are not limited to, the following:

(*1*) The individual in question was employed by the employer on a regular and substantial basis. A determination of a regular and substantial basis is established by a comparison of other workers who are similarly employed by the employer;

(*2*) The individual in question complied with the employer's established and published policy regarding his or her absence;

(*3*) The employer's past history of recalling absent employees for employment indicates a likelihood that the individual in question will resume employment with the employer within a reasonable time in the future;

(*4*) The former position held by the individual in question has not been taken permanently by another worker;

(*5*) The individual in question has not sought or obtained benefits during his or her absence from employment with the employer that are inconsistent with an expectation of resuming employment with the employer within a reasonable time in the future. Such benefits include, but are not limited to, severance and retirement benefits;

(*6*) The financial condition of the employer indicates the ability of the employer to permit the individual in question to resume employment within a reasonable time in the future; or

(*7*) The oral and/or written communication between employer, the employer's supervisory employees and the individual in question indicates that it is reasonably likely that the individual in question will resume employment with the employer within a reasonable time in the future.

(2) *Retention and Inspection of Form I–9.* (i) A paper (with original handwritten signatures), electronic (with acceptable electronic signatures that meet the requirements of paragraphs (h) and (i) of this section or original paper scanned into an electronic format, or a combination of paper and electronic formats that meet the requirements of paragraphs (e), (f), and (g) of this section), or microfilm or microfiche copy of the original signed version of Form I–9 must be retained by an employer or a recruiter or referrer for a fee for the following time periods:

(A) In the case of an employer, three years after the date of the hire or one year after the date the individual's employment is terminated, whichever is later; or

(B) In the case of a recruiter or referrer for a fee, three years after the date of the hire.

(ii) Any person or entity required to retain Forms I–9 in accordance with this section shall be provided with at least three business days notice prior to an inspection of Forms I–9 by officers of an authorized agency of the United States. At the time of inspection, Forms I–9 must be made available in their original paper, electronic form, a paper copy of the electronic form, or on microfilm or microfiche at the location where the request for production was made. If Forms I–9 are kept at another location, the person or entity must inform the officer of the authorized agency of the United States of the location where the forms are kept and make arrangements for the inspection. Inspections may be performed at an office of an authorized agency of the United States. A recruiter or referrer for a fee who has designated an employer to complete the employment verification procedures may present a photocopy or printed electronic image of the Form I–9 in lieu of presenting the Form I–9 in its original paper or electronic form or on microfilm or microfiche, as set forth in paragraph (b)(1)(iv) of this section. Any refusal or delay in presentation of the Forms I–9 for inspection is a violation of the retention requirements as set forth in section 274A(b)(3) of the Act. No Subpoena or warrant shall be required for such inspection, but the use of such enforcement tools is not precluded. In addition, if the person or entity has not complied with a request to present the Forms I–9, any officer listed in 8 CFR 287.4 may compel production of the Forms I–9 and any other relevant documents by issuing a subpoena. Nothing in this section is intended to limit the subpoena power under section 235(d)(4) of the Act.

(iii) The following standards shall apply to Forms I–9 presented on microfilm or microfiche submitted to an officer of the Service, the Special Counsel for Immigration-Related Unfair Employment Practices, or the Department of Labor: Microfilm, when displayed on a microfilm reader (viewer) or reproduced on paper must exhibit a high degree of legibility and readability. For this purpose, legibility is defined as the quality of a letter or numeral which enables the observer to positively and quickly identify it to the exclusion of all other letters or numerals. Readability is defined as the quality of a group of letters or numerals being recognizable as words or whole numbers. A detailed index of all microfilmed data shall be maintained and arranged in such a manner as to permit the immediate location of any particular record. It is the responsibility of the employer, recruiter or referrer for a fee:

(A) To provide for the processing, storage and maintenace of all microfilm, and

(B) To be able to make the contents thereof available as required by law. The person or entity presenting the microfilm will make available a reader-printer at the examination site for the ready reading, location and reproduction of any record or records being maintained on microfilm. Reader-printers made available to an officer of the Service, the Special Counsel for Immigration-Related Unfair Employment Practices, or the Department of Labor shall provide safety features and be in clean condition, properly maintained and in good working order. The reader-printers must have the capacity to display and print a complete page of information. A person or entity who is determined to have failed to comply with the criteria established by this regulation for the presentation of microfilm or microfiche to the Service, the Special Counsel for Immigration-Related Unfair Employment Practices, or the Department of Labor, and at the time of the inspection does not present a properly completed Form I–9 for the employee, is in violation of section 274A(a)(1)(B) of the Act and § 274a.2(b)(2).

(iv) Paragraphs (e), (f), (g), (h), and (i) of this section specify the standards for electronic Forms I–9.

(3) *Copying of documentation.* An employer, or a recruiter or referrer for a fee may, but is not required to, copy or make an electronic image of a document presented by an individual solely for the purpose of complying with the verification requirements of this section. If such a copy or electronic image is made, it must either be retained with the Form I–9 or stored with the employee's records and be retrievable consistent with paragraphs (e), (f), (g), (h), and (i) of this section. The copying or electronic imaging of any such document and retention of the copy or electronic image does not relieve the employer from the requirement to fully complete section 2 of the Form I–9. An employer, recruiter or referrer for a fee

should not, however, copy or electronically image only the documents of individuals of certain national origins or citizenship statuses. To do so may violate section 274B of the Act.

(4) *Limitation on use of Form I–9.* Any information contained in or appended to the Form I–9, including copies or electronic images of documents listed in paragraph (c) of this section used to verify an individual's identity or employment eligibility, may be used only for enforcement of the Act and sections 1001, 1028, 1546, or 1621 of title 18, United States Code.

(c) *Employment verification requirements in the case of hiring an individual who was previously employed.* (1) When an employer hires an individual whom that person or entity has previously employed, if the employer has previously completed the Form I–9 and complied with the verification requirements set forth in paragraph (b) of this section with regard to the individual, the employer may (in lieu of completing a new Form I–9) inspect the previously completed Form I–9 and:

(i) If upon inspection of the Form I–9, the employer determines that the Form I–9 relates to the individual and that the individual is still eligible to work, that previously executed Form I–9 is sufficient for purposes of section 274A(b) of the Act if the individual is hired within three years of the date of the initial execution of the Form I–9 and the employer updates the Form I–9 to reflect the date of rehire; or

(ii) If upon inspection of the Form I–9, the employer determines that the individual's employment authorization has expired, the employer must reverify on the Form I–9 in accordance with paragraph (b)(1)(vii); otherwise the individual may no longer be employed.

(2) For purposes of retention of the Form I–9 by an employer for a previously employed individual hired pursuant to paragraph (c)(1) of this section, the employer shall retain the Form I–9 for a period of three years commencing from the date of the initial execution of the Form I–9 or one year after the individual's employment is terminated, whichever is later.

(d) *Employment verification requirements in the case of recruiting or referring for a fee an individual who was previously recruited or referred.* (1) When a recruiter or referrer for a fee refers an individual for whom that recruiter or referrer for a fee has previously completed a Form I–9 and complied with the verification requirements set forth in paragraph (b) of this section with regard to the individual, the recruiter or referrer may (in lieu of completing a new Form I–9) inspect the previously completed Form I–9 and:

(i) If upon inspection of the Form I–9, the recruiter or referrer for a fee determines that the Form I–9 relates to the individual and that the individual is still eligible to work, that previously executed Form I–9 is sufficient for purposes of section 274A(b) of the Act if the individual is referred within three years of the date of the initial execution of the Form I–9 and the recruiter or referrer for a fee updates the Form I–9 to reflect the date of rehire; or

(ii) If upon inspection of the Form I–9, the recruiter or referrer determines that the individual's employment authorization has expired, the recruiter or referrer for a fee must reverify on the Form I–9 in accordance with paragraph (b)(1)(vii) of this section; otherwise the individual may no longer be recruited or referred.

(2) For purposes of retention of the Form I–9 by a recruiter or referrer for a previously recruited or referred individual pursuant to paragraph (d)(1) of this section, the recruiter or referrer shall retain the Form I–9 for a period of three years from the date of the rehire.

(e) *Standards for electronic retention of Form I–9.* (1) Any person or entity who is required by this section to complete and retain Forms I–9 may complete or retain electronically only those pages of the Form I–9 on which employers and employees enter data in an electronic generation or storage system that includes:

(i) Reasonable controls to ensure the integrity, accuracy and reliability of the electronic generation or storage system;

(ii) Reasonable controls designed to prevent and detect the unauthorized or accidental creation of, addition to, alteration of, deletion of, or deterioration of an electronically completed or stored Form I–9, including the electronic signature if used;

(iii) An inspection and quality assurance program evidenced by regular evaluations of the electronic generation or storage system, including periodic checks of the electronically stored Form I–9, including the electronic signature if used;

(iv) In the case of electronically retained Forms I–9, a retrieval system that includes an indexing system that permits searches consistent with the requirements of paragraph (e)(6) of this section; and

(v) The ability to reproduce legible and readable hardcopies.

(2) All documents reproduced by the electronic retention system must exhibit a high degree of legibility and readability when displayed on a video display terminal or when printed on paper, microfilm, or microfiche. The term "legibility" means the observer must be able to identify all letters and numerals positively and quickly, to the exclusion of all other letters or numerals. The term "readability" means that the observer must be able to recognize any group of letters or numerals that form words or numbers as those words or complete numbers. The employer, or recruiter or referrer for a fee, must ensure that the reproduction process maintains the legibility and readability of the electronically stored document.

(3) An electronic generation or storage system must not be subject, in whole or in part, to any agreement (such as a contract or license) that would limit or restrict access to and use of the electronic generation or storage system by an agency of the United States, on the premises of the employer, recruiter or referrer for a fee (or at any other place where the electronic generation or storage system is maintained), including personnel, hardware, software, files, indexes, and software documentation.

(4) A person or entity who chooses to complete or retain Forms I–9 electronically may use one or more electronic generation or storage systems. Each electronic generation or storage system must meet the requirements of this paragraph, and remain available as long as required by the Act and these regulations. Employers may implement new electronic storage systems provided:

(i) All systems meet the requirements of paragraphs (e), (f), (g), (h) and (i) of this section; and

(ii) Existing Forms I–9 are retained in a system that remains fully accessible.

(5) For each electronic generation or storage system used, the person or entity retaining the Form I–9 must maintain, and make available upon request, complete descriptions of:

(i) The electronic generation and storage system, including all procedures relating to its use; and

(ii) The indexing system.

(6) An "indexing system" for the purposes of paragraphs (e)(1)(iv) and (e)(5) of this section is a system that permits the identification and retrieval for viewing or reproducing of relevant documents and records maintained in an electronic storage system. For example, an indexing system might consist of assigning each electronically stored document a unique identification number and maintaining a separate database that contains descriptions of all electronically stored books and records along with their identification numbers. In addition, any system used to maintain, organize, or coordinate multiple electronic storage systems is treated as an indexing system. The requirement to maintain an indexing system will be satisfied if the indexing system is functionally comparable to a reasonable hardcopy filing system. The requirement to maintain an indexing system does not require that a separate electronically stored documents and records description database be maintained if comparable results can be achieved without a separate description database.

(7) Any person or entity choosing to retain completed Forms I–9 electronically may use reasonable data compression or formatting technologies as part of the electronic storage system as long as the requirements of 8 CFR 274a.2 are satisfied.

(8) At the time of an inspection, the person or entity required to retain completed Forms I–9 must:

(i) Retrieve and reproduce (including printing copies on paper, if requested) only the Forms I–9 electronically retained in the electronic storage system and supporting documentation specifically requested by an agency of the United States, along with associated audit trails. Generally, an audit trail is a record showing who has accessed a computer system and the actions performed within or on the computer system during a given period of time;

(ii) Provide a requesting agency of the United States with the resources (e.g., appropriate hardware and software, personnel and documentation) necessary to locate, retrieve, read, and reproduce (including paper copies) any electronically stored Forms I–9, any supporting documents, and their associated audit trails, reports, and other data used to maintain the authenticity, integrity, and reliability of the records; and

(iii) Provide, if requested, any reasonably available or obtainable electronic summary file(s), such as a spreadsheet, containing all of the information fields on all of the electronically stored Forms I–9 requested by a requesting agency of the United States.

(f) *Documentation.* (1) A person or entity who chooses to complete and/or retain Forms I–9 electronically must maintain and make available to an agency of the United States upon request documentation of the business processes that:

(i) Create the retained Forms I–9;

(ii) Modify and maintain the retained Forms I–9; and

(iii) Establish the authenticity and integrity of the Forms I–9, such as audit trails.

(2) Insufficient or incomplete documentation is a violation of section 274A(a)(1)(B) of the Act.

(3) Any officer listed in 8 CFR 287.4 may issue a subpoena to compel production of any documentation required by 8 CFR 274a.2. Nothing in this section is intended to limit the subpoena power of an agency of the United States under section 235(d)(4) of the Act.

(g) *Security.* (1) Any person or entity who elects to complete or retain Forms I–9 electronically must implement an effective records security program that:

(i) Ensures that only authorized personnel have access to electronic records;

(ii) Provides for backup and recovery of records to protect against information loss, such as power interruptions;

(iii) Ensures that employees are trained to minimize the risk of unauthorized or accidental alteration or erasure of electronic records; and

(iv) Ensure that whenever the electronic record is created, completed, updated, modified, altered, or corrected, a secure and permanent record is created that establishes the date of access, the identity of the individual who accessed the electronic record, and the particular action taken.

(2) An action or inaction resulting in the unauthorized alteration, loss, or erasure of electronic records, if it is known, or reasonably should be known, to be likely to have that effect, is a violation of section 274A(b)(3) of the Act.

(h) *Electronic signatures for employee.* (1) If a Form I–9 is completed electronically, the attestations in Form I–9 must be completed using a system for capturing an electronic signature that meets the standards set forth in this paragraph. The system used to capture the electronic signature must include a method to acknowledge that the attestation to be signed has been read by the signatory. The electronic signature must be attached to, or logically associated with, an electronically completed Form I–9. In addition, the system must:

(i) Affix the electronic signature at the time of the transaction;

(ii) Create and preserve a record verifying the identity of the person producing the signature; and

(iii) Upon request of the employee, provide a printed confirmation of the transaction to the person providing the signature.

(2) Any person or entity who is required to ensure proper completion of a Form I–9 and who chooses electronic signature for a required attestation, but who has failed to comply with the standards set forth in this paragraph, is deemed to have not properly completed the Form I–9, in violation of section 274A(a)(1)(B) of the Act and 8 CFR 274a.2(b)(2).

(i) *Electronic signatures for employer, recruiter or referrer, or representative.* If a Form I–9 is completed electronically, the employer, the recruiter or referrer for a fee, or the representative of the employer or the recruiter or referrer, must attest to the required information in Form I–9. The system used to capture the electronic signature should include a method to acknowledge that the attestation to be signed has been read by the signatory. Any person or entity who has failed to comply with the criteria established by this regulation for electronic signatures, if used, and at the time of inspection does not present a properly completed Form I–9 for the employee, is in violation of section 274A(a)(1)(B) of the Act and 8 CFR 274a.2(b)(2).

[52 FR 16221, May 1, 1987, as amended at 53 FR 8612, Mar. 16, 1988; 55 FR 25932, June 25, 1990; 56 FR 41784, Aug. 23, 1991; 58 FR 48780, Sept. 20, 1993; 61 FR 46537, Sept. 4, 1996; 61 FR 52236, Oct. 7, 1996; 62 FR 51005, Sept. 30, 1997; 64 FR 6189, Feb. 9, 1999; 64 FR 11533, Mar. 9, 1999; 71 FR 34514, June 15, 2006; 73 FR 76511, Dec. 17, 2008; 74 FR 2838, Jan. 16, 2009; 74 FR 7995, Feb. 23, 2009; 74 FR 10455, Mar. 11, 2009; 74 FR 55739, Oct. 28, 2009; 74 FR 62207, Nov. 27, 2009; 75 FR 42578, July 22, 2010; 78 FR 18472, Mar. 27, 2013; 81 FR 82491, Nov. 18, 2016; 82 FR 5289, Jan. 17, 2017]

§274a.3 Continuing employment of unauthorized aliens.

An employer who continues the employment of an employee hired after November 6, 1986, knowing that the employee is or has become an unauthorized alien with respect to that employment, is in violation of section 274A(a)(2) of the Act.

[52 FR 16221, May 1, 1987, as amended at 53 FR 8613, Mar. 16, 1988]

§274a.4 Good faith defense.

An employer or a recruiter or referrer for a fee for employment who shows good faith compliance with the employment verification requirements of §274a.2(b) of this part shall have established a rebuttable affirmative defense that the person or entity has not violated section 274A(a)(1)(A) of the Act with respect to such hiring, recruiting, or referral.

§274a.5 Use of labor through contract.

Any person or entity who uses a contract, subcontract, or exchange entered into, renegotiated, or extended after November 6, 1986 (or, with respect to the Commonwealth of the Northern Mariana Islands, after the transition program effective date as defined in 8 CFR 1.1), to obtain the labor or services of an alien in the United States knowing that the alien is an unauthorized alien with respect to performing such labor or services, shall be considered to have hired the alien for employment in the United States in violation of section 274A(a)(1)(A) of the Act.

[74 FR 55739, Oct. 28, 2009]

§274a.6 State employment agencies.

(a) *General.* Pursuant to sections 274A(a)(5) and 274A(b) of the Act, a state employment agency as defined in §274a.1 of this part may, but is not required to, verify identity and employment eligibility of individuals referred for employment by the agency. However, should a state employment agency choose to do so, it must:

(1) Complete the verification process in accordance with the requirements of §274a.2(b) of this part *provided* that the individual may not present receipts in lieu of documents in order to complete the verification process as otherwise permitted by §274a.2(b)(1)(vi) of this part; and

(2) Complete the verification process prior to referral for all individuals for whom a certification is required to be issued pursuant to paragraph (c) of this section.

(b) *Compliance with the provisions of section 274A of the Act.* A state employment agency which chooses to verify employment eligibility of individuals pursuant to §274a.2(b) of this part shall comply with all provisions of section 274A of the Act and the regulations issued thereunder.

(c) *State employment agency certification.* (1) A state employment agency which chooses to verify employment eligibility pursuant to paragraph (a) of this section shall issue to an employer who hires an individual referred for employment by the agency, a certification as set forth in paragraph (d) of this section. The certification shall be transmitted by the state employment agency directly to the employer, personally by an agency official, or by mail, so that it will be received by the employer within 21 business days of the date that the referred individual is hired. In no case shall the certification be transmitted to the employer from the state employment agency by the individual referred. During this period:

(i) The job order or other appropriate referral form issued by the state employment agency to the employer, on behalf of the individual who is referred and hired, shall serve as evidence, with respect to that individual, of the employer's compliance with the provisions of section 274A(a)(1)(B) of the Act and the regulations issued thereunder.

(ii) In the case of a telephonically authorized job referral by the state employment agency to the employer, an appropriate annotation by the employer shall be made and shall serve as evidence of the job order. The employer should retain the document containing the annotation where the employer retains Forms I–9.

(2) Job orders or other referrals, including telephonic authorizations, which are used as evidence of compliance pursuant to paragraph (c)(1)(i) of this section shall contain:

(i) The name of the referred individual;

(ii) The date of the referral;

(iii) The job order number or other applicable identifying number relating to the referral;

(iv) The name and title of the referring state employment agency official; and

(v) The telephone number and address of the state employment agency.

(3) A state employment agency shall not be required to verify employment eligibility or to issue a certification to an employer to whom the agency referred an individual if the individual is hired for a period of employment not to exceed 3 days in duration. Should a state agency choose to verify employment eligibility and to issue a certification to an employer relating to an individual who is hired for a period of employment not to exceed 3 days in duration, it must verify employment eligibility and issue certifications relating to *all* such individuals. Should a state employment agency choose not to verify employment eligibility or issue certifications to employers who hire, for a period not to exceed 3 days in duration, agency-referred individuals, the agency shall notify employers that, as a matter of policy, it does not perform verifications for individuals hired for that length of time, and that the employers must complete the identity and employment eligibility requirements pursuant to § 274a.2(b) of this part. Such notification may be incorporated into the job order or other referral form utilized by the state employment agency as appropriate.

(4) An employer to whom a state employment agency issues a certification relating to an individual referred by the agency and hired by the employer, shall be deemed to have complied with the verification requirements of § 274a.2(b) of this part provided that the employer:

(i) Reviews the identifying information contained in the certification to ensure that it pertains to the individual hired;

(ii) Observes the signing of the certification by the individual at the time of its receipt by the employer as provided for in paragraph (d)(13) of this section;

(iii) Complies with the provisions of § 274a.2(b)(1)(vii) of this part by either:

(A) Updating the state employment agency certification in lieu of Form I–9, upon expiration of the employment authorization date, if any, which was noted on the certification issued by the state employment agency pursuant to paragraph (d)(11) of this section; or

(B) By no longer employing an individual upon expiration of his or her employment authorization date noted on the certification;

(iv) Retains the certification in the same manner prescribed for Form I–9 in § 274a.2(b)(2) of this part, to wit, three years after the date of the hire or one year after the date the individual's employment is terminated, whichever is later; and

(v) Makes it available for inspection to officers of the Service or the Department of Labor, pursuant to the provisions of section 274A(b)(3) of the Act, and § 274a.2(b)(2) of this part.

(5) Failure by an employer to comply with the provisions of paragraph (c)(4)(iii) of this section shall constitute a violation of section 274A(a)(2) of the Act and shall subject the employer to the penalties contained in section 274A(e)(4) of the Act, and § 274a.10 of this part.

(d) *Standards for state employment agency certifications.* All certifications issued by a state employment agency pursuant to paragraph (c) of this section shall conform to the following standards. They must:

(1) Be issued on official agency letterhead;

(2) Be signed by an appropriately designated official of the agency;

(3) Bear a date of issuance;

(4) Contain the employer's name and address;

(5) State the name and date of birth of the individual referred;

(6) Identify the position or type of employment for which the individual is referred;

(7) Bear a job order number relating to the position or type of employment for which the individual is referred;

(8) Identify the document or documents presented by the individual to the state employment agency for the purposes of identity and employment eligibility verification;

(9) State the identifying number or numbers of the document or documents described in paragraph (d)(8) of this section;

(10) Certify that the agency has complied with the requirements of section 274A(b) of the Act concerning verification of the identity and employment eligibility of the individual referred, and has determined that, to the best of the agency's knowledge, the individual is authorized to work in the United States;

(11) Clearly state any restrictions, conditions, expiration dates or other limitations which relate to the individual's employment eligibility in the United States, or contain an affirmative statement that the employment authorization of the referred individual is not restricted;

(12) State that the employer is not required to verify the individual's identity or employment eligibility, but must retain the certification in lieu of Form I–9;

(13) Contain a space or a line for the signature of the referred individual, requiring the individual under penalty of perjury to sign his or her name before the employer at the time of receipt of the certification by the employer; and

(14) State that counterfeiting, falsification, unauthorized issuance or alteration of the certification constitutes a violation of federal law pursuant to title 18, U.S.C. 1546.

(e) *Retention of Form I–9 by state employment agencies.* A Form I–9 utilized by a state employment agency in verifying the identity and employment eligibility of an individual pursuant to § 274a.2(b) of this part must be retained by a state employment agency for a period of three years from the date that the individual was last referred by the agency and hired by an employer. A state employment agency may retain a Form I–9 either in its original form, or on microfilm or microfiche.

(f) *Retention of state employment agency certifications.* A certification issued by a state employment agency pursuant to this section shall be retained:

(1) By a state employment agency, for a period of three years from the date that the individual was last referred by the agency and hired by an employer, and in a manner to be determined by the agency which will enable the prompt retrieval of the information contained on the original certification for comparison with the relating Form I–9;

(2) By the employer, in the original form, and in the same manner and location as the employer has designated for retention of Forms I–9, and for the period of time provided in paragraph (c)(4)(iv) of this section.

(g) *State employment agency verification requirements in the case of an individual who was previously referred and certified.* When a state employment agency refers an individual for whom the verification requirements have been previously complied with and a Form I–9 completed, the agency shall inspect the previously completed Form I–9:

(1) If, upon inspection of the Form, the agency determines that the Form I–9 pertains to the individual and that

the individual remains authorized to be employed in the United States, no additional verification need be conducted and no new Form I–9 need be completed prior to issuance of a new certification *provided* that the individual is referred by the agency within 3 years of the execution of the initial Form I–9.

(2) If, upon inspection of the Form, the agency determines that the Form I–9 pertains to the individual but that the individual does not appear to be authorized to be employed in the United States based on restrictions, expiration dates or other conditions annotated on the Form I–9, the agency shall not issue a certification unless the agency follows the updating procedures pursuant to § 274a.2(b)(1)(vii) of this part; otherwise the individual may no longer be referred for employment by the state employment agency.

(3) For the purposes of retention of the Form I–9 by a state employment agency pursuant to paragraph (e) of this section, for an individual previously referred and certified, the state employment agency shall retain the Form for a period of 3 years from the date that the individual is last referred and hired.

(h) *Employer verification requirements in the case of an individual who was previously referred and certified.* When an employer rehires an individual for whom the verification and certification requirements have been previously complied with by a state employment agency, the employer shall inspect the previously issued certification.

(1) If, upon inspection of the certification, the employer determines that the certification pertains to the individual and that the individual remains authorized to be employed in the United States, no additional verification need be conducted and no new Form I–9 or certification need be completed *provided* that the individual is rehired by the employer within 3 years of the issuance of the initial certification, and that the employer follows the same procedures for the certification which pertain to Form I–9, as specified in § 274a.2(c)(1)(i) of this part.

(2) If, upon inspection of the certification, the employer determines that the certification pertains to the individual but that the certification reflects restrictions, expiration dates or other conditions which indicate that the individual no longer appears authorized to be employed in the United States, the employer shall verify that the individual remains authorized to be employed and shall follow the updating procedures for the certification which pertain to Form I–9, as specified in § 274a.2(c)(1)(ii) of this part; otherwise the individual may no longer be employed.

(3) For the purposes of retention of the certification by an employer pursuant to this paragraph for an individual previously referred and certified by a state employment agency and rehired by the employer, the employer shall retain the certification for a period of 3 years after the date that the individual is last hired, or one year after the date the individual's employment is terminated, whichever is later.

[52 FR 43053, Nov. 9, 1987]

§ 274a.7 Pre-enactment provisions for employees hired prior to November 7, 1986 or in the CNMI prior to the transition program effective date.

(a) For employees who are continuing in their employment and have a reasonable expectation of employment at all times (as set forth in 8 CFR 274a.2(b)(1)(viii)), except those individuals described in 8 CFR 274a.2(b)(1)(viii)(A)(*7*)(*iii*) and (b)(1)(viii)(A)(*8*):

(1) The penalty provisions set forth in section 274A(e) and (f) of the Act for violations of sections 274A(a)(1)(B) and 274A(a)(2) of the Act shall not apply to employees who were hired prior to November 7, 1986.

(2) The penalty provisions set forth in section 274A(e) and (f) of the Act for violations of section 274A(a)(1)(B) of the Act shall not apply to employees who were hired in the CNMI prior to the transition program effective date as defined in 8 CFR 1.1.

(b) For purposes of this section, an employee who was hired prior to November 7, 1986 (or if hired in the CNMI, prior to the transition program effective date) shall lose his or her pre-enactment status if the employee:

(1) Quits; or

(2) Is terminated by the employer; the term termination shall include, but

is not limited to, situations in which an employee is subject to seasonal employment; or

(3) Is excluded or deported from the United States or departs the United States under a grant of voluntary departure; or

(4) Is no longer continuing his or her employment (or does not have a reasonable expectation of employment at all times) as set forth in § 274a.2(b)(1)(viii).

[52 FR 16221, May 1, 1987, as amended at 53 FR 8613, Mar. 16, 1988; 55 FR 25935, June 25, 1990; 56 FR 41786, Aug. 23, 1991; 74 FR 55740, Oct. 28, 2009]

§ 274a.8 Prohibition of indemnity bonds.

(a) *General.* It is unlawful for a person or other entity, in hiring or recruiting or referring for a fee for employment of an individual, to require the individual to post a bond or security, to pay or agree to pay an amount, or otherwise to provide a financial guarantee or indemnity, against any potential liability arising under this part relating to such hiring, recruiting, or referring of the individual. However, this prohibition does not apply to performance clauses which are stipulated by agreement between contracting parties.

(b) *Penalty.* Any person or other entity who requires any individual to post a bond or security as stated in this section shall, after notice and opportunity for an administrative hearing in accordance with section 274A(e)(3)(B) of the Act, be subject to a civil monetary penalty of $1,000 for each violation before September 29, 1999, of $1,100 for each violation occurring on or after September 29, 1999 but on or before November 2, 2015, and of $2,236 for each violation occurring after November 2, 2015, and to an administrative order requiring the return to the individual of any amounts received in violation of this section or, if the individual cannot be located, to the general fund of the Treasury.

[52 FR 16221, May 1, 1987, as amended at 64 FR 47101, Aug. 30, 1999; 81 FR 43002, July 1, 2016; 82 FR 8580, Jan. 27, 2017; 83 FR 13835, Apr. 2, 2018]

§ 274a.9 Enforcement procedures.

(a) *Procedures for the filing of complaints.* Any person or entity having knowledge of a violation or potential violation of section 274A of the Act may submit a signed, written complaint in person or by mail to the Service office having jurisdiction over the business or residence of the potential violator. The signed, written complaint must contain sufficient information to identify both the complainant and the potential violator, including their names and addresses. The complaint should also contain detailed factual allegations relating to the potential violation including the date, time and place of the alleged violation and the specific act or conduct alleged to constitute a violation of the Act. Written complaints may be delivered either by mail to the appropriate Service office or by personally appearing before any immigration officer at a Service office.

(b) *Investigation.* The Service may conduct investigations for violations on its own initiative and without having received a written complaint. When the Service receives a complaint from a third party, it shall investigate only those complaints that have a reasonable probability of validity. If it is determined after investigation that the person or entity has violated section 274A of the Act, the Service may issue and serve a Notice of Intent to Fine or a Warning Notice upon the alleged violator. Service officers shall have reasonable access to examine any relevant evidence of any person or entity being investigated.

(c) *Warning notice.* The Service and/or the Department of Labor may in their discretion issue a Warning Notice to a person or entity alleged to have violated section 274A of the Act. This Warning Notice will contain a statement of the basis for the violations and the statutory provisions alleged to have been violated.

(d) *Notice of Intent to Fine.* The proceeding to assess administrative penalties under section 274A of the Act is commenced when the Service issues a Notice of Intent to Fine on Form I–763. Service of this Notice shall be accomplished pursuant to part 103 of this chapter. The person or entity identified in the Notice of Intent to Fine shall be known as the respondent. The Notice of Intent to Fine may be issued by an officer defined in § 242.1 of this chapter with concurrence of a Service attorney.

(1) *Contents of the Notice of Intent to Fine.* (i) The Notice of Intent to Fine will contain the basis for the charge(s) against the respondent, the statutory provisions alleged to have been violated, and the penalty that will be imposed.

(ii) The Notice of Intent to Fine will provide the following advisals to the respondent:

(A) That the person or entity has the right to representation by counsel of his or her own choice at no expense to the government;

(B) That any statement given may be used against the person or entity;

(C) That the person or entity has the right to request a hearing before an Administrative Law Judge pursuant to 5 U.S.C. 554–557, and that such request must be made within 30 days from the service of the Notice of Intent to Fine;

(D) That the Service will issue a final order in 45 days if a written request for a hearing is not timely received and that there will be no appeal of the final order.

(2) [Reserved]

(e) *Request for Hearing Before an Administrative Law Judge.* If a respondent contests the issuance of a Notice of Intent to Fine, the respondent must file with the INS, within thirty days of the service of the Notice of Intent to Fine, a written request for a hearing before an Administrative Law Judge. Any written request for a hearing submitted in a foreign language must be accompanied by an English language translation. A request for a hearing is not deemed to be filed until received by the Service office designated in the Notice of Intent to Fine. In computing the thirty day period prescribed by this section, the day of service of the Notice of Intent to Fine shall not be included. If the Notice of Intent to Fine was served by ordinary mail, five days shall be added to the prescribed thirty day period. In the request for a hearing, the respondent may, but is not required to, respond to each allegation listed in the Notice of Intent to Fine.

(f) *Failure to file a request for hearing.* If the respondent does not file a request for a hearing in writing within thirty days of the day of service of the Notice of Intent to Fine (thirty-five days if served by ordinary mail), the INS shall issue a final order from which there is no appeal.

[52 FR 16221, May 1, 1987, as amended at 53 FR 8613, Mar. 16, 1988; 55 FR 25935, June 25, 1990; 56 FR 41786, Aug. 23, 1991; 61 FR 52236, Oct. 7, 1996]

§ 274a.10 Penalties.

(a) *Criminal penalties.* Any person or entity which engages in a pattern or practice of violations of subsection (a)(1)(A) or (a)(2) of the Act shall be fined not more than $3,000 for each unauthorized alien, imprisoned for not more than six months for the entire pattern or practice, or both, notwithstanding the provisions of any other Federal law relating to fine levels.

(b) *Civil penalties.* A person or entity may face civil penalties for a violation of section 274A of the Act. Civil penalties may be imposed by the Service or an administrative law judge for violations under section 274A of the Act. In determining the level of the penalties that will be imposed, a finding of more than one violation in the course of a single proceeding or determination will be counted as a single offense. However, a single offense will include penalties for each unauthorized alien who is determined to have been knowingly hired or recruited or referred for a fee.

(1) A respondent found by the Service or an administrative law judge to have knowingly hired, or to have knowingly recruited or referred for a fee, an unauthorized alien for employment in the United States or to have knowingly continued to employ an unauthorized alien in the United States, shall be subject to the following order:

(i) To cease and desist from such behavior;

(ii) To pay a civil fine according to the following schedule:

(A) First offense—not less than $275 and not more than $2,200 for each unauthorized alien with respect to whom the offense occurred before March 27, 2008; not less than $375 and not exceeding $3,200, for each unauthorized alien with respect to whom the offense occurred occurring on or after March 27,

2008 and on or before November 2, 2015; and not less than $559 and not more than $4,473 for each unauthorized alien with respect to whom the offense occurred occurring after November 2, 2015.

(B) Second offense—not less than $2,200 and not more than $5,500 for each unauthorized alien with respect to whom the second offense occurred before March 27, 2008; not less than $3,200 and not more than $6,500, for each unauthorized alien with respect to whom the second offense occurred on or after March 27, 2008 and on or before November 2, 2015; and not less than $4,473 and not more than $11,181 for each unauthorized alien with respect to whom the second offense occurred after November 2, 2015; or

(C) More than two offenses—not less than $3,300 and not more than $11,000 for each unauthorized alien with respect to whom the third or subsequent offense occurred before March 27, 2008; not less than $4,300 and not exceeding $16,000, for each unauthorized alien with respect to whom the third or subsequent offense occurred on or after March 27, 2008 and on or before November 2, 2015; and not less than $6,709 and not more than $22,363 for each unauthorized alien with respect to whom the third or subsequent offense occurred after November 2, 2015; and

(iii) To comply with the requirements of section 274a.2(b) of this part, and to take such other remedial action as is appropriate.

(2) A respondent determined by the Service (if a respondent fails to request a hearing) or by an administrative law judge, to have failed to comply with the employment verification requirements as set forth in § 274a.2(b), shall be subject to a civil penalty in an amount of not less than $100 and not more than $1,000 for each individual with respect to whom such violation occurred before September 29, 1999; not less than $110 and not more than $1,100 for each individual with respect to whom such violation occurred on or after September 29, 1999 and on or before November 2, 2015; and not less than $224 and not more than $2,236 for each individual with respect to whom such violation occurred after November 2, 2015. In determining the amount of the penalty, consideration shall be given to:

(i) The size of the business of the employer being charged;

(ii) The good faith of the employer;

(iii) The seriousness of the violation;

(iv) Whether or not the individual was an unauthorized alien; and

(v) The history of previous violations of the employer.

(3) Where an order is issued with respect to a respondent composed of distinct, physically separate subdivisions which do their own hiring, or their own recruiting or referring for a fee for employment (without reference to the practices of, and under the control of, or common control with another subdivision) the subdivision shall be considered a separate person or entity.

(c) *Enjoining pattern or practice violations.* If the Attorney General has reasonable cause to believe that a person or entity is engaged in a pattern or practice of employment, recruitment or referral in violation of section 274A(a)(1)(A) or (2) of the Act, the Attorney General may bring civil action in the appropriate United States District Court requesting relief, including a permanent or temporary injunction, restraining order, or other order against the person or entity, as the Attorney General deems necessary.

[52 FR 16221, May 1, 1987, as amended at 55 FR 25935, June 25, 1990; 56 FR 41786, Aug. 23, 1991; 64 FR 47101, Aug. 30, 1999; 73 FR 10136, Feb. 26, 2008; 81 FR 43002, July 1, 2016; 82 FR 8580, Jan. 27, 2017; 83 FR 13835, Apr. 2, 2018]

§ 274a.11 [Reserved]

Subpart B—Employment Authorization

§ 274a.12 Classes of aliens authorized to accept employment.

(a) *Aliens authorized employment incident to status.* Pursuant to the statutory or regulatory reference cited, the following classes of aliens are authorized to be employed in the United States without restrictions as to location or type of employment as a condition of their admission or subsequent change to one of the indicated classes. Any alien who is within a class of aliens described in paragraphs (a)(3), (a)(4), (a)(6)–(a)(8), (a)(10)–(a)(15), or (a)(20) of this section, and who seeks to be employed in the United States, must apply to U.S. Citizenship and Immigration Services (USCIS) for a document evidencing such employment authorization. USCIS may, in its discretion, determine the validity period assigned to any document issued evidencing an alien's authorization to work in the United States.

(1) An alien who is a lawful permanent resident (with or without conditions pursuant to section 216 of the Act), as evidenced by Form I–551 issued by the Service. An expiration date on the Form I–551 reflects only that the card must be renewed, not that the bearer's work authorization has expired;

(2) An alien admitted to the United States as a lawful temporary resident pursuant to sections 245A or 210 of the Act, as evidenced by an employment authorization document issued by the Service;

(3) An alien admitted to the United States as a refugee pursuant to section 207 of the Act for the period of time in that status, as evidenced by an employment authorization document issued by the Service;

(4) An alien paroled into the United States as a refugee for the period of time in that status, as evidenced by an employment authorization document issued by the Service;

(5) An alien granted asylum under section 208 of the Act for the period of time in that status, as evidenced by an employment authorization document, issued by USCIS to the alien. An expiration date on the employment authorization document issued by USCIS reflects only that the document must be renewed, and not that the bearer's work authorization has expired. Evidence of employment authorization shall be granted in increments not exceeding 5 years for the period of time the alien remains in that status.

(6) An alien admitted to the United States as a nonimmigrant fiancé or fiancée pursuant to section 101(a)(15)(K)(i) of the Act, or an alien admitted as a child of such alien, for the period of admission in that status, as evidenced by an employment authorization document issued by the Service;

(7) An alien admitted as a parent (N–8) or dependent child (N–9) of an alien granted permanent residence under section 101(a)(27)(I) of the Act, as evidenced by an employment authorization document issued by the Service;

(8) An alien admitted to the United States as a nonimmigrant pursuant to the Compact of Free Association between the United States and of the Federated States of Micronesia, the Republic of the Marshall Islands, or the Republic of Palau;

(9) Any alien admitted as a nonimmigrant spouse pursuant to section 101(a)(15)(K)(ii) of the Act, or an alien admitted as a child of such alien, for the period of admission in that status, as evidenced by an employment authorization document, with an expiration date issued by the Service;

(10) An alien granted withholding of deportation or removal for the period of time in that status, as evidenced by an employment authorization document issued by the Service;

(11) An alien whose enforced departure from the United States has been deferred in accordance with a directive from the President of the United States to the Secretary. Employment is authorized for the period of time and under the conditions established by the Secretary pursuant to the Presidential directive;

(12) An alien granted Temporary Protected Status under section 244 of the Act for the period of time in that status, as evidenced by an employment authorization document issued by the Service;

(13) An alien granted voluntary departure by the Attorney General under the Family Unity Program established by section 301 of the Immigration Act of 1990, as evidenced by an employment authorization document issued by the Service;

(14) An alien granted Family Unity benefits under section 1504 of the Legal Immigrant Family Equity (LIFE) Act Amendments, Public Law 106–554, and the provisions of 8 CFR part 245a, Subpart C of this chapter, as evidenced by an employment authorization document issued by the Service;

(15) Any alien in V nonimmigrant status as defined in section

101(a)(15)(V) of the Act and 8 CFR 214.15.

(16) Any alien in T–1 nonimmigrant status, pursuant to 8 CFR 214.11, for the period in that status, as evidenced by an employment authorization document issued by USCIS to the alien.

(17)–(18) [Reserved]

(19) Any alien in U–1 nonimmigrant status, pursuant to 8 CFR 214.14, for the period of time in that status, as evidenced by an employment authorization document issued by USCIS to the alien.

(20) Any alien in U–2, U–3, U–4, or U–5 nonimmigrant status, pursuant to 8 CFR 214.14, for the period of time in that status, as evidenced by an employment authorization document issued by USCIS to the alien.

(b) *Aliens authorized for employment with a specific employer incident to status or parole.* The following classes of aliens are authorized to be employed in the United States by the specific employer and subject to any restrictions described in the section(s) of this chapter indicated as a condition of their parole or of their admission in, or subsequent change to, the designated nonimmigrant classification. An alien in one of these classes is not issued an employment authorization document by DHS:

(1) A foreign government official (A–1 or A–2), pursuant to § 214.2(a) of this chapter. An alien in this status may be employed only by the foreign government entity;

(2) An employee of a foreign government official (A–3), pursuant to § 214.2(a) of this chapter. An alien in this status may be employed only by the foreign government official;

(3) A foreign government official in transit (C–2 or C–3), pursuant to § 214.2(c) of this chapter. An alien in this status may be employed only by the foreign government entity;

(4) [Reserved]

(5) A nonimmigrant treaty trader (E–1) or treaty investor (E–2), pursuant to § 214.2(e) of this chapter. An alien in this status may be employed only by the treaty-qualifying company through which the alien attained the status. Employment authorization does not extend to the dependents of the principal treaty trader or treaty investor (also designated "E–1" or "E–2"), other than those specified in paragraph (c)(2) of this section;

(6) A nonimmigrant (F–1) student who is in valid nonimmigrant student status and pursuant to 8 CFR 214.2(f) is seeking:

(i) On-campus employment for not more than twenty hours per week when school is in session or full-time employment when school is not in session if the student intends and is eligible to register for the next term or session. Part-time on-campus employment is authorized by the school and no specific endorsement by a school official or Service officer is necessary;

(ii) [Reserved]

(iii) Curricular practical training (internships, cooperative training programs, or work-study programs which are part of an established curriculum) after having been enrolled full-time in a Service approved institution for one full academic year. Curricular practical training (part-time or full-time) is authorized by the Designated School Official on the student's Form I–20. No Service endorsement is necessary.

(iv) An Employment Authorization Document, Form I–766 or successor form, under paragraph (c)(3)(i)(C) of this section based on a STEM Optional Practical Training extension, and whose timely filed Form I–765 or successor form is pending and employment authorization and accompanying Form I–766 or successor form issued under paragraph (c)(3)(i)(B) of this section have expired. Employment is authorized beginning on the expiration date of the Form I–766 or successor form issued under paragraph (c)(3)(i)(B) of this section and ending on the date of USCIS' written decision on the current Form I–765 or successor form, but not to exceed 180 days. For this same period, such Form I–766 or successor form is automatically extended and is considered unexpired when combined with a Certificate of Eligibility for Nonimmigrant (F–1/M–1) Students, Form I–20 or successor form, endorsed by the Designated School Official recommending such an extension; or

(v) Pursuant to 8 CFR 214.2(h) is seeking H–1B nonimmigrant status and whose duration of status and employment authorization have been extended pursuant to 8 CFR 214.2(f)(5)(vi).

(7) A representative of an international organization (G–1, G–2, G–3, or G–4), pursuant to § 214.2(g) of this chapter. An alien in this status may be employed only by the foreign government entity or the international organization;

(8) A personal employee of an official or representative of an international organization (G–5), pursuant to § 214.2(g) of this chapter. An alien in this status may be employed only by the official or representative of the international organization;

(9) A temporary worker or trainee (H–1, H–2A, H–2B, or H–3), pursuant to § 214.2(h) of this chapter, or a nonimmigrant specialty occupation worker pursuant to section 101(a)(15)(H)(i)(b1) of the Act. An alien in this status may be employed only by the petitioner through whom the status was obtained. In the case of a professional H–2B athlete who is traded from one organization to another organization, employment authorization for the player will automatically continue for a period of 30 days after acquisition by the new organization, within which time the new organization is expected to file a new Form I–129 to petition for H–2B classification. If a new Form I–129 is not filed within 30 days, employment authorization will cease. If a new Form I–129 is filed within 30 days, the professional athlete's employment authorization will continue until the petition is adjudicated. If the new petition is denied, employment authorization will cease. In the case of a nonimmigrant with H–1B status, employment authorization will automatically continue upon the filing of a qualifying petition under 8 CFR 214.2(h)(2)(i)(H) until such petition is adjudicated, in accordance with section 214(n) of the Act and 8 CFR 214.2(h)(2)(i)(H);

(10) An information media representative (I), pursuant to § 214.2(i) of this chapter. An alien in this status may be employed only for the sponsoring foreign news agency or bureau. Employment authorization does not extend to the dependents of an information media representative (also designated "I");

(11) An exchange visitor (J–1), pursuant to § 214.2(j) of this chapter and 22 CFR part 62. An alien in this status may be employed only by the exchange visitor program sponsor or appropriate designee and within the guidelines of the program approved by the Department of State as set forth in the Form DS–2019, Certificate of Eligibility, issued by the program sponsor;

(12) An intra-company transferee (L–1), pursuant to § 214.2(l) of this chapter. An alien in this status may be employed only by the petitioner through whom the status was obtained;

(13) An alien having extraordinary ability in the sciences, arts, education, business, or athletics (O–1), and an accompanying alien (O–2), pursuant to § 214.2(o) of this chapter. An alien in this status may be employed only by the petitioner through whom the status was obtained. In the case of a professional O–1 athlete who is traded from one organization to another organization, employment authorization for the player will automatically continue for a period of 30 days after the acquisition by the new organization, within which time the new organization is expected to file a new Form I–129 petition for O nonimmigrant classification. If a new Form I–129 is not filed within 30 days, employment authorization will cease. If a new Form I–129 is filed within 30 days, the professional athlete's employment authorization will continue until the petition is adjudicated. If the new petition is denied, employment authorization will cease.

(14) An athlete, artist, or entertainer (P–1, P–2, or P–3), pursuant to § 214.2(p) of this chapter. An alien in this status may be employed only by the petitioner through whom the status was obtained. In the case of a professional P–1 athlete who is traded from one organization to another organization, employment authorization for the player will automatically continue for a period of 30 days after the acquisition by the new organization, within which time the new organization is expected to file a new Form I–129 for P–1 nonimmigrant classification. If a new Form I–129 is not filed within 30 days,

employment authorization will cease. If a new Form I–129 is filed within 30 days, the professional athlete's employment authorization will continue until the petition is adjudicated. If the new petition is denied, employment authorization will cease;

(15) An international cultural exchange visitor (Q–1), according to §214.2(q)(1) of this chapter. An alien may only be employed by the petitioner through whom the status was obtained;

(16) An alien having a religious occupation, pursuant to §214.2(r) of this chapter. An alien in this status may be employed only by the religious organization through whom the status was obtained;

(17) Officers and personnel of the armed services of nations of the North Atlantic Treaty Organization, and representatives, officials, and staff employees of NATO (NATO–1, NATO–2, NATO–3, NATO–4, NATO–5 and NATO–6), pursuant to §214.2(o) of this chapter. An alien in this status may be employed only by NATO;

(18) An attendant, servant or personal employee (NATO–7) of an alien admitted as a NATO–1, NATO–2, NATO–3, NATO–4, NATO–5, or NATO–6, pursuant to §214.2(o) of this chapter. An alien admitted under this classification may be employed only by the NATO alien through whom the status was obtained;

(19) A nonimmigrant pursuant to section 214(e) of the Act. An alien in this status must be engaged in business activities at a professional level in accordance with the provisions of Chapter 16 of the North American Free Trade Agreement (NAFTA);

(20) A nonimmigrant alien within the class of aliens described in paragraphs (b)(2), (b)(5), (b)(8), (b)(9), (b)(10), (b)(11), (b)(12), (b)(13), (b)(14), (b)(16), (b)(19), (b)(23) and (b)(25) of this section whose status has expired but on whose behalf an application for an extension of stay was timely filed pursuant to §214.2 or §214.6 of this chapter. These aliens are authorized to continue employment with the same employer for a period not to exceed 240 days beginning on the date of the expiration of the authorized period of stay. Such authorization shall be subject to any conditions and limitations noted on the initial authorization. However, if the district director or service center director adjudicates the application prior to the expiration of this 240 day period and denies the application for extension of stay, the employment authorization under this paragraph shall automatically terminate upon notification of the denial decision;

(21) A nonimmigrant alien within the class of aliens described in 8 CFR 214.2(h)(1)(ii)(C) who filed an application for an extension of stay pursuant to 8 CFR 214.2 during his or her period of admission. Such alien is authorized to be employed by a new employer that has filed an H–2A petition naming the alien as a beneficiary and requesting an extension of stay for the alien for a period not to exceed 120 days beginning from the "Received Date" on Form I–797 (Notice of Action) acknowledging receipt of the petition requesting an extension of stay, provided that the employer has enrolled in and is a participant in good standing in the E-Verify program, as determined by USCIS in its discretion. Such authorization will be subject to any conditions and limitations noted on the initial authorization, except as to the employer and place of employment. However, if the District Director or Service Center director adjudicates the application prior to the expiration of this 120-day period and denies the application for extension of stay, the employment authorization under this paragraph (b)(21) shall automatically terminate upon 15 days after the date of the denial decision. The employment authorization shall also terminate automatically if the employer fails to remain a participant in good standing in the E-Verify program, as determined by USCIS in its discretion;

(22) An alien in E–2 CNMI Investor nonimmigrant status pursuant to 8 CFR 214.2(e)(23). An alien in this status may be employed only by the qualifying company through which the alien attained the status. An alien in E–2 CNMI Investor nonimmigrant status may be employed only in the Commonwealth of the Northern Mariana Islands for a qualifying entity. An alien who attained E–2 CNMI Investor nonimmigrant status based upon a Foreign

Retiree Investment Certificate or Certification is not employment-authorized. Employment authorization does not extend to the dependents of the principal investor (also designated E–2 CNMI Investor nonimmigrants) other than those specified in paragraph (c)(12) of this section;

(23) A Commonwealth of the Northern Mariana Islands transitional worker (CW–1) pursuant to 8 CFR 214.2(w). An alien in this status may be employed only in the CNMI during the transition period, and only by the petitioner through whom the status was obtained, or as otherwise authorized by 8 CFR 214.2(w). An alien who is lawfully present in the CNMI (as defined by 8 CFR 214.2(w)(1)(v)) on or before November 27, 2011, is authorized to be employed in the CNMI, and is so employed in the CNMI by an employer properly filing an application under 8 CFR 214.2(w)(14)(ii) on or before such date for a grant of CW–1 status to its employee in the CNMI for the purpose of the alien continuing the employment, is authorized to continue such employment on or after November 27, 2011, until a decision is made on the application;

(24) An alien who is authorized to be employed in the Commonwealth of the Northern Mariana Islands for a period of up to 2 years following the transition program effective date, under section 6(e)(2) of Public Law 94–241, as added by section 702(a) of Public Law 110–229. Such alien is only authorized to continue in the same employment that he or she had on the transition program effective date as defined in 8 CFR 1.1 until the earlier of the date that is 2 years after the transition program effective date or the date of expiration of the alien's employment authorization, unless the alien had unrestricted employment authorization or was otherwise authorized as of the transition program effective date to change employers, in which case the alien may have such employment privileges as were authorized as of the transition program effective date for up to 2 years;

(25) A nonimmigrant treaty alien in a specialty occupation (E–3) pursuant to section 101(a)(15)(E)(iii) of the Act; or

(26)–(36) [Reserved]

(37) An alien paroled into the United States as an entrepreneur pursuant to 8 CFR 212.19 for the period of authorized parole. An entrepreneur who has timely filed a non-frivolous application requesting re-parole with respect to the same start-up entity in accordance with 8 CFR 212.19 prior to the expiration of his or her parole, but whose authorized parole period expires during the pendency of such application, is authorized to continue employment with the same start-up entity for a period not to exceed 240 days beginning on the date of expiration of parole. Such authorization shall be subject to any conditions and limitations on such expired parole. If DHS adjudicates the application prior to the expiration of this 240-day period and denies the application for re-parole, the employment authorization under this paragraph shall automatically terminate upon notification to the alien of the denial decision.

(c) *Aliens who must apply for employment authorization.* An alien within a class of aliens described in this section must apply for work authorization. If authorized, such an alien may accept employment subject to any restrictions stated in the regulations or cited on the employment authorization document. USCIS, in its discretion, may establish a specific validity period for an employment authorization document, which may include any period when an administrative appeal or judicial review of an application or petition is pending.

(1) An alien spouse or unmarried dependent child; son or daughter of a foreign government official (A–1 or A–2) pursuant to 8 CFR 214.2(a)(2) and who presents an endorsement from an authorized representative of the Department of State;

(2) An alien spouse or unmarried dependent son or daughter of an alien employee of the Coordination Council for North American Affairs (E–1) pursuant to § 214.2(e) of this chapter;

(3) A nonimmigrant (F–1) student who:

(i)(A) Is seeking pre-completion practical training pursuant to 8 CFR 214.2(f)(10)(ii)(A)(*1*) and (*2*);

(B) Is seeking authorization to engage in up to 12 months of post-completion Optional Practical Training (OPT) pursuant to 8 CFR 214.2(f)(10)(ii)(A)(*3*); or

(C) Is seeking a 24-month OPT extension pursuant to 8 CFR 214.2(f)(10)(ii)(C);

(ii) Has been offered employment under the sponsorship of an international organization within the meaning of the International Organization Immunities Act (59 Stat. 669) and who presents a written certification from the international organization that the proposed employment is within the scope of the organization's sponsorship. The F-1 student must also present a Form I-20 ID or SEVIS Form I-20 with employment page completed by DSO certifying eligibility for employment; or

(iii) Is seeking employment because of severe economic hardship pursuant to 8 CFR 214.2(f)(9)(ii)(C) and has filed the Form I-20 ID and Form I-538 (for non-SEVIS schools), or SEVIS Form I-20 with employment page completed by the DSO certifying eligibility, and any other supporting materials such as affidavits which further detail the unforeseen economic circumstances that require the student to seek employment authorization.

(4) An alien spouse or unmarried dependent child; son or daughter of a foreign government official (G-1, G-3 or G-4) pursuant to 8 CFR 214.2(g) and who presents an endorsement from an authorized representative of the Department of State;

(5) An alien spouse or minor child of an exchange visitor (J-2) pursuant to §214.2(j) of this chapter;

(6) A nonimmigrant (M-1) student seeking employment for practical training pursuant to 8 CFR 214.2(m) following completion of studies. The alien may be employed only in an occupation or vocation directly related to his or her course of study as recommended by the endorsement of the designated school official on the I-20 ID;

(7) A dependent of an alien classified as NATO-1 through NATO-7 pursuant to §214.2(n) of this chapter;

(8) An alien who has filed a complete application for asylum or withholding of deportation or removal pursuant to 8 CFR part 208, whose application:

(i) Has not been decided, and who is eligible to apply for employment authorization under §208.7 of this chapter because the 150-day period set forth in that section has expired. Employment authorization may be granted according to the provisions of §208.7 of this chapter in increments to be determined by the Commissioner and shall expire on a specified date; or

(ii) Has been recommended for approval, but who has not yet received a grant of asylum or withholding or deportation or removal;

(9) An alien who has filed an application for adjustment of status to lawful permanent resident pursuant to part 245 of this chapter. For purposes of section 245(c)(8) of the Act, an alien will not be deemed to be an "unauthorized alien" as defined in section 274A(h)(3) of the Act while his or her properly filed Form I-485 application is pending final adjudication, if the alien has otherwise obtained permission from the Service pursuant to 8 CFR 274a.12 to engage in employment, or if the alien had been granted employment authorization prior to the filing of the adjustment application and such authorization does not expire during the pendency of the adjustment application. Upon meeting these conditions, the adjustment applicant need not file an application for employment authorization to continue employment during the period described in the preceding sentence;

(10) An alien who has filed an application for suspension of deportation under section 244 of the Act (as it existed prior to April 1, 1997), cancellation of removal pursuant to section 240A of the Act, or special rule cancellation of removal under section 309(f)(1) of the Illegal Immigration Reform and Immigrant Responsibility Act of 1996, enacted as Pub. L. 104-208 (110 Stat. 3009-625) (as amended by the Nicaraguan Adjustment and Central American Relief Act (NACARA)), title II of Pub. L. 105-100 (111 Stat. 2160, 2193) and whose properly filed application has been accepted by the Service or EOIR.

(11) Except as provided in paragraphs (b)(37) and (c)(34) of this section and §212.19(h)(4) of this chapter, an alien paroled into the United States temporarily for urgent humanitarian reasons

or significant public benefit pursuant to section 212(d)(5) of the Act.

(12) An alien spouse of a long-term investor in the Commonwealth of the Northern Mariana Islands (E–2 CNMI Investor) other than an E–2 CNMI investor who obtained such status based upon a Foreign Retiree Investment Certificate, pursuant to 8 CFR 214.2(e)(23). An alien spouse of an E–2 CNMI Investor is eligible for employment in the CNMI only;

(13) [Reserved]

(14) An alien who has been granted deferred action, an act of administrative convenience to the government which gives some cases lower priority, if the alien establishes an economic necessity for employment;

(15) [Reserved]

(16) Any alien who has filed an application for creation of record of lawful admission for permanent residence pursuant to part 249 of this chapter.

(17) A nonimmigrant visitor for business (B–1) who:

(i) Is a personal or domestic servant who is accompanying or following to join an employer who seeks admission into, or is already in, the United States as a nonimmigrant defined under sections 101(a)(15) (B), (E), (F), (H), (I), (J), (L) or section 214(e) of the Act. The personal or domestic servant shall have a residence abroad which he or she has no intention of abandoning and shall demonstrate at least one year's experience as a personal or domestic servant. The nonimmigrant's employer shall demonstrate that the employer/employee relationship has existed for at least one year prior to the employer's admission to the United States; or, if the employer/employee relationship existed for less than one year, that the employer has regularly employed (either year-round or seasonally) personal or domestic servants over a period of several years preceding the employer's admission to the United States;

(ii) Is a domestic servant of a United States citizen accompanying or following to join his or her United States citizen employer who has a permanent home or is stationed in a foreign country, and who is visiting temporarily in the United States. The employer/employee relationship shall have existed prior to the commencement of the employer's visit to the United States; or

(iii) Is an employee of a foreign airline engaged in international transportation of passengers freight, whose position with the foreign airline would otherwise entitle the employee to classification under section 101(a)(15)(E)(i) of the Immigration and Nationality Act, and who is precluded from such classification solely because the employee is not a national of the country of the airline's nationality or because there is no treaty of commerce and navigation in effect between the United States and the country of the airline's nationality.

(18) An alien against whom a final order of deportation or removal exists and who is released on an order of supervision under the authority contained in section 241(a)(3) of the Act may be granted employment authorization in the discretion of the district director only if the alien cannot be removed due to the refusal of all countries designated by the alien or under section 241 of the Act to receive the alien, or because the removal of the alien is otherwise impracticable or contrary to the public interest. Additional factors which may be considered by the district director in adjudicating the application for employment authorization include, but are not limited to, the following:

(i) The existence of economic necessity to be employed;

(ii) The existence of a dependent spouse and/or children in the United States who rely on the alien for support; and

(iii) The anticipated length of time before the alien can be removed from the United States.

(19) An alien applying for Temporary Protected Status pursuant to section 244 of the Act shall apply for employment authorization only in accordance with the procedures set forth in part 244 of this chapter.

(20) Any alien who has filed a completed legalization application pursuant to section 210 of the Act (and part 210 of this chapter).

(21) A principal nonimmigrant witness or informant in S classification, and qualified dependent family members.

(22) Any alien who has filed a completed legalization application pursuant to section 245A of the Act (and part 245a of this chapter). Employment authorization shall be granted in increments not exceeding 1 year during the period the application is pending (including any period when an administrative appeal is pending) and shall expire on a specified date.

(23) [Reserved]

(24) An alien who has filed an application for adjustment pursuant to section 1104 of the LIFE Act, Public Law 106–553, and the provisions of 8 CFR part 245a, Subpart B of this chapter.

(25) Any alien in T–2, T–3, T–4, T–5, or T–6 nonimmigrant status, pursuant to 8 CFR 214.11, for the period in that status, as evidenced by an employment authorization document issued by USCIS to the alien.

(26) An H–4 nonimmigrant spouse of an H–1B nonimmigrant described as eligible for employment authorization in 8 CFR 214.2(h)(9)(iv).

(27)–(33) [Reserved]

(34) A spouse of an entrepreneur parolee described as eligible for employment authorization in §212.19(h)(3) of this chapter.

(35) An alien who is the principal beneficiary of a valid immigrant petition under section 203(b)(1), 203(b)(2) or 203(b)(3) of the Act described as eligible for employment authorization in 8 CFR 204.5(p).

(36) A spouse or child of a principal beneficiary of a valid immigrant petition under section 203(b)(1), 203(b)(2) or 203(b)(3) of the Act described as eligible for employment authorization in 8 CFR 204.5(p).

(d) An alien lawfully enlisted in one of the Armed Forces, or whose enlistment the Secretary with jurisdiction over such Armed Force has determined would be vital to the national interest under 10 U.S.C. 504(b)(2), is authorized to be employed by that Armed Force in military service, if such employment is not otherwise authorized under this section and the immigration laws. An alien described in this section is not issued an employment authorization document.

(e) *Basic criteria to establish economic necessity.* Title 45—Public Welfare, Poverty Guidelines, 45 CFR 1060.2 should be used as the basic criteria to establish eligibility for employment authorization when the alien's economic necessity is identified as a factor. The alien shall submit an application for employment authorization listing his or her assets, income, and expenses as evidence of his or her economic need to work. Permission to work granted on the basis of the alien's application for employment authorization may be revoked under §274a.14 of this chapter upon a showing that the information contained in the statement was not true and correct.

[52 FR 16221, May 1, 1987]

EDITORIAL NOTE: For FEDERAL REGISTER citations affecting §274a.12, see the List of CFR Sections Affected, which appears in the Finding Aids section of the printed volume and at *www.govinfo.gov*.

§274a.13 Application for employment authorization.

(a) *Application.* An alien requesting employment authorization or an Employment Authorization Document (Form I–766), or both, may be required to apply on a form designated by USCIS with any prescribed fee(s) in accordance with the form instructions. An alien may file such request concurrently with a related benefit request that, if granted, would form the basis for eligibility for employment authorization, only to the extent permitted by the form instructions or as announced by USCIS on its Web site.

(1) The approval of applications filed under 8 CFR 274a.12(c), except for 8 CFR 274a.12(c)(8), are within the discretion of USCIS. Where economic necessity has been identified as a factor, the alien must provide information regarding his or her assets, income, and expenses.

(2) An initial employment authorization request for asylum applicants under 8 CFR 274a.12(c)(8) must be filed on the form designated by USCIS in accordance with the form instructions. The applicant also must submit a copy of the underlying application for asylum or withholding of deportation, together with evidence that the application has been filed in accordance with 8 CFR 208.3 and 208.4. An application for an initial employment authorization or for a renewal of employment

authorization filed in relation to a pending claim for asylum shall be adjudicated in accordance with 8 CFR 208.7. An application for renewal or replacement of employment authorization submitted in relation to a pending claim for asylum, as provided in 8 CFR 208.7, must be filed, with fee or application for waiver of such fee.

(b) *Approval of application.* If the application is granted, the alien shall be notified of the decision and issued an employment authorization document valid for a specific period and subject to any terms and conditions as noted.

(c) *Denial of application.* If the application is denied, the applicant shall be notified in writing of the decision and the reasons for the denial. There shall be no appeal from the denial of the application.

(d) *Renewal application*—(1) *Automatic extension of Employment Authorization Documents.* Except as otherwise provided in this chapter or by law, notwithstanding 8 CFR 274a.14(a)(1)(i), the validity period of an expiring Employment Authorization Document (Form I–766) and, for aliens who are not employment authorized incident to status, also the attendant employment authorization, will be automatically extended for an additional period not to exceed 180 days from the date of such document's and such employment authorization's expiration if a request for renewal on a form designated by USCIS is:

(i) Properly filed as provided by form instructions before the expiration date shown on the face of the Employment Authorization Document, or during the filing period described in the applicable FEDERAL REGISTER notice regarding procedures for obtaining Temporary Protected Status-related EADs;

(ii) Based on the same employment authorization category as shown on the face of the expiring Employment Authorization Document or is for an individual approved for Temporary Protected Status whose EAD was issued pursuant to 8 CFR 274a.12(c)(19); and

(iii) Based on a class of aliens whose eligibility to apply for employment authorization continues notwithstanding expiration of the Employment Authorization Document and is based on an employment authorization category that does not require adjudication of an underlying application or petition before adjudication of the renewal application, including aliens described in 8 CFR 274a.12(a)(12) granted Temporary Protected Status and pending applicants for Temporary Protected Status who are issued an EAD under 8 CFR 274a.12(c)(19), as may be announced on the USCIS Web site.

(2) *Terms and conditions.* Any extension authorized under this paragraph (d) shall be subject to any conditions and limitations noted in the immediately preceding employment authorization.

(3) *Termination.* The period authorized by paragraph (d)(1) of this section will automatically terminate the earlier of up to 180 days after the expiration date of the Employment Authorization Document (Form I–766), or upon issuance of notification of a decision denying the renewal request. Nothing in paragraph (d) of this section will affect DHS's ability to otherwise terminate any employment authorization or Employment Authorization Document, or extension period for such employment or document, by written notice to the applicant, by notice to a class of aliens published in the FEDERAL REGISTER, or as provided by statute or regulation including 8 CFR 274a.14.

(4) *Unexpired Employment Authorization Documents.* An Employment Authorization Document (Form I–766) that has expired on its face is considered unexpired when combined with a Notice of Action (Form I–797C), which demonstrates that the requirements of paragraph (d)(1) of this section have been met.

[52 FR 16221, May 1, 1987, as amended at 55 FR 25937, June 25, 1990; 56 FR 41787, Aug. 23, 1991; 59 FR 33905, July 1, 1994; 59 FR 62303, Dec. 5, 1994; 60 FR 21976, May 4, 1995; 63 FR 39121, July 21, 1998; 64 FR 25773, May 12, 1999; 65 FR 15846, Mar. 24, 2000; 72 FR 53042, Sept. 17, 2007; 74 FR 26940, June 5, 2009; 76 FR 53796, Aug. 29, 2011; 80 FR 10312, Feb. 25, 2015; 81 FR 82491, Nov. 18, 2016]

§ 274a.14 Termination of employment authorization.

(a) *Automatic termination of employment authorization.* (1) Employment authorization granted under § 274a.12(c) of this chapter shall automatically terminate upon the occurrence of one of the following events:

(i) The expiration date specified by the Service on the employment authorization document is reached;

(ii) Exclusion or deportation proceedings are instituted (however, this shall not preclude the authorization of employment pursuant to § 274a.12(c) of this part where appropriate); or

(iii) The alien is granted voluntary departure.

(2) Termination of employment authorization pursuant to this paragraph does not require the service of a notice of intent to revoke; employment authorization terminates upon the occurrence of any event enumerated in paragraph (a)(1) of this section.

However, automatic revocation under this section does not preclude reapplication for employment authorization under § 274.12(c) of this part.

(b) *Revocation of employment authorization*—(1) *Basis for revocation of employment authorization.* Employment authorization granted under § 274a.12(c) of this chapter may be revoked by the district director:

(i) Prior to the expiration date, when it appears that any condition upon which it was granted has not been met or no longer exists, or for good cause shown; or

(ii) Upon a showing that the information contained in the application is not true and correct.

(2) *Notice of intent to revoke employment authorization.* When a district director determines that employment authorization should be revoked prior to the expiration date specified by the Service, he or she shall serve written notice of intent to revoke the employment authorization. The notice will cite the reasons indicating that revocation is warranted. The alien will be granted a period of fifteen days from the date of service of the notice within which to submit countervailing evidence. The decision by the district director shall be final and no appeal shall lie from the decision to revoke the authorization.

(c) *Automatic termination of temporary employment authorization granted prior to June 1, 1987.* (1) Temporary employment authorization granted prior to June 1, 1987, pursuant to 8 CFR 274a.12(c) (§ 109.1(b) contained in the 8 CFR edition revised as of January 1, 1987), shall automatically terminate on the date specified by the Service on the document issued to the alien, or on December 31, 1996, whichever is earlier. Automatic termination of temporary employment authorization does not preclude a subsequent application for temporary employment authorization.

(2) A document issued by the Service prior to June 1, 1987, that authorized temporary employment authorization for any period beyond December 31, 1996, is null and void pursuant to paragraph (c)(1) of this section. The alien shall be issued a new employment authorization document upon application to the Service if the alien is eligible for temporary employment authorization pursuant to 274A.12(c).

(3) No notice of intent to revoke is necessary for the automatic termination of temporary employment authorization pursuant to this part.

[52 FR 16221, May 1, 1987, as amended at 53 FR 8614, Mar. 16, 1988; 53 FR 20087, June 1, 1988; 61 FR 46537, Sept. 4, 1996]

PART 280—IMPOSITION AND COLLECTION OF FINES

Sec.

AUTHORITY: 8 U.S.C. 1103, 1221, 1223, 1227, 1229, 1253, 1281, 1283, 1284, 1285, 1286, 1322, 1323, 1330; 66 Stat. 173, 195, 197, 201, 203, 212, 219,

221–223, 226, 227, 230; Pub. L. 101–410, 104 Stat. 890, as amended by Pub. L. 114–74, 129 Stat. 599.

SOURCE: 22 FR 9807, Dec. 6, 1957, unless otherwise noted.

§ 280.1 Notice of intention to fine; administrative proceedings not exclusive.

Whenever a district director or the Associate Commissioner for Examinations, or the Director for the National Fines Office has reason to believe that any person has violated any of the provisions of the Immigration and Nationality Act and has thereby become liable to the imposition of an administrative fine under the Immigration and Nationality Act, he shall cause a Notice of Intention to Fine, Form I–79, to be served as provided in this part. Nothing in this subchapter shall affect, restrict, or prevent the institution of a civil suit, in the discretion of the Attorney General, under the authority contained in section 280 of the Immigration and Nationality Act.

[22 FR 9807, Dec. 6, 1957, as amended at 54 FR 18649, May 2, 1989]

§ 280.2 Special provisions relating to aircraft.

In any case in which the imposition of a fine is predicated upon an alleged violation of a regulation promulgated under authority of section 239 of the Immigration and Nationality Act, the procedure prescribed in this part shall be followed and the aircraft involved shall not be granted clearance pending determination of the question of liability to the payment of any fine, or while the fine remains unpaid; but clearance may be granted prior to the determination of such question upon the deposit of a sum sufficient to cover such fine or of a bond with sufficient surety to secure the payment thereof, approved by the Commissioner. If the alleged violation was by the owner or person in command of the aircraft, the penalty provided for shall be a lien against the aircraft, which, except as provided in § 280.21, shall be seized by the district director or by an immigration officer designated by the district director, and placed in the custody of the customs officer who is in charge of the port of entry or customs station nearest the place of seizure. If the owner or owners of the airport at which such aircraft is located are the owners of the seized aircraft, the aircraft shall be removed to another suitable place for storage if practicable.

[22 FR 9807, Dec. 6, 1957, as amended at 32 FR 17651, Dec. 12, 1967; 56 FR 26020, June 6, 1991]

§ 280.3 Departure of vessel or aircraft prior to denial of clearance.

If any vessel or aircraft which is subject to the imposition of a fine shall have departed from the United States prior to the denial of clearance by the district director of customs and such vessel or aircraft is subsequently found in the United States, a Notice of Intention to Fine, Form I–79, shall be served as provided in this part, if such form has not been previously served for the same violation. Clearance of such vessel or aircraft shall be withheld by the district director of customs, and the procedure prescribed in this part shall be followed to the same extent and in the same manner as though the vessel or aircraft had not departed from the United States. Aircraft subject to the provisions of § 280.2, which shall have departed from the United States prior to the time of seizure could be effected, shall be subject to all of the provisions of this part, if subsequently found in the United States, to the same extent as though it had not departed from the United States.

[22 FR 9807, Dec. 6, 1957, as amended at 32 FR 17651, Dec. 12, 1967]

§ 280.4 Data concerning cost of transportation.

Within five days after request therefor, transportation companies shall furnish to the district director or the Associate Commissioner for Examinations, or the Director for the National Fines Office pertinent information contained in the original transportation contract of all rejected aliens whose cases are within the purview of any of the provisions of the Immigration and Nationality Act relating to refund of passage monies, and shall specify the exact amounts paid for transportation from the initial point of departure (which point shall be indicated) to the foreign port of embarkation, from the latter to the port of arrival in the

United States and from the port of arrival to the inland point of destination, respectively, and also the amount paid for headtax, if any.

[22 FR 9807, Dec. 6, 1957, as amended at 54 FR 18649, May 2, 1989]

§280.5 Mitigation or remission of fines.

In any case in which mitigation or remission of a fine is authorized by the Immigration and Nationality Act, the party served with Notice of Intention to Fine may apply in writing to the district director or the Associate Commissioner for Examinations, or the Director for the National Fines Office for such mitigation or remission.

[22 FR 9807, Dec. 6, 1957, as amended at 54 FR 18649, May 2, 1989]

§280.6 Bond to obtain clearance; form.

A bond to obtain clearance of a vessel or aircraft under section 231, 237, 239, 243, 251, 253, 254, 255, 256, 272, or 273 of the Immigration and Nationality Act shall be filed on Form I–310.

[22 FR 9807, Dec. 6, 1957, as amended at 54 FR 102, Jan. 4, 1989]

§280.7 Approval of bonds or acceptance of cash deposit to obtain clearance.

The district director of customs is authorized to approve the bond, or accept the sum of money which is being offered for deposit under any provision of the Immigration and Nationality Act or by this chapter for the purpose of obtaining clearance of a vessel or aircraft with the exception of sections 239, 251(d), 255, 256, 272, and 273(d) in which the Commissioner of the Immigration and Naturalization Service is authorized to approve the bond or accept the sum of money which is being offered for deposit.

[22 FR 9807, Dec. 6, 1957, as amended at 32 FR 17651, Dec. 12, 1967; 56 FR 26020, June 6, 1991]

§280.11 Notice of intention to fine; procedure.

Notice of Intention to Fine, Form I–79, shall be prepared in triplicate, with one additional copy for each additional person on whom the service of such notice is contemplated. The notice shall be addressed to any or all of the available persons subject to fine. A copy of the notice shall be served by personal service on each such person. If the notice is delivered personally, the person upon whom it is served shall be requested to acknowledge such service by signing his name to the duplicate and triplicate copies. The officer effecting such service shall attest to the service by signing his name thereon and shall indicate thereon the date and place of service. If the person so served refuses to acknowledge service, or if service is made by leaving it at an office or mailing it, the person making such service shall indicate the method and date on the duplicate and triplicate copies of Form I–79, and shall sign his name upon such copies. The duplicate copy shall be retained by the district director of immigration and naturalization or the Associate Commissioner for Examinations, or the Director for the National Fines Office and the triplicate copy shall be delivered directly to the district director of customs for the district in which the vessel or aircraft is located, and the district director of customs shall withhold clearance until deposit is made or bond furnished as provided in the Immigration and Nationality Act. If the vessel or aircraft is located in a customs district which is outside the jurisdiction of the office of the Service having jurisdiction over the matter, the triplicate copy shall be forwarded to the office of the Service nearest such customs district for delivery to the district director of customs.

[22 FR 9807, Dec. 6, 1957, as amended at 32 FR 17651, Dec. 12, 1967; 37 FR 11471, June 8, 1972; 54 FR 18649, May 2, 1989]

§280.12 Answer and request or order for interview.

Within 30 days following the service of the Notice of Intention to Fine (which period the district director or the Associate Commissioner for Examinations, or the Director for the National Fines Office may extend for an additional period of 30 days upon good cause being shown), any person upon whom a notice under this part has been served may file with the district director or the Associate Commissioner for Examinations, or the Director for the National Fines Office a written defense, in duplicate, under oath setting forth the reasons why a fine should not be imposed, or if imposed, why it should be mitigated or remitted if permitted by the Immigration and Nationality Act, and stating whether a personal appearance is desired. Documentary evidence shall be submitted in support of such defense and a brief may be submitted in support of any argument made. If a personal interview is requested, the evidence in opposition to the imposition of the fine and in support of the request for mitigation or remission may be presented at such interview. An interview shall be conducted if requested by the party as provided hereinabove or, if directed at any time by the Board, the Commissioner, or the district director or the Associate Commissioner for Examinations, or the Director for the National Fines Office.

[22 FR 9807, Dec. 6, 1957, as amended at 54 FR 18649, May 2, 1989]

§ 280.13 Disposition of case.

(a) *Allegations admitted or no answer filed.* If a request for personal appearance is not filed and (1) the answer admits the allegations in the notice, or (2) no answer is filed, the district director or the Associate Commissioner for Examinations, or the Director for the National Fines Office shall enter such order in the case as he deems appropriate and no appeal from his decision may be taken.

(b) *Answer filed; personal appearance.* Upon receipt of an answer asserting a defense to the allegations in the notice without requesting a personal appearance, or if a personal appearance is requested or directed, the case shall be assigned to an immigration officer. The immigration officer shall prepare a report summarizing the evidence and containing his findings and recommendation. The record, including the report and recommendation of the immigration officer, shall be forwarded to the district director or the Associate Commissioner for Examinations, or the Director for the National Fines Office. The district director or the Associate Commissioner for Examinations, or the Director for the National Fines Office shall note on the report of the immigration officer whether he approves or disapproves the recommendation of the immigration officer. The person shall be informed in writing of the decision of the district director or the Associate Commissioner for Examinations, or the Director for the National Fines Office and, if his decision is that a fine shall be imposed or that the requested mitigation or remission shall not be granted, of the reasons for such decision. From the decision of the district director or the Associate Commissioner for Examinations, or the Director for the National Fines Office an appeal may be taken to the Board as provided in 8 CFR part 1003.

[22 FR 9808, Dec. 6, 1957, as amended at 23 FR 9124, Nov. 26, 1958; 54 FR 18649, May 2, 1989; 76 FR 74629, Dec. 1, 2011]

§ 280.14 Record.

The record made under § 280.13 shall include the request for the interview or a reference to the order directing the interview; the medical certificate, if any; a copy of any record of hearing before a Board of Special Inquiry, Hearing Examiner, Hearing Officer, or Special Inquiry Officer which is relevant to the fine proceedings; the duplicate copy of the Notice of Intention to Fine; the evidence upon which such Notice was based; the duplicate of any notices to detain, deport, deliver, or remove aliens; notice to pay expenses; evidence as to whether any deposit was made or bond furnished in accordance with the Immigration and Nationality Act; reports of investigations conducted; documentary evidence and testimony adduced at the interview; the original of any affidavit or brief filed in opposition to the imposition of fine; the application for mitigation or remission; and any other relevant matter.

§ 280.15 Notice of final decision to district director of customs.

At such time as the decision under this part is final, the regional administrative officer shall be furnished a copy of the decision by the district director of immigration and naturalization or the Associate Commissioner for Examinations, or the Director for the National Fines Office. The regional administrative officer shall notify the district director of customs who was furnished a copy of the Notice of Intention to Fine of the final decision made in the case. Such notification need not be made if the regional administrative officer has been previously furnished with a notice of collection of the amount of the penalty by the district director of customs.

[32 FR 17651, Dec. 12, 1967, as amended at 54 FR 18649, May 2, 1989]

§ 280.21 Seizure of aircraft.

Seizure of an aircraft under the authority of section 239 of the Act and § 280.2 will not be made if such aircraft is damaged to an extent that its value is less than the amount of the fine which may be imposed. If seizure of an aircraft for violation of section 239 of the Act is to be made, Form G–297 (Order to Seize Aircraft) and Form G–298 (Public Notice of Seizure) shall be prepared in septuple and the originals furnished to the immigration officer who will effect the seizure. The original of Form G–297, properly endorsed as to date and place of seizure, shall be returned for retention in the relating file after seizure is effected. The original of Form G–298 shall be placed on the seized aircraft and a copy retained in the file. Copies of both forms shall be served upon the owner of the aircraft and the pilot if other than the owner. Copies shall also be furnished the district director of customs and the United States Attorney for the district in which the seizure was made. In addition, immediately upon the seizure of an aircraft, or prior thereto, if circumstances permit, a full report of the facts in the case shall be submitted by the district director to the United States Attorney for the district in which the seizure was made, together with copies of Form G–296 (Report of Violation) and Form I–79 (Notice of Intention to Fine). The report shall include the cost incurred in seizing and guarding the aircraft and an estimate of the further additional cost likely to be incurred.

[29 FR 14433, Oct. 21, 1964, as amended at 32 FR 17651, Dec. 12, 1967]

§ 280.51 Application for mitigation or remission.

(a) *When application may be filed.* An application for mitigation or remission of a fine may be filed as provided under § 280.12 of this part; or, within 30 days after the date of receipt of the district director's or the Associate Commissioner for Examinations, or the Director for the National Fines Office's decision to impose a fine whether or not the applicant responded to the Notice of Intention to Fine.

(b) *Form and contents of application.* An application for mitigation or remission shall be filed in duplicate under oath and shall include information, supported by documentary evidence, as to the basis of the claim to mitigation or remission, and as to the action, if any, which may have been taken by the applicant, or as to the circumstances present in the case which, in the opinion of the applicant, justified the granting of his application.

(c) *Disposition of application.* The application, if filed with the answer, shall be disposed of as provided in § 280.13. In any other case the application shall be considered and decided by the district director or the Associate Commissioner for Examinations, or the Director for the National Fines Office from whose decision an appeal may be taken to the Board as provided in 8 CFR part 1003.

[22 FR 9808, Dec. 6, 1957, as amended at 23 FR 9124, Nov. 26, 1958; 46 FR 28624, May 28, 1981; 54 FR 18649, May 2, 1989; 76 FR 74629, Dec. 1, 2011]

§ 280.52 Payment of fines.

(a) All fines assessed pursuant to sections 231(d); 237(b); 239; 251(d); 254(a); 255; 256; 271(a); 272, 273 and 274(c) of the Act shall be made payable to and collected by the Service.

(b) All fines collected pursuant to sections 271(a) and 273 of the Act shall be deposited in the Immigration User Fee Account established in accordance with the provisions of section 286 of the Act.

(c) From the amounts collected under paragraphs (a) and (b) of this section, the increase in penalties collected resulting from the amendments made by sections 203(b), 543(a), and 544 of the Immigration Act of 1990, shall be credited to the appropriation for activities authorized under section 280(b) of the Act.

[56 FR 26020, June 6, 1991]

§ 280.53 Civil monetary penalties inflation adjustment.

(a) *Statutory authority*. In accordance with the requirements of the Federal Civil Penalties Inflation Adjustment Act of 1990, Public Law 101–410, 104 Stat. 890, as amended by the Federal Civil Penalties Inflation Adjustment Act Improvements Act of 2015, Public Law 114–74, Sec. 701, 129 Stat. 599, the civil monetary penalties listed in paragraph (b) of this section are adjusted as provided in paragraph (b).

(b) *Adjustment of penalties*. For violations occurring on or before November 2, 2015, the penalty amount prior to adjustment applies. For violations occurring after November 2, 2015, the listed penalties are adjusted as follows:

(1) Section 231(g) of the Act, Penalties for non-compliance with arrival and departure manifest requirements for passengers, crewmembers, or occupants transported on commercial vessels or aircraft arriving to or departing from the United States: From $1,333 to $1,360.

(2) Section 234 of the Act, Penalties for non-compliance with landing requirements at designated ports of entry for aircraft transporting aliens: From $3,621 to $3,695.

(3) Section 240B(d) of the Act, Penalties for failure to depart voluntarily: From $1,527 minimum/$7,635 maximum to $1,558 minimum/$7,791 maximum.

(4) Section 243(c)(1)(A) of the Act, Penalties for violations of removal orders relating to aliens transported on vessels or aircraft, under section 241(d) of the Act, or for costs associated with removal under section 241(e) of the Act: From $3,054 to $3,116;

(5) Penalties for failure to remove alien stowaways under section 241(d)(2): From $7,635 to $7,791.

(6) Section 251(d) of the Act, Penalties for failure to report an illegal landing or desertion of alien crewmen, and for each alien not reported on arrival or departure manifest or lists required in accordance with section 251 of the Act: From $362 to $369; and penalties for use of alien crewmen for longshore work in violation of section 251(d) of the Act: From $9,054 to $9,239.

(7) Section 254(a) of the Act, Penalties for failure to control, detain, or remove alien crewmen: From $906 minimum/$5,432 maximum to $924 minimum/$5,543 maximum.

(8) Section 255 of the Act, Penalties for employment on passenger vessels of aliens afflicted with certain disabilities: From $1,811 to $1,848.

(9) Section 256 of the Act, Penalties for discharge of alien crewmen: From $2,716 minimum/$5,432 maximum to $2,771 minimum/$5,543 maximum.

(10) Section 257 of the Act, Penalties for bringing into the United States alien crewmen with intent to evade immigration laws: From $18,107 maximum to $18,477 maximum.

(11) Section 271(a) of the Act, Penalties for failure to prevent the unauthorized landing of aliens: From $5,432 to $5,543.

(12) Section 272(a) of the Act, Penalties for bringing to the United States aliens subject to denial of admission on a health-related ground: From $5,432 to $5,543.

(13) Section 273(b) of the Act, Penalties for bringing to the United States aliens without required documentation: From $5,432 to $5,543.

(14) Section 274D of the Act, Penalties for failure to depart: From $763 to $779, for each day the alien is in violation.

(15) Section 275(b) of the Act, Penalties for improper entry: From $76 minimum/$382 maximum to $78 minimum/$390 maximum, for each entry or attempted entry.

[82 FR 8580, Jan. 27, 2017, as amended at 83 FR 13835, Apr. 2, 2018]

PART 286—IMMIGRATION USER FEE

Sec.

AUTHORITY: 8 U.S.C. 1101, 1103, 1356; Title VII of Public Law 110–229; 8 CFR part 2.

SOURCE: 53 FR 5757, Feb. 26, 1988, unless otherwise noted.

§286.1 Definitions.

The following definitions apply to the following terms in this part:

(a) The term *adjacent islands* means Anguilla, Antigua, Aruba, Bahamas, Barbados, Barbuda, Bermuda, Bonaire, British Virgin Islands, Cayman Islands, Cuba, Curacao, Dominica, the Dominican Republic, Grenada, Guadeloupe, Haiti, Jamaica, Marie-Galante, Martinique, Miquelon, Montserrat, Saba, Saint Barthélemy, Saint Christopher, Saint Eustatius, Saint Kitts-Nevis, Saint Lucia, Saint Maarten, Saint Martin, Saint Pierre, Saint Vincent and Grenadines, Trinidad and Tobago, Turks and Caicos Islands, and other British, French and Netherlands territory or possessions bordering on the Caribbean Sea.

(b) The term *collector* means an air or sea carrier, travel agent, tour wholesaler, or other entity which collects, but may or may not be required to remit, fees pursuant to this part.

(c) The term *commercial aircraft* means any civilian aircraft being used to transport persons or property for compensation or hire.

(d) The term *commercial vessel* means any civilian vessel being used to transport persons or property for compensation or hire.

(e) The term *Assistant Commissioner, Office of Financial Management* means the Office of the Assistant Commissioner, Financial Management, Immigration and Naturalization Service, Room 6307, 425 I Street NW., Washington, DC 20536.

(f) The term *fee* means the immigration user fee.

(g) The term *port of entry* means a port or place designated by the Commissioner at which a person may apply for admission into the United States.

(h) The term *remitter* means an air or sea carrier, travel agent, tour wholesaler, or other entity which collects, including receipt of fees collected by collectors which are not required to remit fees, and remits fees pursuant to this part.

(i) *Territories or possessions of the United States* means American Samoa, Baker Island, Howland Island, Jarvis Island, Johnston Atoll, Kingman Reef, Midway, Swains Island, Palmyra Island, and Wake Island.

(j) The term *document for transportation* means any document accepted by a carrier in return for transportation.

(k) *United States*, when used in a geographical sense, means the continental United States, Alaska, Hawaii, Puerto Rico, Guam, the Virgin Islands of the United States, and the Commonwealth of the Northern Mariana Islands.

[53 FR 5757, Feb. 26, 1988, as amended at 59 FR 49349, Sept. 28, 1994; 63 FR 51272, Sept. 25, 1998; 74 FR 55740, Oct. 28, 2009]

§286.2 Fee for arrival of passengers aboard commercial aircraft or commercial vessels.

(a) A fee, in the amount prescribed in section 286(d) of the Act, per individual is charged and collected by the Commissioner for the immigration inspection of each passenger aboard a commercial aircraft or commercial vessel, arriving at a port-of-entry in the United States, or for the preinspection of a passenger in a place outside the United States prior to such arrival, except as provided in §286.3.

(b) A fee, in the amount prescribed in section 286(e)(3) of the Act, per individual, is charged and collected by the Commissioner for the immigration inspection at a port-of-entry in the United States, or for the preinspection in a place outside the United States of each commercial vessel passenger whose journey originated in the United States, Canada, Mexico, territories or possessions of the United States, or adjacent islands, except as provided in §286.3. All tickets or documents for transportation on voyages that are booked on or after February 27, 2003, will be subject to this immigration user fee.

(c) Each commercial aircraft and vessel carrier or ticket-selling agent whose monthly collections in any month exceed $50,000 shall submit a summary statement showing the amount of user fees collected that month. The summary statement is due on the last business day of the following month. This information shall be forwarded to the Immigration and Naturalization Service, Chief, Analysis and Formulation Branch, 425 I Street,

NW., Room 6307, Washington, DC 20536. For the months of December, March, June, and August, the quarterly remittance and statement required by § 286.5 will serve as the monthly report for those months. Therefore, a monthly report is required for all other months in which monthly collections exceed $50,000.

[59 FR 49348, Sept. 28, 1994, as amended at 63 FR 51272, Sept. 25, 1998; 67 FR 15334, Apr. 1, 2002; 68 FR 4092, Jan. 28, 2003]

§ 286.3 Exceptions.

The fees set forth in §§ 286.2(a) and 286.2(b) shall not be charged or collected from passengers who fall within any one of the following categories:

(a) Persons arriving at designated ports-of-entry by the following vessels, when operating on a regular schedule: Great Lakes international ferries or Great Lakes vessels on the Great Lakes and connecting waterways;

(b) Persons directly connected with the operation, navigation, or business of the commercial aircraft or commercial vessel including working crew, deadheading crew, U.S. Federal Aviation Administration inspectors, sky marshals, and commercial airline or commercial vessel employees on official business;

(c) Persons who are listed as foreign diplomats on the accreditation list maintained by the U.S. Department of State or who are in possession of a diplomatic visa (A–1 and 2, G–1 thru 4) valid for entry into the United States;

(d) Persons who are passengers on any commercial aircraft or commercial vessel owned or operated exclusively by the Government of the United States or a foreign government, including any agency or political subdivision thereof, so long as that aircraft or vessel is not transporting any persons or property for commercial purposes.

(e) Persons who are passengers on commercial aircraft or commercial vessels under contract to the U.S. Department of Defense, if they have been preinspected outside of the United States under a joint Service and U.S. Department of Defense military inspection program;

(f) Persons arriving on an aircraft or vessel due to an emergency or forced landing when the original destination of the aircraft or vessel was not the United States; and

(g) Persons transiting the United States who are not inspected by the Service. Transit without visa passengers who are inspected by the Service are not excepted from payment of the fee under this section.

[53 FR 5757, Feb. 26, 1988, as amended at 59 FR 49348, Sept. 28, 1994; 68 FR 4092, Jan. 28, 2003]

§ 286.4 Fee collection responsibility.

(a) It is the responsibility of the air or sea carriers, travel agents, tour wholesalers, or other parties, which issue tickets or documents for transportation on or after December 1, 1986, to collect the fee set forth in § 286.2 of this part from all passengers transported to the United States who are not excepted under § 286.3 of this part.

(b) Tickets and documents for transportation shall be marked by the collector of the fee to indicate that the required fee has been collected. Such markings shall be in accordance with the procedures set forth in the ARC Industry Agents Handbook, the SATO Ticketing Handbook, or compatible procedures set forth in the operations manual of individual collectors.

(c) It is the responsibility of the carrier transporting a passenger from the United States to collect the fee upon departure, if the passenger was not excepted under § 286.3 of this part and tickets or documents for transportation of the passenger do not reflect collection of the fee at the time of issuance. If at the time of departure such a passenger refuses to pay the fee, the carrier shall record the full name, complete address, nationality, passport number, and alien file number, if any, of the passenger and immediately notify the Associate Commissioner, Finance.

[53 FR 5757, Feb. 26, 1988, as amended at 59 FR 49349, Sept. 28, 1994]

§ 286.5 Remittance and statement procedures.

(a) The air or sea carrier whose ticket stock or document for transportation reflects collection of the fee is responsible for remittance of the fee to the Service. The travel agent, tour wholesaler, or other entity, which issues their own non-carrier related ticket or document for transportation to an air or sea passenger who is not excepted from the fee pursuant to §286.3 of this part, is responsible for remittance of the fee to the Service, unless by contract the carrier will remit the fee.

(b)(1) Fee remittances shall be sent to the Immigration and Naturalization Service, at a designated Treasury depository, for receipt no later than 31 days after the close of the calendar quarter in which the fees are collected, except the fourth quarter payment for fees collected shall be made on the date that is 10 days before the end of the U.S. Government's fiscal year, and the first quarter payment shall include any collections made in the preceding quarter that were not remitted with the previous payment. The fourth quarter payment shall include collections for the months of July and August. The fiscal year referenced is the U.S. Government's fiscal year which begins on October 1 and ends on September 30.

(2) Late payments will be subject to interest, penalty, and handling charges as provided in the Debt Collection Act of 1982 (31 U.S.C. 3717). Refunds by a remitter of fees collected in conjunction with unused tickets or documents for transportation shall be netted against the next subsequent remittance.

(c) Along with the remittance, as set forth in paragraph (b) of this section, each remitter making such remittance shall attach a statement which sets forth the following:

(1) Name and address;

(2) Taxpayer identification number;

(3) Calendar quarter covered by the payment;

(4) Interest and penalty charges; and

(5) Total amount collected and remitted.

(d) Remittances shall be made in U.S. dollars by check or money order through a U.S. bank, to Assistant Commissioner, Office of Financial Management, INS.

(e) Annually, each U.S. based remitter, which retains an independent accountant and which remits $10,000 or more in fees in any one calendar quarter, shall submit to the Assistant Commissioner, Financial Management a report from the independent accountant in accordance with the *Statement on Standards for Attestation Engagements* on the application of Passenger User Fee Collection and Remittance Procedures established by the American Institute of Certified Public Accountants and the Service, to the Assistant Commissioner, Financial Management. Each foreign-based remitter, which retains an independent accountant and which remits $10,000 or more in fees in any one calendar quarter, shall submit a similar report to the Assistant Commissioner, Financial Management from the independent accountant in accordance with generally accepted accounting principles of their respective countries. These reports from the independent accountants are to be submitted for receipt by the Assistant Commissioner, Financial Management no later than ninety (90) days after the close of the fiscal year of each remitter. Each remitter, which does not retain an independent accountant or which does not remit $10,000 or more in any one calendar quarter, shall certify under oath on each statement submitted pursuant to paragraph (c) of this section that they have complied with the applicable statutes and regulations.

(f) The Commissioner reserves the right to conduct an independent audit of any collector or remitter not providing the report or certification required pursuant to paragraph (e) of this section or based upon other information indicating non-compliance in order to assure the accuracy of the remittances of fees collected and remitted and compliance with the applicable statutes and regulations.

(g) In order to enforce compliance with the provisions of this part, the Commissioner may issue a subpoena requiring the production of records, evidence, and witnesses pursuant to the procedures set forth in §287.4 of this chapter. The authority to issue a subpoena pursuant to this section is limited to the Commissioner, Deputy Commissioner, Associate Commissioner for Management, Director for Program Inspection, all Regional Commissioners; and all District Directors.

[53 FR 5757, Feb. 26, 1988, as amended at 55 FR 729, Jan. 9, 1990; 59 FR 49348, 49349, Sept. 28, 1994; 63 FR 51272, Sept. 25, 1998]

§ 286.6 Maintenance of records.

Each collector and remitter shall maintain records necessary for the Service to verify the accuracy of fees collected and remitted and to otherwise determine compliance with the applicable statutes and regulations. Such records shall be maintained for a period of two years from the date of fee collection. Each remitter shall advise the Assistant Commissioner, Office of Financial Management of the name, address, and telephone number of a responsible officer who shall have the authority to verify and produce any records required to be maintained under this part. The Assistant Commissioner, Office of Financial Management shall be promptly notified of any changes of the responsible officer.

[53 FR 5757, Feb. 26, 1988, as amended at 59 FR 49349, Sept. 28, 1994; 63 FR 51272, Sept. 25, 1998]

§ 286.7 Penalties.

Failure of any air or sea carrier to comply with the provisions of section 286 of the Act and this part shall subject it to one or more of the following:

(a) Termination of existing agreements under the provisions of section 238 of the Act; and

(b) Suspension of enroute inspections or preinspections.

§ 286.8 Establishment of pilot programs for the charging of a land border fee for inspection services.

Under the provisions of section 286(q) of the Act, the Service may establish pilot programs at one or more land border ports-of-entry to charge fees for immigration inspection services to be collected by the Commissioner. Individual ports-of-entry selected by the Commissioner to participate in such pilot programs may charge a fee to enhance inspection services and to recover the cost of:

(a) Hiring additional immigration inspectors, including all associated personnel costs such as salary, benefits, and overtime;

(b) Expansion, operation, and maintenance of information systems for nonimmigrant control;

(c) Construction costs, including those associated with adding new primary traffic lanes (with the concurrence of the General Services Administration);

(d) Procuring detection devices and conducting training to identify fraudulent documents used by applicants for entry to the United States;

(e) Other administrative costs associated with the PORTPASS Program; and

(f) Costs associated with the administration of the Land Border Inspection Fee account.

[60 FR 50390, Sept. 29, 1995, as amended at 61 FR 53833, Oct. 16, 1996]

§ 286.9 Fee for processing applications and issuing documentation at land border Ports-of-Entry.

(a) *General.* A fee may be charged and collected by the Commissioner for the processing and issuance of specified Service documents at land border Ports-of-Entry. These fees, as specified in § 103.7(b)(1) of this chapter, shall be dedicated to funding the cost of providing application-processing services at land border ports.

(b) *Forms for which a fee may be charged.* (1) A nonimmigrant alien who is required to be issued, or requests to be issued, Form I–94 (see § 1.4), Arrival/Departure Record, for admission at a land border Port-of-Entry must remit the required fee for issuance of Form I–94 upon determination of admissibility.

(2) A nonimmigrant alien applying for admission at a land border Port-of-Entry as a Visa Waiver Pilot Program applicant pursuant to § 217.2(c) or § 217.3(c) of this chapter must remit the required fee for issuance of Form I–94W upon determination of admissibility.

(3) A Mexican national in possession of a valid Form DSP–150, B–1/B–2 Visa and Border Crossing Card, issued by the DOS, or a passport and combined B–1/B–2 visa and non-biometric BCC (or similar stamp in a passport) issued by the DOS, who is required to be issued Form I–94, Arrival/Departure Record, pursuant to § 235.1(f) of this chapter, must remit the required fee for issuance of Form I–94 upon determination of admissibility.

(4) A citizen or lawful permanent resident alien of the United States or a Canadian citizen or permanent resident of Canada who is a national of a designated Visa Waiver Program country

listed in §217.2(a) of this chapter who requests Form I–68, Canadian Border Boat Landing Permit, pursuant to §235.1(e) of this chapter, for entry to the United States from Canada as an eligible pleasure boater on a designated body of water, must remit the required fee at the time of application for Form I–68.

[60 FR 40069, Aug. 7, 1995, as amended at 62 FR 10390, Mar. 6, 1997; 67 FR 71450, Dec. 2, 2002; 68 FR 5194, Jan. 31, 2003; 78 FR 18472, Mar. 27, 2013]

PART 287—FIELD OFFICERS; POWERS AND DUTIES

Sec.

AUTHORITY: 8 U.S.C. 1103, 1182, 1225, 1226, 1251, 1252, 1357; Homeland Security Act of 2002, Pub. L. 107–296 (6 U.S.C. 1, *et seq.*); 8 CFR part 2.

§287.1 Definitions.

(a)(1) *External boundary.* The term *external boundary,* as used in section 287(a)(3) of the Act, means the land boundaries and the territorial sea of the United States extending 12 nautical miles from the baselines of the United States determined in accordance with international law.

(2) *Reasonable distance.* The term *reasonable distance,* as used in section 287(a) (3) of the Act, means within 100 air miles from any external boundary of the United States or any shorter distance which may be fixed by the chief patrol agent for CBP, or the special agent in charge for ICE, or, so far as the power to board and search aircraft is concerned any distance fixed pursuant to paragraph (b) of this section.

(b) *Reasonable distance; fixing by chief patrol agents and special agents in charge.* In fixing distances not exceeding 100 air miles pursuant to paragraph (a) of this section, chief patrol agents and special agents in charge shall take into consideration topography, confluence of arteries of transportation leading from external boundaries, density of population, possible inconvenience to the traveling public, types of conveyances used, and reliable information as to movements of persons effecting illegal entry into the United States: *Provided,* That whenever in the opinion of a chief patrol agent or special agent in charge a distance in his or her sector or district of more than 100 air miles from any external boundary of the United States would because of unusual circumstances be reasonable, such chief patrol agent or special agent in charge shall forward a complete report with respect to the matter to the Commissioner of CBP, or the Assistant Secretary for ICE, as appropriate, who may, if he determines that such action is justified, declare such distance to be reasonable.

(c) *Patrolling the border.* The phrase *patrolling the border to prevent the illegal entry of aliens into the United States* as used in section 287 of the Immigration and Nationality Act means conducting such activities as are customary, or reasonable and necessary, to prevent the illegal entry of aliens into the United States.

(d) *Arrested by federal, state, or local law enforcement official.* The term *arrested,* as used in section 287(d) of the Act (as amended by section 1701 (Subtitle M) of the Anti-Drug Abuse Act of 1986, Pub. L. 99–509), means that an alien has been—

(1) Physically taken into custody for a criminal violation of the controlled substance laws; and

(2) Subsequently booked, charged or otherwise officially processed; or

(3) Provided an initial appearance before a judicial officer where the alien has been informed of the charges and the right to counsel.

(e) *Law enforcement or other official.* The phrase *law enforcement official (or other official),* as used in section 287(d) of the Act, means an officer or employee of an agency engaged in the administration of criminal justice pursuant to statute or executive order, including (1) courts; (2) a government agency or component which performs the administration of criminal justice as defined in 28 CFR part 20 including performance of any of the following activities: detection, apprehension, detention, pretrial release, post-trial release, prosecution, adjudication, correctional supervision, or rehabilitation of accused persons or criminal offenders.

(f) *Controlled substance.* The term *controlled substance,* as used in section 287(d)(3) of the Act, shall mean the same as that referenced in the Controlled Substances Act, 21 U.S.C. 801 *et seq.*, and shall include any substance contained in Schedules I through V of 21 CFR 1308.1 *et seq.* For the purposes of this chapter, the term *controlled substance* includes controlled substance analogues as defined in 21 U.S.C. 802(23) and 813.

(g) *Basic immigration law enforcement training.* The phrase basic immigration law enforcement training, as used in §§ 287.5 and 287.8, means the successful completion of one of the following courses of training provided at the Immigration Officer Academy or Border Patrol Academy: Immigration Officer Basic Training Course after 1971; Border Patrol Basic Training Course after 1950; Immigration Detention Enforcement Officer Basic Training Course after 1977; and Immigration Customs Enforcement Special Agent Training, after 2002; or training substantially equivalent thereto as determined by the Commissioner of CBP or the Assistant Secretary for ICE with respect to personnel in their respective bureaus. The phrase basic immigration law enforcement training also means the successful completion of the Other than Permanent Full-Time (OTP) Immigration Inspector Basic Training Course after 1991 in the case of individuals who are OTP immigration inspectors. Conversion by OTP immigration to any other status requires training applicable to that position.

(h) References to specific titles of officers mean all individuals holding such positions and any individual acting in such position.

(i) Nothing in this part limits the authority of any DHS officers to act pursuant to any authorities that they may otherwise possess.

[22 FR 9808, Dec. 6, 1957, as amended at 29 FR 13244, Sept. 24, 1964; 53 FR 9283, Mar. 22, 1988; 57 FR 47258, Oct. 15, 1992; 59 FR 42415, Aug. 17, 1994; 68 FR 35276, June 13, 2003]

§ 287.2 Disposition of criminal cases.

Whenever a special agent in charge, port director, or chief patrol agent has reason to believe that there has been a violation punishable under any criminal provision of the immigration and nationality laws administered or enforced by the Department, he or she shall immediately initiate an investigation to determine all the pertinent facts and circumstances and shall take such further action as he or she deems necessary. In no case shall this investigation prejudice the right of an arrested person to be taken without unnecessary delay before a United States magistrate judge, a United States district judge, or, if necessary, a judicial officer empowered in accordance with 18 U.S.C. 3041 to commit persons charged with offenses against the laws of the United States.

[59 FR 42415, Aug. 17, 1994, as amended at 68 FR 35276, June 13, 2003]

§ 287.3 Disposition of cases of aliens arrested without warrant.

(a) *Examination.* An alien arrested without a warrant of arrest under the authority contained in section 287(a)(2) of the Act will be examined by an officer other than the arresting officer. If no other qualified officer is readily available and the taking of the alien before another officer would entail unnecessary delay, the arresting officer, if the conduct of such examination is a part of the duties assigned to him or her, may examine the alien.

(b) *Determination of proceedings.* If the examining officer is satisfied that there is prima facie evidence that the arrested alien was entering, attempting to enter, or is present in the United States in violation of the immigration laws, the examining officer will refer the case to an immigration judge for further inquiry in accordance with 8

CFR parts 235, 239, or 240, order the alien removed as provided for in section 235(b)(1) of the Act and §235.3(b) of this chapter, or take whatever other action may be appropriate or required under the laws or regulations applicable to the particular case.

(c) *Notifications and information.* Except in the case of an alien subject to the expedited removal provisions of section 235(b)(1)(A) of the Act, an alien arrested without warrant and placed in formal proceedings under section 238 or 240 of the Act will be advised of the reasons for his or her arrest and the right to be represented at no expense to the Government. The examining officer will provide the alien with a list of the available free legal services provided by organizations and attorneys qualified under 8 CFR part 1003 and organizations recognized under §292.2 of this chapter or 8 CFR 1292.2 that are located in the district where the hearing will be held. The examining officer shall note on Form I-862 that such a list was provided to the alien. The officer will also advise the alien that any statement made may be used against him or her in a subsequent proceeding.

(d) *Custody procedures.* Unless voluntary departure has been granted pursuant to subpart C of 8 CFR part 240, a determination will be made within 48 hours of the arrest, except in the event of an emergency or other extraordinary circumstance in which case a determination will be made within an additional reasonable period of time, whether the alien will be continued in custody or released on bond or recognizance and whether a notice to appear and warrant of arrest as prescribed in 8 CFR parts 236 and 239 will be issued.

[62 FR 10390, Mar. 6, 1997, as amended at 66 FR 48335, Sept. 20, 2001; 68 FR 35276, June 13, 2003]

§287.4 Subpoena.

(a) *Who may issue*—(1) *Criminal or civil investigations.* All District Directors; Deputy District Directors; Chief Patrol Agents; Deputy Chief Patrol Agents; Assistant Chief Patrol Agents; Officers in Charge; Patrol Agents in Charge; Assistant Patrol Agents in Charge; Field Operations Supervisors; Special Operations Supervisors; Supervisory Border Patrol Agents; Assistant District Directors, Investigations; Supervisory Criminal Investigators, Anti-Smuggling; Regional Directors; Service Center Directors; Assistant District Directors, Examinations; Director, Detention and Removal; Special Agents in Charge; all Special Agents in supervisory positions; Field Office Directors; Deputy Field Office Directors; and any other immigration officer who has been expressly delegated such authority as provided by 8 CFR 2.1 may issue a subpoena requiring the production of records and evidence for use in criminal or civil investigations.

(2) *Proceedings other than naturalization proceedings*—(i) *Prior to commencement of proceedings.* All District Directors; Deputy District Directors; Chief Patrol Agents; Deputy Chief Patrol Agents; Officers in Charge; Director, Detention and Removal; Special Agents in Charge; Deputy Special Agents in Charge; Resident Agents in Charge; District Field Officers; Field Office Directors; Deputy Field Office Directors; and Port Directors may issue a subpoena requiring the attendance of witnesses or the production of documentary evidence, or both, for use in any proceeding under this chapter I, other than under 8 CFR part 335, or any application made ancillary to the proceeding.

(ii) *Subsequent to commencement of any immigration court proceeding.* Procedures for the issuance of a subpoena after the commencement of proceedings, in cases other than those arising under part 335 of this chapter, are set forth at 8 CFR 1003.35(b) and 1287.4.

(b) *Form of subpoena.* All subpoenas shall be issued on Form I-138.

(1) *Criminal or civil investigations.* The subpoena shall command the person or entity to which it is addressed to attend and to give testimony at a time or place specified. A subpoena shall also command the person or entity to which it is addressed to produce the books, papers, or documents specified in the subpoena. A subpoena may direct the taking of a deposition before an immigration officer of the Department.

(2) *Proceedings other than naturalization proceedings.* Every subpoena issued under the provisions of this section shall state the title of the proceeding and shall command the person to whom

it is directed to attend and to give testimony at a time and place specified. A subpoena shall also command the person to whom it is directed to produce the books, papers, or documents specified in the subpoena. A subpoena may direct the taking of a deposition before an immigration officer of the Department.

(c) *Service.* A subpoena issued under this section may be served by any person, over 18 years of age not a party to the case, designated to make such service by the District Director; Deputy District Director; Chief Patrol Agent; Deputy Chief Patrol Agent; Assistant Chief Patrol Agent; Patrol Agent in Charge; Officer in Charge; Assistant District Director, Investigations; Supervisory Criminal Investigator, Anti-Smuggling; Regional Director; Special Agent in Charge; Deputy Special Agent in Charge; Resident Agent in Charge; District Field Officer; Field Office Director; Deputy Field Office Director; Supervisory Deportation Officer; Supervisory Detention and Deportation Officer; and Port Director having administrative jurisdiction over the office in which the subpoena is issued. The Director, Detention and Removal, shall also have the authority to make such designation. Service of the subpoena shall be made by delivering a copy thereof to the person named therein and by tendering to him/her the fee for one day's attendance and the mileage allowed by law by the United States District Court for the district in which the testimony is to be taken. When the subpoena is issued on behalf of the Department, fee and mileage need not be tendered at the time of service. A record of such service shall be made and attached to the original copy of the subpoena.

(d) *Invoking aid of court.* If a witness neglects or refuses to appear and testify as directed by the subpoena served upon him or her in accordance with the provisions of this section, the officer or immigration judge issuing the subpoena shall request the United States Attorney for the district in which the subpoena was issued to report such neglect or refusal to the United States District Court and to request such court to issue an order requiring the witness to appear and testify and to produce the books, papers, or documents designated in the subpoena.

[50 FR 30134, July 24, 1985; 50 FR 47205, Nov. 15, 1985, as amended at 60 FR 56937, Nov. 13, 1995; 62 FR 10390, Mar. 6, 1997; 67 FR 39260, June 7, 2002; 68 FR 35276, June 13, 2003]

§ 287.5 Exercise of power by immigration officers.

(a) *Power and authority to interrogate and administer oaths.* Any immigration officer is hereby authorized and designated to exercise anywhere in or outside the United States the power conferred by:

(1) Section 287(a)(1) of the Act to interrogate, without warrant, any alien or person believed to be an alien concerning his or her right to be, or to remain, in the United States, and

(2) Section 287(b) of the Act to administer oaths and to take and consider evidence concerning the privilege of any person to enter, reenter, pass through, or reside in the United States; or concerning any matter which is material or relevant to the enforcement of the Act and the administration of the immigration and naturalization functions of the Department.

(b) *Power and authority to patrol the border.* The following immigration officers who have successfully completed basic immigration law enforcement training are hereby authorized and designated to exercise the power to patrol the border conferred by section 287(a)(3) of the Act:

(1) Border patrol agents;

(2) Air and marine agents;

(3) Special agents;

(4) CBP officers;

(5) Supervisory and managerial personnel who are responsible for supervising the activities of those officers listed in this paragraph; and

(6) Immigration officers who need the authority to patrol the border under section 287(a)(3) of the Act in order to effectively accomplish their individual missions and who are designated, individually or as a class, by the Commissioner of CBP, or the Assistant Secretary/Director of ICE.

(c) *Power and authority to arrest.* (1) Arrests of aliens under section 287(a)(2) of the Act for immigration violations. The following immigration officers who have successfully completed basic immigration law enforcement training are hereby authorized and designated to exercise the arrest power conferred by section 287(a)(2) of the Act and in accordance with 8 CFR 287.8(c):

(i) Border patrol agents;

(ii) Air and marine agents;

(iii) Special agents;

(iv) Deportation officers;

(v) CBP officers;

(vi) Immigration enforcement agents;

(vii) Supervisory and managerial personnel who are responsible for supervising the activities of those officers listed in this paragraph; and

(viii) Immigration officers who need the authority to arrest aliens under section 287(a)(2) of the Act in order to effectively accomplish their individual missions and who are designated, individually or as a class, by the Commissioner of CBP, the Assistant Secretary/Director of ICE, or the Director of the USCIS.

(2) Arrests of persons under section 287(a)(4) of the Act for felonies regulating the admission or removal of aliens. The following immigration officers who have successfully completed basic immigration law enforcement training are hereby authorized and designated to exercise the arrest power conferred by section 287(a)(4) of the Act and in accordance with 8 CFR 287.8(c):

(i) Border patrol agents;

(ii) Air and marine agents;

(iii) Special agents;

(iv) Deportation officers;

(v) CBP officers;

(vi) Immigration enforcement agents;

(vii) Supervisory and managerial personnel who are responsible for supervising the activities of those officers listed in this paragraph; and

(viii) Immigration officers who need the authority to arrest persons under section 287(a)(4) of the Act in order to effectively accomplish their individual missions and who are designated, individually or as a class, by the Commissioner of CBP, the Assistant Secretary/Director of ICE, or the Director of the USCIS.

(3) Arrests of persons under section 287(a)(5)(A) of the Act for any offense against the United States. The following immigration officers who have successfully completed basic immigration law enforcement training are hereby authorized and designated to exercise the arrest power conferred by section 287(a)(5)(A) of the Act and in accordance with 8 CFR 287.8(c):

(i) Border patrol agents;

(ii) Air and marine agents;

(iii) Special agents;

(iv) Deportation officers;

(v) CBP officers;

(vi) Supervisory and managerial personnel who are responsible for supervising the activities of those officers listed in this paragraph; and

(vii) Immigration officers who need the authority to arrest persons under section 287(a)(5)(A) of the Act in order to effectively accomplish their individual missions and who are designated, individually or as a class, by the Commissioner of CBP, or the Assistant Secretary/Director of ICE.

(4) Arrests of persons under section 287(a)(5)(B) of the Act for any felony. (i) Section 287(a)(5)(B) of the Act authorizes designated immigration officers, as listed in paragraph (c)(4)(iii) of this section, to arrest persons, without warrant, for any felony cognizable under the laws of the United States if:

(A) The immigration officer has reasonable grounds to believe that the person to be arrested has committed or is committing such a felony;

(B) The immigration officer is performing duties relating to the enforcement of the immigration laws at the time of the arrest;

(C) There is a likelihood of the person escaping before a warrant can be obtained for his or her arrest; and

(D) The immigration officer has been certified as successfully completing a training program that covers such arrests and the standards with respect to the immigration enforcement activities of the Department as defined in 8 CFR 287.8.

(ii) The following immigration officers who have successfully completed basic immigration law enforcement training are hereby authorized and designated to exercise the arrest power conferred by section 287(a)(5)(B) of the Act and in accordance with 8 CFR 287.8(c):

(A) Border patrol agents;

(B) Air and marine agents;

(C) Special agents;

(D) Deportation officers;

(E) CBP officers;

(F) Supervisory and managerial personnel who are responsible for supervising the activities of those officers listed in this paragraph; and

(G) Immigration officers who need the authority to arrest persons under section 287(a)(5)(B) of the Act in order to effectively accomplish their individual missions and who are designated, individually or as a class, by the Commissioner of CBP or the Assistant Secretary/Director of ICE.

(iii) Notwithstanding the authorization and designation set forth in paragraph (c)(4)(ii) of this section, no immigration officer is authorized to make an arrest for any felony under the authority of section 287(a)(5)(B) of the Act until such time as he or she has been certified as successfully completing a training course encompassing such arrests and the standards for enforcement activities are defined in 8 CFR 287.8. Such certification will be valid for the duration of the immigration officer's continuous employment, unless it is suspended or revoked by the Commissioner of CBP or the Assistant Secretary/Director of ICE, or their respective designees, for just cause.

(5) Arrests of persons under section 274(a) of the Act who bring in, transport, or harbor certain aliens, or induce them to enter.

(i) Section 274(a) of the Act authorizes designated immigration officers, as listed in paragraph (c)(5)(ii) of this section, to arrest persons who bring in, transport, or harbor aliens, or induce them to enter the United States in violation of law. When making an arrest, the designated immigration officer shall adhere to the provisions of the enforcement standard governing the conduct of arrests in 8 CFR 287.8(c).

(ii) The following immigration officers who have successfully completed basic immigration law enforcement training are authorized and designated to exercise the arrest power conferred by section 274(a) of the Act:

(A) Border patrol agents;

(B) Air and marine agents;

(C) Special agents;

(D) Deportation officers;

(E) CBP officers;

(F) Supervisory and managerial personnel who are responsible for supervising the activities of those officers listed in this paragraph; and

(G) Immigration officers who need the authority to arrest persons under section 274(a) of the Act in order to effectively accomplish their individual missions and who are designated, individually or as a class, by the Commissioner of CBP or the Assistant Secretary/Director of ICE.

(6) Custody and transportation of previously arrested persons. In addition to the authority to arrest pursuant to a warrant of arrest in paragraph (e)(3)(iv) of this section, detention enforcement officers and immigration enforcement agents who have successfully completed basic immigration law enforcement training are hereby authorized and designated to take and maintain custody of and transport any person who has been arrested by an immigration officer pursuant to paragraphs (c)(1) through (c)(5) of this section.

(d) *Power and authority to conduct searches.* The following immigration officers who have successfully completed basic immigration law enforcement training are hereby authorized and designated to exercise the power to conduct searches conferred by section 287(c) of the Act:

(1) Border patrol agents;

(2) Air and marine agents;

(3) Special agents;

(4) Deportation officers;

(5) CBP officers;

(6) Immigration enforcement agents;

(7) Supervisory and managerial personnel who are responsible for supervising the activities of those officers listed in this paragraph; and

(8) Immigration officers who need the authority to conduct searches under section 287(c) of the Act in order to effectively accomplish their individual missions and who are designated, individually or as a class, by the Commissioner of CBP, the Assistant Secretary/Director of ICE, or the Director of USCIS.

(e) *Power and authority to execute warrants*—(1) *Search warrants.* The following immigration officers who have successfully completed basic immigration law enforcement training are hereby authorized and designated to exercise the power conferred by section

287(a) of the Act to execute a search warrant:

(i) Border patrol agents;

(ii) Air and marine agents;

(iii) CBP officers;

(iv) Special agents;

(v) Deportation officers;

(vi) Immigration enforcement agents;

(vii) Supervisory and managerial personnel who are responsible for supervising the activities of those officers listed in this paragraph; and

(viii) Immigration officers who need the authority to execute search warrants under section 287(a) of the Act in order to effectively accomplish their individual missions and who are designated, individually or as a class, by the Commissioner of CBP or the Assistant Secretary/Director of ICE.

(2) *Issuance of arrest warrants for immigration violations.* A warrant of arrest may be issued by any of the following immigration officials who have been authorized or delegated such authority:

(i) District directors (except foreign);

(ii) Deputy district directors (except foreign);

(iii) Assistant district directors for investigations;

(iv) Deputy assistant district directors for investigations;

(v) Assistant district directors for deportation;

(vi) Deputy assistant district directors for deportation;

(vii) Assistant district directors for examinations;

(viii) Deputy assistant district directors for examinations;

(ix) Officers in charge (except foreign);

(x) Assistant officers in charge (except foreign);

(xi) Chief patrol agents;

(xii) Deputy chief patrol agents;

(xiii) Division chiefs;

(xiv) Assistant chief patrol agents;

(xv) Patrol agents in charge;

(xvi) Deputy patrol agents in charge;

(xvii) Border Patrol watch commanders;

(xviii) Special operations supervisors;

(xix) Supervisory border patrol agents;

(xx) Directors of air operations;

(xxi) Directors of marine operations;

(xxii) Supervisory air and marine interdiction agents;

(xxiii) Executive Associate Director of Homeland Security Investigations;

(xxiv) Institutional Hearing Program directors;

(xxv) Director, Field Operations;

(xxvi) Assistant Director, Field Operations;

(xxvii) Port directors;

(xxviii) Assistant port directors;

(xxix) Field operations watch commanders;

(xxx) Field operations chiefs;

(xxxi) Supervisory deportation officers;

(xxxii) Supervisory detention and deportation officers;

(xxxiii) Group Supervisors;

(xxxiv) Director, Office of Detention and Removal Operations;

(xxxv) Special Agents in Charge;

(xxxvi) Deputy Special Agents in Charge;

(xxxvii) Associate Special Agents in Charge;

(xxxviii) Assistant Special Agents in Charge;

(xxxix) Field Office Directors;

(xl) Deputy Field Office Directors;

(xli) District Field Officers;

(xlii) Supervisory immigration services officers;

(xliii) Supervisory immigration officers;

(xliv) Supervisory asylum officers;

(xlv) Supervisory special agents;

(xlvi) Director of investigations;

(xlvii) Directors or officers in charge of detention facilities;

(xlviii) Directors of field operations;

(xlix) Deputy or assistant directors of field operations;

(l) Unit Chief, Law Enforcement Support Center;

(li) Section Chief, Law Enforcement Support Center;

(lii) Immigration Enforcement Agents; or

(liii) Other duly authorized officers or employees of the Department of Homeland Security or the United States who are delegated the authority as provided in 8 CFR 2.1 to issue warrants of arrest, and who have successfully completed any required immigration law enforcement training.

(3) *Service of warrant of arrests for immigration violations.* The following immigration officers who have successfully completed basic immigration law

enforcement training are hereby authorized and designated to exercise the power pursuant to section 287(a) of the Act to execute warrants of arrest for administrative immigration violations issued under section 236 of the Act or to execute warrants of criminal arrest issued under the authority of the United States:

(i) Border patrol agents;

(ii) Air and marine agents;

(iii) Special agents;

(iv) Deportation officers;

(v) Detention enforcement officers or immigration enforcement agents (warrants of arrest for administrative immigration violations only);

(vi) CBP officers;

(vii) Supervisory and managerial personnel who are responsible for supervising the activities of those officers listed in this paragraph; and

(viii) Immigration officers who need the authority to execute arrest warrants for immigration violations under section 287(a) of the Act in order to effectively accomplish their individual missions and who are designated, individually or as a class, by the Commissioner of CBP or the Assistant Secretary/Director of ICE.

(4) *Service of warrant of arrests for non-immigration violations*. The following immigration officers who have successfully completed basic immigration law enforcement training are hereby authorized and designated to exercise the power to execute warrants of criminal arrest for non-immigration violations issued under the authority of the United States:

(i) Border patrol agents;

(ii) Air and marine agents;

(iii) CBP officers

(iv) Special agents;

(v) Deportation officers;

(vi) Immigration enforcement agents;

(vii) Supervisory and managerial personnel who are responsible for supervising the activities of those officers listed in this paragraph; and

(viii) Immigration officers who need the authority to execute warrants of arrest for non-immigration violations under section 287(a) of the Act in order to effectively accomplish their individual missions and who are designated, individually or as a class, by the Commissioner of CBP or the Assistant Secretary/Director of ICE.

(f) *Power and authority to carry firearms*. The following immigration officers who have successfully completed basic immigration enforcement training are hereby authorized and designated to exercise the power conferred by section 287(a) of the Act to carry firearms provided that they are individually qualified by training and experience to handle and safely operate the firearms they are permitted to carry, maintain proficiency in the use of such firearms, and adhere to the provisions of the enforcement standard governing the use of force in 8 CFR 287.8(a):

(1) Border patrol agents;

(2) Air and marine agents;

(3) Special agents;

(4) Deportation officers;

(5) Detention enforcement officers or immigration enforcement agents;

(6) CBP officers;

(7) Supervisory and managerial personnel who are responsible for supervising the activities of those officers listed in this paragraph; and

(8) Immigration officers who need the authority to carry firearms under section 287(a) of the Act in order to effectively accomplish their individual missions and who are designated, individually or as a class, by the Commissioner of CBP or the Assistant Secretary/Director of ICE.

[68 FR 35277, June 13, 2003, as amended at 70 FR 67089, Nov. 4, 2005; 76 FR 53797, Aug. 29, 2011; 81 FR 62356, Sept. 9, 2016]

§ 287.6 Proof of official records.

(a) *Domestic*. In any proceeding under this chapter, an official record or entry therein, when admissible for any purpose, shall be evidenced by an official publication thereof, or by a copy attested by the official having legal custody of the record or by an authorized deputy.

(b) *Foreign: Countries not Signatories to Convention*. (1) In any proceeding under this chapter, an official record or entry therein, when admissible for any purpose, shall be evidenced by an official publication thereof, or by a copy attested by an officer so authorized. This attested copy in turn may but need not be certified by any authorized foreign officer both as to the genuineness of the signature of the attesting officer and as to his/her official position. The signature and official position of this certifying foreign officer may then likewise be certified by any other foreign officer so authorized, thereby creating a chain of certificates.

(2) The attested copy, with the additional foreign certificates if any, must be certified by an officer in the Foreign Service of the United States, stationed in the foreign country where the record is kept. This officer must certify the genuineness of the signature and the official position either of (i) the attesting officer; or (ii) any foreign officer whose certification of genuineness of signature and official position relates directly to the attestation or is in a chain of certificates of genuineness of signature and official position relating to the attestation.

(c) *Foreign: Countries Signatory to Convention Abolishing the Requirement of Legislation for Foreign Public Document.* (1) In any proceeding under this chapter, a public document or entry therein, when admissible for any purpose, may be evidenced by an official publication, or by a copy properly certified under the Convention. To be properly certified, the copy must be accompanied by a certificate in the form dictated by the Convention. This certificate must be signed by a foreign officer so authorized by the signatory country, and it must certify (i) the authenticity of the signature of the person signing the document; (ii) the capacity in which that person acted, and (iii) where appropriate, the identity of the seal or stamp which the document bears.

(2) No certification is needed from an officer in the Foreign Service of public documents.

(3) In accordance with the Convention, the following are deemed to be public documents:

(i) Documents emanating from an authority or an official connected with the courts of tribunals of the state, including those emanating from a public prosecutor, a clerk of a court or a process server;

(ii) Administrative documents;

(iii) Notarial acts; and

(iv) Official certificates which are placed on documents signed by persons in their private capacity, such as official certificates recording the registration of a document or the fact that it was in existence on a certain date, and official and notarial authentication of signatures.

(4) In accordance with the Convention, the following are deemed not to be public documents, and thus are subject to the more stringent requirements of § 287.6(b) above:

(i) Documents executed by diplomatic or consular agents; and

(ii) Administrative documents dealing directly with commercial or customs operations.

(d) *Canada.* In any proceedings under this chapter, an official record or entry therein, issued by a Canadian governmental entity within the geographical boundaries of Canada, when admissible for any purpose, shall be evidenced by a certified copy of the original record attested by the official having legal custody of the record or by an authorized deputy.

[50 FR 37834, Sept. 18, 1985, as amended at 54 FR 39337, Sept. 26, 1989; 54 FR 48851, Nov. 28, 1989]

§ 287.7 Detainer provisions under section 287(d)(3) of the Act.

(a) *Detainers in general.* Detainers are issued pursuant to sections 236 and 287 of the Act and this chapter 1. Any authorized immigration officer may at any time issue a Form I–247, Immigration Detainer-Notice of Action, to any other Federal, State, or local law enforcement agency. A detainer serves to advise another law enforcement agency that the Department seeks custody of an alien presently in the custody of that agency, for the purpose of arresting and removing the alien. The detainer is a request that such agency advise the Department, prior to release of the alien, in order for the Department to arrange to assume custody, in situations when gaining immediate physical custody is either impracticable or impossible.

(b) *Authority to issue detainers.* The following officers are authorized to issue detainers:

(1) Border patrol agents, including aircraft pilots;

(2) Special agents;

(3) Deportation officers;

(4) Immigration inspectors;

(5) Adjudications officers;

(6) Immigration enforcement agents;

(7) Supervisory and managerial personnel who are responsible for supervising the activities of those officers listed in this paragraph; and

(8) Immigration officers who need the authority to issue detainers under section 287(d)(3) of the Act in order to effectively accomplish their individual missions and who are designated individually or as a class, by the Commissioner of CBP, the Assistant Secretary for ICE, or the Director of the USCIS.

(c) *Availability of records.* In order for the Department to accurately determine the propriety of issuing a detainer, serving a notice to appear, or taking custody of an alien in accordance with this section, the criminal justice agency requesting such action or informing the Department of a conviction or act that renders an alien inadmissible or removable under any provision of law shall provide the Department with all documentary records and information available from the agency that reasonably relates to the alien's status in the United States, or that may have an impact on conditions of release.

(d) *Temporary detention at Department request.* Upon a determination by the Department to issue a detainer for an alien not otherwise detained by a criminal justice agency, such agency shall maintain custody of the alien for a period not to exceed 48 hours, excluding Saturdays, Sundays, and holidays in order to permit assumption of custody by the Department.

(e) *Financial responsibility for detention.* No detainer issued as a result of a determination made under this chapter I shall incur any fiscal obligation on the part of the Department, until actual assumption of custody by the Department, except as provided in paragraph (d) of this section.

[68 FR 35279, June 13, 2003, as amended at 76 FR 53797, Aug. 29, 2011]

§ 287.8 Standards for enforcement activities.

The following standards for enforcement activities contained in this section must be adhered to by every immigration officer involved in enforcement activities. Any violation of this section shall be reported to the Office of the Inspector General or such other entity as may be provided for in 8 CFR 287.10.

(a) *Use of force*—(1) *Non-deadly force.* (i) Non-deadly force is any use of force other than that which is considered deadly force as defined in paragraph (a)(2) of this section.

(ii) Non-deadly force may be used only when a designated immigration officer, as listed in paragraph (a)(1)(iv) of this section, has reasonable grounds to believe that such force is necessary.

(iii) A designated immigration officer shall always use the minimum non-deadly force necessary to accomplish the officer's mission and shall escalate to a higher level of non-deadly force only when such higher level of force is warranted by the actions, apparent intentions, and apparent capabilities of the suspect, prisoner, or assailant.

(iv) The following immigration officers who have successfully completed basic immigration law enforcement training are hereby authorized and designated to exercise the power conferred by section 287(a) of the Act to use non-deadly force should circumstances warrant it:

(A) Border patrol agents;

(B) Air and marine agents;

(C) Special agents;

(D) Deportation officers;

(E) Detention enforcement officers or immigration enforcement agents;

(F) CBP officers;

(G) Supervisory and managerial personnel who are responsible for supervising the activities of those officers listed in this paragraph; and

(H) Immigration officers who need the authority to use non-deadly force under section 287(a) of the Act in order to effectively accomplish their individual missions and who are designated, individually or as a class, by the Commissioner of CBP or the Assistant Secretary/Director of ICE.

(2) *Deadly force.* (i) Deadly force is any use of force that is likely to cause death or serious physical injury.

(ii) Deadly force may be used only when a designated immigration officer, as listed in paragraph (a)(2)(iii) of this section, has reasonable grounds to believe that such force is necessary to protect the designated immigration officer or other persons from the imminent danger of death or serious physical injury.

(iii) The following immigration officers who have successfully completed basic immigration law enforcement training are hereby authorized and designated to exercise the power conferred by section 287(a) of the Act to use deadly force should circumstances warrant it:

(A) Border patrol agents;

(B) Air and marine agents;

(C) Special agents

(D) Deportation officers;

(E) Detention enforcement officers or immigration enforcement agents;

(F) CBP officers;

(G) Supervisory and managerial personnel who are responsible for supervising the activities of those officers listed above; and

(H) Immigration officers who need the authority to use deadly force under section 287(a) of the Act in order to effectively accomplish their individual missions and who are designated, individually or as a class, by the Commissioner of CBP or the Assistant Secretary/Director of ICE.

(b) *Interrogation and detention not amounting to arrest.* (1) Interrogation is questioning designed to elicit specific information. An immigration officer, like any other person, has the right to ask questions of anyone as long as the immigration officer does not restrain the freedom of an individual, not under arrest, to walk away.

(2) If the immigration officer has a reasonable suspicion, based on specific articulable facts, that the person being questioned is, or is attempting to be, engaged in an offense against the United States or is an alien illegally in the United States, the immigration officer may briefly detain the person for questioning.

(3) Information obtained from this questioning may provide the basis for a subsequent arrest, which must be effected only by a designated immigration officer, as listed in 8 CFR 287.5(c). The conduct of arrests is specified in paragraph (c) of this section.

(c) *Conduct of arrests*—(1) *Authority.* Only designated immigration officers are authorized to make an arrest. The list of designated immigration officers may vary depending on the type of arrest as listed in § 287.5(c)(1) through (c)(5).

(2) *General procedures.* (i) An arrest shall be made only when the designated immigration officer has reason to believe that the person to be arrested has committed an offense against the United States or is an alien illegally in the United States.

(ii) A warrant of arrest shall be obtained except when the designated immigration officer has reason to believe that the person is likely to escape before a warrant can be obtained.

(iii) At the time of the arrest, the designated immigration officer shall, as soon as it is practical and safe to do so:

(A) Identify himself or herself as an immigration officer who is authorized to execute an arrest; and

(B) State that the person is under arrest and the reason for the arrest.

(iv) With respect to an alien arrested and administratively charged with being in the United States in violation of law, the arresting officer shall adhere to the procedures set forth in 8 CFR 287.3 if the arrest is made without a warrant.

(v) With respect to a person arrested and charged with a criminal violation of the laws of the United States, the arresting officer shall advise the person of the appropriate rights as required by law at the time of the arrest, or as soon thereafter as practicable. It is the duty of the immigration officer to assure that the warnings are given in a language the subject understands, and that the subject acknowledges that the warnings are understood. The fact that a person has been advised of his or her rights shall be documented on appropriate Department forms and made a part of the arrest record.

(vi) Every person arrested and charged with a criminal violation of the laws of the United States shall be brought without unnecessary delay before a United States magistrate judge, a United States district judge or, if necessary, a judicial officer empowered in accordance with 18 U.S.C. 3041 to commit persons charged with such crimes. Accordingly, the immigration officer shall contact an Assistant United States Attorney to arrange for an initial appearance.

(vii) The use of threats, coercion, or physical abuse by the designated immigration officer to induce a suspect to waive his or her rights or to make a statement is prohibited.

(d) *Transportation*—(1) *Vehicle transportation.* All persons will be transported in a manner that ensures the safety of the persons being transported. When persons arrested or detained are being transported by vehicle, each person will be searched as thoroughly as circumstances permit before being placed in the vehicle. The person being transported shall not be handcuffed to the frame or any part of the moving vehicle or an object in the moving vehicle. The person being transported shall not be left unattended during transport unless the immigration officer needs to perform a law enforcement function.

(2) *Airline transportation.* Escorting officers must abide by all Federal Aviation Administration, Transportation Security Administration, and airline carrier rules and regulations pertaining to weapons and the transportation of prisoners.

(e) *Vehicular pursuit.* (1) A vehicular pursuit is an active attempt by a designated immigration officer, as listed in paragraph (e)(2) of this section, in a designated pursuit vehicle to apprehend fleeing suspects who are attempting to avoid apprehension. A designated pursuit vehicle is defined as a vehicle equipped with emergency lights and siren, placed in or on the vehicle, that emit audible and visual signals in order to warn others that emergency law enforcement activities are in progress.

(2) The following immigration officers who have successfully completed basic immigration law enforcement training are hereby authorized and designated to initiate a vehicular pursuit:

(i) Border patrol agents;

(ii) Air and marine agents;

(iii) CBP officers;

(iv) Supervisory personnel who are responsible for supervising the activities of those officers listed in this paragraph; and

(v) Immigration officers who need the authority to initiate a vehicular pursuit in order to effectively accomplish their individual mission and who are designated, individually or as a class, by the Commissioner of CBP or the Assistant Secretary/Director of ICE.

(f) *Site inspections.* (1) Site inspections are Border and Transportation Security Directorate enforcement activities undertaken to locate and identify aliens illegally in the United States, or aliens engaged in unauthorized employment, at locations where there is a reasonable suspicion, based on articulable facts, that such aliens are present.

(2) An immigration officer may not enter into the non-public areas of a business, a residence including the curtilage of such residence, or a farm or other outdoor agricultural operation, except as provided in section 287(a)(3) of the Act, for the purpose of questioning the occupants or employees concerning their right to be or remain in the United States unless the officer has either a warrant or the consent of the owner or other person in control of the site to be inspected. When consent to enter is given, the immigration officer must note on the officer's report that consent was given and, if possible, by whom consent was given. If the immigration officer is denied access to conduct a site inspection, a warrant may be obtained.

(3) Adequate records must be maintained noting the results of every site inspection, including those where no illegal aliens are located.

(4) Nothing in this section prohibits an immigration officer from entering into any area of a business or other activity to which the general public has access or onto open fields that are not farms or other outdoor agricultural operations without a warrant, consent, or any particularized suspicion in order to question any person whom the officer believes to be an alien concerning his or her right to be or remain in the United States.

(g) *Guidelines.* The criminal law enforcement authorities authorized under this part will be exercised in a manner consistent with all applicable guidelines and policies of the Department of

Justice and the Department of Homeland Security.

[68 FR 35280, June 13, 2003, as amended at 81 FR 62357, Sept. 9, 2016]

§287.9 Criminal search warrant and firearms policies.

(a) A search warrant should be obtained prior to conducting a search in a criminal investigation unless a specific exception to the warrant requirement is authorized by statute or recognized by the courts. Such exceptions may include, for example, the consent of the person to be searched, exigent circumstances, searches incident to a lawful arrest, and border searches. The Commissioner of CBP and the Assistant Secretary of ICE shall promulgate guidelines governing officers' conduct relating to search and seizure.

(b) In using a firearm, an immigration officer shall adhere to the standard of conduct set forth in 8 CFR 287.8(a)(2). An immigration officer may carry only firearms (whether Department issued or personally owned) that have been approved pursuant to guidelines promulgated by the Commissioner of CBP or the Assistant Secretary for ICE. These officials shall promulgate guidelines with respect to:

(1) Investigative procedures to be followed after a shooting incident involving an officer;

(2) Loss or theft of an approved firearm;

(3) Maintenance of records with respect to the issuance of firearms and ammunition; and

(4) Procedures for the proper care, storage, and maintenance of firearms, ammunition, and related equipment.

[59 FR 42420, Aug. 17, 1994, as amended at 68 FR 35280, June 13, 2003]

§287.10 Expedited internal review process.

(a) *Violations of standards for enforcement activities.* Alleged violations of the standards for enforcement activities established in accordance with the provisions of §287.8 shall be investigated expeditiously consistent with the policies and procedures of the Department of Homeland Security and pursuant to any guidelines issued by the Secretary.

(b) *Complaints.* Any persons wishing to lodge a complaint pertaining to violations of enforcement standards contained in §287.8 may contact the Department of Homeland Security, Office of the Inspector General, 245 Murray Drive—Building 410, Washington, DC, 20548, or telephone 1–800–323–8603. With respect to employees of the former INS, persons may contact the Office of Internal Audit, Bureau of Immigration and Customs Enforcement, 425 I Street NW., Washington, DC, 20536.

(c) *Expedited processing of complaints.* When an allegation or complaint of violation of §287.8 is lodged against an employee or officer of the Department, the allegation or complaint shall be referred promptly for investigation in accordance with the policies and procedures of the Department. At the conclusion of an investigation of an allegation or complaint of violation of §287.8, the investigative report shall be referred promptly for appropriate action in accordance with the policies and procedures of the Department.

(d) *Unsubstantiated complaints.* When an investigative report does not support the allegation, the employee or officer against whom the allegation was made shall be informed in writing that the matter has been closed as soon as practicable. No reference to the allegation shall be filed in the official's or employee's official personnel file.

(e) *Jurisdiction of Department of Justice organizations.* Nothing in this section alters or limits, is intended to alter or limit, or shall be construed to alter or limit, the jurisdiction or authority conferred upon the Federal Bureau of Investigation, the United States Attorneys, the Criminal Division or the Civil Rights Division, or any other component of the Department of Justice that may have jurisdiction regarding criminal violations of law.

[68 FR 35281, June 13, 2003]

§287.11 Pre-enrolled Access Lane.

(a) *Pre-enrolled Access Lane* (PAL). A PAL is a designated traffic lane located at a Service checkpoint, which, when in operation, may be used exclusively by enrolled participants and their passengers in vehicles authorized by the Service to pass through the checkpoint.

(b) *General requirements for Pre-enrolled Access Lane Program.* (1) Participation in the Pre-enrolled Access Lane program is wholly voluntary and failure to apply or denial of an application does not prevent any person from passing through the checkpoint in the regular traffic lanes.

(2) Only United States citizens and members of the classes of aliens which the Commissioner of the Service or her delegates determine to be eligible may enroll in the PAL program. To participate in the PAL program, an applicant must have a permanent or temporary residence in the United States, and must agree to furnish all information requested on the application.

(3) The applicant must agree to all terms and conditions required for use of a Pre-enrolled Access Lane. Immigration, criminal justice information, and law enforcement records and databases will be checked to assist in determining the applicant's eligibility. The Service may require applicants to submit fingerprints, and the Service may provide those fingerprints to Federal, State, and local government agencies for the purpose of determining eligibility to participate in the PAL program.

(4) Any vehicle used in a Pre-enrolled Access Lane must have current approval from the Service for use in the PAL program.

(5) Enrolled participants may be issued an identification document showing authorization to participate in the PAL program, and, if such a document is issued, participants must have it in their possession whenever using the PAL. In addition, alien participants must be in possession of a valid form constituting evidence of alien registration pursuant to § 264.1(b) of this chapter at all times while using the PAL.

(6) The Service will install any and all equipment, decals, devices, technology, or methodology it deems necessary on registered vehicles to ensure that only authorized persons and vehicles use the PAL.

(7) All devices, decals, or other equipment, methodology, or technology used to identify persons or vehicles using a Pre-enrolled Access Lane remain the property of the United States Government at all times and must be surrendered upon request of the Service. Enrolled participants must abide by the terms set forth by the Service for use of any device, decal, or other equipment, methodology, or technology. If a vehicle is sold or otherwise disposed of, it is the responsibility of the enrolled participant to remove or obliterate any identifying decal or other authorization for participation in the PAL program before or at the time of sale or disposal unless otherwise notified by the Service. If the Service installs an electronic transmitter or similar device on the vehicle, the enrolled participant must have that device removed by the Service at the PAL enrollment center prior to sale or disposal of an authorized vehicle.

(8) Enrolled participants in the PAL program may carry passengers who are not enrolled in the program in their authorized vehicles in the PAL as long as all passengers are United States citizens, lawful permanent residents of the United States, or rightful holders of valid nonimmigrant United States visas.

(c) *Application.* (1) Application for Pre-enrolled Access Lane participation shall be made on Form I–866, Application—Checkpoint Pre-enrolled Access Lane.

(2) Each person wishing to enroll in the Pre-enrolled Access Lane program must submit a separate application.

(3) Applications must be supported by documents establishing identity, United States citizenship or lawful immigration status in the United States, a valid driver's license, and vehicle registration for all vehicles being registered. The Service may require additional documentation where appropriate to substantiate information provided on the application, as well as written permission from the vehicle owner to use any vehicle not owned by the applicant in the PAL.

(4) Each person filing an application may be required to present himself or herself for an interview at a time and place designated by the Service prior to approval of the application.

(5) The Service may inspect any vehicle that a PAL applicant desires to register for use in the PAL to ensure that it does not present evidence of having

been used or prepared to be used to smuggle aliens or controlled substances, and the Service must approve all vehicles prior to use in the PAL. The Service may prohibit the use of certain types of vehicles in the PAL for reasons of safety and law enforcement.

(6) An application may be denied by the Chief Patrol Agent having jurisdiction over the PAL enrollment center where the application is filed. Written notice of the decision on the application shall be given to the applicant or mailed by ordinary mail to the applicant's last known address. There is no appeal from a denial, but denial is without prejudice to reapplying for this program. Re-applications following denial or revocation of the privilege to participate in the PAL program will not be considered by the Service until 90 days after the date of denial or revocation.

(7) Registration in the PAL program is limited to individuals who the Service has determined present a low risk of using the PAL for unlawful purposes. Criteria that will be considered in the decision to approve or deny the application include the following: lawful presence in the United States, criminal history and/or evidence of criminality, employment, residency, prior immigration history, possession of a valid driver's license, vehicle type, registration, and inspection.

(8) Applications approved by the Service will entitle the authorized person and the authorized vehicle to use the PAL for 2 years from the date of approval of the application or until authorization is revoked, whichever occurs first.

(d) *Acknowledgments and agreements.* By signing and submitting the Form I-866 each applicant acknowledges and agrees to all of the conditions for participation in the PAL program and the statements on the Form I-866.

(e) *Violation of conditions of a Pre-enrolled Access Lane and Revocation.* An enrolled participant who violates any condition of the PAL program, or any applicable law or regulation, or who is otherwise determined by an immigration officer to be ineligible to participate in the PAL program, may have his or her authorization and the authorization of his or her vehicle(s) revoked by the Chief Patrol Agent with jurisdiction over the PAL enrollment center where the application is filed and may be subject to other applicable sanctions, such as criminal and/or civil penalties, removal, and/or possible seizure of goods and/or vehicles. If an authorized vehicle is sold, stolen, or otherwise disposed of, authorization to use that vehicle in the PAL is automatically revoked. Within 24 hours of when an authorized vehicle is stolen, or within 7 days of when such vehicle is sold, or otherwise disposed of or the license plates are changed, enrolled participants must give, in person or by facsimile transmission, written notice of such occurrence to the PAL enrollment center at which their application was filed. Failure to do so will result in the automatic revocation of the authorization to use the PAL of the person who registered such vehicle in the PAL program. Unless revocation is automatic, the Service will give notice of revocation to the enrolled PAL participant or mail it by ordinary mail to his or her last known address. However, written notification is not necessary prior to revocation of the privilege to participate in the PAL program. There is no appeal from the revocation of an authorization to participate in the PAL program.

(f) *No benefits or rights conferred.* This section does not, is not intended to, shall not be construed to, and may not be relied upon to confer any immigration benefit or status to any alien or create any rights, substantive or procedural, enforceable in law or equity by any party in any matter.

[62 FR 19025, Apr. 18, 1997]

§ 287.12 Scope.

With regard to this part, these regulations provide internal guidance on specific areas of law enforcement authority. These regulations do not, are not intended to, and shall not be construed to exclude, supplant, or limit otherwise lawful activities of the Department or the Secretary. These regulations do not, are not intended to, shall not be construed to, and may not be relied upon to create any rights, substantive or procedural, enforceable at law by any party in any matter, civil or criminal. The Secretary shall have exclusive authority to enforce these regulations through such administrative and other means as he may deem appropriate.

[68 FR 35282, June 13, 2003]

PART 289—AMERICAN INDIANS BORN IN CANADA

AUTHORITY: Secs. 103, 262, 289, 66 Stat. 173, 224, 234; 8 U.S.C. 1103, 1302, 1359; 45 Stat. 401, 54 Stat. 670; 8 U.S.C. 226a, 451.

§ 289.1 Definition.

The term *American Indian born in Canada* as used in section 289 of the Act includes only persons possessing 50 per centum or more of the blood of the American Indian race. It does not include a person who is the spouse or child of such an Indian or a person whose membership in an Indian tribe or family is created by adoption, unless such person possesses at least 50 per centum or more of such blood.

[29 FR 11494, Aug. 11, 1964]

§ 289.2 Lawful admission for permanent residence.

Any American Indian born in Canada who at the time of entry was entitled to the exemption provided for such person by the Act of April 2, 1928 (45 Stat. 401), or section 289 of the Act, and has maintained residence in the United States since his entry, shall be regarded as having been lawfully admitted for permanent residence. A person who does not possess 50 per centum of the blood of the American Indian race, but who entered the United States prior to December 24, 1952, under the exemption provided by the Act of April 2, 1928, and has maintained his residence in the United States since such entry shall also be regarded as having been lawfully admitted for permanent residence. In the absence of a Service record of arrival in the United States, the record of registration under the Alien Registration Act, of 1940 (54 Stat. 670; 8 U.S.C. 451), or section 262 of the Act, or other satisfactory evidence may be accepted to establish the date of entry.

[29 FR 11494, Aug. 11, 1964]

§ 289.3 Recording the entry of certain American Indians born in Canada.

The lawful admission for permanent residence of an American Indian born in Canada shall be recorded on Form I–181.

[33 FR 7485, May 21, 1968]

PART 292—REPRESENTATION AND APPEARANCES

AUTHORITY: 6 U.S.C. 112; 8 U.S.C. 1103, 1252b, 1362.

§ 292.1 Representation of others.

(a) A person entitled to representation may be represented by any of the following, subject to the limitations in 8 CFR 103.2(a)(3):

(1) *Attorneys in the United States.* Any attorney as defined in8 CFR 1.2.

(2) *Law students and law graduates not yet admitted to the bar.* A law student who is enrolled in an accredited U.S. law school, or a graduate of an accredited U.S. law school who is not yet admitted to the bar, provided that:

(i) He or she is appearing at the request of the person entitled to representation;

(ii) In the case of a law student, he or she has filed a statement that he or she is participating, under the direct supervision of a faculty member, licensed attorney, or accredited representative, in a legal aid program or clinic conducted by a law school or non-profit organization, and that he or she is appearing without direct or indirect remuneration from the alien he or she represents;

(iii) In the case of a law graduate, he or she has filed a statement that he or she is appearing under the supervision of a licensed attorney or accredited representative and that he or she is appearing without direct or indirect remuneration from the alien he or she represents; and

(iv) The law student's or law graduate's appearance is permitted by the DHS official before whom he or she wishes to appear. The DHS official may require that a law student be accompanied by the supervising faculty member, attorney, or accredited representative.

(3) *Reputable individuals.* Any reputable individual of good moral character, provided that:

(i) He is appearing on an individual case basis, at the request of the person entitled to representation;

(ii) He is appearing without direct or indirect renumeration and files a written declaration to that effect;

(iii) He has a pre-existing relationship or connection with the person entitled to representation (e.g., as a relative, neighbor, clergyman, business associate or personal friend), provided that such requirement may be waived, as a matter of administrative discretion, in cases where adequate representation would not otherwise be available; and

(iv) His or her appearance is permitted by the DHS official before whom he or she seeks to appear, provided that such permission will not be granted with respect to any individual who regularly engages in immigration and naturalization practice or preparation, or holds himself or herself out to the public as qualified to do so.

(4) *Accredited representatives.* A person representing an organization described in §292.2 of this chapter who has been accredited by the Board.

(5) *Accredited officials.* An accredited official, in the United States, of the government to which an alien owes allegiance, if the official appears solely in his official capacity and with the alien's consent.

(6) *Attorneys outside the United States.* An attorney, other than one described in 8 CFR 1.2, who is licensed to practice law and is in good standing in a court of general jurisdiction of the country in which he or she resides and who is engaged in such practice, may represent parties in matters before DHS, provided that he or she represents persons only in matters outside the geographical confines of the United States as defined in section 101(a)(38) of the Act, and that the DHS official before whom he or she wishes to appear allows such representation as a matter of discretion.

(b) *Persons formerly authorized to practice.* A person, other than a representative of an organization described in §292.2 of this chapter, who on December 23, 1952, was authorized to practice before the Board and the Service may continue to act as a representative, subject to the provisions of §292.3 of this chapter.

(c) *Former employees.* No person previously employed by the Department of Justice shall be permitted to act as a representative in any case in violation of the provisions of 28 CFR 45.735–7.

(d) *Amicus curiae.* The Board may grant permission to appear, on a case-by-case basis, as amicus curiae, to an attorney or to an organization represented by an attorney, if the public interest will be served thereby.

(e) Except as set forth in this section, no other person or persons shall represent others in any case.

[40 FR 23271, May 29, 1975, as amended at 53 FR 7728, Mar. 10, 1988; 55 FR 49251, Nov. 27, 1990; 61 FR 53610, Oct. 15, 1996; 62 FR 23635, May 1, 1997; 75 FR 5227, Feb. 2, 2010; 76 FR 53797, Aug. 29, 2011]

§292.2 Organizations qualified for recognition; requests for recognition; withdrawal of recognition; accreditation of representatives; roster.

(a) *Qualifications of organizations.* A non-profit religious, charitable, social service, or similar organization established in the United States and recognized as such by the Board may designate a representative or representatives to practice before the Service alone or the Service and the Board (including practice before the Immigration Court). Such organization must establish to the satisfaction of the Board that:

(1) It makes only nominal charges and assesses no excessive membership dues for persons given assistance; and

(2) It has at its disposal adequate knowledge, information and experience.

(b) *Requests for recognition.* An organization having the qualifications prescribed in paragraph (a) of this section may file an application for recognition on a Form G–27 directly with the Board, along with proof of service of a copy of the application on the district director having jurisdiction over the area in which the organization is located. The district director, within 30 days from the date of service, shall forward to the Board a recommendation for approval or disapproval of the application and the reasons therefor, or request a specified period of time in which to conduct an investigation or otherwise obtain relevant information regarding the applicant. The district director shall include proof of service of a copy of such recommendation or request on the organization. The organization shall have 30 days in which to file a response with the Board to a recommendation by a district director that is other than favorable, along with proof of service of a copy of such response on the district director. If the Board approves a request for time to conduct an investigation, or in its discretion remands the application to the district director for further information, the organization shall be advised of the time granted for such purpose. The Service shall promptly forward the results of any investigation or inquiry to the Board, along with its recommendations for approval or disapproval and the reasons therefor, and proof of service of a copy of the submission on the organization. The organization shall have 30 days from the date of such service to file a response with the Board to any matters raised therein, with proof of service of a copy of the response on the district director. Requests for extensions of filing times must be submitted in writing with the reasons therefor and may be granted by the Board in its discretion. Oral argument may be heard before the Board in its discretion at such date and time as the Board may direct. The organization and Service shall be informed by the Board of the action taken regarding an application. Any recognized organization shall promptly notify the Board of any changes in its name, address, or public telephone number.

(c) *Withdrawal of recognition.* The Board may withdraw the recognition of any organization which has failed to maintain the qualifications required by § 292.2(a). Withdrawal of recognition may be accomplished in accordance with the following procedure:

(1) The Service, by the district director within whose jurisdiction the organization is located, may conduct an investigation into any organization it believes no longer meets the standards for recognition.

(2) If the investigation establishes to the satisfaction of the district director that withdrawal proceedings should be instituted, he shall cause a written statement of the grounds upon which withdrawal is sought to be served upon the organization, with notice to show cause why its recognition should not be withdrawn. The notice will call upon the organization to appear before a special inquiry officer for a hearing at a time and place stated, not less than 30 days after service of the notice.

(3) The special inquiry officer shall hold a hearing, receive evidence, make findings of fact, state his recommendations, and forward the complete record to the Board.

(4) The organization and the Service shall have the opportunity of appearing at oral argument before the Board at a time specified by the Board.

(5) The Board shall consider the entire record and render its decision. The order of the Board shall constitute the final disposition of the proceedings.

(d) *Accreditation of representatives.* An organization recognized by the Board under paragraph (b) of this section may apply for accreditation of persons of good moral character as its representatives. An organization may apply to have a representative accredited to practice before the Service alone or the Service and the Board (including practice before immigration judges). An application for accreditation shall fully set forth the nature and extent of the proposed representative's experience and knowledge of immigration and naturalization law and procedure and the category of accreditation sought. No individual may submit an application on his or her own behalf. An application shall be filed directly with the Board, along with proof of service of a copy of the application on the district director having jurisdiction over the area in which the requesting organization is located. The district director, within 30 days from the date of service, shall forward to the Board a recommendation for approval or disapproval of the application and the reasons therefor, or request a specified period of time in which to conduct an investigation or otherwise obtain relevant information regarding the applicant. The district director shall include proof of service of a copy of such recommendation or request on the organization. The organization shall have 30 days in which to file a response with the Board to a recommendation by a distrct director that is other than favorable, with proof of service of a copy of such response on the district director. If the Board approves a request for time to conduct an investigation, or in its discretion remands the application to the district director for further information, the organization shall be advised of the time granted for such purpose. The district director shall promptly forward the results of any investigation or inquiry to the Board, along with a recommendation for approval or disapproval and the reasons therefor, and proof of service of a copy of the submission on the organization. The organization shall have 30 days from the date of service to file a response with the Board to any matters raised therein, with proof or service of a copy of the response on the district director. Requests for extensions of filing times must be submitted in writing with the reasons therefor and may be granted by the Board in its discretion. Oral argument may be heard before the Board in its discretion at such date and time as the Board may direct. The Board may approve or disapprove an application in whole or in part and shall inform the organization and the district director of the action taken with regard to an application. The accreditation of a representative shall be valid for a period of three years only; however, the accreditation shall remain valid pending Board consideration of an application for renewal of accreditation if the application is filed at least 60 days before the third anniversary of the date of the Board's prior accreditation of the representative. Accreditation terminates when the Board's recognition of the organization ceases for any reason or when the representative's employment or other connection with the organization ceases. The organization shall promptly notify the Board of such changes.

(e) *Roster.* The Board shall maintain an alphabetical roster of recognized organizations and their accredited representatives. A copy of the roster shall be furnished to the Commissioner and he shall be advised from time to time of changes therein.

[40 FR 23272, May 29, 1975, as amended at 49 FR 44086, Nov. 2, 1984; 62 FR 9075, Feb. 28, 1997]

§ 292.3 Professional conduct for practitioners—Rules and procedures.

(a) *General provisions*—(1) *Authority to sanction.* An adjudicating official or the Board of Immigration Appeals (Board) may impose disciplinary sanctions against any practitioner if it finds it to be in the public interest to do so. It will be in the public interest to impose disciplinary sanctions against a practitioner who is authorized to practice before DHS when such person has engaged in criminal, unethical, or unprofessional conduct, or in frivolous behavior, as set forth in 8 CFR 1003.102. In accordance with the disciplinary proceedings set forth in 8 CFR part 1003, an adjudicating official or the Board may impose any of the following disciplinary sanctions:

(i) Expulsion which is permanent, from practice before the Board and the Immigration Courts, or DHS, or before all three authorities;

(ii) Suspension, including immediate suspension, from practice before the Board and the Immigration Courts, or DHS, or before all three authorities;

(iii) Public or private censure; or

(iv) Such other disciplinary sanctions as the adjudicating official or the Board deems appropriate.

(2) *Persons subject to sanctions.* Persons subject to sanctions include any practitioner. A practitioner is any attorney as defined in 8 CFR 1.2 who does not represent the federal government,

or any representative as defined in 8 CFR 1.2. Attorneys employed by DHS will be subject to discipline pursuant to paragraph (i) of this section.

(b) *Grounds of discipline.* It is deemed to be in the public interest for the adjudicating official or the Board to impose disciplinary sanctions as described in paragraph (a)(1) of this section against any practitioner who falls within one or more of the categories enumerated in 8 CFR 1003.102. These categories do not constitute the exclusive grounds for which disciplinary sanctions may be imposed in the public interest. Nothing in this regulation should be read to denigrate the practitioner's duty to represent zealously his or her client within the bounds of the law.

(c) *Immediate suspension and summary disciplinary proceedings; duty of practitioner to notify DHS of conviction or discipline.* (1) *Immediate suspension proceedings.* Immediate suspension proceedings will be conducted in accordance with the provisions set forth in 8 CFR 1003.103. DHS shall file a petition with the Board to suspend immediately from practice before DHS any practitioner who has been found guilty of, or pleaded guilty or nolo contendere to, a serious crime, as defined in 8 CFR 1003.102(h), any practitioner who has been suspended or disbarred by, or while a disciplinary investigation or proceeding is pending has resigned from, the highest court of any State, possession, territory, or Commonwealth of the United States, or the District of Columbia, or any Federal court; or who has been placed on an interim suspension pending a final resolution of the underlying disciplinary matter.

(2) *Copies and proof of service.* A copy of the petition will be forwarded to EOIR, which may submit a written request to the Board that entry of any order immediately suspending a practitioner before DHS also apply to the practitioner's authority to practice before the Board and the Immigration Courts. Proof of service on the practitioner of EOIR's request to broaden the scope of any immediate suspension must be filed with the Board.

(3) *Summary disciplinary proceedings.* Summary disciplinary proceedings will be conducted in accordance with the provisions set forth in 8 CFR 1003.103. DHS shall promptly initiate summary disciplinary proceedings against any practitioner described in paragraph (c)(1) of this section by the issuance of a Notice of Intent to Discipline, upon receipt of a certified copy of the order, judgment, and/or record evidencing the underlying criminal conviction, discipline, or resignation, and accompanied by a certified copy of such document. Delays in initiation of summary disciplinary proceedings under this section will not impact an immediate suspension imposed pursuant to paragraph (c)(1) of this section. Any such proceeding will not be concluded until all direct appeals from an underlying criminal conviction have been completed.

(4) *Duty of practitioner to notify DHS of conviction or discipline.* Within 30 days of the issuance of the initial order, even if an appeal of the conviction or discipline is pending, of any conviction or discipline for professional misconduct entered on or after July 27, 2000, a practitioner must notify DHS disciplinary counsel if the practitioner has been: Found guilty of, or pleaded guilty or nolo contendere to, a serious crime, as defined in 8 CFR 1003.102(h); suspended or disbarred by, or while a disciplinary investigation or proceeding is pending has resigned from, the highest court of any State, possession, territory, or Commonwealth of the United States, or the District of Columbia, or any Federal court; or placed on an interim suspension pending a final resolution of the underlying disciplinary matter. Failure to notify DHS disciplinary counsel as required may result in immediate suspension as set forth in paragraph (c)(1) of this section.

(d) *Filing of complaints of misconduct occurring before DHS; preliminary inquiry; resolutions; referral of complaints*—(1) *Filing of complaints of misconduct occurring before DHS.* Complaints of criminal, unethical, or unprofessional conduct, or of frivolous behavior by a practitioner before DHS must be filed with the DHS disciplinary counsel. Disciplinary complaints must be submitted in writing and must state in detail the information that supports the basis for the complaint, including, but not limited to, the names and addresses of the complainant and the practitioner, the date(s) of the conduct or behavior, the nature of the conduct or behavior, the individuals involved, the harm or damages sustained by the complainant, and any other relevant information. The DHS disciplinary counsel will notify EOIR disciplinary counsel of any disciplinary complaint that pertains, in whole or in part, to a matter before the Board or the Immigration Courts.

(2) *Preliminary inquiry.* Upon receipt of a disciplinary complaint or on its own initiative, the DHS disciplinary counsel will initiate a preliminary inquiry. If a complaint is filed by a client or former client, the complainant thereby waives the attorney-client privilege and any other applicable privilege, to the extent necessary to conduct a preliminary inquiry and any subsequent proceeding based thereon. If the DHS disciplinary counsel determines that a complaint is without merit, no further action will be taken. The DHS disciplinary counsel may, in his or her discretion, close a preliminary inquiry if the complainant fails to comply with reasonable requests for assistance, information, or documentation. The complainant and the practitioner will be notified of any such determination in writing.

(3) *Resolutions reached prior to the issuance of a Notice of Intent to Discipline.* The DHS disciplinary counsel may, in his or her discretion, issue warning letters and admonitions, and may enter into agreements in lieu of discipline, prior to the issuance of a Notice of Intent to Discipline.

(e) *Notice of Intent to Discipline*—(1) *Issuance of Notice to Practitioner.* If, upon completion of the preliminary inquiry, the DHS disciplinary counsel determines that sufficient prima facie evidence exists to warrant charging a practitioner with professional misconduct as set forth in 8 CFR 1003.102, it will file with the Board and issue to the practitioner who was the subject of the preliminary inquiry a Notice of Intent to Discipline. Service of this notice will be made upon the practitioner by either certified mail to his or her last known address, as defined in paragraph (e)(2) of this section, or by personal delivery. Such notice shall contain a statement of the charge(s), a copy of the preliminary inquiry report, the proposed disciplinary sanctions to be imposed, the procedure for filing an answer or requesting a hearing, and the mailing address and telephone number of the Board. In summary disciplinary proceedings brought pursuant to §292.3(c), a preliminary inquiry report is not required to be filed with the Notice of Intent to Discipline. Notice of Intent to Discipline proceedings will be conducted in accordance with the provisions set forth in 8 CFR 1003.105 and 1003.106.

(2) *Practitioner's address.* For the purposes of this section, the last known address of a practitioner is the practitioner's address as it appears in DHS records if the practitioner is actively representing an applicant or petitioner before DHS on the date the DHS disciplinary counsel issues the Notice of Intent to Discipline. If the practitioner does not have a matter pending before DHS on the date of the issuance of a Notice of Intent to Discipline, then the last known address for a practitioner will be as follows:

(i) *Attorneys in the United States:* The attorney's address that is on record with a state jurisdiction that licensed the attorney to practice law.

(ii) *Accredited representatives:* The address of a recognized organization with which the accredited representative is affiliated.

(iii) *Accredited officials:* The address of the embassy of the foreign government that employs the accredited official.

(iv) *All other practitioners:* The address for the practitioner that appears in DHS records for the application or petition proceeding in which the DHS official permitted the practitioner to appear.

(3) *Copy of Notice to EOIR; reciprocity of disciplinary sanctions.* A copy of the Notice of Intent to Discipline shall be forwarded to the EOIR disciplinary counsel. Under Department of Justice regulations in 8 CFR chapter V, the EOIR disciplinary counsel may submit a written request to the Board or the adjudicating official requesting that

any discipline imposed upon a practitioner which restricts his or her authority to practice before DHS also apply to the practitioner's authority to practice before the Board and the Immigration Courts. Proof of service on the practitioner of any request to broaden the scope of the proposed discipline must be filed with the Board or the adjudicating official.

(4) *Answer.* The practitioner shall file a written answer or a written request for a hearing to the Notice of Intent to Discipline in accordance with 8 CFR 1003.105. If a practitioner fails to file a timely answer, proceedings will be conducted according to 8 CFR 1003.105.

(f) *Right to be heard and disposition; decision; appeal; and reinstatement after expulsion or suspension.* Upon the filing of an answer, the matter shall be heard, decided, and appeals filed according to the procedures set forth in 8 CFR 1003.106. Reinstatement proceedings after expulsion or suspension shall be conducted according to the procedures set forth in 8 CFR 1003.107.

(g) *Referral.* In addition to, or in lieu of, initiating disciplinary proceedings against a practitioner, the DHS disciplinary counsel may notify any appropriate Federal and/or state disciplinary or regulatory authority of any complaint filed against a practitioner. Any final administrative decision imposing sanctions against a practitioner (other than a private censure) will be reported to any such disciplinary or regulatory authority in every jurisdiction where the disciplined practitioner is admitted or otherwise authorized to practice.

(h) *Confidentiality.* (1) *Complaints and preliminary inquiries.* Except as otherwise provided by law or regulation or as authorized by this regulation, information concerning complaints or preliminary inquiries is confidential. A practitioner whose conduct is the subject of a complaint or preliminary inquiry, however, may waive confidentiality, except that the DHS disciplinary counsel may decline to permit a waiver of confidentiality if it is determined that an ongoing preliminary inquiry may be substantially prejudiced by a public disclosure before the filing of a Notice of Intent to Discipline.

(i) *Disclosure of information for the purpose of protecting the public.* The DHS disciplinary counsel may disclose information concerning a complaint or preliminary inquiry for the protection of the public when the necessity for disclosing information outweighs the necessity for preserving confidentiality in circumstances including, but not limited to, the following:

(A) A practitioner has caused, or is likely to cause, harm to client(s), the public, or the administration of justice, such that the public or specific individuals should be advised of the nature of the allegations. If disclosure of information is made pursuant to this paragraph, the DHS disciplinary counsel may define the scope of information disseminated and may limit the disclosure of information to specified individuals or entities;

(B) A practitioner has committed criminal acts or is under investigation by law enforcement authorities;

(C) A practitioner is under investigation by a disciplinary or regulatory authority, or has committed acts or made omissions that may reasonably result in investigation by such an authority;

(D) A practitioner is the subject of multiple disciplinary complaints and the DHS disciplinary counsel has determined not to pursue all of the complaints. The DHS disciplinary counsel may inform complainants whose allegations have not been pursued of the status of any other preliminary inquiries or the manner in which any other complaint(s) against the practitioner have been resolved.

(ii) *Disclosure of information for the purpose of conducting a preliminary inquiry.* The DHS disciplinary counsel may, in his or her discretion, disclose documents and information concerning complaints and preliminary inquiries to the following individuals or entities:

(A) To witnesses or potential witnesses in conjunction with a complaint or preliminary inquiry;

(B) To other governmental agencies responsible for the enforcement of civil or criminal laws;

(C) To agencies and other jurisdictions responsible for conducting disciplinary investigations or proceedings;

(D) To the complainant or a lawful designee; and

(E) To the practitioner who is the subject of the complaint or preliminary inquiry or the practitioner's counsel of record.

(2) *Resolutions reached prior to the issuance of a Notice of Intent to Discipline.* Resolutions, such as warning letters, admonitions, and agreements in lieu of discipline, reached prior to the issuance of a Notice of Intent to Discipline, will remain confidential. However, such resolutions may become part of the public record if the practitioner becomes subject to a subsequent Notice of Intent to Discipline.

(3) *Notices of Intent to Discipline and action subsequent thereto.* Notices of Intent to Discipline and any action that takes place subsequent to their issuance, except for the imposition of private censures, may be disclosed to the public, except that private censures may become part of the public record if introduced as evidence of a prior record of discipline in any subsequent disciplinary proceeding. Settlement agreements reached after the issuance of a Notice of Intent to Discipline may be disclosed to the public upon final approval by the adjudicating official or the Board. Disciplinary hearings are open to the public, except as noted in 8 CFR 1003.106(a)(v).

(i) *Discipline of government attorneys.* Complaints regarding the conduct or behavior of DHS attorneys shall be directed to the Office of the Inspector General, DHS. If disciplinary action is warranted, it will be administered pursuant to the Department's attorney discipline procedures.

[75 FR 5228, Feb. 2, 2010, as amended at 76 FR 53797, Aug. 29, 2011]

§292.4 Appearances.

(a) *Authority to appear and act.* An appearance must be filed on the appropriate form as prescribed by DHS by the attorney or accredited representative appearing in each case. The form must be properly completed and signed by the petitioner, applicant, or respondent to authorize representation in order for the appearance to be recognized by DHS. The appearance will be recognized by the specific immigration component of DHS in which it was filed until the conclusion of the matter for which it was entered. This does not change the requirement that a new form must be filed with an appeal filed with the Administrative Appeals Office of USCIS. Substitution may be permitted upon the written withdrawal of the attorney or accredited representative of record or upon the filing of a new form by a new attorney or accredited representative. When an appearance is made by a person acting in a representative capacity, his or her personal appearance or signature will constitute a representation that under the provisions of this chapter he or she is authorized and qualified to appear as a representative as provided in 8 CFR 103.2(a)(3) and 292.1. Further proof of authority to act in a representative capacity may be required.

(b) A party to a proceeding and his or her attorney or representative will be permitted to examine the record of proceeding in accordance with 6 CFR part 5.

[23 FR 2673, Apr. 23, 1958, as amended at 32 FR 9633, July 4, 1967; 52 FR 2941, Jan. 29, 1987; 59 FR 1466, Jan. 11, 1994; 75 FR 5230, Feb. 2, 2010; 76 FR 53797, Aug. 29, 2011]

§292.5 Service upon and action by attorney or representative of record.

(a) *Representative capacity.* Whenever a person is required by any of the provisions of this chapter to give or be given notice; to serve or be served with any paper other than a warrant of arrest or a subpoena; to make a motion; to file or submit an application or other document; or to perform or waive the performance of any act, such notice, service, motion, filing, submission, performance, or waiver shall be given by or to, served by or upon, made by, or requested of the attorney or representative of record, or the person himself if unrepresented.

(b) *Right to representation.* Whenever an examination is provided for in this chapter, the person involved shall have the right to be represented by an attorney or representative who shall be permitted to examine or cross-examine such person and witnesses, to introduce evidence, to make objections which shall be stated succinctly and entered on the record, and to submit briefs.

Provided, that nothing in this paragraph shall be construed to provide any applicant for admission in either primary or secondary inspection the right to representation, unless the applicant for admission has become the focus of a criminal investigation and has been taken into custody.

[37 FR 11471, June 8, 1972 and 45 FR 81733, Dec. 12, 1980; 46 FR 2025, Jan. 8, 1981; 58 FR 49911, Sept. 24, 1993]

§ 292.6 Interpretation.

Interpretations of this part will be made by the Board of Immigration Appeals, subject to the provisions of 8 CFR part 1003.

[32 FR 9633, July 4, 1967, as amended at 75 FR 5230, Feb. 2, 2010]

PART 293—DEPOSIT OF AND INTEREST ON CASH RECEIVED TO SECURE IMMIGRATION BONDS

AUTHORITY: 8 U.S.C. 1363.

SOURCE: 36 FR 13677, July 23, 1971, unless otherwise noted.

§ 293.1 Computation of interest.

The Secretary of the Treasury determines the rate at which an immigration bond secured by cash shall bear interest, consistent with 8 CFR 293.2. Interest shall be computed from the deposit date to and including the refund date or breach date of the immigration bond. For purposes of this part, the deposit date shall be the date shown on the receipt for the cash received as security on an immigration bond. The refund date shall be the date upon which the interest is certified to the Treasury Department for payment. The breach date shall be the date the immigration bond was breached as shown on Form I–323—"Notice—Immigration Bond Breached." In counting the number of days for which interest shall be computed, the day on which the cash was deposited shall not be counted; however, the refund date or the breach date shall be counted.

[80 FR 34242, June 16, 2015]

§ 293.2 Interest rate.

Interest on cash deposited to secure immigration bonds will be at the rate as determined by the Secretary of the Treasury, but in no case will exceed 3 per centum per annum or be less than zero. The rate will be published by Treasury on the Treasury Web site or through another mechanism.

[80 FR 34242, June 16, 2015]

§ 293.3 Time of payment.

Interest shall be paid only at time of disposition of principal cash when the immigration bond has been cancelled or declared breached.

[80 FR 34242, June 16, 2015]

PART 299—IMMIGRATION FORMS

AUTHORITY: 8 U.S.C. 1101 and note, 1103; 8 CFR part 2.

§ 299.1 Prescribed forms.

A listing of USCIS, ICE, and CBP approved forms referenced in chapter I can be viewed on the Office of Management and Budget Web site at *http://www.reginfo.gov*. A listing of approved USCIS forms can also be viewed on its Internet Web site.

[76 FR 53797, Aug. 29, 2011]

§ 299.2 Distribution of Service forms.

The distribution of official Immigration and Naturalization applications, petitions, and related forms is as follows:

(a) Any officer or employee of the Service may issue official application or petition and related forms to the person for whose use the form is intended or to a person identified as a representative of the intended user in the quantity required for filing the application or petition and related forms.

(b) A small quantity, twenty-five (25) copies, may be issued to organizations and practitioners who make written request to the Regional Commissioner for the geographic location of the requester if such forms have not been made available for purchase from the Superintendent of Documents, Washington, DC 20402.

(c) Voluntary agencies (VOLAGS) participating in the Outreach Program of the Service who make written request to the Regional Commissioner for the geographic location of the requester may be furnished Service forms gratis in the volumes requested.

[43 FR 14304, Apr. 5, 1978, as amended at 45 FR 6777, Jan. 30, 1980; 45 FR 21611, Apr. 2, 1980]

§ 299.3 [Reserved]

§ 299.4 Reproduction of Public Use Forms by public and private entities.

(a) *Duplication requirements.* All forms required for applying for a specific benefit in compliance with the immigration and naturalization regulations, including those which have been made available for purchase by the Superintendent of Documents as listed in § 299.3, may be printed or otherwise reproduced. Such reproduction must be by an appropriate duplicating process and at the expense of the public or private entity. Forms printed or reproduced by public or private entities shall be:

(1) In black ink or dye that will not fade or "feather" within 20 years, and

(2) Conform to the officially printed forms currently in use with respect to:

(i) Size,

(ii) Wording and language,

(iii) Arrangement, style and size of type, and

(iv) Paper specifications (White, standard copier or typing paper).

(b) *Requirements for electronic generation.* Public or private entities may electronically generate forms required for applying for a specific benefit, in compliance with the immigration and naturalization regulations, at their own expense. This includes forms that have been made available for purchase by the Superintendent of Documents, as listed in § 299.3 provided that each form satisfies the following requirements:

(1) An electronic reproduction must be complete, containing all questions which appear on the official form. The wording and punctuation of all data elements and identifying information must match exactly. No data elements may be added or deleted. The sequence and format for each item on the form must be replicated to mirror the authorized agency form. Each item must be printed on the same page in the same location. Likewise, multiple-part sets may be printed as single sheets provided that the destination of the carbon copy is clearly identified on the bottom of the form. An electronic reproduction of a multi page form does not need to match the head-to-head or head-to-foot printing configuration of the official form. In the case of the Form I–20 A–B/I–20ID, Certificate of Eligibility for Nonimmigrant (F–1) Student Status—For Academic and Language Students, private entities may generate this form in single-page format rather than double-sided format, provided that the student's name, school, and date of birth is printed in a shaded box on the top of page 4 of the form, using the same type size and font style as the body of the form.

(2) The final form must match the design, format, and dimensions of the official form. All blocks must remain the same size and lines must remain the same length. No variations will be permissible.

(c) The accuracy of electronically generated forms is the responsibility of the private entities. Changes to existing forms, as announced by the Service, must be promptly incorporated into the private entity software program application. Deviations from the aforementioned standards may result in the return or denial of the applicant's application/petition for a particular benefit.

(d) Electronic printers that provide for near-letter-quality documents should be used to generate electronic forms. Dot matrix printers that are only capable of producing draft quality documents should not be used for form generation, but may be used for the entry of data in a preprinted form where appropriate.

(e) Any form with poor print quality or other defect which renders it illegible, difficult to read, or displays added or missing data elements, will be rejected by the Service. Any problems regarding the acceptability of a specific electronic version of a particular Service form may be brought to the attention of the Director, Policy Directives and Instructions Branch, 425 "I" Street, NW., Room 4034, Washington, DC 20536, telephone number (202) 514–3048.

[59 FR 25558, May 17, 1994, as amended at 61 FR 47801, Sept. 11, 1996; 65 FR 61260, Oct. 17, 2000]

§ 299.5 [Reserved]

SUBCHAPTER C—NATIONALITY REGULATIONS

PART 301—NATIONALS AND CITIZENS OF THE UNITED STATES AT BIRTH

AUTHORITY: 8 U.S.C. 1103, 1401; 8 CFR part 2.

SOURCE: 62 FR 39927, July 25, 1997, unless otherwise noted.

§ 301.1 Procedures.

(a) *Application.* (1) As provided in 8 CFR part 341, a person residing in the United States who desires to be documented as a United States citizen pursuant to section 301(h) of the Act may apply for a passport at a United States passport agency or may submit an application on the form specified by USCIS in accordance with the form instructions and with the fee prescribed by 8 CFR 103.7(b)(1). The applicant will be notified when and where to appear before a USCIS officer for examination on his or her application.

(2) A person residing outside of the United States who desires to be documented as a United States citizen under section 301(h) of the Act shall make his or her claim at a United States embassy or consulate, in accordance with such regulations as may be prescribed in the Secretary of State.

(b) *Oath of allegiance; issuance of certificate.* Upon determination by the district director that a person is a United States citizen pursuant to section 301(h) of the Act, the person shall take the oath of allegiance, prescribed in 8 CFR part 337, before an officer of the Service designated to administer the oath of allegiance within the United States, and a certificate of citizenship shall be issued. The person shall be considered a United States citizen as of the date of his or her birth.

[62 FR 39927, July 25, 1997, as amended at 74 FR 26940, June 5, 2009; 76 FR 53797, Aug. 29, 2011]

PART 306—SPECIAL CLASSES OF PERSONS WHO MAY BE NATURALIZED: VIRGIN ISLANDERS

AUTHORITY: Secs. 103, 306, 332, 66 Stat. 173, 237, 252; 8 U.S.C. 1103, 1406, 1443.

SOURCE: 22 FR 9812, Dec. 6, 1957, unless otherwise noted.

§ 306.1 Persons eligible.

Any Danish citizen who resided in the Virgin Islands of the United States on January 17, 1917, and in those Islands, Puerto Rico, or the United States on February 25, 1927, and who had preserved his Danish citizenship by making the declaration prescribed by Article VI of the treaty entered into between the United States and Denmark on August 4, 1916, and proclaimed January 25, 1917, may renounce his Danish citizenship before any court of record in the United States irrespective of his place of residence, in accordance with the provisions of this part.

§ 306.2 United States citizenship; when acquired.

Immediately upon making the declaration of renunciation as described in § 306.12 the declarant shall be deemed to be a citizen of the United States. No certificate of naturalization or of citizenship shall be issued by the clerk of court to any person obtaining, or who has obtained citizenship solely under section 306(a)(1) of the Immigration and Nationality Act or under section 1 of the act of February 25, 1927.

§ 306.11 Preliminary application form; filing; examination.

A person of the class described in § 306.1 shall submit to the Service on Form N–350 preliminary application to renounce Danish citizenship, in accordance with the instructions contained therein. The applicant shall be notified in writing when and where to appear before a representative of the Service for examination as to his eligibility to renounce Danish citizenship and for assistance in filing the renunciation.

§ 306.12 Renunciation forms; disposition.

The renunciation shall be made and executed by the applicant under oath, in duplicate, on Form N–351 and filed in the office of the clerk of court. The usual procedural requirements of the Immigration and Nationality Act shall not apply to proceedings under this part. The fee shall be fixed by the court or the clerk thereof in accordance with the law and rules of the court, and no accounting therefor shall be required to be made to the Service. The clerk shall retain the original of Form N–351 as the court record and forward the duplicate to the district director exercising administrative naturalization jurisdiction over the area in which the court is located.

PART 310—NATURALIZATION AUTHORITY

Sec.

AUTHORITY: 8 U.S.C. 1103, 1421, 1443, 1447, 1448; 8 CFR 2.

SOURCE: 56 FR 50480, Oct. 7, 1991, unless otherwise noted.

§ 310.1 Administrative naturalization authority.

(a) *Attorney General.* Commencing October 1, 1991, section 310 of the Act confers the sole authority to naturalize persons as citizens of the United States upon the Attorney General.

(b) *Commissioner of the Immigration and Naturalization Service.* Pursuant to § 2.1 of this chapter, the Commissioner of the Immigration and Naturalization Service is authorized to perform such acts as are necessary and proper to implement the Attorney General's authority under the provisions of section 310 of the Act.

§ 310.2 Jurisdiction to accept applications for naturalization.

USCIS shall accept an application for naturalization from an applicant who is subject to a continuous residence requirement under section 316(a) or 319(a) of the Act as much as three months before the date upon which the applicant would otherwise satisfy such continuous residence requirement in the State or Service district, as defined in 8 CFR 316.1, where residence is to be established for naturalization purposes. At the time of examination on the application, the applicant will be required to prove that he or she satisfies the residence requirements for the residence reflected in the application.

[56 FR 50480, Oct. 7, 1991, as amended at 76 FR 53797, Aug. 29, 2011]

§ 310.3 Administration of the oath of allegiance.

(a) An applicant for naturalization may elect, at the time of filing of, or at the examination on, the application, to have the oath of allegiance and renunciation under section 337(a) of the Act administered in a public ceremony conducted by the Service or by any court described in section 310(b) of the Act, subject to section 310(b)(1)(B) of the Act.

(b) The jurisdiction of all such courts specified to administer the oath of allegiance shall extend only to those persons who are resident within the respective jurisdictional limits of such courts, except as otherwise provided in section 316(f)(2) of the Act. Persons who temporarily reside within the jurisdictional limits of a court in order to pursue an application properly filed pursuant to section 319(b), 328(a), or 329 of the Act or section 405 of the Immigration Act of 1990 are not subject to the exclusive jurisdiction provisions of section 310(b)(1)(B) of the Act.

(c)(1) A court that wishes to exercise exclusive jurisdiction to administer the oath of allegiance for the 45-day period specified in section 310(b)(1)(B) of the Act shall notify, in writing, the district director of the Service office having jurisdiction over the place in which the court is located, of the court's intent to exercise such exclusive jurisdiction.

(2) At least 60 days prior to the holding of any oath administration ceremony referred to in § 337.8 of this chapter, the clerk of court shall give written notice to the appropriate district director of the time, date, and place of such ceremony and of the number of persons who may be accommodated.

(d) A court that has notified the Service pursuant to paragraph (c)(1) of this section shall have exclusive authority to administer the oath of allegiance to persons residing within its jurisdiction for a period of 45 days beginning on the date that the Service notifies the clerk of court of the applicant's eligibility for naturalization. Such exclusive authority shall be effective only if on the date the Service notifies the clerk of court of the applicant's eligibility, the court has notified the Service of the day or days during such 45-day period on which the court has scheduled oath administration ceremonies available to the applicant. The Service must submit the notification of the applicant's eligibility to the clerk of court within 10 days of the approval of the application pursuant to § 337.8 of this chapter.

(e) *Waiver of exclusive authority.* A court exercising exclusive authority to administer the oath of allegiance pursuant to paragraph (c) of this section may waive such exclusive authority when it is determined by the court that the Service failed to notify the court within a reasonable time prior to a scheduled oath ceremony of the applicant's eligibility such that it is impractical for the applicant to appear at that ceremony. The court shall notify the district director in writing of the waiver of exclusive authority as it relates to a specific applicant, and the Service shall promptly notify the applicant. The Service shall then arrange for the administration of the oath of allegiance pursuant to § 337.2 of this chapter.

[58 FR 49911, Sept. 24, 1993, as amended at 66 FR 32144, June 13, 2001]

§ 310.4 Judicial naturalization authority and withdrawal of petitions.

(a) *Jurisdiction.* No court shall have jurisdiction under section 310(a) of the Act, to naturalize a person unless a petition for naturalization with respect to that person was filed with the naturalization court before October 1, 1991.

(b) *Withdrawal of petitions.* (1) In the case of any petition for naturalization which was pending in any court as of November 29, 1990, the petitioner may elect to withdraw such petition, and have the application for naturalization considered under the administrative naturalization process. Such petition must be withdrawn after October 1, 1991, but not later than December 31, 1991.

(2) Except as provided in paragraph (b)(1) of this section, the petitioner shall not be permitted to withdraw his or her petition for naturalization, unless the Attorney General consents to the withdrawal.

(c) *Judicial proceedings.* (1) All pending petitions not withdrawn in the manner and terms described in paragraph (b) of this section, shall be decided, on the merits, by the naturalization court, in conformity with the applicable provisions of the judicial naturalization authority of the prior statute. The reviewing court shall enter a final order.

(2) In cases where the petitioner fails to prosecute his or her petition, the court shall decide the petition upon its merits unless the Attorney General moves that the petition be dismissed for lack of prosecution.

§ 310.5 Judicial review.

(a) *After 120 days following examination.* An applicant for naturalization may seek judicial review of a pending application for naturalization in those instances where the Service fails to make a determination under section 335 of the Act within 120 days after an examination is conducted under part 335 of this chapter. An applicant shall make a proper application for relief to the United States District Court having jurisdiction over the district in which the applicant resides. The court may either determine the issues brought before it on their merits, or remand the matter to the Service with appropriate instructions.

(b) *After denial of an application.* After an application for naturalization is denied following a hearing before a Service officer pursuant to section 336(a) of the Act, the applicant may seek judicial review of the decision pursuant to section 310 of the Act.

PART 312—EDUCATIONAL REQUIREMENTS FOR NATURALIZATION

Sec.

AUTHORITY: 8 U.S.C. 1103, 1423, 1443, 1447, 1448.

SOURCE: 56 FR 50481, Oct. 7, 1991, unless otherwise noted.

§312.1 Literacy requirements.

(a) *General.* Except as otherwise provided in paragraph (b) of this section, no person shall be naturalized as a citizen of the United States upon his or her own application unless that person can demonstrate an understanding of the English language, including an ability to read, write, and speak words in ordinary usage in the English language.

(b) *Exceptions.* The following persons need not demonstrate an ability to read, write and speak words in ordinary usage in the English language:

(1) A person who, on the date of filing of his or her application for naturalization, is over 50 years of age and has been living in the United States for periods totalling at least 20 years subsequent to a lawful admission for permanent residence;

(2) A person who, on the date of filing his or her application for naturalization, is over 55 years of age and has been living in the United States for periods totalling at least 15 years subsequent to a lawful admission for permanent residence; or

(3) The requirements of paragraph(a) of this section shall not apply to any person who is unable, because of a medically determinable physical or mental impairment or combination of impairments which has lasted or is expected to last at least 12 months, to demonstrate an understanding of the English language as noted in paragraph (a) of this section. The loss of any cognitive abilities based on the direct effects of the illegal use of drugs will not be considered in determining whether a person is unable to demonstrate an understanding of the English language. For purposes of this paragraph, the term *medically determinable* means an impairment that results from anatomical, physiological, or psychological abnormalities which can be shown by medically acceptable clinical or laboratory diagnostic techniques to have resulted in functioning so impaired as to render an individual unable to demonstrate an understanding of the English language as required by this section, or that renders the individual unable to fulfill the requirements for English proficiency, even with reasonable modifications to the methods of determining English proficiency, as outlined in paragraph(c) of this section.

(c) *Literacy examination.* (1) *Verbal skills.* The ability of an applicant to speak English will be determined by a designated immigration officer from the applicant's answers to questions normally asked in the course of the examination.

(2) *Reading and writing skills.* Except as noted in 8 CFR 312.3, an applicant's ability to read and write English must be tested in a manner prescribed by USCIS. USCIS will provide a description of test study materials and testing procedures on the USCIS Internet Web site.

[56 FR 50481, Oct. 7, 1991, as amended at 62 FR 12923, Mar. 19, 1997; 62 FR 15751, Apr. 2, 1997; 64 FR 7993, Feb. 18, 1999; 76 FR 53797, Aug. 29, 2011]

§312.2 Knowledge of history and government of the United States.

(a) *General.* No person shall be naturalized as a citizen of the United States upon his or her own application unless that person can demonstrate a knowledge and understanding of the fundamentals of the history, and of the principles and form of government, of the United States. A person who is exempt from the literacy requirement under § 312.1(b) (1) and (2) must still satisfy this requirement.

(b) *Exceptions.* (1) The requirements of paragraph (a) of this section shall not apply to any person who is unable to demonstrate a knowledge and understanding of the fundamentals of the history, and of the principles and form of government of the United States because of a medically determinable physical or mental impairment, that already has or is expected to last at least 12 months. The loss of any cognitive skills based on the direct effects of the illegal use of drugs will not be considered in determining whether an individual may be exempted. For the purposes of this paragraph the term *medically determinable* means an impairment that results from anatomical, physiological, or psychological abnormalities which can be shown by medically acceptable clinical or laboratory diagnosis techniques to have resulted in functioning so impaired as to render an individual to be unable to demonstrate the knowledge required by this section or that renders the individuals unable to participate in the testing procedures for naturalization, even with reasonable modifications.

(2) *Medical certification.* All persons applying for naturalization and seeking an exception from the requirements of § 312.1(a) and paragraph (a) of this section based on the disability exceptions must submit Form N–648, Medical Certification for Disability Exceptions, to be completed by a medical or osteopathic doctor licensed to practice medicine in the United States or a clinical psychologist licensed to practice psychology in the United States (including the United States territories of Guam, Puerto Rico, and the Virgin Islands). Form N–648 must be submitted as an attachment to the applicant's Form N–400, Application for Naturalization. These medical professionals shall be experienced in diagnosing those with physical or mental medically determinable impairments and shall be able to attest to the origin, nature, and extent of the medical condition as it relates to the disability exceptions noted under § 312.1(b)(3) and paragraph (b)(1) of this section. In addition, the medical professionals making the disability determination must sign a statement on the Form N–648 that they have answered all the questions in a complete and truthful manner, that they (and the applicant) agree to the release of all medical records relating to the applicant that may be requested by the Service and that they attest that any knowingly false or misleading statements may subject the medical professional to the penalties for perjury pursuant to title 18, United Stated Code, Section 1546 and to civil penalties under section 274C of the Act. The Service also reserves the right to refer the applicant to another authorized medical source for a supplemental disability determination. This option shall be invoked when the Service has credible doubts about the veracity of a medical certification that has been presented by the applicant. An affidavit or attestation by the applicant, his or her relatives, or guardian on his or her medical condition is not a sufficient medical attestation for purposes of satisfying this requirement.

(c) *History and government examination*—(1) *Procedure.* The examination of an applicant's knowledge of the history and form of government of the United States must be given orally in English by a designated immigration officer, except:

(i) If the applicant is exempt from the English literacy requirement under 8 CFR 312.1(b), the examination may be conducted in the applicant's native language with the assistance of an interpreter selected in accordance with 8 CFR 312.4 but only if the applicant's command of spoken English is insufficient to conduct a valid examination in English;

(ii) The examination may be conducted in the applicant's native language, with the assistance of an interpreter selected in accordance with 8 CFR 312.4, if the applicant is required to satisfy and has satisfied the English literacy requirement under 8 CFR 312.1(a), but the officer conducting the examination determines that an inaccurate or incomplete record of the examination would result if the examination on technical or complex issues were conducted in English, or

(iii) The applicant has met the requirements of 8 CFR 312.3.

(2) *Scope and substance.* The scope of the examination will be limited to subject matters prescribed by USCIS. In choosing the subject matters, in phrasing questions and in evaluating responses, due consideration must be given to the applicant's:

(i) Education,

(ii) Background,

(iii) Age,

(iv) Length of residence in the United States,

(v) Opportunities available and efforts made to acquire the requisite knowledge, and

(vi) Any other elements or factors relevant to an appraisal of the adequacy of the applicant's knowledge and understanding.

(Approved by the Office of Management and Budget under control number 1115–0208)

[56 FR 50481, Oct. 7, 1991, as amended at 58 FR 49912, Sept. 24, 1993; 62 FR 12923, Mar. 19, 1997; 62 FR 15751, Apr. 2, 1997; 64 FR 7993, Feb. 18, 1999; 76 FR 53797, Aug. 29, 2011]

§312.3 Testing of applicants who obtained permanent residence pursuant to section 245A of the Act.

An applicant who has obtained lawful permanent resident alien status pursuant to section 245A of the Act, and who, at that time, demonstrated English language proficiency in reading and writing, and knowledge of the government and history of the United States through either an examination administered by USCIS or the INS or a standardized section 312 test authorized by the USCIS or the INS for use with Legalization applicants as provided in section 245A(b)(1)(D)(iii) of the Act, will not be reexamined on those skills at the time of the naturalization interview. However, such applicant, unless otherwise exempt, must still demonstrate his or her ability to speak and understand English in accordance with 8 CFR 312.1(c)(1) and establish eligibility for naturalization through testimony in the English language.

[76 FR 53798, Aug. 29, 2011]

§312.4 Selection of interpreter.

An interpreter to be used under §312.2 may be selected either by the applicant or by the Service. However, the Service reserves the right to disqualify an interpreter provided by the applicant in order to ensure the integrity of the examination. Where the Service disqualifies an interpreter, the Service must provide another interpreter for the applicant in a timely manner. If rescheduling of the interview is required, then a new date shall be set as soon as practicable so as not to delay unduly the adjudication of the application. The officer who disqualifies an interpreter shall make a written record of the reason(s) for disqualification as part of the record of the application.

[60 FR 6651, Feb. 3, 1995]

§312.5 Failure to meet educational and literacy requirements.

(a) An applicant for naturalization who fails the English literacy or history and government test at the first examination will be afforded a second opportunity to pass the test(s) within 90 days after the first examination during the pendency of the application.

(b) If an applicant who receives notice of the second scheduled examination date fails to appear without good cause for that second examination without prior notification to the Service, the applicant will be deemed to have failed this second examination. Before an applicant may request a postponement of the second examination to a date that is more than 90 days after the initial examination, the applicant must agree in writing to waive the requirement under section 336 of the Act that the Service must render a determination on the application within 120 days from the initial interview, and instead to permit the Service to render a decision within 120 days from the second interview.

[56 FR 50481, Oct. 7, 1991, as amended at 58 FR 49912, Sept. 24, 1993]

PART 313—MEMBERSHIP IN THE COMMUNIST PARTY OR ANY OTHER TOTALITARIAN ORGANIZATIONS

AUTHORITY: 8 U.S.C. 1103, 1424, 1443.

SOURCE: 56 FR 50482, Oct. 7, 1991, unless otherwise noted.

§313.1 Definitions.

For purposes of this part:

Advocate includes, but is not limited to, advising, recommending, furthering by overt act, or admitting a belief in a doctrine, and may include the giving, lending, or promising of support or of money or any thing of value to be used for advocating such doctrine.

Advocating Communism means advocating the establishment of a totalitarian communist dictatorship, including the economic, international, and governmental doctrines of world communism, in all countries of the world through the medium of an internationally coordinated communist revolutionary movement.

Affiliation with an organization includes, but is not limited to, the giving, lending, or promising of support or of money or any thing of value, to that organization to be used for any purpose.

Circulate includes circulating, distributing, or displaying a work.

Communist Party includes:

(1) The Communist Party of the United States;

(2) The Communist Political Association;

(3) The Communist Party of any state of the United States, of any foreign state, or of any political or geographical subdivision of any foreign state;

(4) Any section, subsidiary, branch, affiliate, or subdivision of any such association or party;

(5) The direct predecessors or successors of any such association or party, regardless of what name such group or organization may have used, may now bear, or may hereafter adopt; and

(6) Any communist-action or communist-front organization that is registered or required to be registered under section 786 of title 50 of the United States Code, provided that the applicant knew or had reason to believe, while he or she was a member, that such organization was a communist-front organization.

Organization includes, but is not limited to, an organization, corporation, company, partnership, association, trust, foundation, or fund, and any group of persons, whether incorporated or not, permanently or temporarily associated together for joint action on any subject or subjects.

Publication or *publishing* of a work includes writing or printing a work; permitting, authorizing, or consenting to the writing or printing of a work; and paying for the writing or printing of a work.

Subversive is any individual who advocates or teaches:

(1) Opposition to all organized government;

(2) The overthrow, by force or violence or other unconstitutional means, of the Government of the United States or of all forms of law;

(3) The duty, necessity, or propriety of the unlawful assaulting or killing, either individually or by position, of any officer or officers of the United States or of any other organized government, because of his, her, or their official character;

(4) The unlawful damage, injury, or destruction of property; or

(5) Sabotage.

Totalitarian dictatorship and *totalitarianism* refer to systems of government not representative in fact and characterized by:

(1) The existence of a single political party, organized on a dictatorial basis, with so close an identity between the policies of such party and the government policies of the country in which the party exists that the government and the party constitute an indistinguishable unit; and

(2) The forcible suppression of all opposition to such a party.

Totalitarian party includes:

(1) Any party in the United States which advocates totalitarianism;

(2) Any party in any State of the United States, in any foreign state, or in any political or geographical subdivision of any foreign state which advocates or practices totalitarianism;

(3) Any section, subsidiary, branch, affiliate, or subdivision of any such association or party; and

(4) The direct predecessors or successors of any such association or party, regardless of what name such group or

organization may have used, may now bear, or may hereafter adopt.

[56 FR 50482, Oct. 7, 1991, as amended at 58 FR 49912, Sept. 24, 1993]

§313.2 Prohibitions.

Except as provided in §313.3, no applicant for naturalization shall be naturalized as a citizen of the United States if, within ten years immediately preceding the filing of an application for naturalization or after such filing but before taking the oath of citizenship, such applicant:

(a) Is or has been a member of or affiliated with the Communist Party or any other totalitarian party; or

(b) Is or has advocated communism or the establishment in the United States of a totalitarian dictatorship; or

(c) Is or has been a member of or affiliated with an organization that advocates communism or the establishment in the United States of a totalitarian dictatorship, either through its own utterance or through any written or printed matter published by such organization; or

(d) Is or has been a subversive, or a member of, or affiliated with, a subversive organization; or

(e) Knowingly is publishing or has published any subversive written or printed matter, or written or printed matter advocating communism; or

(f) Knowingly circulates or has circulated, or knowingly possesses or has possessed for the purpose of circulating, subversive written or printed matter, or written or printed matter advocating communism; or

(g) Is or has been a member of, or affiliated with, any organization that publishes or circulates, or that possesses for the purpose of publishing or circulating, any subversive written or printed matter, or any written or printed matter advocating communism.

§313.3 Statutory exemptions.

(a) *General.* An applicant shall bear the burden of establishing that classification in one of the categories listed under §313.2 is not a bar to naturalization.

(b) *Exemptions.* Despite membership in or affiliation with an organization covered by §313.2, an applicant may be naturalized if the applicant establishes that such membership or affiliation is or was:

(1) Involuntary:

(2) Without awareness of the nature or the aims of the organization, and was discontinued if the applicant became aware of the nature or aims of the organization;

(3) Terminated prior to the attainment of age sixteen by the applicant, or more than ten years prior to the filing of the application for naturalization;

(4) By operation of law; or

(5) Necessary for purposes of obtaining employment, food rations, or other essentials of living.

(c) *Awareness and participation*—(1) *Exemption applicable.* The exemption under paragraph (b)(2) of this section may be found to apply only to an applicant whose participation in the activities of an organization covered under §313.2 was minimal in nature, and who establishes that he or she was unaware of the nature of the organization while a member of the organization.

(2) *Exemptions inapplicable.* The exemptions under paragraphs (b)(4) and (b)(5) of this section will not apply to any applicant who served as a functionary of an organization covered under §313.2, or who was aware of and believed in the organization's doctrines.

(d) *Essentials of living*—(1) *Exemption applicable.* The exemption under paragraph (b)(5) of this section may be found to apply only to an applicant who can demonstrate:

(i) That membership in the covered organization was necessary to obtain the essentials of living like food, shelter, clothing, employment, and an education, which were routinely available to the rest of the population—for purposes of this exemption, higher education will qualify as an essential of living only if the applicant can establish the existence of special circumstances which convert the need for higher education into a need as basic as the need for food or employment: and,

(ii) That he or she participated only to the minimal extent necessary to receive the essential of living.

(2) *Exemption inapplicable.* The exemption under paragraph (b)(5) of this section will not be applicable to an applicant who became a member of an organization covered under 313.2 to receive certain benefits:

(i) Without compulsion from the governing body of the relevant country; or

(ii) Which did not qualify as essentials of living.

§313.4 Procedure.

In all cases in which the applicant claims membership or affiliation in any of the organizations covered by §313.2, the applicant shall attach to the application a detailed written statement describing such membership or affiliation, including the periods of membership or affiliation, whether the applicant held any office in the organization, and whether membership or affiliation was voluntary or involuntary. If the applicant alleges that membership or affiliation was involuntary, or that one of the other exemptions in §313.3 applies, the applicant's statement shall set forth the basis of that allegation.

PART 315—PERSONS INELIGIBLE TO CITIZENSHIP: EXEMPTION FROM MILITARY SERVICE

Sec.

AUTHORITY: 8 U.S.C. 1103, 1443.

SOURCE: 56 FR 50483, Oct. 7, 1991, unless otherwise noted.

§315.1 Definitions.

As used in this part:

Exemption from military service means either:

(1) A permanent exemption from induction into the Armed Forces or the National Security Training Corps of the United States for military training or military service; or

(2) The release or discharge from military training or military service in the Armed Forces or in the National Security Training Corps of the United States.

Induction means compulsory entrance into military service of the United States whether by conscription or, after being notified of a pending conscription, by enlistment.

Treaty national means an alien who is a national of a country with which the United States has a treaty relating to the reciprocal exemption of aliens from military training or military service.

§315.2 Ineligibility and exceptions.

(a) *Ineligibility.* Except as provided in paragraph (b) of this section, any alien who has requested, applied for, and obtained an exemption from military service on the ground that he or she is an alien shall be ineligible for approval of his or her application for naturalization as a citizen of the United States.

(b) *Exceptions.* The prohibition in paragraph (a) of this section does not apply to an alien who establishes by clear and convincing evidence that:

(1) At the time that he or she requested an exemption from military service, the applicant had no liability for such service even in the absence of an exemption;

(2) The applicant did not request or apply for the exemption from military service, but such exemption was automatically granted by the United States government;

(3) The exemption from military service was based upon a ground other than the applicant's alienage;

(4) In claiming an exemption from military service, the applicant did not knowingly and intentionally waive his or her eligibility for naturalization because he or she was misled by advice from a competent United States government authority, or from a competent authority of the government of his or her country of nationality, of the consequences of applying for an exemption from military service and was, therefore, unable to make an intelligent choice between exemption and citizenship;

(5) The applicant applied for and received an exemption from military service on the basis of alienage, but was subsequently inducted into the Armed Forces, or the National Security Training Corps, of the United States; however, an applicant who voluntarily enlists in and serves in the Armed Forces of the United States,

after applying for and receiving an exemption from military service on the basis of alienage, does not satisfy this exception to paragraph (a) of this section;

(6) Prior to requesting the exemption from military service:

(i) The applicant was a treaty national who had served in the armed forces of the country of which he or she was a national; however, a treaty national who did not serve in the armed forces of the country of nationality prior to requesting the exemption from military service does not satisfy this exception to paragraph (a) of this section;

(ii) The applicant served a minimum of eighteen months in the armed forces of a nation that was a member of the North Atlantic Treaty Organization at the time of the applicant's service; or

(iii) The applicant served a minimum of twelve months in the armed forces of a nation that was a member of the North Atlantic Treaty Organization at the time of the applicant's service, provided that the applicant applied for registration with the Selective Service Administration after September 28, 1971; or

(7) The applicant is applying for naturalization pursuant to section 329 of the Act.

§315.3 Evidence.

(a) The records of the Selective Service System and the military department under which the alien served shall be conclusive evidence of whether the alien was relieved or discharged from liability for military service because he or she was an alien.

(b) The regulations of the Selective Service Administration and its predecessors will be controlling with respect to the requirement to register for, and liability for, service in the Armed Forces of the United States.

§315.4 Exemption treaties.

(a) The following countries currently have effective treaties providing reciprocal exemption of aliens from military service:

Argentina (Art. X, 10 Stat. 1005, 1009, effective 1853)
Austria (Art. VI, 47 Stat. 1876, 1880, effective 1928)
China (Art. XIV, 63 Stat. 1299, 1311, effective 1946)
Costa Rica (Art. IX, 10 Stat. 916, 921, effective 1851)
Estonia (Art. VI, 44 Stat. 2379, 2381, effective 1925)
Honduras (Art. VI, 45 Stat. 2618, 2622, effective 1927)
Ireland (Art. III, 1 US 785, 789, effective 1950)
Italy (Art. XIII, 63 Stat. 2255, 2272, effective 1948)
Latvia (Art. VI, 45 Stat. 2641, 2643, effective 1928)
Liberia (Art. VI, 54 Stat. 1739, 1742, effective 1938)
Norway (Art. VI, 47 Stat. 2135, 2139, effective 1928)
Paraguay (Art. XI, 12 Stat. 1091, 1096, effective 1859)
Spain (Art. V, 33 Stat. 2105, 2108, effective 1902)
Switzerland (Art. II, 11 Stat. 587, 589, effective 1850)
Yugoslavia (Serbia) (Art. IV, 22 Stat. 963, 964, effective 1881)

(b) The following countries previously had treaties providing for reciprocal exemption of aliens from military service:

El Salvador (Art. VI, 46 Stat. 2817, 2821, effective 1926 to February 8, 1958)
Germany (Art. VI, 44 Stat. 2132, 2136, effective 1923 to June 2, 1954)
Hungary (Art. VI, 44 Stat, 2441, 2445, effective 1925 to July 5, 1952)
Thailand (Siam) (Art. 1, 53 Stat. 1731, 1732, effective 1937 to June 8, 1968)

PART 316—GENERAL REQUIREMENTS FOR NATURALIZATION

AUTHORITY: 8 U.S.C. 1103, 1181, 1182, 1443, 1447; 8 CFR part 2.

SOURCE: 56 FR 50484, Oct. 7, 1991, unless otherwise noted.

§316.1 Definitions.

As used in this part, the term:

Application means any form, as defined in 8 CFR part 1, on which an applicant requests a benefit relating to naturalization.

Residence in the Service district where the application is filed means residence in the geographical area over which a particular local field office of USCIS ordinarily has jurisdiction for purposes of naturalization, regardless of where or how USCIS may require such benefit request to be submitted, or whether jurisdiction for the purpose of adjudication is relocated or internally reassigned to another USCIS office.

Service district means the geographical area over which a particular local field office of USCIS ordinarily has jurisdiction for purposes of naturalization.

[76 FR 53798, Aug. 29, 2011]

§316.2 Eligibility.

(a) *General.* Except as otherwise provided in this chapter, to be eligible for naturalization, an alien must establish that he or she:

(1) Is at least 18 years of age;

(2) Has been lawfully admitted as a permanent resident of the United States;

(3) Has resided continuously within the United States, as defined under §316.5, for a period of at least five years after having been lawfully admitted for permanent residence;

(4) Has been physically present in the United States for at least 30 months of the five years preceding the date of filing the application;

(5) Immediately preceding the filing of an application, or immediately preceding the examination on the application if the application was filed early pursuant to section 334(a) of the Act and the three month period falls within the required period of residence under section 316(a) or 319(a) of the Act, has resided, as defined under §316.5, for at least three months in a State or Service district having jurisdiction over the applicant's actual place of residence;

(6) Has resided continuously within the United States from the date of application for naturalization up to the time of admission to citizenship;

(7) For all relevant time periods under this paragraph, has been and continues to be a person of good moral character, attached to the principles of the Constitution of the United States, and favorably disposed toward the good order and happiness of the United States; and

(8) Is not a person described in Section 314 of the Act relating to deserters of the United States Armed Forces or those persons who departed from the United States to evade military service in the United States Armed Forces.

(b) *Burden of proof.* The applicant shall bear the burden of establishing by a preponderance of the evidence that he or she meets all of the requirements for naturalization, including that the applicant was lawfully admitted as a permanent resident to the United States, in accordance with the immigration laws in effect at the time of the applicant's initial entry or any subsequent reentry.

[56 FR 50484, Oct. 7, 1991, as amended at 58 FR 49912, Sept. 24, 1993; 60 FR 6651, Feb. 3, 1995; 76 FR 53798, Aug. 29, 2011]

§316.3 [Reserved]

§316.4 Application; documents.

(a) The applicant will apply for naturalization in accordance with instructions provided on the form prescribed by USCIS for that purpose.

(b) At the time of the examination on the application for naturalization, the applicant may be required to establish the status of lawful permanent resident by submitting the original evidence, issued by the Service, of lawful permanent residence in the United States. The applicant may be also required to submit any passports, or any other documents that have been used to enter the United States at any time after the original admission for permanent residence.

[56 FR 50484, Oct. 7, 1991, as amended at 58 FR 48780, Sept. 20, 1993; 63 FR 12987, Mar. 17, 1998; 63 FR 70316, Dec. 21, 1998; 76 FR 53798, Aug. 29, 2011]

§316.5 Residence in the United States.

(a) *General.* Unless otherwise specified, for purposes of this chapter, including §316.2 (a)(3), (a)(5), and (a)(6), an alien's residence is the same as that alien's domicile, or principal actual dwelling place, without regard to the alien's intent, and the duration of an alien's residence in a particular location is measured from the moment the alien first establishes residence in that location.

(b) *Residences in specific cases*—(1) *Military personnel.* For applicants who are serving in the Armed Forces of the United States but who do not qualify for naturalization under part 328 of this chapter, the applicant's residence shall be:

(i) The State or Service District where the applicant is physically present for at least three months, immediately preceding the filing of an application for naturalization, or immediately preceding the examination on the application if the application was filed early pursuant to section 334(a) of the Act and the three month period falls within the required period of residence under section 316(a) or 319(a) of the Act;

(ii) The location of the residence of the applicant's spouse and/or minor child(ren); or

(iii) The applicant's home of record as declared to the Armed Forces at the time of enlistment and as currently reflected in the applicant's military personnel file.

(2) *Students.* An applicant who is attending an educational institution in a State or Service District other than the applicant's home residence may apply for naturalization:

(i) Where that institution is located; or

(ii) In the State of the applicant's home residence if the applicant can establish that he or she is financially dependent upon his or her parents at the time that the application is filed and during the naturalization process.

(3) *Commuter aliens.* An applicant who is a commuter alien, as described in §211.5 of this chapter, must establish a principal dwelling place in the United States with the intention of permanently residing there, and must thereafter acquire the requisite period of residence before eligibility for naturalization may be established. Accordingly, a commuter resident alien may not apply for naturalization until he or she has actually taken up permanent residence in the United States and until such residence has continued for the required statutory period. Such an applicant bears the burden of providing evidence to that effect.

(4) *Residence in multiple states.* If an applicant claims residence in more than one State, the residence for purposes of this part shall be determined by reference to the location from which the annual federal income tax returns have been and are being filed.

(5) *Residence during absences of less than one year.* (i) An applicant's residence during any absence of less than one year shall continue to be the State or Service district where the applicant last resided at the time of the applicant's departure abroad.

(ii) *Return to the United States.* If, upon returning to the United States, an applicant returns to the State or Service district where the applicant last resided, the applicant will have complied with the continuous residence requirement specified in §316.2(a)(5) when at least three months have elapsed, including any part of the applicant's absence, from the date on which the applicant first established that residence. If the applicant establishes residence in a State or Service district other than the one in which he or she last resided, the applicant must complete three months at that new residence to be eligible for naturalization.

(6) *Spouse of military personnel.* Pursuant to section 319(e) of the Act, any period of time the spouse of a United States citizen resides abroad will be treated as residence in any State or district of the United States for purposes of naturalization under section 316(a) or 319(a) of the Act if, during the period of time abroad, the applicant establishes that he or she was:

(i) The spouse of a member of the Armed Forces;

(ii) Authorized to accompany and reside abroad with that member of the Armed Forces pursuant to the member's official orders; and

(iii) Accompanying and residing abroad with that member of the Armed

Forces in marital union in accordance with 8 CFR 319.1(b).

(c) *Disruption of continuity of residence*—(1) *Absence from the United States*—(i) *For continuous periods of between six (6) months and one (1) year.* Absences from the United States for continuous periods of between six (6) months and one (1) year during the periods for which continuous residence is required under §316.2 (a)(3) and (a)(6) shall disrupt the continuity of such residence for purposes of this part unless the applicant can establish otherwise to the satisfaction of the Service. This finding remains valid even if the applicant did not apply for or otherwise request a nonresident classification for tax purposes, did not document an abandonment of lawful permanent resident status, and is still considered a lawful permanent resident under immigration laws. The types of documentation which may establish that the applicant did not disrupt the continuity of his or her residence in the United States during an extended absence include, but are not limited to, evidence that during the absence:

(A) The applicant did not terminate his or her employment in the United States;

(B) The applicant's immediate family remained in the United States;

(C) The applicant retained full access to his or her United States abode; or

(D) The applicant did not obtain employment while abroad.

(ii) *For period in excess of one (1) year.* Unless an applicant applies for benefits in accordance with §316.5(d), absences from the United States for a continuous period of one (1) year or more during the period for which continuous residence is required under §316.2 (a)(3) and (a)(5) shall disrupt the continuity of the applicant's residence. An applicant described in this paragraph who must satisfy a five-year statutory residence period may file an application for naturalization four years and one day following the date of the applicant's return to the United States to resume permanent residence. An applicant described in this paragraph who must satisfy a three-year statutory residence period may file an application for naturalization two years and one day following the date of the applicant's return to the United States to resume permanent residence.

(2) *Claim of nonresident alien status for income tax purposes after lawful admission as a permanent resident.* An applicant who is a lawfully admitted permanent resident of the United States, but who voluntarily claims nonresident alien status to qualify for special exemptions from income tax liability, or fails to file either federal or state income tax returns because he or she considers himself or herself to be a nonresident alien, raises a rebuttable presumption that the applicant has relinquished the privileges of permanent resident status in the United States.

(3) *Removal and return.* Any departure from the United States while under an order of removal (including previously issued orders of exclusion or deportation) terminates the applicant's status as a lawful permanent resident and, therefore, disrupts the continuity of residence for purposes of this part.

(4) *Readmission after a deferred inspection or exclusion proceeding.* An applicant who has been readmitted as a lawful permanent resident after a deferred inspection or by the immigration judge during exclusion proceedings shall satisfy the residence and physical presence requirements under §316.2 (a)(3), (a)(4), (a)(5), and (a)(6) in the same manner as any other applicant for naturalization.

(d) *Application for benefits with respect to absences; appeal*—(1) *Preservation of residence under section 316(b) of the Act.* (i) An application for the residence benefits under section 316(b) of the Act to cover an absence from the United States for a continuous period of one year or more shall be submitted to the Service on Form N–470 with the required fee, in accordance with the form's instructions. The application may be filed either before or after the applicant's employment commences, but must be filed before the applicant has been absent from the United States for a continuous period of one year.

(ii) An approval of Form N–470 under section 316(b) of the Act shall cover the spouse and dependent unmarried sons and daughters of the applicant who are residing abroad as members of the applicant's household during the period covered by the application. The notice of approval, Form N–472, shall identify the family members so covered.

(iii) An applicant whose Form N–470 application under section 316(b) of the Act has been approved, but who voluntarily claims nonresident alien status to qualify for special exemptions from income tax liability, raises a rebuttable presumption that the applicant has relinquished a claim of having retained lawful permanent resident status while abroad. The applicant's family members who were covered under section 316(b) of the Act and who were listed on the applicant's Form N–472 will also be subject to the rebuttable presumption that they have relinquished their claims to lawful permanent resident status.

(2) *Preservation of residence under section 317 of the Act.* An application for the residence and physical presence benefits of section 317 of the Act to cover any absences from the United States, whether before or after December 24, 1952, shall be submitted to the Service on Form N–470 with the required fee, in accordance with the form's instructions. The application may be filed either before or after the applicant's absence from the United States or the performance of the functions or services described in section 317 of the Act.

(3) *Approval, denial, and appeal.* The applicant under paragraphs (d)(1) or (d)(2) of this section shall be notified of the Service's disposition of the application on Form N–472. If the application is denied, the Service shall specify the reasons for the denial, and shall inform the applicant of the right to appeal in accordance with the provisions of part 103 of this chapter.

[56 FR 50484, Oct. 7, 1991, as amended at 56 FR 50487, Oct. 7, 1991; 58 FR 49913, Sept. 24, 1993; 60 FR 6651, Feb. 3, 1995; 62 FR 10394, Mar. 6, 1997; 76 FR 53798, Aug. 29, 2011]

§ 316.6 Physical presence for certain spouses of military personnel.

Pursuant to section 319(e) of the Act, any period of time the spouse of a United States citizen resides abroad will be treated as physical presence in any State or district of the United States for purposes of naturalization under section 316(a) or 319(a) of the Act if, during the period of time abroad, the applicant establishes that he or she was:

(a) The spouse of a member of the Armed Forces;

(b) Authorized to accompany and reside abroad with that member of the Armed Forces pursuant to the member's official orders; and

(c) Accompanying and residing abroad with that member of the Armed Forces in marital union in accordance with 8 CFR 319.1(b).

[76 FR 53798, Aug. 29, 2011]

§§ 316.7–316.9 [Reserved]

§ 316.10 Good moral character.

(a) *Requirement of good moral character during the statutory period.* (1) An applicant for naturalization bears the burden of demonstrating that, during the statutorily prescribed period, he or she has been and continues to be a person of good moral character. This includes the period between the examination and the administration of the oath of allegiance.

(2) In accordance with section 101(f) of the Act, the Service shall evaluate claims of good moral character on a case-by-case basis taking into account the elements enumerated in this section and the standards of the average citizen in the community of residence. The Service is not limited to reviewing the applicant's conduct during the five years immediately preceding the filing of the application, but may take into consideration, as a basis for its determination, the applicant's conduct and acts at any time prior to that period, if the conduct of the applicant during the statutory period does not reflect that there has been reform of character from an earlier period or if the earlier conduct and acts appear relevant to a determination of the applicant's present moral character.

(b) *Finding of a lack of good moral character.* (1) An applicant shall be found to lack good moral character, if the applicant has been:

(i) Convicted of murder at any time; or

(ii) Convicted of an aggravated felony as defined in section 101(a)(43) of the Act on or after November 29, 1990.

(2) An applicant shall be found to lack good moral character if during the statutory period the applicant:

(i) Committed one or more crimes involving moral turpitude, other than a purely political offense, for which the applicant was convicted, except as specified in section 212(a)(2)(ii)(II) of the Act;

(ii) Committed two or more offenses for which the applicant was convicted and the aggregate sentence actually imposed was five years or more, provided that, if the offense was committed outside the United States, it was not a purely political offense;

(iii) Violated any law of the United States, any State, or any foreign country relating to a controlled substance, provided that the violation was not a single offense for simple possession of 30 grams or less of marijuana;

(iv) Admits committing any criminal act covered by paragraphs (b)(2) (i), (ii), or (iii) of this section for which there was never a formal charge, indictment, arrest, or conviction, whether committed in the United States or any other country;

(v) Is or was confined to a penal institution for an aggregate of 180 days pursuant to a conviction or convictions (provided that such confinement was not outside the United States due to a conviction outside the United States for a purely political offense);

(vi) Has given false testimony to obtain any benefit from the Act, if the testimony was made under oath or affirmation and with an intent to obtain an immigration benefit; this prohibition applies regardless of whether the information provided in the false testimony was material, in the sense that if given truthfully it would have rendered ineligible for benefits either the applicant or the person on whose behalf the applicant sought the benefit;

(vii) Is or was involved in prostitution or commercialized vice as described in section 212(a)(2)(D) of the Act;

(viii) Is or was involved in the smuggling of a person or persons into the United States as described in section 212(a)(6)(E) of the Act;

(ix) Has practiced or is practicing polygamy;

(x) Committed two or more gambling offenses for which the applicant was convicted;

(xi) Earns his or her income principally from illegal gambling activities; or

(xii) Is or was a habitual drunkard.

(3) Unless the applicant establishes extenuating circumstances, the applicant shall be found to lack good moral character if, during the statutory period, the applicant:

(i) Willfully failed or refused to support dependents;

(ii) Had an extramarital affair which tended to destroy an existing marriage; or

(iii) Committed unlawful acts that adversely reflect upon the applicant's moral character, or was convicted or imprisoned for such acts, although the acts do not fall within the purview of §316.10(b) (1) or (2).

(c) *Proof of good moral character in certain cases*—(1) *Effect of probation or parole.* An applicant who has been on probation, parole, or suspended sentence during all or part of the statutory period is not thereby precluded from establishing good moral character, but such probation, parole, or suspended sentence may be considered by the Service in determining good moral character. An application will not be approved until after the probation, parole, or suspended sentence has been completed.

(2) *Full and unconditional executive pardon*—(i) *Before the statutory period.* An applicant who has received a full and unconditional executive pardon prior to the beginning of the statutory period is not precluded by §316.10(b)(1) from establishing good moral character provided the applicant demonstrates that reformation and rehabilitation occurred prior to the beginning of the statutory period.

(ii) *During the statutory period.* An applicant who receives a full and unconditional executive pardon during the statutory period is not precluded by §316.10(b)(2) (i) and (ii) from establishing good moral character, provided the applicant can demonstrate that extenuating and/or exonerating circumstances exist that would establish his or her good moral character.

(3) *Record expungement*—(i) *Drug offenses.* Where an applicant has had his or her record expunged relating to one of the narcotics offenses under section 212(a)(2)(A)(i)(II) and section 241(a)(2)(B) of the Act, that applicant shall be considered as having been "convicted" within the meaning of §316.10(b)(2)(ii), or, if confined, as having been confined as a result of "conviction" for purposes of §316.10(b)(2)(iv).

(ii) *Moral turpitude.* An applicant who has committed or admits the commission of two or more crimes involving moral turpitude during the statutory period is precluded from establishing good moral character, even though the conviction record of one such offense has been expunged.

[56 FR 50484, Oct. 7, 1991, as amended at 58 FR 49913, Sept. 24, 1993]

§316.11 Attachment to the Constitution; favorable disposition towards the good order and happiness.

(a) *General.* An applicant for naturalization must establish that during the statutorily prescribed period, he or she has been and continues to be attached to the principles of the Constitution of the United States and favorably disposed toward the good order and happiness of the United States. Attachment implies a depth of conviction which would lead to active support of the Constitution. Attachment and favorable disposition relate to mental attitude, and contemplate the exclusion from citizenship of applicants who are hostile to the basic form of government of the United States, or who disbelieve in the principles of the Constitution.

(b) *Advocacy of peaceful change.* At a minimum, the applicant shall satisfy the general standard of paragraph (a) of this section by demonstrating an acceptance of the democratic, representational process established by the Constitution, a willingness to obey the laws which may result from that process, and an understanding of the means for change which are prescribed by the Constitution. The right to work for political change shall be consistent with the standards in paragraph (a) of this section only if the changes advocated would not abrogate the current Government and establish an entirely different form of government.

(c) *Membership in the Communist Party or any other totalitarian organization.* An applicant who is or has been a member of or affiliated with the Communist Party or any other totalitarian organization shall be ineligible for naturalization, unless the applicant's membership meets the exceptions in sections 313 and 335 of the Act and §313.4 of this chapter.

§316.12 Applicant's legal incompetency during statutory period.

(a) *General.* An applicant who is legally competent at the time of the examination on the naturalization application and of the administration of the oath of allegiance may be admitted to citizenship, provided that the applicant fully understands the purpose and responsibilities of the naturalization procedures.

(b) *Legal incompetence.* Naturalization is not precluded if, during part of the statutory period, the applicant was legally incompetent or confined to a mental institution.

(1) There is a presumption that the applicant's good moral character, attachment, and favorable disposition which existed prior to the period of legal incompetency continued through that period. The Service may, however, consider an applicant's actions during a period of legal incompetence, as evidence tending to rebut this presumption.

(2) If the applicant has been declared legally incompetent, the applicant has the burden of establishing that legal competency has been restored. The applicant shall submit legal and medical evidence to determine and establish the claim of legal competency.

(3) The applicant shall bear the burden of establishing that any crimes committed, regardless of whether the applicant was convicted, occurred while the applicant was declared legally incompetent.

§316.13 [Reserved]

§316.14 Adjudication—examination, grant, denial.

(a) *Examination.* The examination on an application for naturalization shall be conducted in accordance with Section 335 of the Act.

(b) *Determination*—(1) *Grant or denial.* Subject to supervisory review, the employee of the Service who conducts the examination under paragraph (a) of this section shall determine whether to grant or deny the application, and shall provide reasons for the determination, as required under section 335(d) of the Act.

(2) *Appeal.* An applicant whose application for naturalization has been denied may request a hearing, which shall be carried out in accordance with section 336 of the Act.

§§ 316.15–316.19 [Reserved]

§ 316.20 American institutions of research, public international organizations, and designations under the International Immunities Act.

(a) *American institutions of research.* The following-listed organizations have been determined to be American Institutions of research recognized by the Attorney General:

African Medical and Research Foundation (AMREF-USA).
Albert Einstein College of Medicine of Yeshiva University (only in relationship to its research programs).
American Friends of the Middle East, Inc.
American Institutes of Research in the Behavioral Sciences (only in relationship to research projects abroad).
American Universities Field Staff, Inc.
American University, The, Cairo, Egypt.
American University of Beirut (Near East College Associations).
Arctic Institute of North America, Inc.
Armour Research Foundation of Illinois Institute of Technology.
Asia Foundation, The (formerly Committee for a Free Asia, Inc.).
Association of Universities for Research in Astronomy (AURA, Inc.), Tucson, AZ.
Atomic Bomb Casualty Commission.
Beirut University College.
Bermuda Biological Station for Research, Inc.
Bernice P. Biship Museum of Polynesian Antiquities, Ethnology and Natural History at Honolulu, HI.
Brookhaven National Laboratory, Associated Universities, Inc.
Brown University (Department of Engineering), Providence, RI.
Buffalo Eye Bank and Research Society, Inc.
Burma Office of Robert N. Nathan Associates, Inc.
California State University at Long Beach, Department of Geological Sciences.
Carleton College (Department of Sociology and Anthropology), Northfield, MN.
Center of Alcohol Studies, Laboratory of Applied Biodynamics of Yale University.
Central Registry of Jewish Losses in Egypt.
College of Engineering, University of Wisconsin.
College of Medicine, State University of New York.
Colorado State University (Research Foundation), Fort Collins, CO.
Colorado University (International Economic Studies Center), Boulder, CO.
Columbia University (Parker School of Foreign and Comparative Law) and (Faculty of Pure Science), New York, NY.
Cornell University (International Agricultural Development, University of the Philippines-Cornell University Graduate Education Program).
Dartmouth Medical School.
Department of French, Department of Scandinavian Languages, and Department of Near Eastern Languages of the University of California, Berkeley, CA.
Duke University.
Environmental Research Laboratory of the University of Arizona.
Fletcher School of Law and Diplomacy, Medford, MA.
Ford Foundation, 477 Madison Avenue, New York, NY.
Free Europe, Inc. (formerly Free Europe Committee, Inc.; National Committee for a Free Europe (including Radio Free Europe)).
Georgetown University.
George Williams Hooper Foundation, San Francisco Medical Center, University of California, San Francisco, CA.
Gorgas Memorial Institute of Tropical and Preventive Medicine, Inc., and its operating unit, the Gorgas Memorial Laboratory.
Graduate Faculty of Political and Social Science Division of the New School for Social Research, New York, NY.
Harvard University (research and educational programs only)
Harvard-Yenching Institute.
Humboldt State University, School of Natural Resources, Wildlife Management Department.
Indiana University at Bloomington, Indianapolis, South Bend, Northwest, Kokomo, Southeast, East, and Fort Wayne
Institute for Development Anthropology, Inc.
Institute of International Education, Inc.
Institute of International Studies, University of California, Berkeley, CA.
International Center for Social Research, New York, NY.
International Development Foundation, Inc.
International Development Services, Inc.

International Research Associates, Inc.
Inter-University Program for Chinese Language Studies (formerly Stanford Center for Chinese Studies) in Taipei, Taiwan.
Iowa State University.
Iran Foundation, Inc., The.
Kossuth Foundation, Inc., The, New York, NY.
Louisiana State University.
Massachusetts Institute of Technology.
Michigan State University, East Lansing, MI.
Missouri Botanical Garden (research and educational programs only)
Natural Science Foundation, Philadelphia, PA.
New York Zoological Society.
Paderewski Foundation, Inc.
Peabody Museum of Natural History of Yale University.
People to People Health Foundation, Inc., The (only in relationship to the scientific research activities that will be carried on abroad by the medical staff of the SS "Hope").
Pierce College (in relationship to research by an instructor, Department of Psychology), Athens, Greece.
Population Council, The, New York, NY.
Radio Liberty Committee, Inc. (formerly American Committee for Liberation, Inc.; American Committee for Liberation of the Peoples of Russia, Inc.; American Committee for Liberation from Bolshevism, Inc.).
Rockefeller Foundation.
Rutgers University, the State University of New Jersey
School of International Relations of the University of Southern California.
SIRIMAR (Societa Internazionale Recerche Marine) Division, Office of the Vice President for Research, Pennsylvania State University.
Social Science Research Council.
Solar Energy Research Institute (SERI).
Stanford Electronic Laboratories, Department of Electrical Engineering, School of Engineering, Stanford University, Stanford, CA.
Stanford Research Institute, Menlo Park, CA.
Stanford University (the George Vanderbilt Foundation), Stanford, CA.
Syracuse University.
Tulane University Graduate School.
Tulane University Medical School.
University of Alabama.
University of Alabama Medical Center.
University of Chicago (as a participant in the International Cooperation Administration Program No. W–74 only).
University of Colorado (Department of History), Boulder, CO.
University of Connecticut, College of Liberal Arts and Science (Department of Germanic and Slavic Languages).
University of Hawaii, Honolulu, HI.
University of Ilinois at Urbana-Champaign, Austria-Illinois Exchange Program.
University of Kansas, Office of International Programs.
University of La Verne (La Verne College of Athens)
University of Michigan (School of Natural Resources), Ann Arbor, MI.
University of Minnesota, Department of Plant Pathology (in relationship to research project abroad).
University of Nebraska Mission in Columbia, South America.
University of North Carolina at Chapel Hill.
University of Notre Dame, Notre Dame, IN.
University of Puerto Rico.
University of Washington (Department of Marketing, Transportation, and International Business) and (The School of Public Health and Community Medicine), Seattle, WA.
Wayne State University, Detroit, MI.
Wenner-Gren Foundation for Anthropological Research, Inc.
Williams College, Economic Department, Williamstown, MA.

(b) *Public international organizations of which the United States is a member by treaty or statute.* The following-listed organizations have been determined to be public international organizations of which the United States is a member by treaty or statute:

The North Atlantic Treaty Organization.
United Nations and all agencies and organizations which are a part thereof.

(c) *International Organizations Immunities Act designations.* The following public international organizations are entitled to enjoy the privileges, exemptions, and immunities provided for in the International Organizations Immunities Act, and are considered as public international organizations of which the United States is a member by treaty or statute within the meaning of section 316(b) of the Act and as public international organizations in which the United States participates by treaty or statute within the meaning of section 319(b) of the Act:

African Development Bank (E.O. 12403, Feb. 8, 1983).
African Development Fund (E.O. 11977, Mar. 14, 1977).
Asian Development Bank (E.O. 11334, Mar. 7, 1967).
Caribbean Organization (E.O. 10983, Dec. 30, 1961).
Criminal Police Organization (E.O. 12425, June 16, 1983).

Customs Cooperation Council (E.O. 11596, June 5, 1971).
European Space Research Organization (ESRO) (E.O. 11760, Jan. 17, 1974).
Food and Agriculture Organization, The (E.O. 9698, Feb 19, 1946).
Great Lakes Fishery Commission (E.O. 11059, Oct. 23, 1962).
Inter-American Defense Board (E.O. 10228, Mar. 26, 1951).
Inter-American Development Bank (E.O. 10873, Apr. 8, 1960).
Inter-American Institute for Cooperation on Agriculture (E.O. 9751, July 11, 1946).
Inter-American Statistical Institute (E.O. 9751, July 11, 1946).
Inter-American Tropical Tuna Commission (E.O. 11059, Oct. 23, 1962).
Intergovernmental Committee for European Migration (formerly the Provisional Intergovernmental Committee for the Movement of Migrants from Europe) (E.O. 10335, Mar. 28, 1952).
Intergovernmental Maritime Consultative Organization (E.O. 10795, Dec. 13, 1958).
International Atomic Energy Agency (E.O. 10727, Aug. 31, 1957).
International Bank for Reconstruction and Development (E.O. 9751, July 11, 1946).
International Centre for Settlement of Investment Disputes (E.O. 11966, Jan. 19, 1977).
International Civil Aviation Organization (E.O. 9863, May 31, 1947).
International Coffee Organization (E.O. 11225, May 22, 1965).
International Cotton Advisory Committee (E.O. 9911, Dec. 19, 1947).
International Development Association (E.O. 11966, Jan. 19, 1977).
International Fertilizer Development Center (E.O. 11977, Mar. 14, 1977).
International Finance Corporation (E.O. 10680, Oct. 2, 1956).
International Food Policy Research Institute (E.O. 12359, Apr. 22, 1982).
International Hydrographic Bureau (E.O. 10769, May 29, 1958).
International Institute for Cotton (E.O. 11283, May 27, 1966).
International Joint Commission—United States and Canada (E.O. 9972, June 25, 1948).
International Labor Organization, The (functions through staff known as The International Labor Office) (E.O. 9698, Feb. 19, 1946).
International Maritime Satellite Organization (E.O. 12238, Sept. 12, 1980).
International Monetary Fund (E.O. 9751, July 11, 1946).
International Pacific Halibut Commission (E.O. 11059, Oct. 23, 1962).
International Secretariat for Volunteer Service (E.O. 11363, July 20, 1967).
International Telecommunication Union (E.O. 9863, May 31, 1947).
International Telecommunications Satellite Organization (INTELSAT) (E.O. 11718, May 14, 1973).
International Wheat Advisory Committee (E.O. 9823, Jan. 24, 1947).
Multinational Force and Observers (E.O. 12359, Apr. 22, 1982).
Organization for European Economic Cooperation (E.O. 10133, June 27, 1950) (Now known as Organization for Economic Cooperation and Development; 28 FR 2959, Mar. 26, 1963).
Organization of African Unity (OAU) (E.O. 11767, Feb. 19, 1974).
Organization of American States (includes Pan American Union) (E.O. 10533, June 3, 1954).
Pan American Health Organization (includes Pan American Sanitary Bureau) (E.O. 10864, Feb. 18, 1960).
Preparatory Commission of the International Atomic Energy Agency (E.O. 10727, Aug. 31, 1957).
Preparatory Commission for the International Refugee Organization and its successor, the International Refugee Organization (E.O. 9887, Aug. 22, 1947).
South Pacific Commission (E.O. 10086, Nov. 25, 1949).
United International Bureau for the Protection of Intellectual Property (BIRPI) (E.O. 11484, Sept. 29, 1969).
United Nations, The (E.O. 9698, Feb. 19, 1946).
United Nations Educational, Scientific, and Cultural Organizations (E.O. 9863, May 31, 1947).
Universal Postal Union (E.O. 10727, Aug. 31, 1957).
World Health Organization (E.O. 10025, Dec. 30, 1948).
World Intellectual Property Organization (E.O. 11866, June 18, 1975).
World Meteorological Organization (E.O. 10676, Sept. 1, 1956).

[32 FR 9634, July 4, 1967]

EDITORIAL NOTE: For FEDERAL REGISTER citations affecting §316.20, see the List of CFR Sections Affected, which appears in the Finding Aids section of the printed volume and at *www.govinfo.gov*.

PART 318—PENDING REMOVAL PROCEEDINGS

AUTHORITY: 8 U.S.C. 1103, 1252, 1429, 1443; 8 CFR part 2.

SOURCE: 62 FR 10394, Mar. 6, 1997, unless otherwise noted.

§318.1 Warrant of arrest.

For the purposes of section 318 of the Act, a notice to appear issued under 8

CFR part 239 (including a charging document issued to commence proceedings under sections 236 or 242 of the Act prior to April 1, 1997) shall be regarded as a warrant of arrest.

PART 319—SPECIAL CLASSES OF PERSONS WHO MAY BE NATURALIZED: SPOUSES OF UNITED STATES CITIZENS

AUTHORITY: 8 U.S.C. 1103, 1430, 1443.

§ 319.1 Persons living in marital union with United States citizen spouse.

(a) *Eligibility.* To be eligible for naturalization under section 319(a) of the Act, the spouse of a United States citizen must establish that he or she:

(1) Has been lawfully admitted for permanent residence to the United States;

(2) Has resided continuously within the United States, as defined under § 316.5 of this chapter, for a period of at least three years after having been lawfully admitted for permanent residence;

(3) Has been living in marital union with the citizen spouse for the three years preceding the date of examination on the application, and the spouse has been a United States citizen for the duration of that three year period;

(4) Has been physically present in the United States for periods totaling at least 18 months;

(5) Has resided, as defined in § 316.5 of this chapter, for at least 3 months immediately preceding the filing of the application, or immediately preceding the examination on the application if the application was filed early pursuant to section 334(a) of the Act and the three month period falls within the required period of residence under section 316(a) or 319(a) of the Act, in the State or Service district having jurisdiction over the alien's actual place of residence;

(6) Has resided continuously within the United States from the date of application for naturalization until the time of admission to citizenship;

(7) For all relevant periods under this paragraph, has been and continues to be a person of good moral character, attached to the principles of the Constitution of the United States, and favorably disposed toward the good order and happiness of the United States; and

(8) Has complied with all other requirements for naturalization as provided in part 316 of this chapter, except for those contained in § 316.2 (a)(3) through (a)(5) of this chapter.

(b) *Marital union*—(1) *General.* An applicant lives in marital union with a citizen spouse if the applicant actually resides with his or her current spouse. The burden is on the applicant to establish, in each individual case, that a particular marital union satisfies the requirements of this part.

(2) *Loss of Marital Union*—(i) *Divorce, death or expatriation.* A person is ineligible for naturalization as the spouse of a United States citizen under section 319(a) of the Act if, before or after the filing of the application, the marital union ceases to exist due to death or divorce, or the citizen spouse has expatriated. Eligibility is not restored to an applicant whose relationship to the citizen spouse terminates before the applicant's admission to citizenship, even though the applicant subsequently marries another United States citizen.

(ii) *Separation*—(A) *Legal separation.* Any legal separation will break the continuity of the marital union required for purposes of this part.

(B) *Informal separation.* Any informal separation that suggests the possibility of marital disunity will be evaluated on a case-by-case basis to determine whether it is sufficient enough to signify the dissolution of the marital union.

(C) *Involuntary separation.* In the event that the applicant and spouse live apart because of circumstances beyond their control, such as military service in the Armed Forces of the United States or essential business or occupational demands, rather than because of voluntary legal or informal separation, the resulting separation, even if prolonged, will not preclude naturalization under this part.

(c) *Physical presence in the United States.* In the event that the alien spouse has never been in the United States, eligibility under this section is not established even though the alien spouse resided abroad in marital union with the citizen spouse during the three year period.

[56 FR 50488, Oct. 7, 1991, as amended at 76 FR 53798, Aug. 29, 2011]

§319.2 Person whose United States citizen spouse is employed abroad.

(a) *Eligibility.* To be eligible for naturalization under section 319(b) of the Act, the alien spouse of a United States citizen must:

(1) Establish that his or her citizen spouse satisfies the requirements under section 319(b)(1) of the Act, including that he or she is regularly stationed abroad. For purposes of this section, a citizen spouse is regularly stationed abroad if he or she proceeds abroad, for a period of not less than one year, pursuant to an employment contract or orders, and assumes the duties of employment;

(2) At the time of examination on the application for naturalization, be present in the United States pursuant to a lawful admission for permanent residence;

(3) At the time of naturalization, be present in the United States;

(4) Declare in good faith, upon naturalization before the Service, an intention:

(i) To reside abroad with the citizen spouse; and

(ii) To take up residence within the United States immediately upon the termination of the citizen spouse's employment abroad;

(5) Be a person of good moral character, attached to the principles of the Constitution of the United States, and favorably disposed toward the good order and happiness of the United States; and

(6) Comply with all other requirements for naturalization as provided in part 316 of this chapter, except for those contained in §316.2(a)(3) through (a)(6) of this chapter.

(b) *Alien spouse's requirement to depart abroad immediately after naturalization.* An alien spouse seeking naturalization under section 319(b) of the Act must:

(1) Establish that he or she will depart to join the citizen spouse within 30 to 45 days after the date of naturalization;

(2) Notify the Service immediately of any delay or cancellation of the citizen spouse's assignment abroad; and

(3) Notify the Service immediately if he or she is unable to reside with the citizen spouse because the citizen spouse is employed abroad in an area of hostilities where dependents may not reside.

(c) *Loss of marital union due to death, divorce, or expatriation of the citizen spouse.* A person is ineligible for naturalization as the spouse of a United States citizen under section 319(b) of the Act if, before or after the filing of the application, the marital union ceases to exist due to death or divorce, or the citizen spouse has expatriated. Eligibility is not restored to an applicant whose relationship to the citizen spouse terminates before the applicant's admission into citizenship, even though the applicant subsequently marries another United States citizen.

[56 FR 50488, Oct. 7, 1991]

§319.3 Surviving spouses of United States citizens who died during a period of honorable service in an active duty status in the Armed Forces of the United States.

(a) *Eligibility.* To be eligible for naturalization under section 319(d) of the Act, the surviving spouse, child, or parent of a United States citizen must:

(1) Establish that his or her citizen spouse, child, or parent died during a period of honorable service in an active duty status in the Armed Forces of the United States and, in the case of a surviving spouse, establish that he or she was living in marital union with the citizen spouse, in accordance with 8

CFR 319.1(b), at the time of the citizen spouse's death;

(2) At the time of examination on the application for naturalization, reside in the United States pursuant to a lawful admission for permanent residence;

(3) Be a person of good moral character, attached to the principles of the Constitution of the United States, and favorably disposed toward the good order and happiness of the United States; and

(4) Comply with all other requirements for naturalization as provided in 8 CFR 316, except for those contained in 8 CFR 316.2(a)(3) through (6).

(b) *Remarriage of the surviving spouse.* The surviving spouse of a United States citizen described under paragraph (a)(1) of this section remains eligible for naturalization under section 319(d) of the Act, even if the surviving spouse remarries.

[56 FR 50488, Oct. 7, 1991, as amended at 76 FR 53798, Aug. 29, 2011]

§319.4 Persons continuously employed for 5 years by United States organizations engaged in disseminating information.

To be eligible for naturalization under section 319(c) of the Act, an applicant must:

(a) Establish that he or she is employed as required under section 319(c)(1) of the Act;

(b) Reside in the United States pursuant to a lawful admission for permanent residence;

(c) Establish that he or she has been employed as required under paragraph (a) of this section continuously for a period of not less than five years after a lawful admission for permanent residence;

(d) File his or her application for naturalization while employed as required under paragraph (a) of this section, or within six months following the termination of such employment;

(e) Be present in the United States at the time of naturalization;

(f) Declare in good faith, upon naturalization before the Service, an intention to take up residence within the United States immediately upon his or her termination of employment;

(g) Be a person of good moral character, attached to the principles of the Constitution of the United States, and favorably disposed toward the good order and happiness of the United States; and

(h) Comply with all other requirements for naturalization as provided in part 316 of this chapter, except for those contained in §316.2(a)(3) through (a)(6) of this chapter.

[56 FR 50489, Oct. 7, 1991]

§319.5 Public international organizations in which the U.S. participates by treaty or statute.

Organizations designated by the President as international organizations pursuant to the International Organizations Immunities Act are considered as public international organizations in which the United States participates by treaty or statute within the meaning of section 319(b) or the Act. For a list of such organizations see §316.20(b) of this chapter. In addition, the following have been determined to be public international organizations within the purview of section 319(b) of the Act:

The North Atlantic Treaty Organization.

The United Nations and all agencies and organizations which are a part thereof.

The regional commissioner shall forward a copy of each decision regarding a public international organization to the Assistant Commissioner, Naturalization.

[32 FR 9635, July 4, 1967. Redesignated at 33 FR 255, Jan. 9, 1968. Further redesignated and amended at 56 FR 50489, Oct. 7, 1991]

§319.6 United States nonprofit organizations engaged abroad in disseminating information which significantly promotes U.S. interests.

The following have been determined to be U.S. incorporated nonprofit organizations principally engaged in conducting abroad through communications media the dissemination of information which significantly promotes U.S. interests abroad within the purview of section 319(c) of the Act:

Free Europe, Inc.; formerly Free Europe Committee, Inc.; National Committee for a Free Europe (including Radio Free Europe)).

Radio Liberty Committee, Inc. (formerly American Committee for Liberation, Inc.;

American Committee for Liberation of the Peoples of Russia, Inc.; American Committee for Liberation from Bolshevism, Inc.).

[33 FR 255, Jan. 9, 1968. Redesignated and amended at 56 FR 50489, Oct. 7, 1991]

§§319.7–319.10 [Reserved]

§319.11 Filing of application.

(a) *General.* An applicant under this part must submit an application for naturalization in accordance with the form instructions with the fee required by 8 CFR 103.7(b)(1). An alien spouse applying for naturalization under section 319(b) of the Act who is described in 8 CFR 319.2 must also submit a statement of intent containing the following information about the citizen spouse's employment and future intent:

(1) The name of the employer and:

(i) The nature of the employer's business; or

(ii) The ministerial, religious, or missionary activity in which the employer is engaged;

(2) Whether the employing entity is owned in whole or in part by United States interests;

(3) Whether the employing entity is engaged in whole or in part in the development of the foreign trade and commerce of the United States;

(4) The nature of the activity in which the citizen spouse is engaged;

(5) The anticipated period of employment abroad;

(6) Whether the alien spouse intends to reside abroad with the citizen spouse; and,

(7) Whether the alien spouse intends to take up residence within the United States immediately upon the termination of such employment abroad of the citizen spouse.

(b) *Applications by military spouses*—(1) *General.* The alien spouses of United States military personnel being assigned abroad must satisfy the basic requirements of section 319(b) of the Act and of paragraph (a) of this section.

(2) *Government expense.* In the event that transportation expenses abroad for the alien spouse are to be paid by military authorities, a properly executed Certificate of Overseas Assignment to Support Application to File Petition for Naturalization, DD Form 1278 will be submitted in lieu of the statement of intent required by paragraph (a) of this section. Any DD Form 1278 issued more than 90 days in advance of departure is unacceptable for purposes of this section.

(3) *Private expense.* In the event that the alien spouse is not authorized to travel abroad at military expense, the alien spouse must submit in lieu of the statement of intent required by paragraph (a) of this section:

(i) A copy of the citizen spouse's military travel orders,

(ii) A letter from the citizen spouse's commanding officer indicating that the military has no objection to the applicant traveling to and residing in the vicinity of the citizen spouse's new duty station; and

(iii) Evidence of transportation arrangements to the new duty station.

[56 FR 50489, Oct. 7, 1991, as amended at 76 FR 53798, Aug. 29, 2011]

PART 320—CHILD BORN OUTSIDE THE UNITED STATES AND RESIDING PERMANENTLY IN THE UNITED STATES; REQUIREMENTS FOR AUTOMATIC ACQUISITION OF CITIZENSHIP

Sec.

AUTHORITY: 8 U.S.C. 1103, 1443; 8 CFR part 2.

SOURCE: 66 FR 32144, June 13, 2001, unless otherwise noted.

§320.1 What definitions are used in this part?

As used in this part, the term:

Adopted means adopted pursuant to a full, final and complete adoption. If a foreign adoption of an orphan was not full and final, was defective, or the unmarried U.S. citizen parent or U.S. citizen parent and spouse jointly did not see and observe the child in person prior to or during the foreign adoption proceedings, the child is not considered to have been fully, finally and completely adopted and must be readopted in the United States. Readoption requirements may be waived if the state of residence of the United States citizen parent(s) recognizes the foreign adoption as full and final under that state's adoption laws.

Adopted child means a person who has been adopted as defined above and who meets the requirements of section 101(b)(1)(E) or (F) of the Act.

Child means a person who meets the requirements of section 101(c)(1) of the Act.

Joint custody, in the case of a child of divorced or legally separated parents, means the award of equal responsibility for and authority over the care, education, religion, medical treatment, and general welfare of a child to both parents by a court of law or other appropriate government entity pursuant to the laws of the state or country of residence.

Legal custody refers to the responsibility for and authority over a child.

(1) For the purpose of the CCA, the Service will presume that a U.S. citizen parent has legal custody of a child, and will recognize that U.S. citizen parent as having lawful authority over the child, absent evidence to the contrary, in the case of:

(i) A biological child who currently resides with both natural parents (who are married to each other, living in marital union, and not separated),

(ii) A biological child who currently resides with a surviving natural parent (if the other parent is deceased), or

(iii) In the case of a biological child born out of wedlock who has been legitimated and currently resides with the natural parent.

(2) In the case of an adopted child, a determination that a U.S. citizen parent has legal custody will be based on the existence of a final adoption decree. In the case of a child of divorced or legally separated parents, the Service will find a U.S. citizen parent to have legal custody of a child, for the purpose of the CCA, where there has been an award of primary care, control, and maintenance of a minor child to a parent by a court of law or other appropriate government entity pursuant to the laws of the state or country of residence. The Service will consider a U.S. citizen parent who has been awarded "joint custody," to have legal custody of a child. There may be other factual circumstances under which the Service will find the U.S. citizen parent to have legal custody for purposes of the CCA.

§ 320.2 Who is eligible for citizenship?

(a) *General.* To be eligible for citizenship under section 320 of the Act, a person must establish that the following conditions have been met after February 26, 2001:

(1) The child has at least one United States citizen parent (by birth or naturalization);

(2) The child is under 18 years of age; and

(3) The child is residing in the United States in the legal and physical custody of the United States citizen parent, pursuant to a lawful admission for permanent residence.

(b) *Additional requirements if child is adopted.* If adopted, the child must meet all of the requirements in paragraph (a) of this section as well as satisfy the requirements applicable to adopted children under section 101(b)(1) of the Act.

§ 320.3 How, where, and what forms and other documents should be filed?

(a) *Application.* Individuals who are applying for a certificate of citizenship on their own behalf should submit the request in accordance with the form instructions on the form prescribed by USCIS for that purpose. An application for a certificate of citizenship under this section on behalf of a child who has not reached the age of 18 years must be submitted by that child's U.S. citizen biological or adoptive parent(s), or legal guardian.

(b) *Evidence.* (1) An applicant under this section must establish eligibility as described in 8 CFR 320.2. An applicant must submit the following supporting evidence unless such evidence is already contained in USCIS administrative file(s):

(i) The child's birth certificate or record;

(ii) Marriage certificate of child's parents (if applicable);

(iii) If the child's parents were married before their marriage to each other, proof of termination of any previous marriage of each parent (e.g., death certificate or divorce decree);

(iv) Evidence of U.S. citizenship of parent, (*i.e.*, birth certificate; naturalization certificate; FS–240, Report of Birth Abroad; a valid unexpired U.S. passport; or certificate of citizenship);

(v) If the child was born out of wedlock, documents verifying legitimation according to the laws of the child's residence or domicile or father's residence or domicile (if applicable);

(vi) In case of divorce, legal separation, or adoption, documentation of legal custody;

(vii) Copy of Permanent Resident Card/Alien Registration Receipt Card or other evidence of lawful permanent resident status (e.g. I–551 stamp in a valid foreign passport or Service-issued travel document);

(viii) If adopted, a copy of the full, final adoption decree and, if the adoption was outside of the United States and the child immigrated as an IR–4 (orphans coming to the United States to be adopted by U.S. citizen parent(s)), evidence that the foreign adoption is recognized by the state where the child is permanently residing; and

(ix) Evidence of all legal name changes, if applicable, for the child and U.S. citizen parent.

(2) If the Service requires any additional documentation to make a decision on the application for certificate of citizenship, applicants may be asked to provide that documentation under separate cover or at the time of interview. Applicants do not need to submit documents that were submitted in connection with: An application for immigrant visa and retained by the American Consulate for inclusion in the immigrant visa package, or an immigrant petition or application and included in a Service administrative file. Applicants should indicate that they wish to rely on such documents and identify the administrative file(s) by name and alien number. The Service will only request the required documentation again if necessary.

[66 FR 32144, June 13, 2001, as amended at 74 FR 26940, June 5, 2009; 76 FR 53799, Aug. 29, 2011]

§ 320.4 Who must appear for an interview on the application for citizenship?

All applicants (and U.S. citizen parent(s) if application filed on behalf of a minor biological or adopted child) must appear for examination unless such examination is waived under the guidelines expressed in § 341.2 of this chapter.

§ 320.5 Decision.

(a) *Approval of application.* If the application for the certificate of citizenship is approved, after the applicant takes the oath of allegiance prescribed in 8 CFR 337.1 (unless the oath is waived), USCIS will issue a certificate of citizenship.

(b) *Denial of application.* If the decision of USCIS is to deny the application for a certificate of citizenship under this section, the applicant will be advised in writing of the reasons for denial and of the right to appeal in accordance with 8 CFR 103.3(a). An applicant may file an appeal within 30 days of service of the decision in accordance with the instructions on the form prescribed by USCIS for that purpose, and with the fee required by 8 CFR 103.7(b)(1).

(c) *Subsequent application.* After an application for a certificate of citizenship has been denied and the time for appeal has expired, USCIS will reject a subsequent application submitted by the same individual and the applicant will be instructed to submit a motion for reopening or reconsideration in accordance with 8 CFR 103.5. The motion must be accompanied by the rejected application and the fee specified in 8 CFR 103.7(b)(1).

[76 FR 53799, Aug. 29, 2011]

PART 322—CHILD BORN OUTSIDE THE UNITED STATES; REQUIREMENTS FOR APPLICATION FOR CERTIFICATE OF CITIZENSHIP

Sec.

AUTHORITY: 8 U.S.C. 1103, 1443; 8 CFR part 2.

SOURCE: 66 FR 32144, June 13, 2001, unless otherwise noted.

§ 322.1 What are the definitions used in this part?

As used in this part the term:

Adopted means adopted pursuant to a full, final and complete adoption. In the case of an orphan adoption, if a foreign adoption was not full and final, was defective, or the unmarried U.S. citizen parent or U.S. citizen parent and spouse jointly did not see and observe the child in person prior to or during the foreign adoption proceedings, an orphan is not considered to have been adopted and must be re-adopted in the United States or satisfy the requirements of section 101(b)(1)(E) of the Act.

Adopted child means a person who has been adopted as defined above and who meets the requirements of section 101(b)(1)(E), (F) or (G) of the Act.

Child means a person who meets the requirements of section 101(c)(1) of the Act.

Lawful admission shall have the same meaning as provided in section 101(a)(13) of the Act.

Joint custody, in the case of a child of divorced or legally separated parents, means the award of equal responsibility for and authority over the care, education, religion, medical treatment and general welfare of a child to both parents by a court of law or other appropriate government entity pursuant to the laws of the state or country of residence.

Legal custody refers to the responsibility for and authority over a child.

(1) For the purpose of the CCA, the Service will presume that a U.S. citizen parent has legal custody of a child, and will recognize that U.S. citizen parent as having lawful authority over the child, absent evidence to the contrary, in the case of:

(i) A biological child who currently resides with both natural parents (who are married to each other, living in marital union, and not separated),

(ii) A biological child who currently resides with a surviving natural parent (if the other parent is deceased), or

(iii) In the case of a biological child born out of wedlock who has been legitimated and currently resides with the natural parent.

(2) In the case of an adopted child, a determination that a U.S. citizen parent has legal custody will be based on the existence of a final adoption decree. In the case of a child of divorced or legally separated parents, the Service will find a U.S. citizen parent to have legal custody of a child, for the purpose of the CCA, where there has been an award of primary care, control, and maintenance of a minor child to a parent by a court of law or other appropriate government entity pursuant to the laws of the state or country of residence. The Service will consider a U.S. citizen parent who has been awarded "joint custody," to have legal custody of a child. There may be other factual circumstances under which the Service will find the U.S. citizen parent to have legal custody for purposes of the CCA.

[66 FR 32144, June 13, 2001, as amended at 76 FR 53799, Aug. 29, 2011]

§ 322.2 Eligibility.

(a) *General*. A child will be eligible for citizenship under section 322 of the Act, if the following conditions have been fulfilled:

(1) The child has at least one United States citizen parent (by birth or naturalization);

(2) The United States citizen parent has been physically present in the United States or its outlying possessions for at least 5 years, at least 2 of which were after the age of 14, or the United States citizen parent has a United States citizen parent who has been physically present in the United States or its outlying possessions for at least 5 years, at least 2 of which were after the age of 14;

(3) The child currently is under 18 years of age;

(4) The child currently is residing outside the United States in the legal and physical custody of the United States citizen parent; and

(5) The child is temporarily present in the United States pursuant to a lawful admission and is maintaining such lawful status in the United States.

(b) *Additional requirements if child is adopted.* If an adopted child, all of the requirements in paragraph (a) of this section must be fulfilled and the child must satisfy the requirements applicable to adopted children under section 101(b)(1) of the Act.

(c) *Exceptions for children of military personnel.* Pursuant to section 322(d) of the Act, a child of a member of the Armed Forces of the United States residing abroad is exempt from the temporary physical presence, lawful admission, and maintenance of lawful status requirements under 8 CFR 322.2(a)(5), if the child:

(1) Is authorized to accompany and reside abroad with the member of the Armed Forces pursuant to the member's official orders; and

(2) Is accompanying and residing abroad with the member of the Armed Forces.

[66 FR 32144, June 13, 2001, as amended at 76 FR 53799, Aug. 29, 2011]

§ 322.3 Application and supporting documents.

(a) *Application.* A U.S. citizen parent of an alien child (including an adopted child) may file an application for the child to become a citizen and obtain a certificate of citizenship under section 322 of the Act by submitting an application on the form prescribed by USCIS in accordance with the form instructions and with the fee prescribed by 8 CFR 103.7(b)(1). If the U.S. citizen parent has died, the child's U.S. citizen grandparent or U.S. citizen legal guardian may submit the application, provided the application is filed not more than 5 years after the death of the U.S. citizen parent.

(b) *Evidence.* (1) An applicant under this section shall establish eligibility under § 322.2. In addition to the forms and the appropriate fee as required in § 103.7(b)(1) of this chapter, an applicant must submit the following required documents unless such documents are already contained in the Service administrative file(s):

(i) The child's birth certificate or record;

(ii) Marriage certificate of child's parents (if applicable);

(iii) If the child's parents were married before their marriage to each other, proof of termination of any previous marriage of each parent (e.g., death certificate or divorce decree);

(iv) Evidence of U.S. citizenship of parent (*i.e.*, birth certificate; naturalization certificate; FS–240, Report of Birth Abroad; a valid unexpired U.S. passport; or certificate of citizenship);

(v) If the child was born out of wedlock, documents verifying legitimation according to the laws of the child's residence or domicile or father's residence or domicile (if applicable);

(vi) In case of divorce, legal separation, or adoption, documentation of legal custody (if applicable);

(vii) Documentation establishing that the U.S. citizen parent or U.S. citizen grandparent meets the required physical presence requirements (e.g., school records, military records, utility bills, medical records, deeds, mortgages, contracts, insurance policies, receipts, or attestations by churches, unions, or other organizations);

(viii) Evidence that the child is present in the United States pursuant to a lawful admission and is maintaining such lawful status, or evidence establishing that the child qualifies for an exception to these requirements as provided in 8 CFR 322.2(c) pursuant to section 322(d) of the Act. Such evidence may be presented at the time of interview when appropriate;

(ix) If adopted, a copy of a full, final adoption decree;

(x) For adopted children (not orphans) applying under section 322 of the Act, evidence that they satisfy the requirements of section 101(b)(1)(E);

(xi) For adopted orphans applying under section 322 of the Act, a copy of notice of approval of the orphan petition and supporting documentation for such petition (except the home study) or evidence that the child has been admitted for lawful permanent residence in the United States with the immigrant classification of IR–3 (Orphan adopted abroad by a U.S. citizen) or IR–4 (Orphan to be adopted by a U.S. citizen);

(xii) For a Hague Convention adoptee applying under section 322 of the Act, a copy of the notice of approval of the Convention adoptee petition and its supporting documentation, or evidence that the child has been admitted for lawful permanent residence in the United States with the immigrant classification of IH–3 (Hague Convention Orphan adopted abroad by a U.S. citizen) or IH–4 (Hague Convention Orphan to be adopted by a U.S. citizen); and

(xiii) Evidence of all legal name changes, if applicable, for the child, U.S. citizen parent, U.S. citizen grandparent, or U.S. citizen legal guardian.

(2) If USCIS requires any additional documentation to make a decision on the application, the parents may be asked to provide that documentation under separate cover or at the time of interview. Parents do not need to submit documents that were submitted in connection with: An application for immigrant visa and retained by the American Consulate for inclusion in the immigrant visa package, or another immigrant petition or application and included in a Service administrative file. Parents should indicate that they wish to rely on such documents and identify the administrative file(s) by name and alien number. The Service will only request the required documentation again if necessary.

[66 FR 32144, June 13, 2001, as amended at 72 FR 56867, Oct. 4, 2007; 74 FR 26940, June 5, 2009; 76 FR 53799, Aug. 29, 2011]

§ 322.4 Interview.

The U.S. citizen parent and the child must appear in person before a USCIS officer for examination on the application under this section. If the U.S. citizen parent is deceased, the child's U.S. citizen grandparent or U.S. citizen legal guardian who filed the application on the child's behalf must appear.

[76 FR 53799, Aug. 29, 2011]

§ 322.5 Decision.

(a) *Approval of application.* If the application for certificate of citizenship is approved, after the applicant takes the oath of allegiance prescribed in 8 CFR 337.1 (unless the oath is waived), USCIS will issue a certificate of citizenship. The child is a citizen as of the date of approval and administration of the oath of allegiance.

(b) *Denial of application.* If the USCIS decision is to deny the application for a certificate of citizenship under this section, the applicant will be furnished with the reasons for denial and advised of the right to appeal in accordance with the provisions of 8 CFR 103.3(a). An applicant may file an appeal within 30 days of service of the decision in accordance with the instructions on the form prescribed by USCIS for that purpose, and with the fee required by 8 CFR 103.7(b)(1).

(c) *Subsequent application.* After an application for a certificate of citizenship has been denied and the time for appeal has expired, USCIS will reject a subsequent application submitted by the same individual and the applicant will be instructed to submit a motion for reopening or reconsideration in accordance with 8 CFR 103.5. The motion must be accompanied by the rejected application and the fee specified in 8 CFR 103.7(b)(1).

[76 FR 53800, Aug. 29, 2011]

PART 324—SPECIAL CLASSES OF PERSONS WHO MAY BE NATURALIZED: WOMEN WHO HAVE LOST UNITED STATES CITIZENSHIP BY MARRIAGE AND FORMER CITIZENS WHOSE NATURALIZATION IS AUTHORIZED BY PRIVATE LAW

Sec.

AUTHORITY: 8 U.S.C. 1103, 1435, 1443, 1448, 1101 note.

§ 324.1 Definitions.

As used in this part:

Oath means the Oath of Allegiance as prescribed in section 337 of the Act.

[56 FR 50490, Oct. 7, 1991]

§324.2 Former citizen at birth or by naturalization.

(a) *Eligibility.* To be eligible for naturalization under section 324(a) of the Act, an applicant must establish that she:

(1) Was formerly a United States citizen;

(2) Lost or may have lost United States citizenship:

(i) Prior to September 22, 1922, by marriage to an alien, or by the loss of United States citizenship of the applicant's spouse; or

(ii) On or after September 22, 1922, by marriage before March 3, 1931 to an alien ineligible to citizenship;

(3) Did not acquire any other nationality by affirmative act other than by marriage;

(4) Either:

(i) Has resided in the United States continuously since the date of the marriage referred to in paragraph (a)(2) of this section; or

(ii) Has been lawfully admitted for permanent residence prior to filing an application for naturalization;

(5) Has been and is a person of good moral character, attached to the principles of the Constitution of the United States, and favorably disposed toward the good order and happiness of the United States, for the period of not less than five years immediately preceding the examination on the application for naturalization up to the time of admission to citizenship; and

(6) Complies with all other requirements for naturalization as provided in part 316 of this chapter, except that:

(i) The applicant is not required to satisfy the residence requirements under §316.2(a)(3) through (a)(6) of this chapter; and,

(ii) The applicant need not set forth an intention to reside permanently within the United States.

(b) *Application.* An applicant for naturalization under this section must submit an application on the form designated by USCIS in accordance with the form instructions and with the fee prescribed in 8 CFR 103.7(b)(1) as required by 8 CFR 316.4. The application must be accompanied by a statement describing the applicant's eligibility as provided in paragraph (a) of this section as well as any available documentation to establish those facts.

[56 FR 50490, Oct. 7, 1991, as amended at 74 FR 26941, June 5, 2009; 76 FR 53800, Aug. 29, 2011; 76 FR 73477, Nov. 29, 2011]

§324.3 Women, citizens of the United States at birth, who lost or are believed to have lost citizenship by marriage and whose marriage has terminated.

(a) *Eligibility.* To be eligible for naturalization under section 324(c) of the Act, an applicant must establish:

(1) That she was formerly a United States citizen by birth;

(2) That she lost or may have lost her United States citizenship:

(i) Prior to September 22, 1922, by marriage to an alien; or

(ii) On or after September 22, 1922, by marriage to an alien ineligible to citizenship before March 3, 1931;

(3) That the marriage specified in paragraph (a)(2) of this section terminated subsequent to January 12, 1941;

(4) That she did not acquire any other nationality by affirmative act other than by marriage; and

(5) That she is not proscribed from naturalization under section 313 of the Act.

(b) *Procedures*—(1) *Application.* An applicant eligible for naturalization pursuant to paragraph (a) of this section, who desires to regain citizenship pursuant to section 324(c) of the Act, shall submit, without fee, an application for naturalization on the form prescribed by USCIS in accordance with the instructions on the form.

(2) *Oath of Allegiance.* The USCIS shall review the applicant's submission, and shall inform the applicant of her eligibility under section 324(c) of the Act to take the oath in conformity with part 337 of this chapter. After the applicant has taken the oath, the applicant will be furnished with a copy of the oath by the clerk of the Court or USCIS, as appropriate, properly certified, for which a fee not exceeding $5 may be charged. The oath may also be taken abroad before any diplomatic or consular officer of the United States, in accordance with such regulations as

may be prescribed by the Secretary of State.

[56 FR 50490, 50491, Oct. 7, 1991, as amended at 74 FR 26941, June 5, 2009; 76 FR 53800, Aug. 29, 2011]

§ 324.4 Women restored to United States citizenship by the act of June 25, 1936, as amended by the act of July 2, 1940.

A woman who was restored to citizenship by the act of June 25, 1936, as amended by the act of July 2, 1940, but who failed to take the oath of allegiance prescribed by the naturalization laws prior to December 24, 1952, may take the oath before any naturalization court or USCIS office within the United States. Such woman shall comply with the procedural requirements of § 324.4(b) and (c) except that a fee not exceeding $1.00 may be charged if the woman requests a copy of the oath.

[22 FR 9814, Dec. 6, 1957. Redesignated and amended at 56 FR 50490, 50491, Oct. 7, 1991; 74 FR 26941, June 5, 2009]

§ 324.5 Former citizen of the United States whose naturalization by taking the oath is authorized by a private law.

A former citizen of the United States whose naturalization by taking the oath before any naturalization court or office of USCIS within the United States is authorized by a private law must submit an application on the form specified by USCIS, without fee, in accordance with the form instructions.

[76 FR 53800, Aug. 29, 2011]

PART 325—NATIONALS BUT NOT CITIZENS OF THE UNITED STATES; RESIDENCE WITHIN OUTLYING POSSESSIONS

Sec.

AUTHORITY: 8 U.S.C. 1103, 1436, 1443.

SOURCE: 56 FR 50491, Oct. 7, 1991, unless otherwise noted.

§ 325.1 [Reserved]

§ 325.2 Eligibility.

An applicant for naturalization under section 325 of the Act who owes permanent allegiance to the United States, and who is otherwise qualified may be naturalized if:

(a) The applicant becomes a resident of any State; and

(b) The applicant complies with all of the applicable requirements in parts 316 or 319 of this chapter, as appropriate, except as modified in this part.

§ 325.3 Residence.

(a) For purposes of applying the residence and physical presence requirements in parts 316 and 319 of this chapter, except as they relate to the required three months' residence in a State or Service district, residence and physical presence in an outlying possession of the United States will count as residence and physical presence in the United States.

(b) An applicant who intends to resume residence in an outlying possession after naturalization will be regarded as having established that he or she intends to reside permanently in the United States.

§ 325.4 Application; documents.

(a) An application for naturalization under this part shall be submitted in compliance with § 316.4(a) of this chapter.

(b) The applicant shall submit with the application:

(1) A birth certificate or other evidence of national status;

(2) Proof of identity; and

(3) Evidence of actual residence in the State or Service district, as defined in 8 CFR 316.1, for three months immediately preceding the filing of the application, or immediately preceding the examination on the application if the application was filed early pursuant to section 334(a) of the Act and the three month period falls within the required period of residence under section 316(a) or 319(a) of the Act.

[56 FR 50491, Oct. 7, 1991, as amended at 76 FR 53800, Aug. 29, 2011]

PART 327—SPECIAL CLASSES OF PERSONS WHO MAY BE NATURALIZED: PERSONS WHO LOST UNITED STATES CITIZENSHIP THROUGH SERVICE IN ARMED FORCES OF FOREIGN COUNTRY DURING WORLD WAR II

AUTHORITY: 8 U.S.C. 1103, 1438, 1443.

§327.1 Eligibility.

To be eligible for naturalization under section 327 of the Act, an applicant must establish that:

(a) The applicant, on or after September 1, 1939 and on or before September 2, 1945:

(1) Served in the military, air or naval forces of any country at war with a country with which the United States was at war after December 7, 1941 and before September 2, 1945; or

(2) Took an oath of allegiance or obligation for purposes of entering or serving in the military, air, or, naval forces of any country at war with a country with which the United States was at war after December 7, 1941 and before September 2, 1945;

(b) The applicant was a United States citizen at the time of the service or oath specified in paragraph (a) of this section;

(c) The applicant lost United States citizenship as a result of the service or oath specified in paragraph (a) of this section;

(d) The applicant has been lawfully admitted for permanent residence and intends to reside permanently in the United States;

(e) The applicant is, and has been for a period of at least five years immediately preceding taking the oath required in §327.2(c), a person of good moral character, attached to the principles of the Constitution of the United States, and favorably disposed toward the good order and happiness of the United States; and

(f) The applicant has complied with all other requirements for naturalization as provided in part 316 of this chapter, except for those contained in §316.2 (a)(3) through (a)(6) of this chapter.

[56 FR 50492, Oct. 7, 1991]

§327.2 Procedure for naturalization.

(a) *Application.* An applicant who is eligible for naturalization pursuant to section 327 of the Act and §327.1 shall submit an Application for Naturalization, Form N–400, in accordance with §316.4 of this chapter. Such application must be accompanied by a statement describing the applicant's eligibility under §327.1 (a), (b), and (c) and any available documentation to establish those facts.

(b) *Oath of Allegiance.* Upon naturalization of the applicant, the district director shall transmit a copy of the oath of allegiance taken by the applicant to the Department of State.

[56 FR 50492, Oct. 7, 1991, as amended at 74 FR 26941, June 5, 2009]

PART 328—SPECIAL CLASSES OF PERSONS WHO MAY BE NATURALIZED: PERSONS WITH 1 YEAR OF SERVICE IN THE UNITED STATES ARMED FORCES

AUTHORITY: 8 U.S.C. 1103, 1439, 1443.

SOURCE: 56 FR 50492, Oct. 7, 1991, unless otherwise noted.

§328.1 Definitions.

As used in this part:

Honorable service means only that military service which is designated as honorable service by the executive department under which the applicant performed that military service. Any service that is designated to be other than honorable will not qualify under this section.

Service in the Armed Forces of the United States means:

(1) Active or reserve service in the United States Army, United States Navy, United States Marines, United States Air Force, or United States Coast Guard; or

(2) Service in a National Guard unit during such time as the unit is Federally recognized as a reserve component of the Armed Forces of the United States.

§ 328.2 Eligibility.

To be eligible for naturalization under section 328(a) of the Act, an applicant must establish that the applicant:

(a) Has served honorably in and, if separated, has been separated honorably from, the Armed Forces of the United States;

(b) Has served under paragraph (a) of this section for a period of 1 or more years, whether that service is continuous or discontinuous;

(c) Is a lawful permanent resident of the United States at the time of the examination on the application;

(d) Has been, during any period within five years preceding the filing of the application for naturalization, or the examination on the application if eligible for early filing under section 334(a) of the Act, and continues to be, of good moral character, attached to the principles of the Constitution of the United States, and favorably disposed toward the good order and happiness of the United States.

(1) An applicant is presumed to satisfy the requirements of this paragraph during periods of honorable service under paragraph (a) of this section.

(2) An applicant must establish that he or she satisfies the requirements of this paragraph from the date of discharge from military until the date of admission to citizenship.

(3) An applicant whose honorable service is discontinuous must also demonstrate that he or she satisfies the requirements of this paragraph for those periods of time when that applicant is not in honorable service.

(e) Has complied with all other requirements for naturalization as provided in part 316 of this chapter, except that:

(1) An applicant who files an application for naturalization while still in honorable service, or within six months after termination of such service, is generally not required to satisfy the residence requirements under § 316.2(a)(3) through (a)(6) of this chapter; however, if the applicant's military service is discontinuous, that applicant must establish, for periods between honorable service during the five years immediately preceding the date of filing the application, or the examination on the application if eligible for early filing under section 334(a) of the Act, that he or she resided in the United States and in the State or Service district in the United States in which the application is filed.

(2) An applicant who files an application for naturalization more than six months after terminating honorable service must satisfy the residence requirements under § 316.2(a)(3) through (a)(6) of this chapter. However, any honorable service by the applicant within the five years immediately preceding the date of filing of the application shall be considered as residence within the United States for purposes of § 316.2(a)(3) of this chapter.

[56 FR 50492, Oct. 7, 1991, as amended at 75 FR 2787, Jan. 19, 2010]

§ 328.3 [Reserved]

§ 328.4 Application and evidence.

(a) *Application.* An applicant for naturalization under section 328 of the Act must submit an application on the form prescribed by USCIS in accordance with the form instructions and as provided in 8 CFR 316.4.

(b) *Evidence.* The applicant's eligibility for naturalization under 8 CFR 328.2(a) or (b) will be established only by the certification of honorable service by the executive department under which the applicant served or is serving.

[76 FR 53800, Aug. 29, 2011]

PART 329—SPECIAL CLASSES OF PERSONS WHO MAY BE NATURALIZED: PERSONS WITH ACTIVE DUTY OR CERTAIN READY RESERVE SERVICE IN THE UNITED STATES ARMED FORCES DURING SPECIFIED PERIODS OF HOSTILITIES

Sec.

329.4 Application and evidence.

AUTHORITY: 8 U.S.C. 1103, 1440, 1443; 8 CFR part 2.

§ 329.1 Definitions.

As used in this part:

Honorable service and separation means service and separation from service which the executive department under which the applicant served determines to be honorable, including:

(1) That such applicant had not been separated from service on account of alienage;

(2) That such applicant was not a conscientious objector who performed no military, air or naval duty; and

(3) That such applicant did not refuse to wear a military uniform.

Service in an active duty status in the Armed Forces of the United States means active service in the following organizations:

(1) United States Army, United States Navy, United States Marines, United States Air Force, United States Coast Guard; or

(2) A National Guard unit during such time as the unit is Federally recognized as a reserve component of the Armed Forces of the United States and that unit is called for active duty.

World War I means the period beginning on April 6, 1917, and ending on November 11, 1918.

[56 FR 50493, Oct. 7, 1991]

§ 329.2 Eligibility.

To be eligible for naturalization under section 329(a) of the Act, an applicant must establish that he or she:

(a) Has served honorably in the Armed Forces of the United States as a member of the Selected Reserve of the Ready Reserve or in an active duty status in the Armed Forces of the United States during:

(1) World War I;

(2) The period beginning on September 1, 1939 and ending on December 31, 1946;

(3) The period beginning on June 25, 1950 and ending on July 1, 1955;

(4) The period beginning on February 28, 1961 and ending on October 15, 1978; or

(5) Any other period as may be designated by the President in an Executive Order pursuant to section 329(a) of the Act;

(b) If separated, has been separated honorably from service in the Armed Forces of the United States under paragraph (a) of this section;

(c) Satisfies the permanent residence requirement in one of the following ways:

(1) Any time after enlistment or induction into the Armed Forces of the United States, the applicant was lawfully admitted to the United States as a permanent resident; or

(2) At the time of enlistment or induction, the applicant was physically present in the geographical territory of the United States, the Canal Zone, American Samoa, Midway Island (prior to August 21, 1959), or Swain's Island, or in the ports, harbors, bays, enclosed sea areas, or the three-mile territorial sea along the coasts of these land areas, whether or not the applicant has been lawfully admitted to the United States as a permanent resident;

(d) Has been, for at least one year prior to filing the application for naturalization, and continues to be, of good moral character, attached to the principles of the Constitution of the United States, and favorably disposed toward the good order and happiness of the United States; and

(e) Has complied with all other requirements for naturalization as provided in part 316 of this chapter, except that:

(1) The applicant may be of any age;

(2) The applicant is not required to satisfy the residence requirements under § 316.2 (a)(3) through (a)(6) of this chapter; and

(3) The applicant may be naturalized even if an outstanding notice to appear pursuant to 8 CFR part 239 (including a charging document issued to commence proceedings under sections 236 or 242 of the Act prior to April 1, 1997) exists.

[56 FR 50493, Oct. 7, 1991, as amended at 58 FR 49913, Sept. 24, 1993; 62 FR 10395, Mar. 6, 1997; 75 FR 2787, Jan. 19, 2010]

§ 329.3 [Reserved]

§ 329.4 Application and evidence.

(a) *Application.* An applicant for naturalization under section 329 of the Act must submit an application on the form prescribed by USCIS in accordance with the form instructions and as provided in 8 CFR 316.4.

(b) *Evidence.* The applicant's eligibility for naturalization under 8 CFR 329.2(a), (b), or (c)(2) will be established only by a certification of honorable service by the executive department under which the applicant served or is serving.

[76 FR 53800, Aug. 29, 2011]

PART 330—SPECIAL CLASSES OF PERSONS WHO MAY BE NATURALIZED: SEAMEN

AUTHORITY: 8 U.S.C. 1103, 1443.

§ 330.1 Eligibility.

To be eligible for naturalization under section 330 of the Act, an applicant must establish that he or she:

(a) Has been lawfully admitted as a permanent resident of the United States;

(b) Has served honorably or with good conduct, during such periods of lawful residence, in a capacity other than as a member of the Armed Forces of the United States, on board:

(1) A vessel operated by the United States, or an agency thereof, the full legal and equitable title to which is in the United States; or

(2) A vessel, whose home port is the United States, and

(i) Which is registered under the laws of the United States; or

(ii) The full legal and equitable title to which is in a citizen of the United States, or a corporation organized under the laws of any of the several States of the United States;

(c) Served in the capacity specified in paragraph (b) of this section within five years immediately preceding the date on which the applicant filed the application for naturalization, or on which the alien is examined, if the application was filed early pursuant to section 334(a) of the Act.

(d) Has been, during the five years preceding the filing of the application for naturalization, or the examination on the application if the application was filed early under section 334(a) of the Act, and continues to be, of good moral character, attached to the principles of the Constitution of the United States, and favorably disposed toward the good order and happiness of the United States.

(1) An applicant is presumed to satisfy the requirements of this paragraph during periods of service in accordance with paragraphs (b) and (c) of this section, as reflected by the records and certificates submitted by the applicant under § 330.2(b).

(2) An applicant must demonstrate that he or she satisfies the requirements of this paragraph for those required periods when that applicant did not perform service in accordance with paragraphs (b) and (c) of this section; and

(e) Has complied with all other requirements for naturalization as provided in part 316 of this chapter, except that, for purposes of the residence requirements under paragraphs § 316.2 (a)(3) and (a)(4) of this chapter, service satisfying the conditions of this section shall be considered as residence and physical presence within the United States.

[56 FR 50493, Oct. 7, 1991]

§ 330.2 Application.

(a) An applicant for naturalization under section 330 of the Act must submit an application on the form designated by USCIS.

(b) An applicant under this part must submit authenticated copies of the records and certificates of either:

(1) The Executive Department or Agencies having custody of records reflecting the applicant's service on a vessel in United States Government Service, if the applicant provided service under § 330.1(b)(1); or

(2) The masters of those vessels maintaining a home port in the United States, and either registered under the laws of the United States or owned by United States citizens or corporations, if the applicant provided service under § 330.1(b)(2).

[56 FR 50493, Oct. 7, 1991, as amended at 74 FR 26941, June 5, 2009; 76 FR 53800, Aug. 29, 2011]

PART 331—ALIEN ENEMIES; NATURALIZATION UNDER SPECIFIED CONDITIONS AND PROCEDURES

AUTHORITY: 8 U.S.C. 1103, 1443.

SOURCE: 56 FR 50494, Oct. 7, 1991, unless otherwise noted.

§331.1 Definitions.

As used in this part:

Alien enemy means any person who is a native, citizen, subject or denizen of any country, state or sovereignty with which the United States is at war, for as long as the United States remains at war, as determined by proclamation of the President or resolution of Congress.

Denizen includes, but is not limited to, any person who has been admitted to residence and is entitled to certain rights in a country other than the one of the person's nationality. A person holding a status in another country equivalent to that of a lawful permanent resident in the United States would be considered to be a denizen.

§331.2 Eligibility.

An alien enemy may be naturalized as a citizen of the United States under section 331 of the Act if:

(a) The alien's application for naturalization is pending at the beginning of the state of war, or the Service has granted the alien an exception from the classification as an alien enemy after conducting an investigation in accordance with §331.3;

(b) The alien's loyalty to the United States is fully established upon investigation by the Service in accordance with §331.3; and

(c) The alien is otherwise entitled to admission to citizenship.

§331.3 Investigation.

The Service shall conduct a full investigation of any alien enemy whose application for naturalization is pending upon declaration of war or at any time thereafter. This investigation may take place either prior to or after the examination on the application. This investigation shall encompass, but not be limited to, the applicant's loyalty to the United States and attachment to the country, state, or sovereignty with which the United States is at war.

§331.4 Procedures.

(a) Upon determining that an applicant for naturalization is an alien enemy, the Service shall notify the applicant in writing of its determination. Upon service of this notice to the applicant, the provisions of section 336(b) of the Act will no longer apply to such applicant, until that applicant is no longer classifiable as an alien enemy.

(b) Upon completion of the investigation described in §331.3, if the Service concludes that the applicant's loyalty and attachment to the United States have been fully established, the application may be granted.

PART 332—NATURALIZATION ADMINISTRATION

AUTHORITY: 8 U.S.C. 1103, 1443, 1447.

§332.1 Designation of USCIS employees to administer oaths and conduct examinations and hearings.

(a) *Examinations.* All USCIS officers are hereby designated to conduct the examination for naturalization required under section 335 of the Act, provided that each officer so designated has received appropriate training.

(b) *Hearings.* Section 336 of the Act authorizes USCIS officers who are designated under paragraph (a) of this section to conduct hearings under that section.

(c) *Depositions.* All USCIS officers who are designated under paragraph (a) of this section are hereby designated to take depositions in matters relating to the administration of naturalization and citizenship laws.

(d) *Oaths and affirmations.* All USCIS officers who are designated under paragraph (a) of this section are hereby designated to administer oaths or affirmations except for the oath of allegiance as provided in 8 CFR 337.2.

[76 FR 53800, Aug. 29, 2011]

§§ 332.2–332.4 [Reserved]

§ 332.5 Official forms for use by clerks of court.

(a) *Official forms essential to exercise of jurisdiction.* Before exercising jurisdiction in naturalization proceedings, the naturalization court shall direct the clerk of such court upon written application to obtain from the Service, in accordance with section 310(c) of the Immigration and Nationality Act, proper forms, records, booked, and supplies required in naturalization proceedings. Such jurisdiction may not be exercised until such official forms, records, and books have been supplied to such court. Only such forms as are supplied shall be used in naturalization proceedings. Where sessions of the court are held at different places, the judge of such court may require the clerk to obtain a separate supply of official forms, records and books for each such place.

(b) *Official forms prescribed for use of clerks of naturalization courts.* Clerks of courts shall use only the forms listed in § 499.1 of this chapter in the exercise of naturalization jurisdiction.

(c) *Initial application for official forms.* Whenever the initial application for forms, records, books and supplies is made by a State court of record, it shall be accompanied by a certificate of the Attorney General of the State, certifying that the said court is a court of record, having a seal, a clerk, and jurisdiction in actions at law or in equity, or at law and in equity, in which the amount in controversy is unlimited.

(d) *Subsequent application for use of official forms.* Included with the initial supply of official forms, records, and books furnished to the various courts by the Service shall be Form N–3 entitled "Requisition for Forms and Binders," and thereafter such forms shall be used by clerks of courts in making requisition for forms, records, books, and supplies for use in naturalization proceedings in their respective courts.

[22 FR 9817, Dec. 6, 1957. Redesignated and amended at 56 FR 50495, Oct. 7, 1991]

PART 333—PHOTOGRAPHS

AUTHORITY: 8 U.S.C. 1103, 1443.

§ 333.1 Description of required photographs.

(a) Every applicant who is required to provide photographs under section 333 of the Act must do so as prescribed by USCIS in its form instructions.

(b) The applicant, except in the case of a child or other person physically incapable of signing his or her name, shall sign each copy of the photograph on the front of the photograph with his or her full true name, in such manner as not to obscure the features. An applicant unable to write may make the signature by a mark. An applicant for naturalization must sign the photographs in the English language, unless the applicant is exempt from the English language requirement of part 312 of this chapter and is unable to sign in English, in which case the photographs may be signed in any language.

(c)(1) If a child is unable to sign his or her name, the photographs must be signed by a parent or guardian, the signature reading "(name of child) by (name of parent or guardian)."

(2) If an adult is physically unable to sign or make a mark, a guardian or the Service employee conducting the interview will sign the photographs as provided in paragraph (c)(1) of this section.

(d) The photographs must be signed when submitted with an application if the instructions accompanying the application so require. If signature is not required by the instructions, the photographs are to be submitted without being signed and shall be signed at such later time during the processing of the application as may be appropriate.

[56 FR 50495, Oct. 7, 1991, as amended at 76 FR 53801, Aug. 29, 2011]

§333.2 Attachment of photographs to documents.

A photograph of the applicant must be securely and permanently attached to each certificate of naturalization or citizenship, or to any other document that requires a photograph, in a manner prescribed by USCIS.

[76 FR 53801, Aug. 29, 2011]

PART 334—APPLICATION FOR NATURALIZATION

AUTHORITY: 8 U.S.C. 1103, 1443; 8 CFR part 2.

§334.1 Filing of application for naturalization.

Any person who is an applicant under sections 316, 319, 324, 325, 327, 328, 329, or 330 of the Act and the corresponding parts of this chapter, may apply for naturalization in accordance with the procedures prescribed in this chapter in accordance with the instructions on the form.

[56 FR 50496, Oct. 7, 1991, as amended at 66 FR 32147, June 13, 2001; 74 FR 26941, June 5, 2009]

§334.2 Application for naturalization.

(a) An applicant may file an application for naturalization with required initial evidence in accordance with the general form instructions for naturalization. The applicant must include the fee as required in 8 CFR 103.7(b)(1).

(b) An application for naturalization may be filed up to 90 days prior to the completion of the required period of residence, which may include the three-month period of residence required to establish jurisdiction under section 316(a) or 319(a) of the Act.

[56 FR 50496, Oct. 7, 1991, as amended at 59 FR 48780, Sept. 20, 1993; 66 FR 32147, June 13, 2001; 76 FR 53801, Aug. 29, 2011]

§334.3 [Reserved]

§334.4 Investigation and report if applicant is sick or disabled.

Whenever it appears that an applicant for naturalization may be unable, because of sickness or other disability, to appear for the initial examination on the application or for any subsequent interview, the district director shall cause an investigation to be conducted to determine the circumstances surrounding the sickness or disability. The district director shall determine, based on available medical evidence, whether the sickness or disability is of a nature which so incapacitates the applicant as to prevent the applicant's appearance at a Service office having jurisdiction over the applicant's place of residence. If so, the district director shall designate another place where the applicant may appear for the requisite naturalization proceedings.

[58 FR 49913, Sept. 24, 1993]

§334.5 Amendment of application for naturalization; reopening proceedings.

(a) *Clerical amendments*—(1) *By applicant.* An applicant may request that the application for naturalization be amended either prior to or subsequent to the administration of the oath of allegiance.

(2) *By Service.* The Service may amend, at any time, an application for naturalization when in receipt of information that clearly indicates that a clerical error has occurred.

(3) *Amendment procedure.* Any amendment will be limited to the correction of clerical errors arising from oversight or omission. If the amendment is approved, the amended application shall be filed with the original application for naturalization.

(b) *Substantive amendments.* Any substantive amendments which affect the jurisdiction or the decision on the merits of the application will not be authorized. When the Service is in receipt of any information that would indicate that an application for naturalization should not have been granted on the merits, the Service may institute proceedings to reopen the application before admission to citizenship, or to revoke the naturalization of a person who has been admitted to citizenship, in accordance with section 340 of the Act and § 335.5 of this chapter.

[56 FR 50496, Oct. 7, 1991]

§§ 334.6–334.10 [Reserved]

§ 334.11 Declaration of intention.

(a) *Application.* Any person who is a lawful permanent resident over 18 years of age may file an application for a declaration of intention to become a citizen of the United States while present in the United States. Such application, with the requisite fee, shall be filed on the form specified by USCIS, in accordance with the form instructions.

(b) *Approval.* If approved, USCIS will retain the application in the file and advise the applicant of the action taken.

(c) *Denial.* If an application is denied, the applicant shall be notified in writing of the reasons for denial. No appeal shall lie from this decision.

[58 FR 49913, Sept. 24, 1993, as amended at 74 FR 26941, June 5, 2009; 76 FR 53801, Aug. 29, 2011]

§§ 334.12–334.15 [Reserved]

PART 335—EXAMINATION ON APPLICATION FOR NATURALIZATION

AUTHORITY: 8 U.S.C. 1103, 1443, 1447.

§ 335.1 Investigation of applicant.

Subsequent to the filing of an application for naturalization, the Service shall conduct an investigation of the applicant. The investigation shall consist, at a minimum, of a review of all pertinent records, police department checks, and a neighborhood investigation in the vicinities where the applicant has resided and has been employed, or engaged in business, for at least the five years immediately preceding the filing of the application. The district director may waive the neighborhood investigation of the applicant provided for in this paragraph.

[56 FR 50497, Oct. 7, 1991]

§ 335.2 Examination of applicant.

(a) *General.* Subsequent to the filing of an application for naturalization, each applicant shall appear in person before a USCIS officer designated to conduct examinations pursuant to 8 CFR 332.1. The examination shall be uniform throughout the United States and shall encompass all factors relating to the applicant's eligibility for naturalization. The applicant may request the presence of an attorney or representative who has filed an appearance in accordance with part 292 of this chapter.

(b) *Completion of criminal background checks before examination.* USCIS will notify applicants for naturalization to appear before a USCIS officer for initial examination on the naturalization application only after the USCIS has received a definitive response from the Federal Bureau of Investigation that a full criminal background check of an applicant has been completed. A definitive response that a full criminal background check on an applicant has been completed includes:

(1) Confirmation from the Federal Bureau of Investigation that an applicant does not have an administrative or a criminal record;

(2) Confirmation from the Federal Bureau of Investigation that an applicant has an administrative or a criminal record; or

(3) Confirmation from the Federal Bureau of Investigation that the fingerprint data submitted for the criminal background check has been rejected.

(c) *Procedure.* Prior to the beginning of the examination, USCIS shall make known to the applicant the official capacity in which the officer is conducting the examination. The applicant shall be questioned, under oath or affirmation, in a setting apart from the public. Whenever necessary, the examining officer shall correct written answers in the application for naturalization to conform to the oral statements made under oath or affirmation. USCIS shall maintain, for the record, brief notations of the examination for naturalization. At a minimum, the notations shall include a record of the test administered to the applicant on English literacy and basic knowledge of the history and government of the United States. USCIS may have a stenographic, mechanical, electronic, or videotaped transcript made, or may prepare an affidavit covering the testimony of the applicant. The questions to the applicant shall be repeated in different form and elaborated, if necessary, until the officer conducting the examination is satisfied that the applicant either fully understands the questions or is unable to understand English. The applicant and USCIS shall have the right to present such oral or documentary evidence and to conduct such cross-examination as may be required for a full and true disclosure of the facts.

(d) *Witnesses.* Witnesses, if called, shall be questioned under oath or affirmation to discover their own credibility and competency, as well as the extent of their personal knowledge of the applicant and his or her qualifications to become a naturalized citizen.

(1) *Issuance of subpoenas.* Subpoenas requiring the attendance of witnesses or the production of documentary evidence, or both, may be issued by the examining officer upon his or her own volition, or upon written request of the applicant or his or her attorney or representative. Such written request shall specify, as nearly as possible, the relevance, materiality, and scope of the testimony or documentary evidence sought and must show affirmatively that the testimony or documentary evidence cannot otherwise be produced. The examining officer shall document in the record his or her refusal to issue a subpoena at the request of the applicant.

(2) *Service of subpoenas.* Subpoenas will be issued on the form designated by USCIS and a record will be made of service. The subpoena may be served by any person over 18 years of age, not a party to the case, designated to make such service by USCIS.

(3) *Witness fees.* Mileage and fees for witnesses subpoenaed under this section shall be paid by the party at whose instance the subpoena is issued, at rates allowed and under conditions prescribed by the Service. Before issuing a subpoena, the officer may require the deposit of an amount adequate to cover the fees and mileage involved.

(4) *Failure to appear.* If the witness subpoenaed neglects or refuses to testify or to produce documentary evidence as directed by the subpoena, the district director shall request that the United States Attorney for the proper district report such neglect or refusal to any District Court of the United States, and file a motion in such court for an order directing the witness to appear and to testify and produce the documentary evidence described in the subpoena.

(5) *Extraterritorial testimony.* The testimony of a witness may be taken outside the United States. The witness's name and address shall be sent to the Service office abroad which has jurisdiction over the witness's residence. The officer taking the statement shall be given express instructions regarding any aspect of the case which may require special development or emphasis during the interrogation of the witness.

(e) *Record of examination.* At the conclusion of the examination, all corrections made on the application form and all supplemental material shall be consecutively numbered and listed in the space provided on the applicant's affidavit contained in the application form. The affidavit must then be subscribed and sworn to, or affirmed, by the applicant and signed by the USCIS officer. The affidavit shall be executed under the following oath (or affirmation): "I swear (affirm) and certify under penalty of perjury under the laws of the United States of America that I know that the contents of this application for naturalization subscribed by me, and the evidence submitted with it, are true and correct to the best of my knowledge and belief." Evidence received by the officer shall be placed into the record for determination of the case. All documentary or written evidence shall be properly identified and introduced into the record as exhibits by number, unless read into the record. A deposition or statement taken by a USCIS officer during the initial examination or any subsequent examination shall be included as part of the record on the application.

(f) *Use of interpreter*. If the use of an interpreter is authorized pursuant to 8 CFR 312.4, the examining officer shall note on the application the use and identity of any interpreter. If the USCIS officer is proficient in the applicant's native language, the USCIS officer may conduct the examination in that language with the consent of the applicant.

[56 FR 50497, Oct. 7, 1991, as amended at 58 FR 49913, Sept. 24, 1993; 63 FR 12987, 12988, Mar. 17, 1998; 76 FR 53801, Aug. 29, 2011]

§ 335.3 Determination on application; continuance of examination.

(a) USCIS shall grant the application if the applicant has complied with all requirements for naturalization under this chapter. A decision to grant or deny the application shall be made at the time of the initial examination or within 120-days after the date of the initial examination of the applicant for naturalization under § 335.2. The applicant shall be notified that the application has been granted or denied and, if the application has been granted, of the procedures to be followed for the administration of the oath of allegiance pursuant to part 337 of this chapter.

(b) Rather than make a determination on the application, USCIS may continue the initial examination on an application for one reexamination, to afford the applicant an opportunity to overcome deficiencies on the application that may arise during the examination. The officer must inform the applicant in writing of the grounds to be overcome or the evidence to be submitted. The applicant shall not be required to appear for a reexamination earlier than 60 days after the first examination. However, the reexamination on the continued case shall be scheduled within the 120-day period after the initial examination, except as otherwise provided under § 312.5(b) of this chapter. If the applicant is unable to overcome the deficiencies in the application, the application shall be denied pursuant to § 336.1 of this chapter.

[56 FR 50497, Oct. 7, 1991, as amended at 58 FR 49914, Sept. 24, 1993; 76 FR 53801, Aug. 29, 2011]

§ 335.4 Use of record of examination.

In the event that an application is denied, the record of the examination on the application for naturalization, including the executed and corrected application form and supplements, affidavits, transcripts of testimony, documents, and other evidence, shall be submitted to the USCIS officer described in 8 CFR 332.1 of this chapter to conduct hearings on denials of applications for naturalization in accordance with part 336 of this chapter. The record of the examination shall be used for examining the petitioner and witnesses, if required to properly dispose of issues raised in the matter.

[56 FR 50498, Oct. 7, 1991, as amended at 76 FR 53801, Aug. 29, 2011]

§ 335.5 Receipt of derogatory information after grant.

In the event that USCIS receives derogatory information concerning an applicant whose application has already been granted as provided in § 335.3(a) of this chapter, but who has not yet taken the oath of allegiance as provided in part 337 of this chapter, USCIS shall remove the applicant's name from any list of granted applications or of applicants scheduled for administration of the oath of allegiance, until such time as the matter can be resolved. USCIS shall notify the applicant in writing of the receipt of the specific derogatory information, with a motion to reopen the previously adjudicated application, giving the applicant 15 days to respond. If the applicant overcomes the derogatory information, the application will be granted and the applicant will be scheduled for administration of the oath of allegiance. Otherwise the motion to reopen will be granted and the application will be denied pursuant to §336.1 of this chapter.

[56 FR 50498, Oct. 7, 1991, as amended at 58 FR 49914, Sept. 24, 1993; 76 FR 53801, Aug. 29, 2011]

§ 335.6 Failure to appear for examination.

(a) An applicant for naturalization shall be deemed to have abandoned his or her application if he or she fails to appear for the examination pursuant to § 335.3 and fails to notify USCIS of the reason for non-appearance within 30 days of the scheduled examination. Such notification shall be in writing and contain a request for rescheduling of the examination. In the absence of a timely notification, USCIS may administratively close the application without making a decision on the merits.

(b) An applicant may reopen an administratively closed application by submitting a written request to USCIS within one (1) year from the date the application was closed. Such reopening shall be without additional fee. The date of the request for reopening shall be the date of filing of the application for purposes of determining eligibility for naturalization.

(c) If the applicant does not request reopening of an administratively closed application within one year from the date the application was closed, USCIS will consider that application to have been abandoned, and shall dismiss the application without further notice to the applicant.

[58 FR 49914, Sept. 24, 1993, as amended at 60 FR 6651, Feb. 3, 1995; 76 FR 53801, Aug. 29, 2011]

§ 335.7 Failure to prosecute application after initial examination.

An applicant for naturalization who has appeared for the examination on his or her application as provided in 8 CFR 335.2 will be considered as failing to prosecute such application if he or she, without good cause being shown, either failed to excuse an absence from a subsequently required appearance, or fails to provide within a reasonable period of time such documents, information, or testimony deemed by USCIS to be necessary to establish his or her eligibility for naturalization. USCIS will deliver notice of requests for appearance or evidence as provided in 8 CFR 103.8. In the event that the applicant fails to respond within 30 days of the date of notification, USCIS will adjudicate the application on the merits pursuant to 8 CFR 336.1.

[76 FR 53801, Aug. 29, 2011]

§ 335.8 [Reserved]

§ 335.9 Transfer of application.

(a) *Request for transfer of application.* An applicant who, after filing an application for naturalization, changes residence, or plans to change residence within three months, may request, in writing, that a pending application be transferred from the current USCISoffice to the USCIS office having jurisdiction over the applicant's new place of residence. The request shall be submitted to the office where the application was originally filed. The request shall include the applicant's name, alien registration number, date of birth, complete current address including name of the county, complete address at the time of filing the application, reason for the request to transfer the application, and the date the applicant moved or intends to move to the new jurisdiction.

(b) *Discretion to authorize transfer.* The USCIS may authorize the transfer of an application for naturalization after such application has been filed. In the event that the USCIS does not consent to the transfer of the application, the application shall be adjudicated on its merits by USCIS office retaining jurisdiction. If upon such adjudication the application is denied, the written decision pursuant to §336.1 of this chapter shall also address the reason(s) for USCIS's decision not to consent to the transfer request.

[56 FR 50498, Oct. 7, 1991, as amended at 58 FR 49914, Sept. 24, 1993; 76 FR 53801, Aug. 29, 2011; 76 FR 73477, Nov. 29, 2011]

§ 335.10 Withdrawal of application.

An applicant may request, in writing, that his or her application, filed with USCIS, be withdrawn. If USCIS consents to the withdrawal, the application will be denied without further notice to the applicant and without prejudice to any future application. The withdrawal by the applicant will constitute a waiver of any review pursuant to part 336 of this chapter. If USCIS does not consent to the withdrawal, the application for naturalization shall be adjudicated on its merits.

[56 FR 50498, Oct. 7, 1991, as amended at 76 FR 53801, Aug. 29, 2011]

PART 336—HEARINGS ON DENIALS OF APPLICATIONS FOR NATURALIZATION

Sec.

AUTHORITY: 8 U.S.C. 1103, 1443, 1447, 1448.

SOURCE: 56 FR 50499, Oct. 7, 1991, unless otherwise noted.

§ 336.1 Denial after section 335 examination.

(a) After completing all examination procedures contained in part 335 of this chapter and determining to deny an application for naturalization, USCIS will serve a written notice of denial upon an applicant for naturalization no later than 120 days after the date of the applicant's first examination on the application.

(b) A notice of denial shall be prepared in a written, narrative format, and shall recite, in clear concise language, the pertinent facts upon which the determination was based, the specific legal section or sections applicable to the finding of ineligibility, and the conclusions of law reached by the examining officer in rendering the decision. Such notice of denial shall also contain a specific statement of the applicant's right either to accept the determination of the examining officer, or request a hearing before an immigration officer.

(c) Service of the notice of denial must be by personal service as described in 8 CFR 103.8, or upon the attorney or representative of record as provided in part 292 of this chapter.

[56 FR 50499, Oct. 7, 1991, as amended at 76 FR 53802, Aug. 29, 2011]

§ 336.2 USCIS hearing.

(a) The applicant, or his or her authorized representative, may request a hearing on the denial of the applicant's application for naturalization by filing a request with USCIS within thirty days after the applicant receives the notice of denial.

(b) Upon receipt of a timely request for a hearing, USCIS will schedule a review hearing, within a reasonable period of time not to exceed 180 days from the date upon which the appeal is filed. The review will be with an officer other than the officer who conducted the original examination or who rendered determination upon which the hearing is based, and who is classified at a grade level equal to or higher than the grade of the examining officer. The reviewing officer will have the authority and discretion to review the application for naturalization, to examine the applicant, and either to affirm the findings and determination of the original examining officer or to re-determine the original decision in whole or in part. The reviewing officer will also have the discretion to review any administrative record which was created as part of the examination procedures as well USCIS files and reports. He or she may receive new evidence or take such additional testimony as may be deemed relevant to the applicant's eligibility for naturalization or which the applicant seeks to provide. Based upon the complexity of the issues to be reviewed or determined, and upon the necessity of conducting further examinations with respect to essential naturalization requirements, such as literacy or civics knowledge, the reviewing immigration officer may, in his or her discretion, conduct a full *de novo* hearing or may utilize a less formal review procedure, as he or she deems reasonable and in the interest of justice.

(c) *Improperly filed request for hearing.* (1) *Request for hearing filed by a person or entity not entitled to file.* (i) *Rejection without refund of filing fee.* A request for hearing filed by a person or entity who is not entitled to file such a request must be rejected as improperly filed. In such a case, any filing fee will not be refunded.

(ii) *Request for hearing by attorney or representative without proper Form G–28.* If a request for hearing is filed by an attorney or representative who has not properly filed a notice of entry of appearance as attorney or representative entitling that person to file the request for hearing, the appeal will be considered as improperly filed. In such a case, any filing fee will not be refunded regardless of the action taken. The reviewing official will ask the attorney or representative to submit a proper notice of entry within 15 days of the request. If such notice is not submitted within the time allowed, the official may, on his or her own motion, under 8 CFR 103.5(a)(5)(i), make a new decision favorable to the affected party without notifying the attorney or representative. The request for hearing may be considered properly filed as of its original filing date if the attorney or representative submits a properly executed notice entitling that person to file the request for hearing.

(2) *Untimely request for hearing.* (i) *Rejection without refund of filing fee.* A request for hearing which is not filed within the time period allowed must be rejected as improperly filed. In such a case, any filing fee will not be refunded.

(ii) *Untimely request for hearing treated as motion.* If an untimely request for hearing meets the requirements of a motion to reopen as described in 8 CFR 103.5(a)(2) or a motion to reconsider as described in 8 CFR 103.5(a)(3), the request for hearing must be treated as a motion and a decision must be made on the merits of the case.

[76 FR 53802, Aug. 29, 2011]

§§ 336.3–336.8 [Reserved]

§ 336.9 Judicial review of denial determinations on applications for naturalization.

(a) *General.* The provisions in part 310 of this chapter shall provide the sole and exclusive procedures for requesting judicial review of final determinations on applications for naturalization made pursuant to section 336(a) of the Act and the provisions of this chapter by USCIS on or after October 1, 1991.

(b) *Filing a petition.* Under these procedures, an applicant must file a petition for review in the United States District Court having jurisdiction over his or her place of residence, in accordance with Chapter 7 of Title 5, United States Code, within a period of not more than 120 days after the USCIS final determination. The petition for review must be brought against USCIS, and service of the petition for review must be made upon DHS and upon the USCIS office where the hearing was held pursuant to 8 CFR 336.2.

(c) *Standard of review.* The review will be *de novo*, and the court will make its own findings of fact and conclusions of law. The court may also conduct, at the request of the petitioner, a hearing *de novo* on the application for naturalization.

(d) *Exhaustion of remedies.* A USCIS determination denying an application for naturalization under section 335(a) of the Act shall not be subject to judicial review until the applicant has exhausted those administrative remedies available to the applicant under section 336 of the Act. Every petition for judicial review shall state whether the validity of the final determination to deny an application for naturalization has been upheld in any prior administrative proceeding and, if so, the nature and date of such proceeding and the forum in which such proceeding took place.

[56 FR 50499, Oct. 7, 1991, as amended at 76 FR 53802, Aug. 29, 2011]

PART 337—OATH OF ALLEGIANCE

Sec.

AUTHORITY: 8 U.S.C. 1103, 1443, 1448; 8 CFR part 2.

§ 337.1 Oath of allegiance.

(a) *Form of oath.* Except as otherwise provided in the Act and after receiving notice from the district director that such applicant is eligible for naturalization pursuant to § 335.3 of this chapter, an applicant for naturalization shall, before being admitted to citizenship, take in a public ceremony held within the United States the following oath of allegiance, to a copy of which the applicant shall affix his or her signature:

I hereby declare, on oath, that I absolutely and entirely renounce and abjure all allegiance and fidelity to any foreign prince, potentate, state, or sovereignty, of whom or which I have heretofore been a subject or citizen; that I will support and defend the Constitution and laws of the United States of America against all enemies, foreign and domestic; that I will bear true faith and allegiance to the same; that I will bear arms on behalf of the United States when required by the law; that I will perform noncombatant service in the Armed Forces of the United States when required by the law; that I will perform work of national importance under civilian direction when required by the law; and that I take this obligation freely, without any mental reservation or purpose of evasion; so help me God.

(b) *Alteration of form of oath; affirmation in lieu of oath.* In those cases in which a petitioner or applicant for naturalization is exempt from taking the oath prescribed in paragraph (a) of this section in its entirety, the inapplicable clauses shall be deleted and the oath shall be taken in such altered form. When a petitioner or applicant for naturalization, by reason of religious training and belief (or individual interpretation thereof), or for other reasons of good conscience, cannot take the oath prescribed in paragraph (a) of this section with the words "on oath" and "so help me God" included, the words "and solemnly affirm" shall be substituted for the words "on oath," the words "so help me God" shall be deleted, and the oath shall be taken in such modified form. Any reference to 'oath of allegiance' in this chapter is understood to mean equally 'affirmation of allegiance' as described in this paragraph.

(c) *Obligations of oath.* A petitioner or applicant for naturalization shall, before being naturalized, establish that it is his or her intention, in good faith, to assume and discharge the obligations of the oath of allegiance, and that his or her attitude toward the Constitution and laws of the United States renders him or her capable of fulfilling the obligations of such oath.

(d) *Renunciation of title or order of nobility.* A petitioner or applicant for naturalization who has borne any hereditary title or has been of any of the orders of nobility in any foreign state shall, in addition to taking the oath of allegiance prescribed in paragraph (a) of this section, make under oath or affirmation in public an express renunciation of such title or order of nobility, in the following form:

(1) I further renounce the title of (give title or titles) which I have heretofore held; or

(2) I further renounce the order of nobility (give the order of nobility) to which I have heretofore belonged.

[22 FR 9824, Dec. 6, 1957, as amended at 24 FR 2584, Apr. 3, 1959; 32 FR 13756, Oct. 3, 1967; 56 FR 50499, Oct. 7, 1991]

§ 337.2 Oath administered by USCIS or EOIR.

(a) *Public ceremony.* An applicant for naturalization who has elected to have his or her oath of allegiance administered by USCIS or an immigration judge and is not subject to the exclusive oath administration authority of an eligible court pursuant to section 310(b) of the Act must appear in person in a public ceremony, unless such appearance is specifically excused under the terms and conditions set forth in this part. Such ceremony will be held at a time and place designated by USCIS or EOIR within the United States (or abroad as permitted for certain applicants in accordance with 8 U.S.C. 1443a) and within the jurisdiction where the application for naturalization was filed, or into which the application for naturalization was transferred pursuant to 8 CFR 335.9. Naturalization ceremonies will be conducted at regular intervals as frequently as necessary to ensure timely naturalization, but in all events at least once monthly where it is required to minimize unreasonable delays. Naturalization ceremonies will be presented in such a manner as to preserve the dignity and significance of the occasion.

(b) *Authority to administer oath of allegiance.* The Secretary may delegate authority to administer the oath of allegiance prescribed in section 337 of the Act to such officials of DHS and to immigration judges or officials designated by the Attorney General as may be necessary for the efficient administration of the naturalization program.

(c) *Execution of questionnaire.* Immediately prior to being administered the oath of allegiance, each applicant must complete the questionnaire on the form designated by USCIS. USCIS will review each completed questionnaire and may further question the applicant regarding the responses provided. If derogatory information is revealed, USCIS will remove the applicant's name from the list of eligible persons as provided in 8 CFR 335.5 and he or she will not be administered the oath.

[76 FR 53802, Aug. 29, 2011]

§ 337.3 Expedited administration of oath of allegiance.

(a) An applicant may be granted an expedited oath administration ceremony by either the court or USCIS upon demonstrating sufficient cause. In determining whether to grant an expedited oath administration ceremony, the court or USCIS shall consider special circumstances of a compelling or humanitarian nature. Special circumstances may include but are not limited to:

(1) The serious illness of the applicant or a member of the applicant's family;

(2) Permanent disability of the applicant sufficiently incapacitating as to prevent the applicant's personal appearance at a scheduled ceremony;

(3) The developmental disability or advanced age of the applicant which would make appearance at a scheduled ceremony inappropriate; or

(4) Urgent or compelling circumstances relating to travel or employment determined by the court or USCIS to be sufficiently meritorious to warrant special consideration.

(b) Courts exercising exclusive authority may either hold an expedited oath administration ceremony or refer the applicant to USCIS in order for either the Immigration Judge or USCIS to conduct an oath administration ceremony, if an expedited judicial oath administration ceremony is impractical. The court shall inform USCIS in writing of its decision to grant the applicant an expedited oath administration ceremony and that the court has relinquished exclusive jurisdiction as to that applicant.

(c) All requests for expedited administration of the oath of allegiance shall be made in writing to either the court or USCIS. Such requests shall contain sufficient information to substantiate the claim of special circumstances to permit either the court or USCIS to properly exercise the discretionary authority to grant the relief sought. The court or USCIS may seek verification of the validity of the information provided in the request. If the applicant submits a written request to USCIS, but is awaiting an oath administration ceremony by a court pursuant to § 337.8, USCIS promptly shall provide the court with a copy of the request without reaching a decision on whether to grant or deny the request.

[60 FR 37804, July 24, 1995, as amended at 76 FR 53803, Aug. 29, 2011]

§ 337.4 When requests for change of name granted.

When the court has granted the petitioner's change of name request, the petitioner shall subscribe his or her new name to the written oath of allegiance.

[56 FR 50500, Oct. 7, 1991]

§§ 337.5–337.6 [Reserved]

§ 337.7 Information and assignment of individuals under exclusive jurisdiction.

(a) No later than at the time of the examination on the application pursuant to § 335.2 of this chapter, an employee of USCIS shall advise the applicant of his or her right to elect the site for the administration of the oath of allegiance, subject to the exclusive jurisdiction provision of § 310.3(d) of this chapter. In order to assist the applicant in making an informed decision, USCIS shall advise the applicant of the upcoming Immigration Judge or USCIS conducted and judicial ceremonies at which the applicant may appear, if found eligible for naturalization.

(b) An applicant whose application has been approved by USCIS who is subject to the exclusive jurisdiction of a court pursuant to § 310.2(d) of this chapter, shall be advised of the next available court ceremony and provided with a written notice to appear at that ceremony. If the applicant is subject to the exclusive jurisdiction of more than one court exercising exclusive jurisdiction, the applicant will be informed of the upcoming ceremonies in each affected court. The applicant shall decide which court he or she wishes to administer the oath of allegiance.

[58 FR 49915, Sept. 24, 1993, as amended at 60 FR 37804, July 24, 1995; 76 FR 53803, Aug. 29, 2011]

§ 337.8 Oath administered by the courts.

(a) *Notification of election.* An applicant for naturalization not subject to the exclusive jurisdiction of 8 CFR 310.2(d) must notify USCIS at the time of the filing of, or no later than at the examination on, the application of his or her election to have the oath of allegiance administered in an appropriate court having jurisdiction over the applicant's place of residence.

(b) *Certificate of eligibility*—(1) *Exclusive jurisdiction.* In those instances falling within the exclusive jurisdiction provision of section 310(b)(1)(B) of the Act, USCIS will notify the court of the applicant's eligibility for admission to United States citizenship by notifying the clerk of the court within 10 days of the approval of the application.

(2) *Non-exclusive jurisdiction.* In those instances in which the applicant has elected to have the oath administered in a court ceremony, USCIS will notify the clerk of the court in writing that the applicant has been determined by the USCIS to be eligible for admission to United States citizenship upon taking the requisite oath of allegiance and renunciation in a public ceremony. If a scheduled hearing date is not available at the time of notification, USCIS will notify the applicant in writing that the applicant has been approved but no ceremony date is yet available.

(c) *Preparation of lists.* (1) At or prior to the oath administration ceremony, the representative attending the ceremony will submit to the court, in duplicate, lists of persons to be administered the oath of allegiance and renunciation. After the ceremony, and after any required amendments and notations have been made to the lists, the clerk of the court will sign the lists.

(2) The originals of all court lists specified in this section will be filed permanently in the court, and the duplicates returned by the clerk of the court to USCIS. The same disposition will be made of any list presented to, but not approved by, the court.

(d) *Personal representation of the government at oath administration ceremonies.* An oath administration ceremony must be attended by a representative of USCIS who will review each completed questionnaire and may further question the applicant regarding the responses provided. If derogatory information is revealed, the USCIS representative will remove the applicant's name from the list of eligible persons as provided in 8 CFR 335.5 and the court will not administer the oath to such applicant.

(e) *Written report in lieu of personal representation.* If it is impractical for a USCIS representative to be present at a judicial oath administration ceremony, written notice of that fact will be given by the USCIS to the court. The list of persons to be administered the oath of allegiance and renunciation, forms, memoranda, and certificates will be transmitted to the clerk of the court, who will submit the appropriate lists to the court.

(f) *Withdrawal from court.* An applicant for naturalization not subject to the exclusive jurisdiction of 8 CFR 310.3(d) who has elected to have the oath administered in a court oath ceremony may, for good cause shown, request that his or her name be removed from the list of persons eligible to be administered the oath at a court oath ceremony and request that the oath be administered by an immigration judge or USCIS. Such request must be in writing to the USCIS office which granted the application and must cite the reasons for the request. USCIS will consider the good cause shown and the best interests of the applicant in making a decision. If it is determined that the applicant will be permitted to withdraw his or her name from the court ceremony, USCIS will give written notice to the court of the applicant's withdrawal, and the applicant will be scheduled for the next available oath ceremony, conducted by an Immigration Judge or USCIS, as if he or she had never elected the court ceremony.

[76 FR 53803, Aug. 29, 2011]

§ 337.9 Effective date of naturalization.

(a) An applicant for naturalization shall be deemed a citizen of the United States as of the date on which the applicant takes the prescribed oath of allegiance in an administrative ceremony or in a ceremony conducted by an appropriate court under § 337.8 of this chapter.

(b) [Reserved]

[56 FR 50500, Oct. 7, 1991, as amended at 60 FR 37804, July 24, 1995; 66 FR 32147, June 13, 2001; 76 FR 53803, Aug. 29, 2011]

§ 337.10 Failure to appear for oath administration ceremony.

An applicant who fails to appear without good cause for more than one oath administration ceremony for which he or she was duly notified shall be presumed to have abandoned his or her intent to be naturalized. Such presumption shall be regarded as the receipt of derogatory information, and the procedures contained in § 335.5 of this chapter shall be followed.

[58 FR 49916, Sept. 24, 1993]

PART 338—CERTIFICATE OF NATURALIZATION

Sec.

AUTHORITY: 8 U.S.C. 1103, 1443; 8 CFR part 2.

§ 338.1 Execution and issuance of certificate.

(a) *Issuance.* When an applicant for naturalization has taken and subscribed to the oath of allegiance in accordance with 8 CFR part 337, USCIS will issue a Certificate of Naturalization at the conclusion of the oath administration ceremony.

(b) *Contents of certificate.* The certificate must be issued to the applicant in accordance with section 338 of the Act in his or her true, full, and correct name as it exists at the time of the administration of the oath of allegiance. The certificate must show, under "country of former nationality," the name of the applicant's last country of citizenship, as shown in the application and USCIS records, even though the applicant may be stateless at the time of admission to citizenship.

[76 FR 53803, Aug. 29, 2011]

§ 338.2 Execution in case name is changed.

Whenever the name of an applicant has been changed by order of a court as a part of a naturalization, the clerk of court, or his or her authorized deputy, shall forward a copy of the order changing the applicant's name with the notifications required by part 339 of this chapter. The Certificate of Naturalization will be issued to the applicant in the name as changed.

[56 FR 50501, Oct. 7, 1991]

§ 338.3 Delivery of certificates.

No Certificate of Naturalization will be delivered in any case in which the naturalized person has not surrendered his or her Permanent Resident Card to USCIS. Upon a finding that the card is destroyed or otherwise unavailable, USCIS may waive the surrender of the card and the Certificate of Naturalization shall then be delivered to the naturalized person.

[56 FR 50501, Oct. 7, 1991, as amended at 63 FR 70316, Dec. 21, 1998; 76 FR 53803, Aug. 29, 2011]

§ 338.4 [Reserved]

§ 338.5 Correction of certificates.

(a) *Application.* Whenever a Certificate of Naturalization has been delivered which does not conform to the facts shown on the application for naturalization, or a clerical error was made in preparing the certificate, an application for issuance of a corrected certificate may be filed, without fee, in accordance with the form instructions.

(b) *Court-issued certificates*. If the certificate was originally issued by a clerk of court under a prior statute and USCIS finds that a correction is justified and can be made without mutilating the certificate, USCIS will authorize the issuing court to make the necessary correction and to place a dated endorsement of the court on the reverse of the certificate explaining the correction. The authorization will be filed with the naturalization record of the court, the corrected certificate will be returned to the naturalized person, and the duplicate will be endorsed to show the date and nature of the correction and endorsement made, and then returned to USCIS. No fee will be charged the naturalized person for the correction.

(c) *USCIS-issued certificates*. If the certificate was originally issued by USCIS (or its predecessor agency), and USCIS finds that a correction was justified, the correction shall be made to the certificate and a dated endorsement made on the reverse of the certificate.

(d) *Administrative actions*. When a correction made pursuant to paragraphs (b) or (c) of this section would or does result in mutilation of a certificate, USCIS will issue a replacement Certificate of Naturalization and destroy the surrendered certificate.

(e) *Data change*. The correction will not be deemed to be justified where the naturalized person later alleges that the name or date of birth which the applicant stated to be his or her correct name or date of birth at the time of naturalization was not in fact his or her name or date of birth at the time of the naturalization.

[76 FR 53803, Aug. 29, 2011]

§§ 338.6–338.10 [Reserved]

PART 339—FUNCTIONS AND DUTIES OF CLERKS OF COURT REGARDING NATURALIZATION PROCEEDINGS

AUTHORITY: 8 U.S.C. 1103, 1443, 1448.

§ 339.1 Administration of oath of allegiance to applicants for naturalization.

It shall be the duty of a judge of a court that administers an oath of allegiance to ensure that such oath is administered to each applicant for naturalization who has chosen to appear before the court. The clerk of court shall issue to each person to whom such oath is administered the Certificate of Naturalization provided by USCIS in accordance with 8 CFR 338.1. The clerk of court shall provide to each person whose name was changed as part of the naturalization proceedings, pursuant to section 336(e) of the Act, certified evidence of such name change.

[58 FR 49916, Sept. 24, 1993, as amended at 76 FR 53804, Aug. 29, 2011]

§ 339.2 Monthly reports.

(a) *Oath administration ceremonies*. Clerks of court will on the first day of each month or immediately following each oath ceremony submit to USCIS a report listing all oath administration ceremonies held and the total number of persons issued the oath at each ceremony, in accordance with USCIS instructions. The report will include a list of persons attending naturalization oath ceremonies during the month, and certified copies of any court orders granting changes of name.

(b) *Petitions filed for de novo hearings*. The clerk of court must submit to USCIS a monthly report of all persons who have filed *de novo* review petitions before the court. The report shall include each petitioner's name, alien registration number, date of filing of the petition for a *de novo* review, and, once an order has been entered, the disposition.

(c) *Other proceedings and orders*. The clerk of court must forward to USCIS copies of the records of such other proceedings and other orders instituted on or issued by the court affecting or relating to the naturalization of any person as may be required from time to time.

(d) *Use of reports for accounting purposes*. State and federal courts may use the reports as a monthly billing document, submitted to USCIS for reimbursement in accordance with section 344(f)(1) of the Act. USCIS will use the information submitted to calculate costs incurred by courts in performing their naturalization functions. State and federal courts will be reimbursed pursuant to terms set forth in annual agreements entered into between DHS and the Administrative Office of United States Courts.

[76 FR 53804, Aug. 29, 2011]

§339.3 Relinquishment of naturalization jurisdiction.

Whenever a court relinquishes naturalization jurisdiction, the clerk of court shall, within ten days following the date of relinquishment, furnish the district director having administrative jurisdiction over the place in which the court is located, a certified copy of the order of court relinquishing jurisdiction. A representative of the Service shall thereafter examine the naturalization records in the office of the clerk of court and shall bind and lock them. The clerk of court shall return all unused forms and blank certificates of naturalization to the district director with his monthly report on Form N–4.

[22 FR 9825, Dec. 6, 1957]

§339.4 Binding of naturalization records.

Whenever a volume of petitions for naturalization, applications to take the oath of allegiance, declarations of intention, orders of court, or other documents affecting or relating to the naturalization of persons is completed, it shall be bound and locked by the clerk of court.

[22 FR 9825, Dec. 6, 1957]

§339.5 Recordkeeping.

The maintenance of records and submission of reports under this chapter may be accomplished by either electronic or paper means.

[56 FR 50502, Oct. 7, 1991]

PART 340—REVOCATION OF NATURALIZATION

AUTHORITY: 8 U.S.C. 1103, 1443.

§340.1 [Reserved]

§340.2 Revocation proceedings pursuant to section 340(a) of the Act.

(a) *Recommendations for institution of revocation proceedings.* Whenever it appears that any grant of naturalization may have been illegally procured or procured by concealment of a material fact or by willful misrepresentation, and a prima facie case exists for revocation pursuant to section 340(a) of the Act, USCIS will make a recommendation regarding revocation.

(b) *Recommendation for criminal prosecution.* If it appears to USCIS that a case described in paragraph (a) of this section is amenable to criminal penalties under 18 U.S.C. 1425 for unlawful procurement of citizenship or naturalization, the facts will be reported to the appropriate United States Attorney for possible criminal prosecution.

[76 FR 53804, Aug. 29, 2011]

PART 341—CERTIFICATES OF CITIZENSHIP

AUTHORITY: Pub. L. 82–414, 66 Stat. 173, 238, 254, 264, as amended; 8 U.S.C. 1103, 1409(c), 1443, 1444, 1448, 1452, 1455; 8 CFR part 2.

SOURCE: 30 FR 5472, Apr. 16, 1965, unless otherwise noted.

§341.1 Application.

An application for a certificate of citizenship by or in behalf of a person who claims to have acquired United States citizenship under section 309(c) of the Act or to have acquired or derived United States citizenship as specified in section 341 of the Act must be submitted on the form designated by USCIS with the fee specified in 8 CFR

103.7(b)(1) and in accordance with the instructions on the form.

[76 FR 53804, Aug. 29, 2011]

§ 341.2 Examination upon application.

(a) *Personal appearance of applicant and parent or guardian*—(1) *When testimony may be omitted.* An application may be processed without interview if the USCIS officer adjudicating the case has in the administrative file(s) all the required documentation necessary to establish the applicant's eligibility for U.S. citizenship, or if the application is accompanied by one of the following:

(i) A Department of State Form FS-240 (Report of Birth Abroad of a Citizen of the United States);

(ii) An unexpired United States passport issued initially for a full five/ten-year period to the applicant as a citizen of the United States, or

(iii) The applicant's parent(s)' naturalization certificate(s).

(2) *Testimony required.* Each applicant, when notified to do so, shall appear in person before an officer for examination under oath or affirmation upon the application. A person under 18 years of age must have a parent or guardian apply, appear, and testify for the applicant, unless one is unavailable and the district director is satisfied that the applicant is old enough to provide reliable testimony. The same rule will apply for incompetent applicants. At the examination the applicant and the acting parent or guardian, if necessary, shall present testimony and evidence pertinent to the claim to citizenship and shall have the right to review and rebut any adverse evidence on file, and to cross-examine witnesses called by the Government.

(b) *Witness*—(1) *Personal appearance.* A witness shall be called to testify under oath or affirmation at the discretion of USCIS only if that person's testimony is needed to prove a particular point, and only if alternative proof is unavailable or more difficult to produce than is the witness.

(2) *Substitution and waiver.* When testimony is deemed necessary by the district director and the presentation of the person or persons through whom citizenship is claimed is precluded by reason of death, refusal to testify, unknown whereabouts, advanced age, mental or physical incapacity, or severe illness or infirmity, another witness or witnesses shall be produced. A substitute witness also may be produced in lieu of such person if such person is a member of the United States Armed Forces serving outside the United States in an area where his testimony could not be taken without imposing extreme hardship upon him, or without unduly delaying action on the application, and no issue is present which can be resolved only by this testimony.

(c) *Proof.* The burden of proof shall be upon the claimant, or his parent or guardian if one is acting in his behalf, to establish the claimed citizenship by a preponderance of the evidence.

(d) *Assignment and authority of officer.* USCIS will conduct the examination provided for in paragraphs (a) and (b) of this section. The assigned officer shall have authority to administer oaths or affirmations; to present and receive evidence; to rule upon offers of proof; to take or cause to be taken depositions or interrogatories; to regulate the course of the examination; to examine and cross-examine all witnesses appearing in the proceedings; to grant or order continuances; to consider and rule upon objections to the introduction of evidence; to make a report and recommendation as to whether the application shall be granted or denied, and to take such other action as may be appropriate to the conduct of the examination and the disposition of the application.

(e) *Conduct of examination.* The assigned officer shall, at the commencement of the examination of the claimant or the acting parent or guardian, advise them of their rights as set forth in paragraphs (a) and (f) of this section, and shall interrogate them under oath or affirmation with regard to each assertion made in the application and any other matter pertinent to the claim to citizenship; in addition, when a witness is deemed necessary, he shall interrogate each witness with regard to pertinent matters within the personal knowledge of the witness, such as the relationship between the claimant and the citizen source or sources; the citizenship of the latter, and any possible expatriatory acts performed by the claimant and the citizen source or sources. He may, in his discretion, have a transcript made of the testimony. At the conclusion of the examination of the claimant or the action parent or guardian, all corrections made on the applications form shall be consecutively numbered and recorded in the space provided therefor in the form. The affidavit shall then be signed and sworn to or affirmed by the claimant or the acting parent or guardian; and the remainder of the affidavit completed and signed by the assigned officer.

(f) *Representation during proceedings.* The claimant shall have the right to representation during the proceedings, as provided in part 292 of this chapter, and such representative shall have the right to examine and cross-examine witnesses appearing in the proceedings; to introduce evidence; to object to the introduction of evidence, which objections shall be stated succinctly and entered on the record, and to submit briefs. If the claimant is not represented by an attorney or representative, the assigned officer shall assist him in the introduction of all evidence available in his behalf.

[30 FR 5472, Apr. 16, 1965; 30 FR 5621, Apr. 21, 1965, as amended at 32 FR 6260, Apr. 21, 1967; 45 FR 84011, Dec. 22, 1980; 51 FR 35629, Oct. 7, 1986; 66 FR 32147, June 13, 2001; 76 FR 53804, Aug. 29, 2011]

§ 341.3 Depositions.

If satisfied that a witness whose testimony is essential is not available for examination in the United States, the assigned officer may authorize the taking of a deposition abroad by written interrogatories beforea DHS or Department of State official.

[30 FR 5472, Apr. 16, 1965, as amended at 76 FR 53804, Aug. 29, 2011]

§ 341.4 Surrender of immigration documents.

Each claimant shall surrender any immigration identification and permanent resident cards in his or her possession.

[30 FR 5472, Apr. 16, 1965, as amended at 63 FR 70316, Dec. 21, 1998]

§ 341.5 Decision.

(a) *Adjudication.* USCIS may adjudicate the application only after the appropriate approving official has reviewed the report, findings, recommendation, and endorsement of the USCIS officer assigned to adjudicate the application.

(b) *Approval.* If the application is granted, USCIS will prepare a certificate of citizenship and, unless the claimant is unable by reason of mental incapacity or young age to understand the meaning of the oath, he or she must take and subscribe to the oath of renunciation and allegiance prescribed by 8 CFR 337 before USCIS within the United States. Except as provided in paragraph (c), delivery of the certificate in accordance with 8 CFR 103.2(b)(19) and 8 CFR 103.8 must be made in the United States to the claimant or the acting parent or guardian.

(c) *Approval pursuant to section 322(d) of the Act.* Persons eligible for naturalization pursuant to section 322(d) of the Act may subscribe to the oath of renunciation and allegiance and may be issued a certificate of citizenship outside of the United States, in accordance with 8 U.S.C. 1443a.

(d) *Denial.* If USCIS denies the application, the applicant will be furnished the reasons for denial and advised of the right to appeal in accordance with 8 CFR 103.3.

(e) *Subsequent application.* After an application for a certificate of citizenship has been denied and the time for appeal has expired, USCIS will reject a subsequent application submitted by the same individual and the applicant will be instructed to submit a motion to reopen or reconsider in accordance with 8 CFR 103.5. The motion must be accompanied by the rejected application and the fee specified in 8 CFR 103.7.

[76 FR 53804, Aug. 29, 2011]

PART 342—ADMINISTRATIVE CANCELLATION OF CERTIFICATES, DOCUMENTS, OR RECORDS

Sec.

AUTHORITY: 8 U.S.C. 1103, 1453.

SOURCE: 28 FR 209, Jan. 9, 1963, unless otherwise noted.

§ 342.1 Notice.

If it shall appear to a district director that a person has illegally or fraudulently obtained or caused to be created a certificate, document, or record described in section 342 of the Act, a notice shall be served upon the person of intention to cancel the certificate, document, or record. The notice shall contain allegations of the reasons for the proposed action and shall advise the person that he may submit, within 60 days of service of the notice, an answer in writing under oath or affirmation showing cause why the certificate, document, or record should not be canceled, that he may appear in person before a naturalization examiner in support of, or in lieu of his written answer, and that he may have present at that time, without expense to the Government, an attorney or representative qualified under part 292 of this chapter. In such proceedings the person shall be known as the respondent.

[29 FR 5511, Apr. 24, 1964, as amended at 37 FR 2767, Feb. 5, 1972]

§ 342.2 Service of notice.

The notice required by 8 CFR 342.1 must be by personal service as described in 8 CFR 103.8(a)(2).

[76 FR 53805, Aug. 29, 2011]

§ 342.3 Allegations admitted; no answer filed; no personal appearance requested.

If the answer admits all material allegations in the notice, or if no answer is filed within the 60-day period or any extension thereof and no personal appearance is requested within such period or periods, it shall be deemed to authorize the district director, without further notice to respondent, to find the facts to be as alleged in the notice and to cancel the certificate, document, or record. No appeal shall lie from such decision. Written notice of the decision shall be served upon the respondent with demand for surrender of the certificate, document, or record forthwith.

§ 342.4 Answer asserting defense; personal appearance requested.

If the respondent files an answer within the prescribed period asserting a defense to the allegations in the notice, or requests a personal appearance, with or without an answer, the district director shall designate a naturalization examiner to consider the case. The respondent shall be notified that he may appear in person or through counsel with any witnesses and evidence in defense of the allegations, and shall be informed of the date, time, and place for such appearance.

§ 342.5 Conduct of examination.

(a) *Authority of naturalization examiner.* The naturalization examiner assigned to consider the case shall have authority to administer oaths or affirmations to respondent and witnesses, issue subpoenas, present and receive evidence, rule upon offers of proof, take or cause depositions or interrogatories to be taken, regulate the course of the examination, take testimony of respondent and witnesses, grant continuances, consider and rule upon objections to the introduction of evidence, make recommendations to the district director as to whether cancellation shall be ordered or the proceedings terminated, and to take any other action as may be appropriate to the conduct and disposition of the case.

(b) *Assignment of additional officer.* The district director may, in his discretion, assign an officer of the Service to examine and cross-examine the respondent and witnesses and to present evidence pertinent to the case. The naturalization examiner designated under § 342.4 may take such part in the proceedings as he may deem necessary.

(c) *Examination.* The naturalization examiner designated under § 342.4 shall, prior to commencement of the examination, make known to the respondent his official capacity and that of any officer assigned pursuant to paragraph

(b) of this section, the nature of the proceedings, his right to representation by counsel, to examine or object to evidence against him, to present evidence in his own behalf, to cross-examine witnesses presented by the Government, and shall read the allegations in the notice to respondent and, if necessary, explain them to him. The respondent shall be asked whether he admits or denies the material allegations in the notice, or any of them, and whether he concedes illegality or fraud. If respondent admits all the material allegations and that the certificate, document, or record was procured by fraud or illegality, and no issue of law or fact remains, the naturalization examiner may determine that fraud or illegality has been established on the basis of the respondent's admissions. The allegations in the notice shall be taken as admitted if respondent, without reasonable cause, fails or refuses to attend or remain in attendance at the examination. The examination shall be recorded verbatim except for statements made off the record with the permission of the naturalization examiner.

(d) *Prior statements.* The naturalization examiner assigned to consider the case may receive in evidence any oral or written statement which is material and relevant to any issue in the case previously made by the respondent or by any other person during any investigation, examination, hearing, trial, proceeding, or interrogation.

[28 FR 209, Jan. 9, 1963, as amended at 32 FR 3340, Feb. 28, 1967]

§ 342.6 Depositions.

Upon good cause shown, the testimony of any witness may be taken by depositions, either orally or upon written interrogatories before a person having authority to administer oaths (affirmations), as may be designated by the naturalization examiner.

[37 FR 2767, Feb. 5, 1972]

§ 342.7 Report and recommendation.

The naturalization examiner shall prepare a report summarizing the evidence, discussing the applicable law, and containing his findings and recommendations. The record, including the report and recommendation, shall be forwarded to the district director, who shall sign the report, either approving or disapproving the recommendation. If the decision of the district director is that the proceedings be terminated, the respondent shall be so informed.

§ 342.8 Appeals.

Should the district director find that the certificate, document, or record was fraudulently or illegally obtained, he shall enter an order that it be cancelled and the certificate or document surrendered to the Service forthwith. Written notification of such action shall be given the respondent, with a copy of the decision, findings and decision of the district director, and he shall be informed of his right of appeal in accordance with the provisions of part 103 of this chapter.

§ 342.9 Notice re 18 U.S.C. 1428.

The notice to surrender a cancelled certificate of citizenship or copy thereof, prescribed by section 1428 of Title 18 of the United States Code, shall be given by the district director in whose district the person who has possession or control of such document resides.

[28 FR 9282, Aug. 23, 1963]

PART 343—CERTIFICATE OF NATURALIZATION OR REPATRIATION; PERSONS WHO RESUMED CITIZENSHIP UNDER SECTION 323 OF THE NATIONALITY ACT OF 1940, AS AMENDED, OR SECTION 4 OF THE ACT OF JUNE 29, 1906

AUTHORITY: 8 U.S.C. 1101, 1103, 1443, 1454, and 1455.

§ 343.1 Application.

A person who lost citizenship of the United States incidental to service in one of the allied armies during World War I or II, or by voting in a political election in a country not at war with the United States during World War II, and who was naturalized under the provisions of section 323 of the Nationality Act of 1940, as amended, or a person who, before January 13, 1941, resumed United States citizenship under the twelfth subdivision of section 4 of the act of June 29, 1906, may obtain a certificate evidencing such citizenship by making application in accordance with USCIS instructions. The applicant shall be required to appear in person before an assigned officer for interrogation under oath or affirmation upon the application. When the application is approved, a certificate of naturalization or repatriation shall be issued and delivered in person, in the United States only, upon the applicant's signed receipt therefor. If the application is denied, the applicant shall be notified of the reasons therefor and his right to appeal in accordance with the provisions of part 103 of this chapter.

[23 FR 9125, Nov. 26, 1958, as amended at 32 FR 9635, July 4, 1967; 76 FR 53805, Aug. 29, 2011]

PART 343a—NATURALIZATION AND CITIZENSHIP PAPERS LOST, MUTILATED, OR DESTROYED; NEW CERTIFICATE IN CHANGED NAME; CERTIFIED COPY OF REPATRIATION PROCEEDINGS

AUTHORITY: 8 U.S.C. 1101 note, 1103, 1435, 1443, 1454, and 1455.

§ 343a.1 Application for replacement of or new papers relating to naturalization, citizenship, or repatriation.

(a) *Lost, mutilated, or destroyed naturalization papers.* A person whose declaration of intention, certificate of naturalization, citizenship, or repatriation, or whose certified copy of proceedings under the act of June 25, 1936, as amended, or under section 317(b) of the Nationality Act of 1940, or under section 324(c) of the Immigration and Nationality Act, or under the provisions of any private law, has been lost, mutilated, or destroyed,must apply on the form designated by USCIS with the fee specified in 8 CFR 103.7(b)(1) and in accordance with the form instructions.

(b) *New certificate in changed name.* A naturalized citizen whose name has been changed after naturalization by order of court or by marriage must apply for a new certificate of naturalization, or of citizenship, in the changed name.

(c) *Adjudication and disposition*—(1) *Interview.* The applicant shall only be required to appear in person for interview under oath or affirmation in specific cases. Those cases which necessitate an interview enabling an officer to properly adjudicate the application at the office having jurisdiction will be determined by USCIS.

(2) *Approval.* If an application for a new certificate of naturalization, citizenship, or repatriation or a new declaration of intention is approved, the new certificate or declaration will be issued and delivered by personal service in accordance with 8 CFR 103.8(a)(2). If an application for a new certified copy of the proceedings under the Act of June 25, 1936, as amended, or under section 317(b) of the Nationality Act of 1940, or under section 324(c) of the Immigration and Nationality Act, or under the provisions of any private law is approved, a certified photocopy of the record of the proceedings will be issued. If, subsequent to naturalization or repatriation, the applicant's name was changed by marriage, the certification of the photocopy will show both the name in which the proceedings were conducted and the changed name. The new certified copy will be delivered to the applicant in accordance with 8 CFR 103.8(a)(2).

(3) *Denial.* If the application is denied, the applicant shall be notified of the reasons for the denial and of the right to appeal in accordance with 8 CFR 103.3.

[23 FR 9125, Nov. 26, 1958, as amended at 32 FR 9635, July 7, 1967; 51 FR 35629, Oct. 7, 1986; 76 FR 53805, Aug. 29, 2011]

§ 343a.2 Return or replacement of surrendered certificate of naturalization or citizenship.

A certificate of naturalization or citizenship which is contained in a USCIS file, and which was surrendered on a finding that loss of nationality occurred directly or through a parent as a result of the application of any of the following sections of law may, upon request, be returned to the person to whom it was originally issued, notwithstanding the fact that he or she has since been naturalized or repatriated in the United States or abroad:

(a) Section 404 (b) or (c) of the Nationality Act of 1940;

(b) Section 352 of the Immigration and Nationality Act, which was invalidated by *Schneider* v. *Rusk*, 377 U.S. 163;

(c) Section 401(e) of the Nationality Act of 1940;

(d) Section 349(a)(5) of the Immigration and Nationality Act, which was invalidated by *Afroyim* v. *Rusk*, 387 U.S. 253;

(e) Section 301(b) of the Immigration and Nationality Act

(f) Section 301(c) of the Immigration and Nationality Act relative to persons born after May 24, 1934, which was invalidated by amendment to section 301(b) on October 27, 1972, Public Law 92–584.

If, after having been surrendered to the Department of State or to USCIS, the certificate was lost, mutilated, or destroyed as a result of action by USCIS or that Department, a replacement certificate may be issued in the name shown in the surrendered certificate without fee and without requiring the submission ofan application. A surrendered certificate shall not be regarded as mutilated and a replacement shall not be issued solely because of holes made in it to accommodate a fastener, unless the citizen declines to accept the return of the surrendered certificate in that condition and insists upon issuance of a replacement. When it is desired that the replacement certificate be furnished in a name other than the one shown in the surrendered certificate, the regular application procedure with payment of fee must be followed.

[51 FR 35629, Oct. 7, 1986, as amended at 76 FR 53805, Aug. 29, 2011]

PART 343b—SPECIAL CERTIFICATE OF NATURALIZATION FOR RECOGNITION BY A FOREIGN STATE

Sec.

AUTHORITY: 8 U.S.C. 1103, 1443, 1454, 1455.

§ 343b.1 Application.

A naturalized citizen who desires to obtain recognition as a citizen of the United States by a foreign state shall submit an application on the form designated by USCIS with the fee specified in 8 CFR 103.7(b)(1) and in accordance with the form instructions. He shall not be furnished with verification of his naturalization for such purpose in any other way. An applicant who is a claimant against a foreign government for property damage pursuant to the provisions of a peace treaty shall not be requested to furnish the name, official title, and address of a foreign official unless such information is available when the investigation of the applicant is conducted. The applicant shall be required to appear in person before an assigned officer for interrogation under oath or affirmation upon the application.

[32 FR 9636, July 4, 1967, as amended at 56 FR 50502, Oct. 7, 1991; 76 FR 53805, Aug. 29, 2011]

§ 343b.2 Number of applications required.

A special certificate of naturalization is delivered to one foreign government official only. An applicant who desires recognition as a U.S. citizen by more than one foreign official, whether in the same country or not, must file a separate application for each certificate required.

[32 FR 9636, July 4, 1967]

§ 343b.3 Interview.

When the application presents a prima facie case, USCIS may issue a certificate without first interviewing the applicant. In all other cases, the applicant must be interviewed. The interviewing officer must provide a complete written report of the interview before forwarding the application for issuance of the certificate.

[76 FR 53805, Aug. 29, 2011]

§ 343b.4 Applicant outside of United States.

If the application is received by a DHS office outside the United States, an officer will, when practicable, interview the applicant before the application is forwarded to USCIS for issuance of the certificate. When an interview is not practicable, or is not conducted because the application is submitted directly to USCIS in the United States, the certificate may nevertheless be issued and the recommendation conditioned upon satisfactory interview by the Department of State. When forwarding the certificate in such a case, USCIS will inform the Secretary of State that the applicant has not been interviewed, and request to have the applicant interviewed regarding identity and possible expatriation. If identity is not established or if expatriation has occurred, the Department of State will return the certificate to USCIS for disposition.

[76 FR 53805, Aug. 29, 2011]

§ 343b.5 Verification of naturalization.

The application shall not be granted without first obtaining verification of the applicant's naturalization.

[32 FR 9636, July 4, 1967]

§ 343b.11 Disposition of application.

(a) *Approval.* If the application is granted, USCIS will prepare a special certificate of naturalization and forward it to the Secretary of State for transmission to the proper authority of the foreign state in accordance with procedures agreed to between DHS and the Department of State, retain the application and a record of the disposition in the DHS file, and notify the applicant of the actions taken.

(b) *Denial.* If the application is denied, the applicant will be notified of the reasons for denial and of the right to appeal in accordance with 8 CFR 103.3.

[76 FR 53806, Aug. 29, 2011]

PART 343c—CERTIFICATIONS FROM RECORDS

AUTHORITY: 5 U.S.C. 552; 8 U.S.C. 1103.

§ 343c.1 Application for certification of naturalization record of court or certificate of naturalization or citizenship.

An application for certification of a naturalization record of any court, or of any part thereof, or of any certificate of naturalization, repatriation, or citizenship, under section 343(e) of the Act for use in complying with any statute, Federal or State, or in any judicial proceeding, shall be made on the form designated by USCIS in accordance with the form instructions.

[40 FR 50703, Oct. 31, 1975, as amended at 76 FR 53806, Aug. 29, 2011]

PART 349—LOSS OF NATIONALITY

AUTHORITY: Sec. 103, 66 Stat. 173; 8 U.S.C. 1103. Interprets or applies 401(i), 54 Stat. 1169; 8 U.S.C. 801, 1946 ed.

§ 349.1 Japanese renunciation of nationality.

A Japanese who renounced United States nationality pursuant to the provisions of section 401(i), Nationality Act of 1940, who claims that his renunciation is void, shall complete Form N–576, Supplemental Affidavit to be Submitted with Applications of Japanese Renunciants. The affidavit shall be submitted to the Assistant Attorney General, Civil Division, Department of Justice, Washington, DC 20530, with a covering letter requesting a determination of the validity of the renunciation.

[32 FR 9636, July 4, 1967]

PART 392—SPECIAL CLASSES OF PERSONS WHO MAY BE NATURALIZED: PERSONS WHO DIE WHILE SERVING ON ACTIVE DUTY WITH THE UNITED STATES ARMED FORCES DURING CERTAIN PERIODS OF HOSTILITIES

Sec.

AUTHORITY: 8 U.S.C. 1103, 1440 and note, and 1440–1; 8 CFR part 2.

SOURCE: 56 FR 22822, May 17, 1991, unless otherwise noted.

§ 392.1 Definitions.

As used in this part:

Active-duty status means full-time duty in the active military service of the United States, and includes full-time training duty, which constitutes qualifying service under section 329(a) of the Act. Active service in the United States Coast Guard during one of the periods of hostilities specified herein shall constitute service in the military, air, or naval forces of the United States. Active-duty status also includes annual training duty and attendance, while in the active military service, at a service school designated by the military authorities under 10 U.S.C. 101(22). The order of a national guardsman into active duty for training under 10 U.S.C. 672 constitutes service in active-duty status in the military forces of the United States. Active duty in a noncombatant capacity is qualifying service.

Decedent means the person on whose behalf an application for a certificate of posthumous citizenship is made.

Induction, enlistment, and *reenlistment,* refer to the decedent's place of entry into active duty military service.

Korean Hostilities relates to the period from June 25, 1950, to July 1, 1955, inclusive.

Lodge Act means the Act of June 30, 1950, which qualified for naturalization nonresident aliens who served honorably for 5 years in the United States Army during specified periods, notwithstanding that they never formally became lawful permanent residents of the United States.

Next-of-kin means the closest surviving blood or legal relative of the decedent in the following order of succession:

(1) The surviving spouse;

(2) The decedent's surviving son or daughter, if the decedent has no surviving spouse;

(3) The decedent's surviving parent, if the decedent has no surviving spouse or sons or daughters; or,

(4) The decedent's surviving brother or sister, if none of the persons described in paragraphs (1) through (3) of this definition survive the decedent.

Other periods of military hostilities means any period designated by the President under Executive Order as a period in which Armed Forces of the United States are or were engaged in military operations involving armed conflict with a hostile foreign force.

Representative means:

(1) The duly appointed executor or administrator of the decedent's estate, including a special administrator appointed for the purpose of seeking the decedent's naturalization; or,

(2) The duly appointed guardian, conservator, or committee of the decedent's next-of-kin; or,

(3) A service organization listed in 38 U.S.C. 3402, or chartered by Congress, or State, or other service organization recognized by the Department of Veterans Affairs.

Vietnam Hostilities relates to the period from February 28, 1961, to October 15, 1978, inclusive.

World War I relates to the period from April 6, 1917, to November 11, 1918, inclusive.

World War II relates to the period from September 1, 1939, to December 31, 1946, inclusive.

§ 392.2 Eligibility for posthumous citizenship.

(a) *General.* Any alien or noncitizen national of the United States is eligible for posthumous United States citizenship who:

(1) Served honorably in an active-duty status with the military, air, or naval forces of the United States during World War I, World War II, the Korean Hostilities, the Vietnam Hostilities, or in other periods of military hostilities designated by the President under Executive Order; and,

(2) Died as a result of injury or disease incurred in or aggravated by service in the United States Armed Forces during a period of military hostilities listed in paragraph (a)(1) of this section. Where the person died subsequent to separation from military service, the death must have resulted from an injury or disease that was sustained, acquired, or exacerbated during active-duty service in a qualifying period of military hostilities as specified in this part.

(b) *Qualifying enlistment.* In conjunction with the qualifying service as described in paragraph (a)(1) of this section, the decedent must have:

(1) Enlisted, reenlisted, or been inducted in the United States, the Canal Zone, American Samoa, or Swains Island;

(2) Been lawfully admitted to the United States for permanent residence, at any time; or,

(3) Enlisted or reenlisted in the United States Army pursuant to the provisions of the Lodge Act. In such case, the decedent shall be considered to have been lawfully admitted to the United States as a permanent resident for purposes of this section, provided he or she:

(i) Entered the United States, its outlying possessions, or the Canal Zone, at some time during the period of army service, pursuant to military orders; and

(ii) Was honorably discharged following completion of at least 5 full years of active duty service, even though the active-duty service may not have occurred during a qualifying period of hostilities specified in section 329(a) of the Act.

(c) *Character of military service.* Where the character of military service is not certified as honorable by the executive department under which the person served, or where the person was dishonorably discharged or discharged under conditions other than honorable, such service shall not satisfy the requirement of paragraph (a)(1) of this section.

(d) *Certification of eligibility.* (1) The executive department under which the decedent served shall determine whether:

(i) The decedent served honorably in an active-duty status;

(ii) The separation from such service was under honorable conditions; and,

(iii) The decedent died as a result of injury or disease incurred in, or aggravated by active duty service during a qualifying period of military hostilities.

(2) The certification required by section 329A(c)(2) of the Act to prove military service and service-connected death must be requested by the applicant on the form designated by USCIS in accordance with the form instructions. The form will also be used to verify the decedent's place of induction, enlistment, or reenlistment.

[56 FR 22822, May 17, 1991, as amended at 76 FR 53806, Aug. 29, 2011]

§ 392.3 Application for posthumous citizenship.

(a) *Persons who may apply.* (1) Only one person who is either the next-of-kin or another representative of the decedent shall be permitted to apply for posthumous citizenship on the decedent's behalf. A person who is a next-of-kin who wishes to apply for posthumous citizenship on behalf of the decedent, shall, if there is a surviving next-of-kin in the line of succession above him or her, be required to obtain authorization to make the application from all surviving next-of-kin in the line of succession above him or her. The authorization shall be in the form of an affidavit stating that the affiant authorizes the requester to apply for posthumous citizenship on behalf of the decedent. The affidavit must include the name and address of the affiant, and the relationship of the affiant to the decedent.

(2) When there is a surviving next-of-kin, an application for posthumous citizenship shall only be accepted from a representative provided authorization has been obtained from all surviving next-of-kin. However, this requirement shall not apply to the executor or administrator of the decedent's estate. In the case of a service organization acting as a representative, authorization must also have been obtained from any appointed representative. A veterans service organization must submit evidence of recognition by the Department of Veterans Affairs. Once USCIS has granted posthumous citizenship to a person, no subsequent applications on his or her behalf shall be approved, nor shall any additional original certificates be issued, except in the case of an application for issuance of a replacement certificate for one lost, mutiliated, or destroyed.

(b) *Application.* An application for posthumous citizenship must be submitted on the form designated by USCIS in accordance with the form instructions.

(c) *Application period.* An application for posthumous citizenship must be filed no later than two years after the date of the decedent's death.

(d) *Denial of application.* When the application is denied, the applicant shall be notified of the decision and the reason(s) for denial. There is no appeal from the denial of an application under this part.

[56 FR 22822, May 17, 1991, as amended at 74 FR 26941, June 5, 2009; 76 FR 53806, Aug. 29, 2011]

§392.4 Issuance of a certificate of citizenship.

(a) *Approval of application.* When an application for posthumous citizenship under this part has been approved, USCIS will issue a Certificate of Citizenship to the applicant in the name of the decedent.

(b) *Delivery of certificate.* Delivery of the Certificate of Citizenship shall be made by registered mail to the address designated by the applicant. If the applicant resides outside the United States, the certificate shall be sent by registered mail to the Service office abroad, if one is located where delivery is to be made; otherwise, it shall be forwarded to the nearest American Embassy or Consulate.

(c) *Effective date of citizenship.* Where the Service has approved an Application for Posthumous Citizenship (Form N–644), the decedent shall be considered a United States citizen as of the date of his or her death.

(d) *Ineligibility for immigration benefits.* The granting of posthumous citizenship under section 329A of the Immigration and Naturalization Act, as amended, and issuance of a certificate under paragraph (a) of this section, shall not entitle the surviving spouse, parent, son, daughter, or other relative of the decedent to any benefit under any provision of the Act. Nor shall such grant make applicable the provisions of section 319(d) of the Act to the surviving spouse.

(e) *Replacement certificate.* An application for a replacement Certificate of Citizenship must be submitted on the form designated by USCIS with the fee specified in 8 CFR 103.7(b)(1) and in accordance with the form instructions.

[56 FR 22822, May 17, 1991, as amended at 76 FR 53806, Aug. 29, 2011]

PARTS 393–499 [RESERVED]

CHAPTER V—EXECUTIVE OFFICE FOR IMMIGRATION REVIEW, DEPARTMENT OF JUSTICE

SUBCHAPTER A—GENERAL PROVISIONS

SUBCHAPTER B—IMMIGRATION REGULATIONS

SUBCHAPTER A—GENERAL PROVISIONS

PART 1000 [RESERVED]

PART 1001—DEFINITIONS

AUTHORITY: 5 U.S.C. 301; 8 U.S.C. 1101, 1103; Pub. L. 107-296, 116 Stat. 2135; Title VII of Pub. L. 110-229.

§ 1001.1 Definitions.

As used in this chapter:

(a) The terms defined in section 101 of the Immigration and Nationality Act (66 Stat. 163) shall have the meanings ascribed to them in that section and as supplemented, explained, and further defined in this chapter.

(b) The term *Act* means the Immigration and Nationality Act, as amended.

(c) The term *Service* means the Immigration and Naturalization Service, as it existed prior to March 1, 2003. Unless otherwise specified, references to the Service on or after that date mean the offices of the Department of Homeland Security to which the functions of the former Service were transferred pursuant to the Homeland Security Act, Public Law 107-296 (Nov. 25, 2002), as provided in 8 CFR chapter I.

(d) The term *Commissioner* means the Commissioner of the Immigration and Naturalization Service prior to March 1, 2003. Unless otherwise specified, references to the Commissioner on or after that date mean those officials of the Department of Homeland Security who have succeeded to the functions of the Commissioner of the former Service, as provided in 8 CFR chapter I.

(e) The term *Board* means the Board of Immigration Appeals.

(f) The term *attorney* means any person who is eligible to practice law in and is a member in good standing of the bar of the highest court of any State, possession, territory, or Commonwealth of the United States, or of the District of Columbia, and is not under any order suspending, enjoining, restraining, disbarring, or otherwise restricting him in the practice of law.

(g) Unless the context otherwise requires, the term *case* means any proceeding arising under any immigration or naturalization law, Executive order, or Presidential proclamation, or preparation for or incident to such proceeding, including preliminary steps by any private person or corporation preliminary to the filing of the application or petition by which any proceeding under the jurisdiction of the Service or the Board is initiated.

(h) The term *day* when computing the period of time for taking any action provided in this chapter including the taking of an appeal, shall include Saturdays, Sundays, and legal holidays, except that when the last day of the period so computed falls on a Saturday, Sunday or a legal holiday, the period shall run until the end of the next day which is not a Saturday, Sunday, nor a legal holiday.

(i) The term *practice* means the act or acts of any person appearing in any case, either in person or through the preparation or filing of any brief or other document, paper, application, or petition on behalf of another person or client before or with DHS, or any immigration judge, or the Board.

(j) The term *representative* refers to a person who is entitled to represent others as provided in §§ 1292.1(a) (2), (3), (4), (5), (6), and 1292.1(b) of this chapter.

(k) The term *preparation*, constituting practice, means the study of the facts of a case and the applicable laws, coupled with the giving of advice and auxiliary activities, including the incidental preparation of papers, but does not include the lawful functions of a notary public or service consisting solely of assistance in the completion of blank spaces on printed Service forms by one whose remuneration, if any, is nominal and who does not hold himself out as qualified in legal matters or in immigration and naturalization procedure.

(l) The term *immigration judge* means an attorney whom the Attorney General appoints as an administrative judge within the Executive Office for Immigration Review, qualified to conduct specified classes of proceedings, including a hearing under section 240 of the Act. An immigration judge shall be subject to such supervision and shall perform such duties as the Attorney

General shall prescribe, but shall not be employed by the Immigration and Naturalization Service.

(m) The term *representation* before the Board and the Service includes practice and preparation as defined in paragraphs (i) and (k) of this section.

(n) The term *Executive Office* means Executive Office for Immigration Review.

(o) The term *Director*, unless otherwise specified, means the Director of the Executive Office for Immigration Review. For a definition of the term *Director* when used in the context of an official with the Department of Homeland Security, *see* 8 CFR 1.1(o).

(p) The term *lawfully admitted for permanent residence* means the status of having been lawfully accorded the privilege of residing permanently in the United States as an immigrant in accordance with the immigration laws, such status not having changed. Such status terminates upon entry of a final administrative order of exclusion, deportation, removal, or rescission.

(q) The term *arriving alien* means an applicant for admission coming or attempting to come into the United States at a port-of-entry, or an alien seeking transit through the United States at a port-of-entry, or an alien interdicted in international or United States waters and brought into the United States by any means, whether or not to a designated port-of-entry, and regardless of the means of transport. An arriving alien remains an arriving alien even if paroled pursuant to section 212(d)(5) of the Act, and even after any such parole is terminated or revoked. However, an arriving alien who was paroled into the United States before April 1, 1997, or who was paroled into the United States on or after April 1, 1997, pursuant to a grant of advance parole which the alien applied for and obtained in the United States prior to the alien's departure from and return to the United States, will not be treated, solely by reason of that grant of parole, as an arriving alien under section 235(b)(1)(A)(i) of the Act.

(r) The term *respondent* means a person named in a Notice to Appear issued in accordance with section 239(a) of the Act, or in an Order to Show Cause issued in accordance with §242.1 of 8 CFR chapter I as it existed prior to April 1, 1997.

(s) The terms *government counsel* or *Service counsel*, in the context of proceedings in which the Department of Homeland Security has appeared, mean any officer assigned to represent the Department of Homeland Security in any proceeding before an immigration judge or the Board of Immigration Appeals.

(t) The term *aggravated felony* means a crime (or a conspiracy or attempt to commit a crime) described in section 101(a)(43) of the Act. This definition is applicable to any proceeding, application, custody determination, or adjudication pending on or after September 30, 1996, but shall apply under section 276(b) of the Act only to violations of section 276(a) of the Act occurring on or after that date.

(u) The term *Department*, unless otherwise specified, means the Department of Justice.

(v) The term *Secretary*, unless otherwise specified, means the Secretary of Homeland Security.

(w) The term *DHS* means the Department of Homeland Security. These rules incorporate by reference the organizational definitions for components of DHS as provided in 8 CFR 1.1.

(x) The term *OLAP* means the Office of Legal Access Programs.

(y) The term *OLAP Director* means the Program Director of the Office of Legal Access Programs.

(aa) [Reserved]

(bb) The term *transition program effective date* as used with respect to extending the immigration laws to the Commonwealth of the Northern Mariana Islands means November 28, 2009.

[23 FR 9115, Nov. 26, 1958]

EDITORIAL NOTE: For FEDERAL REGISTER citations affecting §1001.1, see the List of CFR Sections Affected, which appears in the Finding Aids section of the printed volume and at *www.govinfo.gov*.

PART 1003—EXECUTIVE OFFICE FOR IMMIGRATION REVIEW

Sec.

Subpart A—Board of Immigration Appeals

Subpart B—Office of the Chief Immigration Judge

Subpart C—Immigration Court—Rules of Procedure

Subpart D [Reserved]

Subpart E—List of Pro Bono Legal Service Providers

Subpart F [Reserved]

Subpart G—Professional Conduct for Practitioners—Rules and Procedures

AUTHORITY: 5 U.S.C. 301; 6 U.S.C. 521; 8 U.S.C. 1101, 1103, 1154, 1155, 1158, 1182, 1226, 1229, 1229a, 1229b, 1229c, 1231, 1254a, 1255, 1324d, 1330, 1361, 1362; 28 U.S.C. 509, 510, 1746; sec. 2 Reorg. Plan No. 2 of 1950; 3 CFR, 1949–1953 Comp., p. 1002; section 203 of Pub. L. 105–100, 111 Stat. 2196–200; sections 1506 and 1510 of Pub. L. 106–386, 114 Stat. 1527–29, 1531–32; section 1505 of Pub. L. 106–554, 114 Stat. 2763A-326 to -328.

SOURCE: Redesignated at 68 FR 9830, Feb. 28, 2003.

EDITORIAL NOTE: Nomenclature changes to part 1003 appear at 68 FR 9846, Feb. 28, 2003, and at 68 FR 10350, Mar. 5, 2003.

§ 1003.0 Executive Office for Immigration Review.

(a) *Organization.* Within the Department of Justice, there shall be an Executive Office for Immigration Review (EOIR), headed by a Director who is appointed by the Attorney General. The Director shall be assisted by a Deputy Director and by a General Counsel. EOIR shall include the Board of Immigration Appeals, the Office of the Chief Immigration Judge, the Office of the Chief Administrative Hearing Officer, the Office of Legal Access Programs, and such other staff as the Attorney General or the Director may provide.

(b) *Powers of the Director*—(1) *In general.* The Director shall manage EOIR and its employees and shall be responsible for the direction and supervision of the Board, the Office of the Chief Immigration Judge, and the Office of the Chief Administrative Hearing Officer in the execution of their respective duties pursuant to the Act and the provisions of this chapter. Unless otherwise provided by the Attorney General, the Director shall report to the Deputy Attorney General and the Attorney General. The Director shall have the authority to:

(i) Issue operational instructions and policy, including procedural instructions regarding the implementation of new statutory or regulatory authorities;

(ii) Direct the conduct of all EOIR employees to ensure the efficient disposition of all pending cases, including the power, in his discretion, to set priorities or time frames for the resolution of cases; to direct that the adjudication of certain cases be deferred; to regulate the assignment of adjudicators to cases; and otherwise to manage the docket of matters to be decided by the Board, the immigration judges, the Chief Administrative Hearing Officer, or the administrative law judges;

(iii) Provide for appropriate administrative coordination with the other components of the Department of Justice, with the Department of Homeland Security, and with the Department of State;

(iv) Evaluate the performance of the Board of Immigration Appeals, the Office of the Chief Immigration Judge, the Office of the Chief Administrative Hearing Officer, and other EOIR activities, make appropriate reports and inspections, and take corrective action where needed;

(v) Provide for performance appraisals for immigration judges and Board members while fully respecting their roles as adjudicators, including a process for reporting adjudications that reflect temperament problems or poor decisional quality;

(vi) Administer an examination for newly-appointed immigration judges and Board members with respect to their familiarity with key principles of immigration law before they begin to adjudicate matters, and evaluate the temperament and skills of each new immigration judge or Board member within 2 years of appointment;

(vii) Provide for comprehensive, continuing training and support for Board members, immigration judges, and EOIR staff in order to promote the quality and consistency of adjudications;

(viii) Implement a process for receiving, evaluating, and responding to complaints of inappropriate conduct by EOIR adjudicators; and

(ix) Exercise such other authorities as the Attorney General may provide.

(2) *Delegations.* The Director may delegate the authority given to him by this part or by the Attorney General to the Deputy Director, the General Counsel, the Chairman of the Board of Immigration Appeals, the Chief Immigration Judge, the Chief Administrative Hearing Officer, or any other EOIR employee.

(c) *Limit on the Authority of the Director.* The Director shall have no authority to adjudicate cases arising under the Act or regulations and shall not direct the result of an adjudication assigned to the Board, an immigration judge, the Chief Administrative Hearing Officer, or an Administrative Law Judge; provided, however, that nothing in this part shall be construed to limit the authority of the Director under paragraph (b) of this section.

(d) *Deputy Director.* The Deputy Director shall advise and assist the Director in the management of EOIR and the formulation of policy and guidelines. Unless otherwise limited by law or by order of the Director, the Deputy

Director shall exercise the full authority of the Director in the discharge of his or her duties.

(e) *General Counsel.* Subject to the supervision of the Director, the General Counsel shall serve as the chief legal counsel of EOIR. The General Counsel shall provide legal advice and assistance to the Director, Deputy Director, and heads of the components within EOIR, and shall supervise all legal activities of EOIR not related to adjudications arising under the Act or this chapter.

(1) *Professional standards.* The General Counsel shall administer programs to protect the integrity of immigration proceedings before EOIR, including administering the disciplinary program for practitioners and recognized organizations under subpart G of this part.

(2) *Fraud issues.* The General Counsel shall designate an anti-fraud officer who shall—

(i) Serve as a point of contact relating to concerns about possible fraud upon EOIR, particularly with respect to matters relating to fraudulent applications or documents affecting multiple removal proceedings, applications for relief from removal, appeals, or other proceedings before EOIR;

(ii) Coordinate with investigative authorities of the Department of Homeland Security, the Department of Justice, and other appropriate agencies with respect to the identification of and response to such fraud; and

(iii) Notify the EOIR disciplinary counsel and other appropriate authorities with respect to instances of fraud, misrepresentation, or abuse pertaining to an attorney or accredited representative.

(f) *Office of Legal Access Programs and authorities of the Program Director.* Within EOIR, there shall be an Office of Legal Access Programs (OLAP), consisting of a Program Director and such other staff as the Director deems necessary. Subject to the supervision of the Director, the Program Director of OLAP (the OLAP Director), or the OLAP Director's designee, shall have the authority to:

(1) Develop and administer a system of legal orientation programs to provide education regarding administrative procedures and legal rights under immigration law;

(2) Develop and administer a program to recognize organizations and accredit representatives to provide representation before the Immigration Courts, the Board, and DHS, or DHS alone. The OLAP Director shall determine whether an organization and its representatives meet the eligibility requirements for recognition and accreditation in accordance with this chapter. The OLAP Director shall also have the authority to administratively terminate the recognition of an organization and the accreditation of a representative and to maintain the roster of recognized organizations and their accredited representatives;

(3) Issue guidance and policies regarding the implementation of OLAP's statutory and regulatory authorities; and

(4) Exercise such other authorities as the Director may provide.

(g) *Citizenship Requirement for Employment.* (1) An application to work at EOIR, either as an employee or a volunteer, must include a signed affirmation from the applicant that he or she is a citizen of the United States of America. If requested, the applicant must document United States citizenship.

(2) The Director of EOIR may, by explicit written determination and to the extent permitted by law, authorize the appointment of an alien to an EOIR position when necessary to accomplish the work of EOIR.

[72 FR 53676, Sept. 20, 2007, as amended at 81 FR 92361, Dec. 19, 2016]

Subpart A—Board of Immigration Appeals

§ 1003.1 Organization, jurisdiction, and powers of the Board of Immigration Appeals.

(a)(1) *Organization.* There shall be in the Department of Justice a Board of Immigration Appeals, subject to the general supervision of the Director, Executive Office for Immigration Review (EOIR). The Board members shall be attorneys appointed by the Attorney General to act as the Attorney General's delegates in the cases that come before them. The Board shall consist of

21 members. A vacancy, or the absence or unavailability of a Board member, shall not impair the right of the remaining members to exercise all the powers of the Board.

(2) *Chairman.* The Attorney General shall designate one of the Board members to serve as Chairman. The Attorney General may designate one or two Vice Chairmen to assist the Chairman in the performance of his duties and to exercise all of the powers and duties of the Chairman in the absence or unavailability of the Chairman.

(i) The Chairman, subject to the supervision of the Director, shall direct, supervise, and establish internal operating procedures and policies of the Board. The Chairman shall have authority to:

(A) Issue operational instructions and policy, including procedural instructions regarding the implementation of new statutory or regulatory authorities;

(B) Provide for appropriate training of Board members and staff on the conduct of their powers and duties;

(C) Direct the conduct of all employees assigned to the Board to ensure the efficient disposition of all pending cases, including the power, in his discretion, to set priorities or time frames for the resolution of cases; to direct that the adjudication of certain cases be deferred, to regulate the assignment of Board members to cases, and otherwise to manage the docket of matters to be decided by the Board;

(D) Evaluate the performance of the Board by making appropriate reports and inspections, and take corrective action where needed;

(E) Adjudicate cases as a Board member; and

(F) Exercise such other authorities as the Director may provide.

(ii) The Chairman shall have no authority to direct the result of an adjudication assigned to another Board member or to a panel; provided, however, that nothing in this section shall be construed to limit the management authority of the Chairman under paragraph (a)(2)(i) of this section.

(3) *Panels.* The Chairman shall divide the Board into three-member panels and designate a presiding member of each panel if the Chairman or Vice Chairman is not assigned to the panel. The Chairman may from time to time make changes in the composition of such panels and of presiding members. Each three-member panel shall be empowered to decide cases by majority vote, and a majority of the Board members assigned to the panel shall constitute a quorum for such panel. In addition, the Chairman shall assign any number of Board members, as needed, to serve on the screening panel to implement the case management process as provided in paragraph (e) of this section.

(4) *Temporary Board members.* The Director may in his discretion designate immigration judges, retired Board members, retired immigration judges, and administrative law judges employed within, or retired from, EOIR to act as temporary Board members for terms not to exceed six months. In addition, with the approval of the Deputy Attorney General, the Director may designate one or more senior EOIR attorneys with at least ten years of experience in the field of immigration law to act as temporary Board members for terms not to exceed six months. A temporary Board member shall have the authority of a Board member to adjudicate assigned cases, except that temporary Board members shall not have the authority to vote on any matter decided by the Board *en banc.*

(5) *En banc process.* A majority of the permanent Board members shall constitute a quorum for purposes of convening the Board *en banc.* The Board may on its own motion by a majority vote of the permanent Board members, or by direction of the Chairman, consider any case *en banc*, or reconsider as the Board *en banc* any case that has been considered or decided by a three-member panel. En banc proceedings are not favored, and shall ordinarily be ordered only where necessary to address an issue of particular importance or to secure or maintain consistency of the Board's decisions.

(6) *Board staff.* There shall also be attached to the Board such number of attorneys and other employees as the Deputy Attorney General, upon recommendation of the Director, shall from time to time direct.

(7) [Reserved]

(b) *Appellate jurisdiction.* Appeals may be filed with the Board of Immigration Appeals from the following:

(1) Decisions of Immigration Judges in exclusion cases, as provided in 8 CFR part 240, subpart D.

(2) Decisions of Immigration Judges in deportation cases, as provided in 8 CFR part 1240, subpart E, except that no appeal shall lie seeking review of a length of a period of voluntary departure granted by an Immigration Judge under section 244E of the Act as it existed prior to April 1, 1997.

(3) Decisions of Immigration Judges in removal proceedings, as provided in 8 CFR part 1240, except that no appeal shall lie seeking review of the length of a period of voluntary departure granted by an immigration judge under section 240B of the Act or part 240 of this chapter.

(4) Decisions involving administrative fines and penalties, including mitigation thereof, as provided in part 280 of this chapter.

(5) Decisions on petitions filed in accordance with section 204 of the act (except petitions to accord preference classifications under section 203(a)(3) or section 203(a)(6) of the act, or a petition on behalf of a child described in section 101(b)(1)(F) of the act), and decisions on requests for revalidation and decisions revoking the approval of such petitions, in accordance with section 205 of the act, as provided in parts 204 and 205, respectively, of 8 CFR chapter I or parts 1204 and 1205, respectively, of this chapter.

(6) Decisions on applications for the exercise of the discretionary authority contained in section 212(d)(3) of the act as provided in part 1212 of this chapter.

(7) Determinations relating to bond, parole, or detention of an alien as provided in 8 CFR part 1236, subpart A.

(8) Decisions of Immigration Judges in rescission of adjustment of status cases, as provided in part 1246 of this chapter.

(9) Decisions of Immigration Judges in asylum proceedings pursuant to § 1208.2(b) of this chapter.

(10) Decisions of Immigration Judges relating to Temporary Protected Status as provided in 8 CFR part 1244.

(11) [Reserved]

(12) Decisions of Immigration Judges on applications for adjustment of status referred on a Notice of Certification (Form I-290C) to the Immigration Court in accordance with §§ 1245.13(n)(2) and 1245.15(n)(3) of this chapter or remanded to the Immigration Court in accordance with §§ 1245.13(d)(2) and 1245.15(e)(2) of this chapter.

(13) Decisions of adjudicating officials in disciplinary proceedings involving practitioners or recognized organizations as provided in subpart G of this part.

(14) Decisions of immigration judges regarding custody of aliens subject to a final order of removal made pursuant to § 1241.14 of this chapter.

(c) *Jurisdiction by certification.* The Commissioner, or any other duly authorized officer of the Service, any Immigration Judge, or the Board may in any case arising under paragraph (b) of this section certify such case to the Board. The Board in its discretion may review any such case by certification without regard to the provisions of § 1003.7 if it determines that the parties have already been given a fair opportunity to make representations before the Board regarding the case, including the opportunity request oral argument and to submit a brief.

(d) *Powers of the Board*—(1) *Generally.* The Board shall function as an appellate body charged with the review of those administrative adjudications under the Act that the Attorney General may by regulation assign to it. The Board shall resolve the questions before it in a manner that is timely, impartial, and consistent with the Act and regulations. In addition, the Board, through precedent decisions, shall provide clear and uniform guidance to the Service, the immigration judges, and the general public on the proper interpretation and administration of the Act and its implementing regulations.

(i) The Board shall be governed by the provisions and limitations prescribed by applicable law, regulations, and procedures, and by decisions of the Attorney General (through review of a decision of the Board, by written order, or by determination and ruling pursuant to section 103 of the Act).

(ii) Subject to these governing standards, Board members shall exercise their independent judgment and discretion in considering and determining the cases coming before the Board, and a panel or Board member to whom a case is assigned may take any action consistent with their authorities under the Act and the regulations as is appropriate and necessary for the disposition of the case.

(2) *Summary dismissal of appeals*—(i) *Standards*. A single Board member or panel may summarily dismiss any appeal or portion of any appeal in any case in which:

(A) The party concerned fails to specify the reasons for the appeal on Form EOIR–26 or Form EOIR–29 (Notices of Appeal) or other document filed therewith;

(B) The only reason for the appeal specified by the party concerned involves a finding of fact or a conclusion of law that was conceded by that party at a prior proceeding;

(C) The appeal is from an order that granted the party concerned the relief that had been requested;

(D) The Board is satisfied, from a review of the record, that the appeal is filed for an improper purpose, such as to cause unnecessary delay, or that the appeal lacks an arguable basis in fact or in law unless the Board determines that it is supported by a good faith argument for extension, modification, or reversal of existing law;

(E) The party concerned indicates on Form EOIR–26 or Form EOIR–29 that he or she will file a brief or statement in support of the appeal and, thereafter, does not file such brief or statement, or reasonably explain his or her failure to do so, within the time set for filing;

(F) The appeal does not fall within the Board's jurisdiction, or lies with the Immigration Judge rather than the Board;

(G) The appeal is untimely, or barred by an affirmative waiver of the right of appeal that is clear on the record; or

(H) The appeal fails to meet essential statutory or regulatory requirements or is expressly excluded by statute or regulation.

(ii) *Action by the Board*. The Board's case management screening plan shall promptly identify cases that are subject to summary dismissal pursuant to this paragraph. An order dismissing any appeal pursuant to this paragraph (d)(2) shall constitute the final decision of the Board.

(iii) *Disciplinary consequences*. The filing by a practitioner, as defined in § 1003.101(b), of an appeal that is summarily dismissed under paragraph (d)(2)(i) of this section, may constitute frivolous behavior under § 1003.102(j).Summary dismissal of an appeal under paragraph (d)(2)(i) of this section does not limit the other grounds and procedures for disciplinary action against attorneys or representatives.

(3) *Scope of review*. (i) The Board will not engage in *de novo* review of findings of fact determined by an immigration judge. Facts determined by the immigration judge, including findings as to the credibility of testimony, shall be reviewed only to determine whether the findings of the immigration judge are clearly erroneous.

(ii) The Board may review questions of law, discretion, and judgment and all other issues in appeals from decisions of immigration judges *de novo*.

(iii) The Board may review all questions arising in appeals from decisions issued by Service officers *de novo*.

(iv) Except for taking administrative notice of commonly known facts such as current events or the contents of official documents, the Board will not engage in factfinding in the course of deciding appeals. A party asserting that the Board cannot properly resolve an appeal without further factfinding must file a motion for remand. If further factfinding is needed in a particular case, the Board may remand the proceeding to the immigration judge or, as appropriate, to the Service.

(4) *Rules of practice*. The Board shall have authority, with the approval of the Director, EOIR, to prescribe procedures governing proceedings before it.

(5) *Discipline of practitioners and recognized organizations*. The Board shall have the authority pursuant to § 1003.101 *et seq*. to impose sanctions upon practitioners who appear in a representative capacity before the Board, the Immigration Courts, or DHS, and upon recognized organizations. The

Board shall also have the authority pursuant to § 1003.107 to reinstate disciplined practitioners to appear in a representative capacity before the Board and the Immigration Courts, or DHS, or all three authorities.

(6) *Identity, law enforcement, or security investigations or examinations.* (i) The Board shall not issue a decision affirming or granting to an alien an immigration status, relief or protection from removal, or other immigration benefit, as provided in 8 CFR 1003.47(b), that requires completion of identity, law enforcement, or security investigations or examinations if:

(A) Identity, law enforcement, or security investigations or examinations have not been completed during the proceedings;

(B) DHS reports to the Board that the results of prior identity, law enforcement, or security investigations or examinations are no longer current under the standards established by DHS and must be updated; or

(C) Identity, law enforcement, or security investigations or examinations have uncovered new information bearing on the merits of the alien's application for relief.

(ii) Except as provided in paragraph (d)(6)(iv) of this section, if identity, law enforcement, or security investigations or examinations have not been completed or DHS reports that the results of prior investigations or examinations are no longer current under the standards established by DHS, then the Board will determine the best means to facilitate the final disposition of the case, as follows:

(A) The Board may issue an order remanding the case to the immigration judge with instructions to allow DHS to complete or update the appropriate identity, law enforcement, or security investigations or examinations pursuant to § 1003.47; or

(B) The Board may provide notice to both parties that in order to complete adjudication of the appeal the case is being placed on hold until such time as all identity, law enforcement, or security investigations or examinations are completed or updated and the results have been reported to the Board.

(iii) In any case placed on hold under paragraph (d)(6)(ii)(B) of this section, DHS shall report to the Board promptly when the identity, law enforcement, or security investigations or examinations have been completed or updated. If DHS obtains relevant information as a result of the identity, law enforcement, or security investigations or examinations, or if the applicant fails to comply with necessary procedures for collecting biometrics or other biographical information, DHS may move to remand the record to the immigration judge for consideration of whether, in view of the new information or the alien's failure to comply, the immigration relief should be denied, either on grounds of eligibility or, where applicable, as a matter of discretion.

(iv) The Board is not required to remand or hold a case pursuant to paragraph (d)(6)(ii) of this paragraph if the Board decides to dismiss the respondent's appeal or deny the relief sought.

(v) The immigration relief described in 8 CFR 1003.47(b) and granted by the Board shall take effect as provided in 8 CFR 1003.47(i).

(7) *Finality of decision.* The decision of the Board shall be final except in those cases reviewed by the Attorney General in accordance with paragraph (h) of this section. The Board may return a case to the Service or an immigration judge for such further action as may be appropriate, without entering a final decision on the merits of the case.

(e) *Case management system.* The Chairman shall establish a case management system to screen all cases and to manage the Board's caseload. Unless a case meets the standards for assignment to a three-member panel under paragraph (e)(6) of this section, all cases shall be assigned to a single Board member for disposition. The Chairman, under the supervision of the Director, shall be responsible for the success of the case management system. The Chairman shall designate, from time to time, a screening panel comprising a sufficient number of Board members who are authorized, acting alone, to adjudicate appeals as provided in this paragraph.

(1) *Initial screening.* All cases shall be referred to the screening panel for review. Appeals subject to summary dismissal as provided in paragraph (d)(2)

of this section should be promptly dismissed.

(2) *Miscellaneous dispositions.* A single Board member may grant an unopposed motion or a motion to withdraw an appeal pending before the Board. In addition, a single Board member may adjudicate a Service motion to remand any appeal from the decision of a Service officer where the Service requests that the matter be remanded to the Service for further consideration of the appellant's arguments or evidence raised on appeal; a case where remand is required because of a defective or missing transcript; and other procedural or ministerial issues as provided by the case management plan.

(3) *Merits review.* In any case that has not been summarily dismissed, the case management system shall arrange for the prompt completion of the record of proceedings and transcript, and the issuance of a briefing schedule. A single Board member assigned under the case management system shall determine the appeal on the merits as provided in paragraph (e)(4) or (e)(5) of this section, unless the Board member determines that the case is appropriate for review and decision by a three-member panel under the standards of paragraph (e)(6) of this section. The Board member may summarily dismiss an appeal after completion of the record of proceeding.

(4) *Affirmance without opinion.* (i) The Board member to whom a case is assigned shall affirm the decision of the Service or the immigration judge, without opinion, if the Board member determines that the result reached in the decision under review was correct; that any errors in the decision under review were harmless or nonmaterial; and that

(A) The issues on appeal are squarely controlled by existing Board or federal court precedent and do not involve the application of precedent to a novel factual situation; or

(B) The factual and legal issues raised on appeal are not so substantial that the case warrants the issuance of a written opinion in the case.

(ii) If the Board member determines that the decision should be affirmed without opinion, the Board shall issue an order that reads as follows: "The Board affirms, without opinion, the result of the decision below. The decision below is, therefore, the final agency determination. *See* 8 CFR 3.1(e)(4)." An order affirming without opinion, issued under authority of this provision, shall not include further explanation or reasoning. Such an order approves the result reached in the decision below; it does not necessarily imply approval of all of the reasoning of that decision, but does signify the Board's conclusion that any errors in the decision of the immigration judge or the Service were harmless or nonmaterial.

(5) *Other decisions on the merits by single Board member.* If the Board member to whom an appeal is assigned determines, upon consideration of the merits, that the decision is not appropriate for affirmance without opinion, the Board member shall issue a brief order affirming, modifying, or remanding the decision under review, unless the Board member designates the case for decision by a three-member panel under paragraph (e)(6) of this section under the standards of the case management plan. A single Board member may reverse the decision under review if such reversal is plainly consistent with and required by intervening Board or judicial precedent, by an intervening Act of Congress, or by an intervening final regulation. A motion to reconsider or to reopen a decision that was rendered by a single Board member may be adjudicated by that Board member unless the case is reassigned to a three-member panel as provided under the standards of the case management plan.

(6) *Panel decisions.* Cases may only be assigned for review by a three-member panel if the case presents one of these circumstances:

(i) The need to settle inconsistencies among the rulings of different immigration judges;

(ii) The need to establish a precedent construing the meaning of laws, regulations, or procedures;

(iii) The need to review a decision by an immigration judge or the Service that is not in conformity with the law or with applicable precedents;

(iv) The need to resolve a case or controversy of major national import;

(v) The need to review a clearly erroneous factual determination by an immigration judge; or

(vi) The need to reverse the decision of an immigration judge or the Service, other than a reversal under § 1003.1(e)(5).

(7) *Oral argument.* When an appeal has been taken, a request for oral argument if desired shall be included in the Notice of Appeal. A three-member panel or the Board *en banc* may hear oral argument, as a matter of discretion, at such date and time as is established under the Board's case management plan. Oral argument shall be held at the offices of the Board unless the Deputy Attorney General or his designee authorizes oral argument to be held elsewhere. The Service may be represented before the Board by an officer of the Service designated by the Service. No oral argument will be allowed in a case that is assigned for disposition by a single Board member.

(8) *Timeliness.* As provided under the case management system, the Board shall promptly enter orders of summary dismissal, or other miscellaneous dispositions, in appropriate cases. In other cases, after completion of the record on appeal, including any briefs, motions, or other submissions on appeal, the Board member or panel to which the case is assigned shall issue a decision on the merits as soon as practicable, with a priority for cases or custody appeals involving detained aliens.

(i) Except in exigent circumstances as determined by the Chairman, or as provided in paragraph (d)(6) of this section, the Board shall dispose of all appeals assigned to a single Board member within 90 days of completion of the record on appeal, or within 180 days after an appeal is assigned to a three-member panel (including any additional opinion by a member of the panel).

(ii) In exigent circumstances, the Chairman may grant an extension in particular cases of up to 60 days as a matter of discretion. Except as provided in paragraph (e)(8)(iii) or (iv) of this section, in those cases where the panel is unable to issue a decision within the established time limits, as extended, the Chairman shall either assign the case to himself or a Vice-Chairman for final decision within 14 days or shall refer the case to the Attorney General for decision. If a dissenting or concurring panel member fails to complete his or her opinion by the end of the extension period, the decision of the majority will be issued without the separate opinion.

(iii) In rare circumstances, when an impending decision by the United States Supreme Court or a United States Court of Appeals, or impending Department regulatory amendments, or an impending *en banc* Board decision may substantially determine the outcome of a case or group of cases pending before the Board, the Chairman may hold the case or cases until such decision is rendered, temporarily suspending the time limits described in this paragraph (e)(8).

(iv) For any case ready for adjudication as of September 25, 2002, and that has not been completed within the established time lines, the Chairman may, as a matter of discretion, grant an extension of up to 120 days.

(v) The Chairman shall notify the Director of EOIR and the Attorney General if a Board member consistently fails to meet the assigned deadlines for the disposition of appeals, or otherwise fails to adhere to the standards of the case management system. The Chairman shall also prepare a report assessing the timeliness of the disposition of cases by each Board member on an annual basis.

(vi) The provisions of this paragraph (e)(8) establishing time limits for the adjudication of appeals reflect an internal management directive in favor of timely dispositions, but do not affect the validity of any decision issued by the Board and do not, and shall not be interpreted to, create any substantive or procedural rights enforceable before any immigration judge or the Board, or in any court of law or equity.

(f) *Service of Board decisions.* The decision of the Board shall be in writing and copies thereof shall be transmitted by the Board to the Service and a copy shall be served upon the alien or party affected as provided in part 292 of this chapter.

(g) *Decisions as precedents.* Except as Board decisions may be modified or overruled by the Board or the Attorney

General, decisions of the Board, and decisions of the Attorney General, shall be binding on all officers and employees of the Department of Homeland Security or immigration judges in the administration of the immigration laws of the United States. By majority vote of the permanent Board members, selected decisions of the Board rendered by a three-member panel or by the Board en banc may be designated to serve as precedents in all proceedings involving the same issue or issues. Selected decisions designated by the Board, decisions of the Attorney General, and decisions of the Secretary of Homeland Security to the extent authorized in paragraph (i) of this section, shall serve as precedents in all proceedings involving the same issue or issues.

(h) *Referral of cases to the Attorney General.* (1) The Board shall refer to the Attorney General for review of its decision all cases that:

(i) The Attorney General directs the Board to refer to him.

(ii) The Chairman or a majority of the Board believes should be referred to the Attorney General for review.

(iii) The Secretary of Homeland Security, or specific officials of the Department of Homeland Security designated by the Secretary with the concurrence of the Attorney General, refers to the Attorney General for review.

(2) In any case the Attorney General decides, the Attorney General's decision shall be stated in writing and shall be transmitted to the Board or Secretary, as appropriate, for transmittal and service as provided in paragraph (f) of this section.

(i) *Publication of Secretary's precedent decisions.* The Secretary of Homeland Security, or specific officials of the Department of Homeland Security designated by the Secretary with the concurrence of the Attorney General, may file with the Attorney General decisions relating to the administration of the immigration laws of the United States for publication as precedent in future proceedings, and, upon approval of the Attorney General as to the lawfulness of such decision, the Director of the Executive Office for Immigration Review shall cause such decisions to be published in the same manner as decisions of the Board and the Attorney General.

(j) *Continuation of jurisdiction and procedure.* The jurisdiction of, and procedures before, the Board of Immigration Appeals in exclusion, deportation, removal, rescission, asylum-only, and any other proceedings, shall remain in effect as in effect on February 28, 2003, until the regulations in this chapter are further modified by the Attorney General. Where a decision of an officer of the Immigration and Naturalization Service was, before March 1, 2003, appealable to the Board or to an immigration judge, or an application denied could be renewed in proceedings before an immigration judge, the same authority and procedures shall be followed until further modified by the Attorney General.

[23 FR 9117, Nov. 26, 1958]

EDITORIAL NOTE: For FEDERAL REGISTER citations affecting § 1003.1, see the List of CFR Sections Affected, which appears in the Finding Aids section of the printed volume and at *www.govinfo.gov.*

§ 1003.2 Reopening or reconsideration before the Board of Immigration Appeals.

(a) *General.* The Board may at any time reopen or reconsider on its own motion any case in which it has rendered a decision. A request to reopen or reconsider any case in which a decision has been made by the Board, which request is made by the Service, or by the party affected by the decision, must be in the form of a written motion to the Board. The decision to grant or deny a motion to reopen or reconsider is within the discretion of the Board, subject to the restrictions of this section. The Board has discretion to deny a motion to reopen even if the party moving has made out a *prima facie* case for relief.

(b) *Motion to reconsider.* (1) A motion to reconsider shall state the reasons for the motion by specifying the errors of fact or law in the prior Board decision and shall be supported by pertinent authority. A motion to reconsider a decision rendered by an Immigration Judge or Service officer that is pending when an appeal is filed with the Board, or that is filed subsequent to the filing with the Board of an appeal from the decision sought to be reconsidered, may be deemed a motion to remand the decision for further proceedings before the Immigration Judge or the Service officer from whose decision the appeal was taken. Such motion may be consolidated with, and considered by the Board in connection with the appeal to the Board.

(2) A motion to reconsider a decision must be filed with the Board within 30 days after the mailing of the Board decision or on or before July 31, 1996, whichever is later. A party may file only one motion to reconsider any given decision and may not seek reconsideration of a decision denying a previous motion to reconsider. In removal proceedings pursuant to section 240 of the Act, an alien may file only one motion to reconsider a decision that the alien is removable from the United States.

(3) A motion to reconsider based solely on an argument that the case should not have been affirmed without opinion by a single Board Member, or by a three-Member panel, is barred.

(c) *Motion to reopen.* (1) A motion to reopen proceedings shall state the new facts that will be proven at a hearing to be held if the motion is granted and shall be supported by affidavits or other evidentiary material. A motion to reopen proceedings for the purpose of submitting an application for relief must be accompanied by the appropriate application for relief and all supporting documentation. A motion to reopen proceedings shall not be granted unless it appears to the Board that evidence sought to be offered is material and was not available and could not have been discovered or presented at the former hearing; nor shall any motion to reopen for the purpose of affording the alien an opportunity to apply for any form of discretionary relief be granted if it appears that the alien's right to apply for such relief was fully explained to him or her and an opportunity to apply therefore was afforded at the former hearing, unless the relief is sought on the basis of circumstances that have arisen subsequent to the hearing. Subject to the other requirements and restrictions of this section, and notwithstanding the provisions in § 1001.1(p) of this chapter, a motion to reopen proceedings for consideration or further consideration of an application for relief under section 212(c) of the Act (8 U.S.C. 1182(c)) may be granted if the alien demonstrates that he or she was statutorily eligible for such relief prior to the entry of the administratively final order of deportation.

(2) Except as provided in paragraph (c)(3) of this section, a party may file only one motion to reopen deportation or exclusion proceedings (whether before the Board or the Immigration Judge) and that motion must be filed no later than 90 days after the date on which the final administrative decision was rendered in the proceeding sought to be reopened, or on or before September 30, 1996, whichever is later. Except as provided in paragraph (c)(3) of this section, an alien may file only one motion to reopen removal proceedings (whether before the Board or the Immigration Judge) and that motion must be filed no later than 90 days after the date on which the final administrative decision was rendered in the proceeding sought to be reopened.

(3) In removal proceedings pursuant to section 240 of the Act, the time limitation set forth in paragraph (c)(2) of this section shall not apply to a motion to reopen filed pursuant to the provisions of § 1003.23(b)(4)(ii). The time and numerical limitations set forth in paragraph (c)(2) of this section shall not apply to a motion to reopen proceedings:

(i) Filed pursuant to the provisions of § 1003.23(b)(4)(iii)(A)(*1*) or § 1003.23(b)(4)(iii)(A)(*2*);

(ii) To apply or reapply for asylum or withholding of deportation based on changed circumstances arising in the country of nationality or in the country to which deportation has been ordered, if such evidence is material and was not available and could not have been discovered or presented at the previous hearing;

(iii) Agreed upon by all parties and jointly filed. Notwithstanding such agreement, the parties may contest the issues in a reopened proceeding; or

(iv) Filed by the Service in exclusion or deportation proceedings when the basis of the motion is fraud in the original proceeding or a crime that would support termination of asylum in accordance with § 1208.22(f) of this chapter.

(4) A motion to reopen a decision rendered by an Immigration Judge or Service officer that is pending when an appeal is filed, or that is filed while an appeal is pending before the Board, may be deemed a motion to remand for further proceedings before the Immigration Judge or the Service officer from whose decision the appeal was taken. Such motion may be consolidated with, and considered by the Board in connection with, the appeal to the Board.

(d) *Departure, deportation, or removal.* A motion to reopen or a motion to reconsider shall not be made by or on behalf of a person who is the subject of exclusion, deportation, or removal proceedings subsequent to his or her departure from the United States. Any departure from the United States, including the deportation or removal of a person who is the subject of exclusion, deportation, or removal proceedings, occurring after the filing of a motion to reopen or a motion to reconsider, shall constitute a withdrawal of such motion.

(e) *Judicial proceedings.* Motions to reopen or reconsider shall state whether the validity of the exclusion, deportation, or removal order has been or is the subject of any judicial proceeding and, if so, the nature and date thereof, the court in which such proceeding took place or is pending, and its result or status. In any case in which an exclusion, deportation, or removal order is in effect, any motion to reopen or reconsider such order shall include a statement by or on behalf of the moving party declaring whether the subject of the order is also the subject of any pending criminal proceeding under the Act, and, if so, the current status of that proceeding. If a motion to reopen or reconsider seeks discretionary relief, the motion shall include a statement by or on behalf of the moving party declaring whether the alien for whose relief the motion is being filed is subject to any pending criminal prosecution and, if so, the nature and current status of that prosecution.

(f) *Stay of deportation.* Except where a motion is filed pursuant to the provisions of §§ 1003.23(b)(4)(ii) and 1003.23(b)(4)(iii)(A), the filing of a motion to reopen or a motion to reconsider shall not stay the execution of any decision made in the case. Execution of such decision shall proceed unless a stay of execution is specifically granted by the Board, the Immigration Judge, or an authorized officer of the Service.

(g) *Filing procedures*—(1) *English language, entry of appearance, and proof of service requirements.* A motion and any submission made in conjunction with a motion must be in English or accompanied by a certified English translation. If the moving party, other than the Service, is represented, Form EOIR–27, Notice of Entry of Appearance as Attorney or Representative Before the Board, must be filed with the motion. In all cases, the motion shall include proof of service on the opposing party of the motion and all attachments. If the moving party is not the Service, service of the motion shall be made upon the Office of the District Counsel for the district in which the case was completed before the Immigration Judge.

(2) *Distribution of motion papers.* (i) A motion to reopen or motion to reconsider a decision of the Board pertaining to proceedings before an Immigration Judge shall be filed directly with the Board. Such motion must be accompanied by a check, money order, or fee waiver request in satisfaction of the fee requirements of § 1003.8. The record of proceeding pertaining to such a motion shall be forwarded to the Board upon the request or order of the Board.

(ii) A motion to reopen or a motion to reconsider a decision of the Board pertaining to a matter initially adjudicated by an officer of the Service shall be filed with the officer of the Service having administrative control over the record of proceeding.

(iii) If the motion is made by the Service in proceedings in which the Service has administrative control over the record of proceedings, the record of proceedings in the case and the motion shall be filed directly with the Board. If such motion is filed directly with an office of the Service, the entire record of proceeding shall be forwarded to the Board by the Service officer promptly upon receipt of the briefs of the parties, or upon expiration of the time allowed for the submission of such briefs.

(3) *Briefs and response.* The moving party may file a brief if it is included with the motion. If the motion is filed directly with the Board pursuant to paragraph (g)(2)(i) of this section, the opposing party shall have 13 days from the date of service of the motion to file a brief in opposition to the motion directly with the Board. If the motion is filed with an office of the Service pursuant to paragraph (g)(2)(ii) of this section, the opposing party shall have 13 days from the date of filing of the motion to file a brief in opposition to the motion directly with the office of the Service. In all cases, briefs and any other filings made in conjunction with a motion shall include proof of service on the opposing party. The Board, in its discretion, may extend the time within which such brief is to be submitted and may authorize the filing of a brief directly with the Board. A motion shall be deemed unopposed unless a timely response is made. The Board may, in its discretion, consider a brief filed out of time.

(h) *Oral argument.* A request for oral argument, if desired, shall be incorporated in the motion to reopen or reconsider. The Board, in its discretion, may grant or deny requests for oral argument.

(i) *Ruling on motion.* Rulings upon motions to reopen or motions to reconsider shall be by written order. Any motion for reconsideration or reopening of a decision issued by a single Board member will be referred to the screening panel for disposition by a single Board member, unless the screening panel member determines, in the exercise of judgment, that the motion for reconsideration or reopening should be assigned to a three-member panel under the standards of §1003.1(e)(6). If the order directs a reopening and further proceedings are necessary, the record shall be returned to the Immigration Court or the officer of the Service having administrative control over the place where the reopened proceedings are to be conducted. If the motion to reconsider is granted, the decision upon such reconsideration shall affirm, modify, or reverse the original decision made in the case.

[61 FR 18904, Apr. 29, 1996; 61 FR 32924, June 26, 1996, as amended at 62 FR 10330, Mar. 6, 1997; 64 FR 56142, Oct. 18, 1999; 67 FR 54904, Aug. 26, 2002]

§ 1003.3 Notice of appeal.

(a) *Filing*—(1) *Appeal from decision of an immigration judge.* A party affected by a decision of an immigration judge which may be appealed to the Board under this chapter shall be given notice of the opportunity for filing an appeal. An appeal from a decision of an immigration judge shall be taken by filing a Notice of Appeal from a Decision of an Immigration Judge (Form EOIR–26) directly with the Board, within the time specified in §1003.38. The appealing parties are only those parties who are covered by the decision of an immigration judge and who are specifically named on the Notice of Appeal. The appeal must reflect proof of service of a copy of the appeal and all attachments on the opposing party. An appeal is not properly filed unless it is received at the Board, along with all required documents, fees or fee waiver requests, and proof of service, within the time specified in the governing sections of this chapter. A Notice of Appeal may not be filed by any party who has waived appeal pursuant to §1003.39.

(2) *Appeal from decision of a Service officer.* A party affected by a decision of a Service officer that may be appealed to the Board under this chapter shall be given notice of the opportunity to file an appeal. An appeal from a decision of a Service officer shall be taken by filing a Notice of Appeal to the Board of Immigration Appeals from a Decision of an INS Officer (Form EOIR–29) directly with the office of the Service having administrative control over the record of proceeding within 30 days of the service of the decision being appealed. An appeal is not properly filed until it is received at the appropriate office of the Service, together with all required documents, and the fee provisions of §1003.8 are satisfied.

(3) *General requirements for all appeals.* The appeal must be accompanied by a

check, money order, or fee waiver request in satisfaction of the fee requirements of § 1003.8. If the respondent or applicant is represented, a Notice of Entry of Appearance as Attorney or Representative Before the Board (Form EOIR–27) must be filed with the Notice of Appeal. The appeal and all attachments must be in English or accompanied by a certified English translation.

(b) *Statement of the basis of appeal.* The party taking the appeal must identify the reasons for the appeal in the Notice of Appeal (Form EOIR–26 or Form EOIR–29) or in any attachments thereto, in order to avoid summary dismissal pursuant to § 1003.1(d)(2)(i). The statement must specifically identify the findings of fact, the conclusions of law, or both, that are being challenged. If a question of law is presented, supporting authority must be cited. If the dispute is over the findings of fact, the specific facts contested must be identified. Where the appeal concerns discretionary relief, the appellant must state whether the alleged error relates to statutory grounds of eligibility or to the exercise of discretion and must identify the specific factual and legal finding or findings that are being challenged. The appellant must also indicate in the Notice of Appeal (Form EOIR–26 or Form EOIR–29) whether he or she desires oral argument before the Board and whether he or she will be filing a separate written brief or statement in support of the appeal. An appellant who asserts that the appeal may warrant review by a three-member panel under the standards of § 1003.1(e)(6) may identify in the Notice of Appeal the specific factual or legal basis for that contention.

(c) *Briefs*—(1) *Appeal from decision of an immigration judge.* Briefs in support of or in opposition to an appeal from a decision of an immigration judge shall be filed directly with the Board. In those cases that are transcribed, the briefing schedule shall be set by the Board after the transcript is available. In cases involving aliens in custody, the parties shall be provided 21 days in which to file simultaneous briefs unless a shorter period is specified by the Board, and reply briefs shall be permitted only by leave of the Board. In cases involving aliens who are not in custody, the appellant shall be provided 21 days in which to file a brief, unless a shorter period is specified by the Board. The appellee shall have the same period of time in which to file a reply brief that was initially granted to the appellant to file his or her brief. The time to file a reply brief commences from the date upon which the appellant's brief was due, as originally set or extended by the Board. The Board, upon written motion, may extend the period for filing a brief or a reply brief for up to 90 days for good cause shown. In its discretion, the Board may consider a brief that has been filed out of time. All briefs, filings, and motions filed in conjunction with an appeal shall include proof of service on the opposing party.

(2) *Appeal from decision of a Service officer.* Briefs in support of or in opposition to an appeal from a decision of a Service officer shall be filed directly with the office of the Service having administrative control over the file. The alien and the Service shall be provided 21 days in which to file a brief, unless a shorter period is specified by the Service officer from whose decision the appeal is taken, and reply briefs shall be permitted only by leave of the Board. Upon written request of the alien, the Service officer from whose decision the appeal is taken or the Board may extend the period for filing a brief for good cause shown. The Board may authorize the filing of briefs directly with the Board. In its discretion, the Board may consider a brief that has been filed out of time. All briefs and other documents filed in conjunction with an appeal, unless filed by an alien directly with a Service office, shall include proof of service on the opposing party.

(d) *Effect of certification.* The certification of a case, as provided in this part, shall not relieve the party affected from compliance with the provisions of this section in the event that he or she is entitled and desires to appeal from an initial decision, nor shall it serve to extend the time specified in the applicable parts of this chapter for the taking of an appeal.

(e) *Effect of departure from the United States.* Departure from the United

States of a person who is the subject of deportation proceedings, prior to the taking of an appeal from a decision in his or her case, shall constitute a waiver of his or her right to appeal.

(f) *Application on effective date.* All cases and motions pending on September 25, 2002, shall be adjudicated according to the rules in effect on or after that date, except that § 1003.1(d)(3)(i) shall not apply to appeals filed before September 25, 2002. A party to an appeal or motion pending on August 26, 2002, may, until September 25, 2002, or the expiration of any briefing schedule set by the Board, whichever is later, submit a brief or statement limited to explaining why the appeal or motion does or does not meet the criteria for three-member review under § 1003.1(e)(6).

[61 FR 18906, Apr. 29, 1996, as amended at 66 FR 6445, Jan. 22, 2001; 67 FR 54904, Aug. 26, 2002]

§ 1003.4 Withdrawal of appeal.

In any case in which an appeal has been taken, the party taking the appeal may file a written withdrawal thereof with the office at which the notice of appeal was filed. If the record in the case has not been forwarded to the Board on appeal in accordance with § 1003.5, the decision made in the case shall be final to the same extent as if no appeal had been taken. If the record has been forwarded on appeal, the withdrawal of the appeal shall be forwarded to the Board and, if no decision in the case has been made on the appeal, the record shall be returned and the initial decision shall be final to the same extent as if no appeal had been taken. If a decision on the appeal has been made by the Board in the case, further action shall be taken in accordance therewith. Departure from the United States of a person who is the subject of deportation proceedings subsequent to the taking of an appeal, but prior to a decision thereon, shall constitute a withdrawal of the appeal, and the initial decision in the case shall be final to the same extent as though no appeal had been taken. Departure from the United States of a person who is the subject of deportation or removal proceedings, except for arriving aliens as defined in § 1001.1(q) of this chapter, subsequent to the taking of an appeal, but prior to a decision thereon, shall constitute a withdrawal of the appeal, and the initial decision in the case shall be final to the same extent as though no appeal had been taken.

[61 FR 18907, Apr. 29, 1996, as amended at 62 FR 10331, Mar. 6, 1997]

§ 1003.5 Forwarding of record on appeal.

(a) *Appeal from decision of an immigration judge.* If an appeal is taken from a decision of an immigration judge, the record of proceeding shall be forwarded to the Board upon the request or the order of the Board. Where transcription of an oral decision is required, the immigration judge shall review the transcript and approve the decision within 14 days of receipt, or within 7 days after the immigration judge returns to his or her duty station if the immigration judge was on leave or detailed to another location. The Chairman and the Chief Immigration Judge shall determine the most effective and expeditious way to transcribe proceedings before the immigration judges, and take such steps as necessary to reduce the time required to produce transcripts of those proceedings and improve their quality.

(b) *Appeal from decision of a Service officer.* If an appeal is taken from a decision of a Service officer, the record of proceeding shall be forwarded to the Board by the Service officer promptly upon receipt of the briefs of the parties, or upon expiration of the time allowed for the submission of such briefs. A Service officer need not forward such an appeal to the Board, but may reopen and reconsider any decision made by the officer if the new decision will grant the benefit that has been requested in the appeal. The new decision must be served on the appealing party within 45 days of receipt of any briefs or upon expiration of the time allowed for the submission of any briefs. If the new decision is not served within these time limits or the appealing party does not agree that the new decision disposes of the matter, the record of proceeding shall be immediately forwarded to the Board.

[61 FR 18907, Apr. 29, 1996, as amended at 67 FR 54905, Aug. 26, 2002]

§ 1003.6 Stay of execution of decision.

(a) Except as provided under § 236.1 of this chapter, § 1003.19(i), and paragraph (b) of this section, the decision in any proceeding under this chapter from which an appeal to the Board may be taken shall not be executed during the time allowed for the filing of an appeal unless a waiver of the right to appeal is filed, nor shall such decision be executed while an appeal is pending or while a case is before the Board by way of certification.

(b) The provisions of paragraph (a) of this section shall not apply to an order of an Immigration Judge under § 1003.23 or § 242.22 of 8 CFR chapter I denying a motion to reopen or reconsider or to stay deportation, except where such order expressly grants a stay or where the motion was filed pursuant to the provisions of § 1003.23(b)(4)(iii). The Board may, in its discretion, stay deportation while an appeal is pending from any such order if no stay has been granted by the Immigration Judge or a Service officer.

(c) The following procedures shall be applicable with respect to custody appeals in which DHS has invoked an automatic stay pursuant to 8 CFR 1003.19(i)(2).

(1) The stay shall lapse if DHS fails to file a notice of appeal with the Board within ten business days of the issuance of the order of the immigration judge. DHS should identify the appeal as an automatic stay case. To preserve the automatic stay, the attorney for DHS shall file with the notice of appeal a certification by a senior legal official that—

(i) The official has approved the filing of the notice of appeal according to review procedures established by DHS; and

(ii) The official is satisfied that the contentions justifying the continued detention of the alien have evidentiary support, and the legal arguments are warranted by existing law or by a non-frivolous argument for the extension, modification, or reversal of existing precedent or the establishment of new precedent.

(2) The immigration judge shall prepare a written decision explaining the custody determination within five business days after the immigration judge is advised that DHS has filed a notice of appeal, or, with the approval of the Board in exigent circumstances, as soon as practicable thereafter (not to exceed five additional business days). The immigration court shall prepare and submit the record of proceedings without delay.

(3) The Board will track the progress of each custody appeal which is subject to an automatic stay in order to avoid unnecessary delays in completing the record for decision. Each order issued by the Board should identify the appeal as an automatic stay case. The Board shall notify the parties in a timely manner of the date the automatic stay is scheduled to expire.

(4) If the Board has not acted on the custody appeal, the automatic stay shall lapse 90 days after the filing of the notice of appeal. However, if the Board grants a motion by the alien for an enlargement of the 21-day briefing schedule provided in § 1003.3(c), the Board's order shall also toll the 90-day period of the automatic stay for the same number of days.

(5) DHS may seek a discretionary stay pursuant to 8 CFR 1003.19(i)(1) to stay the immigration judge's order in the event the Board does not issue a decision on the custody appeal within the period of the automatic stay. DHS may submit a motion for discretionary stay at any time after the filing of its notice of appeal of the custody decision, and at a reasonable time before the expiration of the period of the automatic stay, and the motion may incorporate by reference the arguments presented in its brief in support of the need for continued detention of the alien during the pendency of the removal proceedings. If DHS has submitted such a motion and the Board is unable to resolve the custody appeal within the period of the automatic stay, the Board will issue an order granting or denying a motion for discretionary stay pending its decision on the custody appeal. The Board shall issue guidance to ensure prompt adjudication of motions for discretionary stays. If the Board fails to adjudicate a previously-filed stay motion by the end of the 90-day period, the stay will remain in effect (but not more than 30 days) during the time it takes for the

Board to decide whether or not to grant a discretionary stay.

(d) If the Board authorizes an alien's release (on bond or otherwise), denies a motion for discretionary stay, or fails to act on such a motion before the automatic stay period expires, the alien's release shall be automatically stayed for five business days. If, within that five-day period, the Secretary of Homeland Security or other designated official refers the custody case to the Attorney General pursuant to 8 CFR 1003.1(h)(1), the alien's release shall continue to be stayed pending the Attorney General's consideration of the case. The automatic stay will expire 15 business days after the case is referred to the Attorney General. DHS may submit a motion and proposed order for a discretionary stay in connection with referring the case to the Attorney General. For purposes of this paragraph and 8 CFR 1003.1(h)(1), decisions of the Board shall include those cases where the Board fails to act on a motion for discretionary stay. The Attorney General may order a discretionary stay pending the disposition of any custody case by the Attorney General or by the Board.

[61 FR 18907, Apr. 29, 1996; 61 FR 21065, May 9, 1996, as amended at 63 FR 27448, May 19, 1998; 71 FR 57884, Oct. 2, 2006]

§ 1003.7 Notice of certification.

Whenever, in accordance with the provisions of § 1003.1(c), a case is certified to the Board, the alien or other party affected shall be given notice of certification. An Immigration Judge or Service officer may certify a case only after an initial decision has been made and before an appeal has been taken. If it is known at the time the initial decision is rendered that the case will be certified, the notice of certification shall be included in such decision and no further notice of certification shall be required. If it is not known until after the initial decision is rendered that the case will be certified, the office of the Service or the Immigration Court having administrative control over the record of proceeding shall cause a Notice of Certification to be served upon the parties. In either case, the notice shall inform the parties that the case is required to be certified to the Board and that they have the right to make representations before the Board, including the making of a request for oral argument and the submission of a brief. If either party desires to submit a brief, it shall be submitted to the office of the Service or the Immigration Court having administrative control over the record of proceeding for transmittal to the Board within the time prescribed in § 1003.3(c). The case shall be certified and forwarded to the Board by the office of the Service or Immigration Court having administrative jurisdiction over the case upon receipt of the brief, or upon the expiration of the time within which the brief may be submitted, or upon receipt of a written waiver of the right to submit a brief. The Board in its discretion may elect to accept for review or not accept for review any such certified case. If the Board declines to accept a certified case for review, the underlying decision shall become final on the date the Board declined to accept the case.

[61 FR 18907, Apr. 29, 1996]

§ 1003.8 Fees before the Board.

(a) *Appeals and motions before the Board—(1) When a fee is required.* Except as provided in paragraph (a)(2) of this section, a filing fee prescribed in 8 CFR 1103.7, or a fee waiver request pursuant to paragraph (a)(3) of this section, is required in connection with the filing of an appeal, a motion to reopen, or a motion to reconsider before the Board.

(2) *When a fee is not required.* A filing fee is not required in the following instances:

(i) A custody bond appeal filed pursuant to § 1003.1(b)(7);

(ii) A motion to reopen that is based exclusively on an application for relief that does not require a fee;

(iii) A motion to reconsider that is based exclusively on a prior application for relief that did not require a fee;

(iv) A motion filed while an appeal, a motion to reopen, or a motion to reconsider is already pending before the Board;

(v) A motion requesting only a stay of removal, deportation, or exclusion;

(vi) Any appeal or motion filed by the Department of Homeland Security;

(vii) A motion that is agreed upon by all parties and is jointly filed; or

(viii) An appeal or motion filed under a law, regulation, or directive that specifically does not require a filing fee.

(3) *When a fee may be waived.* The Board has the discretion to waive a fee for an appeal, motion to reconsider, or motion to reopen upon a showing that the filing party is unable to pay the fee. Fee waivers shall be requested through the filing of a Fee Waiver Request (Form EOIR–26A), including the declaration to be signed under penalty of perjury substantiating the filing party's inability to pay the fee. The fee waiver request shall be filed along with the Notice of Appeal or the motion. If the fee waiver request does not establish the inability to pay the required fee, the appeal or motion will not be deemed properly filed.

(4) *Method of payment.* When a fee is required for an appeal or motion, the fee shall accompany the appeal or motion.

(i) *In general.* Except as provided in paragraph (a)(4)(ii) of this section, the fee for filing an appeal or motion with the Board shall be paid by check, money order, or electronic payment in a manner and form authorized by the Executive Office for Immigration Review. When paid by check or money order, the fee shall be payable to the "United States Department of Justice," drawn on a bank or other institution that is located within the United States, and payable in United States currency. The check or money order shall bear the full name and alien registration number of the alien. A payment that is uncollectible does not satisfy a fee requirement.

(ii) *Appeals from Department of Homeland Security decisions.* The fee for filing an appeal, within the jurisdiction of the Board, from the decision of a Department of Homeland Security officer shall be paid to the Department of Homeland Security in accordance with 8 CFR 103.7(a).

(b) *Applications for relief.* Fees for applications for relief are not collected by the Board, but instead are paid to the Department of Homeland Security in accordance with 8 CFR 103.7. When a motion before the Board is based upon an application for relief, only the fee for the motion to reopen shall be paid to the Board, and payment of the fee for the application for relief shall not accompany the motion. If the motion is granted and proceedings are remanded to the immigration judge, the application fee shall be paid in the manner specified in 8 CFR 1003.24(c)(1).

[69 FR 44906, July 28, 2004]

Subpart B—Office of the Chief Immigration Judge

SOURCE: 62 FR 10331, Mar. 6, 1997, unless otherwise noted.

§ 1003.9 Office of the Chief Immigration Judge.

(a) *Organization.* Within the Executive Office for Immigration Review, there shall be an Office of the Chief Immigration Judge (OCIJ), consisting of the Chief Immigration Judge, the immigration judges, and such other staff as the Director deems necessary. The Attorney General shall appoint the Chief Immigration Judge. The Director may designate immigration judges to serve as Deputy and Assistant Chief Immigration Judges as may be necessary to assist the Chief Immigration Judge in the management of the OCIJ.

(b) *Powers of the Chief Immigration Judge.* Subject to the supervision of the Director, the Chief Immigration Judge shall be responsible for the supervision, direction, and scheduling of the immigration judges in the conduct of the hearings and duties assigned to them. The Chief Immigration Judge shall have the authority to:

(1) Issue operational instructions and policy, including procedural instructions regarding the implementation of new statutory or regulatory authorities;

(2) Provide for appropriate training of the immigration judges and other OCIJ staff on the conduct of their powers and duties;

(3) Direct the conduct of all employees assigned to OCIJ to ensure the efficient disposition of all pending cases, including the power, in his discretion, to set priorities or time frames for the resolution of cases, to direct that the adjudication of certain cases be deferred, to regulate the assignment of

immigration judges to cases, and otherwise to manage the docket of matters to be decided by the immigration judges;

(4) Evaluate the performance of the Immigration Courts and other OCIJ activities by making appropriate reports and inspections, and take corrective action where needed;

(5) Adjudicate cases as an immigration judge; and

(6) Exercise such other authorities as the Director may provide.

(c) *Limit on the Authority of the Chief Immigration Judge.* The Chief Immigration Judge shall have no authority to direct the result of an adjudication assigned to another immigration judge, provided, however, that nothing in this part shall be construed to limit the authority of the Chief Immigration Judge in paragraph (b) of this section.

(d) *Immigration Court.* The term Immigration Court shall refer to the local sites of the OCIJ where proceedings are held before immigration judges and where the records of those proceedings are created and maintained.

[72 FR 53677, Sept. 20, 2007]

§ 1003.10 Immigration judges.

(a) *Appointment.* The immigration judges are attorneys whom the Attorney General appoints as administrative judges within the Office of the Chief Immigration Judge to conduct specified classes of proceedings, including hearings under section 240 of the Act. Immigration judges shall act as the Attorney General's delegates in the cases that come before them.

(b) *Powers and duties.* In conducting hearings under section 240 of the Act and such other proceedings the Attorney General may assign to them, immigration judges shall exercise the powers and duties delegated to them by the Act and by the Attorney General through regulation. In deciding the individual cases before them, and subject to the applicable governing standards, immigration judges shall exercise their independent judgment and discretion and may take any action consistent with their authorities under the Act and regulations that is appropriate and necessary for the disposition of such cases. Immigration judges shall administer oaths, receive evidence, and interrogate, examine, and cross-examine aliens and any witnesses. Subject to §§ 1003.35 and 1287.4 of this chapter, they may issue administrative subpoenas for the attendance of witnesses and the presentation of evidence. In all cases, immigration judges shall seek to resolve the questions before them in a timely and impartial manner consistent with the Act and regulations.

(c) *Review.* Decisions of immigration judges are subject to review by the Board of Immigration Appeals in any case in which the Board has jurisdiction as provided in 8 CFR 1003.1.

(d) *Governing standards.* Immigration judges shall be governed by the provisions and limitations prescribed by the Act and this chapter, by the decisions of the Board, and by the Attorney General (through review of a decision of the Board, by written order, or by determination and ruling pursuant to section 103 of the Act).

(e) *Temporary immigration judges*—(1) *Designation.* The Director is authorized to designate or select temporary immigration judges as provided in this paragraph (e).

(i) The Director may designate or select, with the approval of the Attorney General, former Board members, former immigration judges, administrative law judges employed within or retired from EOIR, and administrative law judges from other Executive Branch agencies to serve as temporary immigration judges for renewable terms not to exceed six months. Administrative law judges from other Executive Branch agencies must have the consent of their agencies to be designated as temporary immigration judges.

(ii) In addition, the Director may designate, with the approval of the Attorney General, Department of Justice attorneys with at least 10 years of legal experience in the field of immigration law to serve as temporary immigration judges for renewable terms not to exceed six months.

(2) *Authority.* A temporary immigration judge shall have the authority of an immigration judge to adjudicate assigned cases and administer immigration court matters, as provided in the immigration laws and regulations, subject to paragraph (e)(3) of this section.

(3) *Assignment of temporary immigration judges.* The Chief Immigration Judge is responsible for the overall oversight and management of the utilization of temporary immigration judges and for evaluating the results of the process. The Chief Immigration Judge shall ensure that each temporary immigration judge has received a suitable level of training to enable the temporary immigration judge to carry out the duties assigned.

[72 FR 53677, Sept. 20, 2007, as amended at 79 FR 39956, July 11, 2014]

§ 1003.11 Administrative control Immigration Courts.

An administrative control Immigration Court is one that creates and maintains Records of Proceedings for Immigration Courts within an assigned geographical area. All documents and correspondence pertaining to a Record of Proceeding shall be filed with the Immigration Court having administrative control over that Record of Proceeding and shall not be filed with any other Immigration Court. A list of the administrative control Immigration Courts with their assigned geographical areas will be made available to the public at any Immigration Court.

Subpart C—Immigration Court—Rules of Procedure

§ 1003.12 Scope of rules.

These rules are promulgated to assist in the expeditious, fair, and proper resolution of matters coming before Immigration Judges. Except where specifically stated, the rules in this subpart apply to matters before Immigration Judges, including, but not limited to, deportation, exclusion, removal, bond, rescission, departure control, asylum proceedings, and disciplinary proceedings under this part 3. The sole procedures for review of credible fear determinations by Immigration Judges are provided for in § 1003.42.

[57 FR 11571, Apr. 6, 1992, as amended at 62 FR 10331, Mar. 6, 1997; 65 FR 39526, June 27, 2000]

§ 1003.13 Definitions.

As used in this subpart:

Administrative control means custodial responsibility for the Record of Proceeding as specified in § 1003.11.

Charging document means the written instrument which initiates a proceeding before an Immigration Judge. For proceedings initiated prior to April 1, 1997, these documents include an Order to Show Cause, a Notice to Applicant for Admission Detained for Hearing before Immigration Judge, and a Notice of Intention to Rescind and Request for Hearing by Alien. For proceedings initiated after April 1, 1997, these documents include a Notice to Appear, a Notice of Referral to Immigration Judge, and a Notice of Intention to Rescind and Request for Hearing by Alien.

Filing means the actual receipt of a document by the appropriate Immigration Court.

Service means physically presenting or mailing a document to the appropriate party or parties; except that an Order to Show Cause or Notice of Deportation Hearing shall be served in person to the alien, or by certified mail to the alien or the alien's attorney and a Notice to Appear or Notice of Removal Hearing shall be served to the alien in person, or if personal service is not practicable, shall be served by regular mail to the alien or the alien's attorney of record.

[62 FR 10332, Mar. 6, 1997]

§ 1003.14 Jurisdiction and commencement of proceedings.

(a) Jurisdiction vests, and proceedings before an Immigration Judge commence, when a charging document is filed with the Immigration Court by the Service. The charging document must include a certificate showing service on the opposing party pursuant to § 1003.32 which indicates the Immigration Court in which the charging document is filed. However, no charging document is required to be filed with the Immigration Court to commence bond proceedings pursuant to §§ 1003.19, 1236.1(d) and 1240.2(b) of this chapter.

(b) When an Immigration Judge has jurisdiction over an underlying proceeding, sole jurisdiction over applications for asylum shall lie with the Immigration Judge.

(c) Immigration Judges have jurisdiction to administer the oath of allegiance in administrative naturalization ceremonies conducted by the Service in accordance with § 1337.2(b) of this chapter.

(d) The jurisdiction of, and procedures before, immigration judges in exclusion, deportation and removal, rescission, asylum-only, and any other proceedings shall remain in effect as it was in effect on February 28, 2003, until the regulations in this chapter are further modified by the Attorney General. Where a decision of an officer of the Immigration and Naturalization Service was, before March 1, 2003, appealable to the Board or an immigration judge, or an application denied could be renewed in proceedings before an immigration judge, the same authority and procedures shall be followed until further modified by the Attorney General.

[57 FR 11571, Apr. 6, 1992, as amended at 60 FR 34089, June 30, 1995; 62 FR 10332, Mar. 6, 1997. Redesignated and amended at 68 FR 9830, 9832, Feb. 28, 2003]

§ 1003.15 Contents of the order to show cause and notice to appear and notification of change of address.

(a) In the Order to Show Cause, the Service shall provide the following administrative information to the Executive Office for Immigration Review. Omission of any of these items shall not provide the alien with any substantive or procedural rights:

(1) The alien's names and any known aliases;

(2) The alien's address;

(3) The alien's registration number, with any lead alien registration number with which the alien is associated;

(4) The alien's alleged nationality and citizenship;

(5) The language that the alien understands;

(b) The Order to Show Cause and Notice to Appear must also include the following information:

(1) The nature of the proceedings against the alien;

(2) The legal authority under which the proceedings are conducted;

(3) The acts or conduct alleged to be in violation of law;

(4) The charges against the alien and the statutory provisions alleged to have been violated;

(5) Notice that the alien may be represented, at no cost to the government, by counsel or other representative authorized to appear pursuant to 8 CFR 1292.1;

(6) The address of the Immigration Court where the Service will file the Order to Show Cause and Notice to Appear; and

(7) A statement that the alien must advise the Immigration Court having administrative control over the Record of Proceeding of his or her current address and telephone number and a statement that failure to provide such information may result in an *in absentia* hearing in accordance with § 1003.26.

(c) *Contents of the Notice to Appear for removal proceedings.* In the Notice to Appear for removal proceedings, the Service shall provide the following administrative information to the Immigration Court. Failure to provide any of these items shall not be construed as affording the alien any substantive or procedural rights.

(1) The alien's names and any known aliases;

(2) The alien's address;

(3) The alien's registration number, with any lead alien registration number with which the alien is associated;

(4) The alien's alleged nationality and citizenship; and

(5) The language that the alien understands.

(d) *Address and telephone number.* (1) If the alien's address is not provided on the Order to Show Cause or Notice to Appear, or if the address on the Order to Show Cause or Notice to Appear is incorrect, the alien must provide to the Immigration Court where the charging document has been filed, within five days of service of that document, a written notice of an address and telephone number at which the alien can be contacted. The alien may satisfy this requirement by completing and filing Form EOIR–33.

(2) Within five days of any change of address, the alien must provide written notice of the change of address on Form EOIR–33 to the Immigration Court where the charging document

has been filed, or if venue has been changed, to the Immigration Court to which venue has been changed.

[57 FR 11571, Apr. 6, 1992, as amended at 60 FR 34089, June 30, 1995; 62 FR 10332, Mar. 6, 1997]

§ 1003.16 Representation.

(a) The government may be represented in proceedings before an Immigration Judge.

(b) The alien may be represented in proceedings before an Immigration Judge by an attorney or other representative of his or her choice in accordance with 8 CFR part 1292, at no expense to the government.

[52 FR 2936, Jan. 29, 1987. Redesignated at 57 FR 11571, Apr. 6, 1992, as amended at 62 FR 10332, Mar. 6, 1997]

§ 1003.17 Appearances.

(a) In any proceeding before an Immigration Judge in which the alien is represented, the attorney or representative shall file a Notice of Entry of Appearance on Form EOIR–28 with the Immigration Court, and shall serve a copy of the Notice of Entry of Appearance on the DHS as required by 8 CFR 1003.32(a). The entry of appearance of an attorney or representative in a custody or bond proceeding shall be separate and apart from an entry of appearance in any other proceeding before the Immigration Court. An attorney or representative may file an EOIR–28 indicating whether the entry of appearance is for custody or bond proceedings only, any other proceedings only, or for all proceedings. Such Notice of Entry of Appearance must be filed and served even if a separate Notice of Entry of Appearance(s) has previously been filed with the DHS for appearance(s) before the DHS.

(b) Withdrawal or substitution of an attorney or representative may be permitted by an Immigration Judge during proceedings only upon oral or written motion submitted without fee.

[57 FR 11571, Apr. 6, 1992, as amended at 60 FR 34089, June 30, 1995; 62 FR 10332, Mar. 6, 1997; 80 FR 59502, Oct. 1, 2015]

§ 1003.18 Scheduling of cases.

(a) The Immigration Court shall be responsible for scheduling cases and providing notice to the government and the alien of the time, place, and date of hearings.

(b) In removal proceedings pursuant to section 240 of the Act, the Service shall provide in the Notice to Appear, the time, place and date of the initial removal hearing, where practicable. If that information is not contained in the Notice to Appear, the Immigration Court shall be responsible for scheduling the initial removal hearing and providing notice to the government and the alien of the time, place, and date of hearing. In the case of any change or postponement in the time and place of such proceeding, the Immigration Court shall provide written notice to the alien specifying the new time and place of the proceeding and the consequences under section 240(b)(5) of the Act of failing, except under exceptional circumstances as defined in section 240(e)(1) of the Act, to attend such proceeding. No such notice shall be required for an alien not in detention if the alien has failed to provide the address required in section 239(a)(1)(F) of the Act.

[62 FR 10332, Mar. 6, 1997]

§ 1003.19 Custody/bond.

(a) Custody and bond determinations made by the service pursuant to 8 CFR part 1236 may be reviewed by an Immigration Judge pursuant to 8 CFR part 1236.

(b) Application for an initial bond redetermination by a respondent, or his or her attorney or representative, may be made orally, in writing, or, at the discretion of the Immigration Judge, by telephone.

(c) Applications for the exercise of authority to review bond determinations shall be made to one of the following offices, in the designated order:

(1) If the respondent is detained, to the Immigration Court having jurisdiction over the place of detention;

(2) To the Immigration Court having administrative control over the case; or

(3) To the Office of the Chief Immigration Judge for designation of an appropriate Immigration Court.

(d) Consideration by the Immigration Judge of an application or request of a respondent regarding custody or bond under this section shall be separate and apart from, and shall form no part of, any deportation or removal hearing or proceeding. The determination of the Immigration Judge as to custody status or bond may be based upon any information that is available to the Immigration Judge or that is presented to him or her by the alien or the Service.

(e) After an initial bond redetermination, an alien's request for a subsequent bond redetermination shall be made in writing and shall be considered only upon a showing that the alien's circumstances have changed materially since the prior bond redetermination.

(f) The determination of an Immigration Judge with respect to custody status or bond redetermination shall be entered on the appropriate form at the time such decision is made and the parties shall be informed orally or in writing of the reasons for the decision. An appeal from the determination by an Immigration Judge may be taken to the Board of Immigration Appeals pursuant to § 1003.38.

(g) While any proceeding is pending before the Executive Office for Immigration Review, the Service shall immediately advise the Immigration Court having administrative control over the Record of Proceeding of a change in the respondent/applicant's custody location or of release from Service custody, or subsequent taking into Service custody, of a respondent/applicant. This notification shall be in writing and shall state the effective date of the change in custody location or status, and the respondent/applicant's current fixed street address, including zip code.

(h)(1)(i) While the Transition Period Custody Rules (TPCR) set forth in section 303(b)(3) of Div. C of Pub. L. 104–208 remain in effect, an immigration judge may not redetermine conditions of custody imposed by the Service with respect to the following classes of aliens:

(A) Aliens in exclusion proceedings;

(B) Arriving aliens in removal proceedings, including persons paroled after arrival pursuant to section 212(d)(5) of the Act;

(C) Aliens described in section 237(a)(4) of the Act;

(D) Aliens subject to section 303(b)(3)(A) of Pub. L. 104–208 who are not "lawfully admitted" (as defined in § 1236.1(c)(2) of this chapter); or

(E) Aliens designated in § 1236.1(c) of this chapter as ineligible to be considered for release.

(ii) Nothing in this paragraph shall be construed as prohibiting an alien from seeking a redetermination of custody conditions by the Service in accordance with part 1235 or 1236 of this chapter. In addition, with respect to paragraphs (h)(1)(i)(C), (D), and (E) of this section, nothing in this paragraph shall be construed as prohibiting an alien from seeking a determination by an immigration judge that the alien is not properly included within any of those paragraphs.

(2)(i) Upon expiration of the Transition Period Custody Rules set forth in section 303(b)(3) of Div. C. of Pub. L. 104–208, an immigration judge may not redetermine conditions of custody imposed by the Service with respect to the following classes of aliens:

(A) Aliens in exclusion proceedings;

(B) Arriving aliens in removal proceedings, including aliens paroled after arrival pursuant to section 212(d)(5) of the Act;

(C) Aliens described in section 237(a)(4) of the Act;

(D) Aliens in removal proceedings subject to section 236(c)(1) of the Act (as in effect after expiration of the Transition Period Custody Rules); and

(E) Aliens in deportation proceedings subject to section 242(a)(2) of the Act (as in effect prior to April 1, 1997, and as amended by section 440(c) of Pub. L. 104–132).

(ii) Nothing in this paragraph shall be construed as prohibiting an alien from seeking a redetermination of custody conditions by the Service in accordance with part 1235 or 1236 of this chapter. In addition, with respect to paragraphs (h)(2)(i)(C), (D), and (E) of this section, nothing in this paragraph shall be construed as prohibiting an alien from seeking a determination by an immigration judge that the alien is not properly included within any of those paragraphs.

(3) Except as otherwise provided in paragraph (h)(1) of this section, an alien subject to section 303(b)(3)(A) of

Div. C of Pub. L. 104–208 may apply to the Immigration Court, in a manner consistent with paragraphs (c)(1) through (c)(3) of this section, for a redetermination of custody conditions set by the Service. Such an alien must first demonstrate, by clear and convincing evidence, that release would not pose a danger to other persons or to property. If an alien meets this burden, the alien must further demonstrate, by clear and convincing evidence, that the alien is likely to appear for any scheduled proceeding or interview.

(4) *Unremovable aliens.* A determination of a district director (or other official designated by the Commissioner) regarding the exercise of authority under section 303(b)(3)(B)(ii) of Div. C. of Pub. L. 104–208 (concerning release of aliens who cannot be removed because the designated country of removal will not accept their return) is final, and shall not be subject to redetermination by an immigration judge.

(i) *Stay of custody order pending appeal by the government*—(1) *General discretionary stay authority.* The Board of Immigration Appeals (Board) has the authority to stay the order of an immigration judge redetermining the conditions of custody of an alien when the Department of Homeland Security appeals the custody decision or on its own motion. DHS is entitled to seek a discretionary stay (whether or not on an emergency basis) from the Board in connection with such an appeal at any time.

(2) *Automatic stay in certain cases.* In any case in which DHS has determined that an alien should not be released or has set a bond of $10,000 or more, any order of the immigration judge authorizing release (on bond or otherwise) shall be stayed upon DHS's filing of a notice of intent to appeal the custody redetermination (Form EOIR–43) with the immigration court within one business day of the order, and, except as otherwise provided in 8 CFR 1003.6(c), shall remain in abeyance pending decision of the appeal by the Board. The decision whether or not to file Form EOIR–43 is subject to the discretion of the Secretary.

[57 FR 11571, Apr. 6, 1992, as amended at 60 FR 34089, June 30, 1995; 62 FR 10332, Mar. 6, 1997; 63 FR 27448, May 19, 1998; 66 FR 54911, Oct. 31, 2001; 70 FR 4753, Jan. 31, 2005; 71 FR 57884, Oct. 2, 2006]

§ 1003.20 Change of venue.

(a) Venue shall lie at the Immigration Court where jurisdiction vests pursuant to § 1003.14.

(b) The Immigration Judge, for good cause, may change venue only upon motion by one of the parties, after the charging document has been filed with the Immigration Court. The Immigration Judge may grant a change of venue only after the other party has been given notice and an opportunity to respond to the motion to change venue.

(c) No change of venue shall be granted without identification of a fixed street address, including city, state and ZIP code, where the respondent/applicant may be reached for further hearing notification.

[57 FR 11572, Apr. 6, 1992, as amended at 60 FR 34089, June 30, 1995; 62 FR 10332, Mar. 6, 1997]

§ 1003.21 Pre-hearing conferences and statement.

(a) Pre-hearing conferences may be scheduled at the discretion of the Immigration Judge. The conference may be held to narrow issues, to obtain stipulations between the parties, to exchange information voluntarily, and otherwise to simplify and organize the proceeding.

(b) The Immigration Judge may order any party to file a pre-hearing statement of position that may include, but is not limited to: A statement of facts to which both parties have stipulated, together with a statement that the parties have communicated in good faith to stipulate to the fullest extent possible; a list of proposed witnesses and what they will establish; a list of exhibits, copies of exhibits to be introduced, and a statement of the reason for their introduction; the estimated time required to present the case; and, a statement of unresolved issues involved in the proceedings.

(c) If submission of a pre-hearing statement is ordered under paragraph (b) of this section, an Immigration Judge also may require both parties, in writing prior to the hearing, to make any evidentiary objections regarding matters contained in the pre-hearing statement. If objections in writing are required but not received by the date for receipt set by the Immigration Judge, admission of all evidence described in the pre-hearing statement shall be deemed unopposed.

[57 FR 11572, Apr. 6, 1992]

§ 1003.22 Interpreters.

Any person acting as an interpreter in a hearing shall swear or affirm to interpret and translate accurately, unless the interpreter is an employee of the United States Government, in which event no such oath or affirmation shall be required.

[52 FR 2936, Jan. 29, 1987. Redesignated at 57 FR 11571, Apr. 6, 1992]

§ 1003.23 Reopening or reconsideration before the Immigration Court.

(a) *Pre-decision motions.* Unless otherwise permitted by the Immigration Judge, motions submitted prior to the final order of an Immigration Judge shall be in writing and shall state, with particularity the grounds therefore, the relief sought, and the jurisdiction. The Immigration Judge may set and extend time limits for the making of motions and replies thereto. A motion shall be deemed unopposed unless timely response is made.

(b) *Before the Immigration Court*—(1) *In general.* An Immigration Judge may upon his or her own motion at any time, or upon motion of the Service or the alien, reopen or reconsider any case in which he or she has made a decision, unless jurisdiction is vested with the Board of Immigration Appeals. Subject to the exceptions in this paragraph and paragraph (b)(4), a party may file only one motion to reconsider and one motion to reopen proceedings. A motion to reconsider must be filed within 30 days of the date of entry of a final administrative order of removal, deportation, or exclusion, or on or before July 31, 1996, whichever is later. A motion to reopen must be filed within 90 days of the date of entry of a final administrative order of removal, deportation, or exclusion, or on or before September 30, 1996, whichever is later. A motion to reopen or to reconsider shall not be made by or on behalf of a person who is the subject of removal, deportation, or exclusion proceedings subsequent to his or her departure from the United States. Any departure from the United States, including the deportation or removal of a person who is the subject of exclusion, deportation, or removal proceedings, occurring after the filing of a motion to reopen or a motion to reconsider shall constitute a withdrawal of such motion. The time and numerical limitations set forth in this paragraph do not apply to motions by the Service in removal proceedings pursuant to section 240 of the Act. Nor shall such limitations apply to motions by the Service in exclusion or deportation proceedings, when the basis of the motion is fraud in the original proceeding or a crime that would support termination of asylum in accordance with § 1208.22(e) of this chapter.

(i) *Form and contents of the motion.* The motion shall be in writing and signed by the affected party or the attorney or representative of record, if any. The motion and any submission made in conjunction with it must be in English or accompanied by a certified English translation. Motions to reopen or reconsider shall state whether the validity of the exclusion, deportation, or removal order has been or is the subject of any judicial proceeding and, if so, the nature and date thereof, the court in which such proceeding took place or is pending, and its result or status. In any case in which an exclusion, deportation, or removal order is in effect, any motion to reopen or reconsider such order shall include a statement by or on behalf of the moving party declaring whether the subject of the order is also the subject of any pending criminal proceeding under the Act, and, if so, the current status of that proceeding.

(ii) *Filing.* Motions to reopen or reconsider a decision of an Immigration Judge must be filed with the Immigration Court having administrative control over the Record of Proceeding. A motion to reopen or a motion to reconsider shall include a certificate showing service on the opposing party of the motion and all attachments. If the moving party is not the Service, service of the motion shall be made upon the Office of the District Counsel for the district in which the case was completed. If the moving party, other than the Service, is represented, a Form EOIR–28, Notice of Appearance as Attorney or Representative Before an Immigration Judge must be filed with the motion. The motion must be filed in duplicate with the Immigration Court, accompanied by a fee receipt.

(iii) *Assignment to an Immigration Judge.* If the Immigration Judge is unavailable or unable to adjudicate the motion to reopen or reconsider, the Chief Immigration Judge or his or her delegate shall reassign such motion to another Immigration Judge.

(iv) *Replies to motions; decision.* The Immigration Judge may set and extend time limits for replies to motions to reopen or reconsider. A motion shall be deemed unopposed unless timely response is made. The decision to grant or deny a motion to reopen or a motion to reconsider is within the discretion of the Immigration Judge.

(v) *Stays.* Except in cases involving in absentia orders, the filing of a motion to reopen or a motion to reconsider shall not stay the execution of any decision made in the case. Execution of such decision shall proceed unless a stay of execution is specifically granted by the Immigration Judge, the Board, or an authorized officer of the Service.

(2) *Motion to reconsider.* A motion to reconsider shall state the reasons for the motion by specifying the errors of fact or law in the Immigration Judge's prior decision and shall be supported by pertinent authority. Such motion may not seek reconsideration of a decision denying previous motion to reconsider.

(3) *Motion to reopen.* A motion to reopen proceedings shall state the new facts that will be proven at a hearing to be held if the motion is granted and shall be supported by affidavits and other evidentiary material. Any motion to reopen for the purpose of acting on an application for relief must be accompanied by the appropriate application for relief and all supporting documents. A motion to reopen will not be granted unless the Immigration Judge is satisfied that evidence sought to be offered is material and was not available and could not have been discovered or presented at the former hearing. A motion to reopen for the purpose of providing the alien an opportunity to apply for any form of discretionary relief will not be granted if it appears that the alien's right to apply for such relief was fully explained to him or her by the Immigration Judge and an opportunity to apply therefore was afforded at the hearing, unless the relief is sought on the basis of circumstances that have arisen subsequent to the hearing. Pursuant to section 240A(d)(1) of the Act, a motion to reopen proceedings for consideration or further consideration of an application for relief under section 240A(a) (cancellation of removal for certain permanent residents) or 240A(b) (cancellation of removal and adjustment of status for certain nonpermanent residents) may be granted only if the alien demonstrates that he or she was statutorily eligible for such relief prior to the service of a notice to appear, or prior to the commission of an offense referred to in section 212(a)(2) of the Act that renders the alien inadmissible or removable under sections 237(a)(2) of the Act or (a)(4), whichever is earliest. The Immigration Judge has discretion to deny a motion to reopen even if the moving party has established a prima facie case for relief.

(4) *Exceptions to filing deadlines*—(i) *Asylum and withholding of removal.* The time and numerical limitations set forth in paragraph (b)(1) of this section shall not apply if the basis of the motion is to apply for asylum under section 208 of the Act or withholding of removal under section 241(b)(3) of the Act or withholding of removal under the Convention Against Torture, and is based on changed country conditions arising in the country of nationality or the country to which removal has been ordered, if such evidence is material and was not available and could not have been discovered or presented at the previous proceeding. The filing of a motion to reopen under this section

shall not automatically stay the removal of the alien. However, the alien may request a stay and, if granted by the Immigration Judge, the alien shall not be removed pending disposition of the motion by the Immigration Judge. If the original asylum application was denied based upon a finding that it was frivolous, then the alien is ineligible to file either a motion to reopen or reconsider, or for a stay of removal.

(ii) *Order entered in absentia or removal proceedings.* An order of removal entered in absentia or in removal proceedings pursuant to section 240(b)(5) of the Act may be rescinded only upon a motion to reopen filed within 180 days after the date of the order of removal, if the alien demonstrates that the failure to appear was because of exceptional circumstances as defined in section 240(e)(1) of the Act. An order entered in absentia pursuant to section 240(b)(5) may be rescinded upon a motion to reopen filed at any time if the alien demonstrates that he or she did not receive notice in accordance with sections 239(a)(1) or (2) of the Act, or the alien demonstrates that he or she was in Federal or state custody and the failure to appear was through no fault of the alien. However, in accordance with section 240(b)(5)(B) of the Act, no written notice of a change in time or place of proceeding shall be required if the alien has failed to provide the address required under section 239(a)(1)(F) of the Act. The filing of a motion under this paragraph shall stay the removal of the alien pending disposition of the motion by the Immigration Judge. An alien may file only one motion pursuant to this paragraph.

(iii) *Order entered in absentia in deportation or exclusion proceedings.* (A) An order entered in absentia in deportation proceedings may be rescinded only upon a motion to reopen filed:

(*1*) Within 180 days after the date of the order of deportation if the alien demonstrates that the failure to appear was because of exceptional circumstances beyond the control of the alien (e.g., serious illness of the alien or serious illness or death of an immediate relative of the alien, but not including less compelling circumstances); or

(*2*) At any time if the alien demonstrates that he or she did not receive notice or if the alien demonstrates that he or she was in federal or state custody and the failure to appear was through no fault of the alien.

(B) A motion to reopen exclusion hearings on the basis that the Immigration Judge improperly entered an order of exclusion in absentia must be supported by evidence that the alien had reasonable cause for his failure to appear.

(C) The filing of a motion to reopen under paragraph (b)(4)(iii)(A) of this section shall stay the deportation of the alien pending decision on the motion and the adjudication of any properly filed administrative appeal.

(D) The time and numerical limitations set forth in paragraph (b)(1) of this section shall not apply to a motion to reopen filed pursuant to the provisions of paragraph (b)(4)(iii)(A) of this section.

(iv) *Jointly filed motions.* The time and numerical limitations set forth in paragraph (b)(1) of this section shall not apply to a motion to reopen agreed upon by all parties and jointly filed.

[52 FR 2936, Jan. 29, 1987, as amended at 55 FR 30680, July 27, 1990. Redesignated at 57 FR 11571, Apr. 6, 1992, as amended at 60 FR 34089, June 30, 1995; 61 FR 18908, Apr. 29, 1996; 61 FR 19976, May 3, 1996; 61 FR 21228, May 9, 1996; 62 FR 10332, Mar. 6, 1997; 62 FR 15362, Apr. 1, 1997; 62 FR 17048, Apr. 9, 1997; 64 FR 8487, Feb. 19, 1999]

§ 1003.24 Fees pertaining to matters within the jurisdiction of an immigration judge.

(a) *Generally.* All fees for the filing of motions and applications in connection with proceedings before the immigration judges are paid to the Department of Homeland Security in accordance with 8 CFR 103.7, including fees for applications published by the Executive Office for Immigration Review. The immigration court does not collect fees.

(b) *Motions to reopen or reconsider*—(1) *When a fee is required.* Except as provided in paragraph (b)(2) of this section, a filing fee prescribed in 8 CFR 1103.7, or a fee waiver request pursuant to paragraph (d) of this section, is required in connection with the filing of a motion to reopen or a motion to reconsider.

(2) *When a fee is not required.* A filing fee is not required in the following instances:

(i) A motion to reopen that is based exclusively on an application for relief that does not require a fee;

(ii) A motion to reconsider that is based exclusively on a prior application for relief that did not require a fee;

(iii) A motion filed while proceedings are already pending before the immigration court;

(iv) A motion requesting only a stay of removal, deportation, or exclusion;

(v) A motion to reopen a deportation or removal order entered in absentia if the motion is filed pursuant to section 242B(c)(3)(B) of the Act (8 U.S.C. 1252b(c)(3)(B)), as it existed prior to April 1, 1997, or section 240(b)(5)(C)(ii) of the Act (8 U.S.C. 1229a(b)(5)(C)(ii)), as amended;

(vi) Any motion filed by the Department of Homeland Security;

(vii) A motion that is agreed upon by all parties and is jointly filed; or

(viii) A motion filed under a law, regulation, or directive that specifically does not require a filing fee.

(c) *Applications for relief*—(1) *When filed during proceedings.* When an application for relief is filed during the course of proceedings, the fee for that application must be paid in advance to the Department of Homeland Security in accordance with 8 CFR 103.7. The fee receipt must accompany the application when it is filed with the immigration court.

(2) *When submitted with a motion to reopen.* When a motion to reopen is based upon an application for relief, the fee for the motion to reopen shall be paid to the Department of Homeland Security and the fee receipt shall accompany the motion. Payment of the fee for the application for relief must be paid to the Department of Homeland Security within the time specified by the immigration judge.

(d) *Fee waivers.* The immigration judge has the discretion to waive a fee for a motion or application for relief upon a showing that the filing party is unable to pay the fee. The request for a fee waiver must be accompanied by a properly executed affidavit or unsworn declaration made pursuant to 28 U.S.C. 1746 substantiating the filing party's inability to pay the fee. If the request for a fee waiver is denied, the application or motion will not be deemed properly filed.

[69 FR 44906, July 28, 2004]

§ 1003.25 Form of the proceeding.

(a) *Waiver of presence of the parties.* The Immigration Judge may, for good cause, and consistent with section 240(b) of the Act, waive the presence of the alien at a hearing when the alien is represented or when the alien is a minor child at least one of whose parents or whose legal guardian is present. When it is impracticable by reason of an alien's mental incompetency for the alien to be present, the presence of the alien may be waived provided that the alien is represented at the hearing by an attorney or legal representative, a near relative, legal guardian, or friend.

(b) *Stipulated request for order; waiver of hearing.* An Immigration Judge may enter an order of deportation, exclusion or removal stipulated to by the alien (or the alien's representative) and the Service. The Immigration Judge may enter such an order without a hearing and in the absence of the parties based on a review of the charging document, the written stipulation, and supporting documents, if any. If the alien is unrepresented, the Immigration Judge must determine that the alien's waiver is voluntary, knowing, and intelligent. The stipulated request and required waivers shall be signed on behalf of the government and by the alien and his or her attorney or representative, if any. The attorney or representative shall file a Notice of Appearance in accordance with § 1003.16(b). A stipulated order shall constitute a conclusive determination of the alien's deportability or removability from the United States. The stipulation shall include:

(1) An admission that all factual allegations contained in the charging document are true and correct as written;

(2) A concession of deportability or inadmissibility as charged;

(3) A statement that the alien makes no application for relief under the Act;

(4) A designation of a country for deportation or removal under section 241(b)(2)(A)(i) of the Act;

(5) A concession to the introduction of the written stipulation of the alien as an exhibit to the Record of Proceeding;

(6) A statement that the alien understands the consequences of the stipulated request and that the alien enters the request voluntarily, knowingly, and intelligently;

(7) A statement that the alien will accept a written order for his or her deportation, exclusion or removal as a final disposition of the proceedings; and

(8) A waiver of appeal of the written order of deportation or removal.

(c) *Telephonic or video hearings.* An Immigration Judge may conduct hearings through video conference to the same extent as he or she may conduct hearings in person. An Immigration Judge may also conduct a hearing through a telephone conference, but an evidentiary hearing on the merits may only be conducted through a telephone conference with the consent of the alien involved after the alien has been advised of the right to proceed in person or, where available, through a video conference, except that credible fear determinations may be reviewed by the Immigration Judge through a telephone conference without the consent of the alien.

[62 FR 10334, Mar. 6, 1997]

§ 1003.26 In absentia hearings.

(a) In any exclusion proceeding before an Immigration Judge in which the applicant fails to appear, the Immigration Judge shall conduct an *in absentia* hearing if the Immigration Judge is satisfied that notice of the time and place of the proceeding was provided to the applicant on the record at a prior hearing or by written notice to the applicant or to the applicant's counsel of record on the charging document or at the most recent address in the Record of Proceeding.

(b) In any deportation proceeding before an Immigration Judge in which the respondent fails to appear, the Immigration Judge shall order the respondent deported *in absentia* if: (1) The Service establishes by clear, unequivocal and convincing evidence that the respondent is deportable; and (2) the Immigration Judge is satisfied that written notice of the time and place of the proceedings and written notice of the consequences of failure to appear, as set forth in section 242B(c) of the Act (8 U.S.C. 1252b(c)), were provided to the respondent in person or were provided to the respondent or the respondent's counsel of record, if any, by certified mail.

(c) In any removal proceeding before an Immigration Judge in which the alien fails to appear, the Immigration Judge shall order the alien removed *in absentia* if:

(1) The Service establishes by clear, unequivocal, and convincing evidence that the alien is removable; and

(2) The Service establishes by clear, unequivocal, and convincing evidence that written notice of the time and place of proceedings and written notice of the consequences of failure to appear were provided to the alien or the alien's counsel of record.

(d) Written notice to the alien shall be considered sufficient for purposes of this section if it was provided at the most recent address provided by the alien. If the respondent fails to provide his or her address as required under § 1003.15(d), no written notice shall be required for an Immigration Judge to proceed with an *in absentia* hearing. This paragraph shall not apply in the event that the Immigration Judge waives the appearance of an alien under § 1003.25.

[59 FR 1899, Jan. 13, 1994, as amended at 62 FR 10334, Mar. 6, 1997; 62 FR 15362, Apr. 1, 1997]

§ 1003.27 Public access to hearings.

All hearings, other than exclusion hearings, shall be open to the public except that:

(a) Depending upon physical facilities, the Immigration Judge may place reasonable limitations upon the number in attendance at any one time with priority being given to the press over the general public;

(b) For the purpose of protecting witnesses, parties, or the public interest, the Immigration Judge may limit attendance or hold a closed hearing.

(c) In any proceeding before an Immigration Judge concerning an abused alien spouse, the hearing and the Record of Proceeding shall be closed to the public unless the abused spouse agrees that the hearing and the Record of Proceeding shall be open to the public. In any proceeding before an Immigration Judge concerning an abused alien child, the hearing and the Record of Proceeding shall be closed to the public.

(d) Proceedings before an Immigration Judge shall be closed to the public if information subject to a protective order under § 1003.46, which has been filed under seal pursuant to § 1003.31(d), may be considered.

[52 FR 2936, Jan. 29, 1987. Redesignated and amended at 57 FR 11571, 11572, Apr. 6, 1992; 62 FR 10334, Mar. 6, 1997; 67 FR 36802, May 28, 2002]

§ 1003.28 Recording equipment.

The only recording equipment permitted in the proceeding will be the equipment used by the Immigration Judge to create the official record. No other photographic, video, electronic, or similar recording device will be permitted to record any part of the proceeding.

[52 FR 2936, Jan. 29, 1987. Redesignated at 57 FR 11571, Apr. 6, 1992]

§ 1003.29 Continuances.

The Immigration Judge may grant a motion for continuance for good cause shown.

[52 FR 2936, Jan. 29, 1987. Redesignated at 57 FR 11571, Apr. 6, 1992]

§ 1003.30 Additional charges in deportation or removal hearings.

At any time during deportation or removal proceedings, additional or substituted charges of deportability and/or factual allegations may be lodged by the Service in writing. The alien shall be served with a copy of these additional charges and/or allegations and the Immigration Judge shall read them to the alien. The Immigration Judge shall advise the alien, if he or she is not represented by counsel, that the alien may be so represented. The alien may be given a reasonable continuance to respond to the additional factual allegations and charges. Thereafter, the provision of § 1240.10(b) of this chapter relating to pleading shall apply to the additional factual allegations and charges.

[62 FR 10335, Mar. 6, 1997]

§ 1003.31 Filing documents and applications.

(a) All documents and applications that are to be considered in a proceeding before an Immigration Judge must be filed with the Immigration Court having administrative control over the Record of Proceeding.

(b) Except as provided in 8 CFR 1240.11(f), all documents or applications requiring the payment of a fee must be accompanied by a fee receipt from the Service or by an application for a waiver of fees pursuant to 8 CFR 3.24. Except as provided in § 1003.8(a) and (c), any fee relating to Immigration Judge proceedings shall be paid to, and accepted by, any Service office authorized to accept fees for other purposes pursuant to § 1103.7(a) of this chapter.

(c) The Immigration Judge may set and extend time limits for the filing of applications and related documents and responses thereto, if any. If an application or document is not filed within the time set by the Immigration Judge, the opportunity to file that application or document shall be deemed waived.

(d) The Service may file documents under seal by including a cover sheet identifying the contents of the submission as containing information which is being filed under seal. Documents filed under seal shall not be examined by any person except pursuant to authorized access to the administrative record.

[57 FR 11572, Apr. 6, 1992, as amended at 60 FR 34089, June 30, 1995; 61 FR 18908, Apr. 29, 1996; 61 FR 19976, May 3, 1996; 61 FR 21228, May 9, 1996; 61 FR 46374, Sept. 3, 1996; 62 FR 45149, Aug. 26, 1997; 67 FR 36802, May 28, 2002]

§ 1003.32 Service and size of documents.

(a) Except in *in absentia* hearings, a copy of all documents (including proposed exhibits or applications) filed with or presented to the Immigration Judge shall be simultaneously served by the presenting party on the opposing party or parties. Such service shall be in person or by first class mail to the most recent address contained in the Record of Proceeding. A certification showing service on the opposing party or parties on a date certain shall accompany any filing with the Immigration Judge unless service is made on the record during the hearing. Any documents or applications not containing such certification will not be considered by the Immigration Judge unless service is made on the record during a hearing.

(b) Unless otherwise permitted by the Immigration Judge, all written material presented to Immigration Judges including offers of evidence, correspondence, briefs, memoranda, or other documents must be submitted on 8½″ × 11″ size paper. The Immigration Judge may require that exhibits and other written material presented be indexed, paginated, and that a table of contents be provided.

[52 FR 2936, Jan. 29, 1987. Redesignated and amended at 57 FR 11571, 11572, Apr. 6, 1992]

§ 1003.33 Translation of documents.

Any foreign language document offered by a party in a proceeding shall be accompanied by an English language translation and a certification signed by the translator that must be printed legibly or typed. Such certification must include a statement that the translator is competent to translate the document, and that the translation is true and accurate to the best of the translator's abilities.

[59 FR 1900, Jan. 13, 1994]

§ 1003.34 Testimony.

Testimony of witnesses appearing at the hearing shall be under oath or affirmation.

[52 FR 2936, Jan. 29, 1987. Redesignated at 57 FR 11571, Apr. 6, 1992]

§ 1003.35 Depositions and subpoenas.

(a) *Depositions.* If an Immigration Judge is satisfied that a witness is not reasonably available at the place of hearing and that said witness' testimony or other evidence is essential, the Immigration Judge may order the taking of deposition either at his or her own instance or upon application of a party. Such order shall designate the official by whom the deposition shall be taken, may prescribe and limit the content, scope, or manner of taking the deposition, and may direct the production of documentary evidence.

(b) *Subpoenas issued subsequent to commencement of proceedings*—(1) *General.* In any proceeding before an Immigration Judge, other than under 8 CFR part 335, the Immigration Judge shall have exclusive jurisdiction to issue subpoenas requiring the attendance of witnesses or for the production of books, papers and other documentary evidence, or both. An Immigration Judge may issue a subpoena upon his or her own volition or upon application of the Service or the alien.

(2) *Application for subpoena.* A party applying for a subpoena shall be required, as a condition precedent to its issuance, to state in writing or at the proceeding, what he or she expects to prove by such witnesses or documentary evidence, and to show affirmatively that he or she has made diligent effort, without success, to produce the same.

(3) *Issuance of subpoena.* Upon being satisfied that a witness will not appear and testify or produce documentary evidence and that the witness' evidence is essential, the Immigration Judge shall issue a subpoena. The subpoena shall state the title of the proceeding and shall command the person to whom it is directed to attend and to give testimony at a time and place specified. The subpoena may also command the person to whom it is directed to produce the books, papers, or documents specified in the subpoena.

(4) *Appearance of witness.* If the witness is at a distance of more than 100 miles from the place of the proceeding, the subpoena shall provide for the witness' appearance at the Immigration Court nearest to the witness to respond to oral or written interrogatories, unless there is no objection by any party to the witness' appearance at the proceeding.

(5) *Service.* A subpoena issued under this section may be served by any person over 18 years of age not a party to the case.

(6) *Invoking aid of court.* If a witness neglects or refuses to appear and testify as directed by the subpoena served upon him or her in accordance with the

provisions of this section, the Immigration Judge issuing the subpoena shall request the United States Attorney for the district in which the subpoena was issued to report such neglect or refusal to the United States District Court and to request such court to issue an order requiring the witness to appear and testify and to produce the books, papers or documents designated in the subpoena.

[62 FR 10335, Mar. 6, 1997]

§ 1003.36 Record of proceeding.

The Immigration Court shall create and control the Record of Proceeding.

[52 FR 2936, Jan. 29, 1987. Redesignated at 57 FR 11571, Apr. 6, 1992, as amended at 60 FR 34089, June 30, 1995]

§ 1003.37 Decisions.

(a) A decision of the Immigration Judge may be rendered orally or in writing. If the decision is oral, it shall be stated by the Immigration Judge in the presence of the parties and a memorandum summarizing the oral decision shall be served on the parties. If the decision is in writing, it shall be served on the parties by first class mail to the most recent address contained in the Record of Proceeding or by personal service.

(b) A written copy of the decision will not be sent to an alien who has failed to provide a written record of an address.

[57 FR 11573, Apr. 6, 1992, as amended at 59 FR 1900, Jan. 13, 1994]

§ 1003.38 Appeals.

(a) Decisions of Immigration Judges may be appealed to the Board of Immigration Appeals as authorized by 8 CFR 3.1(b).

(b) The Notice of Appeal to the Board of Immigration Appeals of Decision of Immigration Judge (Form EOIR–26) shall be filed directly with the Board of Immigration Appeals within 30 calendar days after the stating of an Immigration Judge's oral decision or the mailing of an Immigration Judge's written decision. If the final date for filing falls on a Saturday, Sunday, or legal holiday, this appeal time shall be extended to the next business day. A Notice of Appeal (Form EOIR–26) may not be filed by any party who has waived appeal.

(c) The date of filing of the Notice of Appeal (Form EOIR–26) shall be the date the Notice is received by the Board.

(d) A Notice of Appeal (Form EOIR–26) must be accompanied by the appropriate fee or by an Appeal Fee Waiver Request (Form EOIR–26A). If the fee is not paid or the Appeal Fee Waiver Request (Form EOIR–26A) is not filed within the specified time period indicated in paragraph (b) of this section, the appeal will not be deemed properly filed and the decision of the Immigration Judge shall be final to the same extent as though no appeal had been taken.

(e) Within five working days of any change of address, an alien must provide written notice of the change of address on Form EOIR–33 to the Board. Where a party is represented, the representative should also provide to the Board written notice of any change in the representative's business mailing address.

(f) Briefs may be filed by both parties pursuant to 8 CFR 3.3(c).

(g) In any proceeding before the Board wherein the respondent/applicant is represented, the attorney or representative shall file a notice of appearance on the appropriate form. Withdrawal or substitution of an attorney or representative may be permitted by the Board during proceedings only upon written motion submitted without fee.

[52 FR 2936, Jan. 29, 1987. Redesignated at 57 FR 11571, Apr. 6, 1992, as amended at 60 FR 34089, June 30, 1995; 61 FR 18908, Apr. 29, 1996]

§ 1003.39 Finality of decision.

Except when certified to the Board, the decision of the Immigration Judge becomes final upon waiver of appeal or upon expiration of the time to appeal if no appeal is taken whichever occurs first.

[52 FR 2936, Jan. 29, 1987. Redesignated and amended at 57 FR 11571, 11573, Apr. 6, 1992]

§ 1003.40 Local operating procedures.

An Immigration Court having administrative control over Records of Proceedings may establish local operating procedures, provided that:

(a) Such operating procedure(s) shall not be inconsistent with any provision of this chapter;

(b) A majority of the judges of the local Immigration Court shall concur in writing therein; and

(c) The Chief Immigration Judge has approved the proposed operating procedure(s) in writing.

[52 FR 2936, Jan. 29, 1987. Redesignated at 57 FR 11571, Apr. 6, 1992, as amended at 60 FR 34090, June 30, 1995]

§ 1003.41 Evidence of criminal conviction.

In any proceeding before an Immigration Judge,

(a) Any of the following documents or records shall be admissible as evidence in proving a criminal conviction:

(1) A record of judgment and conviction;

(2) A record of plea, verdict and sentence;

(3) A docket entry from court records that indicates the existence of a conviction;

(4) Minutes of a court proceeding or a transcript of a hearing that indicates the existence of a conviction;

(5) An abstract of a record of conviction prepared by the court in which the conviction was entered, or by a state official associated with the state's repository of criminal justice records, that indicates the following: The charge or section of law violated, the disposition of the case, the existence and date of conviction, and the sentence;

(6) Any document or record prepared by, or under the direction of, the court in which the conviction was entered that indicates the existence of a conviction.

(b) Any document or record of the types specified in paragraph (a) of this section may be submitted if it complies with the requirement of § 287.6(a) of this chapter, or a copy of any such document or record may be submitted if it is attested in writing by an immigration officer to be a true and correct copy of the original.

(c) Any record of conviction or abstract that has been submitted by electronic means to the Service from a state or court shall be admissible as evidence to prove a criminal conviction if it:

(1) Is certified by a state official associated with the state's repository of criminal justice records as an official record from its repository or by a court official from the court in which conviction was entered as an official record from its repository. Such certification may be by means of a computer-generated signature and statement of authenticity; and,

(2) Is certified in writing by a Service official as having been received electronically from the state's record repository or the court's record repository.

(d) Any other evidence that reasonably indicates the existence of a criminal conviction may be admissible as evidence thereof.

[58 FR 38953, July 21, 1993]

§ 1003.42 Review of credible fear determination.

(a) *Referral.* Jurisdiction for an Immigration Judge to review an adverse credible fear finding by an asylum officer pursuant to section 235(b)(1)(B) of the Act shall commence with the filing by the Service of Form I–863, Notice of Referral to Immigration Judge. The Service shall also file with the notice of referral a copy of the written record of determination as defined in section 235(b)(1)(B)(iii)(II) of the Act, including a copy of the alien's written request for review, if any.

(b) *Record of proceeding.* The Immigration Court shall create a Record of Proceeding for a review of an adverse credible fear determination. This record shall not be merged with any later proceeding pursuant to section 240 of the Act involving the same alien.

(c) *Procedures and evidence.* The Immigration Judge may receive into evidence any oral or written statement which is material and relevant to any issue in the review. The testimony of the alien shall be under oath or affirmation administered by the Immigration Judge. If an interpreter is necessary, one will be provided by the Immigration Court. The Immigration

Judge shall determine whether the review shall be in person, or through telephonic or video connection (where available). The alien may consult with a person or persons of the alien's choosing prior to the review.

(d) *Standard of review.* The immigration judge shall make a *de novo* determination as to whether there is a significant possibility, taking into account the credibility of the statements made by the alien in support of the alien's claim and such other facts as are known to the immigration judge, that the alien could establish eligibility for asylum under section 208 of the Act or withholding under section 241(b)(3) of the Act or withholding under the Convention Against Torture. If the alien is determined to be an alien described in 8 CFR 208.13(c)(3) or 1208.13(c)(3) and is determined to lack a reasonable fear under 8 CFR 208.30(e)(5), the immigration judge shall first review de novo the determination that the alien is described in 8 CFR 208.13(c)(3) or 1208.13(c)(3) prior to any further review of the asylum officer's negative determination.

(e) *Timing.* The Immigration Judge shall conclude the review to the maximum extent practicable within 24 hours, but in no case later than 7 days after the date the supervisory asylum officer has approved the asylum officer's negative credible fear determination issued on Form I–869, Record of Negative Credible Fear Finding and Request for Review.

(f) *Decision.* If an immigration judge determines that an alien has a credible fear of persecution or torture, the immigration judge shall vacate the order entered pursuant to section 235(b)(1)(B)(iii)(I) of the Act. Subsequent to the order being vacated, the Service shall issue and file Form I–862, Notice to Appear, with the Immigration Court to commence removal proceedings. The alien shall have the opportunity to apply for asylum and withholding of removal in the course of removal proceedings pursuant to section 240 of the Act. If an immigration judge determines that an alien does not have a credible fear of persecution or torture, the immigration judge shall affirm the asylum officer's determination and remand the case to the Service for execution of the removal order entered pursuant to section 235(b)(1)(B)(iii)(I) of the Act. No appeal shall lie from a review of an adverse credible fear determination made by an immigration judge.

(g) *Custody.* An Immigration Judge shall have no authority to review an alien's custody status in the course of a review of an adverse credible fear determination made by the Service.

(h) *Safe third country agreement*—(1) *Arriving alien.* An immigration judge has no jurisdiction to review a determination by an asylum officer that an arriving alien is not eligible to apply for asylum pursuant to a bilateral or multilateral agreement (the Agreement) under section 208(a)(2)(A) of the Act and should be returned to a safe third country to pursue his or her claims for asylum or other protection under the laws of that country. See 8 CFR 208.30(e)(6). However, in any case where an asylum officer has found that an arriving alien qualifies for an exception to the Agreement, an immigration judge does have jurisdiction to review a negative credible fear finding made thereafter by the asylum officer as provided in this section.

(2) *Aliens in transit.* An immigration judge has no jurisdiction to review any determination by DHS that an alien being removed from Canada in transit through the United States should be returned to Canada to pursue asylum claims under Canadian law, under the terms of a safe third country agreement with Canada.

[62 FR 10335, Mar. 6, 1997, as amended at 64 FR 8487, Feb. 19, 1999; 69 FR 69496, Nov. 29, 2004; 83 FR 55952, Nov. 9, 2018]

§ 1003.43 Motions to reopen for suspension of deportation and cancellation of removal pursuant to section 203(c) of NACARA and section 1505(c) of the LIFE Act Amendments.

(a) *Standard for Adjudication.* Except as provided in this section, a motion to reopen proceedings under section 309(g) or (h) of the Illegal Immigration Reform and Immigrant Responsibility Act (Pub. L. 104–208) (IIRIRA), as amended by section 203(c) of the Nicaraguan Adjustment and Central American Relief Act (Pub. L. 105–100)

(NACARA) and by section 1505(c) of the Legal Immigration Family Equity Act Amendments (Pub. L. 106–554) (LIFE Act Amendments), respectively, will be adjudicated under applicable statutes and regulations governing motions to reopen.

(b) *Aliens eligible to reopen proceedings under section 203 of NACARA.* A motion to reopen proceedings to apply for suspension of deportation or cancellation of removal under the special rules of section 309(g) of IIRIRA, as amended by section 203(c) of NACARA, must establish that the alien:

(1) Is prima facie eligible for suspension of deportation pursuant to former section 244(a) of the Act (as in effect prior to April 1, 1997) or the special rule for cancellation of removal pursuant to section 309(f) of IIRIRA, as amended by section 203(b) of NACARA;

(2) Was or would be ineligible:

(i) For suspension of deportation by operation of section 309(c)(5) of IIRIRA (as in effect prior to November 19, 1997); or

(ii) For cancellation of removal pursuant to section 240A of the Act, but for operation of section 309(f) of IIRIRA, as amended by section 203(b) of NACARA;

(3) Has not been convicted at any time of an aggravated felony; and

(4) Is within one of the six classes of aliens described in paragraphs (d)(1) through (d)(6) of this section.

(c) *Aliens eligible to reopen proceedings under section 1505(c) of the LIFE Act Amendments.* A motion to reopen proceedings to apply for suspension of deportation or cancellation of removal under the special rules of section 309(h) of IIRIRA, as amended by section 1505(c) of the LIFE Act Amendments, must establish that the alien:

(1) Is prima facie eligible for suspension of deportation pursuant to former section 244(a) of the Act (as in effect prior to April 1, 1997) or cancellation of removal pursuant to section 240A(b) of the Act and section 309(f) of IIRIRA, as amended by section 203(b) of NACARA;

(2) Was or would be ineligible, by operation of section 241(a)(5) of the Act, for suspension of deportation pursuant to former section 244(a) of the Act (as in effect prior to April 1, 1997) or cancellation of removal pursuant to section 240A(b) of the Act and section 309(f) of IIRIRA, as amended by section 203(b) of NACARA, but for enactment of section 1505(c) of the LIFE Act Amendments;

(3) Has not been convicted at any time of an aggravated felony; and

(4) Is within one of the eight classes of aliens described in paragraph (d) of this section.

(d) *Classes of Eligible Aliens*—(1) *Class 1.* A national of El Salvador who:

(i) First entered the United States on or before September 19, 1990;

(ii) Registered for benefits pursuant to the settlement agreement in *American Baptist Churches, et al.* v. *Thornburgh,* 760 F. Supp. 796 (N.D. Cal. 1991) (ABC) on or before October 31, 1991, or applied for Temporary Protected Status (TPS) on or before October 31, 1991; and

(iii) Was not apprehended after December 19, 1990, at time of entry.

(2) *Class 2.* A national of Guatemala who:

(i) First entered the United States on or before October 1, 1990;

(ii) Registered for ABC benefits on or before December 31, 1991; and

(iii) Was not apprehended after December 19, 1990, at time of entry.

(3) *Class 3.* A national of Guatemala or El Salvador who applied for asylum with the Service on or before April 1, 1990.

(4) *Class 4.* An alien who:

(i) Entered the United States on or before December 31, 1990;

(ii) Applied for asylum on or before December 31, 1991; and

(iii) At the time of filing such application for asylum was a national of the Soviet Union, Russia, any republic of the former Soviet Union, Latvia, Estonia, Lithuania, Poland, Czechoslovakia, Romania, Hungary, Bulgaria, Albania, East Germany, Yugoslavia, or any state of the former Yugoslavia.

(5) *Class 5.* The spouse or child of a person who is described in paragraphs (d)(1) through (d)(4) of this section and such person is prima facie eligible for and has applied for suspension of deportation or special rule cancellation of removal under section 203 of NACARA.

(6) *Class 6.* An unmarried son or daughter of a person who is described in paragraphs (d)(1) through (d)(4) of

this section and such person is prima facie eligible for and has applied for suspension of deportation or special rule cancellation of removal under section 203 of NACARA. If the son or daughter is 21 years of age or older, the son or daughter must have entered the United States on or before October 1, 1990.

(7) *Class 7.* An alien who was issued an Order to Show Cause or was in deportation proceedings before April 1, 1997, and who applied for suspension of deportation as a battered alien under former section 244(a)(3) of the Act (as in effect before September 30, 1996).

(8) *Class 8.* An alien:

(i) Who is or was the spouse or child of a person described in paragraphs (d)(1) through (d)(4) of this section:

(A) At the time a decision is rendered to suspend deportation or cancel removal of that person;

(B) At the time that person filed an application for suspension of deportation or cancellation of removal; or

(C) At the time that person registered for ABC benefits, applied for TPS, or applied for asylum; and

(ii) Who has been battered or subjected to extreme cruelty (or the spouse described in paragraph (d)(8)(i) of this section has a child who has been battered or subjected to extreme cruelty) by the person described in paragraphs (d)(1) through (d)(4) of this section.

(e) *Motion to reopen under section 203 of NACARA.* (1) An alien filing a motion to reopen proceedings pursuant to section 309(g) of IIRIRA, as amended by section 203(c) of NACARA, may initially file a motion to reopen without an application for suspension of deportation or cancellation of removal and supporting documents, but the motion must be filed no later than September 11, 1998. An alien may file only one motion to reopen pursuant to section 309(g) of IIRIRA. In such motion to reopen, the alien must address each of the four requirements for eligibility described in paragraph (b) of this section and establish that the alien satisfies each requirement.

(2) A motion to reopen filed pursuant to paragraph (b) of this section shall be considered complete at the time of submission of an application for suspension of deportation or special rule cancellation of removal and accompanying documents. Such application must be submitted no later than November 18, 1999. Aliens described in paragraphs (d)(5) or (d)(6) of this section must include, as part of their submission, proof that their parent or spouse is prima facie eligible and has applied for relief under section 203 of NACARA.

(3) The Service shall have 45 days from the date the alien serves the Immigration Court with either the Form EOIR–40 or the Form I–881 application for suspension of deportation or special rule cancellation of removal to respond to that completed motion. If the alien fails to submit the required application on or before November 18, 1999, the motion will be denied as abandoned.

(f) *Motion to reopen under section 1505(c) of the LIFE Act Amendments.* (1) An alien filing a motion to reopen proceedings pursuant to section 309(h) of IIRIRA, as amended by section 1505(c) of the LIFE Act Amendments, must file a motion to reopen with an application for suspension of deportation or cancellation of removal and supporting documents, on or before October 16, 2001. An alien may file only one motion to reopen proceedings pursuant to section 309(h) of IIRIRA. In such motion to reopen, the alien must address each of the four requirements for eligibility described in paragraph (c) of this section and establish that the alien satisfies each requirement.

(2) A motion to reopen and the accompanying application and supporting documents filed pursuant to paragraph (c) of this section must be submitted on or before October 16, 2001. Aliens described in paragraphs (d)(5) and (d)(6) of this section must include, as part of their submission, proof that their parent or spouse is prima facie eligible and has applied for relief under section 203 of NACARA.

(3) The Service shall have 45 days from the date the alien serves the Immigration Court to respond to that motion to reopen.

(g) *Fee for motion to reopen waived.* No filing fee is required for a motion to reopen to apply for suspension of deportation or cancellation of removal under the special rules of section 309(g) or (h) of IIRIRA, as amended by section 203(c) of NACARA and by section 1505(c) of the LIFE Act Amendments, respectively.

(h) *Jurisdiction over motions to reopen under section 203 of NACARA and remand of appeals.* (1) Notwithstanding any other provisions, any motion to reopen filed pursuant to the special rules of section 309(g) of IIRIRA, as amended by section 203(c) of NACARA, shall be filed with the Immigration Court, even if the Board of Immigration Appeals (Board) issued an order in the case. The Immigration Court that last had jurisdiction over the proceedings will adjudicate the motion.

(2) The Board will remand to the Immigration Court any presently pending appeal in which the alien appears eligible to apply for suspension of deportation or cancellation of removal under the special rules of section 309(g) of IIRIRA, as amended by section 203 of NACARA, and appears prima facie eligible for that relief. The alien will then have the opportunity to apply for suspension or cancellation under the special rules of NACARA before the Immigration Court.

(i) *Jurisdiction over motions to reopen under section 1505(c) of the LIFE Act Amendments and remand of appeals.* (1) Notwithstanding any other provisions, any motion to reopen filed pursuant to paragraph (f) of this section to apply for suspension of deportation or cancellation of removal under section 1505(c) of the LIFE Act Amendments shall be filed with the Immigration Court or the Board, whichever last held jurisdiction over the case. Only an alien with a reinstated final order, or an alien with a newly issued final order that was issued based on the alien having reentered the United States illegally after having been removed or having departed voluntarily under a prior order of removal that was subject to reinstatement under section 241(a)(5) of the Act, may file a motion to reopen with the Immigration Court or the Board pursuant to this section. An alien whose final order has not been reinstated and as to whom a newly issued final order, as described in this section, has not been issued may apply for suspension of deportation or special rule cancellation of removal before the Service pursuant to section 309(h)(1) of IIRIRA, as amended by section 1505(c) of the LIFE Act Amendments, according to the jurisdictional provisions for applications before the Service set forth in 8 CFR 240.62(a) or before the Immigration Court as set forth in 8 CFR 240.62(b).

(2) If the Immigration Court has jurisdiction and grants only the motion to reopen filed pursuant to paragraph (f) of this section, the scope of the reopened proceeding shall be limited to a determination of the alien's eligibility for suspension of deportation or cancellation of removal pursuant to section 309(h)(1) of IIRIRA, as amended by section 1505(c) of the LIFE Act Amendments.

(3) If the Board has jurisdiction and grants only the motion to reopen filed pursuant to paragraph (f) of this section, it shall remand the case to the Immigration Court solely for adjudication of the application for suspension of deportation or cancellation of removal pursuant to section 309(h)(1) of IIRIRA, as amended by section 1505(c) of the LIFE Act Amendments.

(4) Nothing in this section shall be interpreted to preclude or restrict the applicability of any other exceptions regarding motions to reopen that are provided for in 8 CFR 3.2(c)(3) and 3.23(b).

[66 FR 37123, July 17, 2001]

§ 1003.44 Special motion to seek section 212(c) relief for aliens who pleaded guilty or *nolo contendere* to certain crimes before April 1, 1997.

(a) *Standard for adjudication.* This section applies to certain aliens who formerly were lawful permanent residents, who are subject to an administratively final order of deportation or removal, and who are eligible to apply for relief under former section 212(c) of the Act and 8 CFR 1212.3 with respect to convictions obtained by plea agreements reached prior to a verdict at trial prior to April 1, 1997. A special motion to seek relief under section 212(c) of the Act will be adjudicated under the standards of this section and 8 CFR 1212.3. This section is not applicable with respect to any conviction entered after trial.

(b) *General eligibility.* The alien has the burden of establishing eligibility for relief, including the date on which the alien and the prosecution agreed on the plea of guilt or *nolo contendere*. Generally, a special motion under this section to seek section 212(c) relief must establish that the alien:

(1) Was a lawful permanent resident and is now subject to a final order of deportation or removal;

(2) Agreed to plead guilty or *nolo contendere* to an offense rendering the alien deportable or removable, pursuant to a plea agreement made before April 1, 1997;

(3) Had seven consecutive years of lawful unrelinquished domicile in the United States prior to the date of the final administrative order of deportation or removal; and

(4) Is otherwise eligible to apply for section 212(c) relief under the standards that were in effect at the time the alien's plea was made, regardless of when the plea was entered by the court.

(c) *Aggravated felony definition.* For purposes of eligibility to apply for section 212(c) relief under this section and 8 CFR 1212.3, the definition of aggravated felony in section 101(a)(43) of the Act is that in effect at the time the special motion or the application for section 212(c) relief is adjudicated under this section. An alien shall be deemed to be ineligible for section 212(c) relief if he or she has been charged and found deportable or removable on the basis of a crime that is an aggravated felony, except as provided in 8 CFR 1212.3(f)(4).

(d) *Effect of prior denial of section 212(c) relief.* A motion under this section will not be granted with respect to any conviction where an alien has previously been denied section 212(c) relief by an immigration judge or by the Board on discretionary grounds.

(e) *Scope of proceedings.* Proceedings shall be reopened under this section solely for the purpose of adjudicating the application for section 212(c) relief, but if the immigration judge or the Board grants a motion by the alien to reopen the proceedings on other applicable grounds under 8 CFR 1003.2 or 1003.23 of this chapter, all issues encompassed within the reopened proceedings may be considered together, as appropriate.

(f) *Procedure for filing a special motion to seek section 212(c) relief.* An eligible alien shall file a special motion to seek section 212(c) relief with the immigration judge or the Board, whichever last held jurisdiction over the case. An eligible alien must submit a copy of the Form I–191 application, and supporting documents, with the special motion. The motion must contain the notation "special motion to seek section 212(c) relief." The Department of Homeland Security (DHS) shall have 45 days from the date of filing of the special motion to respond. In the event the DHS does not respond to the motion, the DHS retains the right in the proceedings to contest any and all issues raised.

(g) *Relationship to motions to reopen or reconsider on other grounds*—(1) *Other pending motions to reopen or reconsider.* An alien who has previously filed a motion to reopen or reconsider that is still pending before an immigration judge or the Board, other than a motion for section 212(c) relief, must file a separate special motion to seek section 212(c) relief pursuant to this section. The new motion shall specify any other motions currently pending before an immigration judge or the Board. An alien who has previously filed a motion to reopen under 8 CFR 1003.2 or 1003.23 based on *INS* v. *St. Cyr* is not required to file a new special motion under this section, but he or she may supplement the previous motion if it is still pending. Any motion for section 212(c) relief described in this section pending before the Board or an immigration judge on the effective date of this rule that would be barred by the time or number limitations on motions shall be deemed to be a motion filed pursuant to this section, and shall not count against the number restrictions for other motions to reopen.

(2) *Motions previously filed pursuant to prior provision.* If an alien previously filed a motion to apply for section 212(c) relief with an immigration judge or the Board pursuant to the prior provisions of this section, as in effect before October 28, 2004, and the motion is still pending, the motion will be adjudicated pursuant to the standards of this section, both as revised and as previously in effect, and the alien does not

need to file a new special motion pursuant to paragraph (g)(1) of this section. However, if a motion filed under the prior provisions of this section was denied because the alien did not satisfy the requirements contained therein, the alien must file a new special motion pursuant to this section, if eligible, in order to apply for section 212(c) relief based on the requirements established in this section.

(3) *Effect of a prior denial of a motion to reopen or motion to reconsider filed after the St. Cyr decision.* A motion under this section will not be granted where an alien has previously submitted a motion to reopen or motion to reconsider based on the *St. Cyr* decision and that motion was denied by an immigration judge or the Board (except on account of time or number limitations for such motions).

(4) *Limitations for motions.* The filing of a special motion under this section has no effect on the time and number limitations for motions to reopen or reconsider that may be filed on grounds unrelated to section 212(c).

(h) *Deadline to file a special motion to seek section 212(c) relief under this section.* An alien subject to a final administrative order of deportation or removal must file a special motion to seek section 212(c) relief on or before April 26, 2005. An eligible alien may file one special motion to seek section 212(c) relief under this section.

(i) *Fees.* No filing fee is required at the time the alien files a special motion to seek section 212(c) relief under this section. However, if the special motion is granted, and the alien has not previously filed an application for section 212(c) relief, the alien will be required to submit the appropriate fee receipt at the time the alien files the Form I–191 with the immigration court.

(j) *Remands of appeals.* If the Board has jurisdiction and grants the motion to apply for section 212(c) relief pursuant to this section, it shall remand the case to the immigration judge solely for adjudication of the section 212(c) application.

(k) *Limitations on eligibility under this section.* This section does not apply to:

(1) Aliens who have departed the United States and are currently outside the United States;

(2) Aliens issued a final order of deportation or removal who then illegally returned to the United States; or

(3) Aliens who have not been admitted or paroled.

[69 FR 57833, Sept. 28, 2004]

§ 1003.46 Protective orders, sealed submissions in Immigration Courts.

(a) *Authority.* In any immigration or bond proceeding, Immigration Judges may, upon a showing by the Service of a substantial likelihood that specific information submitted under seal or to be submitted under seal will, if disclosed, harm the national security (as defined in section 219(c)(2) of the Act) or law enforcement interests of the United States, issue a protective order barring disclosure of such information.

(b) *Motion by the service.* The Service may at any time after filing a Notice to Appear, or other charging document, file with the Immigration Judge, and serve upon the respondent, a motion for an order to protect specific information it intends to submit or is submitting under seal. The motion shall describe, to the extent practical, the information that the Service seeks to protect from disclosure. The motion shall specify the relief requested in the protective order. The respondent may file a response to the motion within ten days after the motion is served.

(c) *Sealed annex to motion.* In the Service's discretion, the Service may file the specific information as a sealed annex to the motion, which shall not be served upon the respondent. If the Service files a sealed annex, or the Immigration Judge, in his or her discretion, instructs that the information be filed as a sealed annex in order to determine whether to grant or deny the motion, the Immigration Judge shall consider the information only for the purpose of determining whether to grant or deny the motion.

(d) *Due deference.* The Immigration Judge shall give appropriate deference to the expertise of senior officials in law enforcement and national security agencies in any averments in any submitted affidavit in determining whether the disclosure of information will harm the national security or law enforcement interests of the United States.

(e) *Denied motions.* If the motion is denied, any sealed annex shall be returned to the Service, and the Immigration Judge shall give no weight to such information. The Service may immediately appeal denial of the motion to the Board, which shall have jurisdiction to hear the appeal, by filing a Notice of Appeal and the sealed annex with the Board. The Immigration Judge shall hold any further proceedings in abeyance pending resolution of the appeal by the Board.

(f) *Granted motions.* If the motion is granted, the Immigration Judge shall issue an appropriate protective order.

(1) The Immigration Judge shall ensure that the protective order encompasses such witnesses as the respondent demonstrates are reasonably necessary to the presentation of his case. If necessary, the Immigration Judge may impose the requirements of the protective order on any witness before the Immigration Judge to whom such information may be disclosed.

(2) The protective order may require that the respondent, and his or her attorney or accredited representative, if any:

(i) Not divulge any of the information submitted under the protective order, or any information derived therefrom, to any person or entity, other than authorized personnel of the Executive Office for Immigration Review, the Service, or such other persons approved by the Service or the Immigration Judge;

(ii) When transmitting any information under a protective order, or any information derived therefrom, to the Executive Office for Immigration Review or the Service, include a cover sheet identifying the contents of the submission as containing information subject to a protective order under this section;

(iii) Store any information under a protective order, or any information derived therefrom, in a reasonably secure manner, and return all copies of such information to the Service upon completion of proceedings, including judicial review; and

(iv) Such other requirements as the Immigration Judge finds necessary to protect the information from disclosure.

(3) Upon issuance of such protective order, the Service shall serve the respondent with the protective order and the sealed information. A protective order issued under this section shall remain in effect until vacated by the Immigration Judge.

(4) Further review of the protective order before the Board shall only be had pursuant to review of an order of the Immigration Judge resolving all issues of removability and any applications for relief pending in the matter pursuant to 8 CFR 3.1(b). Notwithstanding any other provision of this section, the Immigration Judge shall retain jurisdiction to modify or vacate a protective order upon motion of the Service or the respondent. An Immigration Judge may not grant a motion by the respondent to modify or vacate a protective order until either: the Service files a response to such motion or 10 days after service of such motion on the Service.

(g) *Admissibility as evidence.* The issuance of a protective order shall not prejudice the respondent's right to challenge the admissibility of the information subject to a protective order. The Immigration Judge may not find the information inadmissible solely because it is subject to a protective order.

(h) *Seal.* Any submission to the Immigration Judge, including any briefs, referring to information subject to a protective order shall be filed under seal. Any information submitted subject to a protective order under this paragraph shall remain under seal as part of the administrative record.

(i) *Administrative enforcement.* If the Service establishes that a respondent, or the respondent's attorney or accredited representative, has disclosed information subject to a protective order, the Immigration Judge shall deny all forms of discretionary relief, except bond, unless the respondent fully cooperates with the Service or other law enforcement agencies in any investigation relating to the noncompliance with the protective order and disclosure of the information; and establishes by clear and convincing evidence either that extraordinary and extremely unusual circumstances exist or that failure to comply with the protective order was beyond the control of the respondent and his or her attorney or accredited representative. Failure to comply with a protective order may also result in the suspension of an attorney's or an accredited representative's privilege of appearing before the Executive Office for Immigration Review or before the Service pursuant to 8 CFR part 3, subpart G.

[67 FR 36802, May 28, 2002]

§ 1003.47 Identity, law enforcement, or security investigations or examinations relating to applications for immigration relief, protection, or restriction on removal.

(a) *In general.* The procedures of this section are applicable to any application for immigration relief, protection, or restriction on removal that is subject to the conduct of identity, law enforcement, or security investigations or examinations as described in paragraph (b) of this section, in order to ensure that DHS has completed the appropriate identity, law enforcement, or security investigations or examinations before the adjudication of the application.

(b) *Covered applications.* The requirements of this section apply to the granting of any form of immigration relief in immigration proceedings which permits the alien to reside in the United States, including but not limited to the following forms of relief, protection, or restriction on removal to the extent they are within the authority of an immigration judge or the Board to grant:

(1) Asylum under section 208 of the Act.

(2) Adjustment of status to that of a lawful permanent resident under sections 209 or 245 of the Act, or any other provision of law.

(3) Waiver of inadmissibility or deportability under sections 209(c), 212, or 237 of the Act, or any provision of law.

(4) Permanent resident status on a conditional basis or removal of the conditional basis of permanent resident status under sections 216 or 216A of the Act, or any other provision of law.

(5) Cancellation of removal or suspension of deportation under section 240A or former section 244 of the Act, or any other provision of law.

(6) Relief from removal under former section 212(c) of the Act.

(7) Withholding of removal under section 241(b)(3) of the Act or under the Convention Against Torture.

(8) Registry under section 249 of the Act.

(9) Conditional grants relating to the above, such as for applications seeking asylum pursuant to section 207(a)(5) of the Act or cancellation of removal in light of section 240A(e) of the Act.

(c) *Completion of applications for immigration relief, protection, or restriction on removal.* Failure to file necessary documentation and comply with the requirements to provide biometrics and other biographical information in conformity with the applicable regulations, the instructions to the applications, the biometrics notice, and instructions provided by DHS, within the time allowed by the immigration judge's order, constitutes abandonment of the application and the immigration judge may enter an appropriate order dismissing the application unless the applicant demonstrates that such failure was the result of good cause. Nothing in this section shall be construed to affect the provisions in 8 CFR 1208.4 regarding the timely filing of asylum applications or the determination of a respondent's compliance with any other deadline for initial filing of an application, including the consequences of filing under the Child Status Protection Act.

(d) *Biometrics and other biographical information.* At any hearing at which a respondent expresses an intention to file or files an application for relief for which identity, law enforcement, or security investigations or examinations are required under this section, unless DHS advises the immigration judge that such information is unnecessary in the particular case, DHS shall notify the respondent of the need to provide biometrics and other biographical information and shall provide a biometrics notice and instructions to the respondent for such procedures. The immigration judge shall specify for the record when the respondent receives the biometrics notice and instructions and the consequences for failing to comply with the requirements of this section. Whenever required by DHS, the applicant shall make arrangements with an office of DHS to provide biometrics and other biographical information (including for any other person covered by the same application who is required to provide biometrics and other biographical information) before or as soon as practicable after the filing of the application for relief in the immigration proceedings. Failure to provide biometrics or other biographical information of the applicant or any other covered individual within the time allowed will constitute abandonment of the application or of the other covered individual's participation unless the applicant demonstrates that such failure was the result of good cause. DHS is responsible for obtaining biometrics and other biographical information with respect to any alien in detention.

(e) *Conduct of investigations or examinations.* DHS shall endeavor to initiate all relevant identity, law enforcement, or security investigations or examinations concerning the alien or beneficiaries promptly, to complete those investigations or examinations as promptly as is practicable (considering, among other things, increased demands placed upon such investigations), and to advise the immigration judge of the results in a timely manner, on or before the date of a scheduled hearing on any application for immigration relief filed in the proceedings. The immigration judges, in scheduling hearings, shall allow a period of time for DHS to undertake the necessary identity, law enforcement, or security investigations or examinations prior to the date that an application is scheduled for hearing and disposition, with a view to minimizing the number of cases in which hearings must be continued.

(f) *Continuance for completion of investigations or examinations.* If DHS has not reported on the completion and results of all relevant identity, law enforcement, or security investigations or examinations for an applicant and his or her beneficiaries by the date that the application is scheduled for hearing and disposition, after the time allowed by the immigration judge pursuant to paragraph (e) of this section, the immigration judge may continue proceedings for the purpose of completing the investigations or examinations, or hear the case on the merits. DHS shall attempt to give reasonable notice to the immigration judge of the fact that all relevant identity, law enforcement, or security investigations or examinations have not been completed and the amount of time DHS anticipates is required to complete those investigations or examinations.

(g) *Adjudication after completion of investigations or examinations.* In no case shall an immigration judge grant an application for immigration relief that is subject to the conduct of identity, law enforcement, or security investigations or examinations under this section until after DHS has reported to the immigration judge that the appropriate investigations or examinations have been completed and are current as provided in this section and DHS has reported any relevant information from the investigations or examinations to the immigration judge.

(h) *Adjudication upon remand from the Board.* In any case remanded pursuant to 8 CFR 1003.1(d)(6), the immigration judge shall consider the results of the identity, law enforcement, or security investigations or examinations subject to the provisions of this section. If new information is presented, the immigration judge may hold a further hearing if necessary to consider any legal or factual issues, including issues relating to credibility, if relevant. The immigration judge shall then enter an order granting or denying the immigration relief sought.

(i) *Procedures when immigration relief granted.* At the time that the immigration judge or the Board grants any relief under this section that would entitle the respondent to a new document evidencing such relief, the decision granting such relief shall include advice that the respondent will need to contact an appropriate office of DHS. Information concerning DHS locations and local procedures for document preparation shall be routinely provided to EOIR and updated by DHS. Upon respondent's presentation of a final order from the immigration judge or the Board granting such relief and submission of any biometric and other information necessary, DHS shall prepare such documents in keeping with section 264 of the Act and regulations thereunder and other relevant law.

(j) *Voluntary departure.* The procedures of this section do not apply to the granting of voluntary departure prior to the conclusion of proceedings pursuant to 8 CFR 1240.26(b) or at the conclusion of proceedings pursuant to 8 CFR 1240.26(c). If DHS seeks a continuance in order to complete pending identity, law enforcement, or security investigations or examinations, the immigration judge may grant additional time in the exercise of discretion, and the 30-day period for the immigration judge to grant voluntary departure, as provided in § 1240.26(b)(1)(ii), shall be extended accordingly.

(k) *Custody hearings.* The foregoing provisions of this section do not apply to proceedings seeking the redetermination of conditions of custody of an alien during the pendency of immigration proceedings under section 236 of the Act. In scheduling an initial custody redetermination hearing, the immigration judge shall, to the extent practicable consistent with the expedited nature of such cases, take account of the brief initial period of time needed for DHS to conduct the automated portions of its identity, law enforcement, or security investigations or examinations with respect to aliens detained in connection with immigration proceedings. If at the time of the custody hearing DHS seeks a brief continuance in an appropriate case based on unresolved identity, law enforcement, or security investigations or examinations, the immigration judge in the exercise of discretion may grant one or more continuances for a limited period of time which is reasonable under the circumstances.

[70 FR 4753, Jan. 31, 2005]

Subpart D [Reserved]

Subpart E—List of Pro Bono Legal Service Providers

SOURCE: 62 FR 9073, Feb. 28, 1997, unless otherwise noted.

§ 1003.61 General provisions.

(a) *Definitions*—(1) *Director.* Director means the Director of the Executive Office for Immigration Review (EOIR), pursuant to 8 CFR 1001.1(o), and shall also include any office or official within EOIR to whom the Director delegates authority with respect to subpart E of this part.

(2) *Pro bono legal services.* Pro bono legal services are those uncompensated legal services performed for indigent individuals or the public good without any expectation of either direct or indirect remuneration, including referral fees (other than filing fees or photocopying and mailing expenses), although a representative may be regularly compensated by the firm, organization, or pro bono referral service with which he or she is associated.

(3) *Organization.* A non-profit religious, charitable, social service, or similar group established in the United States.

(4) *Pro bono referral service.* A referral service, offered by a non-profit group, association, or similar organization established in the United States that assists persons in locating pro bono representation by making case referrals to attorneys or organizations that are available to provide pro bono representation.

(5) *Provider.* Any organization, pro bono referral service, or attorney whose name is included on the List of Pro Bono Legal Service Providers.

(b) *Authority.* The Director shall maintain a list, known as the List of Pro Bono Legal Service Providers (List), of organizations, pro bono referral services, and attorneys qualified under this subpart to provide pro bono legal services in immigration proceedings. The List, which shall be updated not less than quarterly, shall be provided to individuals in removal and other proceedings before an immigration court.

(c) *Qualification.* An organization, pro bono referral service, or attorney qualifies to be included on the List if the eligibility requirements under § 1003.62 and the application procedures under § 1003.63 are met.

(d) *Organizations.* Approval of an organization's application to be included on the List under this subpart is not equivalent to recognition under part 1292 of this chapter. Recognition under part 1292 of this chapter does not constitute a successful application for purposes of the List.

[80 FR 59510, Oct. 1, 2015]

§ 1003.62 Eligibility.

(a) *Organizations recognized under part 1292.* An organization that is recognized under part 1292 of this chapter is eligible to apply to have its name included on the List if the organization meets the requirements in paragraphs (a)(1) through (3) of this section.

(1) The organization will provide a minimum of 50 hours per year of pro bono legal services to individuals at each immigration court location where the organization intends to be included on the List, in cases where an attorney or representative of the organization, or an attorney or representative to whom the organization has referred the case for pro bono representation, files a Form EOIR–28 Notice of Entry of Appearance as Attorney or Representative before the Immigration Court (EOIR–28 Notice of Entry of Appearance). When an attorney or representative of the organization represents the individual pro bono before the immigration court location, the organization may count, toward the 50-hour requirement, the attorney's or representative's out-of-court preparation time and in-court time. When the organization refers the case for pro bono legal services outside the organization, the organization may count, toward the 50-hour requirement, time the organization's attorneys and representatives spent providing pro bono legal services, for example conducting an intake interview or mentoring the attorney or representative to whom the case is referred. However, the organization is not permitted to count the time of the attorney or representative to whom the case was referred.

(2) The organization has on its staff at least one attorney, as defined in § 1292.1(a)(1) of this chapter, or at least one representative accredited under part 1292 of this chapter, to practice before the immigration courts and the Board of Immigration Appeals.

(3) No attorney or representative who will provide pro bono legal services on the organization's behalf in cases pending before EOIR is the subject of an order of disbarment under § 1003.101(a)(1) or suspension under § 1003.101(a)(2).

(b) *Organizations not recognized under part 1292.* An organization that is not recognized under part 1292 of this chapter is eligible to apply to have its name included on the List if the organization meets the requirements in paragraphs (b)(1) through (3) of this section.

(1) The organization will provide a minimum of 50 hours per year of pro bono legal services to individuals at each immigration court location where the organization intends to be included on the List, in cases where an attorney or representative of the organization, or an attorney or representative to whom the organization has referred the case for pro bono representation, files a Form EOIR–28 Notice of Entry of Appearance. When an attorney or representative of the organization represents the individual pro bono before the immigration court location, the organization may count, toward the 50-hour requirement, the attorney's or representative's out-of-court preparation time and in-court time. When the organization refers the case for pro bono legal services outside the organization, the organization may count, toward the 50-hour requirement, time the organization's attorneys or representatives spent providing pro bono legal services, for example conducting an intake interview or mentoring the attorney or representative to whom the case is referred. However, the organization is not permitted to count the time of the attorney or representative to whom the case was referred.

(2) The organization has on its staff at least one attorney, as defined in § 1292.1(a)(1) of this chapter.

(3) No attorney or representative who will provide pro bono legal services on the organization's behalf in cases pending before EOIR is the subject of an order of disbarment under

§ 1003.101(a)(1) or suspension under § 1003.101(a)(2).

(c) *Pro bono referral services*. A referral service is eligible to apply to have its name included on the List at each immigration court location where the referral service either refers or plans to refer cases to attorneys or organizations that will provide pro bono legal services to individuals in proceedings before an immigration judge.

(d) *Attorneys*. An attorney, as defined in § 1292.1(a)(1) of this chapter, is eligible to apply to have his or her name included on the List if the attorney meets the requirements in paragraphs (d)(1) through (3) of this section.

(1) The attorney is not the subject of an order of disbarment under § 1003.101(a)(1) or suspension under § 1003.101(a)(2);

(2) The attorney will provide a minimum of 50 hours per year of pro bono legal services to individuals at each immigration court location where the attorney intends to be included on the List, in cases where he or she files a Form EOIR–28 Notice of Entry of Appearance. The attorney may count, toward the requirement, both out-of-court preparation time and in-court time.

(3) The attorney cannot provide pro bono legal services through or in association with an organization or pro bono referral service described in paragraph (a), (b), or (c) of this section because:

(i) Such an organization or referral service is unavailable; or

(ii) The range of services provided by an available organization(s) or referral service(s) is insufficient to address the needs of the community.

[80 FR 59510, Oct. 1, 2015]

§ 1003.63 Applications.

(a) *Generally*. To be included on the List, any organization, pro bono referral service, or attorney that is eligible under § 1003.62 to apply to be included on the List must file an application with the Director. Applications must be received by the Director at least 60 days in advance of the quarterly update in order to be considered. The application must:

(1) Establish by clear and convincing evidence that the applicant qualifies to be on the List pursuant to § 1003.61(c);

(2) Specify how the organization, pro bono referral service, or attorney wants its name and contact information to be set forth on the List; and

(3) Identify each immigration court location where the organization, pro bono referral service, or attorney provides, or plans to provide, pro bono legal services.

(b) *Organizations*. An organization, whether recognized or not under part 1292, must submit with its application a declaration signed by an authorized officer of the organization that states under penalty of perjury:

(1) That it will provide annually at least 50 hours of pro bono legal services to individuals in removal or other proceedings before each immigration court location identified in its application;

(2) That every attorney and accredited representative who will represent clients pro bono before EOIR on behalf of the organization is registered to practice before EOIR under § 1292.1(f);

(3) That no attorney or representative who will provide pro bono legal services on behalf of the organization in cases pending before EOIR:

(i) Is under any order suspending, enjoining, restraining, disbarring, or otherwise restricting him or her in the practice of law; or

(ii) Is the subject of an order of disbarment under § 1003.101(a)(1) or suspension under § 1003.101(a)(2); and

(4) Any specific limitations it has in providing pro bono legal services (e.g., not available to assist detained individuals or those with criminal convictions, or available for asylum cases only).

(c) *Pro bono referral services*. A pro bono referral service must submit with its application a declaration signed by an authorized officer of the referral service that states under penalty of perjury:

(1) That it will offer its referral services to individuals in removal or other proceedings before each immigration court location identified in its application; and

(2) Any specific limitations it has in providing its pro bono referral services

(e.g., not available to assist detained individuals or those with criminal convictions, or available only for asylum cases).

(d) *Attorneys.* An attorney must submit with his or her application a declaration that states under penalty of perjury:

(1) That he or she will provide annually at least 50 hours of pro bono legal services to individuals in removal or other proceedings before each immigration court location identified in his or her application;

(2) Any specific limitations the attorney has in providing pro bono legal services (e.g., not available to assist detained individuals or those with criminal convictions, or available for asylum cases only);

(3) A description of the good-faith efforts he or she made to provide pro bono legal services through an organization or pro bono referral service described in §1003.62(a), (b), or (c) to individuals appearing before each immigration court location listed in the application;

(4) An explanation that any such organization or referral service is unavailable or that the range of services provided by available organization(s) or referral service(s) is insufficient to address the needs of the community;

(5) His or her EOIR registration number;

(6) That he or she is not under any order suspending, enjoining, restraining, disbarring, or otherwise restricting him or her in the practice of law; and

(7) That he or she is not the subject of an order of disbarment under §1003.101(a)(1) or suspension under §1003.101(a)(2).

(e) *Applications approved before* November 30, 2015. Providers whose applications to be included on the List were approved before November 30, 2015 must file an application under this section as follows: Organizations and pro bono referral services, within one year of November 30, 2015; attorneys, within six months of November 30, 2015. The names of providers who do not file an application as required by this paragraph shall be removed from the List following expiration of the application time period, the removal of which will be reflected no later than in the next quarterly update.

(f) *Notice and comments*—(1) *Public notice and comment.* The names of the applicants, whether organizations, pro bono referral services, or individuals, meeting the regulatory requirements to be included on the List shall be publicly posted for 15 days after review of the applications by the Director, and upon request a copy of each application shall be made available for public review. Any individual may forward to the Director comments or a recommendation for approval or disapproval of an application within 30 days from the first date the name of the applicant is publicly posted. The commenting party shall include his or her name and address. A comment or recommendation may be sent to the Director electronically, in which case the Director shall transmit the comment or recommendation to the applicant. A comment or recommendation not sent to the Director electronically must include proof of service on the applicant, in accordance with the definition of "service" set forth in §1003.13.

(2) *Response.* The applicant has 15 days to respond from the date the applicant was served with, or notified by the Director of, the comment. All responses must be filed with the Director and include proof of service of a copy of such response on the commenting party, in accordance with the definition of "service" set forth in §1003.13.

[80 FR 59511, Oct. 1, 2015]

§ 1003.64 Approval and denial of applications.

(a) *Authority.* The Director in his discretion shall have the authority to approve or deny an application to be included on the List of Pro Bono Legal Service Providers. The Director may request additional information from the applicant to determine whether the applicant qualifies to be included on the List.

(b) *Decision.* The applicant shall be notified of the decision in writing. The written notice shall be served in accordance with the definition of "service" set forth in §1003.13, at the address provided on the application unless the applicant subsequently provides a change of address pursuant to §1003.66, or shall be transmitted to the applicant electronically.

(1) *Denials.* If the application is denied, the applicant shall be given a written explanation of the grounds for such denial, and the decision shall be final. Such denial shall be without prejudice to file another application at any time after the next quarterly publication of the List.

(2) *Approval and continuing qualification.* If the application is approved, the applicant's name will be included on the List at the next quarterly update. Every three years from the date of approval, a provider must file with the Director a declaration, under penalty of perjury, stating that the provider remains qualified to be included on the List under § 1003.62(a), (b), (c), or (d). For organizations and attorneys, the declaration must include alien registration numbers of clients in whose cases the provider rendered pro bono legal services under § 1003.62(a)(1), (b)(1), or (d)(2), representing at least 50 hours of pro bono legal services each year since the provider's most recent such declaration, or since the provider was included on the List, whichever was more recent. Organizations must provide, for each case listed, the name of the organization's attorneys or representatives who provided representation or other pro bono legal services, or the name of the attorney, representative, or organization the case was referred to for pro bono legal services. If a provider fails to timely file the declaration or declares that it is no longer qualified to be included on the List, the provider's name will be removed from the List at the next quarterly update. Failure to file a declaration within the applicable time period does not prohibit the filing of a new application to be included on the List.

[80 FR 59512, Oct. 1, 2015]

§ 1003.65 Removal of a provider from the List.

(a) *Automatic removal.* If the Director determines that an attorney on the List is the subject of a final order of disbarment under § 1003.101(a)(1), or an order of suspension under § 1003.101(a)(2), then the Director shall:

(1) Remove the name of the attorney from the List no later than at the next quarterly update; and

(2) Notify the attorney of such removal in writing, at the last known address given by the provider or electronically.

(b) *Requests for removal.* (1) Any provider may, at any time, submit a written request to have the provider's name removed from the List. The written request may include an explanation for the voluntary removal. Upon such written request, the name of the provider shall be removed from the List, and such removal will be reflected no later than in the next quarterly update.

(2) Any provider removed from the List at the provider's request may seek reinstatement to the List upon written notice to the Director. Any request for reinstatement must include a new declaration of eligibility, as set forth under § 1003.63(b), (c), or (d). Reinstatement to the List is at the sole discretion of the Director. Upon the Director's approval of reinstatement, the provider's name shall be included on the List no later than in the next quarterly update. Reinstatement to the List does not affect the requirement under § 1003.64(b)(2) that a provider submit a new declaration of eligibility every three years from the date of the approval of the original application to be included on the List.

(c) *EOIR inquiry in response to complaints.* If EOIR receives complaints that a particular provider on the List may no longer be accepting new pro bono clients, the Director may send a written inquiry to the provider noting that EOIR has received complaints with regard to the provider's acceptance of pro bono clients and allowing an opportunity for the provider to state whether the provider is continuing to comply with the regulations in this subpart or, if appropriate, whether the provider wishes to request voluntary removal from the List as provided in paragraph (b) of this section. The Director may remove a provider from the List for failure to respond to a written inquiry issued under this paragraph within 30 days or such additional time period stated by the Director in the written inquiry.

(d) *Procedures for removing providers from the List.* The following provisions apply in cases not covered by paragraphs (a), (b), or (c) of this section.

(1) *Grounds.* A provider shall be removed from the List if it, he, or she:

(i) Fails to comply with § 1003.66;

(ii) Has filed a false declaration in connection with an application filed pursuant to § 1003.63;

(iii) Improperly uses the List primarily to advertise or solicit clients for compensated legal services; or

(iv) Fails to comply with any and all other requirements of this subpart.

(2) *Notice.* If the Director determines that a provider falls within one or more of the enumerated grounds under paragraph (d)(1) of this section, the Director shall promptly notify the provider in writing, at the address last provided to the Director by the provider or electronically, of the Director's intention to remove the name of the provider from the List.

(3) *Response.* The provider may submit a written answer within 30 days from the date the notice is served, as described in § 1003.13, or is sent to the provider electronically. The provider must establish by clear and convincing evidence that the provider continues to meet the qualifications for inclusion on the List, by declaration under penalty of perjury as to the provider's continued compliance with eligibility requirements under this subchapter, which must include alien registration numbers of clients in whose cases the provider rendered pro bono legal services under § 1003.62(a)(1), (b)(2), or (d)(2), representing at least 50 hours of pro bono legal services each year since the provider's most recent declaration under § 1003.64(b)(2), or since the provider was included on the List, whichever was more recent.

(4) *Decision.* If, after consideration of any response submitted by the provider, the Director determines that the provider is no longer qualified to remain on the List, the Director shall:

(i) Remove the name of the provider from the List no later than in the next quarterly update; and

(ii) Notify the provider of such removal in writing, at the address last provided to the Director by the provider or electronically.

(5) *Disciplinary Action.* Removal from the List pursuant to § 1003.65(a), (b), (c), or (d) shall be without prejudice to the authority to discipline a practitioner under EOIR's rules and procedures for professional conduct for practitioners listed in 8 CFR part 1003, subpart G.

[80 FR 59512, Oct. 1, 2015]

§ 1003.66 Changes in information or status.

All providers with a pending application or currently on the List must notify the Director in writing within ten business days if:

(a) The provider's contact information has changed;

(b) Any specific limitations in providing pro bono legal services under § 1003.63(b)(4), (c)(2), or (d)(2) have changed; or

(c) The provider is no longer eligible under § 1003.62.

[80 FR 59513, Oct. 1, 2015]

Subpart F [Reserved]

Subpart G—Professional Conduct for Practitioners—Rules and Procedures

SOURCE: 65 FR 39526, June 27, 2000, unless otherwise noted.

§ 1003.101 General provisions.

(a) *Authority to sanction.* An adjudicating official or the Board of Immigration Appeals (the Board) may impose disciplinary sanctions against any practitioner if it finds it to be in the public interest to do so. It will be in the public interest to impose disciplinary sanctions against a practitioner who is authorized to practice before the Board and the Immigration Courts when such person has engaged in criminal, unethical, or unprofessional conduct, or in frivolous behavior, as set forth in § 1003.102. In accordance with the disciplinary proceedings set forth in this subpart and outlined below, an adjudicating official or the Board may impose any of the following disciplinary sanctions:

(1) Disbarment, which is permanent, from practice before the Board and the

Immigration Courts or the DHS, or before all three authorities;

(2) Suspension, including immediate suspension, from practice before the Board and the Immigration Courts or the DHS, or before all three authorities;

(3) Public or private censure; or

(4) Such other disciplinary sanctions as the adjudicating official or the Board deems appropriate.

(b) *Persons subject to sanctions.* Persons subject to sanctions include any practitioner. A practitioner is any attorney as defined in § 1001.1(f) of this chapter who does not represent the federal government, or any representative as defined in § 1001.1(j) of this chapter. Attorneys employed by the Department of Justice shall be subject to discipline pursuant to § 1003.109. Nothing in this regulation shall be construed as authorizing persons who do not meet the definition of practitioner to represent individuals before the Board and the Immigration Courts or the DHS.

(c) The administrative termination of a representative's accreditation under 8 CFR 1292.17 after the issuance of a Notice of Intent to Discipline pursuant to § 1003.105(a)(1) shall not preclude the continuation of disciplinary proceedings and the imposition of sanctions, unless counsel for the government moves to withdraw the Notice of Intent to Discipline and the adjudicating official or the Board grants the motion.

[65 FR 39526, June 27, 2000, as amended at 73 FR 76923, Dec. 18, 2008; 77 FR 2014, Jan. 13, 2012; 81 FR 92362, Dec. 19, 2016]

§ 1003.102 Grounds.

It is deemed to be in the public interest for an adjudicating official or the Board to impose disciplinary sanctions against any practitioner who falls within one or more of the categories enumerated in this section, but these categories do not constitute the exclusive grounds for which disciplinary sanctions may be imposed in the public interest. Nothing in this regulation should be read to denigrate the practitioner's duty to represent zealously his or her client within the bounds of the law. A practitioner who falls within one of the following categories shall be subject to disciplinary sanctions in the public interest if he or she:

(a) Charges or receives, either directly or indirectly:

(1) In the case of an attorney, any fee or compensation for specific services rendered for any person that shall be deemed to be grossly excessive. The factors to be considered in determining whether a fee or compensation is grossly excessive include the following: The time and labor required, the novelty and difficulty of the questions involved, and the skill requisite to perform the legal service properly; the likelihood, if apparent to the client, that the acceptance of the particular employment will preclude other employment by the attorney; the fee customarily charged in the locality for similar legal services; the amount involved and the results obtained; the time limitations imposed by the client or by the circumstances; the nature and length of the professional relationship with the client; and the experience, reputation, and ability of the attorney or attorneys performing the services,

(2) In the case of an accredited representative as defined in § 1292.1(a)(4) of this chapter, any fee or compensation for specific services rendered for any person, except that an accredited representative may be regularly compensated by the organization of which he or she is an accredited representative, or

(3) In the case of a law student or law graduate as defined in § 1292.1(a)(2) of this chapter, any fee or compensation for specific services rendered for any person, except that a law student or law graduate may be regularly compensated by the organization or firm with which he or she is associated as long as he or she is appearing without direct or indirect remuneration from the client he or she represents;

(b) Bribes, attempts to bribe, coerces, or attempts to coerce, by any means whatsoever, any person (including a party to a case or an officer or employee of the Department of Justice) to commit any act or to refrain from performing any act in connection with any case;

(c) Knowingly or with reckless disregard makes a false statement of material fact or law, or willfully misleads, misinforms, threatens, or deceives any person (including a party to a case or an officer or employee of the Department of Justice), concerning any material and relevant matter relating to a case, including knowingly or with reckless disregard offering false evidence. If a practitioner has offered material evidence and comes to know of its falsity, the practitioner shall take appropriate remedial measures;

(d) Solicits professional employment, through in-person or live telephone contact or through the use of runners, from a prospective client with whom the practitioner has no family or prior professional relationship, when a significant motive for the practitioner's doing so is the practitioner's pecuniary gain. If the practitioner has no family or prior professional relationship with the prospective client known to be in need of legal services in a particular matter, the practitioner must include the words "Advertising Material" on the outside of the envelope of any written communication and at the beginning and ending of any recorded communication. Such advertising material or similar solicitation documents may not be distributed by any person in or around the premises of any building in which an Immigration Court is located;

(e) Is subject to a final order of disbarment or suspension, or has resigned while a disciplinary investigation or proceeding is pending;

(f) Knowingly or with reckless disregard makes a false or misleading communication about his or her qualifications or services. A communication is false or misleading if it:

(1) Contains a material misrepresentation of fact or law, or omits a fact necessary to make the statement considered as a whole not materially misleading, or,

(2) Contains an assertion about the practitioner or the practitioner's qualifications or services that cannot be substantiated. A practitioner shall not state or imply that the practitioner has been recognized or certified as a specialist in immigration or nationality law unless such certification is granted by the appropriate State regulatory authority or by an organization that has been approved by the appropriate State regulatory authority to grant such certification. An accredited representative shall not state or imply that the accredited representative:

(i) Is approved to practice before the Immigration Courts or the Board, if the representative is only approved as an accredited representative before DHS;

(ii) Is an accredited representative for an organization other than a recognized organization through which the representative acquired accreditation; or

(iii) Is an attorney.

(g) Engages in contumelious or otherwise obnoxious conduct, with regard to a case in which he or she acts in a representative capacity, which would constitute contempt of court in a judicial proceeding;

(h) Has been found guilty of, or pleaded guilty or *nolo contendere* to, a serious crime, in any court of the United States, or of any state, possession, territory, commonwealth, or the District of Columbia. A serious crime includes any felony and also includes any lesser crime, a necessary element of which, as determined by the statutory or common law definition of such crime in the jurisdiction where the judgment was entered, involves interference with the administration of justice, false swearing, misrepresentation, fraud, willful failure to file income tax returns, deceit, dishonesty, bribery, extortion, misappropriation, theft, or an attempt, or a conspiracy or solicitation of another, to commit a serious crime. A plea or verdict of guilty or a conviction after a plea of *nolo contendere* is deemed to be a conviction within the meaning of this section;

(i) Knowingly or with reckless disregard falsely certifies a copy of a document as being a true and complete copy of an original;

(j) Engages in frivolous behavior in a proceeding before an Immigration Court, the Board, or any other administrative appellate body under title II of the Immigration and Nationality Act, provided:

(1) A practitioner engages in frivolous behavior when he or she knows or reasonably should have known that his

or her actions lack an arguable basis in law or in fact, or are taken for an improper purpose, such as to harass or to cause unnecessary delay. Actions that, if taken improperly, may be subject to disciplinary sanctions include, but are not limited to, the making of an argument on any factual or legal question, the submission of an application for discretionary relief, the filing of a motion, or the filing of an appeal. The signature of a practitioner on any filing, application, motion, appeal, brief, or other document constitutes certification by the signer that the signer has read the filing, application, motion, appeal, brief, or other document and that, to the best of the signer's knowledge, information, and belief, formed after inquiry reasonable under the circumstances, the document is well-grounded in fact and is warranted by existing law or by a good faith argument for the extension, modification, or reversal of existing law or the establishment of new law, and is not interposed for any improper purpose.

(2) The imposition of disciplinary sanctions for frivolous behavior under this section in no way limits the authority of the Board to dismiss an appeal summarily pursuant to § 1003.1(d);

(k) Engages in conduct that constitutes ineffective assistance of counsel, as previously determined in a finding by the Board, an immigration judge in an immigration proceeding, or a Federal court judge or panel, and a disciplinary complaint is filed within one year of the finding;

(l) Repeatedly fails to appear for prehearing conferences, scheduled hearings, or case-related meetings in a timely manner without good cause;

(m) Assists any person, other than a practitioner as defined in § 1003.101(b), in the performance of activity that constitutes the unauthorized practice of law. The practice of law before EOIR means engaging in *practice* or *preparation* as those terms are defined in §§ 1001.1(i) and (k);

(n) Engages in conduct that is prejudicial to the administration of justice or undermines the integrity of the adjudicative process. Conduct that will generally be subject to sanctions under this ground includes any action or inaction that seriously impairs or interferes with the adjudicative process when the practitioner should have reasonably known to avoid such conduct;

(o) Fails to provide competent representation to a client. Competent representation requires the legal knowledge, skill, thoroughness, and preparation reasonably necessary for the representation. Competent handling of a particular matter includes inquiry into and analysis of the factual and legal elements of the problem, and use of methods and procedures meeting the standards of competent practitioners;

(p) Fails to abide by a client's decisions concerning the objectives of representation and fails to consult with the client as to the means by which they are to be pursued, in accordance with paragraph (r) of this section. A practitioner may take such action on behalf of the client as is impliedly authorized to carry out the representation;

(q) Fails to act with reasonable diligence and promptness in representing a client.

(1) A practitioner's workload must be controlled and managed so that each matter can be handled competently.

(2) A practitioner has the duty to act with reasonable promptness. This duty includes, but shall not be limited to, complying with all time and filing limitations. This duty, however, does not preclude the practitioner from agreeing to a reasonable request for a postponement that will not prejudice the practitioner's client.

(3) A practitioner should carry through to conclusion all matters undertaken for a client, consistent with the scope of representation as previously determined by the client and practitioner, unless the client terminates the relationship or the practitioner obtains permission to withdraw in compliance with applicable rules and regulations. If a practitioner has handled a proceeding that produced a result adverse to the client and the practitioner and the client have not agreed that the practitioner will handle the matter on appeal, the practitioner must consult with the client about the client's appeal rights and the terms and conditions of possible representation on appeal;

(r) Fails to maintain communication with the client throughout the duration of the client-practitioner relationship. It is the obligation of the practitioner to take reasonable steps to communicate with the client in a language that the client understands. A practitioner is only under the obligation to attempt to communicate with his or her client using addresses or phone numbers known to the practitioner. In order to properly maintain communication, the practitioner should:

(1) Promptly inform and consult with the client concerning any decision or circumstance with respect to which the client's informed consent is reasonably required;

(2) Reasonably consult with the client about the means by which the client's objectives are to be accomplished. Reasonable consultation with the client includes the duty to meet with the client sufficiently in advance of a hearing or other matter to ensure adequate preparation of the client's case and compliance with applicable deadlines;

(3) Keep the client reasonably informed about the status of the matter, such as significant developments affecting the timing or the substance of the representation; and

(4) Promptly comply with reasonable requests for information, except that when a prompt *response* is not feasible, the practitioner, or a member of the practitioner's staff, should acknowledge receipt of the request and advise the client when a *response* may be expected;

(s) Fails to disclose to the adjudicator legal authority in the controlling jurisdiction known to the practitioner to be directly adverse to the position of the client and not disclosed by opposing counsel;

(t) Fails to submit a signed and completed Notice of Entry of Appearance as Attorney or Representative in compliance with applicable rules and regulations when the practitioner:

(1) Has engaged in *practice* or *preparation* as those terms are defined in §§ 1001.1(i) and (k), and

(2) Has been deemed to have engaged in a pattern or practice of failing to submit such forms, in compliance with applicable rules and regulations. Notwithstanding the foregoing, in each case where the respondent is represented, every pleading, application, motion, or other filing shall be signed by the practitioner of record in his or her individual name;

(u) Repeatedly files notices, motions, briefs, or claims that reflect little or no attention to the specific factual or legal issues applicable to a client's case, but rather rely on boilerplate language indicative of a substantial failure to competently and diligently represent the client; or

(v) Acts outside the scope of the representative's approved authority as an accredited representative.

[65 FR 39526, June 27, 2000, as amended at 73 FR 76923, Dec. 18, 2008, 81 FR 92362, Dec. 19, 2016]

§ 1003.103 Immediate suspension and summary disciplinary proceedings; duty of practitioner to notify EOIR of conviction or discipline.

(a) *Immediate Suspension*—(1) *Petition.* The EOIR disciplinary counsel shall file a petition with the Board to suspend immediately from practice before the Board and the Immigration Courts any practitioner who has been found guilty of, or pleaded guilty or nolo contendere to, a serious crime, as defined in § 1003.102(h), or any practitioner who has been suspended or disbarred by, or while a disciplinary investigation or proceeding is pending has resigned from, the highest court of any State, possession, territory, or Commonwealth of the United States, or the District of Columbia, or any Federal court, or who has been placed on an interim suspension pending a final resolution of the underlying disciplinary matter.

(2) DHS petition. DHS may file a petition with the Board to suspend immediately from practice before DHS any practitioner described in paragraph (a)(1) of this section. See 8 CFR 292.3(c).

(3) Copy of petition. A copy of a petition filed by the EOIR disciplinary counsel shall be forwarded to DHS, which may submit a written request to the Board that entry of any order immediately suspending a practitioner before the Board or the Immigration Courts also apply to the practitioner's authority to practice before DHS. A copy of a petition filed by DHS shall be

forwarded to the EOIR disciplinary counsel, who may submit a written request to the Board that entry of any order immediately suspending a practitioner before DHS also apply to the practitioner's authority to practice before the Board and Immigration Courts. Proof of service on the practitioner of any request to broaden the scope of an immediate suspension or proposed discipline must be filed with the Board or the adjudicating official.

(4) *Immediate suspension.* Upon the filing of a petition for immediate suspension pursuant to §§ 1003.103(a)(1) or 1003.103(a)(2), together with a certified copy of a court record finding that a practitioner has been found guilty of, or pleaded guilty or nolo contendere to, a serious crime, or has been disciplined or has resigned, as described in paragraph (a)(1) of this section, the Board shall forthwith enter an order immediately suspending the practitioner from practice before the Board, the Immigration Courts, and/or DHS, notwithstanding the pendency of an appeal, if any, of the underlying disciplinary proceeding, pending final disposition of a summary disciplinary proceeding as provided in paragraph (b) of this section. Such immediate suspension will continue until imposition of a final administrative decision. If an immediate suspension is imposed upon a practitioner, the Board may require that notice of such suspension be posted at the Board, the Immigration Courts, or DHS. Upon good cause shown, the Board may set aside such order of immediate suspension when it appears in the interest of justice to do so. If a final administrative decision includes the imposition of a period of suspension, time spent by the practitioner under immediate suspension pursuant to this paragraph may be credited toward the period of suspension imposed under the final administrative decision.

(b) *Summary disciplinary proceedings.* The EOIR disciplinary counsel (or DHS pursuant to 8 CFR 292.3(c)(3)) shall promptly initiate summary disciplinary proceedings against any practitioner described in paragraph (a) of this section by the issuance of a Notice of Intent to Discipline, upon receipt of a certified copy of the order, judgment, or record evidencing the underlying criminal conviction, discipline, or resignation, and accompanied by a certified copy of such document. However, delays in initiation of summary disciplinary proceedings under this section will not impact an immediate suspension imposed pursuant to paragraph (a) of this section. Summary proceedings shall be conducted in accordance with the provisions set forth in §§ 1003.105 and 1003.106. Any such summary proceeding shall not be concluded until all direct appeals from an underlying criminal conviction shall have been completed.

(1) In matters concerning criminal convictions, a certified copy of the court record, docket entry, or plea shall be conclusive evidence of the commission of the crime in any summary disciplinary proceeding based thereon.

(2) In the case of a summary proceeding based upon a final order of disbarment or suspension, or a resignation while a disciplinary investigation or proceeding is pending (*i.e.*, reciprocal discipline), a certified copy of a judgment or order of discipline shall establish a rebuttable presumption of the professional misconduct. Disciplinary sanctions shall follow in such a proceeding unless the attorney can rebut the presumption by demonstrating clear and convincing evidence that:

(i) The underlying disciplinary proceeding was so lacking in notice or opportunity to be heard as to constitute a deprivation of due process;

(ii) There was such an infirmity of proof establishing the attorney's professional misconduct as to give rise to the clear conviction that the adjudicating official could not, consistent with his or her duty, accept as final the conclusion on that subject; or

(iii) The imposition of discipline by the adjudicating official would result in grave injustice.

(c) *Duty of practitioner and recognized organizations to notify EOIR of conviction or discipline.* A practitioner and if applicable, the authorized officer of each recognized organization with which a practitioner is affiliated must notify the EOIR disciplinary counsel within 30 days of the issuance of the initial order, even if an appeal of the conviction or discipline is pending, when the practitioner has been found guilty of, or pleaded guilty or nolo contendere to, a serious crime, as defined in § 1003.102(h), or has been disbarred or suspended by, or while a disciplinary investigation or proceeding is pending has resigned from, the highest court of any State, possession, territory or Commonwealth of the United States, or the District of Columbia, or any Federal court. A practitioner's failure to do so may result in an immediate suspension as set forth in paragraph (a) of this section and other final discipline. An organization's failure to do so may result in the administrative termination of its recognition for violating the reporting requirement under 8 CFR 1292.14. This duty to notify applies only to convictions for serious crimes and to orders imposing discipline for professional misconduct entered on or after August 28, 2000.

[65 FR 39526, June 27, 2000, as amended at 73 FR 76923, Dec. 18, 2008; 77 FR 2014, Jan. 13, 2012; 81 FR 92362, Dec. 19, 2016]

§ 1003.104 Filing of complaints; preliminary inquiries; resolutions; referral of complaints.

(a) *Filing complaints*—(1) *Practitioners authorized to practice before the Board and the Immigration Courts.* Complaints of criminal, unethical, or unprofessional conduct, or of frivolous behavior by a practitioner who is authorized to practice before the Board and the Immigration Courts shall be filed with the EOIR disciplinary counsel. Disciplinary complaints must be submitted in writing and must state in detail the information that supports the basis for the complaint, including, but not limited to, the names and addresses of the complainant and the practitioner, the date(s) of the conduct or behavior, the nature of the conduct or behavior, the individuals involved, the harm or damages sustained by the complainant, and any other relevant information. Any individual may file a complaint with the EOIR disciplinary counsel using the Form EOIR–44. The EOIR disciplinary counsel shall notify DHS of any disciplinary complaint that pertains, in whole or part, to a matter before DHS.

(2) *Practitioners authorized to practice before DHS.* Complaints of criminal, unethical, or unprofessional conduct, or frivolous behavior by a practitioner who is authorized to practice before DHS shall be filed with DHS pursuant to the procedures set forth in § 292.3(d) of this chapter.

(b) *Preliminary inquiry.* Upon receipt of a disciplinary complaint or on its own initiative, the EOIR disciplinary counsel will initiate a preliminary inquiry. If a complaint is filed by a client or former client, the complainant thereby waives the attorney-client privilege and any other privilege relating to the representation to the extent necessary to conduct a preliminary inquiry and any subsequent proceedings based thereon. If the EOIR disciplinary counsel determines that a complaint is without merit, no further action will be taken. The EOIR disciplinary counsel may, in the disciplinary counsel's discretion, close a preliminary inquiry if the complainant fails to comply with reasonable requests for assistance, information, or documentation. The complainant and the practitioner shall be notified of any such determination in writing.

(c) *Resolution reached prior to the issuance of a Notice of Intent to Discipline.* The EOIR disciplinary counsel, in its discretion, may issue warning letters and admonitions, and may enter into agreements in lieu of discipline, prior to the issuance of a Notice of Intent to Discipline.

(d) *Referral of complaints of criminal conduct.* If the EOIR disciplinary counsel receives credible information or allegations that a practitioner has engaged in criminal conduct, the EOIR disciplinary counsel shall refer the matter to DHS or the appropriate United States Attorney and, if appropriate, to the Inspector General, the Federal Bureau of Investigation, or other law enforcement agency. In such cases, in making the decision to pursue disciplinary sanctions, the EOIR disciplinary counsel shall coordinate in advance with the appropriate investigative and prosecutorial authorities within the Department to ensure that neither the disciplinary process nor criminal prosecutions are jeopardized.

[65 FR 39526, June 27, 2000, as amended at 73 FR 76924, Dec. 18, 2008; 81 FR 92362, Dec. 19, 2016]

§ 1003.105 Notice of Intent to Discipline.

(a) *Issuance of Notice.* (1) If, upon completion of the preliminary inquiry, the EOIR disciplinary counsel determines that sufficient prima facie evidence exists to warrant charging a practitioner with professional misconduct as set forth in § 1003.102 or a recognized organization with misconduct as set forth in § 1003.110, the EOIR disciplinary counsel will file with the Board and issue to the practitioner or organization that was the subject of the preliminary inquiry a Notice of Intent to Discipline. In cases involving practitioners, service of the notice will be made upon the practitioner either by certified mail to the practitioner's last known address, as defined in paragraph (a)(2) of this section, or by personal delivery. In cases involving recognized organizations, service of the notice will be made upon the authorized officer of the organization either by certified mail at the address of the organization or by personal delivery. The notice shall contain a statement of the charge(s), a copy of the preliminary inquiry report, the proposed disciplinary sanctions to be imposed, the procedure for filing an answer or requesting a hearing, and the mailing address and telephone number of the Board. In summary disciplinary proceedings brought pursuant to § 1003.103(b), a preliminary inquiry report is not required to be filed with the Notice of Intent to Discipline. If a Notice of Intent to Discipline is filed against an accredited representative, the EOIR disciplinary counsel shall send a copy of the notice to the authorized officer of the recognized organization through which the representative is accredited at the address of the organization.

(2) For the purposes of this section, the last known address of a practitioner is the practitioner's address as it appears in EOIR's case management system if the practitioner is actively representing a party before EOIR on the date that the EOIR disciplinary counsel issues the Notice of Intent to Discipline. If the practitioner does not have a matter pending before EOIR on the date of the issuance of a Notice of Intent to Discipline, then the last known address for a practitioner will be as follows:

(i) Attorneys in the United States: the attorney's address that is on record with a state jurisdiction that licensed the attorney to practice law.

(ii) Accredited representatives: the address of a recognized organization with which the accredited representative is affiliated.

(iii) Accredited officials: the address of the embassy of the foreign government that employs the accredited official.

(iv) All other practitioners: the address for the practitioner that appears in EOIR's case management system for the most recent matter on which the practitioner represented a party.

(3) *DHS Issuance of Notice to practitioner.* DHS may file a Notice of Intent to Discipline with the Board in accordance with 8 CFR 292.3(e).

(b) *Copy of notice; reciprocity of discipline.* A copy of the Notice of Intent to Discipline filed by the EOIR disciplinary counsel shall be forwarded to DHS, which may submit a written request to the Board or the adjudicating official requesting that any discipline imposed upon a practitioner which restricts his or her authority to practice before the Board and the Immigration Courts also apply to the practitioner's authority to practice before DHS. A copy of the Notice of Intent to Discipline filed by DHS shall be forwarded to the EOIR disciplinary counsel, who may submit a written request to the Board or the adjudicating official requesting that any discipline imposed upon a practitioner that restricts his or her authority to practice before DHS also apply to the practitioner's authority to practice before the Board and the Immigration Courts. Proof of service on the practitioner of any request to broaden the scope of the proposed discipline must be filed with the adjudicating official.

(c) *Answer*—(1) *Filing.* The practitioner or, in cases involving a recognized organization, the organization, shall file a written answer to the Notice of Intent to Discipline with the Board within 30 days of the date of service of the Notice of Intent to Discipline unless, on motion to the Board, an extension of time to answer is granted for good cause. A motion for an extension of time to answer must be received by the Board no later than three (3) working days before the time to answer has expired. A copy of the answer and any such motion shall be served by the practitioner on the counsel for the government.

(2) *Contents.* The answer shall contain a statement of facts which constitute the grounds of defense and shall specifically admit or deny each allegation set forth in the Notice of Intent to Discipline. Every allegation in the Notice of Intent to Discipline which is not denied in the answer shall be deemed to be admitted and may be considered as proved, and no further evidence in respect of such allegation need be adduced. The practitioner or, in cases involving a recognized organization, the organization, may also state affirmatively special matters of defense and may submit supporting documents, including affidavits or statements, along with the answer.

(3) *Request for hearing.* The practitioner or, in cases involving a recognized organization, the organization, shall also state in the answer whether a hearing on the matter is requested. If no such request is made, the opportunity for a hearing will be deemed waived.

(d) *Failure to file an answer.* (1) Failure to file an answer within the time period prescribed in the Notice of Intent to Discipline, except where the time to answer is extended by the Board, shall constitute an admission of the allegations in the Notice of Intent to Discipline and no further evidence with respect to such allegations need be adduced.

(2) Upon such a default by the practitioner or, in cases involving a recognized organization, the organization, the counsel for the government shall submit to the Board proof of service of the Notice of Intent to Discipline. The practitioner or the organization shall be precluded thereafter from requesting a hearing on the matter. The Board shall issue a final order adopting the proposed disciplinary sanctions in the Notice of Intent to Discipline unless to do so would foster a tendency toward inconsistent dispositions for comparable conduct or would otherwise be unwarranted or not in the interests of justice. With the exception of cases in which the Board has already imposed an immediate suspension pursuant to § 1003.103 or that otherwise involve an accredited representative or recognized organization, any final order imposing discipline shall not become effective sooner than 15 days from the date of the order to provide the practitioner opportunity to comply with the terms of such order, including, but not limited to, withdrawing from any pending immigration matters and notifying immigration clients of the imposition of any sanction. Any final order imposing discipline against an accredited representative or recognized organization shall become effective immediately. A practitioner or a recognized organization may file a motion to set aside a final order of discipline issued pursuant to this paragraph, with service of such motion on counsel for the government, provided:

(i) Such a motion is filed within 15 days of the date of service of the final order; and

(ii) The practitioner's or the recognized organization's failure to file an answer was due to exceptional circumstances (such as serious illness of the practitioner or death of an immediate relative of the practitioner, but not including less compelling circumstances) beyond the control of the practitioner or the recognized organization.

[65 FR 39526, June 27, 2000, as amended at 73 FR 76925, Dec. 18, 2008; 77 FR 2014, Jan. 13, 2012; 81 FR 92362, Dec. 19, 2016]

§ 1003.106 Right to be heard and disposition.

(a) *Right to be heard*—(1) *Summary disciplinary proceedings.* A practitioner who is subject to summary disciplinary proceedings pursuant to § 1003.103(b) must make a prima facie showing to the Board in his or her answer that there is a material issue of fact in dispute with regard to the basis for summary disciplinary proceedings, or with one or more of the exceptions set forth in § 1003.103(b)(2)(i) through (iii). If the practitioner files a timely answer and the Board determines that there is a material issue of fact in dispute with regard to the basis for summary disciplinary proceedings, or with one or more of the exceptions set forth in § 1003.103(b)(2)(i) through (iii), then the Board shall refer the case to the Chief Immigration Judge for the appointment of an adjudicating official. If the practitioner fails to make such a prima facie showing, the Board shall retain jurisdiction over the case and issue a final order. Notwithstanding the foregoing, the Board shall refer any case to the Chief Immigration Judge for the appointment of an adjudicating official in which the practitioner has filed a timely answer and the case involves a charge or charges that cannot be adjudicated under the summary disciplinary proceedings provisions in § 1003.103(b). The Board shall refer such a case regardless of whether the practitioner has requested a hearing.

(2) *Procedure.* The procedures set forth in paragraphs (b) through (d) of this section apply to cases in which the practitioner or recognized organization files a timely answer to the Notice of Intent to Discipline, with the exception of cases in which the Board issues a final order pursuant to § 1003.105(d)(2) or § 1003.106(a)(1).

(i) The Chief Immigration Judge shall, upon the filing of an answer, appoint an Immigration Judge as an adjudicating official. At the request of the Chief Immigration Judge, the Chief Administrative Hearing Officer may appoint an Administrative Law Judge as an adjudicating official. The Director may appoint either an Immigration Judge or Administrative Law Judge as an adjudicating official if the Chief Immigration Judge or the Chief Administrative Hearing Officer does not appoint an adjudicating official or if the Director determines it is in the interest of efficiency to do so. An Immigration Judge or Administrative Law Judge shall not serve as the adjudicating official in any case in which the Judge is the complainant, in any case involving a practitioner who regularly appears before the Judge, or in any case involving a recognized organization whose representatives regularly appear before the Judge.

(ii) Upon the practitioner's or, in cases involving a recognized organization, the organization's, request for a hearing, the adjudicating official may designate the time and place of the hearing with due regard to the location of the practitioner's practice or residence or of the recognized organization, the convenience of witnesses, and any other relevant factors. When designating the time and place of a hearing, the adjudicating official shall provide for the service of a notice of hearing, as the term "service" is defined in § 1003.13, on the practitioner or the authorized officer of the recognized organization and the counsel for the government. The practitioner or the recognized organization shall be afforded adequate time to prepare a case in advance of the hearing. Pre-hearing conferences may be scheduled at the discretion of the adjudicating official in order to narrow issues, to obtain stipulations between the parties, to exchange information voluntarily, and otherwise to simplify and organize the proceeding. Settlement agreements reached after the issuance of a Notice of Intent to Discipline are subject to final approval by the adjudicating official or, if the practitioner or organization has not filed an answer, subject to final approval by the Board.

(iii) The practitioner or, in cases involving a recognized organization, the organization, may be represented by counsel at no expense to the government. Counsel for the practitioner or the organization shall file the appropriate Notice of Entry of Appearance (Form EOIR–27 or EOIR–28) in accordance with the procedures set forth in this part. Each party shall have a reasonable opportunity to examine and object to evidence presented by the other party, to present evidence, and to cross-examine witnesses presented by the other party. If the practitioner or the recognized organization files an answer but does not request a hearing, then the adjudicating official shall provide the parties an opportunity to submit briefs and evidence to support or refute any of the charges or affirmative defenses.

(iv) In rendering a decision, the adjudicating official shall consider the following: The complaint, the preliminary inquiry report, the Notice of Intent to Discipline, the answer, any supporting documents, and any other evidence, including pleadings, briefs, and other materials. Counsel for the government shall bear the burden of proving the grounds for disciplinary sanctions enumerated in the Notice of Intent to Discipline by clear and convincing evidence.

(v) The record of proceedings, regardless of whether an immigration judge or an administrative law judge is the adjudicating official, shall conform to the requirements of 8 CFR part 1003, subpart C and 8 CFR 1240.9. Disciplinary hearings shall be conducted in the same manner as Immigration Court proceedings as is appropriate, and shall be open to the public, except that:

(A) Depending upon physical facilities, the adjudicating official may place reasonable limitations upon the number of individuals in attendance at any one time, with priority being given to the press over the general public, and

(B) For the purposes of protecting witnesses, parties, or the public interest, the adjudicating official may limit attendance or hold a closed hearing.

(3) *Failure to appear in proceedings.* If the practitioner or, in cases involving a recognized organization, the organization, requests a hearing as provided in §1003.105(c)(3) but fails to appear, the adjudicating official shall then proceed and decide the case in the absence of the practitioner or the recognized organization in accordance with paragraph (b) of this section, based on the available record, including any additional evidence or arguments presented by the counsel for the government at the hearing. In such a proceeding the counsel for the government shall submit to the adjudicating official proof of service of the Notice of Intent to Discipline as well as the Notice of the Hearing. The practitioner or the recognized organization shall be precluded thereafter from participating further in the proceedings. A final order imposing discipline issued pursuant to this paragraph shall not be subject to further review, except that the practitioner or the recognized organization may file a motion to set aside the order, with service of such motion on counsel for the government, provided:

(i) Such a motion is filed within 15 days of the date of issuance of the final order; and

(ii) The practitioner's or the recognized organization's failure to appear was due to exceptional circumstances (such as serious illness of the practitioner or death of an immediate relative of the practitioner, but not including less compelling circumstances) beyond the control of the practitioner or the recognized organization.

(b) *Decision.* The adjudicating official shall consider the entire record and, as soon as practicable, render a decision. If the adjudicating official finds that one or more grounds for disciplinary sanctions enumerated in the Notice of Intent to Discipline have been established by clear and convincing evidence, the official shall rule that the disciplinary sanctions set forth in the Notice of Intent to Discipline be adopted, modified, or otherwise amended. If the adjudicating official determines that the practitioner should be suspended, the time period for such suspension shall be specified. If the adjudicating official determines that the organization's recognition should be revoked, the official may also identify the persons affiliated with the organization who were directly involved in the conduct that constituted the grounds for revocation. If the adjudicating official determines that the organization's recognition should be terminated, the official shall specify the time restriction, if any, before the organization may submit a new request for recognition. Any grounds for disciplinary sanctions enumerated in the Notice of Intent to Discipline that have not been established by clear and convincing evidence shall be dismissed. The adjudicating official shall provide for service of a written decision or memorandum summarizing an oral decision, as the term "service" is defined in §1003.13, on the practitioner or, in cases involving a recognized organization, on the authorized officer of the organization and on the counsel for the government. Except as provided in paragraph (a)(2) of this section, the adjudicating official's decision becomes final only upon waiver of appeal or expiration of the time for appeal to the Board, whichever comes first, and does not take effect during the pendency of an appeal to the Board as provided in § 1003.6. A final order imposing discipline against an accredited representative or recognized organization shall take effect immediately.

(c) *Appeal.* Upon issuance of a decision by the adjudicating official, either party or both parties may appeal to the Board to conduct a review pursuant to § 1003.1(d)(3). Parties must comply with all pertinent provisions for appeals to the Board, including provisions relating to forms and fees, as set forth in Part 1003, and must use Form EOIR–45. The decision of the Board is the final administrative order as provided in § 1003.1(d)(7), and shall be served upon the practitioner or, in cases involving a recognized organization, the organization, as provided in § 1003.1(f). With the exception of cases in which the Board has already imposed an immediate suspension pursuant to § 1003.103 or cases involving accredited representatives or recognized organizations, any final order imposing discipline shall not become effective sooner than 15 days from the date of the order to provide the practitioner opportunity to comply with the terms of such order, including, but not limited to, withdrawing from any pending immigration matters and notifying immigration clients of the imposition of any sanction. A final order imposing discipline against an accredited representative or recognized organization shall take effect immediately. A copy of the final administrative order of the Board shall be served upon the counsel for the government. If disciplinary sanctions are imposed against a practitioner or a recognized organization (other than a private censure), the Board may require that notice of such sanctions be posted at the Board, the Immigration Courts, or DHS for the period of time during which the sanctions are in effect, or for any other period of time as determined by the Board.

(d) *Referral.* In addition to, or in lieu of, initiating disciplinary proceedings against a practitioner, the EOIR disciplinary counsel may notify an appropriate Federal or state disciplinary or regulatory authority of any complaint filed against a practitioner. Any final administrative decision imposing sanctions against a practitioner (other than a private censure) shall be reported to any such disciplinary or regulatory authority in every jurisdiction where the disciplined practitioner is admitted or otherwise authorized to practice. In addition, the EOIR disciplinary counsel shall transmit notice of all public discipline imposed under this rule to the National Lawyer Regulatory Data Bank maintained by the American Bar Association.

[65 FR 39526, June 27, 2000, as amended at 73 FR 76925, Dec. 18, 2008; 77 FR 2015, Jan. 13, 2012; 81 FR 92363, Dec. 19, 2016]

§ 1003.107 Reinstatement after disbarment or suspension.

(a) *Reinstatement upon expiration of suspension.* (1) Except as provided in paragraph (c)(1) of this section, after the period of suspension has expired, a practitioner who has been suspended and wishes to be reinstated must file a motion to the Board requesting reinstatement to practice before the Board and the Immigration Courts, or DHS, or before all three authorities. The practitioner must demonstrate by clear and convincing evidence that notwithstanding the suspension, the practitioner otherwise meets the definition of attorney or representative as set forth in § 1001.1(f) and (j), respectively, of this chapter. The practitioner must serve a copy of such motion on the EOIR disciplinary counsel. In matters in which the practitioner was ordered suspended from practice before DHS, the practitioner must serve a copy of such motion on the DHS disciplinary counsel.

(2) The EOIR disciplinary counsel and, in matters in which the practitioner was ordered suspended from practice before DHS, the DHS disciplinary counsel, may reply within 13 days of service of the motion in the form of a written response objecting to the reinstatement on the ground that the practitioner failed to comply with the terms of the suspension. The response

must include supporting documentation or evidence of the petitioner's failure to comply with the terms of the suspension. The Board, in its discretion, may afford the parties additional time to file briefs or hold a hearing to determine if the practitioner meets all the requirements for reinstatement.

(3) If a practitioner does not meet the definition of attorney or representative, the Board shall deny the motion for reinstatement without further consideration. If the practitioner failed to comply with the terms of the suspension, the Board shall deny the motion and indicate the circumstances under which the practitioner may apply for reinstatement. If the practitioner meets the definition of attorney or representative and the practitioner otherwise has complied with the terms of the suspension, the Board shall grant the motion and reinstate the practitioner.

(b) *Early reinstatement.* (1) Except as provided in paragraph (c) of this section, a practitioner who has been disbarred or who has been suspended for one year or more may file a petition for reinstatement directly with the Board after one-half of the suspension period has expired or one year has passed, whichever is greater, provided that notwithstanding the suspension, the practitioner otherwise meets the definition of attorney or representative as set forth in §1001.1(f) and (j), respectively, of this chapter. A copy of such a petition shall be served on the EOIR disciplinary counsel. In matters in which the practitioner was ordered disbarred or suspended from practice before DHS, a copy of such petition shall be served on the DHS disciplinary counsel.

(2) A practitioner seeking early reinstatement must demonstrate by clear and convincing evidence that the practitioner possesses the moral and professional qualifications required to appear before the Board, the Immigration Courts, or DHS, and that the practitioner's reinstatement will not be detrimental to the administration of justice. The EOIR disciplinary counsel and, in matters in which the practitioner was ordered disbarred or suspended from practice before DHS, the DHS disciplinary counsel, may reply within 30 days of service of the petition in the form of a written response to the Board, which may include, but is not limited to, documentation or evidence of the practitioner's failure to comply with the terms of the disbarment or suspension or of any complaints filed against the disbarred or suspended practitioner subsequent to the practitioner's disbarment or suspension.

(3) If a practitioner cannot meet the definition of attorney or representative, the Board shall deny the petition for reinstatement without further consideration. If the petition for reinstatement is found to be otherwise inappropriate or unwarranted, the petition shall be denied. Any subsequent petitions for reinstatement may not be filed before the end of one year from the date of the Board's previous denial of reinstatement, unless the practitioner is otherwise eligible for reinstatement under paragraph (a). If the petition for reinstatement is determined to be timely, the practitioner meets the definition of attorney or representative, and the petitioner has otherwise established by the requisite standard of proof that the practitioner possesses the qualifications set forth herein, and that reinstatement will not be detrimental to the administration of justice, the Board shall grant the petition and reinstate the practitioner. The Board, in its discretion, may hold a hearing to determine if the practitioner meets all of the requirements for reinstatement.

(c) *Accredited representatives.* (1) An accredited representative who has been suspended for a period of time greater than the remaining period of validity of the representative's accreditation at the time of the suspension is not eligible to be reinstated under §1003.107(a) or (b). In such circumstances, after the period of suspension has expired, an organization may submit a new request for accreditation pursuant to 8 CFR 1292.13 on behalf of such an individual.

(2) *Disbarment.* An accredited representative who has been disbarred is permanently barred from appearing before the Board, the Immigration Courts, or DHS as an accredited representative and cannot seek reinstatement.

(d) *Appearance after reinstatement.* A practitioner who has been reinstated to practice by the Board must file a new Notice of Entry of Appearance of Attorney or Representative in each case on the form required by applicable rules and regulations, even if the reinstated practitioner previously filed such a form in a proceeding before the practitioner was disciplined.

[65 FR 39526, June 27, 2000, as amended at 73 FR 76926, Dec. 18, 2008; 77 FR 2015, Jan. 13, 2012; 81 FR 92364, Dec. 19, 2016]

§ 1003.108 Confidentiality.

(a) *Complaints and preliminary inquiries.* Except as otherwise provided by law or regulation, information concerning complaints or preliminary inquiries is confidential. A practitioner or recognized organization whose conduct is the subject of a complaint or preliminary inquiry, however, may waive confidentiality, except that the EOIR disciplinary counsel may decline to permit a waiver of confidentiality if it is determined that an ongoing preliminary inquiry may be substantially prejudiced by public disclosure before the filing of a Notice of Intent to Discipline.

(1) *Disclosure of information for the purpose of protecting the public.* The EOIR disciplinary counsel may disclose information concerning a complaint or preliminary inquiry for the protection of the public when the necessity for disclosing information outweighs the necessity for preserving confidentiality in circumstances including, but not limited to, the following:

(i) A practitioner or recognized organization has caused, or is likely to cause, harm to client(s), the public, or the administration of justice, such that the public or specific individuals should be advised of the nature of the allegations. If disclosure of information is made pursuant to this paragraph, the EOIR disciplinary counsel may define the scope of information disseminated and may limit the disclosure of information to specified individuals and entities;

(ii) A practitioner or recognized organization has committed criminal acts or is under investigation by law enforcement authorities;

(iii) A practitioner or recognized organization is under investigation by a disciplinary or regulatory authority, or has committed acts or made omissions that may reasonably result in investigation by such authorities;

(iv) A practitioner or recognized organization is the subject of multiple disciplinary complaints and the EOIR disciplinary counsel has determined not to pursue all of the complaints. The EOIR disciplinary counsel may inform complainants whose allegations have not been pursued of the status of any other preliminary inquiries or the manner in which any other complaint(s) against the practitioner or recognized organization have been resolved.

(2) *Disclosure of information for the purpose of conducting a preliminary inquiry.* The EOIR disciplinary counsel, in the exercise of discretion, may disclose documents and information concerning complaints and preliminary inquiries to the following individuals and entities:

(i) To witnesses or potential witnesses in conjunction with a complaint or preliminary inquiry;

(ii) To other governmental agencies responsible for the enforcement of civil or criminal laws;

(iii) To agencies and other jurisdictions responsible for disciplinary or regulatory investigations and proceedings;

(iv) To the complainant or a lawful designee;

(v) To the practitioner or recognized organization who is the subject of the complaint or preliminary inquiry or the practitioner's or recognized organization's counsel of record.

(3) *Disclosure of information for the purpose of recognition of organizations and accreditation of representatives.* The EOIR disciplinary counsel, in the exercise of discretion, may disclose information concerning complaints or preliminary inquiries regarding applicants for recognition and accreditation, recognized organizations or their authorized officers, or accredited representatives to the OLAP Director for any purpose related to the recognition of organizations and accreditation of representatives.

(b) *Resolutions reached prior to the issuance of a Notice of Intent to Discipline.* Resolutions reached prior to the issuance of a Notice of Intent to Discipline, such as warning letters, admonitions, and agreements in lieu of discipline are confidential, except that resolutions that pertain to an accredited representative may be disclosed to the accredited representative's organization and the OLAP Director. However, all such resolutions may become part of the public record if the practitioner becomes subject to a subsequent Notice of Intent to Discipline.

(c) *Notices of Intent to Discipline and action subsequent thereto.* Notices of Intent to Discipline and any action that takes place subsequent to their issuance, except for the imposition of private censures, may be disclosed to the public, except that private censures may become part of the public record if introduced as evidence of a prior record of discipline in any subsequent disciplinary proceeding. Settlement agreements reached after the issuance of a Notice of Intent to Discipline may be disclosed to the public upon final approval by the adjudicating official or the Board. Disciplinary hearings are open to the public, except as noted in § 1003.106(a)(1)(v).

[65 FR 39526, June 27, 2000, as amended at 73 FR 76926, Dec. 18, 2008; 81 FR 92365, Dec. 19, 2016]

§ 1003.109 Discipline of government attorneys.

Complaints regarding the conduct or behavior of Department attorneys, Immigration Judges, or Board Members shall be directed to the Office of Professional Responsibility, United States Department of Justice. If disciplinary action is warranted, it shall be administered pursuant to the Department's attorney discipline procedures.

§ 1003.110 Sanction of recognized organizations.

(a) *Authority to sanction.* (1) An adjudicating official or the Board may impose disciplinary sanctions against a recognized organization if it is in the public interest to do so. It will be in the public interest to impose disciplinary sanctions if a recognized organization has engaged in the conduct described in paragraph (b) of this section. In accordance with the disciplinary proceedings set forth in this subpart, an adjudicating official or the Board may impose the following sanctions:

(i) Revocation, which removes the organization and its accredited representatives from the recognition and accreditation roster and permanently bars the organization from future recognition;

(ii) Termination, which removes the organization and its accredited representatives from the recognition and accreditation roster but does not bar the organization from future recognition. In terminating recognition under this section, the adjudicating official or the Board may preclude the organization from submitting a new request for recognition under 8 CFR 1292.13 before a specified date; or

(iii) Such other disciplinary sanctions, except a suspension, as the adjudicating official or the Board deems appropriate.

(2) The administrative termination of an organization's recognition under 8 CFR 1292.17 after the issuance of Notice of Intent to Discipline pursuant to § 1003.105(a)(1) shall not preclude the continuation of disciplinary proceedings and the imposition of sanctions, unless counsel for the government moves to dismiss the Notice of Intent to Discipline and the adjudicating official or the Board grants the motion.

(3) The imposition of disciplinary sanctions against a recognized organization does not result in disciplinary sanctions against that organization's accredited representatives; disciplinary sanctions, if any, against an organization's accredited representatives must be imposed separately from disciplinary sanctions against the organization. Termination or revocation of an organization's recognition has the effect of terminating the accreditation of representatives of that organization, but such individuals may retain or seek accreditation through another recognized organization.

(b) *Grounds.* It shall be deemed to be in the public interest for an adjudicating official or the Board to impose disciplinary sanctions against any recognized organization that violates one or more of the grounds specified in this paragraph, except that these grounds do not constitute the exclusive grounds for which disciplinary sanctions may be imposed in the public interest. A recognized organization may be subject to disciplinary sanctions if it:

(1) Knowingly or with reckless disregard provides a false statement or misleading information in applying for recognition or accreditation of its representatives;

(2) Knowingly or with reckless disregard provides false or misleading information to clients or prospective clients regarding the scope of authority of, or the services provided by, the organization or its accredited representatives;

(3) Fails to adequately supervise accredited representatives;

(4) Employs, receives services from, or affiliates with an individual who performs an activity that constitutes the unauthorized practice of law or immigration fraud; or

(5) Engages in the practice of law through staff when it does not have an attorney or accredited representative.

(c) *Joint disciplinary proceedings.* The EOIR disciplinary counsel or DHS disciplinary counsel may file a Notice of Intent to Discipline against a recognized organization and one or more of its accredited representatives pursuant to § 1003.101 *et seq.* Disciplinary proceedings conducted on such notices, if they are filed jointly with the Board, shall be joined and referred to the same adjudicating official pursuant to § 1003.106. An adjudicating official may join related disciplinary proceedings after the filing of a Notice of Intent to Discipline.

[81 FR 92365, Dec. 19, 2016]

§ 1003.111 Interim suspension.

(a) *Petition for interim suspension*—(1) *EOIR Petition.* In conjunction with the filing of a Notice of Intent to Discipline or at any time thereafter during disciplinary proceedings before an adjudicating official, the EOIR disciplinary counsel may file a petition for an interim suspension of an accredited representative. Such suspension, if issued, precludes the representative from practicing before the Board and the Immigration Courts during the pendency of disciplinary proceedings and continues until the issuance of a final order in the disciplinary proceedings.

(2) *DHS Petition.* In conjunction with the filing of a Notice of Intent to Discipline or at any time thereafter during disciplinary proceedings before an adjudicating official, the DHS disciplinary counsel may file a petition for an interim suspension of an accredited representative. Such suspension, if issued, precludes the representative from practicing before DHS during the pendency of disciplinary proceedings and continues until the issuance of a final order in the disciplinary proceedings.

(3) *Contents of the petition.* In the petition, counsel for the government must demonstrate by a preponderance of the evidence that the accredited representative poses a substantial threat of irreparable harm to clients or prospective clients. An accredited representative poses a substantial threat of irreparable harm to clients or prospective clients if the representative committed three or more acts in violation of the grounds of discipline described at § 1003.102, when actual harm or threatened harm is demonstrated, or engages in any other conduct that, if continued, will likely cause irreparable harm to clients or prospective clients. Counsel for the government must serve the petition on the accredited representative, as provided in § 1003.105, and send a copy of the petition to the authorized officer of the recognized organization at the address of the organization through which the representative is accredited.

(4) *Requests to broaden scope.* The EOIR disciplinary counsel or DHS disciplinary counsel may submit a request to broaden the scope of any interim suspension order such that an accredited representative would be precluded from practice before the Board, the Immigration Courts, and DHS.

(b) *Response.* The accredited representative may file a written response to the petition for interim suspension within 30 days of service of the petition.

(c) *Adjudication.* Upon the expiration of the time to respond to the petition for an interim suspension, the adjudicating official will consider the petition for an interim suspension, the accredited representative's response, if any, and any other evidence presented by the parties before determining whether to issue an interim suspension. If the adjudicating official imposes an interim suspension on the representative, the adjudicating official may require that notice of the interim suspension be posted at the Board and the Immigration Courts, or DHS, or all three authorities. Upon good cause shown, the adjudicating official may set aside an order of interim suspension when it appears in the interest of justice to do so. If a final order in the disciplinary proceedings includes the imposition of a period of suspension against an accredited representative, time spent by the representative under an interim suspension pursuant to this section may be credited toward the period of suspension imposed under the final order.

[81 FR 92365, Dec. 19, 2016]

SUBCHAPTER B—IMMIGRATION REGULATIONS

PART 1101—PRESUMPTION OF LAWFUL ADMISSION

AUTHORITY: 8 U.S.C. 1103, 8 CFR part 2.

SOURCE: Duplicated from part 101 at 68 FR 9832, Feb. 28, 2003.

EDITORIAL NOTE: Nomenclature changes to part 1101 appear at 68 FR 9846, Feb. 28, 2003.

§ 1101.1 Presumption of lawful admission.

A member of the following classes shall be presumed to have been lawfully admitted for permanent residence even though a record of his admission cannot be found, except as otherwise provided in this section, unless he abandoned his lawful permanent resident status or subsequently lost that status by operation of law:

(a) *Prior to June 30, 1906.* An alien who establishes that he entered the United States prior to June 30, 1906.

(b) *United States land borders.* An alien who establishes that, while a citizen of Canada or Newfoundland, he entered the United States across the Canadian border prior to October 1, 1906; an alien who establishes that while a citizen of Mexico he entered the United States across the Mexican border prior to July 1, 1908; an alien who establishes that, while a citizen of Mexico, he entered the United States at the port of Presidio, Texas, prior to October 21, 1918, and an alien for whom a record of his actual admission to the United States does not exist but who establishes that he gained admission to the United States prior to July 1, 1924, pursuant to preexamination at a United States immigration station in Canada and that a record of such preexamination exists.

(c) *Virgin Islands.* An alien who establishes that he entered the Virgin Islands of the United States prior to July 1, 1938, even though a record of his admission prior to that date exists as a non-immigrant under the Immigration Act of 1924.

(d) *Asiatic barred zone.* An alien who establishes that he is of a race indigenous to, and a native of a country within, the Asiatic zone defined in section 3 of the Act of February 5, 1917, as amended, that he was a member of a class of aliens exempted from exclusion by the provisions of that section, and that he entered the United States prior to July 1, 1924, provided that a record of his admission exists.

(e) *Chinese and Japanese aliens*—(1) *Prior to July 1, 1924.* A Chinese alien for whom there exists a record of his admission to the United States prior to July 1, 1924, under the laws and regulations formerly applicable to Chinese and who establishes that at the time of his admission he was a merchant, teacher, or student, and his son or daughter under 21 or wife accompanying or following to join him; a traveler for curiosity or pleasure and his accompanying son or daughter under 21 or accompanying wife; a wife of a United States citizen; a returning laborer; and a person erroneously admitted as a United States citizen under section 1993 of the Revised Statutes of the United States, as amended, his father not having resided in the United States prior to his birth.

(2) *On or after July 1, 1924.* A Chinese alien for whom there exists a record of his admission to the United States as a member of one of the following classes; an alien who establishes that he was readmitted between July 1, 1924, and December 16, 1943, inclusive, as a returning Chinese laborer who acquired lawful permanent residence prior to July 1, 1924; a person erroneously admitted between July 1, 1924, and June 6, 1927, inclusive, as a United States citizen under section 1993 of the Revised Statutes of the United States, as amended, his father not having resided in the United States prior to his birth; an alien admitted at any time after

June 30, 1924, under section 4 (b) or (d) of the Immigration Act of 1924; an alien wife of a United States citizen admitted between June 13, 1930, and December 16, 1943, inclusive, under section 4(a) of the Immigration Act of 1924; an alien admitted on or after December 17, 1943, under section 4(f) of the Immigration Act of 1924; an alien admitted on or after December 17, 1943, under section 317(c) of the Nationality Act of 1940, as amended; an alien admitted on or after December 17, 1943, as a preference or nonpreference quota immigrant pursuant to section 2 of that act; and a Chinese or Japanese alien admitted to the United States between July 1, 1924, and December 23, 1952, both dates inclusive, as the wife or minor son or daughter of a treaty merchant admitted before July 1, 1924, if the husband-father was lawfully admitted to the United States as a treaty merchant before July 1, 1924, or, while maintaining another status under which he was admitted before that date, and his status changed to that of a treaty merchant or treaty trader after that date, and was maintaining the changed status at the time his wife or minor son or daughter entered the United States.

(f) *Citizens of the Philippine Islands*—(1) *Entry prior to May 1, 1934*. An alien who establishes that he entered the United States prior to May 1, 1934, and that he was on the date of his entry a citizen of the Philippine Islands, provided that for the purpose of petitioning for naturalization he shall not be regarded as having been lawfully admitted for permanent residence unless he was a citizen of the Commonwealth of the Philippines on July 2, 1946.

(2) *Entry between May 1, 1934, and July 3, 1946*. An alien who establishes that he entered Hawaii between May 1, 1934, and July 3, 1946, inclusive, under the provisions of the last sentence of section 8(a)(1) of the Act of March 24, 1934, as amended, that he was a citizen of the Philippine Islands when he entered, and that a record of such entry exists.

(g) *Temporarily admitted aliens*. The following aliens who when admitted expressed an intention to remain in the United States temporarily or to pass in transit through the United States, for whom records of admission exist, but who remained in the United States: An alien admitted prior to June 3, 1921, except if admitted temporarily under the 9th proviso to section 3 of the Immigration Act of 1917, or as an accredited official of a foreign government, his suite, family, or guest, or as a seaman in pursuit of his calling; an alien admitted under the Act of May 19, 1921, as amended, who was admissible for permanent residence under that Act notwithstanding the quota limitation's thereof and his accompanying wife or unmarried son or daughter under 21 who was admissible for permanent residence under that Act notwithstanding the quota limitations thereof; and an alien admitted under the Act of May 19, 1921, as amended, who was charged under that Act to the proper quota at the time of his admission or subsequently and who remained so charged.

(h) *Citizens of the Trust Territory of the Pacific Islands who entered Guam prior to December 24, 1952*. An alien who establishes that while a citizen of the Trust Territory of the Pacific Islands he entered Guam prior to December 24, 1952, by records, such as Service records subsequent to June 15, 1952, records of the Guamanian Immigration Service, records of the Navy or Air Force, or records of contractors of those agencies, and was residing in Guam on December 24, 1952.

(i) *Aliens admitted to Guam*. An alien who establishes that he was admitted to Guam prior to December 24, 1952, by records such as Service records subsequent to June 15, 1952, records of the Guamanian Immigration Service, records of the Navy or Air Force, or records of contractors of those agencies; that he was not excludable under the Act of February 5, 1917, as amended; and that he continued to reside in Guam until December 24, 1952, and thereafter was not admitted or re-admitted into Guam as a nonimmigrant, provided that the provisions of this paragraph shall not apply to an alien who was exempted from the contract laborer provisions of section 3 of the Immigration Act of February 5, 1917, as amended, through the exercise, expressly or impliedly, of the 4th or 9th provisos to section 3 of that act.

(j) *Erroneous admission as United States citizens or as children of citizens*. (1)(i) An alien for whom there exists a record of admission prior to September 11, 1957, as a United States citizen who establishes that at the time of such admission he was the child of a United States citizen parent; he was erroneously issued a United States passport or included in the United States passport of his citizen parent accompanying him or to whom he was destined; no fraud or misrepresentation was practiced by him in the issuance of the passport or in gaining admission; he was otherwise admissible at the time of entry except for failure to meet visa or passport requirements; and he has maintained a residence in the United States since the date of admission, or (ii) an alien who meets all of the foregoing requirements except that if he were, in fact, a citizen of the United States a passport would not have been required, or it had been individually waived, and was erroneously admitted as a United States citizen by a Service officer. For the purposes of all of the foregoing, the terms *child* and *parent* shall be defined as in section 101(b) of the Immigration and Nationality Act, as amended.

(2) An alien admitted to the United States before July 1, 1948, in possession of a section 4(a) 1924 Act nonquota immigration visa issued in accordance with State Department regulations, including a child of a United States citizen after he reached the age of 21, in the absence of fraud or misrepresentation; a member of a naturalized person's family who was admitted to the United States as a United States citizen or as a section 4(a) 1924 Act nonquota immigrant on the basis of that naturalization, unless he knowingly participated in the unlawful naturalization of the parent or spouse rendered void by cancellation, or knew at any time prior to his admission to the United States of the cancellation; and a member of a naturalized person's family who knew at any time prior to his admission to the United States of the cancellation of the naturalization of his parent or spouse but was admitted to the United States as a United States citizen pursuant to a State Department or Service determination based upon a then prevailing administrative view, provided the State Department or Service knew of the cancellation.

[23 FR 9119, Nov. 26, 1958, as amended at 24 FR 2583, Apr. 3, 1959; 24 FR 6476, Aug. 12, 1959; 25 FR 581, Jan. 23, 1960; 31 FR 535, Jan. 15, 1966]

§1101.2 Presumption of lawful admission; entry under erroneous name or other errors.

An alien who entered the United States as either an immigrant or nonimmigrant under any of the following circumstances shall be regarded as having been lawfully admitted in such status, except as otherwise provided in this part: An alien otherwise admissible whose entry was made and recorded under other than his full true and correct name or whose entry record contains errors in recording sex, names of relatives, or names of foreign places of birth or residence, provided that he establishes by clear, unequivocal, and convincing evidence that the record of the claimed admission relates to him, and, if entry occurred on or after May 22, 1918, if under other than his full, true and correct name that he also establishes that the name was not adopted for the purpose of concealing his identity when obtaining a passport or visa, or for the purpose of using the passport or visa of another person or otherwise evading any provision of the immigration laws, and that the name used at the time of entry was one by which he had been known for a sufficient length of time prior to making application for a passport or visa to have permitted the issuing authority or authorities to have made any necessary investigation concerning him or that his true identity was known to such officials.

[32 FR 9622, July 4, 1967]

§1101.3 Creation of record of lawful permanent resident status for person born under diplomatic status in the United States.

(a) *Person born to foreign diplomat*—(1) *Status of person.* A person born in the United States to a foreign diplomatic officer accredited to the United States, as a matter of international law, is not subject to the jurisdiction of the United States. That person is not a

United States citizen under the Fourteenth Amendment to the Constitution. Such a person may be considered a lawful permanent resident at birth.

(2) *Definition of foreign diplomatic officer. Foreign diplomatic officer* means a person listed in the State Department Diplomatic List, also known as the Blue List. It includes ambassadors, ministers, chargés d'affaires, counselors, secretaries and attachés of embassies and legations as well as members of the Delegation of the Commission of the European Communities. The term also includes individuals with comparable diplomatic status and immunities who are accredited to the United Nations or to the Organization of American States, and other individuals who are also accorded comparable diplomatic status.

(b) *Child born subject to the jurisdiction of the United States.* A child born in the United States is born subject to the jurisdiction of the United States and is a United States citizen if the parent is not a "foreign diplomatic officer" as defined in paragraph (a)(2) of this section. This includes, for example, a child born in the United States to one of the following foreign government officials or employees:

(1) Employees of foreign diplomatic missions whose names appear in the State Department list entitled "Employees of Diplomatic Missions Not Printed in the Diplomatic List," also known as the White List; employees of foreign diplomatic missions accredited to the United Nations or the Organization of American States; or foreign diplomats accredited to other foreign states. The majority of these individuals enjoy certain diplomatic immunities, but they are not "foreign diplomatic officers" as defined in paragraph (a)(2) of this section. The immunities, if any, of their family members are derived from the status of the employees or diplomats.

(2) Foreign government employees with limited or no diplomatic immunity such as consular officials named on the State Department list entitled "Foreign Consular Officers in the United States" and their staffs.

(c) *Voluntary registration as lawful permanent resident of person born to foreign diplomat.* Since a person born in the United States to a foreign diplomatic officer is not subject to the jurisdiction of the United States, his/her registration as a lawful permanent resident of the United States is voluntary. The provisions of section 262 of the Act do not apply to such a person unless and until that person ceases to have the rights, privileges, exemptions, or immunities which may be claimed by a foreign diplomatic officer.

(d) *Retention of lawful permanent residence.* To be eligible for lawful permanent resident status under paragraph (a) of this section, an alien must establish that he/she has not abandoned his/her residence in the United States. One of the tests for retention of lawful permanent resident status is continuous residence, not continuous physical presence, in the United States. Such a person will not be considered to have abandoned his/her residence in the United States solely by having been admitted to the United States in a nonimmigrant classification under paragraph (15)(A) or (15)(G) of section 101(a) of the Act after a temporary stay in a foreign country or countries on one or several occasions.

(Secs. 101(a)(20), 103, 262, 264 of the Immigration and Nationality Act, as amended; 8 U.S.C. 1101(a)(20), 1103, 1302, 1304)

[47 FR 940, Jan. 8, 1982]

§ 1101.4 Registration procedure.

The procedure for an application for creation of a record of lawful permanent residence and a Permanent Resident Card, Form I–551, for a person eligible for presumption of lawful admission for permanent residence under § 1101.1 or § 1101.2 or for lawful permanent residence as a person born in the United States to a foreign diplomatic officer under § 1101.3 is described in § 264.2 of 8 CFR chapter 1.

(Secs. 101(a)(20), 103, 262, 264 of the Immigration and Nationality Act, as amended; 8 U.S.C. 1101(a)(20), 1103, 1302, 1304)

[47 FR 941, Jan. 8, 1982, as amended at 63 FR 70315, Dec. 21, 1998; 68 FR 10351, Mar. 5, 2003]

§ 1101.5 Special immigrant status for certain G–4 nonimmigrants.

(a) *Application.* An application for adjustment to special immigrant status under section 101(a)(27)(I) of the INA shall be made on Form I–485. The application date of the I–485 shall be the date of acceptance by the Service as properly filed. If the application date is other than the fee receipt date it must be noted and initialed by a Service officer. The date of application for adjustment of status is the closing date for computing the residence and physical presence requirement. The applicant must have complied with all requirements as of the date of application.

(b) *Documentation.* All documents must be submitted in accordance with §103.2(b) of this chapter. The application shall be accompanied by documentary evidence establishing the aggregate residence and physical presence required. Documentary evidence may include official employment verification, records of official or personnel transactions or recordings of events occurring during the period of claimed residence and physical presence. Affidavits of credible witnesses may also be accepted. Persons unable to furnish evidence in their own names may furnish evidence in the names of parents or other persons with whom they have been living, if affidavits of the parents or other persons are submitted attesting to the claimed residence and physical presence. The claimed family relationship to the principle G–4 international organization officer or employee must be substantiated by the submission of verifiable civil documents.

(c) *Residence and physical presence requirements.* All applicants applying under sections 101(a)(27)(I) (i), (ii), and (iii) of the INA must have resided and been physically present in the United States for a designated period of time.

For purposes of this section only, an absence from the United States to conduct official business on behalf of the employing organization, or approved customary leave shall not be subtracted from the aggregated period of required residence or physical presence for the current or former G–4 officer or employee or the accompanying spouse and unmarried sons or daughters of such officer or employee, provided residence in the United States is maintained during such absences, and the duty station of the principle G–4 nonimmigrant continues to be in the United States. Absence from the United States by the G–4 spouse or unmarried son or daughter without the principle G–4 shall not be subtracted from the aggregate period of residence and physical presence if on customary leave as recognized by the international organization employer. Absence by the unmarried son or daughter while enrolled in a school outside the United States will not be counted toward the physical presence requirement.

(d) *Maintenance of nonimmigrant status.* Section 101(a)(27)(I) (i), and (ii) requires the applicant to accrue the required period of residence and physical presence in the United States while maintaining status as a G–4 or N nonimmigrant. Section 101(a)(27)(I)(iii) requires such time accrued only in G–4 nonimmigrant status.

Maintaining G–4 status for this purpose is defined as maintaining qualified employment with a "G" international organization or maintaining the qualifying family relationship with the G–4 international organization officer or employee. Maintaining status as an N nonimmigrant for this purpose requires the qualifying family relationship to remain in effect. Unauthorized employment will not remove an otherwise eligible alien from G–4 status for residence and physical presence requirements, provided the qualifying G–4 status is maintained.

[54 FR 5927, Feb. 7, 1989]

PART 1103—APPEALS, RECORDS, AND FEES

Sec.

AUTHORITY: 8 U.S.C. 1101, 1103, 1304, 1356; 31 U.S.C. 9701; 28 U.S.C. 509, 510.

SOURCE: 40 FR 44481, Sept. 26, 1975, unless otherwise noted. Duplicated from part 103 at 68 FR 9833, Feb. 28, 2003.

EDITORIAL NOTE: Nomenclature changes to part 1103 appear at 68 FR 9846, Feb. 28, 2003, and at 68 FR 10351, Mar. 5, 2003.

§ 1103.3 Denials, appeals, and precedent decisions.

(a) *DHS regulations.* The regulations pertaining to denials, appeals, and precedent decisions of the Department of Homeland Security are contained in 8 CFR Chapter I.

(b) [Reserved]

(c) *DHS precedent decisions.* The Secretary of Homeland Security, or specific officials of the Department of Homeland Security designated by the Secretary with the concurrence of the Attorney General, may file with the Attorney General decisions relating to the administration of the immigration laws of the United States for publication as precedent in future proceedings, and upon approval of the Attorney General as to the lawfulness of such decision, the Director of the Executive Office for Immigration Review shall cause such decisions to be published in the same manner as decisions of the Board and the Attorney General.

[31 FR 3062, Feb. 24, 1966, as amended at 37 FR 927, Jan. 21, 1972; 48 FR 36441, Aug. 11, 1983; 49 FR 7355, Feb. 29, 1984; 52 FR 16192, May 1, 1987; 54 FR 29881, July 17, 1989; 55 FR 20769, 20775, May 21, 1990; 55 FR 23345, June 7, 1990; 57 FR 11573, Apr. 6, 1992; 68 FR 9832, Feb. 28, 2003; 81 FR 92366, Dec. 19, 2016]

§ 1103.4 Certifications.

(a) *Certification of other than special agricultural worker and legalization cases*—(1) *General.* The Commissioner or the Commissioner's delegate may direct that any case or class of cases be certified to another Service official for decision. In addition, regional commissioners, regional service center directors, district directors, officers in charge in districts 33 (Bangkok, Thailand), 35 (Mexico City, Mexico), and 37 (Rome, Italy), and the Director, National Fines Office, may certify their decisions to the appropriate appellate authority (as designated in this chapter) when the case involves an unusually complex or novel issue of law or fact.

(2) *Notice to affected party.* When a case is certified to a Service officer, the official certifying the case shall notify the affected party using a Notice of Certification (Form I–290C). The affected party may submit a brief to the officer to whom the case is certified within 30 days after service of the notice. If the affected party does not wish to submit a brief, the affected party may waive the 30-day period.

(3) *Favorable action.* The Service officer to whom a case is certified may suspend the 30-day period for submission of a brief if that officer takes action favorable to the affected party.

(4) *Initial decision.* A case within the appellate jurisdiction of the Associate Commissioner, Examinations, or for which there is no appeal procedure may be certified only after an initial decision is made.

(5) *Certification to AAU.* A case described in paragraph (a)(4) of this section may be certified to the AAU.

(6) *Appeal to Board.* In a case within the Board's appellate jurisdiction, an unfavorable decision of the Service official to whom the case is certified (whether made initially or upon review) is the decision which may be appealed to the Board under § 1003.1(b) of this chapter.

(7) *Other applicable provisions.* The provisions of § 1103.3(a)(2)(x) of this part also apply to decisions on certified cases. The provisions of § 1103.3(b) of this part also apply to requests for oral argument regarding certified cases considered by the AAU.

(b) *Certification of denials of special agricultural worker and legalization applications.* The Regional Processing Facility director or the district director may, in accordance with paragraph (a) of this section, certify a decision to the Associate Commissioner, Examinations (Administrative Appeals Unit) (the appellate authority designated in § 103.1(f)(2)) of this part, when the case involves an unusually complex or novel question of law or fact.

[52 FR 661, Jan. 8, 1987, as amended at 53 FR 43985, Oct. 31, 1988; 55 FR 20770, May 21, 1990]

§ 1103.7 Fees.

(a) *Remittances—(1) In general.* Fees shall be submitted in connection with any formal appeal, motion, or application prescribed in this chapter in the amount prescribed by law or regulation. Payment of any fee under this section does not constitute filing of the appeal, motion, or application with the Board of Immigration Appeals or with the immigration court.

(2) *Board of Immigration Appeals.* The fee for filing an appeal or a motion with the Board of Immigration Appeals shall be paid pursuant to the provisions of 8 CFR 1003.8 when a fee is required.

(3) *All other fees payable in connection with immigration proceedings.* Except as provided in 8 CFR 1003.8, the Executive Office for Immigration Review does not accept the payment of any fee relating to Executive Office for Immigration Review proceedings. Instead, such fees, when required, shall be paid to, and accepted by, an office of the Department of Homeland Security authorized to accept fees, as provided in 8 CFR 103.7(a)(1). The Department of Homeland Security shall return to the payer, at the time of payment, a receipt for any fee paid, and shall also return to the payer any documents, submitted with the fee, relating to any immigration proceeding. The fee receipt and the application or motion shall then be submitted to the Executive Office for Immigration Review. Remittances to the Department of Homeland Security for applications, motions, or forms filed in connection with immigration proceedings shall be payable subject to the provisions of 8 CFR 103.7(a)(2).

(b) *Amounts of fees—(1) Appeals.* For filing an appeal to the Board of Immigration Appeals, when a fee is required pursuant to 8 CFR 1003.8, as follows:

Form EOIR–26. For filing an appeal from a decision of an immigration judge—$110.

Form EOIR–29. For filing an appeal from a decision of an officer of the Department of Homeland Security—$110.

Form EOIR–45. For filing an appeal from a decision of an adjudicating official in a practitioner disciplinary case—$110.

(2) *Motions.* For filing a motion to reopen or a motion to reconsider, when a fee is required pursuant to 8 CFR 1003.8 or 1003.24—$110.

(3) *Multiple parties.* When an appeal or motion is filed on behalf of two or more aliens and the aliens are covered by one decision, only one fee is required.

(4) *Applications for Relief—(i) Forms published by the Executive Office for Immigration Review.* Fees for applications for relief shall be paid in accordance with 8 CFR 1003.8(b) and 1003.24(c) as follows:

Form EOIR–40. Application for Suspension of Deportation—$100.

Form EOIR–42A. Application for Cancellation of Removal for Certain Permanent Residents—$100.

Form EOIR–42B. Application for Cancellation of Removal and Adjustment of Status for Certain Nonpermanent Residents—$100.

(ii) *Forms published by the Department of Homeland Security.* The fees for applications published by the Department of Homeland Security and used in immigration proceedings are governed by 8 CFR 103.7.

(c) *Fee waivers.* For provisions relating to the authority of the Board or the immigration judges to waive any of the fees prescribed in paragraph (b) of this section, see 8 CFR 1003.8 and 1003.24. No waiver may be granted with respect to the fee prescribed for a Department of Homeland Security form or action that is identified as non-waivable in regulations of the Department of Homeland Security.

(d) *Requests for records under the Freedom of Information Act.* Fees for production or disclosure of records under 5 U.S.C. 552 may be waived or reduced in accordance with 28 CFR 16.11.

[69 FR 44907, July 28, 2004]

PART 1204—IMMIGRANT PETITIONS

AUTHORITY: 8 U.S.C. 1101, 1103, 1151, 1153, 1154, 1182, 1186a, 1255, 1641; 8 CFR part 2.

§ 1204.1 Single level of appellate review.

The decision of the Board of Immigration Appeals concerning the denial of a relative visa petition under 8 CFR chapter I, part 204 because the petitioner failed to establish eligibility for the bona fide marriage exemption contained in that part will constitute the single level of appellate review established by statute.

[68 FR 9833, Feb. 28, 2003]

PART 1205—REVOCATION OF APPROVAL OF PETITIONS

AUTHORITY: 8 U.S.C. 1101, 1103, 1151, 1153, 1154, 1155, 1182, and 1186a.

SOURCE: Duplicated from part 205 at 68 FR 9833, Feb. 28, 2003.

EDITORIAL NOTE: Nomenclature changes to part 1205 appear at 68 FR 9846, Feb. 28, 2003.

§ 1205.1 Automatic revocation.

(a) *Reasons for automatic revocation.* The approval of a petition or self-petition made under section 204 of the Act and in accordance with part 204 of 8 CFR chapter I is revoked as of the date of approval:

(1) If the Secretary of State shall terminate the registration of the beneficiary pursuant to the provisions of section 203(e) of the Act before October 1, 1991, or section 203(g) of the Act on or after October 1, 1994;

(2) If the filing fee and associated service charge are not paid within 14 days of the notification to the remitter that his or her check or other financial instrument used to pay the filing fee has been returned as not payable; or

(3) If any of the following circumstances occur before the beneficiary's or self-petitioner's journey to the United States commences or, if the beneficiary or self-petitioner is an applicant for adjustment of status to that of a permanent resident, before the decision on his or her adjustment application becomes final:

(i) *Immediate relative and family-sponsored petitions, other than Amerasian petitions.* (A) Upon written notice of withdrawal filed by the petitioner or self-petitioner with any officer of the Service who is authorized to grant or deny petitions.

(B) Upon the death of the beneficiary or the self-petitioner.

(C) Upon the death of the petitioner, except as provided for in 8 CFR 205.1(a)(3)(i)(C).

(D) Upon the legal termination of the marriage when a citizen or lawful permanent resident of the United States has petitioned to accord his or her spouse immediate relative or family-sponsored preference immigrant classification under section 201(b) or section 203(a)(2) of the Act. The approval of a spousal self-petition based on the relationship to an abusive citizen or lawful permanent resident of the United States filed under section 204(a)(1)(A)(iii) or 204(a)(1)(B)(ii) of the Act, however, will not be revoked solely because of the termination of the marriage to the abuser.

(E) Upon the remarriage of the spouse of an abusive citizen or lawful permanent resident of the United States when the spouse has self-petitioned under section 204(a)(1)(A)(iii) or 204(a)(1)(B)(ii) of the Act for immediate relative classification under section 201(b) of the Act or for preference classification under section 203(a)(2) of the Act.

(F) Upon a child reaching the age of 21, when he or she has been accorded immediate relative status under section 201(b) of the Act. A petition filed on behalf of a child under section 204(a)(1)(A)(i) of the Act or a self-petition filed by a child of an abusive United States citizen under section 204(a)(1)(A)(iv) of the Act, however, will remain valid for the duration of the relationship to accord preference status under section 203(a)(1) of the Act if the beneficiary remains unmarried, or to accord preference status under section 203(a)(3) of the Act if he or she marries.

(G) Upon the marriage of a child, when he or she has been accorded immediate relative status under section 201(b) of the Act. A petition filed on behalf of the child under section 204(a)(1)(A)(i) of the Act or a self-petition filed by a child of an abusive United States citizen under section 204(a)(1)(A)(iv) of the Act, however, will remain valid for the duration of the relationship to accord preference status under section 203(a)(3) of the Act if he or she marries.

(H) Upon the marriage of a person accorded preference status as a son or daughter of a United States citizen under section 203(a)(1) of the Act. A petition filed on behalf of the son or daughter, however, will remain valid for the duration of the relationship to accord preference status under section 203(a)(3) of the Act.

(I) Upon the marriage of a person accorded status as a son or daughter of a lawful permanent resident alien under section 203(a)(2) of the Act.

(J) Upon legal termination of the petitioner's status as an alien admitted for lawful permanent residence in the United States unless the petitioner became a United States citizen. The provisions of 8 CFR 204.2(i)(3) shall apply if the petitioner became a United States citizen.

(ii) *Petition for Pub. L. 97–359 Amerasian.* (A) Upon formal notice of withdrawal filed by the petitioner with the officer who approved the petition.

(B) Upon the death of the beneficiary.

(C) Upon the death or bankruptcy of the sponsor who executed Form I–361, Affidavit of Financial Support and Intent to Petition for Legal Custody for Pub. L. 97–359 Amerasian. In that event, a new petition may be filed in the beneficiary's behalf with the documentary evidence relating to sponsorship and, in the case of a beneficiary under 18 years of age, placement. If the new petition is approved, it will be given the priority date of the previously approved petition.

(D) Upon the death or substitution of the petitioner if other than the beneficiary or sponsor. However, if the petitioner dies or no longer desires or is able to proceed with the petition, and another person 18 years of age or older, an emancipated minor, or a corporation incorporated in the United States desires to be substituted for the deceased or original petitioner, a written request may be submitted to the Service or American consular office where the petition is located to reinstate the petition and restore the original priority date.

(E) Upon the beneficiary's reaching the age of 21 when the beneficiary has been accorded classification under section 201(b) of the Act. Provided that all requirements of section 204(f) of the Act continue to be met, however, the petition is to be considered valid for purposes of according the beneficiary preference classification under section 203(a)(1) of the Act if the beneficiary remains unmarried or under section 203(a)(3) if the beneficiary marries.

(F) Upon the beneficiary's marriage when the beneficiary has been accorded classification under section 201(b) or section 203(a)(1) of the Act. Provided that all requirements of section 204(f) of the Act continue to be met, however, the petition is to be considered valid for purposes of according the beneficiary preference classification under section 203(a)(3) of the Act.

(iii) *Petitions under section 203(b), other than special immigrant juvenile petitions.* (A) Upon invalidation pursuant to 20 CFR Part 656 of the labor certification in support of the petition.

(B) Upon the death of the petitioner or beneficiary.

(C) Upon written notice of withdrawal filed by the petitioner, in employment-based preference cases, with any officer of the Service who is authorized to grant or deny petitions.

(D) Upon termination of the employer's business in an employment-based preference case under section 203(b)(1)(B), 203(b)(1)(C), 203(b)(2), or 203(b)(3) of the Act.

(iv) *Special immigrant juvenile petitions.* Unless the beneficiary met all of the eligibility requirements as of November 29, 1990, and the petition requirements as of November 29, 1990, and the petition for classification as a special immigrant juvenile was filed before June 1, 1994, or unless the change in circumstances resulted from the beneficiary's adoption or placement in a guardianship situation:

(A) Upon the beneficiary reaching the age of 21;

(B) Upon the marriage of the beneficiary;

(C) Upon the termination of the beneficiary's dependency upon the juvenile court;

(D) Upon the termination of the beneficiary's eligibility for long-term foster care; or

(E) Upon the determination in administrative or judicial proceedings that it is in the beneficiary's best interest to be returned to the country of nationality or last habitual residence of the beneficiary or of his or her parent or parents.

(b) *Notice.* When it shall appear to the director that the approval of a petition has been automatically revoked, he or she shall cause a notice of such revocation to be sent promptly to the consular office having jurisdiction over the visa application and a copy of such notice to be mailed to the petitioner's last known address.

[61 FR 13077, Mar. 26, 1996, as amended at 68 FR 10352, Mar. 5, 2003; 71 FR 35757, June 21, 2006]

§ 1205.2 Revocation on notice.

(a) *General.* Any Service officer authorized to approve a petition under section 204 of the Act may revoke the approval of that petition upon notice to the petitioner on any ground other than those specified in §1205.1 when the necessity for the revocation comes to the attention of this Service.

(b) *Notice of intent.* Revocation of the approval of a petition of self-petition under paragraph (a) of this section will be made only on notice to the petitioner or self-petitioner. The petitioner or self-petitioner must be given the opportunity to offer evidence in support of the petition or self-petition and in opposition to the grounds alleged for revocation of the approval.

(c) *Notification of revocation.* If, upon reconsideration, the approval previously granted is revoked, the director shall provide the petitioner or the self-petitioner with a written notification of the decision that explains the specific reasons for the revocation. The director shall notify the consular officer having jurisdiction over the visa application, if applicable, of the revocation of an approval.

(d) *Appeals.* The petitioner or self-petitioner may appeal the decision to revoke the approval within 15 days after the service of notice of the revocation. The appeal must be filed as provided in part 1003 of this chapter, unless the Associate Commissioner for Examinations exercises appellate jurisdiction over the revocation under part 103 of 8 CFR chapter I. Appeals filed with the Associate Commissioner for Examinations must meet the requirements of part 103 of this chapter.

[48 FR 19156, Apr. 28, 1983, as amended at 58 FR 42851, Aug. 12, 1993; 61 FR 13078, Mar. 26, 1996; 68 FR 10352, Mar. 5, 2003]

PART 1207—ADMISSION OF REFUGEES

AUTHORITY: 8 U.S.C. 1101, 1103, 1151, 1157, 1159, 1182; 8 CFR part 2.

§1207.3 Waivers of inadmissibility.

(a) *Authority.* Section 207(c)(3) of the Act sets forth grounds of inadmissibility under section 212(a) of the Act which are not applicable and those which may be waived in the case of an otherwise qualified refugee and the conditions under which such waivers may be approved. Officers in charge of overseas offices are delegated authority to initiate the necessary investigations to establish the facts in each waiver application pending before them and to approve or deny such waivers.

(b) *Filing requirements.* The applicant for a waiver must submit Form I–602, Application by Refugee for Waiver of Grounds of Inadmissibility, with the Service office processing his or her case. The burden is on the applicant to show that the waiver should be granted based upon humanitarian grounds, family unity, or the public interest. The applicant shall be notified in writing of the decision, including the reasons for denial, if the application is denied. There is no appeal from such decision.

[62 FR 10336, Mar. 6, 1997. Duplicated from §207.3 at 68 FR 9833, Feb. 28, 2003]

PART 1208—PROCEDURES FOR ASYLUM AND WITHHOLDING OF REMOVAL

Subpart A—Asylum and Withholding of Removal

Sec.

Subpart B—Credible Fear of Persecution

AUTHORITY: 8 U.S.C. 1101, 1103, 1158, 1226, 1252, 1282; Title VII of Public Law 110–229.

SOURCE: 62 FR 10337, Mar. 6, 1997, unless otherwise noted. Duplicated from part 208 at 68 FR 9834, Feb. 28, 2003.

EDITORIAL NOTE: Nomenclature changes to part 1208 appear at 68 FR 9846, Feb. 28, 2003, and at 68 FR 10352, Mar. 5, 2003.

Subpart A—Asylum and Withholding of Removal

§ 1208.1 General.

(a) *Applicability*—(1) *In general.* Unless otherwise provided in this chapter V, this subpart A shall apply to all applications for asylum under section 208 of the Act or for withholding of deportation or withholding of removal under section 241(b)(3) of the Act, or under the Convention Against Torture, whether before an asylum officer or an immigration judge, regardless of the date of filing. For purposes of this chapter V, withholding of removal shall also mean withholding of deportation under section 243(h) of the Act, as it appeared prior to April 1, 1997, except as provided in § 1208.16(d). Such applications are hereinafter referred to as "asylum applications." The provisions of this part shall not affect the finality or validity of any decision made by a district director, an immigration judge, or the Board of Immigration Appeals in any such case prior to April 1, 1997. No asylum application that was filed with a district director, asylum officer, or immigration judge prior to April 1, 1997, may be reopened or otherwise reconsidered under the provisions of this part except by motion granted in the exercise of discretion by the Board of Immigration Appeals, an immigration judge, or an asylum officer for proper cause shown. Motions to reopen or reconsider must meet the requirements of sections 240(c)(6) and (c)(7) of the Act, and 8 CFR parts 1003 and 1103, where applicable.

(2) *Commonwealth of the Northern Mariana Islands.* The provisions of this subpart A shall not apply prior to January 1, 2015, to an alien physically present in or arriving in the Commonwealth of the Northern Mariana Islands seeking to apply for asylum. No application for asylum may be filed prior to January 1, 2015, pursuant to section 208 of the Act by an alien physically present in or arriving in the Commonwealth of the Northern Mariana Islands. Effective on the transition program effective date, the provisions of this subpart A shall apply to aliens physically present in or arriving in the CNMI with respect to withholding of removal under section 241(b)(3) of the Act and withholding and deferral of removal under the Convention Against Torture.

(b) *Training of asylum officers.* The Director of International Affairs shall ensure that asylum officers receive special training in international human rights law, nonadversarial interview techniques, and other relevant national and international refugee laws and principles. The Director of International Affairs shall also, in cooperation with the Department of State and other appropriate sources, compile and disseminate to asylum officers information concerning the persecution of persons in other countries on account of race, religion, nationality, membership in a particular social group, or political opinion, torture of persons in other countries, and other information relevant to asylum determinations, and shall maintain a documentation center with information on human rights conditions.

[64 FR 8487, Feb. 19, 1999, as amended at 74 FR 55741, Oct. 28, 2009]

§ 1208.2 Jurisdiction.

(a) *Office of International Affairs.* Except as provided in paragraph (b) or (c) of this section, the Office of International Affairs shall have initial jurisdiction over an asylum application filed by an alien physically present in the United States or seeking admission at a port-of-entry. The Office of International Affairs shall also have initial jurisdiction over credible fear determinations under § 1208.30 and reasonable fear determinations under § 1208.31.

(b) *Jurisdiction of Immigration Court in general.* Immigration judges shall have exclusive jurisdiction over asylum applications filed by an alien who has been served a Form I–221, Order to Show Cause; Form I–122, Notice to Applicant for Admission Detained for a Hearing before an Immigration Judge; or Form I–862, Notice to Appear, after the charging document has been filed with the Immigration Court. Immigration judges shall also have jurisdiction over any asylum applications filed prior to April 1, 1997, by alien crewmembers who have remained in the United States longer than authorized, by applicants for admission under the Visa Waiver Pilot Program, and by aliens who have been admitted to the United States under the Visa Waiver Pilot Program. Immigration judges shall also have the authority to review reasonable fear determinations referred to the Immigration Court under § 1208.31, and credible fear determinations referred to the Immigration Court under § 1208.30.

(c) *Certain aliens not entitled to proceedings under section 240 of the Act*—(1) *Asylum applications and withholding of removal applications only.* After Form I–863, Notice of Referral to Immigration Judge, has been filed with the Immigration Court, an immigration judge shall have exclusive jurisdiction over any asylum application filed on or after April 1, 1997, by:

(i) An alien crewmember who:

(A) Is an applicant for a landing permit;

(B) Has been refused permission to land under section 252 of the Act; or

(C) On or after April 1, 1997, was granted permission to land under section 252 of the Act, regardless of whether the alien has remained in the United States longer than authorized;

(ii) An alien stowaway who has been found to have a credible fear of persecution or torture pursuant to the procedures set forth in subpart B of this part;

(iii) An alien who is an applicant for admission pursuant to the Visa Waiver Program under section 217 of the Act, except that if such an alien is an applicant for admission to the Commonwealth of the Northern Mariana Islands, then he or she shall not be eligible for asylum prior to January 1, 2015;

(iv) An alien who was admitted to the United States pursuant to the Visa Waiver Program under section 217 of the Act and has remained longer than authorized or has otherwise violated his or her immigration status, except that if such an alien was admitted to the Commonwealth of the Northern Mariana Islands, then he or she shall not be eligible for asylum in the Commonwealth of the Northern Mariana Islands prior to January 1, 2015;

(v) An alien who has been ordered removed under § 235(c) of the Act, as described in § 235.8(a) of this chapter (applicable only in the event that the alien is referred for proceedings under this paragraph by the Regional Director pursuant to section 235.8(b)(2)(ii) of this chapter);

(vi) An alien who is an applicant for admission, or has been admitted, as an alien classified under section 101(a)(15)(S) of the Act (applicable only in the event that the alien is referred for proceedings under this paragraph by the district director);

(vii) An alien who is an applicant for admission to Guam or the Commonwealth of the Northern Mariana Islands pursuant to the Guam-CNMI Visa Waiver Program under section 212(l) of the Act, except that if such an alien is an applicant for admission to the Commonwealth of the Northern Mariana Islands, then he or she shall not be eligible for asylum prior to January 1, 2015; or

(viii) An alien who was admitted to Guam or the Commonwealth of the Northern Mariana Islands pursuant to the Guam-CNMI Visa Waiver Program under section 212(l) of the Act and has remained longer than authorized or has otherwise violated his or her immigration status, except that if such an alien was admitted to the Commonwealth of the Northern Mariana Islands, then he or she shall not be eligible for asylum in the Commonwealth of the Northern Mariana Islands prior to January 1, 2015.

(2) *Withholding of removal applications only*. After Form I–863, Notice of Referral to Immigration Judge, has been filed with the Immigration Court, an immigration judge shall have exclusive jurisdiction over any application for withholding of removal filed by:

(i) An alien who is the subject of a reinstated removal order pursuant to section 241(a)(5) of the Act; or

(ii) An alien who has been issued an administrative removal order pursuant to section 238 of the Act as an alien convicted of committing an aggravated felony.

(3) *Rules of procedure*—(i) *General*. Except as provided in this section, proceedings falling under the jurisdiction of the immigration judge pursuant to paragraph (c)(1) or (c)(2) of this section shall be conducted in accordance with the same rules of procedure as proceedings conducted under 8 CFR part 1240, subpart A. The scope of review in proceedings conducted pursuant to paragraph (c)(1) of this section shall be limited to a determination of whether the alien is eligible for asylum or withholding or deferral of removal, and whether asylum shall be granted in the exercise of discretion. The scope of review in proceedings conducted pursuant to paragraph (c)(2) of this section shall be limited to a determination of whether the alien is eligible for withholding or deferral of removal. During such proceedings, all parties are prohibited from raising or considering any other issues, including but not limited to issues of admissibility, deportability, eligibility for waivers, and eligibility for any other form of relief.

(ii) *Notice of hearing procedures and in-absentia decisions*. The alien will be provided with notice of the time and place of the proceeding. The request for asylum and withholding of removal submitted by an alien who fails to appear for the hearing shall be denied. The denial of asylum and withholding of removal for failure to appear may be reopened only upon a motion filed with the immigration judge with jurisdiction over the case. Only one motion to reopen may be filed, and it must be filed within 90 days, unless the alien establishes that he or she did not receive notice of the hearing date or was in Federal or State custody on the date directed to appear. The motion must include documentary evidence, which demonstrates that:

(A) The alien did not receive the notice;

(B) The alien was in Federal or State custody and the failure to appear was through no fault of the alien; or

(C) "Exceptional circumstances," as defined in section 240(e)(1) of the Act, caused the failure to appear.

(iii) *Relief*. The filing of a motion to reopen shall not stay removal of the alien unless the immigration judge issues an order granting a stay pending disposition of the motion. An alien who fails to appear for a proceeding under this section shall not be eligible for relief under section 240A, 240B, 245, 248, or 249 of the Act for a period of 10 years after the date of the denial, unless the applicant can show exceptional circumstances resulted in his or her failure to appear.

[65 FR 76130, Dec. 6, 2000, as amended at 74 FR 55741, Oct. 28, 2009]

§ 1208.3 Form of application.

(a) An asylum applicant must file Form I–589, Application for Asylum and for Withholding of Removal, together with any additional supporting evidence in accordance with the instructions on the form. The applicant's spouse and children shall be listed on the application and may be included in the request for asylum if they are in the United States. One additional copy of the principal applicant's Form I–589 must be submitted for each dependent included in the principal's application.

(b) An asylum application shall be deemed to constitute at the same time an application for withholding of removal, unless adjudicated in deportation or exclusion proceedings commenced prior to April 1, 1997. In such instances, the asylum application shall be deemed to constitute an application for withholding of deportation under section 243(h) of the Act, as that section existed prior to April 1, 1997. Where a determination is made that an applicant is ineligible to apply for asylum under section 208(a)(2) of the Act, an asylum application shall be construed as an application for withholding of removal.

(c) Form I–589 shall be filed under the following conditions and shall have the following consequences:

(1) If the application was filed on or after January 4, 1995, information provided in the application may be used as a basis for the initiation of removal proceedings, or to satisfy any burden of proof in exclusion, deportation, or removal proceedings;

(2) The applicant and anyone other than a spouse, parent, son, or daughter of the applicant who assists the applicant in preparing the application must sign the application under penalty of perjury. The applicant's signature establishes a presumption that the applicant is aware of the contents of the application. A person other than a relative specified in this paragraph who assists the applicant in preparing the application also must provide his or her full mailing address;

(3) An asylum application that does not include a response to each of the questions contained in the Form I–589, is unsigned, or is unaccompanied by the required materials specified in paragraph (a) of this section is incomplete. The filing of an incomplete application shall not commence the 150-day period after which the applicant may file an application for employment authorization in accordance with §1208.7. An application that is incomplete shall be returned by mail to the applicant within 30 days of the receipt of the application by the Service. If the Service has not mailed the incomplete application back to the applicant within 30 days, it shall be deemed complete. An application returned to the applicant as incomplete shall be resubmitted by the applicant with the additional information if he or she wishes to have the application considered;

(4) Knowing placement of false information on the application may subject the person placing that information on the application to criminal penalties under title 18 of the United States Code and to civil or criminal penalties under section 274C of the Act; and

(5) Knowingly filing a frivolous application on or after April 1, 1997, so long as the applicant has received the notice required by section 208(d)(4) of the Act, shall render the applicant permanently ineligible for any benefits under the Act pursuant to §1208.20.

[62 FR 10337, Mar. 6, 1997, as amended at 65 FR 76131, Dec. 6, 2000]

§1208.4 Filing the application.

Except as prohibited in paragraph (a) of this section, asylum applications shall be filed in accordance with paragraph (b) of this section.

(a) *Prohibitions on filing.* Section 208(a)(2) of the Act prohibits certain aliens from filing for asylum on or after April 1, 1997, unless the alien can demonstrate to the satisfaction of the Attorney General that one of the exceptions in section 208(a)(2)(D) of the Act applies. Such prohibition applies only to asylum applications under section 208 of the Act and not to applications for withholding of removal under §1208.16. If an applicant files an asylum application and it appears that one or more of the prohibitions contained in section 208(a)(2) of the Act apply, an asylum officer, in an interview, or an immigration judge, in a hearing, shall review the application and give the applicant the opportunity to present any relevant and useful information bearing on any prohibitions on filing to determine if the application should be rejected. For the purpose of making determinations under section 208(a)(2) of the Act, the following rules shall apply:

(1) *Authority.* Only an asylum officer, an immigration judge, or the Board of Immigration Appeals is authorized to make determinations regarding the prohibitions contained in section 208(a)(2)(B) or (C) of the Act.

(2) *One-year filing deadline.* (i) For purposes of section 208(a)(2)(B) of the

Act, an applicant has the burden of proving:

(A) By clear and convincing evidence that the application has been filed within 1 year of the date of the alien's arrival in the United States, or

(B) To the satisfaction of the asylum officer, the immigration judge, or the Board that he or she qualifies for an exception to the 1-year deadline.

(ii) The 1-year period shall be calculated from the date of the alien's last arrival in the United States or April 1, 1997, whichever is later. When the last day of the period so computed falls on a Saturday, Sunday, or legal holiday, the period shall run until the end of the next day that is not a Saturday, Sunday, or legal holiday. For the purpose of making determinations under section 208(a)(2)(B) of the Act only, an application is considered to have been filed on the date it is received by the Service, pursuant to §103.2(a)(7) of 8 CFR chapter I. In a case in which the application has not been received by the Service within 1 year from the applicant's date of entry into the United States, but the applicant provides clear and convincing documentary evidence of mailing the application within the 1-year period, the mailing date shall be considered the filing date. For cases before the Immigration Court in accordance with §1003.13 of this chapter, the application is considered to have been filed on the date it is received by the Immigration Court. For cases before the Board of Immigration Appeals, the application is considered to have been filed on the date it is received by the Board. In the case of an application that appears to have been filed more than a year after the applicant arrived in the United States, the asylum officer, the immigration judge, or the Board will determine whether the applicant qualifies for an exception to the deadline. The failure to have provided required biometrics and other biographical information does not prevent the "filing" of an asylum application for purposes of the one-year filing rule of section 208(a)(2)(B) of the Act. *See* 8 CFR 1003.47. For aliens present in or arriving in the Commonwealth of the Northern Mariana Islands, the 1-year period shall be calculated from January 1, 2015, or from the date of the alien's last arrival in the United States (including the Commonwealth of the Northern Mariana Islands), whichever is later. No period of physical presence in the Commonwealth of the Northern Mariana Islands prior to January 1, 2015, shall count toward the 1-year period. After November 28, 2009, any travel to the Commonwealth of the Northern Mariana Islands from any other State shall not re-start the calculation of the 1-year period.

(3) *Prior denial of application.* For purposes of section 208(a)(2)(C) of the Act, an asylum application has not been denied unless denied by an immigration judge or the Board of Immigration Appeals.

(4) *Changed circumstances.* (i) The term "changed circumstances" in section 208(a)(2)(D) of the Act shall refer to circumstances materially affecting the applicant's eligibility for asylum. They may include, but are not limited to:

(A) Changes in conditions in the applicant's country of nationality or, if the applicant is stateless, country of last habitual residence;

(B) Changes in the applicant's circumstances that materially affect the applicant's eligibility for asylum, including changes in applicable U.S. law and activities the applicant becomes involved in outside the country of feared persecution that place the applicant at risk; or

(C) In the case of an alien who had previously been included as a dependent in another alien's pending asylum application, the loss of the spousal or parent-child relationship to the principal applicant through marriage, divorce, death, or attainment of age 21.

(ii) The applicant shall file an asylum application within a reasonable period given those "changed circumstances." If the applicant can establish that he or she did not become aware of the changed circumstances until after they occurred, such delayed awareness shall be taken into account in determining what constitutes a "reasonable period."

(5) The term "extraordinary circumstances" in section 208(a)(2)(D) of the Act shall refer to events or factors directly related to the failure to meet

the 1-year deadline. Such circumstances may excuse the failure to file within the 1-year period as long as the alien filed the application within a reasonable period given those circumstances. The burden of proof is on the applicant to establish to the satisfaction of the asylum officer, the immigration judge, or the Board of Immigration Appeals that the circumstances were not intentionally created by the alien through his or her own action or inaction, that those circumstances were directly related to the alien's failure to file the application within the 1-year period, and that the delay was reasonable under the circumstances. Those circumstances may include but are not limited to:

(i) Serious illness or mental or physical disability, including any effects of persecution or violent harm suffered in the past, during the 1-year period after arrival;

(ii) Legal disability (e.g., the applicant was an unaccompanied minor or suffered from a mental impairment) during the 1-year period after arrival;

(iii) Ineffective assistance of counsel, provided that:

(A) The alien files an affidavit setting forth in detail the agreement that was entered into with counsel with respect to the actions to be taken and what representations counsel did or did not make to the respondent in this regard;

(B) The counsel whose integrity or competence is being impugned has been informed of the allegations leveled against him or her and given an opportunity to respond; and

(C) The alien indicates whether a complaint has been filed with appropriate disciplinary authorities with respect to any violation of counsel's ethical or legal responsibilities, and if not, why not;

(iv) The applicant maintained Temporary Protected Status, lawful immigrant or nonimmigrant status, or was given parole, until a reasonable period before the filing of the asylum application;

(v) The applicant filed an asylum application prior to the expiration of the 1-year deadline, but that application was rejected by the Service as not properly filed, was returned to the applicant for corrections, and was refiled within a reasonable period thereafter; and

(vi) The death or serious illness or incapacity of the applicant's legal representative or a member of the applicant's immediate family.

(6) *Safe third country agreement.* Immigration judges have authority to consider issues under section 208(a)(2)(A) of the Act, relating to the determination of whether an alien is ineligible to apply for asylum and should be removed to a safe third country pursuant to a bilateral or multilateral agreement, only with respect to aliens whom DHS has chosen to place in removal proceedings under section 240 of the Act, as provided in 8 CFR 1240.11(g). For DHS regulations relating to determinations by asylum officers on this subject, see 8 CFR 208.30(e)(6).

(b) *Filing location*—(1) *With the service center by mail.* Except as provided in paragraphs (b)(2), (b)(3), (b)(4) and (b)(5) of this section, asylum applications shall be filed directly by mail with the service center servicing the asylum office with jurisdiction over the place of the applicant's residence or, in the case of an alien without a United States residence, the applicant's current lodging or the land border port-of-entry through which the alien seeks admission to the United States.

(2) *With the asylum office.* An asylum application shall be filed directly with the asylum office having jurisdiction over the matter in the case of an alien who:

(i) Has received the express consent of the asylum office director or the Director of Asylum to do so, or

(ii) Previously was included in a spouse's or parent's pending application but is no longer eligible to be included as a derivative. In such cases, the derivative should include a cover letter referencing the previous application and explaining that he or she is now independently filing for asylum.

(3) *With the Immigration Court.* Asylum applications shall be filed directly with the Immigration Court having jurisdiction over the case in the following circumstances:

(i) During exclusion, deportation, or removal proceedings, with the Immigration Court having jurisdiction over the underlying proceeding.

(ii) After completion of exclusion, deportation, or removal proceedings, and in conjunction with a motion to reopen pursuant to 8 CFR part 1003 where applicable, with the Immigration Court having jurisdiction over the prior proceeding. Any such motion must reasonably explain the failure to request asylum prior to the completion of the proceedings.

(iii) In asylum proceedings pursuant to § 1208.2(c)(1) and after the Form I–863, Notice of Referral to Immigration Judge, has been served on the alien and filed with the Immigration Court having jurisdiction over the case.

(4) *With the Board of Immigration Appeals.* In conjunction with a motion to remand or reopen pursuant to §§ 1003.2 and 1003.8 of this chapter where applicable, an initial asylum application shall be filed with the Board of Immigration Appeals if jurisdiction over the proceedings is vested in the Board of Immigration Appeals under 8 CFR part 1003. Any such motion must reasonably explain the failure to request asylum prior to the completion of the proceedings.

(5) *With the district director.* In the case of any alien described in § 1208.2(c)(1) and prior to the service on the alien of Form I–863, any asylum application shall be submitted to the district director having jurisdiction pursuant to 8 CFR part 103. If the district director elects to issue the Form I–863, the district director shall forward such asylum application to the appropriate Immigration Court with the Form

(c) *Amending an application after filing.* Upon request of the alien and as a matter of discretion, the asylum officer or immigration judge having jurisdiction may permit an asylum applicant to amend or supplement the application, but any delay caused by such request shall extend the period within which the applicant may not apply for employment authorization in accordance with § 1208.7(a).

[62 FR 10337, Mar. 6, 1997, as amended at 64 FR 8488, Feb. 19, 1999; 64 FR 13881, Mar. 23, 1999; 65 FR 76131, Dec. 6, 2000; 69 FR 69497, Nov. 29, 2004; 70 FR 4754, Jan. 31, 2005; 74 FR 55741, Oct. 28, 2009]

§ 1208.5 Special duties toward aliens in custody of DHS.

(a) *General.* When an alien in the custody of DHS requests asylum or withholding of removal, or expresses a fear of persecution or harm upon return to his or her country of origin or to agents thereof, DHS shall make available the appropriate application forms and shall provide the applicant with the information required by section 208(d)(4) of the Act, except in the case of an alien who is in custody pending a credible fear determination under 8 CFR 1208.30 or a reasonable fear determination pursuant to 8 CFR 1208.31. Although DHS does not have a duty in the case of an alien who is in custody pending a credible fear or reasonable fear determination under either 8 CFR 1208.30 or 8 CFR 1208.31, DHS may provide the appropriate forms, upon request. Where possible, expedited consideration shall be given to applications of detained aliens. Except as provided in paragraph (c) of this section, such alien shall not be excluded, deported, or removed before a decision is rendered on his or her asylum application. Furthermore, except as provided in paragraph (c) of this section, an alien physically present in or arriving in the Commonwealth of the Northern Mariana Islands shall not be excluded, deported, or removed before a decision is rendered on his or her application for withholding of removal pursuant to section 241(b)(3) of the Act and withholding of removal under the Convention Against Torture. No application for asylum may be filed prior to January 1, 2015, pursuant to section 208 of the Act by an alien physically present in or arriving in the Commonwealth of the Northern Mariana Islands.

(b) *Certain aliens aboard vessels.* (1) If an alien crewmember or alien stowaway on board a vessel or other conveyance alleges, claims, or otherwise makes known to an immigration inspector or other official making an examination on the conveyance that he or she is unable or unwilling to return to his or her country of nationality or last habitual residence (if not a national of any country) because of persecution or a fear of persecution in that country on account of race, religion, nationality, membership in a particular social group, or political opinion, or if the alien expresses a fear of torture upon return to that country, the alien shall be promptly removed from the conveyance. If the alien makes such fear known to an official while off such conveyance, the alien shall not be returned to the conveyance but shall be retained in or transferred to the custody of the Service.

(i) An alien stowaway will be referred to an asylum officer for a credible fear determination under § 1208.30.

(ii) An alien crewmember shall be provided the appropriate application forms and information required by section 208(d)(4) of the Act and may then have 10 days within which to submit an asylum application to the district director having jurisdiction over the port-of-entry. The district director may extend the 10-day filing period for good cause. Once the application has been filed, the district director, pursuant to § 1208.4(b), shall serve Form I–863 on the alien and immediately forward any such application to the appropriate Immigration Court with a copy of the Form I–863 being filed with that court.

(iii) An alien crewmember physically present in or arriving in the Commonwealth of the Northern Mariana Islands can request withholding of removal pursuant to section 241(b)(3) of the Act and withholding of removal under the Convention Against Torture. However, such an alien crewmember is not eligible to request asylum pursuant to section 208 of the Act prior to January 1, 2015.

(2) Pending adjudication of the application, and, in the case of a stowaway the credible fear determination and any review thereof, the alien may be detained by the Service or otherwise paroled in accordance with § 1212.5 of this chapter. However, pending the credible fear determination, parole of an alien stowaway may be permitted only when the Attorney General determines, in the exercise of discretion, that parole is required to meet a medical emergency or is necessary for a legitimate law enforcement objective.

(c) *Exception to prohibition on removal.* A motion to reopen or an order to remand accompanied by an asylum application pursuant to § 1208.4(b)(3)(iii) shall not stay execution of a final exclusion, deportation, or removal order unless such stay is specifically granted by the Board of Immigration Appeals or the immigration judge having jurisdiction over the motion.

[62 FR 10337, Mar. 6, 1997, as amended at 64 FR 8488, Feb. 19, 1999; 65 FR 76132, Dec. 6, 2000; 73 FR 55741, Oct. 28, 2009]

§ 1208.6 Disclosure to third parties.

(a) Information contained in or pertaining to any asylum application, records pertaining to any credible fear determination conducted pursuant to § 1208.30, and records pertaining to any reasonable fear determination conducted pursuant to § 1208.31, shall not be disclosed without the written consent of the applicant, except as permitted by this section or at the discretion of the Attorney General.

(b) The confidentiality of other records kept by the Service and the Executive Office for Immigration Review that indicate that a specific alien has applied for asylum, received a credible fear or reasonable fear interview, or received a credible fear or reasonable fear review shall also be protected from disclosure. The Service will coordinate with the Department of State to ensure that the confidentiality of those records is maintained if they are transmitted to Department of State offices in other countries.

(c) This section shall not apply to any disclosure to:

(1) Any United States Government official or contractor having a need to examine information in connection with:

(i) The adjudication of asylum applications;

(ii) The consideration of a request for a credible fear or reasonable fear interview, or a credible fear or reasonable fear review;

(iii) The defense of any legal action arising from the adjudication of, or failure to adjudicate, the asylum application, or from a credible fear determination or reasonable fear determination under § 1208.30 or § 1208.31;

(iv) The defense of any legal action of which the asylum application, credible fear determination, or reasonable fear determination is a part; or

(v) Any United States Government investigation concerning any criminal or civil matter; or

(2) Any Federal, State, or local court in the United States considering any legal action:

(i) Arising from the adjudication of, or failure to adjudicate, the asylum application, or from a credible fear or reasonable fear determination under § 1208.30 or § 1208.31; or

(ii) Arising from the proceedings of which the asylum application, credible fear determination, or reasonable fear determination is a part.

[65 FR 76133, Dec. 6, 2000]

§ 1208.7 Employment authorization.

(a) *Application and approval.* (1) Subject to the restrictions contained in sections 208(d) and 236(a) of the Act, an applicant for asylum who is not an aggravated felon shall be eligible pursuant to §§ 1274a.12(c)(8) and 1274a.13(a) of this chapter to submit a Form I–765, Application for Employment Authorization. Except in the case of an alien whose asylum application has been recommended for approval, or in the case of an alien who filed an asylum application prior to January 4, 1995, the application shall be submitted no earlier than 150 days after the date on which a complete asylum application submitted in accordance with §§ 1208.3 and 1208.4 has been received. In the case of an applicant whose asylum application has been recommended for approval, the applicant may apply for employment authorization when he or she receives notice of the recommended approval. If an asylum application has been returned as incomplete in accordance with § 1208.3(c)(3), the 150-day period will commence upon receipt by the Service of a complete asylum application. An applicant whose asylum application has been denied by an asylum officer or by an immigration judge within the 150-day period shall not be eligible to apply for employment authorization. If an asylum application is denied prior to a decision on the application for employment authorization, the application for employment authorization shall be denied. If the asylum application is not so denied, the Service shall have 30 days from the date of filing of the Form I–765 to grant or deny that application, except that no employment authorization shall be issued to an asylum applicant prior to the expiration of the 180-day period following the filing of the asylum application filed on or after April 1, 1997.

(2) The time periods within which the alien may not apply for employment authorization and within which the Service must respond to any such application and within which the asylum application must be adjudicated pursuant to section 208(d)(5)(A)(iii) of the Act shall begin when the alien has filed a complete asylum application in accordance with §§ 1208.3 and 1208.4. Any delay requested or caused by the applicant shall not be counted as part of these time periods, including delays caused by failure without good cause to follow the requirements for fingerprint processing. Such time periods shall also be extended by the equivalent of the time between issuance of a request for evidence pursuant to § 103.2(b)(8) of 8 CFR chapter I and the receipt of the applicant's response to such request.

(3) The provisions of paragraphs (a)(1) and (a)(2) of this section apply to applications for asylum filed on or after January 4, 1995.

(4) Employment authorization pursuant to § 1274a.12(c)(8) of this chapter may not be granted to an alien who fails to appear for a scheduled interview before an asylum officer or a hearing before an immigration judge, unless the applicant demonstrates that the failure to appear was the result of exceptional circumstances.

(b) *Renewal and termination.* Employment authorization shall be renewable, in increments to be determined by the Commissioner, for the continuous period of time necessary for the asylum officer or immigration judge to decide the asylum application and, if necessary, for completion of any administrative or judicial review.

(1) If the asylum application is denied by the asylum officer, the employment authorization shall terminate at the expiration of the employment authorization document or 60 days after the denial of asylum, whichever is longer.

(2) If the application is denied by the immigration judge, the Board of Immigration Appeals, or a Federal court, the employment authorization terminates upon the expiration of the employment authorization document, unless the applicant has filed an appropriate request for administrative or judicial review.

(c) *Supporting evidence for renewal of employment authorization.* In order for employment authorization to be renewed under this section, the alien must provide the Service (in accordance with the instructions on or attached to the employment authorization application) with a Form I–765, the required fee (unless waived in accordance with § 103.7(c) of this chapter), and (if applicable) proof that he or she has continued to pursue his or her asylum application before an immigration judge or sought administrative or judicial review. For purposes of employment authorization, pursuit of an asylum application is established by presenting to the Service one of the following, depending on the stage of the alien's immigration proceedings:

(1) If the alien's case is pending in proceedings before the immigration judge, and the alien wishes to continue to pursue his or her asylum application, a copy of any asylum denial, referral notice, or charging document placing the alien in such proceedings;

(2) If the immigration judge has denied asylum, a copy of the document issued by the Board of Immigration Appeals to show that a timely appeal has been filed from a denial of the asylum application by the immigration judge; or

(3) If the Board of Immigration Appeals has dismissed the alien's appeal of a denial of asylum, or sustained an appeal by the Service of a grant of asylum, a copy of the petition for judicial review or for habeas corpus pursuant to section 242 of the Act, date stamped by the appropriate court.

(d) In order for employment authorization to be renewed before its expiration, the application for renewal must be received by the Service 90 days prior to expiration of the employment authorization.

[62 FR 10337, Mar. 6, 1997, as amended at 63 FR 12986, Mar. 17, 1998]

§ 1208.8 Limitations on travel outside the United States.

(a) An applicant who leaves the United States without first obtaining advance parole under § 212.5(f) of this chapter shall be presumed to have abandoned his or her application under this section.

(b) An applicant who leaves the United States pursuant to advance parole under § 1212.5(f) of this chapter and returns to the country of claimed persecution shall be presumed to have abandoned his or her application, unless the applicant is able to establish compelling reasons for such return.

[62 FR 10337, Mar. 6, 1997, as amended at 65 FR 82255, Dec. 28, 2000]

§ 1208.9 Procedure for interview before an asylum officer.

(a) The Service shall adjudicate the claim of each asylum applicant whose application is complete within the meaning of § 1208.3(c)(3) and is within the jurisdiction of the Service.

(b) The asylum officer shall conduct the interview in a nonadversarial manner and, except at the request of the applicant, separate and apart from the general public. The purpose of the interview shall be to elicit all relevant and useful information bearing on the applicant's eligibility for asylum. At the time of the interview, the applicant must provide complete information regarding his or her identity, including name, date and place of birth, and nationality, and may be required to register this identity electronically or through any other means designated by the Attorney General. The applicant may have counsel or a representative present, may present witnesses, and may submit affidavits of witnesses and other evidence.

(c) The asylum officer shall have authority to administer oaths, verify the identity of the applicant (including through the use of electronic means), verify the identity of any interpreter, present and receive evidence, and question the applicant and any witnesses.

(d) Upon completion of the interview, the applicant or the applicant's representative shall have an opportunity to make a statement or comment on the evidence presented. The asylum officer may, in his or her discretion, limit the length of such statement or comment and may require its submission in writing. Upon completion of the interview, the applicant shall be informed that he or she must appear in person to receive and to acknowledge receipt of the decision of the asylum officer and any other accompanying material at a time and place designated by the asylum officer, except as otherwise provided by the asylum officer. An applicant's failure to appear to receive and acknowledge receipt of the decision shall be treated as delay caused by the applicant for purposes of § 1208.7(a)(3) and shall extend the period within which the applicant may not apply for employment authorization by the number of days until the applicant does appear to receive and acknowledge receipt of the decision or until the applicant appears before an immigration judge in response to the issuance of a charging document under § 1208.14(c).

(e) The asylum officer shall consider evidence submitted by the applicant together with his or her asylum application, as well as any evidence submitted by the applicant before or at the interview. As a matter of discretion, the asylum officer may grant the applicant a brief extension of time following an interview during which the applicant may submit additional evidence. Any such extension shall extend by an equivalent time the periods specified by § 1208.7 for the filing and adjudication of any employment authorization application.

(f) The asylum application, all supporting information provided by the applicant, any comments submitted by the Department of State or by the Service, and any other information specific to the applicant's case and considered by the asylum officer shall comprise the record.

(g) An applicant unable to proceed with the interview in English must provide, at no expense to the Service, a competent interpreter fluent in both English and the applicant's native language or any other language in which the applicant is fluent. The interpreter must be at least 18 years of age. Neither the applicant's attorney or representative of record, a witness testifying on the applicant's behalf, nor a representative or employee of the applicant's country of nationality, or if stateless, country of last habitual residence, may serve as the applicant's interpreter. Failure without good cause to comply with this paragraph may be considered a failure to appear for the interview for purposes of § 1208.10.

[62 FR 10337, Mar. 6, 1997, as amended at 65 FR 76133, Dec. 6, 2000]

§ 1208.10 Failure to appear at a scheduled hearing before an immigration judge; failure to follow requirements for biometrics and other biographical information processing.

Failure to appear for a scheduled immigration hearing without prior authorization may result in dismissal of the application and the entry of an order of deportation or removal *in absentia*. Failure to comply with processing requirements for biometrics and other biographical information within the time allowed will result in dismissal of the application, unless the applicant demonstrates that such failure was the result of good cause. DHS is responsible for obtaining biometrics and other biographical information with respect to any alien in custody.

[70 FR 4754, Jan. 31, 2005]

§ 1208.11 Comments from the Department of State.

(a) The immigration judge may request, in his or her discretion, specific comments from the Department of State regarding individual cases or types of claims under consideration, or other information the immigration judge deems appropriate.

(b) With respect to any asylum application, the Department of State may provide, at its discretion, to the Immigration Court:

(1) Detailed country conditions information relevant to eligibility for asylum, withholding of removal under section 241(b)(3) of the Act, and withholding of removal under the Convention Against Torture;

(2) An assessment of the accuracy of the applicant's assertions about conditions in the applicant's country of nationality or habitual residence and the applicant's particular situation;

(3) Information about whether persons who are similarly situated to the applicant are persecuted or tortured in the applicant's country of nationality or habitual residence and the frequency of such persecution or torture; or

(4) Such other information as it deems relevant.

(c) Any comments received pursuant to paragraph (b) of this section shall be made part of the record. Unless the comments are classified under an applicable Executive Order, the applicant shall be provided an opportunity to review and respond to such comments prior to the issuance of any decision to deny the application.

[78 FR 19079, Mar. 29, 2013]

§ 1208.12 Reliance on information compiled by other sources.

(a) In deciding an asylum application, or in deciding whether the alien has a credible fear of persecution or torture pursuant to § 1208.30 of this part, or a reasonable fear of persecution or torture pursuant to § 1208.31, the asylum officer may rely on material provided by the Department of State, the Office of International Affairs, other Service offices, or other credible sources, such as international organizations, private voluntary agencies, news organizations, or academic institutions.

(b) Nothing in this part shall be construed to entitle the applicant to conduct discovery directed toward the records, officers, agents, or employees of the Service, the Department of Justice, or the Department of State. Persons may continue to seek documents available through a Freedom of Information Act (FOIA) request pursuant to 28 CFR part 16.

[62 FR 10337, Mar. 6, 1997, as amended at 64 FR 8488, Feb. 19, 1999; 65 FR 76133, Dec. 6, 2000]

§ 1208.13 Establishing asylum eligibility.

(a) *Burden of proof.* The burden of proof is on the applicant for asylum to establish that he or she is a refugee as defined in section 101(a)(42) of the Act. The testimony of the applicant, if credible, may be sufficient to sustain the burden of proof without corroboration. The fact that the applicant previously established a credible fear of persecution for purposes of section 235(b)(1)(B) of the Act does not relieve the alien of the additional burden of establishing eligibility for asylum.

(b) *Eligibility.* The applicant may qualify as a refugee either because he or she has suffered past persecution or because he or she has a well-founded fear of future persecution.

(1) *Past persecution.* An applicant shall be found to be a refugee on the basis of past persecution if the applicant can establish that he or she has suffered persecution in the past in the applicant's country of nationality or, if stateless, in his or her country of last habitual residence, on account of race, religion, nationality, membership in a particular social group, or political opinion, and is unable or unwilling to return to, or avail himself or herself of the protection of, that country owing to such persecution. An applicant who has been found to have established such past persecution shall also be presumed to have a well-founded fear of persecution on the basis of the original claim. That presumption may be rebutted if an asylum officer or immigration judge makes one of the findings described in paragraph (b)(1)(i) of this section. If the applicant's fear of future persecution is unrelated to the past persecution, the applicant bears the burden of establishing that the fear is well-founded.

(i) *Discretionary referral or denial.* Except as provided in paragraph (b)(1)(iii) of this section, an asylum officer shall, in the exercise of his or her discretion, refer or deny, or an immigration judge, in the exercise of his or her discretion, shall deny the asylum application of an alien found to be a refugee on the basis of past persecution if any of the following is found by a preponderance of the evidence:

(A) There has been a fundamental change in circumstances such that the applicant no longer has a well-founded fear of persecution in the applicant's country of nationality or, if stateless, in the applicant's country of last habitual residence, on account of race, religion, nationality, membership in a particular social group, or political opinion; or

(B) The applicant could avoid future persecution by relocating to another part of the applicant's country of nationality or, if stateless, another part of the applicant's country of last habitual residence, and under all the circumstances, it would be reasonable to expect the applicant to do so.

(ii) *Burden of proof.* In cases in which an applicant has demonstrated past persecution under paragraph (b)(1) of this section, the Service shall bear the burden of establishing by a preponderance of the evidence the requirements of paragraphs (b)(1)(i)(A) or (B) of this section.

(iii) *Grant in the absence of well-founded fear of persecution.* An applicant described in paragraph (b)(1)(i) of this section who is not barred from a grant of asylum under paragraph (c) of this section, may be granted asylum, in the exercise of the decision-maker's discretion, if:

(A) The applicant has demonstrated compelling reasons for being unwilling or unable to return to the country arising out of the severity of the past persecution; or

(B) The applicant has established that there is a reasonable possibility that he or she may suffer other serious harm upon removal to that country.

(2) *Well-founded fear of persecution.* (i) An applicant has a well-founded fear of persecution if:

(A) The applicant has a fear of persecution in his or her country of nationality or, if stateless, in his or her country of last habitual residence, on account of race, religion, nationality, membership in a particular social group, or political opinion;

(B) There is a reasonable possibility of suffering such persecution if he or she were to return to that country; and

(C) He or she is unable or unwilling to return to, or avail himself or herself of the protection of, that country because of such fear.

(ii) An applicant does not have a well-founded fear of persecution if the applicant could avoid persecution by relocating to another part of the applicant's country of nationality or, if stateless, another part of the applicant's country of last habitual residence, if under all the circumstances it would be reasonable to expect the applicant to do so.

(iii) In evaluating whether the applicant has sustained the burden of proving that he or she has a well-founded fear of persecution, the asylum officer or immigration judge shall not require the applicant to provide evidence that there is a reasonable possibility he or she would be singled out individually for persecution if:

(A) The applicant establishes that there is a pattern or practice in his or her country of nationality or, if stateless, in his or her country of last habitual residence, of persecution of a group of persons similarly situated to the applicant on account of race, religion, nationality, membership in a particular social group, or political opinion; and

(B) The applicant establishes his or her own inclusion in, and identification with, such group of persons such that his or her fear of persecution upon return is reasonable.

(3) *Reasonableness of internal relocation.* For purposes of determinations under paragraphs (b)(1)(i), (b)(1)(ii), and (b)(2) of this section, adjudicators should consider, but are not limited to considering, whether the applicant would face other serious harm in the place of suggested relocation; any ongoing civil strife within the country; administrative, economic, or judicial infrastructure; geographical limitations; and social and cultural constraints, such as age, gender, health, and social and familial ties. Those factors may, or may not, be relevant, depending on all the circumstances of the case, and are not necessarily determinative of whether it would be reasonable for the applicant to relocate.

(i) In cases in which the applicant has not established past persecution, the applicant shall bear the burden of establishing that it would not be reasonable for him or her to relocate, unless the persecution is by a government or is government-sponsored.

(ii) In cases in which the persecutor is a government or is government-sponsored, or the applicant has established persecution in the past, it shall be presumed that internal relocation would not be reasonable, unless the Service establishes by a preponderance of the evidence that, under all the circumstances, it would be reasonable for the applicant to relocate.

(c) *Mandatory denials*—(1) *Applications filed on or after April 1, 1997*. For applications filed on or after April 1, 1997, an applicant shall not qualify for asylum if section 208(a)(2) or 208(b)(2) of the Act applies to the applicant. If the applicant is found to be ineligible for asylum under either section 208(a)(2) or 208(b)(2) of the Act, the applicant shall be considered for eligibility for withholding of removal under section 241(b)(3) of the Act. The applicant shall also be considered for eligibility for withholding of removal under the Convention Against Torture if the applicant requests such consideration or if the evidence presented by the alien indicates that the alien may be tortured in the country of removal.

(2) *Applications filed before April 1, 1997*. (i) An immigration judge or asylum officer shall not grant asylum to any applicant who filed his or her application before April 1, 1997, if the alien:

(A) Having been convicted by a final judgment of a particularly serious crime in the United States, constitutes a danger to the community;

(B) Has been firmly resettled within the meaning of § 1208.15;

(C) Can reasonably be regarded as a danger to the security of the United States;

(D) Has been convicted of an aggravated felony, as defined in section 101(a)(43) of the Act; or

(E) Ordered, incited, assisted, or otherwise participated in the persecution of any person on account of race, religion, nationality, membership in a particular social group, or political opinion.

(F) Is described within section 212(a)(3)(B)(i)(I),(II), and (III) of the Act as it existed prior to April 1, 1997, and as amended by the Anti-terrorist and Effective Death Penalty Act of 1996 (AEDPA), unless it is determined that there are no reasonable grounds to believe that the individual is a danger to the security of the United States.

(ii) If the evidence indicates that one of the above grounds apply to the applicant, he or she shall have the burden of proving by a preponderance of the evidence that he or she did not so act.

(3) *Additional limitation on eligibility for asylum*. For applications filed after November 9, 2018, an alien shall be ineligible for asylum if the alien is subject to a presidential proclamation or other presidential order suspending or limiting the entry of aliens along the southern border with Mexico that is issued pursuant to subsection 212(f) or 215(a)(1) of the Act on or after November 9, 2018 and the alien enters the United States after the effective date of the proclamation or order contrary to the terms of the proclamation or order. This limitation on eligibility does not apply if the proclamation or order expressly provides that it does not affect eligibility for asylum, or expressly provides for a waiver or exception that makes the suspension or limitation inapplicable to the alien.

[62 FR 10337, Mar. 6, 1997, as amended at 64 FR 8488, Feb. 19, 1999; 65 FR 76133, Dec. 6, 2000; 83 FR 55952, Nov. 9, 2018]

§ 1208.14 Approval, denial, referral, or dismissal of application.

(a) *By an immigration judge*. Unless otherwise prohibited in § 1208.13(c), an immigration judge may grant or deny asylum in the exercise of discretion to an applicant who qualifies as a refugee under section 101(a)(42) of the Act. In no case shall an immigration judge grant asylum without compliance with the requirements of § 1003.47 concerning identity, law enforcement, or security investigations or examinations.

(b) *Approval by an asylum officer*. In any case within the jurisdiction of the Office of International Affairs, unless otherwise prohibited in § 1208.13(c), an asylum officer may grant, in the exercise of his or her discretion, asylum to an applicant who qualifies as a refugee under section 101(a)(42) of the Act, and whose identity has been checked pursuant to section 208(d)(5)(A)(i) of the Act.

(c) *Denial, referral, or dismissal by an asylum officer.* If the asylum officer does not grant asylum to an applicant after an interview conducted in accordance with § 1208.9, or if, as provided in § 1208.10, the applicant is deemed to have waived his or her right to an interview or an adjudication by an asylum officer, the asylum officer shall deny, refer, or dismiss the application, as follows:

(1) *Inadmissible or deportable aliens.* Except as provided in paragraph (c)(4) of this section, in the case of an applicant who appears to be inadmissible or deportable under section 212(a) or 237(a) of the Act, the asylum officer shall refer the application to an immigration judge, together with the appropriate charging document, for adjudication in removal proceedings (or, where charging documents may not be issued, shall dismiss the application).

(2) *Alien in valid status.* In the case of an applicant who is maintaining valid immigrant, nonimmigrant, or Temporary Protected Status at the time the application is decided, the asylum officer shall deny the application for asylum.

(3) *Alien with valid parole.* If an applicant has been paroled into the United States and the parole has not expired or been terminated by the Service, the asylum officer shall deny the application for asylum.

(4) *Alien paroled into the United States whose parole has expired or is terminated*—(i) *Alien paroled prior to April 1, 1997, or with advance authorization for parole.* In the case of an applicant who was paroled into the United States prior to April 1, 1997, or who, prior to departure from the United States, had received an advance authorization for parole, the asylum officer shall refer the application, together with the appropriate charging documents, to an immigration judge for adjudication in removal proceedings if the parole has expired, the Service has terminated parole, or the Service is terminating parole through issuance of the charging documents, pursuant to § 1212.5(d)(2)(i) of this chapter.

(ii) *Alien paroled on or after April 1, 1997, without advance authorization for parole.* In the case of an applicant who is an arriving alien or is otherwise subject to removal under § 1235.3(b) of this chapter, and was paroled into the United States on or after April 1, 1997, without advance authorization for parole prior to departure from the United States, the asylum officer will take the following actions, if the parole has expired or been terminated:

(A) *Inadmissible under section 212(a)(6)(C) or 212(a)(7) of the Act.* If the applicant appears inadmissible to the United States under section 212(a)(6)(C) or 212(a)(7) of the Act and the asylum officer does not intend to lodge any additional charges of inadmissibility, the asylum officer shall proceed in accordance with § 1235.3(b) of this chapter. If such applicant is found to have a credible fear of persecution or torture based on information elicited from the asylum interview, an asylum officer may refer the applicant directly to an immigration judge in removal proceedings under section 240 of the Act, without conducting a separate credible fear interview pursuant to § 1208.30. If such applicant is not found to have a credible fear based on information elicited at the asylum interview, an asylum officer will conduct a credible fear interview and the applicant will be subject to the credible fear process specified at § 1208.30(b).

(B) *Inadmissible on other grounds.* In the case of an applicant who was paroled into the United States on or after April 1, 1997, and will be charged as inadmissible to the United States under provisions of the Act other than, or in addition to, sections 212(a)(6)(C) or 212(a)(7), the asylum officer shall refer the application to an immigration judge for adjudication in removal proceedings.

(d) *Applicability of § 103.2(b) of this chapter.* No application for asylum or withholding of deportation shall be subject to denial pursuant to § 103.2(b) of this chapter.

(e) *Duration.* If the applicant is granted asylum, the grant will be effective for an indefinite period, subject to termination as provided in § 1208.24.

(f) *Effect of denial of principal's application on separate applications by dependents.* The denial of an asylum application filed by a principal applicant for asylum shall also result in the denial of asylum status to any dependents of that principal applicant who are included in that same application. Such denial shall not preclude a grant of asylum for an otherwise eligible dependent who has filed a separate asylum application, nor shall such denial result in an otherwise eligible dependent becoming ineligible to apply for asylum due to the provisions of section 208(a)(2)(C) of the Act.

(g) *Applicants granted lawful permanent residence status.* If an asylum applicant is granted adjustment of status to lawful permanent resident, the Service may provide written notice to the applicant that his or her asylum application will be presumed abandoned and dismissed without prejudice, unless the applicant submits a written request within 30 days of the notice, that the asylum application be adjudicated. If an applicant does not respond within 30 days of the date the written notice was sent or served, the Service may presume the asylum application abandoned and dismiss it without prejudice.

[62 FR 10337, Mar. 6, 1997, as amended at 63 FR 12986, Mar. 17, 1998; 64 FR 27875, May 21, 1999; 65 FR 76134, Dec. 6, 2000; 70 FR 4754, Jan. 31, 2005]

§ 1208.15 Definition of "firm resettlement."

An alien is considered to be firmly resettled if, prior to arrival in the United States, he or she entered into another country with, or while in that country received, an offer of permanent resident status, citizenship, or some other type of permanent resettlement unless he or she establishes:

(a) That his or her entry into that country was a necessary consequence of his or her flight from persecution, that he or she remained in that country only as long as was necessary to arrange onward travel, and that he or she did not establish significant ties in that country; or

(b) That the conditions of his or her residence in that country were so substantially and consciously restricted by the authority of the country of refuge that he or she was not in fact resettled. In making his or her determination, the asylum officer or immigration judge shall consider the conditions under which other residents of the country live; the type of housing, whether permanent or temporary, made available to the refugee; the types and extent of employment available to the refugee; and the extent to which the refugee received permission to hold property and to enjoy other rights and privileges, such as travel documentation that includes a right of entry or reentry, education, public relief, or naturalization, ordinarily available to others resident in the country.

[65 FR 76135, Dec. 6, 2000]

§ 1208.16 Withholding of removal under section 241(b)(3)(B) of the Act and withholding of removal under the Convention Against Torture.

(a) *Consideration of application for withholding of removal.* An asylum officer shall not decide whether the exclusion, deportation, or removal of an alien to a country where the alien's life or freedom would be threatened must be withheld, except in the case of an alien who is otherwise eligible for asylum but is precluded from being granted such status due solely to section 207(a)(5) of the Act. In exclusion, deportation, or removal proceedings, an immigration judge may adjudicate both an asylum claim and a request for withholding of removal whether or not asylum is granted.

(b) *Eligibility for withholding of removal under section 241(b)(3) of the Act; burden of proof.* The burden of proof is on the applicant for withholding of removal under section 241(b)(3) of the Act to establish that his or her life or freedom would be threatened in the proposed country of removal on account of race, religion, nationality, membership in a particular social group, or political opinion. The testimony of the applicant, if credible, may be sufficient to sustain the burden of proof without corroboration. The evidence shall be evaluated as follows:

(1) *Past threat to life or freedom.* (i) If the applicant is determined to have suffered past persecution in the proposed country of removal on account of race, religion, nationality, membership in a particular social group, or political opinion, it shall be presumed that the applicant's life or freedom would be threatened in the future in the country

of removal on the basis of the original claim. This presumption may be rebutted if an asylum officer or immigration judge finds by a preponderance of the evidence:

(A) There has been a fundamental change in circumstances such that the applicant's life or freedom would not be threatened on account of any of the five grounds mentioned in this paragraph upon the applicant's removal to that country; or

(B) The applicant could avoid a future threat to his or her life or freedom by relocating to another part of the proposed country of removal and, under all the circumstances, it would be reasonable to expect the applicant to do so.

(ii) In cases in which the applicant has established past persecution, the Service shall bear the burden of establishing by a preponderance of the evidence the requirements of paragraphs (b)(1)(i)(A) or (b)(1)(i)(B) of this section.

(iii) If the applicant's fear of future threat to life or freedom is unrelated to the past persecution, the applicant bears the burden of establishing that it is more likely than not that he or she would suffer such harm.

(2) *Future threat to life or freedom.* An applicant who has not suffered past persecution may demonstrate that his or her life or freedom would be threatened in the future in a country if he or she can establish that it is more likely than not that he or she would be persecuted on account of race, religion, nationality, membership in a particular social group, or political opinion upon removal to that country. Such an applicant cannot demonstrate that his or her life or freedom would be threatened if the asylum officer or immigration judge finds that the applicant could avoid a future threat to his or her life or freedom by relocating to another part of the proposed country of removal and, under all the circumstances, it would be reasonable to expect the applicant to do so. In evaluating whether it is more likely than not that the applicant's life or freedom would be threatened in a particular country on account of race, religion, nationality, membership in a particular social group, or political opinion, the asylum officer or immigration judge shall not require the applicant to provide evidence that he or she would be singled out individually for such persecution if:

(i) The applicant establishes that in that country there is a pattern or practice of persecution of a group of persons similarly situated to the applicant on account of race, religion, nationality, membership in a particular social group, or political opinion; and

(ii) The applicant establishes his or her own inclusion in and identification with such group of persons such that it is more likely than not that his or her life or freedom would be threatened upon return to that country.

(3) *Reasonableness of internal relocation.* For purposes of determinations under paragraphs (b)(1) and (b)(2) of this section, adjudicators should consider, among other things, whether the applicant would face other serious harm in the place of suggested relocation; any ongoing civil strife within the country; administrative, economic, or judicial infrastructure; geographical limitations; and social and cultural constraints, such as age, gender, health, and social and familial ties. These factors may or may not be relevant, depending on all the circumstances of the case, and are not necessarily determinative of whether it would be reasonable for the applicant to relocate.

(i) In cases in which the applicant has not established past persecution, the applicant shall bear the burden of establishing that it would not be reasonable for him or her to relocate, unless the persecutor is a government or is government-sponsored.

(ii) In cases in which the persecutor is a government or is government-sponsored, or the applicant has established persecution in the past, it shall be presumed that internal relocation would not be reasonable, unless the Service establishes by a preponderance of the evidence that under all the circumstances it would be reasonable for the applicant to relocate.

(c) *Eligibility for withholding of removal under the Convention Against Torture.* (1) For purposes of regulations under Title II of the Act, "Convention Against Torture" shall refer to the United Nations Convention Against

Torture and Other Cruel, Inhuman or Degrading Treatment or Punishment, subject to any reservations, understandings, declarations, and provisos contained in the United States Senate resolution of ratification of the Convention, as implemented by section 2242 of the Foreign Affairs Reform and Restructuring Act of 1998 (Pub. L. 105–277, 112 Stat. 2681, 2681–821). The definition of torture contained in § 1208.18(a) of this part shall govern all decisions made under regulations under Title II of the Act about the applicability of Article 3 of the Convention Against Torture.

(2) The burden of proof is on the applicant for withholding of removal under this paragraph to establish that it is more likely than not that he or she would be tortured if removed to the proposed country of removal. The testimony of the applicant, if credible, may be sufficient to sustain the burden of proof without corroboration.

(3) In assessing whether it is more likely than not that an applicant would be tortured in the proposed country of removal, all evidence relevant to the possibility of future torture shall be considered, including, but not limited to:

(i) Evidence of past torture inflicted upon the applicant;

(ii) Evidence that the applicant could relocate to a part of the country of removal where he or she is not likely to be tortured;

(iii) Evidence of gross, flagrant or mass violations of human rights within the country of removal, where applicable; and

(iv) Other relevant information regarding conditions in the country of removal.

(4) In considering an application for withholding of removal under the Convention Against Torture, the immigration judge shall first determine whether the alien is more likely than not to be tortured in the country of removal. If the immigration judge determines that the alien is more likely than not to be tortured in the country of removal, the alien is entitled to protection under the Convention Against Torture. Protection under the Convention Against Torture will be granted either in the form of withholding of removal or in the form of deferral of removal. An alien entitled to such protection shall be granted withholding of removal unless the alien is subject to mandatory denial of withholding of removal under paragraphs (d)(2) or (d)(3) of this section. If an alien entitled to such protection is subject to mandatory denial of withholding of removal under paragraphs (d)(2) or (d)(3) of this section, the alien's removal shall be deferred under § 1208.17(a).

(d) *Approval or denial of application*—(1) *General.* Subject to paragraphs (d)(2) and (d)(3) of this section, an application for withholding of deportation or removal to a country of proposed removal shall be granted if the applicant's eligibility for withholding is established pursuant to paragraphs (b) or (c) of this section.

(2) *Mandatory denials.* Except as provided in paragraph (d)(3) of this section, an application for withholding of removal under section 241(b)(3) of the Act or under the Convention Against Torture shall be denied if the applicant falls within section 241(b)(3)(B) of the Act or, for applications for withholding of deportation adjudicated in proceedings commenced prior to April 1, 1997, within section 243(h)(2) of the Act as it appeared prior to that date. For purposes of section 241(b)(3)(B)(ii) of the Act, or section 243(h)(2)(B) of the Act as it appeared prior to April 1, 1997, an alien who has been convicted of a particularly serious crime shall be considered to constitute a danger to the community. If the evidence indicates the applicability of one or more of the grounds for denial of withholding enumerated in the Act, the applicant shall have the burden of proving by a preponderance of the evidence that such grounds do not apply.

(3) *Exception to the prohibition on withholding of deportation in certain cases.* Section 243(h)(3) of the Act, as added by section 413 of Pub. L. 104–132 (110 Stat. 1214), shall apply only to applications adjudicated in proceedings commenced before April 1, 1997, and in which final action had not been taken before April 24, 1996. The discretion permitted by that section to override section 243(h)(2) of the Act shall be exercised

only in the case of an applicant convicted of an aggravated felony (or felonies) where he or she was sentenced to an aggregate term of imprisonment of less than 5 years and the immigration judge determines on an individual basis that the crime (or crimes) of which the applicant was convicted does not constitute a particularly serious crime. Nevertheless, it shall be presumed that an alien convicted of an aggravated felony has been convicted of a particularly serious crime. Except in the cases specified in this paragraph, the grounds for denial of withholding of deportation in section 243(h)(2) of the Act as it appeared prior to April 1, 1997, shall be deemed to comply with the Protocol Relating to the Status of Refugees, Jan. 31, 1967, T.I.A.S. No. 6577.

(e) *Reconsideration of discretionary denial of asylum.* In the event that an applicant is denied asylum solely in the exercise of discretion, and the applicant is subsequently granted withholding of deportation or removal under this section, thereby effectively precluding admission of the applicant's spouse or minor children following to join him or her, the denial of asylum shall be reconsidered. Factors to be considered will include the reasons for the denial and reasonable alternatives available to the applicant such as reunification with his or her spouse or minor children in a third country.

(f) *Removal to third country.* Nothing in this section or § 1208.17 shall prevent the Service from removing an alien to a third country other than the country to which removal has been withheld or deferred.

[62 FR 10337, Mar. 6, 1997, as amended at 64 FR 8488, Feb. 19, 1999; 65 FR 76135, Dec. 6, 2000]

§ 1208.17 Deferral of removal under the Convention Against Torture.

(a) *Grant of deferral of removal.* An alien who: has been ordered removed; has been found under § 1208.16(c)(3) to be entitled to protection under the Convention Against Torture; and is subject to the provisions for mandatory denial of withholding of removal under § 1208.16(d)(2) or (d)(3), shall be granted deferral of removal to the country where he or she is more likely than not to be tortured.

(b) *Notice to alien.* (1) After an immigration judge orders an alien described in paragraph (a) of this section removed, the immigration judge shall inform the alien that his or her removal to the country where he or she is more likely than not to be tortured shall be deferred until such time as the deferral is terminated under this section. The immigration judge shall inform the alien that deferral of removal:

(i) Does not confer upon the alien any lawful or permanent immigration status in the United States;

(ii) Will not necessarily result in the alien being released from the custody of the Service if the alien is subject to such custody;

(iii) Is effective only until terminated; and

(iv) Is subject to review and termination if the immigration judge determines that it is not likely that the alien would be tortured in the country to which removal has been deferred, or if the alien requests that deferral be terminated.

(2) The immigration judge shall also inform the alien that removal has been deferred only to the country in which it has been determined that the alien is likely to be tortured, and that the alien may be removed at any time to another country where he or she is not likely to be tortured.

(c) *Detention of an alien granted deferral of removal under this section.* Nothing in this section shall alter the authority of the Service to detain an alien whose removal has been deferred under this section and who is otherwise subject to detention. In the case of such an alien, decisions about the alien's release shall be made according to part 241 of this chapter.

(d) *Termination of deferral of removal.* (1) At any time while deferral of removal is in effect, the INS District Counsel for the District with jurisdiction over an alien whose removal has been deferred under paragraph (a) of this section may file a motion with the Immigration Court having administrative control pursuant to § 1003.11 of this chapter to schedule a hearing to consider whether deferral of removal should be terminated. The Service motion shall be granted if it is accompanied by evidence that is relevant to the possibility that the alien would be tortured in the country to which removal has been deferred and that was not presented at the previous hearing. The Service motion shall not be subject to the requirements for reopening in §§ 3.2 and 3.23 of this chapter.

(2) The Immigration Court shall provide notice to the alien and the Service of the time, place, and date of the termination hearing. Such notice shall inform the alien that the alien may supplement the information in his or her initial application for withholding of removal under the Convention Against Torture and shall provide that the alien must submit any such supplemental information within 10 calendar days of service of such notice (or 13 calendar days if service of such notice was by mail). At the expiration of this 10 or 13 day period, the Immigration Court shall forward a copy of the original application, and any supplemental information the alien or the Service has submitted, to the Department of State, together with notice to the Department of State of the time, place and date of the termination hearing. At its option, the Department of State may provide comments on the case, according to the provisions of § 1208.11 of this part.

(3) The immigration judge shall conduct a hearing and make a *de novo* determination, based on the record of proceeding and initial application in addition to any new evidence submitted by the Service or the alien, as to whether the alien is more likely than not to be tortured in the country to which removal has been deferred. This determination shall be made under the standards for eligibility set out in § 1208.16(c). The burden is on the alien to establish that it is more likely than not that he or she would be tortured in the country to which removal has been deferred.

(4) If the immigration judge determines that the alien is more likely than not to be tortured in the country to which removal has been deferred, the order of deferral shall remain in place. If the immigration judge determines that the alien has not established that he or she is more likely than not to be tortured in the country to which removal has been deferred, the deferral of removal shall be terminated and the alien may be removed to that country. Appeal of the immigration judge's decision shall lie to the Board.

(e) *Termination at the request of the alien.* (1) At any time while deferral of removal is in effect, the alien may make a written request to the Immigration Court having administrative control pursuant to § 1003.11 of this chapter to terminate the deferral order. If satisfied on the basis of the written submission that the alien's request is knowing and voluntary, the immigration judge shall terminate the order of deferral and the alien may be removed.

(2) If necessary the immigration judge may calendar a hearing for the sole purpose of determining whether the alien's request is knowing and voluntary. If the immigration judge determines that the alien's request is knowing and voluntary, the order of deferral shall be terminated. If the immigration judge determines that the alien's request is not knowing and voluntary, the alien's request shall not serve as the basis for terminating the order of deferral.

(f) *Termination pursuant to § 1208.18(c).* At any time while deferral of removal is in effect, the Attorney General may determine whether deferral should be terminated based on diplomatic assurances forwarded by the Secretary of State pursuant to the procedures in § 1208.18(c).

[64 FR 8489, Feb. 19, 1999]

§ 1208.18 Implementation of the Convention Against Torture.

(a) *Definitions.* The definitions in this subsection incorporate the definition of torture contained in Article 1 of the Convention Against Torture, subject to the reservations, understandings, declarations, and provisos contained in the United States Senate resolution of ratification of the Convention.

(1) Torture is defined as any act by which severe pain or suffering, whether physical or mental, is intentionally inflicted on a person for such purposes as obtaining from him or her or a third person information or a confession, punishing him or her for an act he or she or a third person has committed or

is suspected of having committed, or intimidating or coercing him or her or a third person, or for any reason based on discrimination of any kind, when such pain or suffering is inflicted by or at the instigation of or with the consent or acquiescence of a public official or other person acting in an official capacity.

(2) Torture is an extreme form of cruel and inhuman treatment and does not include lesser forms of cruel, inhuman or degrading treatment or punishment that do not amount to torture.

(3) Torture does not include pain or suffering arising only from, inherent in or incidental to lawful sanctions. Lawful sanctions include judicially imposed sanctions and other enforcement actions authorized by law, including the death penalty, but do not include sanctions that defeat the object and purpose of the Convention Against Torture to prohibit torture.

(4) In order to constitute torture, mental pain or suffering must be prolonged mental harm caused by or resulting from:

(i) The intentional infliction or threatened infliction of severe physical pain or suffering;

(ii) The administration or application, or threatened administration or application, of mind altering substances or other procedures calculated to disrupt profoundly the senses or the personality;

(iii) The threat of imminent death; or

(iv) The threat that another person will imminently be subjected to death, severe physical pain or suffering, or the administration or application of mind altering substances or other procedures calculated to disrupt profoundly the sense or personality.

(5) In order to constitute torture, an act must be specifically intended to inflict severe physical or mental pain or suffering. An act that results in unanticipated or unintended severity of pain and suffering is not torture.

(6) In order to constitute torture an act must be directed against a person in the offender's custody or physical control.

(7) Acquiescence of a public official requires that the public official, prior to the activity constituting torture, have awareness of such activity and thereafter breach his or her legal responsibility to intervene to prevent such activity.

(8) Noncompliance with applicable legal procedural standards does not *per se* constitute torture.

(b) *Applicability of §§1208.16(c) and 1208.17(a)*—(1) *Aliens in proceedings on or after March 22, 1999.* An alien who is in exclusion, deportation, or removal proceedings on or after March 22, 1999 may apply for withholding of removal under §1208.16(c), and, if applicable, may be considered for deferral of removal under §1208.17(a).

(2) *Aliens who were ordered removed, or whose removal orders became final, before March 22, 1999.* An alien under a final order of deportation, exclusion, or removal that became final prior to March 22, 1999 may move to reopen proceedings for the sole purpose of seeking protection under §1208.16(c). Such motions shall be governed by §§1003.23 and 1003.2 of this chapter, except that the time and numerical limitations on motions to reopen shall not apply and the alien shall not be required to demonstrate that the evidence sought to be offered was unavailable and could not have been discovered or presented at the former hearing. The motion to reopen shall not be granted unless:

(i) The motion is filed within June 21, 1999; and

(ii) The evidence sought to be offered establishes a prima facie case that the applicant's removal must be withheld or deferred under §§1208.16(c) or 1208.17(a).

(3) *Aliens who, on March 22, 1999, have requests pending with the Service for protection under Article 3 of the Convention Against Torture.* (i) Except as otherwise provided, after March 22, 1999, the Service will not:

(A) Consider, under its pre-regulatory administrative policy to ensure compliance with the Convention Against Torture, whether Article 3 of that Convention prohibits the removal of an alien to a particular country, or

(B) Stay the removal of an alien based on a request filed with the Service for protection under Article 3 of that Convention.

(ii) For each alien who, on or before March 22, 1999, filed a request with the Service for protection under Article 3 of the Convention Against Torture, and whose request has not been finally decided by the Service, the Service shall provide written notice that, after March 22, 1999, consideration for protection under Article 3 can be obtained only through the provisions of this rule.

(A) The notice shall inform an alien who is under an order of removal issued by EOIR that, in order to seek consideration of a claim under §§ 1208.16(c) or 1208.17(a), such an alien must file a motion to reopen with the immigration court or the Board of Immigration Appeals. This notice shall be accompanied by a stay of removal, effective until 30 days after service of the notice on the alien. A motion to reopen filed under this paragraph for the limited purpose of asserting a claim under §§ 1208.16(c) or 1208.17(a) shall not be subject to the requirements for reopening in §§ 1003.2 and 1003.23 of this chapter. Such a motion shall be granted if it is accompanied by a copy of the notice described in paragraph (b)(3)(ii) or by other convincing evidence that the alien had a request pending with the Service for protection under Article 3 of the Convention Against Torture on March 22, 1999. The filing of such a motion shall extend the stay of removal during the pendency of the adjudication of this motion.

(B) The notice shall inform an alien who is under an administrative order of removal issued by the Service under section 238(b) of the Act or an exclusion, deportation, or removal order reinstated by the Service under section 241(a)(5) of the Act that the alien's claim to withholding of removal under § 1208.16(c) or deferral of removal under § 1208.17(a) will be considered under § 1208.31.

(C) The notice shall inform an alien who is under an administrative order of removal issued by the Service under section 235(c) of the Act that the alien's claim to protection under the Convention Against Torture will be decided by the Service as provided in § 1208.18(d) and 1235.8(b)(4) and will not be considered under the provisions of this part relating to consideration or review by an immigration judge, the Board of Immigration Appeals, or an asylum officer.

(4) *Aliens whose claims to protection under the Convention Against Torture were finally decided by the Service prior to March 22, 1999.* Sections 208.16(c) and 208.17 (a) and paragraphs (b)(1) through (b)(3) of this section do not apply to cases in which, prior to March 22, 1999, the Service has made a final administrative determination about the applicability of Article 3 of the Convention Against Torture to the case of an alien who filed a request with the Service for protection under Article 3. If, prior to March 22, 1999, the Service determined that an applicant cannot be removed consistent with the Convention Against Torture, the alien shall be considered to have been granted withholding of removal under § 1208.16(c), unless the alien is subject to mandatory denial of withholding of removal under § 1208.16(d)(2) or (d)(3), in which case the alien will be considered to have been granted deferral of removal under 208.17(a). If, prior to March 22, 1999, the Service determined that an alien can be removed consistent with the Convention Against Torture, the alien will be considered to have been finally denied withholding of removal under § 1208.16(c) and deferral of removal under § 1208.17(a).

(c) *Diplomatic assurances against torture obtained by the Secretary of State.* (1) The Secretary of State may forward to the Attorney General assurances that the Secretary has obtained from the government of a specific country that an alien would not be tortured there if the alien were removed to that country.

(2) If the Secretary of State forwards assurances described in paragraph (c)(1) of this section to the Attorney General for consideration by the Attorney General or her delegates under this paragraph, the Attorney General shall determine, in consultation with the Secretary of State, whether the assurances are sufficiently reliable to allow the alien's removal to that country consistent with Article 3 of the Convention Against Torture. The Attorney General's authority under this paragraph may be exercised by the Deputy Attorney General or by the Commissioner, Immigration and Naturalization Service, but may not be further delegated.

(3) Once assurances are provided under paragraph (c)(2) of this section, the alien's claim for protection under the Convention Against Torture shall not be considered further by an immigration judge, the Board of Immigration Appeals, or an asylum officer.

(d) *Cases involving aliens ordered removed under section 235(c) of the Act.* With respect to an alien terrorist or other alien subject to administrative removal under section 235(c) of the Act who requests protection under Article 3 of the Convention Against Torture, the Service will assess the applicability of Article 3 through the removal process to ensure that a removal order will not be executed under circumstances that would violate the obligations of the United States under Article 3. In such cases, the provisions of Part 208 relating to consideration or review by an immigration judge, the Board of Immigration Appeals, or an asylum officer shall not apply.

(e) *Judicial review of claims for protection from removal under Article 3 of the Convention Against Torture.* (1) Pursuant to the provisions of section 2242(d) of the Foreign Affairs Reform and Restructuring Act of 1998, there shall be no judicial appeal or review of any action, decision, or claim raised under the Convention or that section, except as part of the review of a final order of removal pursuant to section 242 of the Act; provided however, that any appeal or petition regarding an action, decision, or claim under the Convention or under section 2242 of the Foreign Affairs Reform and Restructuring Act of 1998 shall not be deemed to include or authorize the consideration of any administrative order or decision, or portion thereof, the appeal or review of which is restricted or prohibited by the Act.

(2) Except as otherwise expressly provided, nothing in this paragraph shall be construed to create a private right of action or to authorize the consideration or issuance of administrative or judicial relief.

[64 FR 8490, Feb. 19, 1999; 64 FR 13881, Mar. 23, 1999]

§ 1208.19 Decisions.

The decision of an asylum officer to grant or to deny asylum or to refer an asylum application, in accordance with § 1208.14(b) or (c), shall be communicated in writing to the applicant. Pursuant to § 1208.9(d), an applicant must appear in person to receive and to acknowledge receipt of the decision to grant or deny asylum, or to refer an asylum application unless, in the discretion of the asylum office director, service by mail is appropriate. A letter communicating denial of asylum or referral of the application shall state the basis for denial or referral and include an assessment of the applicant's credibility.

[65 FR 76136, Dec. 6, 2000]

§ 1208.20 Determining if an asylum application is frivolous.

For applications filed on or after April 1, 1997, an applicant is subject to the provisions of section 208(d)(6) of the Act only if a final order by an immigration judge or the Board of Immigration Appeals specifically finds that the alien knowingly filed a frivolous asylum application. For purposes of this section, an asylum application is frivolous if any of its material elements is deliberately fabricated. Such finding shall only be made if the immigration judge or the Board is satisfied that the applicant, during the course of the proceedings, has had sufficient opportunity to account for any discrepancies or implausible aspects of the claim. For purposes of this section, a finding that an alien filed a frivolous asylum application shall not preclude the alien from seeking withholding of removal.

[64 FR 8492, Feb. 19, 1999. Redesignated at 65 FR 76136, Dec. 6, 2000]

§ 1208.21 Admission of the asylee's spouse and children.

(a) *Eligibility.* In accordance with section 208(b)(3) of the Act, a spouse, as defined in section 101(a)(35) of the Act, 8 U.S.C. 1101(a)(35), or child, as defined in section 101(b)(1) of the Act, also may be granted asylum if accompanying, or following to join, the principal alien who was granted asylum, unless it is determined that the spouse or child is ineligible for asylum under section 208(b)(2)(A)(i), (ii), (iii), (iv) or (v) of the Act for applications filed on or after April 1, 1997, or under

§ 1208.13(c)(2)(i)(A), (C), (D), (E), or (F) for applications filed before April 1, 1997.

(b) *Relationship.* The relationship of spouse and child as defined in sections 101(a)(35) and 101(b)(1) of the Act must have existed at the time the principal alien's asylum application was approved and must continue to exist at the time of filing for accompanying or following-to-join benefits and at the time of the spouse or child's subsequent admission to the United States. If the asylee proves that the asylee is the parent of a child who was born after asylum was granted, but who was *in utero* on the date of the asylum grant, the child shall be eligible to accompany or follow-to-join the asylee. The child's mother, if not the principal asylee, shall not be eligible to accompany or follow-to-join the principal asylee unless the child's mother was the principal asylee's spouse on the date the principal asylee was granted asylum.

(c) *Spouse or child in the United States.* When a spouse or child of an alien granted asylum is in the United States, but was not included in the asylee's application, the asylee may request accompanying or following-to-join benefits for his/her spouse or child by filing for each qualifying family member a separate Form I–730, Refugee/Asylee Relative Petition, and supporting evidence, with the designated Service office, regardless of the status of that spouse or child in the United States. A recent photograph of each derivative must accompany the Form I–730. The photograph must clearly identify the derivative, and will be made part of the derivative's immigration record for identification purposes. Additionally, a separate Form I–730 must be filed by the asylee for each qualifying family member before February 28, 2000, or within 2 years of the date in which he/she was granted asylum status, whichever is later, unless it is determined by the Service that this period should be extended for humanitarian reasons. Upon approval of the Form I–730, the Service will notify the asylee of such approval on Form I–797, Notice of Action. Employment will be authorized incident to status. To demonstrate employment authorization, the Service will issue a Form I–94, Arrival-Departure Record, which also reflects the derivative's current status as an asylee, or the derivative may apply under § 274a.12(a) of this chapter, using Form I–765, Application for Employment Authorization, and a copy of the Form I–797. The approval of the Form I–730 shall remain valid for the duration of the relationship to the asylee and, in the case of a child, while the child is under 21 years of age and unmarried, provided also that the principal's status has not been revoked. However, the approved Form I–730 will cease to confer immigration benefits after it has been used by the beneficiary for admission to the United States as a derivative of an asylee.

(d) *Spouse or child outside the United States.* When a spouse or child of an alien granted asylum is outside the United States, the asylee may request accompanying or following-to-join benefits for his/her spouse or child(ren) by filing a separate Form I–730 for each qualifying family member with the designated Service office, setting forth the full name, relationship, date and place of birth, and current location of each such person. A recent photograph of each derivative must accompany the Form I–730. The photograph must clearly identify the derivative, and will be made part of the derivative's immigration record for identification purposes. A separate Form I–730 for each qualifying family member must be filed before February 28, 2000, or within 2 years of the date in which the asylee was granted asylum status, whichever is later, unless the Service determines that the filing period should be extended for humanitarian reasons. When the Form I–730 is approved, the Service will notify the asylee of such approval on Form I–797. The approved Form I–730 shall be forwarded by the Service to the Department of State for delivery to the American Embassy or Consulate having jurisdiction over the area in which the asylee's spouse or child is located. The approval of the Form I–730 shall remain valid for the duration of the relationship to the asylee and, in the case of a child, while the child is under 21 years of age and unmarried, provided also that the principal's status has not been revoked. However, the approved Form I–730 will cease to confer immigration benefits after it has been used by the beneficiary for admission to the United States as a derivative of an asylee.

(e) *Denial.* If the spouse or child is found to be ineligible for the status accorded under section 208(c) of the Act, a written notice stating the basis for denial shall be forwarded to the principal alien. No appeal shall lie from this decision.

(f) *Burden of proof.* To establish the claimed relationship of spouse or child as defined in sections 101(a)(35) and 101(b)(1) of the Act, evidence must be submitted with the request as set forth in part 204 of this chapter. Where possible this will consist of the documents specified in § 204.2 (a)(1)(i)(B), (a)(1)(iii)(B), (a)(2), (d)(2), and (d)(5) of 8 CFR chapter I. The burden of proof is on the principal alien to establish by a preponderance of the evidence that any person on whose behalf he or she is making a request under this section is an eligible spouse or child.

(g) *Duration.* The spouse or child qualifying under section 208(c) of the Act shall be granted asylum for an indefinite period unless the principal's status is revoked.

[62 FR 10337, Mar. 6, 1997, as amended at 63 FR 3796, Jan. 27, 1998. Redesignated at 64 FR 8490, Feb. 19, 1999 and further redesignated and amended at 65 FR 76136, Dec. 6, 2000]

§ 1208.22 Effect on exclusion, deportation, and removal proceedings.

An alien who has been granted asylum may not be deported or removed unless his or her asylum status is terminated pursuant to § 1208.24. An alien in exclusion, deportation, or removal proceedings who is granted withholding of removal or deportation, or deferral of removal, may not be deported or removed to the country to which his or her deportation or removal is ordered withheld or deferred unless the withholding order is terminated pursuant to § 1208.24 or deferral is terminated pursuant to § 1208.17(d) or (e).

[64 FR 8492, Feb. 19, 1999. Revised at 65 FR 76136, Dec. 6, 2000]

§ 1208.23 Restoration of status.

An alien who was maintaining his or her nonimmigrant status at the time of filing an asylum application and has such application denied may continue in or be restored to that status, if it has not expired.

[62 FR 10337, Mar. 6, 1997. Redesignated at 64 FR 8490, Feb. 19, 1999 and further redesignated at 65 FR 76136, Dec. 6, 2000]

§ 1208.24 Termination of asylum or withholding of removal or deportation.

(a) *Termination of asylum by the Service.* Except as provided in paragraph (e) of this section, an asylum officer may terminate a grant of asylum made under the jurisdiction of an asylum officer or a district director if following an interview, the asylum officer determines that:

(1) There is a showing of fraud in the alien's application such that he or she was not eligible for asylum at the time it was granted;

(2) As to applications filed on or after April 1, 1997, one or more of the conditions described in section 208(c)(2) of the Act exist; or

(3) As to applications filed before April 1, 1997, the alien no longer has a well-founded fear of persecution upon return due to a change of country conditions in the alien's country of nationality or habitual residence or the alien has committed any act that would have been grounds for denial of asylum under § 1208.13(c)(2).

(b) *Termination of withholding of deportation or removal by the Service.* Except as provided in paragraph (e) of this section, an asylum officer may terminate a grant of withholding of deportation or removal made under the jurisdiction of an asylum officer or a district director if the asylum officer determines, following an interview, that:

(1) The alien is no longer entitled to withholding of deportation or removal because, owing to a fundamental change in circumstances relating to the original claim, the alien's life or freedom no longer would be threatened on account of race, religion, nationality, membership in a particular social group, or political opinion in the country from which deportation or removal was withheld.

(2) There is a showing of fraud in the alien's application such that the alien

was not eligible for withholding of removal at the time it was granted;

(3) The alien has committed any other act that would have been grounds for denial of withholding of removal under section 241(b)(3)(B) of the Act had it occurred prior to the grant of withholding of removal; or

(4) For applications filed in proceedings commenced before April 1, 1997, the alien has committed any act that would have been grounds for denial of withholding of deportation under section 243(h)(2) of the Act.

(c) *Procedure.* Prior to the termination of a grant of asylum or withholding of deportation or removal, the alien shall be given notice of intent to terminate, with the reasons therefor, at least 30 days prior to the interview specified in paragraph (a) of this section before an asylum officer. The alien shall be provided the opportunity to present evidence showing that he or she is still eligible for asylum or withholding of deportation or removal. If the asylum officer determines that the alien is no longer eligible for asylum or withholding of deportation or removal, the alien shall be given written notice that asylum status or withholding of deportation or removal and any employment authorization issued pursuant thereto, are terminated.

(d) *Termination of derivative status.* The termination of asylum status for a person who was the principal applicant shall result in termination of the asylum status of a spouse or child whose status was based on the asylum application of the principal. Such termination shall not preclude the spouse or child of such alien from separately asserting an asylum or withholding of deportation or removal claim.

(e) *Removal proceedings.* When an alien's asylum status or withholding of removal or deportation is terminated under this section, the Service shall initiate removal proceedings, as appropriate, if the alien is not already in exclusion, deportation, or removal proceedings. Removal proceedings may take place in conjunction with a termination hearing scheduled under §1208.24(f).

(f) *Termination of asylum, or withholding of deportation or removal, by an immigration judge or the Board of Immigration Appeals.* An immigration judge or the Board of Immigration Appeals may reopen a case pursuant to §3.2 or §3.23 of this chapter for the purpose of terminating a grant of asylum, or a withholding of deportation or removal. In such a reopened proceeding, the Service must establish, by a preponderance of evidence, one or more of the grounds set forth in paragraphs (a) or (b) of this section. In addition, an immigration judge may terminate a grant of asylum, or a withholding of deportation or removal, made under the jurisdiction of the Service at any time after the alien has been provided a notice of intent to terminate by the Service. Any termination under this paragraph may occur in conjunction with an exclusion, deportation, or removal proceeding.

(g) *Termination of asylum for arriving aliens.* If the Service determines that an applicant for admission who had previously been granted asylum in the United States falls within conditions set forth in §1208.24 and is inadmissible, the Service shall issue a notice of intent to terminate asylum and initiate removal proceedings under section 240 of the Act. The alien shall present his or her response to the intent to terminate during proceedings before the immigration judge.

[62 FR 10337, Mar. 6, 1997. Redesignated at 64 FR 8490, Feb. 19, 1999 and further redesignated and amended at 65 FR 76136, Dec. 6, 2000]

§§ 1208.25–1208.29 [Reserved]

Subpart B—Credible Fear of Persecution

§ 1208.30 Credible fear determinations involving stowaways and applicants for admission who are found inadmissible pursuant to section 212(a)(6)(C) or 212(a)(7) of the Act or whose entry is limited or suspended under section 212(f) or 215(a)(1) of the Act.

(a) *Jurisdiction.* The provisions of this subpart B apply to aliens subject to sections 235(a)(2) and 235(b)(1) of the Act. Pursuant to section 235(b)(1)(B), asylum officers have exclusive jurisdiction to make credible fear determinations, and the immigration judges have exclusive jurisdiction to review such determinations. Prior to January 1, 2015, an alien present in or arriving in the Commonwealth of the Northern Mariana Islands is ineligible to apply for asylum and may only establish eligibility for withholding of removal pursuant to section 241(b)(3) of the Act or withholding or deferral of removal under the Convention Against Torture.

(b) *Treatment of dependents.* A spouse or child of an alien may be included in that alien's credible fear evaluation and determination, if such spouse or child:

(1) Arrived in the United States concurrently with the principal alien; and

(2) Desires to be included in the principal alien's determination. However, any alien may have his or her credible fear evaluation and determination made separately, if he or she expresses such a desire.

(c)–(d) [Reserved]

(e) *Determination.* For the standards and procedures for asylum officers in conducting credible fear interviews and in making positive and negative credible fear determinations, see 8 CFR 208.30. The immigration judges will review such determinations as provided in paragraph (g)(2) of this section and 8 CFR 1003.42.

(f) [Reserved]

(g) *Procedures for a negative credible fear finding*—(1) *Review by immigration judge of a mandatory bar finding.* If the alien is determined to be an alien described in 8 CFR 208.13(c)(3) or 1208.13(c)(3) and is determined to lack a reasonable fear under 8 CFR 208.30(e)(5), the immigration judge shall first review de novo the determination that the alien is described in 8 CFR 208.13(c)(3) or 1208.13(c)(3). If the immigration judge finds that the alien is not described in 8 CFR 208.13(c)(3) or 1208.13(c)(3), then the immigration judge shall vacate the order of the asylum officer, and DHS may commence removal proceedings under section 240 of the Act. If the immigration judge concurs with the credible fear determination that the alien is an alien described in 8 CFR 208.13(c)(3) or 1208.13(c)(3), the immigration judge will then review the asylum officer's negative decision regarding reasonable fear made under 8 CFR 208.30(e)(5) consistent with paragraph (g)(2) of this section, except that the immigration judge will review the findings under the reasonable fear standard instead of the credible fear standard described in paragraph (g)(2).

(2) Review by immigration judge of a negative credible fear finding.

(i) The asylum officer's negative decision regarding credible fear shall be subject to review by an immigration judge upon the applicant's request, or upon the applicant's refusal either to request or to decline the review after being given such opportunity, in accordance with section 235(b)(1)(B)(iii)(III) of the Act.

(ii) The record of the negative credible fear determination, including copies of the Form I–863, the asylum officer's notes, the summary of the material facts, and other materials upon which the determination was based shall be provided to the immigration judge with the negative determination.

(iii) A credible fear hearing shall be closed to the public unless the alien states for the record or submits a written statement that the alien is waiving that requirement; in that event the hearing shall be open to the public, subject to the immigration judge's discretion as provided in § 1003.27.

(iv) Upon review of the asylum officer's negative credible fear determination:

(A) If the immigration judge concurs with the determination of the asylum officer that the alien does not have a credible fear of persecution or torture, the case shall be returned to the Service for removal of the alien. The immigration judge's decision is final and may not be appealed. The Service, however, may reconsider a negative credible fear finding that has been concurred upon by an immigration judge after providing notice of its reconsideration to the immigration judge.

(B) If the immigration judge finds that the alien, other than an alien stowaway, possesses a credible fear of persecution or torture, the immigration judge shall vacate the order of the asylum officer issued on Form I–860 and the Service may commence removal proceedings under section 240 of the Act, during which time the alien may file an application for asylum and withholding of removal in accordance with § 1208.4(b)(3)(i).

(C) If the immigration judge finds that an alien stowaway possesses a credible fear of persecution or torture, the alien shall be allowed to file an application for asylum and withholding of removal before the immigration judge in accordance with § 1208.4(b)(3)(iii). The immigration judge shall decide the application as provided in that section. Such decision may be appealed by either the stowaway or the Service to the Board of Immigration Appeals. If a denial of the application for asylum and for withholding of removal becomes final, the alien shall be removed from the United States in accordance with section 235(a)(2) of the Act. If an approval of the application for asylum or for withholding of removal becomes final, the Service shall terminate removal proceedings under section 235(a)(2) of the Act.

[65 FR 76136, Dec. 6, 2000, as amended at 69 FR 69497, Nov. 29, 2004; 74 FR 55742, Oct. 28, 2009; 83 FR 55952, Nov. 9, 2018]

§ 1208.31 Reasonable fear of persecution or torture determinations involving aliens ordered removed under section 238(b) of the Act and aliens whose removal is reinstated under section 241(a)(5) of the Act.

(a) *Jurisdiction.* This section shall apply to any alien ordered removed under section 238(b) of the Act or whose deportation, exclusion, or removal order is reinstated under section 241(a)(5) of the Act who, in the course of the administrative removal or reinstatement process, expresses a fear of returning to the country of removal. The Service has exclusive jurisdiction to make reasonable fear determinations, and EOIR has exclusive jurisdiction to review such determinations.

(b) *Initiation of reasonable fear determination process.* Upon issuance of a Final Administrative Removal Order under § 238.1 of this chapter, or notice under § 1241.8(b) of this chapter that an alien is subject to removal, an alien described in paragraph (a) of this section shall be referred to an asylum officer for a reasonable fear determination. In the absence of exceptional circumstances, this determination will be conducted within 10 days of the referral.

(c) *Interview and procedure.* The asylum officer shall conduct the interview in a non-adversarial manner, separate and apart from the general public. At the time of the interview, the asylum officer shall determine that the alien has an understanding of the reasonable fear determination process. The alien may be represented by counsel or an accredited representative at the interview, at no expense to the Government, and may present evidence, if available, relevant to the possibility of persecution or torture. The alien's representative may present a statement at the end of the interview. The asylum officer, in his or her discretion, may place reasonable limits on the number of persons who may be present at the interview and the length of the statement. If the alien is unable to proceed effectively in English, and if the asylum officer is unable to proceed competently in a language chosen by the alien, the asylum officer shall arrange for the assistance of an interpreter in conducting the interview. The interpreter may not be a representative or employee of the applicant's country or nationality, or if the applicant is stateless, the applicant's country of last habitual residence. The asylum officer shall create a summary of the material facts as stated by the applicant. At the conclusion of the interview, the officer shall review the summary with the alien and provide the alien with an opportunity to correct errors therein. The asylum officer shall create a written record of his or her determination, including a summary of the material facts as stated by the applicant, any additional facts relied on by the officers, and the officer's determination of whether, in light of such facts, the alien has established a reasonable fear of persecution or torture. The alien shall be determined to have a reasonable fear of persecution or torture if the alien establishes a reasonable possibility that he or she would be persecuted on account of his or her race, religion, nationality, membership in a particular social group or political opinion, or a reasonable possibility that he or she would be tortured in the country of removal. For purposes of the screening determination, the bars to eligibility for withholding of removal under section 241(b)(3)(B) of the Act shall not be considered.

(d) *Authority.* Asylum officers conducting screening determinations under this section shall have the authority described in § 1208.9(c).

(e) *Referral to Immigration Judge.* If an asylum officer determines that an alien described in this section has a reasonable fear of persecution or torture, the officer shall so inform the alien and issue a Form I–863, Notice of Referral to the Immigration Judge, for full consideration of the request for withholding of removal only. Such cases shall be adjudicated by the immigration judge in accordance with the provisions of § 1208.16. Appeal of the immigration judge's decision shall lie to the Board of Immigration Appeals.

(f) *Removal of aliens with no reasonable fear of persecution or torture.* If the asylum officer determines that the alien has not established a reasonable fear of persecution or torture, the asylum officer shall inform the alien in writing of the decision and shall inquire whether the alien wishes to have an immigration judge review the negative decision, using Form I–898, Record of Negative Reasonable Fear Finding and Request for Review by Immigration Judge, on which the alien shall indicate whether he or she desires such review.

(g) *Review by immigration judge.* The asylum officer's negative decision regarding reasonable fear shall be subject to review by an immigration judge upon the alien's request. If the alien requests such review, the asylum officer shall serve him or her with a Form I–863. The record of determination, including copies of the Form I–863, the asylum officer's notes, the summary of the material facts, and other materials upon which the determination was based shall be provided to the immigration judge with the negative determination. In the absence of exceptional circumstances, such review shall be conducted by the immigration judge within 10 days of the filing of the Form I–863 with the immigration court. Upon review of the asylum officer's negative reasonable fear determination:

(1) If the immigration judge concurs with the asylum officer's determination that the alien does not have a reasonable fear of persecution or torture, the case shall be returned to the Service for removal of the alien. No appeal shall lie from the immigration judge's decision.

(2) If the immigration judge finds that the alien has a reasonable fear of persecution or torture, the alien may submit Form I–589, Application for Asylum and Withholding of Removal.

(i) The immigration judge shall consider only the alien's application for withholding of removal under § 1208.16 and shall determine whether the alien's removal to the country of removal must be withheld or deferred.

(ii) Appeal of the immigration judge's decision whether removal must be withheld or deferred lies to the Board of Immigration Appeals. If the alien or the Service appeals the immigration judge's decision, the Board shall review only the immigration judge's decision regarding the alien's eligibility for withholding or deferral of removal under § 1208.16.

[64 FR 8493, Feb. 19, 1999; 64 FR 13881, Mar. 23, 1999]

PART 1209—ADJUSTMENT OF STATUS OF REFUGEES AND ALIENS GRANTED ASYLUM

Sec.

AUTHORITY: 8 U.S.C. 1101, 1103, 1157, 1158, 1159, 1228, 1252, 1282; Title VII of Public Law 110–229.

SOURCE: Duplicated from part 209 at 68 FR 9835, Feb. 28, 2003

EDITORIAL NOTE: Nomenclature changes to part 1209 appear at 68 FR 9846, Feb. 28, 2003.

§ 1209.1 Adjustment of status of refugees.

The provisions of this section shall provide the sole and exclusive procedure for adjustment of status by a refugee admitted under section 207 of the Act whose application is based on his or her refugee status.

(a) *Eligibility.* (1) Every alien in the United States who is classified as a refugee under part 207 of this chapter, whose status has not been terminated, is required to apply to the Service 1 year after entry in order for the Service to determine his or her admissibility under section 212 of the Act.

(2) Every alien processed by the Immigration and Naturalization Service abroad and paroled into the United States as a refugee after April 1, 1980, and before May 18, 1980, shall be considered as having entered the United States as a refugee under section 207(a) of the Act.

(b) *Application.* Upon admission to the United States, every refugee entrant shall be notified of the requirement to submit an application for permanent residence 1 year after entry. An application for the benefits of section 209(a) of the Act shall be filed on Form I–485, without fee, with the director of the appropriate Service office identified in the instructions which accompany the Form I–485. A separate application must be filed by each alien. Every applicant who is 14 years of age or older must submit a completed Form G–325A (Biographical Information) with the Form I–485 application. Following submission of the Form I–485 application, a refugee entrant who is 14 years of age or older will be required to execute a Form FD–258 (Applicant Fingerprint Card) at such time and place as the Service will designate.

(c) *Medical examination.* A refugee seeking adjustment of status under section 209(a) of the Act is not required to repeat the medical examination performed under § 207.2(c) of chapter I, unless there were medical grounds of inadmissibility applicable at the time of admission. The refugee is, however, required to establish compliance with the vaccination requirements described under section 212(a)(1)(A)(ii) of the Act, by submitting with the adjustment of status application a vaccination supplement, completed by a designated civil surgeon in the United States.

(d) *Interview.* The Service director having jurisdiction over the application will determine, on a case-by-case basis, whether an interview by an immigration officer is necessary to determine the applicant's admissibility for permanent resident status under this part.

(e) *Decision.* The director will notify the applicant in writing of the decision of his or her application for admission to permanent residence. If the applicant is determined to be inadmissible or no longer a refugee, the director will deny the application and notify the applicant of the reasons for the denial. The director will, in the same denial notice, inform the applicant of his or her right to renew the request for permanent residence in removal proceedings under section 240 of the Act. There is no appeal of the denial of an application by the director, but such denial will be without prejudice to the alien's right to renew the application in removal proceedings under part 240 of this chapter. If the applicant is found to be admissible for permanent residence under section 209(a) of the Act, the director will approve the application and admit the applicant for lawful permanent residence as of the date of the alien's arrival in the United States. An alien admitted for lawful permanent residence will be issued Form I–551, Alien Registration Receipt Card.

[63 FR 30109, June 3, 1998, as amended at 68 FR 10353, Mar. 5, 2003]

§ 1209.2 Adjustment of status of alien granted asylum.

The provisions of this section shall be the sole and exclusive procedure for adjustment of status by an asylee admitted under section 208 of the Act whose application is based on his or her asylee status.

(a) *Eligibility.* (1) Except as provided in paragraph (a)(2) or (a)(3) of this section, the status of any alien who has been granted asylum in the United States may be adjusted to that of an alien lawfully admitted for permanent residence, provided the alien:

(i) Applies for such adjustment;

(ii) Has been physically present in the United States for at least one year after having been granted asylum;

(iii) Continues to be a refugee within the meaning of section 101(a)(42) of the Act, or is the spouse or child of a refugee;

(iv) Has not been firmly resettled in any foreign country; and

(v) Is admissible to the United States as an immigrant under the Act at the time of examination for adjustment without regard to paragraphs (4), (5)(A), (5)(B), and (7)(A)(i) of section 212(a) of the Act, and (vi) has a refugee number available under section 207(a) of the Act.

If the application for adjustment filed under this part exceeds the refugee numbers available under section 207(a) of the Act for the fiscal year, a waiting list will be established on a priority basis by the date the application was properly filed.

(2) An alien, who was granted asylum in the United States prior to November 29, 1990 (regardless of whether or not such asylum has been terminated under section 208(b) of the Act), and is no longer a refugee due to a change in circumstances in the foreign state where he or she feared persecution, may also have his or her status adjusted by the director to that of an alien lawfully admitted for permanent residence even if he or she is no longer able to demonstrate that he or she continues to be a refugee within the meaning of section 101(a)(42) of the Act, or to be a spouse or child of such a refugee or to have been physically present in the United States for at least one year after being granted asylum, so long as he or she is able to meet the requirements noted in paragraphs (a)(1)(i), (iv), and (v) of this section. Such persons are exempt from the numerical limitations of section 209(b) of the Act. However, the number of aliens who are natives of any foreign state who may adjust status pursuant to this paragraph in any fiscal year shall not exceed the difference between the per country limitation established under section 202(a) of the Act and the number of aliens who are chargeable to that foreign state in the fiscal year under section 202 of the Act. Aliens who applied for adjustment of status under section 209(b) of the Act before June 1, 1990, are also exempt from its numerical limitation without any restrictions.

(3) No alien arriving in or physically present in the Commonwealth of the Northern Mariana Islands may apply to adjust status under section 209(b) of the Act in the Commonwealth of the Northern Mariana Islands prior to January 1, 2015.

(b) *Inadmissible Alien.* An applicant who is inadmissible to the United States under section 212(a) of the Act, may, under section 209(c) of the Act, have the grounds of inadmissibility waived by the director (except for those grounds under paragraphs (27), (29), (33), and so much of (23) as relates to trafficking in narcotics) for humanitarian purposes, to assure family unity, or when it is otherwise in the public interest. An application for the waiver may be filed on Form I–602 (Application by Refugee for Waiver of Grounds of Excludability) with the application for adjustment. An applicant for adjustment who has had the status of an exchange alien nonimmigrant under section 101(a)(15)(J) of the Act, and who is subject to the foreign resident requirement of section 212(e) of the Act, shall be eligible for adjustment without regard to the foreign residence requirement.

(c) *Application.* An application for the benefits of section 209(b) of the Act may be filed on Form I–485, with the correct fee, with the director of the appropriate Service office identified in the instructions to the Form I–485. A separate application must be filed by each alien. Every applicant who is 14 years of age or older must submit a completed Form G–325A (Biographic Information) with the Form I–485 application. Following submission of the Form I–485 application, every applicant who is 14 years of age or older will be required to execute a Form FD–258 (Applicant Fingerprint Card) at such time and place as the Service will designate. Except as provided in paragraph (a)(2) of this section, the application must also be supported by evidence that the applicant has been physically present in the United States for at least 1 year. If an alien has been placed in deportation or exclusion proceedings, the application can be filed and considered only in proceedings under section 240 of the Act.

(d) *Medical examination.* An alien seeking adjustment of status under section 209(b) of the Act 1 year following the grant of asylum under section 208 of the Act shall submit the results of a medical examination to determine whether any grounds of inadmissibility described under section 212(a)(1)(A) of the Act apply. Form I–693, Medical Examination of Aliens Seeking Adjustment of Status, and a vaccination supplement to determine compliance with the vaccination requirements described under section 212(a)(1)(A)(ii) of the Act must be completed by a designed civil surgeon in the United States and submitted at the time of application for adjustment of status.

(e) *Interview.* Each applicant for adjustment of status under this part shall be interviewed by an immigration officer. The interview may be waived for a child under 14 years of age. The Service director having jurisdiction over the application will determine, on a case-by-case basis, whether an interview by an immigration officer is necessary to determine the applicant's admissibility for permanent resident status under this part.

(f) *Decision.* The applicant shall be notified of the decision, and if the application is denied, of the reasons for denial. No appeal shall lie from the denial of an application by the director but such denial will be without prejudice to the alien's right to renew the application in proceedings under part 240 of this chapter. If the application is approved, the director shall record the alien's admission for lawful permanent residence as of the date one year before the date of the approval of the application, but not earlier than the date of the approval for asylum in the case of an applicant approved under paragraph (a)(2) of this section.

[46 FR 45119, Sept. 10, 1981, as amended at 56 FR 26898, June 12, 1991; 57 FR 42883, Sept. 17, 1992; 63 FR 30109, June 3, 1998; 74 FR 55742, Oct. 28, 2009]

PART 1211—DOCUMENTARY REQUIREMENTS: IMMIGRANTS; WAIVERS

AUTHORITY: 8 U.S.C. 1101, 1103, 1181, 1182, 1203, 1225, 1257; 8 CFR part 2.

EDITORIAL NOTE: Nomenclature changes to part 1211 appear at 68 FR 9846, Feb. 28, 2003.

§ 1211.4 Waiver of documents for returning residents.

(a) Pursuant to the authority contained in section 211(b) of the Act, an alien previously lawfully admitted to the United States for permanent residence who, upon return from a temporary absence was inadmissible because of failure to have or to present a valid passport, immigrant visa, reentry permit, border crossing card, or other document required at the time of entry, may be granted a waiver of such requirement in the discretion of the district director if the district director determines that such alien:

(1) Was not otherwise inadmissible at the time of entry, or having been otherwise inadmissible at the time of entry is with respect thereto qualified for an exemption from deportability under section 237(a)(1)(H) of the Act; and

(2) Is not otherwise subject to removal.

(b) Denial of a waiver by the district director is not appealable but shall be without prejudice to renewal of an application and reconsideration in proceedings before the immigration judge.

[62 FR 10346, Mar. 6, 1997. Duplicated from § 211.4 at 68 FR 9835, Feb. 28, 2003]

PART 1212—DOCUMENTARY REQUIREMENTS: NONIMMIGRANTS; WAIVERS; ADMISSION OF CERTAIN INADMISSIBLE ALIENS; PAROLE

Sec.

AUTHORITY: 8 U.S.C. 1101 and note, 1102, 1103, 1182 and note, 1184, 1187, 1223, 1225, 1226, 1227, 1255; 8 U.S.C. 1185 note (section 7209 of Pub. L. 108–458); Title VII of Public Law 110–229.

SOURCE: 17 FR 11484, Dec. 19, 1952, unless otherwise noted. Duplicated from part 212 at 68 FR 9535, Feb. 28, 2003.

EDITORIAL NOTE: Nomenclature changes to part 1212 appear at 68 FR 9846, Feb. 28, 2003, and at 68 FR 10353, Mar. 5, 2003.

§ 1212.1 Documentary requirements for nonimmigrants.

A valid unexpired visa and an unexpired passport, valid for the period set forth in section 212(a)(26) of the Act, shall be presented by each arriving nonimmigrant alien except that the passport validity period for an applicant for admission who is a member of a class described in section 102 of the Act is not required to extend beyond the date of his application for admission if so admitted, and except as otherwise provided in the Act, this chapter, and for the following classes:

(a) *Canadian nationals, and aliens having a common nationality with nationals of Canada or with British subjects in Bermuda, Bahamian nationals or British subjects resident in Bahamas, Cayman Islands, and Turks and Caicos Islands.* A visa is not required of a Canadian national in any case. A passport is not required of such national except after a visit outside of the Western Hemisphere. A visa is not required of an alien having a common nationality with Canadian nationals or with British subjects in Bermuda, who has his or her residence in Canada or Bermuda. A passport is not required of such alien except after a visit outside of the Western Hemisphere. A visa and a passport are required of a Bahamian national or a British subject who has his residence in the Bahamas except that a visa is not required of such an alien who, prior to or at the time of embarkation for the United States on a vessel or aircraft, satisfied the examining U.S. immigration officer at the Bahamas, that he is clearly and beyond a doubt entitled to admission in all other respects. A visa is not required of a British subject who has his residence in, and arrives directly from, the Cayman Islands or the Turks and Caicos Islands and who presents a current certificate from the Clerk of Court of the Cayman Islands or the Turks and Caicos Islands indicating no criminal record.

(b) *Certain Caribbean residents*—(1) *British, French, and Netherlands nationals, and nationals of certain adjacent islands of the Caribbean which are independent countries.* A visa is not required of a British, French, or Netherlands national, or of a national of Barbados, Grenada, Jamaica, or Trinidad and Tobago, who has his or her residence in British, French, or Netherlands territory located in the adjacent islands of the Caribbean area, or in Barbados, Grenada, Jamaica, or Trinidad and Tobago, who:

(i) Is proceeding to the United States as an agricultural worker;

(ii) Is the beneficiary of a valid, unexpired indefinite certification granted by the Department of Labor for employment in the Virgin Islands of the United States and is proceeding to the Virgin Islands of the United States for such purpose, or

(iii) Is the spouse or child of an alien described in paragraph (b)(1)(i) or (b)(1)(ii) of this section, and is accompanying or following to join him or her.

(2) *Nationals of the British Virgin Islands.* A visa is not required of a national of the British Virgin Islands who has his or her residence in the British Virgin Islands, if:

(i) The alien is seeking admission solely to visit the Virgin Islands of the United States; or

(ii) At the time of embarking on an aircraft at St. Thomas, U.S. Virgin Islands, the alien meets each of the following requirements:

(A) The alien is traveling to any other part of the United States by aircraft as a nonimmigrant visitor for business or pleasure (as described in section 101(a)(15)(B) of the Act);

(B) The alien satisfies the examining U.S. Immigration officer at the port-of-entry that he or she is clearly and beyond a doubt entitled to admission in all other respects; and

(C) The alien presents a current *Certificate of Good Conduct* issued by the Royal Virgin Islands Police Department indicating that he or she has no criminal record.

(c) *Mexican nationals*. (1) A visa and a passport are not required of a Mexican national who:

(i) Is in possession of a Form DSP–150, B–1/B–2 Visa and Border Crossing Card, containing a machine-readable biometric identifier, issued by the DOS and is applying for admission as a temporary visitor for business or pleasure from contiguous territory.

(ii) Is a Mexican national entering solely for the purpose of applying for a Mexican passport or other official Mexican document at a Mexican consular office on the United States side of the border.

(2) A visa shall not be required of a Mexican national who:

(i) Is in possession of a Form DSP–150, with a biometric identifier, issued by the DOS, and a passport, and is applying for admission as a temporary visitor for business or pleasure from other than contiguous territory;

(ii) Is a crew member employed on an aircraft belonging to a Mexican company owned carrier authorized to engage in commercial transportation into the United States; or

(iii) Bears a Mexican diplomatic or official passport and who is a military or civilian official of the Federal Government of Mexico entering the United States for 6 months or less for a purpose other than on assignment as a permanent employee to an office of the Mexican Federal Government in the United States, and the official's spouse or any of the official's dependent family members under 19 years of age, bearing diplomatic or official passports, who are in the actual company of such official at the time of admission into the United States. This provision does not apply to the spouse or any of the official's family members classifiable under section 101(a)(15)(F) or (M) of the Act.

(3) A Mexican national who presents a BCC at a POE must present the DOS-issued DSP–150 containing a machine-readable biometric identifier. The alien will not be permitted to cross the border into the United States unless the biometric identifier contained on the card matches the appropriate biometric characteristic of the alien.

(4) Mexican nationals presenting a combination B–1/B–2 nonimmigrant visa and border crossing card (or similar stamp in a passport), issued by DOS prior to April 1, 1998, that does not contain a machine-readable biometric identifier, may be admitted on the basis of the nonimmigrant visa only, provided it has not expired and the alien remains admissible. A passport is also required.

(5) *Aliens entering pursuant to International Boundary and Water Commission Treaty*. A visa and a passport are not required of an alien employed either directly or indirectly on the construction, operation, or maintenance of works in the United States undertaken in accordance with the treaty concluded on February 3, 1944, between the United States and Mexico regarding the functions of the International Boundary and Water Commission, and entering the United States temporarily in connection with such employment.

(d) *Citizens of the Freely Associated States, formerly Trust Territory of the Pacific Islands*. Citizens of the Republic of the Marshall Islands and the Federated States of Micronesia may enter into, lawfully engage in employment, and establish residence in the United States and its territories and possessions without regard to paragraphs (14), (20) and (26) of section 212(a) of the Act pursuant to the terms of Pub. L. 99–239. Pending issuance by the aforementioned governments of travel documents to eligible citizens, travel documents previously issued by the Trust Territory of the Pacific Islands will continue to be accepted for purposes of identification and to establish eligibility for admission into the United States, its territories and possessions.

(e) *Aliens entering Guam pursuant to section 14 of Public Law 99–396, "Omnibus Territories Act" and 8 CFR 212.1(e).* (1) As provided in 8 CFR 212.1(e), until November 28, 2009, a visa is not required of an alien who is a citizen of a country enumerated in 8 CFR 212.1(e)(3) who:

(i) Is classifiable as a visitor for business or pleasure;

(ii) Is solely entering and staying on Guam for a period not to exceed fifteen days;

(iii) Is in possession of a round-trip nonrefundable and nontransferable transportation ticket bearing a confirmed departure date not exceeding fifteen days from the date of admission to Guam;

(iv) Is in possession of a completed and signed Visa Waiver Information Form (Form I–736);

(v) Waives any right to review or appeal the immigration officer's determination of admissibility at the port of entry at Guam; and

(vi) Waives any right to contest any action for deportation, other than on the basis of a request for asylum.

(2) The DHS regulations for waiver of the visa requirement for aliens entering Guam pursuant to section 14 of Public Law 99–396, prior to November 28, 2009, are set forth at 8 CFR 212.1(e).

(3) [Reserved]

(4) Admission under 8 CFR 212.1(e) renders an alien ineligible for:

(i) Adjustment of status to that of a temporary resident or, except under the provisions of section 245(i) of the Act or as an immediate relative as defined in section 201(b), to that of a lawful permanent resident;

(ii) Change of nonimmigrant status; or

(iii) Extension of stay.

(f) *Direct transits*—(1) *Transit without visa.* A passport and visa are not required of an alien who is being transported in immediate and continuous transit through the United States in accordance with the terms of an agreement entered into between the transportation line and the Service under the provisions of section 238(d) of the Act on Form I–426 to insure such immediate and continuous transit through, and departure from, the United States en route to a specifically designated foreign country: *Provided,* That such alien is in possession of a travel document or documents establishing his/her identity and nationality and ability to enter some country other than the United States.

(2) *Unavailability to transit.* This waiver of passport and visa requirement is not available to an alien who is a citizen of Afghanistan, Angola, Bangladesh, Belarus, Bosnia-aherzegovina, Burma, Burundi, Central African Republic, People's Republic of China, Colombia, Congo (Brazzaville), Cuba, India, Iran, Iraq, Libya, Nigeria, North Korea, Pakistan, Serbia, Sierra Leone, Somalia, Sri Lanka, and Sudan.

(3) *Foreign government officials in transit.* If an alien is of the class described in section 212(d)(8) of the Act, only a valid unexpired visa and a travel document valid for entry into a foreign country for at least 30 days from the date of admission to the United States are required.

(g) *Unforeseen emergency.* A nonimmigrant seeking admission to the United States must present an unexpired visa and a passport valid for the amount of time set forth in section 212(a)(7)(B) of the Act or a valid biometric border crossing card, issued by the DOS on Form DSP–150, at the time of application for admission, unless the nonimmigrant satisfies the requirements described in one or more of the paragraphs (a) through (f),(i) or (o) of this section. Upon a nonimmigrant's application on Form I–193, Application for Waiver of Passport and/or Visa, a district director may, in the exercise of his or her discretion, on a case-by-case basis, waive the documentary requirements if satisfied that the nonimmigrant cannot present the required documents because of an unforeseen emergency. The district director or the Deputy Commissioner may at any time revoke a waiver previously authorized pursuant to this paragraph and notify the nonimmigrant in writing to that effect.

(h) *Nonimmigrant spouses, fiancées, fiancés, and children of U.S. citizens.* Notwithstanding any of the provisions of this part, an alien seeking admission as a spouse, fiancée, fiancé, or child of a U.S. citizen, or as a child of the spouse, fiané, or finacée of a U.S. citizen, pursuant to section 101(a)(15)(K) of the Act shall be in possession of an unexpired nonimmigrant visa issued by an American consular officer classifying the alien under that section, or be inadmissible under section 212(a)(7)(B) of the Act.

(i) *Visa Waiver Pilot Program.* A visa is not required of any alien who is eligible to apply for admission to the United States as a Visa Waiver Pilot Program applicant pursuant to the provisions of section 217 of the Act and part 217 of this chapter if such alien is a national of a country designated under the Visa Waiver Pilot Program, who seeks admission to the United States for a period of 90 days or less as a visitor for business or pleasure.

(j) *Officers authorized to act upon recommendations of United States consular officers for waiver of visa and passport requirements.* All district directors, the officers in charge are authorized to act upon recommendations made by United States consular officers or by officers of the Visa Office, Department of State, pursuant to the provisions of 22 CFR 41.7 for waiver of visa and passport requirements under the provisions of section 212(d)(4)(A) of the Act. The District Director at Washington, DC, has jurisdiction in such cases recommended to the Service at the seat of Government level by the Department of State. Neither an application nor fee are required if the concurrence in a passport or visa waiver is requested by a U.S. consular officer or by an officer of the Visa Office. The district director or the Deputy Commissioner, may at any time revoke a waiver previously authorized pursuant to this paragraph and notify the nonimmigrant alien in writing to that effect.

(k) *Cancellation of nonimmigrant visas by immigration officers.* Upon receipt of advice from the Department of State that a nonimmigrant visa has been revoked or invalidated, and request by that Department for such action, immigration officers shall place an appropriate endorsement thereon.

(l) *Treaty traders and investors.* Notwithstanding any of the provisions of this part, an alien seeking admission as a treaty trader or investor under the provisions of Chapter 16 of the North American Free Trade Agreement (NAFTA) pursuant to section 101(a)(15)(E) of the Act, shall be in possession of a nonimmigrant visa issued by an American consular officer classifying the alien under that section.

(m) *Aliens in S classification.* Notwithstanding any of the provisions of this part, an alien seeking admission pursuant to section 101(a)(15)(S) of the Act must be in possession of appropriate documents issued by a United States consular officer classifying the alien under that section.

(n) *Alien in Q–2 classification.* Notwithstanding any of the provisions of this part, an alien seeking admission as a principal according to section 101(a)(15)(Q)(ii) of the Act must be in possession of a Certification Letter issued by the Department of State's Program Administrator documenting participation in the Irish peace process cultural and training programs.

(o) *Alien in T–2 through T–4 classification.* Individuals seeking T–2 through T–4 nonimmigrant status may avail themselves of the provisions of paragraph (g) of this section, except that the authority to waive documentary requirements resides with the Service Center.

(p) [Reserved]

(q) *Aliens admissible under the Guam-CNMI Visa Waiver Program and 8 CFR 212.1(q)*—(1) *Eligibility for Program.* As provided in 8 CFR 212.1(q), in accordance with Public Law 110–229, beginning November 28, 2009, the Secretary of Homeland Security, in consultation with the Secretaries of the Departments of Interior and State, may waive the visa requirement in the case of a nonimmigrant alien who seeks admission to Guam or to the Commonwealth of the Northern Mariana Islands (CNMI) under the Guam-CNMI Visa Waiver Program. To be admissible under the Guam-CNMI Visa Waiver Program, prior to embarking on a carrier for travel to Guam or the CNMI, each nonimmigrant alien must:

(i) Be a national of a country or geographic area listed in 8 CFR 212.1(q)(2);

(ii) Be classifiable as a visitor for business or pleasure;

(iii) Be solely entering and staying on Guam or the CNMI for a period not to exceed forty-five days;

(iv) Be in possession of a round trip ticket that is nonrefundable and nontransferable and bears a confirmed departure date not exceeding forty-five days from the date of admission to Guam or the CNMI. "Round trip ticket" includes any return trip transportation ticket issued by a participating carrier, electronic ticket record, airline employee passes indicating return passage, individual vouchers for return passage, group vouchers for return passage for charter flights, or military travel orders which include military dependents for return to duty stations outside the United States on U.S. military flights;

(v) Be in possession of a completed and signed Guam-CNMI Visa Waiver Information Form (CBP Form I–736);

(vi) Be in possession of a completed and signed I–94, Arrival-Departure Record (CBP Form I–94);

(vii) Be in possession of a valid unexpired ICAO compliant, machine readable passport issued by a country that meets the eligibility requirements of paragraph (q)(2) of this section;

(viii) Have not previously violated the terms of any prior admissions. Prior admissions include those under the Guam-CNMI Visa Waiver Program, the prior Guam Visa Waiver Program, the Visa Waiver Program as described in section 217(a) of the Act and admissions pursuant to any immigrant or nonimmigrant visa;

(ix) Waive any right to review or appeal an immigration officer's determination of admissibility at the port of entry into Guam or the CNMI;

(x) Waive any right to contest any action for deportation or removal, other than on the basis of: an application for withholding of removal under section 241(b)(3) of the INA; withholding of removal under the regulations implementing Article 3 of the United Nations Convention Against Torture and Other Cruel, Inhuman or Degrading Treatment or Punishment; or, an application for asylum if permitted under section 208 of the Act; and

(xi) If a resident of Taiwan, possess a Taiwan National Identity Card and a valid Taiwan passport with a valid reentry permit issued by the Taiwan Ministry of Foreign Affairs.

(2) *Implementing regulations.* The DHS regulations for waiver of the visa requirement for aliens seeking admission to Guam or to the CNMI under the Guam-CNMI Visa Waiver Program are set forth at 8 CFR 212.1(q).

(3) [Reserved]

(4) *Admission under 8 CFR 212.1(q).* Admission under 8 CFR 212.1(q) renders an alien ineligible for:

(i) Adjustment of status to that of a temporary resident or, except as provided by section 245(i) of the Act, other than as an immediate relative as defined in section 201(b) of the Act, to that of a lawful permanent resident;

(ii) Change of nonimmigrant status; or

(iii) Extension of stay.

(5)–(7) [Reserved]

(8) *Inadmissibility and Deportability*—(i) *Determinations of inadmissibility.* (A) An alien who applies for admission under the provisions of the Guam-CNMI Visa Waiver Program, who is determined by an immigration officer to be inadmissible to Guam or the CNMI under one or more of the grounds of inadmissibility listed in section 212 of the Act (other than for lack of a visa), or who is in possession of and presents fraudulent or counterfeit travel documents, will be refused admission into Guam or the CNMI and removed. Such refusal and removal shall be effected without referral of the alien to an immigration judge for further inquiry, examination, or hearing, except that an alien who presents himself or herself as an applicant for admission to Guam under the Guam-CNMI Visa Waiver Program, who applies for asylum, withholding of removal under section 241(b)(3) of the INA or withholding of removal under the regulations implementing Article 3 of the United Nations Convention Against Torture and Other Cruel, Inhuman or Degrading Treatment or Punishment must be issued a Form I–863, Notice of Referral to Immigration Judge, for a proceeding in accordance with 8 CFR 208.2(c)(1) and (2) and 1208.2(c)(1) and (2). The provisions of 8 CFR part 1208 subpart A shall not apply to an alien present or arriving in the CNMI seeking to apply for asylum prior to January 1, 2015. No application for asylum may be filed pursuant to section 208 of the Act by an

alien present or arriving in the CNMI prior to January 1, 2015; however, aliens physically present in the CNMI during the transition period who express a fear of persecution or torture only may establish eligibility for withholding or deferral of removal pursuant to INA 241(b)(3) or pursuant to the regulations implementing Article 3 of the United Nations Convention Against Torture and Other Cruel, Inhuman or Degrading Treatment or Punishment.

(B) [Reserved]

(C) Refusal of admission under this paragraph or 8 CFR 212.1(q)(8)(i) shall not constitute removal for purposes of the Act.

(ii) *Determination of deportability.* (A) An alien who has been admitted to either Guam or the CNMI under the provisions of this section who is determined by an immigration officer to be deportable from either Guam or the CNMI under one or more of the grounds of deportability listed in section 237 of the Act, shall be removed from either Guam or the CNMI to his or her country of nationality or last residence. Such removal will be determined by DHS authority that has jurisdiction over the place where the alien is found, and will be effected without referral of the alien to an immigration judge for a determination of deportability, except that an alien admitted to Guam under the Guam-CNMI Visa Waiver Program who applies for asylum or other form of protection from persecution or torture must be issued a Form I–863 for a proceeding in accordance with 8 CFR 208.2(c)(1) and (2) and 1208.2(c)(1) and (2). The provisions of 8 CFR part 1208 subpart A shall not apply to an alien present or arriving in the CNMI seeking to apply for asylum prior to January 1, 2015. No application for asylum may be filed pursuant to section 208 of the INA by an alien present or arriving in the CNMI prior to January 1, 2015; however, aliens physically present or arriving in the CNMI prior to January 1, 2015, may apply for withholding of removal under section 241(b)(3) of the Act and withholding of removal under the regulations implementing Article 3 of the United Nations Convention Against Torture, Inhuman or Degrading Treatment or Punishment.

(B) Removal by DHS under paragraph (b)(1) of this section or 8 CFR 212.1(q)(8)(ii) is equivalent in all respects and has the same consequences as removal after proceedings conducted under section 240 of the Act.

(iii) [Reserved]

(Secs. 103, 104, 212 of the Immigration and Nationality Act, as amended (8 U.S.C. 1103, 1104, 1132))

[26 FR 12066, Dec. 16, 1961]

EDITORIAL NOTE: For FEDERAL REGISTER citations affecting § 1212.1, see the List of CFR Sections Affected, which appears in the Finding Aids section of the printed volume and at *www.govinfo.gov.*

§ 1212.2 Consent to reapply for admission after deportation, removal or departure at Government expense.

(a) *Evidence.* Any alien who has been deported or removed from the United States is inadmissible to the United States unless the alien has remained outside of the United States for five consecutive years since the date of deportation or removal. If the alien has been convicted of an aggravated felony, he or she must remain outside of the United States for twenty consecutive years from the deportation date before he or she is eligible to re-enter the United States. Any alien who has been deported or removed from the United States and is applying for a visa, admission to the United States, or adjustment of status, must present proof that he or she has remained outside of the United States for the time period required for re-entry after deportation or removal. The examining consular or immigration officer must be satisfied that since the alien's deportation or removal, the alien has remained outside the United States for more than five consecutive years, or twenty consecutive years in the case of an alien convicted of an aggravated felony as defined in section 101(a)(43) of the Act. Any alien who does not satisfactorily present proof of absence from the United States for more than five consecutive years, or twenty consecutive years in the case of an alien convicted of an aggravated felony, to the consular or immigration officer, and any alien who is seeking to enter the United States prior to the completion of the requisite five- or twenty-year absence, must apply for permission to reapply for admission to the United States as provided under this part. A temporary stay in the United States under section 212(d)(3) of the Act does not interrupt the five or twenty consecutive year absence requirement.

(b) *Alien applying to consular officer for nonimmigrant visa or nonresident alien border crossing card.* (1) An alien who is applying to a consular officer for a nonimmigrant visa or a nonresident alien border crossing card, must request permission to reapply for admission to the United States if five years, or twenty years if the alien's deportation was based upon a conviction for an aggravated felony, have not elapsed since the date of deportation or removal. This permission shall be requested in the manner prescribed through the consular officer, and may be granted only in accordance with sections 212(a)(17) and 212(d)(3)(A) of the Act and § 1212.4 of this part. However, the alien may apply for such permission by submitting Form I–212, Application for Permission to Reapply for Admission into the United States after Deportation or Removal, to the consular officer if that officer is willing to accept the application, and recommends to the district director that the alien be permitted to apply.

(2) The consular officer shall forward the Form I–212 to the district director with jurisdiction over the place where the deportation or removal proceedings were held.

(c) *Special provisions for an applicant for nonimmigrant visa under section 101(a)(15)(K) of the Act.* (1) An applicant for a nonimmigrant visa under section 101(a)(15)(K) must:

(i) Be the beneficiary of a valid visa petition approved by the Service; and

(ii) File an application on Form I–212 with the consular officer for permission to reapply for admission to the United States after deportation or removal.

(2) The consular officer must forward the Form I–212 to the Service office with jurisdiction over the area within which the consular officer is located. If the alien is ineligible on grounds which, upon the applicant's marriage to the United States citizen petitioner, may be waived under section 212 (g), (h), or (i) of the Act, the consular officer must also forward a recommendation as to whether the waiver should be granted.

(d) *Applicant for immigrant visa.* Except as provided in paragraph (g)(3) of this section, an applicant for an immigrant visa who is not physically present in the United States and who requires permission to reapply must file Form I–212 with the district director having jurisdiction over the place where the deportation or removal proceedings were held. Except as provided in paragraph (g)(3) of this section, if the applicant also requires a waiver under section 212 (g), (h), or (i) of the Act, Form I–601, Application for Waiver of Grounds of Excludability, must be filed simultaneously with the Form I–212 with the American consul having jurisdiction over the alien's place of residence. The consul must forward these forms to the appropriate Service office abroad with jurisdiction over the area within which the consul is located.

(e) *Applicant for adjustment of status.* An applicant for adjustment of status under section 245 of the Act and part 245 of this chapter must request permission to reapply for entry in conjunction with his or her application for adjustment of status. This request is made by filing an application for permission to reapply, Form I–212, with the district director having jurisdiction over the place where the alien resides. If the application under section 245 of the Act has been initiated, renewed, or is pending in a proceeding before an immigration judge, the district director must refer the Form I–212 to the immigration judge for adjudication.

(f) *Applicant for admission at port of entry.* Within five years of the deportation or removal, or twenty years in the case of an alien convicted of an aggravated felony, an alien may request permission at a port of entry to reapply for admission to the United States. The alien shall file the Form I–212 with the district director having jurisdiction over the port of entry.

(g) *Other applicants.* (1) Any applicant for permission to reapply for admission under circumstances other than those described in paragraphs (b) through (f) of this section must file Form I–212. This form is filed with either:

(i) The district director having jurisdiction over the place where the deportation or removal proceedings were held; or

(ii) The district director who exercised or is exercising jurisdiction over the applicant's most recent proceeding.

(2) If the applicant is physically present in the United States but is ineligible to apply for adjustment of status, he or she must file the application with the district director having jurisdiction over his or her place of residence.

(3) If an alien who is an applicant for parole authorization under § 245.15(t)(2) of 8 CFR chapter I requires consent to reapply for admission after deportation, removal, or departure at Government expense, or a waiver under section 212(g), 212(h), or 212(i) of the Act, he or she may file the requisite Form I–212 or Form I–601 at the Nebraska Service Center concurrently with the Form I–131, Application for Travel Document. If an alien who is an applicant for parole authorization under § 245.13(k)(2) of 8 CFR chapter I requires consent to reapply for admission after deportation, removal, or departure at Government expense, or a waiver under section 212(g), 212(h), or 212(i) of the Act, he or she may file the requisite Form I–212 or Form I–601 at the Texas Service Center concurrently with the Form I–131, Application for Travel Document.

(h) *Decision.* An applicant who has submitted a request for consent to reapply for admission after deportation or removal must be notified of the decision. If the application is denied, the applicant must be notified of the reasons for the denial and of his or her right to appeal as provided in part 103 of this chapter. Except in the case of an applicant seeking to be granted advance permission to reapply for admission prior to his or her departure from the United States, the denial of the application shall be without prejudice to the renewal of the application in the course of proceedings before an immigration judge under section 242 of the Act and this chapter.

(i) *Retroactive approval.* (1) If the alien filed Form I–212 when seeking admission at a port of entry, the approval of the Form I–212 shall be retroactive to either:

(i) The date on which the alien embarked or reembarked at a place outside the United States; or

(ii) The date on which the alien attempted to be admitted from foreign contiguous territory.

(2) If the alien filed Form I–212 in conjunction with an application for adjustment of status under section 245 of the Act, the approval of Form I–212 shall be retroactive to the date on which the alien embarked or reembarked at a place outside the United States.

(j) *Advance approval.* An alien whose departure will execute an order of deportation shall receive a conditional approval depending upon his or her satisfactory departure. However, the grant of permission to reapply does not waive inadmissibility under section 212(a) (16) or (17) of the Act resulting from exclusion, deportation, or removal proceedings which are instituted subsequent to the date permission to reapply is granted.

[56 FR 23212, May 21, 1991, as amended at 64 FR 25766, May 12, 1999; 65 FR 15854, Mar. 24, 2000]

§ 1212.3 Application for the exercise of discretion under former section 212(c).

(a) *Jurisdiction.* An application by an eligible alien for the exercise of discretion under former section 212(c) of the Act (as in effect prior to April 1, 1997), if made in the course of proceedings under section 240 of the Act, or under former sections 235, 236, or 242 of the Act (as in effect prior to April 1, 1997), shall be submitted to the immigration judge by filing Form I–191, Application for Advance Permission to Return to Unrelinquished Domicile.

(b) *Filing of application.* The application may be filed prior to, at the time of, or at any time after the applicant's departure from or arrival into the United States. All material facts or circumstances that the applicant knows or believes apply to the grounds of excludability, deportability, or removability must be described in the application. The applicant must also submit all available documentation relating to such grounds.

(c) [Reserved]

(d) *Validity.* Once an application is approved, that approval is valid indefinitely. However, the approval covers only those specific grounds of excludability, deportability, or removability that were described in the application. An applicant who failed to describe any other grounds of excludability, deportability, or removability, or failed to disclose material facts existing at the time of the approval of the application, remains excludable, deportable, or removable under the previously unidentified grounds. If the applicant is excludable, deportable, or removable based upon any previously unidentified grounds a new application must be filed.

(e) *Filing or renewal of applications before an immigration judge.* (1) An eligible alien may renew or submit an application for the exercise of discretion under former section 212(c) of the Act in proceedings before an immigration judge under section 240 of the Act, or under former sections 235, 236, or 242 of the Act (as it existed prior to April 1, 1997), and under this chapter. Such application shall be adjudicated by the immigration judge, without regard to whether the applicant previously has made application to the district director.

(2) The immigration judge may grant or deny an application for relief under section 212(c), in the exercise of discretion, unless such relief is prohibited by paragraph (f) of this section or as otherwise provided by law.

(3) An alien otherwise entitled to appeal to the Board of Immigration Appeals may appeal the denial by the immigration judge of this application in accordance with the provisions of § 1003.38 of this chapter.

(f) *Limitations on discretion to grant an application under section 212(c) of the Act.* An application for relief under former section 212(c) of the Act shall be denied if:

(1) The alien has not been lawfully admitted for permanent residence;

(2) The alien has not maintained lawful domicile in the United States, as either a lawful permanent resident or a lawful temporary resident pursuant to section 245A or section 210 of the Act, for at least seven consecutive years immediately preceding the filing of the application;

(3) The alien is subject to inadmissibility or exclusion from the United States under paragraphs (3)(A), (3)(B), (3)(C), (3)(E), or (10)(C) of section 212(a) of the Act;

(4) The alien has been charged and found to be deportable or removable on the basis of a crime that is an aggravated felony, as defined in section 101(a)(43) of the Act (as in effect at the time the application for section 212(c) relief is adjudicated), except as follows:

(i) An alien whose convictions for one or more aggravated felonies were entered pursuant to plea agreements made on or after November 29, 1990, but prior to April 24, 1996, is ineligible for section 212(c) relief only if he or she has served a term of imprisonment of five years or more for such aggravated felony or felonies, and

(ii) An alien is not ineligible for section 212(c) relief on account of an aggravated felony conviction entered pursuant to a plea agreement that was made before November 29, 1990; or

(5) The alien is deportable under former section 241 of the Act or removable under section 237 of the Act on a ground which does not have a statutory counterpart in section 212 of the Act.

(g) *Relief for certain aliens who were in deportation proceedings before April 24, 1996.* Section 440(d) of Antiterrorism and Effective Death Penalty Act of 1996 (AEDPA) shall not apply to any applicant for relief under this section whose deportation proceedings were commenced before the Immigration Court before April 24, 1996.

(h) *Availability of section 212(c) relief for aliens who pleaded guilty or nolo contendere to certain crimes.* For purposes of this section, the date of the plea agreement will be considered the date the plea agreement was agreed to by the parties. Aliens are not eligible to apply for section 212(c) relief under the provisions of this paragraph with respect to convictions entered after trial.

(1) *Pleas before April 24, 1996.* Regardless of whether an alien is in exclusion, deportation, or removal proceedings, an eligible alien may apply for relief

under former section 212(c) of the Act, without regard to the amendment made by section 440(d) of the Antiterrorism and Effective Death Penalty Act of 1996, with respect to a conviction if the alien pleaded guilty or *nolo contendere* and the alien's plea agreement was made before April 24, 1996.

(2) *Pleas between April 24, 1996 and April 1, 1997.* Regardless of whether an alien is in exclusion, deportation, or removal proceedings, an eligible alien may apply for relief under former section 212(c) of the Act, as amended by section 440(d) of the Antiterrorism and Effective Death Penalty Act of 1996, with respect to a conviction if the alien pleaded guilty or *nolo contendere* and the alien's plea agreement was made on or after April 24, 1996, and before April 1, 1997.

(3) *Please on or after April 1, 1997.* Section 212(c) relief is not available with respect to convictions arising from plea agreements made on or after April 1, 1997.

[56 FR 50034, Oct. 3, 1991, as amended at 60 FR 34090, June 30, 1995; 61 FR 59825, Nov. 25, 1996; 66 FR 6446, Jan. 22, 2001; 69 FR 57834, Sept. 28, 2004]

§ 1212.4 Applications for the exercise of discretion under section 212(d)(1) and 212(d)(3).

(a) *Applications under section 212(d)(3)(A)*—(1) *General.* District directors and officers in charge outside the United States in the districts of Bangkok, Thailand; Mexico City, Mexico; and Rome, Italy are authorized to act upon recommendations made by consular officers for the exercise of discretion under section 212(d)(3)(A) of the Act. The District Director, Washington, DC, has jurisdiction in such cases recommended to the Service at the seat-of-government level by the Department of State. When a consular officer or other State Department official recommends that the benefits of section 212(d)(3)(A) of the Act be accorded an alien, neither an application nor fee shall be required. The recommendation shall specify:

(i) The reasons for inadmissibility and each section of law under which the alien is inadmissible;

(ii) Each intended date of arrival;

(iii) The length of each proposed stay in the United States;

(iv) The purpose of each stay;

(v) The number of entries which the alien intends to make; and

(vi) The justification for exercising the authority contained in section 212(d)(3) of the Act.

If the alien desires to make multiple entries and the consular officer or other State Department official believes that the circumstances justify the issuance of a visa valid for multiple entries rather than for a specified number of entries, and recommends that the alien be accorded an authorization valid for multiple entries, the information required by items (ii) and (iii) shall be furnished only with respect to the initial entry. Item (ii) does not apply to a bona fide crewman. The consular officer or other State Department official shall be notified of the decision on his recommendation. No appeal by the alien shall lie from an adverse decision made by a Service officer on the recommendation of a consular officer or other State Department official.

(2) *Authority of consular officers to approve section 212(d)(3)(A) recommendations pertaining to aliens inadmissible under section 212(a)(28)(C).* In certain categories of visa cases defined by the Secretary of State, United States consular officers assigned to visa-issuing posts abroad may, on behalf of the Attorney General pursuant to section 212(d)(3)(A) of the Act, approve a recommendation by another consular officer that an alien be admitted temporarily despite visa ineligibility solely because the alien is of the class of aliens defined at section 212(a)(28)(C) of the Act, as a result of presumed or actual membership in, or affiliation with, an organization described in that section. Authorizations for temporary admission granted by consular officers shall be subject to the terms specified in § 1212.4(c) of this chapter. Any recommendation which is not clearly approvable shall, and any recommendation may, be presented to the appropriate official of the Immigration and Naturalization Service for a determination.

(b) *Applications under section 212(d)(3)(B).* An application for the exercise of discretion under section

212(d)(3)(B) of the Act shall be submitted on Form I–192 to the district director in charge of the applicant's intended port of entry prior to the applicant's arrival in the United States. (For Department of State procedure when a visa is required, see 22 CFR 41.95 and paragraph (a) of this section.) If the application is made because the applicant may be inadmissible due to present or past membership in or affiliation with any Communist or other totalitarian party or organization, there shall be attached to the application a written statement of the history of the applicant's membership or affiliation, including the period of such membership or affiliation, whether the applicant held any office in the organization, and whether his membership or affiliation was voluntary or involuntary. If the applicant alleges that his membership or affiliation was involuntary, the statement shall include the basis for that allegation. When the application is made because the applicant may be inadmissible due to disease, mental or physical defect, or disability of any kind, the application shall describe the disease, defect, or disability. If the purpose of seeking admission to the United States is for treatment, there shall be attached to the application statements in writing to establish that satisfactory treatment cannot be obtained outside the United States; that arrangements have been completed for treatment, and where and from whom treatment will be received; what financial arrangements for payment of expenses incurred in connection with the treatment have been made, and that a bond will be available if required. When the application is made because the applicant may be inadmissible due to the conviction of one or more crimes, the designation of each crime, the date and place of its commission and of the conviction thereof, and the sentence or other judgment of the court shall be stated in the application; in such a case the application shall be supplemented by the official record of each conviction, and any other documents relating to commutation of sentence, parole, probation, or pardon. If the application is made at the time of the applicant's arrival to the district director at a port of entry, the applicant shall establish that he was not aware of the ground of inadmissibility and that it could not have been ascertained by the exercise of reasonable diligence, and he shall be in possession of a passport and visa, if required, or have been granted a waiver thereof. The applicant shall be notified of the decision and if the application is denied of the reasons therefor and of his right to appeal to the Board within 15 days after the mailing of the notification of decision in accordance with the Provisions of part 1003 of this chapter. If denied, the denial shall be without prejudice to renewal of the application in the course of proceedings before a special inquiry officer under sections 235 and 236 of the Act and this chapter. When an appeal may not be taken from a decision of a special inquiry officer excluding an alien but the alien has applied for the exercise of discretion under section 212(d)(3)(B) of the Act, the alien may appeal to the Board from a denial of such application in accordance with the provisions of §236.5(b) of this chapter.

(c) *Terms of authorization*—(1) *General.* Except as provided in paragraph (c)(2) of this section, each authorization under section 212(d)(3)(A) or (B) of the Act shall specify:

(i) Each section of law under which the alien is inadmissible;

(ii) The intended date of each arrival, unless the applicant is a bona fide crewman. However, if the authorization is valid for multiple entries rather than for a specified number of entries, this information shall be specified only with respect to the initial entry;

(iii) The length of each stay authorized in the United States, which shall not exceed the period justified and shall be subject to limitations specified in 8 CFR part 214. However, if the authorization is valid for multiple entries rather than for a specified number of entries, this information shall be specified only with respect to the initial entry;

(iv) The purpose of each stay;

(v) The number of entries for which the authorization is valid;

(vi) Subject to the conditions set forth in paragraph (c)(2) of this section, the dates on or between which each application for admission at POEs in the United States is valid;

(vii) The justification for exercising the authority contained in section 212(d)(3) of the Act; and

(viii) That the authorization is subject to revocation at any time.

(2) *Conditions of admission.* (i) For aliens issued an authorization for temporary admission in accordance with this section, admissions pursuant to section 212(d)(3) of the Act shall be subject to the terms and conditions set forth in the authorization.

(ii) The period for which the alien's admission is authorized pursuant to this section shall not exceed the period justified, or the limitations specified, in 8 CFR part 214 for each class of nonimmigrant, whichever is less.

(3) *Validity.* (i) Authorizations granted to crew members may be valid for a maximum period of 2 years for application for admission at U.S. POEs and may be valid for multiple entries.

(ii) An authorization issued in conjunction with an application for a Form DSP–150, B–1/B–2 Visa and Border Crossing Card, issued by the DOS shall be valid for a period not to exceed the validity of the biometric BCC for applications for admission at U.S. POEs and shall be valid for multiple entries.

(iii) A multiple entry authorization for a person other than a crew member or applicant for a Form DSP–150 may be made valid for a maximum period of 5 years for applications for admission at U.S. POEs.

(iv) An authorization that was previously issued in conjunction with Form I–185, Nonresident Alien Canadian Border Crossing Card, and that is noted on the card may remain valid. Although the waiver may remain valid, the non-biometric border crossing card portion of this document is not valid after that date. This waiver authorization shall cease if otherwise revoked or voided.

(v) A single-entry authorization to apply for admission at a U.S. POE shall not be valid for more than 6 months from the date the authorization is issued.

(vi) An authorization may not be revalidated. Upon expiration of the authorization, a new application and authorization are required.

(d) *Admission of groups inadmissible under section 212(a)(28) for attendance at international conferences.* When the Secretary of State recommends that a group of nonimmigrant aliens and their accompanying family members be admitted to attend international conferences notwithstanding their inadmissibility under section 212(a)(28) of the Act, the Deputy Commissioner, may enter an order pursuant to the authority contained in section 212(d)(3)(A) of the Act specifying the terms and conditions of their admission and stay.

(e) *Inadmissibility under section 212(a)(1).* Pursuant to the authority contained in section 212(d)(3) of the Act, the temporary admission of a nonimmigrant visitor is authorized notwithstanding inadmissibility under section 212(a)(1) of the Act, if such alien is accompanied by a member of his/her family, or a guardian who will be responsible for him/her during the period of admission authorized.

(f) *Action upon alien's arrival.* Upon admitting an alien who has been granted the benefits of section 212(d)(3)(A) of the Act, the immigration officer shall be guided by the conditions and limitations imposed in the authorization and noted by the consular officer in the alien's passport. When admitting any alien who has been granted the benefits of section 212(d)(3)(B) of the Act, the Immigration officer shall note on the arrival-departure record, Form I–94, or crewman's landing permit, Form I–95, issued to the alien, the conditions and limitations imposed in the authorization.

(g) *Authorizations issued to crewmen without limitation as to period of validity.* When a crewman who has a valid section 212(d)(3) authorization without any time limitation comes to the attention of the Service, his travel document shall be endorsed to show that the validity of his section 212(d)(3) authorization expires as of a date six months thereafter, and any previously-issued Form I–184 shall be lifted and Form I–95 shall be issued in its place and similarly endorsed.

(h) *Revocation.* The Deputy Commissioner or the district director may at any time revoke a waiver previously authorized under section 212(d)(3) of the Act and shall notify the nonimmigrant in writing to that effect.

(i) *Alien witnesses and informants*—(1) *Waivers under section 212(d)(1) of the Act.* Upon the application of a federal or state law enforcement authority ("LEA"), which shall include a state or federal court or United States Attorney's Office, pursuant to the filing of Form I-854, Inter-Agency Alien Witness and Informant Record, for nonimmigrant classification described in section 101(a)(15)(S) of the Act, the Commissioner shall determine whether a ground of exclusion exists with respect to the alien for whom classification is sought and, if so, whether it is in the national interest to exercise the discretion to waive the ground of excludability, other than section 212(a)(3)(E) of the Act. The Commissioner may at any time revoke a waiver previously authorized under section 212(d)(1) of the Act. In the event the Commissioner decides to revoke a previously authorized waiver for an S nonimmigrant, the Assistant Attorney General, Criminal Division, and the relevant LEA shall be notified in writing to that effect. The Assistant Attorney General, Criminal Division, shall concur in or object to the decision. Unless the Assistant Attorney General, Criminal Division, objects within 7 days, he or she shall be deemed to have concurred in the decision. In the event of an objection by the Assistant Attorney General, Criminal Division, the matter will be expeditiously referred to the Deputy Attorney General for a final resolution. In no circumstances shall the alien or the relevant LEA have a right of appeal from any decision to revoke.

(2) *Grounds of removal.* Nothing shall prohibit the Service from removing from the United States an alien classified pursuant to section 101(a)(15)(S) of the Act for conduct committed after the alien has been admitted to the United States as an S nonimmigrant, or after the alien's change to S classification, or for conduct or a condition undisclosed to the Attorney General prior to the alien's admission in, or change to, S classification, unless such conduct or condition is waived prior to admission and classification. In the event the Commissioner decides to remove an S nonimmigrant from the United States, the Assistant Attorney General, Criminal Division, and the relevant LEA shall be notified in writing to that effect. The Assistant Attorney General, Criminal Division, shall concur in or object to that decision. Unless the Assistant Attorney General, Criminal Division, objects within 7 days, he or she shall be deemed to have concurred in the decision. In the event of an objection by the Assistant Attorney General, Criminal Division, the matter will be expeditiously referred to the Deputy Attorney General for a final resolution. In no circumstances shall the alien or the relevant LEA have a right of appeal from any decision to remove.

[29 FR 15252, Nov. 13, 1964, as amended at 30 FR 12330, Sept. 28, 1965; 31 FR 10413, Aug. 3, 1966; 32 FR 15469, Nov. 7, 1967; 35 FR 3065, Feb. 17, 1970; 35 FR 7637, May 16, 1970; 40 FR 30470, July 21, 1975; 51 FR 32295, Sept. 10, 1986; 53 FR 40867, Oct. 19, 1988; 60 FR 44264, Aug. 25, 1995; 60 FR 52248, Oct. 5, 1995; 67 FR 71448, Dec. 2, 2002]

§ 1212.5 Parole of aliens into the United States.

Procedures and standards for the granting of parole by the Department of Homeland Security can be found at 8 CFR 212.5.

[69 FR 69497, Nov. 29, 2004]

§ 1212.6 Border crossing identification cards.

The regulations of the Department of Homeland Security pertaining to border crossing identification cards can be found at 8 CFR 212.6.

[81 FR 92367, Dec. 19, 2016]

§ 1212.7 Waiver of certain grounds of inadmissibility.

(a) *General*—(1) *Filing procedure*—(i) *Immigrant visa or K nonimmigrant visa applicant.* An applicant for an immigrant visa or "K" nonimmigrant visa who is inadmissible and seeks a waiver of inadmissibility shall file an application on Form I-601 at the consular office considering the visa application. Upon determining that the alien is admissible except for the grounds for which a waiver is sought, the consular officer shall transmit the Form I–601 to the Service for decision.

(ii) *Adjustment of status applicant.* An applicant for adjustment of status who is excludable and seeks a waiver under section 212(h) or (i) of the Act shall file an application on Form I–601 with the director or immigration judge considering the application for adjustment of status.

(iii) *Parole authorization applicant under § 1245.15(t).* An applicant for parole authorization under § 1245.15(t) of this chapter who is inadmissible and seeks a waiver under section 212(h) or (i) of the Act must file an application on Form I–601 with the Director of the Nebraska Service Center considering the Form I–131.

(iv) *Parole authorization applicant under § 1245.13(k)(2) of this chapter.* An applicant for parole authorization under § 1245.13(k)(2) of this chapter who is inadmissible and seeks a waiver under section 212(h) or (i) of the Act must file an application on Form I–601 with the Director of the Texas Service Center adjudicating the Form I–131.

(2) *Termination of application for lack of prosecution.* An applicant may withdraw the application at any time prior to the final decision, whereupon the case will be closed and the consulate notified. If the applicant fails to prosecute the application within a reasonable time either before or after interview the applicant shall be notified that if he or she fails to prosecute the application within 30 days the case will be closed subject to being reopened at the applicant's request. If no action has been taken within the 30-day period immediately thereafter, the case will be closed and the appropriate consul notified.

(3) *Decision.* If the application is approved the director shall complete Form I–607 for inclusion in the alien's file and shall notify the alien of the decision. If the application is denied the applicant shall be notified of the decision, of the reasons therefor, and of the right to appeal in accordance with part 103 of this chapter.

(4) *Validity.* A waiver granted under section 212(h) or section 212(i) of the Act shall apply only to those grounds of excludability and to those crimes, events or incidents specified in the application for waiver. Once granted, the waiver shall be valid indefinitely, even if the recipient of the waiver later abandons or otherwise loses lawful permanent resident status, except that any waiver which is granted to an alien who obtains lawful permanent residence on a conditional basis under section 216 of the Act shall automatically terminate concurrently with the termination of such residence pursuant to the provisions of section 216. Separate notification of the termination of the waiver is not required when an alien is notified of the termination of residence under section 216 of the Act, and no appeal shall lie from the decision to terminate the waiver on this basis. However, if the respondent is found not to be deportable in a deportation proceeding based on the termination, the waiver shall again become effective. Nothing in this subsection shall preclude the director from reconsidering a decision to approve a waiver if the decision is determined to have been made in error.

(b) *Section 212(g) (tuberculosis and certain mental conditions)*—(1) *General.* Any alien who is ineligible for a visa and is excluded from admission into the United States under section 212(a) (1), (3), or (6) of the Act may file an Application for Waiver of Grounds of Excludability (Form I–601) under section 212(g) of the Act at an office designated in paragraph (2). The family member specified in section 212(g) of the Act may file the waiver for the applicant if the applicant is incompetent to file the waiver personally.

(2) *Locations for filing Form I–601.* Form I–601 may be filed at any one of the following offices:

(i) The American consulate where the application for a visa is being considered if the alien is outside the United States;

(ii) The Service office having jurisdiction over the port of entry where the alien is applying for admission into the United States;

(iii) The Service office having jurisdiction over the alien if the alien is in the United States;

(iv) The Nebraska Service Center, if the alien is outside the United States and seeking parole authorization under § 1245.15(t)(2) of this chapter; or

(v) The Texas Service Center if the alien is outside the United States and is seeking parole authorization under § 1245.13(k)(2) of this chapter.

(3) *Section 212(a)(6) (tuberculosis).* If the alien is excludable under section 212(a)(6) of the Act because of tuberculosis, he shall execute Statement A on the reverse of page 1 of Form I–601. In addition, he or his sponsor in the United States is responsible for having Statement B executed by the physician or health facility which has agreed to supply treatment or observation; and, if required, Statement C shall be executed by the appropriate local or State health officer.

(4) *Section 212(a) (1) or (3) (certain mental conditions)*—(i) *Arrangements for submission of medical report.* If the alien is excludable under section 212(a) (1) or (3) (because of mental retardation or because of a past history of mental illness) he or his sponsoring family member shall submit an executed Form I–601 to the consular or Service office with a statement that arrangements have been made for the submission to that office of a medical report. The medical report shall contain a complete medical history of the alien, including details of any hospitalization or institutional care or treatment for any physical or mental condition; findings as to the current physical condition of the alien, including reports of chest X-ray examination and of serologic test for syphilis if the alien is 15 years of age or over, and other pertinent diagnostic tests; and findings as to the current mental condition of the alien, with information as to prognosis and life expectancy and with a report of a psychiatric examination conducted by a psychiatrist who shall, in case of mental retardation, also provide an evaluation of the alien's intelligence. For an alien with a past history of mental illness, the medical report shall also contain available information on which the U.S. Public Health Service can base a finding as to whether the alien has been free of such mental illness for a period of time sufficient in the light of such history to demonstrate recovery. Upon receipt of the medical report, the consular or Service office shall refer it to the U.S. Public Health Service for review.

(ii) *Submission of statement.* Upon being notified that the medical report has been reviewed by the U.S. Public Health Service and determined to be acceptable, the alien or the alien's sponsoring family member shall submit a statement to the consular or Service office. The statement must be from a clinic, hospital, institution, specialized facility, or specialist in the United States approved by the U.S. Public Health Service. The alien or alien's sponsor may be referred to the mental retardation or mental health agency of the state of proposed residence for guidance in selecting a post-arrival medical examining authority who will complete the evaluation and provide an evaluation report to the Centers for Disease Control. The statement must specify the name and address of the specialized facility, or specialist, and must affirm that:

(A) The specified facility or specialist agrees to evaluate the alien's mental status and prepare a complete report of the findings of such evaluation.

(B) The alien, the alien's sponsoring family member, or another responsible person has made complete financial arrangements for payment of any charges that may be incurred after arrival for studies, care, training and service;

(C) The Director, Division of Quarantine, Center for Prevention Services, Centers for Disease Control, Atlanta, GA. 30333 shall be furnished:

(*1*) The report evaluating the alien's mental status within 30 days after the alien's arrival; and

(*2*) Prompt notification of the alien's failure to report to the facility or specialist within 30 days after being notified by the U.S. Public Health Service that the alien has arrived in the United States.

(D) The alien shall be in an outpatient, inpatient, study, or other specified status as determined by the responsible local physcian or specialist during the initial evaluation.

(5) *Assurances: Bonds.* In all cases under paragraph (b) of this section the alien or his or her sponsoring family member shall also submit an assurance that the alien will comply with any special travel requirements as may be specified by the U.S. Public Health Service and that, upon the admission

of the alien into the United States, he or she will proceed directly to the facility or specialist specified for the initial evaluation, and will submit to such further examinations or treatment as may be required, whether in an outpatient, inpatient, or other status. The alien, his or her sponsoring family member, or other responsible person shall provide such assurances or bond as may be required to assure that the necessary expenses of the alien will be met and that he or she will not become a public charge. For procedures relating to cancellation or breaching of bonds, see part 103 of 8 CFR chapter I.

(c) *Section 212(e).* (1) An alien who was admitted to the United States as an exchange visitor, or who acquired that status after admission, is subject to the foreign residence requirement of section 212(e) of the Act if his or her participation in an exchange program was financed in whole or in part, directly or indirectly, by a United States government agency or by the government of the country of his or her nationality or last foreign residence.

(2) An alien is also subject to the foreign residence requirement of section 212(e) of the Act if at the time of admission to the United States as an exchange visitor or at the time of acquisition of exchange visitor status after admission to the United States, the alien was a national or lawful permanent resident of a country which the Director of the United States Information Agency had designated, through public notice in the FEDERAL REGISTER, as clearly requiring the services of persons engaged in the field of specialized knowledge or skill in which the alien was to engage in his or her exchange visitor program.

(3) An alien is also subject to the foreign residence requirement of section 212(e) of the Act if he or she was admitted to the United States as an exchange visitor on or after January 10, 1977 to receive graduate medical education or training, or following admission, acquired such status on or after that date for that purpose. However, an exchange visitor already participating in an exchange program of graduate medical education or training as of January 9, 1977 who was not then subject to the foreign residence requirement of section 212(e) and who proceeds or has proceeded abroad temporarily and is returning to the United States to participate in the same program, continues to be exempt from the foreign residence requirement.

(4) A spouse or child admitted to the United States or accorded status under section 101(a)(15)(J) of the Act to accompany or follow to join an exchange visitor who is subject to the foreign residence requirement of section 212(e) of the Act is also subject to that requirement.

(5) An alien who is subject to the foreign residence requirement and who believes that compliance therewith would impose exceptional hardship upon his/her spouse or child who is a citizen of the United States or a lawful permanent resident alien, or that he or she cannot return to the country of his or her nationality or last residence because he or she will be subject to persecution on account of race, religion, or political opinion, may apply for a waiver on Form I–612. The alien's spouse and minor children, if also subject to the foreign residence requirement, may be included in the application, provided the spouse has not been a participant in an exchange program.

(6) Each application based upon a claim to exceptional hardship must be accompanied by the certificate of marriage between the applicant and his or her spouse and proof of legal termination of all previous marriages of the applicant and spouse; the birth certificate of any child who is a United States citizen or lawful permanent resident alien, if the application is based upon a claim of exceptional hardship to a child, and evidence of the United States citizenship of the applicant's spouse or child, when the application is based upon a claim of exceptional hardship to a spouse or child who is a citizen of the United States.

(7) Evidence of United States citizenship and of status as a lawful permanent resident shall be in the form provided in part 204 of 8 CFR chapter I. An application based upon exceptional hardship shall be supported by a statement, dated and signed by the applicant, giving a detailed explanation of the basis for his or her belief that his

or her compliance with the foreign residence requirement of section 212(e) of the Act, as amended, would impose exceptional hardship upon his or her spouse or child who is a citizen of the United States or a lawful permanent resident thereof. The statement shall include all pertinent information concerning the incomes and savings of the applicant and spouse. If exceptional hardship is claimed upon medical grounds, the applicant shall submit a medical certificate from a qualified physician setting forth in terms understandable to a layman the nature and effect of the illness and prognosis as to the period of time the spouse or child will require care or treatment.

(8) An application based upon the applicant's belief that he or she cannot return to the country of his or her nationality or last residence because the applicant would be subject to persecution on account of race, religion, or political opinion, must be supported by a statement, dated and signed by the applicant, setting forth in detail why the applicant believes he or she would be subject to persecution.

(9) *Waivers under Pub. L. 103–416 based on a request by a State Department of Public Health (or equivalent).* In accordance with section 220 of Pub. L. 103–416, an alien admitted to the United States as a nonimmigrant under section 101(a)(15)(J) of the Act, or who acquired status under section 101(a)(15)(J) of the Act after admission to the United States, to participate in an exchange program of graduate medical education or training (as of January 9, 1977), may apply for a waiver of the 2-year home country residence and physical presence requirement (the "2-year requirement") under section 212(e)(iii) of the Act based on a request by a State Department of Public Health, or its equivalent. To initiate the application for a waiver under Pub. L. 103–416, the Department of Public Health, or its equivalent, or the State in which the foreign medical graduate seeks to practice medicine, must request the Director of USIA to recommend a waiver to the Service. The waiver may be granted only if the Director of USIA provides the Service with a favorable waiver recommendation. Only the Service, however, may grant or deny the waiver application. If granted, such a waiver shall be subject to the terms and conditions imposed under section 214(l) of the Act (as redesignated by section 671(a)(3)(A) of Pub. L. 104–208). Although the alien is not required to submit a separate waiver application to the Service, the burden rests on the alien to establish eligibility for the waiver. If the Service approves a waiver request made under Pub. L. 103–416, the foreign medical graduate (and accompanying dependents) may apply for change of nonimmigrant status, from J–1 to H–1B and, in the case of dependents of such a foreign medical graduate, from J–2 to H–4. Aliens receiving waivers under section 220 of Pub. L. 103–416 are subject, in all cases, to the provisions of section 214(g)(1)(A) of the Act.

(i) *Eligiblity criteria.* J–1 foreign medical graduates (with accompanying J–2 dependents) are eligible to apply for a waiver of the 2-year requirement under Pub. L. 103–416 based on a request by a State Department of Public Health (or its equivalent) if:

(A) They were admitted to the United States under section 101(a)(15)(J) of the Act, or acquired J nonimmigrant status before June 1, 2002, to pursue graduate medical education or training in the United States.

(B) They have entered into a bona fide, full-time employment contract for 3 years to practice medicine at a health care facility located in an area or areas designated by the Secretary of Health and Human Services as having a shortage of health care professionals ("HHS-designated shortage area");

(C) They agree to commence employment within 90 days of receipt of the waiver under this section and agree to practice medicine for 3 years at the facility named in the waiver application and only in HHS-designated shortage areas. The health care facility named in the waiver application may be operated by:

(*1*) An agency of the Government of the United States or of the State in which it is located; or

(*2*) A charitable, educational, or other not-for-profit organization; or

(*3*) Private medical practitioners.

(D) The Department of Public Health, or its equivalent, in the State where the health care facility is located has requested the Director, USIA, to recommend the waiver, and the Director, USIA, submits a favorable waiver recommendation to the Service; and

(E) Approval of the waiver will not cause the number of waivers granted pursuant to Pub. L. 103–416 and this section to foreign medical graduates who will practice medicine in the same state to exceed 20 during the current fiscal year.

(ii) *Decision on waivers under Pub. L. 103–416 and notification to the alien*—(A) *Approval.* If the Director of USIA submits a favorable waiver recommendation on behalf of a foreign medical graduate pursuant to Pub. L. 103–416, and the Service grants the waiver, the alien shall be notified of the approval on Form I–797 (or I–797A or I–797B, as appropriate). The approval notice shall clearly state the terms and conditions imposed on the waiver, and the Service's records shall be noted accordingly.

(B) *Denial.* If the Director of USIA issues a favorable waiver recommendation under Pub. L. 103–416 and the Service denies the waiver, the alien shall be notified of the decision and of the right to appeal under 8 CFR part 1103. However, no appeal shall lie where the basis for denial is that the number of waivers granted to the State in which the foreign medical graduate will be employed would exceed 20 for that fiscal year.

(iii) *Conditions.* The foreign medical graduate must agree to commence employment for the health care facility specified in the waiver application within 90 days of receipt of the waiver under Pub. L. 103–416. The foreign medical graduate may only fulfill the requisite 3-year employment contract as an H–1B nonimmigrant. A foreign medical graduate who receives a waiver under Pub. L. 103–416 based on a request by a State Department of Public Health (or equivalent), and changes his or her nonimmigrant classification from J–1 to H–1B, may not apply for permanent residence or for any other change of nonimmigrant classification unless he or she has fulfilled the 3-year employment contract with the health care facility and in the specified HHS-designated shortage area named in the waiver application.

(iv) *Failure to fulfill the three-year employment contract due to extenuating circumstances.* A foreign medical graduate who fails to meet the terms and conditions imposed on the waiver under section 214(l) of the Act and this paragraph will once again become subject to the 2-year requirement under section 212(e) of the Act.

Under section 214(l)(1)(B) of the Act, however, the Service, in the exercise of discretion, may excuse early termination of the foreign medical graduate's 3-year period of employment with the health care facility named in the waiver application due to extenuating circumstances. Extenuating circumstances may include, but are not limited to, closure of the health care facility or hardship to the alien. In determining whether to excuse such early termination of employment, the Service shall base its decision on the specific facts of each case. In all cases, the burden of establishing eligibility for a favorable exercise of discretion rests with the foreign medical graduate. Depending on the circumstances, closure of the health care facility named in the waiver application may, but need not, be considered an extenuating circumstance excusing early termination of employment. Under no circumstances will a foreign medical graduate be eligible to apply for change of status to another nonimmigrant category, for an immigrant visa or for status as a lawful permanent resident prior to completing the requisite 3-year period of employment for a health care facility located in an HHS-designated shortage area.

(v) *Required evidence.* A foreign medical graduate who seeks to have early termination of employment excused due to extenuating circumstances shall submit documentary evidence establishing such a claim. In all cases, the foreign medical graduate shall submit an employment contract with another health care facility located in an HHS-designated shortage area for the balance of the required 3-year period of employment. A foreign medical graduate claiming extenuating circumstances based on hardship shall also submit evidence establishing that such hardship was caused by unforeseen circumstances beyond his or her control. A foreign medical graduate claiming extenuating circumstances based on closure of the health care facility named in the waiver application shall also submit evidence that the facility has closed or is about to be closed.

(vi) *Notification requirements.* A J–1 foreign medical graduate who has been granted a waiver of the 2-year requirement pursuant to Pub. L. 103–416, is required to comply with the terms and conditions specified in section 214(l) of the Act and the implementing regulations in this section. If the foreign medical graduate subsequently applies for and receives H–1B status, he or she must also comply with the terms and conditions of that nonimmigrant status. Such compliance shall also include notifying the Service of any material change in the terms and conditions of the H–1B employment, by filing either an amended or a new H–1B petition, as required, under §§ 214.2(h)(2)(i)(D), 214.2(h)(2)(i)(E), and 214.2(h)(11) of 8 CFR chapter I.

(A) *Amended H–1B petitions.* The health care facility named in the waiver application and H–1B petition shall file an amended H–1B petition, as required under § 214.2(h)(2)(i)(E) of 8 CFR chapter I, if there are any material changes in the terms and conditions of the beneficiary's employment or eligibility as specified in the waiver application filed under Pub. L. 103–416 and in the subsequent H–1B petition. In such a case, an amended H–1B petition shall be accompanied by evidence that the alien will continue practicing medicine with the original employer in an HHS-designated shortage area.

(B) *New H–1B petitions.* A health care facility seeking to employ a foreign medical graduate who has been granted a waiver under Pub. L. 103–416 (prior to the time the alien has completed his or her 3-year contract with the facility named in the waiver application and original H–1B petition), shall file a new H–1B petition with the Service, as required under §§ 214.2(h)(2)(i) (D) and (E) of 8 CFR chapter I. Although a new waiver application need not be filed, the new H–1B petition shall be accompanied by the documentary evidence generally required under § 214.2(h) of this chapter, and the following additional documents:

(*1*) A copy of Form I–797 (and/or I–797A and I–797B) relating to the waiver and nonimmigrant H status granted under Pub. L. 103–416;

(*2*) An explanation from the foreign medical graduate, with supporting evidence, establishing that extenuating circumstances necessitate a change in employment;

(*3*) An employment contract establishing that the foreign medical graduate will practice medicine at the health care facility named in the new H–1B petition for the balance of the required 3-year period; and

(*4*) Evidence that the geographic area or areas of intended employment indicated in the new H–1B petition are in HHS-designated shortage areas.

(C) *Review of amended and new H–1B petitions for foreign medical graduates granted waivers under Pub. L. 103–416 and who seek to have early termination of employment excused due to extenuating circumstances*—(*1*) *Amended H–1B petitions.* The waiver granted under Pub. L. 103–416 may be affirmed, and the amended H–1B petition may be approved, if the petitioning health care facility establishes that the foreign medical graduate otherwise remains eligible for H–1B classification and that he or she will continue practicing medicine in an HHS-designated shortage area.

(*2*) *New H–1B petitions.* The Service shall review a new H–1B petition filed on behalf of a foreign medical graduate who has not yet fulfilled the required 3-year period of employment with the health care facility named in the waiver application and in the original H–1B petition to determine whether extenuating circumstances exist which warrant a change in employment, and whether the waiver granted under Pub. L. 103–416 should be affirmed. In conducting such a review, the Service shall determine whether the foreign medical graduate will continue practicing medicine in an HHS-designated shortage area, and whether the new H–1B petitioner and the foreign medical graduate have satisfied the remaining H–1B eligibility criteria described under section 101(a)(15)(H) of the Act and § 214.2(h) of 8 CFR chapter I. If these criteria have been satisfied, the waiver granted to the foreign medical graduate under Pub. L. 103–416 may be affirmed, and the new H1–B petition may be approved in the exercise of discretion, thereby permitting the foreign medical graduate to serve the balance of the requisite 3-year employment period at the health care facility named in the new H–1B petition.

(D) *Failure to notify the Service of any material changes in employment.* Foreign medical graduates who have been granted a waiver of the 2-year requirement and who have obtained H–1B status under Pub. L. 103–416 but fail to: Properly notify the Service of any material change in the terms and conditions of their H–1B employment, by having their employer file an amended or a new H–1B petition in accordance with this section and § 214.2(h) of 8 CFR chapter I; or establish continued eligibility for the waiver and H–1B status, shall (together with their dependents) again become subject to the 2-year requirement. Such foreign medical graduates and their accompanying H–4 dependents also become subject to deportation under section 241(a)(1)(C)(i) of the Act.

(10) The applicant and his or her spouse may be interviewed by an immigration officer in connection with the application and consultation may be had with the Director, United States Information Agency and the sponsor of any exchange program in which the applicant has been a participant.

(11) The applicant shall be notified of the decision, and if the application is denied, of the reasons therefor and of the right of appeal in accordance with the provisions of part 103 of this chapter. However, no appeal shall lie from the denial of an application for lack of a favorable recommendation from the Secretary of State. When an interested United States Government agency requests a waiver of the two-year foreign-residence requirement and the Director, United States Information Agency had made a favorable recommendation, the interested agency shall be notified of the decision on its request and, if the request is denied, of the reasons thereof, and of the right of appeal. If the foreign country of the alien's nationality or last residence has furnished statement in writing that it has no objection to his/her being granted a waiver of the foreign residence requirement and the Director, United States Information Agency has made a favorable recommendation, the Director shall be notified of the decision and, if the foreign residence requirement is not waived, of the reasons therefor and of the foregoing right of appeal. However, this "no objection" provision is not applicable to the exchange visitor admitted to the United States on or after January 10, 1977 to receive graduate medical education or training, or who acquired such status on or after that date for such purpose; except that the alien who commenced a program before January 10, 1977 and who was readmitted to the United States on or after that date to continue participation in the same program, is eligible for the "no objection" waiver.

(d) *Criminal grounds of inadmissibility involving violent or dangerous crimes.* The Attorney General, in general, will not favorably exercise discretion under section 212(h)(2) of the Act (8 U.S.C. 1182(h)(2)) to consent to an application or reapplication for a visa, or admission to the United States, or adjustment of status, with respect to immigrant aliens who are inadmissible under section 212(a)(2) of the Act in cases involving violent or dangerous crimes, except in extraordinary circumstances, such as those involving national security or foreign policy considerations, or cases in which an alien clearly demonstrates that the denial of the application for adjustment of status or an immigrant visa or admission as an immigrant would result in exceptional and extremely unusual hardship. Moreover, depending on the gravity of the alien's underlying criminal offense, a showing of extraordinary circumstances might still be insufficient to warrant a favorable exercise of discretion under section 212(h)(2) of the Act.

(Secs. 103, 203, 212 of the Immigration and Nationality Act, as amended by secs. 4, 5, 18 of Pub. L. 97–116, 95 Stat. 1611, 1620, (8 U.S.C. 1103, 1153, 1182)

[29 FR 12584, Sept. 4, 1964]

EDITORIAL NOTE: For FEDERAL REGISTER citations affecting §1212.7, see the List of CFR Sections Affected, which appears in the Finding Aids section of the printed volume and at *www.govinfo.gov*.

§1212.8 Certification requirement of section 212(a)(14).

(a) *General.* The certification requirement of section 212(a)(14) of the Act applies to aliens seeking admission to the United States or adjustment of status under section 245 of the Act for the purpose of performing skilled or unskilled labor, who are preference immigrants as described in section 203(a) (3) or (6) of the Act, or who are nonpreference immigrants as described in section 203(a)(8). The certification requirement shall not be applicable to a nonpreference applicant for admission to the United States or to a nonpreference applicant for adjustment of status under section 245 who establishes that he will not perform skilled or unskilled labor. A native of the Western Hemisphere who established a priority date with a consular officer prior to January 1, 1977 and who was found to be entitled to an exemption from the labor certification requirement of section 212(a)(14) of the Act under the law in effect prior to January 1, 1977 as the parent, spouse or child of a United States citizen or lawful permanent resident alien shall continue to be exempt from that requirement for so long as the relationship upon which the exemption is based continues to exist.

(b) *Aliens not required to obtain labor certifications.* The following persons are not considered to be within the purview of section 212(a)(14) of the Act and do not require a labor certification: (1) A member of the Armed Forces of the United States; (2) a spouse or child accompanying or following to join his spouse or parent who either has a labor certification or is a nondependent alien who does not require such a certification; (3) a female alien who intends to marry a citizen or alien lawful permanent resident of the United States, who establishes satisfactorily that she does not intend to seek employment in the United States and whose fiance has guaranteed her support; (4) an alien who establishes on Form I–526 that he has invested, or is actively in the process of investing, capital totaling at least $40,000 in an enterprise in the United States of which he will be a principal manager and that the enterprise will employ a person or persons in the United States of which he will be a principal manager and that the enterprise will employ a person or persons in the United States who are United States citizens or aliens lawfully admitted for permnanent residence, exclusive of the alien, his spouse and children. A copy of a document submitted in support of Form I–526 may be accepted though unaccompanied by the original, if the copy bears a certification by an attorney, typed or rubber-stamped in the language set forth in §204.2(j) of 8 CFR chapter I. However, the original document shall be submitted, if submittal is requested by the Service.

[31 FR 10021, July 23, 1966; 31 FR 10355, Aug. 22, 1966, as amended at 34 FR 5326, Mar. 18, 1969; 38 FR 31166, Nov. 12, 1973; 41 FR 37566, Sept. 7, 1976; 41 FR 55850, Dec. 23, 1976; 47 FR 44990, Oct. 13, 1982; 48 FR 19157, Apr. 28, 1983]

§1212.9 Applicability of section 212(a)(32) to certain derivative third and sixth preference and nonpreference immigrants.

A derivative beneficiary who is the spouse or child of a qualified third or sixth preference or nonpreference immigrant and who is also a graduate of a medical school as defined by section 101(a)(41) of the Act is not considered to be an alien who is coming to the United States principally to perform services as a member of the medical profession. Therefore, a derivative third or sixth preference or nonpreference immigrant under section 203(a)(8) of the Act, who is also a graduate of a medical school, is eligible for an immigrant visa or for adjustment of status under section 245 of the Act, whether or not such derivative immigrant has passed Parts I and II of the National Board of Medical Examiners Examination or equivalent examination.

(Secs. 103, 203(a)(8), and 212(a)(32), 8 U.S.C 1103, 1153(a)(8), and 1182(a)(32))

[45 FR 63836, Sept. 26, 1980]

§ 1212.10 Section 212(k) waiver.

Any applicant for admission who is in possession of an immigrant visa, and who is excludable under sections 212(a)(14), (20), or (21) of the Act, may apply to the district director at the port of entry for a waiver under section 212(k) of the Act. If the application for waiver is denied by the district director, the application may be renewed in exclusion proceedings before an immigration judge as provided in part 1236 of this chapter.

(Secs. 103, 203, 212 of the Immigration and Nationality Act, as amended by secs. 4, 5, 18 of Pub. L. 97–116, 95 Stat. 1611, 1620, (8 U.S.C. 1103, 1153, 1182)

[47 FR 44236, Oct. 7, 1982]

§ 1212.11 Controlled substance convictions.

In determining the admissibility of an alien who has been convicted of a violation of any law or regulation of a State, the United States, or a foreign country relating to a controlled substance, the term *controlled substance* as used in section 212(a)(23) of the Act, shall mean the same as that referenced in the Controlled Substances Act, 21 U.S.C. 801, *et seq.*, and shall include any substance contained in Schedules I through V of 21 CFR 1308.1, *et seq.* For the purposes of this section, the term *controlled substance* includes controlled substance analogues as defined in 21 U.S.C. 802(23) and 813.

[53 FR 9282, Mar. 22, 1988]

§ 1212.12 Parole determinations and revocations respecting Mariel Cubans.

(a) *Scope.* This section applies to any native of Cuba who last came to the United States between April 15, 1980, and October 20, 1980 (hereinafter referred to as *Mariel Cuban*) and who is being detained by the Immigration and Naturalization Service (hereinafter referred to as the *Service*) pending his or her exclusion hearing, or pending his or her return to Cuba or to another country. It covers Mariel Cubans who have never been paroled as well as those Mariel Cubans whose previous parole has been revoked by the Service. It also applies to any Mariel Cuban, detained under the authority of the Immigration and Nationality Act in any facility, who has not been approved for release or who is currently awaiting movement to a Service or Bureau Of Prisons (BOP) facility. In addition, it covers the revocation of parole for those Mariel Cubans who have been released on parole at any time.

(b) *Parole authority and decision.* The authority to grant parole under section 212(d)(5) of the Act to a detained Mariel Cuban shall be exercised by the Commissioner, acting through the Associate Commissioner for Enforcement, as follows:

(1) *Parole decisions.* The Associate Commissioner for Enforcement may, in the exercise of discretion, grant parole to a detained Mariel Cuban for emergent reasons or for reasons deemed strictly in the public interest. A decision to retain in custody shall briefly set forth the reasons for the continued detention. A decision to release on parole may contain such special conditions as are considered appropriate. A copy of any decision to parole or to detain, with an attached copy translated into Spanish, shall be provided to the detainee. Parole documentation for Mariel Cubans shall be issued by the district director having jurisdiction over the alien, in accordance with the parole determination made by the Associate Commissioner for Enforcement.

(2) *Additional delegation of authority.* All references to the Commissioner and Associate Commissioner for Enforcement in this section shall be deemed to include any person or persons (including a committee) designated in writing by the Commissioner or Associate Commissioner for Enforcement to exercise powers under this section.

(c) *Review Plan Director.* The Associate Commissioner for Enforcement shall appoint a Director of the Cuban Review Plan. The Director shall have authority to establish and maintain appropriate files respecting each Mariel Cuban to be reviewed for possible parole, to determine the order in which the cases shall be reviewed, and to coordinate activities associated with these reviews.

(d) *Recommendations to the Associate Commissioner for Enforcement.* Parole recommendations for detained Mariel

Cubans shall be developed in accordance with the following procedures.

(1) *Review Panels.* The Director shall designate a panel or panels to make parole recommendations to the Associate Commissioner for Enforcement. A Cuban Review Panel shall, except as otherwise provided, consist of two persons. Members of a Review Panel shall be selected from the professional staff of the Service. All recommendations by a two-member Panel shall be unanimous. If the vote of a two-member Panel is split, it shall adjourn its deliberations concerning that particular detainee until a third Panel member is added. A recommendation by a three-member Panel shall be by majority vote. The third member of any Panel shall be the Director of the Cuban Review Plan or his designee.

(2) *Criteria for Review.* Before making any recommendation that a detainee be granted parole, a majority of the Cuban Review Panel members, or the Director in case of a record review, must conclude that:

(i) The detainee is presently a nonviolent person;

(ii) The detainee is likely to remain nonviolent;

(iii) The detainee is not likely to pose a threat to the community following his release; and

(iv) The detainee is not likely to violate the conditions of his parole.

(3) *Factors for consideration.* The following factors should be weighed in considering whether to recommend further detention or release on parole of a detainee:

(i) The nature and number of disciplinary infractions or incident reports received while in custody;

(ii) The detainee's past history of criminal behavior;

(iii) Any psychiatric and psychological reports pertaining to the detainee's mental health;

(iv) Institutional progress relating to participation in work, educational and vocational programs;

(v) His ties to the United States, such as the number of close relatives residing lawfully here;

(vi) The likelihood that he may abscond, such as from any sponsorship program; and

(vii) Any other information which is probative of whether the detainee is likely to adjust to life in a community, is likely to engage in future acts of violence, is likely to engage in future criminal activity, or is likely to violate the conditions of his parole.

(4) *Procedure for review.* The following procedures will govern the review process:

(i) *Record review.* Initially, the Director or a Panel shall review the detainee's file. Upon completion of this record review, the Director or the Panel shall issue a written recommendation that the detainee be released on parole or scheduled for a personal interview.

(ii) *Personal interview.* If a recommendation to grant parole after only a record review is not accepted or if the detainee is not recommended for release, a Panel shall personally interview the detainee. The scheduling of such interviews shall be at the discretion of the Director. The detainee may be accompanied during the interview by a person of his choice, who is able to attend at the time of the scheduled interview, to assist in answering any questions. The detainee may submit to the Panel any information, either orally or in writing, which he believes presents a basis for release on parole.

(iii) *Panel recommendation.* Following completion of the interview and its deliberations, the Panel shall issue a written recommendation that the detainee be released on parole or remain in custody pending deportation or pending further observation and subsequent review. This written recommendation shall include a brief statement of the factors which the Panel deems material to its recommendation. The recommendation and appropriate file material shall be forwarded to the Associate Commissioner for Enforcement, to be considered in the exercise of discretion pursuant to § 1212.12(b).

(e) *Withdrawal of parole approval.* The Associate Commissioner for Enforcement may, in his or her discretion, withdraw approval for parole of any detainee prior to release when, in his or her opinion, the conduct of the detainee, or any other circumstance, indicates that parole would no longer be appropriate.

(f) *Sponsorship*. No detainee may be released on parole until suitable sponsorship or placement has been found for the detainee. The paroled detainee must abide by the parole conditions specified by the Service in relation to his sponsorship or placement. The following sponsorships and placements are suitable:

(1) Placement by the Public Health Service in an approved halfway house or mental health project;

(2) Placement by the Community Relations Service in an approved halfway house or community project; and

(3) Placement with a close relative such as a parent, spouse, child, or sibling who is a lawful permanent resident or a citizen of the United States.

(g) *Timing of reviews*. The timing of review shall be in accordance with the following guidelines.

(1) *Parole revocation cases*. The Director shall schedule the review process in the case of a new or returning detainee whose previous immigration parole has been revoked. The review process will commence with a scheduling of a file review, which will ordinarily be expected to occur within approximately three months after parole is revoked. In the case of a Mariel Cuban who is in the custody of the Service, the Cuban Review Plan Director may, in his or her discretion, suspend or postpone the parole review process if such detainee's prompt deportation is practicable and proper.

(2) *Continued detention cases*. A subsequent review shall be commenced for any detainee within one year of a refusal to grant parole under § 1212.12(b), unless a shorter interval is specified by the Director.

(3) *Discretionary reviews*. The Cuban Review Plan Director, in his discretion, may schedule a review of a detainee at any time when the Director deems such a review to be warranted.

(h) *Revocation of parole*. The Associate Commissioner for Enforcement shall have authority, in the exercise of discretion, to revoke parole in respect to Mariel Cubans. A district director may also revoke parole when, in the district director's opinion, revocation is in the public interest and circumstances do not reasonably permit referral of the case to the Associate Commissioner. Parole may be revoked in the exercise of discretion when, in the opinion of the revoking official:

(1) The purposes of parole have been served;

(2) The Mariel Cuban violates any condition of parole;

(3) It is appropriate to enforce an order of exclusion or to commence proceedings against a Mariel Cuban; or

(4) The period of parole has expired without being renewed.

[52 FR 48802, Dec. 28, 1987, as amended at 59 FR 13870, Mar. 24, 1994; 65 FR 80294, Dec. 21, 2000]

§ 1212.13 [Reserved]

§ 1212.14 Parole determinations for alien witnesses and informants for whom a law enforcement authority ("LEA") will request S classification.

(a) *Parole authority*. Parole authorization under section 212(d)(5) of the Act for aliens whom LEAs seek to bring to the United States as witnesses or informants in criminal/counter terrorism matters and to apply for S classification shall be exercised as follows:

(1) *Grounds of eligibility*. The Commissioner may, in the exercise of discretion, grant parole to an alien (and the alien's family members) needed for law enforcement purposes provided that a state or federal LEA:

(i) Establishes its intention to file, within 30 days after the alien's arrival in the United States, a completed Form I–854, Inter-Agency Alien Witness and Informant Record, with the Assistant Attorney General, Criminal Division, Department of Justice, in accordance with the instructions on or attached to the form, which will include the names of qualified family members for whom parole is sought;

(ii) Specifies the particular operational reasons and basis for the request, and agrees to assume responsibility for the alien during the period of the alien's temporary stay in the United States, including maintaining control and supervision of the alien and the alien's whereabouts and activities, and further specifies any other terms and conditions specified by the Service during the period for which the parole is authorized;

(iii) Agrees to advise the Service of the alien's failure to report quarterly any criminal conduct by the alien, or any other activity or behavior on the alien's part that may constitute a ground of excludability or deportability;

(iv) Assumes responsibility for ensuring the alien's departure on the date of termination of the authorized parole (unless the alien has been admitted in S nonimmigrant classification pursuant to the terms of paragraph (a)(2) of this section), provides any and all assistance needed by the Service, if necessary, to ensure departure, and verifies departure in a manner acceptable to the Service;

(v) Provide LEA seat-of-government certification that parole of the alien is essential to an investigation or prosecution, is in the national interest, and is requested pursuant to the terms and authority of section 212(d)(5) of the Act;

(vi) Agrees that no promises may be, have been, or will be made by the LEA to the alien that the alien will or may:

(A) Remain in the United States in parole status or any other nonimmigrant classification;

(B) Adjust status to that of lawful permanent resident; or

(C) Otherwise attempt to remain beyond the authorized parole. The alien (and any family member of the alien who is 18 years of age or older) shall sign a statement acknowledging an awareness that parole only authorizes a temporary stay in the United States and does not convey the benefits of S nonimmigrant classification, any other nonimmigrant classification, or any entitlement to further benefits under the Act; and

(vii) Provides, in the case of a request for the release of an alien from Service custody, certification that the alien is eligible for parole pursuant to § 1235.3 of this chapter.

(2) *Authorization*. (i) Upon approval of the request for parole, the Commissioner shall notify the Assistant Attorney General, Criminal Division, of the approval.

(ii) Upon notification of approval of a request for parole, the LEA will advise the Commissioner of the date, time, and place of the arrival of the alien. The Commissioner will coordinate the arrival of the alien in parole status with the port director prior to the time of arrival.

(iii) Parole will be authorized for a period of thirty (30) days to commence upon the alien's arrival in the United States in order for the LEA to submit a completed Form I–854 to the Assistant Attorney General, Criminal Division. Upon the submission to the Assistant Attorney General of the Form I–854 requesting S classification, the period of parole will be automatically extended while the request is being reviewed. The Assistant Attorney General, Criminal Division, will notify the Commissioner of the submission of a Form I–854.

(b) *Termination of parole*—(1) *General*. The Commissioner may terminate parole for any alien (including a member of the alien's family) in parole status under this section where termination is in the public interest. A district director may also terminate parole when, in the district director's opinion, termination is in the public interest and circumstances do not reasonably permit referral of the case to the Commissioner. In such a case, the Commissioner shall be notified immediately. In the event the Commissioner, or in the appropriate case, a district director, decides to terminate the parole of an alien witness or informant authorized under the terms of this paragraph, the Assistant Attorney General, Criminal Division, and the relevant LEA shall be notified in writing to that effect. The Assistant Attorney General, Criminal Division, shall concur in or object to that decision. Unless the Assistant Attorney General, Criminal Division, objects within 7 days, he or she shall be deemed to have concurred in the decision. In the event of an objection by the Assistant Attorney General, Criminal Division, the matter will be expeditiously referred to the Deputy Attorney General for a final resolution. In no circumstances shall the alien or the relevant LEA have a right of appeal from any decision to terminate parole.

(2) *Termination of parole and admission in S classification.* When an LEA has filed a request for an alien in authorized parole status to be admitted in S nonimmigrant classification and that request has been approved by the Commissioner pursuant to the procedures outlines in 8 CFR 214.2(t), the Commissioner may, in the exercise of discretion:

(i) Terminate the alien's parole status;

(ii) Determine eligibility for waivers; and

(iii) Admit the alien in S nonimmigrant classification pursuant to the terms and conditions of section 101(a)(15(S) of the Act and 8 CFR 214.2(t).

(c) *Departure.* If the alien's parole has been terminated and the alien has been ordered excluded from the United States, the LEA shall ensure departure from the United States and so inform the district director in whose jurisdiction the alien has last resided. The district director, if necessary, shall oversee the alien's departure from the United States and, in any event, shall notify the Commissioner of the alien's departure. The Commissioner shall be notified in writing of the failure of any alien authorized parole under this paragraph to depart in accordance with an order of exclusion and deportation entered after parole authorized under this paragraph has been terminated.

(d) *Failure to comply with procedures.* Any failure to adhere to the parole procedures contained in this section shall immediately be brought to the attention of the Commissioner, who will notify the Attorney General.

[60 FR 44265, Aug. 25, 1995]

§ 1212.15 Certificates for foreign health care workers.

(a) *Inadmissible aliens.* With the exception of the aliens described in paragraph (b) of this section, any alien coming to the United States for the primary purpose of performing labor in a health care occupation listed in paragraph (c) of this section is inadmissible to the United States unless the alien presents a certificate as described in paragraph (f) of this section.

(b) *Inapplicability of the ground of inadmissibility.* The following aliens are not subject to this ground of inadmissibility:

(1) Aliens seeking admission to the United States to perform services in a non-clinical health care occupation. A non-clinical health-care occupation is one where the alien is not required to perform direct or indirect patient care. Occupations which are considered to be non-clinical include, but are not limited to, medical teachers, medical researchers, managers of health care facilities, and medical consultants to the insurance industry;

(2) The spouse and dependent children of any immigrant alien who is seeking to immigrate in order to accompany or follow to join the principal alien; and

(3) Any alien applying for adjustment of status to that of a permanent resident under any provision of law other than an alien who is seeking to immigrate on the basis of an employment-based immigrant visa petition which was filed for the purpose of obtaining the alien's services in a health care occupation described in paragraph (c) of this section.

(c) *Occupations affected by this provision.* With the exception of the aliens described in paragraph (b) of this section, any alien seeking admission to the United States as an immigrant or any alien applying for adjustment of status to a permanent resident to perform labor in one of the following health care occupations, regardless of where he or she received his or her education or training, is subject to this provision:

(1) Licensed practical nurses, licensed vocational nurses, and registered nurses.

(2) Occupational therapists.

(3) Physical therapists.

(4) Speech-Language Pathologists and Audiologists.

(5) Medical Technologists (Clinical Laboratory Scientists).

(6) Physician Assistants.

(7) Medical Technicians (Clinical Laboratory Technicians).

(d) *Presentation of the certificate.* An alien described in paragraph (a) of this section who is applying for admission as an immigrant seeking to perform labor in a health care occupation as described in this section must present a certificate to a consular officer at the time of visa issuance and to the Service at the time of admission or adjustment of status. The certificate must be valid at the time of visa issuance and admission at a port-of-entry, or, if applicable, at the time of adjustment of status.

(e) *Organizations approved by the Service to issue certificates for health care workers.* (1) The Commission on Graduates of Foreign Nursing Schools may issue certificates pursuant to 8 U.S.C. 1182(a)(5)(C), and section 212(a)(5)(C) of the Act for the occupations of nurse (licensed practical nurse, licensed vocational nurse, and registered nurse), physical therapist, occupational therapist, speech-language pathologist and audiologist, medical technologist (clinical laboratory scientist), physician assistant, and medical technician (clinical laboratory technician).

(2) The National Board for Certification in Occupational Therapy is authorized by the Service to issue certificates under section 343 for the occupation of occupational therapist.

(3) The Foreign Credentialing Commission on Physical Therapy is authorized by the Service to issue certificates under section 343 for the occupation of physical therapist.

(f) *Contents of the certificate.* A certificate must contain the following information:

(1) The name and address of the certifying organization;

(2) A point of contact where the organization may be contacted in order to verify the validity of the certificate;

(3) The date of the certificate was issued;

(4) The occupation for which the certificate was issued;

(5) The alien's name, and date and place of birth;

(6) Verification that the alien's education, training, license, and experience are comparable with that required for an American health care worker of the same type;

(7) Verification that the alien's education, training, license, and experience are authentic and, in the case of a license, unencumbered;

(8) Verification that the alien's education, training, license, and experience meet all applicable statutory and regulatory requirements for admission into the United States as an immigrant under section 203(b) of the Act. This verification is not binding on the Service; and

(9) Verification either that the alien has passed a test predicting success on the occupation's licensing or certification examination, provided such a test is recognized by a majority of States licensing the occupation for which the certificate is issued, or that the alien has passed the occupation's licensing or certification examination.

(g) *English testing requirement.* (1) With the exception of those aliens described in paragraph (g)(2) of this section, every alien must meet certain English language requirements in order to obtain a certificate. The Secretary of Health and Human Services has determined that an alien must have a passing score on one of the two tests listed in paragraph (g)(3) of this section before he or she can be granted a certificate.

(2) *Aliens exempt from the English language requirement.* Aliens who have graduated from a college, university, or professional training school located in Australia, Canada (except Quebec), Ireland, New Zealand, the United Kingdom, and the United States are exempt from the English language requirement.

(3) *Approved testing services.* (i) Michigan English Language Assessment Battery (MELAB). Effective June 30, 2000, the MELAB Oral Interview Speaking Test is no longer being given overseas and is only being administered in the United States and Canada. Applicants may take MELAB Parts 1, 2, and 3, plus the Test of Spoken English offered by the Educational Testing Service.

(ii) Test of English as a Foreign Language, Educational Testing Service (ETS).

(4) *Passing scores for various occupations*—(i) *Occupational and physical therapists.* An alien seeking to perform labor in the United States as an occupational therapist or physical therapist must obtain the following scores on the English tests administered by ETS: Test Of English as a Foreign Language (TOEFL), Paper-Based 560, Computer-Based 220; Test of Written English (TWE): 4.5; Test of Spoken English

(TSE): 50. Certifying organizations shall not accept the results of the MELAB for the occupation of occupational therapist or physical therapist. Aliens seeking to obtain a certificate to work as an occupational or physical therapist must take the test offered by the ETS. The MELAB scores are not acceptable for these occupations.

(ii) *Registered nurses.* An alien coming to the United States to perform labor as a registered nurse must obtain the following scores to obtain a certificate: ETS: TOEFL: Paper-Based 540, Computer-Based 207; TWE: 4.0; TSE: 50; MELAB: Final Score 79; Oral Interview: 3+.

(iii) *Licensed practical nurses and licensed vocational nurses.* An alien coming to the United States to perform labor as a licensed practical nurse or licensed vocational nurse must have the following scores to be issued a certificate: ETS: TOEFL: Paper-Based 530, Computer-Based 197; TWE: 4.0; TSE: 50; MELAB: Final Score 77; Oral Interview: 3+.

(iv) *Speech-language pathologists and Audiologists, medical technologists (clinical laboratory scientists), and physician assistants.* An alien coming to the United States to perform labor as a speech-language pathologist and audiologist, a medical technologist (clinical laboratory scientist), or a physician assistant must have the following scores to be issued a certificate: ETS: TOEFL: Paper-Based 540, Computer-Based 207; TWE: 4.0; TSE: 50; MELAB: Final Score 79; Oral Interview: 3+.

(v) *Medical technicians (clinical laboratory technicians).* An alien coming to the United States to perform labor as a medical technician (clinical laboratory technician) must have the following scores to be issued a certificate: ETS: TOEFL: Paper-Based 530, Computer-Based 197; TWE: 4.0; TSE: 50; MELAB: Final Score 77; Oral Interview: 3+.

[63 FR 55011, Oct. 14, 1998, as amended at 64 FR 23177, Apr. 30, 1999; 66 FR 3444, Jan. 16, 2001]

§ 1212.16 Applications for exercise of discretion relating to T nonimmigrant status.

(a) *Filing the waiver application.* An alien applying for the exercise of discretion under section 212(d)(13) or (d)(3)(B) of the Act (waivers of inadmissibility) in connection with an application for T nonimmigrant status shall submit Form I–192, with the appropriate fee in accordance with § 103.7(b)(1) of this chapter or an application for a fee waiver, to the Service with the completed Form I–914 application package for status under section 101(a)(15)(T)(i) of the Act.

(b) *Treatment of waiver application.* (1) The Service shall determine whether a ground of inadmissibility exists with respect to the alien applying for T nonimmigrant status. If a ground of inadmissibility is found, the Service shall determine if it is in the national interest to exercise discretion to waive the ground of inadmissibility, except for grounds of inadmissibility based upon sections 212(a)(3), 212(a)(10)(C) and 212(a)(10)(E) of the Act, which the Commissioner may not waive. Special consideration will be given to the granting of a waiver of a ground of inadmissibility where the activities rendering the alien inadmissible were caused by or incident to the victimization described under section 101(a)(15)(T)(i) of the Act.

(2) In the case of applicants inadmissible on criminal and related grounds under section 212(a)(2) of the Act, the Service will only exercise its discretion in exceptional cases unless the criminal activities rendering the alien inadmissible were caused by or were incident to the victimization described under section 101(a)(15)(T)(i) of the Act.

(3) An application for waiver of a ground of inadmissibility for T nonimmigrant status (other than under section 212(a)(6) of the Act) will be granted only in exceptional cases when the ground of inadmissibility would prevent or limit the ability of the applicant to adjust to permanent resident status after the conclusion of 3 years.

(4) The Service shall have sole discretion to grant or deny a waiver, and there shall be no appeal of a decision to deny a waiver. However, nothing in this paragraph (b) is intended to prevent an applicant from re-filing a request for a waiver of a ground of inadmissibility in appropriate cases.

(c) *Incident to victimization.* When an applicant for status under section 101(a)(15)(T) of the Act seeks a waiver of a ground of inadmissibility under section 212(d)(13) of the Act on grounds other than those described in sections 212(a)(1) and (a)(4) of the Act, the applicant must establish that the activities rendering him or her inadmissible were caused by, or were incident to, the victimization described in section 101(a)(15)(T)(i)(I) of the Act.

(d) *Revocation.* The Commissioner may at any time revoke a waiver previously authorized under section 212(d) of the Act. Under no circumstances shall the alien or any party acting on his or her behalf have a right to appeal from a decision to revoke a waiver.

[67 FR 4795, Jan. 31, 2002]

PART 1214—REVIEW OF NONIMMIGRANT CLASSES

Sec.

AUTHORITY: 8 U.S.C. 1101, 1102, 1103, 1182, 1184, 1186a, 1187, 1221, 1281, 1282, 1301–1305 and 1372; sec. 643, Pub. L. 104–208, 110 Stat. 3009–708; section 141 of the Compacts of Free Association with the Federated States of Micronesia and the Republic of the Marshall Islands, and with the Government of Palau, 48 U.S.C. 1901, note, and 1931 note, respectively; 8 CFR part 2.

SOURCE: 68 FR 9835, Feb. 28, 2003, unless otherwise noted.

§ 1214.1 Review of requirements for admission, extension, and maintenance of status.

Every nonimmigrant alien who applies for admission to, or an extension of stay in, the United States, shall establish that he or she is admissible to the United States, or that any ground of inadmissibility has been waived under section 212(d)(3) of the Act. Upon application for admission, the alien shall present a valid passport and valid visa unless either or both documents have been waived. However, an alien applying for extension of stay shall present a passport only if requested to do so by the Service. The passport of an alien applying for admission shall be valid for a minimum of six months from the expiration date of the contemplated period of stay, unless otherwise provided in this chapter, and the alien shall agree to abide by the terms and conditions of his or her admission. The passport of an alien applying for extension of stay shall be valid at the time of application for extension, unless otherwise provided in this chapter, and the alien shall agree to maintain the validity of his or her passport and to abide by all the terms and conditions of his extension. The alien shall also agree to depart the United States at the expiration of his or her authorized period of admission or extension, or upon abandonment of his or her authorized nonimmigrant status. At the time a nonimmigrant alien applies for admission or extension of stay he or she shall post a bond on Form I–352 in the sum of not less than $500, to insure the maintenance of his or her nonimmigrant status and departure from the United States, if required to do so by the director, immigration judge or Board of Immigration Appeals.

§ 1214.2 Review of alien victims of severe forms of trafficking in persons; aliens in pending immigration proceedings.

(a) *Applications for T visas while in proceedings.* Individuals who believe they are victims of severe forms of trafficking in persons and who are in pending immigration proceedings must inform the Service if they intend to apply for T nonimmigrant status under this section. With the concurrence of Service counsel, a victim of a severe form of trafficking in persons in proceedings before an immigration judge or the Board of Immigration Appeals may request that the proceedings be administratively closed (or that a motion to reopen or motion to reconsider be indefinitely continued) in order to allow the alien to pursue an application for T nonimmigrant status with the Service. If the alien appears eligible for T nonimmigrant status, the immigration judge or the Board, whichever has jurisdiction, may grant such a request to administratively close the proceeding or continue a motion to reopen or motion to reconsider indefinitely. In the event the Service finds an alien ineligible for T–1 nonimmigrant status, the Service may recommence proceedings that have been administratively closed by filing a motion to re-calendar with the immigration court or a motion to reinstate with the Board. If the alien is in Service custody pending the completion of immigration proceedings, the Service may continue to detain the alien until a decision has been rendered on the application. An alien who is in custody and requests bond or a bond redetermination will be governed by the provisions of part 236 of this chapter.

(b) *Stay of final order of exclusion, deportation, or removal.* A determination by the Service that an application for T–1 nonimmigrant status is bona fide automatically stays the execution of any final order of exclusion, deportation, or removal. This stay shall remain in effect until there is a final decision on the T application. The filing of an application for T nonimmigrant status does not stay the execution of a final order unless the Service has determined that the application is bona fide. Neither an immigration judge nor the Board of Immigration Appeals has jurisdiction to adjudicate an application for a stay of execution, deportation, or removal order, on the basis of the filing of an application for T nonimmigrant status.

§ 1214.3 Certain spouses and children of lawful permanent residents; aliens in proceedings; V visas.

An alien who is already in immigration proceedings and believes that he or she may have become eligible to apply for V nonimmigrant status should request before the immigration judge or the Board of Immigration Appeals, as appropriate, that the proceedings be administratively closed (or before the Board that a previously-filed motion for reopening or reconsideration be indefinitely continued) in order to allow the alien to pursue an application for V nonimmigrant status with the Service. If the alien appears eligible for V nonimmigrant status, the immigration judge or the Board, whichever has jurisdiction, shall administratively close the proceeding or continue the motion indefinitely. In the event that the Service finds an alien eligible for V nonimmigrant status, the Service can adjudicate the change of status under this section. In the event that the Service finds an alien ineligible for V nonimmigrant status, the Service shall recommence proceedings by filing a motion to re-calendar.

PART 1215—CONTROLS OF ALIENS DEPARTING FROM THE UNITED STATES

AUTHORITY: Sec. 104, 66 Stat. 174, Proc. 3004, 18 FR 489; 8 U.S.C. 1104, 3 CFR, 1953 Supp. Interpret or apply sec. 215, 66 Stat. 190; (8 U.S.C. 1185).

SOURCE: 45 FR 65516, Oct. 3, 1980, unless otherwise noted. Duplicated from part 215 at 68 FR 9836, Feb. 28, 2003.

EDITORIAL NOTE: Nomenclature changes to part 1215 appear at 68 FR 9846, Feb. 28, 2003.

§ 1215.1 Definitions.

For the purpose of this part:

(a) The term *alien* means any person who is not a citizen or national of the United States.

(b) The term *Commissioner* means the Commissioner of Immigration and Naturalization.

(c) The term *regional commissioner* means an officer of the Immigration and Naturalization Service duly appointed or designated as a regional commissioner, or an officer who has been designated to act as a regional commissioner.

(d) The term *district director* means an officer of the Immigration and Naturalization Service duly appointed or designated as a district director, or an officer who has been designated to act as a district director.

(e) The term *United States* means the several States, the District of Columbia, the Canal Zone, Puerto Rico, the Virgin Islands, Guam, American Samoa, Swains Island, the Trust Territory of the Pacific Islands, and all other territory and waters, continental and insular, subject to the jurisdiction of the United States.

(f) The term *continental United States* means the District of Columbia and the several States, except Alaska and Hawaii.

(g) The term *geographical part of the United States* means: (1) The continental United States, (2) Alaska, (3) Hawaii, (4) Puerto Rico, (5) the Virgin Islands, (6) Guam, (7) the Canal Zone, (8) American Samoa, (9) Swains Island, or (10) the Trust Teritory of the Pacific Islands.

(h) The term *depart from the United States* means depart by land, water, or air: (1) From the United States for any foreign place, or (2) from one geographical part of the United States for a separate geographical part of the United States: *Provided*, That a trip or journey upon a public ferry, passenger vessel sailing coastwise on a fixed schedule, excursion vessel, or aircraft, having both termini in the continental United States or in any one of the other geographical parts of the United States and not touching any territory or waters under the jurisdiction or control of a foreign power, shall not be deemed a departure from the United States.

(i) The term *departure-control officer* means any immigration officer as defined in the regulations of the Immigration and Naturalization Service who is designated to supervise the departure of aliens, or any officer or employee of the United States designated by the Governor of the Canal Zone, the High Commissioner of the Trust Territory of the Pacific Islands, or the governor of an outlying possession of the United States, to supervise the departure of aliens.

(j) The term *port of departure* means a port in the continental United States, Alaska, Guam, Hawaii, Puerto Rico or the Virgin Islands, designated as a port of entry by the Attorney General or by the Commissioner, or in exceptional circumstances such other place as the departure-control officer may, in his discretion, designate in an individual case, or a port in American Samoa, Swains Island, the Canal Zone, or the Trust Territory of the Pacific Islands, designated as a port of entry by the chief executive officer thereof.

(k) The term *special inquiry officer* shall have the meaning ascribed thereto in section 101(b)(4) of the Immigration and Nationality Act.

§ 1215.2 Authority of departure-control officer to prevent alien's departure from the United States.

(a) No alien shall depart, or attempt to depart, from the United States if his departure would be prejudicial to the interests of the United States under the provisions of § 1215.3. Any departure-control officer who knows or has reason to believe that the case of an alien in the United States comes within the provisions of § 1215.3 shall temporarily prevent the departure of such alien from the United States and shall serve him with a written temporary order directing him not to depart, or attempt to depart, from the United States until notified of the revocation of the order.

(b) The written order temporarily preventing an alien, other than an enemy alien, from departing from the United States shall become final 15 days after the date of service thereof upon the alien, unless prior thereto the alien requests a hearing as hereinafter provided. At such time as the alien is served with an order temporarily preventing his departure from the United States, he shall be notified in writing concerning the provisions of this paragraph, and shall be advised of his right to request a hearing if entitled thereto under § 1215.4. In the case of an enemy alien, the written order preventing departure shall become final on the date of its service upon the alien.

(c) Any alien who seeks to depart from the United States may be required, in the discretion of the departure-control officer, to be examined under oath and to submit for official inspection all documents, articles, and other property in his possession which are being removed from the United States upon, or in connection with, the alien's departure. The departure-control officer may permit certain other persons, including officials of the Department of State and interpreters, to participate in such examination or inspection and may exclude from presence at such examination or inspection any person whose presence would not further the objectives of such examination or inspection. The departure-control officer shall temporarily prevent the departure of any alien who refuses to submit to such examination or inspection, and may, if necessary to the enforcement of this requirement, take possession of the alien's passport or other travel document.

§ 1215.3 Alien whose departure is deemed prejudicial to the interests of the United States.

The departure from the United States of any alien within one or more of the following categories shall be deemed prejudicial to the interests of the United States.

(a) Any alien who is in possession of, and who is believed likely to disclose to unauthorized persons, information concerning the plans, preparation, equipment, or establishments for the national defense and security of the United States.

(b) Any alien who seeks to depart from the United States to engage in, or who is likely to engage in, activities of any kind designed to obstruct, impede, retard, delay or counteract the effectiveness of the national defense of the United States or the measures adopted by the United States or the United Nations for the defense of any other country.

(c) Any alien who seeks to depart from the United States to engage in, or who is likely to engage in, activities which would obstruct, impede, retard, delay, or counteract the effectiveness of any plans made or action taken by any country cooperating with the United States in measures adopted to promote the peace, defense, or safety of the United States or such other country.

(d) Any alien who seeks to depart from the United States for the purpose of organizing, directing, or participating in any rebellion, insurrection, or violent uprising in or against the United States or a country allied with the United States, or of waging war against the United States or its allies, or of destroying, or depriving the United States of sources of supplies or materials vital to the national defense of the United States, or to the effectiveness of the measures adopted by the United States for its defense, or for the defense of any other country allied with the United States.

(e) Any alien who is subject to registration for training and service in the Armed Forces of the United States and who fails to present a Registration Certificate (SSS Form No. 2) showing that he has complied with his obligation to register under the Universal Military Training and Service Act, as amended.

(f) Any alien who is a fugitive from justice on account of an offense punishable in the United States.

(g) Any alien who is needed in the United States as a witness in, or as a party to, any criminal case under investigation or pending in a court in the United States: *Provided,* That any alien who is a witness in, or a party to, any criminal case pending in any criminal court proceeding may be permitted to depart from the United States with the consent of the appropriate prosecuting authority, unless such alien is otherwise prohibited from departing under the provisions of this part.

(h) Any alien who is needed in the United States in connection with any investigation or proceeding being, or soon to be, conducted by any official executive, legislative, or judicial agency in the United States or by any governmental committee, board, bureau, commission, or body in the United States, whether national, state, or local.

(i) Any alien whose technical or scientific training and knowledge might be utilized by an enemy or a potential enemy of the United States to undermine and defeat the military and defensive operations of the United States or of any nation cooperating with the United States in the interests of collective security.

(j) Any alien, where doubt exists whether such alien is departing or seeking to depart from the United States voluntarily except an alien who is departing or seeking to depart subject to an order issued in extradition, exclusion, or deportation proceedings.

(k) Any alien whose case does not fall within any of the categories described in paragraphs (a) to (j), inclusive, of this section, but which involves circumstances of a similar character rendering the alien's departure prejudicial to the interests of the United States.

§ 1215.4 Procedure in case of alien prevented from departing from the United States.

(a) Any alien, other than an enemy alien, whose departure has been temporarily prevented under the provisions of § 1215.2, may, within 15 days of the service upon him of the written order temporarily preventing his departure, request a hearing before a special inquiry officer. The alien's request for a hearing shall be made in writing and shall be addressed to the district director having administrative jurisdiction over the alien's place of residence. If the alien's request for a hearing is timely made, the district director shall schedule a hearing before a special inquiry officer, and notice of such hearing shall be given to the alien. The notice of hearing shall, as specifically as security considerations permit, inform the alien of the nature of the case against him, shall fix the time and place of the hearing, and shall inform the alien of his right to be represented, at no expense to the Government, by counsel of his own choosing.

(b) Every alien for whom a hearing has been scheduled under paragraph (a) of this section shall be entitled: (1) To appear in person before the special inquiry officer, (2) to be represented by counsel of his own choice, (3) to have the opportunity to be heard and to present evidence, (4) to cross-examine the witnesses who appear at the hearing, except that if, in the course of the examination, it appears that further examination may divulge information of a confidential or security nature, the special inquiry officer may, in his discretion, preclude further examination of the witness with respect to such matters, (5) to examine any evidence in possession of the Government which is to be considered in the disposition of the case, provided that such evidence is not of a confidential or security nature the disclosure of which would be prejudicial to the interests of the United States, (6) to have the time and opportunity to produce evidence and witnesses on his own behalf, and (7) to reasonable continuances, upon request, for good cause shown.

(c) Any special inquiry officer who is assigned to conduct the hearing provided for in this section shall have the authority to: (1) Administer oaths and affirmations, (2) present and receive evidence, (3) interrogate, examine, and cross examine under oath or affirmation both the alien and witnesses, (4) rule upon all objections to the introduction of evidence or motions made during the course of the hearing, (5) take or cause depositions to be taken, (6) issue subpoenas, and (7) take any further action consistent with applicable provisions of law, Executive orders, proclamations, and regulations.

§ 1215.5 Hearing procedure before special inquiry officer.

(a) The hearing before the special inquiry officer shall be conducted in accordance with the following procedure:

(1) The special inquiry officer shall advise the alien of the rights and privileges accorded him under the provisions of § 1215.4.

(2) The special inquiry officer shall enter of record: (i) A copy of the order served upon the alien temporarily preventing his departure from the United States, and (ii) a copy of the notice of hearing furnished the alien.

(3) The alien shall be interrogated by the special inquiry officer as to the matters considered pertinent to the proceeding, with opportunity reserved to the alien to testify thereafter in his own behalf, if he so chooses.

(4) The special inquiry officer shall present on behalf of the Government such evidence, including the testimony

of witnesses and the certificates or written statements of Government officials or other persons, as may be necessary and available. In the event such certificates or statements are received in evidence, the alien may request and, in the discretion of the special inquiry officer, be given an opportunity to interrogate such officials or persons, by deposition or otherwise, at a time and place and in a manner fixed by the special inquiry officer: *Provided*, That when in the judgment of the special inquiry officer any evidence relative to the disposition of the case is of a confidential or security nature the disclosure of which would be prejudicial to the interests of the United States, such evidence shall not be presented at the hearing but shall be taken into consideration in arriving at a decision in the case.

(5) The alien may present such additional evidence, including the testimony of witnesses, as is pertinent and available.

(b) A complete verbatim transcript of the hearing, except statements made off the record shall be recorded. The alien shall be entitled, upon request, to the loan of a copy of the transcript, without cost, subject to reasonable conditions governing its use.

(c) Following the completion of the hearing, the special inquiry officer shall make and render a recommended decision in the case, which shall be governed by and based upon the evidence presented at the hearing and any evidence of a confidential or security nature which the Government may have in its possession. The decision of the special inquiry officer shall recommend: (1) That the temporary order preventing the departure of the alien from the United States be made final, or (2) that the temporary order preventing the departure of the alien from the United States be revoked. This recommended decision of the special inquiry officer shall be made in writing and shall set forth the officer's reasons for such decision. The alien concerned shall at his request be furnished a copy of the recommended decision of the special inquiry officer, and shall be allowed a reasonable time, not to exceed 10 days, in which to submit representations with respect thereto in writing.

(d) As soon as practicable after the completion of the hearing and the rendering of a decision by the special inquiry officer, the district director shall forward the entire record of the case, including the recommended decision of the special inquiry officer and any written representations submitted by the alien, to the regional commissioner having jurisdiction over his district. After reviewing the record, the regional commissioner shall render a decision in the case, which shall be based upon the evidence in the record and on any evidence or information of a confidential or security nature which he deems pertinent. Whenever any decision is based in whole or in part on confidential or security information not included in the record, the decision shall state that such information was considered. A copy of the regional commissioner's decision shall be furnished the alien, or his attorney or representative. No administrative appeal shall lie from the regional commissioner's decision.

(e) Notwithstanding any other provision of this part, the Administrator of the Bureau of Security and Consular Affairs referred to in section 104(b) of the Immigration and Nationality Act, or such other officers of the Department of State as he may designate, after consultation with the Commissioner, or such other officers of the Immigration and Naturalization Service as he may designate, may at any time permit the departure of an individual alien or of a group of aliens from the United States if he determines that such action would be in the national interest. If the Administrator specifically requests the Commissioner to prevent the departure of a particular alien or of a group of aliens, the Commissioner shall not permit the departure of such alien or aliens until he has consulted with the Administrator.

(f) In any case arising under §§ 1215.1 to 1215.7, the Administrator shall, at his request, be kept advised, in as much detail as he may indicate is necessary, of the facts and of any action taken or proposed.

§ 1215.6 Departure from the Canal Zone, the Trust Territory of the Pacific Islands, or outlying possessions of the United States.

(a) In addition to the restrictions and prohibitions imposed by the provisions of this part upon the departure of aliens from the United States, any alien who seeks to depart from the Canal Zone, the Trust Territory of the Pacific Islands, or an outlying possession of the United States shall comply with such other restrictions and prohibitions as may be imposed by regulations prescribed, with the concurrence of the Administrator of the Bureau of Security and Consular Affairs and the Commissioner, by the Governor of the Canal Zone, the High Commissioner of the Trust Territory of the Pacific Islands, or by the governor of an outlying possession of the United States, respectively. No alien shall be prevented from departing from such zone, territory, or possession without first being accorded a hearing as provided in §§ 1215.4 and 1215.5.

(b) The Governor of the Canal Zone, the High Commissioner of the Trust Territory of the Pacific Islands, or the governor of any outlying possession of the United States shall have the authority to designate any employee or class of employees of the United States as hearing officers for the purpose of conducting the hearing referred to in paragraph (a) of this section. The hearing officer so designated shall exercise the same powers, duties, and functions as are conferred upon special inquiry officers under the provisions of this part. The chief executive officer of such zone, territory, or possession shall, in lieu of the regional commissioner, review the recommended decision of the hearing officer, and shall render a decision in any case referred to him, basing it on evidence in the record and on any evidence or information of a confidential or a security nature which he deems pertinent.

§ 1215.7 Instructions from the Administrator required in certain cases.

In the absence of appropriate instructions from the Administrator of the Bureau of Security and Consular Affairs, departure-control officers shall not exercise the authority conferred by § 1215.2 in the case of any alien who seeks to depart from the United States in the status of a nonimmigrant under section 101(a)(15) (A) or (G) of the Immigration and Nationality Act, or in the status of a nonimmigrant under section 11(3), 11(4), or 11(5) of the Agreement between the United Nations and the United States of America regarding the Headquarters of the United Nations (61 Stat. 756): *Provided*, That in cases of extreme urgency, where the national security so requires, a departure-control officer may preliminarily exercise the authority conferred by § 1215.2 pending the outcome of consultation with the Administrator, which shall be undertaken immediately. In all cases arising under this section, the decision of the Administrator shall be controlling: *Provided*, That any decision to prevent the departure of an alien shall be based upon a hearing and record as prescribed in this part.

PART 1216—CONDITIONAL BASIS OF LAWFUL PERMANENT RESIDENCE STATUS

Sec.

AUTHORITY: 8 U.S.C. 1101, 1103, 1154, 1184, 1186a, 1186b, and 8 CFR part 2.

SOURCE: 53 FR 30018, Aug. 10, 1988, unless otherwise noted. Duplicated from part 216 at 68 FR 9837, Feb. 28, 2003.

EDITORIAL NOTE: Nomenclature changes to part 1216 appear at 68 FR 9846, Feb. 28, 2003, and at 68 FR 10353, Mar. 5, 2003.

§ 1216.1 Definition of conditional permanent resident.

A *conditional permanent resident* is an alien who has been lawfully admitted for permanent residence within the meaning of section 101(a)(20) of the Act, except that a conditional permanent resident is also subject to the conditions and responsibilities set forth in section 216 or 216A of the Act, whichever is applicable, and part 216 of this chapter. Unless otherwise specified, the rights, privileges, responsibilities and duties which apply to all other lawful permanent residents apply equally to conditional permanent residents, including but not limited to the right to apply for naturalization (if otherwise eligible), the right to file petitions on behalf of qualifying relatives, the privilege of residing permanently in the United States as an immigrant in accordance with the immigration laws, such status not having changed; the duty to register with the Selective Service System, when required; and the responsibility for complying with all laws and regulations of the United States. All references within this chapter to lawful permanent residents apply equally to conditional permanent residents, unless otherwise specified. The conditions of section 216 of the Act shall not apply to lawful permanent resident status based on a self-petitioning relationship under section 204(a)(1)(A)(iii), 204(a)(1)(A)(iv), 204(a)(1)(b)(ii), or 204(a)(1)(B)(iii) of the Act or based on eligibility as the derivative child of a self-petitioning spouse under section 204(a)(1)(A)(iii) or 204(a)(1)(B)(ii) of the Act, regardless of the date on which the marriage to the abusive citizen or lawful permanent resident occurred.

[53 FR 30018, Aug. 10, 1988, as amended at 59 FR 26590, May 23, 1994; 61 FR 13079, Mar. 26, 1996]

§ 1216.2 Notification requirements.

(a) *When alien acquires status of conditional permanent resident.* At the time an alien acquires conditional permanent residence through admission to the United States with an immigrant visa or adjustment of status under section 245 of the Act, the Service shall notify the alien of the conditional basis of the alien's status, of the requirement that the alien apply for removal of the conditions within the ninety days immediately preceding the second anniversary of the alien's having been granted such status, and that failure to apply for removal of the conditions will result in automatic termination of the alien's lawful status in the United States.

(b) *When alien is required to apply for removal of the conditional basis of lawful permanent resident status.* Approximately 90 days before the second anniversary of the date on which the alien obtained conditional permanent residence, the Service should notify the alien a second time of the requirement that the alien and the petitioning spouse or alien entrepreneur must file a petition to remove the conditional basis of the alien's lawful permanent residence. Such notification shall be mailed to the alien's last known address.

(c) *Effect of failure to provide notification.* Failure of the Service to provide notification as required by either paragraph (a) or (b) of this section does not relieve the alien and the petitioning spouse, or alien entrepreneur of the requirement to file a petition to remove conditions within the 90 days immediately preceding the second anniversary of the date on which the alien obtained permanent residence.

[53 FR 30018, Aug. 10, 1988, as amended at 59 FR 26590, May 23, 1994]

§ 1216.3 Termination of conditional resident status.

(a) *During the two-year conditional period.* The director shall send a formal written notice to the conditional permanent resident of the termination of the alien's conditional permanent resident status if the director determines that any of the conditions set forth in section 216(b)(1) or 216A(b)(1) of the Act, whichever is applicable, are true, or it becomes known to the government that an alien entrepreneur who was admitted pursuant to section 203(b)(5) of the Act obtained his or her investment capital through other than legal means (such as through the sale of illegal drugs). If the Service issues a notice of intent to terminate an alien's conditional resident status, the director shall not adjudicate Form I–751 or Form I–829 until it has been determined that the alien's status will not be terminated. During this time, the alien shall continue to be a lawful conditional permanent resident with all the rights, privileges, and responsibilities provided to persons possessing such status. Prior to issuing the notice of termination, the director shall provide the alien with an opportunity to review and rebut the evidence upon which the decision is to be based, in accordance with § 103.2(b)(2) of 8 CFR chapter I. The termination of status, and all of the rights and privileges concomitant thereto (including authorization to accept or continue in employment in this country), shall take effect as of the date of such determination by the director, although the alien may request a review of such determination in removal proceedings. In addition to the notice of termination, the director shall issue a notice to appear in accordance with 8 CFR part 1239. During the ensuing removal proceedings, the alien may submit evidence to rebut the determination of the director. The burden of proof shall be on the Service to establish, by a preponderance of the evidence, that one or more of the conditions in section 216(b)(1) or 216A(b)(1) of the Act, whichever is applicable, are true, or that an alien entrepreneur who was admitted pursuant to section 203(b)(5) of the Act obtained his or her investment capital through other than legal means (such as through the sale of illegal drugs).

(b) *Determination of fraud after two years.* If, subsequent to the removal of the conditional basis of an alien's permanent resident status, the director determines that an alien spouse obtained permanent resident status through a marriage which was entered into for the purpose of evading the immigration laws or an alien entrepreneur obtained permanent resident status through a commercial enterprise which was improper under section 216A(b)(1) of the Act, the director may institute rescission proceedings pursuant to section 246 of the Act (if otherwise appropriate) or removal proceedings under section 240 of the Act.

[62 FR 10349, Mar. 6, 1997]

§ 1216.4 Joint petition to remove conditional basis of lawful permanent resident status for alien spouse.

(a) *Filing the petition*—(1) *General procedures.* Within the 90-day period immediately preceding the second anniversary of the date on which the alien obtained permanent residence, the alien and the alien's spouse who filed the original immigrant visa petition or fiance/fiancee petition through which the alien obtained permanent residence must file a Petition to Remove the Conditions on Residence (Form I–751) with the Service. The petition shall be filed within this time period regardless of the amount of physical presence which the alien has accumulated in the United States. Before Form I–751 may be considered as properly filed, it must be accompanied by the fee required under § 103.7(b) of 8 CFR chapter I and by documentation as described in paragraph (a)(5) of this section, and it must be properly signed by the alien and the alien's spouse. If the joint petition cannot be filed due to the termination of the marriage through annulment, divorce, or the death of the petitioning spouse, or if the petitioning spouse refuses to join in the filing of the petition, the conditional permanent resident may apply for a waiver of the requirement to file the joint petition in accordance with the provisions of § 1216.5 of this part. Upon receipt of a properly filed Form I–751, the alien's conditional permanent resident status shall be extended automatically, if necessary, until such time as the director has adjudicated the petition.

(2) *Dependent children.* Dependent children of a conditional permanent resident who acquired conditional permanent resident status concurrently with the parent may be included in the joint petition filed by the parent and the parent's petitioning spouse. A child shall be deemed to have acquired conditional residence status concurrently with the parent if the child's residence was acquired on the same date or within 90 days thereafter. Children who cannot be included in a joint petition filed by the parent and parent's petitioning spouse due to the child's not having acquired conditional resident status concurrently with the parent, the death of the parent, or other reasons may file a separate Petition to Remove the Conditions on Residence (Form I–751).

(3) *Jurisdiction.* Form I–751 shall be filed with the director of the regional service center having jurisdiction over the alien's place of residence.

(4) *Physical presence at time of filing.* A petition may be filed regardless of whether the alien is physically present in the United States. However, if the alien is outside the United States at the time of filing, he or she must return to the United States, with his or her spouse and dependent children, to comply with the interview requirements contained in the Act. Furthermore, if the documentation submitted in support of the petition includes affidavits of third parties having knowledge of the bona fides of the marital relationship, the petitioner must arrange for the affiants to be present at the interview, at no expense to the government. Once the petition has been properly filed, the alien may travel outside the United States and return if in possession of documentation as set forth in § 1211.1(b)(1) of this chapter, provided the alien and the petitioning spouse comply with the interview requirements described in § 1216.4(b). An alien who is not physically present in the United States during the filing period but subsequently applies for admission to the United States shall be processed in accordance with § 1235.11 of this chapter.

(5) *Documentation.* Form I–751 shall be accompanied by evidence that the marriage was not entered into for the purpose of evading the immigration laws of the United States. Such evidence may include:

(i) Documentation showing joint ownership of property;

(ii) Lease showing joint tenancy of a common residence;

(iii) Documentation showing commingling of financial resources;

(iv) Birth certificates of children born to the marriage;

(v) Affidavits of third parties having knowledge of the bona fides of the marital relationship, or

(vi) Other documentation establishing that the marriage was not entered into in order to evade the immigration laws of the United States.

(6) *Termination of status for failure to file petition.* Failure to properly file Form I–751 within the 90-day period immediately preceding the second anniversary of the date on which the alien obtained lawful permanent residence on a conditional basis shall result in the automatic termination of the alien's permanent residence status and the initiation of proceedings to remove the alien from the United States. In such proceedings the burden shall be on the alien to establish that he or she complied with the requirement to file the joint petition within the designated period. Form I–751 may be filed after the expiration of the 90-day period only if the alien establishes to the satisfaction of the director, in writing, that there was good cause for the failure to file Form I–751 within the required time period. If the joint petition is filed prior to the jurisdiction vesting with the immigration judge in removal proceedings and the director excuses the late filing and approves the petition, he or she shall restore the alien's permanent residence status, remove the conditional basis of such status and cancel any outstanding notice to appear in accordance with § 1239.2 of this chapter. If the joint petition is not filed until after jurisdiction vests with the immigration judge, the immigration judge may terminate the matter upon joint motion by the alien and the Service.

(b) *Interview*—(1) *Authority to waive interview.* The director of the regional service center shall review the Form I–751 filed by the alien and the alien's spouse to determine whether to waive the interview required by the Act. If satisfied that the marriage was not for the purpose of evading the immigration laws, the regional service center director may waive the interview and approve the petition. If not so satisfied, then the regional service center director shall forward the petition to the district director having jurisdiction over the place of the alien's residence so that an interview of both the alien and the alien's spouse may be conducted. The director must either waive the requirement for an interview and adjudicate the petition or arrange for an interview within 90 days of the date on which the petition was properly filed.

(2) *Location of interview.* Unless waived, an interview on the Form I–751 shall be conducted by an immigration examiner or other officer so designated by the district director at the district office, files control office or suboffice

having jurisdiction over the residence of the joint petitioners.

(3) *Termination of status for failure to appear for interview.* If the conditional resident alien and/or the petitioning spouse fail to appear for an interview in connection with the joint petition required by section 216(c) of the Act, the alien's permanent residence status will be automatically terminated as of the second anniversary of the date on which the alien obtained permanent residence. The alien shall be provided with written notification of the termination and the reasons therefor, and a notice to appear shall be issued placing the alien under removal proceedings. The alien may seek review of the decision to terminate his or her status in such proceedings, but the burden shall be on the alien to establish compliance with the interview requirements. If the alien submits a written request that the interview be rescheduled or that the interview be waived, and the director determines that there is good cause for granting the request, the interview may be rescheduled or waived, as appropriate. If the interview is rescheduled at the request of the petitioners, the Service shall not be required to conduct the interview within the 90-day period following the filing of the petition.

(c) *Adjudication of petition.* The director shall adjudicate the petition within 90 days of the date of the interview, unless the interview is waived in accordance with paragraph (b)(1) of this section. In adjudicating the petition the director shall determine whether—

(1) The qualifying marriage was entered into in accordance with the laws of the place where the marriage took place;

(2) The qualifying marriage has been judicially annulled or terminated, other than through the death of a spouse;

(3) The qualifying marriage was entered into for the purpose of procuring permanent residence status for the alien; or

(4) A fee or other consideration was given (other than a fee or other consideration to an attorney for assistance in preparation of a lawful petition) in connection with the filing of the petition through which the alien obtained conditional permanent residence. If derogatory information is determined regarding any of these issues, the director shall offer the petitioners the opportunity to rebut such information. If the petitioners fail to overcome such derogatory information the director may deny the joint petition, terminate the alien's permanent residence, and issue a notice to appear to initiate removal proceedings. If derogatory information not relating to any of these issues is determined during the course of the interview, such information shall be forwarded to the investigations unit for appropriate action. If no unresolved derogatory information is determined relating to these issues, the petition shall be approved and the conditional basis of the alien's permanent residence status removed, regardless of any action taken or contemplated regarding other possible grounds for removal.

(d) *Decision*—(1) *Approval.* If the director approves the joint petition he or she shall provide written notice of the decision to the alien and shall require the alien to report to the appropriate office of the Service for processing for a new Permanent Resident Card (if necessary), at which time the alien shall surrender any Permanent Resident Card previously issued.

(2) *Denial.* If the director denies the joint petition, he or she shall provide written notice to the alien of the decision and the reason(s) therefor and shall issue a notice to appear under section 239 of the Act and 8 CFR part 1239. The alien's lawful permanent resident status shall be terminated as of the date of the director's written decision. The alien shall also be instructed to surrender any Permanent Resident Card previously issued by the Service. No appeal shall lie from the decision of the director; however, the alien may seek review of the decision in removal proceedings. In such proceedings the burden of proof shall be on the Service to establish, by a preponderance of the evidence, that the facts and information set forth by the petitioners are

not true or that the petition was properly denied.

[53 FR 30018, Aug. 10, 1988, as amended at 54 FR 30369, July 20, 1989; 59 FR 26590, May 23, 1994; 62 FR 10349, Mar. 6, 1997; 63 FR 70315, Dec. 21, 1998]

§ 1216.5 Waiver of requirement to file joint petition to remove conditions by alien spouse.

(a) *General.* (1) A conditional resident alien who is unable to meet the requirements under section 216 of the Act for a joint petition for removal of the conditional basis of his or her permanent resident status may file Form I–751, Petition to Remove the Conditions on Residence, if the alien requests a waiver, was not at fault in failing to meet the filing requirement, and the conditional resident alien is able to establish that:

(i) Deportation or removal from the United States would result in extreme hardship;

(ii) The marriage upon which his or her status was based was entered into in good faith by the conditional resident alien, but the marriage was terminated other than by death, and the conditional resident was not at fault in failing to file a timely petition; or

(iii) The qualifying marriage was entered into in good faith by the conditional resident but during the marriage the alien spouse or child was battered by or subjected to extreme cruelty committed by the citizen or permanent resident spouse or parent.

(2) A conditional resident who is in exclusion, deportation, or removal proceedings may apply for the waiver only until such time as there is a final order of exclusion, deportation or removal.

(b) *Fee.* Form I–751 shall be accompanied by the appropriate fee required under § 103.7(b) of 8 CFR chapter I.

(c) *Jurisdiction.* Form I–751 shall be filed with the regional service center director having jurisdiction over the alien's place of residence.

(d) *Interview.* The service center director may refer the application to the appropriate local office and require that the alien appear for an interview in connection with the application for a waiver. The director shall deny the application and initiate removal proceedings if the alien fails to appear for the interview as required, unless the alien establishes good cause for such failure and the interview is rescheduled.

(e) *Adjudication of waiver application*—(1) *Application based on claim of hardship.* In considering an application for a waiver based upon an alien's claim that extreme hardship would result from the alien's removal from the United States, the director shall take into account only those factors that arose subsequent to the alien's entry as a conditional permanent resident. The director shall bear in mind that any removal from the United States is likely to result in a certain degree of hardship, and that only in those cases where the hardship is extreme should the application for a waiver be granted. The burden of establishing that extreme hardship exists rests solely with the applicant.

(2) *Application for waiver based upon the alien's claim that the marriage was entered into in good faith.* In considering whether an alien entered into a qualifying marriage in good faith, the director shall consider evidence relating to the amount of commitment by both parties to the marital relationship. Such evidence may include—

(i) Documentation relating to the degree to which the financial assets and liabilities of the parties were combined;

(ii) Documentation concerning the length of time during which the parties cohabited after the marriage and after the alien obtained permanent residence;

(iii) Birth certificates of children born to the marriage; and

(iv) Other evidence deemed pertinent by the director.

(3) *Application for waiver based on alien's claim of having been battered or subjected to extreme mental cruelty.* A conditional resident who entered into the qualifying marriage in good faith, and who was battered or was the subject of extreme cruelty or whose child was battered by or was the subject of extreme cruelty perpetrated by the United States citizen or permanent resident spouse during the marriage, may request a waiver of the joint filing requirement. The conditional resident parent of a battered or abused child

may apply for the waiver regardless of the child's citizenship or immigration status.

(i) For the purpose of this chapter the phrase "was battered by or was the subject of extreme cruelty" includes, but is not limited to, being the victim of any act or threatened act of violence, including any forceful detention, which results or threatens to result in physical or mental injury. Psychological or sexual abuse or exploitation, including rape, molestation, incest (if the victim is a minor) or forced prostitution shall be considered acts of violence.

(ii) A conditional resident or former conditional resident who has not departed the United States after termination of resident status may apply for the waiver. The conditional resident may apply for the waiver regardless of his or her present marital status. The conditional resident may still be residing with the citizen or permanent resident spouse, or may be divorced or separated.

(iii) Evidence of physical abuse may include, but is not limited to, expert testimony in the form of reports and affidavits from police, judges, medical personnel, school officials and social service agency personnel. The Service must be satisfied with the credibility of the sources of documentation submitted in support of the application.

(iv) The Service is not in a position to evaluate testimony regarding a claim of extreme mental cruelty provided by unlicensed or untrained individuals. Therefore, all waiver applications based upon claims of extreme mental cruelty must be supported by the evaluation of a professional recognized by the Service as an expert in the field. An evaluation which was obtained in the course of the divorce proceedings may be submitted if it was provided by a professional recognized by the Service as an expert in the field.

(v) The evaluation must contain the professional's full name, professional address and license number. It must also identify the licensing, certifying, or registering authority. The Service retains the right to verify the professional's license.

(vi) The Service's decision on extreme mental cruelty waivers will be based upon the evaluation of the recognized professional. The Service reserves the right to request additional evaluations from expert witnesses chosen by the Service. Requests for additional evaluations must be authorized by the Assistant Regional Commissioner for Adjudications.

(vii) Licensed clinical social workers, psychologists, and psychiatrists are professionals recognized by the Service for the purpose of this section. A clinical social worker who is not licensed only because the state in which he or she practices does not provide for licensing will be considered a licensed professional recognized by the Service if he or she is included in the Register of Clinical Social Workers published by the National Association of Social Workers or is certified by the American Board of Examiners in Clinical Social Work.

(viii) As directed by the statute, the information contained in the application and supporting documents shall not be released without a court order or the written consent of the applicant; or, in the case of a child, the written consent of the parent or legal guardian who filed the waiver application on the child's behalf. Information may be released only to the applicant, his or her authorized representative, an officer of the Department of Justice, or any federal or State law enforcement agency. Any information provided under this part may be used for the purposes of enforcement of the Act or in any criminal proceeding.

(f) *Decision.* The director shall provide the alien with written notice of the decision on the application for waiver. If the decision is adverse, the director shall advise the alien of the reasons therefor, notify the alien of the termination of his or her permanent residence status, instruct the alien to surrender any Permanent Resident Card issued by the Service and issue a notice to appear placing the alien in removal proceedings. No appeal shall lie from the decision of the director; however, the alien may seek review of such decision in removal proceedings.

[53 FR 30018, Aug. 10, 1988, as amended at 56 FR 22637, May 16, 1991; 59 FR 26591, May 23, 1994; 62 FR 10350, Mar. 6, 1997; 63 FR 70315, Dec. 21, 1998]

§ 1216.6 Petition by entrepreneur to remove conditional basis of lawful permanent resident status.

(a) *Filing the petition*—(1) *General procedures.* A petition to remove the conditional basis of the permanent resident status of an alien accorded conditional permanent residence pursuant to section 203(b)(5) of the Act must be filed by the alien entrepreneur on Form I–829, Petition by Entrepreneur to Remove Conditions. The alien entrepreneur must file Form I–829 within the 90-day period preceding the second anniversary of his or her admission to the United States as a conditional permanent resident. Before Form I–829 may be considered as properly filed, it must be accompanied by the fee required under § 103.7(b)(1) of 8 CFR chapter I, and by documentation as described in paragraph (a)(4) of this section, and it must be properly signed by the alien. Upon receipt of a properly filed Form I–829, the alien's conditional permanent resident status shall be extended automatically, if necessary, until such time as the director has adjudicated the petition. The entrepreneur's spouse and children should be included in the petition to remove conditions. Children who have reached the age of twenty-one or who have married during the period of conditional permanent residence and the former spouse of an entrepreneur, who was divorced from the entrepreneur during the period of conditional permanent residence, may be included in the alien entrepreneur's petition or may file a separate petition.

(2) *Jurisdiction.* Form I–829 must be filed with the regional service center having jurisdiction over the location of the alien entrepreneur's commercial enterprise in the United States.

(3) *Physical presence at time of filing.* A petition may be filed regardless of whether the alien is physically present in the United States. However, if the alien is outside the United States at the time of filing, he or she must return to the United States, with his or her spouse and children, if necessary, to comply with the interview requirements contained in the Act. Once the petition has been properly filed, the alien may travel outside the United States and return if in possession of documentation as set forth in § 1211.1(b)(1) of this chapter, provided the alien complies with the interview requirements described in paragraph (b) of this section. An alien who is not physically present in the United States during the filing period but subsequently applies for admission to the United States shall be processed in accordance with § 1235.11 of this chapter.

(4) *Documentation.* The petition for removal of conditions must be accompanied by the following evidence:

(i) Evidence that a commercial enterprise was established by the alien. Such evidence may include, but is not limited to, Federal income tax returns;

(ii) Evidence that the alien invested or was actively in the process of investing the requisite capital. Such evidence may include, but is not limited to, an audited financial statement or other probative evidence; and

(iii) Evidence that the alien sustained the actions described in paragraph (a)(4)(i) and (a)(4)(ii) of this section throughout the period of the alien's residence in the United States. The alien will be considered to have sustained the actions required for removal of conditions if he or she has, in good faith, substantially met the capital investment requirement of the statute and continuously maintained his or her capital investment over the two years of conditional residence. Such evidence may include, but is not limited to, bank statements, invoices, receipts, contracts, business licenses, Federal or State income tax returns, and Federal or State quarterly tax statements.

(iv) Evidence that the alien created or can be expected to create within a reasonable time ten full-time jobs for qualifying employees. In the case of a "troubled business" as defined in 8 CFR 204.6(j)(4)(ii), the alien entrepreneur must submit evidence that the commercial enterprise maintained the number of existing employees at no less than the pre-investment level for the period following his or her admission as a conditional permanent resident. Such evidence may include payroll records, relevant tax documents, and Forms I–9.

(5) *Termination of status for failure to file petition.* Failure to properly file

Form I–829 within the 90-day period immediately preceding the second anniversary of the date on which the alien obtained lawful permanent residence on a conditional basis shall result in the automatic termination of the alien's permanent resident status and the initiation of deportation proceedings. The director shall send a written notice of termination and an order to show cause to an alien entrepreneur who fails to timely file a petition for removal of conditions. No appeal shall lie from this decision; however, the alien may request a review of the determination during deportation proceedings. In deportation proceedings, the burden of proof shall rest with the alien to show by a preponderance of the evidence that he or she complied with the requirement to file the petition within the designated period. The director may deem the petition to have been filed prior to the second anniversary of the alien's obtaining conditional permanent resident status and accept and consider a late petition if the alien demonstrates to the director's satisfaction that failure to file a timely petition was for good cause and due to extenuating circumstances. If the late petition is filed prior to jurisdiction vesting with the immigration judge in deportation proceedings and the director excuses the late filing and approves the petition, he or she shall restore the alien's permanent resident status, remove the conditional basis of such status, and cancel any outstanding order to show cause in accordance with § 242.7 of 8 CFR chapter I. If the petition is not filed until after jurisdiction vests with the immigration judge, the immigration judge may terminate the matter upon joint motion by the alien and the Service.

(6) *Death of entrepreneur and effect on spouse and children.* If an entrepreneur dies during the prescribed two-year period of conditional permanent residence, the spouse and children of the entrepreneur will be eligible for removal of conditions if it can be demonstrated that the conditions set forth in paragraph (a)(4) of this section have been met.

(b) *Petition review*—(1) *Authority to waive interview.* The director of the service center shall review the Form I–829 and the supporting documents to determine whether to waive the interview required by the Act. If satisfied that the requirements set forth in paragraph (c)(1) of this section have been met, the service center director may waive the interview and approve the petition. If not so satisfied, then the service center director shall forward the petition to the district director having jurisdiction over the location of the alien entrepreneur's commercial enterprise in the United States so that an interview of the alien entrepreneur may be conducted. The director must either waive the requirement for an interview and adjudicate the petition or arrange for an interview within 90 days of the date on which the petition was properly filed.

(2) *Location of interview.* Unless waived, an interview relating to the Form I–829 shall be conducted by an immigration examiner or other officer so designated by the district director at the district office that has jurisdiction over the location of the alien entrepreneur's commercial enterprise in the United States.

(3) *Termination of status for failure to appear for interview.* If the alien fails to appear for an interview in connection with the petition when requested by the Service, the alien's permanent resident status will be automatically terminated as of the second anniversary of the date on which the alien obtained permanent residence. The alien will be provided with written notification of the termination and the reasons therefore, and an order to show cause shall be issued placing the alien under deportation proceedings. The alien may seek review of the decision to terminate his or her status in such proceedings, but the burden shall be on the alien to establish by a preponderance of the evidence that he or she complied with the interview requirements. If the alien has failed to appear for a scheduled interview, he or she may submit a written request to the district director asking that the interview be rescheduled or that the interview be waived. That request should explain his or her failure to appear for the scheduled interview, and if a request for waiver of the interview, the reasons such waiver

should be granted. If the district director determines that there is good cause for granting the request, the interview may be rescheduled or waived, as appropriate. If the district director waives the interview, he or she shall restore the alien's conditional permanent resident status, cancel any outstanding order to show cause in accordance with §1216.6(a)(5), and proceed to adjudicate the alien's petition. If the district director reschedules that alien's interview, he or she shall restore the alien's conditional permanent resident status, and cancel any outstanding order to show cause in accordance with §1216.6(a)(5). If the interview is rescheduled at the request of the alien, the Service shall not be required to conduct the interview within the 90-day period following the filing of the petition.

(c) *Adjudication of petition*. (1) The decision on the petition shall be made within 90 days of the date of filing or within 90 days of the interview, whichever is later. In adjudicating the petition, the director shall determine whether:

(i) A commercial enterprise was established by the alien;

(ii) The alien invested or was actively in the process of investing the requisite capital; and

(iii) The alien sustained the actions described in paragraphs (c)(1)(i) and (c)(1)(ii) of this section throughout the period of the alien's residence in the United States. The alien will be considered to have sustained the actions required for removal of conditions if he or she has, in good faith, substantially met the capital investment requirement of the statute and continuously maintained his or her capital investment over the two years of conditional residence.

(iv) The alien created or can be expected to create within a reasonable period of time ten full-time jobs to qualifying employees. In the case of a "troubled business" as defined in 8 CFR 204.6(j)(4)(ii), the alien maintained the number of existing employees at no less than the pre-investment level for the previous two years.

(2) If derogatory information is determined regarding any of these issues or it becomes known to the government that the entrepreneur obtained his or her investment funds through other than legal means (such as through the sale of illegal drugs), the director shall offer the alien entrepreneur the opportunity to rebut such information. If the alien entrepreneur fails to overcome such derogatory information or evidence the investment funds were obtained through other than legal means, the director may deny the petition, terminate the alien's permanent resident status, and issue an order to show cause. If derogatory information not relating to any of these issues is determined during the course of the interview, such information shall be forwarded to the investigations unit for appropriate action. If no unresolved derogatory information is determined relating to these issues, the petition shall be approved and the conditional basis of the alien's permanent resident status removed, regardless of any action taken or contemplated regarding other possible grounds for deportation.

(d) *Decision*—(1) *Approval*. If, after initial review or after the interview, the director approves the petition, he or she will remove the conditional basis of the alien's permanent resident status as of the second anniversary of the alien's entry as a conditional permanent resident. He or she shall provide written notice of the decision to the alien and shall require the alien to report to the appropriate district office for processing for a new Permanent Resident Card, Form I–551, at which time the alien shall surrender any Permanent Resident Card previously issued.

(2) *Denial*. If, after initial review or after the interview, the director denies the petition, he or she shall provide written notice to the alien of the decision and the reason(s) therefor, and shall issue an order to show cause why the alien should not be deported from the United States. The alien's lawful permanent resident status and that of his or her spouse and any children shall be terminated as of the date of the director's written decision. The alien shall also be instructed to surrender any Permanent Resident Card previously issued by the Service. No appeal shall lie from this decision; however, the alien may seek review of the

decision in deportation proceedings. In deportation proceedings, the burden shall rest with the Service to establish by a preponderance of the evidence that the facts and information in the alien's petition for removal of conditions are not true and that the petition was properly denied.

[59 FR 26591, May 23, 1994, as amended at 63 FR 70315, Dec. 21, 1998]

PART 1235—INSPECTION OF PERSONS APPLYING FOR ADMISSION

AUTHORITY: 8 U.S.C. 1101 and note, 1103, 1183, 1185 (pursuant to E.O. 13323, 69 FR 241, 3 CFR, 2003 Comp., p. 278), 1201, 1224, 1225, 1226, 1228, 1365a note, 1379, 1731–32; Title VII of Public Law 110–229; 8 U.S.C. 1185 note (section 7209 of Pub. L. 108–458).

SOURCE: Duplicated from part 235 at 68 FR 9837, Feb. 28, 2003.

EDITORIAL NOTE: Nomenclature changes to part 1235 appear at 68 FR 9846, Feb. 28, 2003, and at 68 FR 10354, Mar. 5, 2003.

§ 1235.1 Scope of examination.

(a) *General.* Application to lawfully enter the United States shall be made in person to an immigration officer at a U.S. port-of-entry when the port is open for inspection, or as otherwise designated in this section.

(b) *U.S. citizens.* A person claiming U.S. citizenship must establish that fact to the examining officer's satisfaction and must present a U.S. passport if such passport is required under the provisions of 22 CFR part 53. If such applicant for admission fails to satisfy the examining immigration officer that he or she is a U.S. citizen, he or she shall thereafter be inspected as an alien.

(c) *Alien members of United States Armed Forces and members of a force of a NATO country.* Any alien member of the United States Armed Forces who is in the uniform of, or bears documents identifying him or her as a member of, such Armed Forces, and who is coming to or departing from the United States under official orders or permit of such Armed Forces is not subject to the removal provisions of the Act. A member of the force of a NATO country signatory to Article III of the Status of Forces Agreement seeking to enter the United States under official orders is exempt from the control provision of the Act. Any alien who is a member of either of the foregoing classes may, upon request, be inspected and his or her entry as an alien may be recorded. If the alien does not appear to the examining immigration officer to be clearly and beyond a doubt entitled to enter the United States under the provisions of the Act, the alien shall be so informed and his or her entry shall not be recorded.

(d) *Alien applicants for admission.* (1) Each alien seeking admission at a United States port-of-entry shall present whatever documents are required and shall establish to the satisfaction of the immigration officer that he or she is not subject to removal under the immigration laws, Executive Orders, or Presidential Proclamations and is entitled under all of the applicable provisions of the immigration laws and this chapter to enter the United States. A person claiming to have been lawfully admitted for permanent residence must establish that fact to the satisfaction of the inspecting immigration officer and must present proper documents in accordance with § 211.1 of this chapter.

(2) An alien present in the United States who has not been admitted or paroled or an alien who seeks entry at other than an open, designated port-of-entry, except as otherwise permitted in this section, is subject to the provisions of section 212(a) of the Act and to removal under section 235(b) or 240 of the Act.

(3) An alien who is brought to the United States, whether or not to a designated port-of-entry and regardless of the means of transportation, after having been interdicted in international or United States waters, is considered an applicant for admission and shall be examined under section 235(b) of the Act.

(4) An alien stowaway is not an applicant for admission and may not be admitted to the United States. A stowaway shall be removed from the United States under section 235(a)(2) of the Act. The provisions of section 240 of the Act are not applicable to stowaways, nor is the stowaway entitled to further hearing or review of the removal, except that an alien stowaway who indicates an intention to apply for asylum, or expresses a fear of persecution, a fear of torture, or a fear of return to the country of proposed removal shall be referred to an asylum officer for a determination of credible fear of persecution or torture in accordance with section 235(b)(1)(B) of the Act and § 1208.30 of this chapter. An alien stowaway who is determined to have a credible fear of persecution or torture shall have his or her asylum application adjudicated in accordance with § 1208.2(b)(2) of this chapter.

(e) *U.S. citizens, lawful permanent residents of the United States, and other aliens, entering the United States along the northern border, other than at a Port-of-Entry.* A citizen or lawful permanent resident of the United States, a Canadian national or landed immigrant of Canada having a common nationality with nationals of Canada, or a landed immigrant of Canada who is a national of a country listed in § 217.2(a), may, if in possession of a valid, unexpired, Canadian Border Boat Landing Permit (Form I–68) or evidence of enrollment in any other Service Alternaitve Inspections program (e.g., the Immigration and Naturalization Service Passenger Accelerated Service System (INSPASS) or the Port Passenger Accelerated Service System (PORTPASS)), enter the United States by means of a pleasure craft along the northern border of the United States from time-to-time without further inspection. No persons other than those described in this paragraph may participate in this program. Landed immigrants of Canada who do not share a common nationality with nationals of Canada, but who are nationals of a designated country listed in § 217.2(a) of this chapter (Visa Waiver Pilot Program) must be in possession of a valid, unexpired passport issued by his or her country of nationality, and an unexpired multiple entry Form I–94 or I–94W, Nonimmigrant Visa Waiver Arrival/Departure Form, and a valid unexpired United States visa (if the alien is not in possession of a valid unexpired Form I–94W). When an entry to the United States is made by a person who is a Canadian citizen or a landed immigrant of Canada, entry may be made under this program only for a purpose as described in section 101(a)(15)(B)(ii) of the Act. Persons seeking to enter the United States for any other purpose must do so at a staffed Port-of-Entry. Persons aboard a vessel which has crossed the international boundary between the United States and Canada and who do not intend to land in the United States, other than at a staffed Port-of-Entry, are not required to be in possession of Form I–68 or evidence of enrollment in an Alternative Inspections program merely because they have crossed the international boundary. However, the Service retains the right to conduct inspections or examinations of all persons applying for admission or readmission to or seeking transit through the United States in accordance with the Act.

(1) *Application.* An eligible applicant may apply for a Canadian Border Boat Landing Permit by completing the Form I–68 in triplicate. Application forms will be made readily available through the Internet, from a Service office, or by mail. A family may apply on a single application. For the purposes of this paragraph, a family is defined as a husband, wife, unmarried children under the age of 21, and the parents of either husband or wife, who reside at the same address. In order for the I–68 application to be considered complete, it must be accompanied by the following:

(i) For each person included on the application, evidence of citizenship, and, if not a citizen of the Untied States or Canada, evidence of legal permanent resident status in either the

United States or Canada. Evidence of residency must be submitted by all applicants. It is not required that all persons on the application be of the same nationality; however, they must all be individually eligible to participate in this program.

(ii) If multiple members of a family, as defined in paragraph (e)(1) of this section, are included on a single application, evidence of the familial relationship.

(iii) A fee as prescribed in § 103.7(b)(1) of 8 CFR chapter I.

(iv) A copy of any previously approved Form I–68.

(v) A landed immigrant of Canada who does not have a common nationality with nationals of Canada, but who is a national of a designated country listed in § 217.2(a) of 8 CFR chapter I (Visa Waiver Pilot Program) must also present his or her passport, a valid unexpired multiple entry Form I–94 or I–94W and valid, unexpired nonimmigrant visa if he or she is not in possession of a valid, unexpired multiple entry Form I–94W. Such a landed immigrant of Canada may apply for admission simultaneously with the I–68 application and thereby obtain a Form I–94 or I–94W.

(2) *Submission of Form I–68.* Except as indicated in this paragraph, Form I–68 shall be properly completed and submitted in person, along with the documentary evidence and the required fee as specified in § 103.7(b)(1) of 8 CFR chapter I, to a United States immigration officer at a Canadian border Port-of-Entry located within the district having jurisdiction over the applicant's residence or intended place of landing. Persons previously granted Form I–68 approval may apply by mail to the issuing Service office for renewal if a copy of the previous Form I–68 is included in the application. At the discretion of the district director concerned, any applicant for renewal of Form I–68 may be required to appear for an interview in person if the applicant does not appear to be clearly eligible for renewal.

(3) *Denial of Form I–68.* If the applicant has committed a violation of any immigration or customs regulation or, in the case of an alien, is inadmissible to the United States, approval of the Form I–68 shall be denied. However, if, in the exercise of discretion, the district director waives under section 212(d)(3) of the Act all applicable grounds of inadmissibility, the I–68 application may be approved for such non-citizens. If the Form I–68 application is denied, the applicant shall be given written notice of and the reasons for the denial by letter from the district director. There is no appeal from the denial of the Form I–68 application, but the denial is without prejudice to a subsequent application for this program or any other Service benefit, except that the applicant may not submit a subsequent Form I–68 application for 90 days after the date of the last denial.

(4) *Validity.* Form I–68 shall be valid for 1 year from the date of issuance, or until revoked or violated by the Service.

(5) *Conditions for participation in the I-68 program.* Upon being inspected and positively identified by an immigration officer and found admissible and eligible for participation in the I–68 program, a participant must agree to abide by the following conditions:

(i) Form I–68 may be used only when entering the United States by means of a vessel exclusively used for pleasure, including chartered vessels when such vessel has been chartered by an approved Form I–68 holder. When used by a person who is a not a citizen or a lawful permanent resident of the United States, admission shall be for a period not to exceed 72 hours to visit within 25 miles of the shore line along the northern border of the United States, including the shore line of Lake Michigan and Puget Sound.

(ii) Participants must be in possession of any authorization documents issued for participation in this program or another Service Alternative Inspections program (INSPASS or PORTPASS). Participants over the age of 15 years and who are not in possession of an INSPASS or PORTPASS enrollment card must also be in possession of a photographic identification document issued by a governmental agency. Participants who are landed immigrants of Canada and do not have a common nationality with nationals of Canada, but who are nationals of a designated country listed in § 217.2(a) of

8 CFR chapter I must also be in possession of proper documentation as described in paragraph (e) of this section.

(iii) Participants may not import merchandise or transport controlled or restricted items while entering the United States under this program. The entry of any merchandise or goods must be in accordance with the laws and regulations of all Federal Inspection Services.

(iv) Participants must agree to random checks or inspections that may be conducted by the Service, at any time and at any location, to ensure compliance.

(v) Participants must abide by all Federal, state, and local laws regarding the importation of alcohol or agricultural products or the importation or possession of controlled substances as defined in section 101 of the Controlled Substance Act (21 U.S.C. 802).

(vi) Participants acknowledge that all devices, decals, cards, or other Federal Government supplied identification or technology used to identify or inspect persons or vessels seeking entry via this program remain the property of the United States Government at all times, and must be surrendered upon request by a Border Patrol Agent or any other officer of a Federal Inspection Service.

(vii) The captain, charterer, master, or owner (if aboard) of each vessel bringing persons into the United States is responsible for determining that all persons aboard the vessel are in possession of a valid, unexpired Form I–68 or other evidence of participation in a Service Alternative Inspections program (INSPASS or PORTPASS) prior to entry into the territorial waters of the United States. If any person on board is not in possession of such evidence, the captain, charterer, master, or owner must transport such person to a staffed United States Port-of-Entry for an in-person immigration inspection.

(6) *Revocation.* The district director, the chief patrol agent, or their designated representatives may revoke the designation of any participant who violates any condition of this program, as contained in paragraph (e)(5) of this section, or who has violated any immigration law or regulation, or a law or regulation of the United States Customs Service or other Federal Inspection Service, has abandoned his or her residence in the United States or Canada, is inadmissible to the United States, or who is otherwise determined by an immigration officer to be ineligible for continued participation in this program. Such persons may be subject to other applicable sanctions, such as criminal and/or administrative prosecution or deportation, as well as possible seizure of goods and/or vessels. If permission to participate is revoked, a written request to the district director for restoration of permission to participate may be made. The district director will notify the person of his or her decision and the reasons therefore in writing.

(7) *Compliance checking.* Participation in this program does not relieve the holder from responsibility to comply with all other aspects of United States Immigration, Customs, or other Federal inspection service laws or regulations. To prevent abuse, the United States Immigration and Naturalization Service retains the right to conduct inspections or examinations of all persons applying for admission or readmission to or seeking transit through the United States in accordance with the Immigration and Nationality Act.

(f) *Form I–94, Arrival Departure Record.* (1) Unless otherwise exempted, each arriving nonimmigrant who is admitted to the United States shall be issued, upon payment of a fee prescribed in § 103.7(b)(1) of this chapter for land border admissions, a Form I–94 as evidence of the terms of admission. A Form I–94 issued at a land border port-of-entry shall be considered issued for multiple entries unless specifically annotated for a limited number of entries. A Form I–94 issued at other than a land border port-of-entry, unless issued for multiple entries, must be surrendered upon departure from the United States in accordance with the instructions on the form. Form I–94 is not required by:

(i) Any nonimmigrant alien described in § 1212.1(a) of this chapter and 22 CFR 41.33 who is admitted as a visitor for business or pleasure or admitted to proceed in direct transit through the United States;

(ii) Any nonimmigrant alien residing in the British Virgin Islands who was admitted only to the U.S. Virgin Islands as a visitor for business or pleasure under § 212.1(b) of this chapter;

(iii) Except as provided in paragraph (f)(1)(v) of this section, any Mexican national who is exempt from a visa and passport pursuant to § 1212.1(c)(1) of this chapter, or who is in possession of a passport and valid visa who is admitted as a nonimmigrant visitor for a period not to exceed 72 hours to visit within 25 miles of the border;

(iv) Bearers of Mexican diplomatic or official passports described in § 1212.1(c) of this chapter; or

(v) Any Mexican national who is exempt from a visa and passport pursuant to § 1212.1(c)(1) of this chapter, or is in possession of a passport and valid visa who is admitted as a nonimmigrant visitor at the Mexican border POEs in the State of Arizona at Sasabe, Nogales, Mariposa, Naco, or Douglas for a period not to exceed 72 hours to visit within the State of Arizona and within 75 miles of the border.

(2) *Paroled aliens.* Any alien paroled into the United States under section 212(d)(5) of the Act, including any alien crewmember, shall be issued a completely executed Form I–94, endorsed with the parole stamp.

[62 FR 10353, Mar. 6, 1997, as amended at 62 FR 47751, Sept. 11, 1997; 64 FR 8494, Feb. 19, 1999; 64 FR 36561, July 7, 1999; 64 FR 68617, Dec. 8, 1999; 67 FR 71449, Dec. 2, 2002]

§ 1235.2 Parole for deferred inspection.

(a) A district director may, in his or her discretion, defer the inspection of any vessel or aircraft, or of any alien, to another Service office or port-of-entry. Any alien coming to a United States port from a foreign port, from an outlying possession of the United States, from Guam, Puerto Rico, or the Virgin Islands of the United States, or from another port of the United States at which examination under this part was deferred, shall be regarded as an applicant for admission at that onward port.

(b) An examining immigration officer may defer further examination and refer the alien's case to the district director having jurisdiction over the place where the alien is seeking admission, or over the place of the alien's residence or destination in the United States, if the examining immigration officer has reason to believe that the alien can overcome a finding of inadmissibility by:

(1) Posting a bond under section 213 of the Act;

(2) Seeking and obtaining a waiver under section 211 or 212(d)(3) or (4) of the Act; or

(3) Presenting additional evidence of admissibility not available at the time and place of the initial examination.

(c) Such deferral shall be accomplished pursuant to the provisions of section 212(d)(5) of the Act for the period of time necessary to complete the deferred inspection.

(d) Refusal of a district director to authorize admission under section 213 of the Act, or to grant an application for the benefits of section 211 or section 212(d) (3) or (4) of the Act, shall be without prejudice to the renewal of such application or the authorizing of such admission by the immigration judge without additional fee.

(e) Whenever an alien on arrival is found or believed to be suffering from a disability that renders it impractical to proceed with the examination under the Act, the examination of such alien, members of his or her family concerning whose admissibility it is necessary to have such alien testify, and any accompanying aliens whose protection or guardianship will be required should such alien be found inadmissible shall be deferred for such time and under such conditions as the district director in whose district the port is located imposes.

[62 FR 10355, Mar. 6, 1997]

§ 1235.3 Inadmissible aliens and expedited removal.

(a) *Detention prior to inspection.* All persons arriving at a port-of-entry in the United States by vessel or aircraft shall be detained aboard the vessel or at the airport of arrival by the owner, agent, master, commanding officer, person in charge, purser, or consignee of such vessel or aircraft until admitted or otherwise permitted to land by an officer of the Service. Notice or order to detain shall not be required. The owner, agent, master, commanding officer, person in charge, purser, or consignee of such vessel or aircraft shall deliver every alien requiring examination to an immigration officer for inspection or to a medical officer for examination. The Service will not be liable for any expenses related to such detention or presentation or for any expenses of a passenger who has not been presented for inspection and for whom a determination has not been made concerning admissibility by a Service officer.

(b) *Expedited removal*—(1) *Applicability.* The expedited removal provisions shall apply to the following classes of aliens who are determined to be inadmissible under section 212(a)(6)(C) or (7) of the Act:

(i) Arriving aliens, as defined in § 1001.1(q) of this chapter;

(ii) As specifically designated by the Commissioner, aliens who arrive in, attempt to enter, or have entered the United States without having been admitted or paroled following inspection by an immigration officer at a designated port-of-entry, and who have not established to the satisfaction of the immigration officer that they have been physically present in the United States continuously for the 2-year period immediately prior to the date of determination of inadmissibility. The Commissioner shall have the sole discretion to apply the provisions of section 235(b)(1) of the Act, at any time, to any class of aliens described in this section. The Commissioner's designation shall become effective upon publication of a notice in the FEDERAL REGISTER. However, if the Commissioner determines, in the exercise of discretion, that the delay caused by publication would adversely affect the interests of the United States or the effective enforcement of the immigration laws, the Commissioner's designation shall become effective immediately upon issuance, and shall be published in the FEDERAL REGISTER as soon as practicable thereafter. When these provisions are in effect for aliens who enter without inspection, the burden of proof rests with the alien to affirmatively show that he or she has the required continuous physical presence in the United States. Any absence from the United States shall serve to break the period of continuous physical presence. An alien who was not inspected and admitted or paroled into the United States but who establishes that he or she has been continuously physically present in the United States for the 2-year period immediately prior to the date of determination of inadmissibility shall be detained in accordance with section 235(b)(2) of the Act for a proceeding under section 240 of the Act.

(2) *Determination of inadmissibility*—(i) *Record of proceeding.* An alien who is arriving in the United States, or other alien as designated pursuant to paragraph (b)(1)(ii) of this section, who is determined to be inadmissible under section 212(a)(6)(C) or 212(a)(7) of the Act (except an alien for whom documentary requirements are waived under § 1211.1(b)(3) or § 1212.1 of this chapter), shall be ordered removed from the United States in accordance with section 235(b)(1) of the Act. In every case in which the expedited removal provisions will be applied and before removing an alien from the United States pursuant to this section, the examining immigration officer shall create a record of the facts of the case and statements made by the alien. This shall be accomplished by means of a sworn statement using Form I–867AB, Record of Sworn Statement in Proceedings under Section 235(b)(1) of the Act. The examining immigration officer shall read (or have read) to the alien all information contained on Form I–867A. Following questioning and recording of the alien's statement regarding identity, alienage, and inadmissibility, the examining immigration officer shall record the alien's response to the questions contained on Form I–867B, and have the alien read (or have read to him or her) the statement, and the alien shall sign and initial each page of the statement and each correction. The examining immigration officer shall advise the alien of the charges against him or her on Form I–860, Notice and Order of Expedited Removal, and the alien shall be given an opportunity to respond to those charges in the sworn statement. After obtaining supervisory concurrence in accordance with paragraph (b)(7) of this section, the examining immigration official shall serve the alien

with Form I–860 and the alien shall sign the reverse of the form acknowledging receipt. Interpretative assistance shall be used if necessary to communicate with the alien.

(ii) *No entitlement to hearings and appeals.* Except as otherwise provided in this section, such alien is not entitled to a hearing before an immigration judge in proceedings conducted pursuant to section 240 of the Act, or to an appeal of the expedited removal order to the Board of Immigration Appeals.

(iii) *Detention and parole of alien in expedited removal.* An alien whose inadmissibility is being considered under this section or who has been ordered removed pursuant to this section shall be detained pending determination and removal, except that parole of such alien, in accordance with section 212(d)(5) of the Act, may be permitted only when the Attorney General determines, in the exercise of discretion, that parole is required to meet a medical emergency or is necessary for a legitimate law enforcement objective.

(3) *Additional charges of inadmissibility.* In the expedited removal process, the Service may not charge an alien with any additional grounds of inadmissibility other than section 212(a)(6)(C) or 212(a)(7) of the Act. If an alien appears to be inadmissible under other grounds contained in section 212(a) of the Act, and if the Service wishes to pursue such additional grounds of inadmissibility, the alien shall be detained and referred for a removal hearing before an immigration judge pursuant to sections 235(b)(2) and 240 of the Act for inquiry into all charges. Once the alien is in removal proceedings under section 240 of the Act, the Service is not precluded from lodging additional charges against the alien. Nothing in this paragraph shall preclude the Service from pursuing such additional grounds of inadmissibility against the alien in any subsequent attempt to reenter the United States, provided the additional grounds of inadmissibility still exist.

(4) *Claim of asylum or fear of persecution or torture.* (i) The DHS regulations at 8 CFR 235.3(b)(4) provide for referring an alien to an asylum officer if the alien indicates an intention to apply for asylum or expresses a fear of persecution or torture or a fear of return to his or her country.

(i) *Referral.* The referring officer shall provide the alien with a written disclosure on Form M–444, Information About Credible Fear Interview, describing:

(A) The purpose of the referral and description of the credible fear interview process;

(B) The right to consult with other persons prior to the interview and any review thereof at no expense to the United States Government;

(C) The right to request a review by an immigration judge of the asylum officer's credible fear determination; and

(D) The consequences of failure to establish a credible fear of persecution or torture.

(ii) *Detention pending credible fear interview.* Pending the credible fear determination by an asylum officer and any review of that determination by an immigration judge, the alien shall be detained. Parole of such alien in accordance with section 212(d)(5) of the Act may be permitted only when the Attorney General determines, in the exercise of discretion, that parole is required to meet a medical emergency or is necessary for a legitimate law enforcement objective. Prior to the interview, the alien shall be given time to contact and consult with any person or persons of his or her choosing. Such consultation shall be made available in accordance with the policies and procedures of the detention facility where the alien is detained, shall be at no expense to the government, and shall not unreasonably delay the process.

(5) *Claim to lawful permanent resident, refugee, or asylee status or U.S. citizenship*—(i) *Verification of status.* If an applicant for admission who is subject to expedited removal pursuant to section 235(b)(1) of the Act claims to have been lawfully admitted for permanent residence, admitted as a refugee under section 207 of the Act, granted asylum under section 208 of the Act, or claims to be a U.S. citizen, the immigration officer shall attempt to verify the alien's claim. Such verification shall include a check of all available Service data systems and any other means available to the officer. An alien whose claim to lawful permanent resident,

refugee, asylee status, or U.S. citizen status cannot be verified will be advised of the penalties for perjury, and will be placed under oath or allowed to make a declaration as permitted under 28 U.S.C. 1746, concerning his or her lawful admission for permanent residence, admission as a refugee under section 207 of the Act, grant of asylum status under section 208 of the Act, or claim to U.S. citizenship. A written statement shall be taken from the alien in the alien's own language and handwriting, stating that he or she declares, certifies, verifies, or states that the claim is true and correct. The immigration officer shall issue an expedited order of removal under section 235(b)(1)(A)(i) of the Act and refer the alien to the immigration judge for review of the order in accordance with paragraph (b)(5)(iv) of this section and §1235.6(a)(2)(ii). The person shall be detained pending review of the expedited removal order under this section. Parole of such person, in accordance with section 212(d)(5) of the Act, may be permitted only when the Attorney General determines, in the exercise of discretion, that parole is required to meet a medical emergency or is necessary for a legitimate law enforcement objective.

(ii) *Verified lawful permanent residents.* If the claim to lawful permanent resident status is verified, and such status has not been terminated in exclusion, deportation, or removal proceedings, the examining immigration officer shall not order the alien removed pursuant to section 235(b)(1) of the Act. The examining immigration officer will determine in accordance with section 101(a)(13)(C) of the Act whether the alien is considered to be making an application for admission. If the alien is determined to be seeking admission and the alien is otherwise admissible, except that he or she is not in possession of the required documentation, a discretionary waiver of documentary requirements may be considered in accordance with section 211(b) of the Act and §1211.1(b)(3) of this chapter or the alien's inspection may be deferred to an onward office for presentation of the required documents. If the alien appears to be inadmissible, the immigration officer may initiate removal proceedings against the alien under section 240 of the Act.

(iii) *Verified refugees and asylees.* If a check of Service records or other means indicates that the alien has been granted refugee status or asylee status, and such status has not been terminated in deportation, exclusion, or removal proceedings, the immigration officer shall not order the alien removed pursuant to section 235(b)(1) of the Act. If the alien is not in possession of a valid, unexpired refugee travel document, the examining immigration officer may accept an application for a refugee travel document in accordance with §223.2(b)(2)(ii) of 8 CFR chapter I. If accepted, the immigration officer shall readmit the refugee or asylee in accordance with §223.3(d)(2)(i) of 8 CFR chapter I. If the alien is determined not to be eligible to file an application for a refugee travel document the immigration officer may initiate removal proceedings against the alien under section 240 of the Act.

(iv) *Review of order for claimed lawful permanent residents, refugees, asylees, or U.S. citizens.* A person whose claim to U.S. citizenship has been verified may not be ordered removed. When an alien whose status has not been verified but who is claiming under oath or under penalty of perjury to be a lawful permanent resident, refugee, asylee, or U.S. citizen is ordered removed pursuant to section 235(b)(1) of the Act, the case will be referred to an immigration judge for review of the expedited removal order under section 235(b)(1)(C) of the Act and §1235.6(a)(2)(ii). If the immigration judge determines that the alien has never been admitted as a lawful permanent resident or as a refugee, granted asylum status, or is not a U.S. citizen, the order issued by the immigration officer will be affirmed and the Service will remove the alien. There is no appeal from the decision of the immigration judge. If the immigration judge determines that the alien was once so admitted as a lawful permanent resident or as a refugee, or was granted asylum status, or is a U.S. citizen, and such status has not been terminated by final administrative action, the immigration judge will terminate proceedings and vacate the expedited removal order. The Service may initiate removal proceedings against such an alien, but not against a person determined to be a U.S. citizen, in proceedings under section 240 of the Act. During removal proceedings, the immigration judge may consider any waivers, exceptions, or requests for relief for which the alien is eligible.

(6) *Opportunity for alien to establish that he or she was admitted or paroled into the United States.* If the Commissioner determines that the expedited removal provisions of section 235(b)(1) of the Act shall apply to any or all aliens described in paragraph (b)(2)(ii) of this section, such alien will be given a reasonable opportunity to establish to the satisfaction of the examining immigration officer that he or she was admitted or paroled into the United States following inspection at a port-of-entry. The alien will be allowed to present evidence or provide sufficient information to support the claim. Such evidence may consist of documentation in the possession of the alien, the Service, or a third party. The examining immigration officer will consider all such evidence and information, make further inquiry if necessary, and will attempt to verify the alien's status through a check of all available Service data systems. The burden rests with the alien to satisfy the examining immigration officer of the claim of lawful admission or parole. If the alien establishes that he or she was lawfully admitted or paroled, the case will be examined to determine if grounds of deportability under section 237(a) of the Act are applicable, or if paroled, whether such parole has been, or should be, terminated, and whether the alien is inadmissible under section 212(a) of the Act. An alien who cannot satisfy the examining officer that he or she was lawfully admitted or paroled will be ordered removed pursuant to section 235(b)(1) of the Act.

(7) *Review of expedited removal orders.* Any removal order entered by an examining immigration officer pursuant to section 235(b)(1) of the Act must be reviewed and approved by the appropriate supervisor before the order is considered final. Such supervisory review shall not be delegated below the level of the second line supervisor, or a person acting in that capacity. The supervisory review shall include a review of the sworn statement and any answers and statements made by the alien regarding a fear of removal or return. The supervisory review and approval of an expedited removal order for an alien described in section 235(b)(1)(A)(iii) of the Act must include a review of any claim of lawful admission or parole and any evidence or information presented to support such a claim, prior to approval of the order. In such cases, the supervisor may request additional information from any source and may require further interview of the alien.

(8) *Removal procedures relating to expedited removal.* An alien ordered removed pursuant to section 235(b)(1) of the Act shall be removed from the United States in accordance with section 241(c) of the Act and 8 CFR part 1241.

(9) *Waivers of documentary requirements.* Nothing in this section limits the discretionary authority of the Attorney General, including authority under sections 211(b) or 212(d) of the Act, to waive the documentary requirements for arriving aliens.

(10) *Applicant for admission under section 217 of the Act.* The provisions of § 1235.3(b) do not apply to an applicant for admission under section 217 of the Act.

(c) *Arriving aliens placed in proceedings under section 240 of the Act.* Except as otherwise provided in this chapter, any arriving alien who appears to the inspecting officer to be inadmissible, and who is placed in removal proceedings pursuant to section 240 of the Act shall be detained in accordance with section 235(b) of the Act. Parole of such alien shall only be considered in accordance with § 1212.5(b) of this chapter. This paragraph shall also apply to any alien who arrived before April 1, 1997, and who was placed in exclusion proceedings.

(d) *Service custody.* The Service will assume custody of any alien subject to detention under paragraph (b) or (c) of this section. In its discretion, the Service may require any alien who appears inadmissible and who arrives at a land border port-of-entry from Canada or Mexico, to remain in that country while awaiting a removal hearing. Such alien shall be considered detained for a proceeding within the meaning of section 235(b) of the Act and may be ordered removed in absentia by an immigration judge if the alien fails to appear for the hearing.

(e) *Detention in non-Service facility.* Whenever an alien is taken into Service custody and detained at a facility other than at a Service Processing Center, the public or private entities contracted to perform such service shall have been approved for such use by the Service's Jail Inspection Program or shall be performing such service under contract in compliance with the Standard Statement of Work for Contract Detention Facilities. Both programs are administered by the Detention and Deportation section having jurisdiction over the alien's place of detention. Under no circumstances shall an alien be detained in facilities not meeting the four mandatory criteria for usage. These are:

(1) 24-Hour supervision,

(2) Conformance with safety and emergency codes,

(3) Food service, and

(4) Availability of emergency medical care.

(f) *Privilege of communication.* The mandatory notification requirements of consular and diplomatic officers pursuant to § 1236.1(e) of this chapter apply when an inadmissible alien is detained for removal proceedings, including for purpose of conducting the credible fear determination.

[62 FR 10355, Mar. 6, 1997, as amended at 64 FR 8494, Feb. 19, 1999; 65 FR 82256, Dec. 28, 2000; 69 FR 69497, Nov. 29, 2004; 82 FR 4773, Jan. 17, 2017]

§ 1235.4 Withdrawal of application for admission.

The Attorney General may, in his or her discretion, permit any alien applicant for admission to withdraw his or her application for admission in lieu of removal proceedings under section 240 of the Act or expedited removal under section 235(b)(1) of the Act. The alien's decision to withdraw his or her application for admission must be made voluntarily, but nothing in this section shall be construed as to give an alien the right to withdraw his or her application for admission. Permission to withdraw an application for admission should not normally be granted unless the alien intends and is able to depart the United States immediately. An alien permitted to withdraw his or her application for admission shall normally remain in carrier or Service custody pending departure, unless the district director determines that parole of the alien is warranted in accordance with § 1212.5(b) of this chapter.

[62 FR 10358, Mar. 6, 1997; 62 FR 15363, Apr. 1, 1997; 65 FR 82256, Dec. 28, 2000]

§ 1235.5 Preinspection.

(a) *In United States territories and possessions.* For provisions of the DHS regulations with respect to examinations of passengers and crew in the case of any aircraft proceeding from Guam, the Commonwealth of the Northern Mariana Islands (beginning November 28, 2009), Puerto Rico, or the United States Virgin Islands destined directly and without touching at a foreign port or place, to any other of such places, or to one of the States of the United States or the District of Columbia, *see* 8 CFR 235.5.

(b) *In foreign territory.* In the case of any aircraft, vessel, or train proceeding directly, without stopping, from a port or place in foreign territory to a port-of-entry in the United States, the examination and inspection of passengers and crew required by the Act and final determination of admissibility may be made immediately prior to such departure at the port or place in the foreign territory and shall have the same effect under the Act as though made at the destined port-of-entry in the United States.

[62 FR 10358, Mar. 6, 1997, as amended at 74 FR 55744, Oct. 28, 2009]

§ 1235.6 Referral to immigration judge.

(a) *Notice*—(1) *Referral by Form I–862, Notice to Appear.* An immigration officer or asylum officer will sign and deliver a Form I–862 to an alien in the following cases:

(i) If, in accordance with the provisions of section 235(b)(2)(A) of the Act, the examining immigration officer detains an alien for a proceeding before an immigration judge under section 240 of the Act; or

(ii) If an asylum officer determines that an alien in expedited removal proceedings has a credible fear of persecution or torture and refers the case to the immigration judge for consideration of the application for asylum, except that, prior to January 1, 2015, an alien present in or arriving in the Commonwealth of the Northern Mariana Islands is not eligible to apply for asylum but the immigration judge may consider eligibility for withholding of removal pursuant to section 241(b)(3) of the Act or withholding or deferral of removal under the Convention Against Torture.

(iii) If the immigration judge determines that an alien in expedited removal proceedings has a credible fear of persecution or torture and vacates the expedited removal order issued by the asylum officer, except that, prior to January 1, 2015, an alien physically present in or arriving in the Commonwealth of the Northern Mariana Islands is not eligible to apply for asylum but an immigration judge may consider eligibility for withholding of removal pursuant to section 241(b)(3) of the Act or withholding or deferral of removal under the Convention Against Torture.

(iv) If an immigration officer verifies that an alien subject to expedited removal under section 235(b)(1) of the Act has been admitted as a lawful permanent resident refugee, or asylee, or upon review pursuant to § 1235.3(b)(5)(iv) an immigration judge determines that the alien was once so admitted, provided that such status has not been terminated by final administrative action, and the Service initiates removal proceedings against the alien under section 240 of the Act.

(2) *Referral by Form I–863, Notice of Referral to Immigration Judge.* An immigration officer will sign and deliver a Form I–863 to an alien in the following cases:

(i) If an asylum officer determines that an alien does not have a credible fear of persecution or torture, and the alien requests a review of that determination by an immigration judge; or

(ii) If, in accordance with section 235(b)(1)(C) of the Act, an immigration officer refers an expedited removal order entered on an alien claiming to be a lawful permanent resident, refugee, asylee, or U.S. citizen for whom the officer could not verify such status to an immigration judge for review of the order.

(iii) If an immigration officer refers an applicant described in § 1208.2(b)(1) of this chapter to an immigration judge for an asylum hearing under § 208.2(b)(2) of this chapter.

(b) *Certification for mental condition; medical appeal.* An alien certified under sections 212(a)(1) and 232(b) of the Act shall be advised by the examining immigration officer that he or she may appeal to a board of medical examiners of the United States Public Health Service pursuant to section 232 of the Act. If such appeal is taken, the district director shall arrange for the convening of the medical board.

[62 FR 10358, Mar. 6, 1997, as amended at 64 FR 8494, Feb. 19, 1999; 74 FR 55744, Oct. 28, 2009]

§ 1235.8 Inadmissibility on security and related grounds.

(a) *Report.* When an immigration officer or an immigration judge suspects that an arriving alien appears to be inadmissible under section 212(a)(3)(A) (other than clause (ii)), (B), or (C) of the Act, the immigration officer or immigration judge shall order the alien removed and report the action promptly to the district director who has administrative jurisdiction over the place where the alien has arrived or where the hearing is being held. The immigration officer shall, if possible, take a brief sworn question-and-answer statement from the alien, and the alien shall be notified by personal service of Form I–147, Notice of Temporary Inadmissibility, of the action taken and the right to submit a written statement and additional information for consideration by the Attorney General. The district director shall forward the report to the regional director for further action as provided in paragraph (b) of this section.

(b) *Action by regional director.* (1) In accordance with section 235(c)(2)(B) of the Act, the regional director may deny any further inquiry or hearing by an immigration judge and order the alien removed by personal service of Form I–148, Notice of Permanent Inadmissibility, or issue any other order disposing of the case that the regional director considers appropriate.

(2) If the regional director concludes that the case does not meet the criteria contained in section 235(c)(2)(B) of the Act, the regional director may direct that:

(i) An immigration officer shall conduct a further examination of the alien, concerning the alien's admissibility; or,

(ii) The alien's case be referred to an immigration judge for a hearing, or for the continuation of any prior hearing.

(3) The regional director's decision shall be in writing and shall be signed by the regional director. Unless the written decision contains confidential information, the disclosure of which would be prejudicial to the public interest, safety, or security of the United States, the written decision shall be served on the alien. If the written decision contains such confidential information, the alien shall be served with a separate written order showing the disposition of the case, but with the confidential information deleted.

(4) The Service shall not execute a removal order under this section under circumstances that violate section 241(b)(3) of the Act or Article 3 of the Convention Against Torture. The provisions of part 1208 of this chapter relating to consideration or review by an immigration judge, the Board of Immigration Appeals, or an asylum officer shall not apply.

(c) *Finality of decision.* The regional director's decision under this section is final when it is served upon the alien in accordance with paragraph (b)(3) of this section. There is no administrative appeal from the regional director's decision.

(d) *Hearing by immigration judge.* If the regional director directs that an alien subject to removal under this section be given a hearing or further hearing before an immigration judge, the hearing and all further proceedings in the matter shall be conducted in accordance with the provisions of section 240 of the Act and other applicable sections of the Act to the same extent as though the alien had been referred to an immigration judge by the examining immigration officer. In a case where the immigration judge ordered the alien removed pursuant to paragraph (a) of this section, the Service shall refer the case back to the immigration judge and proceedings shall be automatically reopened upon receipt of the notice of referral. If confidential information, not previously considered in the matter, is presented supporting the inadmissibility of the alien under section 212(a)(3)(A) (other than clause (ii)), (B) or (C) of the Act, the disclosure of which, in the discretion of the immigration judge, may be prejudicial to the public interest, safety, or security, the immigration judge may again order the alien removed under the authority of section 235(c) of the Act and further action shall be taken as provided in this section.

(e) *Nonapplicability.* The provisions of this section shall apply only to arriving aliens, as defined in §1001.1(q) of this chapter. Aliens present in the United States who have not been admitted or paroled may be subject to proceedings under Title V of the Act.

[62 FR 10358, Mar. 6, 1997, as amended at 64 FR 8494, Feb. 19, 1999]

§ 1235.9 Northern Marianas identification card.

During the two-year period that ended July 1, 1990, the Service issued Northern Marianas Identification Cards to aliens who acquired United States citizenship when the Covenant to Establish a Commonwealth of the Northern Mariana Islands in Political Union with the United States entered into force on November 3, 1986. These cards remain valid as evidence of United States citizenship. Although the Service no longer issues these cards, a United States citizen to whom a card was issued may file Form I–777, Application for Issuance or Replacement of Northern Marianas Card, to obtain replacement of a lost, stolen, or mutilated Northern Marianas Identification Card.

[62 FR 10359, Mar. 6, 1997]

§ 1235.10 U.S. Citizen Identification Card.

(a) *General.* Form I–197, U.S. Citizen Identification Card, is no longer issued by the Service but valid existing cards will continue to be acceptable documentation of U.S. citizenship. Possession of the identification card is not mandatory for any purpose. A U.S. Citizen Identification Card remains the property of the United States. Because the identification card is no longer issued, there are no provisions for replacement cards.

(b) *Surrender and voidance*—(1) *Institution of proceeding under section 240 or 342 of the Act.* A U.S. Citizen Identification Card must be surrendered provisionally to a Service office upon notification by the district director that a proceeding under section 240 or 342 of the Act is being instituted against the person to whom the card was issued. The card shall be returned to the person if the final order in the proceeding does not result in voiding the card under this paragraph. A U.S. Citizen Identification Card is automatically void if the person to whom it was issued is determined to be an alien in a proceeding conducted under section 240 of the Act, or if a certificate, document, or record relating to that person is canceled under section 342 of the Act.

(2) *Investigation of validity of identification card.* A U.S. Citizen Identification Card must be surrendered provisionally upon notification by a district director that the validity of the card is being investigated. The card shall be returned to the person who surrendered it if the investigation does not result in a determination adverse to his or her claim to be a United States citizen. When an investigation results in a tentative determination adverse to the applicant's claim to be a United States citizen, the applicant shall be notified by certified mail directed to his or her last known address. The notification shall inform the applicant of the basis for the determination and of the intention of the district director to declare the card void unless within 30 days the applicant objects and demands an opportunity to see and rebut the adverse evidence. Any rebuttal, explanation, or evidence presented by the applicant must be included in the record of proceeding. The determination whether the applicant is a United States citizen must be based on the entire record and the applicant shall be notified of the determination. If it is determined that the applicant is not a United States citizen, the applicant shall be notified of the reasons, and the card deemed void. There is no appeal from the district director's decision.

(3) *Admission of alienage.* A U.S. Citizen Identification Card is void if the person to whom it was issued admits in a statement signed before an immigration officer that he or she is an alien and consents to the voidance of the card. Upon signing the statement the card must be surrendered to the immigration officer.

(4) *Surrender of void card.* A void U.S. Citizen Identification Card which has not been returned to the Service must be surrendered without delay to an immigration officer or to the issuing office of the Service.

(c) *U.S. Citizen Identification Card previously issued on Form I–179.* A valid Form I–179, U.S. Citizen Identification Card, continues to be valid subject to the provisions of this section.

[62 FR 10359, Mar. 6, 1997]

§ 1235.11 Admission of conditional permanent residents.

(a) *General*—(1) *Conditional residence based on family relationship.* An alien seeking admission to the United States with an immigrant visa as the spouse or son or daughter of a United States citizen or lawful permanent resident shall be examined to determine whether the conditions of section 216 of the Act apply. If so, the alien shall be admitted conditionally for a period of 2 years. At the time of admission, the alien shall be notified that the alien and his or her petitioning spouse must file a Form I–751, Petition to Remove the Conditions on Residence, within the 90-day period immediately preceding the second anniversary of the alien's admission for permanent residence.

(2) *Conditional residence based on entrepreneurship.* An alien seeking admission to the United States with an immigrant visa as an alien entrepreneur (as defined in section 216A(f)(1) of the Act) or the spouse or unmarried minor child of an alien entrepreneur shall be admitted conditionally for a period of 2 years. At the time of admission, the alien shall be notified that the principal alien (entrepreneur) must file a

Form I–829, Petition by Entrepreneur to Remove Conditions, within the 90-day period immediately preceding the second anniversary of the alien's admission for permanent residence.

(b) *Correction of endorsement on immigrant visa.* If the alien is subject to the provisions of section 216 of the Act, but the classification endorsed on the immigrant visa does not so indicate, the endorsement shall be corrected and the alien shall be admitted as a lawful permanent resident on a conditional basis, if otherwise admissible. Conversely, if the alien is not subject to the provisions of section 216 of the Act, but the visa classification endorsed on the immigrant visa indicates that the alien is subject thereto (e.g., if the second anniversary of the marriage upon which the immigrant visa is based occurred after the issuance of the visa and prior to the alien's application for admission) the endorsement on the visa shall be corrected and the alien shall be admitted as a lawful permanent resident without conditions, if otherwise admissible.

(c) *Expired conditional permanent resident status.* The lawful permanent resident alien status of a conditional resident automatically terminates if the conditional basis of such status is not removed by the Service through approval of a Form I–751, Petition to Remove the Conditions on Residence or, in the case of an alien entrepreneur (as defined in section 216A(f)(1) of the Act), Form I–829, Petition by Entrepreneur to Remove Conditions. Therefore, an alien who is seeking admission as a returning resident subsequent to the second anniversary of the date on which conditional residence was obtained (except as provided in §1211.1(b)(1) of this chapter) and whose conditional basis of such residence has not been removed pursuant to section 216(c) or 216A(c) of the Act, whichever is applicable, shall be placed under removal proceedings. However, in a case where conditional residence was based on a marriage, removal proceedings may be terminated and the alien may be admitted as a returning resident if the required Form I–751 is filed jointly, or by the alien alone (if appropriate), and approved by the Service. In the case of an alien entrepreneur, removal proceedings may be terminated and the alien admitted as a returning resident if the required Form I–829 is filed by the alien entrepreneur and approved by the Service.

[62 FR 10360, Mar. 6, 1997]

PART 1236—APPREHENSION AND DETENTION OF INADMISSIBLE AND DEPORTABLE ALIENS; REMOVAL OF ALIENS ORDERED REMOVED

Subpart A—Detention of Aliens Prior to Order of Removal

AUTHORITY: 5 U.S.C. 301, 552, 552a; 8 U.S.C. 1103, 1182, 1224, 1225, 1226, 1227, 1231, 1362; 18 U.S.C. 4002, 4013(c)(4); 8 CFR part 2.

SOURCE: 62 FR 10360, Mar. 6, 1997, unless otherwise noted. Duplicated from part 236 at 68 FR 9838, Feb. 28, 2003.

EDITORIAL NOTE: Nomenclature changes to part 1236 appear at 68 FR 9846, Feb. 28, 2003, and at 68 FR 10354, Mar. 5, 2003.

Subpart A—Detention of Aliens Prior to Order of Removal

§1236.1 Apprehension, custody, and detention.

(a) *Detainers.* The issuance of a detainer under this section shall be governed by the provisions of §287.7 of 8 CFR chapter I.

(b) *Warrant of arrest*—(1) *In general.* At the time of issuance of the notice to appear, or at any time thereafter and up to the time removal proceedings are completed, the respondent may be arrested and taken into custody under the authority of Form I–200, Warrant of Arrest. A warrant of arrest may be issued only by those immigration officers listed in §287.5(e)(2) of 8 CFR chapter I and may be served only by those immigration officers listed in §287.5(e)(3) of 8 CFR chapter I.

(2) If, after the issuance of a warrant of arrest, a determination is made not to serve it, any officer authorized to issue such warrant may authorize its cancellation.

(c) *Custody issues and release procedures*—(1) *In general.* (i) After the expiration of the Transition Period Custody Rules (TPCR) set forth in section 303(b)(3) of Div. C of Pub. L. 104–208, no alien described in section 236(c)(1) of the Act may be released from custody during removal proceedings except pursuant to section 236(c)(2) of the Act.

(ii) Paragraph (c)(2) through (c)(8) of this section shall govern custody determinations for aliens subject to the TPCR while they remain in effect. For purposes of this section, an alien "subject to the TPCR" is an alien described in section 303(b)(3)(A) of Div. C of Pub. L. 104–208 who is in deportation proceedings, subject to a final order of deportation, or in removal proceedings. The TPCR do not apply to aliens in exclusion proceedings under former section 236 of the Act, aliens in expedited removal proceedings under section 235(b)(1) of the Act, or aliens subject to a final order of removal.

(2) *Aliens not lawfully admitted.* Subject to paragraph (c)(6)(i) of this section, but notwithstanding any other provision within this section, an alien subject to the TPCR who is not lawfully admitted is not eligible to be considered for release from custody.

(i) An alien who remains in status as an alien lawfully admitted for permanent residence, conditionally admitted for permanent residence, or lawfully admitted for temporary residence is "lawfully admitted" for purposes of this section.

(ii) An alien in removal proceedings, in deportation proceedings, or subject to a final order of deportation, and not described in paragraph (c)(2)(i) of this section, is not "lawfully admitted" for purposes of this section unless the alien last entered the United States lawfully and is not presently an applicant for admission to the United States.

(3) *Criminal aliens eligible to be considered for release.* Except as provided in this section, or otherwise provided by law, an alien subject to the TPCR may be considered for release from custody if lawfully admitted. Such an alien must first demonstrate, by clear and convincing evidence, that release would not pose a danger to the safety of other persons or of property. If an alien meets this burden, the alien must further demonstrate, by clear and convincing evidence, that the alien is likely to appear for any scheduled proceeding (including any appearance required by the Service or EOIR) in order to be considered for release in the exercise of discretion.

(4) *Criminal aliens ineligible to be considered for release except in certain special circumstances.* An alien, other than an alien lawfully admitted for permanent residence, subject to section 303(b)(3)(A) (ii) or (iii) of Div. C. of Pub. L. 104–208 is ineligible to be considered for release if the alien:

(i) Is described in section 241(a)(2)(C) of the Act (as in effect prior to April 1, 1997), or has been convicted of a crime described in section 101(a)(43)(B), (E)(ii) or (F) of the Act (as in effect on April 1, 1997);

(ii) Has been convicted of a crime described in section 101(a)(43)(G) of the Act (as in effect on April 1, 1997) or a crime or crimes involving moral turpitude related to property, and sentenced therefor (including in the aggregate) to at least 3 years' imprisonment;

(iii) Has failed to appear for an immigration proceeding without reasonable cause or has been subject to a bench warrant or similar legal process (unless quashed, withdrawn, or cancelled as improvidently issued);

(iv) Has been convicted of a crime described in section 101(a)(43)(Q) or (T) of the Act (as in effect on April 1, 1997);

(v) Has been convicted in a criminal proceeding of a violation of section 273, 274, 274C, 276, or 277 of the Act, or has admitted the factual elements of such a violation;

(vi) Has overstayed a period granted for voluntary departure;

(vii) Has failed to surrender or report for removal pursuant to an order of exclusion, deportation, or removal;

(viii) Does not wish to pursue, or is statutorily ineligible for, any form of relief from exclusion, deportation, or removal under this chapter or the Act; or

(ix) Is described in paragraphs (c)(5)(i)(A), (B), or (C) of this section but has not been sentenced, including in the aggregate but not including any portions suspended, to at least 2 years' imprisonment, unless the alien was lawfully admitted and has not, since the commencement of proceedings and within the 10 years prior thereto, been convicted of a crime, failed to comply with an order to surrender or a period of voluntary departure, or been subject to a bench warrant or similar legal process (unless quashed, withdrawn, or cancelled as improvidently issued). An alien eligible to be considered for release under this paragraph must meet the burdens described in paragraph (c)(3) of this section in order to be released from custody in the exercise of discretion.

(5) *Criminal aliens ineligible to be considered for release.* (i) A criminal alien subject to section 303(b)(3)(A)(ii) or (iii) of Div. C of Pub. L. 104–208 is ineligible to be considered for release if the alien has been sentenced, including in the aggregate but not including any portions suspended, to at least 2 years' imprisonment, and the alien

(A) Is described in section 237(a)(2)(D)(i) or (ii) of the Act (as in effect on April 1, 1997), or has been convicted of a crime described in section 101(a)(43)(A), (C), (E)(i), (H), (I), (K)(iii), or (L) of the Act (as in effect on April 1, 1997);

(B) Is described in section 237(a)(2)(A)(iv) of the Act; or

(C) Has escaped or attempted to escape from the lawful custody of a local, State, or Federal prison, agency, or officer within the United States.

(ii) Notwithstanding paragraph (c)(5)(i) of this section, a permanent resident alien who has not, since the commencement of proceedings and within the 15 years prior thereto, been convicted of a crime, failed to comply with an order to surrender or a period of voluntary departure, or been subject to a bench warrant or similar legal process (unless quashed, withdrawn, or cancelled as improvidently issued), may be considered for release under paragraph (c)(3) of this section.

(6) *Unremovable aliens and certain long-term detainees.* (i) If the district director determines that an alien subject to section 303(b)(3)(A)(ii) or (iii) of Div. C of Pub. L. 104–208 cannot be removed from the United States because the designated country of removal or deportation will not accept the alien's return, the district director may, in the exercise of discretion, consider release of the alien from custody upon such terms and conditions as the district director may prescribe, without regard to paragraphs (c)(2), (c)(4), and (c)(5) of this section.

(ii) The district director may also, notwithstanding paragraph (c)(5) of this section, consider release from custody, upon such terms and conditions as the district director may prescribe, of any alien described in paragraph (c)(2)(ii) of this section who has been in the Service's custody for six months pursuant to a final order of deportation terminating the alien's status as a lawful permanent resident.

(iii) The district director may release an alien from custody under this paragraph only in accordance with the standards set forth in paragraph (c)(3) of this section and any other applicable provisions of law.

(iv) The district director's custody decision under this paragraph shall not be subject to redetermination by an immigration judge, but, in the case of a custody decision under paragraph (c)(6)(ii) of this section, may be appealed to the Board of Immigration Appeals pursuant to paragraph (d)(3)(iii) of this section.

(7) *Construction.* A reference in this section to a provision in section 241 of the Act as in effect prior to April 1, 1997, shall be deemed to include a reference to the corresponding provision in section 237 of the Act as in effect on April 1, 1997. A reference in this section to a "crime" shall be considered to include a reference to a conspiracy or attempt to commit such a crime. In calculating the 10-year period specified in paragraph (c)(4) of this section and the 15-year period specified in paragraph (c)(5) of this section, no period during which the alien was detained or incarcerated shall count toward the total. References in paragraph (c)(6)(i) of this section to the "district director" shall be deemed to include a reference to any official designated by the Commissioner to exercise custody authority

over aliens covered by that paragraph. Nothing in this part shall be construed as prohibiting an alien from seeking reconsideration of the Service's determination that the alien is within a category barred from release under this part.

(8) Any officer authorized to issue a warrant of arrest may, in the officer's discretion, release an alien not described in section 236(c)(1) of the Act, under the conditions at section 236(a)(2) and (3) of the Act; provided that the alien must demonstrate to the satisfaction of the officer that such release would not pose a danger to property or persons, and that the alien is likely to appear for any future proceeding. Such an officer may also, in the exercise of discretion, release an alien in deportation proceedings pursuant to the authority in section 242 of the Act (as designated prior to April 1, 1997), except as otherwise provided by law.

(9) When an alien who, having been arrested and taken into custody, has been released, such release may be revoked at any time in the discretion of the district director, acting district director, deputy district director, assistant district director for investigations, assistant district director for detention and deportation, or officer in charge (except foreign), in which event the alien may be taken into physical custody and detained. If detained, unless a breach has occurred, any outstanding bond shall be revoked and canceled.

(10) The provisions of § 103.6 of 8 CFR chapter I shall apply to any bonds authorized. Subject to the provisions of this section, the provisions of § 1003.19 of this chapter shall govern availability to the respondent of recourse to other administrative authority for release from custody.

(11) An immigration judge may not exercise the authority provided in this section, and the review process described in paragraph (d) of this section shall not apply, with respect to any alien beyond the custody jurisdiction of the immigration judge as provided in § 1003.19(h) of this chapter.

(d) *Appeals from custody decisions*—(1) *Application to immigration judge.* After an initial custody determination by the district director, including the setting of a bond, the respondent may, at any time before an order under 8 CFR part 1240 becomes final, request amelioration of the conditions under which he or she may be released. Prior to such final order, and except as otherwise provided in this chapter, the immigration judge is authorized to exercise the authority in section 236 of the Act (or section 242(a)(1) of the Act as designated prior to April 1, 1997 in the case of an alien in deportation proceedings) to detain the alien in custody, release the alien, and determine the amount of bond, if any, under which the respondent may be released, as provided in § 1003.19 of this chapter. If the alien has been released from custody, an application for amelioration of the terms of release must be filed within 7 days of release.

(2) *Application to the district director.* After expiration of the 7-day period in paragraph (d)(1) of this section, the respondent may request review by the district director of the conditions of his or her release.

(3) *Appeal to the Board of Immigration Appeals.* An appeal relating to bond and custody determinations may be filed to the Board of Immigration Appeals in the following circumstances:

(i) In accordance with § 1003.38 of this chapter, the alien or the Service may appeal the decision of an immigration judge pursuant to paragraph (d)(1) of this section.

(ii) The alien, within 10 days, may appeal from the district director's decision under paragraph (d)(2)(i) of this section.

(4) *Effect of filing an appeal.* The filing of an appeal from a determination of an immigration judge or district director under this paragraph shall not operate to delay compliance with the order (except as provided in § 1003.19(i)), nor stay the administrative proceedings or removal.

(e) *Privilege of communication.* Every detained alien shall be notified that he or she may communicate with the consular or diplomatic officers of the country of his or her nationality in the United States. Existing treaties with the following countries require immediate communication with appropriate consular or diplomatic officers whenever nationals of the following countries are detained in removal proceedings, whether or not requested by the alien and even if the alien requests that no communication be undertaken in his or her behalf. When notifying consular or diplomatic officials, Service officers shall not reveal the fact that any detained alien has applied for asylum or withholding of removal.

Albania[1]
Antigua
Armenia
Azerbaijan
Bahamas
Barbados
Belarus
Belize
Brunei
Bulgaria
China (People's Republic of)[2]
Costa Rica
Cyprus
Czech Republic
Dominica
Fiji
Gambia, The
Georgia
Ghana
Grenada
Guyana
Hungary
Jamaica
Kazakhstan
Kiribati
Kuwait
Kyrgyzstan
Malaysia
Malta
Mauritius
Moldova
Mongolia
Nigeria
Philippines
Poland
Romania
Russian Federation
St. Kitts/Nevis
St. Lucia
St. Vincent/Grenadines
Seychelles
Sierra Leone
Singapore
Slovak Republic
South Korea
Tajikistan
Tanzania
Tonga
Trinidad/Tobago
Turkmenistan
Tuvalu
Ukraine
United Kingdom[3]
U.S.S.R.[4]
Uzbekistan
Zambia

(f) *Notification to Executive Office for Immigration Review of change in custody status.* The Service shall notify the Immigration Court having administrative control over the Record of Proceeding of any change in custody location or of release from, or subsequent taking into, Service custody of a respondent/applicant pursuant to § 1003.19(g) of this chapter.

[62 FR 10360, Mar. 6, 1997; 62 FR 15363, Apr. 1, 1997, as amended at 63 FR 27449, May 19, 1998; 65 FR 80294, Dec. 21, 2000]

§ 1236.2 Confined aliens, incompetents, and minors.

(a) *Service.* If the respondent is confined, or if he or she is an incompetent, or a minor under the age of 14, the notice to appear, and the warrant of arrest, if issued, shall be served in the manner prescribed in § 1239.1 of this chapter upon the person or persons specified by § 103.5a(c) of 8 CFR chapter I.

(b) *Service custody and cost of maintenance.* An alien confined because of physical or mental disability in an institution or hospital shall not be accepted into physical custody by the Service until an order of removal has been entered and the Service is ready to remove the alien. When such an

[1] Arrangements with these countries provide that U.S. authorities shall notify responsible representatives within 72 hours of the arrest or detention of one of their nationals.

[2] When Taiwan nationals (who carry "Republic of China" passports) are detained, notification should be made to the nearest office of the Taiwan Economic and Cultural Representative's Office, the unofficial entity representing Taiwan's interests in the United States.

[3] British dependencies are also covered by this agreement. They are: Anguilla, British Virgin Islands, Hong Kong, Bermuda, Montserrat, and the Turks and Caicos Islands. Their residents carry British passports.

[4] All U.S.S.R. successor states are covered by this agreement. They are: Armenia, Azerbaijan, Belarus, Georgia, Kazakhstan, Kyrgyzstan, Moldova, Russian Federation, Tajikistan, Turkmenistan, Ukraine, and Uzbekistan.

alien is an inmate of a public or private institution at the time of the commencement of the removal proceedings, expenses for the maintenance of the alien shall not be incurred by the Government until he or she is taken into physical custody by the Service.

§ 1236.3 Detention and release of juveniles.

(a) *Juveniles.* A juvenile is defined as an alien under the age of 18 years.

(b) *Release.* Juveniles for whom bond has been posted, for whom parole has been authorized, or who have been ordered released on recognizance, shall be released pursuant to the following guidelines:

(1) Juveniles shall be released, in order of preference, to:

(i) A parent;

(ii) Legal guardian; or

(iii) An adult relative (brother, sister, aunt, uncle, grandparent) who is not presently in Service detention, unless a determination is made that the detention of such juvenile is required to secure his or her timely appearance before the Service or the Immigration Court or to ensure the juvenile's safety or that of others. In cases where the parent, legal guardian, or adult relative resides at a location distant from where the juvenile is detained, he or she may secure release at a Service office located near the parent, legal guardian, or adult relative.

(2) If an individual specified in paragraphs (b)(1)(i) through (iii) of this section cannot be located to accept custody of a juvenile, and the juvenile has identified a parent, legal guardian, or adult relative in Service detention, simultaneous release of the juvenile and the parent, legal guardian, or adult relative shall be evaluated on a discretionary case-by-case basis.

(3) In cases where the parent or legal guardian is in Service detention or outside the United States, the juvenile may be released to such person as is designated by the parent or legal guardian in a sworn affidavit, executed before an immigration officer or consular officer, as capable and willing to care for the juvenile's well-being. Such person must execute an agreement to care for the juvenile and to ensure the juvenile's presence at all future proceedings before the Service or an immigration judge.

(4) In unusual and compelling circumstances and in the discretion of the Director of the Office of Juvenile Affairs, a juvenile may be released to an adult, other than those identified in paragraphs (b)(1)(i) through (b)(1)(iii) of this section, who executes an agreement to care for the juvenile's well-being and to ensure the juvenile's presence at all future proceedings before the Service or an immigration judge.

(c) *Juvenile coordinator.* The case of a juvenile for whom detention is determined to be necessary should be referred to the "Juvenile Coordinator," whose responsibilities should include, but not be limited to, finding suitable placement of the juvenile in a facility designated for the occupancy of juveniles. These may include juvenile facilities contracted by the Service, state or local juvenile facilities, or other appropriate agencies authorized to accommodate juveniles by the laws of the state or locality.

(d) *Detention.* In the case of a juvenile for whom detention is determined to be necessary, for such interim period of time as is required to locate suitable placement for the juvenile, whether such placement is under paragraph (b) or (c) of this section, the juvenile may be temporarily held by Service authorities or placed in any Service detention facility having separate accommodations for juveniles.

(e) *Refusal of release.* If a parent of a juvenile detained by the Service can be located, and is otherwise suitable to receive custody of the juvenile, and the juvenile indicates a refusal to be released to his or her parent, the parent(s) shall be notified of the juvenile's refusal to be released to the parent(s), and they shall be afforded the opportunity to present their views to the district director, chief patrol agent, Director of the Office of Juvenile Affairs or immigration judge before a custody determination is made.

(f) *Notice to parent of application for relief.* If a juvenile seeks release from detention, voluntary departure, parole, or any form of relief from removal, where it appears that the grant of such relief may effectively terminate some interest inherent in the parent-child relationship and/or the juvenile's rights and interests are adverse with those of the parent, and the parent is presently residing in the United States, the parent shall be given notice of the juvenile's application for relief, and shall be afforded an opportunity to present his or her views and assert his or her interest to the district director, Director of the Office of Juvenile Affairs or immigration judge before a determination is made as to the merits of the request for relief.

(g) *Voluntary departure.* Each juvenile, apprehended in the immediate vicinity of the border, who resides permanently in Mexico or Canada, shall be informed, prior to presentation of the voluntary departure form or being allowed to withdraw his or her application for admission, that he or she may make a telephone call to a parent, close relative, a friend, or to an organization found on the free legal services list. A juvenile who does not reside in Mexico or Canada who is apprehended shall be provided access to a telephone and must in fact communicate either with a parent, adult relative, friend, or with an organization found on the free legal services list prior to presentation of the voluntary departure form. If such juvenile, of his or her own volition, asks to contact a consular officer, and does in fact make such contact, the requirements of this section are satisfied.

(h) *Notice and request for disposition.* When a juvenile alien is apprehended, he or she must be given a Form I–770, Notice of Rights and Disposition. If the juvenile is less than 14 years of age or unable to understand the notice, the notice shall be read and explained to the juvenile in a language he or she understands. In the event a juvenile who has requested a hearing pursuant to the notice subsequently decides to accept voluntary departure or is allowed to withdraw his or her application for admission, a new Form I–770 shall be given to, and signed by the juvenile.

[62 FR 10360, Mar. 6, 1997, as amended at 67 FR 39258, June 7, 2002]

§ 1236.4 Removal of S–5, S–6, and S–7 nonimmigrants.

(a) *Condition of classification.* As a condition of classification and continued stay in classification pursuant to section 101(a)(15)(S) of the Act, nonimmigrants in S classification must have executed Form I–854, Part B, Inter-agency Alien Witness and Informant Record, certifying that they have knowingly waived their right to a removal hearing and right to contest, other than on the basis of an application for withholding of deportation or removal, any removal action, including detention pending deportation or removal, instituted before lawful permanent resident status is obtained.

(b) *Determination of deportability.* (1) A determination to remove a deportable alien classified pursuant to section 101(a)(15)(S) of the Act shall be made by the district director having jurisdiction over the place where the alien is located.

(2) A determination to remove such a deportable alien shall be based on one or more of the grounds of deportability listed in section 237 of the Act based on conduct committed after, or conduct or a condition not disclosed to the Service prior to, the alien's classification as an S nonimmigrant under section 101(a)(15)(S) of the Act, or for a violation of, or failure to adhere to, the particular terms and conditions of status in S nonimmigrant classification.

(c) *Removal procedures.* (1) A district director who determines to remove an alien witness or informant in S nonimmigrant classification shall notify the Commissioner, the Assistant Attorney General, Criminal Division, and the relevant law enforcement agency in writing to that effect. The Assistant Attorney General, Criminal Division, shall concur in or object to that decision. Unless the Assistant Attorney General, Criminal Division, objects within 7 days, he or she shall be deemed to have concurred in the decision. In the event of an objection by the Assistant Attorney General, Criminal Division, the matter will be expeditiously referred to the Deputy Attorney General for a final resolution. In no circumstances shall the alien or the relevant law enforcement agency have a right of appeal from any decision to remove.

(2) A district director who has provided notice as set forth in paragraph (c)(1) of this section and who has been advised by the Commissioner that the Assistant Attorney General, Criminal Division, has not objected shall issue a Warrant of Removal. The alien shall immediately be arrested and taken into custody by the district director initiating the removal. An alien classified under the provisions of section 101(a)(15)(S) of the Act who is determined, pursuant to a warrant issued by a district director, to be deportable from the United States shall be removed from the United States to his or her country of nationality or last residence. The agency that requested the alien's presence in the United States shall ensure departure from the United States and so inform the district director in whose jurisdiction the alien has last resided. The district director, if necessary, shall oversee the alien's departure from the United States and, in any event, shall notify the Commissioner of the alien's departure.

(d) *Withholding of removal*. An alien classified pursuant to section 101(a)(15)(S) of the Act who applies for withholding of removal shall have 10 days from the date the Warrant of Removal is served upon the alien to file an application for such relief with the district director initiating the removal order. The procedures contained in §§ 1208.2 and 1208.16 of this chapter shall apply to such an alien who applies for withholding of removal.

(e) *Inadmissibility*. An alien who applies for admission under the provisions of section 101(a)(15)(S) of the Act who is determined by an immigration officer not to be eligible for admission under that section or to be inadmissible to the United States under one or more of the grounds of inadmissibility listed in section 212 of the Act and which have not been previously waived by the Commissioner will be taken into custody. The district director having jurisdiction over the port-of-entry shall follow the notification procedures specified in paragraph (c)(1) of this section. A district director who has provided such notice and who has been advised by the Commissioner that the Assistant Attorney General, Criminal Division, has not objected shall remove the alien without further hearing. An alien may not contest such removal, other than by applying for withholding of removal.

§ 1236.5 Fingerprints and photographs.

Every alien 14 years of age or older against whom proceedings based on deportability under section 237 of the Act are commenced under this part by service of a notice to appear shall be fingerprinted and photographed. Such fingerprints and photographs shall be made available to Federal, State, and local law enforcement agencies upon request to the district director or chief patrol agent having jurisdiction over the alien's record. Any such alien, regardless of his or her age, shall be photographed and/or fingerprinted if required by any immigration officer authorized to issue a notice to appear. Every alien 14 years of age or older who is found to be inadmissible to the United States and ordered removed by an immigration judge shall be fingerprinted, unless during the preceding year he or she has been fingerprinted at an American consular office.

§ 1236.6 Information regarding detainees.

No person, including any state or local government entity or any privately operated detention facility, that houses, maintains, provides services to, or otherwise holds any detainee on behalf of the Service (whether by contract or otherwise), and no other person who by virtue of any official or contractual relationship with such person obtains information relating to any detainee, shall disclose or otherwise permit to be made public the name of, or other information relating to, such detainee. Such information shall be under the control of the Service and shall be subject to public disclosure only pursuant to the provisions of applicable federal laws, regulations and executive orders. Insofar as any documents or other records contain such information, such documents shall not be public records. This section applies to all persons and information identified or described in it, regardless of when such persons obtained such information, and applies to all requests for public disclosure of such information, including requests that are the subject of proceedings pending as of April 17, 2002.

[67 FR 19511, Apr. 22, 2002]

§§ 1236.7–1236.9 [Reserved]

PART 1238—EXPEDITED REMOVAL OF AGGRAVATED FELONS

AUTHORITY: 8 U.S.C. 1228; 8 CFR part 2.

§ 1238.1 Proceedings under section 238(b) of the Act.

(a) *Definitions.* As used in this part the term:

Deciding Service officer means a district director, chief patrol agent, or another immigration officer designated by a district director, chief patrol agent, the Deputy Executive Associate Commissioner for Detention and Removal, or the Director of the Office of Juvenile Affairs, so long as that person is not the same person as the Issuing Service Officer.

Issuing Service officer means any Service officer listed in § 1239.1 of this chapter as authorized to issue notices to appear.

(b) *Preliminary consideration and Notice of Intent to Issue a Final Administrative Deportation Order; commencement of proceedings*—(1) *Basis of Service charge.* An issuing Service officer shall cause to be served upon an alien a Form I–851, Notice of Intent to Issue a Final Administrative Deportation Order (Notice of Intent), if the officer is satisfied that there is sufficient evidence, based upon questioning of the alien by an immigration officer and upon any other evidence obtained, to support a finding that the individual:

(i) Is an alien;

(ii) Has not been lawfully admitted for permanent residence, or has conditional permanent resident status under section 216 of the Act;

(iii) Has been convicted (as defined in section 101(a)(48) of the Act and as demonstrated by any of the documents or records listed in § 1003.41 of this chapter) of an aggravated felony and such conviction has become final; and

(iv) Is deportable under section 237(a)(2)(A)(iii) of the Act, including an alien who has neither been admitted nor paroled, but who is conclusively presumed deportable under section 237(a)(2)(A)(iii) by operation of section 238(c) of the Act (''Presumption of Deportability'').

(2) *Notice.* (i) Removal proceedings under section 238(b) of the Act shall commence upon personal service of the Notice of Intent upon the alien, as prescribed by §§ 103.5a(a)(2) and 103.5a(c)(2) of 8 CFR chapter I. The Notice of Intent shall set forth the preliminary determinations and inform the alien of the Service's intent to issue a Form I–851A, Final Administrative Removal Order, without a hearing before an immigration judge. The Notice of Intent shall constitute the charging document. The Notice of Intent shall include allegations of fact and conclusions of law. It shall advise that the alien: has the privilege of being represented, at no expense to the government, by counsel of the alien's choosing, as long as counsel is authorized to practice in removal proceedings; may request withholding of removal to a particular country if he or she fears persecution or torture in that country; may inspect the evidence supporting the Notice of Intent; may rebut the charges within 10 calendar days after service of such Notice (or 13 calendar days if service of the Notice was by mail).

(ii) The Notice of Intent also shall advise the alien that he or she may designate in writing, within the rebuttal period, the country to which he or she chooses to be deported in accordance with section 241 of the Act, in the event that a Final Administrative Removal Order is issued, and that the Service will honor such designation only to the extent permitted under the terms, limitations, and conditions of section 241 of the Act.

(iii) The Service must determine that the person served with the Notice of Intent is the person named on the notice.

(iv) The Service shall provide the alien with a list of available free legal services programs qualified under 8

CFR part 1003 and organizations recognized pursuant to 8 CFR part 1292, located within the district or sector where the Notice of Intent is issued.

(v) The Service must either provide the alien with a written translation of the Notice of Intent or explain the contents of the Notice of Intent to the alien in the alien's native language or in a language that the alien understands.

(c) *Alien's response*—(1) *Time for response.* The alien will have 10 calendar days from service of the Notice of Intent or 13 calendar days if service is by mail, to file a response to the Notice of Intent. In the response, the alien may: designate his or her choice of country for removal; submit a written response rebutting the allegations supporting the charge and/or requesting the opportunity to review the Government's evidence; and/or submit a statement indicating an intention to request withholding of removal under 8 CFR 1208.16 of this chapter, and/or request in writing an extension of time for response, stating the specific reasons why such an extension is necessary.

(2) *Nature of rebuttal or request to review evidence.* (i) If an alien chooses to rebut the allegations contained in the Notice of Intent, the alien's written response must indicate which finding(s) are being challenged and should be accompanied by affidavit(s), documentary information, or other specific evidence supporting the challenge.

(ii) If an alien's written response requests the opportunity to review the Government's evidence, the Service shall serve the alien with a copy of the evidence in the record of proceeding upon which the Service is relying to support the charge. The alien may, within 10 calendar days following service of the Government's evidence (13 calendar days if service is by mail), furnish a final response in accordance with paragraph (c)(1) of this section. If the alien's final response is a rebuttal of the allegations, such a final response should be accompanied by affidavit(s), documentary information, or other specific evidence supporting the challenge.

(d) *Determination by deciding Service officer*—(1) *No response submitted or concession of deportability.* If the deciding Service officer does not receive a timely response and the evidence in the record of proceeding establishes deportability by clear, convincing, and unequivocal evidence, or if the alien concedes deportability, then the deciding Service officer shall issue and cause to be served upon the alien a Final Administrative Removal Order that states the reasons for the deportation decision. The alien may, in writing, waive the 14-day waiting period before execution of the final order of removal provided in a paragraph (f) of this section.

(2) *Response submitted*—(i) *Insufficient rebuttal; no genuine issue of material fact.* If the alien timely submits a rebuttal to the allegations, but the deciding Service officer finds that deportability is established by clear, convincing, and unequivocal evidence in the record of proceeding, the deciding Service officer shall issue and cause to be served upon the alien a Final Administrative Removal Order that states the reasons for the decision of deportability.

(ii) *Additional evidence required.* (A) If the deciding Service officer finds that the record of proceeding, including the alien's timely rebuttal, raises a genuine issue of material fact regarding the preliminary findings, the deciding Service officer may either obtain additional evidence from any source, including the alien, or cause to be issued a notice to appear to initiate removal proceedings under section 240 of the Act. The deciding Service officer may also obtain additional evidence from any source, including the alien, if the deciding Service officer deems that such additional evidence may aid the officer in the rendering of a decision.

(B) If the deciding Service officer considers additional evidence from a source other than the alien, that evidence shall be made a part of the record of proceeding, and shall be provided to the alien. If the alien elects to submit a response to such additional evidence, such response must be filed with the Service within 10 calendar days of service of the additional evidence (or 13 calendar days if service is by mail). If the deciding Service officer finds, after considering all additional evidence, that deportability is established by clear, convincing, and unequivocal evidence in the record of proceeding, the deciding Service officer shall issue and cause to be served upon the alien a Final Administrative Removal Order that states the reasons for the decision of deportability.

(iii) *Conversion to proceedings under section 240 of the Act.* If the deciding Service officer finds that the alien is not amenable to removal under section 238 of the Act, the deciding Service officer shall terminate the expedited proceedings under section 238 of the Act and shall, where appropriate, cause to be issued a notice to appear for the purpose of initiating removal proceedings before an immigration judge under section 240 of the Act.

(3) *Termination of proceedings by deciding Service officer.* Only the deciding Service officer may terminate proceedings under section 238 of the Act, in accordance with this section.

(e) *Proceedings commenced under section 240 of the Act.* In any proceeding commenced under section 240 of the Act which is based on deportability under section 237 of the Act, if it appears that the respondent alien is subject to removal pursuant to section 238 of the Act, the immigration judge may, upon the Service's request, terminate the case and, upon such termination, the Service may commence administrative proceedings under section 238 of the Act. However, in the absence of any such request, the immigration judge shall complete the proceeding commenced under section 240 of the Act.

(f) *Executing final removal order of deciding Service officer*—(1) *Time of execution.* Upon the issuance of a Final Administrative Removal Order, the Service shall issue a Warrant of Removal in accordance with § 1241.2 of this chapter; such warrant shall be executed no sooner than 14 calendar days after the date the Final Administrative Removal Order is issued, unless the alien knowingly, voluntarily, and in writing waives the 14-day period.

(2) *Country to which alien is to be removed.* The deciding Service officer shall designate the country of removal in the manner prescribed by section 241 of the Act.

(3) *Withholding of removal.* If the alien has requested withholding of removal under § 1208.16 of this chapter, the deciding officer shall, upon issuance of a Final Administrative Removal Order, immediately refer the alien's case to an asylum officer to conduct a reasonable fear determination in accordance with § 1208.31 of this chapter.

(g) *Arrest and detention.* At the time of issuance of a Notice of Intent or at any time thereafter and up to the time the alien becomes the subject of a Warrant of Removal, the alien may be arrested and taken into custody under the authority of a Warrant of Arrest issued by an officer listed in § 287.5(e)(2) of 8 CFR chapter I. The decision of the Service concerning custody or bond shall not be administratively appealable during proceedings initiated under section 238 of the Act and this part.

(h) *Record of proceeding.* The Service shall maintain a record of proceeding for judicial review of the Final Administrative Removal Order sought by any petition for review. The record of proceeding shall include, but not necessarily be limited to: the charging document (Notice of Intent); the Final Administrative Removal Order (including any supplemental memorandum of decision); the alien's response, if any; all evidence in support of the charge; and any admissible evidence, briefs, or documents submitted by either party respecting deportability. The executed duplicate of the Notice of Intent in the record of proceedings shall be retained as evidence that the individual upon whom the notice for the proceeding was served was, in fact, the alien named in the notice.

[62 FR 10365, Mar. 6, 1997, as amended at 64 FR 8494, Feb. 19, 1999; 67 FR 39258, June 7, 2002. Duplicated from § 238.1 at 68 FR 9838, Feb. 28, 2003, as amended at 68 FR 10355, Mar. 3, 2003]

PART 1239—INITIATION OF REMOVAL PROCEEDINGS

Sec.

AUTHORITY: 8 U.S.C. 1103, 1221, 1229.

SOURCE: 62 FR 10366, Mar. 6, 1997, unless otherwise noted. Duplicated from part 239 at 68 FR 9838, Feb. 28, 2003.

EDITORIAL NOTE: Nomenclature changes to part 1239 appear at 68 FR 9846, Feb. 28, 2003, and at 68 FR 10355, Mar. 3, 2003.

§ 1239.1 Notice to appear.

(a) *Commencement.* Every removal proceeding conducted under section 240 of the Act (8 U.S.C. 1229a) to determine the deportability or inadmissibility of an alien is commenced by the filing of a notice to appear with the immigration court. For provisions relating to the issuance of a notice to appear by an immigration officer, or supervisor thereof, see 8 CFR 239.1(a).

(b) *Service of notice to appear.* Service of the notice to appear shall be in accordance with section 239 of the Act.

[62 FR 10366, Mar. 6, 1997, as amended at 67 FR 39258, June 7, 2002; 69 FR 44907, July 28, 2004]

§ 1239.2 Cancellation of notice to appear.

(a) *Prior to commencement of proceedings.* For provisions relating to the authority of an immigration officer to cancel a notice to appear prior to the vesting of jurisdiction with the immigration judge, see 8 CFR 239.2(a) and (b).

(b) [Reserved]

(c) *Motion to dismiss.* After commencement of proceedings pursuant to 8 CFR 1003.14, government counsel or an officer enumerated in 8 CFR 239.1(a) may move for dismissal of the matter on the grounds set out under 8 CFR 239.2(a). Dismissal of the matter shall be without prejudice to the alien or the Department of Homeland Security.

(d) *Motion for remand.* After commencement of the hearing, government counsel or an officer enumerated in 8 CFR 239.1(a) may move for remand of the matter to the Department of Homeland Security on the ground that the foreign relations of the United States are involved and require further consideration. Remand of the matter shall be without prejudice to the alien or the Department of Homeland Security.

(e) *Warrant of arrest.* When a notice to appear is canceled or proceedings are terminated under this section any outstanding warrant of arrest is canceled.

(f) *Termination of removal proceedings by immigration judge.* An immigration judge may terminate removal proceedings to permit the alien to proceed to a final hearing on a pending application or petition for naturalization when the alien has established prima facie eligibility for naturalization and the matter involves exceptionally appealing or humanitarian factors; in every other case, the removal hearing shall be completed as promptly as possible notwithstanding the pendency of an application for naturalization during any state of the proceedings.

[62 FR 10366, Mar. 6, 1997. Duplicated from part 239 at 68 FR 9838, Feb. 28, 2003, as amended at 69 FR 44907, July 28, 2004]

§ 1239.3 Effect of filing notice to appear.

The filing of a notice to appear shall have no effect in determining periods of unlawful presence as defined in section 212(a)(9)(B) of the Act.

PART 1240—PROCEEDINGS TO DETERMINE REMOVABILITY OF ALIENS IN THE UNITED STATES

Subpart A—Removal Proceedings

Sec.

AUTHORITY: 8 U.S.C. 1103, 1158, 1182, 1186a, 1186b, 1225, 1226, 1227, 1228, 1229a, 1229b, 1229c, 1252 note, 1361, 1362; secs. 202 and 203, Pub. L. 105–100 (111 Stat. 2160, 2193); sec. 902, Pub. L. 105–277 (112 Stat. 2681).

SOURCE: 62 FR 10367, Mar. 6, 1997, unless otherwise noted. Redesignated in part and duplicated in part from part 240 at 68 FR 9838, 9840, Feb. 28, 2003.

EDITORIAL NOTE: Nomenclature changes to part 1240 appear at 68 FR 9846, Feb. 28, 2003, and at 68 FR 10355, Mar. 3, 2003.

Subpart A—Removal Proceedings

§ 1240.1 Immigration judges.

(a) *Authority*. (1) In any removal proceeding pursuant to section 240 of the Act, the immigration judge shall have the authority to:

(i) Determine removability pursuant to section 240(a)(1) of the Act; to make decisions, including orders of removal as provided by section 240(c)(1)(A) of the Act;

(ii) To determine applications under sections 208, 212(a)(2)(F), 212(a)(6)(F)(ii), 212(a)(9)(B)(v), 212(d)(11), 212(d)(12), 212(g), 212(h), 212(i), 212(k), 237(a)(1)(E)(iii), 237(a)(1)(H), 237(a)(3)(C)(ii), 240A(a) and (b), 240B, 245, and 249 of the Act, section 202 of Pub. L. 105–100, section 902 of Pub. L. 105–277, and former section 212(c) of the Act (as it existed prior to April 1, 1997);

(iii) To order withholding of removal pursuant to section 241(b)(3) of the Act and pursuant to the Convention Against Torture; and

(iv) To take any other action consistent with applicable law and regulations as may be appropriate.

(2) An immigration judge may certify his or her decision in any case under section 240 of the Act to the Board of Immigration Appeals when it involves an unusually complex or novel question of law or fact. Nothing contained in this part shall be construed to diminish the authority conferred on immigration judges under sections 101(b)(4) and 103 of the Act.

(b) *Withdrawal and substitution of immigration judges.* The immigration judge assigned to conduct the hearing shall at any time withdraw if he or she deems himself or herself disqualified. If an immigration judge becomes unavailable to complete his or her duties, another immigration judge may be assigned to complete the case. The new immigration judge shall familiarize himself or herself with the record in the case and shall state for the record that he or she has done so.

(c) *Conduct of hearing.* The immigration judge shall receive and consider material and relevant evidence, rule upon objections, and otherwise regulate the course of the hearing.

(d) *Withdrawal of application for admission.* An immigration judge may allow only an arriving alien to withdraw an application for admission. Once the issue of inadmissibility has been resolved, permission to withdraw an application for admission should ordinarily be granted only with the concurrence of the Service. An immigration judge shall not allow an alien to withdraw an application for admission unless the alien, in addition to demonstrating that he or she possesses both the intent and the means to depart immediately from the United States, establishes that factors directly relating to the issue of inadmissibility indicate that the granting of the withdrawal would be in the interest of justice. During the pendency of an appeal from the order of removal, permission to withdraw an application for admission must be obtained from the immigration judge or the Board.

[62 FR 10367, Mar. 6, 1997; 62 FR 15363, Apr. 1, 1997, as amended at 63 FR 27829, May 21, 1998; 64 FR 8495, Feb. 19, 1999; 64 FR 25766, May 12, 1999; 69 FR 57835, Sept. 28, 2004; 72 FR 53678, Sept. 20, 2007]

§ 1240.2 Service counsel.

(a) *Authority.* Service counsel shall present on behalf of the government evidence material to the issues of deportability or inadmissibility and any other issues that may require disposition by the immigration judge. The duties of the Service counsel include, but are not limited to, the presentation of evidence and the interrogation, examination, and cross-examination of the respondent or other witnesses. Nothing contained in this subpart diminishes the authority of an immigration judge to conduct proceedings under this part. The Service counsel is authorized to appeal from a decision of the immigration judge pursuant to § 1003.38 of this chapter and to move for reopening or reconsideration pursuant to § 1003.23 of this chapter.

(b) *Assignment.* In a removal proceeding, the Service shall assign an attorney to each case within the provisions of § 1240.10(d), and to each case in which an unrepresented respondent is incompetent or is under 18 years of age, and is not accompanied by a guardian, relative, or friend. In a case in which the removal proceeding would result in an order of removal, the Service shall assign an attorney to each case in which a respondent's nationality is in issue. A Service attorney shall be assigned in every case in which the Commissioner approves the submission of non-record information under § 1240.11(a)(3). In his or her discretion, whenever he or she deems such assignment necessary or advantageous, the General Counsel may assign a Service attorney to any other case at any stage of the proceeding.

§ 1240.3 Representation by counsel.

The respondent may be represented at the hearing by an attorney or other representative qualified under 8 CFR part 1292.

§ 1240.4 Incompetent respondents.

When it is impracticable for the respondent to be present at the hearing because of mental incompetency, the attorney, legal representative, legal guardian, near relative, or friend who was served with a copy of the notice to appear shall be permitted to appear on behalf of the respondent. If such a person cannot reasonably be found or fails or refuses to appear, the custodian of the respondent shall be requested to appear on behalf of the respondent.

§ 1240.5 Interpreter.

Any person acting as an interpreter in a hearing before an immigration judge under this part shall be sworn to interpret and translate accurately, unless the interpreter is an employee of the United States Government, in which event no such oath shall be required.

§ 1240.6 Postponement and adjournment of hearing.

After the commencement of the hearing, the immigration judge may grant a reasonable adjournment either at his or her own instance or, for good cause shown, upon application by the respondent or the Service.

§ 1240.7 Evidence in removal proceedings under section 240 of the Act.

(a) *Use of prior statements.* The immigration judge may receive in evidence any oral or written statement that is material and relevant to any issue in the case previously made by the respondent or any other person during any investigation, examination, hearing, or trial.

(b) *Testimony.* Testimony of witnesses appearing at the hearing shall be under oath or affirmation administered by the immigration judge.

(c) *Depositions.* The immigration judge may order the taking of depositions pursuant to § 1003.35 of this chapter.

§ 1240.8 Burdens of proof in removal proceedings.

(a) *Deportable aliens.* A respondent charged with deportability shall be found to be removable if the Service proves by clear and convincing evidence that the respondent is deportable as charged.

(b) *Arriving aliens.* In proceedings commenced upon a respondent's arrival in the Untied States or after the revocation or expiration of parole, the respondent must prove that he or she is clearly and beyond a doubt entitled to be admitted to the United States and is not inadmissible as charged.

(c) *Aliens present in the United States without being admitted or paroled.* In the case of a respondent charged as being in the United States without being admitted or paroled, the Service must first establish the alienage of the respondent. Once alienage has been established, unless the respondent demonstrates by clear and convincing evidence that he or she is lawfully in the United States pursuant to a prior admission, the respondent must prove that he or she is clearly and beyond a doubt entitled to be admitted to the United States and is not inadmissible as charged.

(d) *Relief from removal.* The respondent shall have the burden of establishing that he or she is eligible for any requested benefit or privilege and that it should be granted in the exercise of discretion. If the evidence indicates that one or more of the grounds for mandatory denial of the application for relief may apply, the alien shall have the burden of proving by a preponderance of the evidence that such grounds do not apply.

§ 1240.9 Contents of record.

The hearing before the immigration judge, including the testimony, exhibits, applications, proffers, and requests, the immigration judge's decision, and all written orders, motions, appeals, briefs, and other papers filed in the proceedings shall constitute the record in the case. The hearing shall be recorded verbatim except for statements made off the record with the permission of the immigration judge. In his or her discretion, the immigration judge may exclude from the record any arguments made in connection with motions, applications, requests, or objections, but in such event the person affected may submit a brief.

§ 1240.10 Hearing.

(a) *Opening.* In a removal proceeding, the immigration judge shall:

(1) Advise the respondent of his or her right to representation, at no expense to the government, by counsel of his or her own choice authorized to practice in the proceedings and require the respondent to state then and there whether he or she desires representation;

(2) Advise the respondent of the availability of pro bono legal services for the immigration court location at which the hearing will take place, and ascertain that the respondent has received a list of such pro bono legal service providers.

(3) Ascertain that the respondent has received a copy of appeal rights.

(4) Advise the respondent that he or she will have a reasonable opportunity to examine and object to the evidence against him or her, to present evidence in his or her own behalf and to cross-examine witnesses presented by the government (but the respondent shall not be entitled to examine such national security information as the government may proffer in opposition to the respondent's admission to the United States or to an application by the respondent for discretionary relief);

(5) Place the respondent under oath;

(6) Read the factual allegations and the charges in the notice to appear to the respondent and explain them in non-technical language; and

(7) Enter the notice to appear as an exhibit in the Record of Proceeding.

(b) *Public access to hearings.* Removal hearings shall be open to the public, except that the immigration judge may, in his or her discretion, close proceedings as provided in § 1003.27 of this chapter.

(c) *Pleading by respondent.* The immigration judge shall require the respondent to plead to the notice to appear by stating whether he or she admits or denies the factual allegations and his or her removability under the charges contained therein. If the respondent admits the factual allegations and admits his or her removability under the charges and the immigration judge is satisfied that no issues of law or fact remain, the immigration judge may determine that removability as charged has been established by the admissions of the respondent. The immigration judge shall not accept an admission of removability from an unrepresented respondent who is incompetent or under the age of 18 and is not accompanied by an attorney or legal representative, a near relative, legal guardian, or friend; nor from an officer of an institution in which a respondent is an inmate or patient. When, pursuant to this paragraph, the immigration judge does not accept an admission of removability, he or she shall direct a hearing on the issues.

(d) *Issues of removability.* When removability is not determined under the provisions of paragraph (c) of this section, the immigration judge shall request the assignment of an Service counsel, and shall receive evidence as to any unresolved issues, except that no further evidence need be received as to any facts admitted during the pleading. The alien shall provide a court certified copy of a Judicial Recommendation Against Deportation (JRAD) to the immigration judge when such recommendation will be the basis of denying any charge(s) brought by the Service in the proceedings against the alien. No JRAD is effective against a charge of deportability under former section 241(a)(11) of the Act or if the JRAD was granted on or after November 29, 1990.

(e) *Additional charges in removal hearings.* At any time during the proceeding, additional or substituted charges of inadmissibility and/or deportability and/or factual allegations may be lodged by the Service in writing. The alien in removal proceedings shall be served with a copy of these additional charges and allegations. The immigration judge shall read the additional factual allegations and charges to the alien and explain them to him or her. The immigration judge shall advise the alien, if he or she is not represented by counsel, that the alien may be so represented, and that he or she may be given a reasonable continuance to respond to the additional factual allegations and charges. Thereafter, the provision of § 1240.6(b) relating to pleading shall apply to the additional factual allegations and charges.

(f) *Country of removal.* With respect to an arriving alien covered by section 241(b)(1) of the Act, the country, or countries in the alternative, to which the alien may be removed will be determined pursuant to section 241(b)(1) of the Act. In any other case, the immigration judge shall notify the respondent that if he or she is finally ordered removed, the country of removal will in the first instance be the country designated by the respondent, except as otherwise provided under section 241(b)(2) of the Act, and shall afford him or her an opportunity then and there to make such designation. The immigration judge shall also identify for the record a country, or countries in the alternative, to which the alien's removal may be made pursuant to section 241(b)(2) of the Act if the country of the alien's designation will not accept him or her into its territory, or fails to furnish timely notice of acceptance, or if the alien declines to designate a country. In considering alternative countries of removal, acceptance or the existence of a functioning government is not required with respect to an alternative country described in section 241(b)(1)(C)(i)–(iii) of the Act or a removal country described in section 241(b)(2)(E)(i)–(iv) of the Act. *See* 8 CFR 241.15.

[62 FR 10367, Mar. 6, 1997. Redesignated in part and duplicated in part from part 240 at 68 FR 9838, 9840, Feb. 28, 2003; 70 FR 674, Jan. 5, 2005; 80 FR 59513, Oct. 1, 2015]

§ 1240.11 Ancillary matters, applications.

(a) *Creation of the status of an alien lawfully admitted for permanent residence.* (1) In a removal proceeding, an alien may apply to the immigration judge for cancellation of removal under section 240A of the Act, adjustment of status under section 1 of the Act of November 2, 1966 (as modified by section 606 of Pub. L. 104–208), section 101 or 104 of the Act of October 28, 1977, section 202 of Pub. L. 105–100, or section 902 of Pub. L. 105–277, or for the creation of a record of lawful admission for permanent residence under section 249 of the Act. The application shall be subject to the requirements of § 1240.20, and 8 CFR parts 1245 and 1249. The approval of any application made to the immigration judge under section 245 of the Act by an alien spouse (as defined in section 216(g)(1) of the Act) or by an alien entrepreneur (as defined in section 216A(f)(1) of the Act) shall result in the alien's obtaining the status of lawful permanent resident on a conditional basis in accordance with the provisions of section 216 or 216A of the Act, whichever is applicable. However, the Petition to Remove the Conditions on Residence required by section 216(c) of the Act, or the Petition by Entrepreneur to Remove Conditions required by section 216A(c) of the Act shall be made to the director in accordance with 8 CFR part 1216.

(2) In conjunction with any application for creation of status of an alien lawfully admitted for permanent residence made to an immigration judge, if the alien is inadmissible under any provision of section 212(a) of the Act, and believes that he or she meets the eligibility requirements for a waiver of the ground of inadmissibility, he or she may apply to the immigration judge for such waiver. The immigration judge shall inform the alien of his or her apparent eligibility to apply for any of the benefits enumerated in this chapter and shall afford the alien an opportunity to make application during the hearing, in accordance with the provisions of § 1240.8(d). In a relevant case, the immigration judge may adjudicate the sufficiency of an Affidavit of Support Under Section 213A (Form I–864), executed on behalf of an applicant for admission or for adjustment of status, in accordance with the provisions of section 213A of the Act and 8 CFR part 213a.

(3) In exercising discretionary power when considering an application for status as a permanent resident under this chapter, the immigration judge may consider and base the decision on information not contained in the record and not made available for inspection by the alien, provided the Commissioner has determined that such information is relevant and is

classified under the applicable Executive Order as requiring protection from unauthorized disclosure in the interest of national security. Whenever the immigration judge believes that he or she can do so while safeguarding both the information and its source, the immigration judge should inform the alien of the general nature of the information in order that the alien may have an opportunity to offer opposing evidence. A decision based in whole or in part on such classified information shall state that the information is material to the decision.

(b) *Voluntary departure.* The alien may apply to the immigration judge for voluntary departure in lieu of removal pursuant to section 240B of the Act and subpart C of this part. The immigration judge shall advise the alien of the consequences of filing a post-decision motion to reopen or reconsider prior to the expiration of the time specified by the immigration judge for the alien to depart voluntarily.

(c) *Applications for asylum and withholding of removal.* (1) If the alien expresses fear of persecution or harm upon return to any of the countries to which the alien might be removed pursuant to § 1240.10(f), and the alien has not previously filed an application for asylum or withholding of removal that has been referred to the immigration judge by an asylum officer in accordance with § 1208.14 of this chapter, the immigration judge shall:

(i) Advise the alien that he or she may apply for asylum in the United States or withholding of removal to those countries;

(ii) Make available the appropriate application forms; and

(iii) Advise the alien of the privilege of being represented by counsel at no expense to the government and of the consequences, pursuant to section 208(d)(6) of the Act, of knowingly filing a frivolous application for asylum. The immigration judge shall provide to the alien a list of persons who have indicated their availability to represent aliens in asylum proceedings on a *pro bono* basis.

(2) An application for asylum or withholding of removal must be filed with the Immigration Court, pursuant to § 1208.4(b) of this chapter. Upon receipt of an application, the Immigration Court may forward a copy to the Department of State pursuant to § 1208.11 of this chapter and shall calendar the case for a hearing. The reply, if any, from the Department of State, unless classified under an applicable Executive Order, shall be given to both the alien and to DHS counsel and shall be included in the record.

(3) Applications for asylum and withholding of removal so filed will be decided by the immigration judge pursuant to the requirements and standards established in 8 CFR part 1208 of this chapter after an evidentiary hearing to resolve factual issues in dispute. An evidentiary hearing extending beyond issues related to the basis for a mandatory denial of the application pursuant to § 1208.14 or § 1208.16 of this chapter is not necessary once the immigration judge has determined that such a denial is required.

(i) Evidentiary hearings on applications for asylum or withholding of removal will be open to the public unless the alien expressly requests that the hearing be closed pursuant to § 3.27 of this chapter. The immigration judge shall inquire whether the alien requests such closure.

(ii) Nothing in this section is intended to limit the authority of the immigration judge to properly control the scope of any evidentiary hearing.

(iii) During the removal hearing, the alien shall be examined under oath on his or her application and may present evidence and witnesses in his or her own behalf. The alien has the burden of establishing that he or she is a refugee as defined in section 101(a)(42) of the Act pursuant to the standards set forth in § 1208.13 of this chapter.

(iv) Service counsel may call witnesses and present evidence for the record, including information classified under the applicable Executive Order, provided the immigration judge or the Board has determined that such information is relevant to the hearing. When the immigration judge receives such classified information, he or she shall inform the alien. The agency that provides the classified information to the immigration judge may provide an unclassified summary of the information for release to the alien, whenever it determines it can do so consistently with safeguarding both the classified nature of the information and its sources. The summary should be as detailed as possible, in order that the alien may have an opportunity to offer opposing evidence. A decision based in whole or in part on such classified information shall state whether such information is material to the decision.

(4) The decision of an immigration judge to grant or deny asylum or withholding of removal shall be communicated to the alien and to the Service counsel. An adverse decision shall state why asylum or withholding of removal was denied.

(d) *Application for relief under sections 237(a)(1)(H) and 237(a)(1)(E)(iii) of the Act.* The respondent may apply to the immigration judge for relief from removal under sections 237(a)(1)(H) and 237(a)(1)(E)(iii) of the Act.

(e) *General.* An application under this section shall be made only during the hearing and shall not be held to constitute a concession of alienage or deportability in any case in which the respondent does not admit his or her alienage or deportability. However, nothing in this section shall prohibit the Service from using information supplied in an application for asylum or withholding of deportation or removal submitted to the Service on or after January 4, 1995, as the basis for issuance of a charging document or to establish alienage or deportability in a case referred to an immigration judge under § 1208.14(b) of this chapter. The alien shall have the burden of establishing that he or she is eligible for any requested benefit or privilege and that it should be granted in the exercise of discretion. Nothing contained in this section is intended to foreclose the respondent from applying for any benefit or privilege that he or she believes himself or herself eligible to receive in proceedings under this part. Nothing in this section is intended to limit the Attorney General's authority to remove an alien to any country permitted by section 241(b) of the Act.

(f) *Fees.* The alien shall not be required to pay a fee on more than one application within paragraphs (a) and (c) of this section, provided that the minimum fee imposed when more than one application is made shall be determined by the cost of the application with the highest fee. When a motion to reopen or reconsider is made concurrently with an application for relief seeking one of the immigration benefits set forth in paragraphs (a) and (c) of this section, only the fee set forth in § 103.7(b)(1) of 8 CFR chapter I for the motion must accompany the motion and application for relief. If such a motion is granted, the appropriate fee for the application for relief, if any, set forth in 8 CFR 103.7(b)(1), must be paid within the time specified in order to complete the application.

(g) *Safe third country agreement.* (1) The immigration judge has authority to apply section 208(a)(2)(A) of the Act, relating to a determination that an alien may be removed to a safe third country pursuant to a bilateral or multilateral agreement (Agreement), in the case of an alien who is subject to the terms of the Agreement and is placed in proceedings pursuant to section 240 of the Act. In an appropriate case, the immigration judge shall determine whether under the Agreement the alien should be returned to the safe third country, or whether the alien should be permitted to pursue asylum or other protection claims in the United States.

(2) An alien described in paragraph (g)(1) of this section is ineligible to apply for asylum, pursuant to section 208(a)(2)(A) of the Act, unless the immigration judge determines, by preponderance of the evidence, that:

(i) The Agreement does not apply to the alien or does not preclude the alien from applying for asylum in the United States; or

(ii) The alien qualifies for an exception to the Agreement as set forth in paragraph (g)(3) of this section.

(3) The immigration judge shall apply the applicable regulations in deciding whether the alien qualifies for any exception under the Agreement that would permit the United States to exercise authority over the alien's asylum claim. The exceptions under the Agreement are codified at 8 CFR 208.30(e)(6)(iii). The immigration judge shall not review, consider, or decide any issues pertaining to any discretionary determination on whether the

alien should be permitted to pursue an asylum claim in the United States notwithstanding the general terms of the Agreement, as such discretionary public interest determinations are reserved to DHS. However, an alien in removal proceedings who is otherwise ineligible to apply for asylum under the Agreement may apply for asylum if DHS files a written notice in the proceedings before the immigration judge that it has decided in the public interest to allow the alien to pursue claims for asylum or withholding of removal in the United States.

(4) An alien who is found to be ineligible to apply for asylum under section 208(a)(2)(A) of the Act is ineligible to apply for withholding of removal pursuant to section 241(b)(3) of the Act and the Convention against Torture. However, the alien may apply for any other relief from removal for which the alien may be eligible. If an alien who is subject to section 208(a)(2)(A) of the Act is ordered removed, the alien shall be ordered removed to the safe third country in which the alien will be able to pursue his or her claims for asylum or protection against persecution or torture under the laws of that country.

[62 FR 10367, Mar. 6, 1997, as amended at 62 FR 45150, Aug. 26, 1997; 63 FR 27829, May 21, 1998; 64 FR 25766, May 12, 1999; 69 FR 69497, Nov. 29, 2004; 71 FR 35757, June 21, 2006; 73 FR 76937, Dec. 18, 2008; 78 FR 19080, Mar. 29, 2013]

§ 1240.12 Decision of the immigration judge.

(a) *Contents.* The decision of the immigration judge may be oral or written. The decision of the immigration judge shall include a finding as to inadmissibility or deportability. The formal enumeration of findings is not required. The decision shall also contain reasons for granting or denying the request. The decision shall be concluded with the order of the immigration judge.

(b) *Summary decision.* Notwithstanding the provisions of paragraph (a) of this section, in any case where inadmissibility or deportability is determined on the pleadings pursuant to § 1240.10(b) and the respondent does not make an application under § 1240.11, the alien is statutorily ineligible for relief, or the respondent applies for voluntary departure only and the immigration judge grants the application, the immigration judge may enter a summary decision or, if voluntary departure is granted, a summary decision with an alternate order of removal.

(c) *Order of the immigration judge.* The order of the immigration judge shall direct the respondent's removal from the United States, or the termination of the proceedings, or other such disposition of the case as may be appropriate. The immigration judge is authorized to issue orders in the alternative or in combination as he or she may deem necessary.

(d) *Removal.* When a respondent is ordered removed from the United States, the immigration judge shall identify a country, or countries in the alternative, to which the alien's removal may in the first instance be made, pursuant to the provisions of section 241(b) of the Act. In the event that the Department of Homeland Security is unable to remove the alien to the specified or alternative country or countries, the order of the immigration judge does not limit the authority of the Department of Homeland Security to remove the alien to any other country as permitted by section 241(b) of the Act.

[62 FR 10367, Mar. 6, 1997. Redesignated in part and duplicated in part from part 240 at 68 FR 9838, 9840, Feb. 28, 2003; 70 FR 674, Jan. 5, 2005]

§ 1240.13 Notice of decision.

(a) *Written decision.* A written decision shall be served upon the respondent and the Service counsel, together with the notice referred to in § 1003.3 of this chapter. Service by mail is complete upon mailing.

(b) *Oral decision.* An oral decision shall be stated by the immigration judge in the presence of the respondent and the Service counsel, if any, at the conclusion of the hearing. A copy of the summary written order shall be furnished at the request of the respondent or the Service counsel.

(c) *Summary decision.* When the immigration judge renders a summary decision as provided in § 1240.12(b), he or she shall serve a copy thereof upon the respondent and the Service counsel at the conclusion of the hearing.

(d) *Decision to remove.* If the immigration judge decides that the respondent is removable and orders the respondent to be removed, the immigration judge shall advise the respondent of such decision, and of the consequences for failure to depart under the order of removal, including civil and criminal penalties described at sections 274D and 243 of the Act. Unless appeal from the decision is waived, the respondent shall be furnished with Form EOIR–26, Notice of Appeal, and advised of the provisions of § 1240.15.

§ 1240.14 Finality of order.

The order of the immigration judge shall become final in accordance with § 1003.39 of this chapter.

§ 1240.15 Appeals.

Pursuant to 8 CFR part 1003, an appeal shall lie from a decision of an immigration judge to the Board of Immigration Appeals, except that no appeal shall lie from an order of removal entered in absentia. The procedures regarding the filing of a Form EOIR 26, Notice of Appeal, fees, and briefs are set forth in §§ 1003.3, 1003.31, and 1003.38 of this chapter. An appeal shall be filed within 30 calendar days after the mailing of a written decision, the stating of an oral decision, or the service of a summary decision. The filing date is defined as the date of receipt of the Notice of Appeal by the Board of Immigration Appeals. The reasons for the appeal shall be stated in the Notice of Appeal in accordance with the provisions of § 1003.3(b) of this chapter. Failure to do so may constitute a ground for dismissal of the appeal by the Board pursuant to § 1003.1(d)(2) of this chapter.

[62 FR 10367, Mar. 6, 1997, as amended at 66 FR 6446, Jan. 22, 2001]

§ 1240.16 Application of new procedures or termination of proceedings in old proceedings pursuant to section 309(c) of Public Law 104–208.

The Attorney General shall have the sole discretion to apply the provisions of section 309(c) of Public Law 104–208, which provides for the application of new removal procedures to certain cases in exclusion or deportation proceedings and for the termination of certain cases in exclusion or deportation proceedings and initiation of new removal proceedings. The Attorney General's application of the provisions of section 309(c) shall become effective upon publication of a notice in the FEDERAL REGISTER. However, if the Attorney General determines, in the exercise of his or her discretion, that the delay caused by publication would adversely affect the interests of the United States or the effective enforcement of the immigration laws, the Attorney General's application shall become effective immediately upon issuance, and shall be published in the FEDERAL REGISTER as soon as practicable thereafter.

§§ 1240.17–1240.19 [Reserved]

Subpart B—Cancellation of Removal

§ 1240.20 Cancellation of removal and adjustment of status under section 240A of the Act.

(a) *Jurisdiction.* An application for the exercise of discretion under section 240A of the Act shall be submitted on Form EOIR–42, Application for Cancellation of Removal, to the Immigration Court having administrative control over the Record of Proceeding of the underlying removal proceeding under section 240 of the Act. The application must be accompanied by payment of the filing fee as set forth in § 103.7(b) of 8 CFR chapter I or a request for a fee waiver.

(b) *Filing the application.* The application may be filed only with the Immigration Court after jurisdiction has vested pursuant to § 1003.14 of this chapter.

(c) For cases raised under section 240A(b)(2) of the Act, extreme hardship shall be determined as set forth in § 1240.58 of this part.

[62 FR 10367, Mar. 6, 1997, as amended at 64 FR 27875, May 21, 1999]

§ 1240.21 Suspension of deportation and adjustment of status under section 244(a) of the Act (as in effect before April 1, 1997) and cancellation of removal and adjustment of status under section 240A(b) of the Act for certain nonpermanent residents.

(a) *Applicability of annual cap on suspension of deportation or cancellation of removal.* (1) As used in this section, the term *cap* means the numerical limitation of 4,000 grants of suspension of deportation or cancellation of removal in any fiscal year (except fiscal year 1998, which has a limitation of 8,000 grants) pursuant to section 240A(e) of the Act.

(2) The provisions of this section apply to grants of suspension of deportation pursuant to section 244(a) of the Act (as in effect before April 1, 1997) or cancellation of removal pursuant to section 240A(b) of the Act that are subject to a numerical limitation in section 240A(e) of the Act for any fiscal year. This section does not apply to grants of suspension of deportation or cancellation of removal to aliens described in section 309(c)(5)(C)(i) of the Illegal Immigration Reform and Immigrant Responsibility Act (IIRIRA), as amended by section 203(a)(1) of the Nicaraguan Adjustment and Central American Relief Act (NACARA), or aliens in deportation proceedings prior to April 1, 1997, who apply for suspension of deportation pursuant to section 244(a)(3) of the Act (as in effect prior to April 1, 1997). The Immigration Court and the Board shall no longer issue conditional grants of suspension of deportation or cancellation of removal as provided in 8 CFR 240.21 (as in effect prior to September 30, 1998).

(b) [Reserved]

(c) *Grants of suspension of deportation or cancellation of removal in fiscal years subsequent to fiscal year 1998.* On and after October 1, 1998, the Immigration Court and the Board may grant applications for suspension of deportation and adjustment of status under section 244(a) of the Act (as in effect prior to April 1, 1997) or cancellation of removal and adjustment of status under section 240A(b) of the Act that meet the statutory requirements for such relief and warrant a favorable exercise of discretion until the annual numerical limitation has been reached in that fiscal year. The awarding of such relief shall be determined according to the date the order granting such relief becomes final as defined in §§ 1003.1(d)(7) and 1003.39 of this chapter.

(1) *Applicability of the annual limitation.* When grants are no longer available in a fiscal year, further decisions to grant such relief must be reserved until such time as a grant becomes available under the annual limitation in a subsequent fiscal year.

(2) *Aliens applying for additional forms of relief.* Whether or not the cap has been reached, the Immigration Court or the Board shall adjudicate concurrently all other forms of relief for which the alien has applied. Applications for suspension of deportation or cancellation of removal shall be denied in the exercise of discretion if the alien is granted asylum or adjustment of status, including pursuant to section 202 of NACARA, while the suspension of deportation or cancellation of removal application is pending. Where an appeal of a decision granting asylum or adjustment is sustained by the Board, a decision to deny as a matter of discretion an application for suspension of deportation or cancellation of removal on this basis shall be reconsidered.

[63 FR 52138, Sept. 30, 1998, as amended at 66 FR 6446, Jan. 22, 2001; 82 FR 57339, Dec. 5, 2017]

§§ 1240.22–1240.24 [Reserved]

Subpart C—Voluntary Departure

§ 1240.26 Voluntary departure—authority of the Executive Office for Immigration Review.

(a) *Eligibility: general.* An alien previously granted voluntary departure under section 240B of the Act, including by the Service under § 240.25, and who fails to depart voluntarily within the time specified, shall thereafter be ineligible, for a period of ten years, for voluntary departure or for relief under sections 240A, 245, 248, and 249 of the Act.

(b) *Prior to completion of removal proceedings*—(1) *Grant by the immigration judge.* (i) An alien may be granted voluntary departure by an immigration judge pursuant to section 240B(a) of the Act only if the alien:

(A) Makes such request prior to or at the master calendar hearing at which the case is initially calendared for a merits hearing;

(B) Makes no additional requests for relief (or if such requests have been made, such requests are withdrawn prior to any grant of voluntary departure pursuant to this section);

(C) Concedes removability;

(D) Waives appeal of all issues; and

(E) Has not been convicted of a crime described in section 101(a)(43) of the Act and is not deportable under section 237(a)(4).

(ii) The judge may not grant voluntary departure under section 240B(a) of the Act beyond 30 days after the master calendar hearing at which the case is initially calendared for a merits hearing, except pursuant to a stipulation under paragraph (b)(2) of this section.

(2) *Stipulation.* At any time prior to the completion of removal proceedings, the Service counsel may stipulate to a grant of voluntary departure under section 240B(a) of the Act.

(3) *Conditions.* (i) The judge may impose such conditions as he or she deems necessary to ensure the alien's timely departure from the United States, including the posting of a voluntary departure bond to be canceled upon proof that the alien has departed the United States within the time specified. The alien shall be required to present to the Service, for inspection and photocopying, his or her passport or other travel documentation sufficient to assure lawful entry into the country to which the alien is departing, unless:

(A) A travel document is not necessary to return to his or her native country or to which country the alien is departing; or

(B) The document is already in the possession of the Service.

(ii) The Service may hold the passport or documentation for sufficient time to investigate its authenticity. If such documentation is not immediately available to the alien, but the immigration judge is satisfied that the alien is making diligent efforts to secure it, voluntary departure may be granted for a period not to exceed 120 days, subject to the condition that the alien within 60 days must secure such documentation and present it to the Service. The Service in its discretion may extend the period within which the alien must provide such documentation. If the documentation is not presented within the 60-day period or any extension thereof, the voluntary departure order shall vacate automatically and the alternate order of removal will take effect, as if in effect on the date of issuance of the immigration judge order.

(iii) If the alien files a post-decision motion to reopen or reconsider during the period allowed for voluntary departure, the grant of voluntary departure shall be terminated automatically, and the alternate order of removal will take effect immediately. The penalties for failure to depart voluntarily under section 240B(d) of the Act shall not apply if the alien has filed a post-decision motion to reopen or reconsider during the period allowed for voluntary departure. Upon the granting of voluntary departure, the immigration judge shall advise the alien of the provisions of this paragraph (b)(3)(iii).

(iv) The automatic termination of a grant of voluntary departure and the effectiveness of the alternative order of removal shall not affect, in any way, the date that the order of the immigration judge or the Board became administratively final, as determined under the provisions of the applicable regulations in this chapter.

(c) *At the conclusion of the removal proceedings*—(1) *Required findings.* An immigration judge may grant voluntary departure at the conclusion of the removal proceedings under section 240B(b) of the Act, if he or she finds that:

(i) The alien has been physically present in the United States for period of at least one year preceding the date the Notice to Appear was served under section 239(a) of the Act;

(ii) The alien is, and has been, a person of good moral character for at least five years immediately preceding the application;

(iii) The alien has not been convicted of a crime described in section 101(a)(43) of the Act and is not deportable under section 237(a)(4); and

(iv) The alien has established by clear and convincing evidence that the alien has the means to depart the United States and has the intention to do so.

(2) *Travel documentation.* Except as otherwise provided in paragraph (b)(3) of this section, the clear and convincing evidence of the means to depart shall include in all cases presentation by the alien of a passport or other travel documentation sufficient to assure lawful entry into the country to which the alien is departing. The Service shall have full opportunity to inspect and photocopy the documentation, and to challenge its authenticity or sufficiency before voluntary departure is granted.

(3) *Conditions.* The immigration judge may impose such conditions as he or she deems necessary to ensure the alien's timely departure from the United States. The immigration judge shall advise the alien of the conditions set forth in this paragraph (c)(3)(i)–(iii). If the immigration judge imposes conditions beyond those specifically enumerated below, the immigration judge shall advise the alien of such conditions before granting voluntary departure. Upon the conditions being set forth, the alien shall be provided the opportunity to accept the grant of voluntary departure or decline voluntary departure if he or she is unwilling to accept the amount of the bond or other conditions. In all cases under section 240B(b) of the Act:

(i) The alien shall be required to post a voluntary departure bond, in an amount necessary to ensure that the alien departs within the time specified, but in no case less than $500. Before granting voluntary departure, the immigration judge shall advise the alien of the specific amount of the bond to be set and the duty to post the bond with the ICE Field Office Director within 5 business days of the immigration judge's order granting voluntary departure.

(ii) An alien who has been granted voluntary departure shall, within 30 days of filing of an appeal with the Board, submit sufficient proof of having posted the required voluntary departure bond. If the alien does not provide timely proof to the Board that the required voluntary departure bond has been posted with DHS, the Board will not reinstate the period of voluntary departure in its final order.

(iii) Upon granting voluntary departure, the immigration judge shall advise the alien that if the alien files a post-order motion to reopen or reconsider during the period allowed for voluntary departure, the grant of voluntary departure shall terminate automatically and the alternate order of removal will take effect immediately.

(iv) The automatic termination of an order of voluntary departure and the effectiveness of the alternative order of removal shall not impact, in any way, the date that the order of the immigration judge or the Board became administratively final, as determined under the provisions of the applicable regulations in this chapter.

(v) If, after posting the voluntary departure bond the alien satisfies the condition of the bond by departing the United States prior to the expiration of the period granted for voluntary departure, the alien may apply to the ICE Field Office Director for the bond to be canceled, upon submission of proof of the alien's timely departure by such methods as the ICE Field Office Director may prescribe.

(vi) The voluntary departure bond may be canceled by such methods as the ICE Field Office Director may prescribe if the alien is subsequently successful in overturning or remanding the immigration judge's decision regarding removability.

(4) *Provisions relating to bond.* The voluntary departure bond shall be posted with the ICE Field Office Director within 5 business days of the immigration judge's order granting voluntary departure, and the ICE Field Office Director may, at his or her discretion, hold the alien in custody until the bond is posted. Because the purpose of the voluntary departure bond is to ensure that the alien does depart from the United States, as promised, the failure to post the bond, when required, within 5 business days may be considered in evaluating whether the alien should be detained based on risk of flight, and also may be considered as a

negative discretionary factor with respect to any discretionary form of relief. The alien's failure to post the required voluntary departure bond within the time required does not terminate the alien's obligation to depart within the period allowed or exempt the alien from the consequences for failure to depart voluntarily during the period allowed. However, if the alien had waived appeal of the immigration judge's decision, the alien's failure to post the required voluntary departure bond within the period allowed means that the alternate order of removal takes effect immediately pursuant to 8 CFR 1241.1(f), except that an alien granted the privilege of voluntary departure under 8 CFR 1240.26(c) will not be deemed to have departed under an order of removal if the alien:

(i) Departs the United States no later than 25 days following the failure to post bond;

(ii) Provides to DHS such evidence of his or her departure as the ICE Field Office Director may require; and

(iii) Provides evidence DHS deems sufficient that he or she remains outside of the United States.

(d) *Alternate order of removal.* Upon granting a request made for voluntary departure either prior to the completion of proceedings or at the conclusion of proceedings, the immigration judge shall also enter an alternate order or removal.

(e) *Periods of time.* If voluntary departure is granted prior to the completion of removal proceedings, the immigration judge may grant a period not to exceed 120 days. If voluntary departure is granted at the conclusion of proceedings, the immigration judge may grant a period not to exceed 60 days.

(1) *Motion to reopen or reconsider filed during the voluntary departure period.* The filing of a motion to reopen or reconsider prior to the expiration of the period allowed for voluntary departure has the effect of automatically terminating the grant of voluntary departure, and accordingly does not toll, stay, or extend the period allowed for voluntary departure under this section. See paragraphs (b)(3)(iii) and (c)(3)(ii) of this section. If the alien files a post-order motion to reopen or reconsider during the period allowed for voluntary departure, the penalties for failure to depart voluntarily under section 240B(d) of the Act shall not apply. The Board shall advise the alien of the condition provided in this paragraph in writing if it reinstates the immigration judge's grant of voluntary departure.

(2) *Motion to reopen or reconsider filed after the expiration of the period allowed for voluntary departure.* The filing of a motion to reopen or a motion to reconsider after the time allowed for voluntary departure has already expired does not in any way impact the period of time allowed for voluntary departure under this section. The granting of a motion to reopen or reconsider that was filed after the penalties under section 240B(d) of the Act had already taken effect, as a consequence of the alien's prior failure voluntarily to depart within the time allowed, does not have the effect of vitiating or vacating those penalties, except as provided in section 240B(d)(2) of the Act.

(f) *Extension of time to depart.* Authority to extend the time within which to depart voluntarily specified initially by an immigration judge or the Board is only within the jurisdiction of the district director, the Deputy Executive Associate Commissioner for Detention and Removal, or the Director of the Office of Juvenile Affairs. An immigration judge or the Board may reinstate voluntary departure in a removal proceeding that has been reopened for a purpose other than solely making an application for voluntarily departure if reopening was granted prior to the expiration of the original period of voluntary departure. In no event can the total period of time, including any extension, exceed 120 days or 60 days as set forth in section 240B of the Act. The filing of a motion to reopen or reconsider does not toll, stay, or extend the period allowed for voluntary departure. The filing of a petition for review has the effect of automatically terminating the grant of voluntary departure, and accordingly also does not toll, stay, or extend the period allowed for voluntary departure.

(g) *Administrative Appeals.* No appeal shall lie regarding the length of a period of voluntary departure (as distinguished from issues of whether to grant voluntary departure).

(h) *Reinstatement of voluntary departure.* An immigration judge or the Board may reinstate voluntary departure in a removal proceeding that has been reopened for a purpose other than solely making application for voluntary departure, if reopening was granted prior to the expiration of the original period of voluntary departure. In no event can the total period of time, including any extension, exceed 120 days or 60 days as set forth in section 240B of the Act and paragraph (a) of this section.

(i) *Effect of filing a petition for review.* If, prior to departing the United States, the alien files a petition for review pursuant to section 242 of the Act (8 U.S.C. 1252) or any other judicial challenge to the administratively final order, any grant of voluntary departure shall terminate automatically upon the filing of the petition or other judicial challenge and the alternate order of removal entered pursuant to paragraph (d) of this section shall immediately take effect, except that an alien granted the privilege of voluntary departure under 8 CFR 1240.26(c) will not be deemed to have departed under an order of removal if the alien departs the United States no later than 30 days following the filing of a petition for review, provides to DHS such evidence of his or her departure as the ICE Field Office Director may require, and provides evidence DHS deems sufficient that he or she remains outside of the United States. The Board shall advise the alien of the condition provided in this paragraph in writing if it reinstates the immigration judge's grant of voluntary departure. The automatic termination of a grant of voluntary departure and the effectiveness of the alternative order of removal shall not affect, in any way, the date that the order of the immigration judge or the Board became administratively final, as determined under the provisions of the applicable regulations in this chapter. Since the grant of voluntary departure is terminated by the filing of the petition for review, the alien will be subject to the alternate order of removal, but the penalties for failure to depart voluntarily under section 240B(d) of the Act shall not apply to an alien who files a petition for review, and who remains in the United States while the petition for review is pending.

(j) *Penalty for failure to depart.* There shall be a rebuttable presumption that the civil penalty for failure to depart, pursuant to section 240B(d)(1)(A) of the Act, shall be set at $3,000 unless the immigration judge specifically orders a higher or lower amount at the time of granting voluntary departure within the permissible range allowed by law. The immigration judge shall advise the alien of the amount of this civil penalty at the time of granting voluntary departure.

[62 FR 10367, Mar. 6, 1997, as amended at 67 FR 39258, June 7, 2002; 73 FR 76937, Dec. 18, 2008]

§§ 1240.27–1240.29 [Reserved]

Subpart D—Exclusion of Aliens (for Proceedings Commenced Prior to April 1, 1997)

§ 1240.30 Proceedings prior to April 1, 1997.

Subpart D of 8 CFR part 240 applies to exclusion proceedings commenced prior to April 1, 1997, pursuant to the former section 236 of the Act. An exclusion proceeding is commenced by the filing of Form I–122 with the Immigration Court, and an alien is considered to be in exclusion proceedings only upon such filing. All references to the Act contained in this subpart are references to the Act in effect prior to April 1, 1997.

§ 1240.31 Authority of immigration judges.

In determining cases referred for further inquiry as provided in section 235 of the Act, immigration judges shall have the powers and authority conferred upon them by the Act and this chapter, including the adjudication of applications for adjustment of status pursuant to section 202 of Pub. L. 105–100, or section 902 of Pub. L. 105–277. Subject to any specific limitation prescribed by the Act and this chapter, immigration judges shall also exercise the discretion and authority conferred upon the Attorney General by the Act as is appropriate and necessary for the disposition of such cases.

[62 FR 10367, Mar. 6, 1997, as amended at 63 FR 27829, May 21, 1998; 64 FR 25766, May 12, 1999]

§ 1240.32 Hearing.

(a) *Opening*. Exclusion hearings shall be closed to the public, unless the alien at his or her own instance requests that the public, including the press, be permitted to attend; in that event, the hearing shall be open, provided that the alien states for the record that he or she is waiving the requirement in section 236 of the Act that the inquiry shall be kept separate and apart from the public. When the hearing is to be open, depending upon physical facilities, reasonable limitation may be placed upon the number in attendance at any one time, with priority being given to the press over the general public. The immigration judge shall ascertain whether the applicant for admission is the person to whom Form I–122 was previously delivered by the examining immigration officer as provided in 8 CFR part 1235; enter a copy of such form in evidence as an exhibit in the case; inform the applicant of the nature and purpose of the hearing; advise him or her of the privilege of being represented by an attorney of his or her own choice at no expense to the Government; advise him or her of the availability of pro bono legal services for the immigration court location at which the hearing will take place, and ascertain that he or she has received a list of such pro bono legal service providers; and request him or her to ascertain then and there whether he or she desires representation; advise him or her that he or she will have a reasonable opportunity to present evidence in his or her own behalf, to examine and object to evidence against him or her, and to cross-examine witnesses presented by the Government; and place the applicant under oath.

(b) *Procedure*. The immigration judge shall receive and adduce material and relevant evidence, rule upon objections, and otherwise regulate the course of the hearing.

(c) *Attorney for the Service*. The Service shall assign an attorney to each case in which an applicant's nationality is in issue and may assign an attorney to any case in which such assignment is deemed necessary or advantageous. The duties of the Service counsel include, but are not limited to, the presentation of evidence and the interrogation, examination, and cross-examination of the applicant and other witnesses. Nothing contained in this section diminishes the authority of an immigration judge to conduct proceedings under this part.

(d) *Depositions*. The procedures specified in § 1240.48(e) shall apply.

(e) *Record*. The hearing before the immigration judge, including the testimony, exhibits, applications, proffers, and requests, the immigration judge's decision, and all written orders, motions, appeals, and other papers filed in the proceeding shall constitute the record in the case. The hearing shall be recorded verbatim except for statements made off the record with the permission of the immigration judge.

[62 FR 10367, Mar. 6, 1997, as amended at 80 FR 59513, Oct. 1, 2015]

§ 1240.33 Applications for asylum or withholding of deportation.

(a) If the alien expresses fear of persecution or harm upon return to his or her country of origin or to a country to which the alien may be deported after a determination of excludability from the United States pursuant to this subpart, and the alien has not been referred to the immigration judge by an asylum officer in accordance with § 1208.14(b) of this chapter, the immigration judge shall:

(1) Advise the alien that he or she may apply for asylum in the United States or withholding of deportation to that other country; and

(2) Make available the appropriate application forms.

(b) An application for asylum or withholding of deportation must be filed with the Immigration Court, pursuant to § 1208.4(b) of this chapter. Upon receipt of an application, the Immigration Court may forward a copy to the Department of State pursuant to § 1208.11 of this chapter and shall calendar the case for a hearing. The reply, if any, from the Department of State, unless classified under an applicable Executive Order, shall be given to both the applicant and to DHS counsel and shall be included in the record.

(c) Applications for asylum or withholding of deportation so filed will be decided by the immigration judge pursuant to the requirements and standards established in 8 CFR part 1208 after an evidentiary hearing that is necessary to resolve material factual issues in dispute. An evidentiary hearing extending beyond issues related to the basis for a mandatory denial of the application pursuant to § 1208.13(c) of this chapter is not necessary once the immigration judge has determined that such denial is required.

(1) Evidentiary hearings on applications for asylum or withholding of deportation will be closed to the public unless the applicant expressly requests that it be open pursuant to § 1236.3 of this chapter.

(2) Nothing in this section is intended to limit the authority of the immigration judge properly to control the scope of any evidentiary hearing.

(3) During the exclusion hearing, the applicant shall be examined under oath on his or her application and may present evidence and witnesses on his or her own behalf. The applicant has the burden of establishing that he or she is a refugee as defined in section 101(a)(42) of the Act pursuant to the standard set forth in § 1208.13 of this chapter.

(4) The Service counsel for the government may call witnesses and present evidence for the record, including information classified under the applicable Executive Order, provided the immigration judge or the Board has determined that such information is relevant to the hearing. The applicant shall be informed when the immigration judge receives such classified information. The agency that provides the classified information to the immigration judge may provide an unclassified summary of the information for release to the applicant whenever it determines it can do so consistently with safeguarding both the classified nature of the information and its source. The summary should be as detailed as possible, in order that the applicant may have an opportunity to offer opposing evidence. A decision based in whole or in part on such classified information shall state that such information is material to the decision.

(d) The decision of an immigration judge to grant or deny asylum or withholding of deportation shall be communicated to the applicant and to the Service counsel for the government. An adverse decision will state why asylum or withholding of deportation was denied.

[62 FR 10367, Mar. 6, 1997, as amended at 78 FR 19080, Mar. 29, 2013]

§ 1240.34 Renewal of application for adjustment of status under section 245 of the Act.

An adjustment application by an alien paroled under section 212(d)(5) of the Act, which has been denied by the district director, may be renewed in exclusion proceedings under section 236 of the Act (as in effect prior to April 1, 1997) before an immigration judge under the following two conditions: first, the denied application must have been properly filed subsequent to the applicant's earlier inspection and admission to the United States; and second, the applicant's later absence from and return to the United States must have been under the terms of an advance parole authorization on Form I–512 granted to permit the applicant's absence and return to pursue the previously filed adjustment application. In a relevant case, the immigration judge may adjudicate the sufficiency of an Affidavit of Support Under Section 213A (Form I–864), executed on behalf of an applicant for admission or for adjustment of status, in accordance with the provisions of section 213A of the Act and 8 CFR part 213a.

[62 FR 10367, Mar. 6, 1997. Redesignated in part and duplicated in part from part 240 at 68 FR 9838, 9840, Feb. 28, 2003, as amended at 71 FR 35757, June 21, 2006]

§ 1240.35 Decision of the immigration judge; notice to the applicant.

(a) *Decision.* The immigration judge shall inform the applicant of his or her decision in accordance with § 1003.37 of this chapter.

(b) *Advice to alien ordered excluded.* An alien ordered excluded shall be furnished with Form I–296, Notice to Alien Ordered Excluded by Immigration Judge, at the time of an oral decision by the immigration judge or upon service of a written decision.

(c) *Holders of refugee travel documents.* Aliens who are the holders of valid unexpired refugee travel documents may be ordered excluded only if they are found to be inadmissible under section 212(a)(2), 212(a)(3), or 212(a)(6)(E) of the Act, and it is determined that on the basis of the acts for which they are inadmissible there are compelling reasons of national security or public order for their exclusion. If the immigration judge finds that the alien is inadmissible but determines that there are no compelling reasons of national security or public order for exclusion, the immigration judge shall remand the case to the district director for parole.

§ 1240.36 Finality of order.

The decision of the immigration judge shall become final in accordance with § 1003.37 of this chapter.

§ 1240.37 Appeals.

Except for temporary exclusions under section 235(c) of the Act, an appeal from a decision of an Immigration Judge under this part may be taken by either party pursuant to § 1003.38 of this chapter.

§ 1240.38 Fingerprinting of excluded aliens.

Every alien 14 years of age or older who is excluded from admission to the United States by an immigration judge shall be fingerprinted, unless during the preceding year he or she has been fingerprinted at an American consular office.

§ 1240.39 [Reserved]

Subpart E—Proceedings To Determine Deportability of Aliens in the United States: Hearing and Appeal (for Proceedings Commenced Prior to April 1, 1997)

§ 1240.40 Proceedings commenced prior to April 1, 1997.

Subpart E of 8 CFR part 1240 applies only to deportation proceedings commenced prior to April 1, 1997. A deportation proceeding is commenced by the filing of Form I–221 (Order to Show Cause) with the Immigration Court, and an alien is considered to be in deportation proceedings only upon such filing, except in the case of an alien admitted to the United States under the provisions of section 217 of the Act. All references to the Act contained in this subpart pertain to the Act as in effect prior to April 1, 1997.

§ 1240.41 Immigration judges.

(a) *Authority.* In any proceeding conducted under this part the immigration judge shall have the authority to determine deportability and to make decisions, including orders of deportation, as provided by section 242(b) and 242B of the Act; to reinstate orders of deportation as provided by section 242(f) of the Act; to determine applications under sections 208, 212(k), 241(a)(1)(E)(iii), 241(a)(1)(H), 244, 245 and 249 of the Act, section 202 of Pub. L. 105–100, and section 902 of Pub. L. 105–277; to determine the country to which an alien's deportation will be directed in accordance with section 243(a) of the Act; to order temporary withholding of deportation pursuant to section 243(h) of the Act; and to take any other action consistent with applicable law and regulations as may be appropriate. An immigration judge may certify his or her decision in any case to the Board of Immigration Appeals when it involves an unusually complex or novel question of law or fact. Nothing contained in this part shall be construed to diminish the authority conferred on immigration judges under section 103 of the Act.

(b) *Withdrawal and substitution of immigration judges.* The immigration judge assigned to conduct the hearing shall at any time withdraw if he or she deems himself or herself disqualified. If an immigration judge becomes unavailable to complete his or her duties within a reasonable time, or if at any time the respondent consents to a substitution, another immigration judge may be assigned to complete the case. The new immigration judge shall familiarize himself or herself with the record in the case and shall state for the record that he or she has done so.

[62 FR 10367, Mar. 6, 1997, as amended at 63 FR 27829, May 21, 1998; 63 FR 39121, July 21, 1998; 64 FR 25767, May 12, 1999]

§ 1240.42 Representation by counsel.

The respondent may be represented at the hearing by an attorney or other representative qualified under 8 CFR part 1292.

§ 1240.43 Incompetent respondents.

When it is impracticable for the respondent to be present at the hearing because of mental incompetency, the guardian, near relative, or friend who was served with a copy of the order to show cause shall be permitted to appear on behalf of the respondent. If such a person cannot reasonably be found or fails or refuses to appear, the custodian of the respondent shall be requested to appear on behalf of the respondent.

§ 1240.44 Interpreter.

Any person acting as interpreter in a hearing before an immigration judge under this part shall be sworn to interpret and translate accurately, unless the interpreter is an employee of the United States Government, in which event no such oath shall be required.

§ 1240.45 Postponement and adjournment of hearing.

After the commencement of the hearing, the immigration judge may grant a reasonable adjournment either at his or her own instance or, for good cause shown, upon application by the respondent or the Service.

§ 1240.46 Evidence.

(a) *Sufficiency*. A determination of deportability shall not be valid unless it is found by clear, unequivocal, and convincing evidence that the facts alleged as grounds for deportation are true.

(b) *Use of prior statements*. The immigration judge may receive in evidence any oral or written statement that is material and relevant to any issue in the case previously made by the respondent or any other person during any investigation, examination, hearing, or trial.

(c) *Testimony*. Testimony of witnesses appearing at the hearing shall be under oath or affirmation administered by the immigration judge.

(d) *Depositions*. The immigration judge may order the taking of depositions pursuant to § 1003.35 of this chapter.

§ 1240.47 Contents of record.

The hearing before the immigration judge, including the testimony, exhibits, applications, proffers, and requests, the immigration judge's decision, and all written orders, motions, appeals, briefs, and other papers filed in the proceedings shall constitute the record in the case. The hearing shall be recorded verbatim except for statements made off the record with the permission of the immigration judge. In his or her discretion, the immigration judge may exclude from the record any arguments made in connection with motions, applications, requests, or objections, but in such event the person affected may submit a brief.

§ 1240.48 Hearing.

(a) *Opening*. The immigration judge shall advise the respondent of his or her right to representation, at no expense to the Government, by counsel of his or her own choice authorized to practice in the proceedings and require him or her to state then and there whether he or she desires representation; advise the respondent of the availability of pro bono legal services for the immigration court location at which the hearing will take place; ascertain that the respondent has received a list of such pro bono legal service providers, and a copy of Form I–618, Written Notice of Appeal Rights; advise the respondent that he or she will have a reasonable opportunity to examine and object to the evidence against him or her, to present evidence in his or her own behalf and to cross-examine witnesses presented by the Government; place the respondent under oath; read the factual allegations and the charges in the order to show cause to the respondent and explain them in nontechnical language, and enter the order to show cause as an exhibit in the record. Deportation hearings shall be open to the public, except that the immigration judge may, in his or her discretion and for the purpose of protecting witnesses, respondents, or the public interest, direct that the general public or particular individuals shall be excluded from the hearing in any specific case. Depending upon physical facilities, reasonable limitation may be placed upon the number in attendance at any one time, with priority being given to the press over the general public.

(b) *Pleading by respondent.* The immigration judge shall require the respondent to plead to the order to show cause by stating whether he or she admits or denies the factual allegations and his or her deportability under the charges contained therein. If the respondent admits the factual allegations and admits his or her deportability under the charges and the immigration judge is satisfied that no issues of law or fact remain, the immigration judge may determine that deportability as charged has been established by the admissions of the respondent. The immigration judge shall not accept an admission of deportability from an unrepresented respondent who is incompetent or under age 16 and is not accompanied by a guardian, relative, or friend; nor from an officer of an institution in which a respondent is an inmate or patient. When, pursuant to this paragraph, the immigration judge may not accept an admission of deportability, he or she shall direct a hearing on the issues.

(c) *Issues of deportability.* When deportability is not determined under the provisions of paragraph (b) of this section, the immigration judge shall request the assignment of a Service counsel, and shall receive evidence as to any unresolved issues, except that no further evidence need be received as to any facts admitted during the pleading. The respondent shall provide a court certified copy of a Judicial Recommendation Against Deportation (JRAD) to the immigration judge when such recommendation will be the basis of denying any charge(s) brought by the Service in the proceedings against the respondent. No JRAD is effective against a charge of deportability under section 241(a)(11) of the Act or if the JRAD was granted on or after November 29, 1990.

(d) *Additional charges.* The Service may at any time during a hearing lodge additional charges of deportability, including factual allegations, against the respondent. Copies of the additional factual allegations and charges shall be submitted in writing for service on the respondent and entry as an exhibit in the record. The immigration judge shall read the additional factual allegations and charges to the respondent and explain them to him or her. The immigration judge shall advise the respondent if he or she is not represented by counsel that he or she may be so represented and also that he or she may have a reasonable time within which to meet the additional factual allegations and charges. The respondent shall be required to state then and there whether he or she desires a continuance for either of these reasons. Thereafter, the provisions of paragraph (b) of this section shall apply to the additional factual allegations and lodged charges.

[62 FR 10367, Mar. 6, 1997, as amended at 80 FR 59513, Oct. 1, 2015]

§ 1240.49 Ancillary matters, applications.

(a) *Creation of the status of an alien lawfully admitted for permanent residence.* The respondent may apply to the immigration judge for suspension of deportation under section 244(a) of the Act; for adjustment of status under section 245 of the Act, or under section 1 of the Act of November 2, 1966, or under section 101 or 104 of the Act of October 28, 1977; or for the creation of a record of lawful admission for permanent residence under section 249 of the Act. The application shall be subject to the requirements of 8 CFR parts 1240, 1245, and 1249. The approval of any application made to the immigration judge under section 245 of the Act by an alien spouse (as defined in section 216(g)(1) of the Act) or by an alien entrepreneur (as defined in section 216A(f)(1) of the Act), shall result in the alien's obtaining the status of lawful permanent resident on a conditional basis in accordance with the provisions of section 216 or 216A of the Act, whichever is applicable. However, the Petition to Remove the Conditions on Residence required by section 216(c) of the

Act or the Petition by Entrepreneur to Remove Conditions required by section 216A(c) of the Act shall be made to the director in accordance with 8 CFR part 1216. In conjunction with any application for creation of status of an alien lawfully admitted for permanent residence made to an immigration judge, if the respondent is inadmissible under any provision of section 212(a) of the Act and believes that he or she meets the eligibility requirements for a waiver of the ground of inadmissibility, he or she may apply to the immigration judge for such waiver. The immigration judge shall inform the respondent of his or her apparent eligibility to apply for any of the benefits enumerated in this paragraph and shall afford the respondent an opportunity to make application therefor during the hearing. In a relevant case, the immigration judge may adjudicate the sufficiency of an Affidavit of Support Under Section 213A (Form I–864), executed on behalf of an applicant for admission or for adjustment of status, in accordance with the provisions of section 213A of the Act and 8 CFR part 213a. In exercising discretionary power when considering an application under this paragraph, the immigration judge may consider and base the decision on information not contained in the record and not made available for inspection by the respondent, provided the Commissioner has determined that such information is relevant and is classified under the applicable Executive Order as requiring protection from unauthorized disclosure in the interest of national security. Whenever the immigration judge believes that he or she can do so while safeguarding both the information and its source, the immigration judge should inform the respondent of the general nature of the information in order that the respondent may have an opportunity to offer opposing evidence. A decision based in whole or in part on such classified information shall state that the information is material to the decision.

(b) *Voluntary departure.* The respondent may apply to the immigration judge for voluntary departure in lieu of deportation pursuant to section 244(e) of the Act and § 1240.56.

(c) *Applications for asylum or withholding of deportation.* (1) The immigration judge shall notify the respondent that if he or she is finally ordered deported, his or her deportation will in the first instance be directed pursuant to section 243(a) of the Act to the country designated by the respondent and shall afford him or her an opportunity then and there to make such designation. The immigration judge shall then specify and state for the record the country, or countries in the alternative, to which respondent's deportation will be directed pursuant to section 243(a) of the Act if the country of his or her designation will not accept him or her into its territory, or fails to furnish timely notice of acceptance, or if the respondent declines to designate a country.

(2) If the alien expresses fear of persecution or harm upon return to any of the countries to which the alien might be deported pursuant to paragraph (c)(1) of this section, and the alien has not previously filed an application for asylum or withholding of deportation that has been referred to the immigration judge by an asylum officer in accordance with § 1208.14(b) of this chapter, the immigration judge shall:

(i) Advise the alien that he or she may apply for asylum in the United States or withholding of deportation to those countries; and

(ii) Make available the appropriate application forms.

(3) An application for asylum or withholding of deportation must be filed with the Immigration Court, pursuant to § 1208.4(b) of this chapter. Upon receipt of an application, the Immigration Court may forward a copy to the Department of State pursuant to § 1208.11 of this chapter and shall calendar the case for a hearing. The reply, if any, of the Department of State, unless classified under an applicable Executive Order, shall be given to both the applicant and to DHS counsel and shall be included in the record.

(4) Applications for asylum or withholding of deportation so filed will be decided by the immigration judge pursuant to the requirements and standards established in 8 CFR part 1208 after an evidentiary hearing that is necessary to resolve factual issues in

dispute. An evidentiary hearing extending beyond issues related to the basis for a mandatory denial of the application pursuant to § 1208.13 or § 1208.16 of this chapter is not necessary once the immigration judge has determined that such a denial is required.

(i) Evidentiary hearings on applications for asylum or withholding of deportation will be open to the public unless the applicant expressly requests that it be closed.

(ii) Nothing in this section is intended to limit the authority of the immigration judge properly to control the scope of any evidentiary hearing.

(iii) During the deportation hearing, the applicant shall be examined under oath on his or her application and may present evidence and witnesses in his or her own behalf. The applicant has the burden of establishing that he or she is a refugee as defined in section 101(a)(42) of the Act pursuant to the standard set forth in § 1208.13 of this chapter.

(iv) The Service counsel for the government may call witnesses and present evidence for the record, including information classified under the applicable Executive Order, provided the immigration judge or the Board has determined that such information is relevant to the hearing. When the immigration judge receives such classified information he or she shall inform the applicant. The agency that provides the classified information to the immigration judge may provide an unclassified summary of the information for release to the applicant, whenever it determines it can do so consistently with safeguarding both the classified nature of the information and its source. The summary should be as detailed as possible, in order that the applicant may have an opportunity to offer opposing evidence. A decision based in whole or in part on such classified information shall state whether such information is material to the decision.

(5) The decision of an immigration judge to grant or deny asylum or withholding of deportation shall be communicated to the applicant and to the Service counsel for the government. An adverse decision will state why asylum or withholding of deportation was denied.

(d) *Application for relief under sections 241(a)(1)(H) and 241(a)(1)(E)(iii) of the Act.* The respondent may apply to the immigration judge for relief from deportation under sections 241(a)(1)(H) and 241(a)(1)(E)(iii) of the Act.

(e) *General.* An application under this section shall be made only during the hearing and shall not be held to constitute a concession of alienage or deportability in any case in which the respondent does not admit his alienage or deportability. However, nothing in this section shall prohibit the Service from using information supplied in an application for asylum or withholding of deportation submitted to an asylum officer pursuant to § 1208.2 of this chapter on or after January 4, 1995, as the basis for issuance of an order to show cause or a notice to appear to establish alienage or deportability in a case referred to an immigration judge under § 1208.14(b) of this chapter. The respondent shall have the burden of establishing that he or she is eligible for any requested benefit or privilege and that it should be granted in the exercise of discretion. The respondent shall not be required to pay a fee on more than one application within paragraphs (a) and (c) of this section, provided that the minimum fee imposed when more than one application is made shall be determined by the cost of the application with the highest fee. Nothing contained in this section is intended to foreclose the respondent from applying for any benefit or privilege which he or she believes himself or herself eligible to receive in proceedings under this part.

[62 FR 10367, Mar. 6, 1997. Redesignated in part and duplicated in part from part 240 at 68 FR 9838, 9840, Feb. 28, 2003, as amended at 71 FR 35757, June 21, 2006; 78 FR 19080, Mar. 29, 2013]

§ 1240.50 Decision of the immigration judge.

(a) *Contents.* The decision of the immigration judge may be oral or written. Except when deportability is determined on the pleadings pursuant to § 1240.48(b), the decision of the immigration judge shall include a finding as to deportability. The formal enumeration of findings is not required. The decision shall also contain the reasons for granting or denying the request. The decision shall be concluded with the order of the immigration judge.

(b) *Summary decision.* Notwithstanding the provisions of paragraph (a) of this section, in any case where deportability is determined on the pleadings pursuant to § 1240.48(b) and the respondent does not make an application under § 1240.49, or the respondent applies for voluntary departure only and the immigration judge grants the application, the immigration judge may enter a summary decision on Form EOIR–7, Summary Order of Deportation, if deportation is ordered, or on Form EOIR–6, Summary Order of Voluntary Departure, if voluntary departure is granted with an alternate order of deportation.

(c) *Order of the immigration judge.* The order of the immigration judge shall direct the respondent's deportation, or the termination of the proceedings, or such other disposition of the case as may be appropriate. When deportation is ordered, the immigration judge shall specify the country, or countries in the alternate, to which respondent's deportation shall be directed. The immigration judge is authorized to issue orders in the alternative or in combination as he or she may deem necessary.

§ 1240.51 Notice of decision.

(a) *Written decision.* A written decision shall be served upon the respondent and the Service counsel, together with the notice referred to in § 1003.3 of this chapter. Service by mail is complete upon mailing.

(b) *Oral decision.* An oral decision shall be stated by the immigration judge in the presence of the respondent and the trail attorney, if any, at the conclusion of the hearing. Unless appeal from the decision is waived, the respondent shall be furnished with Form EOIR–26, Notice of Appeal, and advised of the provisions of § 1240.53. A printed copy of the oral decision shall be furnished at the request of the respondent or the Service counsel.

(c) *Summary decision.* When the immigration judge renders a summary decision as provided in § 1240.51(b), he or she shall serve a copy thereof upon the respondent at the conclusion of the hearing. Unless appeal from the decision is waived, the respondent shall be furnished with Form EOIR–26, Notice of Appeal, and advised of the provisions of § 1240.54.

§ 1240.52 Finality of order.

The decision of the immigration judge shall become final in accordance with § 1003.39 of this chapter.

§ 1240.53 Appeals.

(a) Pursuant to 8 CFR part 1003, an appeal shall lie from a decision of an immigration judge to the Board, except that no appeal shall lie from an order of deportation entered in absentia. The procedures regarding the filing of a Form EOIR–26, Notice of Appeal, fees, and briefs are set forth in §§ 1003.3, 1003.31, and 1003.38 of this chapter. An appeal shall be filed within 30 calendar days after the mailing of a written decision, the stating of an oral decision, or the service of a summary decision. The filing date is defined as the date of receipt of the Notice of Appeal by the Board. The reasons for the appeal shall be stated in the Form EOIR–26, Notice of Appeal, in accordance with the provisions of § 1003.3(b) of this chapter. Failure to do so may constitute a ground for dismissal of the appeal by the Board pursuant to § 1003.1(d)(2) of this chapter.

(b) *Prohibited appeals; legalization or applications.* An alien respondent defined in § 245a.2(c)(6) or (7) of this chapter who fails to file an application for adjustment of status to that of a temporary resident within the prescribed period(s), and who is thereafter found to be deportable by decision of an immigration judge, shall not be permitted to appeal the finding of deportability based solely on refusal by the immigration judge to entertain such an application in deportation proceedings.

[62 FR 10367, Mar. 6, 1997, as amended at 66 FR 6446, Jan. 22, 2001]

§ 1240.54 [Reserved]

Subpart F—Suspension of Deportation and Voluntary Departure (for Proceedings Commenced Prior to April 1, 1997)

§ 1240.55 Proceedings commenced prior to April 1, 1997.

Subpart F of 8 CFR part 1240 applies to deportation proceedings commenced prior to April 1, 1997. A deportation proceeding is commenced by the filing of Form I–221 (Order to Show Cause) with the Immigration Court, and an alien is considered to be in deportation proceedings only upon such filing, except in the case of an alien admitted to the United States under the provisions of section 217 of the Act. All references to the Act contained in this subpart are references to the Act in effect prior to April 1, 1997.

§ 1240.56 Application.

Notwithstanding any other provision of this chapter, an alien who is deportable because of a conviction on or after November 18, 1988, for an aggravated felony as defined in section 101(a)(43) of the Act, shall not be eligible for voluntary departure as prescribed in 8 CFR part 1240 and section 244 of the Act. Pursuant to subpart F of this part and section 244 of the Act, an immigration judge may authorize the suspension of an alien's deportation; or, if the alien establishes that he or she is willing and has the immediate means with which to depart promptly from the United States, an immigration judge may authorize the alien to depart voluntarily from the United States in lieu of deportation within such time as may be specified by the immigration judge when first authorizing voluntary departure, and under such conditions as the district director shall direct. An application for suspension of deportation shall be made on Form EOIR–40.

§ 1240.57 Extension of time to depart.

Authority to reinstate or extend the time within which to depart voluntarily specified initially by an immigration judge or the Board is within the sole jurisdiction of the district director, except that an immigration judge or the Board may reinstate voluntary departure in a deportation proceeding that has been reopened for a purpose other than solely making an application for voluntary departure. A request by an alien for reinstatement or an extension of time within which to depart voluntarily shall be filed with the district director having jurisdiction over the alien's place of residence. Written notice of the district director's decision shall be served upon the alien and no appeal may be taken therefrom.

§ 1240.58 Extreme hardship.

(a) To be eligible for suspension of deportation under former section 244(a)(1) of the Act, as in effect prior to April 1, 1997, the alien must meet the requirements set forth in the Act, which include a showing that deportation would result in extreme hardship to the alien or to the alien's spouse, parent, or child, who is a citizen of the United States, or an alien lawfully admitted for permanent residence. Extreme hardship is evaluated on a case-by-case basis, taking into account the particular facts and circumstances of each case. Applicants are encouraged to cite and document all applicable factors in their applications, as the presence or absence of any one factor may not be determinative in evaluating extreme hardship. Adjudicators should weigh all relevant factors presented and consider them in light of the totality of the circumstances, but are not required to offer an independent analysis of each listed factor when rendering a decision. Evidence of an extended stay in the United States without fear of deportation and with the benefit of work authorization, when present in a particular case, shall be considered relevant to the determination of whether deportation will result in extreme hardship.

(b) To establish extreme hardship, an applicant must demonstrate that deportation would result in a degree of hardship beyond that typically associated with deportation. Factors that may be considered in evaluating whether deportation would result in extreme hardship to the alien or to the alien's qualified relative include, but are not limited to, the following:

(1) The age of the alien, both at the time of entry to the United States and at the time of application for suspension of deportation;

(2) The age, number, and immigration status of the alien's children and their ability to speak the native language and to adjust to life in the country of return;

(3) The health condition of the alien or the alien's children, spouse, or parents and the availability of any required medical treatment in the country to which the alien would be returned;

(4) The alien's ability to obtain employment in the country to which the alien would be returned;

(5) The length of residence in the United States;

(6) The existence of other family members who are or will be legally residing in the United States;

(7) The financial impact of the alien's departure;

(8) The impact of a disruption of educational opportunities;

(9) The psychological impact of the alien's deportation;

(10) The current political and economic conditions in the country to which the alien would be returned;

(11) Family and other ties to the country to which the alien would be returned;

(12) Contributions to and ties to a community in the United States, including the degree of integration into society;

(13) Immigration history, including authorized residence in the United States; and

(14) The availability of other means of adjusting to permanent resident status.

(c) For cases raised under section 244(a)(3) of the Act, the following factors should be considered in addition to, or in lieu of, the factors listed in paragraph (b) of this section.

(1) The nature and extent of the physical or psychological consequences of abuse;

(2) The impact of loss of access to the United States courts and criminal justice system (including, but not limited to, the ability to obtain and enforce orders of protection, criminal investigations and prosecutions, and family law proceedings or court orders regarding child support, maintenance, child custody, and visitation);

(3) The likelihood that the batterer's family, friends, or others acting on behalf of the batterer in the home country would physically or psychologically harm the applicant or the applicant's child(ren);

(4) The applicant's needs and/or needs of the applicant's child(ren) for social, medical, mental health or other supportive services for victims of domestic violence that are unavailable or not reasonably accessible in the home country;

(5) The existence of laws and social practices in the home country that punish the applicant or the applicant's child(ren) because they have been victims of domestic violence or have taken steps to leave an abusive household; and

(6) The abuser's ability to travel to the home country and the ability and willingness of authorities in the home country to protect the applicant and/or the applicant's children from future abuse.

(d) Nothing in § 1240.58 shall be construed as creating any right, interest, or entitlement that is legally enforceable by or on behalf of any party against the United States or its agencies, officers, or any other person.

[64 FR 27875, May 21, 1999]

Subpart G—Civil Penalties for Failure to Depart [Reserved]

Subpart H—Applications for Suspension of Deportation or Special Rule Cancellation of Removal Under Section 203 of Pub. L. 105–100

SOURCE: 64 FR 27876, May 21, 1999, unless otherwise noted.

§ 1240.60 Definitions.

As used in this subpart the term:

ABC means *American Baptist Churches* v. *Thornburgh*, 760 F. Supp. 796 (N.D. Cal. 1991).

ABC class member refers to:

(1) Any Guatemalan national who first entered the United States on or before October 1, 1990; and

(2) Any Salvadoran national who first entered the United States on or before September 19, 1990.

Asylum application pending adjudication by the Service means any asylum application for which the Service has not served the applicant with a final decision or which has not been referred to the Immigration Court.

Filed an application for asylum means the proper filing of a principal asylum application or filing a derivative asylum application by being properly included as a dependent spouse or child in an asylum application pursuant to the regulations and procedures in effect at the time of filing the principal or derivative asylum application.

IIRIRA means the Illegal Immigration Reform and Immigrant Responsibility Act of 1996, enacted as Pub. L. 104–208 (110 Stat. 3009–625).

NACARA means the Nicaraguan Adjustment and Central American Relief Act (NACARA), enacted as title II of Pub. L. 105–100 (111 Stat. 2160, 2193), as amended by the Technical Corrections to the Nicaraguan Adjustment and Central American Relief Act, Pub. L. 105–139 (111 Stat. 2644).

Registered ABC class member means an ABC class member who:

(1) In the case of an *ABC* class member who is a national of El Salvador, properly submitted an ABC registration form to the Service on or before October 31, 1991, or applied for temporary protected status on or before October 31, 1991; or

(2) In the case of an *ABC* class member who is a national of Guatemala, properly submitted an *ABC* registration form to the Service on or before December 31, 1991.

§ 1240.61 Applicability.

(a) Except as provided in paragraph (b) of this section, this subpart H applies to the following aliens:

(1) A registered *ABC* class member who has not been apprehended at the time of entry after December 19, 1990;

(2) A Guatemalan or Salvadoran national who filed an application for asylum with the Service on or before April 1, 1990, either by filing an application with the Service or filing the application with the Immigration Court and serving a copy of that application on the Service.

(3) An alien who entered the United States on or before December 31, 1990, filed an application for asylum on or before December 31, 1991, and, at the time of filing the application, was a national of the Soviet Union, Russia, any republic of the former Soviet Union, Latvia, Estonia, Lithuania, Poland, Czechoslovakia, Romania, Hungary, Bulgaria, Albania, East Germany, Yugoslavia, or any state of the former Yugoslavia;

(4) An alien who is the spouse or child of an individual described in paragraph (a)(1), (a)(2), or (a)(3) of this section at the time a decision is made to suspend the deportation, or cancel the removal, of the individual described in paragraph (a)(1), (a)(2), or (a)(3) of this section;

(5) An alien who is:

(i) The unmarried son or unmarried daughter of an individual described in paragraph (a)(1), (a)(2), or (a)(3) of this section and is 21 years of age or older at the time a decision is made to suspend the deportation, or cancel the removal, of the parent described in paragraph (a)(1), (a)(2), or (a)(3) of this section; and

(ii) Entered the United States on or before October 1, 1990.

(b) This subpart H does not apply to any alien who has been convicted at any time of an aggravated felony, as defined in section 101(a)(43) of the Act.

§ 1240.62 Jurisdiction.

(a) *Office of International Affairs*. Except as provided in paragraph (b) of this section, the Office of International Affairs shall have initial jurisdiction to grant or refer to the Immigration Court or Board an application for suspension of deportation or special rule cancellation of removal filed by an alien described in § 1240.61, provided:

(1) In the case of a national of El Salvador described in § 1240.61(a)(1), the alien filed a complete asylum application on or before January 31, 1996 (with an administrative grace period extending to February 16, 1996), or otherwise met the asylum application filing deadline pursuant to the *ABC* settlement agreement, and the application is still pending adjudication by the Service;

(2) In the case of a national of Guatemala described in § 1240.61(a)(1), the alien filed a complete asylum application on or before January 3, 1995, or otherwise met the asylum application filing deadline pursuant to the *ABC* settlement agreement, and the application is still pending adjudication by the Service;

(3) In the case of an individual described in § 1240.61(a)(2) or (3), the individual's asylum application is pending adjudication by the Service;

(4) In the case of an individual described in § 1240.61(a)(4) or (5), the individual's parent or spouse has an application pending with the Service under this subpart H or has been granted relief by the Service under this subpart.

(b) *Immigration Court.* The Immigration Court shall have exclusive jurisdiction over an application for suspension of deportation or special rule cancellation of removal filed pursuant to section 309(f)(1)(A) or (B) of IIRIRA, as amended by NACARA, by an alien who has been served Form I–221, Order to Show Cause, or Form I–862, Notice to Appear, after a copy of the charging document has been filed with the Immigration Court, unless the alien is covered by one of the following exceptions:

(1) *Certain ABC class members.* (i) The alien is a registered *ABC* class member for whom proceedings before the Immigration Court or the Board have been administratively closed or continued (including those aliens who had final orders of deportation or removal who have filed and been granted a motion to reopen as required under 8 CFR 1003.43);

(ii) The alien is eligible for benefits of the *ABC* settlement agreement and has not had a *de novo* asylum adjudication pursuant to the settlement agreement; and

(iii) The alien has not moved for and been granted a motion to recalendar proceedings before the Immigration Court or the Board to request suspension of deportation.

(2) *Spouses, children, unmarried sons, and unmarried daughters.* (i) The alien is described in § 1240.61(a) (4) or (5);

(ii) The alien's spouse or parent is described in § 1240.61(a)(1), (a)(2), or (a)(3) and has a Form I–881 pending with the Service; and

(iii) The alien's proceedings before the Immigration Court have been administratively closed, or the alien's proceedings before the Board have been continued, to permit the alien to file an application for suspension of deportation or special rule cancellation of removal with the Service.

§ 1240.63 Application process.

(a) *Form and fees.* Except as provided in paragraph (b) of this section, the application must be made on a Form I–881, Application for Suspension of Deportation or Special Rule Cancellation of Removal (pursuant to section 203 of Public Law 105–100 (NACARA)), and filed in accordance with the instructions for that form. An applicant who submitted to EOIR a completed Form EOIR–40, Application for Suspension of Deportation, before the effective date of the Form I–881 may apply with the Service by submitting the completed Form EOIR–40 attached to a completed first page of the Form I–881. Each application must be filed with the filing and fingerprint fees as provided in § 1103.7(b)(1) of this chapter, or a request for fee waiver, as provided in § 1103.7(c) of this chapter. The fact that an applicant has also applied for asylum does not exempt the applicant from the fingerprinting fees associated with the Form I–881.

(b) *Applications filed with EOIR.* If jurisdiction rests with the Immigration Court under § 260.62(b), the application must be made on the Form I–881, if filed subsequent to June 21, 1999. The application form, along with any supporting documents, must be filed with the Immigration Court and served on the Service's district counsel in accordance with the instructions on or accompanying the form. Applications for suspension of deportation or special rule cancellation of removal filed prior to June 21, 1999 shall be filed on Form EOIR–40.

(c) *Applications filed with the Service.* If jurisdiction rests with the Service under § 1240.62(a), the Form I–881 and supporting documents must be filed at the appropriate Service Center in accordance with the instructions on or accompanying the form.

(d) *Conditions and consequences of filing.* Applications filed under this section shall be filed under the following conditions and shall have the following consequences:

(1) The information provided in the application may be used as a basis for the initiation of removal proceedings, or to satisfy any burden of proof in exclusion, deportation, or removal proceedings;

(2) The applicant and anyone other than a spouse, parent, son, or daughter of the applicant who assists the applicant in preparing the application must sign the application under penalty of perjury. The applicant's signature establishes a presumption that the applicant is aware of the contents of the application. A person other than a relative specified in this paragraph who assists the applicant in preparing the application also must provide his or her full mailing address;

(3) An application that does not include a response to each of the questions contained in the application, is unsigned, or is unaccompanied by the required materials specified in the instructions to the application is incomplete and shall be returned by mail to the applicant within 30 days of receipt of the application by the Service; and

(4) Knowing placement of false information on the application may subject the person supplying that information to criminal penalties under title 18 of the United States Code and to civil penalties under section 274C of the Act.

§ 1240.64 Eligibility—general.

(a) *Burden and standard of proof.* The burden of proof is on the applicant to establish by a preponderance of the evidence that he or she is eligible for suspension of deportation or special rule cancellation of removal and that discretion should be exercised to grant relief.

(b) *Calculation of continuous physical presence and certain breaks in presence.* For purposes of calculating continuous physical presence under this section, section 309(c)(5)(A) of IIRIRA and section 240A(d)(1) of the Act shall not apply to persons described in § 1240.61. For purposes of this subpart H, a single absence of 90 days or less or absences which in the aggregate total no more than 180 days shall be considered brief.

(1) For applications for suspension of deportation made under former section 244 of the Act, as in effect prior to April 1, 1997, the burden of proof is on the applicant to establish that any breaks in continuous physical presence were brief, casual, and innocent and did not meaningfully interrupt the period of continuous physical presence in the United States. For purposes of evaluating whether an absence is brief, single absences in excess of 90 days, or absences that total more than 180 days in the aggregate will be evaluated on a case-by-case basis. An applicant must establish that any absence from the United States was casual and innocent and did not meaningfully interrupt the period of continuous physical presence.

(2) For applications for special rule cancellation of removal made under section 309(f)(1) of IIRIRA, as amended by NACARA, the applicant shall be considered to have failed to maintain continuous physical presence in the United States if he or she has departed from the United States for any period in excess of 90 days or for any periods in the aggregate exceeding 180 days. The applicant must establish that any period of absence less than 90 days was casual and innocent and did not meaningfully interrupt the period of continuous physical presence in the United States.

(3) For all applications made under this subpart, a period of continuous physical presence is terminated whenever an alien is removed from the United States under an order issued pursuant to any provision of the Act or the alien has voluntarily departed under the threat of deportation or when the departure is made for purposes of committing an unlawful act.

(4) The requirements of continuous physical presence in the United States under this subpart shall not apply to an alien who:

(i) Has served for a minimum period of 24 months in an active-duty status in the Armed Forces of the United States and, if separated from such service, was separated under honorable conditions, and

(ii) At the time of the alien's enlistment or induction, was in the United States.

(c) *Factors relevant to extreme hardship.* Except as described in paragraph (d) of this section, extreme hardship shall be determined as set forth in § 1240.58.

(d) *Rebuttable presumption of extreme hardship for certain classes of aliens*—(1) *Presumption of extreme hardship.* An applicant described in paragraphs (a)(1) or (a)(2) of § 1240.61 who has submitted a completed Form I–881 or Form EOIR–40 to either the Service or the Immigration Court, in accordance with § 1240.63, shall be presumed to have established that deportation or removal from the United States would result in extreme hardship to the applicant or to his or her spouse, parent, or child, who is a citizen of the United States or an alien lawfully admitted for permanent residence.

(2) *Rebuttal of presumption.* A presumption of extreme hardship as described in paragraph (d)(1) of this section shall be rebutted if the evidence in the record establishes that it is more likely than not that neither the applicant nor a qualified relative would suffer extreme hardship if the applicant were deported or removed from the United States. In making such a determination, the adjudicator shall consider relevant factors, including those listed in § 1240.58.

(3) *Burden of proof.* In those cases where a presumption of extreme hardship applies, the burden of proof shall be on the Service to establish that it is more likely than not that neither the applicant nor a qualified relative would suffer extreme hardship if the applicant were deported or removed from the United States.

(4) *Effect of rebuttal.* (i) A determination that it is more likely than not that neither the applicant nor a qualified relative would suffer extreme hardship if the applicant were deported or removed from the United States shall be grounds for referral to the Immigration Court or dismissal of an application submitted initially to the Service. The applicant is entitled to a *de novo* adjudication and will again be considered to have a presumption of extreme hardship before the Immigration Court.

(ii) If the Immigration Court determines that extreme hardship will not result from deportation or removal from the United States, the application will be denied.

[64 FR 27876, May 21, 1999; 64 FR 33386, June 23, 1999]

§ 1240.65 Eligibility for suspension of deportation.

(a) *Applicable statutory provisions.* To establish eligibility for suspension of deportation under this section, the applicant must be an individual described in § 1240.61; must establish that he or she is eligible under former section 244 of the Act, as in effect prior to April 1, 1997; must not be subject to any bars to eligibility in former section 242B(e) of the Act, as in effect prior to April 1, 1997, or any other provisions of law; and must not have been convicted of an aggravated felony or be an alien described in former section 241(a)(4)(D) of the Act, as in effect prior to April 1, 1997 (relating to Nazi persecution and genocide).

(b) *General rule.* To establish eligibility for suspension of deportation under former section 244(a)(1) of the Act, as in effect prior to April 1, 1997, an alien must be deportable under any law of the United States, except the provisions specified in paragraph (c) of this section, and must establish:

(1) The alien has been physically present in the United States for a continuous period of not less than 7 years immediately preceding the date the application was filed;

(2) During all of such period the alien was and is a person of good moral character; and

(3) The alien's deportation would, in the opinion of the Attorney General, result in extreme hardship to the alien or to the alien's spouse, parent, or child, who is a citizen of the United States or an alien lawfully admitted for permanent residence.

(c) *Aliens deportable on criminal or certain other grounds.* To establish eligibility for suspension of deportation under former section 244(a)(2) of the Act, as in effect prior to April 1, 1997, an alien who is deportable under former section 241(a) (2), (3), or (4) of the Act, as in effect prior to April 1, 1997 (relating to criminal activity, document fraud, failure to register, and security threats), must establish that:

(1) The alien has been physically present in the United States for a continuous period of not less than 10 years immediately following the commission of an act, or the assumption of a status constituting a ground for deportation;

(2) The alien has been and is a person of good moral character during all of such period; and

(3) The alien's deportation would, in the opinion of the Attorney General, result in exceptional and extremely unusual hardship to the alien, or to the alien's spouse, parent, or child, who is a citizen of the United States or an alien lawfully admitted for permanent residence.

(d) *Battered spouses and children.* To establish eligibility for suspension of deportation under former section 244(a)(3) of the Act, as in effect prior to April 1, 1997, an alien must be deportable under any law of the United States, except under former section 241(a)(1)(G) of the Act, as in effect prior to April 1, 1997 (relating to marriage fraud), and except under the provisions specified in paragraph (c) of this section, and must establish that:

(1) The alien has been physically present in the United States for a continuous period of not less than 3 years immediately preceding the date the application was filed;

(2) The alien has been battered or subjected to extreme cruelty in the United States by a spouse or parent who is a United States citizen or lawful permanent resident (or is the parent of a child of a United States citizen or lawful permanent resident and the child has been battered or subjected to extreme cruelty in the United States by such citizen or permanent resident parent); and

(3) During all of such time in the United States the alien was and is a person of good moral character; and

(4) The alien's deportation would, in the opinion of the Attorney General, result in extreme hardship to the alien or the alien's parent or child.

§ 1240.66 Eligibility for special rule cancellation of removal.

(a) *Applicable statutory provisions.* To establish eligibility for special rule cancellation of removal, the applicant must show he or she is eligible under section 309(f)(1) of IIRIRA, as amended by section 203 of NACARA. The applicant must be described in § 1240.61, must be inadmissible or deportable, must not be subject to any bars to eligibility in sections 240(b)(7), 240A(c), or 240B(d) of the Act, or any other provisions of law, and must not have been convicted of an aggravated felony or be an alien described in section 241(b)(3)(B)(I) of the Act (relating to persecution of others).

(b) *General rule.* To establish eligibility for special rule cancellation of removal under section 309(f)(1)(A) of IIRIRA, as amended by section 203 of NACARA, the alien must establish that:

(1) The alien is not inadmissible under section 212(a)(2) or (3) or deportable under section 237(a)(2), (3) or (4) of the Act (relating to criminal activity, document fraud, failure to register, and security threats);

(2) The alien has been physically present in the United States for a continuous period of 7 years immediately preceding the date the application was filed;

(3) The alien has been a person of good moral character during the required period of continuous physical presence; and

(4) The alien's removal from the United States would result in extreme hardship to the alien, or to the alien's spouse, parent or child who is a United States citizen or an alien lawfully admitted for permanent residence.

(c) *Aliens inadmissible or deportable on criminal or certain other grounds.* To establish eligibility for special rule cancellation of removal under section 309(f)(1)(B) of IIRIRA, as amended by section 203 of NACARA, the alien must be described in § 1240.61 and establish that:

(1) The alien is inadmissible under section 212(a)(2) of the Act (relating to criminal activity), or deportable under paragraphs (a)(2) (other than section 237(a)(2)(A)(iii), relating to aggravated felony convictions), or (a)(3) of section

237 of the Act (relating to criminal activity, document fraud, and failure to register);

(2) The alien has been physically present in the United States for a continuous period of not less than 10 years immediately following the commission of an act, or the assumption of a status constituting a ground for removal;

(3) The alien has been a person of good moral character during the required period of continuous physical presence; and

(4) The alien's removal from the United States would result in exceptional and extremely unusual hardship to the alien or to the alien's spouse, parent, or child, who is a United States citizen or an alien lawfully admitted for permanent residence.

§ 1240.67 Procedure for interview before an asylum officer.

(a) *Fingerprinting requirements.* The Service will notify each applicant 14 years of age or older to appear for an interview only after the applicant has complied with fingerprinting requirements pursuant to § 103.2(e) of 8 CFR chapter I, and the Service has received a definitive response from the FBI that a full criminal background check has been completed. A definitive response that a full criminal background check on an applicant has been completed includes:

(1) Confirmation from the FBI that an applicant does not have an administrative or criminal record;

(2) Confirmation from the FBI that an applicant has an administrative or a criminal record; or

(3) Confirmation from the FBI that two properly prepared fingerprint cards (Form FD–258) have been determined unclassifiable for the purpose of conducting a criminal background check and have been rejected.

(b) *Interview.* (1) The asylum officer shall conduct the interview in a non-adversarial manner and, except at the request of the applicant, separate and apart from the general public. The purpose of the interview shall be to elicit all relevant and useful information bearing on the applicant's eligibility for suspension of deportation or special rule cancellation of removal. If the applicant has an asylum application pending with the Service, the asylum officer may also elicit information relating to the application for asylum in accordance with § 1208.9 of this chapter. At the time of the interview, the applicant must provide complete information regarding the applicant's identity, including name, date and place of birth, and nationality, and may be required to register this identity electronically or through any other means designated by the Attorney General.

(2) The applicant may have counsel or a representative present, may present witnesses, and may submit affidavits of witnesses and other evidence.

(3) An applicant unable to proceed with the interview in English must provide, at no expense to the Service, a competent interpreter fluent in both English and a language in which the applicant is fluent. The interpreter must be at least 18 years of age. The following individuals may not serve as the applicant's interpreter: the applicant's attorney or representative of record; a witness testifying on the applicant's behalf; or, if the applicant also has an asylum application pending with the Service, a representative or employee of the applicant's country of nationality, or, if stateless, country of last habitual residence. Failure without good cause to comply with this paragraph may be considered a failure to appear for the interview for purposes of § 1240.68.

(4) The asylum officer shall have authority to administer oaths, verify the identity of the applicant (including through the use of electronic means), verify the identity of any interpreter, present and receive evidence, and question the applicant and any witnesses.

(5) Upon completion of the interview, the applicant or the applicant's representative shall have an opportunity to make a statement or comment on the evidence presented. The asylum officer may, in the officer's discretion, limit the length of such statement or comment and may require its submission in writing. Upon completion of the interview, and except as otherwise provided by the asylum officer, the applicant shall be informed of the requirement to appear in person to receive and to acknowledge receipt of the decision and any other accompanying material

at a time and place designated by the asylum officer.

(6) The asylum officer shall consider evidence submitted by the applicant with the application, as well as any evidence submitted by the applicant before or at the interview. As a matter of discretion, the asylum officer may grant the applicant a brief extension of time following an interview, during which the applicant may submit additional evidence.

§ 1240.68 Failure to appear at an interview before an asylum officer or failure to follow requirements for fingerprinting.

(a) Failure to appear for a scheduled interview without prior authorization may result in dismissal of the application or waiver of the right to an adjudication by an asylum officer. A written request to reschedule will be granted if it is an initial request and is received by the Asylum Office at least 2 days before the scheduled interview date. All other requests to reschedule the interview, including those submitted after the interview date, will be granted only if the applicant has a reasonable excuse for not appearing, and the excuse was received by the Asylum Office in writing within a reasonable time after the scheduled interview date.

(b) Failure to comply with fingerprint processing requirements without reasonable excuse may result in dismissal of the application or waiver of the right to an adjudication by an asylum officer.

(c) Failure to appear shall be excused if the notice of the interview or fingerprint appointment was not mailed to the applicant's current address and such address had been provided to the Office of International Affairs by the applicant prior to the date of mailing in accordance with section 265 of the Act and Service regulations, unless the asylum officer determines that the applicant received reasonable notice of the interview or fingerprinting appointment.

§ 1240.69 Reliance on information compiled by other sources.

In determining whether an applicant is eligible for suspension of deportation or special rule cancellation of removal, the asylum officer may rely on material described in § 1208.12 of this chapter. Nothing in this subpart shall be construed to entitle the applicant to conduct discovery directed toward records, officers, agents, or employees of the Service, the Department of Justice, or the Department of State.

§ 1240.70 Decision by the Service.

(a) *Service of decision.* Unless the asylum officer has granted the application for suspension of deportation or special rule cancellation of removal at the time of the interview or as otherwise provided by an Asylum Office, the applicant will be required to return to the Asylum Office to receive service of the decision on the applicant's application. If the applicant does not speak English fluently, the applicant shall bring an interpreter when returning to the office to receive service of the decision.

(b) *Grant of suspension of deportation.* An asylum officer may grant suspension of deportation to an applicant eligible to apply for this relief with the Service who qualifies for suspension of deportation under former section 244(a)(1) of the Act, as in effect prior to April 1, 1997, who is not an alien described in former section 241(a)(4)(D) of the Act, as in effect prior to April 1, 1997, and who admits deportability under any law of the United States, excluding former section 241(a)(2), (3), or (4) of the Act, as in effect prior to April 1, 1997. If the Service has made a preliminary decision to grant the applicant suspension of deportation under this subpart, the applicant shall be notified of that decision and will be asked to sign an admission of deportability or inadmissibility. The applicant must sign the admission before the Service may grant the relief sought. If suspension of deportation is granted, the Service shall adjust the status of the alien to lawful permanent resident, effective as of the date that suspension of deportation is granted.

(c) *Grant of cancellation of removal.* An asylum officer may grant cancellation of removal to an applicant who is eligible to apply for this relief with the Service, and who qualifies for cancellation of removal under section

309(f)(1)(A) of IIRIRA, as amended by section 203 of NACARA, and who admits deportability under section 237(a), excluding paragraphs (2), (3), and (4), of the Act, or inadmissibility under section 212(a), excluding paragraphs (2) or (3), of the Act. If the Service has made a preliminary decision to grant the applicant cancellation of removal under this subpart, the applicant shall be notified of that decision and asked to sign an admission of deportability or inadmissibility. The applicant must sign the concession before the Service may grant the relief sought. If the Service grants cancellation of removal, the Service shall adjust the status of the alien to lawful permanent resident, effective as of the date that cancellation of removal is granted.

(d) *Referral of the application.* Except as provided in paragraphs (e) and (f) of this section, and unless the applicant is granted asylum or is in lawful immigrant or non-immigrant status, an asylum officer shall refer the application for suspension of deportation or special rule cancellation of removal to the Immigration Court for adjudication in deportation or removal proceedings, and will provide the applicant with written notice of the statutory or regulatory basis for the referral, if:

(1) The applicant is not clearly eligible for suspension of deportation under former section 244(a)(1) of the Act as in effect prior to April 1, 1997, or for cancellation of removal under section 309(f)(1)(A) of IIRIRA, as amended by NACARA;

(2) The applicant does not appear to merit relief as a matter of discretion;

(3) The applicant appears to be eligible for suspension of deportation or special rule cancellation of removal under this subpart, but does not admit deportability or inadmissibility; or

(4) The applicant failed to appear for a scheduled interview with an asylum officer or failed to comply with fingerprinting processing requirements and such failure was not excused by the Service, unless the application is dismissed.

(e) *Dismissal of the application.* An asylum officer shall dismiss without prejudice an application for suspension of deportation or special rule cancellation of removal submitted by an applicant who has been granted asylum, or who is in lawful immigrant or non-immigrant status. An asylum officer may also dismiss an application for failure to appear, pursuant to § 1240.68. The asylum officer will provide the applicant written notice of the statutory or regulatory basis for the dismissal.

(f) *Special provisions for certain ABC class members whose proceedings before EOIR were administratively closed or continued.* The following provisions shall apply with respect to an *ABC* class member who was in proceedings before the Immigration Court or the Board, and those proceedings were closed or continued pursuant to the *ABC* settlement agreement:

(1) *Suspension of deportation or asylum granted.* If an asylum officer grants asylum or suspension of deportation, the previous proceedings before the Immigration Court or Board shall be terminated as a matter of law on the date relief is granted.

(2) *Asylum denied and application for suspension of deportation not approved.* If an asylum officer denies asylum and does not grant the applicant suspension of deportation, the Service shall move to recalendar proceedings before the Immigration Court or resume proceedings before the Board, whichever is appropriate. The Service shall refer to the Immigration Court or the Board the application for suspension of deportation. In the case where jurisdiction rests with the Board, an application for suspension of deportation that is referred to the Board will be remanded to the Immigration Court for adjudication.

(g) *Special provisions for dependents whose proceedings before EOIR were administratively closed or continued.* If an asylum officer grants suspension of deportation or special rule cancellation of removal to an applicant described in § 1240.61(a)(4) or (a)(5), whose proceedings before EOIR were administratively closed or continued, those proceedings shall terminate as of the date the relief is granted. If suspension of deportation or special rule cancellation of removal is not granted, the Service shall move to recalendar proceedings before the Immigration Court or resume proceedings before the Board, whichever is appropriate. The Service shall refer to the Immigration Court or the Board the application for suspension of deportation or special rule cancellation of removal. In the case where jurisdiction rests with the Board, an application for suspension of deportation or special rule cancellation of removal that is referred to the Board will be remanded to the Immigration Court for adjudication.

(h) *Special provisions for applicants who depart the United States and return under a grant of advance parole while in deportation proceedings.* Notwithstanding paragraphs (f) and (g) of this section, for purposes of adjudicating an application for suspension of deportation or special rule cancellation of removal under this subpart, if an applicant departs and returns to the United States pursuant to a grant of advance parole while in deportation proceedings, including deportation proceedings administratively closed or continued pursuant to the *ABC* settlement agreement, the deportation proceedings will be considered terminated as of the date of applicant's departure from the United States. A decision on the NACARA application shall be issued in accordance with paragraph (a), and paragraphs (c) through (e) of this section.

PART 1241—APPREHENSION AND DETENTION OF ALIENS ORDERED REMOVED

Subpart A—Post-hearing Detention and Removal

Sec.

Subpart B—Deportation of Excluded Aliens (for Hearings Commenced Prior to April 1, 1997)

Subpart C—Deportation of Aliens in the United States (for Hearings Commenced Prior to April 1, 1997)

AUTHORITY: 5 U.S.C. 301, 552, 552a; 8 U.S.C. 1103, 1182, 1223, 1224, 1225, 1226, 1227, 1231, 1251, 1253, 1255, 1330, 1362; 18 U.S.C. 4002, 4013(c)(4).

SOURCE: 62 FR 10378, Mar. 6, 1997, unless otherwise noted. Duplicated from part 241 at 68 FR 9840, Feb. 28, 2003.

EDITORIAL NOTE: Nomenclature changes to part 1241 appear at 68 FR 9846, Feb. 28, 2003, and 68 FR 10357, Mar. 5, 2003.

Subpart A—Post-hearing Detention and Removal

§ 1241.1 Final order of removal.

An order of removal made by the immigration judge at the conclusion of proceedings under section 240 of the Act shall become final:

(a) Upon dismissal of an appeal by the Board of Immigration Appeals;

(b) Upon waiver of appeal by the respondent;

(c) Upon expiration of the time allotted for an appeal if the respondent does not file an appeal within that time;

(d) If certified to the Board or Attorney General, upon the date of the subsequent decision ordering removal;

(e) If an immigration judge orders an alien removed in the alien's absence, immediately upon entry of such order; or

(f) If an immigration judge issues an alternate order of removal in connection with a grant of voluntary departure, upon overstay of the voluntary departure period, or upon the failure to post a required voluntary departure bond within 5 business days. If the respondent has filed a timely appeal with the Board, the order shall become final upon an order of removal by the Board or the Attorney General, or upon overstay of the voluntary departure period granted or reinstated by the Board or the Attorney General.

[62 FR 10378, Mar. 6, 1997, as amended at 73 FR 76938, Dec. 18, 2008]

§1241.2 Warrant of removal; detention of aliens during removal period.

For the regulations of the Department of Homeland Security with respect to the detention and removal of aliens who are subject to a final order of removal, see 8 CFR part 241.

[70 FR 674, Jan. 5, 2005]

§§1241.3–1241.5 [Reserved]

§1241.6 Administrative stay of removal.

(a) An alien under a final order of deportation or removal may seek a stay of deportation or removal from the Department of Homeland Security as provided in 8 CFR 241.6.

(b) A denial of a stay by the Department of Homeland Security shall not preclude an immigration judge or the Board from granting a stay in connection with a previously filed motion to reopen or a motion to reconsider as provided in 8 CFR part 1003.

(c) The Service shall take all reasonable steps to comply with a stay granted by an immigration judge or the Board. However, such a stay shall cease to have effect if granted (or communicated) after the alien has been placed aboard an aircraft or other conveyance for removal and the normal boarding has been completed.

[65 FR 80298, Dec. 21, 2000, as amended at 67 FR 39259, June 7, 2002; 70 FR 674, Jan. 5, 2005]

§1241.7 Self-removal.

Any alien who has departed from the United States while an order of deportation or removal is outstanding shall be considered to have been deported, excluded and deported, or removed, except that an alien who departed before the expiration of the voluntary departure period granted in connection with an alternate order of deportation or removal shall not be considered to be so deported or removed.

[67 FR 39260, June 7, 2002, as amended at 70 FR 674, Jan. 5, 2005]

§1241.8 Reinstatement of removal orders.

(a) *Applicability.* An alien who illegally reenters the United States after having been removed, or having departed voluntarily, while under an order of exclusion, deportation, or removal shall be removed from the United States by reinstating the prior order. The alien has no right to a hearing before an immigration judge in such circumstances. In establishing whether an alien is subject to this section, the immigration officer shall determine the following:

(1) Whether the alien has been subject to a prior order of removal. The immigration officer must obtain the prior order of exclusion, deportation, or removal relating to the alien.

(2) The identity of the alien, *i.e.*, whether the alien is in fact an alien who was previously removed, or who departed voluntarily while under an order of exclusion, deportation, or removal. In disputed cases, verification of identity shall be accomplished by a comparison of fingerprints between those of the previously excluded, deported, or removed alien contained in Service records and those of the subject alien. In the absence of fingerprints in a disputed case the alien shall not be removed pursuant to this paragraph.

(3) Whether the alien unlawfully reentered the United States. In making this determination, the officer shall consider all relevant evidence, including statements made by the alien and any evidence in the alien's possession. The immigration officer shall attempt to verify an alien's claim, if any, that he or she was lawfully admitted, which shall include a check of Service data systems available to the officer.

(b) *Notice.* If an officer determines that an alien is subject to removal under this section, he or she shall provide the alien with written notice of his or her determination. The officer shall advise the alien that he or she may make a written or oral statement contesting the determination. If the alien wishes to make such a statement, the officer shall allow the alien to do so and shall consider whether the alien's statement warrants reconsideration of the determination.

(c) *Order*. If the requirements of paragraph (a) of this section are met, the alien shall be removed under the previous order of exclusion, deportation, or removal in accordance with section 241(a)(5) of the Act.

(d) *Exception for applicants for benefits under section 902 of HRIFA or sections 202 or 203 of NACARA*. If an alien who is otherwise subject to this section has applied for adjustment of status under either section 902 of Division A of Public Law 105–277, the Haitian Refugee Immigrant Fairness Act of 1998 (HRIFA), or section 202 of Public Law 105–100, the Nicaraguan Adjustment and Central American Relief Act (NACARA), the provisions of section 241(a)(5) of the Immigration and Nationality Act shall not apply. The immigration officer may not reinstate the prior order in accordance with this section unless and until a final decision to deny the application for adjustment has been made. If the application for adjustment of status is granted, the prior order shall be rendered moot.

(e) *Exception for withholding of removal*. If an alien whose prior order of removal has been reinstated under this section expresses a fear of returning to the country designated in that order, the alien shall be immediately referred to an asylum officer for an interview to determine whether the alien has a reasonable fear of persecution or torture pursuant to § 1208.31 of this chapter.

(f) *Execution of reinstated order*. Execution of the reinstated order of removal and detention of the alien shall be administered in accordance with this part.

[62 FR 10378, Mar. 6, 1997, as amended at 64 FR 8495, Feb. 19, 1999; 66 FR 29451, May 31, 2001]

§§ 1241.9–1241.13 [Reserved]

§ 1241.14 Continued detention of removable aliens on account of special circumstances.

(a) *Scope*. This section provides for the review of determinations by the Department of Homeland Security to continue the detention of particular removable aliens found to be specially dangerous. See 8 CFR 241.14.

(1) *Applicability*. This section applies to the review of the continued detention of removable aliens because the Department of Homeland Security has determined that release of the alien would pose a special danger to the public, where there is no significant likelihood of removal in the reasonably foreseeable future. This section does not apply to aliens who are not subject to the special review provisions under 8 CFR 241.13.

(2) *Jurisdiction*. The immigration judges and the Board have jurisdiction with respect to determinations as to whether release of an alien would pose a special danger to the public, as provided in paragraphs (f) through (k) of this section.

(b)–(e) [Reserved]

(f) *Detention of aliens determined to be specially dangerous*—(1) *Standard for continued detention*. Subject to the review procedures provided in this section, the Service shall continue to detain an alien if the release of the alien would pose a special danger to the public, because:

(i) The alien has previously committed one or more crimes of violence as defined in 18 U.S.C. 16;

(ii) Due to a mental condition or personality disorder and behavior associated with that condition or disorder, the alien is likely to engage in acts of violence in the future; and

(iii) No conditions of release can reasonably be expected to ensure the safety of the public.

(2) *Determination by the Commissioner*. The Service shall promptly initiate review proceedings under paragraph (g) of this section if the Commissioner has determined in writing that the alien's release would pose a special danger to the public, according to the standards of paragraph (f)(1) of this section.

(3) *Medical or mental health examination*. Before making such a determination, the Commissioner shall arrange for a report by a physician employed or designated by the Public Health Service based on a full medical and psychiatric examination of the alien. The report shall include recommendations pertaining to whether, due to a mental condition or personality disorder and behavior associated with that condition or disorder, the alien is likely to engage in acts of violence in the future.

(4) *Detention pending review.* After the Commissioner or Deputy Commissioner has made a determination under this paragraph, the Service shall continue to detain the alien, unless an immigration judge or the Board issues an administratively final decision dismissing the review proceedings under this section.

(g) *Referral to Immigration Judge.* Jurisdiction for an immigration judge to review a determination by the Service pursuant to paragraph (f) of this section that an alien is specially dangerous shall commence with the filing by the Service of a Notice of Referral to the Immigration Judge (Form I–863) with the Immigration Court having jurisdiction over the place of the alien's custody. The Service shall promptly provide to the alien by personal service a copy of the Notice of Referral to the Immigration Judge and all accompanying documents.

(1) *Factual basis.* The Service shall attach a written statement that contains a summary of the basis for the Commissioner's determination to continue to detain the alien, including a description of the evidence relied upon to reach the determination regarding the alien's special dangerousness. The Service shall attach copies of all relevant documents used to reach its decision to continue to detain the alien.

(2) *Notice of reasonable cause hearing.* The Service shall attach a written notice advising the alien that the Service is initiating proceedings for the continued detention of the alien and informing the alien of the procedures governing the reasonable cause hearing, as set forth at paragraph (h) of this section.

(3) *Notice of alien's rights.* The Service shall also provide written notice advising the alien of his or her rights during the reasonable cause hearing and the merits hearing before the Immigration Court, as follows:

(i) The alien shall be provided with the List of Pro Bono Legal Service Providers for the immigration court at which the hearing is being held, and may be represented by an attorney or other representative of his or her choice in accordance with 8 CFR part 1292, at no expense to the Government;

(ii) The Immigration Court shall provide an interpreter for the alien, if necessary, for the reasonable cause hearing and the merits hearing.

(iii) The alien shall have a reasonable opportunity to examine evidence against the alien, to present evidence in the alien's own behalf, and to cross-examine witnesses presented by the Service; and

(iv) The alien shall have the right, at the merits hearing, to cross-examine the author of any medical or mental health reports used as a basis for the determination under paragraph (f) of this section that the alien is specially dangerous.

(4) *Record.* All proceedings before the immigration judge under this section shall be recorded. The Immigration Court shall create a record of proceeding that shall include all testimony and documents related to the proceedings.

(h) *Reasonable cause hearing.* The immigration judge shall hold a preliminary hearing to determine whether the evidence supporting the Service's determination is sufficient to establish reasonable cause to go forward with a merits hearing under paragraph (i) of this section. A finding of reasonable cause under this section will be sufficient to warrant the alien's continued detention pending the completion of the review proceedings under this section.

(1) *Scheduling of hearing.* The reasonable cause hearing shall be commenced not later than 10 business days after the filing of the Form I–863. The Immigration Court shall provide prompt notice to the alien and to the Service of the time and place of the hearing. The hearing may be continued at the request of the alien or his or her representative.

(2) *Evidence.* The Service must show that there is reasonable cause to conduct a merits hearing under a merits hearing under paragraph (i) of this section. The Service may offer any evidence that is material and relevant to the proceeding. Testimony of witnesses, if any, shall be under oath or affirmation. The alien may, but is not required to, offer evidence on his or her own behalf.

(3) *Decision.* The immigration judge shall render a decision, which should be in summary form, within 5 business days after the close of the record, unless that time is extended by agreement of both parties, by a determination from the Chief Immigration Judge that exceptional circumstances make it impractical to render the decision on a highly expedited basis, or because of delay caused by the alien. If the immigration judge determines that the Service has met its burden of establishing reasonable cause, the immigration judge shall advise the alien and the Service, and shall schedule a merits hearing under paragraph (i) of this section to review the Service's determination that the alien is specially dangerous. If the immigration judge determines that the Service has not met its burden, the immigration judge shall order that the review proceedings under this section be dismissed. The order and any documents offered shall be included in the record of proceedings, and may be relied upon in a subsequent merits hearing.

(4) *Appeal.* If the immigration judge dismisses the review proceedings, the Service may appeal to the Board of Immigration Appeals in accordance with §1003.38 of this chapter, except that the Service must file the Notice of Appeal (Form EOIR–26) with the Board within 2 business days after the immigration judge's order. The Notice of Appeal should state clearly and conspicuously that it is an appeal of a reasonable cause decision under this section.

(i) If the Service reserves appeal of a dismissal of the reasonable cause hearing, the immigration judge's order shall be stayed until the expiration of the time to appeal. Upon the Service's filing of a timely Notice of Appeal, the immigration judge's order shall remain in abeyance pending a final decision of the appeal. The stay shall expire if the Service fails to file a timely Notice of Appeal.

(ii) The Board will decide the Service's appeal, by single Board Member review, based on the record of proceedings before the immigration judge. The Board shall expedite its review as far as practicable, as the highest priority among the appeals filed by detained aliens, and shall determine the issue within 20 business days of the filing of the notice of appeal, unless that time is extended by agreement of both parties, by a determination from the Chairman of the Board that exceptional circumstances make it impractical to render the decision on a highly expedited basis, or because of delay caused by the alien.

(iii) If the Board determines that the Service has met its burden of showing reasonable cause under this paragraph (h), the Board shall remand the case to the immigration judge for the scheduling of a merits hearing under paragraph (i) of this section. If the Board determines that the Service has not met its burden, the Board shall dismiss the review proceedings under this section.

(i) *Merits hearing.* If there is reasonable cause to conduct a merits hearing under this section, the immigration judge shall promptly schedule the hearing and shall expedite the proceedings as far as practicable. The immigration judge shall allow adequate time for the parties to prepare for the merits hearing, but, if requested by the alien, the hearing shall commence within 30 days. The hearing may be continued at the request of the alien or his or her representative, or at the request of the Service upon a showing of exceptional circumstances by the Service.

(1) *Evidence.* The Service shall have the burden of proving, by clear and convincing evidence, that the alien should remain in custody because the alien's release would pose a special danger to the public, under the standards of paragraph (f)(1) of this section. The immigration judge may receive into evidence any oral or written statement that is material and relevant to this determination. Testimony of witnesses shall be under oath or affirmation. The alien may, but is not required to, offer evidence on his or her own behalf.

(2) *Factors for consideration.* In making any determination in a merits hearing under this section, the immigration judge shall consider the following non-exclusive list of factors:

(i) The alien's prior criminal history, particularly the nature and seriousness of any prior crimes involving violence or threats of violence;

(ii) The alien's previous history of recidivism, if any, upon release from either Service or criminal custody;

(iii) The substantiality of the Service's evidence regarding the alien's current mental condition or personality disorder;

(iv) The likelihood that the alien will engage in acts of violence in the future; and

(v) The nature and seriousness of the danger to the public posed by the alien's release.

(3) *Decision.* After the closing of the record, the immigration judge shall render a decision as soon as practicable. The decision may be oral or written. The decision shall state whether or not the Service has met its burden of establishing that the alien should remain in custody because the alien's release would pose a special danger to the public, under the standards of paragraph (f)(1) of this section. The decision shall also include the reasons for the decision under each of the standards of paragraph (f)(1) of this section, although a formal enumeration of findings is not required. Notice of the decision shall be served in accordance with § 1240.13(a) or (b).

(i) If the immigration judge determines that the Service has met its burden, the immigration judge shall enter an order providing for the continued detention of the alien.

(ii) If the immigration judge determines that the Service has failed to meet its burden, the immigration judge shall order that the review proceedings under this section be dismissed.

(4) *Appeal.* Either party may appeal an adverse decision to the Board of Immigration Appeals in accordance with § 3.38 of this chapter, except that, if the immigration judge orders dismissal of the proceedings, the Service shall have only 5 business days to file a Notice of Appeal with the Board. The Notice of Appeal should state clearly and conspicuously that this is an appeal of a merits decision under this section.

(i) If the Service reserves appeal of a dismissal, the immigration judge's order shall be stayed until the expiration of the time to appeal. Upon the Service's filing of a timely Notice of Appeal, the immigration judge's order shall remain in abeyance pending a final decision of the appeal. The stay shall expire if the Service fails to file a timely Notice of Appeal.

(ii) The Board shall conduct its review of the appeal as provided in 8 CFR part 3, but shall expedite its review as far as practicable, as the highest priority among the appeals filed by detained aliens. The decision of the Board shall be final as provided in § 1003.1(d)(3) of this chapter.

(j) *Release of alien upon dismissal of proceedings.* If there is an administratively final decision by the immigration judge or the Board dismissing the review proceedings under this section upon conclusion of the reasonable cause hearing or the merits hearing, the Service shall promptly release the alien on conditions of supervision, as determined by the Service, pursuant to § 1241.13. The conditions of supervision shall not be subject to review by the immigration judge or the Board.

(k) *Subsequent review for aliens whose release would pose a special danger to the public*—(1) *Periodic review.* In any case where the immigration judge or the Board has entered an order providing for the alien to remain in custody after a merits hearing pursuant to paragraph (i) of this section, the Service shall continue to provide an ongoing, periodic review of the alien's continued detention, according to § 1241.4 and paragraphs (f)(1)(ii) and (f)(1)(iii) of this section.

(2) *Alien's request for review.* The alien may also request a review of his or her custody status because of changed circumstances, as provided in this paragraph (k). The request shall be in writing and directed to the HQPDU.

(3) *Time for review.* An alien may only request a review of his or her custody status under this paragraph (k) no earlier than six months after the last decision of the immigration judge under this section or, if the decision was appealed, the decision of the Board.

(4) *Showing of changed circumstances.* The alien shall bear the initial burden to establish a material change in circumstances such that the release of the alien would no longer pose a special danger to the public under the standards of paragraph (f)(1) of this section.

(5) *Review by the Service.* If the Service determines, upon consideration of

the evidence submitted by the alien and other relevant evidence, that the alien is not likely to commit future acts of violence or that the Service will be able to impose adequate conditions of release so that the alien will not pose a special danger to the public, the Service shall release the alien from custody pursuant to the procedures in § 1241.13. If the Service determines that continued detention is needed in order to protect the public, the Service shall provide a written notice to the alien stating the basis for the Service's determination, and provide a copy of the evidence relied upon by the Service. The notice shall also advise the alien of the right to move to set aside the prior review proceedings under this section.

(6) *Motion to set aside determination in prior review proceedings.* If the Service denies the alien's request for release from custody, the alien may file a motion with the Immigration Court that had jurisdiction over the merits hearing to set aside the determination in the prior review proceedings under this section. The immigration judge shall consider any evidence submitted by the alien or relied upon by the Service and shall provide an opportunity for the Service to respond to the motion.

(i) If the immigration judge determines that the alien has provided good reason to believe that, because of a material change in circumstances, releasing the alien would no longer pose a special danger to the public under the standards of paragraph (f)(1) of this section, the immigration judge shall set aside the determination in the prior review proceedings under this section and schedule a new merits hearing as provided in paragraph (i) of this section.

(ii) Unless the immigration judge determines that the alien has satisfied the requirements under paragraph (k)(6)(i) of this section, the immigration judge shall deny the motion. Neither the immigration judge nor the Board may *sua sponte* set aside a determination in prior review proceedings. Notwithstanding 8 CFR 1003.23 or 1003.2 (motions to reopen), the provisions set forth in this paragraph (k) shall be the only vehicle for seeking review based on material changed circumstances.

(iii) The alien may appeal an adverse decision to the Board in accordance with § 1003.38 of this chapter. The Notice of Appeal should state clearly and conspicuously that this is an appeal of a denial of a motion to set aside a prior determination in review proceedings under this section.

[66 FR 56979, Nov. 14, 2001, as amended at 70 FR 674, Jan. 5, 2005; 80 FR 59513, Oct. 1, 2015]

§ 1241.15 Lack of jurisdiction to review other country of removal.

The immigration judges and the Board of Immigration Appeals have no jurisdiction to review any determination by officers of the Department of Homeland Security under 8 CFR 241.15.

[70 FR 675, Jan. 5, 2005]

§§ 1241.16–1241.19 [Reserved]

Subpart B—Deportation of Excluded Aliens (for Hearings Commenced Prior to April 1, 1997)

§ 1241.20 Aliens ordered excluded.

For the regulations of the Department of Homeland Security pertaining to the detention and deportation of excluded aliens, see 8 CFR 241.20 through 241.25.

[70 FR 675, Jan. 5, 2005]

§§ 1241.21–1241.29 [Reserved]

Subpart C—Deportation of Aliens in the United States (for Hearings Commenced Prior to April 1, 1997)

§ 1241.30 Aliens ordered deported.

For the regulations of the Department of Homeland Security pertaining to the detention and deportation of aliens ordered deported, see 8 CFR 241.30 through 241.33.

[70 FR 675, Jan. 5, 2005]

§ 1241.31 Final order of deportation.

Except as otherwise required by section 242(c) of the Act for the specific purposes of that section, an order of deportation, including an alternate order of deportation coupled with an order of voluntary departure, made by the immigration judge in proceedings under 8 CFR part 1240 shall become final upon dismissal of an appeal by the Board of Immigration Appeals, upon waiver of appeal, or upon expiration of the time allotted for an appeal when no appeal is taken; or, if such an order is issued by the Board or approved by the Board upon certification, it shall be final as of the date of the Board's decision.

§ 1241.32 Warrant of deportation.

A Form I–205, Warrant of Deportation, based upon the final administrative order of deportation in the alien's case shall be issued by a district director. The district director shall exercise the authority contained in section 243 of the Act to determine at whose expense the alien shall be deported and whether his or her mental or physical condition requires personal care and attention en route to his or her destination.

§ 1241.33 Expulsion.

(a) *Execution of order.* Except in the exercise of discretion by the district director, and for such reasons as are set forth in § 1212.5(b) of this chapter, once an order of deportation becomes final, an alien shall be taken into custody and the order shall be executed. For the purposes of this part, an order of deportation is final and subject to execution upon the date when any of the following occurs:

(1) A grant of voluntary departure expires;

(2) An immigration judge enters an order of deportation without granting voluntary departure or other relief, and the alien respondent waives his or her right to appeal;

(3) The Board of Immigration Appeals enters an order of deportation on appeal, without granting voluntary departure or other relief; or

(4) A Federal district or appellate court affirms an administrative order of deportation in a petition for review or habeas corpus action.

(b) *Service of decision.* In the case of an order entered by any of the authorities enumerated above, the order shall be executed no sooner than 72 hours after service of the decision, regardless of whether the alien is in Service custody, provided that such period may be waived on the knowing and voluntary request of the alien. Nothing in this paragraph shall be construed, however, to preclude assumption of custody by the Service at the time of issuance of the final order.

[62 FR 10378, Mar. 6, 1997, as amended at 65 FR 82256, Dec. 28, 2000]

PART 1244—TEMPORARY PROTECTED STATUS FOR NATIONALS OF DESIGNATED STATES

Sec.

AUTHORITY: 8 U.S.C. 1103, 1254, 1254a note, 8 CFR part 2.

SOURCE: Duplicated from part 244 at 68 FR 9841, Feb. 28, 2003.

EDITORIAL NOTE: Nomenclature changes to part 1244 appear at 68 FR 9846, Feb. 28, 2003, and 68 FR 10357, Mar. 5, 2003.

§ 1244.1 Definitions.

As used in this part:

Brief, casual, and innocent absence means a departure from the United States that satisfies the following criteria:

(1) Each such absence was of short duration and reasonably calculated to accomplish the purpose(s) for the absence;

(2) The absence was not the result of an order of deportation, an order of voluntary departure, or an administrative grant of voluntary departure without the institution of deportation proceedings; and

(3) The purposes for the absence from the United States or actions while outside of the United States were not contrary to law.

Charging document means the written instrument which initiates a proceeding before an Immigration Judge. For proceedings initiated prior to April 1, 1997, these documents include an Order to Show Cause, a Notice to Applicant for Admission Detained for Hearing before Immigration Judge, and a Notice of Intention to Rescind and Request for Hearing by Alien. For proceedings initiated after April 1, 1997, these documents include a Notice to Appear, a Notice of Referral to Immigration Judge, and a Notice of Intention to Rescind and Request for Hearing by Alien.

Continuously physically present means actual physical presence in the United States for the entire period specified in the regulations. An alien shall not be considered to have failed to maintain continuous physical presence in the United States by virtue of brief, casual, and innocent absences as defined within this section.

Continuously resided means residing in the United States for the entire period specified in the regulations. An alien shall not be considered to have failed to maintain continuous residence in the United States by reason of a brief, casual and innocent absence as defined within this section or due merely to a brief temporary trip abroad required by emergency or extenuating circumstances outside the control of the alien.

Felony means a crime committed in the United States, punishable by imprisonment for a term of more than one year, regardless of the term such alien actually served, if any, except: When the offense is defined by the State as a misdemeanor and the sentence actually imposed is one year or less regardless of the term such alien actually served. Under this exception for purposes of section 244 of the Act, the crime shall be treated as a misdemeanor.

Foreign state means any foreign country or part thereof as designated by the Attorney General pursuant to section 244 of the Act.

Misdemeanor means a crime committed in the United States, either:

(1) Punishable by imprisonment for a term of one year or less, regardless of the term such alien actually served, if any, or

(2) A crime treated as a misdemeanor under the term "felony" of this section.

For purposes of this definition, any crime punishable by imprisonment for a maximum term of five days or less shall not be considered a felony or misdemeanor.

Prima facie means eligibility established with the filing of a completed application for Temporary Protected Status containing factual information that if unrebutted will establish a claim of eligibility under section 244 of the Act.

Register means to properly file, with the director, a completed application, with proper fee, for Temporary Protected Status during the registration period designated under section 244(b) of the Act.

[56 FR 619, Jan. 7, 1991, as amended at 56 FR 23497, May 22, 1991. Redesignated at 62 FR 10367, 10382, Mar. 6, 1997, as amended at 63 FR 63595, Nov. 16, 1998; 64 FR 4781, Feb. 1, 1999]

§ 1244.2 Eligibility.

Except as provided in §§ 1244.3 and 1244.4, an alien may in the discretion of the director be granted Temporary Protected Status if the alien establishes that he or she:

(a) Is a national, as defined in section 101(a)(21) of the Act, of a foreign state designated under section 244(b) of the Act;

(b) Has been continuously physically present in the United States since the effective date of the most recent designation of that foreign state;

(c) Has continuously resided in the United States since such date as the Attorney General may designate;

(d) Is admissible as an immigrant except as provided under § 1244.3;

(e) Is not ineligible under § 1244.4; and

(f)(1) Registers for Temporary Protected Status during the initial registration period announced by public notice in the FEDERAL REGISTER, or

(2) During any subsequent extension of such designation if at the time of the initial registration period:

(i) The applicant is a nonimmigrant or has been granted voluntary departure status or any relief from removal;

(ii) The applicant has an application for change of status, adjustment of status, asylum, voluntary departure, or any relief from removal which is pending or subject to further review or appeal;

(iii) The applicant is a parolee or has a pending request for reparole; or

(iv) The applicant is a spouse or child of an alien currently eligible to be a TPS registrant.

(3) Eligibility for late initial registration in a currently designated foreign state shall also continue until January 15, 1999, for any applicant who would have been eligible to apply previously if paragraph (f)(2) of this section as revised had been in effect before November 16, 1998.

(g) Has filed an application for late registration with the appropriate Service director within a 60-day period immediately following the expiration or termination of conditions described in paragraph (f)(2) of this section.

[63 FR 63595, Nov. 16, 1998]

§ 1244.3 Applicability of grounds of inadmissibility.

(a) *Grounds of inadmissibility not to be applied.* Paragraphs (4), (5) (A) and (B), and (7)(A)(i) of section 212(a) of the Act shall not render an alien ineligible for Temporary Protected Status.

(b) *Waiver of grounds of inadmissibility.* Except as provided in paragraph (c) of this section, the Service may waive any other provision of section 212(a) of the Act in the case of individual aliens for humanitarian purposes, to assure family unity, or when the granting of such a waiver is in the public interest. If an alien is inadmissible on grounds which may be waived as set forth in this paragraph, he or she shall be advised of the procedures for applying for a waiver of grounds of inadmissibility on Form I–601 (Application for waiver of grounds of excludability).

(c) *Grounds of inadmissibility that may not be waived.* The Service may not waive the following provisions of section 212(a) of the Act:

(1) Paragraphs (2)(A)(i), (2)(B), and (2)(C) (relating to criminals and drug offenses);

(2) Paragraphs (3)(A), (3)(B), (3)(C), and (3)(D) (relating to national security); or

(3) Paragraph (3)(E) (relating to those who assisted in the Nazi persecution).

[56 FR 619, Jan. 7, 1991, as amended at 58 FR 58937, Nov. 5, 1993. Redesignated at 62 FR 10367, 10382, Mar. 6, 1997]

§ 1244.4 Ineligible aliens.

An alien is ineligible for Temporary Protected Status if the alien:

(a) Has been convicted of any felony or two or more misdemeanors, as defined in § 1244.1, committed in the United States, or

(b) Is an alien described in section 243(h)(2) of the Act.

[56 FR 619, Jan. 7, 1991, as amended at 56 FR 23497, May 22, 1991. Redesignated at 62 FR 10367, 10382, Mar. 6, 1997, as amended at 63 FR 63596, Nov. 16, 1998]

§ 1244.5 Temporary treatment benefits for eligible aliens.

(a) *Prior to the registration period.* Prior to the registration period established by the Attorney General, a national of a foreign state designated by the Attorney General shall be afforded temporary treatment benefits upon the filing, after the effective date of such designation, of a completed application for Temporary Protected Status which establishes the alien's *prima facie* eligibility for benefits under section 244 of the Act. This application may be filed without fee. Temporary treatment benefits, if granted, shall terminate unless the registration fee is paid or a waiver is sought within the first thirty days of the registration period designated by the Attorney General. If the registration fee is paid or a waiver is sought within such thirty day period, temporary treatment benefits shall continue until terminated under § 1244.13. The denial of temporary treatment benefits prior to the registration period designated by the Attorney General shall be without prejudice to the filing of an application for Temporary Protected Status during such registration period.

(b) *During the registration period.* Upon the filing of an application for Temporary Protected Status, the alien shall be afforded temporary treatment benefits, if the application establishes the alien's *prima facie* eligibility for Temporary Protected Status. Such temporary treatment benefits shall continue until terminated under § 1244.13.

(c) *Denied benefits.* There shall be no appeal from the denial of temporary treatment benefits.

[56 FR 619, May 22, 1991, as amended at 56 FR 23497, May 22, 1991. Redesignated at 62 FR 10367, 10382, Mar. 6, 1997, as amended at 63 FR 63596, Nov. 16, 1998]

§ 1244.6 Application.

An application for Temporary Protected Status must be made in accordance with § 103.2 of this chapter except as provided in this section. Each application must be filed with the fee, as provided in §103.7 of this chapter by each individual seeking temporary protected status, except that the filing fee for the Form I–765 will be charged only for those applicants between the ages of 14 and 65 (inclusive) who are requesting employment authorization. Each application must include a completed Form I–821, Application for Temporary Protected Status, Form I–765, Application for Employment Authorization, two identification photographs (1½″ × 1½″), and supporting evidence as provided in § 1244.9. Every applicant who is 14 years of age or older must be fingerprinted on Form FD–258, Applicant Card, as prescribed in § 103.2(e) of this chapter.

[64 FR 4781, Feb. 1, 1999]

§ 1244.7 Filing the application.

(a) An application for Temporary Protected Status shall be filed with the director having jurisdiction over the applicant's place of residence.

(b) An application for Temporary Protected Status must be filed during the registration period established by the Attorney General, except in the case of an alien described in § 1244.2(f)(2).

(c) Each applicant must pay a fee, as determined at the time of the designation of the foreign state, except as provided in § 1244.5(a).

(d) If the alien has a pending deportation or exclusion proceeding before the immigration judge or Board of Immigration Appeals at the time a foreign state is designated under section 244(b) of the Act, the alien shall be given written notice concerning Temporary Protected Status. Such alien shall have the opportunity to submit an application for Temporary Protected Status to the director under paragraph (a) of this section during the published registration period unless the basis of the charging document, if established, would render the alien ineligible for Temporary Protected Status under § 1244.3(c) or § 1244.4. Eligibility for Temporary Protected Status in the latter instance shall be decided by the Executive Office for Immigration Review during such proceedings.

[63 FR 63596, Nov. 16, 1998]

§ 1244.8 Appearance.

The applicant may be required to appear in person before an immigration officer. The applicant may be required to present documentary evidence to establish his or her eligibility. The applicant may have a representative as defined in § 1292.1 of this chapter present during any examination. Such representative shall not directly participate in the examination; however, such representative may consult with and provide advice to the applicant. The record of examination shall consist of the application, documents relating to the application, and the decision of the director.

[56 FR 619, Jan. 7, 1991, as amended at 56 FR 23497, May 22, 1991. Redesignated at 62 FR 10367, 10382, Mar. 6, 1997, as amended at 63 FR 63596, Nov. 16, 1998]

§ 1244.9 Evidence.

(a) *Documentation.* Applicants shall submit all documentation as required in the instructions or requested by the Service. The Service may require proof of unsuccessful efforts to obtain documents claimed to be unavailable. If any required document is unavailable, an affidavit or other credible evidence may be submitted.

(1) *Evidence of identity and nationality.* Each application must be accompanied by evidence of the applicant's identity and nationality, if available. If these documents are unavailable, the applicant shall file an affidavit showing proof of unsuccessful efforts to obtain such identity documents, explaining why the consular process is unavailable, and affirming that he or she is a national of the designated foreign state. A personal interview before an immigration officer shall be required for each applicant who fails to provide documentary proof of identity or nationality. During this interview, the applicant may present any secondary evidence that he or she feels would be helpful in showing nationality. Acceptable evidence in descending order of preference may consist of:

(i) Passport;

(ii) Birth certificate accompanied by photo identification; and/or

(iii) Any national identity document from the alien's country of origin bearing photo and/or fingerprint.

(2) *Proof of residence.* Evidence to establish proof of continuous residence in the United States during the requisite period of time may consist of any of the following:

(i) Employment records, which may consist of pay stubs, W-2 Forms, certification of the filing of Federal, State, or local income tax returns; letters from employer(s) or, if the applicant has been self employed, letters from banks, and other firms with whom he or she has done business. In all of the above, the name of the alien and the name of the employer or other interested organization must appear on the form or letter, as well as relevant dates. Letters from employers must be in affidavit form, and shall be signed and attested to by the employer under penalty of perjury. Such letters from employers must include:

(A) Alien's address(es) at the time of employment;

(B) Exact period(s) of employment;

(C) Period(s) of layoff; and

(D) Duties with the company.

(ii) Rent receipts, utility bills (gas, electric, telephone, etc.), receipts, or letters from companies showing the dates during which the applicant received service;

(iii) School records (letters, report cards, etc.) from the schools that the applicant or his or her children have attended in the United States showing name of school and period(s) of school attendance;

(iv) Hospital or medical records showing medical treatment or hospitalization of the applicant or his or her children, showing the name of the medical facility or physician as well as the date(s) of the treatment or hospitalization;

(v) Attestations by churches, unions, or other organizations of the applicant's residence by letter which:

(A) Identifies applicant by name;

(B) Is signed by an official whose title is also shown;

(C) Shows inclusive dates of membership;

(D) States the address where applicant resided during the membership period;

(E) Includes the seal of the organization impressed on the letter or is on the letterhead of the organization, if the organization has letterhead stationery;

(F) Establishes how the attestor knows the applicant; and

(G) Establishes the origin of the information being attested to.

(vi) Additional documents to support the applicant's claim, which may include:

(A) Money order receipts for money sent in or out of the country;

(B) Passport entries;

(C) Birth certificates of children born in the United States;

(D) Bank books with dated transactions;

(E) Correspondence between the applicant and other persons or organizations;

(F) Social Security card;

(G) Selective Service card;

(H) Automobile license receipts, title, vehicle registration, etc;

(I) Deeds, mortgages, contracts to which applicant has been a party;

(J) Tax receipts;

(K) Insurance policies, receipts, or letters; and/or

(L) Any other relevant document.

(3) *Evidence of eligibility under section 244(c)(2) of the Act.* An applicant has the burden of showing that he or she is eligible for benefits under this part.

(4) *Evidence of valid immigrant or nonimmigrant status.* In the case of an alien described in § 1244.2(f)(2), Form I–551 or Form I–94 must be submitted by the applicant.

(b) *Sufficiency of evidence.* The sufficiency of all evidence will be judged according to its relevancy, consistency, credibility, and probative value. To meet his or her burden of proof the applicant must provide supporting documentary evidence of eligibility apart from his or her own statements.

(c) *Failure to timely respond.* Failure to timely respond to a request for information, or to appear for a scheduled interview, without good cause, will be deemed an abandonment of the application and will result in a denial of the application for lack of prosecution. Such failure shall be excused if the request for information, or the notice of the interview was not mailed to the applicant's most recent address provided to the Service.

[56 FR 619, Jan. 7, 1991, as amended at 56 FR 23497, May 22, 1991; 58 FR 58937, Nov. 5, 1993. Redesignated at 62 FR 10367, 10382, Mar. 6, 1997, as amended at 63 FR 63596, Nov. 16, 1998]

§ 1244.10 Decision by the director or Administrative Appeals Unit (AAU).

(a) *Temporary treatment benefits.* The director shall grant temporary treatment benefits to the applicant if the applicant establishes *prima facie* eligibility for Temporary Protected Status in accordance with § 1244.5.

(b) *Temporary Protected Status.* Upon review of the evidence presented, the director may approve or deny the application for Temporary Protected Status in the exercise of discretion, consistent with the standards for eligibility in §§ 1244.2, 1244.3, and 1244.4.

(c) *Denial by director.* The decision of the director to deny Temporary Protected Status, a waiver of grounds of inadmissibility, or temporary treatment benefits shall be in writing served in person or by mail to the alien's most recent address provided to the Service and shall state the reason(s) for the denial. Except as otherwise provided in this section, the alien shall be given written notice of his or her right to appeal a decision denying Temporary Protected Status. To exercise such right, the alien shall file a notice of appeal, Form I–290B, with the director who issued the denial. If an appeal is filed, the administrative record shall be forwarded to the AAU for review and decision, pursuant to authority delegated in § 103.1(f)(2), except as otherwise provided in this section.

(1) If the basis for the denial of the Temporary Protected Status constitutes a ground for deportability or excludability which renders the alien ineligible for Temporary Protected Status under § 1244.4 or inadmissible under § 1244.3(c), the decision shall include a charging document which sets forth such ground(s).

(2) If such a charging document is issued, the alien shall not have the right to appeal the director's decision denying Temporary Protected Status as provided in this subsection. The decision shall also apprise the alien of his or her right to a *de novo* determination of his or her eligibility for Temporary Protected Status in deportation or exclusion proceedings pursuant to §§ 1240.11 and 1244.18.

(d) *Decision by AAU.* The decision of the AAU shall be in writing served in person, or by mail to the alien's most recent address provided to the Service, and, if the appeal is dismissed, the decision shall state the reason(s) for the denial.

(1) If the appeal is dismissed by the AAU under § 1240.18(b), the decision shall also apprise the alien of his or her right to a *de novo* determination of eligibility for Temporary Protected Status in deportation or exclusion proceedings.

(2) If the appeal is dismissed by the AAU, the director may issue a charging document if no charging document is presently filed with the Immigration Court.

(3) If a charging document has previously been filed or is pending before the Immigration Court, either party may move to recalendar the case after the decision by the AAU.

(e) *Grant of temporary treatment benefits.* (1) Temporary treatment benefits shall be evidenced by the issuance of an employment authorization document.

The alien shall be given, in English and in the language of the designated foreign state or a language that the alien understands, a notice of the registration requirements for Temporary Protected Status and a notice of the following benefits:

(i) Temporary stay of deportation; and

(ii) Temporary employment authorization.

(2) Unless terminated under § 1244.13, temporary treatment benefits shall remain in effect until a final decision has been made on the application for Temporary Protected Status.

(f) *Grant of temporary protected status.* (1) The decision to grant Temporary Protected Status shall be evidenced by the issuance of an alien registration document. For those aliens requesting employment authorization, the employment authorization document will act as alien registration.

(2) The alien shall be provided with a notice, in English and in the language of the designated foreign state or a language that the alien understands, of the following benefits:

(i) The alien shall not be deported while maintaining Temporary Protected Status;

(ii) Employment authorization;

(iii) The privilege to travel abroad with the prior consent of the director as provided in § 1244.15;

(iv) For the purposes of adjustment of status under section 245 of the Act and change of status under section 248 of the Act, the alien is considered as being in, and maintaining, lawful status as a nonimmigrant while the alien maintains Temporary Protected Status.

(v) An alien eligible to apply for Temporary Protected Status under § 1244.2(f)(2), who was prevented from filing a late application for registration because the regulations failed to provide him or her with this opportunity, will be considered to have been maintaining lawful status as a nonimmigrant until the benefit is granted.

(3) The benefits contained in the notice are the only benefits the alien is entitled to under Temporary Protected Status.

(4) Such notice shall also advise the alien of the following:

(i) The alien must remain eligible for Temporary Protected Status;

(ii) The alien must register annually with the district office or service center having jurisdiction over the alien's place of residence; and

(iii) The alien's failure to comply with paragraphs (f)(4) (i) or (ii) of this section will result in the withdrawal of Temporary Protected Status, including work authorization granted under this Program, and may result in the alien's deportation from the United States.

[56 FR 619, Jan. 7, 1991, as amended at 56 FR 23497, May 22, 1991; 58 FR 58937, Nov. 5, 1993; 60 FR 34090, June 30, 1995. Redesignated at 62 FR 10367, 10382, Mar. 6, 1997, as amended at 63 FR 63596, Nov. 16, 1998; 64 FR 4782, Feb. 1, 1999]

§ 1244.11 Renewal of application; appeal to the Board of Immigration Appeals.

If a charging document is served on the alien with a notice of denial or withdrawal of Temporary Protected Status, an alien may renew the application for Temporary Protected Status in deportation or exclusion proceedings. The decision of the immigration judge as to eligibility for Temporary Protected Status may be appealed to the Board of Immigration Appeals pursuant to § 1003.3 of this chapter. The provisions of this section do not extend the benefits of Temporary Protected Status beyond the termination of a foreign state's designation pursuant to § 1244.19.

[56 FR 619, Jan. 7, 1991, as amended at 56 FR 23497, May 22, 1991. Redesignated at 62 FR 10367, 10382, Mar. 6, 1997, as amended at 63 FR 63596, Nov. 16, 1998]

§ 1244.12 Employment authorization.

(a) Upon approval of an application for Temporary Protected Status, the INS shall grant an employment authorization document valid during the initial period of the foreign state's designation (and any extensions of such period).

(b) If the alien's Temporary Protected Status is withdrawn under § 1244.14, employment authorization expires upon notice of withdrawal or on the date stated on the employment authorization document, whichever occurs later.

(c) If Temporary Protected Status is denied by the INS, employment authorization shall terminate upon notice of denial or at the expiration of the employment authorization document, whichever occurs later.

(d) If the application is renewed or appealed in deportation or exclusion proceedings, or appealed to the Administrative Appeals Unit pursuant to § 1244.18(b), employment authorization will be extended during the pendency of the renewal and/or appeal.

[56 FR 619, Jan. 7, 1991, as amended at 56 FR 23498, May 22, 1991; 60 FR 21975, May 4, 1995. Redesignated at 62 FR 10367, 10382, Mar. 6, 1997, as amended at 63 FR 63596, Nov. 16, 1998; 64 FR 4782, Feb. 1, 1999]

§ 1244.13 Termination of temporary treatment benefits.

(a) Temporary treatment benefits terminate upon a final determination with respect to the alien's eligibility for Temporary Protected Status.

(b) Temporary treatment benefits terminate, in any case, sixty (60) days after the date that notice is published of the termination of a foreign state's designation under section 244(b)(3) of the Act.

[56 FR 619, Jan. 7, 1991. Redesignated at 62 FR 10367, 10382, Mar. 6, 1997, as amended at 63 FR 63596, Nov. 16, 1998]

§ 1244.14 Withdrawal of Temporary Protected Status.

(a) *Authority of director*. The director may withdraw the status of an alien granted Temporary Protected Status under section 244 of the Act at any time upon the occurrence of any of the following:

(1) The alien was not in fact eligible at the time such status was granted, or at any time thereafter becomes ineligible for such status;

(2) The alien has not remained continuously physically present in the United States from the date the alien was first granted Temporary Protected Status under this part. For the purpose of this provision, an alien granted Temporary Protected Status under this part shall be deemed not to have failed to maintain continuous physical presence in the United States if the alien departs the United States after first obtaining permission from the district director to travel pursuant to § 1244.15;

(3) The alien fails without good cause to register with the Attorney General annually within thirty (30) days before the end of each 12-month period after the granting of Temporary Protected Status.

(b) *Decision by director*. (1) Withdrawal of an alien's status under paragraph (a) of this section shall be in writing and served by personal service pursuant to § 103.5(a) of this chapter. If the ground for withdrawal is § 240.14(a)(3), the notice shall provide that the alien has thirty (30) days within which to provide evidence of good cause for failure to register. If the alien fails to respond within thirty (30) days, Temporary Protected Status shall be withdrawn without further notice.

(2) Withdrawal of the alien's Temporary Protected Status under paragraph (b)(1) of this section may subject the applicant to exclusion or deportation proceedings under sections 235, 236, 237, 238, 240, or 241 of the Act as appropriate.

(3) If the basis for the withdrawal of Temporary Protected Status constitutes a ground of deportability or excludability which renders an alien ineligible for Temporary Protected Status under § 1244.4 or inadmissible under § 1244.3(c), the decision shall include a charging document which sets forth such ground(s) with notice of the right of a *de novo* determination of eligibility for Temporary Protected Status in deportation or exclusion proceedings. If the basis for withdrawal does not constitute such a ground, the alien shall be given written notice of his or her right to appeal to the AAU. Upon receipt of an appeal, the administrative record will be forwarded to the AAU for review and decision pursuant to the authority delegated under § 103.1(f)(2). Temporary Protected Status benefits will be extended during the pendency of an appeal.

(c) *Decision by AAU*. If a decision to withdraw Temporary Protected Status is entered by the AAU, the AAU shall notify the alien of the decision and the right to a *de novo* determination of eligibility for Temporary Protected Status in deportation or exclusion proceedings, if the alien is then deportable or excludable, as provided by § 1244.10(d).

[56 FR 619, Jan. 7, 1991, as amended at 56 FR 23498, May 22, 1991. Redesignated at 62 FR 10367, 10382, Mar. 6, 1997, as amended at 63 FR 63596, 63597, Nov. 16, 1998]

§ 1244.15 Travel abroad.

(a) After the grant of Temporary Protected Status, the alien must remain continuously physically present in the United States under the provisions of section 244(c)(3)(B) of the Act. The grant of Temporary Protected Status shall not constitute permission to travel abroad. Permission to travel may be granted by the director pursuant to the Service's advance parole provisions. There is no appeal from a denial of advance parole.

(b) Failure to obtain advance parole prior to the alien's departure from the United States may result in the withdrawal of Temporary Protected Status and/or the institution or recalendering of deportation or exclusion proceedings against the alien.

[56 FR 619, Jan. 7, 1991, as amended at 56 FR 23498, May 22, 1991. Redesignated at 62 FR 10367, 10382, Mar. 6, 1997, as amended at 63 FR 63597, Nov. 16, 1998; 64 FR 4782, Feb. 1, 1999]

§ 1244.16 Confidentiality.

The information contained in the application and supporting documents submitted by an alien shall not be released in any form whatsoever to a third party requester without a court order, or the written consent of the alien. For the purpose of this provision, a third party requester means any requester other than the alien, his or her authorized representative, an officer of the Department of Justice, or any federal or State law enforcement agency. Any information provided under this part may be used for purposes of enforcement of the Act or in any criminal proceeding.

[56 FR 619, Jan. 7, 1991. Redesignated at 62 FR 10367, 10382, Mar. 6, 1997]

§ 1244.17 Annual registration.

(a) Aliens granted Temporary Protected Status must register annually with the INS designated office having jurisdiction over their place of residence. Such registration will apply to nationals of those foreign states designated or redesignated for more than one year by the Attorney General pursuant to section 244(b) of the Act. Registration may be accomplished by mailing or submitting in person, depending on the practice in place at the INS designated office, completed Forms I–821 and I–765 within the thirty (30) day period prior to the anniversary of the grant of Temporary Protected Status (inclusive of such anniversary date). Form I–821 will be filed without fee. Form I–765 will be filed with fee only if the alien is requesting employment authorization. Completing the block on the I–821 attesting to the continued maintenance of the conditions of eligibility will generally preclude the need for supporting documents or evidence. The Service, however, reserves the right to request additional information and/or documentation on a case-by-case basis.

(b) Unless the Service determines otherwise, registration by mail shall suffice to meet the alien's registration requirements. However, as part of the registration process, an alien will generally have to appear in person in order to secure a renewal of employment authorization unless the Service determines that employment authorization will be extended in another fashion due to operational need. The Service may also request that an alien appear in person as part of the registration process. In such cases, failure to appear without good cause shall be deemed a failure to register under this chapter.

(c) Failure to register without good cause will result in the withdrawal of the alien's Temporary Protected Status.

[56 FR 619, Jan. 7, 1991, as amended at 56 FR 23498, May 22, 1991; 60 FR 21975, May 4, 1995. Redesignated at 62 FR 10367, 10382, Mar. 6, 1997, as amended at 63 FR 63597, Nov. 16, 1998]

§ 1244.18 Issuance of charging documents; detention.

(a) A charging document may be issued against an alien granted Temporary Protected Status on grounds of deportability or excludability which would have rendered the alien statutorily ineligible for such status pursuant to §§ 1244.3(c) and 244.4. Aliens shall not be deported for a particular offense for which the Service has expressly granted a waiver. If the alien is deportable on a waivable ground, and no such waiver for the charged offense has been previously granted, then the alien may seek such a waiver in deportation or exclusion proceedings. The charging document shall constitute notice to the alien that his or her status in the United States is subject to withdrawal. A final order of deportation or exclusion against an alien granted Temporary Protected Status shall constitute a withdrawal of such status.

(b) The filing of the charging document by the Service with the Immigration Court renders inapplicable any other administrative, adjudication or review of eligibility for Temporary Protected Status. The alien shall have the right to a *de novo* determination of his or her eligibility for Temporary Protected Status in the deportation or exclusion proceedings. Review by the Board of Immigration Appeals shall be the exclusive administrative appellate review procedure. If an appeal is already pending before the Administrative Appeals Unit, the director shall notify the Administrative Appeals Unit of the filing of the charging document, in which case the pending appeal shall be dismissed and the record of proceeding returned to the jurisdiction where the charging document was filed.

(c) Upon denial of Temporary Protected Status by the Administrative Appeals Unit, the Administrative Appeals Unit shall immediately forward the record of proceeding to the director having jurisdiction over the alien's place of residence. The director shall, as soon as practicable, file a charging document with the Immigration Court if the alien is then deportable or excludable under section 241(a) or section 212(a) of the Act, respectively.

(d) An alien who is determined by the Service to be deportable or excludable upon grounds which would have rendered the alien ineligible for such status as provided in §§ 1240.3(c) and 1240.4 may be detained under the provisions of this chapter pending deportation or exclusion proceedings. Such alien may be removed from the United States upon entry of a final order of deportation or exclusion.

[56 FR 619, Jan. 7, 1991, as amended at 56 FR 23498, May 22, 1991; 60 FR 34090, June 30, 1995. Redesignated at 62 FR 10367, 10382, Mar. 6, 1997, as amended at 63 FR 63597, Nov. 16, 1998; 64 FR 4782, Feb. 1, 1999]

§ 1244.19 Termination of designation.

Upon the termination of designation of a foreign state, those nationals afforded temporary Protected Status shall, upon the sixtieth (60th) day after the date notice of termination is published in the FEDERAL REGISTER, or on the last day of the most recent extension of designation by the Attorney General, automatically and without further notice or right of appeal, lose Temporary Protected Status in the United States. Such termination of a foreign state's designation is not subject to appeal.

[56 FR 619, Jan. 7, 1991. Redesignated at 62 FR 10367, 10382, Mar. 6, 1997, as amended at 63 FR 63597, Nov. 16, 1998]

§ 1244.20 Waiver of fees.

(a) Any of the fees prescribed in 8 CFR 103.7(b) which relate to applications to the district director or service center director for Temporary Protected Status may be waived if the applicant establishes that he or she is unable to pay the prescribed fee. The applicant will have established his or her inability to pay when the adjudicating officer concludes, on the basis of the requisite affidavit and of any other information submitted, that it is more probable than not that:

(1) The applicant's gross income from all sources for the three-month period prior to the filing of the fee waiver request, including income received or earned by any dependent in the United States, was equaled or exceeded by essential expenditures for such three-month period; and

(2) The applicant does not own, possess, or control assets sufficient to pay the fee without substantial hardship.

(b) For purposes of this section, essential expenditures are limited to reasonable expenditures for rent, utilities, food, transportation to and from employment, and any essential extraordinary expenditures, such as essential medical expenses, or expenses for clothing, laundry, and child care, to the extent that the applicant can show that those expenditures made during the three-month period prior to the filing of the fee waiver request were reasonable and essential to his or her physical well-being or to earning a livelihood.

(c) For purposes of this section, the TPS registration fee (including the fee for employment authorization, if applicable) shall be considered an essential expenditure. A fee waiver will be granted if the sum of the fees for TPS registration and employment authorization equals or exceeds income and assets that remain after deducting other essential expenditures.

(d) If an adjudicating officer is satisfied that an applicant has established inability to pay, he or she shall not deny a fee waiver due to the cost of administering the TPS program.

(e) For purposes of this section, the following documentation shall be required:

(1) The applicant seeking a fee waiver must submit an affidavit, under penalty of perjury, setting forth information to establish that he or she satisfies the requirements of this section. The affidavit shall individually list:

(i) The applicant's monthly gross income from each source for each of the three months prior to the filing of the fee waiver request;

(ii) All assets owned, possessed, or controlled by the applicant or by his or her dependents;

(iii) The applicant's essential monthly expenditures, itemized for each of the three months prior to the filing of the fee waiver request, including essential extraordinary expenditures; and

(iv) The applicant's dependents in the United States, his or her relationship to those dependents, the dependents' ages, any income earned or received by those dependents, and the street address of each dependent's place of residence.

(2) The applicant may also submit other documentation tending to substantiate his or her inability to pay.

(f) If the adjudicating officer concludes based upon the totality of their circumstances that the information presented in the affidavit and in any other additional documentation is inaccurate or insufficient, the adjudicating officer may require that the applicant submit the following additional documents prior to the adjudication of a fee waiver:

(1) The applicant's employment records, pay stubs, W-2 forms, letter(s) from employer(s), and proof of filing of a local, state, or federal income tax return. The same documents may also be required from the applicant's dependents in the United States.

(2) The applicant's rent receipts, bills for essential utilities (for example, gas, electricity, telephone, water), food, medical expenses, and receipts for other essential expenditures.

(3) Documentation to show all assets owned, possessed, or controlled by the applicant or by dependents of the applicant.

(4) Evidence of the applicant's living arrangements in the United States (living with relative, living in his or her own house or apartment, etc.), and evidence of whether his or her spouse, children, or other dependents are residing in his or her household in the United States.

(5) Evidence of the applicant's essential extraordinary expenditures or those of his or her dependents residing in the United States.

(g) The adjudicating officer must consider the totality of the information submitted in each case before requiring additional information or rendering a final decision.

(h) All documents submitted by the applicant or required by the adjudicating officer in support of a fee waiver request are subject to verification by the Service.

(i) In requiring additional information, the adjudicating officer should consider that some applicants may have little or no documentation to substantiate their claims. An adjudicating officer may accept other evidence, such as an affidavit from a member of the community of good moral character, but only if the applicant provides an affidavit stating that more direct documentary evidence in unavailable.

[57 FR 34507, Aug. 5, 1992. Redesignated at 62 FR 10367, 10382, Mar. 6, 1997]

PART 1245—ADJUSTMENT OF STATUS TO THAT OF PERSON ADMITTED FOR PERMANENT RESIDENCE

Sec.

AUTHORITY: 8 U.S.C. 1101, 1103, 1182, 1255; section 202, Public Law 105–100, 111 Stat. 2160, 2193; section 902, Public Law 105–277, 112 Stat. 2681; Title VII of Public Law 110–229.

SOURCE: Duplicated from part 245 at 68 FR 9842, Feb. 28, 2003.

EDITORIAL NOTE: Nomenclature changes to part 1245 appear at 68 FR 9846, Feb. 28, 2003, and 68 FR 10357, Mar. 5, 2003.

§ 1245.1 Eligibility.

(a) *General.* Any alien who is physically present in the United States, except for an alien who is ineligible to apply for adjustment of status under paragraph (b) or (c) of this section, may apply for adjustment of status to that of a lawful permanent resident of the United States if the applicant is eligible to receive an immigrant visa and an immigrant visa is immediately available at the time of filing of the application. A special immigrant described under section 101(a)(27)(J) of the Act shall be deemed, for the purpose of applying the adjustment to status provisions of section 245(a) of the Act, to have been paroled into the United States, regardless of the actual method of entry into the United States.

(b) *Restricted aliens.* The following categories of aliens are ineligible to apply for adjustment of status to that of a lawful permanent resident alien under section 245 of the Act, unless the alien establishes eligibility under the provisions of section 245(i) of the Act and § 1245.10, is not included in the categories of aliens prohibited from applying for adjustment of status listed in § 1245.1(c), is eligible to receive an immigrant visa, and has an immigrant visa immediately available at the time of filing the application for adjustment of status:

(1) Any alien who entered the United States in transit without a visa;

(2) Any alien who, on arrival in the United States, was serving in any capacity on board a vessel or aircraft or was destined to join a vessel or aircraft in the United States to serve in any capacity thereon;

(3) Any alien who was not admitted or paroled following inspection by an immigration officer;

(4) Any alien who, on or after January 1, 1977, was employed in the United States without authorization prior to filing an application for adjustment of status. This restriction shall not apply to an alien who is:

(i) An immediate relative as defined in section 201(b) of the Act;

(ii) A special immigrant as defined in section 101(a)(27)(H) or (J) of the Act;

(iii) Eligible for the benefits of Public Law 101–238 (the Immigration Nursing

Relief Act of 1989) and files an application for adjustment of status on or before October 17, 1991; or

(iv) Eligible for the benefits of Public Law 101–238 (the Immigration Nursing Relief Act of 1989), and has not entered into or continued in unauthorized employment on or after November 29, 1990.

(5) Any alien who on or after November 6, 1986 is not in lawful immigration status on the date of filing his or her application for adjustment of status, except an applicant who is an immediate relative as defined in section 201(b) or a special immigrant as defined in section 101(a)(27) (H), (I), or (J).

(6) Any alien who files an application for adjustment of status on or after November 6, 1986, who has failed (other than through no fault of his or her own or for technical reasons) to maintain continuously a lawful status since entry into the United States, except an applicant who is an immediate relative as defined in section 201(b) of the Act or a special immigrant as defined in section 101(a)(27) (H), (I), or (J) of the Act;

(7) Any alien admitted as a visitor under the visa waiver provisions of 8 CFR 212.1(e) or (q), other than an immediate relative as defined in section 201(b) of the Act;

(8) Any alien admitted as a Visa Waiver Pilot Program visitor under the provisions of section 217 of the Act and part 217 of 8 CFR chapter I other than an immediate relative as defined in section 201(b) of the Act;

(9) Any alien who seeks adjustment of status pursuant to an employment-based immigrant visa petition under section 203(b) of the Act and who is not maintaining a lawful nonimmigrant status at the time he or she files an application for adjustment of status; and

(10) Any alien who was ever employed in the United States without the authorization of the Service or who has otherwise at any time violated the terms of his or her admission to the United States as a nonimmigrant, except an alien who is an immediate relative as defined in section 201(b) of the Act or a special immigrant as defined in section 101(a)(27)(H), (I), (J), or (K) of the Act. For purposes of this paragraph, an alien who meets the requirements of § 1274a.12(c)(9) of this chapter shall not be deemed to have engaged in unauthorized employment during the pendency of his or her adjustment application.

(c) *Ineligible aliens.* The following categories of aliens are ineligible to apply for adjustment of status to that of a lawful permanent resident alien under section 245 of the Act:

(1) Any nonpreference alien who is seeking or engaging in gainful employment in the United States who is not the beneficiary of a valid individual or blanket labor certification issued by the Secretary of Labor or who is not exempt from certification requirements under § 1212.8(b) of this chapter;

(2) Except for an alien who is applying for residence under the provisions of section 133 of the Immigration Act of 1990, any alien who has or had the status of an exchange visitor under section 101(a)(15)(J) of the Act and who is subject to the foreign residence requirement of section 212(e) of the Act, unless the alien has complied with the foreign residence requirement or has been granted a waiver of that requirement, under that section. An alien who has been granted a waiver under section 212(e)(iii) of the Act based on a request by a State Department of Health (or its equivalent) under Pub. L. 103–416 shall be ineligible to apply for adjustment of status under section 245 of the Act if the terms and conditions specified in section 214(k) of the Act and § 1212.7(c)(9) of this chapter have not been met;

(3) Any alien who has nonimmigrant status under paragraph (15)(A), (15)(E), or (15)(G) of section 101(a) of the Act, or has an occupational status which would, if the alien were seeking admission to the United States, entitle the alien to nonimmigrant status under those paragraphs, unless the alien first executes and submits the written waiver required by section 247(b) of the Act and part 247 of 8 CFR chapter 1;

(4) Any alien who claims immediate relative status under section 201(b) or preference status under sections 203(a) or 203(b) of the Act, unless the applicant is the beneficiary of a valid unexpired visa petition filed in accordance with part 204 of 8 CFR chapter 1;

(5) Any alien who is already an alien lawfully admitted to the United States

for permanent residence on a conditional basis pursuant to section 216 or 216A of the Act, regardless of any other quota or non-quota immigrant visa classification for which the alien may otherwise be eligible;

(6) Any alien admitted to the United States as a nonimmigrant defined in section 101(a)(15)(K) of the Act, unless:

(i) In the case of a K–1 fianceé(e) under section 101(a)(15)(K)(i) of the Act or the K–2 child of a fianceé(e) under section 101(a)(15)(K)(iii) of the Act, the alien is applying for adjustment of status based upon the marriage of the K–1 fianceé(e) which was contracted within 90 days of entry with the United States citizen who filed a petition on behalf of the K–1 fianceé(e) pursuant to §214.2(k) of 8 CFR chapter 1;

(ii) In the case of a K–3 spouse under section 101(a)(15)(K)(ii) of the Act or the K–4 child of a spouse under section 101(a)(15)(K)(iii) of the Act, the alien is applying for adjustment of status based upon the marriage of the K–3 spouse to the United States citizen who filed a petition on behalf of the K–3 spouse pursuant to §214.2(k) of 8 CFR chapter I;

(7) A nonimmigrant classified pursuant to section 101(a)(15)(S) of the Act, unless the nonimmigrant is applying for adjustment of status pursuant to the request of a law enforcement authority, the provisions of section 101(a)(15)(S) of the Act, and 8 CFR 1245.11;

(8) Any alien who seeks to adjust status based upon a marriage which occurred on or after November 10, 1986, and while the alien was in exclusion, deportation, or removal proceedings, or judicial proceedings relating thereto.

(i) *Commencement of proceedings.* The period during which the alien is in deportation, exclusion, or removal proceedings or judicial proceedings relating thereto, commences:

(A) With the issuance of the Form I–221, Order to Show Cause and Notice of Hearing prior to June 20, 1991;

(B) With the filing of a Form I–221, Order to Show Cause and Notice of Hearing, issued on or after June 20, 1991, with the Immigration Court;

(C) With the issuance of Form I–122, Notice to Applicant for Admission Detained for Hearing Before Immigration Judge, prior to April 1, 1997,

(D) With the filing of a Form I–862, Notice to Appear, with the Immigration Court, or

(E) With the issuance and service of Form I–860, Notice and Order of Expedited Removal.

(ii) *Termination of proceedings.* The period during which the alien is in exclusion, deportation, or removal proceedings, or judicial proceedings relating thereto, terminates:

(A) When the alien departs from the United States while an order of exclusion, deportation, or removal is outstanding or before the expiration of the voluntary departure time granted in connection with an alternate order of deportation or removal;

(B) When the alien is found not to be inadmissible or deportable from the United States;

(C) When the Form I–122, I–221, I–860, or I–862 is canceled;

(D) When proceedings are terminated by the immigration judge or the Board of Immigration Appeals; or

(E) When a petition for review or an action for habeas corpus is granted by a Federal court on judicial review.

(iii) *Exemptions.* This prohibition shall no longer apply if:

(A) The alien is found not to be inadmissible or deportable from the United States;

(B) Form I–122, I–221, I–860, or I–862, is canceled;

(C) Proceedings are terminated by the immigration judge or the Board of Immigration Appeals;

(D) A petition for review or an action for habeas corpus is granted by a Federal court on judicial review;

(E) The alien has resided outside the United States for 2 or more years following the marriage; or

(F) The alien establishes the marriage is bona fide by providing clear and convincing evidence that the marriage was entered into in good faith and in accordance with the laws of the place where the marriage took place, was not entered into for the purpose of procuring the alien's entry as an immigrant, and no fee or other consideration was given (other than to an attorney for assistance in preparation of a lawful petition) for the filing of a petition.

(iv) *Request for exemption.* No application or fee is required to request the exemption under section 245(e) of the Act. The request must be made in writing and submitted with the Form I–485. Application for Permanent Residence. The request must state the basis for requesting consideration for the exemption and must be supported by documentary evidence establishing eligibility for the exemption.

(v) *Evidence to establish eligibility for the bona fide marriage exemption.* Section 204(g) of the Act provides that certain visa petitions based upon marriages entered into during deportation, exclusion or related judicial proceedings may be approved only if the petitioner provides clear and convincing evidence that the marriage is bona fide. Evidence that a visa petition based upon the same marriage was approved under the bona fide marriage exemption to section 204(g) of the Act will be considered primary evidence of eligibility for the bona fide marriage exemption provided in this part. The applicant will not be required to submit additional evidence to qualify for the bona fide marriage exemption provided in this part, unless the district director determines that such additional evidence is needed. In cases where the district director notifies the applicant that additional evidence is required, the applicant must submit documentary evidence which clearly and convincingly establishes that the marriage was entered into in good faith and not entered into for the purpose of procuring the alien's entry as an immigrant. Such evidence may include:

(A) Documentation showing joint ownership of property;

(B) Lease showing joint tenancy of a common residence;

(C) Documentation showing commingling of financial resources;

(D) Birth certificates of children born to the applicant and his or her spouse;

(E) Affidavits of third parties having knowledge of the bona fides of the marital relationship, or

(F) Other documentation establishing that the marriage was not entered into in order to evade the immigration laws of the United States.

(vi) *Decision.* An application for adjustment of status filed during the prohibited period shall be denied, unless the applicant establishes eligibility for an exemption from the general prohibition.

(vii) *Denials.* The denial of an application for adjustment of status because the marriage took place during the prohibited period shall be without prejudice to the consideration of a new application or a motion to reopen a previously denied application, if deportation or exclusion proceedings are terminated while the alien is in the United States. The denial shall also be without prejudice to the consideration of a new application or motion to reopen the adjustment of status application, if the applicant presents clear and convincing evidence establishing eligibility for the bona fide marriage exemption contained in this part.

(viii) *Appeals.* An application for adjustment of status to lawful permanent resident which is denied by the district director solely because the applicant failed to establish eligibility for the bona fide marriage exemption contained in this part may be appealed to the Associate Commissioner, Examinations, in accordance with 8 CFR part 103. The appeal to the Associate Commissioner, Examinations, shall be the single level of appellate review established by statute.

(d) *Definitions*—(1) *Lawful immigration status.* For purposes of section 245(c)(2) of the Act, the term "lawful immigration status" will only describe the immigration status of an individual who is:

(i) In lawful permanent resident status;

(ii) An alien admitted to the United States in nonimmigrant status as defined in section 101(a)(15) of the Act, whose initial period of admission has not expired or whose nonimmigrant status has been extended in accordance with part 214 of 8 CFR chapter I;

(iii) In refugee status under section 207 of the Act, such status not having been revoked;

(iv) In asylee status under section 208 of the Act, such status not having been revoked;

(v) In parole status which has not expired, been revoked or terminated; or

(vi) Eligible for the benefits of Public Law 101–238 (the Immigration Nursing Relief Act of 1989) and files an application for adjustment of status on or before October 17, 1991.

(2) *No fault of the applicant or for technical reasons.* The parenthetical phrase *other than through no fault of his or her own or for technical reasons* shall be limited to:

(i) Inaction of another individual or organization designated by regulation to act on behalf of an individual and over whose actions the individual has no control, if the inaction is acknowledged by that individual or organization (as, for example, where a designated school official certified under § 214.2(f) of 8 CFR chapter I or an exchange propram sponsor under § 214.2(j) of 8 CFR chapter I did not provide required notification to the Service of continuation of status, or did not forward a request for continuation of status to the Service); or

(ii) A technical violation resulting from inaction of the Service (as for example, where an applicant establishes that he or she properly filed a timely request to maintain status and the Service has not yet acted on that request). An individual whose refugee or asylum status has expired through passage of time, but whose status has not been revoked, will be considered to have gone out of status for a technical reason.

(iii) A technical violation caused by the physical inability of the applicant to request an extension of nonimmigrant stay from the Service either in person or by mail (as, for example, an individual who is hospitalized with an illness at the time nonimmigrant stay expires). The explanation of such a technical violation shall be accompanied by a letter explaining the circumstances from the hospital or attending physician.

(iv) A technical violation resulting from the Service's application of the maximum five/six year period of stay for certain H–1 nurses only if the applicant was subsequently reinstated to H–1 status in accordance with the terms of Public Law 101–656 (Immigration Amendments of 1988).

(3) *Effect of departure.* The departure and subsequent reentry of an individual who was employed without authorization in the United States after January 1, 1977 does not erase the bar to adjustment of status in section 245(c)(2) of the Act. Similarly, the departure and subsequent reentry of an individual who has not maintained a lawful immigration status on any previous entry into the United States does not erase the bar to adjustment of status in section 245(c)(2) of the Act for any application filed on or after November 6, 1986.

(e) *Special categories*—(1) *Alien medical graduates.* Any alien who is a medical graduate qualified for special immigrant classification under section 101(a)(27)(H) of the Act and is the beneficiary of an approved petition as required under section 204(a)(1)(E)(i) of the Act is eligible for adjustment of status. An accompanying spouse and children also may apply for adjustment of status under this section. Temporary absences from the United States for 30 days or less, during which the applicant was practicing or studying medicine, do not interrupt the continuous presence requirement. Temporary absences authorized under the Service's advance parole procedures will not be considered interruptive of continuous presence when the alien applies for adjustment of status.

(2) *Adjustment of certain nurses who were in H–1 nonimmigrant status on September 1, 1989 (Pub. L. 101–238)*—(i) *Eligibility.* An alien is eligible to apply for adjustment of status without regard to the numerical limitations of sections 201 and 202 of the Act if:

(A) The applicant was admitted to the United States in, or had been granted a change of status to, nonimmigrant status under section 101(a)(15)(H)(i) of the Act on or before September 1, 1989, to perform services as a registered nurse (regardless of the date upon which the applicant's authorization to remain in the United States expired or will expire), and the applicant had not thereafter been granted a change to status to any other nonimmigrant classification prior to September 1, 1989,

(B) The applicant has been employed in the United States as a registered nurse for an aggregate of three years prior to the date of application for adjustment of status,

(C) The applicant's continued employment as a registered nurse meets the standards established for certification described in section 212(a)(5)(A)(i) of the Act,

(D) The applicant is the beneficiary of:

(*1*) A valid, unexpired visa petition filed prior to October 1, 1991, which has been approved to grant the applicant preference status under section 202(a) (3) or (6) of the Act (as in effect prior to October 1, 1991), and is deemed by operation of the automatic conversion provisions of section 4 of Public Law 102–110 (the Armed Forces Immigration Adjustment Act of 1991), to be effective to grant the applicant preference status under section 203(b) (2) or (3) of the Act (as in effect on and after October 1, 1991) because of his or here occupation as a registered nurse, provided the application for adjustment of status is approved no later than October 1, 1993, or

(*2*) A valid, unexpired visa petition filed on or after October 1, 1991, which has been approved to grant the applicant preference, status under section 203(b) (1), (2), or (3) of this Act (as in effect on and after October 1, 1991) because of his or her occupation as a registered nurse, and

(E) The applicant properly files an application for adjustment of status under the provisions of section 245 of the Act.

(ii) *Application period.* To benefit from the provisions of Public Law 101–238, an alien must properly file an application for adjustments of status under section 245 of the Act on or before March 20, 1995.

(iii) *Application.* An applicant for the benefits of Public Law 101–238 must file an application for adjustment of status on Form I–485, accompanied by the fee and supporting documents described in §1245.2 of this part. Beneficiaries of Public Law 101–238 must also submit:

(A) Evidence that the applicant is the beneficiary of:

(*1*) A valid, unexpired visa petition filed prior to October 1, 1991, which has been approved to grant the applicant preference status under section 203(a) (3) or (6) of the Act (as in effect prior to October 1, 1991) and is deemed by operation of the automatic conversion provisions of section 4 of Public Law 101–110 to be effective to grant the applicant preference status under section 203(b) (2) or (3) of the Act (as in effect on and after October 1, 1991) because of his or her occupation as a registered nurse, provided the application for adjustment of status is approved no later than October 1, 1993, or

(*2*) A valid, unexpired visa petition filed on or after October 1, 1991, which has been approved to grant the applicant preference status under section 203(b) (1), (2), or (3) of the Act (as in effect on and after October 1, 1991) because of his or her occupation as a registered nurse, and

(B) A request, made on Form ETA 750 submitted in duplicate, for a determination by the district director that the alien is qualified for and will engage in the occupation of registered nurse, as currently listed on Schedule A (20 CFR part 656),

(C) Evidence showing that the applicant has been employed in the United States as a registered nurse for an aggregate of three years prior to the date the application for adjustment of status is filed, in the form of:

(*1*) Letters from employers stating the beginning and ending dates of employment as a registered nurse, or

(*2*) Other evidence of employment as a registered nurse, such as pay receipts supported by affidavits of co-workers, which is accompanied by evidence that the nurse has made reasonable efforts to obtain employment letter(s), but has been unable to do so because the current or former employer refuses to issue the letter or has gone out of business,

(D) Evidence that the applicant was licensed, either temporarily or permanently, as a registered nurse during all periods of qualifying employment, and

(E) Evidence which establishes that the applicant was in the United States in H–1 nonimmigrant status for the purpose of performing services as a registered nurse on September 1, 1989.

(iv) *Effect of section 245(c)(2).* An applicant for the benefits of the adjustment of status provisions of Public Law 101–238 must establish eligibility for adjustment of status under all provisions of section 245 unless those provisions have specifically been waived.

(A) *Application for adjustment of status filed on or before October 17, 1991.* An applicant who qualifies for the benefits of Public Law 101–238, who properly files an application for adjustment of status on or before October 17, 1991, may be granted adjustment of status even though the alien has engaged or is engaging in unauthorized employment. For purposes of adjustment of status, the applicant will be considered to have continuously maintained a lawful nonimmigrant status throughout his or her stay in the United States as a nonimmigrant and to be in lawful nonimmigrant status at the time the application is filed.

(B) *Application for adjustment of status filed after October 17, 1991.* An alien who files an application for adjustment of status after October 17, 1991, will not automatically be considered as having maintained lawful nonimmigrant status. An alien who files for adjustment after this date will be subject to the statutory bar of section 245(c)(2) of the Act and will be ineligible to apply for adjustment of status if he or she has failed to continuously maintain lawful nonimmigrant status (other than through no fault of his or her own or for technical reasons); if he or she was not in lawful nonimmigrant status at the time the application was filed; or if he or she was employed without authorization on or after November 29, 1990. Unauthorized employment which has been waived as a basis for ineligibility for adjustment of status may not be used as the basis of a determination that the applicant is ineligible for adjustment of status due to failure to continuously maintain lawful nonimmigrant status.

(C) *Motions to reopen.* Public Law 101–649 (the Immigration Act of 1990), which became law on November 29, 1990, retroactively amended Public Law 101–238 (the Immigration Nursing Relief Act of 1989). An alien whose application for adjustment of status under the provisions of Public Law 101–238 was denied by the district director before November 29, 1990, because of unauthorized employment, failure to continuously maintain a lawful nonimmigrant status, or not being in lawful immigration status at the time of filing, may file a motion to reopen the adjustment application. The motion to reopen must be made in accordance with the provisions of 8 CFR 103.5. The district director will reopen the application for adjustment of status and enter a new decision based upon the provisions of Public Law 101–238, as amended by Public Law 101–649. Any other alien whose application for adjustment of status was denied may file a motion to reopen or reconsider in accordance with normal statutory and regulatory provisions.

(v) *Description of qualifying employment.* Qualifying employment as a registered nurse may have taken place at any time before the alien files the application for adjustment of status. It may have occurred before, on, or after the enactment of Public Law 101–238. All qualifying employment must have occurred in the United States. The qualifying employment as a registered nurse may have occurred while the alien was in any immigration status, provided that the alien had been admitted in or changed to H–1 status for the purpose of performing services as a registered nurse on or before September 1, 1989, and had not thereafter changed from H–1 status to any other status before September 1, 1989. The employment need not have been continuous, provided the applicant can establish that he or she engaged in qualifying employment for a total of three or more years. Qualifying employment may include periods when the applicant possessed a provisional, temporary, interim, or other permit or license authorizing the applicant to perform services as a registered nurse; provided the license or permit was issued or recognized by the State Board of Nursing of the state in which the employment was performed. Qualifying employment may not include periods when the applicant performed duties as a registered nurse in violation of any state law regulating the employment of registered nurses in that state.

(vi) *Effect of enactment on spouse or child*—(A) *Spouse or child accompanying principal alien.* The accompanying spouse or child of an applicant for adjustment of status who benefits from

Public Law 101–238, may also apply for adjustment of status. All benefits and limitations of this section, including those resulting from the implementation of the adjustment of status provisions of section 162(f) of Public Law 101–649, apply equally to the principal applicant and his or her accompanying spouse or child.

(B) *Spouse or child residing outside the United States or ineligible for adjustment of status.* A spouse or child who is ineligible to apply for adjustment of status as an accompanying spouse or child is not immediately eligible for issuance of an immigrant visa under the provisions of Public Law 101–238. However, the spouse or child may be eligible for visa issuance under other provisions of the Act.

(*1*) *Existing relationship.* A spouse or child acquired by the principal alien prior to the approval of the principal's adjustment of status application may be accorded the derivative priority date and preference category of the principal alien. The spouse or child may use the priority date and category when it becomes current, in accordance with existing limitations outlined in sections 201 and 202 of the Act. The priority date is not considered immediately available for these family members under Public Law 101–238.

(*2*) *Relationship entered into after adjustment of status is approved.* An alien who acquires lawful permanent residence under the provisions of Public Law 101–238 may file a petition under section 204 of the Act for an alien spouse, unmarried son or unmarried daughter in accordance with existing laws and regulations. The priority date is not considered immediately available for these family members under Public Law 101–238.

(3) *Special immigrant juveniles.* Any alien qualified for special immigrant classification under section 101(a)(27)(J) of the Act shall be deemed, for the purpose of section 245(a) of the Act, to have been paroled into the United States, regardless of the alien's actual method of entry into the United States. Neither the provisions of section 245(c)(2) nor the exclusion provisions of sections 212(a)(4), (5)(A), or (7)(A) of the Act shall apply to a qualified special immigrant under section 101(a)(27)(J) of the Act. The exclusion provisions of sections 212(a)(2)(A), (2)(B), (2)(C) (except for so much of such paragraph as related to a single offense of simple possession of 30 grams or less of marijuana), (3)(A), (3)(B), (3)(C), or (3)(E) of the Act may not be waived. Any other exclusion provision may be waived on an individual basis for humanitarian purposes, family unity, or when it is otherwise in the public interest; however, the relationship between the alien and the alien's natural parents or prior adoptive parents shall not be considered a factor in a discretionary waiver determination.

(f) *Concurrent applications to overcome grounds of inadmissibility.* Except as provided in 8 CFR parts 1235 and 1249, an application under this part shall be the sole method of requesting the exercise of discretion under sections 212(g), (h), (i), and (k) of the Act, as they relate to the inadmissibility of an alien in the United States. No fee is required for filing an application to overcome the grounds of inadmissibility of the Act if filed concurrently with an application for adjustment of status under the provisions of the Act of October 28, 1977, and of this part.

(g) *Availability of immigrant visas under section 245 and priority dates*—(1) *Availability of immigrant visas under section 245.* An alien is ineligible for the benefits of section 245 of the Act unless an immigrant visa is immediately available to him or her at the time the application is filed. If the applicant is a preference alien, the current Department of State Bureau of Consular Affairs Visa Bulletin will be consulted to determine whether an immigrant visa is immediately available. An immigrant visa is considered available for accepting and processing the application Form I–485 is the preference category applicant has a priority date on the waiting list which is earlier than the date shown in the Bulletin (or the Bulletin shows that numbers for visa applicants in his or her category are current). An immigrant visa is also considered immediately available if the applicant establishes eligibility for the benefits of Public Law 101–238. Information concerning the immediate availability of an immigrant visa may be obtained at any Service office.

(2) *Priority dates.* The priority date of an applicant who is seeking the allotment of an immigrant visa number under one of the preference classes specified in section 203(a) or 203(b) of the Act by virtue of a valid visa petition approved in his or her behalf shall be fixed by the date on which such approved petition was filed.

(h) *Conditional basis of status.* Whenever an alien spouse (as defined in section 216(g)(1) of the Act), an alien son or daughter (as defined in section 216(g)(2) of the Act), an alien entrepreneur (as defined in section 216A(f)(1) of the Act), or an alien spouse or child (as defined in section 216A(f)(2) of the Act) is granted adjustment of status to that of lawful permanent residence, the alien shall be considered to have obtained such status on a conditional basis subject to the provisions of section 216 or 216A of the Act, as appropriate.

(i) *Adjustment of status from K–3/K–4 status.* An alien admitted to the United States as a K–3 under section 101(a)(15)(K)(ii) of the Act may apply for adjustment of status to that of a permanent resident pursuant to section 245 of the Act at any time following the approval of the Form I–130 petition filed on the alien's behalf, by the same citizen who petitioned for the alien's K–3 status. An alien admitted to the United States as a K–4 under section 101(a)(15)(K)(iii) of the Act may apply for adjustment of status to that of permanent residence pursuant to section 245 of the Act at any time following the approval of the Form I–130 petition filed on the alien's behalf, by the same citizen who petitioned for the alien's parent's K–3 status. Upon approval of the application, the director shall record his or her lawful admission for permanent residence in accordance with that section and subject to the conditions prescribed in section 216 of the Act. An alien admitted to the U.S. as a K–3/K–4 alien may not adjust to that of permanent resident status in any way other than as a spouse or child of the U.S. citizen who originally filed the petition for that alien's K–3/K–4 status.

(Title I of Pub. L. 95–145 enacted Oct. 28, 1977 (91 Stat. 1223), sec. 103 of the Immigration and Nationality Act (8 U.S.C. 1103). Interpret or apply secs. 101, 212, 242 and 245 (8 U.S.C. 1101, 1182, 1252 and 1255))

[30 FR 14778, Nov. 30, 1965]

EDITORIAL NOTE: For FEDERAL REGISTER citations affecting § 1245.1, see the List of CFR Sections Affected, which appears in the Finding Aids section of the printed volume and at *www.govinfo.gov*.

§ 1245.2 Application.

(a)*General*—(1) *Jurisdiction*—(i) *In General.* In the case of any alien who has been placed in deportation proceedings or in removal proceedings (other than as an arriving alien), the immigration judge hearing the proceeding has exclusive jurisdiction to adjudicate any application for adjustment of status the alien may file.

(ii) *Arriving Aliens.* In the case of an arriving alien who is placed in removal proceedings, the immigration judge does not have jurisdiction to adjudicate any application for adjustment of status filed by the arriving alien unless:

(A) The alien properly filed the application for adjustment of status with USCIS while the arriving alien was in the United States;

(B) The alien departed from and returned to the United States pursuant to the terms of a grant of advance parole to pursue the previously filed application for adjustment of status;

(C) The application for adjustment of status was denied by USCIS; and

(D) DHS placed the arriving alien in removal proceedings either upon the arriving alien's return to the United States pursuant to the grant of advance parole or after USCIS denied the application.

(2) *Proper filing of application*—(i) *Under section 245.* (A) An immigrant visa must be immediately available in order for an alien to properly file an adjustment application under section 245 of the Act See § 1245.1(g)(1) to determine whether an immigrant visa is immediately available.

(B) If, at the time of filing, approval of a visa petition filed for classification under section 201(b)(2)(A)(i), section

203(a) or section 203(b)(1), (2) or (3) of the Act would make a visa immediately available to the alien beneficiary, the alien beneficiary's adjustment application will be considered properly filed whether submitted concurrently with or subsequent to the visa petition, provided that it meets the filing requirements contained in parts 103 of 8 CFR chapter I and 1245 of this chapter. For any other classification, the alien beneficiary may file the adjustment application only after the Service has approved the visa petition.

(C) A visa petition and an adjustment application are concurrently filed only if:

(*1*) The visa petitioner and adjustment applicant each file their respective form at the same time, bundled together within a single mailer or delivery packet, with the proper filing fees on the same day and at the same Service office, or;

(*2*) the visa petitioner filed the visa petition, for which a visa number has become immediately available, on, before or after July 31, 2002, and the adjustment applicant files the adjustment application, together with the proper filing fee and a copy of the Form I–797, Notice of Action, establishing the receipt and acceptance by the Service of the underlying Form I–140 visa petition, at the same Service office at which the visa petitioner filed the visa petition, or;

(*3*) The visa petitioner filed the visa petition, for which a visa number has become immediately available, on, before, or after July 31, 2002, and the adjustment applicant files the adjustment application, together with proof of payment of the filing fee with the Service and a copy of the Form I–797 Notice of Action establishing the receipt and acceptance by the Service of the underlying Form I–140 visa petition, with the Immigration Court or the Board of Immigration Appeals when jurisdiction lies under paragraph (a)(1) of this section.

(ii) *Under the Act of November 2, 1966.* An application for the benefits of section 1 of the Act of November 2, 1966 is not properly filed unless the applicant was inspected and admitted or paroled into the United States subsequent to January 1, 1959. An applicant is ineligible for the benefits of the Act of November 2, 1966 unless he or she has been physically present in the United States for one year (amended from two years by the Refugee Act of 1980).

(3) *Submission of documents*—(i) *General.* A separate application shall be filed by each applicant for benefits under section 245, or the Act of November 2, 1966. Each application shall be accompanied by an executed Form G–325A, if the applicant has reached his or her 14th birthday. Form G–325A shall be considered part of the application. An application under this part shall be accompanied by the document specified in the instructions which are attached to the application.

(ii) *Under section 245.* An application for adjustment of status is submitted on Form I–485, Application for Permanent Residence. The application must be accompanied by the appropriate fee as explained in the instructions to the application.

(iii) *Under section 245(i).* An alien who seeks adjustment of status under the provisions of section 245(i) of the Act must file Form I–485, with the required fee. The alien must also file Supplement A to Form I–485, with any required additional sum.

(iv) *Under the Act of November 2, 1966.* An application for adjustment of status is made on Form I–485A. The application must be accompanied by Form I–643, Health and Human Services Statistical Data Sheet. The application must include a clearance from the local police jurisdiction for any area in the United States when the applicant has lived for six months or more since his or her 14th birthday.

(4) *Effect of departure*—(i) *General.* The effect of a departure from the United States is dependent upon the law under which the applicant is applying for adjustment.

(ii) *Under section 245 of the Act.* (A) The departure from the United States of an applicant who is under exclusion, deportation, or removal proceedings shall be deemed an abandonment of the application constituting grounds for termination of the proceeding by reason of the departure. Except as provided in paragraph (a)(4)(ii)(B) and (C) of this section, the departure of an applicant who is not under exclusion, deportation, or removal proceedings shall be deemed an abandonment of the application constituting grounds for termination of any pending application for adjustment of status, unless the applicant was previously granted advance parole by the Service for such absences, and was inspected upon returning to the United States. If the adjustment application of an individual granted advance parole is subsequently denied the individual will be treated as an applicant for admission, and subject to the provisions of section 212 and 235 of the Act.

(B) The travel outside of the United States by an applicant for adjustment who is not under exclusion, deportation, or removal proceedings shall not be deemed an abandonment of the application if he or she was previously granted advance parole by the Service for such absences, and was inspected and paroled upon returning to the United States. If the adjustment of status application of such individual is subsequently denied, he or she will be treated as an applicant for admission, and subject to the provisions of section 212 and 235 of the Act.

(C) The travel outside of the United States by an applicant for adjustment of status who is not under exclusion, deportation, or removal proceeding and who is in lawful H–1 or L–1 status shall not be deemed an abandonment of the application if, upon returning to this country, the alien remains eligible for H or L status, is coming to resume employment with the same employer for whom he or she had previously been authorized to work as an H–1 or L–1 nonimmigrant, and, is in possession of a valid H or L visa (if required) and the original I–797 receipt notice for the application for adjustment of status. The travel outside of the United States by an applicant for adjustment of status who is not under exclusion, deportation, or removal proceeding and who is in lawful H–4 or L–2 status shall not be deemed an abandonment of the application if the spouse or parent of such alien through whom the H–4 or L–2 status was obtained is maintaining H–1 or L–1 status and the alien remains otherwise eligible for H–4 or L–2 status, and, the alien is in possession of a valid H–4 or L–2 visa (if required) and the original copy of the I–797 receipt notice for the application for adjustment of status. The travel outside of the United States by an applicant for adjustment of status, who is not under exclusion, deportation, or removal proceeding and who is in lawful K–3 or K–4 status shall not be deemed an abandonment of the application if, upon returning to this country, the alien is in possession of a valid K–3 or K–4 visa and remains eligible for K–3 or K–4 status.

(D) The travel outside of the United States by an applicant for adjustment of status who is not under exclusion, deportation, or removal proceeding and who is in lawful V status shall not be deemed an abandonment of the application if, upon returning to this country, the alien is admissible as a V nonimmigrant.

(iii) *Under the Act of November 2, 1966.* If an applicant who was admitted or paroled subsequent to January 1, 1959, later departs from the United States temporarily with no intention of abandoning his or her residence, and is readmitted or paroled upon return, the temporary absence shall be disregarded for purposes of the applicant's "last arrival" into the United States in regard to cases filed under section 1 of the Act of November 2, 1966.

(5) *Decision*—(i) *General.* The applicant shall be notified of the decision of the director and, if the application is denied, the reasons for the denial.

(ii) *Under section 245 of the Act.* If the application is approved, the applicant's permanent residence shall be recorded as of the date of the order approving the adjustment of status. An application for adjustment of status, as a preference alien, shall not be approved until an immigrant visa number has been allocated by the Department of State, except when the applicant has established eligibility for the benefits of Public Law 101–238. No appeal lies from the denial of an application by the director, but the applicant, if not an arriving alien, retains the right to renew his or her application in proceedings under 8 CFR part 1240. Also, an applicant who is a parolee and meets the two conditions described in

§ 1245.2(a)(1) may renew a denied application in proceedings under 8 CFR part 1240 to determine admissibility. At the time of renewal of the application, an applicant does not need to meet the statutory requirement of section 245(c) of the Act, or § 1245.1(g), if, in fact, those requirements were met at the time the renewed application was initially filed with the director. Nothing in this section shall entitle an alien to proceedings under section 240 of the Act who is not otherwise so entitled.

(iii) *Under the Act of November 2, 1966.* If the application is approved, the applicant's permanent residence shall be recorded in accordance with the provisions of section 1. No appeal lies from the denial of an application by the director, but the applicant, if not an arriving alien, retains the right to renew his or her application in proceedings under 8 CFR part 1240. Also, an applicant who is a parolee and meets the two conditions described in § 1245.2(a)(1) may renew a denied application in proceedings under 8 CFR part 1240 to determine admissibility.

(b) *Application under section 2 of the Act of November 2, 1966.* An application by a native or citizen of Cuba or by his spouse or child residing in the United States with him, who was lawfully admitted to the United States for permanent residence prior to November 2, 1966, and who desires such admission to be recorded as of an earlier date pursuant to section 2 of the Act of November 2, 1966, shall be made on Form I–485A. The application shall be accompanied by the Permanent Resident Card, Form I–151 or I–551, issued to the applicant in connection with his lawful admission for permanent residence, and shall be submitted to the director having jurisdiction over the applicant's place of residence in the United States. The decision on the application shall be made by the director. No appeal shall lie from his decision. If the application is approved, the applicant will be furnished with a replacement of his Form I–151 or I–551 bearing the new date as of which the lawful admission for permanent residence has been recorded.

(c) *Application under section 214(d) of the Act.* An application for permanent resident status pursuant to section 214(d) of the Act shall be filed on Form I–485 with the director having jurisdiction over the applicant's place of residence. A separate application shall be filed by each applicant. If the application is approved, the director shall record the lawful admission of the applicant as of the date of approval. The applicant shall be notified of the decision and, if the application is denied, of the reasons therefor. No appeal shall lie from the denial of an application by the director but such denial shall be without prejudice to the alien's right to renew his or her application in proceedings under 8 CFR part 240.

[30 FR 14778, Nov. 30, 1965]

EDITORIAL NOTE: For FEDERAL REGISTER citations affecting § 1245.2, see the List of CFR Sections Affected, which appears in the Finding Aids section of the printed volume and at *www.govinfo.gov*.

§ 1245.3 Adjustment of status under section 13 of the Act of September 11, 1957, as amended.

Any application for benefits under section 13 of the Act of September 11, 1957, as amended, must be filed on Form I–485 with the director having jurisdiction over the applicant's place of residence. The benefits under section 13 are limited to aliens who were admitted into the United States under section 101, paragraphs (a)(15)(A)(i), (a)(15)(A)(ii), (a)(15)(G)(i), or (a)(15)(G)(ii) of the Immigration and Nationality Act who performed diplomatic or semi-diplomatic duties and to their immediate families, and who establish that there are compelling reasons why the applicant or the member of the applicant's immediate family is unable to return to the country represented by the government which accredited the applicant and that adjustment of the applicant's status to that of an alien lawfully admitted for permanent residence would be in the national interest. Aliens whose duties were of a custodial, clerical, or menial nature, and members of their immediate families, are not eligible for benefits under section 13. In view of the annual limitation of 50 on the number of aliens whose status may be adjusted under section 13, any alien who is prima facie eligible for adjustment of status to that of a lawful permanent resident under another provision of law shall be advised to apply for adjustment pursuant to such other provision of law. An applicant for the benefits of section 13 shall not be subject to the labor certification requirement of section 212(a)(14) of the Immigration and Nationality Act. The applicant shall be notified of the decision and, if the application is denied, of the reasons for the denial and of the right to appeal under the provisions of part 103 of this chapter. Any applications pending with the Service before December 29, 1981 must be resubmitted to comply with the requirements of this section.

(Secs. 103, 245, of the Immigration and Nationality Act, as amended; 71 Stat. 642, as amended, sec. 17, Pub. L. 97–116, 95 Stat. 1619 (8 U.S.C. 1103, 1255, 1255b))

[47 FR 44238, Oct. 7, 1982, as amended at 59 FR 33905, July 1, 1994]

§ 1245.4 Documentary requirements.

The provisions of part 1211 of this chapter relating to the documentary requirements for immigrants shall not apply to an applicant under this part.

(Secs. 103, 214, 245 Immigration and Nationality Act, as amended; (8 U.S.C. 1103, 1184, 8 U.S.C. 1255, Sec. 2, 96 Stat. 1157, 8 U.S.C. 1255 note))

[30 FR 14779, Nov. 30, 1965. Redesignated at 48 FR 4770, Feb. 3, 1983, and further redesignated at 52 FR 6322, Mar. 3, 1982, and further redesignated at 56 FR 49481, Oct. 2, 1991]

§ 1245.5 Medical examination.

Pursuant to section 232(b) of the Act, an applicant for adjustment of status shall be required to have a medical examination by a designated civil surgeon, whose report setting forth the findings of the mental and physical condition of the applicant, including compliance with section 212(a)(1)(A)(ii) of the Act, shall be incorporated into the record. A medical examination shall not be required of an applicant for adjustment of status who entered the United States as a nonimmigrant spouse, fianceé, or fianceeé of a United States citizen or the child of such an alien as defined in section 101(a)(15)(K) of the Act and § 214.2(k) of 8 CFR chapter I if the applicant was medically examined prior to, and as a condition of, the issuance of the nonimmigrant visa; provided that the medical examination must have occurred not more than 1 year prior the date of application for adjustment of status. Any applicant certified under paragraphs (1)(A)(ii) or (1)(A)(iii) of section 212(a) of the Act may appeal to a Board of Medical Officers of the U.S. Public Health Service as provided in section 234 of the Act and part 1235 of this chapter.

[56 FR 49841, Oct. 2, 1991, as amended at 62 FR 10384, Mar. 6, 1997; 66 FR 42595, Aug. 14, 2001]

§ 1245.6 Interview.

Each applicant for adjustment of status under this part shall be interviewed by an immigration officer. This interview may be waived in the case of a child under the age of 14; when the applicant is clearly ineligible under section 245(c) of the Act or § 1245.1 of this chapter; or when it is determined by the Service that an interview is unnecessary.

[57 FR 49375, Nov. 2, 1992]

§ 1245.7 Adjustment of status of certain Soviet and Indochinese parolees under the Foreign Operations Appropriations Act for Fiscal Year 1990 (Pub. L. 101–167).

(a) *Application.* Each person applying for benefits under section 599E of Public Law 101–167 (103 Stat. 1195, 1263) must file Form I–485, Application to Register Permanent Residence or Adjust Status, with the director having jurisdiction over the applicant's place of residence and must pay the appropriate filing and fingerprinting fee, as prescribed in § 103.7 of this chapter. Each application shall be accompanied by Form I–643, Health and Human Services Statistical Data for Refugee/Asylee Adjusting Status, and the results of a medical examination given in accordance with § 1245.8. In addition, if the applicant has reached his or her 14th birthday but is not over 79 years of age, the application shall be accompanied by a completed Form G–325A, Biographic Information, and the applicant shall be fingerprinted on Form FD–258, Applicant Card, as prescribed in § 103.2(e) of this chapter.

(b) *Aliens eligible to apply for adjustment.* The benefits of this section shall only apply to an alien who:

(1) Was a national of the Soviet Union, Vietnam, Laos, or Cambodia, and

(2) Was inspected and granted parole into the United States during the period beginning on August 15, 1988, and ending on September 30, 1990, after being denied refugee status.

(c) *Eligibility*. Benefits under Section 599E of Public Law 101–167 are limited to any alien described in paragraph (b) of this section who:

(1) Applies for such adjustment,

(2) Has been physically present in the United States for at least one year and is physically present in the United States on the date the application for such adjustment is filed,

(3) Is admissible to the United States as an immigrant, except as provided in paragraph (d) of this section, and

(4) Pays a fee for the processing of such application.

(d) *Waiver of certain grounds for inadmissibility*. The provisions of paragraphs (14), (15), (20), (21), (25), (28) (other than subparagraph (F), and (32) of section 212(a) of the Act shall not apply to adjustment under this section. The Attorney General may waive any other provision of section 212(a) (other than paragraph (23)(B), (27), (29), or (33)) with respect to such an adjustment for humanitarian purposes, to assure family unity, or when it is otherwise in the public interest.

(e) *Date of approval*. Upon approval of such an application for adjustment of status, the Attorney General shall create a record of the alien's admission as a lawful permanent resident as of the date of the alien's inspection and parole described in paragraph (b)(2) of this section.

(f) *No offset in number of visas available*. When an alien is granted the status of having been lawfully admitted for permanent residence under this section, the Secretary of State shall not be required to reduce the number of immigrant visas authorized to be issued under the Immigration and Nationality Act.

[55 FR 24860, July 19, 1990. Redesignated at 56 FR 49841, Oct. 2, 1991, as amended at 59 FR 33905, July 1, 1994; 63 FR 12987, Mar. 17, 1998]

§ 1245.8 Adjustment of status as a special immigrant under section 101(a)(27)(K) of the Act.

(a) *Application*. Each person applying for adjustment of status as a special immigrant under section 101(a)(27)(K) of the Act must file a Form I–485, Application to Register Permanent Residence or Adjust Status, with the director having jurisdiction over the applicant's place of residence. Benefits under this section are limited to aliens who have served honorably (or are enlisted to serve) in the Armed Forces of the United States for at least 12 years, and their spouses and children. For purposes of this section, special immigrants described in section 101(a)(27)(K) of the Act and his or her spouse and children shall be deemed to have been paroled into the United States pursuant to section 245(g) of the Act. Each applicant must file a separate application with the appropriate fee.

(b) *Eligibility*. The benefits of this section shall apply only to an alien described in section 101(a)(27)(K) of the Act who applies for such adjustment. The accompanying spouse or child of an applicant for adjustment of status who benefits from Public Law 102–110 may also apply for adjustment of status. The provisions of section 245(c) of the Act do not apply to the principal Armed Forces special immigrant or to his or her spouse or child.

(c) *Interview of the applicant*. Upon completion of the adjustment of status interview for a special immigrant under section 101(a)(27)(K) of the Act, the director shall make a *prima facie* determination regarding eligibility for naturalization benefits if the applicant is to be granted status as an alien lawfully admitted for permanent residence. If the director determines that the applicant is immediately eligible for naturalization under section 328 or 329 of the Act, the director shall advise the applicant that he or she is eligible to apply for naturalization on Form N–400, Application to File Petition for Naturalization. If the applicant wishes to apply for naturalization, the director shall instruct the applicant concerning the requirements for naturalization and provide him or her with the necessary forms.

(d) *Spouse or child outside the United States*. When a spouse or child of an alien granted special immigrant status under section 101(a)(27)(K) of the Act is outside the United States, the principal alien may file Form I–824, Application for Action on an Approved Application or Petition, with the office which approved the original application.

(e) *Removal provisions of section 237 of the Act.* If the Service is made aware by notification from the appropriate executive department or by any other means that a section 101(a)(27)(K) special immigrant who has already been granted permanent residence fails to complete his or her total active duty service obligation for reasons other than an honorable discharge, the alien may become subject to the removal provisions of section 237 of the Act, provided the alien is in one or more of the classes of deportable aliens specified in section 237 of the Act. The Service shall obtain a current Form DD–214, Certificate of Release or Discharge from Active Duty, from the appropriate executive department for verification of the alien's failure to maintain eligibility.

(f) *Rescission proceedings under section 246 of the Act.* If the Service determines that a military special immigrant under section 101(a)(27)(K) of the Act was not in fact eligible for adjustment of status, the Service may pursue rescission proceedings under section 246 of the Act.

[57 FR 33862, July 31, 1992, as amended at 58 FR 50836, Sept. 29, 1993; 62 FR 10384, Mar. 6, 1997]

§ 1245.9 Adjustment of status of certain nationals of the People's Republic of China under Public Law 102–404.

(a) *Principal applicant status.* All nationals of the People's Republic of China who qualify under the provisions of paragraph (b) of this section may apply for adjustment of status as principals in their own right, regardless of age or marital status. Nationals of other countries who meet the requirements of paragraphs (b) and (c) of this section may apply for adjustment of status as qualified family members.

(b) *Aliens eligible to apply for adjustment.* An alien is eligible to apply for adjustment of status under the provisions of Public Law 102–404, if the alien:

(1) Is a national of the People's Republic of China or a qualified family member of an eligible national of the People's Republic of China;

(2) Was in the United States at some time between June 5, 1989, and April 11, 1990, inclusive, or would have been in the United States during this time period except for a brief, casual, and innocent departure from this country;

(3) Has resided continuously in the United States since April 11, 1990, except for brief, casual, and innocent absences;

(4) Was not physically present in the People's Republic of China for more than a cumulative total of 90 days between April 11, 1990, and October 9, 1992;

(5) Is admissible to the United States as an immigrant, unless the basis for excludability has been waived;

(6) Establishes eligibility for adjustment of status under all provisions of section 245 of the Act, unless the basis for ineligibility has been waived; and

(7) Properly files an application for adjustment of status under section 245 of the Act.

(c) *Qualified family member who is not a national of the People's Republic of China.* A qualified family member within the meaning of this section includes the spouse, child, son, or daughter of a national of the People's Republic of China who is eligible for benefits under the provisions of paragraph (b) of this section, provided that:

(1) He or she qualified as the spouse or child (as defined in section 101(b)(1) of the Act) of an eligible national of the People's Republic of China as of April 11, 1990; and

(2) The qualifying relationship continues to exist, or the family member is a son or daughter of an eligible national of the People's Republic of China and the family member was unmarried and under the age of 21 on April 11, 1990.

(d) *Waivers of inadmissibility under section 212(a) of the Act.* An applicant for the benefits of the adjustment of status provisions of Pub. L. 102–404 is automatically exempted from compliance with the requirements of sections 212(a)(5) and 212(a)(7)(A) of the Act. A Pub. L. 102–404 applicant may also apply for one or more waivers of inadmissibility under section 212(a) of the Act, except for inadmissibility under section 212(a)(2)(C), 212(a)(3)(A), 212(a)(3)(B), 212(a)(3)(C) or 212(a)(3)(E) of the Act.

(e) *Waiver of the two-year foreign residence requirement of section 212(e).* An applicant for the benefits of the adjustment of status provisions of Public Law 102–404 is automatically exempted from compliance with the two-year foreign residence requirement of section 212(e) of the Act.

(f) *Waiver of section 245(c) of the Act.* Public Law 102–404 provides that the provisions of section 245(c) of the Act shall not apply to persons applying for the adjustment of status benefits of Public Law 102–404.

(g) *Application.* Each applicant must file an application for adjustment of status on Form I–485, Application to Register Permanent Residence or Adjust Status, accompanied by the prescribed fee, and the supporting documents specified on the instructions to Form I–485 and described in § 1245.2. Secondary evidence may be submitted if the applicant is unable to obtain the required primary evidence. Applicants who are nationals of the People's Republic of China should complete Part 2 of Form I–485 by checking box "h—other" and writing "CSPA—Principal" next to that block. Applicants who are not nationals of the People's Republic of China should complete Part 2 of Form I–485 by checking box "h—other" and writing "CSPA—Qualified Family Member" next to that block. Each applicant for the benefits of Public Law 102–404 must also submit evidence of eligibility for the adjustment of status benefits of Public Law 102–404:

(1) A photocopy of all pages of the applicant's most recent passport or an explanation of why the applicant does not have a passport;

(2) An attachment on a plain piece of paper showing:

(i) The date of the applicant's last arrival in the United States before or on April 11, 1990;

(ii) The date of each departure the applicant made from the United States since that arrival (if the applicant did not depart the United States after the initial date of arrival, the applicant should write "I was in the United States on April 11, 1990, and I have not departed the United States since April 11, 1990");

(iii) The reason for each departure; and

(iv) The date of each return to the United States.

(3) An attachment on a plain piece of paper showing:

(i) The date the applicant arrived in the People's Republic of China; and

(ii) The date the applicant left the People's Republic of China for each trip the applicant made to the People's Republic of China between April 11, 1990, and October 9, 1992 (if the applicant did not travel to the People's Republic of China, the applicant should write "I was not in the People's Republic of China between April 11, 1990, and October 9, 1992");

(4) A copy of evidence showing that the applicant was found eligible for benefits under E.O. 12711, such as deferred enforced departure (DED), employment authorization, and/or waiver of the two-year foreign residence requirement, if the applicant previously applied for benefits under E.O. 12711; and

(5) Primary or secondary evidence of a qualifying family relationship to an eligible national of the People's Republic of China, such as a birth or marriage certificate, if the applicant is a qualified family member who is not a national of the People's Republic of China.

(h) *Secondary evidence.* If any required primary evidence is unavailable, church or school records, or other secondary evidence pertinent to the facts in issue, may be submitted. If such documents are unavailable, affidavits may be submitted. The applicant may submit as many types of secondary evidence as necessary to establish the birth, marriage, or other event. Documentary evidence establishing that primary evidence is unavailable need not accompany secondary evidence of birth or marriage in the People's Republic of China.

(i) *Filing.* The application period begins on July 1, 1993. To benefit from the provisions of Public Law 102–404 (the Chinese Student Protection Act of

1992), an alien must properly file an application for adjustment of status under section 245 of the Act on or before June 30, 1994. All applications for the benefits of Public Law 102–404 must be submitted by mail to the Service Center having jurisdiction over the applicant's place of residence in the United States. Pursuant to the deactivation clause of Public Law 102–404, if the President of the United States determines and certifies to Congress before July 1, 1993, that conditions in the People's Republic of China permit persons covered by Public Law 102–404 to safely return to the People's Republic of China, no applications for lawful permanent resident status under Public Law 102–404 will be processed or granted.

(j) *Immigrant classification and assignment of priority date.* Public Law 102–404 provides eligible applicants with automatic classifications as immigrants under section 203(b)(3)(A)(i) of the Act. No immigrant visa petition is required and applicants need not meet the usual requirements for classification as skilled workers. The applicant's priority date shall be the date his or her application for adjustment of status under Public Law 102–404 is properly filed with the Service.

(k) *Effect of immigrant visa number limitations.* Eligible Public Law 102–404 applicants are exempt from the per-country immigrant visa number limitations of section 202(a)(2) of the Act. Eligible Public Law 102–404 applicants may file an application for adjustment of status under Public Law 102–404 without regard to immigrant visa number limitations of sections 202(a)(2) and 203(b)(3)(A)(i) of the Act. However, the adjustment of status application may not be approved and adjustment of status to that of a lawful permanent resident of the United States may not be granted until a visa number becomes available for the applicant under the worldwide allocation of immigrant visa numbers for employment-based aliens under section 203(b)(3)(A)(i) of the Act. The applicant may request initial or continued employment authorization during this period by filing Form I–765, Application for Employment Authorization. If the applicant needs to travel outside the United States during this period, he or she may file a request for advance parole on Form I–131, Application for Travel Document.

(l) *Decision.* In the case of an application for adjustment of status filed pursuant to the provisions of Public Law 102–404, the authority conferred upon district directors in 8 CFR part 1245 to accept and adjudicate an application for adjustment of status under section 245 of the Act is delegated exclusively to the service center director having jurisdiction over the applicant's place of residence in the United States. If the service center director transfers the application to the district director, authority to adjudicate an application for adjustment of status filed pursuant to the provisions of Public Law 102–404 lies with the district director having jurisdiction over the applicant's place of residence.

(m) *Effect of enactment on family members other than qualified family members.* The adjustment of status benefits and waivers provided by Public Law 102–404 do not apply to a spouse or child who is not a qualified family member as defined in paragraph (c) of this section. However, a spouse or child whose relationship to the principal alien was established prior to the approval of the principal's adjustment-of-status application may be accorded the derivative priority date and preference category of the principal alien, in accordance with the provisions of section 203(d) of the Act. The spouse or child may use the priority date and category when it becomes current, in accordance with the limitations set forth in sections 201 and 202 of the Act.

[58 FR 35838, July 1, 1993, as amended at 62 FR 10384, Mar. 6, 1997; 62 FR 63254, Nov. 28, 1997]

§ 1245.10 Adjustment of status upon payment of additional sum under section 245(i).

(a) *Definitions.* As used in this section the term:

(1)(i) *Grandfathered alien* means an alien who is the beneficiary (including a spouse or child of the alien beneficiary if eligible to receive a visa under section 203(d) of the Act) of:

(A) A petition for classification under section 204 of the Act which was properly filed with the Attorney General on or before April 30, 2001, and which was approvable when filed; or

(B) An application for labor certification under section 212(a)(5)(A) of the Act that was properly filed pursuant to the regulations of the Secretary of Labor on or before April 30, 2001, and which was approvable when filed.

(ii) If the qualifying visa petition or application for labor certification was filed after January 14, 1998, the alien must have been physically present in the United States on December 21, 2000. This requirement does not apply with respect to a spouse or child accompanying or following to join a principal alien who is a grandfathered alien as described in this section.

(2) *Properly filed* means:

(i) With respect to a qualifying immigrant visa petition, that the application was physically received by the Service on or before April 30, 2001, or if mailed, was postmarked on or before April 30, 2001, and accepted for filing as provided in §103.2(a)(1) and (a)(2) of 8 CFR chapter I; and

(ii) With respect to a qualifying application for labor certification, that the application was properly filed and accepted pursuant to the regulations of the Secretary of Labor, 20 CFR 656.21.

(3) *Approvable when filed* means that, as of the date of the filing of the qualifying immigrant visa petition under section 204 of the Act or qualifying application for labor certification, the qualifying petition or application was properly filed, meritorious in fact, and non-frivolous ("frivolous" being defined herein as patently without substance). This determination will be made based on the circumstances that existed at the time the qualifying petition or application was filed. A visa petition that was properly filed on or before April 30, 2001, and was approvable when filed, but was later withdrawn, denied, or revoked due to circumstances that have arisen after the time of filing, will preserve the alien beneficiary's grandfathered status if the alien is otherwise eligible to file an application for adjustment of status under section 245(i) of the Act.

(4) *Circumstances that have arisen after the time of filing* means circumstances similar to those outlined in §1205.1(a)(3)(i) or (a)(3)(ii) of this chapter.

(b) *Eligibility.* An alien who is included in the categories of restricted aliens under §1245.1(b) and meets the definition of a "grandfathered alien" may apply for adjustment of status under section 245 of the Act if the alien meets the requirements of paragraphs (b)(1) through (b)(7) of this section:

(1) Is physically present in the United States;

(2) Is eligible for immigrant classification and has an immigrant visa number immediately available at the time of filing for adjustment of status;

(3) Is not inadmissible from the United States under any provision of section 212 of the Act, or all grounds for inadmissibility have been waived;

(4) Properly files Form I–485, Application to Register Permanent Residence or Adjust Status on or after October 1, 1994, with the required fee for that application;

(5) Properly files Supplement A to Form I–485 on or after October 1, 1994;

(6) Pays an additional sum of $1,000, unless payment of the additional sum is not required under section 245(i) of the Act; and

(7) Will adjust status under section 245 of the Act to that of lawful permanent resident of the United States on or after October 1, 1994.

(c) *Payment of additional sum.* An adjustment applicant filing under the provisions of section 245(i) of the Act must pay the standard adjustment application filing fee as specified in §103.7(b)(1) of this chapter. Each application submitted under the provisions of section 245(i) of the Act must be submitted with an additional sum of $1,000. An applicant must submit the additional sum of $1,000 only once per application for adjustment of status submitted under the provisions of section 245(i) of the Act. However, an applicant filing under the provisions of section 245(i) of the Act is not required to pay the additional sum if, at the time the application for adjustment of status is filed, the alien is:

(1) Unmarried and less than 17 years of age;

(2) The spouse of a legalized alien, qualifies for and has properly filed Form I–817, Application for Voluntary

Departure under the Family Unity Program, and submits a copy of his or her receipt or approval notice for filing Form I–817; or

(3) The child of a legalized alien, is unmarried and less than 21 years of age, qualifies for and has filed Form I–817, and submits a copy of his or her receipt or approval notice for filing Form I–817. Such an alien must pay the additional sum if he or she has reached the age of 21 years at the time of filing for adjustment of status. Such an alien must meet all other conditions for adjustment of status contained in the Act and in this chapter.

(d) *Pending adjustment application with the Service or Executive Office for Immigration Review filed without Supplement A to Form I–485 and additional sum.* An alien who filed an adjustment of status application with the Service in accordance with § 103.2 of 8 CFR chapter I will be allowed the opportunity to amend such an application to request consideration under the provisions of section 245(i) of the Act, if it appears that the alien is not otherwise ineligible for adjustment of status. The Service shall notify the applicant in writing of the Service's intent to deny the adjustment of status application, and any other requests for benefits that derive from the adjustment application, unless Supplement A to Form I–485 and any required additional sum is filed within 30 days of the date of the notice. If the application for adjustment of status is pending before the Executive Office for Immigration Review (EOIR), EOIR will allow the respondent an opportunity to amend an adjustment of status application filed in accordance with § 103.2 of 8 CFR chapter I (to include Supplement A to Form I–485 and proof of remittance to the INS of the required additional sum) in order to request consideration under the provisions of section 245(i) of the Act.

(e) *Applications for Adjustment of Status filed before October 1, 1994.* The provisions of section 245(i) of the Act shall not apply to an application for adjustment of status that was filed before October 1, 1994. The provisions of section 245(i) of the Act also shall not apply to a motion to reopen or reconsider an application for adjustment of status if the application for adjustment of status was filed before October 1, 1994. An applicant whose pre-October 1, 1994, application for adjustment of status has been denied may file a new application for adjustment of status pursuant to section 245(i) of the Act on or after October 1, 1994, provided that such new application is accompanied by: the required fee; Supplement A to Form I–485; the additional sum required by section 245(i) of the Act; and all other required initial and additional evidence.

(f) *Effect of section 245(i) on completed adjustment applications before the Service.* (1) Any motion to reopen or reconsider before the Service alleging availability of section 245(i) of the Act must be filed in accordance with § 103.5 of 8 CFR chapter I. If said motion to reopen with the Service is granted, the alien must remit to the Service Supplement A to Form I–485 and the additional sum required by section 245(i) of the Act. If the alien had previously remitted Supplement A to Form I–485 and the additional sum with the application which is the subject of the motion to reopen, then no additional sum need be remitted upon such reopening.

(2) An alien whose adjustment application was adjudicated and denied by the Service because of ineligibility under section 245(a) or (c) of the Act and now alleges eligibility due to the availability of section 245(i) of the Act may file a new application for adjustment of status pursuant to section 245(i) of the Act, provided that such new application is accompanied by the required fee for the application, Supplement A to Form I–485, additional sum required by section 245(i) of the Act and all other required and additional evidence.

(g) *Aliens deportable under section 237(a)(4)(B) of the Act are ineligible to adjust status.* Section 237(a)(4)(B) of the Act renders any alien who has engaged, is engaged, or at any time after admission engages in any terrorist activity, as defined in section 212(a)(3)(B)(iii) of the Act, deportable. Under section 245(c)(6) of the Act, persons who are deportable under section 237(a)(4)(B) of the Act are ineligible to adjust status under section 245(a) of the Act. Any person who is deportable under section 237(a)(4)(B) of the Act is also ineligible to adjust status under section 245(i) of the Act.

(h) *Asylum or diversity immigrant visa applications.* An asylum application, diversity visa lottery application, or diversity visa lottery-winning letter does not serve to grandfather the alien for purposes of section 245(i) of the Act. However, an otherwise grandfathered alien may use winning a diversity visa as a basis for adjustment.

(i) *Denial, withdrawal, or revocation of the approval of a visa petition or application for labor certification.* The denial, withdrawal, or revocation of the approval of a qualifying immigrant visa petition, or application for labor certification, that was properly filed on or before April 30, 2001, and that was approvable when filed, will not preclude its grandfathered alien (including the grandfathered alien's family members) from seeking adjustment of status under section 245(i) of the Act on the basis of another approved visa petition, a diversity visa, or any other ground for adjustment of status under the Act, as appropriate.

(j) *Substitution of a beneficiary on an application for a labor certification.* Only the alien who was the beneficiary of the application for the labor certification on or before April 30, 2001, will be considered to have been grandfathered for purposes of filing an application for adjustment of status under section 245(i) of the Act. An alien who was previously the beneficiary of the application for the labor certification but was subsequently replaced by another alien on or before April 30, 2001, will not be considered to be a grandfathered alien. An alien who was substituted for the previous beneficiary of the application for the labor certification after April 30, 2001, will not be considered to be a grandfathered alien.

(k) *Changes in employment.* An applicant for adjustment under section 245(i) of the Act who is adjusting status through an employment-based category is not required to work for the petitioner who filed the petition that grandfathered the alien, unless he or she is seeking adjustment based on employment for that same petitioner.

(l) *Effects of grandfathering on an alien's nonimmigrant status.* An alien's nonimmigrant status is not affected by the fact that he or she is a grandfathered alien. Lawful immigration status for a nonimmigrant is defined in § 1245.1(d)(1)(ii).

(m) *Effect of grandfathering on unlawful presence under section 212(a)(9)(B) and (c) of the Act.* If the alien is not in a period of stay authorized by the Attorney General, the fact that he or she is a grandfathered alien does not prevent the alien from accruing unlawful presence under section 212(a)(9)(B) and (C) of the Act.

(n) *Evidentiary requirement to demonstrate physical presence on December 21, 2000.* (1) Unless the qualifying immigrant visa petition or application for labor certification was filed on or before January 14, 1998, a principal grandfathered alien must establish that he or she was physically present in the United States on December 21, 2000, to be eligible to apply to adjust status under section 245(i) of the Act. If no one document establishes the alien's physical presence on December 21, 2000, he or she may submit several documents establishing his or her physical presence in the United States prior to, and after December 21, 2000.

(2) To demonstrate physical presence on December 21, 2000, the alien may submit Service documentation. Examples of acceptable Service documentation include, but are not limited to:

(i) A photocopy of the Form I–94, Arrival-Departure Record, issued upon the alien's arrival in the United States;

(ii) A photocopy of the Form I–862, Notice to Appear;

(iii) A photocopy of the Form I–122, Notice to Applicant for Admission Detained for Hearing before Immigration Judge, issued by the Service on or prior to December 21, 2000, placing the applicant in exclusion proceedings under section 236 of the Act (as in effect prior to April 1, 1997);

(iv) A photocopy of the Form I–221, Order to Show Cause, issued by the Service on or prior to December 21, 2000, placing the applicant in deportation proceedings under section 242 or 242A of the Act (as in effect prior to April 1, 1997);

(v) A photocopy of any application or petition for a benefit under the Act filed by or on behalf of the applicant on or prior to December 21, 2000, which establishes his or her presence in the United States, or a fee receipt issued by the Service for such application or petition.

(3) To demonstrate physical presence on December 21, 2000, the alien may submit other government documentation. Other government documentation issued by a Federal, state, or local authority must bear the signature, seal, or other authenticating instrument of such authority (if the document normally bears such instrument), be dated at the time of issuance, and bear a date of issuance not later than December 21, 2000. For this purpose, the term Federal, state, or local authority includes any governmental, educational, or administrative function operated by Federal, state, county, or municipal officials. Examples of such other documentation include, but are not limited to:

(i) A state driver's license;

(ii) A state identification card;

(iii) A county or municipal hospital record;

(iv) A public college or public school transcript;

(v) Income tax records;

(vi) A certified copy of a Federal, state, or local governmental record which was created on or prior to December 21, 2000, shows that the applicant was present in the United States at the time, and establishes that the applicant sought on his or her own behalf, or some other party sought on the applicant's behalf, a benefit from the Federal, state, or local governmental agency keeping such record;

(vii) A certified copy of a Federal, state, or local governmental record which was created on or prior to December 21, 2000, that shows that the applicant was present in the United States at the time, and establishes that the applicant submitted an income tax return, property tax payment, or similar submission or payment to the Federal, state, or local governmental agency keeping such record;

(viii) A transcript from a private or religious school that is registered with, or approved or licensed by, appropriate State or local authorities, accredited by the State or regional accrediting body, or by the appropriate private school association, or maintains enrollment records in accordance with State or local requirements or standards.

(4) To demonstrate physical presence on December 21, 2000, the alien may submit non-government documentation. Examples of documentation establishing physical presence on December 21, 2000, may include, but are not limited to:

(i) School records;

(ii) Rental receipts;

(iii) Utility bill receipts;

(iv) Any other dated receipts;

(v) Personal checks written by the applicant bearing a bank cancellation stamp;

(vi) Employment records, including pay stubs;

(vii) Credit card statements showing the dates of purchase, payment, or other transaction;

(viii) Certified copies of records maintained by organizations chartered by the Federal or State government, such as public utilities, accredited private and religious schools, and banks;

(ix) If the applicant established that a family unit was in existence and cohabiting in the United States, documents evidencing the presence of another member of the same family unit; and

(x) For applicants who have ongoing correspondence or other interaction with the Service, a list of the types and dates of such correspondence or other contact that the applicant knows to be contained or reflected in Service records.

(5)(i) The adjudicator will evaluate all evidence on a case-by-case basis and will not accept a personal affidavit attesting to physical presence on December 21, 2000, without requiring an interview or additional evidence to validate the affidavit.

(ii) In all cases, any doubts as to the existence, authenticity, veracity, or accuracy of the documentation shall be resolved by the official government record, with records of the Service and the Executive Office for Immigration Review (EOIR) having precedence over the records of other agencies. Furthermore, determinations as to the weight to be given any particular document or item of evidence shall be solely within the discretion of the adjudicating authority (*i.e.*, the Service or EOIR). It shall be the responsibility of the applicant to obtain and submit copies of the records of any other government agency that the applicant desires to be considered in support of his or her application.

[59 FR 51095, Oct. 7, 1994; 59 FR 53020, Oct. 20, 1994, as amended at 62 FR 10384, Mar. 6, 1997; 62 FR 39424, July 23, 1997; 62 FR 55153, Oct. 23, 1997; 66 FR 16388, Mar. 26, 2001]

§ 1245.11 Adjustment of aliens in S nonimmigrant classification.

(a) *Eligibility*. An application on Form I–854, requesting that an alien witness or informant in S nonimmigrant classification be allowed to adjust status to that of lawful permanent resident, may only be filed by the federal or state law enforcement authority ("LEA") (which shall include a federal or state court or a United States Attorney's Office) that originally requested S classification for the alien. The completed application shall be filed with the Assistant Attorney General, Criminal Division, Department of Justice, who will forward only properly certified applications to the Commissioner, Immigration and Naturalization Service, for approval. Upon receipt of an approved Form I–854 allowing the S nonimmigrant to adjust status to that of lawful permanent resident, the alien may proceed to file with that Form, Form I–485, Application to Register Permanent Residence or Adjust Status, pursuant to the following process.

(1) *Request to allow S nonimmigrant to apply for adjustment of status to that of lawful permanent resident*. The LEA that requested S nonimmigrant classification for an S nonimmigrant witness or informant pursuant to section 101(a)(15)(S) of the Act may request that the principal S nonimmigrant be allowed to apply for adjustment of status by filing Form I–854 with the Assistant Attorney General, Criminal Division, in accordance with the instructions on, or attached to, that form and certifying that the alien has fulfilled the terms of his or her admission and classification. The same Form I–854 may be used by the LEA to request that the principals nonimmigrant's spouse, married and unmarried sons and daughters, regardless of age, and parents who are in derivative S nonimmigrant classification and who are qualified family members as described in paragraph (b) of this section similarly be allowed to apply for adjustment of status pursuant to section 101(a)(15)(S) of the Act.

(2) *Certification*. Upon receipt of an LEA's request for the adjustment of an alien in S nonimmigrant classification on Form I–854, the Assistant Attorney General, Criminal Division, shall review the information and determine whether to certify the request to the Commissioner in accordance with the instructions on the form.

(3) *Submission of requests for adjustment of status to the Commissioner*. No application by an LEA on Form I–854 requesting the adjustment to lawful permanent resident status of an S nonimmigrant shall be forwarded to the Commissioner unless first certified by the Assistant Attorney General, Criminal Division.

(4) *Decision on request to allow adjustment of S nonimmigrant*. The Commissioner shall make the final decision on a request to allow an S nonimmigrant to apply for adjustment of status to lawful permanent resident.

(i) In the event the Commissioner decides to deny an application on Form I–854 to allow an S nonimmigrant to apply for adjustment of status, the Assistant Attorney General, Criminal Division, and the relevant LEA shall be notified in writing to that effect. The Assistant Attorney General, Criminal Division, shall concur in or object to that decision. Unless the Assistant Attorney General, Criminal Division, objects within 7 days, he or she shall be deemed to have concurred in the decision. In the event of an objection by the Assistant Attorney General, Criminal Division, the matter will be expeditiously referred to the Deputy Attorney General for a final resolution. In no circumstances shall the alien or the relevant LEA have a right of appeal from any decision to deny.

(ii) Upon approval of the request on Form I–854, the Commissioner shall forward a copy of the approved form to the Assistant Attorney General and the S nonimmigrant, notifying them that the S nonimmigrant may proceed to file Form I–485 and request adjustment of status to that of lawful permanent resident, and that, to be eligible for adjustment of status, the nonimmigrant must otherwise:

(A) Meet the requirements of paragraph (b) of this section, if requesting adjustment as a qualified family member of the certified principal S nonimmigrant witness or informant;

(B) Be admissible to the United States as an immigrant, unless the ground of inadmissibility has been waived;

(C) Establish eligibility for adjustment of status under all provisions of section 245 of the Act, unless the basis for ineligibility has been waived; and

(D) Properly file with his or her Form I–485, Application to Register Permanent Residence or Adjust Status, the approved Form I–854.

(b) *Family members*—(1) *Qualified family members*. A qualified family member of an S nonimmigrant includes the spouse, married or unmarried son or daughter, or parent of a principal S nonimmigrant who meets the requirements of paragraph (a) of this section, provided that:

(i) The family member qualified as the spouse, married or unmarried son or daughter, or parent (as defined in section 101(b) of the Act) of the principal S nonimmigrant when the family member was admitted as or granted a change of status to that of a nonimmigrant under section 101(a)(15)(S) of the Act;

(ii) The family member was admitted in S nonimmigrant classification to accompany, or follow to join, the principal S–5 or S–6 alien pursuant to the LEA's request;

(iii) The family member is not inadmissible from the United States as a participant in Nazi persecution or genocide as described in section 212(a)(3)(E) of the Act;

(iv) The qualifying relationship continues to exist; and

(v) The principal alien has adjusted status, has a pending application for adjustment of status or is concurrently filing an application for adjustment of status under section 101(a)(15)(S) of the Act.

(vi) Paragraphs (b)(1)(iv) and (v) of this section do not apply if the alien witness or informant has died and, in the opinion of the Attorney General, was in compliance with the terms of his or her S classification under section 245(i) (1) and (2) of the Act.

(2) *Other family member*. The adjustment provisions in this section do not apply to a family member who has not been classified as an S nonimmigrant pursuant to a request on Form I–854 or who does not otherwise meet the requirements of paragraph (b) of this section. However, a spouse or an unmarried child who is less than 21 years old, and whose relationship to the principal S nonimmigrant or qualified family member was established prior to the approval of the principal S nonimmigrant's adjustment of status application, may be accorded the priority date and preference category of the principal S nonimmigrant or qualified family member, in accordance with the provisions of section 203(d) of the Act. Such a spouse or child:

(i) May use the principal S nonimmigrant or qualified member's priority date and category when it becomes current, in accordance with the limitations set forth in sections 201 and 202 of the Act;

(ii) May seek immigrant visa issuance abroad or adjustment of status to that of a lawful permanent resident of the United States when the priority date becomes current for the spouse's or child's country of chargeability under the fourth employment-based preference classification;

(iii) Must meet all the requirements for immigrant visa issuance or adjustment of status, unless those requirements have been waived;

(iv) Is not applying for adjustment of status under 101(a)(15)(S) of the Act, is not required to file Form I–854, and is not required to obtain LEA certification; and

(v) Will lose eligibility for benefits if the child marries or has his or her twenty-first birthday before being admitted with an immigrant visa or granted adjustment of status.

(c) *Waivers of inadmissibility*. An alien seeking to adjust status pursuant to the provisions of section 101(a)(15)(S) of the Act may not be denied adjustment of status for conduct or a condition that:

(1) Was disclosed to the Attorney General prior to admission; and

(2) Was specifically waived pursuant to the waiver provisions set forth at section 212(d)(1) and 212(d)(3) of the Act.

(d) *Application.* Each S nonimmigrant requesting adjustment of status under section 101(a)(15)(S) of the Act must:

(1) File Form I–485, with the prescribed fee, accompanied by the approved Form I–854, and the supporting documents specified in the instructions to Form I–485 and described in 8 CFR 1245.2. Secondary evidence may be submitted if the nonimmigrant is unable to obtain the required primary evidence as provided in 8 CFR 103.2(b)(2). The S nonimmigrant applying to adjust must complete Part 2 of Form I-485 by checking box "h-other" and writing "S" or "S-Qualified Family Member." Qualified family members must submit documentary evidence of the relationship to the principal S nonimmigrant witness or informant.

(2) Submit detailed and inclusive evidence of eligibility for the adjustment of status benefits of S classification, which shall include:

(i) A photocopy of all pages of the alien's most recent passport or an explanation of why the alien does not have a passport; or

(ii) An attachment on a plain piece of paper showing the dates of all arrivals and departures from the United States in S nonimmigrant classification and the reason for each departure; and

(iii) Primary evidence of a qualifying relationship to the principal S nonimmigrant, such as birth or marriage certificate. If any required primary evidence is unavailable, church or school records, or other secondary evidence may be submitted. If such documents are unavailable, affidavits may be submitted as provided in 8 CFR 103.2(b)(2).

(e) *Priority date.* The S nonimmigrant's priority date shall be the date his or her application for adjustment of status as an S nonimmigrant is properly filed with the Service.

(f) *Visa number limitation.* An adjustment of status application under section 101(a)(15)(S) of the Act may be filed regardless of the availability of immigrant visa numbers. The adjustment of status application may not, however, be approved and the alien's adjustment of status to that of lawful permanent resident of the United States may not be granted until a visa number becomes available for the alien under the worldwide allocation for employment-based immigrants under section 201(d) and section 203(b)(4) of the Act. The alien may request initial or continued employment authorization while the adjustment application is pending by filing Form I–765, Application for Employment Authorization. If the alien needs to travel outside the United States during this period, he or she may file a request for advance parole on Form I–131, Application for Travel Document.

(g) *Filing and decision.* An application for adjustment of status filed by an S nonimmigrant under section 101(a)(15)(S) of the Act shall be filed with the district director having jurisdiction over the alien's place of residence. Upon approval of adjustment of status under this section, the district director shall record the alien's lawful admission for permanent residence as of the date of such approval. The district director shall notify the Commissioner and the Assistant Attorney General, Criminal Division, of the adjustment.

(h) *Removal under section 237 of the Act.* Nothing in this section shall prevent an alien adjusted pursuant to the terms of these provisions from being removed for conviction of a crime of moral turpitude committed within 10 years after being provided lawful permanent residence under this section or for any other ground under section 237 of the Act.

(i) *Denial of application.* In the event the district director decides to deny an application on Form I–485 and an approved Form I–854 to allow an S nonimmigrant to adjust status, the Assistant Attorney General, Criminal Division, and the relevant LEA shall be notified in writing to that effect. The Assistant Attorney General, Criminal Division, shall concur in or object to that decision. Unless the Assistant Attorney General, Criminal Division, objects within 7 days, he or she shall be deemed to have concurred in the decision. In the event of an objection by the Assistant Attorney General, Criminal Division, the matter will be expeditiously referred to the Deputy Attorney General for a final resolution. In no circumstances shall the alien or the relevant LEA have a right of appeal from any decision to deny. A denial of an adjustment application under this paragraph may not be renewed in subsequent removal proceedings.

[60 FR 44269, Aug. 25, 1995; 60 FR 52248, Oct. 5, 1995, as amended at 62 FR 10384, Mar. 6, 1997]

§ 1245.12 What are the procedures for certain Polish and Hungarian parolees who are adjusting status to that of permanent resident under the Illegal Immigration Reform and Immigrant Responsibility Act of 1996?

(a) *How do I apply for adjustment of status under this section?* (1) Each person applying for adjustment of status, under section 646(b) of Public Law 104–208, must file a completed Form I–485, Application to Register Permanent Residence or Adjust Status, with the correct filing fee, with the Service director having jurisdiction over the applicant's place of residence.

(2) The application must include Form G–325A, Biographic Information and the results of the medical examination made according to § 232.1 of 8 CFR chapter I and § 1245.5.

(3) The application must include evidence to show the applicant was a national of Poland or Hungary who, after being denied refugee status, was inspected and granted parole into the United States between November 1, 1989, and December 31, 1991.

(4) The applicant must have been physically present in the United States for at least 1 year before filing a Form I–485.

(5) After receiving the Form I–485, the adjudicating Service office will notify each applicant who is 14 years old or older of the time and location for the required fingerprinting.

(b) *How is my application for adjustment of status affected if I leave the United States while my application is still pending?* The departure from the United States by an applicant for adjustment of status must be considered an abandonment of the application, as provided in § 1245.2(a)(4)(ii), unless the applicant was previously granted advance parole for such absence, and was reinspected on returning to the United States.

(c) *Which grounds for inadmissibility do not apply or can be waived?* The provisions of section 212(a) (4), (5), and (7)(A) of the Act will not apply to adjustment of status under § 1245.12. In addition, the director may waive any other ground of inadmissibility except section 212(a)(2)(C) or 212(a)(3)(A), (B), (C), or (E) of the Act, for humanitarian purposes, to ensure family unity, or when it is otherwise in the public interest.

(d) *If my application for adjustment of status is approved under § 1245.12, what date will be recorded as my admission to permanent residence?* On approval of the application for adjustment of status, the date of the applicant's admission to permanent resident status will be the date of the applicant's inspection and parole, as described in paragraph (a) of this section.

[65 FR 20070, Apr. 14, 2000]

§ 1245.13 Adjustment of status of certain nationals of Nicaragua and Cuba under Public Law 105–100.

(a) *Aliens eligible to apply for adjustment.* An alien is eligible to apply for adjustment of status under the provisions of section 202 of Pub. L. 105–100 as amended and without regard to section 241(a)(5) of the Act, if the alien:

(1) Is a national of Nicaragua or Cuba;

(2) Except as provided in paragraph (o) of this section, has been physically present in the United States for a continuous period beginning not later than December 1, 1995, and ending not earlier that the date the application for adjustment is granted, excluding:

(i) Any periods of absence from the United States not exceeding 180 days in the aggregate; and

(ii) Any periods of absence for which the applicant received an Advance Authorization for Parole (Form I–512) prior to his or her departure from the United States, provided the applicant returned to the United States in accordance with the conditions of such Advance Authorization for Parole;

(3) Is not inadmissible to the United States for permanent residence under any provisions of section 212(a) of the

Act, with the exception of paragraphs (4), (5), (6)(A), (7)(A) and (9)(B). If available, an applicant may apply for an individual waiver as provided in paragraph (c) of this section;

(4) Is physically present in the United States at the time the application is filed; and

(5) Properly files an application for adjustment of status in accordance with this section.

(b) *Qualified family members*—(1) *Existence of relationship at time of adjustment.* The spouse, child, or unmarried son or daughter of an alien eligible for adjustment of status under the provisions of Pub. L. 105–100 is eligible to apply for benefits as a dependent provided the qualifying relationship existed when the principal beneficiary was granted adjustment of status and the dependent meets all applicable requirements of sections 202(a) and (d) of Pub. L. 105–100.

(2) *Spouse and minor children.* If physically present in the United States, the spouse or minor child of an alien who is eligible for permanent residence under the provisions of Pub. L. 105–100 may also apply for and receive adjustment of status under this section, provided such spouse or child meets the criteria established in paragraph (a) of this section, except for the requirement of continuous physical presence in the United States since December 1, 1995. Such application may be filed concurrently with or subsequent to the filing of the principal's application but may not be approved prior to approval of the principal's application.

(3) *Unmarried adult sons and daughters.* An unmarried son or daughter of an alien who is eligible for permanent residence under the provisions of Pub. L. 105–100 may apply for and receive adjustment under this section, provided such son or daughter meets the criteria established in paragraph (a) of this section.

(c) *Applicability of inadmissibility grounds contained in section 212(a)*—(1) *General.* An applicant for the benefits of the adjustment of status provisions of section 202 of Pub. L. 105–100 need not establish admissibility under paragraphs (4), (5), (6)(A), (7)(A), and (9)(B) of section 212(a) of the Act in order to be able to adjust his or her status to that of permanent resident. An applicant under section 202 of Pub. L. 105–100 may also apply for one or more of the immigrant waivers of inadmissibility under section 212 of the Act, if applicable, in accordance with § 1212.7 of this chapter.

(2) *Special rule for waiver of inadmissibility grounds for NACARA applicants under section 212(a)(9)(A) and 212(a)(9)(C) of the Act.* An applicant for adjustment of status under section 202 of Public Law 105–100 who is inadmissible under section 212(a)(9)(A) or 212(a)(9)(C) of the Act, may apply for a waiver of these grounds of inadmissibility while present in the United States. Such an alien must file a Form I–601, Application for Waiver of Grounds of Excludability, with the director of the Texas Service Center if the application for adjustment is pending at that office, with the district director having jurisdiction over the application if the application for adjustment is pending at a district office, with the Immigration Judge having jurisdiction if the application for adjustment is pending before the Immigration Court, or with the Board of Immigration Appeals if the appeal is pending before the Board.

(d) *General*—(1) *Proceedings pending before an Immigration Court.* Except as provided in paragraph (d)(3) of this section, while an alien is in exclusion, deportation, or removal proceedings pending before an immigration judge, or has a pending motion to reopen or motion to reconsider filed with an immigration judge on or before May 21, 1998, sole jurisdiction over an application for adjustment of status under section 202 of Public Law 105–100 shall lie with the immigration judge. If an alien who has a pending motion to reopen or motion to reconsider filed with an immigration judge on or before May 21, 1998 files an application for adjustment of status under section 202 of Pub. L. 105–100, the immigration judge shall reopen the alien's proceedings for consideration of the adjustment application, unless the alien is clearly ineligible for adjustment of status under section 202 of Pub. L. 105–100. All applications for adjustment of status under section 202 of Pub. L. 105–100 filed with an Immigration Court shall be subject to the requirements of §§ 3.11 and 3.31 of this chapter.

(2) *Proceedings pending before the Board of Immigration Appeals.* Except as provided in paragraph (d)(3) of this section, in cases where a motion to reopen or motion to reconsider filed with the Board on or before May 21, 1998, or an appeal, is pending, the Board shall remand, or reopen and remand, the proceedings to the Immigration Court for the sole purpose of adjudicating an application for adjustment of status under section 202 of Public Law 105–100, unless the alien is clearly ineligible for adjustment of status under section 202 of Public Law 105–100. If the immigration judge denies, or the alien fails to file, the application for adjustment of status under section 202 of Public Law 105–100, the immigration judge shall certify the decision to the Board for consideration in conjunction with the previously pending appeal or motion.

(3) *Administrative closure of pending exclusion, deportation, or removal proceedings.* (i) In the case of an alien who is in exclusion, deportation, or removal proceedings, or has a pending motion to reopen or a motion to reconsider such proceedings filed on or before May 21, 1998, and who appears to be eligible to file an application for adjustment of status under section 202 of Pub. L. 105–100, the Immigration Court having jurisdiction over such proceedings or motion, or if the matter is before the Board on appeal or by motion, the Board, shall, upon request of the alien and with the concurrence of the Service, administratively close the proceedings, or continue indefinitely the motion, to allow the alien to file such application with the Service as prescribed in paragraph (g) of this section.

(ii) In any case not administratively closed in accordance with paragraph (d)(3)(i) of this section, the immigration judge having jurisdiction over the exclusion, deportation, or removal proceedings shall have jurisdiction to accept and adjudicate any application for adjustment of status under section 202 of Pub. L. 105–100 during the course of such proceedings.

(4)(i) *Aliens with final orders of exclusion, deportation, or removal.* An alien who is subject to a final order of exclusion, deportation, or removal, and who has not been denied adjustment of status under section 202 of Public Law 105–100 by the immigration judge or the Board of Immigration Appeals, may apply to the Service for adjustment of status under section 202 of Pub. L. 105–100.

(ii) An alien may file a motion to reopen with the Immigration Court or the Board of Immigration Appeals, whichever had jurisdiction last, if the alien is present in the United States and subject to a final order of exclusion, deportation, or removal and has been denied adjustment of status under section 202 of NACARA by an Immigration Court or the Board or who never applied for adjustment of status on or before March 31, 2000, with either the Service, the Immigration Court or the Board, and who is now eligible for adjustment as a result of section 1505(a)(1) of the Legal Immigration Family Equity Act of 2000 (LIFE) and the LIFE amendments, Public Law 106–553 and Public Law 106–554, respectively. As provided by § 1505(a)(2) of the LIFE Act and its amendments, such a motion to reopen must be filed on or before June 19, 2001.

(5) *Stay of final order of exclusion, deportation, or removal*—(i) *With the Service.* The filing of an application for adjustment under section 202 of Public Law 105–100 with the Service shall not stay the execution of such final order unless the applicant has filed, and the Service has approved an Application for Stay of Removal (Form I–246) in accordance with section 241(c)(2) of the Act and § 241.6 of this chapter. Absent evidence of the applicant's statutory ineligibility for adjustment of status under section 202 of Public Law 105–100 or significant negative discretionary factors, a Form I–246 filed by a bona fide applicant for adjustment under section 202 of Public Law 105–100 shall be approved, and the removal of the applicant shall be stayed until such time as the application for adjustment has been adjudicated in accordance with this section.

(ii) *With EOIR.* When the Service refers a decision to an immigration judge on a Notice of Certification (Form I–290C) in accordance with paragraph (m)(3) of this section, the referral shall not stay the execution of the final order. Execution of such final order shall proceed unless a stay of execution is specifically granted by the immigration judge, the Board, or an authorized Service officer.

(6) *Effect on applications for adjustment under other provisions of the law.* Nothing in this section shall be deemed to allow any alien who is in either exclusion proceedings that commenced prior to April 1, 1997, or removal proceedings as an inadmissible arriving alien that commenced on or after April 1, 1997, and who has not been paroled into the United States, to apply for adjustment of status under any provision of law other than section 202 of Pub. L. 105–100.

(e) *Application and supporting documents.* Each applicant for adjustment of status must file a Form I–485, Application to Register Permanent Residence or Adjust Status. An applicant should complete Part 2 of Form I–485 by checking box "h—other" and writing "NACARA—Principal" or "NACARA—Dependent" next to that block. Each application must be accompanied by:

(1) The fee prescribed in § 103.7(b)(1) of 8 CFR chapter I;

(2) If the applicant is 14 years of age or older, the fee for fingerprinting prescribed in § 103.7(b)(1) of 8 CFR chapter I;

(3) Evidence of commencement of physical presence in the United States at any time on or before December 1, 1995. Such evidence may relate to any time at or after entry and may consist of either:

(i) Documentation evidencing one or more of the activities specified in section 202(b)(2)(A) of Public Law 105–100;

(ii) A copy of the Form I–94, Record of Arrival and Departure, issued to the applicant at the time of his or her inspection and admission or parole;

(iii) Other documentation issued by a Federal, State, or local authority provided such other documentation bears the signature, seal, or other authenticating instrument of such authority (if the document normally bears such instrument), was dated at the time of issuance, and bears a date of issuance not later than December 1, 1995. Examples of such other documentation include, but are not limited to:

(A) A State driver's license;

(B) A State identification card issued in lieu of a driver's license to a non-driver;

(C) A county or municipal hospital record;

(D) A public college or public school transcript; and

(E) Income tax records;

(iv) A copy of a petition on behalf of the applicant that was submitted to the Service on or before December 1, 1995, and that lists the applicant as being physically present in the United States;

(v) A certified copy of a Federal, State, or local governmental record that was created on or prior to December 1, 1995, shows that the applicant was present in the United States at the time, and establishes that the applicant sought on his or her own behalf, or some other party sought on the applicant's behalf, a benefit from the Federal, State, or local governmental agency keeping such record;

(vi) A certified copy of a Federal, State, or local governmental record that was created on or prior to December 1, 1995, shows that the applicant was present in the United States at the time, and establishes that the applicant submitted an income tax return, property tax payment, or similar submission or payment to the Federal, State, or local governmental agency keeping such record; or

(vii) In the case of an applicant who, while under the age of 21, attended a private or religious school in the United States on or prior to December 1, 1995, a transcript from such private or religious school, provided that the school:

(A) Is registered with, approved by, or licensed by, appropriate State or local authorities;

(B) Is accredited by the State or regional accrediting body, or by the appropriate private school association; or

(C) Maintains enrollment records in accordance with State or local requirements or standards;

(4) Evidence of continuity of physical presence in the United States since the last date on or prior to December 1, 1995, on which the applicant established commencement of physical presence in the United States. Such documentation may have been issued by

any governmental or nongovernmental authority, provided such evidence bears the name of the applicant, was dated at the time it was issued, and bears the signature, seal, or other authenticating instrument of the issuing authority or its authorized representative, if the document would normally contain such authenticating instrument. Such documentation may include, but is not limited to:

(i) School records;

(ii) Rental receipts;

(iii) Utility bill receipts;

(iv) Any other dated receipts;

(v) Personal checks written by the applicant bearing a dated bank cancellation stamp;

(vi) Employment records, including pay stubs;

(vii) Credit card statements showing the dates of purchase, payment, or other transaction;

(viii) Certified copies of records maintained by organizations chartered by the government, such as public utilities, accredited private and parochial schools, and banks;

(ix) If the applicant establishes that a family unit was in existence and cohabiting in the United States, documents evidencing the physical presence in the United States of another member of that same family unit; and

(x) If the applicant has had correspondence or other interaction with the Service, a list of the types and dates of such correspondence or other contact that the applicant knows to be contained or reflected in Service records;

(5) A copy of the applicant's birth certificate;

(6) If the applicant is between 14 and 79 years of age, a completed Biographic Information Sheet (Form G–325A);

(7) A report of medical examination, as specified in § 1245.5;

(8) Two photographs, as described in the instructions to Form I–485;

(9) If the applicant is 14 years of age or older, a police clearance from each municipality where the alien has resided for 6 months or longer since arriving in the United States. If there are multiple local law enforcement agencies (e.g., city police and county sheriff) with jurisdiction over the alien's residence, the applicant may obtain a clearance from either agency. If the applicant resides or resided in a State where the State Police maintain a compilation of all local arrests and convictions, a statewide clearance is sufficient. If the applicant presents a letter from the local police agencies involved, or other evidence, to the effect that the applicant attempted to obtain such clearance but was unable to do so because of local or State policy, the director or immigration judge having jurisdiction over the application may waive the local police clearance. Furthermore, if such local police agency has provided the Service or the Immigration Court with a blanket statement that issuance of such police clearance is against local or state policy, the director or immigration judge having jurisdiction over the case may waive the local police clearance requirement regardless of whether the applicant individually submits a letter from that local police agency;

(10) If the applicant is applying as the spouse of another Public Law 105–100 beneficiary, a copy of their certificate of marriage and copies of documents showing the legal termination of all other marriages by the applicant or the other beneficiary;

(11) If the applicant is applying as the child, unmarried son, or unmarried daughter of another (principal) beneficiary under section 202 of Public Law 105–100 who is not the applicant's biological mother, copies of evidence (such as the applicant's parent's marriage certificate and documents showing the legal termination of all other marriages, an adoption decree, or other relevant evidence) to demonstrate the relationship between the applicant and the other beneficiary;

(12) A copy of the Form I–94, Arrival-Departure Record, issued at the time of the applicant's arrival in the United States, if the alien was inspected and admitted or paroled; and

(13) If the applicant has departed from and returned to the United States since December 1, 1995, an attachment on a plain piece of paper showing:

(i) The date of the applicant's last arrival in the United States before or on December 1, 1995;

(ii) The date of each departure from the United States since that arrival;

(iii) The reason for each departure; and

(iv) The date, manner, and place of each return to the United States.

(f) *Secondary evidence.* If the primary evidence required in paragraph (e)(4), (e)(9) or (e)(10 of this section is unavailable, church or school records, or other secondary evidence pertinent to the facts in issue, may be submitted. If such documents are unavailable, affidavits may be submitted. The applicant may submit as many types of secondary evidence as necessary to establish the birth, marriage, or other event. Documentary evidence establishing that primary evidence is unavailable must accompany secondary evidence of birth or marriage in the home country. In adjudicating the application for adjustment of status under section 202 of Public Law 105–100, the Service or immigration judge shall determine the weight to be given such secondary evidence. Secondary evidence may not be submitted in lieu of the documentation specified in paragraphs (e)(2) and (e)(3) of this section. However, subject to verification by the Service, if the documentation specified in paragraphs (e)(2) and (e)(3) is already contained in the Service's file relating to the applicant, the applicant may submit an affidavit to that effect in lieu of the actual documentation.

(g) *Filing.* The application period begins on June 22, 1998. To benefit from the provisions of section 202 of Public Law 105–100, an alien must properly file an application for adjustment of status before April 1, 2000. Except as provided in paragraph (d) of this section, all applications for the benefits of section 202 of Pub. L. 105–100 must be submitted by mail to: USINS Texas Service Center, P.O. Box 851804, Mesquite, TX 75185-1804. All applications must be accompanied by either the correct fee as specified in §103.7(b)(1) of 8 CFR chapter I; or a request for a fee waiver in accordance with §103.7(c) of 8 CFR chapter I. An application received by the Service or Immigration Court before April 1, 2000, that has been properly signed and executed and for which a waiver of the filing fee has been requested shall be regarded as having been filed before the statutory deadline regardless of whether the fee waiver request is denied provided that the applicant submits the required fee within 30 days of the date of any notice that the fee waiver request has been denied. In a case over which the Board has jurisdiction, an application received by the Board before April 1, 2000, that has been properly signed and executed shall be considered filed before the statutory deadline without payment of the fee or submission of a fee waiver request. Upon demand by the Board, the payment of the fee or a request for a fee waiver shall be made upon submission of the application to the Immigration Court in accordance with 8 CFR 1240.11(f). If a request for a fee waiver is denied, the application shall be considered as having been properly filed with the Immigration Court before the statutory deadline provided that the applicant submits the required fee within 30 days of the date of any notice that the fee waiver request has been denied. After proper filing of the application, the Service will notify the applicant to appear for fingerprinting as prescribed in §103.2(e) of 8 CFR chapter I.

(h) *Jurisdiction.* Except as provide din paragraphs (d) and (i) of this section, the director of the Texas Service Center shall have jurisdiction over all applications for adjustment of status under section 202 of Public Law 105–100.

(i) *Interview.* (1) Except as provided in paragraphs (d), (i)(2), and (i)(3) of this section, all applicants for adjustment of status under section 202 of Pub. L. 105–100 must be personally interviewed by an immigration officer at a local office of the Service. In any case in which the director of the Texas Service Center determines that an interview of the applicant is necessary, that director shall forward the case to the appropriate local Service office for interview and adjudication.

(2) In the case of an applicant who has submitted evidence of commencement of physical presence in the United States consisting of one or more of the documents specified in section 202(b)(2)(A)(i) through (v) or section 202(b)(2)(A)(vii) of Pub. L. 105–100 and upon examination of the application, including all other evidence submitted in support of the application, all relevant Service records and all

other relevant law enforcement indices, if the director of the Texas Service Center determines that the alien is clearly eligible for adjustment of status under Pub. L. 105–100 and that an interview of the applicant is not necessary, the director may approve the application.

(3) Upon examination of the application, all supporting documentation, all relevant Service records, and all other relevant law enforcement indices, if the director of the Texas Service Center determines that the alien is clearly ineligible for adjustment of status under Pub. L. 105–100 and that an interview of the applicant is not necessary, the director may deny the application.

(j) *Authorization to be employed in the United States while the application is pending*—(1) *Application.* An applicant for adjustment of status under section 202 of Pub. L. 105–100 who wishes to obtain initial or continued employment authorization during the pendency of the adjustment application must file an Application for Employment authorization (Form I–765), with fee as set forth in §103.7(b)(1) of 8 CFR chapter I. The applicant may submit Form I–765 concurrently with, or subsequent to, the filing of the Form I–485.

(2) *Adjudication and issuance.* In general, employment authorization may not be issued to an applicant for adjustment of status under section 202 of Pub. L. 105–100 until the adjustment application has been pending for 180 days. However, if Service records contain one or more of the documents specified in section 202(b)(2)(A)(i) through (v) and (vii) of Pub. L. 105–100, evidence of the applicant's Nicaraguan or Cuban nationality, and no indication that the applicant is clearly ineligible for adjustment of status under section 202 of Pub. L. 105–100, the application for employment authorization may be approved, and the resulting document issued immediately upon verification that the Service record contains such information. If the Service fails to adjudicate the application for employment authorization upon expiration of the 180-day waiting period or within 90 days of the filing of application for employment authorization, whichever comes later, the alien shall be eligible for interim employment authorization in accordance with §1274a.13(d) of this chapter. Nothing in this section shall preclude an applicant for adjustment of status under Pub. L. 105–100 from being granted an initial employment authorization or an extension of employment authorization under any other provision of law or regulation for which the alien may be eligible.

(k) *Parole authorization for purposes of travel*—(1) *Travel from and return to the United States while the application for adjustment of status is pending.* If an applicant for benefits under section 202 of Pub. L. 105–100 desires to travel outside, and return to, the United States while the application for adjustment of status is pending, he or she must file a request for advance parole authorization on an Application for Travel Document (Form I–131), with fee as set forth in §103.7(b)(1) of 8 CFR chapter I and in accordance with the instructions on the form. If the alien is either in deportation or removal proceedings, or subject to a final order of deportation or removal, the Form I–131 must be submitted to the Assistant Commissioner for International Affairs; otherwise the Form I–131 must be submitted to the director of the Texas Service Center, who shall have jurisdiction over such applications. Unless the applicant files an advance parole request prior to departing from the United States, and the Service approves such request, his or her application for adjustment of status under section 202 of Public Law 105–100 is deemed to be abandoned as of the moment of his or her departure. Parole may only be authorized pursuant to the authority contained in, and the standards prescribed in, section 212(d)(5) of the Act.

(2) *Parole authorization for the purpose of filing an application for adjustment of status under section 202 of Pub. L. 105–100.* An otherwise eligible applicant who is outside the United States and wishes to come to the United States in order to apply for benefits under section 202 of Pub. L. 105–100 may request parole authorization for such purpose by filing an Application for Travel Document (Form I–131) with the Texas Service Center, at P.O. Box 851804, Mesquite, TX 75185–1804. Such application must be supported by a photocopy of the Form I–485 that the alien will file

once he or she has been paroled into the United States. The applicant must include photocopies of all the supporting documentation listed in paragraph (e) of this section, except the filing fee, the medical report, the fingerprint card, and the local police clearances. If the director of the Texas Service Center is satisfied that the alien will be eligible for adjustment of status once the alien has been paroled into the United States and files the application, he or she may issue an Authorization for Parole of an Alien into the United States (Form I–512) to allow the alien to travel to, and be paroled into, the United States for a period of 60 days. The applicant shall have 60 days from the date of parole to file the application for adjustment of status. If the alien files the application for adjustment of status within that 60-day period, the Service may re-parole the alien for such time as is necessary for adjudication of the application. Failure to file such application for adjustment of status within 60 days shall result in the alien being returned to the custody of the Service and being examined as an arriving alien applying for admission. Such examination will be conducted in accordance with the provisions of section 235(b)(1) of the Act if the alien is inadmissible under section 212(a)(6)(C) or 212(a)(7) of the Act, or section 240 of the Act if the alien is inadmissible under any other grounds. Parole may only be authorized pursuant to the authority contained in, and the standards prescribed in, section 212(d)(5) of the Act.

(3) *Effect of departure on an outstanding warrant of exclusion, deportation, or removal.* If an alien who is the subject of an outstanding final order of exclusion, deportation, or removal departs from the United States, with or without an advance parole authorization, such final order shall be executed by the alien's departure. The execution of such final order shall not preclude the applicant from filing an Application for Permission to Reapply for Admission Into the United States After Deportation or Removal (Form I–212) in accordance with § 1212.2 of this chapter.

(l) *Approval.* If the director approves the application for adjustment of status under the provisions of section 202 of Pub. L. 105–100, the director shall record the alien's lawful admission for permanent resident as of the date of such approval and notify the applicant accordingly. The director shall also advise the alien regarding the delivery of his or her Permanent Resident Card and of the process for obtaining temporary evidence of alien registration. If the alien had previously been issued a final order of exclusion, deportation, or removal, such order shall be deemed canceled as of the date of the director's approval of the application for adjustment of status. If the alien had been in exclusion, deportation, or removal proceedings that were administratively closed, such proceedings shall be deemed terminated as of the date of approval of the application for adjustment of status by the director. If an immigration judge grants or if the Board, upon appeal, grants an application for adjustment under the provisions of section 202 of Pub. L. 105–100, the alien's lawful admission for permanent residence shall be as of the date of such grant.

(m) *Denial and review of decision.* (1) If the director denies the application for adjustment of status under the provisions of section 202 of Public Law 105–100, the director shall notify the applicant of the decision. The director shall also:

(i) In the case of an alien who is not maintaining valid nonimmigrant status and who had not previously been placed in exclusion, deportation or removal proceedings, initiate removal proceedings in accordance with § 1239.1 of this chapter during which the alien may renew his or her application for adjustment of status under section 202 of Public Law 105–100; or

(ii) In the case of an alien whose previously initiated exclusion, deportation, or removal proceedings had been administratively closed or continued indefinitely under paragraph (d)(3) of this section, advise the Immigration Court that had administratively closed the proceedings, or the Board, as appropriate, of the denial of the application. Upon a motion to recalendar filed by the Service, the Immigration Court or the Board will then recalendar or reinstate the prior exclusion, deportation or removal proceedings, during which the alien may renew his or her application for adjustment under section 202 of Public Law 105–100; or

(iii) In the case of an alien who is the subject of an outstanding final order of exclusion, deportation, or removal, refer the decision to deny the application by filing a Form I–290C, Notice of Certification, with the Immigration Court that issued the final order for consideration in accordance with paragraph (n) of this section.

(2) Aliens who were denied adjustment of status by the director, but who are now eligible for such adjustment of status pursuant to section 1505(a)(1) of the LIFE Act and amendments, and have not been referred to immigration proceedings as specified in paragraph (m)(1) of this section may file a motion to reopen with the Service. If an alien has been referred to the Immigration Court or has filed an appeal with the Board after an Immigration Court has denied the application for adjustment under NACARA section 202, and proceedings are pending, then the application for adjustment of status will be adjudicated in accordance with section 1505(a) of the LIFE Act and its amendments. An alien present in the United States subject to a final order of removal after his or her application was denied by an Immigration Court or the Board, but who was made eligible for adjustment pursuant to section 1505(a) of the LIFE Act and its amendments may file a motion to reopen with the Immigration Court or the Board, whichever had jurisdiction last. Pursuant to section 1505(a)(2) of the LIFE Act and its amendments, motions to reopen proceedings before the Immigration Court or the Board must be filed on or before June 19, 2001.

(n) *Action of immigration judge upon referral of decision by a Notice of Certification (Form I–290C)*—(1) *General.* Upon the referral by a Notice of Certification (Form I–290C) of a decision to deny the application, in accordance with paragraph (m)(3) of this section, and under the authority contained in § 1003.10 of this chapter, the immigration judge shall conduct a hearing to determine whether the alien is eligible for adjustment of status under section 202 of Public Law 105–100. Such hearing shall be conducted under the same rules of procedure as proceedings conducted under part 1240 of this chapter, except the scope of review shall be limited to a determination on the alien's eligibility for adjustment of status under section 202 of Public Law 105–100. During such proceedings all parties are prohibited from raising or considering any other issues, including but not limited to issues of admissibility, deportability, removability, and eligibility for any form of relief other than adjustment of status under section 202 of Public Law 105–100. Should the alien fail to appear for such hearing, the immigration judge shall deny the application for adjustment under section 202 of Public Law 105–100.

(2) *Appeal of immigration judge decision.* Once the immigration judge issues his or her decision on the application, either the alien or the Service may appeal the decision to the Board. Such appeal must be filed pursuant to the requirements for appeals to the Board from an immigration judge decision set forth in §§ 1003.3 and 1003.8 of this chapter.

(3) *Rescission of the decision of an immigration judge.* The decision of an immigration judge under paragraph (n)(1) of this section denying an application for adjustment under section 202 of Public Law 105–100 for failure to appear may be rescinded only:

(i) Upon a motion to reopen filed within 180 days after the date of the denial if the alien demonstrates that the failure to appear was because of exceptional circumstances as defined in section 240(e)(1) of the Act;

(ii) Upon a motion to reopen filed at any time if the alien demonstrates that the alien did not receive notice of the hearing in person (or, if personal service was not practicable, through service by mail to the alien or to the alien's counsel of record, if any) or the alien demonstrates that the alien was in Federal or State custody and the failure to appear was through no fault of the alien; or

(iii) Upon a motion to reopen filed not later than June 19, 2001, by an alien present in the United States who became eligible for adjustment of status under section 202 of Public Law 105–100, as amended by section 1505, Public Law 106–554.

(o) *Transition period provisions for tolling the physical presence in the United States provision for certain individuals*—(1) *Departure without advance authorization for parole.* In the case of an otherwise eligible applicant who departed the United States on or before December 31, 1997, the physical presence in the United States provision of section 202(b)(1) of Pub. L. 105–100 is tolled as of November 19, 1997, and until July 20, 1998.

(2) *Departure with advance authorization for parole.* In the case of an alien who departed the United States after having been issued an Authorization for parole of an Alien into the United States (Form I–512), and who returns to the United States in accordance with the conditions of that document, the physical presence in the United States requirement of section 202(b)(1) of Pub. L. 105–100 is tolled while the alien is outside the United States pursuant to the issuance of the Form I–512.

(3) *Request for parole authorization from outside the United States.* In the case of an alien who is outside the United States and submits an application for parole authorization in accordance with paragraph (k)(2) of this section, and such application for parole authorization is granted by the Service, the physical presence in the United States provisions of section 202(b)(1) of Pub. L. 105–100 is tilled from the date the application is received at the Texas Service Center until the alien is paroled into the United States pursuant to the issuance of the Form I–512.

(Approved by the Office of Management and Budget under Control Number 1115–0221)

[63 FR 27829, May 21, 1998, as amended at 65 FR 15854, Mar. 24, 2000; 66 FR 29451, May 31, 2001]

§ 1245.14 Adjustment of status of certain health care workers.

An alien applying for adjustment of status to perform labor in a health care occupation as described in 8 CFR 1212.15(c) must present evidence at the time he or she applies for adjustment of status, and, if applicable, at the time of the interview on the application, that he or she has a valid certificate issued by the Commission on Graduates of Foreign Nursing Schools or the National Board of Certification in Occupational Therapy.

[63 FR 55012, Oct. 14, 1998]

§ 1245.15 Adjustment of status of certain Haitian nationals under the Haitian Refugee Immigrant Fairness Act of 1998 (HRIFA).

(a) *Definitions.* As used in this section, the terms:

Abandoned and *abandonment* mean that both parents have, or the sole or surviving parent has, or in the case of a child who has been placed into a guardianship, the child's guardian or guardians have, willfully forsaken all parental or guardianship rights, obligations, and claims to the child, as well as all control over and possession of the child, without intending to transfer these rights to any specific person(s).

Guardian means a person lawfully invested (by order of a competent Federal, State, or local authority) with the power, and charged with the duty, of taking care of, including managing the property, rights, and affairs of, a child.

Orphan and *orphaned* refer to the involuntary detachment or severance of a child from his or her parents due to any of the following:

(1) The death or disappearance of, desertion by, or separation or loss from both parents, as those terms are defined in § 204.3(b) of 8 CFR chapter I;

(2) The irrevocable and written release of all parental rights by the sole parent, as that term is defined in § 204.3(b) of 8 CFR chapter I, based upon the inability of that parent to provide proper care (within the meaning of that phrase in § 204.3(b) of 8 CFR chapter I) for the child, provided that at the time of such irrevocable release such parent is legally obligated to provide such care; or

(3) The death or disappearance, as that term is defined in § 204.3(b) of 8 CFR chapter I, of one parent and the irrevocable and written release of all parental rights by the sole remaining parent based upon the inability of that parent to provide proper care (within the meaning of that phrase in § 204.3(b) of 8 CFR chapter I) for the child, provided that at the time of such irrevocable release such parent is legally obligated to provide such care.

Parent, father, or *mother* means a parent, father, or mother only where the relationship exists by reason of any of the circumstances set forth in paragraphs (A) through (E) of section 101(b)(1) of the Act.

Sole remaining parent means a person who is the child's only parent because:

(1) The child's other parent has died; or

(2) The child's other parent has been certified by competent Haitian authorities to be presumed dead as a result of his or her disappearance, within the meaning of that term as set forth in § 204.3(b) of 8 CFR chapter I.

(b) *Applicability of provisions of section 902 of HRIFA in general.* Section 902 of Division A of Pub. L. 105–277, the Haitian Refugee Immigrant Fairness Act of 1998 (HRIFA), provides special rules for adjustment of status for certain nationals of Haiti, and without regard to section 241(a)(5) of the Act, if they meet the other requirements of HRIFA.

(1) *Principal applicants.* Section 902(b)(1) of HRIFA defines five categories of principal applicants who may apply for adjustment of status, if the alien was physically present in the United States on December 31, 1995:

(i) An alien who filed for asylum before December 31, 1995;

(ii) An alien who was paroled into the United States prior to December 31, 1995, after having been identified as having a credible fear of persecution, or paroled for emergent reasons or reasons deemed strictly in the public interest; or

(iii) An alien who at the time of arrival in the United States and on December 31, 1995, was unmarried and under 21 years of age and who:

(A) Arrived in the United States without parents in the United States and has remained, without parents, in the United States since his or her arrival;

(B) Became orphaned subsequent to arrival in the United States; or

(C) Was abandoned by parents or guardians prior to April 1, 1998, and has remained abandoned since such abandonment.

(2) *Dependents.* Section 902(d) of HRIFA provides for certain Haitian nationals to apply for adjustment of status as the spouse, child, or unmarried son or daughter of a principal HRIFA beneficiary, even if the individual would not otherwise be eligible for adjustment under section 902. The eligibility requirements for dependents are described further in paragraph (d) of this section.

(c) *Eligibility of principal HRIFA applicants.* A Haitian national who is described in paragraph (b)(1) of this section is eligible to apply for adjustment of status under the provisions of section 902 of HRIFA if the alien meets the following requirements:

(1) *Physical presence.* The alien is physically present in the United States at the time the application is filed;

(2) *Proper application.* The alien properly files an application for adjustment of status in accordance with this section, including the evidence described in paragraphs (h), (i), (j), and (k) of this section. For purposes of § 1245.15 of this chapter only, an Application to Register Permanent Residence or Adjust Status (Form I–485) submitted by a principal applicant for benefits under HRIFA may be considered to have been properly filed if it:

(i) Is received not later than March 31, 2000, at the Nebraska Service Center, the Board, or the Immigration Court having jurisdiction;

(ii) Has been properly completed and signed by the applicant;

(iii) Identifies the provision of HRIFA under which the applicant is seeking adjustment of status; and

(iv) Is accompanied by either:

(A) The correct fee as specified in § 103.7(b)(1) of this chapter; or

(B) A request for a fee waiver in accordance with § 103.7(c) of 8 CFR chapter I, provided such fee waiver request is subsequently granted; however, if such a fee waiver request is subsequently denied and the applicant submits the require fee within 30 days of the date of any notice that the fee waiver request had been denied, the application shall be regarded as having been filed before the statutory deadline. In addition, in a case over which the Board has jurisdiction, an application received by the Board before April 1, 2000, that has been properly signed and executed shall be considered filed before the statutory deadline without payment of the fee or submission of a fee waiver request. Upon remand by the Board, the payment of the fee or a request for a fee waiver shall be made upon submission of the application to the Immigration Court in accordance with 8 CFR 1240.11(f). If a request for a fee waiver is denied, the application shall be considered as having been properly filed with the Immigration Court before the statutory deadline provided that the applicant submits the required fee within 30 days of the date of any notice that the fee waiver request has been denied.

(3) *Admissibility.* The alien is not inadmissible to the United States for permanent residence under any provisions of section 212(a) of the Act, except as provided in paragraph (e) of this section; and

(4) *Continuous physical presence.* The alien has been physically present in the United States for a continuous period beginning on December 31, 1995, and ending on the date the application for adjustment is granted, except for the following periods of time:

(i) Any period or periods of absence from the United States not exceeding 180 days in the aggregate; and

(ii) Any periods of absence for which the applicant received an Advance Authorization for Parole (Form I–512) prior to his or her departure from the United States, provided the applicant returned to the United States in accordance with the conditions of such Advance Authorization for Parole.

(iii) Any periods of absence from the United States occurring after October 21, 1998, and before July 12, 1999, provided the applicant departed the United States prior to December 31, 1998.

(d) *Eligibility of dependents of a principal HRIFA beneficiary.* A Haitian national who is the spouse, child, or unmarried son or daughter of a principal beneficiary eligible for adjustment of status under the provisions of HRIFA is eligible to apply for benefits as a dependent, if the dependent alien meets the following requirements:

(1) *Physical presence.* The alien is physically present in the United States at the time the application is filed;

(2) *Proper application.* The alien properly files an application for adjustment of status as a dependent in accordance with this section, including the evidence described in paragraphs (h) and (l) of this section;

(3) *Admissibility.* The alien is not inadmissible to the United States for permanent residence under any provisions of section 212(a) of the Act, except as provided in paragraph (e) of this section;

(4) *Relationship.* The qualifying relationship to the principal alien must have existed at the time the principal was granted adjustment of status and must continue to exist at the time the dependent alien is granted adjustment of status. To establish the qualifying relationship to the principal alien, evidence must be submitted in accordance with §204.2 of this chapter. Such evidence should consist of the documents specified in §204.2(a)(1)(i)(B), (a)(1)(iii)(B), (a)(2), (d)(2), and (d)(5) of 8 CFR chapter I;

(5) *Continuous physical presence.* If the alien is applying as the unmarried son or unmarried daughter of a principal HRIFA beneficiary, he or she must have been physically present in the United States for a continuous period beginning not later than December 31, 1995, and ending on the date the application for adjustment is granted, as provided in paragraphs (c)(4) and (j) of this section.

(e) *Applicability of grounds of inadmissibility contained in section 212(a)*—(1) *Certain grounds of inadmissibility inapplicable to HRIFA applicants.* Paragraphs (4), (5), (6)(A), (7)(A) and (9)(B) of section 212(a) of the Act are inapplicable to HRIFA principal applicants and their dependents. Accordingly, an applicant for adjustment of status under section 902 of HRIFA need not establish admissibility under those provisions in order to be able to adjust his or her status to that of permanent resident.

(2) *Availability of individual waivers.* If a HRIFA applicant is inadmissible under any of the other provisions of section 212(a) of the Act for which an immigrant waiver is available, the applicant may apply for one or more of the immigrant waivers of inadmissibility under section 212 of the Act, in accordance with §1212.7 of this chapter. In considering an application for waiver under section 212(g) of the Act by an

otherwise statutorily eligible applicant for adjustment of status under HRIFA who was paroled into the United States from the U.S. Naval Base at Guantanamo Bay, for the purpose of receiving treatment of an HIV or AIDS condition, the fact that his or her arrival in the United States was the direct result of a government decision to provide such treatment should be viewed as a significant positive factor when weighing discretionary factors. In considering an application for waiver under section 212(i) of the Act by an otherwise statutorily eligible applicant for adjustment of status under HRIFA who used counterfeit documents to travel from Haiti to the United States, the adjudicator shall, when weighing discretionary factors, take into consideration the general lawlessness and corruption which was widespread in Haiti at the time of the alien's departure, the difficulties in obtaining legitimate departure documents at that time, and other factors unique to Haiti at that time which may have induced the alien to commit fraud or make willful misrepresentations.

(3) *Special rule for waiver of inadmissibility grounds for HRIFA applicants under section 212(a)(9)(A) and 212(a)(9)(C) of the Act.* An applicant for adjustment of status under HRIFA who is inadmissible under section 212(a)(9)(A) or 212(a)(9)(C) of the Act, may apply for a waiver of these grounds of inadmissibility while present in the United States. Such an alien must file Form I–601, Application for Waiver of Grounds of Excludability. If the application for adjustment is pending at the Nebraska Service Center, Form I–601 must be filed with the director of that office. If the application for adjustment is pending at a district office, Form I–601 must be filed with the district director having jurisdiction over the application. If the application for adjustment is pending before the immigration court, Form I–601 must be filed with the immigration judge having jurisdiction, or with the Board of Immigration Appeals if the appeal is pending before the Board.

(f) *Time for filing of applications*—(1) *Applications for HRIFA benefits by a principal HRIFA applicant.* The application period begins on June 11, 1999. To benefit from the provisions of section 902 of HRIFA, an alien who is applying for adjustment as a principal applicant must properly file an application for adjustment of status before April 1, 2000.

(2) *Applications by dependent aliens.* The spouse, minor child, or unmarried son or daughter of an alien who is eligible for adjustment of status as a principal beneficiary under HRIFA may file an application for adjustment of status under this section concurrently with or subsequent to the filing of the application of the principal HRIFA beneficiary. An application filed by a dependent may not be approved prior to approval of the principal's application.

(g) *Jurisdiction for filing of applications*—(1) *Filing of applications with the Service.* The Service has jurisdiction over all applications for the benefits of section 902 of HRIFA as a principal applicant or as a dependent under this section, except for applications filed by aliens who are in pending immigration proceedings as provided in paragraph (g)(2) of this section. All applications filed with the Service for the benefits of section 902 of HRIFA must be submitted by mail to: USINS Nebraska Service Center, PO Box 87245, Lincoln, NE 68501–7245. After proper filing of the application, the Service will instruct the applicant to appear for fingerprinting as prescribed in § 103.2(e) of this chapter. The Director of the Nebraska Service Center shall have jurisdiction over all applications filed with the Service for adjustment of status under section 902 of HRIFA, unless the Director refers the applicant for a personal interview at a local Service office as provided in paragraph (o)(1) of this section.

(2) *Filing of applications by aliens in pending exclusion, deportation, or removal proceedings.* An alien who is in exclusion, deportation, or removal proceedings pending before the Immigration Court or the Board, or who has a pending motion to reopen or motion to reconsider filed with the Immigration Court or the Board on or before May 12, 1999, must apply for HRIFA benefits to the Immigration Court or the Board, as provided in paragraph (p)(1) of this section, rather than to the Service. However, an alien whose proceeding has

been administratively closed (see paragraph (p)(4) of this section) may only apply for HRIFA benefits with the Service as provided in paragraph (g)(1) of this section.

(3)(i) *Filing of applications with the Service by aliens who are subject to a final order of exclusion, deportation, or removal.* An alien who is subject to a final order of exclusion, deportation, or removal, and who has not been denied adjustment of status under section 902 of HRIFA by the Immigration Court or the Board, may only apply for HRIFA benefits with the Service as provided in paragraph (g)(1) of this section. This includes applications for HRIFA benefits filed by aliens who have filed a motion to reopen or motion to reconsider a final order after May 12, 1999.

(ii) An alien present in the United States who is subject to a final order of exclusion, deportation, or removal and has been denied adjustment of status under section 902 of HRIFA by the Immigration Court or the Board, or who never applied for adjustment of status with the Service, an Immigration Court, or the Board on or before March 31, 2000, and who was made eligible for HRIFA benefits under the Legal Immigration Family Equity Act of 2000 (LIFE Act) and LIFE amendments, Public Law 106–553 and Public Law 106–554, respectively, may file a motion to reopen with either the Immigration Court or the Board, whichever had jurisdiction last. As provided by the LIFE Act, motions to reopen must be filed on or before June 19, 2001.

(iii) *Stay of final order of exclusion, deportation, or removal.* The filing of an application for adjustment under section 902 of HRIFA with the Service shall not stay the execution of such final order unless the applicant has requested and been granted a stay in connection with the HRIFA application. An alien who has filed a HRIFA application with the Service may file an Application for Stay of Removal (Form I–246) in accordance with section 241(c)(2) of the Act and §1241.6 of this chapter.

(iv) *Grant of stay.* Absent evidence of the applicant's statutory ineligibility for adjustment of status under section 902 of HRIFA or significant negative discretionary factors, a Form I–246 filed by a bona fide applicant for adjustment under section 902 of HRIFA shall be approved and the removal of the applicant shall be stayed until such time as the Service has adjudicated the application for adjustment in accordance with this section.

(h) *Application and supporting documents.* Each applicant for adjustment of status must file an Application to Register Permanent Residence or Adjust Status (Form I–485). An applicant should complete Part 2 of Form I–485 by checking box "h—other" and writing "HRIFA—Principal" or "HRIFA—Dependent" next to that block. Each application must be accompanied by:

(1) *Application fee.* The fee for Form I–485 prescribed in §103.7(b)(1) of 8 CFR chapter I;

(2) *Fingerprinting fee.* If the applicant is 14 years of age or older, the fee for fingerprinting prescribed in §103.7(b)(1) of 8 CFR chapter I;

(3) *Identifying information.* (i) A copy of the applicant's birth certificate or other record of birth as provided in paragraph (m) of this section;

(ii) A completed Biographic Information Sheet (Form G–325A), if the applicant is between 14 and 79 years of age;

(iii) A report of medical examination, as specified in §1245.5 of this chapter; and

(iv) Two photographs, as described in the instructions to Form I–485;

(4) *Arrival-Departure Record.* A copy of the Form I–94, Arrival-Departure Record, issued at the time of the applicant's arrival in the United States, if the alien was inspected and admitted or paroled;

(5) *Police clearances.* If the applicant is 14 years old or older, a police clearance from each municipality where the alien has resided for 6 months or longer since arriving in the United States. If there are multiple local law enforcement agencies (e.g., city police and county sheriff) with jurisdiction over the alien's residence, the applicant may obtain a clearance from either agency. If the applicant resides or resided in a State where the State police maintain a compilation of all local arrests and convictions, a statewide clearance is sufficient. If the applicant presents a letter from the local police agencies involved, or other evidence, to the effect that the applicant attempted

to obtain such clearance but was unable to do so because of local or State policy, the director or immigration judge having jurisdiction over the application may waive the local police clearance. Furthermore, if such local police agency has provided the Service or the Immigration Court with a blanket statement that issuance of such police clearance is against local or State policy, the director or immigration judge having jurisdiction over the case may waive the local police clearance requirement regardless of whether the applicant individually submits a letter from that local police agency;

(6) *Proof of Haitian nationality.* If the applicant acquired Haitian nationality other than through birth in Haiti, a copy of the certificate of naturalization or certificate of citizenship issued by the Haitian government; and

(7) *Additional supporting evidence.* Additional supporting evidence pertaining to the applicant as provided in paragraphs (i) through (l) of this section.

(i) *Evidence of presence in the United States on December 31, 1995.* An alien seeking HRIFA benefits as a principal applicant must provide with the application evidence establishing the alien's presence in the United States on December 31, 1995. Such evidence may consist of the evidence listed in §1245.22.

(j) *Evidence of continuity of presence in the United States since December 31, 1995.* An alien seeking HRIFA benefits as a principal applicant, or as the unmarried son or daughter of a principal applicant, must provide with the application evidence establishing continuity of the alien's physical presence in the United States since December 31, 1995. (This requirement does not apply to a dependent seeking HRIFA benefits as the spouse or minor child of a principal applicant.)

(1) *Evidence establishing presence.* Evidence establishing the continuity of the alien's physical presence in the United States since December 31, 1995, may consist of any documentation issued by any governmental or non-governmental authority, provided such evidence bears the name of the applicant, was dated at the time it was issued, and bears the signature, seal, or other authenticating instrument of the authorized representative of the issuing authority, if the document would normally contain such authenticating instrument.

(2) *Examples.* Documentation establishing continuity of physical presence may include, but is not limited to:

(i) School records;

(ii) Rental receipts;

(iii) Utility bill receipts;

(iv) Any other dated receipts;

(v) Personal checks written by the applicant bearing a dated bank cancellation stamp;

(vi) Employment records, including pay stubs;

(vii) Credit card statements showing the dates of purchase, payment, or other transaction;

(viii) Certified copies of records maintained by organizations chartered by the Federal or State government, such as public utilities, accredited private and religious schools, and banks;

(ix) If the applicant establishes that a family unit was in existence and cohabiting in the United States, documents evidencing presence of another member of that same family unit; and

(x) For applicants who have had ongoing correspondence or other interaction with the Service, a list of the types and dates of such correspondence or other contact that the applicant knows to be contained or reflected in Service records.

(3) *Evidence relating to absences from the United States since December 31, 1995.* If the alien is applying as a principal applicant, or as the unmarried son or daughter of a principal applicant, and has departed from and returned to the United States since December 31, 1995, the alien must provide with the application an attachment on a plain piece of paper showing:

(i) The date of the applicant's last arrival in the United States before December 31, 1995;

(ii) The date of each departure (if any) from the United States since that arrival;

(iii) The reason for each departure; and

(iv) The date, manner, and place of each return to the United States.

(k) *Evidence establishing the alien's eligibility under section 902(b) of HRIFA.* An alien seeking HRIFA benefits as a principal applicant must provide with the application evidence establishing that the alien satisfies one of the eligibility standards described in paragraph (b)(1) of this section.

(1) *Applicant for asylum.* If the alien is a principal applicant who filed for asylum before December 31, 1995, the applicant must provide with the application either:

(i) A photocopy of the first page of the Application for Asylum and Withholding of Removal (Form I–589); or

(ii) If the alien is not in possession of a photocopy of the first page of the Form I–589, a statement to that effect giving the date of filing and the location of the Service office or Immigration Court at which it was filed;

(2) *Parolee.* If the alien is a principal applicant who was paroled into the United States prior to December 31, 1995, after having been identified as having a credible fear of persecution, or paroled for emergent reasons or reasons deemed strictly in the public interest, the applicant must provide with the application either:

(i) A photocopy of the Arrival-Departure Record (Form I–94) issued when he or she was granted parole; or

(ii) If the alien is not in possession of the original Form I–94, a statement to that effect giving the date of parole and the location of the Service port-of-entry at which parole was authorized.

(3) *Child without parents.* If the alien is a principal applicant who arrived in the United States as a child without parents in the United States, the applicant must provide with the application:

(i) Evidence, showing the date, location, and manner of his or her arrival in the United States, such as:

(A) A photocopy of the Form I–94 issued at the time of the alien's arrival in the United States;

(B) A copy of the airline or vessel records showing transportation to the United States;

(C) Other similar documentation; or

(D) If none of the documents in paragraphs (k)(3)(i)(A)–(C) of this section are available, a statement from the applicant, accompanied by whatever evidence the applicant is able to submit in support of that statement; and

(ii) Evidence establishing the absence of the child's parents, which may include either:

(A) Evidence showing the deaths of, or disappearance or desertion by, the applicant's parents; or

(B) Evidence showing that the applicant's parents did not live in the United States with the applicant. Such evidence may include, but is not limited to, documentation or affidavits showing that the applicant's parents have been continuously employed outside the United States, are deceased, disappeared, or abandoned the applicant prior to the applicant's arrival, or were otherwise engaged in activities showing that they were not in the United States, or (if they have been in the United States) that the applicant and his or her parents did not reside together.

(4) *Orphaned child.* If the alien is a principal applicant who is or was a child who became orphaned subsequent to arrival in the United States, the applicant must provide with the application:

(i) Evidence, showing the date, location, and manner of his or her arrival in the United States, such as:

(A) A photocopy of the Form I–94 issued at the time of the alien's arrival in the United States;

(B) A copy of the airline or vessel records showing transportation to the United States;

(C) Other similar documentation; or

(D) If none of the documents in paragraphs (k)(4)(i)(A)–(C) of this section are available, a statement from the applicant, accompanied by whatever evidence the applicant is able to submit in support of that statement; and

(ii) Either:

(A) The death certificates of both parents (or in the case of a child having only one parent, the death certificate of the sole parent) showing that the death or deaths occurred after the date of the applicant's arrival in the United States;

(B) Evidence from a State, local, or other court or governmental authority having jurisdiction and authority to make decisions in matters of child welfare establishing the disappearance of, the separation or loss from, or desertion by, both parents (or, in the case of a child born out of wedlock who has not been legitimated, the sole parent); or

(C) Evidence of:

(*1*) Either:

(*i*) The child having only a sole parent, as that term is defined in § 204.3(b) of this chapter;

(*ii*) The death of one parent; or

(*iii*) Certification by competent Haitian authorities that one parent is presumed dead as a result of his or her disappearance, within the meaning of that term as set forth in § 204.3(b) of this chapter; and

(*2*) A copy of a written statement executed by the sole parent, or the sole remaining parent, irrevocably releasing all parental rights based upon the inability of that parent to provide proper care for the child.

(5) *Abandoned child.* If the alien is a principal applicant who was abandoned by parents or guardians prior to April 1, 1998, and has remained abandoned since such abandonment, the applicant must provide with the application:

(i) Evidence, showing the date, location, and manner of his or her arrival in the United States, such as:

(A) A photocopy of the Form I–94 issued at the time of the alien's arrival in the United States;

(B) A copy of the airline or vessel records showing transportation to the United States;

(C) Other similar documentation; or

(D) If none of the documents in paragraphs (k)(5)(i)(A)–(C) of this section are available, a statement from the applicant, accompanied by whatever evidence the applicant is able to submit in support of that statement; and

(ii) Either:

(A) Evidence from a State, local, or other court or governmental authority having jurisdiction and authority to make decisions in matters of child welfare establishing such abandonment; or

(B) Evidence to establish that the applicant would have been considered to be abandoned according to the laws of the State where he or she resides, or where he or she resided at the time of the abandonment, had the issue been presented to the proper authorities.

(l) *Evidence relating to applications by dependents under section 902(d) of HRIFA*—(1) *Evidence of spousal relationship.* If the alien is applying as the spouse of a principal HRIFA beneficiary, the applicant must provide with the application a copy of their certificate of marriage and copies of documents showing the legal termination of all other marriages by the applicant or the other beneficiary.

(2) *Evidence of parent-child relationship.* If the applicant is applying as the child, unmarried son, or unmarried daughter of a principal HRIFA beneficiary, and the principal beneficiary is not the applicant's biological mother, the applicant must provide with the application evidence to demonstrate the parent-child relationship between the principal beneficiary and the applicant. Such evidence may include copies of the applicant's parent's marriage certificate and documents showing the legal termination of all other marriages, an adoption decree, or other relevant evidence.

(m) *Secondary evidence.* Except as otherwise provided in this paragraph, if the primary evidence required in this section is unavailable, church or school records, or other secondary evidence pertinent to the facts in issue, may be submitted. If such documents are unavailable, affidavits may be submitted. The applicant may submit as many types of secondary evidence as necessary to establish birth, marriage, or other relevant events. Documentary evidence establishing that primary evidence is unavailable must accompany secondary evidence of birth or marriage in the home country. The unavailability of such documents may be shown by submission of a copy of the written request for a copy of such documents which was sent to the official keeper of the records. In adjudicating the application for adjustment of status under section 902 of HRIFA, the Service or immigration judge shall determine the weight to be given such secondary evidence. Secondary evidence may not be submitted in lieu of the documentation specified in paragraphs (i) or (j) of this section. However, subject to verification by the Service, if the documentation specified in this paragraph or in paragraphs (h)(3)(i), (i), (j), (l)(1), and (l)(2) of this section is already contained in the Service's file relating to the applicant, the applicant may submit an affidavit to that effect in lieu of the actual documentation.

(n) *Authorization to be employed in the United States while the application is pending*—(1) *Application for employment authorization.* An applicant for adjustment of status under section 902 of HRIFA who wishes to obtain initial or continued employment authorization during the pendency of the adjustment application must file an Application for Employment Authorization (Form I–765) with the Service, including the fee as set forth in § 103.7(b)(1) of 8 CFR chapter I. The applicant may submit Form I–765 either concurrently with or subsequent to the filing of the application for HRIFA benefits on Form I–485.

(2) *Adjudication and issuance.* Employment authorization may not be issued to an applicant for adjustment of status under section 902 of HRIFA until the adjustment application has been pending for 180 days, unless the Director of the Nebraska Service Center verifies that Service records contain evidence that the applicant meets the criteria set forth in section 902(b) or 902(d) of HRIFA, and determines that there is no indication that the applicant is clearly ineligible for adjustment of status under section 902 of HRIFA, in which case the Director may approve the application for employment authorization, and issue the resulting document, immediately upon such verification. If the Service fails to adjudicate the application for employment authorization upon expiration of the 180-day waiting period, or within 90 days of the filing of application for employment authorization, whichever comes later, the alien shall be eligible for interim employment authorization in accordance with § 1274a.13(d) of this chapter. Nothing in this section shall preclude an applicant for adjustment of status under HRIFA from being granted an initial employment authorization or an extension of employment authorization under any other provision of law or regulation for which the alien may be eligible.

(o) *Adjudication of HRIFA applications filed with the Service*—(1) *Referral for interview.* Except as provided in paragraphs (o)(2) and (o)(3) of this section, all aliens filing applications for adjustment of status with the Service under this section must be personally interviewed by an immigration officer at a local office of the Service. If the Director of the Nebraska Service Center determines that an interview of the applicant is necessary, the Director shall forward the case to the appropriate local Service office for interview and adjudication.

(2) *Approval without interview.* Upon examination of the application, including all other evidence submitted in support of the application, all relevant Service records and all other relevant law enforcement indices, the Director may approve the application without an interview if the Director determines that:

(i) The alien's claim to eligibility for adjustment of status under section 902 of HRIFA is verified through existing Service records; and

(ii) The alien is clearly eligible for adjustment of status.

(3) *Denial without interview.* If, upon examination of the application, all supporting documentation, all relevant Service records, and all other relevant law enforcement indices, the Director determines that the alien is clearly ineligible for adjustment of status under HRIFA and that an interview of the applicant is not necessary, the Director may deny the application.

(p) *Adjudication of HRIFA applications filed in pending exclusion, deportation, or removal proceedings*—(1) *Proceedings pending before an Immigration Court.* Except as provided in paragraph (p)(4) of this section, the Immigration Court shall have sole jurisdiction over an application for adjustment of status under this section filed by an alien who is in exclusion, deportation, or removal proceedings pending before an immigration judge or the Board, or who has a pending motion to reopen or motion to reconsider filed with an immigration judge or the Board on or before May 12, 1999. The immigration judge having jurisdiction over the exclusion, deportation, or removal proceedings shall have jurisdiction to accept and adjudicate any application for adjustment of status under section 902 of HRIFA during the course of such proceedings. All applications for adjustment of status under section 902 of

HRIFA filed with an Immigration Court shall be subject to the requirements of §§ 1003.11 and 1003.31 of this chapter.

(2) *Motion to reopen or motion to reconsider.* If an alien who has a pending motion to reopen or motion to reconsider timely filed with an immigration judge on or before May 12, 1999, files an application for adjustment of status under section 902 of HRIFA, the immigration judge shall reopen the alien's proceedings for consideration of the adjustment application, unless the alien is clearly ineligible for adjustment of status under section 902 of HRIFA.

(3) *Proceedings pending before the Board.* Except as provided in paragraph (d)(4) of this section, in the case of an alien who either has a pending appeal with the Board or has a pending motion to reopen or motion to reconsider timely filed with the Board on or before May 12, 1999, the Board shall remand, or reopen and remand, the proceedings to the Immigration Court for the sole purpose of adjudicating an application for adjustment of status under section 902 of HRIFA, unless the alien is clearly ineligible for adjustment of status under section 902 of HRIFA. If the immigration judge denies, or the alien fails to file, the application for adjustment of status under section 902 of HRIFA, the immigration judge shall certify the decision to the Board for consideration in conjunction with the applicant's previously pending appeal or motion.

(4) *Administrative closure of exclusion, deportation, or removal proceedings.* (i) An alien who is in exclusion, deportation, or removal proceedings, or who has a pending motion to reopen or a motion to reconsider such proceedings filed on or before May 12, 1999, may request that the proceedings be administratively closed, or that the motion be indefinitely continued, in order to allow the alien to file such application with the Service as prescribed in paragraph (g) of this section. If the alien appears to be eligible to file an application for adjustment of status under this section, the Immigration Court or the Board (whichever has jurisdiction) shall, with the concurrence of the Service, administratively close the proceedings or continue indefinitely the motion.

(ii) In the case of an otherwise-eligible alien whose exclusion, deportation, or removal proceedings have been administratively closed for reasons not specified in this section, the alien may only apply before the Service for adjustment of status under this section.

(q) *Approval of HRIFA applications*—(1) *Applications approved by the Service.* If the Service approves the application for adjustment of status under the provisions of section 902 of HRIFA, the director shall record the alien's lawful admission for permanent residence as of the date of such approval and notify the applicant accordingly. The director shall also advise the alien regarding the delivery of his or her Permanent Resident Card and of the process for obtaining temporary evidence of alien registration. If the alien had previously been issued a final order of exclusion, deportation, or removal, such order shall be deemed canceled as of the date of the director's approval of the application for adjustment of status. If the alien had been in exclusion, deportation, or removal proceedings that were administratively closed, such proceedings shall be deemed terminated as of the date of approval of the application for adjustment of status by the director.

(2) *Applications approved by an immigration judge or the Board.* If an immigration judge or (upon appeal) the Board grants an application for adjustment under the provisions of section 902 of HRIFA, the date of the alien's lawful admission for permanent residence shall be the date of such grant.

(r) *Review of decisions by the Service denying HRIFA applications*—(1)(i) *Denial notification.* If the Service denies the application for adjustment of status under the provisions of section 902 of HRIFA, the director shall notify the applicant of the decision and of any right to renew the application in proceedings before the Immigration Court.

(ii) An alien made eligible for adjustment of status under HRIFA by the LIFE Act amendments and whose case has not been referred to EOIR under paragraphs (r)(2) or (r)(3) of this section, may file a motion to reopen with the Service.

(2) *Renewal of application for HRIFA benefits in removal, deportation, or exclusion proceedings.* An alien who is not the subject of a final order of removal, deportation, or exclusion may renew his or her application for adjustment under section 902 of HRIFA during the course of such removal, deportation, or exclusion proceedings.

(i) *Initiation of removal proceedings.* In the case of an alien who is not maintaining valid nonimmigrant status and who had not previously been placed in exclusion, deportation, or removal proceedings, the director shall initiate removal proceedings in accordance with § 1239.1 of this chapter.

(ii) *Recalendaring or reinstatement of prior proceedings.* In the case of an alien whose previously initiated exclusion, deportation, or removal proceeding had been administratively closed or continued indefinitely under paragraph (p)(4) of this section, the director shall make a request for recalendaring or reinstatement to the Immigration Court that had administratively closed the proceeding, or the Board, as appropriate, when the application has been denied. The Immigration Court or the Board will then recalendar or reinstate the prior exclusion, deportation, or removal proceeding.

(iii) *Filing of renewed application.* A principal alien may file a renewed application for HRIFA benefits with the Immigration Court either before or after March 31, 2000, if he or she had filed his or her initial application for such benefits with the Service on or before March 31, 2000. A dependent of a principal applicant may file such renewed application with the Immigration Court either before or after March 31, 2000, regardless of when he or she filed his or her initial application for HRIFA benefits with the Service.

(3) *Aliens with final orders.* In the case of an alien who is the subject of an outstanding final order of exclusion, deportation, or removal, the Service shall refer the decision to deny the application by filing a Notice of Certification (Form I–290C) with the Immigration Court that issued the final order for consideration in accordance with paragraph (s) of this section.

(4)(i) An alien whose case has been referred to the Immigration Court under paragraphs (r)(2) or (r)(3) of this section, or who filed an appeal with the Board after his or her application for adjustment of status under section 902 of HRIFA was denied, and whose proceedings are pending, and who is now eligible for adjustment of status under HRIFA as amended by section 1505(b) of the LIFE Act and its amendments, may renew the application for adjustment of status with either the Immigration Court or the Board, whichever has jurisdiction. The application will be adjudicated in accordance with section 1505(b) of the LIFE Act and its amendments.

(ii) An alien present in the United States who is subject to a final order of exclusion, deportation or removal after his or her HRIFA adjustment application was denied by an Immigration Court or the Board, but who was made eligible for HRIFA adjustment as a result of section 1505(b) of the LIFE Act and its amendments, may file a motion to reopen with either the Immigration Court or the Board, whichever had jurisdiction last. Such motion to reopen must be filed on or before June 19, 2001.

(s) *Action on decisions referred to the Immigration Court by a Notice of Certification (Form I–290C)*—(1) *General.* Upon the referral by a Notice of Certification (Form I–290C) of a decision to deny the application, in accordance with paragraph (r)(3) of this section, the immigration judge shall conduct a hearing, under the authority contained in § 3.10 of this chapter, to determine whether the alien is eligible for adjustment of status under section 902 of HRIFA. Such hearing shall be conducted under the same rules of procedure as proceedings conducted under part 240 of this chapter, except the scope of review shall be limited to a determination of the alien's eligibility for adjustment of status under section 902 of HRIFA. During such proceedings, all parties are prohibited from raising or considering any unrelated issues, including, but not limited to, issues of admissibility, deportability, removability, and eligibility for any remedy other than adjustment of status under section 902 of HRIFA. Should the alien fail to appear for such hearing, the immigration judge shall deny the application for adjustment under section 902 of HRIFA.

(2) *Stay pending review.* When the Service refers a decision to the Immigration Court on a Notice of Certification (Form I–290C) in accordance with paragraph (r)(3) of this section, the referral shall not stay the execution of the final order. Execution of such final order shall proceed unless a stay of execution is specifically granted by the immigration judge, the Board, or an authorized Service officer.

(3) *Appeal of Immigration Court decision.* Once the immigration judge issues his or her decision on the application, either the alien or the Service may appeal the decision to the Board. Such appeal must be filed pursuant to the requirements for appeals to the Board from an Immigration Court decision set forth in §§ 1003.3 and 1003.8 of this chapter.

(4) *Rescission or reopening of the decision of an Immigration Court.* The decision of an Immigration Court under paragraph (s)(1) of this section denying an application for adjustment under section 902 of HRIFA for failure to appear may be rescinded or reopened only:

(i) Upon a motion to reopen filed within 180 days after the date of the denial if the alien demonstrates that the failure to appear was because of exceptional circumstances as defined in section 240(e)(1) of the Act;

(ii) Upon a motion to reopen filed at any time if the alien demonstrates that he or she did not receive notice of the hearing in person (or, if personal service was not practicable, through service by mail to the alien or to the alien's counsel of record, if any) or the alien demonstrates that he or she was in Federal or State custody and the failure to appear was through no fault of the alien; or

(iii) Upon a motion to reopen filed not later than June 19, 2001, by an alien present in the United States who became eligible for adjustment of status under HRIFA, as amended by section 1505, of Public Law 106–554.

(t) *Parole authorization for purposes of travel*—(1) *Travel from and return to the United States while the application for adjustment of status is pending.* If an applicant for benefits under section 902 of HRIFA desires to travel outside, and return to, the United States while the application for adjustment of status is pending, he or she must file a request for advance parole authorization on an Application for Travel Document (Form I–131), with fee as set forth in § 103.7(b)(1) of 8 CFR chapter I and in accordance with the instructions on the form. If the alien is either in deportation or removal proceedings, or subject to a final order of deportation or removal, the Form I–131 must be submitted to the Director, Office of International Affairs; otherwise the Form I–131 must be submitted to the Director of the Nebraska Service Center, who shall have jurisdiction over such applications. Unless the applicant files an advance parole request prior to departing from the United States, and the Service approves such request, his or her application for adjustment of status under section 902 of HRIFA is deemed to be abandoned as of the moment of his or her departure. Parole may only be authorized pursuant to the authority contained in, and the standards prescribed in, section 212(d)(5) of the Act.

(2) *Parole authorization for the purpose of filing an application for adjustment of status under section 902 of HRIFA.* (i) An otherwise eligible applicant who is outside the United States and wishes to come to the United States in order to apply for benefits under section 902 of HRIFA may request parole authorization for such purpose by filing an Application for Travel Document (Form I–131) with the Nebraska Service Center, at P.O. Box 87245, Lincoln, NE 68501–7245. Such application must be supported by a photocopy of the Form I–485 that the alien will file once he or she has been paroled into the United States. The applicant must include photocopies of all the supporting documentation listed in paragraph (h) of this section, except the filing fee, the medical report, the fingerprint card, and the local police clearances.

(ii) If the Director of the Nebraska Service Center is satisfied that the alien will be eligible for adjustment of status once the alien has been paroled into the United States and files the application, he or she may issue an Authorization for Parole of an Alien into the United States (Form I–512) to allow the alien to travel to, and be paroled into, the United States for a period of 60 days.

(iii) The applicant shall have 60 days from the date of parole to file the application for adjustment of status. If the alien files the application for adjustment of status within that 60-day period, the Service may re-parole the alien for such time as is necessary for adjudication of the application. Failure to file such application for adjustment of status within 60 days shall result in the alien being returned to the custody of the Service and being examined as an arriving alien applying for admission. Such examination will be conducted in accordance with the provisions of section 235(b)(1) of the Act if the alien is inadmissible under section 212(a)(6)(C) or 212(a)(7) of the Act, or section 240 of the Act if the alien is inadmissible under any other grounds.

(iv) Parole may only be authorized pursuant to the authority contained in, and the standards prescribed in, section 212(d)(5) of the Act. The authority of the Director of the Nebraska Service Center to authorize parole from outside the United States under this provision shall expire on March 31, 2000.

(3) *Effect of departure on an outstanding warrant of exclusion, deportation, or removal.* If an alien who is the subject of an outstanding final order of exclusion, deportation, or removal departs from the United States, with or without an advance parole authorization, such final order shall be executed by the alien's departure. The execution of such final order shall not preclude the applicant from filing an Application for Permission to Reapply for Admission Into the United States After Deportation or Removal (Form I–212) in accordance with § 1212.2 of this chapter.

(u) *Tolling the physical presence in the United States provision for certain individuals*—(1) *Departure with advance authorization for parole.* In the case of an alien who departed the United States after having been issued an Authorization for Parole of an Alien into the United States (Form I–512), and who returns to the United States in accordance with the conditions of that document, the physical presence in the United States requirement of section 902(b)(1) of HRIFA is tolled while the alien is outside the United States pursuant to the issuance of the Form I–512.

(2) *Request for parole authorization from outside the United States.* In the case of an alien who is outside the United States and submits an application for parole authorization in accordance with paragraph (t)(2) of this section, and such application for parole authorization is granted by the Service, the physical presence requirement contained in section 902(b)(1) of HRIFA is tolled from the date the application is received at the Nebraska Service Center until the alien is paroled into the United States pursuant to the issuance of the Form I–512.

(3) *Departure without advance authorization for parole.* In the case of an otherwise-eligible applicant who departed the United States on or before December 31, 1998, the physical presence in the United States provision of section 902(b)(1) of HRIFA is tolled as of October 21, 1998, and until July 12, 1999.

(v) *Judicial review of HRIFA adjustment of status determinations.* Pursuant to the provisions of section 902(f) of HRIFA, there shall be no judicial appeal or review of any administrative determination as to whether the status of an alien should be adjusted under the provisions of section 902 of HRIFA.

[64 FR 25767, May 12, 1999, as amended at 65 FR 15844, Mar. 24, 2000; 66 FR 29452, May 1, 2001; 67 FR 78673, Dec. 26, 2002]

§ 1245.18 How can physicians (with approved Forms I–140) that are serving in medically underserved areas or at a Veterans Affairs facility adjust status?

(a) *Which physicians are eligible for this benefit?* Any alien physician who has been granted a national interest waiver under § 204.12 of 8 CFR chapter 1 may submit Form I–485 during the 6-year period following Service approval of a second preference employment-based immigrant visa petition.

(b) *Do alien physicians have special time-related requirements for adjustment?* (1) Alien physicians who have been granted a national interest waiver under § 204.12 of 8 CFR chapter I must meet all the adjustment of status requirements of this part.

(2) The Service shall not approve an adjustment application filed by an

alien physician who obtained a waiver under section 203(b)(2)(B)(ii) of the Act until the alien physician has completed the period of required service established in § 204.12 of 8 CFR chapter I.

(c) *Are the filing procedures and documentary requirements different for these particular alien physicians?* Alien physicians submitting adjustment applications upon approval of an immigrant petition are required to follow the procedures outlined within this part with the following modifications.

(1) Delayed fingerprinting. Fingerprinting, as noted in the Form I–485 instructions, will not be scheduled at the time of filing. Fingerprinting will be scheduled upon the physician's completion of the required years of service.

(2) Delayed medical examination. The required medical examination, as specified in § 1245.5, shall not be submitted with Form I–485. The medical examination report shall be submitted with the documentary evidence noting the physician's completion of the required years of service.

(d) *Are alien physicians eligible for Form I–766, Employment Authorization Document?* (1) Once the Service has approved an alien physician's Form I–140 with a national interest waiver based upon full-time clinical practice in an underserved area or at a Veterans Affairs facility, the alien physician should apply for adjustment of status to that of lawful permanent resident on Form I–485, accompanied by an application for an Employment Authorization Document (EAD), Form I–765, as specified in § 274a.12(c)(9) of 8 CFR chapter I.

(2) Since section 203(b)(2)(B)(ii) of the Act requires the alien physician to complete the required employment before the Service can approve the alien physician's adjustment application, an alien physician who was in lawful nonimmigrant status when he or she filed the adjustment application is not required to maintain a nonimmigrant status while the adjustment application remains pending. Even if the alien physician's nonimmigrant status expires, the alien physician shall not be considered to be unlawfully present, so long as the alien physician is practicing medicine in accordance with § 204.5(k)(4)(iii) of 8 CFR chapter I.

(e) *When does the Service begin counting the physician's 5-year or 3-year medical practice requirement?* Except as provided in this paragraph, the 6-year period during which a physician must provide the required 5 years of service begins on the date of the notice approving the Form I–140 and the national interest waiver. Alien physicians who have a 3-year medical practice requirement must complete their service within the 4-year period beginning on that date.

(1) If the physician does not already have employment authorization and so must obtain employment authorization before the physician can begin working, then the period begins on the date the Service issues the employment authorization document.

(2) If the physician formerly held status as a J–1 nonimmigrant, but obtained a waiver of the foreign residence requirement and a change of status to that of an H–1B nonimmigrant, pursuant to section 214(l) of the Act, as amended by section 220 of Public Law 103–416, and § 212.7(c)(9) of 8 CFR chapter I, the period begins on the date of the alien's change from J–1 to H–1B status. The Service will include the alien's compliance with the 3-year period of service required under section 214(l) in calculating the alien's compliance with the period of service required under section 203(b)(2)(B)(ii)(II) of the Act and this section.

(3) An alien may not include any time employed as a J–1 nonimmigrant physician in calculating the alien's compliance with the 5 or 3-year medical practice requirement. If an alien is still in J–1 nonimmigrant status when the Service approves a Form I–140 petition with a national interest job offer waiver, the aggregate period during which the medical practice requirement period must be completed will begin on the date the Service issues an employment authorization document.

(f) *Will the Service provide information to the physician about evidence and supplemental filings?* The Service shall provide the physician with the information and the projected timetables for completing the adjustment process, as described in this paragraph. If the physician either files the Form I–485 concurrently with or waits to subsequently file the Form I–485 while the previously filed Form I–140 is still pending, then the Service will given this information upon approval of the Form I–140. If the physician does not file the adjustment application until after approval of the Form I–140 visa petition, the Service shall provide this information upon receipt of the Form I–485 adjustment application.

(1) The Service shall note the date that the medical service begins (provided the physician already had work authorization at the time the Form I–140 was filed) or the date that an employment authorization document was issued.

(2) A list of the evidence necessary to satisfy the requirements of paragraphs (g) and (h) of this section.

(3) A projected timeline noting the dates that the physician will need to submit preliminary evidence two years and 120 days into his or her medical service in an underserved area or VA facility, and a projected date six years and 120 days in the future on which the physician's final evidence of completed medical service will be due.

(g) *Will physicians be required to file evidence prior to the end of the 5 or 3-year period?* (1) For physicians with a 5-year service requirement, no later than 120 days after the second anniversary of the approval of Petition for Immigrant Worker, Form I–140, the alien physician must submit to the Service Center having jurisdiction over his or her place of employment documentary evidence that proves the physician has in fact fulfilled at least 12 months of qualifying employment. This may be accomplished by submitting the following.

(i) Evidence noted in paragraph (h) of this section that is available at the second anniversary of the I–140 approval.

(ii) Documentation from the employer attesting to the fill-time medical practice and the date on which the physician began his or her medical service.

(2) Physicians with a 3-year service requirement are not required to make a supplemental filing, and must only comply with the requirements of paragraph (h) of this section.

(h) *What evidence is needed to prove final compliance with the service requirement?* No later than 120 days after completion of the service requirement established under §204.12(a) of this section, an alien physician must submit to the Service Center having jurisdiction over his or her place of employment documentary evidence that proves the physician has in fact satisfied the service requirement. Such evidence must include, but is not limited to:

(1) Individual Federal income tax returns, including copies of the alien'sW-2 forms, for the entire 3-year period or the balance years of the 5-year period that follow the submission of the evidence required in paragraph (e) of this section;

(2) Documentation from the employer attesting to the full-time medical service rendered during the required aggregate period. The documentation shall address instances of breaks in employment, other than routine breaks such as paid vacations;

(3) If the physician established his or her own practice, documents noting the actual establishment of the practice, including incorporation of the medical practice (if incorporated), the business license, and the business tax returns and tax withholding documents submitted for the entire 3 year period, or the balance years of the 5-year period that follow the submission of the evidence required in paragraph (e) of this section.

(i) *What if the physician does not comply with the requirements of paragraphs (f) and (g) of this section?* If an alien physician does not submit (in accordance with paragraphs (f) and (g) of this section) proof that he or she has completed the service required under §204.12(a) of 8 CFR chapter I, the Service shall serve the alien physician with a written notice of intent to deny the alien physician's application for adjustment of status and, after the denial is finalized, to revoke approval of the Form I–140 and national interest waiver. The written notice shall require the alien physician to provide the evidence required by paragraph (f) or (g) of this section within 30 days of the date of the written notice. The Service shall not extend this 30-day period. If the alien physician fails to submit the evidence within the 30-day period established by the written notice, the Service shall deny the alien physician's application for adjustment of status and shall revoke approval of the Form I–140 and of the national interest waiver.

(j) *Will a Service officer interview the physician?* (1) Upon submission of the evidence noted in paragraph (h) of this section, the Service shall match the documentary evidence with the pending form I–485 and schedule the alien physician for fingerprinting at an Application Support Center.

(2) The local Service office shall schedule the alien for an adjustment interview with a Service officer, unless the Service waives the interview as provided in § 1245.6. The local Service office shall also notify the alien if supplemental documentation should either be mailed to the office, or brought to the adjustment interview.

(k) *Are alien physicians allowed to travel outside the United States during the mandatory 3 or 5-year service period?* An alien physician who has been granted a national interest waiver under § 204.12 of this chapter and has a pending application for adjustment of status may travel outside of the United States during the required 3 or 5-year service period by obtaining advanced parole prior to traveling. Alien physicians may apply for advanced parole by submitting form I–131, Application for Travel Document, to the Service office having jurisdiction over the alien physician's place of business.

(l) *What if the Service denies the adjustment application?* If the Service denies the adjustment application, the alien physician may renew the application in removal proceedings.

[65 FR 53895, Sept. 6, 2000; 65 FR 57861, Sept. 26, 2000; 65 FR 57944, Sept. 27, 2000; 67 FR 49563, July 31, 2002]

§ 1245.20 Adjustment of status of Syrian asylees under Public Law 106–378.

(a) *Eligibility.* An alien is eligible to apply to adjust status under Public Law 106–378 if the alien is:

(1) A Jewish national of Syria;

(2) Arrived in the United States after December 31, 1991, after being permitted by the Syrian Government to depart from Syria;

(3) Is physically present in the United States at the time of filing the application to adjust status;

(4) Applies for adjustment of status no later than October 26, 2001, or has a pending application for adjustment of status under the Act that was filed with the Service before October 27, 2000;

(5) Has been physically present in the United States for at least 1 year after being granted asylum;

(6) Has not firmly resettled in any foreign country; and

(7) Is admissible as an immigrant under the Act at the time of examination for adjustment.

(b) *Qualified family members.* The spouse, child, or unmarried son or daughter of an alien eligible for adjustment under Public Law 106–378 is eligible to apply for adjustment of status under this section if the alien meets the criteria set forth in paragraphs (a)(4) through (a)(7) of this section.

(c) *Grounds not to be applied and waivers.* The grounds of inadmissibility found at section 212(a)(4) of the Act, relating to public charge, and at section 212(a)(7)(A) of the Act, relating to documentation, do not apply to applicants for adjustment of status under Public Law 106–378. Applicants may also request the waivers found at sections 212(h), (i), and (k) of the Act, to the extent they are eligible.

(d) *Application*—(1) *New applications.* An applicant must submit From I–485, Application to Register Permanent Residence or Adjust Status, along with the appropriate application fee as stated in § 103.7(b)(1) of 8 CFR chapter I, to the Nebraska Service Center. The application must physically be received by the Nebraska Service Center no later than close of business on October 26, 2001. Applicants 14 years of age or older must also submit the fingerprinting service fee provided for in § 103.7(b)(1) of this chapter. Each application filed must be accompanied by two photographs as described in the Form I–485 instructions; a completed Biographic Information Sheet (Form G–325A) if the applicant is between 14 and 79 years of age; and a report of medical examination (Form I–693 and vaccination supplement) as specified in 8 CFR 245.5. On Form I-485, Part 2, question "h", applicants must write "*SYRIAN ASYLEE—P.L. 106–378*" to indicate that they are applying based on this provision.

(2) *Filing of requests to change the basis of a pending Form I-485*—(i) *Request.* An eligible Syrian national with a Form I-485 that is currently pending with the Service may request that the basis of his or her Form I-485 be changed to Public Law 106–378. The alien must submit this request in writing to the Nebraska Service Center. The request may only be granted if the 2,000 adjustment limit specified in paragraph (i) of this section has not yet been reached. The 2,000 adjustment limit includes both new and pending Form I-485 petitions. The applicant should clearly annotate "*SYRIAN ASYLEE P.L. 106–378*" on the envelope to identify the correspondence.

(ii) *Time limit.* If the Form I-485 was filed before October 27, 2000, there is no time limit for requesting a change of basis for adjustment of status. However, if the Form I-485 was filed on or after October 27, 2001, then the Service must receive the request for change of basis no later than October 27, 2001.

(e) *Evidence.* Applicants must submit evidence that demonstrates they are eligible for adjustment of status under Public Law 106–378. Required evidence includes the following:

(1) A copy of the alien's passport;

(2) A copy of the applicant's Arrival-Departure Record (Form I-94) or other evidence of inspection and admission or parole into the United States after December 31, 1991;

(3) Documentation including, but not limited to, those listed at § 1245.15(j)(2) to establish physical presence in the United States for at least 1 year after being granted asylum;

(4) If the applicant is the spouse of a principal alien applying for adjustment, he or she must submit a marriage certificate, if available, or other evidence to demonstrate the marriage; and

(5) If the applicant is the child of a principal alien applying for adjustment of status, he or she must submit a birth certificate, if available, or other evidence to demonstrate the relationship.

(f) *Employment authorization.* Applicants who want to obtain employment authorization based on a pending application for adjustment of status under Public Law 106–378 may submit Form I-765, Application for Employment Authorization, along with the application fee listed in § 103.7(b)(1) of 8 CFR chapter I. If the Service approves the application for employment authorization, the applicant will be issued an employment authorization document.

(g) *Travel while an application to adjust status is pending.* Applicants who wish to travel abroad and re-enter the United States while an application for adjustment of status is pending without being considered to have abandoned that application must obtain advance parole prior to departing the United States. To obtain advance parole, applicants must file Form I-131, Application for a Travel Document, along with the application fee listed in § 103.7(b)(1) of 8 CFR chapter I. If the Service approves Form I-131, the alien will be issued Form I-512, Authorization for the Parole of an Alien into the United States.

(h) *Approval and date of admission as a lawful permanent resident.* When the Service approves an application to adjust status to that of lawful permanent resident based on Public Law 106–378, the applicant will be notified in writing of the Service's decision. In addition, the record of the alien's admission as a lawful permanent resident will be recorded as of the date 1 year before the approval of the application.

(i) *Number of adjustments under Public Law 106–378.* No more than 2,000 aliens may have their status adjusted to that of lawful permanent resident under Public Law 106–378.

(j) *Notice of Denial*—(1) *General.* When the Service denies an application to adjust status to that of lawful permanent resident based on Public Law 106–378, the applicant will be notified of the decision and the reason for the denial in writing.

(2) *Cases involving requests to change the basis of a pending Form I-485.* If an applicant who requested that a pending Form I-485, be considered under Public Law 106–378, is found to be ineligible under Public Law 106–378, but he or she appears eligible for adjustment under

the original section of the Act under which the Form I–485 was filed, the Service will provide the applicant with notice of this fact. Processing the Form I–485 under the original provision of law will resume as appropriate.

(k) *Administrative review.* An alien whose application for adjustment of status under Public Law 106–378 is denied by the Service may not appeal the decision. However, the denial will be without prejudice to the alien's right to renew the application in proceedings under 8 CFR part 1240 provided that the 2,000 statutory limit on such adjustments has not yet been reached.

[66 FR 27448, May 17, 2001]

§ 1245.21 Adjustment of status of certain nationals of Vietnam, Cambodia, and Laos (section 586 of Public Law 106–429).

(a) *Eligibility.* The Service may adjust the status to that of a lawful permanent resident, a native or citizen of Vietnam, Cambodia, or Laos who:

(1) Was inspected and paroled into the United States before October 1, 1997;

(2) Was paroled into the United States from Vietnam under the auspices of the Orderly Departure Program (ODP), a refugee camp in East Asia, or a displaced person camp administered by the United Nations High Commissioner for Refugees (UNHCR) in Thailand;

(3) Was physically present in the United States prior to and on October 1, 1997;

(4) Files an application for adjustment of status in accordance with paragraph (b) of this section during the 3-year application period; and

(5) Is otherwise eligible to receive an immigrant visa and is otherwise admissible as an immigrant to the United States except as provided in paragraphs (e) and (f) of this section.

(b) *Applying for benefits under section 586 of Public Law 106–429*—(1) *Application period.* The application period lasts from January 27, 2003 until January 25, 2006. The Service will accept applications received after the end of the application period, but only if the 5,000 limit on adjustments has not been reached prior to the end of the three-year application period, and the application bears an official postmark dated on or before the final day of the application period. Postmarks will be evaluated in the following manner:

(i) If the postmark is illegible or missing, the Service will consider the application to be timely filed if it is received on or before 3 business days after the end of the application period.

(ii) In all instances, the burden of proof is on the applicant to establish timely filing of an application.

(2) *Application.* An alien must be physically present in the United States to apply for adjustment of status under section 586 of Public Law 106–429. An applicant must submit Form I–485, Application to Register Permanent Residence or Adjust Status, along with the appropriate application fee contained in § 103.7(b)(1) of this chapter. Applicants who are 14 through 79 years of age must also submit the fingerprinting service fee provided for in § 103.7(b)(1) of this chapter. Each application filed must be accompanied by evidence establishing eligibility as provided in paragraph (g) of this section; two photographs as described in the Form I–485 instructions; a completed Biographic Information Sheet (Form G–325A) if the applicant is between 14 and 79 years of age; a report of medical examination (Form I–693 and vaccination supplement) specified in § 1245.5; and, if needed, an application for waiver of inadmissibility. Under Part 2, question h of Form I–485, applicants must write "INDOCHINESE PAROLEE P.L. 106–429". Applications must be sent to: INS Nebraska Service Center, P.O. Box 87485, Lincoln NE 68501–7485.

(c) *Applications from aliens in immigration proceedings.* An alien in pending immigration proceedings who believes he or she is eligible for adjustment of status under section 586 of Public Law 106–429 must apply directly to the Service in accordance with paragraph (b) of this section. An immigration judge or the Board of Immigration Appeals may not adjudicate applications for adjustment of status under this section. An alien who is currently in immigration proceedings who alleges eligibility for adjustment of status under section 586 of Public Law 106–429 may contact

Service counsel after filing an application to request the consent of the Service to the filing of a joint motion for administrative closure. Unless the Service consents to such a motion, the immigration judge or the Board may not defer or dismiss the proceeding in connection with section 586 of Public Law 106–429.

(d) *Applications from aliens with final orders of removal, deportation, or exclusion.* An alien with a final order of removal, deportation, or exclusion who believes he or she is eligible for adjustment of status under section 586 of Public Law 106–429 must apply directly to the Service in accordance with paragraph (b) of this section.

(1) An application under this section does not automatically stay the order of removal, deportation, or exclusion. An alien who is eligible for adjustment of status under section 586 of Public Law 106–429 may request that the district director with jurisdiction over the alien grant a stay of removal during the pendency of the application. The regulations governing such a request are found at 8 CFR 241.6.

(2) The Service in general will exercise its discretion not to grant a stay of removal, deportation, or exclusion with respect to an alien who is inadmissible on any of the grounds specified in paragraph (m)(3) of this section, unless there is substantial reason to believe that the Service will grant the necessary waivers of inadmissibility.

(3) An immigration judge or the Board may not grant a motion to reopen or stay in connection with an application under this section.

(4) If the Service approves the application, the approval will constitute the automatic re-opening of the alien's immigration proceedings, vacating of the final order of removal, deportation, or exclusion, and termination of the reopened proceedings.

(e) *Grounds of inadmissibility that do not apply.* In making a determination of whether an applicant is otherwise eligible for admission to the United States for lawful permanent residence under the provisions of section 586 of Public Law 106–429, the grounds of inadmissibility under sections 212(a)(4), (a)(5), (a)(7)(A), and (a)(9) of the Act shall not apply.

(f) *Waiver of grounds of inadmissibility.* In connection with an application for adjustment of status under this section, the alien may apply for a waiver of the grounds of inadmissibility under sections 212(a)(1), (a)(6)(B), (a)(6)(C), (a)(6)(F), (a)(8)(A), (a)(10)(B), and (a)(10)(D) of the Act as provided in section 586(c) of Public Law 106–429, if the alien demonstrates that a waiver is necessary to prevent extreme hardship to the alien, or to the alien's spouse, parent, son or daughter who is a U.S. citizen or an alien lawfully admitted for permanent residence. In addition, the alien may apply for any other waiver of inadmissibility under section 212 of the Act, if eligible. In order to obtain a waiver for any of these grounds, an applicant must submit Form I–601, Application for Waiver of Grounds of Excludability, with the application for adjustment.

(g) *Evidence.* Applicants must submit evidence that demonstrates they are eligible for adjustment of status under section 586 of Public Law 106–429. Such evidence shall include the following:

(1) A birth certificate or other record of birth;

(2) Documentation to establish that the applicant was physically present in the United States on October 1, 1997, under the standards set forth in § 1245.22 of this chapter.

(3) A copy of the applicant's Arrival-Departure Record (Form I–94) or other evidence that the alien was inspected or paroled into the United States prior to October 1, 1997, from one of the three programs listed in paragraph (a)(2) of this section. Subject to verification, documentation pertaining to paragraph (a)(2) of this section is already contained in Service files and the applicant may submit an affidavit to that effect in lieu of actual documentation.

(h) *Employment authorization.* Applicants who want to obtain employment authorization based on a pending application for adjustment of status under this section may submit Form I–765, Application for Employment Authorization, along with the application fee listed in 8 CFR 103.7(b)(1). If the Service approves the application for employment authorization, the applicant will be issued an employment authorization document.

(i) *Travel while an application to adjust status is pending.* An alien may travel abroad while an application to adjust status is pending. Applicants must obtain advance parole in order to avoid the abandonment of their application to adjust status. An applicant may obtain advance parole by filing Form I–131, Application for a Travel Document, along with the application fee listed in 8 CFR 103.7(b)(1). If the Service approves Form I–131, the alien will be issued Form I–512, Authorization for the Parole of an Alien into the United States. Aliens granted advance parole will still be subject to inspection at a port-of-entry.

(j) *Approval and date of admission as a lawful permanent resident.* When the Service approves an application to adjust status to that of lawful permanent resident based on section 586 of Public Law 106–429, the applicant will be notified in writing of the Service's decision. In addition, the record of the alien's admission as a lawful permanent resident will be recorded as of the date of the alien's inspection and parole into the United States, as described in paragraph (a)(1) of this section.

(k) *Notice of denial.* When the Service denies an application to adjust status to that of lawful permanent resident based on section 586 of Public Law 106–429, the applicant will be notified of the decision in writing.

(l) *Administrative review.* An alien whose application for adjustment of status under section 586 of Public Law 106–429 is denied by the Service may appeal the decision to the Administrative Appeals Office in accordance with 8 CFR 103.3(a)(2).

(m) *Number of adjustments permitted under this section*—(1) *Limit.* No more than 5,000 aliens may have their status adjusted to that of a lawful permanent resident under section 586 of Public Law 106–429.

(2) *Counting procedures.* Each alien granted adjustment of status under this section will count towards the 5,000 limit. The Service will assign a tracking number, ascending chronologically by filing date, to all applications properly filed in accordance with paragraphs (b) and (g) of this section. Except as described in paragraph (m)(3) of this section, the Service will adjudicate applications in that order until it reaches 5,000 approvals under this part. Applications initially denied but pending on administrative appeal will retain their place in the queue by virtue of their tracking number, pending the Service's adjudication of the appeal.

(3) *Applications submitted with a request for the waiver of a ground of inadmissibility.* In the discretion of the Service, applications that do not require adjudication of a waiver of inadmissibility under section 212(a)(2), (a)(6)(B), (a)(6)(F), (a)(8)(A), or (a)(10)(D) of the Act may be approved and assigned numbers within the 5,000 limit before those applications that do require a waiver of inadmissibility under any of those provisions. Applications requiring a waiver of any of those provisions will be assigned a tracking number chronologically by the date of approval of the necessary waivers rather than the date of filing of the application.

(4) *Procedures when the 5,000 limit is reached.* The Service will track the total number of adjustments and stop processing applications after the 5,000 limit has been reached. When the limit is reached, the Service will return any additional applications to applicants with a dated notice encouraging applicants to retain their application package and the notice in the event the 5,000 limit is expanded or eliminated and the alien wishes to apply again. The Service will keep an identifying chronological record of the application for purposes of processing applications under this section if the 5,000 limit subsequently is expanded or eliminated. If at the time the 5,000 limit is reached, it appears that Congress is about to pass legislation to expand or eliminate the cap, the Service retains the discretion to retain such applications and the related fees.

[67 FR 78673, Dec. 26, 2002]

§ 1245.22 Evidence to demonstrate an alien's physical presence in the United States on a specific date.

(a) *Evidence.* Generally, an alien who is required to demonstrate his or her physical presence in the United States on a specific date in connection with an application to adjust status to that of an alien lawfully admitted for permanent residence should submit evidence according to this section. In cases where a more specific regulation relating to a particular adjustment of status provision has been issued in the 8 CFR, such regulation is controlling to the extent that it conflicts with this section.

(b) *The number of documents.* If no one document establishes the alien's physical presence on the required date, he or she may submit several documents establishing his or her physical presence in the United States prior to and after that date.

(c) *Service-issued documentation.* To demonstrate physical presence on a specific date, the alien may submit Service-issued documentation. Examples of acceptable Service documentation include, but are not limited to, photocopies of:

(1) Form I-94, Arrival-Departure Record, issued upon the alien's arrival in the United States;

(2) Form I-862, Notice to Appear, issued by the Service on or before the required date;

(3) Form I-122, Notice to Applicant for Admission Detained for Hearing before Immigration Judge, issued by the Service on or prior to the required date, placing the applicant in exclusion proceedings under section 236 of the Act (as in effect prior to April 1, 1997);

(4) Form I-221, Order to Show Cause, issued by the Service on or prior to the required date, placing the applicant in deportation proceedings under section 242 or 242A (redesignated as section 238) of the Act (as in effect prior to April 1, 1997); or

(5) Any application or petition for a benefit under the Act filed by or on behalf of the applicant on or prior to the required date that establishes his or her presence in the United States, or a fee receipt issued by the Service for such application or petition.

(d) *Government-issued documentation.* To demonstrate physical presence on the required date, the alien may submit other government documentation. Other government documentation issued by a Federal, State, or local authority must bear the signature, seal, or other authenticating instrument of such authority (if the document normally bears such instrument), be dated at the time of issuance, and bear a date of issuance not later than the required date. For this purpose, the term Federal, State, or local authority includes any governmental, educational, or administrative function operated by Federal, State, county, or municipal officials. Examples of such other documentation include, but are not limited to:

(1) A state driver's license;

(2) A state identification card;

(3) A county or municipal hospital record;

(4) A public college or public school transcript;

(5) Income tax records;

(6) A certified copy of a Federal, State, or local governmental record that was created on or prior to the required date, shows that the applicant was present in the United States at the time, and establishes that the applicant sought in his or her own behalf, or some other party sought in the applicant's behalf, a benefit from the Federal, State, or local governmental agency keeping such record;

(7) A certified copy of a Federal, State, or local governmental record that was created on or prior to the required date, that shows that the applicant was present in the United States at the time, and establishes that the applicant submitted an income tax return, property tax payment, or similar submission or payment to the Federal, State, or local governmental agency keeping such record; or

(8) A transcript from a private or religious school that is registered with, or approved or licensed by, appropriate State or local authorities, accredited by the State or regional accrediting body, or by the appropriate private school association, or maintains enrollment records in accordance with State or local requirements or standards. Such evidence will only be accepted to document the physical presence of an alien who was in attendance and under the age of 21 on the specific date that physical presence in the United States is required.

(e) *Copies of records.* It shall be the responsibility of the applicant to obtain and submit copies of the records of any other government agency that the applicant desires to be considered in support of his or her application. If the alien is not in possession of such a document or documents, but believes that a copy is already contained in the Service file relating to him or her, he or she may submit a statement as to the name and location of the issuing Federal, State, or local government agency, the type of document and the date on which it was issued.

(f) *Other relevant document(s) and evaluation of evidence.* The adjudicator will consider any other relevant document(s) as well as evaluate all evidence submitted, on a case-by-case basis. The Service may require an interview when necessary.

(g) *Accuracy of documentation.* In all cases, any doubts as to the existence, authenticity, veracity, or accuracy of the documentation shall be resolved by the official government record, with records of the Service having precedence over the records of other agencies. Furthermore, determinations as to the weight to be given any particular document or item of evidence shall be solely within the discretion of the adjudicating authority.

[67 FR 78674, Dec. 26, 2002]

PART 1246—RESCISSION OF ADJUSTMENT OF STATUS

AUTHORITY: Authority: 8 U.S.C. 1103, 1254, 1255, 1256, 1259; 8 CFR part 2.

SOURCE: 62 FR 10385, Mar. 6, 1997, unless otherwise noted. Duplicated from part 246 at 68 FR 9842, Feb. 28, 2003.

EDITORIAL NOTE: Nomenclature changes to part 1246 appear at 68 FR 9846, Feb. 28, 2003, and 68 FR 10359, Mar. 5, 2003.

§ 1246.1 Notice.

If it appears to a district director that a person residing in his or her district was not in fact eligible for the adjustment of status made in his or her case, or it appears to an asylum office director that a person granted adjustment of status by an asylum officer pursuant to 8 CFR 1240.70 was not in fact eligible for adjustment of status, a proceeding shall be commenced by the personal service upon such person of a notice of intent to rescind, which shall inform him or her of the allegations upon which it is intended to rescind the adjustment of his or her status. In such a proceeding the person shall be known as the respondent. The notice shall also inform the respondent that he or she may submit, within thirty days from the date of service of the notice, an answer in writing under oath setting forth reasons why such rescission shall not be made, and that he or she may, within such period, request a hearing before an immigration judge in support of, or in lieu of, his or her written answer. The respondent shall further be informed that he or she may have the assistance of or be represented by counsel or representative of his or her choice qualified under part 292 of this chapter, at no expense to the Government, in the preparation of his or her answer or in connection with his or her hearing, and that he or she may present such evidence in his or her behalf as may be relevant to the rescission.

[62 FR 10385, Mar. 6, 1997, as amended at 64 FR 27881, May 21, 1999]

§ 1246.2 Allegations admitted; no answer filed; no hearing requested.

If the answer admits the allegations in the notice, or if no answer is filed within the thirty-day period, or if no hearing is requested within such period, the district director or asylum office director shall rescind the adjustment of status previously granted, and no appeal shall lie from his decision.

[62 FR 10385, Mar. 6, 1997, as amended at 64 FR 27881, May 21, 1999]

§ 1246.3 Allegations contested or denied; hearing requested.

If, within the prescribed time following service of the notice pursuant to § 1246.1, the respondent has filed an answer which contests or denies any allegation in the notice, or a hearing is requested, a hearing pursuant to § 1246.5 shall be conducted by an immigration judge, and the requirements contained in §§ 1240.3, 1240.4, 1240.5, 1240.6, 1240.7, and 1240.9 of this chapter shall be followed.

§ 1246.4 Immigration judge's authority; withdrawal and substitution.

In any proceeding conducted under this part, the immigration judge shall have authority to interrogate, examine, and cross-examine the respondent and other witnesses, to present and receive evidence, to determine whether adjustment of status shall be rescinded, to make decisions thereon, including an appropriate order, and to take any other action consistent with applicable provisions of law and regulations as may be appropriate to the disposition of the case. Nothing contained in this part shall be construed to diminish the authority conferred on immigration judges by the Act. The immigration judge assigned to conduct a hearing shall, at any time, withdraw if he or she deems himself or herself disqualified. If a hearing has begun but no evidence has been adduced other than the notice and answer, if any, pursuant to §§ 1246.1 and 1246.2, or if an immigration judge becomes unavailable to complete his or her duties within a reasonable time, or if at any time the respondent consents to a substitution, another immigration judge may be assigned to complete the case. The new immigration judge shall familiarize himself or herself with the record in the case and shall state for the record that he or she is familiar with the record in the case.

§ 1246.5 Hearing.

(a) *Service counsel.* The Government shall be represented at the hearing by a Service counsel who shall have authority to present evidence, and to interrogate, examine, and cross-examine the respondent and other witnesses. The Service counsel is authorized to appeal from a decision of the immigration judge pursuant to § 1246.7 and to move for reopening or reconsideration pursuant to § 1003.23 of this chapter.

(b) *Opening.* The immigration judge shall advise the respondent of the nature of the proceeding and the legal authority under which it is conducted; advise the respondent of his or her right to representation, at no expense to the Government, by counsel or representative of his or her own choice qualified under part 1292 of this chapter and require him or her to state then and there whether he or she desires representation; advise the respondent that he or she will have a reasonable opportunity to examine and object to the evidence against him or her, to present evidence in his or her own behalf, and to cross-examine witnesses presented by the Government; place the respondent under oath; read the allegations in the notice to the respondent and explain them in nontechnical language, and enter the notice and respondent's answer, if any, as exhibits in the record.

(c) *Pleading by respondent.* The immigration judge shall require the respondent to state for the record whether he or she admits or denies the allegations contained in the notice, or any of them, and whether he or she concedes that his or her adjustment of status should be rescinded. If the respondent admits all of the allegations and concedes that the adjustment of status in his or her case should be rescinded under the allegations set forth in the notice, and the immigration judge is satisfied that no issues of law or fact remain, he or she may determine that rescission as alleged has been established by the respondent's admissions. The allegations contained in the notice shall be taken as admitted when the respondent, without reasonable cause, fails or refuses to attend or remain in attendance at the hearing.

§ 1246.6 Decision and order.

The decision of the immigration judge may be oral or written. The formal enumeration of findings is not required. The order shall direct either that the proceeding be terminated or that the adjustment of status be rescinded. Service of the decision and finality of the order of the immigration judge shall be in accordance with, and as stated in §§ 1240.13 (a) and (b) and 1240.14 of this chapter.

§ 1246.7 Appeals.

Pursuant to 8 CFR part 1003, an appeal shall lie from a decision of an immigration judge under this part to the Board of Immigration Appeals. An appeal shall be taken within 30 days after the mailing of a written decision or the stating of an oral decision. The reasons for the appeal shall be specifically identified in the Notice of Appeal (Form EOIR 26); failure to do so may constitute a ground for dismissal of the appeal by the Board.

§ 1246.8 [Reserved]

§ 1246.9 Surrender of Form I–551.

A respondent whose status as a permanent resident has been rescinded in accordance with section 246 of the Act and this part, shall, upon demand, promptly surrender to the district director having administrative jurisdiction over the office in which the action under this part was taken, the Form I–551 issued to him or her at the time of the grant of permanent resident status.

PART 1249—CREATION OF RECORDS OF LAWFUL ADMISSION FOR PERMANENT RESIDENCE

AUTHORITY: 8 U.S.C. 1103, 1182, 1259; 8 CFR part 2.

SOURCE: Duplicated from part 249 at 68 FR 9843, Feb. 28, 2003.

EDITORIAL NOTE: Nomenclature changes to part 1249 appear at 68 FR 9846, Feb. 28, 2003.

§ 1249.1 Waiver of inadmissibility.

In conjunction with an application under section 249 of the Act, an otherwise eligible alien who is inadmissible under paragraph (9), (10), or (12) of section 212(a) of the Act or so much of paragraph (23) of section 212(a) of the Act as relates to a single offense of simple possession of 30 grams or less of marihuana may request a waiver of such ground of inadmissibility under section 212(h) of the Act. Any alien within the classes described in subparagraphs (B) through (H) of section 212(a)(28) of the Act may apply for the benefits of section 212(a)(28)(I)(ii) in conjunction with an application under section 249 of the Act.

[47 FR 44238, Oct. 7, 1982]

§ 1249.2 Application.

(a) *Jurisdiction.* An application by an alien, other than an arriving alien, who has been served with a notice to appear or warrant of arrest shall be considered only in proceedings under 8 CFR part 1240. In any other case, an alien who believes he or she meets the eligibility requirements of section 249 of the Act shall apply to the district director having jurisdiction over his or her place of residence. The application shall be made on Form I–485 and shall be accompanied by Form G–325A, which shall be considered part of the application. The application shall also be accompanied by documentary evidence establishing continuous residence in the United States since prior to January 1, 1972, or since entry and prior to July 1, 1924. All documents must be submitted in accordance with § 103.2(b) of this chapter. Documentary evidence may include any records of official or personal transactions or recordings of events occurring during the period of claimed residence. Affidavits of credible witnesses may also be accepted. Persons unemployed and unable to furnish evidence in their own names may furnish evidence in the names of parents or other persons with whom they have been living, if affidavits of the parents or other persons are submitted attesting to the residence. The numerical limitations of sections 201 and 202 of the Act shall not apply.

(b) *Decision.* The applicant shall be notified of the decision and, if the application is denied, of the reasons therefor. If the application is granted, a Form I–551, showing that the applicant has acquired the status of an alien lawfully admitted for permanent residence, shall not be issued until the applicant surrenders any other document in his or her possession evidencing compliance with the alien registration requirements of former or existing law. No appeal shall lie from the denial of an application by the district director. However, an alien, other than an arriving alien, may renew the denied application in proceedings under 8 CFR part 1240.

[52 FR 6322, Mar. 3, 1987, as amended at 62 FR 10386, Mar. 6, 1997; 68 FR 10359, Mar. 5, 2003]

§ 1249.3 Reopening and reconsideration.

An applicant who alleged entry and residence since prior to July 1, 1924, but in whose case a record was created as of the date of approval of the application because evidence of continuous residence prior to July 1, 1924, was not submitted, may have his case reopened and reconsidered pursuant to § 103.5 of 8 CFR chapter I. Upon the submission of satisfactory evidence, a record of admission as of the date of alleged entry may be created.

[29 FR 11494, Aug. 11, 1964, as amended at 68 FR 10359, Mar. 5, 2003]

PART 1270—PENALTIES FOR DOCUMENT FRAUD

Sec.

AUTHORITY: 8 U.S.C. 1101, 1103, and 1324c; Pub. L. 101–410, 104 Stat. 890, as amended by Pub. L. 104–134, 110 Stat. 1321.

SOURCE: 57 FR 33866, July 31, 1992, unless otherwise noted. Duplicated from part 270 at 68 FR 9843, Feb. 28, 2003.

EDITORIAL NOTE: Nomenclature changes to part 1270 appear at 68 FR 9846, Feb. 28, 2003, and at 68 FR 10359, Mar. 5, 2003.

§ 1270.1 Definitions.

For the purpose of this part—

Document means an instrument on which is recorded, by means of letters, figures, or marks, matters which may be used to fulfill any requirement of the Act. The term "document" includes, but is not limited to, an application required to be filed under the Act and any other accompanying document or material;

Entity means any legal entity, including, but not limited to, a corporation, partnership, joint venture, governmental body, agency, proprietorship, or association, including an agent or anyone acting directly or indirectly in the interest thereof.

§ 1270.2 Enforcement procedures.

(a) *Procedures for the filing of complaints.* Any person or entity having knowledge of a violation or potential violation of section 274C of the Act may submit a signed, written complaint to the Service office having jurisdiction over the business or residence of the potential violator or the location where the violation occurred. The signed, written complaint must contain sufficient information to identify both the complainant and the alleged violator, including their names and addresses. The complaint should also contain detailed factual allegations relating to the potential violation including the date, time and place of the alleged violation and the specific act or conduct alleged to constitute a violation of the Act. Written complaints may be delivered either by mail to the appropriate Service office or by personally appearing before any immigration officer at a Service office.

(b) *Investigation.* When the Service receives complaints from a third party in accordance with paragraph (a) of this section, it shall investigate only those complaints which, on their face, have a substantial probability of validity. The Service may also conduct investigations for violations on its own initiative, and without having received a written complaint. If it is determined after investigation that the person or entity has violated section 274C of the Act, the Service may issue and serve upon the alleged violator a Notice of Intent to Fine.

(c) *Issuance of a subpoena.* Service officers shall have reasonable access to examine any relevant evidence of any person or entity being investigated. The Service may issue subpoenas pursuant to its authority under sections 235(a) and 287 of the Act, in accordance with the procedures set forth in § 1287.4 of this chapter.

(d) *Notice of Intent to Fine.* The proceeding to assess administrative penalties under section 274C of the Act is commenced when the Service issues a Notice of Intent to Fine. Service of this notice shall be accomplished by personal service pursuant to § 103.5a(a)(2) of 8 CFR chapter I. Service is effective upon receipt, as evidenced by the certificate of service or the certified mail return receipt. The person or entity identified in the Notice of Intent to Fine shall be known as the respondent. The Notice of Intent to Fine may be issued by an officer defined in § 242.1 of this chapter or by an INS port director designated by his or her district director.

(e) *Contents of the Notice of Intent to Fine.* (1) The Notice of Intent to Fine shall contain the basis for the charge(s) against the respondent, the statutory provisions alleged to have been violated, and the monetary amount of the penalty the Service intends to impose.

(2) The Notice of Intent to Fine shall provide the following advisals to the respondent:

(i) That the person or entity has the right to representation by counsel of his or her own choice at no expense to the government;

(ii) That any statement given may be used against the person or entity;

(iii) That the person or entity has the right to request a hearing before an administrative law judge pursuant to 5 U.S.C. 554–557, and that such request must be filed with INS within 60 days from the service of the Notice of Intent to Fine; and

(iv) That if a written request for a hearing is not timely filed, the Service will issue a final order from which there is no appeal.

(f) *Request for hearing before an administrative law judge.* If a respondent contests the issuance of a Notice of Intent to Fine, the respondent must file with the INS, within 60 days of the Notice of Intent to Fine, a written request for a hearing before an administrative law judge. Any written request for a hearing submitted in a foreign language must be accompanied by an English language translation. A request for hearing is deemed filed when it is either received by the Service office designated in the Notice of Intent to Fine, or addressed to such office, stamped with the proper postage, and postmarked within the 60-day period. In computing the 60-day period prescribed by this section, the day of service of the Notice of Intent to Fine shall not be included. In the request for a hearing, the respondent may, but is not required to, respond to each allegation listed in the Notice of Intent to Fine. A respondent may waive the 60-day period in which to request a hearing before an administrative law judge and ask that the INS issue a final order from which there is no appeal. Prior to execution of the waiver, a respondent who is not a United States citizen will be advised that a waiver of a section 274C hearing will result in the issuance of a final order and that the respondent will be excludable and/or deportable from the United States pursuant to the Act.

(g) *Failure to file a request for hearing.* If the respondent does not file a written request for a hearing within 60 days of service of the Notice of Intent to Fine, the INS shall issue a final order from which there shall be no appeal.

(h) *Issuance of the final order.* A final order may be issued by an officer defined in § 242.1 of 8 CFR chapter I, by an INS port director designated by his or her district director, or by the Director of the INS National Fines Office.

(i) *Service of the final order*—(1) *Generally.* Service of the final order shall be accomplished by personal service pursuant to § 103.5a(a)(2) of 8 CFR chapter I. Service is effective upon receipt, as evidenced by the certificate of service or the certified mail return receipt.

(2) *Alternative provisions for service in a foreign country.* When service is to be effected upon a party in a foreign country, it is sufficient if service of the final order is made: (i) In the manner prescribed by the law of the foreign country for service in that country in an action in any of its courts of general jurisdiction; or

(ii) As directed by the foreign authority in response to a letter rogatory, when service in either case is reasonably calculated to give actual notice; or

(iii) When applicable, pursuant to § 103.5a(a)(2) of 8 CFR chapter I.

Service is effective upon receipt of the final order. Proof of service may be made as prescribed by the law of the foreign country, or, when service is pursuant to § 103.5a(a)(2) of 8 CFR chapter I, as evidenced by the certificate of service or the certified mail return receipt.

(j) *Declination to file charges for document fraud committed by refugees at the time of entry.* The Service shall not issue a Notice of Intent to Fine for acts of document fraud committed by an alien pursuant to direct departure from a country in which the alien has a well-founded fear of persecution or from which there is a significant danger that the alien would be returned to a country in which the alien would have a well-founded fear of persecution, provided that the alien has presented himself or herself without delay to an INS officer and shown good cause for his or her illegal entry or presence. Other acts of document fraud committed by such an alien may result in the issuance of a Notice of Intent to Fine and the imposition of civil money penalties.

§ 1270.3 Penalties.

(a) *Criminal penalties.* Nothing in section 274C of the Act shall be construed to diminish or qualify any of the penalties available for activities prohibited by this section but proscribed as well in title 18, United States Code.

(b) *Civil penalties.* A person or entity may face civil penalties for a violation of section 274C of the Act. Civil penalties may be imposed by the Service or by an administrative law judge for violations under section 274C of the Act. The Service may charge multiple violations of section 274C of the Act in a single Notice of Intent to Fine, and may impose separate penalties for each such unlawful act in a single proceeding or determination. However, in determining whether an offense is a first offense or a subsequent offense, a finding of more than one violation in the course of a single proceeding or determination will be counted as a single offense.

(1) A respondent found by the Service or an administrative law judge to have violated section 274C of the Act shall be subject to an order:

(i) To cease and desist from such behavior; and

(ii) To pay a civil penalty as follows:

(A) *First offense.* Not less than $250 and not exceeding $2,000 for each fraudulent document or each proscribed activity described in section 274C(a)(1) through (a)(4) of the Act before September 29, 1999, and not less than $275 and not exceeding $2,200, for each fraudulent document or each proscribed activity on or after September 29, 1999.

(B) *Subsequent offenses.* Not less than $2,000 and not more than $5,000 for each fraudulent document or each proscribed activity described in section 274C(a)(1) through (a)(4) of the Act before September 29, 1999, and not less than $2,200 and not exceeding $5,500, for each fraudulent document or each proscribed activity occurring on or after September 29, 1999.

(2) Where an order is issued to a respondent composed of distinct, physically separate subdivisions each of which provides separately for the hiring, recruiting, or referring for a fee for employment (without reference to the practices of, and not under the common control of or common control with, another subdivision), each subdivision shall be considered a separate person or entity.

[57 FR 33866, July 31, 1992, as amended at 64 FR 47101, Aug. 30, 1999]

PART 1274a—CONTROL OF EMPLOYMENT OF ALIENS

Subpart A—Employer Requirements

Sec.

Subpart B [Reserved]

AUTHORITY: 8 U.S.C. 1101, 1103, 1324a.

SOURCE: 52 FR 16221, May 1, 1987, unless otherwise noted. Duplicated from part 274a at 68 FR 9844, Feb. 28, 2003.

EDITORIAL NOTE: Nomenclature changes to part 1274a appear at 68 FR 9846, Feb. 28, 2003, and 68 FR 10359, Mar. 5, 2003.

Subpart A—Employer Requirements

§ 1274a.1 Employer requirements.

(a) *Applicable regulations.* The regulations of the Department of Homeland Security (DHS) relating to the implementation of the employment eligibility and verification provisions of section 274A of the Immigration and Nationality Act (Act) are contained in 8 CFR part 274a.

(b) *Adjudication of civil penalty proceedings.* The procedures for hearings before an administrative law judge relating to civil penalties sought by DHS under section 274A of the Act are contained in 28 CFR part 68. The regulations governing employment eligibility and verification in 8 CFR part 274a are applicable to hearings before an administrative law judge and, to the extent relevant, to cases before an immigration judge or the Board of Immigration Appeals.

[74 FR 2340, Jan. 15, 2009]

§ 1274a.9 Enforcement procedures.

(a)–(d) [Reserved]

(e) *Request for Hearing Before an Administrative Law Judge.* If a respondent contests the issuance of a Notice of Intent to Fine, the respondent must file with the DHS, within thirty days of the service of the Notice of Intent to Fine, a written request for a hearing before an Administrative Law Judge. Any written request for a hearing submitted in a foreign language must be accompanied by an English language translation. A request for a hearing is not deemed to be filed until received by the DHS office designated in the Notice of Intent to Fine. In computing the thirty day period prescribed by this section, the day of service of the Notice of Intent to Fine shall not be included. If the Notice of Intent to Fine was served by ordinary mail, five days shall be added to the prescribed thirty day period. In the request for a hearing, the respondent may, but is not required to, respond to each allegation listed in the Notice of Intent to Fine.

(f) *Failure to file a request for a hearing.* If the respondent does not file a request for a hearing in writing within thirty days of the date of service of a Notice of Intent to Fine (thirty-five days if served by ordinary mail), the final order issued by DHS shall not be subject to a hearing before an administrative law judge under 28 CFR part 68.

[52 FR 16221, May 1, 1987, as amended at 53 FR 8613, Mar. 16, 1988; 55 FR 25935, June 25, 1990; 56 FR 41786, Aug. 23, 1991; 61 FR 52236, Oct. 7, 1996; 74 FR 2340, Jan. 15, 2009]

§ 1274a.10 Penalties.

The regulations pertaining to the imposition of penalties for violations of the provisions of section 274A of the Immigration and Nationality Act are contained in 8 CFR part 274a and 28 CFR part 68.

[73 FR 10136, Feb. 26, 2008]

§ 1274a.11 [Reserved]

Subpart B [Reserved]

PART 1280—IMPOSITION AND COLLECTION OF FINES

AUTHORITY: 8 U.S.C. 1103, 1221, 1223, 1227, 1229, 1253, 1281, 1283, 1284, 1285, 1286, 1322, 1323, 1330; 66 Stat. 173, 195, 197, 201, 203, 212, 219, 221–223, 226, 227, 230; Pub. L. 101–410, 104 Stat. 890, as amended by Pub. L. 104–134, 110 Stat. 1321.

SOURCE: 22 FR 9807, Dec. 6, 1957, unless otherwise noted. Duplicated from part 280 at 68 FR 9844, Feb. 28, 2003.

EDITORIAL NOTE: Nomenclature changes to part 1280 appear at 68 FR 9846, Feb. 28, 2003.

§ 1280.1 Review of fines and civil monetary penalties imposed by DHS.

(a) *Applicable regulations.* The regulations of the Department of Homeland Security (DHS) relating to the imposition of certain fines and civil monetary penalties under provisions of the Immigration and Nationality Act, including sections 231(g), 234, 240B(d), 241(d) and (e), 243(c)(1), 251(d), 254(a), 255, 256, 257, 271(a), 272(a), 273(b), 274D, and 275(b), are contained in 8 CFR part 280.

(b) *Adjudication of civil monetary penalty proceedings.* The Board of Immigration Appeals (Board) has appellate authority to review DHS decisions involving fines and civil monetary penalties imposed under 8 CFR part 280, as provided under 8 CFR part 1003. The regulations in 8 CFR part 280 governing the imposition of certain fines and civil monetary penalties are applicable in such proceedings before the Board.

(c) *Civil monetary penalties under sections 274A, 274B, or 274C.* For regulations relating to civil monetary penalties imposed under sections 274A, 274B, or 274C of the Act, *see* 8 CFR parts 274a and 1274a and 28 CFR part 68.

[76 FR 74630, Dec. 1, 2011]

PART 1287—FIELD OFFICERS; POWERS AND DUTIES

AUTHORITY: 8 U.S.C. 1103, 1182, 1225, 1226, 1251, 1252, 1357.

SOURCE: Duplicated from part 287 at 68 FR 9845, Feb. 28, 2003.

EDITORIAL NOTE: Nomenclature changes to part 1287 appear at 68 FR 9846, Feb. 28, 2003.

§ 1287.4 Subpoena.

(a) *Who may issue—(1) Criminal or civil investigations.* For provisions relating to the authority of immigration officers to issue a subpoena requiring the production of records and evidence for use in criminal or civil investigations, *see* 8 CFR 287.4(a)(1).

(2) *Proceedings other than naturalization proceedings—(i) Prior to commencement of proceedings.* For provisions relating to who may issue a subpoena requiring the attendance of witnesses or the production of documentary evidence, or both, for use in any proceeding under this title, other than under 8 CFR part 335, or any application made ancillary to the proceeding, *see* 8 CFR 287.4(a)(2)(i).

(ii) *Subsequent to commencement of any proceeding.* (A) In any proceeding under this chapter and in any proceeding ancillary thereto, an immigration judge having jurisdiction over the matter may, upon his/her own volition or upon application of government counsel, the alien, or other party affected, issue subpoenas requiring the attendance of witnesses or for the production of books, papers and other documentary evidence, or both.

(B) *Application for subpoena.* A party applying for a subpoena shall be required, as a condition precedent to its issuance, to state in writing or at the proceeding, what he/she expects to prove by such witnesses or documentary evidence, and to show affirmatively that he/she has made diligent effort, without success, to produce the same.

(C) *Issuance of subpoena.* Upon being satisfied that a witness will not appear and testify or produce documentary evidence and that the witness' evidence is essential, the immigration judge shall issue a subpoena.

(D) *Appearance of witness.* If the witness is at a distance of more than 100 miles from the place of the proceeding, the subpoena shall provide for the witnesses' appearance at the Service office nearest to the witness to respond to oral or written interrogatories, unless the Service indicates that there is no objection to bringing the witness the distance required to enable him/her to testify in person.

(b) *Form of subpoena.* All subpoenas shall be issued on Form I–138.

(1) *Criminal or civil investigations.* The subpoena shall command the person or entity to which it is addressed to attend and to give testimony at a time or place specified. A subpoena shall also command the person or entity to which it is addressed to produce the books, papers, or documents specified in the subpoena. A subpoena may direct the taking of a deposition before an officer of the Service.

(2) *Proceedings other than naturalization proceedings.* Every subpoena issued under the provisions of this section shall state the title of the proceeding and shall command the person to whom it is directed to attend and to give testimony at a time and place specified. A subpoena shall also command the person to whom it is directed to produce the books, papers, or documents specified in the subpoena. A subpoena may direct the making of a deposition before an officer of the Service.

(c) *Service.* For provisions relating to who may serve a subpoena issued under this section, *see* 8 CFR 287.4(c).

(d) *Invoking aid of court.* If a witness neglects or refuses to appear and testify as directed by the subpoena served upon him or her in accordance with the provisions of this section, the immigration judge issuing the subpoena shall request the United States Attorney for the district in which the subpoena was issued to report such neglect or refusal to the United States District Court and to request such court to issue an order requiring the witness to appear and testify and to produce the books, papers, or documents designated in the subpoena.

[50 FR 30134, July 24, 1985; 50 FR 47205, Nov. 15, 1985, as amended at 60 FR 56937, Nov. 13, 1995; 62 FR 10390, Mar. 6, 1997; 67 FR 39260, June 7, 2002; 69 FR 44907, July 28, 2004]

§ 1287.6 Proof of official records.

(a) *Domestic.* In any proceeding under this chapter, an official record or entry therein, when admissible for any purpose, shall be evidenced by an official publication thereof, or by a copy attested by the official having legal custody of the record or by an authorized deputy.

(b) *Foreign: Countries not Signatories to Convention.* (1) In any proceeding under this chapter, an official record or entry therein, when admissible for any purpose, shall be evidenced by an official publication thereof, or by a copy attested by an officer so authorized. This attested copy in turn may but need not be certified by any authorized foreign officer both as to the genuineness of the signature of the attesting officer and as to his/her official position. The signature and official position of this certifying foreign officer may then likewise be certified by any other foreign officer so authorized, thereby creating a chain of certificates.

(2) The attested copy, with the additional foreign certificates if any, must be certified by an officer in the Foreign Service of the United States, stationed in the foreign country where the record is kept. This officer must certify the genuineness of the signature and the official position either of (i) the attesting officer; or (ii) any foreign officer whose certification of genuineness of signature and official position relates directly to the attestation or is in a chain of certificates of genuineness of signature and official position relating to the attestation.

(c) *Foreign: Countries Signatory to Convention Abolishing the Requirement of Legislation for Foreign Public Document.* (1) In any proceeding under this chapter, a public document or entry therein, when admissible for any purpose, may be evidenced by an official publication, or by a copy properly certified under the Convention. To be properly certified, the copy must be accompanied by a certificate in the form dictated by the Convention. This certificate must be signed by a foreign officer so authorized by the signatory country, and it must certify (i) the authenticity of the signature of the person signing the document; (ii) the capacity in which that person acted, and (iii) where appropriate, the identity of the seal or stamp which the document bears.

(2) No certification is needed from an officer in the Foreign Service of public documents.

(3) In accordance with the Convention, the following are deemed to be public documents:

(i) Documents emanating from an authority or an official connected with the courts of tribunals of the state, including those emanating from a public prosecutor, a clerk of a court or a process server;

(ii) Administrative documents;

(iii) Notarial acts; and

(iv) Official certificates which are placed on documents signed by persons in their private capacity, such as official certificates recording the registration of a document or the fact that it was in existence on a certain date, and official and notarial authentication of signatures.

(4) In accordance with the Convention, the following are deemed not to be public documents, and thus are subject to the more stringent requirements of § 1287.6(b) above:

(i) Documents executed by diplomatic or consular agents; and

(ii) Administrative documents dealing directly with commercial or customs operations.

(d) *Canada.* In any proceedings under this chapter, an official record or entry therein, issued by a Canadian governmental entity within the geographical boundaries of Canada, when admissible for any purpose, shall be evidenced by a certified copy of the original record attested by the official having legal custody of the record or by an authorized deputy.

[50 FR 37834, Sept. 18, 1985, as amended at 54 FR 39337, Sept. 26, 1989; 54 FR 48851, Nov. 28, 1989]

PART 1292—REPRESENTATION AND APPEARANCES

IN GENERAL

AUTHORITY: 8 U.S.C. 1103, 1362.

SOURCE: Duplicated from part 292 at 68 FR 9845, Feb. 28, 2003.

EDITORIAL NOTE: Nomenclature changes to part 1292 appear at 68 FR 9846, Feb. 28, 2003, and 68 FR 10360, Mar. 5, 2003.

IN GENERAL

§ 1292.1 Representation of others.

(a) A person entitled to representation may be represented by any of the following:

(1) *Attorneys in the United States.* Any attorney as defined in § 1001.1(f) of this chapter and who, once the registration requirements in paragraph (f) of this section have taken effect, is registered to practice with the Executive Office for Immigration Review.

(2) *Law students and law graduates not yet admitted to the bar.* A law student who is enrolled in an accredited U.S. law school, or a graduate of an accredited U.S. law school who is not yet admitted to the bar, provided that:

(i) He or she is appearing at the request of the person entitled to representation;

(ii) In the case of a law student, he or she has filed a statement that he or she is participating, under the direct supervision of a faculty member, licensed attorney, or accredited representative, in a legal aid program or clinic conducted by a law school or non-profit organization, and that he or she is appearing without direct or indirect remuneration from the alien he or she represents;

(iii) In the case of a law graduate, he or she has filed a statement that he or she is appearing under the supervision of a licensed attorney or accredited representative and that he or she is appearing without direct or indirect remuneration from the alien he or she represents; and

(iv) The law student's or law graduate's appearance is permitted by the official before whom he or she wishes to appear (namely an immigration judge, district director, officer-in-charge, regional director, the Commissioner, or the Board). The official or officials may require that a law student be accompanied by the supervising faculty member, attorney, or accredited representative.

(3) *Reputable individuals.* Any reputable individual of good moral character, provided that:

(i) He is appearing on an individual case basis, at the request of the person entitled to representation;

(ii) He is appearing without direct or indirect renumeration and files a written declaration to that effect;

(iii) He has a pre-existing relationship or connection with the person entitled to representation (e.g., as a relative, neighbor, clergyman, business associate or personal friend), provided that such requirement may be waived, as a matter of administrative discretion, in cases where adequate representation would not otherwise be available; and

(iv) His appearance is permitted by the official before whom he wished to appear (namely, a special inquiry officer, district director, officer-in-charge, regional commissioner, the Commissioner, or the Board), provided that such permission shall not be granted with respect to any individual who regularly engages in immigration and naturalization practice or preparation, or holds himself out to the public as qualified to do so.

(4) *Accredited representative.* An individual whom EOIR has authorized to represent immigration clients on behalf of a recognized organization, and whose period of accreditation is current and has not expired. A partially accredited representative is authorized to practice solely before DHS. A fully accredited representative is authorized to practice before DHS, and upon registration, to practice before the Immigration Courts and the Board.

(5) *Accredited officials.* An accredited official, in the United States, of the government to which an alien owes allegiance, if the official appears solely in his official capacity and with the alien's consent.

(b) *Persons formerly authorized to practice.* A person, other than a representative of an organization described in § 1292.2 of this chapter, who on December 23, 1952, was authorized to practice before the Board and the Service may continue to act as a representative, subject to the provisions of § 1292.3 of this chapter.

(c) *Former employees.* No person previously employed by the Department of Justice shall be permitted to act as a representative in any case in violation of the provisions of 28 CFR 45.735–7.

(d) *Amicus curiae.* The Board may grant permission to appear, on a case-by-case basis, as amicus curiae, to an attorney or to an organization represented by an attorney, if the public interest will be served thereby.

(e) Except as set forth in this section, no other person or persons shall represent others in any case.

(f) *Registration requirement for attorneys and accredited representatives.* The Director or his designee is authorized to register, and establish procedures for registering, attorneys and accredited representatives, specified in paragraph (a) of this section, as a condition of practice before immigration judges or the Board of Immigration Appeals. Such registration procedures will include a requirement for electronic registration and that each registrant validate his or her identity by presenting photo identification. The Director or his designee may administratively suspend from practice before the immigration judges and the Board any attorney or accredited representative who fails to provide the following required registration information: name, business address(es), business telephone number(s), date of birth, email address, bar admission information (if applicable), and recognized organization (if applicable), or who, after having provided that information, fails to present photo identification or comply with any other validation requirements implemented by the Director. After such a system has been established, an immigration judge may, under extraordinary and rare circumstances, permit an unregistered attorney or accredited representative to appear at one hearing if the immigration judge first acquires from the attorney or accredited representative, on the record, the required registration information. An unregistered attorney or accredited representative who is permitted to appear at a hearing in such circumstances must complete the electronic registration process without delay after the hearing at which he or she is permitted to appear.

[40 FR 23271, May 29, 1975, as amended at 53 FR 7728, Mar. 10, 1988; 55 FR 49251, Nov. 27, 1990; 61 FR 53610, Oct. 15, 1996; 62 FR 23635, May 1, 1997; 73 FR 76927, Dec. 18, 2008; 78 FR 19408, Apr. 1, 2013; 81 FR 92367, Dec. 19, 2016]

§ 1292.2 [Reserved]

§ 1292.3 Conduct for practitioners and recognized organizations—rules and procedures.

Practitioners, as defined in § 1003.101(b) of this chapter, and recognized organizations are subject to the imposition of sanctions as provided in 8 CFR part 1003, subpart G, § 1003.101 *et seq.*, and 8 CFR 292.3 (pertaining to practice before DHS).

[81 FR 92367, Dec. 19, 2016]

§ 1292.4 Appearances.

(a) An appearance shall be filed on the appropriate form by the attorney or representative appearing in each case. During Immigration Judge or Board proceedings, withdrawal and/or substitution of counsel is permitted only in accordance with §§ 1003.16 and 1003.36 respectively. During proceedings before the Service, substitution may be permitted upon the written withdrawal of the attorney or representative of record, or upon notification of the new attorney or representative. When an appearance is made by a person acting in a representative capacity, his or her personal appearance or signature shall constitute a representation that under the provisions of this chapter he or she is authorized and qualified to represent. Further proof of authority to act in a representative capacity may be required. A notice of appearance entered in application or petition proceedings must be signed by the applicant or petitioner to authorize representation in order for the appearance to be recognized by the Service.

(b) *Availability of records.* During the time a case is pending, and except as otherwise provided in § 103.2(b) of 8 CFR chapter I, a party to a proceeding or his attorney or representative shall be permitted to examine the record of proceeding in a Service office. He may, in conformity with § 103.10 of 8 CFR chapter I, obtain copies of Service records or information therefrom and copies of documents or transcripts of evidence furnished by him. Upon request, he may in addition, be loaned a copy of the testimony and exhibits contained in the record of proceeding upon giving his receipt for such copies and pledging that it will be surrendered upon final disposition of the case or upon demand. If extra copies of exhibits do not exist, they shall not be furnished free on loan; however, they shall be made available for copying or purchase of copies as provided in § 103.10 of 8 CFR chapter I.

[23 FR 2673, Apr. 23, 1958, as amended at 32 FR 9633, July 4, 1967; 52 FR 2941, Jan. 29, 1987; 59 FR 1466, Jan. 11, 1994]

§ 1292.5 Service upon and action by attorney or representative of record.

(a) *Representative capacity.* Whenever a person is required by any of the provisions of this chapter to give or be given notice; to serve or be served with any paper other than a warrant of arrest or a subpoena; to make a motion; to file or submit an application or other document; or to perform or waive the performance of any act, such notice, service, motion, filing, submission, performance, or waiver shall be given by or to, served by or upon, made by, or requested of the attorney or representative of record, or the person himself if unrepresented.

(b) *Right to representation.* Whenever an examination is provided for in this chapter, the person involved shall have the right to be represented by an attorney or representative who shall be permitted to examine or cross-examine such person and witnesses, to introduce evidence, to make objections which shall be stated succinctly and entered on the record, and to submit briefs. Provided, that nothing in this paragraph shall be construed to provide any applicant for admission in either primary or secondary inspection the right to representation, unless the applicant for admission has become the focus of a criminal investigation and has been taken into custody.

[37 FR 11471, June 8, 1972 and 45 FR 81733, Dec. 12, 1980; 46 FR 2025, Jan. 8, 1981; 58 FR 49911, Sept. 24, 1993]

§ 1292.6 Interpretation.

Interpretations of §§ 1292.1 through 1292.6 will be made by the Board, subject to the provisions of part 1003 of this chapter. Interpretations of §§ 1292.11 through 1292.20 will be made by the OLAP Director.

[81 FR 92367, Dec. 19, 2016]

RECOGNITION OF ORGANIZATIONS AND ACCREDITATION OF NON-ATTORNEY REPRESENTATIVES

§ 1292.11 Recognition of an organization.

(a) *In general.* The OLAP Director, in the exercise of discretion, may recognize an eligible organization to provide representation through accredited representatives who appear on behalf of clients before the Immigration Courts, the Board, and DHS, or DHS alone. The OLAP Director will determine whether an organization is eligible for recognition. To be eligible for recognition, the organization must establish that:

(1) The organization is a non-profit religious, charitable, social service, or similar organization that provides immigration legal services primarily to low-income and indigent clients within the United States, and, if the organization charges fees, has a written policy for accommodating clients unable to pay fees for immigration legal services;

(2) The organization is a Federal tax-exempt organization established in the United States;

(3) The organization is simultaneously applying to have at least one employee or volunteer of the organization approved as an accredited representative by the OLAP Director and at least one application for accreditation is concurrently approved, unless the organization is seeking renewal of recognition and has an accredited representative or is seeking renewal of recognition on inactive status as described in § 1292.16(i);

(4) The organization has access to adequate knowledge, information, and experience in all aspects of immigration law and procedure; and

(5) The organization has designated an authorized officer to act on behalf of the organization.

(b) *Proof of status as non-profit religious, charitable, social service, or similar organization established in the United States and service to low-income and indigent clients.* The organization must submit: A copy of its organizing documents, including a statement of its mission or purpose; a declaration from its authorized officer attesting that it serves primarily low-income and indigent clients; a summary of the legal services to be provided; if it charges fees for legal services, fee schedules and organizational policies or guidance regarding fee waivers or reduced fees based on financial need; and its annual budget. The organization may also submit additional documentation to demonstrate non-profit status and service to primarily low-income and indigent individuals, such as reports prepared for funders or information about other free or low-cost immigration-related services that it provides (*e.g.*, educational or outreach events).

(c) *Annual budget.* The organization must submit its annual budget for providing immigration legal services for the current year and, if available, its annual budget for providing immigration legal services for the prior year. If the annual budgets for both the current and prior years are unavailable, the organization must submit its projected annual budget for the upcoming year. The annual budget should describe how the organization is funded and include information about the organization's operating expenses and sources of revenue for providing immigration legal services. Sources of revenue may include, but are not limited to, grants, fees, donations, or dues.

(d) *Proof of tax-exempt status.* The organization must submit a copy of its currently valid IRS tax-exemption determination letter, alternative documentation to establish Federal tax-exempt status, or proof that is has applied for Federal tax-exempt status.

(e) *Proof of knowledge, information, and experience.* The organization must submit: A description of the immigration legal services that the organization seeks to offer; a description of the legal resources to which the organization has access; an organizational chart showing names, titles, and supervisors of immigration legal staff members; a description of the qualifications, experience, and breadth of immigration knowledge of these staff members, including, but not limited to resumes, letters of recommendation, certifications, and a list of all relevant, formal immigration-related trainings attended by staff members; and any agreement or proof of a formal arrangement entered into with non-staff immigration practitioners and recognized organizations for consultations or technical legal assistance.

(f) *Validity period of recognition.* Recognition is valid for a period of six years from the date of the OLAP Director's approval of recognition, unless the organization has been granted conditional recognition. Conditional recognition is granted to an organization that has not been recognized previously, that has Federal tax-exempt status pending, or that has been approved for recognition after recognition was previously terminated pursuant to § 1292.17 or 8 CFR 1003.101 *et seq.* Conditional recognition is valid for two years from the date of the OLAP Director's approval of conditional recognition. Any organization's recognition is subject to being terminated pursuant to § 1292.17 or upon the issuance of disciplinary sanctions (termination or revocation) under 8 CFR 1003.101 *et seq.*

[81 FR 92367, Dec. 19, 2016]

§ 1292.12 Accreditation of representatives.

(a) *In general.* Only recognized organizations, or organizations simultaneously applying for recognition, may request accreditation of individuals. The OLAP Director, in the exercise of discretion, may approve accreditation of an eligible individual as a representative of a recognized organization for either full or partial accreditation. An individual who receives full accreditation may represent clients before the Immigration Courts, the Board, and DHS. An individual who receives partial accreditation may represent clients only before DHS. In the request for accreditation, the organization must specify whether it seeks full or partial accreditation and establish eligibility for accreditation for the individual. To establish eligibility for accreditation, an organization must demonstrate that the individual for whom the organization seeks accreditation:

(1) Has the character and fitness to represent clients before the Immigration Courts and the Board, or DHS, or before all three authorities. Character and fitness includes, but is not limited to, an examination of factors such as: Criminal background; prior acts involving dishonesty, fraud, deceit, or misrepresentation; past history of neglecting professional, financial, or legal obligations; and current immigration status that presents an actual or perceived conflict of interest;

(2) Is employed by or is a volunteer of the organization;

(3) Is not an attorney as defined in 8 CFR 1001.1(f);

(4) Has not resigned while a disciplinary investigation or proceeding is pending and is not subject to any order disbarring, suspending, enjoining, restraining, or otherwise restricting the individual in the practice of law or representation before a court or any administrative agency;

(5) Has not been found guilty of, or pleaded guilty or nolo contendere to, a serious crime, as defined in 8 CFR 1003.102(h), in any court of the United States, or of any State, possession, territory, commonwealth, or the District of Columbia, or of a jurisdiction outside of the United States; and

(6) Possesses broad knowledge and adequate experience in immigration law and procedure. If an organization seeks full accreditation for an individual, it must establish that the individual also possesses skills essential for effective litigation.

(b) *Request for accreditation.* To establish that an individual satisfies the requirements of paragraph (a) of this section, the organization must submit a request for accreditation (Form EOIR–31A and supporting documents). The request for accreditation must be signed by the authorized officer and the individual to be accredited, both attesting that the individual satisfies these requirements.

(c) *Proof of knowledge and experience.* To establish that the individual satisfies the requirement in paragraph (a)(6) of this section, the organization must submit with its request for accreditation, at minimum: A description of the individual's qualifications, including education and immigration law experience; letters of recommendation from at least two persons familiar with the individual's qualifications; and documentation of all relevant, formal immigration-related training, including a course on the fundamentals of immigration law, procedure, and practice.

An organization must also submit documentation that an individual for whom the organization seeks full accreditation has formal training, education, or experience related to trial and appellate advocacy.

(d) *Validity period of accreditation.* Accreditation is valid for a period of three years from the date of the OLAP Director's approval of accreditation, unless the organization's recognition or the representative's accreditation is terminated pursuant to § 1292.17 or the organization or the representative is subject to disciplinary sanctions (termination, revocation, suspension, or disbarment) under 8 CFR 1003.101 *et seq.*

(e) *Change in accreditation.* An organization may request to change the accreditation of a representative from partial to full accreditation at any time during the validity period of accreditation or at renewal. Such a request will be treated as a new, initial request for full accreditation and must comply with this section.

[81 FR 92367, Dec. 19, 2016]

§ 1292.13 Applying for recognition of organizations or accreditation of representatives.

(a) *In general.* An organization applying for recognition or accreditation of a representative must submit a request for recognition (Form EOIR–31) or a request for accreditation (Form EOIR–31A) to the OLAP Director with proof of service of a copy of the request on the appropriate USCIS office(s) in the jurisdictions where the organization offers or intends to offer immigration legal services. An organization must submit a separate request for accreditation (Form EOIR–31A) for each individual for whom it seeks accreditation. To determine whether an organization has established eligibility for recognition or accreditation of a representative, the OLAP Director shall review all information contained in the request for recognition or accreditation and may review any publicly available information or any other information that OLAP may obtain or possess about the organization, its authorized officer, or the proposed representative or may have received pursuant to paragraphs (b), (c), and (d) of this section. Unfavorable information obtained by the OLAP Director that may be relied upon to disapprove a recognition or accreditation request, if not previously served on the organization, shall be disclosed to the organization, and the organization shall be given a reasonable opportunity to respond. Prior to determining whether to approve or disapprove a request for recognition or accreditation, the OLAP Director may request additional information from the organization pertaining to the eligibility requirements for recognition or accreditation. The OLAP Director, in writing, shall inform the organization and each USCIS office in the jurisdictions where the organization offers or intends to offer immigration legal services of the determination approving or disapproving the organization's request for recognition or accreditation of a representative. The OLAP Director may, in the exercise of discretion, extend the deadlines provided in this section. The OLAP Director is authorized to allow requests, notifications, recommendations, and determinations described in this section to be made electronically.

(b) *USCIS recommendation and investigation.* Within 30 days from the date of service of the request for recognition or accreditation, the USCIS office served with the request may submit to the OLAP Director a recommendation for approval or disapproval of the request for recognition or accreditation, including an explanation for the recommendation, or may request from the OLAP Director a specified period of additional time, generally no more than 30 days, in which to conduct an investigation or otherwise obtain relevant information regarding the organization, its authorized officer, or any individual for whom the organization seeks accreditation. The OLAP Director shall inform the organization if the OLAP Director grants a request from USCIS for additional time to conduct an investigation, or if, in the exercise of discretion, the OLAP Director has requested that USCIS conduct an investigation of the organization, its authorized officer, or any individual for whom the organization seeks accreditation. USCIS must submit any recommendation with proof of service of a copy of the recommendation on the organization. Within 30 days of service of an unfavorable recommendation, the organization may file with the OLAP Director a response to the unfavorable recommendation, along with proof of service of a copy of such response on the USCIS office that provided the recommendation.

(c) *ICE recommendation.* Upon receipt of a request for recognition or accreditation, the OLAP Director may request a recommendation or information from ICE in the jurisdictions where the organization offers or intends to offer immigration legal services regarding the organization, its authorized officer, or any individual for whom the organization seeks accreditation. Within 30 days from the date of receipt of the OLAP Director's request, ICE may make a recommendation or disclose information regarding the organization, its authorized officer, or individuals for whom the organization seeks accreditation. ICE must submit any recommendation with proof of service of a copy of the recommendation on the organization. Within 30 days of service of an unfavorable recommendation, the organization may file with the OLAP Director a response to the unfavorable recommendation, along with proof of service of a copy of such response on the ICE office that provided the recommendation. The OLAP Director, in writing, shall inform ICE of the determination approving or disapproving the organization's request for recognition or accreditation of a representative.

(d) *EOIR investigation.* Upon receipt of a request for recognition or accreditation, the OLAP Director may request that the EOIR disciplinary counsel or anti-fraud officer conduct an investigation into the organization, its authorized officer, or any individual for whom the organization seeks accreditation. Within 30 days from the date of receipt of the OLAP Director's request, the EOIR disciplinary counsel or anti-fraud officer may disclose to the OLAP Director information, including complaints, preliminary inquiries, warning letters, and admonitions, relating to the organization, its authorized officer, or any individual for whom the organization seeks accreditation.

(e) *Finality of decision.* The OLAP Director's determination to approve a request for recognition or accreditation is final. An organization whose request for recognition or accreditation was disapproved may make one request for reconsideration of the disapproval within 30 days of the determination. An organization whose request for recognition or accreditation was disapproved, or whose request for reconsideration after disapproval and, if applicable, request for administrative review pursuant to §1292.18 was denied, may submit a new request for recognition or accreditation at any time unless otherwise prohibited.

[81 FR 92367, Dec. 19, 2016]

§1292.14 Reporting, recordkeeping, and posting requirements for recognized organizations.

(a) *Duty to report changes.* A recognized organization has a duty to promptly notify the OLAP Director in writing or electronically of changes in the organization's contact information, changes to any material information the organization provided in Form EOIR–31, Form EOIR–31A, or the documents submitted in support thereof, or changes that otherwise materially relate to the organization's eligibility for recognition or the eligibility for accreditation of any of the organization's accredited representatives. These changes may include alterations to: The organization's name, address, telephone number, Web site address, email address, or the designation of the authorized officer of the organization; an accredited representative's name or employment or volunteer status with the organization; and the organization's structure, including a merger of organizations that have already been individually accorded recognition, or a change in non-profit or Federal tax-exempt status.

(b) *Recordkeeping.* A recognized organization must compile each of the following records in a timely manner, and retain them for a period of six years from the date the record is created, as long as the organization remains recognized:

(1) The organization's immigration legal services fee schedule, if the organization charges any fees for immigration legal services, for each office or location where such services are provided; and

(2) An annual summary of immigration legal services provided by the organization, which includes: The total number of clients served (whether through client intakes, applications prepared and filed with DHS, cases in which its attorneys or accredited representatives appeared before the Immigration Courts or, if applicable, the Board, or referrals to attorneys or other organizations) and clients to whom it provided services at no cost; a general description of the immigration legal services and other immigration-related services (*e.g.*, educational or outreach events) provided; a statement regarding whether services were provided pro bono or clients were charged in accordance with a fee schedule and organizational policies or guidance regarding fee waivers and reduced fees; and a list of the offices or locations where the immigration legal services were provided. The summary should not include any client-specific or client-identifying information. OLAP may require the organization to submit such records to it or DHS upon request.

(c) *Posting.* The OLAP Director shall have the authority to issue public notices regarding recognition and accreditation and to require recognized organizations and accredited representatives to post such public notices. Information contained in the public notices shall be limited to: The names and validity periods of a recognized organization and its accredited representatives, the requirements for recognition and accreditation, and the means to complain about a recognized organization or accredited representative.

[81 FR 92367, Dec. 19, 2016]

§ 1292.15 Extension of recognition and accreditation to multiple offices or locations of an organization.

Upon approving an initial request for recognition or a request for renewal of recognition, or at any other time, the OLAP Director, in the OLAP Director's discretion, may extend the recognition of an organization to any office or location where the organization offers services. To request extension of recognition, an organization that is seeking or has received recognition must submit a Form EOIR–31 that identifies the name and address of the organization's headquarters or designated office and the name and address of each other office or location for which the organization seeks extension of recognition. The organization must also provide a declaration from its authorized officer attesting that it periodically conducts inspections of each such office or location, exercises supervision and control over its accredited representatives at those offices and locations, and provides access to adequate legal resources at each such office or location. OLAP may require an organization to seek separate recognition for an office or location of the organization, for example, when a subordinate office or location has distinct operations, management structure, or funding sources from the organization's headquarters. The OLAP Director's determination to extend recognition to the offices or locations identified in Form EOIR–31 permits the organization's accredited representatives to provide immigration legal services out of those offices or locations. OLAP will post the address of each office or location to which recognition has been extended on the roster of recognized organizations and accredited representatives. The OLAP Director is authorized to allow requests and determinations described in this section to be made electronically.

[81 FR 92367, Dec. 19, 2016]

§ 1292.16 Renewal of recognition and accreditation.

(a) *In general.* To retain its recognition and the accreditation of its representatives after the conclusion of the validity period specified in § 1292.11(f) or § 1292.12(d), an organization must submit a request for renewal of its recognition or the accreditation of its representatives (Form EOIR–31, Form EOIR–31A, and supporting documents). In the exercise of discretion, as provided in paragraph (i) of this section, the OLAP Director may approve an organization's request for renewal of recognition without a currently approved accredited representative.

(b) *Timing of renewal*—(1) *Recognition.* An organization requesting renewal of recognition must submit the request on or before the sixth anniversary date of the organization's last approval or renewal of recognition or, for a conditionally recognized organization, on or before the second anniversary of the approval date of the conditional recognition. Any request must include proof of service of a copy of the request on the appropriate USCIS office(s) in the jurisdictions where the organization offers or intends to offer immigration legal services.

(2) *Accreditation.* An organization requesting renewal of accreditation of its representative must submit the request on or before the third anniversary date of the representative's last approval or renewal of accreditation, with proof of service of a copy of the request on the appropriate USCIS office(s) in the jurisdictions where the organization offers or intends to offer immigration legal services.

(3) The OLAP Director, in the OLAP Director's discretion, may grant additional time to submit a request for renewal or accept a request for renewal filed out of time. The recognition of the organization and the accreditation of any representatives for whom the organization timely requests renewal shall remain valid pending the OLAP Director's consideration of the renewal requests, except in the case of an interim suspension pursuant to 8 CFR 1003.111.

(c) *Renewal requirements*—(1) *Recognition.* The request for renewal of recognition must establish that the organization remains eligible for recognition under §1292.11(a), include the records specified in §1292.14(b) regarding fee schedules and the summary of immigration legal services provided that the organization compiled since the last approval of recognition, and describe any unreported changes that impact eligibility for recognition from the date of the last approval of recognition.

(2) *Accreditation.* Each request for renewal of accreditation must establish that the individual remains eligible for accreditation under §1292.12(a) and has continued to receive formal training in immigration law and procedure commensurate with the services the organization provides and the duration of the representative's accreditation.

(d) *Recommendations and investigations.* Each USCIS office served with a request for renewal of recognition or a request for renewal of accreditation may submit to the OLAP Director a recommendation for approval or disapproval of that request pursuant to §1292.13(b). The OLAP Director may request a recommendation from ICE or an investigation from the EOIR disciplinary counsel or anti-fraud officer, pursuant to §1292.13(c) and (d).

(e) *Renewal process.* The OLAP Director shall review all information contained in the requests and may review any publicly available information or any other information that OLAP may possess about the organization, its authorized officer, or any individual for whom the organization seeks accreditation or renewal of accreditation or that OLAP may have received pursuant to §1292.13(b) through (d). Unfavorable information obtained by the OLAP Director that may be relied upon to disapprove a recognition or accreditation request, if not previously served on the organization, shall be disclosed to the organization, and the organization shall be given a reasonable opportunity to respond. Prior to determining whether to approve or disapprove a request for renewal of recognition or accreditation, the OLAP Director may request additional information from the organization pertaining to the eligibility requirements for recognition or accreditation. The OLAP Director, in writing, shall inform the organization and the appropriate DHS office(s) in the jurisdictions where the organization offers or intends to offer immigration legal services of the determination to approve or disapprove a request for renewal of recognition. If the OLAP Director renews recognition, the OLAP Director shall issue a written determination approving or disapproving each request for accreditation or renewal of accreditation. The OLAP Director is authorized to allow requests, notifications, recommendations, and determinations described in this section to be made electronically.

(f) *Finality of decision.* The OLAP Director's determination to approve a request to renew recognition or accreditation is final. An organization whose request for renewal of recognition or accreditation of its representatives has been disapproved may make one request for reconsideration of the disapproval within 30 days of the determination. The recognition of the organization and the accreditation of any representatives for whom the organization timely requests reconsideration shall remain valid pending the OLAP Director's consideration of the reconsideration request, except in the case of an interim suspension pursuant to 8 CFR 1003.111. An organization whose recognition or accreditation of its representatives is terminated because the organization's request to renew recognition or accreditation is disapproved or whose request for reconsideration after disapproval and, if applicable, request for administrative review pursuant to § 1292.18 was denied, may submit a new request for recognition and accreditation at any time unless otherwise prohibited.

(g) *Validity period of recognition and accreditation after renewal.* After renewal of recognition, the recognition of the organization is valid for a period of six years from the date of the OLAP Director's determination to renew recognition, unless the organization's recognition is terminated pursuant to § 1292.17 or the organization is subject to disciplinary sanctions (*i.e.*, termination or revocation) under 8 CFR 1003.101 *et seq.* After renewal of accreditation, the accreditation of a representative is valid for a period of three years from the date of the OLAP Director's determination to renew accreditation, unless the organization's recognition or the representative's accreditation is terminated pursuant to § 1292.17 or the organization or the representative is subject to disciplinary sanctions (termination, revocation, suspension, or disbarment) under 8 CFR 1003.101 *et seq.*

(h) *Organizations and representatives recognized and accredited prior to January 18, 2017*—(1) *Applicability.* An organization or representative that received recognition or accreditation prior to January 18, 2017, through the Board under former § 1292.2 is subject to the provisions of this part. Such an organization or representative shall continue to be recognized or accredited until the organization is required to request renewal of its recognition and accreditation of its representatives as required by paragraphs (h)(2) and (3) of this section and pending the OLAP Director's determination on the organization's request for renewal if such a request is timely made, unless the organization's recognition or the representative's accreditation is terminated pursuant to § 1292.17 or the organization or the representative is subject to disciplinary sanctions (termination, revocation, suspension, or disbarment) under 8 CFR 1003.101 *et seq.*

(2) *Renewal of recognition.* To retain its recognition, an organization that received recognition prior to January 18, 2017, must request renewal of its recognition pursuant to this section on or before the following dates:

(i) Within 1 year of January 18, 2017, if the organization does not have an accredited representative on the effective date of this regulation;

(ii) Within 2 years of January 18, 2017, if the organization is not required to submit a request for renewal at an earlier date under paragraph (h)(2)(i) of this section, and the organization has been recognized for more than 10 years as of the effective date of this regulation; or

(iii) Within 3 years of January 18, 2017, if the organization is not required to submit a request for renewal at an earlier date under paragraph (h)(2)(i) or (ii) of this section.

(3) *Renewal of accreditation.* To retain the accreditation of its representatives who were accredited prior to January 18, 2017, an organization must request renewal of accreditation of its representatives on or before the date that the representative's accreditation would have expired under the prior rule.

(i) *Inactive status.* An organization shall be placed on inactive status if it has no currently approved accredited representative, and it promptly notified OLAP that it no longer has an accredited representative, as required by § 1292.14(a). An organization on inactive status is precluded from providing immigration legal services unless it has an attorney on staff. An organization shall be on inactive status for two years from the date the organization is placed on inactive status in order for the organization to apply for and have approved the accreditation of one or more representatives. If an organization on inactive status is subject to renewal while on inactive status, the organization must request renewal of recognition at the time required for renewal. The OLAP Director, in the OLAP Director's discretion, may approve a request to renew an organization's recognition without a currently approved accredited representative, provided that the organization satisfies the renewal requirements under § 1292.16(c)(1) and attests that it intends to apply for and have approved the accreditation of one or more representatives within two years from the date of renewal. An organization renewed under such circumstances shall be on inactive status for two years from the date of renewal in order for the organization to apply for and have approved the accreditation of one or more representatives. The OLAP Director, in the OLAP Director's discretion, may grant an organization additional time on inactive status beyond the time limits provided in this paragraph.

[81 FR 92367, Dec. 19, 2016]

§ 1292.17 Administrative termination of recognition and accreditation.

(a) *In general.* The OLAP Director may administratively terminate an organization's recognition or a representative's accreditation and remove the organization or representative from the recognition and accreditation roster. Prior to issuing a determination to administratively terminate recognition or accreditation, the OLAP Director may request, in writing or electronically, information from the organization, representative, DHS, or EOIR, regarding the bases for termination. The OLAP Director, in writing or electronically, shall inform the organization or the representative, as applicable, of the determination to terminate the organization's recognition or the representative's accreditation, and the reasons for the determination.

(b) *Bases for administrative termination of recognition.* The bases for termination of recognition under this section are:

(1) An organization did not submit a request to renew its recognition at the time required for renewal;

(2) An organization's request for renewal of recognition is disapproved or request for reconsideration after disapproval and if applicable, request for administrative review pursuant to § 1292.18 is denied;

(3) All of the organization's accredited representatives have been terminated pursuant to this section or suspended or disbarred pursuant to 8 CFR 1003.101 *et seq.*, and the organization is not on inactive status as described in § 1292.16(i);

(4) An organization submits a written request to the OLAP Director for termination of its recognition;

(5) An organization fails to comply with its reporting, recordkeeping, or posting requirements under § 1292.14, after being notified of the deficiencies and having an opportunity to respond;

(6) An organization fails to maintain eligibility for recognition under § 1292.11, after being notified of the deficiencies and having an opportunity to respond; or

(7) An organization on inactive status fails to have an individual approved as an accredited representative within the time provided under § 1292.16(i).

(c) *Bases for administrative termination of accreditation.* The bases for termination of accreditation under this section are:

(1) An individual's organization has had its recognition terminated pursuant to this section or terminated or revoked pursuant to 8 CFR 1003.101 *et seq.;*

(2) An organization does not submit a request for renewal of the individual's accreditation at the time required for renewal;

(3) An organization's request for renewal of an individual's accreditation is disapproved or request for reconsideration after disapproval and, if applicable, request for administrative review pursuant to § 1292.18, is denied;

(4) An accredited representative submits a written request to the OLAP Director for termination of the representative's accreditation;

(5) An organization submits a written request to the OLAP Director for termination of the accreditation of one or more of its representatives; or

(6) An individual fails to maintain eligibility for accreditation under § 1292.12, after the individual's organization has been notified of the deficiencies and has had an opportunity to respond.

(d) *Request for reconsideration.* An organization whose recognition is terminated pursuant to paragraph (b)(5) or (6) of this section or the accreditation of its representative(s) is terminated pursuant to paragraph (c)(6) of this section may make one request for reconsideration of the disapproval within 30 days of the determination. The recognition of the organization and the accreditation of any representatives for whom the organization timely requests reconsideration shall remain valid pending the OLAP Director's consideration of the reconsideration request. The OLAP Director is authorized to allow requests and determinations described in this paragraph to be made electronically.

(e) *Effect of administrative termination of recognition.* The OLAP Director's determination to terminate recognition is final as of the date of service of the administrative termination notice. Upon service or electronic delivery of an administrative termination of recognition notice to the organization's accredited representatives by OLAP, the organization's representatives shall no longer be authorized to represent clients before the Immigration Courts, the Board, or DHS on behalf of that organization, but the notice shall not affect an individual's accreditation through another recognized organization unless otherwise specified. An organization whose recognition is terminated may submit a new request for recognition at any time after its termination unless otherwise prohibited.

(f) *Effect of administrative termination of accreditation.* The OLAP Director's determination to terminate accreditation is final as of the date of service of the administrative termination notice. Upon service or electronic delivery of an administrative termination of accreditation notice to an accredited representative by OLAP, the individual shall no longer be authorized to represent clients before the Immigration Courts, the Board, or DHS on behalf of that organization, but the notice does not affect the individual's accreditation through another organization unless specified in the determination. An organization may submit a request for accreditation on behalf of any individual whose accreditation has been terminated unless otherwise prohibited.

[81 FR 92367, Dec. 19, 2016]

§ 1292.18 Administrative review of denied requests for reconsideration.

(a) *Authority of the Director.* The Director has the discretionary authority to review a request for reconsideration pursuant to § 1292.13(e), § 1292.16(f), or § 1292.17(d) that has been denied. The Director may delegate this authority to any officer within EOIR, except the OLAP Director.

(1) An organization whose request for reconsideration pursuant to § 1292.13(e), § 1292.16(f), or § 1292.17(d) has been denied may request administrative review from the Director within ten (10) days of the denial, identifying the alleged factual or legal errors in the underlying determination. The request for administrative review shall be submitted to the OLAP Director, who will forward the request to the Director.

(2) The Director may review a request for reconsideration pursuant to § 1292.13(e), § 1292.16(f), or § 1292.17(d) that has been denied on the Director's own initiative by issuing a notification of administrative review within ten (10) days of the denial. This notification shall state the issues to be reviewed.

(3) The recognition of the organization and the accreditation of any representatives that are subject to administrative review as described in this section shall remain valid pending the Director's consideration of the request, except in the case of an interim suspension pursuant to 8 CFR 1003.111.

(b) *Review.* The Director shall review the record before OLAP and the organization's request for administrative review, and, in the Director's discretion, may request additional filings from the organization. The Director may affirm the denial of the request for reconsideration or vacate the denial and return the matter to the OLAP Director for further action consistent with the Director's determination. The Director may not approve a request for recognition or accreditation or renewal thereof.

[81 FR 92367, Dec. 19, 2016]

§ 1292.19 Complaints against recognized organizations and accredited representatives.

(a) *Filing complaints.* Any individual may submit a complaint to EOIR or DHS that a recognized organization or accredited representative has engaged in behavior that is a ground of termination or otherwise contrary to the public interest. Complaints must be submitted in writing or on Form EOIR–44 to the EOIR disciplinary counsel or DHS disciplinary counsel and must state in detail the information that supports the basis for the complaint, including, but not limited to: The name and address of each complainant; the name and address of each recognized organization and accredited representative that is a subject of the complaint; the nature of the conduct or behavior; the individuals involved; and any other relevant information. EOIR disciplinary counsel and DHS disciplinary counsel shall notify each other of any complaint that pertains, in whole or in part, to a matter involving the other agency. EOIR may authorize that complaints submitted to the EOIR disciplinary counsel may be made electronically.

(b) *Preliminary inquiry.* Upon receipt of the complaint, the EOIR disciplinary counsel shall initiate a preliminary inquiry. If a complaint is filed by a client or former client of a recognized organization or any of its accredited representatives, the complainant waives the attorney-client privilege and any other privilege relating to the representation to the extent necessary to conduct a preliminary inquiry and any subsequent proceedings based thereon. If the EOIR disciplinary counsel determines that a complaint is without merit, no further action will be taken. The EOIR disciplinary counsel may also, in the disciplinary counsel's discretion, dismiss a complaint if the complainant fails to comply with reasonable requests for information or documentation. If the EOIR disciplinary counsel determines that a complaint has merit, the EOIR disciplinary counsel may disclose information concerning the complaint or the preliminary inquiry to the OLAP Director pursuant to 8 CFR 1003.108(a)(3) or initiate disciplinary proceedings through the filing of a Notice of Intent to Discipline pursuant to 8 CFR 1003.105. If a complaint involves allegations that a recognized organization or accredited representative engaged in criminal conduct, the EOIR disciplinary counsel shall refer the matter to DHS or the appropriate United States Attorney, and if appropriate, to the Inspector General, the Federal Bureau of Investigation, or other law enforcement agency.

[81 FR 92367, Dec. 19, 2016]

§ 1292.20 Roster of recognized organizations and accredited representatives.

The OLAP Director shall maintain a roster of recognized organizations and their accredited representatives. An electronic copy of the roster shall be made available to the public and updated periodically.

[81 FR 92367, Dec. 19, 2016]

SUBCHAPTER C—NATIONALITY REGULATIONS

PART 1299—IMMIGRATION REVIEW FORMS

AUTHORITY: 8 U.S.C. 1103, 1252, 1429, 1443; Homeland Security Act of 2002, Pub. L. 107–296.

SOURCE: 68 FR 9845, Feb. 28, 2003, unless otherwise noted.

§ 1299.1 Use of immigration forms.

In addition to forms prepared by the Executive Office for Immigration Review, the Executive Office for Immigration Review, immigration judges, the Board of Immigration Appeals, and administrative law judges use forms listed under 8 CFR chapter I, part 299.

§ 1299.2 Specific immigration review forms.

The Director of the Executive Office for Immigration Review may designate the specific version of a form listed in 8 CFR chapter I, part 299, which shall be utilized in filings before the immigration judges, the Board of Immigration Appeals, and administrative law judges.

PART 1337—OATH OF ALLEGIANCE

AUTHORITY: 8 U.S.C. 1103, 1443, 1448; 8 CFR part 2.

SOURCE: Duplicated from part 337 at 68 FR 9845, Feb. 28, 2003.

EDITORIAL NOTE: Nomenclature changes to part 1337 appear at 68 FR 9846, Feb. 28, 2003, and 68 FR 10360, Mar. 5, 2003.

§ 1337.1 Oath of allegiance.

(a) *Form of oath.* Except as otherwise provided in the Act and after receiving notice from the district director that such applicant is eligible for naturalization pursuant to § 335.3 of 8 CFR chapter I, an applicant for naturalization shall, before being admitted to citizenship, take in a public ceremony held within the United States the following oath of allegiance, to a copy of which the applicant shall affix his or her signature:

I hereby declare, on oath, that I absolutely and entirely renounce and abjure all allegiance and fidelity to any foreign prince, potentate, state, or sovereignty, of whom or which I have heretofore been a subject or citizen; that I will support and defend the Constitution and laws of the United States of America against all enemies, foreign and domestic; that I will bear true faith and allegiance to the same; that I will bear arms on behalf of the United States when required by the law; that I will perform noncombatant service in the Armed Forces of the United States when required by the law; that I will perform work of national importance under civilian direction when required by the law; and that I take this obligation freely, without any mental reservation or purpose of evasion; so help me God.

(b) *Alteration of form of oath; affirmation in lieu of oath.* In those cases in which a petitioner or applicant for naturalization is exempt from taking the oath prescribed in paragraph (a) of this section in its entirety, the inapplicable clauses shall be deleted and the oath shall be taken in such altered form. When a petitioner or applicant for naturalization, by reason of religious training and belief (or individual interpretation thereof), or for other reasons of good conscience, cannot take the oath prescribed in paragraph (a) of this section with the words "on oath" and "so help me God" included, the words "and solemnly affirm" shall be substituted for the words "on oath," the words "so help me God" shall be deleted, and the oath shall be taken in such modified form. Any reference to 'oath of allegiance' in 8 CFR chapter I is understood to mean equally 'affirmation of allegiance' as described in this paragraph.

(c) *Obligations of oath.* A petitioner or applicant for naturalization shall, before being naturalized, establish that it is his or her intention, in good faith, to assume and discharge the obligations of the oath of allegiance, and that his or her attitude toward the Constitution and laws of the United States renders him or her capable of fulfilling the obligations of such oath.

(d) *Renunciation of title or order of nobility.* A petitioner or applicant for naturalization who has borne any hereditary title or has been of any of the orders of nobility in any foreign state shall, in addition to taking the oath of allegiance prescribed in paragraph (a) of this section, make under oath or affirmation in public an express renunciation of such title or order of nobility, in the following form:

(1) I further renounce the title of (give title or titles) which I have heretofore held; or

(2) I further renounce the order of nobility (give the order of nobility) to which I have heretofore belonged.

[22 FR 9824, Dec. 6, 1957, as amended at 24 FR 2584, Apr. 3, 1959; 32 FR 13756, Oct. 3, 1967; 56 FR 50499, Oct. 7, 1991]

§ 1337.2 Oath administered by the Immigration and Naturalization Service or an Immigration Judge.

(a) *Public ceremony.* An applicant for naturalization who has elected to have his or her oath of allegiance administered by the Service or an Immigration Judge and is not subject to the exclusive oath administration authority of an eligible court pursuant to section 310(b) of the Act shall appear in person in a public ceremony, unless such appearance is specifically excused under the terms and conditions set forth in this part. Such ceremony shall be held at a time and place designated by the Service or the Executive Office for Immigration Review within the United States and within the jurisdiction where the application for naturalization was filed, or into which the application for naturalization was transferred pursuant to § 335.9 of 8 CFR chapter I. Such ceremonies shall be conducted at regular intervals as frequently as necessary to ensure timely naturalization, but in all events at least once monthly where it is required to minimize unreasonable delays. Such ceremonies shall be presented in such a manner as to preserve the dignity and significance of the occasion. District directors shall ensure that ceremonies conducted by the Service in their districts, inclusive of those held by suboffice managers, are in keeping with the Model Plan for Naturalization Ceremonies. Organizations traditionally involved in activities surrounding the ceremony should be encouraged to participate in Service-administered ceremonies by local arrangement.

(b) *Authority to administer oath of allegiance.* The authority of the Attorney General to administer the oath of allegiance shall be delegated to Immigration Judges and to the following officers of the Service: The Commissioner; district directors; deputy district directors; officers-in-charge; assistant officers-in-charge; or persons acting in behalf of such officers due to their absence or because their positions are vacant. In exceptional cases where the district director or officer-in-charge determines that it is appropriate for employees of a different rank to conduct ceremonies, the district director or officer-in-charge may make a request through the Commissioner to the Assistant Commissioner, Adjudications, for permission to delegate such authority. The request shall furnish the reasons for seeking exemption from the requirements of this paragraph. The Commissioner may delegate such authority to such other officers of the Service or the Department of Justice as he or she may deem appropriate.

(c) *Execution of questionnaire.* Immediately prior to being administered the oath of allegiance, each applicant shall complete the questionnaire on Form N–445. Each completed Form N–445 shall be reviewed by an officer of the Service who may question the applicant regarding the information thereon. If derogatory information is revealed, the applicant's name shall be removed from the list of eligible persons as provided in § 335.5 of 8 CFR chapter I and he or she shall not be administered the oath.

[60 FR 37803, July 24, 1995]

§ 1337.3 Expedited administration of oath of allegiance.

(a) An applicant may be granted an expedited oath administration ceremony by either the court or the Service upon demonstrating sufficient cause. In determining whether to grant an expedited oath administration ceremony, the court or the district director shall consider special circumstances of a compelling or humanitarian nature. Special circumstances may include but are not limited to:

(1) The serious illness of the applicant or a member of the applicant's family;

(2) Permanent disability of the applicant sufficiently incapacitating as to prevent the applicant's personal appearance at a scheduled ceremony;

(3) The developmental disability or advanced age of the applicant which would make appearance at a scheduled ceremony inappropriate; or

(4) Urgent or compelling circumstances relating to travel or employment determined by the court or the Service to be sufficiently meritorious to warrant special consideration.

(b) Courts exercising exclusive authority may either hold an expedited oath administration ceremony or refer the applicant to the Service in order for either the Immigration Judge or the Service to conduct an oath administration ceremony, if an expedited judicial oath administration ceremony is impractical. The court shall inform the district director in writing of its decision to grant the applicant an expedited oath administration ceremony and that the court has relinquished exclusive jurisdiction as to that applicant.

(c) All requests for expedited administration of the oath of allegiance shall be made in writing to either the court or the Service. Such requests shall contain sufficient information to substantiate the claim of special circumstances to permit either the court or the Service to properly exercise the discretionary authority to grant the relief sought. The court or the Service may seek verification of the validity of the information provided in the request. If the applicant submits a written request to the Service, but is awaiting an oath administration ceremony by a court pursuant to § 1337.8, the Service promptly shall provide the court with a copy of the request without reaching a decision on whether to grant or deny the request.

[60 FR 37804, July 24, 1995]

§ 1337.4 When requests for change of name granted.

When the court has granted the petitioner's change of name request, the petitioner shall subscribe his or her new name to the written oath of allegiance.

[56 FR 50500, Oct. 7, 1991]

§§ 1337.5–1337.6 [Reserved]

§ 1337.7 Information and assignment of individuals under exclusive jurisdiction.

(a) No later than at the time of the examination on the application pursuant to § 335.2 of 8 CFR chapter I, an employee of the Service shall advise the applicant of his or her right to elect the site for the administration of the oath of allegiance, subject to the exclusive jurisdiction provision of § 310.3(d) of 8 CFR chapter I. In order to assist the applicant in making an informed decision, the Service shall advise the applicant of the upcoming Immigration Judge or Service conducted and judicial ceremonies at which the applicant may appear, if found eligible for naturalization.

(b) An applicant whose application has been approved by the Service who is subject to the exclusive jurisdiction of a court pursuant to § 310.2(d) of 8 CFR chapter I, shall be advised of the next available court ceremony and provided with a written notice to appear at that ceremony. If the applicant is subject to the exclusive jurisdiction of more than one court exercising exclusive jurisdiction, the applicant will be informed of the upcoming ceremonies in each affected court. The applicant shall decide which court he or she wishes to administer the oath of allegiance.

[58 FR 49915, Sept. 24, 1993, as amended at 60 FR 37804, July 24, 1995]

§ 1337.8 Oath administered by the courts.

(a) *Notification of election.* An applicant for naturalization not subject to the exclusive jurisdiction of § 310.2(d) of 8 CFR chapter I shall notify the Service at the time of the filing of, or no later than at the examination on, the application of his or her election to have the oath of allegiance administered in an appropriate court having jurisdiction over the applicant's place of residence.

(b) *Certification of eligibility*—(1) *Exclusive jurisdiction.* In those instances falling within the exclusive jurisdiction provision of section 310(b)(1)(B) of the Act, the Service shall notify the court of the applicant's eligibility for admission to United States citizenship by submitting to the clerk of court Form N–646 within ten (10) days of the approval of the application.

(2) *Non-exclusive jurisdiction.* In those instances in which the applicant has elected to have the oath administered in a court ceremony, the Service shall notify the clerk of court, in writing, using Form N–646, that the applicant has been determined by the Attorney General to be eligible for admission to United States citizenship upon taking the requisite oath of allegiance and renunciation in a public ceremony. If a scheduled hearing date is not available at the time of the notification, Form N–646 shall indicate that the applicant has not been scheduled for a ceremony and the applicant shall be informed in writing that the application has been approved but no ceremony date is yet available.

(c) *Preparation of lists.* (1) At or prior to the oath administration ceremony the representative attending the ceremony shall submit to the court on Form N–647, in duplicate, lists of persons to be administered the oath of allegiance and renunciation. After the ceremony, and after any required amendments and notations have been made therein, the clerk of court shall sign the lists.

(2) The originals of all court lists specified in this section shall be filed permanently in the court, and the duplicates returned by the clerk of court to the appropriate Service office for retention by such office. The same disposition shall be made of any list presented to, but not approved by, the court.

(d) *Personal representation of the government at oath administration ceremonies.* An oath administration ceremony shall be attended by a representative of the Service, who shall review each applicant's completed questionnaire Form N–445. If necessary, the Service representative shall question the applicant regarding the information thereon. If the questioning reveals derogatory information, the applicant's name shall be removed from the list of eligible persons as provided in § 335.5 of 8 CFR chapter I and the court shall not administer the oath to such applicant.

(e) *Written report in lieu of personal representation.* If it is impracticable for a Service representative to be present at a judicial oath administration ceremony, written notice of that fact shall be given by the Service to the court. The applicants to be administered the oath shall be listed on the appropriate forms prescribed in paragraph (d) of this section. The forms, memoranda, and certificates of naturalization shall be transmitted to the clerk of court, who shall submit the appropriate lists to the court.

(f) *Withdrawal from court.* An applicant for naturalization not subject to the exclusive jurisdiction of § 310.3(d) of 8 CFR chapter I, who has elected to have the oath administered in a court oath ceremony, may, for good cause shown, request that his or her name be removed from the list of persons eligible to be administered the oath at a court oath ceremony and request that the oath be administered in a ceremony conducted by an Immigration Judge or the Service. Such request shall be in writing to the Service office which granted the application and shall cite the reasons for the request. The district director or officer-in-charge shall consider the good cause shown and the best interests of the applicant in making a decision. If it is determined that the applicant shall be permitted to withdraw his or her name from the court ceremony, the Service shall give written notice to the court of the applicant's withdrawal, and the applicant shall be scheduled for the next available oath ceremony, conducted by an Immigration Judge or the Service, as if he or she had never elected the court ceremony.

[58 FR 49915, Sept. 24, 1993, as amended at 60 FR 37804, July 24, 1995]

§ 1337.9 Effective date of naturalization.

(a) An applicant for naturalization shall be deemed a citizen of the United States as of the date on which the applicant takes the prescribed oath of allegiance, administered either by the Service or an Immigration Judge in an administrative ceremony or in a ceremony conducted by an appropriate court under § 1337.8 of 8 CFR chapter I.

(b) [Reserved]

[56 FR 50500, Oct. 7, 1991, as amended at 60 FR 37804, July 24, 1995; 66 FR 32147, June 13, 2001]

§ 1337.10 Failure to appear for oath administration ceremony.

An applicant who fails to appear without good cause for more than one oath administration ceremony for which he or she was duly notified shall be presumed to have abandoned his or her intent to be naturalized. Such presumption shall be regarded as the receipt of derogatory information, and the procedures contained in § 335.5 of 8 CFR chapter I shall be followed.

[58 FR 49916, Sept. 24, 1993]

PARTS 1338–1399 [RESERVED]

FINDING AIDS

A list of CFR titles, subtitles, chapters, subchapters and parts and an alphabetical list of agencies publishing in the CFR are included in the CFR Index and Finding Aids volume to the Code of Federal Regulations which is published separately and revised annually.

Table of CFR Titles and Chapters

(Revised as of January 1, 2019)

Title 1—General Provisions

Title 2—Grants and Agreements

Title 2—Grants and Agreements—Continued

Title 3—The President

Title 4—Accounts

Title 5—Administrative Personnel

Chap.	
XXVIII	Department of Justice (Parts 3800—3899)
XXIX	Federal Communications Commission (Parts 3900—3999)
XXX	Farm Credit System Insurance Corporation (Parts 4000—4099)
XXXI	Farm Credit Administration (Parts 4100—4199)
XXXIII	Overseas Private Investment Corporation (Parts 4300—4399)
XXXIV	Securities and Exchange Commission (Parts 4400—4499)
XXXV	Office of Personnel Management (Parts 4500—4599)
XXXVI	Department of Homeland Security (Parts 4600—4699)
XXXVII	Federal Election Commission (Parts 4700—4799)
XL	Interstate Commerce Commission (Parts 5000—5099)
XLI	Commodity Futures Trading Commission (Parts 5100—5199)
XLII	Department of Labor (Parts 5200—5299)
XLIII	National Science Foundation (Parts 5300—5399)
XLV	Department of Health and Human Services (Parts 5500—5599)
XLVI	Postal Rate Commission (Parts 5600—5699)
XLVII	Federal Trade Commission (Parts 5700—5799)
XLVIII	Nuclear Regulatory Commission (Parts 5800—5899)
XLIX	Federal Labor Relations Authority (Parts 5900—5999)
L	Department of Transportation (Parts 6000—6099)
LII	Export-Import Bank of the United States (Parts 6200—6299)
LIII	Department of Education (Parts 6300—6399)
LIV	Environmental Protection Agency (Parts 6400—6499)
LV	National Endowment for the Arts (Parts 6500—6599)
LVI	National Endowment for the Humanities (Parts 6600—6699)
LVII	General Services Administration (Parts 6700—6799)
LVIII	Board of Governors of the Federal Reserve System (Parts 6800—6899)
LIX	National Aeronautics and Space Administration (Parts 6900—6999)
LX	United States Postal Service (Parts 7000—7099)
LXI	National Labor Relations Board (Parts 7100—7199)
LXII	Equal Employment Opportunity Commission (Parts 7200—7299)
LXIII	Inter-American Foundation (Parts 7300—7399)
LXIV	Merit Systems Protection Board (Parts 7400—7499)
LXV	Department of Housing and Urban Development (Parts 7500—7599)
LXVI	National Archives and Records Administration (Parts 7600—7699)
LXVII	Institute of Museum and Library Services (Parts 7700—7799)
LXVIII	Commission on Civil Rights (Parts 7800—7899)
LXIX	Tennessee Valley Authority (Parts 7900—7999)
LXX	Court Services and Offender Supervision Agency for the District of Columbia (Parts 8000—8099)
LXXI	Consumer Product Safety Commission (Parts 8100—8199)
LXXIII	Department of Agriculture (Parts 8300—8399)

Title 5—Administrative Personnel—Continued

Chap.	
LXXIV	Federal Mine Safety and Health Review Commission (Parts 8400—8499)
LXXVI	Federal Retirement Thrift Investment Board (Parts 8600—8699)
LXXVII	Office of Management and Budget (Parts 8700—8799)
LXXX	Federal Housing Finance Agency (Parts 9000—9099)
LXXXIII	Special Inspector General for Afghanistan Reconstruction (Parts 9300—9399)
LXXXIV	Bureau of Consumer Financial Protection (Parts 9400—9499)
LXXXVI	National Credit Union Administration (Parts 9600—9699)
XCVII	Department of Homeland Security Human Resources Management System (Department of Homeland Security—Office of Personnel Management) (Parts 9700—9799)
XCVIII	Council of the Inspectors General on Integrity and Efficiency (Parts 9800—9899)
XCIX	Military Compensation and Retirement Modernization Commission (Parts 9900—9999)
C	National Council on Disability (Parts 10000—10049)
CI	National Mediation Board (Part 10101)

Title 6—Domestic Security

I	Department of Homeland Security, Office of the Secretary (Parts 1—199)
X	Privacy and Civil Liberties Oversight Board (Parts 1000—1099)

Title 7—Agriculture

	SUBTITLE A—OFFICE OF THE SECRETARY OF AGRICULTURE (PARTS 0—26)
	SUBTITLE B—REGULATIONS OF THE DEPARTMENT OF AGRICULTURE
I	Agricultural Marketing Service (Standards, Inspections, Marketing Practices), Department of Agriculture (Parts 27—209)
II	Food and Nutrition Service, Department of Agriculture (Parts 210—299)
III	Animal and Plant Health Inspection Service, Department of Agriculture (Parts 300—399)
IV	Federal Crop Insurance Corporation, Department of Agriculture (Parts 400—499)
V	Agricultural Research Service, Department of Agriculture (Parts 500—599)
VI	Natural Resources Conservation Service, Department of Agriculture (Parts 600—699)
VII	Farm Service Agency, Department of Agriculture (Parts 700—799)
VIII	Grain Inspection, Packers and Stockyards Administration (Federal Grain Inspection Service), Department of Agriculture (Parts 800—899)

Chap.	
IX	Agricultural Marketing Service (Marketing Agreements and Orders; Fruits, Vegetables, Nuts), Department of Agriculture (Parts 900—999)
X	Agricultural Marketing Service (Marketing Agreements and Orders; Milk), Department of Agriculture (Parts 1000—1199)
XI	Agricultural Marketing Service (Marketing Agreements and Orders; Miscellaneous Commodities), Department of Agriculture (Parts 1200—1299)
XIV	Commodity Credit Corporation, Department of Agriculture (Parts 1400—1499)
XV	Foreign Agricultural Service, Department of Agriculture (Parts 1500—1599)
XVI	Rural Telephone Bank, Department of Agriculture (Parts 1600—1699)
XVII	Rural Utilities Service, Department of Agriculture (Parts 1700—1799)
XVIII	Rural Housing Service, Rural Business-Cooperative Service, Rural Utilities Service, and Farm Service Agency, Department of Agriculture (Parts 1800—2099)
XX	Local Television Loan Guarantee Board (Parts 2200—2299)
XXV	Office of Advocacy and Outreach, Department of Agriculture (Parts 2500—2599)
XXVI	Office of Inspector General, Department of Agriculture (Parts 2600—2699)
XXVII	Office of Information Resources Management, Department of Agriculture (Parts 2700—2799)
XXVIII	Office of Operations, Department of Agriculture (Parts 2800—2899)
XXIX	Office of Energy Policy and New Uses, Department of Agriculture (Parts 2900—2999)
XXX	Office of the Chief Financial Officer, Department of Agriculture (Parts 3000—3099)
XXXI	Office of Environmental Quality, Department of Agriculture (Parts 3100—3199)
XXXII	Office of Procurement and Property Management, Department of Agriculture (Parts 3200—3299)
XXXIII	Office of Transportation, Department of Agriculture (Parts 3300—3399)
XXXIV	National Institute of Food and Agriculture (Parts 3400—3499)
XXXV	Rural Housing Service, Department of Agriculture (Parts 3500—3599)
XXXVI	National Agricultural Statistics Service, Department of Agriculture (Parts 3600—3699)
XXXVII	Economic Research Service, Department of Agriculture (Parts 3700—3799)
XXXVIII	World Agricultural Outlook Board, Department of Agriculture (Parts 3800—3899)
XLI	[Reserved]
XLII	Rural Business-Cooperative Service and Rural Utilities Service, Department of Agriculture (Parts 4200—4299)

Title 8—Aliens and Nationality

Chap.

I Department of Homeland Security (Immigration and Naturalization) (Parts 1—499)

V Executive Office for Immigration Review, Department of Justice (Parts 1000—1399)

Title 9—Animals and Animal Products

I Animal and Plant Health Inspection Service, Department of Agriculture (Parts 1—199)

II Grain Inspection, Packers and Stockyards Administration (Packers and Stockyards Programs), Department of Agriculture (Parts 200—299)

III Food Safety and Inspection Service, Department of Agriculture (Parts 300—599)

Title 10—Energy

I Nuclear Regulatory Commission (Parts 0—199)

II Department of Energy (Parts 200—699)

III Department of Energy (Parts 700—999)

X Department of Energy (General Provisions) (Parts 1000—1099)

XIII Nuclear Waste Technical Review Board (Parts 1300—1399)

XVII Defense Nuclear Facilities Safety Board (Parts 1700—1799)

XVIII Northeast Interstate Low-Level Radioactive Waste Commission (Parts 1800—1899)

Title 11—Federal Elections

I Federal Election Commission (Parts 1—9099)

II Election Assistance Commission (Parts 9400—9499)

Title 12—Banks and Banking

I Comptroller of the Currency, Department of the Treasury (Parts 1—199)

II Federal Reserve System (Parts 200—299)

III Federal Deposit Insurance Corporation (Parts 300—399)

IV Export-Import Bank of the United States (Parts 400—499)

V (Parts 500—599) [Reserved]

VI Farm Credit Administration (Parts 600—699)

VII National Credit Union Administration (Parts 700—799)

VIII Federal Financing Bank (Parts 800—899)

IX Federal Housing Finance Board (Parts 900—999)

X Bureau of Consumer Financial Protection (Parts 1000—1099)

XI Federal Financial Institutions Examination Council (Parts 1100—1199)

XII Federal Housing Finance Agency (Parts 1200—1299)

XIII Financial Stability Oversight Council (Parts 1300—1399)

Title 12—Banks and Banking—Continued

Chap.	
XIV	Farm Credit System Insurance Corporation (Parts 1400—1499)
XV	Department of the Treasury (Parts 1500—1599)
XVI	Office of Financial Research (Parts 1600—1699)
XVII	Office of Federal Housing Enterprise Oversight, Department of Housing and Urban Development (Parts 1700—1799)
XVIII	Community Development Financial Institutions Fund, Department of the Treasury (Parts 1800—1899)

Title 13—Business Credit and Assistance

I	Small Business Administration (Parts 1—199)
III	Economic Development Administration, Department of Commerce (Parts 300—399)
IV	Emergency Steel Guarantee Loan Board (Parts 400—499)
V	Emergency Oil and Gas Guaranteed Loan Board (Parts 500—599)

Title 14—Aeronautics and Space

I	Federal Aviation Administration, Department of Transportation (Parts 1—199)
II	Office of the Secretary, Department of Transportation (Aviation Proceedings) (Parts 200—399)
III	Commercial Space Transportation, Federal Aviation Administration, Department of Transportation (Parts 400—1199)
V	National Aeronautics and Space Administration (Parts 1200—1299)
VI	Air Transportation System Stabilization (Parts 1300—1399)

Title 15—Commerce and Foreign Trade

	SUBTITLE A—OFFICE OF THE SECRETARY OF COMMERCE (PARTS 0—29)
	SUBTITLE B—REGULATIONS RELATING TO COMMERCE AND FOREIGN TRADE
I	Bureau of the Census, Department of Commerce (Parts 30—199)
II	National Institute of Standards and Technology, Department of Commerce (Parts 200—299)
III	International Trade Administration, Department of Commerce (Parts 300—399)
IV	Foreign-Trade Zones Board, Department of Commerce (Parts 400—499)
VII	Bureau of Industry and Security, Department of Commerce (Parts 700—799)
VIII	Bureau of Economic Analysis, Department of Commerce (Parts 800—899)
IX	National Oceanic and Atmospheric Administration, Department of Commerce (Parts 900—999)
XI	National Technical Information Service, Department of Commerce (Parts 1100—1199)

Title 15—Commerce and Foreign Trade—Continued

Chap.	
XIII	East-West Foreign Trade Board (Parts 1300—1399)
XIV	Minority Business Development Agency (Parts 1400—1499)
	SUBTITLE C—REGULATIONS RELATING TO FOREIGN TRADE AGREEMENTS
XX	Office of the United States Trade Representative (Parts 2000—2099)
	SUBTITLE D—REGULATIONS RELATING TO TELECOMMUNICATIONS AND INFORMATION
XXIII	National Telecommunications and Information Administration, Department of Commerce (Parts 2300—2399) [Reserved]

Title 16—Commercial Practices

I	Federal Trade Commission (Parts 0—999)
II	Consumer Product Safety Commission (Parts 1000—1799)

Title 17—Commodity and Securities Exchanges

I	Commodity Futures Trading Commission (Parts 1—199)
II	Securities and Exchange Commission (Parts 200—399)
IV	Department of the Treasury (Parts 400—499)

Title 18—Conservation of Power and Water Resources

I	Federal Energy Regulatory Commission, Department of Energy (Parts 1—399)
III	Delaware River Basin Commission (Parts 400—499)
VI	Water Resources Council (Parts 700—799)
VIII	Susquehanna River Basin Commission (Parts 800—899)
XIII	Tennessee Valley Authority (Parts 1300—1399)

Title 19—Customs Duties

I	U.S. Customs and Border Protection, Department of Homeland Security; Department of the Treasury (Parts 0—199)
II	United States International Trade Commission (Parts 200—299)
III	International Trade Administration, Department of Commerce (Parts 300—399)
IV	U.S. Immigration and Customs Enforcement, Department of Homeland Security (Parts 400—599) [Reserved]

Title 20—Employees' Benefits

I	Office of Workers' Compensation Programs, Department of Labor (Parts 1—199)
II	Railroad Retirement Board (Parts 200—399)
III	Social Security Administration (Parts 400—499)

Chap.

IV Employees' Compensation Appeals Board, Department of Labor (Parts 500—599)

V Employment and Training Administration, Department of Labor (Parts 600—699)

VI Office of Workers' Compensation Programs, Department of Labor (Parts 700—799)

VII Benefits Review Board, Department of Labor (Parts 800—899)

VIII Joint Board for the Enrollment of Actuaries (Parts 900—999)

IX Office of the Assistant Secretary for Veterans' Employment and Training Service, Department of Labor (Parts 1000—1099)

Title 21—Food and Drugs

I Food and Drug Administration, Department of Health and Human Services (Parts 1—1299)

II Drug Enforcement Administration, Department of Justice (Parts 1300—1399)

III Office of National Drug Control Policy (Parts 1400—1499)

Title 22—Foreign Relations

I Department of State (Parts 1—199)

II Agency for International Development (Parts 200—299)

III Peace Corps (Parts 300—399)

IV International Joint Commission, United States and Canada (Parts 400—499)

V Broadcasting Board of Governors (Parts 500—599)

VII Overseas Private Investment Corporation (Parts 700—799)

IX Foreign Service Grievance Board (Parts 900—999)

X Inter-American Foundation (Parts 1000—1099)

XI International Boundary and Water Commission, United States and Mexico, United States Section (Parts 1100—1199)

XII United States International Development Cooperation Agency (Parts 1200—1299)

XIII Millennium Challenge Corporation (Parts 1300—1399)

XIV Foreign Service Labor Relations Board; Federal Labor Relations Authority; General Counsel of the Federal Labor Relations Authority; and the Foreign Service Impasse Disputes Panel (Parts 1400—1499)

XV African Development Foundation (Parts 1500—1599)

XVI Japan-United States Friendship Commission (Parts 1600—1699)

XVII United States Institute of Peace (Parts 1700—1799)

Title 23—Highways

I Federal Highway Administration, Department of Transportation (Parts 1—999)

Title 23—Highways—Continued

Chap.

II National Highway Traffic Safety Administration and Federal Highway Administration, Department of Transportation (Parts 1200—1299)

III National Highway Traffic Safety Administration, Department of Transportation (Parts 1300—1399)

Title 24—Housing and Urban Development

SUBTITLE A—OFFICE OF THE SECRETARY, DEPARTMENT OF HOUSING AND URBAN DEVELOPMENT (PARTS 0—99)

SUBTITLE B—REGULATIONS RELATING TO HOUSING AND URBAN DEVELOPMENT

I Office of Assistant Secretary for Equal Opportunity, Department of Housing and Urban Development (Parts 100—199)

II Office of Assistant Secretary for Housing-Federal Housing Commissioner, Department of Housing and Urban Development (Parts 200—299)

III Government National Mortgage Association, Department of Housing and Urban Development (Parts 300—399)

IV Office of Housing and Office of Multifamily Housing Assistance Restructuring, Department of Housing and Urban Development (Parts 400—499)

V Office of Assistant Secretary for Community Planning and Development, Department of Housing and Urban Development (Parts 500—599)

VI Office of Assistant Secretary for Community Planning and Development, Department of Housing and Urban Development (Parts 600—699) [Reserved]

VII Office of the Secretary, Department of Housing and Urban Development (Housing Assistance Programs and Public and Indian Housing Programs) (Parts 700—799)

VIII Office of the Assistant Secretary for Housing—Federal Housing Commissioner, Department of Housing and Urban Development (Section 8 Housing Assistance Programs, Section 202 Direct Loan Program, Section 202 Supportive Housing for the Elderly Program and Section 811 Supportive Housing for Persons With Disabilities Program) (Parts 800—899)

IX Office of Assistant Secretary for Public and Indian Housing, Department of Housing and Urban Development (Parts 900—1699)

XII Office of Inspector General, Department of Housing and Urban Development (Parts 2000—2099)

XV Emergency Mortgage Insurance and Loan Programs, Department of Housing and Urban Development (Parts 2700—2799) [Reserved]

XX Office of Assistant Secretary for Housing—Federal Housing Commissioner, Department of Housing and Urban Development (Parts 3200—3899)

XXIV Board of Directors of the HOPE for Homeowners Program (Parts 4000—4099) [Reserved]

XXV Neighborhood Reinvestment Corporation (Parts 4100—4199)

Title 25—Indians

Chap.

I Bureau of Indian Affairs, Department of the Interior (Parts 1—299)

II Indian Arts and Crafts Board, Department of the Interior (Parts 300—399)

III National Indian Gaming Commission, Department of the Interior (Parts 500—599)

IV Office of Navajo and Hopi Indian Relocation (Parts 700—899)

V Bureau of Indian Affairs, Department of the Interior, and Indian Health Service, Department of Health and Human Services (Part 900—999)

VI Office of the Assistant Secretary, Indian Affairs, Department of the Interior (Parts 1000—1199)

VII Office of the Special Trustee for American Indians, Department of the Interior (Parts 1200—1299)

Title 26—Internal Revenue

I Internal Revenue Service, Department of the Treasury (Parts 1—End)

Title 27—Alcohol, Tobacco Products and Firearms

I Alcohol and Tobacco Tax and Trade Bureau, Department of the Treasury (Parts 1—399)

II Bureau of Alcohol, Tobacco, Firearms, and Explosives, Department of Justice (Parts 400—699)

Title 28—Judicial Administration

I Department of Justice (Parts 0—299)

III Federal Prison Industries, Inc., Department of Justice (Parts 300—399)

V Bureau of Prisons, Department of Justice (Parts 500—599)

VI Offices of Independent Counsel, Department of Justice (Parts 600—699)

VII Office of Independent Counsel (Parts 700—799)

VIII Court Services and Offender Supervision Agency for the District of Columbia (Parts 800—899)

IX National Crime Prevention and Privacy Compact Council (Parts 900—999)

XI Department of Justice and Department of State (Parts 1100—1199)

Title 29—Labor

SUBTITLE A—OFFICE OF THE SECRETARY OF LABOR (PARTS 0—99)

SUBTITLE B—REGULATIONS RELATING TO LABOR

I National Labor Relations Board (Parts 100—199)

Title 29—Labor—Continued

Chap.	
II	Office of Labor-Management Standards, Department of Labor (Parts 200—299)
III	National Railroad Adjustment Board (Parts 300—399)
IV	Office of Labor-Management Standards, Department of Labor (Parts 400—499)
V	Wage and Hour Division, Department of Labor (Parts 500—899)
IX	Construction Industry Collective Bargaining Commission (Parts 900—999)
X	National Mediation Board (Parts 1200—1299)
XII	Federal Mediation and Conciliation Service (Parts 1400—1499)
XIV	Equal Employment Opportunity Commission (Parts 1600—1699)
XVII	Occupational Safety and Health Administration, Department of Labor (Parts 1900—1999)
XX	Occupational Safety and Health Review Commission (Parts 2200—2499)
XXV	Employee Benefits Security Administration, Department of Labor (Parts 2500—2599)
XXVII	Federal Mine Safety and Health Review Commission (Parts 2700—2799)
XL	Pension Benefit Guaranty Corporation (Parts 4000—4999)

Title 30—Mineral Resources

I	Mine Safety and Health Administration, Department of Labor (Parts 1—199)
II	Bureau of Safety and Environmental Enforcement, Department of the Interior (Parts 200—299)
IV	Geological Survey, Department of the Interior (Parts 400—499)
V	Bureau of Ocean Energy Management, Department of the Interior (Parts 500—599)
VII	Office of Surface Mining Reclamation and Enforcement, Department of the Interior (Parts 700—999)
XII	Office of Natural Resources Revenue, Department of the Interior (Parts 1200—1299)

Title 31—Money and Finance: Treasury

	SUBTITLE A—OFFICE OF THE SECRETARY OF THE TREASURY (PARTS 0—50)
	SUBTITLE B—REGULATIONS RELATING TO MONEY AND FINANCE
I	Monetary Offices, Department of the Treasury (Parts 51—199)
II	Fiscal Service, Department of the Treasury (Parts 200—399)
IV	Secret Service, Department of the Treasury (Parts 400—499)
V	Office of Foreign Assets Control, Department of the Treasury (Parts 500—599)
VI	Bureau of Engraving and Printing, Department of the Treasury (Parts 600—699)
VII	Federal Law Enforcement Training Center, Department of the Treasury (Parts 700—799)

Title 31—Money and Finance: Treasury—Continued

Title 32—National Defense

Title 33—Navigation and Navigable Waters

Title 34—Education

Title 34—Education—Continued

Chap.	
IV	Office of Career, Technical and Adult Education, Department of Education (Parts 400—499)
V	Office of Bilingual Education and Minority Languages Affairs, Department of Education (Parts 500—599) [Reserved]
VI	Office of Postsecondary Education, Department of Education (Parts 600—699)
VII	Office of Educational Research and Improvement, Department of Education (Parts 700—799) [Reserved]
	SUBTITLE C—REGULATIONS RELATING TO EDUCATION
XI	(Parts 1100—1199) [Reserved]
XII	National Council on Disability (Parts 1200—1299)

Title 35 [Reserved]

Title 36—Parks, Forests, and Public Property

I	National Park Service, Department of the Interior (Parts 1—199)
II	Forest Service, Department of Agriculture (Parts 200—299)
III	Corps of Engineers, Department of the Army (Parts 300—399)
IV	American Battle Monuments Commission (Parts 400—499)
V	Smithsonian Institution (Parts 500—599)
VI	[Reserved]
VII	Library of Congress (Parts 700—799)
VIII	Advisory Council on Historic Preservation (Parts 800—899)
IX	Pennsylvania Avenue Development Corporation (Parts 900—999)
X	Presidio Trust (Parts 1000—1099)
XI	Architectural and Transportation Barriers Compliance Board (Parts 1100—1199)
XII	National Archives and Records Administration (Parts 1200—1299)
XV	Oklahoma City National Memorial Trust (Parts 1500—1599)
XVI	Morris K. Udall Scholarship and Excellence in National Environmental Policy Foundation (Parts 1600—1699)

Title 37—Patents, Trademarks, and Copyrights

I	United States Patent and Trademark Office, Department of Commerce (Parts 1—199)
II	U.S. Copyright Office, Library of Congress (Parts 200—299)
III	Copyright Royalty Board, Library of Congress (Parts 300—399)
IV	National Institute of Standards and Technology, Department of Commerce (Parts 400—599)

Title 38—Pensions, Bonuses, and Veterans' Relief

I	Department of Veterans Affairs (Parts 0—199)
II	Armed Forces Retirement Home (Parts 200—299)

Title 39—Postal Service

Title 40—Protection of Environment

Title 41—Public Contracts and Property Management

Title 41—Public Contracts and Property Management—Continued

Title 42—Public Health

Title 43—Public Lands: Interior

Title 44—Emergency Management and Assistance

Title 45—Public Welfare

Title 45—Public Welfare—Continued

Title 46—Shipping

Title 47—Telecommunication

Title 48—Federal Acquisition Regulations System

Chap.

1 Federal Acquisition Regulation (Parts 1—99)

2 Defense Acquisition Regulations System, Department of Defense (Parts 200—299)

3 Department of Health and Human Services (Parts 300—399)

4 Department of Agriculture (Parts 400—499)

5 General Services Administration (Parts 500—599)

6 Department of State (Parts 600—699)

7 Agency for International Development (Parts 700—799)

8 Department of Veterans Affairs (Parts 800—899)

9 Department of Energy (Parts 900—999)

10 Department of the Treasury (Parts 1000—1099)

12 Department of Transportation (Parts 1200—1299)

13 Department of Commerce (Parts 1300—1399)

14 Department of the Interior (Parts 1400—1499)

15 Environmental Protection Agency (Parts 1500—1599)

16 Office of Personnel Management, Federal Employees Health Benefits Acquisition Regulation (Parts 1600—1699)

17 Office of Personnel Management (Parts 1700—1799)

18 National Aeronautics and Space Administration (Parts 1800—1899)

19 Broadcasting Board of Governors (Parts 1900—1999)

20 Nuclear Regulatory Commission (Parts 2000—2099)

21 Office of Personnel Management, Federal Employees Group Life Insurance Federal Acquisition Regulation (Parts 2100—2199)

23 Social Security Administration (Parts 2300—2399)

24 Department of Housing and Urban Development (Parts 2400—2499)

25 National Science Foundation (Parts 2500—2599)

28 Department of Justice (Parts 2800—2899)

29 Department of Labor (Parts 2900—2999)

30 Department of Homeland Security, Homeland Security Acquisition Regulation (HSAR) (Parts 3000—3099)

34 Department of Education Acquisition Regulation (Parts 3400—3499)

51 Department of the Army Acquisition Regulations (Parts 5100—5199)

52 Department of the Navy Acquisition Regulations (Parts 5200—5299)

53 Department of the Air Force Federal Acquisition Regulation Supplement (Parts 5300—5399) [Reserved]

54 Defense Logistics Agency, Department of Defense (Parts 5400—5499)

57 African Development Foundation (Parts 5700—5799)

61 Civilian Board of Contract Appeals, General Services Administration (Parts 6100—6199)

99 Cost Accounting Standards Board, Office of Federal Procurement Policy, Office of Management and Budget (Parts 9900—9999)

Title 49—Transportation

Chap.

SUBTITLE A—OFFICE OF THE SECRETARY OF TRANSPORTATION (PARTS 1—99)

SUBTITLE B—OTHER REGULATIONS RELATING TO TRANSPORTATION

I Pipeline and Hazardous Materials Safety Administration, Department of Transportation (Parts 100—199)

II Federal Railroad Administration, Department of Transportation (Parts 200—299)

III Federal Motor Carrier Safety Administration, Department of Transportation (Parts 300—399)

IV Coast Guard, Department of Homeland Security (Parts 400—499)

V National Highway Traffic Safety Administration, Department of Transportation (Parts 500—599)

VI Federal Transit Administration, Department of Transportation (Parts 600—699)

VII National Railroad Passenger Corporation (AMTRAK) (Parts 700—799)

VIII National Transportation Safety Board (Parts 800—999)

X Surface Transportation Board (Parts 1000—1399)

XI Research and Innovative Technology Administration, Department of Transportation (Parts 1400—1499) [Reserved]

XII Transportation Security Administration, Department of Homeland Security (Parts 1500—1699)

Title 50—Wildlife and Fisheries

I United States Fish and Wildlife Service, Department of the Interior (Parts 1—199)

II National Marine Fisheries Service, National Oceanic and Atmospheric Administration, Department of Commerce (Parts 200—299)

III International Fishing and Related Activities (Parts 300—399)

IV Joint Regulations (United States Fish and Wildlife Service, Department of the Interior and National Marine Fisheries Service, National Oceanic and Atmospheric Administration, Department of Commerce); Endangered Species Committee Regulations (Parts 400—499)

V Marine Mammal Commission (Parts 500—599)

VI Fishery Conservation and Management, National Oceanic and Atmospheric Administration, Department of Commerce (Parts 600—699)

Alphabetical List of Agencies Appearing in the CFR

(Revised as of January 1, 2019)

Agency	CFR Title, Subtitle or Chapter
Administrative Conference of the United States	1, III
Advisory Council on Historic Preservation	36, VIII
Advocacy and Outreach, Office of	7, XXV
Afghanistan Reconstruction, Special Inspector General for	5, LXXXIII
African Development Foundation	22, XV
Federal Acquisition Regulation	48, 57
Agency for International Development	2, VII; 22, II
Federal Acquisition Regulation	48, 7
Agricultural Marketing Service	7, I, IX, X, XI
Agricultural Research Service	7, V
Agriculture, Department of	2, IV; 5, LXXIII
Advocacy and Outreach, Office of	7, XXV
Agricultural Marketing Service	7, I, IX, X, XI
Agricultural Research Service	7, V
Animal and Plant Health Inspection Service	7, III; 9, I
Chief Financial Officer, Office of	7, XXX
Commodity Credit Corporation	7, XIV
Economic Research Service	7, XXXVII
Energy Policy and New Uses, Office of	2, IX; 7, XXIX
Environmental Quality, Office of	7, XXXI
Farm Service Agency	7, VII, XVIII
Federal Acquisition Regulation	48, 4
Federal Crop Insurance Corporation	7, IV
Food and Nutrition Service	7, II
Food Safety and Inspection Service	9, III
Foreign Agricultural Service	7, XV
Forest Service	36, II
Grain Inspection, Packers and Stockyards Administration	7, VIII; 9, II
Information Resources Management, Office of	7, XXVII
Inspector General, Office of	7, XXVI
National Agricultural Library	7, XLI
National Agricultural Statistics Service	7, XXXVI
National Institute of Food and Agriculture	7, XXXIV
Natural Resources Conservation Service	7, VI
Operations, Office of	7, XXVIII
Procurement and Property Management, Office of	7, XXXII
Rural Business-Cooperative Service	7, XVIII, XLII
Rural Development Administration	7, XLII
Rural Housing Service	7, XVIII, XXXV
Rural Telephone Bank	7, XVI
Rural Utilities Service	7, XVII, XVIII, XLII
Secretary of Agriculture, Office of	7, Subtitle A
Transportation, Office of	7, XXXIII
World Agricultural Outlook Board	7, XXXVIII
Air Force, Department of	32, VII
Federal Acquisition Regulation Supplement	48, 53
Air Transportation Stabilization Board	14, VI
Alcohol and Tobacco Tax and Trade Bureau	27, I
Alcohol, Tobacco, Firearms, and Explosives, Bureau of	27, II
AMTRAK	49, VII
American Battle Monuments Commission	36, IV
American Indians, Office of the Special Trustee	25, VII
Animal and Plant Health Inspection Service	7, III; 9, I

Agency	CFR Title, Subtitle or Chapter
Presidential Documents	3
Science and Technology Policy, Office of	32, XXIV; 47, II
Trade Representative, Office of the United States	15, XX
Export-Import Bank of the United States	2, XXXV; 5, LII; 12, IV
Family Assistance, Office of	45, II
Farm Credit Administration	5, XXXI; 12, VI
Farm Credit System Insurance Corporation	5, XXX; 12, XIV
Farm Service Agency	7, VII, XVIII
Federal Acquisition Regulation	48, 1
Federal Aviation Administration	14, I
Commercial Space Transportation	14, III
Federal Claims Collection Standards	31, IX
Federal Communications Commission	5, XXIX; 47, I
Federal Contract Compliance Programs, Office of	41, 60
Federal Crop Insurance Corporation	7, IV
Federal Deposit Insurance Corporation	5, XXII; 12, III
Federal Election Commission	5, XXXVII; 11, I
Federal Emergency Management Agency	44, I
Federal Employees Group Life Insurance Federal Acquisition Regulation	48, 21
Federal Employees Health Benefits Acquisition Regulation	48, 16
Federal Energy Regulatory Commission	5, XXIV; 18, I
Federal Financial Institutions Examination Council	12, XI
Federal Financing Bank	12, VIII
Federal Highway Administration	23, I, II
Federal Home Loan Mortgage Corporation	1, IV
Federal Housing Enterprise Oversight Office	12, XVII
Federal Housing Finance Agency	5, LXXX; 12, XII
Federal Housing Finance Board	12, IX
Federal Labor Relations Authority	5, XIV, XLIX; 22, XIV
Federal Law Enforcement Training Center	31, VII
Federal Management Regulation	41, 102
Federal Maritime Commission	46, IV
Federal Mediation and Conciliation Service	29, XII
Federal Mine Safety and Health Review Commission	5, LXXIV; 29, XXVII
Federal Motor Carrier Safety Administration	49, III
Federal Prison Industries, Inc.	28, III
Federal Procurement Policy Office	48, 99
Federal Property Management Regulations	41, 101
Federal Railroad Administration	49, II
Federal Register, Administrative Committee of	1, I
Federal Register, Office of	1, II
Federal Reserve System	12, II
Board of Governors	5, LVIII
Federal Retirement Thrift Investment Board	5, VI, LXXVI
Federal Service Impasses Panel	5, XIV
Federal Trade Commission	5, XLVII; 16, I
Federal Transit Administration	49, VI
Federal Travel Regulation System	41, Subtitle F
Financial Crimes Enforcement Network	31, X
Financial Research Office	12, XVI
Financial Stability Oversight Council	12, XIII
Fine Arts, Commission of	45, XXI
Fiscal Service	31, II
Fish and Wildlife Service, United States	50, I, IV
Food and Drug Administration	21, I
Food and Nutrition Service	7, II
Food Safety and Inspection Service	9, III
Foreign Agricultural Service	7, XV
Foreign Assets Control, Office of	31, V
Foreign Claims Settlement Commission of the United States	45, V
Foreign Service Grievance Board	22, IX
Foreign Service Impasse Disputes Panel	22, XIV
Foreign Service Labor Relations Board	22, XIV
Foreign-Trade Zones Board	15, IV
Forest Service	36, II
General Services Administration	5, LVII; 41, 105

Agency	CFR Title, Subtitle or Chapter
Contract Appeals, Board of	48, 61
Federal Acquisition Regulation	48, 5
Federal Management Regulation	41, 102
Federal Property Management Regulations	41, 101
Federal Travel Regulation System	41, Subtitle F
General	41, 300
Payment From a Non-Federal Source for Travel Expenses	41, 304
Payment of Expenses Connected With the Death of Certain Employees	41, 303
Relocation Allowances	41, 302
Temporary Duty (TDY) Travel Allowances	41, 301
Geological Survey	30, IV
Government Accountability Office	4, I
Government Ethics, Office of	5, XVI
Government National Mortgage Association	24, III
Grain Inspection, Packers and Stockyards Administration	7, VIII; 9, II
Gulf Coast Ecosystem Restoration Council	2, LIX; 40, VIII
Harry S. Truman Scholarship Foundation	45, XVIII
Health and Human Services, Department of	2, III; 5, XLV; 45, Subtitle A
Centers for Medicare & Medicaid Services	42, IV
Child Support Enforcement, Office of	45, III
Children and Families, Administration for	45, II, III, IV, X, XIII
Community Services, Office of	45, X
Family Assistance, Office of	45, II
Federal Acquisition Regulation	48, 3
Food and Drug Administration	21, I
Indian Health Service	25, V
Inspector General (Health Care), Office of	42, V
Public Health Service	42, I
Refugee Resettlement, Office of	45, IV
Homeland Security, Department of	2, XXX; 5, XXXVI; 6, I; 8, I
Coast Guard	33, I; 46, I; 49, IV
Coast Guard (Great Lakes Pilotage)	46, III
Customs and Border Protection	19, I
Federal Emergency Management Agency	44, I
Human Resources Management and Labor Relations Systems	5, XCVII
Immigration and Customs Enforcement Bureau	19, IV
Transportation Security Administration	49, XII
HOPE for Homeowners Program, Board of Directors of	24, XXIV
Housing and Urban Development, Department of	2, XXIV; 5, LXV; 24, Subtitle B
Community Planning and Development, Office of Assistant Secretary for	24, V, VI
Equal Opportunity, Office of Assistant Secretary for	24, I
Federal Acquisition Regulation	48, 24
Federal Housing Enterprise Oversight, Office of	12, XVII
Government National Mortgage Association	24, III
Housing—Federal Housing Commissioner, Office of Assistant Secretary for	24, II, VIII, X, XX
Housing, Office of, and Multifamily Housing Assistance Restructuring, Office of	24, IV
Inspector General, Office of	24, XII
Public and Indian Housing, Office of Assistant Secretary for	24, IX
Secretary, Office of	24, Subtitle A, VII
Housing—Federal Housing Commissioner, Office of Assistant Secretary for	24, II, VIII, X, XX
Housing, Office of, and Multifamily Housing Assistance Restructuring, Office of	24, IV
Immigration and Customs Enforcement Bureau	19, IV
Immigration Review, Executive Office for	8, V
Independent Counsel, Office of	28, VII
Independent Counsel, Offices of	28, VI
Indian Affairs, Bureau of	25, I, V
Indian Affairs, Office of the Assistant Secretary	25, VI

Agency	CFR Title, Subtitle or Chapter
Indian Arts and Crafts Board	25, II
Indian Health Service	25, V
Industry and Security, Bureau of	15, VII
Information Resources Management, Office of	7, XXVII
Information Security Oversight Office, National Archives and Records Administration	32, XX
Inspector General	
Agriculture Department	7, XXVI
Health and Human Services Department	42, V
Housing and Urban Development Department	24, XII, XV
Institute of Peace, United States	22, XVII
Inter-American Foundation	5, LXIII; 22, X
Interior, Department of	2, XIV
American Indians, Office of the Special Trustee	25, VII
Endangered Species Committee	50, IV
Federal Acquisition Regulation	48, 14
Federal Property Management Regulations System	41, 114
Fish and Wildlife Service, United States	50, I, IV
Geological Survey	30, IV
Indian Affairs, Bureau of	25, I, V
Indian Affairs, Office of the Assistant Secretary	25, VI
Indian Arts and Crafts Board	25, II
Land Management, Bureau of	43, II
National Indian Gaming Commission	25, III
National Park Service	36, I
Natural Resource Revenue, Office of	30, XII
Ocean Energy Management, Bureau of	30, V
Reclamation, Bureau of	43, I
Safety and Enforcement Bureau, Bureau of	30, II
Secretary of the Interior, Office of	2, XIV; 43, Subtitle A
Surface Mining Reclamation and Enforcement, Office of	30, VII
Internal Revenue Service	26, I
International Boundary and Water Commission, United States and Mexico, United States Section	22, XI
International Development, United States Agency for	22, II
Federal Acquisition Regulation	48, 7
International Development Cooperation Agency, United States	22, XII
International Joint Commission, United States and Canada	22, IV
International Organizations Employees Loyalty Board	5, V
International Trade Administration	15, III; 19, III
International Trade Commission, United States	19, II
Interstate Commerce Commission	5, XL
Investment Security, Office of	31, VIII
James Madison Memorial Fellowship Foundation	45, XXIV
Japan–United States Friendship Commission	22, XVI
Joint Board for the Enrollment of Actuaries	20, VIII
Justice, Department of	2, XXVIII; 5, XXVIII; 28, I, XI; 40, IV
Alcohol, Tobacco, Firearms, and Explosives, Bureau of	27, II
Drug Enforcement Administration	21, II
Federal Acquisition Regulation	48, 28
Federal Claims Collection Standards	31, IX
Federal Prison Industries, Inc.	28, III
Foreign Claims Settlement Commission of the United States	45, V
Immigration Review, Executive Office for	8, V
Independent Counsel, Offices of	28, VI
Prisons, Bureau of	28, V
Property Management Regulations	41, 128
Labor, Department of	2, XXIX; 5, XLII
Employee Benefits Security Administration	29, XXV
Employees' Compensation Appeals Board	20, IV
Employment and Training Administration	20, V
Employment Standards Administration	20, VI
Federal Acquisition Regulation	48, 29
Federal Contract Compliance Programs, Office of	41, 60

Agency	CFR Title, Subtitle or Chapter
Federal Procurement Regulations System	41, 50
Labor-Management Standards, Office of	29, II, IV
Mine Safety and Health Administration	30, I
Occupational Safety and Health Administration	29, XVII
Public Contracts	41, 50
Secretary of Labor, Office of	29, Subtitle A
Veterans' Employment and Training Service, Office of the Assistant Secretary for	41, 61; 20, IX
Wage and Hour Division	29, V
Workers' Compensation Programs, Office of	20, I, VII
Labor-Management Standards, Office of	29, II, IV
Land Management, Bureau of	43, II
Legal Services Corporation	45, XVI
Libraries and Information Science, National Commission on	45, XVII
Library of Congress	36, VII
Copyright Royalty Board	37, III
U.S. Copyright Office	37, II
Local Television Loan Guarantee Board	7, XX
Management and Budget, Office of	5, III, LXXVII; 14, VI; 48, 99
Marine Mammal Commission	50, V
Maritime Administration	46, II
Merit Systems Protection Board	5, II, LXIV
Micronesian Status Negotiations, Office for	32, XXVII
Military Compensation and Retirement Modernization Commission	5, XCIX
Millennium Challenge Corporation	22, XIII
Mine Safety and Health Administration	30, I
Minority Business Development Agency	15, XIV
Miscellaneous Agencies	1, IV
Monetary Offices	31, I
Morris K. Udall Scholarship and Excellence in National Environmental Policy Foundation	36, XVI
Museum and Library Services, Institute of	2, XXXI
National Aeronautics and Space Administration	2, XVIII; 5, LIX; 14, V
Federal Acquisition Regulation	48, 18
National Agricultural Library	7, XLI
National Agricultural Statistics Service	7, XXXVI
National and Community Service, Corporation for	2, XXII; 45, XII, XXV
National Archives and Records Administration	2, XXVI; 5, LXVI; 36, XII
Information Security Oversight Office	32, XX
National Capital Planning Commission	1, IV, VI
National Counterintelligence Center	32, XVIII
National Credit Union Administration	5, LXXXVI; 12, VII
National Crime Prevention and Privacy Compact Council	28, IX
National Drug Control Policy, Office of	2, XXXVI; 21, III
National Endowment for the Arts	2, XXXII
National Endowment for the Humanities	2, XXXIII
National Foundation on the Arts and the Humanities	45, XI
National Geospatial-Intelligence Agency	32, I
National Highway Traffic Safety Administration	23, II, III; 47, VI; 49, V
National Imagery and Mapping Agency	32, I
National Indian Gaming Commission	25, III
National Institute of Food and Agriculture	7, XXXIV
National Institute of Standards and Technology	15, II; 37, IV
National Intelligence, Office of Director of	5, IV; 32, XVII
National Labor Relations Board	5, LXI; 29, I
National Marine Fisheries Service	50, II, IV
National Mediation Board	5, CI; 29, X
National Oceanic and Atmospheric Administration	15, IX; 50, II, III, IV, VI
National Park Service	36, I
National Railroad Adjustment Board	29, III
National Railroad Passenger Corporation (AMTRAK)	49, VII
National Science Foundation	2, XXV; 5, XLIII; 45, VI
Federal Acquisition Regulation	48, 25
National Security Council	32, XXI

Agency	CFR Title, Subtitle or Chapter
National Security Council and Office of Science and Technology Policy	47, II
National Technical Information Service	15, XI
National Telecommunications and Information Administration	15, XXIII; 47, III, IV, V
National Transportation Safety Board	49, VIII
Natural Resources Conservation Service	7, VI
Natural Resource Revenue, Office of	30, XII
Navajo and Hopi Indian Relocation, Office of	25, IV
Navy, Department of	32, VI
Federal Acquisition Regulation	48, 52
Neighborhood Reinvestment Corporation	24, XXV
Northeast Interstate Low-Level Radioactive Waste Commission	10, XVIII
Nuclear Regulatory Commission	2, XX; 5, XLVIII; 10, I
Federal Acquisition Regulation	48, 20
Occupational Safety and Health Administration	29, XVII
Occupational Safety and Health Review Commission	29, XX
Ocean Energy Management, Bureau of	30, V
Oklahoma City National Memorial Trust	36, XV
Operations Office	7, XXVIII
Overseas Private Investment Corporation	5, XXXIII; 22, VII
Patent and Trademark Office, United States	37, I
Payment From a Non-Federal Source for Travel Expenses	41, 304
Payment of Expenses Connected With the Death of Certain Employees	41, 303
Peace Corps	2, XXXVII; 22, III
Pennsylvania Avenue Development Corporation	36, IX
Pension Benefit Guaranty Corporation	29, XL
Personnel Management, Office of	5, I, XXXV; 5, IV; 45, VIII
Human Resources Management and Labor Relations Systems, Department of Homeland Security	5, XCVII
Federal Acquisition Regulation	48, 17
Federal Employees Group Life Insurance Federal Acquisition Regulation	48, 21
Federal Employees Health Benefits Acquisition Regulation	48, 16
Pipeline and Hazardous Materials Safety Administration	49, I
Postal Regulatory Commission	5, XLVI; 39, III
Postal Service, United States	5, LX; 39, I
Postsecondary Education, Office of	34, VI
President's Commission on White House Fellowships	1, IV
Presidential Documents	3
Presidio Trust	36, X
Prisons, Bureau of	28, V
Privacy and Civil Liberties Oversight Board	6, X
Procurement and Property Management, Office of	7, XXXII
Public Contracts, Department of Labor	41, 50
Public and Indian Housing, Office of Assistant Secretary for	24, IX
Public Health Service	42, I
Railroad Retirement Board	20, II
Reclamation, Bureau of	43, I
Refugee Resettlement, Office of	45, IV
Relocation Allowances	41, 302
Research and Innovative Technology Administration	49, XI
Rural Business-Cooperative Service	7, XVIII, XLII
Rural Development Administration	7, XLII
Rural Housing Service	7, XVIII, XXXV
Rural Telephone Bank	7, XVI
Rural Utilities Service	7, XVII, XVIII, XLII
Safety and Environmental Enforcement, Bureau of	30, II
Saint Lawrence Seaway Development Corporation	33, IV
Science and Technology Policy, Office of	32, XXIV
Science and Technology Policy, Office of, and National Security Council	47, II
Secret Service	31, IV
Securities and Exchange Commission	5, XXXIV; 17, II

Agency	CFR Title, Subtitle or Chapter
Selective Service System	32, XVI
Small Business Administration	2, XXVII; 13, I
Smithsonian Institution	36, V
Social Security Administration	2, XXIII; 20, III; 48, 23
Soldiers' and Airmen's Home, United States	5, XI
Special Counsel, Office of	5, VIII
Special Education and Rehabilitative Services, Office of	34, III
State, Department of	2, VI; 22, I; 28, XI
Federal Acquisition Regulation	48, 6
Surface Mining Reclamation and Enforcement, Office of	30, VII
Surface Transportation Board	49, X
Susquehanna River Basin Commission	18, VIII
Tennessee Valley Authority	5, LXIX; 18, XIII
Trade Representative, United States, Office of	15, XX
Transportation, Department of	2, XII; 5, L
Commercial Space Transportation	14, III
Emergency Management and Assistance	44, IV
Federal Acquisition Regulation	48, 12
Federal Aviation Administration	14, I
Federal Highway Administration	23, I, II
Federal Motor Carrier Safety Administration	49, III
Federal Railroad Administration	49, II
Federal Transit Administration	49, VI
Maritime Administration	46, II
National Highway Traffic Safety Administration	23, II, III; 47, IV; 49, V
Pipeline and Hazardous Materials Safety Administration	49, I
Saint Lawrence Seaway Development Corporation	33, IV
Secretary of Transportation, Office of	14, II; 49, Subtitle A
Transportation Statistics Bureau	49, XI
Transportation, Office of	7, XXXIII
Transportation Security Administration	49, XII
Transportation Statistics Bureau	49, XI
Travel Allowances, Temporary Duty (TDY)	41, 301
Treasury, Department of the	2, X;5, XXI; 12, XV; 17, IV; 31, IX
Alcohol and Tobacco Tax and Trade Bureau	27, I
Community Development Financial Institutions Fund	12, XVIII
Comptroller of the Currency	12, I
Customs and Border Protection	19, I
Engraving and Printing, Bureau of	31, VI
Federal Acquisition Regulation	48, 10
Federal Claims Collection Standards	31, IX
Federal Law Enforcement Training Center	31, VII
Financial Crimes Enforcement Network	31, X
Fiscal Service	31, II
Foreign Assets Control, Office of	31, V
Internal Revenue Service	26, I
Investment Security, Office of	31, VIII
Monetary Offices	31, I
Secret Service	31, IV
Secretary of the Treasury, Office of	31, Subtitle A
Truman, Harry S. Scholarship Foundation	45, XVIII
United States and Canada, International Joint Commission	22, IV
United States and Mexico, International Boundary and Water Commission, United States Section	22, XI
U.S. Copyright Office	37, II
Utah Reclamation Mitigation and Conservation Commission	43, III
Veterans Affairs, Department of	2, VIII; 38, I
Federal Acquisition Regulation	48, 8
Veterans' Employment and Training Service, Office of the Assistant Secretary for	41, 61; 20, IX
Vice President of the United States, Office of	32, XXVIII
Wage and Hour Division	29, V
Water Resources Council	18, VI
Workers' Compensation Programs, Office of	20, I, VII
World Agricultural Outlook Board	7, XXXVIII

List of CFR Sections Affected

All changes in this volume of the Code of Federal Regulations (CFR) that were made by documents published in the FEDERAL REGISTER since January 1, 2014 are enumerated in the following list. Entries indicate the nature of the changes effected. Page numbers refer to FEDERAL REGISTER pages. The user should consult the entries for chapters, parts and subparts as well as sections for revisions.

For changes to this volume of the CFR prior to this listing, consult the annual edition of the monthly List of CFR Sections Affected (LSA). The LSA is available at *www.govinfo.gov*. For changes to this volume of the CFR prior to 2001, see the "List of CFR Sections Affected, 1949–1963, 1964–1972, 1973–1985, and 1986–2000" published in 11 separate volumes. The "List of CFR Sections Affected 1986–2000" is available at *www.govinfo.gov*.

2014

8 CFR

79 FR Page

Chapter I

100.4 (a) amended 42451
103 Authority citation revised 27174
103.2 (b)(19) revised; eff. 1-27-15 64305
103.7 (b)(1)(ii)(N) added; interim 27174
214 Policy statement 58241
217.2 (a) amended 17854
235 Authority citation revised 27174
235.13 Added; interim 27174

Chapter V

1003.10 (e) added; interim 39956

2015

8 CFR

80 FR Page

Chapter I

100.4 (a) amended 75632
214 Policy statement 63911
214.1 (k) revised; interim 24108
214.2 (h)(9)(iv) revised 10311
(f)(15)(ii) and (m)(17)(ii) revised 23688
(h)(9)(iii)(B) revised; interim 24108
Regulation at 78 FR 24061 confirmed 24183
214.3 (l)(1)(iii) revised 23689
217.5 (d)(3) added; (h)(2) revised 32294

8 CFR—Continued

80 FR Page

Chapter I—Continued

248.1 (c)(1) amended; CFR correction 79459
274a.12 (c)(26) added 10311
274a.13 (d) amended 10312
293 Authority citation revised 34242
293.1 Revised 34242
293.2 Revised 34242
293.3 Revised 34242
293.4 Removed 34242

Chapter V

1003.1 (a)(1) amended; interim 31463
(b)(11) removed 59510
1003.17 (a) revised 59502
1003.61—1003.65 (Subpart E) Heading revised 59510
1003.61 Revised 59510
1003.62 Revised 59510
1003.63 Revised 59511
1003.64 Revised 59512
1003.65 Revised 59512
1003.66 Added 59513
1240.10 (a)(2) and (3) revised 59513
1240.32 (a) amended 59513
1240.48 (a) amended 59513
1241.14 (g)(3)(i) amended 59513
1245.10 (a)(2)(i) amended; CFR correction 79460

2016

8 CFR

81 FR Page

Chapter I

1.4 Regulation at 78 FR 18472 confirmed; eff. 1-18-17 91670

103 Regulation at 79 FR 27174 confirmed 84415

103.2 (a)(2), (3), (b)(6), (7), (9), (10) and (12) amended......................50275

(a)(1), (7) and (b)(9) revised 73328

103.7 (a)(2) and (b)(1) revised 73328

Regulation at 79 FR 27174 confirmed.....................................84415

103.16 (a) amended.........................73331

103.17 (b) revised 73332

204 Authority citation revised 82484

204.5 (i)(3)(ii) and (iii) redesignated as (i)(3)(iii) and (iv); new (i)(3)(ii) added 2083

(d), (e) and (n)(3) revised; (p) added; eff. 1-17-17 82484

204.6 (m)(6) revised.......................73332

205 Authority citation revised 82485

205.1 (a)(2) removed.......................73332

(a)(3)(iii)(C) and (D) revised; eff. 1-17-17 82486

210.4 Regulation at 78 FR 18472 confirmed; eff. 1-18-17...............91670

212 Authority citation revised 72491, 92304

212.1 (b) revised; interim................6433

Introductory text amended 72491

Regulation at 78 FR 18472 confirmed; eff. 1-18-17.....................91670

(o) revised; interim; eff. 1-18-17 92304

212.4 Regulation at 78 FR 18472 confirmed; eff. 1-18-17...............91670

212.6 Regulation at 78 FR 18472 confirmed; eff. 1-18-17...............91670

212.7 (a) heading removed; (e) revised.......................................50275

Regulation at 78 FR 18472 confirmed; eff. 1-18-17.....................91670

212.16 Revised; interim; eff. 1-18-17...92304

214 Authority citation revised....... 2083, 13117, 72491

Policy statement 60581

214.1 (c)(1) amended.......................2083

(a)(3)(i) amended 72491

(l) added; eff. 1-17-17 82486

Regulation at 78 FR 18472 confirmed; eff. 1-18-17.....................91670

(a)(1)(viii) revised; (a)(2) table amended; interim; eff. 1-18-17 92304

8 CFR—Continued

81 FR Page

Chapter I—Continued

(f) revised....................................94234

214.2 (f)(5)(vi), (10)(ii)(A)(*3*), (C), (D), (E), (11) and (12) revised 13117

(h)(19)(vi) removed; (h)(19)(vii) redesignated as new (h)(19)(vi); (h)(2)(i)(H), (8)(ii)(F), (13)(iii)(C), (D), (E), (19)(iii)(D), (E) and (20) added; (h)(4)(v)(C), (13)(i)(A), (19)(i) introductory text, (ii), (iii)(B), (v) and new (vi) revised; (h)(9)(iv) and (19)(iii)(C) amended; eff. 1-17-17 82486

Regulation at 78 FR 18472 confirmed; eff. 1-18-17......................91670

214.3 (g)(2)(ii)(F) revised 13121

214.6 Regulation at 78 FR 18473 confirmed; eff. 1-18-17...............91670

214.7 Regulation at 78 FR 18473 confirmed; eff. 1-18-17...............91670

214.11 Revised; interim; eff. 1-18-17...92304

214.14 Regulation at 78 FR 18473 confirmed; eff. 1-18-17...............91670

214.16 Added; eff. 5-10-16 through 5-10-19.......................................13121

215 Heading and authority citation revised 72491

215.1—215.9 (Subpart A) Designated as Subpart A; heading added.......................................72491

215.1 Introductory text amended 72491

215.8 Regulation at 78 FR 18473 confirmed; eff. 1-18-17...............91670

215.21—215.24 (Subpart B) Added 72491

231.1 Regulation at 78 FR 18473 confirmed; eff. 1-18-17...............91670

231.2 Regulation at 78 FR 18473 confirmed; eff. 1-18-17...............91670

234.2 (a) amended; interim 14953

235 Regulation at 79 FR 27174 confirmed 84415

235.1 Regulation at 78 FR 18473 confirmed; eff. 1-18-17...............91670

235.13 Regulation at 79 FR 27174 confirmed; (c)(6), (f)(2) introductory text, (3), (4), (g)(1), (2) and (h) amended; (f) heading revised......................................84415

236.1 (c)(7), (10), (11), (d)(1), (3)(i), (4) and (f) amended 62355

238.1 (b)(1)(iii) amended 62355

239.1 (a)(1) through (41) revised; (a)(42) through (46) added 62355

8 CFR—Continued

81 FR Page

Chapter I—Continued

240.25 (a) amended....62355
241.2 (a)(1) revised; (a)(2) amended....62355
245.15 (n)(2) revised; eff. 1-17-17....82490
245.15 Regulation at 78 FR 18473 confirmed; eff. 1-18-17....91670
245.21 Regulation at 78 FR 18473 confirmed; eff. 1-18-17....91670
245.23 Regulation at 78 FR 18473 confirmed; eff. 1-18-17....91670
(a)(3) and (b)(2) revised; interim; eff. 1-18-17....92312
245.24 Regulation at 78 FR 18473 confirmed; eff. 1-18-17....91670
245.25 Added; eff. 1-17-17....82490
245a.1 Regulation at 78 FR 18473 confirmed; eff. 1-18-17....91670
245a.2 Regulation at 78 FR 18473 confirmed; eff. 1-18-17....91670
245a.4 Regulation at 78 FR 18473 confirmed; eff. 1-18-17....91670
245a.15 Regulation at 78 FR 18473 confirmed; eff. 1-18-17....91670
247.12 Regulation at 78 FR 18473 confirmed; eff. 1-18-17....91670
248.3 Heading and (a) revised....2084
253.1 Regulation at 78 FR 18473 confirmed; eff. 1-18-17....91670
264.1 Regulation at 78 FR 18473 confirmed; eff. 1-18-17....91670
(f) removed....94234
270 Authority citation revised....43001
270.3 (b)(1)(ii)(A) through (D) revised; interim....43001
273.3 (b)(1)(ii) and (iii) amended; (b)(1)(iv) and (4) added....72493
274a Authority citation revised....43002
274a.2 (b)(1)(vii) revised; eff. 1-17-17....82491
Regulation at 78 FR 18473 confirmed; eff. 1-18-17....91670
274a.8 (b) revised; interim....43002
Corrected from 4a.8....62353
274a.10 (b)(1)(ii)(A), (B), (C) and (iii)(2) revised; interim....43002
(b)(2) correctly revised; interim....57442
274a.12 (b)(9), (20), (23) and (24) amended; (b)(25) added....2084
(b)(6)(iv), (v) and (c)(3)(i) revised....13121
(b)(9) amended; (c)(35) and (36) added; eff. 1-17-17....82491
(a)(16) and (c)(25) revised; interim; eff. 1-18-17....92312

8 CFR—Continued

81 FR Page

Chapter I—Continued

274a.13 (a) introductory text and (d) revised; (a)(1) amended; eff. 1-17-17....82491
280 Authority citation revised....43002
280.53 Revised; interim....43002
286.9 Regulation at 78 FR 18473 confirmed; eff. 1-18-17....91670
287.5 (b)(1) through (6), (c)(1)(i) through (viii), (2)(i) through (viii), (3)(i) through (vii), (4)(ii)(A) through (G), (iii), (5)(ii)(A) through (G), (d)(1) through (8), (e)(1)(i) through (vi), (2)(i) through (l), (3)(i) through (viii), (4)(i) through (vi) and (f)(1) through (8) revised; (e)(1)(vii), (viii), (2)(li), (lii), (liii), (4)(vii) and (viii) added....62356
287.8 (a)(1)(iv)(A) through (H), (2)(iii)(A) through (H), (c)(1), (e)(2)(i), (ii) and (iii) revised; (e)(2)(iv) and (v) added....62357

Chapter V

1001 Authority citation revised....92361
1001.1 (x) and (y) added; eff. 1-18-17....92361
1003.0 (a) and (e)(1) revised; (f) redesignated as (g); new (f) added; eff. 1-18-17....92361
1003.1 (b)(13) and (d)(5) revised; (d)(2)(iii) amended; eff. 1-18-17....92361
1003.101 (c) added; eff. 1-18-17....92362
1003.102 (f)(2) revised; (t)(2) and (u) amended; (v) added; eff. 1-18-17....92362
1003.103 (c) revised; eff. 1-18-17....92362
1003.104 (b) revised; eff. 1-18-17....92362
1003.105 (a) heading, (1), (c)(3), (d)(2) introductory text and (ii) revised; (c)(1) and (2) amended; eff. 1-18-17....92362
1003.106 (a)(2) introductory text, (a)(2)(i), (ii), (iii), (3) introductory text, (ii), (b) and (c) revised; eff. 1-18-17....92363
1003.107 (a) and (b) revised; (c) redesignated as (d); new (c) added; eff. 1-18-17....92364
1003.108 (a) introductory text, (1)(i) through (iv), (2)(v) and (b) revised; (a)(3) added; eff. 1-18-17....92365
1003.110 Added; eff. 1-18-17....92365

8 CFR—Continued

81 FR Page

Chapter V—Continued

1003.111 Added; eff. 1-18-17 92365

1103.3 (a) and (c) revised; (b) removed; eff. 1-18-17 92366

1212.6 Revised; eff. 1-18-17 92367

1292 Authority citation revised...92367

1292.1 Undesignated center heading added; (a)(4) revised; eff. 1-18-17 92367

1292.2 Removed; eff. 1-18-17 92367

1292.3 Revised; eff. 1-18-17 92367

1292.6 Revised; eff. 1-18-17 92367

1292.11 Undesignated center heading and section added; eff. 1-18-17 92367

1292.12 Added; eff. 1-18-17 92367

1292.13 Added; eff. 1-18-17 92367

1292.14 Added; eff. 1-18-17 92367

1292.15 Added; eff. 1-18-17 92367

1292.16 Added; eff. 1-18-17 92367

1292.17 Added; eff. 1-18-17 92367

1292.18 Added; eff. 1-18-17 92367

1292.19 Added; eff. 1-18-17 92367

1292.20 Added; eff. 1-18-17 92367

2017

8 CFR

82 FR Page

Chapter I

103.7 (b)(1)(i)(KKK) added 5286

Regulation at 82 FR 5286 eff. date delayed to 3-14-18......................31887

212 Authority citation revised....... 5286, 41873

Regulation at 82 FR 5286 eff. date delayed to 3-14-18......................31887

212.1 (g) revised............................41873

212.19 Added 5286

Regulation at 82 FR 5286 eff. date delayed to 3-14-18......................31887

214 Policy statement 55493

214.2 (h)(6)(x) added (temporary) 32998

235 Technical correction 8353

235.3 (b)(1)(i) revised.......................4771

270 Regulation at 81 FR 43001 confirmed......................................8579

270.3 Regulation at 81 FR 43001 confirmed; (b)(1)(ii)(A) through (D) revised 8579

274a Regulation at 81 FR 43002 confirmed 8579

8 CFR—Continued

82 FR Page

Chapter I—Continued

274a.2 (b)(1)(v)(A)(*5*) and (C)(*2*) revised; (b)(1)(v)(C)(*3*) removed; (b)(1)(v)(C)(*4*) through (*8*) redesignated as new (b)(1)(v)(C)(*3*) through (*7*)...........5289

Regulation at 82 FR 5289 eff. date delayed to 3-14-18 in part...........31887

274a.8 Regulation at 81 FR 43002 confirmed 8579

(b) revised.....................................8580

274a.10 Regulation at 81 FR 43002 confirmed 8579

(b)(1)(ii)(A), (B), (C) and (2) revised 8580

274a.12 (b) introductory text and (c)(11) revised; (b)(24) and (25) amended; (b)(37) and (c)(34) added 5289

Regulation at 82 FR 5289 eff. date delayed to 3-14-18......................31887

280 Regulation at 81 FR 43002 confirmed......................................8579

280.53 Regulation at 81 FR 43002 confirmed 8579

Revised 8580

Chapter V

1235.3 (b)(1)(i) revised 4773

1240.21 (b) removed; (c) introductory text and (1) revised; eff. 1-4-18 57339

2018

8 CFR

83 FR Page

Chapter I

103 Authority citation revised 44450

103.7 (b)(1)(i)(SS) introductory text amended............................44450

208.13 (c)(3) added; interim 55952

208.30 Heading revised; (e)(5) amended; interim 55952

212.1 Regulation at 81 FR 6433 confirmed 31450

214.2 (h)(6)(x) added (temporary)....................................24917

270.3 (b)(1)(ii)(A) through (D) revised...13834

274a.8 (b) revised..........................13835

274a.10 (b)(1)(ii)(A), (B), (C), and (2) introductory text revised...13835

280.53 (b)(1) through (15) revised...13835

Chapter V

1003.1 (a)(1) amended 8323

8 CFR—Continued

8 CFR—Continued

www.ingramcontent.com/pod-product-compliance
Lightning Source LLC
LaVergne TN
LVHW052200200926
848481LV00001B/1